FIRST CONGRESS

OF PEOPLE'S DEPUTIES

OF THE USSR

Related Titles From
ACADEMIC INTERNATIONAL PRESS

Documents of Soviet History
USSR Documents Annual
USSR Calendar of Events, 1987–1991
Russia & Eurasia Facts & Figures Annual
Sino-Soviet Documents Annual

FIRST CONGRESS

OF

PEOPLE'S DEPUTIES

OF THE

USSR

25 May – 9 June 1989

THE STENOGRAPHIC RECORD

Volume I

EDITED BY

PATRICK J. ROLLINS

Academic International Press

1993

FIRST CONGRESS OF PEOPLE'S DEPUTIES OF THE USSR
25 May – 9 June 1989. Stenographic Record. Volumes 1 and 2
Edited by Patrick J. Rollins

Copyright © 1993 by Academic International Press

All rights reserved. The reproduction or utilization of this work, or any part thereof in any form or by any electronic, mechanical, digital, or other means, now known or hereafter invented, including xeroxgraphy photocopying, and recording, and in any information storage and retrieval system, by any individual, institution or library is forbidden under law without the written permission of the publisher.

ISBN: 0-87569-166-8

Composition by Ethel Chamberlain

Printed in the United States of America

By direct subscription with the publisher

ACADEMIC INTERNATIONAL PRESS
POB 1111 • Gulf Breeze FL 32562–1111 • USA

CONTENTS

VOLUME I

Preface ix

Introduction
　Building Democracy in the USSR by James A. Duran Jr. x

Annotated List of Speeches
　First Session　　25 May 1989　　xvii
　Second Session　25 May 1989　　xviii
　Third Session　　26 May 1989　　xxi
　Fourth Session　 27 May 1989　　xxvi
　Fifth Session　　29 May 1989　　xxx
　Sixth Session　　30 May 1989　　xxxiv
　Seventh Session　31 May 1989　　xxxviii

Stenographic Record
　First and Second Sessions, 25 May 1989
　　Introduction　1
　　Text　4

　Third Session　26 May 1989
　　Introduction　50
　　Text　52

　Fourth Session　27 May 1989
　　Introduction　91
　　Text　92

　Fifth Session　29 May 1989
　　Introduction　139
　　Text　140

　Sixth Session　30 May 1989
　　Introduction　189
　　Text　190

　Seventh Session　31 May 1989
　　Introduction　246
　　Text　247

Notes
　First and Second Sessions　297
　Third Session　300
　Fourth Session　301

CONTENTS

Notes (continued)
    Fifth Session   303
    Sixth Session   306
    Seventh Session   307

Maps and Illustrations
    Structure of the Soviet Government, May 1989   xvi
    The Caucasus Region   6
    The Baltic Region   90

VOLUME II

Annotated List of Speeches

Eighth Session	1 June 1989	iii
Ninth Session	2 June 1989	x
Tenth Session	5–6 June 1989	xiv
Eleventh Session	7 June 1989	xvi
Twelfth Session	8 June 1989	xviii
Thirteenth Session	9 June 1989	xxv

Stenographic Record

Eighth Session   1 June 1989
    Introduction   1
    Text   2

Ninth Session   2 June 1989
    Introduction   61
    Text   61

Tenth Session   5-6 June 1989
    Introduction   113
    Text   114

Eleventh Session   7 June 1989
    Introduction   149
    Text   149

Twelfth Session   8 June 1989
    Introduction   166
    Text   166

Thirteenth Session   9 June 1989
    Introduction   235
    Text   236

Notes

Eighth Session	290
Ninth Session	291
Tenth Session	293
Eleventh Session	295
Twelfth Session	295
Thirteenth Session	296

Works Cited 297

Appendix A: Constitutional Provisions, Laws, and Decrees

1. Constitution (Basic Law) of the USSR: Articles Cited — 298
2. Law on the Election of People's Deputies of the USSR, 1 December 1988 — 304
3. Decree on the Procedure for Organizing and Holding Meetings, Rallies, Street Processions, and Demonstrations in the USSR, 28 July 1988 — 316
4. Law on Criminal Liability for State Crimes (25 December 1958), Articles 7 and 11 as Amended and Supplemented by Decree of the USSR Supreme Soviet Presidium of 8 April 1989 — 317
5. Decree on the Duties and Rights of Internal Troops of the USSR Ministry of Internal Affairs in Safeguarding Public Order, 28 July 1988 (Summary) — 318

Appendix B: Documents of the Congress

1. Provisional Standing Orders for Sessions of the Congress of People's Deputies of the USSR — 320
2. Resolution on Proposals, Statements, and Complaints from Citizens Received by the Congress of People's Deputies — 322
3. Resolution on the Preparation of a USSR Draft Law on the Status of People's Deputies in the USSR — 322
4. Resolution on Basic Guidelines for the Domestic and Foreign Policy of the USSR — 324
5. Findings of the Commission to Investigate the Circumstances Connected with Events in Tbilisi City on 9 April 1989 — 332
6. Resolution of the USSR Congress of People's Deputies on the Report of the Commission to Investigate the Circumstances Connected with Events in Tbilisi City on 9 April 1989 — 338
7. Report of A.N. Yakovlev, Chairman of the Commission on the Political and Legal Assessment of the 1939 Soviet-German Treaty of Non-Aggression, to the Second Congress of USSR People's Deputies, 23 December 1989 — 338

CONTENTS

Appendix B (continued)

    8. Resolution of the USSR Congress of People's Deputies on the Political and Legal Assessment of the Soviet-German Treaty of Non-Aggression of 1939   346

    9. Report of A.S. Dzasokhov, Chairman of the USSR Supreme Soviet Committee on International Affairs, to the Second Congress of USSR People's Deputies on the Political Assessment of the Decision to send Soviet Troops into Afghanistan in December 1979   347

    10. Resolution of the USSR Congress of People's Deputies on the Political Assessment of the Decision to Send Soviet Troops into Afghanistan in December 1979   349

Appendix C: Membership of Executive Organs and Commissions

    1. Presidium of the USSR Congress of People's Deputies   350

    2. Secretariat of the USSR Congress of People's Deputies   350

    3. Credentials Commission   351

    4. Tellers Commission   353

    5. Commission to Investigate the Circumstances Connected with Events in Tbilisi City on 9 April 1989   355

    6. Commission to Verify the Materials Connected with the Activities of the USSR Prosecutor's Office Investigative Group headed by T.Kh. Gdlyan   356

    7. Commission to Prepare the Resolution on Basic Guidelines for the Domestic and Foreign Policy of the USSR   357

    8. Constitutional Commission   359

    9. Commission to Draft Legislation on the Constitutional Oversight Committee of the USSR   363

    10. Commission to Render a Political and Legal Appraisal of the Soviet-German Non-Aggression Treaty of 1939   364

Appendix D: Directory of People's Deputies of the USSR   365

Indexes

    Speakers   455
    Persons   457
    Place Names   464
    Subjects   468

Abbreviations and Acronyms   482

PREFACE

These volumes contain the complete daily record of the thirteen sessions of the First Congress of People's Deputies of the USSR which met in the Kremlin in Moscow between 25 May and 9 June 1989. The records, created by the Congress' Secretariat, first appeared in *Izvestiya* within a day or two of the proceedings they recount. They were translated and printed by the Foreign Broadcast Information Service (FBIS) in June, July, and August 1989 as Supplements to its *Daily Reports* on the Soviet Union, and that is the text reproduced here. A detailed citation of the source material appears in the bibliography at the end of the work.

The USSR Supreme Soviet subsequently published a six-volume collection titled *Pervyi syezd narodnykh deputatov SSSR, 25 maya—9 iyunya 1989 g. Stenograficheskii otchet* (Moskva, 1989-). Since all deputies who wished to address the Congress could not be accommodated, their written statements were added to the record. Volumes 4-6 of the *Pervyi syezd* contain 360 undelivered speeches. Otherwise the texts of the two versions are nearly identical. The principal difference between the two is in the identification of speakers, the later edition being somewhat more accurate. Notes to the present work indicate speakers who were originally mistaken for someone else. The erroneous name is preserved in the *Izvestiya*-FBIS text and in the Annotated List of Speeches, but in the table the correct name is appended in brackets. A speaker's initials are correct in the List if not always in the text.

The later Soviet edition contains two major errors of identification. In *Pervyi syezd*, 1:11, the name of G.Kh. Popov is substituted for that of F.V. Popov for remarks that the liberal Gavril Popov never could have made. Similarly, at 1:99 *Pervyi syezd* inserts "Voice from the floor" in place of A.M. Obolensky who was explaining why he was a candidate for the chairmanship of the Supreme Soviet. Since he was the only candidate, other than Gorbachev, only he could have made that speech. In short, the official *Pervyi syezd* is not an unqualified improvement over the more spontaneous record that first appeared in *Izvestiya*. Our goal, of course, has been to make judicious use of both sources to improve on both.

One aspect of the record can never be improved. The Palace of Congresses was not equipped with microphones except at the dais. Consequently comments shouted from the floor were not always recorded accurately. The crush of speakers and confusion at the front of the hall complicated the work of the stenographers who taped and transcribed the proceedings. They could not always hear clearly, but then, neither could the audience. That chaotic ambience is now also part of the historical record.

In order not to confuse or annoy the reader unnecessarily, editorial material conforms to FBIS spelling conventions, with one exception. The "iy" suffix preferred by FBIS is shortened to "y" or "i" as appropriate in editorial matter. Thus the FBIS rendering of "Mariy ASSR" appears in notes as "Mari," whereas "Zaslavskiy" becomes simply "Zaslavsky."

The Appendices at the end of Volume 2 provide the texts of decrees and legislation of most concern to the deputies. That includes many sections of the USSR Constitution or Fundamental Law, which was amended extensively during 1988-89 to accommodate the legislative and executive restructuring of the Soviet state. The original text of the 1977 Constitution will be of little help to readers trying to follow the debates on constitutional issues, and they should rely on the amended text in Appendix A.1. The general roster of deputies (Appendix D), listed originally according to the Cyrillic alphabet, has been reordered according to the Latin alphabet.

The synopses of individual addresses and remarks in the tables at the front of each volume are comprehensive but not complete in detail. Their purpose is to present a quick sketch of the proceedings and the *main* lines of argument. Used in conjunction with the Indices at the end of the work, they should enable readers readily to find and follow the debate on any particular subject.

The editor acknowledges the support of the Russian and East European Center of the University of Illinois at Champaign-Urbana and the College of Arts and Letters of Old Dominion University.

Patrick J. Rollins

INTRODUCTION
BUILDING DEMOCRACY IN THE USSR
THE FIRST CONGRESS OF USSR PEOPLE'S DEPUTIES
25 MAY–9 JUNE 1989

> The possibility, no matter how remote it may appear at the moment, that ritual and ceremony may some day be replaced by substance should not be ignored. Lifeless legal bodies playing a ritualistic role sometimes come to life under certain conditions and circumstances.
> —Vernon Aspaturian, 1967

The opening of the first Congress of USSR People's Deputies on 25 May 1989 began the institutionalization of a new Soviet system of government. Vigorous debates about the forms that the new political structures were to take had been underway since mid-1988. Mikhail Gorbachev, General Secretary of the Communist Party of the Soviet Union (CPSU), had taken the position that democratization meant the establishment of a check-and-balance system based on the separation of powers among the three branches of government. His reforms had allowed the choice of a majority of deputies through multi-candidate, secret-ballot elections. Within a few hours after the opening gavel it was clear that the legislature was no longer "primarily a decorative structure." Fundamental issues of state policy were openly debated. A political opposition to the policy line of the leaders of the CPSU was allowed to present alternative proposals. The aim of this essay is to provide a basis for understanding the central issues raised by the deputies.

Liberal-democrats had good reason to doubt the general secretary's commitment to changing the fundamental institutions of the party-state. From a Western viewpoint, Soviet rhetoric about democracy had lacked credibility since the initial days of the Bolshevik seizure of power in October 1917. Articles in the USSR constitutions of 1936 and 1977 had given supreme power over all institutions to the USSR Supreme Soviet. Article 4 of the 1977 "Brezhnev" constitution provided that "State organizations, public organizations and officials shall observe the Constitution of the USSR and Soviet laws." In reality, this was not so in the party-state. The "leading role" of the CPSU was guaranteed in Articles 6 and 7 of the same Fundamental Law. National elections were a charade.

Party bosses preselected nominees to the Supreme Soviet according to a quota system designed to give representation to all elements of the population. Voters cast their single-candidate ballots in a way that violated provisions for secrecy. The deputies met briefly each year in two sessions, each lasting a few days. The proceedings were totally dominated by the notables of the *nomenklatura*, that is, the Party elite and their appointees. Pre-approved minor changes were introduced into legislation after scripted speeches were delivered on the floor of the Supreme Soviet. Votes were unanimous.

The CPSU Politburo and Central Committee Secretariat possessed the real policymaking power. No effective check-and-balance system was in place to enforce a rule-of-law state. The numerous departments of the Central Committee undertook to guide virtually every aspect of Soviet life. Through control of appointments to 23,000,000 patronage jobs on the nomenklatura lists, the Party bosses ensured support of key personnel. Statutes were ignored or overridden by the decrees and instructions of the government ministries and departments. Party officials were key plenipotentiaries of the Center and arbitrarily intervened even in micromanagement down to the local level. Through "telephone justice" they used their influence in as many as 5 percent of court cases. This undermined articles of the Constitution guaranteeing human rights and equality before the law. To change this bureaucratic-command system would be to challenge the basic vested interests of an entrenched ruling class that did not have to defend its policies in competitive, free election campaigns in a pluralist political system. Conservatives in 1989 were those who were trying to maintain or to retrieve the essentials of the Brezhnev-type party-state.

INTRODUCTION

GORBACHEV AND PERESTROIKA

Beginning in April 1985, the new general secretary tried to instill a new dynamism into Soviet society through *perestroika* (restructuring). For a Marxist true believer, the failure to overcome the alienation of the masses from the system would call into question the *raison d'etre* of the Revolution. Pragmatically the leaders recognized that the apathy of the Soviet masses had to be broken to overcome the economic stagnation that had become more and more serious after the mid-1970s.

The first stage of perestroika featured reliance essentially on traditional mobilization and administrative methods. The men brought into the leadership during the brief tenure of Yuri Andropov as general secretary had discussed new ideas for policy developed by leading members of the intelligentsia. Emphasis on strengthening workers' discipline, an anti-alcohol campaign, and economic acceleration (*uskorenie*) in key machine-building sectors did not result in a solid growth in GNP. *Glasnost* (openness) facilitated the debate on options and, by revealing past abuses, began the process of undermining the principles basic to the bureaucratic-command system. Gorbachev's personal willingness to admit that he was fallible contrasted with the past practice of the CPSU leadership. He stated frankly that participants in a debate could learn from each other and determine what the best option for action would be. Yet, he still remained committed to preserving the "leading role" of the Party and to the "socialist choice" in economic system. Only at the Twenty-seventh Party Congress (25 February–6 March 1986) did he succeed in replacing many Brezhnevites with men of his generation. Hints at reform in the CPSU Program by no means threatened the nomenklatura.

In January 1987 the general secretary began to move towards a more radical restructuring of the system. The Law on State Enterprise enacted on 30 June 1987 was designed to decentralize economic administration by transferring significant power to enterprise managers. To give the workers a feeling that they had a stake in the economic success of the enterprise, the rights of their collectives to influence plant policy were enhanced, for example, in the selection of directors. In the local elections of June 1987, 5 percent of seats were chosen through multi-candidate, secret-ballot elections. A few of the nomenklatura suffered defeat, but basically the *apparat* (bureaucracy) that controlled the Party machine did not feel that the process had gotten out of control.

Glasnost meanwhile featured a systematic critique of the abuses of the Stalinist "cult of personality" period and the corruption of the Brezhnev " period of stagnation." This was designed not only to discredit individual leaders but also key principles underlying the bureaucratic-command system that had been developing since the late 1920s. Returning to the truths as taught by Lenin remained a constant theme. After negotiations lasting from January to June 1987 the Central Committee agreed to call a Party Conference. The general secretary had to concede that the delegates would not have power to make personnel changes in the ruling organs. It would be the first such meeting since 1941.

Proposals for reforming the political system were the center of controversy during debates on setting the agenda of the Party Conference. At a plenum of the Central Committee on 8 January 1988 the general secretary in a speech entitled "Democratization is the Essence of Perestroika and Socialism" declared that restructuring was to enter a second, revolutionary stage. He and the reformers asserted that political reform was essential to end economic stagnation. Only by giving the people a real voice in policy-making through meaningful participation in the political process would their apathy be ended. When Gorbachev and his allies realized that the central bureaucracy was sabotaging the Law on State Enterprise, they launched a broad campaign against the state and Party bureaucrats who were defending their vested interests in the old system.

THE NINETEENTH PARTY CONFERENCE

In the preparatory stages of the conference Gorbachev demonstrated his tactical political skills by taking a centrist position. The use of democratization and glasnost as means to overcome bureaucratic inertia and the apathy of the masses was very worrisome for many major figures in the apparat. While the leadership publicly maintained a facade of unity, Politburo member Yegor Ligachev emerged as the recognized leader of those advocating cautious reform. Stubborn adherence to the essence of "class-based," Marxist-Leninist dogmas and defense of the past achievements of "socialism," whatever the errors and abuses committed by the leaders, distinguished the conservative tendency.

Under Gorbachev's leadership agreement was reached that, as a rule, delegates to the conference were to be chosen by lower Party bodies in multi-candidate, secret-ballot elections. Generally speaking, the conservative apparatchiki gained a solid majority despite the efforts of Gorbachev's aides in the Secretariat. However, a significant number of radicals would be present to advocate far-reaching reforms.

Resolutions passed at the five-day Nineteenth Party Conference, 28 June–1 July 1988 initiated changes in the fundamental rules of the political game in the USSR. Unprecedented public debate lent high drama to the process of perestroika. With great political skill and marginal concessions, the general secretary gained approval for a major restructuring of both Party and state institutions. The CPSU apparat was to concern itself with broad macro-policy and the organizational work necessary for any political party. The CPSU Secretariat was to be reorganized so as to cease to be a "shadow government" duplicating the functions of state agencies. Its staff was to be cut dramatically in size and no longer to have special branches to intervene in day-to-day governmental administration, especially in various sectors of the economy. The nomenklatura were to be limited to two five-year terms in high Party office. Elders over 65 were expected to retire. No longer were Party leaders to be co-opted from above. Under the new rules, rank-and-file members were to be given a real chance to influence policy by election to office through multi-candidate, secret-ballot elections. Party members also had the right of recall.

Also approved at the Nineteenth Party Conference was the restructuring of state institutions into a check-and-balance system. A new two-tier national legislature with two-thirds of the deputies elected in a competitive, secret-ballot procedure was to have genuine supreme authority. The chairman of the USSR Supreme Soviet would be the head of state, preside over the legislative branch, and possess some powers, especially in foreign affairs, of an independent chief executive. Day-to-day administration was to remain with the Council of Ministers confirmed by the legislative branch. In the judicial sphere, a Constitutional Oversight Committee was to be created with the power to review and to submit legal findings on the conformity of statutes (*zakon*) passed by the national legislature with the USSR Constitution (Fundamental Law). However, this constitutional review body could not suspend all-union statutes. Since the parliament was supreme, legislative action would be necessary either to bring the law into conformity with the Constitution or to amend the Fundamental Law itself. More important for establishing a rule-of-law state in the Soviet context would be the committee's power to suspend the legal effect of decrees and instructions of the ministries that contradicted statutes or the USSR Constitution.

CONSTITUTIONAL AND ELECTORAL REFORM

The first step in implementing the state reforms was to have the USSR Supreme Soviet, scheduled to convene in December, pass appropriate constitutional amendments and a new law on elections. Following Soviet tradition, a period of general public discussion was initiated upon publication on 22 October 1988 of the draft amendments and on the next day of the draft electoral law. The public debate had little effect on the all-union proposals, but the criticisms of the public did shape subsequent legislation on the union-republic level. Essentially, the draft amendments were prepared in the same old pattern the apparatchiki had used in the past, with involvement of the Supreme Soviet committee only at the last stage. Compromises were essential to reassure the nomenklatura who constituted the great majority of the deputies that empowerment of the legislative branch would not mean their loss of influence.

One major concession involved the formation of a two-tier legislature, the USSR Congress of People's Deputies and the smaller, indirectly-elected, full-time USSR Supreme Soviet. The Congress was to consist of 2250 deputies. Following the past pattern, 750 were to be from territorial districts and another 750 from territorial-ethnic districts. Very controversial was the concession offered to the party bosses that an additional 750 deputies were to represent various corporate groups, including 100 from the CPSU and the remainder mainly from front organizations such as the official trade unions, the Communist Youth League (Komsomol), etc. The radical reformers argued that the Brezhnev constitution with alterations in the electoral procedures would be more democratic since all deputies were elected directly and served in the parliament full time. As a result of the proposed formula, some citizens would receive a disproportionate number of votes in the elections. Since the Congress was to choose the members of the smaller USSR Supreme Soviet, the conservatives might use their power in the Congress as a "filter" to ensure a majority favorable to their vested interests in the Soviet.

The radicals also objected to filters in the electoral law that could be manipulated by the apparat. While the draft law had provisions to ensure multi-candidate, secret-ballot elections in the districts, a multi-stage nominating procedure created the opportunity for abuse by the Party bosses. For example, if a district nomination was contested by more than two candidates, a pre-electoral meeting was required to screen the nominees for a place on the ballot. Unfortunately, the procedure for choosing delegates to those meetings and rules for conducting them were very loosely prescribed. Approximately 9000 complaints later were referred to the Central Electoral Commission and the Credentials Commission by the First Congress.

The proposal that the CPSU general secretary be chosen by the Congress of People's Deputies to be the chairman of the USSR Supreme Soviet and therefore head of state was a serious point of contention. Radicals maintained that the office should be filled by direct, popular election. Others suggested that the general secretary should not simultaneously be Party head, for combining the two posts would put too much power in the hands of a single person.

A similar proposal that the Party's first secretary at each lower level be elected chairman of the corresponding legislature aroused fears that the proposal to give real authority to the soviets was only cosmetic. Radicals preferred choice by direct popular vote, but the general secretary and the Party leaders stood firm on this. To sustain the principle of Party discipline meant the continuation of the party-state, albeit in another form. Gorbachev's defense was that having the first secretaries as presiding officers would facilitate empowerment of the soviets. A major modification leading to a separation of powers was to make the heads of executive departments ineligible to serve as deputies with the exception of the chairmen of Republic Councils of Ministers and the lower executive committees (*ispolkom*). No longer were numerous heads of departments to be deputies and thus in a direct position to dominate legislative proceedings as completely as they had in the past. The chairman of a soviet was not to be a member of its executive committee. His function was to take charge of organizing the work of the legislature. Its committees, meanwhile, were to be manned by some full-time deputies responsible for monitoring the work of government agencies.

Constitutional amendments to reform the federal institutions of the Union were put off to a later stage of perestroika. The Balts and other minority leaders seeking to protect their ethnic interests did provoke a controversy that caused a change in some provisions of the proposed constitutional amendments. National and ethnic leaders feared that the two chambers of the USSR Supreme Soviet to be chosen by the Congress would be packed and dominated by deputies from the Russian Republic. Taking the lead, on 16 November 1988 the Estonian Supreme Soviet amended its republic constitution with provisions that rejected the authority of the center in certain fields and asserted their right to overrule all-union laws. Being questioned was the nature of the Union. Major compromises followed. The number of deputies to represent each union republic in the Soviet of Nationalities was raised from 7 to 11. Provision was made for ethnic representation in the other chamber based on territorial districts, the Soviet of the Union. These were initial steps to reform the federal system.

Arguments for establishing a stronger constitutional court than proposed in the draft did not prevail. However, the membership of the USSR Constitutional Oversight Committee was increased from 15 to 22 to guarantee the representation of each republic by at least one judge. This committee was to be an independent agency with members confirmed by the Congress for ten-year terms.

On 20 December 1988 the final session of the old-style USSR Supreme Soviet passed the amendments and the new law on elections. Democratization was evident in this final session dominated by the old political processes. Under pressure, the government withdrew a proposed tax law for later consideration. Five "no" votes and 27 abstentions were recorded as the amendments were passed. The apparat still believed it could manipulate the political process and, though many conservatives grumbled, Party discipline prevailed during the voting.

ELECTING THE PEOPLE'S DEPUTIES

The election campaign during the spring of 1989 was more democratic than any held since the campaigning in November 1917 for the ill-fated Constituent Assembly. The wide-ranging debates on the amendments and the subsequent polemics during the electoral campaign in the spring of 1989 initiated the "revolution from below." By no means was the "playing field" even. Due to its long monopoly of political power, the bosses of the CPSU had tremendous organizational resources. Yet, Party membership was somewhat divided. The Party platform was a litany of broad generalizations in support of perestroika and the retention of the Party's leading role. Belief in the apparat's conversion to "socialist pluralism" was undermined by the way elections to most of the corporate seats were manipulated. Gorbachev himself was one of the Central Committee's one hundred nominees to fill the hundred seats reserved for the CPSU. Inclusion in the non-competitively elected "Red Hundred" severely undermined his legitimacy. The initiator of democratization had never submitted himself to a competitive contest. Only a few public organizations had spirited contests. The Academy of Sciences chose a number of distinguished reformers, including Andrei Sakharov. The Union of Cinematographers was a hotbed of radicalism. Yet these were exceptions. The Party chieftans of most of the eligible front organizations blocked the rank-and-file membership from real influence in the choice of deputies. The overwhelming majority chosen were conservatives.

The elections for the remaining two-thirds of the deputies began a revolution from below as large numbers of opposition activists involved themselves in the electoral process. In the first round, 2895 candidates were on the ballot for 1500 seats. Due to a lack of pluralism in the past, no well-organized opposition political parties existed. Platforms tended to be individual, except in some ethnic areas like the Baltics where nationalists were well-organized. The most successful opposition candidates were supported by the many informal associations that had emerged since 1987. Party bosses, especially in the Ukraine, Belorussia, Central Asia, and in rural areas, utilized the filters provided by the nomination and registration process to keep opponents off the ballot. The Central Electoral Commission did intervene to correct some blatant abuses when appealed, but the time was too short and the staff too small to deal with the problem on a large scale. Challengers benefitted from the provisions that authorized a staff of ten paid by election commission funds. However, no outside contributions were permitted. Gaining access to the media or meeting places was very difficult in many areas for those who opposed candidates endorsed by the Party.

Unlike past elections, the turnout of more than 90 percent of the electorate was not contrived. Where a candidate did not receive 50 percent of the vote cast, a second round had to be held. Even single candidates could lose if a majority of voters crossed out their names. If no clear victor emerged in the second round due to a failure of a majority of eligible voters to cast ballots, the initial nominating stage had to be repeated. Not all seats were filled when the Congress of People's Deputies opened its first session. Of the 166 regional party (*obkom*) first secretaries who ran, 33 were defeated. The top Party leaders in Moscow, Leningrad, and Kiev were particularly humiliated. Approximately four hundred radical deputies eventually were elected, mostly from the large urban areas. The most spectacular victory was that of Boris Yeltsin in a national-territorial district in Moscow. Despite every effort of the Party regulars, Yeltsin began his political ascent by gathering 89 percent of 5.7 million votes to his opponent's 7 percent. As was predicted, the social composition of the legislature changed as candidates won by virtue of their competence to campaign. The former quota system had ensured set percentages for peasants, workers, youth, women, etc. The great majority of the elected deputies were conservatives of various hues. Their ranks included pragmatic conservatives who were willing to listen to suggestions by radicals, to weigh the merits of alternative proposals, and to back major reforms submitted by the general secretary. The dogmatic conservatives, vigorous defenders of the Brezhnevite order, still accepted the principle of Party discipline but were growing increasingly disillusioned with the direction of the general secretary's policies.

The results of the election were very sobering for the Party leaders. According to a report in *Izvestiya* on 27 April 1989 Gorbachev pronounced the elections a victory for perestroika. Elections begun on initiative from above had reached "a decisive stage characterized by a powerful mass movement from below—a movement of the broadest mass of the working people." The people had thrown off their apathy and now the country could move forward to implement reform plans.

REVOLUTIONARY MOMENTUM

The debates leading up to the elections and the abuses experienced in conducting them spurred further measures of democratization. When the republics amended their constitutions and electoral laws in early 1990, they introduced major departures from the central pattern. Some small union republics dropped the two-tier legislature, retaining only a single body. Most either dropped completely or reduced to a minimum seats reserved for corporate bodies. Electoral laws were revised to exclude many of the filters used to deny candidates a place on the ballot. While problems persisted with the apparat in some republics, particularly in Central Asia, Ukraine, Belorussia, and in some rural oblasts, nationalists won a majority in the 1990 elections in seven re- publics, the three Balt, three Transcaucasian, and Moldavia (Moldova). Most significantly, a motley group of radicals won a bare majority in the RSFSR Congress. In the struggle over the new form the Union was to take, the governments of these republics had a greater legitimacy in the sense of a popular mandate than the central government. Party first secretaries had no chance to be elected chairmen of those soviets in which the opposition won majorities. One institutional safeguard for the conservatives thereby was lost.

The election cleared the way for a revolution, that is, a fundamental change in the institutions of political power. So broad are the powers of the USSR Congress of People's Deputies that it might act as a constituent assembly. As amended, Article 108 of the Constitution recognizes the Congress as the "supreme organ of state power" with authority to consider "all questions assigned to the jurisdiction of the USSR." In its exclusive jurisdiction is "the adoption of the Constitution of the USSR and amendments therein." Basic directions of foreign and domestic policy shall receive its approval. It elects the head of state and confirms the head of government (chairman of the USSR Council of Ministers) and can remove both. It chooses the 542 full-time deputies of the two-house USSR Supreme Soviet and the 20 percent of membership that is rotated each year. The Congress can annul any acts of the full-time legislature, which is responsible for the demanding day-to-day tasks of crafting laws. Confirmation of the heads of certain independent agencies, such as the People's Control Committee, the Procurator-General, and key judicial organs are its prerogative. As noted, the full membership of the Constitutional Oversight Committee was within the Congress' jurisdiction. Only one session per year was required, but it was expected that initially there would be two.

As the following proceedings of the First Congress of USSR People's Deputies makes clear, the national legislature ceased to be a rubber-stamp legislature. In place of scripted speeches and ritualistic unanimous endorsement of the leadership's policies, wide-ranging, free, and often chaotic debate on fundamental issues of the polity took place. Party discipline was not invoked in the old manner. Deputy Andrei Sakharov spoke many times. No one could accuse him of mincing words.

General-Secretary Mikhail Gorbachev deserves credit for initiating the processes for establishing a check-and-balance system based on a separation of powers among the three branches of government. The full-time USSR Supreme Soviet really is doing the job of preparing and debating laws. On the floor and through its committees, the deputies are attempting to exercise control over executive agencies. Two sets of constitutional amendments in 1990 created an executive presidency on the French pattern, separate from the legislature. Once again, the general secretary was elected indirectly by the USSR Congress of People's Deputies. Lack of a popular mandate undermined his legitimacy during times of major crises. As in France, the Council of Ministers holds office so long as it has the confidence of the legislative branch, but it also has responsibilities to the president. The Supreme Soviet has refused to confirm ministerial nominations and has caused the government to withdraw major proposals, including economic programs. Steps have been taken to establish an independent judiciary subject only to the law. The Constitutional Oversight Committee has voided presidential decrees and instructions of the central ministries and state committees in sensitive areas. By no means is the delimitation of powers among the branches resolved, but the present system is far different than that of the old party-state.

Indications are that the present Congress of USSR People's Deputies will be the last of its type. The USSR Constitution has been amended to eliminate in future elections the 750 seats reserved for corporate groups. In the Center's proposal for a new treaty of union, the Congress would be abolished. Remaining would be a single-tier, full-time Supreme Soviet composed entirely of directly-elected deputies. Amendment of Articles 6 and 7 have ended the CPSU's formal constitutional monopoly of power. Also on the agenda is upgrading of the Constitutional Oversight Committee to a Constitutional Court with augmented powers of judicial review.

At present, the looming decision about the future nature of the Union has polarized political forces and may threaten the emerging liberal political system. Conservatives still holding crucial positions of power are calling for order to preserve the Soviet empire. Radicals seek either a decentralized federation or even a confederation. Some nationalists aim simply to secede. President Gorbachev attempts to find a middle position but has the declared purpose of maintaining the Union and law-and-order. He has demonstrated time and again that he is reluctant to use force. A polarized and volatile environment is very unfavorable for the continued development of a liberal-democratic form of government in a state with strong authoritarian traditions. Events in the USSR seem to reconfirm Alexis de Tocqueville's wise observation that "the most critical moment for bad governments is the one which witnesses their first step toward reform."

James A. Duran Jr.
Professor Emeritus of History

Canisius College
May 1991

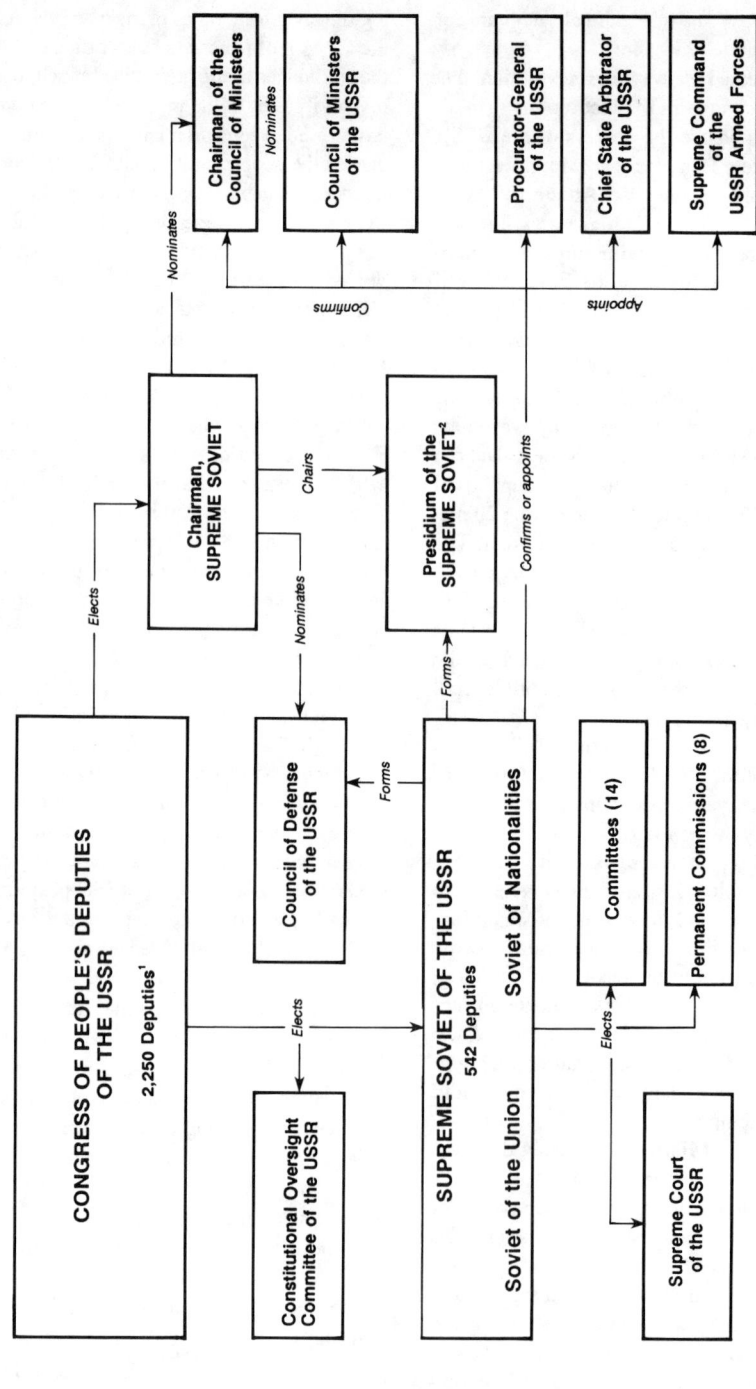

ANNOTATED LIST OF SPEECHES
SESSIONS 1–7, 25–31 MAY 1989

FIRST SESSION
25 MAY 1989

Speaker	Subject	Page
V.P. Orlov	Opens Congress	4a
V.F. Tolpezhnikov	Honors Tbilisi victims, seeks inquiry	5a
V.P. Lukin	Proposes Presidium members	5a
	Election of Presidium	7a
M.S. Gorbachev	Assumes chairmanship of the Congress	7a
N.A. Nazarbayev	Proposes agenda	7a
A.D. Sakharov	Criticizes agenda, opposes transfer of legislative responsibilities to Supreme Soviet, calls on Gorbachev to defend reforms	7b
F.V. Popov	Rebuts Sakharov, defends agenda and electoral method	8b
Ye.N. Meshalkin	Defends agenda and electoral method	9a
M.S. Gorbachev	Reads note announcing A.M. Obolensky's intention to stand for election as Chairman of Supreme Soviet to ensure a contested election	9b
A.M. Obolensky	Proposes postponement of election of Supreme Soviet	10a
V.N. Belyaev	Reports substitutions in Tellers Commission slate	10b
	Tellers Commission elected	11a
Yu.Yu. Boldyrev	Proposes recorded vote on all substantive issues	11a
	Agenda adopted; consideration of Provisional Standing Orders	11a
K.A. Antanavichyus	Recalls unrecorded amendments to Standing Orders	11b
V.V. Landsbergis	Challenges voting procedure, seeks response to Sakharov's proposal to clarify constitutional relationship between Congress and Supreme Soviet	12a
M.S. Gorbachev	Discusses new role of Supreme Soviet and people's deputies	12b
A.V. Levashov	Notes that Electoral Commission chairman is required to preside over First Session	13a
A.A. Plotniyeks	Calls for commission to expand and clarify Standing Orders	13b
S.B. Stankevich	Proposes amendment enabling 100 deputies to require a recorded vote	14b
M.S. Gorbachev	Offers counterproposal requiring a majority of deputies to force a recorded vote (adopted)	14b
M.S. Gorbachev	Reads complaint protesting "pernicious" effort by Sakharov and others to disrupt work of the Congress	15a
Yu.R. Boyars	Urges mechanism to ensure every delegation a voice on major issues, proposes electoral change, moves to give all deputies a role in Supreme Soviet committees and commissions	15b
A.Ye. Sebentsov	Objects to spectators' behavior	17a
G.M. Kurochka	Cites need for microphones among deputies, deplores unresponsiveness of Electoral Commission	17b
A.M. Adamovich	Calls for suspension of decree on demonstrations	17b

Speaker	Subject	Page
Unidentified	Questions ambiguous wording of Article 20	17b
M.S. Gorbachev	Denies that decree on demonstrations impedes work of Congress	17b
A.N. Saunin	Raises objections to Articles 1 and 19	18a
M.S. Gorbachev	Urges deputies to avoid constitutional issues	18b
K.D. Lubenchenko	Recommends commission to consider Standing Orders, calls for formal approval of Gorbachev as chairman of Congress	18b
	Provisional Standing Orders adopted, consideration of Credentials Commission	19a
A.D. Sakharov	Asserts need for professional jurist to lead Credentials Commission	19a
M.S. Gorbachev	Disagrees	19b
S.B. Stankevich	Proposes that commission elect its own officers	19b
V.I. Revnitsev	Supports Gidaspov for chair of Credentials Commission	19b
B.V. Gidaspov	Discusses his qualifications	19b
A.P. Aydak	Calls meeting of all deputies engaged in agriculture	20a
	Credentials Commission elected	20b
	Congress adjourned	

SECOND SESSION
25 MAY 1989

Speaker	Subject	Page
V.I. Vorotnikov	Presides	20a
B.V. Gidaspov	Presents Credentials report, certifies all deputies despite 9000 complaints, notes popular dissatisfaction with electoral commissions, summarizes deputies' characteristics	20a
Unidentified	Inquires about alleged Latvian electoral violations	22b
B.V. Gidaspov	Refers all complaints to Supreme Soviet	23a
	Credentials report approved	23a
N.A. Kutsenko	Reads cable detailing ineligibility of an elected deputy	23b
A.I. Lukyanov	Clarifies disputed deputy's election	23b
E.N. Shengelaya	Seeks circulation of official Georgian Soviet report on Tbilisi events, calls for interrogation of responsible ministers and for expulsion of General Rodionov	23b
V.I. Vorotnikov	Notes intent to form special Tbilisi investigation commission	24a
G.S. Igityan	Calls for investigation of anti-Armenian riot in Sumgait, condemns indifference of Azerbaijani intelligentsia	24b
V.I. Vorotnikov	Urges adherence to agenda	25a
V.I. Alksnis	Sees "Watergate" in creation of disproportionate Latvian electoral districts and official reluctance to investigate, cites Russian voters' disadvantages, proposes inquiry by deputies committee	25a
V.I. Vorotnikov	Suggests that Central Electoral Commission reexamine Alksnis' complaint	25b
M.S. Gorbachev	Notes deputies' mistrust of Electoral Commission, proposes joint investigation with Credentials Commission	25b

ANNOTATED LIST OF SPEECHES

Speaker	Subject	Page
B.V. Gidaspov	Avers ignorance of Latvian irregularities but declares willingness to investigate	26a
	Central Electoral Commission and Credentials Commission ordered to investigate Latvian elections	26b
M.R. Mamedov	Responds to Igityan, asserts Azerbaijani blamelessness	26b
V.I. Vorotnikov	Interrupts Mamedov, cautions restraint	26b
I.I. Zaslavsky	Proposes prompt investigation of the most serious electoral violations	26b
V.I. Vorotnikov	Closes credentials discussion	27b
Ch. Aytmatov	Nominates Gorbachev for chairmanship of Supreme Soviet	27b
V.A. Logunov	Supports Gorbachev candidacy but proposes that he resign party posts	29a
V.L. Bedulya	Supports Gorbachev candidacy, praises his foreign policy	29a
V.A. Yavorivsky	Sees Gorbachev as necessary, Yeltsin as desirable; cites need for direct, popular election of president	29b
B.V. Kryzhkov	Questions Gorbachev on dual posts, party loyalty, and Gdlyan-Ivanov case	29b
Mukhammad-Yusuf	Declares Moslem support for Gorbachev	30a
V.P. Khmel	Supports Gorbachev and combined posts	30a
V.A. Biryukov	Attempts to nominate Yeltsin	30b
M.Y. Lauristan	Supports Gorbachev, asks position on republic self-determination and sovereignty, role of army in civil disturbances, and Politburo responsibility for Tbilisi massacre	30b
V.A. Voblikov	Supports Gorbachev and combined offices as necessary to restructuring of the party	31a
Yu.B. Solovyev	Favors combined offices but urges more vigorous action on domestic issues	31b
A.D. Sakharov	Supports Gorbachev but wants full debate of issues and Gorbachev's response to questions	31b
Unidentified	Supports Gorbachev, anticipates that his domestic program will equal his foreign policy successes	31b
V.I. Vorotnikov	Tries to end discussion	32a
M.S. Gorbachev	Advises continued discussion with speakers limited to one minute	32a
A.A. Shchelkanov	Questions Gorbachev on Crimean dacha, personal attitude toward combined posts, and arbitrary decision making	32a
D.E. Ivans	Seeks Gorbachev's position on national rights and self-determination	32b
Unidentified	Asserts need for Gorbachev as brake on party bureaucrats, deems combined posts essential to survival of democracy	33a
L.I. Sukhov	Compares Gorbachev to Napoleon, cites need to close gap between rich and poor	33a
V.I. Voskoboynikov	Objects to anonymous efforts to end discussion, opposes combined posts	33b
Unidentified	Rebukes Vorotnikov for merging separate questions into one	33b
Ye.L. Golovlev	Opposes combined posts	33b
V.V. Goncharov	Condemns bureaucracy, urges Gorbachev to establish direct contact with people	34a
R.A. Allayarov	Deplores slow pace of Congress and dominance of Moscow, Leningrad, and Baltic deputies; slurs glasnost	34a
T.I. Kayumova	Supports Gorbachev candidacy	34b
N.P. Bekhtereva	Sees absolute need for combined offices, praises Raisa Gorbachev for role in USSR's international successes	34b

SECOND SESSION, 26 MAY 1989

Speaker	Subject	Page
Ye.V. Kogan	Addresses national issues in the Baltic, sees combined posts as too burdensome	34b
S.N. Zvonov	Opposes combined offices on personal and constitutional grounds, challenges Gorbachev to reconcile democracy with April law on state crimes, questions motives of those seeking to end discussion	35a
L.A. Arutyunyan	Cites Armenians' faith in Gorbachev, need for continued struggle for social justice and resolution of Nagorno-Karabakh issue	35b
A.F. Yemelyanenkov	Asks Gorbachev to explain need to combine state and party posts and his role in the adoption of the decree on demonstrations	36a
N.V. Fedorov	Challenges authority of Supreme Soviet Presidium to change content of laws and restrict constitutional rights	36b
K.D. Lubenchenko	Argues need to delimit party and state functions	36b
N.V. Yeseykin	Supports Gorbachev candidacy	37a
M.V. Spiridonov	Supports Gorbachev candidacy	37a
Unidentified	Supports Gorbachev candidacy	37b
S.I. Konev	Favors combined posts until local soviets acquire real power	37b
V.I. Mironenko	Favors combined posts lest party be isolated from the people	37b
P.P. Falk	Begs Congress to resolve national questions	38a
Unidentified	Praises Gorbachev on behalf of women	38a
I.I. Kukhar	Supports Gorbachev candidacy	38a
V.I. Vorotnikov	Seeks to curtail discussion	38b
V.A. Martirosyan	Urges focus on national issues	38b
Ye.P. Velikhov	Expresses confusion over power	39a
M.S. Gorbachev	Addresses issues raised by deputies, stresses difficulties of translating policy into practice and need for political reform, describes his role in Tbilisi events, recognizes need to harmonize ethnic relations, defends combined posts as necessary to ensure party cooperation in restructuring, discusses matter of Crimean dacha, asserts personal dedication to democracy	39a
	Gorbachev admitted to secret ballot	41b
A.M. Obolensky	Nominates self as candidate for chairman of Supreme Soviet, outlines his program	42a
A.A. Korshunov	Castigates Obolensky for wasting time	44a
S.V. Belozertsev	Defends Obolensky and precedent of choice	44a
L.I. Sandulyan	Endorses Obolensky candidacy	44a
A.A. Sobchak	Sees important principle in Obolensky's candidacy	44b
M.Ch. Zalikhanov	Accuses Obolensky of demagoguery	44b
A.M. Obolensky	Explains candidacy	44b
	Obolensky candidacy rejected	45a
G.E. Burbulis	Nominates Yeltsin for chairmanship of Supreme Soviet	45a
V.L. Fomenko	Compares rejection of Obolensky to apparatchiks' rejection of candidates in okrug meetings, rebukes Zalikhanov	45a
S.S. Sulakshin	Observes that open voting on candidacies nullifies secret ballot	45b
A.N. Krayko	Praises Yeltsin but urges him to withdraw	45b
V.A. Chelyshev	Commends Yeltsin but urges withdrawal	46a
R.G. Voronina	Supports Gorbachev in name of working class	46b
B.N. Yeltsin	Withdraws candidacy	46b
V.A. Berezov	Proposes members of counting commission	47a

ANNOTATED LIST OF SPEECHES

Speaker	Subject	Page
A.M. Obolensky	Asks to be removed from counting commission	47a
	Tellers Commission approved	47b
Yu.A. Osipyan	Explains voting procedure	47b
	Congress recesses to vote	48b
Yu.A. Osipyan	Reports Gorbachev's election as Chairman of Supreme Soviet	48b
	Report approved	49a
V.I. Vorotnikov	Announces election of Gorbachev	49a
M.S. Gorbachev	Thanks deputies	49a
	Congress adjourned	49b

THIRD SESSION
26 MAY 1989

Speaker	Subject	Page
M.S. Gorbachev	Opens discussion on election of Supreme Soviet, invites Stroyev to summarize work of conference of deputies	52a
Ye.S. Stroyev	Reports, proposes lists of candidates for secret ballot	52a
T.I. Zaslavskaya	Alleges police interference with lawful voters rally, calls on interior minister to explain, demands suspension of decree on rallies and demonstrations	53a
M.S. Gorbachev	Summons Bakatin to explain police action	53a
V.V. Bakatin	Denies police interference with voter rallies, cites dispersal of one illegal gathering near the Kremlin	53a
Z.Z. Vayshvila	Contends militia presence caused tension	53b
S.B. Stankevich	Reports that militia closely surrounded citizens (*interruptions*), asks Gorbachev to control deputies, requests site for citizenry to meet with deputies during Congress	54a
V.P. Filippov	Defends militia action	54a
A.D. Sakharov	Supports call to suspend decree on demonstrations	54a
Yu.T. Akbarov	Urges end to demagoguery and wasting of time	54b
M.S. Gorbachev	Reads deputy's request for tolerance and patience, supports need to permit public rallies while also maintaining order	54b
Unidentified	Asks for vote to suspend decree on demonstrations	55a
	Proposal defeated	55a
M.S. Gorbachev	Announces Moscow city soviet decision to permit public meetings in Luzhniki Square, notes that very few requests for rally permits are denied	55b
A.S. Samsonov	Asserts that deputies should confine activities to their own constituencies, cites Sakharov and Stankevich	55b
M.S. Gorbachev	Endorses both positions	56a
G.A. Kakaras	Proposes microphones in aisles and more tellers	56a
M.S. Gorbachev	Prefers speakers to use podium but announces that microphones will be installed in hall for questions and brief reports	56a

THIRD SESSION, 26 MAY 1989

Speaker	Subject	Page
I.A. Andreyeva	Asks whether deputies must give up jobs to serve in Supreme Soviet, proposes adoption of an order to prohibit deputies from interfering with speakers	56b
M.S. Gorbachev	Opines that most members of Soviet will serve full time	56b
V.A. Statulyavichyus	Questions method of electing Soviet; Lithuanian delegation proposes vote by republics, amending Article 111; challenges constitutionality of decree on demonstrations	57a
V.L. Ginzburg	Sees need for full time service in Supreme Soviet and need for annual evaluations of deputies, accepts logic of electing Soviet of Nationalities by republic but not Soviet of the Union	57b
V.I. Kirillov	Sees need for republic election of Soviet of Nationalities to protect national minorities while all-union interests of Soviet of Union require vote of all deputies	58a
V.I. Samarin	Doubts that party functionaries can properly perform Soviet duties, challenges propriety of allowing republic executives to serve in Supreme Soviet	58a
M.S. Gorbachev	Cites, disagrees with memos demanding limitations on speakers and complaining that Moscovites are disrupting the Congress	58b
V.I. Borkovets	Offers corrections to candidate list	58b
B.F. Pylin	Calls for creation of third Supreme Soviet chamber to represent social organizations, sees attempt by Moscow contingent to augment their representation	59a
A.I. Konovalov	Urges clarification of deputies' roles before election of Soviet, notes constituents' concern over violation of constitution, questions propriety of voting on persons unknown to electors, complains about lack of information	59b
S.N. Fedorov	Urges Congress to rise above parochialism in election of Soviet and to cooperate in the destruction of the incompetent state apparatus	60a
M.S. Gorbachev	Defends Moscow Group's nomination of candidates in excess of quota, reads notes concerning election procedure and confusion over permanence of Soviet responsibilities	60b
A.N. Boyko	Expresses concern over apparatchiks' control of nominating process, proposes constitutional amendments establishing executive authority of Supreme Soviet and allowing votes of no confidence in government, urges Gorbachev to muzzle those who interrupt speakers	60b
V.P. Zolotukhin	Stresses need to clarify composition and duties of Supreme Soviet and to follow democratic procedures	61b
Ya.Ya. Bezbakh	Reports that deputies elected in runoffs were not considered for election to Supreme Soviet, demands addition of candidates to Ukrainian list	61b
M.S. Gorbachev	Reads letter inquiring whether deputies must resign jobs to serve in Soviet	62a
O.T. Bogomolov	Repeats questions concerning deputy status, proposes equality of deputies of Congress and Soviet, formation of committees by the Congress	62a
A.N. Murashev	Asserts that excess Moscow nominations signal democratic example not power grab, suggests publication of nominees' names to inform voters	62b
A.I. Tkhor	Claims that intelligentsia dominates candidate lists while only workers will uphold workers' interests	63a
A.V. Minzhurenko	Contends that party secretaries dominate delegations, proposes more nominees to contest every seat	63b

ANNOTATED LIST OF SPEECHES

Speaker	Subject	Page
D.N. Kugultinov	Wanted to speak on previous issue	64a
Yu.A. Levykin	Sees quotas as appropriate to Soviet of Nationalities but not Union, favors more candidates, nominations from floor, informed voting	64a
M.S. Gorbachev	Reports memo calling for "no supreme anything" but a Congress of Deputies	64b
V.Ya. Shevlyuga	Sees state-party bureaucracy attempting to dominate nominations, nominates self and colleague	65a
V.V. Guly	Responds to Tkhor, cites bureaucratic abuse of nominating process	65a
I.O. Bisher	States Latvian position that republics should decide their own representation as prescribed by 1924 Constitution; asserts that Latvian list reflects republic's ethnic-social composition, acknowledges disagreement with Moscow Group	66a
F.M. Burlatsky	Calls for alternative candidates and for able, full time deputies to counteract bureaucracy	66b
M.S. Gorbachev	Reports letters demanding end to procedural discussion and limit of one speech per day per deputy; also that critics offer solutions, that apparatchiks show respect for people's representatives, and that Zaslavskaya apologize for slandering the Moscow militia	67b
V.A. Pisarenko	Calls for clear procedure for adopting laws, proposes that deputies elected to Soviet be relieved of other jobs, supports regional quotas	67b
V.P. Grishchuk	Sees need for full time professional work in Soviet, proposes compromise allowing republics to designate 90 percent of membership of Soviet of Union with remainder to be freely elected	68b
S.V. Karaganov	Opposes Guly's candidacy	68b
M.S. Gorbachev	Reads note asking how the two chambers of Supreme Soviet will differ if both are elected on a regional basis	69a
R.Z. Sagdeyev	Sees choice among deputies as between proponents of new and old thinking; argues that candidates for Soviet should be asked to give up full time jobs and that 25 party secretaries of republic and oblast committees should be eliminated as candidates	69a
V.N. Kudryavtsev	Reviews evils of former Supreme Soviet, especially dominance of Presidium; outlines distribution of lawmaking functions between Congress and Soviet, warns that efforts to weaken Soviet perpetuates old system, cites need to limit Supreme Soviet Presidium to promulgation of extraordinary acts, with normative acts reserved to Congress or Soviet; sees important distinctions between deputies of Congress and Soviet	69b
V.A. Giro	Supports quotas in election of Soviet deputies because republics know the people they nominate, declares willingness to sacrifice Tajik party secretaries to cause of perestroika	71a
A.Yu. Smaylis	Proposes three-month hiatus before promulgation of draft laws to allow time for comment and amendment	71b
M.S. Gorbachev	Reads Metropolitan's proposal that requests to speak should be submitted in writing with thrust of remarks stated	71b
	Proposal approved by acclamation	
V.M. Kotlyakov	Distinguishes between election and delegation of deputies to Supreme Soviet, urges augmentation of candidate lists to ensure competitive elections, nominates M.Ch. Zalikhanov (Kabardino-Balkar ASSR)	72a
M.S. Gorbachev	Reviews situation, proposes recess	72b
G.V. Koshlakov	Suggests alternate procedure for electing Soviet	72b
M.S. Gorbachev	Expresses desire to see commissions of Soviet headed and staffed by creative persons with knowledge and experience	73a

THIRD SESSION, 26 MAY 1989

Speaker	Subject	Page
F.M. Burlatsky	Proposes that only those released from regular duties serve in Soviet and that only deputies of Congress head commissions	73a
S.A. Tsyplyayev	Fears that mandatory release from jobs to serve in Soviet will lead to an apparatchik-type organization	73b
	Approval of resolution to release of deputies elected to Supreme Soviet from permanent jobs, "as a rule"; rejection of proposal to require deputies to surrender their jobs in order to serve in the Soviet	73b
M.S. Gorbachev	Promises to clarify meaning of phrase, "as a rule"	74a
M.S. Gorbachev	Summons Lukyanov to present the Presidium's conclusions and proposals	74a
A.I. Lukyanov	Recommends adherence to constitution until commission has examined distribution of powers; defines criteria for identifying candidates to be released from jobs for full time work in Soviet, composition of commissions and committees of the Soviet, consultative role of other deputies, and method of election, with separate list for Moscow	74a
Unidentified	Questions how method of election conforms to constitution	75a
A.I. Lukyanov	Insists that nomination by republics and election by Congress meets constitutional requirements; hears deputy assert that Nagorno-Karabakh delegation was not permitted to nominate its own candidates	76a
V.V. Landsbergis	Asserts principle of national sovereignty in election of representatives, threatens Lithuanian boycott of election	76a
M.S. Gorbachev	Notes crisis situation, appeals for Lithuanian trust and respect	76a
R.A. Medvedev	Expresses personal dislike of quotas, but compares Lithuania to Moscow in lack of sovereignty; appeals to Lithuanians to withdraw ultimatum	76b
M.S. Gorbachev	Stresses that republic interests are protected by nominating process which elections merely confirm	77a
Yu.A. Osipyan	Appeals to Lithuanians and others inclined to support them, reiterates previous argument	77a
A.Y. Burachas	Seeks more time for Lithuanian delegation to consider Gorbachev's statement, offers further explanation of its position, notes incorrect wording in amendment to Standing Orders	77b
A.G. Kuliyev	Supports statements of Lukyanov and Medvedev	78a
S.P. Zalygin	Rebukes Lithuanians, cites need for cooperation	78a
V.D. Romanenko	Makes Ukrainian delegation's appeal to Lithuanians	78b
	Approval of Presidium's report	78b
Ya.S. Kanovich	States that each deputy should vote in accord with his conscience	79a
	Congress recessed to allow delegations to amend or conclude action on candidate lists	79a
V.V. Landsbergis	Expresses regret (as instructed by the Lithuanian delegation) that earlier statement was misinterpreted: intention was to make clear that deputies would vote as individuals according to their consciences	79a
A.I. Lukyanov	Reports on development of candidate lists	79b
M.S. Gorbachev	Opens discussion of candidacies for Soviet of Nationalities	79b
V.I. Vorotnikov	Reports changes in RSFSR candidate list, voices concern that number of candidates exceeds quota	79b
M.A. Lezhnev	Nominates V.M. Rybakov (RSFSR)	80a
S.I. Kolesnikov	Nominates N.A. Demakov and A.A. Kiselev (RSFSR)	80a

ANNOTATED LIST OF SPEECHES

Speaker	Subject	Page
V.I. Kolotov	Nominates A.M. Obolensky and N.V. Ivanov (RSFSR)	80b
A.L. Plotnikov	Nominates V.P. Savinykh (RSFSR)	80b
B.V. Gidaspov	Nominates N.P. Napalkov (RSFSR)	80b
S.I. Novotny	Nominates V.V. Bushuyev in place of Yu.I. Borodin (RSFSR)	80b
S.S. Shushkevich	Nominates A.O. Dobrovolsky, A.G. Zhuravlev, S.A. Gabrusev, and V.N. Korniyenko (Belorussian SSR)	81a
G.M. Kurochka	Nominates self (RSFSR)	81a
A.I. Dubko	Urges rejection of Shushkevich's motion	81b
V.Ye. Karmanovsky	Urges rejection of Kurochka's motion	81b
Unidentified (S.B. Kalyagin)	Nominates A.F. Nasonov (RSFSR)	82a
V.S. Grigoryan	Nominates G.A. Pogosyan and Z.G. Balayan (NKAO-Azerbaijan)	82a
Yu.E. Andreyev	Reports T.I. Zaslavkaya's withdrawal, nominates T.Kh. Gdlyan as replacement; also N.Ya. Petrakov and G.S. Lisichkin (RSFSR)	82a
V.P. Polyanichko	Nominates G.A. Pogosyan and V.Dzh. Dzhafarov (NKAO-Azerbaijan)	82a
V.L. Fomenko	Supports nomination of Korniyenko, Gabrusev, Dobrovolsky, and Zhuravlev; confirms disharmony among Belorussian deputies	82b
R.K. Shchedrin	Nominates N.I. Travkin (RSFSR)	82b
V.V. Sevryukov	Urges election of candidates under age thirty, renominates Kiselev (RSFSR)	82b
N.V. Savchenko	Criticizes selection process, describes method followed in Krasnodar; nominates V.A. Gubarev, V.V. Kasyan, V.V. Khmura, and A.T. Kuzovlev (RSFSR)	83a
T.P. Zhukova	Supports Kiselev's candidacy	83b
V.N. Zubkov	Protests exclusion of Rostov-on-Don's one million citizens from representation, nominates V.Ya. Shevlyuga and self (RSFSR)	83b
M.S. Gorbachev	Offers time for Belorussian and RSFSR delegation to prune candidate lists	84a
Ye.Ye. Sokolov	Declines more time, declares that newly named candidates lack majority support and will be rejected by Belorussian delegation	84a
M.S. Gorbachev	Notes Russian delegation needs more time, declares 30-minute recess	84b
	Congress recessed	
V.I. Vorotnikov	Reports that nomination issues remain unresolved—candidacies still exceed RSFSR and Moscow quotas	84b
M.S. Gorbachev	Conducts vote among Russian delegation: original list of twelve RSFSR candidates is confirmed, additional nominees are excluded; opens discussion on composition of Moscow delegation	85a
Unidentified	Reports Moscow delegates' decision to retain original list without additions or deletions	85b
Unidentified	Repeats distinction between election and delegation of authority, proposes two nominees for each place in Soviet of Nationalities as well as proportional representation for national groups	85b
	Nominations for Supreme Soviet closed	
	Congress recessed to await printing of ballots	86b
M.S. Gorbachev	Reads telegrams: Sochi worker urges Congress to take as much time as needed to allow everyone to speak, while Novokuznetsk worker condemns interference with speakers as insult to voters and deputies	86b

FOURTH SESSION, 27 MAY 1989

Speaker	Subject	Page
Yu.A. Osipyan	Reviews voting procedure and counting options, notes that 29 of 55 Moscow candidates though elected separately will be included in the 146 deputies allotted to the RSFSR	87a
Unidentified	Protests that Nagorno-Karabakh representatives were not allowed to nominate deputies for Soviet of Nationalities	88b
M.S. Gorbachev	Rules that those matters are now settled; holds election of Congress Secretariat; presents, adopts draft resolution "On Citizens' Proposals"	89a
	Congress adjourned	89b

FOURTH SESSION
27 MAY 1989

Speaker	Subject	Page
M.S. Gorbachev	Presiding	92a
Yu.A. Osipyan	Reports election of Soviet of Nationalities (complete list and voting results), defers report on election of Soviet of the Union	92a
	Tellers report adopted	97a
Yu.N. Afanaseyev	Decries election of "Stalinist-Brezhnevian Supreme Soviet," claims CPD is dominated by "aggressively obedient majority," questions Gorbachev's role	97b
M.S. Gorbachev	Departs from agenda, opens floor for responses to Afanaseyev's speech	98a
G.Kh. Popov	Supports Afanaseyev's attack, claims that apparat and Congress majority scorn democracy and pluralism, invites formation of independent Interregional Group of Deputies, sees party as inefficient and no longer capable of leading the nation	98a
V.N. Stepanov	Attacks disruptive tactics of Moscow delegation, calls for return to agenda	100a
M.S. Gorbachev	Challenges Popov's willingness to split Congress into "factions," denies any effort to manipulate the Congress	100b
V.F. Tolpezhnikov	Supports Afanaseyev, proposes ejection of deputies who interfere with speakers, protests Gorbachev's practice of interpreting deputies' statements	100b
A.M. Adamovich	Asserts that restructuring requires popular restraint of party apparatus, control of budget, and protection from excessive concentration of power by means of referenda, impeachment, recall, and votes of no-confidence; condemns the "enthusiasm of obedience"	101a
S.P. Golovin	Demands explanation for omission of deputy Chemodanov as candidate for Soviet of Nationalities	102b
Ye.N. Meshalkin	Characterizes remarks of Afanaseyev and Popov as sour grapes, opposes factionalism, calls for constitutional amendment to ensure continuity during transfer of power	102b
M.R. Mamedov (V.G. Mamedov)	Opposes Afanaseyev and Popov, calls for united action by all	104a
V.I. Kasarev	Asserts that Congress majority has blocked all efforts at reform, demands that Lukyanov apologize for poor organization of Congress	104b

ANNOTATED LIST OF SPEECHES xxvii

Speaker	Subject	Page
M.S. Gorbachev	Defends Lukyanov	105b
T.V. Momotova	Proclaims self independent of apparat and objects to pressure from Moscow Group	105b
Yu.A. Osipyan	Reports election of Soviet of the Union (complete list and voting results), denies responsibility for omission of Chemodanov from ballot	106a
V.I. Vorotnikov	Cites insufficient population as reason for absence of candidates from four RSFSR autonomous republics, contends that Chemodanov's name appeared improperly on Mari ASSR candidates list	109a
M.S. Gorbachev	Adds his explanation	109b
Unidentified	Alleges procedural violations	110a
S.P. Golovin	Wants name of person responsible for removing Chemodanov's name on ballot	110a
Yu.A. Osipyan	Notes that compilation of ballots required several changes	110a
M.S. Gorbachev	Reminds deputies that each republic nominated its own candidates	110b
Unidentified	Seeks amendment to allow public organizations to nominate Supreme Soviet candidates	110b
O.M. Savostyuk	Requests vote on Chemodanov's candidacy	110b
G.A. Pogosyan	Calls on Lukyanov to explain how NKAO list was determined and to defend the Presidium's role	110b
G.V. Starovoytova	Supports Pogosyan's demand, proposes nullification of NKAO Supreme Soviet election	111a
G.A. Posibeyev	Calls for representation of autonomous regions regardless of population, asks Congress to decide validity of Chemodanov's candidacy	111b
A.V. Sharonov	Suggests two methods of settling question of Chemodanov's candidacy, demands to know who removed his name and substituted Veprev's	112a
A.A. Sobchak	Warns that voting irregularities stem from inattention to procedural issues, cites incompetence of RSFSR leadership, calls for expansion of Supreme Soviet by constitutional amendment but, that failing, offers Leningrad seat to NKAO representative	112b
A.V. Oborin	Advises postponement of Chemodanov-Veprev question, calls for commission to oversee procedural compliance, proposes representation for each nationality regardless of size	113a
V.A. Zubanov	Sees method of choosing Supreme Soviet as unresponsive to popular will, cites need to change the status of that body	113a
L.A. Arutyunyan	Protests violation of constitutional rights of Armenian citizens of NKAO, calls for new election of candidates nominated by NKAO's Armenian representatives	114a
V.A. Martirosyan	Supports all measures to satisfy demands of NKAO deputies	114a
M.A. Ibragimov	Defends Azerbaijani treatment of and solicitude for citizens of NKAO	114b
N.N. Vorontsov	Complains of disorganization, supports new elections for Mari ASSR and NKAO	115b
M.S. Gorbachev	Asks RSFSR deputies to confer and advise Congress on Chemodanov candidacy with Azeri and NKAO deputies to do same in consultation with representatives of Presidium, declares question of NKAO representation in Supreme Soviet still open	116a

xxviii FOURTH SESSION, 27 MAY 1989

Speaker	Subject	Page
A.A. Sobchak	Disagrees with Gorbachev, asserts that NKAO representation in Soviet of Nationalities must stand, offers to surrender two Leningrad seats to NKAO delegates	116b
G.A. Yenokyan	Insists on right of NKAO deputies to choose their own representation, calls for Armenian participation if NKAO deputies are required to meet with Azerbaijan delegation	116b
M.S. Gorbachev	Proposes to rule Soviet of Nationalities election valid except for voting on NKAO delegation, invites deputies' approval	117a
E.T. Arutyunyan	Asserts that NKAO deputies should consult with the real authorities in NKAO, not the Azerbaijani delegation	117a
M.S. Gorbachev	Disagrees, deplores divisive comments, asks support for his proposal to nullify the NKAO election	117a
A.Kh. Vezirov	Protests Azeri sincerity in seeking equitable NKAO representation, opposes nullification of election, agrees to seek mutual understanding	117b
S.G. Arutyunyan	Favors annulment of NKAO election	118a
	Election of NKAO deputies to Soviet of Nationalities voided	118b
M.S. Gorbachev	Presents alternatives to resolve issue of Mari representation	118b
	Rotating representation of ASSRs approved by acclamation	
Yu.M. Chemodanov	Agrees with compromise, stakes claim to begin the rotation	118b
M.S. Gorbachev	Declares "Russian crisis" settled, discusses agenda, invites comment	119a
N.S. Sazonov	Suggests curtailment of discussion of Afanaseyev's speech in order to move on	119b
	Congress recessed	119b
A.I. Lukyanov	Reports on Presidium's ongoing effort to resolve question of NKAO representation	120a
O.O. Suleymenov	Praises resolution of Chemodanov candidacy as form of "repentance," sympathizes with Afanaseyev but opposes rhetoric that could split Congress, sees need for dialogue between left and right	120b
Ye.V. Yakovlev	Condones sharp rhetoric as reflective of state of society, criticizes bureaucratic organization of Congress, urges unity over factionalism, questions composition of Supreme Soviet	121a
V.S. Obraz	Urges Congress to abandon struggle for power and address fundamental issues confronting society	122a
N.S. Petruchenko	Condemns passivity of party leadership and political ambitions of Moscovites, calls for more democratic procedures, better discipline, and more effective organization of Congress	123a
L.P. Kravchenko	Condemns intolerance of minority as undemocratic, disparages scare tactics, sees order and discipline as essential to democracy	124b
V.I. Kirillov	Commends Afanaseyev but urges focus on causes of stagnation, attributes all problems to ministerial monopolies	125b
S.I. Konev	Argues that perestroika has consisted of half-measures because administrative-command system remains intact, contends that key is to revamp the political system	126a
A.N. Krayko	Attributes failings and inefficiency to inexperience with democracy	126b
Ch.T. Aytmatov	Criticizes haphazard organization and procedures, calls for orderly consideration of problems	128a
M.S. Gorbachev	Cites notes criticizing deviation from agenda, but defends discussion of Afanaseyev-Popov speeches	129a

ANNOTATED LIST OF SPEECHES

Speaker	Subject	Page
V.A. Palm	Lauds Moscow Group's preparation for Congress, notes inevitable disagreements when interests conflict but calls on progressives to stand united against efforts of apparatus to prevent radical restructuring	129b
A.S. Samsonov	Objects to being identified as member of apparat, calls on deputies to oppose the Moscovite faction and to condemn factionalism generally	130b 131b
M.S. Gorbachev	Proposes to end discussion of Afanaseyev-Popov speeches following remarks of deputy Moshnyaga; deputies approve	131b
T.V. Moshnyaga	Criticizes preparation of Congress, suggests consultation with deputies in setting agenda and schedule, criticizes RSFSR delegation's selection of Supreme Soviet representatives	131b
M.S. Gorbachev	Overrules Congress and self, allows Popov to speak	132b
G.Kh. Popov	Absolves Gorbachev of manipulating speakers, denies factional activity, urges united action	132b
M.S. Gorbachev	Terminates discussion of Afanaseyev-Popov speeches, nominates A.I. Lukyanov to be First Deputy Chairman of USSR Supreme Soviet	133a
A.D. Sakharov	Calls on Lukyanov to explain role in adoption of decrees on public order and state security	133b
G.I. Filshin	Reads telegram denouncing single candidate elections, challenges Lukyanov's uncontested candidacy, sees him unfit for post due to incompetence in preparing for Congress	134a
M.S. Gorbachev	Claims sole constitutional authority to nominate senior government officials	134b
N.G. Dmitriyev	Notes constitutional deficiency that allows Gorbachev and Lukyanov to head Supreme Soviet without being elected to that body	134b
Unidentified	Agrees with Gorbachev's interpretation of constitutional powers, questions Lukyanov's role in adoption of decree on state crimes, complains of haphazard method of being recognized to speak	135a
M.S. Gorbachev	Asks Secretariat to take charge of registering speakers	135b
G.V. Starovoytova	Seeks postponement of vote on First Deputy Chairman in order to hold full discussion of ethnic relations, wants to know role of Lukyanov and central authorities in events in Tbilisi and Sumgait	135b
A.V. Oborin (V.A. Shapovalenko)	Reiterates complaints against Supreme Soviet Presidium and staff concerning organization of Congress, sees no need for prolonging Fourth Session, seeks postponement of Lukyanov's election	136a
	Election of First Deputy Chairman postponed	136b
M.S. Gorbachev	Notes instructions to Presidium to form commissions to investigate Tbilisi events and Gdlyan-Ivanov affair	136b
I.I. Zaslavsky	Asserts that commission should investigate charges made by Gdlyan as well as accusations against him	137a
M.S. Gorbachev	Agrees, invites Gdlyan's views	137a
T.Kh. Gdlyan	Asks to defer statement due to fatigue, but appeals for an investigative commission independent of party apparatus	137b
V.A. Yarin	Supports Gdlyan, calls for independent investigation	137b
V.A. Vrovkov	Stresses need for a Gdlyan commission trusted by deputies and the people—need for the truth, whatever the cost	138a
G.I. Yanayev	Supports independent investigation of Gdlyan affair, but rebukes Gdlyan for reference to "so-called deputies"	138b
M.S. Gorbachev	Charges Presidium to form a commission in consultation with Gdlyan	138b
	Congress adjourned	

FIFTH SESSION
29 MAY 1989

Speaker	Subject	Page
M.S. Gorbachev	Presiding; announces that Secretariat is finally working, advises against proposal to end radio-tv coverage of Congress	140a
A.I. Lukyanov	Responds to questions posed in previous session: disclaims individual responsibility for decrees approved collectively by Presidium, defends need for legislation on demonstrations and use of internal forces, declares opposition to force in inter-ethnic relations, denies foreknowledge of use of army in Tbilisi, defends Congress preparations, declares support for democratization, delimitation of powers, war on crime, judicial and legal reform, and glasnost	140b
Unidentified	Questions Lukyanov on Tbilisi and absence of flag as backdrop to podium	143b
A.I. Lukyanov	Admits breakdown of law and order in Georgia, calls for renewed respect for national symbols	143b
A.A. Shchelkanov	Proposes that candidates respond immediately to questions when posed	143b
A.I. Konovalov	Proposes rules to clarify method of electing First Deputy Chairman	144a
M.S. Gorbachev	Agrees on need but prefers to leave question of elections to next Congress	145a
	Konovalov's motion rejected	145b
M.S. Gorbachev	Appeals to deputies not to derail Congress with procedural issues however important, proposes special session to discuss procedures after election of Lukyanov; a majority agrees	145b
V.P. Nosov	Reads telegram supporting reformers and criticizing Gorbachev for permitting deputies' intolerance, calls for elimination of command structure and bureaucratic apparatus	146b
A.I. Demidov	Chastises Lukyanov for unsatisfactory preparation of Congress, proposes vote by secret ballot	147a
A.G. Zhuravlev	Condemns time wasted on procedural matters	147b
Yu.A. Koltsov	Expresses satisfaction with Lukyanov's views but dissatisfaction with logistics, cites need to clarify deputies' status	148a
Kh.A. Fargiyev	Calls for restoration of Ingush autonomy and rehabilitation of Volga Germans, Crimean Tatars, Chechen, Karachay, Kalmyk, and Balkar peoples; links establishment of rule-of-law state to elimination of effects of Stalin regime	149a
S.B. Aguzarova	Supports Lukyanov candidacy	149b
A.Ye. Sebentsov	Alleges that Presidium voters influence deputies, suggests they vote later; criticizes majority for rejecting Yeltsin against popular will, expresses voters' gratitude and support for democratic reformers and for reelection of RSFSR deputies to Soviet of Nationalities	150a
T.Kh. Gdlyan	Poses questions for Lukyanov on increase in crime, demoralization of law enforcement agencies, and specific cases of bribery and corruption	150b

ANNOTATED LIST OF SPEECHES

Speaker	Subject	Page
A.I. Lukyanov	Declares support for law on deputies' status, favors rehabilitation of peoples repressed by Stalin, notes serious shortcomings in struggle against crime, reviews accomplishments, sees official corruption spreading, declines to discuss particular cases, calls for concerted action against criminal activity	152a
N.V. Ivanov	Urges Lukyanov to be more specific in explaining state policy—wants his personal position on decree on rallies and demonstrations, declares Leningrad group in support of Afanaseyev's position, criticizes "undemocratic" election of Supreme Soviet	154b

Congress recessed

Speaker	Subject	Page
M.S. Gorbachev	Announces that deputy's badges are ready, certificates to be mailed to homes	155a
I.N. Shundeyev	Asks why Lukyanov candidacy is unopposed, why biographies and programs of future ministers are not available, how Gorbachev will cope with two major posts, how party leadership will be rejuvenated, and what is being done to transfer power to local soviets; calls for microphones and for full, free debate of issues	155b
V.N. Kudryavtsev	Praises Lukyanov's qualifications, rebukes Gdlyan	156a
R.A. Medvedev	Wants names of those who allegedly try to subvert Gorbachev's policies when he is absent or distracted, supports Lukyanov candidacy	156b
R.Kh. Solntsev	Questions imprecision in Supreme Soviet Presidium decrees, calls for observance of democratic principles, including contested elections	157b
A. Yakubov	Supports Lukyanov candidacy, questions tardiness of legal reform and delays in investigations of official corruption, proposes Uzbek representation on Gdlyan-Ivanov commission	158a
S.F. Kalashnikov	Challenges Lukyanov on preparations for Congress, claims Komsomol dissatisfaction with his disinterest in issues of concern to young people	159a
A.I. Lukyanov	Describes his policy as the collective policy of the Presidium, denies coverup or attempt to divert official investigations of corruption, sees need for new legislation on legal process, notes youth legislation in progress, admits personal support of controversial clause in decree on rallies, lauds Politburo as source of policy	159b
M.S. Gorbachev	Attempts to end discussion of Lukyanov candidacy, meets various objections	161a
V.K. Starovoytov	Declares majority of Belorussian delegation in support of Lukyanov	162a
E.B. Bichkauskas	Seeks Lukyanov's estimate of bearing of Ribbentrop-Molotov Pact on status of Baltic republics	162a
T.V. Gamkrelidze	States Georgian dissatisfaction with Lukyanov's response to questions concerning events in Tbilisi, sets forth position of Georgian deputies denying validity of 1921 Soviet annexation of the Georgian republic	162a
G.I. Isayev	Reports Azerbaijani support of Lukyanov, constituents' doubt of professional qualifications of G.V. Starovoytova, and Azeris' hostile reaction to speech of G.S. Igityan	163a
S. Negmatulloyev	Reports Tajik deputies' unanimous support of Lukyanov, voices Tajik concerns over water quality and earthquakes	163b
G. Amangeldinova	Rebukes Gdlyan and Ivanov, calls for Congress to support Gorbachev's nominee	164a
R.A. Bazarova	Declares Turkmeni support for Lukyanov	164b
N.P. Kiriyak	Praises Lukyanov, urges state-level study of women's problems	164b

FIFTH SESSION, 29 MAY 1989

Speaker	Subject	Page
A.I. Lukyanov	Defers to appropriate commissions all deputies' questions concerning electoral process, Ribbentrop-Molotov pact, Article 124, and a continuing Georgian prosecution	165a
M.S. Gorbachev	Seeks end to discussion	165b
A.I. Lukyanov	Notes continuing investigation of Karabakh committee; admits legal and party work in Poland, Hungary, and Czechoslovakia in 1956 and 1968	166b
	Lukyanov elected First Deputy Chairman of USSR Supreme Soviet, Chairman's report deferred, Congress recessed	167a
M.S. Gorbachev	Resumes proceedings	167b
A.V. Gorbunov	Apologizes for Secretariat's inability to regulate access to podium, outlines and explains procedure for responding to Gorbachev report (*Several exchanges among deputies, chair, and podium*)	167b
M.S. Gorbachev	Opens discussion of procedural issues	170a
S.N. Khadzhiyev	Proposes resignation of Supreme Soviet Presidium when chairman's term ends, formation of group to organize the Congress, creation of post of master of ceremonies, election of a committee to draft rules of debate, and preparation of an appeal to peoples and parliaments of the world	170b
V.N. Kiselev	Complains of inaccurate reportage, calls for working presidium, equal access to television, popular election of heads of state and government, adherence to constitution, proposes Yeltsin for chair of People's Control Committee	171b
Yu.Ye. Burykh	Alleges voter indignation over method of electing Supreme Soviet, omission of Yeltsin; attributes ineffectiveness of Congress to failure to endow it with exclusive legislative power, calls for commission on legislative initiatives	172b
N.I. Kashnikov	Stresses importance of procedural issues, contested elections, and potential validity of minority positions; proposes time for Moscow Group to respond to Gorbachev's report	174a
O.V. Chernyshev	Characterizes procedural debate as part of secret struggle for democracy in a "congress of missed opportunities"	174b
M.I. Chimpoy	Decries indifference to serious questions; proposes roll-call vote on suspension of decree on demonstrations and on resolutions on Tbilisi, Moldavia, and all matters of national policy	175b
I.I. Zaslavsky	Sees democratic rights and powers as central to reform in all areas, calls for duplication and distribution of documents, for competitive elections, for roll-call vote on important issues, and for one day to be set aside for consideration of social and ecological problems	176a
A.Z. Yastrebov	Complains of lack of microphones in hall, faults Presidium for inefficiency, calls for clarification of status of deputies, demands measures to prevent tampering with candidate lists as in Mari case, wants screening of film on Tbilisi events, cites Lukyanov for inadequate preparation of Congress	177a
N.A. Strukov	Criticizes Presidium, needless repetition of ideas, redundancy of Gdlyan commission, Lukyanov's subservience to party apparatus, and Gorbachev's indifference to effective organization; sees need for commission to reorganize law enforcement agencies and root out apparat corruption and privilege	178a
S.V. Belozertsev	Protests media coverage, rebukes Gorbachev for deferring issues, calls for more information on decrees on disturbances and militia, supports call for roll-call voting, and questions legitimacy of deputies elected by public organizations	179a

ANNOTATED LIST OF SPEECHES

Speaker	Subject	Page
Yu.A. Barashkov	Cites voter dissatisfaction with lack of accomplishment, supports Moscow Group, Afanaseyev, and Popov	180a
V.I. Samarin	Addresses "citizen president"; sees discrepancy in terms of office of Supreme Soviet deputies and the state officials it elects as reason for appointment of top officials by CPD	180a
M.S. Gorbachev	Objects to being addressed as "mister;" terms are clarified	181b
A.M. Obolensky	Notes inaccuracies in stenographic record, cites constituent proposal to abolish leading role of Party, objects to deferral of major issues to Supreme Soviet, calls for commission on legislative proposals, favors refocus of Gdlyan inquest into an investigation of compliance with socialist legality	181b
V.D. Yudin	Claims that procedural irregularities and inconsistencies make CPD a poor model of law and order, sees minority rights as essential to democracy; supports roll-call voting, viewing of Tbilisi film, and co-report by Moscow Group	183a
G.Kh. Popov	Introduces A.I. Kazannik	183b
A.I. Kazannik	Offers to yield seat in Soviet of Nationalities to Yeltsin	184a
M.S. Gorbachev	Seeks legal advice on Kazannik's offer, supports it "in principle"	184b
A.A. Sobchak	Analyzes issue, doubts that deputy can impose conditions and choose his own successor	184b
F.M. Burlatsky	Sees issue as political, notes overwhelming electoral support for Yeltsin	185a
A.P. Yanenko	Asserts that Congress has right to appoint Yeltsin	185a
B.V. Miroshin	Concludes that Yeltsin's popularity warrants approval	185b
A.N. Krayko	Sees Yeltsin's commitment to democracy as added reason to appoint him	185b
M.S. Gorbachev	Proposes that Presidium and Secretariat consider advice and prepare a resolution	185b
Unidentified	Notes possibilities of additional arguments and proposals	186a
M.S. Gorbachev	Advises deputies to submit proposals to Secretariat, seeks legal advice	186b
A.I. Kazannik	Insists on conditional withdrawal to guarantee that conservative majority will not reject Yeltsin	187a
Unidentified	Suggests approval of procedure followed by Kazannik's formal withdrawal	187a
Unidentified	Opines that Supreme Soviet may accept a deputy's withdrawal or that Congress may adopt a procedural amendment	187a
M.S. Gorbachev	Observes that Congress is being confused by lawyers	187b
L.A. Kuznetsov	Cites precedent followed in case of NKAO deputies to allow CPD to replace Kazannik with Yeltsin	187b
M.S. Gorbachev	Proposes that Yeltsin, as next highest vote-getter, is eligible to replace Kazannik	187b
	Kazannik resignation accepted, Yeltsin's election approved	188a
M.S. Gorbachev	Appeals to Armenian and Azeri deputies to find basis for rapprochement	188a
	Congress adjourned	

SIXTH SESSION
30 MAY 1989

Speaker	Subject	Page
R.N. Nishanov	Announces agenda: discussion of basic directions for domestic and foreign policy of the USSR; calls for Gorbachev's report	190a
M.S. Gorbachev	Attributes slow pace of restructuring to market imbalances caused by economic and fiscal mismanagement, poor labor discipline, and inflationary pressures; declares complete reliance on market mechanisms to be socially unacceptable, calls for greater emphasis on consumer goods production, states that rural reform is slowed by lack of understanding and bureaucratic opposition. Identifies major social problems as poverty, health care, environmental protection, housing; youth, women, and veterans' issues; and nomenklatura privileges	190a
	Proposes new directions: reduction of capital investment in heavy industry and conversion of military expenditure to civilian programs—sees greater role for diplomacy in ensuring state security; radical restructuring and downsizing of administrative apparatus as part of national economic reconstruction aimed at increasing productivity and quality of output. Admits lag in creating economic mechanisms to match expectations but renews goal of "full-blooded socialist market" that will protect workers from exploitation or alienation from means of production	
	Praises democratization as main achievement of perestroika, endorses principle of "power to the soviets," calls for delineation of party and state functions with party in role of integrating force, sees restructuring of republic and local governments and redefinition of federative state as next stage of political reform. Declares support for legal and civil rights but denounces lack of social discipline, criminal activity, and mass disturbances; endorses judicial reform and more effective law enforcement; reaffirms "Leninist principle of national self-determination"	
	Outlines benefits of New Thinking and new course of Soviet foreign policy, asserts that persistence of armed forces and alliances no longer prevents qualitative improvement of international relations, sees security maintained politically through "demilitarization, democratization, and humanization of international relations"; envisions larger role for Supreme Soviet in foreign policy	
	Cites need to delimit functions of CPD and Supreme Soviet and between legislative and executive bodies, recognizes need to clarify status of people's deputies, praises pluralism and diversity of opinion but cautions against hasty revision of the Constitution	

Congress recessed

Speaker	Subject	Page
S.T. Melekhin	Surveys housing crisis, poverty, pricing mechanisms; calls for increased investment in consumer goods and nonindustrial construction, for meeting social needs with savings from reduced military spending and administrative cutbacks; proposes that deputies visit Lenin's tomb and lay wreath at tomb of unknown soldier	205a

ANNOTATED LIST OF SPEECHES

Speaker	Subject	Page
Ye.Ye. Sokolov	Questions failure to implement Twenty-seventh CPSU Congress guidelines, cites bureaucratic emasculation of decisions of center, accuses certain elements of using labor collectives to undermine perestroika and sow social and national dissension, supports stronger criminal legislation, urges rapid implementation of measures to increase productivity, supports federalism and strong union	207a
V.A. Masol	Sees democratization and glasnost as chief gains of restructuring to date; ascribes deterioration of conditions in Ukraine to over-industrialization, calls for slowdown of industrial construction with greater emphasis on agricultural development; deplores ethnic strife, poses European Economic Community as model of integration, urges end to export of fuel and fertilizers and their allocation to Soviet agriculture	209a
D.S. Likhachev	Describes deplorable state of national treasures, libraries, museums, and schools; cites low salaries, low morale, and lack of skilled professionals; sees solution in reduction of bloated cultural administration, reduction of foreign aid, and long-range planning for cultural development; proposes that Komsomol assume nationwide responsibility for neglected children	210b
A.P. Yanenko	Urges transfer of general budgetary control and economic oversight from ministries and central apparat to Congress, subordination of Council of Ministers to Supreme Soviet; urges introduction of expert staff to raise quality of decrees and legislation; wants Congress to question ministers responsible for lack of consumer goods, particularly heads of Gosplan and Goskomstat; calls for improvement of rural life and legal-social status of peasants	212b
N.A. Nazarbayev	Attributes lack of progress in restructuring to Goskomstat's erroneous and incomplete data which conceals extent of economic crisis, to wasted planning efforts, to use of archaic indicators and mechanisms that feed inefficiency; condemns central administration for social and ecological devastation of Kazakhstan, including destruction of Aral Sea; urges breakup of ministerial monopolies and empowerment of soviets to protect local health and safety; supports republican sovereignty and economic integration in a Leninist federation	215a
R.N. Nishanov	Reports that 440 deputies have signed up to speak, reads deputy's appeal to hear from grass roots rather than leadership, promises that representatives of each republic will be heard, interrupts discussion of Gorbachev report for report on results of negotiation on NKAO	217b
G.A. Pogosyan	Presents resolution reaffirming the original nomination of (Armenians) Balayan and Pogosyan but also admitting Dzhafarov (an Azerbaijani) as candidates for two NKAO seats in Soviet of Nationalities; praises Sobchak and Denisov for yielding Leningrad seats to NKAO	218a
V.D. Dzhafarov	Objects to new election, protests annulment of his election, asserts right of NKAO's Azerbaijanis to representation in Supreme Soviet, challenges qualifications of Balayan and Pogosyan on basis of residency	218b
R.N. Nishanov	Orders preparation of ballots listing the three candidates, yields to demands from floor for more discussion	219a
L.V. Barusheva	Cautions that heated debate could have explosive consequences in the Caucasus, favors seating an Armenian and an Azerbaijani (Dzhafarov), considers new election inexpedient	219a
S.A. Gabrusev	Proposes referendum in NKAO	219b
M.N. Rakhmanova	Supports original election that gave representation to each nation	219b

SIXTH SESSION, 30 MAY 1989

Speaker	Subject	Page
S.A. Ambartsumyan	Urges support for the proposal worked out by NKAO delegation and Presidium, asserts that interference by either Armenians or Azerbaijanis in NKAO internal affairs is illegal	220a
R.N. Nishanov	Calls for vote on NKAO resolution but then yields to demand for further discussion	220a
L.M. Veyser	Opposes resolution, warns that to annul previous election and install two Armenians would be setting a match to a powder keg	220b
	Nishanov has difficulty controlling access to podium due to crush of deputies eager to speak. A.N. Krayko's appearance at the microphone ignites a noisy reaction from conservatives who continue to harass him as he speaks	
A.N. Krayko	Urges seating in Supreme Soviet of NKAO delegates as well as Sobchak and Denisov	221a
R.N. Nishanov	Denies podium to G.V. Starovoytova	221a
Ye.U. Kim	Proposes that six deputies elected from NKAO serve in Soviet of Nationalities on a rotating basis	221a
R.N. Nishanov	Again denies podium to Starovoytova	221b
I.D. Kobzon	Proposes meeting of elders of both nations to find a solution	221b
A.I. Volsky	Attempts to explain mixup of NKAO candidacies, alleges that Dzhafarov's place was always secure, indicts Vorotnikov's leadership, proposes that next session of Congress add one NKAO representative to Supreme Soviet, pleads for end to discussion so as not to aggravate the situation	221b
	Resolution on NKAO approved	222b
B.V. Gidaspov	Calls meeting of Mandate (Credentials) Commission	222b
V.I. Vorotnikov	Calls meeting of RSFSR members of Supreme Soviet	222b
	Congress recessed	222b
T. Kaipbergenov	Describes ecological crisis in Aral region; appeals for immediate assistance including creation of special deputy group with extraordinary power, reduction of cotton-growing area, ban on expansion of irrigation, official designation of Aral region as disaster zone, and an appeal for international assistance	223a
T.V. Gankrelidze	Recounts details of Tbilisi massacre; charges that authorities and press concealed events, including use of poison gas, and that reactionary forces hostile to democratization subverted the legal machinery; condemns Rodionov and Nikorsky for their roles in the affair	224b
R.A. Bratun	Proposes time at the end of sessions for brief announcements	227a
R.N. Nishanov	Invites General Rodionov to respond to charges	227a
I.N. Rodionov	Quotes extensively from official report of Georgian party's central committee: rejects description of mass rally as peaceful, noting presence of well-trained agitators, national and anti-Russian sloganeering, and incitements of violence against communists; defends role of authorities, police, and army; challenges accuracy of press reports and nationalists' charges—denies use of poison gas; contends that indecisive leadership of reformists was ultimate cause of the disaster	227b
R.N. Nishanov	Presents Presidium's nominees for Tbilisi investigating commission	230b
A.M. Adamovich	Objects to V.V. Karpov as proposed chairman of Tbilisi commission, recommends D.A. Granin	231a
V.P. Tomkus	Compares Tbilisi intervention to military intervention in Vilnius in September 1987, urges replacement of all commission members named "from above" and inclusion of representatives of ethnic minorities	231b

ANNOTATED LIST OF SPEECHES

Speaker	Subject	Page
Yu.F. Karyakin	Opposes appointment of G.A. Borovik to commission, alludes to possibility of official provocateurs	232a
Yu.R. Boyars	Alleges similarities between Riga and Tbilisi in April 1988, questions Rodionov's moral qualifications, asks appointment of lawyer to Tbilisi commission	232a
E.N. Shengelaya	Urges appointment of qualified professionals, recommends several persons	232b
Unidentified	Suggests inclusion of General Govorov	233a
N.S. Petrushenko	Argues for representation of army and interior ministry in Tbilisi commission	233a
Ya.A. Manayenkov	Takes exception to statements of Shengelaya and Medvedev	234a
V.A. Voblikov	Urges Congress to be objective and responsible	234a
D.I. Patiashvili	Recounts events in Tbilisi, charges riot by army and MVD troops, accuses Rodionov of lying	234b
M.S. Gorbachev	Describes his role in events preceding Tbilisi massacre, expresses personal confidence in A.N. Yakovlev as commission member	237a
A.V. Gorbunov	Promises report on work of Congress Presidium and Secretariat at next session	238a
R.N. Nishanov	Tries to dissuade Karpov from speaking	238a
V.V. Karpov	Urges that commission be given access to records of KGB, MVD, defense ministry, and CPSU Central Committee; withdraws name from consideration, recommends A.N. Yakovlev as chairman	238a
G.A. Borovik	Defends his integrity against charges levied by Karyakin, decries use of podium for personal vendettas	238b
R.N. Nishanov	Echoes Borovik's caution against personal attacks, presents list of deputies nominated for Gdlyan-Ivanov investigation commission	238b
B.L. Vasilyev	Asks to switch appointments	239b
R.N. Nishanov	Announces other withdrawals and invitations	239b
N.V. Karlov	Advises inclusion of clergy in Tbilisi commission	240a
V.V. Krychkov	Suggests revision of official title of Gdlyan-Ivanov commission and its expansion, wants to know principles followed by Presidium in nominating members of commissions	240a
R.N. Nishanov	Asserts that no preconceptions guided Presidium in naming commissions, then notes its preference for naming lawyers to the Gdlyan-Ivanov commission and political figures to the Tbilisi commission	240b
T.Kh. Gdlyan	Sees wrangling over commission membership as waste of time, urges deputies to rely on Presidium	240b
R.N. Nishanov	Defends nominations from floor as reflection of will of the Congress	241a
A.A. Zakharov	Nominates ten progressive deputies for appointment to Gdlyan-Ivanov commission	241a
A.D. Sakharov	Supports Zakharov's list, backs L.S. Kudrin for chairman	241a
M.N. Poltoranin	Nominates A.I. Kazannik	241b
T.V. Moshnyaga	Nominates G.P. Gidirin for Tbilisi commission	241b
A.G. Mukhtarov	Rebukes Sakharov, urges rejection of Zakharov's list of nominees	241b
A.V. Belina	Nominates M.M. Yakovlev	242a
Ye.M. Primakov	Asks Presidium to terminate speeches that stray from nominations, urges it to define objectives or procedures of the commissions	242a
R.N. Nishanov	Endorses Primakov's remarks	242a
A.A. Sidorov	Urges rejection of Kudrin due to inexperience and bias	242a
Yu.Yu. Olekas	Nominates E.V. Bichkauskas for Gdlyan-Ivanov commission	242b

Speaker	Subject	Page
R.K. Odzhiyev	Nominates self for Tbilisi commission	242b
G.V. Koshlakov	Stresses need to investigate Gdlyan team itself	242b
V.A. Shapovalenko	Nominates B.V. Miroshin for Gdlyan commission, disagrees with Koshlakov	243a
G.M. Kurochka	Nominates self for Gdlyan commission, cites judicial experience	243a
S.M. Ryabchenko	Protests waste of time, suggests that nominations be screened by Presidium	243a
A.I. Kazannik	Declines nomination	243b
A.O. Dobrovolsky	Nominates N.I. Ignatovich	244a
A.Ya. Eshpay	Urges V.V. Karpov not to withdraw	244a
R.N. Nishanov	Notes three additional names and declares nominations closed	244a
Yu.A. Osipyan	Describes voting procedure	244b
R.N. Nishanov	Concludes session	245b

Congress adjourned

SEVENTH SESSION
31 MAY 1989

Speaker	Subject	Page
A.-M.K. Brazauskas	Presiding; announces continuation of discussion on basic trends of domestic and foreign policy	247a
V.A. Starodubtsev	Compares current conditions to World War II, cites food supply as number one problem and agrarian reform as number one priority, calls for accelerated development of material and technical base of rural society and infrastructure; decries economically destructive policies of central planners, polarization of interests of town and country, loss of peasant work ethic; presents seven-point program of agrarian deputies	247a
V.A. Gontar	Reads statement of 417 agrarian deputies demanding highest priority for resolution of agrarian problems, total reorientation of state investment to raise rural standard of living to urban levels, end to administrative interference, incompetence, and inefficiency; appeals for total democratic reorganization of rural life, radical land reform permitting a wide range of forms of ownership, and measures to realize economic, social, and legal equality of peasantry with urban workers; offers this appeal as draft resolution on agrarian questions	250
A.-M.K. Brazauskas	Refers Gontar's statement to Presidium for consideration	251b
V.I. Kolesnikov	Sees tasks of Congress as completing the October Revolution by creating mechanisms for transfer of power to soviets and transfer of ownership of enterprises to working people; cites need to define status of people's deputies and the relationships of various legislative and administrative organizations, need to adopt a law on elections, and need for openness in legislative process; raises questions concerning Rostov's representation and AIDS outbreak in Elista	251b
R.N. Nishanov	Expresses concern over divisive elements in the Congress, stresses importance of creating an effective democratic mechanism as foundation of rule of law state, recommends restoration of constitutional	253b

Speaker	Subject	Page
	(continued) provision recognizing sovereign rights of union republics, surveys problems of Uzbekistan: political and moral corruption, overemphasis on industrial development and cotton production, inattention to environmental damage, and unbalanced economy; calls for reducing cotton production to levels consistent with national needs; praises Gorbachev's foreign policy, especially rapprochement with China	
A.V. Gorbunov	Submits draft law on constitutional amendments aimed at creating new basis of federation in which sovereign union republics would define their internal political status, exercise full state power on their own territories, control their own resources, and enjoy unlimited economic power	255b
A.N. Mutalibov	Praises democratization, glasnost, and perestroika, but stresses below average standard of living in Azerbaijan; sees remedy in economic independence and sovereignty; distinguishes nationalities seeking genuine socioeconomic progress from those interested only in pressing territorial claims, reviews ecological problems of Sumgait area and Caspian Sea, asserts need for strict adherence to constitution when Supreme Soviet addresses boundaries of republics and autonomous regions	257b
A.-M.K. Brazauskas	Declares that results of vote on NKAO will be announced at conclusion of morning session	260a
B.I. Oleynik	Satirizes conduct of deputies; addresses national questions: favors primacy of native languages, notes paradox of Russians who lack both a communist party and an academy of sciences, calls for protection of environment from "industrial aggression" of central ministries, demands halt to construction of Crimean nuclear power plant and complete shut down of Chernobyl; urges major effort to protect the Ukraine, Belorussia, and western Russia from radiation effects; appeals for compassionate concern for peasants and war widows	260a
Z.P. Pukhova	Urges broad and vigorous governmental attention to problems affecting women and family life, decries "barbaric" employment of women in manual labor, contends that reform lacks legal basis; fears separation of women's concerns from broader issues of economic and social reform and thus urges women's representation on all committees and commissions; appeals to Gorbachev and leadership to translate their rhetoric into effective action	262a
M.S. Gorbachev	Acknowledges ninetieth birthday of writer L.M. Leonov	263b
	Congress recessed	
B.N. Yeltsin	Sees power as basic issue confronting CPD even though party-bureaucratic apparatus has already moved to ensure its monopoly; contends that cumbersome administrative system enables apparat to frustrate reform in face of mounting social problems: social stratification, national conflicts, organized crime, disorganization of the domestic market, inflation, and imminent financial collapse; urges CPD to draft new constitution that will dismantle administrative-command structure, decentralize power and the economy, radically transform productive relations, free peasantry and the press to release society's creative energy, and require direct election of head of state; calls for extraordinary party congress to redefine party's role, redefine and renew restructuring, and replacethe failed central committee; proposes reorganization of economic management with greater freedom for republics, stabilization of the ruble, redrafting	263b

SEVENTH SESSION, 31 MAY 1989

Speaker	Subject	Page
	(continued) of 12th Five-year plan, elimination of elitism, abolition of nomenklatura, and annual referenda on the performance of the head of state	
S.G. Arutyunyan	Endorses regional cost accounting, economic independence and autonomy of republics, but also proposes special status for Armenia enabling it to accept foreign aid and investment; attributes crisis of NKAO to Stalinist nationality policy and its continuation in present leadership's suppression of Armenian dignity and interests; demands popular referendum to decide fate of NKAO, raises issue of genocide, cites legal and constitutional obstacles to resolution of AzeriArmenian conflict	266b
A.M. Ridiger	Links moral renewal of society to restructuring, cites history as proof that noble social theories cannot be realized through coercion, welcomes anticipated law on freedom of worship, presents documents of recent European ecumenical conference	269a
V.I. Bakulin	Proclaims faith in party, resents struggle for power waged by some deputies, and rebukes party loyalists for tolerating attacks and slanders; praises gains of perestroika but sees need for less talk, more action, and a decisive economic policy; criticizes administration's hastily drafted, often conflicting resolutions; sees expansion of construction industry as essential to solution of food, housing, and other basic problems; denounces cooperatives as source of social inequity and crime, warns that economic reform must not worsen the life of the people	270a
V.V. Kazarezov	Links fate of restructuring to improved standard of living, challenges accuracy of government's economic data, and questions competence of Gorbachev's economic advisers; urges accelerated investment in heat and power industries, sees paradox in excessive centralization of economic management and the anarchy plaguing the organization of labor and the integration of technology and industry; supports regional economic accountability and autonomy, recommends conversion of defense factories to experimental labs for scientific institutes, and urges greater efforts to improve conditions of life in Siberia	271b
Yu.A. Osipyan	Announces election of V.V. Dzhafarov and G.A. Pogosyan to Supreme Soviet as result of balloting on NKAO representation	274a
	NKAO election ratified, election of Soviet of Nationalities ratified	274b
A.-M.K. Brazauskas	Addresses several administrative matters	275a
	Congress recessed	
A.I. Lukyanov	Presides temporarily while Brazauskas speaks for Lithuanian delegation	275b
A.-M.K. Brazauskas	Attributes country's straits not to restructuring but to its tragic history and painful quest to create a socialist system; sees roots of conflict between Moscow and republics in excessive centralization—its solution in creation of rule of law state, new union treaties, and constitutional revision; calls for radical economic reform, declares that relations with Lithuania depend on frank acknowledgement of the illegality of Soviet-German treaty of 1939	275b
Yu.P. Vlasov	Describes pollution in Moscow suburb, complains of bias in television coverage, cites responsibility for Tbilisi intervention as demonstrating need for constitutional article on impeachment, declares that leaders responsible for deplorable conditions should resign en masse; warns against rule by force, fear, and intolerance; warns against dependence on single individual and a KGB unchecked by	277b

ANNOTATED LIST OF SPEECHES

Speaker	Subject	Page
	(continued) popular control, recommends deputies commission to bypass corrupted data published by State Committee on Statistics, calls for election of people's deputies every three years, sees previous session's applause for use of force in Tbilisi as reflection of unbridgeable moral division among deputies	
A.M. Masaliyev	Endorses Gorbachev's recommendations, proposes ways to streamline work of legislators, sees key to harmony in balanced economic relations between center and republics, advises republics to focus on local issues, urges restoration of discipline to check nationalist and democratic extremists from further undermining state and party and increasing tensions	280b
P.G. Bunich	Sees economic reform to date as cosmetic failure, warns that emergency measures cannot substitute for genuine reform, denies that Soviet people have lost proprietorial spirit, fixes chief responsibility for continued stagnation on bureaucratic planners and management and a system that penalizes efficiency and rewards inefficiency; describes economic accountability as positive but ineffective as long as enterprises are not self-reliant; favors leasing and sale of public property with collective ownership of whatever remains, praises cooperative system, and proposes six-month ultimatum to finance ministry	282b
K. Makhkamov	Endorses formula of "strong center, strong republics" but argues that self-financing and self-management require reform of wholesale and retail price structure, nationwide conversion to cost accounting, and adoption of a legal framework for regulating interstate economic relations; identifies critical Tajik problems as scarcity of arable land, shortage of electric power, and need for a resettlement policy; describes negative impact of unrestricted supplier monopolies on economic restructuring, urges prompt attention to inter-ethnic relations and laws governing the demarcation of national-territorial boundaries	285b
I.Kh. Toome	Reports Estonian endorsement of decentralized economic management, republican sovereignty, and regional self-management and self-financing; declares republic's intention to proceed with reforms because public would interpret delay as deliberate obstruction of popular will, denies any intent to achieve special status; regrets union ministries' lack of support but asserts Estonia's determination to initiate economic independence on 1 January 1990	288a
P.A. Azizbekova	Reads nominees for commission to draft the CPD resolution on Gorbachev's report	290a
A.-M.K. Brazauskas	Adds name of writer I.A. Vasilyev to editorial commission	291a
G.G. Borovikov	Objects to inclusion of Gorbachev-supporter Chingiz Aytmatov, nominates P.G. Bunich	291a
B.V. Kryzhkov	Objects to absence of engineers, nominates Kuzubov	291a
Unidentified	Nominates economist N.N. Engver	291b
A.L. Plotnikov	Nominates engineer V.M. Minin	291b
V.V. Bushuyev	Reasons that since a fifty-member commission could not draft a report, the draft must already exist, and, therefore, calls for its distribution to all deputies at next session	291b
A.-M.K. Brazauskas	Denies existence of draft report; overrules, without discussion, the motion to exclude Aytmatov from commission; calls for vote on commission as amended	291b
	Editing Commission approved	291b
A.-M.K. Brazauskas	Reads Presidium's nominees for Tbilisi investigation commission	292a

SEVENTH SESSION, 31 MAY 1989

Speaker	Subject	Page
Unidentified	Nominates B.L. Vasilyev	292b
A.N. Tavkhelidze	Declares that commission of the Georgian Supreme Soviet thoroughly investigated the incident, learning everything but who appointed the commander of the operation; alleges that second commission headed by Tarazevich sent from Moscow made superficial investigation and learned nothing, demands that Tarazevich render an account to the Congress	292b
A.-M.K. Brazauskas	Urges speakers to stick to nomination of commission members	293a
A.K. Safonov	Reports Kazakh delegation's insistence on appointment of A.N. Yakovlev to chair Tbilisi commission	293a
Unidentified	Refusing "to cooperate with murderers," resigns as deputy as long as General Rodionov remains in CPD	293a
A.-M.K. Brazauskas	Again urges deputies not to stray from matter at hand	293b
T.M. Shamba	Demands time at next session to defend Abkhazians against charges of guilt in connection with Georgian crisis	293b
A.A. Korshunov	Pleads for restraint and end to discussion	293b
M.N. Poltoranin	Argues that Politburo members (i.e., A.N. Yakovlev) should not be appointed to commissions, seconds nomination of Nazarbayev as chairman	293b
Bishop (Metropolitan) Pitirim	Asks whether deputies can serve on two commissions	294a
Unidentified	Opines that membership in more than one commission is permitted	294a
T.Kh. Gdlyan	Nominates Sakharov	294a
A.-M.K. Brazauskas	States that Sakharov had already refused nomination	294a
N.A. Nazarbayev	Expresses sympathy for Georgian people but contends that film on Tbilisi disaster presented no facts, only opinion of narrator; pledges honest, conscientious effort but states preference to be replaced as chairman by some "neutral" person	294a
A.-M.K. Brazauskas	Observes that no one is without nationality; announces addition of B.L. Vasilyev to commission, seeks vote	294a
R.Sh. Tabukashvili	Insists on Nazarbayev's withdrawal due to bias	294b
Unidentified	Demands names of persons who obstructed Tbilisi investigation	294b
V.F. Tolpezhnikov	Makes third demand for name of person who authorized use of force in Tbilisi, asserts that a government that does not know who ordered destruction of its own people deserves vote of no confidence	294b
A.-M.K. Brazauskas	Proposes separate vote on chairmanship of commission, accepts motion to elect commission and let commission choose its chairman and deputy, calls for vote	294b
	Tbilisi Commission approved	295a
A.M. Mambetov	Begs respect for divergent opinions, invites Bobrikov to apologize to Aytmatov	295a
N.S. Sazonov	Discusses composition of Supreme Soviet committees and commissions	295b
A.I. Lukyanov	Adds information on composition of Supreme Soviet commissions	295b
M.S. Gorbachev	Proposes reducing speeches from fifteen minutes to ten to allow time for representatives of autonomous regions to speak	295b
	Recalls deputy's proposal to set aside one hour for brief statements at end of each session; Congress responds negatively, ratifies original regulation	296a
A.-M.K. Brazauskas	Promises to read deputies' motions during morning session, announces first six speakers, recesses the Congress	296b
	Congress adjourned	

FIRST CONGRESS OF PEOPLE'S DEPUTIES OF THE USSR

FIRST AND SECOND SESSIONS
THURSDAY, 25 MAY 1989
THE KREMLIN PALACE OF CONGRESSES

The Moscow Kremlin had never witnessed a congregation like the 2155 people's deputies called to order in the Palace of Congresses by electoral commissioner V.P. Orlov at 10:00 a.m. on 25 May 1989. No assembly as free or representative had gathered in Russia for seventy-one years. It was five in the morning of 19 January 1918 when Victor Chernov, newly elected president of the Constituent Assembly, had ordered Russian Democracy to take a twelve-hour break. Lenin's decree and Bolshevik bayonets had prolonged that recess for three generations. Now two thousand representatives were about to resume the people's business. That certainly was the hope of millions who witnessed the event on television, despite the fact that 87 percent of the deputies were members of the Communist Party.

The Congress opened with a moment of silence to honor the latest victims of Soviet power nineteen Georgians slain by the army during a demonstration in Tbilisi a month earlier. It was an ironic but altogether appropriate beginning, for although the quality of life had steadily deteriorated, victims was one commodity the regime had produced efficiently over the years.

After that sober start, the deputies turned to the business at hand, which was to organize the Congress, adopt an agenda, and repair the social and economic fabric of the USSR. The first two matters presumably had been settled by the Presidium of the Supreme Soviet and its First Deputy Chairman, Anatoly I. Lukyanov, who was primarily responsible for organizing the Congress. Under its auspices, and with Mikhail S. Gorbachev presiding, a group of 446 deputies, representing various organizations and factions, had met for nine hours on the previous day (24 May) to approve the rules and machinery and to iron out remaining issues.

A QUESTION OF POWER

One problem that the representatives could not readily solve concerned the very nature of the Congress. The plan developed by the Supreme Soviet Presidium within the framework of the 1977 Constitution envisioned the Congress essentially as an assembly of *electors*. The people's deputies were to elect one-fourth of their number to the remodeled Supreme Soviet, the Union's working legislature. They were also slated to approve, with minor amendments at most, the guidelines for economic and political reform already worked out by Gorbachev, his advisors, and the Party leadership. For the majority of deputies, Leninist apparatchiks promoted for the most part from single-candidate districts, it was to be another routine party conference: sit through the reading of the reports, approve the program, elect the new slate, and get back home again.

But there was another view of the role of the Congress. The Moscow group, reformists including Andrei Sakharov, Gavril Popov, V.V. Landsbergis, S.B. Stankevich, Yu.R. Boyars, and about two hundred others, wanted the assembly to function as a genuine parliamentary body, which the Soviet Constitution seemed to allow. In their view, the deputies were not mere electors: the Congress was the sovereign representative of the people and they were the people's law-makers. They would not simply review and perhaps touch up the government's program, they would propose alternatives. Nor would they meekly delegate their responsibility. "The people elected us and sent us to this Congress so that we would take responsibility for the country's destiny," thundered Sakharov. "Our Congress cannot hand legislative power to a fifth of its composition.... It is the exclusive right of the USSR Congress of People's Deputies to pass USSR laws and to appoint the USSR's top officials."

During the pre-Congress assembly on the twenty-fourth, the Moscow Group had been encouraged by the seeming willingness of the conservatives to consider their views. But in the Congress itself, the majority was not so generous. It tried to smother every effort to deviate from the prescribed course. In fairness to the "strict-constructionist" majority, one could argue that an assembly of two thousand, lacking staff support, office facilities, and a committee structure, had neither the administrative capacity nor the investigative resources to produce sound legislation; that, indeed, the task of drafting legislative proposals was properly left to the smaller, more manageable chambers of the Supreme Soviet with their anticipated array of permanent and temporary commissions. The Constitution, after all, empowered the Congress of People's Deputies to review and confer final approval upon legislation adopted by the Supreme Soviet. The reformers, in short, were trying to bypass the Constitution and turn the Congress into a constituent assembly. The issue was power and who was to exercise it.

In an established legislature, rules of procedure and related matters are secondary or peripheral to the legislative process. Custom and practice have long since resolved such matters. But in the First Congress of People's Deputies procedural issues were often the essential ones. That was because spokesmen of the Moscow Group, and then other deputies and delegations too, acted as though they were members of a parliament. Their manner and conduct antagonized the bureaucratic majority whose incivility and ugliness became commonplace. Gorbachev was reluctant to muzzle the progressives: "I do not think we should deprive comrades...of the opportunity to report their views to the Congress." The apparatchiks, however, circumvented the chairman by hounding unwelcome speakers with hoots, whistles, and rhythmic clapping (noted in the transcript as "Noise in the hall" or similar expressions). "Get on with it!" was their battle cry. "Invited guests" state and Party functionaries who packed the balconies rudely supported their comrades on the floor. In that way the First Sitting set the pattern for the twelve days of the Congress. "The confrontation between the majority and the radically-minded minority of deputies," wrote Yegor V. Yakovlev, editor-in-chief of *Moskovskie novosti*, "sometimes brought to mind a dialogue of the deaf and the dumb: one segment could not hear, and the other had no voice."

A QUESTION OF ORDER

The business of the Congress was conducted in a casual, undisciplined, and frequently cavalier manner. It was not a congress of parliamentarians but a people's congress, and it was run accordingly, like the traditional village assembly. Proposals from the floor were sometimes considered, sometimes not. More often than not they were lost in the course of discussion. Meanwhile the chairmen, especially V.I. Vorotnikov who conducted the Second Session, discovered motions in the atmosphere.

The chairman frequently combined multiple issues and voted on them as single propositions. Gorbachev set a pattern of routinely commenting on speeches or engaging the speaker in discussion or argument. Rarely was a proposal or amendment properly offered as a motion. A second was irrelevant, and not one was recorded. Gorbachev replaced Orlov in the chair early in the first meeting, contrary to the Constitution which requires the chairman of the Central Electoral Commission to preside over the First Session and then to give way to the chairman of the Supreme Soviet or his deputy. That sequence was necessary because the new Supreme Soviet did not yet exist, and one of the primary duties of the Congress was to elect that body and its chairman (in that order, another stipulation violated by the organizers of the Congress). Procedural regularity may seem a minor matter, but the creation of a "rule-of-law state" might depend as much on civility and conformity to rules of procedure as it does on the enactment of sweeping constitutional and legislative reform. The Soviet Union has never lacked for laws; its deficiency ever has been in their routine observance.

Although essentially organizational matters consumed the meetings of the first day, members of the Moscow group raised substantive political and constitutional issues at every opportunity. Their effort began with Vilan F. Tolpezhnikov's demand that the government identify the persons responsible for ordering the use of lethal gas against the Tbilisi demonstrators. It was a deputy's right to propose such a question, but the timing was inopportune. Orlov treated it as a rhetorical question and proceeded to the election of the Presidium, following which Gorbachev assumed the chair. Consideration of the agenda enabled Sakharov and Popov to raise fundamental questions about the relationship of the Congress of People's Deputies to the Supreme Soviet of the USSR, about the method of electing the Supreme Soviet and its chairman (the head of state in the revised constitutional structure) as well as the chairman of the Council of Ministers and other all-union officials, and generally about the nature of the representative government under the amended Constitution of the USSR.

The lengthiest debate of the morning session took place over the adoption of the Provisional Standing Orders, twenty articles drafted by the Supreme Soviet Presidium that defined the powers and procedures of the Congress. Gorbachev told the deputies that their representatives had discussed the document "quite intensively" on the preceding day and had made "a lot of interesting additions" before "unanimously" approving the document. A parade of speakers, however, contradicted the chairman: amendments agreed to on the previous day had not been incorporated into the draft. Gorbachev then lamely explained that the Presidium, working all night to revise the document, might have "missed some things." The progressives were suspicious. Under the old system it was not the published law that counted but rather the implementing instructions that were relayed to the ministries and other state organs by the central apparatus. Thus an extraordinary sequence ensued in which several deputies (notably K.A. Antanavichyus, Stankevich, and Boyars) in effect negotiated with Gorbachev to amend the document. At length the revised Provisional Standing Orders were approved, and, after wrangling over the chairmanship of the Credentials Commission, the deputies recessed for lunch.

GORBACHEV FOR PRESIDENT

The main business of the afternoon (which dragged on into the evening) was Gorbachev's scheduled election as Chairman of the USSR Supreme Soviet. His nomination afforded deputies the opportunity to voice their complaints and to question and challenge the General Secretary on numerous issues, including his personal integrity. The focal point of the discussion, however, was whether the posts of party chief and head of state should be held concurrently by one person, a question argued on both constitutional and political grounds. K. D. Lubenchenko, a legal scholar, essentially disposed of the structural issue by observing that whether the offices were combined in one person was irrelevant as long as the country lacked a constitutional separation of powers. The chief argument against his election was the concentration of power and fear of its abuse, an idea bluntly expressed by a Kharkov truck driver, L.I. Sukhov, who compared Gorbachev to Napoleon who "thanks to yes-men and his wife...went from a republic to an empire." But fear was also the reason to entrust both offices to Gorbachev. An unidentified deputy warned that if he gave up the party leadership, "the powerful party bureaucracy which has immense power, the only real power in the country will quickly crush him and drive us all away from here." The compelling reason for Gorbachev's candidacy was simply the lack of an alternative. At length, he was admitted to the ballot with only four absentions.

(The rules of the Congress required the election of the Chairman of the Supreme Soviet by secret ballot. To be inscribed on the ballot, however, a nominee had to win approval of a majority of deputies voting by a show of hands. Thus the nominating procedure nullified the anonymity of the secret ballot, and more than one deputy questioned the logic and propriety of the system.)

For the rest of the session the deputies engaged in "learning democracy." A.M. Obolensky, a member of the Moscow group from the Kola Peninsula, nominated himself in order to establish a precedent of contested elections. After a brief but vigorous debate, the Congress voted to exclude Obolensky from the ballot, although nearly seven hundred deputies supported his cause. Boris Yeltsin's name was then placed in nomination, but he came to the podium to withdraw, wryly noting, however, since he was no longer employed, he was amenable to "some kind of offer." The assembly then recessed so that the deputies could retire to the Granovitaya Hall, there to cast secret ballots for or against the only candidate permitted to run for president. Gorbachev won handily. Only 87 delegates crossed his name off their ballots. The deputies reassembled, heard, and voted to approve the results of the election. Thereupon Vorotnikov made it official. The president-elect then thanked the Congress, and the deputies retired for the night. Crossing Red Square on the way to their hotel, veteran party secretaries no doubt could be heard grousing about the good old days when all this business would have been settled in an hour.

Texts of documents cited during the First and Second Sessions are compiled in Appendices at the end of Volume 2: Constitution (Basic Law) of the USSR, Articles 48, 108, 110, 111, 113, and 120 (Appendix A.1); Law on Elections of USSR People's Deputies, Article 17 (Appendix A.2); Provisional Standing Orders (Appendix B.1); Decree on the Procedure for Organizing and Holding Meetings, Rallies, Street Processions and Demonstrations in the USSR (Appendix A.3); Decree on the Introduction of Amendments and Addenda to the USSR Law "On Criminal Liability for State Crimes" (Appendix A.4) Members of the Presidium, the Secretariat, and the Tellers Commission are listed in Appendices C.1-3.

FIRST AND SECOND SESSIONS
THURSDAY, 25 MAY 1989
STENOGRAPHIC RECORD

Vladimir Pavlovich Orlov, chairman of the Central Electoral Commission: Esteemed comrades, people's deputies of the USSR: I have a great honor. As chairman of the Central Electoral Commission and in accordance with the Constitution of the Union of Soviet Socialist Republics, I have the honor of opening the USSR Congress of People's Deputies. Allow me, first of all, on behalf of the Central Electoral Commission, to cordially congratulate you on your election to the highest organ of state power in our country, as people's deputies of the USSR, with the great trust which the Soviet people have placed in you in that honored and exceptionally responsible mission which is now placed upon you.

The elections and the preparations for them took place in conditions of broad, hitherto unprecedented glasnost and openness, the stormy growth of the working people's political activity. This was particularly convincingly confirmed on Sunday 26 March, when more than 172 million Soviet people, almost 90 percent of the people eligible to vote, went to polling stations, expressing, all the diversity of public opinion, to support restructuring. The elections showed that restructuring has become the business of all our people. Soviet people came out in favor of deepening it further and making changes for the better as soon as possible in all spheres of life. By their novelty and by the high interest of the masses, the elections filled and enriched the face of restructuring. They became a step of fundamental significance in the development of democracy. They moved our society further along the path outlined by the 27th CPSU Congress and the 19th All-Union CPSU Conference. The elections confirmed that the people see in the party of Lenin strength capable of rallying Soviet society, safeguarding its consolidation, finding effective ways to resolve the problems that have come to a head, and overcoming difficulties. We have not yet had a more powerful, nationwide referendum in favor of the Communist Party and its course for renewal.

It can be said today that the elections were a major contribution in the practical implementation of reforming the political system, in affirming the sovereignty of the people. They brought Soviet democracy to a qualitatively new level and will go down in the history of our socialist state as one of the most important levels in the development of all social life. During the course of the election campaign, the Soviet people acquired unique political experience. At a new and extremely crucial and difficult stage of our country's democratic development, candidate deputies were nominated from the bottom up. Thousands of contenders took part in the election, which presented a choice. Millions of voters have only now truly sensed that their vote means a great deal in solving big state issues in the sociopolitical development of the country. The current election campaign presented by no means one single picture. It reflected the diversity of the positions, points of view, and opinions that exist in our society. It became a unique testing ground in which the new tenets of the USSR Constitution were set into motion for the first time and a principally new law on elections was tested. It mainly enabled the elections to be carried out on a truly democratic basis and a new election practice to be acquired. At pre-election meetings, in works collectives, and in the mass media, desires were expressed about the need to amend certain norms and procedures set out in the law. They all deserve attention and require analysis.

Taking into account the experience acquired, it is important to make the necessary alterations to the legislation on the elections so that it may meet more fully the interests of the development of socialist democracy and of strengthening our statehood. All the proposals on these questions which have arrived addressed to the Central Electoral Commission will be passed on by it to the USSR Supreme Soviet.

Today, 2,155 people's deputies of the USSR of the 2,249 who were elected are present at the congress. Detailed information about the results of the elections and the composition of he deputies will be provided by the Credentials Commission which the congress will elect and to whom the Central Electoral Commission will pass on all the documentation necessary to check the deputies' powers.

I would like to say that in this hall today are workers, kolkhozniks, captains of industry, scientists, cultural figures, military servicemen, people from various professions, people from various generations, representatives of the people who possess great political and intellectual potential. The composition of the deputies reflects the multinational character of our country. In their ranks are representatives of 65 nations and ethnic groups.

The present corps of deputies is faced with solving tasks of state-wide importance. These tasks are entrusted by our constitution, first and foremost to the Congress of People's Deputies, which as the supreme body of state power, is authorized to examine any question attributed to the jurisdiction of the USSR and determines the main policy of the activity of the Supreme Soviet and all other state bodies.

First Session
25 May 1989

The attention and thoughts of all working people are now focused on the USSR Congress of People's Deputies. Much is expected from it, above all an answer to the questions people are concerned about, questions connected with the further course of restructuring. Together with your mandates as deputies, the voters gave you, comrade deputies, their belief in a better life, in a prospering and mighty Soviet socialist state.

Allow me to voice the conviction that the Congress of People's Deputies will justify the people's aspirations and that every deputy will contribute his experience, knowledge, and effort to the joint efforts aimed at our society attaining new heights in socioeconomic and spiritual progress.

Comrades, in accordance with Article 110 of the USSR Constitution, I declare the first session of the USSR Congress of People's Deputies open. (Applause).

Tolpezhnikov: Before we begin our session, I ask you to honor the memory of those who died in Tbilisi. (All stand. A minute's silence.) Thank you.

A deputy's question. On instruction from my electors, I demand that it be stated for all to hear now at the USSR Congress of People's Deputies who gave the order to attack peaceful demonstrators in the city of Tbilisi on 9 April 1989 and use poisonous substances against them, and that the nature of these poisonous substances be stated. Tolpezhnikov, a USSR people's deputy from the 293d national territorial Proletarskiy constituency of the city of Riga, Latvia. (Applause).

Orlov: Comrades, proposals on the election of the presidium of our congress have been submitted by many deputies. These proposals have been supported by the assembly of representatives of groups of USSR people's deputies. The floor for proposals on behalf of the assembly of representatives on the composition of the presidium of the congress is given to Deputy Lukin.

Lukin: Esteemed comrades: As you know, the USSR Supreme Soviet Presidium was given the responsibility of organizing and preparing for the USSR Congress of People's Deputies and the USSR Supreme Soviet session. As you know, the work has been done. The assembly of representatives of deputies' groups is putting forward the proposal to elect to the Congress of People's Deputies Presidium: Comrade Mikhail Sergeyevich Gorbachev, chairman of the USSR Supreme Soviet Presidium and general secretary of the CPSU Central Committee; (applause) and Comrade Anatoliy Ivanovich Lukyanov, first deputy chairman of the USSR Supreme Soviet Presidium. (Applause).

There is also a proposal to elect to the congress presidium Comrade Vladimir Pavlovich Orlov, chairman of the Central Electoral Commission. (Applause). In accordance with the USSR Constitution, he opened the first session of the congress. It was decided at the assembly of deputies's groups to send one representative from each republic as a delegate to the congress presidium. The following comrades have been proposed for the congress presidium by the assemblies of deputies from the republics:

Azizbekova, Pyusta Azizagakyzy, director of the Museum for the History of Azerbaijan under the Azerbaijan Soviet Socialist Republic [SSR] Academy of Sciences;

Aytmatov, Chingiz, chairman of the board of the Kirgiz SSR Union of Writers and editor in chief of the magazine INOSTRANNAYA LITERATURA;

Ambartsumyan, Viktor Amazaspovich, president of the Armenian SSR Academy of Sciences;

Brazauskas, Algirdas-Mikolas Kaze, first secretary of the Lithuanian Communist Party Central Committee;

Vorotnikov, Vitaliy Ivanovich, member of the CPSU Central Committee Politburo and chairman of the Presidium of the Russian Soviet Federated Socialist Republic [RSFSR] Supreme Soviet;

Gorbunov, Anatoliy Valeriyanovich, chairman of the Latvian SSR Supreme Soviet Presidium;

Ishanov, Khekim, chief engineer at the Turkmenneft production association in the Turkmen SSR;

Kozhakhmetov, Ibraimzhan, chairman of the Kirov Kolkhoz, Panfilovskiy Rayon, Taldy-Kurgan Oblast, Kazakh SSR;

Kiseleva, Valentina Adamovna, machine operator at the Grodno 60th Anniversary of the USSR Khimvolokno production association in the Belorussian SSR;

Kurashvili, Zeynab Giviyevna, sewing machine operator at the Tbilisi Gldani knitwear production association, Georgian SSR;

Lippmaa, Endel Teodorovich, director of the Institute of Chemical and Biological Physics of the Estonian SSR Academy of Sciences;

Mukhabatova, Soniyabibi Kushvakhtova, livestock unit team leader at Khayeti-Nav Sovkhoz, Garmskiy Rayon, Tajik SSR;

Nishanov, Rafik Nishanovich, first secretary of the Uzbekistan Communist Party Central Committee;

Paton, Boris Yevgenyevich, president of the Ukrainian SSR Academy of Sciences;

Rotar, Svetlana Anatolyevna, mechanized milking foreman at the Moldova Kolkhoz, Dondyushany Rayon, Moldavian SSR.

STENOGRAPHIC RECORD

The CAUCASUS REGION

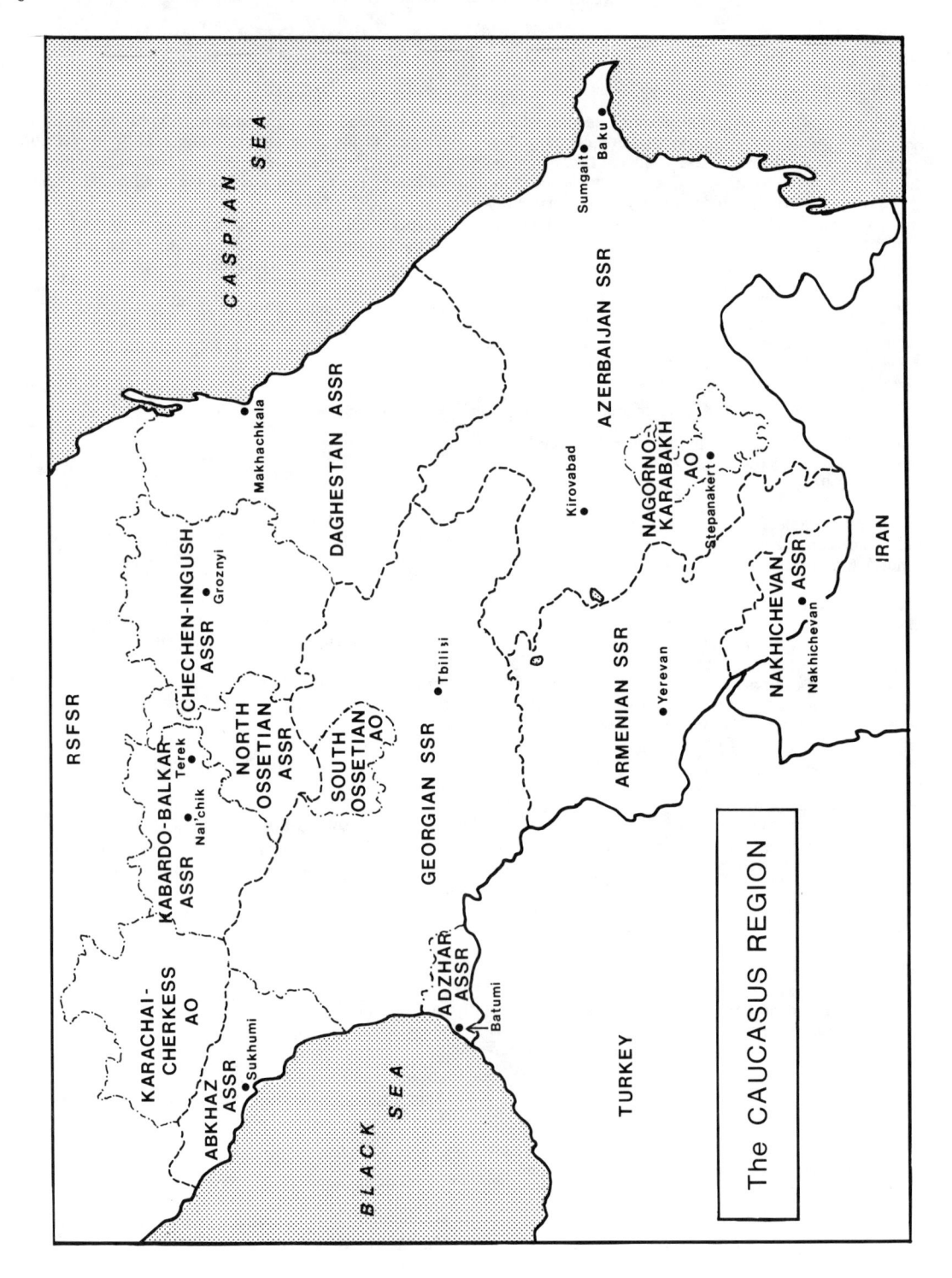

First Session

25 May 1989

Thus, in all 18 comrades are being proposed for the body of the congress presidium.

Orlov: Allow me to put the proposal to a vote. Everyone in favor of the proposal, of the composition of the proposed presidium, please raise your hands.

You can use your mandates. Do you want to take the vote again using mandates? Everyone in favor of electing the proposed composition of the presidium please raise your mandates. Please lower them. Against. Abstentions.

Right, the motion is carried virtually [prakticheski] unanimously. I didn't see a single one.

Would the deputies elected please take their seats in the congress presidium.

Gorbachev: On behalf of the congress presidium, allow me to thank you for the trust you have shown. We will try.... (Applause). We will try to work in full contact—I am confident in this, all the members of the presidium support me—with the congress, with the purpose of successfully conducting this vessel toward the goals that have been set. We need to endorse the agenda and the working procedure of the congress. I would like to inform USSR people's deputies and the congress that yesterday, on your authorization, representatives of delegations—446 people—held a meeting for 9 hours and they discussed these questions in the most thorough way to prepare proposals for you on those issues. On behalf of the meeting of representatives, the floor is given to Deputy Nazarbayev, Kazakhstan, on the issue of the agenda and the working procedures of the congress. Please.

Nazerbayev: Esteemed comrades people's deputies: Yesterday, at a meeting of representatives of groups of people's deputies, the question of the agenda of the USSR Congress of People's Deputies was comprehensively discussed. Different views on the issue were voiced at the meeting. Following a thorough discussion, a proposal was worked out to put the following questions on the agenda:

1. To elect the mandate commission of the congress.
2. To elect the chairman of the USSR Supreme Soviet.
3. To elect the USSR Supreme Soviet.
4. To elect the first deputy chairman of the USSR Supreme Soviet.
5. On the main guidelines of the USSR's domestic and foreign policy, a report by the chairman of the USSR Supreme Soviet.
6. A program for the forthcoming activity of the USSR Government. A report by the chairman of the USSR Council of Ministers.
7. To approve the chairman of the USSR Council of Ministers.
8. To elect the USSR Committee for Constitution Supervision.
9. To approve the chairman of the USSR People's Control Committee, the chairman of the USSR Supreme Court, the USSR procurator general, and the USSR chief state arbiter.
10. Miscellanea.

On behalf of the meeting of representatives of people's deputies groups, I propose to approve this agenda of the USSR Congress of People's Deputies. As to the congress' working procedures, it is proposed to examine issues in the sequence they were included in the agenda.

Gorbachev: Thank you, thank you. So, there are the proposals from the conference of representatives.

Sakharov: I ask to be given the floor.

Gorbachev: You are welcome. Andrey Dmitriyevich Sakharov, people's deputy, please. (Applause).

Sakharov: Esteemed deputies: I would like to speak in defense of two theses of principle which were laid down in the foundation of a draft agenda elaborated by a group of Moscow deputies after prolonged work, which was also seconded by a number of deputies from the country's other regions. We proceed from the fact that this congress is a historic event in our country's history.

Electors and the people elected us and sent us to this congress so that we would take responsibility for the country's destiny, for the problems it is facing now, and for the prospects of its development. Therefore, our congress cannot be...cannot start from elections. Otherwise, it would turn it into a congress of electors. Our congress cannot hand legislative power to a fifth of its composition. The fact that rotation has been stipulated does not change anything; the more so as, apparently in a haste, the rotation was drafted in such a way that only as few as 36 percent—I am proceeding from the Constitution—only 36 percent of the deputies have a chance to be included in the composition of the Supreme Soviet.

It is in connection with this that the first and principled thesis of the proposal contained in the draft was set forth by the Moscow group.

I propose to take as one of the first points of the congress agenda a decree of the USSR Congress of People's Deputies. We are going through a revolution. Restructuring is a revolution. And the word decree is the most germane in the given instance. It is the exclusive right of the USSR Congress of People's Deputies to pass USSR laws and to appoint the USSR's top officials, including the chairman of the USSR Council of Ministers, the chairman of the Committee for People's Control, the chairman of the USSR Supreme Court, the USSR procurator general, and the USSR chief arbiter. In line with this, amendments should be made to those articles of the USSR's Constitution that deal with the rights of the USSR Supreme Soviet. In particular, this goes for Articles 108 and 111.

STENOGRAPHIC RECORD

First Session

25 May 1989

The second principled matter which we face is whether we can—whether we have the right—to elect the head of state, the chairman of the USSR Supreme Soviet, before there has been debate and discussion of the whole gamut of political issues, which determine the destiny of our country, that we are obliged to examine.

Order always exists, from the start of the discussion, the initial presentation of candidates and their platforms, and then the elections. We would disgrace ourselves in front of our entire people—and this is my profound conviction—if we do otherwise. We cannot do this. (Applause). In my speeches I have, on several occasions, voiced support for the candidacy of Mikhail Sergeyevich Gorbachev. (Applause). I still maintain that position now, inasmuch as I do not see another person who could lead our country. I do not see it at the present time. My support is of a conditional nature. I think discussion is necessary. We need a report from the candidates because I think that in principle we should bear in mind the alternative principle for all elections at this congress, including for elections of the chairman of the Supreme Soviet. That is why I use the word "candidates" although I consider it fully possible that there will not be other candidates. But if there are any, then we will be talking in the plural. The candidates should present their political platform.

Mikhail Sergeyevich Gorbachev, the forefather of restructuring—the beginning of the process of restructuring is connected with his name, as is the leadership of the country during a 4-year period—should also talk about what has happened in our country over those 4 years. He should speak both about the achievements and about the mistakes self-critically. Our standpoint will also depend on that. And, most importantly, he should say what he—and if there are other candidates, then they also should say—what they intend to do in the near future to overcome the extremely difficult situation in our country, and what they will do in the long term. (Noise in the hall.)

Gorbachev, interrupting: Let's reach an agreement on the order of discussion. Speakers should have up to 5 minutes to express themselves, maximum.

Sakharov: I'm just finishing. I will not list all the questions which I consider necessary for discussion. They are contained in our draft. And I hope that our delegates are familiar with this draft. I end by saying that I hope that the congress will be worthy of the great mission which it faces and that it will democratically approach the tasks which it faces.

Gorbachev: Just a minute, comrades! I think we are at the final stage now. We have discussed all the questions with fairly great desire and without indifference. And these questions have basically been formulated. But I do not think we should deprive comrades who spoke at earlier stages of the opportunity to report their view to the congress. The business of the congress is to adopt a decision. The main proposal has been submitted on behalf of all delegations, therefore I ask you, comrades, to express yourselves briefly. Comrade Popov, please.

Popov: Comrades, yesterday, in a fully democratic atmosphere, at the conference of representatives of delegations, an agenda was adopted which has been reported on here today. We took part in the discussion. We were all given the opportunity to express ourselves. There was voting. Fifteen percent of participants in the conference of representatives expressed themselves in favor of our proposal which we were putting forward. But as Mikhail Sergeyevich rightly said, democracy is democracy and we have the possibility also of addressing the congress. Essentially, the essence of the problem lies in one of the points on the agenda, to put it accurately, and that is whether to conduct discussion and debate and the report before the election of the Supreme Soviet or after the election of the Supreme Soviet. There was the proposal which Andrey Dmitriyevich talked about, and there was a second proposal which was voted on yesterday, that Mikhail Sergeyevich's report should be heard out as a third point on the agenda after his election—from which proceeds today's idea that election by the congress of the Supreme Soviet should take place immediately.

The idea proceeds from two assumptions. The first assumption is that both of these assumptions are not anybody's invention, or ill will, nor a wish to neglect the machinery of voting, and so on. They are dicated by the logic of our Constitution, and it is fully understandable that the comrades have put forward these proposals. According to the Constitution we should indeed wait until the Supreme Soviet confirms the chairman of the Council of Ministers, the general procurator, and the chairman of the People's Control Committee. Then these candidatures should come to us, and we should vote. In this event the logic offered by the agenda is natural, but we think that an amendment to the Constitution is essential here—which Andrey Dmitriyevich talked about—to the effect that the chairman of the Council of Ministers, the chairman of the People's Control Committee, the general procurator, the chairman of the Supreme Court, and the chief arbiter, should be elected here by us at the congress in order to raise the role of the congress as the highest body of power in the country. If this amendment is adopted, there will be no need of any kind for a preliminary and early election of the Supreme Soviet in order to give it the opportunity to work and to put forward the candidatures.

The second assumption at the basis of the agenda is that in essence the election of deputies for the Supreme Soviet does not require a debate over their points of view, positions, and so on. It is being proposed in essence that we move away from such principles of democracy as real secret voting and election among alternative candidatures. It is proposed to us that we vote on a list of candidates whose number corresponds to the number of allocated places.

STENOGRAPHIC RECORD

First Session

25 May 1989

Why has such an idea arisen? Again, not because somebody wants to trample on democracy. Once again there is logic here, and once again this is the logic of our Constitution. It is written in it that the Soviet of the Union should be formed by taking into account the regional principle, and all the consequences have arisen from this. Once you have the regional principle, then consequently you have quotas. Quotas, which are the natural thing for the Soviet of Nationalities, were extended to the Soviet of the Union, and as a result every region, perfectly naturally, is striving to implement its quota. But a situation arises which requires attention. You see, there are various deputies in every region today. I don't know the situation in many places, but, for example, they are fully familiar to me for Moscow Oblast. Such a well-known figure of our restucturing as Nikolay Travkin won in the elections in Moscow Oblast. In the list of representatives from Moscow Oblast, I don't see him as a deputy for the Supreme Soviet. I, for example, consider his participation in the Supreme Soviet essential for restructuring.

Gorbachev: Finish up.

Popov: The last thing. Consequently, it is being proposed to us that we simply adopt as a basis what is being proposed by every region. It seems to me that we have all found ourselves in this hall only because there were new elections, elections with a choice of candidates, elections with programs, and so on. The principle of choice needs to be spread to elections for the Supreme Soviet. If this principle is adopted—the principle of choice—then everything will fall into place.

Then there is the possibility of, indeed—on the third point of the agenda—hearing out the report and organizing debates. Yesterday our delegation sat in session for a very long time, until late. And with a majority of votes, with three abstentions and with two against, it adopted a decision to appeal to the congress with a full list of candidates, which we are putting forward and which significantly exceeds the number of places made for us. We ask all of you to follow our example and to defend the new democracy. (Applause).

Gorbachev: Good. The floor is given to People's Deputy Meshalkin, an academician from Novosibirsk.

Meshalkin: Deeply respected comrade deputies, this is the first time that I have had the occasion to speak to such an important and huge forum. Forgive me it I am somewhat flustered. But it seems to me that in gathering today to confirm the agenda, there must, of course, be a justification for the agenda, and there must also be a perfectly responsible posing of the questions on the agenda, which was proposed here and approved yesterday by the majority of delegations.

The key point of that agenda is to immediately elect the chairman of the Supreme Soviet, or first of all to listen to him. It seems to me that in order to listen to the future chairman of the Supreme Soviet, we need first of all to invest him with authority, because not only a statement of today, but also an analysis of what can be done, underpinned by the supreme power—that is, the Supreme Soviet, with which, of course, the chairman will discuss his report—are absolutely essential for this. After all, we cannot just listen to empty promises. We need something which will be underpinned by deeds. (Applause).

Representatives of the Moscow group of deputies, in particular Academician Sakharov, have confirmed that they see no alternative to the person of Mikhail Sergeyevich Gorbachev. When it is a question of a claimant to the post of chairman or president, then his figure is determined not by what he will say now, but what determined his deeds prior to these elections. Surely we know the prior deeds with which the future claimant to the post of chairman characterized his previous—if only 4 years'—activity. After all, no one makes the U.S. President make promises to the public or to the Senate right before the election. There is a lengthy, 4 or 6 month election campaign which paints the deeds of the future president and his promises, and so I suggest that, with a view to the fact that we wanted to have a truly businesslike report, a true analysis of what needs to be done and of what needs to be carried out to complete restructuring in our country, we should first of all invest the chairman of the Supreme Soviet Presidium with the authority of chairman, and then listen to the report. That is my viewpoint.

Voices in the auditorium: Right! (Applause).

Meshalkin: That's the first thing. (Applause). I also propose that the report should be heard after holding elections for the Supreme Soviet. No one is preventing an alternative candidacy from being raised. And the discussion of candidates for the Supreme Soviet is the second question on the agenda, but not the first, and it must not now be submitted. I propose that our first session of the congress should now restrict itself to confirming the agenda and giving the opportunity, in accordance with that agenda, of deciding all the points therein; and on each point of the agenda, when its turn comes to be examined, debates should be organized, as I was just saying. I call for a vote in favor of the agenda which was confirmed yesterday by the majority—85 percent, Comrade Popov says, more than 85 percent. The voting was almost unanimous. The representatives of the delegations confirmed this agenda. Thank you. (Applause).

Gorbachev: Good. Comrades, shall we continue the debates? (Sounds of approval from hall). One moment, comrades. Shall we continue the debates, or have two points of view formed, and we can discuss them and decide the question of which one we will take? Who is in favor of concluding on this exchange of opinions? Who proposes in support? (Shouts from hall). One moment. (He reads a note handed to him): Fulfilling the mandate of my electors concerning the fact that any elections at

STENOGRAPHIC RECORD

First Session

25 May 1989

the congress must absolutely be on a competitive basis, and on the basis of Articles 48 and 120 of the Constitution, I put forward my own candidacy for election to the post of chairman of the USSR Supreme Soviet. I am prepared to speak and set forth my program. Obolenskiy, Aleksandr Mitrofanovich, people's deputy for the Leningrad Rural National Territorial Constituency No 20 of the RSFSR. (Applause).

Mitrofanovich: I have an alternative proposal. I agree that we should first elect Mikhail Sergeyevich as chairman of the Supreme Soviet because we know him. We know him for what he has done, for his daily activities involving all kinds of work. I profoundly agree with this.

But I do not agree that we should elect the Supreme Soviet immediately, because there are many people who gather there whom we do not know. In our lives we are now getting back to common sense. To elect people with whom we are basically not acquainted, who are still frequently changing in front of our eyes.... I would like to see how they prove their worth here, what their positions are, what sort of civic spirit they have, how bold they are. And only then, once I have listened to them and had a look at them, will I vote for them.

I would like to submit an alternative proposal: First elect the chairman of the Supreme Soviet—I agree with the arguments which have been put forward here—but I would like to propose that the election of the Supreme Soviet itself be postponed until after the debate. (Applause).

Gorbachev: Still, I will steer our ship in the following way: Who is in favor of ending the exchange of opinions on this question? Please vote. Please lower your hands. Who is against? Fine. For the moment I would ask those who are against to lower their hands. We will have to work out the mechanism.

A proposal is submitted to the effect that we make a count of the votes in open voting and instruct a group of people's deputies to do this as follows:

Head of the group: Deputy Aleksandr Grigoryevich Kostenyuk, chairman of the Orenburg Oblast Executive Committee. His assistants: comrades Platonov, academician, president of the Belorussian SSR Academy of Sciences; Sokolov, senior scientific worker at the Voronezh Elektronika Scientific Production Association.

It is also proposed that the following deputies be part of the group: Amangeldinova, a secondary school teacher in Pavlodar; Vidiker, director of the Suvorovskiy Sovkhoz, Kazakhstan; Akhunov, deputy director at No 4 School, Uzbekistan; Baranov, chairman of a trade union committee at the Izhorskiy Zavod Production Association, Leningrad; Andreyev, chief engineer of the Moscow State Planning and Surveying Institute, Mosgiprotrans; Yaroshenko, deputy general director of the scientific-production association for tractor building, Moscow;

Babich, chairman of the Kiev City Committee of the Agro-Industrial Complex Workers' Trade Union; Bichkauskas, investigator for especially grave cases of the procuracy of the Lithuanian SSR; Giro, commander of a Tu-154 aircraft, Tajikistan; Ibragimov, driller from the Neftyanyye Kamni Marine Directorate of drilling operations, Azerbaijan SSR; Margvelashvili, senior lecturer from Tbilisi State University; (Burskiy), chairman of the Brest Oblast Executive Committee; Reshetnikov, deputy chief of a shop at the Kaluga Engine-Building Production Association; Nazarov, first secretary of the Russkopolyanskiy Rayon Party Committee, Omsk Oblast; Yerokhin, deputy commander of a subunit of the Kiev Military District Army unit; Shlyakota, director of the Vecumi Sovkhoz, Latvia; Aasmyae, head of a sector of the Estonia design and construction bureau; and Belyayev, dean of the Moscow Physical Engineering Institute. These are comrades whom we have examined and whom we are proposing. Are there objections to these comrades?

Voices from the auditorium: No, no.

Gorbachev: No. I put them to the vote. Those in favor of approving the deputies acting as tellers for counting votes in open ballot, please raise your mandates. Please, lower them. Anybody against? No. Abstentions? No. One vote. Whom do you propose? Come here and speak.

Belyaev: Two comrades fell ill today, and they are absent. I am Belyayev, from the eighth district, Moscow. Two comrades have fallen ill. We have two sectors which are not covered. At that conference, two comrades from the reserves were nominated. I would ask the chairman of the voting commission simply to announce these names so that they can be endorsed today by the whole congress.

Gorbachev: All right. So, who can announce these two names? Who can report on the changes Moscow has introduced? Comrade Kostenyuk. Please, make your announcement regarding the two comrades.

Kostenyuk: Mikhail Sergeyevich and comrade deputies, we have a reserve in the persons of Comrade Karasev....

Gorbachev, interrupting: Where from?

Kostenyuk: He is head of a department at the Kramatorsk Industrial Institute, the Ukrainian SSR.

Gorbachev: And the other?

Kostenyuk: Comrade Belenkov Yuriy Nikitich, director of the All-Union Cardiology Scientific Center of the USSR Academy of Medical Sciences.

Gorbachev: Comrades, do you accept this replacement?

Voices: Yes.

STENOGRAPHIC RECORD

First Session

25 May 1989

Gorbachev: We are voting for the replacement. Please, raise your mandates. Please lower. Anybody against? Abstentions? So, this has been decided. You would like to say something regarding the voting, please. We will now be counting votes against.

Boldyrev: Deputy Boldyrev, No 54 constituency from Leningrad. I have a proposal on the mechanism of voting. The fact is that far from all deputies will be able to speak over the time of the congress. Electors must have the right to assess how their representatives have performed at this congress. Electors must have the right to know how their deputies voted on this or that issue, apart from personal ones. For that reason, I submit the proposal of organizing a registered vote [fiksirovannoye golosovaniye] on all issues apart from personal ones. I think that all the technical matters can be resolved. (Applause).

Gorbachev: I think that this proposal is one of the attempts to draw us into things that the congress should not get involved in. (Applause). Now, relying on the experience of open voting which we have, we have selected tellers, and we can move on. But since such a proposal has been made, I have to determine this one way or the other. And so, the first proposal submitted by the presidium. Will all those who are in favor of this voting mechanism please raise their mandate cards? Put them down. Those against? One, 2, 3, 4, 5, 6, 7, 8, 9, 10, 11, 12, 13, 14, 15, 16, 17, 18, 19, 20, 21, 22, 23, 24, 25, 26, 27, 28, 29, 30, 31.

Lukyanov: And that one, and that one?

Gorbachev: No, I have counted those. All you comrades sitting in the stalls, we have counted you. Thirty-one deputies against. Abstentions? Any abstentions? One, 2, 3, 4, 5, 6, 7, 8, 9, 10, 11, 12, 13, 14, 15, 16, 17, 18, 19, 20 abstentions. The matter is settled. And so, we have a voting commission [schetnaya kommissiya]. I will ask the comrades to get down to work, and I will return to who is in favor of endorsing the agenda that Comrade Nazarbayev submitted on behalf of the conference of representatives of delegations as it stands, and discussion—at the same time he gave an order of discussion—in the order that the issues are in. I ask the deputies to raise their mandate cards. Put them down. Who is against? Count them, comrades. So, who abstains on this matter, comrades? How many abstentions on this question?

Kostenyuk: Can we give our report, Mikhail Sergeyevich?

Gorbachev: Please go ahead.

Kostenyuk: The results of the voting, then: Against, 379. Abstentions 9. (Applause).

Gorbachev: Then the matter has been decided. (Laughter). The matter has been decided.

On the question of the order, what was proposed was put to a vote. It gained overwhelming support. At the same time this decides the fate of the other proposals, for the congress cannot work under two agendas at one time. It has already been determined. That's it. All right. Comrade Shchedrin asks that we vote on his alternative proposal. Do you consider it necessary? Don't worry, I know what needs to be done. Who is in favor of our confining ourselves to this, that the examination of the agenda should be regarded as decided and thus that we should not embark upon consideration of the other alternative proposals? I ask deputies to vote. Please put your hands down. Are there any against? Clearly a minority. In this case this is not required it is of no significance. We won't make a count. It was an absolute, overwhelming majority. We've decided. The agenda of the USSR Congress of People's Deputies has been approved.

I will now decide one more question, and then I will raise a question which some comrades here have raised with me. It deals with the order of our work. On behalf of the meeting of representatives, Deputy Nazarbayev submitted the proposal that the issues be examined in the order in which they have been included in the agenda. I included that in the first point in the voting and we voted on it. But the question is that there are now the standing orders. As you know, the Constitution provides for the adoption of the standing orders by the USSR Congress of People's Deputies and the Supreme Soviet, the task of which is to define in detail the whole procedure of the activity of the supreme bodies of power. We naturally do not have such standing orders now. We have to adopt them and evidently the congress, at the appropriate time, must adopt a decision and entrust the Supreme Soviet with the task of working out these standing orders in draft form, and of presenting them for confirmation by a regular congress, which today is the autumn congress. Clearly that is how we are going to proceed. Before the permanently operating standing orders are adopted it would be expedient to adopt a provisional document determining the procedure of the work of the congress. This task is resolved by the provisional standing orders of the congress session, a draft of which is in your hands. It includes all the norms of the USSR Constitution on the work of the congress, and also the rules that issue from them. The provisional standing orders have been examined by the USSR Suprem Soviet Presidium and at the group yesterday we discussed them—quite intensively, moveover—and a lot of interesting additions were incorporated. And in my opinion, there were none who objected here, and all approved them unanimously. Here, therefore, are your draft standing orders, our draft. They are in your hands. Can I put them to the vote, if the comrade deputies are in agreement with the proposals which have been made in this connection by the meeting of representatives? Please take the floor. Please introduce yourself first.

Antanavichyus: Deputy Antanavichyus, 22d national constituency. The standing orders which we received today make no mention of the amendments introduced

STENOGRAPHIC RECORD

First Session

25 May 1989

yesterday. For instance, an amendment was adopted on point 19 to the effect that the statements, declarations, and addresses introduced at the congress by no less than 20 deputies are distributed by the congress as official documents of the congress. Further, an amendment was introduced into Article 15 to the effect that in a decision regarding the question of ending a debate, deputies elected from a union republic have the right to insist upon the continuation of the debate on questions concerning the republic provided such a proposal is supported by at least two-thirds of the deputies elected from that republic. And there was more. However, I did not make any more proposals. Therefore, I think that their authors will also speak out.

Gorbachev: First of all, I see that point 15 says a debate is ended on the decision of the Congress of People's Deputies adopted by a majority of no less than two-thirds of the overall number of people's deputies. In deciding the question of ending a debate, deputies elected from the union republics have the right to insist that the floor be given to one of the deputies of the given republic, provided such a proposal is supported by at least two-thirds of the deputies elected from that republic.

Antanavichyus: Then the question arises, why did these representatives meet yesterday? Yesterday, we agreed that a debate continues on the demand of at least two-thirds of the delegates of the republic. That is an essential—the essence of the change. Not one deputy, but the debate continues, and as you, Mikhail Sergeyvich, said yesterday, until the second ballot.

Gorbachev: Alright, let us have this amplification. I agree with this. Let us elaborate. There won't be any objections? Ballot? I think, comrades, that this is all acceptable. The mechanism has been thought out. The congress can always intervene in that process if things begin to get drawn out and if speculation begins on that legal norm. It can put an end to that business by repeat ballotting.

Now, as far as your second proposal is concerned. I consider that we came to an agreement, and I remember that just as you do. We voted, but so that all these things are not distributed by the delegations themselves, but through the Supreme Soviet presidium, a document is distributed. I think that what we agreed upon at the meeting has to be confirmed. You know, they worked till dawn last night and missed something. Please, Comrade Landsbergis. Now, where is that comrade who wanted to speak? Oh, there he is. I shall give you the floor. There you are. Introduce yourself, please.

Landsbergis: Deputy Landsbergis, 245th constituency, the town of Panevezys. I asked for the floor a bit earlier, but even now I would like to draw your attention, esteemed delegates, to the fact that the method of voting which we are adopting here, which has already been adopted, and which was adopted yesterday, can be regarded as an improper one. That is because whenever there are alternative proposals, it would be more proper to vote for the first proposal, and then for the second proposal, and not the way we do it. I suggest we reflect on that.

At the same time, I would like to draw your attention to the fact that Academician Sakharov made two proposals on the agenda, and the first proposal on the decree of the congress has so far been passed over in silence.

Gorbachev: Let us examine! As for the questions of the agenda, they have been decided. We have already resolved the. The congress decided collectively. I do not think we will go back to that again. Let us move on.

As for the question raised by Academician Sakharov about a decree, let us instruct the presidium to examine this proposal. That is not contrary to the agenda. It has more to do with the hierarchy of the supreme organs of power, and that is more a matter for the congress than the Supreme Soviet. And it can decide more accurately. This subject was the main one yesterday, and incidentally we reached a very interesting proposal. I mean that we will apparently be proposing (but this comes later) to hold two congresses a year, after all. And not as it was planned, but for the Supreme Soviet basically to become a working organ, albeit a solid, high-ranking organ, with considerable rights, but all the same, basically to work for the congress. And for the main laws, apart from those that do not require a decision of congress (we will detail this), to be adopted, ultimately, by the congress after all. (Applause).

We agreed that those deputies who do not get onto the Supreme Soviet should not feel that they are invited once a year, or even twice, and are then left to stew in their own juice. No. We thought about this. It should all be viewed comprehensively. As yet it has only been examined as an idea, on a preliminary basis. I sensed from conversations with many deputies that many, if not all, are worried about the future of the people's deputy. And we agreed that, first, the commissions should include, say, 50 percent Supreme Soviet members and 50 percent other people's deputies. Thus this will immediately widen the deputies' opportunities to take part in the commissions' work.

We also agreed that the Supreme Soviet, carrying out its current work in the chambers and commissions, will send the people's deputies the work schedule and the schedule for commission sessions. Therefore all the deputies will know what questions are being discussed, and every deputy, when it is necessary and when he considers it possible to participate in the discussion and express his view on a particular question, will come and take part in the work of a given commission or a chamber session. And we agreed that this must be decided here, at this congress.

STENOGRAPHIC RECORD

First Session

25 May 1989

Apart from that, there will be a status—today it is temporary; for the Supreme Soviet deputy this will be a new status which, generally, is bound to elevate our USSR people's deputy in comparison with his position in accordance with the present status. We shall work on that and make a decision on that at the autumn congress.

Therefore, comrades, through the realization of these ideas—and as we work our way through them, others, I think, will appear—we will achieve a situation in which the people's deputy, in the framework of his powers and the terms of those powers, will participate efficiently in the entire work. And at a certain stage, we will provide instructions on all of these issues. Right, let us instruct the Presidium, regarding the proposal by Academician Sakharov, to take its stand and offer its ideas to you. All right? I do not think that requires a vote, just an agreement. Now one of the deputies has come to me and said: Mikhail Sergeyevich, it is not right that you should be conducting the congress, because it should be conducted by the chairman of the Central Electoral Commission. Is it my lack of democracy or something which is making some people unhappy? I do not know, but according to the Constitution, yes indeed, I will say it all now, as you say. We discussed this question, comrades, and it was recognized that there should be representatives on the working presidium, both from the Supreme Soviet Presidium, which was entrusted with opening it, the chairman of the Central Electoral Commission, who was instructed to open it, and from the republics, so that it would be a working, full blooded, representative, democratic body which could meet and discuss how the congress is going, what considerations need working out, and if something crops up they would report it to you, and so forth. All the deputies, both in the discussion in groups of deputies and at the assembly of representatives, agreed with this, and this proposal was submitted. Probably they want to overthrow me, or something. But don't worry, we agreed that all the presidium members will be conducting business in turn....

Unidentified deputy: The Central Electoral Commission....

Gorbachev: Please introduce yourself.

Levashov: Deputy Levashov, Kolpinskiy Territorial Constituency No 52. Comrade deputies, the thing is that according to Article 110 of the Constitution, the first session following the elections of the Congress of People's Deputies is conducted by the chairman of the Central Electoral Commission. If not, then all the decisions made now, the votes and acts, have no legal force. We need to reopen the congress. There is a very serious question here. This is the question I put to the presidium. Thank you for listening. (Isolated applause).

Gorbachev: I believe that the congress, the congress at the preparatory stage, worked out the proposals and democratically decided the question of the presidium. In that way the congress today has constituted everything as it is. Shall we take it from there? (Sounds of agreement from the hall). Does anyone object on that score? (Sounds of "no" from the hall). No. Good.

So, we have started discussing the standing orders. If you please. Please introduce yourself. Comrade Plotniyeks, no?

Plotniyeks: A.A. Plotniyeks, No 304 National-Territorial Electoral Constituency. Esteemed comrade people's deputies! The question of the standing orders, temporary or permanent, might at first seem a purely technical matter. But I have come to the rostrum because I think that this is a matter of primary importance. And today, drafting or refining this or that varient of the standing orders, we are laying the foundations for the more successful or less successful work of our congress. In connection with this, I am, as it were, beginning with the final conclusion: I propose the election of or the formation of a commission from among the USSR people's deputies, who will now over a couple of days put the final touches to these temporary standing orders, which the congress will endorse. Our legal status, the form of our activities immediately after the congress closes, and the possibilities of using deputies' rights will depend on what this document will be like.

In connection with this, there is the following, as well. Today we find ourselves at the second stage of the reform of the political system. This stage presupposes that we will restructure the federation and take into account the real sovereignty of the union republics; that in turn means that there will be very intensive legislative activity. The draft temporary standing orders talk about this. They talk of who has the right of initiating legislation, how laws are passed, and so on. But a whole range of issues remain open, particularly the question of which laws will be passed by the congress and which by the Supreme Soviet. The Constitution gives us no reply to this question. If you compare the powers of the congress and those of the Supreme Soviet, they partially overlap. And so, in the standing orders, we must somehow or other stipulate which laws we will be discussing, and perhaps provide for some possibility of convening not an extraordinary but a regular congress wich would engage in legislative work. Further, I propose, in this connection, that we consider that it might be sensible to have the laws adopted by the Supreme Soviet to be endorsed at a regular congress. That would be democratic; it would not take a lot of time, but at least the people, in the person of the people's deputies, would—so to speak—give its approval to the work that has been done by the Supreme Soviet in a given period.

The question of regulating the legislative work of the congress is also a very interesting matter. For example, from the standing orders, there is no mention of what the time frames are for the preparation of drafts in standing commissions and committees, what the procedure for making amendments to them is, nor how participation of deputies—both those elected in the Supreme Soviet and

STENOGRAPHIC RECORD

First Session
25 May 1989

those not elected—in the work of these standing commissions is expressed. This is extremely important; it is the machinery, the legislative machinery. But depending on how much we manage to work out these rules, we will be able to provide laws which are technically better or worse laws. Mikhail Sergeyevich has already spoken of the desirability of allowing people's deputies not elected to the Supreme Soviet to work in the standing commissions. There is nothing in the standing orders about this. It seems to me that this should definitely be included, so that in cases where special knowledge is required, we can come and speak, because there will be no chance to speak at the congress, but everyone wants to make whatever contribution they can to legislative activity.

Finally, it seems to me that today's experience already shows that we need organizational forms. There is the beginning of them, too, here, but so far there are too few. Imagine, such a gigantic collective of people. How are we to organize it? Evidently, it should be organized by union republic, and evidently the deputies from a union republic should figure in the standing orders as some association, be it a group, delegation, whatever we want. And it should be clearly registered how work is organized and how deputies speak here—then there will be no lack of coordination; there will be greater organization and greater efficiency. Thank you for your attention. (Applause).

Gorbachev: Good. May I express my reaction to what I think was a very substantive speech? So, we—evidently this is the fate of a first congress—are faced with the need for standing orders. We have to draft them. But until we have drafted and endorsed standing orders, we have to live on and work. To this end there is, as it were, a transitional stage: the temporary standing orders.

This is what has been proposed, so that we might be able to work, move ahead, and tackle the issues. But I have already said that we must draw up standing orders, and they should be the object of in-depth discussion at the congress. That is the first thing. In the second place, of the many matters that the comrade deputy correctly raised, I would say—judging by what one can glean at once from what one hears—the majority, by and large, deserves attention. And in particular, I believe that the standing orders will change greatly, given that the delegates support the idea of the need to go back and more precisely apportion the hierarchy between congress and the Supreme Soviet and, thus, the participation of deputies in various forms, including in commissions. All of this must be implemented in the standing orders. And so, therefore, if we keep our feet firmly on the ground, the actual situation is this: For the congress to be able to work and tackle the issues, we must now support and go along with the provisional standing orders and all the other matters, including those which you mentioned before—true, some of them are, as it turns out, included, such as the participation of deputies in the work of the standing commissions, regardless of whether they are in the Supreme Soviet. That is mentioned, but that is not the point. That is, all the remaining issues are within the context of the fact that, generally speaking, we will decide the question of two congresses—as yet we have just the one planned—and that we need to clarify the jurisdiction of the congress and the Supreme Soviet. Moreover, it will probably turn out that not every law, for example, ratification—well, there are laws that require only the Supreme Soviet to convene and decide the matter, but there are laws, including perhaps a ratification law, that require the congress to meet, when the matter affects the destiny of the state. And so, we must work on this. And all of this will be reflected later in the permanent standing orders that we will put forward for approval by the next congress.

I believe we must move ahead in that direction, on the basis of this discussion. What about it, comrades? (Noise from hall). Right. Please go ahead, Comrade Stankevich. Comrade Stankevich, a deputy from Moscow.

Stankevich: Deputy Stankevich, Cheremushki Constituency No 26, Moscow city. I wish to propose an amendment to Article 18 of the provisional standing orders. I agree that a more serious review of the regulations can wait. A special commission needs to be set up to make a serious study of this. But, in my opinion, it would make sense to include this proposal, which I submit for your examination, in the provisional standing orders of the congress. We can't manage without it. I am talking about Article 18, in which the sequence of the voting procedure is determined. The thing is, it makes no provision for a registered vote. During my election campaign, and from chatting to voters in Moscow and other towns, it became perfectly clear to me that the overwhelming majority of the electorate wants to know how the representatives at the congress are voting. Moreover—excuse me, excuse me—this is an amendment to the standing orders which we are discussing. And moreover, deputies now have sufficient convenient opportunity, thanks to anonymous voting, to reject serious proposals and serious draft bills which the electorate is anticipating, and consequently—subsequently—to bear no responsibility toward the electorate. Well, I would like to avoid this convenient opportunity of anonymous voting. I am well aware that, since we have technical difficulties in the country and we cannot permit ourselves such a luxury as an electronic voting system—we are unable to in this situation—we are forced to seek other ways. Let's suppose the majority of the voting is simply carried out by a raising of hands. So, let's proceed with this archaic method. But on the more fundamental proposals and the more fundamental draft bills, on the demand of, say, no less than 100 deputies, we can proceed with such a luxury as a registered vote. Therefore, the crux of the proposal follows. This is my formula: to supplement Article 18 of the provisional regulations with the following clause: On request of no less than 100 congress deputies, a registered vote may be carried out. Thank you. (Applause).

Gorbachev: Permit me to present my attitude to this and, in this connection, to consult with you. I believe that Comrade Stankevich's proposal is worth attention.

First Session
25 May 1989

comrades. Let's remind ourselves, that voting by name took place on the Peace of Brest, so to speak. Such things happen in our country, they may even become turning points, when each deputy, weighing everything up, has to engage in voting by name.

But I would only disagree with Comrade Stankevich's formula about the request of 100 deputies. By a decision of the congress, the congress should determine, and not 100 deputies whether voting by name is necessary or not. Therefore, I would say that, by a decision of the congress, voting by name can be conducted. In my opinion, this is a very important and serious addendum.

And so, Comrade Stankevich's first proposal: voting by name on the initiative of a minimum of 100 deputies. Those in favor of deputy Stankevich's proposal, please raise your mandates. Please count them. One moment, please lower them. In the order submitted, a proposal is being put to the vote, as worded by Deputy Stankevich, as follows: Voting by name may be carried out at the congress on the initiative of no less than 100 deputies. (Indistinct interjection from floor). No, but there is still a proposal.

The second proposal is the one which I have submitted: Voting by name may be carried out by decision of the congress. The first proposal was by Deputy Stankevich. No, but I think that we should proceed as laid out in the democratic process. The first proposal is from deputy Stankevich: He proposes, his formula is as follows: that the congress may carry out voting by name if such a proposal is submitted by no less than 100 deputies. Is that correct, Comrade Stankevich? Those in favor of his proposal, please vote. Please count the votes.

Gorbachev: First and second sectors, report.

Vote counter: I report 431 in favor.

Gorbachev: What?

Vote counter: Four hundred and thirty-one people voted in favor.

Gorbachev: All right, Who is against? (Several interjections from the floor). For the second? Who is in favor of the second proposal, that the congress can conduct a nominal vote on its decision. All right, you can put your hands down. Is it necessary to count in this case?

Voices: No.

Gorbachev: But only in the event that everyone agrees to it. Then we shall not count...the overwhelming majority...there is no need? No one insists on a count? No one. Then the question has been resolved. Your proposal is being accepted with an amendment, with an amendment.

STENOGRAPHIC RECORD

Now, comrades, I want to make public the request of deputies Gorinov and Karpochev, deputies from the Mari ASSR [Autonomous Soviet Socialist Republic], I think. They write that the attempts by some deputies to divert the congress to the discussion of procedures, procedures issues, is a very pernicious thing. It does not give prestige to our congress in the eyes of the electorate, even those voters who elected Comrades Sakharov, Boldyrev, and others. The people are waiting to see how the congress will decide fundamental questions, of our way of life. Therefore, one must appeal to the congress as to whether those who are actively introducing disorganization into the work of the congress should be given the floor three or four times. (Applause).

For my part, I will comment on this in the following way. Many substantial questions were posed here, many. Therefore, I think that everything that has been done up to now in this hour—an hour and a half already, one and a half—is substantial. We have approved the agenda. We have practically approved the standing orders. And all our activity should be based on that. And finally we have had exchanges with one another the questions which are already appearing in an outline. For all that, I have in mind Academician Sakharov's idea. And the fact that I am drawing up this suggestion—I developed the fact that it is already time for us to think about the presidium preparing, drawing on the participation of the deputies, questions regarding the powers of the congress and the Supreme Soviet, the functioning of all that complicated representative mechanism of ours. Therefore I would say that everything that has been discussed here was not just negative work. Mainly, it was, nevertheless, positive, but a warning like that and such a desire is pertinent and I think democratic as well. They took advantage of their right to express such a comment.

So please introduce yourself.

Bojars: Fedir Rudolfovich Bojars, constituency No 303, Dobele. Well, I have no doubt that the standing orders presented by the presidium can be adopted as a basis, and I would vote for this with pleasure. But, obviously, apart from this, we still need to adopt some small amendments so that we can with a clear conscience move forward. And for some republics and delegations, these amendments clearly are of considerable importance. The more so, in what I am about to say. We basically, Mikhail Sergeyevich—I probably assume that you won't let me be interupted—that we talked about it yesterday and somehow more or less agreed on it. So, this is my proposal. Concerning small delegations, in particular the Baltic republics, it is worrying that the basic political debates they—in our very big mass of basically constructively minded comrades who all want to speak—may not be heard at all. For this reason, we had a proposal yesterday...no, comrades, this is serious, there is no er, um, yes, no. I have no criticism. So it is a small request: that we should vote that every delegation, every republic should have at least a guaranteed minimum of speeches—three speeches at the basic political debates.

First Session
25 May 1989

Gorbachev: Right.

Bojars: This is very important.

Gorbachev: Right. Comrades, I confirm the question. The deputy is right. It was discussed at the conference of representatives, and we agreed, and let's write it in, to instruct the presidium to collegially determine the list of speakers, so that the interests of all the republics, krays, and oblasts, are taken into account, first and foremost I place the republics—after all, we are a union—and probably to some extent there should be representatives also of the various strata. So, unless you object, we can instruct the presidium with the following formula: to keep track of the speeches to ensure a minimum participation of representatives of all republics, krays, and oblasts, and the respective groups.

Bojars: So, my next proposal, comrades.

Gorbachev: And of public organizations.

Bojars: Yesterday we also more or less agreed—and a whole series of comrades from the Russian Federation and also from Moscow made this proposal—that we should vote nevertheless to nominate our representatives to the congress. And this should obviously be registered according to groups in the standing orders, because we think that we, in our group, spent a whole day in Riga discussing whom to nominate and in what way, taking into account the work and personal qualities and even the potential of each. Professor Plotnieks, who spoke before me, has—pardon me for saying so—also his own personal matters of concern. At home he has a young child and a mother whom he has to look after. We take this into account in our group, but other comrades cannot be aware of this. This is why we have an absolutely precise proposal. We are nominating our list and we shall stand for it. And later we shall change it, because, well, why should I interfere in the matters of the Russian Federation and determine who should represent the Russian Federation? I would consider this to be even immodest. And this is our second proposal in regard of which we already agreed yesterday.

Gorbachev: Yes, this does not have anything to do with standing orders, but this relates to the voting procedure, yes?

Bojars: It is registered here. And for the next matter, concerning the proposal of Professor Plotnieks, this is what we need here at the congress. We are firstly legislators and people who determine our state' policy. This is why one of the most important tasks of our congress is evidently, at least, the compilation of a basic list of the laws which should be adopted in a most urgent way. And it is evidently necessary to vote on this. And in the course of the congress this work must evidently be done and in order to do this it is necessary to create an appropriate commission, which would deal with these laws and with the proposals on draft laws. This work is, as they say at international meetings, essential and important. And this is my second proposal.

Gorbachev: And so, in the first part there is a proposal to include, to instruct the presidium to keep track of and to regulate the speeches so that the representation of the republics, regions, and public organizations would be ensured in the debates as a minumum. As far as the second group of questions is concerned, let's instruct the presidium to organize a study of these questions and on this account submit a proposal for subsequent examination. They are of a very important nature.

Bojars: Now, as for the laws, Comrades Mikhail Sergeyevich remarked very correctly that there are laws and laws. But as far as the so-called functional laws are concerned, I still have a motion: to vote on all laws, that is, to pass all laws at the congress or to approve them at the congress. In the intervals between regular sessions of the congress—however we decide, once or twice a year—a law adopted by the Supreme Soviet will be in force, but if the congress does not approve a law, it is not valid. That is the motion.

Gorbachev: Well, I believe, that is along the lines of what I said, and all of these issues should be resolved at the stage of the basic standing orders where we will delimit the basic hierarchies, rights, and correlations and decide there, to what extent and which particular laws will be resolved finally in the Supreme Soviet, which ones at the congress, or which ones require being brought to the attention of the congress or approved by it. That is, we will dot our i's. For these are major legal issues of fundamental importance.

Bojars: And a small amendment which we, after all, agreed upon yesterday. I believe we unequivocally resolved that. Have a look at the amendment to the standing orders, item 19, the very last paragraph at the bottom of the page. We have agreed that people's deputies will have the right to take part not only in the work of the chambers, but also in the work of commissions and committees, with the right of consultative vote. I motion to place it on record; and as important for the status of people's deputy.

Gorbachev: All right; let us place that on record. Even more so, because in the preliminary study we proceeded from the fact.... Just a moment! No, we are dealing with commissions here.

Bojars: We agreed on the consultative vote yesterday.

Gorbachev: The point is that the commissions will include approximately 50 percent Supreme Soviet members and 50 percent people's deputies with a consultative vote. With a decisive vote on the commissions, and with a consultative vote on the Supreme Soviet organs.

STENOGRAPHIC RECORD

First Session
25 May 1989

Boyars: And the last thing, comrades, we are all very concerned with moving forward somehow all the time, without getting stuck in the very complex issues and discussions which we will not be able to resolve, if we are to deal with such a great mass of them. That is why I doubt very much that it is worth voting by a roll call here. If we had the electronic machinery, which is used at some international conferences, then we could proceed quickly. But if we vote by roll call on this mass of issues, a single issue would take a day. I doubt very much that it is worth it. That is why this decision whereby the congress....

Gorbachev, interrupting: Generally speaking, for the benefit of the deputies, I would like to say that such instructions have been given and a draft is being drawn, because each deputy's working position should be properly prepared. That draft is being studied. And it will be decided. Comrades, shall we finish the discussion? Yes.

Unidentified deputy: (Inaudible).

Gorbachev: Comrades, the issue is a major one. We discussed it thoroughly yesterday at the conference of representatives, very thoroughly. The 446 people who are among us here can confirm that. Today's discussion confirms the fact that it is indeed a major issue. And I believe that we should act on the basis of the Constitution, according to which the congress elects the Supreme Soviet. The Supreme Soviet is elected, and not formed in the way it was formed when there were congresses of soviets. Then, the lower echelons of the Soviets delegated their deputies higher, and the process of shaping the congress of Soviets proceeded in that way.

In this particular case, proposals are sent from the localities, from the delegations, but decisions are made by vote at the congress itself. I believe there are issues here which we should consider, on how to combine them. And the issue, so to speak, of combining that right of the congress to determine, to pass the final decision on the composition of the Supreme Soviet, taking into account the opinion of the republics—that issue needs at further stages to be—so to speak—refined. I believe we have discussed it; your remark was heard by all that these nuances, I think, will be refined. The only thing is, I would not like us to suspect each other of doing something; that's the only thing. And I hope we can rid ourselves from suspicion.

Sebentsov: Deputy Sebentsov, 19th Territorial Constituency. Comrades. I have a proposal regarding the 20th article of the provisional standing orders. It concerns the procedure for conducting our congress. Under Article 20 the congress session is open; representatives of state and other organizations are invited to it, as well as other individuals. I would like to suggest the following addition to that article. The invited parties do not have the right to interfere with the work of the congress by showing their opinion through shouting, applause, and other such means. (Applause).

Gorbachev: I think it is necessary to express this wish on behalf of the congress, to all those invited today and in the future. All deputies here are sitting in the stalls. And there is nobody here apart from them.

Sebentsov: Yes, but we have already heard yells from the balcony. And another question. I would like to make use of my right of legislative initiative and propose a draft law on the status of the people's deputy of the USSR so that this draft be reproduced and presented to all deputies present at the congress.

Gorbachev: Comrades! Now we will allow half a minute each for speeches.

Korochka: I propose that microphones be placed between rows; otherwise it is awkward to work. That is the first thing. And the second thing, the second proposal. At the very beginning I handed in a note to the chairman of the Central Electoral Commission. But for some reason there has not been any answer, although it contains questions which concern many deputies. That is all.

Gorbachev: All right. Please Ales Adamovich. In a minute, in a minute. You will all go through, comrades.

Adamovich: Deputy Adamovich. We have been in session here for 2 hours, and for 2 hours millions of people have been watching us. So there you are, our people are thinking: Good, but we want to support the congress, and express our opinion on the issues raised at the congress. So let us think. People will go out now to express their opinions somehow, and what will they encounter? Surely they cannot encounter that law on demonstrations and meetings that has been passed? Don't we need somehow, for the time of the congress and for the time of elections, to suspend the effect of this law, so that the people can participate actively in our work? (Applause).

Gorbachev: Please.

Unidentified speaker: Amendment to Article 20. There has already been talk about this article here, but not very importantly. The last part was noted. It says at the start of the formulation of this point that representatives of state organizations are invited to the session. Why "are invited"? We are building a law-governed state. The term "are invited" is not at all a legal formula. And it essentially legalizes the judgement of the organizers of one congress or another. The formula by which representatives of state organizations, work collectives, of the press, television, mass media have the right to be present must be envisaged. Otherwise we shall not fulfill the directives of the 19th party conference on the development of glasnost and the resolutions on glasnost.

Gorbachev: Let us first define our position on this. I think that there is no doubt that we will return to the theme raised by Comrade Adamovich.

STENOGRAPHIC RECORD

First Session

25 May 1989

As for the proposal to adopt a decision now and suspend the Decree on Demonstrations and Rallies, I do not think we can go down that road at all. The next step would be to suspend something else. Then we will say: Let us suspend the Constitution—and so passions will flare up. I believe the procedure we have today—with all its failings, which no doubt deputies will mention—allows rallies to be held both for and against, but linked with the congress, so to speak. And this does not present an obstacle. And now the issue has been raised of the need to abolish everything and stop it. I would not tackle this matter in such a dramatic way. But then we come to these matters, I believe we will discuss them. Do you insist on voting on the issue? I believe what there is gives the opportunity for discussion. And, incidentally, in the runup to the congress you were at rallies in two or three places, and everything was fine. You were listened to. And so I don't know what you're talking about. Very well. There's a written question here: Is there a direct broadcast of the session being shown? Yes, there is. Yes, there is. Everything is being seen. The whole country and the whole world can see. Is there a guarantee that the broadcasting of the session will not be broken off? Yes, there is a guarantee. There is a guarantee.

Yes, go ahead. Thirty seconds.

Saunin: Saunin, Anatoliy Nikolayevich, from Makeyevak Territorial Constituency No 443.

The first thing I would like to say is that I get the impression that some delegates—pardon me, deputies—here are racing to catch a train that is just about to leave. And those proposals depart from the agenda and from those problems that we are discussing.

The second thing, regarding the standing orders: We want to build a state based on the rule of law, and so presumably we want to live in accordance with laws and decisions. Any haste in adopting standing orders and other documents could mean that we will again have to return to them, to their imperfectness and their unfinished state, just as we did before. And, therefore, I believe that the democratic process is a difficult one. We have to gather our patience, and thoughtfully and attentively listen to all points of view—both for and against—and then make the decision.

On the standing orders, article one of the provisional standing orders states that a congress is to be held once a year. Mikhail Sergeyevich seemed to say that we should plan for two, but we don't actually hear it. And so, twice a year should be written in the standing orders.

Then again, I don't like Article 19, the final lines, where we—people's deputies, the plenipotentiary and equal representatives of the people—are divided into those deputies with the right to a deciding vote, and those with a right to a consultative vote. I believe this is tied up with what Mikhail Sergeyevich was talking about—it is a change in the status of the USSR Supreme Soviet, turning it from an organ of state power into an organ of the Congress of People's Deputies. And I propost that we remove this article.

Gorbachev: All right. I am coming back again to what we talked about. I think that until we have introduced amendments to the constitution—and it says once a year—we cannot enter this into the standing orders, as they must not be at variance with the Constitution. But we all arrived—and I see that the congress is arriving at this, too—yesterday, at the meeting of representatives; we all agreed that this subject—the subject of a congress of the Supreme Soviet, its time limits, the frequency and regularity of congresses—must be studied by us; we must introduce the corresponding amendments into the constitution and enter them in new standing orders. Let us do this that way, comrades. Meanwhile, let us solve the issue of the provisional standing orders so that we can act. So, everything will be taken into account. I am sure that you have proposals which touch upon precisely such problems which are clear to us to a great extent, on the whole. Just 30 seconds—each speaker will be given ½ a minute.

Lubenchenko: Well, comrades, we are all calling on one another to have high political standards.

Gorbachev: Introduce yourself.

Lubenchenko: Lubenchenko, Territorial Constituency No 40. Unfortunately we are not really demonstrating this, demonstrating this on our live transmission. It seems to me that if we are talking about the standing orders, then this is such an ultracomplex document, which we have to work out very thoroughly and over a period of many months. We cannot resolve it now. But, apart from this, we also want to include in these standing orders a whole series of substantive matters and specific legislation, and each one of us wants to express, in general, a sea of all kinds of thoughts, a sea, and this sea will simply swamp us. We are now examining one issue, the issue of the temporary standing orders. The congress possesses such supreme juridical force that, on the whole, temporary standing orders are no obstacle. And during examination of whatever questions, we can instantly and immediately introduce changes to it if they bother us. However, if we now devote time to including all these matters into the standing orders, then we will achieve nothing. Therefore, it seems to me that we now need to raise the question, perhaps, of an editorial commission which could immediately deal with matters and with summing up this mass of all these remarks that are coming in, so that we do not all have to come out to the rostrum and speak about this.

Gorbachev: That's it, your time is up.

Lubenchenko: And one last thing, if you will allow me. The last comment was made to us here on point 11, that after the elections the chairman of the Central Electoral Commission is the first to conduct the session of the

STENOGRAPHIC RECORD

First Session

25 May 1989

congress, and then the chairman of the USSR Supreme Soviet. But in order for us not to violate the constitution, it seems to me that we should confirm by a vote of the congress the right to conduct the congress, which was entrusted to Mikhail Sergeyevich Gorbachev by the presidium, and thus the question of violations of the Constitution will be procedurally removed.

Gorbachev: As though I decided this matter and legalized it. Yes. Why, would you like to vote? All right then, so as to reinforce straightaway what has begun, and so that no one gets the idea that I am a usurper. Please go ahead. (Laughter). Please put down your hands. Against? Good. We've reached unanimity, comrades. (Laughter and applause). But what about abstentions? One moment. Abstentions? Two, three, four. Four. Five abstentions. There are five abstentions. Good. We've decided. Then allow me to push off from the idea expressed by comrade.... Do you also wish to speak about the standing orders? On the standing orders? No? Then just wait a minute. Allow me to conclude this discussion on the standing orders with the following—using as a basis the proposals made by the last people's deputy, and to put the question in the following way: To endorse the standing orders, the provisional standing orders, including the addenda about which we have already adopted decisions in every specific case here, and, naturally, to instruct the presidium to submit proposals to the commission so that it can already start working on summing up all the proposals for the standing orders, and so that this work can already get under way, and to edit these standing orders, taking account of the remarks. Those in favor of adopting the provisional standing orders with the addenda to have adopted please raise your mandates. Please lower them. Who is against, comrades? I do not see anyone. Do the vote counters see anyone? No. Any abstentions? There are abstentions; please count them.

Have you counted, comrades? Who has abstained?

Vote counter: Mikhail Sergeyevich, 17 persons have abstained.

Gorbachev: Fine, that means we have adopted the standing orders with 17 abstentions. Now, comrades, in accordance with the constitution, we have to form the Credentials Commission of the congress in order to check the authorization of the elected deputies. You have these proposals in your hands; they have been submitted by delegations and by a meeting of representatives of delegations. This has been agreed in general, but, nevertheless, some questions of other proposals may arise at the congress. What comments are there on the personnel? Andrey Dmitriyevich, if you please.

Sakharov: I consider that the office of chairman of the Credentials Commission is an extremely important office, and it should be discussed personally, and not as a section of a general list. My proposal is that a professional jurist, in line with the particular nature of this work, should be in this office.

Gorbachev: So, the question of chairman—Comrade Gidaspov, Boris Veniaminovich, general director of a scientific production association, chairman of the board of the Tekhnokhim interbranch state association in the city of Leningrad. I would like to say that this nomination arose directly at the conference of representatives. This was a unanimous view. I also think that Andrey Dmitriyevich spoke in favor of this. But he probably gave it some thought. Something has arisen, and maybe it would be sensible to discuss his proposal since we are talking about the person of chairman. Incidentally, there are jurists here. Well, I don't think this is an occasion where you necessarily have to have a jurist. Comrade Stankevich, if you please. We shall continue our debate.

Stankevich: Deputy Stankevich, Cheremushkinskiy Constituency Number 26, Moscow. I would like to submit the following proposal: to give the commission itself the opportunity to elect the chairman and to vote only on the composition of the commission. Let the commission decide on its own who will be the chairman, who will be deputy chairmen, who will be a secretary. Thank you.

Gorbachev: If it makes no difference to us. This topic was examined at a conference of representatives and this has been proposed, but everybody thought that this is the prerogative of the congress and not only of the commission itself. Thus, comrades from Leningrad, what can you say about Comrade Gidaspov; and Comrade Gidaspov, where is he sitting? And you (he turns to another deputy) you obviously want to say something?

Revnivtsev: Deputy Revnivtsev, Leningrad. I think that in order to elect the chairman, the basic characteristics have to be decency and honesty. The Leningrad delegation, having examined the question, believes that Comrade Gidaspov has these qualities. And there are jurists there. And the proper juridicial composition quorum for the commission will be ensured, I think. (Applause).

Gorbachev: Good. Does anybody doubt this? Comrade Gidaspov, where is he, come here! Tell us a little about yourself.

Gidaspov: Comrades! I am indeed not a jurist. I have had a technical education and I have attended two or three sessions, and I understand that such an education is now against me. I was graduated from a polytechnic and then taught for a long time at high schools and went on to become deputy head of a department, and, at present, I am a corresponding member of the Academy of Sciences, the director of a large institute, and chairman of an inter-branch association set-up in Leningrad for the first time.

Indistinct voices: We can't hear you.

Second Session

25 May 1989

Gidaspov: My attitude, Aleksandrovich, let me note, is correct and normal. That is, we consider that we have got as much out of the elections as we put into them. (Applause).

Gorbachev: Good, sit down. Are there are more questions? (Laughter). Introduce yourself, Comrade Aydak.

Aydak: Thank you.

Gorbachev: Is there time? Comrade Aydak, please, one minute, okay? Deputy Aydak.

Aydak: The 689th National Territorial Constituency of Chuvashiya, Aydak. It is, of course, very incidental, but what can one do? Two days ago, dear comrades, on the initiative of the peasant commission of the Committee for the Salvation of the Volga and a group of chairmen of collective farms, a conference of chairmen of collective farms and directors of state farms was held. We are very grateful to Mikhail Sergeyevich Gorbachev, Nikolay Ivanovich Ryzhkov, and Yegor Kuzmich Ligachev that they found more than 2 hours of their time for the meeting and the examination of all the vital problems of the countryside with us. Yesterday, the chairman of collective farms and directors of state farms met again, and thanks to our country's leadership's good advice—that is, to turn to the congress with our problems, and without appeal—and yesterday a group of chairmen of collective farms, some 70 people, decided that this appeal must be examined not only with chairmen and directors of state farms but all deputies—agriculturists.

Gorbachev: Comrade Aydak, are you talking about the credentials commission?

Aydak: No. (Laughter). I mean—I am asking all those connected with agricultural production to stay here in this hall immediately after the break to discuss this appeal. (Laughter). In this hall! All stay here!

Gorbachev: Enough.

Aydak: Thank you.

Gorbachev: If there are no other comments, no other views on the credentials commission, then I can put its composition to a vote. Who is in favor of the proposed composition of the credentials commission? Please raise your mandates; please lower them. Who is against? Two. Who abstained? One, two, three; three abstained. The composition of the credentials commission has been solved with two against and three abstentions.

Now it is necessary to give the floor straight away to the chairman of the credentials commission to report.

Gidaspov: I am asking members of the credentials commission, when the work of this session is over, to go to the Grandvitaya Palace where we shall hold a sesion. This means, if anybody needs help, I shall wait on the fourth floor on the right from here. Thank you.

Gorbachev: Comrades, awaiting this, it would appear that they need some 3-4 hours. So, I am asking your agreement to continue working here and to meet here at 1600. It is 1210 now, right? A break till 1600.

SECOND SESSION

V.I. Vorotnikov, chairman of the Russian Soviet Federated Socialist Republic [RSFSR] Supreme Soviet Presidium, is presiding.

V.I. Vorotnikov: Comrade Deputies, let us continue our work. I give the floor to Deputy Gidaspov, chairman of the Credentials Commission, to deliver the report of the Credentials Commission.

B.V. Gidaspov: Comrade deputies! The elections of USSR people's deputies which have taken place complete one of the most important stages of the reform of the USSR's political system.

For the first time in many decades truly democratic elections have been held in our country. Millions of people throughout the country have taken the most committed part in the nomination of candidates and the election debate.

The past election campaign affected the complex underlying processes of our life and helped to reveal public opinion on a broad range of questions of domestic and foreign policy. The voters and public organizations gave the people's deputies thousands of mandates and proposals. The elections merged organically into the process of restructuring and became a nationwide referendum in its support.

Comrades! The Congress Credentials Commission elected with 47 members, guided by article 110 of the USSR Constitution, has verified the powers of the USSR

Second Session

25 May 1989

people's deputies elected in March, April, and May 1989 and submits the result of this work for your examination.

In accordance with the USSR Constitution and the election law, elections of USSR people's deputies were held in 750 territorial and 750 national-territorial okrugs and for the first time directly from all-union public organizations, which were given 750 deputies' seats.

According to the report from the Central Electoral Commission delivered by its chairman, Comrade V.P. Orlov, the electoral okrugs and public organizations created the necessary conditions for holding elections in accordance with the USSR Constitution and the Law on Elections.

As is well known, the election law expanded the opportunities for the labor collectives and public organizations to nominate candidate deputies. This right was granted for the first time to voters at their place of residence.

Okrug election meetings were held in 836 electoral okrugs to discuss the candidates who had been nominated and their election programs and to take decisions on submitting candidates for registration.

The election measures as a rule took place in an atmosphere of openness and glasnost. On election day the candidate deputies' agents, representatives of the labor collectives and public organizations, and workers of the mass media were present at the electoral wards and sessions of the electoral commissions while the votes were counted and the results of the elections established.

In all 9,505 people were nominated as candidate people's deputies for 2,250 seats. Here 282 candidate deputies were nominated by meetings of voters at their place of residence. Of the tens of thousands of candidacies proposed by the grass-roots collectives, 923 candidate deputies were nominated from the public organizations. The foundation was thus laid for the practise of elections providing a real choice.

Some 5,074 people were registered as candidate USSR people's deputies, 2,195 of them for territorial okrugs, 1,967 for national-territorial okrugs, and 912 from public organizations. In 399 okrugs just one candidate deputy ran.

The Congress Credentials Commission, having checked the electoral commissions' protocols submitted to it on the registration of candidate deputies and their statements agreeing to run for the relevant okrugs and public organizations, deems the registration of all candidates to be legal.

Some 172.8 million voters, or 89.8 percent of the number of those on the lists, took part in the elections of USSR people's deputies 26 March this year. For the first time in our electoral practice runoffs and repeat elections were held within the framework of a single election campaign in 76 and 198 okrugs respectively. Elections to replace a deceased deputy were held in territorial electoral okrug No 619 in the Kazakh Soviet Socialist Republic [SSR].

Some 16,200 voters, or 84.2 percent of the total number on the lists, took part in elections from all-union public organizations. Repeat elections were held in five public organizations.

On the basis of the electoral commissions' protocols the Central Electoral Commission registered 2,249 elected candidates.

In summing up the results of the elections it must be noted that the Central Electoral Commission, okrug and ward electoral commissions, and public organizations' electoral commissions as a whole ensured that the elections were conducted in accordance with the demands of the Constitution and the Law on Elections.

At the same time the Credentials Commission considers it essential to report to the Congress that during the term of its activity the Central Electoral Commission received over 8,000 letters and telegrams and about 1,000 citizens visited reception with questions about the organization of the elections.

Citizens expressed dissatisfaction with the work of the electoral commission, the organization of the nomination of candidates, and the holding of okrug electoral meetings. There were also critical comments leveled against the Central Electoral Commission. There were indications of the inconsistent application in a number of places of some of the provisions of the electoral law. Complaints came in of the unjustified refusal to register candidate deputies.

The Central Electoral Commission also examine complaints of unequal conditions for candidates' participation in electoral events, in particular complaints about how some of them had broader opportunities for using the mass media.

Instances were reported of the incorrect attitude of candidates and their agents toward each other, of attempts to put pressure on the voters. Attention was drawn to the bias in covering the preparation for elections in individual electoral okrugs.

The credentials commission has examined information from the Central Electoral Commission on the results of the checking of statements and complaints sent to it on questions of the legitimacy of the election of individual candidates. A number of them cast doubts on the results of the election of USSR people's deputies.

All these appeals were examined by the Central Electoral Commission. The Central Electoral Commission established no violations of the law casting doubt on the results of the elections. The Credentials Commission considers it possible to agree with this conclusion.

FIRST CONGRESS OF PEOPLE'S DEPUTIES OF THE USSR

Second Session

25 May 1989

At the same time the members of the Credentials Commission noted that existing shortcomings in preparing and holding the elections were caused to a certain degree by the imperfection of individual norms of the Law on Elections.

There was also an examination of the letters and statements which had arrived at the Credentials Commission. They express individual citizens' disagreement with the results of the elections. Negative assessments are expressed of the elected deputies' political, professional, and moral qualities. Some letters suggest not recognizing the powers of deputies whose speeches contained, in the citizens' opinion, positions which do not accord with the USSR Constitution and Soviet laws and for other reasons.

Having checked these appeals, the commission failed to establish violations of legislation on the elections while other questions are not within its competence. The commission considers it possible to recognize the powers of all USSR people's deputies and these letters and statements are to be passed on to the newly elected USSR Supreme Soviet.

As a result the Credentials Commission is submitting a proposal that the powers of all 2,249 USSR people's deputies be recognized. At the elections they received, as required, the necessary number of votes from voters and participants in congresses, conferences, and plenums of all-union organs and public organizations which took part in the voting.

Thus, if the commission's proposal is accepted, as of today there is just one electoral okrug in which no deputy has been elected.

Comrades!

In the union republics, taking into account the results of the elections from public organizations, the following groups of USSR people's deputies have formed. In the Russian Soviet Federated Socialist Republic—1,099 people's deputies, in the Ukrainian SSR—262, in the Belorussian SSR—94, in the Uzbek SSR—108, in the Kazakh SSR—99, in the Georgian SSR—91, in the Azerbaijan SSR—72, in the Lithuanian SSR—58, in the Moldavian SSR—55, in the Latvian SSR—52, in the Kirghiz SSR—53, in the Tajik SSR—57, in the Armenian SSR—53, in the Turkmen SSR—48, and in the Estonian SSR—48 people's deputies. All the autonomous republics, autonomous oblasts, and autonomous okrugs are represented at the Congress. Representatives of 65 nationalities have been elected USSR people's deputies.

Of all the people's deputies 88.1 percent have been elected for the first time to the country's supreme representative organ of state power. Some 1,957 people's deputies, or 87 percent, are CPSU members and candidate members.

Our Congress reflects sufficiently fully the socioprofessional structure of Soviet society.

Of the Congress membership 557 people's deputies, or 24.8 percent, are workers in industry, construction, transport, and communications, and 425 people's deputies, or 18.9 percent, are agricultural workers. Among us we have 532, or 23.7 percent, who are workers and ordinary kolkhoz members, those who by their labor and specific deeds are implementing the program for our society's renewal.

A considerable number of deputies' seats—616, or 27.4 percent—were given by voters to representatives of the scientific and creative intelligentsia. Some 1,806 deputies, or 80.3 percent, are aged between 30 and 60 while 187 deputies are under 30, 9 of them being 21 years old. Some 133 people's deputies are members of the All-Union Leninist Communist Youth League. Some 352 women have been elected people's deputies.

The general educational level of the deputies elected to the supreme organ of state power is characterized by the following figures. Some 1,702 people's deputies, or 75.7 percent, have higher and incomplete higher education, one in five has an academic degree or academic title, and they include 140 academicians and corresponding members of the academies of sciences of the USSR and the union republics. Some 528 deputies, or 23.5 percent, have general secondary and specialized secondary education.

Among the people's deputies 152, or 6.8 percent, are leaders of industrial associations and enterprises and 192, or 8.5 percent, are leaders of kolkhozes, sovkhozes, and agro-industrial associations.

The deputies include 316 scientific, higher school, and educational workers, 96 national health workers, 146 cultural and arts workers, and 58 mass media workers.

The people's deputies include 237 party workers. They are secretaries of the CPSU Central Committee and union republic communist party central committees, secretaries of kray, oblast, okrug, city, and rayon party committees, and of primary party organizations. Every other deputy has experience of work in soviets of people's deputies.

The USSR Armed Forces are represented by 80 people's deputies. For the first time 7 religious figures have been elected people's deputies.

As can be seen from the figures cited above, the composition of the USSR people's deputies ensures the opportunity for the effective work of the new supreme organs of state power.

Comrades!

The Congress Credentials Commission expresses the conviction that the USSR people's deputies will honorably justify this lofty title and will always be up to the demands made on the deputy by the people.

Chairman: Comrade Deputies! Are there any questions for the speaker?

From the floor: I submitted a deputy's question to the Congress Credentials Commission the day before yesterday concerning violations of the Election Law in the Latvian Soviet Socialist Republic [SSR].

STENOGRAPHIC RECORD

First Congress of People's Deputies of the USSR

Second Session

25 May 1989

B.V. Gidaspov: The Central Electoral Commission has examined all the questions it has received, and it has received a large number of them. We have examined the results of the Central Electoral Commission's work, and we agree with these results. The Central Electoral Commission and the Credentials Commission have received 60 letters and appeals from working people, including one bearing many signatures addressed to 43 people's deputies. The electoral commission has not had a chance to examine them all and deems it advisable to submit them to the USSR Supreme Soviet. We entered in the minutes that we considered it advisable in a number of cases to create special groups of deputies to examine the aforementioned questions. As the letters do not contain any information about election violations, and because the enclosed documents illustrate that they were not violated in any way, these questions fall outside the competence of the Credentials Commission.

Chairman: We will perhaps, comrades, examine similar questions after we have decided the question of the Credentials Commission's specific functions. Here are the questions that have arisen—here is a note from Comrade Shengeliya, who asks to be given the floor to make a statement—we will examine others and determine our stand and make the appropriate decisions on them. If these questions require the participation of and examination by the Congress and the creation of any congress commissions to examine and resolve these questions or submit these questions for consideration, that is exactly what we will do.

But now let us examine specific questions having to do with the competence of the Credentials Commission.

Chairman: Comrades, Deputy Gidaspov has read out the Congress draft resolution on recognizing the credentials of USSR people's deputies.

Are there any comments and proposals on the draft that Comrade Gidaspov has read out?

Voices from the floor: No.

Chairman: No. Permit me then to put this question to the vote. I ask you to prepare your credentials cards. Those in favor of adopting the resolution submitted by the Credentials Commission raise your credentials cards. Lower them. Those against? Count the votes, comrades.

From the floor: There are 21 people against.

Chairman: Twenty-one. What about abstentions, comrades? I do not see any. I ask the tellers to count. Can the seventh sector report, please? So, there are 21 against, and 11 deputies abstain. The Congress resolution on recognizing the credentials of USSR people's deputies has been passed. (Applause).

Allow me, comrades, to cordially congratulate all of us on the ratification of the credentials of USSR's people's deputies. (Applause).

Does anyone want to make a statement? Comrade Nikolay Antonovich Kutsenko, a deputy from Poltava Oblast, has the floor.

STENOGRAPHIC RECORD

N.A. Kutsenko, legal adviser at Kremenchugskiy House Construction Combine No 3 (Poltavskiy National-Territorial Okrug No 54, Ukrainian SSR): I received a cable yesterday from Mirgorod, Poltava Oblast, to read out at the congress. "Tell the congress the following. Myakota, secretary of the Poltava Oblast party committee [obkom], was not entitled to be a candidate in the elections because he is a deputy to two soviets. That is a gross violation of Article 96 of the new constitutional Law on Elections. The congress does not have the right to approve him as a Supreme Soviet deputy, and the instructions that have been concealed from the people and distributed to okrug commissions are anticonstitutional, born of the bureaucratic apparatus in the interest of bureaucrats, in the same way that hundreds of antipopular instructions arise. I ask you to inform Mirgorod of the receipt of the cable." Signed Pensioner Kulikov, history teacher.

This is the question. Comrade Myakota is indeed a deputy to the oblast soviet of people's deputies and the Ukrainian SSR Supreme Soviet, and he is now a USSR people's deputy. In this connection the congress needs to make a decision in order to give voters a precise and clear answer.

Chairman: One minute, have you finished?

N.A. Kutsenko: Yes.

Chairman: Thank you. Comrade A.I. Lukyanov now has the floor to provide clarification.

A.I. Lukyanov: Comrades! Under Article 96 of the USSR Constitution "...citizens of the USSR cannot be a people's deputy to more than two soviets of people's deputies at the same time." The question was correct. But, his credentials had not as yet been approved. Comrade Myakota's credentials have now been approved at a third soviet of people's deputies, and he should set aside his credentials for one of the other soviets. That's the whole story, so that his credentials can be recognized. (Applause).

Chairman: Is that clear, Comrades? Comrade Shengeliya, a deputy from the USSR Union of Cinematographers, has the floor.

E.N. Shengeliya, director and producer at the "Gruzhinfilm" film studio (USSR Union of Cinematographers): Comrade deputies! I have already been introduced, and I won't introduce myself again.

I will discuss questions linked with the incident that occurred in Tbilisi. In this connection I want to make the following statement: The Georgian SSR Supreme Soviet commission has been in effect since the moment the incident occurred. This commission's materials have been drawn up. I ask for you to allow these materials to be circulated; they include an appeal to you, the conclusions of the medical commission and the chemical and toxicological commission, and the examination of the conditions whereby the curfew was declared. These documents will in many respects help you understand the situation and the ensuing consequences. That is why I ask your permission to circulate this document. That is the first point.

Second Session

25 May 1989

Second. We are putting three questions to deputies: to Yazov, the defense minister; to Kochetov, USSR first deputy defense minister; and to Bakatin, USSR minister of internal affairs. We ask them to give us an official answer to our questions when this matter is discussed.

Third. We have made a video which I believe you should look at to see for yourselves what happened. In view of the fact—and this is what we have, unfortunately, noted—that the central press and the "Vremya" television program misinformed the country's public in many respects, I think that it would be right if you saw this in its entirety and if the organizers of the congress helped us show you this video. It lasts 1 hour. Public misinformation is a bad thing, and it is a bad thing when the country's president does not obtain totally correct information, which is why his statements contain inaccuracies. I would ask Mikhail Sergeyevich and the Congress Presidium to also watch this video. This is very important.

Last, as a result of this military punitive action—I can find no other word for it—21 people have died to date, more than 4,000 people have requested medical treatment, more than 3,000 people have been poisoned, and hundreds were maimed and injured. General Rodionov was in charge of this action. I do not think our congress wants such a deputy within our ranks. That is what I wanted to say. I will say this to the congress Presidium. Thank you. (Applause).

Chairman: Esteemed comrades! Comrade Shengeliya has indeed raised a very important question which is troubling and affecting not only the people of Georgia but also the entire Soviet people. That is why a proposal in this connection has been put forward—on behalf of the Congress—to instruct the Presidium to form a special commission—to be ratified by a decision of the congress—to examine and study during the congress' period of work the entire range of questions raised here and which may arise again in connection with the Tbilisi events, and to task this commission with conducting a more thorough and detailed investigation of all aspects of this tragedy, and with reporting back to the congress. Are there any objections to this proposal?

M.S. Gorbachev. If the commission has the time it can report to the congress, if not it can report to the Supreme Soviet. I believe the documents should be distributed so that our comrades can examine them.

Chairman: Because several questions have been raised, they should be studied thoroughly and in detail and reported to the congress.

Do you agree with this proposal? Is there any point in voting, or shall we vote? We will. I ask those in favor of this proposal to raise their mandate cards or credentials cards. Please lower them. Who is against? No one. Any abstentions? None.

M.S. Gorbachev: Comrades, this is such a painful issue that it has affected all of us. Let the Presidium work, then the commission's personnel will submit their findings for ratification by the congress. A commission must be set up to which we will entrust everything. This must all be brought to a conclusion.

Chairman: We think that we have decided this matter. Yes? We have.

G.S. Igityan, general director of the Republic Aesthetic Education Center and director of the Museum of Armenian Modern Art, Yerevan city (from the USSR Union of Artists): I am wholly in agreement with what Deputy Shengeliya said. As a deputy I have visited Tbilisi and familiarized myself with all the issues. This was indeed a monstrous tragedy with violence and brutality. I do not want to go any further in describing this, but I do want to draw the attention of the congress, for the first time from this rostrum, to a serious incident that took place in Sumgait. When the Armenian people appeared bearing slogans proclaiming "Lenin, Party, Gorbachev," following Mikhail Sergeyevich Gorbachev's Appeal to the Peoples of Azerbaijan and Armenia, a monstrous and most brutal reaction followed in response in Sumgait, one that cost many lives. This had never happened before on our country's territory apart from during the years of enemy invasions. There were numerous instances of violence, killing, the burning of crosses, and pogroms in Sumgait. I believe today's congress should examine this entire question very earnestly, for this happened a 30-minute journey from Baku, the capital of the union republic, over several days. A political assessment has not yet been made of Sumgait, but I believe it is the start of a barbarity which—if we do not stop and curb it—will go a very long way.

We have all lived through the great patriotic war, and we were all brothers in that war. We cannot permit this manifest vandalism to not be given a political assessment during the time of restructuring when the party is appealing to our peoples. We believe that the tragedy in Tbilisi, like the tragedy in Sumgait, should be condemned to forever prevent such manifestations from again occurring in our Soviet land. I believe that all the union republics will support us. Moreover, I must say that we did not feel that the progressive part of Azerbaijan—its intelligentsia—condemned this act of violence. If Armenians had done this, I would have stood up and asked for forgiveness before the entire Soviet people and the whole world. But for some reason this was not what we heard. We only heard Vezirov, secretary of the Azerbaijan Communist Party Central Committee, speak of namus during the discussion of this problem. Namus, comrades, is conscience. Can one speak of conscience after the manifestation of such brutal violence? I ask all of you, all the fraternal republics of the Soviet Union, and I also ask honest Azerbaijanis to support my position. Thank you.

STENOGRAPHIC RECORD

FIRST CONGRESS OF PEOPLE'S DEPUTIES OF THE USSR

Second Session

25 May 1989

V.I. Vorotnikov: Let us end with a question which is under discussion in accordance with our agenda. We may have many correct and objective statements arise here which we will examine in accordance with the agenda in the course of our business. I am referring to a whole series of questions that we will discuss during our session—this was discussed yesterday at a meeting of group representatives. It is necessary to discuss a whole series of questions which may be resolved at the congress—or the Supreme Soviet, the government, or other organizations may be given instructions concerning these questions. That is why I am asking that we proceed in accordance with the standing orders and the agenda that have been adopted. Do you have any comments on the Credentials Commission minutes?

Lieutenant Colonel V.I. Alksnis, senior engineer and inspector at troop unit 13703, Baltic Military District (Yuglskiy National-Territorial Electoral Okrug, Latvian SSR): The chairman of the Credentials Commission has misled the congress. The day before yesterday I submitted a deputy's question to the Congress of USSR People's Deputies Credentials Commission. Allow me to read it aloud. "During the elections of USSR people's deputies in national-territorial okrugs within the Latvian SSR, there were flagrant violations of Article 17 of the Law on the Election of USSR People's Deputies. In violation of the terms of Article 17, which states that national-territorial okrugs are to be formed with an equal number of voters throughout the territory of the corresponding union republic, okrugs were created in the Latvian SSR with differing numbers of voters: These range from 28,800 people in Okrug No 308 to 127,300 people in Okrug No 290. That is, one okrug was four times the size of the other. The average designated number of voters in each of the republic's national-territorial electoral okrugs, given the overall figure, should be approximately 62,000 people. Small national-territorial electoral okrugs were formed mainly in the republic's rural regions, which ensured that most deputy mandates came from these regions, despite the fact that the majority of the population (71 percent) live in the cities. This substantially restricted the opportunities of the working class and also the republic's Russian-speaking population to be elected as USSR people's deputies. It is typical that many leading lights of the Latvian People's Front [LPF] stood for deputy in these small okrugs and were elected, which definitely attests to a possible deliberate violation of Article 17 of the Law on Elections of USSR People's Deputies in favor of LPF representatives. Ten of the eleven members of the LPF Council stood for deputy in these small okrugs."

This year on 14 April I proposed forming a commission of deputies at a meeting of deputies at the Latvian Communist Party Central Committee, in order to investigate this violation of the law. However, this proposal did not meet with support. I submitted a deputy's question on 4 May to the USSR general prosecutor on this question, but I have not received an answer. I also sent a similar letter on 11 May to the USSR Supreme Soviet Presidium reception office. The USSR Supreme Soviet Presidium sent this letter to the body about which I was complaining—the Latvian SSR Supreme Soviet Presidium—in the spirit of the old stagnation times, and I obtained a purely formal reply from them.

I am submitting the following proposal to the congress. Yes, we have recognized deputies' credentials, but I propose creating a commission of deputies to investigate and clarify what happened in this situation.

I see this as a real "Watergate"—in terms of the situation that took shape and in terms of how I was silenced. Even here in Moscow people have also tried to shut me up. The Central Electoral Commission tried to persuade me not to raise this question. However, I believe that a rule-of-law state cannot be built on a foundation of lawlessness and lies. If we do not restore order to this question now, we will be threatened with trouble in the future. That is what I wanted to tell you. (Applause).

V.I. Vorotnikov: Comrades, maybe we should decide on this and instruct the Central Electoral Commission to examine this question again.

M.S. Gorbachev: And the Credentials Commission.

V.I. Vorotnikov: The Credentials Commission should also examine this question again if it proves necessary. Are there any objections?

M.S. Gorbachev: No, my understanding is that our comrades no longer trust one commission—the electoral commission—in the sense that it has already tackled this.

From the floor: Correct!

M.S. Gorbachev: But we do have the Credentials Commission. They could examine everything in this wad of papers and report back. If we are not satisfied, we could create a special group of deputies.

V.I. Vorotnikov: Comrades, are there any objections to this proposal? No.

From the floor: Yes!

V.I. Vorotnikov: There are? What is your objection?

From the floor: We did not hear.

M.S. Gorbachev: No, the Credentials Commission was not involved before; we are adding it.

V.I. Vorotnikov: Comrades, the Credentials Commission together with the Central Electoral Commission will report back to the congress when it reaches some decision.

Maybe we should give the chairman of the Credentials Commission another chance to speak.

STENOGRAPHIC RECORD

Second Session

25 May 1989

B.V. Gidaspov: I will give you information again. The Credentials Commission has not examined this material. We have only examined the election commission's minutes on the appeals and petitions it has received. If this kind of specific question exists, I did not see it, but I believe that the Credentials Commission along with the Central Electoral Commission can carry out the investigation.

V.I. Vorotnikov: I believe the proposal deserves attention. The Credentials Commissions at the congress will be working the whole time, and that is why some more proposals and comments may arise. It will examine these questions, and it will then certainly be correct to ensure that the Credentials Commission examines this question—together, naturally, with the Central Electoral Commission—and submits the results to the congress for examination. Shall we have a vote on this proposal?

V.I. Vorotnikov: Well, let us be totally democratic. The question has been raised of first voting for the first proposal—concerning the creation of a group of deputies to examine these questions. The second proposal is that this question should be examined by the Credentials Commission along with the Central Electoral Commission. Two proposals. Those in favor of the first proposal raise your credential cards.

I would like to repeat once again: The first proposal, which was submitted by the deputy, concerns creating a group of deputies to examine the violations that, in his view, have occurred in the formation of okrugs.

The second proposal is that this question be entrusted on behalf of the congress to the Credentials Commission to be examined together with the okrug electoral commission. Those are the two proposals.

From the floor: With the Central Electoral Commission?

V.I. Vorotnikov: With the Central Electoral Commission. An amendment is needed: that the Credentials Commission alone examines this. If the need arises, it will invite representatives of the Central Electoral Commission to hear the considerations on which this commission based its decision.

The first question is the one submitted by the deputy on creating a group of deputies or a commission of deputies. Those in favor of the first proposal raise your mandate cards!

Comrade tellers, count the votes!

(The votes are counted).

V.I. Vorotnikov: Allow me to announce the results of the vote: 246 deputies have voted in favor of the first proposal. Who is in favor of adopting the second proposal, that is, entrusting the examination of this question to the Credentials Commission? Would you raise your credentials cards, please. A clear majority. I do not think there is any need to count the votes. Consequently, the Credentials Commission is instructed to examine this question.

Before I give the floor to the next speaker, I would like to say the following: Would the comrades who wish to speak confine their contributions to the work of the Credentials Commission. If anyone has any other proposals, we ought to seek advice on whether, apart from the agreed agenda, there should be an additional discussion of the problem. Let us give the floor to the next speaker and seek advice.

M.R. Mamedov, first secretary of Baku Azerbaijan Communist Party city committee [gorkom] (Bakinskiy-Oktyabrskiy National-Territorial Electoral Okrug, Azerbaijan SSR): Esteemed people's deputies! It was the irresponsible speech by People's Deputy Igityan which brought me to this rostrum. The point is that all those expressions, which I would not like to repeat or address to anyone sitting in the hall or to any representative of the Soviet peoples, are an insult. This is hurtful to my people, to proletarian Baku, and to the people who themselves made a sufficiently critical assessment of what happened in Sumgait. Everything that was done subsequently in the Azerbaijan party organization and in the Azerbaijan SSR bears out that we never sought confrontation. We never sought pretexts for hostility between the two peoples. Everything goes to demonstrate precisely that we are trying to find a compromise solution. In condemning what happened in Sumgait I would like to ask: Does Igityan not know that of 165,000 Azerbaijanis, not one remains in Armenia today? Does Igityan not know how many Azerbaijanis were killed in Armenia?

V.I. Vorotnikov: Esteemed Comrade Deputy! I must ask you to stop. I believe, comrades, that this is not the time or the place for such mutual recriminations. We have gathered here as a united family, representatives of 65 peoples and nationalities of the Soviet Union, to rally and unite, to elaborate the program for our further progress toward restructuring. Therefore, there clearly is no need for mutual reproaches and accusations from one or the other or a third side. Otherwise, who knows where we will end up. It is necessary, all the same, to exercise restraint, to have a sense of responsibility in the face of any statements. I am asking you, therefore, to conclude your contribution. (Applause).

Comrade Zaslavskiy has the floor for a statement on the Credentials Commission. After Comrade Zaslavskiy's contribution, I will put to the vote the question of whether the debate on the Credentials Commission should continue.

I.I. Zaslavskiy, scientific associate at the Moscow A.N. Kosygin Textile Institute (Oktyabrskiy Territorial Electoral Okrug, Moscow city):

FIRST CONGRESS OF PEOPLE'S DEPUTIES OF THE USSR

Second Session

25 May 1989

This is what I would like to say: We have organized elections on a competitive basis. It is important to ensure that in the future they take place without any deviations from the law. A great many complaints have accumulated here in respect to all kind of violations of the law connected with the work of electoral commissions, and I have raised this question in some of the most serious cases, specifically as concerns Proletarskiy Okrug in Moscow city and Smolenskiy National-Territorial Okrug No 27. There were a great number of complaints from citizens claiming that several ballot papers per person were issued, as well as other complaints. In general, this has to be investigated. We decided at the time to pass this matter on to the Supreme Soviet, but because the Credentials Commission will be working here, maybe two or three of the most serious cases should be examined during the course of the congress with a view to making the relevant decision and ascertaining whether the complaints are justified. If they are justified, specific decisions must then be adopted to ensure that when there are elections to republic or local soviets everyone knows that there is nothing to be gained from deviations from the law, or from pressuring voters. And if something that is not quite in order occurs again, it will again have to be investigated. (Applause).

V.I. Vorotnikov: There is a proposal to put Comrade Zaslavskiy's report on record.

I.I. Zaslavskiy: I will attach the corresponding proposal to the protocol of the commission.

V.I. Vorotnikov: Let us vote. Who is in favor of here concluding the discussion on the question concerning the work of the Credentials Commission and continuing on to the next item on the agenda? Would you please vote? Who is in favor? You may lower your credential cards. Who is against? Please count the votes. Three people are opposed. The proposal is adopted.

Comrade Deputies! The next item on the agenda is the election of the chairman of the USSR Supreme Soviet.

Deputy Aytmatov has the floor.

Ch. Aytmatov, writer, chairman of the Kirghiz SSR Writers Union Board, and chief editor of the journal INOSTRANNAYA LITERATURA (from the CPSU).

Ch. Aytmatov. By virtue of my age and length of service as a deputy I belong to the older generation of the parliamentarians in this hall. For that reason, it will be permissible for me to share a few observations with you.

Quite recently, at sittings of the Supreme Soviet, there reigned a totally different atmosphere from the democratically stormy one that preceded the days leading up to the congress, and especially today at our first meeting and at the present moment. Previously, on the Olympus of the Supreme Soviet, it was quiet, convenient, and not in the least burdensome for the leadership, apart from the fact that, about twice a year, it was necessary, as though in a theater, to sit through the hours of ritual at meetings that their rank required of them. The reason for this was that, from the first days of its existence, the country's Supreme Soviet found itself under the irresistible pressure of authoritarian regimes that reduced the role of the supreme legislative body to that of a formal appendage to the party apparatus, an impeccably obedient institution that advertised the virtual absence of democracy. Everyone knew this, but no one ever ventured to draw attention to the damage that was being done to society by such a state of affairs. It seems to have been a very simple matter to decorate citizens with orders and medals. That too lay beyond the powers of the Supreme Soviet.

As the rest--parliamentary debates, ironing out the contradictions in searches for constructive solutions to the problems of the life of the people, everything that should constitute the chief essence of a democratic image of government--there's no point in talking about it, as the saying goes, since the dialectic of parliamentary struggle was totally excluded from the practice and consciousness of a featureless system of popular representation.

But then a man came and he disturbed the slumbering realm of stagnation. He did not come from somewhere outside, but appeared from within that very system, possibly, as a chance for survival through renewal, since from the point of view of its historical status, the period of stagnation, just like a snowball, was picking up more and more of the destructive force of inertia and conservatism, a force which is dangerous both to society itself from within and to the surrounding external world. This man, by the will of destiny, assumed the leadership just in time. He need not have bothered. He could have calmly presided at ceremonial occasions and read from platforms the texts written by his secretariat, and everything would have proceeded along the well-worn path.

However, he ventured to take what seemed to be impossible--a revolution of minds while retaining a socialist organization of society. And that, as we can all testify, is an immensely difficult task, requiring enormous responsibility. He ventured to take on this task not through vanity, but because he had perceived the worsening sickness in society of totalitarian dogmatism and economic crisis that was emerging like an increasingly bare iceberg from the depths of the stagnant past. He ventured on to the path of social renewal and stands on it, in the stiff wind of restructuring.

STENOGRAPHIC RECORD

Second Session

25 May 1989

Everyone realizes, of course, that we are talking about Mikhail Sergeyevich Gorbachev. It is, however, a paradox of today that now, when we have admitted the spirit of freedom and democracy, when restructuring and glasnost have opened up new visions of the world for us as individuals, when the spiritual ascent of society has revealed more and more forcefully the former lack of freedom and our economic and technological backwardness, and when we have started to speak openly of this, rather than engaging in distracting speculation, pointing toward space, where we are supposed to be enjoying endless successes--which is virtually the main meaning of life for us--when the intellectual regeneration of society brings to the fore everyday more new and active forces in the most varied social strata, when we have become unrecognizable, striking people to the outside world, when we are venerated everywhere as the bearers and originators of new global thinking, our critical views and demands have grown so much in these conditions that, like the spray of a stormy sea, these waves have moved against the very creator of this historic movement.

Today our criticism touches Gorbachev, too. Well, all right, this is quite understandable and fully in the spirit of real genuine democracy. This is how it should be. Society is regaining its health and is undergoing the democracy treatment. I am not saying this for the purpose of show some sympathy for, or even more, defending Gorbachev in some way. No, he has absolutely no need of this. I am saying this in order to outline the range of changes in our psychology, which was crushed and distorted in the past by the long-term dictatorships of personal power and their products--political repressions, the hounding of dissenters, the forcible expulsion of whole peoples from their lands, since time immemorial, and the cult of military intimidation and great-power complacency.

All this has passed and is receding like a terrible dream. We are now breathing the intoxicating air of the new democracy, and we have the bold, seething energy of reformers. To his honor, Gorbachev, indeed, in this uncustomary situation of social unfetteredness, produced by restructuring and glasnost, when a young deputy may shout out from the balcony his ardent disagreement with him as an equal to an equal, displays striking flexibility and wisdom, since having himself assumed total responsibility for the fate of the work that has been started he, more than anyone else, realizes the full value of the rebirth of the people, and himself serves as the generator and conduit of this very complex process. Herein resides his strength and novelty as a politician of a fundamentally new reforming quality.

We are now facing a new reality in the fatherland, which has been unprecedentedly complicated as a result of the colossal effect on the attitudes of people of the ideology and practice of restructuring. Now we are facing a world reality that, despite threats and expansions, is given to ever-strengthened hopes for the survival of mankind, which have again been produced by a breakthrough in world consciousness--the new historical thinking, with priority of common human ideals over all other ideas and goals. At the junction and the crossroads of these global tendencies of the 20th century we stand dependent on the historical experience that we have acquired together with Gorbachev in the difficult age of restructuring.

In our own interests and in the interest of humanization and further democratization, it is necessary to use this experience to the maximum, improving and enriching it in the course of social development. As long as this person is full of energy, as long as his thinking embraces in its totality the global problems of peace and the daily needs of the people's existence as a single vital reality, and as long as he is capable of illumination and large-scale political generalization, it seems to me that we should be alongside him, and he with us, in order to tackle, seek, and find ways to fundamentally improve the material and spiritual life of the multinational Soviet people. [applause]

I would not like my words to be misinterpreted. I am at heart and, I think, in social practice, an opponent of all kinds of authoritarian regimes and political idols. But in this case, taking account of the fact that we do not live along on the globe, at this first Congress of People's Deputies, with full awareness of the matter and being confident that the political credo of our leader is crystal clear, and that it is the concept of the new thinking, I consider it necessary and appropriate to pay tribute to Mikhail Sergeyevich Gorbachev in order that he may with even greater energy service Soviet society, given that fact that we note also serious miscalculations in the course of restructuring, concerning primarily the calamitous economic situation in the country, and also the exacerbated problems relating to interethnic relations.

But this is a specific point for discussion. As we have come to this, then all of us together, and quite probably our social system itself, are to blame for this. Moreover,

I do not rule out the idea that, in the process of our joint work, differences may appear on certain matters of public life, too. But at the same time, I have no doubt whatsoever that these differences can be overcome during a search for a general solutions to the problems concerned. I ask that all I have said be considered a

preamble to an official proposal. Comrades, I have been charged, on behalf of the meeting of the representatives of the deputies' groups, and also taking into account the unanimous opinion of the party meeting of the people's deputies, to introduce the proposal that Comrade Mikhail Sergeyevich Gorbachev be elected chairman of the USSR Supreme Soviet. [loud applause]

FIRST CONGRESS OF PEOPLE'S DEPUTIES OF THE USSR

Second Session

25 May 1989

Thank you for your attention. In concluding, I would like to reserve an opportunity to speak later, along with others, on the matters which are of interest to me as a deputy.

V.I. Vorotnikov: Comrades! Who has something to say about Comrade Gorbachev's candidacy? Is there anyone who wishes to speak on this question? I repeat: so far only on Gorbachev's candidacy; we will discuss other candidacies as they come up.

V.A. Logunov, deputy editor of MOSKOVSKAYA PRAVDA (Kuntsevskiy Territorial Electoral Okrug, Moscow city): I support Mikhail Sergeyevich Gorbachev's candidacy. However, in the course of the election campaign I frequently received advice from voters. It consisted of this: In order to protect our people and the USSR Supreme Soviet chairman from the partocracy and from the influence of the party apparatus, and in order to avoid his being hamstrung by party discipline, I propose that Mikhail Sergeyevich Gorbachev resign from the post of general secretary and Politburo member.

V.I. Vorotnikov: Who else wants to have a say? Go ahead, please.

V.L. Bedulya, chairman of the "Sovetskaya Belorussiya" collective farm [kolkhoz], Belorussian SSR. (From the Soviet Peace Fund allied with eight Soviet committees advocating peace, solidarity, and international cooperation): Esteemed comrades! Last year, as part of a 10-member delegation from the Belorussian SSR, I was able to visit the United States for 3 weeks. I also had the opportunity to experience the impact of our restructuring abroad. What does the restoration of mutual understanding and trust between peoples mean?

There were dozens of meetings and discussions, but we felt at ease. We felt at ease because there had been the meetings in Geneva, Reykjavik, Washington, and Moscow. We felt at ease because the withdrawal of Soviet forces from Afghanistan was in full swing. We felt at ease because the practical reduction of nuclear weapons had already begun. We felt at ease because the celebrations connected with the millennium of Christianity in Russia had taken place and because our people and the people of the whole planet had been able to take a look at our history and culture from a different angle.

Therefore, when considering the proposal, the following should also be borne in mind. It is impossible to overestimate the success of our restructuring in foreign policy questions and in questions of the struggle for peace and detente. I would also like to add the example of the latest visit to China, the normalization of relations with China, and many, many other steps whose significance cannot be overestimated.

Comrades! This is the first time that we, as freely elected deputies, have gathered. The first and decisive step toward changing the political system and creating the mechanism of people's power has been taken. A congress has been convened whose will, common sense, and responsibility will determine our future. A resolute revolutionary breakthrough in our history has been achieved peacefully. It is impossible here to not pay tribute to Mikhail Sergeyevich Gorbachev, a politician who consistently advocates mutual understanding instead of bitterness, unity instead of strife, and democracy instead of extremism. The guarantee of the success of restructuring lies in the efficient and conscientious work of all of us without exception.

In conclusion, I would like to once again express support for the candidacy of Mikhail Sergeyevich Gorbachev and express confidence that the great and responsible tasks facing our society will be successfully resolved under his leadership.

V.I. Vorotnikov: I would like to ask you, comrades, because these are statements rather than proper speeches, to keep them brief.

V.A. Yavorivskiy, writer, secretary of the Ukranian Writers Union Board, Kiev city (Minskiy Territorial Electoral Okrug, Kiev city): Dear comrades! The ideal situation, a situation which would firmly establish our progress toward democracy, would, of course, be a situation in which we would today be choosing from among several candidacies. I will not praise Gorbachev; there is no time for that. It is necessary to push the country away from the brink of the precipice. We will vote for Gorbachev (I mean the Ukrainian delegation), but despite this, we will not forget Yeltsin.

And let me nonetheless tell the people that this is the last time we are doing this; the last time. And let me say one more thing: If what is happening today at the tip of the pyramid finds its way down to the base, and if, what is more, it is distorted, if caricatured versions of it appear—which is quite possible—the people will turn away from us; they will again revert to silence, vodka, and anecdotes. Anecdotes about both, you, Mikhail Sergeyevich, and about us, the deputies.

Let us think about how we can ensure that at the next elections the president of our country is elected in a nationwide election, and meanwhile, we will today give our votes to Gorbachev.

B.V. Kryzhkov, assistant production manager of the Dzerzhinsk "Kaprolaktam" production association (Dzerzhinskiy Territorial Electoral Okrug, Gorkiy Oblast). I would like to know Comrade Gorbachev's stand on the following question: In the past, it was the practice in our country to combine the posts of general secretary and Supreme Soviet chairman in order to provide access to the international arena for the general secretary. This by no means served to promote people's power but rather led to cults and the subsequent posthumous criticism of leaders.

FIRST CONGRESS OF PEOPLE'S DEPUTIES OF THE USSR

Second Session

25 May 1989

The country is tired of that. At the same time, if we really want our congress to be of supreme importance, if we want to ensure that the administration of the country is carried out by working Communists rather than the party apparatus, I then believe that the post of general secretary should after all be relinquished upon election as chairman of the Supreme Soviet.

There have already been precedents when it was suggested to our group of the Gorkiy delegation that if Communists do not agree with the decisions of the 19th Party Conference then they may have to part with their party cards. I treasure my party card, but I also treasure the voters' trust. Therefore I would like to obtain an unequivocal answer here.

Comrade Adamovich, who spoke the day before yesterday, said that this sort of situation may lead to the emergence of a new Stalin. But the point is that this is possible even in the current situation. I am totally baffled by the situation which has arisen in connection with Gdlyan and Ivanov. It also smacks of the political trials of the thirties. This question has not yet been raised here, but I believe that it too demands an unequivocal assessment, and I would like Comrade Gorbachev to answer this question.

And I would like to submit another proposal. I would like to hear Comrade Yeltsin's viewpoint on these questions. Thank you. (Applause).

V.I. Vorotnikov: Let us give the floor to a representative of the clergy. Go ahead, please.

Mukhammad-Yusuf Mukhammad-Sodik, chairman of the Spiritual Administration of Moslems of Central Asia and Kazakhstan, Tashkent City (Tashkentsko-Kirovskiy Territorial Electoral Okrug, Tashkent Oblast, Uzbek SSR): Dear Comrades, People's Deputies! I am People's Deputy Mufti Mukhammad, chairman of the Spiritual Administration of Moslems of Central Asia and Kazakhstan. On behalf of the many million Moslems who live in our country I call on you to vote for the candidacy of Mikhail Sergeyevich Gorbachev, a man who has done so much for our people and will, we hope, do a lot more in the times to come. (Applause).

V.P. Khmel, leader of a composite team of painters and decorators at the Angarskiy Construction Trust No. 5 construction and installation administration, Irkutsk Oblast, Angarsk City (From the CPSU): I thought that we, on the gallery, we Siberians, would never be given the floor. Moscow and Leningrad, Moscow and Leningrad keep coming forward, and we have been silent for the 3d day in succession.

Comrades! We are all living in difficult times today. Life is difficult for everyone. It is difficult for us Siberians, too. Probably more difficult for us Siberians than anyone. However, we are halfway through with our plans, with what we have begun. Today we have arrived at the midpoint watershed. And so, comrades, let us make a sensible decision. Let us pause and think so that we do not have to start restructuring from the beginning again, so that we do not have to restructure ourselves again. Let us take it through to the end, let us bring it to fruition.

Therefore on behalf of the Siberians I propose that we vote for Mikhail Sergeyevich Gorbachev and for combining the posts of general secretary and Supreme Soviet Presidium chairman. (Applause).

V.I. Vorotnikov: Please bear in mind that proposals to end the speeches are coming in. So be very brief, please.

V.A. Biryukov, fitter at the A.K. Serov Metallurgical Plant (Serovskiy Territorial Electoral Okrug, Sverdlovsk Oblast): Comrade deputies of the Land of the Soviets! I speak on behalf of the Sverdlovsk Oblast group of deputies and their voters. Esteemed Mikhail Sergeyevich! Their mandate to the Congress of People's Deputies is to propose Boris Nikolayevich Yeltsin for the office of chairman of the USSR Supreme Soviet.

Boris Nikolayevich was a Supreme Soviet deputy from the okrug I represent. (Applause). Let me have my say. (Animation in the hall.)

V.I. Vorotnikov: Comrades, may I have your attention! Esteemed comrade deputy, the point is that we are now discussing Gorbachev's candidacy. We will then move on to discuss other candidates. (Voice from the hall: To the nomination.) To nominate other candidates. You will be given an opportunity to nominate Ivanov, Petrov, Sidorov, Yeltsin and so on. No objections, please. But for the time being we are talking about Gorbachev. About the candidate nominated by Comrade Aytmatov.

M.Y. Lauristin, chief of department at Tartu State University (Tartuskiy Territorial Electoral Okrug, Estonian SSR): I am a deputy from No 750 Territorial Electoral Okrug, Estonia. I would like to say that, from the very beginning, the people's democratic movements in defense of restructuring in the Baltic republics perceived Mikhail Sergeyevich Gorbachev as a democratic leader and now we perceive no alternative to his candidacy. But we, and I personally, do have several questions which I would like answered before I can vote with peace of mind. I hope that Mikhail Sergeyevich will find an opportunity to answer them. And the first question is: What political and juridical guarantees for the self-determination of nations and for the protection of republics' sovereignty would you, as chairman of the Supreme Soviet, deem necessary to see in the Soviet Union's Constitution?

The second question: Do you personally perceive the use of the army for punitive operations against the civilian

Second Session
25 May 1989

population compatible with the development of democracy and a rule-of-law state in our country? We all share to a great extent the tragedy in Tbilisi. And I think that mothers would not like, on the one hand, to see their sons become killers while serving in the ranks of the army and, on the other hand, to know that their daughters are threatened by that terrible death which befell the young girls in Tbilisi. And in this context, what is your attitude toward the demand to abolish the "emergency"-role troops in a democratic state?

The third question: Which of the members of the CPSU Central Committee Politburo were notified in advance of the intention to use troops in Tbilisi? It would probably be very important for us all to know when you personally learned about this. And how do you, as chairman of the Supreme Soviet, intend to guarantee that such a tragedy will not recur anywhere else and at any other time? (Applause).

V.A. Voblikov, chief of Baltiysk CPSU Gorkom Organizational Department (Chernyakhovskiy Territorial Electoral Okrug, Kaliningrad Oblast): I highly respect and value Mikhail Sergeyevich Gorbachev as a courageous man. I also respect our Chingiz Aytmatov. Nonetheless, I do believe that it is not worth showering anyone with too many words and too much praise. Even though Aytmatov did make the reservation that we must not create idols. Yes, we must not create idols. We need a man, a courageous and effective man, we realize and understand this. I support Mikhail Sergeyevich Gorbachev's candidacy. Many of us who were elected from territorial okrugs and fought a most complex struggle in complex conditions have hastened to help Mikhail Sergeyevich. So that he would not be alone in bearing responsibility for the country's destiny. So that all together we could share this destiny. So that the people could share this destiny. We thus take part of the responsibility off Mikhail Sergeyevich's shoulders. And he will act more boldly.

This is why I believe that the combination of offices is very important at the present moment. The present situation is such that it does not allow us to relieve Mikhail Sergeyevich Gorbachev of his duties as general secretary. Because we need restructuring within the party more than ever before. It is with Mikhail Sergeyevich Gorbachev that I associate the hope that relations within the party apparatus will change for the better and we will thereby move forward.

In supporting Mikhail Sergeyevich Gorbachev's candidacy I advocate political stability. We know that he is constantly and steadily advocating a better future for our country. I cannot say what sort of stability we would have and what path we would take if we opted for a different candidacy. I might even be pleased to see some more radical measures, but I still believe that stage-by-stage progress in politics is more reliable than unpredictability. (Applause).

Yu.B. Solovyev, chairman of the USSR Designers' Union Board (from the USSR Designers' Union): The previous deputy partly said what I wanted to say. I believe that it would be a gross mistake to separate the offices of chairman of the Supreme Soviet and general secretary of the CPSU Central Committee today. It would be a gross mistake if we were to do this.

But I do have grievances against Mikhail Sergeyevich. I must say that recently the brilliant successes in the international arena of which our country can be proud have not been accompanied by corresponding successes inside the country. And I note that recently Mikhail Sergeyevich's speeches have lacked the clarity and boldness that used to characterize them.

I think, Mikhail Sergeyevich, that now that you have so many like-minded supporters (this is a very awkward situation for me actually: I'm addressing Mikhail Sergeyevich but I should be addressing the auditorium), the overwhelming majority of whom support your candidacy, we expect you to take radical and vigorous action which we will all share and in which we will most actively participate. (Applause).

A.D. Sakharov: First and foremost, I want to say that I personally support wholeheartedly the restructuring policy begun at the initiative of Comrade Mikhail Sergeyevich Gorbachev. At the same time, I want to return to what I said this morning. My support for Gorbachev personally in today's election is conditional. I made it dependent on the way in which the debate is held on the main political questions and on Mikhail Sergeyevich's reaction to what he has to hear during this debate. (Applause) I think that this is a question of profound principle. We cannot allow elections to be held in a formal manner. In these conditions I do not consider it possible to participate in this election.

V.I. Vorotnikov: Comrades, many notes are coming in about concluding the discussion of this issue. Let us give the floor to the final comrade and finish on that point.

From the floor: Comrade deputies, we all know that Mikhail Sergeyevich Gorbachev only recently filled the post of president. I remember that when Mikhail Sergeyevich Gorbachev became general secretary and did not hold the post of president, unlike his predecessors, many correspondents asked: "Why do you not hold that post?" He replied: So much work has piled up in our party that there's more than enough to cope with. But then, when he started work and delved into the process, it transpired that the country was indeed in a very serious situation. The general secretary made the only correct decision: to also hold this post so as to really place the running of the state in one pair of hands. I'm a worker representing Alma-Ata city; I call on everyone with a cool head but a passionate heart to support Mikhail Sergeyevich Gorbachev's candidacy. And if we have achieved colossal successes in international relations, of course, Mikhail Sergeyevich Gorbachev will try to do everything to ensure that there is

STENOGRAPHIC RECORD

FIRST CONGRESS OF PEOPLE'S DEPUTIES OF THE USSR

Second Session

25 May 1989

equal success domestically. We passionately want this and hope for it. I want to call on you to support this candidate. (Applause).

V.I. Vorotnikov: Just a moment. Comrades, there are very many suggestions that we end the discussion about Comrade Gorbachev's candidacy. I am putting the question to a vote. (From the floor: It's a very important question.) Yes, it is. (From the floor: I ask to be heard.) But we must listen to the voice of the masses; can you sense the reaction in the auditorium? Let us listen not just to those who, so to speak, want to take the floor, but to the entire congress. That is why I am putting the question to a vote. Who is in favor of ending the discussion on Comrade Gorbachev's candidacy and including it on the ballot paper for the secret ballot for the election of chairman of the USSR Supreme Soviet? Have I formulated the question clearly? (From the floor: Yes.) Please raise your credentials cards. (Animation in the auditorium.) Or perhaps we should let one more comrade speak? (From the floor: No!)

V.I. Vorotnikov: Let us consult once again, comrades. Mikhail Sergeyevich is asking to speak.

M.S. Gorbachev: This may be somewhat awkward for me, but nonetheless I would perhaps feel even worse if I did not state my own opinion on this matter. I think that the question is, of course, decisive. What can I say? We have been discussing all aspects of this matter for 3 days now. And if comrades have something to say to the candidate or, even more, if there are still questions and I have to react to them at least in some way, then I would ask the congress to at least give comrades 1 minute each. (Applause). Bearing in mind that this is a fundamental question involving great passions—even though the matter is now clear to the majority—I would ask that we be patient and respectful. Let comrades express their attitude or ask questions; then we can proceed. Other candidates are also a possibility—and there would again be a discussion. And I would be forced to speak once again, for people would ask me direct questions.

A.A. Shchelkanov, loader at the Leningrad "Berezka" trading firm's No 20 Store (Kirovskiy Territorial Electoral Okrug, RSFSR):

Esteemed comrade deputies, Mikhail Sergeyevich. Today I am representing here roughly 400,000 inhabitants of Leningrad, of whom around 270,000 are voters. I am today responsible for the decisions we will all have to make. It is from this standpoint that I am speaking here. Today we are not used to putting questions to the person who will become our president tomorrow. We are not used to working in the way that we will start working tomorrow. However, we all have to realize that now is the time for annoying questions, but it is not the time to be annoyed by them. That is why, Mikhail Sergeyevich, I am asking you questions which I want to hear answered before making my decision—questions which are today in people's minds and on their lips.

First question: There was a lot of talk in late 1987 and 1988 about the construction of a dacha in the Crimea. Today I would either like to hear you deny this or to hear from you about it. Perhaps it was a provocation or perhaps it was gossip, but the millions now watching on TV should be given a straight answer, and only you can give it.

My second question, Mikhail Sergeyevich, concerns your personal attitude to the possibility of standing down as general secretary. The 19th party conference resolution is currently just a party conference resolution, and it is not the opinion of our country's entire population. Moreover, I know from my contacts with voters that most people do not support this decision. I want to know your question [as published] about combining these two posts.

And my last question. There is a great deal of confusion when the public learns about the appearance of documents bearing your signature such as the 17 November 1988 CPSU Central Committee and USSR Council of Ministers resolution No 1328 on the procedure for material and consumer provision for persons released from the party and administrative apparatus. Documents such as the 15 March 1989 CPSU Central Committee and USSR Council of Ministers resolution on the suspension of certain social programs. Also, I would like to know why these resolutions and why the matters they cover are not first discussed with collectives, not to mention all of society or the entire population. And, I want to tell you that the presence of your signature on them raises doubts in people's hearts and minds.

Today we need the closest contact between our president—who must be a man of utter probity—and the mighty people's movement that is beginning and which emerged in the election process. I'll be able to make my decision after hearing an answer to these questions. (Applause).

V.I. Vorotnikov: Next, please.

D.E. Ivans, chairman of the Latvian People's Front (Madonskiy National-Territorial Electoral Okrug, Latvian SSR):

We must not forget that today we are not electing a boss [vozhd]; we are electing a leader, our colleague. If we are going to talk about boldness, I think that Gorbachev's boldness depends on our boldness. At the Forum of the Peoples of Latvia, we put forward the following idea: In order to help Gorbachev, we ourselves must be more like Gorbachev than he is himself.

STENOGRAPHIC RECORD

Second Session
25 May 1989

Our people are very agitated about their future destiny, and we read with great agitation the things that Mikhail Sergeyevich and other leaders say about the further development of equal sovereign states within our union, as well as what they say about the self-determination of nations and ethnic groups. And so I must ask Mikhail Sergeyevich the following perturbing question: How does he view the further defense of Soviet nations' rights to self-determination; how does he see the possibility of preserving small peoples who are already on humanity's list of endangered species and who were treated quite inhumanly in the past? At the same time, I must apologize before the people for the speech by Deputy Alksnis, because most of our delegation does not feel like he does.

From the floor: Comrade USSR people's deputies! There are those among you who were not desired as candidates by the apparatus and who during the election campaign felt the full force, power, craftiness, cruelty, and treachery of the party bureaucracy, which prevented us from conducting the election campaign. Therefore, it would be an unforgivable mistake on the part of us deputies to insist and push Mikhail Sergeyevich Gorbachev into standing down as general secretary of the CPSU. He is now participating in controlling this apparatus. I'm not totally sure that he is controlling it, but he is taking part in one way or another. When he gives this up, the powerful party bureaucracy—which has immense power, the only real power in the country—will quickly crush him and drive us all away from here. (Applause).

L.I. Sukhov, driver at the Kharkov motor transport enterprise No 16301 (Kharkovskiy-Leninskiy Territorial Electoral Okrug, Kharkov Oblast):

I would like to mention the telegram I sent Mikhail Sergeyevich at the 19th party conference. It contained, I think, the aspirations of my voters, and this telegram was the wave that has brought me here.

I wrote: "On listening to your correct, fiery speeches, even those that began tactlessly and cut speakers short, I compare you not to Lenin and Stalin but rather to the great Napoleon, who, fearing neither bullets nor death, led the people to victories. But, thanks to yes-men and his wife, he went from a republic to an empire. Put me to death, if you like, but I fear this path, and if this is so, the cause of the revolution is doomed to failure." Evidently, even you cannot avoid flattery and the influence of your wife. It has never yet happened in history that the rich and the poor sat at the same table. Some ate chicken, while others licked their fingers clean and simultaneously made the same old speeches. The majority of the people will not go for such restructuring. This telegram expresses the fact that a stratification is truly now beginning to take place. And so, Mikhail Sergeyevich, I will vote for you in all sincerity; but take these remarks into account, so that the people really believe that we will come to the idea of the communist movement, of bringing the badly-off closer to the better-off. This is the idea of the whole communist movement, and so I will vote for you if you implement these ideas. Thank you for your attention.

V.I. Voskoboynikov, Mi-8 helicopter flight mechanic (Novourengoyskiy Territorial Electoral Okrug No 324, Tyumen Oblast): I certainly have not come out here to discuss Gorbachev's candidacy. I wanted only to say that if proposals are put to the Presidium that the debate must be stopped, it is necessary to read out who they come from. We are all struggling against anonymous letters, but for some reason not a single name has been heard here with regard to who specifically made these proposals to close the debate. My personal belief is that any deputy must be afforded an opportunity to speak. Each of us is an elected representative of the people, and mouths must not be stilled up here. I believe that the practice of "slamming shut" is not a practice that can be approved by the people now sitting before their television sets. I am ashamed of the hall now. This is my personal feeling. As for Mikhail Sergeyevich's candidacy, I will vote for him, but I believe that it is necessary to separate the posts of general secretary and Supreme Soviet chairman. (Applause).

V.I. Vorotnikov: Quickly, please; make a request quickly.

From the floor: Deeply esteemed colleagues! A purely technical remark and a request to the chairman; to the present one and to all subsequent ones. One and the same formal, logical mistake has been made three times in the hall today. Fortunately, this took place without particular consequences. Our dear, esteemed colleagues in the chair, let us put just one question to the vote, for two questions must not be combined in one. We almost voted just now to include Mikhail Sergeyevich on the list and, at the same time, to close the debate. These are two questions, but only one is being voted on. But I am for Mikhail Sergeyevich Gorbachev. I am for You [initial "y" is capitalized to indicate that it is Gorbachev who is being addressed]. (Applause).

Ye.L. Golovlev, laboratory chief at the Institute of Biochemistry and Physiology of Microorganisms, Pushchino city (Serpukhovskiy Territorial Electoral Okrug No 41, Moscow Oblast): I believe that there is now no alternative in the country to Mikhail Sergeyevich as president, as chairman of the Supreme Soviet. I believe that the situation in the party is now very serious and grave. The penultimate April plenum showed that there is no considered, scientific concept in the party, no concept of restructuring, no concept of the party-state relationship, or no concept of the ruling party. Therefore, the duties of the general secretary are just as great as the president's. Because of this, I believe that the proposal to combine these two posts was a serious mistake by Mikhail Sergeyevich. I think it is wrong to reckon that combining the two posts will somehow make it possible to block the impact of the party apparatus on soviet organs.

STENOGRAPHIC RECORD

Second Session

25 May 1989

V.V. Goncharov, first secretary of Yenakiyevo All-Union Leninist Communist Youth League City Committee (Yenakiyevskiy Territorial Electoral Okrug No 437, Donetsk Oblast): Comrades! I ran a very long election marathon, one on the order of 180 meetings. Also, I am not expressing only my own viewpoint here. The people have very great faith in you, Mikhail Sergeyevich Gorbachev, but it has been shaken recently. It has been shaken, I believe, precisely because of the policy of the middle link—the bureaucratic apparatus, of which we have spoken here. And I believe that this is not a proposal or a wish today but rather a demand: Direct access to the people is needed. You, Mikhail Sergeyevich, need the same kind of access as we people's deputies have had to communicate with the people. After you have been elected, but not just afterwards. A president must communicate with the people. I believe that the mass media must make use of this. There must be monthly television addresses and television and radio contacts. This is the voters' demand because I, in particular, try to explain a very great deal that the people do not understand about your policies and about your positions. I, however, have been unable to do this. Therefore, it is necessary to explain all this to people, and then this faith will be strengthened and our faith in restructuring will also be strengthened.

R.A. Allayarov, chairman of the Kalinin Kolkhoz, Tashauzskiy Rayon, Tashauz Oblast (Tezebazarskiy National Territorial Electoral Okrug No 443, Turkmen SSR): Comrades! I was induced to come out here and have my say because certain groups of Moscow and Leningrad deputies and representatives of the fraternal Baltic republics have had very many opportunities to express their opinions. However, except for two Caucasian representatives, neither Central Asia, nor Siberia, nor the Far East have yet taken advantage of this high rostrum. This is the 4th day we have been working, but we have not yet decided anything, you might say. We have only approved the standing orders and the agenda. We have only gotten on to the second item. And this item, if we continue like this, will take us another day. So, comrades, I beg your attention.

It is Lenin's principle that we, the union republics and the national republics must also represent our quorum here. The opinion has even been expressed that the Moscow delegation is asking for 55 seats, not 30. Let they themselves choose 30 of these 55, but the national republics must be represented in just the same way. It seems to me that this will be right.

However, the candidacy for the post of Supreme Soviet chairman is being discussed here. Comrades, our delegation unanimously votes for Mikhail Sergeyevich Gorbachev.

V.I. Vorotnikov: Thank you.

R.A. Allayarov: I beg your pardon. I have something else to say. Our main achievement is democracy and glasnost. You have all begun freely expounding your opinions here. This must subsequently result in our having an abundance of them. Thank you, comrades, for your attention.

V.I. Vorotnikov: I propose giving women an opportunity to speak.

T.I. Kayumova, teacher at the Lunacharskiy No 33 School, Ishtykhanskiy Rayon (Bulungurskiy Territorial Electoral Okrug No 586, Samarkand Oblast): Esteemed comrade deputies. I am an Uzbek, a nonparty person, and a deputy for Territorial Okrug No 586. I do not understand one thing: You and I—our society's most progressive face—have gathered here today to discuss our current situation. As a nonparty person, I repeat once more, I respect my party and speak on behalf of the Uzbek deputies and my voters. We support Comrade Gorbachev's candidacy, and our voters wish him only health in this great and difficult work. That is all I have to say. (Applause).

N.P. Bekhtereva, academician and director of the USSR Academy of Medical Sciences Scientific Research Institute of Experimental Medicine, Leningrad city (from scientific societies and associations under the USSR Academy of Sciences): Esteemed comrades! I said in the party group that I am for Mikhail Sergeyevich. I will not repeat myself, but I want to say now that we should, in fact, have demanded that Mikhail Sergeyevich combine the two posts in view of today's situation. And he should have refused or agreed. The situation is serious. You all know perfectly well what elections we have been through. You know the situation in the country. You know the absolute need to combine these two posts. It seems to me that there cannot be another opinion.

Second. I would despise myself if I did not speak today, as a woman, about Raisa Maksimovna's tremendous role in our country's international successes, in our government's international successes.

Ye.V. Kogan, chief of the heat engineering laboratory at the "Estrybprom" Association, Tallinn city (Tallinnskiy-Kalininskiy National-Territorial Electoral Okrug No 450, Estonian SSR): Dear comrades! I represent National-Territorial Okrug No 450 in Tallinn city. There is doubtless no need to remind you of Mikhail Sergeyevich's services to the cause of democratization, for most of us owe our election to these very changes. However, I would like to draw your attention to the fact that the nationalities question intervenes, unfortunately, and powerfully so, in our restructuring processes. This question has become unprecedentedly acute. We can say that there have been a whole series of incidents that have really made all of us shudder. These processes are currently continuing, and they have not stopped. In this

STENOGRAPHIC RECORD

Second Session
25 May 1989

respect the Baltic region is also a region where everything is very involved, although, perhaps, in a less temperamental way and without such turbulent manifestations.

I would like to say to Mikhail Sergeyevich Gorbachev that in the sphere of interethnic relations, the utmost tact is necessary. I want to warn you that in the Baltic region your name is often used as a cover for extremely unpopular decisions among the Russian-speaking population. In particular, this is on laws like the law on language, and to some extent, on the concepts that still have to be discussed here.

Now, in view of the fact that I will not be able to speak often, I would like to take this opportunity to say another thing. I would like to hear Mikhail Sergeyevich's answer as to his attitude to these language problems, as well as on whether, in adopting these laws on languages that divide us up into petty princedoms—if we want to remain within a single mighty power (and I think the majority of us do want that)—we should think about a law on language, on the federal language, the all-union language. This may be very painstaking and prolonged work, but we must do it.

I would, of course, like to know Mikhail Sergeyevich Gorbachev's attitude to these questions. I want to say one last thing: It seems to me that historical experience does, after all, suggest that to combine the two highest posts in the party and state is an excessive burden for an individual. And when someone falls between two stools, you know, nothing good can come of it.

With that, I would like to conclude the discussion of Mikhail Sergeyevich's candidacy. I also want to simply say that progress along the path of democracy must, of course, be slow. And I would like to believe that perhaps our next elections will be different—with the congress nominating several candidates, who will engage in a contest, and the question will be decided by direct ballot throughout the Land of the Soviets. That, in my view, will be the final victory for democracy in our country. Thank you for your attention. (Applause).

Vorotnikov, V.I.: Perhaps we could limit ourselves....

S.N. Zvonov, director of the Ivanovo Passenger Motor Transport Enterprise No 2 (from the All-Union Leninist Komsomol): I would like to speak about the question of combining posts. I have thought about this for a long time, and, as is usual in tackling such questions, I started counting up the pros and cons.

Let us consider the "cons" of combining posts. First. I do not understand how it is physically possible to combine these functions. Today I am an enterprise director and at the same time a deputy, an ordinary deputy. And I have absolutely not enough time. And let us add it up: March—a plenum, April—a plenum, May— a plenum,

June—the congress continues, another session; and in the fall there will be the congress again, the trip to China, and so forth. You cannot grasp it all. I think it is simply a physical impossibility to very effectively perform your duties in both posts.

Second, I believe that combining the posts, that is, concentrating twofold power in one person's hands, in a single individual, is, in my view, contrary to the principles of the rule-of-law state and democracy.

Third, the possibility emerges here of political methods of leadership turning into administrative methods, which I also consider negative. The only weighty argument was that a serious situation has arisen in the party. Comrades! Is there really no one in the Politburo who could head this work?

From the auditorium: There is no one today.

Zvonov: In that case, comrades, the Communists should perhaps give some consideration to this. How can it be that there is no one in the party who could do the work in the party? This question must be tackled, but these matters are not for the deputies. After all, the people elected us to tackle affairs of state, not party, importance. I would like to say something else. I am interested to know, Mikhail Sergeyevich, how you combine the concepts of democracy with the April decree, in particular Article 11 (the note). And one last thing. I cannot understand it when they ask us to cut short the debate. Did we come here to run the 100-meter dash? When we were leaving for Moscow, we were told: Stay at the congress a month if you like, but resolve everything as is necessary in the end. And let us give everyone the opportunity to express their opinion and make decisions. That is all I have to say. (Applause).

L.A. Arutyunyan, faculty chief at Yerevan State University (from the women's councils united by the Soviet Women's Committee): Dear deputies! In our country's history we have the unsuccessful experiment in social reformism in the sixties. And if we want to achieve success along the path of restructuring, then we must analyze why that experiment failed. We pin our hopes on the new leader for taking the new social reform to its conclusion. In this instance, the Armenian delegation pins its hopes on the name of Mikhail Sergeyevich Gorbachev, for he has shown himself to be the man who can lead the cause of restructuring. However, we have a number of problems in this sphere.

The first problem is not to allow the field of restructuring to be narrowed. Restructuring is not a narrow rut in a well-marked road but rather a wide river that will lead our country into the mainstream of civilization. From this viewpoint we have no right to restrict our tasks today. In particular, I am talking about the problem of national relations. Restructuring has roused the people. We have no right to disappoint the peoples' hopes.

STENOGRAPHIC RECORD

Second Session

25 May 1989

Restructuring is the assertion of social justice and the deepening of social justice. Can we shrug aside the peoples' expectations for the assertion of social justice in the nationalities sphere? Therefore, we pin on the name of Mikhail Gorbachev the hope of pursuing restructuring in all areas of public life.

The next question that greatly interests me is that of the escalation of violence. Restructuring cannot be compatible with the escalation of violence. From this viewpoint we expect from the new leader a consistently peace-loving approach not only in external, but also in internal relations. The people and government should live by dialogue. Collaboration can only mean dialogue. This system is not based on monologue, but on dialogue. From this viewpoint we ask, we expect, and we instruct Mikhail Sergeyevich to continue the line of dialogue with the people and to take account of the people's opinion in his further activity.

The next question I would like to raise is that in a civilized state, the leader's wife also fulfills state functions. Let us not be a backward country, and let us not speak about things that ought not to be spoken of in this great auditorium. On the contrary, we should promote the opportunity for the civilized representation of our state and our society. Only in this way can we attain civilization.

One last thing. Mikhail Sergeyevich, the Armenian people pin on you their hopes for the resolution of the Nagorno-Karabakh Oblast problem. You cannot fail to resolve these problems, and you cannot make the people of Nagorno-Karabakh Oblast continue living in the condition they are living in. (Applause).

Yemelyanenkov, A.F., deputy chief editor of the weekly SOBESEDNIK, Moscow city (Primorskiy Territorial Electoral Okrug No 121): I am one of the deputies who were elected at the very last moment. And as a colleague of mine, a young deputy, said, we rushed straight here to the congress to help Mikhail Sergeyevich implement his ideas and plans, and not to listen to eulogies of him such as today's by esteemed Chingiz Aytmatov and Vladimir Bedulya. I do not think Mikhail Sergeyevich needs this today. What he needs is honest and truthful words, and the opinion of the many thousands of voters we met with on the eve of the election campaign. In this connection, I think that the question that is being raised very often from this platform on combining the post of party leader and head of state at the central and local levels, is the starting point from which we today have to jump off, and from which—as I understand it, and as many Communists understand it, including those in our okrug—we have to resolve the tasks of the future separation of party and state power in our country. Therefore, it is not only my wish as a deputy, but, I think, the desire of all the voters who are watching on television, to hear from Mikhail Sergeyevich's own lips the justifications and motives that explain the need to today combine these two functions. I think the following point should be added to the questions put to the general secretary, to which we would like to hear the answer today: How did the aforementioned 9 April decree come about, with Mikhail Sergeyevich Gorbachev's signature on it; how did it appear on the eve of the congress; and why did it take effect with no discussion? Once again I stress that it was mainly Communists who asked me this. They realize, in any case, that it is offensive to Mikhail Sergeyevich himself to formulate the matter thus: that if he vacates the post of general secretary, there is not one person in the party, in the entire party, in the Central Committee, who could head these processes of improving the party. I do not think this is the case; I believe such a person can be found, and that there is plenty of work in both posts. We remember (our memory is long) Mikhail Sergeyevich's own speech in April 1985, when the need for one person to concentrate on party work and another on work in the soviets was validated. It seems to me that we will get there in the end all the same. If we do not do it at this congress, then we will be forced to at some time in the future. Thank you for your attention. (Applause).

N.V. Fedorov, senior teacher at Chuvash State University (Moskovskiy Electoral Okrug No 681): I too must ask Mikhail Sergeyevich Gorbachev one very fundamental question. Under the current Constitution, the USSR Supreme Soviet Presidium does not have the power to change the content of laws by means of its decrees. Nonetheless, we recently have seen such decrees appearing particularly intensively (some of them have been mentioned) in the sphere of criminal legislation, labor legislation, and on a number of other issues. I and my voters would like to know: Will the USSR Supreme Soviet Presidium continue, without having the constitutional power to do so, to change the content of laws, restrict the sphere of operation of constitutional rights, and continue the practice that has hitherto existed? The fact that this practice is for you and me, and for the majority of us very familiar does not make it any less pernicious, unconstitutional, or unlawful. Thank you. (Applause).

K.D. Lubenchenko, lecturer at the law faculty at Moscow M.V. Lomonosov State University (Ramenskiy Territorial Electoral Okrug No 40): Comrades! I want to give you my personal opinion; I am not speaking on behalf of Moscow Oblast. I have no right personally to demand that Mikhail Sergeyevich tell me something now, for which I will give him my vote. Therefore, I would like to draw attention first of all to questions of principle that have been raised here, questions that I cannot disregard from a professional point of view.

We are making a great many complaints now, but far more complaints against others than against ourselves. We make complaints against the country's president,

Second Session
25 May 1989

too. But from a legal point of view we have never had a president of the country, and we do not yet have one. And we have now gathered here precisely in order to resolve the question of the birth of the country's president. The kind of prerogatives that we now want to enshrine in the future candidacy do not yet exist. We should create such prerogatives now, and then we will be able to direct appropriate complaints to the country's future president: Gorbachev.

Now for the question of combining party and state posts. From my point of view, I think that combining the posts of state leader and party leader is only possible under conditions of the separation of powers, conditions that now exist in a number of Western countries. But in our country the separation of powers does not yet exist. Therefore, we have gathered here to express the voters' will and to resolve, at the congress and in the work of the Supreme Soviet, the problem of the separation of powers and the creation of a rule-of-law state.

But now we are again trying to combine party and state functions. However, if we are to work on the basis of a rule-of-law state, let us render unto God that which is God's, and unto Caesar that which is Caesar's. Then let us, if we are bold enough, raise questions like this one here, at the congress: Why do we, like the party members, lack the boldness to raise this question within the framework of a social organization? To raise it within the framework of the party, within the framework of the congress, and resolve the question of the delimitation of party and state functions there, in that sphere, the sphere of the party organization. I ask you to consider these circumstances.

N.V. Yeseykin, machine operator in a lease subunit at the "Dobrovolets" Kolkhoz, Shilovskiy Rayon, Ryazan Oblast (Sasovskiy Territorial Electoral Okrug, Ryazan Oblast): Comrade deputies! This is what I would like to say. First, various groupings—almost parties—have recently begun to spring up, but as yet we have only one party in our country. Mikhail Sergeyevich is our leader, and I think he should remain in his post as head of the party and also serve as president of our country. And that is not only my personal opinion, but the opinion of the Ryazan Oblast delegates.

V.I. Vorotnikov: Deputy Spiridonov has the floor.

M.V. Spiridonov, chairman of the 22d Party Congress Kolkhoz, Orlovskiy Rayon, Orel Oblast (from the kolkhozes united by the Union Kolkhoz Council): On the instructions of my group of deputies, I would like to say that we warmly support the proposal to nominate Mikhail Sergeyevich to the high post of chairman of the USSR Supreme Soviet, for all the positive changes in our country are associated with his name. We had the honor of receiving Mikhail Sergeyevich on our farm, and people approved his of policy, both domestic and foreign, with love and respect. We associate with his name the further progress of restructuring, the resolution of the agrarian question, and the revival of the villages and countryside of our native Non-Chernozem.

A deputy (who did not introduce himself): I will not speak for long. I vote for Mikhail Sergeyevich Gorbachev with both hands—if only because he was born in Stavropol, and I am from the Kuban. That is enough for me. Comrades, it has been said here that Mikhail Sergeyevich is a true Leninist, and that is indeed the case. Let us remember, did not Lenin combine the post of Council of Ministers chairman and general secretary? That is all I have to say.

V.I. Vorotnikov: Next, please.

S.I. Konev, clinical physician at the infectious diseases faculty of the Dnepropetrovsk Medical Institute (Dneprodzerzhinskiy Territorial Electoral Okrug, Dnepropetrovsk Oblast): I represent Dneprodzerzhinsk, the birthplace, so to speak, of stagnation. (Animation in the auditorium.) I wish to express my view on combining the two posts. In principle I can see nothing but promise in the separation of these posts. But at the moment, for the time being, I share the view of combining them in the person of Mikhail Sergeyevich. How do I justify this? Because it is necessary to ensure democratic elections at all vertical levels. At present, in effect, the party apparatus is developing undivided power in the republics and oblasts and in the localities.

Until such time as we hold democratic elections and eliminate all the defects and distortions in practice that existed during the previous stage, he should hold this post. When the soviets are the real organs of power locally, then I think Mikhail Sergeyevich will himself renounce this post. That is his right to choose. Thank you for your attention.

V.I. Mironenko, first secretary of the Komsomol Central Committee (from the All-Union Leninist Komsomol): Esteemed Comrade Chairman! Esteemed comrade deputies! I would like to say two things only. For all my profound respect for Chingiz Aytmatov and some other deputies who have spoken here, I must say it seems to me that there is no need to praise Mikhail Sergeyevich. It seems to me that this belittles this man, this major political and state leader who is at the head of our party. (Animation in the auditorium. Applause.) Do you think I have praised him myself? (Applause). All the same, I wanted to say the first thing I have said, and all the same, there is no need to praise him.

And the second thing: As a Communist, I feel I must say this. Deputy Loginov's speech contained remarks on how Gorbachev must be safeguarded against the partocracy, and to that end he should renounce his duties as general secretary and member of the Politburo of the

STENOGRAPHIC RECORD

Second Session
25 May 1989

CPSU Central Committee. I remember what one deputy said at the party group conference, that we are not children who need to be led by the hand. It is indeed unpleasant if people lead you by the hand. But it is perhaps equally unpleasant when they try to lead you by the nose. It seems to me that something is present, perhaps unconsciously, in the proposals to separate Gorbachev from the party or to separate the party from Gorbachev, the thoughts that are expressed in one way or another—directly or indirectly—on separating the party from the people—these are by no means to the benefit of restructuring. They cannot benefit restructuring. Furthermore, I am convinced that if we permit this, we will be doing enormous, indisputable damage to restructuring. Thank you.

P.P. Falk, Air Force lieutenant colonel and senior navigator (Buzulukskiy Territorial Electoral Okrug No 246, Orenburg Oblast): I represent a people more than 2 million strong, the Soviet Germans. The political accusation made against this people by Stalin in 1941 is now being lifted. The question of their political rehabilitation is now being resolved, and therefore I wish to make just one request: I request that the problem of the revival of the republic and national rayons in the Soviet Union be resolved in full. (Applause).

Voice from the floor: Dear comrade deputies. In all, in the last 4 days we have heard good and bad. I want to say one thing: Please tell me, who does not stumble and who does not make mistakes in a new and very difficult task? Yes, Gorbachev has made mistakes; there are plenty of them concerning cooperatives and women's questions. (Animation in the auditorium.) At the moment I am criticizing, not praising him. We women very much hope that he will receive all-around support. Yes, he must be given all-around support; we must not simply praise him eloquently, speak eloquently, and write eloquent letters. There are more problems in the USSR than anywhere else. But tell me, please, who first started to combat drunkenness? Who first started to oppose those who are robbing us? Tell me, please, who first made us all bold and opened our eyes to many things? And I could go on! Vote for him! I think he will realize his mistakes.

I.I. Kukhar, chairman of the Vladimir Ilich Kolkhoz, Leninskiy Rayon, Moscow Oblast (from the kolkhozes united by the Union Council of Kolkhozes): Comrade deputies! Today the Union Council of Kolkhozes unites more than 25,500 kolkhozes, with more than 26 million kolkhoz members. And today our kolkhoz workers expect from us, comrades, big decisions, the resolution of agrarian policy, and the resolution of the Food Program.

Today more than ever before the question of food production is foremost. We hope that Comrade Mikhail Sergeyevich Gorbachev, being a specialist in agrarian policy, will, together with us, do everything to bring agriculture out of its current grave situation. And we vote for Comrade Gorbachev. As a Communist, as a party member, comrades, I say to you today that at this stage the combination of the posts of chairman of the USSR Supreme Soviet and general secretary of the party Central Committee is necessary.

V.I. Vorotnikov: I wish to consult with you, comrades. In the notes and rejoinders people are asking to have the discussions curtailed; the waiting line for the podium is growing. Therefore we have this suggestion: Give Mikhail Sergeyevich a chance to speak. Because essentially the speeches are being repeated. And therefore, perhaps, the discussion should be curtailed and then we could vote on including Mikhail Sergeyevich on the list.

From the floor: Give the floor to the colonel and Velikhov and let that be it.

V.I. Vorotnikov: All right? Good. Go ahead.

V.A. Martirosyan, military unit commander, Carpathian Military District (Rovno territorial electoral okrug No 509): Dear Comrades, I am Col Martirosyan Vilen Arutyunovich. As you can see, I am an Armenian by nationality, but I was born and grew up in Azerbaijan. The Ukrainian people nominated me as deputy. I am an internationalist. (Applause). Thank you.

Comrades, you know that during the most difficult times we had a placard that said: "The motherland calls!" Our tasks now, as representatives of all nationalities, is to decide the fate of our state, and the rest of the problems we shall solve later.

If at this time each of us begins to raise only his own crucial issues we shall get away from the main thing. And the main thing now is to resolve the most crucial issues which affect the interests of all of our Soviet nation. The main thing is that we all see in Mikhail Sergeyevich Gorbachev a man who is worthy of being the chairman of the Supreme Soviet. I do not think that there is even any point in discussing alternatives. This candidate can be selected even by open voting. This is a person who has proved through his work that he deserves this.

I think that the first thing we should do is reconcile all Armenian and Azerbaijani deputies who are present so that they will leave here as friends. (Applause).

We must resolve the most crucial issue with respect to Georgia. When the commission is created I wish to be included on it as a military person. We must resolve the Baltic issues. Comrade Balts! I appeal to you as a military person. You are good people but today you can no longer think only of your own personal interests. Let us first resolve statewide issues right now and then we shall resolve yours as well. I fully support the candidacy of Mikhail Sergeyevich Gorbachev. Thank you. (Applause).

STENOGRAPHIC RECORD

Second Session
25 May 1989

Ye.P. Velikhov, vice president of the USSR Academy of Sciences (from the CPSU): Comrade deputies! We are discussing the question of combining and dividing up power. What power are you speaking about? Today there is still no full-fledged Soviet power! When we turn the power over to the soviets we shall strengthen this power, and then will come the time for questions of the party in the state and combining and dividing up power. Today let us take the question of turning it over and resolve that. (Applause).

V.I. Vorotnikov: Comrade Mikhail Sergeyevich Gorbachev has the floor.

M.S. Gorbachev: The present events in this hall are unusual for all us. Using the strictest yardsticks and given all the nuances I would assess this as the most convincing fact that restructuring is progressing. I would like to assure you above all in principled terms that I am devoted to this path on which we have embarked: restructuring and the renewal of our society on the principles of democracy, glasnost, a respectful attitude to man, and the elevation of every individual in our society. I am devoted to this line and cannot implement any other policy. My comrades should know that. I am not referring to specific things now. When you are deciding an issue and an election is held, then there will probably be talk of specifics. I want to voice my position now in a principled way.

I thank my comrades for their support. I sense it, it was also expressed here. I assure you—you have possibly been able to see this for yourselves, observing my style of work—that I find any bureaucratic fuss, bureaucratism, alienation from the people, and exclusivity unacceptable. I do not accept them because of my internal convictions. I am implementing these convictions, as far as I am able, in my work. I favor dialogue within the country, dialogue within the party, with all strata, all public movements—which are sometimes difficult when they forget about the main values and our main gains. Nevertheless we must conduct dialogue on everything that is happening in our country. The main thing is to utilize everything.

When people sometimes level at me the accusation that our country is somewhat reminiscent of a discussion club. I want to say the following: We are still learning democracy, we are all learning. We are still shaping our political culture. We are still mastering all the mechanisms of democracy.

Certainly we have made many blunders. Many emotions are coming out. Some people are exploiting this situation to satisfy their political ambitions, acting from careerist positions or other considerations. But they are not the people who are determining the situation. I do not think that we can act in any other way. Otherwise that would mean that we do not believe in our people and we do not believe in socialism, and the essence of socialism is that it is the working people's system for the working people.

That is why we must proceed along this path and gain experience.

Of course, restructuring is proceeding with difficulty. I assure you, comrades, and I also want to disabuse those of you who believe that information does not reach me and that I do not know what is going on within the country. I am even aware of the following case: Veterans are traveling in Moscow's last bus and bringing the following "visual agitation" with them—a portrait of Brezhnev with medals and a portrait of Gorbachev with ration cards. I know everything. I maybe even know more than you. If you are all taken together, I know less, but in comparison with each of you individually I know more...

The tension of the situation is not getting me down, because we have entered the most difficult phase of restructuring. There was policy, there were rallies, there were debates—difficult, interesting, and important ones. We molded this policy in principle on the main aspects. It requires development and deepening in all areas. But we do have this policy. The most difficult thing is to overcome our principle of leaving things to the last minute... We have begun to unite our concept—notwithstanding all its shortcomings—with life and have seen how difficult it is for this process to penetrate the densely-packed layers and with what difficulty it was perceived at the level of policy and objectives.

This policy is not abstract now. It is affecting people. In the economy it is affecting the working class, above all those who were accustomed to leveling and pay inducements. It is affecting economic managers who are unable to work in conditions of economic accountability because they are incompetent. People see this and want to replace them because economic accountability means living by end results and by your ability to work and people need intelligent leaders.

This policy is affecting the management apparatus, which we are cutting back thoroughly, and some people, who have lived a considerable part of their life, are having to find turning points and change their lifestyle. Is that easy? Are the processes that are under way within the party really easy?

What about when we transferred science to economic accountability instead of simply running it on a budget, although some scientists had often failed to produce a single invention or a single innovation in 10 years? Was that really easy?

What about the army? We have tackled it thoroughly. It has as many problems there. Was that really easy?

Let us take a look at the spiritual sphere. Moreover when we tackled this, we saw how our structure that had taken shape over decades resists and how the system itself resists. We realized the need for change and progression, but the system did not allow us. Then political reform

STENOGRAPHIC RECORD

Second Session
25 May 1989

and democratization came along and we set these processes in motion in order to put man in the arena via the processes of democracy and make him a decisive force.

The congress is the first stage of the reform and it shows that we were not mistaken on the main point. One can talk about whether a law is good or not and in which district someone has "duped" someone else. And I am sorry, but I can also say who has talked a great deal of nonsense and that has also happened, you realize. Some people in our country have obtained mandates possibly by acting as follows: By particularly throwing themselves into the critical aspect and abusing the management we can entrust you with... Well, this has happened. But that does not cancel out the main point which is that we have here on the whole a body of cadres and deputies, which, I am sure, can assume responsibility at this crucial phase, the most difficult phase of restructuring. Responsibility for the country's future.

I want to say, certainly, comrades, we have gone a long way in many respects, especially in our perception of ourselves—what we are, what is going on around us throughout the world, and how we should transform it both in our internal policy and in our views of the world. I believe that we have proposed the correct strategic direction for our country. We have also put forward initiatives for the world, which have directly changed the whole world's attitude toward us.

There have been mistakes and great serious miscalculations. I think that the chairman of the Supreme Soviet and, particularly, the leader of our government should also talk about these because our amendments will not be made to our policy without this fruitful discussion and the elaboration of decisions. That is the main point.

Certainly, comrades, many questions have been raised here, including with regard to the fact that there are great miscalculations and calamities here which we have experienced. Some of them could have been avoided. Yes, they could have been avoided. I also feel this deeply.

I do not think that you suspect me of wanting things to be worse. I think that we are still only taking the situation in hand. We are taking it in hand but it is still escaping our grasp. Reform is breaking loose, the political process is breaking loose. Everything has only just begun in the spiritual sphere. The realization has now appeared after such head-on skirmishes that it is time for consolidation for the sake of our supreme interests, the country's interests, and for the sake of achieving these goals. I think that we have reached this stage, we will do what is necessary for economic reform. We must ponder how we are to advance political reform at the second stage. We must ponder how we are to rally the people via the ideology of renewal, the triumph of morality, the triumph of our values, to which we all swear allegiance. Above all this will occur in life itself.

I want to answer the questions, but without going into details, since there are many questions particularly from Estonia's deputies; Comrade Lauristin, for instance, raised many questions, I am replying here in a principled way. I think that within the framework of this congress we should answer all these painful questions and examine what is what. I cannot fail to speak now when there is a discussion under way and you want to know Gorbachev's opinion. Can we act in such a way whereby the army is employed to restore order and carry out actions as happened in Tbilisi? Although this entire matter still has to be investigated. Let me be blunt and say: The army must do its own job. That is the view held by the Politburo and the government. We must all ensure that it never comes to this. People are saying: How was it that troops appeared there? You are aware, I think, that we should probably discuss when we invite our troops to help the militia ensure that events like those in Sumgait do not happen and somehow preserve order. It should be discussed. We proceeded on the premise that the situation had to be contained somehow in this case! People delayed 4 hours before imposing the curfew and somehow taking the situation in hand—and look what happened. That is why we need to consider the mechanisms so that no one should suspect anyone of thinking about moving in the army to calm the people. No. But we will, where necessary, employ all forces to maintain stability—political, organizational, militia, the aktiv, and the people. Everyone. Let us consider all these mechanisms when we form the supreme organs. Everything must be done on the basis of discussion and decisions adopted by the Supreme Soviet and the USSR Congress of People's Deputies on most important questions, when the country's future is at stake.

We learned what happened in Tbilisi at 1000 the following day. The day before, Saturday, I was told at the airport about the situation in Tbilisi on returning to Moscow after a visit. And we agreed right there, at the airport, that despite all the trials of the visit—we had visited three countries—Comrade Shevardnadze and Comrade Razumovskiy should go there immediately. The aircraft was ready to take off. But a call came from Tbilisi and Comrade Shevardnadze was told that it was not necessary for him to come, that the situation was normalizing, so to speak. I was briefed. And on Sunday I learned what had happened.

Let us thoroughly investigate everything. A prosecutor's office investigation is already under way there, a republic commission and a commission sent from the center are at work. It is necessary to make all these materials public and to hand them over to our commission which we will set up at the congress. Let it examine everything. If necessary it will go and investigate on the spot and report to us. We all have a lesson to learn from this. We must not sidestep it.

Comrades have touched on the interethnic question. I believe that in our Union where so many peoples and ethnic groups live together, we will not achieve anything if either the big or the small peoples feel ill at ease. By means of a whole series of interconnected steps and legislative enactments we must embark during the second stage of the reform on the harmonization of interethnic relations and the realization of the sovereignty of union republics so that

STENOGRAPHIC RECORD

Second Session
25 May 1989

they really are union republics. And to enhance their independence, and consequently also their responsibility.

Comrades, we must achieve a situation in which all citizens feel at ease, irrespective of their nationality, no matter where they live. In Russia, in the Baltic republics, in Transcaucasia—everywhere. If we adopt a different approach, if we start separating our peoples and ethnic groups now, drawing dividing lines, if we start recarving our country, it will be the road to disaster, I assure you. Everything can be resolved only on the basis of respect, equality, realization of sovereignty, mutual links, broad development of cultures and languages and exchanges between them, mutual contacts, and cooperation. I am confident that within the framework of the democratic process which is under way in the country and which is engendering new structures capable of perceiving interests, discussing them, identifying them, and implementing them in policy and practice, we will find the solution to these questions. Let me assure everyone that we will find answers to these very important and burning issues.

On the subject of combining posts. In the context of the current situation, at the present stage of the development of society, I am convinced that the 19th All-Union Party Conference adopted the correct recommendation. This is what is needed today. I am deeply convinced of this, comrades. This is because the process of restructuring, of political reform, the process of the separation of functions, the realization by the party of its role of the political vanguard of society and its liberation from state and economic functions—this process is only just beginning. It is important to grasp here that without the position of the party, without being able to lean on the party, so to speak, this process will go badly. I have said this before and I remain convinced that today this is necessary. There is no other way. I am confident that this topic will be one of the main ones when we embark on new elections. And maybe even earlier. Perhaps the congress, too, will return to the discussion of this question. Most probably, the congress will follow the same train of thought as the 19th conference. I am convinced that in the present context this is the right road.

Last, comrades, there is much that we have to sort out. Personal matters were touched upon here. I have tried to give some explanations in the press. I would like to once again return to the question concerning the dacha, since it has been raised. Neither I, nor any member of my family, have ever owned a dacha. State dachas are put at the disposal of the current leadership and not only the leadership. There are dachas in our country for academicians, writers, and so forth.

About the dacha in the Crimea. It is true that we have completed the construction of the dachas that were planned. Now another process has started. We have carried out a review and have already handed over some 10 dachas to the health service, to veterans, for cultural purposes, and so forth. We will examine the further development of this process. Anything that can be made available, that is not needed for representational purposes and for providing services to the leadership must be made available bearing in mind the democratic processes, but state dachas must nonleess be provided for the top leadership, that is a limited circle of people, while they are in office. But it really is a problem.

I would put it this way: Privileges exist everywhere. Heroes [of the Soviet Union] have their privileges, miners have their privileges, in the North there are privileges, academicians have privileges, trade unions and enterprises have their privileges. Today I heard Comrade Postnikov from my native region say on the radio that they are going to pay pensioners an additional R70 from their profits, those who had worked there for 20-30 years. In our country medical services were also developed under departments. Ministries have their own holiday homes and sanatoria. Some of our enterprises have facilities which others would not even dream of. I would like to make a proposal. I may repeat it later if I am called upon to deliver a report. Let us set up a Supreme Soviet commission, let us take stock, let us see what we have and how it has come about, let us discuss everything sensibly and adopt a decision on the whole range of these questions.

These are the specific matters which I wanted to mention. Thank you for the words of great support. I accept businesslike, critical remarks as being comradely. I welcome this. You may rest assured that I will use neither my present nor my future position in order to do something that I have myself struggled against. I will continue to struggle and will devote myself wholly to this, insofar as I am instructed by the people and the party to do so. I will strive to steer the course of democracy to the end so that things that once happened in our lives can never repeat themselves.

V.I. Vorotnikov: Dear Comrade deputies! Although we are working for longer than is specified in the regulations, we still must finish with this issue before we break. Agreed?

Audience: Agreed.

V.I. Vorotnikov: I vote for curtailing the discussion of the question of the nomination of Mikhail Gorbachev. Everyone in favor of this please raise your hands. Lower them. Those against? No. There are two deputies. Any more? There are two against. How many abstentions? None. Let us close the discussion.

Now raised for your vote is a motion to include on the ballot the candidacy of Comrade Mikhail Sergeyevich Gorbachev for a secret vote for the election of the chairman of the USSR Supreme Soviet. Those in favor of this motion please raise your hands. Lower your hands. Those against? Will the vote counter please count the votes.

(The votes are counted.)

V.I. Vorotnikov: Here is the report. Against—zero. (Applause). Who has abstained? Please count them, comrades.

STENOGRAPHIC RECORD

Second Session
25 May 1989

From the floor: Comrade deputies, here is the report: Four deputies abstained.

V.I. Vorotnikov: Good, thank you. Thus Comrade Gorbachev's candidacy is included on the ballot for secret voting. (Applause).

Comrades, the people's deputy from the Leningrad rural national-territorial okrug No 20, Aleksandr Mitrofanivoch Obolenskiy, has submitted to the congress an application on his candidacy to the post of chairman of the USSR Supreme Soviet and asks for the opportunity to speak. Please, Comrade Obolenskiy. (Applause).

A.M. Obolenskiy: Dear comrades, I shall try to confine myself to 20 minutes as Mikhail Sergeyevich did. You will excuse me in advance since it will be very difficult for me to present my entire program in such a short period of time. You knew all of his work so it was easier for him.

From the floor: Who are you?

A.M. Obolenskiy: Let me introduce myself. I an an engineer-designer. I live and work in the city of Apatita. I work at the Polar Geophysical Institute of the Kola Scientific Center of the USSR Academy of Sciences. I was born in 1943 in Orel. I grew up there, finished school with a gold medal, and went to work at the plant. I worked for a year as a lathe operator in the machine-building plant. Then came training at Leningrad University. In my second year I was drafted into the army. I served for 3 years in the Group of Soviet Forces in Germany. Since being discharged I have lived and worked on the Kola Peninsula. I was a member of the trade union committee and handled housing and domestic problems. After that I was the people's assessor of the city court and a member of the voluntary society for contributing to perestroyka in our city. I am a Russian, a nonparty member, I am married and have three children, and I have never been convicted of a crime. That is all I have to say about myself.

Now about my program. I think that in the next few years our main task will be to build a rule-of-law state, a task set by Mikhail Sergeyevich Gorbachev. I shall not explain: We all know that this is one of our primary tasks.

First. This is the prohibition of departmental norm setting. The only basis for our living in this country should be the laws adopted by legislative authority. (Applause). Departmental normative acts, which are being adopted to this day, should have the force of recommendations. It is all right to have them but they should not have the force of law. If we do not do this perestroyka will just spin its wheels.

Second. This is the institution of a constitutional court. As you can understand, this is more important than the Committee for Constitutional Supervision. The Committee for Constitutional Supervision is an instrument for solving problems from the stagnant administrative-command era. Is it worthwhile to drag it into the future?

The next thing is to provide for real independence of the courts. So far I do not know of a better procedure than trial by jury.

I shall move on to the political section. In order for the Constitution to be the Basic Law, it must be revised. I suggest that it be shortened; 174 articles are too many. We should keep only those which actually reinforce the foundations of our life and define its basic aspects. And the main thing is that it should be adopted through a series of nationwide referendums. The Basic Law should be taken out from the control of any representative agencies at all. Only then will we be confident of our future and begin to realize the slogan proclaimed at the congress concerning the changeover from power on behalf of the people to power of the people.

Further—the agricultural and food problem. This is very important to everyone. There have been many debates about how to motivate the peasant to work the land, how to turn him to the land. Various forms of leasing have been proposed and suggestions have been made about time periods. The right to the land has been granted for 5 years, for 50 years, indefinitely, and even through heredity. I do not think that this is the root of the problem because even if we now adopt a law on inheriting the right to the land, it will still not change anything. The rank-and-file worker has no confidence in the stability of the decision. He has learned too well from the experience of preceding generations: If we adopt a law today, within a week or half a year it can be changed again. There are plenty of examples. But if the right to lease is established in the Constitution, which is adopted by the people themselves, there will be confidence. This pertains also to industry, the right to lease enterprises, and so forth.

In the political part of my program is the realization of the principle of separation of state power. I have in mind independent legislative, executive, and judicial power. The principle of independence is that the agencies of power are formed by the people independently of one another. Now we have a sequential chain.

Further. We like the slogan "all power to the soviets" very much and we all welcome it. I wish to add the following refinement to it: "all power to the local soviets." We are speaking about that same local self-management of the soviets about which a point was included in the program of the RSDRP [Russian Social Democratic Workers' Party] when it came to power. I understand it this way: A decision of the local soviet adopted for the territory which it governs and by which it was elected takes priority. It cannot be overridden by any higher soviet, right up to the Supreme Soviet. If the

Second Session
25 May 1989

decision is made in violation of the law, the only path is through the courts, as is proper in a rule-of-law state.

The "economics" section includes immediate elimination of branch ministries. I think they comprise one of the main impediments to restructuring along the path of economic accountability and other of our undertakings. I consider the question of the budget very important in the sphere of economics. I would ask you to return to this question later and discuss it because I consider it inadmissible for our country to continue to live with this deficit in the future. This is my program and that of Otto Rudolfovich Latsis, who was my last opponent on the path to this podium. We are both in favor of getting rid of this deficit.

We are the legislative power and we must solve the problem of the deficit in principle. But how to eliminate it—this is primarily the business of the executive power. If our finance minister is unable to conduct this operation properly, he should probably be removed. Perhaps we could call in a Japanese? Excuse me.

Comrades! This, of course, is not a simple issue, and if I may I shall discuss it in a little greater detail. For everyone sitting in this hall deals with the budget twice a month. Some of us probably solve the difficult problem of how to live from one paycheck to the next. And we are able to make ends meet without going into debt. Can we imagine this situation: We have piled up debts throughout the year and then we smile nicely at the creditor and "gladden" his heart: "I am not going to pay." It is understandable that he will be disturbed. Then we "smooth things over": "I shall not pay, but do not worry—you will get my children, who are still only knee high, and they will grow up and pay for me. I think that this is an immoral situation and such a thought never entered any of our heads. We are not our children's enemies. But now let us think about what we are doing on the scale of the country. The deficit is nothing other than a debt taken out against the money of the next generation. I think this is inadmissible. In principle we must make a decision and learn, however difficult it may be, to live within our means. (Applause).

I shall not touch upon the rest of the sections of my economic program. I shall say simply that I am very glad about the numerous sections that we have formed: the state sector, cooperation, individual activity—both in agriculture and in industry. For the first time our worker has been given the freedom of choice of where he can apply his ability, knowledge, and labor skills with the greatest effectiveness for his family. And this means for the society as well.

And, finally, my program contains a section on the standard of living of the people. It has a number of points. I shall touch upon only two of them. Mikhail Sergeyevich Gorbachev already touched upon them in his speech. First is the fight against privileges. It would be more correct to say—against abuses of job position. Because there are no privileges under the law. All this is done behind our backs. But we all know that it is being done, and the people know it too. These questions are asked at every meeting.

Why do I consider this question important? Because through the system of privileges our bureaucratic class solves three main problems. First. It separates from you and me the most capable and enterprising people. Second. Corrupting them with the system of privileges, it creates material interest in preserving the existing situation. Third. This is a comfortable place from which to control them.

There should be special concern for the situation of the most impoverished categories of our compatriots: invalids, pensioners, the underpaid. I do not think that our country has the moral right to call itself socialist until it can create at least the minimum standard of living for these people. There is no need to explain to you that it is impossible to live on R23 a month and less. We ourselves push some of our compatriots onto the semilegal path of making a living. Not all of those old people who trade in alcohol and make home brew on the sly do this because of a sporting interest. Many are forced by need. How do we resolve this problem?

Finally, we must determine the real minimum standard of living. Discussions about this have been going on for a long time. We must stop talking and start acting. I do not think that this is so difficult.

Briefly about pensions. Of course revision of pension legislation is a fairly complicated matter. I think it necessary to adopt an additional decision to make additional payments from the state budget to all who receive less than this level. Simply an additional payment. What else can you call it? A poverty stipend? Whatever you like. The name is not important. But we must find this money, however difficult it may be. And I do not think that this matter can be put off until later. Let us get by with fewer plans for the longer range. Perhaps we need not satisfy our space appetites so fully. This is also for the future, but we must get on our feet.

Two words about how I ended up at this podium. I am, after all, quite well aware that I have no chances of winning against Mikhail Sergeyevich Gorbachev. In our history and practice I want us to have a precedent for holding elections. Even if it is not an alternative basis, they are still elections. The voters who elected me demand this. I promised them and I shall keep my promise. Thank you. (Applause).

STENOGRAPHIC RECORD

Second Session

25 May 1989

V.I. Vorotnikov: Comrades, what is your opinion? Who wants to speak in response to Comrade Obolenskiy? Please.

A.A. Korshunov, brigade leader of the Tashkent Aviation Production Association imeni V.P. Chkalov (On behalf of the USSR trade unions): I am categorically against keeping people from speaking up when they are talking business. But I am also categorically against turning democracy into a game of democracy.

I value the comrade's courage and I apologize for not remembering his name. He is undoubtedly a courageous person. But we are gathered at the highest congress—our highest agency of power. People are waiting outside the gates, outside the walls of this palace to hear the decisions we make. Not which slogans, not which set of slogans, as the comrade has presented, but what we will say to the people when we return from the congress. What will we say to the elderly who are half starving? What will we say to the disabled; what will we say to the Soviet people? I do not mean that I am condemning him; I do not think I could do that. This is simply an appeal to the comrade deputies to save time, not only their own, but also that of our Soviet people. The country is on the brink and here we are starting to engage in empty talk. My own personal opinion is that this candidacy is in no way suitable for the position of president of the country. (Turbulent applause)

S.V. Belozertsev, senior instructor of the Karelian State University, Petrozavodsk (Kalinin national territorial electoral okrug): I was surprised to hear the debates regarding the new regulations. It seems to me that many of us absolutely do not understand why we were debating. Look, Mikhail Sergeyevich has had to answer many questions, essentially to give a mini-report. If we had had the report sooner, all of these questions, all of these speeches would have been eliminated. But precisely this agenda was stubbornly imposed on us.

As concerns the alternative candidate, we were sent here to hold democratic elections, so that we would have a democratic procedure for the future. Therefore I call upon you to vote in favor of including Comrade Obolenskiy as a candidate on the list for the position of the country's president. No, he will not make it. But this will set a procedure. This will create a precedent which we need, a precedent of choice. This is not a game; we are talking about principles. (Applause).

L.I. Sandulyan, department head of the biology faculty of Chernovtsy State University (Chernovtsy territorial electoral okrug): Dear comrade deputies! Here today and in the party group one could hear expressions like "enough playing children's games." My voters who sent me here do not think that perestroyka is a game; it is serious and irreversible. (Applause).

Mikhail Sergeyevich Gorbachev deserves a great deal of credit in our country. There is no doubt that he is an outstanding politician of modernity, but he is our only one. Or is he?

It is simply that we do not know the others. Because we have not had the opportunity to get to know them. Thanks to Comrade Gorbachev we know that there are people running for the highest government position in the country. I ask you to include on the list for the secret vote Comrade Obolenskiy who nominated himself for this position. (Applause).

A.A. Sobchak, department head of the faculty of Leningrad State University, Leningrad (Vasileostrov territorial electoral okrug): Over decades, since Stalin's time, a situation has developed in which any position in our country, any government position, beginning with the chairman of the rural soviet, not to mention chairman of the Council of Ministers or a minister, has been filled only by members of the Communist Party. I think that in our new constitution, the edition of the constitution we are to approve today, we should introduce a fundamental point that each Soviet person, regardless of the party to which he belongs or whether he belongs to a party or not, should have the right to run for any government position. In principle. This is why I think that we should include on the list for the secret vote for the position of chairman of the Supreme Soviet Comrade Obolenskiy who does not belong to a party. (Applause).

M.Ch. Zalikhanov, director of the Vosokogornyy Geophysical Institute, Nalchik (Elbrus national-territorial electoral okrug of the Karbadino-Balkar ASSR [Autonomous Soviet Socialist Republic]): Comrades, today I have been hearing many comrades and I recall how in my youth I read in some magazine that one can always find someone who lives on the equator who will advise an eskimo about how best to fight against the cold. I am convinced of this today. We have many advisers like this here in the hall and outside it. Does Mikhail Sergeyevich really not know about the difficulties, about the matters Obolenskiy discussed here today? I wish to say that I feel very sorry for those voters who sent such a demagogue here. (Applause).

A.M. Obolenskiy: I shall take literally 20 seconds. Because I must express my viewpoint regarding what I consider important in the question of the discussion and nomination today. I have no doubt that Mikhail Sergeyevich Gorbachev will win. I shall vote for him. But I hope that there will be elections in the republic where there will actually be alternative candidates who are perhaps more worthy and this will not be a bad example. (Applause).

V.I. Vorotnikov: Dear comrades, I understand your attitude and I shall place the vote on the question of including Comrade Obolenskiy's candidacy on the ballot

Second Session

25 May 1989

for secret voting first on the list of issues. I ask those in favor of this to vote. I repeat—in favor of including Comrade Obolenskiy on the list for secret voting. Please count them.

From the floor: Comrade deputies, permit me to report; 689 deputies voted "for."

I shall bring the second motion to a vote. Who is against including Comrade Obolenskiy on the list for secret voting. Please vote.

From the floor: Comrade deputies! Voting against, 1,415. Who has abstained? Please, I ask you to vote. (From the floor. Comrade deputies! Abstaining, 33 deputies.) Thus, comrades, in keeping with the results of the voting, the candidacy of Deputy Obolenskiy will not be included on the secret ballot. (Applause).

Are there any other motions for different candidacies? Please speak now. Please, who wishes to take the floor?

G.E. Burbulis, deputy director of the All-Union Institute for Increasing Qualifications of Specialists of the USSR Ministry of Nonferrous Metallurgy, Sverdlovsk (Lenin territorial electoral okrug): At one time, when the events of April 1985 were gathering speed, Mikhail Sergeyevich made this statement: We have kept our people outside of politics for too long. This was the whole truth. We, the party, have kept people outside of politics for a long time; that is, for decades; that is, we have had our own system of means and ends. Four years have passed. If anyone were to say that nothing has changed he would be deeply mistaken. Our voters and our workers have become politicians. I support the suggestion made today by my colleague, the deputy from Serov, Vitaliy Biryukov, and am conveying to the congress my instructions from the voters: to recommend for the position of chairman of the USSR Supreme Soviet Boris Nikolayevich Yeltsin... (Applause).

V.L. Fomenko, deputy shop chief of the Artificial Fiber Plant imeni V.V. Kuybyshev of the Mogilev Khimvolokno Production Association imeni V.I. Lenin (Mogilev city territorial electoral okrug): A couple of words in response. I think that now the congress, having eliminated the candidacy of the second comrade, has acted approximately the way the okrug meetings acted by unjustifiably rejecting candidates for deputies. This is my first remark. (Applause). If we proceed like this, we can get rid of other candidacies according to the same principle.

Further, I think it is unseemly for one deputy to go up to the podium and call another deputy a demagogue. We are all equals here and let us choose our words carefully. (Applause).

V.I. Vorotnikov: A request is being made regarding the proposed candidacy. This is what we are discussing now. Let us conclude with the formation of the ballot for secret voting.

S.S. Sulakshin, laboratory chief of the Scientific Research Institute of Nuclear Physics (Tomsk territorial electoral okrug): I have a small remark regarding the procedure we are engaged in now. Comrades, when we decide the issue of including one or another nominated candidate on the ballot, we can do this either on the basis of a substantiated rejection or a withdrawal of one's own nomination. Otherwise we are replacing the procedure of secret voting, which is determined by normative documents, with the procedure of open voting.

I call upon you not to commit this violation. I propose including all nominated candidates on the ballot for secret—I emphasize this—voting unless someone withdraws his own nomination or there is a substantiated rejection. (Applause).

A.N. Krayko, department chief of the division of the Central Institute of Aircraft Engine Construction imeni P.I. Baranov (Bauman territorial electoral okrug, Moscow): I have deep respect for Boris Nikolayevich Yeltsin. Moreover, I am deeply convinced that his alienation from political activity, real political activity, should not continue in the future. I think he should be enlisted for active participation in our political life.

Nonetheless I would be happy if Boris Nikolayevich Yeltsin would withdraw his own nomination. I shall explain why. Recently my constituents sent me a letter with the following content: "Dear Aleksandr Nikolayevich! The elections of 26 March inspired in us the hope that the course of affairs in our country would no longer be determined by anyone other than ourselves, that we would now be able to influence the development of events through our deputies. But new concerns appeared. A large number of the people's deputies are representatives of the administrative-party apparatus. How will the congress act when resolving the most important issues? And we consider the most important issue to be the election of the chairman of the Supreme Soviet and, apparently, the president of the country. We are familiar with various positions and viewpoints concerning the current process of transformations. We attend meetings of the Moscow People's Front and Memorial, we have communicated with representatives of various informal associations, and we read the leaflets, pamphlets, and the newspaper NOVOYE DELO. And we see: In spite of the fact that the opinion that we should elect Gorbachev as president is very widespread—Sakharov, for example, mentions this—it is still not unanimous. Some people may not excuse him for signing ukases that are not fully worked out or some people do not think he is decisive enough, comparing Yeltsin's boldness to his.

Second Session

25 May 1989

"We cannot but respect Boris Nikolayevich's courageous statements. We supported him during the electoral campaign. But is decisiveness the main merit of a leader now?

"It all reduces down to the opinion that we need a peaceful path of reform and transformations. And the peaceful path is the path of compromises, dialogue, and, possibly, certain concessions. And on this path the most appropriate leader is Gorbachev. In the first place, he has demonstrated his ability to steer the 'ship' by tacking. Over 4 years through gradual actions he has managed to achieve what has never been achieved all at once. This is the expansion of glasnost, attempts to create a free market, and the gradual reform of the electoral system. In the second place, Gorbachev has a great deal of international authority. In the third place, Mikhail Sergeyevich occupies the highest level of the party hierarchy, and this makes his candidacy more acceptable to party functionaries. And, of course, Gorbachev's main opponents are by no means the idols of the People's Front. Speaking at preelection meetings, a candidate for people's deputy Shatov noted that the statements at the April Plenum showed that there are many Nina Andreyevas in the Central Committee and it cannot be ruled out that in the developing battle for the president's position they will try to put through someone who will not act on principles and will at best halt the process of transformations or, more likely, will turn it back. Taking into account the real alignment of forces, this variant is quite probable. Therefore it seems to us extremely expedient at this point to oppose them with Gorbachev and the more progressive candidates. In the current stage we have a goal in common with Gorbachev—perestroyka and gradual but steady progress along the path of democratization of the society. We, your constituents, ask you to support Gorbachev's candidacy in the elections for chairman of the Supreme Soviet and promise all kinds of support in organizing rallies, conferences, and so forth."

Comrades, I wish to say once again that Boris Nikolayevich was nominated as people's deputy by thousands of enterprises, he gathered 5 million votes, and he should be in our political system, and here when you mention his name voices start to hum. But now resoluteness is not the main merit of a leader, and I would be glad if Boris Nikolayevich would withdraw his nomination. (Applause).

V.A. Chelyshev, senior correspondent of the newspaper INDUSTRIALNOYE ZAPOROZHYE (Zaporozhye—Zhovtnev territorial electoral okrug, Zaporozhye): I am very sympathetic to Boris Nikolayevich Yeltsin's program. I am sympathetic not only to its economic aspects: I am sympathetic to the fact that he has showed himself to be a fighter against the privileges that exist in the higher echelons, because there are third category dining rooms that serve first category food. We have all this. And that is not all. He is a sober politician but I do not like it when Gorbachev is juxtaposed to Yeltsin. They are two different wings of perestroyka. And, excuse me, there is no need for them to butt heads. They are two different wings of perestroyka, both of which are needed to keep it aloft. And therefore I think that Boris Nikolayevich should withdraw his candidacy now. I shall vote for Mikhail Sergeyevich Gorbachev. I think that there should be a very significant and very important post for Yeltsin. It could be an alternative candidacy for the post of chairman of the USSR Council of Ministers. That is all.

V.I. Vorotnikov: Perhaps this is enough? We have been in session for 4 hours and have violated the regulations. I should probably be relieved of my responsibilities.

R.G. Voronina, glass blower at the Ryazan Production Association for Electronic Instruments (on behalf of the USSR trade unions): I represent here his majesty the working class. Before leaving for the congress I visited three of the largest enterprises of my city. And everywhere they all told me: "Raisa Grigoryevna, you will be representing the working class at that large forum and we ask you to cast our vote for Mikhail Sergeyevich Gorbachev. He is our political leader and we can see no other." This is what the working class said. (Applause).

V.I. Vorotnikov: There are two motions... Does Boris Nikolayevich Yeltsin want to speak? Please. (Applause).

B.N. Yeltsin (Moscow city national territorial electoral okrug, RSFSR [Russian Soviet Federated Socialist Republic]): Dear comrade deputies! I thank the comrades for nominating me. But at the same time I think that in this situation it is necessary to take into account the decisions of the 19th Party Conference concerning combining positions and the decisions of the May Plenum of the party Central Committee which recommended Mikhail Sergeyevich for this position. At the plenum I was simply asked whether I would carry out the decisions of the May Plenum of the party Central Committee. And I answered: Of course, as a communist I shall carry it out because I am in favor of perestroyka and in favor of proceeding with it—only through more resolute, aggressive actions. I abstained during the voting at that time, thinking that in any case it would be necessary to propose certain alternative candidacies if only for an example, if only to educate our youth, subsequently to take certain additional steps forward in this matter. Since I have been unemployed since yesterday, I could accept some kind of offer, working seriously and acknowledging perestroyka. But now I withdraw my name from nomination. (Applause).

V.I. Vorotnikov: There is probably no further need to discuss this. There is a motion to honor Comrade Yeltsin's request. I ask for the vote. Those in favor of accepting Comrade Yeltsin's withdrawal from nomination please vote. Please lower your hands. Those against? The count please.

Second Session
25 May 1989

From the floor: Comrade deputies! The results of the voting: against—14 votes. And who has abstained? (From the floor—one).

V.I. Vorotnikov: Will the vote counters please pick up the pace. (From the floor—7 abstentions). Are there any other candidates on the list for voting? No? Good. Comrades! We still have to nominate the counting commission and then we will have a long break. Are there any objections? No.

Before turning the floor over to the counting commission I should like to remind you, comrades, that the voting is secret, that the chairman of the USSR Supreme Soviet is elected from the people's deputies by a secret vote. The ballot for the secret vote will include those candidates who have been approved by the congress. It is also stipulated—I ask you to pay attention to this—that the ballot is invalid if two or more candidacies are left on it. The chairman of the counting commission will announce the voting rules.

Is there any need for us to vote on this issue? No?

Then allow me to turn the floor over to Deputy Berezov.

V.A. Berezov, second secretary of the Central Committee of the Communist Party of Lithuania (Taurage national territorial okrug, Lithuanian SSR [Soviet Socialist Republic]): Comrade deputies! In keeping with the procedure for secret voting and the determination of its results at the USSR Congress of People's Deputies and on instructions from the meeting of representatives of groups of people's deputies, we introduce for your consideration the proposal to elect a congress counting commission consisting of 75 members.

V.I. Vorotnikov: Are there any other suggestions regarding the number of members. No. You have the list in your hands.

V.A. Berezov: It is suggested that the counting commission include 25 deputies from territorial and national-territorial electoral okrugs and social organizations. These are representatives of all union republics. Among them are workers, kolkhoz [collective farm] workers, engineering and technical personnel, representatives of the creative intelligentsia, physicians, teachers, military servicemen, and others. The deputies have proposals concerning the personal composition and I have been told that the changes introduced at the meeting of representatives have been made on this list.

V.I. Vorotnikov: Are there any comments regarding the personal composition of the counting commission?

A.M. Obolenskiy: Comrades! I beg your pardon for taking your time once again, but I must say that I figure in this composition. It would have been unethical to include me on it while we were competing. But that is not the main thing. The main thing is that nobody asked my permission. I learned about this only today. As I understand it, this counting commission will conduct elections for the Supreme Soviet as well. I cannot rule out the possibility that I shall run for that as well, and therefore I ask that my name be withdrawn.

V.I. Vorotnikov: There is a motion to comply with this request. A motion has been made by representatives of Murmansk Oblast to include their representative. Are there any objections? There is another motion to include Lieutenant Colonel Sychev. Who is in favor of having Obolenskiy's candidacy replaced by Sychev's and approving the entire composition of the counting commission. Please raise your certification.

Lower it. Is anyone against? None are against. Are there any abstentions? One person abstains.

Thus the counting commission has been elected. We request that the deputies who have been elected to the counting commission gather after the break in Granovitaya Chamber of the Great Kremlin Palace.

Our next meeting will be devoted to this vote. We shall break until 9 o'clock.

V.I. Vorotnikov: Dear comrade deputies! Let us continue our work. The floor is turned over to the chairman of the congress counting commission, Deputy Osipyan.

Yu.A. Osipyan, academician, vice president of the USSR Academy of Sciences, director of the Institute of Solid State Physics of the USSR Academy of Sciences, Moscow (on behalf of the USSR Academy of Sciences): Dear comrade deputies! During the break there was a meeting of the counting commission elected by the USSR Congress of People's Deputies, and the chairmanship of the counting commission was entrusted to me.

People's deputy Vladimir Petrovich Anishchev, second secretary of the Central Committee of the Communist Party of Uzbekistan, was elected secretary of the counting commission.

You are aware of the procedure for conducting the secret voting which we adopted this morning and so there is no need to report on that. At the same time I should like to draw your attention to certain issues related to the procedure for conducting secret voting for the election of the chairman of the USSR Supreme Soviet.

Each deputy will be given a ballot for electing the chairman of the USSR Supreme Soviet. In keeping with the way we voted, this ballot will include the name of Mikhail Sergeyevich Gorbachev.

Now regarding the voting itself. The ballots will be distributed in Georgiyevskiy Hall of the Great Kremlin

STENOGRAPHIC RECORD

Second Session

25 May 1989

Palace. The members of the counting commission will issue these ballots upon presentation of certification as a USSR people's deputy.

There will be 21 tables set up in Georgiyevskiy Hall. The initials of the deputies will be placed on them. The ballots will be issued there and the appropriate marks will be made on them. Again I draw your attention to the fact that the voting deputies are distributed in alphabetical order of their names, regardless of how they were elected.

And so you will receive your ballots, after which you can complete the act of voting itself. We have set up 44 booths for secret voting in the hall for this.

After receiving his ballot, each deputy will go into any free booth and complete the act there—he fills out the ballot; that is, either leaves or crosses out the candidate on it.

Then upon leaving the booth he drops the ballot in the secret voting box. These boxes are placed in a row on the side of the booths where you come out after passing through them.

I repeat again that it is possible to deposit the ballot only after going through the booth. Members of the counting commission will check to make sure that people do not go around the sides or vote in any other way. It is possible to drop off the ballot only by going through the booth. In each booth there is a shelf on which there is a small container with a pencil and a marker, and you can do your voting there.

After voting, the people's deputies can exit the Great Kremlin Palace to Sobornaya Square or they can go downstairs and leave through Georgiyevskiy Hall.

I draw your attention to the fact that the passageway here is fairly narrow and people should be walking in only one direction; therefore the people's deputies who are going to vote will cross over on the third floor and they must go out onto the street or to the first floor and then return to the foyer. Because we will have to wait while the counting takes place and then we will certify the results. According to the procedure, this is to be done today because of the great political significance of this act. The entire world is awaiting the results of our voting.

Now, comrades, we must determine the policy for leaving the hall because the passageway is narrow and the speed of the voting depends on the speed of the distribution of the ballots. This procedure is suggested: The deputies sitting in the 21st row and beyond are to leave through the door at the end of the hall. After that (there will be signs) they must go to the Great Kremlin Palace and there, in Georgiyevskiy Hall, they are to vote.

STENOGRAPHIC RECORD

Comrades, in order not to return to the question of today's voting, I shall say the following: The procedure is clear to us and we shall count the votes, and there will be no, as it were, alternative variants. But the instructions concerning the elections to the Supreme Soviet given to you for your consideration in which the policy for conducting the secret voting is outlined were drawn up in very general form; that is, at the end, after the counting of the votes, you understand there can be various variants. There is a motion to discuss this issue and inform you of it before the voting for the Supreme Soviet, but not today. Otherwise you will forget it in a day or two. And it would be better to freshen your memory at the time. I shall close here.

Vorotnikov, V.I.: Just one second. I must detain you. Are there any questions for the counting commission? Is everything clear? So the break will be continuous—for the voting and for the counting. I ask you not to leave, to stay here, so that you can approve the report of the counting commission today. This will be at approximately 11 o'clock. We hope that it will be no later.

That is all. I ask that you begin voting.

V.I. Vorotnikov: Dear comrade deputies! Let us continue our work. The floor is turned over to the chairman of the congress counting commission, Deputy Osipyan. Please.

Yu.A. Osipyan, academician, vice president of the USSR Academy of Sciences, director of the Institute of Solid State Physics of the USSR Academy of Sciences, Moscow (on behalf of the USSR Academy of Sciences): Comrade deputies! In keeping with the policy approved by the congress for secret voting and determination of its results at the USSR Congress of People's Deputies, the counting commission has counted the votes cast in the election of the chairman of the USSR Supreme Soviet and has established the ballot for secret voting for election of the chairman of the USSR Supreme Soviet included the candidacy of USSR People's Deputy Mikhail Sergeyevich Gorbachev. For the voting 2,221 ballots were issued. When the ballot boxes were closed there were 2,210 ballots. There were no invalid ballots. The votes were distributed as follows. There were 2,123 votes in favor of Comrade Gorbachev. There were 87 against him. Thus in the election for chairman of the USSR Supreme Soviet 95.6 percent of the votes of those participating in the secret voting were for Comrade Gorbachev. (Turbulent and prolonged applause)

Thus USSR People's Deputy Comrade Mikhail Sergeyevich Gorbachev was elected chairman of the USSR Supreme Soviet. (Turbulent applause)

V.I. Vorotnikov: Are there questions for the chairman of the counting commission? No questions. A motion is made to approve the counting commission report.

Second Session

25 May 1989

All those in favor of this motion raise your hands. Lower them. Those against? I do not see any. Are there any abstentions? No. The counting commission report is approved.

Thus, according to the results of the secret voting, the Congress of People's Deputies of the Union of Soviet Socialist Republics adopts the following decree "On the Chairman of the USSR Supreme Soviet": "The USSR Congress of People's Deputies hereby decrees: To elect Chairman of the USSR Supreme Soviet Comrade Mikhail Sergeyevich Gorbachev." (Applause).

The floor is turned over to Mikhail Sergeyevich Gorbachev.

M.S. Gorbachev: It is now clear that I must report to you, but I would like to express my deep gratitude for the high confidence you representatives of the Soviet people have placed in me. Thank you very much. (Applause).

I perceive my new duties as an incentive to work with you, the new body of USSR people's deputies, relying on the support we received from the workers in the election, to take advantage of all I have at my disposal, my new opportunities and obligations, to do everything possible to advance our great cause of perestroyka in the interests of the renewal of our society, the development and strengthening of democracy, glasnost, and the improvement of the life and position of man in our society. It is precisely for this and not for anything else that I shall use that which is given to me by my new duties. Have no doubt of that.

And another thing. I regard the results of the voting and the confidence you have shown me today as support for the cause we are championing. And this is an immense motivation to proceed more confidently forward. Let us do it better than we have up to now and let us devote the days of work of the congress and the Supreme Soviet precisely to searching for the most effective ways of moving forward along the path of perestroyka so that in the near future we can find solutions to crucial problems and, of course, lay a solid foundation for our country's advancement along the path to a renewed society. I hope that we shall manage to do this since we now have experience and immense desire and the support of the people. Thank you. (Applause).

V.I. Vorotnikov: Dear comrade deputies! There will be a break until 10 am tomorrow.

FIRST CONGRESS OF PEOPLE'S DEPUTIES OF THE USSR
THIRD SESSION
FRIDAY, 26 MAY 1989
THE KREMLIN PALACE OF CONGRESSES

The main business of the second day of the Congress was the election of the bicameral Supreme Soviet of the USSR. The May 24 pre-Congress assembly of representatives of republic and oblast deputies (dominated, to be sure, by Party secretaries) had already nominated the candidates. The first secretary of the Orel oblast central committee, Yegor S. Stroyev, was designated to present the candidate lists and open the discussion. At the conclusion of Stroyev's report, however, Moscow deputy Tatyana I. Zaslavskaya, director of the Center for the Study of Public Opinion and one of Gorbachev's personal advisers on social matters, raised a different issue.

Citing unidentified informants, Zaslavskaya charged that on the previous evening the militia had dispersed a peaceful crowd of citizens who had gathered to meet with deputies. Using her prerogative as a deputy, she called on the Minister of Internal Affairs to make a formal explanation of the action of the police. She also called on the chairman to put to a vote a pending proposal to suspend the decree on rallies for the duration of the Congress. V.V. Bakatin, the minister, came immediately to the podium to defend the policy of the government and the activities of his subordinates. Rallies and meetings in connection with the Congress had been held without interference in many cities, he reported, and nowhere had there been any arrests. The militia not only had orders not to interfere with meetings of citizens and deputies but, on the contrary, had been instructed to facilitate them. Accordingly, on the previous evening the police had allowed an unauthorized rally in Pushkin Square near the Lira cafe. But, he declared, they had also prevented a crowd, awaiting the appearance of deputies who had been delayed, from advancing on the Borovitsky Gate of the Kremlin or from entering Red Square, where public demonstrations are never permitted.

Several deputies who followed Bakatin to the podium tried without success to discredit his statement while seconding Zaslavskaya's demand to suspend the decree on rallies. It was apparent that the militia, though deployed in force, had done nothing more draconian than mop up drunks drawn to the action. The only excesses that took place seem to have occurred in the imaginations of some constables who perceived two thousand Muscovites strolling toward the Kremlin as descendants of the mob that stormed the Bastille. The effort to besmirch the forces of law and order ignited the wrath of the conservatives who were already in an ugly mood. Gorbachev had to intervene so that Stankevich could finish his remarks. In the end the Congress refused to suspend the decree. The liberals had made their point, however. For the rest of the day from across the empire came telegrams condemning the boorish, undemocratic conduct of the communist elite.

ISSUES IN ELECTING THE SUPREME SOVIET

The election of the Supreme Soviet raised two issues that engaged the Congress well into the evening. One was whether members of the Soviet were to be full time parliamentarians, who therefore would have to quit or be released from their jobs if elected. Article 124 of the constitution provided that deputies elected to the Soviet "can be" freed of their duties "for the entire period" of service. The discussion of that provision disclosed a number of concerns and a range of opinion on the nature of the Soviet and its relation to the Congress of People's Deputies. The issue was most thoughtfully analyzed by Professor V.N. Kudryavtsev, director of the Institute of State and Law, who insisted that the new Supreme Soviet had to be a full-time, working parliament. To weaken it or to establish the Congress of People's Deputies as a biannual legislature would only perpetuate the old system by reducing either or both to a rubber stamp for decrees prepared by the central apparat and issued by its presidium. The Supreme Soviet Presidium, he argued, had to be confined to issuing extraordinary decrees and resolutions, leaving only the Soviet and the Congress to deal with normative acts, each in its own sphere. As for the proposition that all deputies are equal that, he contended, was a lofty but unworkable notion. The distinctions, which he enumerated, were several, but all stemmed from the fact that election to the Soviet conferred responsibilities quite different from those of deputies in general.

The latter could enjoy at best only a consultative voice in the Soviet.

Chairman Gorbachev afforded some insight into his political method when he noted the need to involve experts from various disciplines as consultants to the Soviet. "People who are already generating progressive ideas" should head those advisory groups, but unfortunately "few such people have been elected deputies." To be able to invite such people to fill those roles, he explained, was the reason for amending Article 124 to read that "as a rule" some but not all people would be released from their duties. That was the formula finally adopted by the Congress. But if Gorbachev's goal was to create a more professional legislature, the modification "as a rule" served another purpose as well. It enabled party secretaries, including Gorbachev himself, to serve as deputies while retaining their fulltime state and party posts. Thus in the rule-of-law state, party leaders were to continue to be more equal than mere citizens.

The other major question had to do with the method of electing the Supreme Soviet. The controlling law was Article 111 of the constitution which entrusted the election of both chambers of the Soviet to "a general vote" of the people's deputies. Each chamber was to be elected on the basis of a quota. The quota for the Soviet of Nationalities was prescribed: eleven deputies for each union republic, four for each autonomous republic, two for each autonomous oblast, and one for each autonomous okrug. Population distribution determined quotas for the Soviet of the Union one deputy for each 771,000 citizens. At that ratio Russia, the largest republic, would elect 146 deputies, including 29 who were specifically allocated to the city of Moscow. Much time was wasted by deputies, weaned on Leninist-style single-candidate elections and mistrustful of Muscovites, who could not grasp how the Moscow delegation could nominate 55 candidates for 29 slots and then boldly deny that they meant to exceed their quota.

The Muscovites deliberately "over-nominated" in order to demonstrate their commitment to democratic processes by showing how elections should be held. Their strategy backfired, however, because of the system of negative voting. Under that method, one did not vote for candidates but rather against them by crossing their names off the ballot. Such a system creates a natural bias in favor of the obscure candidate, because those who are well known are more likely to be crossed off. That, in fact, was what happened. The best known Muscovites, including Boris Yeltsin, failed to win election.

Bureaucratic control of the nominating process, which prevailed in most regions, was attacked or ridiculed by several speakers. Deputies like V.P. Zolotukhin and others noted that republic and oblast executives dominated their delegations' lists of nominees. Some, like A.V. Minzhurenko, complained of having "absolutely no chance of bypassing the obkom first secretary and getting onto the Supreme Soviet, any more than there was in the old days." The Congress applauded V.A. Giro, an airline pilot from Tajikistan, who, tongue-in-cheek, solemnly proclaimed that in the interests of perestroika, his delegation was "prepared to sacrifice both the first and second secretaries of the Tajik Communist Party." Ya.Ya. Bezbakh revealed a deficiency of a different kind when he reported that deputies elected in runoffs held after mid-May had been excluded from consideration for the Supreme Soviet. The general antidote, recommended by several deputies, was to contest the elections by expanding candidate lists with nominations from the floor. That was tried, but in the end the strength of the apparatchiks prevailed. At one point Belorussian party chief Yefrem Ye. Sokolov brusquely refused Gorbachev's offer of time to allow his delegation to consider adding deputies nominated from the floor. The persons who made the nominations, declared Sokolov, represented a minority among the delegation, and he curtly advised Gorbachev to "draw your conclusions on that basis."

THE LITHUANIAN CHALLENGE

The climax of the session came late in the afternoon when the Lithuanians' threatened to boycott the election. A number of speakers, including representatives from the Baltic, had been challenging the method prescribed for electing the Soviet of the Union. One view was that a quota-based election meant that there was no difference in the manner of choosing the Soviet of the Union and the Soviet of Nationalities. Another held that as long as candidates were chosen by territorial or public units and presented in single-candidate lists, the Congress would not be electing but merely confirming or delegating deputies to the Soviet (hence the demand to expand the lists and make the process competitive). The extreme view was advanced by the Lithuanian delegation.

The Lithuanian position was first stated during the morning session by V.A. Statulyavichyus, director of the Institute of Mathematics and Cybernetics of the Lithuanian Academy of Sciences. Statulyavichyus argued and then offered an amendment to the effect that delegates to both chambers should be elected by their republics with those elections subsequently ratified by the Congress of People's Deputies. The system prescribed by Article 111 is a charade, he contended, because the deputies cannot hope to know the candidates they are voting for and thus can only pose, dishonestly, as electors.

When V.V. Landsbergis came to the podium in the afternoon, he bluntly confronted the issue that everyone had cautiously been avoiding. The election of representatives, he declared, "is an internal matter touching upon a republic's sovereignty." Just as Lithuania has no right to "interfere" in the affairs of Tajikistan or "trespass on the sovereignty of Moscow," neither does it want their participation in its affairs. Therefore, "do not be surprised that we will be unable to take part in the voting." Gorbachev, clearly shocked, characterized Landsbergis's statement as an ultimatum, proclaimed a "crisis," and appealed to the Lithuanians to reconsider. Others rushed to the podium to second his plea, but the fragility of the liberal coalition on national questions stood exposed. A recess was ordered. Gorbachev and some of his advisers met with the Lithuanians. When the proceedings resumed, Landsbergis expressed regret that his remarks had been misinterpreted. Thus the crisis passed, and the deputies eventually got around to casting their ballots.

Texts of documents cited during the Third Session are compiled in Appendices at the end of volume 2: Constitution (Basic Law) of the USSR, Articles 111, 112, 113, 119, and 124 (Appendix A.1); Decree on the Procedure for Organizing and Holding Meetings, Rallies, Street Processions and Demonstrations in the USSR (Appendix A.3). Members of the Secretariat are listed in Appendix C.2.

THIRD SESSION
FRIDAY, 26 MAY 1989
STENOGRAPHIC RECORD

M.S. Gorbachev, chairman of the USSR Supreme Soviet, is in the chair.

M.S. Gorbachev: Comrades, I declare the sitting open. Let us move on to the next item on the agenda. There are requests from Comrade Zaslavskaya and Comrade Samarin, and I will let them speak later.

The next item on the agenda is the question of electing the USSR Supreme Soviet. A conference of representatives did some work on the eve of the congress. We agreed to hand out what we had worked out to the deputies, so they could have everything on hand and see the lists. But the conference of representatives agreed to have someone speak to describe the candidacies and proposals for the Soviet of the Union and Soviet of Nationalities.

On behalf of the conference of representatives, Deputy Stroyev will speak for the proposal regarding candidates for election to the USSR Supreme Soviet Soviet of the Union.... These will be brief reports. We will listen to them, and then I will give you the floor, Tatyana Ivanovna. Please go ahead, Comrade Stroyev.

Ye.S. Stroyev, first secretary of Orel CPSU Oblast Party Committee [obkom] (Livenskiy Territorial Electoral Okrug, Orel Oblast): Comrade Deputies! According to the USSR Constitution, the Soviet of the Union is elected from among the USSR people's deputies from territorial electoral okrugs and the USSR people's deputies from social organizations while taking into account the number of voters in the union republic or region.

The Soviet of the Union and Soviet of Nationalities are to be equal in size. In view of this 271 USSR people's deputies must be elected to the Soviet of the Union. Candidacies for the Supreme Soviet have been thoroughly discussed at meetings of USSR people's deputies in republics, krays, and oblasts and the people's deputies recommended to serve on the Soviet of the Union have been nominated. These candidacies were approved at the meeting of representatives of the groups of people's deputies held 24 May. The candidates for election to the Soviet of the Union include workers, peasants, representatives of the intelligentsia, prominent figures from science and the arts, and servicemen. The candidates include women, representatives of young people, and war and labor veterans. Thus all social strata and groups of our society and all leading regions of the country will be widely represented in this chamber of the Supreme Soviet. On the instructions of the meeting of representatives, I submit the proposal that the candidates on the list in your possession be included on the ballot paper for the secret ballot on the elections of the Soviet of the Union. If you have looked at this list, you clearly will have noted that more candidates than are to be elected in accordance with the number of voters have been nominated from certain regions, in particular, from Moscow. In other regions the number coincides. The meeting of representatives asks that the list of candidates agreed at its session be examined.

M.S. Gorbachev: Fine.... But I think there's a question. Please go ahead.

From the floor: What about Russia?

Ye.S. Stroyev: So far as Russia is concerned two oblasts have put forward "extra" candidates. Sakhalin has nominated two candidates instead of the one envisaged by

FIRST CONGRESS OF PEOPLE'S DEPUTIES OF THE USSR

Third Session

26 May 1989

the quota. And 55 have been nominated for Moscow instead of 29.

M.S. Gorbachev: This is what we are going to discuss now, comrades. Thank you. Deputy Zaslavskaya has the floor.

T.I. Zaslavskaya, academician and director of the All-Union Center for the Study of Public Opinion on Socioeconomic Questions under the All-Union Central Council of Trade Unions [AUCCTU] and the USSR State Committee for Labor and Social Problems, Moscow, (from scientific societies and associations under the USSR Academy of Sciences): Esteemed comrades. I want to make an extraordinary announcement to you. At midnight yesterday my voters called me and reported that the participants in a rally who had assembled on Pushkin Square in order to meet with deputies (several deputies had promised to meet with the voters, but they were delayed and did not go) went to the Borovitskiy Gate in order to meet with the deputies there. From the reports that were passed on to me I learned that special troops were used to disperse this rally and there were arrests.

As you recall, yesterday Deputy Adamovich put a proposal before us that the operation of the well-known decrees be suspended for the duration of the congress' work, in particular, until such time as the congress can fully analyze these decrees and adopt a final decision. Unfortunately this question was not put to the vote. As you can see, the results are unpleasant. Already here I have heard that something similar happened near the "Lira" cafe. Presumably this could also have happened elsewhere in the country. So I would like to ask the minister of internal affairs to explain the situation to us. Why were such measures taken? That is the first point. The second point. I believe that the question of suspending the operation of the antidemocratic decrees for the entire period of the congress' work should be put to the vote so we can decide it. And, third, we must without fail decide this question and finally make a substantive examination of it, clearly under the heading "Any Other Business" of the agenda we have adopted. That is what I wanted to say. Thank you for your attention. (Applause).

M.S. Gorbachev: The proposal is: In view of Comrade Zaslavskaya's speech, to instruct the minister of internal affairs to give an answer, and during the afternoon. Is Minister Comrade Bakatin here? Here? Can you make a report now? Please go ahead.

V.V. Bakatin, USSR minister of internal affairs: Esteemed comrade deputies! In connection with Comrade Zaslavskaya's request I can report that on the whole in the country the 1st day of the congress' work was greeted very positively, but not always unequivocally. In many regions of the country—I will not list them—impromptu voters' meetings were held, so to speak. People discussed the course of the congress, which, as you know, was relayed in full. Nowhere, in no place, was anyone arrested, anyone dispersed, or any special troops used for that purpose. I state that with total responsibility.

As for the unsanctioned rally that Moscow citizens in advance wanted to hold near the "Lira" cafe in Pushkin Square, on this matter I can report the following. Yesterday in Moscow announcements were posted up near the subway station inviting comrades to this rally. The rally was not authorized by the Moscow City Soviet, and the Moscow militia was told to prohibit the holding of it. We conferred among ourselves in the Ministry of Internal Affairs and decided: Let them hold the rally. The comrades did hold the rally, and the militia did not intervene, did not take any action, and arrested no one. One deputy, I think it was Stankevich but I may be wrong, was there, and I think he spoke. And Comrade Sakharov was there. I don't know, did the militia prevent you from meeting?

Clear instructions were issued that not only were people not to be prevented from meeting with deputies but, on the contrary, this was to be facilitated. At a certain moment a crowd—it may be unpleasant to say it, but we will say it—of citizens decided to go to the Borovitskiy Gate, to the Kremlin, clearly in order to meet with deputies. These actions were stopped. They were simply not admitted, because a specific regime applies to Red Square and the venue for the sittings—the Kremlin Palace of Congresses—and we must safeguard that regime, which is approved by those who are responsible for security during the holding of the Congress of People's Deputies. (Applause).

M.S. Gorbachev: Any questions for Comrade Bakatin? No questions.

From the floor: (Inaudible).

Bakatin: As for hotels, you know there are no militia in hotels.

M.S. Gorbachev: Thank you, Comrade Bakatin.

Z.Z. Vayshvila, senior lecturer at the Lithuanian Council of Ministers Institute for Improving the Qualifications of Leading Cadres and Specialists of the National Economy, (Mazhekskiy National-Territorial Electoral Okrug, Lithuanian Soviet Socialist Republic [SSR]): Yesterday, just after midnight, we two Lithuanian deputies were at the rally. We had heard that it would be held, so we went along to have a look. I can't say anything specific about arrests. But the militia's actions caused tension. Why? The square was surrounded and no one was allowed in to join the participants in the rally. Such behavior on the part of the militia causes resentment and clashes. I draw attention to that fact.

STENOGRAPHIC RECORD

Third Session
26 May 1989

M.S. Gorbachev: Comrade Stankevich, please go ahead.

S.B. Stankevich, senior scientific staffer at the USSR Academy of Sciences General History Institute, (Cheremushkinskiy Territorial Electoral Okrug, Moscow): I will give a very brief report. I was indeed at the rally, after midnight, it is true. I can't say what happened earlier. There were about 2,000 people. They were standing in the square and were indeed very densely surrounded by militia. I am describing the actual situation, comrades. (Murmuring in the hall, applause)

I officially ask the chairman to stop an antidemocratic practice that unfortunately seems to be becoming fashionable at this congress. (Applause). It is disgusting. I was sent here by 380,000 voters, you have no right to shut me up.

M.S. Gorbachev: Comrades! I think we should nevertheless respect the standing orders which we approved, the congress presidium that you elected. I will try to conduct the congress sitting in an organized fashion so it does not degenerate into a farce. Comrade Stankevich, finish your report.

S.B. Stankevich: I'm finishing it. Thus I did indeed not see the milita disperse the participants in the rally. Nevertheless, I think that some actions must be taken. An appropriate place in Moscow must be set aside where citizens could gather, learn the news, and meet with deputies—that is absolutely necessary for normal work by the congress. I make the corresponding request. (Applause).

M.S. Gorbachev: Good. Please go ahead, Comrade Filippov.

V.P. Filippov, director of the PechorNIPIneft [expansion unknown] Institute, (Timanskiy National-Territorial Electoral Okrug, Komi Autonomous Soviet Socialist Republic [ASSR]): Yesterday I unexpectedly found myself witnessing the rally, and I cannot refrain from assessing the remarks that have been made today. I saw and watched the whole thing: The militia did indeed detain people, but they detained drunks who could not stand on their feet. I think that the militia's actions yesterday were correct. (Applause). In general, comrades, you know, this is an unnecessary charging of the atmosphere—it is hampering the normal work of our congress. (Applause).

M.S. Gorbachev: Andrey Dmitriyevich, please.

A.D. Sakharov, academician, chief scientific staffer at the P.N. Lebedev Physics Institute (from the USSR Academy of Sciences): A girl rang me from that rally yesterday—she was weeping because people were surrounded by the militia. I could not come at once, for I did not feel very well yesterday. But still I came, only after Stankevich. And I spoke with those people, with those who still remained there. It was a very good and substantive discussion on the problems of the congress and, in general, about things that concern people. This is our youth, our future, people with an active interest in the congress, with an active interest in everything. And they asked us to come to them in that square, to that very place every day after the congress ends.

Every deputy who wants to meet with our young people can do so. There will be questions, there will be discussions, perhaps there will be arguments, but this is what we must strive for. We cannot move away from the people, and we cannot surround the people with the Dzerzhinskiy Division, the very one that was in Tbilisi and that is now showing its potential strength—in this instance, potential—but we know what they did there. And girls and boys are receiving a negative lesson in Soviet democracy. We cannot allow this.

I subscribe to Deputy Zaslavskaya's proposal to suspend the undemocratic laws on rallies and demonstrations for the duration of the congress and to ensure order, but not to stand in the way of these rallies and demonstrations, at any rate during the congress. And we must discuss what to do next. But there must be no obstacles now, during the congress. By this we also compromise the congress. (Applause).

M.S. Gorbachev: Let us hand over to another deputy, and then we will discuss the question of whether to continue the discussion. Please.

Yu.T. Akbarov, driver for the No 2 Motor Vehicle Combine, Tashkent City (Tashkentskiy-Akmal-Ikramovskiy Territorial Electoral Okrug): Dear comrade deputies. I am a driver. During my shift I convey a large number of people of different nationalities, different origins, and different specialties in a day. And I have heard from every mouth that so many problems face our people which we must resolve today. But we are engaging in demagoguery here. After all, we have come here to work, not to cultivate demagoguery.

Comrades, think better of it: What are you doing? For our precious time is being wasted absolutely uselessly. After all, we must do what has to be done. We must work, comrades. (Applause).

M.S. Gorbachev: Deputy Zubanov writes: "I beg the hall not to 'shut out' speakers on delicate questions of the nationalities policy and the holding of rallies but to calmly hear them out and allow the chairman calmly to find a way out of complex situations."

So, shall we continue discussing this question or not? I will put it to the vote. Whoever is in favor of stopping the discussion, please raise your mandate cards. Please lower them.

STENOGRAPHIC RECORD

Third Session

26 May 1989

Who is against? Who has abstained? A clear minority.

Now there is a proposal to take into consideration the reply of the USSR minister of internal affairs to Deputy Zaslavskaya's question. No objections? No.

And again. There is a proposal to entrust the Moscow City Soviet, with regard to this debate, with finding an opportunity to hold rallies, for example, in the Luzhniki region. Rallies gathered there, incidentally, before the congress, until very recently. I believe that the Moscow City Soviet must resolve this question, so that people know where they can gather, meet with deputies, and ask them questions. This is the first point. And, second, let us consider that we do not cast doubt on the question now. This is a special question, and we will discuss it as we agreed at the congress, what to do about and with the aforesaid decrees. I believe that we must agree with the fact that rallies will be held, but on condition that order is observed and that this does not harm anything, including the city's life. (Applause).

If you do not object, let the comrades in Moscow realize these practical assignments of ours.

From the floor: Mikhail Sergeyevich, we, the Lithuanian SSR delegation, beg to put a question to the vote.

M.S. Gorbachev: Which question?

From the floor: To suspend the USSR Supreme Soviet Presidium decree "On the Procedure for Organizing and Holding Meetings, Rallies, Street Processions, and Demonstrations in the USSR" of 28 July 1988.

M.S. Gorbachev: Do you propose suspending the decree on rallies for the duration of the congress? Since this topic is present here all the time, I will put this question to the vote. Whoever is in favor of suspending the decree relating to rallies during the work of the congress, please vote.

Yu.A. Osipyan, chairman of the Tellers Commission: Comrade deputies! Results of the vote: "For"—831.

M.S. Gorbachev: Who is against? While the comrades are counting, I will tell you that Comrade Zaykov writes that the question of holding rallies was discussed at the Moscow City Soviet this morning. A decision was adopted to permit the holding of a rally in Luzhniki during the congress. (Applause).

Yu.A. Osipyan: Results of the vote: Against—1,261. (Applause).

M.S. Gorbachev: Who abstained? Count them. Comrades, we are asking speakers not to repeat themselves and to stick to the point. We must now resolve urgent questions. We must find a sensible solution with regard to yesterday and today.

Yu.A. Osipyan: Thirty people abstained.

M.S. Gorbachev: The question is decided. But what does decided mean, comrades? We do not suspend the decrees, but the decrees do not prevent the holding of rallies. It should not look as though the congress is supplementing this decree with something new. And I must say: For all our criticism of this decree, refusals and bans make up 5 or 6 percent. Clearly, questions arise with regard to individual rallies. This is the point at issue.

A.S. Samsonov, director of the First Moscow S.M. Kirov Clock and Watch Plant (Proletarskiy Territorial Electoral Okrug, Moscow City): I am not in favor of deputies discussing here what happened, but I am in favor of there being some elementary order. With regard to yesterday's rally. I address the deputies, primarily from Moscow and its oblast, who, in addition to the internal affairs organs, must ensure order in Moscow. (Applause).

The first and most important question. Some rally was held yesterday. Comrades Sakharov and Stankevich, why did you not tell me yesterday that this rally was being held? Am I not a deputy? Can I not participate in it? And, second, I was elected from the 20th, Proletarskiy Okrug, and Comrade Stankevich, as I understand it, from Cheremushkinskiy Rayon. Why do you suddenly turn up in Pushkin Square? You should occupy yourself with your own voters.

I submit a specific proposal on this question. There is a territorial okrug. We have organized things like this: There is a voters' club, where they await the deputy's report on what is being done at the congress. Yesterday they waited for me until 8 o'clock, they listened to the relay and realized that I would not be able to be present. But today we have agreed to meet, in the dinner break for example, when it is convenient. For we are perfectly well aware that we must not close our eyes to all these things and that we can try to influence the voters as is necessary.

M.S. Gorbachev: I believe we must synthesize two proposals: Above all, of course, there are voters' clubs in okrugs, and I think that every deputy, particularly in Moscow, having an invitation from the spot, must go to these clubs, meet, and chat. But this does not do away with the procedure that a deputy can participate in meetings wherever he wants to. I believe that both are democratic. But Comrade Samsonov's advice is correct—it is necessary to work with one's own deputies and not forget them.

Comrades are standing next to the rostrum, waiting to speak, and I feel even uncomfortable in front of them.

STENOGRAPHIC RECORD

Third Session
26 May 1989

But let us reach an agreement. Are we going to move ahead on the chief question? Let us discuss. It is true I have a debt from yesterday: I promised to hand over to a deputy from the Baltic republics.

But for now I wish to put the question like this: Will we vote, or will we continue after this speech the discussion of the chief question? So, do we discuss the chief question?

From the floor: Yes.

M.S. Gorbachev: So, whoever is in the line wishing to speak not on the chief question, please take your seats and...sit quietly. If anyone wishes to discuss the question of the Soviet of the Union, please write notes or raise your hand. And I also ask the comrades on the secretariat to place about 10 chairs in the aisles by the rostrum. Those who are standing here, waiting to speak, sometimes get in the way of other deputies. Let us place 10 chairs, and comrades will approach and occupy them. So there will be no need to move representatives of the press. You yourselves insisted on broad coverage of the congress....

Good, good.... We will hand over to you, but please introduce yourself.

G.-I.A. Kakaras, chief of the astronomical observatory of the Lithuanian SSR Academy of Sciences Physics Institute (Ukmergskiy National Territorial Okrug, Lithuanian SSR): Deeply esteemed deputies! I wanted to congratulate you on the start of the academic year in the 5-year polytechnical institute in the "democratization by parliamentary means" faculty. We have made a good start. And a Lithuanian proverb states: "A good beginning is half the work." To ensure that its second half is no worse—and I believe we will work not just 1 or 2 days and not just 1 or 2 years—I have two proposals.

First, I propose setting up several microphones in all the aisles, so that we feel identically equal. Both the presidium and the whole congress. So that, because of polite little rejoinders and questions, we do not have to run the length of the hall or shout as in a forest with little hope of being heard.

The second proposal. The voting is proceeding OK here. But when particularly important alternative variants start to be decided, when opinion divides around the 50-percent mark, I believe that one vote teller in each sector will not be enough. He might make a mistake. Therefore I propose allocating three or, at the very least, two deputies in each sector. Thank you for your attention.

M.S. Gorbachev: This is what I think: Let us still conduct the main work through this rostrum. Let us not organize a bazaar. Because I see, nonetheless, that this is to some extent what we have. We must rule this out. The congress' work as a whole yesterday is, I know, perceived as a very great event proceeding in a form that is open to the people. But there are already comments too—will the deputies get down to business soon?

I believe that we are, of course, getting down to business. But it is, nonetheless, clearly a question of form. And we must be organized here.

Now as regards microphones. Still, if the question arises, I think we must organize them by Monday—this is what we agreed. And, as questions arise, entrust the services group of the presidium secretariat with handing a microphone to those who wish to ask something. But no speeches are to be made over these microphones. Speeches are to be made from the rostrum. Someone has put a question and introduced himself. If we deem it necessary, we will hand over—then speak.

How suitable is this, comrades? Because there are also more drastic proposals. If I read everything out, there will be a storm here now.... I am summing up ideas so that we do not suspect each other of anything. Thus, we will implement the first part of your proposal—with regard to microphones.

I.A. Andreyeva, chief art critic at the All-Union House of Clothes Patterns, secretary of the board of the USSR Designers Union (from the USSR Designers' Union): This is my question. I have familiarized myself with the lists which we have received today—for the Soviet of Nationalities and the Soviet of the Union. Long, interesting lists. Although it is a pity there are no alternative ones. But I have a question to put to the presidium, although partly also to the congress. Do people who have agreed to nominate their candidacy for the Supreme Soviet really believe that they must leave their work? And must they leave their work in order to be professional parliamentarians, so to speak? This question occurred to me in connection with the list. I have a small proposal. It must be entered in our standing orders that people not bang to stop speakers. Let them raise their hand, and the chairman will let them speak. I believe that will be simpler.

M.S. Gorbachev: Comrades! As regards the first part, clearly this is very important. Because everyone is weighing up whether or not to have to do with the Supreme Soviet. We proceed from the premise that a significant part, the bulk of the Supreme Soviet, will work on a permanent basis. These are the people who head the chambers and their deputies, and those who head the commissions and committees and their deputies. But, in addition, quite a substantial group in each commission must also be permanent. So, evidently, the bulk of those who join the Supreme Soviet will work on a permanent basis. I will now explain why not all. Because we are interested in not losing those who do not wish to leave some job, while the presence of this competent person would be useful in the Supreme Soviet. This is my

STENOGRAPHIC RECORD

Third Session

26 May 1989

reasoning. But in general, as the saying goes, we must go further, and then everything will be cleared up. I believe that not even Comrade Burlatskiy will give an answer to this now. Even though he has expressed a proposal here, and thought about these questions, I believe we will acquire experience, comrades. But still the bulk will be permanent. And the others will also have to devote a considerable part of their time to participating in the work of the Supreme Soviet.

M.S. Gorbachev [repeated name as published]: Do you wish to speak on this question, comrade?

V.A. Statulyavichyus, vice president of the Lithuanian SSR Academy of Sciences, director of the Lithuanian SSR Academy of Sciences Institute of Mathematics and Cybernetics, Vilnius City (Utenskiy National Territorial Electoral Okrug, Lithuanian SSR): Yes.

M.S. Gorbachev: Fine, speak.

V.A. Statulyavichyus: I believe that before discussing candidacies we must without fail resolve the question of the voting procedure. As the senior person, I put forward this proposal on behalf of the entire Lithuanian delegation: Voting for both chambers of the Supreme Soviet should be conducted by republics. And only then should the voting protocols be approved. Why? Because in our time of restructuring the most important thing, I believe, is honesty. This is the 3d or 4th day now that we have been discussing the system of our elections, voting, and so forth. But how can we vote for unknown people? I believe this is dishonest.

I was at the meeting of representatives. There, too, you understand, it was a little bit formal. Lists giving people's posts were read out, then a great many comments were made from the auditorium on the need to speed up the procedure, and to that end to read out only the surnames. But what do surnames signify, especially now? Suppose that even for Moscow we have to strike out the superfluous candidates, and suppose I know my colleagues. But there is a revolution going on here. I do not know how their views have changed over the last 2-3 years: whether they are active fighters for restructuring or are only hampering it (I do not think there is anyone like that among the deputies). If we are to vote honestly, to strike out names or leave them on, then all these people must be heard here. We must listen to their platforms. Otherwise it would be a procedure of the stagnation type. But we do not have time for this, and therefore we have to trust the republics.

I think, Mikhail Sergeyevich, that the presidium's proposal is based on the assumption that we trust the republics. And since we are trusting them, let the republics vote. Therefore I propose an amendment to Article 111 of the existing USSR Constitution. Paragraph 2 should read: "The USSR Supreme Soviet is elected by groups from the republics from among USSR people's deputies at the Congress of USSR People's Deputies and is ratified by the Congress, remaining subordinate to it."

Since I will not be appearing on this platform again, I would like to ask Mikhail Sergeyevich something.

All of us deputies from the Baltic region met to discuss the decree, and the majority voted in favor of suspending it. But in our letter (the USSR Supreme Soviet has it) the reasoning was that this decree is contrary to the existing USSR Constitution. I propose that our representatives meet with lawyers and discuss the matter. If there are no contradictions with the USSR Constitution, leave it alone. But if it is contrary to the Constitution...

M.S. Gorbachev: Let us include this question in "Miscellaneous," as we said yesterday. We will come back to it later and we will all discuss it.

V.A. Statulyavichyus: I thought sooner....

M.S. Gorbachev: Yes, I understand. I have to give the floor, let the comrades who are standing (they have chosen that method for themselves) forgive me, but I have to give the floor to Deputy Ginzburg, because his note arrived earlier, and then to Comrade Kirillov, who asked yesterday to speak on the composition of the Supreme Soviet.

V.L. Ginzburg, academician, adviser to the directorate of the P.N. Lebedev Physics Institute of the USSR Academy of Sciences, Moscow (from the USSR Academy of Sciences): I wish to recall that under Article 112 of the USSR Constitution the Supreme Soviet is convened every year for spring and fall sessions of 3-4 months duration each. There may be extraordinary sessions. There are very many questions now, and it is clear that the Supreme Soviet should sit permanently and spend, so to speak, a great deal of time at work. It seems to me that the point of dividing us into the Supreme Soviet and all the other deputies, although we are equal, is precisely to single out some kind of group to work actively all the time. A Soviet parliament, as has been said. Therefore it seems to me that we should elect to the Supreme Soviet people who really consciously seek this and can devote a considerable proportion of their time to working here.

Second. The following is a very important proposal. In a year's time we will elect part of the Supreme Soviet again. I would like there to be reports in a year's time on how the Supreme Soviet members have carried out their duties. When we carry out this rotation, what will it be based on? It is very important to base it on how a person has worked, and to remove those who have done poor work.

Third. I was not intending to speak about this. But I strongly disagree with the previous speaker. Elections to the Soviet of Nationalities are, of course, a different

Third Session
26 May 1989

matter. It represents individual republics. But the Soviet of the Union is an all-union organ, and the stronger its unionwide unity the better. Yet we want to introduce some kind of separatism.

M.S. Gorbachev: Fine. A philosophical exchange is now under way; next it will be down to personalities. I give the floor to Deputy Kirillov.

V.I. Kirillov, senior scientific staffer at the Voronezh Polytechnical Institute (Leninskiy Territorial Electoral Okrug, Voronezh City): From the viewpoint of democracy, it is of fundamental importance that a two-chamber parliament has not only different candidates, but different voters, too. If in the elections to the Soviet of Nationalities, which provides guarantees for national minorities in the USSR, the only voters, in accordance with the proposed procedure, are representatives of the delegations—and that is correct—then in the elections to the Soviet of the Union—whose task is to safeguard unionwide interests, the interests of all citizens of a region regardless of their nationalities—then all the delegates should vote.

In the elections to the Soviet of the Union it is necessary to ensure that the principle of alternatives is observed. How can this be done without infringing the rights of regions? A certain number of seats should be reserved for each region, as is clear from the USSR Constitution. The region nominates all candidates, with the exception of those who have withdrawn of their own accord. The Congress votes. Those elected are the candidates who have collected more votes than the other representatives of that delegation who laid claim to the given number of places reserved for it. Only in this way will we be able to take account of the interests of citizens of nonindigenous nationality in the national republics and okrugs. That is all. Thank you.

M.S. Gorbachev: Comrade Samarin registered on this question too. Comrade Samarin, where are you?

V.I. Samarin, own correspondent for the newspaper ORLOVSKAYA PRAVDA, Orel City (Orlovskiy Territorial Electoral Okrug, RSFSR [Russian Soviet Federated Socialist Republic]): I have a question that directly concerns the formation of the Soviet of the Union and the Soviet of Nationalities. Much has already been said today about the fact that these organs should be working organs, that they should work permanently for at least 8 months, if not more. Therefore the appearance in both the Soviet of the Union and the Soviet of Nationalities of a large number of people who at the same time hold high, responsible party posts means that they will not be able to fulfill these functions properly. I can give you a real example from our own Orel Oblast. We arrived here, and at the very last, the very latest moment Deputy Yegor Semenovich Stroyev arrived—the first secretary of the party obkom. He said: "Comrades, every day I spend in the oblast is precious to me." And if a party obkom first secretary spends 8 months, or even 6, at sessions of the Supreme Soviet chambers, I can imagine what will happen in the oblast.

My proposal is to examine this question. That does not mean that we do not trust the party. There are party committee secretaries and party raykom [rayon committee] secretaries too. But a party obkom secretary, the leader of a large party organization, is elected at a party conference and all the oblast's Communists place their trust in him. I believe that this question must be discussed here and considered.

And a second proposal: On the Soviet of the Union and the Soviet of Nationalities there are, strange as it may seem, representatives of not union, but republican executive power. In one way or another they find their way, of course, onto committees and commissions on problems that they themselves are involved with, because they are professionals in their field. But I think that in that case the laws they draft will be drafted with a view to how far these laws will suit them. There are two such representatives on the Soviet of the Union and six representatives on the Soviet of Nationaltiies. I think we should submit for discussion by the Congress these important questions—the representation of party leaders, major leaders, leaders of republic Communist Party Central Committee and party obkoms and kraykoms [kray committees], and the representation, or rather the undesirable representation, of people who hold executive posts. This proposal is, in my view, very important. I would like to hear a competent opinion on this score.

M.S. Gorbachev: Fine. There are many notes here, comrades. I must say this. The notes I have set aside say that the congress should operate strictly according to the standing orders and no one should depart from them. Let me remind you that some comrades have already used the right to speak more than once in a single day, and the standing orders provide for only two speeches. But I think that in this case, in the discussion of this question, it is rather a different matter. In discussing a report—yes, but in discussing candidacies, you cannot avoid repeated interventions. But this is what they write; I will read it: "Esteemed Mikhail Sergeyevich, when will the Moscow group of deputies stop causing disorganization and confusion in the congress' work? The standing orders should be applied to them too. They are dragging out the work of the congress. Is this not deliberate? Deputies Kislitsyn, Karpochev, Gorinov." (Applause.) That is for the deputies from Moscow to think about. I do not think this is some kind of reprimand or anything of that nature. It is information, for consideration. (Applause.)

Borkovets, V.I., team leader at the "Sayanmramor" Production Association, Sayanogorsk City (Khakasskiy Territorial Electoral Okrug, RSFSR): On 24 May at the council of representatives the question of candidates for

STENOGRAPHIC RECORD

Third Session

26 May 1989

all the chambers was discussed, in particular those from Krasnoyarsk Kray. Three candidacies were submitted. Comrade Vorotnikov stated that Krasnoyarsk Kray had not exceeded its quota, and everything was in order. Nonetheless we discovered on the lists that we are one candidate short, namely Arkadiy Filimonovich Veprev. We insist that the third candidacy from Krasnoyarsk Kray be included.

B.F. Pylin, lieutenant colonel, senior instructor at the Kacha Myasnikov Higher Military Pilots' School, Volgograd City (Sovetskiy Territorial Electoral Okrug, RSFSR): Comrade deputies! For 3 days before the congress we discussed the question of elections, but we confined ourselves mainly to when to hold the elections to the Supreme Soviet—at the beginning, in the middle, or at the end of the congress' work—but it seems to me that we should have discussed the question of how to hold them. And here, in my view, not everything is yet clear. We now represent three major contingents—deputies elected from territorial okrugs, national-territorial okrugs, and social organizations. But now within the framework of the existing USSR Constitution we are forced to create only two soviets, not three—there is no provision for a Soviet of Social Organizations.

What is the way out of this situation? It is this, comrades, it seems to me—to create a Supreme Soviet of not 542 people, but 812, and thus we will spare ourselves the need for yet another cohort of deputies who will occupy some kind of intermediate position, that is, who will not be Supreme Soviet deputies, but will work on the commissions.

I propose that a quota of a total of 270 people be allocated to the social organizations, and that they be elected as follows—36 deputies each from the Communist Party, the trade unions, and the cooperative unions, and 27 each from the other social organizations. The elections should be held in two stages, by secret ballot. At the first stage there should be elections by regions, that is, not only republics, but oblasts; too. The RSFSR is so big that we do not know all the deputies. There should be separate elections for the social organizations. The Communist Party, for instance, should elect 36 deputies to the Supreme Soviet out of its 100 deputies, and so forth. And the rotation should proceed on this basis.

To conclude. At the second stage there should be a general ballot of deputies, and if a given deputy does not secure two-thirds of the vote, then the social organization or region, accordingly, puts forward a new deputy. As it is, comrades, I perceive an attempt by the Moscow deputies to get a larger number onto the Supreme Soviet, because if they now strike out all the other deputies, they will receive the biggest number, and all 56 of those proposed will get onto the Supreme Soviet. We should not permit that, either.

M.S. Gorbachev: Fine. The next registered is Comrade Fedorov.

A.I. Konovalov, rector of Kazan State University (Vakhitovskiy National-Territorial Electoral Okrug, Tatar ASSR): Esteemed chairman, esteemed deputies! You see, I am not from the Moscow group, but perhaps some people may feel that what I am going to say is dragging out the work of our forum. But I think it is too soon to discuss the list of names. For several days we have been saying that it is necessary to define what the Supreme Soviet is and what the congress is.

It is necessary to define the status of deputy: what rights an ordinary congress deputy will have, what rights a Supreme Soviet deputy will have. We know nothing about this; we do not know about the composition of the committees, the composition of the commissions; we have not made that decision.

Of course, there were correct assurances, I understand, that these questions will be examined and resolved. By whom? And when?

I believe that these questions should be decided here, and before the Supreme Soviet is elected, because the elections must be held quite consciously in the light of who is going to work where, how, and in what way. There are a lot of people here who are in a hurry, forgive me, but I think that after all, we are really discussing fundamental questions. I do not know about many of those present, but I am aware of the attention and the pressure that there is now from the voters. I, for instance, am already receiving questions from voters asking why Article 110 of the USSR Constitution has been violated. In the name of the principle of expediency we all proclaimed the principle of a rule-of-law state, but nonetheless we violated a matter of principle; I will not go back to that.

A second question. Again from voters. Surely you are not going once again to turn yourselves into representatives of an all-union okrug meeting? Surely you are not going to vote on a list, one by one, without discussion, without knowing the people who will be elected or in what form? That should have been considered beforehand. It should have been considered and discussed at the meetings that took place with people's deputies. Not the formal, futile kind of meeting, but real working meetings.

Now about the work of the congress. As yet we do not have any documents or information from individual delegations. Documents were handed over yesterday for distribution among the deputies, but we don't have them. We don't have even elementary things. Anybody who goes to a scientific congress immediately receives a list of all the participants—but we don't have a list of deputies.

A great deal is determined from above, of course, and the resultant line is implemented; we can feel it. But for all

STENOGRAPHIC RECORD

Third Session
26 May 1989

that let us be aware that we are the people's representatives, as we have repeatedly said. The people hold us responsible and consider that it is not always the case that a CPSU Central Committee Plenum decision corresponds to the people's opinion. We became convinced of this when the question of Yeltsin arose. We became convinced of it when the people were discussing the "party hundred" [the 100 deputies elected from the CPSU]. So let us not decide the question today on the basis of our congress "500." Thank you for your attention. (Applause).

M.S. Gorbachev: I got the impression that there were no specific proposals. But the question was put. So comrades who speak hereafter should take this into account and enrich the question under discussion with specific arguments.

S.N. Fedorov, general director of the "Ocular Microsurgery" intersector scientific and technical complex and chairman of the Soviet Charity and Health Foundation (from the CPSU): Dear comrade deputies! I have listened to several speeches here, and it seems to me that we are still living in a country divided into little princedoms in which the princedoms are fighting each other, and so each one wants to choose an emissary of its own to defend its interests here in Moscow.

It seems to me that the task of all elections, the task of the entire people is to elect to the Supreme Soviet—precisely the Supreme Soviet—not representatives of regions, not some incomprehensible name with no meaning behind it (why has Smolensk teamed up with Bryansk, and Tambov with some place else?) What we have here are totally incomprehensible geographical principles. I consider that we must elect to the Supreme Soviet the intellect of the nation; this was the principle on which the people elected us. And if we do believe that we should elect not people with a civic attitude, not honest and noble people who will tackle the problems of the entire country, but merely defenders of some single region, some locality—well, the Soviet of Nationalities exists for that. We must not resolve merely regions' egoistical interests here; we must resolve common interests, and we must integrate these interests.

We must make restructuring on the basis of restructuring. We created a state based on state monopoly ownership which we now wish to restructure, and the first words of the party's appeal to the peoples are as follows: The development of diverse forms of ownership, the enhancement of the role of the individual, and the transformation of the person from an appendage of the state technological machine into an individual, a free man. The principles of Marxism—a free man engaged in free labor—must be translated into reality in the Soviet Union. But today we are an appendage of an enormous state machine and incomprehensible ministries, which in my view are destroying the country, an appendage of various other structures; and evidently only intelligent people united in the Supreme Soviet can smash this machine, which nobody needs and which has not justified itself, and create a free state. (Applause).

M.S. Gorbachev: It would be desirable for comrades who are going to speak subsequently to heed the thoughts expressed on these questions....

S.N. Fedorov: This is why the Moscow delegation decided that simply the entire congress would choose who will be Muscovites' representatives from among the 55 candidates. Choose who you like. Whether you want sensible people or not is up to you.

M.S. Gorbachev: No, comrades. I wish to defend the Muscovites; I also belong to the Moscow group. Moscow nominated 50-plus people, but it has a quota of 29. And they agreed that Moscow would be singled out on the ballot paper, which will state that its quota is 29 deputies but 55 are put forward. Those who vote will choose who to leave out. They are relying on the will of the congress.

Comrades, I have two notes. On these questions.

The first note: "Elections to the Soviet of the Union and Soviet of Nationalities should be conducted secretly by republic and region. Second, the results of these elections should be ratified at the congress, having passed through the Credentials Commission first. Third, we should move on to the third item on the agenda."

Heed that.

The second note: "At the meeting of the Moscow deputies group it was stated: 'Let every deputy state definitely whether he agreeable to leaving his job to work permanently on the Supreme Soviet.' Given these conditions deputies who are leaders of creative unions or major figures active in culture and science withdrew their candidacies from the list of candidates for membership of the Supreme Soviet. Today you have expressed a different notion of the work of a Supreme Soviet member which would also have a substantial impact on the Moscow list. I ask you to read this out. Platonov."

I have read out these notes to sum up all the ideas on this question, so to speak.

A.N. Boyko, head of department at Donetsk State University (Donetskiy-Voroshilovskiy Territorial Electoral Okrug, Ukrainian SSR): Esteemed comrades! As you can see, colossal procedural difficulties lie ahead of us in resolving this question, and passions are becoming heated. I am convinced that we will have as many variant options as we have people coming up here to speak and notes being passed to the platform. How is this problem to be resolved?

It is first necessary to ascertain the factors and then, naturally, seek solutions. There are two factors here. We

STENOGRAPHIC RECORD

Third Session
26 May 1989

have obviously already talked about one of them—the inequality of deputies, which naturally arises in connection with this two-tier approach. And the second factor has also been talked about, but maybe not very clearly. I wish to say that in many republics—not all, but many—the apparatus method of nomination was used. We are very well aware what this apparatus method of nomination is. We also know its results. In this connection a proportion of deputies—an extremely significant proportion, I think—are also worried on this score. So what decision can be made to lessen the tension here and facilitate the solution of this question?

Back during the preliminary stages the group of deputies from Donetsk Oblast made a suggestion, and I would like to repeat it. It seems to me that we are making very poor use of an extremely radical means which we possess, namely making amendments to the USSR Constitution. Look, Article 111 states: "The USSR Supreme Soviet is the permanently functioning legislative, administrative [rasporyaditelnyy], and monitoring organ of USSR state power." All we have to do now it to vote to insert the following wording: that "...it is the permanently functioning, working, executive [ispolnitelnyy], and monitoring organ of USSR state power," and then, I am sure, the fuss over this question will abate sharply. And the principle of what deputies represent—a territory, men, women, organizations, or whatever—will not be of substantial significance for the simple reason that everyone will be placed in an equal position. It's just that some will be permanent members of commissions or committees, while others won't be permanent. But they will have an absolutely equal voice. Then there will be no infringement of status. That is the solution I would propose, and I request that the question be put to the vote.

A second point. Since it's not so easy to get to this rostrum, I will jump ahead and submit an amendment on another question. Since we wish to assert the full power of the soviets, we definitely need to include in Article 113 of the USSR Constitution a point on the possibility of votes of no confidence in the USSR Government and members of the government. I request a vote on this amendment. But, I repeat, this relates to another question.

And finally, I would like to ask Mikhail Sergeyevich Gorbachev to put a stop to the "gagging" methods which some comrades here are allowing themselves. And to express my extreme indignation at the statement of that "people's representative" who is already demanding today that he be shielded from the people by a "wall of China." (Applause).

M.S. Gorbachev: I'm going to sort out those who have written notes and those who want to speak from the floor. Comrade Zolotukhin says that he has already written four notes. I've got the fourth one, and so I give the floor to Comrade Zolotukhin.

V.P. Zolotukhin, permanent correspondent of the Turkestan Military District newspaper FRUNZEVETS (Tashkentskiy-Kuybyshevskiy Electoral Okrug, Uzbek SSR). Comrades, I agree with the previous speaker that as yet we have not determined precisely what we are electing: a working organ or a parliament which will adopt laws and determine our country's life. I therefore consider it important, before we start voting and discussing candidacies, to adopt Comrade Sakharov's proposal that the congress adopt a Decree on the Congress of People's Deputies, and have it determined by the supreme organ of state power in our country. Since this question has still not been resolved yet, the question of the composition of the Supreme Soviet assumes fundamental significance.

Yesterday there was a great deal of talk about combining jobs. If we are talking about the job of head of state, that is a political question. The current question is purely practical. Who is going to work on the USSR Supreme Soviet, and whether he will be able to work at full capacity, is of very great importance. I am worried about this because, for example, the people being proposed for election to the Supreme Soviet from our republic delegation include the first secretary of the republic Communist Party Central Committee, the chairman of the republic Supreme Soviet Presidium, the first deputy chairman of the republic Council of Ministers, the chairman of the republic State Planning Commission, the chairman of the republic People's Control Committee, and three obkom first secretaries. I am very worried about how these comrades are going to combine their jobs. (Applause).

And another point. I felt somewhat insulted by the statement that our country's intellect is concentrated in Moscow. What does this mean, that only stupid people live in Uzbekistan? This is not so. Therefore I believe that we still must proceed from the premise that republics should be assigned quotas and their delegations should vote on the matter. But here we must also rule out any chance of an undemocratic principle in the shaping of deputies' groups. So far, the proposal by our republic is not the collectively elaborated viewpoint of the Uzbek delegation. Not even a formal vote was taken in our republic on these candidacies.

Therefore I propose, first of all, that when voting congress deputies should show respect for the republics' proposals on candidacies and trust them. And in order to democratically formulate these proposals, it is absolutely necessary to have a discussion and secret ballot in the republics for election to the USSR Supreme Soviet. This is all I have to say. (Applause).

Ya.Ya. Bezbakh, team leader at the Nizhnedneprovskiy K. Liebknecht Pipe-Rolling Plant open-hearth shop basic production section (Industrialnyy Territorial Okrug, Dnepropetrovsk City): I have a brief address to the Congress. We USSR people's deputies elected at

STENOGRAPHIC RECORD

Third Session
26 May 1989

runoffs after 14 May 1989 found ourselves at a disadvantage compared with the other people's deputies, since the nomination of candidates for the USSR Supreme Soviet at meetings of representatives was done without our participation.

We found out only today, when we received the documents, that the opportunity for choice in the nomination of candidates from the Ukraine was ruled out; in other words, 52 candidates were nominated for the proposed 52 seats in the Supreme Soviet. In order to restore justice, we demand: Before coming to the vote on the Supreme Soviet's composition, our republic's delegation should be given an opportunity, with our participation, to add to or amend the initial list of candidates suggested for election to the Supreme Soviet. Should this opportunity be denied, we demand the inclusion of all the following candidates on the ballot papers for the secret vote from the Ukrainian SSR. There are six of us, and we handed the lists to the presidium yesterday. (Applause).

M.S. Gorbachev: Comrade Deputy Gabrusev wrote the following letter: "I ask that the question of a deputy's status be put to the vote—should he retain his main job or not, in the event of being elected to the Supreme Soviet? If we resolve the question of USSR people's deputies resigning their main jobs, then the formation of the Supreme Soviet will be immediately simplified, since by no means everyone would give up a cushy job for the sake of restructuring. (Applause). Only then should we go on to elect. I ask that this be read at voters' request."

Comrades, even though we are now clarifying the philosophical aspect, specific questions are also being raised. And so, Comrade Bogomolov, we are implementing what was stated in your note [as published].

O.T. Bogomolov, director of the USSR Academy of Sciences Economics of the World Socialist System Institute (Sevastopolskiy Territorial Electoral Okrug, Moscow City): I would like to say how difficult it is for us to make a choice today without having clarified the distribution of functions between the Congress of People's Deputies and the Supreme Soviet, and also without having introduced sufficient clarity as regards the activity of the Supreme Soviet and the deputies who will not be elected to the Supreme Soviet.

With his speech yesterday Mikhail Sergeyevich quelled many deputies' fears that they might end up only as electors [vyborshchik] and participants in annual parliamentary debates unless they are elected to the Supreme Soviet. But I still feel that some things are still unclear.

Under the Constitution the congress is the supreme organ of state power and is vested with legislative and monitoring functions, since the Supreme Soviet is subordinate to it. But in contrast to the Supreme Soviet, the Constitution makes no provision for parliamentary mechanisms which would ensure that the congress can perform these functions, as the commissions of the chambers and the committees for the most important matters of state will be formed from among Supreme Soviet deputies by the Supreme Soviet with participation by congress deputies—but it is unclear whether they will have a vote or a consultative voice.

My proposal is that the congress should form committees for the most important matters of state on the principle that there is parity between Supreme Soviet members and congress deputies not elected to the Supreme Soviet, with both having a vote. It seems to me that, maybe in contrast to the Supreme Soviet, these committees should not work in continuous sessions lasting 3 or 4 months but should assemble several times a year for shorter sessions to examine the most important matters of state.

And one more consideration in this context. It is very important to ensure that these committees should bring together truly professional people familiar with various problems, and that these people should be able to work throughout the duration of their term, so that one-fifth of these committees' membership is not renewed every year, as responsibility for the elaboration of decisions and the high standards of professionalism demand that members of these committees should work on them for a long enough period. I would ask that these considerations be taken into account.

M.S. Gorbachev: Go ahead, Comrade Murashev.

A.N. Murashev, scientific associate of the USSR Academy of Sciences High Temperatures Institute (Timiryazevskiy Territorial Electoral Okrug, Moscow City): Comrades, here is what I would like to say. It seems to me that a kind of neurotic and unhealthy atmosphere has developed around the Moscow delegation and its proposals. And what was said by the lieutenant colonel who spoke here indicates that maybe not everyone has actually understood the essence of these proposals.

We do not claim a single extra seat on the Supreme Soviet Soviet of the Union. Our quota of 29 seats will be rigorously observed whatever happens. The list of Moscow deputies containing more names than the quota is an act of good will; it is an act expressing confidence in the congress to prevent the approval of already compiled lists. After all, any quota principles and any elections by republics are remnants of past mistrust of one another. We wanted to create a precedent of trust, and we do not claim a single seat.

In this context, I propose the following amendment to the secret ballot procedure: To accept as valid also any

STENOGRAPHIC RECORD

Third Session

26 May 1989

ballot papers which contain the names of more than 271 candidates. In this way, people who deem it impossible on ethical grounds to interfere in the choice between people from other regions and republics who are unknown to them could freely refrain from doing so.

And one last point. We have simply "distanced" the voters from the procedure of electing the Supreme Soviet. Could it be worth while at least informing them, by publishing in IZVESTIYA the lists of candidates for the Supreme Soviet? I wanted to say something else, but Vitaliy Lazarevich Ginzburg got in before me: When nominating the additional candidates we proceeded from the premise that the best people—maybe from Moscow—who were not included on this list should under no circumstances be excluded from work on the Supreme Soviet. We are talking about professional legislative work, and this is why our list contains the names of only those who have consented to give up their main jobs and devote all their time to work on the Supreme Soviet. Thank you for your attention. (Applause).

M.S. Gorbachev: Comrade Aleksey Ivanovich Tkhor, deputy from the Ukraine.

A.I. Tkhor, leader of a team of breakage face miners at the "Rovenkiantratsit" Production Association's M.V. Frunze Mine Administration, Voroshilovgrad Oblast, Antratsit City (from the USSR Trade Unions): Esteemed comrade deputies! Having seen the list of candidates for the USSR Supreme Soviet, I thought to myself: Our country consists of nothing but intellectuals, scientists, academicians, and professors. So why is it that we miners still have a shovel in our hands? (Applause).

This is one question. Here is another: The slogan on our banner reads: "All Power to the Soviets of Workers and Peasants!" Have we by any chance abandoned this slogan and the gains of October? Being a working man, I say: No. And the same would be said by all my voters.

One more question—actually about the election procedure in question. I know Moscow's importance and I am aware of what Moscow means for us. But we won't give up a single one of our seats! Under the quota system Moscow may even be entitled not to 29 but to fewer seats. Moscow is represented by 55 people. And I believe that we in our collectives ought to work things out for our own republics and our own regions.

And the working class must not be considered a faceless mass which cannot stand up for itself. The interests of miners, the interests of workers will not be upheld by some professor; they will be upheld only by a worker. This is what I wanted to say. Thank you for your attention. (Applause).

M.S. Gorbachev: A note has been received requesting that the floor be given to a Tajik SSR representative. Two of their three candidates are the first and second secretaries of the Tajik Communist Party Central Committee. (Stir in the hall)

A.V. Minzhurenko, head of department at the Omsk State Teacher Training Institute (Tsentralnyy Territorial Electoral Okrug, Omsk City): I would like to speak about the mechanism for the selection—yes, the selection and not the election—of Supreme Soviet deputies. It seems to me that there are major defects in the system being proposed to us. In any event, this is a breach of the prerogative of the congress itself, and this aspect has been even more pronounced in some of the speeches here. It is being suggested to us that we split into delegations and fix, as it were, the question of Supreme Soviet deputies. In effect this does away with the need for our joint session. And so? The point is that this system infringes the rights of the minority. And it will no longer be democratic if we elect the Supreme Soviet by regions.

I will not touch on a delicate question like the republic quotas. But it seems to me that oblast quotas are unnecessary in our Russia. There is absolutely no need to proceed from such jingoism (and we actually heard it here: We won't give up a single one of our seats, it was said—he may not be perfect, but at least he's one of us); there is no need to go round in circles within this system. There are 11 people in our delegation. It turns out that out of respect for the obkom first secretary, who is a member of our delegation, five or six people vote the same way as he does, automatically. So in effect everything is decided by one man. I am not saying this as a reproach to him, but as a reproach to the system. It appears that in our delegation there is absolutely no chance of bypassing the obkom first secretary and getting onto the Supreme Soviet, any more than there was in the old days.

True, there is a hint that if you behave yourself well, the first secretary could appoint you to the Supreme Soviet. Is that how it is? Because out of the 11, 6-7 places are immediately, so to speak, in the pocket of this one man. That is undemocratic, comrades, and that is why voting by regions is damaging to minority rights.

That is why a debate was necessary, comrades. A debate before the elections, so that we would all be "illuminated," so that we would know who is who. That is why I voted with the minority, for the debate to precede the elections. This is very important. In our party group several comrades spoke, and I know quite clearly whom I will strike out. I am grateful that the party group meeting was held. But if there had also been a debate, I would have had a clear opinion of a great many people.

Therefore, a specific proposal: Submit even more candidacies, so that the list is longer and the elections are

STENOGRAPHIC RECORD

Third Session

26 May 1989

contested. And there is no need to insist on backing one's own people! I, for instance, comrades—perhaps our delegation will not support me—but I am willing to let the whole of our Omsk quota go, for the sake of one progressive Muscovite. Let him make a 30th. For the good of the cause.

M.S. Gorbachev: First, I have a note saying this: "We support the proposal to vote for the renunciation of official duties in the event of election as a deputy to the Supreme Soviet." Signed by three deputies.

Deputy Kugultinov has the floor.

D.N. Kugultinov, writer, chairman of the Kalmyk ASSR Writers' Union Board, Elista City (Iki-Burulskiy National-Territorial Electoral Okrug): It is a pity there are no microphones in the auditorium. Mikhail Sergeyevich, I asked to speak in the debate after your report. Thank you.

M.S. Gorbachev: But it does not say that here.

D.N. Kugultinov: My mistake.

M.S. Gorbachev: No, it does not say it, and since I received a note, I decided to give you the floor. Fine. In that case Comrade Levykin has the floor.

Yu.A. Levykin, scientific staffer at the USSR Academy of Sciences Spectroscopy Institute, Troitsk City (Podolskiy Territorial Electoral Okrug): I would like to say this. Yes, we are now engaged in an extremely important task—the formation of the USSR Supreme Soviet. Generally speaking, I agree in principle with the quota approach in forming the Soviet of Nationalities, but unfortunately I cannot agree with that approach in forming the Soviet of the Union. A good many views have already been expressed in support of this same opinion, so I will not enlarge on this theme. It seems to me that the Soviet of the Union was devised precisely so that we would not try to manipulate all-union interests to suit our local angles. And therefore it should preferably be formed on the basis of some kind of general list that should not be voted on individually, by republics. But I also have a number of proposals that I am sure would suit a great many people.

First. I think each delegation, or rather the number of candidates for each delegation, should be enlarged.

Second. It seems to me that it is entirely permissible to nominate candidates directly from the auditorium now. And the secret ballot procedure should not be preceded by an open ballot procedure on inclusion or noninclusion on the list.

Third. A great many people are now asking how, for instance, Latvians can vote for Uzbeks whom they do not know, and vice versa. Indeed, it is very difficult. How can we make use of the enormous number of votes we have (271 for each chamber), when the number of people we know is extremely small—10, 20, or 30.

So should we perhaps change the actual voting system? After all, the point is that we have not yet discussed the proposed secret ballot procedure at all, or adopted it. So in principle we have a free hand.

What do I propose? I propose a system of so-called proportional representation. Each deputy casts a certain number of votes. And you will not want to cast a great many. Say, not more than 30. And you will only vote for the people you know very well. I will speak about the advantages of this. Well, first, in this case the qualitative composition of the chamber deputies will be improved dramatically. Second, not only will the majority receive the majority of their places, but a minority can also be represented. Thus the necessary political stability will be ensured in the future, too. Otherwise there will be unnecessary friction. And the quota system could also be satisfied in the best possible way. And there is one last aspect I would like to highlight.

Yes, we put forward candidates by delegations. But people have already described how the nomination took place, and in order not to make the esteemed public laugh, I will not tell you how the nomination, discussion, and voting took place in our Moscow Oblast. In principle I disagree with this procedure.

I have spoken about the advantages of a different system, and we need not really discuss the question of whether or not we understand this system. The proposed voting procedure is even simpler than the one we have. We have to search the lists for the people we do not want to see there. In the former option we will only be looking for those we want to see. Counting votes is a matter for experts. We have to evaluate either the merits or the shortcomings of a given system. Whether or not to elect on a majority basis, that is what we should discuss, not the actual procedure.

M.S. Gorbachev: I am reading out proposals as we go along, so that we have all the options. Here are two proposals.

First. "If it is clearly stipulated that every USSR people's deputy will be a member of the Supreme Soviet at least once in the course of 5 years, I think many misgivings will disappear. Comrade Minasbekyan."

And another proposal, more categorical. "What do we want to create? In effect, two supreme soviets—the congress and the soviet—or a real working organ of people's deputies? There should be a presidium of the

STENOGRAPHIC RECORD

FIRST CONGRESS OF PEOPLE'S DEPUTIES OF THE USSR

Third Session

26 May 1989

Congress of People's Deputies and no supreme anythings—and two sessions of the congress. Klokov, deputy from the veterans."

I give the floor to Comrade Shevlyuga, deputy from Rostov.

V.Ya. Shevlyuga, molder at the "Rostselmash" Production Association, Rostov-na-Donu City (Proletarskiy Electoral Okrug): Comrade deputies, you can all see that in the course of the nomination of deputies to the USSR Supreme Soviet a clear line can be perceived—the party and soviet apparatus is again proposing that we elect the Supreme Soviet by the old system.

I propose first that we consider the fact that today you and I are not professors, generals, or priests; today we are the chosen representatives of the people. Before making any decision, let us first reflect that today we represent not only ourselves, but all the Soviet people, the voters who voted for us. Therefore the remarks that have been made today, what I would call the improper remarks, are offensive first and foremost to our voters.

As for my specific statement, we, USSR People's Deputies Vladimir Nikolayevich Zubkov (Territorial Okrug 267) and Vladimir Yakovlevich Shevlyuga (Territorial Okrug 269), taking into account the norm of representation on the USSR Supreme Soviet, and also guided by the fact that the city of Rostov-na-Donu—which has more than a million inhabitants and three territorial electoral okrugs, and which was, because of devious maneuvering, deprived of the opportunity to delegate a deputy to the USSR Supreme Soviet—have decided to resort in practice to self-nomination. We ask the congress to add to the list of proposed members of the USSR Supreme Soviet Vladimir Nikolayevich Zubkov, chief physician at maternity association No 5, CPSU member, deputy from Leninskiy Electoral Okrug No 267, Rostov-na-Donu City.

With a view to observing the norms of representation, we consider it expedient to submit Zubkov's candidacy as part of the total number of deputies from Rostov Oblast.

As for the remarks made here by certain speakers on the incompetence and inability of deputies to resolve questions on the USSR Supreme Soviet, I consider them invalid. We were all elected by the people, and the people cannot be wrong about their deputies. Thank you for your attention.

V.V. Guliy, special correspondent of the newspaper SOVETSKIY SAKHALIN, Yuzhno-Sakhalinsk City (Yuzhno-Sakhalinskiy Territorial Electoral Okrug): The miner deputy is wrong to worry that the interests of the working class will not be defended. If I get onto the Supreme Soviet I will defend his interests, as I have always defended the interests of miners, fishermen, and agricultural workers, as a journalist myself. There is no need to regard the intelligentsia and the working class as being in opposition. (Applause.)

In our delegation, two representatives from Sakhalin were put on the Supreme Soviet lists. Why was this? The situation is not so simple as it may at first appear. In all, we have four deputies from Sakhalin Oblast, two from territorial okrugs—myself and Ivan Andreyevich Zhdakayev—and two from social organizations: the trade unions and the Leninist Communist Youth League [Komsomol]. I will say at once that we do not lay claim to an additional place to the detriment of others in the Soviet of the Union. So why have we submitted two candidacies? In principle all four of us believe that the elections should be contested, but in this case different motives underlie the situation. A few days ago, at the conference of people's deputies from the RSFSR, Comrade Vorotnikov, reading out the list of candidacies for the Supreme Soviet, mentioned, among others, the name of Ivan Andreyevich Zhdakayev, USSR people's deputy from Tymovskiy Electoral Okrug No 291. According to Comrade Vorotnikov, Zhdakayev's candidacy was recommended from the localities. For me, as a representative of our delegation, this was news, and it also came as a surprise to Ivan Andreyevich Zhdakayev himself.

How did it come about that a decision was taken without taking into account the opinion of the two deputies from territorial okrugs? Who dared to assume this responsibility? I think you have guessed—our boldest people—the apparatus workers. But, strange as it may seem, in this case they were helped, wittingly or unwittingly, by the people's deputies from the trade unions, Comrade Kapustin, and the Komsomol, Comrade Karaganov, who did not consider it necessary to ascertain the opinion of the people's deputies from territorial okrugs. At the same time our opinion was formed long ago, after careful consideration of the potential of each person and of other circumstances. And we had decided to recommend for work on the first convocation of the Supreme Soviet People's Deputy from Yuzhno-Sakhalinskiy Territorial Okrug No 290 Vitaliy Valentinovich Guliy, that is to say, me. Yes. I am bound by this promise to my voters and consider myself obliged to fulfill their will.

In conclusion I wish to say that we have not yet perfected the nomination mechanism. We held a secret ballot. Again, opinions were divided, two and two. And that will go on to infinity. What is the solution? Who should be the arbiter? The congress? So be it. But we thought our voters could also have a say. We telephoned the voters: They sent a mass of telegrams; I have them here. There are telegrams from labor collectives, voters, and social organizations, but not from party and soviet organs. There are even some from orthodox believers, who, incidentally, send you their deep respects, Mikhail Sergeyevich, and say that they will pray for you and wish you all the best.

STENOGRAPHIC RECORD

Third Session

26 May 1989

The nomination mechanism must be perfected. The social organizations have an advantage—they vote twice, nominate twice from their social organizations, and have the legal right of the casting vote. But we—the territorial representatives—are impeded. This must be resolved somehow. That is all I have to say.

M.S. Gorbachev: The floor is given to Comrade Bisher, deputy from National-Territorial Electoral Okrug No 317.

I.O. Bisher, professor at the Stuchka Latvian State University, Riga City (Stuchkinskiy National-Territorial Okrug, Latvian SSR): We, the Latvian deputies, adhere to the principles of a rule-of-law state, and therefore respect our Constitution and the decisions adopted by the congress, although in a number of cases they might not be to our liking. First, last year there were a whole series of amendments to the Constitution and the electoral law then being proposd that were not to our liking. Using democratic methods of struggle, we tried to change them. In some cases we succeeded, in others not. But as the election practice showed, in particular, our struggle against the preelection meetings was not without justification.

We also expressed doubts about the division of deputies into congress deputies and Supreme Soviet members. Now we wanted these questions of dividing deputies and appointing them to the Supreme Soviet to be decided after we had discussed the Constitution and perhaps changed it in some respects. But the congress voted that questions concerning the Constitution be put to the vote after we have elected the Supreme Soviet. This also put us in some difficulties, but we must submit to the decision of congress. And therefore we believe that since the congress has decided, we must not return to this question now. The Constitution clearly states that the union republics, first, have 11 places on the Soviet of Nationalities, and a place on the Soviet of the Union according to the size of the republic's population. And it must be said that the quota that no one has yet approved, but that is being proposed here, suits us. We have approximately 1 percent of the population, and we are allocated three seats—that is also approximately 1 percent.

The next question. How should these seats be distributed? We believe that since these seats are allocated to the republic, the republic should decide who is authorized to represent it. And therefore we ask for the proposals we have put forward on this question to be adopted.

Something was said here about petty princedoms. I do not think we have any petty princedoms, but since we are a federal state, we have union republics, members of the Union, who must be respected. If we say that we will all vote together for the Soviet of the Union, with no quotas, it could mean that the Russian Federation, which has more than 1,000 deputies, will "outvote" the Latvian delegation, which has 50 votes. I think that would be not only undemocratic, but not in accordance with the Constitution.

Then it was said in one of the speeches here that this is because of the need to protect the national minorities in the union republics. Since that person was Russian, no doubt he wants to protect the Russian population of our republic. Unfortunately some people have gained the impression, not without the help of certain press publications published in Moscow, that in our republic representatives of other nationalities are underprivileged.

I should say that I regard the spread of such information here, from the congress platform, as improper at best, especially if no concrete evidence is produced. If you read our list you will see that this list is drawn up in such a way that all the nationalities that there are among our deputies are represented. There are Latvians, Russians; there is a Jew who was elected as one of our deputies. We tried to ensure that all social groups are represented. We have professors and workers. I do not believe that I cannot defend the interests of workers because I am a professor. I was not given my seat by professors, but by workers and peasants. I think a worker can defend my interests, too. I trust the workers to look after their own interests.

We held our elections democratically, we discussed many candidacies, and therefore we in the republic believe that we adopted the optimum decision so as to cover numerically all the commissions that are envisaged and provide for the question of rotation. I do not think anyone can do this better. Unfortunately we cannot help the Moscow comrades if they themselves cannot tell which of the 55 deputies on the list are capable of representing their interests. We are not going to strike out candidates for them. I think, all the same, we should make use of some experience. In the days when we had real elections (this was in the twenties, under the 1924 Constitution), this procedure was adopted: Candidates were elected by the republic, and the congress approved them. I think we should preserve this procedure (it is not contrary to our Constitution), and any delegate, I think, could protest the elections only when evidence is presented to the congress that the elections were undemocratic, in which case the congress could annul them. We did this democratically; all the problems were discussed in the republican press, and the voters supported our proposals. (Applause.)

M.S. Gorbachev: Comrades, Comrade Burlatskiy will now speak, after which we will take a break. The speaker will remember that he is allowed 3 minutes.

F.M. Burlatskiy, LITERATURNAYA GAZETA political observer, Moscow City (from the Soviet Peace Fund in conjunction with eight Soviet committees campaigning for peace, solidarity, and international cooperation): Comrade deputies! Today we have come up against a

Third Session

26 May 1989

fact of exceptional importance. This fact is not only the difference of opinions, but the difference of interests of various strata and various nationalities. How should we act? Should we engage in gang warfare, or should we seek to combine our interests and compromise? I think we should now create a model of the combination of interests and the quest for compromise. Some of my proposals stem from this.

The first is about the quota. I understand the feelings of the comrades from the localities, and particularly from the republics. For a long time they were under pressure from Moscow, from the center, and now, of course, they want to defend their interests. But on the other hand, the last time there was a quota from the localities and from organizations was in the 17th century, at the Ecumenical Council. Therefore we must be able to combine the territorial principle with a sensible principle of personal selection. That is the first thing.

Second. Whom are we electing? We are not electing a parliament; we ourselves are the parliament. We are electing the executive, working part of the parliament. This determines the principles of selection. We should select those who will carry out your will, and carry it out professionally. Those who will know how to write laws, how to uphold your interests, how to counter the bureaucracy.

Third. This relates to whether people are to work on a permanent or nonpermanent basis on the parliament's executive organ. If we leave the loophole and send some people there as "celebrities," many working leaders will rush there. We must not allow that. Then we would get the situation we had in the last parliament. I want to say this to those comrades who are interested in doing this. They have already satisfied their own prestige by being elected people's deputies. Election to the Supreme Soviet will add nothing to that prestige. On the contrary, they impose responsibility on themselves and add to their work. It is a source of great concern to me that many of my comrades in the Moscow delegation—economists, political specialists, and experts in environmental problems—have refused to enter the parliament. They are concerned that they will have to give up their job. That is why I am earnestly asking the people who will be standing for election, I am earnestly asking all of you to consider that fact. I support Mikhail Sergeyevich's proposal to put the question I have mentioned to the vote: Only those deputies who are completely relieved of their work for this period should be elected to the executive section of the parliament. We must also vote on that. Even if the majority does not vote in favor of this, I urge you all to vote taking this fact into consideration.

Last, a word about alternatives: We elected Mikhail Sergeyevich Gorbachev without an alternative candidate. Why? Because there was no alternative candidate. The frivolous proposals that we heard from many people could not, so to speak, convince us to include any rival candidate on the secret ballot paper. But there are alternative people here! No one—either in the Soviet Union or abroad—will understand us if we approve a firm list now without alternative candidates. That is why (I proposed this during the session of the Moscow group of deputies, despite the fact that I was included on the list at first) we decided to nominate a large list—55 people—although our quota—let's call it that—was 29. Let other delegations nominate a large number of people. What is to be done with those people who win a majority but do not enter the Supreme Soviet? I propose, comrades, that they be put on immediate reserve for the next rotation in the Supreme Soviet. Thank you for your attention. (Applause).

M.S. Gorbachev: Recess for 20 minutes.

M.S. Gorbachev: Comrades! Since there are many people wanting to speak, it is maybe worth us spending another 2 hours and then giving the presidium a chance to think over and sum up what has been said and submit some proposals in order for us to progress. Because it is a question of the Supreme Soviet's position in its relations with the congress and of how this entire mechanism will function—this is not a question of procedure.

Moreover, comrades, we are also receiving letters and people are asking for them to be read out. Some people are writing that the congress should be protected against attempts to impose a discussion of procedural questions and that we should strictly follow the standing orders for speeches by scientists and economists criticizing our economic reform without proposing anything in return. "They must be elected to the Supreme Soviet; let them prove their capabilities in action." And: "Don't give speakers the floor more than once a day." Then: "Urge respectable deputies from the center to show elementary respect for the working class and the national republics. There is no need to pin labels on people." I believe that no one should do this at all: neither side.

"We demand that Deputy Zaslavskaya apologize to the Moscow militia for her impolite speech." I think that things have not reached that point here. She raised a question and we discussed and removed this problem. We also decided the matter that was put to the vote. Let us not dramatize any question, comrades. I think it is useful that opinions were exchanged and some things were taken into consideration while others were rejected and went further. So, I have fulfilled your request: A large group from Kazakhstan demanded that I read out the letters to the presidium.

Comrade Pisarenko from Altay Kray has the floor. Then Comrade Grishchuk is to speak.

Colonel V.A. Pisarenko, first deputy chief of the Siberian Military District Air Force Political Department (Kamenskiy Territorial Electoral Okrug, Altay Kray): Comrade people's deputies! It is a good thing that we are maximalists. We want to do everything more quickly and we want to show the fruits of our labor more quickly; but

STENOGRAPHIC RECORD

Third Session
26 May 1989

that is certainly complex in a power like ours. That is why I would like to raise my first question to do with lawmaking. We must take a very serious line on it, especially as regards the Constitution. Of course, the congress can change any clause of the Constitution: It can add or change anything and make addenda. But, comrades, we must think about the guarantees that we will give to our people. If there are 2 congresses every year—10 congresses in 5 years—we may change the Constitution so much that the people will then say: "What are we to believe in? You are in session and you are making decisions but whom do these decisions affect? The working class and the peasantry." I think that we need to first draw up a law on the procedure for adopting laws. We do not have that kind of procedure. If this procedure and this law did exist, many problems here today would not be so acute.

Second question. I consider it impossible to govern the state with people holding down more than one job. That is why I am proposing that the people's deputies who are to work in the Supreme Soviet be completely discharged of their official duties so that they can channel all their efforts, endeavors, knowledge, and skill into their work in the Supreme Soviet.

Next. People's deputies who will work in the localities must leave the congress, as they have a chance to work with their voters. The last problem is as follows, comrades. It is written in the temporary standing orders that we must obtain documents 2 weeks before the congress. Of course, this is not a very long period, especially if a serious law is proposed so that a deputy needs to discuss it with his voters, collect popular wisdom, and bring the people's collective reason to the congress. At least 2 months are needed. I would like us not to neglect a single proposal or a single speech—very many fundamental wishes and proposals have been voiced. I would like them to be considered during the work of the Supreme Soviet, so that every people's deputy knows when he brings his proposal to the congress that it will not remain unnoticed. If this is a promising proposal, use will be made of it. Very many programs were born during the election struggle. Each one contains serious proposals and ways of solving particular problems. I think these programs should be collected in from all the people's deputies, generalized, and the priority areas in them singled out so that the programs can be utilized in the future, in planning.

A word about elections to the Supreme Soviet, comrades. I think that every one of us sitting here realizes that our voters consider us to be most worthy. Naturally, regions must be allocated quotas. Let people in every region, oblast, or republic decide how their deputies are to be elected—by a secret ballot or by a show of hands. I think this will be the most reliable lesson in democracy and it will be to our advantage. If we are mistaken today, we will meet for another congress in a year and we will carry out the rotation—it will determine most objectively in whom we were mistaken and who proved worthy. Thank you for your attention.

M.S. Gorbachev: I give the floor to Deputy Grishchuk. Please go ahead. And then Comrade Karaganov.

V.P. Grishchuk, associate professor at Kiev's T.G. Shevchenko State University. (Dneprovskiy Territorial Electoral Okrug, Ukrainian SSR). The country needs professional politicians. That is why the Supreme Soviet should be a place for full-time work. Many people have already said that and it seems that no one objects. Now a word about quotas. Groups I respect—both the Moscow deputies and deputies from the Baltic republics—have diametrically opposing viewpoints. Comrades, we have to seek compromises. I propose the following: I propose that we leave the quota for the Soviet of Nationalities as it is, but make the quota for the Soviet of the Union 90 percent of the current quota. I propose that republics decide the question of the 90-percent quota, and the remaining 10 percent (approximately 27 people) can be made into a "free market" and thus implement the Muscovites' proposals. (Applause). I can be even more specific. Seats will not be taken away from those republics with a quota of less than 10 people in the Soviet of the Union. This "free market" will then consist of a total of 20 people.

Now a few words about rotation. Rotation should not be an end in itself. We must approach this in a very well-considered fashion. We should above all consider deputies' personal requests and conduct an objective assessment of a deputy's work in the Supreme Soviet. Thank you. (Applause).

M.S. Gorbachev: Good. I give the floor to Sergey Vasilyevich Karaganov. And then to Comrade Sagdeyev.

S.V. Karaganov, director of No 6 Secondary Vocational and Technical School, Sakhalin Oblast, Okha City. (From the Komsomol): Esteemed comrades! I love my island—the island of Sakhalin. I am profoundly interested in who represents our oblast in the USSR Supreme Soviet. That is why I cannot understand the speech made before the recess by my fellow islander, Sakhalin Deputy Comrade Guliy. Comrade Vitaliy Valentinovich Guliy is a correspondent for the oblast newspaper, and is insistently and doggedly proposing his own candidacy. I advocate multiple-candidate elections and I am especially in favor of a deputy proposing himself. If this is backed up by specific actions and constructive proposals and—and this is the most important thing—by his own stance on the questions under discussion. But it is this that Comrade Guliy is lacking.

I fully agree that we need to seek grains of reason in the positions of various groups of deputies, be they from Leningrad, Moscow, or so on. But useful things [poleznyye vzkhody] can only emerge from one's own judgement and understanding of a question. I reckon that Comrade Ivan Andreyevich Zhdakayev, a bulldozer operator from a timber procurement establishment and a pretty competent and principled man, should be elected to the USSR Supreme Soviet. That is why I propose not

STENOGRAPHIC RECORD

Third Session

26 May 1989

including Comrade Guliy on the secret ballot papers. and if he is included, I will vote for Ivan Andreyevich Zhdakayev. Thank you for your attention. (Applause).

M.S. Gorbachev: Let me read out a note: "Esteemed comrade chairman! What are we talking about? If the procedure for elections to the Supreme Soviet is the same as that to the Soviet of Nationalities, how will the former differ from the latter? Both are determined on the regional principle. What about the Constitution? Deputy Zalygin, writer."

Academician R.Z. Sagdeyev, leader of the USSR Academy of Sciences Space Studies Institute Analytical Studies Scientific and Methodological Center, Moscow City. (From the USSR Academy of Sciences): Comrade deputies! I can indeed sense passions heating up. We will send the best people to the Supreme Soviet—the most worthy representatives of those people elected by the people, those who can carry out concrete work between congresses and who are our instrument.

I think that the flareup of passions is to some degree attributable to our customary mentality, shaped during the years of chronic shortages, whereby we saw a waiting line and immediately stood in it without finding out what people were standing in line for. A whole number of deputies are insistently proposing that we come to an agreement on the nature of a people's deputy and the nature of a Supreme Soviet deputy. If we clearly established our position on this problem, things would be much easier for us: We should either stand in line or put the most suitable people in line.

I would like to try to somewhat alleviate the awkwardness and irritability that also arose on another question. I am referring to the confrontation and verbal skirmishes between Moscow and regions outside Moscow. Comrades, I want to assure all of you—workers, engineers, and peasants alike—that, when necessary, we Muscovites and professors also knuckle down to hard work. (Stir in the hall). I am referring, in particular, to agriculture. But also to construction work.

Our task today is to elect people not so much on intellect and not, as my esteemed comrade Fedorov said somewhat unfortunately, "choose between wise men and numbskulls." I think that other people have come here. If there is some dividing line between us, I hope it is not very serious. This dividing line runs between the new thinking and the old thinking. We need to elect people to the Supreme Soviet by conscience. To ensure (I am addressing Comrade Tkhor) that you never have a sapper's shovel brandished at you. (Applause).

Comrades! Permit me now to submit some specific proposals on behalf of some of the Moscow delegates. Let us seek a compromise. Moscow has already said that the the capital by no means aspires to a larger quota than has been agreed. During the polemics of the last few days we simply wanted to propose candidacies for multiple-candidate voting to the Soviet of the Union. But now I want to continue with the following. The debate that unfolded here will possibly help us to resolve the question somewhat differently and find a broader platform for compromise. I add my voice to those who are insisting that Supreme Soviet deputies should be full-time professional parliamentarians. Let us now take a look at the list that the regions have proposed. This list numbers 25 first secretaries of republic Communist Party central committees and party obkoms. I will not speak of party conscience. I would simply like to ask them the following question: What will they say to their party organizations? Are they abandoning their work there in order to work full time in Moscow? If so, we can calmly consider whether to vote for them or not. If they are not going to do this, I must warn you that I personally will vote against them.

But I would like us include the exclusion of such candidates from the ballot papers in our procedure. Incidentally, all candidates on this ballot paper should be asked to give up their full-time work. If you think this proposal is reasonable, there could be another vote [peregolovaniye], after, of course, a candidate's position is clear as to whether he is in favor of full-time work or not. Thank you. (Applause).

M.S. Gorbachev: I give the floor to Deputy Academician Kudryavtsev.

M.S. Gorbachev [repeated name as published]: Good, please go ahead.

V.N. Kudryavtsev, vice president of the USSR Academy of Sciences, director of the USSR Academy of Sciences Institute of State and Law (from the CPSU). What was bad about the former Supreme Soviet and the system in which we worked? It contained a great many bad elements. The main one was the pro forma voting and approval of previously adopted or—more correctly—previously prepared draft laws when the Supreme Soviet met once or twice a year. This gave rise to two things. First, as comrades know, it was practically impossible to discuss a law. Second. Decrees were adopted in the interval between Supreme Soviet sessions which there was no other way to adopt apart from in intervals. In approximately 1 year the presidium would adopt 50 or 60 decrees, while in the same year the Supreme Soviet would only adopt 1 or 2 laws. Why am I saying this? Because I think that we are now creating a full-time parliament in our country for the first time in over 70 years. I do not fully agree with you, Fedor Mikhaylovich Burlatskiy, when you said that all of us who are sitting here—2,500 people—comprise this full-time parliament. That is a profound misconception, and if that is what you think, you want to return to the previous structure. Because if the Congress of USSR People's Deputies

STENOGRAPHIC RECORD

Third Session
26 May 1989

meets twice a year and rubberstamps, excuse me, laws previously prepared by the apparatus, you will be returning to the the old system. Excuse me, but there is another way out of this.

F.M. Burlatskiy: (Inaudible).

V.N. Kudryavtsev: That is another matter, but it is not a working part of the parliament, as you describe the Supreme Soviet. It should be a working parliament, a full-time parliament, which should be elected by our congress.

Three facts follow from this. The first arises from the Constitution. The presidium that will exist will be unable to issue normative-type decrees. That is a very important fact. Because all the misunderstandings on political questions that were discussed yesterday and today applied, as you know, to decrees. The second fact is that people should work in this parliament on a full-time basis—many people have said this here, Comrade Sagdeyev, among others. When we discussed this at the Academy of Sciences, for instance, many people refused to take part in this parliament because they were unable to give up their work. In my opinion, we only have three people who agreed to this work. But the third fact, which should be implemented, arises since the Constitution does indeed speak of a legislative organ in the context of both the Supreme Soviet and the congress; in my opinion, this was not formulated very well at all, and we must fully implement this idea and distribute lawmaking functions between them—between the congress and the Supreme Soviet. I cannot fully agree with those people who said yesterday that laws should only be adopted here, at the congress. This, of course, would involve a devaluation of the Supreme Soviet. This is a return to the old system. Thus, we need to do something else. We need to provide the congress with an opportunity of adopting only certain laws.

I think that the structure here should be quite simple. It is obvious. First. The congress can change the Constitution. Only the congress and no one else. Second. The congress can be given the right to adopt fundamentals of legislation for the USSR and the union republics (we now have six or seven of these fundamentals of legislation for various sectors of the law). This a kind of all-union act. Third. The congress can be given the following, so to speak, delaying property. The congress has the right to revise or criticize any law adopted by the Supreme Soviet before. If the congress does not do this, then the law adopted by the Supreme Soviet is valid. But as the supreme organ the congress can, of course, also repeal or halt the operation of a law. In other words, to conclude this part of my speech, I must say that the Supreme Soviet should be strong. All attempts to weaken it will lead to the former system. That is my profound conviction.

Another two small points. The following thesis was voiced here yesterday: All of us deputies are equal. You know that I took a somewhat critical view of this because this is a good slogan; it is emotional and puts us all in a lofty position; we can take pride in this. But we should in fact ourselves realize why we are working here. If we do elect a circle of people to enter the Supreme Soviet, that means that people who are in the Supreme Soviet will have different functions from those who are not. We must look at this frankly with our eyes open and not see anything shameful in the fact that a particular person will not be elected to the Supreme Soviet. I calculated that we are equal on five points (I have a passion for mathematical calculations since I work in the Academy of Sciences. People there say that where there is no mathematics there is no science.)

First. Are we equal with respect to voters? Fully equal. Second. We should be equal, I think, with respect to Supreme Soviet commissions. We can join any Supreme Soviet commission not on a consultative basis but with a vote—just like those in the Supreme Soviet. Third. We can set up committees of the congress itself, up to and including investigative committees and the various commissions discussed yesterday. Here we are all also completely equal. Fourth. We are equal as regards rotation, since we are all entitled to stake a claim to a seat on the Supreme Soviet after 1 year. As for the Supreme Soviet itself, I think we cannot claim equality in that respect. Equality in what sense? Yesterday it was said that we can all go to the Supreme Soviet and have a vote there. But that, of course, is a devaluation and a ridiculous picture in general. It would mean that if we disliked someone we could assemble a group of our Moscow deputies—195 people, go over to the Supreme Soviet, and, having a vote, obstruct any resolution. Would that be right? No, it wouldn't. As you know, I am not putting myself forward for election to the Supreme Soviet. I think that we should not claim a vote in the Supreme Soviet. A consultative voice is a different matter.

The last thing I would like to say is that I want to support Comrade Zalygin, who stated in his note to you, Mikhail Sergeyevich, that we should not elect two Soviets of Nationalities, as seems to be the case now, when comrades insist on quotas for republics. There should be a difference. The Constitution exists, and we should take account of a law that exists. Article 11 of the Constitution makes a distinction between elections to the Soviet of Nationalities on the basis of quotas and elections to the Soviet of the Union, where there are no quotas—even though they are needed, bearing in mind the size of the population. It seems to me that this is a very simple matter. This proposal has already been raised here many times. We should simply follow the line of expanding this list somewhat.

As to the nomination of additional alternative candidates for the Supreme Soviet, if two people from Sakhalin are arguing about this between themselves, then

STENOGRAPHIC RECORD

Third Session

26 May 1989

another two should be added, and we will listen to all four of you and decide who will and who won't be elected.

I have also been asked another question. Comrade Kudryavtsev should comment on the status of Article 199 of the Constitution: The Supreme Soviet Presidium issues decrees and adopts resolutions. I can comment. Indeed, it does issue decrees of a nonnormative nature. And, incidentally, this should have been somehow hammered home yet again, Anatoliy Ivanovich, since this article was used when the amendment to the Constitution was adopted at the last session. Such non-normative decrees as, for instance, the appointment of an ambassador to another country should be carried out by presidium decree. Or, for instance, the awarding of an order or an honorary title.... These are non-normative decrees. Only acts which are adopted by the Supreme Soviet or the congress should be of a normative nature. If we go down the old path we will return to the apparatus system with all its drawbacks. That is why it seems to me that we should clarify this point, if only for our own satisfaction, and I will explain to Fedor Mikhaylovich Burlatskiy privately where he's going wrong. (Applause).

M.S. Gorbachev: The floor passes to Deputy Vladimir Anatolyevich Giro from Tajikistan. He will be followed by Comrade Khomyakov.

V.A. Giro, captain of a Tu-154 aircraft with the Tajik Civil Aviation Administration. (Dushanbinskiy Zheleznodorozhnyy National-Territorial Electoral Okrug, Tajik SSR): I am forced to speak, to address the people's deputies because of the assessment I have heard here of the nomination of candidates for the Supreme Soviet from the Tajik delegation.... What can be said about it? Comrades, I think, first, that we nonetheless need to become more closely acquainted with the procedure for electing the Supreme Soviet before we do elect it. And the fact that each delegation has nominated its own candidates does not show some kind of division by region or the creation of some separate princedoms. The point is that all of us, having gone through the procedure of the first, truly democratic elections, have received the greatest trust from our people. The people nominated and elected those they know. In this case we are reinforcing this procedure in electing our Supreme Soviet. Well, you might say, how can I vote for Lithuania? I might choose, let's suppose, the well-known movie actor Adomaytis from Lithuania, Pauls from Latvia, and Yeltsin and Fedorov from Moscow. And the rest I can strike off with a clear conscience, for example. What right do I have? That is why each delegation, when discussing the candidates for the Supreme Soviet, did what our people did in the elections—it nominated those it knows.

As for the fact that the Supreme Soviet will demand complete devotion in people's work, this is not just worrying us. It is worrying the entire people. How can the first secretary of the Tajik Communist Party Central Committee also work on the USSR Supreme Soviet? Well, as far as our leading officials are concerned, I can officially state on the delegation's behalf that we chose the people we know and, in order to ensure that the ship of restructuring stays on course, we are prepared to sacrifice both the first and second secretaries of the Tajik Communist Party Central Committee (applause), to which I have their consent in principle. So we are happy for them to be here. That is the way that all candidates for the Supreme Soviet should act. Everyone should weigh up now just what they value most and decide unambiguously for themselves whether to withdraw their candidacy or whether to go forward and work in our supreme organ. Additionally, of course, we need an alternative. I think that everyone is free to nominate their candidacy for the Supreme Soviet, and we will discuss the candidacy, above all in the delegation concerned (I don't want to talk about dividing things up again, but this quota is nonetheless fair). This is democratization—from the standpoint that we know, or should know, whom we are nominating. For my part, I would like to say that I have also been asked my view of this matter. Believe you me, it is just as hard for a Tu-154 captain to leave his job—any pilot will know that—as it is for the president of the Academy of Sciences, for instance. I had refused, but in order to demonstrate the democratic nature of this election, I propose myself as a candidate for next year's Supreme Soviet. Thank you. (Applause).

M.S. Gorbachev: I had announced Comrade Khomyakov, but he has remarks to make on the composition of the Soviet of Nationalities. We can probably wait for that; let us nonetheless conclude our, figuratively speaking, philosophical section. Here is Comrade Smaylis, from electoral okrug No 239 in Lithuania. He, too, would like to put forward some views on this point.

A.Yu. Smaylis, laboratory chief at the Z. Yanushkyavichus Cardio-Vascular System Physiology and Pathology Scientific Research Institute (Kaunasskiy Rural National-Territorial Electoral Okrug): Highly esteemed chairman! Highly esteemed deputies! Draft laws will be worked out in the Supreme Soviet. And if, of course, these laws possibly fail to completely suit all Supreme Soviet deputies, I propose leaving a so-called "vacatio legis" in this respect. "Vacatio legis" is a 3-month adjournment before a law is adopted in order to allow congress delegates to familiarize themselves with the law. During this period it is possible to submit amendments. The amended draft law returns to the Supreme Soviet. If the Supreme Soviet finds that the amendments are unacceptable, the law must be discussed at the congress of deputies. Thank you for your attention. (Applause).

M.S. Gorbachev: The presidium has received an interesting request. I will read the note: "Clearly, we need to determine the procedure for holding discussions, giving opinions, submitting amendments and other questions,

STENOGRAPHIC RECORD

Third Session

26 May 1989

and the procedure for holding meetings under established international regulations. First, requests to speak should be made in writing. The deputies have official notepads for this purpose.

"Second. The request should state the speaker's name, the issue and thrust of the speech, and whether it is 'for' or 'against' or an 'amendment to a point.' This should be put in writing. Third, the length of the speech should be stated, and this should be strictly observed, up to and including having the microphone cut off. A certain emancipation of delegates is very positive, but spontaneity and disorganization can compromise a meeting. The line waiting beside the presidium is an unusual thing. It would be better for notes to be handed to the presidium not by the deputies themselves but through special officials drawn from the service personnel who would stand in the aisles and take the notes from the floor. Thank you. Metropolitan Pitirim (Deputy Nechayev)." (Applause).

Everyone's applauding. That is good. In that case, please would everyone who wants to speak take their seats and write notes. Let's start that way. I will give people the floor on the basis of the notes I receive. As for the time, let's limit a discussion, unless it's a report, to 3 minutes. And let's keep to the point. I have also been told that the chairman should be seated, as is always the case at such forums. What do you think? Should I be seated?

From the floor: Yes.

M.S. Gorbachev: Let's go on. The floor passes to Deputy Vladimir Mikhaylovich Kotlyakov.

V.M. Kotlyakov, corresponding member of the USSR Academy of Sciences, director of the USSR Academy of Sciences Geography Institute (from USSR Academy of Sciences scientific societies and associations): Dear comrades! Today is a very portentous day for those present. We are building the framework of our congress' future work. And the fact that we are spending a lot of time discussing procedural and other matters is justifiable.

At the same time, it is very important to bring the discussion we are having today to a logical conclusion.

The fact is that many proposals are being expressed here, and deputies are not clear about how they are recorded or how they will be summed up. The word "philosophy" which you have used several times, Mikhail Sergeyevich, diminishes the level of our discussion to a certain extent. It is not philosophical. It is a discussion of the real procedure which will we be following for the next 5 years. I think that the differences between the two chambers and multiple-candidate elections are both very important points in this procedure. What we are currently seeing on the list of candidates for the Supreme Soviet is, if not a violation of the Constitution, at least not an accurate interpretation of it. The Basic Law states that we must elect the Supreme Soviet and that there must be elections. But it is being suggested to us that we essentially simply delegate deputies to the Supreme Soviet.

That is why it is very important to supplement the list right now. As a specific proposal, I suggest including on the list of candidates for the Soviet of Nationalities from the Kabardino-Balkar Autonomous Republic Deputy Mikhail Chokkayevich Zalikhanov, who spoke here yesterday; you saw him. I think that many people know him. He is a deputy to the Kabardino-Balkar Republic Supreme Soviet and chairman of that soviet's Nature Conservancy Commission, which is well known throughout the North Caucasus and probably throughout our country. The fact that he is not on the list of candidates is a great loss. Such amendments, I think, should be made for all other republics.

M.S. Gorbachev: Comrades, you have probably felt that to a certain extent we have already revealed deputies' opinions. All of them, using various arguments, support one point of view or another. This boils down to a desire to define the relationship between the congress and the Supreme Soviet and to clarify whether Supreme Soviet deputies are released for the period of their work in the Supreme Soviet and leave their former posts, or whether some of them will work permanently in the Supreme Soviet while others combine two jobs. We will resolve this question and everything will fall into place.

The other question concerns the right of deputies to participate in commissions. As for the commissions, we have already said that it would be expedient for them to comprise members of the Supreme Soviet and other congress deputies on an equal footing. And they would have identical rights.

The question has been asked as to how voting will take place in the elections for the Supreme Soviet. Perhaps we could do the following. We could have a break until 1500 [as published]. This would give deputies time to consult with each other on clarifications to the lists of candidates. During this time the presidium will try to reach its own conclusions and then submit them for discussion, summing up the proposals from deputies. What do you think, comrades? Shall we break until 1600? Don't go away yet.

G.V. Koshlakov, first deputy chairman of the Tajik SSR Council of Ministers. (Gorno-Badakhshan Autonomous Oblast):

Comrades, the main requirement in the election is that of deputies' competence. We naturally do not know everyone and therefore we cannot competently elect a Supreme Soviet. That is why I have the following proposals on election procedure. First, we should decide the question of whether Supreme Soviet deputies should be released from their other duties or not. This will reduce the number of candidates. Moreover, the number of

Third Session

26 May 1989

candidates on the list should not be limited. Even self-nominations should be accepted. Delegation quotas should be retained. All deputies should note on the list five deputies whom they trust and know. Naturally, a candidate from Belorussia should not be included on the Lithuanian list, and so forth. At the same time, any deputy retains the opportunity to vote for an individual—that is, for the most outstanding people.

Furthermore, delegates within each republic's quota who obtain the most votes shall be deemed to have been elected. That is, those who receive the most votes in a given delegation will go forward. If some candidates receive identical numbers of votes from a given delegation, and some of them cannot join the Supreme Soviet owing to the quota, the deputies will be chosen by ballot. People will be chosen on the same basis for the Soviet of Nationalities.

M.S. Gorbachev: Forgive me, could we hang on a little longer? There are comrades who insist on speaking. Shall we give them a minute each?

From the auditorium (inaudible, noise): No, that's enough.

M.S. Gorbachev: Alright, we have two proposals, but I would like to comment on them briefly before putting them to a vote.

Of course, the Supreme Soviet, within the framework of the work of chambers, committees, and commissions, is entitled to enlist all our country's intellectuals; and, moreover, our scientists, representatives of the working class, and major economic leaders with the relevant knowledge and experience always participate in this work, and even complain that they are little consulted. So this question can nonetheless be resolved by setting up some kinds of sections or consultative councils attached to the commissions or working groups, and drawn from the most talented people who cannot leave science or their work. But, on the other hand, one would like them to be headed by people who are already generating progressive ideas that find a response in society, and setting the direction for thinking in various spheres. Few such people have been elected deputies, and it would be very desirable, of course, to invite them to head up or join certain commissions. That was our intention in proposing the formula: "As a rule, people shall be released...." Would not the standard of the commissions' work be affected if we strictly decided that there would be no exceptions? Let's think about it.

The floor passes to Comrade Burlatskiy.

F.M. Burlatskiy: Comrades, I want to put to a vote the question that only those who are completely released from their work can be elected to the Supreme Soviet. But in order to resolve the problem raised by Mikhail Sergeyevich, I would propose that the committees or even the commissions set up by the congress and comprising both Supreme Soviet deputies and people's deputies should be headed by people's deputies rather than by members of the Supreme Soviet. This will solve the entire problem.

M.S. Gorbachev: This is again the same thing that Comrade Kudryavtsev said. We want a standing parliament that is able to prepare high-quality, well-prepared, and considered documents in order to avoid what was permitted in the first few years, when the content of our documents did not satisfy us and the documents were not of a very high legal quality.

From the floor: There is a second part to that. If people agree and want to work in the Supreme Soviet, are elected to it, and then rotation begins after a year and they have no job left, what are they going to do?

M.S. Gorbachev: That question will be resolved.

S.A. Tsyplyayev, scientific secretary at the S.I. Vavilov State Optical Institute, Leningrad City (from the Komsomol): Esteemed comrade deputies, I would like to request your attention so that you can take one other point into consideration. If we proceed from the formal principle of mandatory release, gearing our thinking on this purely to party committee first secretaries, then we must take into account the fact that we will thereby be cutting off very many people who have an opportunity to take part in the work of USSR Supreme Soviet organs but cannot do so as a result of having a certain position or a certain job. We thereby run the risk of setting up a purely apparatus-style organ. We are very concerned about apparatus-style organs maturing here and there, and many comrades are now speaking out against these things.

M.S. Gorbachev: So, there are two proposals.... The first proposal is that deputies elected to the Supreme Soviet should, as a rule, be released from their permanent jobs (voices from the floor objecting). Respect the congress, I have to carry out its will.... Thus, the second proposal is that all comrade deputies elected to the Supreme Soviet shall be released from their work. Temporarily, of course.

I call for a vote—who is in favor of the first proposal?

(The votes are counted).

Yu.A. Osipyan: Comrade deputies! The result of the vote is that 1,419 were in favor.

M.S. Gorbachev: This means that we shall retain the constitutional position. It is clear that the majority favor the first proposal. Who is in favor of the second? Take the count, please.

STENOGRAPHIC RECORD

FIRST CONGRESS OF PEOPLE'S DEPUTIES OF THE USSR

Third Session
26 May 1989

Deputies raised the following point and have put it to me. The proposal I have submitted is essentially enshrined in the Constitution, although I did not formulate it quite accurately. But the second proposal would be an amendment to the Constitution. If we adopt the first proposal, then we will retain the constitutional position. If the congress opts for the second proposal, then we would have to amend Article 124 of the Constitution. Therefore, we're talking about consultation. I may not have put this in strictly legal terms, but, following your criticism, comrades, I will clarify this.

Comrades have said that this formula—"as a rule"—should be commented upon, and some kind of normative basis would thereby be proposed. We will do that at the next stage.

Yu.A. Osipyan: The results of the vote for the second proposal: 636 in favor.

M.S. Gorbachev: That means Article 124 of the Constitution stands.

Interval until 1600.

26 May 1989. Kremlin Palace of Congresses. 1600.

Under the chairmanship of M.S. Gorbachev, chairman of the USSR Supreme Soviet.

M.S. Gorbachev: Let us continue our work, comrades.

The congress presidium has elaborated certain ideas on the basis of the discussion at the congress' morning session which we deem it necessary to submit to the congress for its examination, and on their basis it will be possible to start compiling the list of candidates and then proceed to voting.

Comrade Lukyanov is called upon to speak on the presidium's behalf.

A.I. Lukyanov (deputy from the CPSU): Comrade deputies, after carefully analyzing the proposals submitted here today the congress presidium has instructed me to report its thoughts on the results of the discussion, and it proposes to draw the following conclusions and to be governed by them in further work.

1. In forming the USSR Supreme Soviet chambers to adhere to the existing USSR Constitution and that which is laid down in it. To adhere also to the procedure for forming the chambers in accordance with the Constitution. Necessary modifications can and should, of course, subsequently be made to the Constitution. A special commission will be set up for this purpose. But, while the Constitution is in effect, it should be fully observed. Likewise, Article 110 on the principles of forming the chambers should be fully observed.

2. In proposing candidates for the Supreme Soviet the presidium would also consider it expedient to proceed from the provision of the Constitution which states that members of the USSR Supreme Soviet elected to it may, in accordance with Article 124 of the USSR Constitution, be released from their official and production duties. The Constitution says "they may," and, as follows from this, they will—in observance of this rule—be released from their duties. However, this naturally does not mean all of them, but rather only that section of workers who will combine their duties both at the local level and in union republic supreme soviet presidiums to ensure close liaison between the Supreme Soviet and the local level.

3. Both members of the USSR Supreme Soviet and deputies not belonging to the Supreme Soviet are (we will be proceeding from this principle) to be elected to the commissions of the chambers and the committees of the USSR Supreme Soviet. Their ratio will be roughly fifty-fifty. The commissions and committees are to be headed by members of the USSR Supreme Soviet. All deputies elected to a commission—both members of the Supreme Soviet and other deputies—possess an equal right to vote in commissions.

4. People's deputies not elected to the USSR Supreme Soviet or to committees and commissions may take part in sessions of the chambers of the Supreme Soviet and committees and commissions on questions of interest to them, with the right to speak but not to vote. They shall also have at their disposal all necessary information and documents on those questions.

This constitutes the response to the first question on the status of the Supreme Soviet and the correlation of powers. Here, as we have agreed, a commission, namely [v tom chisle] a Constitutional Committee, will be set up, which will carefully examine once again all questions concerning the correlation of the powers of the Congress of People's Deputies and the Supreme Soviet of the USSR. A number of delimitations on these powers will be defined in the Constitution, and some in the Standing Orders of the USSR Supreme Soviet and the Congress of People's Deputies and in other legislative documents. These questions demand careful study and cannot be resolved quickly. However, the congress retains the right to consider any question falling within USSR jurisdiction and also retains, in accordance with the USSR Constitution, the right to repeal or alter any document, any legislative act, and any decision adopted by the USSR Supreme Soviet.

These are the principles of delimitation and the conclusions to which the congress presidium has come.

* The following are the conclusions on how we should now form the Supreme Soviet that we wish to propose to the congress on behalf of the presidium.

STENOGRAPHIC RECORD

FIRST CONGRESS OF PEOPLE'S DEPUTIES OF THE USSR

Third Session

26 May 1989

The presidium has instructed me to report to you that it would be expedient when compiling the list of candidates for election to the USSR Supreme Soviet to adopt as its basis the proposal which the assembly of representatives of groups of people's deputies today formulated and which you have in your possession.

Today it would have been possible at the congress to agree to augment the lists submitted or to alter them according to the opinion of deputies elected from the appropriate regions, in order to finalize them and then place them on the ballot for a secret vote.

We discussed this for a long time in the presidium and came to the conclusion that the following rule, a proposal on which was circulated to you yesterday, must be retained. Deputies who obtain more than 50 percent of the vote and relatively more than other deputy candidates will be considered elected to the Supreme Soviet.

Here the counting of votes will be carried out as follows: for the Soviet of the Union—separately for Moscow and separately for the RSFSR and the other (14) union republics. That is to say, there will be 16 such lists. If in some places the list is incomplete or, on the contrary, too many [bolshe] deputies—upon obtaining 50 percent of the vote—are elected, then in that event the deputies of that single republic alone will vote again from a single list only.

In this regard, in our opinion (and we also had a long discussion on this) it would be possible to establish rules, which were submitted and distributed to USSR people's deputies yesterday, concerning the procedure for holding secret votes and for determining its results. This would naturally be with account taken of the opinion of all deputies. If the congress agrees these principles which we have drawn up, it would now be possible to proceed to the discussion of the lists of candidates to each of the chambers of the USSR Supreme Soviet.

M.S. Gorbachev: Are there any questions for Comrade Lukyanov? If you would, please.

From the floor: Tell us again: What is the procedure for voting? If it is 50 percent and more, then where is the guarantee that we will not vote for everyone? This wording must be included in the Procedure for the Conduct of Voting.

A.I. Lukyanov: I beg your pardon, comrade. I would ask you to look once again at the Procedure. Naturally a candidate member of the Supreme Soviet should obtain more than half the vote to be elected to the Supreme Soviet. That is clear. On the other hand, those who obtain relatively more votes than other candidates will also become members. That is all there is to it. But the 50-percent principle should be retained. It was retained in the the "Law on the Election of USSR People's Deputies," and it is retained everywhere in our public and state practice. We believe it should be retained here, too. Also, it is reflected in the proposal that we have submitted.

M.S. Gorbachev: That is to say, if in some places there are too many [bolshe] candidates and an alternative is needed, then 29 will be selected, as in Moscow. And those who have obtained more than 50 percent, but—by a relative majority of votes—will be selected. Are there any further questions?

From the floor: Comrades, how are people to vote? The question has arisen here of how to elect, in particular, the Soviet of Nationalities; or, elect the Supreme Soviet only, say, by the deputies of each republic. If such a rule were established, we would be breaking the article of the Constitution which enshrines that the USSR Supreme Soviet is elected by the Congress of USSR People's Deputies. If we agree not to deviate from the principles of the Constitution, then we should observe every letter of them.

M.S. Gorbachev: Please clarify this part of the nomination.

A.I. Lukyanov: As far as the proposal for nominating candidates from republics and deputies in terms of regions is concerned, it has, as far as I can recall, been elaborated three times. Deputies from some republics have carried out the election of candidates by secret ballot. Therefore, of course, if they replace a candidacy (and they know that candidacy best of all), they will in that case have to speak on it. If some further candidacies are proposed here, which is perfectly feasible, it would be a good thing to hear the opinion of the representatives of the region or republic.

M.S. Gorbachev: And, finally, if the deputies of a republic do not reach their quota in respect to Supreme Soviet candidates, then they themselves must submit new proposals. When another vote is taken, it is the region and the republic which draws up the list.

A.I. Lukyanov: In short, we have proceeded from the principle, comrades, that we now possess dual knowledge. First, there is the knowledge that the republic or region possesses of the deputies who have been nominated and who have waged persistent campaigns—that's one thing. On the other hand, there is the knowledge of the position held by many people's deputies that we have acquired as a result of the congress' 2 days of work.

M.S. Gorbachev: Are there any other questions? Briefly, another question.

From the floor: (inaudible).

M.S. Gorbachev: Would you repeat that, please?

STENOGRAPHIC RECORD

Third Session

26 May 1989

A.I. Lukyanov: The comrade says that the Nagorno-Karabakh delegation did not nominate candidates, but they have appeared on the list. Do you agree with those candidates? If so, then it is certainly necessary that you get together, is it not?

M.S. Gorbachev: Okay. That means we first of all have the presidium's proposals.

I understood that Deputy Landsbergis of the Lithuanian delegation wishes to speak on this question or enter a rejoinder concerning the election procedure.

V.V. Landsbergis, professor of the Lithuanian SSR State Conservatory (Panevezhskiy city National-Territorial Electoral Okrug, Lithuanian SSR): Esteemed Chairman, esteemed deputies. I feel obliged to clarify the position of the Lithuanian delegation and, as far as I am aware, the Latvian delegation, concerning the adopted voting procedure, and more than the procedure—the very principle. A number of deputies have tried to explain—yesterday Deputy Boryas, and today Zolotukhin and our senior member— that we have no right to vote for and elect people who are practically unknown. That is to say that we consider that we are not entitled to vote "in the dark." That would be possible if every candidate explained his platform here. That, as you yourselves appreciate, is a "reductio ad absurdum" of the mistake previously made when adopting the Election Standing Orders, which have been enshrined in the Constitution—a bad constitution—which we have now agreed to idolize, as it were. Although we have the right here and now to now refine it.

That being so, we believe we have no right to interfere in the affairs of, say, Tajikistan, in electing its deputies That is an internal matter touching upon a republic's sovereignty, and we do not have that moral right. Nor do we trespass on the sovereignty of Moscow in the shape of its group of deputies. But we do not want them to vote for us either, without knowing us. Be that as it may, I hope that our position is clear. This position is rather one of morality and principle. We believe that we do not have the moral right to vote blindly. We therefore ask you not be surprised that we will be unable to take part in the voting. Thank you.

M.S. Gorbachev: Thus there is the proposal that we have submitted for examination on behalf of the presidium, but there is also the stand of our comrades from Lithuania (I, it is true, do not know whether this is the common view of the delegation or not). Our situation is, frankly, one of crisis. And we therefore need to define our position. In point of fact the comrades have issued an ultimatum: If we do not adopt their proposals, then they will refuse to take part in the voting, although everything that is submitted here has been done as such on the basis of the Constitution. The arguments regarding what we know or do not know about candidates are, I think, scarcely convincing, because there are necessary and sufficient bounds to knowledge, and, in particular, there is the trust upon which we earlier decided many questions and are doing so now.

I therefore regard the proposal as some kind of demonstration, comrades. I would ask the comrades from Lithuania to heed us, and I invite them to participate in the voting because the main thing, in my opinion, is what Comrade Lukyanov has proposed on the presidium's behalf. That is also our united opinion. It contains two very significant features: The proposals derive from below and are thereby based on maximum knowledge, and on the other hand they are voted on by the whole congress, as laid down in the Constitution. And there is also the element of great trust. That also, incidentally, stimulates the trend toward rapprochement, trust, and consolidation rather than the reverse. We respect the Lithuanian comrades' stand, but, I think, they are also bound to heed us and treat us with respect. And when their list has been discussed and refined, let them think again. Perhaps we can even begin with this, for it affects us all. If you agree with me, I would ask you to accede to my appeal and not only my appeal but also that of the congress—if, of course, you support the proposal that the comrades consider our appeal. (Applause).

Comrade Medvedev has asked to speak in connection with the proposal put forward by the deputy from Lithuania. Comrade Medvedev, go ahead, please.

R.A. Medvedev, writer (Voroshilovskiy Territorial Electoral Okrug, Moscow city): What I have to say may appear somewhat involved to you, but I think that in principle you will understand. The voting procedure submitted to the presidium is not perfect, of course, even though it accords with the Constitution. However, for example during the elections to the Soviet of the Union, the election by quotas essentially follows the same procedure as the election to the Soviet of Nationalities. I do not like this type of voting for it is considerably to the disadvatage of the interests of Moscow, where more candidates than stipulated by the quota have been put forward. So, it is more than likely that many of the candidates from Moscow will be crossed off, but I cannot imagine the Moscow delegation presenting an ultimatum—either you accept our list or we deputies from Moscow will refuse to vote. After all, such a policy of ultimatums and refusals to vote disrupts the whole structure of our supreme organ of power.

We are not electing the Lithuanian Supreme Soviet; we are electing the USSR Supreme Soviet. I am totally baffled by the remark of the Lithuanian representative when he said: We will not encroach on the sovereignty of Moscow city. Moscow has no sovereignty, and I believe that I will be expressing the thoughts of all delegates and Moscow city deputies when I say: If you object to a specific person on Moscow's list—and there are many people here who are known throughout the Union for their good points or otherwise—you are perfectly free to

Third Session

26 May 1989

cross off the name of whoever you do not like. And this applies equally to a comrade from Kazakhstan or a comrade who happens to live in the Ukraine. Sitting next to me are comrades from Moscow who worked in Lithuania for many years, and they know many of the Lithuanian deputies. If they leave in those whom they do not know, and cross off those whom they know well, that is their affair.

Therefore, I fail to understand why, if we are electing the Supreme Soviet of the Soviet Union, we should be speaking about the sovereignty of each individual republic and voting only for our own candidates and not the candidates from Tajikistan or Uzbekistan. Would that not mean that if I read the list submitted by the Ukraine and I object to someone on that list, I would not have the right to cross him off? In my opinion, we all have this right, both under the Constitution and simply due to common sense. Otherwise, why should we have gathered for the Congress of USSR People's Deputies? Therefore, I would like to ask the comrades from Lithuania to allow themselves to be guided by common sense and not to wreck the tremendous amount of work which has been carried out to date to promote the democratization of our society and implement the new electoral reform and the—partially—new Constitution, work which is of the utmost importance for the whole of the Soviet Union, including the Baltic republics. I ask them to withdraw their ultimatum because otherwise our work could be wrecked and reduced to naught. Why are we gathered here? (Applause).

M.S. Gorbachev: I would like, furthermore, to emphasize once again: We are talking about voting here, whereas the nomination, as I keep emphasizing all the time, has been left for each republic to decide. And if another vote must be held because a candidate fails to win support, because the list of a specific republic fails to win support, it will again be the republic itself which will submit its proposals to the congress and name those whom it sees fit. Therefore, I believe that in this case there is harmony between the wishes of a republic as to whom it wants to have in the Supreme Soviet and the interests of the Union as a whole.

Comrade Osipyan, go ahead, please.

Academician A.Yu. Osipyan, vice president of the USSR Academy of Sciences, director of the USSR Academy of Sciences Institute of Solid State Physics, Moscow city (from the USSR Academy of Sciences): Comrades! I would like to propose that we express support for the voting procedure put forward on behalf of the presidium as the only possible one concerning the voting mechanism. And, I would like to appeal to the Lithuanian delegation and other delegations which appear to be supporting the ultimatum demand.

I would like to draw everyone's attention, and the attention of the Lithuanian delegation in particular, to the fact that the sovereignty of republics is fully guaranteed due to the fact that the nomination of candidates is carried out solely by the delegation of the republic in question. Nobody nominates any candidates on the Lithuanian list in addition to those nominated by the Lithuanian delegation itself. Therefore, it is merely a question of voting. The motives for the way each candidate votes may depend on how well informed he is. But, the possibility of voting in accordance with the level of one's information exists in respect to every delegate.

If we all know whoever we are voting for, we vote. If we do not know them, we can turn to the delegation in question or to people whom we trust. We can ask for this information because any other method proposed by the Lithuanian delegation, as Deputy Medvedev has said, is totally at variance with the Constitution. We are truly ensuring the election of the USSR Supreme Soviet by the Congress of USSR People's Deputies, as Mikhail Sergeyevich Gorbachev has said.

Therefore, on behalf of many deputies who support this viewpoint, I earnestly appeal to the Lithuanian delegation to withdraw its proposal and join the consensus that the USSR Supreme Soviet is elected by the Congress of USSR People's Deputies as a whole.

M.S. Gorbachev: Introduce yourself, please.

A.Y. Burachas, chairman of the scientific and technical information council under the Lithuanian SSR Academy of Sciences Presidium, Vilnius city. (Alitusskiy Territorial Electoral Okrug): Esteemed Chairman, esteemed deputies! Essentially, the greater part of our delegation has discussed the proposal made by Mikhail Sergeyevich Gorbachev, and we have decided to make use of this proposal and to discuss it in greater detail. Let me say a few words in this context. It is a question of the principles in a rule-of-law state. I personally also believe that the proposal of Anatoliy Ivanovich Lukyanov, as an essential but insufficient condition, represents an important advance in the solution of this problem arising under the current USSR Constitution. In actual fact, if we do not vote for republic quotas, this creates a fictitious choice. Many options of procedural solutions have been proposed here. A fictitious choice essentially leads to a vicious circle. A temporary solution has been proposed here, but where do the problems really lie?

The stand of the Lithuanian delegate was received as a categorical rejection of the presidium's proposal. But there is a difference between fictitious and real juridical acts, if you think about it. After all, what really happens—and this was mentioned here—is that we are voting for people whom we do not know. It seems that we are voting, but in reality we are not. Therefore, we only confirm or otherwise; but we vote only for individual people, we vote only in exceptional cases. Therefore, it is a question here of a principle in action. Either we are going to vote, or we are merely going to confirm something that has been voted on. Juridically, there is a difference here.

STENOGRAPHIC RECORD

Third Session

26 May 1989

I would also like to avail myself of this opportunity as I do not believe that I will be speaking later. I would like to draw attention to the fact that the juridical acts of our session are unfortunately being incorrectly reflected, for instance in the press. The Temporary Standing Orders inaccurately reflect previous materials and decisions. Mikhail Sergeyevich Gorbachev agreed to the group representatives' proposal —as Antanavichyus reminded us—to amend Article 19, that statements, declarations, or appeals submitted at the congress by at least 20 deputies are circulated by the congress as official documents. Mikhail Sergeyevich Gorbachev stated it quite clearly. We voted in favor of all these documents being circulated with the clarification that this takes place via the USSR Supreme Soviet Presidium.

In the Temporary Standing Orders published in the press the modality has been changed. It is essentially a totally different matter. It is stated there that the USSR Supreme Soviet Presidium may, at the proposal of no less than 20 people's deputies, circulate as official documents materials which they have drafted. Consequently, this is possible via the presidium, and also, it appears via the delegations. This constitutes an alternative. Your wording, Mikhail Sergeyevich, and the wording accepted at the congress, have been changed. Attention was also drawn to this by esteemed Comrade Otsason of the Estonian delegation. Thank you for your attention.

M.S. Gorbachev: Fine. What do you have to say on the main question?

A.Y. Burachas: What I said at the beginning. We need time to consult the whole delegation and decide together.

M.S. Gorbachev: So you want to consult?

A.Y. Burachas: Yes.

M.S. Gorbachev: Fine. Let me see. There are more comrades who wish to speak. Go ahead, please.

A.G. Kuliyev, Azerbaijan Union of Consumer Trade Cooperatives [Potrebsoyuz] department chief, Baku city (from the All-Union Organization of War and Labor Veterans): Comrades! I do not consider opting out of a general vote, as the Lithuanian delegation proposes, to be an acceptable option. I support the proposal of Comrade Anatoliy Ivanovich Lukyanov and Comrade Medvedev.

M.S. Gorbachev: Go ahead, Comrade Zalygin.

S.P. Zalygin, writer, chief editor of the journal NOVYY MIR, and secretary of the USSR Writers' Union Board, Moscow city (from the USSR Writers' Union): I think that our Lithuanian colleagues will now consult with each other. But maybe they would still be interested to know the opinion of other deputies, too. I would like to express one such opinion.

Could it be the case that all the ideas of restructuring, everything new that has come into our lives in the past few years, came to us from Lithuania? It came from Moscow, you know, from here. So there is some need to value what we have obtained. And if today we are all going to do our own thing, it means that in general you are already putting our entire policy in doubt. This is where restructuring is right now. This is where things stand. Who is taking advantage of this? And how? We must take account of this. This is what I would like to say to you, my dear friends with whom I have had many past encounters in the Baltic region; and I still have many ties there. This should not be forgotten. (Applause).

M.S. Gorbachev: Comrade Romanenko from the Ukraine; Deputy Romanenko.

V.D. Romanenko, director of the Ukrainian Academy of Sciences Institute of Hydrobiology, Kiev city (from the USSR Trade Unions): Esteemed comrades! Voting is an act of trust, in this instance an act of trust by one republic with respect to another. We have to adopt very many various laws relating to various republics and voters living in various republics. I am a representative from the Soviet trade unions and an academician from the Ukrainian Academy of Sciences. The people's deputies from the Ukraine have asked me to express their attitude, our attitude, and to ask our colleagues—the deputies from Latvia, Lithuania, and Estonia—to change their attitude and to agree to vote. We want to express trust in you through the act of voting, and, like deputies from other republics, we also wish to receive an act of trust from you.

M.S. Gorbachev: One moment, comrades. Can I put to a vote the arguments, principles, and considerations put forward by Comrade Lukyanov? Fine. Those in favor of supporting them, please vote. Please lower your hands. Against? Count them, please.

(The votes are counted)

M.S. Gorbachev: Comrades, I don't think that now, when we are still coming to grips with things, is yet the time to call a savage halt to everything. I think that we are gradually beginning to see that we work better when we don't have people rushing about, waiting in line, and so forth. Let us slip gradually into the groove and absorb this experience. I wouldn't like tough interference by the presidium at this time...

Voice from the floor: (inaudible).

M.S. Gorbachev: Fine. One moment. Comrades, while there's no debate going on, have you finished counting?

Yu.A. Osipyan: Yes. There were 72 votes against.

M.S. Gorbachev: And abstentions?

Voice from the floor: They didn't say.

FIRST CONGRESS OF PEOPLE'S DEPUTIES OF THE USSR

Third Session

26 May 1989

M.S. Gorbachev: I don't understand.

Yu.A. Osipyan: People didn't say if they were abstaining.

M.S. Gorbachev: So who did abstain? Let me ask the deputies.

Ya.S. Kanovich, writer, Vilnius city. (Vilyusskiy-Pashilaychskiy National-Territorial Electoral Okrug): I think that we, our delegation, would be doing the right thing if each person voted in accordance with his conscience and his voters' instructions. (Applause).

M.S. Gorbachev: So, comrades, do you have the figure for the number of abstentions?

Voice from the floor: There were 63 abstentions.

M.S. Gorbachev: That means we have decided the matter. Now I want to say this, comrades. We have a list here in the presidium. It contains deputies' requests to make specific comments on the personnel. And some comrades have already spoken and made proposals in the course of the speeches. Perhaps this is what we should do. As we are combining two principles, and each delegation from a republic or region is deciding on its final, collective candidacies for the list (whether by secret or open ballot), and in view of the fact that there are a great many observations, it seems to me that we should now take a 30-minute break, so that each delegation can make a final decision, formulate its proposals, and report its views to the presidium. And the oblasts of Russia too, comrades. Any comments?

We will break for 30 minutes.

M.S. Gorbachev [resumes]: Comrade Landsbergis wants to speak on behalf of the Lithuanian deputies. Go ahead.

V.V. Landsbergis: Esteemed chairman! Esteemed deputies! The Lithuanian delegation has instructed me to say this. We regret that what I said earlier was misunderstood and misinterpreted. The only purpose of my statement was to explain our fundamental moral principle. We are not seizing or assuming the right to decide for other republics who should represent them on the Supreme Soviet. We deemed it necessary to explain this before the vote, so that the motivation for the personal decision by any particular deputy of ours is clear to his fellow deputies. Thank you! (Applause).

M.S. Gorbachev: Now I give the floor to Comrade Lukyanov.

A.I. Lukyanov: Comrades! I will simply say what has been done so far. It is very good that the deputies elected from the republics have responded so effectively to the call for unity. We have received a full list from Belorussia, with minor amendments. The deputies from Uzbekistan have also reported their amendments, and their list is fully agreed. The deputies from Azerbaijan have sumitted two lists—one for the Soviet of the Union and one for the Soviet of Nationalities. The deputies from Tajikistan have reported that they have no comments to make. The Kirov group of deputies, the Turkmen delegation, and the Moldavian delegation have made minor amendments, the Komi delegation...

M.S. Gorbachev: Are you talking about the Soviet of the Union?

A.I. Lukyanov: No, no, about both chambers. We now have approximately one-third of the delegations which have agreed on everything and prepared lists that are to be put to the vote. Latvia has no changes, nor the Ukraine, nor Lithuania.

M.S. Gorbachev: Three substitutions within the quota.

A.I. Lukyanov: Yes, in the group of deputies from the Ukraine there are three substitutions within the quota. In Kirghizia, none. In Moscow, none. In Armenia, none. Vitaliy Ivanovich [Vorotnikov] was in charge of coordination for the Russian Federation.

M.S. Gorbachev: Comrades! After hearing the short report from Comrade Stroyev on the Soviet of the Union, we became involved in resolving the main question, which was an obstacle to the discussion of the personnel for the Soviet of the Union and the Soviet of Nationalities. Therefore, a certain lack of coordination arose, in the sense that the report on behalf of the meeting of representatives on the composition of the Soviet of Nationalities has not been heard, although you have the lists in your hands. But I want to say: Because we have exchanged opinions in general on the approaches to this problem, we have thereby covered many of the issues. Nonetheless, by virtue of legal principles, I should once again specifically ask the question in connection with the Soviet of Nationalities: Does anyone have any comment on this score? They say there were comments on the Russian Federation's lists and proposals. Well, Vitaliy Ivanovich, do you want to report? Go ahead.

I. Vorotnikov: I should say that a norm was set—11 candidacies from each union republic. On the list for discussion at the meeting held by the group of representatives of deputies elected for national-territorial okrugs in the RSFSR, there were 13 people instead of the 11 allowed under the quota. One deputy, Comrade Mikhail Ivanovich Sorokin, a deputy defense minister, withdrew, and at the start of the opening of this session we were left with 12 people instead of 11. But additional proposals have just come in to include Comrade Nikolay Andreyevich Demakov from Novosibirsk on the list of candidate members of the Supreme Soviet. Incidentally, Novosibirsk also has an extra deputy, in addition to the quota, for the Soviet of the Union. Comrade Aleksandr Aleksandrovich Kiselev, second secretary of Volgograd Komsomol Obkom, and Comrade Vitaliy Makarovich

STENOGRAPHIC RECORD

Third Session

26 May 1989

Ryabkov, rector of the Magnitogorsk Mining and Metallurgical Institute, are also proposed. This is signed on behalf of the deputies by Deputy Kolesnikov from Irkutsk. He is not entitled to do that.

The Chelyabinsk deputies also propose to include on the secret ballot list for the Soviet of Nationalities Vitaliy Makarovich Ryabkov, rector of the Magnitogorsk Mining and Metallurgical Institute and deputy from Chelyabinsk and Kurgan Oblasts. This proposal is submitted by Deputy Lezhnev in his own name.

M.S. Gorbachev: What do you think about this?

V.I. Vorotnikov: I think these proposals have not been discussed and are not substantiated. Deputy Gidaspov has also sent in an addition.

Voice from the floor: The Leningrad delegation?

V.I. Vorotnikov: Leningrad. He asks for the inclusion among the candidates for the Soviet of Nationalities of Nikolay Pavlovich Napalkov, people's deputy from the All-Union "Znaniye" Society. That makes 17 people.

Voice from the floor: I would like to speak!

M.S. Gorbachev: On this question? Go ahead.

M.A. Lezhnev (Traktozavodskiy Territorial Electoral Okrug, Chelyabinsk Oblast): We Chelyabinsk Oblast delegates discussed it and decided to include on the secret ballot list Vitaliy Makarovich Ryabkov, born in 1938, rector of the mining and metallurgical institute, doctor of sciences, and professor. Incidentally, esteemed comrade deputies from the Russian Federation, he had to come a long way in the elections—three rounds. He was elected from Kurgan and Chelyabinsk Oblasts. I request that the candidacy of Vitaliy Makarovich Ryabkov be supported and that he be included on the secret ballot list.

M.S. Gorbachev: Understood.

S.I. Kolesnikov, chairman of the presidium of the East Siberian Branch of the Siberian Department of the USSR Academy of Medical Sciences, Irkutsk city (Irkutskiy National-Territorial Electoral Okrug, RSFSR): Esteemed comrades! I proposed the inclusion of Nikolay Andreyevich Demakov and Aleksandr Aleksandrovich Kiselev on the list for the ballot for the Soviet of Nationalities. This proposal was discussed yesterday evening and today with representatives of the national-territorial okrugs of Chelyabinsk, Novosibirsk, Irkutsk, Omsk, Dalnevostochnyy Okrug, Kalininskiy, and Ivanovskiy. Therefore, I do not think it is quite correct to say that I am not entitled to nominate these people as candidates for the Soviet of Nationalities. The fact is that when we discussed the original list it was rather different, and that the deputies from the RSFSR national-territorial okrugs were not again called together to discuss it, so additional proposals arose.

Thank you for your attention.

V.I. Kolotov, editor of the newspaper VYBORGSKIY KOMMUNIST (Vyborgskiy Territorial Electoral Okrug, RSFSR): Comrade deputies! A group of Leningrad deputies was, as you know, elected on 14 and 19 May, and it could not participate in the selection of candidates for the Supreme Soviet. But so as to remove this discrimination, I propose on behalf of this group that Aleksandr Mitrofanovich Obolenskiy, deputy from Leningradskiy Rural National-Territorial Okrug No 20, and Nikolay Veniaminovich Ivanov, deputy from Leningradskiy National-Territorial Okrug No 19, be added to the secret ballot list from the RSFSR for the Soviet of Nationalities.

A.L. Plotnikov, foreman, at the Kirovo-Chepetsk machine repair plant, RSFSR, Kirov Oblast, Kirovo-Chepetsk city (From the All-Union Leninist Komsomol): Comrade deputies! We sent a note to the presidium from Kirov and Kostroma Oblasts, but for some reason it was not read out. It concerns Viktor Petrovich Savinykh. We all know that the Supreme Soviet is a working body. That means that it needs real workhorses, right? Viktor Petrovich Savinykh—we know how he worked in space—will not, I think, let us down here. He is willing. Therefore, I ask that his candidacy be considered attentively and supported. In addition, I support Aleksandr Kiselev from Volgograd.

M.S. Gorbachev: Comrade Gidaspov, please.

V.B. Gidaspov, general director of the "GIPKh" Science and Production Association, chairman of the board of the "Tekhnokhim" intersector state association, Leningrad city (Petrogradskiy Territorial Electoral Okrug, Leningrad city): Comrade deputies, during the break there was a conference of the Leningrad deputation, virtually the whole of it. We held an open vote on the candidacies that it would be expedient to submit for the Soviet of Nationalities. I wish to draw your attention to the fact that it is traditional to have a Leningrad deputy on the Soviet of Nationalities. If you examine this list carefully, you will see that there is no such candidate on it. Having conferred and voted, we reached this conclusion: The vast majority of votes went to Nikolay Pavlovich Napalkov, who has been mentioned here. He is a major Soviet scientist, director of the Leningrad oncology center, a medical academician, and a man of high moral qualities. On behalf of all the Leningraders, I ask you to support his candidacy in the vote. Thank you.

S.I. Novotnyy, general director of the "Adron" Science and Production Association research institute, Novosibirsk city (Zayeltsovskiy Territorial Electoral Okrug, RSFSR): Vitaliy Ivanovich, at the conference of

Third Session

26 May 1989

representatives we submitted amendments on three people, but for some reason these amendments did not reach you; they must have been delayed somewhere.

Today I submitted to Anatoliy Ivanovich [Lukyanov] the last amendment, in connection with the fact that Academician Yuriy Ivanovich Borodin wishes to withdraw. If his request is satisfied, we propose from the Novosibirsk Oblast delegation that Vitaliy Vasilyevich Bushuyev be included in the Supreme Soviet, for the chamber of the Soviet of the Union.

Voice from the floor: Could you not read out all the candidacies?

S.I. Novotnyy: I can say this: Yuriy Ivanovich Borodin, Nina Mikhaylovna Piryazeva, and Yuriy Yakovlevich Shmal. Yuriy Ivanovich Borodin has asked to withdraw; he sent a note to the presidium. If his withdrawal is accepted, Vitaliy Vasilyevich Bushuyev is proposed instead of Yuriy Ivanovich Borodin.

Voice from the floor: And if it is not accepted, Borodin remains?

S.I. Novotnyy: As the congress decides.

M.S. Gorbachev: Understood.

S.S. Shushkevich, prorector of the V.I. Lenin Belorussian State University (Minskiy Moskovskiy Territorial Electoral Okrug, Belorussian SSR): Esteemed comrades, for us in the Belorussian group of deputies everything is by no means as harmonious as it may seem from the list you have been given. I speak on behalf of four deputies—Comrades Stepanenko, Voronezhtsev, Fomenko, and myself. We believe that elections that are not contested will not allow us to form a worthy representation on the USSR Supreme Soviet, and therefore on behalf of these deputies I submit a proposal to include on the secret ballot list and nominate as candidates for the Soviet of the Union Aleksandr Olgertovich Dobrovolskiy (Minsk) and Aleksandr Grigoryevich Zhuravlev (Minsk), and for the Soviet of Nationalities Sergey Artemovich Gabrusev (Mogilev) and Viktor Nikolayevich Korneyenko (Gomel).

I will not give a portrait of each of them individually. I will only say that they are worthy representatives—from the highly qualified professor of economics Comrade Zhuravlev to the highly skilled worker Comrade Korneyenko from Gomel. I think the presence of such people on the list will make the elections more democratic and worthy.

Thank you for your attention.

G.M. Kurochka, chairman of the Komi Autonomous Soviet Socialist Republic Supreme Court permanent session. (Vorkutinskiy National-Territorial Electoral Okrug, Komi ASSR): I am not fond of speaking for a long time. My first question concerns the crisis situation that arose with regard to Lithuania. I think that there is a third compromise option.

From the floor: There is no need.

G.M. Kurochka: No need? All right. Then I will move on to my second question. I am a deputy from the Vorkuta National-Territorial Okrug. Deputies from the Komi ASSR did not include me on the list of candidates which should be entered on the ballot. But the congress presidium should now have no less than five cables from the people of Vorkuta and collectives asking for my candidacy to be included on this list.

Why am I so persistent and insistent on my candidacy? Because I am a lawyer with 12 years' service. We intend to build a rule-of-law state, and a lawyer with 12 years' service will certainly help this. Second, Comrades, Vorkuta has its own features, and if miners reckon that it is I who must defend their interests here, then what is bad about that? I appeal to the Congress and propose that this question be resolved at your discretion. That is all I have to say. (Applause).

A.I. Dubko, chairman of the "Progress" agro-industrial kolkhoz combine, Belorussian SSR, Grodno Oblast. (From the kolkhozes united in the All-Union Kolkhoz Council): People's deputies from Belorussia nominated candidates to the Supreme Soviet at their meeting. This problem was also resolved regionally. Candidates to the USSR Supreme Soviet were first elected in oblasts by a show of hands, and the meeting of Belorussian people's deputies then determined these candidacies as a whole. That is why I would ask you to consider the opinion expressed by a Belorussian deputy on behalf of four deputies as his personal opinion. The absolute majority is in favor of the candidacies proposed by the meeting. I would ask the congress to decline the request by the people's deputy from Belorussia concerning addenda to the lists with the presidium. Thank you.

V.Ye. Karmanovskiy, chief of the "Komitermneft" Oil and Gas Extraction Administration (Intinskiy National-Territorial Electoral Okrug, Komi ASSR). Anatoliy Ivanovich Lukyanov is indeed correct when he said that we have already "rehashed" our lists several times and that we began the discussion on 26 April. The original recommended list has undergone changes. It was also changed after the final elections that took place on 21 May. Of five people whose names were put forward at first, two of the proposed candidates have withdrawn their candidacies. We replaced them with a newly elected comrade and another man. However, during the voting in our area, 16 of the 17 delegates voted in favor of this proposal, while only Comrade Kurochka voted against it.

That is why I have a big request to ask of the congress: Decline Comrade Kurochka's request. I believe that it is not totally normal when deputies enlist support during

Third Session

26 May 1989

their election effort by saying that they will then be elected to the Supreme Soviet, and that that is why they recommend that people vote for them.

We reckon that our deputies have worked quite earnestly and adopted the following decision: On their behalf I ask you you to reject Comrade Kurochka and not vote for him.

Voice from the floor: Esteemed Comrade Deputies! I represent Territorial Okrug No 258, Perm city. I am submitting an additional candidacy from the RSFSR to the USSR Supreme Soviet Soviet of Nationalities for your consideration—namely Aleksandr Filippovich Nasonov, chief of the "Permgrazhdanstroy" Design and Construction Association. Aleksandr Filippovich was elected from an okrug with more than 2 million voters. He went through the repeat election procedure and a runoff—that is, he won in a very great struggle. I believe that alternatives in voting are a boon and that there is no point in rejecting those candidacies that do not have objections from the hall in principle. Thank you for your attention.

V.S. Grigoryan, first secretary of the Martuninskiy party Raykom, Nagorno-Karabakh Autonomous Oblast [NKAO]. (Martuninskiy National-Territorial Electoral Okrug, NKAO): On behalf of the NKAO group of deputies I am submitting a proposal that Comrades Genrikh Andreyevich Pogosyan and Zoriy Gaykovich Balayan be included on the secret ballot list. We concluded that three of the five NKAO deputies are party raykom first secretaries. Comrade Pogosyan lives in Moscow and has every opportunity to participate in the work of the USSR Supreme Soviet Soviet of Nationalities. Comrade Zoriy Gaykovich Balayan also has an opportunity to take an active part in it. That is why our group concluded that everyone should be included on the secret ballot paper. Thank you.

Yu.A. Andreyev, chief engineer at the "Mosgiprotrans" Moscow State Transport Construction Design and Research Institute (Babushkinskiy Territorial Electoral Okrug, Moscow city): I did not hear that the Moscow group would allow changes. When we met here, Tatyana Ivanovna Zaslavskaya expressed a wish to withdraw her candidacy. That was my understanding. But we did not hear this, so I have come to provide clarification. In connection with the fact that Tatyana Ivanovna has withdrawn her candidacy, I propose including Telman Khorenovich Gdlyan, deputy from Moscow City Territorial Electoral Okrug No 25, in the secret ballot paper for elections to the Soviet of the Union. He has a juridical higher education and was born in 1940. Moreover, I propose including Comrades Petrakov and Lisichkin on the secret ballot paper for election to the Soviet of the Union. That is all I have to say. (Applause).

V.P. Polyanichko, second secretary of the Azerbaijan Communist Party Central Committee. (Khachmasskiy Territorial Electoral Okrug, Azerbaijan SSR): I want to provide you with a small piece of information. In accordance with the procedure for nominating candidates for election to the Supreme Soviet chambers, our republic's deputies, who have a supremely respectful attitude toward the NKAO's Armenian and Azerbaijani populations, supported two candidacies: Comrades Pogosyan and Dzhafarov. Therefore, we sought to take another real step toward rapprochement and mutual understanding. The day before yesterday, at the meeting of USSR people's deputies in which representatives of Azerbaijan, Armenia, and the NKAO took part, these candidacies caused no comment. We do not see any grounds for revising our proposals. We have just consulted deputies from our republic and NKAO deputies once again: If the decisions that we adopt over these few days are wise then our actions should also be wise. (Applause).

V.L. Fomenko, deputy shop chief at the V.V. Kuybyshev artifical fiber plant of the V.I. Lenin "Khimvolokno" Production Association in Mogilev. (Mogilevskiy City Territorial Electoral Okrug, Mogilev Oblast): Comrades, the following situation has taken shape within the Belorussian delegation: Most of us are proceeding on the premise that the quota of Belorussian representation in the USSR Supreme Soviet signifies our quota for nominating candidates. I reckon that these are two different things. The representation quota is enshrined in the USSR Constitution, but we can nominate a larger number of candidates. That is why I am confirming our proposal regarding the nomination of an additional list of candidates to the USSR Supreme Soviet. This list includes Comrades Korniyenko, Gabrusev, Dobrovolskiy, and Zhuravlev. I reckon that the withdrawal of their candidacy is unmotivated and unwarranted, and that there is interference from the Belorussian delegation in the congress' prerogatives to elect the USSR Supreme Soviet.

R.K. Shchedrin, composer and chairman of the RSFSR Union of Composers Board. (from the USSR Union of Composers): I want to submit a proposal: to add Nikolay Ilich Travkin to the list of candidates for the USSR Supreme Soviet Soviet of the Union. I think that many of you have seen him on television. I think that he is a man of natural gifts with a most interesting and impressive way of thinking. He is a construction worker, one who has experienced the great and complex school of life. I think that his involvement in the work of the USSR Supreme Soviet could be of great benefit, and I am pleased to do this because a musician is proposing a worker.

V.V. Sevryukov, deputy chief of youth work and secretary of the Black Sea Steamship Company's Komsomol Committee. (from the Komsomol): Two questions, Comrades. The question of young people is a very important question, and after the speeches, it will be discussed in detail in the debate on the report. If we now look at the list of candidates in the elections for the USSR Supreme Soviet, only 5 percent of them are young people age 30 or under. Bearing in mind the fact that it

Third Session

26 May 1989

is those deputies who win more than 50 percent of the vote in general who will be elected to the Supreme Soviet. I ask you to pay serious attention to this. We should make sure that we do not elect other deputies at the expense of young people. I repeat, young people make up just 5 percent!

My second question comes from the Komsomol delegation. I would nonetheless ask you to support the candidacy of Aleksandr Kiselev from Volgograd. (Applause).

N.V. Savchenko, chairman of Krasnodar Kray's "Chernomorets" fishing kolkhoz. (from the All-Union Association of Fishing Kolkhozes): I'm speaking in general at the behest of our Krasnodar group, because we are not quite clear as to what is currently happening. Each deputy leaves his own group of deputies and cannot decide the question of which of them will be in the Supreme Soviet. What do you think we should be deciding, comrades? If you cannot choose someone out of 30 people when you know them, we, too, find it very hard to choose from among such a number of people.

Take the Moscow group, for instance. I have great respect for it, but I don't understand: You have even set up a club in which you have been discussing matters for more than 2 months, and you still cannot choose people. Why? Why do you not trust each other? After all, we have a single program and a single aim: These are our people, these are our voters, and we are talking about improving their lives and all areas of our life. Why do we take this attitude to each other?

I would like to mention how we in Krasnodar made our choice: We decided the matter long before coming to Moscow. Admittedly, not all of us were well-known deputies. Six of our people had not been elected before. But we immediately reserved one seat for them, to ensure that people who were elected at the last minute also had a chance of joining the Supreme Soviet.

We took the view that all delegates representing our Kuban in the Supreme Soviet should have a single correct aim. That is, they should do everything possible to carry out our voters' wishes.

We chose the candidates for the USSR Supreme Soviet ourselves—the first secretary of the party kraykom and the chairman of the krayispolkom. But they declined the nomination and had reasons for so doing. We chose four people: Viktor Andreyevich Gubarev, deputy director of the "Neftetermmash" prototype-experimental machine building plant; Vladimir Vasilyevich Kasyan, administrator of a sovkhoz department; Valeriy Vasilyevich Khmura, chairman of the Primorsko-Akhtarskiy Rayon's Olginskaya Rural Soviet Ispolkom; and Anatoliy Tikhonovich Kuzovlev, chairman of a kolkhoz board.

I ask the congress to support the candidates we have chosen. As for other oblasts' delegations, I think that they need to work out the question themselves. We should trust them in that respect and support the candidates they put forward. (Applause).

T.P. Zhukova, teacher at the Moscow Oblast Children's Home, (from the Komsomol): You know, you have already heard this request, but I insistently ask you once again to pay attention to Aleksandr Kiselev's candidacy. I think that Aleksandr Kiselev has currently won prestige among young people and in the Komsomol, and that he is indeed worthy of it. And who better than young people to protect their interests in the USSR Supreme Soviet? (Applause).

M.S. Gorbachev: Do you also have a specific proposal? Go ahead.

V.N. Zubkov, chief physician at the No 5 Maternity Association, Rostov-na-Donu city. (Leninskiy Territorial Okrug, Rostov Oblast): Comrade deputies! Look how complex the situation is. We are all saying that we need to choose representatives for the Soviet of the Union from regions, oblasts, and krays. At the same time, we are saying that there should be a norm for representation. As Vitaliy Ivanovich Vorotnikov said, there should be 1 deputy per 771,000 persons. I am now turning to you for help—for collective help, so to speak. In our city of Rostov we have 1 million inhabitants, if not more. We have three deputies. And now our democracy, our Constitution, has led to not one of us three being listed as candidates for the Supreme Soviet. Deputies representing the oblast were listed.

Before lunch today a worker from the "Rostselmash" plant spoke. He, too, was worried, and he asked for me to be included, as an exception, on the list of future members of the Supreme Soviet. Now, after the interval, we have not reached a clear answer, and I would like to make the reverse proposal. I therefore ask you to include on the list of candidates for the USSR Supreme Soviet the worker from Rostov-na-Donu city. I have swapped places with him, for we need someone in Rostov-na-Donu to protect the interests of the city rather than of the oblast as a whole. We have all been talking about regions, and you can see the situation.

And so we USSR people's deputies, myself, Vladimir Nikolayevich Zubkov, and Vladimir Yakovlevich Shevlyuga—bearing in mind the norms for representation in the USSR Supreme Soviet, and guided by the fact that Rostov-na-Donu (a city with over 1 million inhabitants and three territorial electoral okrugs, two of which we represent) has been deprived by numerous maneuvers of the possibility of delegating a deputy to the Supreme Soviet—we have both decided (because the third deputy from Rostov-na-Donu city did not support us very strongly) to essentially resort to self-nomination. To which end we ask you, the congress, to include Deputy Shevlyuga on the list of proposed members of the USSR

STENOGRAPHIC RECORD

Third Session
26 May 1989

Supreme Soviet. Before lunch he mentioned me. We therefore ask you to perhaps put both of us on the list... (noise in the auditorium) That's the way it is. I ask the congress to support our statement.

M.S. Gorbachev: Before giving the floor to other comrades, I want to submit the following proposal: If Russia and Belorussia, which will have twice the number of candidates for the Soviet of Nationalities as was originally proposed by the delegation, consider this acceptable, the proposals can be adopted by the congress. If they want to consult with each other and they need time, then we must give them time. Let them meet during the break and discuss the matter, because ultimately we must reach a common denominator. If they ask us, we must respect them, because I have seen very many proposals from various Russian oblasts. And, for instance, two speakers from Belorussia have essentially advocated the same opinion—supplementing the list of candidates.

That is why I want to ask, Vitaliy Ivanovich (addressing V.I. Vorotnikov), whether you need time or whether we can adopt all these proposals and include these people on the list.

V.N. Zubkov: The point is that many oblast representatives object to these candidacies; that is why we should discuss them all.

M.S. Gorbachev: You need to consult. Comrades from Belorussia! Do you need to consult on the question of additions? Comrade Sokolov?

Ye.Ye. Sokolov, first secretary of the Belorussian Communist Party Central Committee, Minsk city. (Kobrinskiy Territorial Electoral Okrug, Brest Oblast): Dear Comrades! This congress includes 94 people from the Belorussian SSR, 60 of whom were elected from national-territorial and territorial electoral okrugs. We have examined on three occasions the question of whom to recommend as candidates on the list for election to the USSR Supreme Soviet, twice in Minsk and the last time literally just before this session began. We examined this at the oblast level, and all the lists we have submitted here were supported by an overwhelming majority of deputies, with the exception of four. The comrades who have submitted an additional proposal do not reflect the general opinion of the Belorussian delegation. I would ask you to draw your conclusions on that basis.

M.S. Gorbachev: So you are not asking for a break?

Ye.Ye. Sokolov: No.

M.S. Gorbachev: You are clear about everything?

Ye.Ye. Sokolov: Yes.

M.S. Gorbachev: But your proposal is not to be adopted?

Ye.Ye. Sokolov: No.

M.S. Gorbachev: Understood. Fine. The comrades from Russia, and that is more than 1,000 delegates, ask us to give them time to confer. I do not think we can ignore one-half of the deputies. I would suggest that as we are about to take a break, let the Russian Federation stay in the auditorium and hold a discussion. Then they can come and tell us what they have decided. The Belorussian comrades, because the time is available, can also discuss this and let us know. And all the other delegations where questions arise, do not raise them from the platform; instead, decide them during the break. And then if your proposals are agreed on, submit them to us.

Comrades, if we take this path, what do you think? Is it the right one?

Voices from the floor: Yes.

M.S. Gorbachev: No objections?

Voices from the floor: No.

M.S. Gorbachev: Then I announce a break for half an hour. The deputies from the Russian Federation will remain in the auditorium.

M.S. Gorbachev [resumes]: Let us hear the report on the results of work by the Russian Federation deputies.

V.I. Vorotnikov: Esteemed comrades! The deputies from the Russian Federation displayed a very high level of activity in the last few minutes, and we were unable to decide the matter in the time remaining for the break. Therefore, we are forced to request permission to resolve some of our questions in the presence of all the congress deputies.

It is a question, comrades, first, of proposals for people's deputies included on the Russian Federation's list for the Soviet of Nationalities. Under the USSR Constitution the Russian Federation, like any other union republic, has a quota: 11 people are to be submitted to the Soviet of Nationalities from the national-territorial okrugs and social organizations.

On the eve of the congress we had a meeting of the deputies who were elected for national-territorial okrugs (true, not all of them—a few people were absent) and representatives from the social organizations. A list of proposals was drawn up, which you have in your hands. This list—I will not read out the names—includes 12 candidacies for 11 places. After instructions were given to the groups of deputies from the union republics and from the oblasts of the Russian Federation to reexamine the proposals both for the Soviet of the Union and for the Soviet of Nationalities, additional proposals were made by some deputies individually and by some groups of deputies. Such proposals came from Novosibirskiy Okrug for the inclusion of an additional candidate,

STENOGRAPHIC RECORD

Third Session
26 May 1989

Deputy Nikolay Andreyevich Demakov, on the list, from Volgogradskiy Okrug for the additional inclusion of Aleksandr Aleksandrovich Kiselev, and from Chelyabinsk on the inclusion of Vitaliy Makarovich Ryabkov. A proposal was submitted by Comrade Obolenskiy. He submitted a proposal on Comrade Ivanov, who was elected for Leningradskiy National-Territorial Okrug. A proposal was submitted on Comrade Savinykh, who was elected for Kirovskiy National-Territorial Okrug—he is rector of the Institute of Geodesy, Aerial Photography, and Cartography, from Moscow city; a proposal from Perm on Comrade Nasonov; and another from Leningrad on Comrade Nikolay Pavlovich Napalkov. That is to say, the list increased from 12 people to 20. During the break we tried to resolve this question, but we did not have enough time. Therefore, we consider it necessary to put this question to the vote in order to decide: Shall we agree to the list that was drawn up, coordinated, and voted on by representatives from Russia's national-territorial okrugs (as I told you, 12 were named, including 7 from national-territorial okrugs and 5 from social organizations)? Or, shall we begin to discuss the additional candidacies and decide the question of their inclusion on the list? That is the first question. In addition, proposals have come in from the Moscow city deputies....

M.S. Gorbachev: Now, this is for the Soviet of the Union?

V.I. Vorotnikov: Yes. Proposals have come in for a further increase in the list of candidacies for inclusion on the ballot paper for election to the Soviet of the Union. We are talking about Comrades Petrakov, Lisichkin, Gdlyan, Travkin, and others. I believe the Moscow group of deputies met to discuss this. At the same time, we have received withdrawals from some comrades, in particular Comrade Borovik and that same Comrade Lisichkin. I think the Moscow comrades should clarify the list of candidacies in some way, so that it is finalized. That is the crux of the matter.

M.S. Gorbachev: Fine. In general, basically, if we follow the logic of Comrade Vorotnikov's speech, we should begin to examine the question of candidates for the Soviet of Nationalities. They have the original list of candidacies, the list that was discussed at the meeting of representatives and added to, amended, and submitted to the congress today. With a quota of 11, they had a list of 12. Now, as a result of the initiative movement, the list has grown to 20. That is how I understand your proposal, which you did not have time to vote on. And we should help you to do this—that is, the Russian Federation deputies should vote in the presence of everyone. The question should be put to the vote, in their presence: whether to agree on the original proposals, or whether to extend the list of candidacies and discuss those candidacies that were submitted additionally. But I want to ask (although in this case it is a question of the Soviet of Nationalities, it does affect the regions), should the entire body of deputies therefore take part in the vote?

V.I. Vorotnikov: The entire body of deputies from Russia.

M.S. Gorbachev: Well then, comrades, we have two proposals: Do we continue the debate on Russia's behalf (Russia has already had a debate) or do we simply vote? We vote? Fine.

In that case I put the first proposal to the vote. Who is in favor of confirming the first proposal, which we have had here since this morning—the list of 12 people? I ask you to raise your credentials cards. Only the RSFSR deputies are voting. Please count. Yes, I am also voting for the first proposal.

From the floor: Comrade deputies! Results of the vote: Out of the 1,059 Russian Federation deputies, 726 voted "for." (applause.)

M.S. Gorbachev: Who is against? Unless you want the full breakdown: Who is "against" and who "abstains"? Then that is all; the question is decided. The first proposal is adopted, meaning the first option—12 people remain on the list.

From the floor: (inaudible).

M.S. Gorbachev: Who is against the first option and for the second? Let us count. Well, there is clearly a minority.

Yu.A. Osipyan, academician, vice president of the USSR Academy of Sciences, and director of the USSR Academy of Sciences Institute of Solid State Physics (from the USSR Academy of Sciences): Results of the vote on the second proposal: 265 deputies voted "for."

M.S. Gorbachev: So we have clarified the matter. Now we have a question from the delegation of Moscow deputies. Which of you wants the floor? A question on the Soviet of the Union. I should have added, on the Soviet of the Union.

People's deputy (does not introduce himself): Comrade deputies! As you know, the Moscow delegation, the Moscow deputies proposed to the congress an alternative option for the election of deputies to the USSR Supreme Soviet. Now, during the break, we have had a session of the Moscow group of deputies. The vast majority were present. There was a vote, and the delegates from Moscow asked me to inform the congress that Moscow wishes to keep the list that was submitted this morning. (Applause).

People's deputy (who did not introduce himself): Esteemed comrade deputies, I wish to draw your attention to a problem. In my view the difficulties that have now arisen in nominating candidates from national-territorial okrugs for the Soviet of Nationalities stem from the fact that we are trying to combine things that are basically incompatible: namely, elections and delegating [delegirovaniye]. If we retain the procedure we

FIRST CONGRESS OF PEOPLE'S DEPUTIES OF THE USSR

Third Session

26 May 1989

have now decided upon—that is, a republic decides on 11 candidates for 11 places—then the elections by the congress become a fiction. On the other hand, it is naturally necessary to make provisions for the republics' sovereign rights. In my view, the way out of this situation is this: to instruct every delegation and every republic to nominate a minimum of two candidates for each place on the Soviet of Nationalities, which will enable the congress, for its part, also to hold elections, without the whole thing coming down to empty approval, which cost us dearly enough in the past.

And a second proposal, dear comrades. Because we have no single-nation republics, although some people have recently been trying to convince us of this, as our republics are inhabited by various national groups whose interests often, unfortunately, lead to certain contradictions, it seems to me that in nominating candidacies for the Soviet of Nationalities (among the 24 candidacies that are nominated), the principle of proportionality should be observed, as was envisaged by the 19th party conference.

Thank you for your attention.

It is true that I would like this proposal to be considered by the deputies. And if not this time, when we have virtually completed the procedure, then it should be taken into account next time.

M.S. Gorbachev: Comrades, shall we continue?

Fine. Those in favor of now ending the discussion of the question of the nomination of candidacies to the Soviet of the Union and Soviet of Nationalities, please raise your mandate cards. Please lower them. Who is against this? Count. (The votes are counted).

M.S. Gorbachev: Eight. So the question is decided.

Now we have to organize the voting. But before we vote, we have to establish the voting procedure. We have a proposal on this question. Indeed, you have it. Do we need a report?

Voices from the floor: No.

M.S. Gorbachev: In the course of the explanations, especially as regards the first part, although the comrades do not like what I am saying—the philosophy of the matter—in the course of the explanations we have clarified all the general questions. And it seems that much that was unclear and could have arisen in the course of discussion of the draft on the procedure for conducting the secret ballot for elections to the Supreme Soviet and Soviet of Nationalities is now clear.

But perhaps there are still some matters that are not clear.

Voices from the floor: No.

M.S. Gorbachev: We can put it to the vote whether or not to adopt this procedure.

Those in favor of adopting the proposed draft, taking into account the exchange of opinions and interpretations, please raise your hands. Please lower them.

Anyone against? Please count.

Eight against.

Abstentions? For the record.

M.S. Gorbachev [resumes]: In general, the question is decided. Now the tellers' commission must begin its work. Before it begins, the floor is given to Comrade Osipyan. Go ahead. The chairman of the tellers' commission:

Yu.A. Osipyan: Comrade deputies! We now have to print 2,200 ballot papers, something like that, on each of which, you realize, there will be 250-270 or even 300 candidates. That will take some time, and so we must now start printing the ballot papers after all the questions have been decided. In approximately 2 hours, the voting will begin.

M.S. Gorbachev: Comrades! The sensible thing would be to vote at 2100 today, and then hear the results tomorrow.

Yu.A. Osipyan: Comrades! You can imagine that the tallying, when there are 2,200 ballot papers with 500 candidates on each of them, will take some time, perhaps 10 hours or so. Therefore, if we vote today, we can do the counting during the night and part of tomorrow, and then the work of the congress can continue. Otherwise, it will be broken off for a long time.

M.S. Gorbachev: After the explanation, no one insists on anything else?

The auditorium: No.

M.S. Gorbachev: Therefore, I declare a break for the work of the tellers' commission, until 2100 hours.

M.S. Gorbachev: I shall read a telegram to you while we are assembling. Deputy Borovikov from Sochi received the following telegram: "We believe that everyone should have the opportunity to speak. You shouldn't keep the kind of people in a hurry to get home or who have no time. Work at least a year, as long as you have to. The workers will pay for your labor." (Applause).

In general the telegrams keep coming in....

A telegram from Novokuznetsk: "I ask Novokuznetskiy Territorial Electoral Okrug Deputy Medikov to read it out to the congress. What democratization can there be in the country if there is no democratization at the congress? Slow hand clapping, refusal to hear a deputy, depriving him of his right to speak. That's democracy?

STENOGRAPHIC RECORD

Third Session
26 May 1989

You must not only know how to speak, you must know how to listen to everyone. It's an insult to the voters and deputies or boorishness. Installation worker Poroshin, nonparty member. Novokuznetsk." (Applause).

Yu.A. Osipyan: Comrades! You can see how much time the printing of the ballot papers has taken. The papers are complicated, there is an enormous number of them, they are very large and unwieldy because there is a large number of candidacies. You can imagine that their complexity is in direct proportion to the greater time today's papers have taken to print than previous ones. And we will take longer to count. So the tellers' commission will work for a long time.

Now the thrust of the matter: The procedure for voting or rather going to the place to vote, obtaining ballot papers, and voting... Just as yesterday, you will have to cross out the candidacies which you believe must be crossed out. But today there is a special feature. Each of you will receive two ballot papers. There will be pens in the booths. And the voting mechanism will be the same. You will receive two thick ballot papers—for voting for candidacies to the Soviet of the Union and for voting on candidacies for the Soviet of Nationalities. They are of different colors: white for the Soviet of the Union and blue for the Soviet of Nationalities.

On each ballot paper the candidacies will be in the same order as they figure in your reference information. About the order in which the candidacies for the Soviet of the Union are set out. First there is Moscow City and then all the union republics. The order of candidacies for the Soviet of Nationalities includes all the union republics including, where they exist, the autonomous republics, autonomous oblasts, and national okrugs. Under each heading the candidates will be listed in alphabetic order. The ballot paper indicates the quota for each republic, autonomous oblast, and national okrug.

You have the right to cross out as many candidacies as you consider necessary and also to leave as many as you consider necessary.

Now—how will the votes be counted and how will the results of the voting be assessed? I want to dwell specially on this point.

There can be various options. There are an enormous number of possible options.

First. The voting procedure which you have to hand contains phrases which define what will have to be done. Candidates who have received the largest number of votes among the candidates for a particular union republic and over half the votes from the total number of USSR people's deputies are considered to be elected to the Soviet of the Union and the Soviet of Nationalities. Candidates who have received the greatest number of votes are also considered to have been elected to the Soviet of Nationalities. If the number of candidates who have received over 50 percent of votes is larger than the quota, then the first in terms of the largest number of votes are considered to have been elected.

But it is immediately clear that there can be all kinds of variations. For instance, all candidates for a particular union republic (and there are republics which have a number of candidates equal to the quota) receive 100 percent of the votes. That means they are all elected. If, for a given union republic, the number of candidates is more than the quota (and they all receive 100 percent of the votes) there will be a runoff for all candidates.

That is the first variation. The second is as follows. For instance, a certain number of candidates receives the largest number of votes necessary to be elected. For instance, 8 candidates are left out of 11. Three seats remain unfilled. It immediately transpires that there are four candidates who are runners up, having received an equal number of votes. Consequently a runoff has to be held only for these four candidates to fill the three remaining seats.

There is also the following option: Some eight people have received the necessary number of votes, the remainder less than 50 percent of the votes. The eight are considered to have been elected and a runoff will be held for the runners up, for the same candidacies.

It is also possible that during a runoff no one will have received over 50 percent of the votes. Then one more runoff may be held. But it is also possible to hold a new discussion of the question and to nominate new candidates.

That is, I want to say that the phrase in the procedure, to wit, that if, as a result of voting for the Soviet of the Union or the Soviet of Nationalities for either the okrugs or the republics, the number of elected candidates is more or less than the quota stipulated for the specific republic, then a runoff is held following a decision of the Congress. That is a general phrase which includes all kinds of possible options and simply indicates that there are different situations when there will be a runoff.

We will thus probably have to take decisions on each situation which takes shape. The presidium will submit the question for examination by the Congress and it will be decided how to carry out the runoff.

Now we must hold the first vote.

M.S. Gorbachev: Comrades, I ask everyone to remain seated.

Yu.A. Osipyan: The main thing which should be borne in mind is that in accordance with the USSR Constitution all decisions of the Congress on both general and personal questions must be taken by a majority of votes. As

Third Session
26 May 1989

you know, during the elections of people's deputies at the last stage, when deputies failed to receive the necessary number of votes, it was enough simply to beat their rival by any number of votes. We cannot have this at the Congress. That is why we will either have to hold as many rounds as necessary for a candidate to receive over 50 percent of the votes or, following a Congress decision, have a new discussion and nominate other candidates, for instance.

That is the rather complex situation. We are faced with a serious vote. The possibility of repeat elections is not ruled out either.

M.S. Gorbachev: Comrades, are there questions for the commission chairman?

Yu.S. Osipyan: Yes, how to get to the voting place? There is one question here. As you recall, yesterday the main thing which took up our time was getting the ballot papers; the actual act of voting was very swift. You passed through the booth, you could do nothing with the ballot paper and then simply drop it into the box or you could cross out names or write something on the paper. But now when you have a ballot paper in your hands (two ballot papers) with about 600 names and you have to do something with it, most of the time will be spent working on your paper. Where are you to do this? The simplest solution would be for you to be able to enter a booth and spend 10 or 15 minutes in the booth with the ballot paper. But an enormous line of people would form behind you because it is still quicker to get a ballot paper than to fill it in. So we suggest that it will probably not be a contravention if, once you have received your ballot paper, you go to one side with it and go down to another floor. But, comrades, before putting your ballot paper in the box, you will have to pass through a booth. You can return and pass through the booth so that everyone has an opportunity to enter the booth.

So we will probably do it like this: We shall use some of the booths for people to go into and work with their ballot papers in the booth and some booths will simply be for those who have marked their ballot papers elsewhere and want to go through the booth and drop the paper into the box.

It now only remains for me, comrades, to show you the ballot papers themselves and what they will look like.

The paper for elections to the Soviet of the Union is white. What does it look like? At the top is the first group, the candidates from Moscow. And it is written: First paragraph—Russian Soviet Federated Socialist Republic [RSFSR], 146 deputies are being elected, 176 are running as candidates. The first group consists of the candidates from Moscow. The names are in alphabetical order here. There is also a reminder that 29 are being elected and 55 are running. That is the basis on which you can do what you want with the list.

Then there is the RSFSR and the autonomous republics, krays, and oblasts of the RSFSR. There is a similar list for the Ukraine—52 deputies with 52 running, while the list for Belorussia is 10 and 10 respectively, for Uzbekistan 14 and 14, and so forth. You are all well aware of this.

Now the ballot paper for elections to the Soviet of Nationalities. This is easy to understand, the RSFSR, the Ukraine, Belorussia, Uzbekistan, are set out in a column... So that everything should be clear there is written information for all the union republics too. As you know, 11 people must be elected from each and on some lists there are 12 people, on others 11—it's all explained for each republic. Everything has been done the same way for the autonomous republics, autonomous oblasts, and, finally the national okrugs.

That's really all. Now a request to the presidium: How to regulate the flow. People will move more slowly now so perhaps not the first 20 rows but let's say the first 10 rows at first will go out, then the next 10.

M.S. Gorbachev: Good, thank you. A question for the chairman? Please go ahead.

Voice from the auditorium: Forgive me, I have one question, how will the results of the voting for candidates from Moscow City be summed up? In accordance with the Standing Order the results are summed up for the republic as a whole and these candidates are thus on the overall list for the RSFSR.

Yu.A. Osipyan: No.

Voice from the auditorium: In accordance with the Standing Order that is exactly how it is since the candidates who have received the largest number of votes among the candidates for a particular union republic are considered to have been elected to the Soviet of the Union. And Moscow City is not singled out in any way in the Standing Order. And I should like an explanation.

Yu.A. Osipyan: We have the following figures for the elections to the Soviet of the Union: The Russian Federation—146 deputies are elected and 176 are running as candidates. That means that we must ultimately elect 146 deputies from this overall list for the Russian Federation. That is the main Regulation for deputies from the Russian Federation. We are obliged to meet this regulation. So there cannot be a greater or lesser number of elected deputies in the final outcome.

In line with the decision taken by the congress, when it singled out Moscow in a separate list, here too it is singled out. It indicates that 29 deputies are being elected and 55 are running as candidates. These 29 deputies together with the remaining 117 will make up the 146 deputies who are standing as candidates under the standing order.

M.S. Gorbachev: That is fine. Is that all, comrades? A question? Go ahead.

Voice from the auditorium: Comrade Osipyan, Nagorno-Karabakh Autonomous Oblast [NKAO] has

Third Session
26 May 1989

not nominated deputies for election to the Soviet of Nationalities. Our oblast is deprived of these rights. This has been done for us by the republic, although it is clearly stated here that this is the prerogative of the oblast. I think, comrade deputies, that although we only began this work yesterday we are already committing breaches of the law, because that is the prerogative of the oblast. Every oblast present here appointed for itself those persons it felt necessary to include on the list. Consequently, I believe that we do not have any candidates from the NKAO and I call upon all those who believe that the foundations of legal relations must primarily be laid by us here to consider that our candidates are not on the list. Thank you.

M.S. Gorbachev: I think we have already discussed this question, if you remember. Every republic was instructed (on the basis of the exchange of opinions and proposals expressed) to clarify its position in the interval and submit its proposals. I repeat, every republic, apart from Moscow, for which an exception has been made. That is what the comrades have done. Everything said by every republic has been incorporated in this report. I do not think there is any justification for reviewing the lists now. What do you think, comrades? Otherwise we will have to start all over again.

Yu.A. Osipyan: That is not a question for the tellers commission but for the presidium.

M.S. Gorbachev: Fine, thank you.

Comrades, may I ask you to give 3 minutes to decide important questions raised by deputies?

The first point. It is proposed that a congress secretariat be formed. When this idea was suggested, we asked that proposals be formulated. The preliminary proposals are as follows. I will read out the names of deputies and the republic they represent.

Comrades: Apostol—chief producer of the Kishinev Russian Drama Theater; Bocharov—director of the Butovskiy Construction Materials Combine, Moscow City; Vare—leading scientific associate of the Estonian Soviet Socialist Republic [SSR] Academy of Sciences History Institute; Yeraliyev—director of the 30th Anniversary of the October Revolution State Farm [sovkhoz], Chimkent City; Igrunov—second secretary of the Belorussian Communist Party Central Committee; Kapto—chief of the CPSU Central Committee Ideology Department; Krylova—chief editor of the journal RABOTNITSA; Kudarauskas—head of department at the Kaunas Polytechnical Institute, Lithuania; Mamedov—first secretary of the Kirovabad city party committee (gorkom), Azerbaijan; Margvelashvili—senior lecturer in physics theory at the Tbilisi State University; Medvedev—director of the Kirghiz Mining and Metallurgy Combine; Nazarov—Tajik minister of public education; Nazaryan—chairman of the "Maralik" Collective Farm [kolkhoz] agrarian firm in Armenia; Orazmuradova—pediatrician at the Serakhskiy Rayon Hospital, Turkmenia; Plotniyeks—professor at the Stuchka Latvian State University; Shcherbak—writer,

secretary of the board of the Ukrainian Writers Union; and Usmanov—Russian language and literature teacher at School No 20, Uzbekistan.

Voice from the floor: The deputy from Georgia has already been elected as a teller.

M.S. Gorbachev: Then we must replace the comrade from Georgia. Perhaps you could suggest someone?

From the floor: (Inaudible remark).

M.S. Gorbachev: I can't hear you. Never mind, we will establish who represents the delegation. Can we vote for the secretariat as it is?

Voices from the floor: Yes.

M.S. Gorbachev: I put it to the vote. Those in favor of the proposed secretariat, I ask you to raise your cards. Now put them down. Is there anyone against? No. Abstentions? No.

A draft resolution has also been proposed, if you have no objection, "On Citizens' Proposals, Statements, and Complaints Addressed to the Congress of People's Deputies."

The Congress of USSR People's Deputies resolves:

"1. To instruct the Presidium and Secretariat of the Congress of USSR People's Deputies to promptly examine and take into account citizens' proposals addressed to the congress during the preparation of the relevant items and decisions.
"2. To forward citizens' requests and complaints of a personal nature addressed to the congress for examination by the appropriate state and social bodies within the established legal procedure. Measures taken to resolve issues raised in citizens' appeals must be communicated to the petitioners and to the USSR Supreme Soviet Presidium."

That is the brief resolution. As citizens' appeals are still coming in and are going to increase in number, there must also be work in this direction. Is that acceptable, comrades? We will make a start and, if we should need to include some more mechanisms, we will proceed further. Are there any other proposals?

Voices from the floor: No.

M.S. Gorbachev: I put the proposed draft to the vote. Those in favor, I ask you to raise your cards. Now put them down. Any against? Abstentions? No. So it is decided, comrades. Thank you for everything.

Perhaps we could start work tomorrow at 1100? Or at 1200? The first suggestion is for 1100. All those in favor of continuing work at 1100 tomorrow, I ask you to raise your hands. Now put them down. Anyone against? Clearly a minority. So we will start at 1100. Goodbye.

STENOGRAPHIC RECORD

The BALTIC REGION

FIRST CONGRESS OF PEOPLE'S DEPUTIES OF THE USSR
FOURTH SESSION
SATURDAY, 27 MAY 1989
THE KREMLIN PALACE OF CONGRESSES

The third day's agenda called for the Congress to ratify the election of the Supreme Soviet and elect Anatoly I. Lukyanov to be its First Deputy Chairman. Hope for a speedy session faded when Yuri Osipyan, chairman of the Tellers' Commission, going strictly by the book, insisted not only on reading the names of all nominees for the Soviet of Nationalities but then on repeating the process, this time giving the votes cast for and against each candidate. (For the record, the leading vote-getter was G.A. Chernykh who was elected from the Komi ASSR with only 12 negative votes.) Since, outside of Moscow, only four seats were contested, the exercise was tedious and rather bizarre. It was later repeated for the election of the Soviet of the Union.

The somnolent tranquility of the hall was shattered, however, by the declaration of war delivered for the democratic minority by historian Yuri Afanasyev who characterized the newly elected Soviet as a "Stalinist-Brezhnevian" body. An "aggressive and obedient majority" that included Gorbachev himself was determined to retain power, frustrate the aspirations of the people, and ignore their needs. Economist Gavril Popov followed Afanasyev to the podium and continued the attack. The democratic minority, he declared, had opted to play a constructive, not an oppositionist, role in the Congress, but the apparatchiks had displayed no respect for pluralism. He concluded with an invitation to those who were not under will of the apparatus to join in forming an independent, Interregional Group of Deputies, which would formulate and present alternatives through minority reports ("co-reports").

Several conservatives heard Popov raise the specter of factionalism and reacted accordingly. To good Leninists factionalism was no matter to be taken lightly. The Tenth Party Congress of 1921 had made it a crime punishable by expulsion. A decade later Stalin upped the penalty to death by shooting and used it to decimate the Old Bolsheviks. Although Popov's appeal fell short of the formal definition, it came close enough. That explains the vigorous reaction of a number of party faithful as well as his own effort at the end of the session to temper his remarks.

The debate precipitated by the Afanasyev-Popov theses brought out some of the fundamental values at stake. Belorussian film producer Ales Adamovich identified the aspirations of most liberals when he called for popular control of the party apparatus and constitutional protection against an excessive concentration of power. On the other side, Baku deputy M.R. Mamedov struck at the basic failing of glasnost when he chided the liberals for offering no constructive advice: "They don't talk about how things should be fixed; all we know is that they've got to have freedom." That theme was revisited many times in the next several days by speakers demanding order and a restoration of discipline.

The residue of the Supreme Soviet elections contained two cases of apparent tinkering with candidate slates. One concerned the RSFSR, the other the NKAO. In the former, either by mistake or malice the name of Yuri Chemodanov was mysteriously replaced by that of another. The issue was resolved by a practical compromise that showed what could be accomplished when good will prevailed. The intense ethnic enmities in Nagorno-Karabakh left no room for compromise, however. The Congress had elected to the Soviet of Nationalities, an Armenian (Pogosyan) and an Azeri (Dzhafarov), the slate proposed by the Azerbaijan delegation. But in assembling the ballot the Presidium had ignored the two Armenian candidates (Pogosyan and Balayan) nominated by the oblast representatives. At length the Congress agreed to annul that election and hold another.

Gorbachev's nomination of Lukyanov as First Deputy Chairman of the Supreme Soviet was challenged on two counts, the propriety if not the legality of the nomination and the integrity of the candidate. The general secretary's hope of rushing through the election was frustrated by the extent of the criticism and questions about Lukyanov's role in setting and executing policy. Consequently his election had to be postponed to the next meeting.

Texts of documents cited in the Fourth Session are compiled in Appendices at the end of volume 2: Decree on the Procedure for Organizing and Holding Meetings, Rallies, Street Processions and Demonstrations in the USSR (Appendix A.3); Decree on the Introduction of Amendments and Addenda to the USSR Law "on Criminal Liability for State Crimes" (Appendix A.4); Decree on the Duties and Rights of USSR MVD Internal Troops in the Protection of Public Order (Summary) (Appendix A.5).

FOURTH SESSION
SATURDAY, 27 MAY 1989
STENOGRAPHIC RECORD

M.S. Gorbachev, chairman of the USSR Supreme Soviet, is in the chair.

M.S. Gorbachev: Comrades, there are several urgent notes, two or three. Let us open the session and give the floor to Deputy Osipyan, chairman of the Tellers' Commission, to speak on one of the main items on our agenda while we prepare ourselves on these notes. They contain urgent requests.

Please, Comrade Osipyan.

Yu.A. Osipyan: Comrade people's deputies! At its latest session, which continued without a break until the very last moment, the Tellers' Commission determined the results of the vote to elect the USSR Supreme Soviet, separately from the Soviet of the Union election and the Soviet of Nationalities election. When counting the votes for election to the Soviet of the Union, just as those for election to the Soviet of Nationalities, the Tellers' Commission, in accordance with the Election Regulations, was guided by the material passed on to it by the congress presidium. This material, the personal composition of nominated candidates, listed the surnames of candidates who were discussed at the initial sessions of delegations and at the sessions of representatives. This list was subsequently amended in the course of the congress, and as a result, in accordance with the congress regulations, and in accordance with procedural rules, all the material passed on to the Tellers' Commission constituted the contents of the ballot papers which you all received yesterday and used for the secret ballot.

Allow me first to read the minutes of the USSR Congress of People's Deputies Tellers' Commission on the results of the vote to elect the USSR Supreme Soviet Soviet of Nationalities, dated 26 May 1989. In accordance with the procedure approved by the congress for holding a secret ballot and determining its results at the USSR Congress of People's Deputies, the Tellers' Commission counted the number of votes cast to elect the USSR Supreme Soviet Soviet of Nationalities, and established that the following USSR people's deputies were listed on the ballot paper for the secret ballot to elect the Soviet of Nationalities:

From the Russian Soviet Federated Socialist Republic [RSFSR]:
V.I. Belov, N.V. Bosenko, V.I. Vorotnikov, Ye.A. Gayer, B.N. Yeltsin, A.I. Kazannik, A.A. Likhanov, V.P. Lukin, L.I. Matyukhin, S.I. Nevolin, V.S. Podziruk, V.M. Falin. 12 candidates.

From the Ukrainian Soviet Socialist Republic [SSR]:
V.S. Venglovskaya, V.V. Gnatyuk, I.A. Zabrodin, V.A. Ivashko, A.S. Kapto, S.M. Katilevskiy, V.T. Kurilenko, G.F. Lezhenko, B.I. Oleynik, V.D. Romanenko, V.S. Shevchenko.

From the Belorussian SSR:
V.S. Bolbasov, V.Ye. Golovnev, A.I. Dubko, N.I. Ignatovich, A.P. Kucheyko, V.A. Kiseleva, V.A. Labunov, Z.K. Mateushuk, T.V. Momotova, G.S. Tarazevich, V.V. Yakushkin.

From the Uzbek SSR:
V.T. Adylov, A.R. Atadzhanov, P. Badalbayeva, N. Davranov, A.S. Yefimov, M.Z. Zokirov, A.A. Korshunov, R.N. Nishanov, F. Sefershayev, R.M. Khudaybergenova, V.I. Tso.

From the Kazakh SSR:
Ye.N. Auyelbekov, R.S. Akhmetova, L.M. Veyser, V.I. Vidiker, M.D. Dzhumatova, P.M. Klishchuk, I. Kozhakhmetov, K.U. Medeubekov, Ye. Rakhmadiyev, K.Z. Romazanov, G.G. Shtoyk.

From the Azerbaijan SSR:
Ya.I. Abbasov, P.A. Azizbekova, R.M. Aleskerova, L.V. Barusheva, A.Kh. Vezirov, M.M. Gadzhiyev, G.R. Ibragimov, T.K. Ismailov, E.M. Kafarova, V.G. Mamedov, A.A. Namazova.

From the Lithuanian SSR:
E.V. Bichkauskas, E.Y. Vilkas, B.K. Genzyalis, R.V. Gudaytis, K.V. Zaletskas, S.Y. Kudarauskas, Yu.Y. Kuplyauskene, N.N. Medvedev, K.V. Moteka, Yu.Yu. Olekas, K.K. Uoka.

From the Georgian SSR:
V.S. Advadze, Sh.A. Amonashvili, A.V. Bakradze, D.I. Guguchiya, G.G. Gumbaridze, A.D. Dikhtyar, Z.G.

Fourth Session
27 May 1989

Kurashvili, T.N. Menteshashvili, T.M. Spanderashvili, T.S. Stepnadze, R.Sh. Tabukashvili.

From the Moldavian SSR:
Ye.D. Doga, I.P. Drutse, M.F. Zamanyagra, A.M. Kanarovskaya, N.P. Kiriyak, N.A. Kostishin, T.V. Moshnyaga, B.T. Palagnyuk, M.K. Pashaly, S.I. Platon, M.I. Chimpoy.

From the Latvian SSR:
I.O. Bisher, M.G. Vulfson, V.S. Klibik, M.G. Kostenetskaya, R.A. Kukayn, Ya.P. Lutsans, N.V. Neyland, K.I. Nyuksha, Ya.Ya. Peters, A.P. Rubiks, A.M. Shamikhin.

From the Kirghiz SSR:
Ch. Aytmatov, U.K. Akmataliyeva, T. Akmatov, A. Akayev, V.I. Barabanov, Z. Beyshekeyeva, A.I. Zanokha, I.I. Isakov, G.I. Kiselev, M.S. Kuldyshev, U.Sh. Orozova.

From the Armenian SSR:
Kh.B. Abramyan, V.A. Ambartsumyan, S.A. Ambartsumyan, L.A. Arutyunyan, E.T. Arutyunyan, R.P. Vardanyan, G.A. Yenokyan, G.S. Igityan, B.G. Mnatsakanyan, R.G. Oganesyan, S.N. Khanzadyan.

From the Tajik SSR:
N.V. Britvin, Z.S. Gulova, B.K. Kodyrov, N.M. Manko, R.K. Odzhiyev, G. Pallayev, B.F. Rakhimova, B.S. Safarov, G. Safiyeva, M. Fatullayev, M.A. Khusanbayev.

From the Turkmen SSR:
G.M. Akmamedov, R.A. Allayarov, A. Annamukhamedov, Kh. Atdayev, R.A. Bazarova, N.F. Baleshev, Ya.P. Gundogdyyev, Kh. Ishanov, A. Kurbanova, K. Melzev, A.B. Shalyyev.

From the Estonian SSR:
Yu.Y. Aare, M.L. Bronshteyn, Yu.V. Vooglayd, I.N. Gryazin, S.U. Kallas, Yu.Kh. Kakhn, T.R. Kyabin, Yu.I. Nugis, T.K. Pupkevich, A.F. Ryuytel, K.S. Khallik.

From the Abkhaz Autonomous Soviet Socialist Republic [ASSR]:
V.G. Ardzinba, R.A. Arshba, R.G. Salukvadze, K.S. Cholokyan.

From the Adzhar ASSR:
N.U. Badzhelidze, T.P. Buachidze, A.R. Gogeshvili, I.B. Sakandelidze.

From the Bashkir ASSR:
V.V. Nikolayev, V.I. Prokushev, M.M. Safin, Yu.K. Sharipov.

From the Buryat ASSR:
S.V. Angapov, V.Ya. Kalashnikov, G.N. Litvintseva, G.S. Stepanova.

From the Dagestan ASSR:
A.G. Gorbachev, D.G. Zaynalkhanov, K.Z. Kakhirov, G.M. Magomedov.

From the Kabardino-Balkar ASSR:
L.T. Zhigunova, V.F. Karpenko, S.O. Kuliyev, A.M. Umerenkov.

From the Kalmyk ASSR:
I.Z. Burayev, D.N. Kugultinov, V.V. Nikitin, V.N. Ochirov.

From the Kara-Kalpak ASSR:
Sh. Abdimuratova, M.I. Ibragimov, T. Kaipbergenov, A.L. Pershin.

From the Karelian ASSR:
L.V. Afanasyeva, A.A. Genchev, M.V. Demidov, S.V. Pilnikov.

From the Komi ASSR:
S.V. Ignatov, S.G. Lushchikov, V.N. Maksimov, G.A. Chernykh.

From the Mariy ASSR:
Z.A. Vedenkina, V.A. Karpochev, R.I. Nikitin, N.A. Samsonov.

From the Mordovian ASSR:
N.I. Aliluyev, Ye.A. Kulikov, V.A. Levakin, A.P. Maslakova.

From the Nakhichevan ASSR:
K.A. Abasov, G.I. Isayev, D.A. Kerimov, R.Sh. Nagiyev.

From the North Osetian ASSR:
S.B. Aguzarova, V.Y. Byazyrova, G.D. Ikayev, A.I. Nyrkov.

From the Tatar ASSR:
G.V. Buravov, G.N. Kamenshchikova, T.A. Mainullin, M.T. Mukhametzyanov.

From the Udmurt ASSR:
S.N. Danilov, V.V. Korobkin, V.K. Murashov, N.I. Engver.

From the Tuva ASSR:
D.B. Kara-Sal, Yu.T. Komarov, V.L. Lapygin, A.S. Sanchat.

From the Chechen-Ingush ASSR:
M.Yu. Darsigov, Ye.I. Nemtsev, S.Z. Umalatova, V.K. Fateyev.

From the Chuvash ASSR:
L.F. Valentinov, A.A. Dmitriyev, L.I. Mikhaylova, N.V. Fedorov.

FIRST CONGRESS OF PEOPLE'S DEPUTIES OF THE USSR

Fourth Session
27 May 1989

From the Yakutsk ASSR:
S.V. Boykov, V.P. Larionov, M.A. Mikheyev, P.D. Osipov.

From the Adyge Autonomous Oblast:
V.V. Dmitriyev, I.Sh. Mashbashev.

From the Gorno-Altay Autonomous Oblast:
V.K. Yerelina, D.S. Mironova.

From the Gorno-Badakhshan Autonomous Oblast:
Sh. Navruzov, D. Khudonazarov.

From the Jewish Autonomous Oblast:
N.I. Danilyuk, P.A. Khitrov.

From the Karachayevo-Cherkess Autonomous Oblast:
A.Ya. Kangliyev, L.N. Petrova.

From the Nagorno-Karabakh Autonomous Oblast:
V.D. Dzhafarov, G.A. Pogosyan.

From the Khakass Autonomous Oblast:
L.I. Batynskaya, I.N. Botandayev.

From the South Osetian Autonomous Oblast:
L.R. Tedeyev, D.V. Khugayeva.

From the Aga Buryat Autonomous Okrug:
Ts. Nimbuyev.

From the Komi-Permyak Autonomous Okrug:
A.I. Khomyakov.

From the Koryak Autonomous Okrug:
V.V. Kosygin.

From the Nenetsk Autonomous Okrug:
A.I. Vyucheyskiy.

From the Taymyr Autonomous Okrug:
S.Ya. Palchin.

From the Ust-Orda Buryat Autonomous Okrug:
A.B. Batorov.

From the Khanti-Mansiysk Autonomous Okrug:
Ye.D. Aypin.

From the Chukotsk Autonomous Okrug:
V.M. Yetylen.

From the Evenki Autonomous Okrug:
M.I. Mongo.

From the Yamalo-Nenetsk Autonomous Okrug:
R.P. Rugin.

A total of 2,159 ballot papers were distributed among USSR people's deputies for voting purposes. 2,149 ballot papers were produced when the ballot boxes were opened. In other words, the situation is exactly the same as during the election the day before yesterday.

2,149 ballot papers were deemed valid; there were no invalid ballot papers. The votes were cast as follows:

From the RSFSR:
V.I. Belov: 1,984 for, 165 against; N.V. Bosenko: 1,925 for, 224 against; V.I. Vorotnikov: 1,388 for, 761 against; Ye.A. Gayer: 2,032 for, 117 against; B.N. Yeltsin: 1,185 for, 964 against; A.I. Kazannik: 2,078 for, 71 against; A.A. Likhanov: 2,002 for, 147 against; V.P. Lukin: 2,088 for, 61 against; L.I. Matyukhin: 2,018 for, 131 against; S.I. Nevolin: 2,080 for, 69 against; V.S. Podziruk: 1,978 for, 171 against; V.M. Falin: 1,776 for, 373 against.

From the Ukrainian SSR:
V.S. Venglovskaya: 2,106 for, 43 against; V.V. Gnatyuk: 2,127 for, 22 against; I.A. Zabrodin: 1,954 for, 195 against; V.A. Ivashko: 1,905 for, 244 against; A.S. Kapto: 1,867 for, 282 against; S.M. Katilevskiy: 2,115 for, 34 against; V.T. Kurilenko: 2,115 for, 34 against; G.F. Lezhenko: 2,115 for, 34 against; B.I. Oleynik: 2,082 for, 67 against; V.D. Romanenko: 2,104 for, 45 against; V.S. Shevchenko: 1,922 for, 227 against.

From the Belorussian SSR:
V.S. Bolbasov: 2,129 for, 20 against; V.Ye. Golovnev: 2,213 for, 36 against; A.I. Dubko: 2,099 for, 50 against; N.I. Ignatovich: 2,102 for, 47 against; A.P. Kucheyko: 2,120 for, 29 against; V.A. Kiseleva: 2,113 for, 36 against; V.A. Labunov: 2,093 for, 56 against; Z.K. Mateushuk: 2,106 for, 43 against; T.V. Momotova: 2,121 for, 28 against; G.S. Tarazevich: 1,898 for, 259 against; V.V. Yakushkin: 2,123 for, 26 against.

From the Uzbek SSR:
V.T. Adylov: 2,084 for, 65 against; A.R. Atadzhanov: 1,916 for, 233 against; P. Badalbayeva: 2,121 for, 28 against; N. Davranov: 2,125 for, 24 against; A.S. Yefimov: 1,978 for, 171 against; M.Z. Zokirov: 2,097 for, 52 against; A.A. Korshunov: 2,117 for, 32 against; R.N. Nishanov: 1,860 for, 289 against; F. Sefershayev: 2,112 for, 37 against; R.M. Khudaybergenova: 1,907 for, 242 against; V.I. Tso: 2,100 for, 39 against [figures for V.I. Tso as published].

From the Kazakh SSR:
Ye.N. Auyelbekov: 1,888 for, 261 against; R.S. Akhmetova: 2,123 for, 26 against; L.M. Veyser: 2,124 for, 25 against; V.I. Vidiker: 2,119 for, 30 against; M.D. Dzhumatova: 2,127 for, 22 against; P.M. Klishchuk: 2,113 for, 36 against; I. Kozhakhmetov: 2,118 for, 31 against; K.U. Medeubekov: 2,054 for, 95 against; Ye. Rakhmadiyev: 2,106 for, 43 against; K.Z. Romazanov: 2,118 for, 31 against; G.G. Shtoyk: 2,113 for, 36 against.

From the Georgian SSR:
V.S. Advadze: 2,119 for, 30 against; Sh.A. Amonashvili: 2,123 for, 26 against; A.V. Bakradze: 2,119 for, 30 against; D.I. Guguchiya: 2,113 for, 36 against; G.G.

Fourth Session
27 May 1989

Gumbaridze: 1,927 for, 222 against; A.D. Dikhtyar: 2,126 for, 23 against; Z.G. Kurashvili: 2,128 for, 21 against; T.N. Menteshashvili: 1,937 for, 212 against; T.M. Spanderashvili: 2,115 for, 34 against; T.S. Stepnadze: 2,123 for, 26 against; R.Sh. Tabukashvili: 2,114 for, 35 against.

From the Azerbaijan SSR:
Ya.I. Abbasov: 2,090 for, 59 against; P.A. Azizbekova: 2,046 for, 103 against; R.M. Aleskerova: 2,072 for, 77 against; L.V. Barusheva: 2,103 for, 46 against; A.Kh. Vezirov: 1,824 for, 325 against; M.M. Gadzhiyev: 2,105 for, 44 against; G.R. Ibragimov: 2,095 for, 54 against; T.K. Ismailov: 2,080 for, 69 against; E.M. Kafarova: 1,936 for, 213 against; V.G. Mamedov: 1,977 for, 172 against; A.A. Namazova: 2,099 for, 50 against.

From the Lithuanian SSR:
E.V. Bichkauskas: 2,072 for, 77 against; E.Y. Vilkas: 2,074 for, 75 against; B.K. Genzyalis: 2,061 for, 88 against; R.V. Gudaytis: 2,073 for, 76 against; K.V. Zaletskas: 2,003 for, 146 against; S.Y. Kudarauskas: 2,086 for, 63 against; Yu.Y. Kuplyauskene: 2,079 for, 70 against; N.N. Medvedev: 2,100 for, 149 against; K.V. Moteka: 2,042 for, 87 against; Yu.Yu. Olekas: 2,086 for, 63 against; K.K. Uoka: 2,091 for, 58 against.

From the Moldavian SSR:
Ye.D. Doga: 2,117 for, 32 against; I.P. Drutse: 2,078 for, 71 against; M.F. Zamanyagra: 2,125 for, 24 against; A.M. Kanarovskaya: 2,114 for, 35 against; N.P. Kiriyak: 1,987 for, 162 against; N.A. Kostishin: 2,121 for, 128 against; T.V. Moshnyaga: 2,130 for, 19 against; B.T. Palagnyuk: 2,115 for, 34 against; M.K. Pashaly: 2,108 for, 41 against; S.I. Platon: 2,057 for, 92 against; M.I. Chimpoy: 2,104 for, 45 against.

From the Latvian SSR:
I.O. Bisher: 2,069 for, 80 against; M.G. Vulfson: 2,048 for, 102 against; V.S. Klibik: 2,030 for, 119 against; M.G. Kostenetskaya: 2,090 for, 59 against; R.A. Kukayn: 2,080 for, 69 against; Ya.P. Lutsans: 2,096 for, 53 against; N.V. Neyland: 2,051 for, 98 against; K.I. Nyuksha: 2,107 for, 42 against; Ya.Ya. Peters: 2,069 for, 80 against; A.P. Rubiks: 2,048 for, 101 against; A.M. Shamikhin: 2,089 for, 66 against [figures for A.M. Shamikhin as published].

From the Kirghiz SSR:
Ch. Aytmatov: 2,018 for, 131 against; U.K. Akmataliyeva: 2,115 for, 34 against; T. Akmatov: 1,974 for, 115 against [figures for T. Akmatov as published]; A. Akayev: 2,071 for, 78 against; V.I. Barabanov: 2,116 for, 33 against; Z. Beyshekeyeva: 2,102 for, 47 against; A.I. Zanokha: 2,121 for, 28 against; I.I. Isakov: 2,103 for, 46 against; G.I. Kiselev: 1,961 for, 188 against; M.S. Kuldyshev: 2,123 for, 26 against; U.Sh. Orozova: 2,080 for, 69 against.

From the Tajik SSR:
N.V. Britvin: 1,997 for, 152 against; Z.S. Gulova: 2,119 for, 30 against; B.K. Kodyrov: 2,113 for, 36 against; N.M. Manko: 2,122 for, 27 against; R.K. Odzhiyev: 2,120 for, 29 against; G. Pallayev: 1,945 for, 204 against; B.F. Rakhimova: 1,270 for, 179 against [figures for B.F. Rakhimova as published]; B.S. Safarov: 2,119 for, 30 against; G. Safiyeva: 2,109 for, 40 against; M. Fatullayev: 2,130 for, 19 against; M.A. Khusanbayev: 2,118 for, 31 against.

From the Armenian SSR:
Kh.B. Abramyan: 2,051 for, 98 against; V.A. Ambartsumyan: 2,004 for, 145 against; S.A. Ambartsumyan: 2,024 for, 125 against; L.A. Arutyunyan: 2,075 for, 74 against; E.T. Arutyunyan: 2,043 for, 106 against; R.P. Vardanyan: 2,080 for, 69 against; G.A. Yenokyan: 2,075 for, 75 against; G.S. Igityan: 2,058 for, 91 against; B.G. Mnatsakanyan: 2,065 for, 84 against; R.G. Oganesyan: 2,098 for, 51 against; S.N. Khanzadyan: 2,029 for, 120 against.

From the Turkmen SSR:
G.M. Akmamedov: 2,121 for, 21 against [figures for G.M. Akmamedov as published]; R.A. Allayarov: 2,121 for, 28 against; A. Annamukhamedov: 2,122 for, 27 against; Kh. Atdayev: 2,119 for, 30 against; R.A. Bazarova: 1,969 for, 180 against; N.F. Baleshev: 1,959 for, 190 against; Ya.P. Gundogdyyev: 1,987 for, 162 against; Kh. Ishanov: 2,115 for, 34 against; A. Kurbanova: 2,116 for, 33 against; K. Melzev: 2,125 for, 24 against; A.B. Shalyyev: 2,107 for, 42 against.

From the Estonian SSR:
Yu.Y. Aare: 2,064 for, 85 against; M.L. Bronshteyn: 2,036 for, 113 against; Yu.V. Vooglayd: 2,082 for, 67 against; I.N. Gryazin: 2,091 for, 58 against; S.U. Kallas: 2,065 for, 84 against; Yu.Kh. Kakhn: 2,090 for, 59 against; T.R. Kyabin: 2,084 for, 65 against; Yu.I. Nugis: 2,091 for, 58 against; T.K. Pupkevich: 2,103 for, 46 against; A.F. Ryuytel: 1,982 for, 167 against; K.S. Khallik: 2,070 for, 79 against.

From the Abkhaz ASSR:
V.G. Ardzinba: 2,129 for, 20 against; R.A. Arshba: 2,126 for, 23 against; R.G. Salukvadze: 2,128 for, 21 against; K.S. Cholokyan: 2,122 for, 27 against.

From the Adzhar ASSR:
N.U. Badzhelidze: 2,126 for, 23 against; T.P. Buachidze: 2,115 for, 34 against; A.R. Gogeshvili: 2,126 for, 23 against; I.B. Sakandelidze: 2,122 for, 27 against.

From the Bashkir ASSR:
V.V. Nikolayev: 2,115 for, 34 against; V.I. Prokushev: 2,121 for, 28 against; M.M. Safin: 2,112 for, 37 against; Yu.K. Sharipov: 2,092 for, 57 against.

From the Buryat ASSR:
S.V. Angapov: 2,043 for, 106 against; V.Ya. Kalashnikov: 2,117 for, 32 against; G.N. Litvintseva: 2,119 for, 30 against; G.S. Stepanova: 2,118 for, 31 against.

STENOGRAPHIC RECORD

Fourth Session
27 May 1989

From the Dagestan ASSR:
A.G. Gorbachev: 2,116 for, 33 against; D.G. Zaynalkhanov: 2,127 for, 22 against; K.Z. Kakhirov: 2,127 for, 22 against; G.M. Magomedov: 2,030 for, 119 against.

From the Kabardino-Balkar ASSR:
L.T. Zhigunova: 2,124 for, 25 against; V.F. Karpenko: 2,114 for, 35 against; S.O. Kuliyev: 2,120 for, 29 against; A.M. Umerenkov: 2,119 for, 30 against.

From the Kalmyk ASSR:
I.Z. Burayev: 2,126 for, 23 against; D.N. Kugultinov: 2,087 for, 62 against; V.V. Nikitin: 1,996 for, 153 against; V.N. Ochirov: 2,097 for, 52 against.

From the Kara-Kalpak ASSR:
Sh. Abdimuratova: 2,133 for, 16 against; M.I. Ibragimov: 2,020 for, 129 against; T. Kaipbergenov: 2,119 for, 30 against; A.L. Pershin: 2,130 for, 19 against.

From the Karelian ASSR:
L.V. Afanasyeva: 2,136 for, 13 against; A.A. Genchev: 2,130 for, 19 against; M.V. Demidov: 2,023 for, 126 against; S.V. Pilnikov: 2,131 for, 18 against.

From the Komi ASSR:
S.V. Ignatov: 2,134 for, 15 against; S.G. Lushchikov: 2,079 for, 70 against; V.N. Maksimov: 2,124 for, 25 against; G.A. Chernykh: 2,137 for, 12 against.

From the Mari ASSR:
Z.A. Vedenkina: 2,120 for, 29 against; V.A. Karpochev: 2,127 for, 22 against; R.I. Nikitin: 2,103 for, 46 against; N.A. Samsonov: 2,113 for, 36 against.

From the Mordovian ASSR:
N.I. Aliluyev: 2,120 for, 29 against; Ye.A. Kulikov: 2,110 for, 39 against; V.A. Levakin: 2,107 for, 42 against; A.P. Maslakova: 2,126 for, 23 against.

From the Nakhichevan ASSR:
K.A.K. Abasov: 2,098 for, 51 against; G.I. Isayev: 2,024 for, 125 against; D.A. Kerimov: 2,085 for, 64 against; R.Sh. Nagiyev: 2,114 for, 35 against.

From the North Osetian ASSR:
S.B. Aguzarova: 2,119 for, 30 against; V.Y. Byazyrova: 2,128 for, 21 against; G.D. Ikayev: 2,022 for, 127 against; A.I. Nyrkov: 2,131 for, 18 against.

From the Tatar ASSR:
G.V. Buravov: 2,114 for, 35 against; G.N. Kamenshchikova: 2,127 for, 22 against; T.A. Miniullin [name as published]: 2,107 for, 42 against; M.T. Mukhametzyanov: 2,120 for, 29 against.

From the Tuva ASSR:
D.B. Kara-Sal: 2,128 for, 21 against; Yu.T. Komarov: 2,107 for, 42 against; V.L. Lapygin: 2,083 for, 66 against; A.S. Sanchat: 2,064 for, 85 against.

From the Udmurt ASSR:
S.N. Danilov: 2,128 for, 21 against; V.V. Korobkin: 2,126 for, 23 against; V.K. Murashov: 2,117 for, 32 against; N.N. Engver: 2,135 for, 14 against.

From the Chechen-Ingush ASSR:
M.Yu. Darsigov: 2,122 for, 27 against; Ye.I. Nemtsev: 2,125 for, 24 against; S.Z. Umalatova: 2,126 for, 23 against; V.K. Foteyev: 1,964 for, 185 against.

From the Chuvash ASSR:
L.F. Valentinov: 2,120 for, 29 against; A.A. Dmitriyev: 2,115 for, 34 against; L.I. Mikhaylova: 2,133 for, 16 against; N.V. Fedorov: 2,133 for, 16 against.

From the Yakutsk ASSR:
S.V. Boykov: 2,132 for, 17 against; V.P. Larionov: 2,126 for, 23 against; M.A. Mikheyev: 2,126 for, 23 against; P.D. Osipov: 2,084 for, 65 against.

From the Adyge Autonomous Oblast:
V.V Dmitriyev: 2,122 for, 27 against; I.Sh. Mashbashev: 2,124 for, 25 against.

From the Gorno-Altay Autonomous Oblast:
V.K. Yerelina: 2,133 for, 16 against; D.S. Mironova: 2,109 for, 40 against.

From the Gorno-Badakhshan Autonomous Oblast:
Sh. Navruzov: 2,127 for, 22 against; D. Khudonazarov: 2,123 for, 26 against.

From the Jewish Autonomous Oblast:
N.I. Danilyuk: 2,042 for, 107 against; P.A. Khitron: 2,115 for, 34 against.

From the Karachayevo-Cherkess Autonomous Oblast:
A.Ya. Kangliyev: 2,127 for, 22 against; L.N. Petrova: 2,103 for, 46 against.

From the Nagorno-Karabakh Autonomous Oblast:
V.D. Dzhafarov: 1,912 for, 237 against; G.A. Pogosyan: 1,956 for, 193 against.

From the Khakass Autonomous Oblast:
L.I. Batynskaya: 2,115 for, 34 against; I.N. Botandayev: 2,117 fr, 32 against.

From the South Osetian Autonomous Oblast:
L.R. Tedeyev: 2,126 for, 23 against; D.V. Khugayeva: 2,128 for, 21 against.

From the Aga Buryat Autonomous Okrug:
Ts. Nimbuyev: 2,118 for, 31 against.

From the Komi-Permyak Autonomous Okrug:
A.I. Khomyakov: 2,128 for, 21 against.

From the Koryak Autonomous Okrug:
V.V. Kosygin: 2,119 for, 30 against.

FIRST CONGRESS OF PEOPLE'S DEPUTIES OF THE USSR

Fourth Session

27 May 1989

From the Nenetsk Autonomous Okrug:
A.I. Vyucheyskiy: 2,130 for, 19 against.

From the Taymyr Autonomous Okrug:
S.Ya. Palchin: 2,130 for, 19 against.

From the Ust-Orda Buryat Autonomous Okrug:
A.B. Batorov: 2,078 for, 71 against.

From the Khanti-Mansiysk Autonomous Okrug:
Ye.D. Aypin: 2,130 for, 19 against.

From the Chukotsk Autonomous Okrug:
V.M. Yetylen: 2,123 for, 26 against.

From the Evenki Autonomous Okrug:
M.I. Mongo: 2,119 for, 30 against.

From the Yamalo-Nenetsk Autonomous Okrug:
R.P. Rugin: 2,129 for, 20 against.

Thus the following USSR people's deputies have been elected to the USSR Supreme Soviet Soviet of Nationalities:

From the RSFSR:
V.I. Belov, N.V. Bosenko, V.I. Vorotnikov, Ye.A. Gayer, A.I. Kazannik, A.A. Likhanov, V.P. Lukin, L.I. Matyukhin, S.I. Nevolin, V.S. Podziruk, and V.M. Falin.

Furthermore, comrades, all the candidates on all remaining lists have been elected from all the union republics and all the autonomous republics, autonomous oblasts, and national okrugs. Unless required, I will not read them out. (Applause.)

M.S. Gorbachev: Have you finished?

Yu.A. Osipyan: Yes. The minutes have been signed by the chairman, secretary, and all the members of the Tellers' Commission.

M.S. Gorbachev: Any questions for the chairman of the Tellers' Commission, comrades? Yes or no?

From the floor: No.

M.S. Gorbachev: So, the proposal is to approve the Tellers' Commission minutes on the results of the voting in the elections to the Soviet of Nationalities. All those in favor of adopting such a decision, please vote. Please lower your hands.

Who is against? Count them please.

Yu.A. Osipyan: Esteemed deputies! 15 deputies voted against.

M.S. Gorbachev: Who abstained? Please raise your mandate cards.

Yu.A. Osipyan: Esteemed deputies! 15 deputies abstained.

M.S. Gorbachev: Fine. Approved. Yuriy Andreyevich, did you want to say something about the Soviet of the Union?

Yu.A. Osipyan: Comrades! I have to tell you that a very great deal of intensive work has been done. We worked all night without sleep, nobody went home, there was a great deal of counting to do, and unfortunately as yet we have not managed to finalize the results in the form of a final protocol on the results of the elections to the Soviet of the Union. The only thing I can say is that the counting is complete and the elections were carried out in full accordance with the requirements, and I wish to give you the gratifying news that there will be no further voting. (Applause). Allow me to read out these minutes in a few moments when they have been printed.

M.S. Gorbachev: Granted.

Yu.A. Osipyan: Thank you very much.

M.S. Gorbachev: Comrades, urgent requests from deputies have accumulated here. Yuriy Nikolayevich Afanasyev, people's deputy from the Noginsk Territorial Electoral Okrug No 36, is asking to have the floor in the course of the congress. Go ahead.

Yu.N. Afanasyev, rector of the Moscow State History and Archives Institute (Noginsk Territorial Electoral Okrug, Moscow Oblast): Dear comrade deputies! All of us are called upon to take a critical view of the situation in our country. I believe that we are supposed to take as critical a view of our own activities at the congress. In that sense, yesterday's proceedings of our congress made a dispiriting impression on me for many reasons, which I am here to talk about.

First, after midnight we failed to hear the voice of the Karabakh delegation, or, more precisely, failed to respond to it in any manner. As a result, it was left without any reaction at all on our part. Somewhat earlier, all of us together essentially put in a position of political isolation the Lithuanian delegation, which had submitted, as I see it, a quite poorly formulated proposal, but, nonetheless, a proposal which is substantive. So, we set in motion the customary machine. After several moralizing and stigmatizing speeches, including those by Zalygin and Medvedev, whom I respect, the numbing majority votes followed. (Applause).

Even before that, we hastily put together the membership of the Supreme Soviet. In our haste, we failed to hear an entire array of what I believe were businesslike proposals, including the voice of Rodion Shchedrin. As a result, the voice of Rodion Shchedrin disappeared, and with it Deputy Travkin, who was mentioned, sunk into

STENOGRAPHIC RECORD

Fourth Session
27 May 1989

oblivion. Subsequently, as many of us here, I attended a conference of the Russian [RSFSR] delegation, which essentially did not come to any normal conclusions; it was held hastily, and could not discuss in a regular manner many important issues. Comrades, I believe that everyone is free to voice his opinion here, this is why I am talking.

I examined the composition of our Supreme Soviet attentively once again. I am duty-bound to say this, because this is what I think, and this is what I am convinced of: If we take into account the level of skills of the deputies, in view of the problems this Supreme Soviet will have to solve, if we take into account the level of their professionalism, which is needed under these difficult conditions for our country, then we have formed a Stalinist-Brezhnevian Supreme Soviet.... (Noise on the floor, applause). Now about the majority which has formed....

M.S. Gorbachev: Yuriy Nikolayevich, your 3 minutes are up.

Yu.N. Afanasyev: I am already finishing it at this congress. This is exactly the depressing thing which I wanted to talk about. I address you, what I would call the aggressively obedient majority, which yesterday torpedoed all the resolutions of the congress which the people are expecting of us.... (Noise on the floor).

M.S. Gorbachev: Quiet, comrades! I believe a serious conversation is under way.

Yu.N. Afanasyev: I am about done. However, I would ask you not to clap your hands and yell, because this is exactly what I have come here to say. So, our esteemed aggressively obedient majority, and you, Mikhail Sergeyevich, who either listens attentively to this majority, or skillfully exerts influence on it. We may go on working like that. We may be obedient, stop lining up, and pass on our notes neatly. We can be serene, as Father Pitirim has called on us to be. Still, let us not forget for a minute about those who sent us to this congress. They did not send us here in order for us to behave serenely, but in order for us to change the situation in the country resolutely. (Applause).

M.S. Gorbachev: Does anyone want to take the floor? Will we share our opinions concerning comrade Afanasyev's speech? Let us speak for 2 or 3 minutes each about this.

G.Kh. Popov, editor-in-chief of the journal VOPROSY EKONOMIKI (from the USSR Union of Scientific and Engineering Associations): I object to 3-minute speeches. We have adopted a 15-minute time limit.

M.S. Gorbachev: All right. In this case, I withdraw my proposal, and let us operate in keeping with the time limit, comrades. Yes? All right.

G.Kh. Popov: Comrades! The first 2 days of the work of the congress require that we make serious decisions concerning its future work. Inevitably, deputies with a democratic orientation had to be in a minority at this congress. We proceeded from this. We understood that it was going to be that way. Still, we came to our congress with much enthusiasm.

We had two variants of actions. The first variant was to begin to play the role of some kind of opposition, and the second variant was to join the constructive work of the congress. We opted for the second variant. We understood that the situation in the country is too difficult for us to allow ourselves to toy with some oppositions, standoffs, coalitions, and so forth. We should unite all creative forces which exist in the country, all disagreements regarding various approaches toward the main tasks of our perestroyka notwithstanding. This is what the main task of our congress is: tapping new reserves of restructuring.

We created working groups and began preparing materials for the forthcoming congress because we had not received any materials from the apparatus of the presidium of the Supreme Soviet. We worked sparing no effort, worked day and night; a package of our proposals was prepared. However, our work encountered serious mistrust and even some kind of bias from the very beginning. The presidium of the Supreme Soviet could not even find a room for us, could not allocate paper for us. The materials prepared by us still have not been run off officially and distributed to the deputies of the congress. This was not understandable, but we still believed that our joint work would begin.

I think that all of you are now aware that an entire array of suggestions, which we have made, have not been acted on, in particular suggestions on equipping this hall of ours with a regular electronic voting system, for installing microphones at every work station. All the more so, our apprehension that opening the proceedings with elections is far from what the country is expecting us to do has been confirmed.

However, once again we were inspired by the fact that we were supported by the Moscow City Committee of the party, and the Moscow Soviet. Lev Nikolayevich Zaykov helped us and allocated us a room so that we could work. We were seriously encouraged by the Moscow delegation not setting in motion the machine of voting, as was the case in many delegations. When representatives were elected for the Moscow delegation, they were elected for the spheres and sections which had emerged in our delegations. This is why at the conference of representatives the Moscow delegation reflected the spectrum of opinions which existed in it. This very much disposed us to creative work in the future.

We hoped that the congress as well would carry on this principle of pluralism, that the minority would be represented in a regular manner at all stages of its work,

FIRST CONGRESS OF PEOPLE'S DEPUTIES OF THE USSR

Fourth Session

27 May 1989

without claiming definitive influence, but in order to work in a regular, creative manner.

If groups had been created at this congress of deputies in line with the interests and approaches, if every such group had been given an opportunity to nominate its own candidates, yesterday would not have happened, when people stood up and nominated additional candidacies for almost one-third of the oblasts. This was the very minority with which the present majority does not wish to reckon.

Certainly, they can go on disregarding the minority; this is a way quite common in the practice of political life. However, yesterday a machine of voting by a perfunctory majority was actually set in motion. The deputies whose views differed from the opinions of their delegations were simply left out. The lists were put together on this very principle.

The congress which has been elected on an alternative basis, in a competitive system, by secret ballot, has in essence embarked on the path of nominating the number of candidates corresponding to the number of seats. In general, as Levsha in the well-known novel by Leskov said in his time: We know what that snow coming down on us is all about.

You saw that we strove to work together; we supported the candidacy of Mikhail Sergeyevich vigorously and resolutely. Still, it is becoming clear to us all the time that the apparatus is definitely trying to take its revenge, is definitely trying to directly influence the course of the congress. Under these conditions, continued compliance with the procedures which we kept at the beginning would not be understandable either for us, our voters, or our country.

Why was all of this done, why was it necessary to set this perfunctory voting in motion? There can be only one answer—only in order to put together a Supreme Soviet obedient to the will of the apparatus, and to continue bringing pressure to bear on the progressive wing of the leadership of our country, this time on behalf of the Supreme Soviet.

This is why we are left thinking about a change in position. First, the group of regional Moscow deputies from scientific organizations and creative arts unions considers it necessary to leave the all-Moscow delegation. We propose considering the formation of an interregional independent deputy group, and we invite all comrade deputies to join this group. (Applause).

We believe that this group should be given an opportunity to deliver co-reports to the report which we will hear on Monday, a regular co-report, 30 minutes long, as was envisaged by us, and a co-report to the government report which is to be made in the future. We invite all people's deputies to think about such a group during the break, and pass its list to the presidium of our congress.

Certainly, at the elections to the Supreme Soviet which we are now witnessing, which proceed before our very eyes, the apparatus has definitely triumphed. However, generally speaking, it is not that difficult to gain the upper hand here, in this hall, as you understand. However, who is going to get the upper hand over inflation in our country, empty stores, and the incompetence of the leadership? (Applause). We have come here to handle this very issue.

However, if we were to look precisely for the most instructive example of what is happening here, it is how we worked yesterday, and how we have worked over these 2 days.

Look at this hall: complete lack of skill in organizing elementary work. We have forgotten about our procedures, given up the principle of finishing up by 1800 hours, and are working "as the spirit moves us," if I might say so. We talked about time limit of 15 minutes, and 7 minutes for follow-up statements, and we have forgotten about all of this. We reduced the time limit to 1 or 2 minutes; five or six persons speak, and then we wait for the vote for 15 or 20 minutes. If we were to count—and I tried doing that yesterday—in 12 hours of overall work we really worked not more than 3 or 4 hours.

Notes coming to the presidium are not registered. Some of these notes, and some of the proposals, are lost. Some proposals are not put to a vote. The abbreviated information TASS disseminates about the work of our congress is not reviewed by us. For example, I have not seen the version of my speech at all, in the form in which it went to TASS. It is not known who has done versions for PRAVDA and other newspapers.

I do not think we can work like that. Did we really have to sit around for 4 hours not knowing what to do? Was there a dearth of other issues to consider? Three or four halls could have been provided for the deputies to gather and share their opinions on the issues of concern to them—ecology, the economy, and some other things—while our counting commission was at work.

If I were to speak honestly, I am afraid. If people cannot organize the work of a single hall, what can they do with the country? (Noise. Applause).

If someone hopes that he is going to change the situation in the country with the help of perfunctory voting and the majority, with the help of the Supreme Soviet and other bodies thus put together, he is in grave error. The apparatus has held power for decades, and we have not gone beyond the impasse as a result of such leadership. If the apparatus yet again prevents those elected by the

STENOGRAPHIC RECORD

Fourth Session
27 May 1989

people from solving problems, if it yet again attempts to assume responsibility for the situation in the country, then I can say with absolute certainty: Nothing will work out for you. (Applause).

We can be patient. We have been patient for decades when we have not been reckoned with. We can go on just playing the role of opposition. Just one thing bothers me: How long are our people going to be patient? Thank you for your attention. (Applause).

M.S. Gorbachev: Introduce yourself. Are you speaking in conjunction with Comrade Afanasyev's speech?

V.N. Stepanov, director of the Vidlitskiy fur animal farm in Olonetskiy Rayon (Petrozavodsk Electoral Okrug, Karelian ASSR [Autonomous Soviet Socialist Republic]): Yes, comrades, we are present at an unusual congress. This is the first such congress. However, as perhaps all of you understand, today we are trying to harness a new horse to an old cart very fast. I think that the Moscow delegation is trying here, by using us, to set the people against the congress and put pressure on such sore spots as Georgia, Nagorno-Karabakh, the Baltic area, and others, shared at present with us by the entire people. Yes, we know that many legal acts need to be changed. We will have to take up the constitution in a major way. However, all of this is not done all at once. We also do not quite like the procedures for the operation of the congress, the fact that we sometimes waste time here, state time which the people are paying for. However, the Muscovites have misled all of Russia, the entire people, through leasing, cooperatives, and so forth. Are you not the ones who propose these ideas to the Politburo and the Central Committee without having consulted the people? (Applause). I believe that Comrade Afanasyev insulted a considerable segment of the deputies who are represented here.

From the floor: Right. (Applause).

Let us not forget that Moscow is not the entire people yet. I doubt whether the workers of Moscow support comrades Afanasyev, Popov, and the like. The fact that today you have proposed that the congress create factions is madness! Come to your senses; what you are going to do! We should feed the people; we should make the economy healthy! Instead, you have thus far brought about disorder in the proceedings of the congress and distracted it from acute problems. I would suggest that we not stray from the agenda. There will be a report. Yes, I personally took the floor at the council of representatives and told Mikhail Sergeyevich it was my opinion that we needed not a report, but a statement, so to speak, a program declaration. And we need to have alternative candidacies. However, the mechanism did not work. Fine, let us have peace today. Apparently, this is how it is going to be in the future. We should make corresponding amendments in our Constitution. However, comrades, we cannot work like this. Let us not deviate from the agenda. There will be a report, there will be a discussion. I believe we cannot depart from the agenda; otherwise, the congress will never come to a close. Thank you for your attention. (Applause).

M.S. Gorbachev: Just a minute. Take your seat for a while. Here is Deputy Tolpezhnikov (293d okrug), who is asking for a minute to respond to the speeches of comrades Afanasyev and Popov. Subsequently, Comrade Adamovich is asking to be given the floor.

Before Comrade Tolpeznikov begins to speak.... I think we should not be in a hurry in conjunction with what Comrade Afanasyev has said here. Comrade Popov has raised the issue, and formulated it in particular when he started toward splitting the congress, toward a faction. This is serious. Let us not simplify it. This is what we need to discuss, because this is a critical point in the work of our congress. The comrades know what they are doing. Perhaps, they have many more variants prepared, but we should sort this out. I do not think we should reject everything: what Comrade Afanasyev has said and what Comrade Popov has said. No, I do not think so. However, there are things which we cannot accept. I am not saying now what I mean. I have a definite opinion. However, since the comrade accuses me of sort of manipulating the majority, I will still try somehow to sum up the statements of deputies after they are made, and state my own attitude. I would ask you not to suspect me. I would consider my mission worthless if we were to tear this congress to pieces, the first congress created as a result of such an election campaign, and deprive it of the opportunity to work fruitfully in the name of advancing restructuring, and advancing the entire country, solving pent-up problems.

Please. Excuse me. Go ahead.

V.F. Tolpezhnikov, office chief at the 1st N. Burdenko city clinic of the ambulance service, city of Riga (Proletarskiy National-Territorial Electoral Okrug). Deputy Afanasyev spoke harshly, but he put it very well. If we are going to talk about that sincerely, and say what we think, say what we have been sent here to say, we may come closer to the truth. Only he who is not confident of himself can be insulted by this statement. We have nothing to fear from hearing out an opinion.

I have a very specific suggestion. Yesterday, we failed to give a really earnest hearing to the declaration of Deputy Landsbergis from the Lithuanian delegation, which described the very essence of how elections ought to be handled. We were still unable to receive this in a timely manner and evaluate this properly. However, let us proceed without haste; we have nowhere to hurry to; we should grasp the meaning. This is why I have a specific proposal: Deputies who make noise during the speech of another deputy should be ejected from the hall. (Applause).

STENOGRAPHIC RECORD

Fourth Session
27 May 1989

Second, we respect Mikhail Sergeyevich Gorbachev very much. We know no other leader in the country. However, I resolutely protest his interference with the statements of candidates. Thank you.

M.S. Gorbachev: Deputy Adamovich is given the floor, and then Deputy Meshalkin.

A.M. Adamovich, director of the All-Union Research Institute of Cinema Art, city of Moscow (from the Union of Cinema Producers of the USSR): Dear comrade deputies! In the speech of Afanasyev, I disagree with just one statement. When Mikhail Sergeyevich Gorbachev is behind me, I feel confident, and I know that what this side of the hall would not do to me—what it did when Comrade Vorotnikov was there—that this would not happen to me. (Applause). I am in favor of consolidation. I am not a Muscovite, I am Belorussian, but I am asking for my 15 minutes. I am Belorussian. I have heard the Muscovites say: "Comrades, all delegates will come; let us somehow unite. Let us work together, let us go to them. This is what we have developed; let us show this to them." I have heard it, I have heard this as an observer.

I will start this talk from a somewhat broader perspective, but I am likely to arrive at the same thing which was already discussed. On one occasion, I heard the following: "The people have stopped drinking, sobered up some, looked around, and asked: 'Where is the tsar?'" As they say, people have awakened. During the war, as I saw myself and as I later heard from others, people suddenly fell asleep, dropped off to sleep out of fear. Around him, people were being killed, as in the Khatyns of Belorussia, and the man had fallen asleep, was sleeping—a defensive reaction of the organism, a psychological reaction. This is how one segment of the people was being killed in turn in the 1920's, 1930's, and 1940's, and the rest were benumbed. They slept unnaturally, to cheerful tunes like "...get up, curly head, greet the day..." What have we found after waking up from the self-delusion that, supposedly, we were a normal, even progressive, state and society, a model for all, and a progressive economy? We have found something like an underdeveloped superpower, which was losing its ability to develop into the bargain. As we have found out, it is an extremely difficult task to reform an administrative-command moron into a normal social organism, to create anew an economy which works. We will not get out from underneath the avalanche of economic problems unless we restructure the political system profoundly, rather than merely do a face-lift. Our people pin tremendous hopes on this congress. Do we justify these hopes, do we take a detached view of ourselves to a sufficient degree, do we see how we look here, what we have found and what we have lost during these 3 days of meetings? Won't we have to buy dark glasses in order to sneak past the crowds which every day wait for us over there at the exit from the Kremlin after the congress is closed? (Applause).

The supreme power in the country should belong to the Congress of People's Deputies. What does this mean? What does the power of people's deputies mean, when all of us know well that power belongs to the party, and, more precisely, the party apparatus and the departments? If the supreme power in the country is handed over to the Congress of People's Deputies, the issue of control over all other sources of power will immediately arise; yes indeed, the issue which thus far appears blasphemous to some, the issue of people's control over the party apparatus. (Applause).

Control over the budget is the most important lever of power. Without having the right to such control and corresponding mechanisms, the congress will not accomplish much; it will not be able to bring to a halt the absurd process of producing for the sake of production, when increasing quantities of steel are being produced in order to build machines for producing steel, while people have nothing to wash themselves with. Ten times or so—Yuriy Chernichenko will know better—more tractors and combine harvesters are produced than are needed, but we purchase agricultural products. The state is getting rich while the people literally slide below the poverty line. However, this is advantageous and necessary for someone, since this absurdity is going on, and it is not possible to get rid of it in any manner. How should all forms and sources of power in the country be placed under the control of the people?

I believe that under specific, current conditions this is impossible without the powerful and independent position of the president and his cabinet (in this I support Burlatskiy), or, as we call him, the chairman of the Supreme Soviet, who in the immediate future is to be elected by a direct vote of all people and is to receive his mandate for power from the people themselves. However, the issue of protection from the excessive concentration of power in the same hands will immediately arise. We already know what all of this can lead to. Here we are coming to the main right of the people's deputies at the congress—the right and duty to call referendums. First, when the need arises to protect the head of state from those whose power should inevitably be reduced. Apparently, the Lithuanians have a proverb: "Stay away from the hooves of a mortally wounded ox." Meanwhile, our ox—that is, the command-administrative system—is far from dying. You can expect any surprises and convulsions. So much for protecting the head of state. However, a reliable mechanism for protecting society from the head of state himself should be created in case he begins to have Stalin's dreams. The Americans have a law and procedures for stripping the president of power before the appointed time: "impeachment." We cannot go on without this as well. It goes without saying that the Congress of People's Deputies should have the right to give the government, the Council of Ministers, a vote of no confidence if they clearly fail to cope with their responsibilities. In the shop windows of the West, they have merchandise. It would be nice to hang the portraits of ministers in our shop windows: in the butcher shop, the minister of agriculture; in the shoe store, the minister of light industry, and so on. (Applause).

STENOGRAPHIC RECORD

Fourth Session

27 May 1989

For a start, we should, perhaps, call a referendum as early as this congress on the following most significant issue. Do the people really believe that the collective and state farms are indeed capable of feeding the country—even if we tinker with this some, and call it intra-collective farm leasing? Even poets have stopped composing odes to the collective farms, and they do not miss too much when it comes to this. The lyre they have dropped has been picked up by some of our major party functionaries who are in charge of the new agrarian program. Are we not being put to sleep again by old tunes? We cannot sleep by any means, or else we will wake up in the embrace of a new dictator. An iron fist will be needed to deal with famine uprisings, and this will be it for the agrarian program, and curtains for restructuring. After all, the Stalinist forms of agriculture have robbed the country of the farmer. Is it conceivable to bring back the farmer within the framework of these forms as the main ones, even if all kinds of other forms exist? I still remember Fedor Abramov yelling into the phone to me after we saw in Leningrad a performance of "Wooden Horses" directed by Lyubimov: "What idiot..."—this is quoted verbatim—"...convinced us that it is absolutely necessary to digest the peasant in an industrial pot, to cook the peasant?"

A country without farmers is like a planet without air. What happened in our country? The smart high-caliber politicians announced that this air—that is, the peasant—is too petty bourgeois; let's pump it out and pump in scientifically new, collective-farm air. So, we are choking. The economy is choking because of the absence of the farmer. We will not bring man back to earth unless we announce (here I am addressing directly Aleksandr Nikolayevich Yakovlev, chairman of the rehabilitation commission) that all repressions against the peasant families in the 1920's and 1930's, the so-called expropriation of the kulaks, were a crying act of lawlessness, just as were the decisions of all "three-member panels" and special boards in the 1930's. (Applause). Of course, this is not enough. We need an article in the Constitution which will give the peasant, farmer, or cooperative member certainty that they will not be treated to a new round of kulak expropriation as an expression of gratitude after they have fed the country. After all, those who are full are always ungrateful.

I have some other proposals here, but I am not going to take too much time. For example, if the Supreme Soviet which we have elected here, for better or worse, and which we will renew through rotation—what if it does not satisfy the expectations of the people? Do we have the right to use impeachment—that is, recall before the appointed time—with regard to it as well? I liked the concept of Yuriy Karyakin—so the people see us for what we are here. What if the voters are already beginning to think: Is not the term of 5 years too long for this membership of the congress? Could we ourselves, before the people ask us to, and if we feel that the time is passing us by, recall ourselves in 3 rather than 5 years? So to say, "impeach" ourselves in 3 rather than 5 years? (Applause).

I began to write my speech during the first days of work of our congress with much faith in the historic mission of our congress. I end it, as you can see, with much doubt. Have they not misjudged us when electing us to this body? We have brought to this hall all the ills of our society. They are a part of us. These ills make us feverish even here. Observing us here, one intelligent person (it is not Afanasyev, it is a professor of the University of Kazan) mentioned the enthusiasm of obedience. I would say, the aggressiveness of obedience. Indeed, there are belligerently obedient people who furiously fight to preserve their obedience. Say, this cry, which has been heard: Protect us from the public, the people who are waiting for us so much—is an impassioned plea for anticipating the thinking of the higher-ups. Is the energy of a considerable segment of the membership of our congress channeled in the right direction? Is it up to accepting power as it is, and does it deserve power? I believe that very soon we will hear the answers from the people themselves rather than from Afanasyev. I wish we would not turn from the favorites and hope of our voters into something completely opposite. After all, we are not going to live in the Kremlin, but among our people. Let us not forget this. (Applause).

M.S. Gorbachev: What is your name? I will give you the floor now.

S.P. Golovin, adjuster of radio equipment at the Mari Machine-Building Plant, city of Yoshkar-Ola (Yoshkar-Ola Territorial Electoral Okrug): Yesterday lists were endorsed for secret balloting to the Council of the Union. At the council of representatives, the candidacy of Yuriy Chemodanov, people's deputy from the VLKSM [All-Union Leninist Communist Youth Union] was mentioned. When we examined the final lists for voting, the name of Chemodanov was not there. Another name, Veprev, appeared. I am asking the congress to sort this issue out. (Applause).

M.S. Gorbachev: The floor is given to Deputy Meshalkin; after him Deputy Karasev will speak. Comrades, I am sorting the notes which have arrived earlier. They are here in front of me. However, this situation has arisen following the speech of Comrade Afanasyev and we must resolve it. Your speeches will come later.

Ye.N. Meshalkin, director of the Research Institute for Pathology and Blood Circulation of the RSFSR [Russian Soviet Federated Socialist Republic] Ministry of Health Care, city of Novosibirsk (from the peace movement united under the Soviet Committee for the Defense of Peace jointly with the USSR Association for the United Nations): Comrade deputies! We Siberians sit at the top level of the hall. The Siberian oblasts are far away, but there are lots of us Siberians there. We sit there and treat

Fourth Session

27 May 1989

the Moscow delegation with respect; we think it will act reasonably, and appreciate its responsibilities. However, I am not the only one surprised by what is happening here. I am addressing primarily the young deputies, the ones who are elected for the first time and will work 10 years, not 5, as we will, because in another 5 years we will not get elected. We will be too old, but you will begin working for 10 years on the creation of our new society. Tell me, where are we in a hurry to get to at present? Why do we want everything to be immediately changed right now, this very minute? I view the speeches by Deputies Afanasyev and Popov as dissatisfaction with their position at the congress. They turned out to be in a minority, and this cannot satisfy them. They thought that they would be able to rally us all just as at the meetings in Luzhniki [Stadium], and immediately wipe out everything that interferes with their heading the congress.

I see no other explanation for that. (Applause). The dissatisfaction with ending up in a minority is clearly seen. They want to set up a faction, counting on the factional work, in which they are experienced, making it possible for them to capture a majority at the congress. I am not a politician. I am present for the first time at such a lively exchange of opinions and statements behind which there are many ulterior motives. Not all of what is said here is said sincerely. This is politics, and this is how it should be interpreted.

I believe that we should organize the working bodies first, and begin to work methodically within them. Much of what is happening here is due to the absence of a protocol, of a detailed description of the sequence of our actions at the meetings, because there was no one to prepare the protocol, because there were no organs yet which the Congress of People's Deputies had to elect. The congress is electing such bodies right now. Let us not interfere with our election of these bodies in order to let them work. These working bodies are not elected for 100 years. They will be augmented and added to every year. Nobody will interfere with any deputy—Popov, Afanasyev, or whoever—entering these forums, stating their opinion there, and arguing their points. This is where they should work instead of calling on the congress to come down on the chairman and take his powers away. They have already started talking about impeachment, self-dissolution, and what have you. This is more than nonsense; this is, pardon me, delirium. Comrades, we cannot work like that! (Applause).

I would like to say once again that our seats are in the back of the hall. What kind of influence is Mikhail Sergeyevich exerting on us? Has someone come from him and said: Comrades, this is how you have got to speak? Meanwhile, the "Moscow" faction does such work everyday. You are the ones conducting factional work aimed at splitting the congress, and not Mikhail Sergeyevich. He should not be accused of that. In general, comrade deputies, is it not the time to give everyone equal rights? Why should Siberia sit in the gallery, and you here, in the front rows? (Applause).

Maybe, we should do rotation during the break? Let us ask the first 20 rows to move back and 20 back rows to move forward.

Comrades, I am concerned with the situation in the country no less than you are. However, those who scream about poor work have not submitted any constructive suggestions; they don't talk about how things should be fixed; all we know is that that they've got to have freedom. (Applause).

I do not understand this; do we really have to behave like pirates who have seized the ship of state and set out to destroy it with all superstructures, the control console, and power plant, and later, having broken everything down into regional pieces, embark on sailing on these pieces through the rough seas of the world? Maybe we can still preserve unity and consolidation?

I believe it is incorrect to lay the course for a split and polarization at present. This does not become those who indeed think in terms of state, and intend to work in the manner of state. Plurality of opinions is mandatory, but do you really think that plurality of actions is? There has got to be unity in actions. If there is a reasonable majority at the congress, and if this reasonable majority would not be led astray, this does not at all mean that the majority should subordinate itself to the minority and renounce its right to evaluate what is going on here. Comrades, I believe that the congress should think hard. This is the second critical situation at our congress. The first one occurred on 25 May when we gathered for the first meeting. For 13 hours our country did not have a head of state because at 1000 hours Mikhail Sergeyevich Gorbachev surrendered his powers as the chairman of the presidium of the Supreme Soviet, and we elected him only at 2300 hours. For 13 hours we did not have a head of state!

You recall that in his statement Mikhail Sergeyevich told us that they were several hours late with vigorous actions in Sumgait, that they were a little bit late in Tbilisi. After all, these are minor emergencies compared to what can happen to our country, which has tens of thousands kilometers of frontiers. If this had happened during the critical 13 hours, who would have made active decisions and led our country out of the critical situation? The congress? With the kind of debates we've witnessed, the congress would have made a decision in 2 weeks. Meanwhile, the country would have perished. This is why we need to develop not only the protocol and changes in the Constitution; we should also develop ways of continuity, of transferring power.

Comrades, it is very difficult to talk over the first 10 rows which do not want to listen to this. But I think that over there, in the back, they still hear me because of the microphones. I am asking you to be reasonable and to give us an opportunity to bring to completion all structural changes which are planned by us and put on the

STENOGRAPHIC RECORD

Fourth Session

27 May 1989

agenda. If we are to talk about a co-report, it should be presented as a co-report of the chairman of the Council of Ministers, and not in the form of factional reports which they are trying to foist on us. (Applause).

M.S. Gorbachev: Deputy Mamedov, from a national-territorial okrug in Azerbaijan. Comrade Karasev is to prepare.

Deputy Mamedov, first secretary of the 26 Commissars of Baku rayon committee of the Communist Party of Azerbaijan, city of Baku (26 Commissars of Baku National-Territorial Electoral Okrug, city of Baku):

Dear Mikhail Sergeyevich! Dear deputies! I would like to express my categorical disagreement with the comrades who were the first to speak about the results of voting; that is, comrades Afanasyev and Popov.

I believe all of us agree that they and several more people make statements, they are constantly given the floor. There are very many deputies who would like to be given the floor, but they beat them to it and obscure the issues. I think it is altogether unbecoming for us, deputies, to accuse the other side. We have many complaints on the Karabakh issue, and many other issues. However, let us agree that we need to establish rapprochement, establish an alliance, establish a contract, and the contract should be fulfilled. I think we should take this path. We are advancing in an adequately democratic manner, though many comrades are sidetracking us and are trying to delay the discussion of the main issues through various procedural points.

Many different bodies should be elected in which we can actually solve problems. Excuse me, but I would like to talk about a meeting at Luzhniki which Comrade Popov chaired. I am a citizen of Baku, and possibly I made a mistake in introducing myself as a secretary of the rayon party committee. I was not given the floor. People who stood next to you (addresses Deputy Popov) asked me: Are you a representative of the People's Front? I told them: "We have one front—the Communist Party of Azerbaijan." "Then wait." What does that show?

Let us come to our senses. We are also in favor of things new, of a qualitative, serious renewal of the laws, procedures, and cadres. However, let us proceed in this matter in a businesslike manner.

A couple more words about meetings. We, so to speak, got gray hair over the issue of meetings in Baku. I am also a secretary in whose rayon the very main square is located. The 20 days we spent at the square taught us a lot. Do you know who drags us to the meetings? Either those who gravely err, or, pardon me, those who have ulterior motives. Because at a meeting, when you do not know each other, when only your throat is at work, and your ear is not, this can lead to anything at all. (Applause).

We opted for the following method: discuss issues in student, labor, and other collectives where all people know each other, where a break can be made and specialists can be invited, where we can come to an agreement and work out some platform, elucidate issues, and make joint decisions. Excuse me, but I will say it straightforwardly: Demagogic rhetoric is not going to advance us. Beware of the people who—I vouch for this—have ulterior motives for dragging us in this or that direction. Beware: The people see everything. Are you not going to incur their wrath? (Applause). Thank you. Mikhail Sergeyevich, I think we should move forward that way. We are on the right track, although it is a long and difficult journey. Although we are advancing slowly, I believe it is right. Thank you for your attention.

M.S. Gorbachev: Deputy Karasev is given the floor.

V.I. Karasev, head of chair at the Kramatorsk Industrial Institute, city of Kramatorsk (Kramatorsk Territorial Electoral Okrug, Ukrainian SSR): Dear comrades, I am not a Muscovite. Nonetheless, here is what I want to say. It is good at the initial stages that we have high words and discussions here. Let the people speak their minds. We, just as the entire people, are speaking our minds here for the first time. However, the time comes to speak to the point. The point is that we were indeed sent here by the voters in order to solve a problem for the people. In the process, they, as well as we, proceeded from this: We were elected to this body, the body which has the status of supreme power of the state. Therefore, the task of legislating, of creating the law, is the first and foremost task of it.

Now let us sort out the results of these 2 days quietly and without emotions. What has the legislative organ done? Nothing. Beginning with the speech at the party group, I, and also Comrade Burykh from the Donetsk delegation, submitted proposals on constitutional amendments which should have changed, or at any rate, raised the issue of changing the status of the Supreme Soviet, Congress of People's Deputies, and the status of people's deputies. This was rejected by the majority in the course of our congress. The first act of legislative initiative was not carried out. The second act which could be settled at our congress is to adopt such an agenda which would provide for real choices on the USSR Supreme Soviet, of its chairman and his first deputy. This would provide for debates, discussions, consideration, and preliminary familiarization of the deputies with each other. This was not done. This is why our legislative initiative was ignored here as a result.

The next question: What has happened? It happened that by the firm and confident hand of the majority we have turned ourselves into a congress of electors. We will leave without a statute, without constitutional amendments—we will leave being the same as the deputies of the Supreme Soviet used to be, whom we criticized for that. This is the first point.

STENOGRAPHIC RECORD

Fourth Session
27 May 1989

The second point, dear comrades. In our preelection speeches, all of us called for a professional parliament. As of now, these should be knowledgeable and skillful politicians to whom we will entrust our fate. This is the foremost, vital necessity. What is the result? Let me quote the data for the Ukraine. The results of elections to the Supreme Soviet: 35 percent of workers, 21 percent of ranking apparatus functionaries. Actually, our republic, which has a tremendous scientific-technical potential, produced 1.5 percent of economists. This is the one and only Deputy Saunin from Donetsk Oblast, and not one scientist in the field of the state, politics, and law. If this ratio is maintained, what kind of professionalism in the parliament can there be? (Applause).

The next point, dear comrades. I am concerned with nondemocratic tendencies surfacing not only with regard to legislative initiatives. They surface in the procedures for the conduct of our congress. Let me quote two examples from the regulations which we also adopted by a majority vote. It is laid down in the regulations that all materials for the proceedings of the congress should be provided to us no later than 2 weeks in advance. Actually, we received all materials only on the day of the meeting. Moreover, yesterday we got lists for perusal at 11 pm, literally before voting. Was it conceivable to sort these lists out despite the many debates being held? The picture yesterday was such that people went and put their ballots in without crossing out.

The next point. For 2 days we have been violating regulations in the course of the proceedings of the congress. We work a lot beyond the appointed hours. There is nothing wrong with working a lot provided you get results! There are no results.

One more issue. Yesterday at 11 pm Comrade Lukyanov came out and said that there was a delay with the lists, and we had to wait for 20 minutes. Twenty minutes turned out to be 4 hours. I was, in a human way, expecting the first words of Comrade Lukyanov to be: "Dear comrade-deputies, I apologize for what has happened."

Comrades, we did not elect the presidium in order for it to sit pretty here. We elected the presidium in order for it to work. Since it was elected, it should bear the responsibility.

This is how I would like to finish—to call on everybody to work. Working means producing results. As of now, there are none.

I would also like to express my opinion that it is necessary for the chair to make an official apology to the USSR Congress of People's Deputies on behalf of the presidium for poor organization and dragged-out proceedings during the first 2 days. Thank you for your attention. (Applause).

M.S. Gorbachev: I will say outright that there is no justification for that, and I take the remarks made as fair. They were also stated yesterday. However, I am grateful that the deputies still showed much tenacity under the circumstances and were guided by superior interests. I apologize for the delay yesterday. (Applause).

The floor is given to Deputy Momotova.

T.V. Momotova, deputy chief engineer of the Zhlobin fake fur production association (Zhlobin National-Territorial Election Okrug, Belorussian SSR): Dear comrade deputies! I am a representative of Belorussia from the city of Zhlobin in Gomel Oblast. According to what Comrade Afanasyev has said, you are looking at a representative of the Brezhnevian-Stalinist apparatus. Do I look like one? Comrades, I am responding to you quite officially—no. I was not an obedient individual manipulated by someone else whatever the times were, and voters in my okrug know this. Our first secretary of the city committee ran against me and we had a very difficult struggle with him. In the course of this struggle I had very many questions addressed to, among others, the apparatus. This is why I am saddened when they call me a representative of the Brezhnevian-Stalinist apparatus.

I have attentively familiarized myself with the position of the Moscow delegation. I find some aspects of this position acceptable, and some unacceptable; I am trying to study some of the aspects. To my mind, this is normal. However, I am surprised by the stand of the Moscow delegation, which is trying to bring pressure to bear on the deputies from other regions. It turns out that if deputies do not completely agree with the position of the Moscow delegation and do not support it, they are representatives of the time of stagnation. The question is why?

All of us have worked out a firm position at meetings with our voters. I for one do not make it a custom to change it rapidly, no matter whose opinion contradicts it—that of an academician, a scientist, or whoever. I deliberately agreed to run for deputy; I deliberately failed to reject the inclusion of my name on the lists of deputies to the Supreme Soviet. This is why I am simply offended by the Moscow delegation putting such pressure on us. (Applause). I would like the Moscow delegation, as well as Comrades Popov and Afanasyev, whom I respect very much, to draw the necessary conclusions and understand that we do not express the opinion of any apparatus, that this is our personal opinion, our position, which is different from theirs. I say this in order for them to take a sober view of the situation in this hall, if for no other reason. I also disagree with many things in the procedure of conducting the congress: there are many breaks and delays. However, comrades, this is not the main point today. One may send a note about this to the presidium, and incidentally I have already prepared it. However, I am calling on all deputies to work constructively and not

STENOGRAPHIC RECORD

FIRST CONGRESS OF PEOPLE'S DEPUTIES OF THE USSR

Fourth Session

27 May 1989

to get wrapped up in minor issues. I still hope that in the future the scientists will not set themselves off against us, representatives of the working class and the intelligentsia, in this manner. After all, we hope to receive help from them. When I was elected to the Supreme Soviet, I very much hoped to get their help. Thank you for your attention. (Applause).

M.S. Gorbachev: Comrades, would you object if the chairman of the counting commission reports on the results after all, and then we will proceed with speeches?

Yu.A. Osipyan: Comrade deputies! Permit me to read out the protocol of the USSR Congress of People's Deputies Tellers' Commission on the results of the voting in the elections to the USSR Supreme Soviet Soviet of the Union, 27 May 1989.

In accordance with the secret balloting procedure ratified by the congress and the determination of its results at the USSR Congress of People's Deputies, the Tellers' Commission has produced a summary of the votes cast in the election to the USSR Supreme Soviet Soviet of the Union and has established that the following candidacies from USSR people's deputies were submitted on the secret ballot paper for the election to the Soviet of the Union....

M.S. Gorbachev: Do you insist this be read out?

Auditorium: No.

M.S. Gorbachev: Let us allow the chairman himself to get his bearings so as to avoid any confusion.

Yu.A. Osipyan: Comrades, I would nonetheless beg leave to read out the full figures, because we need to know the number of votes "for" in order to get our bearings. I think this will suit everyone.

2,159 ballot papers were issued to USSR people's deputies for the vote. When the ballot boxes were opened they contained 2,149 ballot papers, none of which were spoiled. The votes cast were as follows:

RUSSIAN SOVIET FEDERATED SOCIALIST REPUBLIC [RSFSR], Moscow City: Yu.E. Andreyev: 919 for, 1,230 against; Yu.N. Belenkov: 1,261 for, 888 against; V.N. Belyayev: 1,101 for, 1,048 against; G.A. Borovik: 1,154 for, 995 against; M.A. Bocharov: 1,621 for, 528 against; F.M. Burlatskiy: 1,310 for, 839 against; Ye.P. Velikhov: 1,661 for, 488 against; A.P. Vladislavlev: 1,107 for, 1,042 against; N.N. Vorontsov: 1,229 for, 920 against; N.S. Glazkov: 1,576 for, 573 against; A.I. Golyakov: 1,451 for, 698 against; V.V. Gorbatko: 1,519 for, 630 against; N.N. Gritsenko: 1,319 for, 830 against; V.I. Dikul: 1,629 for, 520 against; Yu.V. Drunina: 1,328 for, 821 against; A.M. Yemelyanov: 1,475 for, 674 against; T.I. Zaslavskaya: 591 for, 1,558 against; I.I. Zaslavskiy: 829 for, 1,320 against; V.V. Ivanov: 1,163 for, 986 against; D.M. Iovlev: 1,575 for, 574 against; V.I. Kisin: 1,510 for, 639 against; A.N. Krayko: 975 for, 1,174 against; A.N. Kuzmin: 1,227 for, 922 against; V.G. Kulikov: 1,410 for, 739 against; I.D. Laptev: 1,376 for, 773 against; V.A. Logunov: 1,111 for, 1,038 against; V.A. Lunev: 1,653 for, 496 against; Ye.K. Malkova: 1,472 for, 677 against; I.I. Maltsev: 1,604 for, 546 against; R.A. Medvedev: 1,293 for, 856 against; A.N. Murashev: 1,201 for, 948 against; A.Ya. Neumyvakin: 1,318 for, 831 against; M.A. Pamfilova: 1,487 for, 662 against; M.N. Poltoranin: 1,184 for, 965 against; G.Kh. Popov: 1,007 for, 1,142 against (applause); Ye.M. Primakov: 1,483 for, 666 against; Z.P. Pukhova: 1,521 for, 628 against; Ye.N. Rogatin: 1,264 for, 885 against; Yu.A. Ryzhov: 1,304 for, 845 against; S.Ye. Savitskaya: 1,480 for, 669 against; O.M. Savostyuk: 1,281 for, 868 against; A.Ye. Sebentsov: 1,189 for, 960 against; Yu.Yu. Sokolova: 1,405 for, 744 against; S.B. Stankevich: 806 for, 1,343 against; V.S. Sysoyev: 1,034 for, 1,115 against; N.Ya. Sychev: 1,216 for, 933 against; V.A. Tikhonov: 630 for, 1,519 against; A.V. Firsov: 1,227 for, 922 against; K.V. Frolov: 1,518 for, 631 against; V.A. Tsyurupa: 1,527 for, 622 against; Yu.D. Chernichenko: 1,086 for, 1,063 against; S.G. Shuvalov: 1,044 for, 1,105 against; V.P. Shcherbakov: 1,172 for, 977 against; A.V. Yablokov: 1,156 for, 993 against; V.N. Yaroshenko: 1,124 for, 1,025 against.

RSFSR, AUTONOMOUS REPUBLICS, KRAYS, AND OBLASTS:

S.S. Alekseyev: 1,974 for, 174 against; V.G. Afonin: 1,658 for, 491 against; Ye.Kh. Blayev: 2,040 for, 109 against; L.Ye. Bliznov: 2,065 for, 84 against; Ye.F. Bobyleva: 1,957 for, 192 against; I.M. Bogdanov: 2,096 for, 53 against; Yu.A. Bogomolov: 2,084 for, 65 against; V.A. Borovkov: 2,066 for, 83 against; Yu.I. Borodin: 2,033 for, 116 against; A.F. Veprev: 2,097 for, 52 against; M.I. Vlazneva: 2,007 for, 142 against; I.S. Vnebrachnyy: 2,039 for, 110 against; V.A. Volkov: 2,011 for, 138 against; V.V. Volodichev: 2,095 for, 54 against; V.I. Voskoboynikov: 2,082 for, 67 against; R.G. Gamzatov: 1,858 for, 291 against; Yu.V. Golik: 2,047 for, 102 against; N.P. Grachev: 2,100 for, 49 against; V.I. Gross: 1,994 for, 155 against; A.I. Grudinina: 2,096 for, 51 against; V.A. Gubarev: 2,094 for, 55 against; V.G. Gudilina: 2,106 for, 43 against; V.V Guliy: 1,617 for, 532 against; N.I. Gutskalov: 2,087 for, 62 against; A.A. Denisov: 2,052 for, 97 against; I.V. Dorokhov: 1,905 for, 244 against; P.A. Druz: 1,791 for, 358 against; I.N. Dyakov: 1,839 for, 310 against; O.M. Yegorov : 2,112 for, 37 against; A.S. Yezhelev: 1,984 for, 165 against; G.M. Yermolayev: 2,087 for, 62 against; N.V. Yefimov: 2,091 for, 58 against; I.A. Zhdakayev: 2,042 for, 107 against; Yu.I. Zubov: 2,089 for, 60 against; K.Ye. Ivanov: 2,033 for, 116 against; I.M. Ivchenko: 2,095 for, 54 against; A.A Kazarin: 2,088 for, 61 against; P.P. Kazachenko: 2,088 for, 61 against; V.I. Kalashnikov: 1,719 for, 430 against; Yu.Kh. Kalmykov: 2,073 for, 76 against; V.V. Kasyan: 2,073 for, 76 against; Ye.U. Kim:

Fourth Session
27 May 1989

2,051 for, 98 against; M.M. Klimov: 2,090 for, 59 against; N.I. Konkov: 1,850 for, 299 against; A.V. Kopylova: 2,086 for, 63 against; N.M. Kopysov: 2,078 for, 71 against; A.A. Korenev: 2,087 for, 62 against; N.N. Koryugin: 2,109 for, 60 against; Ye.I. Krasnokutskiy: 2,080 for, 69 against; N.A. Kryuchenkova: 2,111 for, 38 against; A.T. Kuzovlev: 2,083 for, 66 against; V.Ye. Kurteshin: 2,062 for, 87 against; V.A. Leonchev: 2,087 for, 62 against; K.D. Lubenchenko: 2,042 for, 107 against; V.P. Lushnikov: 2,098 for, 81 against; V.A. Mayboroda: 2,077 for, 72 against; Yu.A. Manayenkov: 1,975 for, 174 against; O.I. Markov: 2,089 for, 62 against; V.I. Matviyenko: 1,944 for, 205 against; V.Ya. Medikov: 2,105 for, 44 against; A.D. Menshatov: 2,084 for, 65 against; S.A. Militenko: 2,108 for, 41 against; V.M. Minin: 2,126 for, 23 against; F.F. Mikhedov: 2,107 for, 42 against; A.K. Mukhametzyanov: 2,042 for, 107 against; S.Ya. Naumov: 2,112 for, 37 against; Yu.V. Neyelov: 2,078 for, 71 against; I.A. Nikanorov: 2,090 for, 59 against; Ye.N. Nikolskiy: 1,991 for, 158 against; V.P. Nuzhnyy: 2,093 for, 56 against; A.P. Orekhov: 2,034 for, 115 against; V.A. Ostroukhov: 2,053 for, 96 against; N.V. Panteleyev: 2,108 for, 41 against; A.N. Penyagin: 2,098 for, 51 against; N.D. Pivovarov: 1,946 for, 203 against; N.M. Piryazeva: 2,058 for, 91 against; V.I. Postnikov: 2,053 for, 96 against; G.S. Pokhodnya: 2,097 for, 52 against; N.N. Prybylova: 2,089 for, 60 against; M.G. Rakhimov: 2,069 for, 80 against; M.N. Rakhmanova: 2,092 for, 57 against; A.V. Reshetnikov: 2,119 for, 30 against; V.A. Rogozhina: 2,109 for, 40 against; V.V. Ryumin: 2,069 for, 80 against; N.S. Sazonov: 2,034 for, 115 against; Yu.G. Samsonov: 1,769 for, 380 against; A.A. Sapegin: 2,088 for, 61 against; A.T. Sarakayev: 2,109 for, 40 against; V.B. Svatkovskiy: 2,091 for, 58 against; V.V. Skvortsov: 2,122 for, 27 against; S.Ye. Sleptsov: 2,098 for, 51 against; I.M. Smorodin: 2,097 for, 52 against; A.A. Sobchak: 1,966 for, 183 against; N.I. Sotnikov: 2,096 for, 63 against; V.Ya. Stadnik: 2,073 for, 76 against; V.N. Stepanov: 2,121 for, 28 against; G.I. Stoumova: 2,103 for, 46 against; V.A. Titenov: 2,097 for, 51 against [figures as published]; V.M. Timchenko: 2,097 for, 52 against; M.A. Timchenko: 2,110 for, 39 against; N.D. Tutov: 2,048 for, 101 against; N.A. Usilina: 2,107 for, 42 against; G.I. Filshin: 2,065 for, 84 against; V.V. Finogenov: 2,106 for, 43 against; S.N. Khadzhiyev: 1,997 for, 152 against; V.V. Khmura: 2,065 for, 84 against; S.A. Tsyplyayev: 2,082 for, 67 against; N.F. Chernyayev: 2,095 for, 54 against; Yu.M. Chichik: 2,071 for, 78 against; M.I. Shaydulin: 1,900 for, 249 against; L.V. Sharin: 1,836 for, 313 against; A.V. Shashkov: 2,110 for, 39 against; V.A. Shekhovtsov: 2,063 for, 86 against; V.A. Shishov: 2,108 for, 41 against; Yu.Ya. Shmal: 2,043 for, 106 against; V.I. Shtepo: 2,010 for, 139 against; A.S. Shukshin: 2,106 for, 43 against; V.D. Yudin: 2,069 for, 80 against; V.S. Yakutis: 2,033 for, 115 against; V.A. Yarin: 2,072 for, 77 against; O.P. Yarovaya: 2,032 for, 117 against.

UKRAINIAN SOVIET SOCIALIST REPUBLIC [SSR]:

N.M. Amosov: 2,035 for, 114 against; N.I. Babchenko: 2,035 for, 114 against; B.S. Breurosh: 2,113 for, 36 against; I.A. Vakarchuk: 2,129 for, 20 against; A.N. Vasilets: 2,117 for, 32 against; N.P. Vasilchuk: 2,048 for, 101 against; V.M. Vologzhin: 2,104 for, 45 against; A.S. Vuychitskiy: 2,116 for, 33 against; N.F. German: 2,123 for, 26 against; Ya.Ya. Gil: 2,123 for, 26 against; A.V. Grib: 2,119 for, 30 against; V.N. Danilov: 2,130 for 19 against; F.M. Demchenko: 2,122 for, 27 against; I.P. Zelinskiy: 2,116 for, 33 against; A.F. Kasyanov: 2,101 for, 48 against; V.A. Kravets: 1,984 for, 165 against; V.G. Kucherenko: 2,004 for, 145 against; Ya.S. Lesyuk: 2,076 for, 73 against; S.I. Matveychuk: 2,120 for, 29 against; L.T. Matiyko: 2,114 for, 35 against; G.S. Moskalenko: 2,109 for, 40 against; M.N. Moskalik: 2,098 for, 51 against; D.K. Motornyy: 2,087 for 62 against; V.A. Nozdrya: 2,125 for, 24 against; V.A. Opolinskiy: 2,121 for, 28 against; I.B. Pavlevich: 2,114 for, 35 against; A.A. Pavliy: 2,051 for, 98 against; V.A. Plyutinskiy: 2,090 for, 59 against; Z.S. Prikhodko: 1,966 for, 186 against [figures as published]; G.I. Revenko: 1,919 for, 230 against; S.M. Ryabchenko: 2,121 for, 28 against; A.N. Saunin: 2,120 for, 29 against; A.M. Sbitnev: 2,121 for, 28 against; T.V. Sidorchuk: 2,109 for, 40 against; D.G. Smirnov: 2,133 for, 16 against; L.I. Sukhov: 2,106 for, 43 against; B.I. Sushko: 2,119 for, 30 against; V.I. Trefilov: 2,104 for, 45 against; G.A. Tyminskiy: 2,109 for, 40 against; G.P. Kharchenko: 1,897 for, 252 against; Yu.S. Tsavro: 2,130 for, 19 against; A.L. Tsarevskiy: 2,092 for, 57 against; V.I. Tsybukh: 1,941 for, 208 against; A.I. Chabanov: 2,130 for, 19 against; N.I. Chentsov: 2,112 for, 37 against; M.A. Chepurnaya: 2,113 for, 36 against; S.V. Chervonopiskiy: 2,006 for, 143 against; V.M. Shabanov: 2,133 for, 16 against; G.I. Sharyy: 2,121 for, 28 against; A.A. Shust: 2,109 for, 40 against; Yu.N. Shcherbak: 2,098 for, 41 against; A.N. Yakimenko: 2,122 for, 27 against.

BELORUSSIAN SSR:

N.G. Bobritskiy: 2,123 for, 26 against; T.N. Dudko: 2,054 for, 95 against; S.F. Kalashnikov: 2,124 for, 95 against; I.M. Luchenok: 2,108 for, 41 against; A.K. Miloserdnyy: 2,110 for, 39 against; G.P. Piskunovich: 2,116 for, 33 against; V.I. Semukha: 2,043 for, 106 against; Ye.Ye. Sokolov: 1,856 for, 293 against; N.S. Feskov: 2,121 for, 28 against; P.V. Shetko: 2,058 for, 91 against.

UZBEK SSR:

Yu.T. Akbarov: 2,100 for, 49 against; A.K. Arslonov: 2,114 for, 35 against; T. Zhurbayeva: 2,124 for, 25 against; T.B. Kirgizbayeva: 2,105 for, 44 against; N.I. Kucherskiy: 2,105 for, 44 against; M.M. Mirkasymov: 1,858 for, 291 against; A.G. Mukhtarov: 2,087 for, 62

FIRST CONGRESS OF PEOPLE'S DEPUTIES OF THE USSR

Fourth Session
27 May 1989

against; V.I. Ogarok: 1,901 for, 248 against; A.S. Pavlov: 1,957 for, 192 against; A. Rakhimov: 2,109 for, 40 against; K. Salykov: 1,883 for, 266 against; R.A. Ubaydullayeva: 2,085 for, 64 against; B.M. Ergashev: 2,103 for, 46 against; E.Yu. Yusupov: 2,107 for, 42 against.

KAZAKH SSR:

A.T. Dzhanasbayev: 2,116 for, 33 against; Ya.A. Donchak: 2,112 for, 37 against; B.S. Iskakova: 2,122 for, 27 against; G.V. Kolbin: 1,885 for, 264 against; Ye. V. Krivoruchko: 2,106 for, 43 against; A.V. Milkin: 1,921 for, 228 against; O.M. Pal: 2,106 for, 43 against; M.R. Sagdiyev: 1,924 for, 225 against; A.V. Semenikhin: 2,067 for, 82 against; O.O. Suleymenov: 2,093 for, 56 against; V.N. Fominykh: 2,118 for, 31 against; P.M. Chursina: 2,108 for, 41 against; M.Shakhanov: 2,109 for, 40 against; K.A. Shopanayev: 2,103 for, 46 against.

GEORGIAN SSR:

N.S. Amaglobeli: 2,109 for, 40 against; G.Sh. Kvaratskhelia: 2,119 for, 30 against; M.R. Kontselidze: 2,118 for, 31 against; V.V. Kublashvili: 2,120 for, 29 against; N.M. Mgaloblishvili: 2,125 for, 24 against.

AZERBAIJAN SSR:

A.M. Amanov: 2,082 for, 67 against; D.G. Gilalzade: 2,090 for, 59 against; A.D. Melikov: 2,094 for, 55 against; A.R. Rzayev: 2,059 for, 90 against; A.Kh. Salimov: 2,086 for, 63 against.

LITHUANIAN SSR:

V.V. Antanaytis: 2,047 for, 102 against; A.-M.K. Brazauskas: 1,942 for, 207 against; A.Y. Burachas: 2,048 for, 101 against; K.D.P. Prunskene: 2,067 for, 82 against.

MOLDAVIAN SSR:

S.F. Akhromeyev: 1,927 for, 222 against; S.K. Grossu: 1,839 for, 310 against; V.A. Katrinich: 2,120 for, 29 against; A.A. Mokanu: 1,948 for, 201 against.

LATVIAN SSR:

Ya.Ya. Vagris: 1,930 for, 219 against; A.V. Gorbunov: 1,995 for, 154 against; D.O. Skulme: 2,045 for, 104 against.

KIRGHIZ SSR:

L.N. Druzhinina: 2,103 for, 46 against; T.A. Kerimbekov: 2,103 for, 46 against; A.M. Masaliyev: 1,895 for, 254 against.

TAJIK SSR:

M. Kanoatov: 2,066 for, 83 against; K. Makhkamov: 1,902 for, 247 against; S. Saydaliyev: 2,094 for, 55 against.

ARMENIAN SSR:

S.G. Arutyunyan: 1,833 for, 316 against; G.M. Voskanyan: 1,879 for, 270 against; A.B. Kirakosyan: 2,081 for, 68 against.

TURKMEN SSR:

M.B. Amanova: 2,112 for, 37 against; S.A. Niyazov: 1,844 for, 305 against; D. Shaklycheva: 2,117 for, 32 against.

ESTONIAN SSR:

V.I. Vare: 2,030 for, 119 against; M.Y. Lauristin: 2,036 for, 113 against.

Comrades! At this point I shall probably ask you to resolve the question the easy way, as they say.

M.S. Gorbachev: Yes, submit the proposal.

Yu.A. Osipyan: In accordance with the quota established for Moscow, there were 29 vacancies to be filled, right? Let me read out all 29 names of the elected deputies.

For the Russian Federation it turned out that there were 4 more candidate deputies for the Soviet of the Union than was stipulated by the quota. Therefore I will read out the names of the four deputies who were not elected.

Voice from the floor: We didn't hear Chemodanov's name mentioned.

Yu.A. Osipyan: I could not read out Chemodanov's name because he was not on the lists which the Tellers' Commission was handling. This is not a question for me. Finally I can say that all the candidate deputies nominated for the quotas of the remaining union republics were elected. Thus the number of candidates coincided with the number of quota places. So you will probably allow me to refrain from reading them out. (Applause).

Thus, the following deputies were elected for the City of Moscow; I will read the out in alphabetical order: M.A. Bocharov, F.M. Burlatskiy, Ye.P. Velikhov, N.S. Glazkov, A.I. Golyakov, V.V. Gorbatko, N.N. Gritsenko, V.I. Dikul, Yu.V. Drunina, A.M. Yemelyanov, D.M. Iovlev, V.I. Kisin, V.G. Kulikov, I.D. Laptev, V.A. Lunev, Ye.K. Malkova, I.I. Maltsev, R.A. Medvedev, A.Ya. Neumyvakin, I.A. Pamfilova, Ye.M. Primakov, Z.P. Pukhova, B.N. Rogatin, Yu.A. Ryzhov, S.Ye. Savitskaya, O.M. Savostyuk, Yu.Yu. Sokolova, K.V. Frolov, and V.A. Tsyurupa.

For the vacant oblast and autonomous republic places, that is, the remainder of the Russian Federation, all the candidates were elected with the exception of candidates V.G. Afonin, V.V. Guliy, V.I. Kalashnikov, and Yu.G. Samsonov.

All the other candidates for the Russian Federation's quota of seats were elected.

STENOGRAPHIC RECORD

Fourth Session

27 May 1989

M.S. Gorbachev: Yuriy Andreyevich, is that all you've got to say? Is your report complete?

Yu.A. Osipyan: Yes, I have finished, comrades.

M.S. Gorbachev: What are the questions for the chairman of the counting commission?

From the floor: (Inaudible).

M.S. Gorbachev: Good, then we will have to approve the minutes of the counting commission.

From the floor: (Inaudible).

M.S. Gorbachev: Good.

Yu.A. Osipyan: I cannot answer.

M.S. Gorbachev: Answer, please.

Yu.A. Osipyan: Comrades, here the comrade now asks me a question regarding the candidacy of Deputy Chemodanov. I can only repeat once more what I said at the beginning of the report of the counting commission. The counting commission had in its possession materials that were given to us, to the counting commission, for the compilation of a ballot of the presidium of the congress. The presidium of the congress operated with materials given to us by delegates of the union republics, and also of other delegations, well, let us say, of the Moscow delegation, because delegate conferences were repeatedly going on and these lists were being edited. All questions relating to how the delegations formulated their lists should be addressed to the delegates.

M.S. Gorbachev: Good.

Yu.A. Osipyan: I repeat once more, comrades. If you were present at a meeting of the delegates of the Russian Federation, then address yourselves to that delegation.

M.S. Gorbachev: Confirm? Or, still, first clarify? Good. Comrade Vorotnikov has the floor.

V.I. Vorotnikov: Dear comrade deputies, I will try to explain this question. In considering the list of candidates from the Russian Federation to membership in the Council of the Union from the oblasts, krays, and autonomous republics at the general meeting of all the deputies on 22 May, a preliminary list of the names of these candidates coordinated with the representatives of krays, oblasts, and ASSR's was read out and promulgated. Candidates of four autonomous republics to the Council of the Union were not on the list. These are the Buryat ASSR, Mariy ASSR, Tuva ASSR, and the Kalmyk ASSR. We explained this situation as follows: In connection with the fact that instead of 10, we are submitting a significantly greater number of mandates for election to membership to the Council of the Union of the USSR Supreme Soviet from Moscow, and considering the norm—one deputy for each 712,000 voters—the number of candidates was reduced for these autonomous republics and quite a few other krays and oblasts. In this connection Deputy Posibeyev asked whether it was possible, nonetheless, to nominate a candidate from the Mariy ASSR to the Council of the Union. It was explained to him that there were 535,000 voters in the Mariy Autonomous Republic. This was not enough to elect their own representative. But, then, the republic is fully represented in the Council of Nationalities. The same situation applies to Buryatiya, which has more than 660,000 voters, and in Kalmykiya and Tuva. After this Deputy Eshpay came out at the meeting with the very same kind of proposal. Explanations were also given to him. Both deputies were satisfied.

Afterwards, at a meeting of the representatives in the Kremlin, there was another discussion of all of the candidates, and no proposals came from the Mariy ASSR. However, for some unknown reason, and without the knowledge of the presidium, the name of Comrade Chemodanov appeared on the list of deputies that was submitted. It was announced in this connection that inasmuch as there was a need for a replacement and a rearrangement, the candidates should come to the table of the presidium of the congress and make the necessary changes. Many of the representatives of delegations approached the table and changed candidacies. Representatives of the Mariy delegation also came up. They were told again that the quota for the Mariy, Buryat, Tuva, and Kalmyk Autonomous Republics is not being changed, but that it should not be forgotten that in connection with the proposed rotation it is envisioned that there should be representatives from these four republics on the Council of the Union in the next composition of the USSR Supreme Soviet. There were no objections from the Buryat, Tuva, and Kalmyk deputies, but the deputies from the Mariy Republic kept insisting.

M.S. Gorbachev: If the participants of the meeting of representatives will recall, we had a big discussion. The comrades from the Kuban spoke and calculated that for their 3.6 million voters, they were short two candidates at a minimum. Comrades from Rostov calculated about the same. Many other comrades from large electoral okrugs also introduced proposals. This question was debated for a long time, and they still considered it possible—and, in my opinion, the general opinion of the meeting of the representatives was accepted by all of the republics—they deemed it possible to resolve this question, taking into account that Moscow is the capital and that it absorbs a lot of creative forces that arrive here from everywhere. Take even this list, which went around Moscow for voting. Two-thirds of the list are those who started their lives in other regions. But this is a feature of Moscow. Therefore, we felt also that the Russian Federation should agree to an increase in the number of representatives of Moscow. It is difficult to think any

STENOGRAPHIC RECORD

Fourth Session
27 May 1989

other way here. That, basically, is the action they took. But this problem remained and kept coming up. And now, when the right was given to the republic to make a final decision, we have come to this situation. It is very likely that the imperfection of our electoral system has an effect here; it would be difficult to think otherwise. And they agreed, keeping in mind that when we implement rotation, we will take the fact into account that these republics are to be represented in the Council of the Union. So, we drew up the final lists on the basis of these clarifications, and the counting commission operated with them. What shall we do, comrades?

Deputy (did not introduce himself): Dear comrades, we must once and for all agree on the accuracy of procedural questions. Honestly, it is embarrassing when we have to analyze questions like this. I was embarrassed by yesterday's meeting of representatives of the Russian Federation delegation, and I was embarrassed for Chemodanov that he found out that he was not on the list only after receiving the ballot for secret voting. We do not think about people. But paragraph 4 of the Instructions on Secret Balloting clearly stipulates: "The ballot lists all candidates for secret voting who were approved by the congress." Can any one of you, the deputies, recall that the congress did not approve Chemodanov's candidacy which was placed on the list? This simply did not happen. We are once more violating instructions that we approve. I think we have to put an end to this.

Moreover, dear chairman, this morning Comrade Vorotnikov was given a deputy's inquiry from the deputies. It has not been read at the meeting. It concerns the candidacy of Comrade Chemodanov. I would suggest that all inquiries on procedural questions that concern deputies' inquiries should be read out if they have a direct connection to questions under examination. And before this, a note was submitted in a similar situation concerning comrades Uvarov and Tsegelnikov. At a meeting of the Kalinin delegation (I was there on instructions of a group of deputies from the VLKSM), it was said: If the elections of the Russian Federation are to be competitive, then the voting lists must carry two candidacies, one of whom is Comrade Uvarov. But his name did not appear on the list. And we have many such discrepancies. Our congress is a rather great event. And it seems to me that it is absolutely embarrassing to "become impatient" about such minutiae. I would ask the presidium and the secretariat of the congress to set up an exact order for these procedural questions. (Applause).

M.S. Gorbachev: Next, please.

S.P. Golovin, radio equipment adjuster from the Mariysk machine construction plant (Yoshkar-Ola Territorial Electoral Okrug): But still I would like to know who specifically, from the list we approved, erased the name of Chemodanov and included Comrade Veprev. Specifically. (Applause).

Yu.A. Osipyan: I should say, comrades, that the list underwent changes not only in connection with the exclusion of Chemodanov, but also for a number of other candidacies. You saw, representatives from delegations came up and proposed making changes. We made the changes on this basis.

M.S. Gorbachev: I remind you that the principle which we assume as a basis are the proposals of the republic delegations of deputies, but inside the republics they are the oblast delegations. Remember, this is the situation that arose: Apart from the proposals made by Belorussia, four deputies were introduced. Therefore, we had a break so that all of the republics could, as the saying goes, have the matter out, since it was found that there were proposals on replacing individual candidates, or someone removed his own, not wanting to participate, because there was no chance of becoming a member of the Supreme Soviet. We arrived at an understanding that each republic would finally complete this process within the framework of the instructions of the congress. If we talk about the fact that comrades are making comments about the presidium of the congress concerning procedural matters, then, I think, this has to be taken into account and conclusions have to be derived from this.

Deputy (did not introduce himself): Comrade deputies! So that such excesses will never again be repeated, there is a proposal to make an amendment to the Law on Elections to make it possible for public organizations themselves to nominate candidates to the USSR Supreme Soviet. Then we will also retain the one-third quota—since we agreed to elections from public organizations and territorial and national-territorial okrugs. It is very likely apparent to public organizations and the deputies who should represent them in the USSR Supreme Soviet.

O.M. Savostyuk, graphic artist, secretary of the board of the Union of USSR Artists, chairman of the board of the organization of the Union of RSFSR Artists, city of Moscow (from the Union of USSR Artists): I propose that we correct in the following way this very grave error which we all committed: Put Deputy Chemodanov's candidacy to a vote.

G.A. Pogosyan, pensioner. (Stepanakert Electoral Okrug, Nagorno-Karabakh Autonomous Oblast [NKAO]): I would like to make a short statement before the break; otherwise my statement will not have a very great effect. Two deputies should be listed from the NKAO for membership in the USSR Supreme Soviet according to the quota. Yesterday, when we received the lists of candidates to the USSR Supreme Soviet, two deputies from Nagorno-Karabakh figured there, but not one of the candidacies from the group of deputies was coordinated. Although all of these candidacies were reviewed in the preliminary plan, there was no final decision. When we were given a break in order to consider and introduce our amendments, all of the deputies discussed the candidacies and nominated two new ones. Deputy Comrade Grigoryan submitted these proposals to the

FIRST CONGRESS OF PEOPLE'S DEPUTIES OF THE USSR

Fourth Session
27 May 1989

presidium. After this, Deputy Comrade Polyanichko from the Azerbaijani group of deputies and our autonomous oblast made his own counterproposals, which did not fully correspond with our proposals. Yesterday, during the voting, we found out that Comrade Polyanichko's proposal passed, and not the proposal from our group.

I would like Comrade Lukyanov to explain here and now straightforwardly: In the final analysis, who has the priority right to nominate candidates to electoral organs, and did the presidium act properly, adopting a list for execution that was submitted by the republic and not by the oblast? If I am right, and this prerogative belongs to us, then in what way did the presidium of the congress allow Azerbaijan to usurp our right to nominate candidates, and what guarantees can the presidium now give that this will not be repeated in the future? Thank you. (Applause).

M.S. Gorbachev: Comrade Galina Vasilyevna Starovoytova, please.

G.V. Starovoytova, senior researcher in the Center of the Study of Inter-ethnic Relations of the presidium of the USSR Academy of Sciences, city of Moscow. (Yerevan Soviet National-Territorial Electoral Okrug, Armenian SSR): I would like to draw your attention to the question that was raised here by Genrikh Andreyevich Pogosyan. Democratic principles presuppose the nomination of candidates for deputies to the Supreme Soviet from below, by delegates themselves from local administrative formations. And, I think, that this principle should be adhered to with particular consistency in regard to NKAO. As we know, it was the infringement of the national rights of the main ethnic majority of this oblast that led to the dramatic situation that developed there, and which has still not normalized.

The main reason for the tension, I think, is that the country does not listen much to the voice of Karabakh, and knows little about the true processes that are occurring there. Unfortunately, the congress also did not hear the voice of the Karabakh deputies, although they were right to expect a special sensitivity and tact with respect to a national minority. I would also like to draw your attention here to the well-known Moscow centrism in the approach to similar problems. Deputy Zalygin, whom I respect, yesterday tried to teach the Lithuanian delegation that all progressive ideas come from Moscow, and that Lithuania and other republics should thank Moscow for the spirit of these ideas. I fear that many national minorities today became dissatisfied with the progress of the review, in particular, with the decision on the question of the nomination of proxy deputies to the Supreme Soviet from Karabakh. I think that the congress can still correct the mistake. It is a very serious mistake, which can lead to a further escalation of tension in the Transcaucasus region. I think that the congress can now adopt the competitive list that was proposed by Karabakh. It includes famous people—Genrikh Andreyevich Pogosyan and Zoriya Balayana, a well-known publicist and writer and a Karabakh by birth. I understand that voting is a very cumbersome and difficult procedure. And the deputies who are kept in a state of lack of sleep, not only by the presidium but also by our voters, are tired, and they do not want to go to Georgievskiy Hall again to vote. However, the results of this voting place too great a responsibility on us: How will Nagorno-Karabakh live in the next 5 years with those deputies that it did not elect to the Supreme Soviet? Who will protect their interests? Therefore, I propose that the results of the voting on the NKAO nomination to the Supreme Soviet be considered inoperative in view of the undemocratic procedure for nominating these deputies. I further propose approval of a new list to be nominated by the NKAO itself. To accept the decision of the congress—the congress has the authority to make such a decision—on the possibility of conducting an open vote, and that new ballots not be printed, and then to vote on the list of deputies that was submitted by Nagorno-Karabakh itself. Thank you. (Applause).

M.S. Gorbachev: A 30-minute break.

M.S. Gorbachev: And so we must conclude the discussion of two problems in connection with the publication of the results of the voting for the Council of the Union. Two problems have been raised: One is the Mariy ASSR delegation on Comrade Chemodanov, and the other is in connection with NKAO representation. I ask that this discussion be continued in order to clarify the questions. First, about the Mariy republic. Were the comrades able to work out some approach? It seems that Comrade Sharanov is ready to speak? Or you, Comrade Posibeyev?

K.A. Posibeyev, first secretary of the Mariy CPSU Obkom, city of Yoshkar-Ola (Sovetskiy Territorial Electoral Okrug, Mariy ASSR): Dear comrade deputies! The fact that four autonomous republics do not have even one representative in the Council of the Union, obviously, is the result of the imperfections of our system of elections to the Supreme Soviet from regions of the country and from national formations. Well, you yourselves understand what an autonomous republic is—it is a people, it is a culture, it is a language, and it is problems. I think that it matters to each autonomous republic whether someone represents it or not in the Council of Nationalities. It is apparent that this problem has to be solved for the future. But it is not our fault that our quota, so to speak, does not make it possible to have one representative. What is our republic guilty of? Or, let us say, Checheno-Ingushetiya or Tuva? Obviously, there should be some kind of a stipulation or annotation—or whatever you want—that in the event that an autonomous republic or any other region does not have the required number of voters, then one seat will be set aside for this republic or region, nonetheless. And, perhaps, we should resolve this question today. I do not know the point of view of the delegations of other republics but, maybe, with respect to the exclusion, these four autonomous republics should be given an opportunity to hold a vote today? This is the first point.

STENOGRAPHIC RECORD

Fourth Session
27 May 1989

Second. Perhaps we would not have reacted this way, if we had gotten an immediate reply to the inquiry we sent to Comrade Vitaliy Ivanovich Vorotnikov. But as Veprev's candidacy appeared instead of Chemodanov's, perhaps the questions should be decided in an open vote. I also think that the congress should do this. Thank you for your attention.

M.S. Gorbachev: But this proposal did not move us very far.... Please, Comrade Sharonov, the VLKSM deputy, has the floor.

A.V. Sharonov, chairman of the Kozmodemyansk city people's court of the Ufa Ordzhonikidze Aviation Institute, Bashkir ASSR, city of Ufa (From the All-Union Leninist Communist Youth League): We met for the first time with a group of Komsomol deputies, and we would like to submit for your review what seems to us to be an acceptable proposal for getting out of this contentious situation with Chemodanov. What specifically? We see two variants here. The first variant is to arrange a new vote, apparently, a secret one, on the two candidates: Veprev and Chemodanov. The second variant. Hold a secret vote on one of the candidacies, Chemodanov's candidacy, and include the results of the voting in the general ballot for secret voting and see how the situation changes in this case. If Chemodanov comes out last then he will not get into the Soviet of the Union. If it is someone else, then we will in such an event review the results of the voting.

There is one more point. I would like to establish clearly, here at the congress, the basis for and who placed the candidacy of Comrade Veprev, which was not approved by the congress, on the ballot. And on what grounds and by whom was the candidacy of Chemodanov, which the conference of representatives proposed and the congress approved, removed from this ballot. This question is not just a personal question, and it concerns not only Chemodanov and the Mariy Republic; it is a question of principle. So that we could say that the congress decided everything, and that there was not someone deciding for the congress.

As for the situation with Nagorno-Karabakh, we are ready to review it in the same way; that is, to hold another vote. Thank you.

M.S. Gorbachev: Good. Perhaps we will make a determination on the Mariy Republic, and then we will go to the second part—the NKAO. Do you, Comrade Sobchak, want to speak on this question? Please.

From the floor: (Inaudible).

M.S. Gorbachev: Comrades, we will examine the deputies' inquiries at the end of the conference and give instructions.

A.A. Sobchak, head of a department of the juridical faculty at Leningrad State University (Vasileostrov Territorial Electoral Okrug, city of Leningrad): Dear comrade deputies! The contentious situation—I would say, crisis situation—with respect to the results of the voting arose from the fact that many of the deputies have not yet perceived the full importance of the events taking place today in this hall. The fact is that we are not simply deciding some kind of procedural questions, we are laying the foundation for a new political system. And it is natural that in laying this foundation we can make mistakes—we do not have the experience of democratic traditions. This is the way it is. It is precisely because of inattention to these legal technical questions which, at first glance, appear to be secondary, that this special case arose, and that we fell into such a complicated situation. As a lawyer, I can say that in strict conformity with the Constitution, after we have already practically unanimously approved the report of the counting commission, there is only one way out. The necessity arose for another vote on the entire list. But I am a realist, and I understand that all of the people's deputies should not be compelled to spend time on this again because of errors of this kind.

Therefore, I have a proposal. Violations have appeared not only with respect to the Council of Nationalities—I have in mind the infringement of the interests of the NKAO—but also of the Council of the Union—I have in mind the situation with Comrade Chemodanov, which, in my opinion, arose because of complete professional incompetence on th part of those who presided during the conduct of our Russian Federation conferences. (Applause). I think that the way out of the situation is the following. We have to adopt an amendment to the Constitution, to Article 111, and to increase both the Council of Nationalities and the Council of the Union simultaneously. We would thereby guarantee the interests of the NKAO and assure the opportunity to vote for Deputy Chemodanov, who was nominated but who for some reason did not appear on the rolls for secret balloting. Moreover, this will make it possible additionally to nominate one more candidate. The mandatory increase by two seats of the Council of the Union is dictated by the fact that membership in both houses has to be the same. The question cannot be resolved by increasing the seats in the Council of Nationalities by less than two seats. And, finally, if my proposal is not accepted, I am fully authorized by Professor Denisov, deputy from Leningrad—we are prepared to give up our deputy authority (and both of us have been elected) in favor of the deputies from NKAO. (Applause). I think that the Leningrad voters will understand our step correctly. The unity of all nationalities of our countries and a resolution of the Nagorno-Karabakh problem are far more important than our two extra deputy seats for Leningrad. I ask for a vote. (Applause).

M.A. Gorbachev: Please.

Fourth Session

27 May 1989

A.V. Oborin, chairman of the Kozmodemyansk city people's court (Gorno-Mariy National-Territorial Okrug): Dear chairman and dear parliamentarians! Our discussion has disclosed that the Constitution in force today is not perfect. But we are not beginning the work of the first congress with nothing at all, and, however bad it is, the Constitution exists. If we both take the path of instantaneous reaction to amendments to the Constitution of the USSR, then it will be according to the proverb: The further one goes into a forest, the more wood there is. This is unquestionable.

Amendments to the Constitution are a serious step in legislative activity. They have to be interpreted very soberly, in a businesslike atmosphere, with the involvement of a wide circle of professional jurists, politicians, etc. Therefore, I see a way out of today's situation in the following. The question with Chemodanov and Veprev, who appeared outside the list, in my view, has to be postponed until the autumn session, when we will again assemble with you. It is a pressing question, and the congress will resolve it. The Supreme Soviet will not collapse without two persons. I have no doubt about this. This is the first thing.

To avoid similar errors, we have to create a commission which will work with the Constitution and simultaneously keep a watch so that all infractions of procedural questions—and, incidentally, there are very serious ones—are investigated, and that specific parties guilty of "disappearances" and "appearances" of candidacies are exposed so this could be reported to the congress and so we could have the opportunity to decide.

Further: In connection with the situation that arose on quotas, I propose, and ask, that this be examined as a legislative proposal, which does not concern today's forum, and to introduce it in the future in the next amendment to the Constitution: Each autonomous republic, and each nationality, no matter how small it is, must have its own seat in such a forum, having the right of a deciding vote. If we look at the practice of the world community, we find that San Marino and the United States of America have equal rights in the United Nations. But this is only a proposal. This has to be discussed.

Thank you for your attention. (Applause).

V.A. Zubanov, secretary of the party committee of the Khartsyzsk steel rope and cable plant (Makeyev-Gornyatsk Territorial Electoral Okrug, Donetsk Oblast): Comrades, our passions are heating up. This is inappropriate at such a forum. To start with I want to say that there were speeches and remarks on the qualitative composition of our Supreme Soviet. Will it be able to work—will it not be able to work? There were hot-tempered speeches about whether we would elect intelligent or unintelligent people.... I am categorically against such a "division" of deputies. We are all here in the same role; we all received a vote of confidence from the voters; and we are all honorable.

I work as a secretary of a party committee of a rather large plant. I would like you to hear the opinions of one of those party apparatchiks, whom many here criticize.

Our voting was secret. But, unfortunately, the secrecy of this vote was not assured. We assembled in groups, exchanged advice, and counselled each other, as to who to cross off and who to leave. I have 24 party organizations, and any party committee on the next day would call the "secrecy" of such voting invalid, and they would also reprimand the secretary of the party organization.

Second. Here we talked about alternatives in placing republic candidates on lists. I think that the present election system in no way allows the implementation of the principle of alternatives, that it does not conform to logic. Why? The deputies from the Russian Federation did the right thing! Implementing this principle, they submitted four more persons. And we applauded. But look at what the voting showed: Of the four, three secretaries of the party obkom did not pass. This is why we so insistently and stubbornly dropped the principle of alternatives.

Now the situation in the country is such that all nuances and all shortcomings are associated with the work of managerial organs, and I am confident enough to assure you that this is not always so. Not knowing these people, these secretaries of the obkoms, I believe that we, nonetheless, did not come to the right conclusion. Just as in the case of Chemodanov. We did not forget deputy Chemodanov; we forgot the 330,000 voters who are behind him.

Comrades, we are not playing games here. The country is watching us. Not knowing the deputies, we up and crossed them off the list. We crossed off that same Yeltsin for whom 6 million Muscovites voted. Who gave us the right to ignore this? No one gave us this kind of right. (Applause).

Third, comrades. As we already see, a fifth of the deputies elected to the Supreme Soviet will have legislative functions. A fifth! Four-fifths have not gotten there. And we already see a differentiation in the degree of inequality among the deputies. I am confident that the deputies, which these four-fifths will comprise, will not resign themselves to this situation. If the deputies resign themselves to this, then their voters will not resign themselves to the fact that four-fifths of those elected will have unequal oppportunities by comparison with those who are elected to the Supreme Soviet.

Mikhail Sergeyevich Gorbachev said at the first meetings that we should assemble a congress twice a year, and that the Supreme Soviet should be given the status of a

STENOGRAPHIC RECORD

Fourth Session

27 May 1989

working body, that it will adopt laws and ratify treaties. But we did not do this. We have turned back now. Why? I raise the question directly. We transmitted a note to the presidium. Maybe it got lost, there is a mountain of paper still.... I propose, not immediately, but after discussions, to weigh all possibilities and change the status of the Supreme Soviet.

Finally, I ask—maybe this is not very proper—Mikhail Sergeyevich Gorbachev, nevertheless, to think about this question on the status of the Supreme Soviet. Because we all see, the whole country sees, that there is today a mood among the deputies wherein the hall reacts to whatever way Mikhail Sergeyevich comments on matters, or whichever way he turns. Thank you for your attention. (Applause).

L.A. Arutyunyan, head of a department of the Yerevan State University (from the women's soviets united under the Committee of Soviet Women): Dear choices of the people! Numerous telegrams have arrived from Armenia which contain demands that the deputies fulfill their mission. Yesterday there was a violation of the constitutional rights of the people of the Nagorno-Karabakh Autonomous Oblast, which was not able to nominate its deputies to the Supreme Soviet. We voted, unfortunately, for this violation of constitutional rights. But it is not too late because we are only learning, and our conscience should not permit these rights to be violated any longer. The USSR Supreme Soviet made a decision about the special status of this oblast, and we should honor our own decisions. This special status has not been annulled by anyone yet. This means we have to take this into account when nominating deputies.

I ask that you examine our statement not as a discussion about persons, but as a discussion about principles. We should adhere to principles, and we should establish a legal reality. Words are not enough; actions are needed. And in this indicated case action was taken in the direction of discrimination against the rights of Nagorno-Karabakh. In this connection, I propose, through open voting, to resolve the question of recognizing as inoperative the results of the voting of the deputies from Nagorno-Karabakh. We have to express in an open vote our opinion with respect to new candidacies who will be proposed only from the deputies of Nagorno-Karabakh. No side should interfere in this.

Next. We ask the delegates of Azerbaijan henceforth not to violate the constitutional rights of NKAO and not to put the congress in a difficult situation. There is a contentious situation there, and our congress should promote peace in this region, not inflame passions. And the last thing. An amendment to the Constitution is not needed. It is necessary that the representatives to the Supreme Soviet be proposed by the NKAO deputies. Thank you. (Applause).

V.A. Martirosyan, colonel, commander of military unit 70425, Transcaucasus Military District, city of Rovno (Rovno Territorial Electoral Okrug, Ukranian SSR): Dear comrades! The most exhausted people today are the residents of Nagorno-Karabakh. I think that the residents of Nagorno-Karabakh have earned our introduction today of specific changes in order not to offend the deputies of Azerbaijan and give aid to the deputies of the Armenian people. I see these changes in the following. So that the residents of Nagorno-Karabakh do not think that there is no concern for them, we should today introduce any additions or changes to the USSR Constitution in order to satisfy the request of the deputies from Nagorno-Karabakh. But we should not start voting at the beginning; we should not begin now with removing Azerbaijanis or others, etc. We simply have to satisfy the request of the deputies from Nagorno-Karabakh and let the people living in Nagorno-Karabakh know that their fate is of concern to us, the people's deputies who are taking an active part in the discussion. And this, I believe, will be a gift to Nagorno-Karabakh.

Comrades. Those are the changes which we, I think, will introduce. And I turn to Mikhail Sergeyevich Gorbachev with a request to support me on this question. These changes will be a sign of solidarity, a sign of giving aid to the residents of the long-suffering Nagorno-Karabakh. Let us all support this proposal so they will know that their interests will not remain unattended. Thank you. (Applause).

M.S. Gorbachev: Deputy Ibragimov has the floor.

M.A. Ibragimov, writer, head of a department of the Nizami Institute of Literature of the Academy of Sciences of the Azerbaijan SSR, city of Baku (Nakhichevan Territorial Electoral Okrug, Azerbaijan SSR): Dear comrades, friends! I do not know if there is anything on earth, on our planet, that is more precious than friendship, most of all the friendship of people. Our congress is important because there are representatives here of practically all the people and nationalities of our great and mighty country. It is the sacred duty of every Communist and of every Soviet person to support and strengthen this friendship, and not to drag out some kind of far-fetched contentious questions in order, so to speak, to break the harmony of this friendship, the harmony among peoples.

Much has been said here about Nagorno-Karabakh. My dear friends, I turn to you, and I urge you strongly, before talking about the problem of Nagorno-Karabakh, you must study the problem. There are comrades speaking for Nagorno-Karabakh who have never set foot on that land. On the basis of rumors, instigations, and at the request of others, they begin to repeat such things that are absolutely contradictory to the truth, justice, and honesty of a person. I do not want to take up your time any longer. I only want to say that Azerbaijan has always treated, and now treats Nagorno-Karabakh as sacred land, as a land that gives birth to Azerbaijanis and Armenians. They live and have lived as neighbors in Nagorno-Karabakh for decades and centuries. Their

STENOGRAPHIC RECORD

Fourth Session

27 May 1989

sons and daughters intermarry—an Azerbaijani man to an Armenian woman, an Armenian man to an Azerbaijani woman. Nagorno-Karabakh is a very complicated problem, very. It is so important because it is precisely here that we have to reinforce friendship in a real way. We, I assure you, are aspiring to this. I am a writer, and for me, a writer, friendship is a great cause. I will take up a little more time and say that I translated Khachatur Abovyan into the Azerbaijani language. I read his story "Turkish Woman" with tears in my eyes—it is written with such warmth. I wrote many articles that were repeatedly printed in Russian, as well as individual books in Armenian about Khachatur Abovyan, about Isvakyan, and about Tumanyan.

Comrades! Many Armenian writers have written about us. As far back as the 1920's, Azat Vshtuni said: "Yey, Azerbaijan, yey, dzhan, salam, Azerbaijan!" We were brought up on him. Where did the extremists come from who created this contradiction? I do not want to take up your time. I know that Comrade Gorbachev gets upset when we talk a long time because he has to manage this, so to speak, large body. I want to say to you that when we nominated candidates to the Council of Nationalities (which is already approved) we proceeded specifically from a desire not to create contradictions among people. We proceeded from the fact that we would bring these people closer together so that the extremists would not be able to take advantage of the trustfulness of the people and to play with their destiny. There was an Azerbaijani man....

Voice from the floor: Deputy of Nagorno-Karabakh and not Azerbaijan.

M.A. Ibragimov: I ask that you not make rejoinders and have the courage to listen. I listened to everyone very attentively and then there is a need for ethics; some kind of ethics has to be observed, comrades. For us Communists, ethics is a very important matter.

Thus, Nagorno-Karabakh, comrades. Think about it, Azerbaijani deputies are assembling in the Central Committee of the Azerbaijan Communist Party, but no comrades from Nagorno-Karabakh appear. The first secretary of the Central Committee of the Azerbaijan Communist Party goes to Nagorno-Karabakh in order to talk and find out what they need and what should be done. They do not want to meet with the secretary of the Central Committee. Is this the way? Does this lead to friendship? Does this lead to mutual understanding? No, comrades. This is the way of a provocateur, of people there who pour kerosene on a fire that should be put out. This is the problem.

Therefore, I ask that the decision on the Council of Nationalities be left as it is, as we have already approved it. There is no reason for us to turn back. Azerbaijan is a republic, after all, and the Azerbaijani party organization has always been internationalist. There is nothing to add here, for the Baku party organization is internationalism, for as far back as 1905, in the first Russian revolution, Azerbaijanis, Armenians, and Russians who lived there came out hand in hand. I assure you that it will be proper if we let our decision remain in force. (Applause).

M.S. Gorbachev: Comrade Vorontsov has the floor. Afterwards we will continue the discussion. In my opinion, there is already something to discuss here, and we can come to some kind of effective decisions. Please, Comrade Vorontsov.

N.N. Vornotsov, doctor of biological sciences, research associate of the H.K. Koltsov Institute of Biological Development of the USSR Academy of Sciences, city of Moscow (from the scientific societies and associations attached to the USSR Academy of Sciences): Comrade deputies! I want to touch on these questions. First of all, about certain pressing measures on the organization of the normal work of the congress. They are very simple. We here, in this very same palace, held an international conference of geneticists 10 years ago at which there were 6,000 persons. On the opening day of the congress, each person received a full list of the participants. We still do not have a list of the deputies. This is absolutely abnormal. I see it this way, that here the apparatus of the presidium of the USSR Supreme Soviet did not do its work.

The comrades from Lithuania did a great job. They brought nameplates with them. We get to know who they are, but we would also like to get to know others as well. I do not think that in the work experience demonstrated to us by the apparatus of the presidium that it will be able to handle this matter in the days remaining and make the same kind of plastic nameplates for the rest of the deputies such as the deputies from Lithuania have. But I want to ask that all deputies receive nameplates at least for the autumn session. This will make it easier for us to get acquainted with each other. This is an elementary thing.

Now, with respect to the elections. The Central Electoral Commission has all of the biographic data on each of the deputies. But how did we vote? We voted blindly. I understand that we will not be able to correct this now. But I ask that it be taken as a rule that in the preparation of the next elections to the congress we have brief biographical data on each deputy. This is a very elementary thing.

Now, with respect to the problems facing us in connection with the elections. I think that we have to agree with the proposal of the deputies of the Mariy Republic and conduct at least a partial new vote. Consequently we cannot approve the procedures on the Council of the Union. This is a pity, but we cannot create an erroneous precedent, comrade deputies.

Further, I would like to say several words with respect to the problems of NKAO—not about everything, but about what is happening. I would like to tell the comrades from the Azerbaijani delegation, the Armenian

STENOGRAPHIC RECORD

Fourth Session
27 May 1989

delegation, and the Georgian delegation that as a member of an expedition in the last four field seasons, I worked in the Transcaucasus and therefore, so to speak, while not knowing the language, I have some feel for the problems. I was in the NKAO during an expedition in 1987. I now ask the comrades from the Azerbaijani delegation to display statesmanship, to show that the Azerbaijani people are really internationalist, and to reject the proposal that was tabled not on behalf of the Azerbaijani people, but on an old apparatus level. These are absolutely different matters. I propose not to approve the minutes of the counting commission for the Council of Nationalities with respect to the part on the NKAO delegation, and to allow the NKAO delegation to nominate their own deputies. Unfortunately if we follow the wise, good, and broad proposal of Deputy Sobchak and give this autonomous oblast four seats, then we will infringe on the rights of other autonomous oblasts. Is this not so? That is all. Thus, I propose not to approve the minutes of the counting commission for the Council of Nationalities with respect to the part on the NKAO. This is an addendum.

M.S. Gorbachev: You are limiting my possibilities and at the same time are asking something from me. Therefore, I will seek some kind of middle ground so that the points of view are represented and the atmosphere is retained. In my opinion, this is the major concern. But still I think the moment has now arrived when we, perhaps, will resolve this important question.

As for the Mariy Autonomous Republic, this question relates to the entire Russian Federation, for Russia, its share of deputies, determines the quotas for each region. But the Mariy Republic did not have a quota.

There should have been an agreement earlier that Comrade Chemodanov be on the lists. Because a quota exists, to add to the list, it is necessary to reduce the quota somewhere else. There was some talk about Krasnoyarsk. There Comrade Veprev was put on the list, and, they say, from the very beginning. The comrades did not finish the work; some kind of contact was lost here. Inasmuch as this affects all of Russia, it should also get its own quota. The Russian delegation should get together and submit its proposals to us. I think that we at the congress will not debate for Russia, otherwise we will compel it to do something. We proceeded from this, discussing the question.

On NKAO. The members of the presidium discussed it during the break, how to find a way out. There are two points of view. But apparently not everything was considered in a proper way. Perhaps we should do this—this is my proposal on behalf of the members of the presidium—that the comrades from one side and the other—from the NKAO and from Azerbaijan—try to get closer in their positions, and that they submit their proposals about another vote. And we, in the part that concerns approval of the results of the voting in the Council of Nationalities, would consider the position open. The question we have is about the NKAO. We have already approved the minutes for the Council of Nationalities. Therefore, not changing our decision in general, we add to it with respect to the NKAO part, and propose that the comrades from Azerbaijan meet with the participation of the NKAO deputies. We agreed that if there will be such a decision of the congress, to delegate members of the presidium to this discussion—Comrade Nishanov and Comrade Paton. Let the deputies of Azerbaijan and the NKAO work together with presidium representatives and submit their proposals. In other words, we will in this way come out with a vote on this part.

That is the first proposal.

Now about Russia. Apparently Russia has to work on this. Nonetheless, in all preparatory phases the Mariy Republic did not have a quota, comrades. I am not making a slip, because the proposal was based on the quota, and this quota was determined with respect to each region. Perhaps now the deputies of Russia will meet, talk, and confirm that they should agree with what has taken place. But in the future, in connection with rotation, give them an opportunity to resolve this question immediately in the next phase. There are two such proposals.

A.A. Sobchak (from the floor): Comrade Gorbachev, I think that what you just said with respect to the NKAO is incorrect. The train has already left. One representative of Armenian nationality and one representative of Azerbaijani nationality have been elected. If we today submit.... (What is said further is not intelligible). We do not understand: Either an Azerbaijani comrade will be left, or an Armenian.

From the floor: Correct, correct.

A.A. Sobchak: Mikhail Sergeyevich, the problem is resolved. The Nagorno-Karabakh Autonomous Oblast will be represented in the Council of Nationalities by those who have already been elected. It will receive two additional seats in the Council of the Union. This is such an imortant problem.... (Applause).

G.A. Yenokin, general director of the Yerevan clothing production association (Yerevan-Spandaryanskiy NAtional-Territorial Electoral Okrug, Armenian SSR): Comrade deputies! Excuse me, please. I have not been able to put in two words since this morning. The question here is about discrimination against the rights of NKAO deputies. If the question has already passed that everyone has a right to elect deputies from their own okrugs, why should not the NKAO itself have submitted its own candidacy. Understand me correctly: It does not matter to us who will be on the list. But let these people be nominated only from the NKAO deputies. The question is only about this, only about the discrimination of

Fourth Session

27 May 1989

the rights of deputies. Because tomorrow these people will not be able to go back to their republic, because even here, in the congress, only those from the NKAO were not approved as deputies. This is the only question. Understand it correctly. Thank you.

M.S. Gorbachev: One minute. We will still continue.

G.A. Yenokin: Pardon me a thousand times. Mikhail Sergeyevich said that the deputies of Azerbaijan and the NKAO should decide together. I find this to be irregular. If there will be deputies of Azerbaijan and the NKAO then, excuse me, let the Armenian deputies also be present. But in general this question should be decided only by the NKAO deputies.

M.S. Gorbachev: One minute. I think that we still have to come to a conclusion. It seems to me that the question on the situation with the NKAO has been cleared up, nonetheless. This is the way it looks. The part of the minutes on the voting to the Council of Nationalities should be annulled, not affecting the other parts. Here we have to go back to the initial position. Let the comrades, together with our participation from the presidium—and if someone else wants to participate, then let him come also—talk about all of this in a comradely, friendly way, and then they will submit proposals. We will ask the comrades to come back to the question. If it becomes necessary, I am also ready to take part. Or Comrade Lukyanov will go together with members of the presidium to discuss everything in detail the way it should be. But, still, go for a new vote. (Applause).

E.T. Arutyunyan, foreman of a tool and die maker group of the Yerevan production association Elektropribor, city of Yerevan (Yerevan-Shaumyanovsk National-Territorial Electoral Okrug, Armenian SSR): Dear comrades, apparently not all deputies know that a decision was made at the beginning of January to introduce a special form of management in the NKAO. Proceeding from this, I believe that NKAO deputies should coordinate their actions, not with Azerbaijan, but with the management of NKAO.... (Noise in the hall).

M.S. Gorbachev: I think, comrades, that in the preceding speech of the deputy from Armenia, his proposal that the question on another vote should be discussed and conducted within the scope of the NKAO, without the participation of and contacts with Azerbaijan, is incorrect.

In the first place, it is incorrect legally inasmuch as the NKAO did not put forth the special procedure from Azerbaijan.

Second, and this is the most important point, I think we have to rely on common sense and on a sense of friendship that is maintained at every turn. But the proposals directed at division will only complicate the entire process. The presidium will participate in a discussion of the question. I think that this will be a comradely conversation. A conversation that should, nonetheless, be conducted in a friendly manner.

And then, Azerbaijanis also live in the NKAO. An isolated conversation, in my opinion, would worsen the situation.

Dear comrades, the NKAO is our common painful problem. It affects the interests of Azerbaijan and Armenia. We are all emotionally involved and want to find the kind of answer that would lead to harmony, even though not immediately. We have to sit together now, to sit a while and try to come to an agreement about the proposals that could be submitted to the congress for a new vote. Right, comrades?

From the hall: Right.

M.S. Gorbachev: Who is for the proposal, for annulling that part respecting the results of the voting to the Council of Nationalities relating to the NKAO, but not affecting the rest; for asking the comrades from Azerbaijan and the NKAO, with the participation of members of the presidium, to meet, work over the proposals, and report their ideas on this account, so that we could ensure a new vote?

There were many speeches. They concerned various approaches: leave everything as is, as was approved; there were proposals that only the NKAO deputies should meet, and that no one should interfere; etc., etc. There were the proposals of Comrade Sobchak.... There were many proposals. If you wish us to make a full inventory of these proposals and decide question by question—this is one approach. Or, summarizing the entire discussion—because this was a discussion after all—perhaps we can come out for this proposal?

What do you think, comrades? What, Comrade Vezirov?

A.-R.Kh. Vezirov, first secretary of the Central Committee of the Azerbaijan Communist Party, city of Baku (Imishli National-Territorial Electoral Okrug, Azerbaijan SSR): Dear comrades, you know it is the third day of our congress, and questions are being raised continuously, and not on the initiative of the deputies of our republic, in connection with the NKAO—along with other questions that, frankly speaking, do not lead us along the path of cooperation and along the path of mutual understanding. And we should only go along this path. Talking about this problem, I want to assure all deputies of the congress that we made every effort to find at least an opportunity to meet, discuss, and determine our overall possition. And when the question was raised about nominating two candidates—in particular, comrades Pogosyan and Dzhafarov—we talked about it with the chairman and the members of the special control committee.

STENOGRAPHIC RECORD

Fourth Session
27 May 1989

We proceeded in this case from one fact: There should be one Armenian and one Azerbaijani in the membership of deputies to the Council of Nationalities inasmuch as these two peoples live in the NKAO. Of course, there will be a rotation, there will be changes, and we wanted to come to this kind of a decision. I would like, Mikhail Sergeyevich, to amend your proposal. Not to annul the results of the voting with respect to the NKAO, but to make it possible to discuss and reach a mutual understanding. We agree with and welcome this approach. We think that what you proposed is very correct—that we find a common language and meet once more. We continuously have in the past and will continue in the future to follow the path of a search for compromise, a search for a way to resolve qestions and to show flexibility. We will do this—I assure the delegates of the congress. It makes sense to give us an opportunity to meet with members of the presidium of the congress, with Mikhail Sergeyevich, and if you are busy, with Anatoliy Ivanovich. We want to meet with each other, to talk, and calmly consider the question, and then the members of the presidium will report the results of our meeting to the congress. Thank you. (Applause).

M.S. Gorbachev: You can proceed that way, comrades....

From the floor: After the break....

S.G. Arutyunyan, first secretary of the Central Committee of the Armenian Communist Party (Leninakan Territorial Electoral Okrug, Armenian SSR): Comrades, I did not intend to speak, but after the speech of Comrade Vezirov, I would like to express my point of view. I think it is apparent to each deputy sitting in this hall that the rights of the NKAO have been violated. In the complicated and explosive situation that has developed in the oblast, I suggest that it is impossible and impermissible to treat the opinion of the NKAO deputies in this way. If we do not make a proper decision today, I do not know how and in what direction events in this region will unfold on the whole.

Therefore, I propose supporting the proposal of Mikhail Sergeyevich that the results of the voting on the NKAO be annulled. And, first and foremost, to take the opinion of the NKAO deputies into account when nominating candidates to the USSR Supreme Soviet. (Applause).

M.S. Gorbachev: So, perhaps we can still return to that which I, in summarizing, submitted. Then we will examine those proposals presented by comrades Vezirov and Arutyunyan. The gist of the proposals is that (and we exchanged opinions on them in the presidium during the break): It is necessary that the deputies of Nagorno-Karabakh and Azerbaijan, together with the participation of the presidium of the congress, table new proposals in connection with a new vote. As for the results of the secret voting on the part on NKAO, they should be annulled. This is the first proposal. I put it to a vote.

Who is for this proposal—please raise your hands. Please lower them. Andrey Dmitriyevich (he turns to Deputy Sakharov), you missed something that I said?

From the floor: (Inaudible).

M.S. Gorbachev: No, you see what the problem is....

From the floor: (Inaudible).

M.S. Gorbachev: No, Andrey Dmitriyevich, we must declare the result void in order for the people to have the opportunity to prepare proposals for revoting; what else can we do?

So, who is in favor of the proposal I formulated—to void the results of the voting for the Council of Nationalities as pertains to the NKAO? Please lower your hands. Who is against? Count them please.

(The votes are counted).

From the floor: Dear comrades, 86 voted "against."

M.S. Gorbachev: Who abstained?

From the floor: There were 45 abstentions.

M.S. Gorbachev: The question has been decided. Now the question of the representation of the Mariy Autonomous Republic which—you understand—we cannot consider separately from the results of the voting on the Russian Federation. Therefore, if we reach a point where the group of deputies from the Mariy republic do not withdraw their objections and proposals and do insist on them, we must conduct a repeat vote for all the candidates for Russia.

So, either we proceed, having agreed upon the results reported to us by the counting commission, and, on behalf of the congress, certify this republic and the other autonomous republics which have not yet had the opportunity to be represented in the Supreme Soviet, for now, if the deputies from the Mariy ASSR insist, the others will also raise this issue.... Or we can take the other path: Here we guarantee that upon rotation all these autonomous republics will have the opportunity to be represented in the Supreme Soviet. (Applause, general noise, voices). So, comrades, shall we consider this with the full congress? (Voices from the floor: Full congress.). Or shall we entrust it to the Russian delegation? Please, who from the Mariy republic wishes to say something?

Yu.M. Chemodanov, teacher at the Kuanpamash incomplete-grade secondary school, Mariy ASSR, Novotoryalskiy Rayon, Kuanpamash, (on behalf of the All-Union Lenin Communist Youth Union): I suggest this variant: This time we leave the list as it is, but next year the

Fourth Session

27 May 1989

rotation should begin taking the Mariy ASSR into account, namely with me. (Applause).

M.S. Gorbachev: The "Russian crisis"—that is, our crisis—is settled. (Stirring in the hall, applause). Then we can vote and approve the results reported by the counting commission for the Council of the Union. Those in favor of approving them please so certify by raising your hands. Please lower them. Who is against approval? Count them, please.

While the comrades are counting I suggested that, since we formed a secretariat of the congress yesterday, in the future all notes and documents be sent to the secretariat. The secretariat will work on the third floor in the "diplomatic office," and we shall maintain constant live contact with them—we agreed on this in the presidium—Comrade Gorbunov, if you have questions you can drop in at the secretariat and have them answered. We ask the secretariat to keep a record, accept documents, and give them back to us after they have been put in order. Thus we want to use the secretariat to take some of the load off, since they are supposed to help the presidium. Are there any objections?

Voices: No.

M.S. Gorbachev: At the meeting of representatives of groups of people's deputies we agreed that it was necessary to sign up for participation in the discussions of the report of the chairman of the USSR Supreme Soviet when the report was made. Nonetheless, we already have two files full of notes. There is a proposal to turn these files over to the secretariat. Or perhaps we should declare these notes void? Let us discuss it. Are there any remarks regarding this proposal? I raise the question: When should we open the record of the discussions of the report? After the report?

Those in favor of having the record updated after the report please vote. Please lower your hands. Are there any against? Abstentions? A few. There is no need for a count in this case. The question has been decided.

Now the comrades are interested in when the report will take place—Monday morning.

Now you, Comrade Osipyan, must report the results of the voting to us.

Yu.A. Osipyan: 19 deputies voted "against."

M.S. Gorbachev: Abstentions? (Voices from the floor). Good.... Comrades, we must think about this question. We have halted the exchange of opinions because of Comrade Afanasyev's speech, which, as I understand it, was developed by comrades Popov and Adamovich, since they gave developed, as it were, prepared, thought-out proposals. I think that the subjects they touched upon are so serious that we should return to them and devote at least one meeting to them. Therefore, I would like to consult with you: What should we do? We can now take a break for an hour and then meet again from 5 to 7 pm. But we are always breaking the rules. We could take a break for 2 hours for dinner and work from 6 to 8 pm. So, the first proposal: to take a break for an hour, from 4 to 5 pm and then conduct one session and exchange opinions on the speeches of comrades Afanasyev, Popov, and Adamovich. We shall not work tomorrow. Tomorrow we shall have off.

From the floor: (Inaudible).

M.S. Gorbachev: I said the report would be on Monday. So, comrades, regarding the break—an hour. Those in favor of having an hour break please raise you hands.... So, I ask for a vote: Who is in favor of an hour break? Please lower your hands. Who is against? Well, a minority. Just a minute. A deputy thinks that he can use one minute to express his opinion on the subject. He sent in a note.

N.S. Sazonov, secretary of the party committee of the automatic lathe production of the Kama Automotive Plant, Naberezhnyye Chelny, (Naberezhnyye Chelny Territorial Electoral Okrug, Tatar ASSR): I asked this morning to submit a request from numerous voters who are following the course of the congress. They say they are tired of all the tongue wagging. When are you going to get down to business? What do I want to say? I fully agree with Comrade Afanasyev, but I suggest cutting short the discussion of this speech, and there is no need to create a stir. He expressed an opinion which I personally support. This is simply an opinion.

I think that if at the beginning of the congress we had supported the program proposed by the Moscow group (the Baltic republics also participated in the preparation of this program and so did I), then there would have been none of these questions and we would not have made these mistakes. Therefore, I suggest curtailing the discussion of Afanasyev's speech and getting on with things.

M.S. Gorbachev: Comrades, I think we can take under advisement that the deputy from Naberezhnyye Chelny agrees with Comrade Afanasyev. This is his position. But I think that we must also give the floor to other deputies who either agree with him or have their own opinions. This would be useful to Comrades Afanasyev and Popov, and me, and you, and all of us. I declare a recess for an hour.

(Break).

M.S. Gorbachev: Now, comrades, Comrade Lukyanov has a couple of words to say, and then we shall continue our discussion. Please.

FIRST CONGRESS OF PEOPLE'S DEPUTIES OF THE USSR

Fourth Session

27 May 1989

A.I. Lukyanov (on behalf of the CPSU): Comrade deputies! During the entire break we conducted painstaking and very friendly negotiations with the deputies elected from Nagorno-Karabakh. What is so difficult about this problem? The fact is that the deputies from Nagorno-Karabakh were to have nominated a certain number of candidates for two positions on the Council of Nationalities. In principle, all of the deputies from Nagorno-Karabakh did not reach an agreement of opinions. One of them was absent; he was on a trip abroad. In general, they did not reach an agreement as they should have. A certain agreement was reached here at the congress.

You know that only two people can be elected from Nagorno-Karabakh to the Council of Nationalities. You know that in this small, I would say, long-suffering area more than 75 percent of the citizens are of Armenian nationality and the rest are Azerbaijani. Therefore, it is a very painful issue, and everything must be carefully taken into account, displaying the greatest tact.

The preliminary agreement was as follows: The deputies would nominate Comrade Pogosyan, a deputy of Armenian nationality, and Comrade Dzhafarov—the first secretary of the Shushinskiy Party Raykom where the Azerbaijani population live. That is, they proceeded from the understanding that the population in the NKAO was of two nationalities and the majority are Armenians. The deputies also wanted to reach an agreement with the Azerbaijani delegation for one of the Armenian deputies to be nominated to the Council of the Union from the Azerbaijani delegation. Unfortunately, this nomination was not made.

Apparently it was necessary to take other interests into account as well. Therefore, we are not forced to continue discussion of this issue.

The question is complicated. It must be resolved in the interests of people of both nationalities so as not to create an explosive situation, and it is very tense in Nagorno-Karabakh and Armenia, and to some degree in Azerbaijan. We are counting on assistance and, as it were, a recognition of the peculiarities of the problem from both the Azerbaijan delegation and the delegation from Nagorno-Karabakh. I must tell you, comrades, that, having reached an agreement with the Azerbaijani delegation, we three representatives of the presidium held a conversation with all of the deputies elected from Nagorno-Karabakh. In general, the discussion was calm. It is still difficult to reach an agreement, but we shall continue these consultations and only after completing them shall we introduce for the congress's consideration a proposal concerning how to resolve this issue, how to untie this knot. Believe me, the question is extremely complicated and difficult, and we must use maximum tact in everything pertaining to the national issue.

M.S. Gorbachev: Are there no remarks? Let the consultations continue; in any case we must find an outcome involving all the interested parties. Does nobody insist on opening the debates on this issue now? No.

Let us return to the subjects of the discussion we interrupted in order to complete the discussion of the voting issues. The floor is turned over to Deputy Suleymenov. Then Deputy Yakovlev, editor of the newspaper MOSKOVSKIYE NOVOSTI, will speak.

O.O. Suleymenov, writer, first secretary of the board of the Union of Writers of Kazakhstan (Ayaguz Territorial Electoral Okrug, Kazakh SSR): Dear comrade chairman, dear comrades! I wanted to speak this morning right after the speeches of Comrades Afanasyev and Popov. But there were procedural issues which took away some of our enthusiasm, time, and attention, and the problem of the "mythical" Chemodanov arose. I should like to return to Chemodanov because there was a very great spiritual meaning to the way we attentively discussed this issue. When Comrade Chemodanov suddenly resolved the problem a relieved applause broke out. We all applauded him from our hearts, and this expressed not only our desire to avoid more elections, but also a kind of repentance, the repentance of large, great nations, the penitence of the state before the small nations of the Soviet Union, who have born such a heavy burden all these years. We are now seeing clearly that there is nothing higher than the interests of each person, each nation, each nationality.

Now let us move on to a subject that is difficult for me—Comrade Afanasyev's speech. Yuriy Nikolayevich Afanasyev is a eminent historian and commentator. I have known him for a long time, and I love him. We have been friends for about 10 years, and I share many of his views. But I do not agree with this evaluation of the Supreme Soviet, with this phrase: the "Stalinist-Brezhnevite Supreme Soviet."

These are very strong words. They could bring anyone to his feet, arouse a crowd, arouse the people. But are they fair? Yes, a certain number of party workers have been elected to the Supreme Soviet. But they are in approximately the same if not a smaller proportion than they are in our congress. If the Supreme Soviet is to be called "Stalinist-Brezhnevite" then our congress deserves the same judgment.

When we divide up the deputies.... How strangely we have actually taken our places: to the right of me now are the leftists, and the rightists seem to be to my left. In the center are Moscow and Russia—as they should be. So we have a certain aggressively subdued majority and a democratic minority.

From the history of prerevolutionary party congresses we know how factions have originated, how they divided into the majority and minority, into Bolsheviks and

STENOGRAPHIC RECORD

Fourth Session

27 May 1989

Mensheviks. Now it is being suggested that a faction be organized on the basis of the Moscow and certain other delegations. And now it is being suggested that we organize some kind of faction of our own: Perhaps Central Asia should unite with Siberia; we are sitting next to one another. I think that such appeals, although they enliven the process of democratization which is gathering force in our country, will not help us to solve all the problems the people are expecting us to solve. They could split the congress apart and, taking into account that millions of our voters are now watching us, they could bring confusion into the hearts and consciousness of all of our people.

We have all noticed that the left wing flaps more frequently than the right, the left oar dips into the water more frequently. But if we row too strongly with the left oar, the boat being steered with this oar will turn sharply to the right. There is such a paradoxical law. Our task now is to maintain dialogue, to prolong and not curtail it. Thus we shall contribute to the development of democracy. We should not arouse those forces that are standing ready. Those forces that clearly poison the atmosphere which reigns over our congress. Resolute challenges and appeals directly to the people, and calls for demonstrations can destabilize the situation, which will only impede the work both of our congress and our restructuring as a whole.

I call upon you, dear comrades, to remember that democracy is still a maiden, as it were. To demand that she satisfy all of our passions without being given a chance to grow up is simply criminal. (Stirring in the hall).

Let her grow up, let the fruit ripen. We must not pick the green apples; we should not expect immediate solutions to our problems, in this forum, during these days. Thank you. (Applause).

M.S. Gorbachev: The floor goes to Deputy Yakovlev, and then comes Deputy Vasiliy Sidorovich Obraz from the All-Union Organization of Veterans of War and Labor.

Ye.V. Yakovlev, editor-in-chief of the newspaper MOSKOVSKIYE NOVOSTI, Moscow (on behalf of the USSR Union of Cinematographers): When Yuriy Nikolayevich Afanasyev and then Gavriil Kharitonovich Popov spoke this morning it seemed that the question had been raised to the highest level of acuteness. But we returned to the question and, in my opinion, it was even more acute. Such, apparently, is our congress, and such is our life today. But if we are to speak about the speeches of Yuriy Nikolayevich Afnasyev and Gavriil Kharitonovich Popov, I agree with Mikhail Sergeyevich that there is a good deal that is rational in their words. Only a generally prejudiced person would not want to see this rational part. But I agree with them on far from everything. Just as I do not agree with the deputy who accused the Muscovites of "imposing" sedition on the party leadership in the form of leasing and cooperatives. Unfortunately, I did not impose it, but I am very sorry not to be the author of these excellent ideas.

I think, comrades, that in general we should not be frightened and fall into some kind of animosity concerning the speeches of the comrades who said what they think. I think the condition of our hall precisely reflects the condition of our society. Complicated processes are taking place in society, and some people hold one opinion while others hold another. That this kind of discussion is taking place is, in general, right and the way it should be. But to blame one side or the other is the same as blaming the society in which you live, or blaming the mirror if your face is all crooked.

I think we must perceive this normally and think of how to get out of the situation. Of course, it is necessary to get out of the situation of the generally unsuitably organized work of the congress. Out of a situation which above all, in my opinion, produces many unnecessary experiences, like the experience of Comrade Meshalkin concerning the fact that the Novosibirsk representatives are sitting in the 20th row. I am prepared to relinquish my seat in the 12th row to Comrade Meshalkin, but I want to warn you that in the 12th row there are three Yakovlevs in alphabetical order. Also sitting nearby is the writer Karpov and the chess player Karpov. The bureaucrat's dream has triumphed: Everyone is sitting in alphabetical order, everyone is distributed according to letters.

We all remarked that the secretaries and members of the Politburo who left the stage moved into the hall. I think this is the beginning of their path to the deputies, as the deputies from other social organizations are seated with the deputies from the region in which they live. Sooner or later, all of us Muscovites will simply be sitting together. Then, Roy Aleksandrovich Medvedev will be sitting next to Vadim Andreyevich Medvedev, and the rector of the Moscow Aviation Institute—Ryzhov—next to the Chairman of the Council of Ministers Ryzhkov. (Applause).

The second issue, comrades, which I should like to touch upon here. I think that the statement of the question of factions is, in general, unnecessary. Of course, a faction is an unusual thing for us; it is almost romantic. It reminds me of one person who had been in a children's home who told me that all his life he had read Dickens and had never understood what a sandwich was. A faction for us is approximately the same thing. I do not think that we have by any means exhausted the possibility of consolidation, and I think we should use our energy not for joining factions but for looking for ways of consolidation.

I wish to discuss only two issues. I am very sorry, for example, that we did not pass the suggestion from one of

STENOGRAPHIC RECORD

Fourth Session

27 May 1989

the deputies—I do not remember which—that we should vote by name if no less than 100 deputies wish this. This would be the first guarantee of the possibility of having the minority influence the work of the congress. I am not a jurist but it seems to me that for the next congress we should think about the possibility of minority guarantees for a number of issues. And we should spend energy on that and not on creating factions.

Another issue: Let us say that in general I am not satisfied with the composition of the Supreme Soviet. Concerning discharging members of the Supreme Soviet they used the phrase "as a rule." At the end of the congress I would like very much to hear from the Supreme Soviet who will be working there permanently and who will be working "as a rule." (Applause). I would still like to establish a quota, which you, Mikhail Sergeyevich, also mentioned, I believe. A quota so that, say, 10 percent will not be discharged, but there should be such a quota, and if it is more than 10 percent, in the fall there can be a rotation of these "more than 10 percent." Because we have still conducted an electoral campaign so that there will be a permanent parliament and we cannot back away from this. I have simply given two examples, and I do not think there is a single conflict which we could not peacefully resolve together. I am simply asking the other speakers, if the discussion of this issue continues, not to say: Moscow is to blame, or Siberia is to blame. Let us look for a solution to each concrete problem that bothers us. (Applause).

M.S. Gorbachev: The floor is turned over to the deputy from the veterans, Obraz, and then Deputy Petrushenko from Leningrad will speak.

V.S. Obraz, pensioner, Ukrainian SSR, Poltava. (On behalf of the All-Union Organization of Veterans of War and Labor):

Comrade deputies! After the speeches of comrades Afanesyev and Popov, and also the discussions in the corridors with the participation of Academician Sakharov, to which I was an involuntary witness, I got the idea and the impression that we do not have a clear understanding of the degree of tension there is in our country or the degree to which our public opinion is emotional and psychological. It seems to me that we do not understand that in our age everything that takes place at the congress—i.e. stratification, and so forth—is immediately conveyed to the masses. It seems to me that we do not understand that we are not dealing with what we should be dealing with here. For my constituents—and I was elected from an all-union organization—sent me here to resolve fundamental issues. That is, to form our leadership agencies and immediately resolve at least one problem: feeding and providing the basic conditions for the life of those people who have lived through industrialization, collectivization, repressions, the Great Patriotic War, and the restoration of the national economy.

I shall not mention the conditions under which a considerable number of the people I call war veterans live. We are dealing with procedural issues now. In a number of the speeches I can see attempts simply to split the congress apart. In practice this means to split our society apart. For I hear there is a conversation to the effect the we, comrades, after this should go to Luzhniki, to a rally. Listen, in all times a rally has called either for a great event or for overthrowing the government. Our television viewers, our country, cannot but note that what is starting here is a scramble for power and not for resolving those crucial issues for which our people elected us. (Applause).

We cannot work that way! You cannot do anything without hearing merciless criticism. Can it really work like this? The fledgling was barely able to stand on its feet before we started criticizing: It is not right, you understand; the congress is proceeding poorly; it is not well thought out.

Comrades, one of the deputies here was right when he said that our democracy, which we are studying, is an innocent virgin, and we are throwing rocks at her from all directions. I see a direct continuity in the link between this phenomenon and the criticism of the past in which we have become involved. The criticism stems from there and is transferred to the present day. Some people cannot resist the urge to criticize. I appeal to writers, journalists, and commentators to recall the words uttered recently by a Western journalist. He said the Soviet Union is the only country in the world with an unpredictable past. Let us think about that, comrades.

I evaluate the present day as follows: During the postwar period I do not recall, comrades, a single time when a maximum consolidation of all society's forces was required of us. I do not recall such a period. I wish to take this idea to the point where during the course of the consolidation and concentration of our forces on resolving the major issues, we must forego national, religious, group, and even class ambitions in places where they are beginning to be manifested. Otherwise we shall not resolve these problems.

We must concentrate our attention on what we must do so that our people will love to work. The party has earmarked a number of measures for this.

What must we do so that the education of the Soviet person is placed on the necessary level? I daresay that nobody in our country has dealt with education since the time of Peter I. We have not developed the concept of this education. Yes, the nobility had a system—they educated the nobility and not the people. We do not have such a concept yet. There was a pathetic attempt to create one in the form of a moral code for the construction of communism, you understand. But that was it. Religion during the postrevolution got away from moral teaching. And we are floundering any which way we can.

STENOGRAPHIC RECORD

Fourth Session

27 May 1989

If we are to build a socialist society we should have developed certain measures, views, and mechanisms. I suggest beginning immediately to develop a concept of the education of the individual in a socialist society. To do this we must enlist the best intellectual efforts of our philosophers, historians, political scientists, educators, and psychologists. And we must ultimately put an end to this purely Russian "perhaps." For because of this "perhaps" we have Chernobyl and other disasters about which you know. Everything depends on education. We must think: Why are the Japanese so disciplined? Or the Germans? We should not be ashamed to adopt their experience.

Comrades! I appeal to all of you to put aside all trivial and unessential issues. Moreover, you must take into account that for national problems we have the plenum of the party Central Committee where this issue will be resolved in a fundamental way.

Let us ultimately get away from rallies. What does a rally do for us, comrades? I am simply surprised, you understand, that Comrade Sakharov said that he foresees strikes in the country's future. What is this? What is this—joy or something? Is he glad that we are going to have strikes? Do any good decisions really come as a result of strikes? To work! We must work! In the most real way—everyone. I thank you for your attention. (Applause).

M.S. Gorbachev: The floor goes to Deputy Petrushenko. The next to speak will be Deputy Kravchenko.

N.S. Petruchenko, lieutenant colonel, Central Asian Military District. (Leninogorsk Territorial Electoral Okrug, Kazakh SSR): Dear comrade chairman, dear comrade deputies! Developing the idea expressed from the podium by Olzhas Suleymenov, my esteemed colleague in the deputy corps, I could say that I am one of that unique category, that unique part of the deputies of our deputy corps, who could be included in the left wing and the right wing of the deputies equally well. To the very left, for during the course of the pre-election struggle I nominated myself, and I experienced pressure from the apparatus. Participating in the discussions of the Moscow deputies' club and in their main pre-congress meeting, I am fairly familiar with the Moscow deputies' kitchen from the inside. But as concerns the right wing itself, and this apparently pertains to our entire delegation from Kazakhstan, having already rephrased the words spoken here, I can say that I am in the very right wing: Figuratively speaking, the only thing to the right of me is the wall of the Kremlin Palace of Congresses. But still I would not include myself in the very right wing, but would sit in the middle today—with respect to calling our deputy corps to reconciliation.

It seems to me that the situation in our hall largely reflects the situation that has developed in the society and the country. I should like to ask the deputies first of all to understand how difficult it is to run such a country and how difficult it is to control such a nonstandard congress, which is experiencing a "childhood disease" of democracy.

Out of fairness one should recognize that the factors leading to confrontation in the congress, for instance between the Muscovites and the periphery, are largely objective. These factors were apparently conditioned by the passivity of the staff of the USSR Supreme Soviet, which acted slowly during the responsible period of preparation for the congress. This alarmed those of us who are afraid of party games, and our Moscow colleagues in the deputy corps worked during the period of preparation and came to the congress with proposals at which we are looking anxiously. But personal ambitions are also having their effect, including those of the Moscow deputies. We deputies from the periphery who have only just entered the arena of political games could not help but notice this. These games are largely motivated by the desire of a number of deputies to be sure to be a part of the USSR Supreme Soviet, and the same aspirations on the party of our voters. I, too, am receiving telegrams and phone calls from my constituents who definitely want to see us, the people they have elected, in the USSR Supreme Soviet.

I think that the confrontation in our hall is a result of the fact that the processes of democratization in the hall of congresses largely lag behind the processes of democratization in each union republic.

We deputies who have come from the periphery find it difficult to figure out the situation in a short period of time, but we have enough a political sense to see through the political maneuvers surrounding the constructive proposals of the Moscow deputies. I mention this because, in addition to good, businesslike proposals from the Moscow deputies, we also frequently hear such epithets as "temporary," "temporary government," "temporary Supreme Soviet," "temporary regulariton," "temporary presidium" and "temporary congress guard."

I, as a Communist and deputy whom the Leninogorsk territrial okrug entrusted to represent almost a quarter of a million voters here, am alarmed by the fact that at pre-election meetings and in political discussion clubs, whether we like it or not, there has been a dividing up of political portfolios. I should like to remind the deputies from Moscow, whom I deeply respect for the initiative they showed in preparing for the Congress of People's Deputies, that it is not only for them but for all of us deputies to divide up the portfolios of the chairman of the presidium and the Procurator General, and the chairman of the committee for constitutional supervision. And this should be done here in this hall, and not at a meeting in Luzhniki, in which I also participated and spoke. (Applause).

Fourth Session

27 May 1989

I think that our Muscovite colleagues have gotten a little bit carried away. Those who, deliberately or not, are challenging us to a confrontation have also gotten carried away. What must the congress do to avoid further development of the "childhood disease" of the democracy of our congress? I should like to appeal to the deputies to think about my proposal concerning this and reject the harmful, politically erroneous idea of confrontation of the congress and the formation of factions suggested by my esteemed colleagues comrades Popov and Afanasyev. The voters will not forgive a single deputy who now abandons his deputy post in the delegation and enters into some faction. I am here as part of a multinational Kazakh delegation, and sitting next to me are Germans, Kazakhs, Dungans, and representatives of other ethnic groups. I myself am a Belorussian, the only Belorussian elected in Kazakhstan, and I think that if I were even to commit a tactless act, it is a national trait of the Kazakh people that they would never tell me to my face. But I would not want for the division into factions that has been proposed to us to lead to the destruction of our multinational deputy groups. Whether we like each other or not, comrade Muscovites, since fate has brought us together in this Palace of Congresses, we must think about the country's future, about how we can through joint efforts find a way out of this most difficult situation which has developed today, both in the congress and in the country.

I would still suggest trying to neutralize the confrontation that has arisen in the congress through a more democratic procedure for forming its commissions and committees which, in my opinion, are called upon precisely to take care of the dissatisfaction that is being manifested today by representatives of the Moscow deputies because of the results of the elections to the USSR Supreme Soviet. Apparently the presidium should strengthen the discipline of the congress, which will enable it itself to be more responsible and take a more responsible approach to our proposals. This would not be a bad idea for the Moscow deputies whose club meeting I attended. I am surprised, for example, that the chairman of the USSR Supreme Soviet does not have a computer with which he could find out in a moment which region is represented by which deputy. The Moscow club has such a computer, which can also be used for reproducing numerous slogans and leaflets.

I think, comrades, that the congress regulations should also envision reinforcing the procedure and status of the deputy conference—regional, republic, and oblast—so that these conferences will be conducted with mandatory observance of the procedural norms and with minutes being kept. Then in the future we shall not have a situation like the one in which we were placed by the esteemed delegation from the Russian Federation.

I think, comrades, that today we still must complete the elections with the selection of the deputy chairman of the USSR Supreme Soviet and let the USSR Supreme Soviet we have elected get to work. And the mandate commission should replace our temporary credentials with permanent ones so that, even if it is a formal act, every one of us will have a sense of responsibility for belonging to the deputy corps of the country of the soviets. Thank you for your attention. (Applause).

M.S. Gorbachev: The floor goes to Deputy Kravchenko and then Deputy Kirillov will speak.

L.P. Kravchenko, general director of TASS (on behalf of the USSR Union of Journalists): More and more frequently from this podium one hears words about the Muscovites and the Moscow faction. I must assure you that such a faction does not exist, and I am confident that it will not be created. We are all made of different stuff, and you will be convinced of this after my speech.

Neither the speech of Comrade Afanasyev nor that of Comrade Popov was a surprise to me. I happened to be in the United States of America recently, and there I had to lead a discussion about whether a united opposition faction consisting of approximately 350-400 people would speak at the congress. In the United States, for some reason, they were able to figure this out in advance. Fortunately, we have not reached this point yet, and I hope that we never shall. But there they were discussing not only the size of the group but also who would represent it. Attentively reading the responses from the foreign press in TASS each day, I discovered after the first day of work of the congress that, in the opinion of Western agencies, even on the first day the "radicals" tried to impose their viewpoint in the discussion of procedural issues. The question was asked: "Will they succeed in imposing their viewpoint when all other key issues are being resolved at this congress?" Honestly speaking, I would like very much not to believe all this, but here we have heard these speeches.

Of course I am struck by phrases like the "Stalinist-Brezhnevite wing." I know comrades who say this as consistent proponents of democracy. And yet democracy presupposes tolerance of others' ideas! And when this kind of intolerance is shown not only toward people with different ideas but toward the majority with different ideas, I cannot but question whether they are consistently upholding the principle of democracy. (Applause).

It seems to me that this is a case where certain comrades are openly imposing their will, including one of the speakers who said here that he supports the viewpoint of Comrade Popov and therefore thinks that there is no more need to discuss this issue. You can see how people sometimes understand democracy and pluralism of opinions.

The scare tactics to which certain comrades occasionally resort seem futile to me as well. I mean you, Ales

STENOGRAPHIC RECORD

Fourth Session

27 May 1989

Adamovich. I deeply respect you as an eminent commentator who in numerous statements on radio, television, and in the press has criticized Stalin, Stalinism, and repression. I do not think there is a single person in this hall who does not share my viewpoint. But I am beginning to feel more and more that we are being intimidated by Stalinism. It is becomming the talk of the town. We even have a new term now—the "Stalinist-Brezhnevite wing." Why, one asks, should we be frightened? Each one of the people's deputies who has been elected has his head on his shoulders and has a sense of his personal worth. Proponents of democracy must have a clear understanding of this. Otherwise things could get awkward later.

I can assure you that during the years preceding the Congress of People's Deputies, Comrade Afanasyev, Comrade Popov, Comrade Adamovich, and others—I do not wish to give more names—were given the privilege to speak their mind in the press, on television, and on radio many more times than anyone else. But here we must be concerned about equal rights of deputies to present their viewpoints. We should think about this today as well. (Applause).

I assume that no arguments will arise from these words. Certain deputies are hampered by a feeling of heightened ambitions (both personal and political) and are sometimes hampered to such a degree that their zeal causes disruptions. And certain people leap to the conclusion that a struggle for power has begun. Perhaps we have not reached this point yet, but political ambitions have already come into play. This is a fact, and apparently we must speak about developing the political and general culture which—as I have been convinced at this congress—many of us are lacking. Otherwise they would neither storm the podium nor storm the presidium, but would write down notes and deposit them in the boxes that have been placed here for this purpose.

Order is needed in everything, order and discipline; democracy stands only to gain from this. It cannot be destructive. Democracy must be fruitful. And we must keep democracy as the apple of our eye. And when all around us we see calls to strikes, rallies, and national feuds, many people naturally wonder whether or not this is fruitful. But it is not democracy that is to blame for this but those who use it incorrectly.

The last thing I would like to discuss: We have given a fairly complete answer to the question: "Who is to blame?" The time has come to answer these questions: "What should we do?" and "How should we do it?" Today we heard from the podium an appeal for the ability to work well to be the main thing in our lives. Because unless we learn to work well we shall never solve the key problems of strengthening our society's economic might and we shall not carry out the social programs which we shall be discussing today. Thank you. (Applause).

M.S. Gorbachev: Deputy Kirillov has the floor. Next will be Deputy Konev (the Ukraine).

V.I. Kirillov, senior scientific associate of the Voronezh Politechnical Institute (Leninskiy Territorial Electoral Okrug, Voronezh): I wish to say that I was among those who applauded Yuriy Nikolayevich Afanaseyev for his speech. I largely agree with him. But at the same time I wish to draw your attention to the fact that Yuriy Nikolayevich did not call for dividing our congress into factions. This appeal came from someone no less respected by me than Gavriil Kharitonovich Popov. What is the difference? The difference is that Yuriy Nikolayevich, like myself, was elected by a territorial okrug. Both he and I feel our constituents breathing hotly down our necks; they are always checking on us. I have no intention of offending the deputies from social organizations, whom I respect. I wish only to note the lack of perfection of our electoral system.

The people, who have entrusted the deputies' mandates to us, are placing their hopes in us. They think that they have entrusted them to real politicians. But what is politics? Politics is the art of achieving the possible. And this should be our primary point of departure. Can we see at this time what our possibilities are? Boris Nikolayevich Yeltsin, whom I respect, said that he had been left without a job. At the present time he has left the post of minister. I think that in fact he is performing a very important job in our society by determining the present level of democracy in our country. It is possible to go through a very simple procedure to determine the present level of democracy in our society. Simply compare the number of people at the congress who voted against Boris Nikolayevich Yeltsin with the overall number who voted. We receive 45 percent. Let us take this as a point of departure, comrades. Our democracy is very young. We are merely proceeding along the path of democratization of the society. Let us proceed from the figure given above.

Taking this into account, I call upon all democratic forces at this congress and all deputies not to waste the gift of time on fruitless discussions but to move on more rapidly to a constructive discussion of the main cause of stagnation in our society, the cause of all our problems, namely: monopolies in the economy, departmental monopolies. This is the cause of the self-stimulating growth of prices in our country, the deficit that is eating away at our society and tearing it apart, and, as a result, the increased crime rate. The poor quality of our goods, the halting of the scientific-technical and technological revolution in our country, and the transformation of our country into an appendage of developed countries that provides them with raw materials—these are the result of the aforementioned monopolies. We have met with an ecological catastrophe—essentially genocide by means of ecocide. Dear comrades from the national republics, I also wish to draw your attention to the fact that it is existence of monopolies in the economy that is the main

STENOGRAPHIC RECORD

Fourth Session

27 May 1989

reason for the growth of interethnic tension in the country. Therefore I consider it necessary to bring up as a primary issue for discussion at the congress the development of an antimonopoly policy in our country. It is necessary to create a special commission for the antimonopoly policy and instruct it to prepare for the Congress of People's Deputies that will be held in the fall a plan of antimonopoly measures, including antimonopoly legislation.

Yesterdy I asked Mikhail Sergeyevich Gorbachev a question about antimonopoly legislation in our country. He said that these questions would be dealt with in his report. I appeal to you, comrades: Let us listen to the report from Mikhail Sergeyevich Gorbachev, and after that, during the discussion of it, let us move on to solving the main problem. This is what the voters who are behind us expect of us. They expect us to find a way out of the stagnation. Thank you for your attention. (Applause).

M.S. Gorbachev: The floor is turned over to Deputy Konev from the Ukraine. Next will be Comrade Krayko.

S.I. Konev, clinical house surgeon of the department of infectious diseases of the Dnepetrovsk Medical Institute (Dneprodzherzhinsk Electoral Okrug, Dnepropetrovsk Oblast): I wish to express my opinion regarding the speech of Yuriy Nikolayevich Afanasyev. I was simply alarmed that we no sooner began this discussion than they were trying to end it as quickly as possible. Voices are ringing out here: let us get to work. The fact is that appeals like "let us get to work" have been heard for, perhaps, more than 70 years. The preceding speaker put the question correctly: What is keeping us from working? Why is there no response to these appeals?

I think it is because for some reason the backbone of the administrative-command system has been very carefully preserved for 4 years. All of the laws that have been adopted have been half measures.

At the same time the country is approaching the edge of an economic and ecological abyss and undesireable sociopolitical processes are growing. And if we do not take radical measures in the economy and halt the processes about which I am speaking, it could get worse. We know what happened in Poland. And how difficult it was later to restore anything through appeals.

There are many reproaches against the Baltic republics. I would like to express my ideas about this. In the first place they are frequently accused of separatism, of self-isolation, when in principle they are speaking about the republic's sovereignty. They have developed an eocnomic system—I am fairly well acquainted with it since I read the press from the Baltic republics. Unfortunately, there is an impediment which keeps them from carrying out the reform earmarked in these countries. "Moscow centrism" is having its effect, and there are other factors as well.

I wish to discuss the most significant thing that bothers me. I consider it necessary for our forum to make all the refinements, get moving on solving the radical economic problems, and completely break the administrative-command system. It goes without saying that it is impossible to make any progress without resolving the political issue.

Certain of us deputies have been reproached for being power hungry. I heard these reproaches while I was still in Dneprodzerzhinsk where I was nominated as deputy candidate by 19 labor collectives. In such cases I responded to certain comrades: "If I am hungry for power, you have already taken hold of it and you are in no hurry to let go." (Applause).

I think it necessary, comrades, to move on to the constructive part of our discussion. Here I should like to hear from the economists of the Baltic republics. Let them discuss in detail their plans and what is now being done. What is Academician Bronshteyn doing in the area of solving ecological problems? Perhaps there are some positive strides in other regions as well.

As concerns the ecology, our Dneprodzerzhinsk has already gone beyond the permissible limit. Unfortunately we were not listened to in the country since information about our problems does not get to the outside. We have one of the highest rates of malignant tumors in children. And nonetheless we continue as before to build and operate facilities without purification installations. The success of restructuring will depend primarily on how realistically we can now turn our attention to the needs of the people. I have in mind protection of disabled people, protection of mothers with children and pensioners. If restructuring does not show that we have turned our attention to man this will have a negative effect on all processes in the future. Therefore I think that the time has now come to begin to consider this problem. I thank you for your attention. (Applause).

M.S. Gorbachev: Deputy Krayko has the floor; Deputy Aytmatov will be next.

A.N. Krayko, department chief of a division of the P.I. Baranov Central Institute of Aircraft Engine Construction (Aauman Electoral Okrug, Moscow): From the ruckus that arose when I was first announced I already understood that I am known. So I do not think there is any need to introduce myself. I wish to say that I am of practically the same generation as Mikhail Sergeyevich. He is just a little older than I.

Apparently the cries about one speech or another and the remarks that some people are hungry for power pertain

Fourth Session
27 May 1989

to me as well, if one also takes into account the fact that I am a part of the Moscow delegation. In this connection I can note that, in the first place, if I have ever been power hungry it was probably 30 years ago when I should have entered the party, but I, in spite of my firm conviction that the party is the only power we now have which can lead the country along the path of renewal, remained outside the party. I never entered the party no matter how many times I was invited. This is the first thing.

The second thing: The Muscovites' charges that their ambitions were not fulfilled, that they were not elected to the Supreme Soviet, you see, are stupid to say the least for the simple reason that by exceeding our quota we doomed ourselves to failure. Therefore it was understood quite unambiguously: anyone who spoke at the congress would not be elected. So I do not think there is any justification for calling us ambitious.

But I did not come here to answer all these charges. I wish to say that I personally and the majority, at least, of those with whom I am in touch, are interested in consolidation. Yes, we are learning democracy. And this is not a disease; it is simply that we want it to become the normal condition of our society. And the presidium's accusations that the regulations are not being observed are by no means accusations of some deliberate evil coming from the presidium. The presidium does not have enough experience either.

We have a great deal to learn. We did not know, for example, how much time it would take to print the ballots, to count the votes and so forth. But I hope that this congress will teach us a great deal.

We hear objections that some people are given the floor while others are not, that some people speak too long and others not long enough. Comrades, be so kind as to write all this down. If you have something to say, there has probably not been a case where the floor was turned over to a Muscovite instead of to someone else. If they do not turn over the floor, this applies in the same way to everyone, do you understand? Taking into account the fact that time is passing. If you have ideas—say so. I, for example, am always glad when other people speak. Sometimes they express my ideas and there is no longer any need for me to speak.

It is surprising that nobody objects to the numerous speeches of Academician Meshalkin. The Muscovites did not start to object immediately and there was no noise in the hall. But as soon as, for instance, Ales Adamovich goes up to the podium the noise begins. Why this selectivity? I think we should make noise when Academician Meshalkin speaks as well. But in general I am against this kind of noise.

Now about another point, which I think is more important. Yes, it is necessary for this congress to become the congress of consolidation. But consolidation on the basis of principle, consolidation precisely of pluralistic viewpoints. I should like for the presidium to hear the opinion of the minority, including the minority, say, that is comprised of the party delegations. We have gotten used to always having the presidium above us, but the presidium should not be above us; it should listen to what is being said. And if this were the case today we would not have had such a long discussion of the problem of Nagorno-Karabakh. For this question was raised yesterday.

I am very bothered by the fact that not all forces in the country or even at this congress will be really working in the Supreme Soviet. Concerning Moscow, for example, I personally was not bothered a bit by that; I will still come here about questions that interest me, and you can be sure that I will speak. And not in order to force myself in; I am already resigned to not being a member of the Supreme Soviet. And all the members of the Politburo have been eliminated from active work in the Supreme Soviet. This bothers me.

Yesterday I exerted what might be called colossal efforts so that not one but two members of the Politburo would be in the Supreme Soviet. Were it not for these efforts I am afraid that Vitaliy Ivanovich would not be there. I should like to work precisely with him. Here someone said: "Sit with him in the hall." Yegor Kuzmich should sit behind me. But so far he has not been in his place. Of course it would be good if he would sit with me and we could exchange opinions. Now I exchange opinions with Ivan Ivanovich Kukhar.

There is another very serious problem about which for some reason we have not spoken, although apparently it is one of the reasons why these debates have begun today and why all Soviet people are following this meeting, unlike yesterday's, with such interest. This is the problem of the failure to elect Boris Nikolayevich Yeltsin to the Supreme Soviet.

Comrades, we must understand that Boris Nikolayevich Yeltsin, as it actually turned out, is the first candidate of the RSFSR [Russian Soviet Federated Socialist Republic]. It is not only that 5 million Muscovites voted for him. More than a thousand and, as far as I know, almost 2,000 enterprises nominated him. In this case it is impossible to ignore the opinion of the people. Excuse me, but it is to the discredit of the congress that this happened. We are also to blame for this. We did not see at once that there were 12 people on the list and that this exceeded the quota. For some reason we did not pay attention to this immediately. And it was clear that he would not get in over the quota. (Noise in the hall). No

STENOGRAPHIC RECORD

Fourth Session

27 May 1989

more interrupting me. comrades! I am backed by 120,000 voters. I think that in order to make sure that there is no confrontation between us and the people, so that we can really join together, our presidium and our leadership should make certain efforts so that people like Boris Mikhaylovich will participate actively in political life. And not somewhere at meetings but right here. And I appeal to Mikhail Sergeyevich for this. And I hope that members of the Politburo will come here as I have, for example, to the Supreme Soviet and that we shall work productively with them. I thank you for your attention. (Applause).

M.S. Gorbachev: Chingiz Aytmatov has the floor. The next to speak will be Comrade Lalm from Estonia.

Ch.T. Aytmatov, writer, chairman of the board of the Union of Writers of the Kirghiz SSR, editor-in-chief of the magazine INOSTRANNAYA LITERATURA, Frunze (on behalf of the Communist Party of the Soviet Union): Dear comrades! I intended to speak after our chairman's report but today by way of a rejoinder I shall allow myself to take a little of your time.

I cannot shake the feeling that our congress is going, to be honest, in the way I, for example, had envisioned it. A certain spontaneity, a certain jerkiness, and organizational improvisation are always disturbing our work. As concerns the speeches that follow one after the other, they seem to be more impromptu and not finished statements, not well thought out. There are still outbursts of emotion in them. Nonetheless since we have gathered here and we represent the Soviet parliament, apparently, we must make do with what we have. We must be tolerant of one another and we must find the most correct and reasonable paths to dialogue and general advice and general discussion.

I imagined the work this way: After all of our organizational measures we hear the report of the Chairman of the USSR Supreme Soviet who will give us justification for later developing debates concerning his report. Then everyone could go up and present his viewpoint regarding this. And, moreover, if certain large, important problems that are crucial to us were not elucidated in the report we would have the opportunity to augment this report or enter into polemics with it. This is all in the order of things.

Unfortunately, that is not the way it has turned out. We are not giving ourselves the chance somehow to work within the system so that one thing would follow from another. We are getting ahead of ourselves. We have not been able to resolve all of our disputed procedural issues here before we begin to throw out certain ideas related to problems and concepts having to do with very large and serious problems. I am very disturbed by the fact that in the first half of our work today we have heard the very serious and alarming speeches both of Afanasyev and of other comrades. Not that I do not agree with them. On the contrary , I agree with everything they say. I agree with them in that they are showing us all of the large, painful, key aspects of our public, economic, and social life which present really serious concern and, moreover, danger to us.

I understand that we do not have time to discuss this subject now. We are harvesting the bitter fruits of great mistakes and delusions of those who preceded us. The French have a saying: "The fathers ate the sour grapes but the children have the bitter taste left in their mouths." This is the way it is now. I understand my comrades, to whom I really feel very close, I understand their concern, their alarm, even the, as it were, excessive pointedness of their statements, since in industry, agriculture, social security, and political leadership we have much that no longer suits us. That which is outdated, that which no longer meets the requirements of the day, that which is becoming anachronistic. All this cannot but bother us, and on this plane I agree with them. The only thing I should like to note now is that they are prematurely casting these ideas into this environment, into this hall, because everything should still have a certain sequence. Let us first solve certain problems and then take up others. And still I should like to note one other aspect of these critical remarks.

They are very strong at the level of self-criticism. Yes, now everywhere you look, as soon as you leave the gates of the Kremlin wall you encounter our reality, which presents you with problem after problem. And we are drowning in these problems everywhere. We can see no way out. It has almost become the fashion to speak this way. But, comrades, when we come up to this podium, the podium of the country, not that the attention of all the people, of the Soviet society, is fixed on us, let us also suggest ways of solving these problems. Let us not talk only about what is bad and alarming and then go no further. But let us also talk about what should come next. If you see these causes, you must earmark some actions, set some goals. And there should be some kind of constructive suggestion for everyone together, for all of the people. This is not happening. We have one-sided simple criticism of our activity, with which, once again, I agree.

Here sits my friend—Ales. I am addressing Adamovich. We are old friends; we can take a hint from one another. So tell us, please, if we bring this congress to a point where there appear certain factions, certain groups, certain unacceptable relations among us, will this save us, will this put us on the path to curing the society? No. Factions cannot solve our problems now; I see no positive principle or energy in factions. If this were the case, if I were convinced that if we were to divide up into factions now and each were to be separate, each were to have its own political program, this would be to our advantage—when leaving this podium I would immediately come and sit beside you.

STENOGRAPHIC RECORD

Fourth Session

27 May 1989

This is what we are talking about. Therefore this is not the time, dear Ales, to tear ourselves away from each other and introduce certain discord. I appeal to you. I wish to say that 5 years ago when you and I were languishing in the grip of voicelessness an immense amount of courage was required to go up to the podium and conduct the congress of the Union of Writers in the way we managed to do it. But it took so much effort, the atmosphere was such, it was so heavy, it was so depressing because the gloom of stagnation had fallen over everyone and everything. And what was our tragedy? It was one thing that we could think and reason in private and quite another that the public expression of our thoughts and ideas always led to some large difference. That was our tragedy and that was our embarrassment. And now when I do not compare this with the way we lived that inner life which existed before this and now when there is the possibility of coming up to this podium and, moreover, through the mass media, through radio and television, introduce ourselves and express our ideas, express our concerns, why should we now rake everything together, all of our concerns and problems, and throw them into the maelstrom of divisiveness, the maelstrom which is still to be created.

It seems to me that we are being a bit hasty. I am simply addressing you, Ales, because through you I am addressing all my friends who are radicals, with whom I....

From the floor: (Inaudible)

Ch. Aytmatov: Yes, Yes. Now I seem to have become agitated and I cannot explain to you. That is I wish for us to remain friends who are deeply concerned about our society, our culture, and our politics. But I want this to be reasonable, I want us to solve our problems in an orderly fashion without getting ahead of ourselves and without trying to do things for which we are not yet ready.

The fact is that if we continue our congress in this spirit, when our attitudes and emotions sometimes flare up, I do not think it will be to the advantage of restructuring. On the contrary. And those people who gloat over this, who are watching to see us fail, who are still unable to get away from the old thinking and the old idea about justice and socialism in general—they are the ones for whom we are putting the oil on the fire today. In this case today we are providing grist for their mill. And I should like for us to turn our efforts and spirit in the opposite direction, for us to leave here as renewed people, and for certain hopes to sparkle in the eyes of our compatriots. (Applause).

M.S. Gorbachev: Comrades, I am receiving notes. In particular, they are saying that with my help we are failing to stick to the agenda. And some people are even adding that it is on my initiative. But I did not ask Comrade Afanasyev to forget about sleep and prepare, or Comrade Popov to put everything else aside and prepare his speech. I did not ask them to do this; I did not show initiative. They spoke on their own initiative.

But since they have raised the problem I consider it my duty to address you. Because we could not simply leave after approving the minutes, leaving everything like this without reaching an understanding or exchanging opinions. It seemed to me that this would be a mistake. I suggested it and you decided to do it the way we are doing it. I could not have made that decision by myself. I am not sorry about this, comrades, I am not sorry. I simply think that we should do what we agreed upon. We said that we would devote 2 hours, one meeting and that would be all. Because I have so many notes here. Here they are.... And so many people have spoken. Therefore let us do what we agreed upon. Let us finish the meeting and then we shall sum up. Are there any objections, comrades? Good.

The floor goes to Viktor Alekseyevich Palm, the deputy from Estonia.

V.A. Palm, faculty head of Tartu State University (Keylas National Territorial Okrug, Estonian SSR): Excuse me, my voice is not very good but I shall try to make myself understood. Dear comrades, throughout my adult life I have been engaged in science and therefore I am well aware that my desires, the desires of other people, emotions, and demands can change nothing if there are other, more powerful processes taking place in reality. Therefore I have the suggestion that henceforth in our work we not proceed from the model that there are deputies with ill will and deputies with good will among us. This does not mean that all the deputies are of the same opinion and it does not mean that they can agree on all issues, nor does it mean that we shall not have conflicts. They already exist. But let us be aware that here we are not expressing our own will or our own interests. We are expressing the interests of the voters. But the voters are not a solid gray mass. Among them are various strata, various social groups, people from various nations, and so forth. These interests are real and their confrontation, which sometimes does not even mean differences, is also a reality, and we need a good deal of common sense and the suppression of our own personal emotions in order to deal with these interests and find constructive solutions.

It seems to me that if we agree not to display our personal emotions anymore we shall move forward more productively.

The question of the Moscow group is now being discussed here. I should like to say this, comrades: Whether we like it or not, this group of Moscow deputies has worked long, attentively, purposefully, and skillfully just

STENOGRAPHIC RECORD

Fourth Session
27 May 1989

in order to deal with these real problems of our society and prepare for the congress. I too had the opportunity to keep abreast of their work and participate in it, although not very actively. This is perhaps the only real preparation with the participation of many deputies from various regions. This is very important, and not only for Moscow but for this congress. Unfortunately there was no other center where the others could be united. Therefore this group inevitably submitted its wishes concerning the agenda and the sequence of actions in this theater, which are taking place in front of hundreds and probably millions of people, and they introduced a number of draft laws and constructive proposals on their own behalf and also in cooperation with others. It was impossible to wave this work aside. It was very unpleasant and regrettable to me that the preliminary meeting of delegation representatives did not take this preparatory work into account sufficiently. Therefore we have ended up now with a somewhat absurd situation. We are discussing Mikhail Sergeyevich's report, which we have not yet heard. You see, events forced us to discuss the essential first. Let us learn this lesson.

Now regarding confrontation and consolidation. We in Estonia and also in the other Baltic republics have almost 2 years' worth of experience in mass participation of the population in politics. In an increasingly deliberate and organized way. We have lived through periods of outbursts of emotion. We have lived through very critical periods when it was impossible to predict what would happen in a week or even the next day. As you can see, we have already emerged from this situation. And in the context of what we are now discussing I should like to share some conclusions. It is impossible to avoid confrontations when interests differ. Therefore let us abandon the hope that everything will proceed for us according to the formula: "Boys, let us live together as friends." You all know that this will not happen. But this must be a politically decorous confrontation, with mutual respect, without the desire to keep anyone from expressing his opinion, but as concerns imposing one's opinions—nobody is forbidden to persuade.

On the other hand I should like very much (here I shall switch from reality to my wishes, excuse me for contradicting what I said in the beginning somewhat) for there to be consolidation of all those progressive forces which, only by working together and mustering all of their strength, can bring our country out of the situation in which we have found ourselves.

I should not like to have a confrontation. I still recall when I was two and a half years old my parents were divorced and it was absolutely impossible for me to choose between my mother and my father. And now how can I choose between Mikhail Sergeyevich and Yuriy Afanasyev? I do not wish to; I reject this confrontation if it is to occur. Let us give all of our efforts to restructuring, to a radical restructuring which goes against the attempts of the apparatus, and such attempts are being made all the time. And to a significant degree they left their mark on the pre-election campaign.

Let us recall what happened in Leningrad. We have followed these events holding our breath. We must frustrate the attempts of the apparatus. We must overcome its resistance through all forces that are progressive and express the interests of the people who have earned their living by labor, regardless of whether it was at a computer or in a mine or at a machine tool. These people must consolidate (if only until we get over this snag). We must find a common language in this sense. Let us at least set this as a goal.

Here I cannot but note how they are separating us. I shall give just one example. I do not wish to have a long discussion here. PRAVDA (the newspaper is called PRAVDA) published the fabrications of a member of the Estonian SSR Academy of Sciences, Nan, about what is taking place in Estonia with the clear intention of showing "see how it is there." PRAVDA published this. A unanimous decision was made by the general assembly of the Academy of Sciences (it was adopted by all academicians and corresponding members) which said that because of the fact that there were clear signs of a deliberate information blockade from the central means of mass propaganda, we demand, the academy demands that our decision be published. I could continue, and continue, and continue. An incorrect image was created of entire peoples and the republic. This is what leads to confrontation. This work is not for consolidation. I hope very much that a direct transmmission of our congress will put an end to such things.

Thank you for your attention.

(Applause).

M.S. Gorbachev: The floor goes to Deputy Samsonov from Moscow. Then it will be turned over to Deputy Moshnyage from Kishinev.

A.S. Samsonov, director of the First Moscow S.M. Kirov Clock Plant, Moscow (Proletarskiy Territorial Electoral Okrug):

Dear deputies! I spoke here yesterday. Yesterday I said to the Moscow group of deputies and also deputies from Moscow Oblast that the policy I would like for us to have depends to a decisive degree on these delegations and these deputies. True, one comrade said to me: "Do not bring Moscow Oblast into this. We have everything in order." Therefore today I am addressing the deputies of the city of Moscow regarding the rallies and demonstrations that are taking place. And I wish again to address the fact that each of us who has been elected in some territorial okrug has worked with the voters, has done the necessary work, and is responsible for the state of order.

Fourth Session

27 May 1989

Somebody sent me a note from the hall: But what about the deputies who came here from Kamchatka? Are we supposed to go back to our voters? I invite you, comrades from Kamchatka, if you like, to join me. We shall go to our 20th Proletarskiy Okrug and talk with the voters who elected me.

But what then. You will see what is happening. I barely managed to get back to my office at the plant before I was met by a group who said: "You seem to be generally apolitical. In general you are acting undemocratically. You are generally against everything." Some committee was found (somewhere, somebody's) which is now organizing feedback, and today they have come to stuff leaflets everywhere saying that I am a representative from the Communist Party apparatus. And this is nonsense. But if we conduct ourselves this way....

Why am I saying all this today? All this is a direct result of today's conversation. Along with everything that is good in the Moscow organization there are also factions, which we discussed today and which we must condemn. I would ask the deputies today not to join all those deputies of the Moscow organization in this faction wing. (Applause). I do not want this label. I do not intend, Comrade Afanasyev, to raise my hand to vote for something with which I do not agree. I have my own particular opinion and I have told my voters about this.

Here they have begun to talk about power. When I voted I said that I would not work in a permanent agency of the Supreme Soviet. I have an enterprise where I will do everything that works for perestroyka.

Regarding Comrade Popov's speech. I say that I do not agree with all this absolutely. Today we are speaking about democracy and about business, but are beginning to talk democratic nonsense. (Applause).

Dear Comrade Popov, I invite you to visit my plant. I shall give you a certain work section and you organize for me, please, that which you are proclaiming. (Applause). In order to speak to our voters today, to speak about what is lacking in the stores.... In order for them to come here today? So that henceforth everything will be the way it should be. And there is no need to persuade anyone that empty shelves are bad, we all understand that.

But we still do not have a clearcut decision about how to act, what to do. And we are beginning to conduct a discussion of this—here I support Comrade Afanasyev all the way.

Let us now discuss whether or not it is possible for a normal person to sit at this table for 4 hours in a row without moving. And there are enough discussions literally for an entire day. We must simply observe the regulations.

STENOGRAPHIC RECORD

From the floor: (Inaudible).

A.S. Samsonov: I have nothing to say about the idea that the Moscow deputies did a poor job of preparing.... No, none of that is true. But we are speaking now about factions. We want all of this to just go away, but let us look the truth in the face. After all, we have people who simply cannot live without factions. They would get sick tomorrow if that possibility were taken away. (Applause). I think that this should be condemned. Officers have an officers' court of honor. I suggest introducing a deputies' court of honor so that people will not have to be trained here, where we are conducting business, but can be called there and let them train them as they will. Thank you for your attention. (Applause).

M.S. Gorbachev: I wish to consult with you. The speech of Comrade Mishnyaga, the deputy from Moldavia, has been announced. Let us give him the floor and then end the speeches. Do you agree, comrades?

From the floor: We agree.

M.S. Gorbachev: It seems that this question requires a decision since I see some people are insisting on something else. (Noise in the hall) I raise the question for a vote. Who is in favor of stopping the debates after the announced speech of Deputy Moshnyaga? I ask for a vote. Who is in favor? Lower your hands. Are there any against? Abstentions? We shall go by the majority of the votes. The floor is yours, Comrade Moshnyaga.

T.V. Moshnyaga, head physician of the republic clinical hospital, Kishinev (Leninskiy National Territorial Electoral Okrug, Moldavian SSR): Deeply esteemed comrade deputies! Deeply esteemed chairman of the country's Supreme Soviet! The Moldavian group of deputies does not intend to enter into a discussion of this subject. It intends to speak aobut the main report on the work of the Congress of People's Deputies pertaining to the situation in our country which, we expect, will reflect questions of the economy and sociopolitical, interethnic, linguistic, ecological, and other questions.

I decided to speak today about questions that arise on more of an organizational plane. Indeed, there have been serious organizational blunders in the work of the congress both in the preparatory stage and in the stage that just ended with today's work. In fact we do not even yet have the proper organization or the proper work experience. Well, we are learning democracy. In this connection I should like to make three proposals at the same time.

First. Regarding the work schedule. There have been discussions of it on the first and subsequent days. Apparently it is necessary to circulate a questionnaire of all people's deputies in order for them to express their opinions about this. This should be done either with

Fourth Session

27 May 1989

questionnaires or in some other way that is convenient for the deputies. I do not think there is any other way for us to hear the opinion of all or even the majority of deputies regarding this. The same thing should be done regarding the ways and means of voting. For the subject of today's discussion actually arose because of the incomplete work on the process of preparing for and conducting the voting itself. There should be questionnaires regarding this issue as well.

Since I have already been elected a member of the Supreme Soviet I have the fear that similar problems may be repeated in the work of the Supreme Soviet—in the Council of Nationalities and the Council of the Union. And so before the Supreme Soviet goes to work, before it begins to consider legislative issues and so forth, it is extremely necessary to demarcate them: either by defining the status of the deputy or through some other act. It is necessary to demarcate the activity of the Congress of People's Deputies and determine the list of issues it will consider in the future, and to determine the issues that are within the purview of the Supreme Soviet. Moreover, I think, Mikhail Sergeyevich, that before the Supreme Soviet takes up procedural issues and the development and adoption of individual legislative acts, it is necessary to introduce a computer system and install it so that it can be used for the voting. I have the same request with respect to information about the composition of the Supreme Soviet, the occupations of the deputies, and so forth.

The next question. Is it correct that, as was stated in the corridors, the Supreme Soviet does not include a number of eminent personalities, renowned economists, political scientists, jurists, historians, and so forth? I think, comrades, that that is the fault of the poor work of the delegations from Moscow and the Russian Federation. Comrades spoke here today and referred to the proposals of the Lithuanian delegation. Indeed the Lithuanian delegation has made a sensible suggestion. But the quota that was determined should have been worked out in the group of deputies, including, if necessary, recounting votes, repeated, and even secret votes in order to reach a unanimous opinion. Who knows better than the deputies from each republic—union, autonomous, and so forth—the skills, possibilities, capabilities, and knowledge of its deputies in order to delegate them to the Supreme Soviet in one chamber or the other or to the appropriate commissions or committees of the Supreme Soviet. Thus I do not want to say anything bad about the Moscow group or other groupings, not to mention factions, but it is clear whom the Muscovites did not appoint, that the Supreme Soviet will be deprived of Shmelev and Chernichenko and Abalkin, and so forth and so on. This obviously cannot be allowed in the future when we again work on the question of the re-election of the Supreme Soviet at subsequent congresses.

And the last thing I wish to say has to do with the unity of our congress. I have in mind the appeals uttered today concerning the creation of factions, whether they be from Moscow, the Russian Federation, or the union republics.

I, comrade Muscovites, am not offended, but as a physician and a specialist, a medical expert from Moldavia, I wish to express my viewpoint. We are frequently oriented toward the center because the best medical institutions; the best methods of therapy, say, in public health, which is my specialty and which I know very well, come from you. We are oriented toward the Muscovites toward the central scientific research institutes and so forth, and I wish to say that the role of the center is very large. But today you are not providing us with a good example, today you are not showing us the center or the role of the center which is as skilled and intelligent as it is in medicine. You want to impose factions on the work of our congress. At the same time you want to evoke resistance from the union and autonomous republics. Is this right? Does this inspire respect for Moscow, the capital of our Soviet Homeland? Therefore I support the opinion of the deputies who have spoken here and those who have not spoken yet but are of the same opinion. In the corridors we have consulted with many delegations and agree that the main thing we must preserve in our Congress of People's Deputies is unity! This is the only way our country will get over the bad place it is in today. Thank you for your attention. (Applause).

M.S. Gorbachev: Comrades, I forgot to announce that Deputy Popov has requested the floor for 2 or 3 minutes.

From the floor: (Inaudible).

M.S. Gorbachev: No. I had to agree with you and I think that since he wishes, as it were, to react and express himself we must give him the floor. After all, the discussion here concerns his speech, comrades.

G.Kh. Popov, editor-in-chief of the newspaper VOPROSY EKONOMIKI, Moscow. (From the USSR Union of Scientific and Engineering Societies): Comrades! First of all I should like to say that the accusations against Mikhail Sergeyevich of some kind of manipulation of the speakers here are clearly contradictory. If, on the one hand, he is accused of encouraging the speeches of those we might call the traditional deputies, then he has a strange kind of logic. That would mean that he is also encouraging Afanasyev and me if we are to be logical. I still think we should thank our chairman for the democratic way in which he is conducting this discussion. (Applause).

Nobody here has any interests except the interests of restructuring. And if I criticize someone and do not agree with someone that is not because I suspect them of not wanting restructuring. Our discussions are about something else. What is better for restructuring, which path is more effective? This is why we have gathered here, and this discussion, in my view, is quite natural.

I did not even mention the word "faction" in my speech. I do not know why certain people have to take the

Fourth Session

27 May 1989

group's attempt to work out a certain issue and necessarily reduce it to a desire for factions.

(Noise in the hall).

M.S. Gorbachev: Comrades! Let us listen to this, it is important.

G.Kh. Popov: The next question. It seems to me that the main thing now—and here I completely agree with many of the speakers—is to concentrate on creative suggestions. Where should we go from here? From this perspective I should like to say just a couple of words about the speech of my Moscow colleague, Deputy Samsonov. You understand, comrade director, that I too was new to the shop and that I too had worked in the Moscow Council of the National Economy [Sovnarkhoz]. And when I began to work in the shop, very quickly, after a couple of years I understood that some of the problems we encountered could not be solved in the shop no matter how much you beat your brains. It was necessary to take care of the problems of the plants. And here it became clear after a couple of years that no matter what you do, no matter what you try, that again the problems could not be solved. After that I wrote some articles about the branches, which you have also probably read. And if now I arrive at the conclusion that, in order to solve the problems of the shop, the region, the branch, and all the rest, it is necessary to deal with the problems of the country's entire economic mechanism, this is simply experience from life. Of course I should like to solve the problems of the shop if this were possible. But I am deeply convinced that if we restrict ourselves to the framework of the enterprise or the shop we shall not have what the country needs. I do not know what products your plant produces, Comrade Samsonov, I do not know who wears your watches. But on the other hand I wish to say that in the rayon in which you cast your vote, as a result of a law which we have, an outstanding person, for example, the clergyman Gleb Yakunin, was not registered by the okrug assembly as a candidate for deputy. And this, comrades, is what I wish to discuss. I agree with the ideas expressed here by the esteemed Chingiz Aytmatov. I think that as long as we have even the slightest possibility of working together we must work together. And I am deeply convinced that this possibility exists. Therefore I should like for there to be no more talk of factions. Since we are ready to work, let us get to work. (Applause).

M.S. Gorbachev: Are no resolutions required? No. This has been a useful discussion. Let us go on to the next question. We are discussing resolving the issue of the First Deputy Chairman of the USSR Supreme Soviet. Here I shall take advantage of my constitutional authority and this will not start with me. My choice is Comrade Anatoliy Ivanovich Lukyanov and I ask you to support this choice. (Applause). Good, Andrey Dmitriyevich, good. One minute. I have not yet completed my argument supporting my proposal.

I proceed from the idea that in Comrade Lukyanov we have a person who is trained theoretically and politically and trained also with respect to experience in state and Soviet construction. Now that we have entered a new stage in the development of our democracy and the restoration of agencies of Soviet power, now that we are dealing with new agencies, the highest agencies of authority in the country, this experience is useful and necessary and comprises a value. In recent months I have had the opportunity to observe Comrade Lukyanov right in his work and you have also had the opportunity to observe him, and I think that you are competent to judge. It seems to me that in this case we can proceed to his election. This election will be held by open vote. That is my proposal. Is there any need to present the details of Comrade Lukyanov's career?

Now I should like to ask who would like to speak or make a motion. As I understood, Deputy Sakharov would like to be first to say something. Or did you not ask for the floor? Then, as I understood it, you move to open discussion. Yes, Andrey Dmitriyevich, go ahead.

A.D. Sakharov, academician and head of the scientific association of the P.N. Lebedev Physics Institute of the USSR Academy of Sciences, Moscow (on behalf of the USSR Academy of Sciences): The question I would like to raise pertains to the following: Last year in our country we adopted a number of laws and decrees that are causing a good deal of concern among the public. We are not fully aware of the mechanism for developing these laws or, moreover, how the legislative activity has taken place in our country. Many legal experts have even written that they do not know in which stage or in which places the law is drawn up in its final form. But the legislative acts about which we are speaking have indeed caused a good deal of concern in the community. These are decrees on rallies and demonstrations and on the rights and responsibilities of internal forces for preserving public order, which were adopted last October.

In my opinion these decrees represent a step backward in the democratization of our country and a step backward in comparison to those international commitments that our state has made. They reflect a fear of the will of the people, a fear of the free democratic activity of the people, and embedded in them was that explosive material that was manifested in Minsk, in the village of Lenino in the Crimea, in Krasnoyarsk, in Kuropaty, and in many other places. The apogee of all this were the tragic events in Tbilisi which we are discussing. I would like to know Comrade Lukyanov's role in the development of these decrees, whether or not he sanctioned them, and what his personal attitude toward these decrees is. This is my first question.

STENOGRAPHIC RECORD

Fourth Session
27 May 1989

My second is the question of the decree of the USSR Supreme Soviet Presidium adopted on 8 April. In my opinion, it also contradicts the principles of democracy. There is a most important principle which was also formulated in the General Declaration of Human Rights adopted in 1948, and by such an international organization as "Amnesty International." The principle states that no acts related to convictions, unless they involve violence or the call for violence, can be the subject of criminal prosecution. This is a key principle which lies at the basis of a democratic legal system. And this key word "violence" does not appear in the wording of the decree of 8 April. Therefore, I find it unsatisfactory. But, moreover, there also appeared an additional Article 11-1, which is known to everyone and which, unfortunately—since the decree has begun to be applied—has already been used to convict people. A clarification was required from the USSR Supreme Court, but it also seems to me to be incomplete and unsatisfactory. The main thing is that it is very bad when a law or a decree requires clarification. A law should not allow ambiguous interpretation, for this is fraught with many dangers. I am speaking of this now because this is the demand of many voters, many groups of voters; and therefore I have the right to speak about it. But I would again like to ask—and this is my question for Comrade Lukyanov—how he feels about these decrees and whether he participated in their development. (Applause).

M.S. Gorbachev: Introduce yourself, please.

G.I. Filshin, department chief of the Institute of Economics and Organization of Industrial Production of the Siberian Branch of the USSR Academy of Sciences (Irkutsk Territorial Electoral Okrug, RSFSR): Comrades, among the many telegrams addressed to me and to the other deputy from Irkutsk I received today there was this one: "I ask that you announce this at the congress: Unless the congress reaches a decision that it is possible to vote for any candidate who has not withdrawn his own nomination for the post of chairman of the Supreme Soviet, I consider the congress to be antidemocratic. The question of a national referendum for electing the country's president should be decided immediately. If we wait until the next congress to decide this issue, the bureaucracy will become entrenched in its positions once and for all. Give Obolenskiy a chance to participate in the elections. Voter Anatoliy Presnyakov, worker."

Why do I bring up this telegram? I think we have taken a great false step by already starting to exclude people. Incidentally, a satire from the end of the 19th century called our country exceptional in that we do not do anything according to the law and that we do everything as an exception. Today as an exception we are electing the first deputy chairman of the USSR Supreme Soviet without any alternative candidate, and tomorrow it will be the chairman of the USSR Council of Ministers. But when will we do what we promised the voters? It is time to ask ourselves that question. (Applause).

This is the first reason why, in my opinion, we cannot discuss this question today. We have not prepared an alternative candidacy, and Comrade Lukyanov has not presented to us his program or his report on his past activities. (Applause). And we must attentively listen to this report, and here is why: because the congress was not satisfactorily prepared for. And the reason—incidentally, there are many discussions about this—is the unsatisfactory preparation for the congress by the USSR Supreme Soviet Presidium and Comrade Lukyanov personally. Do you see what we have here? Here we are sitting in the gallery; I have already sent my third note and still cannot make my way to the podium. I was forced to come here.... For the 3d day in a row now we have raised the question of microphones, but the question has not been resolved. See how they have prepared for the congress. Not a single one of us had a precise idea about the program, the agenda, or the documents!

What kind of preparation is this? If Comrade Lukyanov thinks that he can continue to work like this, I think we should by no means elect him deputy chairman of the Supreme Soviet.... Here is my first proposal: Do not allow any further election of the highest leaders of the country without alternative candidates. (Applause). Second. The question is not prepared and it cannot be resolved today. And, incidentally, we are all tired. Does it have anything to do with our fatigue that we are now voting on everything? Such things, in my opinion, must not be permitted. And third. In general we must not allow any more elections without alternative candidacies. These are my proposals. (Applause).

M.S. Gorbachev: I must disagree with you. You may agree or disagree with the proposals made by the chairman of the USSR Supreme Soviet, but I have the constitutional authority to make proposals, starting with the first deputy chairman of the Supreme Soviet. And it is probably not without reason that this was written into the Constitution, discussed by all the people, adopted, and approved. It is not without reason that we conceived this post of chairman of the Supreme Soviet, that we thought we needed such a post, and that we wanted it to be the way we approved it—this is why these broad rights were granted. Therefore I make a proposal, and it will be this way for the other candidates as well. You may discuss it and accept it or not, but if my proposal is rejected, the chairman will again be asked to make his proposals. Therefore alternatives can come from me—after you reject or refuse to accept my proposal. Therefore, I ask the the congress to discuss my proposal of Comrade Lukyanov. Please....

Just a minute (he addresses one of the deputies), sit down, please; I shall give you the floor.

N.G. Dmitriyev, acting chairman of the presidium of the branch of the V.I. Lenin All-Union Academy of Agricultural Sciences for the Non-Chernozem Zone of the RSFSR, director of the All-Union Scientific Research Institute of Propagation and Genetics of Agricultural

Fourth Session

27 May 1989

Animals, Pushkin (on behalf of the V.I. Lenin All-Union Academy of Sciences): I have a question for Mikhail Sergeyevich Gorbachev. We have elected you chairman of the Supreme Soviet, and now we shall elect the deputy chairman of the Supreme Soviet.

M.S. Gorbachev: First deputy chairman.

N.G. Dmitriyev: First deputy. I have just looked at the Constitution and it turns out that it is nowhere stipulated that you and he must be deputies of the Supreme Soviet. How would you explain this situation? It would seem to be inconvenient. Well, all right, the question concerning you is decided. Now for Lukyanov. Let us say that there is a meeting of the Supreme Soviet and that you were ill. It would then be led by someone who is not a deputy of the Supreme Soviet.

M.S. Gorbachev: What do you mean? He is a deputy.

N.G. Dmitriyev: We have not elected Lukyanov to the Supreme Soviet.

M.S. Gorbachev: But he is a people's deputy.

N.G. Dmitriyev: But we have two categories today: deputies to the Supreme Soviet and....

M.S. Gorbachev: No, we have only deputies.

N.G. Dmitriyev: I asked the question: Do you think that is normal?

M.S. Gorbachev: It is normal; everything is constitutional and correct.... Please wait, Comrade Starovoytova.

From the podium (the deputy has not introduced himself): I fully agree with Mikhail Sergeyevich Gorbachev that it is his right to nominate the candidate. We vote, and if the candidate is not approved, then the chairman nominates another one. But I personally am inclined to think that if Mikhail Sergeyevich Gorbachev nominates him this means it is someone with whom he can work. We elected the chairman almost unanimously, and it is his right to nominate the candidate for the post of first deputy. There is just one thing for which I would like an answer: There have been two decrees, especially the last decree, of 8 April. Were they signed by Comrade Lukyanov with the knowledge of Mikhail Sergeyevich Gorbachev? If it was with his knowledge, I shall vote for Lukyanov. This means that Mikhail Sergeyevich Gorbachev gave his "okay" and that he signed it. But if it was signed without the knowledge of the chairman, then I shall vote against him. This is because I object to certain individual features of this decree.

But frankly, that is not why I came up here. Mikhail Sergeyevich, this is the 3d day, but some people have spoken for 20 minutes and some for 5. At 1200 I sent in a note; I am bursting to speak. Well, let us also, as it were, speak. We cannot let people from the same region speak all the time.

M.S. Gorbachev: You are right. I still ask the secretariat of the presidium to take charge of recording the speeches and to give the record to me. And you can send your applications to speak there. Turn in your applications and I will place them in a pile and give the floor to people in the order that they apply—right where you can see it.

From the podium: I do not know. At 1200 I sent a note through the rows; I think my turn would come after 7 hours.... I still insist that you give me the floor for this vote after the break or on the next day. I think I have something interesting to say to the people's deputies, and I ask you to give me the floor the day after tomorrow or today after the break, when it is convenient for the people's deputies.

M.S. Gorbachev: Why?

From the podium: Everyone is tired now.

M.S. Gorbachev: Regarding the election, yes?

From the podium: No, not regarding the election, regarding the voting that has already taken place. I have what I think is something interesting to say.

M.S. Gorbachev: All right.

From the podium: Thank you.

M.S. Gorbachev: So. Comrade Starovoytova.

G.V. Starovoytova, senior scientific associate at the Center for the Study of Interethnic Relations under the presidium of the USSR Academy of Sciences, Moscow (Yerevanskiy—Sovetskiy National Territorial Electoral Okrug): Dear comrades! It seems to me that the question of the election of the first deputy chairman of the Supreme Soviet is a very important issue, and it would be inexpedient for us to resolve it in our current condition. It is a question on which the country's entire domestic policy depends to a significant degree. We understand how busy Mikhail Sergeyevich Gorbachev is with the immense complex of problems related to foreign and interethnic policy. It seems to me that our shortcomings—I would even call them blunders—in our domestic policy are linked to the apparatus today surrounding Mikhail Sergeyevich and to the degree of competence of this apparatus. (Applause). They are related to the competence of the expert evaluations of various issues: legal ones, which have already been discussed; but I am bothered more by ethnic issues because I am a specialist in ethnic relations. There are many problems and issues

STENOGRAPHIC RECORD

Fourth Session
27 May 1989

here which I could address to the presidium and particularly Anatoliy Ivanovich Lukyanov. I know he is also involved in Transcaucasian affairs, but—I repeat—I ask to put up for a vote the question of putting off these important issues until Monday. (Applause).

But in addition, because I am not likely to gain the floor again in these debates, I would like to ask Anatoliy Ivanovich several questions. In particular, when did he learn about the events in Tbilisi? Did he participate in making the decision concerning these events? And why did the apparatus surrounding Mikhail Sergeyevich not make him aware of these events until 1000 when the decision regarding them had been made the night before? I would like to hear answers to these questions.

And the second question. I, who am also a specialist in ethnic affairs, was pained, Mikhail Sergeyevich, to hear yesterday, and not for the first time (I can imagine how it was for the many millions of Armenian people to hear about this) that our troops were 3 or 4 hours late in arriving in Sumgait. I know for a fact that they were several days late in getting there. I would also like to know where you get information such as that. Who is misinforming you and thus discrediting such an important post and function? I address this question to Anatoliy Ivanovich Lukyanov as well.

Finally, how does Anatoliy Ivanovich feel about alternative elections and who does he see as a candidate for his post besides himself? (Applause).

M.S. Gorbachev: All right. Comrade Oborin.

A.V. Oborin, chairman of the Kozmodemyansk city people's court, Kozmodemyansk (Gornomariyskiy National Territorial Okrug, Mariy ASSR): I wish to say at the outset that I will vote for Anatoliy Ivanovich, although, as those who were at the meeting of representatives of groups of people's deputies will remember, I voted against his candidacy there. But I shall not withdraw my complaints against the USSR Supreme Soviet Presidium and the apparatus of which it is in charge. I am alarmed by the fact that for the 3d day in a row during voting we are driving into a corner and that we are sitting for several hours without a break. We are granting more and more breaks for unimportant reasons and then we are too tired to think. Do not fear, Mikhail Sergeyevich; we will still vote and solidarity is possible, but there is no need to keep us here so long.

As for the complaints against the staff, I wish to say this: I have already told Mikhail Sergeyevich when we met that I personally tried to beat my way through to someone, if not the leadership then to officials of the presidium; but it was useless. The wall is so thick that you could never get through it. There I saw people without legs, disabled people. And I saw people who were absolutely indifferent, who did not want anything changed. I was involved in deputy activity. With the letters and complaints sent by the presidium of the Supreme Soviet back to the local areas, to those about whom the complaints were made. This disturbs the people, and they cannot forgive this.

Now there is talk of reducing the apparatus. We say that it should be reduced, but opinion is that if there are not enough people on the presidium, let there be more of them. We will feed them, just as long as they react more sensitively and solve all the problems themselves and not send everything back to the local areas.

And now for why I say I will vote for Anatoliy Ivanovich. In the first place, everything looks a little different from a distance. Now I, too, have seen how they work, and I think that when he hears what you are dissatisfied with he is somewhat uncomfortable and takes all this into account. Still, his experience is probably good, unless, of course, other deputies have more serious complaints than those that have already been expressed. Therefore, I have only one request: Let us still put off voting until Monday. (Applause).

M.S. Gorbachev: Comrades! The question arises: Either take a break and continue afterwards or recess until Monday.

From the floor: Wait until Monday.

M.S. Gorbachev: Comrades, let us figure this out. If we decided on today, then we can take a break and return to this question.

Voices: No.

M.S. Gorbachev: And so let us vote for the first proposal—to today conclude the question of the candidacy of the first deputy. Those favoring this proposal please raise your credentials. Lower them. Those against? That is all. The question is postponed until Monday.

Before we say goodbye to you, at the insistence—and I think it is justified—of many deputies (this was heard even in the meeting of representatives and during the course of the congress, as well as in notes, conversations, and addresses), we are submitting a proposal on the following two issues.

To instruct the presidium, in coordination with groups of deputies from the union republics and regions, to submit to the congress proposals concerning the creation from the USSR people's deputies:

First. Commissions for investigating the circumstances that led to the tragic events in the city of Tbilisi on 9 April 1989 and the nature of these events. That is, to give instructions to the presidium to prepare proposals for the composition of the commissions and then to form such a commission. I think that all the comrades suggested this. So this is the first proposal.

Fourth Session

27 May 1989

Second. Because of the fact that both at the meeting of representatives and in the mandate commission there arose the question of Deputy Gdlyan, and because a certain situation arose in the USSR Procurator's Office with respect to the investigation of certain affairs, the deputies have expressed their proposals. In spite of the fact that these questions were dealt with along various lines, including with the participation of people's deputies in the last stage, this work has not been completed. Since this causes a certain amount of concern both among the deputies and among the workers, I suggest instructing the presidium to prepare proposals and, in this connection, to form a commission for objective consideration of these issues.

Both commissions are to be deputy commissions that are made up of USSR people's deputies. And I have in mind that in this case there should be representation for all groups so that they can provide an in-depth and objective study of the questions and then report to the congress.

If you have no objections against having us give these instructions to the presidium we can vote now, and later the presidium will bring up for your consideration the personal composition of the commissions on the basis of consultations with the deputy groups.

From the floor: Let us add also Ivanov—Gdlyan and Ivanov.

M.S. Gorbachev: Well, that is the same thing, comrades. (Laughter in the hall). I did not mean that as a joke but that there would be only one investigation group. What about it, comrades? Let us give the instruction: to make proposals regarding the composition of the commission. And to develop proposals, let us hold consultation regarding these issues.

Please, Comrade Zaslavskiy.

I.I. Zaslavskiy, scientific associate of the Moscow A.N. Kosygin Textile Institute (Oktyabrskiy Territorial Electoral Okrug, Moscow): I should like to reiterate the proposals made by the mandate commission to the effect that if we create a commission regarding the Gdlyan issue—and this commission must be created in order to figure out all the circumstances of the affair objectively—it must be created not only for the Gdlyan affair and the accusations raised against Gdlyan, but also the accusations being raised in turn by Gdlyan. And all this must be straightened out objectively.

M.S. Gorbachev: I have all this in mind, comrades. Including all the complaints that were officially registered on behalf of the investigatory group concerning a number of specific people. All this must be studied together.

What about you, Comrade Gdlyan, do you want this?

T.Kh. Gdlyan, senior investigator for especially important cases under the USSR Procurator General (Tushinskiy Territorial Electoral Okrug, Moscow): Comrades! You are all tired, but this is a very serious discussion. I know the deputies' opinions regarding this extremely touchy issue, but I cannot state my position today for just one reason—the question must be discussed with a clear head. And this cannot be done in haste since new candidates are being imposed on us at the end of the day, the third day already. We are deciding the fate of apparatus and also this issue.... Therefore this is the only thing I should like to ask: We have already had it up to our ears with these deputies. We already had deputies who figured out in 6 days the immense amount of work it took us 6 years to do. Not even 6 days....

I should like to ask one more thing, comrade deputies, that this commission include people who are absolutely independent and not apparatchiks. And for the apparatus not to impose its own people on us once again as it did on the preceding commission, because it will be necessary to unmask the preceding commission—what they were up to and whose will they were following in their nonobjectivity. I ask that the commission not only be independent but also have authority, comrades. Therefore I think it will be necessary to create an initiative group out of that category of deputies who without the apparatus and without instructions from above will determine the number and candidacies of deputies who under no circumstances will compromise their conscience as did the commission headed by the Procurator General and other so-called deputies, so that they will determine....

From the floor: (Inaudible).

T.Kh. Gdlyan: All right. We shall submit such a list.... I am in favor of just one thing—the soviet trial should be a trial by jury. Comrades, there will be no real justice in the country if the people who make the decisions.... They must have a base of confidence. Here as well. Our side should express confidence to the members of the commission. Do you understand? Therefore I again suggest creating an initiative group, and let it create the commission and submit a list of its members.

M.S. Gorbachev: Telman Khorenovich, are you against creating the commission?

T.Kh. Gdlyan: I am in favor of it.

M.S. Gorbachev: Good, comrades.

V.A. Yarin, operator at the Nizhnyy Tagil V.I. Lenin Metallurgical Combine (Nizhniy Tagil Territorial Electoral Okrug, Sverdlovsk Oblast): I am from a weary city which today, I can tell you, leads a life in which not to know the truth of the Gdlyan affair means not to live anymore. Today in Tagil planned operations are being scrapped, there are not enough medications, and at the same time the newspapers are peppered with information

STENOGRAPHIC RECORD

Fourth Session
27 May 1989

about such financial power concentrated in certain people's hands through illegal means! Therefore, speaking at the meeting of the elders, I said: "The Gdlyan affair is on the table! Tell the people the truth. Gdlyan is guilty—he should answer. But if a commission created of independent people's deputies establishes that someone has disgraced the country and the party—they should answer! (Applause). I fully support People's Deputy Gdlyan. Calmly, without emotion. Without these soul-wrenching emotions that some are experiencing and without attempts to keep certain things from being said.... Such a commission should be created, but not in haste. (Applause).

V.A. Vrovkov, fitter for machine assembly work of the Kirovskiy Zavod Production Association, Leningrad (on behalf of USSR trade unions): The Ivanov and Gdlyan issue has grown into more than just a problem to be considered at the congress today. Since we in Leningrad nominated Comrade Ivanov, our telephones have been ringing constantly. And this debate has become so much a part of our lives that we are beginning to be defined in terms of how we relate to this issue. Whom are you for—are you on this side or that? Therefore, Mikhail Sergeyevich, we are making a request—I did not coordinate this question and I am not speaking for everybody, but I see the nods—the commission must not only be competent but apparently it must be approved right here, so that we can place our trust in specifically these people.

The comrade who spoke last said that the answer should be for us to go and tell everything to all the people who are working at the plants and not at meetings. Because at meetings their opinions are already clear. But at the plants the workers have questions; there is much that they do not know and they are wavering in various directions: in SOVETSKAYA ROSSIYA we read one thing and in LITERATURKA [LITERATUNAYA GAZETA], another. We must tell the truth. I would not like to suggest, as the emotional comrade here put it—to whomever, wherever, as they say, around any corner, but we must tell the truth to all the people together. Either they will believe us or they will call us idle talkers. Thank you.

M.S. Gorbachev: Is that all? Sit down, please.

G.I. Yanayev, secretary of the AUCCTU (on behalf of the trade unions of the USSR, Moscow): Mikhail Sergeyevich, I asked for the floor according to standard procedure. And I should like to point out that there is an international procedure according to which if a person asks for the floor, he has the right to it in order to make a brief response. I should like to take advantage of that right and state the following.

First. Yes, I think that we must straighten out the Gdlyan-Ivanov affair with utmost care. But I should like, Mikhail Sergeyevich, for this to take place now, under conditions where the delegates are both physically and emotionally exhausted after today's extremely serious discussion, when we have been on the verge of a crisis several times. I support your suggestion that a commission should be created of independent deputies. But I should like to make a remark to Comrade Gdlyan regarding his incorrect statement with respect to the "so-called deputies." This is incorrect, Comrade Gdlyan.

M.S. Gorbachev: Comrades, I think I clearly stated: The plenum would like only to receive instructions to begin work on the basis of consultations, including with Deputy Gldyan. And then submit proposals to the congress. And what we at the congress decide is what will happen. We shall take it that you have given us these instructions. Who is in favor of these instructions going to two commissions? I ask for a vote. Lower your hands, please. Who is against this? A few. The question has been decided. I declare a recess until 10 am on Monday.

FIRST CONGRESS OF PEOPLE'S DEPUTIES OF THE USSR
FIFTH SESSION
MONDAY, 29 MAY 1989
THE KREMLIN PALACE OF CONGRESSES

Deputies reassembling after Sunday's respite found bulletins reporting that since the opening of the Congress the Secretariat had received 21,300 letters and telegrams from individuals and organizations. The morning edition of *Izvestiya*, meanwhile, carried the results of a survey of 1347 deputies conducted by sociologists of the CPSU CC Academy of Social Sciences and the All-Union Scientific Research Institute of Soviet State Building and Legislation. The study classified deputies into three groups on the basis of their expectations and satisfaction with the work of the Congress. The "more radical and least satisfied" numbered 25-30 percent of the deputies surveyed; "balanced" assessments characterized 40-55 percent; and those deemed "moderate and relatively satisfied" numbered 15-20 percent of the sample. The deputies' greatest concerns were to raise the nation's standard of living (74 percent) and maintain law and order (56 percent). Nearly 75 percent doubted that the process of democratization had become irreversible.

The principal business of the morning session was the election of A.I. Lukyanov as First Deputy Chairman of the Supreme Soviet, and for the second time Soviet citizens were able to see one of their leaders answer for his actions and describe his policies. The process was something less than the interpellation of a minister, however, for the candidate took up questions in blocks and there was no opportunity to probe an issue beyond his response. Generally Lukyanov portrayed himself as a member of a collective leadership with which he agreed on all essential matters: the decrees on rallies and demonstrations, on state crimes, and on the use of internal troops; questions of republican sovereignty and national self-determination, etc. On only two issues was he explicit. He had learned of the intervention of troops in Tbilisi six hours after the event (and therefore had not ordered it), and as a member of the Supreme Soviet Presidium he had voted for the controversial Article 11-1 of the decree amending the law on state crimes, which he defended as reasonable and necessary. Lukyanov accepted responsibility for some of the often remarked shortcomings in the organization of the Congress. They resulted, he explained, from a deliberate decision not to rely on the party apparatus but to use instead the regional and local soviets, the implication being that the soviets were much less efficient than the party. Ironically the Constitution, amended largely under Lukyanov's direction to accommodate the new institutions, neglected to stipulate the method of electing the First Deputy Chairman. At Gorbachev's prompting the Congress agreed to an open ballot, and Lukyanov was duly elected, although 179 deputies voted against him and 137 abstained.

The evening session was devoted, as promised, to procedural matters. Fifteen deputies spoke on a variety of issues, most of which had been discussed previously. That was precisely the point made by Kursk deputy N.A. Strukov. The apparatus could have created a working environment for the Congress, he argued, but instead "the presidium has allowed us to be drawn into unnecessary debates," while the deputies themselves remain "an amorphous mass trying to get to the dais, rushing to say (their) piece, more often than not without a subject, chaotically repeating the same thoughts on the same problems...." The reason for this is the electoral law and Lukyanov's leadership which have guaranteed the overwhelming majority of the party apparatus that has and is deciding the main issue, the issue of power. "They simply will not give other tasks for the congress to resolve. Under a call for the renewal of power they are preserving their earlier makeup, without offering an alternative to Gorbachev...resolving all matters without alternatives. I think that we shall not have alternatives in this country while this order, or rather disorder, is preserved."

The name of Boris Yeltsin had been mentioned several times during the day in connection with the Congress's rejection of his candidacy for the Supreme Soviet. Meanwhile disgruntled citizens had flooded the Secretariat with calls and telegrams condemning the Congress for ignoring the popular will by rejecting the country's most popular politician. Then as the session was drawing to a close, A. I. Kazannik, from the faculty of Omsk University, came forward to offer his seat in the Soviet of Nationalities to Yeltsin. Gorbachev wanted to study the matter and suggested a commission, but he yielded to the argument that the Congress had the power to make the substitution, and so it was done.

Texts of documents cited during the Fifth Session are compiled in Appendices at the end of Volume 2: Decree on the Introduction of Amendments and Addenda to the USSR Law on "Criminal Liability for State Crimes" and Certain Other USSR Legislative Acts (Appendix A.4); Constitution (Basic Law) of the USSR, Article 124 (Appendix A.1); Law on Elections of USSR People's Deputies (Appendix A.2).

FIFTH SESSION

MONDAY, 29 MAY 1989

STENOGRAPHIC RECORD

M.S. Gorbachev, Chairman of the USSR Supreme Soviet, presiding.

M.S. Gorbachev: Dear comrade deputies! I would like to declare the morning session of our congress open. First, I would like to make two announcements that might be of great importance for organizing the work of the congress. After our secretariat has begun to feel at home and has begun to work, we request that you send to the secretariat all the materials that you want to send elsewhere. The secretariat desk is over here. I can see Comrades Bocharov, Krylov, and others. That is where all your the memoranda, requests, and materials that a particular delegation or delegate wants to disseminate should go. There has been a general wish that all the materials to to the presidium by way of the congress secretariat. The congress presidium maintains constant communication with the secretariat by way of special representative Comrade Gorbunov, and therefore we shall be constantly informed about the work of the secretariat. If it becomes necessary for you to meet with anyone from the congress secretariat, you will have to go to the third floor, where all the secretariat services are located.

Now to discuss another matter: I did not mention this on Saturday, at the height of the discussion, because that would have introduced an unnecessary element. Nevertheless I must inform you that certain deputies have sent memoranda to the effect that it might be desirable for the congress to return to the question of broadcasting its work. They feel that open broadcasting to the entire country, to the entire world, is leading to a situation in which the deputies' statements contain a very large amount of self-advertising. Nevertheless I would ask the deputies not to insist on this proposal. Even if this does happen for each of us when we are giving the arguments for a particular point of view, we are certainly seeking those arguments that might have an effect in the auditorium, and that might also cause some kind of reaction in public opinion. Therefore all of this is normal, and I would ask the comrades to remove that question and to move in the direction in which we have have been moving, and ask them, as they acquire experience, to get rid of any specific details or any lack of organization, if such should occur—and, of course, that does occur, including at the fault of the congress presidium. The presidium is also gaining experience. And in general all of this is a unique phenomenon, the procedural factors of which must still be worked out. Therefore, in my opinion, it is necessary to retain the most important thing— the openness of the congress—and we will work out everything else as we go. That's why we are sitting here. What do you think, comrades? (Applause). Good!

Inasmuch as, on Saturday, we began to discuss the candidacy for the position of first deputy and the proposal that I had made as chairman of the USSR Supreme Soviet, and certain comrades had already spoken on that question, it became obvious that we still had questions and that some other things remained to be said with regard to this proposal. We decided at that time to interrupt our session and to reconvene today. Inasmuch as the views of several deputies were expressed immediately, and the speakers raised questions that required an answer by Comrade Lukyanov and he should be allowed to express his position, I shall begin by giving the floor to Comrade Anatoliy Ivanovich Lukyanov, and then we shall continue the discussion on this topic.

Voice from the floor: (Inaudible).

M.S. Gorbachev: All right, then. I have already given the floor to Lukyanov, and then we shall begin the discussion immediately.

A.I. Lukyanov (from the Communist Party of the Soviet Union): Comrades, at the last session I was asked a number of questions. There were statements both "pro" and "con." Therefore, while expressing my gratitude to those comrades and those deputies who supported me, I would like to say with all frankness that the attitude that

Fifth Session

29 May 1989

I take to the criticism that was expressed here—regardless of how sharp that criticism was—is an attitude of complete responsibility.

As for the questions that were asked of me at the last session, I can say the following. I shall discuss the basic questions. The decress of the presidium of the USSR Supreme Soviet, according to our Constitution—and those desrees were mentioned at the last session—cannot be enacted by a single person. This is done jointly by means of a vote in which the 39 presidium members participate. All 39 must vote, and it is only in such an instance that the decree is enacted. Consequently, desrees appear not on the basis of anyone's whim, but are linked with the realities of our life. They are developed by many of our departments, as a rule with the participation of scientific institutions. It was stated here that in recent months before the congress, the presidium of the USSR Supreme Soviet was working hurriedly to enact new decrees. Comrades, that is not so. On the contrary, the presidium of the Supreme Soviet refrained from enacting a number of new legislative acts which had been given to us, and at its 23 May session the presidium decided to submit all the decrees that had been enacted by it for the consideration and approval of the USSR people's deputies.

We are not idealizing these documents. To state the situation outright, time moves quickly, and many laws and decrees often become obsolete almost immediately after they are enacted. I think that this is in general a completely natural phenomenon during the transitional period that restructuring is. We shall have to recast some of the legislative acts into a new form. In particular, in my opinion, it is necessary to enact not an decree, but a law governing demonstrations and mass meetings. All the questions about the functions of the internal forces that were raised—and they were at first regulated simply by a decree of the USSR government—all these questions about the functions of the internal forces should be resolved in the law that is currently being prepared and that will be approved by the Supreme Soviet and the people's deputies, and in the Law Governing the Soviet Militia; that is, we need another form. That is completely obvious to me as a jurist.

As for the 8 April decree, with a consideration of the opinions expressed by the public, the presidium of the USSR Supreme Soviet, at its last session, came to the conclusion concerning the desirability of resolving the fate of Article 11-1, by removing from it the concept "discreditation." On the whole, of course, it is possible to argue over and over again with regard to the quality of these decrees and the formulations of individual articles, but certainly we must all understand that the democratization process that is becoming deeper in the course of restructuring, the process that is increasing in size, must not only be developed, but also must undoubtedly be defended. We do not have another path.

I was asked here about my position in resolving questions of interethnic relations. Our party's overall position with regard to this question—and I definitely adhere to this position—has been set forth in recent documents of the party's Central Committee. That position will be given in extended form at the forthcoming plenum of the CPSU Central Committee. I shall say only that after that plenum it will undoubtedly be necessary to carry out a very large amount of legislative work, including the work of re-examining the USSR Constitution. In particular, it will be necessary to provide in the Constitution an exhaustive, rather than open, list of the powers of the Union of Soviet Socialist Republics. There are no doubts about this. I have had detailed discussions about this with representatives of the people's fronts of Latvia and Estonia and with member-delegates of the Lithuanian Sajudis and representatives of the Transcaucasian republics. Everything must take on the strictest juridical forms that are linked both with the republic's sovereignty and with the self-determination of nations. One thing is obvious: that, in order to resolve interethnic problems, it is not acceptable to use methods of force such as those that were employed in Tbilisi. Like other comrades of mine in the Politburo, I learned of these methods six hours after they occurred.

I am convinced that in interethnic relations most of the questions can and must be resolved only by means of the painstaking, very delicate, very consistent work of untying all kinds of knots and removing all kinds of prejudices. Including, of course, those that occur also in the Supreme Soviet where, undoubtedly, it is necessary to create for this purpose perhaps not one commission, but a system of commissions, in the Soviet of Nationalities. Incidentally, something that is specifically linked with the multiethnic structure of our state and the expression of that structure in the Supreme Soviet, is the fact that the chairman of the Supreme Soviet and his first deputy are elected by the congress separately from the Supreme Soviet. If they are elected to the Soviet of Nationalities, it would disrupt the balance of the republics (from what republic, then, would they be elected?); if they are elected in the Soviet of the Union, it would disturb the equal rights of the houses. So it was in consideration of this that the appropriate norms in the USSR Constitution were formulated.

Now the subject of the shortcomings in organizing the preparation and conducting of the congress: I think that all the comments that were expressed here by the deputies are just and lawful. Many of the purely organizational problems are explained by the fact that the apparatus of the presidium of the USSR Supreme Soviet, practically speaking, did not interfere at all in the preparation of the drafts of the congress materials, as a very, very large number of deputies had requested. There was a guarded attitude toward the apparatus, and I must tell you this frankly. Although one and a half months ago, immediately after the publication of the decree governing the convocation of the congress—literally the very

STENOGRAPHIC RECORD

Fifth Session

29 May 1989

next day—a package of proposals was sent to the outlying areas by way of the presidiums of the republic supreme soviets and the kray and oblast ispolkoms—that is, by way of the soviet agencies. Those proposals had been prepared by the presidium on the basis of the constitutional requirements, and there were a large number of them. But I will state outright that they were not always or not everywhere made properly known to the people's deputies, but the intention had been a simple one: Do nothing by way of the apparatus, but in all matters rest upon the deputies' initiative.

As for the procedure for conducting the congress, I think that, of course, we did have a large number of surprises, and certainly one should simply consider the fact that we have never had this kind of congress before. And inasmuch as our congress, from my point of view as a jurist, is not very similar to a strictly parliamentarian institution, but, rather, is a broad people's congress where legislative formulas are at times combined with emotions, an inquiry is confused with a question, not very parliamentary expressions are encountered, etc. But it is a forum that provides the opportunity to complete in some manner the very active process that occurred during the election. And, in my opinion, this is not frightening, but perhaps is even completely natural, since, properly speaking, this is exactly the way that the 19th all-union party conference also was conducted, or, for example, the congresses of trade unions, kolkhoz members, and teachers. We were all witnesses to the same kind of tempestuous onslaught. In my opinion this is good. This corresponds to the development of our democracy. In this regard, of course, it must be said that all this is linked with the very state of our society and with the processes that are occurring in it. It is only important for the apparatus of the presidium of the Supreme Soviet, the apparatus of the Supreme Soviet, that has become accustomed to the excessively organized sessions, to be today at the level of those changes. It will be difficult to do this. During the past half-year—I have been working only a half-year in this apparatus—it has had to be renewed by almost one-fourth. More than 100 persons were retired, and it was necessary to change the functions and the structure of the apparatus.

The Scientific-Research Institute of Soviet State Construction and Legislation was formed under the Supreme Soviet, and proposals were prepared concerning the creation of an information center linked with the data banks of all the economic and other departments. Technical documentation has been developed for installing electronic equipment to conduct the voting, including nominal voting. Incidentally, when people began thinking about installing electronic equipment in this auditorium, it turned out that it would take about a year's work to do this. But in the auditorium where sessions of the Supreme Soviet are held, it is easier to do this with our equipment. But on the whole, of course, this is the beginning of a large amount of complicated work to create all the mechanisms for rendering assistance to the deputy, for supporting the deputy's initiative in every way to assure that the main figure is not the apparatus, but the deputy himself.

In general, comrades, in carrying out the political reform we have no less a need for innovation and no fewer difficulties than in resolving many of the other tasks of restructuring. This pertains in full measure to those problems that I have had to work on in the party's Central Committee and recently in the Supreme Soviet. I was asked here what kind of program I have in this regard. I have already explained this program many times—to my constituents (and it has been published), at meetings with Moscow deputies, with veterans, with young people, with trade-union deputies, and at many other meetings. I shall mention only the main features.

First. It is necessary to put an end, once and for all, to the position of our country's highest agency of authority—a position that has come down to us from the times of the personality cult and of stagnation, a position that is formal, submissive, and I would even say debased and frequently only ceremonial. This agency must be an efficient, working, demanding agency that makes it possible to compare various points of view and alternative drafts—that is, to ascertain the entire spectrum, the entire sum of the opinions of the people and the voters. But, most important, it is necessary to have the opportunity here to give a ruthless evaluation, a realistic evaluation of what is occurring in society and to search for effective ways to resolve all the problems that have come to a head. That will be the most important thing.

Second. There cannot be and there must not be any important problems in the development of our society that are are closed to discussion and resolution at the Congress of People's Deputies or the Supreme Soviet. The turning of the economy toward man; the elimination of disproportions; the channeling of appropriations; the granting of loans; price determinations; interethnic relations; the ecological situation; the use of military contingents outside the confines of the country; the true status of various strata of society, regions, and branches of the economy; and, most importantly, the responsibility, and once again the responsibility, borne by any state agency or official—all this must be under the constant scrutiny of the highest agencies of authority. There can be no other way. Otherwise they would cease to be agencies of authority.

Third. It is completely obvious that our congress and our Supreme Soviet are only the tip of the entire pyramid of the corps of 50,000 persons constituting the soviets in our country. And that includes the local soviets. And if, right now, the Supreme Soviet does not show concern about these agencies, factually speaking we will simply be deprived of our roots. This has necessitated the radical reinforcement of the material-financial base of the soviets, and the sharp demarcation of powers among the union, republic, and local agencies, and especially between the rural and settlement soviets, which have

STENOGRAPHIC RECORD

Fifth Session
29 May 1989

literally been bled white in our country. And all of this must be firmly established in the Law within the very near future, before the election, of course, so that it will be armed with a new law governing local administration and self-government of the local management.

Fourth. In any democratic state, the law must rule. We have become too accustomed to all kinds of instructional guides, to all kinds of decrees issued by executive agencies that are regulating the very important questions. It is necessary to discuss carefully the most important laws, and to bring them before national discussion and a referendum. Comrades, a colossal amount of work will be required. The absolutely minimal computations attest to the fact that this will require approximately 50 new legislative acts. I would mention first of all the following ones: pension legislation, which has completely lagged behind; labor legislation; legislation about young people's rights; housing legislation; land legislation which, in my opinion, is currently at the level that it was in the past century; tax legislation; and, finally, a number of legislative acts dealing with human rights, the rights of the citizen. These include the freedom of the press, voluntary societies, trade unions, etc. It is necessary to a very great deal in this area, especially in increasing the court's role in determining a person's relations with the official and the state agency.

Fifth. The Congress of People's Deputies and the Supreme Soviet must become the epicenter of the monitoring of the activities of the executive and other state agencies. A tremendous role here must belong to our commissions and to the Committee for Constitutional Overview. But, most importantly, we must resolve the critical cadre questions in this area—the assignments to all positions in our state.

Sixth. The mechanisms for protecting our democracy must start operating at full capacity. Moreover, it seems to me that we need a union-wide state program not simply for fighting crime, but waging war against it. And this brings us right now to the immediate acceleration of all the work of carrying out the court and legal reform.

And, finally, the last. The work of the congress, the Supreme Soviet, and its agencies is impossible without glasnost or without democracy. In general this must be the standard for democracy, organizational integrity, and effectiveness. And consequently we need the closest contact with the voters. Perhaps the creation of commissions dealing with rights, dealing with communications from the citizens, and of deputy commissions. And, most importantly, it is according to our congress and according to the Supreme Soviet that the people will judge the questions of unity, solidarity, and directedness toward the job at hand. Therefore it seems to me that the tasks of consolidating society are tasks that pertain directly to the deputy, and we bear absolutely the first responsibility for them. (Applause).

Voice from the floor: Anatoliy Ivanovich, if the presidium of the Supreme Soviet learns about events of this scope in a union republic, doesn't that mean that the presidium is not in control of the situation in the country?

Voice from the floor: (Inaudible).

M.S. Gorbachev: Would you ask the question, please?

Voice from the floor: I asked the question: If the presidium of the Supreme Soviet learns about events of the scope that occurred in Georgia only six hours after they occurred, doesn't that mean that it simply was not in control of the situation in the country? (Applause).

And I'd like to ask a second question also, if I may. Do you not think, Anatoliy Ivanovich, that the USSR State Flag ought to be hanging on the wall behind the chairman of the USSR Supreme Soviet, or else we might soon forget how it looks? (Applause).

A.I. Lukyanov: I'll answer your question immediately, comrade. I feel that what happened in Georgia was disorder. But that is a fact. It's the truth. Because we are telling you that truth. And it is necessary to put an end, once and for all, to such impotence on the part of central agencies with regard to such acute questions.

As for our symbols—the seal, the flag, and the anthem—unfortunately it will be necessary for us to change our positions fundamentally, because, it seems to me, in any self-respecting country its flag, anthem, and seal are high symbols. Starting when the schoolchild is in the very first grade, our teachers begin to imbue in that child respect for that flag or other symbols. Unfortunately, in our country this has proven to be disparaged. The defense of the flag and the anthem, unfortunately, has been disparaged even in criminal law and in our other legislative acts. I have absolutely no doubt that this must be reconsidered.

M.S. Gorbachev: Good. Would you sit down, please. Do you have a question for Comrade Lukyanov?

Voice from the floor: In accordance with procedure....

M.S. Gorbachev: Good. Please ask your question. I have promised to discuss the question in accordance with procedure, and we are always discussing things out of turn. Please ask the question.

A.A. Shchelkanov, freight loader, store No 20, Berezka Trade Firm in Leningrad (Kirov Territorial Electoral District, Leningrad): I would like to make one comment pertaining to procedure. Comrade deputies! Comrade chairman! We are gradually working out the process of

STENOGRAPHIC RECORD

Fifth Session

29 May 1989

discussing the candidacies of persons seeking the highest administrative positions in the country, in particular, by way of the mechanism of asking a question. But it must be noted that the practice that is generally accepted as of today possesses the substantial shortcoming that all the questions that are asked in turn by the deputies are complied by us into a single large package that subsequently is submitted for answers. That package is assembled until there are no more persons who wish to ask questions, or any more questions themselves. In the process of providing a single, overall answer to these questions, some of them are lost, and some disappear in the overall stream that we also encountered when discussing the candidacy of the chairman of the Supreme Soviet and of Comrade Lukyanov.

In order to increase the effectivness of discussing the candidacies, I consider it to be necessary to correct the procedure by introducing into it requirements that the answers to questions asked by each of the deputies be given immediately after they have been formulated. (Applause). In the event of disagreement with this proposal, please put the question to a vote.

M.S. Gorbachev: Well, then, let's decide it. Let's decide how we shall deal with questions as they arise. But I must warn you that there has been a flood of questions both in written form and in oral form. I assume that you are dealing with oral questions.

Voice from the floor: (Inaudible).

M.S. Gorbachev: Well, that is of a slightly different nature. Let's see, then, whether we can make a decision. There is a specific question and it is possible, so to speak, to give an answer to it. If there are no other opinions, one can assume that we have agreed with it. Is that right, comrades? That's right. Good.

Voice from the floor: (Inaudible).

M.S. Gorbachev: We have stipulated, comrades, that as far as questions of procedure are concerned, we will hear a person out. There are always brief questions that must be considered. For example, I see right here in front of me a pile of questions dealing with the statement made by Comrade Lukyanov.... Please, make your statement.

A.I. Konovalov, rector of Kazan State University (Vakhitov National-Territorial Electoral District): I was registered in accordance with procedure. So far as I know, I was second, but nevertheless I was forced, to my great regret, to approach the rostrum here in order to ask for the floor. It seems to me that problems sometimes arise in us and we get the sense of a certain mutual distrust because of the fact that, as used to be the situation, neither the procedural questions nor the standing rules for discussing and resolving these questions have not been completely worked out. But for the democratic conducting of a congress, it is extremely important for them to be worked out precisely.

It seems to me that we must have definite standing rules for electing the first deputy chairman of the USSR Supreme Soviet. Of course, I am somewhat tardy with that proposal now, but at one time I assumed that a certain procedure with regard to this matter would be proposed to us from the presidium, but it was not proposed. Therefore I make a proposal from a group of deputies that we adopt the following standard operating procedure for electing the first deputy chairman of the USSR Supreme Soviet.

First. The chairman of the USSR Supreme Soviet submits to the congress the candidacy for election to the position of first deputy chairman of the USSR Supreme Soviet. In his oral statement he completely describes the candidate and gives the well-argumented reasons for his choice. All the USSR people's deputies receive in advance a printed statement about the candidate.

Second. After the chairman of the USSR Supreme Soviet answers the questions asked by the USSR people's deputies, the congress, by open voting, makes a decision concerning the acceptance or nonacceptance of the candidacy for consideration at the congress.

Third. In the event of an affirmative decision by the congress, the candidate nominated for the position of first deputy chairman of the USSR Supreme Soviet makes a report on the future directions that he will take in his future actions (the report is not improvised).

Fourth. After the candidate replies to questions asked by the USSR people's deputies, the congress conducts a discussion of the candidacy, which discussion ends with the making of a decision concerning the form of voting: open or secret. As is well known, it is stated in the USSR Constitution that this is done simply by a vote, and consequently the question must be resolved by the congress.

Fifth. Voting.

Sixth. In the event of affirmative results in the voting, the congress enacts a resolution concerning the election of the first deputy chairman of USSR Supreme Soviet.

Seventh. In the event of negative results in the voting, the congress once again carries out work in accordance with the standing rules. Repeated nomination of the same candidacy for the position of first deputy chairman of USSR Supreme Soviet is not authorized.

Fifth Session

29 May 1989

I think that if we adopt a strictly definite procedure, standing rules for our work with regard to various questions, this will promote the effective work of our congress.

Dear deputies, I feel that if some kind of decision is made a bit later, this scheme can also be applied when discussing and electing other candidates. And from that point of view I think that the consideration of the proposed standing rules is not belated. (Applause).

M.S. Gorbachev: I think that we must react without any postponement to this very serious proposal. It seems to me that of course—and we all feel this—if we do not have any ready-made documents concerning the functioning of the congress or the standing rules for carrying out the work of the Supreme Soviet, just as we do not have any concerning the status of deputy, we will constantly come up against this. Therefore it would seem to be necessary to show patience and to continue the work, deciding question after question. But right now, if one speaks about adopting, on the run, standing rules for electing candidates, I, for example, am not ready. I do not know: What do you think, comrades? It is necessary to think carefully about all of this. If we take this path, then we must immediately stop everything, discontinue the congress, create a commission, and give it, as a minimum, the responsibility of having the comrades work out the question and make some kind of proposals. But this, I must say, is not the first question that can arise. Questions may also arise later. Perhaps we must nevertheless take into consideration the realities that by the next congress we will have all these documents. I have in mind the autumn congress. Then we will have the standing rules, etc. Therefore let's discuss this. In general I welcome the idea that has been suggested. But should we be drawn into it now, when we are discussing Comrade Lukyanov's candidacy? Won't it be as though all of us are jerking back and forth from one side to another?

Question from the floor: (Inaudible).

M.S. Gorbachev: I have something I would like to say in this regard. Why don't we present the question about the proposed standing rules for elections to the next congress? We can approve it there, and that will be for the future. Life will go on and people will change. So we will need this kind of standing rules.

Should we have a debate on this question? An exchange of opinions? The question seems to me to be clear. I present for a vote the proposal that was made by Comrade Konovalov. It has also been signed by Comrade Yeremenko, Comrade Gavrilov, Comrade Romanov, Comrade Kotov, and Comrade Krasilnikov. They are are district deputies. This is their proposal. Who is in favor of having us engage now in working out the standing rules for electing the first deputy chairman of the USSR Supreme Soviet? But apparently, then, the question about a standing rules for electing other persons will also arise. All right, then, who is in favor of this? Then we shall decide whether or not a commission is needed. That is a subordinate question.

Voice from the floor: (Inaudible).

M.S. Gorbachev: The question is clear. The comrades have stated that we will not open the discussion. Have I understood that correctly? Therefore I am putting up the question for a vote. Who is in favor of accepting the proposal made by the group of deputies and of working out the standing rules right now? Please raise your mandates. Please count them.

(Votes are counted).

A.G. Kostenyuk: Dear deputies! "Aye" votes—851 deputies.

M.S. Gorbachev: Who voted "nay"?

A.G. Kostenyuk: Dear deputies! "Nay" votes—1130 deputies. (Applause).

M.S. Gorbachev: Who abstained? Please count them.

A.G. Kostenyuk: Comrade deputies! Abstentions—47 deputies.

M.S. Gorbachev: The question has been decided. But this is what I assume: It has been decided with the understanding that these questions, in and of themselves, are important and they must all be implemented. This will remain in the materials in order to prepare the documents. Or maybe even....

Voice from the floor: (Inaudible).

M.S. Gorbachev: I want to resolve this question now, comrades. In general I have been receiving information that there are a few people who want to develop a tactic of putting a spoke in the congress wheels by bringing up procedural questions, etc. I have been getting that information. But I will tell you that I am not at the marketplace, but before the congress. If this had any foundation, it would be a very serious mistake—in such a serious situation a mistake that even the congress ought to evaluate.

I have simply shared this with you in order for us to avoid this. I think nevertheless that we will have to maintain our counsel. And we should not try to put everything into a Procrustean bed even before we have had any experience, or mechanisms, or procedural documents, or to carry out everything now in an ideal situation. There will probably be opinions from the outlying areas. Nevertheless I want to ask, comrades, that this not be used in order to put a spoke in the congress wheels. (Applause).

STENOGRAPHIC RECORD

Fifth Session
29 May 1989

Maybe now we can do this. Still, all these deputy comrades want to make a comment about procedure, about the organization. Yes, with regard to organizing the work of the congress. It would seem that we ought to look at this first of all.

Voice from the floor: Here, too—here, by way of the secretariat, also....

M.S. Gorbachev: Here, by way of the secretariat, there have also been comments dealing with procedure. But this is what I want to say, comrades....

Voice from the floor: Mikhail Sergeyevich, this will never end.... An assault on the rostrum should not be made like this....

M.S. Gorbachev: This is how I would think, comrades: We have been accumulating a file of procedural questions—there have been comments. I would ask these comrades to register their names with Comrades Bocharov. Just a minute. Please hear me out. My proposal is: Organize this file of comments, let the comrades wait a while: we will decide this question and organize it, and we will allocate time especially for discussion, so that everything can be heard. Otherwise, as the expression goes, we'll be jerked back and forth from one problem to another. This—and I will tell you this outright—has been hampering the work of the congress. This is my impression. If you insist on continuing things the way everything has been going, then I will tell you that in the final analysis I will submit, but I am expressing my opinion.

Comrades! Inasmuch as this situation has arisen, the proposal is: Continue the discussion of Comrade Lukyanov's candidacy, and all the comrades who want to speak on procedural questions can go to Comrade Bocharov and to the comrades from the secretariat, in order to register. They will prepare a list. Then we can discuss all these procedural questions. That is my proposal.

Whoever is in favor of this approach, please raise your mandates. Please lower them.

And who is against?

Well, it's an obvious minority. There is no need to count the votes, is there, comrades? This does not have any importance.

The question has been decided. Let us get on with things, comrades. I ask you to do this. Now the secretariat has transferred memoranda directly here to me. Let me read what they are. The secretary has put numbers on them.

First. Deputy Nosov from the Nizhnepechorsk Electoral District asks to be given the floor to make a brief statement. Then Comrade Demidov.

V.P. Nosov, chief of the "Tsilemskiy" State Farm's Mechanical Repair Workshop, Trusovo Village, Ust-Tsilemskiy Rayon (Nizhnepechorskiy National-Territorial Electoral Okrug, Komi Autonomous Soviet Socialist Republic [ASSR]): Esteemed deputies, permit met to read out a telegram from my voters: "We ask you to support the position of Deputies Popov, Afanasyev, and Adamovich and to read out our telegram at the congress. We support Deputy Popov's speech at the congress. According to generally accepted norms, all people—not to mention groups of people—are entitled to their views and concepts and to the freedom to express them and uphold them. We are tired of harmonious, unanimous parliaments; we condemn the attacks on Deputies Afanasyev, Popov, and Adamovich, who rejected Stalinism and Brezhnevism. At the congress there should be diversity of ideas and programs, respect for opponents, and protection for all from the pressure of the old system. The latter can only lead to 'witch hunts.' Comrade Gorbachev! Responsibility before the people for the manifestations at the congress of a lack of democracy and intolerance of others' opinions lies with you as the session chairman. Comrade deputies! We call on you to protect the shoots of democracy and not to return to something we wish to escape. Signed: Leonenkov, Flotnikov, Semyashkin, Boka." (Applause).

Comrades! For 3 days we have been listening to speeches and sitting in session, but you get the impression that we're beating about the bush and scared of "taking the bull by the horns." It is time to do just that. It is time to do the main job that the people sent us here to do. It is a fact that democracy and glasnost are already in action. It is a fact that we—ordinary representatives of the people—are here. So democracy is no longer a "little girl," as someone here said. (Applause).

Comrades! In our northern way, I would make a comparison to illustrate democracy. You know, when the sun warms the ants in the forest they all climb out onto the anthill, and you can't tell what is the ants and what is the anthill. This is exactly the case now. The party Central Committee April plenum warmed our country, and the entire people began to stir and talk. As of yet this is the main thing; we have not gotten down to business yet—but comrades, it is time to "take the bull by the horns." (Noise in the auditorium). We have developed the world's most powerful administrative apparatus in terms of size. We have more ministers in proportion to the population that any other country, but do we benefit? Over 40 years after the war, in peacetime, when not a single hectare of our land is under the fascists, we have reached the point of issuing ration coupons. This makes our state look bad. So this question must be resolved. What does a peasant do when he has a big ox that eats a lot but works badly? Comrades, the peasant kills it and

Fifth Session
29 May 1989

trains a young ox to take its place. (Noise in the auditorium).

M.S. Gorbachev: Quiet, comrades, quiet.

V.P. Nosov: Comrades! We must eliminate the command and bureaucratic apparatus and create a new, creative, bold, enterprising, and businesslike apparatus in order to ensure that restructuring is resolved more rapidly and that life improves. In this sphere, comrades, an absolutely correct decision was adopted by the party Central Committee March (1989) plenum on agriculture, and it should be fulfilled. We are talking about a rule-of-law state—it should be created in our country. The Land of the Soviets should indeed be such a state, a rule-of-law state, so that never again in our country are "enemies of the people" shot in their millions or political prisoners jailed in their millions. This must not be allowed. Once is enough.

In a rule-of-law state the laws must be observed. How are they observed in our country at the moment? There is the Law on the State Enterprise, but so many instructions and provisions have been dreamed up in addition to this law that it is the instructions that are in force rather than the law. We have a good nature conservation law. But how does it operate? It is gathering dust. But I will discuss this, comrades, after Comrade Mikhail Sergeyevich Gorbachev's report.

I support Comrade Lukyanov's candidacy.

M.S. Gorbachev: I wish to remind comrades that according to our provisional standing orders speeches on candidacies may last up to 5 minutes. Deputy Demidov has the floor.

A.I. Demidov, senior lecturer at the "Leningradskiy Metallicheskiy Zavod" Turbine Manufacturing Production Association's Higher Technical Education Plant (Kalininskiy Territorial Electoral Okrug, Leningrad City): Comrade chairman, comrade deputies! Today we are discussing the candidate for what is, to all intents and purposes, the number two job in our state. It is no exaggeration to say that his role in the state's life and in activities to lead the USSR Supreme Soviet is extremely great, and in a situation where Comrade Gorbachev combines the jobs of chairman of the USSR Supreme Soviet and general secretary of the CPSU Central Committee, it is even greater still. Undoubtedly, the contender for this post should be a specialist in the field of state building and a generator of constructive ideas in this field. Undoubtedly, he should be a popular person in our country. Undoubtedly, he should be a talented organizer of the work of the Supreme Soviet and its apparatus—work which is very complex and very necessary.

Exercising the right granted him by the USSR Constitution, Mikhail Sergeyevich Gorbachev has proposed Deputy Anatoliy Ivanovich Lukyanov for this post. I think that there is a question mark against Comrade Lukyanov's candidacy. I, like, clearly, many other deputies, can judge his capacities and capabilities from the preparations for our congress and the organization of its work. These, in my view, have been unsatisfactory. In particular, many important documents were not ready for the start of the congress, such as the new draft Law on the Status of People's Deputies, bearing in mind that some deputies will be working in the Supreme Soviet but the majority of them will not. There is still no draft provision on the rotation of deputies in the Supreme Soviet. The overall list of deputies was not drawn up in good time. As is well known, we received it only today.

I do not think that the placing of deputies in the auditorium is entirely successful. On the one hand, comrades, it is very good that the seats for special deputies, members of the CPSU Central Committee Politburo and other high-ranking comrades, have finally been removed from the Palace of Congresses. And now we are not having played out before us the daily ritual of the "appearance of the leaders [vozhdi] before the people," accompanied by the obligatory standing ovation, as was the case until quite recently. On the other hand, comrades, it is bad that Politburo members still sit apart. Their special status at our congress is thereby willy-nilly emphasized. (Applause). I think that here in this auditorium all people's deputies are equal. So it would clearly be better if these deputies took their seats in the auditorium along with the appropriate delegations. This would be in a spirit of democratization.

The congress is already into its 4th day, but no work is being done to find out whether deputies want to work in this or that commission or committee. It is time we began to get to know the contenders for ministerial posts—to get to know them in good time. It is in the resolution of these and other issues that Comrade Lukyanov should have shown his mettle. But as yet they are not being resolved as we would like.

Comrade deputies! Attaching the greatest importance to the post of first deputy chairman of the USSR Supreme Soviet, and bearing in mind the instructions of my Leningrad voters, I propose a secret ballot for the election to this post. Thank you for your attention. (Applause).

M.S. Gorbachev: We will decide the voting procedure later, when we have agreed on the candidacy. Deputy Aleksandr Grigoryevich Zhuravlev has the floor.

A.G. Zhuravlev, professor of the Republic Intersectoral Institute for Enhancing the Qualifications of Leading Workers and Specialists, Minsk City, (Minskiy-Sovetskiy Territorial Electoral Okrug, Belorussian Soviet Socialist Republic [SSR]): Esteemed comrades! I was forced to ask to speak by the stream of telegrams and

Fifth Session

29 May 1989

phone calls, which I suppose we all have been getting from our local areas. Let us nonetheless try to hear the voice of our voters. They are appealing to our reason and our responsibility. I may be wrong, I may have misheard my voters. They will put me right. But I get the feeling that maybe when I go home many of them will no longer be in the land of the living. Because some of them are dying from indignation and the others from laughter. (Applause). Right. Of course, we can discuss procedural questions for a very long time. We can. That's our right. But no one gave us the right to waste time on such discussions now. And I'll explain why. Yes, we can find fault with esteemed Comrade Lukyanov and with any of us. There are ancient churches here on Kremlin territory, and we can set some of them aside as confessionals and ask Father Pitirim to give us absolution. (Applause).

Okay, I propose agreeing with the proposal submitted on the election of Comrade Lukyanov as first deputy chairman of the Supreme Soviet and continuing our congress' work. That is the first point. (Applause).

Second, when I came here, very many of my voters insisted that I hand their letters personally to you, Mikhail Sergeyevich. I have decided to pass on one of these letters. It was written before I came here. It is a letter from the worker Aleksandr Valentinovich Vydrin. If you consider it possible, Mikhail Sergeyevich, publish the letter after you've read it: It is a letter to us all, a letter-cum-meditation, a letter that shows anguish over what is happening in our country. Please, let us take a responsible attitude to what is happening now. Let us stop debating and get down to work. (Applause).

M.S. Gorbachev: People's Deputy Comrade Koltsov has the floor.

Yu.A. Koltsov, colonel, Odessa Military District (Kerchenskiy Territorial Electoral Okrug, Crimea Oblast): Esteemed comrade chairman! Esteemed comrade deputies! Deputy Koltsov from Kerchenskiy Territorial Okrug No 483 reporting. During the recent elections, and now during the discussion of candidacies at the congress, the candidates' attitudes to restructuring have been decisive. That was why it was easy for us to elect Mikhail Sergeyevich to the post of chairman of the USSR Supreme Soviet. We were electing and elected the acknowledged leader of restructuring. Now we are examining a candidacy for the post of first deputy chairman of the USSR Supreme Soviet. This is a post which determines the working style of the USSR Supreme Soviet apparatus. My proposal was that we listen to Anatoliy Ivanovich Lukyanov's views on ways of restructuring the Supreme Soviet apparatus. I heard his reply, and it satisfied me.

But one question still remains unclear; it is formulated somewhat vaguely. This is the question of the provision of equipment for the deputies' seats. In order for the congress to move on in its work and not keep coming back to this question, I consider it necessary for the congress to instruct the USSR Supreme Soviet Presidium, in the period before the next USSR Congress of People's Deputies, to fit the auditorium with equipment to speed up the voting process and enable deputies to make speeches from the floor. This instruction could be put to a vote, but if the chairman of the USSR Supreme Soviet considers it possible to accept the instruction without a vote, in view of its obviousness, a vote could be dispensed with.

One further remark: Deputies at the congress need well-documented urgent communications with their local voters and labor collectives. We have no such communications at present. For instance, during the entire opening day of the congress I was unable to send a telex message. I would also like the work of the apparatus to be better organized as regards deputies' questions and appeals. We have already experienced a case at the beginning of the congress when a deputy's question from Comrade Alksnis was mislaid. Incidentally, during the opening of the congress, deputies from the Crimea sent a deputy's question to the minister of nuclear power generation on the question of the conversion of the Crimean Nuclear Power Station. The time for the reply to be received expires today; we are waiting for it. The content of the reply will determine the position of Crimean deputies when ratifying the list of USSR ministers.

One last point. We all see Anatoliy Ivanovich Lukyanov as a major specialist in the theory and practice of jurisprudence. In this respect it is somewhat unusual that the USSR Supreme Soviet Presidium seems to pay no attention to the legal discrepancy between two laws—the USSR Constitution and the Law on the Status of People's Deputies in the USSR. Currently the law on their status wholly lacks the concept of USSR people's deputy introduced by the Constitution. Discussion of the new law on status is being moved to the end of the congress, and time is passing. The law may not be created during the congress, although deputies now have to hand proposals and versions of a new law on status. But we are obliged to bring the law on status into line with the USSR Constitution during the congress. Otherwise it would be the case that the congress lacked a legislative basis. This should not happen.

One final point. I propose instructing the newly elected first deputy chairman of the USSR Supreme Soviet to organize during the congress the study of proposals to eradicate the discrepancies between the law on status and the USSR Constitution, and to submit these proposals for examination and ratification by the congress. In my view, this could be done simply in the form of a brief additional fifth section to the law on status. I am prepared to participate in this work. Thank you for your attention.

M.S. Gorbachev: Deputy Fargiyev will take the floor. Then Comrade Aguzarova.

STENOGRAPHIC RECORD

Fifth Session
29 May 1989

Kh.A. Fargiyev, teacher, Secondary School No 18, Malgobek, Chechen-Ingush ASSR (Sunzhenskiy Territorial Electoral District, RSFSR): Dear deputies! As a USSR people's deputy, I have been asked by my constituents to pose the question of restoring the autonomy of Ingushetia that was illegally abolished in 1934. A delegation of the Ingush nation is currently here in the city of Moscow. In 1928 Stalin made his first attempt to abolish Ingush autonomy....

Voice from the floor: Keep to the subject.

Kh.A. Fargiyev: I definitely am keeping to the subject. My question is a question that is not national and is not territorial. It is the question of creating a rule-of-law state. I feel that the creation of a rule-of-law state is impossible without eliminating the consequences of the personality cult.

If a nation was illegally repressed, then it must have its rights restored. If the individuals who were repressed in 1934 have been rehabilitated, why has there been no rehabilitation of the Ingush nation, which was entirely repressed?

This is the inquiry that I am making.

The foundation for the genocide directed against the Ingush nation was laid long before the carrying out of the act of forced resettlement itself in 1944. The constitutional right of the Ingush nation was violated as early as 1934. Without taking into consideration the national interests, without considering the public opinion.

At the present time the opinion of the Ingush nation with regard to this matter has been expressed in two appeals: in October 1988 and in April 1989. The total number of persons who signed these appeals was 60,000. That is the absolute majority of the Ingush nation. The Ingush nation feels that, without the restoration of Ingush autonomy, the further development of that nation is impossible in any way—culturally, political, or economically. In this regard I request the USSR Congress of People's Deputies to consider the question of restoring Ingush autonomy. Once again I repeat that this question is not a national or a territorial one. It is a question of creating a rule-of-law state.

At the same time I request the congress to consider the question of the complete legal rehabilitation of the Volga Germans, the Crimean Tatars, and the Chechen, Karachay, Kalmyk, and Balkar nations. Why is this so important? Because none of us needs another incendiary crisis situation in the country.

The situation in Chechen-Ingushetia is very complicated. Apparently victorious reports have been coming here, and the situation is very difficult—at any moment something that we do not need might occur—because the party's obkom in Northern Osetia, and the party's obkom in Chechen-Ingushetia, are engaged in creating a nervous situation. For that reason I want to say clearly that a very large role has been played here by Kh.Kh. Bokov, chairman of the presidium of the Chechen-Ingush ASSR Supreme Soviet, and by D.K. Bezuglyy, editor of the GROZNENSKIY RABOCHIY newspaper, who on 14 December 1988, at a plenum of the board of governors of the USSR Writers Union, said that anti-Russian moods are maturing in Chechen-Ingushetia. As an Ingush who lives in the midst of Russians, Chechens, and Ingush, in Chechen-Ingushetia, I assert that this is a shameless lie. There are no anti-Russian moods, but those moods are being incited.

Once more, I repeat: We cannot permit the creation of yet another hot spot in our country. I have registered my name to speak on this question during the discussion period for the report. Thank you for your attention.

M.S. Gorbachev: Fine. The floor is given to Stella Borisovna Aguzarova from North Osetia. She will be followed by Deputy Sebentsov.

S.B. Aguzarova, assembly worker at the Ordzhonikidze 50th Anniversary of the Komsomol Electric Lamp Plant, Ordzhonikidze City (Sovetskiy National-Territorial Electoral Okrug, RSFSR): You know, comrades, for all the importance of the procedural issues being discussed, I still think that we need to make more rapid progress and move faster through the congress agenda.

Now to the essence of the matter. The things I value most in a statesman and politician are professional knowledge and a civic stance. So I have deeply sympathized with the pointed, exacting calls made at our congress to nominate worthy people for elected posts and the structures of our country's highest legislative body.

During these last few days we have really got to know one another better, so it is with great conviction that I support the nomination of Comrade Anatoliy Ivanovich Lukyanov for the post of first deputy chairman of the USSR Supreme Soviet. The logic behind my stand is as follows.

First. He is a doctor of juridical sciences in the field of state building, which, incidentally, has been mentioned at earlier sessions by many legal experts.

Second. His commitment to the concept of restructuring.

And third. His patience and ability to listen to others' opinions.

My modest experience, including in the field of social work, tells me how important compatibility between people is in a common cause—their psychological, human, and professional compatibility. It is for this reason I feel that the recommendation by Comrade

STENOGRAPHIC RECORD

Fifth Session

29 May 1989

Mikhail Sergeyevich Gorbachev must be a very important factor for us, because he already has experience of working with Anatoliy Ivanovich Lukyanov.

And the last point. As we are professing democracy, we should obviously also show concern and protect the sovereign constitutional rights of the chairman of the Supreme Soviet and support his proposal. (Applause).

M.S. Gorbachev: Deputy Sebentsov has the floor. He will be followed by Deputy Gdlyan.

A.Ye. Sebentsov, head of department at the Moscow Searchlight Plant, Moscow City (Perovskiy Territorial Electoral Okrug, RSFSR): Comrade chairman! Comrade deputies! First of all I would like to make a small protest against Comrade A.G. Zhuravlev's unethical joke.

Okay, now for what I wanted to say. During the congress's examination of the candidacy of Anatoliy Ivanovich Lukyanov, proposed for the post of first deputy chairman of the Supreme Soviet by the Central Committee plenum and Comrade Gorbachev, several complaints have been made about Comrade Lukyanov, including with regard to organization of the congress. Enough has been said about these complaints today. The course of the congress' work is also a source of complaints. One gets the impression that the congress is only working at all thanks to skillful leadership on the part of Mikhail Sergeyevich Gorbachev.

On the evening of 26 May I was approached in the street by a voter who asked me to tell Comrade Gorbachev that television viewers have noticed that the way the presidium votes clearly influences the course of the voting in the hall, and suggested that the presidium be given the opportunity to cast its vote a little bit later, so that all the rest can express their own opinion first. (Applause).

The delay with the voting, resulting from the long time taken to prepare the ballot papers, prompted a question from me, which I address to Comrade Gdlyan: How long should a person under investigation be detained before it is convenient to deal with him? The results of the 27 May elections, which left Boris Nikolayevich Yeltsin outside the Supreme Soviet, and the subsequent course of the congress, have led me to think that there are no mistakes or incompetence in the preparation and staging of the congress, but that there is a very definite iron will—a will that has no need of a working parliament. (Applause).

I would like to quote two remarks by Lenin in this connection: "A person's shortcomings are, as it were, the extension of his merits. But if merits extend beyond the appropriate point and are not displayed at the right time and in the right place, they are shortcomings." (V.I. Lenin, Complete Collected Works, vol 44, p 323). And the other remark: "A political leader is responsible not only for how he leads but also for the actions of those he leads. He sometimes does not know this and often does not want this, but the responsibility rests with him nevertheless." (V.I. Lenin, Complete Collected Works, vol 42, p 218). Mikhail Sergeyevich Gorbachev is a strong political leader and I think he is entitled to propose the candidacy of the person whom he can best work with, and who has already demonstrated his merits and qualities. For this reason I invite you to vote in support of Comrade A.I. Lukyanov.

I would also like to add a few words. I, too, have received a considerable number of appeals from voters demanding that Soviet power be saved; otherwise, they say, we will recall you. This is the kind of reaction prompted by what is happening in this auditorium. Voters ask me to convey their appeal to the congress, and I would like to read out a few lines of it: "We are closely following the congress and express gratitude to the groups of people's deputies from Moscow, Leningrad, the Baltic republics, the Ukraine, and Belorussia, who are honestly abiding by their oath to the people and consistently and courageously pursuing the policy of the people's masses. We now know clearly that we were not mistaken in our choice of elected people's representatives. We would like to express our deep gratitude and support to Deputy Obolenskiy, who bravely and at the cost of his own reputation has tried to close the embrasure of antidemocracy and create an alternative in the elections for the leader of our country. We would like the Congress of People's Deputies to rectify its mistakes before new ones are made."

In numerous appeals, voters rank as one of the main mistakes the fact that Boris Nikolayevich Yeltsin has not been included in the USSR Supreme Soviet Soviet of Nationalities, although he was nominated in hundreds of electoral okrugs and secured the votes of many millions of people from multinational Moscow. Voters believe—and I am voicing their opinion in this case—that the congress would be sensible to adopt a decision to hold new elections to the Soviet of Nationalities from the RSFSR. Thank you for your attention.

M.S. Gorbachev: The floor is now given to Deputy Gdlyan, who will be followed by Comrade Ivanov, from Leningrad City National-Territorial Okrug. (Animation in the auditorium). This is what the secretariat has decided—I have nothing to do with it.

T.Kh. Gdlyan, senior investigator for especially important cases under the USSR prosecutor general (Tushinskiy Territorial Okrug, Moscow City): Last time, it was on Saturday, you heard me use the phrase "so-called deputies." Please take into account that what I meant to say was "so-called commission," but it came out as "so-called deputies." You yourselves know how wrong that is, so I apologize.

I have specific questions with regard to the subject being discussed—Lukyanov's candidacy for the position of first deputy chairman of the USSR Supreme Soviet.

Fifth Session

29 May 1989

Anatoliy Ivanovich, in the course of discussing your candidacy for the second most important position in the structure of state authority, I would like to ascertain your role and position with regard to the following fundamental questions.

First. For a number of years you were secretary of the CPSU Central Committee, and you directly monitored the activity of the law-enforcement agencies. It was precisely during that period that there was a sharp increase in crime throughout the country. How do you evaluate your role in the failure of the party policy with regard to legal questions, and should you bear party responsibility for the obvious breakdown in the work sector assigned to you?

Second. Recently you occupied the position of first deputy chairman of the USSR Supreme Soviet and, naturally, were responsible in the most direct manner for the condition of legality and law and order in the state. It is generally known that at the present time the law-enforcement agencies are in a state of complete demoralization and have not been properly executing the functions that have been entrusted to them—the protection of the citizens' rights and freedoms. The country has been literally inundated with crime, especially organized crime. Who, besides yourself, should bear the personal responsibility for the breakdown of the work in the law-enforcement system on a country-wide scale?

Third. Do you dispute the fact that there exist in this country mafia groups that have concentrated in their hands the political and economic levers of power? If not, what regions are most infected by this criminal disease? What is your position with regard to the existence of organized criminal groups in Moscow? Can you present to the congress a concrete large-scale program for ridding society of lawlessness within the next few years?

Fourth. It is generally known that two years ago, also under the pretext that violations of socialist legality had allegedly occurred, former USSR General Procurator Rekunkov gave short shrift to the investigation group of the USSR Procuracy, which was headed by Nagonyuk, investigator for especially important cases, under the USSR General Procurator. That group had been so bold as to carry out a thorough investigation of large-scale thefts and the bribery involved with them in the gold-mining industry system. A number of highly-placed officials in the city of Moscow came into the orbit of the investigation. Rekunkov, guided by subjective motives, and having a personal self-interest, illegally disbanded the investigation group and issued the instruction to discontinue the "gold case" and to initiate two criminal cases against the investigation, which were subsequently dropped. All these facts became the object of discussion, with your participation, at the CPSU Central Committee, but the illegality and injustice with respect to the investigation group have not been corrected. What is your position with respect to such a vitally important case, that affects the economic foundation of the state, inasmuch as this involved the country's currency fund? If you did not agree with the actions of the general procurator, why did you not use your high official position as secretary of CPSU Central Committee and your authority in order, first, to prevent the illegality with regard to this extremely important case, and, second, to defend the honest and well-principled investigators who were "guilty" only of having defended the global interests of our state? And, third, hasn't the time come for reinstituting the investigation of the case involving the gold?

Fifth. On the threshold of the USSR Congress of People's Deputies, in April-May 1989, the mass media began an unprecedentedly broad political campaign to discredit the activities of the investigation group of the USSR Procuracy. At a meeting in which you participated in early May 1989, the question was raised concerning the granting to us of opportunities to give well-argued replies to the unsubstantiated and unproven accusations also in the mass media. That request was refused, with the reason being given that, prior to the completion of the commission's work, neither side would be given the right to make such statements. However, the information boom to discredit the investigation was continued. The methods used in this large-scale persecution were the most unscrupulous ones of providing disinformation to develop public opinion and to create the image of the "enemy" such as was created in 1937. At the same time censorship deprives us of the opportunity to speak the truth and, on the basis of the facts, bring to public disclosure those who, while executing the social demand of their bosses, carry out illegal actions to defeat a case. In this regard I would like to ascertain your position with regard to the following questions: Do you not feel that the unprecedented persecution and defamation of the investigation group in all types of the mass media is an action that has been precisely planned and that has been skillfully directed by certain individuals with the purpose of protecting the Moscow bribe-takers? Do the stern bans that have been placed by censorship on the statements made by USSR people's deputies who are attempting to defend their principles, their case materials, and their honor conform to the principles of democracy and glasnost? And finally, if you are elected vice-president of the country, will you provide us with the opportunity to make a statement in the central press and on television, and to tell the nation the whole truth with regard to the case involving the corruption of officials in Uzbekistan and in Moscow?

Sixth. When you occupied the position of secretary of the CPSU Central Committee, you repeatedly received from the USSR Procuracy, and from us personally, information that the materials in the case being investigated by us contained data concerning bribes paid to responsible workers in the CPSU Central Committee. You received similar information in 1987 from the members of a CPSU Central Committee commission who were investigating the criminal case involving the corruption of

STENOGRAPHIC RECORD

Fifth Session

29 May 1989

administrative workers in Uzbekistan and Moscow. What measures did you, as the secretary of CPSU Central Committee, carry out with regard to these facts?

Seventh. In April-May 1989, under the leadership of Sukharev, USSR General Procurator, responsible workers of the USSR KGB and the central apparatus of the USSR Procuracy began the planned breakdown of the proof with regard to the highly-placed officials in the city of Moscow who had been exposed as bribe-takers. The investigation group of the USSR Procuracy, behind whose back all of this occurred, repeatedly sent requests in written form personally to you, asking you to interfere immediately and to stop the illegal actions and the destruction of the six-year investigation that were being carried out by the workers of the Procuracy and the KGB. Similar requests were sent to you by the labor collectives of Moscow and Leningrad. How do you explain that you, as a representative of the country's supreme authority, displayed absolute indifference toward all these legal and completely just appeals, and by your failure to interfere you objectively promoted the breakdown of the case?

And, finally, the last question, the eighth. Do you have the moral right, after these facts have been stated, to occupy such a high position in the state? What is your opinion? (Applause.)

M.S. Gorbachev: I do not know whether Comrade Lukyanov will be able to answer all this immediately. Will you be able to now? All right, then. The floor is given to Comrade Lukyanov.

A.I. Lukyanov: I will first answer some of the questions that came in earlier and that were asked by persons who spoke here. Then I will answer Comrade Gdlyan.

Mention was made here of putting the Law Governing the State of the People's Deputies into conformity with the Constitution. Comrade Koltsov, a deputy from Crimea Oblast, made a statement. I think that it is a correct proposal if we can succeed in preparing this very complicated law promptly. We received a good draft of the law that had been written by the deputy. I read through the draft attentively, and I think that it contains a number of moot points. And so, until we finish working on that law, I think that we will have to return fundamentally, over and over again, to certain principles in it. The Law Governing Status, which currently exists and which actually does not contain the concept "USSR people's deputy," took a year and a half to work out, to prepare. I will also say that when amendments were being made in the Constitution, a special chapter was devoted to the USSR People's Deputy. Currently the Constitution has a new chapter that contains a principle dealing with the USSR People's Deputy and that, in some way, overlaps the norms of the Law Governing

Status. If there is an opportunity for this during the congress, it would of course be good to do this. I am ready to take part in this.

Several deputies spoke about rehabilitating the nations that had been illegally repressed during the Stalin years, in particular the Chechens, the Ingush, the Crimean Tatars, etc. I myself have the opportunity on several occasions, in the reception room of the presidium, to meet representatives of those nations. Recently I had a very long conversation with Meskhet Turks, the Turkish population that used to live on the border between Soviet Russia and Turkey, and on the border of Georgia. I must say that these problems are very painful. I am definitely in favor of the most complete rehabilitation of those illegally repressed nations. But this must be decided in an extremely cautious manner, in order not to cause an even greater heating up of the interethnic relations.

With regard to what Deputy Gdlyan has written, one could answer all day. I want to speak briefly. Deputy Gdlyan has raised what is in my opinion a serious question: my role and position with regard to questions of the fight against crime, and the reinforcement of socialist legality. I had the occasion of working in this sector one and a half years in the party's Central Committee. It must be said that previously that position—the Central Committee secretary who dealt with such question—did not exist at the Central Committee. There are a vast number of shortcomings in the fight against crime, and it must be said that their roots go back primarily to our economic and social mess and to the poor work performed by the law-enforcement agencies, which proved to be unready to operate under conditions of democratization and glasnost. At first it simply was not clear from what angle to approach those problems. Then we introduced into the secretariat of the party's Central Committee the concept of court and legal reform, which concept had been worked out over a long period of time, with the participation of a very large number of persons engaged in legal practice and scientists, and which was approved at the 19th party conference.

Nevertheless, during the year and ½ when I was involved in this work, a few things were done. A draft of the Law Governing the Status of Judges, which increases their independence, was prepared; and, finally, the draft of a decree concerning the improvement of their material status was submitted to the Council of Ministers. This is a colossally difficult question, because it is linked with the large turnover rate of judicial cadres: soon we will not have any judges in the outlying areas. Second, the work was completed on the draft version of the Principles of Criminal Legislation, and there is a possibility of renewing all our criminal legislation by the beginning of next year. Third, we have begun to publish crime statistics. You know what stresses and arguments this caused among the public. We took that action and the Central

STENOGRAPHIC RECORD

Fifth Session
29 May 1989

Committee supported us. The Law Governing the Legal Profession was prepared and is currently ready. That law expands the rights of the lawyer, including the right to participate in a case at an early stage of investigation. There has been a new act governing arbitration, which is now being brought closer to the economic court. It was a difficult process, but a Statute Governing Psychiatric Assistance to the Public has been enacted. That statute finally brought a number of psychiatric hospitals out from under subordination to MVD. Here, too, a line aimed at observing the international agreements that we have concluded has been maintained. A number of steps have been taken to change the conditions in corrective-labor colonies. The main principle here is not to keep in places of incarceration any persons who are guilty of minor crimes. We used to have a very large number of them, but at the present time only a few remain in places of incarceration. But in no instance are we lessening the punishment for repeat offenders, murderers, rapists, or robbers. The point of view that I have—regardless of what the comrades have said about humanization—is absolutely unambiguous: There can be no indulgence toward these elements. (Applause).

I have been and I remain a decisive proponent of recognizing the existence of organized crime in our society. I answer this question firmly that it was upon our initiative that materials were published concerning organized crime, and that point of view was supported. So far as I know, that question was discussed in the most serious manner at the Commission of CPSU Central Committee. I shall say something else: The recent court processes demonstrate that both a regional organization, in both Moscow and a number of republics, and, if you will, a new type of crime is beginning to crystallize—crime that is linked with the direct use of bribes by definite individuals to get the cooperation of officials. We have been coming up against this, comrades. It is growing. Serious attention is required. We need a very large amount of very serious work. Therefore, on our initiative—and also, I must say, not without difficulties—in the draft of the Principles of the Criminal Legislation of the USSR and the Union Republics, which was published recently, participation in organized criminal groups is included among the circumstances that aggravate the blame. This also is very serious.

I shall state it outright: Crime is growing. There are many reasons. Of course, there have been instances of insufficient work performed both by the party agencies and other agencies, but the main causes are the overall weakening of labor and social discipline; the growing shortages of all kinds, which the criminal world takes advantage of; the diversion of the militia forces to preserve public order—we were forced to a considerable degree to do that; the new outburst of drunken crime, which was on the point of going into a decline, but which now is on the rise again; and the consistently high rate of recidivism (one-fourth of all the criminals who are released return again to places of confinement). And, I must add, the very weak work that is done at people's places of residence and in labor collectives with those who are returning from places of confinement. I could mention even more causes. But the main thing, of course, is cadres. Recently, during the same period that Comrade Gdlyan mentions, during a period of a year and ½ it was necessary to replace all the procurators of the union republics and 50 percent of the oblast and rayon procurators. The renewing of the cadres in the militia is measured in the hundreds of thousands. That, comrades, is the course that had to be taken, and it is necessary to speak outright about it, because it is not only themselves who are leaving. We are getting rid of our unsavory individuals, just as Lenin spoke about. (See "Poln. sobr. soch." [Complete Collected Works], Vol 44, pp 397-398). The unfortunate thing is that highly trained, honest people are also begun leaving the law-enforcement agencies, and in greater and greater quantity. Jurists are leaving—and there are 217,000 of them in the country—to go into cooperatives, into easier work, and sometimes under the pressure of—please forgive me—the nonobjectivity in the press.

I am in favor of having the harshest criticism of shortcomings, but the defamation of the jurists and legal experts, our comrades in the law-enforcement agencies, is a serious matter. And it is a large problem. Of course, not only I myself, but also other workers in the party, soviet, and law-enforcement agencies bear the responsibility for this situation. I shall not touch upon any specific cases—for example, the case of A.N. Nagornyuk that arose prior to my time, the case of the "golden boys," or the Pechora cartel, or other cases. Recently we have held firmly to the principle: The Politburo, the Central Committee Secretariat, and the party agencies must transfer to the procurator's and judicial agencies everything that pertains to court cases and the observance of legality—and those agencies will make the final decision. Otherwise our words to the effect that "telephone law" exists, that pressure on the judges on the part of party agencies exists, will be at variance with the deed. We cannot allow this. I shall say to you, Telman Khorenovich, that I shall not go into a detailed analysis now of all your documents. I think that they should be handed over to a commission that we shall create. You and I met twice, we had a detailed conversation, and I said the very same thing that you were told by Mikhail Sergeyevich Gorbachev at a meeting in Moscow. If you feel calm about everything, if your conscience is clear, then you can allow anyone who wants to check to do so: no one will besmirch your name or your work. And that, I think, is how one should raise that question. (Applause).

Second. If we are going to talk about all this, then there are many things that I tried to do, taking advantage, so to speak, of my position as deputy chairman of the presidium of the USSR Supreme Soviet. Telman Khorenovich

Fifth Session
29 May 1989

called me on the telephone and said, "I do not want the Khint case to be considered in the presence of Terebilov. I don't trust Terebilov (former chairman of the Supreme Court)." Telman Khorenovich, I kept my word: Terebilov retired on pension. The question was considered in the absence of Terebilov in the Supreme Court, and 38 judges acquitted Khint. Let's be objective. (Applause).

I am in favor of having only the competent agencies, and only the group of deputies that we elect, engage in this. Deputy Yarin spoke here very actively. His heart aches for this case. So let's include him in the commission. Let those people whose hearts ache for this case, for this so-called "Uzbek" case—I beg for forgiveness by our Uzbek comrades, because it should not be called this, because there is no such case, there is only a group of criminals—let them investigate this case to the ground, to the end, wherever its threads may lead. That is the position of the Politburo and that is the position of the presidium of the Supreme Soviet.

But in general, comrades, I shall speak outright: Whatever a person may be, whether he be a veritable Solomon, whether he be an excellent investigator or an excellent procurator, he cannot cope by himself alone in the fight against crime if society as a whole does not join in the job. This is a very profound social matter. We need a program that declares outright war on crime, a war in which the Komsomol, the party, and all the economic levers will be used. It is impossible to resolve this dilemma in any other way.

So far as I know, the CPSU Central Committee's Commission on Legal Questions recently engaged in this very thoroughly. I am not part of that commission, but I know that all the questions of fighting crime have been concentrated there, on instructions from the Central Committee.

As to whether, Telman Khorenovich, I have the right to occupy a high position, judge not me, but the party's Central Committee and our congress. I have said the whole truth. I have felt and I still feel that the fight against crime is a matter for the entire party and our entire country. One person cannot do much here, regardless of the high position that he occupies.

Do you think that this might be enough, Mikhail Sergeyevich? There are more memoranda, and I can keep on answering and answering.

M.S. Gorbachev: All right. Please take your seat.

(Applause).

We can listen to some more statements before the break, inasmuch as we have alloted five minutes for each. I give the floor to Deputy Ivanov from the Leningrad National-Territorial District. After his statement we will probably take a break.

N.V. Ivanov, investigator for especially important cases, under the USSR General Procurator (Leningrad City National-Territorial Electoral District, RSFSR, city of Moscow): I also have a number of questions to ask the candidate for the position of first deputy chairman of USSR Supreme Soviet, Deputy Lukyanov.

Recently one has noted throughout the country an obvious shift to the right and a departure from democratic gains. The actions of the party apparatus during the election campaign, the latest appearance of the "Yeltsin case," the enactment of the obviously undemocratic 8 April 1988 decree, the slaughter in Tbilisi, the unprecedented political persecution by the entire apparatus of the law-enforcement agencies of the absolutely minuscule investigation group, and other factors—all these things attest to this. You, Anatoliy Ivanovich, are responsible for the domestic policy in the country. We have not heard in your answers any concern with regard to this. I would like for you to answer all these questions more concretely.

Anatoliy Ivanovich, you work as a member of the Politburo. We are constantly assured that unity of opinions and approaches exists in the Politburo. If this is actually so, then your positions and your views do not differ in any way from Comrade Ligachev's views and positions. Is that so?

There is something else. At the present time the state policy is the policy of the complete discontinuation of the fight against crime, regardless of what is said here. The facts attest to that. This process gradually began in approximately 1986. First it was gradually, but now it is proceeding in a thorough-going manner. As of today, you cannot name a single case that has not been completed, localized, or discontinued. At the same time there has been an increase in serious crimes and a reduction in the rate of exposing them. How do you explain that this has become, as of today, the state policy?

Anatoliy Ivanovich, you have not answered the question concerning your attitude to an alternative candidate for this position. Well, in evaluating what has been occurring at the congress over the three-day period, I must state, on behalf of a group of Leningrad delegates, that we completely support Comrade Afanasyev's position, which was given at the last session and in a number of other statements. We feel that time will put everything in its proper place.

Voice from the floor: Who did you name?

STENOGRAPHIC RECORD

Fifth Session
29 May 1989

N.V. Ivanov: I named a number of deputies from Leningrad. There is no need to cause a sensation. Naturally, it is not the entire delegation.

Voice from the floor: (Inaudible).

N.V. Ivanov: A question was asked about the 8 April decree. Did you vote for the enactment of this undemocratic decree or did you not vote? That is, you personally, rather than 39 people as a whole.

One last item: Much has been said here to the effect that, from now on, the party will not interfere in functions that are not within its competency, including the administration of justice. Actually, we have been observing the unceremonious interference into all spheres of activity, including the sphere of investigation. Just read the recent documents. Even what the press has published on the so-called "case of Gdlyan and Ivanov." First there was the Central Committee and KPK [Party Control Committee] commission headed by Comrade Pugo. Then it was transformed into a commission of the presidium of the USSR Supreme Soviet. And then the USSR people's deputies appeared. So I would like to hear more concrete, more precise answers to these questions.

And finally, the voters of Leningrad and Moscow has asked to raise the question of how the undemocratic procedure for holding elections to the USSR Supreme Soviet has led to a situation in which the Soviet of Nationalties does not have a single representative from Moscow or Leningrad, although they were nominated. Naturally, I cannot talk about myself, inasmuch as I will never, under any circumstances, be allowed into that membership. I am perfectly aware that for me this is the last congress. But I also know something else. I have clean hands. I am a person who is convinced of the rightness of his cause, and I know perfectly what course I am taking and what I am saying. Thank you for your attention.

M.S. Gorbachev: Comrades, we will now take a 30-minute break.

(Recess).

M.S. Gorbachev: While the comrades take their seats there will be an opportunity to make an announcement. As you know, after the approval of his credentials every people's deputy is issued with a people's deputy's certificate and badge. The badges are ready. They can be obtained today during the recess in the Georgiyevskiy Hall of the Great Kremlin Palace following the same procedure as for registration. As for the certificates, comrades, there have already been complaints on this score, but you should know that the production of certificates requires a specific technology. There must be photographs and the production process must be observed. A certain amount of time will be required, comrades, because this is a special production. You will apparently receive your certificates once you are back home. That is what I wanted to say. And now we can continue.

Deputy Shundeyev has the floor.

I.N. Shundeyev, director of the "Koyeglinskiy" State Farm, Yetkulskiy Rayon (Kopeyskiy Territorial Electoral Okrug, Chelyabinsk Oblast): Comrade deputies! We are now receiving telephone calls and letters from our voters. When seeing us off here they expected much from us: that we would examine the questions which perturb them. That is why they have asked for answers to three questions.

First. Why is the congress departing from electoral democracy? Why is there no alternative to the candidacy of Anatoliy Ivanovich Lukyanov? Why have we not heard his autobiography and program? A reliable crew should be chosen for the ship of restructuring. But it is not only the captain but also the passengers who must know where our ship will proceed and how when it has run aground. Our future depends on its course.

So I propose that the government be appointed and elected only when deputies have full information about particular candidacies. We must duplicate the biographies and programs of future ministers right now.

Second. The voters also ask you, Mikhail Sergeyevich, to give an answer at the end of the congress about your holding of two responsible posts. How will you cope, where will your activity be focused, who will take your place as general secretary and chairman of the Supreme Soviet if you fall ill? If there is no candidacy, then why? Is that an error, or is it the system?

Stalin shot promising young cadres, Nikita Sergeyevich fired them, Leonid Ilich failed to notice them. Mikhail Sergeyevich does notice them but does not promote them. In 4 years the Politburo has been renewed but has not been rejuvenated in relation to the general secretary. I believe that there should be a continuous succession of young people. Then there will be no artificial shortage of cadres for top posts and no cult figures will be created.

I am amazed at Mikhail Sergeyevich's courage. The party has been losing prestige recently. The same is happening to the Komsomol. Thousands of Communists are leaving the party. An enormous amount of scrupulous work is needed to serry the Communists' ranks and raise the party's prestige. The country is in a grave and

STENOGRAPHIC RECORD

Fifth Session
29 May 1989

protracted economic crisis. A gigantic amount of extreme effort will be needed to lead the country out of economic stagnation. What measures do you propose? Our voters also asked you to talk about that.

And another thing. What document is being prepared to hand over power to the soviets locally, to the local soviets?

And one final thing. The work of the congress is well in hand. The presidium has understood that pressure is not the best method of democracy. That is why I propose that we not depart from the agenda, not be hasty, not direct or control the auditorium. To this end we ask for the second time now that microphones be set up in the gangways and that they be given to the tellers. Everyone must be given the freedom to speak on the agenda.

The standing orders must be observed. Retorts like "demagogue" and so forth must not be hurled. Deputies must be given full information. All members of the presidium should chair the session in turn. Thank you for your attention.

M.S. Gorbachev: Deputy Kudryavtsev has the floor.

V.N. Kudryavtsev, vice president of the USSR Academy of Sciences and director of the USSR Academy of Sciences Institute of State and Law, Moscow City (from the CPSU): Comrades! I am satisfied with Anatoliy Ivanovich Lukyanov's statements so I shall not say anything. It seems to me that the president is assembling his own crew. That is how it is done in many countries. So it seems to me that we have a good and suitable first crew member. He is a lawyer with top qualifications. (Applause). He is a doctor of juridical sciences. I should say that he did not defend his doctorate with us. (He is not a lawyer in the same field as me: I am a criminologist, he is a political scientist.) He defended his doctorate at Moscow State University. I don't know how he manages to engage in scientific work, because as far as I know his work day is 16 hours. And in my opinion, Anatoliy Ivanovich, unless I am wrong, you are violating labor legislation in the most flagrant manner, because you have probably had no leave since 1985. But that is a shortcoming of the president's work. The president should allow his deputies to go on leave.

As for the growth of crime, I shall also say nothing about that; now is neither the place nor the time. But I want to say that in this auditorium probably, if you take people of my age, then in my opinion at least 10 percent have had relatives who were once repressed. I should not personally like a repetition of this picture in the eighties and nineties. That is what worries me in all this story about crime and legality. We do not need a mafia, we do not need racketeering, we do not need robbers and bandits. Nor do we need investigators who interrogate us in contravention of legality; we do not need people who can arrest our relatives and children and demand that a man incriminate himself. (Tumultuous applause).

M.S. Gorbachev: Deputy Medvedev has the floor.

Voice from the floor: Krasnoyarsk.

R.A. Medvedev, author, Moscow (Voroshilovskiy Territorial Electoral District, Moscow): First of all I want to say that I do not consider it to be necessary for a deputy chairman of the Supreme Soviet to discuss his own program that differs from the program of the chairman of the Supreme Soviet. (Applause). One of the previous speakers here told us that if we have elected a person who will sail our ship of state, we must also, with complete knowledge, select this kind of crew. But I would add that it is the kind of crew that will sail that ship of state (when, for example, the captain is resting) in the same direction, rather than in the opposite direction. Because during the past three years, as a historian, I have observed that as soon as Mikhail Sergeyevich Gorbachev, who previously, as the head of the party, had actually been the head of the government, goes on a vacation or makes a trip abroad, the entire state policy, both in the area of ideology and in many other areas, changes, and it changes by 50, 60, or sometimes even 180 degrees. (Applause).

That's how it was in 1987, when Mikhail Sergeyevich's vacation was extended because he was writing a book. It was then that articles began appearing in our newspapers (not only in SOVETSKAYA ROSSIYA, but even in PRAVDA)—articles that are completely in agreement with Andreyeva's article "I Cannot Waive My Principles." In August, September, and early October 1987 the entire intelligentsia was concerned about what was happening. Had our party begun to carry out a completely different policy? It was only when Mikhail Sergeyevich returned to his desk that the intelligentsia began breathing more freely—the policy that began to be continued was the previous one.

But in December Mikhail Sergeyevich flew to Washington to sign the Soviet-American Treaty and he stayed over in Washington. And at that time, in December, strange things began to happen in our ideological work. One member of the CPSU Central Committee's Politburo gathered together the representatives of the mass media and gave them certain instructions, and a week later another Politburo member gathered the representatives of the mass media and gave them completely opposite instructions. And we all observed this in the press, and we saw everything. For example, in December the rehabilitations of Bukharin and the entire group linked with Bukharin, which had already been planned by the USSR Supreme Court, were postponed until a definite time. As an historian, I knew that those rehabilitations would occur, but I could not wait to see them. They occurred only after the negotiations in Washington

STENOGRAPHIC RECORD

Fifth Session

29 May 1989

ended and Comrade Gorbachev returned from Washington to Moscow. In March Comrade Gorbachev flew to Yugoslavia, and Comrade Yakovlev flew to Mongolia, and after about a week, once again, the policy of our party and our government, both in the ideological area and in all other areas, changed. And what appeared was not an article by Nina Andreyeva, but the policy of Nina Andreyeva, which introduced divisiveness and doubts into all the ideological services and into our country's intelligentsia. And it was necessary for Comrade Gorbachev to return from Yugoslavia and for Comrade Yakovlev to return from Mongolia, and for rather large-scale, sharp, and dramatic meetings to occur before, finally, the policy of restructuring triumphed. So we need the kind of deputy who will continue our ship's movement along the assigned course, rather than having it veer from side to side. (Applause). And even quite recently, when Mikhail Sergeyevich flew to Cuba and England and had just returned, dramatic events, in violation of the Constitution, occurred in Georgia on the night of 8-9 April. A state of martial law was imposed in violation of the USSR Constitution by the local authorities, rather than by the USSR Supreme Soviet, as is supposed to be the procedure. A few people were in a very big hurry and said, "Gorbachev is sleeping, so let's break up the demonstration now." That is certainly what happened, because we still do not know who in Moscow gave such a sanction, but certainly someone in Moscow had indeed given such a sanction. If it was not Lukyanov and it was not Gorbachev, as they have said, then there are probably present right here in this auditorium people who were informed about what was happening in Tbilisi, but who are remaining silent today. I would like to know who these people are.

Therefore, when selecting the head of state, which, in general, is not such an uninfluential position as the chairman of the presidium of the Supreme Soviet and his deputy used to be (as, of course, we know, that was a purely formal position), and when granting tremendous powers to these people, we must actually select persons who completely trust one another. Mikhail Sergeyevich has been a bit shy here. He said that he knows Comrade Lukyanov from having worked together over the course of the past few months. As an historian, I can say that I have had the occasion to read many old newspapers, and I have come across evidence that they have been acquainted for a much longer period of time. Even when examining the bound volumes of the MOSKOVSKIY UNIVERSITET newspaper for 1950-1955, I came across several curious items in which both Lukyanov's name and Gorbachev's name appear. There was, for example, an item stating that a Komsomol meeting in the Law School had elected a Komsomol committee in which, in the training and indoctrination sector, the person who was elected chairman was student Lukyanov, and the person who was elected his deputy was student Gorbachev. (Applause). As was the student custom at that time, the newspaper did not mention their names and patronymics, but I think that I would not be making a mistake by saying that these are the very same Lukyanov and Gorbachev whom we are electing today in a different order. Therefore I feel that we must unanimously elect Comrade Lukyanov. (Applause).

M.S. Gorbachev: Deputy Solntsev has the floor.

R.Kh. Solntsev, writer, Krasnoyarsk City (Kirovskiy Territorial Electoral Okrug, Krasnoyarsk Kray): Good day, good evening, I'm losing track. The difference between here and Krasnoyarsk is 4-5 hours, comrades. We are receiving telephone calls from Siberia around the clock. Last night, too, the Siberians called. In general, we go to sleep at 0100 hours or 0200 hours. Moscow time, and wake up at 0400 hours or 0500 hours. By that time people at home in Siberia are already up and about. So it is not surprising that our heads ache; we constantly receive instructions, and our pockets are full of telegrams. But we are not let up here, probably because we are sitting a long way away and, moreover, we are not bold enough, or something. However, we all know what happens when petroleum, gas, gold, fur pelts, and so forth are needed; we recall the fine words of the great man who said that Siberia will make the might of the Russian state grow, yet when we want to say something, all our notes get lost. I think I am only the second person from our region to be given the floor, and I am very grateful to the congress presidium for this opportunity.

Now about Anatoliy Ivanovich Lukyanov's candidacy. It goes without saying that Mikhail Sergeyevich Gorbachev has the unquestioned right to present his deputy to us, a man who stands in for him when he is away, a man with whom he finds it easy to work and on whom he can rely. But I believe that here, at the first USSR Congress of People's Deputies, we must be frank with each other (just like at the Last Judgement); we must speak to each other honestly and openly. It would be wrong to simply vote; if something is bothering you, you should get it off your chest. I recall Academician Sakharov's statement the day before yesterday, and I would like to go along with his quiet yet very strict words and add three points of my own. What about? About the discrepancies in the decrees in question, imprecise terms, and incorrect formulations, although they were drawn up by jurists and Anatoliy Ivanovich himself is a highly educated jurist with a brilliant command of language. We have only just heard him speak, he is a truly remarkable speaker. But why in these decrees does one article contradict another, and why are there, or rather were there, phrases whose presence was simply incomprehensible, because they were an insult to the age of restructuring? I ask myself, could this be an oversight? There is a great deal of work; Comrade Lukyanov has not been in his post long. But it is strange to presume an oversight or inattention on the part of a man vested with such tremendous power. So it probably must be the result of endless compromises, yes? We understand, there is no complete unanimity, nor should there be; there is pressure from the left, pressure from the right. Clearly, the constantly arising need for changes and amendments means that the end result is neither fish, flesh, nor fowl—in practice the decree can be interpreted any way you like.

Fifth Session
29 May 1989

And last but not least, perhaps this is done on purpose so people can act as they see fit. If the leadership in a specific place is noble, it will accordingly make noble use of the decree, but if it is in the Stalinist mold, it will hit out wildly, as we have witnessed recently in some parts of our country. These are the three points which I wanted to make because I cannot understand the reasons for the imprecision in all these decrees of the last year. This is all I would like to know.

And one more thing. I would be very reluctant to see us speaking on behalf of each other. Academician Meshalkin has spoken several times here; he seems to be more congenial somehow. However, I do not want him to speak on behalf of all the Siberians. (Applause). I would also like to say that I, too, have received many telegrams, and I would like to read you one of them. Probably I will not have another opportunity to come up here, but perhaps we will be given a chance to have a say on Mikhail Sergeyevich's report? The Siberians have a great deal to say. Some people may think that out there in Siberia, working in the wind and the frost, we merely wave our arms about shouting "Heave ho!" or "Hoist!" and that we have nothing to say. This is not correct, in my view. Let me read this: "We voters elected the deputies not because of their names, party membership, or posts; what we elected was a program. And we cannot understand what this full consolidation is all about. We expect observance of democratic principles and we did not empower deputies to put pressure on alternative candidates. This is illegal and unethical. The feeling is that the deputies doing the pressurizing should be recalled right now. We can do without the cultivation of another person 'loved and respected by all, full of creative powers,' and so on. I would say in this connection that I voted and would vote again for Mikhail Sergeyevich Gorbachev. Other candidates on our ship are a different matter. Let us take a risk for once in our lives and let there be alternatives. Are there no other clever, able, fine, educated doctors of sciences and so on? Do we only have Anatoliy Ivanovich? A remarkable man, a clever man, but is there no one else? (Applause). Nikolay Gumilev wrote: The sun has been halted by words and words have occupied cities. We judge not by words, but by actions. I have tried to assess Anatoliy Ivanovich by his actions. Finally, comrades, please don't send all the country's dregs, if you will excuse the expression, to us in Siberia. (Applause).

M.S. Gorbachev: Comrade Yakubov, deputy from Uzbekistan, has the floor.

A. Yakubov, first secretary of the Uzbekistan Writers Union Board, Tashkent (from the USSR Writers Union): Dear comrades! I will say right away that I, like the majority of deputies from Uzbekistan (I say majority and not everyone, because one deputy here told me that he does not support Comrade Lukyanov as candidate for the post of the country's vice president), support Comrade Lukyanov's candidacy, if only because he was nominated by Mikhail Sergeyevich Gorbachev, whom we unanimously elected head of state. I have some questions for Anatoliy Ivanovich. We talk a lot about a rule-of-law state; we have been talking about it for some years, and we are now tired of talking about it. Our entire press, scientists, and the creative intelligentsia are requesting the speedier adoption of laws on the institution of the defense attorney, on the independence of judges, and on removing investigators from oversight by the prosecutor's office. Why has this grand and noble matter, so essential to the people, been postponed, why is the adoption of these laws being delayed? It is a question that concerns our entire public, particularly people who know from their own bitter experience what a breach of the rule of law is. Much has been said in the press about investigations sometimes dragging on for 5 years or more and being sanctioned by the USSR Supreme Soviet Presidium, in which you are number two. It has also been written that the Supreme Soviet Presidium has no right to do this. It is not something I am saying, it has been said many times in the press. What would you say about it? That is my second question.

Judging by the newspapers this kind of illegality was also manifested in the so-called "Uzbek affair." Today Anatoliy Ivanovich Lukyanov even said, with some embarrassment, that the affair had been turned into the "Uzbek affair"—a case of embezzlers. I agree that the actions of both sides—both the embezzlers and those who are supposed to judge them—must be based on the law and on the law alone. (Noise in the hall). Perhaps I have not put it very grammatically; please excuse me, I am not a Russian....

But the report published in the press under the rubric "At The Supreme Soviet Presidium" regarding the work of the commission on this affair makes nothing clear, comrades. Everything is shrouded in a kind of strange mist. What is going on? If you do not want to answer this question it would be a good idea if one of the members of the Supreme Soviet commission were to answer it before we set up the commission today.

And since I will be unable to mount this lofty platform again today I want to say a couple more words. We Uzbeks are not a vindictive people; we are a quiet, submissive, shy people. Both Gdlyan and Ivanov know this. I think that in any other republic—if this orgy had taken place in some other region, the people there would have behaved differently. But since the "Uzbek affair" has been stirred up, there should also be deputies from Uzbekistan on the commission. We want an honest solution of this very complex affair. Made more complex by the fact that it has been said several times in the press that since the big publicity for Gdlyan and Ivanov on television and radio, investigators have begun to compete in the press. Why, they say, can they imprison and expose people and achieve amazing results and we can't? You will agree this is very dangerous, comrades, for society. So I propose two of our deputies—Erkin Yusupovich Yusupov, vice president of the Uzbek SSR Academy of Sciences, and Akhmedzhan Gulyamovich

Fifth Session
29 May 1989

Mukhtarov, first secretary of the Uzbekistan Journalists Union—as members of the commission. They are honest and, I repeat, unprejudiced people who will adopt a totally (Comrade Gdlyan need not worry) honest position, who will not take sides and are capable of being completely objective. I make this proposal on behalf of, on this occasion, the absolute majority of deputies from Uzbekistan. Thank you. (Applause).

M.S. Gorbachev: Deputy Kalashnikov has the floor.

From the floor: We can't hear.

S.F. Kalashnikov, deputy director for work with young people at the Bobruysk F.E. Dzerzhinskiy Sewn Goods Factory, Belorussian SSR, Mogilev Oblast, Bobruysk City (from the Komsomol): Esteemed comrade chairman of the USSR Supreme Soviet, esteemed comrade people's deputies! On instructions from the Komsomol and a number of young deputies from the territories I would like to set forth to the congress our positions on the candidacy of the first deputy chairman of the Supreme Soviet now under discussion.

While not doubting in principle the correctness of the choice of Comrade Lukyanov for this post, we would like to express our doubt with regard to one of Comrade Lukyanov's statements, which in our opinion is of fundamental importance and which has been reflected in the course of the congress itself. In response to a question about the reasons for such uneven work at the congress Comrade Lukyanov voiced the thesis that the presidium gave freedom for initiative in preparing pre-congress documents to local delegates. We also prepared for the congress, and for this purpose we held a 10-day consultative meeting of 120 young deputies at which a series of proposals was elaborated on questions of the agenda, the standing orders, and the mechanism for forming the congress working organs and its commissions and committees. They were all passed on in written form to the USSR Supreme Soviet Presidium.

During the young deputies' talk with Comrade Lukyanov we were promised that our proposals would be taken into consideration. And the comment was made that the Supreme Soviet Presidium should not be deprived of its right to prepare the congress. We agreed with that comment. But as far as we know not one of our comments or proposals was taken into consideration. Nonetheless we continued to work and we are now ready to put on the presidium table a number of specific proposals, for instance our draft statute on a committee for youth affairs. You yourselves can understand how much this perturbs us. But we have no certainty now that these proposals of ours will not be buried by the presidium, as has happened with individual proposals of ours and the proposals of individual deputies at the congress.

We have rejected what were in my view sensible proposals that Comrade Gorbachev's report be heard and that he then be elected. As a result we have gotten a variation on Mikhail Sergeyevich Gorbachev's report in question and answer form. We rejected the proposal on the principle for forming the Supreme Soviet: Does a deputy have the right in principle to put forward his own candidacy for the Supreme Soviet, or is that only the right of the territorial group of deputies, although the Constitution has nothing to say on the subject and gives us complete freedom here? As a result we got the problem of the group of deputies from Nagorno-Karabakh. Today we rejected what was in my view a sensible proposal for the procedure for the nomination of people for our country's top state posts. And as a result we have gotten what is in my view a highly dubious mechanism for elections to these top echelons of power. And I ask you not to forget that we will all no longer be able to tell our voters: Dear comrades, you know we took part in this. And this coincidence may be pure chance, but in my view it makes us very suspicious. And this is above all a question for you, Comrade Lukyanov, as the man who prepared the congress and exerts the most direct influence on the progress and movement of the congress' work.

And another thing. So that we deputies from the young people can vote for you with awareness, Comrade Lukyanov, we must know how deep your understanding is of the very serious political and socioeconomic problems of our country's young people, and how far you are prepared to go to meet deputies from young people in resolving these problems. Because our first meeting with you has so far failed to dispel our doubts. As a proposal (so that Anatoliy Ivanovich does not have to stand up again to answer our questions) I am prepared to have a working discussion of these questions with him, together with a group of young deputies. Thank you for your attention. (Applause).

M.S. Gorbachev: The floor is given to Comrade Lukyanov to answer the questions.

A.I. Lukyanov: Some of the questions have been asked in the statements, and some of the questions have been presented in memoranda. I would like, if possible, simply to answer briefly, in order to save your time.

Deputy Ivanov from Leningrad says that I am responsible for the domestic policy in the country. I must tell you, comrades, that the responsibility for the domestic policy in our country is borne by the Politburo, by our government, by the presidium as a whole, and that the first deputy has many other functions, but that only our congress can be responsible for domestic policy as a whole, and only our government can be responsible.

But when Comrade Ivanov says that we have a state policy aimed at discontinuing the fight against crime, please forgive me, but I categorically disagree with that. On the contrary, our entire policy currently must be concentrated not on discontinuing, but on extending the fight against crime. And that is the firm position of the Politburo, of the presidium of the Supreme Soviet, and

STENOGRAPHIC RECORD

Fifth Session

29 May 1989

of the government. I want to say only that in this sense no one has a self-interest in discontinuing any legal proceedings or exerting pressure on anyone. The only thing we want is to work with clean hands. That is the most important thing.

You say that pressure was exerted on the Telman Gdlyan group, but I, on the other hand, say that the offer was made twice to Comrade Gdlyan, to Deputy Gdlyan, to give a statement in response to these questions—both in PRAVDA and in IZVESTIYA. That was reported in our newspapers. No such statement followed. And there were no published items about their group between the announcement of the creation of the committee and the report on its results.

I am very grateful to Comrade Kudryavtsev, who mentioned here the rehabilitation of persons who had been illegally repressed. I am a member of that commission, and I consider it by duty to assure that everyone who was illegally repressed during the Stalin years has all his rights restored. I shall say only that recently that commission has been receiving a rather large number—no less than 5 percent—of complaints from persons who would like to be rehabilitated, but who had been hirelings of the fascists, had been members of bandit groups, etc. The Central Committee's commission cannot take such action, and you understand the reasons why.

Incidentally, comrades, I am very grateful to Comrade Solntsev from Krasnoyarsk, who says, "Don't send all these worthless individuals to us in Siberia." It turns out that entire areas are jam-packed with these people and then it is very difficult to establish order there.

I want to answer individually Comrade Yakubov with regard to questions concerning the fact that for a long period of time the presidium sanctioned the extension of the periods for keeping prisoners under guard by more than nine months. Actually, that practice did exist. True, it was gradually reduced. It was reduced, and it went down from hundreds to probably dozens of instances, but nevertheless this practice of extending the time periods for maintaining people under guard did exist, including for these kinds of difficult and complicated cases. Because difficulties often arise when a case consisting of many volumes has to fit within the time frame for both the procuracy and the investigator. Recently, on the insistence of Mikhail Sergeyevich Gorbachev, we rejected this practice, despite all the pressure that is being exerted on us. But I feel that if such cases occur (and, as a jurist, I know that they will), then it is necessary to do this not by a procedure of making exceptions to the law, but on the basis of a law that the Supreme Soviet will enact.

Comrade Kalashnikov spoke here about a consultative meeting with deputies from the All-Union Komsomol. Actually, we did have a meeting. We took into consideration some of the things in their proposals, and we failed to take into consideration some other things. But I want to say that we are planning to create a USSR Supreme Soviet committee on youth matters. This is already known to the deputies. In addition, we took action and agreed that one of the first laws that would be enacted by the Supreme Soviet will be the USSR Law on Youth. Although the expenditures for that law, according to our first computations, constitute a very considerable, very large amount of month. It will be necessary to calculate the cost of the law. It will be necessary for us in general to calculate the cost of laws. How much do they cost? How much do promises cost? How much do mandates cost? We have always become accustomed to considering this.

"During the time when you were working as Central Committee secretary, did you ever receive any complaints and warning reports, or any other information, about mistakes and abuses, as was reported in the press, concerning the case of the Gdlyan group?" That question is asked by Comrade Kim—a deputy.

Yes, comrades, we did receive them. We received a rather large number of them. I must say that at the first stage we trusted that group very much. Therefore a few announcements were prepared. But then it became clear that some of the announcements had not been sent to us, but were still sitting around in that group. When that process changed over from quantity to quality, at that time there had only been created at first a KPK commission under the CPSU Central Committee. But as soon as it touched upon questions of procedural matters, it immediately transferred all the questions to a special commission under the leadership of the general procurator, about which you read. So they were received.

"What is your personal attitude toward Article 11-1 that was adopted on 8 April?" I voted in favor of that article in the version in which it exists. But when people began to think more deeply about it, to find out whether it provided the authorities with a free hand, we realized there was a definite free hand here, and that therefore the article had to be corrected. The legislator never gives a promissory note that he will not become wiser. That is correct.

It is asked here that when Article 11-1 is corrected (comrades Deputy Kazannik and Deputy Solntsev asked the question), will it be necessary to preserve it at all? I feel that the article in this decree that deals with actions that are linked with the propagandizing of violence and the overthrowing of the Soviet authority—and we are speaking not about propagandizing, but specifically about actions—and another article, dealing with actions linked with the incitement of interethnic enmity—these article should be preserved in the version in which they exist. It is possible to make a few corrections there, as Andrey Dmitriyevich has said here, if one is dealing specifically with the deliberate, violent overthrow of the Soviet authority. But I think that the word "overthrow" itself implies violent actions.

STENOGRAPHIC RECORD

FIRST CONGRESS OF PEOPLE'S DEPUTIES OF THE USSR

Fifth Session

29 May 1989

"What is your attitude personally to the possibility of an alternative holding of an election?" It is generally known that there are no irreplaceable individuals, and that the possibility of an alternative is, from my point of view, a necessary principle in a democratic society. I think that both the Politburo and the Central Committee plenum apparently chose possible versions before making the proposal that they did, and I take a respectful and obliging attitude toward that proposal. (Applause).

And, comrades, this is the last thing that I want to say. There have been several questions here about what the correlation is between the party and the agencies of state authority: "How will you, as the first deputy chairman, construct the interrelationships with the Politburo?" "What is your attitude toward the Politburo at this stage of restructuring?" "What is the role of the Supreme Soviet and the Politburo?" etc.

I will tell you plainly, comrades, that it is the correlation between policy and authority. The Politburo defines the main line along which we are traveling. The problems linked with the actions of the Politburo are the problems of restructuring, the directions to be taken by restructuring, and the discovery of the very term and concept of restructuring. That is policy. And that policy must be defined in the plan, in the budget, in the laws. This is the activity of the highest agencies of authority. Therefore, if we are to talk seriously, whoever wants in some way to introduce discord into the interrelationships between the party and the Supreme Soviet, between the Communists at our congress and the Communists in the Supreme Soviet, is acting, to put it mildly, rashly. It is only thanks to this party that this policy was worked out. It is only thanks to this party that the single Union of Soviet Socialist Republics exists, because no other force can unite it (applause) and only in that party, our Politburo, that there is an opportunity (thank God, I have also seen the work of other compositions of the Politburo), there is an opportunity to argue freely, to compare positions freely, but to develop a single policy. It is only thanks to the party and its unity, and under its leadership, that we can go forward. Only then will our state authority, and the Congress of Soviets, and the Supreme Soviet, work in a real manner. (Applause).

M.S. Gorbachev: I must inform you about a situation that happened at 1300 hours. I am enabled to do this by all the notes that have been transmitted to be from the secretariat, including one memorandum.

Some of the comrades have spoken. There are three more packages. These are the persons who have registered to make a statement. I have announced the statement by Comrade Starovoytov, and now we shall decide what to do after that. I am publicizing the contents of a letter from the deputies from Kazakhstan. They feel that the question about the first deputy as a result of the discussion has now been clarified, and that it might be possible to determine our position and make a decision on this question. In view of the fundamental nature of the question, let us now arrive at an answer so that we will be united in this matter.

Shall we discontinue the exchange of opinions on this question, comrades? Those who agree with this decision, please raise your credentials. Please lower them. Who is against it? There are some, a few. Who has abstained? There are some, but an obvious minority. The question is decided.

Voice from the floor: (Inaudible).

M.S. Gorbachev: You are putting me in an awkward position.

Voice from the floor: (Inaudible).

M.S. Gorbachev: Please turn on the first microphone.

V.A. Palm, department head, Tartu State University, Tartu (Keyla National-Territorial Electoral District, Estonian SSR): There are memoranda there, in which questions have been asked. Simply questions that have been briefly formulated. I also have a question there. I think that it would be proper of answers were given to all the questions.

M.S. Gorbachev: I understand. You would like, when making a statement, to ask questions, but requests like that....

V.A. Palm: I do not want to make a statement. The question is written there. I simply want to get an answer to the question. A brief answer to a brief question.

M.S. Gorbachev: All right. But let's consider that we have made the decision. Now there is a request....

Voice from the floor: The Lithuanian deputies request the floor.

M.S. Gorbachev: Do you insist? All right.

Comrades, in principle, then, the question has been resolved. We still have three problems remaining. There is a written question which Anatoliy Ivanovich has been asked to answer. Now the deputies of Lithuania, as I understand it, by two-thirds insist, as we have given the right according to the standing rules, that they nevertheless be allowed to speak. And, finally, the deputies from Georgia also insist on being given the floor. From the deputies from Azerbaijan, the presidium member is now talking about making a statement....

P.A. Azizbekova, director of the Museum of the History of Azerbaijan, Baku (Baku-Azizbekov National-Territorial District, Azerbaijan SSR): It is not myself personally....

STENOGRAPHIC RECORD

Fifth Session

29 May 1989

M.S. Gorbachev: Yes, yes, it's a request from the delegation. Therefore this is how the situation looks: We can feel that the question has been decided, but now, in conformity with the standing rules, we must give the floor to the deputies from Lithuania, to the deputies from Georgia, and must answer the written question, as I understand it, from the Estonian group of deputies and give the floor to the deputy from Azerbaijan. This, if you will recall, corresponds to our Standing Rules, and we must implement this. Isn't that so? All right. Let us then give the floor to the representative of Lithuania. (Commotion in the auditorium).

M.S. Gorbachev: Forgive me, comrades. The floor is given to Deputy Starovoytov, and then the deputy from Lithuania will make a statement.

V.K. Starovoytov, chairman of the Rassvet Orlovskiy Collective Farm, Belorussian SSR, Mogilev Oblast, Kirovskiy Rayon (from the All-Union Organization of War and Labor Veterans): Dear comrade deputies! I am on the side of those who agree with the point of view that the person who should be the first deputy chairman of the Supreme Soviet is the candidate who is proposed by Mikhail Sergeyevich Gorbachev. That is the majority of the opinions of the delegates from Belorussia. Thank you for your attention. (Applause).

M.S. Gorbachev: The deputy from Lithuania will now please take the floor.

E.B. Bichkauskas, investigator for especially important cases, Lithuanian SSR Procuracy, Vilnius (Shilute National-Territorial Electoral District, Lithuanian SSR): Dear congress! Dear Anatoliy Ivanovich! Perhaps my question will be incomprehensible to the majority of the deputies, but your answer will certainly largely explain the processes that have been occurring in the Baltic area, processes that are being reflected in an obvious incomplete and incorrect way in the central press, and will also explain the position of the majority of the deputies from Lithuania. The answer to this question is extremely important for the entire Baltic area, for our voters, and is extremely important when creating a rule-of-law state, which should not be created on illegal foundations.

Before voting, the deputies from Lithuania and, I think, from a number of other republics, would like to learn your position relative to the Ribbentrop-Molotov pact and the additional secret agreements between the USSR and fascist Germany, as a consequence of which, in 1940, sovereign Lithuania and the other Baltic republics were occupied and incorporated into the USSR, thus losing their independent statehood. (Applause).

M.S. Gorbachev: The next speaker will be the deputy from Georgia.

T.V. Gamkrelidze, director of the Institute of Eastern Studies, Georgian SSR Academy of Sciences, Tbilisi (Akhalshenskiy National-Territorial Electoral District, Adzhar ASSR): We, a group of USSR people's deputies from Georgia, feel that that an unsatisfactory reply was given by Comrade Anatoliy Ivanovich Lukyanov to the question concerning the events in Tbilisi, relative to the fact that the presidium of the USSR Supreme Soviet did not know anything, and did not find out about the events until 6 hours after the tragedy that had occurred in Tbilisi. I propose to tell about this in my special statement.

But at the present time we feel that it is necessary, at this stage in the work of our congress, to set forth the "Position of the USSR People's Deputies from Georgia to the First Congress."

The USSR people's deputies from the Georgian republic feel that the tragedy that occurred in Tbilisi on 9 April 1989 is a crime not only against the Georgian nation, but also against all the nations of the Soviet Union and against mankind in general. This question must become the object of special discussion at the USSR Congress of People's Deputies.

The fundamental restructuring of the social and economic life of the USSR depends upon a substantial change in the country's entire political structure. In the light of this principle, with respect to Georgian SSR the questions that arise first of all are the following questions of a fundamental nature. Namely, censuring the annexation of the independent, democratic Georgian republic in February 1921, as a crude violation of the 7 May 1920 Treaty that had been approved by Vladimir Ilich Lenin, which Treaty had been concluded between completely equal, sovereign states: democratic Georgia and Soviet Russia. The recognition of the absolutely fundamental principles of that Treaty as being legally valid and, under the present-day conditions, as a guarantee for assuring the real and complete sovereignty of the Georgian Soviet Republic.

In the Georgian SSR all the interethnic questions must be resolved by proceeding from the interests of all the nationalities residing in the republic, on the basis of brotherhood, mutual respect, and political, economic, and social justice. (This group of questions, Anatoliy Ivanovich, apparently includes the question of the Meskhet Turks, which you touched upon here.)

Taking into consideration the mandates of their constituents, the deputies from Georgia feel that there is a vital need to resolve immediately the question of the performance of military duties by the young people residing on the territory of Georgian SSR, in accordance with their desire, within the confines of their own republic. (Applause).

It is necessary in every way to support all the positive processes of restructuring and glasnost that are aimed at the democratization of social life and the creation of a rule-of-law state.

Fifth Session

29 May 1989

We hope that these questions will become the object of discussion in the activities of the first deputy chairman of the USSR Supreme Soviet immediately after his possible election. Thank you. (Applause).

M.S. Gorbachev: I think we are now going to give the floor to the deputies from Azerbaijan, but a representative of Tajikistan here is firmly insisting that they also have a two-thirds majority and requests that Negmatulloyev be allowed to speak afterwards. That is all in keeping with our standing orders. Please introduce yourself.

G.I. Isayev, first secretary of Nakhichevan Azerbaijan Communist Party Oblast Committee, Nakhichevan City (Vanandskiy National-Territorial Electoral Okrug, Nakhichevan ASSR): Esteemed comrade deputies, on behalf of the people's deputies of the Azerbaijan SSR I have been instructed to call on you to support Mikhail Sergeyevich Gorbachev's request that Comrade Anatoliy Ivanovich Lukyanov be confirmed as first deputy chairman of the USSR Supreme Soviet.

Comrade Lukyanov is well known as one of the country's leading statesmen. He has devoted many years to work to improve the Soviet Union's state system and possesses great experience and deep theoretical knowledge in the sphere of Soviet state building. All this wealth of practical and theoretical knowledge will undoubtedly be useful in his activity as first deputy chairman of the USSR Supreme Soviet. Comrade Lukyanov's answers to the questions put to him confirm once again his high level of professional competence and great sense of responsibility to the people.

In describing Anatoliy Ivanovich his personal qualities have to be noted. He is a man of great erudition and practical experience and exceptional kindness, decency, and principle. All the aforementioned allows us to ask you to confirm Anatoliy Ivanovich Lukyanov as first deputy chairman of the USSR Supreme Soviet.

I would like to use this opportunity to convey to you briefly the content of the thousands upon thousands of telegrams and telephone calls which we deputies are receiving from our voters. The telegrams and telephone calls express bewilderment over the statements made by Deputy Starovoytova, scientific staffer from Moscow and deputy from Yerevan. I will venture to observe that her obstinate presentation of herself as a specialist on interethnic relations is scarcely justified. At any rate her attempts to analyze the problems of the Nagorno-Karabakh Autonomous Oblast cannot be adjudged a success. We are also receiving thousands of telegrams from our voters who are offended by the unprecedentedly provocative nature of Deputy Igityan's speech. That speech has caused serious complications in the situation in the republic which could have unpredictable consequences. Party, state, and public organizations in the republic are making enormous efforts to restore the normal rhythm of life. Such statements and speeches make you think that some people want to drag us into fruitless debates and divert us from discussing the items on the congress agenda. (Applause).

M.S. Gorbachev: Deputy Negmatulloyev of the Tajik SSR has the floor.

S.Kh. Negmatulloyev, president of the Tajik SSR Academy of Sciences, Dushanbe City (Kurgan-Tyubinskiy Territorial Electoral Okrug, Tajik SSR): Esteemed deputies, on Saturday we were unable to define our position and, I can honestly confess to you, we were somewhat at a loss, so to speak, and unable to give our voters a clear answer to the question—who will be elected? We knew that the president should, of course, pick his own team. We were aware that there are principles of compatability. And we know that this principle is always observed in such major posts of responsibility. We knew that Comrade Lukyanov took part in the drafting of the concept of the rule-of-law state. And we all remember that all this was approved at the 19th all-union party conference. And even the fact that we have assembled here is also a feature of the implementation of that concept. And today, when we heard Anatoliy Ivanovich Lukyanov's speech and answers to questions, all our deputation unanimously came to the conclusion that we would cast our votes for him and enjoin everyone to support his candidacy.

I would like to use this opportunity to say that we too are constantly receiving instructions from our voters. The first thing we are told is: "Speed up the solution of the procedural processes and move on to practical work." The principal thing that worries my voters is that Tajikistan, where the major rivers of Central Asia have their source and where there are colossal stocks of drinking water and huge glaciers, nevertheless has whole regions which are not not provided with ordinary drinking water.

The second problem, and I think that a number of delegations will support me here, is that we live in very active seismic areas, and the recent tragedy in Armenia and Tajikistan has shown that we nevertheless do not work and live in very safe buildings. I therefore urge deputies to adopt a law ensuring the safety of people living in seismically active regions.

Once again, on behalf of the Tajik delegation, I would prevail upon you to vote for Anatoliy Ivanovich Lukyanov. Thank you for your attention. (Applause).

M.S. Gorbachev: Comrades, following the example of Lithuania, an envoy of the Kazakhstan deputies has been here. They insist not by a two-thirds majority but unanimously that they be allowed to take the floor. Comrade Gorbunov, our representative in charge of liaison with the secretariat, reports that the deputies from Turkmenistan are also insisting that they be allowed to speak. We

Fifth Session

29 May 1989

should allow them to do so, albeit briefly. Deputy Galina Aleksandrovna Amangeldinova from Kazakhstan will then speak, followed by Roza Bazarova from Turkmenistan.

G.A. Amangeldinova, teacher at Secondary School No 22, Kazakh SSR, Pavlodar City (from USSR trade unions): Esteemed comrade chairman of the Supreme Soviet! Esteemed comrade deputies! You know that Anatoliy Ivanovich Lukyanov has not been working in this post for long. But the situation has changed radically with Comrade Lukyanov's arrival. You have heard this quite well for yourselves. I think that there is no alternative for the post of first deputy. That is why I shall mention this once more. In addition Comrade Lukyanov is a doctor of juridical sciences, he has a great deal of experience, the most tremendous experience of political work.

But I want to draw your attention to something toward which some speakers are pushing us. And not for the first day. I want to say, Comrade Gdlyan, that when you spoke it did you no particular credit. Of course, we have all followed the progress of the cases of which you were in charge and you had tremendous authority there. But today you looked rather insipid with your questions. I also want to say that Comrade Ivanov delivered an ignorant statement today. (Applause).

I don't think that many Leningraders or Muscovites will fall into the abyss into which you are drawing them. After all, the question is being raised of repealing laws which guarantee order when they are observed. We are being pushed toward disorders, toward lack of control, and this is being spoken of as democracy. Tell me, comrades, how should this be understood? As a condition where no one will have guarantees or protection—neither ordinary people nor we, the people's deputies? But in other countries there are such laws and order is safeguarded. Yet in our country order is obviously not to everyone's liking. There are even statements suggesting that the Politburo members should not sit there. But is the question of where the Politburo sits such an important question today? They are sitting there, so let them sit there. For instance, I.... (Noise in the auditorium). In the situation which has taken shape at the congress, as a woman I am even afraid to sit among those Moscow delegates who spoke in the 1st 3 days. (Animation in the hall).

Comrade deputies, in our overwhelming majority we elected the chairman of the USSR Supreme Soviet and thereby put our trust in him. So, in accordance with the Constitution, it is his right to propose his own deputy. He has proposed him and I urge you, comrades, to support Mikhail Sergeyevich Gorbachev's proposal and give him our support as deputies. (Applause).

And now I have something else to say—on behalf of many women. Comrade men and deputies, if we work at this rate.... The vacation is beginning in the schools and we women have to go home, so let's work in a businesslike way. (Applause).

M.S. Gorbachev: The floor is given to Deputy Bazarova. While Comrade Bazarova is on her way I should tell you that a similar demand has come from Moldavia.

R.A. Bazarova, chairman of the Turkmen SSR Supreme Soviet Presidium, Ashkhabad City (Kunya-Urgenchskiy National-Territorial Okrug): Dear comrades. I wanted to tell you that since yesterday we have received numerous telegrams and had numerous telephone calls from voters in the Turkmen Republic. And now on instructions from the people's deputies from the Turkmen SSR I want to say that we fully support Mikhail Sergeyevich Gorbachev's proposal regarding the candidacy of Comrade Anatoliy Ivanovich Lukyanov for the post of first deputy chairman of the USSR Supreme Soviet. As people have already said here, Anatoliy Ivanovich Lukyanov is a major specialist, a scientist. He has done a very great deal in elaborating the fundamental avenues of the political reform which democracy and glasnost are asserting today.

I personally have met many times with Anatoliy Ivanovich in the course of my work. And I must say that we are always very grateful for his help and support in many questions, especially in the solution of legal questions in our republic. That is why on behalf of our republic I want to reaffirm once more that we support Comrade Lukyanov's candidacy. (Applause).

M.S. Gorbachev. The floor is given to Deputy Kiriyak from the group of Moldavian deputies.

N.P. Kiriyak, secretary of the Moldavian SSR Supreme Soviet Presidium, Kishinev City (from women's councils united in the Committee of Soviet Women): Esteemed comrade deputies! Long before the congress and throughout the congress I have been thinking that I would be expressing the opinion of a very great many deputies and we are constantly thinking that we are in this auditorium only because restructuring has begun, of which our party has become the father. Or to be more precise its father is Mikhail Sergeyevich Gorbachev. Yet Mikhail Sergeyevich Gorbachev did not begin restructuring alone. He had and still has people who think like him, loyal assistants experienced in the business of restructuring, one of whom is Anatoliy Ivanovich Lukyanov.

And if we deputies almost unanimously entrusted Mikhail Sergeyevich Gorbachev with the destiny of the country, the destiny of the restructuring which has been begun, the destiny of our activity as deputies and even of our personal lives, and if we were all eager to become deputies to help restructuring and to help Mikhail Sergeyevich, then let's be consistent to the end and trust Mikhail Sergeyevich Gorbachev to appoint his own assistants in the USSR Supreme Soviet.

As a practical soviet worker I can testify that Comrade Lukyanov is an eminent scientist in the field of soviet building who is elaborating fundamental directions of the development of legislation on the soviets at all levels.

Fifth Session

29 May 1989

And, particularly important for our life today, Comrade Lukyanov has revealed the strong and weak sides of the functioning of our Soviet representational system and has made new generalizations on a theoretical and practical plane. In addition Comrade Lukyanov is one of the authors and executors of the reform of the political system and its functioning under contemporary conditions and of ways of creating a Soviet rule-of-law state. And he is not only a propagandist but also an implementer of Lenin's ideas of the power of the people (applause) and of the introduction of Lenin's principles of glasnost and the consideration of public opinion into the activity of the soviets, public organizations, and the entire Soviet political system. So in Comrade Lukyanov as first deputy chairman of the USSR Supreme Soviet we will have a leader who has worked on a whole complex of theoretical and practical problems.

Comrade deputies! I speak on behalf of the deputies of Moldavia so I ask for another 30 seconds. I cannot fail to mention one problem on behalf of women, the Committee of Soviet Women, and the deputies from the national-territorial okrugs. We would like to express the wish to the deputies and probably above all to our Supreme Soviet that women's problems, problems which are not purely women's problems but the problems of the future of our society, should begin to be studied at state level. I think the acquaintance which deputies from the Committee of Soviet Women have with Comrade Lukyanov and the study, in the Committee of Soviet Women, of the problems of the forthcoming congress and the role of our congress, the role of the soviets, and the role of women in our society enable me to conclude that Comrade Lukyanov is the first deputy chairman of the USSR Supreme Soviet whom we need during the assertion of the real power of the soviets. Thank you.

M.S. Gorbachev: And now, as we have agreed, I give the floor to Comrade Lukyanov in order for him to reply.

Voice from the floor: Why aren't the microphones working, so that we can ask questions of the speaker? What is this, anyway?

M.S. Gorbachev: All right. We'll see about it right away.

Voice from the floor: I submitted a memorandum with a proposal.

M.S. Gorbachev: Would you please give your answer?

A.I. Lukyanov: Comrades! I am answering the memoranda very briefly. I received a memorandum from Comrade Palm. Actually, it arrived somewhat later. How many people's deputies have been elected from districts in which there was a preliminary selection at district meetings, or how many candidates were refused registration despite the voters' protests? According to my information, there 910 such districts. The total number of candidates nominated there was 5711. The Central Electoral Commission received a total of approximately 800 complaints. And of them 20-30 complaints were received at the Central Electoral Commission concerning the fact that the district meetings had failed to register various candidates. I want to tell you that work was done at the Central Electoral Commission to deal with each of these complaints. We transferred them to the Central Electoral Commission and then made a decision which, as you know, was reconsidered again by the Credentials Commission.

I have been asked a question about the fate of the Molotov-Ribbentrop Pact, and about my attitude to that problem. I feel that the fate of the Molotov-Ribbentrop Pact is a very complicated question that affects not only the fate of the peoples of Lithuania, Latvia, and Estonia, but also, for example, the Western Ukraine and certain other regions and, as a whole, comrades, the entire country—the Soviet Union. Therefore a commission has currently been created at the party's Central Committee to deal with this question. And it seems to me that it would be correct for us to return to this question at that point in the agenda that is called "miscellaneous."

M.S. Gorbachev: Are there any questions?

A.I. Lukyanov: There is one more question, Mikhail Sergeyevich. People have been asking why there exists a discrepancy in the formulation "as a rule"—"The USSR people's deputies who have been elected to the Supreme Soviet, as a rule, are relieved from permanent work." That was in our ballot, which was issued to the deputies, and is encompassed by the formulation of Article 124 of the Constitution. Article 124 of the Constitution remains in effect. It is within its confines that these questions will be decided.

There are two memoranda which, unfortunately, were not signed. I could fail to answer them.

M.S. Gorbachev: All right.

A.I. Lukyanov: With regard to Georgia there is a memorandum about the specific fate of a person who participated in the Georgian events. There is also a question that is part of an overall series of questions and that will also be considered by the commission. What answers, then, should I give now? I hope that the commission will resolve everything objectively and will report to us. Why, then, should we guess now about what that answer will be? As for that personal question, the question about the fate of one person in Georgia, please allow me to say that we will take care of it. We will see what is involved.

M.S. Gorbachev: Comrades, I, of course, understand the dissatisfaction of certain deputies, and I do not want even the emotional posing of the questions to be perceived as something of a provocative nature. Probably we have a few things that are not quite right, although I am attempting to see that we move ahead, collectively making decisions about how to take the next step. And this is the next step: We have agreed that, with this, we

Fifth Session

29 May 1989

shall stop the discussion. Is there anyone who has not had the opportunity to speak? I no longer know what to do. Now we are working together with the secretariat. Comrade Gorbunov has constant contact with the presidium. It is probably necessary both for us and for the presidium secretariat to see whether we will have enough time to do all this. This comment is probably a natural one. Nevertheless I am attempting to give people the floor in the order in which they registered, that is, so to speak, to raise the questions "live." I feel that we must listen to all the different opinions. I am attempting to assure you that there is a diversity of opinions. But there is a very acute question that has been posed here—the comrades are dissatisfied, and since this morning they have sent memoranda but have not been included among the persons to give a two-minute or three-minute statement each. And Comrade Obolenskiy raises the question.... There probably have been certain miscalculations. We have all agreed, later on, to discuss the entire series of procedural questions. If your statement pertains directly to the discussion of the candidacy or if you have something that is very unusual.... I do not know. Should we make an exception, or shouldn't we?... No. We have voted on that.

You do feel that I am presenting for discussion the things that you are proposing. Should we stand by our decision, or should we give the floor to the three comrades who ask to have the discussion continued? (Commotion in the auditorium).

Voice from the floor: (Inaudible).

M.S. Gorbachev: Shall we give the floor to Comrade Lukyanov?

Voice from the floor: Yes.

M.S. Gorbachev: Please turn on the first microphone.

Voice from the floor: Comrade Lukyanov, please excuse us if those two memoranda that were sent to you proved to be unsigned. They are from a group of deputies from Armenia, in particular, Sakisyan, Starovoytova, and a few other deputies. We would like very much for you to answer our questions.

M.S. Gorbachev: All right.

Voice from the floor: Would you please allow me to say a few words?

M.S. Gorbachev: Just a minute. Do you have a statement?

Voice from the floor: It deals with the candidacy.

M.S. Gorbachev: The statements have already been ended. Comrade Lukyanov, will you please answer the questions?

A.I. Lukyanov: The first question deals with the fate of the persons from the Karabakh Committee who were arrested, the leaders of the informal democratic movement. We are informed about this problem. It was dealt with by the USSR Procuracy. Investigation is under way, and it may end by the middle of this year. But I want to say that we can resolve here a number of questions that are linked with preventive restrictions. The union and republic procuracies must deal with such questions in the legally established procedure.

The next question that is asked is: Did you participate in the events in Hungary, Czechoslovakia, Poland, and Novocherkassk? (Stirring in the auditorium). I can say that I never have been in Novocherkassk, and I do not know. As for the 1956 Polish events, and then the Hungarian events, I happened to participate there in concluding treaties dealing with legal assistance, which were necessary at that time. As for Czechoslovakia, at that time we were helping the Czechoslovakian party and Komsomol workers, and many of us from the party's Central Committee traveled to the site. That was not linked with any events. We were dealing with the restoration of the activities of the Czechoslovakian party, state, and youth organizations. I do not have any more memoranda.

M.S. Gorbachev: Shall we stop?

Voices from the floor: Yes.

M.S. Gorbachev: Comrades, shall we stop the questions also?

Voices from the floor: Yes.

M.S. Gorbachev: All right. That's all.

A.I. Lukyanov: There are no more questions being asked of me, Mikhail Sergeyevich. I have answered all that I had.

M.S. Gorbachev: Comrades! We have discussed in a fairly thorough manner the question of the election of the first deputy chairman of the Supreme Soviet. And in this regard.... (Commotion in the auditorium). Comrades, please respect the congress. If you do not respect me, then please respect the congress.

Voice from the floor: (Inaudible).

M.S. Gorbachev: A reply to your question will be given by Comrade Lukyanov, but, as he has just told me, he does not know how this matter is being resolved.

Comrades! We are approaching the resolution of the question on the agenda. I want once again to ask the congress to support my proposal. There exists a certain logic. There exists, don't you know, a certain kind of

STENOGRAPHIC RECORD

Fifth Session

29 May 1989

overall idea, the same one that Comrade Burlitskiy spoke about—a cabinet. We must take this into consideration, and I ask you to support my proposal.

How shall we vote in this instance? Inasmuch as there is no stipulation in the Constitution that this is to be done by secret vote, one assumes that there is the possibility of an open vote. Who is in favor of resolving the question of electing the first deputy chairman of the USSR Supreme Soviet by open vote? Please raise your credentials. Please lower them. Who is against? Would you please count them?

A.G. Kostenyuk: Comrade delegates, 290 deputies voted "nay."

M.S. Gorbachev: Who abstained?

A.G. Kostenyuk: Thirty-eight deputies abstained.

M.S. Gorbachev: The question has been decided. Someone sent me a memorandum and he writes correctly that if one totals the "aye" votes, the "nay" votes, and the abstentions, the result is not always the total number. Consequently, some comrades feel that they have the right also not to vote. But we must know the deputies' position, whatever it might be.

Comrades, I am putting the question to a vote—I have in mind my own proposal, which was the first to be made, concerning the election of Comrade Anatoliy Ivanovich Lukyanov as first deputy chairman of the USSR Supreme Soviet. Whoever is in favor of that proposal, please raise your credentials. Please lower them. Who is against? Please count them.

A.G. Kostenyuk: "Nay," 179 votes.

M.S. Gorbachev: Who abstained?

A.G. Kostenyuk: Abstentions, 137 deputies.

M.S. Gorbachev: All right. Thus, the Congress of People's Deputies adopts a resolution concerning the election of Comrade Anatoliy Ivanovich Lukyanov as first deputy chairman of the USSR Supreme Soviet. (Applause).

Comrades! We have to take a break now, but I want to ask you for your advice. As you recall, at the beginning of the session we asked the secretariat to formulate the requests made by deputies who want to make a statement concerning the need to discuss procedural questions pertaining to the conducting and the progress of the congress. This would seem to have been already predecided. What shall we do? Should we announce a two-hour break, and discuss the procedural questions later, or should we listen to the report?

Voices: The report.

M.S. Gorbachev: But maybe we ought to keep our promise and give time for the discussion of the procedural questions? And then listen to the report in the morning? (Commotion in the auditorium).

All right, comrades, two proposals are being formulated. The first proposal is to listen to the report two hours from now. The second proposal is to keep to our word that we gave this morning, and to discuss the procedural questions. Two hours will be enough time for that. Then tomorrow, with a clear head, we can listen to the report. (Applause). This requires a decision.

Whoever is in favor of scheduling the question of the report for tomorrow, please raise your credentials. Please lower them. Who is against? An obvious minority.

Thus, the report is scheduled for tomorrow. There will be a break until 1600 hours.

Yes, comrades, the agrarians request their colleagues in the agrarian sector to remain in the auditorium for a while.

29 May 1989. Kremlin Palace of Congresses. 1600

Session chaired by M.S. Gorbachev, chairman of the USSR Supreme Soviet.

M.S. Gorbachev: Respected comrade deputies! The evening session of our congress is now open. We have arranged to devote the evening session to procedural matters that have accumulated up to this time. First I would like to give the floor to presidium member Comrade Gorbunov, who will set forth certain matters relating to this subject, and then we shall move on to the speeches of the comrades who have been scheduled to speak on these matters.

A.V. Gorbunov, chairman of the Latvian SSR [Soviet Socialist Republic] Supreme Soviet Presidium (Tsessiskiy Territorial Electoral Okrug): Dear comrade deputies. Many critical comments have been addressed to the secretariat and to me personally, connected with the fact that at the morning session the secretariat was unable to organize in a clear-cut way the registration of the lists and requests, particularly requests on statements on the matters that were discussed here before the recess. The criticisms were justified, and all I can do is explain why this happened. You yourselves saw how at first, unfortunately, we started the work imprecisely, and the notes were set in two rows. One went to the secretariat, and the other to the presidium. When we tried to combine the two, the numeration of the requests to speak was, unfortunately, confused. Now, during registration everyone has had an opportunity to obtain special blank forms that can be filled out if you wish to speak on any particular issue. There are, in our opinion, two very important notes that should be made: the time of presentation of your statement and the note of the secretariat. This will make it possible to determine the sequence of statements precisely.

STENOGRAPHIC RECORD

Fifth Session

29 May 1989

It must be said that the secretariat has received a great deal of material, and everyone in the secretariat is now busy analyzing these materials. Tomorrow morning at the start of the congress' work, if it has the opportunity, the secretariat will briefly inform you about what it has received today and what it is doing to deal with particular documents.

A few words about the procedure for the upcoming discussion of the report from the chairman of the USSR Supreme Soviet—first, giving due consideration to the importance of matter under review, in accordance with paragraph 14 of the Provisional Rules, the congress presidium will take into account the requests of deputies representing republic delegations. Second, we have arranged—and this is also stated in the Provisional Regulations for the congress—that at least three delegates from each all-union republic delegation will be given time to speak. But this quota will be increased depending on the numerical makeup of the republic delegation. Accordingly, each republic may offer any number of speakers in a sequence that is desirable for the delegation. We ask the leaders of delegations to pass a list of speakers to the congress secretariat. In this case these proposals will be considered to be the basis for organization of the discussions.

Third, there is a proposal to give the floor to speakers in the order that the all-union republics are listed in the USSR Constitution. Here, after every third speaker one deputy, either from a region of the RSFSR [Russian Soviet Federated Socialist Republic] or from the public organizations will be given an opportunity to speak. There is another request that in order to ensure procedure in the discussions, we ask all those who wish to express their opinions on any particular issue to make use of the blank forms that have been prepared by the secretariat.

M.S. Gorbachev: Are there any questions for Comrade Gorbunov? There are, Comrade Skokov, please.

Yu.V. Skokov: (Inaudible).

A.V. Gorbunov: Comrades, we are not forcing anyone to fill in blank forms over and over to speak just because he has not filled out the form. We shall consider literally all requests received, whether or not on the forms. However, for the sake of order I would very much like to appeal to the deputies from the republics. I understand that now the problem of the RSFSR is again arising. But the order for giving the floor to deputies from regions of the RSFSR or from the public organizations after every three speeches to some extent blunts this problem, if I may put it that way. But I would like deputies from the republics to decide for themselves at least the first and second speakers since the number of speakers is not restricted. Notwithstanding, it is essential that we have some kind of organizational foundation, and then we shall see.

STENOGRAPHIC RECORD

M.S. Gorbachev: Comrade Shalayev, please, the question.

S.A. Shalayev: (Inaudible).

M.S. Gorbachev: Comrade Gorbunov is now repeating what it is about.

A.V. Gorbunov: Permit me once again. In my opinion the public organizations here will be given greater opportunities. Because, first, the republic representatives themselves will not forget the public organizations, and moreover, within the republics there are deputies from the public organizations. Let me say it again: It is proposed after every three speeches to offer one deputy either from a region of the RSFSR or from the public organizations the opportunity to speak.

From the hall: There is a proposal that a report be made at the morning session through the secretariat on which deputies will be given the floor, so as not to cause a crush by the wall near the dais. If anyone does not agree then it will be decided by the secretariat. Thank you.

M.S. Gorbachev: Comrade Krayko, please. You have a question?

A.N. Krayko, sector chief in the P.I. Baranov Central Institute of Aviation Engine Building (Baumanskiy Territorial Electoral Okrug, Moscow city): Yes, the deputies from Russia make up almost half the number and so let one speak—this is a correct proposal—one or perhaps two of them should be given the floor, because otherwise there may be extended speeches from the republic.

M.S. Gorbachev: Fine, please, what is your opinion?

From the hall: I make bold to state that there will be no extended speeches from Latvia or from the other republics.

M.S. Gorbachev: Permit me, speaking from the chair and on the basis of our general opinion, nevertheless to make the following accurate remark: We cannot set one deputy against another. Let us cast this aside, stop pinning labels on people, along with all suspicions and all doubts, you understand me? Each person has his own viewpoint, good, bad, ill-considered or not, and let us respect them. (Applause). I think that we shall all support such a position so that all long-windedness is taken into account. What if we do have to spend another day if we see that this is needed so that deputies can speak? So tell me, what does it cost us to add time? (Applause). This is within our power. It is a question of holding the congress in such a way that the voices of all the republics and all the public organizations are heard. This is what it is really about! I think that we have allocated time enough for the discussions, which will enable deputies to speak.

FIRST CONGRESS OF PEOPLE'S DEPUTIES OF THE USSR

Fifth Session

29 May 1989

From the hall: (Inaudible).

A.G. Kostenyuk, chairman of the Orenburg Oblast soviet of people's deputies ispolkom [executive committee] (Buguruslanskiy Territorial Electoral Okrug, Orenburg Oblast): Quite right. What the secretariat has announced is only for an organizational start, because we have to start somehow, more systematically, as Mikhail Sergeyevich has said, so that the republics and the public organizations and the regions of Russia all have their say. But this does not exclude the possibility that the lists may be long or that each deputy will be able to submit his request. And the secretariat will register it and accept it and there need be no questions about it here.

M.S. Gorbachev: Please.

From the hall: The day before yesterday we voted to have the lists with the requests to speak annulled until after the speech of the chairman of the USSR Supreme Soviet, and to submit them after the report. If we announce these lists then we might just as well not have voted. Then we shall have to vote all over again.

A.V. Gorbunov: Comrades, we really do have a problem here, but the secretariat is not to blame. Yes, an announcement was indeed made that we shall start the lists after the report. However, we have 80 requests. People started to submit them yesterday toward the end of the day, and a particularly large number have been submitted today, from this morning. And so we can decide how to act. So what is your specific proposal?

From the hall: Consider either the requests received after the first day, or those submitted after the report. (Remainder inaudible).

A.V. Gorbunov: "Either...or" is impossible. Is this your specific proposal?

From the hall: It was decided to annul them. We voted in favor of all requests.... (Remainder inaudible).

M.S. Gorbachev: Then let me help. Comrades, this is obviously what must be done: We shall confirm our general opinion that the list should be opened at the start of the report.

From the hall: Correct.

A.V. Gorbunov: The secretariat will be very grateful for this solution.

M.S. Gorbachev: Shall we confirm this? Those in favor please signify. Please put down your hands. Against? Abstentions? Well if there are they are very few.

So, we confirm it: The list is opened again from scratch, using the blank forms, starting tomorrow with the speech. We have resolved the issue. But the other matter that Comrade Gorbunov proposed concerning long-windedness during the discussions is worth supporting,

comrades. And this does not exclude the possibility that during the course of the debates we may decide to limit time.... Yes, we have not made a final decision on this; we shall decide together when to wind up the debates. Is there anything else?

From the hall: I would like.... (Inaudible).

M.S. Gorbachev: In general this will not interfere with what has been suggested. And there the opportunity is ensured for statements from public organizations and from scientists; it can be combined. And at the same time equality, the equal position of deputies, will not be infringed upon....

One moment.... Please.

From the hall: I have the following question. Comrade Gorbunov has said that the delegation leader will decide the order of speakers and the number of speakers. I do not really understand all this terminology. We are not delegates, but sovereign delegates. And what do you have in mind when you talk about a delegation? What does delegation mean? What does delegation leader mean? Please explain for us: Are we delegates or deputies, sovereign and answerable only to our electorate, rather than to the leaders of the delegations? And in general, can we even use this expression—delegation leader? (Applause).

A.V. Gorbunov: First, I did not say that the leader of a delegation will decide who speaks. I am repeating what I wrote, so I can repeat it accurately: We ask the leaders of delegations to pass a list of speakers to the congress secretariat. I said this so that we might have some kind of organizational start for the first speeches. And it seemed to me that a delegation, at least a delegation from a republic, would be able to determine who (just the first two) would speak so as to avoid claims and in order that we could choose who was to be third or fourth. I again emphasize that each deputy is of course sovereign, independent, and so forth.

From the hall: Can you please explain what you mean by delegation leader? What is this?

M.S. Gorbachev: Comrades! Let us dismiss this altogether. You register your names. The secretariat and presidium will determine the order of speaking, and we will try to observe democracy, and long-windedness and diversity of opinion will be accepted. Of course we shall be criticized; there will be more criticism of us. But evidently this cannot be avoided.

From the hall: (Inaudible).

M.S. Gorbachev: All right. This is how we will do it.

The deputy groups from each republic are doing their work. Up to now they have resolved all questions and have put forward collective proposals. Let the deputy

STENOGRAPHIC RECORD

Fifth Session

29 May 1989

groups also decide and choose those from among themselves who will speak. And let the deputy groups pass on their proposals to the secretariat. Is this acceptable?

From the hall: Yes.

M.S. Gorbachev: It is. Then perhaps we can resolve it in this way. Comrade Stankevich, do you have anything to say on this matter? Anything to add? Fine. Please.

S.V. Stankevich, senior scientific associate at the USSR Academy of Sciences Institute of General History (Cheremushkinskiy Territorial Electoral Okrug, Moscow city): There is a proposal to introduce a problematical principle into our debate on tomorrow's report. It seems to me that it will not be quite right if first we have statements on literature and then on economics and then on national questions, and then again on literature. Perhaps in the requests that we shall be submitting we should indicate at least approximately the field, the problem field, on which a deputy intends to speak.

From the hall: (Commotion in the hall).

M.S. Gorbachev: But this is a matter for the deputy! We shall only accept this in the presidium and secretariat if you describe the problems on which you wish to speak. This would not be bad. But is is, so to speak, dependent on the good will of the deputy. Can we consider that we are agreed on the proposals that Comrade Gorbunov has put forward, even though they are of somewhat limited import? Fine, we are agreed.

Now, comrades, let us move on to what we promised, to the discussions with reference to procedural matters concerning their conduct and order, and other matters on which we have agreed to conduct the debates during the course of this meeting.

So, Comrade Salambek Naibovich Khadzhiyev from the Groznenskiy Territorial Okrug No 396 complains that we have for a long time been ignoring his request. Please.

And Comrade Kiselev from Kamchatka, even though it seems that we have heard him and have exchanged opinions with him during every recess, seems to be saying that Kamchatka is not being given the floor.... Well, let us agree as follows: You are next, and then we shall move on to the congress secretariat list as written: comrades Burykh, Kashnikov, Chernyshev, Chimpoy, Zaslavskiy and others. Please.

Let us make just one stipulation: Statements on procedural matters should not be allowed to last 15 minutes as for the Rules, but 5.... Let us not make claims against the presidium. I think that 5 minutes is adequate for these matters. So? To the point, on procedural matters, motives for voting, and requests submitted, the time will be 3 minutes. But I think that here what we are dealing with is not quite procedural matters. Let us set 5 minutes, based on the fact that otherwise we shall have to add extra time. Is this acceptable?

From the hall: Yes.

M.S. Gorbachev: So, 5 minutes. Those in favor please raise your hands. Thank you. Against? Abstentions? Well, we are agreed. Please, proceed on this basis.

S.N. Khadzhiyev, general director of the "Grosneftekhim" Scientific Production Association, Groznyy city (the Groznenskiy Territorial Electoral Okrug, the Checheno-Ingush ASSR [Autonomous Soviet Socialist Republic]): I am immediately beset by difficulties; they have been building up over the 4 days that I have been trying to get to the dais. I do not know how to restructure a report just immediately, but I shall try.

First, on procedure. I would like to substantiate some of the points in my own statement, which was why I wanted to do this, although in the main I want to speak after the report. I think that it occurred first because it is high time that each of us deputies should, in my opinion, define aloud his own position at the congress so that his electorate can know it. The congress is complex, you see.

Even though it is now considered bad form to say anything good about the leaders, this is how it is, notwithstanding the group of delegates from Checheno-Ingush is convinced that many of the positive processes taking place in our country are associated largely with Mikhail Sergeyevich and his colleagues. And we understand the complexity in which he finds himself. On the one hand there is pressure from the right, when everyone says that there is anarchy in the country and the people are falling apart. On the other hand, you have seen the pressure from the left. There is in principle, naturally, an overwhelming majority, and I include myself in that number, who all support Mikhail Sergeyevich and his actions.

Notwithstanding I have a sense of concern that with each passing day the congress is shifting increasingly toward the right. I would like to think that this is nothing but a feeling.

The second reason for my statement is that I am convinced that we shall achieve the aims of restructuring only on condition that, while giving Mikhail Sergeyevich every possible kind of support, we of necessity subject his actions to well-considered and constructive criticism. Mankind has not invented and cannot think of a better way to avoid error than collective discussion and serious, benevolent, mutual criticism. This is the kind of criticism that I would like to make, but since I have little time remaining I would like, without going into it deeply, to offer five proposals. I shall just read them and then pass them to the presidium: There is no time.

Fifth Session

29 May 1989

First proposal. At the expiration of the term of the chairman of the Supreme Soviet, leading workers in the presidium should submit their resignations and have the newly elected chairman of the Supreme Soviet select and appoint presidium workers at his own discretion. The first to resign among leading workers in the presidium should be the chairman of the Supreme Soviet at the conclusion of our congress. You know that the start of the congress has been a mess, but notwithstanding we must afford the president the right to such actions. I know that he has power enough to remove them, and to spare. But it is one thing when he removes power and quite another when this is done in accordance with the law. In a rule-of-law state everything should be done according to the law.

Second proposal. To create, starting from today, an organizational group for the congress, made up of cadre deputies, 20 people—one from each of the all-union republics, 2 from Moscow and 3 from workers in the Supreme Soviet and CPSU Central Committee; and to assign this organizational group the task of immediately taking up matters concerned with the organization of this congress and subsequent congresses. We must have this kind of organizational group since the secretariat can deal only with a small range of matters while a colossal group of questions still remains on the side, including matters of an informational nature.

Third. To institute the post of master of ceremonies for the congress sessions. To submit to the presidium proposals on candidates for the post of master of ceremonies of the congress sessions. To have the apparatus of the Supreme Soviet Presidium provide by the morning of the 30th a place for a master of ceremonies of the congress sessions. (Commotion in the hall). One moment; let me explain. You are aware that we are uncomfortable; we have elected a president and the entire world is watching us. And now all the time we are, in general, somehow with him.... So I left, uncomfortable; this is not the way the world does it. The master of ceremonies of the congress should sit with a hefty gavel and two powerful aides. Then I shall not leave. What will you do with me, call in the militia? This is accepted the world over....

M.S. Gorbachev: And we have Comrade Vlasov sitting among us.

S.N. Khadzhiyev: Since he had the power to do it—but I have jumped at the chance and will stay. Nevertheless, I think that there should be a master of ceremonies for the congress, and the presidium should carry out other functions. The members of the presidium should listen to the debate and then discuss it among themselves and offer us a well-considered proposal of generalized formulations for voting. And the fact that the president of the greatest power of all time is sitting here among us as we argue is, in my opinion, not proper. We have been taught from childhood that with the authorities.... In short, I think that this should be done.

Fourth proposal. To elect a procedural group of 10 people and assign them the task of preparing by 30 May a draft procedure for conducting the debates and adopting decisions. Apart from this one question, we still have an earlier question that has not been declared, and no one is in principle prepared to move into this confusion. There must be clear-cut procedures: How to bring up a matter, who brings up a matter, how much time is allotted for discussion. I, for example, am a categorical opponent of having a vote by a majority preventing people from speaking; this does not occur in a normal parliament. Other matters should be prepared by this procedural commission in time for the fall session of the congress. But we should at least make a start on them now.

And finally. This is our first congress. The entire world is watching us. It has seemed to me that it would be proper, Mikhail Sergeyevich—and I hope that the people's deputies will support this—if we prepared on behalf of the congress an appeal to all peoples and parliaments of the world, setting forth our position on the most important issues.

So there you have it, the fifth proposal that I would like to introduce. Thank you. (Applause).

M.S. Gorbachev: Comrades, let us pass the proposals to the presidium as a matter of importance, and at appropriate stages in the work of the congress express our opinion on these very important and interesting issues. Are there any objections? So resolved.

Comrade Kiselev will be the next to have the floor. And then Comrade Burykh.

V.N. Kiselev, engineer in the organizational-legal section of the V.I. Lenin Fish Farming Collective Farm [kolkhoz], Petropavlovsk-Kamchatka city (Kamchatka Territorial Electoral Okrug, Kamchatka Oblast): Respected comrade people's deputies of the USSR. Before making my statement I would like to ask you to open bulletin No 3 at page 20. We all say that under the conditions of glasnost and democracy we cannot hold back the truth in the history of our state. Today we are making history. Look at what is written at the bottom of page 20, what Fedorov said. We all remember his speech. There has been a hail of telegrams: Voters are asking that he make a public apology, but the bulletin writes that Comrade Fedorov said: "Vote for whomever you please. If you want clever people, fine, if you do not, fine." But in the speech he used the expression "if you want fools." This kind of bulletin also causes mistrust about all decisions. In this connection I ask that the name of the person who permitted this inaccuracy be disclosed. And the names of the deputies who prepared it should appear beneath every law, beneath every program. (Applause).

Comrade people's deputies. We are all indignant about the procedure that has taken shape at the congress, when they "slam the door" on a people's deputy making a

STENOGRAPHIC RECORD

Fifth Session
29 May 1989

statement. I consider this kind of conduct improper. Moreover, according to all the rules, it is impossible to speak out to criticize a speaker. I can express my own opinion and only discuss the report. Why are we acting in this way? Each deputy has the right to express his opinion, and we shall decide whose positive to support.

Next question. I believe that today our working presidium is more for show. And in this connection I propose that the following factors be added to the working presidium. Today the working presidium must strictly observe that today's work be conducted according to the rules. It is necessary to formulate more precisely whose statements should be heard. We have seen the special blank forms that have been prepared and have now been distributed to us. And at the same time, whoever has not spoken has the right to submit his statement to the secretariat so that it can be duplicated and circulated among all people's deputies on the next day.

I have repeatedly submitted written requests to the secretariat (for 2 days I had no vote at the congress) asking them to give us the materials from the meeting of the council of representatives of the deputies, where many issues were resolved, and from the meeting of the party group, where Comrade Shekhovtsov challenged the candidature of the chairman of the Constitutional Oversight Committee. All deputies should know about this. For some reason the materials have still not been distributed to us.

Next question. I believe that all delegations should have an equal opportunity to appear on central television, offer its assessment to the congress, and appear in print in the press. Unfortunately, the country knows all the celebrities and they continue to speak out. This is fundamentally wrong and it brings discredit to the work of the other people's deputies.

Next question—a procedural one. I believe that in order to avoid mistakes in the future (and we do have the elections to the all-union republics coming up) all the people should elect the head of state and head of government, not us, just a certain part of the representatives of the people.

Next. I believe that the head of government and the head of state should take an oath to the people. It is essential to set some age qualification for appointment to state posts. We have already elected a chairman for the Supreme Soviet and the chairman's first deputy. I do not object to Anatoliy Ivanovich; he and I have talked about having these points in the draft of a new constitution. My request is to Mikhail Sergeyevich and to the people's deputies, and is as follows. In accordance with the Provisional Rules that have been proposed here, the chairman will recommend to us the names of candidates for the Constitutional Oversight Committee. And who then will monitor the activity of the Supreme Soviet and recommend and name a procurator general and a chairman for the People's Control Committee? In this connection I suggest, Mikhail Sergeyevich, that perhaps our opinions will coincide, but you should know the opinions both of the voters and of the people's deputies. As you said at the 19th all-union party conference, today we must not dictate, but must hold discussions and carry on a dialogue, respect the opinions of the voters, and introduce proposals on the basis of of those opinions. But our opinions probably will coincide with respect to Ryzhkov and other comrades.

In concluding my statement I would like to bring to your attention certain telegrams that I have selected from the larger mass of telegrams. "In turning down your own program for the creation of a rule-of-law state you have violated the Constitution. Where is your courage? There is no Supreme Soviet or accountability report, yet a chairman has been elected."

This, comrades, is not my opinion, but the opinion of the voters.

Many voters, myself included—and in conversation with Mikhail Sergeyevich we have discussed this matter—have come to the common opinion that today Boris Nikolayevich Yeltsin should also be taking part in the country's public and political life. Since I feel that I will have no further opportunity to speak, I propose that Boris Nikolayevich Yeltsin be considered for the post of chairman of the People's Control Committee. Thank you for your attention. (Applause).

M.S. Gorbachev: Deputy Burykh has the floor. Next will be Comrade Kashnikov.

Yu.Ye. Burykh, chief of the technical department at the Gorlovka Chemical Plant, Gorlovka city (the Gorlovka Territorial Electoral Okrug, Donetsk Oblast): Respected chairman, respected colleagues. I shall lose my self-respect and the trust of the voters, and we shall all lose it, if we are not candid and proper. In connection with the work of the congress and its first results, the political situation in the capital, and indeed throughout the country, is ambiguous. On Saturday after the congress work was completed we, the group of deputies from Donetsk Oblast, met indignant Muscovites at the Moskva hotel, who literally demanded explanations about the results of the elections to the Supreme Soviet, and demanded explanations about the failure to elect Deputy Yeltsin. The Muscovites were dissatisfied with our answer and they invited us to their meeting on Sunday. I was there. And what happened? There was intense dissipation of political indifference and apathy. This is healthy. Society is being revived and people are learning to discuss very important state affairs. But this learning is going on, at least in Moscow, without alternative opinions, in a somewhat one-sided fashion.

STENOGRAPHIC RECORD

FIRST CONGRESS OF PEOPLE'S DEPUTIES OF THE USSR

Fifth Session
29 May 1989

Yesterday at the meeting I tried to express opinions that I knew beforehand would not be approved by some of those present. My objections were directed toward the wisdom of the Muscovites, their common sense, and toward movement in constitutional positions. The rapture of democracy and glasnost that has grown up among us, and dissatisfaction with the results of the elections to the Supreme Soviet, have led some comrades to the conclusion that urgent and extreme measures are needed. Who will explain to the people that there are other democratic ways to influence public opinion about the work of the congress? Can no one prove to the Muscovites the correctness of the outcome of the elections to the Supreme Soviet? This, I think, is where appeals and arguments from deputies Meshalkin and Samsonov would be useful.

I was extremely surprised not to see soviet or party workers among those speaking at the meeting. People are saying candidly that political leaders do not want to hear the people. What are they waiting for?

Respected members of the Politburo, you are also people's deputies, so go out among the people, look at party history and practice. The Bolsheviks went to the meetings and demonstrations, into the regiments and barracks, even when they no longer controlled a situation. They convinced the people and took them along with them. Let us remember that Lenin called alienation from the people communist self-conceit. Otherwise your failure to participate in political discussion may be regarded as a withdrawal from the discussion of urgent problems.

Let us look the truth in the eyes. If we favor the building of a rule-of-law state not in words but in deeds, then we should recognize in a number of cases that we are retreating from the USSR Constitution. The results of the ballot on the elections to the Supreme Soviet have in general not been understood among the people, nor in the congress. What I saw during the course of the voting was group voting by show of hands, when, standing or sitting, in groups of two or three, people compared the bulletin with the lists of candidates. For the bulletins did not indicate job or place of work. We are complaining to the congress and proposing that a commission be set up on the violations during the course of the election of people's deputies at the local level, to conduct a careful investigation of individual instances of this. And now here we are at the congress, violating the ballot procedure and causing mistrust. If the voters could see the voting procedure, you and I would not be sitting here in the Kremlin Palace of Congresses.

Mikhail Sergeyevich really does not want one of the deputies to write in his memoirs 30 years from now that at the 1st Congress of People's Deputies it was noted that there were violations of the Fundamental Law—the Constitution of the USSR—and that they were not put right. Our people are tired of the stresses resulting from revelations made after the fact. It would be proper to consider the possibility of voting again on the makeup of the Supreme Soviet. In this way we would affirm loyalty to the Constitution and calm the voters. Now, with the experience that has been gained, there would be no time for that. I think that the respected chairman of the congress presidium should take a more well-considered attitude toward statements about the occurrence of a conflict situation, split and crisis. Our work is difficult and complex, but nevertheless we are moving ahead. For me there is no crisis in the congress and this will not happen. Whoever has passed through the crucible of the election struggle and has been truly elected from a whole list of candidates, has not been shaken by the statements from deputies Afanasyev, Popov and Adamovich. Their courageous, sharply critical, and emotional view of the course of the congress shocked those who had a relatively smooth election campaign. And there is no need to feel offended, comrades.

It is a secret to no one that deputies vary with respect to the strategy of restructuring. Some are for making restructuring according to a plan from above, others favor doing it through permanent and valid consultation with the people, through living practice and common sense—that is, favor democratic restructuring. In one case this is the earlier monopoly on the truth, with an obedient, resigned people, and in the other it is checking the course of restructuring and the practical work and opportunity of all Soviet people. There is no need to rush to proclaim the delirium of the thoughts and proposals of deputies. There is no need to proclaim as critical political careerists those who think otherwise: On the one hand they are in no way "enemies of the people"; on the other hand, we ourselves might become "careerists." But I make bold to assert that the main thing is that the entire mess of problems in the work of the congress has come about not because of the actions of a minority, but in connection with the retreat from the problem of confirming the key role of the congress of people's deputies in exercising the highest level of state power and by amendments or decree, strengthening the exclusive right of the congress to adopt USSR laws. Here it must be pointed out on a mandatory basis that the Supreme Soviet is a working organ executing the will of the congress.

Unfortunately, up to now this kind of proposal, heard from some deputies from Moscow and Donetsk oblasts, has remained unanswered, and has not even been put to the vote, even partially. This is what happened with the proposal on voting again for the makeup of the Council of Nationalities, put forward at the previous session.

I think that it would now be useful to assign to the presidium the task of setting up a commission on legislative initiatives made by people's deputies during the course of the discussions, so that they may be reviewed at the end of the work of the congress. Thank you for your attention. (Applause).

M.S. Gorbachev: Deputy Kashnikov has the floor. Next to speak will be Comrade Chernyshev.

Fifth Session
29 May 1989

N.I. Kashnikov, senior teacher in a department of the Kumertauskiy evening faculty of the Ufa Sergo Ordzhonikidze Aviation Institute (Kumertauskiy Territorial Electoral Okrug, Bashkir ASSR): Respected chairman. Respected deputies. In a number of the statements by deputies the thought has crept in that there should be no further discussion of procedural matters. It seems to me that M.S. Gorbachev is profoundly correct when he proposes that the discussion continue on these, if you like, fundamental questions.

It has been said here that some voters will die from indignation and others from laughing at the exaggeration of these matters by Muscovites, Leningraders and other deputies. It seems to me that the voters have every cause for indignation if some deputies underestimate these key problems of our first congress. For it is precisely today, at this congress, that a mechanism will be created for our highest organs of power; it is precisely today that, thanks entirely to the procedure that is devised, we shall either obtain capable, competent organs, or after the congress there will be disillusioned voters. Let me give you just one illustration. Here today the peripheral deputies are justifiably indignant that the places in the hall do not make for equal opportunity when we speak. As it has been said here, we are "out in Kamchatka," far away from the dais and the microphone. But this situation is also the result of procedure, a procedure that has made it a complicated matter to express our opinions, while it has made it simple for others. And the ability or inability to represent a particular viewpoint that may influence the adoption of the best decisions depends on this. That is what happened during the formation of the highest organs of power: Thanks to the procedures for their formation, they can be more or less restructured. Our task is to make them more restructured. Accordingly, there should henceforth be a real choice of alternative candidates, both for the post of chairman and for the seats on the Supreme Soviet. And today we should listen to all viewpoints on procedure for shaping true democracy.

Comrades. The failure of the group of deputies from Moscow to accept many of the peripheral deputies is largely explained, it seems to me, on psychological grounds. Without going into the essential nature of what is proposed by deputies from Moscow, but assessing their activity as demagoguery in procedural matters, as a claim to monopoly of the congress, many of us "provincials" have an adverse attitude toward the Muscovites. This is precisely why many of the Muscovites favor the features of the Supreme Soviet. It seems to me that this kind of approach by the Muscovites is incorrect. Yes, today they make up a minority, but they are not alone. Many of the "provincials" are sharing their constitutional views. I also share their constructive views.

History shows that the minority is not always wrong. Remember Lenin. Lenin was several times in a minority but was ultimately shown to be right. I do not exclude the possibility that today the Muscovites are right in many, but not all, questions. And what if something of value can be extracted from their programs for the national state program to bring the country out of its critical situation? I therefore propose that the group of Moscow deputies should be given half-an-hour for a co-report after Comrade Gorbachev or after the report from Comrade Ryzhkov. (Applause). Why should we deprive them of this right just because they have their own views on ways to deal with the critical situation in the country if they really have done their work? I propose that time be allotted for the group of Moscow deputies for a co-report, or statement, as you wish. And if we find anything that is personally acceptable for adoption, then it should be adopted. This is normal parliamentary practice and we must start to shape democratic traditions. Thank you for your attention. (Applause).

M.S. Gorbachev: Deputy Chernyshev, for the USSR Union of Designers, has the floor. The following speaker will be Deputy Chimpoy.

O.V. Chernyshev, chief of the design department at the Belorussian State Theatrical-Artistic Institute, Minsk city (for the USSR Union of Designers): Respected comrade deputies, respected comrade voters and the many millions now watching this on television. The philosophy of Marxism contains the proposition that history develops in a dialectic fashion according to dialectic laws. But dialectics must wait a very long time for history. Today we have been waiting for the historical chance and we have received it from the hands of Mikhail Sergeyevich. It is an historical chance that will perhaps give us an opportunity to save the country in the full meaning of the word. But the fact is that it is not only the supporters of restructuring who have been given this chance, but also its opponents. And therefore a fierce struggle—I do not fear to use this word—is under way, a fierce, internal and hidden struggle. There was a fierce struggle during the process of the election campaign and there is one here, at the congress. Our society is seriously ill. The disease has spread throughout almost all levels in the structure of its organization. We are well aware of this from material in the press, and indeed from life itself. These are the bleeding wounds on the body of our society—national questions, questions of the ecology and the economy, questions of inflation, and so forth. And we should remember that there are wounds on our bodies, on every one of us. But the strangest thing is that many of the wounds are the marks of the act of our political surgeons who have learned very well the article of cutting, but have not learned the article of sewing and joining together. I say this because the lesson of our congress is now being received by people throughout the country. How the congress goes, so too will go life. This, our democratic congress, will be duplicated in the form that we today decide, and millions and millions of copies will be made.

Lenin said that whoever tries to solve particular questions without solving general questions will always be stumbling over them and going back to them, and thus

Fifth Session

29 May 1989

any advance will be hampered. Therefore, questions concerning the Rules are question number one, the most important questions, because only the Rules can reflect democracy in living form. From where did we start? We started from questions of the agenda. For logic demands this: We have come here for the many, many millions of voters. The voters have given us their instructions. That is, we are not just simply Sidorovs and Petrovs and Ivanovs. We are the bearers of the people's will. And we must all therefore recognize the real problems, which are sometimes glossed over. And we see that Mikhail Sergeyevich does not always see these living wounds accurately or in high relief. That is, he is given information that has already been somewhat biased. So that if we were to discuss these problems we would reveal the most important problems, and their causes, and draw up a program of action, and elect people who would engage in these actions under our vigilant eye, and with our help. This has not happened, because the congress has been making somersaults on the first questions that we must resolve right from the start. It must therefore be said that the 1st Congress of People's Deputies is a congress of missed opportunities. Yes, its efficiency is greater than all preceding congresses, but much less than the opportunities that through us should be representing our people. The fact is that the procedures that we have already implemented are an example of how easily and imperceptibly—sometimes under merry commotion, sometimes intoxicated by the air of these Kremlin walls, by the fact that we, simple people from among the people, are even here, and under the influence of this facile and even somewhat euphoric mood—we have resolved some issues, and, moreover, technical, procedural issues, in our present situation today. We have elected a head of state—that is, the chairman of the Supreme Soviet— a Supreme Soviet, and a deputy chairman of the Supreme Soviet. Tell me, please, how anyone here could think that Mikhail Sergeyevich Gorbachev could fail to be elected if there were only three other candidates? Personally I have no doubts that if this had happened there would have been a national riot. I am convinced of this. But you understand what has happened: We used to have this leader, and we still have him. We used to have a traditional agenda, and we still have it. We used to have a Supreme Soviet, elected traditionally, and in principle appointed, and so the republics voted, not the congress. Because wherever the votes accurately matched the quota, no one was introduced there. All we have paid for all this with democracy. Is this not too high a price? (Applause). Because both the letter and the spirit of the law have been violated. But the fact is that as soon as we touch the letter the spirit goes out of the law. And this is always what happens. Here I observe very dangerous trends. I have been forced to rush along. Marx said that if it is not consciously directed but is random, culture leaves behind a desert. I believe that the actions against Sakharov that took place here is already the beginning of that desert. We may obliterate all the things we hold dear in this way. It would be.... There is no need for commotion. It would be as if the Vysotskiy had appeared today. These are people, they are the conscience of our nation. (Applause).

Comrades, do not applaud, my time is short.

M.S. Gorbachev: Your time has run out.

O.V. Chernyshev: One second only. I.... The fact is that everything is so quick.

M.S. Gorbachev: Please.

O.V. Chernyshev: I ask, comrades, that we be able to speak for as long as we wish. One second. For the fact is that what this is is a collection of the popular wisdom. If a person wants to speak for a long time, let him. Next time he will say nothing at all. Because the time spent here will be time given back for restructuring. The more we sit here and make use of this wisdom, the better we shall know how to act. They are calling us to work.

M.S. Gorbachev: That is all. Deputy Chimpoy has the floor. The following speaker will be comrade Ilya Iosifovich Zaslavskiy.

M.I. Chimpoy, writer, secretary of the Moldavian SSR Writer's Union, Kishinev city (Kishinev-Dnestrovsk National-Territorial Electoral Okrug, Moldavian SSR): Respected comrade chairman. Respected comrade deputies. I am very disturbed by the course of this congress. During the first 4 days there were undoubtedly bright democratic elements. But it is also beyond dispute that we are passing over very important problems. It might even be said that we are steamrolling over them. The initiatives of Latvia and many of the businesslike initiatives of Moscow, and other ideas, have been crushed. I therefore propose the creation of a commission to study the platform of the group of Moscow deputies. We must necessarily urgently define the status of people's deputy, giving due consideration to the fact that some of our colleagues, as, for example, Dumitru Matkovskiy from Moldavia, have already become the tragic victims of strange road accidents. The antirestructuring decision against suspending the decree on meetings and demonstrations lies like a dense shadow over our congress. Voters are telephoning me constantly about this, and calling our congress antipopular. Will it not be, dear colleagues, that we come to the Kremlin as people's deputies but will leave as antipopular deputies? (Applause). In order to restore immediately the congress's lost prestige I propose that the question of suspending the decree of 8 April be put to a roll-call vote. And the list of those voting in favor of and against be made public. (Applause). For it may happen that we shall fight for a long time to save people who will be thrown into prison simply because they participated in discussion of the work of our congress. Up to now we still do

Fifth Session
29 May 1989

not know the sponsor of the 8 April decree. So it is an anonymous decree. And as you know, we have no truck with anonymity. (Applause).

We must also conduct a full vote on a resolution of the tragedy in Tbilisi. We must do this right now, and hear without delay an answer to the request of the Latvian delegate on the tragedy in Tbilisi, and to the request of some of the Moldavian group of deputies about the eight innocent citizens, who took part the 12 March demonstration, being held along with criminals, and to other similar requests. This is very important because we must vote for a procurator general and other high officials. I would like to hear the attitude of Comrade Sukharev on all these problems.

To continue, our congress is dealing with national questions in a way that has in recent times become generally accepted in our country. They are either debated for a long time and made artificially complicated, or they go unremarked, ignored. The error with the Nagorno-Karabakh Autonomous Oblast in the voting procedure was very eloquent in this regard. Thank God that it was revealed immediately and in a constructive way. I think that from this moment on it is essential to prepare a clear-cut resolution on national problems, in particular on statehood and on the functioning of national languages. I propose the following deputies from Moldavia to work on this resolution: Drutse, Viera, and Lari. And I ask my colleagues from the republics to support their nomination. I believe that the historic mission that has been laid on our congress simply obliges it to be a true model of democratism, and that it must in no way pass over the important problems, no matter what the procedural formulas.

There is another factor just as important. If we offer criticism that criticism should be constructive. We must beware of the eulogizing, dithyrambic tone that we heard, for example, in the speech of our colleague from Moldavia, Nelli Pavlovna Kiriyak. I would very much like our congress to be not like a young virgin, as my colleague from Kazakhstan, Olzhas Suleymenov said, but like a serious and mature man.

M.S. Gorbachev: Deputy Zaslavskiy from Territorial Electoral Okrug No 17, Moscow, has the floor. The following speaker will be Comrade Yastrebov from Udmurtiya.

I.I. Zaslavskiy, scientific associate at the Moscow A.N. Kosygin Textile Institute (Oktyabrskiy Electoral Okrug, Moscow): Respected chairman, respected congress deputies. I waged my election campaign and came here in order to raise questions about the disabled and the safeguarding of their interests. However, this is now the third time that I have spoken on procedural matters. I am speaking because experience in dealing with social problems shows graphically that the one depends upon the other. Social questions depend on economic questions, and economic questions on political questions.

And political questions cannot be resolved without real rights and powers for those elected by the people. And it is therefore essential that procedure be regulated properly, and that all deputies have an opportunity to express their opinions and make their contribution to the general decision of the congress and participate actively in the work of its organs.

I suggest that to some extent it is procedural matters that have determined the complex situation that came about yesterday, since everyone said that much work was needed, and I fully agree with that. But people who have worked a great deal, for almost 2 months, preparing proposals, have been unable to familiarize themselves with the congress proposals. Why? Because a procedural matter was violated. They decided that documents submitted by delegations should be duplicated and distributed. But up to now this has not been done.

Because of this, people have not known about our materials beforehand, and have only seen one node of problems, and this has created the complexity. It seems to me that it is very important that the congress now show in its further work the lessons of demonstrable democracy, so as to remove all accusations of being antidemocratic. This can be achieved only if our further elections take place on an alternative basis.

Naturally, there arise here complexities connected with the Constitution, since the head of state must propose candidates, but the Constitution does not stipulate the possibility that he may propose only one candidate. In principle it is possible to conduct ballots of several candidates proposed by the head of state. At the same time it would also make sense to elect the first deputies here at the congress for the top workers confirmed here, such as, for example the chairman of the Supreme Court or the chairman of the Council of Ministers, giving due consideration to the interests of the all-union republics. This would be proper and correct, it seems to me, and would again offer an example of democracy at our congress.

I therefore propose alternative elections for the posts of chairman of the Council of Ministers and chairman of the Supreme Court, and for other leading workers, who should be confirmed by our congress or elected by it. I also propose (and this is not my proposal alone, but the proposal of the voters who have sent me to the congress, a proposal with almost 1,100 signatures) that each deputy have an opportunity to speak at the congress if he submits a request to do so, since each of us represents a large number of voters and their pains and desires, so that life may be better. Naturally, time limits are a given, but we should have first discussed the possibility of, for example, publishing in the central press the statements that are not heard at the congress. This has still not been done.

It seems to me that this must be done, and I offer the following proposal. Our bulletin is being circulated only

Fifth Session

29 May 1989

among deputies, but voters have a right to know what viewpoint their deputy is expressing and what he is defending here.

It seems to me that from this standpoint it is very important that as soon we can do it, from the technical angle, we should conduct a roll-call vote and introduce for each of us some kind of registration list where we shall note what we voted for and what we voted against. A people's deputy has been given the trust of an enormous number of people, and naturally he will write the truth on his own list since it will not be automatically monitored. We ourselves must monitor ourselves. This would be right, and the results of those lists should be published so that people would know who voted for what. And if some different reading appears then that, it seems to me, would be interesting. This is the second proposal.

And the last proposal that I would like to introduce. It seems to me that tomorrow, when the debate on the report takes place, it should be conducted, as Sergey Borisovich Stankevich has said, according to subject—that is, a separate subject for each section of the report, so that one statement may dispute with another. Ultimately the collective wisdom of the congress would arrive at some specific proposal. I support the proposal on the co-report. It will provide an opportunity to consider the great preparatory work done before the congress by many deputies who from the very first day have been trying to prepare sometimes and work and offer their own contribution to the congress treasure house. They have also been trying to publish an appeal to all other deputies in the newspaper IZVESTIYA. Unfortunately, this initiative has not been published. Because of this we have a situation in which some have participated in the preparatory activity while some have not.

I propose that one day of the congress be set aside specially for social and ecology problems because these are problems on which our society now rests, problems that are very acute, problems to which people are very sensitive. We must discuss them seriously and define at least some basic directions along which the country should move. This is my third and final proposal. Thank you for your attention. (Applause).

M.S. Gorbachev: Comrade Aleksey Zakharovich Yastrebov, deputy for the 394th Territorial Electoral Okrug, has the floor. The following speaker will be Comrade Nikolay Alekseyevich Strukov from Kursk.

A.Z. Yastrebov, deputy chief technologist at the Sarapul Ordzhonikidze Radio Plant, Sarapul city (Kamskiy Territorial Electoral Okrug, Udmurt ASSR): Honored guests of the congress. Respected colleague deputies. Taking advantage of the fact that the speaker before me was a representative of the Moscow group of deputies, I cannot help but note the following paradox: just as it was when the Rus used to lead us, any initiative is punishable, and the Moscow group, like no other group, was working actively in the 2 months before the congress and has prepared a package of specific and well-worked proposals. We must criticize not this Moscow group, but all the other groups that have come empty-handed to the congress. (Applause). And next time the work of the group of deputies should be assessed precisely by the following principle: if you come empty-handed and without a package of proposals, that is how you will be assessed.

On the specific subject of procedure. I am disturbed by the following: We do have microphones in the hall, but have they just been placed along the aisles as a decorative framing for the congress? These microphones should be switched on whenever deputies are given the opportunity to ask questions on the essence of the problems on the agenda that are being considered. These questions will not be at all topical and will lose their meaning if an hour, or even half-an-hour has passed. It is essential to provide an opportunity for the microphones to be used when questions are asked.

Next proposal. I have the impression that our presidium is not a worker presidium, as we have called it, but an honorary presidium. Essentially just the chairman is working. Of course, he is just one person, despite all his capabilities and opportunities, and he cannot keep up with everything and oversee everything. I propose a small test for our working presidium. This morning we had a proposal from one of the deputies—the draft rules on voting and on the election of future candidates; let the working presidium over the next two or three days work on this draft and bring it to the congress. If our working presidium—what I have in mind is the 15 representatives from our all-union republics—fails to cope with this task, let another presidium be elected. (Applause).

This is what is happening here: for every new question that is raised we are setting up a commission. If we are all busy working in commissions there will be no congress.

It is necessary to entrust the presidium, and first and foremost the first deputy chairman, with the task of working on and examining all proposals on changing the law on the status of deputies, and on who will speak for groups of deputies and for individual deputies—and this should be done by the last day of the congress. You and I will not leave the congress until we obtain at least the basic amendments to the existing law on the status of deputies. (Applause).

The new law on status must be drawn up carefully and adopted, perhaps, in the fall. But amendments must be adopted here at this congress.

Next remark. The Supreme Soviet will soon begin to set up the committees and commissions. I have the following misgiving on this score. You and I have witnessed how the representative of the Mariy ASSR was omitted from the officially published lists of Supreme Soviet candidates. Perhaps it was an accident, and perhaps it was not. We have received no answer to the question of

Fifth Session

29 May 1989

who struck out that name, and why. I shall not name the name; everyone knows it. I do not speak for that person. The fact is that if we do not now make a specific assessment of whoever did this, then the thing may be repeated with any of us when we are elected to the commissions and committees. (Applause).

Further—and you have drawn attention to this—there are frequent recesses in the work of the congress, and they are not so short either. There is reason, good reason, to organize during one of these recesses a screening of the television film of the events in Tbilisi. (Applause).

I think that this will be quite easy to organize technically. There are two video recorders and four television sets. We should certainly see it.

Finally, permit me to organize a small procedure. I would like to explain thoroughly one question.

Respected deputies and groups of deputies. The question concerns the following procedure: Which of you, which groups, before leaving for Moscow, had received drafts of the documents on the preparations for and holding of today's congress? If you did, then take them out, please, let us see them. There are none. This is precisely why I would like to remark that when Anatoliy Ivanovich talked to us on this matter he was not quite accurate.

Thank you for your attention. (Applause).

M.S. Gorbachev: Deputy Nikolay Alekseyevich Strukov has the floor. The following speaker will be Comrade Belozertsev from Petrozavodsk.

N.A. Strukov, senior investigator of the procurator's office for Kursk Oblast, Kursk city (Kursk Territorial Electoral Okrug, Kursk Oblast): The apparatus has a perfect procedural technology and could if it wished ensure a working atmosphere for the congress, and it must do so. Without order and discipline I do not need democracy. The presidium has allowed us to be drawn into unnecessary debates about nonexistent factions, pinning on labels and so forth. We, the potential workers of the congress, have become an amorphous mass trying to get to the dais, rushing to say our piece, more often than not without a subject, chaotically repeating the same thoughts on some problems, and more often than not, it seems, because of a fear of not being heard, as we discuss opinions and try to get closer to the truth. So whither are we rushing?

The day before yesterday, for example, before the work was completed on the discussion of the nomination of candidate Lukyanov, Mikhail Sergeyevich set the quite unnecessary task for the congress of setting up a commission to investigate possible crimes by Gdlyan, outraging the better sensibilities of Ligachev and the Politburo. Today lawyer Lukyanov's statement is murderous: Let whoever wants to consider this matter. And who wanted to throw himself into these investigations? Extrajudicial trials are illegal here.

The leadership of the courts, the procuracy, the MVD, and the KGB have created in the country the kind of mess that the entire congress could not sort out in a year. What we need a hundred times more is a commission to bring order to the country and organize the work of the law enforcement agencies. These are the things that must be asked, but the leadership of these agencies is now setting the congress the task of the Gdlyan case, rather than the question of privileges and the inaccessibility of the courts to the top people, where information about bribe-taking by delegates to the 19th all-union party conference, and about organized crime, is lost. It is to this that the congress should turn its attention and react.

What is the reason for these shortcomings in the work of the congress? On the basis of the excuse for a law on the elections, and under the leadership of Comrade Lukyanov, an overwhelming majority has been created here, and it has decided and is deciding the main question of the party apparatus, namely, the question of power. They simply will not give other tasks for the congress to resolve. (Applause). Under a call for the renewal of power they are preserving their earlier makeup, without offering an alternative to Gorbachev, maintaining him in the post of general secretary, resolving all matters without alternatives; I think that we shall not have alternatives in the country while this order, or rather disorder, is preserved.

We are throwing the impotent people's deputies with their badges into a sea of complaints from people and indignation on the part of the people. Are we to be the buffer? Not all of us, of course, but the majority, are encountering a wall of China made up of subordinates. When Mikhail Sergeyevich referred to his right to name Lukyanov as his deputy, the person next to me—the party obkom first secretary Seleznev—burst out happily with: "Now we have power." Who? And you are against factions, respected apparatchiki. (Applause). Seleznev should learn, and learn quickly, that power should lie with the congress. And today it must be clearly consolidated by decree, as Sakharov proposed. Otherwise the invisible iron will that we are talking about today will give us cause for concern in the future.

When I compare the work of the congress to the operation of a factory—forgive me for the comparison—I think that its output should be the priority programs, ways and means to implement them promptly, and responsible monitoring of them. We have elected a fine director and leader, and together with him we should have determined our—the deputies'—work program and our status, and have specified rights and obligations. But the comrade president is in no hurry to do this; he is in no hurry to organize good work for the congress.

First it has been necessary to form all the structural subdivisions of the congress; it is a question of the

Fifth Session
29 May 1989

commissions. For today, when he raised the question of the Rules, Mikhail Sergeyevich himself said "the congress should not be interrupted." If we had done this right at the start and formed a structure for the congress, and for its working organs, there would be no need to interrupt it. This should have been considered at the start, but as soon as we failed to form the subdivisions and commissions the result has been chaos. We are again working without a system, irresponsibly, incompetently. For some reason our luminaries are silent. Their word is weighty. And when a "non-Meshalkin" come to the dais there will be no time for empty debates. (Applause).

I propose that we deem a number of the decisions of the credentials and counting commission (of which, incidentally, I am a member) illegal, and annul them. After a commission has been set up, all the commissions under the programs, we must define their priority tasks. The report should be made not on the main directions. We have had more than enough of those reports. The report should be made on the program. And then all those presenting co-reports should introduce proposals on a specific program. And they should be worked on until the next congress, so that it can approve these programs. The people and the deputies must be perplexed [as published]; otherwise once again we shall have no work or concrete results. (Applause).

The party apparatus must give the congress control, and a mechanism that in fact ensures for it the conditions for working in the interests of the people, for we are all saying that we are for the people, but for some reason we are altogether unable to bring the country out of this impasse situation, out of its crises. (Applause).

M.S. Gorbachev: Sergey Vladimirovich Belozertsev from Petrozavodsk, the 570th okrug, has the floor. Deputy Barashkov will be next.

S.V. Belozertsev, senior teacher at the Karelian State Pedagogical Institute, Petrozavodsk city (Kalininskiy National-Territorial Okrug, Karelian ASSR): On behalf of my own voters and the Moscow voters I am making a protest about the way that information about the congress is being presented by the [television] program "Vremya," and even in the newspaper IZVESTIYA, where summarized stenographic records are being carried. The voters believe that in the evening it is essential to repeat the work of the congress for those who during the morning and afternoon were unable to watch it, or to totally abandon the tendentious transmission of material.

There is more. Mikhail Sergeyevich, I call on you to abandon the formula "let is take this under advisement," with which the hall must be regaled, with reference to time. They say that a decision on an issue is being delayed because of the discussion of procedural matters for the congress, and they say there are objections. Why not clearly resolve the "ayes" and "nays" and let the congress itself decide by vote what it will accept or reject?

I would like to share my thoughts on the matter of voting on the decrees on items 504 and 505 of the "Records." I submitted a request to the presidium, but like many other requests, it appears to have disappeared somewhere. The fact is that the overwhelming majority of those present have no information about the content of these decrees. If this information were available, particularly for the comrade agrarians, then they would not be saying that they are doing the plowing while we are holding the endless discussions. They would understand the purpose of those decrees. Much has been said about Decree 504 being antidemocratic, but Decree 505 is an anti-Soviet decree. It removes special-purpose troops from the subordination of the organs of Soviet power. Through this decree we have lost the inviolability of our homes; now anyone may come in just on suspicion, according to its formulation, and without the sanction of the procurator's office and not in response to a court order. And according to this decree, weapons may be used against women and children if they make an armed attack on a colleague.

A poll of MVD representatives, conducted by Leningrad sociologists, showed that a very large proportion of them believe that the child who threatened an MVD worker with a rock is engaging in armed attack. This is quite a dangerous understanding of the vague formulations of this decree. I would like to make a request as a deputy, even if only verbally: My voters and I would like to know all the names of the people who subscribed to this decree, both this one, 504, and Decree 505.

Furthermore, I would like to join Comrade Zaslavskiy on the question of a roll-call vote. Since we have rejected this in favor of a show of hands, then in fact we can have recourse to a procedure whereby one or two people record all those voting for or against on basic issues, so that later the voters will have an opportunity to monitor the people who have violated their interests, and can then be recalled in accordance with procedure for the recall of deputies worked out at our congress. (Applause).

Comrade deputies. I would like to say to you that at their meetings the voters of Moscow are expecting a great deal from you. They want to know your opinions. This is what a small circle at a meeting yesterday assigned me to say: "Comrades, the question is why did Yeltsin leave the Supreme Soviet? This is a fundamental question. Let all those who did not strike out this name on the voting paper wear this badge so that the voters can pose their questions to them. And for anyone who is not wearing it, so that they can learn the arguments on this score. [no end quotation marks] (Commotion in the hall).

M.S. Gorbachev: Never mind, continue.

STENOGRAPHIC RECORD

Fifth Session

29 May 1989

S.V. Belozertsev: The fact is that at the meeting in the Luzhniki, for example, they very much wanted to see representatives of the deputies from the CPSU, and also our respected deputies from the Central Asian republics, for whom all voted as one. The voters want to know their position. What else did I want to say here? We have discerned a certain connection between what is being said from this dais. I do not want to exaggerate any contradictions between those who were elected for territorial or national-territorial okrugs and those elected from the public organizations. Eulogies and praise are due the comrades from the public organizations. I do not hold up the academicians as an example here. They, of course, are not included in this category, as are certain other deputies.

In this connection, giving due consideration to the statements of a number of people from the public organizations, in working out the status of the deputy and the recall procedure, provision should be made for the possibility of the people recalling these delegates and for obliging them to deal with the affairs of the people rather than merely defending the interests of their own public organizations. Otherwise they should have a different status. It is essential for them so that during the transition and the elections for the local soviets (I think that an absolute majority of voters will support me here), we abandon one-third and abandon the holding of several posts, because locally in some regions restructuring may come to an end if several posts are held.

Thank you for your attention.

M.S. Gorbachev: Deputy Barashkov has the floor. The following speaker will be Comrade Samarin.

Yu.A. Barashkov, faculty docent at the Arkhangelsk Timber Institute, Arkhangelsk city (Arkhangelsk Territorial Electoral Okrug, Arkhangelsk Oblast): Respected chairman, respected deputies. Since our last session there have been telephone calls and telegrams without end from Arkhangelsk city, which I represent. The inhabitants of Arkhangelsk are not satisfied in general with our work and they are saying so in their telephone calls and telegrams. Permit be briefly to read one to you: "Comrade people's deputies. I am one of those who you are representing at the congress. We have sent you to the congress to determine the country's fate. The first thing, therefore, is not to fear discussion; do not allow yourself to be pushed in the back or rush to reach decisions. Weigh things, doubt them, come to the truth through dispute. In this way you will achieve a grad advance toward the common goal. This is your work, too crucial to hurry—to be all the time pushing. Be patient and tolerant but do not permit yourselves to be pushed about by appeals of the kind made by one of the deputies (the name is mentioned but I shall not quote it): "There is more than enough idle talk, get to work!" There is a secret appeal: "Listen to the older ones"; an attempt to push your work back onto the old rails. We have already been that way. Second, approach the elections to the highest organs of power with a greater sense of responsibility than you did during the forming of the Supreme Soviet. Do not fear to waste time discussing every candidate. We have enough unprofessional stewards and incompetent politicians at all levels. The professional political unsuitability of the government is exactly what you should not allow this time. Third. Do not allow phrases like "we must feed the country," that were heard here on the third day of the congress, to confuse or bewilder you. All of us who support restructuring understand that without the creation of new, progressive political structures in the country, economic renewal will also be impossible. And now everyday practice prompts this. What we need is not simply a piece of bread and sausage bought with tokens, but a full-blooded democratic burgeoning of Soviet society. And it is your duty to lay the foundations of our rule-of-law state. Precisely at this congress. Fourth. I would like to remind you that at the first people's congress we elected you under the slogan "All power to the soviets." But up to now this has not sounded out at the congress. Establishing soviet power in the country was the task set by Lenin for the Bolsheviks in 1917.

And this last position comes directly from letter after letter. Here is a fragment from another letter: "The bureaucratic apparatus will win again; the transfer of real power to the soviets is in doubt." And so forth.

After the congress each of us will have to render an accounting. It is very important that each of us who has been delegated should know our possibilities. I am asked continuously: What did you vote for? I support the Muscovites and I support the statements by Popov and Afanasyev. I voted in favor of there being debate first and then a vote, and so forth. I shall not be ashamed to look my voters in the eye. (Applause).

M.S. Gorbachev: Deputy Samarin has the floor. The following speaker will be Comrade Obolenskiy.

V.I. Samarin, staff correspondent for the newspaper ORLOVSKAYA PRAVDA, Orel city (Orel Territorial Electoral Okrug, Orel Oblast): Respected colleagues. Respected citizen president. (Commotion in the hall). Well, what is so special here? Since we have been discussing procedural matters, I would like to deal with this. More than once I have heard the following question at this congress: "When shall we get down to business? When shall we start to discuss the very important issues in the life of society, the economic and social reforms, and so forth?" But just consider for a moment: Without the creation of a serious, proper, mobile governmental machinery, how is it possible to create those reforms and implement them? I think that it is impossible. Therefore, on behalf of our delegation from Orel, I welcome first the election of Mikhail Sergeyevich Gorbachev to the post of president (for some reason this has not pleased everyone, but I think it was a most proper appointment), and to the post of chairman of the USSR Supreme Soviet. Here on

Fifth Session

29 May 1989

the organizational plane we have made a very sure and correct step. And we made it virtually unanimously.

It is another matter with the elections to the USSR Supreme Soviet, since we do not know each other very well, or each other's positions, and, of course, we have approached the formation of this very important organ to some extent formally. And it is understandable that things have not turned out as they might have done.

With regard to the other organs: Today we have elected the first deputy chairman of the USSR Supreme Soviet. I personally also voted for Anatoliy Ivanovich Lukyanov, even though I think that there could have been alternative nominations in the congress. Our present Constitution contains two articles, numbers 108 and 121. Article 108 states that it is the exclusive prerogative of the Congress of People's Deputies "to elect the chairman of the USSR Supreme Soviet and the first deputy chairman of the USSR Supreme Soviet."

And then it suddenly goes on to say "confirmation of the chairman of the USSR Council of Ministers and confirmation of the chairman of the USSR People's Control Committee, the chairman of the USSR Supreme Court, the USSR Procurator General, and the USSR Chief State Arbiter." And again "the election of the USSR Constitutional Oversight Committee."

If, of course, you just take a quick glance there is nothing strange in this. But the fact is that the appointments to all these high positions will be done by the USSR Supreme Soviet, and as you know, one-fifth of the composition of the Supreme Soviet will be changed each year. And so what we have is the following interesting story: We shall elect the highest officials for 5 years, and the chairman of the Constitutional Oversight Committee for 10 years, but after two or three years the Supreme Soviet will be quite different in composition, and will perhaps have quite different opinions on these top state dignitaries.

What will follow from this? I believe that the appointment or election (we are already saying this) of all top state officials—what I have in mind is the chairman of the USSR Supreme Court, the chairman of the People's Control Committee, the USSR Procurator General, and the Chief State Arbiter—all these things should be the prerogative of the Congress of People's Deputies, which is elected for 5 years and which for 5 years will carefully monitor the work of those state officials. I think that this is essential.

There has been much talk here about the Muscovites. In principle I agree with the position of many of Moscow's deputies. Of course, emotion did sometimes gain the upper hand in the statements of Gavriil Popov and particularly Yuriy Nikolayevich Afanasyev. In their place I would never appeal for withdrawal from the Moscow group or the Moscow delegation, but would call for the consolidation of all democratic forces, for their assembly. I tell you candidly that we do not have a Moscow trend, we have a democratic trend, a trend that we shall call well-considered. So that we have more people's deputies in the democratic camp—and I appeal to all of you for this. Thank you. (Applause).

M.S. Gorbachev: Comrade Samarin, you will, notwithstanding, withdraw the "mister." We all heard....

V.I. Samarin: I said "Citizen President...."

From the hall: Citizen....

M.S. Gorbachev: I beg your pardon.

V.I. Samarin: I was surprised that everyone reacted so. "Citizen President" of course, Mikhail Sergeyevich....

M.S. Gorbachev: I call you comrade, you call me mister. Fine. We are agreed. Deputy Obolenskiy has the floor. The following speaker will be Comrade Yudin.

A.M. Obolenskiy, design engineer at the USSR Academy of Sciences Polar Geophysics Institute at the Kolskiy Such Center, Apatity city (Leningrad Rural National-Territorial Electoral Okrug, RSFSR): Respected deputies. Before getting to the nub of the matter I would like to appeal to those who have already spoken from this dais. Please, check that your statement is correct in the stenographic record. In my statement one paragraph was entirely missing, the one in which I made critical remarks about our chairman. Moreover, in the stenographic account published in IZVESTIYA a remark from the hall that I did not make was attributed to me. So check in any event while everything is still fresh in your head. And now I shall discuss how, what, and why.

At our forum we are hearing frequent references to the Constitution, and people are saying that we have the right to stand above the powers not peculiar to the congress and to appropriate them for ourselves. Let me remind you of Article 108, second paragraph: "The Congress of People's Deputies is empowered to make its own examination and resolve any matter relating to the authority of the USSR." You understand: any!

Now to procedure. I recall that in 1917 one of the first decrees of the 2nd Congress of Soviets was the Decree on Power. I believe that at our congress, too, this is also a key issue. "All Power to the Soviets." This slogan is heard quite often everywhere in the country. And willy-nilly this issue has been raised here with us. The first to propose adoption of the decree was Academician Sakharov. It was not adopted. Then the issue of power came up when we were discussing the question of whether or not the post of general secretary could be combined with the post of Supreme Soviet chairman. We did not resolve the matter in principle at that time, although it was resolved indirectly by electing Mikhail Sergeyevich without any kind of reservations to the post of Supreme Soviet chairman. This means that we voted for it. But in my opinion, those who think that Mikhail

STENOGRAPHIC RECORD

Fifth Session

29 May 1989

Sergeyevich will direct the party in the Politburo are mistaken. The Politburo is a collective organ, and why not admit that it will be under the control of the party apparatus? This is understood, is it not? Accordingly, since we have already avoided these two factors, I think that this question should again be raised for the congress. Incidentally, I received yesterday a collective letter signed by 170 people on this subject, from the city of Apatity, containing a proposal to raise the question of abolishing or fundamentally changing Article 6 of the Constitution, since the leading and guiding role of the CPSU affirmed in it will sound like an additional argument in favor of its subordination to Politburo decisions. The Constitution must be observed.... (Applause).

And now something that they are telling us we have not dealt with. So many businesslike proposals have been made from this dais that their number exceeds several, nay ten earlier sessions of the Supreme Soviet (I am ready to answer for that). But this is what seems strange to me. Our deputies, all of us, simply do not know how, have not become accustomed to using our own right of legislative initiative. For in fact a proposal from a deputy is a proposal to make a legislative decision on a specific matter. But we do not know how to stand our ground here. We offer our ideas obediently to the presidium and then we have the formula "we shall consider it, take it under advisement, work on it, and the Supreme Soviet will decide at the next congress...." But you are not allowing for the fact that there may not be another congress, that it may be dissolved, as at one time the inaugural meeting was, and will our people's power end with that? (Applause).

I believe that in no case should our congress end until fundamental decisions have been made.

Further, it is necessary to set up a commission on legislative proposals. If I am so entrusted I am ready to be part of it. And to introduce a general rule: for example, after a day, the clearly formulated proposals submitted today to the commission should be put to the vote. This will not be a law, it will be a decision or decree of the congress on key issues. A law could come later, on their basis, drawn up by the Supreme Soviet. It will be a guideline.

Furthermore. We are in a great hurry. We are resolving things morning and evening. But let us stop for a while and get to know each other, and think about things. I propose that our meetings be split. In the morning, while heads are still clear, a general meeting. After lunch meetings, say, of sections, or groups, as you like. So that in their own interests deputies would become acquainted without, in general, wasting time. Perhaps certain key directions could be established for the commissions, already worked on by experts and interested people. And after lunch it would be possible to hold parallel meetings of the working commissions.

And finally, I believe that the commission on the Gdlyan and Ivanov cases should be set up urgently so that they can set to work. Our congress does not have the right to break up until a principled decision has been reached on this matter. They say that this is unrealistic.... But consider: We must elect a procurator general. I think it is understood who will be proposed. Sukharev, obviously. And the way in which this matter will be resolved will depend on whether or not he is the procurator. This is my opinion. Although it is difficult, I understand.

M.S. Gorbachev: Have you finished?

A.M. Obolenskiy: I am just finishing; give me a second.

M.S. Gorbachev: You can have a minute.

A.M. Obolenskiy: I would like only to propose that this commission then be transformed into a commission on compliance with socialist legality. Tomorrow I shall submit an official request to Comrade Sukharev. A voter has appealed to me with reference to two young people who have been held for 8 months on suspicion of attempted rape. It appears from the copies they have been given that socialist legality has been violated. There is another case for you. (Commotion in the hall). And finally.

M.S. Gorbachev: No, you have already gone over your time, comrade.

A.M. Obolenskiy: I was only about to state the names.

M.S. Gorbachev: No, you are a minute-and-a-half over time. It is not necessary.

A.M. Obolenskiy: Comrades. (Commotion in the hall).

M.S. Gorbachev: One minute. OK. Go ahead.

A.M. Obolenskiy: I shall just name the names. There were indignant exclamations from the Leningrad delegate when Ivanov spoke. My comrades have asked me, and taking advantage of this I shall just the same name those who are in solidarity with what he said in support of Afanasyev. Ivanov, Shchelkanov, Levashev, Obolenskiy, Kolotov, Petrov, Granin, Zhuk, Sychov. Thank you.

M.S. Gorbachev: Fine.

A.M. Obolenskiy: I apologize publicly to Comrade Granin; it seems that I was in error.

M.S. Gorbachev: Deputy Yudin has the floor. Comrade Popov will be next.

A.M. Obolenskiy: Forgive me, Comrade Petrov is also dissociating himself from this. One moment. The fact is

Fifth Session
29 May 1989

that I misstated it. In this text that I was asked to make public, it stated that these comrades support Afanasyev's statement.

M.S. Gorbachev: So, Comrade Yudin, please.

V.D. Yudin, chief of the Central Geochemical Party in the Central Geophysics Expedition of the Northeast Production Geological Association. Khasyn city, Khasynskiy Rayon (Magadan Territorial Electoral Okrug, Magadan Oblast): We are now discussing procedural matters. Permit me to recall those who are familiar with the information and report to those who are not. According to the results of sociological studies, 57 percent of the deputies here present consider one essential condition for good work to be an obligatory consideration of the opinions of all USSR people's deputies during the adoption of legislative decisions; 54 percent are dissatisfied with procedural decisions; and 56 percent think that maintaining law and order in the country is very important. But law and order in the country begins with our congress, comrades. And I draw your attention to the fact that today we have voted for the second time to cancel the preliminary list for statements to be made after the report. What kind of order is this? We quite calmly reverse questions resolved in the Constitution, while in other cases we support the Constitution even where it is not specifically indicated. I have in mind the first day session when Mikhail Sergeyevich Gorbachev chaired a half-day meeting without having the authority under the Constitution to do so, while we confirmed that right for him after the event. I think that we should be dealing with these matters in a more principled manner. Before moving on to my statement proper, I must not forget to ask all deputies to set forth factual material very clearly. We have just seen a good example of this with Comrade Obolenskiy, and before him, with Deputy Belozertsev, if I am not mistaken, who showed us a red study book. Comrades, I was at the meeting. The red study book has a different formulation. I do not remember exactly what, but it is different. I ask all who attend this meeting to provide an accurate formulation so that people are not led into error.

Further, I would like to draw your attention to the fact that the entire session of our representative body is taking place under the sign of democracy. But, comrades, democracy has its own preferences. One is that the majority really does carry through its decisions. Notwithstanding, I believe that one inseparable preference of a democratic meeting is the right of the minority to speak and defend its own opinion.

You are aware that I was defeated for inflexible and unconditionally different thinking—what we today call having a pluralist opinion— being rejected in the voting for the Supreme Soviet and in the list of the RSFSR delegation for the Council of Nationalities. All the deputies who expressed quite sharp but essentially correct opinions received a majority of minuses, and have no opportunity to defend their viewpoint in the Supreme Soviet.

I therefore think that the question of a roll-call vote is of fundamental importance for us today, from the standpoint of enhancing the sense of responsibility of a deputy to his voters. The version for which we voted, proposed by Mikhail Sergeyevich Gorbachev, essentially did not make sense. What is the sense of a majority insisting on a roll-call vote when the decision has already been reached and the majority regarded it as law? As a method for a roll-call vote, before the hall is equipped with a computer, I see the following scenario. Each deputy would be given some kind of roll-call check book. We know the number of the session, and the number of the issue being resolved. The deputy writes in his viewpoint. Those in a minority are passed to the secretariat.

I believe that we must adhere more rigidly to the procedure on deputies' requests and deputies' notes. On the day of the elections to the Supreme Soviet I submitted a list with a proposal that deputies be shown film of the events in Tbilisi, because those events are evoking extensive interest in the country, and each of us must complete and carry out explanatory work on the basis of the facts. I received neither an answer to that note nor any proposal about when the film might be shown. Even though, you will recall, on that day we spent 4 hours looking for something to do, and one hour would have been ample to look at this important document quite calmly.

I remind you that deputy (I beg your pardon if I have the name wrong) Alksins made a very serious request to the Credential Commission about the correctness of forming okrugs in one of the Baltic republics. Today it has now been 3 days since the deputy submitted his request, and I see no possibility of receiving an answer to that request from the Credentials Commission.

And finally, one very important matter. We spent an entire day discussing possible opposition at this congress. Comrades, why is there not today a formally constituted deputy group studying the administrative principle that we are today criticizing in the press, and which does not meet the urgent demands of today's congress and the demands of most deputies? I think that the formation of deputy groups is mandatory and necessary for us. I support the proposal to give the Moscow group the opportunity to present a co-report. (Applause).

M.S. Gorbachev: Comrade Popov, deputy from Moscow, has the floor. Time for the evening session is running out, and I shall not announce the following speaker. We shall talk about it later....

STENOGRAPHIC RECORD

Fifth Session
29 May 1989

G.Kh. Popov, chief editor of the journal VOPROSY EKONOMIKI, Moscow city (from the USSR Union of Scientific and Engineering Societies): Comrades, on Friday we evidently agreed that work would be conducted normally and in a spirit of cooperation. And I would like to propose to you one version that it seems to me could now become a basis for resolving one serious issue.

As you know, in the election of deputies in the RSFSR there were 11 seats, as laid down by the Constitution. Twelve candidates were nominated for those 11 seats. The last on the list was Boris Nikolayevich Yeltsin, even though he collected 50 percent of the votes—that is, could have passed.

On the same day, as you also know, two deputies from our favorite Leningrad, comrades Sobchak and Denisov, had already put forward the idea of resigning from the Supreme Soviet in order to resolve the question of Nagorno-Karabakh. In my opinion a more correct decision could have been made on the Karabakh problem. And the question has now arisen of resolving the problem of representation in the Soviet of Nationalities for the more than 6 million voters of Moscow. I would also like to say that this kind of example, demonstrated here by the Leningraders, is also being demonstrated by Deputy Aleksey Ivanovich Kazannik, representative from our glorious Siberia, whom I now ask to speak—the deputy from Omsk National-Territorial Electoral Okrug, a docent at Omsk State University. He has been entered on the list of 11 winning deputies, and he asks for your considering the question of withdrawing his nomination for the Soviet of Nationalities, so that the next majority of votes for the Council of Nationalities might include Boris Nikolayevich Yeltsin. Thank you. (Applause). I ask you to hear Deputy Aleksey Ivanovich Kazannik.

M.S. Gorbachev: Comrade Kazannik, do you wish to speak? Do you confirm this? (Applause).

A.I. Kazannik, docent at Omsk State University (Omsk National-Territorial Electoral Okrug, RSFSR): Respected comrade deputies. The fact is that I suggested my own nomination as an alternative. And three times I spoke at the meeting of representatives, asking that my name be included in the composition of the USSR Supreme Soviet. I say in fact that I very much want to work there. The fact is, I am a lawyer, and had intended to work professionally in the USSR Supreme Soviet. I say that I am interested in working during precisely the first year because it will be concerning itself with about 50 very important laws, that will determine the fate of our country perhaps even through the year 2000. But when the elections to the USSR Supreme Soviet took place and I saw that because of our political shortsightedness we had "axed" outstanding scholars, and that because of our improvidence we had not allowed the politicians in, I made what was in my opinion the only correct decision: namely that Boris Nikolayevich Yeltsin should work in the USSR Supreme Soviet, or more accurately, in the Soviet of Nationalities. (Applause).

If I were the first secretary of a party obkom I might not have reached that decision, but would have boldly returned to my native land and have been guarded in my obkom by a border of militiamen—and not one single voter would have come near me. But if I go back like this I will be ashamed to look them in the eyes. I therefore request that you include Boris Nikolayevich Yeltsin in the composition of the Soviet of Nationalities, without a vote, on condition that he assume my nomination, and only on this condition. I fear, comrades, that if a second vote is taken Boris Nikolayevich will again be "blocked," and this is quite impermissible. This is how I look at this problem. (Applause).

M.S. Gorbachev: Comrades, I am no great lawyer, and it is therefore necessary that we consult as to whether or not we can do this. I am certain that we can issue a statement on the constitution of the powers of a deputy. But I am not sure that we can simply include an empty seat in the Soviet of Nationalities from Russia when we take into account the results of a previous vote. (Commotion in the hall). Wait, it is essential that by doing this we do not commit some stupidity. I therefore ask that either we provide an opportunity tomorrow for study of this problem, and bring it up for discussion, or if anyone has a clear idea on this, let let him give us his ideas.

Comrade Sobchak? Please.

From the hall: Do you support it...?

M.S. Gorbachev: In principle I support this proposal....

A.A. Sobchak, department chief in the faculty of law at the Leningrad State University (Vasileoostrovskiy Territorial Electoral Okrug, Leningrad city): I believe that Comrade Kazannik has committed a serious legal error here. The error is that, whereas any elected deputy may withdraw his nomination and refuse a nomination to the Supreme Soviet, there is no doubt that a candidate may not impose conditions on that refusal. This is, so to speak, true both in our legislation and in world legal practice. Therefore we may now discuss Comrade Kazannik's refusal only if he withdraws his condition that he will decline the nomination only if Comrade Yeltsin take his place as, for example, a deputy who is a member of the Council of Nationalities. That is the first issue.

The second issue is that of who should take over the seat vacated in the Council of Nationalities as a result of Comrade Kazannik's withdrawal. This issue is not directly addressed in our legislation, because all previous practice in elections to the Supreme Soviet has simply excluded such a situation.

Fifth Session

29 May 1989

World legal practice varies in different countries. Here, only two variants are possible. If the withdrawal takes place, then the candidate who polled the next largest number of votes under the procedure that has already taken place automatically becomes a member of the appropriate chamber of the Supreme Soviet. (Applause).

This is the first variant. And the second is that there will be a vote for all those wishing to be nominated for the post—say, who have already been nominated and who have already voted—and the question of representation will be resolved according to the result of that new vote.

In my opinion the former procedure is more correct. And if we are satisfied that Comrade Kazannik is withdrawing unconditionally, then the next deputy should be the one who polled the largest number of votes, in this case without an alternative. But in order for this solution to take effect, a congress vote will be needed because, I repeat, no provision is made in our legislation for either procedure. We must therefore first decide which variant we will choose.

M.S. Gorbachev: Does any other lawyer wish to speak? Comrade Burlatskiy.

F.M. Burlatskiy, political observer for LITERATURNAYA GAZETA, Moscow city (from the Soviet Peace Foundation jointly with the 8 Soviet committees for peace, solidarity and international cooperation): Comrades, I believe that this issue is not only a legal one, but also political. What we need to do here is not look for some precedent or form, but move to the essence of the matter. I express only my own personal opinion; I disagree with Boris Nikolayevich Yeltsin on many issues and and ready to enter into dispute with him, but, giving due consideration to the fact that Moscow has by an overwhelming majority voted for that candidate, it is essential to deal reasonably with this. I therefore propose, comrades, that since there is a person who has announced his withdrawal, that seat should automatically be assumed by Boris Nikolayevich Yeltsin. Thank you. (Applause).

A.P. Yanenko, rector of the Novosibirsk Construction Engineering Institute (Oktyabrskiy Territorial Electoral Okrug, Novosibirsk Oblast): I would like to remind you, dear colleagues, that when the first session of our congress opened, Mikhail Sergeyevich Gorbachev took the chair. According to the Constitution, it should have been chaired by the chairman of the Central Electoral Commission. But the congress decided to confirm Mikhail Sergeyevich Gorbachev as congress chairman. I therefore suggest that the congress has a real right to decide that Boris Nikolayevich Yeltsin be in the composition of the USSR Supreme Soviet, after a proposal to that effect has been adopted. (Applause).

B.V. Miroshin, chairman of Sovetskiy Rayispolkom, Orsk city (Orsk Territorial Electoral Okrug, RSFSR): Respected comrades, I work as a rayispolkom chairman and am by education a lawyer. I have had an opportunity to see the reaction of the Muscovites in the election campaign, I know the results of the voting in Moscow for Boris Nikolayevich Yeltsin, and I personally voted for him in the voting for the Soviet of Nationalities. I am aware of the mood of the people of Orenburg, particularly my own fellow townspeople, my voters, who favor Boris Nikolayevich Yeltsin. Last Saturday on Revolution Square I met a large number of Muscovites and guests of the city, and was there from 2200 in the evening until 0130 the next morning answering questions, including questions about Boris Nikolayevich Yeltsin. The viewpoint has already been expressed, comrades, and I support it, that we make the only reasonable and correct decision—to give the vacant seat to Boris Nikolayevich Yeltsin. (Applause).

M.S. Gorbachev: Comrade Krayko, please. (Commotion in the hall). Comrades, we need consultation.

A.N. Krayko, section chief in the P.I. Baranov Central Institute of Aviation Engine Building, Moscow city (Baumanskiy Territory Electoral Okrug, Moscow city): Comrades, the question is in the main clear, since everyone is expressing himself in one mind, and it will be correct if we so decide about Comrade Yeltsin. But I would like simply to draw your attention to one factor. The fact is that everyone is asking the following question: As the list of candidates contained 12 people rather than 11, how did the alternative appear? Everyone can see the machinations of the apparatus in this. I would like to say that this then became clear: The fact that the list contained 12 names was on the initiative of Boris Nikolayevich. It testifies exactly to his honesty and probity, and to the fact that he serves the purpose for which we have elected him. The fact is that Boris Nikolayevich insisted that there be an alternative in the elections for other posts, and naturally he could not make an exception for himself. So there it is; I have explained it for him and for Comrade Vorotnikov, and it really is so—Yeltsin insisted that the list contain 12 names. It is another matter that we could not immediately imagine that someone would withdraw. I therefore support the proposal, and I have offered this explanation so that the whole country may know about it. I think the fact that Boris Nikolayevich acted in this way is an additional argument in favor of his being in the Soviet of Nationalities.

M.S. Gorbachev: So, comrades, there has been an exchange of opinions. We have been discussing procedural matters for 2 hours and our time has run out. We are limited to these statements. Permit me to avail myself of the counsel from the comrades who have spoken here and sum up the debate, even though it is

STENOGRAPHIC RECORD

Fifth Session
29 May 1989

difficult to always find a line of conduct in this heated discussion. I think—and I would like to assure you that I am sticking to the main issue—that the atmosphere at our congress has remained democratic, that there has been a great diversity and pluralism of opinions on all matters discussed, and that it is from this that we here in the presidium will proceed. But this is not so simple given the enormous number of initiatives from deputies and given that, in addition to the agenda, to which it would seem we should strictly adhere, many issues have been raised to which we have had to respond. I think that we are gaining experience but are not changing the main issues, and although we do adhere to the agenda, we are at the same time resolving questions that arise so as to preserve the democratic atmosphere. That is first.

Now, comrades, permit me to propose the following to you. Perhaps we should act thus. Very many important issues have been raised here. Let us assign the presidium and the secretariat the task of extracting from all the statements the proposals of a substantive nature. There are many of them. If I were to start listing only those that I have noted from comrades' statements, we would be dragged into another long discussion. I think that we must categorize the most substantive proposals and let the presidium and secretariat consider what should be done about particular proposals. In one form or another the categorized proposals will be passed to the deputies and then a determination will be made of how we should proceed with particular matters. Certainly we have now set the kind of consideration that no other approach is possible, otherwise there will be a muddle and the entire discussion will have to be repeated. If you have no objections, then we shall assign the congress presidium and secretariat the task of generalizing the comments that have been made by deputies and of submitting these proposals to each deputy, while at the same time considering how to implement them. Who is in favor of this proposal, if there are no others, comrades? This is what I think: this must all be generalized tomorrow, and by the end of the day generalized proposals circulated, and the presidium will determine in, say, 2 days, what kind of commission is needed to implement these and other assignments provided for in the documents.

From the hall: Mikhail Sergeyevich, the question of Yeltsin....

M.S. Gorbachev: We are resolving Yeltsin now.

From the hall: (Inaudible).

M.S. Gorbachev: Microphone No 1 is next to you. Switch it on.

From the hall: In my opinion we must add one other proposal to yours. Many substantive proposals have not been voiced since there has been no time under the Rules. But there may be very specific and fine proposals.

M.S. Gorbachev: I agree. So we must include the following point: Comrades who consider it necessary to put forward specific proposals may submit them to the congress secretariat.

From the hall: Then how can each deputy exercise his right of legislative initiative? How shall we act in this case? Deputies have specific proposals....

M.S. Gorbachev: You know that we here in the presidium have already discussed this issue and have concluded that perhaps during the course of the congress work we must have a special commission of deputies. This is not a standing institution but a working commission. We can consider and introduce proposals in it.

From the hall: I have received many telegrams on various subjects. In particular, one telegram states that if we do not have direct secret balloting then we shall look like an okrug meeting.... And Yeltsin would have been elected to the Supreme Soviet right from the start.

M.S. Gorbachev: Comrades, I am putting to the vote the proposal that was put forward, with one very important addition: Those comrades who have been unable to speak but who have proposals may pass them to the congress secretariat. I ask those in favor of this resolution to raise their hands. Thank you. Against? No. Abstentions? The resolution is carried.

Let us turn to the question that Comrade Popov raised, on the basis of which we held our consultation....

From the hall: (Inaudible).

M.S. Gorbachev: The question is resolved. Resolved by the congress.

From the hall: (Inaudible).

M.S. Gorbachev: The next problem that has been raised. When it was raised it was done so by Comrade Popov, and I asked the lawyers to give their opinions about the possibilities available to us here, and about what kind of legal basis we have here for adopting any particular decision. I think that in principle we are favorably inclined resolving the matter. But let us do it in parts. First. The withdrawal of Deputy Kazannik—we can accept this.

From the hall: Mikhail Sergeyevich, it seems to me.... (Inaudible).

M.S. Gorbachev: So, everything is clear. Comrade Kazannik. You wanted to say something? Switch on the second microphone. It is necessary that you withdraw all conditions.

Fifth Session

29 May 1989

A.I. Kazannik: Comrades, I cannot withdraw the conditions. And do you know why? I fear that if I now relinquish my powers Mikhail Sergeyevich Gorbachev will say: "Who, comrades, is in favor of Boris Nikolayevich Yeltsin being on the USSR Supreme Soviet Soviet of Nationalities?" To judge from how we elected the Supreme Soviet, I fear that a majority in this hall will vote against Boris Nikolayevich Yeltsin. I would therefore like to put forward a proposal. If I withdraw my nomination I reason further that Boris Nikolayevich Yeltsin will automatically become a member of the USSR Supreme Soviet Soviet of Nationalities, since he has obtained an absolute majority of the votes. I do not see why it depends here on the fact that I first withdraw without any conditions, and that we then put it to the vote and elect him. I fear that the opposite may happen....

M.S. Gorbachev: Very well.

From the hall: Comrades, there is no problem here. The sequence must be changed. First we vote on whether or not we accept the procedural proposal that in the event that one of those elected withdraws, then his place will be taken by the person with the next largest number of votes. (Applause).

And the withdrawal is the second question. Then it is up to the comrade as to whether or not he will withdraw his nomination, according to the result of the first vote. (Applause).

From the hall: Wonderful, I fully agree.

M.S. Gorbachev: Let us consider what happens if we reverse this pyramid. Yes, Comrade (name inaudible). I fear that the main thing would be that in our haste we would get it wrong and not do the proper thing.

Deputy (not introduced): Respected comrades. The existing status of the people's deputies provides for the following procedure for the early relinquishing of the powers of deputy. The powers of a deputy may be withdrawn early at the decision of the Soviet. We have adopted no changes, in connection with the congress, on the personal statement of a deputy with respect to him relinquishing his powers of deputy because of circumstances that prevent their exercise. Consequently.... (Commotion in the hall).

Thank you very much for the prompting; I would like to return to the following. A procedure does exist within the framework of the status. Consequently, in order for us now to reach a decision, we can decide either by chance, on impulse—and then, consequently, we can do anything we like here—or we should now provide an opportunity for preparing tomorrow a procedural amendment, which I have already mentioned here, on the possibility of not simply a deputy but a member of the Supreme Soviet withdrawing, and then whoever is next in line should take that seat. There you have it. (Commotion in the hall).

M.S. Gorbachev: If anyone is confusing us, comrades, well, they are lawyers.

L.A. Kuznetsov, senior teacher in the botany department at the Leningrad A.I. Gertsen State Pedagogical Institute, Leningrad city (from the societies and associations of the USSR Academy of Sciences): I propose that this problem, which everyone obviously wants to resolve, be resolved in the following manner. We do have a precedent, so let us act in accordance with the precedent with respect to the Soviet of the Union. We rescinded our decision on the confirmation there with respect to the Nagorno-Karabakh Autonomous Republic. Here, in the same way, we can rescind our decision with respect to the RSFSR, after which Deputy Kazannik can then withdraw his nomination and Boris Nikolayevich Yeltsin will automatically take his seat. I believe that we can act in this way from precedent.

M.S. Gorbachev: Comrades, what if, despite all out desires to find a positive solution to this question, you allow the presidium together with the lawyers to work on this question, and have the matter introduced tomorrow so that it can be resolved?

Then let us go into recess. Fine, then I shall take the risk that of availing myself of the fact that there is no organ higher than the congress. I am a convinced advocate of our not tampering with the present Constitution; everything should be decided very carefully, without haste. But in this case we shall not affect the Constitution.

From the hall: No.

M.S. Gorbachev: It is a matter of, so to speak, an election law, a matter of elections and of unregulated matters. We must, perhaps, ourselves create precedent here. If, I think, it had been a matter of Comrade Yeltsin slipping by without obtaining half or more of the votes, then the question would no longer arise; it would simply be voted on and we would not have been able to use the vacancy that would be opened up because of the withdrawal of Deputy Kazannik. But since we do have a statement to that effect and an opportunity is opening up for us, then we will be able to resort to the following procedure: Because Comrade Yeltsin obtained more than half of the votes, then he should occupy the seat that becomes vacant. And then, naturally, there will be no need for another vote. So, let us start with the proposal to adopt the proposal of, I think, Comrade Palm, in his formulation. I have repeated its sense.

Those in favor of the proposal raise their hands. Thank you. Against? Any abstentions? Well, comrades, just a few. So, the matter is resolved.

STENOGRAPHIC RECORD

Fifth Session

29 May 1989

Then we must satisfy the request of member of the Supreme Soviet Deputy Kazannik on relinquishing his powers, and welcome his initiative. (Applause).

Let me put this question to the vote. All those in favor of satisfying the request of Deputy Kazannik that he relinquish his duties as a member of the Soviet of Nationalities, please raise their hands. Thank you. Against? There are several. Abstentions? The matter is resolved. (Applause).

So, taking into account the report of the chairman of the counting commission on all candidates, and giving due consideration to these present decisions, we can now adopt a resolution confirming the minutes of the counting commission, adding the changes stemming from these decisions. (Applause).

From the hall: (Inaudible).

M.S. Gorbachev: There is no need to vote on the RSFSR, that is until we leave the matter and consider it regulated.

We still have one matter on the Nagorno-Karabakh Autonomous Republic. But we have already run over 30 minutes. I think that we can return to that question. But let comrades be ready to make their proposals. One more thing: as there was tension here after the statement by one of the representatives of the deputy group from Azerbaijan, and representatives of the deputy group from Armenia also wanted to speak, I would like to say the following. Again tension has arisen among us and again, so to speak, mutual claims are being made. I therefore once again appeal to the group of deputies from Armenia and the group of deputies from Azerbaijan to maintain friendly relations and to look for ways of rapprochement. And finally, the discussion must not be turned upside down. The comrades from Armenia have agreed to my request, and also with what I will say. I would like once again to remark, comrades, that at the congress we must approach everything with a great sense of responsibility, and especially this subject, since it has been brought up.

I think that we can end our meeting today. The meeting is closed. If anyone has unresolved questions he should come here. Until tomorrow at 1000 hours.

STENOGRAPHIC RECORD

FIRST CONGRESS OF PEOPLE'S DEPUTIES OF THE USSR
SIXTH SESSION
TUESDAY, 30 MAY 1989
THE KREMLIN PALACE OF CONGRESSES

The long-anticipated report of the general secretary was delivered on the fifth day of the Congress. In *Izvestiya*'s estimation the speech "contained nothing deliberately designed for effect, nothing to capture the imagination, and nothing to elicit applause." It was, in other words, a "downer." If the Congress and the nation were expecting a call to action to fulfill a bold new agenda, they had dialed the wrong channel. The essence of Gorbachev's message was that the country faced a number of problems and something had to be done about them. The state was continuing to live beyond its means, wages were outstripping productivity, the distribution system was in chaos, agrarian reform was foundering on misunderstanding and bureaucratic opposition. The critical social issues were poverty, health care, housing, the environment, and nomenklatura privilege, while the groups needing special attention were youth, women, and veterans. A free market was out of the question; the goal remained "a full-blooded socialist market" that would protect workers from exploitation and alienation from the means of production. Capital investment would be shifted from heavy industry and arms production to civilian programs and the production of consumer goods. The state bureaucracy would be reorganized and streamlined.

As an indication either of its seriousness or the audience's disappointment, the speech was interrupted by applause only nine times. The issues that elicited visceral approval were Gorbachev's call for a special commission to review all social benefits and privileges, his announcement of a 14 percent reduction in military spending, his vindication of the Communist Party as the harmonizing force in the renewal of socialism, and his calls for legal protection of the individual, judicial reform, more effective law enforcement, and a restoration of order and discipline. His mention of the normalization of relations with China drew applause, while, interestingly, his reference to nuclear arms reduction, the easing of tensions in Europe, and the withdrawal from Afghanistan did not.

Following a brief recess, the first of a number of "co-reporters" began their litany of the country's ills and their suggestions for ameliorating them. The relative calm of the morning was interrupted, however, by G.A. Pogosyan's introduction of a resolution on Nagorno-Karabakh's representation in the Soviet of Nationalities. In its third session, the Congress had annulled the NKAO election, because the candidates, the Armenian Pogosyan and the Azerbaijani V.D. Dzhafarov, were the nominees of the Azerbaijan SSR. (Although predominantly Armenian, the NKAO is a subdivision of Azerbaijan.) The NKAO, however, had its own nominees, both Armenian, Pogosyan and Z.G. Balayan. The Armenians claimed that the people of an oblast had the right to choose their own representatives. The Congress had agreed and voided the election, but the two sides had been advised to meet with the Presidium and come to an agreement. Their agreement was to hold another election, with three candidates Pogosyan, Balayan, and Dzhafarov competing for the two seats. After an intense debate during which the chairman, R.N. Nishanov, nearly lost control of the podium, the resolution was adopted and the election scheduled for the evening.

The evening session opened with Kara-Kalpak deputy T. Kaipbergenov's depressing tale of the ecological destruction of the Aral Sea region, but the Armenian question resurfaced and dominated the proceedings for the rest of the evening. It began when Tamaz Gankrelidze of the Georgian Academy of Sciences, having detailed the Tbilisi tragedy of 9 April 1989, placed a major share of the blame on the commander of the Transcaucasus Military District, General I.N. Rodionov, and declared him morally and legally unfit to be a people's deputy. Rodionov then took the podium, denounced all one-sided distortions of the truth, and gave his version and interpretation of events. The deputies then wrangled over the composition of the commission named by the Presidium to investigate the Tbilisi affair and, when Nishanov presented the proposed roster of the Gdlyan-Ivanov investigating commission, the debate extended to the membership of that group. At length the Congress adjourned in order to vote on the NKAO representatives to the Soviet of Nationalities. See Appendix B.5, B.6, C.5, C.6.

SIXTH SESSION
TUESDAY, 30 MAY 1989
STENOGRAPHIC RECORD

USSR People's Deputy R.N. Nishanov, presiding.

Nishanov: Dear comrade people's deputies! We are continuing the work of the congress. Let us turn to the next question on the agenda of our congress: "On the Basic Directions for the Domestic and Foreign Policy of the Union of Soviet Socialist Republics." The floor is given to Comrade Mikhail Sergeyevich Gorbachev, USSR Supreme Soviet Chairman, CPSU Central Committee General Secretary, for a report. (Applause).

[Report by Mikhail Sergeyevich Gorbachev, general secretary of the CPSU Central Committee and chairman of the USSR Supreme Soviet, at the Congress of People's Deputies held in the Kremlin Palace of Congresses—live]

[Text] Esteemed comrade deputies, it has been declared from this rostrum more than once that universal attention is riveted on what is happening in this hall of the Kremlin. We will not calculate in which cases this reflects reality and corresponds with the real state of affairs, and in which cases we pass off what we desire as reality. Nevertheless, I believe that today we have every right, relying on what we know, to assert that the attention of all the Soviet people and all the world public is riveted on our congress.

Events are taking place in the Kremlin these days which signify that the political history of the Soviet Union is entering a new democratic stage, in the throes, in the struggle with the difficulties and complexities. Out of the contradictions and hard clashes a new Soviet parliament is coming into being, a new system of the state mechanism is being formed which in practice includes all citizens in the difficult labor of self-government. This is the view of our Czechoslovak friends, expressed in RUDE PRAVO.

Our congress is in its 5th day of work, and for the 5th day passions are boiling in this hall. I believe we are all agreed that the work of the congress is proceeding on the wavelength of the democratic renewal of life and of the deep revolutionary processes in society. There is scarcely any need today to offer proof that the congress itself and everything that preceded it, and the character of the debates that have begun, are a convincing victory for restructuring, and in essence a fresh page in the destiny of our state. Grasping truth by all of us together and by each of us is no easy process but, comrade deputies, it is a vital necessity for us. It is quite natural that in the frank examination of all our affairs and the impartial analysis of the causes of the situation that has formed and of the progress of the transformations which have begun, all of this is liberating society from the fetters of apathy and indifference, and is engendering a ferment of minds and clashes of stances and proposals.

However varied the opinions, the debates at the session are in keeping with the fundamental ideas put forward by the CPSU since April 1985—especially at the 19th party conference—and with the party's preelection program. I state this with immense satisfaction, since I see in this an expression of important popular support for the restructuring policy. Even in its first days our congress has clearly reflected the complex and contradictory processes under way in the country, and it could not have been otherwise. By the beginning of the 1980's, as a result of long years of stagnation, the country found itself in a state of serious crisis, which embraced all spheres of life. The situation demanded of the party a sharp turn. This was a most responsible choice, and the party made it. Today we can all see the correctness of this choice. The wave of renewal has woken up the country.

A process of assimilating new forms of public life has begun, comrades, in the economy, politics, and culture. The congress has once again demonstrated the profound understanding of the fact that restructuring is our destiny. It is a chance given us by history. It cannot and must not be missed. However varied and contradictory the opinions, a kind of nationwide accord has formed that there is no alternative to the political course of renewal, of fundamental renewal of socialism. All that is so. But today the country expects of the congress a truthful analysis of how restructuring is being implemented, what it has brought, where and why it has not yet justified the expectations, where difficulties and problems have arisen, and what they are. Most importantly, people are expecting specific decisions which provide for forward progress. That is why the talk that has begun at the congress, which has set the tone for the freedom and emancipation in its work, is so important. Difficult decisions await us all. We have all to bear responsibility for them before the Soviet people. But I am confident that the congress will display circumspection and statesmanlike wisdom in assessing the situation and determining practical measures.

Of course, we must not expect instantaneous changes in all spheres of life. Right now we must urgently focus all our efforts to resolve striking problems as soon as possible. I regard this as one of the chief tasks of the congress, the Supreme Soviet, and the new government. The foundations of restructuring, and a decisive factor in achieving its goals, are the profound transformations in the economic and social spheres. The point of all work in this sphere is to turn the economy toward the people, and to create working and living conditions for Soviet people that are worthy of our times. We are dealing first and foremost with such processes and matters as foodstuffs, housing, services, health care, environmental protection, and improving education, science, and culture. We have to understand the situation that has come about collectively, approaching the assessment of it from truthful, realistic and exacting positions. It is important to see the whole picture as it is in order to consolidate and give greater dynamism and stability to all the positive things that have been achieved, and at the same time rid oneself decisively of what was the result of errors made in policies and the practical work both in the center and in the localities.

I believe that we are entitled to talk about the actual process that has begun for the reorientation of the economy toward the social needs of the people. The average annual volume of housing construction in the last 3 years has been increased by 15 percent compared with the previous 5-Year Plan. This means that the Soviet people have received approximately 900,000 apartments. Last year R1.9 billion were allocated in credit for individual housing construction, which is six times higher than in 1985. Housing construction in the country is expanding.

Under difficult economic conditions R6 billion of additional funds were found in the 5-Year Plan for health care, and more than R6 billion for education. Teachers' pay has been increased, and the pay of doctors and other medical staff continues to rise. As a result of the measures taken, 39 percent more polyclinics, 37 percent more schools, 14 percent more children's preschool establishments, 20 percent more hospitals, and 54 percent more culture clubs and houses have been opened in an average year of this 5-Year Plan than in the previous one. As many residential homes for the aged and the disabled have been constructed as were constructed in the whole of the previous 5-Year Plan.

For the first time in our economic history the increase in the production of consumer goods is outstripping the development of industry as a whole for the 2d consecutive year. The services sector is expanding twice as fast as in previous years, by 15 pecent every year. In the last 3 years more than 5 million families have received land for gardening plots, collective gardens, and kitchen gardens.

Already in the first years of restructuring we were faced with the problem of increasing labor productivity through accelerating scientific and technological progress, since it is only on this basis that one can build realistic plans for the development of the economy and for improvement of people's life. For all the shortage of resources, in the 12th 5-year-plan period virtually twice as much capital investment was allocated for the development of priority sectors of machine building and electronics than in the previous 5 years. It was necessary to do this because we are a great deal behind in these spheres.

In our investment policy we emphasize tackling social issues. But we strive not to lose time for creating groundwork connected with enhancing the scientific and technological level of the national economy, so as to have resources available, in the future too, for the improvement of the people's life. We have not yet perceived any substantial return from these undertakings. My conversations with many people's deputies are constantly dwelling on the subject of the shortage of progressive machinery and equipment, something which is holding back the modernization of our national economy. Nevertheless, the pace of renewing the output of machine building has started to grow. The growth of labor productivity has been accelerated. A real reduction in the number of those engaged in the sphere of material production has started. This is also for the first time in the history of our economy.

Why am I talking about this? Not, you understand, in order to embellish the state of our affairs, or present them in rosy colors. This, simply, would not have been serious. I have in mind both those who are sitting in this hall and those millions of people who are following carefully the proceedings of our congress. This is necessary in order to gain an in-depth understanding of the process underway, to identify the sore points, the kind of knots of tension that have emerged on the path of the positive tendencies and processes that have arisen.

What is the matter? Why are we not yet aware even of those positive things that have been done? Above all because the country's financial system has become seriously upset and the consumer market uncoordinated. Shortages of all kinds and a panic for goods arouse among people acute and legitimate discontent and cause social tension in society. There are various causes for this. They include the difficult legacy of the past, the great losses brought about by the fall of world prices for fuel and raw materials, the Chernobyl tragedy, and natural disasters.

But it is also true that the economic situation is greatly connected with our own actions, and sometimes inaction, already during the years of restructuring. Let's start with the fact that the state continues living beyond its means. Expenditure is growing faster than national income during this 5-year-plan period. Hence the budget deficit is rising. Economically, this is simply impermissible, and cannot be considered other than a serious miscalculation in the economic policy, for which first

Sixth Session
30 May 1989

and foremost the USSR Finance Minister and its apparatus bear responsibility. The backlog of incompleted work in the sphere of capital construction has not only failed to decrease, as had been envisaged in the decisions of the 27th congress, but has on the contrary considerably increased, by R30 billion. Both Gosplan and the USSR State Committee for Construction [Gosstroy] have failed to stand up to the pressure of departments and local bodies, while the government has failed to show appropriate exactingness. Such a radical question in the economic reform as the creation of a mechanism for regulating and coordinating the end results of labor with the fund of payment for it has not been resolved—something without which it is impossible to advance in the economic sphere. Situations are arising in which expenditure on wages is growing much faster than labor productivity. We are all in favor of people earning good money, and of their wages growing steadily. But this must be bound up with the actual final results of their labor. Otherwise there will be too much money and too few goods—a difficult situation. This is indeed the case.

So, comrades, we have to get down straightaway to drawing up an economic mechanism for resolving this problem. The first few steps have been taken; initial proposals in this respect have been made. I am counting on a profound and competent discussion of these problems here at the congress.

No analysis of the causes of the existing situation would be complete unless it pointed out that great losses are still being incurred through mismanagement and poor labor discipline. This is also connected with the mastering of the new mechanism, of course, but this mastering, too, is occurring in different ways: some people have properly adopted financial-autonomy relations, which is already producing results, while others continue to live in the old way, or else are simply marking time. Here there is the question of the responsibility of cadres at all levels, of their degree of competence, of whether they meet today's requirements. All our shortcomings, mistakes, and misfortunes have come together in the one main problem of today: the imbalance of the market. It is this that is bringing to naught the positive shifts that have now begun in the economy and the social sphere, small though they may be as yet. This issue has assumed a political nature.

The most urgent task for today is to halt immediately the buildup of adverse phenomena and primarily to normalize the market situation. The most important thing here is a rapid increase in the production of goods and services, in order to ensure that goods stocks increase more rapidly than money incomes. There are, admittedly, other viewpoints: Some believe that, whether we like it or not, this problem must be solved by switching on full the mechanisms of a market economy—let the market sort everything out. We do not share this approach, since it would immediately destroy the entire social situation and disrupt all the processes in the country.

For this year the task has been set of increasing goods production by more than R37 billion, and to substantially improve the situation next year scientists and specialists reckon that this increase will have to be raised to R55-60 billion. In accordance with this, a great deal of work has been under way in the industries and republics. Tremendous or, it could be said, exceptional efforts will be required from the center, the regions, and the labor collectives. But the work on this problem shows that we do possess real capabilities for doing this. Use must be made here not only of the resources, of the capabilities of light industry, food industry, and agriculture, but of all sectors of our economy, including heavy industry and defense enterprises. In a word, all the production capacities that can now be converted to produce the consumer goods required by the population must be used.

Many suggestions are being put forward from the localities on how to put existing reserves to work and saturate the market with goods. The newly constituted government with the republics' participation should complete this work, draw up a specific plan of action, and submit this plan to the USSR Supreme Soviet. As for the shortages of everyday goods, we ought, evidently, to hear a concrete reply from our government on this at the congress.

Of course, the most decisive measures must be taken to improve finances and put money circulation in the country into order. We shall not be able to manage here without making the necessary corrections to the country's entire economic activity, and without drawing up a strict and exceptional [chrezvychaynyy] economy-drive budget. The congress could obviously give special instructions to the government on this matter.

Finally, one must not discount the possibilities of imports, both for developing the light and food industries, and for stocking up the market with consumer goods, subject to the provisos that have already been repeatedly mentioned.

Fulfillment of the decisions of the March Central Committee plenum on issues relating to agrarian policy and the food problem should be singled out as a task of prime importance, both because it is an urgent matter which demands nationwide efforts, and because the restructuring of economic relations in the countryside, and the transition to the new conditions of management, are proceeding, shall we say, with great difficulty, meeting with both a lack of complete understanding and, not infrequently, direct opposition. Let us once again discuss this issue, which is an issue of state importance, taking into account the political directives of the March plenum and the requirements of life.

STENOGRAPHIC RECORD

Sixth Session
30 May 1989

We have all come to the conclusion that without a radical restructuring of economic relations in the countryside, things will not move ahead, and we will be unable to solve the food problem as we want to. No matter how much money we direct there, this will not have the required effect unless this fundamental issue is resolved. But if we are agreed on this, what is it all about, then? This agreement was indeed reached; it was established on the eve of the plenum and found reflection in the decisions of the plenum itself.

Over the past few days I have several times talked to deputies who work in the agrarian sector; they have also held many meetings here, as you are aware. A somewhat curious and contradictory picture emerges: When you talk to the managers and specialists of collective farms [kolkhozes] and state farms [sovkhozes], you hear that there must be more machinery and capital investment, and social amenities in the countryside must be provided more rapidly. That is indeed so, and we did indeed speak about this at the March plenum. With regard to the social development of the countryside, everything must be done to create normal conditions of life for the rural laborer. This must not only be done urgently: We should already have done it considerably better, and sooner. But I felt that some comrades among economists and specialists are not particularly disposed toward the transition to new forms of economic management, to setting up cooperatives, to leasing, to peasant farms. One even said to me: Whoever gave you the idea of bringing in leasing, Mikhail Sergeyevich?

But when you talk to lessees—there are also lessees present here, USSR people's deputies—they are of a different opinion. They are in favor of restructuring economic relations in the countryside, and have an interest in supporting the decisions of the March Central Committee plenum in this regard. At the same time, however, they say that despite these decisions, despite the decree on leasing and the corresponding government decisions, the new forms of management are being held up and are coming up against all sorts of bureaucratic impediments.

The leaseholders say that the local bodies continue to give orders to the kolkhozes and sovkhozes, while the managers and specialists of kolkhozes and sovkhozes in turn do not want to give up the same command methods toward the peasants themselves and the employees of the sovkhozes. Many of them prefer to conduct matters in the old way. They prevent the expansion of financial autonomy relations in rural areas, referring to the unwillingness of peasants to lease land and the means of production. I have heard this here, taking part in one of the conversations. This is the view of the economic planners. Evidently differing interests are clashing here. We have to exchange views about this, comrades, and discuss bluntly what is necessary to ensure that the important decisions of the plenum do not hang in mid-air, and most importantly that the foodstuffs situation improves. Indeed the point of the political directives and the decisions of the Central Committee March plenum is to return man to the land through new forms of economic management, hand him the means of production, make him the master of the land, and thus awaken his personal interest and strengthen the material state in increasing agricultural produce.

Alongside this I want to stress the need to engage immediately in providing the countryside with social amenities and developing in rural areas the trade network, housing construction, public services, the whole infrastructure, and particularly roads. In all regions of the country rural inhabitants are pointedly raising the issue of the provision of gas supplies. As we have huge possibilities at our disposal, we do not have the right to dodge resolution of these matters either.

The USSR people's deputies representing the agrarian sector say that the ministries and departments producing equipment and fertilizers for rural areas are restructuring themselves very slowly. We must investigate this. On the one hand a lot of equipment is being produced in the country, and on the other there is an outcry all over that there is not enough. That means that the right equipment is not being produced. So let's finally make the necessary adjustments to our program so as to organize in the next few years the production of a system of machinery which is needed by the farms, the lease-holders, and the private subsidiary plots of all regions, and which is also affordable—a matter of no small importance. Agrarian sector representatives say that the machine builders have literally hiked up the prices on all equipment, despite the fact that it has changed little on a practical basis in terms of quality and output capabilities.

Comrades, it is also essential to confer on other social policy priorities for the upcoming period. The matter of raising the standard of living of the less well-off section of the population, pensioners, large families, orphans and the disabled, should be placed among those at the top of the list. This problem is of great sociopolitical significance in present-day conditions. Indeed, it involves more than 40 million people on low incomes. However difficult it may be to tackle it, given the present difficult financial situation, this must be done, and as soon as possible. Among the most important measures in this area is the introduction of the new law on pensions, a draft of which is being prepared by the government. It will be presented to the USSR Supreme Soviet and submitted for nationwide discussion. I assume that a law of such importance should then be adopted at the Congress of USSR People's Deputies.

The quality of medical care affects the interests of everyone; a nation's health is a major condition for success in everything. Let us spare no effort, comrades,

STENOGRAPHIC RECORD

Sixth Session
30 May 1989

in ensuring that a network of hospitals and polyclinics equipped with modern machines is developed throughout the country, and that the problem of medical supplies to the population is solved once and for all.

Despite all the difficulties, we are finding, and I hope will find, resources for these purposes. But as regards the assimilation of these resources, the situation has so far been extremely unsatisfactory, though we are really only beginning to create a health care base, a modern health care base in the country. The fault here lies with the builders and, in my view, the local authorities. And one other point: Because of the radical economic reform, financial and material resources are accumulating in enterprises and in the local administrative bodies. It seems to me that labor collectives could unite their efforts to expand the health care base for the population. All these issues have to be strictly monitored by the deputies. In establishing a healthy way of life, particular attention must be paid to environmental protection and, as they say nowadays, to ecological security. The state of affairs here is worrying, to say the least. In just over 100 of the country's cities the quantity of hazardous substances in the atmosphere exceeds the permissible norms; there is a severe situation regarding the protection of water resources, the major rivers and forests, and the use of natural minerals. The problem of land preservation, even of irrigated land, is acute everywhere. Immediate action must be taken.

As I see things, there are two paths we should take; first, we need a clear-cut program for resolving the problems that have already accumulated; this concerns industry, agriculture, water resources, and forests—in short, the entire habitable environment. It seems to me that the drawing up of a national program for this is being dragged out. At this congress we must express definite, quite definite, demands that this work be speeded up. Furthermore, it is important that the resources allocated for this be fully assimilated. We have been saying that many problems have accumulated and that they must be tackled without delay, just like the issues of housing, food, and goods. This is correct, because unless we begin working on the habitable environment now, a disaster awaits us. It's already on the threshold; we have already come face to face with it, so to speak. But just take a look: We are saying that we allocate too few resources, though they are actually increasing each year. But comrades, the resources allocated for environmental protection purposes are only half used. So, comrades, let us not only raise these issues by way of criticism but get down to concrete work, tackle them in practice. On the whole, we neeed to be more businesslike and exacting, I would say—exacting.

The second, and no less important, direction is that we have to arrange things so that all schemes and scientific-technical solutions ensure ecological security. And for this they must be strictly tested for ecological purity. Very...[changes thought] We are continuing to push through unsuitable plans—from the point of view of ecological security—to surprise...[corrects himself] to reduce the cost of various projects. For example, I was speaking to a deputy from Komsomolsk-na-Amur, which I once visited, where the working people are very concerned that they have to import furniture from the center. They reached an agreement with the minister—Comrade Belousov was the minister at the time—and he said that it is possible to produce R20 milion worth of furniture and that they would do everything, even buy equipment abroad, to double the output of furniture for people. It was a good idea and they began to put it into effect. They bought the equipment but they didn't buy the pollution control devices. This is a living example, so to speak, of how it happens, comrades. What kind of a saving is that? Who needs it? And now there are rallies in Komsomolsk-na-Amur because of it.

I repeat that, overall, all projects must undergo strict monitoring for ecological cleanliness. As you know, during the election campaign there was acute discussion of the issues of constructing a number of canals, atomic power stations, and chemical enterprises from the viewpoint of ecological safety. The Congress Presidium is now receiving such inquiries, too, or simply notes. Obviously, the USSR Supreme Soviet and its relevant commissions will immediately have to accept these issues for careful consideration and solution. In doing so, it must pay attention to both ecological requirements and the interests of the further development of the eocnomy, without which it is impossible to satisfy the vital needs of the people.

In connection with the examination of social questions, I would like to express confidence that the congress will endorse the political directive of the 27th party congress aimed at resolving the housing problem to provide every family with an individual apartment or house by the year 2000. It is a task that is very, very far from easy. But it has to be addressed, comrades. I am convinced, and have become even more convinced, of the rightness of such a formulation, of the solid grounds for such a formulation, during my meetings with working people in all regions of the country. I will tell you bluntly: During my conversations, the main, the first question that the working people raise is the housing question, not even the food supply question, not even the question of goods.

The housing question: It is a task that is very, very far from easy. But taking account of the acuteness of this problem for millions of people in towns and rural areas, we clearly have to reassess the plans already outlined and find new possibilities for expanding the scale of housing construction. We have instructions to study the situation and determine our position: What is required to definitely reach a solution to this problem, so that, having taken on such a commitment to the people, we should not end up bankrupt? I should remind you: In the 11th 5-year Plan period, 550 million square meters of housing were built. In the 12th 5-year Plan period the task has

Sixth Session
30 May 1989

been set to bring housing construction up to 650 million square meters. We will meet this task; that is already clear. For the 13th 5-year Plan period the task is being put forward in the preliminary drafts to bring the volume of housing construction up to 820 million square meters, but it is now clear by all accounts that we shall need to reach 900 million, and then, to reach 1 billion square meters in the 14th 5-year Plan period. Then we can speak of the reality of fulfilling the set task.

Of course, all reserves have to be brought in for this, all the possibilities of enterprises and of individual and cooperative housing construction. There is no shortage of initiative. People want to build housing. But what is it that is holding up things today? It is, of course, the shortage of building materials, plumbing fixtures, and everything that is essential for fitting out housing with facilities. Complaints come in from all sides on this score, and it is not only a matter of measures which have to be taken at the center, although they must unfailingly be reflected in our plans. We must all together bring our weight to bear on resolving the task of housing construction, using all local reserves. I would say that this is one of the most important acts of republican and local organs of power, and of their economic organizations. I hope that in the course of the debates we shall deepen the discussion of this theme, and that the congress will give special instructions to the Supreme Soviet and to the new government.

Comrades, social policy cannot be effective if it does not respond to the interests of different strata, social strata, of society. Our society has a vital interest in ensuring better starting conditions for the new generations entering independent life, so that they have everything necessary to reveal their creative abilities, to display the energy of youth, and to take an active part in affairs of state. A considerable number of problems have accumulated here. As you know, the Komsomol Central Committee has prepared a draft law on young people and has submitted it for examination by the USSR Supreme Soviet as a legislative initiative. However, matters cannot, of course, be reduced to the adoption of one law, even the best one. It is necessary that attention everywhere be focused on the problems of training the young generation and of creating the necessary social and other preconditions for it to be involved in life at large in a normal manner. A large amount of constant work is required in this area, and we await a constructive contribution both from the young deputies and, of course, from all people's deputies in the dicussion of questions of social policy with regard to the country's young people.

We are obliged to urgently set about solving the numerous acute problems faced by women. Here, too, an integrated system of measures is needed, including maternity care, protection of women's work and health,
and the easing of domestic work and everyday life. In the election campaign a very great deal was said on this count by voters, and these issues were widely included in the programs of virtually all people's deputies. These questions must be examined in the most careful manner and in detail, taking our potential into account, of course, but nevertheless with due attention to these problems. These are all major issues. So many problems have accumulated here that we will probably be unable to get by without examining them on the basis of a comprehensive approach, because partial solutions alone are not enough here. The Supreme Soviet should evidently have permanent commissions which would be solidly engaged in working through all these issues, or it could be a committee. It is worth having consultations on this. In general, the kinds of conditions, the kinds of structures must be created which would prepare serious proposals for the Supreme Soviet and the congress.

It is our moral duty and obligation to take constant care of veterans of war and labor, those who defended our motherland's independence in the Great Patriotic War, who raised the country's economy and strengthened its industrial might in difficult years, and to whom we all owe all that we have. Among the people's deputies there are our older comrades who know the veterans' aspirations and needs better than the rest. We must listen to their voice and provide just solutions for the issues which life is raising today.

Here I would also like to say this, comrades: There are many simple everyday issues which must be resolved by local bodies, and especially by republican bodies, without any procrastination or waiting for instructions from above, and all the more so without directives from the Congress of People's Deputies. All the more so since-...[Gorbachev changes thought] In addition, there are relevant decisions by government bodies on this count, decisions which make it an obligation to take care of veterans of war and labor, and to solve their vital problems as a matter of primacy.

Nor can I fail to mention that the invalids and all the participants in the Afghan war are in need in an aspect which is of the greatest sensitivity to them.

In tackling the problems of the country's socioeconomic development we must proceed from the consistent implementation of the principle of social justice. It isn't enough to proclaim it. We must also bring into effect the socioeconomic machinery which will make it possible to remove the main brake on our development, unwarranted leveling down, and the psychology of parasitism, which have become deeply rooted. I have already had occasion at the congress to refer in passing to the problems of social advantages and privileges. To what I have said I will add the following:

STENOGRAPHIC RECORD

FIRST CONGRESS OF PEOPLE'S DEPUTIES OF THE USSR

Sixth Session

30 May 1989

The system of advantages has taken shape over many decades, whether it is a matter of differentiations in pension or leave, health care or housing, or the material and cultural provision of various social, age or professional groups of the population, and of territories as well as various departments. Evidently, these issues must be approached in such a way that, on the one hand, talent and highly productive labor are stimulated, and, on the other hand, help is given to those groups in the population in need of it. Of course, any distortions and especially abuses in this sphere must be decisively ruled out.

Hence I propose that a special commission of the USSR Supreme Soviet be instructed to carry out a sort of revision on the basis of these criteria of all benefits and privileges, and to submit appropriate proposals. [applause]

My first attempts to understand how it emerged and what this system represents have encountered the need for this problem to be thoroughly discussed. All this is not that simple. We can see, comrade deputies, how many problems have accumulated in the social sphere. Requests and wishes from everywhere can be heard about meeting various needs. But of course one has to measure all this against our real possibilities.

What should one think about here? First and foremost, about redistribution of the existing resources in the interests of tackling the most vital problems. A great deal of resources can be released through improving the state of affairs in the country's investment complex and through sharply reducing the volume of capital investments in the sphere of production construction. Various figure are mentioned for this reduction, from very moderate to those running into tens of percent. Incidentally, the first steps have been taken in this direction. I consider it desirable that the newly formed government should submit its proposals on this score to the USSR Supreme Soviet. They could be studied thoroughly by the commissions, involving specialists, practical workers, and scientists, and on this basis appropriate corrections could be introduced to the program for capital construction.

We will have to adopt difficult but necessary decisions, concentrating on some points and giving up others. But even now I would express the following judgment: We must adhere to the rule most rigidly so that the volume of capital construction can correspond to the capacities, material, and labor resources available. Only in this case will we be able to do away with the construction fever, and to overcome the diktat and irresponsibility of construction departments and organizations.

Another source of resources for implementing social programs is the reduction of military spending, ensuring the conversion connected with the utilization of the powerful potential of defense sectors for civilian purposes. For our people who have experienced the severe war, reliable defense has been and remains a question of life and of vital importance, just as our Soviet Army has been and remains an object of special concern. But in the modern world the possibilities are increasing for security to be safeguarded by political and diplomatic means. This enables miliary spending to be cut on the basis of giving a new quality to the USSR Armed Forces without any detriment to the country's defense capability. In 1987-88 military spending was frozen; this made a savings in the budget, in comparison with the 5-year plan, of R10 billion. In 1989 military spending amounts to R77.3 billion. Here I am announcing to the congress this real figure for military spending: R77.3 billion. There is a proposal being made to reduce military spending as early as 1990-91 by another R10 billion, that is by 14 percent; and for the Supreme Soviet to tackle further work on this entire complicated complex, taking account both of internal problems and requirements, and the tasks of ensuring the country's reliable defense capability. [applause]

Expenditure on the space program has already been partially cut. This is not so great, either. You will be able to familiarize yourselves with it later, worked out specifically. We must seek more possibilities in this direction. But at the same time we must bear in mind and take into consideration that we obtain unique technology from the latest space developments. It is sufficient to say that the lastest developments made during the Buran project alone could have significant benefit—worth billions of rubles—if they are passed on to the national economic enterprises and organizations. Only in this case will be be able to end...[changes thought] I'm sorry. One must bear in mind that only if that happens will the money we spend to master space will be justified.

Immense possibilities lie in using in the civilian sector the unique technology developed at the defense ministry enterprises. Conditions have been created today to put an end to the irrational secrecy, finishing up with the so-called internal COCOM [Coordinating Committee on Export Controls of NATO].

Quite a few possibilities for redistributing resources for social benefit lie in cuts in administrative spending. The new conditions of economic management make it possible to radically restructure the administrative system. This also needs to be studied thoroughly by the Supreme Soviet. This is why in the past few years there have been important changes in the upper level of administration, and new ones are planned that will be reported by the government. As for the local administrative structures, especially at the level of associations and enterprises, to date the number of administrative staff there has not only not been cut, but has even increased. That is, the granting of economic independence is being accompanied by growth in the number of staff. And every sixth person working is a manager, a specialist. That means it is to someone's advantage. We are spending no more and no less than about R40 billion a year to maintain the administrative apparatus and, what is more, R2.5 billion to maintain bodies of state administration. Here, too, we must clear up this problem.

Sixth Session

30 May 1989

Other possibilities exist for the reallocation of national economic resources in the interests of solving social problems. The people's deputies will probably supplement this part, like other ideas in the report, during their discussion. All these reserves must be used. But primarily, comrades, we must raise production efficiency and the quality of output, and improve the use of all production factors on the basis of radical national economic reconstruction.

We must realize quite clearly that we can solve the immediate social problems and lay the groundwork for the future only by means of scientific and technical progress, by ensuring the development of fundamental science at an outstripping rate, and ensuring the development and application of state-of-the-art technologies. Something else must be made clear: To drag the economy out of the quagmire is impossible without radical economic reform, without the changeover of all ecoomic links to complete financial autonomy and self-financing, and without the extensive development of leasing and cooperatives. We must arrive at a new economic model via radical economic reform.

Fierce discussions—let's not beat around the bush—are now being held in society about the economic reform, about what it has given us, about the problems that have occurred during is implementation. Bearing this in mind, the course of the reforms has been analyzed quite thoroughly in the Central Committee. There have been quite a few meetings on this question with scientists and economists, managers and specialists, and representatives of production collectives. The general conclusion is this: The strategic idea of the reform and its basic directions have been correctly determined. But a lot of inconsistencies, indecisiveness, half-baked measures, zig-zags, and even deviations are being allowed to occur at all levels in the practical implementation of the reform. The main thing is that we are only very slowly, and much later than we should, solving the question of how to work out the economic mechanisms and put them into operation. In other words, we are falling behind in creating an economic medium under the conditions of which alone the reform can gain strength, expand, and produce the awaited results. In essence it is here, in the absence of such economic mechanisms, that the further advance of the reform is being held up. In this situation differing opinions have surfaced about the fate of the reform. You can hear the opinion that many of our economic troubles are born from the new economic management methods, that it is wrong to rush with reform. We cannot agree with this. The Central Committee and the government consider that the main line to national economic development is the consistent development of economic reform.

In this area we consider it necessary to readjust our economic policy and practical activities. Experience shows that reform cannot be carried out as a unique act. It is a complex business to transfer the economy from one mode of operation to another. To weather it more successfully, it is essential to speed up the devising and implementing of a series of interlinked steps aimed at consistent changes in planning methods, financial levers, prices, taxation, working conditions, wages, and all the other links in the economic mechanism. And a lot of this must be done even before the 13th 5-year plan comes into effect.

Another thing, comrades: Life has convincingly shown that economic reform is simply impossible without a radical renewal of socialist ownership and the development and combination of its various forms. We advocate the creation of flexible and efficient relations for the use of public property so each form of ownership can prove its vitality and right to existence in living competition, in a fair contest. The only condition that must be set is the prevention of exploitation or the alienation of workers from the means of production.

Another crucial area of the economic reform is also inseparably linked to this ownership approach—the evolution of a full-blooded socialist market. It goes without saying that the market is not omnipotent, but mankind has not devised any more efficient or democratic mechanism of management. The socialist planned economy cannot do without it, comrades, and this has to be acknowledged. We believe that as the reform intensifies, a system of economic relations will take shape that could be described as a law governed economy [pravovaya ekonomika].

It will be founded not on administrative commands or orders but on relations regulated by law. There will be a clear-cut division between state direction of the economy and economic management. Enterprises, concerns, joint stock societies, and cooperatives should become the main economic forces. To tackle common tasks and to coordinate their efforts, they will, I guess, move to set up, on a voluntary basis, combines, unions, and associations to which the economic management functions currently performed by the ministries will pass. Both our experience and worldwide economic development trends convince us that this is the right approach.

This approach does not mean belittling the role of the state, as long as one doesn't confuse it with the ministries, of course, or economic management with state direction. The latter is shedding the functions of direct intervention in the day-to-day running of economic units and concentrating on creating overall normative frameworks and the conditions for their operation. Its natural spheres will remain the key areas of scientific and technical progress; the infrastructure; environmental protection; the monitoring of social security provisions for people; and the financial system, including its tax instruments and economic legislation, which will involve, among other things, legislation against monopolization and its adverse social consequences. By adopting the law on the state enterprise association and the law on cooperatives we have taken an important—but only the first—step toward such an economy. These laws need

STENOGRAPHIC RECORD

Sixth Session
30 May 1989

All the great amount of work on the judicial reform is, of course, needed not just for the sake of it, but in the interests of strengthening law and order in our country. This task has become particularly topical because of the increase in the number of crimes, including such dangerous ones as corruption, the mafia, extortion, and bribe-taking. A topical problem is the combatting of hooliganism which undermines the normal conditions for people's lives, work, and relaxation. I believe that the deputies will agree that we have to strengthen and support the law enforcement bodies but also demand from them effective measures to eradicate crime.

Democracy can exist only if everyone—the state, public organizations, every collective, and every citizen—exercises clearly their rights and obligations. This is an axiom. I cannot help saying a few words about that which is at present an object of growing concern among our people. I have in mind the attempts by individuals and groups to attain their personal or group aims by way of organizing mass disturbances and provoking acts of violence. Such things cannot be tolerated in a law governed state.

Lawful aims can and must be attained by lawful means, whereas unlawful ones must be stopped. If we are unable to protect democracy and glasnost, this could affect on the fate of the country and the people in the most dramatic way. In a word, it is necessary for all unlawful actions to be opposed not only by rational arguments, appeals to conscience, and public opinion—which must be, of course, in the forefront—but also the force of the law. This is the only way in which a democratic society can live and develop. [applause]

Nor can our congress fail to consider or to deal with a matter about which society is becoming seriously concerned. I have in mind the current state of discipline and order. Putting it bluntly, it fails to satisfy us. It requires a resolute change for the better. A lack of discipline and poor fulfillment of official duties means that we suffer great losses, both economic and moral, and above all in the sphere of labor. This affects extremely negatively our whole society. Irresponsibility and disorder have a disorganizing effect on people's everyday life, introduce unnecessary tension to it, and to put it plainly, drive people out of their minds, and arouse their discontent.

At the same time, it has become shameful for some reason to raise the question of discipline in society and to demand order. Some people discern in these very timid attempts almost the undermining of democracy and the aspiration to restore a system of command and a slave mentality in people. Perhaps for some people the talk about discipline is nothing more than nostalgia for the old days. This probably exists, comrades. It is beyond doubt. They talk about discipline while thinking about a strong hand and about how a command is to be obeyed without question. This probably exists. But comrades, different things are important now. We can all sense the effects brought about by a lack of discipline and poor order. Therefore we must take a firm position at our congress. Without discipline and order the cause of restructuring will not advance. This is the view of people too, incidentally. [applause]

Democratization needs an enhancement of discipline on the basis of a growth in the level of peoples' social activity. We must counter any lack of order with a high level of responsibility for the work that has been entrusted to us and not be afraid to be more exacting over discipline and order.

Comrades, the very first days of the congress proceedings showed again the acute nature of the nationalities question and the complexity of relations between nationalities. Multi-ethnicity is indeed a unique quality of our state and society. On the one hand, it is a source of its strength. On the other, given the smallest distortions of the nationalities policy, it could also become a cause of weakening the state and of social instability, with unpredictably grave consequences.

The times emphasize the correctness of the nationalities policy elaborated by Vladimir Ilyich Lenin. The results it has brought to all of our peoples cannot be overestimated. A huge amout of work has been done to overcome national oppression and inequality, to raise the economy, and to develop the culture of all nations inhabiting the country. Interest has been shown throughout the world in our experience, and this must under no circumstances be forgotten. But in the 1930's Lenin's nationalities policy was subjected to the most gross distortions and deformations, practically all peoples felt their effect. An oversimplified understanding of the multifaceted nature of relations between nationalities, encouragement of unitarian tendencies, a denial of the specifics of national development, political accusations against whole nations with the subsequent arbitrariness and lawlessness, an intolerable identification of people's national feelings with nationalist manifestations—we have had all of this in our lives. Here, as they say, you can neither add anything nor take anything away.

We inherited a very difficult legacy. Moreover, in the times of stagnation the negative processes in relations between nationalities were either ignored or driven below the surface, and this meant that they were increasingly exacerbated. Sooner or later they were bound to come to the surface. Democratization and glasnost enabled the whole truth to be told and a start to be made toward rectifying the distortions that had been committed and eliminating injustices. But it must be admitted that at the beginning of restructuring we far from fully appreciated the necessity of renewing the nationalities policy. There was also probably a delay in resolving a number of urgent matters. In the meantime, natural dissatisfaction with economic and social problems that had piled up began to be interpreted as an encroachment on ethnic interests.

Sixth Session
30 May 1989

Speculating on these general difficulties, certain elements strove to make the situation even more complicated. This led to excesses in a number of republics, and produced the tragic consequences, entailing loss of life, that everyone knows about. Allow me from this tribune, the tribune of our first Congress of People's Deputies, to express our common sorrow and pain in connection with the death of innocent people. This must not recur.

It is clear that we are obliged to radically improve national relations. To free them from everything that contradicts our morality, our ideology and the humanitarian principles of socialism. Speaking of the renewal of the nationality policy, we have in mind the necessity of aligning it with today's realities. The demography has changed, the economy has changed, and so have the demography, the social and national structure of all the republics. National self-awareness has increased, new spiritual needs have surfaced. Many facets of internationality relations face us today in a new light.

It can now be said that a political mechanism is being created in order to ensure a rational and just approach to the questions of internationality relations, and the establishment of such relations as will accord with the interests of each Soviet nation and with the general people's interests. I am thinking both of the already published draft laws on this question, and of the great preparatory work of the Central Committee plenum which was specially devoted to it, which will be specially devoted to discussing them...[Gorbachev corrects himself]

And what is particularly important is the future work of the Supreme Soviet and its commissions in whose framework the nationality problems must find an all round and all embracing solution. The principle of national self-determination set out by Lenin was, and still is, one of the main elements of the nationalities policy of the Communist Party. It was the foundation of socialist statehood during the creation of the Union of Soviet Socialist Republics. And arguments of a historical nature, and economic calculations, and political awareness, and simply common sense and the experience of the peoples, speak of the vital necessity for the development of all the Soviet nations in the framework of a federative union state. Restructuring is the most weighty argument in favor of this, for it creates the conditions to correct any mistakes and deformations committed in the past, to genuinely harmonize relations between nationalities, and allows for the normal national feeling of every person wherever he was born, lives or works.

But now we should give the federative state system real political and economic content so that this form entirely satisfies the requirements and aspirations of the nations and meets the realities of modern times. On the whole, we see the focal points of the nationalities policy of restructuring as follows: In the political sphere, it is the extension of the rights of union and autonomous republics and of other national formations; the transfer to the localities of an increasing circle of administrative functions; the strengthening of the independence and accountability of republican and local organs. In a federative state things relating to the competence of the union and things which are the sovereign right of the republic's autonomy must be clearly defined. It is essential to work out a legal machinery to resolve clashes which might arise in their mutual relations.

In the economic sphere it is essential to harmonize relations between the union and the republics on the basis of the intrinsic fusion of their economic independence and their active participation in the nationwide division of labor. It is from this angle that the control of the country's unified national economic complex should be restructured, by organically incorporating the switch made by republics, regions, krays and oblasts to self-management and self-financing in the general process of the renewal of the Soviet economy.

It is fundamentally important that the new approach to developing the republic's economies and local self-management should not lead to autarky, which looks like an anachronism in the contemporary world, but that it should contribute to the deepening of cooperation, which corresponds to the interests of every republic and the whole country.

Demographic and ecological problems are closely affiliated to economic problems. Here, too, it is necessary to skillfully combine all-union and republican regional interests. In the spiritual sphere we proceed from the recognition of the diversity of national cultures as a very great social and historical valuable, and a unique possession of our entire union. We have no right to undervalue or, worse still, lose a single one of them, because each one is unique. We are in favor of the free and comprehensive development of every people, national language and culture, and in favor of equal and friendly relations between all nations and ethnic and national groups.

The Congress of People's Deputies and the USSR Supreme Soviet will have to resolve a considerable number of very complex issues in the sphere of interethnic relations. Let me express my certainty that their in-depth work will allow us to enrich Leninist national policy in application to today's realities of the Soviet multinational state and thus to create the most reliable political basis for further development, confident development of the country.

Comrades, restructuring in the Soviet Union could not help being reflected in all our international activity, but it could not be implemented if the previous foreign policy were maintained.

The fundamental change in the foreign policy course is connected with the new political thinking that was gradually developed with the liberation from dogmatic ideas and from conclusions which were only correct in their own time and which had ceased to correspond to

Sixth Session
30 May 1989

the realities of our days. New thinking is a dynamic concept which is continuing to develop and deepen, but its main starting point remains the conclusion of the 27th CPSU Congress about the lethal danger which nuclear weapons and the arms race present to mankind's existence, about the integrity and interdependence of the modern world, about the change in the nature of its contradictions, and about the substance of world progress.

At the basis of the new thinking lies a recognition of the priority of human interests and values, of generally accepted norms of morality as the obligatory criterion of all policy, freedom of sociopolitical choice which rules out interference in the affairs of any state and the need for de-ideologization of relations between states. Despite the profound differences between social systems, objective possibilities have appeared in each of them for moving on to a fundamentally new, peaceful period in the history of mankind.

In the reality around us there are any number of cases that do not, it appears, follow the direction taken by the new thinking. There are the forces of the past and contradictions inherited from the past. Thus we cannot renounce our army and say a farewell to arms. The same can be said of military alliances, the preservation of which depends not on us alone. But however necessary the old forms and means may still be, we must not allow them to block the new approaches to the construction of international relations. Therein lies the wisdom of all high politics, and therein lies the qualitative difference of foreign policy in the period of restructuring.

We can now defend it by drawing on real results. Much has already become habitual and seems normal, but where would we be if everything had remained as before? The fever of international tension has abated. There is no direct threat of nuclear war. People of different countries have, as it were, looked each other in the face and realized how absurd enmity is. The reduction of nuclear arsenals has started. The Europeans have embarked on the lowering of the most dangerous military confrontation in the world. We have pulled our troops out of Afghanistan, and have started to withdraw them from the allied countries. The country has opened up to the outside world to take a fitting place in the international division of labor and enjoy its advantages. The restrictions and prejudices hampering our effective involvement in the tackling of global problems and scientific and cultural exchange have been removed.

Our foreign policy is turned to the whole world, but each instance naturally has its specifics and its special and important accents, both in a bilateral context and from the viewpoint of regional and international significance. This concerns the socialist countries in the first place. Mutual relations with them reflect a very crucial stage in the development of the socialist world. We sensed this in full measure during our visit to our great neighbor, the People's Republic of China, the normalization of relations with which was an event of worldwide importance. [applause]

There are and there can be difficulties in the formation of a new type of relations between socialist countries. They lie in the objective realities of the difficult and contradictory processes occurring in different countries. But these difficulties can be overcome. The main condition here is mutual respect, noninterference in one another's affairs, friendly mutual understanding, profound interest in the experience of each other, the need for cooperation and the readiness for joint patient work. We have all this right now.

A major area of our foreign policy work is participation in the building of a common European home. The fundamental ideas are well known. They have come into use in public opinion and negotiating practice. The foundations for healthy relations in the spirit of restructuring with all states participating in the Helsinki process have been laid and are gaining momentum. We will steadfastly continue the Vladivostok line in the Asian-Pacific region. The diversity of the tasks here is even greater. Both the agenda and an amicable, constructive and respectful tone of relations have been determined with many countries. Here as everywhere we will continue to devote special attention to relations with countries. First and foremost this means the great India.

We all understand that Soviet-U.S. relations are of primary importance for world policy. We are ready to interact with the United States on a predictable and stable basis. We are ready to move forward combining continuity with fresh ideas.

We have discovered over these years extraordinary opportunities for closer and more productive ties with Latin America and Africa. Here too there are both common problems and specific features relating to individual states. Strengthening good neighborliness with all neighboring states remains of paramount concern to us.

The Congress of People's Deputies is to consider and legislatively approve the principles of our foreign policy course for the years ahead. I believe that the following should be involved:

The country's security should be maintained above all by political means as an integral part of universal and equal security, in the process of demilitarization, democratization and humanization of international relations, with reliance on the prestige and possibilities of the United Nations. Nuclear weapons should be eliminated in the course of a negotiation process geared to disarmament and the reduction of the defense potential of states to the limits of reasonable sufficiency. [applause]

Sixth Session

30 May 1989

The use of force and the threat of force for the purposes of attaining any kind of political, economic or other goals are impermissible. In relations with other countries, respect for sovereignty, independence, and territorial intregrity is immutable. Dialogue and negotiations oriented toward a balance of interests, not confrontation, should become the sole method of resolving international problems and settling conflicts. We are in favor of bringing the Soviet economy into the world economy on mutually advantageous and equal foundations and of active involvement in the formulation and observance of the rules of modern international division of labor, scientific and technical exchange and trade. We are in favor of cooperation with all who are prepared for it.

Approval by the USSR Congress of People's Deputies of the above-stated principles is of no simple legal significance, but it is of enormous international and domestic political significance.

There is another fundamental matter. In the past our foreign policy practice in certain instances ran counter to the proclaimed exalted principles of socialist foreign policy. Abritrary actions were carried out that caused serious harm to the country and had a negative impact on its international prestige. It was the consequence of the same command-based system and the secretive decision making that was characteristic of it. One of the important tasks of the political system as it is being reconstructed by us is to exclude such systems and methods. In the future all significant foreign policy decisions should be adopted only after they have been thoroughly discussed in the Supreme Soviet and its commissions, while the most major ones, for instance those connected with allied relations and the conclusion of the most important treaties, should also be submitted for consideration by the Congress of People's Deputies. [applause]

Far from everyone in the West, comrades, believes that we have chosen this foreign policy course once and for all and that we do not intend to change it. And here in our country, too, not everyone yet understands the fundamental essence of foreign policy based upon the new thinking. Some people regard it as a sort of tactic, a temporary zig-zag or even a concession to the West. This—I want to stress, and I hope the congress will support this statement—this is our strategic policy which is profoundly well-grounded and which expresses the interests of the Soviet people and which, we are convinced, corresponds to the interests of all mankind.

At the congress itself, I think it was yesterday, a proposal was voiced to dispatch a message from our congress to the peoples of the world. I think that we do have something to say to the people of the planet. [applause] Comrade deputies, as we can see, our field of activity is vast in all areas—in socioeconomic policy, and in state and legal policy, and national policy, and international policy, a great many major tasks of a revolutionary character are to be resolved. There are far more problems than those I have set out in my report, and I am sure that the discussion at this congress will show this.

Quite understandably, the success of the task depends in decisive measure on how we manage to organize our own work, on how soon the new supreme organs of power can assume the functions incumbent upon them, and can take the lead in all the work of reform in the country. Discussion on this topic has already started, in effect. A number of fundamental issues on which there should be consultation have come to the forefront of this discussion.

The first of these is the delimitation of the functions of the congress and the USSR Supreme Soviet. This is no simple issue because the structure of the supreme organs of power currently being introduced in our country is based upon the desire organically to combine our Soviet tradition, born in the socialist revolution, with the experience of the work representative organs generally recognized throughout the world. The Congress of People's Deputies itself, first and foremost, is a unique organ in our system. It is essentially a congress [Gorbachev stumbles over text], and its task is not to operate continuously. This is something we must sort out, I think, and we seem to have made progress in this direction already. It is to assemble, as we arranged, no less than twice a year, in order to adopt the laws and decisions most important for the country on fundamental issues of the state's internal and foreign policy; in order to evaluate and monitor the work of other organs of power; and where necessary to make amendments to the constitution and alter the political system itself. The Supreme Soviet should, in its new form, according to the intention of the political reform, be a permanently operating organ of power, carrying out both legislative and the basic administrative functions.

And now for the relations between the legislative and the executive power. This is a very important issue which requires special elaboration and study. But one can already say today that the relations between the chambers, commissions and committees of the Supreme Soviet, on the one hand, and the executive organs on the other, must be substantially changed, compared to the way things were done up until now. The commissions and committees of the Supreme Soviet should evidently examine the targets of state plans and the articles of the budget, and evalutate them in accordance with the fundamental directions of the Congress of People's Deputies and the Supreme Soviet itself.

The second important task to be settled by the commissions is to consider the candidacies for key state functions—ministers and ambassadors to foreign countries and so on, for example.

It is not hard to see that both of these functions will enable our parliament to hold in its hands the real levers of power. In supervising the activity of the government

STENOGRAPHIC RECORD

Sixth Session

30 May 1989

in issues of strategic importance, the congress and Supreme Soviet should take care that the government is enabled in full measure to solve the tasks of state government within the framework of the constitution and that it assumes the entirety of responsibility.

According to the planned reform, the Committee for Constitutional Compliance—which should in effect act as a Constitutional Court—is intended to play an important role in our political system. Looking ahead, I shall say that the development of judicial supervision over the activities of the administrative organs at all levels should evidently become one of the inalienable elements of socialist law-governed statehood. [applause]

During the preceding days at the congress there has been vigorous discussion of the question of the status of the USSR people's deputy. We already agreed with you that it is necessary to work out a new document regulating a deputy's position, his rights and obligations, and submit it to the congress. But there are some fundamental points on which it is necessary to agree and to adopt a decision so all the comrades can get involved in active work. What should one bear in mind here? First, the unity of the corps of deputies. All deputies, regardless of whether they were elected by territorial or national territorial constituencies or by public organizations, have equal rights. The next point relates to distribution of labor among the deputies. Naturally, the deputies elected to the Supreme Soviet by the congress will bear additional commitments. They must have the appropriate additional possibilities to implement the obligations being placed on them.

Bestowing special functions on a Supreme Soviet member must not by any means belittle the role of other people's deputies. First and foremost, every one of them still has the possibility of being elected to the Supreme Soviet when 20 percent of it is renewed annually. Many deputies will be members of the Supreme Soviet commissions and committees and enjoy the right of a decisive vote there.

It seems sensible—we were thinking about this over recent days—that they should be able to be involved in leading the commissions and committees representing, as it were, in the leadership of the commissions, say, as deputy chairmen of commissions or committees, 50 percent of people's deputies. [sentence as heard] As I understand, we have all agreed that every USSR people's deputy may take part, if he wishes, in the work of various commissions or committees and in the sessions of the Supreme Soviet chambers. Everyone must be given full information about the current work of the Supreme Soviet, the government, and other organs of power. Finally, everyone has the possibility to carry out active political work in his own region or public organization, maintaining a constant connection with his electors and addressing various questions and proposals to local and central organs of power. Deputies must have the necessary conditions to receive citizens and to meet the electorate, and the local bodies must take care of this. Moreover, all these issues must be resolved promptly. [applause]

Thus we will be able to preserve a most valuable equality of the supreme system: constant communication between people's representatives and all of the working people. To put it in the words of Vladimir Ilyich Lenin, to combine the advantages of parliamentarism with the advantages of direct and immediate democracy.

A couple of words about the organization of the work of the congress and the Supreme Soviet. People's deputies have brought here to the Kremlin a diversity of views and life experience, behind which stand various interests: social, ethnic, professional, age related, and regional. It is natural that joint work cannot avoid divergences of opinion, arguments, and discussions. Such discussions began on the first day, if not the first hour, of the congress, and I don't see anything bad in this. On the contrary, pluralism of views broadens the range of possible solutions and enables us to gain a fuller idea of the object under examination. And of course, divergence of opinion should not become an obstacle to sensible decision making.

As was rightly said by one of the comrades here, we may have diverse views, but we should have only one policy: that of revolutionary restructuring. [applause] For this reason it is essential to do everything to achieve accord, to try and understand one another, to make some mutual concessions in the interests of the cause. Only when this proves impossible, the last word, of course, remains with the majority. Such is the law of democracy.

In conclusion, one more very important factor that has also been touched on here. On various grounds, deputies have proposed introducing one or another amendment to the USSR Constitution. I add my voice to those who caution against hasty amendment of the basic law. The constitution is too important a political document to adapt it to a particular situation that may arise. It is another matter and on this, I think, we are united at least. This is how I perceive the mood of the congress. We need to elaborate and adopt a new constitution for the country. The consolidation therein of the revolutionary reforms being implemented in the course of restructuring will form one of the most important guarantees of their irreversibility. But now, at the height of the reform it is not yet possible to take account of the whole complex of issues that must be reflected in the new basic law.

Comrades, this, in a nutshell, is my evaluation of the situation in the country, my main thoughts regarding the main directions of our state's future domestic and foreign policy, and on the work of the congress. This is what I wanted to report to you.

Sixth Session

30 May 1989

What do I want to say in conclusion? We are not beginning our work from scratch. We have formed a concept of restructuring, of economic and political reform. In one form or another, with one or another degree of depth and criticism, these matters have been examined at various forums of party, state, and public organizations. They have been discussed in labor collectives and in the media—definite, practical steps have been taken. But time quickly changes the situation, new tasks and new needs arise. And I would like to express confidence that our congress, expressing the collective reason of the people, will be able to produce an effective agenda for the Soviet state in the coming years and will give new energy to the whole process of the revolutionary renewal of our society. Thank you. [applause]

Nishanov: The report having been completed, perhaps we can agree with the opinion, to submit questions in written form. Are there any objections? The motion is accepted. A 30-minute break is declared. (Break).

Nishanov: Comrade deputies, please sit down. Take your seats. Let us move on to discussion of the report. The floor is granted to Deputy Sergey Tikhonovich Melekhin of Sverdlovsk Oblast, and Comrade Yefrem Yevsevich Sokolov is to prepare himself.

S.T. Melekhin, operator at the Nizhnetagilskiy V.I. Lenin Metallurgical Combine, RSFSR, Sverdlovsk Oblast, Nizhnyy Tagil (from the USSR Trade Unions): Comrade deputies! The report by USSR Supreme Soviet Chairman Mikhail Sergeevich Gorbachev provides an analysis and evaluation of the urgent problems we are to solve in this forum. We are dividing them up. By authority of the deputies from the trade unions I would also like to speak about the most critical social problems.

What is troubling the Soviet people most of all? One of the most acute problems is—housing. About 5,000,000 people currently have dilapidated, emergency or barrack-type housing. One has to wait in long lines for 10-15 years for improved housing conditions. Soviet and party organs are taking measures to correct the situation. The working collectives are doing a great deal, and there is a government resolution. However, in spite of this, the average annual increase in introduction of housing for the 3 years of the 5-year plan amounts to only 15 percent. In our opinion this is clearly inadequate, inasmuch as at that rate, we shall not solve the housing problem by the year 2000. Our mandate to the new government, and to you, Mikhail Sergeyevich, is to search out new possibilities for unconditionally carrying out the planned program—at the same time observing social and regional fairness, so that housing would be constructed on an equal basis throughout the country, and not concentrated in a single city somewhere.

Along with the problem of where to live, the deputies from the trade unions give equal standing to the problem of what to live on. Nearly 40,000,000 Soviet citizens of which the report spoke have an income of less than 75 rubles. We are now saying that these people are living on the edge of poverty; but we are not saying how one can live beyond this line itself. Pensioners, families with lots of children, invalids, and students belong to this category. Moreover, it is very disturbing that the acuteness of the problem is growing like a snowball rolling down a mountain—the closer it gets to the bottom, the bigger it is. For we all know full well how persistently prices are rising and how vitally needed articles are disappearing from the store shelves with equal persistence. A portion of them turn up later in the hands of people who trade for them for fabulous prices at the market. Another portion fall into the category of contract prices, which devour the family budget no less painfully. Finally, the third portion consists of such goods as soap, detergents and so on, which disappear without a trace.

The cooperatives are contributing as best they can to the formation of the snowball. The Soviet people had anticipated that efficient operators, by virtue of manufacturing goods the people need, or by raising cattle, would replenish the needs of the market. But that seems all too simple. Goods are being bought up wholesale and retail according to state prices and are then offered for sale—but then at cooperative prices. I can understand how a cooperator buys a calf or a piglet, raises it, and offers it on the market. Naturally, it is more expensive, because of his expenses; but that is, comrades, additional meat. There are losses, for example, at an enterprise. An enterprising person enters a contract, organizes production of goods in high demand, and offers them for sale. Thus, in both cases, it is a question of bringing additional goods to the market. But the reality of the cooperative movement of today is so distorted, that in many cases it arouses the just indignation of the people.

Nor is the idea of contract prices well understood. Who is it that makes contracts with someone behind the backs of the consumers and at the expense of the family budget? Quite often we see the following picture: A person comes into a store and notes that a kilogram of cucumbers cost 2.50 the day before, and 4.50 today. To the reasonable question, why, the salesperson responds, as a rule: "Read, it says the prices are contracted." One would think that this is not a gap, but a gate flung wide open, through which certain business managers are trying to recover their business affairs. There is no choice: Take it, or leave it.

On one hand there is the price increase—inflation; on the other, the minimum wage has not been re-examined for 17 years. As before, the pensions of the majority of the veterans are at a low level. Finally, no mechanism exists to tie in price increases and inflation with an increase in wages, pensions, benefits, and stipends. There is a great obligation for state loans, for which veterans above all should be considered, who could by

STENOGRAPHIC RECORD

Sixth Session
30 May 1989

means of such loans restore their budget. Under these conditions the new Law on Pensions takes on special significance. We must find a means, as early as the coming year, to raise the minimum amounts of pensions.

We must make special mention, comrades, of our Soviet women. We say a lot of eloquent words about them, but thus far there is no progress. We are talking about improving their working conditions; relieving women from night shifts; increasing, upon their request, partly paid leave in order to look after their children; and offering them the opportunity for part-time work. But what are needed are ways to solve them. One would think that one of them would be—when enterprises or manufacturing plants are being reconstructed or new shops put into operation—normatives should be laid down in such a way that they would envisage the possibilty of women working less than a full day, or less than a full week; otherwise we will once again be drowning in appeals. Many deputies, and trade-union representatives among them, have been given a mandate by the voters—to radically improve medical services. Attempts have been made more than once to fundamentally improve them; however, thus far there are no tangible results. In this connection one cannot agree with the opinion of certain economists who are speaking out for expanding paid medical treatment, or with the opinion of Candidate of Medical Sciences, Comrade Kaplan, who proposed in PRAVDA (24 May) to pay for treatment at the expense of the enterprises. You yourselves understand, that in this case there can be no firm guarantees; for first of all an enterprise would transfer its profits to the state budget, a second portion to its next-higher authority, and only then will allot what is left to itself. Deputies from the trade unions insist on free medical services, and high quality as well. The question arises, where can one find the means. Comrades, they can be found. We are submitting a suggestion to the country's new government—to re-examine the distribution of the national income. The proportion for consumption and non-industrial construction in it must be increased to 86-87 percent.

We often have to listen to statements like, "There's not enough there"; or, "there's a shortage here." Well, with such management we will have to hear these "objective" arguments for a long time yet. Judge for yourselves, comrade deputies: There are more than 300,000 square meters of empty manufacturing space in our country. It would seem that, according to the logic of things, we should immediately install equipment there and put out the products the people need so badly. Instead, we start to erect more and more new boxes. Last year the number of new construction starts increased by 40 percent. Now uncompleted construction amounts to an enormous sum—150 billion rubles. Just try to imagine such a figure, and try to picture for a second, just how many burning problems of a social nature could be resolved, if these frozen assets could be applied to the needs of the people. It is painful to look at how manufacturing accommodations that have been erected but not completed are becoming dilapidated and spoiled; how the equipment rusts and becomes unusable—quite often imported equipment; and thus one wants to say—gold. But who is responsible for this, and what conclusions have been made? We cannot go on this way. The people's money has an altogether real owner—the people. Accordingly, instead of the existing system, which permits squandering, we need a system which permits sensibly utilizing the material valuables in the interests of the Soviet people. At its core there must be a sense of responsibility. The deputies from the trade unions have been authorized to submit a mandate to the government: In the next 2 years the amount of uncompleted construction must be reduced by 40-50 billion rubles. This is an altogether realistic task. These assets would be sufficient to introduce laws on pensions and leave, and to allocate the necessary funds to poor families.

A second proposal: To strive with great persistence to achieve a relaxation of international tensions, and on this basis continue to work for the reduction of military expenditures; moreover, in a reciprocal direction. This, too, will provide us additional billions of rubles.

We have already heard in the report, comrades, about the necessity to reduce the administrative apparat. In spite of repeated appeals and resolutions, its numbers are not declining; on they contrary, they are growing. Sensible reduction—this, comrades, is also a great reserve; and I stress, sensible; for just to issue an order and cite a number—that is only half the job. It must be determined sensibly, where and how much to reduce.

If I were to sum up all the proposals, it would be that there are billions of additonal rubles which could be directed toward solving social needs. In a word, comrades, the time has come for extensive public discussion of the widest variety of extraordinary programs for restoring the financial health of the economy and for radically improving matters in the social sphere. In order to prepare a draft for this problem it would be sensible to establish a special—I would say extraordinary—commission, either at the congress or at the Supreme Soviet, and give it the necessary authority and rights. I would like to emphasize once again, that the workers are expecting of our congress, and of the Supreme Soviet, practical solutions and concrete results, and we must prove worthy of their trust. We must act in such a way, that our country will have more socialism; that in the future no one will ever have an opportunity to assert, or even say these words aloud here: "The past of our motherland was unpredictable."

Comrades! I have a proposal: that all the deputies choose a time during breaks in the work of our congress, pay a visit to Vladimir Ilich Lenin's tomb, and lay a wreath at

Sixth Session

30 May 1989

the tomb and at the tomb of the unknown soldier. (Applause).

R.N. Nishanov offers the floor to Deputy Sokolov. Deputy Masol is to get ready.

Ye.Ye. Sokolov, first secretary of the Belorussian Communist Party Central Committee (Kobrinskiy Territorial Electoral Okrug, Brest Oblast): Dear comrades! Our difficult time is so compressed under the weight of problems inherited from the past or that have arisen in recent years that you have a very acute understanding of how vitally important and how vitally necessary everyone's personal responsibility for the fate of restructuring really is. One of the reasons why it has been marking time in a number of areas is that, in the intoxicating atmosphere and the stormy waves of democratization, the concepts of "organization," "responsibility," and "discipline" have become overshadowed and have begun to be forgotten in both lower and upper echelons.

At the meetings in the runup to the elections, working people rightly asked questions, even with some bewilderment: Why are the 27th CPSU Congress guidelines on changing investment policy and comprehensively developing a region, city, or enterprise not being implemented? Why are new plants still being built without housing and other sociocultural projects? Excessive enthusiasm for building production projects to the detriment of shaping the infrastructure willy-nilly creates the preconditions for ensuring that even newly commissioned plants operate, as a rule, on a one-shift basis, at half strength. In other words, it is continuing the worthless practice of dissipating and burying national resources and freezing fixed state assets. This is happening at a time when areas connected with vital questions of meeting people's basic needs require greater attention. And, in a number of cases, not simply vital but urgent. Such as the task of eliminating the consequences of the Chernobyl disaster, for example.

Time will not dull the pain in the hearts of people living in Belorussia, where 18 percent of agricultural land has been subjected to radioactive pollution. Whereas in the initial stages a union-level governmental commission was working on this problem, now its efforts are barely noticeable. In 3 years the commission has not been able to develop a convincing, properly thought out concept of a safe existence that will guarantee the health of future generations. In our opinion, the position here should be perfectly clear. People should not live in places where it is impossible to use the produce from their own land. This is not an area where we should try to economize.

Another natural question is why are decisions made by higher bodies so emasculated by the time they actually reach departmental offices that there is hardly anything left of them? Why is it that in these very same offices USSR laws are sometimes manipulated to such an extent that you find yourself exclaiming in spite of yourself: "Was there really a law?" Now, in the conditions of democracy and socialist pluralism of opinions, exactingness must be valued as never before—and valued everywhere: From the CPSU Central Committee to party groups, from the USSR Council of Ministers to labor collectives. Recently they, the labor collectives, have become a subject of close attention for those who are trying—by hiding behind restructuring slogans and pouring scorn upon law and order—to sow hatred and enmity between peoples and whip up social and political tension. It is now quite obvious that in some places forces are taking shape which have consciously chosen a path of confrontation, destabilization of the situation, and discrediting of the party line. Confrontation is not simply irresponsible, it is socially dangerous, because it distracts people from real work and undermines their moral world by forcing out warmth, amicability, and a respectful attitude to others regardless of their social status, nationality, or religious beliefs.

Perhaps our congress should adopt a special political resolution on increasing Soviet citizens' responsibility for the fate of restructuring. It would be advisable for this resolution to clearly stipulate that genuine democracy is possible only within the framework of the law and with the supremacy of the law. Only the law, which reflects the will of the people, can serve as a criterion of responsibility. The public has rightly raised the question of changing the correlation between the law and the state and eliminating the primacy of the state over the law. But alongside the concept of a "law-abiding state" there must definitely stand another concept—the "law-abiding citizen."

The development of the cooperative movement and individual labor activity sometimes attracts not only honest workers but also various swindlers and people on the make. Essentially, these people are also opponents of restructuring, who are undermining useful initiatives and trying to incline public opinion toward clearly leftist positions and disorder. As far as they are concerned, the humanization of justice primarily means protection of those who break the law. Now the pages of some newspapers and journals are plastered with reports from places not so very remote—from the world of criminals and drug addicts. What is more, sympathy and charity are mainly shown to those who have committed a crime, while virtually no mention is made of their victims. Yes, we are in favor of the humanization and democratization of legislation. But this humanization and democratization must have one aim only—to protect honest people and not those who encroach on our rights and freedoms, on citizens' personal interests, and on the interests of society. Is this not the main moral principle of a rule-of-law state?

The newly elected USSR Supreme Soviet is faced with the task of adopting the law "On the Basic Principles of

Sixth Session
30 May 1989

Criminal Legislation," and it is important to ensure in this respect that the opinions of broad sections of the public are taken into account. I would, incidentally, like to point out that our country has not developed the institution of forecasting legislation, studying the effectiveness of current legal norms, and seeking new ones. This leads, on the one hand, to the accumulation of a vast number of dead laws and, on the other, to an absence of legal backing for developing social relations.

Each stage of restructuring sets us a new test. But there is one test which society must pass as soon as possible. I am referring to improvement of the economy. While supporting the extensive measures to improve the economic situation contained in Mikhail Sergeyevich Gorbachev's report, I feel it necessary to voice a number of considerations.

The process of achieving a healthier economy is moving through the three "d's," if I may express it as such: democratization, demonopolization, and decentralization. But these processes are developing unevenly. Demonopolization, for example, is only just beginning. It could be speeded up by changes in organizational structures—within the framework of the country's national economy, regions, and also individual sectors. This should be taken into consideration when drafting the 13th 5-year plan. I believe that, in addition to questions concerning the social sphere and defense, its priorities should definitely include the problems of saving resources. Everything should be geared to speeding up the introduction of new, waste-free, resource-saving technologies: scientific research, improvement of the economic mechanism and forms of labor and production organization, development of lease-cooperative relations, and financial levers. If this is not done, it will not just be difficult but impossible to enhance production efficiency and more rapidly resolve social problems.

Youth problems are also a priority—whatever form they take and in whatever specific instance advice may be given. One thing is clear, however: When drafting the 13th 5-year plan, it would be advisable to give a separate section to youth problems and the questions of forming a harmonious personality, beginning from childhood. Today's investment in youth problems is an investment in tomorrow's intellectual, moral, and cadre potential of our socialist fatherland.

However, neither well-considered measures nor fine plans will produce the necessary result if we do not improve matters directly at grassroots level. Relations within society are now changing very rapidly—so rapidly that public opinion cannot keep up and is sometimes left behind in the old, conservative attitudes. Because of the inertia of past years, public opinion is not averse to heaping the whole blame for our shortcomings even onto those who were responsible for initiating restructuring and who, together with the party and the people, have tackled the difficult job of purification and renewal. Of course, no one is absolving the center of blame. But have we at local level made full use of the rights and opportunities offered us by restructuring and begun to work so well that we can forget about self-criticism? It must be admitted that parasitical attitudes and group ambitions are being eradicated more slowly than the mood of criticism is growing. This is a source of serious concern and puts us on our guard. The principle of "seeing a mote in your brother's eye but not the beam in your own" is futile, as stated by popular wisdom.

Here in our republic we link improvement in the situation with a revival of full soviet power, transition to the principle of territorial self-financing, and an increase in discipline generally and labor discipline in particular. Of course, with the introduction of territorial self-financing, regional consciousness and decentralist attitudes will increase. For this reason, when giving legal foundation to the formula "a strong center, strong republics" we should, in my view, clearly define all areas of economic and economic management activity where the word of the republic will be final and not liable to appeal, as they say. Naturally, as long as this is not to the detriment of the country's national interests.

Relations between republics also need legal foundation. But, while strengthening republics' independence and sovereignty, we must also do our utmost to strengthen the supreme sovereignty of the union. As soon as any republic begins to pull more of the blanket over itself, the Leninist foundations of the federation of Soviet peoples inevitably start to disintegrate. Many USSR people's deputies from Belorussia have been given mandates from voters to protect our common home and do everything possible to ensure that it becomes the kind of home Vladimir Ilich Lenin imagined in his dreams. Yes, restructuring is a struggle, but a struggle of the new with the old, progress with stagnation, the progressive with the conservative. And those people who wish to turn it into confrontation between individual republics and the center and between one people and another are maliciously sidetracking us from the main issues. We must not forget about this, nor do we have the right to.

As a representative of a republic whose memories of the last war and the Chernobyl tragedy will never die, I would like to express support for broad international cooperation in the sphere of building a safe world and protecting the environment. It is gratifying that the new quality of the Soviet state's foreign policy, its dynamism, and bold rejection of ossified dogma in favor of a healthy perception of arising realities are finding a positive response throughout the world. And it is our duty, esteemed comrades, the duty of every deputy and every voter to every day do everything necessary to ensure that the decisions of our congress serve the glory of our socialist fatherland and are to the good and happiness of every Soviet citizen. Thank you. (Applause).

STENOGRAPHIC RECORD

Sixth Session

30 May 1989

R.N. Nishanov: Vitaliy Andreyevich Masol has the floor. Let Deputy Likhachev, academician from Leningrad city, get ready.

V.A. Masol, chairman of the Ukrainian Council of Ministers, Kiev City (Donetskiy-Leninskiy Territorial Electoral Okrug, Ukrainian SSR): Esteemed Comrade People's Deputies! All of us—the participants in the first USSR Congress of People's Deputies—evidently agree that the events in the country's life at this crucial period are of tremendous abiding significance for our multiethnic homeland and for the future of the present and future generations.

Glancing back over the path that we have covered since April 1985, it is particularly obvious that the rapidly developing processes in the country's economic, political, and spiritual life have abruptly changed its social and moral climate. For the party and the people the last 4 years have been a time of active questing, the introduction of new forms and methods of political leadership of society, the development of popular initiative and glasnost, the renewal and restructuring of all aspects of the socialist economy. A great deal has been done in this area. But greater and more crucial tasks in the practical implementation of the restructuring course lie ahead of us in the immediate future. Their successful resolution will in many respects depend on the USSR people's deputies, our active stance—yours and ours—and the effective activity of the supreme organ of state power.

I think that key questions of economic reform will also hold a predominant position in the work of the new Supreme Soviet and the USSR Government in the coming period. In this connection it is particularly important to try to grasp and establish what we have achieved in the last 3-4 years and assess correctly the results of what has been done.

So, what have we succeeded in achieving? If we assess the sociopolitical situation that has taken shape at the present time in our republic, I must say outright that the ideas of restructuring have taken hold of the minds and hearts of most of the population. They are winning ever-increasing support every day. The intensification and deepening of restructuring processes, the unprecedented increase in people's social activeness, and the development of democratization and glasnost are the most significant results of the last few years.

In the sphere of socioeconomic development we have succeeded not only in overcoming the tendency for production and labor productivity growth rates to fall but also in ensuring an increase in the Ukraine's resource potential and making it function more fully for the solution of social tasks.

Nonetheless the positive results that have been achieved are still making a poor impact on meeting our people's needs and requirements and are not relieving the acuteness of many problems. That is why we still do not regard the incipient slight progress as a success but rather as the first signs of a gradual improvement in the prevailing situation, the start of our efforts to overcome the crisis recession and inertia of stagnation in the development of the social sphere.

We realize that the situation here will not be simple over the next few years and considerable efforts will be needed to radically improve the state of affairs.

We reckon that the new government should firmly and with greater consistency implement the line of the 19th All-Union Party Conference regarding the social reorientation of the economy. This should be the pivotal question of structural and investment policy, the cornerstone for shaping the targeted plan guidelines for the 13th 5-Year Plan period and the draft concept for the development of the country for the period through 2005. We fully support the terms of the report delivered by Mikhail Sergeyevich Gorbachev, chairman of the USSR Supreme Soviet, on this.

While studying questions of the republic's future comprehensive economic and social development and considering the siting of its productive forces, we need to consider regional factors more fully today. And, as a rule they also in many respects determine the dynamics of the indicators being forecast.

What are these factors? Above all it is a question of the fact that technology-generated pressures have increased sharply in the Ukrainian SSR, which occupies less than 3 percent of USSR territory but produces almost one-fifth of its gross social product. This has been caused by the fact that over a long period chemical and petrochemical industries and ferrous and nonferrous metallurgy enterprises developed rapidly within the republic and thermal and nuclear electric power stations were constructed at intensified rates.

We sense this particularly today. The high concentration of water-intensive production units has brought about a drastic deterioration of the situation with regard to the provision of water for the economy and the population. It is also extremely disquieting that the environmental situation in a number of areas of the republic is becoming complex and that the construction front is becoming overextended. Suffice it to say that since the beginning of this 5-year plan more than 1,000 new major construction sites at an overall estimated cost of almost R21 billion have been counted in our republic. Hundreds of transient construction units totaling R46 billion must be added to these. Under these conditions our construction workers are simply incapable of mastering the proposed volumes. Hence the long periods for the construction of facilities and the large volumes of incomplete construction work.

STENOGRAPHIC RECORD

Sixth Session
30 May 1989

The republic has adopted the firm line of eliminating these distortions in the proportion of "A" and "B" group sectors and overcoming the lag in the development of the consumer-oriented sector of the economy. In 4 years the production of nonfood goods will increase by almost one-third; moreover the growth rates will outstrip by a factor of 1.5 the increase in industrial production as a whole. We have planned to reorient approximately 70 defense sector enterprises to the production of consumer goods by the end of this 5-year plan.

We think that along with us the newly-elected USSR Supreme Soviet and its chambers' appropriate standing commissions must tackle in earnest the examination of the problems of every region's rational utilization of natural, raw material, and climatic conditions on the basis of specialization and the division of labor.

The Ukraine is, for instance, a unique agricultural region in the country for the cultivation of sugar beet and oilseed crops, which do not grow in more northerly regions. Today we produce 50-60 percent of the country's overall production of sunflower oil and sugar. At the same time soil and climatic conditions are by no means being fully utilized owing to technology-generated pressures.

In this connection we reckon that only production units which are not energy-intensive, water-intensive, and land-intensive should be sited in our republic in the immediate future. This will give us an opportunity to considerably expand the cultivation of agricultural crops and increase capacities for processing them.

Of course, we realize that all these questions are closely and indissolubly linked with the introduction of the idea of regional economic accountability [khozraschet] into the practice of interrepublican relations soon. We also realize that this can only have tangible and weighty results after a review of wholesale and purchase prices given full efficiency of economic accountability within every livestock unit, enterprise, and association.

This problem is very topical now and is being discussed extensively. That is why I would like to share some ideas with you on this score. It is our firm conviction that territories can only develop in a balanced and effective way within the framework of the country's single economic complex. No exclusive economic model and artificial extra-economic measures for protecting the intrarepublican market will produce the due effectiveness in economic management and will not provide the requisite return.

I can say with confidence that a temporary gain from the introduction of restrictions on interregional exchanges and cooperation in future will by no means cover the purely economic losses, not to mention the tremendous political damage and the increase in mutual mistrust and division between the fraternal peoples.

It is a correct understanding of the essence of regional economic accountability that opens up possibilities for consolidating the interests and aims of the union republic's peoples. Tasks of boosting the effectiveness of production and people's living standards cannot be resolved in isolation from one another but only on the basis of mutually advantageous equivalent exchange and active participation in the implementation of all-union programs.

I believe that, during the impending discussion of these questions at the USSR Supreme Soviet, we should make full use of the rich experience that the world economy has accumulated. It is no coincidence that all the EEC countries do not shut themselves away within their national borders. On the contrary, further integration is occurring within its framework and the community is proceeding with increasing confidence to introduce a single currency and remove customs restrictions.

We think that our economic and legal science should provide more in-depth, reasoned recommendations and scientifically conclusive answers to these difficult and sometimes very complex questions of interethnic economic intercourse. (Applause). The main thing is to ensure that these answers are precise and timely.

Comrade deputies, I am concerned by the following question. We have said a great deal about increasing agricultural production, while at the same time we are reducing the allocation to agriculture of material, technical, and financial resources every year. I have a question: How are we then to resolve the food problem under these conditions? I would like our government to direct particular attention to this and not sell mineral fertilizers and fuel abroad but allocate them primarily to our agriculture. (Applause).

Esteemed comrades, the people are saying that one good deed is better than a million fine words. It is our real concrete actions to restructure and renew socialist society and the resolute changes for the better in all spheres of public life that will be the most weighty argument. Allow me to wish you every success in this.

D.S. Likhachev, academician, head of sector, Russian Literature Institute (Pushkin House) of the USSR Academy of Sciences, chairman of the board of the Soviet Culture Foundation, Leningrad (from the Soviet Culture Foundation): Dear Comrade President. Dear comrade deputies. I shall speak only of the state of culture in our country and, mainly, its humanitarian, its human side. I made a close study of the electoral platforms of the deputies. I was astounded that the overwhelming majority of them did not even mention the word "culture." At the congress itself the word "culture" was mentioned in passing only on the 3d day. Mikhail Sergeyevich Gorbachev spoke on this subject at that time.

STENOGRAPHIC RECORD

Sixth Session

30 May 1989

Yet, without culture in a society there is no morality. Without basic morality the social laws and the economic laws will not function; ukases will not be implemented, and no contemporary science can exist, for it is difficult, for example, to check experiments that cost millions, huge plans for "construction projects of the century," and so on.

The low cultural standard of our country adversely affects our social life, the work of the government, and relations among nationalities, for a low cultural standard is one of the reasons for national hostility. People with a high cultural standard are not hostile toward other national groups or other people's views and are not aggressive. (Applause). Ignorance of basic formal logic and the elements of law and lack of social tactfulness, which is developed through culture, adversely affect the work of our congress. I believe this needs no explanation.

Unfortunately, the "residual" principle is still functioning in the case of culture. This is confirmed even by the Academy of Sciences of the Soviet Union, where humanitarian culture has been assigned the lowest priority. Look at the directory of the Academy of Sciences. It has virtually no listings for Russian culture.

The extremely low level of culture in our country is confirmed, to begin with, by the condition of cultural and historical monuments. This is obvious to all, and thus I shall not discuss it. The second is the condition of libraries and archives. About the latter, incidentally, the penultimate issue of SOVETSKAYA KULTURA adequately wrote about it. There as well this situation prevails in the largest and the small, rural, libraries. Third, the condition of museums, the condition of education, secondary and primary above all, where the individual's culture is developed.

Let me start with the libraries. The library is the most important part of culture. There may be no universities, institutes, or scientific institutions, but if there are libraries, if such libraries do not burn down or are not flooded, if they have premises equipped with modern facilities, if they are headed not by people off the street but by professionals, culture will not perish in that country. (Applause). Nonetheless, our most important libraries in Moscow, Leningrad, and other cities are burning down like candles. This particularly applies to Leningrad. Water is poured on them, they lack modern fire extinguishing devices, they have no modern equipment, and they have extremely small premises. Let me cite a single example: As early as 1900 Leningrad University Library raised the question of a space shortage. To this day, however, no single addition has been built. None has been built in our country. Even in the main library, which is fully equipped with modern library facilities, even in the main V.I. Lenin National Library, about which I am particularly concerned, although I have been insulted there, small fires break out. Compare this to the Library of Congress of the United States.

What can we say about the rural libraries? Rayon libraries are frequently closed down (in Moscow, for example, this applies to the Nekrasov Library) because premises are needed for other purposes. The same occurs in Leningrad.

Library workers dealing directly with the public—and I emphasize that I am speaking not of administrators but of the officials who deal directly with the readers—that is, those who should be able to recommend a book, have no time themselves to read and be familiar with books and journals, for they lead a life of semi-poverty. Take a look at the 23 April (1950) issue of SOVETSKAYA KULTURA. It says everything accurately. The average salary of a librarian was 110 rubles. The average wage (in 1948) was 220 rubles. The rural rayon librarians, who should be the main authorities in the countryside and who educate people and recommend books, earn 50 rubles. Yet, despite the myth of its alleged backwardness, 19th century Russia was the most advanced country in the world in terms of libraries. I claim this but I am unable to prove it today. Let me remind you that in 1918-1920, at the meetings of the Sovnarkom the question of libraries was considered on 31 occasions and, by the Sovnarkom commissions, more than 50 times.

Now as to the museums. The picture here is similar: antediluvian technical equipment. The salaries of workers who deal with the public and with the items—not administrators but restorers, custodians and guides, is inadmissibly low. Yet it is they precisely who are the true enthusiasts, as are the "low-level" library workers. Particularly unsatisfactory is the calamitous situation of restorers, unless they do hack work. In that kind of work they can earn a great deal, particularly as members of cooperatives.

We have an incalculable museum wealth despite all of our sales, which are partially continuing to this day. However, the condition of cultural monuments is poor and we are forced to invite restoration workers from Poland, Bulgaria and Finland, which is much more expensive. At the Russian Museum in Leningrad which, incidentally, is much bigger than the Tretyakov, there is a shortage of master restorers, for they cannot subsist on their miserable salaries. The situation of the restorers of the Kremlin is the same. Yesterday I visited the restoration workshop of the Kremlin during the lunch break, crawling up an iron step-ladder to an attic premise. It would be interesting to know whether any minister of culture has ever visited these workshops? I believe that they would find it difficult even to get there. A restorer first class of the Moscow Kremlin has a salary of 150 rubles. What does first category restorer mean? It is the equivalent of a doctor of sciences. The same requirements must be met by a first category restorer. The Russian Museum in Leningrad does not have any restorer trainees, for students do not go into restoration work: the salary is too low.

Sixth Session
30 May 1989

The same or even a worse situation prevails in our schools. Today we must simply protect children and educators. School teachers have no authority. They have no time to add to their own knowledge. I could but will not cite examples. Teaching is based on a variety of curricula which duplicate the command-administrative methods of the past, with regulatory instructions and low-quality methods. Teaching in secondary schools means above all educating. This is a creative work of the educator and creativity cannot exist without freedom. It demands freedom. For that reason the teacher must, in addition to the curriculum, have the possibility to tell the students about that which he himself loves and values. He must promote in them love for literature, art and so on.

Let me point out that the students themselves notice these serious shortcomings in our press. Teachers in Russia have always ruled the minds of the young. Today's teacher does not have enough funds to subsist or to dress more or less adequately.

You may ask, where to find the money to raise the living standard of the people whose professions are turned to man, to man precisely, and not to objects? I am a realist. At the risk of turning into enemies many of my comrades, I shall tell you. First: We must reduce, quite decisively at that, the exceptionally inflated and well-paid administrative apparatus of all cultural and ministerial institutions. (Applause). Let those who draft the methods themselves go into teaching according to their methods and implement their own instructions. Let them protect the monuments. Let them guide tourists— that is, let ministry workers work.

Museums should be given funds from Inturist income, which it earns from our poorly preserved cultural values. I was told yesterday that Inturist is ready to contribute 20 percent of its income for the restoration of monuments. This is a splendid Inturist initiative. It must be thoroughly supported and praised and must not remain in words only. (Applause). It is necessary to appropriate for culture more funds as a result of the reduction of military expenditures, as mentioned by Mikhail Sergeyevich Gorbachev, by reducing aid given to other countries, aid coming out of our people's funds, and about which we know little. (Applause).

Culture cannot operate on a cost accounting basis. Returns from culture to the people and the country are immeasurably greater than from possible direct income earned by libraries, archives and museums or by any other economic and technical area. I assert this. However, such returns do not come immediately. The low status of culture and morality, and the growth of crime make all of our efforts in any area sterile and useless. We shall not be able to reform the economy, science or public life and we will be obstructing perestroyka if our culture remains on its present level.

The work of the Ministry of Culture must be substantially improved. People are constantly turning to us, to the Soviet Culture Foundation, with problems which the ministries of culture are not solving. The ministries of culture must be concerned with the peripheral areas as well. We send a great deal of exhibits abroad. However, we have not sent exhibits to our peripheral cities. Our museums have tremendous reserves. However, the organization of exhibits using such reserves for the benefit of peripheral cities, in order to enhance the cultural standards and interests of the people, is very infrequent and very poorly implemented.

Particular attention should be paid to the peripheral museums and to peripheral and rural libraries. Permanent peripheral exhibits based on our reserve stock must be organized.

We must formulate a long-term program for the development of culture in our country. To the best of my knowledge, no such program exists. It is only in such a case that there will be no more national disputes which confirm the low cultural standard. Instead, there will be a normal economic life and the crime rate will decline. In particular, public figures will become more honest.

Allow me to read to you an excerpt from a letter addressed to our Komsomol, which should be particularly concerned with enhancing the cultural standard. This letter expresses the view of millions of our mothers and educators. I quote: "Since the Komsomol is trying by all possible means to prove its expediency and the need for its very existence precisely as a social organization, its apparat and the people's deputies elected by the Komsomol should assume full responsibility for the state of affairs in the country related to the increased number of neglected children. In my view, these comrades should not rest until even a single minor citizen is subject to abuse and coercion on the part of adults corrupted by our society and who are now corrupting other adolescents. It is time for many citizens, comrades, to drop their mercantile concerns and comfortable positions and literally go into entrance halls and basements and, perhaps, go even deeper, in order actively to participate in their life and with a view to putting an end to processes of corrupting minors, which are taking place everywhere."

The fate of the fatherland is in your hands, and the fatherland is in danger. Thank you for your attention. (Applause).

Nishanov: Deputy Yanenko has the floor. Comrade Nazarbayev is to get ready.

A.P. Yanenko, rector of the Novosibirsk Engineering and Construction Institute, Novosibirsk (Oktyabrskiy Territorial District, RSFSR): Esteemed comrade deputies! We have just heard the report of the Chairman of the USSR Supreme Soviet. It is your task and mine to

Sixth Session
30 May 1989

discuss this report and express our comments and suggestions. Evidently all this taken together will then serve as the basis for our subsequent work. I am confident that in the process of the presentations there will be many a great many questions of those who are heard today and in the days to come. But these questions, from my point of view, will vary in terms of their significance. Some of them will be examined by commissions, in committees and at Supreme Soviet sessions; and part will require examination right here, at the Congress of People's Deputies. One such question, from point of view is the question of the functions of the Soviets of People's Deputies. Yes, it is namely we who must cause the Soviets to become a genuine popular organ of power. The first major step in this direction, from my point of view, will be adopting a resolution, in accordance with which the people's deputies would distribute the state budget. The people's deputies of the country—that is, we—would distribute the state budget; deputies of the republic, the republic budget; and so on. Then in accordance with the existing budget, they would draw up and approve the plan for the country's socio-economic development; that is, taking into consideration those sums which the country or the republic have.

Amazing things would happen under such a scheme. Exactly what? It would not be the deputy who goes to the minister with his hand held out, and I apologize for my choice of words—but the minister, who would appeal to the deputies, requesting their approval of the budget or estimated costs for his ministry, specifically, for certain purposes. And a year later, he would be reporting back, on how these moneys were spent. (Applause).

In this connection I propose that the following sentence be added to Point Five, Article 108, of our country's Constitution: "The Congress of People's Deputies shall approve long-range state plans, and shall also approve and distribute the state budget." That is my proposal. (Applause).

The next question which, from my point of view, we must discuss at this congress—is the question of the work of the USSR Council of Ministers. I know full well that Nikolay Ivanovich Ryzhkov has yet to give his speech; but today we are discussing the report of our country's Supreme Soviet chairman. I shall cite Article 113; in Point Five, the following is written: "...Regularly receive reports from organs formed by or assembled by it." That is, our country's Supreme Soviet must control the work of the USSR Council of Ministers. Unfortunately, thus far we have not observed this.

As is well known, the CPSU works out the general strategic policy for our country's development. And it is the task of the Council of Ministers to put this policy into effect. Perhaps I am mistaken, and this is purely my own personal point of view, but the present make-up of the USSR Council of Ministers is not coping with this task. (Applause). The state of affairs in our economy testifies to this; the ever-increasing deficit in the state budget testifies to this; and the empty shelves in our stores testifies to this. And the numerous resolutions and instructions prepared and issued by the Council of Ministers, which contain many poorly-thought-out decisions, testifies to this.

But what should we do, that our Council of Ministers would operate with precision and effectiveness? I think that, first of all, the Council of Ministers should think about its prestige. Why? Because any state document must be flawless; so that, pardon the expression, "a mosquito couldn't sharpen his nose on it." But, there are often many complaints after a government document is published, and many unclear features and inaccuracies.

Why does this happen? I repeat once again; this takes place because who do not have a council; there is no Council of Ministers. And transcripts of the sessions of the Council of Ministers have convinced me of the truth of these words.

What do we observe? We observe the following: when the adoption of this or that resolution or decision takes place, our ministers amiably raise their hands; not one of them opposes it; not one of them objects. And there is our misfortune; there is our problem. (Applause).

This takes place because many of the ministers, before becoming a minister, passed through the great school of apparat work, where the habit became ingrained of working with one eye on the higher authority. And this habit leads to a situation in which the higher authority, with the passage of time, becomes convinced of his own genius. And whatever the higher authority proposes, it always meets with general approval. This is the first factor.

The second factor is that the lower authority begins to think less, because someone else is doing his thinking for him. We must do everything we can, that this does not happen.

How can we do this? I think that in order for a sensible collective decision to be made, we must present our ministers, our Supreme Soviet and Congress of People's Deputies with alternative solutions. I think it would be sensible for us to introduce a so-called department of experts at the USSR Council of Ministers and Supreme Soviet. Some one would prepare a resolution (either the Council of Ministers or the Supreme Soviet); then, at the next stage, when the draft of this resolution is already prepared, it should be given to the department of experts. And the department would invite for expert analysis, scientists or other persons, who had not taken part in the preparation of this resolution or decision. And then different opinions would be worked out and presented to the Council of Ministers, the Supreme Soviet or the congress, for their verdict. And it would be our task to choose the best solution from among a large number of opinions. If this were the case, the most clear-cut and the best-thought-out decision would always

STENOGRAPHIC RECORD

Sixth Session
30 May 1989

be taken. But at the same time, as was already stated at the congress, I believe that the voting should be replaced with mandates. And this, we should write down. The voting must be secret. I believe that it would not be hard at all to equip every chair in the hall with a button, connected to an electronic computer. Precise, clear, and good.

Now, since I have touched on the Council of Ministers, I would like to say a few words about those who work there. I consider it necessary and wise if five or six ministers would speak here, at our congress—those, whose enterprises have permitted a radical reduction in the production of consumer goods (applause), so that we could then express our own opinion; but could the given minister lead this ministry in the future? And in the future we should make every effort to ensure that several ministers would always speak at the congress.

As I have touched on the question of having the ministers speak, I personally would very much like to hear the speeches of two chairmen—the chairman of Gosplan and the chairman of Goskomstat. The Gosplan chairman could describe to us just how they have planned and are planning, so that sewing machines and refrigerators disappear from the stores; and how a great many other things have disappeared, which even five or seven years ago were on the shelves. And naturally, the question arises: if Gosplan is unable to plan—then pardon me, but why should we keep it? That's the first thing.

Second: The chairman of Goskomstat, from my point of view, must share his secret: How are such cunning reference books compiled? Glancing tin the latest handbook which was given to the deputies, we see that our state of affairs is brilliant. In 1988, as compared with 1985, there was an increase in consumer, goods; and an increase in the most important foodstuffs. But pardon me, we cannot see them on the shelves of our stores. Perhaps there was an increase at the snack bars or cafeterias of Goskomstat, but not at our place. (Applause).

I believe that the People's Deputies of the USSR must know the true state of affairs in the country. And passing out handbooks with false data borders on the criminal. Therefore we must deal with this question very carefully.

At this time I would like to offer yet another suggestion. I believe that we should adopt a resolution, in accordance with which we would make public the authors of this or that suggestion, in order that there be no anonymous authors. What am I leading up to? Here's what: A great many comrades propose this or that solution, knowing that even if it results in colossal losses, they will never have to answer for it. So I am offering the suggestion that the press should publish who it was that offered a given proposal. Next time he would be extremely careful and would act thoughtfully.

Now I would like to touch on several questions, not connected with one another; but I believe they require our attention.

The first question—about people who live in the countryside. Mikhail Sergeyevich's report spoke of the fact that greater attention must be devoted to agriculture. I am in complete agreement with this. In my district there were three rural rayons. But you know, before talking about economic reform in the countryside, I believe we must restore obligations to our rural area. In what sense must we restore them? (Applause). We must create normal conditions there, such as those which urban residents have. Only then do we have the right to make demands on them. You have already heard that enterprises in our country have increased production of agricultural machinery; but they have also increased the purchase price two and three-fold. But the peasant, as before, sells his product at the same price that existed five or ten years ago. This is not right. This must be re-examined. (Applause).

While meeting with my constituents I became convinced that social injustice exists with respect to the kolkhoznik. What do I have in mind? It turns out that if I have worked on a kolkhoz for five or six years and I go to a factory, I am not given credit for continued work experience. I believe that our country is one, and that everyone should enjoy identical rights and laws. (Applause).

The next question. We often read in the newspapers of the fact that Siberian gas has come to the villages and cities of the European part of the country. We are very happy for our comrades, but are waiting impatiently for the time that Siberian gas comes to the villages of Siberia. I believe that this most certainly must be done, and I submit this proposal.

The next question. A trend is observed in the country to reject the administrative-command style of leadership. But you see the latest decision on the fact that taxes from transport must be used for building the roads of the Nechernozem is, I believe, a return to the command-administrative style. (Applause).

How could such a decision be made, not knowing the condition of the other roads in the country? I submit the suggestion, that the authors of this decision set out in October on an auto trip along the route Omsk-Novosibirsk-Krasnoyarsk-Irkutsk-Chita. And send a documentary film crew with them, so that they can show us films on the condition of our roads. Then they would be convinced of whether or not to spend all the funds on the Nerchernozem zone, or whether it would be better to allocate money to where it is also needed.

And the last: This question concerns the city of Moscow, and I believe that it must be touched. I ask the forgiveness of our Muscovites, but here is the question: From my point of view, everyone in our country should have

STENOGRAPHIC RECORD

Sixth Session

30 May 1989

identical conditions. But how has it turned out? I will cite only an incident of last year. Last year, the Central Committee, headed by Mikhail Sergeevich Gorbachev, examined the question of supplying the city of Moscow with vegetables. The next day I went into one of our stores to see for myself; apparently we have an abundance? But it turned out not to be so. And what happened after that. It turned out that after that, those trains which were to have gone to Siberia and somewhere else also, had gone to Moscow. And so, when making such decisions, one must think about everyone.

A second question. While I was on a business trip to Moscow last January, I learned with amazement that it turns out that a citizen of Moscow, having paid a visit to a physician, can get a medical certificate for ten days. But a citizen of Novosibirsk does not have that opportunity. I could cite a lot more such examples, but I shall not dwell on this. I believe that in our state, everyone should be equal. Thank you. (Applause).

Nishanov: Deputy Nazarbayev has the floor. Next to speak will be Deputy Kampbergenov.

N.A. Nazarbayev, chairman of the Kazakh SSR Council of Ministers, Alma-Ata (Alma-Ata-Ili Territorial Electoral District): Esteemed comrade deputies! During the course of our congress, numerous reasons have been cited for the lack of progress in the restructuring process, by the previous comrade as well. I would like to continue this idea.

I would support the statements of Comrades Popov, Adamovich and others in the part in which they sharply criticize the empty shelves, the increase in prices, the deficit and other shortcomings. We all understand, sense, and see these things, and this criticism is just. Pluralism of opinions was supported by Lenin himself: "We do not pretend that Marx or Marxists know the path to socialism in all its specificity. That is nonsense. We know the direction of this path; we know what kind of class forces lead to it; but in concrete and practical terms, this is shown only by the experience of the millions, when they get down to business."

Does it not seem to you, esteemed deputies, that we are indeed the representatives of the millions who have gotten down to business; who are expecting from us the decisions which will transform our society for the better within the framework of socialist choice. In my view the root of our troubles lies in solving the main problem—in healing the sickness of the basis, the economy. For this we need an accurate diagnosis. Having been employed by virtue of my duties with questions of practical economy, I can say that we do not have a reliable picture of the situation in the country's economy. I shall single out the conclusions from a PRAVDA report in May on the results of the Council of Ministers session. In my view, it successfully depicted the worsening crisis in the economy. Judge for yourselves: According to data from Goskomstat USSR, production output in the country has not increased, and the shelves are empty. The decisions taken on economic reform have sharply increased the flow of unearned money, and the cheap assortment is being washed away. Plans are being fulfilled, and the state of the economy is getting worse. The necessary growth of food production in the country is not taking place, and agricultural income is growing. Why? Many such "whys" have accumulated. We must at last define the entire depth of the crisis in the economy and work out a clear-cut path for overcoming it.

In this connection the deputies are correct in appealing to the scientists, whom I respect, of whom there are quite a few among the deputies. We know that during the period of stagnation, the opinions of the scientists were not considered, nor were ours. The apparat controlled everyone, and did its own thing. But from the very beginning of restructuring a commission was established in the government for improving the economic mechanism. The backbone of this commission, its scientific section, represents the flower of our economic science, the generators of the scientific ideas of reform. And the government, having taken counsel with them, is making decisions. But what do we have in fact? Today we have had the first, second and third models of cost accounting [khozraschet]; no doubt there will also be a fourth. But you see, cost accounting does not in fact exist! (Applause).

There once was an old regulator—average wages; we have done away with it, and rightly so. But we have not thought of a new one. Thereby we have doubled the issuance of currency, and have impaired the already-unbalanced financial situation in the country. The 12th 5-Year Plan was drawn up in the very worst traditions of the stagnation. In order to at least outwardly correct it, it was stated in all the documents that the indicator for commodity production is taken as an estimate for analytical purposes. But who believes this? Growth rates are lagging; wages, just as before, have been tied to volume in rubles; and gross output is cranked up by means of repeating the counts and the costs, and getting one's wages without producing goods, and without completing projects: We have learned to do this long ago and continue to do so. And this indicator, which was condemned at the 27th party conference and the June 1986 Central Committee Plenum, continues to live. Gross output in rubles, and not in goods, has become even more powerful in the 12th 5-Year Plan, and has achieved its apogee. Satisfying the needs of the people and not the indicators of the agencies also remains a slogan. And now we are forced to return to the most archaic indicator—the correlation between labor productivity and average wages, which has been introduced by four respected agencies. I hope I do not offend them, but at the enterprises this document bears the title, "Letters from the Gang of Four." (Applause).

Comrades! The given indicator cannot work, because labor productivity has a significant influence on the price level; that is, the higher the price the higher the

STENOGRAPHIC RECORD

Sixth Session
30 May 1989

labor productivity. After all, according to the fundamentals of Marxist-Leninist political economy, increasing labor productivity reduces prices; but with us for now the opposite is true—growth of prices increases labor productivity and wages. The entire economy has gone over to self-financing, and wholesale prices were not re-examined. Right now the profitability of milk and meat is low, products which we now badly need, and we want to hang the old obligations of the village on the necks of the tenants. Wholesale trade is not developed, and there are no resources. We know from the mass information media of the fact that in the entire world it is accepted that, if someone introduces a proposal and manages to have it accepted—and that if it turns out in fact to be bankrupt, a bust—then the authors are retired. And so we too, deputies, ought to know who in fact drew up such a five-year plan, and whose ideas are being carried out in the course of our restructuring?

We have rejected anonymity. Therefore, let us put a stop to anonymity for the authors of the various models of khosraschet, and reform in the villages. We must know our heroes, know who's who. (Applause). We must work out, together with the scientists, various alternative variants of administration in the branches and the republics; of course, in accordance with uniform principles and taking into consideration the specific features of each region. And this will form the basis of republic scientific khozraschet. At the same time one must take into consideration that at today's prices, this will nevertheless build the economy on a foundation of sand. At first all the republics agreed on this khozraschet, and then certain of them rejected it. In think that one should carefully consider all suggestions without exception, to include the Moscow group of deputies.

Departmental diktat has led to the situation that while it is one of the richest in terms of raw material resources, which enjoy great demand on the world market, our republic finds itself in a tough situation in its social development, and is on the brink of an ecological crisis. Acting like a bull in a china shop, the ministry has destroyed the Aral Sea. Ekibastuz is becoming covered with ash. Oil does not serve those who are extracting it. In various regions herdsmen have been put off the land, and there is no talk of compensation.

I would especially like to speak about the Semipalatinsk nuclear test range, which has been in operation since 1949, and which began its bursts at first in the atmosphere. Since that time the surrounding population has increased fourfold. But the military are ready to try to convince us that the tests are almost beneficial to the people's health. We understand that testing today is a state necessity. But we must conduct a genuine in-depth analysis of the influence of atomic explosions on the surrounding environment, and tell the people about it. Not to mention certain expenditures to improve the lives of those who live there.

Four years of restructuring have gone by, and the union-level ministries do not yet permit the enterprises to make use of even above-plan production; or even industrial wastes and secondary resources, oil and coal. All the rest, which Kazakhstan has been permitted to keep, comprises merely 7.0 percent of the volume of industry, while from the 93, only 1.0 percent is deducted from its profits for the republic. How long will the republic have to walk around in Moscow offices with its hand stretched out? (Applause).

Comrade deputies! The creative genius of man has created Baikonur, and the splendid city of Leninsk. But you could hardly know that the gateway to the nation's space port, Tyura Tam, remains the squalid refuge of the local population, who are not allowed, as Chingiz Aitmatov wrote in "Burannyy Polustanok," even to the burial places of their ancestors. The Maykain deposits gave the country a billion rubles in gold, but the life of the population of this village remains primitive. And I could cite many such examples. Our government, with the help of scientists, must propose measures for balancing the economy. Whatever they like; but, we must begin to live within our means. There is a decree, that unbalanced plans shall not be accepted in the country. But this decree must be carried out. And we must reduce production losses in the country which take place because of the lack of processing equipment.

The defense industry branches, which have been instructed to create the latest equipment for [food] processing and preserving, are making a mess of the resolution. Once again, no one is to blame. I must say, that in Kazakhstan alone, we lose 20-30 percent of our meat, milk and vegetables every year, just like in the rest of the country. Look where our food resources are! Because of the ministries, comrades. Neither you nor I know today what would take the place of the ministries. I would like to say, that while I know many ministers personally, they are not the ones who were there in 1984. Many of them have been replaced. These are yesterday's top managers at major enterprises, and specialists. I think we should not rush from one extreme to another. But even these new ministers have been unable to break up the monopolism, and change the role of the departments. We must create major firms, associations, and concerns which would themselves select their own organs in Moscow for long-range coordination. But we shall never overcome our illness, by not carrying out, and not answering for failure to carry out, good decisions.

The realization of the slogan, "All Power to the Soviets," has been dragged out. In actual fact, today the Soviets do not yet have the capability to independently resolve questions on the comprehensive development of their territory: they have neither the legal, nor the material-technical, nor the financial, nor the cadre base with which to do this. The adoption of the Law on Local Self-Administration must be accelerated. What sort of power can one speak of today, although we have been talking for four years already! In fact it does not exist!

Sixth Session

30 May 1989

We must also give the local Soviets from the rayon to the republic level the legal authority to suspend the decision of any agency of any rank in instances in which they would lead to ecological complications, or threaten the safety and health of the populace in a given region. (Applause).

We must genuinely increase the responsibility of administrators in the oblasts, republics and ministries for improving the lives of the populace in the localities. Unfortunately, we have not had much to say about just what in the localities, and just what in the rayon, the oblast, the republic, the kolkhoz, the sovkhoz, and the enterprise is slowing down the cause of restructuring today. Restructuring has already given us many opportunities; but we must skillfully take advantage of them. People must at last understand that it is not the government that feeds them, but the other way around: they are feeding everyone. I support the thesis in Mikhail Sergeevich Gorbachev's speech on the fact that specific deeds are required, right now. For this discipline is required, in production and in society. I think that destabilization is beneficial only to the anti-restructuring forces. We must strengthen legality, elevate the role of administrative organs, and carry out the Soviet laws.

In the stormy processes of these days, we must not forget about the fact that the past 70 years did not consist of failures alone, and that the existing economic potential did not descend from heaven, but is the result of the labor of the older generations and the efforts of all the nations. We do not need autarchy; we need to strengthen our economic conveyer; and the entire world is now occupied with integration.

The deputies spoke figuratively of the danger of the break-up of a ship on the ocean. I would use that image also for the friendship of nations in our country. The Supreme Soviet must find a mechanism for an integral state on a new Leninist basis. The diktat issued from the agencies located in Moscow, in the consciousness of certain people, is associated with Russia, with the Russian people. I do not agree with this. Russia herself has suffered from this a good deal. Are they really not speaking about the Nechernozem and its ecological problems, which are even more severe than in other republics? But you see no one can say that Russia had at one time pulled all the blankets over itself alone. I believe that Russia's prestige must also be raised. (Applause).

At the same time, comrades, only a strong republic can be the basis of a strong center. We must in fact expand the rights of all republics as equal, sovereign members of a federated union in its Leninist conception. An effective mechanism must be developed for realizing the authority of the republics; a monopoly at the nucleus as the exclusive property of the Union must be within sensible limits, and their reworking must be advantageous for the republics as well. It is necessary to guarantee a worthy government of national republics, with leadership of all federal organs, including the legal, defense and foreign-policy organs. (Applause).

With all due respect, Mikhail Sergeyevich, I cannot help but speak of yet another sore spot for Kazakhs. I quote from my own notes, your speech at the Politburo in May 1987: "I would like to state principally, that Kazakhstan was at a high level in December 1986. There was no political crisis in Kazakhstan. I would not like to place internationalism in Kazakhstan under suspicion."

These words were my principal response to the numerous questions of my constituents, and won the hearty approval of everyone. The 34 academicians, the writers and cinematographers, and the very flower of the Soviet intelligentsia, who in the war years were forced to work in Kazakhstan, could also testify to the internationalism of the Kazakh people. The pioneers on the virgin lands and today's people's deputies, who represent all of multinational Kazakhstan, could also testify to this. Right now everything is being done in the republic to more fully consider the interests of all the nations which dwell in Kazakhstan, for the purpose of strengthening their traditional friendship.

Each of the deputies speaking at the congress has his own attitude to that which is taking place in country. One would think that this does not divide us, but rather unites us all. I am in favor of the formula described in Mikhail Sergeyevich Gorbachev's report. There can be a variety of opinions, but we have one policy, and that is—restructuring. Thank you for your attention. (Applause).

Nishanov: Comrade deputies! I think that if you have no objections, Deputy Kampbergenov, the writer and our comrade, will speak after the intermission. But now we must take counsel together on a number of questions. Several deputies are asking us to tell them when they will be offered the floor for a speech at the debates. In this connection I should evidently inform you, my dear comrades, that 440 people have signed up for speeches at the debates for this hour. The secretariat of the congress is preparing a corresponding suggestion for the presidium, but to say right now, who may speak and when; well, you can understand that is rather difficult right now. But we can promise you: we shall hold the discussion in a democratic manner, and in detail. Deputy Andreeva has made a small comment and suggestion. She writes, "We are always hearing from the top people in the republic; therefore, their reports are not very useful for the congress. What are needed are new proposals and new points of view." (Applause).

Comrades, comrades! Just a moment! We took counsel together with you, and we agreed, considering the multinational nature and federated make-up of the Soviet Union, that each republic be given an opportunity. But look, during the speeches of a number of republic leaders

Sixth Session

30 May 1989

you became convinced that there were no self-serving speeches, but there was very interesting criticism, creative criticism. (Applause). Therefore, we shall take our turns. Thank you for your support. (Applause).

Comrades! As you will recall, we have authorized the members of the presidium of the congress to hold consultations with a group of deputies elected from Nagorno-Karabakh Autonomous Oblast in connection with the fact that the results of the elections to the Soviet of Nationalities from this oblast have not been confirmed. Such consultations were held. At this time I would like to offer the floor to Deputy Pogosyan, on this question.

G.A. Pogosyan, pensioner (Stepanakert National-Territorial Electoral District, Nagorno-Karabakh Autonomous Oblast): Esteemed deputies! On behalf of the group of deputies from NKAO, I would like to express my deep gratitude for the interested and objective examination of the incident which arose among the groups of deputies from the Azerbaijan republic and the oblast with respect to the gross violation of the rights of the latter to themselves resolve questions of representation in the Supreme Soviet. I would also like to express our gratitude to Mikhail Sergeevich Gorbachev, who found it possible to personally take part in the meeting of the parties on investigation of the conflict.

We are especially grateful to the representatives of the workers of the glorious city of Leningrad—Comrade Sobchak, Anatoliy Aleksandrovich; and Comrade Denisov, Anatoliy Alekseevich—who from the kindest of motives, decided to give up their seats in the Supreme Soviet in favor of the people of Nagorno-Karabakh. We consider representation in this organ of the deputies from the ever-revolutionary Leningrad much more important and useful than ours. We are morally satisfied already by the fact that after properly understanding and evaluating the situation, the deputies have practically protected our rights from another encroachment by the republic.

Having taken counsel, the group decided to propose for inclusion in the bulletin of the repeat election, the deputies whom we had previously nominated: Comrade Balayan and Comrade Pogosyan. However, considering the fact that Comrade Dzhafarov found himself in a difficult situation which was not his fault, we believed it necessary to include him on the list as well. Thus, we propose including the following candidates in the bulletin: Comrade Zoriy Gaykovich Balayan, Comrade Vagif Dzhafarovich Dzhafarov, and Pogosyan. I am confident that the deputies will be able to make the correct choice for the two seats allocated to us according to the quota. If for some reason the voting will be open, I would asked the presidium of the congress to refrain from taking part in the voting, in order not to obliquely influence its results. Thank you. (Applause).

Nishanov: I believe that the presidium of the congress is conducting itself in a highly democratic manner, which we have thus far no reason to doubt. All right, Comrade Dzhafarov, a deputy, is asking for the floor. Please, Comrade Dzhafarov:

V.D. Dzhafarov, first secretary of the Shushinskiy Rayon Party Committee, city of Shusha (Shushinskiy National-Territorial Electoral District, Nagorno-Karabakh Autonomous Oblast): Esteemed cOmrade chairman! Esteemed comrade deputies! Inasmuch as on Saturday the question of the representation of the NKAO in the Soviet of Nationalities caused, as they say here, a crisis situation, I believe it is necessary to make the following statement. I think that the decision taken to annul the results of the election in the NKAO is a consequence of the deputies' lack of information on the true state of affairs. I also believe that my rights were grossly violated, inasmuch as the results of secret balloting were annulled by an open vote and thereby repudiated the expression of the will of almost 2,000 delegates who had cast their ballots for me.

But that is not the main thing. I would like to tell you how it came about that my candidature was included in the election bulletin. I was born, live and work in Shushinskiy Rayon of Nagorno-Karabakh, where over 90 percent of the populace is Azerbaijani. Azerbaijanis live in practically all the 220 populated places in the oblast, and in 53 of them they comprise an overwhelming majority; thus, more than one-fourth of the voters who took part in the elections in the NKAO are Azerbaijanis. And as a representative of this portion of the population of the oblast, I am a member of the Special Administration Committee of Nagornyy Karabakh.

Prior to the beginning of the work of the congress, a conference of deputies from NKAO was held in Stepanakert. Taking part in it were three deputies out of the five. Balayan was in America, and Grigoryan had gone to Yerevan to take part in meetings taking place there. In addition, also taking part in the conference was Dadamyan, elected on a quota not from NKAO but from the Azerbaijan SSR. We reached an agreement to send to the Soviet of Nationalities two people, and my candidature. In this connection the assertion of the deputies from Armenia of somekind of usurpation is nothing other than disinformation.

And now about the other candidatures spoken of here: Balayan and Pogosyan. Zoriy Balayan is a permanent resident of Armenia; Pogosyan at the present time does not live in NKAO either, having moved to Moscow. Therefore, it is being proposed to make persons who do not live or work in NKAO its representatives in the Soviet of Nationalities.

And finally, I have the legal and moral right to be nominated to the Soviet of Nationalities from the NKAO of Azerbaijan SSR. I want you to understand me correctly. I am motivated by the firm conviction, that the

Sixth Session

30 May 1989

presence in the Soviet of Nationalities of representatives from Nagorno-Karabakh Autonomous Oblast of the two nations which live in the oblast answers our principal task—to achieve mutual understanding and stabilization, and to meet one another halfway. Therefore I consider it unacceptable to hold another election. Thank you for your attention. (Applause).

Nishanov: My dear comrades, of course we all understand the exceptionally delicate nature of this question. We, the participants in the congress and its presidium believe that we are all united in the opinion to help the NKAO and the Azerbaijan and Armenian republics to peacefully solve this problem. Therefore, of course, additional people are signing up to speak, and so on. Perhaps we can limit the speeches of these two comrades, and if you agree, include all three comrades on the bulletin for secret balloting? This evening we shall vote, and whatever the results will be, we shall agree to them. Will that be correct?

From the hall: Correct.

Nishanov: Are there any more proposals?

From the audience: No.

Nishanov: Please prepare the mandates.

From the audience: (Noise in hall; inaudible remark).

Nishanov: Does everyone agree with this proposal?

From the audience: (Inaudible).

Nishanov: Then, who is in favor of including all three comrades?... Who is opposed? One moment... Comrades, a moment. It has become necessary to continue the exchange of opinions. Please, Deputy Barusheva wants to speak.

L.V. Barusheva, seamstress at the Baku Volodarskiy Sewing Factory (Bakinskiy-Nasiminskiy National-Territorial Electoral District, Azerbaijan SSR): Comrade deputies! I call your attention to the exceptional importance of the decision which you are now taking. I do not want to dramatize the situation in the least, but I ask you to believe me, that peace in an explosive region depends upon this step. It is unfortunate, but this is the objective reality. Only one thoughtless statement by one of the deputies on the day the congress opened heated up the situation in the city of Baku.

I live a long way from Nagorno-Karabakh, and have not personally experienced, nor have my close relatives experienced the absurdity and the cruelty of national enmity; yet many people lightly hand off their prescriptions for resolving the problem. We do not have the right to deprive the Azerbaijani populace of the oblast to have its own representative in the USSR Supreme Soviet. After all, it comprises more than one-fourth of the population of Nagorno-Karabakh. Nor must we forget the fact that Nagorno-Karabakh Autonomous Oblast is a constituent part of Azerbaijan SSR. What would be wrong with seating two residents of Karabakh—an Armenian and an Azerbaijani here together? Could one really find a deputy who would not like to put an end to an unnatural situation, which has already kept at a fever pitch for two years not only two republics, but the entire country. And so, why complicate the situation further? Deputy Dzhafarov was born, grew up, and works in Nagorno-Karabakh. He is well-known and respected there; and he is a member of the Special Administration Committee. I appeal to all of you, Comrade Deputies, to take a well-reasoned decision, and to vote for equal representation, and thereby vote for justice and peace for tens of thousands of people. And it is namely therefore that I consider it inexpedient to conduct a second election. I request that you support my proposal. (Applause).

Nishanov: Who would also like to take part in the discussion of this question? Please, come forward.

S.A. Gabrusev, chief of synthetic fiber production at the Khimvolokno V.I. Lenin Production Association in Mogilev (Mogilev City National-Territorial Electoral District, Belorussian SSR): Esteemed deputies! Your question is being discussed at the highest levels. Since in the given situation we are the electors, we do not have the right to take upon ourselves the responsibility for resolving it. Therefore, I propose holding a referendum in NKAO on this problem, after preparing variants which have been heard from one side and the other. Let us hold a referendum in Nagorno-Karabakh Oblast. (Applause).

Nishanov: One moment please, Sergey Aleksandrovich. The lady is asking for the floor, and then you can speak. Please, come forward.

M.N. Rakhmanova, chief of the polyclinic pedatrics department at the Orenburg Medical Institute (from the V.I. Lenin Soviet Children's Fund): Esteemed deputies! I live a long way from Nagornyy Karabakh, in Orenburg Oblast. But, believe me, I say this with all seriousness: We too are disturbed by what is taking place there. Truly, we read with alarm in the press about the events in that oblast. It seems to me that what Academician Likhachev was saying today should somehow summon us somewhat to properly evaluate the situation. Truly, the situation arose completely unexpectedly for all of us. But, in my view it would be an absolutely proper decision in the sense that both the Armenian part of the populace and the Azerbaijan part of the populace should be represented. I am not acquainted with Zorkiy Balayan. As far as I know, he is my colleague, a physician, a journalist, who lives in Yerevan and works at LITERATURNAYA GAZETA in Moscow. That is, there are no problems here at all. But it does seem to me that we should right now, in this growing crisis situation, take the proper decision. Academician Likhachev has just spoke well of

STENOGRAPHIC RECORD

Sixth Session

30 May 1989

the role of culture in international relations; of public consciousness and of public tact. And so, are we not violating this tact by the fact that we manifest beforehand a certain lack of confidence in those candidates who were initially nominated? It seems to me that we should retain these two candidatures. And I as a women, as a person, who understands that behind this crisis situation there stands the actual fate, and perhaps even the lives of the people, call upon you to vote just so, displaying public tact. (Applause).

Nishanov: Comrade Sergey Aleksandrovich Ambartsumyan has the floor. (Applause).

S.A. Ambartsumyan, rector of Yerevan State University (Yerevanskiy-Myasnikyanskiy National-Territorial Electoral District, Armenian SSR): Academician Likhachev spoke eloquent words about culture in general, and parliamentary culture as well, incidentally. And I think that any speech, whether prepared or unprepared, impromptu, should contain more culture. That is the first thing. Secondly, the congress has already decided to vote again. That decision was taken on a majority vote of the deputies. Plus the right of an autonomous oblast where there is today a special situation, and special rule, introduced by decision of the CPSU Central Committee and the Supreme Soviet Presidium. I consider interference by either the Azerbaijan republic or the Armenian republic, illegal. In the given situation, this question must be decided by the deputies from NKAO. I believe that the consultations which were held with the participation of Mikhail Sergeevich and other members of the presidium, in which we proposed to hold these consultations with the deputies from NKAO, have in essence led to a proposal such as that made by Comrade Pogosyan. I believe it would be natural for us to vote right now for the proposal made by NKAO. If you were to ask the opinion of the deputies from Armenia, we would propose something entirely different. But because this is an internal affair of the NKAO, we shall make no other proposals, and we advise the Azerbaijan SSR not to do so either. (Applause).

Nishanov: Comrades, perhaps, we can end the exchange of opinons on this? Let us go ahead and decide. Forgive me, please. Please sit down... After you others will come and other comrades will also say, "Let me speak." Please take your seats. We shall now take counsel. We have after all agreed, that we would decide by majority, but without oppressing the minority.

The question is truly a delicate one. We have spoken a great deal with the comrades and representatives from NKAO and the representatives of Azerbaijan and Armenia. Here Comrade Pogosyan has introduced a proposal. Perhaps we should vote on it? But in the sense that another secret ballot should be conducted, the question has already been decided. We have already voted the day-before-yesterday. And that question about a referendum, and so forth. Thesa are already outside the framework of our decision. I put it up for a vote.

From the audience: There is a proposal from a number of deputies to continue the discussion. (Inaudible).

Nishanov: Would you like to speak? Please. You come up; and you sit down please: sit here, please.

L.M. Veyser, Komsomol committee secretary, Masanchi Secondary School, Kazakh SSR, Dzhambul Oblast, Kurdayskiy Rayon, village of Masanchi (from the All-Union Leninist Communist Youth Society): Esteemed comrade deputies! I am a completely neutral person. I have served for more than four and a half years in the Transcaucasus, in the city of Leninakan, and I know the people of Azerbaijan extremely well. I have been to NKAO, and I know the friendly nation of Armenia extremely well; and here is what I want to say. Esteemed Comrade Deputies! Today, in voting for one or the other decision, we are deciding the fate of two fraternal republics. I consider it completely proper that among the deputies from NKAO there should be an Azerbaijani. Why? By electing two Armenians we thereby are provoking the Azerbaijanis to demonstrate. Here we must make a very well-reasoned decision, which would overturn the preceding secret ballot. I am categorically opposed to that.

Nishanov: It was not the presidium that took that decision, but the congress.

Veyser: You proposed that. I shall vote against it. With all respect to those sitting here, and knowing that right now both in NKAO and in the fraternal republics, Azerbaijanis and Armenians are listening to this speech, I want to appeal to you, comrades. Comrade Azerbaijanis, Comrade Armenians! A great request to you: Please, do not take offense at one another; for upon you, and your precipitate speeches, both on the part of Armenia, and on the part of Azerbaijan, depends... The people are there, you understand, and such a tense situation. One incautious word, and that is like touching a spark to a powder keg. That is all I have, comrades. (Applause).

Nishanov: Thank you. One moment. Please take your seat.

A.N. Krayko, department chief at the P.I. Baranov Central Institute of Aviation Engine Building (Baumanskiy Territorial Electoral District, Moscow): (Noise in the hall).

Comrades, you all understand how complex is the situation in Azerbaijan. (Noise in the hall, applause). Look, I am not leaving. (Noise in the hall, applause). If I were going to propose something that had already been proposed, I would not have begun to speak.... (Applause). In my opinion, you should nevertheless listen.... (Applause).

Nishanov: Comrades, a moment. Patience. Let the deputy introduce his proposal and sit down.

From the audience: (Inaudible). (Noise in the hall).

STENOGRAPHIC RECORD

Sixth Session
30 May 1989

Nishanov: Very well, sit down please. Why bother, if they do not want....

Krayko: I was given the floor.... (Noise).

Nishanov: One moment, a moment, patience.

Krayko: So. I believe we should make the following decision, which would satisfy everyone. And there is such a decision. Look, if instead of treating me with such disrespect you would treat the representatives of both sides that way, you would stop clapping, I would say.... I believe that we must find a decision which would permit all four to be in the Soviet of Nationalities. There is such a way out. Wait.... You see, there was the famous example of Sobchak and Denisov. I believe that all four persons should be put on the bulletin, and those who did not come with them. Moreover, I, for example, will vote for all four, because I do not consider it necessary to interfere in this dispute; and I hope, I believe—that if I were a member of the Supreme Soviet from the Soviet of Nationalities, I would decline my, so to speak, membership. I am sure that two persons will be found; and I hope that they will be Russians, who also decline such membership. The fact that anyone who lives in our country, in any republic, can be a representative here—that is an altogether different matter.

Nishanov: Comrade Starovoytova, you have spoken a great deal; please sit down for a minute, sit down please.

Ye.U. Kim, senior scientific associate, Omsk State University, Omsk (Sovetskiy Territorial Electoral District, Omsk Oblast): Comrades, here is my suggestion. Inasmuch as the Soviet of Nationalities' quota for NKAO is two people, and five people have been elected from the national-territorial district, plus Comrade Dadamyan from the social organization—obviously all six people could work in the Soviet of Nationalities on a rotating basis. Therefore, I propose: that all six of them should get together right now and make up a schedule of who would work in the Soviet of Nationalities and in which years. Do you understand? You see, here the situation inevitably arises that in the course of one year two Armenians will be working together, well, say Comrades Balayan and Grigoryan; then next year, Pogosyan and Grigoryan; and for still another year, let's say, Comrades Dzhafarov and Balayan would work. Comrade Volskiy was also elected from the national-territorial district. Right? Do you understand? Perhaps he too could work there. That's what I think; that if, you see, everything were scheduled this way, agreed in advance, then no one would be slighted. You understand, after all, that it is not important just who enters the Soviet of Nationalities right now. In a year or two, they will work there in the very same "bunch." And that is my proposal.

Nishanov: Comrades, just a minute please. Comrade Starovoytova, I respect you very much, and I do not want to insult you. But, by the audience reaction, you must sense.... You have already spoken twice, and here hundreds of deputies have not yet come to the rostrum once.... You must respect the congress. Please, sit down. (Applause).

Comrades, Deputy Kobzon is submitting a proposal that the commission continue its work. Just a minute, please, comrades. I will also explain. Do you want to add something? Please.

I.D. Kobzon, artist of Moskontsert, Moscow (from the USSR Trade Unions): Comrades! I have been to NKAO. It was the first concerts after the crisis there, which began last year. I met with workers in all rayons and with comrades from the Special Administration Committee. I do not know who deprived the Committee and the representatives of these two nations today of deciding the given problem. I believe that there is still another potential opportunity not used for solving the crisis which has come up on this question, this problem: We should now invite the elders [aksakaly] from both sides and have a talk with them. Depending upon what they propose in this situation—either to adopt the suggestion, if reasonable, which they express, or continue the consultation. Otherwise we will now once again adopt a hasty decision. Let them continue consultations on this acute national problem.

Nishanov: Comrades, a moment, one moment please. Comrade Volskiy is asking for the floor.

A.I. Volskiy, chairman of the Special Administration Committee, Nagorno-Karabakh Autonomous Oblast, a CPSU Central Committee department chief, of Moscow (Stepanakert Territorial District, Azerbaijan SSR): Dear comrades! I permit myself to speak to the "Other" category on the agenda, to describe those problems and perhaps certain proposals which we have worked out, working for a year already in Nagornyy Karabakh by your authority, being a representative of the CPSU Central Committee and the USSR Supreme Soviet. And now I would ask you to hear me out for two minutes.

The situation in NKAO is very complex, and it is not homogeneous. Since 3 May strikes have been going on in Nagornyy Karabakh. There are daily clashes on an inter-ethnic basis. Emotion has the upper hand over reason literally everywhere. All appeals, all requests, talks with the aksakals and elders, are thus far not yielding the desired result. But there is are hopeful prospects: certain proposals are being worked out in the republics—both in one and the other. But you see right now, with the heated emotions of today, it would only cause harm. I can say this unequivocally. Certain rayons of Azerbaijan as well as Armenia have been boiling for two days not, and not even of their own will. It has not been peaceful in NKAO, neither today nor yesterday, especially after these debates. Everyone accepted the decision of the congress to cancel the elections for NKAO as an absolutely sensible decision. Why were they cancelled? I want everyone to understand. The situation

STENOGRAPHIC RECORD

Sixth Session
30 May 1989

was like this. When the NKAO delegation got together, the comrades in the Special Administration Committee spoke out for Comrade Dzhafarov to become a part of the corps of deputies of the USSR Supreme Soviet and be elected to the Soviet of Nationalities, an Azerbaijani I stress; and Comrade Pogosyan, former, NKAO party first secretary. These proposals were practically unanimously worked out among the NKAO deputies. I consider them exceptionally sensible. Everyone was in complete unanimity and agreed. But later, for some reason, the candidature of Pogosyan was switched for the candidature of Comrade Gabrielyan, first secretary of the Mardakertskiy Rayon Party Committee. By morning we had already received the list, in which new candidatures were inserted, without considering the opinion of the meeting of the NKAO deputies (That is, the candidature of Gabrielyan and Dzhafarov). You have held it in our hands. Dzhafarov had always, under all circumstances, remained. I do not understand the emotion of Vagiv Dzhafarovich Dzhafarov. He had always, under all circumstances, remained. This caused a reaction in the NKAO delegation, why we had not been considered. There was Pogosyan, Gabrielyan came, and so on. After this, a meeting was held, a rather emotional one, among the delegation. They put forth the following idea: Since you have not consulted with us, that means there will be the candidature of Comrade Balayan and Comrade Pogosyan, without the candidature of Dzhafarov. This emotional outburst came on the first day after the distribution of the lists.

Then I must say that Mikhail Sergeevich and Comrade Lukyanov displayed their wisdom and met with both delegations of NKAO and Azerbaijan. Anatoliy Ivanovich met with them separately once more; yesterday there were talks once again, separately; and today, once again separate talks. At last, a certain rather fragile equilibrium was established: to offer up for your judgment, for your verdict, three candidatures; those which had been introduced and not examined here. I must certify that Vitaliy Ivanovich Vorotnikov did not put up to a vote the question which Nagornyy Karabakh introduced. This is the fault of the chairmanship. I believe that under these circumstances it was necessary to vote.

Today there is an opportunity to take a sensible approach on all three candidates. I have in mind, that if one appeals to a sense of order, in three months ask the comrades, at the next session let's say, to accept one more seat. But there is also another way. If they do not want that, then it will be necessary to vote, to vote calmly, and to weigh what we are all saying. But now, I beg you, do not continue the discussion. We are being watched by both Nagornyy Karabakh, and Azerbaijan, and Armenia. Every careless word could once again be turned against the women, the children, the old people, against the entire population. Every careless word. I beg of you, not to continue the discussion on this subject. (Applause).

Nishanov: Dear comrades! In sum, one proposal stands out, the one introduced by Comrade Pogosyan: Include three candidates on the list for secret balloting. Whoever is in favor of this proposal, I ask you to prepare your mandates and vote. Please lower your hands. Who is opposed? The counters will now report. But seven [hands] are still visible from the presidium.... Voting against were 17 deputies. Who has abstained? I request you count them, comrades... Abstaining were 99 deputies.

Nishanov: Comrades! Thus, the candidatures of Comrades Pogosyan, Dzhafarov, and Balayan shall be included in the bulletin for secret balloting. It is proposed to hold the secret balloting this evening, after the session is over. I ask the counting commission to make all necessary preparations for voting, and to assemble at this time in the Granovitaya Chamber. And one more announcement: the comrades are requesting a meeting of the Mandate Commission during the lunch break. You may now come to an agreement in the Granovitaya Chamber. Please, you make the announcement yourselves, so that there won't be any false rumors.

Gidaspov: I beg the pardon of the deputies. We must assemble the Mandate Commission. There are already a number of questions that must be examined. Therefore, after our plenary session is over, all members of the Mandate Commission are requested to meet in the Supreme Soviet Presidium building, in the Small Hall.

Nishanov: Very well.

Gidaspov: I would like very much for Vladimir Pavlovich Orlov and Anatoliy Valeryanovich Gorbunov to take part in the session of the Mandate Commission, as we agreed. And I ask that the deputy chairmen and secretaries, and Comrade Yakovlev come to me.

Nishanov: Vitaliy Ivanovich Vorotnikov has the floor for a brief announcement.

Vorotnikov, V.I., member of the CPSU Central Committee Politburo, chairman of the RSFSR Supreme Soviet Presidium, from Moscow (Voronezh National-Territorial Electoral District, RSFSR): Comrades, I request that the members of the Supreme Soviet—both the Soviet of the Union and the Soviet of Nationalities of the Russian Federation, including Moscow and Leningrad—remain here in the hall for a few minutes for information, after intermission is called.

Nishanov: Comrades, an intermission is declared until 1600.

Sixth Session
30 May 1989

30 May 1989. Kremlin Palace of Congresses. 1600.

Comrade R.N. Nishanov is chairman.

R.N. Nishanov: Comrade deputies! We are continuing the work of our congress. Deputy Kaipbergenov has the floor.

T. Kaipbergenov, writer, chairman of the board of the Karakalpak ASSR [Autonomous Soviet Socialist Republic] (Khodzheyliyskiy National Territorial Electoral Okrug, Karakalpak ASSR): Esteemed Comrade Chairman! Esteemed comrade deputies! Mikhail Sergeyevich Gorbachev mentioned the imminent ecological crisis in his report as though in passing—that is, among the country's other problems. I should announce that the ecological catastrophe that has taken place and is taking place today in the Aral, in terms of its scale and prolonged consequences, is comparable to the latest large world catastrophes. There are victims, there are people who will be cripples for the rest of their lives. There is poisoned, mutilated land; there are abandoned and destroyed villages. If you fly in an airplane over the expanses of the Aral area, you will see white, lifeless salt marshes. They have covered the land like snow. According to specialists, for every 1 hectare of land in Karakalpakiya, Khoreziya, and Tashauz Oblast in Turkmenia, 540 kgs of salty sand fall annually, carried from the dried-out former water area of the Aral Sea.

It is dangerous to grow fruits and vegetables on our land today.... The land that fed us has been poisoned and destroyed once and for all. Science has not yet been able to purify a single clump of land in Karakalpakiya from herbicides, pesticides, and defoliants which have been applied by the ton on each hectare over past years. If you take our soil into your hands today it no longer smells like soil; it smells of chemicals, and it crumbles between your fingers. From the upper reaches of the Amudarya, all the used water that runs off irrigated land is discharged back into the Amudarya. The residuals of toxic chemicals in the river have reached such a life-threatening level that fish die in this water. In the Aral area people are dying unnatural deaths and are doomed to extinction—the huge doses of toxic chemicals that penetrate our organisms with dust and salt water destroy man's genetics. There has been a sharp increase in the percentage of deformed newborn babies. According to incomplete data from outpatient examinations conducted in the autonomous republic, two of every three people examined have been ill, mainly with typhoid, intestinal cancer, and hepatitis. There are also cases of cholera.

The strangest thing is that the majority of the ill people are children. Disability is constantly increasing. In certain regions of Karakalpakiya, physicians do not recommend feeding children mother's milk—it is toxic. This is hard to believe: Mother's milk has turned into a poison.

In this situation it is difficult to say with confidence whether or not there will be a single healthy person left in the Aral area by the beginning of the next century. In the near future the area will become a habitat of dependent people who are not capable of feeding themselves. Life in the epicenter of the ecological catastrophe is deteriorating from day to day. Fruits and vegetables are saturated with toxic chemicals. The provision of the basic food products in the country is somewhat lower than the average for the country.

At each meeting the voters assault me with questions: Tell us, is there a country on the planet that will allow its own population to be poisoned?

We have come to this place in life not out of our own will but because of the central planning agencies. This is essentially a consequence of the extremely criminal economic policy.

It can be objected that the government is concerned about us, that it adopted the decree of the CPSU Central Committee and the USSR Council of Ministers of 19 September 1988 "On Measures for Radical Improvement of the Ecological and Sanitary Situation in the Region of the Aral Sea, Increasing the Effectiveness of the Utilization and Stepping Up the Protection of the Water and Land Resources in Its Basin." Yes, this decree does exist. But, in the first place, it does not fully solve the problem when we are speaking about—treating a fatal illness. Any half-measures are not therapy but simply a postponement the burial time. I wish to recall that Comrade Gorbachev, in a meeting with the residents of Tashkent on 7 April 1988, responded to the question of the fate of the Aral by saying that variants are being developed for restoration of the Aral Sea. But the decree does not say a word about the restoration of the sea. In the second place, these decrees are intended for the long term, and we need immediate assistance. Finally, this decree is working poorly so far. This year not a single liter, not a single drop of the 8 cubic kilometers of water necessary for sanitation has been put into the Aral Sea. The Aral tragedy has become the most popular, almost a fashionable problem. It is written about frequently and willingly in the press and discussed at all kinds of meetings, conferences, and symposiums. New meetings and speeches at them by individual leaders are beginning to remind one of the tale of Scheherazade from the "Thousand and One Nights." But there the heroine wins one more day of life with each tale, whereas our comforting meetings, at which nothing is decided, on the contrary bring us closer to death. My speech is not a pathetic cry about our impoverished situation. The Aral needs not tears but water. We must not forget that the death of the Aral threatens death to more than just all of Central Asia. It will entail unpredictable, most likely catastrophic, changes in the climate over an immense part of the country. It is already threatened with global disaster.

Sixth Session
30 May 1989

It is generally known that in Central Asia farming exists because of two rivers: the Syrdarya and the Amudarya, which bring their water to the Aral. The dozens of cubic meters of moisture that evaporate from the sea each year are returned in the form of snow to the glaciers of Tyan-shan and the Pamir. Now the natural cycle has been disturbed. If we do not save the Aral, where will we get the water in the rivers that flow from the Pamir and Tyan-shan?

Early frosts in the autumn and late spring have become customary. The salt and dust storm that raged on 29 April of this year is also the result of the sharp reduction of the water area of the Aral Sea. Previously the air currents over it became a shield on the path of the cold winds from the Arctic. The current disaster of Central Asia, with snow falling in May and almost all the planted areas dying out, is another threat of destruction. Immediate resolute actions are needed.

First: In Uzbekistan there is a deputy group for checking on the implementation of government decisions. But the destiny of the Aral depends on more than the republics of Central Asia and Kazakhstan. Therefore, I demand that we create a special deputy group of the USSR Congress of People's Deputies with extraordinary authority, as not a single one of the republics can resolve this ecological disaster by itself. (Applause).

Second: The areas planted to cotton must be reduced rapidly and sharply. Yes, we know that cotton is not only textile raw material but also a strategic product. Apparently we will have to keep the strategic cotton, but we must get rid of the textile cotton. In no case should cotton be exported. At this point to trade in cotton is literally to trade in the health of our compatriots. (Applause).

Third: It is time to put an end to the extensive methods of farming. We need a law for assigning criminal liability for expansion of areas planted on irrigated land. There is no other way of dealing with people who want extra hectares—and this means extra irrigation—to fulfill the plan. We must immediately introduce payment for water, and it is time to start keeping track of it.

The last thing: As we ourselves cannot yet cope with the ecological catastrophe, we should not hide it, but honestly tell the world about it. We must officially declare the Aral zone an ecological disaster and call for help from the world community.

As we have already been convinced, when it comes to misfortune we have something to learn from the foreign specialists, and we have something for which to thank the kind residents of other countries. But up to this point the shores of the Aral, this forbidden zone, this secret territory, reminds one of a reservation. Foreign journalists and specialists are not allowed there.

I wish to make another suggestion: Each month and each quarter to publish information about the number of people who have died from diseases related to the ecological catastrophe; the amount of water put into the Aral; and the continuing decline of the level of the sea and the sizes of its water area.

In concluding my speech I wish to announce the orders of my constituents. They hope that in the near future the first leader of the country will come to their land.

I repeat, our catastrophe was made by human hands. Man must rectify it. Thank you for your attention. (Applause).

R.N. Nishanov: The floor is turned over to Deputy Tamaz Valerianovich Gankrelidze, director of the Institute of Orientology of the Georgian SSR Academy of Sciences. After Comrade Gankrelidze finishes, I shall tell you the order of business. Comrade Starodubtsev is to prepare.

T.V. Gankrelidze, director of the Institute of Orientology of the Georgian SSR Academy of Sciences, Tbilisi (Akhalshenskiy National Territorial Electoral Okrug, Adzhar ASSR): Esteemed comrade deputies! In my speech I wish to touch upon events which have been raised repeatedly in one form or another at our congress. The congress actually began with paying homage to the memory of the innocent victims of the events of 9 April 1989 in Tbilisi. This is no accident. The Tbilisi tragedy shook us all and was a terrible blow to human values about which so much has been said at this congress, a blow whose social and political consequences are difficult to assess at this time.

I shall deal with questions that affect the very basis of the new course of our state which is called "restructuring," "renewal," "democratization," and "glasnost," on whose implementation, in the final analysis, the form and character of the further existence of our multinational country and, possibly, our entire planet, depend.

I shall touch upon the tragic events of 9 April in Tbilisi and try to give an interpretation to these events from the standpoint of the functioning of the legal mechanism in our state and from the standpoint of existing constitutional law.

We must reveal the whole truth and tell it all. Only then is it possible to obtain a certain legal guarantee that nothing similar to these tragic events will be repeated in the future.

FIRST CONGRESS OF PEOPLE'S DEPUTIES OF THE USSR

Sixth Session
30 May 1989

The country and the entire international community know that on April of this year at 4 in the morning, under the pretext of dispersing an unsanctioned rally, there was a mass assault, unprecedented in its cruelty, involving human casualties, against innocent people participating in a peaceful demonstration in Tbilisi. The rally, at which up to 10,000 people had gathered, was peaceful; there was no violence, and there were no calls for violence. When tanks and armored personnel carriers appeared on the square in front of the government house, people, sensing the danger, stood with lit candles, sang old songs, and prayed. This entire picture can be reproduced precisely and in all the details from available video and photographic materials and from numerous eye-witness accounts of victims and other participants in the rally. (As far as I know, these video materials will be shown today at 1900.)

In addition to nightsticks, the military units used trenching tools and poisonous chemical substances, which was officially announced at a special commission of the Georgian SSR Ministry of Public Health, in whose work experts from Moscow and Leningrad participated, and later by international experts, physicians, and toxicologists who were invited here from Switzerland, the FRG, France, and the United States of America.

This military operation which was led by Colonel General Rodionov, the troop commander of the Transcaucasian Military District, was conceived, obviously, not as an operation for dispersing a peaceful rally but as a previously planned punitive operation for destroying people, because before the beginning of the operation there were no warning appeals or actions by the members of punitive expedition. Soldiers blocked the passageways, surrounded the citizens, and hit them with nightsticks and trenching tools, and they showed no mercy for the hungry people there, the girls and elderly women, the physicians and Red Cross workers; they pursued those who were fleeing, they caught up with those who were wounded and took them out of the hands of medical personnel, and they dealt blows to the local police workers who, performing their civic duty, were saving the lives of the citizens.

According to official information, 16 people died at the scene of the tragedy, 14 of whom were women. The oldest was 70 and the youngest 15. Three of them died in the hospital.

Later the central and military press and even PIONERSKAYA PRAVDA wrote that Georgian men had killed their own women and children, and the soldiers, you see, tried to save them and protect them from the attacks of their furious husbands. In general it is disturbing that the mass media, particularly with central press and television, and the "Vremya" program covered the events falsely and in a typical television way, asserting that the people were victims of a "throng that arose" out of nowhere. All this impresses us because of the incompetence and primitive handling.

One is especially shaken by the use of poisonous chemical substances against the demonstrators. All this is incompatible with the moral and legal norms adopted in a civilized society and should be regarded as a crime against the people themselves and humanity in general. It is a crime to use poisonous chemical substances, but it was no less of a crime to cover up this fact for a long time; this caused complications in the condition of or the death of victims poisoned by the gas because they could not be given the appropriate medical assistance promptly. Moreover, having concealed the use of poisonous chemical substances and not promptly conducted degasification of the region where the punitive detachments operated, the military authorities thus contributed to further mass poisoning of people, particularly children and adolescents, for 2-3 weeks after the tragic events of 9 April. For understandable reasons the military authorities stubbornly refused for a long time to admit to the use of poisonous chemical substances. The use of so-called "cheremukhi"—the tear-inducing substance chloroacetophenone—was admitted only on 14 April, and the utilization of the highly toxic substance CS—which is sadly known from Vietnam—was not admitted until the end of the month, and then only under real pressure from the community and people's deputies from Moscow, Kiev, and Saratov.

Foreign toxicologists recently established that among the poisonous chemical substances that were applied there was another strong, asphyxiating poison—chloropicrin, which was used during World War I.

From the very beginning the physicians lacked information about the composition and structure of the poisonous substances, and this made treatment extremely difficult and caused general agitation and indignation among the population. A large group of those who suffered declared a hunger strike over this.

As a result of an investigation it became clear that the chemical poisonous substances were used not only on the square in front of the government house but also in the adjacent areas. The soldiers threw poisonous capsules into buildings where people were hiding from persecution.

As of today 3,500 people have come to medical institutions with symptoms of poisoning; up to 500 of these are in the hospital for treatment, and some are still in serious condition. These figures are confirmed by representatives of the International Red Cross and a group of experts from the United States—"Physicians for Human Rights"—and experts from France—"Physicians Without Borders."

Events developed no less tragically after 9 April. The introduction of a curfew in Tbilisi, about which the population was notified a couple of minutes before it went into effect, entailed serious consequences. A half hour after the declaration of the curfew a young person

STENOGRAPHIC RECORD

Sixth Session

30 May 1989

was killed by a bullet through the windshield of a car and several people were wounded, including a 12-year-old boy who was riding on a bicycle.

The negative consequences of the tragic events of 9 April are being felt to this day, particularly among children and adolescents, in whom foreign experts have established the syndrome of so-called "mass psychogenic reaction to a catastrophe."

We are registering an exceptionally high level of tension in the republic, which can develop into various unpredictable actions at any moment. Only complete openness full and punishment of the guilty parties can prevent the catastrophic influence of this tragedy on the behavior and moral condition of our compatriots throughout the entire territory of the country.

The tragedy of 9 April in the city of Tbilisi and its consequences are perceived by all Georgian people as a universal national disaster whose significance goes beyond the national framework and affects the human principles of the rights and freedoms of nations.

How could it happen that in a rule-of-law socialist state, tragic events played themselves out in violation of the basic constitutional rights of the people and generally recognized principles of human behavior? In the tragedy of 9 April in Tbilisi, one could see the complete bankruptcy of the legal mechanism currently in effect in the USSR whereby not only the destinies of people but the destiny of an entire republic can be attacked by irresponsible reactionary forces that are hostile to the process of democratization and progress. Do the people who gave the order to use the sharpened shovels and poisonous chemical substances against peaceful demonstrators understand that they are killing the spirit of an entire generation, of an entire people, and dealing an irreversible blow to interethnic relations, a blow whose consequences it is difficult to overestimate?

A legal analysis of the legitimacy of decisions made by party, soviet, and military departments regarding the events in Tbilisi on 9 April leaves no doubt that we frequently have irresponsible violations of the sovereign constitutional rights of peoples and that the process of forming a rule-of-law state in our country is still in the embryonic stage. We are calling for an open, public, and responsible investigation of this bloody battle in Tbilisi and the consequences of "bloody Sunday" of 9 April 1989 and for the disclosure of the real parties guilty of this crime and their punishment, even if they are among the highest echelons of military and political power.

If the guilty parties are not punished the public will perceive autocracy of the highest party apparatus and military command. It is necessary to give a political evaluation to the events that took place. The country's entire highest leadership should be aware of a planned action of this scale, with these political consequences.

Colonel General Rodionov in his justification of the punitive operation conducted on 9 April in Tbilisi refers to the sadly known ukase of the Presidium of the USSR Supreme Soviet of 26 July 1986, "On the Rights and Responsibilities of Internal Forces of the USSR MVD [Ministry of Internal Affairs] in Preserving Public Order." The tragic events in Tbilisi clearly showed how dangerous this ukase is when it is arbitrarily interpreted and placed on the agenda the need for its revision or even complete abolition, as was the case, incidentally, with certain other legislative acts, for example, that of 5 April, which strikingly coincided with the time of the tragic events of 9 April in Tbilisi. Related to this, in particular, is the question of the legal status of the so-called "special purpose" units and the actually specialized units—as they are called by the people—of professional killers who, when conducting the Tbilisi operations distinguished themselves by special cruelty and inhumanity.

During the investigation of the tragedy of 9 April and the subsequent period, the ignoble role in these events of Boris Nikorskiy, the second secretary of the Communist Party of Georgia Central Committee, became apparent. He did not even appear before the Georgian SSR Supreme Soviet commission for investigating the events of 9 April. Therefore, it seems expedient for me to raise here, at the USSR Congress of People's Deputies, the question of the role and function in the union republics of the so-called "Second Secretary" sent and appointed from the center.

The practice of creating such an institution of "governor general" was associated with the time of "stagnation" or even with the preceding period and cannot be justified under the current conditions of political reforms and the growing sovereignty in the union republics. These people, as a rule, are not familiar with the national traditions, the culture, or the language of the indigenous population of the republic, which causes dissatisfaction among the broad public and a lack of confidence on the part of the people in this kind of leader. It seems that such an institution of "governor generals" is an anachronism under current conditions and should be abolished. All the leadership of the union republic should be elected exclusively from the local population, taking into account national ceilings and the national merit of the people populating the republic.

It is a manifestation of the highest degree of cynicism that insults the national feeling of the entire population of our republic that, for example, Colonel General Rodionov still sits on the USSR Congress of People's Deputies as someone elected by and representing the Georgian people despite the fact that his constituents have already expressed a lack of confidence in him as a deputy and recalled him in keeping with the existing constitution. (Noise in the hall). Colonel General Rodionov has neither the moral nor the legal right to remain a USSR

STENOGRAPHIC RECORD

Sixth Session
30 May 1989

people's deputy from Georgia. The people's deputy should still be aware that he is elected by the people and protects their interests and not those who punish the people. (Applause).

Completing my speech regarding the tragic events in Tbilisi and their consequences for all the Georgian people I wish to quote the words the Catholicos—patriarch of all Georgia, the most holy and blessed Iliya II—uttered in a conversation with a member of the commission for investigating the events of 9 April, Academician A.D. Sakharov: "It happened that it was the Georgian people who bore this heavy cross and thus delivered other people from similar severe trials. Such a thing should never happen anywhere again." (Applause, some of the deputies stand).

R.N. Nishanov: Are you next? Please. The deputy asked for the floor for discussion. Introduce yourself, please. (Applause continues). Please come to the podium, Comrade Deputy. (Applause continues).

From the floor: Rodionov to the podium.

R.N. Nishanov: Comrades, please. There will be a report from Rodionov.

R.A. Bratun, writer, Lvov (Lvovskiy—Zaliznichnyy Territorial Electoral Okrug, Lvov Oblast): Esteemed Comrade Chairman! Esteemed deputies! I shall give a brief statement on my own behalf and on behalf of the deputies from Kiev: Chernyak and Yavorvskiy. We came here directly from barricades of the pre-election battles. We are afraid that our constituents will think we are dead, since we have not said anything from the podium. We sent notes to the presidium previously, but they were lost somewhere. I do not see any evil intent in this. But today we did not write notes knowing that the list of speakers was astronomically long. We are bringing the following proposal for your consideration: At the end of each work day we should allot an hour for brief announcements, important orders from constituents, references, and other orders—3-5 minutes each for those deputies who have something to say. Otherwise, it will be very difficult for us to report in our local areas. I think that long speeches are very good. But still, perhaps an hour should be given to the rest of us so that we can take advantage of this strict regulation and make brief announcements. Thank you for your attention.

R.N. Nishanov: I think that we should consult on this issue and work out some procedure at the end of the meeting.

There were several voices from the hall demanding that General Rodionov, the troop commander of the Transcaucasian Military District and deputy, express his attitude toward the events in Tbilisi. We shall now hear him; I asked that he prepare. I would also like to remind you that at the beginning of our meeting a question was asked of the minister of defense regarding this issue. I think there should be an answer to this question. Or should we hear Comrade Rodionov?

From the floor: (Inaudible).

R.N. Nishanov: Shall we hear Comrade Rodionov?

Voices from the hall: Yes.

R.N. Nishanov: All right. Comrade Rodionov, I invite you to the podium.

I.N. Rodionov, colonel general, troop commander of the Krasnoznanennyy Transcaucasian Military District (Borzhonskiy Territorial Electoral Okrug, Georgian SSR): Comrade, I might not be able to keep this within the allotted time....

R.N. Nishanov: I ask all the speakers to adhere strictly to the regulations. Just now I refused a note concerning the speech of Tamaz Valerianovich Gankrelidze asking why he was given 20 minutes. I ask you to stay within the allotted time.

I.N. Rodionov: But I did not ask for the floor.

R.N. Nishanov: Please.

M.S. Gorbachev: We shall look and see. This is such a complicated issue.

I.N. Rodionov: Esteemed comrades! Let us get down to brass tacks. I think it necessary to give a political evaluation to what happened in Tbilisi. Without a political evaluation it is impossible to interpret and give a correct evaluation to what happened, the consequences—and the consequences are terrible. Therefore, allow me to remind you of what the deputy who spoke before me said here: The rally was peaceful (I am reading from the appeal to you), the rally was peaceful without the application of violence, without appeals for violence, the slogans did not contradict the existing constitution, when on Rustaveli Prospekt there appeared armored personnel carriers, and so forth.

Verbatim from ZARYA VOSTOKA, the organ of the Communist Party of Georgia Central Committee, for 14 April: "Human material, live people, among whom there were women and adolescents, were needed by the leaders of extremist groupings not only to propagandize their anti-Soviet, antistate, and antisocialist views but also—even more dangerous—to carry out their subversive antistate activities."

Those who now, after the tragedy, speak about the peaceful nature of the rally forget that at the very time over the central square of the city day and night there were vile appeals for physical violence against communists, and anti-Russian and nationalistic attitudes were being fanned. (Noise in the hall).

Sixth Session

30 May 1989

R.N. Nishanov: Just a minute, we have given over the floor, there is a regulation, let us allow him to say what he has to say, and then we will continue the discussion.

I.N. Rodionov: I heard you, comrades: This is the way they refused to let me speak at the Communist Party of Georgia Central Committee Plenum after the tragedy. Why? I shall discuss this at the end. Because it was a double.... (Noise in the hall).

I.N. Rodionov: Allow me to continue. Anti-Russian and nationalistic attitudes flared up, I quote the newspaper of the Central Committee. The evaluation was given immediately after the events of 14 April. Groups of well-trained and organized people forced their way into enterprises, halted the work of hundreds and thousands of people, returned passenger buses to the parks, broke windows, desecrated monuments, and sent shock detachments to other regions of the republic, sowing dissension, discord, and disorder everywhere. There were real threats of taking over vitally important facilities in the republic. This is the way, comrade deputies, the political situation was assessed by the republic leadership. A majority of members of the city party aktiv and a majority of people's deputies of Georgia were participants in the meeting of the city party aktiv at midnight on 8 April.

The party aktiv supported the decision of the bureau that the situation was becoming extremely explosive, with unpredictable consequences. All measures of influence and appeal to reason have been exhausted and there remained the extreme measure—to apply force. Thus, when extreme measures are applied, the consequences can be extremely severe.

Further (from ZARYA VOSTOKA in the assessment of what took place): It was not the introduction of troops that complicated the situation, but the complication of the situation that called for the introduction of troops. One must now question the republic leadership—who went for help? This could put an end to it. But allow me to discuss certain questions that are bothering you and make certain suggestions.

On 6 April at the rally (in front of 6,000 people) under the leadership of the leaders of the Tseleteli Society they read and approved an address to the president and Congress of the United States and to the NATO countries, which suggested:

1. To devote a UN meeting to the day of Georgian sovereignty—26 May.

2. To declare 25 February 1921 the day of occupation of Georgia by the bolshevik forces of Russia.

3. To render help to Georgia in seceding from the union, including through the use of NATO or UN forces.

I shall read out the slogans that were the most widespread throughout the city and especially in the region of the government house, including in English: "Down with Russian communism!" "Russian oppressors, out of Georgia!" "Down with the decadent Russian empire!" "Down with the communist regime!" "The USSR is the prison of the people!" Beyond these, there were open calls for violence against all who were not in favor of these slogans. This is the Georgian variant of restructuring and pluralism of opinions. This is the only variant that suits those who signed the appeal to the congress on behalf of the Georgian people who, incidentally, are continuing to live honestly and work, and are not participating in these orgies. But everything possible is being done to draw the workers in as well.

Now, comrades, a couple of words about the text of the "Appeal to the USSR Congress of People's Deputies From the Commission of the Georgian Supreme Soviet."

We have done everything to avoid casualties.

I continue to read verbatim: "...Such a large number of people at 4 in the morning on the 9th is explained by the fact that during the day of 8 April, along the main street of the city, armored equipment passed through the thick of the people at the rally. This caused a general feeling of alarm and a desire on the part of the citizens, including women and middle-aged men, not to leave their young compatriots alone in the disaster....."

This was done so that people would disperse and there would be no serious consequences.

Further in the text: "There were no warning words or actions by the authorities or military personnel. The soldiers blocked the passageways, surrounded the citizens, and beat them with clubs and trenching tools."

In the front there were internal forces armed with nightsticks and shields, and they advanced slowly. I must tell you that all approaches to Rustaveli Prospekt and the adjacent streets were promptly blocked with dump trucks loaded with reinforced concrete, rocks, and gravel, and buses—the air was let out of all the tires. The barricades made of motor vehicles were in three rows. There were troops from the Soviet Army, an airborne regiment that had come from Kirovabad; its task was to advance after the internal forces that were clearing Rustaveli Prospekt, take the government house and the Communist Party of Georgia Central Committee under guard, and block Rustaveli Prospekt until morning to prevent any assemblies there. The situation was very difficult, and I am sure that the person who spoke here was not there on the Prospekt. I was there from 3 am and stayed as long as necessary, and I saw everything with my own eyes.

About the trenching tools. Comrades, soldiers were going there to prevent gunfire, and it could have broken out in this situation, and we took away all of our personnel's

STENOGRAPHIC RECORD

Sixth Session

30 May 1989

arms; only the officers and noncommissioned officers had firearms. The personnel had trenching tools as part of their equipment. Some people held their trenching tools in their hands because a soldier needs something with which to protect himself. I shall discuss this further.

There were mistakes on our side. We were in a hurry, as we had the experience of Sumgait, Kirovabad, Nakhichevan, and Zvartnots, and there were casualties everywhere. This is why we sent our equipment through, because the casualties had not been gathered up, and the time was early—4 in the morning. What could we do? In front of us were the internal forces, without any firearms. I have already said that among the Soviet Army only the officers and noncommissioned officers had firearms. We slowly pushed the crowd to one side, and nobody was surrounded. Not a single shot was fired on the square. Through the megaphones we warned people to disperse. We did not count on having such strong and stubborn resistance. Both barricades and armed detachments of fighting men. Incidentally, 172 military servicemen were wounded and 25 were hospitalized, and they were wearing helmets, bulletproof vests, and they had shields. So many helmets and so many bulletproof vests that were not effective....

But here is the main thing: Come to see us in Tbilisi when these rallies are being conducted and you will see with your own eyes. Incidentally, comrades, according to official information, 16 people died at the site of the tragedy. I ask you here, before the deputies, to give their names and the cause of each death. But I am telling you (and this is where we began our discussion), not a single one of the people who were gathered up—and the square was cleared by 6 am (from 4 to 6)—not a single one had a cut or a stab wound. Not one of the 16. (Noise in the hall). Do not interrupt me. The investigation agencies have gone into this. You understand, everything is emotional here, but I have already heard so many rumors of all kinds: how the paratroopers forced a 70-year-old woman to walk 3 kms and finally dumped her somewhere in the bushes, and so forth. There are so many rumors. Just now, when I heard the speaker before me I sat quietly and, though disturbed, recalled our magic Russian words.... I ask you to read their names.... (Applause). Read them one by one, and what each one died of. In 2 hours, 16 people were gathered up.

Since there was not a single wound on any of the bodies, they began to talk about gases. But what kind of gases could be used in 2 hours when nobody had gas masks or other means of protection? So all this reduces down to the fact that people were walking with candles and saying prayers. Yes, there were prayers. The esteemed head of the church asked the people to disperse; he appealed to their reason, but the microphone was ripped out of his hands, and they would not let him speak, and through this microphone they called the crowd of people to resist. This is why I say that this is a provocation and not a popular gathering.

From the hall: (Inaudible).

I.N. Rodionov: Yes, three people died in the hospital, and one of those who died had cuts on his head. But he could have been injured some other way, a 34-year-old man. There were many people like this.

From the floor: Wind it up, please.

I.N. Rodionov: Yes, I will, but this question is very fundamental for me.... Give me a chance to speak.

I am especially disturbed, comrades, by discussions of the use of chemicals. This was done by special agencies, and I asked for the representative of the investigation agencies to report the results to you, both about those who died and about the application of chemical substances. So as not to hold your attention too long I should say that Major General Yefimov, who is in charge of the internal forces, appeared on television twice to explain what they were using. Again, to prevent more serious consequences they used a tear gas-like Cheremukha, which the internal forces have. Again, it was not used by the Army. But twice he tried to speak on television, and twice they would not let him speak. Let us try to figure out why. Let the comrades answer.

After all, if we had used chemicals they would have come into direct contact with a large number of military servicemen, and in the crowd there were also workers of the militia and the state security committee who had changed clothes. But only 19 people went for help—with slight traces of toxic substances of the irritant type.

The curfew is a matter of principle. The situation in the city after this tragedy was very complicated, very serious and explosive, with unpredictable consequences. By 7 pm, the bureau of the Communist Party of Georgia Central Committee had convened. Comrades Shevardnadze and Razumovskiy had already come to Tbilisi. The troops who were coming in were used to protect the avenues, facilities, and streets, and on the whole they encompassed the city to calm the population and to prevent unpredictable serious consequences. We were fully ready to enforce the curfew and declare the city in a state of emergency by 11 pm. At 8 pm, I was sent from the bureau to announce this. I arrived at the television studio and immediately sat in front of a camera, but again for incomprehensible reasons the announcement was made at 10:50 pm, 10 minutes before the beginning of the curfew. Please check with the television studio to see what time my statement was made. But why was it postponed until 10:50 pm?

Then there were the children. People write about how they were gathering flowers. But it was not children who were gathering flowers but mainly militia in disguise, and not a single one of them suffered when they were picking up the flowers after the funeral in front of the government house.

STENOGRAPHIC RECORD

Sixth Session

30 May 1989

I am coming to the end, comrades. I appeal to the commission that is now working and ask them to figure out the cause of the 180-degree change in the coverage of events for the mass media.

Second, why at the very beginning of the investigation were the victims declared innocent, and why was the many-hour anti-Soviet orgy called a folk celebration?

Third, why at the very beginning of the investigation were the main people pushed away from the leadership of the republic and party and new ones appointed who immediately declared that everything had been decided without them and that they knew nothing about it? An example: On 22 April, at a conference of party and soviet workers in Tbilisi the newly elected first secretary of the Central Committee of the Communist Party of Georgia, Comrade Gumbaridze (he is here), announced that at the bureau of the Central Committee, when adopting a decision about the events (from here it is verbatim): "An opinion was expressed that if necessary...(I emphasize—if necessary; and the decision was simple, and the party aktiv said that all measures had been exhausted and it was necessary to act only by force; otherwise, the consequences could be serious) to introduce special provisions. But I cannot but note that the majority of members of the bureau, including you personally, did not know the plan, the time, the forms, or the means of concrete implementation of this measure. I thought and I still think that it is never permissible and there is no justification for making such crucial decisions in a small group of people. I want you to understand me correctly." This is verbatim. But at the time of these events Comrade Gumbaridze occupied the post of chairman of the State Security Committee of Georgia and was a member of the bureau of the Central Committee. So, with whom could he work, and who could tell the truth here?

The former leaders are silent, and the new ones have denied everything. The mass media quickly changed their tune and began to distort the events and make fools of the people. It turns out in the end that the internal forces and the Soviet Army, on their own initiative, broke into the square where people were praying, singing songs, and dancing, and slaughtered people when they were left alone and committed other criminal acts. Where were the lawyers who so scrupulously accused the military servicemen of violating the rights and laws as well as the constitution before this tragedy (although it would be better to call it a provocation)? What did the people's deputies sitting in Georgia do to prevent the adoption of extreme measures and to report the truth to the congress after this? I suggest that the elected Supreme Soviet straighten out all of what happened in our republic, in Georgia.

I have been the commander of the military district there for a year. In May it was exactly a year since I arrived there. There were already problems in Azerbaijan, Armenia, and the NKAO [Nagornyy Karabakh Autonomous Oblast]. It was quiet in Georgia, and everybody was happy and proud of the fact that everything was peaceful in Georgia. But over the course of a year, as a result of this work of ours Georgia reached a point of adopting extreme measures.

I shall tell you another thing: Here we are talking about how bad 1937 was, but I think it is worse now than in 1937. Now people can talk about you on television, write about your newspapers, and the mass media can defame you however they wish and without justification. To address my constituents about this tragedy in an open letter, I had to disseminate this open letter as they did during the war over enemy territory—using aircraft and helicopters. In places where the military tried to paste it up the local police came along and ripped it down. This is the situation in Georgia, comrade deputies.

The most malicious newspaper in Georgia recently is MOLODEZH GRUZII. It has published more provocatory libel, in which it tries to defame the highest military and political leadership in the country. Incidentally, I am confident that the provocation was prepared for this.

Here is the result of the neglect: Neglect the political situation in the republic for a year before the crisis, take absolutely no effective measures, do not utilize the authority and opportunities granted to you, and then avoid responsibility for criminal inactivity, draw the Army in, and place all the responsibility on the highest political and military leadership in the country, on the eve of our congress, and then say nothing yourself, deny everything, and falsify everything that happened.

I ask the commission of the Supreme Soviet to deal with the provocatory publication of MOLODEZH GRUZII. I shall end my speech, comrades, again with words from ZARYA VOSTOKA of 14 April: "Those who flirted with, entered into double dealing, and made political capital from the complications, those who along with others bear direct responsibility for what happened today, are making more noise than anyone else, trying to cover up their fear."

I have nothing to add to this. I thank you. (Prolonged applause).

R.N. Nishanov: Dear comrade deputies! After two speeches one gets the feeling that it really is necessary to go into this very deeply, calmly, and completely.

A list for the commission that the congress is to form to deal with this matter has been distributed to the deputies. But for those who are seeing and hearing us on television and the radio I shall read off the members of the commission. The Estonian comrades ask that the name of one of their comrades be added to it.

As of today there are answers to requests from General Yazov, the minister of defense; General Kochetov, the first deputy minister of defense; Comrade Trushin, the first deputy minister of internal affairs; and also the

Sixth Session

30 May 1989

materials of the commission of the Georgian SSR Supreme Soviet. All these materials were turned over to this commission. Moreover, I would like to make you aware that today after 7 pm in the hall for meetings of the Supreme Soviet there will be a film on the events which was brought by the deputies from the Georgian SSR and also a film taken by the curfew group.

Now, about the composition of the commission. I propose a draft decree of the USSR Congress of People's Deputies concerning the formation of a commission for investigating the circumstances associated with the event in the city of Tbilisi on 9 April 1989. The chairman of the commission would be Vladimir Vasilyevich Karpov, first secretary of the USSR Union of Writers, Moscow. Members of the commission would include: Sergey Andreyevich Andronati, director of the A.V. Bogatskiy Physics and Chemistry Institute of the Ukrainian SSR Academy of Sciences, Odessa; Khardo Yulovich Aasmyae, sector chief of the Planning and Design Bureau Maynor, Estonian SSR; Natalya Petrovna Bekhtereva, director of the Scientific Research Institute of Experimental Medicine of the USSR Academy of Medical Sciences, Leningrad; Genrikh Aviezerovich Borovik, chairman of the Soviet Committee for the Protection of Peace, Moscow; Aleksandr Ivanovich Golyakov, first deputy chairman of the All-Union Council of Veterans of War and Labor, Moscow; Dmitriy Sergeyevich Likhachev, sector chief of the Institute of Russian Literature of the USSR Academy of Sciences, Leningrad (Dmitriy Sergeyevich spoke here; you note him also as the chairman of the board of the Soviet Fund for Culture); Vladimir Petrovich Lukin, gas torch cutter of the V.V. Kuybyshev Kolomensk Steam Engine Construction Plant, Moscow Oblast; Oleg Metveyevich Nefedov, vice president of the USSR Academy of Sciences, Moscow; Roald Zinnurovich Sagdeyev, leader of the Scientific Methods Center for Analytical Research of the Institute of Space Research of the USSR Academy of Sciences, Moscow; Andrey Dmitriyevich Sakharov, head scientific associate of the P.N. Levedev Physics Institute of the USSR Academy of Sciences, Moscow; Valentina Ivanovna Fedotiva, editor in chief of the magazine SOVETSKAYA ZHENSHCHINA, Moscow; Elbar Nikolayevich Shengelaya, chairman of the Union of Cinematographers of Georgia, Tbilisi; Pavel Vadimovich Shetko, lecturer of the Department of Propaganda of the Minsk Obkom of the Komsomol of Belorussia. Of course, all members of the commission are deputies.

Those in favor of this composition of the commission I ask to prepare their mandates....

From the floor: (Inaudible).

R.N. Nishanov: Just one minute, I will give you the floor. Comrade Adamovich has an objection.

A.N. Adamovich, director of the All-Union Scientific Research Institute of Cinematography, Moscow (on behalf of the USSR Union of Cinematographers): The comrade general's speech might have sounded convincing to me as well were it not for the events in Minsk, where there were neither these slogans nor the demands from the division from Belorussia; there was nothing, but there was also gas and then the big lie. This is why I asked to withdraw the chairman of the commission that is being created, the esteemed Vladimir Vasilyevich Karpov, my immediate superior in the Union of Writers, and to withdraw his name from these considerations. We see how easily he gives in to emotions. The Georgian deputy spoke, and we applauded; the general spoke, and we applauded even more loudly. It is easy to get into emotions, and therefore the commission must be absolutely disinterested, absolutely objective.

Karpov cannot be such an objective figure, and these are the reasons why:

In the first place, he is a member of the Central Committee, and this means he will be directly subjected to pressure from those party figures who in one way or another are involved. He was a military person in the past, a person who has an especially loving attitude toward the military, and therefore he cannot be objective here either. I am not casting doubt on any of his human qualities. But I suggest as a candidate Daniil Aleksandrovich Granin.

R.N. Nishanov: Please, the floor is yours.

V.P. Tomkus, journalist, Vilnius (Panevezhskiy Territorial Electoral Okrug, Lithuanian SSR): Esteemed comrades! I appeal to you as members of the highest authority of the country. I ask you to put state affairs aside for just a minute and before creating this commission straighten out the things that are now being done in the country that are causing pain to the people.

The Lithuanian people were especially disturbed by the tragedy in Tbilisi. Here is why: The fact is that almost the same events almost took place last year in Lithuania, in Vilnius, in Gediminas Square. On 28 September internal forces and specialized divisions were sent in against defenseless people. Only at the last minute was a confrontation between the troops and the population averted, although there were those who suffered. I consider both these occurrences and the events in Tbilisi to be provocatory, and here is why: In Lithuania, before the unsanctioned rally, nowhere in the mass media was it announced that the rally was unsanctioned. The people could go to it, although the troops had been brought out. As we now know, permission to call out the specialized subdivisions was requested from Lithuania 2 days before the beginning of the event. So one can state that they had prepared for the event ahead of time.

Therefore I suggest:

1. Eliminate the members of the commission that was imposed on us "from above" and anonymously.

STENOGRAPHIC RECORD

Sixth Session

30 May 1989

2. Create a commission which would include representatives of ethnic minorities.

3. Now, without waiting, discover and make public the guilty parties who gave the order to the troops. Otherwise, we are not insured against another tragedy!

R.N. Nishanov: Let us not discuss this issue for 2 days. Those who have objections to candidacies, please.

Yu.F. Karyakin, senior scientific associate of the International Labor Movement of the USSR Academy of Sciences, Moscow (on behalf of the USSR Academy of Sciences): Two remarks—first, I wish to reject the candidacy of Borovik for the commission. Unlike Karpov, about whose conscientiousness I have no doubt, as is also true with Adamovich, I do have doubts about the conscientiousness of Borovik. He is one of the most dependent people I know. That is first. (Applause).

Second: I would be less than honest if I did not recall one story from 1968 when under similar conditions I heard with my own ears in the presence of witnesses how a person who had come to Moscow before August of 1968 said that he was sent to Czechoslovakia to print anti-Soviet leaflets. The Czechs will excuse me for not being able to say this at the time. I am raising the hypothesis of provocation. Everything R. Medvedev has discussed coincides too well. Everything coincides too well.

R.N. Nishanov: A proposal? Please.

Yu.R. Boyars, docent of P. Stuchka Latvian State University, Riga (Doverskiy National Territorial Electoral Okrug, Latvian SSR): Esteemed deputies! I would suggest that you not be in such a hurry with the applause and be more vigilant, as we were advised by an antifascist writer whom we know very well. I must tell you, unfortunately, that at the same time it is possible that the same thing was being prepared in Latvia. Because it was precisely during those days that we received in the Presidium of the Latvian Soviet amendments to our constitution and election legislation. I must say that at that time the leadership of the People's Front was invited to a meeting with our generals. I was invited with them to this meeting. But when I arrived there or, rather, when I was on the way to the meeting, I saw armored personnel carriers on the streets of Riga. If there had been demonstrations or some kind of unrest in Riga at the time I think it is quite possible that something quite similar would have happened there. Therefore, comrades, I would like to ask Comrade Rodionov, first, whether he knows what international human rights are and how soldiers are supposed to deal with women and noncombatants, and whether he explained this to his soldiers before they went to suppress this conflict. This is a very important question, and I wish to receive an answer from him. Further, we request that the commission include a lawyer, since it does not include one now.

R.N. Nishanov: Please, Comrade Shengelaya.

E.N. Shengelaya, director and producer of the film studio Gruziyafilm, Tbilisi (on behalf of the USSR Union of Cinematographers): If you will recall, on the first day of the congress I suggested that you look at the videocassette which you will apparently see today. I am very sorry that you did not see this cassette before you began to discuss this matter. Because the documentary film could orient us very correctly. But you can do this today. But still I ask for you not to hurry, not to hurry with conclusions. I ask that we create a really serious commission today. Because with a competent commission, any lie, regardless of what it might, will be short-lived. The commission will study this problem in all directions and can report the real truth to you.

Yesterday when a legal question came up in the evening, Mikhail Sergeyevich called legal experts to the podium. This was logical, naturally, and correct. Therefore, it seems to me that the commission that is being created should include people not according to the principle we usually use—a worker, a female kolkhoz worker, a member of the intelligentsia, and so forth—but people who are professionally able to really figure all this out. Therefore, I suggest that this commission include Anatoliy Aleksandrovich Sovchak, Aleksandr Maksimovich Yakovlev....

From the floor: (Inaudible).

E.N. Shengelaya: If you, Comrade Yakovlev, cannot do it, then the commission should necessarily include a legal expert of the same rank as Yakovlev.

I suggest including on the commission Deputy Toltezhnikov, Larustin, and Ignatovich. It is very important that this commission include Yegor Vladimirovich Yakovlev and Boris Lvovich Vasilyev, who were in Tbilisi as late as 12 April and, as has been said, saw everything that happened with their own eyes.

Moreover, it seems to me that we should include on the commission several deputies from the Commission of the Georgian SSR Supreme Soviet who have worked for a month and already know all the details and can help the commission. These are Deputies Margvelashvili and Gankrelidze. Of course, I think that it would be very correct if this commission were headed by a member of the Politburo, CPSU Central Committee secretary Aleksandr Nikolayevich Yakovlev. (Applause).

This is important because some time ago, in February, also in a difficult and tense time, he was in Tbilisi and held a certain position, spoke on television, and his speech was received very well by all formal and informal groups throughout society. Therefore, it would be correct if he would agree to head this commission.

I would not be in a hurry with all kinds of emotions, because the people who were killed and suffered are reflected in the medical investigation report, and many materials will be turned over to the commission. The

Sixth Session

30 May 1989

commission should not wait until the next congress to report the truth to the Supreme Soviet and draw the political, moral, and ethical conclusions. This is important for all of us, for our children, for our families, and for our future. Thank you.

R.N. Nishanov: You are welcome.

From the floor: Give us the floor.

R.N. Nishanov: Yes, I will give you the floor now. Just a minute, comrades, everything is proceeding normally here.

From the floor: (Inaudible).

R.N. Nishanov: I wrote down your suggestion.

From the podium (the deputy did not introduce himself): Dear comrades, there are many candidates on the list for the commission to investigate the events in Tbilisi. But since great complaints will be made against military personnel, I suggest including on the commission Army General Govorov.

R.N. Nishanov: Comrade Lieutenant Colonel, wait please.

N.S. Petrushenko, lieutenant colonel, instructor in propaganda and agitation of the political provision of the military unit (Leningrad Territorial Electoral Okrug, Vostochno-Kazakhstanskaya Oblast): Esteemed Comrade Chairman! Esteemed comrade deputies! I signed up for a statement concerning the personnel on the commission as early as this morning, as soon as I received the proposed draft for the composition of the commission. I am very sorry and I apologized to the congress and the presidium for having to take a turn, that is, violate the order for which I myself voted and in support of which many deputies have spoken. But one recalls the words of Vladimir Ilich Lenin to the effect that there never has been and probably never will be a human search for the truth without human emotions.

Therefore, I have no doubt that the proposed composition of the commission selected from deputies with principles and competence consists of people capable of objectively studying all the circumstances of the tragic events. But they will not only have to give an answer, and a conclusion about what happened, but also suggest a package of recommendations intended to avoid such tragedies in the future. As a military person I cannot but see that, judging from the publications and speeches of General Rodionov, whom I know personally, who has received many reprimands from him but also many thanks, the tragic events were used to pound a wedge between the Army and the people. It is unpleasant for us to perform police functions ourselves. But we military people would not like to be reproached in the Hall of the Congresses for being people who are called upon to be constantly in a state of military readiness and sometimes, unfortunately, are late in preventing such tragedies. The dialectic of the development of democracy, unfortunately, is apparently such that it would be correct to include in the commission, taking into account the nature of the tasks it will have to carry out, also deputies who are military servicemen. It seems that in the Hall of Congresses we have no deputies who are representatives of the USSR Ministry of Internal Affairs. If there are any, they should also be included on the commission, because in addition to the proposal from the deputies concerning the revocation of existing ukases that determine the utilization of MVD [Ministry of Internal Affairs] forces, there are also, to our misfortune and shame, objective conditions in which it is impossible to do without them, without special-purpose troops.

I would assume that it would be necessary to ask the presidium and you, comrade deputies, to include on the commission deputies who are military servicemen and specific army officers. For example, Colonel Martirosyan, who spoke here earlier, and Deputy Govorov. Taking into account the serious conclusions that have been confronted here, specifically in the speech yesterday by Roy Medvedev when discussing the candidacy of the first deputy chairman of the USSR Supreme Soviet, I make this proposal: to include on the commission Deputy Miroshnik from Kazakhstan, who holds a position of chairman of the republic's State Security Committee. I think that since we entrust the holy of holies, state security, to these people, we should trust them to look with a competent and experienced eye at the holy of holies of those forces that have prepared this provocation. For I feel that this was a provocation with far-reaching goals.

Taking advantage of the forum of the congress and without waiting for the official investigation by the authorized deputy commission, I should like to make some serious accusations against Deputy Rodionov. The deputies have materials from the investigation of the Georgian tragedy and I would like to familiarize the deputies with the answer I received from the Ministry of Internal Affairs yesterday when, having become familiar with the materials of the Georgian incident, I sent a request to the Ministry of Internal Affairs to answer a basic question: why in the materials of the investigation does it indicate civilians who were killed and wounded but says nothing about the nature of the harm caused to our soldiers who performed military functions that we find undesirable. I would ask to have this document reproduced and distributed to all the deputies as an official response.

Esteemed deputies! I would ask for one minute for a procedural question. I assume that it would be expedient in all documents that are offered to us to indicate:

1. The okrug from which one deputy or another was elected. For it turns out that the commission proposed by the presidium was 90 percent representative of social

STENOGRAPHIC RECORD

Sixth Session

30 May 1989

organizations which, in my opinion, is not altogether correct. I do not wish to cast a shadow on the esteemed deputies from the social organizations, but I would like for the presidium of our congress to indicate the electoral okrug, position, and, obviously, who recommended them. Because I personally do not think that we can agree with this procedure. The more so since certain members of this commission have already been in Tbilisi on private business as it were and this makes me doubt the expediency of this principle or method of forming our high-level commission. (Applause.)

R.N. Nishanov: The floor goes to Comrade Manayenkov.

Yu.A. Manayenkov, first secretary of the Lipetsk CPSU Obkom from the city of Lipetsk (Lebedyanskiy Territorial Electoral Okrug, Lipetsk Oblast): Esteemed comrades! I have just a couple of remarks about procedural issues. When our constituents sent us here to the Supreme Soviet, they gave us a mandate to conduct ourselves, in addition to everything else, objectively and morally with respect to one another. The comrade from Georgia whose film we shall see at 7 pm spoke here and said that the commission should include serious people. Well, excuse me please, since when are academicians Sakharov, Likhachev and Sagdeyev not serious people? It would be good for him to make apologies. I should also like to respond to Comrade Adamovich. We are free to express our opinion about each proposed candidate. But we must justify and substantiate this opinion. But Comrade Karpov is blamed because he is favorably disposed toward military personnel. After all, he is also a hero of the Soviet Union. If we blame him for this, what is left of our spiritual life? (Applause). In my opinion it is quite stupid to blame a person because he is a member of the CPSU Central Committee. (Applause).

I would like to say a little about the speech a couple of days ago by the historian and writer Roy Medvedev. He said that there is something wrong in the Politburo of the CPSU Central Committee, there is no unity. This is the sixth year I have been working as first secretary of the CPSU obkom. I am very frequently in the CPSU Central Committee. At least last year I spent 90 days there. I did not see and do not know of a case where there was anything wrong there. On the contrary, it is a very dynamic, very busy, and very charged atmosphere, an atmosphere of striving. Where do these insinuations come from? It is simple, in reality they are some kind of desire somehow to get rid of our highest political leadership. This, in my view, is unworthy. (Applause.)

R.N. Nishanov: Please, introduce yourself.

V.A. Voblikov, head of the organization section of the Baltysk CPSU Gorkom, Baltysk (Chernyakhovskiy Territorial Electoral Okrug, Kaliningrad Oblast): Comrade deputies, I would like to speak briefly about this. The fact is that we do not have experience in parliamentary work. Many deputies have come here with the struggle they have just been through and brought their rally agitation with them. But still we are working for the entire country. I think that this is fraught with serious circumstances. Because any ill-considered word that is cast out...if we have these kinds of emotions, I can imagine what is happening in Georgia now. Therefore I think that in the Parliament we should learn political work and should be objective. Of course it is impossible to search for the truth without emotions, as Lenin said. But on the other hand, we must build our statements on facts and arguments and, I repeat, they should be weighed, because we have responsibility, for the entire country and for the situation in it. I should like to direct this to the congress.

R.N. Nishanov: Deputy Dzhumber Ilich Patiashvili has the floor. Perhaps after Comrade Patiashvili's speech we shall consult about making a decision concerning the candidates?

I ask the rest of the comrades to sit down. Please sit down. We are discussing a serious problem, comrades. We are creating a commission. If somebody has to be replaced, let us replace him. Everything will be normal.

D.I. Patiashvili, Tbilisi (Tbilisi—Pervomaysk Electoral Okrug, Georgian SSR): Esteemed deputies! From this podium I shall tell all the available truth about the tragedy in Tbilisi. That which I know, since the comrades who are speaking here.... I do not wish to compare some to others now, but the situation that existed requires clarification so that we can know why this tragedy occurred. After what has happened, everyone is now wiser, everyone is second-guessing, and certain people are escaping responsibility, and certain others are coming forward, but this is not the main thing. The main thing is that a tragedy occurred which will remain a black spot in the history of Georgia and the country.

At the same time, I would like to tell the deputies the truth, that there were attempts to direct the investigation of events, some in one direction and some in another. The commissions worked and the union commission worked. Unfortunately, I do not know the decisions about the results but in principle all representatives of the ministries are trying to avoid responsibility. I personally did not and am not avoiding responsibility.

The first remark that was directed to me when I was no longer working as first secretary and was not even a remark but a great mistake, was that we entrusted the leadership of the operation to Commanding General Rodionov. Therefore I would like to say that the bureau of the Central Committee of the Republic Communist Party did not appoint him or instruct him to do this. This was done after Colonel General Rodionov personally, along with the USSR first deputy minister of defense, Army General Kochetov, came to the Central

Sixth Session
30 May 1989

Committee, came to my office and said that the leadership had been assigned to Rodionov. I knew that you would ask this question. Unfortunately, I did not ask that question at that time but I am asking that question today....

In reality, the events developed as follows: in the republic and specifically in Tbilisi, the situation was complicated. I informed the Central Committee about these problems and informed the secretaries of the Central Committee Comrade Razumovskiy and Comrade Chebrikov, I informed them that a difficult situation at an unsanctioned rally in Tbilisi had continued for several days already. But at the same time, in the Abkhaz Autonomous Republic, we also had a difficult situation related to the adoption of a decision by leaders of the autonomous republic to create a union republic and secede from Georgia. Therefore all forces we had in the capital and in Georgia were mobilized to Abkhaziya in order to prevent possible interethnic conflicts and, I would say, there was a danger of that.

On 7 April just at the beginning of the bureau meeting I received a call from the defense minister, Army General Yazov, and was told that in 15-20 minutes the first deputy minister, Army General Kochetov, would be arriving at the Central Committee—I didn't even know he was in the republic—along with Colonel General Rodionov who, according to our information, was in Armenia. On the 7th of April the former chairman of the republic KGB, Gumbaridze, told me that he had spoken with the center and that a detachment of KGB troops would be arriving in Tbilisi. In the bureau we discussed the situation with the military people and came to the decision that additional MVD forces would be needed in order to maintain order in the city and we reported this officially with a coded message to the CPSU Central Committee.

On the next day, 8 April, comrades Kochetov and Rodionov arrived and the latter stated that he had been put in charge of all the troops on the territory of Georgia. On the 8th of April there was a meeting of the republic party aktiv which General Rodionov discussed here, as well as of the Central Committee bureau and the Defense Council.

In his speech Mikhail Sergeyevich mentioned that there were such instructions or a phone call. Yes, there was a conversation with Comrade Shevardnadze. And regarding this question I should like to say that as concerns the arrival of Comrade Shevardnadze and Comrade Razumovskiy, I considered their arrival inexpedient at that time because the situation had begun to stabilize. The only task was to free the square in front of the government house and, according to the assurances of the comrades, this task presented no special difficulties. When our aktiv discussed the decisions concerning the situation in the republic, a plan of measures was adopted to stabilize the situation in the republic, including measures, as I have said, to free the square in front of the government house using the militia, MVD troops, and subdivisions of the Transcaucasian Military District. And after this at the bureau we confirmed the commander of the Transcaucasian Military District, Colonel General Rodionov, as leader of the operation. Unfortunately, I repeat, it was on the morning of 8 April that Comrades Kochetov and Rodionov (they are here) came in and said that Rodionov had been placed in charge of leading the troops and that the bureau, after the meeting of the aktiv, they had approved a decision with two points: to free the square in front of the government house and to put Comrade Rodionov in charge.

Unfortunately, during the time of the meeting of the republic aktiv, as was mentioned here, the military drove armored personnel carriers to the square where the rally was being held. This action led to the opposite reaction, and during the night of 9 April, as we have said, there were several thousand people left on the square. At the bureau and in the Defense Council on 8 April.... I can give you the tape recording of the minutes here. Unfortunately, it has not been typed up because when the commission asks why all these documents have not been typed up one must say that nobody thought about the minutes at the time. There are recordings of the minutes that were taped by the general who is secretary of the Defense Council which include assurances that the square in front of the government house would be freed without causing any casualties, that is, the armed forces have only shields and nightsticks. I emphasize that that was stipulated at the beginning, that the troops, and not only the troops but also the militia and the MVD—should be armed only with shields and nightsticks.

After that, under the leadership of the commander, a plan was drawn up for an operation in conjunction with representatives of the USSR MVD who were in our republic. A half hour before the beginning of the operation the commander telephoned me from the square and reported that he was ready. And the information was that there were many people there. Igor Nikolayevich can confirm this and I asked then: "Perhaps the operation can be put off for a while?" He said firmly that he was on the spot and assured me that there would be no complications. To our great misfortune, instead of dispersal of the unsanctioned rally as they promised, the demonstrators were surrounded and beaten unmercifully. Instead of implementing the decision to free the square—and this is the main question, and those who were in Tbilisi know: the square was not large at all, but the main task was to free the square in front of the government house and the troops, unfortunately, after this chased the people throughout Rustaveli Prospekt. You will see this. And they broke into homes. Several people were killed near the Iveriya Hospital (it is located at a distance of 800 meters to 1 kilometer from the square) or sustained serious injuries. More than 3,000 people were poisoned. When at 3 am it was announced that two people had died, I went to the bureau—several members of the bureau are present here, they are deputies—and I turned in my resignation since I did not think

Sixth Session
30 May 1989

that I had the right to head the party organization any longer. At that time I did not suspect that entrenching tools and toxic chemicals were being used for otherwise, and I say this frankly and sincerely, I would certainly not have turned in my resignation. Perhaps, or probably after this, I would have had more of a punishment, but I would by no means have gone into retirement since all of this was a great trauma for every one of us. After this I had practically abandoned by position. But on 9 April comrades Shevardnadze and Razhumovskiy had already arrived....

Voices from the hall: (Inaudible).

D.I. Patiashvili: Comrades, I will not be speaking here any more, and therefore you will agree that I have a couple of words left.

Voices from the hall: (Inaudible).

D.I. Patiashvili: What character are you asking about?

Voices from the hall: (Inaudible).

D.I. Patiashvili: I shall tell you about the consequences, about the rally, and you will see....

Voices from the hall: (Inaudible).

D.I. Patiashvili: I am speaking specifically: When in the morning they announced that people had been killed and that entrenching tools had been used, Comrade Rodionov categorically denied it. He said that there were no entrenching tools and that they had not been used. Unfortunately, even after numbers of the Politburo arrived in the republic the comrades did not admit this. Only on the third day did they admit that entrenching tools had been used. And regarding gases—that was later, at the end of April. In order to obtain information about how you were informed, leading toxicologists from Moscow, Leningrad and foreign countries were invited.

Voices from the hall: (Inaudible).

D.I. Patiashvili: I am saying that the rally that took place in our city is like rallies that take place here and everywhere. Therefore....

(Noise in the hall).

D.I. Patiashvili: Comrades, we are speaking about something else....

Voice from the floor: Why did you not address the people?... (Inaudible).

D.I. Patiashvili: I am explaining and I am speaking of my own guilt, because the bureau of the Central Committee and I personally did what we could and that which we could not do—for that I have been punished and I will be punished for my guilt. But, comrades, it is not the point that....

Voices from the hall: (Inaudible).

D.I. Patiashvili: Therefore I take personal responsibility, I take responsibility as first secretary. I do not blame anyone, I do not accuse anyone, I am saying that the operation was conducted incorrectly, that the information was incorrect, that in no case should entrenching tools have been used, in no case should there have been gases or chemical substances, this is what we are speaking about. (Noise in the hall).

Voices from the hall: (Inaudible).

R.N. Mishanov: Comrades, comrades, just a minute.

D.I. Patiashvili: Such is the tragic story.... (Noise in the hall).

It was incorrect what happened according to the program "Vremya," that the commander refused.... This was written and therefore our press does not always write the truth. In no case.... I am telling you directly, here they discussed that this was not work for the troops and therefore MVD troops were the ones that were used, and after that.... (Noise in the hall). I again say, as Comrade Rodionov said when speaking on television that he was.... (Noise in the hall).

R.N. Nishanov: Dzhumber Ilich, finish up, please....

D.I. Patiashvili: Such as the tragic history and it is impossible to determine the scope of immense political and moral....

Voice from the floor: I have a question. Where were you yourself during this time?

D.I. Patiashvili: At that time I was on the phone with the commander and was at home. (Noise in the hall). I have questions also, comrades. Specifically I would like to ask those who gave the order to use the entrenching tools and the toxic substances. You ask me. Right? Right. I agreed to this. But what decision was made about the degree of cruelty against the population?

R.N. Nishanov: Comrades, just a minute, attention. Here are the deputies—Comrade Vasilyev, Borovik, Dzasokhov, Ivanov, and many others are asking for the floor. Wait just a minute, I am still speaking. Just wait. I ask you to sit down. Sit down. (Applause). Sit down, please. Sit down. Get away. Well, that is bad.... Do not disgrace yourselves.... Go away. (Noise in the hall). Comrades, this suggestion was being made: Taking into account that we have heard many comrades and there

Sixth Session

30 May 1989

are many aspects that we have to figure out very attentively (the comrades have made many suggestions concerning candidates for the commission), therefore, if you have no objections, let us instruct the presidium, taking all of today's proposals into account, to think over the question of the composition of the commission during the night and tomorrow bring it up for voting. Do you agree? (Noise in the hall). Those in favor please raise your mandate. Lower them. Who is against? (Noise in the hall). So it is adopted. (Prolonged applause). Comrades, I ask everyone to calm down, sit down. Sit down please, we shall give you the opportunity to speak as well, everything here is proceeding normally, everything is proceeding normally.

So, comrades, we have already adopted the decree regarding this issue, give me a chance to play my role out to the end. Thank you dear comrades. (Commotion in the hall). We have made a decision regarding this issue. Now Mikhail Sergeyevich has the floor.

M.S. Gorbachev: Comrades! I do not think that we should oversimplify the issue. No. And I do not think that this is being done here. But even what we have heard now confirms previous intentions, namely, we must look into other things thoroughly and get to the bottom of things. The question is large, special, deep, political, and it pertains, as it were, to the very foundations of our country's existence. Therefore I, for example, informed you—and now I confirm this—and at the same time it was stated in the Politburo of the CPSU Central Committee that it is necessary to get to the bottom of this. We now have materials in the procurator's office—it is conducting an investigation. There are the materials of the local republic commissions. There is Comrade Tarazevich's commission and it has gone to Tbilisi. Other comrades have also made trips. I must say that the picture is still very contradictory. In general, what led to this? Therefore I think we are on the correct path. We must not oversimplify and, I must say, the country is interested in this and the Georgian people are interested in this—they demand respect from us. Now we must not cast doubt on either the one or the other. We need the truth, we must get to the bottom of things regardless of what may be affected, and we must make decisions that will correspond to the truth. (Applause.)

Vladimir Vasilyevich (he addresses Deputy Karpov): There is no need to protect the others, we are having an exchange of opinions. I had begun to protect myself yesterday when for 2 hours I was deliberately worked over. But I thank the deputies because this proved that democracy exists in the congress. (Applause.) But this certainly does not mean that Gorbachev does not see, I see everything. (Laughter and applause in the hall.) And I am in favor of our being and working together and moving forward together.

Comrades! I also want you to devote a couple of minutes to this matter. I am returning to November of last year, to the eve of the session when we were making constitutional amendments. The situation in Georgia was very heated at that time.

I shall not hide anything. I know this republic and I have known these people for a long time. They know me. I love them and I hope that they have respect for me. When I heard that in November the leadership had begun to produce television programs expressing the opinion that a curfew was necessary in order to contain the situation, I told Comrade Shevardnadze directly that during the night he should quickly convey my appeal, an oral one, to the Georgian intelligentsia (they can now tell you whether this is true or not) and to the people that I asked to solve the problem and to remove the curfew. I said: I know that if we resort to this action in Georgia, we will insult the fighting Georgians who will never put up with anything like this. At that time that relieved the tension. I am very thankful that my words got to them. And by 4 am (also at 4 am, you understand) we took care of the problem. Therefore the idea of imposing order without doing everything in order to arrange contact, live communication and discussion of the problems appeared there in November. This is why I say that it is necessary to figure this out, comrades. The question is how we shall go on from here, how we shall conduct a dialogue in the country, how we shall preserve democracy, and how we shall maintain and protect this democracy—this very mean which is the only one in which a healthy person can live and feel like a human being. We have been proceeding toward this for so many decades.

Therefore I do not wish to oversimplify anything, the problem is very complex, and let us think about it as we agreed. I did not participate in forming the commission, but nonetheless I was consulted as to whether someone from the Politburo should be included on the commission. Today I named Comrade Yakovlev. If there are no objections, we could include both Yakovlev and whoever you want. This is your problem and you can solve it. If necessary, we can include Yakovlev and let him be in charge. We will discuss it and decide. There is no problem here. Therefore let us tell the people who are listening to us in the country and in Georgia that the congress was taking correct positions and is interested in the truth, and that the congress was given instructions which will provide for obtaining the truth and on the basis of this we shall draw conclusions which will dictate the results of this investigation. (Applause).

R.N. Nishanov: Comrades, Comrade Starodubtsev, whose speech we have announced, will speak tomorrow morning, and now I should like to consult briefly on a couple of questions.

First Comrade Gorbunov will make a brief announcement about the work of the presidium and the secretariat and certain proposals. Then a couple of more general questions and with this we shall probably complete our work for today.

Voice from the floor: (Inaudible).

M.S. Gorbachev: We will give you the floor tomorrow, Vladimir Vasilyevich. (He turns to Karpov).

STENOGRAPHIC RECORD

Sixth Session

30 May 1989

R.N. Nishanov: We will give you the floor tomorrow, Vladimir Vasilyevich. Please, Comrade Gorbunov. While Comrade Gorbunov is coming up, comrades, we asked members of the counting commission to go into Georgiyevskiy Hall in the large Kremlin Palace.

A.V. Gorbunov, chairman of the Presidium of the Latvian SSR Supreme Soviet, Riga (Tsesisskiy Territorial Electoral Okrug, Latvian SSR): Esteemed comrade deputies! Unfortunately, I am not able to speak very briefly. But I sense the mood of the hall and perhaps we can arrange it so that the report on our work and its directions, how we are carrying out your wishes that you expressed can be printed and distributed to everyone tomorrow morning? Or I need 15 minutes. Tomorrow, yes? Good.

R.N. Nishanov: Now, comrades, we have again decided to speak about the commissions, and we shall take another 5 minutes. All the deputies have been given material regarding the formation.... Vladimir Vasilyevich (he turns to Karpov), I have told you several times: we will give you the floor tomorrow. Do you not agree? But none of the rest of them have had the floor either. Why do you claim a special role?

M.S. Gorbachev: We have already agreed to give you the floor tomorrow.

R.N. Nishanov: We have agreed, tomorrow we will give you the floor.

V.V. Karpov, writer, first secretary of the Board of the USSR Union of Writers, Moscow (from the Communist Party of the Soviet Union): This is what I want to say for tomorrow. In the morning, like all of you I received this list. I did not know anything and received a draft of the composition of the commission. Here certain duties were already to be assigned to me and I, of course, was thinking about what to do and how to do it. Regardless of whether or not I am the chairman or a member of the commission, I wish to suggest two points so that they will be taken into account when preparing the decree, this is a very serious matter. It is necessary for this decree to include not only the list of members of the commission, but also the point that the commission has the right to become familiar with all documents pertaining to the incident in the KGB [Commission for State Security], MVD, Ministry of Defense, CPSU Central Committee, and the staff of the Supreme Soviet, and all these documents should be turned over. (Applause).

It was said here that I am a member of the Central Committee. I anticipated this. The commission should report the results of the work not the Central Committee but to the Presidium of the Supreme Soviet, and at joint meetings of the Council of the Union of Supreme Soviets and the Council of Nationalities so that nobody will exert influence on them beforehand.

I should also add that the commissions should include the metropolitan of Leningrad Aleksiy, since questions related to religious affairs will also be involved. I have spoken with him and he has agreed. That is all, and I withdraw my candidacy; Comrade Yakovlev, a member of the Politburo of the CPSU Central Committee, should be chairman.

G.A. Borovik, writer, political observer of the USSR State Committee for Television and Radio Broadcasting, chairman of the Soviet Committee for the Protection of Peace, Moscow (from the Movement for Peace, the Combined Soviet Committee for the Protection of Peace in conjunction with the Association for Contributing to UN Organizations in the USSR): I took the floor to make a correction, comrades! I understand that the small amount of vituperation that has been expressed at this podium is nothing in comparison to the immense disaster that took place in Tbilisi. But I still wish to say that there is a relationship between man and his own convictions, his group, and his vanity. I depend on my own convictions. I think that my transmissions, say, concerning Karabakh, might not be without shortcomings but this hardly proves that anybody gave me any instructions as to how to do them.

Second. Recently I have been under fire, both from right-wing organizations like Pamyat and our extreme left-wing comrades. This confirms the idea that the extreme left and the extreme right join together and nurture one another.

Third. The comrade who spoke about me here and spoke with me saying that I had something to do with the provocations in Czechoslovakia, and that certain of my comrades, to my amazement, understood that I was in Czechoslovakia and was distributing inflammatory leaflets. Did they understand this? (Noise in the hall.) That is a plain lie! I was first in Czechoslovakia 2 years ago and at that time—in 1968—I was on a business trip in the United States, working for the press agency Novosti, and this can be verified from my articles. And the last reason I took the floor: I request that you do not let the congress podium be used for settling personal accounts, and we do have personal differences and insults. (Applause.)

R.N. Nishanov: Dear comrades! We are taking the information given by deputies Borovik and Karpov under advisement and the commission and presidium will take it into account. But at the end of the meeting I should also like to say something about the last words of Comrade Borovik: Let us never use this high tribune, this responsible tribune, for any mutual attacks or insults. We are being heard by millions of people and they expect from us the most reasonable words in order to solve our crucial problems.

Since we have devoted this evening to our commission, materials regarding the second commission have been distributed to the deputies—the Commission of the

STENOGRAPHIC RECORD

FIRST CONGRESS OF PEOPLE'S DEPUTIES OF THE USSR

Sixth Session

30 May 1989

Congress of People's Deputies for verifying the materials related to the activity of the investigatory group of the USSR Procurator's Office headed by Gdlyan.

Just a minute, just a minute, let me finish what I have to say and then you can stand up. Sit down, I will give you the floor in just a minute, allow me to finish what I have to say.

Since many comrades have been invited here and people are hearing and seeing us throughout the country, I would like to read out the composition of the commission. But before reading it I would like to obtain from the deputies agreement for the following change in this list.

For personal reasons People's Deputy Comrade Zenskova wishes not to be included on this commission. She is nursing a child and it is difficult for her to get away for very long. Therefore the deputies suggest replacing Comrade Zenskova on the commission with Deputy Sergey Nikolayevich Zvonov, director of the Ivanovo Passenger Transportation Enterprise, a law student. With this change I would like to read this list. And after I read the list, if anybody has any objections or additions, they may express them briefly without long speeches. Do you have a suggestion concerning the list, Comrade Vasilyev?

From the floor: (Inaudible).

R.N. Nishanov: Just a moment, I will read the list and then you can withdraw your name. All right?

The decree of the USSR Congress of People's Deputies concerning the formation of a commission for verifying materials related to the activity of the investigatory group of the USSR Procurator's Office headed by Telman Khorenovich Gdlyan.

The USSR Congress of People's Deputies hereby decrees:

In order to verify the materials related to the activity of the investigatory group of the USSR Procurator's Office headed by Telman Khorenovich Gdlyan, to form a commission consisting of the following USSR people's deputies (I shall read them first since the material has been distributed and then we will hear withdrawals): Boris Lvovich Vasilyev, chairman of the commission, movie dramatist, the city of Moscow.

Members of the commission: deputies Valeriy Grigoryevich Aleksandrin, chairman of the Yoshkar-Ola city people's court, Mary ASSR; Ilmar Olgertovich Bisher, professor at the Latvian State University imeni P. Stuchka; Yuriy Vladimirovich Golik, dean of the law faculty of Kemerovo State University (we agreed that he would replace Comrade Zemskova); Dzhangir Ali Abbas Ogly Kerimov, department head of the Academy of Social Sciences under the CPSU Central Committee; Vladimir Nikolayevich Kudryavetsov, vice president of the USSR Academy of Sciences; Vitaliy Aleksandrovich Semenov, senior scientific associate of the Institute of Technical Mechanics of the Ukrainian SSR Academy of Sciences; Igor Viktorovich Sorokin, senior operative for criminal investigations of the line militia division, Kuybyshev Oblast; Viktor Nikolayevich Shorokhov, chief of the Tula Machine-Building Plant imeni V.M. Ryabikov; Erkin Yusupovich Yusupov, vice president of the Uzbek SSR Academy of Sciences; Aleksandr Maksimovich Yakovlev, sector chief of the Institute of State and Law of the USSR Academy of Sciences, Moscow; Veniamin Aleksandrovich Yarin, operator of the Nizhniy Tagil Metallurgical Combine imeni V.I. Lenin, Sverdlovsk Oblast.

Now, Comrade Vasilyev, go ahead. The presidium has certain other withdrawals, and I will read them later. Go ahead, Comrade Vasilyev.

B.L. Vasilyev, movie dramatist, Moscow (from the USSR Union of Cinematographers): Comrade deputies! I thank you for the high honor conferred on me by the fact that you included me as the chairman of such a responsible commission. But for a month and a half now I have been feeling like a person with a guilty conscience. If I may express it this way, somewhat figuratively, I feel like my conscience took a blow from a nightstick in Tbilisi. It hit me hard. I do not know how I have stayed alive for 65 years. It was not my wish to be in Tbilisi—I was sent there by a collective who selected me. I know the Tbilisi material, I have spoken with a large number of people and also I was with a group of deputies—also not at my own request—in the MVD division whose regiment participated in the MVD division whose regiment participated in the events in Tbilisi. Moreover, I am a movie dramatist and also a writer and commentator. The subject of Tbilisi has become a painful one for me and for my creative work. Regardless of whether or not you include me on the commission to investigate the Tbilisi incident I will still work at this subject as a commentator. I ask you very sincerely to exclude me from the commission on questions related to comrades Gdlyan and Ivanov and to include me on the commission concerning the Tbilisi affair. Thank you. (Applause.)

R.N. Nishanov: Good, I think that is a reasonable request. We will keep this in mind upon final consideration. Are there any other requests? Now I shall give you the floor. For the record, there are other withdrawals, I shall announce them and then give you the floor. So, deputies Kudryavtsev, Kerimov, and Yakovlev have asked not to be included on the commission since they already worked on the preceding commission and have expressed their opinion regarding this issue. I think we can grant their request.

Therefore we might ask the following deputies to be included on the commission. Comrades Konstantin Dmitriyevich Lubenchenko, docent of the Law School of Moscow State University; Comrade Roy Aleksandrovich Medvedev, writer, historian, commentator, you know

STENOGRAPHIC RECORD

Sixth Session

30 May 1989

him because he has spoken; Comrade Anatoliy Aleksandrovich Sobchak, department head, who has also spoken and you know him well. The Estonian comrades nominate: Comrade Vello Paulovich Pokhla, a member of the editorial board of ESTONSKIY TELEFILM.

Go ahead, you have the floor.

N.V. Karlov, first founding member of the USSR Academy of Sciences, rector of the Moscow Physics-Technical Institute, Moscow (from the USSR Academy of Sciences): I have a suggestion: As this issue includes also the ethical-moral issue, I ask the esteemed and worthy clergy who are among us to participate in the work of this commission. I cannot, I do not have the right simply to suggest specific names and physicians corresponding to these names, but I ask that when the commission is being formed you take into account the idea that the clergy be included: both the Orthodox hierarchy and worthy representatives of the Muslim religion, and possibly the Georgian patriarch and the Armenian Catholicos. And not only people's deputies. And not only people's deputies. This is my proposal.

V.V. Krychkov, deputy production chief of the Dzerzhinsk Kaprolaktam Production Association, Dzerzhinsk (Dzerzhinsk Territorial Electoral Okrug, Gorkiy Oblast): Comrades, I have a suggestion to augment the text of the name of the commission with this point: "For the Formation of the Commission to Verify Materials Related to the Activity of the Investigatory Group of the USSR Procurator's Office Headed by Comrade Gdlyan and Verification of the Statements of Comrades Gdlyan and Ivanov." The fact is that Gdlyan and Ivanov have made statements which have affected workers of the Central Committee and Moscow and it is necessary in addition to checking on their activity, to check on their statements.

In this connection I suggest expanding the commission, because the 13 people who are represented here are quite inadequate to encompass the second issue, the more so since this issue is very significant. We have already suggested Comrade Sobchak. I suggest also Comrade Strukov from Kursk, who spoke very well yesterday. And in relation to this I would then like to hear from the presidium the principles of the formation of the commission, that is, what it proceeds from in forming the commission. This has not been addressed in the delegation. Here there are some lawyers and some other people, and four people from Moscow, but now the composition has changed somewhat. I do not know how it will be formed. Further, I suggest removing Comrade Kudryavtsev....

From the floor: Comrade Kudryavtsev has removed himself.

V.V. Kryzhkov: He has? That is all, I withdraw my suggestion. Thank you for your attention.

R.N. Nishanov: Just a minute, I will answer a small question. First, the presidium has no preconceived ideas or preliminary considerations of any kind. When forming the commission they simply proceeded from the idea that this group should have a majority of lawyers, since they can figure things out while in the first group there were more political figures. We are now exchanging opinions. We are not suggesting a vote. The exchange of opinions is in progress. Whoever you want can be removed.

Wait just a minute, please. Telman Khorenovich Gdlyan is asking for the floor, and then I will give all three the floor, Andrey Dmitriyevich also.

T. Kh. Gdlyan, senior investigator for especially important cases under the USSR Procurator General, Moscow (Tusha Territorial Electoral Okrug, Moscow): Comrades, why did I come up here myself to speak? Because we are complicating our lives, which are complicated to begin with. Because, probably, the apparatus principle is manifesting itself in us and is prevailing. Pay attention—we are creating two commissions: there are difficulties both here and there. And what are they? They are elementary. These questions, you will understand, are very difficult to resolve. We must create a certain working group, say, with the same presidium of the congress. But the only thing that we had to do was create one, say, for the "Georgian question." You will recall that I got up and spoke at that time: according to the jury principle so that there would be confidence. We asked our Georgian comrade such-and-such. And that was all. We read the list so that everyone could confirm it.

The same thing here. We would discuss and coordinate these issues and the presidium would present the composition of the commissions. Otherwise we will never reach a conclusion, you understand, without endless talking. Dozens of more people could speak, each differently. There is (just a moment!) a specific point, there is a specific point, comrades. How do we figure out what is what? I am very well aware (I do not know who said it, maybe Comrade Karpov said it) of the suggestion that, comrades, it is necessary to include in the decree: all KGB documents, party, militia, procurator, and so forth and so on—on the table. How can we figure it out if there are no documents?

Here, naturally, we must change the formulation because it turns out that we are speaking about Gdlyan and Ivanov. But we were supposed to be speaking about the materials of the criminal case pertaining to the criminal activity not only of those who have been brought up here today but also those who have violated the law recently. This is what we were talking about. Therefore I would ask you, comrades, to close the discussion now. Because we will never get anywhere this way. Then, in conjunction with the comrades from the presidium, we should

Sixth Session

30 May 1989

discuss and coordinate the list, present it and confirm it so as not to lose time. This is reasonable. This is what I wanted to ask. I ask you to accept this suggestion. Thank you.

R.N. Nishanov: A small explanation. First, the presidium has followed the congress's instruction. The congress adopted a decision that the presidium should make a proposal regarding this issue. Therefore there is no independence here, we are following the will of the congress.

M.S. Gorbachev: Let the comrades introduce the proposals.

R.N. Nishanov: Please, introduce whatever proposals you have, please.

A.A. Zakharov, team leader of the comprehensive brigade of finishers of Construction Administration No 15 of the Sverdlovskiy Domostroitelnyy Kombinat imeni 60-Letiye Soyuza SSR Association, Sverdlovsk (Kirov Territorial Electoral Okrug, Sverdlovsk Oblast): On behalf of the initiative group composed of congress deputies, we suggest adding the following comrades to the list: Oleg Petrovich Borodin, staff correspondent of the newspaper IZVESTIYA for the Yakut ASSR; Viktor Nikolayevich Kiselev, engineer of the organizational-legal division of the Fishing Kolkhoz imeni V. I. Lenin, Petropavlovsk-Kamchatskiy; Vladimir Dmitriyevich Yudin, chief of the Central Geochemical Expedition in the village of Khasyn; Vitaliy Valentinovich Guliy, special correspondent of the newspaper SOVETSKIY SAKHALIN; Igor Viktorovich Sorokin, senior operative for criminal investigation, Kuybyshev; Boris Vladimirovich Miroshin, chairman of the Sovetskiy Rayispolkom [Rayon Executive Committee], Orsk; Makar Makarovich Yakovlev, chief of the investigation section of the procurator of the Yakut ASSR, Yakutsk; Leonid Sergeyevich Kudrin, loader for one-ton labor agreements, former people's judge, Sverdlovsk; Ilya Iosifovich Zaslavskiy, Moscow Group of Deputies; Vladimir Aleksandrovich Norikhin, radio equipment adjuster, Vladimir. Thank you for your attention.

R.N. Nishanov: All right, Andrey Dmitriyevich, go ahead.

A.D. Sakharov, academician, head scientific associate of the Physics Institute imeni P.M. Lebedev of the USSR Academy of Sciences, Moscow (from the USSR Academy of Sciences): My task has been simplified a great deal because of the preceding speech. The fact is that I wanted to speak in support of this list. In particular, I think that Comrade Kudrin is a person who could be recommended for heading this commission because of his biography and because of the fact that he is at the same time a lawyer and a representative of our country's working class. This is a very rare combination and it is of immense psychological significance. The fact is that the Gdlyan affair is an affair that has two sides. It is not only an investigation of the activity of this investigatory group, in which it is quite possible that there were serious violations. It is also an investigation of the accusations that have been cast at high levels of our apparatus, our society, and in order to restore confidence in our country it is extremely important for both sides of this conflict to be simultaneously and objectively investigated. And a person with the kind of biography that Comrade Kudrin has, it seems to me, is suitable to head such a responsible political commission. It is actually a political commission. And the country is awaiting the conclusions of this commission. I was at two rallies where 100,000 people were demanding an investigation. And we are meeting these demands, the demands of the people.

N.N. Poltoranin, political observer of the Novosti Press Agency, Moscow (from the USSR Union of Journalists): People have said here that the matter which we are discussing requires principled people. But yesterday evening Comrade Aleksey Ivanovich Kazannik from Omsk demonstrated how principled he is. You will recall that he withdrew his candidacy. I nominate Aleksey Ivanovich Kazannik to be included in the commission.

T.D. Moshnyaga, head physician of the republic clinical hospital, Kishinev (Kishinevskiy-Leninskiy National Territorial Electoral Okrug, Moldavian SSR): I suggest including on the commission for investigating the events that took place in Tbilisi a medical expert, a professor of medicine and department head of the Kishinev Medical Institute, Deputy Georgiy Petrovich Gidirin.

A.G. Mukhtarov, editor of the republic newspaper KISHLOK KHAKIKATI ("Rural Truth"), Uzbek SSR (from the USSR Union of Journalists): First of all, forgive me, I have advice for Academician Andrey Dmitriyevich Sakharov. These questions should not be considered in rallies in Luzhniki; Academician Sakharov should visit Uzbekistan and learn about the real state of affairs there, and then make his suggestions. (Applause).

The question, comrades, is very serious. It pertains to the entire republic, the large union multinational republic. Therefore I ask the presidium: the commission should be objective, authoritative, competent, multinational, and multiprofile. It should include lawyers, party workers, and representatives of other categories and segments of the population. I suggest rejecting the proposal of the comrade who read the long list of candidates. It includes several of my journalist colleagues. I ask that journalists not be included in it because comrades Gdlyan and Ivanov are very cozy with my dear colleagues from Moscow. (Applause). I suggest including on the commission a deputy from Kazakhstan, Olzhas Suleymenov. (Applause).

R.N. Nishanov: Please. Next you, Yevgeniy Maksimovich.

Sixth Session

30 May 1989

A.D. Belina, teacher at the Ytyk-Kyuel Secondary School, Yakut ASSR (Megino-Kangalasskiy National Territorial Electoral Okrug): I received a telegram from my constituents and submitted it to the secretariat but it has not read it, apparently it is lost somewhere. Therefore I must come up to this podium and express my will. The voters sent me a telegram and asked that I convey to the congress that this commission absolutely must include Makar Makarovich Yakovlev, incidentally, for some reason he ended up on the list, but that is good. Makar Makorovich Yakovlev is a lawyer by education and he received the absolute majority of the votes at the elections. In general he received a large number of votes throughout Yakutiya. So I think that he can be trusted. I ask you to take this into account.

R.N. Nishanov: The floor goes to Deputy Yevgeniy Maksimovich Primanov.

Ye.M. Primakov, director of the Institute of World Economics and International Relations of the USSR Academy of Sciences, Moscow (from the Communist Party of the Soviet Union): Comrades, I think that during the time of the work of the commission, both of them, we should not speak from the podium regarding the essence of their work. I think that when a question of the commission is discussed there should be no speeches about what they are working on. Let the commission do its work. I suggest that the presidium simply stop any speeches from this podium regarding the essence of the questions during the whole time the commissions are working.

R.N. Nishanov: I request that the speakers follow the suggestion of Deputy Ye.Me. Primakov. Make your suggestions and in the meantime we will form the commission. Introduce yourself, please.

A.A. Sidorov, pensioner, RSFSR, Sverdlovsk (from the All-Union Organization of Veterans of War and Labor): Perhaps this will not make me look very good, but I consider it my duty and responsibility to reject in front of all present the proposal to choose Comrade Kudrin as part of this commission. Not to mention its chairman. Apparently I do not have the right to say anything bad against this comrade. The voters have shown high confidence in him by electing him a people's deputy, but in any case it would be wrong to link him to the business we are now discussing. Comrade Kudrin is a young person and has completed two educational institutions, including the law institute. But he has not been a people's judge for a very long time. His popularity today is associated with his investigation of the business of rallies. You know that it has been reported in the press that injustice was done to him. There is that fact, but there is also another. In one case the press reported that he was right and in another that he was wrong. I assume that in this case he exchanged his principles for his legal knowledge. He threw away his party card and voluntarily left legal work. Now he works as a loader. I assume that this is his.... Again, I stipulate that I do not want to characterize him as an unworthy person, but in questions related to these legal affairs it would be wrong to include him on the commission. Moreover, he is like the offended party....

Again, comrades, I say that there was an offense against him. Is it possible for a person with such qualities to make such a correct decision about such a complicated issue? I suggest that he not be included on the commission. (Applause).

Yu.Yu. Olekaf, senior scientific associate of the Laboratory for Problem Microsurgery of Vilnius State University, Vilnius (Vilkavishkskiy National Territorial Electoral Okrug, Lithuanian SSR): On behalf of the Lithuanian delegation I suggest including on the commission to verify the materials related to the activity of the investigatory group Egidiyus Vitautovich Bichkhauskas, investigator for especially important cases of the Lithuanian SSR Procurator's Office.

R.K. Odzhiyev, deputy chairman of the Cooperative Association Internatsionalist, Tajik SSR, Dushanbe (from the All-Union Lenin Communist Youth League): Comrades, quiet please. I am the only person who is not involved either in the party or in Soviet power or in state institutions, I am a cooperator. (Laughter in the hall).I see that you have relaxed a little bit. We understand all the responsibility of the matter under discussion here; I have in mind what took place in Tbilisi, and we understand all the responsibility to the internationalist servicemen, I myself am an internationalist serviceman. Now we understand all the responsibility to such a force of modernity, as it were, as cooperation. I ask you to include me on this list and I announce at this high tribune that my participation on this commission will be useful.

R.N. Nishanov: Now you, please.

G.Z. Koshlakov, first deputy chairman of the Tajik SSR Council of Ministers, Dushanbe (Rushanskiy National Territorial Electoral Okrug, Tajik SSR): Although we were asked not to speak about the essence of the issue here, I should still like to respond to Comrade Gdlyan and that will be it. Forgive me. Comrade Gdlyan, who spoke first from this podium, said that today in the press there was an unprecedented campaign for persecuting his brigade. One might just as well say that during the course of the investigation there was an unprecedented campaign of support for a still-undecided criminal case. Before the trial dozens of people were declared criminal. And therefore today, when the press is speaking in the opposite direction, it is necessary to investigate the actions of the Gdlyan brigade itself. And if no violations of the law are found in its actions, then it is possible to go on, but if they confirm what appeared on the pages of the press today, the conclusions should be simple.

STENOGRAPHIC RECORD

Sixth Session

30 May 1989

V.A. Shapovalenko, laboratory chief of the Volga-Ural Scientific Research and Planning Institute for Extraction and Processing of Hydrogen Sulfide Gases of the Orenburggazprom Production Association, Orenburg (Orenburg City Territorial Electoral Okrug, RSFSR): I just want to suggest a candidate, who for some reason has not appeared on this list, who prepared for the presidium. Just yesterday we were consulting and suggested a lawyer from Orenburg Oblast who was given a mandate from his constituents and the Muscovites who have addressed him here today. I have in mind Boris Vladimirovich Miroshin. He is a lawyer by education and has spoken here. I suggest including his name on the Gdlyan commission. At the same time I cannot but respond to the comrades. There has already been an attack here and nobody knows who is getting the upper hand. Representatives from Uzbekistan invite us: come and see what Sakharov has done. You say that it is different from what appeared in the press. Well, what was it then? Was it not Gdlyan who brought in those millions of rubles that were shown to us throughout the entire country? Or was it Gdlyan who hid them away? No! We must figure out once and for all who is guilty. Where did this money come from, and what next? (Applause).

R.N. Nishanov: Comrades! We must figure all this out as deeply as possible and give everyone a turn. All the scoundrels must get what they deserve. That is clear.

G.N. Kurochka, chairman of the Permanent Session of the Komi ASSR Supreme Court, Vorkuta (Vorkuta National Territorial Electoral Okrug, Komi ASSR): I have requested that you include me on the list of candidates for USSR Supreme Soviet. My proposal was not accepted at that time. Now I wish to propose my candidacy for the commission for verification of the materials related to the activity of the investigatory group of the USSR Procurator's Office headed by T.Kh. Gdlyan. I shall briefly explain why. I do not know what guided the presidium when discussing candidacies, but if we want to look at this matter objectively and establish whether the investigation went correctly or not, which violations were procedural and which were violations of criminal legislation by this group, if there were none, then I can do the best job of figuring this out—I have been a judge for 12 years and a member of the Komy ASSR Supreme Court. You can find out about my business qualities and qualifications in 15 minutes by telephoning the RSFSR Ministry of Justice or the RSFSR Supreme Court (activity in the hall.) They will tell you about my qualifications and my business qualities. I ask that you include me on the commission.

R.N. Nishanov: Just a minute of your attention, Comrade Kazannik. I will give you the floor later. Deputy Ryabchenko, please.

S.M. Ryabchenko, laboratory chief of the Institute of Physics of the Ukrainian SSR Academy of Sciences, Kiev (Moskovskiy Territorial Electoral Okrug, Kiev, Ukrainian SSR: I wish again to express complaints against the secretariat of our congress and our attention to the fact that we, having saved time at the beginning with procedural issues, are now losing it again. You understand, comrades, that if we all come up to the podium with our suggestions and discuss everything in front of the entire congress we will never get anywhere. When the question was raised about creating these commissions, our Ukrainian delegation gathered at 9:45 on Sunday—75 percent of the deputies were present—and discussed the possible candidates, voted for them, and as a result nominated two candidates: Comrade Andronati to the commission for investigating the events in Tbilisi, and Comrade Semenov—for the other commission. We submitted these candidacies to the presidium. I do not think that each delegation absolutely must achieve such a unity. There can be proposals from individual groups and individual deputies as well. But they should be submitted to the secretariat, and the secretariat should bring them up for discussion and then we should vote. This is a 5-minute matter and we have already spent an entire hour on it. Therefore I suggest: send all suggestions to the secretariat with the justification so that it can be shown who is recommended by the delegation, who is nominating himself and on what basis. They will read this list to us or distribute it in printed form, and then we can vote. Otherwise we will never get through.

R.N. Nishanov: Deputy Kazannik, please.

A.N. Kazannik, department docent of Omsk State University, Omsk (Omskiy National Territorial Electoral Okrug, RSFSR): Esteemed comrade deputies: You may not have any doubt that I am objective and dispassionate, but still I perceive from the principle that "a cobbler mends shoes and a pie baker bakes pies." And there are various kinds of lawyers. I am a specialist in economic law and I can do very, very little for this commission. It should include specialists in criminal law and procedure, and especially in criminology. If one looks attentively at the list of USSR people's deputies, I think that from the body of deputies one can form such a highly qualified commission. You have no idea what a case this is. It has been going on for more than 6 years. This is an extremely immense mass of documents. And I think that it is necessary to form a good working commission and give it the opportunity to enlist on its own initiative highly skilled specialists regardless of where they may work, for otherwise we may never get out of this situation. And, of course, Comrade Gdlyan should act according to principle here as he said with a "trial by jury." If people suggested for the commission seem suspicious to him, we should give him the right to have them withdrawn so that it will be completely dispassionate. Thank you, comrades.

R.N. Nishanov: Introduce yourself, please.

STENOGRAPHIC RECORD

FIRST CONGRESS OF PEOPLE'S DEPUTIES OF THE USSR

Sixth Session

30 May 1989

A.O. Dobrovolskiy, engineer-designer of the Design Bureau for Precision Electronic Machine Building, Minsk (Minkiy-Leninskiy Territorial Electoral Okrug, BSSR): I shall be so bold as to suggest a candidate not in writing but from this podium, because I have written regarding this issue, but, unfortunately, had to wait in line. You yourself can see how difficult it sometimes is to get the floor.

Fulfilling the mandate of the voters, I would nominate Nikolay Ivanovich Ignatovich. He is known in Belorussia as an honest and principled person and, moreover, his high qualifications—senior justice adviser—enable him to delve seriously and deeply into the essence of the matter. Thank you.

R.N. Nishanov: Deputy Eshpay has the floor. If possible let us end here. Just a minute, we will consult now.

A.Ya. Eshpay, composer, secretary of the board of the USSR Union of Composers, Moscow (from the USSR Union of Composers): Vladimir Vasilyevich Karpov, a most courageous and honest person, has declined to be included on the commission. You know that 2 centuries ago there existed an Institution of Satisfaction when an indiscreet, not to mention insulting word, could cause a person to lose his life. There was such an institution, which has now been lost. Therefore people think that it is possible to say whatever they want. Having reacted to what was said, Vladimir Vasilyevich Karpov withdrew his name. I think that since he has remarkable human qualities and experience he can bring a great deal to the activity of such an important and serious commission for an issue which bothers our entire community and all of our people, such as the question of the events in Georgia. Then, it seems to me, this is the first issue and I want us to ask Vladimir Vasilyevich to remain on the commission. And I also heartily support the candidacy of Professor Yakovlev. We have already heard here from the deputies representing Georgia itself that this person has authority throughout the country. And the fact that Professor Yakovlev has already been in Georgia means that he is familiar with these affairs. He has a great deal of authority in the republic. I think it is extremely reasonable to include him on the commission.

R.N. Nishanov: Just a minute, comrades. Shall we stop? Yes? No? That is it, we have decided. Comrades! Just a couple of more notes. Comrade Kim nominates Comrade Sergey Sergeyevich Alekseyev and Comrade Avdeyev dominates Comrade Isul Gamzatov if Rasul agrees. Regarding Comrade Vichkauskas, we already have a proposal. Regarding the candidacy of Comrade Kurochkin, who nominated himself, a note has come. I shall read it later. Regarding Comrade Pokhol, we have already decided. Thus all the nominations made by people's deputies have been registered. The presidium will study the nominations and then present a draft for your consideration.

The counting commission will now have to do its work. I give the floor to the chairman of the counting commission, Comrade Yuriy Andreyevich Osipyan.

Yu.A. Osipyan: Comrade deputies! The counting commission, having gathered at its regular meeting, approved the form of the ballot for voting for candidates for the Council of Nationalities of the USSR Supreme Soviet from Nagornyy Karabakh. Reform of the ballot is this. There will be a ballot, I will not read the heading. You will see it. It has three names in alphabetical order. These are the names of the people's deputies Balayan, Dzhaforov, and Pogoyan. Right here on the ballot it is written that two deputies are to be selected out of the three. This will not mean that a ballot will be declared invalid if two candidates are not left. You can vote arbitrarily, and the two elected candidates are determined as a result of counting the votes.

The voting will take place the way it did with the election of the chairman of the USSR Supreme Soviet. I emphasize that it was possible to cross out or leave the names of the candidates only while in the booth. Voting outside the booth where there are ballots with a large number of candidates is not allowed this time. It is necessary to go into the booth, cross out or leave the necessary names, and then go and put the ballot in the box. Actually, this is all.

Now we can begin the voting. But I ask another minute of your attention. When publishing the results of the voting in the newspaper IZVESTIYA and also with the next ballot you will receive, unfortunately, there are some typographical errors and mistakes. Next to the names of the candidates it is not clear (there are several cases of this) how many votes were "for," particularly for Deputy Rakhimov from Tajikistan, who came up to me almost in tears because he had received more than 1900 votes and there it was indicated 1200. And this was published in the republic newspaper. Do you understand? Therefore I wish to say that the only precise document is the record from the counting commission.

If you wish, tomorrow morning it will be possible to indicate these mistakes. If not, I assure you that all the deputies were elected by a considerable majority of the votes. No more than 300 were against. We can make a correction if that is your decision. All the figures are indicated correctly on the ballot. There is a difference between the ballot which the counting commission published and the material published in the press.

R.N. Nishanov: Comrades! Are there questions for the chairman of the counting commission? No.

Yu.A. Osipyan: All the ballots with the established form are valid. I wish to explain one other thing: if candidates

Sixth Session

30 May 1989

are included on the ballot for a single vacancy, then it is possible to declare the ballot invalid if more than one name has been left. In all cases where candidates are included for several vacancies (more than one as was the case with the elections to the Supreme Soviet) all ballots with the established form will be valid regardless of how many names are left. When will the results of the voting be announced?

R.N. Nishanov: We shall probably announce the results of the voting tomorrow morning. Thank you, Yuriy Andreyevich. Now a couple of small announcements. Regarding the first issue, the commissions, we have completed our work. But later four notes came in with which I should like to familiarize you. Comrade Borovkov, the deputy from Leningrad, suggests including on the commission we discussed last Comrade Varanov from the Izhorsk Plant. The delegation from the Komi ASSR asked not to accept the self-nomination of Kurochka for this commission. The delegation from the Ukrainian SSR suggests including Academician Andronata on the commission. On the commission for considering the events in Tbilisi, Comrade Borontsov suggests including Deputy Gazenko.

We shall take this under consideration.

The meeting is ended for this evening. Now everyone must go and vote.

I declare recesses until 1000 tomorrow.

STENOGRAPHIC RECORD

FIRST CONGRESS OF PEOPLE'S DEPUTIES OF THE USSR
SEVENTH SESSION
WEDNESDAY, 31 MAY 1989
THE KREMLIN PALACE OF CONGRESSES

Speeches by representatives of Soviet republics and major public organizations dominated the proceedings of the Seventh and Eighth Sessions. The agenda called for discussion of Gorbachev's outline of Soviet policy with a view toward drafting a document to guide the work of the new Supreme Soviet. Only a few speakers, however, alluded to the general secretary's statement, and fewer still addressed any part of it directly. They did, however, lend substance and detail to Gorbachev's speech by portraying a demoralized society in an advanced state of decay. The monopolistic oppression of the ministries was the target of every speaker who addressed the economy or the environment. Over-centralization of power was the bugbear of every nationalist. The environmental movement, powerfully galvanized by the disaster at Chernobyl, was often the genesis and everywhere a major component of the movement for democratization in the USSR. The ecological devastation wreaked by the central ministries inspired the alliance of environmentalism and nationalism. In the main the speakers illustrated the community of interests that united environmentalists, nationalists, and democrats against the traditional administrative-command structure.

Deputies V.A. Starodubtsev and V.A. Gontar led with descriptions of the desperate conditions of rural life. Gontar presented a resolution, endorsed by over four hundred peasant deputies, which appealed for a massive infusion of capital to raise the rural standard of living to urban levels and which called for other measures to give peasants economic, social, and legal equality with urban workers. R.N. Nishanov then described the consequences of overindustrialization in Uzbekistan. A.N. Mutalibov conveyed the concerns of the Azerbaijanis and reviewed the industrial contamination of Sumgait and the Caspian Sea. Poet Boris Oleynik, representing the Ukraine, called for reform to protect the environment from "industrial aggression" and warned that a major effort was needed to protect the Ukraine, Belorussia, and western Russia from the effects of radiation unleashed by the Chernobyl disaster. Concluding the morning session, Zoya Pukhova of the Soviet Women's Committee protested the "barbaric" employment of women as manual laborers and urged that women's concerns not become separated from broader issues of economic and social reform.

Boris Yeltsin, who led the second round of speakers, focused on the question of power and bureaucratic inertia and summoned the Congress to write a new constitution that would dismantle the old system, abolish the nomenklatura, and release the creative energies of society. In contrast, Valentin Bakulin chastised his comrades for silently tolerating attacks and slanders against the party. Urging less talk and more action, Bakulin declared intolerable any economic reform that further reduced the people's standard of living. Similarly, Novosibirsk party secretary Vladimir Kazarezov, who questioned the competence of Gorbachev's economic advisors, cautioned that perestroika would fail if people did not soon experience an improvement in their standard of living.

Besides Mutabilov, four deputies spoke for disaffected republics. S.G. Arutyunyan proposed special status that would enable Armenia to accept foreign aid and investment directly, and he demanded a referendum to decide the future of Nagorno-Karabakh. Latvian Supreme Soviet chairman A.V. Gorbunov presented several constitutional amendments aimed at restoring the sovereignty of the union republics. Algirdas Brazauskas asserted that the key to a workable federal relationship was to end the excessive centralization of the present system. He warned that the USSR's relationship with Lithuania depended on Moscow's unambiguous acknowledgement of the illegality of the territorial provisions of the Nazi-Soviet pact. I.K. Toome, Chairman of the Council of Ministers of Estonia, announced his country's determination to inaugurate its economic independence on the first of the year.

The appointment of commissions concluded the day's work. The editing commission to draft resolutions in response to Gorbachev's report was approved with comparatively little difficulty. The task of naming the Tbilisi investigating commission, however, rekindled latent tensions. An unidentified overwrought deputy, who could not "cooperate with murderers," resigned as a deputy "for as long as General Rodionov will remain among us." Latvian deputy V.F. Tolpezhnikov repeated the demand he made at the opening of the Congress that the government identify the person or persons who ordered the military intervention. "Do you think that our government does not know who issued the order?" he asked. "If so, who needs such a government?" And he called for a vote of no confidence in a regime that "does not know who within it ordered the destruction of its own people." The chair ignored the motion and the Congress finally approved the membership of the commission. Since it had been unable to agree on a chairman, that decision was left to the committee.

Texts of documents cited during the Seventh Session are compiled in Appendices at the end of Volume 2: Constitution (Basic Law) of the USSR, Articles 11, 70, 73, 74, 76, 78, 174 (Appendix A.1); Decree on the Introduction of Amendments and Addenda to the USSR Law on "Criminal Liability for State Crimes" and Certain Other USSR Legislative Acts, Article 11-1 (Appendix 1.4).

SEVENTH SESSION
WEDNESDAY, 31 MAY 1989
STENOGRAPHIC RECORD

The session is chaired by USSR People's Deputy A.-M.K. Brazauskas.

A.-M.K. Brazauskas: Comrades, let us begin our morning session. We are continuing the discussion on the basic trends of domestic and foreign policy of the USSR. As was already announced, Deputy Vasiliy Aleksandrovich Starodubtsev, deputy from kolkhozes [collective farms] united within the Union Council of Kolkhozes, has the floor. The next speaker will be Comrade Vladimir Ivanovich Kolesnikov.

V.A. Starodubtsev, chairman of the V.I. Lenin Kolkhoz Breeding Farm, RSFSR, Tula Oblast, Novomoskovskiy Rayon, Sokolniki (from the kolkhozes united within the Union Council of Kolkhozes): Comrade deputies, this is the sixth day of proceedings of the congress. We are discussing one of the major items on the agenda. The report "On the Basic Trends of USSR Domestic and Foreign Policy" has been submitted for consideration by the deputies. It provides a political assessment of the distance we have covered and earmarks a program for the future. However, this is no time to be enthused and hastily engage in high praises. If one looks at each line of the program, if one weighs and compares the past to the present and the future, one is unwittingly concerned. Is this the way we are solving the problem? Is this the path we are following? I recently toured stores in Tula and in some oblast cities. The shelves were half-empty and there were tense lines even for items which until recently were available. Colleagues from other oblasts say that their situation is even worse. What have we come up to? It is almost as bad as was the situation during wartime: Soap is being issued and even not everywhere are rationing points for meat products backed by resources. We can no longer live this way.

Everyone realizes that the country will not come out of the impasse unless the food problem has been solved. The people have been repeatedly promised that the situation will be corrected. However, there have been no noticeable changes, and the situation has clearly deteriorated in the case of many items.

Today we are essentially issuing the latest promissory note. It is my conviction, however, that such assurances may share the fate of the previous programs, for no serious economic foundations have been laid under the new promises. This is the common concern of more than 400 agricultural deputies who have instructed me to speak out at this congress.

All the time we keep claiming that we are eliminating the disparity between town and country. The disparity remains and the countryside is being wiped off! It is mind boggling: Over the past 20 years more than 100,000 villages have disappeared from the face of the earth. This process is continuing. Every year in Russia alone 3,000 settlements die out. Many of them, although still alive, are leading a pitiful existence. The problems of modern production are snowballing behind these dangerous processes. This perfectly reflects the state policy toward our agriculture. Based on all past and present experience we must acknowledge that in this case tactics and strategy suffer from major errors. To this day, with one campaign following another, it is hardly possible to expect any stability in the work. This too creates fertile grounds for irresponsibility on all management levels. Furthermore, the initiative on reorganization, coming from above, is only leading to a change in shingles with practically no improvements in production affairs.

All of us agree that restructuring will not develop unless we can feed the people. Many are those who agree that the time has come to give real help to the peasant. Furthermore, many of the deputies who attended the work of the 19th All-Union Party Conference mentioned

Seventh Session

31 May 1989

this openly. Its resolutions, as you will recall, ascribed prime significance to the development of the agroindustrial complex. Unfortunately, this remained nothing more than a political appeal. No serious steps were taken to implement it in practice. Furthermore, many party and soviet managers, scientists, and the press are promoting the view that the only reason for the shortage of food is that our peasant works poorly, that he has become lazy and has lost his sense of ownership. Unquestionably, all this has taken place but, speaking frankly, to the same extent as in other economic sectors, from small plants to outer space.

It has been known ever since Marx's time that the productivity of farm labor has a decisive influence on any society. This concept is equally relevant today. But what happens actually? Seventy percent of the total amount of work in agriculture involves hard manual labor. It is no accident that the per capita power facilities available to our farmers average 35 hp, compared to 140 hp per American farmer. It is legitimate, therefore, with such a base that for the time being both cost accounting and leasing or any other forms of farming function poorly.

The administrative-pressure system, which does not take into consideration economic laws and does not ensure proper competence in the management of this important sector, remains a major obstruction. No one would conceive of advising a surgeon how to operate; in agriculture, however, in the agrarian economy, everyone considers himself a major specialist. Here, in the halls of this congress we agrarians gathered during an intermission, to exchange views. A deputy unfamiliar to me asked to speak and began to give advice on most complex agricultural problems. We found out very quickly that he was a leading specialist in the field of design.

Naturally, the agrarian sector suffers from numerous shortcomings and from negligence. The outlay mechanism and elements of dependency are still alive. All of this does exist. However, the problem lies elsewhere. We do not know of any other country in the world which could feed its population without creating a favorable, I emphasize favorable, attitude toward the peasant, which would not engage in systematically solving the problems of agrarian policy. For example, decisions to change material and technical supplies and to make them part of the USSR Gossnab [State Committee for Material and Technical Supply] system are being made without seeking any advice from the peasant or the farm manager. It is claimed that this is being done to help agriculture. But comrades, today we know the way agriculture is being supplied by such materials and equipment through the USSR Gossnab system. Not even ordinary paint can be bought. How could such an important national economic complex be left without a material supply system? The picture which indeed obtains is the following: All agrarians unanimously object, while others try to convince us that this will make it better for us. Whoever accepted such concepts and what they are based on no one can explain. Above all, there is no one responsible for such decisions.

Now, according to the resolutions of the March 1989 CPSU Central Committee Plenum, we have come to the crossroads of economic relations in the countryside. This was a timely, a necessary step. Naturally, all of this cannot be described as radical measures to improve agriculture. On this level, many of those who work in the agroindustrial complex feel an inner dissatisfaction with the steps which were formulated at the Central Committee Plenum. In my view, no radical forward steps were taken and, once again, everything is being reduced to half-way measures. Let us introduce leasing, it is said, and matters will improve, we shall create peasant farming system and ensure a substantial increase in food resources.

Unquestionably, there will be some increase. Already now, however, in order to satisfy market demand, we must increase food resources by a minimum of 30 billion rubles' worth. This is no more and no less than one-sixth of what is available. In this case, as the saying goes, we should double or triple the rpms.

How do we see the solution to this impasse? I believe that we need a serious reorientation of the entire national economy in favor of the accelerated development of the material and technical base of the countryside and its infrastructure. It is entirely understandable that this is no simple step, for we shall have substantially to curtail programs affecting other national economic complexes. We may have to reduce expenditures for defense and other projects. Also inevitable will be the organized resettlement of the able-bodied population from the towns into areas where the population has lost the capacity for self-reproduction. There is simply no other way.

Every citizen in our country must clearly realize that agriculture is today the backbone of the economy of the entire society. Perhaps it would be worth to have a national referendum on the formulation of radical ways for agricultural upsurge. I believe that the people would show a great deal of understanding for such a step and will not stand aside in the solution of such most difficult problems.

You must understand, comrades, that this step must be taken. Otherwise, the difficult situation with food supplies will bring about unpredictable social tension.

The next feature: We lack a clear concept consistent with the economic laws governing the development of society. Unfortunately, for some reason this is not being mentioned, although this is precisely both the reason for and the key to the solution of many problems. One of the Baltic deputies expressed what is in my view a very important thought: Interest is the basis of everything. This is a concept which Marx himself formulated but, unfortunately, which has now been forgotten. The city gives the country unsuitable equipment the prices of which are growing unrestrainedly. Industrial monopoly is becoming the Moloch which is ruining the countryside.

STENOGRAPHIC RECORD

Seventh Session

31 May 1989

Unfortunately, this state of affairs continued even after the March party central committee plenum. This year, state centralized capital investments and budget appropriations for their financing, totaling 540 million rubles, were transferred from the Agricultural Committee for the Nonchernozem to the development of other sectors of the Soviet national economy. Long-term credits totaling 630 million rubles less than last year were appropriated in 1989 for the farms in the nonchernozem zone, along with short-term loans totaling 2.65 billion rubles. This is a total of 3.28 billion rubles. The USSR Council of Ministers passed a resolution on paying the farms' interest owed to the bank on loans the repayment of which was postponed on the basis of separate governmental resolutions, ranging from 1 to 5 percent, which will increase the costs to the farms in the nonchernozem zone by an additional 211 million rubles. Starting with 1 April of this year, the interest rate for the use of short-term loans was set at 15 percent instead of the previous 1.2-3.0 percent. Other documents were also passed, which obviously conflict with the resolution of the March CPSU Central Committee Plenum.

Here is yet another deputy question: By Resolution No 25 of 5 May 1989 on improving (what a blasphemous word!) the country's economy in 1989, the USSR Gosplan [State Planning Committee] removed from the agro-industrial sector 20,000 tractors, 10,000 trucks, 1,100 excavators, and 1,677 bulldozers, which were subsequently delivered to Tsentrosoyuz for sale to the cooperatives. Comrade farm managers, who are sitting in this hall, we have dreamed for years of tractors and bulldozers and have been unable to obtain them. Now, apparently, we shall not obtain them at all.

Comrade deputies, what is happening? The polarization between the interests of town and country is increasing. Group egotism is growing. This was manifested quite rapidly after the laws on the state enterprise and the cooperative were passed. It was precisely during that period that prices jumped incredibly. Why so? Socialism calls for bringing urban interests closer to those of the country. A variety of ways to obtain this objective exists. One of them is to improve commodity-monetary and market relations. If we take this path, we must develop profoundly and comprehensively the mechanism for combining the interests of the city with that of the countryside. This pertains above all to investment policy, economics, price setting, and crediting. The impression is created that someone simply wishes to spoil relations between the working class and the peasantry.

Finally, we must accept the simple truth: Combining interests is the foundation for success. "A society in which a class difference remains between worker and peasant is neither communist nor socialist," Vladimir Ilich Lenin wrote ("*Poln. Sobr. Soch.*" [Complete Collected Works], vol 38, p 353).

Nor do we have a firm concept on the further development of kolkhoz-sovkhoz [state farm] production.

Appeals to abolish the kolkhoz system have been sounded in periodicals, television programs, and even from the rostrum of this congress. It is being accused of failure to feed the people. Name one peasantry in a single country which would be able to withstand such a pressure for elimination. The countryside has been treated as a colony. The peasant was deprived of juridical, social, and economic rights. A great deal of this remains to this day. The fact that kolkhozes have survived this situation proves, yet once again, the great vital force of this system. (Applause).

What could one say today to the opponents of kolkhozes? You would like to strike a final blow at the peasant and thus condemn the people to semi-hungry rations for many long years. Yes, we have learned how to destroy. But how are we to build the peasant farms? Where to find the billions of rubles? Where to find the type of peasant who would like to work without adequate mechanization facilities, from dawn to dawn? There is also a further difficulty: The link between peasant generations has been broken and its restoration will take decades.

Comrades! The agrarian deputies submit the following to the congress:

Measures must be formulated to limit the monopoly of departments and gigantic plants;

The debts of kolkhozes and sovkhozes, caused by price increases and other arbitrary decisions, must be written off;

State orders must be reduced to the 25-30 percent level;

Economically set prices of produce must be established for all farms;

The quality of land must be assessed and fair taxes levied on this basis;

Rural homes must be provided with natural gas and electric power on an equal basis as the towns and at equal rates.

We suggest that a permanent authority—a committee on agrarian problems—be set up by the USSR Supreme Soviet, to defend the interests of the Soviet peasant, a committee which should report directly to the congress and be absolutely independent of departments. (Applause). Naturally, it is very important for the responsibility for such a complex program and problem to be assumed by the chairman of the USSR Council of Ministers. (Applause).

Comrades, the Congress of People's Deputies of the country is an entirely new phenomenon in our life. The entire course of the electoral campaign and its political

Seventh Session

31 May 1989

relevance and high degree of activeness in which it took place generated in the people tremendous hope for this congress. Indeed, this forum is the culminating aspect of democratization of society. If we are able to find a way to solve urgent problems, we shall advance. If we fail to do so, we would doom the country not simply to stagnation but to faster lagging. The people, however, would not forgive us for this. (Applause).

I ask the chair to allow a few minutes for an address to the congress. (Applause).

A.-M.K. Brazauskas: Do go on, comrades. You will allot time, yes?

From the hall: Yes.

A.-M.K. Brazauskas: Does the congress agree? Can we have more time?

From the hall: Yes.

A.-M.K. Brazauskas: Please, proceed.

V.A. Gontar, chairman of the Shlyakh do Kommunizmu Kolkhoz, Ukrainian SSR [Soviet Socialist Republic], Cherkassy Oblast, Chernobayevskiy Rayon, Novoukrainka Village (representing kolkhozes united within the Union Council of Kolkhozes): Dear Mikhail Sergeyevich! Dear people's deputies! On behalf and on the instruction of the 417 agrarian deputies, I ask to be allowed to read an address to the congress.

Address to the USSR Congress of People's Deputies:

To you, the representatives of the people, we turn today with pain and concern. The people of our country have become infinitely tired of empty shelves, endless scarcity, and lines. Under our very eyes, on the 45th year of peaceful life, a rationing system is making its way.

The food problem has become the main yardstick of restructuring. The people rate us on the basis of what they have on their tables. On behalf of those who grow the grain, who love the land, we demand of you, the people's deputies the following: Commit the country's leadership to truly giving priority to the problem of the countryside in the political life of society and thus allow the people to feed themselves. (Applause). Not 10 years hence, but right now.

How to do this? Listen to us, the peasants, and understand and help the countryside. If it is bad for the peasant it is bad for the country. This has been confirmed by the entire experience of both world and domestic history. For many decades everything, to the last drop, has been extracted from the countryside. So far, the March 1989 CPSU Central Committee Plenum has not yielded expected results.

The peasant who is a respected and prestigious figure throughout the world, remains so far in our country a lower category person in terms of pensions, supplies, and living conditions. The desertion of the countryside is continuing. The land is getting poorer and billions in investments are yielding no returns.

The reasons for this are numerous. To this day the life of the peasant is worse than that of the urban resident, even despite his income from his private plot. His life span is shorter than that of the urban resident. The state provides the urban resident with a free apartment with all conveniences, while the peasant must build his own home at his own expense and with his own hands, cut his wood, draw and heat his own water, and procure his own produce. Everything in the countryside is worse: education, medicine, culture, and consumer services. (Applause).

For a number of years the departments, which were wrecking the countryside with their management, have taken even brides away from rural grooms, by destroying the industries and small enterprises which gave jobs to women.

To this day supplies to the villages are based on the residual principle. The villages are supplied with low-grade metal and equipment. How long will this go on? Why do the consumers of agricultural commodities think that the countryside should tolerate this?

As in the past, the peasant does not own the land. The production structure, volume, and state orders are determined from above through a policy of monopoly prices. Under such circumstances the government finds nothing better than to lower capital investments in the development of agriculture. It is revising national economic ratios under a scarcity of food products improperly, mistakenly.

We urgently demand the immediate and sharp turning of the country's economy around, such as to face the needs of the countryside, starting with the present congress. In the next few years the living standards in the country must be raised to a level close to that of the towns. The continuing large-scale industrial construction, defense expenditures, space, and other prestige projects must be sharply curtailed; the further expansion of the cities must be halted and an end must be put to the urbanization of the country. The thus released funds, materials, and manpower must be channeled into improving peasant housing and farms, roads, schools, hospitals, and the entire social area. It is not the peasants alone who must deal with this but this should be accomplished primarily with budget funds. Pensions and social security for all categories of rural workers and urban residents must be guaranteed and equalized. The workloads of the rural teacher, physician, and other categories of working people in the countryside must be revised. The villages must be supplied with natural gas, water, heat, and electric power as good as those of the towns and for the same

Seventh Session

31 May 1989

rates. Supplies to the countryside of all the necessary goods should be no worse than in the cities.

Probably in no other country in the world is there such a gap between the prices of agricultural and industrial commodities, to the detriment of the countryside. In no civilized country is peasant labor valued so low. The prices of resources coming from the cities are increasing with every passing year while the quality of the equipment is declining. It is not astounding that the peasantry is unable to get rid of its debts. We work and work and then the industrial ministry, with the favorable neutrality of the USSR State Committee for Prices, hits us with the next price increase and, once again, the muzhik is in debt up to his ears. (Applause).

At this congress, we are now suggesting that instructions be issued to formulate steps to limit the monopoly status of departments and huge plants. We suggest that the debts caused by price increases and other arbitrary exaggerations to be written off the kolkhozes and sovkhozes. (Applause). In any case, the countryside will be unable to repay them and the lessee will not assume them.

We suggest that the production of contemporary agricultural machinery, equipment and tools be organized at defense plants, so that the call of "beating swords into plowshares" be indeed implemented. (Applause). Construction organizations and enterprises for the production of construction materials working for the countryside must be created immediately and ubiquitously. A considerable share of the urban construction potential should be channeled into the countryside.

For many years the villages were ordered around arbitrarily, even by nonprofessionals. The feeling of ownership has long been beaten out of the peasant. Today it has become easier. Nonetheless, the rural labor collective has no right to handle the produce it grows. Virtually everything is taken away from kolkhozes and sovkhozes on the basis of state orders, all the produce that can be sold. As in the past, the plan is based on the level reached. It is those who make better use of their opportunities that particularly suffer from this.

We suggest that state orders be substantially reduced and placed strictly on the basis of mutually acceptable contractual conditions. We must establish in principle uniform prices of goods by large area of specialization, applicable to all farms. We must knowledgeably assess the quality of the land and, on this basis, levy fair taxes. A land inventory must be taken throughout the country. The land must be taken away from bankrupt enterprises and given to the local soviets, and let them, on the basis of competition, give the land to kolkhozes, sovkhozes, lessees, cooperatives, peasant families, and farmers. We reject the incompetent leadership of agriculture and demand that it be conducted on a strictly scientific and democratic basis, that the role of science be increased and that modern scientific material and technical facilities be created.

We reject any interference from above or from the side in defining the forms of farming and demand the strict observance of the Leninist principle that no one should dare to order the peasant! (Applause.) Whereas in the past criminal coercion was applied, today it would be unreasonable to decide where and how should the peasant live.

We reject the slogan of dismantling kolkhozes and of restraining the leasing movement. We believe that under the conditions of our country kolkhozes, state farms, cooperatives, and peasant farms could and should exist. Let them compete on the basis of a strictly observed legal and economic equality. It is the peasant alone who must make such decisions. (Applause).

We demand a radical land reform—a Law on the Land— and a real variety of forms of ownership and farming.

We suggest that a permanent authority under the Supreme Soviet—a Committee on Agrarian Problems— consisting of USSR people's deputies, be set up to protect the interests of the peasantry, with its own system, independent of other departments, maintained by the kolkhozes and sovkhozes which will be answerable to the committee only. The Committee on Agrarian Problems should report exclusively to the Supreme Soviet, and no authorities and departments could make any decisions affecting agriculture and the condition of the peasantry without its agreement. (Applause). The committee should have the right to initiate legislation.

Actually, all of our suggestions may be reduced to a single thing: Peasant work must become the most prestigious and respected, as it is in all developed countries in the world. (Applause). The peasant must assume a worthy status in our society. It is in the interest of the entire society for the state to change its attitude toward the peasantry as a class. The peasantry must become the equal of workers and employees, economically, socially, and legally, with no exception, as stipulated in the USSR Constitution.

We request that our appeal be considered a draft resolution of the congress on agrarian problems. (Applause).

A.-M.K. Brazauskas: Comrades, the following motion has been made: The presidium should consider this appeal and, after the session, suggest in what way, how to work with this document, and what instructions to be submitted to the congress.

Let us pursue our debates. Comrade Vladimir Ivanovich Kolesnikov, department head at the Rostov Institute of Railroad Transportation Engineers, Territorial District No 268, has the floor. The next speaker will be Comrade Nishanov.

V.I. Kolesnikov, department head, Rostov Institute of Railroad Transportation Engineers, Rostov-na-Donu (Oktyabrskiy Territorial Electoral District, RSFSR): Dear comrade deputies, I consider the importance of this

STENOGRAPHIC RECORD

Seventh Session
31 May 1989

congress in the fact that, for the first time in our history, it raises the question not only of the fact that a person must work, incidentally, we have been raising this question for the past 70 years, but of the sake for which he should work and who should benefit from the results of his labor.

Today we are going back to the slogan of the October Revolution, "All power to the soviets!" However, we must remember that Lenin combined this slogan with two others: "Land to the peasant!" and "Plants and factories to the workers!" However, we did not carry out in full the behests of the October revolution, for the command-administrative system deprived the people of power and ownership. Let me start with the following example:

We, deputies from Rostov Oblast, were instructed by the voters to raise the question of guaranteeing the safety of the Rostov nuclear power plant, built on the coast of the Tsimlyan Sea, on loose soil. I believe that this problem affects not only the people of Rostov. We have submitted to the Presidium of this congress tens of thousands of written appeals by our voters on this matter. We are amazed that that the USSR Council of Ministers has shown no concern for this problem. We understand that the problems of the power industry must be dealt with by the state. However, they must be solved in a statesman-like fashion.

To begin with, the population must be confident of the safety of the nuclear power plant on the basis of nondepartmental expertise. Second, its economic expediency must be proved. It is only then that, together with the people, the question of starting it should be settled.

It seems to me that these facts are related not only to the building of nuclear power plants but also that other plants as well would not exist had the local soviet been the true master of its territory. That is why the primary, the very first task of the congress should be to establish the mechanism for transfer of power to the soviets. We, the people's deputies, must formulate this mechanism. Furthermore, today the local system of soviets is not given material support. What is the solution to this situation? It is for the industrial enterprises to lease the land and the natural, manpower, and other resources form the local soviets. In such a case the enterprises will have to discuss with the local soviets the conditions under which they will operate on its territory. In my view, the task of the people's deputies here is to formulate a mechanism for withholdings for the local budget and to ratify it with a law.

The question that arises is how to combine the slogan of "All power to the soviets!" with those of "The land to the peasant!" and "The plants and factories to the worker!?" In the course of the debates here it was already pointed out the way managers of enterprises and chairmen of executive committees go to Moscow making the rounds hat in hand, asking for money and materials. Let me merely add to this that the faultiness of this system lies also in the fact that sometimes those display greater shrewdness are more successful than those who work better.

Today we must clearly realize that as long as we, as the legislative authority, have not drafted the laws according to which the true masters of the land and the enterprises will be those who work on and in them, we shall be unable to solve a single economic problem. Understandably, the solution of such problems is also related to social tasks: housing, transportation, pensions, medical services, science, education, etc. Furthermore, I am convinced that by solving social problems we shall also greatly ease national tension. All of this is, unquestionably, important and necessary. However, comrade deputies, I would like to draw your attention to the following feature: The moment we have made the soviets the real local power, we could anticipate manifestations of parochialism and attempts at tearing our state apart. In that case the role of the people's deputies will be to prevent this, to be able to rise above local interests, however important they may be.

In my view, a more difficult problem is that of transferring ownership of the enterprises to the working people. We know that some labor collectives, which have already been given independence, have taken the path of increasing their wages without increasing profits, and instead of upgrading labor productivity and mastering the new technology. As a result, we are not getting any richer but merely encouraging inflation and increasing the prices of goods. What is the solution? In my view the solution rests in the need to settle the question of transferring the power to the soviets and giving enterprises autonomy, as closely related to the questions of ownership in its various aspects as possible. Such ownership must be sacred and inviolable. Only in that case could we bring the working person closer to the land, the means of production and the results of his toil.

Comrades, everything seems to indicate that this is a fundamental, a Union problem which we cannot resolve on the level of the plant shop, as has been suggested here by some deputies. This problem must be solved above all at our fora, using to this effect the entire intellectual and, let me emphasize, the civic potential of the country. Furthermore, we also need caution, daring, and resolve as well as legal foundations for the work of the people's deputy, i.e., for his status.

I second the suggestion of many deputies on setting up a commission of people's deputies to draft this status. However, I also favor the formulation of a regulation on relations between the people's deputy and the Supreme Soviet and its commissions; between the people's deputy and ministries, departments, and officials; and between the people's deputy and the party authorities. In the past everything was simple. The Supreme Soviet was an authority directly elected by the people. Now the people have elected people's deputies. There is no power higher than the USSR Congress of People's Deputies. The Supreme Soviet means supremacy. Over what and over

Seventh Session

31 May 1989

whom? Is this accurate? I am confident that in the future we will develop a mechanism for the implementation of the principle which will ensure the maximal manifestation of the will of the people—that is, a principle according to which the power of the deputy has been granted directly by the people and not delegated to anyone. This is natural.

We are all learning and improving ourselves, and the questions we are facing are numerous. This involves rotation in the Supreme Soviet, consensus vote, in which the manifestation of the aggressiveness of a majority or a minority is excluded, the possibility of which we have repeatedly realized in this hall. It also involves the mechanism for convening an extraordinary congress both from above, by the Supreme Soviet, as well as from below, on the demand of the deputies. This also includes the right to deny the government a vote of confidence.

Another major question is drafting a Law on Elections. Elections for republic and soviets are not too far off and we do not know today entirely how to conduct this campaign. I am in favor of elections on an alternative basis, elections after which even this congress will feel the voters breathing down its neck. In this case as well I am deeply convinced that if all elections are of this nature, there would be a greater reciprocal understanding in our own congress. (Applause). I believe that we must eliminate pre-electoral district meetings, for they limit the expression of the will of the voters. (Applause). I believe that candidates nominated by public organization should be elected by the population as a general principle, based on territorial features and alternate choices. (Applause).

I am against factions and favor bringing together the deputies on the basis of certain problems, regardless of their delegations. We know that full unity means stagnation, something which we have already seen. We are not as yet fully acquainted with each other and we have been separated into territorial groups. Yet, I am convinced, that our task is for the deputies to abandon the geographic and land origin principle and to choose for themselves a problem and rally on the basis of the common problems they will have to deal with. (Applause).

When I speak of the problems of the deputies, I link them to the views of the electorate. In the future, therefore, when our parliament will be equipped with technical facilities, we must not reject the the roll-call vote system. The voters must know what their deputy is voting for and what laws he is proposing. And for the deputy to be able to propose such laws, a system must exist for submitting and discussing draft bills. The main thing here is not to exclude any options and to be specific: The people must know who the author or groups of authors of one law or another is, and at that point there would be no question of who could possibly be the author of Article 11.1. Who is the author of the Ukase on demonstrations and meetings? This is quite important. It would make it possible, in drafting a bill, to be particularly cautious, watchful, and responsible. Let me bluntly say that my electorate has instructed me to support the deletion of Article 11.1. I too support Mikhail Sergeyevich Gorbachev's suggestion that the most important laws must be passed on the basis of nationwide referenda.

My voters would like a public answer to the following: Why is it that out of the three deputies sent by the million-strong population of Rostov-na-Donu one of them is a member of the Supreme Soviet, and how do I feel about this? I consider this a basic question, for which reason I shall answer it. When the congress passed the resolution on the nomination of candidacies for the Supreme Soviet by territorial groups of deputies, I suggested Deputy Vladimir Yakovlevich Shevlyuga, a Rostselmash worker. As a result of the open vote, however, the 19 deputies from Rostov Oblast nominated other representatives. I basically consider that the electoral system is imperfect and that instead of having elections, as the USSR Constitution stipulates, we are essentially delegating deputies from our group, although the people elected independent deputies and not delegates.

Comrades, let me mention yet another problem which affects all of us. It is the problems AIDS. We know about its outbreak in the city of Elista. Now there is also AIDS in Rostov and in Volgograd. But when will our hospitals be supplied with disposable syringes? I suggest that a group of deputies who are medical workers be set up to resolve this very important state problem.

Comrade deputies, finally, I would like to draw your attention to a problem which is of vital importance and of prime significance in all areas and sectors of the national economy, a problem whose importance will grow in the future: that of transportation, including by rail. The deputy railroad workers have asked the USSR Council of Ministers to report on the steps planned by the Soviet government on the further development of railroad transportation. I thank you for your attention. (Applause).

A.-M.K. Brazauskas: Thank you. The next speaker is Comrade Rafik Nishanovich Nishanov, first secretary of the Uzbek Communist Party Central Committee.

R.N. Nishanov, first secretary, Uzbek Communist Party Central Committee, Tashkent (Leningradskiy National-Territorial Electoral District, Uzbek SSR): Dear comrade deputies, our congress can be considered with full justification the congress of the peoples of the Soviet Union. The virtually entire country, all Soviet people, are participating in its work. There is absolutely no question that it will implement its historical role of providing a new impetus to the further democratic transformation of socialism and formulate ways of solving urgent problems.

As to problems, we have more than enough. The speech by Comrade Mikhail Sergeyevich Gorbachev dealt in

Seventh Session

31 May 1989

substantial detail with the course of restructuring, changes, errors, and obstacles on the way to its implementation, and primary tasks.

All of us, dear comrades, see that irreversible steps have been taken on the path of restructuring. We have been able to turn society from stagnation to motion, from dogmatism to realism, and to restoring the Leninist approaches and Leninist views of social development. The people expect and demand of restructuring real results. Such results, however, will come about only if the foundations of popular rule and law and order are firmly strengthened and if we can totally reject the command-bureaucratic management methods.

In my view, as a whole, a constructive and practical discussion on such problems is taking place at the congress. I am distressed, however, by isolated bursts and shameless labeling and classifying deputies into progressive and conservative, and the efforts on the part of individual comrades to set the congress against the party workers.

Yesterday, for example, an attack was mounted against the institution of second secretaries. All of this does not contribute to our consolidation but destroys our unity. Individual deputies contaminated, I would say, by the bacillus of arrogance, have allowed themselves to launch insulting sallies against deputies representing Central Asian republics, indiscriminately accusing them of obediently following some kind of orders and instructions. We firmly reject such sallies. (Applause).

Dear comrades, we do not have first-class or second-class deputies. We do not have very responsible or irresponsible deputies any more than we have broad-minded and narrow-minded deputies. All of us are equal and equally responsible to our own electorate and to the country. I believe that we all need a very calm, and reciprocal patient, considered, and competent interpretation of processes and a choice of proper directions and ways of progress, and the consolidation of all groups and all regions, for we are engaged in the pursuit of a common cause. We live with the concerns of the country and the congress, with the concerns of the people. I and my party fellow-workers, like many participants in the congress, are quite seriously concerned, for example, by problems of drafting legal and legislative acts. We know that a building rests on its foundations. A thoroughly developed mechanism for democracy, and profoundly considered laws must become the foundation without which a rule of law state is inconceivable. Some 150 years ago Vissarion Grigoryevich Belinskiy noted that our country needs not sermons but sensible laws and their strictest possible observance. Yet, for the time being we still do not have a thoroughly developed technology for law-making and a procedure for the formulation, discussion, and passing of laws. Some laws, passed of late, are not working as was intended; others develop accretions which reduce their meaning to naught; others again have revealed the controversial nature of some concepts immediately after their promulgation. The authorities and the law must watch over the interests of society, the interests of the people. This was well put in the report.

Problems of relations between the center and the republics require legislative codification as well. As we know, the 1924 Soviet Constitution, which was drafted with the participation of Vladimir Ilich Lenin, included the title "On the Sovereign Rights of Union Republics and On Union Citizenship." The 1936 Constitution, like the current one, does not include such a title. The lack of a legislative stipulation has led to the fact that in the 1940s entire peoples, including the Crimean Tatars, the Meskhet Turks, and others were deprived of their native land and, until recently, any mention of the need to take into consideration the national features and normal patriotic concern for the development of the native language and true national culture was frequently identified with nationalism which, as was accurately mentioned in the report, triggered feelings of bitter hurt and was rather painfully reflected on national self-awareness. (Applause).

I believe it entirely justified if in the drafting of the new Soviet Constitution this title is restored, naturally in accordance with the new requirements. The time has also come to legislatively codify the rights of small ethnic groups as we consider, for example, the concept of a Law on National Groups. (Applause).

Restructuring brought to light a number of sharp and neglected ills in the republics. Yet the events which have taken place in recent years in a number of areas have clearly indicated how far unsolved problems could lead us. The sources of such manifestations may be different but in their majority they are closely related to distortions in national policy in previous decades, gross distortions and exaggerations in economic development, and neglect of the social and cultural areas. The party organization and all working people of Uzbekistan were left a difficult legacy from the period of stagnation. Gross errors and distortions were committed in party and ideological work. There were disproportions in industry and agriculture. A moral decline and the corruption of a number of leading personnel, who are now under party and criminal indictment, were detected. The Uzbek Communist Party Central Committee Buro is engaged in a decisive struggle against corrupt elements of all kinds, and such work will be carried out to its completion. The solution of all such and other radical problems has initiated the practical implementation of the complex process of restructuring which is taking place in the Republic in the course of the difficult struggle between the old and the new, the difficult elimination of existing stereotypes and dogmas, and the difficult mastery of new styles and methods of work and new way of thinking. All of us are learning the restructuring approaches to economic, social, and political problems. This too is not easy to achieve. The structure of public production on the sectorial and territorial levels has been disrupted in the Republic. For many years its development took place essentially without

Seventh Session

31 May 1989

control, and one-sidedly. For many long years the emphasis was on the development of sectors oriented toward the production of raw materials and semi-finished goods, the share of which reached 60 percent in the overall volume of output. Production facilities with an insignificant number of new jobs and a low share of wages in production costs were created at an insanely accelerated pace. This worsened the already grave problem of employment and hindered the growth of the population's monetary income. Huge funds were wasted on the building of extremely big complexes for the extraction and primary processing of raw materials, including for the chemical and petrochemical industries and nonferrous metallurgy, which consume substantial amounts of water, which is scarce under our circumstances, and which seriously affects the ecological situation. Meanwhile, capacities for the production of finished goods and processing agricultural commodities were virtually not developed. But is it admissible for us to process no more than 10 percent of the cotton grown in the Republic? This single crop, inflated to monstrous volumes, became not only a hindrance but the real calamity of our entire area, resulting in the exhaustion of land and water resources, excessively high chemicalization of fields, and mass diseases among the population. As was already said here, the Aral is a clear example of this. Currently, with the help of the Union authorities, we have been able somewhat to reduce the areas in cotton and to expand the areas in fodder crops and fruits, vegetables, and vineyards. However, in order to put a final and total end to the grossest possible distortions and arbitrariness in cotton growing and, therefore, increase the production of foodstuffs, both we and the Union authorities will have to consider further steps to reduce the amounts of cotton and reduce it to the level of the real needs of our country. (Applause).

The growing of cotton, dear comrades, is a most difficult and exhausting type of work which demands tremendous physical and moral efforts. I think that we are still using the cotton quite wastefully. We think little about replacing it with chemical fibers, something which has long been practiced abroad. Judge for yourselves, comrade deputies: Of the total amount of cotton produced in the Soviet Union, approximately 2.5 million tons, or nearly 700,000-800,000 tons, are exported while the rest is kept for domestic consumption. We have the virtually highest use of cotton for industrial purposes in the world, 14 percent, compared to 3 percent in Japan and even less than 1 percent in the United States. In the Soviet Union the production of cotton fabrics per capita is more than double that of other countries; meanwhile, the share of chemical staples in the overall volume of its consumption is the lowest—under 30 percent—which is one half to one third less than in the FRG, Italy, and Japan. We can supply our friends in the socialist community as much cotton as they may require for their own needs.

All of this, dear comrades, urgently calls for developing a scientific Union-wide "Cotton" Program, which would take into consideration the actual needs of the country for cotton staple and which would make it possible firmly to change the production specialization and structure of crops in favor of solving, above all, the food problem. On this matter we agree with the leadership of the USSR Gosplan and I believe that we shall be able to formulate such a program.

Comrade deputies, let me note, in conclusion, that on the eve of our congress a number of events of international significance took place. One of the most outstanding among them was Mikhail Sergeyevich Gorbachev's trip to the PRC. Our large-scale foreign policy action was successful and a beginning was laid to a new era of reciprocal relations between the two great nations—the Soviet and the Chinese. We fully support the foreign policy course charted by our party's Central Committee and all of us are ready to contribute our own efforts in this direction. I thank you very much for your attention. (Applause).

A.-M.K. Brazauskas: Deputy Gorbunov has the floor.

A.V. Gorbunov, chairman of the Presidium of the Latvian SSR Supreme Soviet (Tsesisskiy Territorial Electoral District, Latvian SSR): Dear chairman, dear comrade deputies. One of the most difficult problems in the restructuring and democratization of the Soviet political system is its legal support. However, this clashes with obsolete laws whenever efforts are made to carry out radical changes in a given area. In short, a paradoxical situation develops. One may work inefficiently but in accordance with obviously obsolete norms of the current law. One could passively wait for the new USSR Constitution. It will take more than a year before it can be completed. In that area as well we must truly not be in a hurry. However, there is also another way: tirelessly to advance restructuring and, at the same time, take more decisive timely steps in the legislative area. It is true that we heard here, at the congress, claims that we will not be understood unless we start immediately to introduce amendments to the USSR Constitution.

The Latvian deputies are of a different opinion. Our electorate will not understand if the congress, after working for 2 weeks, fails to introduce a single amendment to the USSR Constitution, even if only in articles which are clearly hindering progress today such as, for example, the development of our federation in the interest of a qualitatively new political and economic sovereignty of Union republics. (Applause). The Republic's legislators are actively making new laws, without which the further democratization of our political system and the legislative solution of still existing problems are impossible.

I am deeply convinced that today we cannot work while constantly facing obsolete Union laws; nor can we agree at all with stagnation requirements according to which the accuracy of the new legal norms should fully coincide with the obsolete stipulations of the Constitution. Therefore, on behalf of the group of deputies of Soviet Latvia, I submit to the consideration of the congress a draft USSR Law on Constitutional Amendments. We are suggesting amendments which apply to what we consider

Seventh Session

31 May 1989

no more than a few essential articles. We ask the congress to set up a commission of competent jurists and deputies representing all republics to formulate the final drafts.

Now, as to the essence of our proposals: They are aimed at restoring the sovereignty of Union Soviet socialist republics. Only a few years ago the problems of granting state sovereignty to Union republics seemed infinitely distant to many citizens and totally unrelated to their daily life and concerns. Now everything has changed. No one is asked any more to prove that restoring the sovereignty of Union republics and the search for an optimal interrelationship among republics and between the Union and the individual republics requires not only the revision of the old dogmas and the understanding of the new situation but also taking entirely specific practical steps.

Let us consider the economy of the Latvian SSR. A number of examples could be cited of unjustified management centralization leading to a total inconsistency between some production facilities and the interests of the republic in which they are located and their peoples for the satisfaction of whose needs they were created. For example, we are completely unable to explain to the Latvian population why, when the republic has four large enterprises for agricultural machine building, our peasants are not equipped with even the basics—a good plow or a sowing machine.

Excessive centralization and neglecting the national interests of Union republics, oblasts, and krays for decades have led to major distortions in their economic development. Thus, for example, the unjustified construction of large and extremely large enterprises, frequently regardless of economic and social consequences and despite lack of power, raw materials, and manpower, led to excessive and uncontrolled migration processes. This entailed not only catastrophic changes in the national and demographic structure of the population of a number of Union republics and oblasts but also to a worsening of the sociocultural infrastructure.

Let us add to this that the same type of deformations in the development of the Latvian national economy was the reason for a sharp worsening of the ecological situation and the decline in the 1970s and 1980s of the living standards and the health of the population. A threat to the future full development of national culture and science arose; the scope and use of the national language shrank. The existing situation demands urgent changes.

We must create an entirely new type of federation. Such was the instruction given to us by our voters. Naturally, in terms of its nature this is a revolutionary and extremely complex matter. An entire array of problems must be solved in a new and unusual fashion. The key among them, in our view, are the decisive decentralization of the Union by demarcating and reassigning rights in favor of Union republics, and establishing an efficient legal mechanism for the coordination of interests between the USSR and the Union republics.

Dear deputies, allow me to cite a few examples of the specific nature of our proposals. Let us begin with the fact that Article 76 of the USSR Constitution, which stipulates that a Union republic is a sovereign Soviet socialist state, clearly conflicts with other articles in that same Constitution. An example of this is Article 73, which interprets the competence of the USSR so loosely that virtually all rights could be interpreted as applicable on the federal level, as well as Article 74, according to which any Soviet law, even if it has been promulgated on problems pertaining exclusively to the competence of a Union republic, is legally superior to any law of a Union republic.

In order somehow to eliminate even this contradiction alone, we suggest that Article 74 be amended as follows: "The laws of the USSR on problems which are within the competence of the Union will have the same power on the territory of all Union republics." Furthermore, we believe that a sovereign state, such as a Union republic, should also have legal guarantees for this sovereignty, the right to ratify the USSR Constitution and its amendments in particular.

Let us now consider Article 174 which defines the procedure for amending the Constitution of the USSR by decision of the Congress of People's Deputies of the USSR. It is formulated in such a way that even if all deputies of a Union republic in the USSR Congress of People's Deputies would vote against amendments and they would be rejected by the supreme legislator of the republic, the law on amending the USSR Constitution would nonetheless be enacted on the territory of all Union republics. The result, therefore, is that the conditions according to which, according to the Constitution there are "sovereign Soviet socialist states," i.e., Union republics, united within the USSR, could be amended not only without their agreement but even against their will.

Today one frequently hears views about centrifugal trends and accusations of separatism. Sometimes even the mention of words such as autonomy, sovereignty, and independence are immediately interpreted as appeals to withdraw from the USSR. I believe that in this area there are many misunderstandings and unnecessary suspicion or simply ignorance.

Nonetheless, what kind of independence are we discussing, and what do we mean by this term?

First, it means an acknowledgment of the fact that our state is constituted by sovereign Union republics, which have the right freely, without any outside pressure, to define their domestic and internal political status. Hence our motion of redrafting Article 70 of the USSR Constitution to read as follows: "The Union of Soviet Socialist Republics is a Union multinational state formed on the basis of a Union treaty as a result of the voluntary unification of equal Soviet socialist republics. This unification is based on the principle of the free self-determination of nations."

STENOGRAPHIC RECORD

Seventh Session

31 May 1989

Second, it means acknowledging the need for the reapportionment of state powers in such a way that Union republics could themselves, on their own territory, exercise full state power. (Applause). In this case we proceed from the fact that the Union republics are primary and the federation is their resultant. The republics alone can grant to the Union or recover a specific right rather than vice versa, for it is the republics that made the Union. (Applause).

Third, a republic cannot be considered a sovereign state unless it has the right independently to handle its territory and resources. According to Article 11 of the USSR Constitution, the land, the soil, waters, forests, and basic means of production are the exclusive property of the state, i.e., the common property of the Soviet people. However, it is difficult to imagine the possible type of economic independence of a republic if constitutionally the land, the soil, water, timber, and any other resources created or located on the territory of a given republic has not been constitutionally codified as the property of the people of that same Union republic.

Fourth, and last, a sovereign state cannot be limited in its economic activities. In this connection, we appeal to the people's deputies of the USSR. The current Constitution gives us the right at this congress to pass laws on everything. But if we think about it, however, this clashes with the principle of the sovereignty of the republics. Let us hope that in their legislative activities both the USSR Congress of People's Deputies and the Supreme Soviet will limit themselves to problems of federative relations, leaving the rest to the republic legislators. (Applause).

What conclusion can be drawn from all this? The conclusion is that one of the decisive aspects in the implementation of the Leninist ideas of Soviet federalism is respect for the right of nations to self-determination. Without this we cannot achieve reciprocal understanding and trust in our multinational Union state. We must not forget that sovereignty is the inalienable right of the people and the state. Let us behave toward this right sensibly and respectfully.

If we are to be honest, we must admit that occasionally we are short of displaying a sensible and respectful attitude. That precisely is the basis of the tension among nationalities in Latvia, which sometimes assumes a nationalistic or chauvinistic aspect. However much we may condemn such shameful phenomena, they will remain unless we eliminate the social roots of tension among nationalities.

Therefore, economic and political autonomy are not a self-seeking aim but a means of improving the living environments not only of the Latvian people but of the entire population in our Republic. In Latvia there is a uniform understanding of problems of economics, culture, and language. However, the ways to solve them are sometimes drastically different. Sometimes priority is given to subjective considerations of specific population groups.

In our hard-earned practice we proceed from the fact that national problems cannot be solved through referenda. They can be solved only through patient search and mutually acceptable decisions. For no single nation can be happy if its happiness is built on the misfortune of another. (Applause).

Therefore, the main question is how to seek such a mutual acceptance? Should it be through ultimata, strikes or a political dialogue based on mutual respect? The Latvian Communist Party Central Committee and the Latvian SSR Supreme Soviet firmly stated both at the plenum and the session that political problems can be solved only through political means. (Applause).

We believe that the sovereignty of Latvia, allied with other republics, is consistent with the interests of people of all nationalities who have linked their destinies to the fate of our Republic. We shall observe this principle strictly. I thank you for your attention. (Applause).

A.-M.K. Brazauskas: Deputy Mutalibov has the floor.

A.N. Mutalibov, chairman of the Council of Ministers of the Azerbaijan SSR (Kubatlinskiy National-Territorial Electoral District, Azerbaijan SSR): Dear Mikhail Sergeyevich! Dear comrade deputies. Hardly anyone today doubts that democratization and glasnost, which were born of restructuring, have become irreversible. This is confirmed by the entire atmosphere, the entire situation in which our congress is being held. The working people of Soviet Azerbaijan and the people's deputies in our delegation accepted the report submitted by Mikhail Sergeyevich Gorbachev as a thorough and self-critical analysis of accomplishments during the period of restructuring and as a program for our further joint work. Despite the difficult and rather complex problems which exist in the country, restructuring has set our society on the move. The question is only of the speed and efficiency with which it is moving, what should our attention be concentrated on in the immediate future, and with what we should begin. The problems which have accumulated in the country and in all its areas apply, to one extent or another, to Azerbaijan as well. Disproportions and the errors which were made in the past have created a stressed economic situation in the Republic. Inherent in Azerbaijan are a monopoly in agriculture, and an industry oriented toward the extraction of raw materials and the production and procurement of semi-finished goods. Consequently, in terms of per capita production the Republic has reached a quite high indicator. Nonetheless, in terms of problems of social insurance or, more accurately, of anything which defines the living standard of the people, we have fallen seriously behind the average Union indicators which, as I understand it, no longer satisfy the Soviet people.

Naturally, this type of economic structure does not ensure today the solution of the most topical, the most vital problems related, in particular, to the production of

Seventh Session

31 May 1989

consumer goods and a wide range of services. This causes an imbalance in monetary circulation and other negative phenomena.

Such a social background demanded of us the formulation and taking of efficient steps and nonstandard decisions. This is helped by the restructuring taking place in the country. I do not wish to be accused of making self-serving reports, but, comrades, within a relatively short time a decisive turn has been taken in implementing tasks in the social area, which was the most lagging and most worrisome for the working people of Azerbaijan. For example, the volume of individual housing construction doubled and we intend to increase its pace. There has been activity in food supplies and medical services, and a program of computerization is being implemented, along with improving the structure of industrial production aimed at the development of sectors with the help of which we can solve problems of using the surplus manpower. Comrades, a struggle is being waged and is intensifying against corruption and the illegal economy and all types of crime. These are merely the first indications of restructuring, merely the beginning of the work.

We can reach higher standards only by efficiently mastering new economic management methods and implementing the measures suggested in Comrade Mikhail Sergeyevich Gorbachev's report. We consider territorial cost accounting the shortest way to an upsurge in the Republic's production forces. That is why we fully support the line of broadening economic independence and increasing the sovereignty of Union republics. In this connection, I suggest that we speed up the formulation of the law on self-management and self-financing of Union republics and not to experiment but to master these principles as a whole in all republics, for all of them are interested in this.

I would also like to emphasize that the new system of economic interrelationships must not erode the principles of Soviet federalism but contribute to their strengthening. There can be no strong union republics without a strong center, and vice versa. Nonetheless, of late attempts have been made to apply the concept of regional cost accounting as a kind of screen to conceal autarchic trends. This is fraught with the danger of the disruption of economic relations among Union republics. Incidentally, let me point out that long before the conversion to territorial cost accounting, as planned for 1989, as you know, more than 50 percent of the output going into the national economy and its use were based on direct contracts. We have tremendous difficulties which can be expressed through the single concept of the diktat of labor collectives: I sign a contract if I want to and I do not if I do not want to. For that reason this very year industry is in a feverish state, in our Republic in particular. In all likelihood, this applies to other areas as well.

This must not be allowed under the conditions of a state structured on the basis of the principles of a voluntary alliance among sovereign republics, closely linked with economic and cultural ties, sharing a common history and a political system. The unified national economic complex is a tremendous accomplishment of the social system and, comrades, it should not go to waste. This is our view. Today integration processes are a common global trend. Can we ignore it?

Development is impossible without extensive equivalent exchange of goods. We acknowledge the need for sensible specialization and cooperation. However, we must not allow the one-sided development of the national economy of one republic or another, or its conversion to or use as a raw material appendage.

We must consider the right of the republics to market independently goods produced above the limit of state orders along with raw materials and production waste which can be used with a view to supplying the republic markets with consumer goods through trade. This will make it possible to reduce our appealing to the central authorities.

It may not have been necessary to mention this today if we had not felt in actual economic practices the aspiration of the center to direct the republics into self-support, on the one hand, and occasionally to increase the production of goods which distort the structure of the local economy, aggravate the ecological situation, and trigger an imbalance in monetary circulation, on the other.

Today we are trying to solve such problems relying on our own forces as well. We try to eliminate feelings of dependency. However, there also are problems in which we need the support of the center. In particular, this includes important matters, such as perfecting the structure of our republic's industry and creating new jobs because of the very grave demographic situation. In this connection, I use this opportunity to express my disagreement, for example, with the decision (however difficult the financial situation in the country may be today) to halt the building of a number of industrial enterprises, such as the plant for personal computers in Baku, the automotive plant in Kirovabad, where two-thirds of the capital investments have already been made, and the carpets combine in Nakhichevan, the construction of which is essentially completed. Such activities on the part of the central departments, which are in the spirit of administrative-command management methods, comrades, are unacceptable today.

The commissioning of these projects would make it possible, among others, to reduce the commodity shortage and provide jobs for tens of thousands of people. For in addition to the already employed population, we must provide jobs to another 65,000 able-bodied people among those who have come to our Republic as a result of the familiar events in the Armenian SSR. In this connection, we deem necessary to request of the new government to consider with great attention the problem of a labor surplus in the Republic, surplus which is the basic resource for the production forces in our country.

Seventh Session
31 May 1989

Comrade deputies, through joint efforts we must also solve the problem of the touchy aspects of relations among nationalities, including the problem of Nagornyy Karabakh. Although they may be quite specific, essentially they are typical of many parts of the country. They are based on the deformation which was allowed to occur in the past in the system of social relations and the fact that socioeconomic and moral-psychological problems remained unsolved. Such problems must be solved in a tranquil atmosphere and not through strikes, power pressure or violations of the sovereign rights of republics. The decree of the CPSU Central Committee and USSR Council of Ministers on radically improving the situation in the NKAO called for the appropriation of substantial funds to this effect. Everything possible must be done to make use of this help. However, there still are many forces which, as they pursue their specific objectives, are blocking positive changes and preventing the elimination of ethnic confrontations.

It is time to draw a clear line between those who indeed are aspiring to an improvement in relations among nationalities and the socioeconomic transformation of this area, and those who do nothing but formulate territorial claims. They have already caused a great deal of trouble and harm! We believe, as was said by many people during the proceedings of this congress and, apparently, more will be said on the subject, that the laws must be strictly observed and applied in ensuring order, guaranteeing the security and the defense of all people wherever they may live and whatever their nationality. In his report the respected Mikhail Sergeyevich particularly emphasized this thought which we support entirely. Our voters demand that we turn from appeals to decisive action in the application of the laws which, incidentally, were passed by the Soviet people in defense of their interests.

Comrades, of late ecological problems have assumed particular gravity. We too are particularly affected by them. The authors of a motion picture which was recently shown on central television described Sumgait as a dead zone. Here chemical works have taken over from man and led the city into an ecological crisis. Many such cities exist both in our Republic and throughout the country. The situation which has developed in them is related to departmental egotism and scorn for the interests of man. Nonetheless, we must also point out that this is the result of the irresponsibility of the labor collectives themselves and their immediate superiors and all of us, comrades. A great deal has already been said on this subject and now specific action is needed!

We are doing a great deal of work which, incidentally, is monitored by our entire public. We are not following the path of confrontation with Union ministries or closing down chemically and ecologically harmful production facilities for, as I understand it, our country's national economy cannot do without them.

Let me cite as an example the interesting work which we have been doing of late with the managers of our ministries and the USSR Council of Ministers. Let me mention Comrade Vladimir Kuzmich Gusev, who has repeatedly come to our Republic to discuss such matters, and Comrade Ministers Bespalov and Olshanskiy. It is only in such unity that we see a solution to all problems which concern us.

Considering that problems of ecology are today holding the attention of the entire public, our delegation deems necessary to submit the motion of setting up within the USSR Supreme Soviet a special environmental protection commission.

Comrades, the solution of economic problems requires interregional integration. Take, for example, the question of the Caspian Sea, the cleanliness of which we can never achieve by ourselves, without cooperating with the various oblasts along the Volga, Daghestan, and the Kazakh and Turkmen SSRs. To this purpose we suggest the creation of a Caspian Institute, which could help us to join efforts.

Comrades, ensuring the population with food is problem number one. Its solution depends on a number of factors. I would like today to single out that of reclamation. An antireclamation mood has been growing in the country of late. Without excusing in the least the numerous distortions, I believe that today it is impossible to farm in a way guaranteed to block the influence of nature without reclamation.

Comrades, the restructuring under way in the country has drawn near yet another significant stage: the drafting of laws which define the rights of the USSR, Union republics, and autonomous formations. Can it be considered normal that out of the innumerable number of legal acts which regulate economic regulations it is only an insignificant part, literally isolated units, that are in the form of laws? This is by no means a formal feature, for in the absence of a law which has a supreme juridical force, we have regulations adopted by executive authorities—that is, by the same administrative apparatus.

Let me also mention our attitude toward improving the activities of the Council of Nationalities. Let me take one aspect. The question is raised for all problems relative to interrepublic and internationality relations which may be submitted to the Congress of People's Deputies for its consideration to be considered by the USSR Supreme Soviet. We believe that such problems must be mandatorily coordinated with the Union republics, particularly those which affect changing the borders, and establishing new autonomous formations. The decisions which are passed in such cases must be strictly based on Article 78 of the USSR Constitution. (Applause).

STENOGRAPHIC RECORD

Seventh Session

31 May 1989

A.-M.K. Brazauskas: I ask the comrades to observe the rules. Here is another announcement: We receive here letters, some motions, and even questions. Deputies are asking when will the results of the vote on the NKAO be made public. I am hereby reporting that the Presidium intends to do this at the end of our morning session. This will be approximately at 1:40. Therefore, please have this in mind. Now Deputy Boris Ilich Oleynik, secretary of the board, Union of Writers of the Ukrainian SSR has the floor. The next speaker will be Comrade Zoya Pavlovna Pukhova.

B.I. Oleynik, poet, secretary of the board of the Ukrainian SSR Writers Union, Kiev (from the Communist Party of the Soviet Union): Dear chairman and comrade deputies, although I am speaking, as you have probably noticed, on behalf of the most humble and loyal Republic, I am not particularly shocked by the excited activeness and emotionalism of the deputies who, without waiting to be called by the chair, march on to the rostrum. We are merely beginning to learn democracy and the standards of parliamentarianism. Nonetheless, I have to point out that in the natural aspiration to prove their activeness to the electorate glued to their television screens, in the first days we primarily showed them not our inspired faces but, forgive me, our backs. I am touched to tears on the way trustingly, intimately opening up to the people's deputies and, consequently, to our entire domestic and global community, we literally leaned on the shoulder of the head of the state, obviously sharing with him our most intimate thoughts. (Laughter, applause).

This generosity of our character and simplicity of mores have been noted not only by the excited domestic viewer but also the foreign public, shaken up by such democracy. (Laughter). I address such observations above all to myself, comrades. For in my village, Zachepilovka, there has not been any consulate with its protocol department. Therefore, we are learning from each other.

Naturally, we would like to solve all problems immediately. I realize that everyone is answerable to his voters, who expect of us something real, and to let them down would be the equivalent of certifying to our own insolvency. However, in order not to disappoint them we should not deceive ourselves in trying hastily to solve all problems.

It would be worth to consider several specific problems and solve them here. Otherwise we would find it difficult to look our voters in the eyes. Here are, in my view, some of them.

Above all, we must find ways, even by eliminating some overall alluring programs, to add, albeit a little bit, to the wages and pensions of people who live below or on the line of poverty, in order not to burn with national shame. (Applause).

The biggest tangle of problems is in the area of nationalities. Let us firmly and frankly say that such tangles can be unraveled only by strictly professing the ideas of federalism, according to which each republic and it alone should be both the subject and the sovereign body in correcting the accumulated deformations. The solution of the linguistic problem in kindergartens, schools, PTU, technical colleges, and VUZs, in office work or science or, in short, in all material and spiritual structures, should be achieved in such a way that the language of the native nation not be like a subservient day worker but a first-class proud master of his native home. (Applause).

In short, I favor the model and idea of the Baltic republics, supported by the prime minister of Kazakhstan: Strong republics mean a strong center, for it is the roots that nourish the crown and not vice versa. Naturally, as we raise the national self-awareness—the sacred feeling of love for the history and laws of our ancestors—to the same extent we must develop within ourselves respect for all nations, for national isolation, as Oles Gonchar has pointed out, is the most terrible thing in this interrelated and interdependent world. However, formalism and equalization are absolutely unacceptable in such a sensitive area. Naturally, we also have common general difficulties and, at the same time, each republic has its own specific problems. For example, in the Ukraine and Belorussia the right of parents to choose the language in which their children will be educated is by no means all that ideal as it may be for other republics, perhaps for the fact alone that in some cities there simply is no choice, for there are no Belorussian and Ukrainian schools at all. In such exceptional cases, in addition to said parental rights we must also stipulate the right of nations to self-defense. For example, we favor granting the Ukrainian language the status of a state language, having emphasized that on such a state level we must contribute to the development of the languages of all nationalities living in the Ukraine. Naturally, this includes Russian, as the tried instrument of international communication.

Of late, however, and not without the participation of central television, the idea is being increasingly promoted of giving the Russian language the status of a state language, along with the national language. I believe that such a step would be a direct retreat from the initial idea which was supported by the overwhelming majority of republic voters. (Applause). In the final account, has anyone ever asked whether the Russians themselves want this? I am confident that the overwhelming majority of Russians will consider this an insulting mistrust in their powerful language which for many decades has been used voluntarily by the peoples of our country as a reliable bridge of brotherhood.

But is it not a paradox for the great Russian people themselves to be the worst harmed from the national aspect point of view, having neither their own communist party nor academy of sciences. Furthermore Russia

STENOGRAPHIC RECORD

Seventh Session

31 May 1989

which, together with Belorussia and the Ukraine, endured just about the heaviest burden of the Great Patriotic War, is not even represented in the United Nations. (Applause).

As to the term "bilingualism" itself: If it is true that the language is the soul of the people, does it not seem to you that this combination of words deliberately leads to another less seemly one? (Applause). I would ask the government and the Politburo to pay attention to and make an example of punishing officials, particularly local ones, who are fiercely opposing restructuring in the area of relations among nationalities and are persecuting, to put it bluntly, the members of the Ukrainian Language Society imeni Taras Grigoryevich Shevchenko.

One should not immediately clutch at one's heart at the sight of an ancient symbol, shall we say in Tallinn or Lvov. For the sources which feed the river of popular history are not to be blamed if, along any part of that river, garbage has been thrown in it. The river must be cleaned, for it is precisely out of this river that future generations will satisfy their thirst for knowledge as to who are their fathers and whose children we are.

A problem directly related to strengthening the sovereignty of republics is that of protecting the habitat and defending it from the invasions of central departments which are building with impunity nuclear power plants, chemical monsters, and all sorts of canals wherever they deem fit. And since, as a rule, the departments present their unwanted gifts to humanized cultural and historical centers, which have been inhabited for centuries, such as Kiev, Chigirin, Kanev, Zaporozhye, Rovno, and Khmelnitskiy, and since such mines are being laid not only under national holies but also under the entire republic, the struggle against these newly hatched industrial aggressors emerges on the forefront. Indeed, one or two more Chernobyls, God forbid, and there will be no one left to fight for language or culture in general. (Applause).

We must point out that in this sometimes uneven struggle initial victories have already been scored. The governmental resolution, which was recently published in the republic press, signed by Nikolay Ivanovich Ryzhkov, on halting the building of the Chigirin nuclear power plant, triggered nationwide rejoicing in the Ukraine. But what about the Crimean one? For there is no single nuclear power plant in the world where such a threatening combination of geophysical dangers, specifically the possibility of earthquakes as high as 10 points, tsunami, the shifting of large masses of water of the Azov Sea, and ground shifts caused by active tectonic breaks, and gas and mud volcanism and sliding clay of the dome on which rests the Crimean nuclear power plant has come together.

Dear comrades from the Politburo and colleagues from the Supreme Soviet! This enumeration alone gives us grounds here to pass a resolution on immediately halting the building of the Crimean nuclear power plant. (Applause). The more as since all four task forces of the governmental commission have reached, by overwhelming majority vote, the conclusion that the planned seismicity of the station of seven points has been inadmissibly lowered. Comrades, without outside consultants, let us combine our spirit and, for the sake of life on earth, halt by ourselves the building of the Crimean nuclear power plant.

After the Chernobyl tragedy, on Belorussian territory alone, not to mention in the Ukraine, more than 520,000 people were exposed to radiation. To this day the Chernobyl nuclear power plant is a nursery of radioactive contamination with unforeseeable results. In order to put out this source, which is a threat to all mankind, we must as of now take the only sensible decision of closing down definitively the Chernobyl nuclear power plant. (Applause).

I must tell you that the radioactive situation, the assertions of the Ministry of Atomic Power and Ministry of Health notwithstanding, is very difficult. To this day there are people living on a territory with a pollution in excess of 15 curies per square kilometer. Judging by the maps published in PRAVDA, the contamination is even higher in Belorussia, in some Bryansk areas. I therefore firmly support the appeal to the present congress addressed by the collective of the Institute of Geological Sciences of the Republic's Academy of Sciences, which asks, in particular, that information on the ecological situation including radiation, be assessed for each oblast, rayon, and settlement. An end must be put to the practice of having departments review existing standards in connection with changing situations and publish temporary admissible standards (VDU) of radioactive contamination, accepted by the Ministry of Health for the post-breakdown period. We must demand of the government to find ways and means of urgently removing the population from areas under strict radiation regime.

Based on the universal human principles of humanism and charity, and taking into consideration the real threat to the genetic stock of the Ukraine, Belorussia, and some Russian oblasts as a result of the accident, we must develop a national program for the protection of children, with mandatory organization of medical-sanatorium "mother and child" complexes, to treat the children from the afflicted territories.

We must draft and pass a law on the criminal liability of officials who conceal or distort information on the ecological and, specifically, the radiation situation and its effect on the population's health, for through their actions they grossly violate human rights and threaten human existence itself. (Applause). Until such a law has been passed, we must consider the question of the official involvement of leading personnel of different departments and commissions responsible for the existing situation.

Seventh Session

31 May 1989

I call upon those who have taken the Hippocratic Oath: Do not commit blasphemy by accusing the people of radiophobia. If such radiophobia has been noticed, it has come above all from the radio, on which the people are being falsely deceived, lulling them with false information. This sin is as unforgivable as the one of building reactors and burial sites for particularly dangerous substances secretly from the people. In this connection, I would like to obtain an explanation on the building of new blocks at the South Ukrainian and Rovno nuclear power plants where, as it were, the operating units are already short of water.

I would urgently request that rumors be either confirmed or denied of installing facilities for the burial of harmful waste within the 30-km plant area between Khmelnitskiy and Vinnitsa Oblasts. I have already presented the congress with the appeal, bearing hundreds of signatures by the population of Derazhnyanskiy Rayon on this subject.

Briefly, all departments, including the nuclear, must finally realize that before building their latest reactor, they should ask the permission of the people and the government of the respective sovereign socialist republic.

We shall be unable to solve these and other no less grave problems without proper consideration of the countryside, to which our state owes a great deal and will owe a great deal for quite some time. Already now, however, we must start by doing perhaps the minimum, equalizing the peasant with the worker in terms of pensions. This applies to the peasant who, in the course of his difficult 70 years does not know the meaning of a free day, paid leave, and a rest home, not to mention sanatorium, who spends his entire life in the mud of roadlessness, degradingly begging the bosses for a cord of word, and not even suspecting that in the vicinity of his village there are pipes carrying gas for the city. I believe that this endlessly patient laborer deserves to live a human life at least in his old age. (Applause).

I am not even mentioning the war widows, who plow the lean soil with their cows, who fed all fronts and the rear and who, crippled and alone, raised us, the half-orphans, as decent people and taught us how to live by the dictates of our conscience, and who received, for all this, a few miserable pennies. Unless we have lost our last bits of conscience, God himself would demand that they be given all the benefits of front line veterans. I thank you for your attention. (Applause).

A.-M.K. Brazauskas: Comrade Zoya Pavlovna Pukhova, chairman, Soviet Women's Committee, has the floor.

Z.P. Pukhova, chairman, Soviet Women's Committee, Moscow (for the women's councils united within the Soviet Women's Committee): Dear comrade deputies, I speak as a deputy representing the women's councils. I speak on behalf of the women, on behalf of those whose voices frequently remain unheard. Yet the questions which we raise are some of the most pressing and sensitive ones affecting our society. They affect the interests of one-half of the population of our country, one-half of those employed in the national economy.

What is it that concerns us, what do the women expect of this congress? They expect a real improvement in their situation. Not endless discussions, such as have become fashionable on how difficult it is for our women, but specific actions, practical steps to improve their life. In his report, Mikhail Sergeyevich stated that the women must be helped. So far, however, there has been no policy aimed at improving the situation of the women. There has been no governmental, overall, unified policies which would take into consideration national and regional features. Meanwhile the problems remain.

Comrades, let us ask ourselves: Why is it that there are more women than men working the night shift, and are there are more women performing hard manual labor and working in industries harmful to the health? What about the protection of motherhood? The family as well is waiting for real help. This is only part of the problem, the tip of the iceberg. And how much remains still under the surface? All such problems are interrelated. Therefore, they can be solved only comprehensively, through a unified state policy.

Today we must establish which are the priority tasks. We are confident that priority must be given to the entire set of problems which affect the interests of women and the family. Naturally, a strong social policy demands substantial funds. Such funds should be sought above all by bringing order in our planning and putting an end to irresponsibility in the country. We expect that the funds released as a result of reductions in the military budget will be part of those used for such purposes. The deputies who said here that we must live according to our means, assessing such means thoroughly, carefully, and sensibly, are right.

Comrade deputies, I assume that the reason for which many of you included the solution of the women's problem in your electoral programs was not merely to obtain the votes of the women. Today the women expect your actions so that the state of affairs can be changed in its essence.

The newly elected Supreme Soviet is setting up a committee on women's affairs. In no case should this committee become a women's commission in which women alone will solve their problems. This, comrades, is not a women's council under the Supreme Soviet. The establishment of such a committee should be based not on sex but on the fact that this is a general social problem, a problem of governmental significance.

We see it as a committee with legislative and control functions. We have many good laws the strict observance of which could substantially change the state of affairs. It

Seventh Session

31 May 1989

is time, finally, to supervise their implementation by ministries and departments which, ignoring the laws, are continuing barbarically to use women's manual labor, considering this less bothersome and more profitable than the application of the achievements of scientific and technical progress.

Reality calls for the formulation of new legislation which would enable us promptly to react to changes which are inevitable in our dynamic times, above all in the area of economics.

Under the conditions of the economic reform, enterprises and some republics have the possibility of directing some of their profits to help the various social groups among the population, including families with children. This would apply, for example, to wages and extending the leave of women to care for newborn children. However, so far we have no legal foundation for this. Could it turn out that such initiatives, which are needed in our society, prove to be illegal?

Comrades, we have an even greater fear. Could it be that it would be exclusively the Committee on Women's Affairs that would be dealing with such problems? Let us consider the protection of motherhood and childhood. In the final account, this ensures the health of the generations. Is it possible for such questions not to be the concern of the committee on health or ecological problems? For this, too, affects the health of our children, our future.

Here is another aspect of the matter: The active work of women who are people's deputies is necessary in all committees and commissions without exception: financial-budgetary, international relations, and international affairs. We appeal to you as well, Mikhail Sergeyevich, as chairman of the Supreme Soviet. We would like to hear in your speeches and in the speeches of the other heads of the party and the government, a more profound formulation of the question of the status of women in our country.

At the 19th All-Union Party Conference you called the women's problem a problem of governmental significance. Therefore, the approach to the problem as well must be governmental. In this connection, we would also like to turn to the USSR Council of Ministers and its chairman. A great deal in solving the women's problem depends on your actions. In particular, this applies to the decision to create a governmental mechanism on women's affairs. It is shameful to admit that in such matters we are behind not only the developed but many developing countries. A great deal was said about this 1 year ago, at the 19th All-Union Party Conference. Meanwhile, no resolutions were passed then and nor are there any now.

Here is another problem: It is extremely regrettable that the number of women among the people's deputies is quite modest. Women account for no more than 17 percent of the deputies. Naturally, to a certain extent this is our fault as well. However, it is a common problem, for in elections based on territorial and national-territorial districts, there were entire oblasts and even Union republics which neither nominated nor elected a single woman. Furthermore, how many women have been nominated by the party, the Komsomol or the other public organizations? The result is that women can work alongside the men and even in night shifts, and engage in hard and occasionally unhealthy type of work, but when it comes to participating in deciding the future of the country and handling their own destinies and those of their children, they are not given such an opportunity.

In conclusion, let me say this as well: Today there is considerable tension in the society. It comes out in debates, meetings, and even the proceedings of our congress. I am confident, however, that a solution does exist. It is found in conducting a respectful dialogue, in engaging in the joint search for decisions and the aspiration not only to formulate claims but also to listen to one another and to join forces. I thank you for your attention. (Applause).

M.S. Gorbachev: Dear comrades, today our outstanding Russian writer Leonid Maksimovich Leonov is celebrating his 90th birthday. Let us wish him well on behalf of our congress. (Applause, all rise).

A.-M.K. Brazauskas: Comrades, I announce an intermission of 30 minutes.

(Intermission).

A.-M.K. Brazauskas: Comrades, let us continue our work. Comrade Boris Nikolayevich Yeltsin has the floor.

B.N. Yeltsin (Moscow City National-Territorial Electoral District, RSFSR): Dear comrade deputies! Dear voters of Moscow and other parts of the country! This congress is solving the main problem which will determine the future of our society. It is the question of power which must justifiably belong to the people represented by its supreme legislative authority, i.e., the Congress of People's Deputies.

My motion of a real transfer, precisely at this first congress, of the power from the party to the soviets, was not supported at the CPSU Central Committee Plenum held on the eve. The decision was made to recommend to leading positions those same individuals who had failed to take the society out of the crises in politics, economics, finances, and living standards. Added to this are the agenda and the procedure for the congress, drafted without taking the views of the deputies into consideration. I believe that this approach belittles the role of those elected by the entire people.

STENOGRAPHIC RECORD

Seventh Session

31 May 1989

Paradoxical though it might be, this congress, which must assume the power and responsibility for restructuring and the reorganization of society, has turned out to be the hostage of the laws and resolutions passed by the preceding Supreme Soviet, which was established during the period of stagnation.

The most important problems of state power and management which, by the logic of the laws should be considered by the congress itself, were predetermined before the congress yet we are asked to vote for them. The rights of the congress in establishing the supreme power authorities and filling positions are extremely reduced. The only independent election was that of chairman of the USSR Supreme Soviet. The Presidium of the Supreme Soviet will no longer be elected. There is no choice. Under these circumstances, the danger is not excluded that the Supreme Soviet, together with its Presidium, may turn out into an apparatus or, shall we say, a semi-apparatus under the chairman.

Meanwhile, the situation in the country remains extremely alarming. Anti-restructuring forces have become stronger and more consolidated; the second economy and corruption are developing; crime is rising; the moral foundations of society are being eroded; the problems of young people, who need the political confidence of our entire society, for the future belongs to them, are becoming aggravated.

The stratification of society on the basis of wealth is intensifying. The principles of social justice and social equality are not being implemented. The number of poor people is growing and the faith of the Soviet people in the real results of restructuring is declining. Contradictions in relations among nationalities are becoming aggravated. Obviously, we must create a Supreme Soviet commission on small nationalities.

The solution of the food problem is dragging out. The cumbersome administrative superstructure in agriculture remains. All that has changed is the names, and functions have been reassigned. How can one simultaneously restructure and hammer out anti-restructuring laws? In the year after the party conference, which supported a course of democratization, we struck with a single Ukase meetings and demonstrations; another Ukase hit at glasnost and yet another allowed the use of special troops against our own people. Naturally, there is also the unfortunate Article 11.1, the author of which we are still unable to identify and who, possibly, is sitting among us.

It is precisely in an atmosphere of such a prohibiting legislation, particularly of late, that crimes become possible such as those committed in Tbilisi. I was there and I realized that this precisely was a crime, a crime against our own people. In addition to the creation of a commission to investigate the Tbilisi events, in order somehow to calm the people down, the congress must be told who, nonetheless, made the decision in the center. (Applause). For this is something known to the leadership.

Today the broadest possible popular masses have not truly become involved in the management of the state. Our press, which did so much during the first steps of restructuring, continues to remain under the control of a group of individuals and does not reflect the entire variety of opinions of the members of our society. The governmental and social institutions are not being subjected to any whatsoever serious changes and are not being reduced. Their cumbersomeness is an unbearable burden to society.

The creators of stagnation have set legislative areas which remain outside the reach of the law. Organized crime has penetrated all social structures, including its superior echelons and the party. The domestic market has become disorganized. Inflation has increased. There are lines and rationing, and the threat of a financial collapse has become real.

The administrative-command system has not been eliminated. As in the past, the power belongs to the party-bureaucratic apparat. Like any revolution from above, as it develops and intensifies, restructuring affects all social strata. However, it affects most essentially the interests of the apparat itself as the power system. Hence the lack of resolve and the halfway nature of the decisions which are being made, running idle before taking any single step forward, shifts to the right and the left or even backpedaling. Hence the complicated, unnatural and, sometimes, even distorted decisions, encrusted with instructions. Many examples of this can be cited. The cumbersome power system suits exclusively the apparat. It gives it space for maneuvering and allows it, based on its experience and organization, and benefiting from the inexperience and disorganization of the deputies, to influence their decisions.

Comrades, the planned program and the promises given over the 4 years of restructuring, have not been fulfilled. The life of the people has worsened. Such is, in my view, the political evaluation of the present times. A certain self-criticism included in the speech by Comrade Gorbachev does not eliminate his responsibility for all this.

Let me say very briefly what and how, in my view, matters should be carried out for restructuring to move ahead. Above all, the USSR Congress of People's Deputies should consider the targets and tasks of the society and, taking them into consideration, set up commissions and begin to draft the new Constitution.

I believe that one of the tasks is firmly to decentralize the power and the economy, and to dismantle the command-administrative system. It is precisely from this that comes today the danger that society may return to the

STENOGRAPHIC RECORD

Seventh Session

31 May 1989

past. Laws must be drafted to lay the foundations for the reorganization of society and for ensuring a radical change in production relations.

"The land to the peasant!" Yes, we must finally implement this slogan and the peasants themselves must determine the ways and means of farming and management. I fully support today the appeal of those who work in the countryside. (Applause). Unquestionably, not only the government and the Central Committee but the entire people must help the peasants. It is only then that we shall be able to move ahead in ensuring the country's food supply.

We must provide guarantees for the broadest possible democratization and glasnost and not hinder them, something which is already taking place. In order to accomplish this we must pass a law on the press. The mass information media should not belong on a mass basis to the party authorities. They must become increasingly independent. Today society has an urgent need for a collective search of ways to surmount the crisis. We must consult with the people. We must bring to light their tremendous creative and intellectual potential. We need a brain center of talented scientists, political experts, and economists who would formulate a strategy for the development of society, including a strategy for the development of the countryside.

The working people must be constitutionally given the right to elect the head of state from several candidates through universal, equal, and direct elections. Above all, we must solve the question of the role and place of the party in society. The formulation and adoption of the law on the party is an urgent task. Such a law would define the range of competencies and rights in decision making by the party authorities.

These are critical times and we cannot wait. The processes of party democratization are falling seriously behind the pace of democratization of society. The authority of the party among the masses is declining. In my view, the state of affairs in the party can be corrected by holding an extraordinary 28th CPSU Congress, the delegates to which should represent the entire party, chosen through alternate and direct elections held by primary organizations. Such a party congress should also consider problems of the general concept of restructuring, its strategy and tactics, and the purity of party ranks, and elect a new membership of the Central Committee, for its present one has failed to solve the formulated assignments within this period. (Applause).

I deem it necessary to touch upon such internal party problems at the Congress of People's Deputies, taking into consideration the special role and significance of our party in our society and its initiative in restructuring. Understandably, without a radical restructuring in the party the process of changes in society will not advance any further. The reform of the political system presumes radical changes in the structure of the authorities in charge of management, their functions and their rights. In 4 years nothing essential has been accomplished in this respect. The monopoly interests of departments are a restraining factor in restructuring. We must decisively reorganize the structure of the management authorities on the basis of the principles of cost accounting and voluntary unification of commodity producers and socialist competition. The center should retain only the right to define the overall ratios and to control production through the policy of investments, taxation, and other economic methods.

The rate of exchange of the ruble must be stabilized in order to ensure the successful implementation of the economic reform and surplus paper money not secured by commodities should be withdrawn from circulation. How can this be accomplished? I suggest, as one of the approaches, that temporarily, for the next few years, to reduce by 30 percent and not by 5-7-8 percent as has been suggested, the volume of centralized capitalist investments for industrial construction and withdraw from circulation the corresponding equivalent in currency. The rate of the ruble can be stabilized by other means as well. Suggestions on this account exist. This would solve three problems: It would take care of 30 billion in unfinished construction; it would strengthen the rate of exchange of the ruble and would make it possible of the enterprises to use their earned funds, for the construction workers would be looking for customers. Supply would exceed demand and the possibility would appear of providing more goods to the domestic market. Naturally, this is only part of the program. The number of ministries must be reduced in a way more decisive than is currently taking place; those who remain must be converted to a cost accounting basis, I have in mind the apparat, rather than financing them out of the state budget. (Applause).

Today progress in the economic reform is held back by the plans and the frequently erroneous rates set for the 12th 5-year period. I believe that the only acceptable option is not to lose one more year, but to define the new plans, programs, and rates for several years, starting with 1990 and 1991, and limit this 5-year period to 4 years.

In order for the reform to advance, greater political rights must be granted along with economic and financial independence and cost accounting to each Union republic which must be given territorial sovereignty. I support in its essence the motion submitted by Deputy Gorbunov on behalf of the Baltic republics, which includes the introduction of bilingualism. (Applause). The center should retain the right to coordinate the problems affecting the interests of the state and society at large.

Laws must be passed on pensions, poverty, ecology, and forms of ownership, without delay. Under the developing conditions, the congress must, above all, adopt a state program for taking the country out of the crisis. Such a program must be in the nature of emergency

Seventh Session

31 May 1989

measures. In more than 70 years we have been unable to advance in solving the problem of achieving some kind of social justice. All the proper reasons exist to speak of the existence of a system of elitism in our society which is building socialism. (Applause). Why is it that in the country there are dozens of millions of people living below any kind of poverty line while others are swimming in luxury? Protecting the interests of the poorest and socially defenseless social strata must become a principle of social justice. Perhaps we should begin, taking into consideration the scarcity, by eliminating all illegal privileges from the nomenclatura and, in general, remove from our vocabulary the word "nomenclatura." (Applause). This would enhance the moral condition of society. We must set an official subsistence wage.

This very congress should solve perhaps one specific social problem, otherwise the people would not understand us. Let us mention free availability of medical drugs and free urban transportation for the disabled and for people living below the poverty line and solving the pension problem, albeit partially. I shall submit to the Presidium the draft decree as a legislative initiative, formulated by a rather large group of deputies. Until we have been able to solve all problems of health care, I suggest that the Fourth Main Administration of the USSR Ministry of Health be directed into providing services for motherhood and childhood, for which it has very well-qualified people. (Applause). We need this for the sake of our future, in order to avoid living in conditions according to which infant mortality in the USSR is twice that of any civilized country.

I have a few remarks on the work of the congress. I must express yet another concern. The present congress, the Constitution, and the party have granted the head of state exceptionally broad rights. We see here a rather alarming trend: Against the background of an overall worsening of the economic situation and the aggravation of national problems there is a growth of personal influence and power in the hands of the head of state. Such a gap could lead to the temptation of solving our difficult problems through power methods. We could find ourselves once again, imperceptibly, trapped by a new authoritarian regime, a new dictatorship, the more so since in 70 years we have failed to gain experience in party, parliamentary or popular control over the activities of the head of state. I believe that within the framework of building a rule of law state the present congress must create corresponding collectively operating mechanisms. I suggest as one of the elements of such a mechanism that we pass a law on an annual referendum on the subject of a vote of confidence for the chairman of the USSR Supreme Soviet. (Applause).

Comrades, the working people of the country, who have sent us to this congress, expect of us radical decisions, decisive actions in restructuring and real results. We must not disappoint them. (Applause).

A.-M.K. Brazauskas: Comrade Suren Gurgenovich Arutyunyan, first secretary of the Armenian Communist Party Central Committee, has the floor.

S.G. Arutyunyan, first secretary of the Armenian Communist Party Central Committee, Yerevan (Leninakanskiy Territorial Electoral District, Armenian SSR): Dear comrade deputies, I would like to single out among the wide range of problems raised in Mikhail Sergeyevich Gorbachev's speech those of national development and relations among nationalities, for it is precisely they that are today in the epicenter of the republic's sociopolitical life and it is precisely about them that I was instructed by the voters who sent me here to speak at the congress.

Today a most complex tangle of problems has developed in Armenia. The burden of socioeconomic difficulties and the aggravated dissatisfaction of the people, the unabated pain of historical memory and outbreaks of national self-awareness and sincere aspirations for democracy and occasional undemocratic forms of their manifestation, problems which took decades to accumulate, and the limited possibilities of solving problems which painfully affect the dignity of the people and, finally, the unparalleled earthquake which cut short the lives of hundreds of thousands of people, have created an extremely tense situation. They have triggered, a national stress, if you wish.

Anyone who visited the earthquake zone was able to see the brink of the precipice on which our people, our Republic found themselves. During the difficult hour of trial we were given a helping hand by all fraternal peoples, by the entire global community. The Armenian pain and concern became the pain and concern of the entire country. Our people will never forget this. During those tragic days we felt with particular strength the great achievement which the fraternal peoples of the USSR is.

The Armenian people have repeatedly stood on the brink of disappearance. Every time, however, they have risen, rebuilding from the ruins and ashes their cities and villages and ancient culture. The earthquake once again faced us with this task of unparalleled scale. In order to solve it we need an overall program for the revival of the Republic, a set of urgent measures for the social rehabilitation of the population and for surmounting negative demographic consequences of the elements and protecting the genetic stock of the nation.

We support regional cost accounting, economic independence, and sovereignty of republics. However, considering the extraordinary situation in which Armenia found itself, we also need new nonstandard decisions.

The interest of foreign countries, companies, and organizations in economic, scientific and technical, and monetary-credit cooperation with the Republic

Seventh Session

31 May 1989

increased sharply after the earthquake. The Armenian diaspora is ready to give us substantial help. It is an inseparable part of our people, with roots are deeply linked to the homeland.

Under these circumstances, the Republic could set up a zone of joint enterprise with the extensive involvement of foreign investments, not only in order to rebuild what was destroyed but also to solve a number of technical problems which are of interest to the entire country.

We believe that this is quite important in order to accelerate the recovery of the Republic from its condition of crisis. It is a step toward developing a mechanism for new forms of direct relations between Union republics and foreign countries. As a whole, in our view, it is necessary legislatively to define the rights of Union republics in establishing business and humanitarian relations with foreign countries in which live communities ethnically related to the nations and nationalities in our country.

Comrade deputies, the renovation processes affect the deep layers of common and global as well as local and regional interests. Reality has proved that any regional problem, unless solved on time, inevitably assumes a global nature and adversely affects the country as a whole.

For the past 18 months the drastically aggravating problem of Nagornyy Karabakh has been shaking up or Republic and our entire area and is echoing throughout the country. Here as well, in the Palace of Congresses, it was repeatedly heard these days. It tragically highlighted the entire sharp facets of relations between nationalities. For decades we repeated the high truth of Leninist national policy, that all peoples in our country are equal. For decades methodically the live shoots of relations among nationalities were cut short by officialdom.

Attempts are still being made to this day to replace a serious and honest study of the problem with high-sounding phrases about friendship and brotherhood and to reduce the aggravated nature of relations between nationalities merely, and I repeat merely, to intrigues of extremists and machinations of corrupt circles.

Confusing causes with consequences and heavy pressure on the part of the mass information media, manipulations of public opinion, and appeals for reciprocal understanding, not backed by real steps, can only aggravate the situation.

We must call things by their proper names. We are dealing with the consequences of the Stalinist anti-democratic approach to determining the destinies of nations. To acknowledge the inviolability of such decisions means to acknowledge as just and substantiated the activities of that regime which led socialism into a condition of grave deformations. I and other deputies from our Republic have been directly asked by the voters why, if today historical justice is being restored for individuals who suffered in the past, the same cannot be done when it comes to entire nations? (Applause).

Truth must be stared in the eyes. Despite the unsupported statement by Comrade Aliyev at the April 1989 CPSU Central Committee Plenum, for decades the national dignity and the social and spiritual demands of the Armenian population have been suppressed in the Nagorno-Karabakh Autonomous Oblast. Even the minimal rights granted by the Constitution to an autonomous oblast were violated. The clear and open injustice in relations between nationalities was precisely what led to the present crisis situation in the area.

Unfortunately, to this day, when it is particularly important to block even the slightest steps which lead to international discord and mistrust, frequently actions are committed which pit the interests of the Azeris against those of the Armenians in the NKAO.

We are trying to promote a normalizing of the situation, a dialogue, and a search for constructive decisions. However, we come across a variety of obstacles in establishing the natural relations between Armenia and Nagornyy Karabakh. The solution of any problem, whether economic, social or cultural, almost becomes a political problem. I do not even mention the trips by the leadership to our Republic. Men of science and culture cannot freely visit Nagornyy Karabakh.

In other words, to this day there have seen repeated occurrences of the old way of thinking and the old approaches.

For a number of years we absolutized class solidarity. We used it to lull ourselves. We see today that if national problems are neglected, national feelings may prevail in the life of a nation and an outburst of national solidarity triggered. In Armenia, the problem of Nagornyy Karabakh has become a nationwide idea, which has sunk so deeply into the hearts of the people that even the unparalleled natural catastrophe was unable to overshadow it.

The creation of the Committee for Special Administration of the NKAO is a compromise dictated by the real situation. Unfortunately, the committee inherited the legal imperfections of oblast autonomy and did not become an independent management system which would lead the autonomous oblast to the direct jurisdiction of the center. A mistrust in the committee developed among the people, the situation in the NKAO became once again aggravated, turning into a fuse worsening the situation in our Republic as well.

It is important, as was pointed out at a recent session of the CPSU Central Committee Politburo Commission on Problems of Nationalities to broaden the rights of the

Special Management Committee, and to grant it real rights independently to solve all the vitally important problems of the autonomous oblast.

At the same time, we also clearly see the need to restore the functions of the oblast authorities—the party obkom, and the oblast soviet—so that they could subsequently assume the full power and the right to be under central jurisdiction.

The country's leadership is paying great attention to the problem of Nagorno-Karabakh. Its problem has been repeatedly considered by the CPSU Central Committee Politburo, the USSR Supreme Soviet Presidium, and the government. As in the past, however, the problem remains pressing and the blood-draining wound is not healing.

Our congress has the important right of making decisions on holding referenda. I believe that the congress could exercise this right in the case of Nagornyy Karabakh. Let the population of that autonomous oblast decide its own fate freely, through the free manifestation of its will.

Each nation has its "sensitive spots." Such spots can be not only present but also historical. To the Armenian people, such a "sensitive spot" is the unhealing wound of the 1915 genocide, committed on the territory of western Armenia. In expressing the expectations of the Armenian people, the Republic's Supreme Soviet passed a law condemning genocide and addressed corresponding suggestions to the USSR Supreme Soviet Presidium.

Once again we turn to the USSR Supreme Soviet with the urgent request to react to our proposals. Genocide, as a monstrous crime committed against mankind, must not be left without condemnation. (Applause).

The Sumgait tragedy, which was not properly assessed, triggered an explosion of protest and created the most difficult problem of refugees. Today we have 200,000 Armenian refugees from Azerbaijan in our republic. Tens of thousands of Azeris have left Armenia. Add 200,000 Armenian refugees and 530,000 people who found themselves without a roof after the earthquake, you can imagine the entire drama of the situation. Nearly one-third of the republic's population is without housing and many people are without jobs.

Nor can I fail to mention the helplessness shown by the law enforcement authorities and the union and republic commissions in determining the reasons and culprits for the mass poisoning of people at work, which has been going on for the past few months.

Delays in solving a number of pressing problems disrupt the republic, disorient the people, and create feelings of social and national defenselessness and a crisis of confidence in the republic's leadership.

The report justifiably noted the underestimating, at the start of restructuring, of the national problem. We are paying a high price for delays in solving some problems of relations among nationalities and for our slowness and halfway nature of the decisions which are being made.

The serious confrontation between the Armenian and Azeri people is a sad fact of our reality. It cannot be ignored. Our people will continue to live side by side. Preventing the worsening of the crisis in relations between the two nations and eliminating the conflict situation is a problem of exceptional importance. For that reason both republics and, above all, the communist parties of Armenia and Azerbaijan, must make use of all opportunities to eliminate the alienation and to restore an atmosphere of reciprocal understanding and trust.

Many difficulties in settling relations between nationalities are related to the lack of a legal mechanism for their democratic resolution and imperfections in the USSR Constitution, in which one article conflicts with another: some parts were drafted under new conditions while other, the majority, remain the legacy of the period of stagnation.

In our view, it would be useful for the congress to formulate a view on this matter and to determine how to make the fundamental law of the state consistent with present realities, including problems of relations among nationalities.

We are justly revising a great many things in this area. A course has been charted toward enriching the democratic principles in relations between the center and union republics, strengthening republic sovereignty, and solving problems of economic, social, and cultural life.

I believe that under these circumstances it is more important than ever to have a clear guideline, a reliable criterion which would help us to avoid equivocal steps and undesirable extremes. Such a guideline and criterion could be strengthening our Soviet state as a federation of sovereign republics.

Yes, our home must be renovated. This is a truth experienced by our society. Nonetheless, all our ideas and steps must be aimed at strengthening this home and building higher forms of integration among our republics and our peoples.

Comrades, I do not agree with those who are trying to cast aspersions on the work of our congress. Regardless of what it may cost us and the difficulties, it is taking place on a broad democratic basis. This is our first opportunity to engage in an open and honest discussion of our problems, compare various views, and state our positions. I believe this is a great accomplishment of the congress. It lays a good foundation for a fruitful search for a solution of the most difficult problems posed by this very responsible stage in the life of the country. (Applause).

Seventh Session

31 May 1989

A.-M.K. Brazauskas: Metropolitan Aleksey, member of the Holy Synod of the Russian Orthodox Church, bishop of Leningrad and Novgorod, has the floor.

The next speaker will be Comrade Valentin Ivanovich Bakulin, head of a fitters brigade in Ivanovo.

A.M. Ridiger, member of the Russian Orthodox Church Holy Synod, Metropolitan Aleksey of Leningrad and Novgorod, Leningrad City (from the Soviet Charity and Health Foundation): Esteemed presidium, esteemed people's deputies! I believe this is the first time a religious figure has spoken from this high rostrum of our country. I would like first to thank Mikhail Sergeyevich for his report and the concept he proposed to us as a way out of the crisis situation. Of course, this concept will be enriched by deputies' speeches, and we should by joint effort find a means of escaping from the crisis situation in which our country and our society find themselves.

From this high platform I would like to say that Orthodox people and all our country's believers not only wholeheartedly support restructuring in the broad sense of the word but also see the processes of renewal being implemented as the real embodiment of their hopes and aspirations. We realize the complexity of the restructuring process, which must affect all spheres of our life—it is sometimes easier to build anew than to restructure. The progress of restructuring presupposes radical economic reform designed to turn the economy toward man, the democratization of internal life, and the moral renewal of our society. I would like to dwell on this last point in somewhat more detail.

The most important lesson that our country has derived from its recent past is the realization of the underlying linkage between morality and society's social development. As is well known, our history has confirmed the ancient truism that you cannot implement the most splendid social ideas by coercion without appealing to man's morality, his conscience, reason, moral choice, and inner freedom. That is why the grave situation in which our economy has found itself, and many aspects of public life, have their initial cause not only in someone's ill will and mistakes by specialists but also in the spiritual impoverishment that has afflicted our society. Our century has seen an unprecedented acceleration in scientific and technical progress—a sphere of mankind's activity which is on the whole exempt from morality. And look what has happened. Today as never before people are spiritually alienated from one another. They are indifferent to one another. This is in a world where man is receiving a hitherto unprecedented amount of information about the life of his colleagues in every part of the world via the most diverse technical channels and means of communication.

Ethics and moral principles are called upon to be that powerful means which will enable us to overcome people's disunity and spiritual alienation and will thus unite us as brothers and sisters to build a happy future for ourselves and our descendants. It is our restored sense of morality that is rendering us tolerant toward one another, charitable to all those who are suffering, the sick, invalids, the elderly, and the lonely, charitable to nature—a scornful and predatory attitude to the latter is a direct consequences of egoism and the unhealthy state of the human soul. (Applause).

I would like to urge all people's deputies from this rostrum to consolidate our efforts to resolve together the common questions with which we are faced. Crises in contemporary society are linked with the moral crisis, and because of this responsibility for moral education falls on all of us, on our entire society. Each person should build his relations with those around him, with society, and with nature on the foundation of a general human moral code. We must all realize that there is a direct link and a direct dependence between morality and survival. That is why the question of the moral education and improvement of all members of our society is very acute today. Academician Dmitriy Sergeyevich Likhachev put this very well from this rostrum; he was speaking about culture, but culture and morality are interconnected.

The church and religious associations are prepared to take part in this process of ensuring the moral renewal of our society, and we await with hope the adoption in the near future of a law on freedom of worship which would give the church greater opportunities for taking part in the social life of our society. (Applause).

Our congress is taking place at a remarkable time which may fundamentally change the course of the country's development. The international situation today is also promoting this. Two days before our congress began I returned from the Swiss city of Basel where the European Christian Ecumenical "Peace and Justice" Assembly had taken place. This meeting was virtually beyond compare. Representatives of all European Christian churches gathered together to discuss burning issues of the day—peace, disarmament, justice, and the preservation of our natural environment. We discussed these questions for a week and reached a unanimous decision, after setting out our solutions in a general document. It touches on all problems facing mankind today. Europe's Christians expressed readiness to work together without procrastination, as Prof Carl von Weizsaecker urged them: "There's no time to lose." We have to work together to ensure mankind's survival and the preservation of peace, justice, and our natural environment. Permit me to convey this assembly's documents to the head of our state. (Applause). (He hands documents to the presidium).

A.-M.K. Brazauskas: Comrade Valentin Ivanovich Bakulin, head of a fitters brigade, Ivanovo Spinning-Finishing Factory, has the floor. The next speaker will be Comrade Vladimir Vasilyevich Kazarezov.

STENOGRAPHIC RECORD

Seventh Session

31 May 1989

V.I. Bakulin, head of a fitters brigade, Krasnaya Talka Spinning-Finishing Factory, Ivanovo, RSFSR (from the USSR trade unions): Comrades, I, a people's deputy from the workers city of Ivanovo, am very pleased to note that the time of proceedings of our congress coincides with the 84th anniversary of the establishment of the Ivanovo-Voznesensk all-city soviet of worker deputies, the first of its kind in Russia. (Applause). This was an initial political effort which proved that the voice of the workers is very important in solving major governmental problems.

Today, as we feel the revolutionary spirit which restructuring in the activities of the soviets carries with it, we sharply feel our personal responsibility for the future of the country. The attention and thoughts of all working people, of those who have entrusted us with the mandate of representing the people, are turned to the congress. A great deal is expected of us, above all to provide answers to questions related to the further course of restructuring and, therefore, to improving our living standard. This is the main thing. I have always believed that the present congress must not be reduced to meeting-style speeches, attempts to mix everything and to introduce confusion and division and prevent the deputies from discussing the most serious problems of domestic and foreign policy. (Applause).

I am in constant touch with the people of Ivanovo, who are particularly concerned by the fact that some deputies have mounted an open struggle for political power through a variety of methods, going as far as to resort to insults, threats, and labeling. The voters object to this. They believe that such an atmosphere in the congress can only worsen the situation in our country. I, a rank and file party member, am worried by the mood of deputies whose speeches and actions are aimed at belittling the role and significance of the CPSU and of the restructuring processes under way. Efforts are being made to drive a wedge between the party and the people: Clearly, such people have their far-reaching political objectives. Is it difficult to understand that it is precisely as a result of the party's initiative, of its Central Committee and Politburo, that changes are taking place in the country's economy and social life and that it is not a matter of indifference to us, comrades, who will lead restructuring on. We do not see any force other than the Communist Party and we shall support its policies. (Applause).

I am amazed at the silence which the party workers are keeping at the congress. Why are they not rebuffing the clearly extremist attacks on the party? If the ideas of restructuring are dear to us...(applause) we, communists, must not stand aside and avoid discussions. In supporting the stipulation in the report submitted by Mikhail Sergeyevich Gorbachev, let me assert that despite all difficulties restructuring is yielding a positive result. We see this through our own examples: Democratization and glasnost are gathering strength; the people's initiative is being released; work in industry is improving, albeit not as it should. Although very slowly, matters are also improving in agriculture. This instills confidence in the accuracy of the course chosen by the party. Nonetheless, some manifestations of stagnation and unsolved problems are also characteristic among us, the people of Ivanovo. Let me frankly say that there is a pressing need for everyone not simply to contribute to the work but to work with all his forces to come out of the swamp, to pull himself out, even if someone may find this quite painful. The working class is seriously concerned about not talking restructuring out to death. Actually, every time we hear that the 27th Party Congress was a critical moment; the 19th All-Union Conference was critical; the various plenums have been critical. This congress is also critical; that is the way we live. We are breaking things and fighting battles. (Stirring in the hall). As a worker, let me say that the people have become tired of many words and promises. They want action and a clearer line in economic policy.

Bearing in mind that the Congress of People's Deputies is formulating a program for action by our government, let me present my own views on a number of basic problems of socioeconomic policy, which define the interests of the working people. In our view, they need immediate resolution. I would like to propose as an instruction to the country's Supreme Soviet, to approach more profoundly, with greater consideration and balance, the formulation and adoption of economic decisions and programs. During the period of restructuring so many resolutions have been passed that their implementation should have drastically enhanced the economy; in practice, however, we draw up a program, we set deadlines and levels, we give people promises and guarantees and at the same time we violate them and we even backpedal. Let me consider two features which, by virtue of the nature of the work, are the closest to me. A great many hopes were generated in the textile workers by the resolution on radically upgrading the technical standards of domestic machine building. We thought that technical progress in textile machine building would enable us to come up to world standards, facilitate the work of our respected and dear women and improve the quality of the goods. Obviously, this did not happen. Instead of highly productive and highly electronized equipment, we witnessed the birth of two other resolutions issued by the central authorities on the unsatisfactory and extremely unsatisfactory implementation of previous resolutions. In this case, as we know, no one was held responsible, neither the authors of the documents nor those who executed them. It seems to me that the Supreme Soviet must find the necessary instruments drastically to upgrade responsibility for the implementation of resolutions, including the firing of the specific culprits. I am firmly convinced that if we fail to strengthen performing discipline in the immediate future, ranging from worker to member of the government, we shall be unable to reach the highest possible labor productivity or even make any essential improvement whatsoever in the country. (Applause).

The problem of supplying the people with goods has become aggravated to its extreme. Major governmental

Seventh Session

31 May 1989

leaders have repeatedly referred to the salutary step taken in solving this problem by the March 1988 party Central Committee and USSR Council of Ministers decree, which calls for the construction, reconstruction, and retooling of hundreds of enterprises in our sector. However, the very first year of application of this most firm document proved its unbalanced nature. One of the construction projects included our Krasnaya Talka factory. The deadline for the designs came and neither the Gosplan nor the Union Ministry of Light Industry can or even promised to solve the question of who will be rebuilding the enterprise, costing tens of millions of rubles in construction and installation? We cannot understand why, even with a governmental decision, one must try to prove that this decision must be implemented. When will there be respect for state resolutions? When shall we put an end to making the rounds of ministries and departments hat in hand? I deem it necessary, before it is too late, for the respective authorities to draw up a kind of inventory of already passed resolutions. In promoting the priority development of a given sector in one resolution we speak, in another, of the need to stop, to freeze, and so on.... This is an indication of the hastiness with which resolutions are drawn up, resolutions which affect the destinies of collectives of thousands of people.

It is also important to eliminate the practice of adopting conflicting documents which, today, has become virtually the norm. A number of resolutions have been issued by the superior authorities which prohibit the development of industrial construction in the nonchernozem. Meanwhile, one after another, resolutions are being passed on the building of new plants, ignoring the opinion of the local population.

In my view, the Supreme Soviet and the country's government must concentrate, on a priority basis, material and financial resources on the development of the material and technical base of the construction industry, for without it we cannot solve food, housing or other problems. Already now the textile workers in the oblast have accumulated more than 100 million rubles in the production and social development funds and are unable to use them because of lack of material resources and capacities of contracting organizations. Our people wait for an apartment between 15 to 18 years. Without developing this sector we cannot hope to solve the political problem which has been formulated, that of providing every family with housing by the year 2000.

As chairman of the labor collective council of the enterprise, want it or not, I must deal with problems of economics. I have extensively read the writings of Comrades Abalkin, Selyunin, Shmelev, Popov, and others. But what, comrade scientists, comes out of all this? The authors keep criticizing each other. One says that "we must promote an economic reform;" another says that "the time has not come, our masses have not matured for this." What is the solution? Whatever course the implementation of the economic reform may take, there must be no worsening of the life of the people. I would think that this question should be clear to everyone. However, every day we see the empty shelves of stores, unrestrained speculations, and price increases. It is time for the leading economists to turn from debates to the formulation of specific ways of treating our economy. (Applause). And as healers, they must bear responsibility for its fastest possible recovery. (Applause).

Nor should I fail to point out that the working class today is concerned with the development of the cooperative system. At first we expected that the market would be saturated with the necessary goods, that the problem of shortages will be resolved, and that there would be a healthy competition with the state sector. What actually happened? We see that the cooperatives have caused social injustice, a decline in discipline, and an increase in the crime rate. They have dipped their hands into the pockets of workers and retirees, and have created an uncontrolled channel for converting cashless into cash funds mostly without any additional output of goods. Against this background there has been a sharp stratification in society. On the one hand, we have people who earn thousands. On the other, millions of people are not ensured even a minimum wage. Particularly hurt are those who, with their toil, built the country during its hardest times. The legislative authorities must urgently complete work on problems related to the development of the cooperatives and see to it that they indeed become a need and not a phenomenon in our lives.

Comrade deputies, I would like to see the Supreme Soviet and the government prove their activities by steadily improving the life of the single Soviet people and for the reputation of our country to grow steadily not only abroad and, above all, that the pride felt by our own people in their homeland in the most just, humane, and progressive socialist system of ours be revived. I address myself to the working people of the country, to the workers of Moscow and Leningrad: Remember, do not forget the words of Vladimir Ilich Lenin: "The proletariat of Moscow, Peter, and Ivanovo-Voznesensk... proved in action that it will not surrender the gains of the revolution for anything." Today we must firmly hold onto these positions. (Prolonged applause).

A.-M.K. Brazauskas: Comrade Vladimir Vasilyevich Kazarezov, first secretary of the Novosibirsk Obkom, has the floor.

V.V. Kazarezov, first secretary of the Novosibirsk Oblast CPSU Committee, (Tatarskiy Territorial Electoral Okrug, Novosibirsk Oblast): Comrade deputies! As a party worker, I should perhaps talk more today about the political aspects of restructuring, but I will be dwelling on the economic aspects, because there has unquestionably been progress in the political sphere.

It is quite obvious to me that if there is no improvement in the people's standard of living in the near future and if urgent social programs are not implemented, people

Seventh Session
31 May 1989

will start to lose faith in the possibility of any positive changes at all. And this would mean the end of restructuring, from whichever direction it came—from the left or from the right. (Applause).

The economy is ill with a serious, chronic disease and I, at least, can see no signs of improvement at present. It seems to me that we have not properly assessed the real depth of the economic crisis. As far as the most recent period is concerned, official assessments have clearly tried to embellish the true state of affairs. This is quite intolerable. Studies conducted by Siberian economists have shown that in the first 3 years of the 5-year period the growth in industrial output has not been 13 percent, as statistical reports would have us believe, but only just over 4 percent—and only 1 percent in 1988. It seems that the remainder of the increase, or, to be more precise, the appearance of an increase has been achieved through concealed price rises and flawed statistics. (Applause).

It is possible that our scientists are overdramatizing the situation, but I do not think that this is to any significant degree. So, I would like to conclude this theory in my speech with an appeal for a totally accurate assessment of the socioeconomic situation in the country, and consequently feel it possible to instruct the newly elected Supreme Soviet and the appropriate commissions to look more deeply into the situation and inform deputies and the population. But it seems more important to establish the reasons for the increasing deterioration in the situation, and more important still to look for ways out of this situation. I could, at this point, talk about our national economy's unreceptiveness to scientific and technical progress, or about how economic reform is marking time and so forth, but a great deal has already been said on the subject and, I am sure, will be said yet. I do not want to deprive scientists and economists of their living. I would like to talk about something else—and on this I am in agreement with the previous speaker—namely, about the low level of competence and weak scientific study when substantiating major decisions in our country, and also about the half-hearted, timid, inconsistent approach to putting these decisions into practice.

You can judge for yourselves the kind of impression that could have been created by the formulation of the task ahead 3 years ago: To ensure that 80-95 percent of basic output is manufactured to world standards by 1990, or, in other words, ensure the kind of leap forward that would make your head spin. It was a bitter, painful experience for the country's leadership when, at every step, people showed amazement at such an unrealistic task, to put it mildly, and, after all, we have been obliged to motivate party organizations and collectives to fulfill this task. Where is this incompetence coming from? I would like to ask you, Mikhail Sergeyevich, to consider what kind of advisers suggest these kind of decisions. Take a really recent decision. The state order for agricultural output is to be conveyed to republics and oblasts but not to individual economic units. In my view, this approach is not only incorrect and illogical, it is also immoral. There must be either one thing or another: Either we abandon the state order from top to bottom, if we are ready for this, or we retain it for a while—again from top to bottom. Otherwise we end up with a conflict between oblast- and rayon-level leadership, on the one hand, and the direct producers of agricultural output on the other, while the center takes a highly respectable democratic position.

There is more. It seems to me that we are causing problems by our ill-considered approach to changing investment policy under the guise of reorientation toward the social sphere. Here, too, I have an example. It is planned to reduce investments in the development of the heat and electric power industry together with other industrial ministries. I will not attempt to judge the situation in the country as a whole (although it is now our duty to think of the country as a whole), but for Novosibirsk Oblast this will mean an impasse situation in social development. Look at what is happening. Last year a USSR Council of Ministers resolution was adopted on the development of the power industry in Novosibirsk Oblast, which envisaged almost doubling capital investments in the Ministry of Power and Electrification in 1990 in comparison to the 1988 level. It has been estimated that the shortage of heat for Novosibirsk alone amounts to 1,000 kilocalories. There is also a considerable shortage of electricity. But it is in fact planned to reduce investments for 1990 to below the present level. Anatoliy Ivanovich Mayorets, minister of power and electrification, explains this as a reduction in capital investments in the power industry within the framework of the general reduction of industrial construction in the country. I would not just call this a shortsighted policy—it is something worse. We are talking about the social sphere, but just try to name a more social sector than heat and electricity generation! When there is no meat you can substitute potatoes and pasta for it for a while; when there is no soap you can get by for a few days, washing without it. (A stir in the audience). But how, in Siberia, with temperatures of minus 40 degrees, can you live if it is cold in your apartment and at work? How are we to heat new housing, schools, kindergartens, and hospitals, which we are now building in greater numbers (and we are indeed building them in greater numbers, comrades), if there is not enough heat to go around, once they are built? We will be forced to curtail our social programs. And the reality of building 1 billion square meters of housing per year across the country, which Mikhail Sergeyevich talked about in his report, is a great problem in this connection. That is why I talk of an impasse situation and urge deputies, particularly those who will be working on the relevant commissions, to help to speed up the development of the heat and electric power industry.

Furthermore, a paradoxical situation has developed in our country. On the one hand, there is excessive centralization in economic management and, on the other, the

STENOGRAPHIC RECORD

Seventh Session

31 May 1989

center is completely powerless when it comes to organizing the division of labor and integrating production and scientific potentials. I see this as one of the main reasons for our lagging behind. After all, in my opinion, in terms of the degree of cooperation and specialization in industry, particularly in machine building, and in terms of certain other indicators, we are at the level of premonopolist capitalism. Take a look at our country's machine-building plants. Each one represents a combine with a selection of virtually every technology available. There is everything here: casting, forging, welding, machine-tool, and other production operations. They have virtually every type of instrument, spare part, industrial holder and fastener, and standard fitting; each one makes them for itself. I am sure that if all this were produced at specialized enterprises, the prime cost of machine-building output would be sharply reduced, the quality and technical standard of this output improved, and the amount of materials used in the process reduced. Comrades, I have studied the documents of party congresses, beginning with the 23d congress. Like an incantation, they have repeated the thesis on the need to develop production specialization and cooperation, but the process has in fact gone in the opposite direction. Four years of restructuring have produced nothing and the situation has only got worse.

Or, take this situation: Realizing it is futile to hope for centralized organization of the production and supply to villages of machinery and equipment they so need, such as silage combines, hay-making equipment, cranes, and so forth (agricultural workers here in the hall know that they certainly do not have enough of all these things—not to mention supplies of new equipment for agriculture), we decided to organize the production of all these things ourselves in the oblast, scattering assemblies and components to dozens of plants. Moscow has given us a pat on the back for this. But what kind of pat on the back do they deserve, when the machinery is going to be several times more expensive and the quality several times more inferior? This is quite barbaric: Each oblast making its own agricultural machinery when the country has such a powerful machine-building potential! And I know that Sverdlovsk, Voronezh, and other oblasts are doing the same as us. But we are ruining the country, comrades, with this kind of approach! How can we talk seriously of restructuring in the economy in view of this? On the whole, as I see it, this is restructuring back to front.

I would like to say a few words about regional economic accountability and self-management. I, like the overwhelming majority of people, am categorically in favor of this. I can understand how this is viewed at union republic level. But what about us, the krays and oblasts—are we each supposed to withdraw into our own cocoon? It seems to me that we should be thinking about making the transition to a region-based administrative system—for example, the Urals, West Siberia, the Far East, the Center, and so forth—and, perhaps, give these regions the rights enjoyed by the union republics in economic respects. (Applause).

A few more words about regional economic accountability. It should be total. It is thought, for example, that investments in science yield the greatest effect. If that were so with regard to the region where science is located, Novosibirsk Oblast would be the most prosperous in the whole country, because in terms of strength of scientific potential we cede place only to Moscow and Leningrad—and possibly Kiev. We have three academy branches here: the USSR Academy of Sciences, the V.I. Lenin All-Union Academy of Agricultural Sciences, and the USSR Academy of Medical Sciences. The fact that they are concentrated in one city is, in my opinion, wrong, but it is too late to talk about that now. We will take the view that history has ordained it so. But in that case it should be to our advantage to develop science, receiving an appropriate percentage for the local budget from the results of scientists' work (and, what is more, work financed from the budget and work based on an economic contract) introduced not only here but elsewhere in the country and sold abroad. Then, firstly, it would be clear exactly what kind of feedback we are getting from our three branches. And, secondly, if the feedback from investments in science really proves to be the most profitable, we will give it priority development at the expense of other sectors and programs, meaning by this that we will resolve many local social problems by using the dividends from science.

A few more words about science. It really does need to very seriously review its attitude to itself. We have outstanding scientific cadres and scientific results of world standard. But it is a thorny path from ideas to practice. The main thing here, apart from the ineffectual economic mechanism, is the weakness of our experimental base, which has already been much discussed. How can the situation be put right? The presidium of the Siberian Branch of the USSR Academy of Sciences takes a traditional approach to this: It is proposing the construction of new institute buildings (the same old extensive course of action again), which means a further increase in the number of new building projects. What can I say? I myself have an allergy to new construction work. And with regard to this particular issue, the position is this: First, building new premises and fitting them out with equipment, thereby investing millions and millions of rubles, is not the same thing as creating an experimental base for institutes. And who is going to work in these premises? Second, for us it will mean setting aside the solution of vital social problems, which, naturally, is something we cannot agree to.

So what is the solution? A solution does exist. In connection with the cuts in arms expenditure and the conversion of defense enterprises, a number of plants in defense sectors should be placed at the disposal of science for use as an experimental base. (Applause). These plants' output would then be redistributed among other enterprises. This is no simple matter, of course, but it would be the sensible thing to do from the state's point of view and would also represent a restructuring of attitudes in these very important areas.

STENOGRAPHIC RECORD

Seventh Session

31 May 1989

The last point, esteemed comrades deputies. I would like to say a few words about Siberia. We have already heard the words of our great ancestor, Mikhail Lomonosov, in this hall, about how Russian might would be increased by Siberia. What can I add to this? The accelerated development of Siberia's productive forces is an important component of CPSU strategy, but this strategy is not being implemented satisfactorily. The main thing is that there is no mechanism to stimulate the accelerated development of regions of Siberia. But if we recall the end of the last century and the beginning of this one, there was a massive resettlement to Siberia—voluntary, not forced—from the center of the country, the Ukraine, Belorussia, and other regions. It was Stolypin, a now undeservedly forgotten Russian statesman, who initiated the reform which ensured this resettlement, without which Siberia's present level of development would not have been possible.

Where are the statesmen of today who could offer something similar, which would make it possible for our country to more actively engage Siberia's powerful potential to the benefit of all the people? (Applause). Many incentives could be considered. But the main point is that only a substantially higher standard of living in Siberia can ensure an influx of fresh forces and stop the indigenous population from leaving for the country's western regions.

Siberian scientists now estimate that at present the level of consumption and use of the most important benefits and services in Siberia, including food, housing, and units in the non-production infrastructure, is below average for the republic. The shortfall will be even more serious if you consider the need to compensate for the harsher natural and climatic conditions, which require a minimum increase of 20-40 percent in the consumer budget in Siberia's southern regions and an increase of 1.5-2 times in its northern regions in comparison to the country's central regions. I ask you to see my speech as raising the question of increasing Siberia's zonal differentiation coefficient. I am sure that giving priority to raising the population's living standard in Siberian regions not only accords with the principles of social justice but is also an essential condition of implementing very important all-union economic programs. Thank you for your attention. (Applause).

A.-M.K. Brazauskas: So, comrades, the following motion has been made: to terminate debates by dinner time and solve some problems.

Yesterday a vote was taken on elections to the Council of Nationalities from the Nagorno-Karabakh Autonomous Oblast. Deputy Yuriy Andreyevich Osipyan, chairman of the vote tallying commission, will report on the results of the vote.

Yu.A. Osipyan: Comrade deputies, in accordance with the procedure approved by the congress, a secret vote was taken and its results were tallied by the commission at the USSR Congress of People's Deputies, counting the votes cast for the elections to the Council of Nationalities of the USSR Supreme Soviet from the Nagorno-Karabakh Autonomous Oblast and determined that the following candidacies of people's deputies of the USSR, listed alphabetically, were included in the slate for a secret vote on elections to the Council of Nationalities from the Nagorno-Karabakh Autonomous Oblast: Z.G. Balayan, V.D. Dzhafarov, and G.A. Pogosyan. Two thousand one hundred and thirty ballots were issued for the vote on USSR people's deputies. The ballot boxes were opened, and a total of 2,109 ballots were counted. A total of 2,108 ballots were declared valid, and one was judged invalid. It was destroyed. The votes were broken down as follows: Z.G. Balayan: 726 for and 1,382 against; V.D. Dzhafarov: 1,884 for and 224 against; G.A. Pogosyan: 1,437 for and 671 against.

Therefore, the following USSR people's deputies were elected to the Council of Nationalities from the Nagorno-Karabakh Autonomous Oblast: Dzhafarov, V.D. and Pogosyan, G.A.

A.-M.K. Brazauskas: Are there any questions for Comrade Osipyan? No questions? Comrades we must ratify the results of the vote on the Nagorno-Karabakh Autonomous Oblast.

I put the matter to a vote. Those in favor of the ratification of these results please say so. Thank you. You may lower your hands. Opponents? Please count the votes, comrades. Abstentions? (Votes are counted).

A.G. Kostenyuk: Dear delegates, following are the results of the vote: "Nay," zero; abstained, five deputies. (Applause).

A.-M.K. Brazauskas: Therefore, the protocol is approved. There is one more vote to be taken. We can now definitively, I emphasize, definitively ratify the protocol of the ballot counting commission for elections to the Council of Nationalities, taking into consideration elections for the Nagorno-Karabakh Autonomous Oblast and our previous resolution to approve the voluntary withdrawal of the candidacy of Deputy A.I. Kazannik and the election to this chamber of Deputy B.N. Yeltsin.

Today we must take a final vote on the entire membership of the Council of Nationalities. Let us vote. Those in favor, please raise your certificates. Thank you.

Who is against? Please count the votes. Whoever is against raise your hands higher. (Votes are counted).

A.G. Kostenyuk. Dear deputies, seven votes were cast against.

A.-M.K. Brazauskas: There were seven against. Are there any questions? Are there abstentions? Please raise your certificates.

Seventh Session

31 May 1989

A.G. Kostenyuk: Two deputies abstained.

A.-M.K. Brazauskas: Two deputies abstained. Therefore, the protocol of the ballot counting commission for elections to the Council of Nationalities is approved. The matter is closed.

Now a few announcements, communications, and motions. Several deputies have expressed to the presidium the wish to meet with the heads of some ministries and departments. As you know, all members of the government and heads of organizations and departments are present here. Therefore, we suggest that the ministers and heads of central departments be approached during intermissions. This can be done in writing as well. The requests may be submitted to the Secretariat which will organize the contact between deputies and the heads of ministries and departments. Is this motion acceptable? Thank you. This matter is closed.

Next, People's Deputy Statulyavichyus asks why deputy questions are not published in the congress' bulletin? He asks that they be published. Let me inform you that, all told, today the secretariat has received 14 questions posed by deputies to the government, ministries, departments, and other. Tomorrow data on such questions and instructions will be considered and distributed by the secretariat to the deputies. There is another motion. Several deputies have asked what has become of their motions. Deputies or representatives of individual groups of deputies or republics could go to the third floor, where the Secretariat is located, and check whether their mandate, suggestions, and so on, are there. It is important for all of them to be recorded and properly duplicated and distributed among the deputies.

A couple of other matters remain. There is a note here according to which Deputies Comrades Nosov, Umarkhodzhayev, and others suggest that debate speeches be limited to 10 minutes. We must report this to the congress and seek the advice of everyone how to proceed. As you know, in our regulation we approved a 15-minute limit. Shall we change it or leave it as is? (Stirring in the hall). Perhaps we should vote? Well, in order to deal with this item, the following motion has been made....

From the hall: (Unintelligible).

A.-M.K. Brazauskas: So, we shall not vote then? (From the hall: No.) That is all, the motion is withdrawn. Here are a few small announcements. Ivan Denisovich Stefanenko, deputy from the All-Union Organization of War and Labor Veterans, writes that some speakers try to distract the congress from the solution of the basic problems. He is offering his services in preventing this from happening. I believe that all of us will take this into consideration in the future, in our addresses. Obviously, his remark is just.

Yet another interesting motion has been made. It has been submitted by Comrade Yuriy Vasilyevich Popov from Leningrad, deputy director for scientific affairs of the Leningrad Scientific Research Institute of Psychoneurology imeni V.M. Bekhterev. He writes, I shall read here a very short note, and he will not have to speak. "Please give me, before the intermission, the possibility to address an appeal to the World Health Organization to adopt 31 May as Nonsmoking Day!" (Applause). Allow me to read the note in full: "Throughout the world the attitude toward this problem is extremely serious. The television is transmitting not only the sessions of the congress but also talks during intermissions where one can probably see people smoking. It would be shameful to display to the entire world the fact that the USSR people's deputies are ignoring the appeals of this authoritative world organization." (Applause). We shall take this into consideration.

Here is another small motion. Comrades, just a minute, we heard here a very important and interesting appeal by deputies, essentially farmworkers, although it has been signed by many people who are not agricultural workers, but which is very serious. There is a motion, from the Presidium, that, to begin with, it be duplicated and distributed among all deputies and, second, that the Supreme Soviet and the corresponding commission, which we shall define, currently it is known as the commission in charge of food supplies, and we do have such a commission, and it could be given a different name, we shall determine this and also submit it to the government, to the USSR Council of Ministers, for such problems to be considered in great detail before the autumn and that corresponding motions be drafted, which would be officially submitted to the consideration of the next congress. Do the deputies second this motion? Is no vote required? It is not. That is all. All announcements have been made, and I declare an intermission until 1600.

Chair: A.I. Lukyanov, first deputy chairman of the USSR Supreme Soviet.

A.I. Lukyanov: Comrade deputies, we are continuing our debates on the basic directions of domestic and foreign policy of the USSR. Deputy Brazauskas, first secretary of the Lithuanian Communist Party Central Committee, has the floor.

A.-M.K. Brazauskas, first secretary of the Lithuanian Communist Party Central Committee, Vilnyus (Vilnyus-Leninskiy Territorial Electoral District, Lithuanian SSR): Dear congress, dear comrades, by the will of the people we are turning a new page in the history of our country. The development of the state once again demands of us to give all power to the soviets. It is for that sake that we were elected and that is what we must discuss. Today we must invest in this slogan a qualitatively new content. Over the past 7 decades we have repeatedly proclaimed full power to the soviets, occasionally depicting wishes as reality. Restructuring, which

Seventh Session

31 May 1989

began in April 1985, took us to a decisive historical line. The sociopolitical situation which developed demands of us to review some values and take another look at the content of political categories, such as the socialist state, ownership, sovereignty, and union. For the sake of fairness we must point out that the current difficult situation in the country is not the result of restructuring only, something of which we are frequently accused. It is the result of our entire complex and tragic history and painful search for the creation of a political and economic system consistent with the ideals of socialism. Today hardly anyone could deny that the country is on the threshold of economic and, consequently, and perhaps imminent political crisis. For that reason real steps must be taken to come out of the developing situation. The people have become tired of theoretical debates. They want to feel changes for the better in their daily lives.

We consider as the main way for solving the problems which have accumulated to be the full solution of the crucial problems presented in the speech by the Supreme Soviet chairman and the speeches of the deputies, and the stipulations of the 19th All-Union Party Conference. Contradictions between the center and the republics and among sectorial interests in the area of national relations developed as a result of excessive centralization in the Soviet Union. Let us also recall the events in Georgia, Karabakh, and Armenia and many events in our Baltic area. The solution of these contradictions, in our view, is possible only through the exercise of the rights of the sovereign peoples as the foundation for the creation of a rule of law society. The USSR, as the unification of these sovereign peoples, must, in this case, be based on the respective implementation of other necessary treaties: economic and interrepublic. Harmony in relations among Union authorities and republic authorities must be based on the efficient and just demarcation of these competencies. In this case we must establish the precise limits of what is exclusively within the competence of the USSR and the exclusive competence of Union republics, and only in individual cases should there be a matter pertaining to joint competence. A multinational union becomes such only by abandoning the existing stipulations of unification in all areas. Above all, the fundamental law of the USSR must clearly define the very concept of the Union of Soviet Socialist Republics. It must reflect the principles governing its establishment and functioning and the legal acceptance of ethnic, political, and economic variety. The current Constitution has become a hindrance to the implementation of such changes. Today the republics are virtually deprived of the possibility of solving problems of the development of the economy and the accumulated problems of ecology and sociopolitical life, which the center, as reality has indicated, is unable to solve properly. This situation objectively introduces a certain tension in the field of relations among nationalities throughout the country as well as within the individual republics. At the last session of the Republic's Supreme Soviet, we were forced to amend some articles of our Constitution, thus making it possible to improve production and social relations. We believe that such a legislative initiative does not conflict with the present spirit of restructuring.

Lines, shortages, empty shelves.... These are words which are not disappearing from our vocabulary. Naturally, from the viewpoint of economics this situation as well has its historical origins. The economic reforms which have been carried out in the country over the past quarter of a century failed to yield desired results essentially because the old methods used to improve the country's economy had become obsolete. We must not deal merely with decorating the facade when a basic capital repair is needed. We need a true revolutionary economic reform, the implementation of which we consider possible through the economic independence of the individual republics, above all. Unfortunately, foot dragging, dashing around, and secrecy in making vitally important decisions are still characteristic of the work style of many Union departments. We are limited in opportunities to maneuver and make independent decisions in an entire array of cases. Interpreting ministerial instructions, taking regional conditions and the level of economic development into consideration, is not always either possible or acceptable.

Several months ago we published a draft Republic concept of economic autonomy, which was supported by the broad population strata. Last February we submitted our considerations on matters of economic autonomy to the CPSU Central Committee and, subsequently, to the Council of Ministers and, hence, to the USSR Gosplan. Unfortunately, all that saw the light were the "General Principles...." which, I hope, are familiar to all deputies. Once again they standardize and lead to unanimous concepts applicable to all republics. Naturally, we cannot understand such a fear of a good initiative. Naturally, also puzzling is the behavior of the country's Gosplan. I doubt the existence in this hall of even a few deputies who think that we would be able to free our economic ship from the rock on which it has been stuck for more than 1 year through the old economic management methods.

We must point out that standardization is inherent in the overwhelming majority of documents coming from the center. Meanwhile, on different levels it is being acknowledged and emphasized that the political and economic situation is not the same for all republics. Taking all of this into consideration, at the latest session of the Republic's Supreme Soviet we passed a law on the foundations of economic autonomy, which is not a copy of the "General Principles...." In our opinion, it will help us to solve a number of pressing problems of departmental diktat. It will contribute to improving relations and free the Republic's constructive potential. It is my view that the implementation of this law could be a model for enhancing our Republic's economy. Such models have been drafted by other republics as well and, naturally, with the least possible risk to the entire country. At the same time, a group of Baltic deputies have formulated a

STENOGRAPHIC RECORD

Seventh Session

31 May 1989

draft USSR Law on Economic Independence of Union Republics. Its purpose is to democratize the USSR and ensure the restructuring of economic policies. Its fundamental principle is that if there are strong republics there will be a strong center, a strong Union. I hope that the stipulations of this draft will meet with the attention of the congress and the Supreme Soviet which, I assume, will consider such problems, as well as with the understanding of Union economic departments. Speaking of the status of a Union republic within the USSR and of upgrading economic autonomy, problems of state-legal guarantees of this sovereignty on the Union level are bound to appear. Unfortunately, our common history dating from Stalinist times has led to the development of a number of tangles of mistrust among republics. This complicates on the sociopolitical level the implementation of radical reforms in all areas of Union activities.

One such tangle is problems of the historical circumstances under which the Lithuanian SSR was established. We know that the 1939 treaty between the USSR and Germany and the secret protocol attached to it predetermined at that time the fate of the independent Lithuanian, Latvian, and Estonian republics. After they became public knowledge, these historical facts and documents triggered sharp political discussions which led to an enhancement of the emotional tension and stress. Vagueness on this matter greatly weakens the positions of the Lithuanian Communist Party. We need an official governmental declaration which would provide a political assessment of these international documents. Restructuring and the process of creating a rule of law state, which are taking place, simply demand the condemnation of the power methods used by Stalinist foreign policy. The open acknowledgment of the illegality of said concept is necessary. This must be accomplished for the sake of historical justice and for the sake of the future of the Lithuanian and the other Baltic nations (applause), the more so since we are on the eve of the 50th anniversary of the signing of these treaties. This will not only help to increase trust and the cohesion of the peoples within the USSR but will also enhance its international reputation. It will also help the more extensive participation of Union republics in shaping and exercising Soviet foreign policy. A faulty practice has developed in which the interests of Union republics abroad in the areas of economics, culture, science, and other are represented by numerous central departments which frequently do not study or not even have the possibility of understanding such needs and their specifics. Based on the announced new thinking in international affairs, specific business relations must be established with the positive segment of the emigres. To this effect we must involve more extensively representatives of Union republics in diplomatic work, particularly in countries in which many of our compatriots live. The Union republics must be given the opportunity to establish with them direct consular relations in the immediate future. The formulation and implementation of an active, flexible, and differentiated foreign and domestic policy, which would combine the Union interests with those of the individual republics, is a most important factor for further progress in restructuring and renovation in the country.

The government established by Lenin was considered the best educated and most intelligent in the world for its time. It successfully solved the very difficult problems of the establishment of the state. We could say without exaggerating that today we have a highly educated and very active deputy membership. This instills the hope that today's most difficult problems as well will be resolved successfully. (Applause).

A.-M.K. Brazauskas: Deputy Yuriy Petrovich Vlasov, Moscow, has the floor. Deputy Masaliyev will be the next speaker.

Yu.P. Vlasov, writer, Moscow (Lyublinskiy Territorial Electoral District, RSFSR): Dear chairman and deputies, I represent Lyublinskiy Rayon in Moscow. From a dacha suburb it has become one of the most unhealthy areas. Dozens of plants are concentrated here, one of which is the AZLK.

The air over the rayon is polluted, and so is its water. Swimming in the river is dangerous. All standards of hygiene have been violated. Nonetheless, recently a cement elevator was completed, and an asphalt-concrete plant is under construction. What are the people to breathe? The smoke from the smokestacks?

The housing problem is grave.... Briefly, this is one of the most deprived areas of Moscow. A casting-machine plant, the main production process of which has not changed since prerevolutionary times, operates in the center of the rayon. This is a crime against the workers, the women in particular, and a crime against all of Moscow.

The state has become accustomed to take from the people their strength and health, offering stingy, sometimes insulting, and extremely miserly compensations. This applies to wages, pensions, and medical facilities. Incidentally, the price of drugs, in general, should be reduced, immediately at that. Occasionally, the people have no money to pay for medicines.

We are proclaiming great principles but essentially we are exploiting the people. The people are totally fed up with promises of a better life and firmly demand change. The worker does not wish to allow and will not allow any further decline in the living standard. That is why we are here. For the time being, the people still have faith in us. The people do not demand a great deal. They want one thing only: to be treated like human beings.

Dear deputies, I am not an economist. The main topic of my address is the democratization of our life. Democracy can feed and clothe us as really as does economics. This is natural, for these two phenomena are organically

Seventh Session
31 May 1989

interlinked. Democracy provides scope for life. It develops economic relations. As to the way democracy is being depicted as a scarecrow, this is a different matter.

My address has not been prescribed by anyone. I have not attended the meetings of the Moscow group. Nor do I like meetings. This statement is not one of the semifinished products mentioned by Deputy Gorbachev in connection with the Moscow group. However, I am part of the Moscow group and with the Moscow group. This is a fact, and I am proud of it!

Here is another minor remark: Due to the fact that on Saturday, 27 May, we finished our work relatively early, I had the opportunity to watch the television report (not a newscast, but the report) on the congress. On that day the speech by Yuriy Nikolayevich Afanasyev was the focal point of the day. His speech and the speech by Deputy Popov and all speeches in support of their statements were given in their abridged versions—that is, with substantial gaps. It was very difficult to gain a clear logical concept of their views. Conversely, the opposite viewpoint was presented in detail, speech after speech by the deputies themselves.

I am addressing myself to those who are in charge of the "Time" Program. Are you not aware that this is a distortion? This is what you are reporting in that same program, on that same day and hour, about 62 percent of the people who, according to a survey, are against blocking the motions of the Moscow group by the congress. And, as you report this, you immediately engage in a forgery, i.e., you stand up against the majority of the people, against these same 62 percent.

I am not a supporter of division. However, it would be erroneous to think that any kind of malice is encouraging a division within the congress. Things are simpler: To any action there is an opposite reaction. In this case this is a reciprocal process.

Incidentally, let me make yet another remark. The position of chairman of Gosteleradio is so important that it would be difficult to overestimate it. The influence of television on the mind is striking and comprehensive. There is no more powerful means of restructuring than that. We must consent to the appointment of someone to, let us say, a responsible position such as chairman of the Constitutional Supervision Committee. I suggest that such consent should also include any candidate for the position of Gosteleradio chairman. (Applause). Such an appointment must be the prerogative—that is, the exclusive right of the congress. For the same reasons I suggest that the position of editor in chief of IZVESTIYA be made the prerogative of the congress. (Applause). Such important positions should not be left to be handled by the apparat.

We agreed not to mention the Tbilisi event until the report of the commission, which ties our hands. All right, we can postpone expressing our views and wait. However, another fact emerges in this tragic history, which should not be kept silent. From the very first days of the proceedings of the congress here, in the hall, there has been a mute question addressed to the leading governmental and party officials in the country: Who issued the order of reprisals? The answer by Deputy Gorbachev led to the need for setting up the present commission. Under no circumstances can we allow for the head of state to be unfamiliar with all the circumstances of the matter. Otherwise what kind of head of state is he? It is equally impossible to assume that to this day the members of the Politburo remain uninformed about this matter.

Please note that no one has answered the persistent questions which have been asked by probably a good dozen of deputies, although the silence itself is an answer. (Applause). No, it is not a question of concealing an important fact from the Congress of People's Deputies. It is a question of something else: of the need to include in our Constitution articles on impeachment, i.e., of depriving the chairman of the Supreme Soviet of his plenary powers because of concealing the truth from the people. (Applause). What I am saying is of essential significance for the future. The head of state must fully know who he is with: with the corporations or with the people. (Applause).

Now as to the responsibility of the government. This was already mentioned. Fears were expressed here caused by the fact that for 10 hours we were without a ruling authority, until the head of state had been elected. During those hours the country was under the threat of possible attack. Most of us realized who Brezhnev was and the way he ruled the country. Lack of principle and complicity in illegal actions and frequently fear forced the people to keep silent and not to consider the possible difficulties, although one of them turned into the misfortune of war. Brezhnev could have been absent not 10 hours but 10 years and hardly anyone would have noted this.

During those years the overwhelming majority of the present members of the Politburo and the members of the government held quite high positions. However, as you know, today all responsibility is written off with a single capacious sentence: "All of us have come out of those times." I categorically disagree with this. Not all! However, I am not talking about this now. Restructuring started 4 years ago and everything that is taking place in the country now is largely the result of the direct activities of our leadership. This richest country in the world is using vouchers, which are the equivalent of rationing cards, in time of peace. Even the most basic staple products are lacking. Our ruble is pitiful compared to any other currency. There is a great deal of corruption, illegality, and arbitrariness in the country. The country is drowning in irresponsible decisions. A great country has been humiliated. It cannot sink any lower, for if it were

Seventh Session

31 May 1989

this would mean disintegration. Usually, individuals who are responsible for such a turn of affairs resign, not singly but as a group, as people who have made a mess of things. (Applause). In any case, that is the custom the world over.

It was said here that normal activities by the government are impossible without strict control. The Supreme Soviet has such rights. It is the executive, the managing authority. The deputies must ask how to pose questions.... they must pose questions to the government. For example, each 2 or 3 weeks the government would report at the sessions about its activities and in front of the television cameras about domestic and foreign policy, economics, and various appointments. There should be no secrets from the people. And everyone must appear in front of them as he truly is.

As we can see, even with the present turn of affairs, the government will not submit its resignation. There are serious reasons for this: The power based on the entire apparat system has always supported the supreme authority.

How could Brezhnev rule our country? No, it was not Brezhnev who ruled. He was merely the symbol. What ruled was force. It was established in our country as the only legal norm. Force, fear, intolerance, and cruelty... imbued our lives and were the nerve of life which are still preventing us to stand tall to this day.

There is intolerance in this hall as well, as a mark of all those years. It is found in the catcalls and aspiration to shut the speaker's mouth. To the people restructuring (along with surmounting the economic crisis) means the elimination of the apparat system. This system developed entirely on the basis of the suppression of the individual and the rightlessness of everyone in particular; rightlessness and, consequently, defenselessness. We have had in our lives all too many lies.

Yes, there is glasnost today but the fact that it was given to us as a gift will not make us freeze in a state of grateful reverence. Democracy must be developed.

It is the guarantee of our strength and, above all, our future.

We cannot, we must not make our future dependent on the moral qualities of a single individual. We must give the people democratic management based on the law and surmount the economic crisis. This is possible only if we establish an efficient legislative right, the right to make demands on people who are here, in this hall, representing the government. We must address demands to them and to those who are behind them. This will be the demand of the people. (Applause).

From the address of a group of voters: "The weekly SEMYA and Central Television described and showed the places where the victims of mass repressions were buried. They included the Don cemetery and the Kalitnikovskoye and Rogozhskoye cemeteries in Moscow. In the place where the dust of tens of thousands of our fellow citizens was buried, on 6 January of this year, at a meeting with workers in science and culture at the CPSU Central Committee, Comrade Gorbachev said that we must single out these places, put them in order, and erect monuments. A respective CPSU Central Committee resolution was passed. However, no real steps to this effect were taken in our city. Why? The search led to other places as well, where there were thousands of skulls and bones. We must honor the memory of our fellow citizens who were the victims of excesses and executions. These were tens of thousands of innocent people who were executed. The history of mankind knows of no other such crimes. Unquestionably, a substantial help in the further investigation could be provided by the files of the KGB. To this day, however, they are tightly sealed. Meanwhile, hundreds of thousands of our families are unable to pay their respects to the memory of unjustly executed or tortured individuals. Is it not time to settle this matter?..."

In order to restrict the power of the apparat, we must organize control by the people over one of the powerful principles of its viability. One wing of the KGB protects the people from external enemies while another, incomparably more powerful, is engaged in a separate specific function. No, I do not have in mind the struggle against corruption. After the hard lessons of the past, after millions of people killed, all of them without exception with the direct involvement of the Cheka-MGB, to this day the threats to democracy must not be considered mythical.

Under the circumstances of the initial steps on the road to democracy and, at the same time, the desire to suppress, it, a power such as the KGB assumes a particular meaning, for the KGB obeys the apparat alone; the KGB has been taken out of the control by the people. It is the most concealed, the most secret of all governmental institutions. Naturally, I do not even think of casting aspersions on the personnel of this department. I am speaking of its role in our life.

Deep secrecy, justified as a feature of its occupation, ensures the actual lack of control over the KGB, although its actions are sometimes quite questionable. No truth can be found in the course of such clashes with the KGB. To seek the truth is dangerous. Manipulations involving alleged mental abnormality can to this day threaten the people who present a danger to the apparat.

The democratic renovation of the country has not changed the position of the KGB in the political system. This committee provides comprehensive control over society and over every separate individual. Within the system of ministerial relations, it clearly stands above the state, obeying only a narrow group of the apparat. The appointment of the chairman of the KGB must go through the Congress of People's Deputies. The people's

STENOGRAPHIC RECORD

Seventh Session

31 May 1989

deputies must know the size of this organization and demand accountability for all violations of the law and be familiar with its budget. (Applause). It would also be better to move the KGB service from Dzerzhinskiy Square. We have quite an unforgettable bloody history of the main building where the "sword defending the people" rests. From here for decades orders were issued for the destruction or persecution of millions of people. Grief, moaning, and pain were sown by this service over our native land. Within this building people were tortured and hurt, people who, as a rule, were the best, the pride, and the flower of our nations. The very complex of these buildings, so unexplainably monumentally huge, somehow confirm who in reality holds the power in the country. Such a complex is unsuitable for the center of Moscow. It would be fair for the KGB to surrender these buildings (the need for premises in our city is tremendous) perhaps baking them a book repository, and build a modest building for itself in the suburbs, but not one like its hospital in Pokrovskoye-Streshnevo. This hospital is surrounded by a pine forest and is an ultramodern huge building, linked by subway to the center. Next to it is the rayon tuberculosis hospital, which is simply a wretched building. The KGB is not a service but a real underground empire which has as yet not surrendered its secrets, for the deepest ones have only been identified. Despite such a past, this service maintains its special, its exclusive status. It is the most powerful of all the existing instruments of the apparat. It is unequal in terms of efficiency and impeccable functioning. A Defense and State Security Commission is being planned under the Supreme Soviet. Let us hope that this will deal with the activities of the MVD and KGB (the MVD as well has not left the best of traces in our history). This commission must be given a new content and engage in efficient control. This is one of the essential tasks which, it is true, would be difficult to accomplish both by the USSR Supreme Soviet and the future Congresses of People's Deputies.

The voters in my district have yet another appeal which I received yesterday. It deals with state statistics. "The Congress of People's Deputies believes that in recent years the USSR State Committee for Statistics was one of the state organizations whose activities contributed to the manipulating of public opinion with false figures which embellished reality. To this day the USSR State Committee for Statistics has not shown its ability to reduce the flow of questionable accountability which the state authorities impose upon enterprises and establishments. The congress resolves (a draft motion) the following: to set up a commission of people's deputies within the framework of the Supreme Soviet to determine the true situation of affairs in the economy, particularly in establishing the true dynamics of the national income, inflation processes, size of monetary emissions, growth of labor productivity, and reduction of the state apparatus. The people must be informed of the results of the commission."

The election of people's deputies not every 5 but 3 years is of essential significance. Such elections must be universal, direct, and secret. The political development of the people is maintaining a pace such that the present composition of the congress will no longer reflect such changes and, metaphorically speaking, the "5-year term" will block a number of important decisions which are so necessary for the people.

We have reached a critical point in our development.

Petr Chaadayev, an original Russian philosopher and friend of Pushkin wrote 150 years ago: "We are an exceptional people. We are one of those nations which somehow are not part of mankind but exist only for the sake of teaching the world some kind of terrible lesson...."

There should no longer be any more "terrible lessons." (Applause).

Let me now say a few words on yesterday's ovations heard in the hall on the use of force in Tbilisi. It is criminal to kill for convictions. Slogans and political alienation, speaking of dissidence, cannot be justifications for murder. Such a position comes close to the one which led our country to commit murders unparalleled in the world and which we are still unable to comprehend with our minds and consciences. After these ovations it is clear to me that a separation is virtually inevitable; more things divide than unite us. These are differences in understanding the very foundations of life. (Sustained applause).

A.-M.K. Brazauskas: Deputy Masaliyev has the floor.

A.M. Masaliyev, first secretary, Kirghiz Communist Party Central Committee (Issyk-Kulskiy Territorial Electoral District, Kirghiz SSR): Dear people's deputies, our electorate expects of us sensible approaches to the solution of the pressing problems, a surfeit of which have accumulated in all areas of life. Things will not improve as a result of emotions, meetings or malicious speeches. We need practical actions. This was mentioned in the report submitted by Mikhail Sergeyevich Gorbachev and in the speeches of many deputies. I fully agree with them.

Inasmuch as the entire power is transferred to the soviets, naturally the role and responsibilities of the USSR Supreme Soviet and its standing authorities will increase. What to do for the Supreme Soviet to exert a real influence on improving the social atmosphere and accelerating the solution of socioeconomic problems? All of us must think about this. Strictly speaking, this is precisely the purpose of the reform in the political system.

I would like to express my own considerations. Bearing in mind that the Congress of People's Deputies will meet twice annually, we should review both the nature and duration of the work of the Supreme Soviet and the

Seventh Session

31 May 1989

congresses, and establish the term and length of the spring and autumn sessions. As to the permanent commissions and committees, they should work as much as is necessary in order thoroughly to prepare the various items before submitting them to the Supreme Soviet.

In my view, two congresses and two sessions annually is excessive. The main thing in the work of the supreme authority, as of the congress, should be greater practicality and concreteness and common sense. In this case a great deal depends on us, deputies. For the time being, emotional discussions rather than practical thoughts predominate.

Here is another problem related to the authority of the deputies and the activities of the Supreme Soviet. It affects work with motions and critical remarks submitted by the deputies. We need an efficient mechanism for their summation, evaluation, and consideration, such that no single suggestion submitted by a people's deputy is ignored. Such a mechanism could be provided, for example, by a specially created Supreme Soviet commission or, perhaps, a commission of the congress, which would consider all suggestions submitted by deputies and issue respective recommendations on their development and application and supervise their practical implementation. Such an approach would largely prevent formal replies, as was the case in the past. The people would like to see their deputies not only as people who criticize one and all but also who are actively working and making their personal contributions to restructuring, to solving the problem of food supplies to the population and organizing the implementation of resolutions and laws which we have been entrusted to pass.

Let me say a few words on relations among nationalities. This matter, actually, is a most complex, touchy, and, let us frankly say, insufficiently studied. As we already pointed out, it will be considered at the Central Committee plenum. It is natural that a great deal of attention to this problem has been paid by the congress as well. As we know, on the initiative of the party's Central Committee and with the active participation of all areas of the country, a search is under way for constructive approaches aimed at uniting society and broadening the sovereignty and independence of the republics. We, deputies representing the Kirghiz SSR, support these steps and hope that they will be embodied in specific legal acts. Above all, it is necessary to settle on a just basis relations in the realm of economics, both between the republic and the center as well as among Union republics. A great deal of distortions exist in this area. For example, a one-sided economic development based on extracting and raw material sectors has developed in Kirghizia, adversely affecting the shaping of the budget and the solution of social problems. In connection with preparations by the Republic for converting to cost accounting and self-management, we must thoroughly consider and solve all such problems. It is our profound conviction that the way of the further development of nations and nationalities passes not through isolation but through organically combining republic autonomy with national interests. Indeed, a strong Union means strong republics and a strong center, and sincere trust and reciprocal respect by our peoples toward each other. That is why as we solve our regional problems we, people's deputies, nonetheless must remember our tremendous responsibility to our descendants in protecting the cohesion of the multinational land of the soviets. For different approaches would, in the final account, cause serious harm to each region and its ethnic groups. Lenin taught us to approach each phenomenon specifically and historically. Taking this into consideration, we believe that at the present difficult stage in the country's development, it is important to focus our efforts not on revising existing national-state forms or remapping the territory of one republic or another, for this would destroy the existing economic relations and result in new economic difficulties, more than enough of which already exist in our country. Naturally, the problems of the republics must be considered and resolved. Today we must establish order in the local areas. Moscow will not do this for us. Each republic has major opportunities and rights to surmount many manifestations of social injustice, to eliminate distortions in its linguistic policy, and to develop culture, education, and other areas.

I cannot avoid the question of democratization of our social life. Unquestionably, the democratic processes taking place are major gains of restructuring. They should be welcomed and consolidated. Nonetheless, we must not forget even for a minute the need to strengthen conscious discipline. Unfortunately, we have unjustifiably weakened this important work. It is no accident that on the crest of the wave of democracy extremist elements have emerged, which are fanning nationalistic moods and deliberately undermining the authority of the Soviet state and the Communist Party and its policy and ideology. As the facts confirm, here and there matters have reached the level of blasphemous encroachments on values we consider sacred. There have been appeals to "turn back from October to February." Aspersions have been cast even on Lenin.

Yes, we can only agree with Comrade Yeltsin in that during the years of restructuring problems of improving food supplies to the population have not been solved; there is a scarcity of housing and goods. Nonetheless, all of us are adults. We understand that such difficult problems cannot be solved in 4 years. All deputies must be well familiar with this fact. However, to say that "nothing has been done and the present composition of the Central Committee and the government will be unable to solve the problems," although this sound attractive to the naive, remains, nonetheless, unfair. There have been changes in the economy, culture, and other areas. Is this not confirmed by the past elections and the proceedings of our congress? (Applause).

Speculating on democracy, some individuals are building their political careers by defaming noted party and state leaders, using to this effect the press, television, and

STENOGRAPHIC RECORD

Seventh Session

31 May 1989

radio which, as the deputies have said, are not always objective. To a certain extent they have been able to develop in the society a negative attitude toward the personnel of party committees as being bureaucratic. Naturally, they include bureaucrats and irresponsible people but are such people also not found among the intelligentsia and among people working in other areas of activity? The party apparatus as well suffers from many shortcomings and distortions. This was accurately mentioned by the deputies. We must draw conclusions: We must more rapidly restructure the style and methods of its work and achieve real results. However, we also see that in addition to the criticism of the apparatus, a frontal attack has been mounted against the party, and Lenin's stipulation that no single party could exist even a single day without an apparat is being rejected. We hope that the Law on the Press, which is now being drafted, will define the rights and obligations of the personnel of the mass information media and will help those who, to repeat Lenin's words, cloud their mind with the freedom of the press, with its brilliant swamp fire (see *"Poln. Sobr. Soch."* [Complete Collected Works], vol 44, p 83), preaching a so-called "pure democracy," and trying to take the press out of control. In our society, as Comrade Gorbachev has frequently repeated, all agencies, public organizations, and leading party and state personalities must be controlled by the people. In recent years some economists have become firmly "established" in newspapers and journals. They regularly speak on television and discuss failures in the economy and financial difficulties. This is being discussed at the congress. However, no sensible solution to the situation is being offered. Do they live outside society? (Applause).

Voice from the hall: They do make suggestions.

A.M. Masaliyev: You are making suggestions but we, the sovereign Kirghiz Republic, have not seen a single scientist during those years. We have not received a single suggestion from you. (Applause). It is time for all of us to join efforts and develop a constructive basis for our activities, directing them to the practical solution of topical problems.

As you and I know, a difficult situation is developing in a number of areas. This is seriously influencing the country's sociopolitical atmosphere. Let us frankly say that in frequent cases the various groups and associations which have appeared here cause social conflicts and instigate the people to engage in confrontation with the party and soviet authorities and provoke the development of relations among nationalities in dangerous ways, involving the population in a "democracy by meetings," and calling for strikes. All of this is doing tremendous harm to restructuring and causes suffering to the toiling people.

Some people have shown such a great liking for meetings and demonstrations that even during the proceedings of the congress they have not put a stop to them. Why? For what purpose? It is clear that it is not for the sake of consolidating the society but for increasing political tension. It is as though the worse it is for the country, the better it is for them. Yet, today all opportunities exist to consider and solve any arising conflicts calmly and efficiently at each enterprise where councils of labor collectives have been created on a democratic basis, headed by authoritative people. Other democratic instruments to this effect exist as well.

We heard in this hall voices calling for the creation of factions even among the corps of deputies. This, too, is presented as a requirement of democracy. This is the first time that people have truly experienced democracy, but there are already those who would like to turn it into anarchy and describe the ukases passed by the Supreme Soviet Presidium for purposes of bringing order, antidemocratic. Possibly such legislative acts may be as yet imperfect. However, in the interest of the overwhelming majority of the people they must be functional and we support them. (Applause).

Finally, some speakers, as we already mentioned, have accused the deputies from the Central Asian republics as being obedient and voting as a block for everything. To say the least, this is not serious. Let us not impose our unacceptable opinions on others.

In turn, we would like for Moscow, the capital of the USSR, and for Leningrad, the cradle of the October revolution, to be in the vanguard of the struggle for restructuring and for the communists, the working class, and the intelligentsia of these the largest economic, scientific, and cultural centers, to set the example of organization and order. We hope that the Moscow and Leningrad groups of deputies will also work in this direction. Thank you for your attention. (Applause).

A.-M.K. Brazauskas: Deputy Bunich has the floor.

P.G. Bunich, corresponding member of the USSR Academy of Sciences and faculty chief at the Moscow S. Ordzhonikidze Institute of Management (from the USSR Academy of Sciences): Esteemed chairman, esteemed deputies! Society is currently showing an unprecedented interest in our congress. This upsurge of interest is the first since the celebrated Congress of Soviets that adopted the Decrees on Peace and Land. The country has declared a kind of sit-down strike—everyone who can goes to work, but does no work; everyone watches television. This is not a show; it reflects the fact that the people pin their hopes on us. And this hope is, for us, a supreme law, higher even than the Constitution.

No one expects us to do everything immediately, to resolve all the problems at once. All we have to do is to move the ship off the sandbank. It has been said here that if you pull on the right-hand oar, you go to the left, and if you pull on the left-hand oar, you go to the right. It seems to me that if the ship is sitting on a sandbank

STENOGRAPHIC RECORD

Seventh Session

31 May 1989

and some people on the extreme right and left start rowing and waving their oars about, it will not move from the spot at all, it will only sink in more deeply. And even overturn.

But when the economic interest of every person throughout our society is involved, and when every person, by virtue of that interest, jettisons the huge ballast that weighs him down, the ship will set off on course for the first time. Then we will gain high world rankings in terms of prosperity, and will lose the high world rankings that we would like to lose.

In particular, we hold one of the highest rankings in the world in terms of expenditure and recovery of oil. We rank first in the world, perhaps, in terms of percentage plan fulfillment. Where we are rich is in this percentage, rather than in what lies behind it. We hold a high world ranking in the number of resolutions, and their length is unique. An enormous number of managers work on these resolutions and according to them. We now hold, so to speak, clear leading positions in waiting lines, the number of people carrying bags, the size of each bag, and the quantity of air it holds. In the attempt to rectify matters we deprive ourselves even of the dubious distinction of leadership in terms of rallies.

Since restructuring began we have constantly acknowledged that it is going slowly, and we have even worked out a formula: more slowly than we would like. This formula is inadequate, although it is a bit better than the one we had before, when we used to profess the concept of isolated shortcomings. Everyone knows that there is no such thing as an isolated shortcoming.

However, all this does nothing to make us more radical. In the sphere of foreign relations we have clear, acknowledged achievements. In the sphere of glasnost the congress itself testifies that here too we have achievements. But in the economic sphere our changes have been almost exclusively cosmetic.

I would like to name some of these. There are the state orders, which are not state orders at all, but are only a camouflaged, inferior name for the old state targets. There is pseudo-wholesale trade, pseudo-self-financing instead of real self-financing. There are the concerns, which in principle should differ from ministries, but in practice are no different. There is marketing, which we have begun to talk about a lot now and to call for, forgetting that in any marketing textbook the first line is this: Trade arises when supply is greater than demand.

But that is not all. There is evidence of a backlash, especially in recent times. A clear trend has developed to manage the economy by means of bans, a trend toward bans rather than incentives. And this is done in the guise of emergency measures. Many examples could be cited. Two of them: The normative relationship between the growth of labor productivity and the average wage, which was introduced in its strict form comparatively recently. As everyone is well aware, this has done no good. In my view this measure is fundamentally inadequate, because our inflation has deeper roots. Then there is the "shooting down" of the cooperative system that occurs, the vacillation, whereby first we create privileged conditions for it, then we start inflicting undeserved wounds.

The real emergency measures, in my view, are simply radical measures. It is necessary to begin a real reform, not to engage in emergency measures, as we have been doing for all the years of Soviet power, including the last 4 years. And when we are called upon to adopt solely these draconian measures, personally it frightens me. I am afraid that the really important creative work will not take place at the same time, and once again the most important thing will be postponed. The main shortage is the shortage of radical measures, both as regards their formulation, and even more, I would say, as regards their implementation.

Who is to blame? There are people who say that implementing the NEP [new economic policy] was all very well. At that time people were, so to speak, not yet genetically ruined; at that time the fire of enterprise was still in them, they had not yet forgotten that they can be the masters, that they can show initiative.

It is claimed that we are in a far worse position now. Perhaps that is true, but I think at least that it is a gross exaggeration to say that people have lost the proprietorial sense. This sense can be revived very rapidly, and the cooperative system is the proof. Perhaps that system has not yet assembled all the best people, perhaps the decent person has only half-heartedly joined in as yet, but nonetheless we can see what energy this form of activity shows.

They say that economic leaders are to blame. I wish to say that those to whom reform is advantageous cannot be to blame. It is advantageous to the people, and on the whole it is advantageous to economic leaders. And today, in any case, it is not a question of economic leaders. Because even if they very badly wanted revolutionary changes, they can do virtually nothing. Nearly everything is simply forbidden for them. In the future we will indeed come up against the problem of economic leaders of enterprises, and also the training of collectives. And that will be perhaps our most belatedly tackled task, and our most difficult. So who, then, is to blame?

For 4 years we have been saying (recently both party and government leaders, but first and foremost party leaders, have begun to say this) that the blame rests mainly with the central departments. More precisely, the central economic departments, which are afraid of responsibility, afraid of making radical decisions.

Seventh Session

31 May 1989

After all, in our country not one person has ever been penalized for going too slowly, only for going too fast. And this danger, the personal danger, holds back everything, under cover of state security.

Moreover the central economic departments are, it must be admitted, losing their position as the main component in the economy, the main component in the country, the position they held under the edict system, and even losing their places. It has been said here today and yesterday that those who came through the elections for territorial okrugs underwent great tempering and have many instructions from the voters. I must say that there were territorial elections where everything was very difficult, but there were also those where everything was very easy. There were social organizations where it was also difficult, and others where it was easy. At the Academy of Sciences, as you know, we went through purgatory. Our voters said to us that as long as the economy is in the hands of leaders like Gostev and Pavlov, restructuring will not happen. (Applause).

I should also say that there is no sign of an improvement, but everything is fine at the State Committee for Labor and Social Questions. Recently the Gosplan proposed the extension of this whole present-day existence of ours not only for the remaining 18 months of this 5-year plan, but for another 2 years. This proposal naturally met with the support of the State Committee for Construction Affairs [Gosstroy], which is now extending its "unfinished construction work" to the whole of society. I should say quite objectively that Nikolay Ivanovich Ryzhkov did not accept these proposals, did not support them. To some extent I find that encouraging.... It is a pity that in our country it is not a crime to discredit the Soviet economy.

What is to be done?

The picture today is like this: If an enterprise makes a loss, it receives the same wages as a profitable one; if an enterprise works five times better, it receives the same wages as if it worked five times worse. That is in the state sector. Thus, the situation in the country is that we have too many who work poorly (loss-making enterprises, and officially 15 percent of our enterprises are loss-making), and if you add the low-profit ones (these are also loss-making, but in a less critical form, and I think they account for 50 percent). [sentence as published] And if you look at the profit-making enterprises, assessed by our excessive Soviet prices, and assess them by any other (world) prices, they too appear to have extremely low profits.... So all this is the reason why when a person works less well, things are better for him. He earns more per unit of labor. Therefore in our country, instead of an urge to rise up from the bottom, there is an urge to sink down to the bottom. And the vast majority of our enterprises are, to an increasing extent, lying at the bottom, where life is easy, quiet, and crowded.

This is what I would say: "He who does not work, eats him who works." That is how it is. Unfortunately we live better than we work, although we live very badly. Because we are eating our children's food. Because we are slipping into debt to other countries. Because we are ruining the ecology, because we are ruining our children's health, because we teach them badly and ruin their education. Because we are eating into the accumulations fund and at the same time technical progress, but they, the future generations, will have nothing to eat into, they will have to take more out of themselves than at present. (Applause).

The main means of resolving our problems was correctly defined 4 years ago. It is economic accountability, when everyone will know that everything he has done belongs to him, minus taxes. When everyone will know that everything he has failed to do, is at his own expense, and that socialism is not social security. And then very few will drown. Because you drown when you know that there is a life belt, when there is a state that will fish out any drowning man. When there is no life belt, everyone will swim—slowly, poorly, but they will not drown. A few will drown, but those who drown will deserve to drown. (Applause).

But instead of all this, stubbornly, with a persistence worthy of a better cause, we are introducing the first and second models of economic accountability. These are both patently old models, although they are passed off as new. Recently one speaker said on the television that there is a "big" difference between them: In the first model you measure the height of a building from the floor to the ceiling, in the second—from the ceiling to the floor. That is the only difference between them. (Applause).

But the main point is not that they are identical, but that they are identically bad. The solution is really to transfer enterprises to self-reliance [samosoderzhaniye], to relying on what they have earned. Then, at first they will have to pay turnover tax, and later tax on the wage fund, which unfortunately does not yet exist. Interest must also be paid to the bank: That is a normal phenomenon. And insurance payments must be made, not today's, but higher, and insurance against commercial risk must be introduced, which we are unfamiliar with, because no one takes any risks. But if everyone is taking risks, they will not do so without such insurance. Lease payments must also be introduced....

Incidentally, on the subject of the lease—some people are beginning to say: Let us hand over the factories to the workers. Let us hand them over. Then, people who work, for instance, in Aeroflot will receive, perhaps, a million rubles per person. And people who work at a hairdresser's will receive the scissors, and nothing else. Let us hand over this auditorium. To whom shall we hand it over when we leave? To the 10, 20, or 30 technical workers?

STENOGRAPHIC RECORD

Seventh Session

31 May 1989

The country has taken taxes from all of us on identical terms, and created a common pot, but has not distributed from that pot on identical terms. And therefore we cannot hand out the property, but we should offer the opportunity to lease it, or for those who so wish, to buy it. Incidentally, leasing is a necessity, in this way, both for large enterprises and for small ones. Among agriculturalists, I have come across this view: Leasing is necessary only for the individual peasant farm. And that a large enterprise should not be leased, and that it cannot, in principle, be leased.... There is the concept of state ownership, it cannot operate in its present form. The property cannot be handed out. So the lease system remains wherever there is state ownership.

Then, after the lease, everything should belong to the collective alone. It can no longer be tied by any strings from above. (Incidentally, these strings from above remind me of the rope, the noose.) But all this is only possible on one condition: that the enterprise is absolutely autonomous, not partially, but absolutely. This does not mean that we are such ignorant people as to propose a free market. It is simply that in present-day conditions the market always incorporates the role of the state. The relationship changes, there is a castling move: At the bottom is the market, the basis is the market, and everything that the market cannot do or does worse than the state—all this is done by the state by market methods, methods that do not damage, break, or destroy our main strength—the strength of economic accountability.

Finally I would like to say that in the near future nonstate property will clearly arise at every state enterprise. After all, if I am on a lease system and I have a development fund that I have earned, after paying to the state everything I owe to it, the projects I have built from that fund are mine. That is, cooperative, or joint-stock, property arises, which will be distributed on the basis of shares. Everyone will have an interest in accumulations, everyone will really strive not to eat up everything today, but to set something aside for the future.

Another thing: Say I take out a loan. I use it to build a shop, a plant, whatever you like. Whose is it? Mine, and mine alone. Say I lease a tractor for 5 years. It does 7 years' service. For 2 years it is absolutely mine.... I want to emphasize this idea of creating cooperative ownership simultaneously at every state enterprise. And as long as our Ministry of Finance does not stifle the enterprises with savage taxes or eat up this development fund, we will indeed have this hybrid, strong combination.

This restores the individual's interest. And that is the most important thing. It could all be legalized in a single law on the enterprise and the cooperative, which Mikhail Sergeyevich has spoken of. The new general law should be based on the Law on the Cooperative System, which is viable. But today, when two different laws exist, the cooperative system is to some extent plundering the state sector.

Different blood groups cannot be compatible. The healthy ruble, the living ruble, will conquer the dead ruble of our sleeping bear, our state sector. And the people will flee the state sector. After just over a year there are 2 million people in the cooperative system, as against 150,000 before. The state sector lost 1 million of these.

They are not the worst people, they are those who can go, and those who do not go stay behind and grumble at the cooperative system. (Applause). If a girl leaves her fiance for another, the likelihood is that the first boyfriend's hidden flaws were to blame. Therefore we should not curse the cooperative system, but impose order in the cooperative system—that is the first thing. And when that order has been created, extend it to the state sector. That is the second thing.

Whose idea was all this? I have heard it said here that it was the Muscovites' idea. I am all in favor of the Muscovites. I would have great pleasure in agreeing that it was our idea. But it was mankind's idea, it came from his wise experience, including the experience of socialist development. Remember our own NEP, remember China, and much more besides.

It is now planned that we should go on living for another 18 months in this system. But please, tell me this, if we can go over to a new system in 18 months' time, why do we have to wait for 18 months? What is there that we cannot do today? (Applause). Is it not enough that we have already been waiting for 3 and $^1\!/_2$ years?

At the beginning of that time, a dilemma was proclaimed—the 5-year plan or restructuring. The useless 5-year plan, or proper restructuring. And then we chose the 5-year plan. I propose—and I proposed this before, some years ago—that we begin to introduce restructuring without delay. Mikhail Sergeyevich has said that many things must be done during this 5-year plan. That is a new position, because formerly it was proposed to postpone everything to the next 5-year plan. Let us at once give the Ministry of Finance one last chance, let us give it 6 months to set things to rights, let it introduce all the necessary taxes and remove the remaining regulators of our economic life. Thank you for your attention. (Applause).

A.-M.K. Brazauskas: Comrade Makhramov has the floor. Comrade Toome will be the next speaker.

K. Makhkamov, first secretary, Tadzhik Communist Party Central Committee, Dushanbe (Dushanbe Territorial Electoral District, Tadzhik SSR): Comrade chairman, comrade deputies, as a USSR people's deputy, representing the interests of the voters of the capital of Tadzhikistan, I support the idea of the formula for the development of the Soviet federation: "strong center—strong republics." Nonetheless, I would like to express some considerations on the practical implementation of this profoundly meaningful thesis.

STENOGRAPHIC RECORD

Seventh Session

31 May 1989

Of late the press has published a number of materials on the restructuring of economic relations among the individual regions in the country. These and many other official discussions quite clearly reveal the thought that the so-called "raw material" republics are silently boycotting the application of the principles of territorial cost accounting. I emphasize, the principles. This is radically untrue. Although we support as a whole the concepts of self-financing and self-management of the republics, nonetheless their implementation mandatorily must meet three conditions:

First. Mandatory reform of wholesale and purchase prices.

Second. Conversion to the principles of cost accounting only on a nationwide basis. On this level we believe accurate the view expressed at the congress about the impossibility of solving basic economic problems within the boundaries of separate economic units. Third and final. The creation of a legal foundation in the guise of a law on economic relations among territories within the system of the state federation.

I believe that we would hardly be able to achieve our objective without solving these three problems. We know that of late ecology has become one of the greatest concerns of the press, radio, and television. Along with a number of sectors of the national economy, it is quite frequently related to hydraulic power construction. The significance of ecological problems, naturally, is not denied by anyone. However, society cannot do without the steady increase in a power base. This, too, is axiomatic.

In the next few years more than 150,000 new jobs must be created in the republic to ensure the employment of ever increasing manpower resources. Under the conditions of scarcity of land, when there are no more than 0.11 hectares of irrigated land per capita, this problem can be resolved essentially through the creation of new production facilities. How can this be achieved without electric power?

In this connection, let me say a few words about the Rigun hydraulic power plant which is being built in the republic on the Vakhsh River. This construction project has triggered a number of questions and heated arguments on the height of the dam, the area to be flooded, and, in particular, the further fate of the resettled people. Currently they are being considered and solved within the framework of economic and ecological expediency. However, we must point out that for quite some time we have felt the need to review the existing rates of compensation for people resettled from flooded areas, for their gardens, vineyards, and others, for these are some of the sources of income for those people. It is no secret that these rates, which are 20 or 30 years old, are totally inconsistent with reality. We believe that the people are raising entirely justified and reasonable demands, and we have no right to ignore them.

This problem has another aspect as well. For a number of years the Republic has been unable to develop small-scale hydraulic power production. Today this problem becomes particularly relevant, and here is why: In the 1930s and 1940s, in order to solve the problem of the country's cotton independence, hundreds of thousands of people who lived in the mountain areas of the Republic were resettled in the uninhabited valleys to grow cotton. Today, when the food problem is pressing, once again we must develop the mountain territories, for which reason some of the excess population in the valleys must be resettled to the mountain areas.

Hundreds of new settlements will appear. As a rule, they will be created in the valleys bordering rivers and streams. Under these circumstances, the question is what is more expedient: to string across mountain ridges and ravines hundreds of kilometers of power cables or build local hydraulic power plants, using the energy resources provided by nature itself? We know that in many countries, such as Sweden, Austria, and others, such resources are used virtually 100 percent. I already raised this question at the 27th Party Conference. More than 3 years have passed since but not a single step forward has been taken. Apparently gigantomania and the diktat of departmental interests have not been surmounted. For the time being, the prospects in this area are discouraging. To the best of our knowledge, Minenergomash does not even intend to undertake the production of low-power hydraulic turbines. Meanwhile, in our Republic alone there is an urgent and substantiated need for the construction of 27 low-power hydroelectric power plants to serve hundreds of settlements, the population of which today is deprived of electric power and everything that it provides. I believe that this matter affects not our Republic alone, and that it must be solved on a national scale.

Let me draw the attention of the people's deputies to yet another matter, the urgency of which is steadily growing. The course of restructuring in economic relations among enterprises, territories, and sectors, based on commodity-monetary relations, is unquestionably strategically correct. By granting autonomy to labor collectives and extensively developing the variety of forms of labor organization, converting to wholesale trade and other steps would mandatorily yield and are already yielding efficient economic results. However, in addition to strategic tasks there also are problems of a tactical nature which, occasionally, require a temporary retreat in order to achieve general success. I am referring above all to the currently developing system of material and technical procurements. The point is that conversion to wholesale trade and the significant expansion of so-called direct relations are taking place today under circumstances marked by the gravest possible scarcity of the absolute majority of items. The monopoly status of suppliers is totally unrestricted. Competing companies have not been created as yet. All of this leads to an even stricter diktat exercised by the owners of scarce products, compared to the past.

Seventh Session

31 May 1989

The army of legitimized fixers has grown sharply and, with them, let us be honest, so has group egotism. By this I mean excessive demands made by suppliers in signing contracts for the delivery of construction materials, food, transport facilities, and others. Here is an example: In Tadzhikistan a gold mining combine is being built, the completion of the first part of which is planned for next year. Therefore, in order to ensure the completion of the project on time, equipment and materials are needed on the basis of direct relations; problems of their manufacturing and procurement within the required deadlines must be solved, involving 40 manufacturing plants of five Union ministries. What is the result? Many plants refuse to sign contracts, referring to the lack of long-term relations. How can such relations be developed by an enterprise which is only under construction? Others demand, in exchange, goods which are in particular short supply: cement, trucks, bridge cranes, rolled metal goods, and millions of rubles of contributions to the development fund.

The Gossnab enterprises are engaged in wholesale trade under conditions of limited resources, compared to the volume of work. Thus, for example, for the majority of building organizations most items are assessed in terms of "million," and it is within such a range, if one could say so, that "resources" are being sold. You must agree that to classify such relationship as trade is simply not serious. In this case the small enterprises and projects under construction find themselves in particularly difficult circumstances. In this connection, a motion has been filed to revise the system of material-technical procurements and, for a while, to return, for certain items, which are in extreme short supply, to a strictly centralized allocation of resources, with strict penalties for a failure to deliver items or with good incentives if contracts are fulfilled. Such a temporary retreat would be justified. It would bring success and make it possible to solve subsequently strategic problems. For in order to win, occasionally one must retreat, otherwise unfinished production will increase and assets will become frozen. Debates have been going on for nearly 20 years in the country on how to lower the volume of unfinished construction without the problem being solved. This was quite pointedly mentioned in Mikhail Sergeyevich Gorbachev's report. Therefore, is it not time, once and for all, to make consistent the volumes of capital investment with the available material resources in the country and thus end all debates?

Comrade deputies! In the course of the congress we have all become aware of how many complexities and acute problems have accumulated in interethnic relations. All this is a result of the fact that we were prisoners of complacency, when wishes posed as deeds. These are the serious consequences of previous times which we must all overcome together. We are convinced that this must be done by joint efforts, in an atmosphere of amicability and the ability to listen to and understand one another. In particular, we in Tajikistan are still running up against the consequences of an inadequately conceived solution for questions connected with national-territorial demarcation in Central Asia. The mistakes made then are still affecting us. There are problems which we are solving on the spot. And there are problems which we cannot solve on the spot. Here is one of them, a tiny example. Many Tajiks and some Uzbeks who live in Tajikistan and Uzbekistan have long been asking about the correcting of passport entries on nationality, because distortions were committed in the past. This problem could have been sorted out a long time ago just by amending the 1974 provision on establishing national affiliation. Back in November last year Tajik and Uzbek leaders petitioned the USSR Council of Ministers on this score. A positive conclusion was apparently arrived at by the competent bodies, but the problem still has not been resolved. At the same time we and the leaders of Uzbekistan are doing all we can so that our peoples strengthen their friendship and solve together the issues that arise. We have begun to implement a joint program of practical measures to develop interethnic links between our republics, including both economic and cultural aspects. But now, in our opinion, it is time for a more profound approach to questions of improving the national state structure on an all-union scale. In order to broaden legal guarantees and meet the national-cultural needs of citizens living outside their national state formations, or if such formations simply do not exist, it seems necessary to resolve the issue of creating, in places where there is a concentration of inhabitants of a particular nationality, national regions with their own soviets and their own representation in the republics' highest state organs. As a whole the newly formed USSR Supreme Soviet should pay particular attention to questions of interethnic relations by resolving all the arising problems in a timely and considered manner.

Comrades, yesterday a Georgian deputy raised the question about the institution of second secretaries of union republic communist party central committees. I support Deputy Ishanov on this issue. I believe that if our Georgian comrades have a problem, then let them solve it for themselves. It is not necessary to spread the problem to other republics.

In the course of the congress some deputies' speeches from this platform have contained reproaches—undeserved in my opinion, and, I hope, not just in mine—against our party. Have there been mistakes and errors on the part of the party? Yes, there have. But was it not the party that led the October revolution? Was it not the party that raised up the entire multinational Soviet people and led them to victory in the Great Patriotic War? Today it has once again started a revolutionary restructuring of society. So, comrade deputies, let us all together help the party win a new victory which will determine the future of our country and of all socialism. Thank you for your attention. (Applause).

A.-M.K. Brazauskas: Comrade Toome has the floor.

STENOGRAPHIC RECORD

FIRST CONGRESS OF PEOPLE'S DEPUTIES OF THE USSR

Seventh Session

31 May 1989

I.Kh. Toome, chairman of the Council of Ministers of the Estonian SSR (Vyruskiy National-Territorial Electoral District, Estonian SSR): Dear chairman and deputies: The numerous vital problems facing the country and our congress have one key problem. The critical condition of our economy, which was repeatedly mentioned here. Despite the entire difference of views and opinions, I am confident that all of us will agree that the country's economic system requires radical change. The question, however, is what type of change and to what extent such change could be the same for all parts of our huge country. The past year-year and a half have convincingly proved that the initial assumption that the country and all its areas will be restructured more or less evenly, on the basis of a single scenario, did not prove justified. However, I think that it would be also thoughtless to demand of the government of the union and the Gosplan to formulate ways and solutions for each republic, oblast or kray. We, too, must become involved and thus assume responsibility.

The deputies from the Estonian SSR came to the congress after the recently held session of the Republic's Supreme Soviet. In the area of political decisions, the session simply condemned the 1939 Hitler-Stalin agreement on the division of Europe, which sharply changed the destinies of many nations, including the Estonian. The session also deemed it necessary to address itself to the USSR Supreme Soviet with a question on the outcome of our legislative initiative and draft USSR Law on Extrajudiciary Mass Repressions of the Period of Stalinism, which was submitted as early as last December. The session turned to the USSR Congress of People's Deputies with the appeal to take steps which would exclude any possibility of a repetition of anything resembling the tragic events in Tbilisi. However, the main question discussed at our session was that of finding ways of pulling the Republic's economy out of its stagnation. Entirely in accordance with the resolutions of the 19th All-Union Party Conference we consider regional cost accounting, the economic sovereignty of the Republic, combined with full responsibility to its people and the entire country for the results of economic management and the living standard, as being such a way.

Why did the people demand of us the elaboration of a concept of cost accounting for the Estonian SSR? Why did they follow so attentively each stage of this work and participated themselves in this process actively? Because they were dissatisfied with half-heartedness, one-sidedness, and lack of comprehensiveness and of necessary radicalism in the implementation of the economic reform and the lack of tangible results from the reform. It became clear that we should not rely, as in the past, exclusively on the center to present us with ready-made decisions which would be equally consistent with both the interests of the country and the Republic, the more so since the old administrative-sectorial approach remains prevalent while the reforms are being cautious and partial. An example of this may be found in the latest notes by the USSR Council of Ministers on further improvements in national economic management. Although the idea of reducing the number of Union ministries, committees, and departments is unquestionably correct, we see here absolutely clearly the aspiration to preserve and even to strengthen centralized management and to intensify the sectorial principle. The intention is to simplify the management structure essentially through the redistribution of the same old functions.

I believe that by now it is clear to everyone that the existing supercentralized economic mechanism has totally exhausted its possibilities, for which reason it has no future whatsoever. Any efforts at preserving it, whatever arguments may be brought forth, could only lead to an aggravation of the economic and political situation both in the country at large and in its individual areas.

We are convinced that a radical restructuring of the economy can be based only on the principle of decentralization of management, republic sovereignty, and regional self-management and self-financing. For the time being, our critics are unable to offer any sensible alternative to this idea.

The Estonian SSR formulated its cost accounting concept with the participation of Republic scientists and many major scientific centers in the country, economic managers, jurists, and practical specialists, prior to its approval by the Estonian SSR Supreme Soviet; it successfully passed the strict test of nationwide discussion. The session approved and is submitting as legislative initiative for your consideration the draft USSR Law on the Conversion of the Estonian SSR to Republic Cost Accounting, related to the concept. Such documents reflect the readiness of the Estonian people to assume full responsibility for the efficient management of the Republic's economy and, thereby, for increasing its contribution to the solution of union-wide problems.

Why is it that these questions cannot wait until the next congress? Above all because the idea of republic cost accounting involved in the revolutionary restructuring of society the broad masses, which consider any delay with the introduction of cost accounting a deliberate obstruction of popular initiative. Second, we intend to start the cost accounting system as of 1 January 1990 and this must be preceded by tremendous preparatory work which cannot be initiated without a legislative base. The deputies who were able to study our suggestions may have noticed that the concept does not have anything unnatural other than the realized aspiration to combine as an entity the Republic's economy, which is today divided into sectorial fragments.

The essence of the concept, without getting into details, is that we wish to live according to our means and spend no more than what we are able to earn ourselves. This in no case means the desire somehow to separate, to lock ourselves in, to abandon all-Union concerns, as we are being accused. Such a charge, to say the least, is not serious, for a closed economy would be fatal. Conversely,

Seventh Session
31 May 1989

the integration among republics and areas must increase and assume a new content rather than remain based on the old distribution principles governing funds and ceilings. The Union republics and regions are a natural market for our products and for purchasing the raw materials and machines we need. On that market equal partnership must be organized instead of a diktat by departments and officials. Regional cost accounting presumes an equivalent and mutually profitable trade, which is possible only under conditions of normal direct economic relations and with the existence of an all-union market in which all of us are interested. Therefore, we shall create it!

Let me repeat once again that we do not seek any privileges for ourselves. We would like to be as poor or as rich as we truly are. This should depend exclusively on us, on the way we are able to work and to organize our economy. We would like to pay for our expenditures out of our income while, naturally, fulfilling our obligations toward the Union budget. Participation in all-Union expenditures and financing governmental development programs are an inseparable part of the budgetary outlays of a cost accounting republic. We, the people's deputies must, naturally, jointly decide how to spend such funds, the entire budget of the country, including military expenditures, and demand full budget accountability.

Cost accounting puts us in a situation in which we simply cannot afford to manage wastefully. We do not expect an easy life. Thus, the forthcoming price increase of raw materials will put the cost accounting republic in a difficult position. Nonetheless, this forces us to truly practice resource conservation and to seek ways of lowering production costs and improving quality.

There are those who tend to believe that we are trying to replace departmental diktat from the center with diktat by bureaucrats from Tallinn. We are also being suspected of wishing to restrict the legitimate rights of enterprises, particularly those under Union jurisdiction. Such is not the case. Our purpose is to reduce administrative management methods and use economic instruments in influencing economic activities without harming in any way but, conversely, expanding the autonomy of labor collectives. This has been clearly codified in our documents. The number of bureaucrats must be reduced both in the center and in the local areas and their functions should be curtailed. For example, according to our plans, internal Republic decentralization of power would allow us to reduce the number of ministries by more than one-half. We are planning to give the enterprises the full right to sell their goods independently on any market and create, on the basis of economic interests, producer associations.

Finally, we would like to close the logical chain, so that the same principles of self-management and self-financing be applicable to all of our cities and rayons and so that rights and full responsibility be delegated to their local soviets. Some of the approaches included in our documents adopted at the session are noticeably different from the general principles of self-management and self-financing which were submitted to nationwide discussion, specifically on matters of sovereignty, state budget, taxation, financial-credit policy, ownership, banking, and others. Perhaps, however, this precisely is what is good. We believe, and reality has repeatedly proved it, that if conditions are different a model applicable to all cannot be efficient. It is the republic alone which can formulate the mechanisms and forms of cost accounting consistent with its historical and cultural traditions and unique economic circumstances. Let there be several models of cost accounting simultaneously functioning in the country. In any case, variety is better than uniformity. In our view, in order to sum up the study of this comprehensive experience and, on this basis, to formulate a strategy for the economic development of the entire country, a Supreme Soviet committee for economic policy should be set up. In the structure for deputy commissions and committees suggested to us no such committee is included.

Union ministries and departments have already given us their initial response to our documents. There is a great deal in them that they do not like. We can understand that but cannot agree with them. We want radical changes and see no other way for converting from the mechanism for economic management of a formally sovereign republic to a mechanism of economic management of a truly sovereign republic. It is only under the conditions of true sovereignty of Union republics that our Union, rallied by the unity of interests and objectives, can be strong. Sovereignty and equality are the foundations for reciprocal respect and trust which cannot exist between those who are equal and those who are more equal than others. For that reason our Republic has submitted the legislative initiative which calls for including in the agenda of the congress and, subsequently adopt, a USSR Law on the Conversion of the Estonian SSR to Republic Cost Accounting (Economic Independence). Such a law should provide the necessary legal guarantees so that as of 1 January 1990 the Republic could work and live in a new way. This will meet the interests of our Republic as well as those of the entire country.

Our congress has been called upon to become a congress which must create the future aspect of the Union. Its main task is to formulate constructive nonstandard decisions. That is why, dear deputies, we trust that you will give us your support. Thank you for your attention. (Applause).

A.-M.K. Brazauskas: Dear deputies, according to our agenda, today the debates were scheduled to end at 1830. We have still not heard speakers from Moldavia and Turkmeniya. A motion has been filed to let them speak tomorrow morning. So? The congress agrees. It will be necessary, in order to formulate the draft decree on this

Seventh Session
31 May 1989

matter, to choose an editorial commission. Deputy Azizbekov has the floor to submit a motion on the structure of that commission. Please.

P.A. Azizbekov, director of the history museum of Azerbaijan, Baku (Baku-Azizbekovskiy National-Territorial Electoral District, Azerbaijan SSR): The editorial commission in charge of formulating the draft resolution of the USSR Congress of People's Deputies, based on the report submitted by the USSR Supreme Soviet chairman "On Basic Directions in the Domestic and Foreign Policy of the USSR": commission chairman: Vadim Andreyevich Medvedev, CPSU Central Committee Politburo member, CPSU Central Committee secretary. Commission members: Leonid Ivanovich Abalkin, director, USSR Academy of Sciences Institute of Economics; Aleksandr Mikhaylovich Adamovich, director of the All-Union Scientific Research Cinematography Institute; Chingiz Aytmatov, writer, chairman of the board of the Kirghiz SSR Writers Union; Rukhi Mursal kyzy Aleskerova, chairman, executive committee, Lagichskiy Settlement Soviet of People's Deputies, Ismaillinskiy Rayon, Azerbaijan SSR; Nazhmiddin Ayubov, director of the Frunze Interkolkhoz Complex, Gissarskiy Rayon, Tadzhik SSR; Roza Atamuradovna Bazarova, chairman of the Turkmen SSR Supreme Soviet Presidium; Vyacheslav Aleksandrovich Borovkov, fitter, Kirovskiy Zavod Production Association, Leningrad; Vanda Sergeyevna Venglovskaya, weaver, 60-Letiya Velikoy Oktyabrskoy Sotsialisticheskoy Revolyutsii Flax Combine, Zhitomir, Ukrainian SSR; Arkadiy Ivanovich Volskiy, chairman, Committee for Special Administration of the Nagorno-Karabakh Autonomous Oblast, CPSU Central Committee department head; Grant Mushegovich Voskanyan, chairman of the Presidium of the Armenian SSR Supreme Soviet; Andrey Petrovich Gavrilov, editor of the newspaper VECHERNYAYA KAZAN, Tatar ASSR; Anatoliy Valeryanovich Gorbunov, chairman, Latvian SSR Supreme Soviet Presidium; Semen Kuzmich Grossu, first secretary of the Moldavian Communist Party Central Committee; Tamara Nikolayevna Dudko, chairman, executive committee, Partizanskiy Rayon Soviet of People's Deputies, Minsk, Belorussian SSR; Boris Nikolayevich Yeltsin, CPSU Central Committee member, Moscow; Lev Nikolayevich Zaykov, CPSU Central Committee Politburo member, CPSU Central Committee secretary, and first secretary of the Moscow CPSU Gorkom; Mirazolim Ibragimovich Ibragimov, chairman, Uzbek SSR Supreme Soviet Presidium; Daynis Evaldovich Ivans, chairman, Latvian People's Front; Tulepbergen Kaipbergenov, chairman of the board, Karakalpak ASSR Writers Union; Chary Kakadzhikov, brigade leader, 40 Let TSSR Kolkhoz, Ashkhabadskiy Rayon, Turkmen SSR; Vladimir Ivanovich Kolesnikov, department head, Rostov Railroad Transportation Engineers Institute; Marina Rizayevna Kontselidze, kolkhoz citrus grower, Khala Village, Kobletskiy Rayon, Georgian SSR; Nadezhda Aleksandrovna Kryuchenkova, teacher, Inzhavinov Secondary School No 2, Tambov Oblast; Ionas Pyatrovich Kubilyus, rector, Vilnyus State University, Lithuanian SSR; Vladimir Nikolayevich Kudryavtsev, vice president, USSR Academy of Sciences, director of the USSR Academy of Sciences Institute of the State and Law; Kirill Yuryevich Lavrov, actor, Leningrad Gorkiy Academic Bolshoy Drama Theater, chairman of the board of the USSR Union of Theater Workers; Ivan Dmitriyevich Laptev, editor in chief of the newspaper IZVESTIYA SOVETOV NARODNYKH DEPUTATOV SSSR; Maryu Yokhannesovna Lauristin, department head, Tartu State University, Estonian SSR; Dmitriy Sergeyevich Likhachev, academician, head of sector, USSR Academy of Sciences Institute of Russian Literature, chairman of the board of the Soviet Culture Foundation; Anatoliy Ivanovich Lukyanov, first deputy chairman of the USSR Supreme Soviet, CPSU Central Committee Politburo candidate member; Kirill Trofimovich Mazurov, chairman, All-Union Council of War and Labor Veterans; Guriy Ivanovich Marchuk, president of the USSR Academy of Sciences; Vitaliy Andreyevich Masol, chairman, Ukrainian SSR Council of Ministers; Vyacheslav Nikolayevich Matyukha, head of a comprehensive brigade, Construction Administration No 36, Mamontovneftepromstroy Trust, Tyumen Oblast; Roy Aleksandrovich Medvedev, writer; Sergey Tikhonovich Melekhin, machine tool operator, large-sections shop, Nizhnyy Tagil Metallurgical Combine, Sverdlovsk Oblast; Mikhail Alekseyevich Moiseyev, chief of general staff of the USSR Armed Forces, USSR first deputy minister of defense; Nursultan Abishevich Nazarbayev, chairman of the Kazakh SSR Council of Ministers; Konstantin Vladimirovich Nechayev, bishop of Volokolamsk and Yuryev Pitirim, chairman, publishing department, Moscow Patriarchy; Nadezhda Petrovna Nechetnaya, spinning worker at the Lenin Factory, Bryansk Oblast; Gaibnazar Pallayev, chairman, Tadzhik SSR Supreme Soviet Presidium; Nikolay Dmitriyevich Pivovarov, chairman, executive committee, Rostov Oblast Soviet of People's Deputies; Semen Ivanovich Platon, chairman, executive committee, Kagul City Soviet of People's Deputies, Moldavian SSR; Gavriil Kharitonovich Popov, editor in chief of the journal VOPROSY EKONOMIKI; Yevgeniy Maksimovich Primakov, director of the USSR Academy of Sciences Institute of World Economics and International Relations; Tadeush Karlovich Pupkevich, machine operator, rocking excavator, Narvskiy Open Pit, Estonslanets Production Association, Sillamyaz City, Estonian SSR; Georgiy Petrovich Razumovskiy, CPSU Central Committee Politburo candidate member and CPSU Central Committee secretary; Murtaza Gubaydullovich Rakhimov, director, Ufa XXII Syezda KPSS Petroleum Refinery, Bashkir ASSR; Nikolay Ivanovich Ryzhkov, chairman, USSR Council of Ministers, CPSU Central Committee Politburo member; Nazira Sabirova, brigade leader, Yangiabad Sovkhoz, Gurlenskiy Rayon, Khorezma Oblast, Uzbek SSR; Anatoliy Mitrofanovich Sbitnev, steel smelter, Kommunarsk Metallurgical Combine, Voroshilovgrad Oblast; Yefrem Yevseyevich Sokolov, first secretary, Belorussian Communist Party Central Committee; Vasiliy Aleksandrovich Starodubtsev, chairman, Lenin Kolkhoz-Breeding

Seventh Session

31 May 1989

Farm, Novomoskovskiy Rayon, Tula Oblast; Galina Ivanovna Stoumova, chief of shop, Gatchinskiy Sovkhoz, Leningrad Oblast; Yekaterina Davydovna Stupina, rayon hospital pediatrician, Tavricheskiy Rayon, Omsk Oblast; Olzhas Omarovich Suleymenov, writer, first secretary of the board, Kazakhstan Writers Union; Valentina Vladimirovna Tereshkova, Presidium chairman, Union of Soviet Societies for Friendship and Cultural Relations With Foreign Countries; Viktor Ivanovich Trefilov, vice president of the Ukrainian SSR Academy of Sciences, director of the Ukrainian SSR Academy of Sciences Institute of Material Science Problems; Vilesha Khachaturovich Khachatryan, motor vehicle driver, Zangezur Copper-Molybdenum Combine, Armenian SSR; Adamali Koshokovich Yusupov, head of the face breakage mining link, Mine imeni Leninskiy Komsomol, Kyzyl-Kiyskoye Mine Administration, Kirghiz SSR; Aleksandr Nikolayevich Yakovlev, CPSU Central Committee Politburo member, CPSU Central Committee secretary; and Arkadiy Petrovich Yamenko, rector, Novosibirsk Engineering-Construction Institute.

A.-M.K. Brazauskas: Thank you. I must make a small addition to those names. Comrade Ivan Afanasyevich Vasilyev, writer, Pskov Oblast, was also nominated member of the commission. Comrade Azizbekov may have simply omitted his name. I am therefore adding it.

Are there motions concerning the membership of the editorial commission? Are there supplements? Do you wish to nominate someone?

G.G. Borovikov, work superintendent, specialized mechanized operations administration No 10, Sochispetsstroy Territorial Construction Association (Sochinskiy Territorial Electoral District): In order not to set up a precedent in praising our CPSU Central Committee General Secretary and USSR Supreme Soviet Chairman Mikhail Sergeyevich Gorbachev, I object to Chingiz Aytmatov. (Applause). I nominate Bunich.

A.-M.K. Brazauskas: Please continue.

B.V. Kryzhkov, deputy production chief, Dzerzhinsk Kaprolaktam Production Association (Dzerzhinskiy Territorial Electoral District): Comrades, I simply wish to make a rejoinder on the microphone but I do not understand why the microphone is not turned on? Is it just for decoration? This is an interpolation. I listened carefully and I may be wrong but I did not hear the nomination of a single engineer. Naturally, it is possible that it was not contemplated that an engineer may turn out to be also a delegate. I believe, however, that it is time to realize that an engineer as well could be a delegate and obviously an engineer would have to be present among 60 people.

A.-M.K. Brazauskas: Do you have a specific motion?

B.V. Kryzhkov: Kuzubov, chief of shop, Gorkiy Oblast.

A.-M.K. Brazauskas: One minute, please, order.

From the hall: I nominate economist Nikolay Nikolayevich Engver, doctor of sciences, representative of the Udmurt Autonomous Republic.

A.-M.K. Brazauskas: Please.

A.L. Plotnikov, foreman, Kirovo-Chepetsk Machine Repair Plant (from the All-Union Komsomol): Since we do not find in the list a single representative of young people and engineers, and it was said here that there are none, I have a motion: to include in the list Viktor Mikhaylovich Minin, machine shop chief, Glebovskoye Production Poultry Association, Istrinskiy Rayon, Moscow Oblast.

A.-M.K. Brazauskas: Please.

V.N. Bushuyev, director, Siberian Scientific Research Power Industry Institute, Novosibirsk (from the USSR Union of Scientific and Engineering Societies): I believe that such a composition of the commission, numbering more than 50 people, would be unable independently to draft any document. Therefore, there is a draft for such a document. I motion that it be distributed tomorrow to all the deputies. Then that commission could receive our suggestions. (Applause).

A.-M.K. Brazauskas: No one has written any such special draft. In this case a great deal is based on the results of the debates. We can draw up a new list today, tomorrow, and so on. At that point we would probably spend half the time talking and arguing about the individual candidates. If there is any specific motion, we could consider it. Four nominations were submitted here. If supported by the congress, we could include them and vote for the commission. (Stirring in the hall).

Now, as to the rejection of Comrade Aytmatov. (Stirring in the hall). I believe that it is not mandatory for others to speak in favor of Comrade Aytmatov. Chingiz Aytmatov has not asked for help in this matter. I believe that we could leave the name of Chingiz Aytmatov as a deputy in this list.

A motion has been filed of adding to this list, which was read, Comrades Bunich, Kuzubov, Engver, and Minin, suggested by the comrades. Does the congress support the motion?

From the hall: (Unintelligible).

A.-M.K. Brazauskas: I then put the matter to a vote. Those in favor of this list with the additions, please raise your hands.

Thank you. You may lower your hands.

Who is against? Please count the votes.

Seventh Session

31 May 1989

A.G. Kostenyuk: Dear deputies, 30 deputies voted against.

A.-M.K. Brazauskas: Thus, 30 deputies were against. Abstentions? Please count.

A.G. Kostenyuk: Twenty-four deputies abstained.

A.-M.K. Brazauskas: I beg your pardon, how many?

A.G. Kostenyuk: Twenty-four.

A.-M.K. Brazauskas: Twenty-four abstained. Therefore, by majority vote we approved the commission's membership.

We have two more commissions that we have to set up. In this case matters may be more difficult. Thus, on your instruction, the Presidium of this congress closely considered all the motions which were received on the membership of the commission and held additional consultations. This is in relation to the commission on Tbilisi.

Therefore, deputies who, in your opinion, could study and evaluate all the materials on such problems independently and objectively were nominated.

The motion has been filed of including the following deputies in the commission to investigate the circumstances related to the Tbilisi events of 9 April. Since constant changes are being made in the membership of the commission, allow me to read the names. This would take no more than 5 minutes, perhaps even 4.

Commission chairman: Nursultan Abishevich Nazarbayev, chairman of the Council of Ministers of the Kazakh SSR. Commission members: Khardo Yulovich Aasmyaz, head of sector at the Maynor Design-Engineering Bureau, Estlegprom Association, Tallinn; Sergey Andreyevich Andronati, director of the A.V. Bogatskiy Physics-Chemistry Institute, Ukrainian SSR Academy of Sciences, Odessa; Oleg Georgiyevich Gazenko, academician, adviser at the office of the Institute of Medical-Biological Problems, USSR Ministry of Health, Moscow; Natalya Petrovna Bekhtereva, academician, director of the Scientific Research Institute of Experimental Medicine, USSR Academy of Medical Sciences, Leningrad; Genrikh Aviezerovich Borovik, writer, political commentator, USSR State Committee for Television and Radio Broadcasting, chairman of the Soviet Peace Committee, Moscow; Aleksandr Ivanovich Golyakov, first deputy chairman of the All-Union Council of War and Labor Veterans, Moscow; Vladimir Leonidovich Goborov, army general, chief of civil defense, USSR deputy minister of defense, Moscow; Dmitriy Sergeyevich Likhachev, academician, head of sector, Institute of Russian Literature (Pushkin House), USSR Academy of Sciences, chairman of the board of the Soviet Cultural Foundation, Leningrad; Vladimir Petrovich Lukin, gas cutter, Kolomna V.V. Kuybyshev Diesel Locomotives Manufacturing Plant, Moscow Oblast; Vilen Arutyunovich Martirosyan, colonel, commander of Army Unit 70425, Carpathian Military District, Rovno; Viktor Mikhaylovich Miroshnik, major general, chairman, Committee for State Security, Kazakh SSR, Alma-Ata; Konstantin Vladimirovich Nechayev, Volokolamsk and Yuryev Pitirim bishop, chairman of the publishing department, Moscow Patriarchate, Moscow; Rizoali Kadamshoyevich Odzhiyev, deputy chairman, Internatsionalist Cooperative Association, Tadzhik SSR, Dushanbe; Roald Zinnurovich Sagdeyev, academician, head of the Scientific-Methodical Center for Analytical Research, Institute of Space Research, USSR Academy of Sciences, Moscow; Anatoliy Aleksandrovich Sobchan, department head, Law School, Leningrad State University, Leningrad; Sergey Borisovich Stankevich, senior scientific associate, Institute of General History, USSR Academy of Sciences, Moscow; Vilen Fedorovich Tolpezhnikov, head of office, First Riga City N. Burdenko Clinical Hospital for Urgent Medical Aid, Riga; Vitas Pyatrovich Tomkus, journalist, Vilnius; Valentina Ivanovna Fedotova, editor in chief of the journal SOVETSKAYA ZHENSHCHINA, Moscow; Eldar Nikolayevich Shengelaya, Gruziya-Film Movie Studio director, Tbilisi; Pavel Vadimovich Shetko, lecturer, propaganda department, Minsk Oblast Komsomol Committee, Belorussian SSR, Minsk; Aleksandr Maksimovich Yakovlev, doctor of juridical sciences, head of sector, Institute of the State and Law, USSR Academy of Science, Moscow.

This is the membership of the commission appointed to investigate the Tbilisi events of 9 April, suggested by the Presidium.

Please, comrades, do not be in a hurry.

Are there any other motions concerning the membership of the commission?

From the hall: Vasilyev.

M.S. Gorbachev: The way I understand it he wanted to switch from another commission to this one.

A.-M.K. Brazauskas: Do we include Comrade Vasilyev?

A.N. Tavkhelidze, president of the Academy of Sciences of the Georgian SSR, Tbilisi (Shukhumi Rural National-Territorial District, Abkhaz ASSR): Deeply honored deputies: Let me inform you of the following: The moment the 9 April tragedy occurred, the Georgian scientific public and the Georgian public came out with a suggestion, and a commission was appointed by the Georgian SSR Supreme Soviet. It included outstanding Georgian scientists in the areas of law, medicine, and political studies. The commission did a tremendous amount of work. Let me say that the commission worked with the great support of the scientific and general public in Georgia. There is a conclusion on the part of this commission on the subject of legal and medical problems

Seventh Session
31 May 1989

and the chemical problem. All of this is at your disposal. The only thing we do not know is, to put it simply, who is it that appointed our deputy to head this operation? I forget his name.... Well, military commanders, who appointed him? Rodionov?

Mikhail Sergeyevich, on the second day or 2 or 3 days later, a new commission was appointed, headed by Deputy Tarazevich. The commission came to Tbilisi and worked there. It did not meet a single time with the deputies or with the other commission and did not take into consideration the opinion of the public. (Stirring in the hall).

Voice: That is why a commission is set up.

A.N. Tavkhelidze: Wait, wait.... How many times could a commission be set up? Let me just say that the commission worked, that there is such a commission. If our purpose is to draw the attention away, then you are right. In that case let Tarazevich answer why his commission was unable to establish the truth and why we are wasting people's money on assignments? What did they do, stay for a while in Tbilisi and leave? (Stirring in the hall). Let me just say that the only question remaining is the legality of imposing a curfew. Please, I beg of you, let Tarazevich answer us why his commission was unable to determine what was happening? (Stirring in the hall).

Voice: You are wrong!

A.N. Tavkhelidze: Why am I wrong? Let Tarazevich answer why he did not find out. Are we children or what? (Stirring in the hall).

A.-M.K. Brazauskas: Comrades, a motion has been filed to set up a commission, to do something.... Later one could already.... Comrades, there is a request to speak out only on the subject of the commission. Let us stick to that.

A.K. Safonov, chief of the Design-Construction Association, Alma-Ata House Building Combine (Alma-Ata-Alatauskiy Territorial District, Alma-Ata): I believe that the head of the commission cannot be a representative of any one of the republics. In my view, this would not be entirely objective. A motion was made yesterday to appoint Comrade Yakovlev, Politburo member, chairman of the commission. The Kazakh delegation insists on it. (Applause).

Deputy (name not given): I would like to make a statement to Deputy Gorbachev, Supreme Soviet chairman. Despite the demands of the voters, General Rodionov continues to attend the session. His address of yesterday indicated his belief in the legitimacy of the act of political assassination he committed. (Stirring in the hall).

My conscience and convictions. (Applause) do not allow me to cooperate with murderers. (Stirring in the hall). I therefore resign as deputy for as long as General Rodionov will remain among us. (Stirring in the hall).

A.-M.K. Brazauskas: Comrades, one thing at a time. (Stirring in the hall). Comrades, let us deal with the matter at hand. We are creating a commission, let us discuss the commission members.

T.M. Shamba, party committee secretary, CPSU Central Committee Academy of Social Sciences, Moscow (Gudautskiy Rural National-Territorial District, Abkhaz ASSR): Dear comrades, 2 days prior to the congress and for 5 days during the congress I have asked to speak on a variety of matters, so that I could express my views. I must tell you that the events we are discussing are related to the Abkhaz problem. I therefore would like, I request and insist, that tomorrow the floor be given to the representative of the Abkhaz ASSR to clear up the matter of the "guilt" of the Abkhaz people in these events.

A.A. Korshunov, brigade leader, Tashkent Aviation Production Association imeni V.P. Chkalov, Uzbek SSR, Tashkent (from the USSR trade unions): Yesterday all of you or many of you saw that film. Yesterday for several hours we discussed the matter of this commission. Volskiy said the right things here but only on an entirely different subject. This was so painful and so sensitive that today once again we are beginning to stir up passions in the hall. You can now imagine what is taking place there, in Tbilisi, in Georgia, and everywhere else. I beg of you, I conjure you not to stir up such passions! We are discussing a commission. This commission is quite extensive. All strata of our society are represented in it. Let us now put an end to the discussion on this topic and allow this commission to work! (Tempestuous applause). It includes many people, different people, and they will tell us and the entire Soviet people the truth, let us stop fanning the fire on this topic! (Applause).

A.-M.K. Brazauskas: Anyone else? Please. Do you have a motion? About the commission? Please.

M.N. Poltoranin, political commentator, NOVOSTI Press Agency, Moscow (from the USSR Union of Journalists): On the subject of the motions which were made here: to include Aleksandr Nikolayevich Yakovlev in the commission. We are setting up our first commissions and shall have to set up many other commissions. I believe that we should not include in such commissions Politburo members. As to the motion concerning Chairman Nazarbayev I, for instance, have known him for the past 20 years. He is a very objective comrade and he can make a full investigation. I would like you to second this motion.

A.-M.K. Brazauskas: Please to turn on Bishop Pitirim's microphone.

STENOGRAPHIC RECORD

Seventh Session
31 May 1989

Bishop Pitirim: Please excuse me, I would like to address a question to the chairman. Is it in order for members of another commission to participate in this commission? (Stirring in the hall).

From the hall: These are different commissions. If there are no objections to the deputies who were nominated here, we believe this to be possible, the more so since there will be no time conflict and they will be able to do their job. If there are resignations, let us hear them. (Stirring in the hall).

A.-M.K. Brazauskas: So, comrades, I see by the reaction in the hall that we must already vote on the commission. The last deputy.

T.Kh. Gdlyan, senior investigator for particularly important cases under the USSR Prosecutor General, Moscow (Tushinskiy Territorial Electoral District, Moscow): Academician Andrey Dmitriyevich Sakharov has participated in all the stages in the work of the commission investigating the Tbilisi tragedy. I move that Academician Sakharov be made part of this commission as well.

A.-M.K. Brazauskas: According to our data, Academician Sakharov has refused. That is the reason for which he is not in it.

T.Kh. Gdlyan: In that case, please excuse me.

A.-M.K. Brazauskas: Comrade Nazarbayev. He probably has the right to speak, for he is a member of that commission. Please.

N.A. Nazarbayev, chairman of the Council of Ministers of the Kazakh SSR (Alma-Ata-Iliyskiy Territorial Electoral District): I thank the Presidium for its trust. We are solving difficult problems. It would be wrong if everyone to whom such problems are assigned would begin to refuse them. The Kazakh people respect the Georgian people profoundly. Their pain is shared by all of us. Yesterday, having heard the Georgian side, we realized that the Georgians are firmly defending their opinion. We developed a different view after listening to General Rodionov. We saw the film yesterday from beginning to end. I beg the comrades to excuse me but the impression we gathered was that it presented no facts whatsoever other than the opinion of the announcer. (Applause). For that reason, dear comrade deputies, if I am given such an assignment I pledge to carry it out honestly and conscientiously. Nonetheless, bearing in mind that it is a question of national republics, I would still ask that a neutral person be appointed. (Stirring in the hall).

A.-M.K. Brazauskas: The entire list consists of people with a nationality, there is not a single person without nationality. (Applause).

N.A. Nazarbayev: Second, this entire matter must be investigated. For example, Comrade Tarazevich was there and investigated. The new chairman will have to investigate all of these problems all over again. You must decide. I have expressed my view and would like you to take it into consideration.

A.-M.K. Brazauskas: So, comrades, I put the matter to a vote. The name of Comrade Lev Borisovich Vasilyev has been added to the names of the members of th commission.

From the hall: Boris Lvovich.

From the hall: (Unintelligible).

R.Sh. Tabukashvili, head of the Gruziya-Film Motion Picture Studio Scenario Association (Batumi National-Territorial Electoral District, Georgian SSR): Taking into consideration that now the future chairman of the commission has already predetermined his attitude toward the events, I categorically insist that he withdraw his candidacy—that is, that we honor his request of withdrawing his candidacy. (Applause).

A.-M.K. Brazauskas: How, comrades?

From the hall: Please submit a motion to name the people who are obstructing the investigation.

V.F. Tolpezhnikov, head of office, First Riga State Clinical Hospital for Urgent Medical Aid imeni N. Burdenko (Proletarskiy National-Territorial Electoral District, Latvian SSR): I fully second the motion of my colleague for Lithuania. How many more commissions should there be? I have asked an entirely specific question: Who sanctioned this murder? (Stirring in the hall).

A.-M.K. Brazauskas: The commission will answer.

V.F. Tolpezhnikov (from his seat): I asked my question on the 25th. Yesterday I repeated my question again. So far there has been no answer. Do you think that our government does not know who issued the order? If such is the case, who needs such a government. (Stirring in the hall). I ask that we express our lack of confidence in our government which does not know who within it ordered the destruction of its own people. (Applause).

A.-M.K. Brazauskas: Quiet, comrades, quiet. What are you suggesting?

From the hall: (Unintelligible).

A.-M.K. Brazauskas: Comrades, let us have silence and quiet. We are repeating our discussion of yesterday, in the same spirit. Since the question concerning the chairman has come up, I would suggest to the congress to vote on the chairman. On the chairman, separately and then on all members of the commission. Is this motion seconded?

Seventh Session

31 May 1989

From the hall: (Unintelligible).

A.-M.K. Brazauskas: I did not gather that Comrade Nazarbayev has withdrawn his candidacy. That is not the way we understood it.

From the hall: (Unintelligible).

A.-M.K. Brazauskas: Comrades, there is yet another motion. Pay attention. There is another motion: not to choose a chairman now, let the commission itself choose its chairman and his deputy. Comrade Nazarbayev, do you insist that your name be withdrawn? Or will you remain member of the commission? Comrade Nazarbayev remains member of the commission. Therefore, a motion has been made not to single out a chairman but to vote for the list which I read, adding Comrade Boris Lvovich Vasilyev to it. This will be the membership of the commission. I put the matter to a vote. Those in favor of this commission, please say so. Thank you. Who is against? Please count the votes.

A.G. Kostenyuk: Dear deputies, there were 21 against.

A.-M.K. Brazauskas: Against, 21. Abstentions? Please raise your certificates.

A.G. Kostenyuk: Seventy-four deputies abstained.

A.-M.K. Brazauskas: Thus, the membership of the commission has been approved by majority vote. The commission will choose its chairman.

M.S. Gorbachev: With the participation of the Presidium.

A.-M.K. Brazauskas: With the participation, naturally, of the Presidium, if this becomes necessary. Thus, we have approved the commission. Thank you. Now a few remarks on procedural matters. Comrade Mambetov has the floor.

A.M. Mambetov, artistic director, Drama Theater imeni M. Auezov, chairman of the board of the Union of Theater Workers of Kazakhstan (from the Union of USSR Theater Workers): Comrades, there is in our congress pluralism of opinions, criticism, and self-criticism. All of this is good. However, I would request that the personality of the artist, of the man, not be insulted. This affects us, creative workers, profoundly. (Applause). In this case I am referring to what was said about Chingiz Aytmatov. For if the comrade who spoke has the necessary courage, let him apologize to Chingiz Aytmatov. In the future, I ask the people's deputies, as Academician Likhachev said, that proper standards be maintained in the debates. I thank you for your attention. (Applause).

A.-M.K. Brazauskas: Thank you. Still on procedural matters, Comrade Sazonov has the floor. Please.

N.S. Sazonov, party committee secretary, automated machine tool production, Kama Motor Vehicles Plant (Naberezhno-Chelninskiy Territorial Electoral District, Tatar ASSR): Dear deputies, naturally, we have been working for 6 days, and we are somewhat tired. I call upon you, however, to pay close attention. This morning all of you received a form, a paper on registrations for committees and commissions, i.e., the draft structure of the USSR Supreme Soviet, which was not discussed. We believe that this draft triggers a number of doubts and does not reflect the key directions in the development of our society. We therefore suggest the following: first, to halt registrations on this draft; second, to set up a task force consisting of one deputy per republic and one for Moscow and Leningrad each, to formulate a draft structure of the USSR Supreme Soviet; third, to discuss and approve it and only then resume the registration. Why? We already made a grave error in setting up the USSR Supreme Soviet, which includes 231 members among the first leaders of party, soviet, and economic authorities who, as a rule, will not be present and our parliament will not be a permanent one. That is why I submit this motion.

Finally, I would like to voice a certain objection to the Presidium for the harm caused to autonomous republics, oblasts, and districts: We have been discussing for the past 2 days and not one person has spoken on behalf of the autonomous republics. I thank you for your attention.

A.-M.K. Brazauskas: We shall take into consideration the remarks made by the comrades.

A.I. Lukyanov, first deputy chairman of the USSR Supreme Soviet: Comrades, a significant percentage of the deputies have already expressed their wish as to the commissions in which they would like to participate. I believe that we must finish with this work and submit our motions. A number of deputies have suggestions as to the structure, names of the commissions, and so on. For example, Deputy Stankevich has suggested a somewhat different structure of the commissions themselves. Once we have collected all the suggestions, we could meet with the group of deputies who have suggested changes, and thus work further on the composition of such commissions and submit them to you for your final consideration. And also this: The list which has been offered to you takes extensively into consideration the suggestions of the deputies themselves. A great many of them have made suggestions and they have been taken into consideration in this list.

M.S. Gorbachev: Comrades, the question of statements by representatives of autonomous areas is quite serious. As you can see, not even all Union republics have been able to speak. You have noted—information on this subject, in my view, was distributed—that 469 people have already put their names down to speak.

From the hall: And 250 have spoken.

STENOGRAPHIC RECORD

Seventh Session

31 May 1989

M.S. Gorbachev: From the very beginning, there have been 250. Once again the comrades are asking a question which was already asked in the past: In order not to deprive anyone, that all representatives of republics speak 15 minutes each, i.e., tomorrow allocate 15 minutes each to the representatives of Moldavia and Turkmeniya and then, perhaps, reduce the speeches by 5 minutes: speak for 10 minutes each. We have approved a regulation. Although temporary, this is already our program. Should we change it? I never hurry to change something once we have approved it. However, the congress has the right to decide. The situation is as follows: Many people have put their names down and it is desirable—everything seems to indicate this, comrades—for the maximum possible number of people to speak. If the comrades can consider their speeches and say everything in 10 minutes, as was done by Comrade Pukhova, we would welcome this. Do you agree? Not to change anything so far?

From the hall: Not to.

M.S. Gorbachev: Now, as to the autonomous areas. Comrade Kugultinov, I am about to finish. Or do you wish to ask a question?

From the hall: (Unintelligible).

M.S. Gorbachev: No, Comrade Kugultinov, on the contrary. The congress ratifies the regulation. Now, comrades, another question. "Yesterday at the evening session," Deputy Bratun said, "I submitted a motion that at the end of each session 1 hour be set aside for brief statements, declarations, and so on, strictly limited to 3-5 minutes. So far there has been no answer and I ask that this be determined."

From the hall: (Unintelligible).

M.S. Gorbachev: This will be a supplement to our regulation, comrades. For that reason we must set aside: Either work until 6 and add another hour, to 7 pm, for answers, or else allocate 1 hour, from 5 to 6, for short statements. Shall we change or not?

From the hall: No.

M.S. Gorbachev: Therefore, we ratify the regulation?

From the hall: Yes.

M.S. Gorbachev: That is all, thank you.

A.-M.K. Brazauskas: That is all, comrades. All the questions which were raised.... (Stirring in the hall). What is happening?

From the hall: Comrade chairman, you promised to read at the end of the session (Further unintelligible; noise in the hall).

A.-M.K. Brazauskas: I promised to pass on your motions. We could read them at the morning session. Sit down, comrades. Let me name them: Brutsa, Mitin, Niyazov, Likhanov, Chernichenko, and Khmura—those deputies will speak tomorrow, during the first session. I wish you a pleasant rest. Until tomorrow, 1000.

NOTES TO THE FIRST AND SECOND SESSIONS

1a ...2155 people's deputies: The enabling legislation authorized 2250 deputies; 2249 were actually elected, but a number failed to attend for personal reasons.

1b ...Moscow Group: Although Moscow was the residence of most members of the faction, the term actually identified those deputies who favored progressive reforms regardless of their place of residence. This element formed the core of the broader liberal-democratic coalition, the Interregional Group of Deputies.

The organization began on 12 October 1988 as a discussion group of about a hundred liberal political activists who took the name *Moskovskaya tribuna*—Moscow Tribune. The founders included Yuri Afanaseyev, Ales Adamovich, Yuri Burtin, Yuri Chernichenko, Gavril Popov, Tatyana Zaslavskaya, Lev Zaykov, and others. Zaykov was First Secretary of the Moscow City Party Committee and ally of Gorbachev as member of the Politburo and secretary of the CPSU Central Committee. He provided meeting rooms and office facilities for Moscow Tribune in the House of Political Enlightenment on Trubnaya Square. The group was officially registered as an "unofficial organization" (i.e., nonparty) early in February 1989. The weekly *Moskovskie novosti*—Moscow News printed the views of several of its most prominent members, and those columns became in effect the political platform of those members who ran for election to the Congress of People's Deputies. By the early Spring of 1989, the Moscow Tribune had forged links with the popular front movements in the Baltic and the Caucasus, and it had informally allied itself with Boris Yeltsin. Cf. *Moscow News*, January-March 1989; Michael E. Urban, *More Power to the Soviets: The Democratic Revolution in the USSR* (Edward Elgar, 1990), pp. 62 and 105; and see the speeches by Popov, 1: 98-100; and Chernichenko, 2: 19-22.

2a ...their comrades on the floor: The deputies were generally seated in blocks of republics and territorial subdivisions. Central Party leaders, however, sat in a separate section, apart from the other deputies.

2a ...the other had no voice: *Moscow News*, 19 June 1989.

5a ...those who died in Tbilisi: Nineteen men and women were killed on 9 April 1989 when MVD and Soviet assault troops used shovels and poison gas to break up a demonstration by about ten thousand Georgian nationalists. See below, note to 18b.

11a ...a registered vote (fiksirovannoye golosovaniye) on all issues apart from personal ones: I.e., a roll-call vote except in elections.

11a ...A.M. Obolensky: "Unidentified deputy" in *Pervyi syezd narodnykh deputatov SSSR: Stenograficheskii otchet*, 6 tt. (Moskva, 1989) 1: 15.

11a ...Yu.Yu. Boldyrev: Identified as V.N. Belyaev, dean of the Moscow Physical Engineering Institute in *Pervyi syezd*, 1: 17.

11b ...Don't worry, I know what needs to be done: From time to time Gorbachev privately addressed colleagues on the rostrum for advice on conducting the meeting. The microphone picked up his words but not those of his interlocutor, and the transcript does not distinguish those asides from words directed to the Congress.

12a ...Deputy Landsbergis: Vitautis Vitautovich Landsbergis, leader of the Lithuanian People's Front in Support of Perestroika, more commonly known as "Sajudis"—the Movement. On 10 March 1990 Landsbergis was elected chairman of the Lithuanian Supreme Council (formerly the Lithuanian Supreme Soviet) or head of state of the newly proclaimed Republic of Lithuania (no longer either "Soviet" or "Socialist").

13b ...which laws will be passed by the Congress and which by the Supreme Soviet: The powers of the USSR Congress of People's Deputies and the USSR Supreme Soviet are generally delimited in Articles 108 through 114 of the Law on Amendments and Additions to the USSR Constitution (Basic Law) approved by the Supreme Soviet on 1 December 1988. They are reproduced in Appendix A.1.

Article 108 declares the Congress of People's Deputies to be "the supreme organ of USSR state power," while Article 111 describes the Supreme Soviet as "the standing legislative, administrative, and monitoring organ of USSR state power" and makes it subordinate to the Congress of People's Deputies. The Constitution seems to envision the Congress as the nation's remote shaper and arbiter of state policy and personnel. Article 113-20 specifically empowers the Supreme Soviet to "adopt USSR laws and resolutions." The Congress of Deputies has no unambiguous legislative authority. It can either do everything—or practically nothing. It has the power to examine and decide "any question within the jurisdiction of the USSR" (Art. 108) and can also "repeal acts adopted by the USSR Supreme Soviet." (Art. 108-12) On the other hand, it adopts "laws and resolutions by a majority of votes." (Art. 108-13) To make matters murkier, Article 114 affords the "right to initiate legislation" in either the Congress or the Soviet to practically every elected or appointed official or commission, including the state prosecutor and the Academy of Sciences. The legislative sections of the document epitomize the best and worst of glasnost—a cacophony of democracy and chaos.

15a ...No, but I think that we should proceed as laid out in the democratic process: Another aside. With two proposals on the floor simultaneously, someone at the rostrum apparently asked whether the chairman wanted to consider them separately.

16a ...republics, krays, and oblasts: Administrative-territorial units of the USSR in descending order of size and importance are union republics, autonomous republics, krays (territories), administrative and autonomous oblasts (regions), national okrugs, and rayons (districts), cities, towns, villages, and settlements. Rayons are generally organized to reflect agricultural or industrial connections; cities over 100,000 usually contain two or more rayons. Autonomous or national units are based on homogeneous linguistic groups. All six krays, all ten national okrugs, and most autonomous republics (ASSRs) and autonomous oblasts (AOs), are located in the RSFSR. Outside Russian territory are the Nakhichevan ASSR and the Nagorno-Karabakh AO in Azerbaijan, the Abkhazian and Adzharian ASSRs and the South-Ossetian AO of Georgia, the Kara-Kalpak ASSR in Uzbekistan, and the Gorno-Badakhshan AO in Tadzhikistan. All autonomous or national units have constitutions, supreme soviets and courts, and ministries; they are directly subordinate to union republics, and no ASSR or AO contains another national unit.

17b ...law on demonstrations and meetings: A reference to the Decree on the Procedure for Organizing and Holding Meetings, Rallies, Street Processions and Demonstrations in the USSR which is reproduced in Appendix A.3.

17b ...Unidentified speaker: There were no microphones among the deputies. Every speaker had to line up for his or, occasionally, her brief moment at the podium. Sometimes a remark or statement shouted from the floor was heard and recorded. Frequently the presiding officer responded to a phantom question or remark.

18a ...a guarantee that the broadcasting of the session will not be broken off: Soviet radio and television provided live coverage of all sessions of the First Congress throughout the day and evening. Television coverage reached 70 percent of the territory of the USSR. Surveys subsequently indicated that worker productivity dropped about 20 percent when the Congress was in session. When the Second Congress convened in December, the meetings were taped for broadcast in the evening, after most citizens had completed their workday.

19b ...there are jurists here: Unlike western legislatures, which tend to be dominated by lawyers, active jurists constituted less than 1 percent of the deputies.

23b ...the conclusions of the medical commission and the chemical and toxicological commission: The Supreme Soviet of the Georgian Republic formed a commission to investigate the use of force against the citizenry of Tbilisi on 9 April 1989. The report of the chemical-toxological subcommission was published on 24 May 1989. It found that several toxic substances in addition to tear gas had been used against the population. Those toxins included amine derivatives which when highly concentrated inflict prolonged nervous disorders or death. The commission found that the troops had used substances far more toxic than anything admitted to the press and that a large area of the city had been contaminated. The situation was aggravated, moreover, because when the troops withdrew they left behind canisters and cartridges that continued to infect the area. Efforts to treat the afflicted had been complicated by the refusal of military authorities to identify the chemical agents. The chemical-toxological team concluded that the troops had "committed a wholly unwarranted barbaric action ...using toxic substances that they had no moral or legal right to use." The medical subcommission reported that autopsies performed on seventeen of the nineteen persons killed on April 9 revealed that twelve had died from asphyxiation, three from injuries, and two as a result of heart attacks precipitated by gassing. It also reported that 3515 persons had been treated as outpatients for injuries or gas poisoning while 584 others remained hospitalized. *Zarya Vostok* (Yerevan), 24 and 25 May 1989, in the *Current Digest of the Soviet Press* (28 June 1989): 19-20 (cited below as CDSP).

24a ...form a special commission (to investigate the Tbilisi tragedy): The stormy debate over the formation of this commission took place at the end of the Seventh Session on 31 May 1989. See 230-47 and 292-95.

24b ...a serious incident that took place in Sumgait: Located a dozen miles northwest of Baku at the base of the Apsheron peninsula, Sumgait was the scene of three days of rioting in February 1988. Thirty-two persons, including twenty-six Armenians, were killed and four hundred were seriously injured while two hundred homes and apartments belonging mainly to Armenians were looted and burned. The Armenian press characterized the violence as an act of genocide conducted by Azeri extremists. On 19 October 1988, *Pravda* reported the opening (in Moscow) of the trial of three Azeris "guilty of participation in the mass riots in Sumgait." One of the accused was ultimately sentenced to death by shooting, but the arrest and conviction of a mere three rioters hardly appeased the outrage and anger of the Armenian community. FBIS-SOV 88-228 (28 November 88): 67.

25a ...members of the LPF Council stood for deputy in these small okrugs: The speaker was a Russian citizen of Latvia. His charge that "safe" rural electoral districts were created for members of the Latvian People's Front touched on one of the most serious problems confronting the USSR in general and Latvia in particular. Interethnic relations in the Latvian republic were particularly tense, because Letts, who comprised about 52 percent of Latvia's population, were in danger of becoming a minority in their own homeland due to the influx of neighboring Russians into industrial centers. The program of the LPF, adopted in July 1988, demanded a sovereign Latvia within the framework of the USSR in order to ensure national survival against a steady flood of Russian immigrants. The most extreme demands of the LPF were its insistence that all immigration be terminated immediately, that Latvian be made the single official language of the republic, and that native Latvians be guaranteed majority representation in all local soviets regardless of the ethnic composition of the locality. On 4 May 1990 the Latvian Supreme Soviet reasserted the independence of Latvia and called for a transitional period of unspecified duration.

Colonel Alksnis subsequently led the conservative faction *Soyuz* in the Supreme Soviet.

29b ...we will not forget Yeltsin: Boris Yeltsin, Gorbachev's *bete noire* on the left. Former First Secretary of the central committee of the Moscow party organization and Gorbachev ally, in October 1987 Yeltsin was expelled from the Politburo for his intemperate attacks on party leaders lackadaisical in their commitment or pursuit of perestroika. Persecution made Yeltsin a national hero. He was elected a people's deputy from Moscow by winning 90 percent of the vote against his official opponent. To avoid defeat by Yeltsin, the ineffectual Vitaly Vorotnikov, Politburo member and chairman of the RSFSR Supreme Soviet Presidium, ran for election in a safe provincial district. Yeltsin was subsequently elected President of the RSFSR.

30a ...Gdlyan and Ivanov: See below, p. 137a.

35b ...the April decree: On 8 April 1989, the USSR Supreme Soviet Presidium altered sections of the Criminal Code dealing with crimes against the state (see Appendix A.4). The amendments provided imprisonment or fines for persons who publicly called for the overthrow or alteration of the Soviet state and social system by unconstitutional means. It also specified penalties for persons who deliberately kindled ethnic or racial hostility or impaired citizens' rights because of their race or nationality. The amended law superseded sections of the 1958 Criminal Code directed against "anti-Soviet agitation and propaganda," which were widely used against human rights activists. It is subsequently referred to as the decree of April 8 (the date of its adoption) or the decree of April 9 (the date of its promulgation).

38a ...Soviet Germans: Known historically as Volga Germans, they are the descendants of Germans who were invited into Russia by Catherine the Great and who successfully resisted assimilation by retaining their language, culture, and lands. In 1924 the first Soviet constitution created the Volga German ASSR. In September 1941, however, following the German invasion, thousands of Volga Germans were arrested on charges of espionage and sabotage, and the entire nation was resettled in Siberia and Kazakhstan. According to official MVD records, as of 1 January 1953, of a total of 2,753,356 people who had been exiled to "special localities," Germans numbered 1,224,931. (*Argumenty i fakty* [30 Sept-6 Oct 1989]: 8.) A 1964 decree absolved the Volga Germans of the "sweeping accusations" of 1941 but did not allow them to return to their ancestral lands. The census of 1979 recorded 1.9 million Soviet German citizens of whom 57 percent reported German as their primary language.

45b ...the Moscow People's Front and Memorial: The Moscow Popular (or People's) Front was one of many Popular Fronts in Support of Perestroika formed in 1988 to mobilize popular support for Gorbachev. The Moscow organization and several others eventually gravitated toward Yeltsin.

Memorial—the All-Union Historical-Educational Society "Memorial" (not to be confused with the Russian neofascist group *Pamyat*—Memory) was established in 1987 for the purpose of organizing public support for a memorial to Stalin's victims. By 1989 it claimed thousands of members and chapters in 110 cities. Its leadership included Vitaly Korotich, editor of *Ogonyok*; Georgy Baklanov, editor of *Znamye*; Andrei Sakharov, actor Mikhail Ulyanov, a frequent portrayer of Lenin; historians Yuri Afanaseyev and Roy Medvedev, writers V.V. Bykov and Anatoly Rybakov; poets Yevgeny Yevtushenko, Andrei Vosnesensky, and Ales Adamovich; and others.

46a ...many Nina Andreyevnas: A Leningrad chemistry teacher, Andreyevna gained notoriety for her defense of Stalin and assault on liberal trends in Soviet society which appeared in the 13 March 1988 edition of *Sovetskaya Rossiya*. Thought to have been published with the blessing of Yegor Ligachev to signal a reversal of policy, the letter initially cowed the supporters of perestroika. They remained in confused silence and disarray until 5 April when a *Pravda* editorial denounced Andreyevna's arguments and characterized her letter as the "manifesto of the anti-perestroika forces."

NOTES TO THE THIRD SESSION

55b ...permit the holding of a rally in Luzhniki: Perhaps as many as 70,000 people assembled on the grounds of the Luzhniki Stadium on Saturday, 27 May, in an exuberant celebration of glasnost. Deputies, representatives of the Moscow party organization, members of unofficial movements and associations, and ordinary citizens voiced their concerns and aspirations. A relatively small contingent of militia unobtrusively patrolled the periphery, and the event took place without incident.

57a ...an amendment to Article 111: The passage in question reads: "The USSR Supreme Soviet is elected by secret vote from among the USSR people's deputies by the USSR Congress of People's Deputies and is accountable to the latter." See Appendix A.1.

59b ...why Article 110 of the USSR Constitution has been violated: A reference to the requirement that the chairman of the Central Electoral Commission preside over the First Session of the Congress; Gorbachev assumed the chair soon after the Congress opened. See the Headnote to the First and Second Sessions.

61a ...Article 113 of the USSR Constitution: That article enumerates the powers of the USSR Supreme Soviet. See Appendix A.1.

61b ...Sakharov's proposal: I.e., that the Congress of People's Deputies exercise its legislative powers and not delegate them to the Supreme Soviet. See above, p. 1.

70b ...Article 11: Article 111, as cited above. The stenographer evidently had difficulty hearing speakers due to the activity and movement around the podium.

71a ...Article 199: Another error; the speaker refers to Article 119 which delimits the powers of the USSR Supreme Soviet Presidium. See Appendix A.1.

73a ...our intention in proposing the formula: I.e., as an amendment to Article 124 of the constitution.

76a ...Deputy Boryas: Evidently a reference to Yu.R. Boyars.

76a ...the sovereignty of Moscow: In Eastern Europe, with its history of multinational states and mixed polities, the concept of sovereignty does not possess the absolute qualities accorded it in western law. See above the note to p. 25a.

81b ...a Belorussian deputy: S.S. Shushkevich (above).

82a ...Unidentified: Identified as S.B. Kalyagin, an engineer from Sverdlovsk, Perm Oblast, in *Pervyi syezd*, 1: 181.

NOTES TO THE FOURTH SESSION

87 ...Lev Nikolayevich Zaykov: See above, note to 1b.

99a ...Levsha in the well-known novel by Leskov: *Levsha* (Lefty: The Tale of the Cross-Eyed Left-Handed Craftsman of Tula and the Steel Flea) (1881) is the satirical story of a Russian gunsmith who seeks to demonstrate Russian genius by shoeing a life-sized steel flea which the British have made in order to flaunt their own technical skill. Levsha succeeds but ruins the delicate mechanism; the newly shod flea can no longer hop because the shoes are too heavy. Nikolay Semenovich Leskov (1831-95), a prolific satirist, is perhaps best known for the tale "Lady Macbeth of Mtsensk District," retold in 1934 as an opera by Dmitry Shostakovich and revived thirty years later as "Katerina Izmailova."

100a ...leasing, cooperatives, and so forth: The Supreme Soviet adopted the "Law on Cooperatives" on 26 May 1988 to take effect on 1 July 1988; in June 1988, twenty thousand cooperatives were registered in the USSR, about one-third of them having been formed since the publication of the draft legislation. By January 1990, the number had increased to 193,400. Although a genuine cooperative movement had flourished in prerevolutionary Russia, most of the new organizations were actually small private enterprises and were widely resented as such.

Under consideration since 1987, the "Principles of Legislation of the USSR and the Union Republics on Leasing and Leasing Relations in the USSR" were finally approved by the Supreme Soviet on 23 November 1989. According to prime minister N.I. Ryzhkov (CDSP [15 November 1989]: 15), the government chose to enact "principles" rather than law so that the republics could adapt legislation to local conditions. That solution reflected the legislators' inability to agree on distinctions between socialist and private property. The "Principles," for example, avoided any reference to dissolving collective farms. Earlier, on 9 April 1989, a decree of the Supreme Soviet, described as an "experimental document," allowed both collectives and individuals to lease land, equipment, buildings, and other property for periods of fifty years and more. FBIS-SOV 89-067 (10 April 1989): 44.

101b ...Yuriy Chernichenko will know better: Yu.D. Chernichenko, commentator on agriculture for Soviet Central Television and the magazine *Znamye*, a leading figure in the Moscow Group and subsequently the Interregional Group of Deputies.

102a ...Fedor Abramov..."Wooden Horses": Abramov's short story *Derevyannie koni* (Wooden Horses) describes a conscientious farmer who toils honestly and achieves modest prosperity only to be denounced as a kulak and parasite. Abramov has been persistent critic of those writers who have curried official favor by glorifying collective farm life and celebrating the destruction of traditional peasant values. In 1960 he resigned from the Chair of Russian Literature at Leningrad State University in order to devote himself exclusively to writing. Among his works is *Pryaslini* (The Pryaslins, 1975), a novel about the struggle of an indomitable peasant family to survive Stalinism and the Second World War.

102a ...Lyubimov: Yuri Petrovich Lyubimov (b. 1917) directed Moscow's Taganka Theater from its inception in 1964 until his dismissal in March 1984. Under his leadership the Taganka asserted a civic spirit and candor that continually antagonized the Brezhnev bureaucracy. Finally in July 1984, condemned for "systematic activity hostile to the USSR," Lyubimov was deprived of his citizenship and expelled. For the next five years he staged productions in England, Sweden, the United States, and Israel. In March 1989, however, his citizenship was restored and in December he was reappointed to his old post.

102a ...rehabilitation commission: At its October 1987 plenary session the CPSU Central Committee called on the Politburo to form a Commission on the Additional Study of Materials Connected with the Repressions that Took Place in the 1930s, the 1940s, and the Early 1950s. On 10 November 1988 the Politburo reorganized the commission and replaced its original chairman, M.S. Solomentsev, with A.N. Yakovlev. The nine-member panel included A.I. Lukyanov and KGB director V.M. Chebrikov. A presidential decree of 13 August 1990, which finally rehabilitated "all the victims of the political repressions from the 1920s to the 1950s," was Yakovlev's last accomplishment before his resignation from the communist leadership. On several occasions during 1989-90 he publicly complained that certain members of the commission, never identified, were resisting a general exoneration of the victims of collectivization and Stalin's terror. *Pravda* (11 November 1988): 1; CDSP (7 December 1988): 19; *Moscow News* (5 January 1990): 6-7; Radio Liberty/Radio Free Europe, *Report on the USSR* (21 September 1990): 8-9 (cited below as RL/RFE Report).

102a ... the concept of Yuriy Karyakin: Yu.F. Karyakin, a senior member of the Institute of the International Workers' Movement.

104a ... M.R. Mamedov: Identified as V.R. Mamedov in *Pervyi syezd*, 1: 237.

110b ... G.A. Pogosyan, pensioner: Genrikh Andreyevich Pogosyan was removed from the post of first secretary of the NKAO provincial party committee and retired "for reasons of health" in January 1989 when Moscow assumed direct control over the region. See below the note at 117a.

111a ... Zoriya Balayana: a mistranslation; the NKAO nominee was Zory Gaikovich Balayan; see above, Grigoryan's speech, 82.

112b ... those who presided during the conduct of our Russian Federation conferences: V.I. Vorotnikov and his minions.

117a ... a special form of management in the NKAO: On 12 January 1989 the Presidium of the USSR Supreme Soviet transferred all legislative and executive power to an eight-member Committee for the Special Administration of the Nagorno-Karabakh Autonomous Province headed by A.I. Volsky. While the committee was enjoined to "take into account the opinion of the Azerbaijan Republic Council of Ministers," it was directly responsible to President Gorbachev and the USSR Council of Ministers. CDSP (8 February 1989): 4-5 and 7.

Arkady Ivanovich Volsky was originally sent to the NKAO in July 1988 as a trouble-shooter for the CPSU Central Committee. Before heading the CPSU CC department of machinery under Gorbachev, he had served as an assistant to General Secretaries Yuri Andropov and Konstantin Chernenko. CDSP (24 August 1988): 19.

121b ... the writer Karpov and the chess player Karpov: Vladimir Vasilyevich Karpov was author of the prize-winning novella *Polkovodets* (The General) and in 1986 was named First Secretary of the USSR Writers Union. The chess player was Anatoly Yevgenyevich Karpov, the world champion from 1975 to 1985.

127b ... Vitaly Ivanovich: V.I. Vorotnikov, Chairman of the Presidium of the RSFSR Supreme Soviet.

128a ... Boris Mikhaylovich: Obviously referring to Yeltsin, the speaker has misstated his patronymic (Nikolayevich).

133b ... rights and responsibilities of internal forces: The Decree on the Duties and Rights of USSR Ministry of Internal Affairs Internal Troops in the Protection of Public Order is summarized in Appendix A.5.

134a ... the decree of 8 April: The revision of the Criminal Code concerning crimes against the state; see Appendix A.4, and above, note 35b.

134a ... Article 11-1: That section of the code reads as follows: "The public insulting or defamation of the USSR supreme organs of state power and government, other state organs constituted or elected by the USSR Congress of People's Deputies or the USSR Supreme Soviet, or officials appointed, elected, or approved in office by the USSR Congress of People's Deputies or the USSR Supreme Soviet, or public organizations and their all-Union organs constituted according to law and acting in conformity with the USSR Constitution—is punishable by deprivation of freedom for a period of up to 3 years or a fine of up to R2,000."

136a ... A.V. Oborin: Identified as V.A. Shapovalenko in *Pervyi syezd*, 1: 317.

137a ... the question of Deputy Gdlyan: Former state prosecutor T.Kh. Gdlyan led the task force that exposed a long-standing web of corruption in Uzbekistan. N.V. Ivanov was his deputy. Among the sixty-two officials arrested and charged (thirty-five were actually brought to trial) with falsifying cotton production figures, bribery, and other crimes was Yuri Churbanov, son-in-law of former First Secretary Leonid Brezhnev. In the summer of 1988 Gdlyan and Ivanov leveled accusations of corruption against a number of senior party officials who had served under Yegor Ligachev and then publicly complained when the state prosecutor's office would not issue warrants for their arrest. In a television interview on 12 May 1989, Ivanov declared that Ligachev and two former Politburo colleagues, Gregory V. Romanov and Mikhail S. Solomentsev, were part of a corrupt Soviet "mafia". Within days Gdlyan and Ivanov and their team of over two hundred investigators were fired, and the USSR Prosecutor General announced a criminal investigation into "violations of legality," entailing threats, intimidation, and torture, employed by Gdlyan and his associates. Despite energetic efforts to discredit them, Gdlyan and Ivanov enjoyed broad popular support.

In March 1990 the report of the commission of inquiry created by the Congress of People's Deputies essentially confirmed the charges of abuse of power against Gdlyan and his associates. Although it censured Gdlyan's superiors for improperly monitoring and supervising the work of his group, it also concluded that "Gdlyan, taking advantage of the lack of control and connivance on the part of the leadership of the USSR Prosecutor's Office, rejected every attempt to put his work under proper supervision." The commission found no evidence to support public accusations of Gdlyan and Ivanov against the Prosecutor General's Office or their charges against Ligachev. (CDSP [4 April 1990]: 12, 32.) In their own defense, Gdlyan and Ivanov argued before the Second Session of the Congress of People's Deputies that they had found themselves in an utterly lawless situation in Uzbekistan where even the local law-enforcement agencies were part of a network of corruption that extended to Moscow and the highest levels of state and Party. (CDSP [11 April 1990]: 11-12.) A Supreme Soviet resolution adopted 18 April 1990 marked a conclusion of sorts to the Gdlyan-Ivanov affair. It condemned the pair's unsubstantiated charges and warned them to cease lest the Soviet take steps to deprive them of their immunity as people's deputies. It concurred with their dismissals but enjoined them to cooperate with the state's continuing investigations of corruption and bribery. CDSP (6 June 1990): 19.

Gdlyan and Ivanov refused to remain silent, however. Their renegade campaign to expose corruption and malfeasance suffered no loss of public credence or support, for, as jurist K.D. Lubenchenko explained, "The many known instances of squandering of the state's money and embezzlement and the use of unjustifiable privileges by a whole series of leaders give rise to well-founded suspicion among the people and a desire to see those responsible for the stagnation sitting in the dock. There was every reason to demand that the rumors concerning leaders such as Grishin, Romanov, Aliyev, Solomentsev, Promyslov and others be confirmed" by our highest state and party leaders, but that was not done. Hence, Gdlyan and Ivanov. For decades our country has existed under a system of "'telephone law' and interference in the affairs of the courts, the prosecutor's office, the police, and the State Security Committee (which) still persists to this day. Hence the demoralized state of our entire system of law-enforcement. Hence the corruption, and hence the scale of organized crime that we now have ..." CDSP (6 June 1990): 18.

Find additional information in articles by Julia Wishnevsky in RL/RFE Report (30 June 1989): 1-7; and (9 March 1990): 6-8; and in the weekly summary for 27 April 1990, pp. 27-28. See also CDSP (14 June 1989): 9; (11 October 1989): 22; (18 October 1989): 2; (18 October 1989): 4; and (1 November 1989): 11.

138a ...V.A. Vrovkov: Identified as A.I. Baranov in *Pervyi syezd*, 1: 321.

NOTES TO THE FIFTH SESSION

141a ...Article 11-1: See above, note, 134a.

142a ...19th all-union party conference: Meeting from 28 June to 2 July 1988, the Nineteenth Party Conference, the first in forty-seven years, is considered to have formally launched the "Gorbachev revolution." The decisions of the conference were embodied in six resolutions on restructuring, democratization and political reform, anti-bureaucratism, nationality relations, legal reform, and glasnost (openness). See generally, CDSP (1988) Nos. 17-39.

147a ...decision of the Central Committee March (1989) plenum on agriculture: The plenum, meeting on 15-16 March, called for expanded cooperation between industrial and agricultural enterprises, including a fivefold increase in the defense industry's production of food-processing equipment; for strengthening family farming operations and for increased output of equipment needed by family farms as part of a general program of strengthening family farming as well as collective gardening and truck farming; for improvement of infrastructure, capital formation, price restructuring, etc. CDSP (12 April 1989): 1 and (26 April 1989): 28-29; Gorbachev's speech reviewing the history of Soviet agriculture and outlining his agrarian policy is reported in CDSP (12 April 1989): 3-6, continued (19 April 1989): 10-16.

147a ...Law on the State Enterprise: Adopted by the USSR Supreme Soviet on 30 June 1987, the object of the law was to "strengthen state (public) ownership of the means of production in industry, construction, the agro-industrial complex, and other branches ...(and to) deepen the principle of centralization ...of the national economy as a single whole .... Complete text: CDSP (26 August 1987): 8-13 and (2 September 1987): 10-17. By late 1989 this law had been emasculated by a number of amendments.

148b ...a deputy's question from Comrade Alksnis was mislaid: See above, p. 25.

148b ...the time for the reply to be received expires today: Article 17 of the Provisional Standing Orders, pursuant to Article 124 of the Constitution, requires Soviet officials to respond to formal queries by people's deputies within three days.

148b ...Law on the Status of People's Deputies: The draft of the Law on the Status of People's Deputies of the USSR was finally approved by the Supreme Soviet on 27 November 1989 and submitted for ratification to the Second Congress of People's Deputies.

149a ...the autonomy of Ingushia that was illegally abolished in 1934: In 1934 the Ingush and Chechen Autonomous Oblasts were merged to form the Chechen-Ingush AO (reconstituted in 1936 as the Chechen-Ingush Autonomous Republic). In 1937-38 a purge decimated the political and intellectual leadership of the republic. In February 1944 the Chechen and Ingush nations were falsely denounced as traitors and Nazi collaborators, their republic was dissolved, and the entire population of about a half million people was forcibly dispersed throughout Soviet Central Asia. The Chechens and Ingush were rehabilitated in 1956, and a Chechen-Ingush ASSR was restored in January 1957, although the Progorodny district of former Ingushia was transferred to Northern Ossetia. Ethnic violence accompanied the return of the deportees to their homeland, much of which had been resettled by Russians who praised Stalin's nationalities policy and called on the government to end the repatriation of Chechens and Ingush. In 1989, 51,000 Ingushis petitioned for restoration of autonomy within the 1934 borders. See Bahdan Nahaylo and Victor Swoboda, *Soviet Disunion* (New York, 1989), 80, 96, 125-26; CDSP (11 April 1990): 30.

150a ...Zhuravlev's unethical joke: Above, p. 147b.

150b ...Obolensky, who...tried to close the embrasure of anti-democracy: A.M. Obolensky opposed Gorbachev for chairmanship of the Supreme Soviet during the First Session (above, pp. 42-45).

150b..."so-called deputies": In Gdlyan's speech at the end of the Fourth Session; the remarks that follow Gdlyan detail some aspects of his controversial investigation of corruption in Uzbekistan. See above, note to p. 125b.

151a ...mafia groups: A general term for organized crime in the USSR; also used to describe the nomenklatura.

151a...Rekunkov: A.M. Rekunkov, former USSR Prosecutor General, was relieved in May 1988 and subsequently resigned from the CPSU Central Committee.

152a ...Sukharev: A.Ye. Sukharev (b. 1923) succeeded Rekunkov as USSR Prosecutor General in May 1988. Sukharev was appointed USSR First Deputy Minister of Justice in 1970, Minister of Justice of the RSFSR in 1984, and USSR First Deputy Prosecutor General in February 1988.

152b ...Law on the Status of Judges: Approved by the USSR Supreme Soviet in November 1989.

152b ...Principles of Criminal Legislation: Still under consideration at the end of 1989; revision of the Principles of Criminal Procedure was completed in June 1990.

152b ...we have begun to publish crime statistics: In the fall of 1988 the State Committee on Statistics was authorized to organize a section on moral statistics to collect, analyze, and publish data on crime and other socially dangerous phenomena (alcoholism, drug addiction, prostitution, vagrancy, suicide, etc.) Reports began appearing in 1989. In July, for example, the Ministry of Internal Affairs released unprecedented information revealing that, during the first six months of 1989, the crime rate increased by 32 percent over the same period in 1988.

153a ...a new act governing arbitration: Law on Procedures for Resolving Collective Labor Disputes (Conflicts), approved by the USSR Supreme Soviet on 9 October 1989.

153a ...steps to change the conditions in corrective-labor colonies: According to the director of the Chief Administration for Correctional Affairs, between 1986 and 1989 a more humane judicial policy had reduced the number of convicts in labor colonies by 40 percent; around two hundred camps had been closed or converted to "therapy-and-labor rehabilitation centers." CDSP (5 July 1989): 25-26.

154a ...CPSU Central Committee's Commission on Legal Questions: Decisions of the Nineteenth Party Conference led to the creation of six CPSU CC commissions including the Commission on Questions of Legal Policy under the chairmanship of V.M. Chebrikov.

156b ...we do not need people who can arrest our relatives and children: A reference to the investigative tactics of T.Kh. Gdlyan; see above, note to p. 137a.

156b ...Andreyevna's article: See above, note to p. 39b.

158a ...Nikolay Gumilev: N.S. Gumilev (1886-1921), poet; married Anna Akhmatova in 1910; executed by the Bolsheviks for alleged participation in an anti-Soviet conspiracy.

162b ...annexation of the Georgian republic in violation of the 7 May 1920 Treaty: The independent

Republic of Georgia was established in May 1918. In May 1920 it repelled the invasion of G.K. Ordzhonikidze's army which had just seized Baku and occupied Azerbaijan. In the treaty of 7 May 1920, Lenin's Russia recognized Georgia's independence and sovereignty. In February 1921, however, Ordzhonikidze, ignoring Lenin's instructions, invaded and conquered Georgia and immediately submerged it into the Transcaucasian Soviet Federative Socialist Republic (one of the four entities that formally established the USSR on 31 January 1924). At the time of its conquest, Georgia had been recognized by twenty-one nations, including Britain and France. Under the Stalin Constitution of 1936 Georgia acquired the status of union republic.

163a ...statements made by Deputy Starovoytova: Above, p. 135b.

163a ...Deputy Igityan's speech: Above, p. 24b.

165b ...Molotov-Ribbentrop Pact...commission: The CPSU CC Commission on Questions of International Policy under the chairmanship of A.N. Yakovlev. Yakovlev also chaired the investigative commission created by the Congress of People's Deputies in the Eighth Session, below.

165b ...Article 124: The relevant passage reads: "USSR people's deputies are released from performing official or production duties for the specific period necessary to carry out their activity as deputies in the USSR Congress of People's Deputies, the USSR Supreme Soviet, its chambers, commissions, and committees, and also among the population. USSR people's deputies elected to the USSR Supreme Soviet can be released from performing official or production duties for the entire period of their powers in the USSR Supreme Soviet."

In the Third Session, the Congress defeated a proposal to require deputies to surrender their jobs in order to serve in the Supreme Soviet and approved a resolution to release deputies from their jobs "as a rule." Gorbachev promised to clarify the meaning of the phrase. See above, pp. 73-74.

166b ...Hungary, Czechoslovakia, Poland, and Novocherkassk: Areas that experienced armed intervention: Hungary and Poland in 1956 and Czechoslovakia in 1968, and the southern Ukrainian city of Novocherkassk where in June 1962, troops were used to suppress a strike of workers and students. Estimates of the number killed range from 70 or 80 to several hundred. The injured and wounded were denied medical treatment, and their families were exiled to Siberia. In ensuing trials, nine strikers were sentenced to death and executed. Mikhail Heller and Aleksandr M. Nekrich, *Utopia in Power* (New York, 1986), 592-97.

171b ...he used the expression, "if you want fools": Both Russian sources record the statement as, "*Khotitye umnykh, khotitye nyet, eto vashe dyelo.*" *Izvestiya*, 1 June 1989; *Pervyi syezd*, 1: 130. Fedorov's complete statement, above, p. 60b.

175b ...the Vysotsky: An ancient people, belonging to the late Bronze or early Iron Age in the western Ukraine, the vestiges of whose culture were discovered near the village of Vysotskoye, Lvov Oblast.

176a ...the 12 March demonstration (in Moldavia): An unauthorized rally in the center of Kishinev by about 20,000 people demanding official use of the Moldavian (Romanian) language and the replacement of Cyrillic by the Latin alphabet. The demonstrators clashed with police; there were rumors of beatings and deaths, and a number of people were arrested. CDSP (26 April 1989): 7-9.

177a ...when the Rus used to lead us: The enigmatic Rus gave their name to Russia sometime after the mid-ninth century.

179a ...a "non-Meshalkin": Ye.N. Meshalkin, a conservative, spoke in the First and Fourth Sessions, pp. 9 and 102-3.

179b ...items 504 and 505 of the "Records": In material distributed to deputies, 504 referred to the decree of 9 April 1989 amending the law on state crimes (Appendix A.4); 505 was the decree on the use of internal troops (Appendix A.5).

183b ...pardon if I have the name wrong) Alksins: Colonel V.I. Alksnis

NOTES TO THE SIXTH SESSION

195a ...13th 5-Year Plan: Covering the years 1991-95; the 14th would run through 2000.

195b ...the psychology of parasitism: "Parasitism" was introduced into Soviet administrative law in 1957 as part of Nikita Khrushchev's efforts to mobilize Soviet society and reinforce social conformity. A "parasite" is an able-bodied adult who deliberately avoids work, reaps unearned income by exploiting others (by begging, black-market operations, bribery, extortion, etc.), or who merely leads "an anti-social parasitic way of life"—an amendment introduced in 1961 to deal with dissidents. In 1970 the administrative offense of parasitism was elevated to the rank of state crime by Article 209-1 of the USSR Criminal Code. Repeat offenders and dissidents were subject to a maximum of five years at forced labor in remote regions.

196b ...COCOM (Coordinating Committee on Export Controls of NATO): Created in November 1949 to prevent the transfer of strategic technology to the USSR and its allies. COCOM was founded by Belgium, France, Italy, Luxembourg, The Netherlands, United Kingdom, and the United States. By 1953 they had been joined by Norway, Denmark, Canada, West Germany, Portugal, Japan, Greece, and Turkey.

213b ...we do not have a council: The translator or typist confused "council" and "counsel," as in legal or technical advisor.

214a ...chairman of Gosplan: In February 1988, Yuri Maslyukov succeeded Nikolay Talyzin who had directed the State Planning Committee since 1985.

214a ...chairman of Goskomstat: M.A. Korolev directed the State Committee on Statistics.

214b ...Nechernozem zone: The non-chernozem zone—roughly the area adjacent to the rich black-soil (chernozem) zone, which stretches from the Ukraine to Lake Baikal in Siberia. In general, the population east of the Urals is concentrated in the black soil region, which is bisected by the Trans-Siberian Railway or, as the speaker says, the route from Omsk to Chita by way of Novosibirsk, Krasnoyarsk, and Irkutsk.

215b ...12th 5-Year Plan: 1986-90.

216b ...Maykain deposits: A rich copper-bearing lode in Pavlodar Oblast north of Karaganda.

216b ...Baikonur: The Soviet space center, located about 400 km northeast of the Aral Sea.

218b ...the Special Administration Committee of Nagornyy Karabakh: See above the note to p. 117a.

226b ...ukase... On the Rights and Responsibilities of Internal Forces: See summary, Appendix A.5.

231b ...the events in Minsk: On 30 October 1988, police and internal security troops dispersed a rally of about five thousand supporters of The Belorussian Martyrology, an unofficial association dedicated to exposing the crimes and criminals of the Stalin era, assisting the victims who survived it, and building a memorial at Kuropaty, the woods near Minsk where thousands of persons were shot and buried in 1937-41. Having initially authorized the rally, local authorities changed their minds and canceled it. They apparently feared that the Martyrology society was or would become the nucleus of a separatist movement.

The interior ministry subsequently denied demonstrators' allegations that clubs, tear gas, and water cannons had been used to break up the rally; seventy demonstrators who were arrested were released within three hours. Spokesmen for Martyrology claimed that hundreds of persons were beaten and blinded by tear gas. A special commission of the Belorussian Supreme Soviet concluded that the executive committee of the local soviet and the rally organizers had both used bad judgment, the former by revoking the rally permit without cause, the latter by deliberately violating the law by assembling without permission. The commission was unable to verify any case of beating, gassing, or excessive force. After a separate investigation, the USSR State Prosecutor's Office and USSR Ministry of Internal Affairs concluded that no tear gas had been issued to police or internal security forces. CDSP (8 Feb 1989): 17-18.

232a ...everything R. Medvedev has discussed: Above, pp. 156-57.

241a ...Kudrin is a person who could be recommended: In August 1988, L.S. Kudrin, then a people's judge in Sverdlovsk, was ordered by his superior to impose short jail terms on several persons arrested for alleged participation in an unauthorized rally. Instead he investigated and subsequently dismissed the case. When

ANNOTATED LIST OF SPEECHES
SESSIONS 8–13, 1–9 JUNE 1989

EIGHTH SESSION
1 JUNE 1989

Speaker	Subject	Page
B.Ye. Paton	Presiding; recognizes USSR's first Children's Protection Day, returns to agenda—continued discussion of basic direction of domestic and foreign policy	2a
I.P. Drutse	Claims title of "homeland of stagnation" for Moldavia, explains; sees intimidation in voting procedure of Congress, advocates dismissal of authorities incapable of communicating with masses, proposes ban on use of troops in local disturbances in order to compel authorities to find political solutions, challenges deputies to revitalize nation's leadership, questions effectiveness of investigative commissions, calls on Gorbachev to clarify position on national questions, defends national languages—opposes bilingualism, sees future being decided either by representatives of the people or by state-party apparatchiks	2a
B.S. Mitin	Addresses problems of education—warns that educational system is presently unable to support perestroika, calls for doubling expenditure with emphasis on computerization, points to threat to education from new cost accounting system, comments on low status of teachers, proposes committee on education, asks some member of Russian leadership to describe impact of restructuring on Russia	5a
S.A. Niyazov	Affirms guiding efficacy of Marxism-Leninism and defends healthy forces within the state-party apparatus, sees no single solution to problems of a multinational state, defends bilingualism as appropriate to Turmenistan; surveys, defines republic's problems as high infant mortality, low status of women, rural backwardness, unbalanced industrialization, ecological degradation, below average supply of consumer goods, distorted market relations, and the disadvantage of being a primary source and supplier of raw material; praises efforts to improve relations with Iran and Afghanistan	6b
A.A. Likhanov	Pleads for support of Children's Fund, surveys its activities, plans for network of infant and children's homes, obstructions of Ministry of Education, crisis of family life, infanticide, delinquency, suicide; appeals for presidential leadership, proposes law on children's rights, urges ratification of UN convention on children's rights, recommends separation of women's issues from those of children and family life	9a
Yu.K. Sharipov	Notes low visibility of Bashkir delegation and deputies from other autonomous republics; addresses shortage of telephones (fifteen million outstanding orders) and inadequate measures to overcome it, recommends a market system supplied by state, collective, and cooperative enterprises; faults central planners for continued stagnation, warns against indirect effects of strikes, doubts effectiveness of regional cost accounting without guaranteeing republics	11b

EIGHTH SESSION, 1 JUNE 1989

Speaker	Subject	Page
	(continued) control of their social and material resources, sees need for laws on enterprises, local management, land tenure, and regional cost accounting; asserts economic equality of autonomous regions and republics, proposes comprehensive legislation on conservation and use of natural resources and a special congress of people's deputies on interethnic relations	
B.Ye. Paton	Reminds deputies of time limit on speeches	13b
V.I. Belov	Deplores rudeness toward president, labels irresponsible deputies who yielded Supreme Soviet seats; asserts that people want improved electoral system, decentralization of power, and private ownership of land; denounces Minvodkhoz for squandering wealth, destroying land, and bringing agriculture to brink of disaster; attributes russophobia to favored political-economic status of RSFSR, attacks self-serving interests of mass media and incompetence of Moscovite economists and academicians, accuses urban elite of promoting vulgarization of culture, alcoholism, drug abuse, and profligacy; demands end to irresponsible or cynical sell-out to foreign capital through concessions, leases, and joint enterprises; calls for immediate national referendum on nuclear energy, warns that power does not yet rest with people's deputies but with those who control mass communications	13b
G.I. Stoumova	Describes rural labor shortage and need for modern equipment, cites specific rural needs: extended maternity leave, higher ceiling on outside income for pensioners, credit for kolhkoz work in computation of state farm workers' pensions, early retirement for certain female construction workers, housing, and freedom for local soviets to address social needs	16a
	Congress recessed	
V.P. Larionov	Addresses constitutional requirements of autonomous republics, oblasts, and districts: questions unequal status of large autonomous regions and small union republics, notes under-representation of recognized nationalities and need for comprehensive review of principles defining national and territorial formations, accuses central ministries of impeding regional development, calls for freedom of union and autonomous republics to manage their own domestic and foreign economic relations, cites special ecological and ethnic problems of northern regions, favors regional cost accounting to reverse ravages of overindustrialization and end artificially low prices paid for energy resources and precious metals; stresses importance of science in Siberian development but calls for shift of emphasis from economic to ecological problems, defends construction of Amur-Yakut Mainline as key investment in Siberian development	17a
Yu.D. Chernichenko	Describes evolution of Moscow Group, charges defeat of popular initiative by party's manipulation of commissions and agendas, contends that millions who awakened to political life condemn the formula of "divide and rule"; compares perestroika to NEP, blames failure of Soviet agriculture on political system, and warns that Stalinism in agriculture is destroying perestroika; ridicules incompetence of Murakhovsky and Ligachev; charges that bureaucracy humiliates USSR with oil exports, grain and food imports, and technological backwardness; sees adoption of new land law as the critical requirement, notes that Moscow Group enjoys nationwide representation and issues open invitation to all	19b

ANNOTATED LIST OF SPEECHES

Speaker	Subject	Page
V.N. Kalish	Cautions against divisiveness; recommends shift of resources from ferrous metals industry to rural development, warns of uselessness of pollution control investment in antiquated Zaporozhye metallurgical complex which must be completely rebuilt using modern technology; criticizes cooperatives for producing little but private wealth, legalizing money obtained illegally, and drawing skilled labor from state enterprises; complains that Muscovites buy goods at state prices while others must pay cooperative prices; defends apparatchiks as conscientious workers, notes that it was scientists who created and "palmed off plans on the Politburo"	22a
K.T. Mazurov	Describes impoverishment of millions of World War II veterans, ex-partisans and widows, presents petition of seventy-five veteran deputies for funding of pensions to subsistence level with allocations made on social instead of regional basis; commends prominent artists' appeal for support of veterans, deplores widespread disrespect toward veterans, urges proper burial of dead soldiers and preservation and restoration of graves and monuments, reports veterans' indignation that Moscow still has no victory monument Condemns leisure orientation of younger generation, urges development of comprehensive program for labor, moral and cultural education of youth with emphasis on physical labor; urges rebuff to those who propose capitalist market relations and multiparty system which would deprive people of social protection and lead to anarchy; contends that restructuring requires order, precision and discipline which only communist leadership can provide	24a
A.A. Grakhovsky	Surveys effects of Chernobyl disaster, particularly in Gomel oblast; sees no substantial improvement for several years, cites need for fourth resettlement program, appeals to scientific community to intensify research in Chernobyl area; enumerates specific problems: difficulties of supplying food and resulting social tension, lack of effective action by central authorities, especially difficult condition of pensioners, shortage of medical equipment, medicine, personal radiation meters and other monitoring devices, shortage of firewood and peat due to contamination, inadequate housing and social services; complains that authorities focus on power station and ignore surrounding area Rebukes "rally-style democrats" for diverting attention from critical issues, approves of democratization and glasnost only if accompanied by self-discipline, collective spirit, and sense of personal responsibility; condemns rush to legislate before legislative mechanisms are in place, resents wholesale disparagement of party cadres, sees attacks as self-defeating	26b
B.Ye. Paton	Interrupts order of speakers to allow Estonian deputy Lippmaa to present proposal	28b
E.T. Lippmaa	Proposes commission to appraise Soviet-German treaty of 1939 and secret protocol, lists members with Ch. Aytmatov as chairman	28b
V.I. Yarovoy	Protests against bias of commission named by Lippmaa, charges anti-Russian mood in Estonia	29b
E.T. Lippmaa	Declares that aim of commission is to clarify situation not kindle disagreements	29b
Zh.I. Alferov	Asserts that treaty lost validity when war began in 1941, questions need for commission	29b
V.V. Ivanov	Urges approval of commission by consensus, opposes division into majority and minority	30a

EIGHTH SESSION, 1 JUNE 1989

Speaker	Subject	Page
V.M. Semenov	Proposes that Supreme Soviet take up the issue	30a
Unidentified	Endorses referral of secondary issues to Supreme Soviet—more important to set up commission on Chernobyl	30a
V.A. Berezov	Stresses importance of commission to Baltic deputies, notes that main issue is not treaty but the secret protocols	30a
I.Ya. Kezbers	Urges approval of commission	30b
I.N. Gryazin	Reads text of secret protocol of 23 August 1939 creating spheres of influence in Baltic and anticipating the partition of Poland, asserts that text raises legal questions that need to be settled by a commission	30b
E.E. Inkens	Stresses special significance of treaty for Baltic peoples, notes that Soviet agreement with Polish government in exile after 1941 nullified part of treaty, implying a question of its continued validity	31a
Yu.Yu. Boldyrev	Challenges deputies' moral right to question motives or actions of other deputies—sees that as task for voters, supports proposal to form a commission to investigate and report to Congress	31a
R.A. Medvedev	Observes that Russians admit to conquest of Siberia, Central Asia and northern Caucasus but cling to lie that Baltic republics voluntarily joined USSR, supports need for commission to assess the agreements but suggests review and revision of its membership	31a
M.S. Gorbachev	Describes failure to locate original copies of 1939 treaty and protocols, supports creation of commission on a broader basis than proposed, argues that it should render a political and legal evaluation of the treaty but not the secret protocol, advises consultation with Presidium to identify competent people, interprets applause as acclamation Replies to question from floor that foreign minister Shevardnadze, not being a deputy, is ineligible to serve on commission, suggests Yakovlev; supported by applause	31b
B.Ye. Paton	Declares that proposal to form commission is approved, denies demand for a vote on grounds that only membership, not advisability of a commission, is being reconsidered; notes that Presidium has 500 requests to speak, reads letter calling for subsequent speakers to focus on solutions to problems, another recommending that undelivered speeches be printed in newspapers and incorporated into stenographic record of the Congress; makes administrative announcements and declares recess	32b

Congress recessed

Speaker	Subject	Page
B.Ye. Paton	Announces speakers for evening session	33a
A.Ya. Neumyvakin	Pleads consideration of more than seven million disabled persons, asks increase of minimum pension, recommends savings through reduced military spending and joint space ventures, supports specific legislation on organizations of disabled, seeks higher quotas and protection of jobs for disabled, describes economic straits and administrative indifference affecting handicapped persons, recalls that 1989 is Year of Charity	33b
A.A. Korshunov	Defends party but criticizes party members who work secretly against restructuring, condemns Andreyeva, "Memorial," and the Democratic Union while praising Moscow Group and Baltic representatives; warns against counterrevolution; cites plight of pensioners, inflation, scarcity of goods and services; demands that Ryzhkov explain "shameful" mess, including failure of cooperatives to improve domestic market and continued producer domination of retail	36b

ANNOTATED LIST OF SPEECHES

Speaker	Subject	Page
	(continued) prices; invites deputies to develop specific program of restructuring and urges end to personal recrimination	
A.Ye. Karpov	Presents Soviet Peace Foundation proposals for expediting conversion of industry from military to civilian production, describes inadequacy of programs for disabled, including 1.5 million veterans; endorses increase in minimum pension to level of minimum wage, calls for free public transportation for disabled, poor and senior citizens; warns against profusion of foundations, proposes curriculum revision to strengthen national unity and national tolerance, calls for power to soviets, land to peasants, and dignity to individuals	39a
Ye.A. Yevtushenko	Proposes legislation to criminalize ethnic slander, protect peasantry and rural communities from state oppression, exonerate "kulaks" from all illegal judgments and expropriations, guarantee free choice of labor, end special privileges for nomenklatura, ensure equal access of all citizens to all state offices, overturn the sentences of all dissidents, limit the licenses of psychiatrists who engaged in medical mistreatment, establish supremacy of soviets of people's deputies, prohibit use of army against any nation, annul decree of 8 April, and institute direct, popular election of all officials; defines perestroika as second Great Patriotic War against nuclear, natural, ethnic, economic, ecological and bureaucratic evils and misfortunes	41b
P.A. Azizbekova	Calls for preservation of multinational state with diverse political institutions and economic models, warns that national isolation will weaken entire union, distort economic relations, and destroy Soviet culture; blames Armenian nationalists for destabilizing the Caucasus and creating 300,000 refugees, urges legal protection and compensation to victims and strict observance of letter and spirit of law; sees possible resolution of crisis and compromise being blocked by "anti-restructuring forces"; calls for rejection of principle that national interests must supersede social interests, endorses appeal for restoration of status quo, and expresses confidence in Gorbachev's leadership	44a
V.V. Gustov	Describes deplorable conditions in Tyumen oblast: 17,500 oil-worker families in temporary housing with inadequate medical facilities, schools, social and cultural services; wasteful extraction methods, obsolete equipment, bureaucratic confusion and mismanagement, overdevelopment, and destruction of environment; proposes transfer of responsibility for environmental protection from Council of Ministers to Supreme Soviet, reconsideration of decision to locate petrochemical industry in the Tyumen, right to use profits to purchase equipment abroad, right to circumvent ministries to address social problems, and right to form regional associations of energy-producing industries in order to achieve greater efficiency under new cost-accounting system; reports that Tyumen agricultural workers support peasants' appeal to the Congress	46a
V.V. Landsbergis	Identifies sovereignty of Baltic republics with goals of perestroika, characterizes old relations between center and republics as outmoded, notes that democratization and rule of law should secure the vital rights of republics, proposes constitutional amendment requiring consent of republics to give force to USSR laws, repeats Baltics' appeal to restrict use of armed forces to defense of USSR and to disband the "dishonored" military units that attacked civilians in Tbilisi, calls for limiting special forces and emergency	47b

EIGHTH SESSION, 1 JUNE 1989

Speaker	Subject	Page
	(continued) powers and for rescinding recent legislation on state crimes, wants issue of secret protocols clearly on agenda of commission on Nazi-Soviet pact, envisions voluntary union of republics incorporating best of Lenin's legacy and nothing of Stalin's	
B.Ye. Paton	Proposes postponing two speeches in order to deal with organizational questions; deputies approve	49b
A.I. Lukyanov	Reviews Tbilisi background—reads three telegrams of April 1989 from Georgian Communist Party First Secretary Patiashvili purporting to describe deteriorating situation due to demands of Abkhazian and Georgian nationalists and calling repeatedly for permission to declare state of emergency and curfew in Tbilisi; telegram of 9 April reports use of security forces and troops to break up demonstration, repeats appeal for permission to institute curfew; asserts that only then did Moscow dispatch Shevardnadze and Razumovsky to Tbilisi	49b
M.S. Gorbachev	Endorses investigation to assure people of no cover-up	51b
F.V. Dovlatyan	Demands response to Armenian deputies' appeals concerning Sumgait and NKAO	52a
B.Ye. Paton	Defers response to the morrow; invites Gidaspov to give Credentials Commission's report on Alksnis' complaint of Latvian electoral irregularities	52a
B.V. Gidaspov	Describes complaints received by commission, confirms Alksnis' complaint of great disparities in numbers of voters in Latvian electoral districts but validates election of all Latvian deputies, recommends that proper authorities see that republics comply with electoral law in creating election districts	52a
Unidentified	Charges Credentials Commission with failing duty to investigate admitted violations of the electoral law	53a
B.V. Gidaspov	Defends commission's action, notes Alksnis's personal satisfaction	53a
B.Ye. Paton	Rules acceptance of Credentials Commission report, calls for show of hands when some deputies protest, notes approval by clear majority; denies podium to unidentified deputy, admits Nishanov	53b
R.N. Nishanov	Describes principles of selection and announces composition of commission on the Gdlyan-Ivanov affair with Medvedev as chair	53b
Unidentified	Wants to know why Yakovlev was excluded	54b
Unidentified	Notes absence of Komsomol representative, proposes Norikhin	54b
B.Ye. Paton	Explains exclusion of Yakovlev	54b
N.V. Ivanov	Questions need for still another Tbilisi commission when only unresolved question is who gave orders from Moscow, observes that successive commissions have nearly succeeded in destroying criminal proceedings in Uzbekistan case, notes release on that day of three officials charged with corruption, attributes delay and new investigation to conspiracy to relieve Moscow bribe-takers of responsibility and perpetuate abuse of power [*several interruptions during speech*]	54b
V.S. Shevchenko	Notes anonymous campaign to enlist deputies' support for Gdlyan and Ivanov; questions right of Gdlyan and Ivanov to veto appointment of a deputy (Semenov) endorsed by the entire Ukrainian delegation	55b
E.Yu. Yusupov	Objects to campaign in defense of Gdlyan and Ivanov, opposes Medvedev as chairman due to bias	56a

ANNOTATED LIST OF SPEECHES

Speaker	Subject	Page
N.A. Strukov	Declares that only courts of law can establish guilt and therefore refuses to serve without constitutional amendment empowering the commission; insists on due process despite Gdlyan's "irresponsible methods"	56a
B.Ye. Paton	States that deputies demanded the commission, opines that judicial matters will be referred to an appropriate court	56b
Unidentified	Asserts need for truth due to widespread embezzlement and bribery that are eroding moral foundation of society	57a
A.G. Mukhtarov	Notes "tens of thousands" subjected to false arrest and imprisonment by Gdlyan prosecutors, opposes chairmanship of Medvedev, proposes election of chair by commission members	57a
Z.K. Rustamova	Objects to commissioning incompetent deputies to investigate and make judgments on intricate criminal procedure, recommends special investigators trained in law to investigate and bring charges if warranted for adjudication by court of law	57a
S.V. Belozertsev	Reports constituents' appeal for newspaper space and television time for Gdlyan and Ivanov to justify themselves, recommends that commission hire its own lawyers	57b
A.U. Khusanov	Favors composition of commission as proposed but wants investigation extended to include prosecutor who allegedly jailed twenty people illegally	57b
Yu.A. Levykin	Proposes that, before appointing commission members, Congress should first charge commission, define its power, and draft its standing orders	58a
A.A. Sobchak	Asserts that purpose of commission is not to investigate case of Gdlyan and Ivanov but to determine whether they should be deprived of parliamentary immunity, not to investigate alleged violations of Gdlyan and Ivanov but the validity of their accusations against state and party officials; urges focus on composition of commission	58a
B.Ye. Paton	Reminds Congress that commission is empowered to obtain any documents it needs	58b
G.M. Kurochka	Reports voters' impatience with Congress' inability to form an objective commission, cites need for appointment of legal specialists	58b
N.A. Kutsenko	Proposes end to "ballyhoo" by assigning both Tbilisi and Gdlyan-Ivanov investigations to Constitutional Oversight Committee of Supreme Soviet	58b
S.S. Sulakshin	Noting general fatigue, urges postponement of question until next session, supports right of Gdlyan and Ivanov to veto commission members but not to nominate them	59a
Unidentified	Interprets Ivanov's speech, questions selection process, especially nomination of Baranov; supports Gdlyan and Ivanov's participation in selection of members	59a
Unidentified	Supports Baranov's candidacy	59a
B.Ye. Paton	Reviews details and calls for vote on composition of commission, leaving selection of chairman to commission itself; notes voluntary withdrawal of Shorokhov	59b
A.D. Sakharov	Wants discussion of earlier proposal	59b
Unidentified	Questions omission of Miroshin, proposes his appointment in place of Shorokhov	59b
R.N. Nishanov	Explains absence of Miroshin from list	59b
	Gdlyan-Ivanov Commission approved	60a

Speaker	Subject	Page
B.Ye. Paton	Opens floor to three-minute comments, first registered speaker declines	60a
A.A. Likhanov	Corrects A.Ye. Karpov's alleged errors on Children Fund expenditures	60a
B.Ye. Paton	Concludes session	60b
	Congress adjourned	

NINTH SESSION
2 JUNE 1989

Speaker	Subject	Page
A.I. Lukyanov	Presiding	61a
A.A. Makanu	Endorses territorial cost accounting and economic autonomy, surveys prerequisites; calls for fresh look at national formations, enlarged role of union republic, language questions, constitutional reform; criticizes inflammatory press coverage of Moldavian affairs	62a
V.V. Khmura	Calls for clearer economic relations between village soviet and local enterprises, equal living standards in village and cities, and transfer of land use control to local soviets; describes ecological problems of the Kuban, economic problem of rural communities; praises positive contributions of Party	64a
V.V. Dyusembayev	Addresses conditions in mining and metallurgical industries, ecology; criticizes trade policy, energy policy, and privatization movement; praises army	66b
Sh.A. Amonashvili	Expresses confidence in Tbilisi investigation; decries authoritarianism and standardized curriculum of schools; advises skepticism toward Rodionov's version of Tbilisi events and pleads for friendship over force in all-union relations	68a
Ch. Aytmatov	Applauds progress toward democratic institutions but sees need for more definite economic program, including introduction of new forms of ownership and productive relations; proposes quest for western credit and establishment of sovereign union republics; endorses bilingualism, condemns press irresponsibility in national issues, urges constitutional protection of national minorities	69b
V.I. Sergiyenko	Urges constitutional separation of powers; disagrees with Chernichenko, defends Ligachev, challenges Ivanov; favors economic and social reform and improved central regulation of a socialist market with tax concessions to socially desirable activities but also endorses proposal to separate state administration from economic direction; urges genuine financial and legal powers for local organs and end to "colonial policy" of central agencies; sees need to ascertain status of autonomous oblasts as national entities	72b
A.I. Trudolyubov	Describes desperate plight of non-chernozem zone, need for economic and social investment; calls for end to industrial development, which depopulates farms and villages; urges support for draft law on youth	75a

ANNOTATED LIST OF SPEECHES

Speaker	Subject	Page
Yu.P. Platonov	Relays recommendations of architects concerning urban planning and construction, portrays chief obstacle to rational urban development as the monopolies of central departments and the contract system	77a
A.I. Lukyanov	Announces that the Congress will not meet on Saturday (June 3)	79b
	Congress in recess	
Z.N. Tkacheva	Describes health effects of Chernobyl disaster in Mogilev-Gomel regions, demands resettlement and compensation, proposes fundraising for facilities for orphaned children and children of Chernobyl; requests response to appeal of Belorussian delegation	80a
V.G. Ardzinba	Surveys history of Abkhazia, seeks adherence to 1921 treaty respecting Abkhazian sovereignty, notes Georgian opposition, proposes formation of deputies' and Supreme Soviet commissions to study problems of autonomous entities	81b
Ya.Ya. Peters	Enumerates Latvian concerns over "colonization" by Russians and Moscow, links to other Soviet nations, economic and environmental degradation; analyzes de jure constitution of USSR noting responsibility of center to protect its constituents from tyranny; demands official denunciation of 1939 Soviet-German treaty; reminds Presidium of pending question concerning Crimean Tatars	84b
V.A. Ambartsumyan	Expresses Armenians' gratitude for assistance to earthquake victims; cites Azeri violence against Armenians to demand resolute action by Moscow, declares self-determination the only solution to NKAO crisis, seeks condemnation of Turkish genocide against Armenians in 1915, lauds sacrifices of Russian people	86b
D. Khudonazarov	Charges official irresponsibility and electoral inequities, deplores tension between workers and intelligentsia, calls for tolerance and democracy in interethnic relations, surveys economic and national problems of Pamir region, proposes that members of Supreme Soviet committees and commissions have consultative role in CPSU Central Committee plenums	88a
S.V. Chervonopisky	Cites older generation for failure to create a legacy of ideas on which youth can build their lives, criticizes Gorbachev for not discussing Afghan war responsibility, defends youth work of veteran-led military patriotic clubs, asserts innocence of troops in Tbilisi riot; scorns leaders of Georgian and Baltic volunteer militias and popular fronts, condemns media persecution of the army; attacks Sakharov for defaming army in interview with Canadian journalists; affirms loyalty to communism	90b
P.V. Shetko	Demands thorough investigation to determine officials responsible for committing troops to Afghanistan, insists on publication of names of all war dead, pleads for aid to disabled veterans and families of war dead	92b
A.D. Sakharov	Denies insulting Soviet Army, reviews opposition to Afghan war, explains statement made to Canadian newsmen that encircled Soviet troops were killed to prevent their capture	93a
V.N. Ochirov	Accuses Sakharov of lying and of slandering the army	93b
A.V. Eyzan	Responds to Chervonopisky's attack on Baltic leaders	93b
V.V. Yakushkin	Finds Sakharov's defense unconvincing	94a
Unidentified	Attests to service of Latvians in Afghanistan	94a

NINTH SESSION, 2 JUNE 1989

Speaker	Subject	Page
S.F. Akhromeyev	Denies Sakharov allegation that General Staff or Ministry of Defense ordered encircled troops killed to prevent capture	94a
G.I. Kravchenko	Rebukes Sakharov	94a
N.A. Polikarpov	Accuses Sakharov of slander	94b
T.K. Kazakova	Declares contempt for Sakharov	94b
	Congress recessed	
G.N. Gorbunov	Wants legislation to prevent national hostility and end economic and social crises, calls for budget policy to be reoriented to solution of social problems; seeks coordinated attack on ecological problems and an end to grandiose engineering projects; opposes price increases to increase availability of consumer goods; favors industrial development at expense of defense industry, joint enterprises with foreign concerns, socially oriented tax structure, increased labor and production discipline, freedom of production centers from control by scientific-technical centers; reviews alleged mistakes made to date under restructuring	94b
Kh. Atdayev	Reviews and approves of electoral process but questions aspects of economic reform and asks immediate attention to question of water supply in Aral region	97b
Yu.F. Karyakin	Discusses changed position of general secretary; calls for publication of records of Central Committee sessions, for restoration of Solzhenitsyn's citizenship, and for removal of Lenin's corpse to family grave as he requested; reads constituent letters condemning and praising Sakharov	99a
Unidentified	Wants enforcement of alleged proposal to bar any more Muscovites from speaking	100b
A.S. Dzasokhov	Calls for holistic approach to constitutional and structural reform, for generalized results from social scientists, for synchronization of the restructuring process, for integration of labor into socio-political sphere; advocates creation of center for interethnic relations, urges participation in global economic system	100b
V.P. Shcherbakov	Contends that socialist achievements have been underrated and that the potential of socialism is not being used; attributes economic crisis to failure of accountability; charges that high officials profit from the cooperative movement and that their uncontrolled connivance is source of economic and financial crises, shortages, and crime; makes specific proposals for fiscal, monetary, and economic reform; supports diversion of funds from armaments to pensioners and indexing of wages, benefits, and pensions to cost of living	102b
A.I. Lukyanov	Shifts discussion to organizational matters; presents Presidium proposal of commission to examine 1939 Soviet-German treaty (approved by Congress) Reports on disposition of deputy requests for information on the following issues: Tbilisi events of 9 April 1989, Gdlyan-Ivanov inquiry, nuclear power generation in the Ukraine, Crimean nuclear plant, Semipalatinsk test range, ecological situation of Frunze, Southern Urals Power Project, Kirishi biochemical plant, Leningrad pumped-storage power plant, Zavolsky chemical plant, consequences of Chernobyl disaster, medical equipment, wages in Eastern	104

ANNOTATED LIST OF SPEECHES

Speaker	Subject	Page
	(continued)	
	Siberia, public health system finances, pensions, rail equipment in Ekibastuz, individual housing, Kansk-Achinsk fuel-power project, law on state enterprise, financing of public education, protection of children and youth, children's rights, draft law on nuclear power, crime, national and ethnic relations involving Abkhazians, Soviet Germans, Crimean Tatars, Ingush, and Gagauz	
	Gives current tallies on correspondence received, speeches, and participation by deputies	
G.M. Khodryrev	Notes cursory, generally unsatisfactory response to deputies' requests by heads of departments and ministries; contends that radio-television coverage of Congress is not accessible everywhere to workers	108b
N.S. Sazanov	Questions implementation of procedural rules, recommends extension of the Congress	108b
N.N. Medvedev	Protests attacks on Baltic delegations, asserts non-violent nature and aims of volunteer people's militias	109a
V.F. Derevyanko	Describes ecological deterioration of Black Sea	109a
R.A. Ubaydullayeva	Complains that presidium ignores requests, asks for publication in press of speeches that could not be delivered	109b
A.I. Lukyanov	Reviews procedural rules adopted by Congress	110a
V.A. Leonchev	Describes deaths and health effects of chemical contamination at Novokuybyshevsk	110a
Yu.B. Solovyev	(Interrupted by Lukyanov) Argues need for consumer durables designed specifically for use in rural areas	110b
A.A. Zgerskaya (Yaroshinskaya)	Advises deputies of videocassette depicting radiation contamination in Zhitomir oblast	110b
M.I. Umarkhodzhayev	Calls for 150 percent increase in price of cotton and measures to reduce unemployment in Uzbekistan and Central Asia	111a
V.P. Malyshev	Inquires about deputy's request concerning construction of Rostov nuclear power plant	111a
P.A. Akhunov	Wants Uzbek minority's views heard	111b
N.A. Kasyan	Denies invitation to delegates, appeals for mutual respect	112a
A.I. Lukyanov	Announces schedule, adjourns session	112a
	Congress adjourned	

TENTH SESSION
5-6 JUNE 1989

Speaker	Subject	Page
	5 June 1989	
M.S. Gorbachev	Reports on gas pipeline disaster in Bashkir ASSR, extends condolences to victims' families, hints at incompetence while noting that an investigative commission is at work; proposes adjournment in consideration of national day of mourning, Congress agrees; reads and associates himself with Moscow, Leningrad, and Baltic deputies' plea for end to bloodshed in Fergana and Nagorno-Karabakh	114a

Congress adjourned

Speaker	Subject	Page
	6 June 1989	
A.V. Gorbunov	Presiding, resumes Tenth Session and discussion of Gorbachev's policy report, lists the day's speakers	115a
Ye.A. Gayer	Questions omission from list of speakers	115b
B.V. Dadamyan	Reviews history of NKAO since 1921; accuses Azerbaijan authorities of withholding capital funds, calls for end to "selective de-Stalinization" and for implementation of Leninist self-determination, presents Armenian demands for measures to unite NKAO with Armenia; presents draft resolution calling for central government to rule NKAO, restore local government, and organize a referendum to decide oblast's fate	116a
A.A. Sokolov	Argues for displacement of central bureaucracies by local soviets strengthened with genuine material and financial resources, for shift of capital investment from industrial expansion to rural development, for shutting down major industrial polluters when necessary, for legislation controlling nuclear power development in interests of safety and human welfare, and for a tax on profits to benefit children and veterans; deplores attacks on Ligachev and on Lenin's memory	118b
K.S. Khallik	Surveys national relations, attributes current problems to Lenin's failure to create a federation and Stalin's imperialism, contends that modern experience favors international integration not centralization and subordination, links success of restructuring and renewal of socialism to abandonment of false notion of class struggle of workers against peasants and intelligentsia, calls for special agency of the Soviet of Nationalities to protect endangered and other minorities, favors a policy to restore cultural diversity	121a
M.I. Mongo	Observes that uneven economic, social, and demographic development and environmental problems aggravate interethnic relations; contends that true conditions of peoples of the North have been hidden from view, calls for range of laws to protect interests of twenty-six national minorities who inhabit Far North, Siberia, and Far East; proposes permanent commission of Soviet of Nationalities on affairs of northern ethnic and national groups, stronger representation and powers for autonomous formations, and a bicameral RSFSR Supreme Soviet to give voice to national minorities	123b

ANNOTATED LIST OF SPEECHES

Speaker	Subject	Page
N.A. Kasyan	Condemns lack of decorum of some deputies, panders to majority's sentiments during lengthy self-advertisement, urges Congress not to waste time	126a
T.A. Minnullin	Describes local interests of constituents, all reflecting desire for improved quality of life; stresses urgency of status of Tatars and need for equality in representation of national groups, cites inequities imposed on lesser nationalities, wants total equality of all Soviet peoples, end to differences between union and autonomous republics, legislation to protect national languages and promote their development, and an end to "paper internationalism"	128b
A.I. Seleznev	Rebukes speakers who criticized party, self, and KGB; maintains that solution of food problem requires total reorientation of attitude and policy toward needs of rural society, calls for radical social reorganization of villages to make rural life appealing and for slower pace in development of mining and power generation in order to redirect funds into revitalization of the countryside; cites need for land improvement in chernozem zone, criticizes current program	131a
A.V. Gorbunov	Presents presidium's draft statement on events in China, stressing internal nature of the situation and expressing hope for a speedy solution "worthy of the great Chinese people"	132b
	Congress adopts statement, recesses	
D.N. Kugultinov	Discusses impact of Lenin's "mistake" (Stalin) in survey of interethnic relations, calls for restoration of Crimean Tatar autonomy and Volga German republic and for law guaranteeing the rights of peoples; appeals for concern for AIDS victims	133a
A.D. Lizichev	Reviews restructuring of the armed forces: new doctrine, arms reduction, modernization and training, force reductions, discipline, crime, conscription, role of army in Afghanistan and in disaster relief; urges deputies to withhold judgment on military role in Tbilisi events; appeals for assistance in resettlement and employment of military families dislocated by force reductions and for improved housing and schools for those still in service	134b
S.S. Alekseyev	Sees Congress's goal as creation of first-class legal system, including a tested legislative policy, a genuine constitution, and laws creating an effective economic system; defends decision to entrust law-making to Supreme Soviet rather than Congress of People's Deputies	137a
V.G. Rasputin	Favors electoral reform, sees need for restraint to preserve democracy, decries "pluralism of morality" and decadence of Soviet society, wants legislation to secure and protect morality; compares current power struggle to prerevolutionary liberal efforts to undermine tsarist government; suggests that Russia could regain its spiritual identity by withdrawing from USSR, contends that russophobia is misplaced, that common enemy is the administrative-industrial machine that is also responsible for wholesale environmental destruction; charges Ryzhkov with irresponsibility in approval of Katun power station	138b
V.I. Yarovoy	Argues for preservation of union; accuses Baltic deputies of sowing mistrust, charges Estonians with oppressing non-Estonians and destroying Party organizations, belittling Soviet institutions, and seeking independence as part of a neutralized region; proposes declaration of principles reinforcing Soviet socialist federation and USSR constitution; reads veterans' appeal for adequate housing	141b
V.I. Goldansky	Proposes rules of conduct for deputies	145a

Speaker	Subject	Page
M. Shakhanov	Presents Kazakh appeal for investigation of violent suppression of Alma-Ata demonstrators in 1986, denounces pejorative accusation of "nationalism," proposes decree clarifying status of national languages	145b
A.P Aydak	Wants more access to podium for agrarian deputies, urges adoption of appeal of agrarian deputies as decision of the Congress	146b
A.L. Plotnik	Offers plan to include people's deputies in staffing Supreme Soviet committees	147a
Ye.A. Gayer	Reports constituent support for Sakharov	147b
A.V. Gorbunov	Cuts off speaker, makes closing announcements	148a

Congress adjourned

ELEVENTH SESSION
7 JUNE 1989

Speaker	Subject	Page
M.S. Gorbachev	Reports commission at work in Uzbekistan to restore order, that situation is under control but still not stable; asks deputies to appeal to Uzbeks to remain calm; announces Supreme Soviet's appointment of Ryzhkov as Chairman of Council of Ministers and Kolbin as Chairman of People's Control Commission; presents Ryzhkov to report on government's policies	149a
N.I. Ryzhkov	Acknowledges that economic crisis is more serious than anticipated due to inertia and failure on a number of fronts; reviews radical economic aims elaborated in 1987, including democratization of management, organizational restructuring of the national economy, and reorientation of the economy toward satisfaction of social needs; sees the latter as most difficult of all tasks because it requires massive overhaul of industrial sector and enhancement of the fiscal and economic powers of republic and local authorities	150b

Reports reduction of state bureaucracy by 600,000 but cites state monopolies as the major obstacle to restructuring; identifies next tasks as introduction of regional cost-accounting into republic and local soviets, introduction of various forms of ownership, creation of modern methods of managing market relations, and development of an adequate tax policy; claims substantial progress but warns that major transformation of basic economic and investment structures is necessary and will prove difficult and painful

Surveys aims of government's social policy in food supply, consumer goods and services, housing, health care, education, spiritual development, and environmental protection; stresses immediate need for new law on pensions to assist almost 40 million people living below the poverty line, notes intent to equalize access to health care, medical treatment, and vacation facilities

Cites food production as area of special concern due to declining growth rate in 1980s (to zero in 1988); admits need to revise decree on leasing with aim of giving peasants the ability to choose from various forms of ownership and administration of property;

ANNOTATED LIST OF SPEECHES xvii

Speaker	Subject	Page

(continued)

declares that decisions concerning water resources must be decentralized with infamous Ministry of Land Reclamation and Water Resources limited to construction

Announces two-stage financial recovery program to halt inflation and increase productivity: envisions near-term increase in output of consumer goods financed by reductions of capital investment in defense and industry, reduction of cost of administrative apparatus, and other economies, with elimination of budget deficit as main goal of second stage (13th Five-Year Plan)

Defines goals of investment policy as rapid increase in development of social and cultural material base, with particular emphasis on social needs of rural population, to be accompanied by basic restructuring of all economic sectors engaged in providing direct services to people

Calls for strict cost-accounting and self-financing in research and design work, noting unwarranted wage increases and irresponsibly high cost of products; notes that environmental problems are so immense that short-term solutions are impossible, announces 45 billion ruble expenditure on environmental protection in each of next three five-year plans vs. 15 billion in current plan; calls upon new Supreme Soviet to examine issues of nuclear and hydroelectric power and aftermath of Chernobyl disaster; acknowledges strength of centrifugal forces, declares government's commitment to defend human rights, legality, and democratic freedoms of all peoples

Announces policy of reducing defense expenditure by one-third to one-half by 1995, stresses need to speed up conversion of military production to civilian uses, anticipates that consumer goods production will account for 60 percent of defense complex output in 1995, defends technical and economic benefits of investment in space technology

Admits to serious problems in foreign trade and balance of payments due in part to collapse of world oil prices, admits dependence on foreign consumer goods and foodstuffs with result that hard-currency payments exceed revenues by more than 100 percent, notes that annual interest on foreign debt exceeds 25 percent of all foreign payments making the USSR a poor credit risk; strategy for foreign economic relations involves breaking with past and engaging in broadest range of scientific, technical and industrial cooperation, increasing the proportion of finished goods among Soviet exports, strengthening relations with socialist countries, and improving socialist economic integration

| M.S. Gorbachev | Presents agenda for remainder of Congress and for second sitting of Supreme Soviet | 164b |

Agenda approved. Congress adjourned

TWELFTH SESSION
8 JUNE 1989

Speaker	Subject	Page
A.-M.K. Brazauskas	Presides, opens session	166a
G.V. Bykov	Reports popular dissatisfaction with pace of restructuring; proposes nationwide union of workers and periodic review of ministries' functions; sees technical retooling as essential to restructuring, wants limits on urban growth and improved life in non-urban areas, wants cooperatives on equal footing with other enterprises, increased power for local government, longer vacations for workers; opposes reinterment of Lenin's corpse	167a
N.P. Shmelev	Expresses optimism over long-term prospects for economic development but concern over short-term, predicting economic collapse in 2-3 years if present course is unchanged; doubts that government appreciates the danger, recounts its errors; sees solution in restoring balance between supply of goods and money supply, restoring value of ruble, and creating supply of goods in excess of demand; warns against price reform and confiscation of excess money under current social conditions; outlines his solution including moratorium on import of equipment for gigantic projects, end to Cuban subsidy, sale or lease of land and other property, reduction of capital investment in industry and defense, end to budget deficit, etc.	168b
K.D.P. Prunskene	Argues that revitalization of economy requires decentralization and local solutions, direct relations between republic enterprises, return to regionalism, diversity, economic and political independence of republics, and protection of human and economic rights; challenges Ryzhkov's statements on the profitability of the Baltics and his failure to recognize the need for economic independence	172a
I.A. Nazarov	Surveys rural problems, supports appeal of agrarian deputies, favors Supreme Soviet committee on agrarian questions, describes visit to typical farm village as trip into the last century, complains of center's neglect of Siberia which needs major capital investment to provide basic social services and infrastructure, approves of Party decision to allow farmers choices of organization and tenure, notes peasants' distrust of management of labor collectives, favors regional cost accounting and local self-government, conveys voters' concern over deterioration of labor and social discipline and termination of anti-alcohol policy, defends Omsk delegation's process of nominating Supreme Soviet candidates	174b
I.A. Yegorova	Discusses social problems of Altay kray, calls for local control of budget and greater independence of local soviets, welcomes Ryzhkov's plan to transfer control of public health budget to republic and regional authorities, wants broader participation in restructuring of public health system, recommends reduced work load and great technical support for physicians, calls for greater efficiency in production and distribution of medical supplies and equipment, urges greater respect and concern for women and motherhood, urges decision to resolve uncertainty concerning Katun hydroelectric station and demands halt to nuclear testing at Semipalatinsk	177b

ANNOTATED LIST OF SPEECHES

Speaker	Subject	Page
A.-M.K. Brazauskas	Lists scheduled speakers	180b
A.M. Yemelyanov	Deplores inconsistencies in policy, cites examples; notes persistence of bureaucratic apparat at all levels, calls for elimination of all management agencies not essential to support lower levels of production, attacks elite privileges; argues that irreversibility of restructuring needs to be guaranteed by separation of powers of state and party, proposes to ensure that by equalizing electoral process for all deputies, by prohibiting any candidate from running unopposed, by direct election of president, and by democratizing the party	180b
Ye.A. Gayer	Surveys problems of people of the Far East and Far North; cites destruction of way of life wrought by "invasion" of timber industry, disregard of natives' rights in pursuit of economic exploitation of traditional forest and marine resources, failure of funds committed to social development to reach intended consumers, need for statute defining rights of people, inequities in wage coefficients and need to apply coefficients to pensions, stipends, and grants; recommends provision for second deputy to represent large number of military constituents, seeks bonus for military personnel being demobilized, notes inaccuracy of official bulletins	183b
A.-M.K. Brazauskas	Injects announcements	186b
	Congress recessed	
G.G. Gumbaridze	Revisits Tbilisi demonstration and its suppression, characterizes April meetings and demonstrations as political actions aimed at national self-determination and decision to use force as a political error; interprets hostility not as anti-Russian but as anti-bureaucratic, sees use of paratroops in civil action as inexcusable and calls on leadership not to degrade army in such a way; attributes coverup to excessive zeal of local officials; finds ultimate cause of unrest in abuse of federal principles and Stalinist assault on Georgian intelligentsia, calls for reexamination of process of incorporating Georgia into Soviet federation in 1918-21; defines goal of constitutional revision as harmonizing relations with center while establishing political and economic sovereignty of republic, acknowledges seriousness of Abkhazian demands and need for new basis of national relations	186b
A.V. Yablokov	Addresses ecological concerns, attributes environmental degradation to weakness of local and regional soviets, contending that ministries and departments have no economic incentive to conserve resources, sees cause also in false belief that socialist management automatically ensures rational utilization of nature; notes lack of information on state of environment, concludes that party must take lead in improving conditions by restoring local power to soviets and enforcing principle that polluters must pay for damage to nature and man; calls for comprehensive ecological investigation and planning, for environmental studies before large projects are approved, for end to ministerial environmental abuse, for entrusting responsibility for environmental protection to Supreme Soviet, for increasing expenditure on environmental protection; urges Congress to adopt resolution of principle on environment and create Supreme Soviet committee on ecology	189b
A.I. Chabanov	Sermonizes on comportment of true communists; sees little new in Ryzhkov's report, asserts confidence in superiority of socialism	192b

Speaker	Subject	Page
	(continued) over capitalism, sees no problem as insuperable, perceives ministries primarily as think tanks, recommends that departments be allowed to switch affiliations while retaining state orders, urges creation of arbitration commission to regulate enterprises' economic arrangements	
S.P. Zalygin	Sees periodic reappearance of reform movement, each time ignoring historical experience and beginning anew; cites destruction of Aral Sea, contends that local farmers could utilize resources more effectively than Ministry of Land Reclamation and Water Resources, notes that environmental legislation cannot be adopted until issues of ownership have been resolved, asserts that bureaucrats fear nothing and that Gosplan has become the prisoner of the ministries it purports to command	195b
V.M. Gvozdez	Regrets lack of discipline, deplores the interpretation of democracy as negation of responsibility, blames media for that attitude; expresses total confidence in party's policies and leadership, concern for lagging social development and declining standard of living	197a
O.O. Suleymenov	Condemns atomic testing and government's disregard for health and welfare of persons in test zones, welcomes moratorium on testing; calls for formal condemnation of Stalinist crimes against socialism and humanity and for full documentation of sources of ethnic conflict as basis for mutual understanding and sympathy	199a
A.-M.K. Brazauskas	Reads announcements, reports tally on speakers	200b
Unidentified	Announces that deputies who supported roll-call vote (which was defeated) will proceed to make votes known for publication in the press, invites others to join in	201a
	Congress recessed	
M.S. Gorbachev	Presiding, invites deputies to confirm Ryzhkov in post of Chairman of USSR Council of Ministers, notes that questions concerning Ryzhkov's policy statement will be answered after discussion of the speech	201a
	Congress confirms N.I. Ryzhkov as Chairman of USSR Council of Ministers	
N.I. Ryzhkov	Expresses confidence that government, guided by decisions of the Congress, will find the correct solution to major problems of the day, thanks deputies and Soviet people for their trust	201b
M.S. Gorbachev	Submits Constitutional Oversight Committee for approval by Congress, notes care exercised in selection of members, proposes V.N. Kudryavtsev as chairman, B.M. Lazarev as deputy, invites comments	202a
N.N. Vorontsov	Notes that all proposed members are party members, hopes that other committees and commissions will reflect heterogeneous nature of society	202b
V.I. Kolotov	Characterizes Kudryavtsev as yes-man, opposes his candidacy	203a
R.V. Gudaytis	Opposes creation of committee under present unitary state based on "Stalinist imperialist model," proposes constitutional amendment empowering union republic representatives with a veto; presents petition, endorsed by large number of Baltic deputies, explaining their refusal to participate in election of oversight committee	203a
A.O. Dobrovolsky	Opposes candidacy of Belorussian jurist Yemenov, proposes V.G. Tikhin, demands separate vote on the Belorussian representative	203b

ANNOTATED LIST OF SPEECHES

Speaker	Subject	Page
Z.G. Balayan	Seeks Kudryavtsev's explanation of why, contrary to his 1982 commentary on USSR constitution, the NKAO bears a geographical designation rather than national name required by the constitution	204a
S.B. Kalagin	Requests discussion of alternate candidates for chairmanship of oversight committee	204a
D.A. Kerinov	Defends Kudryavtsev's independence and integrity	204b
A.M. Yakovlev	Seeks to allay concern that proposed committee would prevent revision of present constitution, cites two examples of Kudryavtsev's independence	204b
A.M. Obolensky	Objects to nominating procedure, anonymous resolution, violation of regulation on timeliness, and lack of information on candidates; proposes as legislative initiative under USSR constitution that election be postponed to second Congress with possibility of additional nominees	205b
Ye.V. Kogan	Objects to Deputy Gudaytis' attempt to speak for all Baltic deputies, hopes oversight committee will begin work in Estonia by reviewing constitutionality of legislative action of November 1988	206a
A.A. Plotyaneks	Expresses confidence in candidates, proposes constitutional amendment to prohibit oversight committee from ruling on republic constitutions	207a
Yu.V. Golik	Stresses necessity of oversight committee, denounces Baltic deputies' ultimatum, endorses Kudryavtsev for chairman	208a
G.S. Tarazevich	Endorses Yevmenov as Belorussian representative	208a
D.G. Smirnov	Protests that oversight committee is governed by nonexistent law on constitutional control, proposes postponement of election of committee	208b
A.T. Kruglov	Prefers a younger committee	208b
N.V. Fedorov	Objects to haste and lack of preparation; nominates V.Ye. Guliyev	209a
N.I. Timashova	Agrees on urgency of electing oversight committee but proposes one-day postponement in order to select a candidate from the autonomous republics	209a
Unidentified	Objects to two or three deputies who presume to represent all Russian-speaking residents of the Baltic; favors postponing election of oversight committee to fall	209b
Yu.Yu. Voldyrev	Condemns haphazard preparations for election of oversight committee, supports postponement	210a
L.M. Sandulik	Favors postponement to allow sufficient time for deliberation; anticipates and opposes Kolbin as chairman of People's Control Committee	210a
Ye.A. Yevtushenko	Doubts Kudryavtsev's commitment to justice and human rights, wants to know what he did to save people from jails, camps, and mental institutions; wants people younger than Gorbachev to lead the committee	210b
Unidentified	Supports presidium's proposal and nominees, endorses Kazakh representative	211a
V.I. Alksnis	Warns that Baltic deputies speak of federation but intend confederation, that Latvian People's Front has begun campaign to secede from USSR; welcomes oversight committee to verify execution of constitution and Soviet law in the Baltic	211b
R.A. Bratun	Detects no secession in Baltics' tactics, favors postponement to fall to allow for consultation	212a
I.N. Gryazin	Prefers postponement to examine constitutional status of committee itself	212a

TWELFTH SESSION, 8 JUNE 1989

Speaker	Subject	Page
I.V. Sorokin	Favors creation of committee, wants to know more about candidates, favors competitive selection, nominates A.A. Sobchak	212b
A.Ya. Tsirulis	Endorses Alksnis' proposal to invite international observers to witness situation in the Baltic	212b
R.A. Medvedev	Cites Lenin to justify postponement to fall of selection of oversight committee	213a
V.N. Kudryavtsev	Answers questions and charges: acknowledges that NKAO is improperly named, defends role of his institute in protecting dissidents from prosecution and confinement; admits to being old but asserts his determination to meet responsibilities; sees committee as necessary and as capable of functioning in interests of democracy and citizens' rights, favors return to Leninist principles of federation	213b
M.S. Gorbachev	Defends creation of oversight committee, discounts concern that it might block further constitutional development, sees immediate need to validate recent legislation and check departmental interpretations and regulations, notes that alternative is Supreme Soviet Presidium which already exercises legislative-executive authority, envisions committee participating in formulation of new legislation, urges deputies to avoid ultimatums; defends ten-year term for oversight committee as standard and necessary for stability, notes that members cannot also serve as people's deputies; denies precipitate action, asserts that Presidium considered and debated composition of committee for three months; questions motives of some deputies, appeals for amicable cooperation for political reform without winners or losers	215a
Unidentified	Proposes election of committee for purpose of defining its status with composition deferred to fall session	217a
V.N. Korneyenko	Disputes Tarazevich's right to nominate Yemenov since Belorussian delegation has not discussed the matter	217a
M.S. Gorbachev	Defers discussion of personnel, puts issues to a vote	217b
	Congress votes to create Constitutional Oversight Committee immediately (433 deputies oppose, 61 abstain); 50 Lithuanian deputies do not vote and walk out when vote is counted	
M.S. Gorbachev	Seeks deputies' advice on next step	218a
Unidentified	Disputes right to create a constitutional committee not authorized by a statute, proposes creation of a commission to define status of oversight committee	218a
F.M. Burlatsky	Proposes postponement of issue to allow Gorbachev and Presidium to consult with Lithuanians	218a
T.V. Moshnyaga	Noting that constitutional oversight affects interests of union republics, proposes deferral of issue for further discussion	218a
M.S. Gorbachev	Endorses Burlatsky's proposal, deputies approve by acclamation	218b
Yu.Yu. Bredikis	Asks whether decision to defer discussion nullifies previous vote	218b
M.S. Gorbachev	Opines that for the moment the vote stands	219a
	Congress recessed	
M.S. Gorbachev	Presents Ye.A. Smolentsev for confirmation as Chairman of USSR Supreme Soviet, invites questions	219a
I.V. Aparin	Seeks Smolentsev's opinion, as former deputy chairman of USSR Supreme Court, on whether the Supreme Court, which approved convictions prepared by Gdlyan group, was also responsible for violations that occurred	219a

ANNOTATED LIST OF SPEECHES

Speaker	Subject	Page
Ye.A. Smolentsev	Claims not to have been involved in court's decisions in Uzbek cases	219b
	Congress confirms appointment of Ye.A. Smolentsev as Chairman of USSR Supreme Soviet with 14 nays and 77 abstentions	
M.S. Gorbachev	Presents Yu.G. Matveyev for post of USSR Chief State Arbiter	220a
	Congress approves Yu.G. Matveyev as USSR Chief State Arbiter with 6 deputies opposed and 28 abstaining	
M.S. Gorbachev	Presents G.V. Kolbin for post of Chairman of USSR People's Control Committee, alludes to "extensive and principled" discussion of candidate by the Supreme Soviet	220a
G.V. Kolbin	Denies "high-handedness" or interference in legal proceedings in previous positions	220a
Unidentified	Attests to good character of Kolbin	220b
A.K. Izmodenov	Questions Kolbin on lack of opposition to virtually all Kazakh obkom first secretaries running for election as people's deputies	220b
G.V. Kolbin	Answers that lack of opposition was matter of "chance" and "people's will"; denies any violation of democracy or constitution	221a
Unidentified	Expresses dissatisfaction with answer, seeks Kolbin's view on role of People's Control Committee	221a
G.V. Kolbin	Observes that forty organizations are involved in interdepartmental control, has no answer at the moment	221a
L.I. Sukhov	Presses Kolbin on how he will supervise subordinates	221a
G.V. Kolbin	States that question requires study	221b
N.N. Koryugin	Wants explanation of Smolentsev's statement that Kolbin's handling of money had been "unlawful"	221b
G.V. Kolbin	Responds that actions were executions of court decisions and therefore legal	221b
Sh.A. Amonashvili	Declares Georgian delegation's support for Kolbin	221b
R.A. Medvedev	Opposes confirmation of Kolbin for lack of firmness and principle, doubts his ability to exercise independent judgment, to oppose decisions of CPSU Central Committee	221b
	Congress confirms G.V. Kolbin as Chairman of USSR People's Control Commission; 252 deputies oppose, 138 abstain	
M.S. Gorbachev	Presents A.Ya. Sukharev for confirmation as USSR General Prosecutor, notes Supreme Soviet's "heated" discussion of his candidacy but overwhelming approval	222a
V.V. Guly	Poses four questions for Sukharev	222b
A.Ya. Sukharev	Responding to Guly, sees need to amend law governing prosecutor's office in view of democratization, admits possibility of alternative candidates for local prosecutors to be discussed before being appointed by general prosecutor, advocates new law to cover growing number of complaints to general prosecutor's office	222b
A.L. Markevich	Question Sukharev on organized crime	223a
A.Ya. Sukharev	Acknowledges growth, hitherto underestimated, of organized crime but doubts that it has gained control of organs of power; notes that need for special committee is being considered	223b
N.V. Ivanov	Charges Sukharev as part of Politburo conspiracy with lying and misleading public in the "Uzbek case," accuses him of being an accomplice of Ligachev and of tampering with witnesses	223b
A.Ya. Sukharev	Responds at length, denying all accusations as baseless and totally unsubstantiated	223b

TWELFTH SESSION, 8 JUNE 1989

Speaker	Subject	Page
A.A. Yarshinskaya	Complains about dilatory investigation of alleged election irregularities in Zhitomir	226b
A.Ya. Sukharev	Apologizes, refers to overload of complaints, promises to look into the matter	227a
Yu.N. Afanaseyev	Complains of inattention to deputies' query about preventive restrictions on members of Karabakh committee, seeks explanation for failure to carry out court decision in case of one Surgutsky	227a
A.Ya. Sukharev	Responds as before about workload but notes resolution of Karabakh question, pleads ignorance of Surgutsky case but promises to investigate	227b
A.B. Demin	Questions inaction in case of person illegally attacked by militiamen	227b
A.Ya. Sukharev	Begs for time, promises to dispense with red tape and punish any guilty party	228a
M.S. Gorbachev	Queries deputies, finds near majority favor continuing the questioning	228a
A.D. Sakharov	Poses series of questions concerning conduct of prosecutor's office and certain colleagues	228b
A.Ya. Sukharev	Responds to Sakharov, states preference for removing investigative apparatus from prosecutor's office, leaving prosecutor to supervise criminal and civil proceedings; considers it essential to involve attorneys in investigation stage, agrees that period of detention should be extended only in exceptional cases, admits callousness in many prosecutors' response to letters appealing unjust convictions but notes change for the better, defends performance of subordinates Katusev and Galkin	229a
A.N. Boyko	Inquires about review of cases involving possible psychiatric abuse	229b
A.Ya. Sukharev	Reports creation of special team to investigate such cases with view toward rectifying any injustice	230a
Unidentified	Asks Sukharev's role in exile of poet Josef Brodsky and trial of five protesters of Czech invasion	230a
A.Ya. Sukharev	Admits to heading CPSU CC department charged with prosecuting cases brought by Ministry of Internal Affairs, claims no connection with Brodsky case, evades answering question concerning five protesters	230b
Unidentified	Asks why, though a resident of Moscow, Sukharev was elected deputy from Checheno-Ingush ASSR	230b
A.Ya. Sukharev	Identifies self as representative of seventh national-territorial okrug which includes Checheno-Ingush ASSR but otherwise neglects to explain how or why	230b
	Gorbachev recognizes T.Kh. Gdlyan and they engage in a lengthy dialogue, Gdlyan trying to "responsibly expose" Sukharev for allegedly suppressing the Kremlin links to the "Uzbek mafia," Gorbachev insisting that Gdlyan may only question Sukharev	231a
A.Ya. Sukharev	Responds to several of Gdlyan's questions in same vein as to Ivanov's; justifies firing of 65 of the 209 investigators because some were engaged only part-time and many were doing no work at all	232b
M.S. Gorbachev	Observes that commission has been formed to investigate Gdlyan-Ivanov charges of high-level bribe-taking and malfeasance by general prosecutor and that proper conclusions will be drawn in due course; meanwhile proposes to act on Supreme Soviet's decision to appoint Sukharev	234a
	Congress agrees to end questioning of A.Ya. Sukharev, votes to confirm him as USSR General Prosecutor, with 330 deputies opposing and 273 abstaining	

ANNOTATED LIST OF SPEECHES

Speaker	Subject	Page
M.S. Gorbachev	Orders new vote counting those "for," because presidium detects some deputies voting both against and abstaining; then announces short, closed session and orders hall cleared of spectators and press	234b

THIRTEENTH SESSION
9 JUNE 1989

Speaker	Subject	Page
A.I. Lukyanov	Presiding, announces continuation of discussion of basic guidelines of domestic and foreign policy and government's program	236a
Z. Beyshekeyeva	Expresses Kirghiz satisfaction with results of Gorbachev's visit to China; describes conditions and concerns of livestock workers, seeks improved wage coefficient, lower pension age for shepherds, and higher prices for wool and meat; complains of environmental damage to Lake Issyk-Kul and of negative reporting and disinformation by mass media	236a
G.Kh. Popov	Questions government's economic strategies and policies, declares that emphasis on production is doomed to failure without reform of existing social, economic, and political relations; asserts irrelevance of Marx's analysis of capitalism, recommends Keynes and neo-Keynesianism, warns that emergency measures will not lead to genuine or permanent solution of financial crisis; favors structure in which the center establishes general economic principles and leaves their implementation to the republics	237a
	Congress gives Popov an additional ten minutes to speak	
	Questions current socio-economic models, recommends raising autonomous republics to status of union republics, doubts that Marxism requires highly centralized system of USSR, supports investment in space as economically sound, compares current agrarian policy with nineteenth-century tsarist policy in its distrust of peasant independence, urges market competition to improve efficiency; favors indexing of wages and pensions to cost of living rather than one-shot payments, sees ultimate solution in giving everyone who wants to work the opportunity to work efficiently, sees ultimate solutions in a system that develops self-reliance	
A. Yakubov	Sees unfavorable comparison of social and material benefits between unrewarding cotton culture of Uzbekistan and Old South in America, urges liberation of region from domination of monoculture	241b
V.A. Ostroukhov	Defends responsible cooperative leadership and practices, recommends measures to improve laws on cooperatives and state enterprises; complains of government's exploitation of Siberia and neglect of the needs of its people, voices confidence in party and its leadership and appeals for trust and support	243a
R.A. Bykov	Urges more thought and concern for human relations as the ultimate objective of restructuring and reform, appeals for genuine commitment, instead of lip-service to the needs of children	244b
V.-E.G. Bresis	Contends that central control of production inhibits economic development and produces apathy, favors republic economic accountability as basis of an all-union market and efficient division of labor, urges	246b

THIRTEENTH SESSION, 9 JUNE 1989

Speaker	Subject	Page
	(continued) abandonment of outmoded dogmas and more receptivity to world experience, favors diverse forms of ownership but particularly private farms, wants debts of state enterprises canceled so that peasants or leaseholders can acquire unencumbered land	
Yu.M. Marinichev	Stresses importance of consumer cooperatives, especially for peasants; discusses shortcomings of law on cooperatives, sees Gosplan and other ministries as attempting to restrict independence of cooperatives and bring them under state control, provides examples; urges government to resolve those issues and act on draft decree aimed at enhancing role of consumer cooperatives in social development of countryside	248b
A.I. Lukyanov	Reports 792 requests to speak and several requests to end discussion; calls for vote on ending discussion	251a
	Congress votes to end discussion of domestic and foreign policy	
	Declares discussion ended, notes that those unable to speak may submit speeches for inclusion in record of the Congress; yields rostrum to N. I. Ryzhkov for his concluding remarks	
N.I. Ryzhkov	Addresses questions raised by deputies: notes serious need for power generation but evades deputies's concerns over construction of nuclear power plants, favors "powerful" government and Supreme Soviet environmental committees, defends construction of West Tyumen gas and chemical complex, admits that chemical industry lacks pollution controls, claims decision on Katun hydroelectric project still under consideration	251b
	Agrees that wage and price controls are not effective and invites aid in finding the "ideal system," declares satisfaction with retail prices but concern for wholesale prices, especially agricultural products; rejects suggestions to terminate current five-year plan due to commitments, good or bad; observes that time is needed to develop and prepare ground for new plan, including establishment of "complete financial autonomy" of union republics	
	Reports foreign debt of R34 billion and additional shortfall of about R10 billion in current year	
	Congress is recessed	
M.S. Gorbachev	Identifies CPD as "major event" in Soviet history, appraises bitter rhetoric as reflecting the seriousness of national problems, finds justifiable "much" of the criticism leveled at center, sees Congress as barometer of people's evaluation of perestroika, noting that deputies' proposals are more radical than the government's	255a
	Calls for restructuring of property relations in such a way as to preserve social ownership of property while giving collectives and individuals control and complete responsibility for its use through leasing arrangements, thus transforming lessors into independent producers for the socialist market; disagrees, however, that free market system can solve everything, notes that even capitalist markets are regulated	
	Wants measures to allow freedom of action for agrarian collectives and individual peasants while noting that legislation is lagging and hindering social transformations, reports that major resources are being directed to rural social amenities and that rural people should soon feel real improvements in living conditions	
	Calls for tact, respect, and broad dialogue in ethnic relations while rejecting illegal action, sees agreement between center and republics in two areas: need to strengthen USSR as a multinational	

Speaker	Subject	Page
	(continued)	
	socialist state and need to ensure the autonomy of republics and rights of individuals of all nations	
	Declares law and order and conscious sense of discipline essential to restructuring and democracy, demands exhaustive efforts and measures to combat crime	
	Reaffirms Marxism-Leninism as scientific socialism, stresses party's capability and responsibility to tackle new theoretical problems through scientific analysis, affirms possibility of many socialist models while rejecting past distortions of dogmatism and arbitrariness; expresses confidence in "boundless possibilities of socialism" and commitment to Soviet rather than borrowed solutions	
	Accepts criticism for slowness of perestroika, particularly in dismantling obsolete management structures and in attacking urgent matters with outdated methods; admits to more sober expectations, now sees restructuring as long-term process but rejects gradualism	
	Sees restoration of normal political life as one result of perestroika, distinguishes apparatus from administrative-command structure, sees need for new apparatus that is qualified, competent, and well-organized; seeks to allay concerns over excessive concentration of power, declares for himself no other policy than restructuring, democratization, and glasnost	
	Rejects attacks on party while affirming that it is responsible for its policies and not above criticism, admits that CPSU, like society, needs restructuring but recalls that party was the initiator of restructuring; denies danger of coup	
	Attributes foreign policy success to changed world conditions and abandonment of musty old policies, not to changes in concepts or doctrines	
V.A. Medvedev	Formally introduces draft resolution "On the Basic Guidelines of the USSR's Domestic and Foreign Policy" to the Congress, summarizes work of editorial commission noting that it received 702 proposals and questions, reports at length on additions and changes subsequently proposed by editing group	262b
	Congress adopts draft resolution as basis of discussion	
A.I. Lukyanov	Reports 29 requests to speak on draft resolution	265a
	Congress is recessed	
M.S. Gorbachev	Presiding; calls for discussion with speakers limited to three minutes	265a
G.N. Podberezsky	Proposes consideration of unified people's control system by next Congress, questions which republics are shifting to regional cost accounting, prefers amending old constitution to writing a new one	265a
N.E. Ternyuk	Offers six amendments including a constitutional guarantee of basic rights and freedoms for all Soviet citizens	265b
I.I. Zaslavsky	Proposes several amendments concerning treatment of disabled persons	266a
V.N. Stepanov	Offers changes concerning banks, citizens' rights, and local autonomy	267a
A.A. Shchelkanov	Questions statement on restructuring, proposes changes concerning pensions, veterans, economy, and rights and freedoms	267b
F.M. Burlatsky	Suggests amendments on purpose, human rights, and statement on Afghanistan	268a
M.S. Minasbekyan	Wants statements calling for referendum in NKAO and condemnation of Turks' for genocide against Armenians in 1915	268b
M.N. Poltoranin	Seeks more precise language in place of certain generalities, asks publication of draft law prepared by 50 journalist deputies	269a

THIRTEENTH SESSION, 9 JUNE 1989

Speaker	Subject	Page
N.G. Dimitriyev	Questions purpose of oral proposals, since none are being voted on; recommends submitting all proposals to the Presidium	269b
M.S. Gorbachev	Agrees with Dimitriyev, calls for vote on requiring proposals to be submitted in writing, sees "overwhelming majority" in favor; seeks Congress's opinion on how final document should be prepared and concludes that deputies will make final review	269b
A.G. Grigoryan	Detects slander of Armenians in Kazakh deputy's speech, wants criminal liability for ecological crimes, wants committee on NKAO	270a
V.I. Ginzburg	Wants proposals published and distributed to deputies	270b
M.T. Abasov	Observes that government has already decided to leave NKAO within Azerbaijan and that Azerbaijanis have also suffered at the hands of Armenians	270b
M.S. Gorbachev	Proposes establishment of Constitutional Committee, reads nominations from Ukrainian and Belorussian delegations, accepts Congress's approval by acclamation; reads letter from A.M. Obolensky seeking inclusion on commission, puts question to a vote	271a
	Congress favors Obolensky's request 943-903 with 114 abstentions	
M.S. Gorbachev	Rules that Obolensky's candidacy fails for lack of majority; accepts Kirghiz nomination by acclamation, admits representative of peoples of Far North and refuses to submit question to a vote as demanded by some deputies	271b
R.Z. Sagdeyev	Nominates Sakharov	272a
M.S. Gorbachev	Hears no objections, notes that Congress will eventually vote on commission as a whole	272a
Yu.E. Andreyev	Objects to Samsonov's alleged reactionary views, proposes M.A. Bocharov in his stead	272a
M.S. Gorbachev	Solicits other views from Moscow delegation	272a
Unidentified	Calls for Samsonov's removal	272b
Unidentified	Alleges violation in election of Samsonov	272b
Unidentified	Expresses support for Bocharov	272b
Unidentified	Finds Samsonov unsuitable for constitutional commission	273a
A.S. Samsonov	Attributes opposition to allegations of electoral violation	273a
N.T. Knyaznyev	Reports that Credentials Commission twice reviewed voting results in Samsonov's district and found flagrant violations of electoral law consisting of attempts to obstruct Samsonov's election, concludes that he is being hounded	273b
V.A. Logunov	Confirms electoral violations in Samsonov's district	273b
Unidentified	Wants Moscow delegation alone to resolve issue	273b
Zh.I. Alferov	Contends that Samsonov withdrew his own name	273b
M.S. Gorbachev	Orders vote on excluding Samsonov	274a
	Motion to exclude Samsonov is defeated 1,188 to 555 with 101 abstentions	
O.P. Borodoin	Reports that 55 percent of the candidates represent top party leadership, proposes alternate commission and two draft constitutions to choose between	274a
V.M. Minin	Proposes Zvonov for commission	274a
Yu.V. Golik	Proposes Yevtyukhin for commission	274b
L.I. Sukhov	Objects to haste, nominates Vlasov and Yevtushenko	274b
M.S. Gorbachev	Calls for vote on Yevtushenko	275a

ANNOTATED LIST OF SPEECHES

Speaker	Subject	Page
A.D. Sakharov	Expects to be in minority on all fundamental issues concerning the draft constitution, wants agreement in advance that commission will produce majority and minority drafts	275a
	Yevtushenko's candidacy receives only 449 votes, and the "no" votes are not counted; Vlasov's candidacy is rejected 934-830	
M.A. Mikheyev	Resents Borodoin's lack of trust in obkom secretaries	275a
Unidentified	Calls for vote on each candidate on the list	275b
M.S. Gorbachev	Resolves voting procedure and calls for vote	275b
	Congress approves Constitutional Commission with 106 "nays" and 94 abstentions	
	Announces compromise with Lithuanian and Estonian deputies on formation of a commission to prepare a draft law on the USSR Constitutional Oversight Committee, reads proposed membership, puts question to a vote	275b
	Congress approves commission; 10 deputies oppose, 25 abstain	
	Congress is recessed	
M.S. Gorbachev	Proposes that editorial commission and Presidium consider deputies' amendments insofar as possible and complete and publish the document on domestic and foreign policy without further consultation	276b
Yu.Yu. Boldyrev	Argues that controversial proposals must be voted on lest the resolution be merely the work of the editorial commission	276b
M.S. Gorbachev	Explains that effect of Boldyrev's proposal is to prolong the work of the Congress; calls for vote on initial proposal to have editorial commission and Presidium complete and publish the document in ten days, relays Sakharov's recommendation that once the resolution has been completed with changes, each deputy could comment individually on changes	277a
	Congress agrees to allow editorial commission and Presidium to complete and publish the resolution on domestic and foreign policy; 121 deputies oppose, 32 abstain	
Unidentified	Asks whether all proposals will be received	277a
M.S. Gorbachev	Answers affirmatively while reminding deputies that many proposals duplicate and overlap each other; yields rostrum to Lukyanov to handle Other Business	277b
A.I. Lukyanov	Reviews work of the Congress, notes that several of twenty proposals have been covered in the policy resolution or effected by commissions formed by the Congress, defines three remaining tasks: draft law on status of deputies, resolution on instructions to Supreme Soviet, and draft law on constitutional oversight	277b
Unidentified	Inquires about draft law on taxation	279a
A.I. Lukyanov	Identifies drafts as material for consideration by Supreme Soviet	279a
A.Ye. Antifeyev	Proposes that Congress elect editor of *Izvestiya*	279a
Yu.A. Levykhin	Wants Congress to rescind Article 11 of April 8 decree	279b
B.N. Nikolsky	Proposes creation of commission to investigate Soviet intervention in Afghanistan	279b
V.A. Martirosyan	Seeks ruling on use of deputies' support groups and advisors, wants permanent space allocated for deputies' use	279b
A.G. Zhuralev	Proposes changes in electoral law for consideration under Other Business	279b
A.A. Sobchak	Proposes resolution to protest judicial decision and rehabilitate persons condemned in Novocherkassk strikes and riots in 1962	280a

THIRTEENTH SESSION, 9 JUNE 1989

Speaker	Subject	Page
A.L. Plotnik	Supports proposals to elect heads of media organizations	280a
I.A. Andreyeva	Questions means of publicizing Supreme Soviet's agenda, seeks temporary suspension and ultimate revision of decrees on demonstrations and use of internal troops, wants list of legislative priorities, and requests time for announcements and statements by groups and individuals	280b
A.V. Levashev	Submits draft resolution on improving the condition of low-income persons	280b
I.B. Shamshev	Wants Supreme Soviet to investigate involvement in Afghan war and assess responsibility, proposes resolution to prohibit dispatch of Soviet forces beyond boundaries of USSR without Supreme Soviet approval	281a
V.I. Kirillov	Wants to require regional referendums on ecological questions until law on referendums is adopted	281a
K.A. Antanavichyus	Wants consideration of draft law on economic autonomy submitted by 109 deputies, sees discussion of restructuring as limited to management and inadequate, supports Sakharov's proposal for empowering the soviets and Rasputin's call for a referendum on nuclear power	281a
G.I. Yanayev	Notes long line of speakers and observes that time will not permit consideration of all topics already identified, proposes to end proposals and open discussion of issues already admitted under Other Business	281b
M.S. Gorbachev	Welcomes proposal, puts question to vote of the Congress, rules that decision is to cut off proposals, and then reviews with deputies the issues to be discussed; eliminates proposal to elect *Izvestiya* editor and tv-radio head, suggests leaving Afghan war, electoral law, and Novocherkassk for Supreme Soviet to consider, thus reduces agenda to consideration of Article 11.1 and three issues submitted by the Presidium; Congress agrees	281b
A.N. Krayko	Submits amendments, prepared by Moscow deputies, to draft law on deputy status: spells out material requirements and legislative autonomy	283a
A.I. Lukyanov	Asks cost of Krayko's proposal; brief exchange follows	283b
M.S. Gorbachev	Agrees on basic needs of deputy including transportation costs (but not private cars) and that everything required immediately should be approved but that law itself should be prepared by Supreme Soviet not the Congress; urges Congress to reject the proposal while adopting many of its provisions; deputies agree	283b
A.V. Minzhurenko	Seeks permission for deputies to entrust notarized authorizations [power of attorney] to their authorized representatives to be used in their absence	284a
M.S. Gorbachev	Rules that practice impermissible, because a deputy's power is derived from the people and cannot be delegated; declares no vote needed on that question	284a
V.A. Zubanov	Seeks Gorbachev's clarification of how deputies who are not members of committees, commissions, or Supreme Soviet can express their views on issues and how deputies in rural areas lacking public transportation are to get around their constituencies	284b
M.S. Gorbachev	Explains that deputies serving on committees and commissions are to have same rights and material support as Supreme Soviet members; deputies will be informed of work of Soviet and may communicate with Supreme Soviet Presidium, leaves other matters to take care of themselves until resolved by law	284b

ANNOTATED LIST OF SPEECHES

Speaker	Subject	Page
V.A. Shapovalenko	Expresses disappointment with Congress's achievements, attributes failures to inadequate advance preparation and deputies' intolerance for others' views; announces establishment of interregional group of deputies to prepare for next Congress	285a
A.I. Lukyanov	Reports Supreme Soviet Presidium opinion on 8 April decree holding that public appeal for violent overthrow of social and state system is punishable under criminal law but that Congress ought to rescind Article 11.1	285b
S.M. Ryabchenko	Wants Article 11.1 rescinded "at the insistence of the congress"	285b
	Congress rescinds Article 11.1 of April 8 decree; seven deputies oppose, six abstain	
M.S. Gorbachev	Announces Sakharov's "urgent request" to speak for fifteen minutes, asks deputies to approve five minutes, rules majority approval	286a
A.D. Sakharov	Deplores Congress's failure to assert its power, proposes "decree on power" calling for abolition of CPSU political monopoly, for confiding full legislative and appointive powers in CPD, for restricting KGB to international security matters, for reducing term of military service as step toward creation of a professional army, and for creation of a federal system	286a
M.S. Gorbachev	Appeals to Sakharov to conclude, finally terminates his speech	287b
A.Ya. Troitsky	Complains about Sakharov's repeated access to rostrum	287b
M.S. Gorbachev	Moves to final item on agenda	287b
V.A. Kiseleva	Reads "Message of the USSR Congress of People's Deputies to the Peoples of the World"	287b
M.S. Gorbachev	Notes approval of Message with two abstentions; gives personal assessment of achievements and significance of CPD, closes the Congress	288b
	Congress concludes with the playing of the National Anthem	

FIRST CONGRESS OF PEOPLE'S DEPUTIES OF THE USSR
EIGHTH SESSION
THURSDAY, 1 JUNE 1989
THE KREMLIN PALACE OF CONGRESSES

The discussion of the Gorbachev report continued as nineteen speakers ranged over disparate subjects. From the director of the Moscow Aviation Engineering Institute, B.S. Mitin, deputies learned that the Soviet education system was so deficient in computer technology that it could not support the goals of perestroika. From Albert Likhanov, the director of the Soviet Children's Fund, they heard a report of appalling social and governmental indifference to homelessness, infanticide, delinquency, suicide, and the general breakdown of family life. They heard shop steward Galina Stoumova's moving description of the rigors and hopelessness of rural life, Gomel oblast chairman Alexander Grakhovsky's bitter and pessimistic survey of the aftermath of Chernobyl, poet Yevgeny Yevtushenko's engaging but earnest appeal for national tolerance and compassion, and so on.

There was an occasional lighter moment, however, as when commentator Yuri Chernichenko stooped to slander conservative leader Yegor Ligachev as "a man who understands nothing of [agriculture] and who has failed in ideology," or when S.A. Niyazov, an obsequious Turkmen functionary, rejoiced that the Congress had reached "a unanimous decision supported by an absolute majority."

In order to rebut the charge that the central government was responsible for the deaths of the Georgian demonstrators in Tbilisi and defuse the issue of a coverup, A.I. Lukyanov read three telegrams allegedly sent to the Politburo by Dzhumbar Patiashvili, Georgian Communist Party Central Committee First Secretary, on the seventh, eighth, and ninth of April 1989. They indicated that no one in Moscow had ordered the use of force, let alone lethal force. Patiashvili already had accepted responsibility and been fired, but Gorbachev strongly backed the formation of a commission to "get to the bottom of everything." Gorbachev and others apparently suspected that conservatives in Georgia and Moscow had conspired to discredit Gorbachev and perestroika. The commission created by the Congress was unable to find evidence for a definite conclusion, although Ligachev apparently was its prime suspect. In February 1990 he declared that the decision to adopt force was taken by the full Politburo on 7 April 1989. Shevardnadze contended that there had been no full meeting of the Politburo on that day.

1939 NON-AGGRESSION PACT

Estonian deputy Endel Lippmaa ignited another controversial issue when he proposed, on behalf of the Baltic republics, the creation of a commission to conduct a "political and legal appraisal of the Soviet-German non-aggression treaty of 1939 and the secret additional protocol that is, the protocol on territorial and political reorganization in Eastern Europe, in particular the Baltic area and Poland and related documents." The latter referred to Soviet-German friendship treaty of 28 September 1939 by which the USSR purchased the right to Lithuania from Germany. Lippmaa's proposal was not welcome to the Russian leaders. At the time the official Soviet position was that the three republics had joined the union in 1940 voluntarily, out of self-interest engendered by historic ties and fear of German expansionism. In June 1989 the USSR did not even acknowledge the existence of the secret protocol. That explains Gorbachev's discourse on the subject and his contention that there was no authentic document to evaluate—after I.N. Gryazin had read the text from the rostrum. Then Gorbachev, having usurped the chair, arbitrarily limited the focus of the inquiry to the treaty proper and avoided further discussion and a vote on the issue by declaring his "motion" adopted by acclamation. The Balts also had to accept revisions in the composition of the commission, which they had packed with confederates. In August 1989 the Soviet government finally acknowledged the existence of the secret protocol; it continued to insist, however, that the Baltics voluntarily joined the USSR to restore a historic union and avoid German aggression. Material related to the commission's report to the Second Congress of People's Deputies can be found in Appendix B.5.

LATVIAN ELECTION IRREGULARITIES

The heavy hand of the chair again was felt later in the session when Boris Gidaspov, the chairman of the Mandate Commission, confirmed the complaint lodged by Viktor Alksnis at the opening of the Congress that many Latvian electoral districts had been rigged to favor pro-independence nationalist candidates. Despite those violations, the commission confirmed all the elections while warning authorities to be more careful in the future. When a deputy protested the commission's cavalier disposal of the matter, Gidaspov replied that Alksnis himself was satisfied with the result, as though it were merely a personal matter. Boris Paton, the presiding officer, then broke in, declared that the commission's report was approved, and cut off any further protest or discussion.

The meeting concluded with the appointment of the Gdlyan-Ivanov commission whose purpose was to determine and advise the Congress on whether the two prosecutors should be deprived of parliamentary immunity in order to be prosecuted themselves for abuse of power. The lengthy argument over the constitution, chairmanship, and mandate of the committee reflected the political character of the entire affair.

Texts of documents cited during the Eighth Session are compiled in Appendices at the end of this volume: Constitution (Basic Law) of the USSR, Articles 6, 9, 19, 22, 31, 35, 40, 74, 113, 151 (Appendix A.1); Law on Elections of USSR People's Deputies, Article 17 (Appendix A.2).

EIGHTH SESSION

THURSDAY, 1 JUNE 1989

STENOGRAPHIC RECORD

Session chaired by USSR People's Deputy B.Ye. Paton, president of the Ukrainian Soviet Socialist Republic [SSR] Academy of Sciences and director of the Ye.O. Paton Institute of Electric Welding.

B.Ye. Paton: Respected deputies! "Today is the first Children's Protection Day. Today the 10th graders of the entire nation have sat down at their desks to write a composition. This is their first exam for the nation. Let us wish them creative inspiration and success in school and life. A great and complex life lies ahead of them. All the deputies should remember that we are working for our children, for them. Deputies from Tula Oblast." (Applause).

Respected comrade deputies, we are continuing the discussion of the question of the "Basic Directions of USSR Domestic and Foreign Policy." The floor is turned over to Deputy Ion Panteleyevich Drutse, a writer. The next to speak will be Boris Sergeyevich Mitin.

I.P. Drutse, writer, Moscow (Drokiya National-Territorial Electoral District, Moldavia): Respected comrade president! Respected colleague deputies! I would like to begin by making a protest against the Dnepropetrovsk deputy who from this rostrum claimed that he was the representative of the "homeland of stagnation." The entire world knows that this is not the case. Everyone knows that stagnation got off the ground in the Moldavian hills. (Stir in the auditorium).

In truth, it must be said that we acquired our renown in a completely unexpected manner. The problem was that, at an advanced age and while extremely ill, Josef Vissarionovich [Stalin] wrote on a slip of paper: "We must immediately help the Moldavian comrades in strengthening their leading cadres." This slip of paper lay in the appropriate file for appointing leading cadres—a file which, it must be said, had little to offer for mortals who saw it with their own eyes. And so Leonid Ilich Brezhnev was appointed to Kishinev as the first secretary, and then followed a chain of appointments: Shchelokov, Chernenko, and Trapeznikov. You all are well aware of how this ended.

We held our funerals, we did what we had to without stirring up too much, as they say, and thought that was the end of it. But all of a sudden, even in the time of restructuring, several years ago, in digging in that file, they discovered the slip of paper on which was written help must be given to the Moldavian comrades in strengthening the leading cadres. And they sent to us Comrade Smirnov as second secretary of the Moldavian Party Central Committee. What could we do? Moscow is Moscow. It, as they say, has big eyes, and they see far. Voices flew about, everything was on the point of collapse, and speeches came one after the other. Well, we lived through that. Now the press has announced to the entire world that it turns out that the second secretary of the Moldavian Party Central Committee has committed grievous crimes and must be deprived of all powers and arrested. And again Moldavia becomes famous throughout the world. Everyone is looking at us, and wondering what are you doing here? And actually, what are you doing? After some more time, a new statement in the "Presidium of the USSR Supreme Soviet." It turns out that Comrade Smirnov was not guilty of anything, that it was a major mistake and again our Moldavia is famous throughout the world. The man was not guilty of anything and they—that is, you—in Kishinev were undermining him. I want to request the leadership of our nation and Mikhail Sergeyevich to write on this slip of paper—done. And do not send us anyone anymore to Kishinev to strengthen the leading cadres. During the years

Eighth Session
1 June 1989

of Soviet power, we, Mikhail Sergeyevich, have grown up and we have our own worthy young people, and generally speaking, somehow we will muddle through. (Applause).

The second problem: We would like to ask Moscow to help us get rid of the ruins of stagnation. Of course, you can say that this is our problem. But we do not know how to get a handle on this question, and, to tell the truth, we do not have a box big enough to send all of it back to Moscow.

Now, if I can move on to a question on procedures which has been discussed here many times—for instance, voting has been discussed many times. Dear comrades, I want to tell you that it is embarrassing for me when the president of the world's first nation to send a man into space counts from the Presidium how many are "for," how many are "against," and how many "abstentions." This is unworthy of our great nation. But this is only part of the problem.

The second part of the problem consists in the fact that we are still confronted with the state-party apparatus which controls us very well and which thinks as follows: We must somehow contain the expressions of deputy will. It must be said that among us are many people holding major state posts. Next to them sit people from the very same region. Whether they want to or not, they must give some thought to how they vote. The neighbor sees this. In addition, there is, as they say, the pressure of the masses. Everyone has peripheral vision; you can see how many hands are raised, and you wonder whether you should raise your hand or not. They say that it will take a year to provide individual voting. I want to turn to our technicians, engineers, scientists and ask them: Dear comrades, think up some method for us so that by the end of this congress so that we could in an individual manner vote on all the vitally important problems of our state.

We have been discussing the question of status for a long time. We have been meeting now for how many days, but in practical terms we still do not know our personal status or the status of our Congress of People's Deputies. To be blunt about it, I am not even certain whether we have the right to give General Rodionov an "order out of turn." If we come back (and in any event we will return) to the Tbilisi problem, it seems to me that it would be good if we heard at least briefly the minister of defense. And if the truth be known, I would also like to question the president of our—the chairman of the defense committee.

Dear Mikhail Sergeyevich, in the report you wrote that a period of disarmament is beginning and that we should resolve many acute political problems by peaceful means. But these, as they say, are our external affairs. But what about internal affairs? Are we really incapable today of resolving by peaceful means the conflicts which arise inside our country? Are we going to go on all our life working out two policies: one, as they say, for the West, and another policy for domestic consumption? I feel that if the authorities of one or another region, oblast, republic or city turn out to be incapable of managing the masses, the emotions and problems of their population, then they of course should be retired and their places taken by those persons who will be capable of finding a common tongue with their population.

In this context I submit for your review a draft decree on the use of force against our own citizens and this states: to ban in the future the use of military force, having in mind regular troop units as well as the special detachments of the Interior Troops, obliging the local authorities to resolve all problems by political means. (Applause).

But let us return again to the Dnepropetrovsk-Moldavian affairs. What is stagnation? We have been fighting against it for countless years and we still cannot establish what stagnation is. From my viewpoint stagnation is the disintegration of the nation by the recruitment and confirmation of personnel following the negative principle in the sense that a person is less worthy of his position the more strongly he holds onto his chair and does not release it under any circumstances. (Applause).

For how many years have we been playing charades? Let us assume that the place of the minister of culture has become vacant. We have a cultivated country, many people read, and everyone is wondering: Who do you think it will be? There is one possibility, a second, a third, but no one fills the post, and there is no minister for 6 months. Well, we grow accustomed to this, and ultimately the deputy minister is not bad. All of a sudden, after a major football match, when everyone has forgotten about this, there is a small release in the "On the Presidium of the Supreme Soviet." Comrade Pilyulkin has been appointed USSR minister of culture. Then, 6 months later, it turns out that Comrade Pilyulkin is a very well known person, but has difficulty distinguishing between the dramatic theater and the opera, and we are put under conditions where the culture figures of the gigantic nation try to help him so that he can master the job he has been appointed to fill. In truth, among them are magnificent students. Everyone recalls the deceased Yekaterina Alekseyevna Furtseva, who also had little knowledge of opera and drama but later on came to the defense of our culture and was generally a fine leader in this area. But this should not become a system. Or, let us assume, the position of the minister of water management and reclamation has come vacant. Everyone is perfectly aware that water problems are the most acute both in the south and in the center of Russia and for all cities. But there is no appointment. For a long time there is no one. Later, suddenly among the graduates of the Higher Party School they find one who was a water transport worker. Without fail he is appointed the minister of water management. (Applause). Further years-long debates begin. The flower of our nation debates water problems with him but for him, the poor man, water remains an enigma.

I want to say that if the Congress of People's Deputies does not establish a special commission for the recruitment, placement, and approval of leading cadres for our nation, then we are not worth a farthing and we have assembled here in vain. Because again each morning we

STENOGRAPHIC RECORD

Eighth Session
1 June 1989

will puzzle out the same charades and suddenly discover that the ambassador to the Ivory Coast is also to serve as the ambassador in Paris. We will sit there wondering what caused this.

Let me return again to the major question of Tbilisi. Of course, we have set up a commission. I should say that it is a major danger that we are constantly setting up commissions. Something happens and a commission is established as some sort of exorcism, and something else and again another commission. Comrades, did the Chernobyl commission settle anything much? Did not the same ulcers as before remain after the formation of this high-level commission? The main problem, from my viewpoint, of Tbilisi is the following: We all should decide—and no commission will decide this—what happened in Tbilisi. What went on there? If this was a revolt in the borderland of a major state, then it actually should be brought to heal. Or was this a holiday of national rebirth? Then we must not move against this with combat engineer shovels or gas tanks.

Personally, I feel—and Mikhail Sergeyevich, speaking in Kiev, said—that this is a national rebirth. We must find our own final attitude toward this because the nation is in turmoil and we are all looking and listening. Approximately the same situations existed in Riga, Kishinev, Lvov, Kiev, and elsewhere. Don't forget that we have many republics and don't forget that we have many military districts. In addition to the Transcaucasian, we also have the Odessa Military District as well as the Carpathian and Baltic Military Districts, and heaven forbid that at our next session we must hear from this rostrum the explanations of the district commanders on what happened in Riga, Vilnius, Kiev, Kishinev, Lvov, and so forth. (Applause). For precisely this reason, without disbanding the established commission, I again invite you to return and work out your attitude to what happened in Tbilisi—a revolt or a holiday of national rebirth.

Now on the language question: This is precisely what now concerns virtually all our national republics. It must be said that the Russian-speaking population has rather nervously received our concern about language, be this in the Baltic, Moldavia, or other regions. Everyone is asking how did this get started? I want to say that all of this started, as Metropolitan Aleksey said yesterday in his, from my viewpoint, excellent speech, from spiritual impoverishment. I would say, with spiritual degradation. And it has involved not only our republics but has also Russia to a varying degree. The Russian language has suffered as much as our minority languages have suffered. Every cultivated man knows that between the Russian language of Chekhov and Tolstoy and the current Russian language of the newspaper PRAVDA or any other of our newspapers, there is approximately the same difference as between the tsarist gold ruble and our present paper ruble.

So the degraded part of this language plus the every-day obscenities and swearing poured into the linguistic elements of our republics and formed what the Belorussians widely called "trasyanka"—that is, a mixture of wheat and chaff. This is precisely in what we converse in in nearly all the republics—in Belorussia, Moldavia, and the Baltics. Why does this bother us? Many people have passed through the world and perished without leaving a trace. Much has been written about the reasons for their demise. The Old Testament states on this issue: There is life and death in language. The ancient Jews established that the weakest, most painful and delicate place of any people is their language—that is, that bridge by which our terrestrial element moves into the spiritual. Of course, our concern for language is dictated primarily by the fact that no living thing can accept its death. A living organism cannot accept its death, and a living nation also cannot accept the degradation of its language. We are grateful for the fact that the center has somehow understood this concern of ours, and in many republics the language of the indigenous nationality has already been declared the state language and the others should also immediately be established in this quality. In truth, a delicate problem has arisen and was raised here yesterday by Deputy Oleynik from the Ukraine; it is bilingualism.

In actuality, we must employ a state mechanism for saving the national languages. At present, no other means will do. But the declaring of both languages to be equal official ones means "a tribute to your grandmother." And this means that they spoke a mixture and you will speak a mixture. (Applause).

Moreover, I feel that the great Russian language—and I consider it my second native language after Moldavian—has moved and is moving throughout the world upon its own authority, upon its own flight, and it is unlikely that anything would be added to Russian if in each of our 14 republics it is given the status of an official language.

In conclusion I would like to say that we, the deputies who underwent direct elections—and very complicated ones—should state to our deputy friends who were elected from the state institutions that we, although standing before you in ordinary clothes, we all, dear friends, are scarred and wounded. It was very heavy "fighting" and the fighting did not come from the local population. It was precisely due to their support that we are now in this auditorium. We fought against the apparatus. (Applause).

And for goodness' sake, don't think that the apparatus is just several state leaders who drive around in Chaykas. Of course, this is also the apparatus. But the apparatus is the brigade leader from a distant village, the party organizer, and the person who does not know what function he is to perform and who holds the entire mass of the people in his hands and before whom the people quake. Today, when we are meeting here, it, this apparatus, is spreading throughout the nation that the results of the elections are to be explained by the consumption of a surplus amount of nitrate in the vegetables and by the early sunny spring which caused the complete debauch of the genetic system. Because of this nonsense,

Eighth Session
1 June 1989

you realize, the people emerged from their obedience and elected us their deputies. Yes, I am ending.

At present our voter stands in front of these local authorities and must ask if there is any milk and what he needs on the farm and is told: And for whom did you vote, blockhead? Well then, go to him and let him give it to you. (Applause).

I feel that if we truly are the representatives of the people and a higher power, then we certainly should take these simple persons under our protection.

And, finally, two forces which formed this spring—the awakened people in the form of the Congress of People's Deputies and the party-state apparatus. I am finishing....

I feel that Mikhail Sergeyevich is confronted with the difficult task of choosing one of these two: either or. I profoundly respect Mikhail Sergeyevich; I am fond of him and hope that he will side with the offspring of his life, restructuring. (Applause).

B.Ye. Paton: Comrade deputies, the floor is turned over to Deputy Mitin. The next to speak is Comrade Niyazov.

B.S. Mitin, rector of the Moscow K.E. Tsiolkovskiy Aviation Engineering Institute, Moscow (from the USSR Trade Unions): Comrades, I have been elected from the trade unions but I am speaking here on behalf of the more than 200 delegates who are the representatives of the education sphere at our congress. We have devoted a great deal of time to debates on the political portion of restructuring and to its economic aspects, as this truly is a crucial moment. But the general plan of restructuring states that the basic means for achieving these goals will be an acceleration of scientific-technical progress and an accelerated introduction of its achievements into the national economy. Education is to play the determining role in this process.

Yesterday a group of deputies from the education sphere distributed among you a brief statement on the state of education in the nation and its tasks. Since possibly not all deputies had an opportunity to become familiar with this and the television viewers certainly did not, I will read only a brief excerpt. In 1963, some 25 years ago, the U.S. Commission on Science and Technology wrote the president that the prosperity and defense capability of the nation were determined not by raw materials, and not by mineral natural resources or even by capital. The decisive source of economic growth more and more was becoming knowledge, as well as the individual ability to use it. The agents and sources of new knowledge are the scientists, designers, engineers, physicians, teachers and other specialists, and for this reason the center of gravity in the political, military and economic rivalry of the world powers is shifting more and more into the educational sphere. A nation which does not possess an educational system capable of training highly skilled personnel inevitably will fall behind in equipment and technology. It has no chance of success in a political rivalry.

I, comrades, can tell you officially that the state of our educational sphere cannot support the strategic tasks of restructuring. At present, the leading nations of the world spend 10-12 percent of their state budget on educational purposes. And we spent 5-6 percent both in 1956 and at present. Our education sphere is in a very severe state. But in the most severe are its inferior levels, particularly the rural school. I will not give all the depressing figures but will say just one thing: Two-thirds of the rural schools do not have elementary amenities, without mentioning all the rest. For this reason, we are right to pose before both the government and the party the question that we must immediately double expenditures on education. These will not be empty outlays. (Applause).

A majority of us consider ourselves to be the direct heirs of October. I would like to remind you of a decision of the People's Commissariat of Education in 1918. I do not feel that at that time the situation of the Soviet Republic was easier than it is now. But then the Sovnarkom [Council of People's Commissars] decided not to cut back on the expenditures of the People's Commissariat of Education but resolve to give some consideration on how it could reduce expenditures of the other departments in favor of education. And this policy was actually carried out. Regardless of all the repressions which our people suffered before the war, the surviving portion of the intelligentsia made an inestimable contribution toward ensuring our victory in the Great Patriotic War. (Applause).

The question always arises of "where is the money to come from?" I, comrades, would be very cautious in determining from this rostrum the spheres where something must be cut. We don't want the next generations to say of us: "They were evil people and they solved their problems at our expense." The main source of funds which we should obtain can be seen in reducing our losses from mismanagement, and there are scores of billions here. (Applause).

Comrades, the next question is the computerization of education. I cannot even say what our place is in the world for this question. But it is clearly in one of the last. Regardless of the government's decree on the necessity of strengthening our industrial ministries by the accelerated computerization of our education sphere, this task will not be carried out over the next 5 years. And it must be carried out immediately. The USSR minister, Comrade Peregudov, at a meeting with workers from the education sphere before the congress said that there is a real agreement with an American firm for solving this problem in 12-18 months. One billion dollars will be required to carry out this agreement.

Yes, this is a major investment. If it is made, we will not obtain an improvement in the situation on the consumer market tomorrow. But if this is not done, then we and our children will be wearing foreign-made clothing and footwear for the rest of our life. The most important thing is to purchase the foreign machines and this we are doing.

Eighth Session

1 June 1989

Where is the money to come from? Here it is an easier question. According to the data of Goskomstat [State Statistics Committee] which is suspected of concealing data, last year alone uninstalled imported equipment froze 5 billion gold rubles. And if we recall that we have our own petrodollars, then we will understand that they were not invested here. For this reason, regardless of all the seeming enormity of the amount, I request, comrades, support for this proposal and above all to computerize the school and the humanities sphere of the higher school. The technical VUZ's are endeavoring to earn the money themselves if there will be a normal economic mechanism. (Applause).

A third question: We are speaking about cost accounting. What does cost accounting now mean for the educational sphere? It is a shame to say, but individual leaders of the local soviets are already beginning to enter into cost accounting relations with the schools. They are required to pay even for the transporting of firewood. So here, comrades, is a major question for you. Under conditions of cost accounting, to provide the possibility for the normal development of the education sphere using legislative, legal measures.

A last question, comrades. What is the status of teachers in our society? Of course, after those facts which were given here by Academician Likhanov on what the status is of our comrades working in museums, libraries and so forth, seemingly the situation of the teacher whom we call "people's" would be much better. But still, comrades, the moral state of a society can be judged from how it considers a person who has been entrusted with the upbringing and education of children. In our nation the wages of teachers are below the national average. And I feel that it is our common task to see to it that this not be the case. A teacher has no other additional sources of income. He cannot join a cooperative, and he cannot, as a rule, engage in a private trade. He does not have the time for this and possibly neither the ability. He is destined for something else. For this reason when a society distributes benefits, it should give some thought to whom these benefits should actually go.

During all my life I have never heard an announcement where a certain city or rayon had built even a simple 5-story modular building specially for teachers or nursery workers. This has never happened. Nevertheless, even now, including in Moscow, they continue to build highly comfortable, full-amenity buildings for workers of the management sphere. When people compare these two facts, then they can determine what priorities have been selected by our leadership. A teacher has an opportunity to have leave once in 35 years. Again we do not build sanitoriums specially for teachers and so forth. Now Mikhail Sergeyevich has stated that a commission will be set up for privileges. I consider that this is correct, such a commission should exist. Then we will see that we can find many reserves among the already existing recreational facilities. I request support for our proposal that a portion of these be allocated completely for workers of the educational sphere. (Applause).

One last thing about privileges. There is one, in my view, most unjust privilege that we are again extending to the leading workers in the management sphere. As a result of this privilege, a book—the source of knowledge and its best examples—come under house arrest. What I mean is that there are persons who from a list can order and receive monthly the finest books. I am a deputy from the social organizations. I happen to travel throughout the entire nation, and I hear that the first complaint of the teacher is not even that he lives poorly and that his wages are low, but that he cannot buy a book which he needs for working with children. So, comrades, this privilege is used by approximately several tens of thousands of our citizens. I feel that if we were to redirect this list to the rural libraries, then we could even now really aid the cause of education. This would not even require any material expenditures. I also have a proposal for the congress delegates: Let us try with ourselves (in truth, I do not have this list) and see how difficult it is to give up privileges. Approximately 500 persons at our congress have such lists. Forward them now to the rural schools so that even before the end of the congress we will have received telegrams of thanks that they have reached there and will be used. (Applause).

Comrades! I have been assigned to request the congress to support the proposal of setting up a separate education committee. I have said that there are over 200 of us. Some 17 have been elected to the Supreme Soviet and they have given their agreement to work on this committee. And it should be a committee because it would be intercameral. Because of the lack of time I will not take up the issue of what a role is played by the educational sphere in resolving nationality questions.

Comrades, I have made my report as I was instructed. But I still have a minute for personal comments. I am deeply grateful to Boris Ilich Oleynik and to other comrade deputies who recalled Russia. Yesterday before the end of our session I was profoundly concerned by the statement of our respected chairman, Comrade Brazauskas, that we have not turned over the floor to two other republics—Moldavia and Turkmenia. But what about Russia? Will the representatives of Russia speak, and what awaits Russia under the conditions of restructuring? Here I would like to hear comments by either Comrade Vorotnikov or Comrade Vlasov. Because, for example, the idea of the Baltic comrades of regional cost accounting as applied to Russia and for a number of other questions seems very attractive to me. Thank you for your attention. (Applause).

V.Ye. Paton: The floor is now turned over to Deputy Niyazov. Deputy Likhanov will speak after him.

S.A. Niyazov, first secretary of the Turkmen CP Central Committee (Ashkhabad Rural Territorial Electoral District): Respected comrade chairman, respected people's deputies! The representatives of our republic are acutely experiencing the process of establishing the new Soviet parliament. We all wanted there to be a business-like discussion at our congress, that various ways be

Eighth Session

1 June 1989

proposed and optimum decisions taken on the most crucial questions. What at first glance seemed to be nonstop disputes obviously was a natural process on the path to unity and consolidation. This was the case for virtually all questions and as a result we have reached a unanimous decision supported by an absolute majority of the deputies and in fact we can report that our congress is a congress of the nation's soviets. We must—we are obliged to—work out uniform tactics considering the interests, particular features, and specific conditions of the regions.

Marxism is based on facts and not possibilities, said V.I. Lenin. If we see that the rebirth of the party's authority is possible only by the uniting of party and state power in the hands of the leader of restructuring, then we say that these are the tactics which we require now. If we see that the exacerbation of interethnic relations and the clashing interests of various strata of society are a fact of our life, then we choose the tactics of unity and consolidation. If we see that except for the party there is no real force capable of advancing restructuring, then we vote for its consistent line of democratizing society.

Here there has been criticism of the so-called majority. Attempts to explain its position by obedience and dependence upon the apparatus are naive and, I would say, nondialectical. Why do certain comrades so want to mix up yesterday and today? Why do they not want to see that with all the imperfection of our apparatus it does have sober, healthy forces which must be supported by careful and painstaking work? Why is there this humiliating overtone which is invested in the word apparatus if not to reap political dividends and manipulate public opinion?

Mikhail Sergeyevich Gorbachev put it correctly in his report: We must proceed from the realities of today. We will not take a single step forward if we do not incorporate in our tactics a consideration of the political diversity of the moment. Specific social processes are occurring in each region and in each republic. It would be a major error to reduce these to some uniformity. But today we can feel a tendency for a leveling of the restructuring processes and at times even the imposing of political models.

We respect the search of the Baltic republics, their search for a sovereign path of development, and we respect the position of all deputies who starkly pose the problems of society and the problems of our congress. However, along with all of this we would like to see the presence of a more weighed, more systematized, differentiated approach to the problems of a multinational state. Certainly, the Central Asian region is not all the same. Each republic in its own way is implementing political, social and economic programs. I have in mind those deep vital seams which in each region are developing under the impact of historical, territorial and national-psychological features.

Not characteristic of our people is a desire for national exclusiveness, and there are no historical roots for this. The consolidation of the Turkmen nation occurred after October, and our development was aided virtually by all of Russia, by all the peoples of the nation, and particularly by the Russian people. We have developed a strong bilingualism. I do not agree with Comrade Drutse when he compares the bilingualism of the different regions and makes an assessment for the nation as a whole. We feel that for us bilingualism is the most appropriate, as living in our republic are 12 percent Russians, 7 percent Uzbeks, 3 percent Kazakhs, from 1 to 2 percent Armenians, Azeris, and Ukrainians, and others. At present, we consider it ill-advised to split the republic, declaring the status of a certain language. On this question we have sought the advice of our people.

We share that particular concern with which certain deputies have spoken of the social disasters of the nation. They are also a severe burden for our republic. Our scourge is high infant mortality, the social backwardness of the countryside, and the demographic defects. And possibly as nowhere else the status of woman is difficult. In the republic a serious disproportion has developed in the structure of the national economy and industry. Sectors of union specialization were developed predominantly, and these were focused on producing and supplying other union republics with gas, oil, chemical products and cotton. Their development was carried out often to the detriment of the ecological situation. At the same time, the sectors which should have served the internal requirements of the republic economy and population developed extremely slowly, and this led to a substantial lag behind the supply level of consumer goods, in terms of the development level of the social and production infrastructure. On a per capita basis, we produce consumer goods worth only 353 rubles. This is 3 1/2-fold less than the union average. The republic's population has a shortage of cotton textiles, although Turkmenia holds first place among the cotton-growing republics in terms of per capita cotton production and just 3-5 percent of the produced cotton is processed here.

Our republic promptly fills its obligations to the fraternal republics in terms of the delivery of cotton fiber, natural gas, petroleum product, chemical, vegetable, melon, and other product; however, we are frequently confronted with the fact when, by referring to a decision of the labor collective councils, our enterprises are partially or completely refused delivery under allocation of raw materials for light industry which are essential for the Turkmen enterprises. For example, this applies to cotton thread and leather goods, as well as machinery and equipment and other products. Even those to whom we deliver our raw materials refuse. For example, we send 35,000 tons of cotton fiber to the Ukraine, but this year we were unable, according to the allocations, to receive 230 tons of thread which, incidentally, was produced from our cotton fiber.

STENOGRAPHIC RECORD

Eighth Session

1 June 1989

We realize that the development of market relations, and particularly with the conversion of regions to self-management and self-financing, is more and more being determined by contractual relations concluded under mutually advantageous conditions as well as equivalent exchange. But at present there is no such mechanism. There is state regulation of the deliveries of many types of products by using allocations but this procedure is not observed. The republic workers do not understand how this is possible in a nation and in a unified national economic complex to put the republic dependent upon whether an enterprise wants to carry out its duties and deliver its products to the region. We feel that such a situation is abnormal and we are hopeful that the new government which we are electing will take a special look at these questions. Both we and a certain portion of our leaders for this reason have proposed seeking consumers for our products overseas and purchasing the goods and raw materials we need there.

The imperfection of the structure is also felt on the employment of the able-bodied republic population and on the size and skill level of the working class. At present in the republic, for every 1,000 persons there are just 69 persons employed in industry, in comparison with 130 as the national average. The social division of labor should not lead to economic damage in the development of the economy of the individual regions, or to a reduction in the standard of living of the population. The existing procedure for calculating national income puts in a disadvantaged position those regions which produce and deliver raw products and semifactures in relation to the regions which produce finished products. In our view, there must be an adjustment of this method and above all in the method of calculating the turnover tax. The turnover tax should be levied at the point where the taxable product is produced. However, there should be a redistribution of the turnover tax between the suppliers of the agricultural raw materials and the producers of the finished product.

Now several questions related to the integrated development of the regions. The union ministries approach the utilization of natural resources often from purely departmental interests, permitting irretrievable losses of many valuable side-products. As part of the natural gas produced in the republic, each year over 1 million tonnes of ethane, a raw material for producing polyethylene, is extracted and not effectively used. With the aim of increasing the integrated use of natural resources, we consider it advisable to institute a payment for natural resources. One of the elements of this mechanism could be the setting of deposit prices which would consider all the components comprising it.

Respected deputies! A unity of social goals in the development of the nation as a whole presupposes the necessity of a guaranteed minimum of material support for the citizens as well as national employment of the labor resources. In our republic these questions are very acute. In line with the conversion of all enterprises to cost accounting, the problem of ensuring employment for the labor resources is becoming even more acute. In our view, the functions of supervising the ensuring of a guaranteed level of material goods and establishing the necessary number of jobs should be assumed by the Supreme Soviet and particularly the Soviet of Nationalities. Using funds from the union budget, long-term specific programs should be financed for the social development of the individual territories. A solution to the questions of the internal union division of labor between the republics is closely tied to a solution to the problems of forming an equivalent interrepublic exchange of product. This will determine the prospective specialization of the region and the standard of living of its population. A solution to these questions will make it possible to overcome possible contradictions in the interethnic ties.

We must also grant the union republics the right themselves to dispose of above-planned product. For example, this year we produced 30,000 tonnes of cotton fiber above the plan. This is the equivalent of producing 10,000-12,000 tonnes of dressed meat. In selling the above-planned share of cotton fiber—for example, in the socialist countries—the republics could have improved the supply of consumer goods for the republic using the foreign exchange earned by this, as well as solved other financial and economic questions.

When the union ministries and departments are working out the initial data for planning the production volumes for their enterprises located on the territory of a republic, we must strengthen the role of the union republics. We feel that these indicators, even before the elaboration of the five-year plan, should be coordinated with the union republic councils of ministers. And, of course, it cannot be considered normal that our union enterprises deduct 1 percent of the obtained profit into our republic's budget while the proportional amount of capital investments channeled by them into social development is 6-8 percent of the volume of production construction.

Comrades! We have set out to rectify the anomalies which have been left to us as a heritage by distant and not distant history. But can we correct everything in a single rush, in a single sweep? We would be bad strategists and politicians if we forgot about tactics and about carrying out our economic, social and nationality policies, now on the basis of possibilities.

Democratization raises the question of deepening the independence of the republics and their greater responsibility for the fate of our union. But here, I feel, we often forget the dialectical priority of unity. This is our political concept. The previous dogmatic interpretation of this is now hopelessly out of date. We need new approaches, and new tactics, and it is for this reason that restructuring is under way. In a condensed form this was spoken of in the report of Mikhail Sergeyevich Gorbachev as well as in the speeches of comrades.

Eighth Session

1 June 1989

We support the provision of the report on the election by the congress of a commission to review proposals concerning supplements and amendments to individual points of the USSR Constitution and, having worked through them, to submit them to the USSR Supreme Soviet for subsequent review at the next Congress of People's Deputies.

In concluding my speech, I would like to voice profound satisfaction with the efficient activities of the CPSU Central Committee and the government, and Mikhail Sergeyevich personally, in carrying out our foreign policy course and in strengthening good-neighborly relations with all countries and particularly with adjacent states. Turkmenistan, in bordering Iran and Afghanistan, is particularly interested in this. We are confident that the constructive steps by our nation on international questions will provide us an opportunity on a mutually advantageous basis of cultural and economic collaboration on many problems related to improving the utilization of natural and raw material resources of our countries. I thank you for the attention. (Applause).

B.Ye. Paton: The floor is turned over to Deputy Likhanov. Deputy Sharipov will speak next.

A.A. Likhanov, writer and chairman of the Board of the V.I. Lenin Soviet Children's Fund (from the V.I. Lenin Soviet Children's Fund): Comrade deputies! And certainly we are deputies who are second and third in line while first in line are the daughters and sons, the mothers and fathers, the grandmothers and grandfathers! Why are we so willing to wean ourselves from starting over, from our initial purpose of ever more democracy, and possibly start from humanity from what parents and children we are, and dispense with the makeup and pomp in everything even down, so to speak, to the petty details—although I personally do not consider these petty details. Should we not now be ashamed of the cheerful juvenile couplets at the congresses, and other adult entertainments which include a certain good humor and moderate criticism of the leadership apparatus, an unworthy amusement for party members fatigued by logomachy? Children are never to blame; it is always the adults who are to blame and who permit the dependent part of society to indulge their feeling of parental concern for the small forces.

I would propose changing one of the clinging traditions, when at the Mausoleum during demonstrations, to touching applause, our leaders are presented with bouquets of flowers by model youths, and who then in exchange receive red boxes of candy and then, with their gifts, run to nearby rostrums to their excited and proud parents. The saying is correct that everything begins from childhood. Including lies. In purging such "details" with the truth, let us, without changing the procedure, have on the Mausoleum not anonymous symbols of prosperity but rather children beset by disaster. Possibly they could be given something more tangible, and instead ask their address, and a half year later, on the eve of a new demonstration, scribble a card to such a stripling; what do you think, comrade leaders? That is not so much trouble, according to the new electoral rules, and for each there would be no more than 2-score such godchildren, but quite a lot if we measured our life by such a human unit of measurement as the child's heart and the boy's eyes.

All my life I have dreamed that all our serious congresses and conferences of a fundamental, principled sort would start with statistics showing how the life of children and elderly had changed for the better—or for the worse! I have dreamed of a time when the annual and 5-year statistical reports along with tons of cast metal and square meters of new housing would print the sobering figures of our failures: how many children were in hospitals, how many children due to parental divorce had been left semiorphans—incidentally, 700,000 each year, comrades!—how many children we, the adults, had brought into the world who were unviable due to drunken barbarism, for medical skills, genetic problems and other adult sins. I greatly missed the concern for these disasters when I listened to your report, Mikhail Sergeyevich. There are 83 million children in the nation, almost one-third of society. But education is unstable and does not hold a prominent place in the budget, and I am not even mentioning morality and upbringing—so many pains and problems are there here. And again, as at the 19th party conference, there was only a hint of this in the report. Let the report last another 30 minutes, but the entire nation wants to hear the ideas of the authorities on this key question.

For many years we assured ourselves and continue to ensure ourselves with the happy notion that children are our future. But forgive me if we use the pronoun "our" then the children are our present. The discussions of the future of childhood have allowed us to put off until later the immediacy of the present disasters. Six thousand children die each year from cancer at present, and tomorrow even more of them will die if instead of the 800 beds for children with cancer the 3,000 required ones do not appear. The government has supported the proposal of the Children's Fund for building a rehabilitation Children's Oncological Center, and we have formed the public Program Hope to aid such children and their mothers, but so much kind-heartedness is required in this sadly tragic work, and where are we to find so much affection and self-denial? If there is blood donating, the transfusing of blood from one person to another, then it is a matter of honor for our society of a complete reworking of our conscience to establish spiritual donating, that is, help not in words but in deeds, a mature transfusion of strength and faith from the strong to the weak, from the old to the young.

In our nation—and unprejudiced common sense is to be thanked for this—charity is being restored. It is curious that the suffering child and our Children's Fund was first supported by the not-weli-off part of our society—the

Eighth Session
1 June 1989

elderly and the sick. Entire cloth sheets with frayed ends and tears were received from humble pensioners and from inhabitants of modern almshouses, and we realize that misfortune is best understood by those who have tasted it. Alas, some but very few leaders of culture and science have come to our side, those members of the Association of the Soviet Intelligentsia in the Defense of Childhood. Let me say frankly that there have been few of the marshals of our spiritual world. The worker collectives help actively. But most importantly, there are few average citizens. I do not blame them. Scientists debate the rise in prices and suddenly soap disappears, although industry produced 7 percent more than last year and charity is the victim. We were hoping for the working, active person and the cooperatives, and they did begin helping us, but then the draft law appeared on the taxation of such property, and I am afraid that again practical charity has been turned into fine words. But the children do not wait. They will grow up or not grow up. They need immediate social, moral, legal, medical and pedagogical aid. We hold an infamous leadership among the developed countries in terms of infant mortality, in competing for this bitter statistic, not with America, not with Japan or Sweden, but rather the state of Mauritius, where in addition the rate of improvement in these matters is treble ours. They are at work on it.

Last year, a special team from the Children's Fund and the USSR Ministry of Health worked 80 days in Central Asia, Kazakhstan and certain oblasts of Russia. We saved the lives of 9,000 children. This is just the first steps, but I want to thank the 2,000 medical workers, basically women, for their voluntary charity and, in taking advantage of this TV forum, to urge physicians, feldshers [middle-level medical personnel] and nurses in whom civil dedication, thank God, has not been extinguished, to come to the aid of the children this summer. (Applause). Incidentally, about glasnost. During those 80 days last year, how many words in the press and on television were there about restructuring, about the need for a better life? But there were just a few comments on the quiet but charitable efforts of the 2,000 medical workers. But surely this work is a real patriotic feat worthy of support and analysis?

I would like to point out that—thank God!—we are developing not bad working relations with the USSR Minzdrav [Ministry of Health]. We have established the International Circle for Aiding the Young Victims of the Armenian Earthquake. Hundreds of children who experienced this are spending their summer vacations by invitation of foreign charitable organizations who are our partners. We are also proceeding on the programs "Children of Chernobyl" and "Children and AIDS." How terrible this is! Recently, we visited the children and mothers from Elista infected with AIDS. They are in a Moscow hospital. The children obviously don't understand what has happened, but for the mothers their despair knows no limit. And they, in essence, are completely unwanted. How long will this enforced seclusion go on—it is terrible to think—perhaps all their lives? What is the social status of these people? How will they live? Where? How will they work? With whom will they have contact, as people flee from them as from the plague? The wound, as they say, is open and bleeding, and as yet our society has no answer to the questions of the innocently suffering children. The old saying that a child does not cry, a mother does not understand should in our times be rephrased. The child cries—and this is well known to all, as twice in recent years the Central Committee and Council of Ministers adopted fundamental documents on orphans at the end of the 20th century—but the maternal power of the local soviets still does not understand that it is not enough to dress a foundling in new clothes and feed it; its life must also be cheered and warmed by humanity.

In olden times they reasoned as follows about help to orphans: Don't build seven churches—find a place for seven children. Now the orphan and generally the idle child, after a public-supported institution, is a public outcast if at first given some food—in essence is homeless. Where should they go? Who goes where? A majority to the vocational-technical school and, if there is a slight hitch, to the "dumbhouse," the so-called boarding school for the mentally retarded. I do not believe in the terrifying figure of 1,185,000 mentally incompetent children, although just a few days ago we were involved with the fate of a 22-year-old Muscovite, Igor Chernikov—he has permitted us to use his name. His mother abandoned him at the maternity home; the young fellow was disabled with a physical defect, but for disobedience, when he had grown up, the benevolent teachers enrolled him in a mental boarding school. And now for 20 years the normal fellow has been in a psychiatric boarding school for veterans and and disabled. He found strength in himself and got out, and we helped him with housing and his rights, but in essence, isn't this proof of our lack of sympathy? Here is a man without an education, without employment, with 26 rubles of pension for everything, and not a single relative around.

The USSR Council of Ministers has supported our idea of establishing family children's homes—to put it more accurately, guardian families and hostels. Today, on Protect the Children Day in Razan Oblast, the Children's Fund, together with the newspaper TRUD, is laying the foundation of the first such hostel. In Lithuania, Rostov and Saratov, the "families" of the fund, are already at work and thriving, but then the Public Education Committee has been unable to approve even a provisional regulation and things have clearly been held up. The traditions of the old Ministry of Education are clearly strong.

Over the last 3 years, the plans for building children's homes in the nation have been fulfilled by 44 percent, and infant homes by 40 percent. I wonder if we have any other quota in construction which has been fulfilled with such shameless neglect! At a recent session of the Bureau of the USSR Council of Ministers on social development, comrades Chekharin (Russian Council of Ministers), Makhamadaliyev (Uzbek Council of Ministers), and Sviridov

Eighth Session
1 June 1989

(Turkmen Council of Ministers) stated that the boarding facilities which are planned for the five-year plan will still be built, but it is hard to believe this. A great deal can—and must!—be said about the children's disasters, to our great lament. What yesterday was simply overlooked or shamelessly crossed out now is becoming a catalyzing means in our general humanization. And it should! It is sad to admit, but we have fallen behind our social opponents not only in the area of motor vehicle building and services but primarily in the area of the practical realization of the finest human feelings. Just look how unsmiling we are, and how adroitly we elbow aside the weak and the silent, how uncourteous we are to women—incidentally, the enormous mass of men flees from the family if a disabled child is born, and the mothers are strangled by impotence and a lack of money, and as a result the state institutions in this area are full of beings who are completely abandoned. Where is our social humanism if over the last 5 years 1,795 women have intentionally killed their newborn children? The children leave home and become missing. You will agree that missing, in peacetime and—in addition—children, this is certainly a disaster.

Some 900,000 juveniles every year are apprehended for violating the law and vagrancy. The homeless children ["besprizorniki"] have reappeared. Child crime is growing. The children of the peoples of the north are dying from tuberculosis. Large families are suffering. I would like for the first time to release two truly tragic figures. In 1987, 1,299 children and juveniles were killed and another 2,194 ended their lives by suicide. In the spring, the Belorussian newspapers decried the fate of the 3d grader from Minsk, Sasha Anufriyev. He was killed in broad daylight. He was killed by a woman, the former wife of Sasha's stepfather, in revenge for having left her for another. Some have been offended by these comments, and some have considered this story a fact of a criminal story. But why do we so willingly waste millions of lines on the most unseemly issues, on trifles not worth the indignation of the entire world? Why have we, having quickly learned meeting-house democracy, not turned the burial of this child into a protest march against cruelty, into a march which would be transmitted by television throughout the nation?

Mikhail Sergeyevich, I turn to you, as the president, with a proposal for a weekly television appeal to the nation. Here we must thoroughly broaden the range of subjects of these appeals, having paid particular attention to the main moral questions of society. (Applause).

We will not restructure our life until we have reduced the pain threshold of our sensations. The most abandoned sphere of inner human relations in our nation is conscience. Having hastily rejected common human morality, we have not created a new morality for the simple reason that all moral underpinnings were already conceived a thousand years before us.

The well-being of the people cannot be instituted at the expense of conscience. Childhood is particularly brittle in terms of adult lack of conscience. For this reason we, the deputies from the Children's Fund, officially submit to the Congress as a legislative initiative a proposal to prepare a USSR Law Governing the Rights of the Child, and are ready to head this practical work. (Applause).

Let me inform the deputies that in the very near future the Supreme Soviet should ratify an international convention on the rights of the child, and this has already been prepared by the United Nations. At the same time, we do not have any analog. Generally speaking, our legislation is greatly in debt to childhood and the family, particularly large families. We also propose not to run together the concept "maternity" and "childhood"—since ancient times an inactive stereotype, but rather establish separately a Committee for Women's Affairs, and separately a Committee for Defending the Interests of Childhood and the Family, as a joint Committee of the Soviet of the Union and the Soviet of Nationalities. This is supported by the women deputies. We also propose, in addition to the USSR Law on the Rights of the Child, to instruct this Committee to prepare a written report to the Congress of People's Deputies on the status of children in the USSR. Support, comrades, these proposals! Let me say again that children are our present. They can become the future only if we help them now. Tomorrow will be too late. (Applause).

B.Ye. Paton: The floor is given over to Deputy Sharipov. After him, Deputy Belov will speak.

Yu.K. Sharipov, general director of the Ufa S.M. Kirov Production Association, Ufa (from the National-Territorial Electoral District): Hello, comrade deputies! Hello, our dear voters. Our Bashkir delegation has empowered me to speak today. We are 29 persons here. And I would like to say that we have received notes and we have been phoned with the complaint that we are working poorly at the congress because we are not being shown on television. We are seated very far away, way to the back, and we are generally speaking a humble people, particularly from the autonomous republics. We do not stand around the microphones but this certainly does not mean that our deputies, including the Bashkir deputies, are not at work. I am making this statement to our voters from the Bashkir Autonomous Republic. This probably also concerns many other deputies who have not had the fortunate opportunity as I to stand here, on the rostrum, so I can be seen, and after this it is concluded that I am at work while the remaining 25 are supposedly not working.

Comrades, there are more than 2,000 of us, and certainly the nation has equally as many problems. So let each of us assume the share which he can of our common work. I promised in my program that I personally would work to see it that each Soviet family had a telephone. I do not know how things are with the other deputies, but in our delegation there are comrade deputies who have no telephone at all. Incidentally, raise your hands if you do not have a telephone. So you see, even deputies who should do a lot of work at home, unfortunately, have no telephone.

FIRST CONGRESS OF PEOPLE'S DEPUTIES OF THE USSR

Eighth Session

1 June 1989

I, as the leader of an association which produces communications equipment, including modern electronic telephone exchanges, know that this is not so easy to do, as well as what problems have accumulated here. Some 30 percent of urban homes have telephones. In the countryside, it is just 10 percent. In order to pass on a message from village to village, one has to ride a horse or a tractor. There are 14.9 million unsatisfied applications, including over a million from disabled persons.

At the same time, I realize that the level of telephone service is one of the most important indicators for the social development of society, and this is an important prerequisite in developing information science and modern management in the country.

The telephone, if you wish, contributes to the development of glasnost and democracy. When our television invites us to take part in direct broadcasts on various problems, in announcing the telephone number of the studio, I am painfully aware that three-quarters of the population has no such opportunity. Incidentally, a large amount of the population does not see these broadcasts, as many regions and villages are deprived of such an opportunity.

Comrades, this year our association will increase the output of automatic telephone exchanges by 2.3-fold. By 1991, we should again double it, and by 1995 we will be able ourselves to provide telephones for 1.8 million apartments. With this amount it is possible to provide full telephone service for seven cities with a population of a million. But even now our associated enterprises cannot keep up with us, and primarily the enterprises of the electronics industry. The Minelektrotekhprom [Ministry of Electrical Equipment Industry] is keeping the communications workers on starvation rations in terms of telephone cable. As an economist, I realize perfectly well that the providing of telephone service requires certain outlays. But with our "trishkinization," from the famous "Trishka's caftan" [pull a thread and unravel the sweater] with its well-known methods of repair, our budget will always lack funds, including for communications. We can find the many billions for the BAM [Baykal-Amur Mainline] and for reversing the course of rivers, but for this, no. But I propose using conversion in the MEP [Ministry of Electric Industry] and the Minelektrotekhprom [Ministry of the Electrical Equipment Industry], having focused the freed capacity on the needs of resolving this social problem. I propose setting up a number of firms, including one on the basis of our association, which would be fully engaged in producing communications equipment, "turnkey" installation and services. I also propose setting up a deputy initiative group for a national telephone service; I will take a most active part in its work and, if you have the confidence, I can even lead it.

A few ideas on improving the operation of enterprises. Without going into a criticism of the existing Law Governing Enterprises, let me say that its new version should proceed from the principle that the labor collective is the real master of the enterprise. In my view, there should be three types of enterprises: state-owned (this would include primarily defense enterprises and transport); the second type leased, which over time can be bought out completely by the collectives and become joint-stock; and the third the well-known cooperatives. I agree with the comrades who said that the law for all types of enterprises should be standard. Everyone pays taxes to the state budget, to the republic budget, and to the local budget. The amount of taxes should be set solely by law. For excluding the negative influence of the existing monopolies on the nation's economy, we probably also require an antitrust law.

Comrades! The basic regulator in the union economy and in the enterprise economy should, naturally, be the market, and for this we must first of all establish the market infrastructure and a network of commercial supply and marketing organizations. The question of the enterprise is inseparably linked to the work of the ministries. There is a proposal by a group of Moscow deputies concerning their further functioning. While they may not be indisputable, in my view, they are basically correct, all the more as at present we do not have at hand and do not see any alternative proposal from the USSR Council of Ministers. We have Moscow proposals, Estonian ones, but we simply do not know what the government is proposing. Possibly they have a better idea.

Comrades, I am concerned by the fact that the existing ministries, in my view, have prematurely moved away from the questions of supply, referring to the direct ties and wholesale trade. But wholesale trade has still gotten nowhere, and there is no order in the direct ties and, in my view, this cannot be instilled in a day. A recent decree of the Gosplan [State Planning Committee], the Gossnab [State Committee for Supply], and Gosarbitrazh [State Arbitration Committee] has permitted suppliers to keep the delivery volumes on last year's level. This is the truest stagnation.

How can we proceed, what can we do with the new articles which do not go through centralized distribution? For this reason, until wholesale trade is a reality, the organization of material and technical supply for the enterprise should be the most important function of the center.

Here mention has already been made that democracy can exist with a respect of the citizens for the law and for discipline. I feel that this is particularly pertinent in the economy and in production. If we do not master this, there will be new Chernobyls, new Nakhimovs.

Moreover, while Comrade Deputy Zaslavskiy has not enrolled me in the "Black Hundred," I will endeavor to be tactful. Strikes today have become a reality. So let the comrades who resolve their problems with the aid of strikes realize that they are bringing a heap of inconveniences for the comrades who want to work at this time

Eighth Session

1 June 1989

but cannot because of the interruption in deliveries; they lose wages and must then work in the evenings and on Sundays. (Applause).

About certain problems in Bashkiria and cost accounting for an autonomous republic. Far from all the social problems have been resolved in our republic. Although recently more housing has been going up, the production of consumer goods is increasing and more food is being produced. For example, republic meat production has annually increased in recent years by 9 percent. But this is far from sufficient and this has led to definite social tension. We feel that with the changeover to real cost accounting, Bashkiria with its strong industrial and agricultural potential would be able to rectify this situation. Without going into the essence of the published plan for restructuring of the republic economy and on which we previously have submitted our comments and proposals to the Russian Soviet Federated Socialist Republic [RSFSR] Council of Ministers, let me say that for realizing real cost accounting we must have amendments of the USSR Constitution in those areas where the status of the autonomous republics is determined. We agree with the political status. As for the economy, we feel that the Constitution should provide a provision according to which the republic should be the real master on its territory. At present, Article 83 states that the republic carries out the decisions of the USSR and union republic state bodies. This is clearly a provision from the period of stagnation which obliges us to carry out the decisions of the apparatus. In the same article an autonomous republic coordinates and monitors the activities of the union and republic enterprises and organizations. In what manner?

I personally understand the position of the enterprise leaders who are supervised and coordinated both by the ministers and by local authorities. For me it is not a question of whom they should obey now, as the one with the resources does the managing. And at present, the ministries have the resources. Article 82 states that a republic, "outside the limits" of the laws of the USSR and the union republics, independently resolve questions related to its running. But in practice this "outside the limits" leaves nothing for the republic. In Bashkiria, 97 percent is made up of the industry of the union and union-republic levels. We would propose that there be a constitutional provision that the republic be responsible for satisfying its social, material and spiritual needs.

For relieving the center of managing the same economy which is to be turned over to be run by the union and autonomous republics, the congress should, in my view, adopt four fundamental laws: a Law on the Enterprise (this has already been mentioned), a Law on Local Self-Management, and a Law on Land Tenure—these laws determine the possibilities of republic cost accounting and as a whole will make it possible to adopt a fourth, corresponding law. As the basis they might adopt the Law on Cost Accounting in Estonia. For us the political status may be different, but the economic status should be equal. We have a population of 4 million and a product volume of 15 billion.

Comrades! I would also like to take up the questions of ecology. Ufa started up a series of ecological demonstrations and meetings, and these were subsequently held in other regions of the nation. Since in accord with Point 7 of Article 113 of the Constitution, the Supreme Soviet provides legislation for protecting the environment and the use of natural resources, I propose working out and adopting a law on conservation and utilization of nature which would make it possible on a comprehensive basis to resolve the questions of ecology in the nation, and I also propose that the Goskompriroda [State Committee for Protection of Nature] provide a preliminary organization responsible solely to the Supreme Soviet. (Applause).

Comrades! I would like to take up one more question and conclude here. There have been speeches on interethnic questions. This question concerns not only the union republics but also the autonomous republics. We have good relations. For example, in Tataria we are now holding a 10-day festival for the literature and art of Bashkiria. But at the same time, there are also problems. I propose that we devote a special congress of people's deputies to interethnic questions after the CPSU Central Committee Plenum has been held on these same questions. Lastly, I would like to make one request. May I have a minute? Thank you, everyone.

B.Ye. Paton: Respected comrade deputies! Let me remind you that yesterday the 10-minute rule was relaxed. In an extreme case up to 15 minutes. At present, as a rule, all the speeches exceed the rule. Please adhere to the rules. The floor is now turned over....

From the audience: We cannot hear.

B.Ye. Paton: The floor is turned over to the Deputy Vasiliy Ivanovich Belov. Deputy Stoumova will speak after.

V.I. Belov, writer, secretary of the Board of the RSFSR Writers' Union (from the CPSU): I would like to begin my comments by saying that I do not understand and do not accept yesterday's two or three rude attacks on the newly elected president (applause). Even the Americans, a noisy people, do not demand impeachment on the second day after electing the president. They respect their president. (Applause).

Generally, I wonder, are we really the people's deputies? If we are truly the people's, then to what degree? I understand the nobility of Deputy Kazannik. I also recall the spirit of the two Leningrad deputies who offered to give up their candidacies in favor of another republic. But if I were in the place of the Leningrad voters, I would not vote for such deputies who abandon their rights with such ease. (Applause). We are obliged to carry out the will of our voters. Even the time of the deputy is now becoming the property of the people, and for this reason we must be aware of the hierarchy of values.

Eighth Session

1 June 1989

In political fighting there are the most diverse procedures. One of them is very simple and reliable, and this is the method of filling in time. For example, for entire days it is possible to discuss a procedural question or some secondary and simply unnecessary law. We can be very easily provoked into a drawn-out, fatiguing discussion of some completely haphazard issue, and then we merely waste our energy.

The orders of the voters are clearly and precisely expressed in the thousands of letters from readers and telegrams of voters. They dictate to me the hierarchy of my deputy values. In my view, it is essential to immediately work out and clarify the Basic Law. Here, in the first place, it is particularly important to bring about a further improvement in the electoral system; second, to establish broadened rights for the soviets by decentralizing power; and third—and this is the most important in my view—our Constitution should stipulate that along with collective farm [kolkhoz]-state farm [sovkhoz] ownership of land, there should finally appear and exist private ownership with the right to inherit. I am convinced that we can and must resolve this at the current congress.

A law which along with kolkhoz ownership also permits private, farmstead and private farmer ownership of the land is essential for all the peoples inhabiting our great state. The adoption of such a law would be proof that we are seriously concerned with the future. It is not merely a matter that we are fed up with begging grain from other states. It is a fact that a new law on land tenure would to a significant degree smooth out many of the economic and particularly the nationality contradictions. It would also contribute to an ecological improvement and, in addition, to the linguistic and cultural rebirth of all the peoples of our multinational state.

I propose calling the Food Commission the Commission on Land Tenure. Certainly I am not a supporter of those hotheads who propose completely eliminating kolkhoz and sovkhoz ownership of the land. The fact that many of our kolkhozes have been plundered and devastated by the state is still not grounds for their immediate liquidation. (Applause). On the contrary, we must halt this plundering and eliminate not the kolkhozes themselves but rather Murakhovskiy's department [State Agro-Industrial Committee]. (Applause).

Land and water should be disposed of not by the department but rather by the people in the form of their local soviets, with the aid of the all-union laws. The USSR Minvodkhoz [Ministry of Land Reclamation and Water Resources], which over the last 20 years has spent some 150 billion of the people's rubles and destroyed millions of hectares of the best land, has brought agriculture to the brink of disaster. It was the ministry, together with the hydroproject builders and chemists which plundered a great river, on the banks of which scores of different peoples lived for centuries! I mean the Volga.

The course of destroying the economy with the aid of departmental decisions is continuing. Recently Murakhovskiy forwarded to the Politburo a note proposing that by the year 2005 the area of irrigated land be increased to 40 million hectares. For these destructive purposes, the Minvodkhoz has again requested some 230 billion rubles from us. We must not give them! (Applause). With this money we could build 500,000 km of roads, 10 million full-amenity rural homes, hundreds of thousands of schools, hospitals and stores. With these billions we could keep the personnel in the countryside and effectively eliminate the food crisis. But for some reason we do not want to recognize our mistakes.

The Minvodkhoz, which recently made a fool of itself in 1988, received thousands of excavators and bulldozers. At the same time, several hundred units of this equipment planned for the Program "Roads of the Non-Chernozem Zone" were not received by the RSFSR Minavtodor [Ministry of Highways]. Generally speaking, it would be a good thing to speak about the political, economic and financial equality of the Soviet Union republics. The unequal political status of the RSFSR in the union of our republics is becoming, in the view of experts, a source of russophobia. Since the RSFSR lacks such important bodies as a central committee, many state committees, and an academy of sciences, it is assumed that these functions are supposedly carried out by the all-union bodies. Is is not for this reason that the all-union bodies are perceived as Russian bodies? Their mistakes and failings, all the flaws of our system in which all our peoples live, are perceived as the errors of the Russians. The inequality of the republics is also felt in the forming of the all-union budget, and in the policy of procurement prices, subsidies and distributed funds. The long years of inequality are confirmed by the demographic situation. It, this situation, is bad not only in the RSFSR, the Ukraine and Belorussia, but also in Estonia, Latvia and Lithuania. However, the economic inequality is particularly characteristic of Siberia and the so-called Non-Chernozem Zone. A majority of the deputies from our congress simply do not know the depressing statistical data on this question. In order to avoid an emotional outburst, I will not read the figures. I will merely give one: Before the revolution, the Russians and Ukrainians had the highest increment in the population. Now both are confronted with the threat of depopulation. In the nation they continue to vote with their feet. I do not envy the governments of the three Baltic republics, where the increase in population is occurring due to immigrants and not from an increased birthrate of the indigenous population. Is this normal? I profoundly believe that the deputies of the Transcaucasus, the Central Asian republics, and the Baltic, as well as the deputies from the autonomous Russian republics, will correctly understand this part of my speech. But I am in no way confident that the so-called "democratic minority," actually the press, will not stick some label on me. At one time, MOSKOVSKIYE NOVOSTI, in six languages, called me a "misanthrope." Of course, the abuse does not stick. If certain members of the Politburo and

Eighth Session
1 June 1989

Mikhail Sergeyevich Gorbachev himself have learned to tolerate badmouthing, then we, mere mortals, have nothing to complain of. But I am still greatly concerned by the fact that the mass information media, particularly television, are in certain hands, and often reflect the interests not of all the people but rather the interests of certain, capital groups. (Applause). Here pluralism as yet has not even found its ground. Judging from the speeches, the Moscow group relies largely on science. In actuality, in no other nation is there such a number of academicians as in ours. In Moscow, academicians are a dime a dozen, space and all sorts. But why in my village does the peasant still mow hay in the same method as he did in the 12th century? (Applause). And what is the result of modern economic science? The result, in my opinion, is still just one. This is the Riga Market in Moscow. Over the 4 years of restructuring, the Moscow and other economists have not thought up anything except urban cooperatives, which should start not in the city but in the countryside. (Applause). And how can we respect such a science which gave us Chernobyl? I am in no way against science as such, but we must not think merely about our academy interests. A majority of the intelligentsia lives in cities. In my home kolkhoz, for 15 years now, the school has not taught a foreign language, as there is no instructor. And can a village graduate gain admission to a university or institute, if the school does not even teach a required subject? Just around 8 percent of the total number of students is peasant children. And we should not forget that the world is governed by literate people....

Here they have mentioned the danger of hooliganism and extremism for our young democracy. And who is to blame, you might ask? Certainly it is not us, certainly it is not television, not the pop tour and not the movies which propagandize the cult of cruelty and violence? (Applause).

The centralizing of cultural policy and turning it over for complete control to the same, free-and-easy people does not produce anything good. Let me read an excerpt from a telegram: "We request that you tell the congress not to allow the vulgarization of culture. The commercial movie, pop music, pornography, the vanguard, alcohol, and drugs destroy the hope of rebirth." Incidentally, about alcoholics. The nonfulfillment of the 1985 law caused disappointment in the people in the actions of the Politburo. It was not a bad law. But the law came and went. Let me read one more telegram, actually an excerpt from the Urals. A woman writes: "I myself have divorced my husband because of his drunkenness. Alone she raised her son, kept a cow, two calves and a sheep. I worked the entire war at a factory while raising my son and for 5 years have been a nurse. Now I am barely able to keep the farm. I deliver milk to the state with a fat content of 4.1. On election day the leadership sent a bus with a voting urn and in the bus everyone was given a drink—just vote. And this is what holds the people together. There are two peasants in the village and they are too drunk to make sense." Now I turn to the Politburo members. You, probably, like all of us, go during the break to the buffet. There they sell fine fermented milk, but, if this woman were to go on a drinking binge, I don't know what would remain in the Kremlin buffet. (Applause). It is time for us to understand the simple truth that a sober economy is impossible with a drunken budget. Those who now complain of the severe budget deficit, we might ask: And why did this happen? Might it not be because the nation has 18 million managers? What does the support of such personnel cost? And what about the war in Afghanistan? And Cuba, Nicaragua and Ethiopia? And what about space? How much do our great festivals, olympiads and international forums cost? How much do those canals of the Minvodkhoz cost? Small wonder that there is a budget deficit with such ministers as Vasilyev and Murakhovskiy. They have squandered billions and things seem no better for the immediate future. (Applause).

I am forced to quote an excerpt from one other letter to me and Valentin Grigoryevich Rasputin. "We request that you come forward with a legislative initiative on having the Supreme Soviet cancel all deals involving the leasing of parts of Soviet territory to foreign and mixed firms. There must be the prohibiting of similar deals in the future as well as the canceling of all other concessions and leases. At present, there seems to be some sort of mercenary frenzy. Some are ready to sell themselves lock, stock and barrel, and here even spit on their motherland. It is bad enough that there has been trade in living articles (athletes numbered like at beauty contests). It is bad enough that the domestic do-gooders are ready to clear out all the riches of the nation for dollars. It is bad enough that the Soviet Union is being turned into a dumping ground for radioactive waste and hazardous products, and now it has come down to bartering away the territories of our own land." (Applause).

I continue quoting: "Just what is this—an extreme degree of political feeble-mindedness, an extreme degree of irresponsibility, a concealed hate for one's country, or a cynical sell-out? Having learned to take bribes in rubles, are they now going for dollars? We are not setting things aside for our motherland. Here it is for our children, our grandchildren and our great-grandchildren to live. This is their land. With what authority does the gorispolkom [city executive committee] or oblispolkom [oblast executive committee], with what authority do these people command our national wealth? Such questions should be settled only by the Supreme Soviet or the Congress of People's Deputies. The shameful deals should be cancelled. The shameful deals to turn our nation into a dumping ground for radioactive wastes should also be publicized and cancelled.

It is hard not to agree with these authors, but I would add here the demand to publish and discuss the conditions of all international treaties and publish the details. Why are these conditions accepted and signed by a narrow group of persons? I propose to the congress and the congress Presidium that we submit to voting by the congress the

Eighth Session

1 June 1989

question of the immediate preparing and holding of a referendum on nuclear energy. (Applause).

Respected deputies! From the congress rostrum several times we have heard proud, even exulting voices about power. Supposedly from now on power forever rests with the people's deputies. But I do not share such deputy optimism. Don't hurry up to hurry, as they say in Odessa! We still do not have power; it belongs to others, sometimes to persons not even known to us. It is in the hands, it is in those hands, in the hands of those who have the television cameras and newspaper editors. It belongs to those who sit closer to the rostrum and those who have already learned to use a Xerox machine. Even here, at the congress, power belongs precisely to such people. There are people who dream about all sorts of disorder, they dream about chaos. Do not forget this, please. It is essential to live and work with ever-growing responsibility.

Thank you for patiently hearing me out. (Applause).

B.Ye. Paton: The floor is turned over to Deputy Galina Ivanovna Stoumova.

G.I. Stoumova, shop chief of the Gatchinskiy Voskhoz, Gatchinskiy Rayon (Gatchina Territorial Electoral District, Leningrad Oblast): Comrade deputies! Since I am an agricultural worker and have been employed in this sector for 30 years, I would like to devote my speech largely to this question. But, having listened to the speech of Vasiliy Aleksandrovich Starodubtsev and the appeal which I also signed, in order not to repeat myself, I will take up only such questions as aid to the rural inhabitants, in particular in Leningrad Oblast, since certain regions of our nation are not having difficulties here and I will also mention several demands of my voters.

Over scores of years, around large cities they have established zones raising vegetables and potatoes. The city has always helped the countryside since we are able to harvest only one-quarter of the area with our own forces. I understand what harm the state suffers when machines at plants and factories stand idle. But since we move people from the countryside to the city, since there exists a great inequality in the social sphere between city and countryside, and as long as the village is not provided with highly productive equipment, we are forced to turn to the city for help. But under conditions of the covering of costs and self-financing, the question related to help from the city has changed sharply and not in favor of the countryside. It is bad enough that the sponsors do not come and for those who are sent to the kolkhozes and sovkhozes the sponsors require 50 or 60 rubles for each man day. The students have come out with the slogan "an academic year without agricultural work"; school children can come to the sovkhoz only on a volunteer basis. But we know the "volunteer ideas" of the children and their parents and for this reason it is difficult to expect their aid for the sovkhozes. I want to ask whether the members of the Politburo and the Council of Ministers are aware that last year in Leningrad Oblast because of the manpower shortage a portion of the fields was plowed under together with unharvested cabbage and carrots, dill, sorrel and lettuce. And no one was held responsible for this. How can one punish the farm leader if it is impossible to embrace and unembraceable?

This year we expect a repetition of last year's situation. We have already overtaxed our people with heavy manual physical labor. But each sovkhoz worker, be they milkmaid, pig tender, specialist or director, in addition to the main job, and this is often done without days off, by a decision of the labor collective council, has been given the duty of weeding five-hundredths [of area] of root crops, loading hay in the barn, and in the autumn harvesting cabbage. There is a way to eliminate these negative phenomena in the future. In Leningrad Oblast in one agrarian combine there is highly productive equipment from France and the Netherlands. City industry has already manufactured examples of this equipment. Now there must be help from the Council of Ministers in serially producing this equipment so that the individual regions do not produce it by artisan, expensive methods. For now such equipment does not exist and I appeal to the workers of industrial enterprises in large cities—I feel that the Moscow sovkhozes also have a need for this—to provide us with help. And I also turn to the USSR Council of Ministers so that a decree be passed to allocate funds from the state budget to compensate for the expenditures on bringing in the crop, as was the case last year. But it must be considered that planting this year was done 3 weeks earlier than last year.

I am somewhat repeating myself, but I cannot help but mention women. Article 35 of the Constitution proclaims the equality of men and women. We, the women, are in favor of equal rights but we are against the equal right to heavy physical labor, to equal leave time, and to the same length of the work day. Finally, we must provide an opportunity for a woman to be concerned with what is predetermined for her by nature herself, that is, the raising of children and maternity. (Applause). For this reason I feel that there is a great need to extend the leave for taking care of an infant up to 3 years. I will not repeat myself and speak about the fate of our war and labor veterans and pensioners. Much has been said at this congress about these people, particularly the kolkhoz pensioners, and I will mention only the instructions about them to the congress. Here are the instructions.

To review the questions of lifting the restrictions on wages and pensions as now the ceiling is R300. Certain pensioners could still continue to work, in particular, on kolkhozes, particularly as we are experiencing such a shortage of experienced personnel. They still could be working but because of the wage restriction they do not go to work. Secondly, the length of employment on a kolkhoz should be considered in the total length of labor employment in figuring a pension. It is very painful to watch a person who has worked 36 years, including 29

STENOGRAPHIC RECORD

Eighth Session

1 June 1989

years on a kolkhoz and 9 on a sovkhoz, and who will receive a pension for only the 9 years of labor employment. Thirdly, female construction workers who are employed in finishing work involving the use of paints and varnishes have strongly urged that we state at the congress that these harmful conditions must be considered and with 15 years experience in this work provide the right to retire on a pension at age 50.

Several words about the housing program in the countryside. It is essential that the city face the problem of rural construction, but now everything is turned backwards. Construction committees have been set up and they, in particular in our Leningrad, we feel will carry out basic construction only in the city. Why? I will tell you. Under the program, by 1990, just in our Gachinskiy Rayon, we plan to build 90,000 m^2 of housing. As of now we have succeeded in "pushing out" only 12,000 m^2. For this reason it is hard to say how the housing program will be carried out in the countryside.

There is one other instruction. We must prevent the departments from carrying out their ideas on the territory of the soviets, prevent their fleecing, and provide the soviets with an opportunity to control their own budget with a focus on improving the social sphere. I thank you for your attention. (Applause).

B.Ye. Paton: Comrade deputies, a 30-minute break is hereby declared.

B.Ye. Paton: Comrade deputies, let us continue our work. The floor is now given to Deputy Larionov. The next to speak will be Deputy Chernichenko.

V.P. Larionov, deputy chairman of the Presidium of the Yakutsk Scientific Center under the Siberian Department of the USSR Academy of Sciences and director of the Institute for Physical-Technical Problems of the North (from the CPSU): Deeply respected chairman of the nation's Supreme Soviet! Deeply respected chairman of the session! Dear comrade people's deputies! The deputies of the Yakut Autonomous Republic have difficulties similar to those of the Bashkir delegation. All the people's deputies representing the Yakut Republic at the congress would like to speak from this rostrum and undoubtedly each has something to say. But our northern tactfulness does not permit us to elbow our way to the rostrum although many of our comrades would actually like to speak and voice their position.

I feel that our deputies will be given an opportunity to state their positions on the Supreme Soviet Commissions and the committees of people's deputies, by participating in working out the congress documents as well as through the mass information media.

I would like to take up certain questions of improving our state structure, the harmonizing of nationality relations and developing a regional economy. In the process of preparing our nation's new Constitution which, it seems, should be adopted by our sitting of USSR people's deputies, very complex questions arise concerning the structure of our nationality-state and territorial formations. The existing structure which was adopted in organizing our union was justified at a certain historical stage in building a socialist state. However, at the present stage of our development, when priority has been given to common human values and the necessity of establishing a state under the law, in terms of our fundamental basis for the status of the union and autonomous republics, the autonomous oblasts and autonomous districts, there are questions requiring a clear answer. It would be better to ask them now when we intend to begin creating a new Constitution for the nation.

I, for example (although a different opinion has also been voiced from this rostrum), find it completely incomprehensible why Tataria has a lower level of statehood than, for instance, the highly esteemed republic of ancient culture, Armenia. Why do the 4 million of Bashkiria hold such a lower status, in comparison, for example, with Estonia? Here the basic distinguishing feature is the presence of frontiers with foreign countries and for me, for example, this is far from persuasive. Certainly in essence we have laid down the bases not for separation but rather unification of our peoples on equal grounds. In terms of such peoples and ethnic groups as the Evens, Yukagirs, Nivkhi, Nanytsy and many others, our state system virtually does not consider their presence.

The problem of the harmonious unity of our multinational state, it seems to me, has not been settled on the principles of the currently existing structure of nationality-state and territorial formations. The questions related to the state organization of the nationality-territorial formations require a profound study and extensive discussion of thoughtful and balanced decisions. For precisely this reason an immediate task for the Commission on Interethnic Relations of the Soviet of Nationalities under the USSR Supreme Soviet is the working out of draft laws for the extensive discussion in the nation of the questions of reshaping the structure of the nationality-state and territorial formations.

Now on the question of improving the electoral system. It seems to me that here we must have a formula which would provide guarantees for the representation of all the country's nations and nationalities in the USSR Congress of People's Deputies. This is fundamentally important in terms of the ethnoses which do not have nationality-administrative formations. The legal powers of the northern nationalities could be realized through their social association which could be established within the framework of the reform of the political system as well as through the Committee of the Council of Nationalities on Northern and Arctic Peoples.

The fact that representatives of just 69 nations and nationalities were proposed in the first stage as candidate USSR people's deputies and even fewer were elected and are present in this auditorium (there are representatives

FIRST CONGRESS OF PEOPLE'S DEPUTIES OF THE USSR

Eighth Session

1 June 1989

of 65 nationalities) shows the seriousness of this problem. It would be worth recalling that according to the 1926 census, 194 nations, nationalities and ethnic groups were recorded, and later by the method of simple unification over 100 nationalities were recognized as living in our nation.

In the sphere of nationality relations, the economic aspect holds an important place. Even before the adoption of the new legislation on the Principles of Nationality-State Formations, even now we must determine the economic rights and duties of the union and autonomous republics, including in the area of foreign economic ties, and we must clearly define the basic principles for economic and financial relations of the central and regional organizations. The dictating of terms by the all-union ministries, which is presently generally recognized and which widely follows its own enforceable enactments discrediting laws [as published], depersonify the local authorities and are a factor in impeding regional development.

On this level the problem of the development of the north requires particular attention. It must be admitted that the Soviet north in demographic terms is overburdened, and ecologically is little protected. The intensive industrial development of the northern regions has been accompanied by an irreversible destruction of the ecosystem with its growing immunodeficiency.

The unsound exploitation of natural resources by the extracting industry ends up with a dead lunar landscape and thousands of square kilometers of flooded, felled and fire-devastated taiga. Around the industrial centers of Yakutia on a territory with an area of 2,400 km^2, there has been a sharp decline in the hunting and fishing stocks, and reindeer raising has virtually disappeared here.

In a number of instances, a threat has arisen for the survival of the ethnic groups. For this reason it is essential to work out a scientific and humane concept for the development of the north, and give up assigning the north the role of just a raw material fief.

In planning the socioeconomic development of the northern regions, it is essential to consider the demographic factors as an important element in the policy and on the nationality question. For example, in the economy of the Yakut Republic the ore-mining industry prevails, and this sector has developed traditionally employing extensive methods. The republic is a supplier of raw material resources, and this from the very start has determined the unprofitability of its economy, primarily as a consequence of the existing price policy for raw materials. This is a public fact. Here, in terms of the level of social amenities and in terms of the condition of schools, hospitals and clubs and, in particular, in rural localities where basically the indigenous population lives, the republic holds one of the last places in the RSFSR. There are many reasons for this. One of them is the high migration of the population. Over the last 20 years, according to estimates of the statistical services, more than 1 million persons have moved into Yakutia and up to 1 million persons have moved out. At present, the entire republic population is a little more than a million persons.

An unique phenomenon has been established of a provisionality with a low production return per worker unit. The economic outlays of the uncontrolled moving in of migrants into new industrial development regions are enormous, while the moral ones are merely hard to comprehend, particularly in the sphere of interethnic relations. For overcoming the migration processes and stabilizing the population, for example in the Yakut Republic, it is essential to have fundamental development for the sectors of raw materials processing, to achieve the instituting of just prices for the delivery of the products of the extracting sectors as well as the sectors of the traditional economy, and to completely solve the problems of the social and domestic spheres and pension support considering the harsh natural and climatic conditions of the habitat. These questions are characteristic for all the northern regions of the nation.

The Yakut ASSR is part of the Far Eastern Economic Region. Our economic region provides the nation with 96 percent of the mined diamonds, the basic portion of gold, tin, polymetals, antimony, gas, and oil mined in our nation. The fur, lumber and fishing sectors of industry have developed. At the same time, the narrow raw-material focus of the economy in the Yakut Republic has predetermined the growth rate of the industrial complex, which is out of balance with the development of the social sphere, and the excessive burden of the mineral and raw material complex on the natural environment with the absence of resource-saving ecologically clean production methods.

For this reason, resting on us, the people's deputies, is a responsibility on the matter of working out the legal, legislative and economic bases and a new socioeconomic policy for developing the northern territories. This includes in the area of an active and effective social policy aimed at providing a full range of vital conditions for man, satisfying his material and spiritual values, and protecting the health of the population in compensating for the negative consequences of the climatic factors, the remoteness and undevelopment of the territory.

Here, achieving the real sovereignty of the nationality-territorial formations on the basis of their economic independence and effective mechanisms for controlling the demographic situation; active participation in economic integration, in foreign economic and overseas cultural ties; the elaboration of legal enactments which protect the priority interests of the indigenous population in the industrial development of the territories of their traditional habitat—these and other areas should be a matter of activity for the appropriate commissions

Eighth Session
1 June 1989

and committees of the USSR Supreme Soviet and the USSR Congress of People's Deputies.

A most important, vitally important Law Governing Local Self-Government and the Local Economy, by which we plan to set off on the real path of exercising power by the local soviets as a whole for the nation, should consider the level and character of development of the productive forces in a specific economic region, and the specific conditions of management and human activity. In the area of price formation, the prime difficulty for our republic is the economically unsound, understated prices for fuel and energy resources and for precious metals. Here the republic receives nothing from the profits of selling the end manufactured product, and the very rich region is constantly playing the role of a beggar. The violating of the price parity between industry and agriculture, the growing gap between the level of state, cooperative, market, and speculative prices for agricultural products undermine the bases for realizing real cost accounting in the complex agro-industrial system of the North, under the harsh natural climatic conditions. The realization of regional cost accounting which would provide for the economic independence of the republic and territories would serve as a basis for strengthening the self-awareness and dignity of the people, morality in society, and for raising discipline and efficiency of labor, which at present we clearly lack.

At the same time, I agree with those speeches by deputies who caution us against the centrifugal trends arising around the "prosperity of nationality apartments." These trends at times contradict the interests of economic integration and political consolidation of our entire society.

Comrades! I feel that everyone realizes the necessity of strengthening the role of science in adopting crucial decisions on the statewide and regional level. The organization of the Siberian Department of the USSR Academy of Sciences in 1957, and later the Urals and Far Eastern Regional departments of the USSR Academy of Sciences, created the essential prerequisite for raising the intellectual potential of the regions. At the same time, I agree with Deputy Kazarezov that the excessive centralization of science does not increase its effectiveness.

In line with the wide-scale industrial development with the eastern and northern regions, it is essential to undertake new fundamental steps to strengthen the scientific centers of these regions. It is essential to propose new organizational and economic mechanisms in the aim of strengthening the scientific approach in solving complex national economic tasks in the north, and confirm the primacy of solving ecological questions over the economic one.

Each region of the nation has its own priority problems. In our republic the crucial condition for life support is transport, the crux of all economic and social policy. With each passing year the problems which depend completely upon the delivery of national economic freight grow worse. And at present these needs are only 60-70 percent satisfied, and this seriously impedes the achieving of a rhythmical life for the entire republic. Moreover, the seasonal nature of freight shipments carried out chiefly by river and maritime routes leads to the stockpiling and, consequently, to the freezing of a large amount of valuable materials en route and at the transshipping depots.

In light of this, the construction of the Amur-Yakut Mainline [AYaM] has assumed exceptionally important significance for the further socioeconomic development of our republic. The necessity and effectiveness of building the AYaM is shown by the experience of operating the first sector of the meridional railroad called the Little BAM. In a situation where, unfortunately, our main BAM has in fact still not gone into operation, the Little BAM from Tynda to Berkakit—Neryungra, according to the data of the Yakut Scientific Center—has already paid for itself and each provides a profit for the nation.

At present, the realization of the AYaM Project (the first stage to the town of Tommot) is threatened due to the shortage of financing for the work being done here. We realize the importance and acute need for saving money, but for all considerations, even the most justified, this cannot be achieved at the expense of curtailing work on the AYaM. In light of the completely valid idea in the report of Mikhail Sergeyevich Gorbachev, it must be emphasized that the AYaM construction capacity which has already been established exceeds the amount of capital investments allocated up to now, and could significantly accelerate the construction of this important project.

In all the stages of our socialist construction, we have worked under the slogan "Everything for the Sake of Man!" However, the deformations of our socialist principles often brought us the reverse results. To find the real ways for overcoming this, in my view, is the main duty of the corps of people's deputies. And it is important to find these paths in the brief interval of time allocated to us. Any delay costs the nation too dearly. And the more we delay the more we must pay. Thank you for your attention. (Applause).

B.Ye. Paton: The floor is given over to Deputy Chernichenko. Deputy Kalish will speak next.

Yu.D. Chernichenko, commentator of the Agriculture Section of Central Television (Gagarinskiy Territorial Electoral District, Moscow): I was born in a place where even in the 1960's you could hear a grandmother comforting her grandchild: "Dear, the Muscovite is coming, the Muscovite is coming." There was no underlying national slur here. The good woman merely wanted to frighten her disobedient child. But when the pre-congress period began, and after the euphoria of the elections—there were 12 people for each place—we got into a squeeze, into a situation of dictated lists and unannounced programs, when there was a real struggle of

Eighth Session

1 June 1989

power for power seemingly honestly and openly chosen by the people, and then there arose the image of the "Muscovite," the bug-bear, the troublemaker from the capital. He set off to capture the rather zealous minds which were predisposed for this. The poorhouse of political education on Trubnaya Square—and in 5 weeks it in fact became a house of political education! There people assembled who were known throughout the nation. And during the night they forged, so to speak, inadmissible things—the general concept and program of this congress!

It makes no sense to involve the leadership (we must live together) but I should secretly report that sitting in with us were both Lev Nikolayevich Zaykov, the first Moscow secretary, and even Anatoliy Ivanovich Lukyanov.

What we hatched up, put together, what seems such a danger for us, was duplicated and sent out to the deputies at a meeting of the RSFSR delegation, not without serious resistance. Who, it might be asked, allowed you?

The story of the Moscow group is fear of a real political initiative. And the initiative evoked a counterinitiative of punishment. Having sensitively picked up the half-voice command, some proposed that the professor be reforged in a shop—a purely Mao Zedong strategem—a second brought up the question of the deficit, while a third point out "this is where all the trouble about leasing and cooperatives comes from!" A charming female deputy from Kazakhstan even deprived them of her female disposition.

Obedient indignation, let us recall, quite recently belittled Pasternak, slandered Tvardovskiy, and hounded Sakharov with "crucify him." But older people, somewhat more experienced than the difficult female delegate, should have a sympathy for the academician or writer who swears constantly when he has given way to weakness and signed a base document. But there is nothing to be done; you cannot shake this in the people's memory or in history. And as a result—on the Supreme Soviet—for one reason or another we lack the economists Abalkin, Bogmolov, Shelev, Tikhonov, Petrakhov, and Popov, and, naturally, the sociologist Zaslavskaya and the historian Afanasyev are not to be found there. There are virtually no lawyers. There is not a single public affairs writer—I ask you to consider—who is widely read by the nation! What is this, an outburst of the Cultural Revolution? Or "the Moor has done his duty, let him go?" Only please, don't talk to me about rotation. Everyone realizes that here there is no random chance, and the old kolkhoz saying is correct: "The machine does not go itself but the tractor operator drives the machine." (Applause).

The new wine of selective enthusiasm has been poured into the old wineskins of the party dictatorship, and this is the heart of the problem. I am an old Communist; I have been a member for around 40 years. In translation "party" means a "part." And when the part becomes bigger than the whole, the need arises of danger and conspiracy. Elections were never communist things. The people clearly separated the party and the bureaucratic ruling apparatus. But during the pre-congress time, the apparatus silently took revenge and began to approve at the Central Committee plenum even the leaders of the parliamentary commissions, giving rise to disobedience of the most pliable, and reading lists which none of the officials had drawn up. The anonymity of initiative, the behind-the-scenes deals—what an anachronism! How this was savored by the vengeful orators of the April plenum who considered themselves the first, but in the elections emerged last.

If the millions of those who have awakened to political life reject the okrug meetings as the initial step of bureaucracy, then they will never approve the final filters, the practice of the broken firing pin, the method of stipulating "as a rule" and "as an exception," whereby the problems are dissipated to the winds. "Divide and rule!" does not work anymore. If you want to rule productively, then combine and achieve the goal! (Applause).

But it is not I who says this. "You elected us? For what? In order for us to argue, reason and decide. But if in all disputes one sees deviations, then it would be better to use dolls or dummies. But who then would think for these dummies?" These are the words of Aleksey Ivanovich Rykov, the first chairman of the Council of People's Commissars after Lenin! (Applause).

Restructuring has proven itself. We have survived. If according to the count of Lenin's NEP [New Economic Policy] of 1921, then we are already living in 1925, and by this time the nation was fed, shod, and the People's Commissar Kraski had not been able to export the Russian grain for gold. "Tell Gorbachev to feed the people!" exclaims one very zealous admirer of restructuring over there, on the other side of the cordon. He clearly has tsarist views, and he feels, like many of us, that this can be done by one man. We, thank heavens, have concluded that "no one will provide us with deliverance—neither God, tsar nor hero." And a coercive agricultural system will never feed the people!

We have spent a good deal on our approach to the truth, and this is quite natural. We cannot blame either nature, which in our regions has created all the natural and climatic zones of the world, nor our unfortunate soil, which contains almost 190 million hectares of Chernozem, an adornment of our planet. There is only one guilty party: the causes of human poverty and the dying of our arable land, and these are exclusively political factors. (Applause).

Stalinism in agriculture is an economic vendee. It is not merely capable of torpedoing restructuring, but is already doing this. We must not exploit the word "plan." A plan which is methodically not carried out, which

Eighth Session
1 June 1989

somehow drags along by completely unacceptable confiscations from another sector, or from hidden bloodsucking, so to speak, by exchanging our oil for the grain of others—this is not a plan. This is something else, and we must find a word for it, then provide it with the word "Gos" or something "Gosplan."

No matter how you try, you would never be able to explain to an intelligent person an economy which produces on a per capita basis 5-fold more tractors and 10-fold more combines than the United States, but produces almost 2-fold less grain. But that is only half of the problem. It produces 3 times as many shoes (it would be better if it did not produce them!) than the United States. But there are other things. For example, sugar. Thank goodness my grandson has learned to take his ration card and go stand in line for sugar. We have 31 kg of it on a per capita basis, while the United States has 22 and there is no line and no ration coupons (now there are coupons in Moscow). But in comparison with industry, we produce 6 times more ore than the United States but 6-fold less modern synthetic resins and plastics than the U.S. Why such an industry?

Or for electronics. Present here is the respected, and our top counter, Comrade Osipyan. I learned with terror that he—a leading electronics expert and a great specialist in physics—used an abacus for calculating. This, I feel, will go down in history. (Applause). Yes, the system which seemed arrested in 1926 by the ruble and by the commanding but not responsible apparatus has led to national humiliation. Let us not be the children who think that Buratino, a wooden puppet, their favorite, moves by himself. Behind him stands the puppeteer. We have literally agreed (because this is the 7th day we are meeting and there has not been a single word about the complete dictatorship of the party apparatus) that not a single hair will fall from the cow without the approval or command of the Central Committee Agriculture Department!

We do not accept this although we beat upon Murakhovskiy. I must admit I am a defender of Murakhovskiy. At 168 electoral and writer meetings I said that Comrade Murakhovskiy is not guilty of anything. Over the door of his office you could write as in an American saloon: "Please don't shoot the pianist, he is playing the best he knows how." Because up to 8 deputies and ministers are sitting in the office and reception room of the deputy head of the Central Committee department. Everyone knows this but this need not be said. In a well-brought up society, this is considered impolite.

I am a great fan of television, and now I watch with enormous interest the television educational programs of Yegor Kuzmich Ligachev. He travels about the country, and he learns a great deal clearly because this is a new sector for him (applause) and he willingly shares it with us. I am crazy about this. Such cultural propaganda, and he is taking away the livelihood of many television journalists, and this is fine. I merely want to say, I want to ask, as I was asked 168 times, why in a politically essential sector, a sector which determines the possibility and future of restructuring, have they placed a man who understands nothing of this, and who has failed in ideology? How can this happen?! (Applause). I do not know.

I am aware that bureaucracy is supranational, and the Russian official also was the same type as the Marxist Prussian functionary and he equally esteemed the miracle, secrecy, and authority. But a concrete nation, a given society, a given association of nations can be humiliated by the bureaucracy, and very productively so. In my view, the bureaucracy humiliates it in a minimum of three ways. As for the total of nations—I do not want to become involved in these disputes because this concerns all of us.

And the first, which alas was not mentioned at this congress, is our shameful exports. We export 200 million tonnes of oil. Who has not stood by his car with an empty gas tank? Some 200 million tonnes of oil a year and predominantly crude! Are our heads being turned by the glory of the emirates? Certainly this is the squandering of our grandchildren's heritage. A true master could not do this. This is an humiliation of me before my grandson. I do not know what I will have to pass on to him.

The opposite bothers me, too. I am humiliated by our imports. The importing of what is grown on our own lands, things and materials which are completely replaceable, the importing of grain, meat and fats is extremely advantageous to the person who sells this and disruptive for the person who buys it.

Do not believe, respected audience, do not believe, deputies, that we purchase some second-rate, some unnecessary grain. Nothing of the sort! Last year according to Goskomstat [State Statistics Committee], we purchased 21 million tonnes of wheat. Name someone who could explain why these 21 million tonnes were purchased when the nation produces the same wheat and 2-fold more than it itself requires? Where is the schizophrenia, and where is the logic? And after this how can you call the Gosplan an authoritative institution? This has lasted not a year but decades. Last year I counted 25 years, a quarter-century jubilee for this antinational practice. And when I am asked: "Does Murakhovskiy believe in kolkhozes?" I say: "Between you and me, no." "Does he believe in sovkhozes?" I say: "In no manner." "Why?" Well, because he would have paid his own first, and over the 25 years everything would have been grown at home, in our nation. Because Kazan, Ryazan, the Kuban, and Kulunda would long have adjusted to these monstrous billions, and the nation of socialism would not appear as an international sponger, as it now does abroad.

Finally, the third and last stage of humiliation. This is a technical humiliation. We have become backward people everywhere, do you realize? The Estonians have the word "Russian work," and this can exist between neighbors. This "Russian work" is bad but, unfortunately, the Estonian article and the Karakalpak are also bad. Are we to blame for this? Are we genetically this way? No! The political system is to blame which can lead but without

STENOGRAPHIC RECORD

Eighth Session
1 June 1989

being responsible for this. At present, I simply can't keep within the time....

I participated in the agrarian note—in that extensive and, in my view, very business-like note—which was read to you yesterday by the respected agrarian deputies. This is also an example of a group and there is nothing wrong with this.

I merely request one thing in these last seconds. Don't mix up, don't tie up everything in "later—later." "Tomorrow, tomorrow and not today" are words not only of lazy persons, but also said by political masters who can make things far removed so that at present short circuits do not arise. They are not short but rather very long! We are on the edge of such dissatisfaction, the edge of such irritation! The poisons of lines and family irritations have so stuffed the national liver that we can expect the most unpleasant of things.

I am a conciliator. I want to lead people from the meeting to work, I want to divert them from conversations or from strikes. You have everything, you are rich. You have been given land. I propose along with the Moscow group that a Land Law be adopted. Let us repeat out loud Lenin's words "from food requisitioning to a food tax," which were the most revolutionary after the words "All power to the soviets!" in the sense of national salvation and the calming of passions, in the sense of eliminating the food shortage in 2 or 3 years. Now, and not sometime later! If we at the next session, our autumn meeting, do not solemnly pass, with the singing of the national anthems, a Land Law, then we are not worth a brass farthing. There will be no more trust in us.

About the Moscow group: Let us remove the word "Moscow." We have just as many people from Chelyabinsk and Orenburg who are asking for a human dialogue, from Kamchatka and Chukotka, from Kursk and who knows where.... We, it seems, have been granted the Small Auditorium in the Presidium of the Supreme Soviet. We invite everyone, including Meshalkin. It is a pity that Nina Andreyeva is not here; we would invite her with great satisfaction as an indicator of innovation. Thank you! (Applause).

B.Ye. Paton: The floor is turned over to Deputy Kalish. The next to speak will be Deputy Mazurov.

V.N. Kalish, steelcaster at the A.N. Kuzmin Dneprospetsstal [Dnieper Special Steel] Electrometallurgical Plant, the Ukraine, Zaporozhye (from the CPSU): Respected deputies, it is a great honor for a worker to come up on this rostrum. I thank the Presidium for granting such an opportunity. But I find it difficult to speak from this rostrum of this first congress. A great responsibility has been placed in our hands. For this reason I immediately want to tell you, comrades: We must not divide up here into deputies who have come to the congress from the territorial or nationality districts and deputies from the social organizations.

I feel that my electors would find it unpleasant to hear if I were called such a deputy. We cannot be divided into a minority and majority. This happened outside your desire. The people expect a great deal from us and from the congress. And we do not have the right to deceive their hopes.

Of course, with the end of the congress there will be no more meat or consumer goods on the store shelves, but we must outline a realistic path for escaping from the arising crisis situation. In working out the tactics of these solutions we should employ everything reasonable that has been brought here by the "majority" as well as the offended "minority." Each of us represents a definite region of the nation with its troubles, misfortunes and problems. I, having become a deputy from the CPSU, here represent workers from Zaporozhye. A majority of us used as the basis of our pre-election program the Appeal of the CPSU Central Committee to the Party and to the Soviet People. In the pre-election meetings we promised the people to use all our deputies' powers to provide the best possible solution to the food problem, the housing problem, the problem of consumer goods production, and ecological problems.

The report of Comrade Gorbachev provided an analysis of realizing these problems on a national scale. Many speakers also made their own proposals. It is my opinion that while at present we can note shifts in housing construction, virtually no progress has been made in solving the Food Program. This also is true of the production of consumer goods, and here things are even worse. My contacts with the peasantry provide grounds for stating that the decisions of the March plenum, which everyone was expecting so eagerly, have not been borne out. People are stating directly that the people cannot be fed by leasing alone. Here I support the agrarian specialists and their appeal to the congress. The countryside must be helped, or, as the press noisily put it, we must repay our debts to the countryside. I realize that it will be difficult to find the funds in the nation required for this, but find them we must; otherwise restructuring will collapse. For 4 years we have been talking and holding meetings, but nothing has happened. My proposal is to instruct the government, beginning in 1990, to stop issuing the ferrous metallurgical enterprises a 100-percent state order, but rather draw this up within the limits of 80 percent. The remaining 20 percent and everything produced above the plan would be turned over to the needs of the countryside and, first of all, for resolving such fundamental problems as water supply and gas supply of the villages. (Applause).

Among the many problems which beset our life, one has appeared which in terms of acuteness has in a number of places entered the category of primary. This is the ecological problem. Linked to it is the appearance of

Eighth Session

1 June 1989

various informal associations, spontaneous and organized meetings, demonstrations, and various ultimatums. This problem has arisen with particular acuteness in Zaporozhye, which is on the list of cities with an elevated level of atmospheric pollution. The question is not a new one, and it has been raised repeatedly from the rostrum of the last sitting of the Supreme Soviet. It has been raised on the pages of newspapers and magazines as well as on the Zaporozhye-Moscow telelink.

I do not want to give the number of tonnes of dust, gases and carcinogenic substances which fall on the heads of the people of Zaporozhye as well as the illnesses related to this. I will say one thing: Decisive measures are required not only by us but also by the government. We are told: Here is money for you, take it and build treatment facilities. But that is not the problem. The Zaporozhye Metallurgical Combine was built in the 1930's by the entire nation for the needs of the entire nation. In the 1940's, all the enterprises rose from the ruins of the war, incidentally, on the same foundations and with the same prewar equipment. All of this led to an extreme degree of backwardness, and the plant was at the end of the line. No treatment facilities would help things. A fundamental reconstruction of all the enterprises of ferrous and nonferrous metallurgy was required on the basis of employing new waste-free or low-waste, ecologically clean production methods. The entire nation needs our products, and for this reason we request aid from the government, realizing all the difficulties related to this. Possibly, as an exception, the Zaporozhye enterprises should be permitted to conclude contracts for reconstruction with foreign firms under the conditions of subsequent repayment in metal or other types of products produced in the oblast. If the experiment is a success, it could be repeated in other cities. Sooner or later life itself will force us to take this step.

A third question which I would like to raise. It is a question of social justice. In the press, as is seen from the debates at our congress, certain comrades primitively reduce this merely to depriving the so-called bureaucrats of their illegally obtained goods. We are pleased that Mikhail Sergeyevich in his report proposed establishing a commission to review all these benefits. I do not want to reduce the essence of the question merely to this. I would like to ask the question of why, regardless of the constant propaganda by our press for the various types of cooperatives, the working class is largely hostile to them. Because the cooperatives have not produced tangible fruits. And the possibility of obtaining enormous income has caused excitement in the minds of many people. As a result, we are observing a clear outflow of skilled manpower from the state enterprises. Incidentally, this is skilled—I would even say the most skilled. Here it has been said that it is the smart ones leaving there. They leave for where they can earn more money quickly. I, as a steelcaster, cannot earn such money, and for this reason I want to say: What would happen if we, the skilled steelcasters, left for cooperatives? Then who would produce the high-quality metal for you? Where would you obtain metal for aircraft and satellites? For normal equipment, so that here they did not complain of the combines and other machines? Would you find them in cooperatives? I feel that here it is an issue of the collapse of state enterprises. (Applause). As for the cooperatives, Mikhail Sergeyevich, here, in this auditorium, at the 19th party conference, on the Commission for Preparing a Draft Resolution, you stated to us that you would not allow the cooperatives to steal from the pockets of the workers. I want to report to you that they are not only stealing from our pockets but are undressing us, trying to make off with our very skins. (Applause).

As a consequence of this there has been a polarization: at one end the Soviet millionaires, and at the other, the workers who can barely make ends meet. (Applause). The cooperatives have become a convenient form for legalizing stolen money. (Applause).

Or take another question concerning social justice. Don't let the people of Moscow, Kiev and other inhabitants of capitals take offense here. In Moscow and in the other capital cities, meat and sausages are sold at the state price. Why should I, a steelcaster, and thousands like me, purchase all of this at cooperative prices, although I know that all of this is shipped off to Moscow from my oblast? (Applause). I would like to hear advice from the economists on how to feed people justly.

One last thing. As a Communist, a steelcaster with 30 years experience, and holding an activist position in life all the time, I cannot help but take up one important, in my view, problem. It is the question of the party apparatus. I would request that we not attack it so. Respected Deputy Drutse went so far as to say that I, a brigade leader of the steelcasters, am also a party apparatchik. How can one do such a thing? It is impossible to attack "in general." We were not sent here by the voters to hang labels on one another or sink to interfering in the activities of the State Security Committee and insulting it. We came here to work on our problems. (Applause).

The party apparachiks. How many have I seen! All of them came from the worker collectives. We promoted to the apparatus those who conscientiously carried out their duties. And now they have been left absolutely socially unprotected. (Applause).

I say this because I frequently meet with them. I know many of them. And they tell me: Do you know, Vitaliy, it is hard for us now; we barely even dare admit where we work. Although they are literally being "executed," and "put up against the wall" for the shortage of soap and matches, salt, meat and milk. And who would choose all of this for us to at least feed the people? Comrades, we must not confuse one with the other, we must not cover up and, believe me, we, the working class will understand.

Respected comrade scientists. It is you who created the plans, it is you who palmed off the plans on the Politburo. (Applause). And we fulfilled them. Why, then, have I not heard your constructive proposals here? Although the Moscow group to some degree presented

Eighth Session

1 June 1989

them. But you merely criticize. And whom? Criticize yourselves. Let us begin to see to it that we do not make up and do not force the fulfillment of bad plans. Production must not work for the mere sake of production.

Due to the press, certain hotheads have endeavored to link all the difficulties of restructuring to these fellows from the party apparatus. Probably it is a question of something else, something larger. Having begun with the cadres of the party apparatus, more and more blows are being directed against the party itself. I feel that the fire which has been opened up by the bodies of the CPSU Central Committee against the party staffs cannot be viewed other than as a shot in the back. (Applause).

Comrade deputies! The working class is in favor of restructuring, and there is no return to stagnation. The guarantee for the success of restructuring should be the unity of our actions. We do not have the right to permit ethnic discord, to set one people against the other or isolate one from the other. It is essential to strengthen the Union of Soviet Socialist Republics. Thank you for the attention. (Applause).

B.Ye. Paton: The floor is given to Deputy Kirill Trofimovich Mazurov, chairman of the All-Union War and Labor Veterans Council. Deputy Grakhovskiy will speak next.

K.T. Mazurov, pensioner, chairman of the All-Union War and Labor Veterans Council, Moscow (from the All-Union War and Labor Veterans Organization): Comrade deputies! In our nation and society we have accumulated numerous shortages. Here they have mentioned, in addition to such scarcities as sugar, soap and other goods, also an immune insufficiency. We all realize that all these shortages must be eliminated. But I would like to take up one shortage which no one has mentioned: the shortage of gratitude for the veterans who ensured the victory in the Great Patriotic War and who provided for all of us and our children a peaceful life. And they are living, forgive me, under very harsh conditions. (Applause).

My comrades and I, some 75 people's deputies, represent over 50 million pensioners, veterans of the war and labor, the party, and the Armed Forces. In the past, this social group was not considered as a political force. Unfortunately, the inertia of such thinking is still found today. There are even scientific works where respected scientists, in examining the forces of restructuring, put our brother in the same group as the declassed elements. These scientists are unaware that of these 50 million, 10 million war and labor veterans—elderly people—are working and are producing material goods. And an even larger number of persons would still be working if they would eliminate the various impediments such as the so-called "ceilings" on wages and so forth.

The veterans are in no way invalids. They have earned the right to a normal attitude from society. When the All-Union Veterans Organization was organized, the All-Union Veterans Council in 1967 decided to check on how the veterans were living. With the aid of other social organizations and with support from the party and soviet bodies, we checked on the lives of more than 30 million persons. This check showed a gloomy picture, comrades. Over 22 million of our war and labor veterans receive a pension of R60 a month and less. Of this number, 10 million are individuals alone who have no other sources of existence. You can imagine what a life it is for them who have guaranteed our current democracy.

Thousands of letters have been sent to all levels, to the All-Union Veteran Council and to the congress and to the press organs; these letters complain about the state of affairs which has developed in our nation for the older generation. I will not abuse your attention but will merely give certain excerpts from one letter which was received yesterday. It is a collective letter from Yoshkar-Ola, the Mari ASSR [Autonomous Soviet Socialist Republic], and which was signed by a large group of war participants. Here is what they write: "Some 44 years have passed since Victory Day. And many victors eke out a meager existence on miserly pensions which have been earned twice by military service and peaceful labor. For decades we have produced and we still repeat fine slogans such as 'No one has forgotten us' and 'Each has been awarded according to merit' and that we are all in an unpaid debt to the war veterans. But when will we pay these debts? In a humane socialist society this is inhumane and antihumane. The solution to this question must not be put off to tomorrow. Certainly we are building and at present are restructuring the most humane and highly moral socialist society in the world. What example we set and how we are able to care for the elderly, particularly the defenders of the motherland, determine not only the moral climate of all society but primarily the attitude toward us of the younger generation, its moral health, and an understanding of the real values of true socialism. It must always be remembered that we reap what we sow and we are sowing.... Let us make a proposal: The year 1990 is to be declared a year of war and labor veterans, and we will actually do everything to free the old soldiers of the ordeals and troubles, the soldiers who seek a pitiable handout from our common table while they themselves made a major contribution to this long ago through their unstinting labor. We must not take from them their last health and belief in those ideals for which they fought, so that at the end of their years, before departing from life, none of them bears hard thoughts or an insult from the state. (Loskutov, Senatorov, Mosunov, Fedorin, Shvetsov, Mitin, Savelyev, Semenov, Cherkasov, Krylov, Medvedev and others)...."

The All-Union Veterans Council has repeatedly examined these questions and submitted proposals to the central leadership bodies. A number of decisions has been taken. I must tell the truth. After April 1985, the Central Committee and government have done a good deal in this regard. But all of these have been less than fundamental measures. The veterans are demanding a fundamental solution to the question. We must feed these people primarily; we must show affection primarily for them. And recently the situation has developed in

Eighth Session

1 June 1989

such a way that as a consequence of the uncontrolled rise in prices for goods and the erosion of cheap goods, the situation of the war and labor veterans and those who have earned a special attitude towards themselves has recently become simply intolerable.

I feel that far from all the deputies have any idea of in what a calamitous state the veterans of the Great Patriotic War live. It is essential to solve this painful problem. We, the 75 people's deputies of the veteran organization, have submitted concrete proposals to the congress, and request that they be reviewed either by a special commission or instruct the Supreme Soviet this very year to resolve the following questions:

1. To find, already this year, R400 million in order to bring the pensions up to a subsistence minimum for the war veterans and the military widows who receive R50 a month and less. (Applause).

2. In the new pension law, review the question of providing the veterans and partisans with a priority status and grounds for receiving increased pensions. We are the only nation of our allies which participated in World War II where the veterans, the fighters of the front and the partisan rear, have not received special pensions, but have received working pensions and the lowest ones.

3. We should begin carrying out the new law in 1990, even before its ratification. And in 1990, we should not begin by regions, as has always been done before, but rather by social groups in increasing the pensions to a subsistance minimum, primarily for the participants in the war and the labor veterans who receive pensions under R60 a month.

I propose that the congress support this proposal.

But this is not the only question. The veterans have not been shown sincere attention. Particularly valuable in this regard are the statements recently published in the newspaper SOVETSKAYA KULTURA by the well known artists Lyudmila Zykina, Yuriy Nikulin, Alla Pugacheva, Irma Sakhadze, Gennadiy Khazanov, and other of our well-known cultural figures, under the motto "The Warmth of Our Hearts for the Veterans." They have urged writers, composers, scientists, artists, and actors to participate in the life of the veterans, particularly those who live in residential homes and our almshouses, and to deduct from fees and from concerts certain amounts directly for these veteran homes as well as to the charity and health fund which has also been organized for these purposes. They write in their appeal: "However, man does not live by bread alone. We are thousands, if not hundreds of thousands. If each of us just once a year would visit the veterans, this would be a continuous line of an unending noble deed—this will be our contribution to great restructuring which has aroused the finest traditions of humanism in the Russian and Soviet multinational culture." We feel that this noble movement should touch the hearts not only of the creative intelligentsia.

The next question. We, the frontline veterans and the partisans who with each passing year are fewer and fewer (approximately 400,000 leave us forever each year), are bothered and insulted not only by the callous attitude of the bureaucrats, but also by the frequently appearing insulting and disrespectful attitude by a certain portion of our citizens. Certain partisans and frontline veterans are reticent to wear their combat orders. They put them on only on 9 May because they do not want to hear insulting comments in the store lines, on streetcars and buses. Such an immoral attitude toward the war veterans, unfortunately, is fostered by frequent publications in our press in which the 70-year history of our country is represented as a solid chain of mistakes and crimes, and the entire older generation is to blame for these crimes.

It is inadmissible when, in analyzing the military period of our history, some draw irresponsible conclusions, blackening the military feat of the people, giving humiliating descriptions of the Red Army Command, and mocking the Soviet soldier, although they should bow down to the ground to him for the fact that they live free. (Applause).

Soon it will be 45 years since the war ended, and still thousands of unknown Soviet soldiers still remain unburied, their bones turning white in trenches overgrown by brush, in the forests and swamps of Novgorod, Leningrad and certain other oblasts, where the hottest fighting against the Nazis occurred. Many fraternal graves and monuments have been abandoned, and in some places they have simply been torn down. Our thanks to the Komsomol for being actively concerned with research work and seeking out the war heroes, but it is not the job of the Komsomol any more than the old veterans to commit the remains of the dead to the ground or to properly bury deceased veterans. This is a matter for the corresponding executive committees of the soviets who have forgotten these sacred duties of theirs.

The veterans are also indignant over the fact that up to now Moscow has no monument to the Great Victory. (Applause). The Museum of the Great Patriotic War and the Victory Park are being turned into a long drawn-out project and significant amounts of money collected by the people have been wasted.

Comrades, we must show particular concern for our younger generation. Comrade Gorbachev and other deputies have already said here that there are numerous negative phenomena among our youth. Our young people live in inactivity. It is paradoxical, but still a fact, that in our state the children working in a majority of families are raised for "doing nothing." The question of labor in our country is overshadowed by the question of leisure. Both in the countryside and in the city the juveniles often grow up under conditions of idleness; they roam about the streets, deafening their ears with rock music, strumming on guitars, humming senseless tunes, and giving vent to unspent youthful energy.

The Komsomol has submitted a proposal to adopt a Youth Law. But it seems to me that the question is more

STENOGRAPHIC RECORD

Eighth Session
1 June 1989

complex. I would like to make a proposal to instruct the Supreme Soviet to work out an overall plan for the comprehensive labor, moral, and cultural education of the younger generation, with a priority for socially useful physical labor (applause) and bring this problem to the level of state policy.

A few words on the course of discussing our restructuring processes. May I request one more minute of attention?

Restructuring to which the party has raised our people is a very serious undertaking. A difficult undertaking. Each step requires a thoughtful, competent approach. But as before, we often show incompetence and a hurry in adopting new decisions and laws, and this is no guarantee against new mistakes.

We are constantly urging each to work at full strength in his job. These appeals remain mere good intentions without increasing the demands placed on each of us by society. Each should work at full strength under the control of all! This is the sort of slogan that is needed.

The crisis phenomena in the economy and in providing the people with everything essential are explained not only by the timidity of the legislators and the conservatism of the apparatus. The shortcomings in carrying out economic reform are to be explained by banal lack of discipline, by the absence of order and exactingness, and even, I would say, by certain concessions by our state bodies.

In society not only have ideas appeared, but also the prophets and the structures are forming, which repudiate socialism and argue in favor of capitalist-type market relations and even a multiparty system. These are prophets who are incompatible with our ideology, but they are not being given a proper rebuff. If we do not have laws which provide social protection for the people, which strictly regulate socialist law and order and protect the rights of the individual, including the leaders who have the trust of the people, and if we do not ensure their strict execution by each citizen, then we will receive not the flourishing of democracy but rather the tyranny of permissiveness and anarchy.

We, the people's deputies, bear great responsibility in preventing such things. Comrade Gorbachev has spoken here about the consolidation of forces. This is a correct slogan. Not the fanning of passions at the congress itself and among the voters, but rather a comradely comparison of opinions and the adoption of the most effective decisions—this is the law of our congress and all our deputies.

Under the conditions of the active involvement of the broad masses of workers in all spheres of life, and under the conditions of the diversity of opinions and the learning of the rudiments of democracy by the people, only under the leadership of the Communist Party can the people realize restructuring. There is no other way. Thank you. (Applause).

STENOGRAPHIC RECORD

B.Ye. Paton: The floor is turned over to Deputy Aleksandr Adamovich Grakhovskiy.

A.A. Grakhovskiy, chairman of the ispolkom [executive committee] of Gomel Oblast Soviet of People's Deputies (Rechitsa National-Territorial Electoral District, Belorussian SSR): Dear comrade deputies! I would like to devote the bulk of my statement to our national tragedy—the accident at the Chernobyl AES. And I would ask your forgiveness for beginning with a situation that is so sad and simultaneously so shameful for us. With every passing day the accident recedes farther and farther into history, but it has not lost its seriousness. Today it is one of the most painful situations in our public life. But first of all it is the heartfelt pain, the unrest, and the tribulations of the population that has suffered. Because the alarm and the concern that we heard in the statement made by a poet whom we respect, Boris Ilich Oleynik, is closer to us and more understandable by us than by anyone else.

I would also like to dwell on this question because the elimination of the consequences of the accident requires not only, and not so much, local efforts, but primarily the participation of the entire country.

We suffered this misfortune from the very first days of the accident. And today we carry the brunt of its consequences on our shoulders. Our burden is certainly no light one, since, with regard to the percentage of the contaminated territory in the European part of the USSR, Gomel Oblast occupies the leading place.

I would like you to understand the following. I am speaking from this high rostrum as one of the direct participants in the work on eliminating the consequences of the accident. I am speaking about this not with the purpose of advertising myself, but so that you can be completely aware of our everyday concerns and alarms.

At first we did not remain in bitter solitude. The entire country came to our assistance, thanks to which a series of operations were carried out to resolve the first-priority tasks. However, the steps that are being taken are not removing the seriousness of the situation. The radiation situation on the territory of the oblast remains complicated. Practical experience and scientific prognosis indicate that we should not expect any substantial improvement of the situation within the next few years.

We carried out the evacuation of the population in three stages. As of today, there are inhabited places in the oblast where the carrying out of agricultural reclamation measures in combination with engineer decontamination and the improvement of services and utilities does not guarantee people's safe residence. It will be necessary to carry out a fourth resettlement. But in order for it to be the last one, it is necessary to consider in the most

Eighth Session

1 June 1989

serious manner the radiation situation and the possible dosage loads that have been placed on each individual inhabited place.

Nor can we remove from the agenda the problems in the social and everyday spheres. The USSR Ministry of Public Health, within the shortest period of time, must make a determination with regard to this problem, and must make the appropriate recommendation to us. I feel that it is appropriate to turn to scientists as a whole. And to appeal to you, our respected scientific comrades, to increase considerably the intensity of scientific-research work as a whole in our Chernobyl area, which—implying no offense to you—was the result also of your activity. Here I completely share the point of view of respected Vasiliy Ivanovich Belov. Unfortunately, during the three years since the accident, we have not received an effective technological scheme, or any mechanisms or means to decontaminate the inhabited places or the agricultural land, and a number of other problems and questions continue to be unresolved.

As a result of the isolation of a considerable amount of the land, and also the need to supply the population in the contaminated territory with shipped-in meat and dairy products, the food question in the oblast has become seriously complicated. The losses incurred by the oblast, and its needs to provide the population with food products in conformity with the scientifically substantiated standards, are not being taken into consideration by the planning agencies.

As you can see, the situation is obviously abnormal, and it is creating increased social tension. We constantly raised these questions at USSR Gosplan and USSR Gosagroprom, and the Politburo of CPSU Central Committee issued instructions to deal with them, but so far no practical measures have been taken. We feel that the union shipments should be adjusted in order to taken into consideration our losses and the additional need to supply the population in the territory that has suffered. Our population has found itself in a disastrous situation not of its own fault, and its interests must be defended.

The questions of providing monetary grants to the population as a result of the limitation of the consumption of food products from the citizens' private plots have not been completely resolved. Persons of retirement age have proven to be in an especially difficult situation. More than 40,000 retirees who have been affected by the misfortune at Chernobyl have pensions that are below the average minimum income—approximately R50, or, more accurately, R47. Even under normal conditions it is very difficult to live on this kind of income, and under our conditions it is even more difficult. The resolution this question as rapidly as possible is our duty and, of course, our conscience.

You are well aware of how critical the question of providing highly qualified medical services to our population is. The necessary construction to create the appropriate medical institutions is under way, but there is nothing to fill them with: There continues to be a shortage of medical equipment, instruments, and medicines. With the current approaches, we shall not receive Soviet-produced equipment soon. The only way out is to purchase it abroad. We are well aware that the country does not have any extra currency, but, taking the unusual nature of the situation into consideration, it must be found somewhere.

There are problems in improving the health of the population, and especially that of children. We have begun to create our own base outside the confines of the oblast, but without assistance from outside, we will not be able to resolve this task. Questions of providing the population with personal radiation meters and other monitoring devices have been raised repeatedly. Instructions with regard to this question have also been issued by Politburo of the CPSU Central Committee, but the radiation meters and devices continue to be nonexistent. It seems to us that the time has come to ask several individuals to give a serious accounting of their lack of action.

Because of the contamination of a considerable amount of the forest area and peat bogs, there has been an annual reduction in the procurement of firewood and in the production of peat briquets. The shortage of fuel produced by the oblast will be more than 40 percent by the middle of the 13th Five-Year Plan. This circumstance, as well the medical and sanitation conditions in the territory, require the taking of immediate steps to decontaminate the entire oblast. In order to resolve promptly the Chernobyl and other serious social problems, we must carry out in a considerably more dynamic manner the construction of housing and of structures in the social and personal-services sphere. We do not ask to have construction workers sent to us from other parts of the country. But in this situation we feel that it necessary, starting next year, to release us from the construction of housing in Tyumen and, practically speaking, to stop the industrial construction in the oblast.

The list of unresolved questions and problems is a large one, but it could be considerably shorter if the USSR governmental commission on eliminating the consequences of the accident at the Chernobyl AES were to work more dynamically, and if it dealt not only with the nuclear power station, but also with the entire territory that has suffered. At the present time this list must be brought into the system. It is necessary for each point to determine the measures, time limits, executors, and funds. Taking into consideration the fact that the elimination of the consequences of the accident at the Chernobyl AES is something that will take a long time, the participation of union agencies is mandatory. We feel that there is a critical need during the current year, on the basis of an analysis of what has been done and also of the scientific forecasts, to develop in the country a Comprehensive USSR State Program for Eliminating the Consequences of the Accident at the Chernobyl AES. And in order for this document to be mandatory for everyone, it must be approved at USSR Supreme Soviet.

STENOGRAPHIC RECORD

Eighth Session

1 June 1989

This major measure will have a positive effect on the safety of the population and on the sociopolitical mood of a large part of the country, and will preclude a large number of approaches and primarily the speculation on the misfortune at Chernobyl. It will make it possible in a more meaningful manner to move forward along the path of fundamental socioeconomic and political reforms.

Comrades! The course of our congress, like the processes that have been occurring in the outlying areas, invite each of us to make very profound reflections. On the one hand, one can understand the attempt of the deputies to guarantee the stable and irreversible development of democracy and glasnost, and the most rapid resolution of the socioeconomic, interethnic, ecological, and other problems. On the other hand, one cannot fail to note that certain deputies are attempting to lead us away from the cardinal resolutions of the critical questions, and are making the attempt to force their point of view, which is at times a dubious one, on us. Instead of thoroughly studying the deeply underlying causes of a particular negative process and working out practical measures to resolve it, they call for rally-style democracy and for prolonged discussions and conversations which are necessary and which at times do little to help the situation.

I accept democratization and glasnost only if people have high self-discipline, organizational spirit, and responsibility for the job assigned to them, and if the person is completely aware of his role in society. In all their other manifestations, they take the form of demagoguery, with elements of anarchy and laxity. (Applause.)

Therefore I want to support the appeals that have been made in this auditorium—appeals for more constructive work, for the consolidation of all our efforts, and the responsible attitude of the deputies toward the resolution of the problems confronting us. Comrades, this is exceptionally important. Our congress must become, for the nation, a model, a school of an efficient, creative, profoundly interpreted approach to bringing our country out of its present condition.

I cannot agree with individual deputies who propose immediately, even before forming agencies of the congress or the government, to start to adopt laws and decrees. Of course we need laws. But I propose that developing a good legislative draft is no simple matter. Speed is not necessary here. Today it is completely obvious that, even earlier, much that was well thought-out, as a result of the hastiness in making a number of decisions and the failure to evaluate completely the possible socioeconomic consequences, received distorted development. This can be said about the weak aspects of the Law Governing the State Enterprise and the Law Governing the Cooperative System, and also about the measures to combat drunkenness and alcoholism.

Therefore, when developing the legislative drafts, it is more intelligent to rely on qualified legal thinking, on the national traditions and territorial peculiarities, the wisdom of all the peoples in our country, and the experience existing in the outlying areas. That is why I support the broad representation of all the social segments of the population in the USSR Supreme Soviet. Its formation simply according to the principle of the professionalism of the deputies cannot be a guarantee of the perfection of its functions. Each of us can participate constantly in the work of the Supreme Soviet, while maintaining a connection with his representation. And in this instance none of us should be insulted or vilified.

As a Communist and as a citizen, I am especially concerned that wholesale disparagement of the party cadres has begun. They were subjected to massive attacks during the election campaign, and we must not close our eyes to this. Their opponents did not balk at anything. They used false rumors, the falsification of the actual state of affairs, and other methods. I do not remove the responsibility from them, just as I do not remove it from any category of workers, for the miscalculations that they make or for the major shortcomings in society. We are all collectively guilty, and we must all work together to bring society to a new qualitative level. But the chosen method can lead to a loss of efficient cadres, and it is causing a large amount of harm to the party as a whole. And this will only harm our common cause. (Applause.)

B.Ye. Paton: Comrade deputies, inasmuch as time is running short, let us agree that Deputy Neumyvakin, who has already been scheduled to speak, will be given the floor after a lunch break. Are there any objections?

Voices from the floor: No.

B.Ye. Paton: Let us move on. On the instructions of the congress Presidium, Deputy Endel Teodorovich Lippmaa of the Estonian SSR will take the floor to make a proposal.

E.T. Lippmaa, director of the Estonian SSR Academy of Sciences Institute of Chemical and Biological Physics, Tallinn (Tallinnskiy-Tsentralnyy Electoral Okrug, Estonian SSR): Esteemed congress and esteemed guests! Many delegations and many speeches here have raised the question of the 1939 treaties with Nazi Germany. We are submitting a draft resolution for the analysis of these most complex problems. The draft runs as follows: "USSR Congress of People's Deputies resolution on setting up a commission to legally appraise the Soviet-German nonaggression treaty of 1939, the so-called Molotov-Ribbentrop pact, and the secret additional protocol to the pact." The USSR Congress of People's Deputies decrees: First, to make a political and legal appraisal of the Soviet-German nonaggression treaty of 1939 and the secret additional protocol—that is, the protocol on territorial and political reorganization in Eastern Europe, in particular in the Baltic area and Poland—and related documents, a commission should be set up comprising the following USSR people's deputies: Commission members: Lyudmila Akopovna Arutyunyan, department head at the Yerevan State University, Yerevan; Georgiy Arkadyevich Arbatov, director of

FIRST CONGRESS OF PEOPLE'S DEPUTIES OF THE USSR

Eighth Session

1 June 1989

the United States of America and Canada Institute; Yuriy Nikolayevich Afanasyev, rector of the Moscow State Historical Archives Institute, Moscow; Ilmar Olgertovich Bisher, professor at the Latvian Stuchka State University, Riga; Mavrik Germanovich Vulfson, senior teacher at the Latvian Academy of Arts, Riga; Igor Nikolayevich Gryazin, department chief at the Estonian SSR Academy of Sciences Institute of Philosophy, Sociology, and Law, Tartu; Aleksey Ivanovich Kazannik, department lecturer at Omsk State University, Omsk; Vitaliy Alekseyevich Korotich, chief editor of the journal OGONEK, Moscow; Vitautas Vitautovich Landsbergis, professor at the Lithuanian SSR State Conservatory, Vilnius; Maryu Yokhannesovna Lauristin, department head at Tartu State University, Tartu; Endel Teodorovich Lippmaa, director of the Estonian SSR Academy of Sciences Institute of Chemical and Biological Physics, Tallinn; Kazimir Vladislavovich Moteka, lawyer at the 1st Vilnius Legal Consultancy, Vilnius; Nikolay Vasilyevich Neyland, Latvian SSR deputy foreign minister, Riga; Edgar Elmarovich Savisaar, deputy director of the "Maynor" Special Planning and Design Bureau, Tallinn; Zita Leonovna Shlichite, lawyer at the Klaypeda Legal Consultancy, Klaypeda; Aleksey Mikhaylovich Ridiger, Metropolitan Aleksiy of Leningrad and Novgorod, Leningrad; and Valentin Mikhaylovich Falin, chief of the CPSU Central Committee International Department. Also one representative each for the Ukrainian, Belorussian, and Moldavian delegations. Incidentally, we also had suggestions on three possible candidates from the Ukraine, Belorussia, and Moldavia. Although, of course, it is a matter for their delegations, they were: Vladimir Ilarionovich Shinkaruk, director of the Institute of Philosophy; Vasiliy Vladimirovich Bykov, writer; and Ion Panteleyevich Drutse, writer. We propose Chingiz Aytmatov, writer, Frunze, as chairman of the commission. That is number one.

Second, the USSR Foreign Ministry and other departments and archives are to make available to the commission all the essential materials.

Third, the commission is to present its conclusion to the USSR Supreme Soviet by the end of this June and publish the results of its activity.

The question remains: Why such haste? Because 23 August this year is the 50th anniversary of the agreement with Hitler on the partitioning of Europe. Therefore we must do something right away. Moreover, there were proposals that the pact should be immediately denounced from the moment it was signed. This is not a bad proposal but, in the first place, many of our deputies do not know the text and, in the second place, this is not enough. Conclusions must be drawn fromn this. Declaring invalidity alone is not enough. Much flows from this, so the commission must be set up anyway. This draft was drawn up by deputies from the Estonian delegation with the active participation of Lithuania and Latvia, but, above all, our Presidium.

B.Ye. Paton: Comrade deputies, if there are no objections, let us approve the proposal put to us and vote. Any objections?

From the floor: No.

B.Ye. Paton: And the title of the commission? Deputy Yarovoy.

V.I. Yarovoy, director of the "'Dvigatel' State V.I. Lenin Union Plant," Tallinn (Tallinnskiy-Lasnamyaeskiy National-Territorial Electoral Okrug): Comrade deputies! There is much talk about this pact in the country as a whole and particularly in the Baltic region. For 18 months the indigenous population has actually been indoctrinated concerning this pact, and distrust has been aroused if the Estonian section of the population. As a result the non-Estonian part has been turned into "occupiers," "colonialists," and who knows what else. I believe that the commission which has been drawn up on the initiative of the Estonian deputies should not be allowed to consider the issue, because they have a stake in the solution of this question. (Applause).

B.Ye. Paton: Any more proposals, anyone else want to speak?

M.S. Gorbachev: There was a question comrades wanted to ask.

B.Ye. Paton: They ask for the title of the commission, the aim of the commission.

E.T. Lippmaa: The commission's aim is simple. So that there are no misunderstandings, so that we can move forward well and effectively. Not to kindle disagreements, but to solve the question, so that there is no superfluous discussion and we can work in a businesslike way.

B.Ye. Paton: Question, please.

Academician Zh.I. Alferov, director of the USSR Academy of Sciences A.F. Ioffe Physical and Technical Institute, Leningrad (from the USSR Academy of Sciences): I have a purely legal question about the treaty having lost its validity. I understood that the Molotov-Ribbentrop treaty lost its validity with the start of the war, on 22 June. (Applause).

One can forumulate one's attitude to the treaty very clearly. Like many others, I believe that the treaty was a disgraceful phenomenon in our history. But do we really need to discuss whether it has ceased to be valid or not? It ceased to be valid on 22 June, when the war started. (Applause).

STENOGRAPHIC RECORD

Eighth Session
1 June 1989

V.V. Ivanov, doctor of philological sciences, sector chief at the USSR Academy of Sciences Institute of Slavic and Balkan Studies, Moscow (from the USSR Academy of Sciences): I want to make a proposal on the procedure for discussing this question. The question is extremely important—perhaps one of the most important we are discussing at this session, and I would like to draw attention to the actual discussion procedure. Delegations from three republics have made a proposal. Of course, we could reject it by an absolute majority and thereby plunge ourselves into yet another very significant conflict within our federative state. I suggest using the method of consensus, which we use too little anyway. We do not need to bother with majority and minority. It is a method that has historically shown itself to be incorrect. We must seek a consensus. And it seems to me that proposals from three republics are enough for the congress to adopt this proposal by consensus. (Applause).

V.M. Semenov, secretary of Grodno Belorussian Communist Party Oblast Committee, Grodno (Grodnenskiy Territorial Electoral Okrug, Belorussian SSR): Comrades! As you can see, I am from western Belorussia. I am speaking on a procedural issue. We could end up with too many proposals, including urgent, serious, and important ones. We must not put all questions to the congress alone. I have a proposal: Instruct the newly elected Supreme Soviet to consider this issue.

Deputy (he did not give his name): Esteemed deputies, esteemed comrades in the Presidium. I support the comrade from western Belorussia and I want to say that we must set up a commission on Chernobyl, on the tragedy that occurred. And these secondary issues can wait. Because it was not only Belorussia and the Ukraine that were affected, but Russia too. The Supreme Soviet Presidium could decide these issues and submit them to our congress for its decision. And let us be constructive and businesslike in our approach to issues. Let us solve these issues. After all, the electorate expects really concrete action from us.

V.A. Berezov, second secretary of the Lithuanian Communist Party Central Committee, Vilnius (Tauragskiy National Territorial Electoral Okrug, Lithuanian SSR): I am a Russian. I ask you, deputies, to support this commission. It is the most painful issue for the Baltic peoples. And these problems must be solved. Because we are not discussing the Molotov-Ribbentrop pact. You have received the Lithuanian SSR Supreme Soviet's appeal. It has been distributed to everyone. The Lithuanian SSR Supreme Soviet is calling for a solution to this problem. It is a question not of the pact itself, but of the secret Molotov-Ribbentrop treaties. These secret treaties are being talked about all the time: They do not exist, they have been lost, and so on. And we deputies from Lithuania, Latvia, and Estonia cannot go home without solving this question. I beg you to back the commission. (Applause).

B.Ye. Paton: Please, go ahead.

I.Ya. Kezbers, Latvian Communist Party Central Committee Secretary, Riga (Kuldigskiy Territorial Electoral Okrug, Latvian SSR): Esteemed colleagues, there are many urgent questions, urgent issues. I represent Latvia. As we often say, that is one percent in many indicators. That is true. But our history is as dear to us as the entire history of our socialist homeland. I believe that it is necessary to back this commission and the idea of investigating this question, and we must at last give our people an answer: Yes, there have been black spots and blank spaces, but we are assessing them fairly. Therefore I ask you to support the proposal that has been made. (Applause).

I.N. Gryazin, department chief at the Estonian SSR Institute of Philosophy, Sociology, and Law, Tartu (Pyarnuskiy National-Territorial Okrug, Estonian SSR): This question has already been touched on: What to do with these treaties and protocols? It is a legal question. Denounce or not denounce? Annul or not annul? Incidentally, some suggested the rather original idea that part of the treaties lost their validity in 1941. An original idea, which also deserves consideration. And that is why the commission is being set up.

What are we talking about? Excuse me, but these eight lines of text need to be read out loud. "Moscow, 23 August 1939. Point one. In the event of territorial and political transformations in areas belonging to the Baltic states—Finland, Estonia, Latvia, Lithuania—the northern border of Lithuania will be the line separating the spheres of influence of Germany and the USSR. In this connection Lithuania's stake in the Vilno area is recognized by both sides. Second, in the event of territorial and political transformations in areas belonging to the Polish state, the spheres of influence of Germany and the USSR will be demarcated approximately by a line following the Narew, Wisla, and San rivers."

Further on there is a very interesting bit: "The question of whether it is desirable in the interests of both sides to preserve the independence of the Polish state and the question of the borders of that state can only be finally decided by the course of future political events. In any case, the two governments will resolve this question by means of a friendly agreement. Third. Concerning Southeast Europe. The Soviet side has indicated its interest in Bessarabia. The German side has clearly stated its total lack of interest politically in these territories. Fourth. This protocol is regarded as strictly secret by both sides. Signed by Joachim von Ribbentrop for the Government of Germany and by Vyacheslav Molotov, plenipotentiary representative of the Government of the USSR."

There is the text. That is what we are talking about. Correct or incorrect? What do we do with it? The commission is needed for this purpose. We cannot decide now; we need a commission. I ask you to vote for the commission. Thank you. (Applause. Noise in the hall).

STENOGRAPHIC RECORD

FIRST CONGRESS OF PEOPLE'S DEPUTIES OF THE USSR

Eighth Session

1 June 1989

E.E. Inkens, senior editor in the Latvian SSR State Committee for Television and Radio Broadcasting main television news editorial office, Riga (Tsesiskiy National-Territorial Electoral Okrug, Latvian SSR): I want to talk about the special significance these treaties have for the Baltic region. What we are saying here today is unprecedented. The whole world knows full well that these protocols exist. We in the Baltic area have also know this for a long time. And the reluctance to examine them here is like covering your ears when the truth is being told. And another thing. This treaty has not been eliminated, because, despite the outbreak of war in 1941, the Soviet Union concluded a special treaty with the emigre Polish government (in London) on the partial denunciation of this treaty. So, unfortunately, it still has some influence. And most importantly, the pernicious part of the treaty relates to the period 1939-1940. That is the period of annexations in the Baltic area.

Yu.Yu. Boldyrev, senior engineer at the Central Scientific Research Istitute of Marine Electrical Engineering and Technology, Leningrad (Moskovskiy Territorial Electoral Okrug, Leningrad, RSFSR): Esteemed comrades! I do not have a vested interest. I doubt whether there is any need at all to persuade you of the importance of this issue. But I want to draw your attention to the results of today's and yesterday's sessions. What we are doing is absolutely intolerable. Esteemed deputies, none of us, in my view, has the moral right to assess and challenge other deputies. Only our voters should have the right to assess us. Passions are being fueled here at the moment, yet in fact a perfectly concrete and clear proposal has been made: Decide nothing here; set up a commission to examine the issue and have the results of the commission's work submitted for our perusal. In this situation, it seems to me, it is quite out of order to challenge these people and say that they have a vested interest. I believe that if anyone sees fit to add their own representatives to the commission, this must be done. Thank you for listening.

B.Ye. Paton: Esteemed comrade, just one moment. I can see nine more wanting to speak. Let us give them each a minute. Please.

R.A. Medvedev, writer (Voroshilovskiy Territorial Electoral Okrug, Moscow): Comrades, I think our tempestuous reaction is due not only to the fact that a commission has been proposed. I have no doubt that the commission is necessary. It is a matter of the membership of the commission. As a historian, I must tell you that we Soviet historians are not ashamed to say that Russia conquered Central Asia. We are not ashamed to say that Russia conquered even the North Caucasus. We are not ashamed to hang the celebrated picture "Yermak's Conquest of Siberia" in our museums. But hitherto, in our official works of history, in our articles, in our publications appearing in Moscow, we have written that Estonia, Latvia, and Lithuania joined the Soviet Union voluntarily, that it was a people's revolution, that there was no violence and there were no threats, and that it was a full, voluntary expression of the will of the Lithuanian, Estonian, and Latvian peoples. This is untrue. It was, of course, an action that occurred when an imperialist war was taking place and when no one—not just the Soviet Union but Germany, Japan, Britain, and France—showed any respect for the rights of small countries and peoples, and when problems were being tackled without regard for the neutrality of Belgium, the Netherlands, Finland, or other countries. So the commission must be set up and we must finally make a correct assessment of these treaties. But the commission must include not only authoritative representatives from Estonia, Latvia, and Lithuania. The commission must have other state figures from our country on it. I am surprised to hear comrades proposing, for example, Chingiz Aytmatov, a man respected by me and by all of us, as chairman of the commission, and not Foreign Minister Shevardnadze, for example. That is, I propose that the decisions be made to set up the commission, but that its membership be looked at again by the deputies from the Estonian and Latvian SSR's, in conjunction with the congress Presidium and members of the Soviet Government and Politburo. (Applause).

M.S. Gorbachev: Comrades, may I speak out of turn? Just to make this issue somewhat clearer. It is an old problem, one that has been discussed and studied by historians, by political scientists, and by the relevant departments. And I have to say that while we have been holding scientific discussions in certain departments, all the documents, including the secret appendix to the treaty, have been published everywhere. The Baltic press has published everything. But all efforts to find the original of the secret treaty have failed. Those who are dealing with these matters will note that I broached the matter in conversation with the Polish comrades and with the Polish press, and in my concluding remarks on the topic following my meeting with the Polish intelligentsia.

We have been dealing with this question for a long time. There are no originals. There are copies, but it is not known what they are copies of. They are signed, but what creates doubts, particularly for us, is the fact that Molotov's signature is in German letters. When Chancellor Kohl was here—it was, as they say, a one-on-one discussion, but since the issue is turning out this way it obviously must be said, and I do not think the chancellor will be very offended if I reveal this secret—there were matters of a purely confidential nature, one-on-one. In particular, I asked him: Do you have the originals of these treaties, the appendix? He replied that they had them. I said: Then would you please give them to us. And on the basis of that understanding we sent Foreign Ministry representatives. Eduard Amvrosiyevich? Yes. But the originals were not found there, either.

This is, so to speak, information to mull over. A serious question that requires scientific and political analysis. I do not want to oversimplify the issue; it must be discussed and evaluated, as the comrades have proposed. So I would advocate the creation of a commission, since it has been requested by several delegations. But I would ask the comrades to look again at who should be on the commission. I think this commission should be

STENOGRAPHIC RECORD

Eighth Session

1 June 1989

expanded, and therefore the congress and the Presidium, which made the proposal, should be asked to provide the time for this. On the basis of consultations with our scientists and with the Academy of Sciences competent people should be placed on the commission, because it is a very serious question. That is number one.

Number two: In view of the special information I have provided, including the conversations with Mr Kohl, I would not at this early stage call the proposal "On the formation of a commission...." In the first place there are different interpretations. The proposal is on the elaboration of a political and legal appraisal, and it is called: "On a legal appraisal of the Soviet-German nonaggression treaty and the secret additional protocol to the pact...." We do not have the secret protocol at the moment, so we cannot evaluate it. But I do think there should be a commission; I would certainly go along with that. It must elaborate a political and legal appraisal of this nonaggression treaty without mentioning the secret protocol, since all the archives we have rummaged through here have not provided an answer. Although I will tell you that the historians know and would tell you that what happened was that two powerful forces were moving toward one another, and at some point this coming into contact came to a complete halt. Something lay at the basis of it. But all we are doing is debating at the moment. So it requires an investigation, an analysis of all the documents, of the entire situation as it occurred, including the way the Soviet Government dealt with the treaty when the war started.... What we did was deem it invalid.

This full range of issues, I think, must be evaluated, because the Baltic republics are frantically discussing these issues, and, as a result, it is being questioned whether the will of the people came into it at all when they joined the Soviet Union. That is scarcely the case. All this must be studied. So I would have the congress set up a commission to provide a political and legal appraisal of the Soviet-German treaty, and after it has been formed at the relevant level, let it get down to work and give its competent judgment on this issue. I do not even know if it will get at the truth in its first attempt. It is no simple matter, but since it exists I believe that we must not try to duck it. Let us not duck it; let us get on and study it. As we have said, in the course of restructuring there are very many acute problems. If the comrades consider it necessary to obtain some more information before making a decision on the composition of the commission, to have some preliminary ideas from the Foreign Ministry, we can ask Comrade Shevardnadze to speak on the matter. But I think the chief thing is to set up the commission correctly, for it to get to work, and then either the Supreme Soviet or all the deputies will be informed of the results of the commission's work. That is my clarification. We might confine ourselves to it now, and if the comrades support the idea of creating a commission, then the Presidium should be given time to continue consultations, to provide it with competent people. Is that right, comrades?

From the hall: Right!

M.S. Gorbachev: Fine, settled, then.

From the hall: (Inaudible).

M.S. Gorbachev: No, comrades, Eduard Amvrosiyevich Shevardnadze is not a deputy. Ministers are not deputies. Let us instruct some deputies. There are two international affairs experts from our Central Committee and from the Politburo there is Comrade Yakovlev. Let us have Yakovlev on the commission. OK? (Applause).

B.Ye. Paton: Comrade deputies! As I see it, the proposal on the advisability of setting up a commission is therefore accepted by everyone. As for the membership, Mikhail Sergeyevich has made a proposal. I think we all accept this proposal: To instruct the Baltic delegations and the Presidium to consider the matter further, since the commission must include more professionals and experts on this issue.

Is the proposal accepted? Thank you.

(Noise in the hall).

B.Ye. Paton: You want a vote? Vote for what? For the advisability of setting up a commission? I mean, we cannot vote for the members as they stand. So it is just the advisability of a commission. I think no one objects to that? Accepted?

From the hall: Accepted.

B.Ye. Paton: Esteemed comrade deputies! The Presidium has received many requests and comments on the fact that many deputies have not been given the floor, that lists are being changed, and so on. I am authorized by the Presidium to announce that around 500 requests to speak in the debate have been received. That is number one. Number two, the Presidium looks at the lists of speakers twice a day to ensure that all regions, republics, public organizations, and so on are represented, so that no one is offended. During the dinner break the list will be drawn up for the evening session. It seems to us that this is the only possible solution in such a complex situation.

I also want to announce that the Presidium receives memoranda that are more or less identical. I will read out a very short one. It is from Valentin Fedorovich Romanov of Magnitogorsk: "Notes on debate procedure: One. It seems to me that during the debates we often display particular inspiration and a splenetic single-mindedness in exposing shortcomings by the spadeful. Although criticism cannot be made in strict doses, the time has come to change the emphasis from the viewpoint of seeking proper ways out of the present situation and not simply stating shortcomings which are familiar to us all. And the criticism must be courteous and benevolent. Two, the tactic of

FIRST CONGRESS OF PEOPLE'S DEPUTIES OF THE USSR

Eighth Session

1 June 1989

trying to intimidate the congress, where certain speeches end with the words 'there could be unforeseen consequences,' must be abandoned. We are building a state in which the consequences must be foreseeable, so ultimatums are not our way." (Applause). There have been similar memoranda from groups of deputies and I am not going to read them out.

Since the situation concerning those wishing to speak is so strained, let me read out a memorandum to the congress Presidium from Deputy Vasilyev: "Please read out the proposals. For the USSR people's deputies who, because of the lack of time, do not have the chance to speak from the congress platform, but would like the pages of the central newspapers to be used as a platform and these newspaper items published during the congress to be regarded as speeches at the congress itself and entered in the stenographic record for the relevant day." This is not a bad idea, I think.

Let me make some very brief announcements now, comrades.

First, since there have been questions about registering to speak on the USSR Council of Ministers chairman's report, the Presidium has authorized me to inform you that registration will begin after the Council of Ministers chairman's speech.

Editorial commission chairman Vadim Andreyevich Medvedev has asked me to inform the commission members that the editorial commission will meet at the start of the break in the Hall of Mirrors and asks the commission members to make their way there.

A request from the doctors: To announce a meeting of all doctor-deputies here, in the hall, at the start of the long interval. There is a similar request from people's deputies working in industry. But it does not specify where and when they want to meet.

Finally, what is in my view a very interesting memorandum to the effect that People's Deputy Nikolay Andreyevich Kasyan, whom we all know very well, is prepared to give medical assistance to any participant of our congress. (Applause).

Allow me to announce that we are taking a break until 1600.

Eighth Session

1 June 1989. Kremlin Palace of Congresses. 1600.

USSR People's Deputy B.Ye. Paton presiding.

B.Ye. Paton: Dear comrade deputies, we are continuing the discussion of the question of the "Basic Directions for the Domestic and Foreign Policy of the USSR." In conformity with the understanding, the congress Presidium has discussed and is making known to you a list of the speakers who have been scheduled for today's evening session:

Aleksandr Yakovlevich Neumyvakin, chairman of the Central Board of the All-Russian Society of the Blind;
Aleksandr Aleksandrovich Korshunov, brigade leader, Tashkent Chkalov Aviation Production Association, Uzbekistan;
Anatoliy Yevgenyevich Karpov, chairman of the Board of the Soviet Peace Foundation;
Yevgeniy Aleksandrovich Yevtushenko, secretary of the Board of the USSR Writers Union;
Pyusta Azizaga kyzy Azizbekova, director of the Museum of the History of Azerbaijan;
Nikolay Semenovich Glazkov, foreman and brigade leader, Moscow Artistic Clock Plant;
Vitautas Vitautovich Landsbergis, professor, Lithuanian SSR State Conservatory;
Aleksandr Aleksandrovich Mokan, Chairman of the Presidium of MSSR Supreme Soviet; and
Valeriy Vasilyevich Khmur, chairman of the ispolkom of the Olginskiy Village Soviet, Krasnodark Kray.

If everyone adheres to the rules, we will be able to give the floor to all of them.

Please allow me to give the floor to Aleksandr Yakovlevich Neumyvakin.

A.Ya. Neumyvakin, chairman of the Central Board of the All-Russian Society of the Blind, (from the Soviet Charity and Health Foundation): Dear comrade chairman! Dear comrade deputies! Comrades! This is the first time that the opportunity to speak from this high state rostrum has been given to a representative from public organizations of the disabled, from the founders of the Soviet Charity and Health Foundation. This attests to the positive changes occurring in our country which we have been discussing today at the congress. This is the first time that we have been given the opportunity to mention our critical problems, which are so numerous that it is necessary to take the most decisive steps.

Restructuring is under way in all social segments of our society. It is also under way in the societies of the disabled. We also have among us opponents of restructuring, conservatives, fault-finders, who do not propose anything themselves, but who accuse everyone of being unable to resolve the problems that have been accumulating over the years. The labor collectives of the societies of the disabled completely support restructuring both for the country as a whole, and within the confines of their own societies. For dozens of years we pretended that there was no problem with regard to the disabled. The mass media considered it to be incompatible with our understanding of humanitarianism to discuss the life of the disabled, or to show them on the television screens. But there were problems. They kept accumulating and becoming increasingly acute, until now more than 7 million disabled persons await major decisions from the deputies.

STENOGRAPHIC RECORD

Eighth Session

1 June 1989

First of all, as my constituents feel and as I feel myself, it is necessary to resolve the question of pension payments. The miserly pension paid to disabled individuals and retirees who ended their labor activity long ago can no longer guarantee them a normal standard of living. It is necessary to raise the lowest limit of the pensions and grants-in-aid to a minimum of R100 and to do so immediately, beginning in 1990, if only for the disabled, prior to the promulgation of the Pension Law. Of course this will require funds, and, naturally, it will be necessary for all of us, comrades, to work together. And we are well aware of this. And especially, of course, it will be necessary for the minister of finance to work with the proposals concerning this question. But nevertheless I support here everyone who states that the question can also be resolved by means of the intelligent reduction of the defense expenditures; by also—and I hope that my former colleagues will not be offended at me for saying so—conquering space jointly with other countries, which will prove to be less expensive; and by reducing the administrative apparatus and limiting the implementation of the idea of those enthusiasts who want to use state funds to divert the flow of rivers and to build stupendous canals that destroy the ecology, thus exerting an influence on people's health and, in the final analysis, leading to an increase in the number of disabled persons.

I completely support the idea of creating a Committee for Affairs of Veterans and Disabled Individuals. That committee must develop a draft of the Law Governing Organizations of the Disabled, since they have been dropped completely from the draft of the Law Governing Social Organizations. This will prevent a repetition of what is currently occurring, when, as various normative acts are published, our organizations are simply forgotten, or at best are equated to societies of anglers, philatelists, etc. You must realize that we understand the importance of these social organizations, but the disabled require a different approach. And this is not selfishness, but a vital necessity.

But you would not believe the obstacles that await us when we attempt to correct the situation! The Society of the Disabled proves to be in a situation when you simply do not know which God to pray to. For example, Decree 824, dated 17 July 1987, concerning the reduction of the administrative apparatus, was not extended to us. Later, by another decree, the reduction was carried out, but we were not granted the right to use the funds that had been made available, nor were we given the right to form a table of organization. For ten years the Society of the Blind attempted to remove the limitation on the earnings of Group II disabled individuals, which could not exceed R120 without affecting their pensions. Finally we achieved this. But the decision proved to be only a halfway measure that divided the disabled into two categories. The persons who received the right to get the benefits were those who work at production-training enterprises of societies of the blind, but the disabled persons working in state enterprises and in institutions did not receive that benefit. One can easily discern here the bureaucratic attitude of the apparatus, the workers of which, when preparing the documents, do not consider it to be necessary to coordinate the final version with those who are asking those questions.

The same thing occurred with the preparation of the Law Governing Public Organizations. My inquiries to the USSR Ministry of Justice and to the Institute of State and Law concerning this question have remained unanswered. Because of this attitude, and also relying upon the processes of restructuring, I began to disregard the so-called subordination of administrative levels, and sent our questions directly to Comrade Ryzhkov, Chairman of the USSR Council of Ministers. So, Nikolay Ivanovich, it was I who who always bothered you. But it was only on your instructions that the societies in the republics managed to resolve as many as a dozen problems that had not been resolved previously.

The competency of the republic Councils of Ministers in resolving many questions is limited, and therefore we are forced to proceed—if you will pardon the expression—in battering-ram fashion, since we do not have any union agency. Here is an example. The percentage of reduction of passenger-car motor transportation that was established for the All-Russian Society of the Blind is the same as for any ministry. In Russia, 70 blind administrators of oblast, kray, autonomous, and republic boards of governors and 18 institutions each have one unit of transportation. For almost a year I attempted to prove that I cannot take away a car from a blind administrator in Tula, but allow one in Smolensk to keep his. And it was only on the basis of Nikolay Ivanovich's personal instructions that people began looking into our situation. And what do you think? They gave us allocations on the basis of the standards, and even more than I had fought for.

A person who has fallen upon hard times, who has become disabled, needs social rehabilitation. In recent years we have been given a large "replenishment" of internationalist fighting men. It is necessary first of all to help a person find his place in life, to help him feel that he is a worthy member of society, a person who is necessary to society—and for this purpose he needs a specialty; he needs work. Until recently there were public organizations only for persons who were disabled only in sight and hearing. About a year ago a society that unites the disabled in other categories was created, but for absolutely all disabled individuals, the problem of finding a job is an extremely important and acute one.

The legislation that is in effect has established for disabled individuals a reservation—2 percent of the jobs. But even within the confines of that reservation the administrators at enterprises and institutions do not want to give jobs to the disabled. Quotas for finding jobs for the disabled exist in many countries, but in those countries they are reinforced by penalty sanctions with respect to the enterprises that fail to meet them. Those fines are paid into a special fund for the disabled. I feel that it is time to change over to

STENOGRAPHIC RECORD

Eighth Session

1 June 1989

economic sanctions in our country also, so that the problems of the disabled can be resolved not only by the disabled individuals themselves, but also at the governmental level, by everyone. The persons with sight disability include the professor and instructor staff, teachers, jurists, and mathematician-programmers working at state enterprises and in institutions. These people request the leadership of the societies to provide their work stations with computers and other equipment that is designed to enable the blind to work normally and effectively. But they are afraid to direct these requests to the administrators of enterprises or organizations, lest conditions be created for them that will make it necessary to fire them. Are we really supposed to believe that a plant or an NII [scientific-research institute] is incapable of buying a computer—even if it has to be bought in exchange for currency—or of creating the normal working conditions for a disabled person?

The societies of the blind and the deaf in all the union republics have their own enterprises. For example, the enterprise of the All-Russian Society of the Blind produces output with a total value of one billion rubles a year. More than 860 state plants and 41 ministries operate cooperatively with our enterprises. But the crux of the matter is not how many millions of rubles worth of output we produce—although this, too, is of no small importance for the country—but the tremendous amount of labor—and I am not exaggerating this—that the disabled have to expend in order to earn additional rubles to supplement their miserly pensions, in order at least to bring their income, on the whole, up to the average level of earnings in the country.

Involving disabled persons in socially beneficial labor proves to be a very difficult struggle at all administrative levels. Wherein is this expressed? First of all, it is necessary to select articles that would guarantee efficient working conditions for disabled persons, and we have selected them. For four years the recommendations from all the republic societies for the blind concerning the priority right for the production of those articles by disabled persons have been shelved. The ministries give as their reason the Law Governing the Enterprise, and put the blame on the rights of the labor collectives, and the labor collectives, in their turn, very frequently demonstrate both individual and group selfishness. What kind of charity is this? What kind of concern? Under such conditions, how is the administrator of the society supposed to act? How is he supposed to explain to the disabled persons the situation that has developed?

For example, the Ekran Plant in Kuybyshev, and the Chapayev Plant, as a result of the reduction of production of output for the defense industry, decided that the workers who had been made available should be kept busy with articles that disabled persons were making on the basis of cooperative efforts with the plant. Two months ago we were informed that, starting with the fourth quarter, the contract would be annulled. Two hundred disabled persons remain without work. Our enterprise is losing R19 million of volume of commercial output, with all the accompanying economic consequences. I would recommend that the plant engage in the production of other consumer goods, rather than taking work away from disabled persons. That would be much more beneficial both for the country and for Kuybyshev Oblast. It is possible to cite dozens of similar examples today. We are required to fulfill the plan just as any other ministry is required to, and we have more than enough controllers. But how do they guarantee our production? Exclusively according to the leftover principle. We are given, for the most part, obsolete equipment that has proven to be unneeded by enterprises in state industry—but there is not even enough of this, and yet we are responsible for the quality. Or I would like to cite an example with the provision of transportation. For 191 enterprises in the All-Russian Society of the Blind that are situated from Vladivostok to Kaliningrad, Gosplan provides 5-6 motor buses a year for transporting disabled persons to their place of work. Not a single electronic computer could help me to divide them. And you can imagine the difficulties that disabled people have in making their way to the enterprise on public transportation, especially during the wintertime. Recently—literally the day before yesterday—the Ministry of Trade delighted us by allocating for the society workers five motor vehicles, for sale to society workers. But I assume that we had so few vehicles allocated to us because they feel that blind people do not have to sit behind the steering wheel. I think that the Ministry of Trade is making a mistake, because we have people who have been working hand in hand with an unsighted person for 30 years, and we have veterans who deserve to be able, after accumulating the money needed, to buy a car. I think that, as I am speaking, the Ministry of Trade is reconsidering the decision that will add about a dozen units to the Society of the Blind. (Applause). Thank you.

Since 1951 the Society of the Blind has been living without any state subsidy, and everything that it does is done with money that has been earned by its own labor. And the society has done quite a bit. It has built enterprises, houses of culture, sanitoriums, special libraries, and apartment houses. But the income tax levied on the society's enterprises is the same that is levied on everyone else—35 percent. In our opinion, when resolving social problems, it is necessary to free disabled persons from paying this task. We could channel those funds into meeting the social needs of the disabled.

For a definite category of the disabled, work at home is acceptable. But just imagine a family of disabled persons living in a single room and also working there. They need housing.

Financial limits of R25 million a year are planned for the All-Russian Society of the Blind for capital construction. Of that amount, R16 million is for housing. But even this total, which is miserly for the RSFSR, also has to be divided among the collectives.

STENOGRAPHIC RECORD

Eighth Session
1 June 1989

Normative documents have determined that 8 percent of the housing area is to be withdrawn by the local agencies to meet the city's needs. That is correct. But the situation that actually occurs in different. The Ulyanov Oblast Ispolkom wants to resolve the housing problem within the confines of its famous Zabota [Concern] program by withdrawing from the organizations of the disabled as much as 20 percent of the housing area constructed with the disabled persons's money. The Pskov and Novosibirsk ispolkoms have gone even farther. They want to take away more than 30 percent. The people in Rostov require, for each thousand of the financial limits for housing, R1400 of limits for developing the municipal management.

I request the Presidium to allow me to finish my statement.

Considering the fact that the limits are not being allocated any more to the society for these purposes, the claims of the ispolkom can only be satisfied at the expense of housing construction—if you do not like these terms, we will not include you in the share, and you won't get anything at all.... That's the entire concern shown for the disabled.

The Moscow City Oblispolkom owes 5000 square meters of housing area, but it refuses to allocate it, since the disabled persons were put on the waiting list later than the persons on the rayon's waiting list. But don't people realize that it is incomparably more difficult for a disabled person to live in a communal apartment? It is necessary to reconsider the benefits for disabled persons in this question. And also to decide the question, so that not a single construction plan is accepted without taking into consideration the specific nature of the disabled person's situation.

A very important problem that can be resolved at the state level is the providing of disabled persons with equipment that helps them to compensate for their physical shortcoming, that enables them to live and work to their fullest. As of today, we do not have enough of even the most elementary things. If one speaks about the blind, we lack the simplest dictaphones and high-grade paper for printing books in Braille. The quality of the production of these books is very low. The normal printing-house base does not exist. I am not even mentioning computers with voice or Braille output, which could be very helpful in providing jobs for the blind.

There are not enough special devices to enhance the hearing of deaf persons. And what about the problems of making prosthetic devices and of manufacturing wheelchairs? When are we going to stop applauding the Western companies and learn how to make these things ourselves? Where are our designers? How long is the minister of social security going to act in the role of a suppliant, or attempt by himself to get the leather, metal, and wood for the prosthetic devices? Incidentally, for purposes of an example, out of the wood that has been allocated, only 16 percent is suitable for prosthetic devices, and the rest is suitable only for use as firewood.

Good programs have been adopted to resolve these problems, but they are not being fulfilled. The "people at the bottom" are waiting for additional instructions, and the "people at the top" feel that everything is taking its course. When will we stop deceiving one another? It is necessary without delay, and in a real way, to achieve the elimination of the shortage of equipment that is vitally important for disabled persons.

Comrades, I have mentioned only a few of the problem. Because of the lack of time, I have not touched upon the topic of disabled children, or of disabled senior citizens who became disabled while working on kolkhozes or sovkhozes or at enterprises and for whom, only because they became members of the Society of Disabled Persons, the collectives have withdrawn all concern.

In conclusion I would like to appeal to our respected writers and journalists. In my opinion, it is time to stop arguing on the pages of the press about who used to take what position in the past. Because we need historical truth, we need works about present-day problems, about the present-day state of affairs. And I would like for the problems of the disabled to be illuminated objectively.

Just as new sprouts come out to replace the branches that have been broken off by the wind, just as everything living turns after the first rain toward the light and the heat, so do we disabled persons. For us, restructuring is the abundant rain, and the light and the heat are our hearts, your understanding. So please give some of the heat of your heats and your souls to the disabled. Help them to become truly equal members of society.

The year 1989 has been declared by the Soviet Charity and Health Foundation to be the Year of Charity. I call upon all of you, my dear deputies and voters, to join actively in this humanitarian movement. Thank you for your attention. (Applause).

B.Ye. Paton: The floor is given to Deputy Aleksandr Aleksandrovich Korshunov. The next to speak will be Deputy Karpov.

A.A. Korshunov, brigade leader at the Tashkent V.P. Chkalov Air Production Association, Uzbek USSR, city of Tashkent (from the USSR Trade Unions): Comrade chairman, comrade deputies! My dear countrymen! I am a representative of the apparatus—an apparatus numbering 140 million persons—of Soviet trade unions. I am one of the representatives in the army of more than 20 million Soviet Communists. And I am forced to begin my statement not with what I had planned to speak about.

Certain speakers have attempted to convey the idea that the chief culprit for all our woes, for all our misfortunes, is the fact that, as is stated in Article 6 of the USSR Constitution, the guiding and directing force of Soviet society, the nucleus of its political system, is the CPSU. This has manifested itself especially clearly at the numerous rallies. I happened to be present at some of them. In the statements made by individual speakers, one hears a

Eighth Session

1 June 1989

direct appeal: Separate the party from the management of the country, give physical reprisals to the Communists. It is not necessary to give physical reprisals to anyone. We have already gone through this, and so have our fathers and grandfathers. It is not necessary to give physical reprisals to people for their convictions. But separation from management is necessary, except that it should not be the party, but those who have penetrated into the party, those who, while hiding behind the party identification card, are obviously and secretly doing everything to prevent our restructuring from happening. (Applause).

There is no need to applaud, comrades. Otherwise I will not be able to say everything within my alloted time, and I will be asked to leave the rostrum. It would be better if you wait until later.

Yes, the party, like the other social institutions in our country, is living through a complicated time of renewal, of reinterpreting its role in the life of our country. Yes, the party and every communist bears a share of the responsibility for why, and with what, we have come to this congress, the responsibility for our failure in economics, for failures in the political area, responsibility for the crisis, for the aggravation of the interethnic relations, for the collapse of the financial system, and for many other things. Communists, of course, bear the responsibility for this. But, comrade deputies, the 1935 Communist deputies who are present here in this auditorium constitute 86 percent. Haven't the Communist Party and its leadership promoted the idea of restructuring our society, the idea of returning to Leninist principles, to democratization and glasnost, to the ideas of building a democratic, rule-of-law state? Do we have the right to forget that, thanks to April 1985, thanks to the 19th all-union party conference, it became possible to hold the election as a result of which we have proven to be here in this auditorium, and, in the final analysis, to conduct this congress? Who, if not the party, provided the impetus for the political and civic awakening of our society, of all the masses of the people, the impetus for the possibility of freely stating and defending any convictions?

There exist forces—and they are real ones—that are attempting to cross out our great, but simultaneously tragic, history. Those forces are attempting to dismember our union, to redesign the map of the country, to throw the country into the abyss of chaos and internecine struggle—and, in the muddy water of the anarchy of complete permissiveness, they are attempting to make political profit for themselves. They are rushing headlong to power, thinking least of all about the interests of our long-suffering nation. They have completely different goals. Nina Andreyeva, "Memorial," and the Democratic Union have nothing in common with democracy.

I would like to say two words about the Moscow group of deputies. For some reason, a few people are attempting to include them in this category. That is incorrect. I assert—and I think that I will be supported by a very large number of deputies—that the work of our Moscow comrades is largely helping us to understand how important it is not to be indifferent. From the delegations of the Baltic republics we are learning parliamentarianism, the culture of parliamentarianism. We all thank you greatly for this. (Applause).

A revolution is occurring in the country, and if that is so, then there is also a counterrevolution. Things must be called by their real names. It is the task of the congress to defend the revolution, and to prevent either the leftists or the rightists from killing the country's renewal, born with such difficulty, so agonizingly. Unfortunately, the process of restructuring has not yet become irreversible. And we, the highest agencies of power in the country, must work to create the mechanism for that irreversibility. I personally have apprehensions that the recently elected president of our country is not completely capable of implementing those ideas of restructuring, those very important structures of the rule-of-law state of which he himself is the author, and which have been supported by our entire society. I hope to God that I am mistaken! But I am not the only person who thinks this way.

There are forces that are preventing our president from implementing people's hopes. This manifests itself if only in the fact that all his precise, clear conceptions of restructuring are becoming bogged down in documents, beginning with the Council of Ministers and ending with the rayon executive committees. It is necessary to create a mechanism that makes a repetition of October 1964 impossible. The president of the country was elected by the congress, and it is only the congress that can release him from that job. The president of the country was elected by the congress, and the president must be accountable to the congress. We must not repeat our numerous cults in the Stalin or Brezhnev version. There is certainly little probability that Gorbachev has been subjected to this. But, nevertheless, first of all, he is not eternal, and, secondly, it is the law that must operate, rather than a good tsar or a kind administrator. (Applause).

Our society paid an immeasurably great price for allowing the power to be, for all practical purposes, in the hands of a single person. The entire fullness of the power must belong to us, to the Congress of People's Deputies. I am a deputy from the trade unions, and therefore I feel that the activity of the entire deputy corps—and especially its trade-union group—must be channeled, in the final analysis, toward the protection of the workers' rights, toward the improvement of the economy, and toward the creation of the conditions for the worthy, comfortable life of all segments of our society.

Comrades! Recently here in Moscow I met—this was not the first meeting, but, rather, there were many such meetings—with an elderly, poorly dressed woman. Seeing my deputy's lapel pin, she said to me, "You'll be there, and you will all keep talking and talking. But we were promised on television that we would get a raise in our pension. For 30 years I worked on a kolkhoz, and my

STENOGRAPHIC RECORD

Eighth Session
1 June 1989

son has moved to Moscow so that he can look after his granddaughter. Then, when he didn't need me anymore, he left me. The amount authorized for a man, a person who has died, is R36. How is a person supposed to live on that? I thought that I would get a raise in my pension, at least to pay for the burial expenses and to buy a mourning dress, but I don't think I can live that long. It's a good thing that my neighbors show Christian mercy in giving me things, in sharing their old clothes with me."

Believe me that it is shameful and painful to listen to this elderly woman, who has endured all the difficulties of our society and who has remained so hapless. It is terrible that in the city of Moscow alone, more than 100,000 retirees receive this so-called pension of less than R50 a month. It is terrible that there are more than 10 million of them in the Soviet Union.

There has been an uncontrollable rise in prices, a washing away of the inexpensive assortment of commodities, and a worsening of their quality. Every day we see more and more empty shelves in the stores. According to statistical information, the unpaid and unsatisfied demand for commodities and services has reached R70 billion. But that is according to statistics. Our statistics can do anything. But according to estimates made by our scientists, that demand has exceeded 100 billion. Inflation constitutes approximately 5 percent a year, according to official data. And what about the real income? The State Committee for Statistics cheerfully asserts that during the past three years the real income in our country has increased by 8.3 percent.

One more question: For whom has it increased? It has become possible, without doing practically anything, to make superprofits. On the other hand, the highest economic agencies are making attempts to hold down the wages of the workers at the state enterprise. Panic has seized some of the population. It is completely impossible to imagine that it is is impossible to find, and in the capital of our motherland, too, such commodities as salt, matches, and soap. It is impossible to explain this by the years of stagnation. It is impossible to explain it by common sense.

The ecological catastrophe engulfing cities and entire regions. I shall not repeat a discussion of this. An excellent report on this was made by the representative from Soviet Uzbekistan, from Soviet Karakalpakia. Despite the solemn assurances of Comrade Chazov, USSR minister of public health, almost nothing is being done to improve the health of our people. Today these serious shortcomings can no longer be explained by the era of stagnation. One can see evidence of obvious failures in planning and in administration and of the imperfection of the economic mechanism.

In this regard I would like to make an oral deputy inquiry to Deputy Nikolay Ivanovich Ryzhkov, Chairman of the USSR Council of Ministers: Does our government have a clear-cut and concrete program for bringing our country out of the shameful position that has been created?

Why is it that in the state sector of the economy the wages have been practically frozen until the end of the five-year plan, thus burying the cost accountability that has not yet had time to be born? Why is it that our cooperative system, which has been called upon to resolve the bottlenecks in production that were formed in the state sector and to saturate the markets with new and needed commodities and services, in many instances at the present time is living parasitically on our economic disorders? Essentially speaking, having produced (according to data provided by the same State Committee for Statistics) last year a total of R6 billion worth of commodities and services—which is a decent total—it has done absolutely nothing to improve the situation in our domestic market. The only things we see so far are kiosks filled with dubious pictures and figurines that corrupt the morality of our children, and not just our children. So far these are extravagant T-shirts, which, incidentally, are state-produced, onto which an appropriate design is slapped down and which are sold at outrageously high prices. How many times can one try to convince these fake cooperative members—I do not consider all of them to be such, because there also are honest ones—that they should not buy up in the state trade system meat and other scarce commodities? However, things happen as in the old saying, "Vaska listens, but keeps eating." In this instance, in my opinion, there are two ways out of the situation that has been created: Either chase Vaska away, or replace the cook. (Applause). The workers are in favor of the cooperative system, but one that will serve the interests of the nation. They are in favor of the civilized cooperative system that Ilich dreamed about.

The repeated statements by Comrade Komin, First Deputy Chairman of Goskomtsen [State Committee on Prices], and many of our respected scientists—Comrades Abalkin, Aganbegyan, Zaslavskaya—who spoke out in favor of the need for a reform in pricing without infringing on the rights of the consumers, have not yet led to anything good. The diktat of the producers manifests itself to an increasingly large degree precisely in the retail prices. May one ask where the work of observing a retail-price policy is being carried out? For the time being, our policy, Comrade Pavlov, only has a detrimental effect on the already empty pockets of the Soviet worker. I can judge from my own budget: three family members, R600 of earnings, are completely sufficient. The earnings have not been increasing, but my family's cost of living in the past two-three years increased on the average of 25-30 percent.

Taking into consideration the extraordinary economic situation in the country, as a worker deputy representing a deputy group of trade unions that defends the workers' interests, I demand the consideration, as early as the first session of the USSR Supreme Soviet, of the Pension Law, and the gradual putting of that law into effect starting 1 January 1990. A comrade has spoken here just now, and it was impossible to listen to him without feeling pain. It is necessary first of all—absolutely first of

STENOGRAPHIC RECORD

Eighth Session

1 June 1989

all—to increase the size of the pensions paid to workers, employees, disabled persons, and participants of the Great Patriotic War, and to bring their minimum amount up to the living wage. It is necessary to create a mechanism to assure that the minimum living wage is always observed and taken into consideration as the inflation and prices rise.

Comrade deputies! We must constantly be aware that the Soviet nation expects from us, from the congress, specific decisions dealing with the most vitally important questions. It expects us to carry away from this congress a centrally controlled schedule for restructuring, a schedule that will consist not of slogans, but of specific assignments dealing with a specific question.

I was elected to our country's Supreme Soviet. I do not consider myself to be a 'gray mass,' as certain people imagine with respect to the working class. I have something to say. I have something to include in the agenda of the congress and the Supreme Soviet. And I have something to defend there. I feel that the other workers and kolkhoz members who are present here could do exactly the same thing.

Comrades! I call upon our congress to consolidate, to assure that there will be no more settling of personal accounts or insults here. The nation expects real decisions and real deeds from us because the country is standing on the line. (Applause).

B.Ye. Paton: The floor is given to Anatoliy Yevgenyevich Karpov. The next to speak after him will be Deputy Yevtushenko.

A.Ye. Karpov, chairman of the board of the Soviet Peace Foundation, Moscow (from the Soviet Peace Foundation jointly with five Soviet committees that are in favor of peace, solidarity, and international cooperation): Dear chairman! Dear deputies! Our congress is a model one both in the literal and in the figurative sense. Our countrymen are looking at us, and all of us together are attempting to consider yesterday's history, today's, and even tomorrow's. It is difficult, very difficult, to learn democracy, or the rules that govern good form in the 72nd year of the life of the state organism.

For the sake of illustration, I shall tell how the nomination of persons from Moscow to the Supreme Soviet of People's Deputies. There are 195 of us, and we received 29 of the places in the Soviet of the Union. It would seem that there would be nothing simpler than to select the best of the best and to give them our blessing. But we acted differently. We carried out a survey asking who wanted and who was able to work in the Supreme Soviet. That does not mean that we forgot the high honor of being in the Supreme Soviet. But being is one thing, and working is something completely different. Many of us have interesting work that we live, and leaving all of that suddenly.... Putting it more briefly, as you know, 55 persons expressed this desire. As a result, it was immediately proposed both to us and to you that the choice be made from the 195, but from the 55. The surplus principle triumphed—the persons who were candidates were not as many as were necessary, but as many as could be candidates and wanted to be. We left it for the congress to choose from them.

I would now like to discuss a few of the burning questions in the work of the Soviet Peace Foundation that I represent here.

First, the participation of the foundation in the conversion program, in other words, the reorientation of production from military to civilian. How does this seem to the nonspecialist? Yesterday the plant produced gunpowder, and a month later it produces nitrocellulose lacquers and viscose, since the raw materials are the same. Alas, everything is much more complicated. It is necessary to re-equip the production fundamentally, to change the technological scheme, and to retrain the cadres. All this requires not only funds, not only time, but also scientific substantiation. It is precisely that substantiation that finds the most economical, the most rapid path to conversion. Consequently, it makes sense to invest money, primarily into the scientific substantiation, in order to win both time and funds, and to assure that the conversion lasts not five to ten years, as certain specialists coolly consider, but perhaps two to three years.

We are engaging in this and are financing scientific developments. But here is something that is strange. The scientists are proceeding along this path as though it is being traveled for the first time, although actually the road has been well-traveled for a long time. As long ago as the 1940's, after the Great Patriotic War, a state agency for conversion was created in our country, and under its guidance our industry was able to restructure itself. You will say that during these years production has moved far ahead. Yes, that is correct. But the principles of conversion remain unchanged. So have the ideas, but they are kept carefully hidden by the notorious secrecy. Only a few people have access, but the number of production entities being restructured is in the hundreds, and thousands of specialists will deal with them. It would seem that there is no need to prove anything here. These materials must be opened up for them. Proceeding from this hypothesis, I propose that the Supreme Soviet immediately engage in developing a law governing conversion, and that it simultaneously instruct the government to create a Conversion Planning and Support Council, that possesses high powers and the opportunity to coordinate the resolution of this problem in a comprehensive manner. The departmental approach here is simply ruinous, as well as impossible.

For purposes of information, I can say that in the United States a bill concerning conversion was introduced in Congress for the first time in 1963, and since that time it has been repeatedly discussed at various levels. And

Eighth Session

1 June 1989

recently the question of creating a Conversion Planning and Support Council was considered.

Second. I shall not explain the kind of poverty our disabled people are living in. Everyone knows this. There are 7 million of them in the country, of whom 1.5 million are disabled war veterans. The number of the latter is actually considerably greater, inasmuch as, according to physicians, today practically every participant in the Great Patriotic War has grounds for qualifying as a disabled individual. And how many disabled children are there?

It may be that not all of you know that in 1988 the USSR Council of Ministers issued a decree to increase the standard expenditures for food and medicines at boarding homes for senior citizens and the disabled. It had previously been proposed to do that in late 1990. For us who are strong and healthy, waiting two years is no problem. But what about those people for whom every day of their life is being counted? Are they supposed to wait two years until they are fed, or until a nurse brings them a pill at their first request? And so, while the government is gathering momentum, the Soviet Peace Foundation decided: The decree will go into effect as of January 1989, but with funds from the foundation—because we are already subsidizing the construction of hospitals for veterans and internationalist fighting men; a social assistance center for single individuals, senior citizens, and soldiers' widows; and the development of the production of prosthetic devices for adults and children.

But how annoying it is if there is a good idea and there is money, but nothing is being done! For example, for many years no one has been able to resolve the question of constructing a therapeutic center for victims of the blockade in Leningrad. The question of building a hospital for disabled war veterans and internationalist fighting men in Alma-Ata has drowned in a flood of papers.

The problems of improving the living conditions for disabled persons and for low-income retirees are our common pain, our common concern, and they must be resolved immediately. In this regard I would like to support Deputy Korshunov and make to specific proposals.

First. We should resolve the question of establishing the minimum pension level to R75 for all categories of our country's population, including the rural population. (Applause).

You might ask, why 75 rubles? Well, it is because that is the minimum living wage in our country.

Second. At one time our party's program stated that by 1980 all the citizens of the country could travel on urban transportation free of charge. Well, then, let's fulfill that promise ten years later, at least for disabled person, persons with low income, and senior citizens! The funds for this purpose must be sought, of course, by the government. On my part I want to say that our foundation is ready to cooperate actively in resolving these questions, both with the government and with public organizations and foundations.

We have already had experience in this kind of cooperation. True, it has taken different directions. For example, two years ago we decreed that R120 million would be allocated to help homes for orphaned children. But at exactly the same time the Lenin Children's Foundation, that is well known to you, was being born, and we thought it would be an excellent thing if our help to the orphans went through their hands. Because it is not important who among us will do it; what is important is that there is a result. And we did not doubt for even a minute that there would not be a result, inasmuch as the Children's Foundation is headed by our associate Albert Anatolyevich Likhanov, a well-known and respected person who has done a lot for children. Since that time, I will remind you, two years have passed. But we have been completely unable to obtain the address of even a single children's home to which we could send our money. Currently a large number of new problems have arisen, and Deputy Likhanov has spoken in an anxious and ardent manner about them. But we hope that our money will finally get to the children.

On my part I would like to say that our foundation is also ready in the future to take the most active part in protecting childhood.

Since the subject has swung around to foundations, I would like to allow myself a small comment. Recently a large number of them have been formed. It has become fashionable: whatever it is, give us a foundation and democracy.... It would seem that we ought to be pleased by this, because any foundation is a noble movement. But whereas we have already matured for this politically, economically we are by no means ready for it. Because any foundation is people's contributions. And how much can a person contribute if he is barely able to make ends meet? Consequently, however noble the ideas of many new foundations may be, they are doomed from the start to vegetate. And a poor foundation is nonsense. If it does not have any money with which to fulfill its function, why is it needed? We have several large-scale, strong foundations: culture, children's, charity, peace.... Why not open up for them special-purpose accounts, instead of organizing a new foundation every time?

And, finally, a topic which for several days has been disturbing our congress and which I also cannot ignore, as it is because of this topic that the Peace Foundation was created. It is internationalism, or, to put it more precisely, the brotherhood of people who are united by the idea of creating the common weal. We have attended all its universities, we have been proud of it, and we have convinced ourselves and others that universal brotherhood is a law in our life. Suddenly blow followed blow: the problem of Karabakh, the tragic events in Sumgait and Tbilisi.... It would seem that those are the places

STENOGRAPHIC RECORD

Eighth Session

1 June 1989

where we could have learned the difficult lessons that could have aroused us and forced us to look at everything realistically. But no, we did not learn anything. We keep talking and talking—we do nothing but keep talking, as though we can use words to persuade an Estonian to defend his history differently, and can use words to reconcile the Azerbaijanis and the Armenians.

What, then, can I recommend in this regard?

First. It is necessary to reconsider fundamentally the curriculum for educating and instructing children in schools and nonschool institutions, and to provide to children and to young men and women broad access to the spiritual wealth of our country's nations, to their traditions, history, culture, and faith. Otherwise we shall have a paradoxical situation in which our children have a better knowledge about faraway Australia than they do of a neighboring republic. But most importantly, it is necessary to return to all nations a genuine, rather than petty-bourgeois, nationalistic interpretation of the concept "the citizen's national dignity," and a Leninist interpretation that was succinctly and clearly formulated in his excellent work "The National Pride of the Great Russians."

As long as I have touched upon this topic, I would like to allow myself a small digression. I miss, for example, at our historic constituent congress—behind the presidium—a map of our great, long-suffering homeland, a homeland that was created by many generations of our ancestors who were directed by the hand of history.

And in conclusion I would like to say: Yes, we are all learning democracy, but it is important for us not to keep sitting in noisy primary classrooms, but, having passed at our congress the examination for the right to be called a people's deputy, we must take more energetic steps to achieve the practical resolution of the vitally important tasks of restructuring.

My statement does not include an exposition of my concept or program for this extraordinarily complicated process of renewal. But I would like to touch upon three problems.

First. In 1917 we demanded the transfer of power to the soviets, guaranteeing that the land would be given back to the peasants. We must fulfill the promise that was made to the nation by the party.

Second. For several years we have been caught in the quagmire of phrase-mongering, as we were growing some special kind of spirituality. Every nation has the right to its uniqueness, a right that has been gained by millenia of sufferings, and, one might say, a genetic right. So we shall respect that part of a nation's being, that part of its culture.

And third. It is time to put an end to the mean trick that annihilates the individual—the name of which is across-the-board leveling—because the time that has been alloted to us by history is running considerably faster than the chess player's timer. And the nation wants to believe us, wants to believe that our team is capable of beating the clock at this historic point in history. Thank you. (Applause).

B.Ye. Paton: The floor is granted to Deputy Yevgeniy Aleksandrovich Yevtushenko, secretary of the board of the USSR Writers Union. The next person to speak after him will be Deputy Azizbekova.

Ye.A. Yevtushenko, (Kharkov-Dzerzhinskiy Electoral District, Ukrainian SSR): My dear comrades, it is no easy matter to sow the seeds of restructuring in soil with cracks of national enmity. What good are toasts to the friendship of nations when, under the legs of the banquet table, blood is flowing! The friendship of nations must be begun even before a child enters school. It must begin as early as the kindergarten, the street, the bus, and the store, where, to our shame, it is still possible from time to time to hear insulting terms applied to people of other nationalities—terms such as "khokhlyandiya," "katsap," "zhid," "armyashka," "chuchmek," "chukhonet," "katsoshka," etc.

To develop the idea expressed by deputies Likhachev, Gorbunov, and Oleynik, I propose a new article in Chapter 9 of the USSR Constitution: "The sovereignty and national dignity of each republic of the USSR are guaranteed by all the other republics. The insulting of any nation, even the smallest one, or disrespect for its language, laws, culture, economy, customs, beliefs, and expression of its will, are considered to be the criminally punishable insulting of all the Soviet nations." (Applause).

It is impossible to wash oneself clean of the past if there is no soap.

The so-called "strong hand" is always ready to grow ominously onto the breakable body of a weak economy. If there is no democracy in the economy, then democracy is threatened everywhere. The undemocratic nature of the economy is explained first of all by a personality cult that has never ended in our country—the cult of the personality of the state. The document that was read aloud here in the name of our long-suffering peasantry is a cry from the land itself, a land that is being raped by the endless decrees that contradict one another, decrees concerning how that land should live, what that land should do, and what it should not do. With regard to this point I share the deep pain of my long-time opponent Vasily Belov, but with regard to other points we are still arguing. Continuing Adamovich's idea, I propose overruling, by a special decree of the Supreme Soviet, absolutely all verdicts applied to the "expropriated kulaks," thus admitting finally the fault of our society, a society that criminally allowed the taking away of the land from its true owners. (Applause). Supporting Starodubtsev, I propose removing from Article 19

Eighth Session
1 June 1989

of the USSR Constitution the insulting and foolish formulation concerning the need to erase the boundaries between the city and the village, a formulation which actually has erased so many villages from the face of the earth. I propose throwing out of the Constitution completely Article 22, concerning the conversion of rural labor into a variety of industrial labor, which is something that belittles and primitivizes the great poetic profession of farmer. (Applause).

The cult of the personality of the state also had a detrimental influence on industry, which long ago became not only a long-term construction project, but a perpetual construction project for the "happy future."

Bridge builders add salt to the construction mortar so that the mortar will "grab." But if they hurriedly put in too much salt, it will subsequently erode the iron armature. Our economy is like that kind of oversalted bridge that has been eroded by corrosion, a bridge whose interminable repairs have exceeded the cost of the bridge itself. The branch ministries are like inflated repair-and-construction offices, and Gosplan is sometimes like a gigantic shop where minor repairs are made to clothing worn by the emperor without clothes. (Stirring in the auditorium, applause). The cult of the personality of the state led to state monopolism. The state, having monopolized all the basic production—from paper clips to missiles—began to resemble a clumsy dinosaur with rickety legs bending under the weight of its body, and with a tiny brain in its head, situated too far from the tail. The state's monopoly on enterprises and the land is not the socialism that had been envisaged by Lenin, but instead is some kind of semifeudal, antistate state capitalism. It is antistate because it is not profitable for the state itself. The indicator of the strength of the state is not the number of those who have a spoon, but the standard of living of those who have a wooden plow. To be as poor as we are, despite all this phenomenal natural wealth, is indisputable proof of the lack of prospects for the cult of the personality of the state, of state monopolism. It is necessary to give freedom to creativity, including economic creativity, not only to the intellectuals, but to all the workers, peasants, employees, and the intellectuals.

Article 40 of the Constitution, which begins with the words "The citizens of the USSR have the right to work," is not only primitive, but also insulting. Even prisoners are citizens, and they also have the right to work.

I propose a new wording for Article 40: "The citizens of the USSR have the right to free labor. Free labor means the free choice of labor: collective, family, individual, state, kolkhoz, cooperative, joint-stock, or lease. Free labor means the right to purchase producer goods from the state, as well as the right to produce producer goods. Farmers have the right to own the land as their basic means of production. Land is provided by the local soviets for a term of up to one hundred years, with the right of inheritance. Free labor is the right to sell the products of one's labor at a price determined by the producer wherever the producer himself decides. Free labor is the right of the producers, after paying state taxes, to determine for themselves the wage fund and the development. Free labor is the right to produce not what has been forcibly dictated from above, but what is dictated by the needs of the market, by the nation's needs."

I propose removing from the preamble of the USSR Constitution the boastful, jingoistic formulation: "A developed socialist society has been constructed in the USSR." It is necessary first to construct it, and then to brag about it. It would be desirable to reduce, and in a number of instances to discontinue, the aid provided to the poorly developed countries until our own country becomes highly developed. (Applause).

My constitutents are from the city of Kharkov, which is a kind of Leningrad of the Ukraine, a place where the intellectual working class and the truly worker's intelligentsia have given me a mandate—a stern mandate—to introduce into Chapter 7 of the Constitution the following article: "Citizens of the USSR, irrespective of their party, state, or social status, possess only equal rights with all other workers in the sphere of trade services and in the sphere of public health. The existence in open or concealed form of privileged special stores, special drug stores, or special hospitals is considered to be an unconstitutional violation of the principles of socialist equality." (Applause).

Comrades! Of course there must be deputy privileges. With today's situation with tickets, we unfortunately need deputy cash offices, and we need to be assured of finding a room quickly in hotels, because of the importance of the people's assignments. But, comrades, having luxurious deputy rooms at airports and train stations when, right nearby, women, children, and old men are sleeping side by side on the floor, is absolutely shameful! (Applause). We all make up the Congress of People's Deputies—the highest agency of power. Let us, with the authorization of the presiding officer at this meeting, carry out now at least one tiny, modest piece of magic for democracy. Let us vote to have all the deputy rooms turned over for use as rooms for mothers with children and for senior citizens. (Applause. The speaker holds up his identification card. The audience supports him.) Thank you for your support!

Lenin, in a speech at a meeting dedicated to his 50th birthday, prophetically stated, "...our party may possibly find itself in a very dangerous position, I believe—namely the position of a person who has become conceited. That position is rather stupid, shameful, and ridiculous." (V.I. Lenin, PSS [Complete Collected Works], Vol 40, pp 326-327.)

But, comrades, didn't we have that conceit, that party self-decoration, that party self-glorification, when the portraits of leaders, the slogans "Glory to the CPSU," etc., were contrasted with the murders of millions of workers, with personal corruption, with the collapse of the economy, and with the death of our irreplaceable boys in Afghanistan?

Eighth Session

1 June 1989

The historical merit of the creative segment of the party and of M.S. Gorbachev personally is that they bravely took a course based on a new way of thinking. But the new way of thinking is incompatible with the previous inert party monopolism on promoting soviet and state administrative cadres. Our country has approximately 20 million party members. But we have approximately 100 million non-party adults! They constitute an inexhaustible golden reserve of potential administrative cadres, but we are continuing to play with this same greasy pack of nomenklatura cards. The country does not have a single non-party USSR minister. You can look high and low, but you won't find a non-party general director. So far as I know, the entire country has only one non-party minister on the republic level—Raymond Pauls—and only one non-party editor of an all-union magazine—Sergey Zalygin, both of whom, at any rate, ought to be included in the Red Book. I could not comprehend here the statements about attacks on the party that had allegedly been organized by the "dark forces" at our congress. There are a total of 292 non-party members here, that is, less than 13 percent. What has been said here, comrades, is, practically speaking, only an intraparty discussion! Neither Academician Likhachev, nor Father Pitirim, spoke against the party. We've had enough of this "enemy-mania"! Those 38 party committee secretaries who were not elected also should not explain this by attacks on the party. It was simply the nation's negative evaluation of their personal actions. (Applause).

We respect the party for all the best things that it has done and is doing, and we believe that it can do a lot more, but we do not need anyone's new individual personality cult, or a party cult.

Mikhail Sergeyevich, you remember that now you are not only the General Secretary of the CPSU Central Committee, but also the president of the party of 100 million non-party members, and we non-party members ask you not to allow in the future this kind of cadre suppression in our country. All of us—party members and non-party members—must be in a single indivisible party—the party of the nation!

I propose an additional article in Chapter 7 of the USSR Constitution: "Citizens of the USSR, irrespective of their status as party member or non-party member, have the right to complete equality when being nominated to fill any Soviet state positions, including the highest ones."

I also propose changing the text of Article 6 to read as follows: "In accordance with the Bolsheviks' historic slogan 'All power to the soviets,' the chief guiding and directing force of Soviet society is the soviets of people's deputies—a completely equal union of party members and non-party members on the basis of the ideas of socialism. The highest agency of power is the Congress of People's Deputies."

I propose, by means of a special decree of the USSR Supreme Soviet, the overruling of the sentences dealing with all the so-called dissident trials. I propose returning Soviet citizenship to all those from whom it was unjustly taken away. I propose limiting the rights to practicing medicine for all psychiatrists who, violating their Hippocratic oath, labeled normal free-thinking people as dissidents and crammed them into mental hospitals.

In developing Drutse's proposal, and proceeding from my own deep respect for our Army, I propose adding the following amendment to Article 31 of the USSR Constitution, to read: "By its blood the Soviet Army has earned the noble reputation of the saviour of the world from fascism, and no one has the right to force it to be used in punitive actions either against the Soviet nations, or against other nations. State officials who issue such unconstitutional orders must be taken to court."

I propose canceling not only Article 11.1 of the 8 April decree, according to which it is possible to make criminally accountable any superior individuals who have made justified criticism, but also to reconsider completely this extremely sloppy and dangerous decree. It contains, for example, a ludicrous "spy-mania" paragraph concerning so-called "foreign copying equipment," as though all our stores are crammed full of our own Soviet-produced Xerox machines. We might note that the thesis of acceleration, in general, has almost disappeared, and even Mikhail Sergeyevich does not repeat it any more. Why? Well, it is because there are no means of acceleration, and Xerox is one of them. So, instead of Vasiliy Ivanovich Belov's vigilant thesis, which is approximately that "Every Xerox machine must be kept under scrutiny," I propose the thesis: "Every Soviet citizen should have his own personal Xerox machine." It may be that a Xerox machine will help even Vasiliy Ivanovich in his work as a writer. (Applause).

I shall be finishing soon, comrades. I still have three minutes remaining. I propose opening up as the official newsletter of the Congress of People's Deputies a permanent union-wide newspaper, GOLOS DEPUTATA [Voice of the Deputy], with an unlimited subscription. This newspaper should be made the responsibility of an editor who is a non-party member, if only for the sake of conducting a unique experiment.

I recommend announcing a competition for a new Anthem of the Soviet Union, since the words in the current one have become hopelessly obsolete.

I propose the following changes in the Election Law: "The election must be universal, equal, direct, and secret. There must be no district meetings. All single-mandate elections, including elections of the chairman of the Supreme Soviet, will henceforth be considered invalid. All organizations, including the party, have the right only to nominate candidates. The right to elect is retained by the chief organization—the nation."

STENOGRAPHIC RECORD

Eighth Session

1 June 1989

Comrades! Why did we win the Great Patriotic War? Because we all had both the desire to achieve a common victory and a sense of having a common enemy. Let us not look for enemies in one another, since we all have common enemies. They are the threat of a nuclear war, terrible natural calamities, ethnic conflicts, economic depression, ecological misfortunes, and the bureaucratic quagmire.

Restructuring is not only our spiritual revolution, but is our second Great Patriotic War. We do not have the right not to be victorious in it, but that victory must not cost us any human victims. Thank you. (Applause).

B.Ye. Paton: The floor is granted to Deputy Pyusta Azizaga kyzy Azizbekova. The next person to speak will be Deputy Gustov.

P.A. Azizbekova, director of the Museum of the History of Azerbaijan, Baku (Baku-Azizbekovskiy National-Territorial Electoral District, Azerbaijan SSR): Comrade deputies! I obviously have been unlucky. Not only have a small number of women deputies been given the floor, but I have been scheduled after such an emotional speaker as our favorite poet Yevtushenko. But I think that you will help me.

M.S. Gorbachev: Women always have a difficult position.

P.A. Azizbekova: Yes. Things in general are not so easy for us nowadays. It is not so easy to give birth to a Soviet Parliament, to form the mechanism of democracy. Sometimes the work of the congress, as we have all seen, is shaken up by sharp discussions. We need conflicts between various positions and points of view. Every day, every session, convinces us of how important, how necessary, it is to search for the answers to questions that will determine our fate. What will our future life be like? How can we move ahead in these difficult times, when the nation is attentively observing our work, when people are waiting for us to provide an answer to all the questions that are troubling them? There are a very large number of questions, in all spheres of life.

I would like, comrade deputies, to dwell on certain problems that were raised in Mikhail Seregeyevich Gorbachev's report. They are ethnic questions. The social, political, and civic participation of our people, who have been aroused by restructuring and glasnost, is a great force. And yet the inertia of the stagnation has by no means been overcome—this is attested to by literally every statement made by deputies—and it takes considerable efforts to assure that the energy of ideas is converted into the energy of movements. True, this is a hackneyed expression, but it must be said here today. It is necessary to place in the service of this idea all the opportunities, all the potential that our all nations and nationalities have, including my own nation, the Azerbaijani nation. No one doubts that each of the national republics that form the Soviet Union has its own specific peculiarities, which find reflection in the variety of its economic, social, and spiritual development. Hence the obvious conclusion: We should not copy one another in creating various political institutions or economic models. But there is a persistent need to create union-wide laws that precisely regulate the combining of the interests both of the USSR and our national union republics. The general principles of restructuring the management of the economy are creating the foundations on which the all-union legislation in this direction should develop. And I would like very much, comrade deputies, for the laws that will be developed by us to be long-lived.

Today one hears increasingly frequent appeals, essentially speaking, to dismantle the foundations of the very constitutional structure of our multinational state. However, all those who make such declarations, it seems to me, express not common-ethnic interests, but group ones. And therefore the question arises: Doesn't this lead to a breaking of ties not only with the center, but also among the republics, to the distortion of the economic relations that have formed, and to the destruction of the unique Soviet culture, which is a very important factor in developing and integrating the socialist nations? Our descendants will not forgive us if we allow a global spiritual "autonomization," or national self-isolation, which will inevitably lead to alienation, and to the weakening of the entire union and each republic individually.

Today, comrade deputies, we are facing the fact of serious nationalistic manifestations in certain regions of the country, including our region. From our own bitter experience we know the misfortune to which the attempts to estrange people on the basis of nationality lead. Simply the asking of the question of redrawing the borders, the unsubstantiated demands to include NKAO in Armenian SSR, became the reason for the destablization of the situation in the region and led to an interethnic conflict. The economic ties and the traditional bonds of friendship were broken. The misfortune that occurred in the region will have an effect for a long time on the fates of people and of entire generations. The scope of the tragedy is too great. Approximately 300,000 refugees from both republics—Armenia and Azerbaijan—have been left without a roof over their heads. Currently 50,000 Armenian inhabitants who left Azerbaijan have returned to their previous places of residence, and we are very glad. We want very much for the 165,000 Azerbaijanis who are living in Armenia but who currently have concentrated among us in Azerbaijan to return to their previous places of residence. The refugees today are a frightening picture, and this is not a regional problem, comrades. The inhabitants of the nonindigenous nationality in other republics where the interethnic conflicts are coming to a head may also find themselves in the position of refugees. It is urgently necessary to involve in this problem the country's legislative agencies; it is necessary to restore the justice that has been trampled upon, to guarantee legal protection to those who have suffered, and to compensate them for the material

Eighth Session

1 June 1989

losses that they have incurred. The problem of the refugees can be resolved, but only if there is the strictest observance of the letter and spirit of the law. We adhere to this principle only.

Despite the entire complexity of the situation in NKAO and all the difficulties and road blocks on the path of normalizing it, I am convinced that this is a resolvable problem. For purposes of normalizing the situation in NKAO, a specific form of administration has been introduced and a Committee of Special Administration has been created. We feel that, in the situation that has been created, the correct compromise decision was made—a decision that is capable of playing a positive role in overcoming the interethnic conflict and in normalizing the interethnic relations in the oblast. During the period that has elapsed, the committee has done a large amount of work on this path, but its activity could be more effective if it were not openly hampered by the anti-restructuring forces that inspire strikes, and the obstruction of the decisions made by the central agencies. Many deputies who spoke at the congress spoke bitterly and painfully about the serious economic and financial situation that has developed in the country. But under these conditions, the amount of money allocated to meet the needs of the oblast and to develop the NKAO of Azerbaijan SSR was—take note of this—a half billion rubles. However, for unexplainable reasons, that help, practically speaking, is being rejected. We need good will and a genuine desire to collaborate if effective use is to be made of the opportunities granted for normalizing the situation and for accelerating the development of the oblast. Creative work is needed.

A fundamental question that requires just as fundamental an answer is an idea that was expressed here—the idea that national feelings, national interests, must dominate over class solidarity. This is a dangerous opposing of two absolutely fundamental factors in our political philosophy. Wherever it is proposed to select one principle out of two, there is obviously a lack of any precise fundamental delineation between the genuine national interests, which never can be opposed to ideas of the solidarity and unity of nations or to nationalistic distortions.

In the history of our nations of the Transcaucasus, there have already been tragic events that were provoked by frenzied nationalists. During those tragic moments there were leaders who were capable of reconciling the fraternal nations that had lived in friendship and harmony for centuries. I am proud that they included my own own grandfather, Meshadi Azizbekov—one of the 26 Baku commissars.

Continuing these traditions, I call upon everyone to reinforce the friendship, and to reconcile those who have forgotten about the bread and salt that our nations shared for centuries and that strengthened our friendship and sacred brotherhood. It would be naive to assume that the conflict will resolve itself. This will require the carrying out of prolonged and painstaking joint work by the healthy patriotic forces of the two nations, the most delicate political actions of party organizations, and the purposeful unification of the efforts of the deputies from Armenia and Azerbaijan, who have been freed of the heavy load of reciprocal insults and prejudices, and who are capable of boldly opposing the blackmail of the anti-restructuring forces.

I want to convey words of genuine gratitude from our voters, and from the entire Azerbaijani nation, to the deputies—Metropolitan Pitirim, M.N. Rakhmanova, and others—who, having penetrated deeply into the complexity of the situation in our region, raised their voices in a heartfelt and wise appeal to reason, restraint, and mutual understanding. The numerous telegrams and telephone calls from our voters enable me to assure you that their words are finding a direct response in the hearts of people who found themselves, for reasons that were not under their control, in the maelstrom of the complicated dramatic events.

Comrade deputies! The seriousness of the situation that has developed can be judged if only from the fact that even such sacred words for us as "the friendship and brotherhood of nations" and "internationalism" seem to others to be but empty phrases. Concern for the fates of the republic and the entire country permeates the letter sent by the deputies from Azerbaijan to Comrade Gorbachev, General Secretary of CPSU Central Committee. Included among the signatures at the bottom of that letter is my own. I am returning to this document because I want everyone to know what we are striving for. We are demanding that, in practice, the supremacy of the law be carried out. We are striving for the taking of decisive steps to stop the attempts to destabilize the situation, regardless of who originates those attempts.

In our republic, the prerequisites have been created for a constructive dialogue within the confines of the Constitution that is in effect, and for a mutual striving to eliminate the conflict that is unnatural for a socialist society. Today the center of gravity must be shifted, to use Lenin's words, "not so much to describing what we have experienced, as to pointing out the experience that we are obtaining and that we must obtain for our direct practical activity" ("Poln. sobr. soch." [Complete Collected Works], Vol 39, p 342). Comrade deputies, you can be assured: The Azerbaijani nation, true to its friendship with all the fraternal nations of the USSR, will always remain a genuine and true internationalist.

One last word: Comrade deputies, I support the opinion expressed by author Deputy Belov concerning the respectful attitude to the president of our great state. But I cannot share the opinion of those who assume that Mikhail Sergeyevich is standing off to one side of restructuring. Comrade Gorbachev has been and still is, has been marching and still is marching, in the vanguard of the revolutionary restructuring of our society. Thank you for your attention. (Applause).

STENOGRAPHIC RECORD

Eighth Session

1 June 1989

B.Ye. Paton: I give the floor to Deputy Gustov.

V.V. Gustov, oil and gas production foreman in the Mamontovneft Oil and Gas Production Administration, Yugaskneftegaz Production Association, Nefteyugansk City, Tyumen Oblast, Russian Soviet Federated Socialist Republic [RSFSR] (from the trade unions of the USSR): Comrade deputies! Tyumen Oblast has finally made it to the rostrum. I did not have to notify Tyumen to close the valves on the gas pipelines.... Comrades, I will not explain what Tyumen Oblast is and what it means to our whole country, in particular the economy. Everyone knows about it. But I do want the country's parliament finally to realize something, namely that the country's main oilfield is on the verge of its latest crisis. It's as if many problems were piling up on each other in this vast region. Especially acute is the social problem. Some 17,500 families of oil workers are huddled in huts and other temporary structures. Under the conditions of the Far North and its marshes! Medical services leave much to be desired. The CPSU Central Committee and USSR Council of Ministers Decree No 797, adopted in 1985, is not being implemented. The construction organizations which were sent in accordance with the decree to deal with the problem of housing and social, cultural, and service facilities, are leaving. The oil workers' trade unions are very disturbed by this, and we demand an answer. Against this background, the petrochemical industry that is being brought into the region has a kind of negative look to it. Without having solved one problem we immediately pile on another. In short, we already have people without homes, and immediately start breeding others. A total of 41 billion rubles will go to build new chemical enterprises. It is calculated that this will require bringing at least 700,000 persons into the region, and there are already over 3.5 million persons in the oblast—more than twice the growth of 20 years. As a result, oil workers' facilities will have to be cut back.

Who comes up with these ideas? I think it must be people who are ill-informed and not fully competent, people who conduct armchair strategies; it is evidently they who are thoroughly confused as to whether the northern fields need to be developed or not. Just think, they assume, how many billions of rubles have been dumped here already. Hundreds of thousands of people have been forced to live and work under terrible conditions.

What has the effect been? The gusher period in Western Siberia has given rise to a sloppy attitude toward fuel. Trading in oil, we have failed to ensure the competitiveness of our machine-building products in foreign markets. The conclusion is to cut back capital investments in the Tyumen oil fields. But do we have anything today that we can substitute for "black gold" on the foreign markets? For some reason, science has been silent, turning the possibility of judging our affairs over to people who are not adequately in possession of the facts, although science, with all the facts at its disposal, should have said whether, for example, the state could earn foreign currency from something other than Tyumen oil. Having produced 149 billion foreign currency rubles' worth of oil for export in the past six years, the oil workers have been left with nothing.

On 5 January, MOSKOVSKAYA PRAVDA printed an interview with Comrade Salmanov, first deputy minister of geology of the USSR, under the heading "Is the Earth Running Out?" It is a timely question. As is well known, we are extracting 600 million tonnes of oil and selling a considerable portion of it abroad. This is disquieting. Against this background, Comrade Salmanov's claim that our country is fabulously rich in oil and gas, which is not backed up by any serious arguments, sounds strange. It creates the false notion of an unlimited supply of valuable fuel and raw materials. Also doubtful is the esteemed geologist's claim that if we produce 700 million tonnes of oil per year it will eliminate lines at the gasoline pumps. Why this ballyhoo? We are no longer fabulously rich at all and are at the limit of profitability. I have been working in the oil fields for more than 20 years and I can see what this leads to. Do we really want to be in the situation that developed in late 1983 and early 1984? At the time we forgot about everything and, under the slogan "Oil at any cost" we pursued our cherished goal. One million tonnes of Tyumen oil per day. Yes, we did produce a million tonnes per day, but only for a day, and then we rolled back, because there was emptiness ahead; there was no material base. People were pushed into the background, with oil in the forefront. In short, we lacked a strong infrastructure, namely social, cultural, and service facilities, housing, and working conditions. And that immediately affected the whole country.

In September 1985, the oblast was visited by Mikhail Sergeyevich Gorbachev. He brought with him many ministers, including those of the machine-building industry. They saw the kind of equipment we were working with, metal-intensive and obsolete equipment.

At this point let me say a word about the ecology. What are we going to leave to our posterity? Oil-covered taigas, marshes, rivers, and lakes. I support Comrade Sharipov's proposal that the Committee for Environmental Protection be made subordinate to the USSR Supreme Soviet rather than the Council of Ministers.

The program for the technical retooling of the oil sector of Western Siberia, which was mapped out in Surgut in that same September of 1985 with the participation of executives of the key machine-building ministries, has in effect been stymied. Out of 64 types of new equipment of cardinal importance to the oil and gas complex, we have been given only one new item—a monitoring-measurement device. Of three highly productive gas lift stations of the Sumy Association of the Ministry of Chemical and Petroleum Machine Building, which were supposed to go into operation in 1987-1988, not one is in operation because of flaws in design. More than 100 million rubles are frozen. These problems could have been solved if our enterprise had had the chance to purchase equipment from abroad, as the Law on the State Enterprise permits. Although this chance was given to other enterprises by the Bureau for the Fuel-Energy Complex, acting for the USSR

Eighth Session

1 June 1989

Council of Ministers, the oil sector was deprived of this right. A condition was set forth: The oil enterprises could export 20 percent of their above-plan output if all the ministries met the target as a whole. A typical example of coverup [krugovaya poruka]. Today it is hampering the initiative of even the successful enterprises. If it were not for the ministerial veto, these enterprises could help the lagging ones. Everyone would gain.

If we had the hard currency, we ourselves could deal with many social tasks without having to go through all the higher echelons, but these issues keep getting bogged down in the echelons, as if they were the Tyumen marshes. What is the matter? Who will explain it? Although we have repeatedly appealed to comrades Ryzhkov and Maslyukov, the question remains unanswered.

Technical backwardness defines the intensive development of the region's oil sector. Let me tell you from my own experience. In the brigade where I work, labor productivity is rising, except it's not from automation and new equipment—we don't get any; we have achieved it by increasing the number of servicing facilities. They keep demanding more and more oil from us, and the 1989 state target already exceeds the original one that was stipulated in the five-year plan. Besides that, there are additional targets for centralized deliveries. Theoretically the Tyumen oil deposits are capable of that kind of output, but the trouble is you can't get that oil with your bare hands.

A word about state orders [goszakaz]. The oil workers have a 100-percent order. For most of our suppliers, however, it is set at 30 percent. And now many of them have informed us that they are taking items which we have ordered out of production. With the transition to cost accounting, these items are no longer profitable. Others have set forth demands that cannot be met—asking for construction materials, cranes, and passenger vehicles in exchange. And the Mytishchi Plant has decided to make the oil workers pay for its dump trucks with hard currency. But if we did have hard currency, we would probably not run to them with outstretched hands. Let state orders be just that for all suppliers, 100 percent.

Comrade deputies! Tyumen Oblast today is one of the least well provided with housing, hospitals, schools, preschool child care institutions, and cultural facilities. It is sufficient to note that the city of Nizhnevartovsk, with a population of 240,000, whose oil fields are producing more oil than all the associations of the country's European region, has only one movie theater, which was built in the 20th year of the city's existence. There is no drama theater in the city. Very little progress has been made in the development of the social sphere of the other cities of the Tyumen North, especially Nefteyugansk, which has no construction industry base of its own at all, and the construction units of the Ministry of Power and Electrification are leaving the city and the region. Thousands of oil workers are still living in temporary structures. Builders, geologists, and workers of other sectors ought to be brought in. The fact that social problems have not been resolved is the main reason for the precrisis situation in the region's oil sector. In light of this, we cannot understand the government's decision to reassign the construction units of the Ministry for the Construction of Petroleum and Gas Industry Enterprises and the ministries of USSR Gosstroy [State Committee for Construction] to gas complex projects.

In conclusion, comrade deputies, I would like to make this point. There is probably not a single republic or oblast today which is not getting Tyumen oil and gas. Yes, nature saw fit to endow our harsh land with that wealth, and we consider it our duty to share it with all the regions of the country. At a price which is not very high—23 rubles per tonne. The world price is 17 dollars per barrel—that is, five times as much. In return, we are getting drilling rigs and equipment from Sverdlovsk and Volgograd, pipes from the Ukraine, and oilfield equipment from Azerbaijan. Rotating brigades come to work with us from Tataria, Bashkiria, Belorussia, and other republics. We work harmoniously and do not quarrel. Under cost accounting [khozraschet], however, it is necessary to calculate just what each region gives and gets, like any good managers.

The problems I have touched upon here affect others besides Tyumen. They are typical of all other regions in which so-called strategic sectors predominate—oil, coal, gas. In the context of examining problems of regional cost accounting and the restructuring of the administration of the national economy, it would be advisable to review the priority creation of consortium-type economic associations in such regions, exercising broad economic and management powers.

Comrade deputies, the deputies from Tyumen also include agricultural workers; they have asked me to say that they took part in formulating the appeal to the congress. With their peasants' group they fully and wholly support the appeal and hope that it will be passed by the congress and that all its provisions will be given the force of law in the near future. Thank you for your attention. (Applause).

B.Ye. Paton: Comrade deputies, the floor is turned over to Vitautas Vitautovich Landsbergis.

V.V. Landsbergis, professor in the State Conservatory, Vilnius, Lithuanian Soviet Socialist Republic [SSR] (Panevezhis City National-Territorial District, Lithuanian SSR): Honored congress, esteemed chairman! All of us here ought to try to understand one another, to perceive the common goals and appreciate the noble aspirations of each. This will reflect political culture as a component of the people's all-around culture.

The Baltic republics' striving to strengthen their sovereignty and develop and regain statehood is the way to

Eighth Session

1 June 1989

emancipate the people's creative forces, one of the goals of restructuring. A gain along this path is a gain for everyone—just as it is with, for example, the concept of the republics' economic independence that has been formulated in the Baltic region. This concept has already acquired the force of law in Lithuania and Estonia, and has now been submitted to the congress in the form of an all-union bill which, the way we see it, is useful to all the republics. It would be a shame for it to languish in a heap under the heading "Miscellaneous."

The problem of mankind's survival, which Mikhail Gorbachev has placed higher than individual state, class, and ideological interests, is coming to be realized more deeply. Nevertheless, it is being dealt with in a specific place—in Lithuania, for example, which already finds itself under the axe of ecological catastrophe. And the problem of survival is coming to be understood by people of all nationalities, just as cost accounting, the struggle against inflation, and a more stable and more secure life are understood. This is why the attempts of the anti-restructuring forces among us to sow suspicion, fear, and ethnic strife have been relatively ineffective.

Restructuring, alas, is accompanied by the heavy burden of the old domestic political thinking. The new thinking is, rather, for export so far. Perhaps the domestic "market," smothered under quotas, is not yet ripe for it. Or perhaps it withered during the prolonged stagnation. The old thinking weighs especially heavy on a range of ideas relating to the rights of peoples and republics. It is not by chance that these problems have been most neglected on the theoretical plane, while the practical pronouncements of the central leaders, unfortunately, have not been free of psychological errors.

The wisdom of the Russian people "got wise to" this method of thinking long ago, characterizing it with the bitter sarcasm of folk sayings like "the bosses know best" and "power doesn't need brains." The insight and generalizing capaciousness of these sayings with regard to state policies—for example, with regard to the convulsions of the economy, or the tragedy of Afghanistan—are worth many years of effort by social science institutes. Relations between the center and the republics, conducted on the customary pattern of "bosses and underlings," have long since become outmoded morally, politically, and practically.

Democratization cannot be manifested only in the sphere of the rights of the individual or the production collective, the sphere of the freedom of conscience, speech, or economic freedoms. It inevitably also poses questions about the freedom of peoples and the rights of republics. But if we interpret democracy in a distorted manner as the power of the majority over the minority, it will set traps for restructuring. For this reason, the democratization of such a complex country must provide guarantees that the republics will not be encroached upon by any pseudodemocratic procedure of majority voting. And since we are moving from a state of force to a state of law, we need guarantees that not one union republic will sense itself to be in a position of constant danger with regard to matters of its vital rights to its own land and its own laws. Considering the poorly developed legislation, the inertia of great-power thinking, and other vices of the present union, this will require the immediate formulation of a protective parliamentary mechanism for the states and peoples of the union.

For example, legislative-control functions could be implemented by a chamber of the Soviet of Nationalities created on a parity basis. Moreover, passing a law binding on all the republics would require the consent of each one and the approval and registration of the law by the republic's Supreme Soviet. So far, however, there is no such all-union parliamentary mechanism. Naturally, the more independently minded republics have undertaken to create mechanims of legal self-defense at home. Thus, the Lithuanian SSR Supreme Soviet on 18 May of this year passed an amendment (one of several) to Article 70 of the Lithuanian SSR Constitution, which now reads, in particular: "The laws of the USSR and the legal acts of the organs of state authority and administration of the USSR shall be in effect within the territory of the Lithuanian SSR only after being ratified by the Lithuanian SSR Supreme Soviet and registered in accordance with established procedures" (I am quoting from SOVETSKAYA LITVA). The same thing is emphasized in the Declaration of the Lithuanian SSR Supreme Soviet, adopted the same day, concerning Lithuania's state sovereignty. I quote: "From now on, from the time the amendment to Article 70 of the Lithuanian SSR Constitution is passed, only those laws which have been passed and ratified by the Lithuanian SSR Supreme Soviet shall be in force in the Lithuanian SSR." Thinking about how to avoid unnecessary political tensions and collisions with the obsolete Brezhnevian All-Union Constitution, we propose to the congress to introduce an amendment to Article 74 of the present USSR Constitution, so that it reads in full as follows: "The laws of the USSR shall be in force within the territories of the union republics after they are passed and registered by the union republic's supreme soviet." (Applause). I take this opportunity to submit this proposal, in the form of a legislative initiative, to the congress from the group of deputies from Lithuania.

The democratization of the country must also provide for the defense of the process of democratization. In connection with this, I would like to mention the appeal to the USSR Congress of People's Deputies, which was adopted in Tallinn on 14 May of this year by the Baltic Assembly of People's Fronts—which included the Lithuanian Sajudis—concerning the threat of war by the state against its own people. This appeal should be read separately and distributed as a document of the congress calling for defining the function of the Armed Forces as exclusively defensive, to be used only in the event of an attack from without. These provisions also form part of

Eighth Session
1 June 1989

a more detailed appeal to the USSR Congress of People's Deputies, signed by 50 deputies from Latvia, Lithuania, and Estonia. As a legislative initiative, it calls for adopting a decision of the USSR Supreme Soviet which also includes a paragraph about disbanding the military units which took part in the murders and violence against the civilian population in Tbilisi, as having dishonored themselves. (Noise in the hall).

From these documents you can see that our hopes and concerns affect everyone. We desire that no gas weapons be tested on people, especially in peacetime. And the congress, which today is responsible for the fate of democracy, must deprive any possible "Napoleonic" or "Pinochetian" coup of any semblance of legality. We are talking about the formal right of the internal affairs minister to decide on his own whether to use special forces, and the right of the USSR Supreme Soviet Presidium to declare a state of emergency over the territory of the whole country all at once—that is, for example, to take Mikhail Sergeyevich prisoner and openly declare itself the ruling junta.

Do we really consent to confer such extraordinary powers on them without any kind of people's control? Do you really consent to the presence on your doorstep of a specter with a bad Constitution in one hand and a bloody shovel in the other—do you consent to that kind of power of the law? (Noise in the hall). Lithuania, at any rate, does not so consent. Please accept these remarks as a proposal to the congress and to each deputy personally to take thought, to return to the discussion, and again put to the vote the question of rescinding these decrees as well as the latest addenda to the criminal legislation, especially the passage on state crimes. We also need to think about what we have done and what position we have taken. Recently, Deputy Rodionov was pining for 1937, and many deputies clapped their hands in agreement. Think, comrade deputies, what you were applauding.

And we are all affected by such a dark and bloody stain on the history of the USSR as the Stalin-Hitler pact, concerning which a serious discussion has already been started here. The existence of the secret protocols is proved not only by the Nuremberg copies but also by the scrupulous compliance with those secret protocols in 1939-1941. Mikhail Sergeyevich himself, in my opinion, does not doubt that they did exist. And I propose defining the task of the commission by something like this designation: "On the pact and the problem of the secret protocols." The purpose of the commission is spelled out clearly in the Lithuanian SSR Supreme Soviet's appeal to us: "Condemn the aforementioned secret deals signed by the Soviet government of that time, and declare them to be illegal and not in force from the moment they were signed." There is no doubt that this will be done, but it is better for all of us not to stretch this ambiguous rubber band.

Which way should we be looking today, in what direction? Restructuring also entails restoring the true meaning to words. Union [soyuz] does not mean "absorption" [priyuz] nor yet "subordination" [podyuz]; a union is an association of union members who have joined together—not by force but voluntarily—for the sake of common goals on the basis of consent and benefits. The journey to such a union is not a short one, but it can be made. It can be done thanks to restructuring, by helping restructuring.

New concepts are needed, concepts which incorporate the best of the Lenin legacy and nothing from the Stalin legacy. Let us envision a union of states and a union of fatherlands. If the spiritual rebirth of the nation gains in strength and produces a material result, it will again take the form of fatherlands, including Russia—the form of self-governing people's states growing out of the principle of people's sovereignty, inseminated by the will of the people, who are masters of their own lives. And then it will be up to them—the peoples and states—as to what reciprocal agreements and alliances to conclude. Such a concept is capable of encompassing whole regions, whether in eastern or northern Europe, joining them together and opening up more realistic prospects for the celebrated European homeland—and who knows, perhaps even building a road to the spiritual rapprochement of Europe and Asia, Christianity and Islam.

Of course, the European homeland would then appear not in the form of a hostel under the authority of an all-knowing and all-suspicious commandant, but rather in the form of a peace-loving community where no one is afraid of anyone, where people can simply share their labor, their goods, their help, and their songs of good-neighborliness. I thank you. (Applause).

B.Ye. Paton: Esteemed comrade deputies! Seven deputies have spoken at the evening session. Two more are scheduled, but we need to decide several organizational matters. It is proposed, therefore, that the discussion be discontinued at this point. Any other proposals?

Voices from the floor: No.

B.Ye. Paton: Thank you. The floor is turned over to Deputy Anatoliy Ivanovich Lukyanov, first deputy chairman of the USSR Supreme Soviet Presidium.

A.I. Lukyanov: Comrade deputies! The Supreme Soviet Presidium and the congress Presidium have directed me to acquaint you with a number of documents. The fact is that you have heard here a number of speeches which included mention of the responsibility of our country's highest levels for what happened in Georgia. There was a hint of just that in the recent speech. A letter has also arrived from public figures in the Georgian SSR, addressed to Mikhail Sergeyevich Gorbachev, asking him to meet with them on these very matters.

M.S. Gorbachev: I will do so.

STENOGRAPHIC RECORD

Eighth Session
1 June 1989

A.I. Lukyanov: I would not like to comment in detail here on these documents; I only want to read them so you may get an objective picture of what took place during those days. The only thing that I will recount in brief is about two telegrams sent from the Georgian SSR by the first secretary of the Georgian Communist Party Central Committee at 1100 on 26 November and at 1900 on 26 November, when the well-known events took place in Georgia in connection with the discussion of the draft amendments to the USSR Constitution. Mikhail Sergeyevich has told about them here. These are the two documents; they conclude with words to the effect that Georgia's public, party, and soviet organs had not managed to normalize the situation, that it was heating up and becoming increasingly unmanageable and out of control, and that the only possibility of stabilizing things and preventing serious conflicts and excesses was to institute a curfew, at least in the republic's capital city. The second document is the same, except that it is dated 19:50 on the 26th: "On the whole, the situation in the capital city has deteriorated during the past 24 hours, and we again insist on instituting a curfew."

From the floor: Who signed it? (Noise in the hall).

A.I. Lukyanov: They were signed by Georgian Communist Party Central Committee First Secretary Patiashvili. That was in November. After that, as you know, Mikhail Sergeyevich addressed an oral message to the Georgian intelligentsia. The negotiations went on all night, and the tension was finally eased. So the first appeals were of just that kind. I will not read all the telegrams here. But I do want the congress delegates to know the three latest telegrams in full.

The first telegram, dated 7 April—please note, 7 April, 2040. It reads as follows: "The situation in the republic has badly deteriorated recently. It is practically out of control. The cause of it was a rally on 18 March in the village of Lykhny, Abkhazian Autonomous SSR [ASSR], which raised the issue of the autonomous republic's secession from the Georgian SSR. But the events have gone beyond those limits. Extremist elements are fanning nationalistic sentiments, calling for strikes and disobedience to the authorities, organizing disturbances, and discrediting party and soviet organs. Under the circumstances, extraordinary measures need to be taken.

"We deem it immediately essential to institute criminal and administrative proceedings against extremists who are coming out with anti-Soviet, anti-socialist, and anti-party slogans and calls to action. There are legal grounds for this.

"Secondly, we deem it essential to declare a state of emergency and institute curfew in Tbilisi, enlisting additional forces of the Ministry of Internal Affairs [MVD] and Transcaucasion Military District [ZakVO].

"Thirdly, we deem it essential to implement a complex of political, organizational, and administrative measures, using the forces of the party, soviet, and economic aktiv, to stabilize the situation. It is essential not to allow publications in the all-union or republic mass media which would complicate the situation.

"Dzhumber Patiashvili, secretary of the Georgian Communist Party Central Committee, 7 April, 2040." That is the original telegram.

The next day, 8 April, 2050. Just 6 hours before the tragedy, as you see.

"This is to report that the situation in Tbilisi continues tense. A rally of many thousands of people is taking place in front of Government House, and their slogans are the same as before: secession from the USSR, creation of an independent Georgia, liquidation of the autonomies, and so on.

"A rally by 3,500 people of Georgian nationality was held in the Abkhazian ASSR, directed against Abkhazia's separation from the Georgian SSR.

"In a number of VUZes, some of the students have declared a hunger strike in support of the rally participants. On the whole, the Georgian Communist Party Central Committee, the government, and local party and soviet organs are in command of the situation and are taking the necessary measures to stabilize it. Yesterday, 7 April, the Georgian Communist Party Central Committee Buro met, and today the republic's party aktiv met and endorsed the measures taken by party, soviet, and law enforcement organs to step up political, organizational, and upbringing work among the labor collectives and in places of residence; it also adopted an Appeal of the Georgian Communist Party Central Committee, Supreme Soviet, and Council of Ministers to the republic's communists and working people. In particular, it mapped out plans to hold aktivs in all the regions of the republic, with the participation of Georgian Communist Party Central Committee and Buro members, also meetings of primary party organizations, where practical plans of action have been worked out in pursuit of the measures to be taken.

"A series of television and radio speeches by prominent figures in the sciences and culture of the republic and representatives of the working class and the peasantry has been organized. The VUZes are holding round tables and meetings with young people on topical questions of Georgia's social life, the harmfulness of illegal actions, measures of reponsibility for anything committed, and the necessity of strengthening order and discipline in order to further develop democracy and glasnost. After the aktiv, everyone went out to the localities, into the labor collectives, to explain the materials of the aktiv, the party's policies under present conditions, the unity of the party and the people, and the implementation of the tasks of restructuring. Workers' squads were formed in 111 enterprises and institutions of Tbilisi, numbering 4684 persons, to maintain discipline and organization. Concrete plans have been drawn up and are being

Eighth Session
1 June 1989

implemented in collaboration with the MVD and ZakVO to enforce law and order and, if necessary, to take exhaustive measures to prevent rioting and illegal actions. The entire apparatus of the Central Committee, the Supreme Soviet, the Council of Ministers, and the Tbilisi Gorkom [ciyt party committee] and Gorispolkom [city soviet executive committee] is carrying out its functions meticulously and doing active work among the population and the rally participants. At present no measures on the part of the CPSU Central Committee and the USSR government, additional to those already taken, are necessary.

"This report is by way of information. Dzhumber Patiashvili.

"Dated 8 April, 2050."

So there was no necessity—I make no comment here—of taking any action from the Center after that telegram.

Now the final telegram that I want to acquaint you with.

The 9th of April, 1025. Now the events have taken place. This is why members of the Politburo, Mikhail Sergeyevich, and now I myself have had to do this, to name the time—1025. This is the telegram. I'll read it: "CPSU Central Committee. On the night of 8 April 1989, in Tbilisi, after 2100, despite all the measures taken by party, soviet, and law enforcement organs, the situation at the rally in front of Government House, participated in by about 15,000 persons, also in other parts of the city, began to be heated up to the limit by extremists and got out of control. In addition to anti-Soviet, anti-socialist, and anti-Russian slogans they began to hand out the extremists' calls for physical reprisals against communists, republic leaders, and members of their families. The rally participants, among whom there were many drunks and persons using narcotics, called for organizing a strike of the entire population of the republic, civil disobedience, and reprisals against those who did not support them. They began to delegate groups of extremists and other participants in the rally to nearby cities and rayons of the republic. In the city of Rustavi there was an attempt to seize the metallurgy plant. The leaders of the so-called national-liberation movement began to announce plans to seize power in the republic.

"In this situation, in order to ensure public safety and prevent unforeseeable consequences, the decision was made at 0400 to use force to clear the rally participants from the square in front of Government House. In accordance with the plan that had been drawn up beforehand by competent organs, subunits of the republic's MVD and ZakVO were used. As they approached the site of the rally, its participants (they numbered about 8,000 by this time) were frequently appealed to by the republic's leaders, members of the Communist Party Central Committee, the party and soviet aktiv, and Georgian Catholicos Ilya II to halt the rally and disperse peaceably. The rally participants, however, did not respond. In turn, the organizers of the rally inflamed people's passions to the point of psychosis, calling upon them not to spare their own blood and life in resisting the forces of law and order. Subunits of the MVD and troops of ZakVO did not use firearms or cold weapons. They followed instructions strictly with regard to careful treatment of women and adolescents. As the first ranks of the rally participants were driven back, despite the ferocious resistance of extremists using sticks and stones, the crowd became unmanageable and moved toward the young people who had declared a hunger strike and were lying on the sidewalk. Moreover, there were many provocateurs in the crowd who were using cold weapons. As a result of the crush that developed, 16 persons died: 13 young women and 3 men. More than 100 persons received wounds of varying degrees of severity, including 22 military personnel, 13 of whom are hospitalized. Persons who were hurt have been given emergency medical aid. At present, the square in front of Government House has been cleared of rally participants and is under guard by the troops. Necessary measures are being taken to apprehend and arrest anyone who instigates disturbances and to prevent any new rallies or demonstrations. In connection with the tragic consequences of the measures that were taken, a government commission has been formed, headed by Georgian SSR Council of Ministers Chairman Chkheidze.

"Today the Georgian Communist Party Central Committee Plenum is to examine the situation and determine the meaures stemming from it. To prevent mass disorders and to stabilize the situation we request permission to institute curfew in Tbilisi starting today.

"9 April, 1025. Georgian Communist Party Secretary Patiashvili." Original copy.

I do not want to comment. We knew how the Georgian people, the Georgian population might react to such things after that. Comrades Shevardnadze and Razumovskiy flew there immediately.

M.S. Gorbachev: Why I think we are on the right track by creating the commission. This whole mechanism must be broken down by hours and summarized. The comrades from Georgia have appealed to me.... When I was meeting with the Moscow group of deputies they asked me the first question. Who gave the command? These are the events, this is how they developed. The fact that there was no confidence there was obvious. It was obvious that the situation there was tense, not a promenade as someone here tried to tell us. A promenade, a street festival—it was just not so. Or at the time it was all wrong, understand? Look at these telegrams.

In short, we must get to the bottom of everything, and therefore we have acted correctly in presenting them at this

Eighth Session
1 June 1989

point, so that, taking account of the information, the people will not have a sour aftertaste and the impression that something is being covered up here. No, we really are counting on getting to the bottom of these events. Everything must be clarified, reported to the Supreme Soviet, and a determination made as to what decisions to make in this case. That will be the right thing, in my opinion.

B.Ye. Paton: Comrades, in accordance with the customary time limit the speakers will be given up to three minutes.

F.V. Dovlatyan, artistic director of Armenfilm Studio, city of Yerevan (Yerevan-Mashtots National-Territorial Election District, Armenian SSR): Esteemed deputies! Honored President! I understand that in this difficult struggle for the Constitution, for a just Constitution, in this struggle for power—comprehensible to us or not—our bleeding wounds, of course, give us no peace, and I ask you to give me one minute to express myself. Hear my protest to the secretariat and the presidium. For four days now the Armenian deputies' group has made appeals, demands, and so on and so forth, but we have not received any answer. I consider this to be unjust. We want to know, at long last, why you are not responding to our requests. They are very serious, urgent, and extremely anxious ones. I remind you that our first request was to classify the events in Sumgait as genocide. The second request dealt with Nagorno-Karabakh Autonomous Oblast [NKAO], the referendum in NKAO. We have simply not been able to get, to receive an answer. Why has there been no response to our requests?

B.Ye. Paton: Comrades! It is proposed that the presidium be instructed to respond to the requests tomorrow. Let us examine another organizational matter.

Comrades! On 25 May, the congress directed the Mandate Commission to give a ruling on Deputy Alksnis's request. The floor is turned over to Deputy Boris Veniaminovich Gidaspov, chairman of the Mandate Commission.

B.V. Gidaspov, general director of GIPKh Scientific-Production Association, chairman of the board of the Tekhnokhim Inter-Sectorial State Association, city of Leningrad (Petrograd Territorial District, Leningrad): Esteemed Chairman, esteemed deputies! A brief report on the activities of the Mandate Commission. In the last few days, the congress Presidium and the Mandate Commission have continued to receive direct appeals, letters, and telegrams, the number of which now approaches 100. The spectrum of regions and oblasts of the Soviet Union is broad; letters are coming in from Moscow, Smolensk, Tbilisi, NKAO, Leningrad, Ust-Kamenogorsk, Naberezhnyye Chelny, and other cities and regions. All of these letters can be divided into two approximately equal groups.

In the letters of the first group, the voters complain of violations of the Law and procedures of the Law on Elections (mainly, Article 13). We have generalized these letters, analyzed them, sent them to the Central Electoral Commission, and are continuing to send them there to be reviewed. Some of them are being reviewed in the presence of the chairman of the district commissions from the places I have mentioned, who were invited specially to Moscow. Based on the findings of the review of these letters, the Mandate Commission will be able to provide additional information in two or three days.

The second group of letters contains additional information about the elected deputies. There are about 50 such letters. They report negative political, business, and personal qualities of the deputies. A review of these letters is outside the jurisdiction of the Mandate Commission; I am here addressing the voters of the whole Soviet Union. But we are generalizing these letters, analyzing them, and will turn them over to the Supreme Soviet to be used in the work of the Commission, which will prepare a new Law on Elections.

Summarizing what I have said, I must note that, as many deputies here have already said, these letters reflect, as in a drop of water, all the shortcomings of the Law on Elections that is in force today. There is not the slightest doubt that the Law needs to be seriously revised or even repealed.

The second question deals with the specific request that was made orally at the congress by Deputy V.I. Alksnis. Deputy Alksnis has raised a fair question concerning deviations from Article 17 of the Law on Elections. This article deals with the formation of national-territorial election districts. Having heard the report of Vladimir Pavlovich Orlov, chairman of the Central Electoral Commission, and Anatoliy Valeryanovich Gorbunov, chairman of the presidium of the Latvian SSR Supreme Soviet, the Mandate Commission notes that such deviations did indeed take place. At the meeting of the Mandate Commission, accordingly, instances of the formation of national-territorial election districts with unequal numbers of voters were cited in the territories of other union republics as well. I have a whole list and, if necessary, I can submit additional examples in regard to this matter.

As for the matter being discussed—violations and deviations from the norm of the law concerning equal numbers of voters in the national-territorial election districts—in fact, as the examination has shown, the number of voters in the national-territorial election districts of the Latvian SSR ranges from 28,800 to 127,300. I must caution at this point that the Mandate Commission cannot examine the totality of the election districts. We review the mandate of each deputy individually. Every deputy from the Latvian SSR has been elected in accordance with the law. The Mandate Commission confirms that the mandates held by the deputies present in this hall are genuine. At the same time, in order to prevent such violations—I am reading here for

Eighth Session

1 June 1989

the sake of accuracy—in order to prevent such violations, the Mandate Commission urges the congress to direct the attention of the Central Electoral Commission and the presidiums of the supreme soviets of the union republics to the necessity of complying strictly with the requirements of the legislation on elections when forming election districts.

And, most important: From now on the Central Electoral Commission must publish lists of election districts with an indication of the number of voters in each district. The Mandate Commission requests that you support our proposal. (Applause).

B.Ye. Paton: Comrade deputies! Are there any questions for Comrade Gidaspov?

From the floor: That's not what we commissioned you to do! Remember, when the declaration and protest came in the proposal was made to look into or create a commission of the congress, but Mikhail Sergeyevich supported and insisted that the Mandate Commission be assigned to look into it. And now you say that you're only looking into the question of credentials [polnomochiya]. You have confirmed the credentials of all the deputies to us all at once. In my opinion, you took the wrong route. What I wonder now is whether you did this deliberately or you simply didn't understand what we wanted you to do.

B.V. Gidaspov: May I respond?

From the floor: The subject was violations, there were violations there, the speaker acknowledges that there were violations, yet he says that the Mandate Commission does not have the right to look into it. But we decided then at the congress to assign the commission to look into it.

B.V. Gidaspov: May I respond to you? I think that the comrade deputy, whose name I did not catch, is a little excited. The fact is that we were directed to respond to Comrade Alksnis's request. The gist of his request dealt with the fact that there were deviations from Article 17 of the Law on Elections of people's deputies of the USSR, and violations of the article having to do with the formation and population of districts in the Latvian SSR. This matter has been examined. The results of the elections give no grounds for depriving anyone of his mandate. The Mandate Commission has confirmed this. Comrade Alksnis was present at the meeting of the Mandate Commission, and he was satisfied with the decision.

(Noise in the hall).

B.V. Gidaspov: Comrades! I have been asked a question, which I here repeat: "You were given documents having to do with Bryansk, Smolensk, and Kaluga...," and also, as I already mentioned, Tbilisi, Naberezhnyye Chelny, Leningrad, and many other cities. These documents have been reviewed by the Mandate Commission and turned over to the Central Electoral Commission, which is supposed to give us a written statement concerning properly conducted verification, summoning the chairmen of the district commissions when necessary. We have in part already heard them in the Mandate Commission, and we will continue this work.

(Noise in the hall).

B.Ye. Paton: Any questions?

From the hall: No.

B.Ye. Paton: It is proposed, comrades, that we take into consideration the report of the chairman of the Mandate Commission. (Applause). Any objections?

Carried. (To the hall): Just a moment. (Noise in the hall).

M.S. Gorbachev: You ought to agree on when to leave. (Noise in the hall). (Applause).

B.Ye. Paton: Comrades, if you're dissatisfied with what in my opinion was a unanimously adopted proposal, let's take a vote. Wait a minute, there can be separate discussion of the other issue. I put it to a vote. Whoever is in favor of taking into consideration the report of the chairman of the Mandate Commission, please raise your cards. I think it's clear that there is an absolute majority. There is no need to vote. Anyone against?

From the hall: No.

B.Ye. Paton: Thank you. (Applause). Comrade deputies. There is a question, shall we yield the floor?

From the hall: No.

B.Ye. Paton: Comrade deputies, our work is not done yet, please sit down. The whole congress has voted against giving you the floor. (Noise in the hall).

M.S. Gorbachev: Please respect the congress.

B.Ye. Paton: Comrade deputies, on your instructions the congress presidium has drawn up a proposal on the composition of the commission to investigate materials relating to the activity of the USSR Prosecutor's Office investigation group headed by Deputy Gdlyan. Deputy Rafik Nishanovich Nishanov has the floor on this question.

R.N. Nishanov, first secretary of the Uzbekistan Communist Party Central Committee (Leningradskiy National-Territorial Electoral Okrug, Uzbek Soviet Socialist Republic): Esteemed comrade deputies! In the course of the preparation of this proposal a number of comrades withdrew. At the same time a total of 30 new candidates were

Eighth Session

1 June 1989

proposed. The congress presidium held consultations with deputies from various union republics and regions, including comrades Telman Khorenovich Gdlyan and Nikolay Veniaminovich Ivanov. All the comrades are agreed that the commission should include deputies from various union republics and regions who have not previously associated themselves in any way with assessments of the work of the investigation group. For this reason it is not expedient for the commission to include either representatives of the former commission, which has played its part, or those deputies who have made various statements on the work of the investigation group.

It is deemed expedient also to refrain from including on the commission workers of the USSR Prosecutor's Office, since this department's work is in question. At the same time we must support the proposal that the commission should be able to involve in its work (in the capacity of experts) consultants and specialists in various spheres. So that is the general principle, and now the composition of the commission:

Chairman of the commission: Roy Aleksandrovich Medvedev.

Members of the commission: Vladimir Tuychiyevich Adylov, lathe operators' team leader at the Tashkent V.P. Chkalov Aircraft Production Association; Valeriy Grigoryevich Aleksandrin, chairman of Yoshkar-Ola City People's Court, Mari autonomous republic; Aleksandr Ivanovich Baranov, chairman of the "Izhorskiy Zavod" Production Association trade union committee, Leningrad City, Kolpino City; Ilmar Olgertovich Bisher, professor at the P. Stuchka Latvian State University; Egidiyus Vitautovich Bichkauskas, Lithuanian SSR Prosecutor's Office investigator for important cases; Yuriy Vladimirovich Golik, dean of Kemerovo State University Law Faculty; Nikolay Ivanovich Ignatovich, Belorussian SSR Prosecutor's Office investigator for important cases; Konstantin Dmitriyevich Lubenchenko, lecturer at Moscow State University Law Faculty; Vello Paulovich Pokhla, member of the editorial collegium of the "Estonskiy Telefilm" Main Editorial Office, Estonian SSR State Committee for Television and Radio Broadcasting, Tallinn City; Vitaliy Aleksandrovich Semenov, senior scientific staffer at the Ukrainian SSR Academy of Sciences Institute of Technical Mechanics, Dnepropetrovsk City; Igor Viktorovich Sorokin, senior superintendent of criminal investigations at the Kuybyshev Station railroad internal affairs department; Nikolay Alekseyevich Strukov, senior investigator of the Kursk Oblast Prosecutor's Office; Olzhas Omarovich Suleymenov, writer, first secretary of the Kazakhstan Writers' Union Board, Alma-Ata City; Svyatoslav Nikolayevich Fedorov, general director of the "Mikrokhirurgiya Glaza" multisector scientific and technical complex; Viktor Nikolayevich Shorokhov, fitter at the Tula V.M. Ryabikov Machine Building Plant; and Veniamin Aleksandrovich Yarin, operator at the Nizhniy Tagil V.I. Lenin Metallurgical Combine, Sverdlovsk Oblast.

Both on the congress presidium and on the secretariat, we considered this matter very carefully and selected these 17 candidates, and I would ask you to approve this composition.

B.Ye. Paton: Any questions for Rafik Nishanovich? (Disturbance in the auditorium).

B.Ye. Paton: No questions?

Voices from the floor: No.

From the floor: I have a question.

B.Ye. Paton: Go ahead. (Disturbance in the auditorium).

From the floor: We nominated Yakovlev. The Yakutsk delegation proposed Yakovlev. Why was he excluded? (Disturbance in the auditorium).

B.Ye. Paton: Go ahead, please, your question.

From the floor: (Inaudible).

From the floor: Please listen to me, comrade deputies, for a minute. Our delegates agree entirely with the opinion on the selection of this commission. But we think that the working class is equally conscious, and moreover there is not a single Komsomol [Leninist Communist Youth League] representative here. I therefore propose—as was proposed earlier in a note—that Vladimir Norikhin be included—he is a controller, from Vladimir City. He is a deputy from the Komsomol and a principled comrade. I ask your support for our proposal.

R.N. Nishanov: Let me answer the question about Comrade Yakovlev from Yakutia. When we were drawing up the list, Comrade Yakovlev's candidacy was also proposed by Comrades Gdlyan and Ivanov. But there were six people on the list. We agreed on the basis of parity that those whom we are investigating cannot form the commission themselves. Therefore I asked for three people to be chosen. The comrades proposed three names, which I included on the list—it is all very logical.

One last point. All the deputies on this list have good credentials, they are all upright, no one has discredited any of them, they are all conscientious, and I am convinced that they will study any question objectively. (Applause).

From the floor: Let us vote!

N.V. Ivanov, preliminary investigator [sledovatel] for especially important matters, USSR General Procuracy

Eighth Session

1 June 1989

(Leningrad City National-Territorial Election District, RSFSR): So, comrades, just a moment. You have probably noticed a peculiar feature. Namely, a serious question has been presented to us at the end of the day, when everyone is tired, and as if by the way.

The ancient Romans, when they undertook an inquiry, always said that it was necessary to answer the question: Whom does this benefit?

(Noise in the hall). Just a moment, let me speak. We are supposed to have a democracy here, after all. Please notice that two commissions are being created here. Two commissions have been the subject all the time. The commission concerning the events in Tbilisi, and the commission concerning a criminal case of corruption. Whom did it benefit, incidentally, to form one more commission on Tbilisi, although there were two questions there that needed to be answered: Who gave the commands from Moscow? Just a moment, I'll answer. No need to manifest, so to speak, enhanced intellect. (Applause).

From the floor: We can't hear you. (Noise in the hall).

N.V. Ivanov: I hope you have calmed down, comrades.

B.Ye. Paton: It is proposed that the speech be halted or allowed to be completed. Let's take a vote. All those in favor of stopping the speech please raise your hands.

Voices from the floor: Let him speak!

M.S. Gorbachev: Comrade Ivanov, please formulate your ideas....

N.V. Ivanov: I have done so. Please have the patience to hear me out, comrades. Here we have a third commission being created, and meanwhile the process of wrecking the criminal case is nearing completion. Here sits People's Deputy Sukharev, whose efforts have resulted in the expulsion of 64 investigators of the group. After this, just try and prove to me or anyone else sitting here in the hall that anyone is interested in completing the case. Today while the congress was in session, Osetrov, the former second secretary of the Uzbekistan Communist Party Central Committee, Orlov, the former vice president of Uzbekistan, along with Smirnov, were released from custody. What for, one wonders? Because a number of goals scheduled for today.... As the saying goes, "Vaska the Cat listens but keeps on eating."

And while we sit here dealing with problems supposedly by democratic means, what will the commission be looking at next? In order for the commission to examine things from the time the decision is made, it must get all the materials, all of them, and not just those which were received by the preceding commission, some kind of stooges. (Noise in the hall). And now about the creation of the commission.

Come on, let's not do it this way. Please, prepare a list, and not just ten minutes before the end of the meeting, so that we can sit down, look at it, and think about who and how. (Noise in the hall). Well I will answer the question, if somebody doesn't shut the microphones off now. Will somebody please say why we need three commissions? The first one is the CPSU Central Committee and Party Control Committee Commission—an illegal one, because the party here is not supposed to interfere in the administration of justice anymore. The second is the USSR Supreme Soviet Presidium Commission, which has wasted a month and a half of investigation, and meanwhile it is being wrecked. And what for? Because by today the process is completed....

Voice: (Inaudible).

N.V. Ivanov: Wait, don't interfere, please. The process of curtailing the struggle against organized crime is nearing completion; attempts are being made to relieve the Moscow bribe-takers of responsibility. And this is also unequivocal: to leave a stain on the region of Uzbekistan and remove, whitewash the stain on Moscow, because look, the Russian bribe-takers are being released from custody. (Noise in the hall). Wait, comrades. Look, now, five minutes before the end of the congress, some kind of roster is suddenly submitted. What can I say offhand about this or that person? They seem to be decent people. I'm very sorry and, incidentally, all those present will, after a while, be quite ashamed over what took place in this hall. Incidentally, the report has gone on two days; for two days I have had a note on my desk saying that I have to speak. Comrades, these are questions of principle we are dealing with.

We have all digressed from the question of authority, the central question. We've talked about all kinds of things. And, again, in the same way, by way of an aggressively obedient majority, by waving our cards, we are deciding all the subsequent issues. Time will pass and many of those present here will be ashamed about what took place here. And the fact that you won't give me the floor, you keep getting off the subject, and you won't give me the opportunity to state my position fully, please understand, it does not do you credit. For this reason, I will not say any more or present arguments. Decide how you will; time will put everything in its place. But, comrades, if Comrade Gdlyan and I, along with 64 investigators of the group, were removed from our posts during the period of the work, why not think about removing comrades Ligachev and a number of other persons from their posts for the period of the commission's work? Thank you for your attention.

(Applause). **V.S. Shevchenko,** chairman of the Ukrainian SSR Supreme Soviet Presidium, Kiev City (Kiyevskiy Rural National-Territorial Electoral Okrug, Ukrainian SSR): Esteemed comrade deputies! This morning many deputies found notes to this effect at the doors of their hotel rooms: "Comrades, we ask you to support comrades Gdlyan and Ivanov." We regard this as an attempt to put pressure on deputies.

STENOGRAPHIC RECORD

Eighth Session

1 June 1989

The decision to form a commission was decided at the congress on Saturday. On Sunday, at 1000 hours, the entire body of deputies from the Ukrainian SSR, and there are 262 of us, met almost in full, and we discussed this question. The delegation decided together whom to recommend for the commission. Several candidacies were put forward. The entire delegation settled on Comrade Semenov's candidacy. And we gave him this instruction: Examine everything honorably and conscientiously. Vindicate the innocent, punish the guilty. We have every trust in the deputy whom we recommended for the commission, and we believe that neither Comrade Gdlyan nor Comrade Ivanov has the right to withdraw a deputy who was recommended by an entire delegation. (Applause).

E.Yu. Yusupov, vice president of the Uzbek SSR Academy of Sciences, Tashkent City (from the All-Union "Znaniye" Society): An organization in defense of Gdlyan and Ivanov is at work in Moscow. It is operating very efficiently. There is not one deputy who has not received an anonymous letter and message in praise of Gdlyan. Drunken young people are walking around everywhere carrying placards, stopping delegates and claiming that if Gdlyan is vindicated, the Food Program in the country will be resolved. When we asked one of them, why are you campaigning for a man you have probably never set eyes on, he replied: I do not know him, but I have been instructed to do this. This is not honest, I think it is a provocation.

Moreover, comrades, you have doubtless read a lot about the activity of the investigation team in Uzbekistan. The facts you have learned are only the tip of a huge iceberg, and we have not yet studied what lies beneath the surface. Let the commission examine it and tell us everything. And another comment. I am opposed to Roy Medvedev's candidacy as chairman, because he is one of the handful of journalists who are involved in creating the myth of Gdlyan and Ivanov. (Applause).

N.A. Strukov, senior investigator of the Kursk Oblast Prosecutor's Office (Kursk Territorial Electoral Okrug, RSFSR): Comrades, we are talking now about a man's guilt. But you have forgotten the most important thing: In accordance with our Constitution, guilt can only be established by the court (Article 151 of the Constitution). Therefore, in order to discuss the formation of a commission, we must think about making an amendment to the Constitution on the question of forming a commission. On this basis I, as a specialist, do not refuse to participate in the commission, but I request that its formation be given constitutional backing.

Moving from the general to the particular, I propose that the question of the actions of the investigation group be examined from the viewpoint of the imposition of law and order. The examination of the question should proceed in two dialectically interconnected directions. First, to establish whether the group operated on the basis of the principles of the rule of law, or of lawlessness. After all, in 6 years Gdlyan and the others entangled many officials, up to the level of the USSR Supreme Soviet, in an endless, irresponsible chain of impermissible methods. For the sake of their political career, they are prepared to do anything in the guise of the protection of law and order, spurred on by the journalists' loathsome praise, in the past, of Gdlyan and his deputy, not of all 209 members of their group. Incidentally, a number of them have already expressed their opinion on the matter. Let us not annoy the people with superfluous talk.

Second. The mafia is still the mafia, and if Gdlyan had not wounded the very foundations of its existence, no violations of the rule of law on his part would be under examination now; it would all have remained in the shadows. (Applause). If we are to debunk the Gdlyan phenomenon, let it be only through the court in accordance with the Constitution. Our parliament is not professional in this respect. There are only a very small number of representatives of legal science on the proposed commission.

But we cannot allow the verdicts that were pronounced, and their legality, to be discredited—that is the most important thing. There were millions of rubles, there were givers and receivers of bribes. There were bribers and bribe-takers, and this campaign is, in my view, aimed at distracting public opinion from the problem of the mafia and preventing investigation of the so-called "sharks."

We will only preserve faith in the rule of law by observing the due process of criminal law. Not many people know that criminal proceedings have now been instituted in the case of the Gdlyan group. But neither he nor the general prosecutor is in any hurry to inform the congress of this. I consider it unlawful to conduct a judicial investigation and an unprofessional investigation by people's deputies in parallel. You cannot build the framework of a rule-of-law state on unlawful foundations. Clearly incompetence of this kind is what leads to casualties in Tbilisi and other regions.

The Constitution must not be violated, and therefore only on condition that an amendment to the Constitution is adopted to provide for the creation of a commission, am I prepared to take part in the examination of this question.

B.Ye. Paton: Comrades, one moment. I want to remind you that the proposal to set up a commission was put forward by the deputies themselves. Questions that come under the jurisdiction of the court may arise in the course of the commission's work. Naturally, these will be handed over to the court. I think that is quite clear.

STENOGRAPHIC RECORD

FIRST CONGRESS OF PEOPLE'S DEPUTIES OF THE USSR

Eighth Session

1 June 1989

Voice from the floor (the deputy did not introduce himself): Comrades, I did not want to seize the microphone, but in the course of the election campaign, at every meeting the voters asked me the same question: Are Gdlyan and Ivanov right or wrong? This is a very serious question, and should not be settled by the methods appropriate to a collective farm [kolkhoz] meeting. (Applause).

Embezzlement and bribery have reached a large scale in our state. You know this very well, and we have to combat this evil. This evil is eating like rust into the moral foundations of Soviet man. And people want to know the truth. Therefore I ask that this question be approached seriously, without fuss or protestations. And if Comrades Ivanov and Gdlyan want to ask the deputies for help to find justice, once again I say—let us approach this seriously. And if Gdlyan and Ivanov are guilty, they should be punished. But if they turn out to be right, the consequences, comrades, will be unpredictable. There is a mafia at work here. Let us approach it seriously. (Applause).

A.G. Mukhtarov, editor of the republican newspaper KISHLAK KHAKIKATI ("RURAL TRUTH"), Uzbek SSR, Tashkent City (from the USSR Journalists' Union): Interesting things are happening here, comrades. To form one congress commission, a commission of deputies, has taken so many debates, so much fuss, so many votes, and so forth. But why were tens of thousands of innocent people from Uzbekistan arrested and put in prison, where they languished for a year, 2, 3, 5, 6 years? I have a telegram here: A man from Tashkent Oblast has been in prison for 8 years.

Comrades, if Gdlyan and Ivanov are not guilty, they should not be opposed to the formation of a commission. I wholly support the composition of the deputies' commission. I have only one proposal: The commission chairman should be elected from among the commission by those who are part of it. But not Comrade Medvedev. That is my earnest request. We have our reasons for this.

Z.K. Rustamova, member of Syr-Darya Oblast People's Court, Uzbek SSR, Syr-Darya Oblast, Gulistan City (from the USSR trade unions): On the question of the formation of the commission, since the deputies have decided to form one, we must approach it with the utmost seriousness.

I am very well aware that the lawyers—investigators and attorneys—who are present here know very well that in 6 years Gdlyan's group did an enormous amount of work. They were investigating criminal cases in a particularly complex category, and each criminal case is not just one or two volumes—it is a criminal file of dozens of volumes. In the oblast courts we have received criminal files of 150 volumes. If a commission is set up it will have access to the numerous complaints made against the investigation group. Let us assume it is to study the complaints. But that will mean that it will be necessary to study the actual criminal cases. Yet the deputies nominated to the commission, our Comrade Adylov, for instance, who works in an entirely different sphere, and then a writer, an apparatchik—from what angle will they approach the study of a criminal case? I am an experienced lawyer, but even for me, it would take a very long time. It is necessary to have a thorough knowledge, by heart, of the norms of the criminal procedure code and the norms of the criminal code. You do not simply open the file, take a look, leaf through it, and decide: Here there was a violation, here Comrade Gdlyan did so-and-so, and so forth. No, even with practical experience you simply cannot do that. And even we lawyers often come unstuck, most often precisely when it comes to the norms of criminal procedure legislation. Yet you want to include heaven knows who on the commission. They will not be able to form their own opinion, offer their own conclusions; they will rely on competent comrades, and they themselves will only nod their heads obediently. I do not understand why we need such a commission. If there really are a vast number of complaints of abuses on the part of Gdlyan's group, as many inhabitants of Uzbekistan assert, then in that case I support the previous comrade's proposal that the matter should be investigated not by a deputies' commission, but by a special investigation group. If abuses are found, then criminal proceedings must be brought and the case investigated and handed over to the court. And only the court can determine their guilt. If the court does not establish guilt, the case will be dropped. The results will be reported to the congress. But what can our incompetent commission decide? (Applause).

S.V. Belozertsev, senior teacher at the Karelian State University, Petrozavodsk City (Kalininskiy National-Territorial Electoral Okrug, Karelian ASSR): I wish to say a few words. Today I submitted to the secretariat an appeal from 419 inhabitants of Karelia to the effect that Gdlyan and Ivanov should be given space in the newspapers and time on television to justify themselves. Some kind of one-sided game is going on in the newspapers. If you look at it, it is not surprising that those who are defending them—informal groups and other support groups—are trying to support them by some means of their own. Including pamphlets. That is only natural.

And about the commission. Lawyers are indeed needed, but not only lawyer deputies; independent lawyers must be brought in from outside. The secretariat has two telegrams from Petrozavodsk and Murmansk. I hope you will heed them.

A.U. Khusanov, executive secretary of the oblast newspaper KOMMUNA, Fergana City (Ferganskiy National-Territorial Electoral Okrug, Uzbek SSR): Esteemed deputies! Esteemed chairman! First the deputies who are defending Gdlyan and Ivanov themselves proposed setting up a commission and investigating everything thoroughly. Now they do not want the commission to work.

Eighth Session

1 June 1989

I wish to say that I approve the proposed composition of the commission. Let this commission investigate, as well as Gdlyan and Ivanov, the case of investigator Galkin, who in the course of 1987 was conducting cases at the Fergana Oblast Prosecutor's Office and in the course of a year unlawfully jailed 20 innocent people.

I wrote an article on this. It was 100 percent confirmed, but this Galkin was not punished in any way. They presented him with flowers and sent him off to Sverdlovsk. In Sverdlovsk he is working as prosecutor, and also, doubtless, working with equal "success."

I request that the commission investigate the case of investigator Galkin.

Yu.A. Levykin, scientific staffer of the USSR Academy of Sciences Institute of Spectroscopy (Podolskiy Territorial Electoral Okrug, Moscow Oblast): It was said here recently that certain deputies have received anonymous letters calling on them to help Gdlyan. I have received letters from my voters, workers at Podolsk plants. The letters have hundreds of signatures. People demand that this case be objectively examined. I will hand these letters over to the presidium, but now I want to talk about something else.

This is the point. We are now forming our third commission, but we are forgetting the most important things. Namely, the powers of the commission and its standing orders. But this is very important, because these things will determine how effective the commission is. What do I have in mind? Well, even such a simple thing as this—who actually goes to whom: the commission to the official, or the other way round, the official to the commission? And another thing. If someone is summoned and fails to attend the commission session, what will happen to him? What enforcement measures can be applied? And again. The people participating in the commission must be able to obtain access to documents, and I do not rule out secret documents. Here, obviously, conflict situations of some kind could arise. it seems to me that the standing orders and powers of the commission should rank above departmental norms, since they are set by the USSR Congress of People's Deputies.

And many other questions must be decided before setting up such a commission. Therefore I have a proposal: Before discussing the personnel of the commission, it seems to me, a working party should be set up; after all, we do not yet have experience of the formation and utilization of such groups and commissions. And only after we have defined and approved the powers and standing orders of the commissions' work will it be possible to set them up. Otherwise the commissions will be simply futile. They will be shown various out-of-date materials, and perhaps they will be favored with interviews by a few of the chiefs. And that is all.

A.A. Sobchak, department chief at the Leningrad State University Law Faculty (Vasileostrovskiy Territorial Electoral Okrug, Leningrad City): Comrade deputies! I have mounted this platform in order to give some explanations, and first of all to express my disagreement with the two colleagues, the judge and the investigator, who have already expressed their attitude to the formation of this commission. Let us be clear about this. We are setting up a parliamentary commission, not a commission to investigate the case of Gdlyan and Ivanov. And they are USSR people's deputies, and we have to decide the question of whether to deprive them of their deputies' immunity or, conversely, to refuse to do so. Therefore we will have to set up a commission in any case.

A second question. What are we creating this commission for? I think the commission must be set up first and foremost to investigate the accusations that Comrades Gdlyan and Ivanov made against a number of state and party workers. That should be the purpose of the commission's work, and not to investigate what violations, if any, were committed in the course of the activity of Gdlyan and Ivanov. (Disturbance in the auditorium).

Your attention, please. Only after investigation—this will be quite correct legally—only after investigation of the accusations made by Comrades Gdlyan and Ivanov, and depending on the results of that investigation, should the commission investigate the activity of the investigation group itself. And to that end the commission, like any parliamentary commission of investigation, should be invested with the widest powers, the right to study any documents, and the right to summon any official. And from that viewpoint I now propose that we discuss only the proposed composition of the commission. If there are specific objections to specific individuals—let us discuss them. If not—let us approve the commission, and make it possible for it to work. (Applause).

B.Ye. Paton: Comrades, I would like.... (Disturbance in the auditorium). Please, let me speak, let me speak.... I would like to remind you that provision was made for the possibility of obtaining any documents that the commission demands. And now, please, go ahead.

G.M. Kurochka, chairman of the permanent session of the Komi ASSR Supreme Court (Vorkutinskiy National-Territorial Electoral Okrug, Komi ASSR): People have said here that various charming anonymous "documents" have been sent to various people, and that someone is behind Gdlyan. I speak on behalf of the miners of Vorkuta City. In our presidium now, if they look, they will find at least 10 telegrams from Vorkuta alone to the congress and to me, expressing indignation that we cannot form an objective commission and decide the question of the protection of two investigators. If we are to form a commission, it must include specialists, otherwise people will not understand us. We do not claim to check on how medics carry out operations, we do not investigate teachers. Why should a teacher investigate the work of investigators?

N.A. Kutsenko, jurisconsult at the Kremenchug House Building Combine No 3, Kremenchug City (Poltavskiy

Eighth Session
1 June 1989

National-Territorial Electoral Okrug, Ukrainian SSR): This is my proposal. Everyone is tired of the arguing, and it seems to me that there is a simple solution. We should wait a little while for the formation of the Constitutional Oversight Committee at the USSR Supreme Soviet, and hand over in full to this committee the powers to investigate both the events in Tbilisi and the Gdlyan case. That would be according to the Constitution. And it would at the same time be a test of the reliability of the new committee. Otherwise all the ballyhoo will simply continue here.

S.S. Sulakshin, laboratory chief at the Scientific Research Institute of Nuclear Physics, Tomsk City (Tomskiy Territorial Electoral Okrug, Tomsk Oblast): Emotions have flared up, not only in this auditorium, but countrywide. Do not forget the millions of Soviet citizens who are even more concerned about this question than we are. I think everyone is too tired now to resolve this serious question. Therefore I propose: First—that the question be postponed until tomorrow. Second—that the proposed list be regarded as a working group to prepare the brief for the commission, and third—to grant Gdlyan and Ivanov the right, not to nominate members of the commission, but to reject them. The point is that the whole country should have confidence in this group, so that emotions do not flare up later in the country and so that people do not start saying that once again an unlawful and inadequate commission has been set up. (Applause).

Deputy (did not introduce himself): Comrade deputies! I did not take Deputy Ivanov's speech to mean that he is opposed to the formation of a commission. I do not think he is opposed to it. From his speech, or rather, from the part of his speech we were able to hear, since the rest was interrupted by rude shouting from the left, we understood that he is in favor of a commission, but a commission that should include people whose objectivity and impartiality he does not doubt.

The esteemed Ukrainian delegation spoke just now and said that they discussed and discussed for a long time the person they are proposing for the commission. But how did the others get there? (Disturbance in the auditorium).

Excuse me! For instance, Comrade Aleksandr Ivanovich Baranov, representative of the Leningrad delegation, was not discussed at the group meeting. And I do not know how Comrade Baranov came to be on the commission. You understand, comrades, Ivanov and Gdlyan should, of course, have a right of consent, so that only objective, impartial people get onto the commission. We cannot hurry this matter now. They should speak, they should be given the right to speak without interruptions or noise and to express doubts, if they exist, on each candidacy. I think that is the right way to resolve the question. (Applause).

From the floor: Comrades! Give me a minute. Ivanov was elected for a national okrug, from Leningrad City. We are receiving many telegrams, telephone calls, and letters asking us to support Gdlyan here. I wish to say that Comrade Sobchak was on the previous list. We did not object to that. But a proposal came in: Since Comrade Ivanov was elected from our okrug, we proposed to add another, alternative candidacy from the trade unions, from the workers. From the workers who supported Comrade Ivanov by electing him deputy from our national-territorial electoral okrug. That is why I support Comrade Baranov's candidacy, and I ask you, too, to support his candidacy.

B.Ye. Paton: Understood. Comrades, let us put the question to the vote, since our congress has every right to form a parliamentary commission, first. Second, provision has been made for the possibility of obtaining the necessary materials to enable the commission to operate. Third, the commission has the right, as necessary, to bring in professionals whom it considers necessary to its work. Consequently there are no infringements of rights here. So it is proposed that a vote be taken. But, as we did yesterday, not to elect the commission chairman, but to give the commission itself the right to elect its own chairman.

M.S. Gorbachev: Has someone withdrawn?

B.Ye. Paton: Comrade Shorokhov has withdrawn, since he considers himself unqualified to work on the commission; he asks that his place be taken by a professional lawyer. "I have no other reason," he writes. I think we can accept this withdrawal.

So, if there are no objections, let us put to the vote the composition of the commission, without preliminary election of the chairman. Those in favor of this proposal, please raise your credentials cards.

B.Ye. Paton [resuming]: Against? Count those against, please.

A.D. Sakharov (from the floor): I was waving, waving my hand. Why has what I proposed yesterday not been discussed? I have two questions.

From the floor: The list was discussed.

From the floor: Comrade chairman! We nominated a lawyer, why was the Orenburg delegation's candidate, Comrade Miroshin, not taken into account? I request that he be included, instead of Shorokhov.

M.S. Gorbachev: What does the comrade have to say?

R.N. Nishanov (from the floor): I can answer that question. Comrade Miroshin—chairman of the Orsk City Rayispolkom [rayon soviet executive committee], people's deputy—was included on the list submitted to the presidium by Comrade Gdlyan and Comrade Ivanov.

STENOGRAPHIC RECORD

Eighth Session

1 June 1989

Comrade Miroshin does not yet have his legal education; he is studying at the law institute. When I proposed to Deputies Gdlyan and Ivanov that three of the six be selected for the commission, Comrade Miroshin's candidacy was dropped. There is nothing unnatural about that. It is all legitimate.

B.Ye. Paton: Comrades, I say again, first those who are in favor of the proposed composition of the commission voted, and then those who are against. We asked the commission to count those against, since the overwhelming majority, it was plain to see, are in favor.

A.G. Kostenyuk: Esteemed comrade deputies! There were 61 votes against.

B.Ye. Paton: Who abstains?

From the floor: I simply have an announcement to make. The Supreme Soviet Presidium cordially invites the Moscow delegation and all those wishing to attend, to assemble in the Malyy Hall. That is what I wanted to say. In the Malyy Hall in the Supreme Soviet Presidium building, by the Spasskaya Tower. Half an hour after the end of the sitting.

B.Ye. Paton: Have the abstentions been counted?

A.G. Kostenyuk: There were 93 abstentions.

B.Ye. Paton: Thank you. So, comrades, the commission is approved by congress.

B.Ye. Paton: At the beginning of the evening session, two deputies asked for the floor for comments [spravka]. Let me remind you that, according to regulations, no more than three minutes are allowed for comments. Allow me to turn the floor over to Deputy Yuriy Borisovich Solovyev from the Designers Union.

(Noise in the hall).

B.Ye. Paton: You decline? In that case, the floor is turned over to Deputy Albert Anatolyevich Likhanov for comments on Deputy A. Ye. Karpov's speech.

A.A. Likhanov, writer, chairman of the board of the V.I. Lenin Soviet Children's Fund, Moscow (from the V.I. Lenin Soviet Children's Fund): Comrades, I realize that it is somewhat risky to speak at the end of the day. I have come here unwillingly. But I must respond to the unobjective information that was unfortunately included in the speech by Deputy Anatoliy Yevgenyevich Karpov, whom I respect.

I regret to say that in preparing his speech, his remarks on the Children's Fund, he evidently didn't even look at the newspaper SEMYA—that's our Fund's publication—which regularly prints estimates of our expenditures. Here, then. The funds that have been turned over to us have been spent for: purchasing buses for children's homes, a medical expedition to save children's lives in Uzbekistan, and to break up groups into smaller units in children's homes all over the Soviet Union. Not all of the money has been spent, of course. We are planning some major programs. The materials of one of the programs were published in IZVESTIYA TsK KPSS No 4. If you read them you will know it involves the construction of a large sanatorium for orphaned children in the Crimea—a mini-Artek.

For this reason, I would like to urge all of us to be more considerate, so to speak, when preparing our speeches, and to keep in mind our mutual dignity and honor. Especially when discussing funds. We have nothing to quarrel about; we are not trotters at the race track; we are not in competition with one another. And we have so many problems in our society that there is plenty of work to do.

B.Ye. Paton: Thank you. It is proposed that this information be taken into consideration.

Comrades, allow me to give three short announcements that I have been asked to make.

"People's deputies elected from women's councils and other social organizations are requested to remain immediately after the meeting." This was written by Comrade Pukhova.

The second announcement. "Please make the following announcement: After the meeting, all deputies from the Komsomol and young deputies elected from the districts are requested to assemble for 15 minutes in the hall under the balcony."

The final announcement. "Please announce: People's deputies working in industry, officials of industrial enterprises, and economic scientists are to remain in this hall after the meeting to draw up proposals for the formation of a Committee 'On the Economy and Problems of Industry.'" Signed by Deputy Mironov.

Thank you. At this point, the evening session is declared closed.

The session will start tomorrow morning at ten o'clock.

STENOGRAPHIC RECORD

FIRST CONGRESS OF PEOPLE'S DEPUTIES OF THE USSR
NINTH SESSION
FRIDAY, 2 JUNE 1989
THE KREMLIN PALACE OF CONGRESSES

After more than a week of frustration party conservatives and apparatchiks finally got the opportunity to vent their resentment and fury. Their liberator was the first speaker of the afternoon session, S. V. Chervonopisky, a veteran who had lost both of his legs in Afghanistan. In fact Chervonopisky, a Komsomol leader, was generally critical of Gorbachev and the Communist Party, but he clearly touched the deepest sentiments of a vast majority of deputies with his defense of the army, country, and communism and his stinging rebuke to Sakharov for defaming the armed forces in a February interview with a Canadian newspaper. The ovation he received as he left the rostrum was the longest and loudest accorded any speaker—"a furious outburst of patriotism and resentment," according to *New York Times* correspondent Francis X. Clines. When Sakharov mounted the podium to defend himself, he was jeered and taunted with cries of "Shame!" At issue was a charge published in *The Ottawa Citizen* that encircled Soviet soldiers had been gunned down by Soviet helicopters to prevent them from surrendering to rebel Afghan forces. Sakharov denied having slandered the army, but his defense was feeble and unconvincing. He had merely repeated western reports, he said. The charges were still under investigation, and he was "still receiving facts supporting my view." But he had none to offer. The well of the auditorium filled with deputies eager to denounce him. None of his liberal associates rose to support him. Turan Kazakova, a teacher from Tashkent, capped the attack. "By one act you have eradicated all your activities. You have insulted the entire army, the entire people, all our fallen who gave up their lives." And as she screamed, "I have nothing but contempt—you should be ashamed," the Politburo members seated in the auditorium rose cheering and applauding, and they soon were joined by nearly the entire Congress. At that point Lukyanov ordered a recess and put an end to Sakharov's excoriation.

Deputies attending the Ninth Session heard forty-one speakers address the usual array of topics: economic and fiscal policy, the political and administrative relation of the center to the republics and local soviets, industrial policy, and social welfare. Environmental issues formed the major theme of ten speeches, with national questions and interethnic relations the focus of eight.

Texts of documents cited during the Ninth Session are compiled in Appendices at the end of this volume: Constitution (Basic Law) of the USSR, Articles 76, 80, and 81 (Appendix A.1); Law on Elections of USSR People's Deputies (Appendix A.2); Provisional Standing Orders (Appendix B.1).

NINTH SESSION
FRIDAY, 2 JUNE 1989
STENOGRAPHIC RECORD

A.I. Lukyanov, first deputy chairman of the USSR Supreme Soviet, in the chair.

A.I. Lukyanov: Comrade deputies! The work of the congress continues. Today the work of the congress is being participated in by 1,965 deputies that have registered. I would like to inform you that a total of more than 300 deputies have spoken at the congress on voting matters [motivy] and various issues, and a considerable number have taken part in the debates [preniya]. We will try to work it so that today, if everything goes as planned, representatives of all the union republics and a large number of the autonomous republics will speak a second time (representatives of all the union republics have already spoken once). And representatives of the various social organizations as well.

Ninth Session

2 June 1989

On behalf of the presidium, which is in session and has reviewed the list of speakers once more to ensure, as far as possible, proportional opportunity for the republics and segments of the population to speak, it is hereby announced that the following deputies will speak at today's morning session: Mokanu, Moldavia; Khmura, Krasnodar Kray; Dyusembayev, a mining foreman from Kazakhstan; Amonashvili, Georgia; Aytmatov, Kirghizia; Sergiyenko, Krasnoyarsk Kray; Trudolyubov, Smolensk Oblast non-chernozem region, from the Komsomol; and Platonov, first secretary of the USSR Architects Union.

As at previous sessions, we think that all requests and remarks should be given at the end of the session. Any objections?

From the hall: No.

A.I. Lukyanov: In that case, the floor is turned over to Comrade Mokanu for a discussion of the basic directions of the USSR's domestic and foreign policies. Comrade Khmura will be next up.

A.A. Mokanu, chairman of the Moldavian SSR Supreme Soviet Presidium (Kotovsk Territorial Election District, Moldavian SSR): Esteemed comrade deputies! We all agree that the USSR Congress of People's Deputies opens a new stage in the development of our country. Its task is to reactivate the potential of people's rule and the interests of restructuring. The congress is an important landmark in the establishment of a state of law, in the effective functioning of the economic system of the country and of each republic.

Today, regional and national problems are especially, closely intertwined. The transition to territorial cost-accounting is of fundamental importance. In Moldavia, a concept of the restructuring of the management of the economy and the social sphere, based on principles of self-administration and self-financing, has been drawn up on the basis of multiple-variant studies which take account of drafts of general principles and propositions. By way of practical experiment, the methodological principles of their application are being worked out on the basis of individual rayons. We are coming to see that this is a rather complex matter. Moreover, public discussion has shown that certain propositions of the draft "General Principles of Restructuring the Management of the Economy and the Social Sphere in the Union Republics on the Basis of Expanding Their Sovereign Rights, Self-Administration, and Self-Financing" cannot be considered indisputable.

Probably some attention should be focused on the proposal to transfer to republic jurisdiction all enterprises of the construction materials industry and some enterprises of agricultural machine building that are not narrowly specialized, and enterprises of household chemicals and biological products. The dictatorship of the all-union departments here gives rise to serious problems, as we have seen in the case of our cement plants. As it happens, we built them and then had them taken away from us, despite our categorical objections.

It is also necessary to expand the rights of the republics with regard to agreeing on the products list of civilian goods produced in enterprises of all-union affiliation located in the respective territories.

It is difficult to convert to territorial cost-accounting without an accurate, balanced system of prices. Fundamental reform in this matter is an essential condition for accomplishing the task. In terms of its potential, the agro-industrial complex in Moldavia is a key sector in the republic's economy. But it is moving backward in terms of finance. There is, for example, a substantial difference between the prices on agricultural goods and prices on the means of production for the agro-industrial complex. This results in a situation where enterprises having nothing to do with the republic's resources, with its natural and climatic potential, are "beneficial" to Moldavia. We are not against having all-union organs retain the right of shaping the strategy of price-formation. At the same time, we need to greatly expand the rights of the union republics in regard to establishing and regulating prices. Not only on goods that are sold in the republic but also on those which are exported outside, if they are relevant to the republic's specialization.

The rights of the republics in regard to the use of credit resources are considerably restricted. We are unequivocal in our position that all credit resources that are formed in the republic should belong to the republic, with the exception of payments to the all-union fund as determined by normatives.

Our opinion is that in revising all-union principles of restructuring, proposals by the republics should be taken account of to the maximum extent. If we want to have a strong state, we must above all have republics that are strong, independent, and economically developed.

Restructuring is also accompanied by complicated, difficult problems of interethnic relations. It is not just today that we have begun to suffer losses in this sphere. The roots are deeper. Thanks to openness, glasnost, we have today a rather more clear idea about them. But that's not enough.

Restructuring necessitates the search for optimal forms of national-state construction. To be sure, this should not merely turn into new campaigns. It cannot progress without precise criteria in deciding such matters as the creation of new national formations for people and ethnic groups who live compactly and do not have other national formations of their own in the country. Nationalities of this sort, for example, include the Gagauzes living in our republic, who are raising the issue of autonomy more and more insistently today.

Much in the regulation of interethnic relations will depend on the effectiveness of the work of the Soviet of Nationalities of the USSR Supreme Soviet. It is essential that this

Ninth Session

2 June 1989

soviet not duplicate the Soviet of the Union, as was the case until recently. Naturally, a fundamental role in implementing national policy must be assigned to the supreme organs of power of the USSR and, of course, the republics.

One of the factors which complicate ethnic relations is the ecological situation in the country and its individual regions. One can observe a striving to look elsewhere for the guilty, to remedy the situation at the expense of others. More and more frequently one hears calls for removing dirty technology outside the borders of one's own republic. But where? It is impossible to resolve economic issues—and many others besides—confined to the shell of isolation; many such issues today go beyond even the borders of the country and are becoming international problems.

In this connection, I cannot refrain from touching upon one of the most urgent issues in our republic, where, as is well known, the ecological situation is especially complex. In light of the fate of the River Prut on the border, which is in a deplorable state today, I believe that it will be necessary to work out and adopt a governmental agreement between the two countries not only to save the river itself but also to open it up to the people, by creating well-developed recreation zones, among other things. This is not just a proposal but one of the mandates of my constituents. The people have been waiting for a resolution of this matter for some time.

There are other local problems as well which need to be dealt with on the all-union level. I am talking particularly about conferring official status on the relevant languages. In connection with this I believe that the time has come to secure the rights of the union republics in the sphere of resolving language problems on a constitutional basis. The lack of a unified approach, and substantial differences in the republics' practices, have not been beneficial to interethnic relations and have led to tension.

It is of fundamental importance to strengthen the sovereignty of state authority and reinforce the rule of law. These are two interrelated processes along the path of forming a state of law. Without a modern legal system we will not be able to solve problems and strengthen law and order in the country. The range of social relations in which it is necessary to perfect legal regulation is very broad. I would like to focus on the regulation of property relations. Practical experience in applying the laws on the state enterprise (association) and the cooperative system has shown that the institution of property has not been promoted to the necessary extent. Its potential has not been utilized adequately to accelerate socioeconomic develoment. In the context of restructuring, the USSR Constitution's provisions concerning the types and forms of ownership are also clearly inadequate. It does not, for example, take into account all the varieties of ownership, including joint enterprises participated in by Soviet organizations and foreign firms. The legislative basis for the emergence of new forms of ownership has yet to be created. Hence, appropriate changes are needed in the Constitution, the adoption of a law on property in the USSR. It is necessary to bring the entire text of the USSR Constitution into line with the present stage of development.

It is advisable to adopt a program, on the highest levels of state authority, to enhance the political and legal culture of the masses, to strengthen the prognosticative aspects of law-making. On the whole, I believe that the program-goal approach to resolving the country's most urgent problems should be the decisive one in the activities of the congress and the Supreme Soviet, on the basis of presenting alternative programs by various groups of deputies, specialists, and experts.

Another matter: Reform of the political system, naturally, is a task of exceptional complexity which cannot be accomplished, as the saying goes, in one sitting. For this reason, it is essential to perceive the entire scope and character of the work facing us. The basic content of the first stage of the reform, as is well known, is the renovation of the structure of the soviets, the procedures for shaping the activities of the supreme organs of authority, and the electoral system. Reorganization of local authority is another stage of the reform. We must all be concerned to create the material and legal prerequisites to ensure that the soviets do in fact cope with all problems of local life and are reborn as fully empowered organs of people's self-government.

You must agree, however, that the process of preparing an all-union law on local self-goverment and local economy is clearly lagging. Existing legislation, moreover, has for some time failed to ensure the necessary differentiation of the powers of the local soviets. Considering the vast amount of work ahead, I would like to endorse the proposals voiced in the report to hold the elections of people's deputies, including those to the local soviets of the republics, in the spring of next year.

There is one other problem that requires serious attention: We need to think today about who is going to be working in those soviets. We need to support them on the material plane. Because of low salaries, it is becoming increasingly harder to select qualified cadres for the organs of the soviets, especially local soviets. I think that this problem needs to be resolved on the all-union level, and the sooner the better. We need fundamentally new approaches to consolidating the legal status of the deputies. It is a matter of substantially widening their rights and securing guarantees that they can carry out their obligations. The recent election campaign brought to light the inadequacy of many forms of the law on elections. All of this must be taken into account when adopting the relevant republic legislation. We cannot today allow restructuring to get bogged down because of unreliable legal security; we cannot allow the democratic potential of the soviets to be less than fully realized.

One final item I would like to speak about—the press. It is performing a major, essential role in restructuring. It

Ninth Session
2 June 1989

seems to me, moreover, that the press is in the vanguard of restructuring. For this we owe it a debt of thanks, for its valor and boldness. At the risk of falling out of favor with the press, however, I will say the following: Recently, many of the central newspapers have been focusing special attention on our republic. Almost all the publications can be characterized by one phrase: "Oh, the things that are going on in Moldavia!" The same old facts migrate from newspaper to newspaper, except with new interpretations. One would like to think that it comes from a desire to help. But whom? Inflamed passions, an agitated population, tension, an explosive situation! It would all be comprehensible if it were not for the sense of a strange consistency, the approval of one aspect and the disapproval of another.

The correspondents get indignant, give advice and instructions. Even in IZVESTIYA's report on the May day demonstration in Kishinev, along with a few portions of disinformation, the correspondent shed an ostentatious tear over the fact that the students were not allowed to parade in a separate column.

And how are we to take an article in SOVETSKAYA KULTURA, which has divided the republic into two? On one side of the "barricades" is the people; on the other, the leadership. Is this supposed to help stabilize the situation, which is indeed complex?

There are those who probably thought, well, here's another leader who hates criticism. But there is criticism and then there is criticism. I am in favor of constructive criticism that can help resolve difficult issues. But I think you will agree that no publication, no author ought to encroach upon the dignity of an individual, a group of people, or a republic, a sovereign republic.

I am not addressing just authors and editorial boards. It is not a mere formality, after all, that every newspaper carries the designation "newspaper of the CPSU Central Committee," "published by the USSR Supreme Soviet Presidium," "organ of the Komsomol Central Committee," and so on. Is the meaning that resides in these words always observed in practice? I believe that this problem is not an exceptional one. In the near future we will have to discuss and adopt a law on the press. In addition to protecting the rights and interests of the corps of journalists, we will have to deal with other aspects of the activities of the press under conditions of the establishment of a state of law.

Thank you for your attention. (Applause).

A.I. Lukyanov: The floor is turned over to Deputy Khmura. Next up will be Comrade Dyusembayev.

V.V. Khmura, chairman of the ispolkom [executive committee], Olginskaya Village Soviet of People's Deputies. Primorsko-Akhtarskiy Rayon, Olginskaya Stanitsa [Cossack village] (Timashevskiy Territorial Election District, Krasnodar Kray): Esteemed chairman of the presidium! Esteemed deputies! I represent on this high rostrum a category of the leaders of the broadest mass organs of people's rule, on whom, as I understand it, the deputies do not hesitate to confer full authority.

I am the chairman of a village soviet ispolkom. Local soviets, as is well known, are always working with people. They know people's concerns and needs better than anyone else. We all listened attentively to Mikhail Sergeyevich Gorbachev's report. In it he sketched the present state of our society in a correct and realistic manner. No matter where you turn, we really have many problems today.

The speaker invited us to debate, to search for ways to resolve urgent problems and to eradicate our shortcomings, which we inherited from the past and which we have managed to accumulate during restructuring.

Our constituents expect us to come up with constructive solutions. The congress must make decisions which will enable our people to live and work better, tomorrow and in the years to come.

I share the position of the report and the statements of many speakers who have discussed a number of serious shortcomings we have and proposed concrete ways to do away with them. The essence of our congress, the way I see it, is to rid socialism of the deformations that afflict it.

When I was getting ready for the congress, I had many meetings with my colleagues. We all are concerned about the position of the village and settlement soviets of people's deputies. People who live within the village soviets come to us with all their needs. But the soviets today have no rights; they are in the position of poor relations; frankly, they perform the role of supplicants to the leaders (and now the labor collective councils have been added as well). I believe this situation needs to be ended, and as soon as possible. Legislative action needs to be taken to resolve the question of the status of the village soviet and its economic relations with all enterprises. It will not be hard to resolve this matter if we talk seriously about turning our policies around to human beings.

Every enterprise ought to make a contribution for each worker on the basic of a normative determined by the soviet. This should constitute the basis of the village budget. Then the village soviet would be concerned to ensure that all enterprises worked as effectively as possible, and all workers living within the soviet's territory would be interested in improving the work of the enterprises. We have already come to terms on such contributions, on a democratic basis: 200 rubles per worker. This has enabled us in part to enhance the authority of the village soviet, and now our constituents have something to come to us for. It is clear, however, that the amount is too small. It

Ninth Session

2 June 1989

does not enable us to cope with the village's social problems, meet the needs and requirements of its inhabitants, especially young people and the aged.

But this has been a guerrilla action on our part, and it needs to be legalized. This is especially important in the Kuban region. Every day, the enterprises of various ministries transport hundreds of thousands of people from the stanitsas to the plants and construction projects of the cities, on the so-called rotation method [vakhtovyy metod]. They're transporting them to Tyumen, Urengoy, and other cities of Siberia and the North.

I heartily endorse the agrarian deputies who day before yesterday raised before the congress the issue that people in the villages ought to be provided for at least as well as and perhaps even better than people in the cities. After all, besides working on the social-sector farms the peasants have to engage in individual farming as well. It is a disgrace when village inhabitants have to go to the city for groceries. It does not benefit the city either.

In our kray we are currently working to ensure that all the rayons and stanitsas are self-sufficient in food. We are actively developing individual household farming [podvorye]; we are setting up procurement and industrial trade organizations [zagotpromtorgi] in every stanitsa, which purchase surplus products produced by the population on household plots, process the goods right there, and sell them to the population. There are now more than 400 such zagotpromtorgi in the kray. By the end of the year they will be functioning in every stanitsa. But the problem of feeds and pastures is a tough one, and for this reason it is necessary to pass a law on land use. The land should be at the disposal of the village soviet, which should have the discretionary ability to provide the population with hayfields, pastures, and all the feeds they need, regardless of the mood or desires of any kolkhoz chairman or other leader. This approach will provide the country with more foodstuffs and enable village inhabitants to live more interesting and meaningful lives.

Comrade deputies, I don't know if any of you have gone into a village soviet building lately; if so, it probably gave you an unpleasant impression.

The buildings are old, shabby, and adapted for other purposes. No one provides furniture for the facilities; they are equipped very poorly; most chairmen have no transportation, or if they do it is a LuAZ or Moskvich that has been "beaten to pieces." Yet, as the saying goes, people are judged by their appearance. Let us think about ensuring that the appearance of the village soviet is consistent with the local authority conferred upon it.

For example, a decision was made concerning the salary fund for the apparatus of state administration, formed with savings from the wage fund. It would be interesting to ask the author of this document what I'm supposed to do to raise my workers' wages. Am I supposed to dismiss two or three workers, form this savings fund, and then raise wages? That's nonsense.

Comrade deputies, the ecology problem was mentioned in the pre-election program of practically every deputy. For the Kuban, this problem has two sides. One is irrigation on large areas, irrigation without drainage— and that's the trouble. Roads are being built without drainage holes [propusknyye prokoly]. Over many decades, starting before the revolution, more than 2,500 levees and dams have been built on the rivers of the steppes. As a result, the rivers have silted up and are overgrown with reeds. Heavy equipment has compacted the chernozem to a depth of about one meter. And now the soil no longer works on the permeation principle.

Increasing cultivated lands to an impossible degree and sowing skimpy tracts of perennial grasses have disrupted the structure of the chernozem. Money has been invested in the land on the principle of "give it to the one who dug the hole and refuse it to the one who has to fill it in." At present, about 400,000 hectares of Kuban chernozem land needs to be saved from inundation. Hundreds of stanitsas are flooded. A long-range drainage program is needed. Equipment is needed. Construction materials are needed. We develop the non-chernozem zone, and the Kuban chernozem lands are being inundated. Is that good management? The kraykom and krayispolkom have collaborated with scientific institutions to prepare a program to save the cultivated land and stanitsas. We are very fearful that the program will get lost in the offices of the now-liquidated agro-industrial committee. All of the fields in the territory of the Olginskaya Village Soviet, Primorsko-Akhtarskiy Rayon, are flooded, cellars are full of water, and every yard is flooded. In Timashevskiy and Bryukhovetskiy rayons—that's my election district—there are kolkhozes where half the cultivated land is under water. The new Council of Ministers has got to take a very serious look at this problem.

The other side of the problem is the rise in the number of industrial enterprises in the Kuban. Land is being taken out of cultivation for their construction. Although treatment facilities are being built, they are not being built well. As a result, industrial wastes are poisoning valuable species of fish and polluting the waters. Added to this are the chemicals used to protect vegetation, which we have not yet learned to deal with and lack the proper equipment—we apply them using home-made equipment, without laboratory analysis, by guesswork. You can imagine the situation today and what it will be like tomorrow.

There are real paradoxes at work here. Kolkhoz craftsmen have developed equipment that makes it possible to grow rice without herbicides, but the state does not want to pay for it as a net product; it will only pay for the allotted quota [otvedennaya kvota]. These inventions

Ninth Session

2 June 1989

should be made use of and rewarded, but people turn their backs on them. This seems to translate as: Don't raise a good-quality product. The kolkhozes of the Kuban do not have shops for processing vegetables and fruit, packing materials, and storage facilities, yet every farm ought to have these items. This would boost production output by 25-30 percent just by eliminating losses, quite aside from assortment and quality concerns.

We ought to think about what we are leaving our posterity, for the Kuban is not only a breadbasket but also a sanatorium. Every year, about 15 million people come there from all parts of the country to recover their health and take a vacation, but because of all the smog, chemicals, and barbarous felling of the forests they not only fail to recover their health, but also their diseases get worse. The Kuban ought to remain the country's breadbasket and sanatorium. It is essential to protect our mineral springs and develop a healthy environment.

Comrades! I avail myself of this rostrum to call upon all deputies to work to protect the country's fish resources. We have already exploited them to the point that all kinds of valuable species of fish are now missing from our waters. We live next to the sea and can observe how many fish are floating belly-up, have gone blind, and are asphyxiated. Taken altogether, it has hurt fish stocks. Compared with the 1950's, the number of fish in the Azov Sea has been reduced to one thirty-sixth. We are keeping water levels 1.5 to 2 meters above normal, which to a large extent causes flooding and reduces the flow of fresh water into the sea. For this reason, we will have to refrain from building livestock complexes in the coastal zone and near rivers and other bodies of water; we will have to cut down on amounts of chemical treatment. All the people must condemn the mistakes that have been made in environmental use and allocate as many funds as necessary to repair the damage and implement environmental protection.

We, the people's elected deputies, must use all our powers to resolve the key problems of the villages: the construction of public facilities and, in particular, the development of sources of fuel supply, gas pipelines, and the construction of rural roads. Efforts to solve the rural housing problem must be constantly monitored, and loans must be made available. Comrades, a decision has been made concerning this, but there are no funds, and there are long lines of people waiting for loans for private construction. Special attention must be focused on the revival of khutors [hamlets] and auls [mountain villages]—that is, on building well-appointed housing with all the conveniences, including the building of roads and installation of gas. Unless we do this today, there will be no one to work in the villages tomorrow. Let me cite an example from my own soviet. In recent years, more than 2500 persons have left the stanitsa, and there's no one to do the work. But the country needs to be fed. Who's going to do it? For this reason, I propose some kind of revision of allocations. A substantial portion should be given to the villages. The congress ought at least to make a start on overcoming the differences between the city and the village—not by words but deeds—and examine the question of retirement security, especially for kolkhoz members, who constitute that category of people who worked for a pittance, carried the burden of the war on their shoulders, and are now receiving pensions of no more than 50 rubles.

Many speakers have asked where the funds are coming from, where we can economize. That is the business of government rather than scientists. Let them think and act, although there have already been many proposals. It seems to me, however, that we at the congress need to determine what needs to be addressed first of all and channel all funds there. There will be results: the people will believe in restructuring.

Comrades, the authority of the party, as the initiator of restructuring, is rising. At present anyone who feels like it attacks the party and its cadres and the Politburo, often for no reason. Because they carried the most difficult problems on their shoulders, raised the people up, and built the country on raw enthusiasm? The party should not be attacked but rather thanked, both for what it has done and for its present course of restructuring. Let's think about it, take a look around. There is no other power in the country that can take the place of the party. The crybabies can neither build the country up nor feed the people, I'm sure of that. (Applause). And you, comrade communist-deputies, also ought to think about that, unless your party conscience has gone to sleep.

Another matter: Our kray has a population made up of 101 nationalities. We live and work in multinational collectives, and we have nothing to quarrel about in the Kuban. What problems we can solve, we do. It is necessary to raise the status of the autonomous oblasts, but there is a problem which the state must solve. That is the problem of the Crimean Tatars. It exists, and we cannot stand aloof from it. The sooner we solve it the better. I say this in the name of all the deputies from the Kuban.

A final matter. Day before yesterday, the deputy from Sochi addressed our esteemed Chingiz Aytmatov in a disrespectful and tactless manner. We of the Kuban group of deputies extend to you our apologies, esteemed Comrade Aytmatov. Be assured that we do not think that of you. (Applause). And we apologize for the sad mistake of our colleague. Thank you for your attention. (Applause).

A.I. Lukyanov: The floor is turned over to Deputy Dyusembayev. Next up will be Deputy Amonashvili.

V.V. Dyusembayev, mine foreman in the drilling and blasting section of the Tishinskiy Mine, Leninogorsk Polymetals Combine, Leninogorsk (Zaysanskiy National-Territorial Election District, Kazakh SSR): Honored chairman, esteemed deputies, and dear esteemed constituents! During

Ninth Session

2 June 1989

these intensive days of the work of the congress, we deputies have had the chance to listen to and compare many points of view. If you assume that the width of the horizon depends on the elevation of the observer, then maybe more problems can be seen from the height of the Moscow academic institutes, and more ways out of the country's difficult economic situation can be seen. But I was more pleased by the proposals of those who stand firmly on the ground—our agricultural people in the person of Starodubtsev, public affairs writer Chernichenko, and writer Belov.

I avail myself of the high rostrum of the USSR Congress of People's Deputies to present the viewpoint of those in the depths of the mines who do not have the opportunity to look down upon our everyday problems from on high. I represent the miners, the metallurgists, and the concentration mill workers. The miners are the vanguard of the working class, and I am proud of that. I take this opportunity to focus the attenion of the Congress of People's Deputies on how our miners are living and working today. Having worked in the mines for 20 years, I can say that there are no signs of improvement in the miners' working conditions and wages. Conditions are getting worse, and we are having to go ever deeper into the earth. The metal content in the ore is falling, just like the professional prestige of the miners who provide the country with nonferrous and rare metals. We talk of environmental ecology, spiritual ecology, and moral ecology, but we do not talk about human ecology. The man working in the mine today is wearing himself out. Dust levels, gas fumes, poor medical services, occupational diseases, and short lifespans attest that it is essential to take decisive measures immediately to improve the state of affairs in the mining and metallurgy industry.

During the pre-election campaign, problems of environmental ecology were brought to the forefront by every deputy from our oblast. The adoption of a special decree regarding East Kazakhstan Oblast did not solve the problem. The Leninogorsk Polymetals Combine has been producing ore for 70 years. Now, with the transition to cost-accounting and self-financing, the combine's labor collective, like other labor collectives, must confront its own problems one-on-one. But perhaps there are not enough forces in the oblast to correct the situation. In this connection, I believe that the transition to regional cost-accounting definitely needs to be preceded by a reform of prices on raw materials. I believe that the State Committee for Environmental Protection, which is headed by Comrade Morgun, needs to prepare and submit to the Supreme Soviet a register of the cities and regions of our country that are the worst off in terms of ecology. On the basis of such a register, the USSR Supreme Soviet ought to determine the priority sequence of measures to save the Aral Sea, for example, Lake Baykal, and East Kazakhstan Oblast.

Our constituents want to know why our departments are selling raw materials abroad, why the statistics are silent about the cost of the zinc and lead that are sold, the production of which is based on ecologically harmful technologies—that is, why we get to keep the polluted water, air, and soil in exchange for equipment to mine the ore. I would like every one of our people's deputies to be given statistical collections concerning foreign trade. I now address the scientists of the defense complex: You have developed lunar vehicles that have walked on the moon; how about developing tunneling combines for the mines? Only not for the same price as a lunar vehicle. Because now we are on cost-accounting.

Today we are discussing the question of closing down nuclear power plants, but we have our own problems. In East Kazakhstan Oblast there is the Ulba GES [hydroelectric power station], which was built in accordance with the GOELRO [State Plan for the Electrification of Russia] and is not functioning today. Matters of this sort need to be reviewed, and small GES's like that need to be reactivated.

My pre-election campaign came to an end just before the congress. Probably this is why there have been such vigorous requests not to come back from the congress without decisions guaranteeing the power of the local soviets. To start with, I think that we ought to decide that all above-plan output should remain at the disposal of the collectives and the local soviets. By way of a temporary decision, probably, we ought to set a percentage for contributions to the budget of the local soviets so that they can start right now to build up their own economic base. I want to say something about heavy industry which is producing consumer goods. These consumer goods (around 50 percent of them) should be supplied first to the industry's own region.

Comrades, I cannot refrain from expressing my disquiet over the proposal to sell the land for private use, because I fear that instead of oranges dropping in price to the level of potatoes, miners will have to buy potatoes at the same price as oranges. I must also say something about my attitude toward the idea of buying back enterprises on lease. It's true that there are several billion free rubles around the country, but not in the hands of the workers. Workers today don't have the money to make such purchases, but they do have the power and the organization to prevent the dispersal of the nation's wealth throughout the private apartments of the Mafia and the corrupt cooperative businessmen—that is, those who do have the money. (Applause).

In conclusion, a few words about the party. I myself am a communist who joined the party during the period of restructuring, and I view my victory in the elections as a testimony to the party's authority. But one gets the impression at the congress that if we added up to less than 80 percent, perhaps some communists (including certain ones holding high posts and party jobs) would cherish the authority and trust of the party more,

Ninth Session

2 June 1989

because I don't think communist voters would empower them to introduce a split in the ranks of the deputies.

Much has been said today about the army, but I personally cannot refrain from stating my opinion as a working man. Indeed it does have its shortcomings, and plenty of them. Indeed it does have its problems. But the army is the child of the people, and one must not betray or fail to love one's child! Why? Because we exist and are alive today only thanks to our army, which has defended us and maintained the peace for over forty years since the war. (Applause).

Knowing the hospitality of the Kazakh people, I take the opportunity to invite you, Mikhail Sergeyevich, to visit our East Kazakhstan—because no other national leaders except for Sergey Mironovich Kirov have ever come to see us in Leninogorsk, the forge of nonferrous metallurgy. Thank you for your attention. (Applause).

A.I. Lukyanov: The floor is turned over to Comrade Amonashvili. Next up is Comrade Aytmatov.

Sh.A. Amonashvili, general director of the Experimental Scientific-Production Pedagogical Association of the Georgian SSR Ministry of Public Education, Tbilisi (from the trade unions of the USSR): Esteemed chairman of the USSR Supreme Soviet! Esteemed deputies! Yesterday the deputies from Georgia met with Mikhail Sergeyevich Gorbachev. It was a very open meeting, with frank discussion, where we were able to speak our thoughts and feelings and explain certain phenomena. In turn, Mikhail Sergeyevich also explained a great deal to us. I am confident that the commission which you, the congress, have set up will get to the bottom of everything and render the necessary, correct, the only correct decision. And this truth will be spoken. Everyone needs the truth—you need it, we need it, because in our country, which is being built on the basis of new principles, principles of humanization, the democratization of society, and glasnost—this truth will be a weapon in our hands to fight to save the soul of the people.

Things are very difficult for us now. I will not overdramatize the situation that we have experienced. Perhaps it is not worthwhile now to speak of all the events, but I would like to examine them from the standpoint of the upbringing of the future generation.

First I would like to say that the telegrams that were read here were unknown to us. Most important, I simply want to assure you, dear deputies, that the claim that narcotics addicts and alcoholics were assembled on the square is not in accord with the truth. Perhaps there were some extremists and others of a different persuasion among the thousands of people who were there, but in the main these were talented young people striving to attain the republic's sovereignty.

I would like to say a couple of words about the state of the schools, which are generating many of our problems and will continue to do so. Our schools have become extremely authoritarian. This is evidently a logical phenomenon, because for many long years authoritarianism itself dominated all over our country. And this authoritarianism was reflected, mirrorlike, in the schools as well. Pressure on the children, the end of freedom, no thinking, no living thoughts. Yet the teacher stands as the main figure, the authoritarian, in front of the children. And, incidentally, this paradox emerges: On the one hand, the teacher is the most frightened person in our country, because he has always had looming over him a very broad network and system consisting of the inspectorate, orders, and decrees. All of this has restricted the teacher's progress toward living thinking. On the other hand, this frightened person frightens his own pupils in class.

We need to divest ourselves of this kind of school situation. And if there is no democratism or glasnost in the schools, if there is no humane approach to the child, the child's personality, we will lose our soul in the schools.

At present we are talking a great deal about the restructuring of the schools, about outfitting the schools with new equipment. It is essential to allocate considerably more funds for education—double the amount, triple, quadruple the amount. But it is essential to be aware, at the same time, that without a good educator, one who knows how to approach people, there will be no upbringing in the schools. And sometimes this good person should be free to sit under a tree with his pupil and there forge his soul.

It is authoritarianism, evidently, that brought about the events that took place in Tbilisi, as well as other places, because a child who has been brought up under such conditions is letting loose his feelings, and this liberty is manifested in various aspects and in various spheres.

There is one other major problem relating to the national schools. We often say that in our schools instruction is conducted in the native language. This is true. This is an achievement of the Revolution, and the national language is becoming the language of instruction for every republic. It must be kept in mind, at the same time, that instruction in the Georgian language, for example, still by no means entails that our school is both a national and a Georgian school. When you consider that all the other content of the instruction is nothing more than a translation from Russian to Georgian.

Consider such a problem as the teaching of history in the schools. Which history do our children study? As far as Georgia is concerned, what we mainly study is the

STENOGRAPHIC RECORD

Ninth Session

2 June 1989

history of the USSR. And what does this history entail? Our Georgian children know more about events in Russia and about what took place from ancient times to the present than about events and phenomena in Georgia itself. And the history of Georgia is barely squeezed into the syllabi; it was even forbidden to allocate more hours to this subject. It seems to me that every republic has its own vast culture and extensive past. That is one of the achievements of our Union. For this reason, it is on these principles that we ought to structure not only history, not only literature, but also, probably, all the other subjects. Standardization [odnotipnost] of our schools is destroying them: standardized curricula, standardized texts, standardized teacher training—everything standardized, and in the end what we get is a person who is also, as a form, molded in the spirit of standardized thinking. So now that freedom is granted, we are surprised when a person acts in a way that is perhaps less than fully restrained.

National sentiments are like delicate heartstrings in a person, very delicate heartstrings that must be approached very carefully. I know that my remarks now are being heard in Tbilisi, and various events are taking place there. For that reason, I would like people in Tbilisi also to know what I am telling you now. The article in the newspaper, to which General Rodionov referred, was written during the time of the curfew. I beg you please not to think that events took place the way they are portrayed in the newspaper. A commission has been set up. It is this commission which will ascertain the whole picture, everything that took place there.

I would also like to say the following. Under present conditions, I may say courageous conditions of restructuring, many complex problems have come to light in relations. And you will probably agree with me when I say that our Union must hold together in the future not on the basis of force but on the basis of spiritual community, friendship. If this friendship is infringed upon in any way, very serious complications could develop between us, and that would lead to no good.

Hence my appeal to the deputies—forgive me, please, for being so bold as to say this—let those who come to speak on this rostrum be extremely careful, let them weigh every word that has to do with nationality. I have received many telegrams these days—from Armenia, from Azerbaijan, and from Georgia. They include many lines like these: It is necessary to weigh every word so as not to hurt the profound structure that is of such concern to people. (Applause).

In conclusion: Perhaps what I am about to say will not be supported, but I would certainly like it to be. We have a multinational country, but there are basic languages in our country—let's say, the languages in which our republics live, speak, and work. It would probably not be a bad idea if the congress were to work in these different languages. Let the Azerbaijani, Armenian, Georgian,

Latvian, and other languages be heard from time to time from this rostrum. We must let our ears become accustomed to the sound of the national languages. That would do no harm to our relations. (Applause).

And so, in order that this be done for the first time today, allow me to say a couple of words in Georgian. They will be addressed to our young people in Tbilisi. Would you also please listen to the sound. I assure you I will say nothing that might split us apart or destroy our community, our love. Dear comrades, I want you to know that Georgia has never drawn nourishment from nationalism, and it will never do so. (Applause). It is said that during the Tbilisi events there were anti-Russian statements; it is claimed that there were calls for secession, and so on. It may be that there were a few such calls, but they do not reflect the Georgian soul, which is free and strives for frienship. If you come to see us, our hospitality will certainly take you into its embrace. Perhaps I offend our government, but let me say that there will be both wine and vodka on the table. (Applause). These are the Georgian words which I address to my fellow countrymen.

(The orator speaks in Georgian).

[Begin Georgian passage] Dear fellow countrymen, young people! I address every one of you in the name of the deputies from Georgia. The congress has taken our problems to its heart and created a commission which will determine the truth. Yesterday we met with Mikhail Gorbachev, who believes that everyone who is guilty must be punished severely. I beg you to remain calm and show patience. Let all of us, young people and the older generation alike, work together, joining forces to build Georgia's future and together contemplate Georgia's sovereignty. [end of Georgian passage]

Dear fellow countrymen, young people! I address every one of you in the name of the deputies from Georgia. The congress is taking our problems to heart. A commission has been created to determine the truth. Yesterday we met with Mikhail Sergeyevich, who also believes that all of those who are guilty must be punished severely. I beg you to remain calm and show patience. And let us together—the younger and the older generations—join forces to build Georgia's future and its sovereignty. (Author's translation from Georgian to Russian).

Thank you very much for your attention. (Thunderous applause).

A.I. Lukyanov: The floor is turned over to Deputy Aytmatov. Up next will be Comrade Sergiyenko.

Ch. Aytmatov, writer, chairman of the board of the Kirghiz SSR Writers Union, editor-in-chief of INOSTRANNAYA LITERATURA, Frunze (from the CPSU): There is an expression, "and so we meet." This phrase marks a certain stage in a difficult talk between people. I

Ninth Session

2 June 1989

would like to use it today in addressing you. And so we meet. Just so, on this building site, where we are erecting together an edifice of new democracy, there is as yet a bit too much of a crush, lack of organization and restraint. Naturally, you endure. All these days, my emotions and pains, and hopes, have never left me; nevertheless (for whatever happens, the work goes forward), the walls are rising, and that's the main thing.

From the first moment of the congress all of us have been concerned about the question of what the forum of people's deputies should be. Can it acquire the unconditional imperative of a supreme organ of independent people's rule, or will it again fall at the feet of a ruling bureaucracy, an obedient and convenient instrument? By now we can state confidently that the congress, overcoming the brambles of skirmishing, polemics, and feuding, and thinking and rethinking its past and present, has in the process of its work taken on the character of a fundamentally new democratic phenomenon in the entire arena of our history, in our self-awareness and in the opinion of the world community.

After dozens of years of people's silence, after dozens of years of abstract promises about the triumph of an abstract communism, after a grave and spiritual enslavement, after ideological and economic totalitarianism, self-deception, and lies, our democratic aspirations are finally coming to be realized in civilized law-making. Although this may only be the beginning, it is already difficult to exaggerate the significance of this phenomenon not only for the fate of the fatherland but also for the entire world as a whole. For we are a part of mankind's mainland, and the extent to which we recover our health, the extent to which we are truly able to find ways to get out of our difficult economic crisis, the extent to which we are engrossed in constructive actions to build a state of law and secure individual liberty, the extent to which we succeed in settling interethnic relations, the extent to which we are able to integrate ourselves harmoniously in the living, interactive structure of the world community, the extent to which we are able to develop in ourselves an understanding of the priority of values common to all mankind and free ourselves of the barbaric doctrine of world revolution, the extent to which we become less dogmatic and less aggressive in our judgments and ideological opposition to other worlds—to that extent we will alleviate the lot of modern mankind and, naturally, our own. Everywhere, in all the countries around us, the people are glued to their television sets, feeling and nourishing in their hearts a hope for the better. That's as it should be. We are a great multinational power from which positive impulses and positive experience should proceed, even when we are occupied with purely domestic affairs, even when it comes to the social disasters that have befallen us.

How shall we live in the future? How are we to get out of the situation while the whole world watches? This is on everyone's mind. Allow me to say something about the matter.

The economy. The country lacks a clear economic concept. And that is the stumbling block. A very dangerous situation has gone too far. Against a background of mass dissatisfaction and censure, of course, it is not especially hard to prance about on the horse of criticism and catch the attention of television viewers. In this sense we are all succeeding, except that how, in practice, are we to increase the quantity and improve the quality of the products of labor, by what means are we to achieve this on the scale of a great country? No one knows.

Elated with the spirit of restructuring and glasnost, we are now beginning to see our way clearly on the edge of a gaping material crisis. And if we rightly presume that it is chiefly short-sighted, incompetent leadership and ineffective reform that are to blame for our plight, the inconsistency of restructuring, that is by no means everything. You won't travel very far in a cart without wheels, no matter how much you whip the horses.

The transition from essentially forced labor, from the legacy of barracks socialism which categorically ruled out man's independent initiative, enterprise, and competitiveness as being intolerable from the class standpoint, an unacceptable counteraction against egalitarian, standardized, impersonal policies, could not be otherwise. This legacy itself gave birth to a frightful evil. Its name is universal alienation, the total alienation of everyone from everything: the government from the people, the people from the government. Until very recently, the people were isolated from real politics, and now before our very eyes a breakthrough is taking place, the people themselves are making a massive breakthrough in the contemplation of their place in society. And for this reason, in my opinion, the time has come to contemplate the path of rebirth. How to rid each one of us and society as a whole of the years of entrenched mentality of alienation and the servile attitude of grabbing as much as possible and working as little as possible.

To do this we need to think about the system of society itself, its root properties, its flaws. Life itself suggests that it is time to place on the agenda the necessity of a skillful combination of various forms of ownership, a combination of various forms of production relations under the maximally allowable conditions of socialism. Incidentally, concerning socialism, that holy of holies of our theoretical doctrines: We must not turn the concept of socialism into an icon. We should not pray to socialism; rather, socialism—in an increasingly well-equipped and elaborated form—should serve people in the cause of creation and prosperity. While we conjectured, ordained, and expatiated as to what socialism should or should not be, other peoples have already got it, built it, and are enjoying its fruits... whereas we, with our experience, have done them a good favor, showing how not to build socialism. I have in mind the flourishing, law-governed societies of Sweden, Austria, Finland, Norway, Holland, Spain, and, across the ocean, Canada. I say nothing here about Switzerland, which is a model. The working man in these countries earns an average of four

Ninth Session

2 June 1989

to five times more than our workers. The social security and level of wellbeing of the working people in those countries are something we can only dream about. That is real and, if you will, workers' trade-union socialism, although these countries do not call themselves socialist, but they are none the worse for that.

How we have tied ourselves down to the immobility of our own socialism! Why does our miner have to declare a hunger strike in order to get them to sell him a car, which in the aforementioned countries is there to be selected, like footwear? Why does our shepherd have to seek an audience with the chairman of the republic's Council of Ministers just to fall on his knees and beg for tires for his old UAZik [vehicle produced by the Ulyanovsk Automotive Plant]?

The essence of socialism does not lie in terminology but in this essence itself. When I said as much once in the editorial offices of one of our major newspapers, the person I was talking to frowned and sadly shook his gray head: "In 1937 you would have been put up against the wall on the spot for saying that." I do not doubt it, especially since I have my own family experience on that account. And now from that dead-end, excuse me, reactionary state of ours the explosion of restructuring has brought us here, to this congress. So let us take thought and decide whether Stalinist socialism can move us forward. No, we are already certain about that. We need to borrow all that is positive, the whole positive experience that is applicable to our own big, specific country, from the advanced, highly developed civilized countries, the experience of states based on law. If we ourselves do not know how, we must learn how others have learned to live and work under real, genuine socialism. And in this connection, comrades, I have two small, concrete proposals.

First, and this is forced upon us but inescapable, we must obtain large credits from the West and reduce the deficit. I know, I know, debts and servitude. But we have vast potential capabilities; we will pay them off and settle accounts in time. Obtain credits before it's too late—that's a priority, emergency measure.

Further: Yesterday we heard a speech and an address on matters of agriculture. It was a universal lament for the countryside. One feels like weeping, especially one who himself sprang from peasant soil. The peasantry needs help from everyone. I propose, by analogy with the possibilities of an alternative choice to military service in the European countries, where a young man, because of his moral objections, commits himself to working off his military obligation in onerous jobs, for example, as a medical orderly in a cancer hospital—if we could permit something similar: Let any draftees who so desire work off their military obligation on the farm. Especially considering that the practice of universal conscription is not our finest feature. (Applause). It seems to me, in any case, that we ought to contemplate this matter.

Right after the economy, the second urgent problem is our national relations. It's good that the commission on Tbilisi has been set up; in any case, a legal guarantee must be worked out to protect the people of our country against violence. On the whole I share the idea of the full-fledged socialist sovereignty of the union republics; without it, federal status becomes a fiction. In my opinion, sovereignty needs to be accomplished methodically, in a well-considered and consistent manner, via statutes rather than emotions; we must not be in a hurry to dot all the i's in one pass. What we have is too precious, and what we want is too serious.

The problems of the national languages are also very close to me, and I would like to dwell on them briefly as well.

It concerns the concept of state languages in the republics and the necessity of providing the legal foundations for this process. Surely, the general model needs to be well considered. I believe that the federal nature of the state should also integrate the federal nature of the country's languages in the sense that the languages of the indigenous peoples of the union republics should function as state languages. In this context, again, it seems to me that we need to maintain a reasonable, logical sequence, and reasonable, convincing, concerted action. In short, the national languages of the republics, which were long ignored locally, must be given most favored linguistic status in order that, being reborn, they may take their rightful place. This is an issue that is very complex, especially in Central Asia. Many of our fellow citizens who are unaccustomed to the presence of the language of the indigenous peoples in official affairs take it to be in opposition to Russian. Let us get clear about this.

The genius of the Russian language has served all of us well, and I personally cannot imagine life without this shared spiritual wealth of ours. In this sense the Russian language is unshakeable and universal. Nothing threatens it within the whole country. But by virtue of its historical spread, it must not crowd out the other languages of the indigenous peoples that exist side by side with it. In this connection, it is essential to realize that every nation remains a nation so long as it has its own language; in this lies its cultural sovereignty. And as soon as it is deprived of the opportunity, for any reason, to use and cultivate its language, it ceases to be what it was and should be.

Hence the task of harmonizing the languages, primarily on the basis of the concept of bilingualism [dvuyazychiye] with priority to most favored status for the languages of the indigenous peoples endowed with official rights. As yet, not all of us are ready to perceive this truth. What is needed is compromise, dialogue, mutual drawing together, and everything must be resolved on the basis of mutual benefits and mutual respect.

Excuse me, could I have another couple of minutes?

A.I. Lukyanov: Shall we give him 2 minutes more?

STENOGRAPHIC RECORD

Ninth Session
2 June 1989

From the hall: Yes.

Ch. Aytmatov: Unfortunately, the mass media do not always promote this process, especially the Central press. It has become all but fashionable to levy the charge of nationalism and parochialism against any citizen who stands up for his natural national needs and, at the same time, to encourage nihilism and the denial of one's own nation as a nation, to accuse normal, patriotic people of nationalism. These manifestations in the press (whether the authors intend it or not) artificially inflame undesirable, negative sentiments in places where the people have lived peaceably and could peaceably share one another's concerns and problems. When it comes to national questions, the press and television must weigh their words very carefully. KOMSOMOLSKAYA PRAVDA, for example, very seriously wrote that the events in Alma-Ata were almost certainly caused by the fact that many young people still attend separate schools in their native language. How are we to take this, and what can we call it?

Nor can the sovereign rights of a socialist republic be circumvented in Kazakhstan. This republic cannot be made an exception to the rule, because it's not the fault of the Kazakh nation—one of the most ancient ethnoses in that territory—that the country needed grain and it was necessary to relocate many millions of people from the European territories to the Virgin Lands, which had a negative effect on the ratio of the newcomers to the indigenous population. And now, at every opportunity, the indigenous people are stood in the corner and reminded of their place. (Applause).

The law, the Constitution, must safeguard the cultural uniqueness of each nation, considering the fact that the indigenous peoples, of Central Asia, for example, including the Kazakh people, do not have their own ethnic analogs outside the borders of their own regions, which would theoretically make it possible to retain the language and culture of the given nation, somewhere else if not here, abroad.

Every nation is unique in itself. Our press and television, in my opinion, are also guilty of tactlessness with regard to the Uzbek people when they pander to the philistines by smacking their lips over the so-called "Uzbek Affair." What do the Uzbeks have to do with it? Why this insult? Because this uniquely labor-loving nation has devoted its life to the thankless job of raising cotton? Because for decades cotton has served, among other things, as one of the main items bringing net currency into the state's treasury? If organized crime does exist in particular places, let the system of justice deal with it and leave the people's national dignity alone. (Applause). I would like to say the same thing in defense of the Crimean Tatars. Excuse me.

A.I. Lukyanov: Time. Please finish.

Ch. Aytmatov: How long are we going to avoid dealing with this glaringly tragic national fate? Yet in this context, the mass media (in particular TASS) continue to portray the matter as if that nation all but deserved the inhuman, genocidal act that took place. That is absurd. By what right is such an opinion shaped, a judgment handed down upon an entire nation? Who gives them that right? The Lord God Himself does not have that right. Was it only the Crimean Tatars who were found to include traitors and defectors during the war years, while other nations were guiltless? There's no such thing. War is war. It is a struggle, it is heroism and suffering, it is chaos and atrocities. It is captivity and betrayal. It is triumph and defeat. And all of this can affect any people, and we must deal with it dialectically rather than demeaning the honor of an entire nation. (Applause).

I cannot refrain from mentioning the injustice—which persists to this day—in regard to the German population of our country. Banished, scattered, and humiliated during the war years, they still suffer from political discrimination. Cultural and administrative autonomy for the Soviet Germans would benefit not only them but all of us. I have no doubt that German autonomy would set an example for all of us. (Applause).

Let us learn a lesson from our terrible past, so that it does not happen again in the future. We need to work out constitutional guarantees of the categorical inviolability of peoples as ethnic wholes, a categorical ban against deporting peoples for any political, official, or racial reasons or motives whatsoever, in order to guarantee equal justice for all. The place of every nation must be the place where it historically sprang up.

A.I. Lukyanov: Deputy Sergiyenko has the floor. Deputy Trudolyubov should get ready.

V.I. Sergiyenko, chairman of Krasnoyarsk Kray Soviet Executive Committee (Minusinskiy Territorial Electoral Okrug, Krasnoyarsk Kray): Comrades! While supporting in principle the basic guidelines for domestic and foreign policy presented in Comrade Gorbachev's report to the Congress of People's Deputies, I would like to put forward some thoughts on my own understanding of the problems facing our society that we have to tackle. Recently, at the congress and elsewhere, we have heard a good many very harsh assessments of our history and reality. I think we have had quite enough of this to be able to move on to formulating proposals for rectifying the situation. In considering the question of power, many people see the main evil in the machinations of the apparatus. But since it is impossible to do without the apparatus entirely, and replacing some apparatus workers with others is hardly likely to amend matters significantly, I see it as one of the main tasks of the USSR Supreme Soviet and our congress not simply to formulate individual laws, however good and however necessary, but radically to improve our legislation with a view to creating a genuine mechanism of people's power, and to separate the legislative, executive, and judicial powers.

STENOGRAPHIC RECORD

Ninth Session

2 June 1989

As an agrarian specialist I share and sympathize with the concerns and needs of our peasantry. Of course, I support the appeal of the group of people's deputies to the congress on this matter. But I cannot share the enthusiasm or the arguments of Comrade Chernichenko or many of his assessments and conclusions. I do not understand why such a serious journalist has to embellish his speech by accusing a party Central Committee secretary, in passing and without any serious arguments, of incompetence. (Applause).

From the congress platform there have unfortunately been many offensive remarks about individual deputies. And if in some cases apologies have followed, this is to some extent understandable. But the direct and as yet unsubstantiated accusation of a grave crime that was leveled again yesterday by Comrade Ivanov against a Politburo member is a more than serious matter. I know well Comrade Ligachev's selflessness, purposefulness, and energy in his work, and his modesty in personal life. I think the congress has a right to demand serious, substantiated arguments on the basis of which Comrade Ivanov makes this accusation. Otherwise it can be assessed not only as outright defamation of a party leader, but as another attempt to cast aspersions on the party itself. (Applause). On a party that has assumed full responsibility for the past and has proposed and taken the lead in the policy of restructuring and renewal.

In the course of further implementing radical restructuring of our economy, in my opinion, we need to make full use (as is proposed in Comrade Gorbachev's report) of both new approaches that have been tested in world economic practice and the principles of management that have proved themselves and are in use at the present time. In this connection I would like to emphasize that we do not have the right to dismiss the proposals of our scientists, the scientists of Moscow and the representatives of the Baltic republics. We must consolidate the congress not by subordinating one group to another but through the constructive use of everything proposed by the scientists and the group of deputies from Moscow and the Baltic republics. I propose that the USSR Supreme Soviet and the government need to direct their efforts toward the formulation and adoption of decisions which will in practice enable us to create a socially oriented and highly effective economy. This will naturally require converting to the new model of economic mechanism based on a variety of forms of ownership, cost-accounting, leasing relations, radical reform of the banking system, and further democratization of the system of economic administration. For all the importance and urgency of doing away with the disproportions that have developed in the social sphere, in my opinion, further development must not be based on patching holes and shifting resources from one social problem to another one that is even more neglected. I think that under present circumstances we need a long-term social program based on the end goals of restructuring—that is, a unified program for radically improving the people's standard of living, to include all its variegated components. It requires radical changes in content and the creation of working conditions worthy of a citizen in socialist society. It requires full, effective employment of the population, better health for the people, enhancing the population's culture in the broadest sense. None of these, of course, are easy matters. Only by dealing with them in an integrated manner, however, can we qualitatively raise the Soviet people's standard of living.

Considering the state of the economy today, we can obviously not do without a program of extraordinary measures to restore it to health. At the same time, despite the urgency of the economic situation, we must do everything possible to resolve the most vital task—that of meeting all of the people's food, consumer goods, and housing requirements in the next few years and cleaning up the ecological situation.

In [Krasnoyarsk] Kray we have formulated programs along these lines. With the support of Mikhail Sergeyevich Gorbachev, they have been approved in USSR Gosplan and in the RSFSR Council of Ministers. We are doing work to implement them. Implementing these programs, however, will largely depend on the extent to which the USSR Government and Supreme Soviet, in their practical activities, especially in drawing up and approving the budget, focus attention on speeding the solution to social problems. Although I do not doubt the necessity of restricting capital investment (one of the most important measures in restoring the economy to health), I still think that we must not restrict volumes of capital investment to be carried out with the local soviets, because this capital investment is earmarked almost totally for the implementation of social programs.

I believe that the Supreme Soviet will have to do a lot of work to perfect the economic mechanism further. Life itself has put forward a number of vital issues that need to be resolved in practice. They include perfecting methods of centralized regulation, establishing a socialist market, restoring the financial health of the national economy, and further perfecting the organizational structure of production and administration. On the concrete plane, I think, radical improvements are needed in the practical formulation and setting of state orders [gosudarstvennyy zakaz], the system of payments for resources, and long-term economic normatives, in particular special-purpose tax breaks to stimulate highly effective activities and promote resource-conserving and ecologically clean technologies. I believe that in the context of the economic situation developing today we will have to set aside retail price reform for a while, make adjustments in decisions taken previously, implement a program of measures (by way of preliminary conditions) to restore the economy to health, in particular saturate the consumers' market finally with goods and services, work out and implement a system of social guarantees, in particular for the less well-off strata of the population,

Ninth Session

2 June 1989

introduce a new pension law, raise the minimum wage, and increase aid to children and other benefits for families with many children.

The problem is so acute that we are simply obligated to find the funds for these needs in order to truly raise the standard of living of these categories of our citizens.

A vital constituent link in economic reform is the restructuring of the organizational structure of administration. I endorse the proposition in the report concerning the necessity of separating state administration of the economy from the functions of immediate management, the transition to primarily lateral links and relations, rational distribution of powers among all-union, republic, and local organs in order to provide conditions for territorial cost-accounting and self-administration.

As an officer in the soviets I take the slogan "All Power to the Soviets" primarily as a resolute reinforcement of the legal and financial base of the local organs of authority. Outwardly, the soviets already have considerable rights in dealing with all matters within their territory. In practice, however, any higher-level echelon has the right, claiming economic ineffectiveness, to reject practically any proposal by local soviets. The ispolkoms of the local soviets are constantly forced into the role of supplicants not only before the ministers but also before the enterprises located in their own territory. To a large extent this has brought about what we in Siberia, in particular Krasnoyarsk Kray, call the departments' colonial policy. It has brought about the rapid development of energy-intensive, ecologically dirty extractive operations and, at the same time, a serious lag in the development of the social sphere, light industry, food, and other sectors of industry that affect human beings. This is why I attach top authority to the Supreme Soviet's task of drawing up a number of legislative acts which will make the local soviets the true masters and plenipotentiary defenders of state and regional interests. In this context I believe that the present draft of the Law on Local Self-Administration and Local Economy is in need of very serious and detailed revision and perfection. Naturally, overcoming the disproportions in the development of the economy of our kray will require considerable effort and time. But there is one matter that is of fundamental importance to the kray's entire rural population, one which, it seems to us, the USSR Council of Ministers could settle without delay. I'm talking about the introduction of reduced rates on electricity supplied for the social and domestic needs of the countryside. In the context of the gigantic scale of energy construction that has been and is being carried out in the kray and which, let's be frank, does not always benefit the local population, we have the right to count on understanding and support in this matter, especially considering that this is one of the main mandates given to the many people's deputies from Krasnoyarsk by our constituents. I submit that serious adjustments are also needed in the practice of forming local budgets, as has been stated many times on this rostrum. Considering that the territory of the kray as a whole annually generates about five billion rubles in profit and turnover tax, and that the kray's budget is just a little over one billion rubles, it is hard even to understand why this is happening, let alone explain it to the people. Of course, such a situation clearly does not constitute a stimulus to improve work.

Also in a difficult position today is routine administration within the territory of a kray where industrial units of all-union subordination predominate. The main planning-economic administrations of the ispolkoms of the kray and oblast soviets that have been created deal mainly only with matters of long-range and operational planning. It was thought that conversion to full cost-accounting and self-financing would automatically solve all problems stemming from the implementation of current plans. Practical experience has shown, however, that that has not happened yet. Quite the contrary: Administration of the region's economy has become considerable more difficult. Moreover, in addition to regional matters of transport, material support, and other inter-sectorial problems, fundamental new problems have arisen in the process of coping with new economic methods of management—those having to do with the territories' financial situation, issuing money, paying for trade turnover with resources, and increasing the production of consumer goods. And these matters are not being dealt with in the ispolkoms of the local soviets, not so much because of the absence of an appropriate apparatus—that is a problem which is very easy to resolve—but chiefly because there is no unified, integral concept, no legal normative base for territorial cost-accounting and regional administration of the economy. And this problem of ours is further aggravated by the necessity of seeking solutions in regard to administering the huge territoral-production complexes that have been created in the kray's territory.

I submit that drawing up legislative acts of this kind should also be one of the tasks of the Supreme Soviet and the government. Among the problems requiring immediate handling is that of a radical clean-up of the ecological situation that has developed in the kray as well as in a number of other regions of Siberia and the country as a whole. The approach here should be well-considered, of course, taking account of a great variety of aspects of the problem. In the case of a number of enterprises of the USSR Ministry of Nonferrous Metallurgy, the Ministry of Power and Electrification, the Ministry of Chemical Industry, and the Ministry of Timber Industry located in the kray, however, it is simply no longer possible to put off decisions, including such as restricting the capacity or restricting the construction, for example, of major hydroelectric plants. I believe that in its practical activities, the USSR Council of Ministers will have to become more deeply and objectively involved in matters of the ecology.

The composition of the kray includes three autonomous territorial formations, which impose their own characteristics on processes of administration. In light of this, it is necessary to ascertain the status of the autonomous

Ninth Session

2 June 1989

oblast, in particular with regard to expanding its prerogatives in implementing the integrated economic and social development of the territory. The problem of the socioeconomic development of the autonomous okrugs of the far north is especially acute. Essentially it is a matter of the survival of the nationalities living in these territories. For this reason, we expect the Supreme Soviet and the government to make radical decisions, backed up materially and economically, to promote fundamental changes for the better in the situation that has developed in the autonomous okrugs of the Far North. Among the mandates and requests which my constituents gave me as a deputy is the following: The time has come for practical work, a time requiring excellent discipline, responsibility, concrete deeds and concrete results in improving the life of every Soviet citizen. I consider it my duty to comply with this mandate. Thank you. (Applause).

A.I. Lukyanov: The floor is turned over to Deputy Aleksandr Ivanovich Trudolyubov. Next up will be Comrade Platonov.

A.I. Trudolyubov, chairman of Dnepr Kolkhoz, Smolensk Oblast, Kholm-Zhirkovskiy Rayon, village of Steshino, RSFSR (from the All-Union Komsomol): Esteemed comrades! There is a good old principle: If you don't agree, object; if you object, propose; if you propose, act. Everyone ought to follow that principle. (Applause). Life's experience shows, after all, that we have plenty of people who do not agree and no fewer people who object, and our greatest shortage is of people who actually do something. Therefore, in dealing with the tasks that face us today we cannot for one minute forget about people's day-to-day concerns. Today the people are counting on an improved supply of provisions, industrial goods, and housing; they demand the restructuring of public education, health care, culture, and solutions to a number of socioeconomic problems.

One of the speakers before me was Vasiliy Aleksandrovich Starodubtsev. In his speech he said a lot that was correct. He expressed the thinking and aspirations of people in the villages. I would also like to dwell on the villages, but from a somewhat different angle. I would like to discuss the problem of the non-chernozem zone.

I am firmly convinced—this was mentioned also in Mikhail Sergeyevich's report and by many deputies who have spoken—that the main thing for us, of course, is to deal with the Food Program. If we can't feed the people, there will be no restructuring.

It is a disgrace that along these lines—resolving the food problem—numerous decisions have been made, the people have been getting promises that we would feed them, but no decisive changes have taken place. And the food problem, in particular for us of the non-chernozem zone, is more than just another economic problem—it is a social-political problem. At present the villages of the non-chernozem zone stand at the brink. This is not a metaphor, not an exaggeration, and I am afraid we might take one more step forward. I am not overdramatizing the situation. It is really so. Resolution measures are needed.

The non-chernozem zone of Russia is not homogeneous. Smolensk Oblast is one of 29 oblasts. Therefore our oblast, mirror-like, reflects the problems of this vast region of the country where about half the population of the RSFSR lives. Concentrated there is a substantial proportion of the industry and cultural treasures of our Motherland.

Our region has also been getting attention. In the past 14 years, three decrees have been adopted on accelerating the region's development; this has to some extent made it possible to strengthen the production-economic potential of the non-chernozem zone's agro-industrial complex. Nevertheless, no radical breakthrough at all has taken place in the transformation of the countryside. It is not because our peasants are loafers and do not know how to work. It's not that at all. It is just that for a long time, other problems have been solved at the expense of the non-chernozem zone, in particular the development of the industrial centers of Russia's huge cities. And today, the villages of the non-chernozem zone have become essentially deserted.

Every year, 20,000 persons leave the communities and villages in our oblast alone; of them, only 10,000 move to the cities of Smolensk Oblast. The rest of them move to Moscow Oblast, Belorussia, Leningrad Oblast, and elsewhere. The intellectual potential is being eroded in the Smolensk countryside and a number of villages of the non-chernozem zone. And the deficit is being made up by people who are not needed in Moscow. I can cite examples from my own farm. They send people to the Smolensk region by the Chinese method, so to speak, for retraining, and these people bring with them their bad habits and their specific outlook on life. This poses a danger. I would even say it is worse than the ecological danger. They are ruining our peasants, let's put it that way.

The Smolensk region suffered terrible losses during the war years, but it suffered even more terribly from the decision concerning nonpromising villages [neperspektivnyye derevni]. I have always wondered who came up with the idea of foisting this proposal on the nonpromising villages on the government. (Applause).

The result in our region was that in 20 years, from 1965 through 1985, 2072 population centers disappeared from the face of the earth—places that had their own history, where people had lived and tilled the soil for a long time. Now they are no longer. It should be said, though, that the Smolensk area is a historical region. Aleksey Bodrenkov put it very well: "Before there was a Russian state, smoke rose from the forests at dawn, and before the rise of the cupolas of Moscow, Smolensk had risen on the Dnepr."

FIRST CONGRESS OF PEOPLE'S DEPUTIES OF THE USSR

Ninth Session
2 June 1989

The fate of our Russia was very often decided in the Smolensk region. During the years of the Great Patriotic War, our fathers, grandfathers, and older brothers did not choose where they went to their grave. They found their final resting place in the Smolensk region: Russians and Tajiks, Armenians and Azerbaijanis, Georgians, Ossetians.... They did not spare their own lives in the defense of our land. What about now? That which they kept from the enemy, we are abandoning: The fields are growing wild, the villages are deserted, no one is left. Therefore I now appeal to all deputies: Comrades, colleagues, friends, anyone who has relatives who perished in the Smolensk region, come and see us, look upon this land and help us any way you can.

And now, on this point, a specific proposal. We have a number of benefits for the families of those who died, a number of benefits for veterans of the Great Patriotic War. But I would like to introduce one other benefit: the opportunity, once a year, to visit the grave of your fallen father, grandfather, or other relative. To me that's very important.

In addition to the neglect of the social sphere at present, the production base in the villages of the non-chernozem zone—the kolkhozes and sovkhozes [state farms]—is also very weak. One third of the livestock facilities in our rayon, for example, are in a dilapidated state and do not even have a book value. In short, comrades, the lack of elementary working and living conditions is literally driving people from the countryside.

It has been estimated that to make up the loss of one able-bodied rural inhabitant it is necessary to spend 20,000 rubles for the technical retooling of production. From 1975 on our oblast would require more than 2.5 billion rubles for these purposes. In fact, however, the growth of fixed productive capital in agriculture during that period totals only 1.3 billion rubles. On the whole, moreover, the level of available resources is very low. We have worked out a program which is called "Rebirth." It is a program which spells out the ways, means, and paths by which we may to some extent raise up our oblast, our non-chernozem zone. And in the first stage of this "Rebirth" program plans call for building up 52 of the most backward farms, which will require about a quarter of a billion rubles. I want to tell you that this program has found support among the people. Some 1500 Komsomol members are ready to go out to the lagging farms, and efforts are underway to attract funds from enterprises, organizations, and voluntary public contributions. At present, about 10 million rubles earned on subbotniks [volunteer Saturday work] have come in to a special account, and people are contributing from their own savings.

We understand that we ourselves will have to earn most of the funds to carry out our program, but this might postpone the accomplishment of the task set before us to a later date and further aggravate the situation in the countryside.

Therefore, on behalf of all the inhabitants of the Smolensk region I appeal to the new government to grant an additional 500 million rubles for the social development of the Smolensk countryside.

Please understand, comrades, that we do not want to display ourselves in the skimpy blanket of our budget, but it is simply necessary. It is calculated that these 52 farms alone, once they begin operating normally, can produce 100 million per year. And I think in addition that there should be a temporary halt to the construction of industrial enterprises in the territory of the oblast. On the one hand, this will make it possible to reduce the migration from the villages; on the other hand, it will help channel the forces of the contracting organizations into construction on the kolkhozes and sovkhozes.

What I have said by no means implies that I am against industrial development. Stagnation is equally unacceptable, especially for a mighty power like ours. But the main emphasis, I think, should be placed on remodeling and modernizing industrial enterprises. Meanwhile the ministries, through Gosplan, continue under varius pretexts to impose more and more new projects on us. There are about 3000 of them in the oblast's territory today. The balance of the estimated cost comes to more than 2 billion rubles. Just to complete all these projects will require about five years. Meanwhile, we have calculated that for my own out-of-the-way Kholm-Zhirkovskiy Rayon it will take 50 years at the present pace of construction to build the minimum roads we need.

Meanwhile, another proposal has been made. The ministries have decided to expand practically all of our major enterprises. To man the planned facilities will require 35,000 to 40,000 persons, again at the expense of the villages. As STROITELNAYA GAZETA aptly put it recently, the Smolensk region has fallen under the wheels of industrial expansion.

One more matter that I would like to consider is the work of the soviets. The work of the soviets has also been the subject of a number of generally rather good decrees. But most of the fundamental provisions of these decrees have not been backed up by legislative acts. This has made itself felt especially now, when the enterprises have converted to full cost-accounting and self-financing. According to legislation presently in force, the soviet is supposed to provide for integrated social and economic development within its territory, but it does not have the necessary funds. This is especially true of the village soviets. For this reason, I endorse the proposal that has been made by a number of deputies to the effect that 10 to 15 percent of the deductions of capital investments of industrial enterprises and other enterprises should go into the fund of the village soviets.

There is one other matter I would like to bring up—namely, the issue of social justice. Our oblast produces about 674 kilograms of milk and almost 90 kilograms of meat per inhabitant. This is one of the best statistics in

STENOGRAPHIC RECORD

Ninth Session
2 June 1989

Russia. In terms of consumption of these products, however, we rank far below first place. This is primarily because more than half of state milk deliveries and about the same amount of meat deliveries are shipped to other regions; for the republic as a whole, these indicators are barely over half that. And so, "the injured winds up carrying the uninjured." These conditions were laid down a long time ago and do not take account of the fact that the oblast's growing industrialization alone increased the number of workers by 100,000, quite apart from the urban population as a whole, yet food stocks have remained unchanged. Frankly, our neighbors in Belorussia and the Baltic region live much better. And every day it becomes much harder to explain to the people why this is. But perhaps it is not necessary to explain. It would probably be much better to resolve this issue once and for all through legislation. Everyone should contribute equally to all-union stocks depending on their resource potential. In this way, people will be genuinely interested in the end results. Whoever works better should live better.

A final matter, comrades, so that I might not take any more time. I am a deputy from the Komsomol and, naturally, I am very concerned about the problems of youth. These problems are reflected in condensed form in the draft of the USSR Law on Youth and state youth policies. Some of you have studied it and some have not. Let me say one thing. This law stipulates practically no special benefits for young people. I would call it a law on the future. It is a law which gives young people a start so that they may get involved sooner in our social production, so that they may benefit our country and our people sooner. Therefore I ask all deputies to study it carefully and not reject it out of hand. Look at it carefully so that this law may be passed at the next session of the Supreme Soviet or the autumn session of the congress. Thank you for your attention. (Applause).

A.I. Lukyanov: The floor is turned over to Deputy Platonov. Next up will be Deputy Kiseleva.

Yu.P. Platonov, first secretary of the board of the USSR Architects Union (from the USSR Architects Union): Esteemed comrade deputies! Concerning the country's architecture and city planning, how do things stand? Not very good. The new cities and villages are monotonous, lack character, and are unlivable. Naturally, there have been some successes in a big country like this. We always look for them in order to award State and Lenin Prizes. There is Kiev, and Minsk, and Lithuania, and others. The so-called successful projects of recent years have been accomplished at the cost of enormous difficulty, slowly, at considerable cost, and not thanks to but in spite of. None of the other arts are tied so closely to production and the economy as is architecture. This makes architectural creation even more crucial to society and the state.

Comrade deputies! I beg you to return in fancy to your own cities, communities, and villages. Not to the downtown sections, which are sometimes decently clean and where the main buildings and amenities have been put up with unbelievable care through the concentration of resources and manpower from the enterprises and institutions. I mean the old districts of the cities, worn out from so-called exploitation and from the senseless painting of pedestals for every big celebration, with their broken-down facades and mutilated entryways, with their headless churches awaiting restoration. Return in fancy to the new projects, the boundless proving grounds of the products of the building construction combines, where the people are able to pick out their own entrances by individual features known only to them—sidewalk curbstones turned upside-down, puddles, doors with smashed windows. Recall these districts without landmarks, without information, without cultural and recreational facilities.

You and I know that the rate of social disorders, crime rates, and the rate of uncared-for children are higher there, as was remarked upon here by Comrade Likhanov. Among many other factors, the spiritual barrenness of the environment is to blame.

Architecture is always an objective portrait of its time. However sad it is to acknowledge, the architecture of many of our cities and villages is also an objective portrait of our attitudes toward people, human beings. It is a portrait of our attitudes toward ourselves, our own culture. What we need is revolutionary changes in the condition of the cities, settlements, and villages. This position has been voiced in many letters to our deputy group.

Thus, the Council of Chief Architects of the Country's Cities, which assembled in conference in Riga on 25-26 May of this year—that is, during the days of the congress—writes as follows: "...we request that you speak at the congress and focus attention on the necessity of changing present practices of city planning, in which narrowly departmental interests are placed above universal human interests. Numerous examples confirm the necessity of an integrated, thoroughly considered, comprehensively substantiated set of decisions in matters of urban development, decisions which will rule out disruption of the ecological balance and degradation of the existing ecosystem and cultural potential of individual regions, cities, and communities."

The Council of Chief Architects of the Country's Cities has raised the issue of the necessity of adopting national legislation on urban development, to be linked obligatorily with the law on local self-administration. The council points out that it is necessary to stipulate by law the actual rights of the chief architects of cities under conditions of raising the responsibility of the local soviets.

The council of chief architects goes on to point out: "It is necessary to raise the issue of revising the long-range program of housing construction, to be linked with the program's actual material-technical foundation, without damaging the architectural-esthetic quality of the environment to be created."

Ninth Session

2 June 1989

Another thing. This is from a note sent to me by Deputy Yeraliyev from Alma-Ata. He writes: "Designs for the new types of housing are not being adopted because the builders are not interested. The reason stems from present economic relations." He points out their complete indifference to the social and climatic characteristics of a region. Take, for example, the city of Gulsary, Guryev Oblast. It experiences frequent dust storms and temperatures of 40 degress above and 40 degress below zero with high winds. To this day, however, the city does not have a single residential building designed especially for the region, despite the explicit decisions of the chairman of USSR Gosstroy that were taken back in 1987. In conclusion, the deputy from Alma-Ata writes: "The country's construction complex needs to be reorganized immediately. The way things stand today, the Housing-2000 Program could be a failure."

In his report, Mikhail Sergeyevich Gorbachev stated that housing is one of the most vital problems and that we must tackle it with everything we have. We must find the funds and resources and accomplish the program "An Apartment or House for Every Family." But it is more than just a matter of housing. It is the whole infrastructure, both technical and social, kindergartens, schools, hospitals, clubs, sports facilities and so on, parks, squares, roads, and, finally, the restoration of historic places—the entire manmade environment, i.e. the architecture in the midst of which we are born, live, and work. It must be an esthetically designed environment for life.

What is to be done? In his report the speaker mentioned the dictatorship of the contract system, the departments; this theme also runs through excerpts from the letters I have read. The economic and production mechanism we have inherited from previous years, the mechanism of carrying out architectural and urban development designs, is based on the embarrassingly backward technologies of the long-ago 1930s and 1940s, standardized, monotonous designs producing defective construction all over the country. Recently a group of American architects inspected construction projects in Moscow. Their reaction was that this kind of construction cannot be; the American economy would not stand for that kind of construction. Projects that drag on for years, wastage of materials, lack of technology. But how to accomplish the task? It is very dangerous to say, "First we do the meters, then you'll get your architecture." The pressure is strong, everything is in the hands of the contractor, and his powerful technical base—mainly panel housing construction—is geared to "gross output." If you don't simply chop out the brambles, they will all grow back. There is no other base; we have to work with it and we must get moving. But a thorough modernization of this industry is necessary and possible. People in the world have long since learned how to do first-class building, including the use of panels—in France, for example. This work must be done on the go, so to speak. We must also restore to the arsenal of construction the use of framing, on-site casting, brick, stone, wooden, and metal techniques. World practice demonstrates that interweaving these systems in urban development makes it possible to create complex, multifaceted cities, communities, and buildings, and spaces commensurate with man to restore to him the feeling that, This is my home, my street, my courtyard, and in this way to restore the vital feeling of patriotism.

The thesis of the report concerning the necessity of shifting funds from defense and utilizing the technological capabilities of the special sectors and imports for the most urgent social needs also ought to be channeled into architecture and construction, into attaining a modern level of construction practice. Simultaneously it is essential to remodel the very system of organization of the construction contract and the construction industry. It is also necessary to decentralize the contract system, project planning, and orders. We need alternative systems of organization; we need competition, not in order to destroy but to strengthen; we need to find the best possible organization of the country's construction complex, get rid of the unwieldy, multi-level construction committees, and break up the pyramid of the all-union contract system in civilian construction. Every city, every village, every community ought to have its own contract system.

This process is already underway. A system of small organizations which make it possible to react quickly to orders is beginning to take shape. The USSR Architects Union is itself actively developing a system of design bureaus and organizations of the Arkhproyekt All-Union Association; there are already about 200. In less than a year, the volume of completed project-planning work in the state valuation system has risen to 50 million rubles. This organizational system simultaneously makes it possible to make more effective use of the architect and his labors in our country, and we have only one fifth or one sixth as many architects per 100,000 inhabitants as in the highly developed countries.

We have also thought about and begun to create small, mobile construction firms known as Arkhstroy. They have already begun to operate jointly with state organizations and foreign firms in Georgia and in the Moscow area, for example. They, together with the forces of the production cooperatives, plus all the other kinds of contract organizations, ought to become a serious force in resolving the problem of housing construction. Because we will never accomplish the "2000" Program via the state system alone.

We need to return to clear and simple truths. The cities and villages cannot be built for the arithmetical average man on behalf of the arithmetical average client or yet the sometimes subordinate contractor, as has happened in Moscow, for example.

The city, the village, the house must have its master, its client (the soviet, collective, cooperative, or citizen) and its specific architect, its specific builder. Look, whose interests are hurt? No one's. Who's indifferent or anonymous? No one. That's morality; that's economics.

STENOGRAPHIC RECORD

Ninth Session

2 June 1989

When that terrible earthquake struck Armenia, my observations caused me to reflect that the buildings that stood up were those bearing the name of the architect, the client, and the builder; the structures that stood up had been built in both the prerevolutionary period and the Soviet period. The ones that fell were no one's. What stood up was responsibility.

A shelter bears special responsibility toward people. A shelter should protect them. It must hold up under extreme conditions until people leave it. Herein lies the supreme purpose of the architect's remarkable profession. People have assigned and entrusted it to him. Yet we have distorted this purpose, having placed funds above the goal.

I began this discussion with the subject of the funds necessary to accomplish the task because the lack of them and backwardness in construction technologies constitute an obstacle to the development of architecture and urban development; they make it difficult to carry out the "2000" Program. But the chief obstacle to the rational development of our cities and communities is the lack of a law, legislation on urban development, which would block the monopolies of the departments and the contract system. It is time to give the force of law to the architectural project design in this country. Approved by soviet authority, it will be subject to execution. Then what ought to happen will happen. The department, the contractor, and the industry will have to exert themselves, seek ways and means to carry out the project, and both architecture and construction will begin to develop. Reflecting as it does a social task, the project design is simultaneously the sole engine of progress in construction. I want to tell you that in recent times our potential capabilties in architecture have been very high. We are winning in an endless number of international contests, yet we can't do anything here at home. At present any project design, frequently even a rather talented one, is subject to various changes.

After the design is accepted by the soviet, the architect takes it to the contractor for consultation, and the latter adjusts it to fit his capabilities. And that's the whole trouble! None of us want that kind of construction, but it bypasses our will. Imagine for a moment the same kind of situation in aviation. If it were like that in aviation, we would still be flying around in PO-2 airplanes. It is time to overthrow this monopoly by law.

The architects union has started working on architectural-urban development legislation. It turns out that we are the only developed country without such legislation, yet our work is regulated by 14,000 legally binding acts, SNiPs [Construction Norms and Regulations], and directives, but where there is no law, as we know, there is lawlessness. This legislation will have to cover the investment relations of the client, the architect, and the builder, coordinate their activities, and protect their interests, in particular author's rights. And, especially, this legislation will become an instrument of authority in the hands of the soviets.

This work has come from above and from below. Following Kiev, a number of cities have adopted a scale of land prices. This is an excellent tool in the hands of the soviets.

We are presently collaborating with the Institute of State and Law on draft legislation, and we are studying world experience. In the United States, for example, there is a well-developed functioning system of legal documents relating to these matters; there are laws on the federal, state, and city level. It is interesting to note, for example, that San Francisco and other cities of America do not permit the construction of two identical buildings. Also in America there is a strict system which protects society against unprofessional interference. In the sphere of architecture, this function is performed, by law, only by the American Architects Union. We are sorely in need of such a law!

Here among the cathedrals of the Kremlin, we understand, I think, that architecture is more than a product of cement; it is above all the product of spirit and lofty ideas.

I would like to conclude with an ancient thought that comes from Greece: Only he who constantly feels the hand of his grandson in his own hand has the right to engage in architecture. That's responsibility to the future!

Architect deputies make the following proposal (there are 13 of us here—10 from the architects union, one from the Academy of Arts, one from the territory, and one, as you know from the newspapers, is the chief architect of restructuring): We believe that the problems of architecture, of the integrated development of cities and villages, must be dealt with constantly in the USSR Supreme Soviet's Committee for urban planning and architecture. In this connection, a request to the government: Nikolay Ivanovich, take your time in adopting new decrees designed to improve architecture and construction. We members of a creative workers' union want to and will be in the center of this work in the parliament, with the government and the party. (Applause).

A.I. Lukyanov: Comrade deputies, before declaring recess, I want to announce the following. A request has come from Deputy Shamikhin: "I request that the presidium announce the schedule of the congress and the Supreme Soviet for Saturday." This is of interest to many.

What are the plans for this Saturday? The congress has worked hard, so we think that most of the participants in the congress, deputies, ought to take a rest on Saturday.

Tomorrow, Saturday, in accordance with the wishes of many deputies, plans have been made for the people's deputies, if they wish, to visit a number of rayons,

Ninth Session

2 June 1989

enterprises, and institutions in Moscow and Moscow Oblast, and to meet with representatives of labor collectives. I should tell you that many labor collectives would like to meet with the deputies from various regions of the country.

Plans call for organizing a visit to a residential microrayon, a sports complex in the Krylatskoye, and a number of enterprises and organizations in several rayons around Moscow. Announcements can be found at the registration places. You have seen them, so we ask you to make your wishes known during the break so that we can organize these excursions.

In addition, there will be an announcement about an exhibtion of space technology, where, incidentally, deputies can get information about, first of all, how much it costs, what the money is being spent for, and what our space technology is working on.

Deputies desiring to take part in all these events are requested to register.... We hereby take a recess of 30 minutes.

(Recess).

A.I. Lukyanov: Comrade deputies, we have to save time. Our session continues. The Belorussian delegation has made a substitution: The floor is turned over to Deputy Tkacheva. Next up will be Comrade Ardzinba.

Z.N. Tkacheva, department head, Slavgorod Central Rayon Hospital, city of Slavgorod (Krichev Territorial Election District, Mogilev Oblast): Esteemed comrade deputies! I am speaking at the behest of the deputies of Mogilev and Gomel oblasts as well as other districts—Momotova, Zhukovskaya, Golovnevo, Feskovo, and others, also on behalf of our constituents who live in the contaminated rayons of these oblasts.

A bit about myselfa: I am a pediatrician with 20 years of service. I could not respect myself if I did not raise the following issues from this rostrum today. As of the present day we, the inhabitants of these rayons, have had our clean land, water, air, forests, and meadows taken away from us, things without which man cannot live but can only exist. The press, the official statements of the Ministry of Health, and the 29 May 1989 edition of PRAVDA fail to reflect adequate concern for people's health and the fate of future generations. It is the first time such a accident has happened, after all, and so there is no observation experience in world practice. It's true there have been no substantial changes as yet in the overall morbidity pattern, although the first portents are already there: Children being born with congenital cataracts; impaired vision; lowered immunity; higher levels of anemia; myocardial infarction. It is still too early now to go by figures; we will do that in 10 to 15 years from now. What we have to do now is focus on the qualitative side of illnesses, that is, their course. And in my opinion, as of the present day this question has not been studied at all, because it is not reflected in a single report. In order to study the behavior of animals, biologists move in next to them and live with them for years. That's what medical doctors ought to do. After all, the complaints being brought in to us by the people of these rayons—excessive fatigue, lack of energy, headaches, and dryness of the mouth—do not fit into a single nosological disease classification.

I believe that scientists have failed to deal with the task that is entrusted to them. This applies both to medical doctors and biophysicists. And I wonder if it wouldn't be better for us to turn for help to foreign scientists, whose equipment is more reliable and whose experience is greater. After all, it is not just the fate of a particular region but of the Belorussian nation as a whole that is being decided today.

It has to be said that practicing physicians' assessment of the health of the people living in the contaminated rayons is increasingly at odds with the assessment by medical scientists and officials of the country's health care system. I can compare the discrepancy, because I have been living in this territory many years and I can see the changes in people's health before and since the accident. Specialists who come to see us, especially those of high rank, spend a few hours or days with us and then try to persuade us that the people's health is not getting worse. They attribute the changes to whatever suits them. Nitrates, poor nutrition, or the lack of breastfeeding, but not to the presence of the radioactive factor. But all of those things were present before. And we could tell them that although these factors might aggravate the harmful effect of the radiation, they are by no means the cause of that effect.

The tension of the psychological atmosphere has been aggravated in a number of cases by the publication of conflicting data and sometimes simple rumors. This is fostered by differences of opinion that have arisen among scientists. To put an end to these differences of opinion, our academicians must speak with authority.

Unfortunately, the USSR Academy of Sciences and the coordination center affiliated with its presidium have distanced themselves from this complex and very crucial problem. The organization and provision of medical services leave much to be desired. To this day we have received no help in regard to improving the supply of medical equipment, medicines, gear, and cadres. The parent institutes have failed to provide us with special methods of observation enabling us to diagnose the early and long-term consequences of radiation. We lack recommendations as to the particulars of the treatment and prevention of somatic disorders against the background of the effect of various doses of radiation.

This is quite aside from the obligatory recommendation that the population be supplied with clean foodstuffs. Obligatory recommendations on sending children outside the republic every year to recover their health are

Ninth Session

2 June 1989

not being complied with either. Like the other deputies, I think that at present we cannot provide guarantees that it is safe to live within the territory of the contaminated rayons. Moreover, scientists of the Biophysics Institute of the USSR Ministry of Health are predicting an additional rise in malignant forms (leukemia, birth defects), although not in a very high percentage of cases. For everyone who lives there, a minimum fraction of a percent is quite sufficient.

All of this creates a tense atmosphere in these areas. We deem it advisable to implement a planned, stage-by-stage resettlement of people from the contaminated rayons, because practical experience shows that it is not we who are controlling the situation, however much we may desire it; the situation is controlling us. At meetings with our constituents, the people demanded that the resettlement issue be resolved; at present, people are still living in places where the total radiation dosage exceeds the safety concept by 35 rem. I cannot forget the eyes of my constituents at these meetings, when they demanded immediate resettlement. We offer them state sausage, individual dosimeters, and tractors with hermetically sealed cabs. They don't want any of that. They ask to be moved out as soon as possible in order to live a normal life, have their own household plot, and engage in farming. It's frightening just to think about it.

The people want to be compensated by the state for the losses they suffered as a result of the Chernobyl accident. They demand that a shorter work service life be set for people working in plants, organizations, medical facilities, schools, kolkhozes, and sovkhozes, based on the conditions of the harm of radioactive damage. They demand additional pay from ministry and departmental funds, in the amount of 10 percent of salaries or wage rates for every year worked, starting as of 1 May 1986, for all workers and employees in the territories of the contaminated rayons. They want additional pay from the state budget for nonworking pensioners and non-working members of families, in the amount of 30 rubles per month. They want additional pay for working pensioners in the amount of 25 percent of wage rates or salaries, to come from ministry and departmental funds. Mothers with children up to the age of three, preschool institutions and schools with students up to the age of 14, along with their teachers, cooks, and medical personnel, must, on completion of the school year, be taken out of the contaminated zone for health treatment for a period of three months, to be paid out of the state budget; a health recovery center must be built in the uncontaminated zone for all workers in the contaminated zone, at state expense. Only those foodstuffs which are free of radioactivity must be supplied; decontamination work must be made more effective; the construction of roads, powerlines, and gas pipelines must be accelerated; and major resources and funds must be channeled into the effort.

We are completing the draft of a state program for 1990-1995 which calls for resettling people from areas where it is impossible to live, and implementing a complex of measures to convert to normal living conditions. We hope that the newly created government will examine and approve this program. Carrying it out will require considerable capital investments which, under the difficult circumstances, the republic is not in a position to handle. In connection with this we request that the CPSU Central Committee and the USSR Council of Ministers provide us the necessary help. Considering the special importance and the long-term nature of problems associated with liquidating the consequences of the accident at the Chernobyl AES [nuclear electric power station], it seems to us that a permanent organ needs to be created in the country in order to ensure that these problems do not have to be dealt with by volunteer efforts [na obshchestvennykh nachalakh], as is being done now. It could comprise an extraordinary commission and a deputy chairman of the USSR Council of Ministers for these matters.

I support Deputy Konstantin Aleksandrovich Khlebtsov's proposal on the creation of such an organ within the USSR Supreme Soviet, one having legislative authority.

I hereby submit to the congress for discussion the proposal by Albert Likhanov, chairman of the board of the V. I. Lenin Soviet Children's Fund, that another all-union subbotnik be held on 1 June and that all the proceeds be used to help the children of Chernobyl, Armenia, and Azerbaijan, to organize family-style children's homes, and to build a health recovery complex in the Crimea for orphaned children and the children of Chernobyl. (Applause).

These matters are reflected in my constituents' appeal to the congress, which was adopted at a rally held during our work. Allow me to submit this appeal to the presidium of the congress. I also request that a response be made during the congress to the requests of the Belorussian deputies on this matter, which have been turned over to the secretariat of the congress.

Thank you for your attention. (Applause).

Z.N. Tkacheva hands the document to the presidium of the congress.

From the floor: (Inaudible).

A.I. Lukyanov: Comrades, let's please maintain order.

From the floor: (Inaudible).

A.I. Lukyanov: Excuse me, let's please respect the congress and ourselves.

The floor is turned over to Deputy Vladislav Grigoryevich Ardzinba. Next up will be Deputy Peters.

V.G. Ardzinba, doctor of historical sciences, director of the D.I. Gulia Abkhazian Institute of Language, Literature, and History, Georgian SSR Academy of Sciences,

STENOGRAPHIC RECORD

Ninth Session

2 June 1989

city of Sukhumi (Gudauta City National-Territorial Election District, Abkhazian ASSR): Esteemed comrade deputies! It should hardly be necessary to argue the point that the future of every nation in our great Motherland depends on resolving a number of the country's shared problems, because all parts of this unitary whole are interconnected and interdependent. One may single out a number of problems, among which, it seems to me, special importance must attach to the creation of a state of law. At the same time, I cannot in any way agree with certain assertions that have been voiced at our congress to the effect that the problems of individual regions must be set aside in the interests of concerns affecting the whole state, assertions that they must wait.

It is unthinkable that concerns of the whole state can be dealt with without taking account of the problems and interests of all the regions of the country, regardless of where they lie. I draw your attention to this problem because only a few of the speeches that have been made in this hall have touched upon the problems of the smaller nations, that is, peoples having small populations. Basically the discussion has been about the union republics, the restructuring of their relations with the Center and the expansion of their rights. In this connection, something has to be said about the fact that any realization of the idea of the greatest possible sovereignty for the union republics, "strong union republics," it seems to me, is cause for definite disquiet among all the peoples which have not made it into the group of 15 "strong republics," the total number of which adds up to 65 in this hall alone; they add up to even more in the country as a whole. Some of them have their own forms of national-state structure, while others are deprived of any forms of national-cultural autonomy whatsoever. Moreover, a mass of problems arises for a non-native [inonatsionalnyy] population living outside the borders of its own national territory. Hence, the restructuring of interethnic relations must encompass a whole complex of problems. Otherwise, serious difficulties are inevitable, sharp conflicts on an ethnic basis. The legal status of an autonomous republic as stipulated in the present Constitution leads in effect to national inequality and lack of equal rights. This kind of ranking of nations is the direct "legacy" of Stalinism as well as an administrative-command system which in effect leads to homogenization, and this is especially detrimental to the autonomous entities. This situation can be illustrated by the example of the development of the Soviet statehood of the Abkhazian people, similar to that of other autonomous entities.

Soviet power was established in Abkhazia on 4 March 1921. The Soviet Socialist Republic of Abkhazia was proclaimed. Under pressure from Stalin, in December 1921 the Soviet Socialist Republic of Abkhazia concluded a treaty of alliance with the Soviet Socialist Republic of Georgia, which was in force until 1931. In legal terms, this alliance meant the creation of a federation based on the equal rights and sovereignty of both republics. Thus, for example, Article 4 of the Abkhazian Constitution states: "The Soviet Socialist Republic of Abkhazia shall exercise independent state authority within its territory, since this authority is not restricted by treaty relations with the Soviet Socialist Republic of Georgia and the constitutions of the Transcaucasian Soviet Federative Socialist Republic and the Union of Soviet Socialist Republics." This sovereignty was also reflected in the existence of Abkhazia's own code of arms, flag, and a number of legal codes and legislative acts. In reality, however, the treaty marked the beginning of the liquidation of Abkhazia's sovereignty.

In 1931, the treaty-based Abkhazia was converted into a mere autonomous republic within the Georgian SSR. In this way, Abkhazia became practically the only republic whose political status was changed, at Stalin's will, from the top down rather than from the bottom up.

Today we know a great deal about the mass repressions against the Soviet people and whole nations during the years of the cult of personality. In the history of the Abkhazian people, the years 1937 through 1953 marked a period in which the question of the liquidation of the nation as such was a real one. The fact that this question was actually raised and dealt with is attested by a whole aggregate of repressive actions against the Abkhazians. The nation was rendered leaderless; all of the most prominent state and party leaders of Abkhazia were destroyed, along with the intelligentsia that was just then emerging. The peasantry suffered mass repressions. Starting in 1940, the Abkhazian nation was no longer called "the Abkhazian nation." Starting in 1941, radio broadcasts in Abkhazian were halted. In 1945-1946, Abkhazian schools were closed and the teachers were shut out. There were practically no Abkhazians in the party and soviet organs of leadership. Forcible massive migration to Abkhazia was begun. Vast sums were spent on this resettlement, which was not halted even during the difficult years of 1941-1942. Greeks, Turks, and other peoples were moved out of Abkhazia, and their homes were turned over to settlers from rayons in Georgia. Because of this artificial population growth, Abkhazians became a minority in their own ancient homeland. The ancient names of places in Abkhazia were subjected to repressions. Between 1948 and 1951 alone, 147 place names were changed in that manner. Concerning the nature of policies during that time, Eduard Amvrosiyevich Shevardnadze, who used to be first secretary of the Georgian Communist Party Central Committee, has said: "It must be stated frankly that in the past, during the period you all know, the Abkhazian people were subjected to policies which must be characterized as in effect chauvinistic—let's call things by their right names—which were radically in conflict with the interests of the Georgian people as well as the interests of the Abkhazian people, the interests of strengthening the Leninist friendship of the Soviet peoples."

Meanwhile, the official denunciation of the "cult of personality" at the 20th Party Congrss did not result in the liquidation of the "legacy" of Stalinism. This

STENOGRAPHIC RECORD

Ninth Session

2 June 1989

"legacy" is making itself felt to this day. Serious violations in the sphere of national policies with respect to the Abkhazian people were recounted in collective and individual letters sent to the Central party and soviet organs by representatives of various segments of the Abkhazian people—the intelligentsia, the working class, and the peasantry—in 1947, 1957, 1967, 1978, and 1988.

In the first stages after such appeals, certain measures were taken to improve the situation that had developed in the autonomous republic. Some time later, however, one would observe a reversion to the situation which the representatives of the Abkhazian people had complained about.

The situation became especially difficult in late 1988. At rallies in Tbilisi there were calls to liquidate the already truncated Abkhazian autonomy. One of the informal societies drew up a special program to fight the Abkhazian nation and its cultural institutions. It is curious to note that this society, whose members consider themselves fighters for democracy, proclaim in this program they have drawn up that "the years 1936-1954 witnessed an end to the domination of the separatists and the violence of the Apsui (author's note: That's what they call the Abkhazians) against other nations living in the Abkhazian ASSR." From the standpoint of these "democrats," in other words, the best years were those when the Abkhazian nation was being destroyed. Representatives of these "democrats" headed for Abkhazia to foment anti-Abkhazian sentiments among the local Georgian population. And by December of last year they managed to organize an unauthorized rally in Sukhumi and marches around the city.

Not only the Abkhazians but also other inhabitants of the republic were seriously disturbed by the drafting and discussion of the draft state program for the development of the Georgian language, which calls for the use of Georgian as the only official language in all institutions, and for compulsory teaching of it to every inhabitant of the republic. Again, this reopened unhealed wounds and reminded us of the gross distortions of the history of the Abkhazian nation and the trampled rights of Abkhazian autonomy.

Abkhazian society was especially disturbed by the fact that these actions were not properly assessed by the leadership of the union republic.

All of this taken together brought it about that an authorized rally was held on 18 March 1989 in the village of Lykhny, on the historic square where issues vital to the fate of the nation have been resolved since ancient times, during which an appeal was adopted and sent to the General Secretary of the CPSU Central Committee, the chairman of the USSR Council of Ministers, and a number of other institutions. Affixed to it were the signatures of about 32,000 persons, including officials of a number of higher party and soviet organs and all deputies of Abkhazian nationality. The appeal was also signed by more than 5000 Russians, Armenians, Greeks, Georgians, and representatives of other peoples. The appeal requested that the status of a Soviet Socialist Republic, which Abkhazia had had in 1921 while V. I. Lenin was alive, be reinstated.

Contrary to some claims, this does not entail the secession but rather the reinstatement of the status of "Treaty-Based Abkhazia." According to the 1921 treaty between the Soviet Socialist Republic of Abkhazia and the Soviet Socialist Republic of Georgia, that status gave Abkhazia the ability to decide its own fate independently in the event that the question of another union republic's secession from the USSR should arise, because the Abkhazian people believe that membership in the USSR is the only possible way to preserve their national distinctiveness. (Applause). I believe that this alliance treaty experience can be utilized in drafting normative acts that regulate relations between other autonomous formations and the particular republics they form part of.

The purpose of the appeal was to expand the republic's rights in the interests of all the multinational population of the Abkhazian ASSR, and it does not confer privileges on any people. The appeal is in no way directed against the Georgian people, with whom we desire to continue to live in peace and friendship.

Statements from the rostrum of the Georgian SSR Supreme Soviet on 29 March 1989 assessing this appeal as contrary to the spirit of the decisions of the 27th party congress and the orientation of the 19th all-union party conference are absolutely groundless. It would seem the Abkhazian people did not have a legal right to express their opinion; the organs of the union republic had decided the fate of Abkhazian autonomy long before the CPSU Central Committee Plenum on interethnic relations. The assessments by the union republic's leadership fomented an even bigger campaign which has not died down to this day, as is attested, in particular, by articles appearing in the press even as the congress is in session.

At meetings with officials who came to Tbilisi after the tragic events, representatives of the Georgian intelligentsia attempted to claim that the cause of what had happened was the "Lykhny Appeal," although the events in Tbilisi were caused by other things and pursued other goals. We are very sorry about the tragedy that took place in Tbilisi, we are deeply sympathetic, and we believe that these events must be thoroughly and completely investigated and that the guilty must get what they deserve.

The restoration of Georgian statehood was observed in the Abkhazian ASSR on 26 May 1988. It is the job of historians to assess the significance of this event in the life of the Georgian nation. In the history of the Abkhazian nation, meanwhile, these events are linked with a state system which in 1918 drowned the Abkhazian Bolshevik Commune in blood and then instituted terror in the villages of Abkhazia. This celebration has led the Abkhazian and Georgian population of the autonomous republic to the brink of conflict. According to numerous

Ninth Session

2 June 1989

telegrams, telephone messages, and other reports that have been coming in to us, the situation in Abkhazia remains tense to this day. Unless urgent measures are taken, something irreparable could happen.

Unfortunately, the CPSU Central Committee and the USSR Council of Ministers have maintained silence in the face of the request of a group of deputies from the Abkhazian ASSR, which was submitted on 25 May of this year. We urgently request that all people's deputies of the USSR support our proposal to create a special commission, made up of people's deputies, to study the situation in the sphere of interethnic relations in Abkhazia.

It would be desirable to have a permanent commission, made up of people's deputies of the USSR, to study the problems of the autonomous formations, in order to relieve tensions in the most difficult regions and not allow things to reach the point of conflict. Our request, which relates to the Abkhazian ASSR, is dictated by the fact that extremist forces have shifted the epicenter of tension to Abkhazia in order, we think, to provoke people to conflict and then blame it on our people. To make us the guilty ones is not difficult, because the mass propaganda media are purveying one-sided information, and representatives of the Abkhazian people are deprived of the right to express their point of view. I would like to note that the people understand the necessity of maximum restraint and calm, because the future of restructuring, the future of our great Motherland, depends on it. And we deputies are doing and are obligated to do everything we can along those lines.

A few more concrete proposals. First, to institute a system of public hearings and scientific appraisals in the chambers and commissions of the Supreme Soviet on questions of interethnic relations in the USSR.

Second, to create a commission on national groups and national minorities in the Chamber of Nationalities of the USSR Supreme Soviet and the supreme soviets of the union republics.

Third, it is essential to return to the original principles of Soviet rule, to the Leninist resolution of the national question, which is based on the "Declaration of the Rights of the Peoples of Russia." A decision to create a deputies' commission to study the situation in the Abkhazian ASSR will introduce calm in the hearts of the people and restore their faith in the triumph of justice.

A.I. Lukyanov: The floor is turned over to deputy Yanis Yanovich Peters. Next up will be Viktor Amazaspovich Ambartsumyan.

I see by the clock that the preceding speaker spoke for 14 and a half minutes. Please observe the time limits.

Ya.Ya. Peters, writer, chairman of the Latvian SSR Writers' Union Board, Riga City (Valmiyerskiy National-Territorial Electoral Okrug, Latvian SSR): Esteemed chairman, people of like mind, people not of like mind, comrade deputies! (Stir in the auditorium, applause).

In the very center of Moscow, greeting the participants in the Congress of People's Deputies and the Muscovites, there hangs a banner which says: "Restructuring—the rebirth of the Leninist face of socialism." I read this fine phrase, and shuddered. What if this is just another flight of poetic fancy—a watchword that we will regard tomorrow with the same bitter irony as the promise that the present generation of Soviet people will live under communism?

I look at the sole historical territory of my forebears, my homeland—Latvia, and I think bitterly: How can it be made into a state that is not even Leninist, but simply normal, not humiliated by all-union monopolies, not poisoned by irresponsible economic activity on the part of irresponsible authorities that are subordinate to no one? How can we ensure that the USSR Council of Ministers allocates, for instance, to the city of Ventspils a mere 1 percent of the currency from the huge proportion of income that it contributes to the all-union budget, paying for it with terrible diseases and deaths among its inhabitants, including abnormalities in pregnant women and their offspring?!

I look at Latvia and I think not so much of "rebirth" as of how to stop the death of my people, because the results of pragmatic, economically invalid actions are already visible. Because of spontaneous migration, the numbers of the indigenous nation in their own territory are approaching the critical minority point. Each people belongs not only to itself. Each people belongs to the world, and the peoples have a shared blood supply.

When this blood supply is disrupted, the entire organism falls sick. That this is so, is indicated by a telegram I received the other day, which I consider it my duty as a deputy to read out:

"To USSR People's Deputies Yanis Peters and Valentin Rasputin, Congress of People's Deputies, Moscow. Please raise the question of the expediency of the construction of the Katunskaya Hydroelectric Power Station, which is a threat to the survival of the Altai ethnic group. [Signed] V. Kydyyev, journalist; Gyuzel Yelemova, poet; S. Kergilov, teacher; M. Tolbina, scientific staffer; A. Tolkachekov, trainer; A. Tadinov, artist; V. Tolkachenov, physician; A. Tyukhteneva, physician."

It is terrible to read such a text, but it is even more terrible to realize that aggressive planning is continuing its crusade against the existence of peoples.

In speaking of the tragedy in Latvia we should, of course, seek the roots in the tragedy of the Russians, Belorussians, Ukrainians, the tragedy of other peoples of the Soviet Union. It is not just for the fun of it that people

Ninth Session

2 June 1989

leave Russian or Belorussian socially oppressed territories, their own sacred lands, and take refuge in the Baltic region, where, without being personally culpable, they are drawn against their will into the creation of a demographic imbalance and an ethnopsychologically unhealthy climate, and the destruction of the national identity and statehood of the union republics. All this destabilizes the political situation and reduces the prestige of the communist parties of Latvia, Lithuania, and Estonia.

It must be admitted that for decades the USSR Government and the Latvian SSR Government violated Article 76 of the USSR Constitution, which states very simply: "A union republic is a sovereign Soviet socialist state that has united with other Soviet republics in the Union of Soviet Socialist Repbulics." I can already hear people saying: "But things are even worse in Russia—Baykal is dying, the birth rate is falling, disease is on the increase, morality is dying...." Yes; I do not deny it, and I believe that the all-union administrative team, including the USSR State Planning Committee [Gosplan], also violates the sovereignty of the RSFSR and the interests of all the peoples of Russia, including the interests of the Russian people and the aforementioned Altai. But the fact that things are even worse in Russia is no consolation for the Latvians, Lithuanians, and Estonians, and no reason to expect equally bad times in the Baltic region. Why should we be compared with less developed regions? Compare us with Finland, Sweden, Norway, Denmark. And if we do not want anti-Russian, anti-Latvian, anti-Lithuanian, anti-Estonian, anti-Semitic, anti-Armenian, anti-Georgian, even anti-Islamic, or anti-anything else feelings to develop, let us really carry out radical restructuring on questions of interethnic relations and the status of the union republic as a sovereign state.

Every schoolboy who has studied grammar knows that sovereignty is virtually synonymous with "independence." So why are we so afraid of this word? Why is Russia afraid of becoming independent of all-union diktat? Why is official Latvia afraid of it? (Unofficial Latvia is no longer afraid of anyone or anything.) Why have we begun to be officially afraid of each other? Why are we afraid of what we ourselves wrote into the Constitution—I quote Article 80: "A union republic has the right to enter into relations with foreign states, conclude treaties with them and exchange diplomatic and consular missions, and participate in the activity of international organizations"?

We are not used to it? Let us admit that at the moment this is true. But I think the time is not far off when Article 81 of the USSR Constitution will also be brought into play—it states: "The sovereign rights of the union republics are protected by the USSR." I am convinced that the USSR should not shrink from coming out in defense of the sovereignty, that is, the independence of the union republics. After all, what is the USSR? It is you and I, each of the 15 constitutionally—but unfortunately, as yet only theoretically—independent states. Only the true independence of these states, with certain restrictions on independence, as is observed in all federal unions, can bring us out of the political, economic, ecological, and national crisis, out of the impasse of moral decline, at this historic moment. The national potential of each people could give a decisive boost to a general economic revival, because national self-awareness, national statehood consists first and foremost of the devout feelings of sons and daughters toward their mother, the motherland, the people who are your family. But the family has the right to lay down order in its own home, and to define the place in that home for its dear relatives, who are, moreover, not relatives at all according to the ethnic principle. In the Baltic family this principle has never dominated. Russian, Belorussian, German, Jewish, Polish, Swedish, and Finnish blood flows in our veins. All we want is not to become lodgers in our own home.

If the center is strong, it should protect us strongly against tyranny, otherwise all it does is to demonstrate strongly its weakness. The new USSR Supreme Soviet should justify on legal principles the stationing of the Army in the union republics. If it has not yet become possible to reduce to a minimum the strength of Army subunits and naval bases in Latvia, Lithuania, and Estonia, or to do away with them entirely in the name of disarmament, then the situation can only be improved by means of an open [glasnyy] contract between the USSR Defense Ministry on the one hand and the union republic Council of Ministers on the other. This contract should stipulate openly what category of troops, in which places, in what numbers, and for what period are deployed in the republic. The concluded contract should be submitted to the republic Supreme Soviet for ratification. New articles should be introduced accordingly into the USSR Constitution and the union republic constitutions, on the relations between the Army and the supreme power in each union republic. Official statutes should be drawn up in addition on the economic, ecological, and cultural behavior of Army subunits, institutions, and departments, soldiers, and officers. I think the military should pass a test in the minimum basic knoweldge of the history, traditions, and way of life of the people among whom they will be living for a certain time under the contract. The contract should guarantee a ban on the show of strength for the purposes of psychological intimidation of citizens. Otherwise the mentality of a citizen of the military district, rather than the country, develops among servicemen.

Comrade deputies! As a result of the February and October 1917 revolution, Latvia, Lithuania, and Estonia acquired national statehood. In 1940 Stalin and his emissaries, Vyshinskiy, Dekanozov, and Zhdanov, the butchers of the peoples, including the Russian people, promised us socialist happiness. It turned out that this was the crude, savage Stalin-Hitler deal on the distribution of spheres of influence. We all are very well aware

STENOGRAPHIC RECORD

Ninth Session

2 June 1989

that you cannot go back to 1939 and start over, but we also are aware that socialism should be synonymous with self-determination for nations and independence for states. It is characteristic that on 25 May, the opening day of the Congress of People's Deputies, PRAVDA published the theses drawn up by the commission of scientists from the USSR and Poland, which say: "In the process of adoption and implementation of decisions, including the 28 September treaty, the Soviet Government committed serious violations of international legal norms. First and foremost we note that the 28 September treaty, which stipulated the extreme eastern limit of the Wehrmacht's advance with a commitment on the part of Germany at state level, was called not only a treaty on the 'border,' but also a 'friendship' treaty, which provided grounds for speaking of 'friendly' relations between the USSR and fascist Germany, in effect whitewashed fascism, distorted class principles in the public and individual consciousness, and had grave consequences for both Poland and the USSR; the treaty flouted Leninist principles and struck a blow against the international workers' movement."

Comrades! Our delegations simply have no right to go back to Riga, Vilnius, and Tallinn without a promise that the USSR's highest legislators will instruct the USSR Government to take all the necessary measures to denounce the unlawful international legal document of 1939, because it is a question of Mankurtism, that phenomenon that was so precisely defined by Chingiz Aytmatov. Remember, a Mankurt is a man who has lost his memory, and is therefore ready to shoot his own mother dead, because he does not recognize her.

The whole world is watching today to see whether the Latvian will shoot his mother Latvia, whether the Lithuanian will shoot his mother Lithuania and the Estonian his mother Estonia, by renouncing their own true history under pressure. The whole world will also watch the commission we have set up, which is called upon to restore the historical memory of the peoples, not in the name of the glorious gains of Russia, but in the name of the preservation of life and the rights of national self-determination for the three peace-loving peoples on the shores of the Baltic Sea.

I appeal to Comrades Gorbachev, Yakovlev, and Shevardnadze right now, at the time of the rebirth of the new society that we all so badly need, to become personally involved in unraveling this historical knot.

And in conclusion—although this is not a congress of communists—about the party. Yes, the party won a victory in the elections, but it also suffered a defeat. It is characteristic that the vast majority of those who became people's deputies are those communists who linked their future with the people's and civil movements for democracy, and also with the idea of national rebirth.

Why was Mikhail Sergeyevich Gorbachev elected president of the USSR almost without an alternative candidacy? Obviously the secret is very simple—the leader of the Soviet Union's communists has resolutely taken the people's side and occupied a position of democratic transformations, and is trying to turn the party into a champion of the peoples' interests and to make the party's activity an integral part of the people's movement. Obviously this is the only way for communists if they wish to claim the role of a progressive political force.

This is also indicated by the phenomenon of the disobedient communist, Boris Nikolayevich Yeltsin, for whom we found a place on the Supreme Soviet after all.

But how can we say that the nonparty candidates lost the elections? When we see today among the most respected and genuine people's deputies the conscience of the Russian intelligentsia, Andrey Dmitriyevich Sakharov, what right do we have to speak of a defeat for the nonparty people? So who won, in the end? I will dare to take the responsibility for saying that for the first time after decades of humiliation, it was a victory for the people, democracy, and the desire to begin the creation of an association of independent rule-of-law states.

One last thing: I would like to remind the presidium that a question from Latvian SSR deputies on the fate of the Crimean Tatars has been in the presidium for some days now. Thank you. (Applause).

A.I. Lukyanov: Deputy Viktor Amazaspovich Ambartsumyan has the floor. Comrade Khudonazarov should prepare himself.

V.A. Ambartsumyan, president of the Armenian SSR Academy of Sciences (Ashtarakskiy National-Territorial Electoral Okrug, Armenian SSR): Comrade deputies! At the end of last year Soviet Armenia suffered a disaster on a gigantic scale. An earthquake of enormous destructive power afflicted the whole area from Leninakan to Kirovakan and all the adjoining regions. Nearly half a million people were left homeless as a result of the tragedy. Winters in the Leninakan region—I say this for the benefit of those who have no idea that Armenia is terribly diverse in terms of climatic zones—can be severe, and the situation was extremely grave. In that difficult, troubled time we received generous assistance from all the republics and oblasts of the Soviet Union. All the peoples of the world, states, and governments gave Armenia moral and material support, which we will never forget.

Since the whole of our country and the whole world are watching our first Congress of People's Deputies closely, I will take this opportunity to express most profound gratitude to all the Soviet peoples and the citizens of the world for this mighty and, I would say, unprecedented manifestation of human solidarity. (Applause).

Ninth Session

2 June 1989

The city of Spitak—the epicenter of the earthquake of which nothing remains—has become a symbol of human goodness.

Armenia bows to you, people of the planet. Unfortunately, we also experienced much else that was distressing last year, we had other grave trials, too. In early March 1988 we received thousands of refugees who were fleeing not an earthquake, but the violence in Sumgait. Many people see the name of that city as a symbol of national enmity. I do not want it to be like that, because I very much respect the labor of many thousands of Azerbaijanis, Russians, and Armenians who together built this young industrial center, which, incidentally, has its problems, too. But we must ensure that Sumgait does not happen again.

Esteemed Deputy Azizbekova has sketched a picture of Azerbaijani-Armenian friendship. This friendship has indeed had a long history, but she omitted to say how the events in Sumgait fit in with this friendship. It must be recognized that internationalism is not only a matter of words; it only gains strength from real deeds.

Throughout last year and the early part of this year we learned daily of the troubles of the people of Nagorno-Karabakh, whose oppression has lasted for decades, and which was removed unlawfully from Armenia.

All this is a grave blow against the unity of the Soviet Union's peoples. Yet that unity is the guarantee, the main guarantee, of our country's future. And comrades, let us cherish and strengthen this unity. And although what I have said also implies criticism of our country's central organs, which do not do enough to protect our society against interethnic clashes and oppression, all the same I do not advocate the weakening of central organs. But I demand that they work better and stop helping those forces that seek to weaken the unity of our peoples.

Furthermore, it seems to me that the argument about the rights that should belong to the center and to the periphery—the great discussion about this—is not being conducted quite correctly. After all, the leadership and the apparatus of power are created solely to serve the people. That is their sacred duty. And in order to fulfill their duties well they should be clearly defined and separated. A clear and precise allocation of duties and functions is absolutely essential. We must know precisely what each of us is responsible for.

And what happens? When any shortcoming is uncovered in our work, when anything bad happens, as is so frequently the case, the same question always arises: Who is to blame? If everyone knew precisely what he is responsible for, that is, knew his duties precisely, then after such an event we would see a resignation, the resignation of the civil servant concerned, that is, the one with the relevant duties. Incidentally, for some reason we regard "civil servant" ["chinovnik"] as a rude word. But no, a civil servant is first and foremost a person who carries out quite specific duties that are entrusted to him. For some reason we have come to accept their renaming. And they have begun increasingly to forget that they have duties; they are glad that they are no longer called civil servants, and they think more about their rights than their duties.

At the same time the distribution of duties should be in accordance with the people's needs, and should not arouse their suspicion. When a clear demarcation of duties is set between the center and the republics, then it will be possible to distribute rights in accordance with duties—and this should be done. I do not mean that duties alone are needed first, and rights only later. This is, of course, a single process. But duties should be clarified first and foremost with regard to the people. And then it should be decided, so to speak, what rights are necessary for the fulfillment of these duties, and only these duties.

If you go into the Karabakh question, the reason for the dispute becomes clear. In the consciousness of the Armenian people the unlawful, unconditional removal of Karabakh from Armenia in the twenties was also based on the principle that the most important thing is to gain rights. To begin the de-Armenianization of that territory. And when the de-Armenianization is completed, as has already been done in Nakhichevan, then let them say what they like. All the same, it will be a fait accompli by then. The question of the final normalization of the situation in Nagorno-Karabakh can only be resolved on the basis of the principle of the peoples' self-determination. Life itself has shown that the Leninist principle of self-determination of nations is the only means of resolving such issues. And this will, of course, be in the spirit of restructuring.

Comrades, great significance is attached to the foreign policy questions to which the second part of Mikhail Sergeyevich's report was devoted. Here our country has achieved successes on a truly worldwide scale. These arose from the introduction of the new thinking. This thinking and its introduction led to the lessening of tension throughout the world. That is greatly to our country's credit.

Our troops have been withdrawn from Afghanistan. I believe that throughout this sphere full approval of our government's activity can be expressed. (Applause). But we ask our government also constantly to take into account the fact that not only the Union as a whole, but each of the Union's peoples, has its own external interests, not only economically, but also politically. Some examples.

First. When Foreign Minister (former, of course) Molotov once declared on behalf of the Armenian people that they renounce their claims to the restoration of the Kars region [now in Turkey] and the territory where, as the whole world knows, the 1915 genocide was carried out, he was not telling the truth. He mercilessly flouted the feelings and

STENOGRAPHIC RECORD

Ninth Session

2 June 1989

interests of one of the peoples of the Soviet Union. The Armenian people are in favor of peace. No one proposes to use force on this matter, but we hope that the question will find a peaceful solution in the future.

Another example. A number of foreign states, as well as the European Parliament, have officially acknowledged and condemned the genocide of Armenians in 1915 by Ottoman Turkey. The Armenian SSR Supreme Soviet recently adopted a decision to request that the USSR Supreme Soviet officially condemn the extermination of the Armenian people in Turkey in 1915. That would be as just as the condemnation of the deportation of the Tatars from the Crimea.

I wish to make one more brief, but important observation here. Many of us representatives of outlying republics have spoken here about our peoples' national feelings, and in particular of cases where national consciousness has been injured. Yes, there is much suffering and many injuries in our shared history. But in this atmosphere of justified demands and reminders of our own grief, it is incumbent on us to pay due tribute to the amazing staunchness of the Russian people—the people who suffered numerous losses in the Great Patriotic War and endured the horrors of depeasantization and de-Cossackization, showing exemplary industriousness, creative initiative, and love for other peoples. Whether we like it or not, the Russian people are placed in a position where they bear the heaviest burden, the heaviest duties, which they cannot shrug off, by virtue of their position. At a congress such as the present first Congress of People's Deputies, this observation on the part of representatives of all the peoples living in the union republics will, I hope, be deemed entirely apposite. (Applause).

Comrades, allow me to express the hope that at least some of the questions we have raised will be resolved in the process of this congress' work. (Applause).

A.I. Lukyanov: The floor is turned over to Deputy Khudonazarov. Next up will be Deputy Chervonopiskiy.

D. Khudonazarov, first secretary of the board of the Tajik SSR Cinematographers Union, city of Dushanbe (Khorog National-Territorial Election District, Gorno-Badakhshan Autonomous Oblast): Esteemed Comrade Chairman! Esteemed comrade deputies! I have the distinct honor of representing, along with other deputies here, the Gorno-Badakhshan Autonomous Oblast, which is located in the Pamirs. Allow me first of all to address a few words directly to my constituents.

Dear countrymen! Believe me, I have not forgotten our problems, our troubles, our discomposure. But I won't be speaking of them today. Today I need to talk about what concerns and unites our whole Union, the worries and hopes we share. Along with our credentials, we have been given by you constituents the responsibility for the fate of every one of you and all of us together.

Responsibility—that's what I want to focus on first. Day before yesterday, Deputy Yu. P. Vlasov voiced the idea of the possibility of calling anyone to account before the people's representatives (that is, before all of society), regardless of the post he holds. But how are we to exercise this requirement when we lack the mechanism by which legislative authority, which guarantees public order in the state, might control the executive organs of that authority? Without a mechanism of control, we enable any official to shift responsibility for concrete actions onto a subordinate. As a result, a decision concerning actions that have consequences for the whole state can be taken at any level. And then there is the possibility, at any level, to "wash one's hands."

If we look at the tragedy of 9 April from this standpoint, we can see that for all the dissimilarity in the specific circumstances and people involved, the events in Tbilisi are of the same order with Chernobyl, the Aral Sea, Sumgait, and Lake Baykal. There is no guarantee that this sad series will not be extended.

The responsibility which we took upon ourselves when we received the mandates of authority from the people must also be extended to all our executive organs and each individual executive officer. Only by doing so and finding the mechanism to demand equally from them and from ourselves can we manifest genuine respect for the principle of collective authority and for the personality of the state official. I ask that you examine the formation of the USSR Committee for Constitutional Supervision through this prism.

Secondly, a matter of great urgency: It is essential right now, while the events are still fresh, to review the experience of the recent elections, to take account of all defects, errors, and violations. Many, very many of our constituents are bitter about the candidates' lack of equal rights. For some candidates, the apparatus rolled out the red carpet; for others, it erected hurdles. Far from being punished, those who violated the principle of equal rights—the fundamental principle of democracy—have not even been charged. The first lessons of our new electoral system must be taken account of immediately in order to guarantee genuine democratic conditions for elections to the supreme soviets of the republics and the local soviets. (Applause).

Local authority is most visible to the people; millions are in touch with it, and trust in the higher levels of authority starts there. The more competently and freely the local deputies express the will of the constitutents, the more effective our and your activities will be. The bitter experience of history proves that puppets do not help the government, they tie its hands. Right now, at this congress, we must pass an amendment to the Law on Elections of People's Deputies of the USSR. We must reject district assemblies which serve as filters for candidates who are undesirable to the apparatus. (Applause). Recent experience has shown that only through direct elections in two rounds can we protect

Ninth Session

2 June 1989

against the despotism and injustice which give rise to social apathy, feelings of bitterness and frustration, distrust of authority, and deepening crisis.

My proposal: to include under Miscellaneous on the agenda a discussion of the Law on Elections and amend it in accordance with the experience we have gained.

Thirdly, we have elected a USSR Supreme Soviet at the present congress. I was also deeply saddened by the fact that many deputies who showed themselves to be competent politicians during the pre-congress period were left out of the Supreme Soviet. During the proceedings of congress we have all experienced an acute shortage of jurists in our ranks. There should be considerably more of them. Whenever we hit a snag, we look around for Deputy A. A. Sobchak. By autumn we will have accumulated the minimum experience to enable us to begin rotation without waiting for the following year. It is essential that the Supreme Soviet become a genuine, vigorous organ of state authority so that in the course of five years our ranks will produce workers, peasants, and members of the intelligentsia who have proved themselves as real politicians. In connection with this, I urge you, my colleagues, not to engage any more in artificially opposing the workers to the intelligentsia. It could create a new nucleus of senseless tension. (Applause).

Further, I agree with Deputy Sh.A. Amonashvili that national sensibilities and interethnic relations are the most troublesome sore points in the social organism. This applies both to the larger and the smaller peoples. An insult to national honor is incomparably greater than an insult to an individual. It is tantamount to an insult to our parents and our children at the same time, an insult to the whole cycle of generations in the past and the future. Interethnic tension in many areas of our country did not come into being today or 70 years ago; sometimes it has grown over the centuries. Such conflicts are caused not only by ethnic but also religious, territorial, and psychological factors. Any so-called "preventive measures" in this sphere must be undertaken with extreme caution! Any coercion, any aggression immediately provokes a reaction whose potential energy has been accumulating for centuries. The only permissible preventive measure is democracy—that is, tolerance, willingness to listen to and understand the other person, openness to any investigation and discussion, local self-government and effective guarantees to protect sovereignty on the part of Central authority.

In contemplating the recent tragedies in the sphere of national policies and interethnic relations, I am increasingly worried because we have neither a genuinely historical nor a long-range concept in this sphere, and, consequently, we do not have legislative guarantees or effective levers for resolving conflicts. Even the simple truth that national and econoimc relations are interconnected is ignored because of the shortsightedness of many local (and not just local) officials.

I think it is necessary to cite two examples of how tension in regional and national relations is born and built up. It is inseparable from economic and political problems. The Pamirs make up the highest mountain region in the country, where the average elevation of inhabited territory is more than 3000 meters above sea level, where mountain peaks top out above 7000 meters, and minimum temperatures go down to -63 degrees Celsius. People live in extreme conditions almost all year round. Added to these natural difficulties is economic and social deprivation. The road that links the oblast to Dushanbe, the capital of Tajikistan, is closed throughout the long winter. Difficult meteorological conditions the year round lead to irregularity in air connections. For this reason, it has been decided to build another road connecting Khorog, Kalai-Khumb, and Kulyab. But at the rate the construction is going—it has been under construction for 10 years now—it will not be completed until the third millenium. Yet old-timers recall how, a half-century ago, with the help of fraternal peoples, they built a road to Dushanbe almost by hand in... 110 days. The indifference of the Central ministry not only deprives the region of a vitally essential link with the country but also creates a cluster of problems in which negative energy is building up.

Another example. At present, an average of 93 percent of the population of the Pamirs watches the Central Television program via the space satellite system. But Pamirians are deprived of the opportunity to watch Tajik Television, and in Murgab Rayon, which is inhabited by Kirghiz as well, there is no reception of broadcasts from Kirghiz Television. Not only that, there are no special correspondents for republic television in the Pamirs, correspondents who could report regularly to the whole region on the life, social problems, and cultural wealth of the Pamir districts. As a result, there is an increasing gap between the two parts of a single nation. It is aggravated by the fact that, while the Pamirians and the lowland Tajiks have common ethnic roots, they speak different languages. Normal cultural communications used to foster the multilingualism that was common to regions of Central Asia. Now, however, the Pamirians are not always perceived by the lowland Tajiks as being a kindred part of the nation with equal rights. In the mountains, on the other hand, fewer people know the common Tajik language, which creates additional difficulties in schooling, in labor, and in the distribution of material, social, and cultural benefits. Meanwhile, broadcasting republic television programs via satellite to Gornyy Badakhshan, to the rest of the territory of Tajikistan, and to the other republics of Central Asia would obviously cost less in every respect than the present mutual isolation.

Thus, economic short-sightedness has brought about growing national problems. And errors in national policies have brought about economic backwardness. It is obvious now that it is impossible to solve economic problems without raising social awareness, and the latter is impossible without shaping national awareness.

STENOGRAPHIC RECORD

Ninth Session
2 June 1989

National awareness embodies a force of enormous magnitude, comparable to nuclear energy. But, like nuclear energy, it can be used to build or to destroy. Neglectfulness, carelessness, or unwise playing upon selfish interests in this sphere can lead to catastrophes comparable to Chernobyl. We have already learned several tragic lessons. Any escalation of nationalist tendencies, insistence on one's superiority and exclusiveness, and any absence of national self-criticism can lead to self-oblivion rather than self-awareness. And, again, the only salvation from explosion is the further development of democracy. Democracy means more than pluralism of opinions and complete freedom to discuss them; it also requires the ability to reach the kind of compromise that satisfies all sides. It is the art of achieving unity, but not a unity that is mechanical and homogenizes the multiplicity of interests and aspirations. Democracy is also self-discipline. There are those who interpret discipline as obedience, but in fact it is the readiness to take responsibilty upon oneself, to answer for the consequences of one's actions in accordance with conscience and the law. One leader of the human rights movement in America has said: "If you're not ready to be part of the solution, you are almost certainly part of the problem." In considering the necessity of broad discussion of the entire complex of interethnic problems in their theoretical, political, legislative, and economic aspects, it must be deemed essential that the work of the CPSU Central Committee Plenum on National Questions be participated in by communist deputies, members of the future commission on interethnic relations. From now on, in my opinion, it should be a rule that members of certain commissions and committees of the USSR Supreme Soviet routinely take part, with the right of a consultative vote, in Central Committee plenums concerning these themes.

For the first time in many decades, the people are touching the levers of state power directly through their representatives. We are standing on the threshold of the house of a state of law. With our very first steps we must restore the rights of one more category. It is classified among those universal human values which the chairman of our Supreme Soviet has mentioned repeatedly as one of the highest criteria of our new life. I refer to the category of honor. It cannot be introduced legislatively; it can be acknowledged voluntarily as a moral principle. Honor and responsibility are inseparable. If you refuse to avow responsibility, you acknowledge the permissibility of shifting your own possible dishonor onto others who are less guilty or absolutely innocent, and in the long run, onto your state, your people. Woe unto us if we again consent to this! Finally in recent years, party and law enforcement organs have carried out broad rehabilitation of the victims of the potentates who cynically rejected honor as a personal or state category. Among the millions of peasants, workers, and members of the intelligentsia who perished innocently, there were many delegates to eight all-union congresses of soviets, and almost all the members of their central executive committees. They departed this life as "enemies of the people." I cannot help thinking that the agony of dishonor was more terrible to them than physical torment. Death in dishonor must have horrified them, because honor is more precious than life. After we have restored legal and political innocence to the martyrs, we people's deputies must restore honor to all our fellow citizens who perished innocently, and hence to ourselves and our children as well. By doing so we will swear fidelity to the inner moral law of honor without which our state cannot flourish.

I ask the chairman to propose that everyone in this hall signify by standing that they swear fidelity to the inner law of honor, without which our country cannot flourish. (Applause).

A.I. Lukyanov: The floor is turned over to Deputy Chervonopiskiy, internationalist soldier [Afghan veteran] and representative of the Komsomol [All-Union Leninist Communist Youth League]. (Applause).

S.V. Chervonopiskiy, first secretary of the Cherkassy Komsomol Gorkom [city party committee] of the Ukraine, Ukrainian Soviet Socialist Republic [SSR], Cherkassy (from the Komsomol): Comrades! I would first of all like to express my gratitude for the fact that after several days of work the representatives of the youth have finally begun to be given the floor. This is one of those complaints which I am forced to voice since our voters are telephoning and are demanding that we bring their instructions to you.

Comrades! While in the Congress Hall, more and more often I recall the phrase said by one of the heroes of our well-known film hit "The White Sun of the Desert," the customs officer Vereshchagin: "It is an insult to the state!" It is an insult to have rationing coupons in the 72d year of Soviet power, it is an insult in the collapse in the economy, the devastated villages, the at times savage interethnic relations, the fishless rivers and the cities with chemical smog. In truth, we certainly do have things to be proud of. In my opinion, in addition to the world's largest computers, we also have the world's greatest nonconstructive criticism.

But there is something which is the most insulting for me, for the Komsomol, for some say, bureaucrat, and is clearly felt by those 143 deputies who voted against my candidacy to the Supreme Soviet. Incidentally, let me give them my direct telephone number: the city of Cherkassy, 47-28-19. And let them try, if they can, catch me in the first disability group in my office.

So let me say that the most insulting thing is that you, the senior comrades, our fathers and grandfathers, have not left for us, for the youth, even any acceptable ideas by which we can build our lives, that we can work for, fight for, and by which we can educate the youth.

As for the Komsomol, the comrades who without grounds criticize it clearly are judging from those times when they themselves were working there or, more

Ninth Session
2 June 1989

accurately, were not working. At present, even over the last 5 years, the situation has changed appreciably. Centers of scientific-technical creativity for the youth, with attendance in the millions, have arisen, as have youth housing projects which are prototypes for the socialist community, recreational centers, labor production associations, and military-sports clubs. The Komsomol has set out to do concrete deeds. In truth, you must not think that this is already the case everywhere. Quite the contrary. Nevertheless, this is a reality. Just a year ago in Sevastopol, a city of undying Russian glory, the representatives of 100,000 Afghaners [Afghan veterans] of the Ukraine elected me the chairman of the republic reserve personnel council. They called me, as we say in the Ukraine, their father. With full right on their behalf, I presently state the following.

In the first place. In the report of Mikhail Sergeyevich Gorbachev there was no political assessment of the Afghan War, which was expected by all of us and possibly by the entire nation and the entire world.

Second, it is embarrassing to the point of tears that those who came under dushman fire, who hit Italian mines or were hit by American Stingers, must at times hear from the mouths of the bureaucrats from the party, the soviet Komsomol and other bodies the words which have almost become a popular saying: "I did not send you to Afghanistan." It is an insult to wait in the so-called preferential lines for a children's baby carriage when the child is already in school, to wait until the year 2000 for an apartment—and as for the furniture and other articles of household luxury, we will have to wait for these obviously until the times when everyone is living well in Russia. I am not speaking here about my crippled brothers. Certainly our prosthetics industry continues to remain at a Stone Age level.

Comrades, I will speak without beating around the bush. My prostheses were manufactured on equipment at one of the two prosthetics plants which were given to us after the war by Churchill's wife. Yes, respected scientists, it is possible to mow with a 12th century model scythe, and even do a good job with it, but I would not even wish it upon my enemies to have to move around with such a deformity at the end of the 20th century. (Applause).

Third, the people have already voiced their trust in us, the former internationalist soldiers. Present in the hall today are 120 people's deputies who underwent the school of hardship, difficulties, courage and military valor in the hard-suffering Afghan land. As you know, the most honest people since time immemorial are our children. So you have tens of thousands of juveniles ripped from the clutches of alcoholism, drug addiction, crime, including organized crime—and there are specific examples of this if you wish to take a look—who are studying today in the military patriotic clubs. I will give a specific example. In our small Cherkassy, there are almost 15 clubs with 800 students. These clubs are run by the former internationalist soldiers. These are involved not in the production of "cannon fodder," as some have tried to accuse us, but rather in educating physically strong, mentally tempered citizens of our socialist motherland who are ready for any difficulties, and whose hands will build that renewed society the foundation of which is being laid today by you and me, comrade deputies. Yes, these clubs do have a lot of problems. They are often misunderstood and not supported by the bureaucrats from DOSAAF [Voluntary Society for the Promotion of the Army, Aviation, and Navy], and public education, the sports bosses who under the most diverse pretexts stubbornly resist turning over to these really effectively operating clubs even the meager athletic equipment which is at their disposal. For now the students often must study precariously in school gymnasiums, and even in barns and basements which do not meet any sanitary requirements and standards. It is an amazing paradox. At the dawn of Soviet power, palaces were given to the children. Now we are driving them into basements. The clubs do not have even elementary facilities, supplies, athletic goods, or training aids. The leaders, basically workers and students, in working 4 or 5 days a week with juveniles, do not receive anything for this except the jitters, and problems on the job and in the family. For this reason I propose that the given question be paid the most serious attention on the state level. We must not limit ourselves to ambiguous directives for the Armed Forces, but rather organize effective sponsorship.

A few words about the Tbilisi tragedy. I, as a person who—and I hope that none of you would have to endure this—has had to say farewell forever to my brothers, my combat friends, among whom were Belorussians, Lithuanians, Gagauz, Tatars, Dargins and Russians, to the depth of my soul hate war and death. Even now I cannot state a definite opinion on this, what is clearly the most shameful and disgraceful provocation of our modern history, and which somehow evokes particular doubt in me. That very airborne regiment from Kirovabad that was discussed here was one of the last to pull out of Afghanistan and end this contradictory war. So I am convinced that the men who even in combat rescued Afghan women and children could never become murderers and butchers, as they have been styled (applause) by politicians from Georgia and the Baltic, who themselves have long been engaged in preparing their own assault detachments (applause), the role of which we are well aware of in the history of certain states. So now they do not put on the badges of the USSR people's deputies, preferring the symbols of their people's fronts. (Applause).

I support without hesitation the idea of republic cost accountability; but when stores sell goods only to persons with a Baltic registry, then this, in my mind, can be called republic nationalistic selfishness. (Applause).

We are still seriously concerned by the unprecedented persecution of the Soviet Army which has been initiated in the mass information media. (Applause).

STENOGRAPHIC RECORD

Ninth Session

2 June 1989

Completely incomprehensible to me are the purpose and sense of the irresponsible statements by Deputy Sakharov on the issue of Afghanistan, and the malicious persecution of the valiant soldiers by the TV broadcast "View" [Vzglyad]. Forgive me, but I would like to interrupt my speech and read to you one small appeal. "To the Presidium of the USSR Congress of People's Deputies. To the Chairman of the USSR Supreme Soviet, the Secretary General of the CPSU Central Committee, and to the Chairman of the National Defense Council, Comrade Mikhail Sergeyevich Gorbachev.

"We, the soldiers, sergeants and officers of the many-thousand-strong troop collective of the Red Banner Orders of Lenin and Kutuzov "60-letiye SSSR" Second Degree Airborne Formation, which for 9 years carried out its international duty in Afghanistan, strongly urge you to provide from the rostrum of the congress an explanation to the people's deputies as to on what grounds or upon whose authorization the USSR People's Deputy Sakharov gave an interview to the journalists of the Canadian newspaper OTTAWA CITIZEN that in Afghanistan Soviet pilots fired on our own Soviet soldiers, who were surrounded, so that they could not be taken prisoner. To the depths of our souls we are indignant over this irresponsible, provocative trick by a well-known scientist, and view his impersonal accusation as an ill-intentioned attack on the Soviet Armed Forces. We view their discrediting as a regular attempt to breach the sacred unity of the Army, the party, and the people. We view this as a belittling of the honor, dignity and memory of those sons of our motherland who to the end carried out its orders: Heroes of the Soviet Union, Airbornemen Mironenko, Chepik, Koryavin, Zadorozhnyy and Yurasov. For us, their example is a symbol of the patriotism and wholehearted loyalty to their military and international duty.

"The congress delegates should know that the airborne troops, contrary to the attempts of Sakharov and other like him, in the future will securely defend the interests of our multinational motherland." (Applause).

I support this appeal because I myself, a former major in the Airborne Troops, served in this formation. The given appeal was signed by Major General Bocharov, Lieutenant Colonel Popov, Major Petrov, Lt Col Yarkov, Captain Turchak, Sergeant Fetisov, Sgt Martynov, Private Solovyev, and Senior Lt Batyuk. They all have been awarded orders and medals of the Soviet Union. (Applause).

Comrade delegates, I am ready to debate the ideas voiced by me today, but I warn you that these are to be debates and not shouting matches as has already occurred here.

One last thing. In the auditorium are more than 80 percent Communists. Very many of them have already spoken. But no one, even in the report, has mentioned the word communism. I am a convinced opponent of slogans and sham. But the three words for which, I feel, we must all fight for I can state now: these are "the state, the motherland and communism." (Applause. The deputies rise.)

Comrade chairman! Since I have saved several minutes in my speech, I would like to give 2 minutes from my speech to my brother from Belorussia Pavel Shetko. Please. (Applause).

A.I. Lukyanov: Give him the floor?

From the floor: Yes!

A.I. Lukyanov: You may speak.

P.V. Shetko, lecturer from the Propaganda Section of the Minsk Komsomol Obkom [oblast party committee] of Belorussia, Belorussian SSR, Minsk (from the Komsomol): Respected people's deputies, respected guests of the congress! I support what Sergey [Chervonopiskiy] has stated from the rostrum. The phrase which one hears now from the bureaucrat—"I did not send you to Afghanistan"—will probably be heard in the future. How else could this be? And today what we glimpse in the newspapers disturbs us. There are the verses of Yevtushenko, such as "Little Wizard," "The Afghan Ant," and others. We, the internationalist soldiers, demand a thorough assessment of the commitment of troops to Afghanistan. We know the truth about Afghanistan and we want you all to know it. We realize that it will not be easy to do this, considering the complexity of the situation. But, comrades, we must not delay. The confidential letter of the CPSU Central Committee has given rise to differing interpretations of the essence of the question, and the worst thing would be a loss of faith in the state which sent us abroad for war. We do not want to be the victims of a political mistake. We will intensify the struggle for peace and for making certain that no one would dare send our children outside our motherland without the permission of the highest body. (Applause).

We know that the General Staff of the Ministry of Defense is at work on creating a "Kniga Pamyati" [Commemorative Book]. Considering the difficulty of this work and its vastness, it will take many months and possibly years. But we still are insisting on the publication of the lists of killed in order to involve both the Komsomol and party bodies and public organizations in this work. In reflecting on the "Kniga Pamyati," we want our soldiers to be remembered, and not only those who carried out their military duty and perished in Afghanistan, but also in other countries.

At present, our nation has been shaken by numerous events, including Chernobyl, Georgia, Tajikistan and Armenia. And everywhere, our soldiers, the so-called Afghaners, have proven to be true internationalists. They have learned to value true friendship and fraternity, and in donating blood they have not asked what nationality the wounded man is to whom they have given

Ninth Session

2 June 1989

blood. And in me there is much blood of my fellows. In the same ranks with the veterans of the Patriotic War, and with the thousands of juveniles from our clubs, we have taken an active part in the sociopolitical life of the nation, but our comrades presently need our help. They need good prostheses and recuperation centers. The pension for a young disabled person without an arm or without a leg is 46 rubles, while the average wage is 217 rubles in our country. Many need housing. Aid, and most importantly attention, are needed by the families of the deceased. Of course, no one can return a mother's son. That is true. But we do not have any moral right to belittle this mother in a store or at work. Even in order to erect a tombstone for her son she must shed tears and grovel. Is this really merciful?

I propose verification of the execution of all decisions and decrees and a strengthening of personal responsibility for those persons who should answer for their fulfillment. Supervision of this should be entrusted to the Committee for Youth Affairs where internationalist soldiers will be working. They are already helping to instill proper order!

We offer to restructuring our experience, an activist position in life and authority. Thank you. (Applause).

A.D. Sakharov, academician and chief science associate at the L.M. Lebedev Physics Institute of the USSR Academy of Sciences, Moscow (from the USSR Academy of Sciences): Least of all (noise in the auditorium) have I sought to insult the Soviet Army. I profoundly respect the Soviet Army and the Soviet soldier who defended our motherland in the Great Patriotic War. But when it is a question of the Afghan War, I again do not insult the soldier who shed his blood there and who heroically carried out his orders. That is not the issue here. It is an issue that the war itself in Afghanistan was a criminal one, a criminal adventure taken...(stir in the auditorium) undertaken by unknown persons, and we also do not know who bears responsibility for this enormous crime against the motherland. This crime cost the lives of almost a million Afghans, a war of destruction was waged against an entire people, and a million persons were killed. And this is what rests on us as a terrible sin, a terrible rebuke. We must wash from ourselves precisely this infamy which lies on our leadership, which committed this act of aggression, against the people and against the Army. This is what I want...(stir in the auditorium). I came out against sending Soviet troops into Afghanistan, and for this I was exiled to Gorkiy (stir in the auditorium). Precisely this was the main reason. I am proud of this, I am proud of this exile to Gorkiy as a decoration which I received.... This is the first thing that I want to say.

Second.... The subject of the interview was quite different, and I have already explained this to KOMSOMOL-SKAYA PRAVDA, but let me repeat: It was a question of the return of Soviet prisoners of war who were in Pakistan. And I also said that the only method of resolving this problem was direct talks between the Soviet side, the Kabul government, and the Afghan partisans who must be recognized as a belligerent, as they were defending the independence of their motherland. And this gives them the right to consider themselves its defenders. Only in this manner is it possible to resolve this problem, only by an exchange, only by a direct recognition of them.... In replying to this question, I mentioned those announcements which were known to me from the foreign radio broadcasts, that is, the fact of the execution (stir in the auditorium), "with the aim," as was written in this letter which I received, "with the aim of avoiding being captured." These words "the exclusion of capture" were a sentence for those who wrote to me—this was a purely Stalinist sentence copied from secret orders. At present, this question is being investigated, and before this question is clear, no one has the right to accuse me that I have said a mistruth. Not before this question has been subjected to an objective and strict investigation. And I am receiving constantly new facts.

For now that is all I want to say. I do not apologize to the entire Soviet Army, as I have not insulted it. I have not insulted the Soviet Army nor the Soviet soldier (applause, stir in the auditorium), but I have insulted those who gave this criminal order to send Soviet troops into Afghanistan. (Applause, stir in the auditorium.)

A.I. Lukyanov: For inquiry? Three minutes. Comrades, attention, up to 3 minutes for inquiry.

V.N. Ochirov, colonel, commander of an air regiment (University National-Territorial Electoral District, Kalmyk Autonomous Soviet Socialist Republic [ASSR]): I am a colonel, the commander of an air regiment who at one time, while still being a captain and a major, twice served in Afghanistan. I read this information which was given by Comrade Sakharov, and I also was angry on behalf of my fellow servicemen, and for the justice of those who did not return, and those who could not return, I state that this is a slander and a lie against our soldiers, against the honor of our people and our Soviet Army. (Applause).

Under the harshest conditions, whatever the circumstances were—at times we had to rescue even one or two wounded soldiers or the dead—when the situation developed that there was not a single chance under heavy fire for the helicopter crew to make a landing or take-off, we still did this, helping out our comrades regardless of nationality. This was our common family of peoples. (Applause).

A.I. Lukyanov: Wait a minute. Three minutes.

A.V. Eyzan, deputy chief physician at the Ventspils Central Rayon Hospital (Ventspils National-Territorial Electoral District, Latvia): Comrade deputies. On behalf of the Baltic republic, I should first state to the congress that in the Baltic the pain of the "Afghaners" is felt just as strongly as in all the other corners of the Soviet Union. Secondly, let me assure you with all responsibility that

Ninth Session
2 June 1989

none of the Baltic republics has even any idea of organizing assault detachments. There are none and will be none! Thank you. (Applause).

V.V. Yakushkin, teacher from the Secondary Vocational-Technical School No 147, Vitebsk (Vitebsk City National-Territorial Electoral District, Belorussia): I myself am an Afghaner. It so happened that we were among the first troops in, in 1979, and we who were there were not only not moved but, even worse, were profoundly angered by all that was said by Academician Sakharov. Here a specific question was posed: Where did the information come from, and who was the source? If a person states something from this high rostrum, he should say who provided him with this information. We request that this be announced to the congress. And I will say for a point of information that as for our helicopter troops, they were killed more than we, as they were more unprotected, and how many helicopters had to seek us out and rescue our pilots.

A.I. Lukyanov: One minute, Sergey Fedorovich [Akhromeyev].

Deputy (not identified): Comrades, I also served in Afghanistan, also in 1979-1980, and I can speak about our brothers, our Latvians. I served with these fellows, and they also, with the Russians and remaining nationalities, did their duty. For this reason, if there are any doubts about the Latvians, I have personally the brightest and best feelings for this nation. Thank you. (Applause).

S.F. Akhromeyev, advisor to the chairman of the presidium of the USSR Supreme Soviet (Beltsy Territorial Electoral District, Moldavia): I must also participate in this debate with Academician Sakharov. I carried out the duties of the first deputy chief of the General Staff and chief of the General Staff during the entire period of the Afghan events. I can report to you with full responsibility (during the 2 ½ years I carried out my military duty in Afghanistan), that not a single order or anything like it was issued at the General Staff and the Ministry of Defense, and we did not receive any such savage instructions from the political leadership of our nation, to destroy our own soldiers who had fallen in an encirclement. All of this is a pure lie, a deliberate untruth, and Academician Sakharov will not find any documents to substantiate it. (Applause).

A.I. Lukyanov: Identify yourself.

G.I. Kravchenko, brigade leader of the Pioner State Farm [sovkhoz] in Sudogodskiy Rayon, Vladimir Oblast (Gus-Khrustalnyy Territorial Electoral District): Comrade deputies! I address myself to our great scientist, Comrade Sakharov, and ask who gave him the right to insult our children? I have two sons. One has already done his service and the other soon will. And so I would like to know precisely who gave him the right to insult our children, who actually gave up everything, possibly their lives, their families, and their youth. And to say such a thing! I would assume that this could be said by a worker who actually did not understand...(stir in the auditorium) out of his ignorance, possibly, learned this somewhere from rumors. But, comrades, such a major scientist! This angers me greatly. During the pre-election campaign I was asked: "How do you relate to the activities, to the policy of Comrade Sakharov?" Well, I replied that it is very difficult for me to judge his activities and his politics as I am a working man. But now, being here at the congress, I have clearly understood that I have a completely different opinion of this man. (Applause).

A.I. Lukyanov: One minute. (Stir in the auditorium). And we will stop. One minute.

N.A. Polikarpov, director of the Yelizavetinskiy Sovkhoz, Moshanskiy Rayon (Oktyabrskiy Territorial Electoral District, Penza Oblast): Comrade deputies! I lost my 23-year-old brother, a military pilot, in Afghanistan. Up to now neither I nor anyone knows why he died or under what circumstances. I agree with the notion made here that in the future a Soviet soldier should never die for interests incomprehensible to us. But, comrades, the statement which was made here about our Soviet Army I consider to be slander. Thank you for your attention. (Applause).

Voices: (Inaudible).

A.I. Lukyanov: Now, comrades, we will end this.

T.D. Kazakova, teacher at the G. Gulyam Secondary School No 22, Gazalkent (Chirchik Territorial Electoral District, Tashkent Oblast): Comrade academician! By one action you have eradicated all your activities. You have insulted the entire Army, the entire people, all our fallen who gave up their lives. I have nothing but contempt. You should be ashamed! (Applause).

A.I. Lukyanov: A break is announced until 1600 hours.

* * *

2 June 1989. Kremlin Palace of Congresses. 1600.

USSR People's Deputy A.I. Lukyanov presiding.

A.I. Lukyanov: Comrade deputies! Let us continue the work of the congress. The floor is given to Deputy Garbunov. Deputy Atdayev is to speak next.

G.N. Gorbunov, director of the Irkutsk "60-letiye SSSR" Aviation Plant, Irkutsk (Leninskiy Territorial Electoral District, Russian Soviet Socialist Republic [RSFSR]): Respected comrades, some time has passed since the start of the radical reforms announced by revolutionary restructuring. I, like all the deputies of our oblast, at this unique congress, must answer two questions for our voters. What do we have in this period? What should be done further?

Ninth Session

2 June 1989

There are indisputable successes in the area of humanitarian order, as well as very high foreign policy activity which is previously unprecedented. This we can approve. But what about the second—the increased deficit in the state budget, the inflation, the embodiment of which are the empty store shelves, the sharp gap in earnings between a small portion of the population and the basic mass who live on one wage, the moral stratification of society, and the deepening of the causes of interethnic problems which have surfaced? All of this is the cause and the consequence of the growing social tension in society. We cannot help but notice this. What should we do?

I feel that having decided on a fundamental restructuring of our own home, we, the people's deputies, should firmly say to each member of our society that for this we need peaceful conditions, and the opportunity to work in an interesting job and freely voice one's opinion. I consider it valid that the next congress adopt a series of laws aimed at preventing interethnic hostility and preventing the heightening of crisis phenomena in the economic and social spheres of our life.

Comrades! Concern for man should become the main goal. We must give him even greater priority in social policy and concentrate all efforts on three, in my opinion, most important areas: supplying food and industrial goods, development of the service sphere, and housing construction. For these purposes we must seek out significantly more funds, also by sharply reducing the development of production for the sake of production, and abandoning the gigantic, inefficient construction projects by which we have grown accustomed to measuring our success. And this question must be resolved rapidly, without waiting until the end of the five-year plan.

I consider it essential precisely at this congress to revise the State Budget by changing investment policy, directing it to the solution of primarily social problems. Otherwise, the course of restructuring will be blocked in the future. And here—I will not hide it—what comes to mind are the words of Clausewitz who, as is known, was highly regarded by Vladimir Ilich Lenin: "Russia is not a country which can actually be conquered. Such a country can be conquered only by inner weakness and by the action of internal discord." We must not allow this. (Applause).

Comrades! Each of us in the course of the electoral campaign came out with his program, but as a whole all programs had man at the center, that is, his life, future and happiness. I am a Siberian, but, unfortunately, I cannot now offer you Siberian help, for our ecological problems in Irkutsk Oblast have become extremely aggrevated, particularly in the towns of Shelekhov, Angarsk, Bratsk and Baykalsk. In the densely populated individual regions of the oblast, due to the concentration of chemical, lumber processing, ore-mining and metallurgical enterprises, the PDK [maximum tolerable concentration] and PDV [maximum tolerable discharge] for a number of vitally important indicators are in excess by 10, 100 and more times. We must share the concern of people for the acute ecological problem which, according to universal recognition, has become the most threatening. At present, the resolution of ecological problems has become one of the main criteria for the humaneness of society and for the level of its technical and scientific development. For this reason it would be advisable, in my view, to instruct the government on a nationwide scale to determine the ecological crisis zones. With the participation of representatives from the local community, the Academy of Sciences, Minzdrav [Ministry of Public Health], Goskomprirody [State Committee for the Protection of Nature] and the AUCCTU [All-Union Central Council of Trade Unions], we must effectively work out integrated programs and instruct the appropriate departments to eliminate the threat to human health. We must also establish an ecological fund or bank where the local authorities could obtain the required funds on credit for solving these problems. It is time to stop squandering our national riches, and it is time to halt the lumber felling and exploitation of deposits and the deliveries of oil and gas for the benefit of foreign citizens, all of which can be explained only by bungling. It is essential to adopt a law on ecological responsibility, as this would erect a barrier against the grandiose projects of the century.

It has long been high time to advance a broad front against the mass ecological illiteracy of people. I feel that the forming of ecological culture as a part of general human culture should begin at preschool age, in the nursery. We must not permit the younger generation to be raised with an attitude toward nature following the textbooks and methods in which the leitmotiv is still the Michurin words: "We cannot wait for charity from nature. It is our task to take this from her." We have fleeced her enough.

In the schools, technical schools and VUZ's we must incorporate in the curriculum an obligatory special ecological course. This work must be carried out through all forms of educational activity. We must more fully utilize the mass information media and shape public opinion on the inadmissibility of an ecological disaster both as a result of mismanagement and out of ecological illiteracy; the children must be educated by words, while enterprises and individual citizens who violate the nature conservation legislation will naturally be educated by the force of the ruble.

Life indicates that this will be both intelligible and persuasive, and there will be funds to at least partially compensate for the damage caused to nature. I propose that at the next congress we hear the Supreme Soviet on a decision for ecological questions. (Applause).

Respected comrades, I, like a majority of my voters, am concerned by the situation developing in the nation over the erosion of cheap, accessible consumer goods by the tendency for an increase in price, particularly in food products and vital necessities. What is going on? What is

Ninth Session

2 June 1989

the matter? The problem is as follows. In the drive to carry out additional quotas for producing consumer goods—which, incidentally, in a number of instances are not provided with the material and technical resources—a product is chosen that is expensive and advantageous for the enterprise in order to fulfill the increased volumes. I feel that here there is not a sufficiently scientific approach, and the question cannot always be rectified by mere desire and by command-administrative methods. But our consumer remains without inexpensive goods. Undoubtedly, it is essential to increase the volume of consumer goods. But it is also essential to make the study considering a balancing of resources and local interests.

Comrades, I support the policy of our party to reduce the military budget and to lower the level of defense orders for a number of industrial sectors. This ultimately should produce a positive effect in increasing capacity, and employing this capacity for the social sphere. But at present the mere replacemnt of a military order by a civilian one does not solve the problem. There is also the question of how the conversion can be financed. The progress in disarmament has been identified with the disbursal of the liberated money to all sufferers. But clearly the released portion of the military budget would better be employed for the respecialization of these same enterprises. Only then could one realistically count on their true and complete repayment. For this reason I feel that one of the most effective variations is not a gradual or partial respecialization of the enterprises but rather doing this completely, under the condition of creating enterprises producing scientific and technological products and, possibly, doing this together with foreign partners.

Furthermore, there is one thing we cannot help but mention. Under the new management conditions, the cost accounting income is at times distributed according to standards that are centrally set. This very imperfect tool—and here I completely share the viewpoint of Deputy Bunich—introduces into economic practice many injustices, although it should guarantee the conditions for the self-financing of the production and social processes. Clearly independence is not produced. We again have remained in the clutches of the ministries and departments. I feel that the nation should introduce a unified differentiated tax system which would skillfully direct the work of the enterprises in the interests of society. All of this cannot help but retard a rise in the level in industry as a whole. (Applause).

Comrades, we are all concerned, as has been repeatedly stated here and as has been stated here today, by the slow pace of restructuring. We must not shut our eyes to what we still have not been able to do or what errors we have made in the course of restructuring. Comrades, that is my opinion. At present, we have not achieved a situation where each member of our society not in words but in fact supports and contributes to restructuring. And there are many comrades who, riding the wave of our democracy, have shown ambitions and encouraged extremist attitudes. All of this, undoubtedly, costs the state dearly.

The nation must be protected against this. Furthermore, let us raise the level of labor and production discipline, combining this with an interest in the end results. The press has somehow avoided this question. It is not without interest. I support the comments of Yevgeniy Aleksandrovich Yevtushenko that actually there must be free labor, but I would also add this should be obligatory labor. (Applause). We clearly must always remember this because in our nation there are very many for whom labor is a burden. Furthermore, there is an absence of enterprise independence. I cannot help but mention this. There has been a reduction in the number of ministries but the functions have remained. Instead of the glavkas [main administrations], we have now made a two-shift system virtually everywhere. We have set up NTT's [scientific-technical centers] with the sole difference that they bear virtually no responsibility for enterprise operations but control the actuating levers. Here I feel there should not be half-way measures. The reform must be carried out completely so that it can work and so that it can work for restructuring.

Furthermore, many mistakes have been made by the leading bodies. I understand that here we should now also press claims against our economic science in the personage of Academician Aganbegyan, Comrade Abalkin and others. Mistakes have been made. And in the time of restructuring, they are painful for us. Thus, we very rashly, I would say, took the decision to prohibit wine and liquor products and to cut down the vineyards. Now the network of Berezka stores has been prohibited. All of this means money. The budget loses income. I feel that we should make fewer such errors.

Here is an example which shows the essence of the mistakes made by the leadership. Decree No 1,113 of September 1986 on systematizing salaries was far from well thought out; it was faceless and insufficient work was done on it. While in essence the idea was seemingly not bad, we have carried it out in an organized manner. Salaries were raised to a sufficient level but we did not receive additions on top of this increase, thereby allowing an even greater gap between the available cash in the hands of the public and the available supply of commodities. Would it not have been better, on the contrary, to increase the volume of goods in the stores and then carry out the second part?

I have as an acquaintance a construction worker who is employed in a design institute (before my departure we exchanged opinions), and he says: "Gennadiy Nikolayevich [Gorbunov], I am ashamed to receive a wage of 700 and more rubles (note that this in a design institute) for the same work I was doing before." Similar words, comrades, can be heard from many mouths. This is now this decree has worked. I proposed we carefully study the effect of the designated document and make proposals considering the situation as it develops in the nation. In the future we must promulgate decrees being prepared

STENOGRAPHIC RECORD

Ninth Session

2 June 1989

according to this scheme, and ensure their actual assistance. I would like to propose that at least twice a year a report be made to the Supreme Soviet on their implementation and effectiveness.

Comrades! I cannot help but voice my concern over the exceptionally poor social protection in the Siberian area. Judge for yourselves, in terms of the proportional amount of the contribution of the production volumes to the republic budget, for instance, Irkutsk Oblast is in 20th place, but in terms of the absolute majority of criteria for social goods, such as the availability of housing, service facilities, trade, schools and medical institutions, it is in one of the last places of the 73 Russian oblasts. This injustice must be quickly corrected by the corresponding enforceable enactments. Furthermore, in reviewing the pension law, I would like to introduce a proposal to provide additional benefits for the workers of our region. This is logical, correct, and just, as the living conditions of the Siberians are harsh.

One other detail. At the 26th congress of our party they announced, and this was reflected in the documents, additional wages and coefficients for Irkutsk Oblast and Krasnoyarsk Kray. A good deal of time has passed, the people are waiting, but there are no explanations, while we, the people's deputies, find it hard to reply and justify ourselves. This is one of the examples when mistrust is instilled and passivity engendered, and at times even opposition. Let us change the attitude toward the authority of our party and people's power; let us raise these in the eyes of the voters. Where decisions have been made and promises given, they must be carried out, and if things do not happen, this must be said openly, explaining the truth to the people, and the people will then understand. We have sent a request from Irkutsk Oblast on this question and I request that it be answered.

Comrades! Restructuring and democratization in the nation were started by the party. The party disclosed those sore points which most afflict society. Of course, we are right at present to lay claims against a portion of the workers in the apparatus, and there is dissatisfaction over individual decrees. That is a fact. But, comrades, under the guise of combating bureaucratic power, we must not wage an offensive against the party and split the party and the people. One can scarcely contemplate that even at this congress a wedge might be openly driven between the Communists present here and the party leaders. Understandably, this is being done not by true supporters of restructuring but rather by persons with a different ultimate purpose. The party should and will steer the ship of restructuring! (Applause).

Comrades! The honor shown us is great but the demands placed are corresponding. We must work honestly, reliably and worthily, including vis-a-vis one another.

I would very must like to see quicker results from our work on matters which ensure a better quality of life for our people. This is our high duty and obligation to society. Thank you for your attention. (Applause).

A.I. Lukyanov: Comrades, I strongly urge you to adhere to the rules, to respect the congress, to respect yourselves and to respect our agreement.

The floor is turned over to Deputy Atdayev.

Kh. Atdayev, blacksmith at the Ashkhabad "50-letiye SSSR" Petroleum Machine Building Plant (Ashkhabad, Zheleznodorozhnyy National-Territorial Electoral District, Turkmenia): Respected comrades! First of all, on behalf of the deputies from Turkmenia, I would like to express agreement with the content and provisions of the report given by Mikhail Sergeyevich Gorbachev. But I am also convinced that at present it is not enough to assess one or another phenomenon. There must be active actions to implement what has been planned. The people have entrusted us with the fate of restructuring. This is confirmed by the numerous telegrams from our voters sent to the congress, and we cannot deceive their hopes.

Those who are participating in the work of the congress have had the particular honor and responsibility after the truly democratic elections which attracted the attention of the entire world to take one other major step in carrying out the political reform of Soviet society as outlined by the 19th All-Union CPSU Conference and elect completely new national governing bodies.

At present many are saying, and are saying with alarm, that in the membership of the USSR people's deputies there is a proportionally small number of workers and collective farm [kolkhoz] members; attempts are being made to give the reasons for this, and voices are being heard that in the next elections a certain number of deputy mandates should be reserved for the representatives of the working class and kolkhoz peasantry in order to ensure their sufficient representation. I feel that the working class does not need artificially eased conditions.

The main reason for what happened in our first democratic elections, in my view, is the lack of experience. At individual places they were very concerned with defending the interests of small groups and at times even individuals, opposing their interests to a larger portion of society. It is not without pride that I say that among the deputies from Turkmenia over half are representatives of the workers and kolkhoz members.

A word about myself. I did not become a deputy in a completely ordinary manner. At the pre-election meeting, when other candidacies were being discussed as well as the programs proposed by them, I decided to propose my own candidacy for discussion and described what I would do if the comrades put their trust in me. In the elections I received a majority of the votes by the voters in competition with the other candidate deputy. And I do not agree with those deputies who have stated that the workers of the party apparatus were an obstacle for us. I obtained only support and help.

STENOGRAPHIC RECORD

Ninth Session

2 June 1989

Generally, it must be said that the past elections brought about a marked revival in the sociopolitical activeness of the workers and forced them, as the real masters of the nation, to take a new look at our reality and the urgent problems. The republic workers, having taken an active part in carrying out the party's course of restructuring and renewal, have given special attention to socioeconomic development, as it was precisely during the years of stagnation that we fell behind the national level for many indicators. Over the 3 years of the five-year plan there has been a significant rise in the volume of national income and real per capita income. Labor productivity has been steadily rising, and the situation in capital construction has been improving. This has made it possible to complete hundreds of thousands of square meters of housing above the plan. We have overfulfilled the quotas for the construction of schools, preschool institutions, hospitals and polyclinics.

Our party's policy is encountering ever-wider understanding and support in the labor collectives, which are endeavoring to materialize it in concrete undertakings. One can realize this in the example of the enterprise where I have been employed for 23 years now, the petroleum machine-building plant, the product of which (an industrial fan for water cooling towers) is delivered to many enterprises, both in our nation and abroad. The plant was one of the first to convert to operation under state acceptance conditions. The enterprise is converting to cost accountabilty and the director was chosen on a competitive basis.

Here, comrades, I would like to say a few words about state acceptance. If an enterprise converts to self-financing, to cost accounting and covering of costs, here state acceptance, in my opinion, has no place. It is completely unnecessary because the workers themselves control the quality of the produced product.

All these signs of the times are directly related to the process of restructuring and democratization of life, to the increased political and civil self-awareness of the workers, and to the establishment of the principle of social justice and glasnost. The USSR Supreme Soviet and its bodies have great work to do in extending these processes. They have also been reflected in the instructions given to us by our electors. They express the sincere concern of the workers for a rapid solution to social problems. In this context, I would like to draw your attention to several of them.

The course of the economic reform is causing serious concern. As before, prior to the passage of the Law on the State Enterprise, the ministries and departments operated by administrative methods. They confiscated from the collective's fund a large portion of the profit, and this impeded and even made impossible their conversion to full cost accounting and self-financing, and slowed down production development.

Precisely such a situation developed, in particular, in a number of collectives of the republic gosagroprom [state agro-industrial committee]. The superior departments confiscate over 70 percent of the income. I feel that as a whole for the nation one could find numerous examples of such ministerial tyranny which prevents the introduction of new forms and methods of management. The USSR Supreme Soviet and the government should certainly supervise more strictly the course of the economic reform, and promptly dampen the administrative ardor of the leaders of the ministries and departments which violates the enterprise rights.

I would like to voice certain ideas also on the question of the concept of regional cost accounting. To put it briefly, we are in favor. But I feel that it is essential to give a more definite role to economic methods which would establish a reliable basis for restructuring the republic economy management. There also is a need to return to price formation for certain products, particularly raw materials such as oil, gas and cotton.

The construction of new enterprises and particularly labor-intensive industrial sectors will make it possible to resolve the urgent problem for our republic of rationally utilizing the free labor resources and above all women of indigenous nationality. On this question help from the center is indispensable for us. We are asking the USSR Council of Ministers to allocate the necessary funds and equipment as a special grant for the republic to organize an additional 20,000-30,000 jobs.

One other problem. Tashauz Oblast, which is part of the Aral Sea Zone, is bad in ecological terms, with a low water consumption rate and a high percentage of infectious diseases in the population. Very acute is the question of providing high-quality drinking water. The CPSU Central Committee and the government have adopted a decree on the Aral, and this resolves the question of providing water for the oblast's population, but only by the end of the 13th Five-Year Plan. Considering the already existing bad situation, we request that the appropriate bodies be instructed to adopt a decision for beginning construction on the water line in Tashauz Oblast in 1990 and provide the necessary capital investments and resources. As for resolving individual questions provided in the decree on the Aral, we support the proposal that a deputy commission should assume control and provide assistance in its immediate fulfillment.

There are the unresolved questions of individual housing construction and central gas supply for our towns and settlements, although the republic holds second place in the nation for gas output. The main reason here is the extreme insufficiency of resources and credit provided by the USSR Sberbank [Savings Bank].

On behalf of the USSR people's deputies from Turkmenia, I would like to assure you that we are approaching with all responsibility the exercising of our deputy powers and we will forthrightly and consistently make our

Ninth Session

2 June 1989

contribution to actually implementing the decisions of the 19th All-Union Party Conference and the current USSR Congress of People's Deputies. Thank you for your attention. (Applause).

A.I. Lukyanov: The floor is turned over to the Deputy Yuriy Fedorovich Karyakin. Deputy Dzasokhov is to prepare to speak next.

Yu.F. Karyakin, senior science associate at the Institute of the International Worker Movement of the USSR Academy of Sciences, Moscow (from the USSR Academy of Sciences): Comrade president, people's deputies and voters! Where have the times gone when our General Secretary and president became thrice Hero of the Soviet Union and received the Order of Victory for the fact that his feats in a film were brilliantly portrayed by an actor who for this performance was given the title of Hero of Socialist Labor? Where have those times gone when books were written for Brezhnev and he received the Lenin Prize for literature for them and this prize was presented to him by Markov and then Markov himself received the title of Hero of Socialist Labor from the recently decorated winner? Where have those times gone when you could make a career with books about the general secretaries, where even Chernenko published a work on the triumph of human rights in the Soviet Union and one of the best known journalists went into ecstasy over this work?

If a person who did not know about all of this happened to attend our congress now, I feel he would be dumbfounded, and evidently he would decide that no one was more to blame for all our misfortunes than our general secretary.

Such a trend has arisen. Our congress has already demonstrated this. This is an unprecedented burst in establishing normal relations between power and the people through the deputies. For the first time everything is happening before the very eyes of the entire people, and this is a real forum. The process of the demystification of power has accelerated sharply. However, a dangerous trend has arisen. Previously, people were so accustomed to fawn on the general secretary that now they consider it obligatory to be rude to the new one (applause), although at present there are many bootlickers. Incidentally, one of them, having seen Mikhail Sergeyevich [Gorbachev] shake my hand last month in farewell, immediately decided to offer me the post of editor-in-chief of a very serious journal. (Applause).

When I speak about boorishness I honestly, and particularly here, have no one in mind. I merely see or feel this trend and am very, very afraid. It would be a good thing, having spotted it, to put an end to it at the very outset. The criterion of progressiveness lies not in indiscriminate criticism of Gorbachev but rather in constructive help to our cause in fact and not in fiction. All the more as we ourselves have seen that actually there are no restricted zones for criticism.

I would very much support Gorbachev's initiative, if I have understood it correctly, at the next to last, the April plenum, of publishing the Central Committee sessions fully. (Applause). If I correctly understand this, the party has no secrets from the people, and the Central Committee cannot have any secrets from the party and the people, just as the Politburo cannot from the Central Committee, and so forth, with the exception, certainly, of certain state secrets. It seems to me that this will help us to find constructive paths of unification, that very difficult unification between the people's soviet power and party power, because the problem of separation does exist and we cannot escape from it. Let us not foster the illusions that we are the power and just who are you, comrades from the Politburo? Certainly here there should be some very constructive and not nihilistic solution.

I greatly respect Yuriy Vlasov. But the demand of impeachment, this to me, honestly speaking, seems out of the realm of dreams. Our impeachment in the old times was determined as follows: We have a monarchy limited by the noose, do you remember? And our current impeachment is something like 14 October 1964. And that was in the best interest, if we are to be completely truthful about it. In my opinion, we should not forget this. In any event, at the Leningrad plenum in April, and even in the one about which I spoke, the elements of such a 14 October were visible to the naked eye. And our congress, as I understand it, elected Gorbachev president in order to defend and accelerate restructuring. (Applause).

Mikhail Sergeyevich! I have a request of you as president. I would like our congress to support it. The request as as follows: To return our Russian citizenship to a person who was the first to dare to say the truth about Stalinism, who was the first to urge both himself and ourselves not to lie, the great writer of the Russian land, the great humanist Solzhenitsyn. (Applause).

You have found a common tongue with the Iron Lady, you have found a common tongue with Bush and Reagan, you have found a common tongue with the Pope in Rome—and they have not ceased to be anticommunist—you found this language on the grounds of humanism. Will we not find a common tongue on these grounds with Solzhenitsyn, the great humanist?

Just think, what if Pushkin, Dostoyevskiy or Tolstoy were living now, would we really like them? So what? Would we exile them for this? It seems to me that we will not forgive ourselves (the notion is not mine but voiced for the first time by Astafyev), we will never forgive ourselves and our offspring will not forgive us if we do not do this.

I have long been troubled by one other question. People have tried to dissuade me from mentioning it. Forgive me but I, of course, am determined. Even in my childhood I learned a very quiet, almost totally forgotten fact. Lenin himself wanted to be buried beside the grave of his

Ninth Session

2 June 1989

mother at the Volkov Cemetery in St. Petersburg. Naturally, Nadezhda Konstantinovna [Krupskaya] and Mariya Ilinichna, his sister, wanted this also. But they did not listen to him or to them. What happened happened. And this was yet another, not immediately recognized, not immediately felt moment in our dehumanization, of course. Not only was the last political will of Lenin flaunted but so was his last personal human will. Of course, in the name of Lenin.

You can just imagine what he would say, what he would do to those who did this. He was lying down there and up above the butcher in soft boots was walking about and then he himself was lying nearby. There still was a buffet there and later they removed it. It was the time of the rule of the devil. The Mausoleum with the body of Lenin was not Lenin's mausoleum but even before it was Stalin's Mausoleum.

One could give thousands of ideological and political arguments against this. But there is not a single human argument. I have been warned that the people will not understand this. The people will understand! I assure you, they will understand. This one quiet, forgotten fact that Lenin wanted to rest in a human manner—do we really not understand this?

Tanks roll across Red Square and the body vibrates. Scientists and artists touch up his face—this is a nightmare. In order to create appearances—but there is nothing there and it is terrible to bring this up. So let us bury this body where he, Lenin, would have wished. If I were a believer and if the soul were immortal, it would say thank you to us. (Applause).

One other even more heretical idea. If we have not lost our memory, if we have not murdered our conscience and conscience is conscience, then on Lubyanka, on that building, we should inscribe precisely there the names of the 40 (we do not know the precise figure) millions of dead because of...in line with...under orders of Lubyanka. If that blood were to flow and descend on Lubyanka, it would carry it away. And our national, social and human honor demands this, and I am convinced that this will be.

How much time do I have? Three minutes?

I have received a letter. They propose adopting a congress resolution condemning Academician Sakharov. The letter contains the following words: "Mr. Sakharov, all your accomplishments have been wiped out by your one blasphemous statement. Yes, you were one of the developers of the hydrogen bomb, without which there could not have been the might of our great power. Yes, you rightly wore the decorations of the motherland which thrice made you Hero of Socialist Labor. Yes, you are one of the initiators of a ban on nuclear testing underground, at ground level and in the air. Yes, you were against the entry of our troops into Afghanistan. Yes, you were a defender of democracy and glasnost, but all of this has now been wiped out. And say thank you that we are not sending you back to Gorkiy or not sending you abroad." The second letter was given to me when I was on my way here. "Each day, the Afghan War killed and maimed scores of our people and hundreds of Afghans. The shortening of it, even by 1 day, saved them from this plight. On behalf of all the persons who remained alive, their mothers, wives, fiancees, and on behalf of their future children—Russians and Afghans—great thanks to you, Mikhail Sergeyevich [Gorbachev], and to you, Andrey Dimitriyevich [Sakharov]! (Applause).

"The Brezhnev clique commenced the war in Afghanistan and now in order to conceal its criminal role; it is shifting the people's attention away from itself." That is it. (Applause).

A.I. Lukyanov: The floor is now given to Deputy Aleksandr Sergeyevich Dzasokhov. Deputy Shcherbakov is to get ready.

Voice from the auditorium: There is a proposal not to allow the Muscovites to have the floor...(remainder inaudible).

A.S. Dzasokhov, first secretary of the North Osetian CPSU Obkom, Ordzhonikidze (Ordzhonikidze Territorial Electoral District, North Osetian ASSR): Respected chairman of the Supreme Soviet, respected deputies! Our first congress of people's deputies possesses, it seems to me, many distinguishing features. One of them which brings us all together is an unusual awareness of our unbroken spiritual and moral tie with our electors. For all the following 5 years, this will remain one of our main duties. In carrying out their will, during these days, the congress has provided extensive political and social scope for active involvement in solving the basic problems of our society, and that which was justly criticized over the years of stagnation. The report of the chairman of the Supreme Soviet submitted to the congress contains an analysis of the essence of the changes. It is perceived as a sharply critical exchange with our people, with their mood and aspirations. This makes it possible for us to realistically assess and disclose the sore points, primarily in the sphere of the national economy and in the management sphere, as well as in interethnic relations. We feel that the experience of the congress, regardless of its emotional charge, will greatly enrich the political strategy of scientific socialism. For this reason, as a people's deputy and simultaneously as a party worker, I view our congress as a real laboratory for the intellectual creativity of the people's deputies.

On this level I would like to voice a number of proposals aimed at giving the political reform a greater dynamism and ethical strength. In the first place, the question discussed at the congress of the real restoration of power to the soviets has gained universal approval. The hopes of the workers, of quickly releasing the previously fettered potential of our society, are naturally fully tied to this process. But still, comrades, it seems to me, in the course of debate on this question extremes have crept in. I have in mind the raising of the question of the role of

Ninth Session

2 June 1989

the soviets, but without an organic link to the other sociopolitical structures of our society. The accent is put predominantly on the delimitation and even the separation of the functions of the soviet and party bodies, with a clear underestimating of the forms and methods of cooperation and coordination between them. In the speeches of a number of the people's deputies, the place of the party has been spoken of in a polemical form, and this is natural because we are working in a creative situation. Here attempts were made, it seems to me, to play down its role in identifying a criticism of the disclosed existing shortcomings with the party itself, with the party cadres as a whole.

In this context, comrades, I would like to draw attention to the profound process of political reforms which are being carried out within the party itself and the start to which was made by the 19th party conference. This has been carried out through a significant curtailment in the party personnel and released workers from all structures—from the Central Committee down to the party obkoms. This can also be traced in that highly open information which we receive from the pages of the Information Bulletin of the CPSU Central Committee. I propose that in working out the updated constitutional and enforceable provisions concerning all levels of the soviets, considering the various approaches it would be advisable to pay particular attention to the question of the interaction of all our society's structures.

Second, comrades! All strata of our society, as we have become convinced recently, are properly aware of the boldness and decisiveness which have been shown in assessing our dramatic past and bringing out the paralyzing roots and prerequisites for the time of stagnation. However, as before, in maintaining the sharply critical intensity in assessing past events, we now, it seems to me, are in great need of generalizing the positive experience which does exist, which is still of humble scale but can become an important incentive for our advance along the path of restructuring. In this context I would like to direct a number of critical considerations on the role of social science. The people's deputies, particularly those of us who work in the field, are interested in obtaining generalized research from our scientists and scientific collectives on such crucial questions as particular features of political culture under the conditions of the qualitatively new state of our society, on the problems of the individual and society, the diversity of opinions under conditions of socialist pluralism, the dialectics of interethnic relations, and other urgent problems. I feel that a thorough elaboration of the questions with the requisite consideration of practical experience is an important condition for realizing the idea of the full power of the soviets. I would like, comrades, to recall the well-known idea of Lenin that the ability to govern does not fall from the sky and does not come by holy spirit, and that the people who have emerged into the arena of active political creativity are not immediately capable of governing.

Third, the political scope opened in the present-day strategy of restructuring places fundamentally new demands on the interaction between the executive bodies and the broad strata of the population. Practice indicates that in certain critical situations it is very difficult to correctly assess the situation and find optimum decisions. As a result at times our comrades, in being dedicated to the ideas and goals of restructuring, are unable to delve deeply into the essence of the problem and master the situation. This, unfortunately, leads to insufficiently thought out decisions. Possibly this is a consequence of the fact that we do not fully consider the potential and absolute primacy of the political decisions as was persuasively described in the report. It is essential, if we can put it this way, to have a synchronization of the process of restructuring in society as a whole and its individual elements and structures.

Fourth, it is essential, it seems to me, to recognize that social activeness has been apparent predominantly up to now in the sociopolitical sphere. Unfortunately, the sphere of labor activity has still been little touched. The representative of Irkutsk Oblast is correct when he spoke about this at our afternoon session. The deformation of socialism is not merely the tyranny of the bureaucracy and the voluntarism of the departmental structures. The virus of inhibition, unfortunately, has essentially touched the entire society. This is manifested in an antisocial, parasitic psychology, in the avoidance of socially useful labor, and in the mass phenomena of theft and corruption, or in the connivance with these negative phenomena. It is not easy to overcome all of this. For this reason I share the opinion that not all levels of soviets should be actively involved in this sphere in order to raise up all our society and its labor enthusiasm through free effective creative and active labor. Possibly, an appeal could be made on this question, and which would be an effective unification of our aspirations with the broad masses of people.

Fifth, the problems of interethnic relations have occupied a major place in the congress' work. I will not speak thoroughly on this on the eve of the Central Committee plenum. I would like to merely point out that the questions of improving interethnic relations in theory as well as in practice have at times erroneously been interpreted as a certain process of a weakening of the international factor. This ignores the humanitarian content which is present in the Marxist-Leninist concept of the nationality question. From the standpoint of an objective assessment of the past, we recognize that major errors were made in resolving the nationality question, and that there was a prevalence of administrative methods, incompetence, and a reticence to delve deeply into the occurring processes. In our days, when real scope is opening up for improving interethnic relations, it is vitally important, respected deputies, to carefully study, generalize and skillfully integrate into creative goals the natural and largely objective process of the increased ethnic awareness of the different nations and nationalities in our country.

It would be advisable, in my opinion, to set up a national center for interethnic relations. This, it seems to me,

Ninth Session

2 June 1989

should not squeeze together and integrate into a system the academy institutions, but rather this should be done like the type of well-known scientific centers, for example in the United States, where exclusively the requests of the U.S. Senate and Congress are carried out. As a whole, we need a people's tribune for interethnic relations. It would make sense to resume the journal which was published at the beginning of the 1920's, that is, during the life of Lenin, and which was named ZHIZN NATSIONALNOSTEY. Major tasks, and here I share the opinion of the delegates, also rest on the Soviet of Nationalities.

Finally, comrades, brief ideas on the foreign policy question. The provisions of the report with great force confirm the close linkage between our domestic restructuring and our policy on the international scene. Even now it is apparent that the breakthrough of the Soviet state to new positions will allow us to hold a worthy place in the world community. Here, to be just, I should point out and recognize that previously our actions in the global community were not always commensurate with our national interests and our capabilities as well. In the course of the debate at our congress, the idea has been repeatedly voiced that Soviet foreign policy, in contrast to domestic, is more advanced and more effective. Is there not some contradiction in this? I feel, comrade deputies, that there is not. The logic of revolutionary restructuring demands the establishing of a maximum favorable climate for implementing our creative plans inside the nation and for the active emergence of our nation in the world economic sphere. I should, comrades, point out that, relying on my own humble experience in foreign policy activities, without active participation in world economic relations, we will not resolve many of our problems. Let me mention the following figure. We produce 1/5 of the world's industrial product, but only 4 percent of this product has an opportunity to be sold for export. The notion of the new political thinking also encourages an improvement of our relations with developing countries.

Major foreign policy actions have been carried out over the period of the last months and the last years. In the most prominent place I would put the straightening out of our relations with China. Here also I would like to turn to the question of Afghanistan and say that the Soviet people with enormous gratitude have received the decision of the political leadership to withdraw the limited contingent of our Armed Forces from the Republic of Afghanistan. There was rejoicing in the families of hundreds of thousands. But while recognizing this gratitude, we should maintain enormous sympathy for our own Soviet Army, where the sons of all the peoples of our multinational motherland undergo patriotic schooling and patriotic training. (Applause).

We all are the generation of the first sitting of people's deputies. This is the particular feature of our situation. In maintaining the highly demanding nature of our views and convictions, at the same time it seems to me that we should also endeavor to achieve inner human solidarity and cultivate a respectful attitude toward one another and raise the level of trust. I am in favor of maintaining the sharply critical atmosphere, but on a basis of greater confidence. We have debated much and heatedly so and we will do so in the future, and before the very eyes of all our people. The question might arise—what are our common ideals, our generally important values? We have probably asked this question ourselves many times. I am profoundly convinced, respected deputies, that each of us will remain loyal to the ideals of the fraternity of peoples, humanism and socialism. Thank you. (Applause).

A.I. Lukyanov: Deputy Shcherbakov has the floor. Deputy Dadamyan should get ready.

V.P. Shcherbakov, chairman of the Moscow City Trade Unions Council, Moscow City (from USSR trade unions): Esteemed comrade deputies! We all know the enormous attention with which Soviet people are following the course of the congress. We are saying a lot about where things are bad and why. But we are keeping shamefacedly quiet about the achievements of socialism, to which there is no alternative in any social system. And proof of this is to be found primarily in the political biographies of all those sitting in this auditorium, beginning with the president. These biographies are impossible under any other political system.

Soviet people are proud of the very great gains of October and the equality and fraternity of all peoples. This alliance must be safeguarded and strengthened. And it is particularly painful today that the potential of socialism is not being used. It is becoming increasingly hard to explain why, despite the decisions which have been taken and the measures which are being implemented for the economy's social reorientation, the working people's living standard is declining. Some people are trying to speculate on these difficulties, to justify their political claims, such as, for instance, the leaders of the Democratic Union, openly calling for civil disobedience to the authorities, for demonstrations and strikes. They stated: "When the stores are empty, when the plants come to a halt, the authorities will fall of their own accord."

The rapid increase in wages, which is outstripping labor productivity growth, is now being cited as one reason for the crisis phenomena in the economy. It is understandable that this phenomenon is abnormal and perturbing, but to seek here the root for economic disorders, for the imbalance in the market, and for the shortage of goods is wrong, to say the least. The real reason is that the main element of the economic reform—economic accountability [khozraschet]—has not worked. It does not exist in teams, on sectors, or in shops. Enterprises have no real independence. Many of the decisions taken formerly to normalize the economy have done nothing to help this, rather the reverse. One example is the transition of industrial enterprises to the new conditions of remuneration of labor, rates, and salaries. In the process of preparing for this

Ninth Session

2 June 1989

crucial step, the labor collectives accumulated a wages fund. Was there no calculation of what this resolution would cost the state when wage rates and salaries were raised? All the Moscow enterprises took an active part in elaborating the "Progress-95" program, which is to ensure the solution of many tasks, including social ones. It will use its own funds here. The implementation of this program has already begun. Many enterprises, using economic independence, are on their own initiative paying for additional leave and child care leave, and are giving grants to badly off families and labor veterans—that is, they are beginning to implement an active social policy without counting on aid from above. But the finance organs are subjecting this policy to criticism.

It is an erroneous opinion that Moscow lives at the expense of other regions. I can say that the capital puts R16 billion in profit into the state budget every year, yet its own budget is R4.2 billion. Today the growth of wages is being artificially limited at many state enterprises. At the same time income in the cooperative sector is not restricted by anything. Why should similar sanctions not be applied to cooperative members? Or does the law so important for state enterprises not operate here?

Everyone knows the story of the "Tekhnika" cooperative which caused such a sensation. Producing nothing, playing mainly on shortages and prices, people there receive wages sometimes hundreds of times greater than the wages of academicians and scientists and statesmen and politicians. I am not opposed to high wages, but one way or another the remuneration of labor should comply with its outlays. The development of the cooperative movement is undoubtedly a necessary matter, but it is a bad thing when this development proceeds without control, with direct connivance from the Ministry of Finance, not unbeknownst to whom the cooperative members are now so successfully transforming state enterprises' noncash funds into cash. Last year Moscow's cooperative members took R311 million out of Moscow's banks and invested R12 million. In the first 5 months of this year they have taken R976 million and invested R38 million. Unless their appetites are moderated, then in the course of the year they will take over R4 billion from Moscow alone. Incidentally, the monthly wages for all workers in Moscow is R1.1 billion, and I remind you that the annual budget for Moscow's municipal economy is R4.2 billion.

I am worried not only by this fact in itself, but by why the financiers and economists are keeping silent, why they are not shouting for help. The working class is directly asking: Who stands to gain? Who is pandering to this? (Applause).

PRAVDA wrote that eight staffers of the USSR Ministry of Justice Institute, including a close relation of O. Soroka, USSR deputy prosecutor general, took part in sharing out the revenue from the "Tekhnika" cooperative. Does that not answer the question of why the cooperatives are under such heavy legal protection? (Applause).

The money which the cooperative members have taken from the banks would be enough to increase the minimum pensions for 20 million badly-off pensioners or to institute 24 days of paid leave right now for all the country's working people. Yet we are seeking funds in terms of crumbs, of kopeks, to help badly-off families, invalids, and pensioners. Here attempts are still being made to reduce appropriations for social needs. Unless the siphoning of funds from enterprises to cooperatives is halted there will be a financial catastrophe. There is already a common saying to the effect that we have achieved the highest labor productivity in printing money. But what have the cooperatives given the working class? In their mass they have engaged in middleman activity, buying up reserve raw material, semifinished materials, and consumer goods. This aggravates the shortage of commodities, leaves store shelves empty, and intensifies corruption, bribery, speculation, and the growth of organized crime. People are asking when this will be stopped.

In this connection I cannot but share the alarm of the group of people's deputies from the trade unions at the aggravating situation with regard to crime in the country voiced in their request to the government. After all, a favorable economic base has now been created for the growth of crime.

Today there is an increasingly acute ring to the question of why we have not achieved the pace for restructuring on which we were counting. Of course, it is impossible to predict the full depth of problems, but there is much which we were obliged to envisage and resolve more vigorously. Here, too, it is appropriate to ask not only our government but also our economic science: Where have you taken us? Behind the keenly critical speeches addressed to the management and apparatus we have somehow forgotten that no adequately clear economic model for the future has been elaborated. New economic methods, before they have even gone into operation, are being sharply criticized, including from this rostrum, and are being recognized as imperfect. Practical workers have been caught up in experiments. Can our economic science really offer nothing more suitable than purely market relations, the transfer of state enterprises into private hands, and the creation of a free manpower market, which some well-known scientists are advocating? The representatives of the Moscow group of delegates do have such proposals, although they are 25-30 people out of Moscow's 195 deputies. I would like to draw your attention to this, because not all that group's proposals and opinions can represent the opinion of all the capital's deputies. (Applause).

Everything the economists are proposing now is not new; it has been solemnly borrowed from capitalism's experience, but where are the laws of development of the socialist economy? Unfortunately, today we have no

STENOGRAPHIC RECORD

Ninth Session

2 June 1989

scientifically substantiated economic concept of restructuring. Many people understand restructuring in their own way, each as they choose, but there should be no different interpretations here. Economic scientists must pool their efforts in elaborating the economic concept of restructuring, and not waver. Measure seven times and cut once. That folk saying should become the principle of the economists' work. (Applause).

Specific measures are needed to normalize the economy. In addition to the sensible reduction of expenses on defense, the maintenance of the apparatus, and capital construction, the foremost, the main task is financial normalization. It is essential to immediately carry out a monetary reform which will not affect the interests of the honest worker but which will remove from circulation funds acquired by unjust means, to introduce more rapidly a progressive tax on income, and to put state enterprises and cooperatives on an equal footing, giving them the opportunity to compete openly. We must immediately forbid state enterprises from settling accounts with cooperatives out of the production development and social development funds and capital repair funds, whatever arguments may be cited. Accounts should be settled with them only from the material incentive fund. That will increase economic leaders' responsibility to the labor collectives for every ruble spent. (Applause).

The market cannot be saturated with high-quality goods if light industry receives only 3.7 percent of all fixed capital for the entire country. It is essential to redistribute state budget funds and to alter substantially, not by 1 percent but several times over, the correlation of capital investments in favor of the development of group "B" sectors. We should not appeal for this, which is what we have done for years, but introduce an economic mechanism which would interest machine-building and defense enterprises and enterprises of other sectors; we should have a state order for the production of consumer goods in volumes no lower than the annual wages fund. Otherwise the Karacharovo mechanical plant will produce consumer goods worth just 5 kopeks for every ruble of wages, the Sergo Ordzhonikidze plant will produce goods worth 6 kopeks, the Vladimir Ilich plant goods worth 35 kopeks, and so forth. Is it not clear to the leaders of the State Planning Committee and the Ministry of Finance that until there is a direct connection between these concepts, and until economic leaders' wages depend on an increase in the volumes of consumer goods production, we will never get out of this vicious circle?

I support Mikhail Sergeyevich's proposal to create a special Supreme Soviet commission which would revise all benefits and privileges and examine the problems of the fair distribution of social consumption funds. We cannot fail to see that they have gradually become the means for redistributing benefits in favor of the most affluent groups of the population. On average, receipts from these funds for workers and employees per member of the family with an income of under R50 are nearly three times smaller than in affluent families. We talk too much about the plight of our health care and about social injustice in the use of various benefits. We must ask: Why do some people enjoying position and power have the opportunity for treatment in a sanatorium every year while others, if you take the travel vouchers normatives, wait for years for such an opportunity? Some people are fed in hospitals for R1.50, others for R3. I think we should decide to redistribute social consumption funds in favor of the badly off.

During the congress the question of resolutely improving pension provisions has been frequently raised. This axiom requires no proof. One of the first laws which should be adopted is the Law on Pensions. Funds are needed for that. I believe that the R10 billion which are being released as a result of the reduction of expenses on armament should be purposefully given to pensioners. The state has the duty to pay its debt to those who have given their labor for the benefit of the motherland. (Applause).

I suggest instructing the Supreme Soviet to finally find out what the minimum living wage is in our country, and to make these figures public. As a whole we must review the entire system of social and legal protection of working people. The existing system provides no protection against inflation and the rise in prices (as though it did not exist in our country). It is essential to introduce a cost of living index and to amend wages, grants, benefits, and pensions when it changes. I consider it absurd and economically harmful to impose restrictions on the payment of pensions and wages to working pensioners. We are short of manpower, and thousands of enterprises are working just one shift, yet we are excluding from social production millions of highly qualified workers and specialists, doctors, and teachers. (Applause). And restrictions for invalids look quite flagrantly unfair. After all, it is not enough that they cannot always find work; the total sum of their wages and pension is limited by law. It is time to remove these restrictions; invalids have a hard life as it is. (Applause).

The congress must take decisions which would enable every person to feel that social justice is being restored. (Applause).

A.I. Lukyanov: Comrades, I have received several notes that we usually draw out the congress sessions, ending them after 0600 or 0700 hours, violating the rules. Comrade Boris Vartanovich Dadamyan from the NKAO [Nagorno-Karabakh Autonomous Oblast] has written us a note again, but possibly we will ask him to speak tomorrow, at the next morning session. Now let us move on to organizational questions and to points of information. Is anyone against this?

From the floor: No.

FIRST CONGRESS OF PEOPLE'S DEPUTIES OF THE USSR

Ninth Session

2 June 1989

A.I. Lukyanov: Boris Vartanovich, then you will speak tomorrow morning. The first assignment which the deputies have given the presidium, along with delegations of the union republics, is the formation of a commission on the political and legal evaluation of the Soviet-German Nonaggression Pact in 1939. The presidium, along with the delegations, together with the deputies from the Baltic Republics, the Ukraine, Moldavia and a number of other republics, have agreed on the membership of the commission. If you will permit, I will read the prepared draft of the decree on this question:

" 'Decree of the USSR Congress of People's Deputies 'On Forming a Commission on a Political and Legal Evaluation of the Soviet-German Nonaggression Pact of 1939.' The USSR Congress of People's Deputies decrees:

"For working out a political and legal assessment of the Soviet-German Nonaggression Pact concluded in 1939 as well as the related documents, a commission is to be organized with the following membership of USSR people's deputies: commission chairman—Aleksandr Nikolayevich Yakovlev, Politburo member, secretary of the CPSU Central Committee; commission members, Chingiz Aytmatov, writer, chairman of the Board of the Kirghizia Writers' Union; Georgiy Arkadyevich Arbatov, director of the Institute for the United States and Canada under the USSR Academy of Sciences; Lyudmila Akopovna Arutyunyan, chair head at the Yerevan State University; Yuriy Nikolayevich Afanasyev, rector of the Moscow State Historical Archives Institute; Vasiliy Vladimirovich Bykov, writer, secretary of the Board of the USSR Writers' Union, Minsk; Mavrik Germanovich Volfson, senior instructor at the Latvian Academy of Arts, Riga; Igor Nikolayevich Gryazin, section head at the Institute for Philosophy, Sociology and Law of the Estonian Academy of Sciences, Tartu; Ion Panteleyevich Drutse, writer, Moldavia; Grigoriy Isidorovich Yeremey, chairman of the Moldavian Republic Trade Union Council; Aleksey Ivanovich Kazannik, docent on the chair of the Omsk State University; Ivan Yanovich Kezbers, secretary of the Latvian Communist Party Central Committee; Vitaliy Alekseyevich Korotich, editor in chief of the journal OGONEK; Vladimir Alekseyevich Kravets, Ukrainian Minister of Foreign Affairs; Sergey Borisovich Lavrov, chair head of Leningrad State University; Vitautas Vitautovich Landsberis, professor of the Lithuanian State Conservatory; Maryu Yokhannesovna Lauristin, chair head of the Tartu State University; Endel Teodorovich Lippmaa, director of the Institute for Chemical and Biological Physics of the Estonian Academy of Sciences; Yustinas Moteyevich Martsinkivichyus, writer, Lithuania; Kazimir Vladimirovich Moteka, lawyer at the First Vilnius Legal Consulting Office; Nikolay Vasilyevich Neyland, Latvian deputy minister of foreign affairs; Aleksey Mikhaylovich Ridiger, metropolitan of Leningrad and Novgorod, Aleksey; Edgar Elmarovich Savisaar, deputy director of the Maynor Special Design Buro, Tallinn; Valentin Mikhaylovich Falin, head of the International Section of the CPSU Central Committee; Vladimir Ilarionovich Shinkarak, director of the Philosophy Institute of the Ukrainian Academy of Sciences; and Zita Leonovna Shichite, lawyer at the Klaypeda Legal Consulting Offices."

This list, comrades, has been fully agreed upon by all delegations. And, as you see, it includes representatives from all the Baltic Republics and from those cities, for example Klaypeda, which were the first to suffer in 1939, as well as the representatives of Belorussia, the Ukraine, Moldavia and, finally, the Russian Federation. The presidium feels that the membership of this commission can investigate this very complex historical and political question which is to be studied.

Are there any proposals? It is moved to approve this membership.

Then I request a vote. Those in favor of the proposal will please raise their cards.

Who is against? I ask you to look, comrades, who is against. Is there anyone? Respected deputies, six have voted against.

Who has abstained?

A.G. Kostenyuk: Seven deputies have abstained.

A.I. Lukyanov: Thus, comrades, the Decree of the USSR Congress of People's Deputies "On Forming a Commission on a Political and Legal Evaluation of the Soviet-German Nonaggression Pact of 1939" is adopted by a majority of votes.

Comrade deputies! The presidium has instructed me to raise one question.

A week of the congress's work has passed. As is known, and you heard this yourselves, a number of deputies, speaking at the congress, have made deputy requests, and certain requests were turned over to the secretariat in a written form. According to the Constitution and the existing practices, by a deputy request one understands a request addressed by a deputy or group of deputies to a body or official. This is a request to give an official explanation or set out a position on a certain problem relating to the competence of the appropriate state body. A deputy request, of course, must be distinguished from questions, and I must say that in a predominant majority of cases even a lawyer would find it difficult to distinguish where is a question and where is a request. But we consider this rather serious in endeavoring to somehow separate requests from questions, comments and proposals which are addressed to the state bodies, the information media, the presidium itself and so forth.

What do I want to say about requests? As a total today around 20 documents termed deputy requests have been

Ninth Session

2 June 1989

received from the people's deputies. These take up a broad range of problems of an economic, social and ecological nature and the development of the national economic sectors. Many people's deputies, in particular comrades Vasnetsov, Igityan, Kurbanov, Tolpezhnikov and others, have submitted requests related to the events of 9 April 1989 in Tbilisi. Since a deputy commission has been set up on the given question by the congress, it has been proposed that these documents be turned over to this commission for review. Thus, the congress presidium considers it advisable to proceed in the same way with requests received over the Soviet-German Pact. We have just set up a commission. And for inspecting the activities of the group of investigators headed by Deputy Gdlyan, we have formed a similar commission. Here I should say that a protest has been received from the Orenburg delegation that we did not include representatives from this delegation in this commission. But it seems to me that we have already published the membership of this commission and does it make any sense for us to revise it. No.

The next question. I would like to inform you about the fate of other deputy documents of the request or question types. A group of people's deputies including Lukyanenko, Demchuk, Matveychuk and Sidor, has raised the question of the correctness of increasing nuclear power capacity in the Ukraine, and in particular at the Rovno and Khmelnitskiy power plants. This is a serious question, an actually major question.

A group of people's deputies from Crimea Oblast, including Ivanov, Baranovskiy, Koltsov and others, has forwarded a request concerning the advisability of building the Crimean Nuclear Plant. It is proposed that these requests be forwarded to the government and that the USSR Minister of Nuclear Power Lukonin prepare an answer for them.

Deputies Merkulov, Aksenov and Mironova forwarded a request on the prospects of operating the Semipalatinsk Range. You heard about this in the speech by Olzhas Suleymenov. This request was forwarded to the USSR Minister of Defense, Comrade Yazov, and to President of the Academy of Sciences Marchuk.

Thirdly, the request of the group of deputies from Kirghizia and certain public organizations (comrades Komarov, Aytmatov, Druzhinin, Shipitko and others) provides information on the extremely bad ecological situation existing in the city of Frunze. This was forwarded to Chairman of the USSR Gosplan Maslyukov and to Minister of the Gas Industry Chernomyrdin.

A group of deputies from Nikolayev Oblast (deputies Lisnichiy, Opolinskiy, Pogorelov and Lisitskiy) have submitted a request on the reasons for the major violations of the nature conservation legislation in the oblast and the continuation of work on building the Southern Urals Power Project. The request was forwarded to the USSR Council of Ministers. The request of Deputy Sokolov (Tikhvin Territorial District No 54) on the Kirishi Biochemical Plant and the Leningrad GAES [Pumped Storage Power Plant] has been sent to the USSR Council of Ministers. Well, you know, so many have written about Kirishi. A group of people's deputies (Comrades Gelman, Zalygin and others) have forwarded to the USSR Council of Ministers a request on halting construction on the second stage of the Zavolzhskiy Chemical Plant. I should say that the appropriate commission of the last Supreme Soviet already carefully studied this question. This was published.

Deputies Goncharik, Kashperk and others have forwarded a request on eliminating the consequences of the disaster at the Chernobyl AES. All these requests have also been forwarded to the government.

Deputies Studenkin, Klimov, Kolesnikov and others have forwarded to ministers Bykov (Minmedbioprom [Ministry of Medical and Microbiological Industry]), Shkabardnya (Minpribor [Ministry of Instrument Making, Automation Equipment and Control Systems]), and Panichev (Minstankoprom [Ministry of Machine Tool and Tool Building Industry]) a request on the date for resolving the problem of producing the necessary amount of disposable syringes and systems for blood transfusion. The comrades read of the chaotic situation in this area and the concern of the deputies is valid.

Deputy Filshin from Irkutsk Oblast has submitted a request to the Chairman of the Goskomtrud [State Committee for Labor and Social Problems] Gladkiy on the reasons for the delay in settling the question of introducing surpayments for the number of years served in the southern regions of Eastern Siberia as well as increasing the coefficients considering the differences in the living conditions in these regions.

The request of Deputy Shcherbak on the state of financing the public health system in the USSR and the measures to improve public health has been forwarded to USSR Minister of Public Health Comrade Chazov.

Deputy Korotich has submitted a request to the USSR Council of Ministers concerning a rise in the low pensions. We have heard here about the pensions in certain speeches by deputies.

The request of Deputy Mukishev on the reasons for the unsatisfactory operation of the Ministry of Railroads to provide gondolas for Ekibastuz was forwarded to the USSR Council of Ministers.

The request of Deputy Vasilyeva on the reasons for increased prices for public services in the area of building individual housing was forwarded to the Chairman of the USSR Gosstroy, Comrade Batalin.

Ninth Session

2 June 1989

I can tell you, comrades, that such requests and questions and wishes continue to be received. If we include all of these requests, as is stated in our procedural rules, in the congress agenda, then we will be unable to discuss the problems related to the report and the pending questions which have been included in the congress agenda. We will stray far away from this agenda. For this reason, the presidium submits for your review the proposal that it would be more correct that the government and ministries provide written answers to the deputies on all these requests. And these replies, to the degree that they should be known to the entire congress, would be brought to the attention of all the deputies participating in the congress by the distributing of appropriate documents.

Let me also provide information to you on questions and other appeals which have come in from the deputies. Here we would put the statements and other appeals addressed specifically to the leaders of certain ministries and departments and relating to particular questions. We do not consider it essential to publicize or report on the work being done with such appeals. We forward them directly through the secretariat to the appropriate ministers, to the ministries and departments, and they are all being forwarded for taking measures and will then be reviewed by the Supreme Soviet elected by you, in its committees and commissions, so that these committees and commissions are, so to speak, a means of monitoring those questions which the deputies have raised. The deputies will be informed correspondingly.

What questions have been posed here? Here are problems of radical economic reform, improving the political system, raising the level of prosperity of the people and developing the social sphere. But there are also particular, so to speak, pinpoint problems such as environmental conservation and so forth. Questions have been raised concerning the life of certain regions of the nation, collectives, groups of people and individual citizens. The need has been expressed of immediately helping someone—and such telegrams have been received—and we have taken measures immediately. All of them, these problems, could not be overlooked, and the appropriate assignments have been given for all received and incoming appeals sent to the congress. All the documents are carefully considered and are forwarded to executors and the deputies are to be informed about them in accord with the law governing the current status.

A significant number of appeals has been received from the people's deputies on the problems of nationality relations. You today heard the speech by Deputy Ardzinba, and several other deputies from the Abkhazian ASSR have also requested to speak. They consider it essential to set up an integrated commission of the Supreme Soviet to study the situation which has arisen here. Deputies from Latvia, such as Ivans, Zakis and others, a total of ten deputies, have made a number of proposals to restore the historical truth concerning the Soviet Germans and the Crimean Tatars. This was taken up today. Deputies Yarin and Tso have forwarded an appeal to the congress from their electors on these questions. Deputy Fargiyev has requested the congress to review the question of creating an Ingush ASSR and you also heard this. Deputy Anufriyev raised the question of the situation of the Gagauz in Moldavia.

What decision is proposed? All these proposals and questions require, as you realize, an extended and very substantial, very careful and tactful study. It is proposed that they be turned over for review to the USSR Supreme Soviet which is to be elected by you as well as to the commission which is currently preparing for the plenum of the CPSU Central Committee on interethnic questions.

The proposal of Deputy Veprev to accelerate the adopting of a program for the scientific and technical development of the KATEK [Kansk-Achinsk Fuel-Power Project] and other questions concerning the region's socioeconomic development has been forwarded to Minister of the Coal Industry Shchadov. A group of deputies including Stadnik, Kurtashin, Levykin and others is demanding a revision of the amount of timber felling in the Greater Moscow Area. There have also been very many letters in both the Moscow and central press about this. These are the green lungs of the capital. Deputy Petrakov has proposed a revision in the procedure for making major economic decisions, particularly those concerning the construction of national economic projects requiring significant capital investments. Deputy Zbykovskiy, in our view, has correctly raised the question of updating the Law Governing State Enterprise. A very large group of questions concerns the social sphere, particularly the life of the war and labor veterans. Here the people's deputies Gromov, Temnogrudova, Konkov and others have spoken on this question. Over 60 persons sent proposals to review and carry out measures to raise the standard of living of elderly citizens, and this was just mentioned from the congress rostrum.

A group of deputies including Ryzhov, Belyayev, Kartashov and others has proposed increasing the amount of money allocated for the development of public education. The presidium discussed this question. We propose that the correct thing to do is to turn over these requests from the deputies to the Supreme Soviet to the appropriate commissions for study and for supervising their implementation.

A significant portion of the appeals from the deputies has been devoted to improving Soviet legislation. In particular, Deputy Bogdanov has proposed working out a law on the protection of children and youth. Such a proposal has also been submitted by speakers. A group of Ukrainian deputies has proposed working out a draft law on nuclear power and submitting it for national discussion. Deputy Likhanov and others have submitted a proposal on adopting a law on defending child rights.

STENOGRAPHIC RECORD

Ninth Session
2 June 1989

Many deputies have also raised other questions relating to social, economic and management development. We propose that all of these and other questions become a matter of thorough investigation by the Supreme Soviet, its commissions and committees. Here it is no longer a matter of request but rather proposals made by the deputies.

Let me draw attention to the fact that a number of deputies (Babchenko, Luchenok, Pamfilova and Safiullin) have very sharply raised questions relating to crime in the nation and its increase. They have raised the question of having the government take immediate measures. Clearly we must support their opinion and request Minister of Internal Affairs Bakatin to report on this question and the planned measures to the USSR Supreme Soviet. This is a question of prime importance.

This, comrades, is a brief report by the presidium and secretariat of the congress on the flow of appeals which have reached us this week. I should also add there were telegrams. As of today, we have received 64,300 letters and telegrams from labor collectives, individual voters and so forth. That is, each day the congress receives an average of 9,500 appeals from the citizens. Certain deputies have proposed publicizing these telegrams but this would simply be impossible. We have also received telegrams where the voters demand that their deputies be included on the list of speakers. (Stir in the auditorium). Probably in this instance we should restrict ourselves to brief information in the form of a condensation of the letters and telegrams received and this would be issued every other day to the congress deputies. We physically simply do not have the possibility of making these telegrams public. (Voices: "Correct.").

I would also like to report to you that over the period from 25 May through 2 June, deputies have spoken 407 times on various questions at the Congress of People's Deputies. As of today, 65 deputies have spoken in the debates on the report. Certain deputies in discussing various questions have taken the floor several times and one of the deputies has carefully estimated what has happened for the delegations. I do not want to read this as the picture is not very balanced. In this context the Presidium should do something so that both the regions and the republics be represented. For example, it has turned out that around 30 deputies have spoken two and more times.

So here we have reported to you on all that has occurred. If you have no argument and support such practices, this can be taken on advisement and we can continue to work in the same spirit. If there are proposals on these questions, then let us agree as follows. Up to 3 minutes, and no more, will be given to each speaker for points of information and proposals. I cannot help but respect the procedural rules as here it is stated that up to 3 minutes will be provided for speaking on the question of the running of the session, reasons for voting and points of information. So please do not take offense.

G.M. Khodyrev, first secretary of the Gorkiy CPSU Obkom (Pavlovskiy Territorial Electoral District, Gorkiy Oblast): Anatoliy Ivanovich [Lukyanov] has set out a clear program for handling the requests of the voters. This we do not dispute. Both the consideration and handling of the requests have been correctly organized. But I would like to draw attention, Anatoliy Ivanovich, of the presidium and secretariat to the not very effective and rash replies of the departments. In particular, the deputies from Gorkiy Oblast, some 18 persons, sent a request to the Council of Ministers on the question of the fate of a central heating supply plant which is being built 5 km away from Gorkiy. Here is what Comrade Shcherbina has replied to us: Central heating supply for population points employing nuclear fuel has been provided in our nation for more than 10 years now. Here we have demonstrated high efficiency and complete safety.

It is as if Chernobyl had not happened and as if there was no public anxiety over the question of nuclear power.

It seems to me that the leaders of the ministries and departments should show greater sense of responsibility in approaching the replies to requests from the deputies.

Second, our voters have again requested an examination of the possibility of changing the procedure for providing information on the course of the congress. The problem is that the Second Program is watched by people who are engaged on one shift in time-based labor, by engineers, technicians, scientific and design organizations. The working class cannot view these broadcasts. For some reason the radio broadcasts are only on the Mayak [Beacon] Program while three-program receivers do not exist in the entire nation and not everyone has them even within a single population point. For this reason we ask that some thought be given to see whether the Vremya [Time] Program could not be extended and the congress be broadcast over the First Radio Program. (Applause).

N.S. Sazonov, secretary of the Party Committee for Automatic Lathe Operations at the Kama Motor Vehicle Plant (Naberezhnyye Chelny Territorial Electoral District, Tatar ASSR): Respected deputies! Respected voters! I speak here as the leader of a group of deputies from the Tatar Autonomous Republic, on behalf of this group which represents not only the 7-million-strong Tatar nation but also the over 100 nations and nationalities living in the autonomous republic. Our voters criticize us for not speaking and merely making procedural comments. Why? I address this question to the presidium. Why not give the floor to all the autonomous republics? There are 20 of them but only 4 have been given the floor.

Why are the deputies here divided into first and second grade? The union is the first and the autonomous is second. Why do you, respected presidium members, consider my comments as two speeches and the remarks

Ninth Session

2 June 1989

of Aleksandr Ivanovich Konovalov as four? According to Article 13 of the Congress Procedural Rules, this is a point of reference merely on the course of running the congress. This is unfounded!

Now for my concerns. Why don't Tikhonov, Shmelev, Abalkin and Burlatskiy speak here? Much has been said, comrades, but there is no economic base to materialize the proposals which have come up in the course of the debates. I feel that for achieving this goal the best proposal was made by Comrade Bunich. And let us remember that no attention was given to two speakers. Yanenko, rector of Novosibirsk University, said: The minister should come to the parliament to make a request. Yeltsin said: The parliament should make the distribution. This is the most important condition for achieving the goal and for implementing the proposals which were voiced.

Comrade deputies! I feel that we must extend the congress. On Saturday and Sunday we should cancel the excursions and continue discussing the political reports. Whoever is in a hurry should order an Il-86 airbus and head home.

N.N. Medvedev, sector chief at the Kaunas Scientific Research Institute for Radio Metering Equipment (Kaunas-Panyamunskiy National-Territorial Electoral District, Lithuania): Respected president, respected chairman! We would like to voice a decisive protest against the insulting attacks heard from the high rostrum of the congress against the delegations of the three Baltic Republics and at the same time against the peoples represented by them, and we censure the chairperson at the session who let these insults pass without comment. We feel that such attacks are aimed at splitting and undermining the congress. We came here for collaboration—however, the fanning of anti-Baltic chauvinism makes this collaboration impossible. I can only add that when mention was made here of assault detachments, I feel that one of these is myself. In contrast to the volunteer people's militias, we can be rallied at any time of the day and night and we move, we hurry, having learned that somewhere, someone is being harmed, be he a Russian, Lithuanian, Jew, or Tatar. We are armed from head to foot and our weapon is words; we have unlimited rights; and we can come to blows when someone is insulted morally and physically. Possibly for this reason we have meetings some 200,000-strong which are not encircled by the police, we are visited by the respected Secretary Brazauskas, the Second Secretary Berezov, we argue, make peace, go our ways, and again come back together to meet. We are searching for the truth. We do not have drunks and hooligans at these meetings. And we do this on Saturdays and Sundays.

Thank you for your attention. (Applause).

V.F. Derevyanko, editor of the newspaper VECHERNYAYA ODESSA (Odessa, Primorskiy Territorial Electoral District, Odessa Oblast): You are well aware that the Ukraine is a borderland and in the Ukraine there is also its own borderland, and this is Odessa. Odessa is never remembered or almost never. Boris Ilich Oleynik has spoken strongly about the disasters which the Ukraine has experienced; he has done this completely correctly and we thank you, Boris Ilich. But he forgot to say one thing. Comrades, in 5 or 10 years, we will enter the Black Sea in the Red Book. What is today happening with the Black Sea and in our Black Sea Area makes it no longer a national health resort, no longer a resort but rather a deception. Here they have established a testing range for the successful—and incidentally, they are successfully testing all means to destroy the environment. Today there are pickets in the city against unloading a diesel vessel which has delivered phosphorites. Our laboratories have estimated that in the cargo, it turns out, there are alpha particles that are 15-fold above the tolerable standard, and even more of other particles. To put it briefly, uranium is now being delivered to us.

Last year, anyone who visited the Black Sea could not go swimming. For this reason, I feel it essential to state all of this. The Black Sea is not our problem, it is your problem. There is one centimeter of Black Sea for each person. We, incidentally, submitted a request, it was broken up into parts for us, and what happened was no longer a single request.

R.A. Ubaydullayeva, director of the Economics Institute of the Uzbek Academy of Sciences, Tashkent (from the women's councils brought together under the Soviet Women's Committee): I would like to state from this rostrum that our delegation has submitted very many requests to the presidium but for some reason these requests today, Anatoliy Ivanovich, were not to be found in your list.

I personally submitted a request on introducing an additional wage coefficient for employment under hot climate conditions for women working in the cotton-growing republics. I submitted a proposal to work out a new concept of locating the productive forces considering the demographic situation and the available labor resources in order to solve the problem of unemployment which exists in the cotton-growing republics. I submitted a request on reviewing the standards weights by women and which at present have been set at 7 tonnes, as well as a number of other questions. I would have liked for these and a number of other proposals to be given and examined.

Furthermore, Mikhail Sergeyevich [Gorbachev], the women of Uzbekistan have phoned and written me with their support for your candidacy for the position of chairman of the USSR Supreme Soviet and I do this. And they requested that we congratulate you, Mikhail Sergeyevich.

One last thing. I have a proposal: Some 500 persons have signed up to speak on the report of Mikhail Sergeyevich

STENOGRAPHIC RECORD

FIRST CONGRESS OF PEOPLE'S DEPUTIES OF THE USSR

Ninth Session

2 June 1989

Gorbachev. I request that the list of deputies who signed up be publicized and published in the press. I also request that our proposals be taken into account and that we publish in the central press the speeches of those deputies who were unable to speak here. Thank you.

A.I. Lukyanov: Let me repeat: In the first place, let us observe the procedural rules of 3 minutes. Second, there is an agreement that all the deputy speeches will be published; this is stated in our procedural rules and we are obliged to do this. Third, if there are comments that the deputy requests have not reached the ministries and departments we will see to it that they do.

V.A. Leonchev, brigade leader of machinists from the Novokuybyshevsk "50-letiye SSSR" Petrochemical Combine, Novokuybyshevsk (Novokuybyshevsk Territorial Electoral District, RSFSR): Here are 16,000 signatures. Our voters requested that I address the congress. It is a question of the colliding of the vital interests of each of us and the most important political decisions of our state. "Respected comrade USSR People's Deputies! The inhabitants of the town of Chapayevsk and other population points located near the plant being built to destroy chemical weapons are turning to you. We support the course of the party and government of fighting for peace, for disarmament, and for destroying weapons of mass destruction, including chemical ones. This course expresses the will of all honest persons in the world and it is dictated by a concern for man and the future of our civilization. Concern for man must always be shown, including in erecting such major facilities as the plant for destroying toxic substances.

"However, even in a superficial analysis it turns out that in designing and selecting the location for the construction of the plant, the interests of the people have been considered last. At present, the situation has developed in such a manner that for many years directly in the city three rather large chemical enterprises have been operating and these are involved in explosive production. These enterprises also systematically pollute the environment. Over the last 4 years here, three accidents have occurred with explosions and human casualties. The last explosion which occurred on 27 November 1988 carried off six human lives. Scrubber facilities exist only at one plant, they are extremely overloaded, and untreated waste products get into the Chapayevka River and then the Volga. In comparison with average data, infant mortality in the oblast is 2.5-fold higher in the city. A number of illnesses of the blood, the upper respiratory tract, the heart, and oncological ailments are characteristic features for the inhabitants of the town of Chapayevsk. Under these complicated ecological conditions, some 10 km from the town, in a rather densely populated zone, they are preparing to operate a plant for destroying toxins. Information on this plant is very contradictory and this evokes natural concern among the local inhabitants. Academician Kuntsevich in his first meeting with the inhabitants of Chapayevsk on 2 February 1989 stated that the plant will destroy toxins manufactured by the local enterprises...."

A.I. Lukyanov: You can hand over those two pages of text as we are ready to distribute it to the deputies, but don't read it now. Wait a bit, Comrade Yaroshenko, sit down, please. Be patient, Deputy Solovyev has signed up also, and I will give you the floor. Please give us the text and we will send it out. Comrade Solovyev, please.

Yu.B. Solovyev, chairman of the Board of the USSR Designers Union, Moscow (from the USSR Union of Designers): Yesterday evening I was sorry for you, comrades, who were denied the floor. And now I scarcely made it to the rostrum. In a very good speech by Deputy Starodubtsev, it was pointed out with indignation that outside specialists are giving advice to landholders. The specialist was myself. And I want to say that I did give advice because this concerns scores of millions of people. In the appeal of the landholders it was stated that the supply of the countryside should be on the city level. This is all for the good but not sufficient. The countryside should receive specific goods for the countryside, and these are not of use in the cities as certainly urban goods are not always fit for the countryside. Let me give three examples....

A.I. Lukyanov: Let us wait for the three examples. I again request, comrades, that you make the proposals.

Yu.B. Solovyev: I have a specific proposal.

A.I. Lukyanov: Then please.

Yu.B. Solovyev: I feel that this appeal should include....

A.I. Lukyanov: Yuriy Borisovich [Solovyev], please be brief. I beg you.

Yu.B. Solovyev: Just one minute.

A.I. Lukyanov: Please.

Yu.B. Solovyev: The appeal should contain the addition: It is essential to organize the production of consumer durables specially for the countryside. This would include ecological toilets, special refrigerators. Urban refrigerators do not work in the countryside. There there should be large individual refrigerators and so forth.

A.I. Lukyanov: Please, the next.

A.A. Zgerskaya (Yaroshinskaya), correspondent from the newspaper RADYANSKA ZHITOMIRSHCHINA, Zhitomir (Zhitomir Territorial District, the Ukraine): Respected comrades! I have a great request of our presidium as well as for you, deputies. What I am about to say concerns not only me and my voters. This is, so to speak, a common human problem. The issue is that our

Ninth Session

2 June 1989

Zhitomir Oblast is in the zone of particularly hard radiation. It is a matter of Narodichskiy Rayon in Zhitomir Oblast which is in the zone of particularly hard radiation. It is being turned into a zone of particularly deep silence. As a journalist, for 18 months I have been unable to publish anywhere the materials on what is occurring in the rayon. While immediately there were 18 villages which were in the zone of particularly hard radiation, at present 3 years later, there are around 90 such villages. While previously only Narodichskiy Rayon was contaminated by radiation, at present another four such rayons have been added.

And then Ukrainian Minister of Public Health Romanenko tells us who live in this zone that it is almost a Swiss resort. This is simply angering. If you view those frames which were taken by the documentary filmmakers from Moscow, you can actually see what is happening. And this concerns all of us. Yes, there is Tbilisi, yes, there are other events. But what is happening here, comrades, is very important. Let me make a great request from the presidium. There is a video cassette and I would greatly appreciate it if the presidium would provide an opportunity for all the people's deputies to view this video cassette. It contains the truth about Narodichskiy Rayon. Thank you.

A.I. Lukyanov: Please.

M.I. Umarkhodzhayev, rector of the Andizhan State Pedagogical Institute in Andizhan (Andizhan National-Territorial District, Uzbekistan): On 31 May, we (more than 70 persons) submitted a statement which for some reason was not read. This is the angst of all the cotton-growing republics. Not only Uzbekistan, but also Kirghizia, Turkmenia and Tajikistan. The first request is to increase the purchasing prices for cotton by 1.5-fold. (Applause). If this is not done then our standard of living will not rise.

Second, the birthrate, as you know, in Uzbekistan and generally in Central Asia, is very high. At present, our children are leaving school. However, the situation in the republic is very difficult in the area of job placement. We must give some very serious thought to this. At present, there are 760,000 persons unemployed in the republic socialized economy. Soon there will be millions. For this reason we and the government must give serious concern to this. I request this on behalf of all the Central Asian delegations. Thank you.

V.P. Malyshev, director of the Pobeda Sovkhoz, Volgodonskiy Rayon in Rostov Oblast, Pobeda (Volgodonsk Territorial Electoral District, Rostov Oblast): We from the Rostov delegation have submitted a deputy request on the construction of the Rostov Nuclear Power Plant. Unfortunately, we have not heard where our request has gone. The situation is very serious, comrades. You are aware that the Atommash [Nuclear Machine Building] Plant and a satellite city are being built. Since there is subsiding soil there, one multistory building has collapsed and many have slipped. The cooling pool is in the sea itself and the plant is located 13 km from the town of Volgodonsk. People are very concerned. The presidium has a petition with 58,000 signatures. The people are requesting an investigation of the construction of this nuclear plant and are insisting that a nondepartmental independent commission be set up which would travel to Volgodonsk and decide whether or not this plant should be built.

A.I. Lukyanov: Good. I will watch the clock, 3 minutes. You recall, comrades, we offered you such short speeches. The congress did not agree. Let us be patient, we will listen another 15 minutes. (Stir in the hall). Well, should we break off?

From the auditorium: Yes!

A.I. Lukyanov: Let us at least hear five more comrades.

From the auditorium: No!

A.I. Lukyanov: No. Then I will put it to a vote.

From the floor: Let one more person!

A.I. Lukyanov: Let the person have the floor as he is already on the rostrum.

P.A. Akhunov, deputy director for educational work at School No 4, Uzbekistan, Andizhan Oblast, Moskovskiy Rayon, the town of Shakhrikhin (from the Komsomol): Three days ago I wanted to make a protest. The problem is that from the Uzbekistan delegation they give the floor only to representatives whose views and estimates are just alike. I requested at the next session that the floor be granted to that minority which has its own view on the state of affairs in the republic. Why are we not allowed to speak about the catastrophic situation in the republic, Mikhail Sergeyevich? The people of Uzbekistan have linked their hopes to restructuring, and that we will finally escape from monocropping. Nothing, unfortunately, is happening. The planted areas in Uzbekistan are enormous, and they must be reduced by 50 percent. I have a great deal to say and I request that I be given the floor in the next session.

A.I. Lukyanov: Comrades, let us respect one another. Well, should we stop? I request a vote.

(Stir in the auditorium).

A.I. Lukyanov: Well, should we give someone the floor or not?

From the audience: No.

(Stir in the auditorium).

STENOGRAPHIC RECORD

Ninth Session

2 June 1989

A.I. Lukyanov: Comrades, the floor is requested by the very respected Kasyan.... (Stir in the auditorium). Should we give Kasyan the floor?

N.A. Kasyan, department head from the Leshchinovskiy Boarding School, the Ukraine, Poltava Oblast, Kobeliki (from the Soviet Charity and Health Fund): This is what I want to say. Yesterday it was announced that I had written a note that I would receive all the delegates. I did not write this note. It was announced over National Radio and Television. Now you can imagine what is happening. (Stir, noise in the auditorium). I today received some 200 persons. That is impossible.

I also have something else to say. Comrades! I am the deputy from charity. Let us be kind, let us respect one another. What are we doing? There was yesterday's speech by Vlasov. It was particularly distasteful to me. He may have suffered some insults. I have also endured insults from the Ukrainian Ministry of Public Health. I was also summoned three times to the republic procurator's office. But why bring up all this dirt which is simply shameful to hear? (Applause). You understand it is very shameful for me to hear such things. I respect our party. I am a nonparty person. But my wife is a party member. (Stir in the auditorium). And we get on well together. Our party and people are united. (Stir in the auditorium. Applause.).

A.I. Lukyanov: I feel that we should give Kasyan the floor separately. Now on this good note let us vote.... Who is in favor of breaking off debates now?

Who is against? Do we need to count? It is a clear minority. (Stir in the auditorium). Then let me say what we will be doing tomorrow, the day after and so forth.

First of all, our cosmonauts (Comrade Ryumin) have invited us to an exhibit of space technology. Those desiring to visit the exhibit "The Introduction of the Achievements of Missile and Space Technology Into the National Economy" should sign up today at the Congress Document Issuing Desk with Deputy Ryumin. The departure tomorrow is at 0930 hours from the Hotel Moskva. The excursion will last to approximately 1600 hours. For the deputies who will be working on Saturday, a trip is offered on Sunday. We want you to take a look and see just what this equipment is, how much it costs, and what it has provided us. That is the first thing.

Second, I want to remind the deputies who are members of the Council of Elders that the session of the Council of Elders will be held tomorrow at 1000 hours in the morning in the Chamber Session Auditorium.

The first organizational session of the Soviet of the Union is to be held tomorrow at 1500 hours also in the Chamber Session Hall of the USSR Supreme Soviet. There will be a session of the Soviet of Nationalities on Monday.

The next session of the congress will be held on Monday, 5 June, at 1000. As for when we are planning to end the work, it will be easier if you ask me the question later. I wish you all the best.

STENOGRAPHIC RECORD

FIRST CONGRESS OF PEOPLE'S DEPUTIES OF THE USSR
TENTH SESSION
MONDAY–TUESDAY, 5–6 JUNE 1989
THE KREMLIN PALACE OF CONGRESSES

At 11:07 p.m. on Sunday, June 3, a gas pipeline running along the Chelyabinsk-Ufa railway in the Bashkir ASSR ruptured as two trains with nearly 1300 passengers were passing. The gas exploded with a force of about 300 tons of TNT. A huge fireball consumed 433 people and severely burned 732 others. More than a third of the victims were children. Hospitals as far away as Leningrad were filled with burn victims in serious or critical condition. A team of thirty American specialists was dispatched with equipment and medicine to Ufa where the most severely burned survivors were taken. Reports issued in the course of an official investigation disclosed that pipeline ruptures were common and explosions none too rare. The Bashkir section alone had experienced forty "incidents" within the past few years; indeed, that very section of the pipeline had just been reopened on June 2. Sobered by his visit to the site on Sunday, General Secretary Gorbachev addressed the Congress of People's Deputies briefly on June 5 before ordering a recess out of respect for the victims of the disaster. While noting that an investigation was underway, Gorbachev left little doubt that he suspected incompetence and irresponsibility.

The Tenth Session resumed on the following day with Anatoly V. Gorbunov, Chairman of the Presidium of the Latvian Supreme Soviet, in the chair. Except for the trifling remarks of the fatuous Dr. Kasyan, a popular physical therapist, the deputies who mounted the rostrum generally continued a new trend of proposing specific reforms in place of the usual slogans and platitudes or generalized calls for "change." The well-reasoned arguments of two Estonian deputies, K. S. Khallik and V. I. Yarovoy, gave the audience clear but conflicting perspectives on Baltic independence from the vantages of Balts and Russians. The Russian national view was also championed by writer Valentin Rasputin, who renewed his appeal for a moral revival and claimed for Russians the same right as others to defend their national honor and dignity. Russians might be better off, he argued, and better able to preserve their cultural and spiritual identity if Russia itself withdrew from the USSR! But he also reminded his non-Russian compatriots that their enemy was not Russia but the administrative-industrial machine that plundered and destroyed their lands.

The Soviet leadership chose to use the Congress of People's Deputies to nurture its rapprochement with the leaders of the People's Republic of China. The Congress approved without discussion a "statement on events in China" submitted by the Presidium. Carefully avoiding any judgment of the Beijing regime's bloody suppression of the Tiananmen Square demonstrators, the Congress expressed the hope that "wisdom, common sense, and a carefully weighed approach" would lead to "a solution worthy of the great Chinese people."

Texts of Articles 36, 109, 111, 118 of the Constitution (Basic Law) of the USSR, cited during the Tenth Session, can be found in Appendix A.1 at the end of this volume.

TENTH SESSION

MONDAY–TUESDAY, 5–6 JUNE 1989

STENOGRAPHIC RECORD

M.S. Gorbachev, chairman of the USSR Supreme Soviet, in the chair.

M.S. Gorbachev: Comrade deputies! As you know, on the night of 3-4 June a major accident occurred at a liquefied gas pipeline near the Chelyabinsk-Ufa Railroad, on the territory of the Bashkirian Autonomous Soviet Socialist Republic, near the border of Chelyabinsk Oblast. A large number of people were killed in the accident. According to preliminary figures, the number is several hundred people. They include a group of children en route to a vacation in the south.

I propose that our congress observe a minute's silence in memory of the deceased. (All rise).

I propose on behalf of the congress that we express our profound condolences to the families, relatives, and friends of those killed in the accident.

Yesterday Comrade Ryzhkov and I flew to the scene of the accident. From the very first minute local people there had immediately gone to aid the victims. It is a remote spot, far from any large settlements. The largest population center—the town of Asha in Chelyabinsk Oblast—is 15 km away. The local population, seeing and hearing that something had happened, went to the scene of the explosion. When they saw everything, they passed on information about what had happened, to Ufa, rayon centers, and Chelyabinsk. The local population were rescuing people all night. Literally in the first few minutes and hours 100 first-aid teams traveled out from Ufa. It is difficult to know how many people are still alive. Yesterday, when we were on the scene, there were more than 580 people alive, but many of them were in serious condition. Several people died yesterday.

It is a great tragedy—even hard to imagine. The pipeline is a kilometer away from the railroad. We went there and had a look. You still cannot approach the area, fires are still burning—the gas is being burned off. Clearly, the pipeline had been holed in the area where the burning continues. The gas itself drifted down the slope to the railroad. Since the weather had been warm recently the gas built up and filled the hollow. There was clearly a massive buildup of explosive material. Consequently, the explosion was so terrible that the forest and everything else was instantly destroyed over a large area. The rails were twisted. In general, the people were involved in a disaster so terrible that it is hard even to contemplate.

It happened at 0200 local time. Most people were asleep, but some of them witnessed what happened. There were several dozen people who received immediate first aid and were able to talk. They talked about everything that happened.

I do not intend now to judge the causes, so as not to preempt the conclusions of the government commission and investigative organs, which are now on the spot and have started work. But a drop in pressure in the pipeline was discovered at 2000 Moscow time—3 hours before the events happened. I do not intend to pass judgment on how people should have acted, but common sense suggests that people should have found out what was happening and why. The investigative organs have now taken control of all the equipment which records the parameters of the pipeline's work. But on the basis of initial information—although this too remains to be clarified—the personnel switched on the pumps to boost pressure without investigating what was happening. Clearly they pumped gas into the pipe, it escaped through the leak, and built up in the hollow. And when a lot had built up and risen up to the level of the contact wires, it only needed a spark to set it all off. That's what happened.

What has happened has caused me very great concern. The question is: Why were these two trains there together? As is well known, they were not supposed to meet at that station. In any event, there must be an investigation. We talked with local residents, too. People are saying that everything must be investigated—so as to prevent a recurrence of incompetence, irresponsibility, mismanagement, and scandal. Things will not work in our country if carelessness leads to such human tragedies, not to mention the economic consequences.

The commission is at work now. Doctors headed by Comrade Chazov are there. All the country's major burns-treatment centers have been mobilized, the leading specialists have been mobilized, and they are all working there. People are donating blood. Generally speaking people are doing all they can, but the situation is very difficult. We must draw very rigorous lessons from this.

Before flying out there yesterday we consulted with comrades from the Politburo and agreed that they should go around to the hotels and inform the deputies. During these conversations many people expressed the wish that all deputies, out of a sense of charity, should donate their day's pay to a charity fund for the families involved. Of course you cannot replace relatives or children, but you must be beside people. I think that we will respond to that.

Tenth Session

5–6 June 1989

Here is another point. We have declared today a day of mourning. Our opinion is that today should be a recess. There will be a session of the congress at 1000 hours tomorrow and a session of the Soviet of Nationalities at 1600 hours. But the time available today could be used by deputies to go to the government, the Central Committee, and the ministries with their unresolved questions or, conversely, to check on how questions are being resolved.

I think that we should do that. Agreed, comrades?

From the floor: Yes.

M.S. Gorbachev: Then I will wind things up here. But we have an appeal from a group of deputies. There is concern at the situation in Fergana and Nagorno-Karabakh, and a group of deputies asks that this letter be read out on behalf of the congress: "We, people's deputies of the USSR, urge those who have been taking part in interethnic clashes to heed the voice of reason and stop the bloodshed. Injustices and problems have accumulated in interethnic relations and were ignored for years, but that does not mean that painful issues cannot be resolved in principle. A knot of problems cannot be unraveled by mutual confrontations. Think about those innocent people against whom the hand has been raised, think about the women, children, and old people. Stay that hand, prevent the injustices. We urge you to resolve the problems that have occurred by peaceful means, by means of the law." There is a large group of deputies from Leningrad, Moscow, and the Baltic region here.

I would support this appeal from our congress. This worries us all. We all feel it: This theme is at the center of our discussion and we are looking now for ways to resolve these questions in the future. Well, comrades? Shall we publish this? People are listening to us and, I think, will heed our voice and our appeal for reason. We will publish this appeal on behalf of the congress.

At this point we take our leave of one another today.

Tenth Session

6 June 1989. Kremlin Palace of Congresses. 1000.

USSR People's Deputy A.V. Gorbunov in the chair.

A.V. Gorbunov: Comrade deputies! Our congress is now back in session. Allow me to announce the deputy registration results for the morning session of 6 June. Two thousand one hundred nineteen deputies registered.

We are continuing discussion of the issue "On the Basic Directions of the USSR's Foreign and Domestic Policy." In keeping with our tradition, there has been a motion to announce the agenda for the morning session and to list the speakers designated by the Presidium of our congress: Dadamyan, general director of the Stepanakert Motor Transport Production Association, Nagorno-Karabakh; Sokolov, chairman of the executive committee of the Gorkiy Oblast Soviet of People's Deputies; Khallik, lead scientific associate of the Institute of Philosophy, Sociology, and Law of the Estonian Soviet Socialist Republic [SSR] Academy of Sciences; Mongo, director of the department for affairs of nationalities of the north and the Arctic of the Krasnoyarsk Kray Executive Committee; Kasyan, division director of the Leshchinovskiy Boarding School, Poltava Oblast; Minnullin, chairman of the board of the Tatar Autonomous Soviet Socialist Republic [ASSR] Writers Union; Seleznev, first secretary of the Kursk Oblast CPSU Committee; Kugultinov, writer, chairman of the board of the Kalmyk ASSR Writers Union; Lizichev, chief of the Main Political Directorate of the Soviet Army and Navy; Alekseyev, director of the Institute of Philosophy and Law; Rasputin, writer; Yarovoy, director of the Dvigatel Production Association, city of Tallinn; Sharik, first secretary of the Amur Oblast CPSU Committee; Borovik, writer, chairman of the Soviet Peace Committee; Lavrov, performer from the Gorkiy Leningrad Theater, chairman of the board of the USSR Union of Theater Officials; Arbatov, academician, director of the Institute of the USA and Canada of the USSR Academy of Sciences; Bykov, art director of the Yunost and Mosfilm associations, secretary of the board of the USSR Union of Cinematographers; Suleymenov, writer, first secretary of the board of the Kazakhstan Writers Union; Ugarov, artist, president of the USSR Artists Academy.

Such is the agenda planned by the presidium for our morning session and for the entire day of our work here together.

The floor is given to Comrade Boris Vartanovich Dadamyan....

Ye.A. Gayer, scientific associate of the Institute of History, Archeology, and Ethnography of the Far Eastern Department of the USSR Academy of Sciences, Vladivostok (Far Eastern National-Territorial Election District, Russian Soviet Federated Socialist Republic [RSFSR]): I have been waiting for a chance to speak for 3 days. I was told on Thursday [1 June] that you would give me an opportunity to speak, on Friday I was told I would be given an opportunity to speak, and today I was told the same thing. My name does not appear on the list today. What is going on? Could you please explain? For the first time in the country's history I was selected as a representative of an indigenous people to the USSR Supreme Soviet, and I am unable to get the floor in order to say something. I ask for the floor today.

A.V. Gorbunov: Respected colleague, please come up here to the presidium during the break. And so, the floor is given to Comrade Dadamyan. Comrade Sokolov, prepare yourself.

From the floor: On behalf of 270 agrarian deputies I ask for the floor....

STENOGRAPHIC RECORD

Tenth Session
5–6 June 1989

A.V. Gorbunov: Excuse me, comrade colleague deputy, the chair will not yield to you.

B.V. Dadamyan, general director of the Stepanakert Motor Transport Production Association, Stepanakert (Stepanakert National-Territorial Election District, Azerbaijan SSR): Dear comrades! The tragedy in the Bashkir ASSR has shaken the citizens of Karabakh, the pain it has caused in our hearts is a familiar one. Together with the entire country we mourn the death of the many hundreds of losses.

Dear friends! You are not alone in your misfortune and sufferings. Brothers of the same blood are with you throughout the entire union. Faced by terrible misfortune, and stricken by their own recent tragedy, the citizens of Karabakh grieve for the victims, recognize the losses to be irretrievable and irreplaceable, and mourn them. In this grim hour of trial, we wish our suffering brethren courage and patience.

One cannot grieve alone, and it is only in a truly equal, unified family of fraternal peoples, relying on sympathy and support, that we can endure this terrible blow. The people of Karabakh offer their condolences. Let me report that representatives of the benevolent society of Armenia and Karabakh have already left for the place of the tragedy with the R50,000 they collected and 40 boxes of medicine. (Applause).

Respected chairmen, respected deputies! In his speech to the congress, when he spoke about national problems, Mikhail Sergeyevich employed the image of a plow. If we begin to establish lines of demarcation, if we begin marking off our land with a plow, this would mean our destruction. That is all quite true! But let's ask ourselves honestly, who was it that drew the plow over the destiny of the people of Nagorno-Karabakh? On 4 July 1921 a decision was made by the plenum of the Caucasian Bureau of the RKP(b) [Russian Communist Party (of Bolsheviks)] to incorporate Nagorno-Karabakh (a part of the ancient Armenian land of Artsy) into Soviet Armenia. But on the very next day, at a new session of the Caucasian Bureau, by Stalin's will the Armenian people were divided into two parts, and an area with a 95 percent Armenian population was transferred to the Azerbaijan SSR on the following grounds, and I quote: "...on the basis of the need for national peace between Armenians and Muslims...." Later on a line was drawn between the Armenian and Azerbaijan SSR in such a way that Nagorno-Karabakh did not possess a common border with Armenia. A 5 km sanitation zone was deliberately formed between the two parts of the Armenian people.

Those who drew the lines knew quite well what they wanted! What was behind this? Short-sightedness, or a policy of "divide and conquer"? At any rate they separated, tore apart, and incorporated. What was the result, what followed? What followed was a policy of discrimination against the Armenian population of the Nagorno-Karabakh Autonomous Oblast and their expulsion from their native land. The leaders of the Azerbaijan SSR changed, and the words and the slogans changed, but this policy remained unchanged. Discrimination encompassed all spheres: economics, jobs, education, culture. The Nagorno-Karabakh Autonomous Oblast has been transformed into a raw material-supplying appendage of Azerbaijan, and the people have abandoned their land. Today around 3,000 Armenians—Karabakh emigrants who had been forced to move away—reside outside Nagorno-Karabakh. In the period from 1970 to 1979 only one out of every 10 Armenians born here stayed in Nagorno-Karabakh; the rest were forced to migrate. Any attempt to establish cultural and spiritual ties with Armenia were brutally suppressed. An attempt was made to take away not only the future of the Armenians, but also their past.

The "history of Armenia" was expunged from Armenian schools. Ancient monuments of Armenian culture and architecture—stone witnesses to our people's ownership of our land—were destroyed and defamed. Even the ancient Armenian khachkary—stone crosses—were proclaimed to be monuments of Azerbaijani ancestors. Things went so far that Armenians began to be persuaded that they were not at all Armenians, but Armenianized Albanians. There was but one goal to such historical and ideological aggression—to prove that the Armenians were immigrants, that they were foreigners on this land.

It has not been a day or two, but decades that the national worth of Karabakh Armenians has been scorned. And the national peace promised by the Caucasian Bureau is nonexistent. The tragic fate of Nakhichevan is an example for Armenians of Nagorno-Karabakh to see. At the demand of Turkey and in compliance with a treaty signed in 1921 between Russia and Turkey, this ancient Armenian land was transferred to Azerbaijan, which administered it in its own way. Today there are practically no Armenians in this autonomous republic, which is located entirely on Armenian territory sharing no borders with Azerbaijan but contained within it. The idea of a national liberation movement dominated the thoughts of Karabakh Armenians throughout all of these decades. The people of the NKAO [Nagorno-Karabakh Autonomous Oblast] rose against national oppression several times. But all uprisings were brutally crushed.

Restructuring generated hope. Expressing the will of its people, in February 1988 the oblast soviet of the Nagorno-Karabakh Autonomous Oblast appealed to the supreme soviets of the Azerbaijan and Armenian SSRs and to the USSR Supreme Soviet with a request to examine and resolve the issue of the reannexation of Nagorno-Karabakh to Armenia. It is the sad truth that whenever complex problems arise, people in our country

Tenth Session

5–6 June 1989

make decisions that are from the best from the very beginning. Or they follow the golden rule of stagnation—shuffle the problem aside, avoid solving it. And so it was with the problem of Nagorno-Karabakh. When it embarked upon restructuring, the country's leadership knew of course that it would not be able to avoid nationality problems. Difficulties were anticipated. This is precisely why the events in the NKAO were perceived not in and of themselves, in their real essence, but as a dangerous precedent, as a possible threat to restructuring. Hence the first reactions of the authorities were to impose prohibitions, hence the erroneous decision of the Politburo on 21 February 1988, and hence the half-measures in the 18 July decree of the Presidium of the USSR Supreme Soviet. These decisions did not account for the complexity and the reality of the situation.

Artificial postponement of the problem's solution sharply aggravated the interethnic situation in the region. It was only following many months that it came to be recognized that the problem exists, and that it arose on the soil of discriminatory, and even inhumane relations, as Mikhail Sergeyevich Gorbachev so aptly defined them, toward us on the part of the former leadership of Azerbaijan.

Attempts are being made to represent the political problem of Nagorno-Karabakh as an economic problem. Of course, the economy of the NKAO is extremely depressed. And we do favor improvement of the economy, and establishment of regional cost accounting. But the main thing for us is to solve the political problem within the framework of self-determination! The fact that the economy will continue to limp along without a political solution is demonstrated by those R450 million that were allocated by Moscow to the NKAO but which were side-tracked en route in Baku. We have yet to see this money. Moreover, you all know that money ceases to be just paper only after it assumes the form of capital, particularly construction materials and equipment, and the lion's share of this capital should be coming from Baku. It should, but it is not!

The Karabakh movement raised many issues which still remain unresolved. The main thing here is this: Do we recognize Lenin's principle of self- determination of nations? It is our belief, Lenin emphasized, that it would be a betrayal of socialism to deny self-determination of nations under socialism. Today, at the end of the 20th century, contrary to recognized international rules of law and the practice of self-determination, clear and unambiguous expression of the people's will concerning the annexation of Nagorno-Karabakh to Armenia is interpreted as unlawful aspiration for restructuring the borders, as something fundamentally impermissible and asocial.

Should we in Nagorno-Karabakh take this to mean that the party has in fact distanced itself from the principles of self-determination of nations? In his report to the congress Mikhail Sergeyevich Gorbachev said: "The principle of national self-determination proposed by Lenin was and remains one of the chief elements of the nationality policy of the Communist Party."

How are the people of Nagorno-Karabakh to interpret these words? As consent to rejoin the two parts of the Armenian people, or as a "Yes, but..." type of political slogan?

Eighty-five percent of us in this hall are Communists, and to a certain degree we represent the face of the party. Let's ask ourselves why, in behalf of what lofty principles must the Armenian people of Karabakh suffer. What sort of self-determination is it when a smaller nation must seek permission for self-determination from a larger nation? The latter may charitably grant permission, or arrogantly refuse. What kind of self-determination is this when it requires the permission of a big power? The time has come to bring our constitution into line with Lenin's conception of self-determination!

Respected deputies! I would like to focus your attention on the practice of selective de-Stalinization. Why is it that as we rid ourselves of Stalin's legacy in other areas of our life, we leave inviolable the arbitrary decisions that were made in regard to the principles and structure of the federated system adopted under pressure from Stalin? The existing status of autonomy, you see, is essentially a semifeudal institution, a means of consolidating a hierarchy of nations! Under these conditions the concept itself of equal nations becomes a fiction!

And now let us move from the proud slogans of self-determination to reality, and consider what Nagorno-Karabakh actually gets in place of self-determination. It received a special form of administration: The power of the oblast soviet of people's deputies, the soviet of labor collectives, and the party oblast committee were curtailed. Local soviet rule was actually abolished. The decision to create a special administrative committee was served up to the public as a compromise which infringed upon no one's interests, as one capable of stabilizing the situation in the region. But this is not so. This special form of administration rests upon a strong military presence, which unfortunately does not keep the leadership of Azerbaijan from pursuing an even more brutal line of discrimination against the Armenian people; the interethnic conflict continues to deepen. Are we cognizant of the fact that in the NKAO, the Azerbaijani leadership is implementing a variant of the "Cypriot model"? The region is split on an ethnic basis into two opposing communities—this is what the desire to postpone solution of the problem of Nagorno-Karabakh has led to! It was our duty to predict this development of events, rather than instilling fear and making references to "unpredictable consequences."

The crime of Sumgait is a special issue. Without going into it, I would like to note that political assessment of

Tenth Session
5–6 June 1989

the crime of Sumgait is important not only for the Armenians but also the Azerbaijani people. I would like to assure you on my part that we have no intention of laying blame for this malicious act upon the Azerbaijani people, and we deeply regret that its true instigators and organizers have not yet been revealed.

Concluding my statement, complying with instructions from my constituents I would like to transmit the demands of the Armenian people of Nagorno-Karabakh to the congress. We demand:

First: Immediate restoration of the oblast CPSU committee and oblast executive committee of the NKAO. Return soviet rule to Karabakh soil!

Second: Repeal the 5 July 1921 decision of the Caucasian Bureau as being contrary to law.

Third: Create a commission of the Supreme Soviet to regulate the procedure of the NKAO's reunification.

If you would permit me, I have 2 minutes left, and I would like to read a resolution of the Congress of People's Deputies, a draft of which we propose here.

A.V. Gorbunov: Respected colleague, it is to me that you direct your request if you wish additional time.... Boris Vartanovich requests 2 minutes to read the resolution.

B.V. Dadamyan: "On the Situation in the Nagorno-Karabakh Autonomous Oblast." This is the draft resolution which we propose.

First. Create a deputy commission to comprehensively and objectively study the situation and to prepare a national referendum in the NKAO on the basis of paragraphs 2 and 13, Article 108, and Paragraph 12, Article 73.

In compliance with Paragraph 6, Article 119 of the USSR Constitution, the USSR Supreme Soviet must organize and conduct a referendum in the Nagorno-Karabakh Autonomous Oblast.

Second. Before the referendum is carried out, grant the NKAO special administrative committee powers which would make the oblast directly subordinant to the central government in fact.

Third. Deem it suitable to restore the functions of local government organs.

This document bears the signatures of 33 deputies. I request.... (Applause).

A.V. Gorbunov: The floor is given over to Deputy Sokolov. Deputy Khallik will speak next.

From the floor: (Inaudible).

A.V. Gorbunov Comrades, please understand me correctly. If each of the 400 who have not spoken all come up to the microphone now and explain the reasons for their desire to speak, we will not make any headway. Therefore I suggest that you come to the presidium table during the break, at 1200, and we will discuss these questions.

A.A. Sokolov, chairman of the executive committee of the Gorkiy Oblast Soviet of People's Deputies (Sergachskiy Territorial Election District, Gorkiy): Comrade deputies! The discussion that has evolved at the congress shows that there are many problems in our country, in society, and in each republic and territory that trouble the people and require immediate solution. But no matter what the problems might be, not only the supreme organ of power but also the entire system of soviets—from supreme to rural—will play a dominant role in their solution.

During the recent elections we all sensed how strongly the people feel about the issue of their day-to-day life. The people demand that the soviets, which are elected by the people, become the true masters of their territory, and that the abnormal situation when bureaucracies play the main role in resolving many important issues affecting local interests be forever abolished. However, despite the decisions and appeals, the power of the soviets is not experiencing any real increase. To make matters worse, now that a number of laws have been enacted, including the "Law on the State Enterprise (Association)," this power has weakened even more. The imperfections and incompleteness of certain articles and provisions of legislative and normative acts adopted by the USSR Supreme Soviet and the government are being capitalized on by a number of enterprises, and especially cooperatives, for the selfish ends of their own collectives; they are one of the reasons for the unjustified increase in wages, for the erosion of inexpensive goods, and for worsening of financial position, as has already been discussed here. In general, as has already been emphasized, the financial status of the soviets, and of the country as a whole, is the main issue, the key issue. Both the elimination of inflation and the financing of all of our programs—the housing, food, and other social programs—depend on its resolution. Therefore I feel that the Supreme Soviet and the new Council of Ministers must examine all of the proposals that have been submitted in cooperation with deputies, and find a solution to this situation at all costs, treating this as a most acute, most fundamental issue.

As far as the Food Program is concerned, our delegation fully supports the proposals of the agrarian deputies, and feels them to be the basis for developing the necessary measures. We feel that we must mothball half of the industrial facilities presently under construction, and

Tenth Session

5–6 June 1989

transfer the released finances and material resources to the rural areas. We have made such decisions in the oblast, but this has led to obstructionism on the part of a number of departments. The situation regarding provision of goods and services to the public remains tense. The course of the election meetings and the situation we observed during the elections revealed general unrest, a growing lack of confidence in the possibilities for swift and complete satisfaction of the population's demand for consumer goods. The list of scarce goods is not decreasing. Speedy elimination of the deficit is problematic. There are many reasons for this. And one of them is the monopolistic power of the departments which determine what is to be made by a given enterprise in what quantities, without consideration for local interests.

The influence of local soviets on placement of orders for consumer goods and paid services manifests itself only as that of coordinators, statisticians, or critics. I think that the law should define more clearly the role of the soviets in resolution of these issues as well. The right thing to do would be to legalize principles in accordance with which the right to place a state order for the production of goods for local consumption and for paid services would be possessed by kray (oblast) executive committees, while the union ministries would retain the right and responsibility to place a state order for the production of complex household appliances and articles, and to determine technical policy.

We cannot fail to note that questions concerning state discipline and the discipline of deliveries have become secondary in many collectives, taking a back seat to various business deals and to finding the most profitable consumer. All of this has placed material and technical supply of the national economy, and chiefly the construction organizations that are building social facilities, especially in rural areas, in a highly difficult position. Frequently the capital that is allocated never goes beyond the paperwork stage. Let me say in this connection that no matter where our representatives go, they are always confronted by demands to produce more motor vehicles. Is this right? Also in this connection, it seems to me that the transition to wholesale trade in production implements and raw materials is not justified in all places, and it is premature.

I would also like to give my support to the principle stated in the report that developing democracy should in no way lead to a decline of discipline in all of its aspects—state, production, and especially the discipline of the rule of law. A legal state must be based on conscious execution of laws and conscious discipline. This is precisely why questions of discipline, and especially of responsibility, must take priority today both in the legislative and in the executive sphere, and especially in regard to persons who have committed particular deviations.

Comrade deputies! All of us are united by the enormous responsibility before the voters, who presented us with a mandate of trust in us as representatives in the supreme organ of power. And among the issues that must be examined, those of ecology and living conditions are the most urgent. No matter how deplorable it may seem, we must recognize that because of the unchecked monopoly of the ministries and departments, and the government's unrestricted support of them, an intolerable ecological situation has been created in the cities of Gorkiy, Dzerzhinsk, Kstovo, and Balakhna, and the elementary conditions of human habitation are absent. Industry is concentrated in such a way that toxic atmospheric discharges, the anthropogenic load on the environment and its influence exceed permissible limits by three or four times, and in some cases even more. This is especially intolerable, as I have said, in these cities. We believe that we will have to act and find solutions more aggressively in this area, going as far as shutting down certain production operations.

The state of waterways, especially the Oka and Volga, which are city water sources, remains no less acute. Under these conditions we feel that any further filling of Cheboksarskoye reservoir is absolutely impermissible. Our positions, and the positions of the Mari ASSR, are supported by the RSFSR government and an expert commission, but there has not yet been any resolution of the matter. As you can see, the situation is extremely tense. And added to it is the stress being suffered by the citizens of Gorkiy from the consequences that may arise if construction of a nuclear power plant at the outskirts of the city, near which 2 million persons reside, is not halted.

This is why we are not satisfied with Comrade Shcherbin's responses to our requests and proposals as deputies, as was discussed in the speech by Gennadiy Maksimovich Khodyrev. Letters from residents on these issues are sent to the central organs, and there they are forwarded to the oblast, which is then instructed to reply to the writers. What sort of reply can be given if the people responsible for this area are unable to formulate it clearly?

Considering that after Chernobyl the problems of nuclear power engineering trouble not just us alone, we feel that a law on nuclear power engineering that must account for all issues troubling the population, and especially safety issues, should be adopted. At the same time we must emphasize the need for independent economic and ecological expert examination of any decisions and plans that are adopted. There have been too many impermissible mistakes. Just in our oblast I can cite examples of thoughtless development of a number of chemical production operations, and of almost R200 million wasted on establishing an operation producing laminated welded tubing in Vyksa. And consider the economic and moral harm that has been done by the

Tenth Session
5–6 June 1989

"theory" of eliminating unpromising villages! This has already been discussed here, but no person has been found to bear the responsibility, no one has been punished, even though many of the authors of this theory are here, and some of them have remodeled themselves into active supporters of restructuring. (Applause). We need to support the proposal to create such an expert commission in the Supreme Soviet.

Or take another matter: The draft law on the basic principles of restructuring management of the economy and of the social sphere in the union republics on the basis of expansion of their sovereign rights, self-government, and self-financing has now been published. In order to increase the power of the soviets, it proposes transferring a number of sectors of the national economy to it—personal services, the housing fund, municipal management, and others. This doubtlessly needs to be done. But this would hardly increase the economic independence of the soviets, since all of these sectors operate at a loss, and they are in a neglected state. And who is going to pay their debts? Who is going to settle accounts on the unfinished and abandoned water, heat, and sewage networks, and for the delays in development of public health, the road network, and passenger transport? We cannot but support comrades who spoke before me on this issue. The citizens of Gorkiy also sense an acute shortage of such facilities. Substantial debts have accumulated, since the citizens of Gorkiy have directed their efforts for many years on industrialization, on attaining victory, on rehabilitating the devastated national economy, and on strengthening the defensive power of our motherland. The citizens of Nizhegorodskiy Rayon did their duty, reconciling themselves to the numerous deprivations. While it occupies a leading place in the country's industrial potential, in terms of social development the oblast's place in the RSFSR is in the fifties. We contribute R4 billion in profit and turnover tax to the union- republic budget, leaving up to 10 percent in our budget. Therefore deductions into local budgets, payments from the profits of enterprises, payments for productive capital and for use of land, labor resources and nature-related enterprises located within the soviet's territory, and the solid standards for these deductions must be established with regard for the state of the local infrastructure and the developmental problems it has accumulated. Deduction standards must be established on the basis of an assessment of an individual's subsistence wage which, incidentally, it would not be bad to determine for the entire country as a whole as well. That is, we need to determine the debt to society and the territory, and we must do this with the active participation of territorial administrative organs.

In this connection the problems of decentralizing the planning of capital construction are especially acute. As before, dictatorship of the ministries and departments persists in this area. We understand that many industrial sectors must enjoy priority in development. They are needed by the country. But we can no longer tolerate the fact that industrial construction is not decreasing in the oblast, and construction organizations do not have enough capacities remaining for facilities of the agro-industrial complex, for housing and for social, cultural, and personal service facilities. Complying with the decisions that have been adopted, in recent years we have been carefully drawing up plans for contracted work, with the assumption that these plans would stand. But they return from Moscow unrecognizable. Russia's special status in relation to a large number of issues has been discussed in this forum. In capital construction such a situation is illegal, and it is felt especially strongly. In contrast to what happens in other republics, union ministries operate in the RSFSR, and union organs draw up the plans. And I must say frankly that in such a situation the influence of territorial organs is essentially very weak. We need more decisive, clear, and consistent actions. Most difficulties of regional administration stem precisely from the absence of clear economic mutual relations between sectors and territories. We have a special need for strengthening the material and financial base of the lowest organs of government, and of town and village soviets. Under the existing conditions, in which, save for the "symbol" of power and the seal carried in the chairman's pocket, they have neither financial nor material resources, they could hardly ensure integrated economic and social development of their territories. In a word, the principle of self-management, self-financing, cost recovery, and mutual coordination of regional with state interests must be reliably secured in the law. Together with these issues, we need to implement measures to raise the prestige of soviet workers and their equipment support.

And finally. Enough has already been said here on the status of socially unprotected groups of children, especially disabled children, their mothers, and veterans. Supporting the proposal that these issues must be resolved without delay and, in my opinion, right during this congress, I submit a proposal to introduce mandatory deductions from the profit of every enterprise and every cooperative for the improvement of the life of this category of people. I think that for these purposes we also need to establish a maximum wage which, when exceeded, would sharply increase income tax benefiting children and veterans. Emotions are inevitably stirred when one recalls the brilliant speech by soldier-internationalist Deputy Chervonopiskiy, and the statement by Comrade Mazurov. One is compelled to think about how to make things so that there would no longer be any justified reproaches for long waits for housing and for solving other social problems of disabled persons, the families of servicemen killed in action, and of categories of individuals equal to them.

But the real situation is such that after introduction of the Law on the State Enterprise (Association), deductions for these purposes have been halved. Rather than decreasing, the waiting line is growing. The volume of housing presently being built on the basis of the title lists of local soviets can in no way cover this demand. Then there is the dilapidated housing fund, and the 12 other

Tenth Session

5–6 June 1989

waiting lines for privileges, besides the usual lines, in which the most poorly paid categories of citizens must stand. In all of this, the soviet stands alone, essentially in a hopeless situation. In my opinion we need to immediately repeal the thoughtless legislative provisions, considering that the 45th anniversary of the victory is approaching. These people defended the entire nation, and the entire nation and all enterprises still owe them a debt. (Applause).

Comrade deputies! There are many acute problems in our life today, and we are talking about them not just to savor them and demonstrate our bankruptcy but to find ways of resolving them. At the same time, the denial of what has been achieved and the besmirching of the past cannot conceal a clear-cut aim of trying to erode socialism and deny the party's leading role. Today's attacks on the party are aimed not at rectifying mistakes but at pooling forces to undermine confidence in the party and its organs and to break its ties with the people. In this respect we do not understand the point of the attacks on Politburo member Yegor Kuzmich Ligachev, whom we know as an active worker. Blasphemous words—I cannot call them anything else—have been said here with regard to the Lenin mausoleum and the memory of Vladimir Ilich. (Applause).

Boldly revealing distortions and learning from mistakes, the party is restructuring the political system for the sake of Soviet people and to improve their lives. And I am sure that it will overcome the difficulties in the current period of restructuring. (Applause).

A.V. Gorbunov: The floor is given to Deputy Khallik. Deputy Mongo, prepare yourself.

K.S. Khallik, lead scientific associate of the Institute of Philosophy, Sociology, and Law of the Estonian SSR Academy of Sciences, Tallinn (Tallinn-Mustamyaeskiy National-Territorial Election District, Estonian SSR): Respected comrade chairman! Comrade deputies! At this congress, this is the first time after a break of 66 years following the 12th party congress that ethnic relations in our country are being openly discussed. This discussion proves that all of those apprehensions against which Lenin cautioned in his commandments have come to pass. The reasons behind what has occurred have already been named at the congress. They include the flaws of state bureaucratic socialism and the unnatural and antidemocratic nature of the tenacious habits of imperial rule. This system infringes upon the interests of all nations, including the largest in population—the Russian nation.

When restructuring began, neither its principal architects nor the public at large were prepared for the possible advent of national movements. And even today, not everyone perceives them as something inevitable. We experienced this ourselves after the well-known sovereignty declaration of the Estonian Supreme Soviet on 16 November of last year. On one hand there was support from the democratic public, while on the other hand we were labeled with creeping counterrevolution, separatism, nationalism, and antisocialism. The authors of today's document, which has been passed out to the deputies deliberately after the congress actually began its work, appeal for introduction of a special form of government in Estonia. We were told in November: "Why are you pushing your national affairs so? Let's finish restructuring, and then your turn will come." And at the congress we heard appeals such as: "First let's settle the affairs of the state, and then national affairs." But now we have come to understand that the state must not have any affairs which are not also the affairs of the people.

As we analyze national policy, we uncover many bitter truths, for the perception of which many are psychologically unprepared. Nonetheless, we must try to comprehend the causes of today's national tensions. Only this would make it possible to determine the place of national democratic movements in restructuring.

First. The main reason for our national conflicts today is that Lenin's attempt to organize the union as a federation was unsuccessful. Stalin created an empire, disdaining not even the resources of imperial foreign policy. He created a unitary state in a federated package, without local self-management, in which the outlands were subordinated to the center in all things. This reality, and nothing else, can explain both the national injustice and, as a reaction to it, the constant reproduction of centrifugal aspirations. How do we act today in the conditions of democratization? We were reminded here, in words that immediately send up red flags, that the central power has the priority in this area. But I think that it is already obvious to everyone that it is impossible to maintain the integrity of the state by the methods which had been used to maintain it previously. These methods will encounter increasingly greater resistance from all peoples. We have no solution other than to really restore the right of nations to self-determination, and to impart to the union both the content and form of a union of equal sovereign states, and ensure broad national-territorial and national-cultural self-government by people who presently do not possess their own statehood. It is precisely the right to self-determination, and not leftover rights bestowed by a strong center, that must become the source of sovereignty of the republics, and it is the treaty that must become the source of federal law. In other words we are faced with constitutional reform of the union in order to ensure a return to Lenin's ideas of federalism.

In this connection I would like to say a couple of words concerning the other side of the so-called "Russian coin," which has already been discussed by Deputies Oleynik and Belov. Because of the truncated structure of the Russian national state, and because of administration of Russia not as a country but as a conglomerate of

STENOGRAPHIC RECORD

oblasts, national self-consciousness is being eroded, to be substituted by an all-Soviet identity. In today's conditions this is inhibiting national rebirth, and as a result the struggle of other republics against bureaucratic centralism are perceived by many in Russia as a struggle against Russia. Creation of all of the political institutions of Russia would make the majority of union departments and organizations unnecessary. They would be replaced by direct, mutually advantageous, and equal ties between republics. And perhaps we would then be able to count how many "Russian" nations there really are in this country: one, or 15 with regard for the number of union republics, or 35 with regard for autonomous republics. This absence of clarity is the source of tense national relations in the republics. Incidentally, yesterday's SOVETSKAYA ESTONIYA reflected the real support possessed by some comrades who claim to fully represent all of the non-Estonian, or so-called Russian-language, population of the republic.

The union's constitutional reform is called upon not only to settle the national issue but also to alter the countenance of socialism in the direction of a self-managing democratic society. This is something all nations, both large and small, equally need.

Second. Recently we have been getting away from believing ourselves to be the wisest and the most farsighted, and we are beginning to consider world experience, albeit selectively for the moment. World experience demonstrates that the path of modern civilization is one of international integration, and not a path of centralization and subordination. Free peoples whose interests as sovereign subjects of historical action are coordinated and not subordinated may undergo integration. But the kind of centralization and central subordination that has evolved in our country is in deep conflict with the objective tendency of integration processes lying in the plane of national structures. Russia, and all the more so Moscow, cannot claim to be the center of even the Slavic languages, not to mention Turkic, Baltic, or Finno-Ugric languages. As we can see, the role of the church and religion is not diminishing in the modern world. In this respect only the center of the Russian Orthodox Church coincides with the traditional center of the state. For the followers of Islam these centers are located beyond the state, as is true for Catholics and some other Christians. The cultural system of Latvians and Estonians, for example, gravitates toward the culture of Scandinavian peoples and the Baltic basin. As we know, in terms of kinship the Estonian language has its roots in Finland. What I am getting at is that the uniqueness and repeatability of our peoples is not only the product of their internal self-development but also the result of the wealth and variety of interethnic interactions. Opening ourselves up to the world and claiming a proper place for our state in the development of the world economy, protecting the living environment, and developing human culture, we must also grant this right to all nations in conformity with their historical and cultural features.

Unequal socioeconomic development of nations and countries is a reality of world experience. This phenomenon is designated in the political lexicon by the concepts "North-South" and "West-East." These polarities are also represented in our state: For example we have institutes of the USA and Canada, and of the countries of Asia and Africa, but we do not have an institute of Central Asia and the ethnic groups of the Soviet North and East. This problem has never been seriously entertained, even though Lenin and the decisions of the 10th party congress, which bear his imprint, encouraged meticulous consideration of these realities in nationality policy.

Inasmuch as the topic of national relations appeared later than others in restructuring, we are not yet ready to analyze them in the commonly accepted terms and concepts of policy. More often than in application to other phenomena, in this area we employ metaphors and invocations such as "common home," "indestructible friendship," "a strong center" and "strong republics." Let's talk incidentally about a strong center: What is this? Has a 16th republic appeared in our midst? If so, then it came into being on its own, without being voted in by all of the other fifteen. I would like to leave my modest mark upon these concepts, and introduce into this matter and develop the concept of a "common blanket" proposed by Deputy Sokolov. It does not take any special insight to see that this "common blanket" is stitched together out of swatches of different strength, and that drafts have already been circulating beneath it for a long time. Perhaps everything would be better if each had his own blanket—a down comforter in the North, and a light lap robe in the South.

And the third aspect. What must we do in order to direct national resources into deepening restructuring and renewing socialism? We need measures which would make it possible to restore the society's viability. First of all we need to surmount the destructive consequences of the so-called class struggle against the peasantry and intelligentsia. It is precisely the peasantry that has always been the caretaker of national cultural roots, and of balanced and caring relationships with nature. Alienation of the people from their past, from the natural environment must be curtailed. And this can be done only by peoples, and not by a population, even one possessing ethnic features. Second. The dominance of monopolies in the national republics and krays has disturbed the social integrity of a number of nations. Management by monopoly has put some of them into the position of a social stratum employed in agriculture or in other subsidiary sectors. Unrestrained extensive industrial development has also jeopardized the internal balance of the structure of the Estonian nation. It is transforming into a people with an incomplete social structure. In order to halt this process, we need an abrupt

Tenth Session

5–6 June 1989

turn in the conception of economic development of regions and republics, and we must account for the national consequences of all economic measures. This incidentally is the national meaning of our conception of republic cost accounting.

Special mention should be made of the minor peoples of the North and East. For centuries they have adapted themselves to the severe and at the same time fragile and readily wounded natural conditions; they have created a unique and thrifty culture of interaction between man and nature; they have preserved a viable natural environment for present generations and for the country. In gratitude for this, our state repeated one of the greatest disgraces of European civilization, which annihilated the American Indians. We repeated this at the threshold of the 20th century in a country which refers to itself as socialist. All is not yet lost; and the state must atone for its fault before the minor nationalities of the North, and not only the North. A special organ should be created in the Soviet of Nationalities to protect minorities, to develop a state program and to gain public support in resurrecting a normal working life, and through it, both the human and national worth of the minorities.

I have before me an appeal from minorities, adopted at an international meeting of writers of Finno-Ugric nations, as well as of the Kurdish people, the Crimean Tartars, the Gagauz people, and some others, which I propose entering in the record of the congressional proceedings.

Next, I suggest that cultural policy must turn toward restoration of our country's cultural diversity. This is a complex task, since the integrity of the cultural systems of many peoples has been disturbed. In a number of cases this happened due to displacement of national languages from science, from politics, and from higher and even secondary education. The languages of even some peoples numbering in the many millions are gradually transforming into backwoods speech of which people in the cities are ashamed. World experience and our own experience suggests that loss of national and ethnic cultural roots makes the culture defenseless against the onslaught of commercial culture, and leads to a decline of spirituality and erosion of the moral tenets of the human community.

These are all grounds for concluding that the present state of national relations in the country is explainable not by particular mistakes and certain omissions, numerous though they may be. It is the result of the entire system of administrative state socialism. Attempts to remove nations as historical subjects from the life of society have been found to be devastating not only to these nations and to the society as a whole. The society has expended enormous social energy in its struggle against national characteristics. In order to restore the viability of our society, nationality policy must be fundamentally altered. If this does not happen, the structure of administrative government will be preserved to a significant extent, and consequently the anti-restructuring base will also be preserved both centrally and locally.

Renewal of nationality policy must be based on international agreements on the rights of nations. The entire world is citing the words of Mikhail Sergeyevich, who said that every nation must have the right to its own historical choice. Our state is also a unique organization of united nations, one which may develop as a civilized society only in the presence of the legal and political guarantees of national rights and liberties.

In conclusion I would like to once again state my support for yesterday's announcement of an appeal to seek peaceful political and democratic forms of settling all of the national conflicts that have evolved in our country over many long years. Thank you for your attention. (Applause).

A.V. Gorbunov: The floor is given to Deputy Mongo. Deputy Kasyan will speak next.

M.I. Mongo, director of the Department for the Affairs of the Peoples of the North and the Arctic of the Krasnoyarsk Kray Executive Committee (Evenki National-Territorial Election District): Respected people's deputies! Respected voters! Our country is inhabited not only by great nations and large nationalities. Dozens of small nationalities and national groups reside in it. And we cannot resolve a single matter, a single problem while neglecting the interests of even the smallest national group. This was clearly voiced in Mikhail Sergeyevich Gorbachev's report and in the statements of deputies to the congress.

Democratization of Soviet society entails more than just allowing the exercise of the most complete rights and liberties of every person of every nationality. It entails providing chiefly economic rights and broad political liberties to each nation and nationality, and elevating the legal status of union and autonomous republics, and of oblasts and okrugs.

I am speaking at this congress in behalf of people's deputies of most of the autonomous okrugs of the Russian Federation. We have all been elected to the Soviet of Nationalities of the USSR Supreme Soviet. By this action, we have done more than comply with the constitutional right of autonomous formations to have their own representatives in higher organs of government; in this way, the overwhelming majority of people's deputies have once again confirmed that they are convinced internationalists. And internationalism presupposes, first of all, deep respect for the right of each nation and nationality to have its own authorized representatives in all soviets, including in the USSR Supreme Soviet. Such representation is all the more necessary because interethnic relations have grown acute in the country. And as many deputies have mentioned here, they have assumed considerable proportions, and they must be resolved integrally.

The problems of interethnic relations are associated primarily with imbalanced economic and social development of individual regions, with disturbance of the ecological situation and with complication of the demographic situation. It is becoming all the more obvious today that swift industrial development of these regions has come into sharp conflict with the traditional way of life of the indigenous national population. While it was authoritatively declared from this lofty podium on certain dates that we no longer have "national districts" in our country and that they will no longer undergo socio-economic development, they did exist before, and they will continue to do so.

For many years we have hidden the truth from the Soviet people about the life of peoples of the North and of the minorities, and the northerners themselves we have deprived of elementary concern for their life. The realities have often been distorted and glossed over. The conception of "unprecedented flourishing" of our nationalities prevailed, and there was talk of swift "leaps," "jumps," and "lunges" in a society of developed socialism. Problems that became acute were given the silent treatment, or they were allowed to fall by the wayside.

"Having leaped across the centuries" in the sense of social organization and education, the indigenous population of the northern regions is a decade behind in social development. Thus, the average life span of nationalities residing in this region is 16-18 years shorter than in the country as a whole, the incidence of tuberculosis is 5-6 times higher, and child mortality is 2-3 times greater than the unionwide level. There is an average 3-4 square meters of housing space for every indigenous resident—that is, a little more than is required for a person in the "lower," as Evenks say, "world beyond the grave."

More than 3,000 families—and this is more than 13,000 people—continue to maintain a nomadic way of life. Even in 50-degree frost they live in skin, bark, or fabric tents and not just because the kind of work they do requires this. All of these families have, as they say, "neither house nor home" in the towns. Teachers, doctors, agricultural and cultural workers, aviators, builders, geologists, war and labor veterans, and others living and working in these severe conditions have an urgent need for housing.

In all of the North, including the Tyumen North, where the country's chief drilling rigs are located, only 3 percent of the towns have been supplied with gas, 4 percent have water lines, and 0.1 percent have central heating. There are no sewage systems and water intakes in most towns. In short, people of the taiga and tundra are living in near-primitive conditions, but with television sets, as was stated in a certain Soviet press publication. We say thanks to the creators of the Orbita system, owing to which our constituents can confirm that what we northerners say from this lofty podium is sad but true.

I support the proposal for a special increase in the minimum income of pensioners, war and labor veterans, and disabled persons. But believe us deputies from the autonomous okrugs, and verify this if need be, that we have more impoverished people than do the small nationalities residing in the country's northeast. And therefore we are certain that people's deputies will support us both in asserting the facts and in the efforts to implement the proposals we suggest for improving their life. So what is it we are asserting, and what is it we are proposing in behalf of the nationalities of the North and other ethnic groups?

The territory in which 26 small nationalities of the Far North, Siberia, and the Far East reside is somewhere close to 11 million square kilometers—that is, half the territory of the USSR. And almost all of this enormous territory has been essentially transformed into a raw material-providing appendage of other, more highly developed regions of the country. The lion's share of oil, gas, phosphates, rare and nonferrous metals, and other minerals are extracted there. The entire country has lived off of all of this in part, but half of its territory has transformed intensively into a "dead zone." Thus for example the level of air pollution by industrial enterprises exceeds the maximum permissible concentrations by many orders of magnitude on the Kola and Taymyr peninsulas. In the Tyumen, Tomsk and Yenisey North, and on Sakhalin, Kamchatka, and the Chukchi Peninsula oilmen, geologists and loggers have ruined hundreds of fish-filled rivers and lakes. Their demise is having a deleterious effect on the climate of Siberian rivers—the Ob, Yenisey, Angara, and others blocked by giant dams.

Despite public protests and the authoritative opinion of scientists, the Ministry of Power and Electrification plans to build yet another hydroelectric power plant, and once again a giant—the Turukhanskaya hydroelectric power station [GES] on the Nizhnyaya Tunguska. If it is built, the reservoir will inundate almost all of the vitally important territory of the Evenki Autonomous Okrug. There are also plans for erecting the Amguemskaya GES on the Chukchi Peninsula, and the Iokanskaya GES in Murmansk Oblast, where the majority of the indigenous national population resides.

Each year hundreds of thousands of hectares of Siberian forest are logged or burned down, extremely valuable cedar groves and hunting lands are destroyed, and the felling is creeping ever-northward, all the way up to the tundra. In the European and Siberian North and in the Far East, according to official data over 34 million

FIRST CONGRESS OF PEOPLE'S DEPUTIES OF THE USSR

Tenth Session

5–6 June 1989

hectares—that is, a tenth of the reindeer pasturelands—were removed from turnover in just the last 15 years. But in reality this figure is much greater.

Today, much is properly being said about the priorities of human values, but primarily in application to spiritual and cultural values. However, the Siberian taiga (which is an "oxygen factory" for the entire planet) and all of the unique Siberian and northern nature are the property of all civilization, and yet it is being intensively destroyed by industrial "invaders." The dominance of departmental monopolism and the need for antimonopoly legislation have already been discussed here. Numerous "extracting" ministries and departments are systematically polluting the North's fragile ecosystem—chiefly because an enormous part of the gas is being burned off, oil is being spilled over the land and during transportation, and timber is clogging the river channels.

From my point of view the time has come to develop and implement a special law on responsibility for mismanagement and carelessness. How many explosions such as the one that occurred this week can the country endure? Such a law is needed by the entire country, but chiefly by its most vulnerable regions—the Far North and the Arctic.

I also feel it necessary to secure constitutional rights of priority land use of hunting lands and reindeer pasturelands, as well as coastal waters, rivers and lakes (as the basis for traditional forms of livelihood) for the small nationalities, and thus solve our acute problem of full employment for the indigenous national population. Otherwise the habitat of the northern nationalities and national groups is threatened not only by ecological but also ethnic catastrophe.

Comrades! We have implemented effective measures to protect polar and brown bears, and other exotic animals and birds on the list of endangered species. But we also need to enact a law to defend the right of the indigenous national populations of our state's outlying districts to live on their own ancient land. All of the minorities of Siberia, the Far North, and the Far East, which number 180,000 persons, are steadily approaching a danger point—total assimilation. Take for example Evenks, of whom I am a representative. In the late 19th century there were over 70,000 of them, while according to the latest census a few more than 20,000 remain. And representatives of nationalities such as the Entsy, Yukagiris, Kets, Aleuts, Tofalars, Nganasans, Negidals, and others number from 300 to 1,000. The proportion of the indigenous population is declining dramatically in all 10 autonomous okrugs, and it is now from 23 percent in the Koryak Autonomous Okrug to 3 percent in Khanty-Mansiysk Autonomous Okrug.

What is the principal cause of such meager numbers? Primarily the fact that the environment itself of northern and other nationalities is being physically destroyed. Second, economic, housing, and cultural construction is proceeding extremely slowly there. The availability of housing, hospitals, and schools is 70 percent of the unionwide level. It must be recognized that even we have not been undertaking decisive measures locally to improve the living conditions of northerers until recently. And third—one of the main causes from my point of view, the minorities have long ceased to be the masters of their vast land. The status of the autonomous okrugs, which has been granted to 10 nationalities, is itself essentially nothing more than a declaration. When it comes to budget allocations, the autonomous okrugs are even equated to ordinary rayons, and they experience perpetual petty wardship of kray or oblast organs, and intense pressure from various union and republic ministries and departments. The time has apparently come to create, or more accurately resurrect, a special organ under the government of the Russian Federation—a state committee similar to the Committee for Assistance to Northern Nationalities, which existed since the early 1920s and which was groundlessly abolished in 1935.

We also need statewide protection of the rights and interests of small nationalities. In this connection it would be proper to create a permanent commission for the affairs of northern nationalities and national groups in the Soviet of Nationalities of the USSR Supreme Soviet. If we wish to continue to improve national relations in application to the minorities, and rescue them from total disappearance from the face of the earth, we could not do without such a statewide organ. The Law on Small Nationalities and National Groups, which was discussed earlier, particularly by Comrade Nishanov and other people's deputies, would also be helpful in this.

This permanent commission must possess both legislative and monitoring functions. Otherwise what happens, comrades? In the last 30 plus years, for example, three major decrees have been adopted on further economic and social development of the regions in which northern nationalities reside. All of them doubtlessly played a positive role. In these years many scientific conceptions and specific-purpose programs for the development of these regions have been developed, and dozens of dissertations have been defended. But as with the preceding ones, new decrees and new conceptions would hardly be implemented, because we do not have a statewide legislative organ which would monitor fulfillment of all of these good programs and decrees.

Judge for yourselves, comrades. For example 42 union ministries and 36 ministries and departments of the Russian Federation took part in the writing and implementation of the CPSU Central Committee and USSR Council of Ministers decree "On Measures for Further Economic and Social Development of the Regions of Residence of Northern Nationalities" dated 7 February 1980. No committee—neither of union nor, all the more so, of republic significance—would be able to monitor their activity. This is why we propose:

STENOGRAPHIC RECORD

Tenth Session

5–6 June 1989

1. Creating a permanent commission for the affairs of northern nationalities and national groups possessing legislative and monitoring functions under the Soviet of Nationalities. We, the people's deputies from the autonomous okrugs, are prepared to take a direct part in its work.

2. Preserving, in accordance with the USSR Constitution, representation of the indigenous national population (irrespective of its numbers) of autonomous okrugs in the Soviet of Nationalities of the USSR Supreme Soviet. The governmental and legal status of autonomous formations must be raised, and new autonomous okrugs, as well as national regions and national rural soviets, in which nationalities not possessing their own autonomy reside, must be created. Autonomous okrugs must be granted the right of legislative initiative at the union and republic level, and development of national culture and languages must be promoted.

3. The population of all of our union republics, especially of the Russian Federation, is multinational and multilingual. Therefore in order to further harmonize interethnic relations, I propose creating two chambers in the RSFSR Supreme Soviet—a Republic Soviet and a Soviet of Nationalities, in order that each nationality and national group would have its own representatives in the supreme organ of republic power.

As far as other union republics are concerned, this would be exclusively their prerogative. All of these measures would become a specific contribution of our congress to the further improvement of interethnic relations in our common home—the Union of Soviet Socialist Republics. Thank you for your attention. (Applause).

A.V. Gorbunov: The floor is given to Deputy Kasyan. Deputy Minnullin will speak next.

N.A. Kasyan, division director of the Leshchinovskiy boarding school of the city of Kobelyaki, Poltava Oblast, Ukrainian SSR (from the Soviet Charity and Health Fund): Dear comrade deputies! Respected presidium! First of all permit me to acquaint you with the text of a telegram I received the day before yesterday from Donetsk.

"Congress, telegraph message, Moscow, the Kremlin, USSR Congress of People's Deputies, Deputy Nikolay Andreyevich Kasyan. All of your patients, colleagues, and friends await your statement at the congress. Down with the party! Long live restructuring! All power to the Soviets! Your student from Donetsk, Ivan Ivanovich Griboyedov. 34010, Donetsk-100, Shevchenko Boulevard, Building 6, Apartment 14."

Let me reply. I do not know you, and I do not desire to know you. (Applause). Even if you show me a certificate signed by me and the director of the Kobelyaki Polyclinic that you had served an apprenticeship with me. The only Griboyedov I know is the one who wrote the famous "Woe From Wit." (Applause).

On arriving in Moscow for the Congress of People's Deputies, to be honest I did not prepare myself to speak from this lofty podium. My thoughts were these: There are great people among the deputies, there are greater people—scientists, of whom there are more, and there are those who are the greatest. It is probably to them that this podium will be offered. And you know, I deeply erred, I simply did not expect that the process of restructuring had opened the door so widely to real democracy, to such enormous and broad freedom of speech and freedom of action.

The floor was given to some representatives in good will, while others themselves took the floor, forcing themselves up to the podium and lining up at it. Some simply shouted from the floor, attempting to attract the attention of not only the quietly sitting deputies but also, of course, television. Foolish or not, such an act will be seen throughout the country and beyond its borders. (Applause).

This unwittingly brought to mind Nikita Sergeyevich Khrushchev's performance at the UN General Assembly, when, demonstrating Soviet "culture," he took off his shoe and pounded it on the podium with the words "kuzkina mat" ["Kuzkin's mother"?]. Of course this "cultural" tactic cost our state an extremely substantial fine, and shameful condemnation by representatives of the whole world. We have not yet gone this far in our congress, though it would not bother me to employ such a sanction, or a similar one, against certain deputies. (Applause).

Comrades! It was we, after all, who elected the presidium, who voted for it, who voted for Mikhail Sergeyevich and for his first deputy. Then why are we not showing respect to our presidium, why are we not respecting all who are sitting in the hall? Why is it that those of you who are so diligently striving to disobey the chairman and get yourselves on camera do not respect either the presidium, or those present in the hall, or yourselves? Is it really that much fun to come up to the podium in your nice clean suits and ties, and demonstrate your lack of culture?

I am a deputy from the Soviet Charity and Health Fund. Doing others good is my main goal. Could it really be that you do not desire the same thing? Could it really be that you are unable to behave in a cultured manner, so that people out there in other countries would say proudly: Yes, that's what the Soviets are like! And despite the fact that they have survived a revolution, collectivization, war, humiliation, defilement and outrage, they still remain Soviet people. (Applause).

Numerous are our shortcomings, mistakes and omissions, many bad things have we done to our people "in someone else's name" and "on the basis of someone else's instructions." There were Stalin and his accomplices. There was the faithful "Leninist" Nikita Sergeyevich and his retinue, under whom we "overtook"

Tenth Session

5–6 June 1989

America in meat and milk and have already been living under communism since 1980. There was the Dnepropetrovsk era of Leonid Ilich Brezhnev and his faithful helpers, some of whom still occupy ministerial chairs and are striving to restructure themselves but having been unable to do so yet. But by whom, and on what basis, were we given the right to outrage the communist party, to withhold our trust from it? By whom were we given the right to outrage the nation or the republic? By whom were we given the right to outrage or at least cast a shadow of mistrust upon our Soviet Army, upon the Committee for State Security? (Applause).

I, a simple doctor, was elected a people's deputy. I was elected never expecting this, and never even dreaming that someday I would become a deputy. I know that there were some who were very much against making Kasyan a deputy. Telephone calls were made to Moscow, to the election commission, to the Soviet Charity and Health Fund to find out if there was still a chance that Kasyan might not get the necessary number of votes. What they heard was no, Kasyan would be voted in.

But I am not resentful of such leaders. "God will forgive them," was what was said to me in reference to the like by The Most Holy Catholicos of All Armenians Vazgen I. I also forgive them, and I will never harbor ill feelings against them. If only they would join the restructuring effort more quickly, and do everything necessary in order to build the Manual Therapy Center in Kobelyaki, so greatly needed by all Soviet people and by all who come to Kobelyaki from abroad for treatment. (Applause).

In this hall, and I mean right in this hall, there are not less than 200 persons to whom Kasyan had once provided medical care long ago. And if we consider that in Kobelyaki I receive 400-450 patients each day, and that every time I come to Moscow on "important" and "very important" matters, every day, or more accurately every early morning, I receive 250 or 300 persons, we find that our entire country is now fervently beseeching the USSR State Planning Committee [Gosplan], the Ministry of Health, and the Ministry of Finance with approximately these words: "Dear, kind ministers! Please resolve the issue of building this center in Kobelyaki more quickly. And if the cost of this construction climbs beyond R4-5 million, we are certain that the USSR Council of Ministers, Gosplan, and the USSR Ministry of Health would throw in another 2-3 million. And in 1992 you will all be able to say proudly: 'You people watching over the project and you, Doctor Kasyan, be joyful, take this Manual Therapy Center and put it to use, together with its hospital, polyclinic, vacation hotel, dining room, and quarters for medical personnel. We are charitable as well, and we have shown this to you'." (Applause).

Yesterday, or more accurately the day before yesterday, I was met at the hotel entrance by an extremely elegantly dressed man, who said: "Nikolay Andreyevich, you are a very popular fellow among Muskovites, and we would like it very much if you could speak in support of our program at a rally in Luzhniki." I replied evenly: "Look, I don't like rallies, and I don't like wasting precious time. Early Monday morning it would be better for me to receive patients, do them some good, and then quietly go to the Palace of Congresses and speak from its podium when the floor is given to me. I'm not about to fight the crowds in your rally, or shout myself hoarse. And I will be both heard and seen by many more people than in your rally."

Let me also say this. Dear comrades, dear deputies! Let's respect the Congress of USSR People's Deputies. We've already spilt all of the dirt we have. I would imagine we put foreign journalists of some countries who were hoping to find this dirt on their own out of a job. And they witnessed our "unusual culture," "our respect for the presidium." And some of them have already "pulled in their fishing lines" and have gone home to seek other work, because there is no longer anything here for them to seek. (Applause). Rather than throwing all kinds of dirt, let's decide how to get ourselves out of the current situation, and what priority tasks we must accomplish in order to get the country out of its crisis. It is for this reason that economists and other ministers are present here today.

And anyway, don't we have anything good that could be said from this podium? Are we really so broken down and ruined that we should be the focus of someone's venomous laughter? We are Soviet people, after all, and in many areas we have been and are being heroic. Even here at the congress we have proven so. Take for example the action taken by Deputy Kazannik, who voluntarily gave up his seat in the Soviet of Nationalities in favor of Deputy Yeltsin.

Some people can be so lucky! But I have not been so lucky. One would think that I wield authority, and at national scale at that. But the truth is otherwise. Let me tell you in confidence that rather than going to meetings, I should be treating patients, and returning life and the joy of labor to them. But there is not enough of me for them, and I do not have enough spare parts by which to maintain my own health. And when it comes to students, real students, they are few, I can count them on the fingers of my hands, while token students are very numerous—in the hundreds. These token students work in cooperatives, they print calling cards stating that they are supposedly students of Doctor Kasyan, and they take money from sick people and live with this refrain: "Restructuring's done well by us, thanks, my dear, to Kasyan's fuss." (Laughter in the hall, applause).

So it is that Kasyan fought for the triumph of manual therapy, he was subjected to all kinds of inspections hundreds of times, thrice he was charged with criminal wrongdoing, and each time without adequate grounds. And now they proudly call themselves his students, and rake in the money from the misfortunes of others. They

Tenth Session
5–6 June 1989

even go so far as to exhibit certificates attesting that they had undergone apprenticeship with Doctor Kasyan. Look at these photographs, they say, here's a picture of Kasyan and me.

My dear doctors of manual therapy! Listen to my words from this podium: One is a student of Kasyan if Kasyan himself is able to see and recognize his student.

Comrades! We touched upon the issue of Vladimir Ilich Lenin's Mausoleum here. Leave our leader alone, let the archives rest. Millions of people from the entire planet go to him, in the mausoleum. We live with him and, when we visit the mausoleum, perhaps our own mistakes come to mind on occasion, and we find the ways to correct them. (Applause).

Much has been said here about the hard life of our rural areas. And we would not have talked so much about this, had there been less aimless running back and forth. Those who argued that rural villages lack a future are probably still living in good health; they are living, but the villages have been destroyed. (Applause).

We go on creating and then pulling down, one after another, first the MTS [automotive-tractor station], then the selkhoztekhnika, then the rapo [rayon agro-industrial association], then the oblapo [oblast agro-industrial association], then the agroprom [agro-industrial committee], then the agrokhimiya [agricultural-chemical], and then some other "selkhoz," and we can't seem to ever arrive at a common denominator. We sit in ministerial chairs, think up our schemes, write, propose, argue, enact laws and decrees, and then repeal them, we dream, but never come up with anything good. In my opinion this is something very easy to do. It would be good for certain administrative workers to get out of their chairs for awhile and visit the countryside. (Applause). Roll up their sleeves, and take up a hoe or shovel. Then sit at the helm of a Rostselmash combine, communicate substantially with the peasants, and then begin drafting their decrees. After doing so, they will come to understand what a plan entails, how it is to be fulfilled, how pensions for the elderly are to be increased, and how to feed the peasant. (Applause).

Comrades! It will be our job to elect the chairman of the Council of Ministers. You already know that Comrade Nikolay Ivanovich Ryzhkov has been recommended for this position by the CPSU Central Committee. We are aware of his shortcomings and mistakes, but we also know of his services and his good deeds. Comrade Ryzhkov earned special love and respect during his visit to Armenia at the time of its misfortune. (Applause).

I appeal to all of you to behave calmly, to vote earnestly for Comrade Ryzhkov as chairman of the USSR Council of Ministers, like I will. Kasyan never makes mistakes about people. (Applause). The only thing is that there are still people around who do not understand Kasyan. But that's all right—someday they will!

Let me ask you once again to behave in a cultured manner, to keep your tempers in check, and preserve the health of those in attendance here. To protect your gallbladders from all mental overloads. Restructuring must proceed in a cultured manner. The entire country and all of mankind are watching us. And the people are making their conclusions about individuals or about certain leaders on the basis of their behavior, on the basis of their personal culture, on the basis of their working qualities, and not on the basis of hot air. (Applause).

And finally, let me appeal to all Soviet people. Come to your senses, people, you can't feed the country with rallies. We can find a solution to our problems only through honest labor and clear thinking. Every minute is precious at the plants and enterprises and in the organizations, collective farms [kolkhozes], and state farms [sovkhozes]. Do not lose precious time. Thank you for your attention. (Applause).

A.V. Gorbunov: The floor is given to Deputy Tufan Abdullovich Minnullin, a writer. Deputy Seleznev will speak next.

T.A. Minnullin, secretary of the board of the USSR Writers Union (Kukmor National-Territorial Election District, Tatar ASSR): Respected comrade president, respected comrade deputies! The delegation of USSR people's deputies from the Tatar ASSR grieves together with all others for the tragedy that occurred in fraternal Bashkiria, and expresses its deep sympathy to the victims and to the families of the deceased. We have distributed our appeal concerning this matter among the deputies. We ask that you support us.

Comrades! With the help of certain deputies, the voters have divided us into active and passive. This is obviously because those who are said to be passive are not perpetually standing in line for the microphones. If this were all we had to do, then we would stand in line as well, but standing in lines is not something all of us would wish to become accustomed to. I think that people's deputies do have other forms of showing themselves to be active. And activeness is something that we need. There are very, very many problems that we have to solve.

On the day after the elections, when I learned that I had been elected a people's deputy, I was naturally pleased with the trust shown by the voters. But after that I was gradually engulfed by a sense of anxiety. My question was this: What was to be done next? It was with this question that I arrived at the congress. During the election campaign we made an abundance of promises, and we were inundated with mandates. How are we to fulfill them? The numerous letters from voters contain questions upon questions. How are they to be answered? And all of them are waiting for answers.

STENOGRAPHIC RECORD

FIRST CONGRESS OF PEOPLE'S DEPUTIES OF THE USSR

Tenth Session

5–6 June 1989

Many of our deputies were elected by rural residents. Of course, the rural resident is more patient than the urban dweller. He had calmly endured many deprivations, and he endures them now. So long as there would be no war, we'll solve the rest of it somehow—so say the aksakaly [translation unknown]. Yes, owing to our state's sensible foreign policy the threat of war is not hanging suspended over our souls, and it is not constraining our will. We can examine our domestic affairs with all seriousness.

As I said, there are more than enough problems here. From implementation of the slogan "All power to the soviets" to the pension for war veteran Gayfutdin Badrutdinov from Sabinskiy Rayon. "At the front, when we went into battle, we were not asked where we worked," he writes, "but now for some reason the pension awarded to a kolkhoz farmer is not equal to that enjoyed by others." I brought this letter with me. The veteran awaits an answer. And together with him wait millions of pensioners whose pensions are less than R50.

I discussed the legal state in meetings with my constituents. They listened to me attentively, they voiced their agreement, and then in a chorus they demanded gas. If I would personally help get gas for at least three villages in each of eight rayons, they promised to even elect me for a second term.

The voters and I also came to an agreement on the general problems of ecology, but they are less prone to discuss this topic abstractly. They are concerned by the death struggle of the great river Volga, and by construction of a nuclear power plant on the Kama. It is being built in the center of the republic's densely populated industrial region. Despite numerous protests from scientists as to the extremely unfortunate choice of location from a geological and geographic point of view, construction is under way.

Of course, an expert commission has been created by the USSR Council of Ministers in response to an appeal from the republic's leadership and the public, but it does not seem to be in any hurry to begin work, while at the same time construction organizations do not have sufficient productive capacities to build hospitals and schools. The voters are patiently awaiting concrete resolution of this issue as well. They also want the fastest possible transition of the republic to cost accounting, they want to live on the money they earn.

What I am saying, comrades, is nothing new, nothing original, and I know that I am repeating others. But the voters, who are watching the progress of our congress on television, want to hear answers to their questions from their deputy. What am I to say to them in reply? Will I be able to answer them in a year, in two, in five?

The nationality issue was also included on the election agenda of Tatar deputies. I would like to dwell in greater detail on this problem, since it is especially urgent today, and it requires immediate solution. As we have all become persuaded, the sweet, kindergarten interpretation of friendship among peoples is now colliding with the real conditions in which the peoples of our country find themselves. Today, as a result of a dogmatic relationship to the problem, and because of violation of Lenin's nationality policy, cracks have appeared in the monolith of selfless friendship achieved by the October Revolution, something that was our chief weapon in the years of the Great Patriotic War. This phenomenon requires deep scientific study. It seems to me that one of the main causes is a failure to practice equality.

We all know the truth that only equals can be friends. This is why this truth has been written into our constitution, and is secured by Article 36. But then, this truth is placed under doubt in that same basic law, in articles 109, 111, 118.

Why, for example, do union republics select 32 deputies from the national- territorial okrugs, and only 11 from the autonomous okrugs? Why are some republics represented in the Soviet of Nationalities by 11 deputies, while others are represented by four? Where is the logic here? What essentially is the difference between union and autonomous republics? Even at our congress, union republics are elevated to a special rank. We in the meantime are relegated to the role of auditors. Why has such a contradiction existed for so many years?

This is not, after all, just a question of prestige. Such inequality has spread throughout our life as a hidden, dangerous disease. It is noticeable primarily in the area of national culture. A territorial-administrative relationship to culture has resulted in a privileged position for some peoples, and a condescending attitude toward others. Why, for example, are the Tatar people, who number in the seven million, forbidden to have their own motion picture industry? Could it be that the republic's economy is not developed well enough? I wouldn't say so. The republic's present gross social product is R23 billion. Could it be that movie makers are not to be found among the indigenous population? No, there are plenty of them. Why is it, for example, that Tatar, Bashkir, Chuvash, Mari, and other autonomous radio and television studios are offered by far less time for their broadcasts than the union republics?

I am speaking here now, and my constituents can watch me on television, but had I been speaking on republic television, they would not have been able to see their deputy. One hundred twenty kilometers from the capital of their republic, people are deprived of the possibility of seeing broadcasts of their own television. This is explained by production, technical, and economic causes, but I am compelled to see other causes here; I see this phenomenon from a political point of view. This is precisely the way tens of thousands of the republic's rural residents see it. I could go on with publication of books, newspapers, and journals, but I am not going to go into it—I don't want to evoke pity.

STENOGRAPHIC RECORD

Tenth Session

5–6 June 1989

What is it that we propose as a way out of this humiliating situation? We need to legislatively abolish the administrative and territorial obstacles that stand in the way of total equality of all peoples of the Soviet Union. I feel it necessary to equate the status of all national republics, without dividing them into union and autonomous republics. (Applause).

There may be other ways to deal with this as well; we need to think about them, and discuss them. The one thing we can't do is leave the question open or, more accurately, closed. Friendship and unity are more precious than anything on earth. I'm not talking about laundry detergent and soap. To keep our souls clean, we need more-effective "washing agents." We will survive our economic crisis. But if a crisis begins in our relations, we would hardly come out of it alive and healthy.

The perniciousness of an administrative-territorial relationship toward culture manifests itself especially in regard to our people. The fact is that only a fourth of the Tatar population resides within its own republic. For practical purposes the rest are estranged from the center of concentration of the main forces of national culture, where the nation's public thought forms. Before, the natural desire of Tatars living outside the republic to preserve their distinct way of life was assessed as something close to brazen nationalism. And our desire to acquaint them with our own culture was viewed as something close to interference into the internal affairs of a foreign state. Even the republic's Ministry of Personal Services, it seems to me, had a broader area for its activity than the republic ministries of culture and public education. Today things seem to be returning to the right track. But what meaning have words without a material basis and without legal reinforcement?

Tatar Muskovites have not been giving me any rest these days. There are over 160,000 of them living in the capital. It has now been several years that they have been asking to make Moscow their cultural center. The city authorities listen to them, but they do not hear. Tatar Muskovites are demanding that I say something about this at the congress. And so I speak. I hope that the comrades from the Moscow City Soviet are hearing me, and that they will think about resolving this very important issue.

There is another problem which does not have administrative and territorial boundaries. It is causing concern among all nationalities. Even though this topic has been discussed in the report to the congress and in the statements of deputies, I cannot pass up Hamlet's question: "To be or not to be?" I am not about to philosophize on the need for knowing one's native language. Do we need a natural mother or not? Is this a topic that could even be debated at all? Nor is there any need to prove the necessity of knowing Russian as the language of international communication. But how is this to be reconciled? It is not all that easy to offer recipes, but something has to be done. And it must be done soon at the statewide level. We in our republic are trying to implement some measures, but they are nothing more than a stop-gap. It is impossible to solve this problem through amateurish education efforts. Unionwide legislative acts protecting the national languages and promoting their development are needed.

Interethnic relations in our republic are not as volatile as in some regions, but this does not give us the right to relax. Every fact associated with this problem requires especial attention and study. For example, just prior to my departure for the congress one of my constituents asked me this: Why was not a single representative of the indigenous nationality elected as a deputy in any of the six election districts in the republic's capital, Kazan? It is not at all a simple question, but we deputies are obligated to find an answer. It would be nice if such questions need not be asked. I hope that we will return to the best that was proclaimed by the October Revolution, and that our unity will continue to be the main source of our power.

Last week our republic celebrated Bashkir Culture Days. To the peoples of the two large republics this event was a holiday of friendship and a concrete attempt to strengthen the sacred traditions of brotherhood. In this connection I wish to reproach the central press, radio, and television organs. They do not provide adequate attention to such events, and they do not do enough to publicize the principles of friendship with positive examples.

I understand my journalist friends. We have long been praising "paper internationalism," but times are changing, and holidays are now acquiring other significance. This should be made note of as well. There are many among us today who are angry and dissatisfied, and we talk about them a great deal. This is natural in today's conditions, but we should also not forget that anger and dissatisfaction should be not destructive but constructive.

How we love extremes! At the forums of a decade ago, speakers competed to outdo one another in praising each and every thing. Today a number of deputies are competing in who would say more that is bad and painful. Unfortunately some orators have even conspired to suggest that our value is less than what it should be. I think that in any case, if we claim objectivity, we must know how to provide balanced assessments of our actions. Both bad and good.

We need to restore the lost faith in our future, since otherwise it would be difficult for us to live a normal life. And we must live on, dear comrades! Thank you for your attention. (Applause).

A.V. Gorbunov: The floor is given to Deputy Seleznev. Deputy Kugultinov will speak next.

Tenth Session
5–6 June 1989

A.I. Seleznev, first secretary of the Kursk Oblast CPSU Committee (Lgov Territorial Election District, Kursk Oblast): Respected comrade deputies! If one watches and listens to the work of our congress attentively, one may doubtlessly assert that the congress reflects the processes of democratic renewal and of revolutionary transformation that are occurring today in our society. Numerous meetings with the electorate demonstrate that our people give the party and the Central Committee their due for shaking the society out of its apolitical, lethargic sleep, and that they support the policy of restructuring. And at the same time they demand, with full grounds, a strict accounting from party committees and specific workers for their mistakes and for retarded economic and social development, and they demand fundamental solutions that would eliminate the difficulties and problems. Our local party committees are experiencing difficult processes today. They were burdened by people with an unclean conscience who abused their official position, and who may reappear today. But the people can see that the party is undergoing self-purification, that its body is becoming healthier, and in my opinion those who are inciting groundless suspicion of party members, attaching all kinds of labels to them, are treading on dangerous ground. The accusation flung from this podium toward Central Committee Secretary Yegor Kuzmich Ligachev is also dictated by nothing more than a desire to cast a shadow upon the Politburo.

In my opinion such actions cannot be treated as anything but a desire to undermine the people's trust in party workers without analyzing who is working how. There is but one goal here, and that is to compromise someone's reputation. So it was that a deputy from our oblast, who spoke on 29 May, raised suspicions about me for some sort of intrigues in relation to the congress; to be blunt, he assumed a path of fabricating and spreading things allegedly said about me in a manner that is unacceptable in communication between people.

Accusations were voiced here against the Committee for State Security. It stands to reason that the people do not forgive, and will never forgive, those workers who were to blame for the death of people tortured and maimed not only physically but morally as well. But to say this and nothing more would mean telling only part of the truth. The whole truth is that thousands of Chekists and agents devoted to their people and to the cause of the revolution have contributed and continue to contribute their knowledge and often even their life in behalf of the people's salvation. It is owing to their efforts that many large-scale misfortunes have been averted. Could it be that anyone would really want us to forget all of this? Put your faith not in your words or the words of others, put your faith in your actions and those of others. This is what Lev Nikolayevich Tolstoy asked us to do.

There is one other item I would like to talk about. During the congress proceedings we often hear the words president and the country's parliament. Even the newly elected chairman of the new chamber, the Soviet of the Union, made constant use of the word parliament during the first session. But these words do not in any way reflect the essence of our government. If this is just a naive misconception, or just a desire to use a foreign word, then this is only half the matter, half the trouble. We are proud of the power of the soviets, born of October, we are proud of our people's deputies. (Applause).

Next, comrades, let me dwell on one of the problems raised in the report by Mikhail Sergeyevich Gorbachev, and namely the agrarian problem. I do not feel it to be an economic problem—I feel it to be a political one. The fact that an entire conglomerate of issues requiring fundamental, statewide resolution has now formed in the countryside has already been discussed. Still, there are two issues which in my opinion are central: the issue of land, and the issue of people. Concerning people, and namely the status of the modern peasantry, I would like to say the following. I completely share and support the premise in the report that implementation of the decisions of the March plenum of the CPSU Central Committee and the new agrarian policy will make it possible to go a long way in returning the peasant to his place as the master of his land, and raise the prestige of rural labor, which has always served as a moral necessity and a yardstick of the personal worth of the individual. But at the same time I am also deeply convinced that without a fundamental turn in the course of the party and state and, if you wish, of all the people, toward the needs of the countryside, without fundamentally changing investment policy, and without bringing it more in line with the production, personal, social, cultural, and spiritual needs of the rural resident, you will have to agree that we will not be able to solve the food problem.

We must implement a system of measures for radical and, by necessity, integral social reorganization of the village. I would like to focus attention on the point that this pertains chiefly to Russia. It is in Russia that rural problems have mushroomed the most acutely and insistently. Much has been said about this both prior to the congress and in the days of its work. As an illustration of this let me cite just a few data on a Russian oblast located in the highly rich lands of central Russia, which has suffered ruin not of its own doing—I am speaking of my own Kursk Oblast. In the last 20 years the rural population has decreased here by almost half, around 300 villages have ceased to exist, the countryside has aged considerably, and the average age of inhabitants has risen to the half-century mark. There are fewer employable persons in our oblast than pensioners, and the most alarming fact is that the number of children has decreased threefold. I suggest that this situation is also typical of many other Russian oblasts. Abandonment of the Russian countryside has not occurred accidentally, after all: Too much time is being taken to solve the problems associated with life support and with improvement of working conditions. Rural areas still lack consistently adequate roads, there are not enough schools and preschool institutions, and in many population centers—all of you are of course well aware of this—the most elementary things are lacking: stores, medical care, personal services. I think that such an impoverished situation is not encountered in very many republics. We have already discussed the problems of gasifying rural settlements. This is a statewide problem. And I propose that the USSR Council of Ministers be instructed to examine it and find a favorable solution to it literally in the next few years. I share the concern voiced at the congress in regard to pension support to the peasants. You see, the size of the pensions of most of them does not exceed R50. And I feel that we need to immediately repeal, as being unjust, the statute on pensions for kolkhoz farmers approved by the USSR Council of Ministers back in 1954. I propose introducing a new law on pension support for discussion at the congress as early as this year.

Here is something else I would like to talk about. In the last three decades our oblast, and the entire region of the Kursk magnetic anomaly as well, has been working to a greater extent for the whole country, leaving many of its own needs unsatisfied. The oblast's economy depends today on the widely known Mikhaylovskiy mining and concentrating combine together with its concentrating mill, an atomic power plant, and large production associations. We can and must be proud of them, but they are the ones that have attracted half a million persons to the cities, and absorbed, and continue to absorb, the best of the young rural population. This is why I would suggest that it would be suitable to temporarily slacken the pace of extensive development of mining industry and power engineering, which spend hundreds of millions of rubles yearly, and channel the released resources into social reorganization of the countryside and creation of a modern agricultural raw material storage and processing base—in short, into solving the food problem.

There is one other problem I would like to touch upon. We, the country's people's deputies, could not but be troubled by the state of our Chernozem which, according to Dokuchayev's definition, is the king of soil, and was, is and will be Russia's breadbasket. How is the country using this wealth? Let me say bluntly—far from prudently. In 60 years the thousand-year experience of careful land use and the social mechanism of its transfer from generation to generation have disappeared in many ways: In the race for further profits, the country often ignores the laws of nature and society, and neglects the principles of equivalent exchange. Let me cite just two figures as a confirmation of this. In 100 years the loss of humus in the Chernozem regions has exceeded its utilization by 20 times, and in a number of places by 50 times. In the vicinity of the Kursk magnetic anomaly, soil erosion has attained dangerous proportions. Intensive application of mineral fertilizers and chemicals has led to acidification of half the area, and has aggravated the ecological situation, spreading the negative effects to man himself as well. The question the deputies naturally ask is probably this: What is the solution? There is an answer. It can be found in cooperation between scientists and producers. We need to seriously get involved with land improvement. But let me emphasize, not the kind which results in the interment of material and financial resources, but the kind which does in fact improve the land. For the moment, things are not at all progressing as they would under good government.

Judge for yourselves. The integrated program for raising soil fertility in the period to the year 2000 calls for investing almost R200 billion into irrigation and drainage, while 14 times less is to be invested into forest land improvement, hydraulic engineering, and erosion control measures. I am convinced that this conception of managing the economy is ecologically damaging and ineffective, and I suggest that it be fundamentally reexamined. Today, now that the problem of land use has reared up to its full height, it appears suitable to prepare and adopt a corresponding land law, and to encourage the country's best forces to develop regional scientific farming conceptions which would maximally account for natural, economic, and social conditions and for the new forms of management. Many problems, including the most acute problems of economic use of the land itself, must be solved within the framework of this conception.

As we solve the problems of the present, of today, I propose that we make it a requirement that peasant problems must be worked out into the deep future. In particular it seems that we need to prepare various models of the rural settlement of the 21st century, ones which we can use as the basis for planning new production relations, a new management structure, and a new way of life; models which could be utilized with regard for the features and traditions of a specific locale.

Finally, comrades, many of the problems of agricultural development are being solved more poorly in the Russian Federation than in other union republics. I suggest that the reason for this, among others, is that the existing system of state and economic control is not in keeping with its scale and its multifacetedness; it cannot fully account for and encompass all features of this territory. Therefore I feel it suitable to ask the Central Committee and the Supreme Soviet to think up a system of state and economic control of Russia. In conclusion I would like to say that the deputies from Kursk Oblast, who express the mood of their constituents, were deeply moved by the concern for the state of affairs in the country expressed in Mikhail Sergeyevich Gorbachev's report, and that they support his constructive proposals. Thank you for your attention. (Applause).

A.V. Gorbunov: Comrade deputies! Before the recess, the presidium offers the following draft statement. Permit me to read this statement.

Statement on events in China. Dramatic events have occurred in neighboring China. The Soviet people were promptly and extensively informed about them. The situation has become especially acute in recent days. According to reports from Chinese mass media, clashes

Tenth Session
5–6 June 1989

have occurred in China's capital, Beijing, between participants of the mass demonstrations of young people and troops; weapons have been fired, and human lives have been lost. This is not the time for ill-conceived, hasty conclusions and statements. No matter how high emotions might sometimes rise, it is important to patiently seek adequate solutions which would be in keeping with the goals of consolidating society. Of course, the events that have now unfolded in China are an internal matter of the country. Any attempts at outside pressure would be impertinent here. Such attempts would only inflame passions, and they will in no way help to stabilize the situation. We hope that wisdom, common sense, and a carefully weighed approach will prevail, and that a solution worthy of the great Chinese people will be found in the current situation. We sincerely wish that the friendly Chinese people will turn this tragic page of their history over as quickly as possible and move forward on the road of economic and political transformations, on the road of building a strong, peace-loving, free socialist China, a great country enjoying the respect and sympathy of its neighbors, and of all mankind.

What sort of objections or proposals do you have in this connection, comrades? There is a motion to adopt this statement in the name of the congress. Are there remarks of an editorial nature, are there any wishes?

If there are no other wishes or remarks, allow me to poll the assembly on the text of the statement. Please raise your certificates. Thank you. Who is against? One. Who abstains? An overwhelming minority. Thus the congress adopts this statement. An overwhelming minority abstained. There will now be a 30 minute recess.

A.V. Gorbunov: Respected comrade deputies! We continue the work of the congress. The floor is given to Deputy Kugultinov. Deputy Lizichev will speak next.

D.N. Kugultinov, chairman of the board of the Kalmyk ASSR Writers Union, Elista (Iki-Burulskiy National-Territorial Election District, Kalmyk ASSR): Dear comrades! Although Friedrich Engels referred to the event respectfully—"His Majesty," nonetheless it was a wonderful event. I am a Kalmyk. Today is 6 June 1989. The entire country and the entire world are celebrating the 190th anniversary of the birth of Aleksandr Sergeyevich Pushkin. I am the one to whom he once referred:

"Word of me will spread over all of Russia the Great, and my name will be spoken in every language existing within it, the proud grandson of the Slavs, the Finn, the still wild Tungus and the friend of the steppes the Kalmyk." (Applause).

What is a genius? God, a prophet, a seer? But how could he predict that on the day of the 190th anniversary of his birth, at the first Congress of People's Deputies of a great power, I, a Kalmyk, would be greeting him and all who are—I am convinced of this—heirs of his soul! (Applause).

When Pushkin said "and the friend of the steppes the Kalmyk," he selected the names of peoples not because he needed a rhyme for the word "language." Finding a rhyme for any word was no difficulty for Pushkin. But Pushkin named these minorities, equating them with all others. And if Pushkin were sitting in the presidium of our congress, I would dare to say that he would have given the floor first not to a representative of the great Russian people, because the great Russian people do not need the kind of assistance needed by, let us say, a Nivkh, a Yukaghir, or a Kalmyk—he would have summoned Rytkheu or some other poet from the minorities to the podium.

Pushkin was wonderful. He was the concentrtion of everything noble about the great Russian people, who created their state initially as a multinational state, and the experience of interethnic relations accumulated by Russia—unique experience found nowhere else, among no other people or power in the world—was unfortunately cancelled by the people's commissar of nationalities, by the "great" expert on "national questions," by the "father of the peoples" Stalin. Great is the experience of Russia, which endured great wars with the assistance of all peoples, and was even victorious over Charles: In 1709, Kalmyks fighting together with Cossacks came very close to taking Mazepa and Charles XII prisoner, and in 1812 Kalmyk cavalry and a camel regiment entered Paris.... Bashkirs, Circassians and all peoples were one in the fatherland, and to all of them, Russia was both a fatherland and a mother. But how is it that today we are speaking from this podium about real misfortunes, and not fabricated ones? My heart overflows, and my soul is pained when we speak about Nagorno-Karabakh, when we speak about Azerbaijanis, when we speak about Turks. My soul is pained, and I do not know how, when and at what time all of this came to be so.

Dear comrades, this is, after all, the ultimate question. I know that these questions have spilled out like from an erupting abscess, precisely right now, in our days—the days of the great congress, a truly historical congress. I have been thinking these past few days that yes, the congress, the first Congress of People's Deputies, will go down in history. I have even sensed the presence of great figures in history. To my mind, Peter I is seated somewhere here. He is watching with satisfaction and saying: "Well done, my descendants. You are speaking as I would have wished—not as if quoting from books, and with everyone able to see who's who." On the right I see Vladimir Ilich Lenin on the steps with his notebook. He is listening to us with alarm and sorrow, and he is saying: "How can there be no soap? How can there be no matches? How many years have passed?" He is told: "It's now 1989." And Lenin thinks: "What has happened, why is this so?—This is not what I taught them. How has it happened?" And it seems to me that he must be horrified by the idea that he had made a mistake. I heard about Lenin's mistake when I was 23—at that young age when the words "Lenin" and "mistake," or "Stalin" and "bad" would leave people in a mystical horror. But then

STENOGRAPHIC RECORD

Tenth Session

5–6 June 1989

in jail cells, on journeys, and in camps I heard about it again and again from old Leninist Bolsheviks. I realized that yes, Lenin had made a mistake, and his mistake was the following. I thought this when I was sitting in this auditorium on the first 2 or 3 days before the election of the chairman of the Supreme Soviet. His mistake, the old Bolsheviks told me, was that Lenin, working in the Council of People's Commissars, left everything else to Stalin, and in the space of 2-3 years Stalin concentrated power within his own hands to such an extent that even Lenin's note about the lover of hot dishes and the need to transfer him was not acted on at the well-known congress. And it was the Stalin years that prevailed in our country and led to all the problems that we now cannot resolve. That was the mistake. I am afraid now—in our transitional period when we are deciding what our state will be like—that we may be seduced by the beauties of democracy and suddenly distracted by highfalutin words, and say: "Comrade Gorbachev, deal with the soviets! Comrade (I don't know who), deal with the party!" And then something might suddenly happen again.

I, who survived the Great Patriotic War, I, who survived the prisons and the camps, I, a graying Kalmyk, whose people have been decimated, have absolutely no intention of flattering Mikhail Sergeyevich Gorbachev here. Actually, however, no matter how bitter it might be for us, no matter how shameful it might be for us, another leader such as he is not to be found today in either our country or even the entire world. And here is why. When the results of the election were announced, when 96 percent of the votes went to Mikhail Sergeyevich Gorbachev, to be honest I had an urge to embrace and kiss each one of you, to ask forgiveness in that perhaps I had thought a little too badly of you. As it turns out, 96 percent are persons of like mind with me, my brothers. 96 percent of our congress are motivated by a single goal, by a single great objective: to make our country wealthy, to make our people fortunate. Probably everyone here experienced this feeling when the election results were announced. Ninety-six percent: This represents hundreds upon hundreds of thousands of voters behind each one of us. This means that all of our Soviet people are for restructuring.

Dear comrades! I have spoken about my people, who have been resurrected, and the Kalmyk ASSR has been resurrected, but I would like to talk here about other peoples that have not yet come back. I left on my seat a folder full of telegrams from the Crimean Tatars, from Germans from the Volga Republic, from Turks who were deported from the southern borders of Georgia, and from many peoples who tearfully turn to each of us, each deputy, to ensure that we are not complacent and that when we talk about the equality of all the peoples and about the brotherhood of all the peoples we also remember those who are not represented at this congress—those peoples whose lands have not been returned, those peoples whom Stalin condemned to long years of sorrow and long years of second-class citizen status. There must be no status in the Land of the Soviets—a socialist country, a communist country—whereby people are classed as the wrong sort just because of the shape of their eyes or the color of their hair. This should not happen! And I want to propose that we should do something about it at this very congress. We should adopt a law restoring the Crimea's autonomy. We should adopt a law restoring the Volga German Republic. We should adopt a law which would give each of them wings, and on these wings they would invisibly attend the congress tomorrow and applaud each of us, saying: "Yes, every deputy has a heart and understands the sorrow and truth of other people." (Applause).

I would like to submit a proposal that at this congress we adopt a law under which not a single people in our country would ever be subjected to such actions as they had been subjected to under Stalin. We need to adopt a law on the rights of peoples. I do not know how the lawyers will word it, but our conscience will formulate these laws, and make our country one of truly exemplary friendship among all peoples!

Now a few words about the Kalmyk ASSR. Pushkin said so many things so well. We are fortunate, remember Pushkin: "Farewell, my gentle Kalmyk girl." Do you remember? (A stirring in the audience).

"To the ill luck of my adventures, it was the habit of good behavior that kept me from pursuing your kibitka over the steppes...."

And this gentle Kalmyk girl, who now lies suffering from AIDS with her child on Sokolina Hill, telephoned me. Yesterday our entire delegation visited this sole hospital in Moscow in which AIDS is treated. And we were astounded by the squalor of this hospital. This is a shopworn, second-rate hospital, and it is supposed to carry on the fight against the plague of mankind—AIDS. This is terrible. I recently returned from the United States of America. I saw how AIDS is being fought there, and I would like to turn all of your attention to this. Of course, I do understand: We have a time limit, but when I speak about AIDS in children, about mothers suffering from AIDS, and deputies shout "Enough," somehow I begin to feel uncomfortable. Thank you. (Applause).

A.V. Gorbunov: The floor is given to Deputy Aleksey Dmitriyevich Lizichev. Comrade Alekseyev will speak next.

A.D. Lizichev, Army general, chief of the Main Political Directorate of the Soviet Army and Navy, Moscow (from the CPSU): Respected comrade chairman! Respected comrade people's deputies! The Armed Forces are called upon to maintain strategic stability in the world and to guarantee the security of the Soviet State and its allies against aggression. This is the fourth year that I am a member of the country's Defense Council, and I am able to report to the people's deputies that in all of these years the Defense Council has been

Tenth Session

5–6 June 1989

comprehensively, deeply, and competently examining the basic problems of the country's defense and development of the military with the participation of prominent specialists, scientists, and designers, and the decisions that have been adopted in regard to restructuring the Armed Forces are both weighted and far-reaching.

Judge for yourselves: In these years we have developed and adopted a new defense doctrine, the principle of reasonable sufficiency for defense was adopted and has begun to operate, over 1,200 intermediate- and shorter-range missiles have been destroyed, the Armed Forces are being reduced, and withdrawal of our troops from friendly countries is beginning. Vienna talks on conventional arms reduction are proceeding, and the quantitative composition of the Army and Navy, the number of servicemen in the armed services, and the country's military budget have been made public. Observers and inspection groups come to our country for major military exercises, and we go to theirs.

Today this is a reality, this is the result of a new way of political thinking in defense policy, and of firm day-to-day leadership of the Armed Forces on the part of our party, its Central Committee, and its Politburo. In the Armed Forces themselves, restructuring is being staked primarily on the qualitative parameters of their development, on the basis of a weighted assessment of the military-political situation, and the country's real possibilities.

Measures are being implemented to raise combat readiness, the troops and fleets are being equipped with modern armaments, operational art and tactics are being adjusted appropriately, and operational, combat, and political training are improving. A solid legal foundation is being laid beneath all military restructuring work. I am certain that the recently created Committee for Defense and Security Questions and development and adoption of the USSR Law on Defense will strengthen the legal basis of restructuring of our Armed Forces even more.

The party principles concerned with the style and methods of work of personnel, and of their selection and placement are being followed firmly. The permanent staff of the central apparatus of the Ministry of Defense and the absolute majority of commanders in chief and commanders have grown younger and been turned over by half. Almost 1,400 general positions and 11,000 colonel positions have been abolished. These processes have not been painless and easy. They have affected the destinies of people. But we undertook them anyway, and now we can see that we had made the right choice.

The Armed Forces are also actively participating today in the country's economic life. In particular, the volume of our capital construction is almost R4 billion. Our subsidiary farms and military state farms [sovkhozes] supply meat and vegetables to all personnel for 3 months out of the year. We are conducting extensive road building projects through our own efforts, employing more than 20 formations in the Russian Non-Chernozem Zone. The railroad troops are carrying out great national economic tasks. Each year the Army and Navy participate in the harvest. Our military builders carry out tasks in behalf of over 10 union ministries, often in the harshest and, at times, extreme conditions.

A tendency for party work to become more active and for improvement of the rule of law and discipline has been noted. Discipline has grown stricter. In the last 3 years the crime rate has been reduced by more than a third. We are eradicating dedovshchina [bullying], we have taken a strong stand against it, and the procuracy conducts investigations on every incident. The number of persons sentenced by the courts of military tribunals has decreased by over 50 percent. However, the fundamental improvement of discipline required today from us by the party Central Committee and restructuring has not yet been achieved. And public criticism of us in this matter is entirely right.

On one hand comprehensive analysis of the demographic situation in the country shows that, comrades, we have practically no possibilities for selecting conscripts today. We thought that such a possibility might arise in connection with the reduction of forces, but there came a need to postpone call-up of students. This was doubtlessly the right decision. And so we are once again calling up sizable numbers of young people who already have police records, who suffer both physical and moral flaws, and who have become acquainted with both drugs and alcohol, chiefly in the construction troops. But these are, after all, our fellow countrymen. Therefore as they say in our Army, we will welcome them into our unified combat formation. We concurrently ask the ministries and departments possessing facilities at which railroad and especially construction troops are working to treat them not as stepchildren but rather to display real concern for their personal lives and labor organization.

On the other hand, comrades, the labor of soldiers and officers is generally becoming increasingly more stressful mentally and difficult both psychologically and physically, in view of the fact that we are being armed with new technology characterized by complex electronic systems, radio and video technology, and new control and monitoring systems. In addition we must keep in mind that over two-thirds of our soldiers are serving along the entire perimeter of our country and beyond its borders, often in still-unpopulated places, and personnel of forces serving combat duty must spend days at missile and radar consoles and at the controls of airplanes, helicopters, and ships. And not all are always able to withstand the nervous and physical load of such service.

But given all of the shortcomings we have in the Armed Forces, as the chief of the Main Political Directorate I can report to the congress with full justification that the Armed Forces are living together with the people, they are living the life of our people. They fully support the

STENOGRAPHIC RECORD

party's course toward restructuring, and the bulk of the privates, seamen, and officers are conscientiously fulfilling their duty. Hundreds of thousands of them fought in Afghanistan, no one "celebrated the coward," no one evaded orders, they all served conscientiously, and they returned from there patriots of the motherland, without griping over the shortcomings, but as warriors of justice, as warriors of restructuring. And the officers did not hide behind the backs of their soldiers: One out of every five killed and one out of every six wounded there were officers. And no one has the right to soil their military biography with dark words. (Applause).

Comrades! I think that Ukrainian and Belorussian deputies have good memories of the soldiers who helped to clean up after the accident at the Chernobyl Nuclear Power Plant. These soldiers are remembered well by the citizens of Sverdlovsk and Gorkiy, and now of the Bashkir ASSR in connection with disaster control following the railroad explosions. The Armenian and Tajik peoples remember the actions of the soldiers in those grave hours and days of the earthquakes and recovery from them.

Yes, as with any school, the Army has its disobedient pupils, and it has not only inexperienced but also negligent teachers. The flight of that airplane to Moscow, the accident in the Navy, the incidents in the Air Force, and the improper relations, especially in construction units, have not done anything to increase our authority. This is why the increase in discipline is not very large either. But I would like to assure you that the course toward reinforcement of combat readiness and discipline, reinforcement of one-man command, and improvement of political education work is a sure course, and it will be followed firmly.

Comrades, we accept positive criticism, and we will make the proper conclusions from it, we will correct the state of affairs. But I cannot help voicing certain concerns in connection with the fact that agitators have appeared in a number of our country's regions who see only the bad, who are striving to compromise the Army and its veterans, and undermine the authority of the Armed Forces among the people. Prophets envisioning a time when no army would be needed, and a transition to its manning on the basis of mercenary principles, have appeared, and demands for tearing the Armed Forces apart and dragging off the separate pieces to nationally defined lairs, giving no thought to the consequences of such reasoning, have even been voiced. In some places it goes as far as gross violation of the law in relation to officers and their families. Privates, seamen, and officers are often referred to as invaders, and told to go home. Housing is not allocated to them, and obstacles are created in passport matters, in gaining treatment in local hospitals, and in finding work or schools for family members. When the rising cost of living is compounded by moral pressures and insults, comrades, it is difficult to serve. And the misfortune is that a mature party assessment is not always made locally of such insinuations, slander, and insults.

All of us, including the people in the military, are troubled by the events in Tbilisi. The congress has created an authoritative commission, we have furnished it with all materials available to us, and we are ready to answer any questions. Let's wait for the results of its works, rather than indiscriminately laying all of the blame entirely on the Army, as some have been trying to do. Our main task is to teach the troops that which they would need in war. And we fully support the premise stated here by Mikhail Sergeyevich Gorbachev that the Army must do its work. (Applause).

What has always determined the goal of the work of military people has been not personal profit but the highest responsibility for the fate of the fatherland and for its security. This position will continue to be the basis of all of our educational and party-political work. We feel that our Army must be a cadre army, nurtured in the spirit of patriotism, the friendship of peoples of the USSR and socialist internationalism, in the spirit of glorious combat traditions, and manned on the basis of universal compulsory military service and extraterritorial service. Being a socialist Army, it is closely associated with the people, and it is devoted to the cause of the party, the cause of restructuring. We are in favor of the unity of the country, we are in favor of the unity of the Army, of consolidation of Soviet socialist society. (Applause).

Dear comrades! Life shows that our theoretical front has fallen seriously behind today from the rate of politization of society. Our social scientists are unable to keep up with the pace of change both in our country and among our friends and allies. Sometimes the opinion that everything in our country is bad surfaces in the social consciousness, and especially among the young. And as we know, creative power and patriotism do not do especially well on such a substrate.

Attempts to erode the Marxist-Leninist teaching on war and the Army and the Leninist position on the role of the Armed Forces in defense of the socialist fatherland have grown more frequent. The stakes are too high to hasten to accept such conclusions.

Comrades! The Army has now begun undergoing reduction. Out of 500,000, almost 150,000 are officers and shore-based and seagoing warrant officers. Together with the children and women, this is over half a million persons. To them, the reduction process is far from easy, and sometimes it is even painful. People have to be resettled, provided employment and housing, and so on. The government has adopted the appropriate decisions. We would ask the people's deputies to always treat the problems of providing housing and employment to servicemen discharged into the reserves as objects of your concern, and to resolve their destinies on the basis of the principles of social justice. In the way, for example, that the problems of providing assistance to internationalist soldiers and disabled war veterans are treated in the Ukraine, in Belorussia, and in Azerbaijan.

Tenth Session

5–6 June 1989

So much for those being discharged. But those who are remaining in the service have many problems as well. Over a hundred thousand officers have not yet found a home for themselves. Many wives of officers and of shore-based and seagoing warrant officers are unable to find jobs. There is an acute lack of preschool institutions. Many people's deputies have included solution of these problems on their agenda. Thank you! On our part, comrades, let me say that the leadership of the Ministry of Defense and the Main Political Directorate, our commanders and the more than million-strong party organization of the Army and Navy will carry out all of the tasks posed to them by our congress, and do everything to make our Army always modern, dependable, and strong.

Thank you. (Applause).

A.V. Gorbunov: The floor is given to Deputy Alekseyev. Deputy Rasputin will speak next.

S.S. Alekseyev, corresponding member of the USSR Academy of Sciences, director of the Institute of Philosophy and Law of the Ural Department of the USSR Academy of Sciences, Sverdlovsk (from the USSR Academy of Sciences): Respected comrade chairman! Respected comrade deputies! Permit me to share with you some of my ideas on the main thing we are called upon to consider—legislation.

My first idea is a decisive one—it concerns the strategy of legislation. So that our legislation would follow a scientifically thought-out, clear, and tested line. The task we face, after all, is of the greatest proportions. We must create a progressive, perfected, top-class legal system, one which would be in keeping with the standards of a legal state. How do we begin?

There are already over 40 bills in the portfolio of the Supreme Soviet. And we in our promises, in our platforms, certainly vowed to do no less. In our meetings we have heard 10-15 proposals for new laws. How do we deal with this mountain of proposals? What do we do, submit them all for examination together? Or create the kind of queue we love so much? Or perhaps we could consider some great act, an act of the greatest, global significance? If I may be excused for saying so, our economic reform would not have gotten into the situation it now is, had we worked out its formula from the very beginning with clarity of general design. It is only now that we're beginning to comprehend that this formula is one of a transition from bureaucratic management to a socialistically variegated commodity-market economy.

For this, we need a tested legislative policy, we need a clear, strict legislative strategy. All laws are important, and of course, each speaker will say that his law must be placed first. But I think that we need to soberly and objectively determine the priorities.

On one hand I would point out three such priorities—this is the most important thing I would like to talk about. The first priority may be labeled "urgent" and "immediate"—these are legislative measures which must be adopted without delay in the next session of the Supreme Soviet. They include the status of the deputy, the standing order, and mandatorily the referendum. And perhaps a few other laws. I feel that we could adopt a strike law in order to lay a normative foundation beneath this matter, and a law on public associations; we could repeal or update those ukases and those normative acts which have not enjoyed the support of our public, of our people.

The second priority, labeled "of highest importance," has to do with the preparation of the constitution. I paused before that word in order to turn your attention to the fact that I did not say a new constitution. I feel that all four preceding constitutions—four of them!—were not an adornment to our society. These were basically political declarations. Such documents were doubtlessly necessary in 1918 and 1924, when our state was being constituted. But the constitutions of 1936 and 1977.... Their declarative nature had already become in many ways a farce, and, if you excuse my saying so, to some degree a lie.

I think that we must create our first real legal constitution, one which documents, in tight, clear, and perhaps aphoristic language, the existence of our state as a free state, a constitution which would document the free, secure existence of each individual.

It seems to me that future measures aimed at deepening our political reform must be implemented within the context of preparing this constitution. So that we are not jumping all over the place, addressing first one, and then another issue, losing sight of what is most important—the core of our constitutional development.

The third priority would be labeled "a most insistent problem." I feel that after we adopt the immediate legislative measures and make the decision to prepare a constitution, we should turn all of our effort to drafting laws on our economic system with the goal of preparing a package of acts, or a complex of acts, a system of acts in order to transform our economy into an effective, well-running one. Fantastic though this might sound, we could do this in the immediate future, by the first of January of next year.

I say in the immediate future, within half a year, within a few months, because time will not wait. We will be unable to solve a single problem—neither food, nor pension support, nor library affairs, nothing, unless we possess an effective, well-running national economic mechanism. We will continue to concern ourselves with distribution of the products of the money printing press. What we need to adopt in this case is precisely a complex of laws, because experience shows that a bureaucratic administrative system adapts very quickly and agilely to

STENOGRAPHIC RECORD

isolated laws. We must make a single legislative attack, publish a system of laws, change property relations, and introduce variegated relations in order to abruptly alter the situation in our national economy. Do we have the substrate for such laws? Yes, we do.

I think that of course it would be better to adopt one law—on the socialist enterprise. But in the immediate future we could for the moment introduce amendments into two laws—the Law on the State Enterprise and the Law on Cooperation.

Following this is another very important law (I will name seven laws in all), number three. This is the Law on Leasing. It is my deep conviction (on this point I am 100 percent in agreement with Bunich, we are of like mind) that there is no other means of surmounting the main obstacle to establishing a commodity-market economy other than that of establishing leasing, real leasing relations.

Incidentally, certain normative acts have already been adopted. We somehow became stuck on the ukases of 8 April, and it was on 7 April that normative acts on leasing were adopted. It was at that time that I conducted a little survey of my colleagues and friends, asking them what it contained that was new. And you know, in my opinion it documents the most serious revolutionary measures! It states that every labor collective may be transformed into an organization of leaseholders. And we in the Urals want to implement this right away, initiate a mass movement. The products of such a leaseholders' organization become its own property as soon as it is able to increase its collective property. I know of no more abrupt, more serious revolutionary measure in economics. Months have passed, but we have not taken a single step in order to implement these great revolutionary measures.

Next follows the Law on Property. All types and forms of property ownership except that associated with exploitation of one man by another must be documented. A Law on Management. The substrate for this one exists as well. The objective would be to establish a permissive management apparatus doing strictly defined work.

A Law on the Market. Even if it is a minor law, it will become the basis for wholesale trade. And finally, that which Leninist cost accounting began in the early 1920s—a unified tax system—is important. Because that which presently exists—the taxes, the collections, the standards and other withdrawals—in the presence of such a system, no cost accounting, commodity-market, and variegated economy is fundamentally possible.

To this let me add the following. It is my deep conviction that implementation of these laws would be the main blow against the system of dictatorial administration, which presides over this bureaucratic state property.

We have become much obsessed by the problems of power, we keep working around these problems, we digress, and our passions swell. But what we need to do is resolve the issue fundamentally; after that, in my opinion, the economic problem would be fundamentally solved. Such is the nature of the strategic problem.... (Applause).

Literally just a few words about reorganizing legislation. Though I understand the national and psychological underpinnings of the proposal for the Congress of People's Deputies to enact all laws, I am somewhat dismayed by it. You must excuse me, but I found the suggestion appalling: If we make it so that the Congress of People's Deputies would enact laws, the whole idea of a legislative system would collapse. We would end up rubber-stamping laws, or bogging down in disputes over a particular term or some particular issue. And in the meantime the departments would go on publishing normative acts. We would wind up back where we started. You see, the whole idea of a permanent—excuse my choice of word—parliament, and of our permanent Supreme Soviet is that their would be a first reading, there would be discussion in committees, there would be alternatives, there would be a second reading, and then mandatory item-by-item passage of the bill. That is the way to get quality laws. And only a permanently working organ that commits all of its energy, rather than passing bills on the fly, would be capable of accomplishing this. I feel that clarity needs to be introduced into this matter.

And now the definite finale. Comrades! We have very many holidays. On some Sundays we celebrate two or three holidays together. There is a holiday for chemists, and there is one for the land improvers.... But we do not have a holiday of democracy and law. Could we perhaps make the twenty-fifth of May the holiday of democracy and law? The twenty-fifth—a noteworthy revolutionary date. Thank you. (Applause).

A.V. Gorbunov: The floor is given to Valentin Grigoryevich Rasputin, with Deputy Yarovoy speaking next.

V.G. Rasputin, writer, secretary of the board of the USSR Writers Union, Irkutsk (from the USSR Writers Union): Esteemed comrade deputies! We have unwittingly revealed the contrast between us—between those who came through competitive, multicandidate campaigns, and those who were returned by social organizations. I have repeatedly heard it said over the past few days that the former are the people's choice, while the latter have been planted to impede the activeness of restructuring. I, too, think that the Law on Elections is imperfect and should eventually be altered to favor an okrug system only. Is it normal for some people to vote twice, three times, or even four times: in their own okrug, somewhere at the Cultural Foundation, at the Writers Union, and then again at the Academy of Sciences? Naturally, this should not be the case. (Applause). However, the further our discussions go, the more I am convinced that representatives from social

Tenth Session
5–6 June 1989

organizations have been needed at the initial stage of our democratic elections. They have been needed for the sake of pluralism, which we have been discussing a great deal as a condition of democratic existence, because restructuring has now entered a stage of social development and reached a high point inhabited by hawks who are trying to monopolize it. And anyone who disagrees with them is called an enemy of restructuring.

The expression most commonly used at the congress has been "antirestructuring forces." We have heard that if restructuring is a revolution there is bound to be a counterrevolution, too. The discussion about counterrevolution, as you yourselves understand, is a special one without any pluralism. When the hawks come to power they will try to set up a state system for suppressing counterrevolution, and now on the road to power a system of social suppression is being introduced—and quite successfully at that.

It is not a question of the differences which inevitably appear in the development process and which can be narrowed or removed as development proceeds. It is a question of something much greater: the fate of restructuring and democracy. I was pleased to hear Olzhas Suleymenov's idea: If you always row a boat on the left you invariably move to the right. That is not just an image but a law of action for any dynamic [povorotnyy] mechanism, including a social mechanism. The ancient Greek philosopher Plato had something marvelous to say about this. I quote: "Tyranny emerges, of course, from no system other than democracy. In other words, extreme freedom leads to supreme and brutal slavery." So in order to prevent this and ensure that democracy is established in our country once and for all, there is nothing reprehensible about society's needing to restrain the "madness of the brave." Singing the praises of this madness has led in the past to tragic consequences. Now it may propel us from the brink of one abyss to another. So we should treat antirestructuring forces more cautiously. By all logic, you, above all, should be included in that category.

Pluralism is possible as an expression of the variety and diversity of public and political opinions. We have imposed a pluralism of morality upon the country. This is more dangerous than any bomb. The society either supports morality, or it does not support it. There can be no third alternative. The timid voices that have been raised here concerning the primary significance of culture and spirituality in any civilized country have in my opinion fallen on deaf ears. We are more interested in various legislative chicanery. God save me from wise amendments to the constitution and the laws. I would only be amazed if a new constitution following the Stalin and Brezhnev constitutions would be a Yevtushenko constitution. (Applause). I repeat, I am not against any reasonable amendments.... That is precisely what we have gathered together for. Only they have not yet been in the name of the spirit, the worth, and the cultural and moral countenance of the people. Bread and entertainment—that's what they've now quietly written on the banners of restructuring.

Of entertainment we have already had plenty, and entertainment of the most doubtful characteristics at that. We are observing almost open propaganda of sex, violence, and liberation from all moral norms. This is a time of tragedies which for some reason are following one after the other. But have you noticed one thing that happens every time? Just as the voice of the announcer fades away after reporting human misfortunes and sacrifices, the television screen becomes filled with a cacophony of frenzied music. But it's all the same to us, we are free of morality and of sympathy. Where does it go from here? A children's sex encyclopedia containing pictures which would make even an adult uncomfortable is being printed in a succession of issues of the weekly SEMYA, an organ of the Lenin Children's Fund. The fund chairman and the journal editor probably see such education as part of their mission of saving deprived children. "There is no limit to evil," was what they said long ago, and this truth is being confirmed, it is being confirmed over and over again. I don't know how the Georgian delegation feels, but I found it uncomfortable, and I felt it to be a sacrilege when bathing beauties participating in one of our beauty contests froze coquettishly in a minute of silence in memory of victims of the April events. Doesn't such a circus insult your national sentiments?

When it comes to entertainment, as you can see, everything is in order. But if we add to this the bread, kneaded not out of sweat and morality, but acquired in a full assortment in a sale of national wealth, a repetition of the fate of the Roman Empire would not be far behind. You might recall here that someone had severely chastised Comrade Lukyanov for the rise in crime. The causes are many, what can we say? But one of the main ones, and perhaps the most important one, is the moral permissiveness and lustfulness, the unscrupulousness and sensationalism of the mass media, especially of youth publications and programs. (Applause). All of this has engulfed books, movies, and the theater in a muddy flow, and is feeding an entertainment industry parasitizing upon human flaws. Our young people perished senselessly in Afghanistan, and they are being maimed just as senselessly in the undeclared war against morality. Appeals to better behavior are insufficient in such cases: We need a law which would secure and protect morality, and prohibit the propaganda of evil, violence, and flaws. There will come a time when we will regret ignoring social psychology, a science of such importance in this time of change. A knowledge of this science, which makes it possible to account for the mood of the people, is capable of producing the most unexpected and surprising results.

In addition to healthy activity, our society has recently been experiencing activity from which Soviet patriotic content is being leached out and which is being directed

Tenth Session

5–6 June 1989

into the channel of nihilism and arrogant claims. The unjust, as we know, is always more active and more organized. During the election campaign certain candidates captured the mood of certain groups with the sensitivity of a barometer. As soon as one of them would display his party card, his popularity would immediately rise as if on wings. (Applause). I am not a member of the party, and I have deliberately avoided joining it, observing how many self-interested people of various sorts are fighting to get in. It used to be profitable to be in the party. This is why it has lost its authority. It is now unprofitable to be in the party, and even dangerous at that. And abandoning it at such a moment is not at all an act of courage, as it is being portrayed to the uninformed: It is just as calculating an act as the one which had earlier opened the door into the party. (Applause). This would have been courageous 10, or even 5 years ago, only don't you think that you are jumping ship a little too early, are you not being led down the garden path by the feelings of those who believe the ship to be doomed? (Applause). There was a time when lawyers explained to us such subtleties of their subject and demonstrated such expert knowledge of the law that it brought joy to our hearts. Such specialists do exist, and we are not far away from a legal state, but what can be said, comrade lawyers, in a situation far from subtlety, in which a colleague of yours wishing to be elected a deputy resorts to sensationalism, tying in a name from the highest echelon of power with criminality? Does the secrecy of investigation no longer exist, has presumption of innocence, or whatever it is you call it, been already repealed? (Applause).

In the nonlegal state in which we had existed for so long, a general and a member of the Politburo could feel himself to be safe, but in the legal state into which you are leading us, judging from everything, neither people in high places nor the simplest individual will be free of either physical or moral destruction the moment he offers a differing opinion or does something not to the liking of another. They will not be free of slander and of the machine of public dishonor, which are in no way better than the machine of drawing and quartering and which, it seems, have already been placed into motion. (Applause). And does it matter at all what the condemned perishes from—from state terror, or from the terror of the environment in a state in which written laws begin to be observed in formal terms only?

Unfortunately, Mikhail Sergeyevich, you did not offer any answer to Deputy Roy Medvedev, who suggested that every time you leave Moscow, and your absence coincides with the absence of Aleksandr Nikolayevich Yakovlev, a situation close to a revolution arises. I would like to ask you in this connection: Is this so? And did the danger of a revolution arise once again during your visit to China, where you went together with Aleksandr Nikolayevich? If such a malefactor exists in the Politburo, why is the Politburo tolerating him? And if Deputy Medvedev's accusations are groundless, why do you not say so? Is it not evident that in the struggle for power, which is no secret to anyone here, there is a prime target of elimination, against which a lengthy organized campaign has been waged? There is no need to remind you who will be next. (Applause). Alas, respected comrade deputies, all of this has already happened before.

There is all too much in the atmosphere of our congress that is recognizable. We now have our own Kerenskyites—Milyukov, Guchkov, Chkheidze, and I hope that the Georgian delegation will not associate that Georgian name with itself. Others will become visible in time as well. Sometimes we hear appeals for a State Duma, the same old dances with procedural matters which interrupt discussion of important affairs, the same old desire to impose one's own position on others, the same old passion for strong language. You might remember that at first they accused the war minister of betraying the state, and when this came to naught, they accused the empress of the same thing, and the rest was history. Let me repeat here some famous words spoken by another, slightly edited: "You, sirs, need great upheavals—we need a great country." (Applause).

About the country. Never since the war had its power been subjected to such trials and upheavals as today. We Russians are respectful and understanding of the national sentiments and problems of all peoples and nationalities of our country without exception. But we also want to be understood. The chauvinism and blind pride of Russians are but fabrications of those who are playing upon your national sentiments, respected brothers. And I would have to say that they are playing with them very competently. Russophobia has spread into the Baltic countries and Georgia, and it is penetrating into other republics, less into some and more into others, but noticeably almost everywhere. Anti-Soviet slogans are being combined with anti-Russian ones. Emissaries from Lithuania and Estonia are carrying them to Georgia, creating a united front. From there, local agitators are being sent to Armenia and Azerbaijan. This is not a struggle against the bureaucratic mechanism, it is something else. The activities of the Baltic deputies, who are attempting to introduce, by parliamentary means, amendments to the constitution which would allow them to part from this country, are readily noticeable here at the congress. It is not for me to give advice in such cases. You will decide your own fate, naturally in accordance with the law and your conscience. But in regard to the Russian habit of coming to the rescue, my thoughts are these: Would it perhaps be better for Russia to leave the union (Applause), considering that you blame it for all of your misfortunes, and considering that its weak development and awkwardness are what are burdening your progressive aspirations? Perhaps that would be better? This incidentally would also help us solve many of our own problems, both present and future. (Applause). We still have a few natural and human resources left, our power has not yet withered away. We could then utter the word "Russian" and talk about national self-consciousness without the fear of being labeled nationalistic. We could then counter the mass spiritual degeneration of the young that we see before us. And, finally, we could

Tenth Session
5–6 June 1989

create our own Academy of Sciences, one which would favor Russian interests and deal with the problems of morality. We would be able to gather the people together into a unified spiritual body.

Believe me when I say that we are tired of being the scapegoats, and of enduring the treachery and the slurs. We are told that this is our cross to bear. (Applause). But this cross is becoming increasingly more unwieldy. We are very grateful to Boris Oleynik, Ion Drutse, and other delegates from the republics who said those kind words about the Russian language and Russia. For them, this is permitted, for us, it is unforgiveable.

It is impossible right now to explain in detail what you yourselves should know anyway—that the blame for your misfortunes lies not with Russia but with that common burden of the administrative-industrial machine, which has turned out to be more terrible to all of us than the Mongolian yoke, and which has humiliated and plundered Russia as well, to a point of near-suffocation. There is no need for detailed explanations, but let me ask this of you: Live with us or not, just as you like, but do not behave arrogantly in relation to us, do not harbor ill for those who have not earned it. But it would be best of all for us to rectify the situation together. It seems to me that all of the possibilities exist for this today. (Applause).

Also true is the fact that this industrial machine that is destroying nature is to blame in many ways today for the interethnic complexities. I am in agreement with those who proposed here not to frighten the deputies, and consequently the whole country as well, which remains glued to television sets, with the gravity of our situation without special need. There is no need to frighten anyone. But there is one most important, fundamental aspect of our existence in relation to which all else fades, no matter what you say, no matter how you try to exaggerate the picture. I am referring to ecology. Nature itself has already written out this word for us not in green but in black paint long ago. We are attempting to build a new, just state. And what reason is there to build it if our years are numbered, considering such a relationship to nature? The State Committee for Protection of Nature has not been up to its functions, and given the nature of its subordination, it cannot carry them out. Before it is too late, we must extricate it from its present situation, in which it lacks any rights, and transfer it to the Supreme Soviet. (Applause).

All of the large-scale nature-transforming projects must be discussed in a commission of the Supreme Soviet and submitted for final approval to the congress. Otherwise we will perish, otherwise we will see more and more government decrees adopted in secret, without the knowledge of the people, such as for example the decree on construction of five petroleum, gas, and chemical complexes in Tyumen Oblast, which are devastating to the country, extremely deleterious to nature, but probably advantageous to foreign firms. Otherwise we will not be able to put an end to the practice of adopting projects without ecological expert examination.

And in conclusion I would like to turn to Nikolay Ivanovich Ryzhkov. Being from Altay Kray, it seems to me that you, Nilolay Ivanovich, who were misled by the ramrods for construction of the Katunskaya hydroelectric power station [GES], have publicly voiced your opinion to the entire country that yes, it should be built. Then in a meeting of the kray party committee you made the qualification: on the condition of a positive ecological expert assessment. However, these words of yours were heard only by those who do not wish to hear them, while your initial statement, which was carried by television, was adopted by the leadership as a signal to act. Many of us deputies are being inundated with telegrams and letters bearing thousands of signatures of the indigenous Altay population and tens of thousands of signatures of those who feel for Altay, we are being inundated precisely because an expert commission of the Siberian Department of the Academy of Sciences and the RSFSR State Planning Committee [Gosplan] will be making a decision this week on approving the construction, and thus the destruction of the last unique natural complex in Siberia. We ask you to consider the Katunskaya affair carefully. Some of us deputies who are participating in the Baikal movement to protect the lake's water had to leave the congress for 2 days in order to attend a regular meeting of this international movement. We saw a film there, presented by the Japanese, about the sickness that is caused by organic mercury. The film was awesome, and the terrible pictures showing the torment and the scale of the misery made one's hair stand on end. There are mercury deposits in the vicinity of the Katunskaya GES. They created doubt in the minds of scientists, but I fear that these doubts disappeared after your unwitting interference, Nikolay Ivanovich.

Out our way on the Angara, water has been descending through hydroelectric power plants for several years. We have more electric power than we know what to do with. Perhaps rather than drowning the Katun, we could transfer this power to Altay? And there are other ways as well, after all.

I would like to end with the comment that if we are now making national referendums a regular practice, then it would be good for the first referendum to be on the issue of the existence of nuclear power plants. Thank you. (Applause).

A.V. Gorbunov: The floor is given to Deputy Vladimir Ivanovich Yarovoy.

V.I. Yarovoy, director of the V.I. Lenin State Union Dvigatel Plant Production Association, Tallinn (Tallinn-Lasnamyaeskiy National- Territorial Election District): Respected comrade deputies! Respected presidium! Sending us off to the congress, our constituents entrusted

Tenth Session

5–6 June 1989

us with a mandate of trust, and simultaneously imposed upon us the responsibility for working out a program of action by which to extricate ourselves from the complex economic and political situation which our country has found itself in as a result of the lengthy period of stagnation. Many of the speakers have suggested their own models of solutions to this problem, with every deputy building his model in accordance with his interpretation of the conception of restructuring. Some see the solution to the problem in radical economic reform, while others see the existing bureaucratic apparatus as the root of all evil. Still others lay primary emphasis on sovereignty of the republics. All of these are important, timely issues that require resolution. But I would not be entirely honest and principled if I did not focus, in the name of my constituents, the attention of deputies on the situation in our common home—the Union of Soviet Socialist Republics, on the need for protecting it from possible division into individual, isolated national states. After that, none of the suggested models would be possible. Does such a danger really exist, you might ask. Am I looking at the situation too dramatically? No, comrades. I dare to assure you that these are the thoughts of my constituents—laborers of large associations and enterprises contained within the United Council of Estonian Labor Collectives, in which I was elected presidium chairman.

Let's look at how quickly the pressure is falling on the country's political barometer. New regions in which the situation is tense and unstable are appearing all the time. Conflicts are flaring up here and there, chiefly on an ethnic basis. The chorus of voices is becoming louder and more unified as they sing out their ultimatum to the center to reexamine the state structure of the country, the agreement to form the union, the USSR Constitution and other legislative acts regulating relations between republics and the USSR. Even at our congress the chairman of the Lithuanian delegation attempted to organize a *demarche* during discussion of the issue of elections to the USSR Supreme Soviet. Utilizing restructuring as a shield, and confusing democracy with demagoguery, numerous groupings and organizations of an extremist persuasion are operating increasingly more openly and rashly. Having joined together under the banner of a national liberation movement, they are subjecting the indigenous population to mass brainwashing essentially unhindered, striving to sow mistrust among people in the existing structure, the party and government, and to promote enmity in relation to the foreign-language population. But from whom or from what do they wish to liberate themselves? From the dictatorship of central departments and sector ministries? Or in part from their own people speaking a different language? The legislative acts being adopted by the republics and the course of events suggest the latter. Not satisfied with their successes in their own republic, these latter-day missionaries are actively propagandizing their viewpoints and aspirations in many regions of the country. They are carrying on this propaganda here at the congress, in the hotel, and in the streets of the city of Moscow. Powerful pressure is being exerted upon party and state organs and upon the republic's Supreme Soviet, compelling the latter to make concessions even to those in relation to whom firmness is needed. In turn, the perpetual yielding by the leadership and the loss of initiative have led to a situation when restructuring has turned into a one-way street in Estonia, when the majority of the non-Estonian population, which does not support the cult of priority of ethnic groups, now finds itself without a place (Applause).

Legislative activity has begun bearing an increasingly more illegal nature. The republic violated Article 74 of the USSR Constitution for the first time back on 16 November of last year, when a session of the Estonian SSR Supreme Soviet adopted the well-known amendments to the constitution and the Declaration on Sovereignty. The presidium of the USSR Supreme Soviet deemed them to be ineffective, thus giving a negative assessment to such actions. It would have been logical for the republic's leadership to insist on repeal of the unconstitutional articles, but this never occurred. The decision of the presidium was only taken under consideration. A legal conflict arose between the union republic and the union state, one which has not yet been resolved. Moreover, on 18 May of this year this conflict was deepened when a session of the Estonian Supreme Soviet adopted the Law on Principles of Cost Accounting in the Estonian SSR, which is based on the above-mentioned amendments, which goes even farther along the road of rejection of the constitution of the Soviet Union, and which creates an obstacle on the republic's territory to the action of the union labor code, the USSR Law on the State Enterprise, and a number of other legislative acts. A paradoxical situation has evolved, where we, citizens of the Soviet Union, do not know what laws we are living under. Under such conditions can we seriously talk about aspirations for a legal state, which is something that is always declared whenever the republic's government must adopt a particular decision? Can we seriously believe in the assurances of the leadership concerning the socialist nature of the transformations that are occurring, and concerning a desire to develop and fortify the socialist federation, when the reverse is occurring before our eyes—creative unions, social organizations, and voluntary societies of Estonia are tearing their ties with their central organs, and alternative structures are arising? The Pioneer organization has ceased to exist in the republic, the Komsomol is at the brink of dissolution, and the question of making the Estonian Communist Party autonomous is being persistently exaggerated.

Look at how quickly the mass media have restructured themselves. Petty bourgeois ideals and values are being propagandized and exalted with envious scope among the population, and concurrently a disdain for all that is Soviet is being nurtured in the people. I could cite examples of incitement of anti-Soviet and anti-Russian moods. Take for example the article by Kherbert Vayn published in the Tallinn City Party Committee's newspaper VECHERNIY TALLINN on 30 May, literally

Tenth Session
5-6 June 1989

right during the work of the congress. Let me read verbatim: "If Stalin (his nationality is of no significance) replaced Lenin's plan for a federation by unitary Russian central power, and if the Russian people allowed him to do this and to proclaim himself to be unique and great throughout all of the Soviet Union, this means that in the eyes of the minorities the responsibility for the distorted Stalinist nationality policy is laid not only upon the Stalinist regime and the regime of stagnation, but also upon the Russian nation. You might not like hearing this, but it is a fact. And if we Communists are made responsible as members of the ruling party for the crimes of Stalinism and for the marching in place during the period of stagnation, irrespective of what our personal role had been, then Russian Communists bear double responsibility for the distorted Stalinist nationality policy." One can find as many articles of this sort as one desires in the last half year.

It is perpetually suggested that Estonia's entry into the Soviet Union was an act of violence and occupation, one which brought misfortune to the Estonian people, who might have been living better today than neighboring Finland. This is why some ideologists of the People's Front are so persistently pressuring Moscow to recognize the pact signed between Molotov and Ribbentrop on 23 August 1939 and the secret protocols attached to it as being ineffective from the moment of their signing. No, such persistence is being displayed not for the sake of restoring historical truth but with the purpose of returning the republic to what it was in 1939. And while this was formerly discussed in whispers, in tiny cafes, in the silence of art studios, now it is being declared loudly enough for all the world to hear.

On 14 May of this year the so-called Baltic Assembly, which was convened in Tallinn with the participation of leaders of the People's Fronts of Lithuania, Latvia, and Estonia, conclusively dispelled the myth behind the true purposes of these movements. And although one of the resolutions addressed to Mikhail Sergeyevich Gorbachev offers assurances of adherence to the course of restructuring and expresses support to the Soviet leadership, the main idea is contained in another document, which I cite: "The Baltic Assembly expresses the aspiration of its nations for state sovereignty in a neutral and demilitarized Baltoscandia."

Comrades, why am I saying all of this? Mainly because every deputy present in this hall has felt the real threat upon our federation, and has come to understand that in the person of those who dream of a return to the times of a bourgeois republic we have a serious, well organized force capable of the most extreme steps in the pursuit of its goals. Let me note incidentally that there are among us around 60 national deputies who participated in the proceedings of the Baltic Assembly, and who voted for its resolutions. The CPSU Central Committee and the presidium of the Supreme Soviet are well aware of the development of events in the Baltic countries. However, the numerous appeals of labor collectives, primary party organizations, and individual citizens expressing alarm and concern for the future of Estonia remain without attention. The impression is created that rescue of this sinking ship is being left to the sinking ship itself. Can we say that such a position is correct when we remember the woeful experience of Sumgait, Nagorno-Karabakh, and now Tbilisi and Fergana?

Because my speaking time is limited I am unable to present all facts, materials, and documents confirming the grounds for our alarm over the fate of the Soviet state. Therefore I submit the materials to the presidium and concurrently suggest the following proposal to the congress.

First. To write and adopt, at this very congress, a declaration on the basic principles and stages of reinforcing the Soviet socialist federation, for which purpose a special commission should be formed out of deputies representing all union and autonomous republics, krays and oblasts, and including prominent Soviet scientists and specialists in the area of state and law.

Second. To instruct the USSR Supreme Soviet to write, and submit for national discussion, a draft USSR law on federation concurrently with the text of amendments and supplements to the constitution—the Basic Law. This law should be adopted at the Second Congress of People's Deputies. I feel that it would be suitable to foresee in the bill a provision promoting equalization of the conditions, rights, and real possibilities of the republics, including the RSFSR, ensuring dynamic, comprehensive development of all regions in proportion to their economic potential and population size. The legal status of national minorities residing not in their own national-territorial formations must be clearly documented.

Third. To hasten the writing of draft USSR laws on citizenship and on the problems of delimiting the powers of the USSR and the union republics, reinforcing the legal status of the autonomous republics, krays, and oblasts, and promoting free development and equal utilization of the languages of the peoples of the USSR. The new Supreme Soviet must ensure preferential development of legal acts of unionwide significance providing an opportunity to discuss and coordinate these acts with all union and autonomous republics, krays and oblasts back during the working stage.

Comrade deputies! I would like to state one more idea. Serious debates are proceeding at our congress, criticism is being addressed toward certain individuals, and mistrust is being voiced. This has happened to our respected Chingiz Aytmatov, our president, and the Politburo. I feel that what has been said in relation to Vladimir Ilich Lenin's Mausoleum is blasphemy. However, deputies speaking subsequently restored justice, and we in this hall supported them in unity. I feel that it is both my duty and a demand of my constituents to restore justice in connection with one of the statements made by the deputies in the group from Estonia. This was on 27 May,

STENOGRAPHIC RECORD

Tenth Session

5–6 June 1989

when I attempted to gain the floor. Brazen, unproven criticism was addressed at that time at Academician Gustav Naan and the newspaper PRAVDA. We were flooded by messages on this account from our constituents, disturbed by this statement and its suggestion that confrontation is a norm of relations. Restructuring in Estonia, in which confrontation is supposedly not a hindrance to preserving normal relations, was cited as an example of such a norm. Yes, this is in part true. We have not in fact had any direct collisions, there have been no pogroms, there have been no refugees, no tanks, armored personnel carriers, and black berets. But real opposition exists, and growing alienation and mistrust between two large population groups exist. Strike committees demanding aggressive action have been created in our country, and citizen committees demanding secession from the Soviet Union have been created in our country. Voices calling for the creation of an administrative-territorial unit out of northeastern Estonia, in which the majority of the non-Estonian part of the population is concentrated, are being heard in our country with increasingly greater frequency. Is this really what we should be striving for?

This is the other side of the truth, in relation to which the speaker remained silent. Moreover he also remained silent in regard to how confrontation is in fact associated with respect for Gustav Naan, a person, one among a few, who permitted himself to present a scientifically justified position on the demographic situation refuting fabrications concerning the demise of the Estonian nation. Unable to find arguments by which to refute Naan, as if on command the local press began a real hate campaign against the academician, creating about him the halo of an enemy of the Estonian nation. The reaction was soon to follow. The academician was literally inundated by numerous telephone calls, letters, threats, and insults. This is why I take the opportunity to express, from this podium, my disagreement with this statement by one of our deputies, and rise to the defense of Estonian Academician Gustav Naan. (Applause). PRAVDA probably does not need the protection of my constituents. Therefore I am extremely grateful to it, and in the name of my constituents I acknowledge PRAVDA's editor in chief Afanasyev, and the editors in chief of KOMSOMOLSKAYA PRAVDA, IZVESTIYA, and TRUD as well, for finding the boldness to express on the pages of their newspapers the truth about the events occurring in Estonia.

Comrade deputies! I came up to the podium with only one purpose. It is concerned with the fact that certain people in the republic are not listening to the voice of my constituents, to the voice of the majority of the laborers, to the voice of the majority of the working class that is working in enterprises in the United Council of Labor Collectives, and that they do not wish that the voice of my constituents would be heard from this podium today.

Vladimir Ilich Lenin wrote that there is a need for publishing a statewide law on the basis of which any measure which would grant privileges of any kind to one nation that would disturb the equality of nations or the rights of a national minority would be pronounced illegal, null and void, and any citizen of the state would have the right to demand repeal of such a measure as being unconstitutional, and criminal punishment for those who had begun implementing it. Today, striving to eliminate the distortions in nationality policy which were created in the periods of Stalinism and stagnation in relation to the union republics, we have managed to create distortions in interethnic relations within the republic itself, within the region in an instant, even faster than usual, because we failed to account for the altered demographic situation and the structure of the population. What we are now talking about is not a single person, but tens of thousands of voters, over a hundred thousand who work at enterprises within the Council of Labor Collectives. And if we include their families, then we are talking about hundreds of thousands. This is something we probably will have to reckon with. Thank you for your attention. (Applause).

V.I. Yarovoy: Comrade deputies! Respected chairman, I request a minute or so for a point of information...an appeal....

From the floor: (Noise).

V.I. Yarovoy: An appeal of veterans of the Armed Forces of the Soviet Union in the city of Tallinn to the Congress of People's Deputies.

"Respected comrade deputies! It is difficult to communicate the situation of absence of rights, poverty, and humiliation experienced in the Estonian SSR by hundreds of families of Armed Forces veterans discharged into the reserves. For years on end we have been deprived of housing and of the right to travel to our selected place of residence, contrary to existing union and republic legislative acts. Our appeals to all levels of authority in local government organs demanding compliance with the law in the provision of housing to us have been unfruitful. We are forced to note that complaints submitted to the presidium of the USSR Supreme Soviet on 4 January and 18 April 1989 and to the USSR Procuracy on 28 March 1989 have also been unable to produce any results. These complaints were returned to republic organs. In our opinion such a method of solving the problems only encourages republic government organs to ignore union legislative acts that have become entrenched in the practice of the Estonian SSR, and equally so, the rights and needs of Armed Forces veterans.

"Under these conditions, Armed Forces veterans who had devoted their lives to the defense of the motherland have found themselves in their declining years without a nook and a roof over their heads, without social rights and protections. We feel that we do not deserve such treatment. Armed Forces veterans wholly support

Tenth Session

5–6 June 1989

restructuring being implemented by the CPSU and the Soviet people, and they are taking part in the society's renewal within the bounds of their capabilities.

"At the same time we are certain that the more frequently violations of the existing laws are tolerated, the more difficult it will be for our society to travel the path of restructuring, and the greater the losses will be.

"A general meeting of Armed Forces veterans of the city of Tallinn instructs the people's deputies from the Estonian SSR, Comrades Yarovoy and Kogan, to present this appeal to the congress and submit the text of the appeal to the constitutional watchdog committee to be created.

"Acting in behalf of the general meeting of veterans of the city of Tallinn held 27 May, Veterans' Council Chairman Captain 1st Rank Ratsis and secretary Captain Felivovich."

Thank you. (Applause).

A.V. Gorbunov: Comrades, we have around 10 minutes left for points of information. Many comrades have signed up here, but I think that we should begin examining these statements without losing time, or comrades will simply begin leaving the hall.

The floor is given first to Comrade Vitaliy Iosifovich Goldanskiy. Mukhtar Shakhanov will be next.

I ask as a big favor that the statements be limited to 2 minutes if possible.

V.I. Goldanskiy, director of the N.N. Semenov Institute of Chemical Physics of the USSR Academy of Sciences, chairman of the Soviet Paguoshskiy Committee, Moscow (from the Soviet Peace Fund jointly with eight Soviet committees for peace, solidarity, and international cooperation): I will try to keep it down to three.

A.V. Gorbunov: Three—otherwise we'll not get anything done here.

V.I. Goldanskiy: Comrades, I sought the floor in accordance with the procedures for conducting this session of the congress. According to the rules I should have 3 minutes. I will try to fit my statement into less.

Dear comrade deputies, there is no doubt, and it is universally recognized, that our restructuring has produced tangible positive results for the moment only in the sociopolitical sphere. Chiefly in international relations, in foreign policy.

The successes of our foreign policy are based on the main thesis of the new way of political thinking—priority of human values over all others. But this is at the foundation. What has also played an extremely important practical role is the fact that in recent years our foreign policy has acquired a number of properties, a number of qualities that were totally alien to it before.

Here are these properties, these qualities. First. The ability to hear out the arguments of the other side, even if they are totally divergent from one's own opinion.

Second. The ability to persuade the other side as to the righteousness of one's own arguments. And I mean persuade, rather than resorting to force.

Third. The ability to seek and find mutually acceptable solutions to disputed issues, to strive for consensus and unanimity in the name of constructive effort.

These qualities are necessary attributes of international relations in a civilized world. But all of these qualities are just as mandatory in all mutual relations between civilized people.

In particular, they are an indispensible prerequisite of normal activities of deputies. And consequently as a minimum we must hear each other out, and respect the right of each deputy to possess and state his own opinion. Neither the majority nor the minority possesses a monopoly on the truth. In the Bible, it was the majority that shouted "Crucify Him!". Half a century ago a majority in our country wrathfully demanded the heads of innocents judged by outrageous kangaroo courts. It is easier of course for a majority to outshout a minority. Though a minority can also sometimes be rather loud.

This is precisely why we must persuade and not outshout one another. We have clearly not yet learned to do so. And the whole world has become witness to our intolerance of the opinions of others, the hissing, the shouts, the clapping, something very close to foot-stamping, and the occasional personal insults voiced in this hall. Through such actions we diminish our authority as deputies and the authority of the entire congress.

Much of course depends on the session chairmen, but it is all in our hands, after all, and we are all responsible for this. And in order to better guarantee that our debates would be constructive, I propose writing rules of behavior and submitting them to the congress for a vote so that we would be sure to observe them. (Applause).

A.V. Gorbunov: The floor is given to Comrade Mukhtar Shakhanov. Comrade Arkadiy Pavlovich Aydak will speak next.

M. Shakhanov, writer, editor in chief of the journal ZHALYN, secretary of the board of the Kazakh SSR Writers Union, Alma-Ata (Alma-Ata-Talgar Territorial-Election District): Exalted congress! I would like to present the following statement in behalf of the 19 USSR people's deputies of Kazakhstan in an effort to avoid new outbursts of international discord, considering the acute situation that has evolved in the republic.

Tenth Session
5–6 June 1989

After the issue as to the events in Georgia was raised at the congress, the group of delegates from Kazakhstan received a mass of telegrams and group letters from their constituents. They are displeased by the fact that even in the presence of such glasnost and openness at the congress we have not raised the issue as to the events that occurred in Alma-Ata in December 1986, when sapper's shovels and police dogs were used against peaceful demonstrators for the first time in the country, and young girls were beaten with clubs and kicked with tarpaulin boots. All of this happened in a time before the existence of the commonly known ukase on demonstrations and rallies. The number of victims among the demonstrators is still being concealed from the public. According to incomplete data around 2,000 persons were arrested. Many of them were sentenced to lengthy prison terms. Thousands were expelled from educational institutions, and fired from their jobs.

In response to the first attack upon it, the era of stagnation has bared its teeth with a vengeance, causing misfortune to hundreds of politically unprepared young men and women whose lives have been forever shattered.

For the sake of justice it must be noted that the republic's party organization, headed by the noted international figure of Comrade Kolbin, devoted considerable effort to improving the situation. However, the truth about the events in Alma-Ata and about the unlawful actions by soldiers of the internal troops still remains classified. This is why various unhealthy rumors are circulating in our country, casting a shadow upon the friendship of peoples and acting as a source of some national enmity.

In this connection we make a strong plea for the creation of a commission out of people's deputies representing different regions and nationalities in order to clarify the real truth about the December events in Alma-Ata.

After the events described above, the CPSU Central Committee published the decree "On the Work of the Kazakh Republic Party Organization on International and Patriotic Education of Laborers." In this decree the event was called a manifestation of Kazakh nationalism. We could accuse five thousand people, ten thousand or one hundred thousand, but we cannot accuse all of the Kazakh people of nationalism. The term "Kazakh nationalism" is an accusation of all of the Kazakh people. Therefore we request that justice be established, and that the severe and undeserved accusations against the people be withdrawn.

The Kazakh people have demonstrated their faithfulness to the friendship of peoples many times by their history and with their blood. A CPSU Central Committee plenum on interethnic problems will soon be held. Many interested people's deputies will not be able to participate in this forum, since they are not members of the Central Committee. Therefore the group of Kazakh deputies proposes that we should adopt a decree prior to the plenum, and precisely during our congress, on the status of the state language of the indigenous nationality of union and autonomous republics, autonomous oblasts, national okrugs and minorities, and resolve the very acute questions as to the destiny of Soviet Turks and Crimean Tatars, who to this date feel themselves to be exiles from their own country.

Allow me to communicate to the presidium some of the demands of the voters, including letters to the congress signed by known writers, scientists, and young people in the republic. Thank you for your attention. (Applause).

A.V. Gorbunov: Arkadiy Pavlovich Aydak now has the floor, and Comrade Plotnikov will speak next.

A.P. Aydak, chairman of the Leninskaya Iskra Collective Farm [kolkhoz], Yadrinskiy Rayon (Yadrinskiy National-Territorial Election District, Chuvash ASSR): I have 3 minutes. Dear comrades! The tragedy in the Bashkir ASSR affects us all, since after all, we are brothers in a single family. Our kolkhoz will donate R5,000 in aid of the victims.

To go on, here is the first thing I wish to say. Food is still the main problem today. Therefore I think that the floor should be given to agrarian deputies to a greater extent than previously. I am certain that the acuity of the problems that have been discussed so much at the congress will decrease if the food situation improves.

Second. After the appeal of the 417 deputies was read to the congress, the chairman announced that creation of a committee on agrarian issues—one of the principal ideas of the appeal—needed to be postponed to the autumn session. Last Friday [2 June] 270 agrarian deputies decided at a meeting, and I am speaking at their instruction, that we need to create a committee on agrarian issues under the Supreme Soviet—prior to the conclusion of the congress work at that—and not a food commission under the Soviet of the Union. On Saturday the Soviet of the Elders was able to decide positively on the creation of precisely this committee, but when I asked the Soviet of the Elders if the rights of the committee would be as stated in the appeal, no guarantee was offered. In this connection I would like to say the following.

In order that creation of the committee would not degenerate into just another formality, we need to adopt the appeal of the 417 at this very congress as a decision of the congress on agrarian issues. This means that we ourselves, the agrarian deputies, will elect the committee with all of the rights stated in the appeal. This will serve as material fulfillment of Lenin's commandment: "Do not dare to command the peasant." (Applause).

May I speak for another minute?

A.V. Gorbunov: Arkadiy Pavlovich, you requested time for a point of information, for a short statement.

FIRST CONGRESS OF PEOPLE'S DEPUTIES OF THE USSR

Tenth Session

5–6 June 1989

A.P. Aydak: That's all I have. I am reaching the end. Our requests to assemble agrarian deputies for meetings are not being announced, except in one case—by Mikhail Sergeyevich—in contrast to the meetings of deputies representing other sectors. Moreover we even have to beg persistently for a microphone to use at the meetings. Here as well, we should not treat peasants as second-rate people, as it is stated in the appeal of the 417.

Mikhail Sergeyevich, we voted for you, and we share with you the responsibility for solving the food problem. Therefore we ask that you heed our opinion. Thank you. (Applause).

A.V. Gorbunov: The last to speak in the "points of information" phase is Comrade Andrey Leonidovich Plotnikov.

A.L. Plotnikov, foreman of the Kirovo-Chepetsk Mechanical Repair Plant, Kirov Oblast (from the All-Union Lenin Communist Youth League): Respected comrade chairman, comrade deputies! As I see it, very soon the Supreme Soviet will have to resolve an important issue concerning the staffing of permanent commissions and committees. During the congress we have already witnessed the loss of a number of candidates during elections to the Soviet of the Union.

Besides the name of Yuriy Chemodanov so painfully familiar to all of us today, which has already disappeared from the secret ballot, the opinions of oblast delegations concerning the candidacy of our young deputies Tsigelnikov and Uvarov were ignored when the list of candidates was being drawn up. Even at this moment certain changes are still being made in this picture. We find that in staffing the Youth Affairs Committee, once again the names of a number of deputies have disappeared—particularly those of Gubin and Minin. This might be a coincidence, but I would prefer to avoid such coincidences, all the more so because in filling out the questionnaire on commissions and committees, a large number of deputies signed up for several of them together—that is, what is operating here is the duplication principle, which is in no way acceptable in the resolution of such important matters.

Comrade deputies, I am certain that none of you have any doubts that tomorrow, after the question of the staffing of the committees is resolved in a joint meeting of the chambers of the USSR Supreme Soviet, debates will necessarily arise over minor procedural matters. In order to avoid them, we suggest what is from our point of view a clear procedure for forming the personnel composition of the committees, which would be the prerogative of the congress. I emphasize—of the Congress of USSR People's Deputies, since in accordance with the constitution, these committees will be staffed not only by members of the Supreme Soviet but also by other USSR people's deputies.

Now I will dare to propose that if this matter is not resolved promptly, mistakes will subsequently arise similar to those made during the elections to the USSR Supreme Soviet.

Comrades, we can and must learn from our own errors, but we must at least strive to not repeat these errors later on. They cost us too dearly. I have in my hands a draft resolution of the Congress of USSR People's Deputies drawn up by a group of deputies from the Komsomol on the procedures for staffing the committees of the USSR Supreme Soviet. In compliance with the provisionary regulations of the congress the proposed draft must be duplicated—that is my opinion, since it was signed by 20 deputies—and distributed to all deputies for detailed examination. If necessary, we can create a working group on this issue right now, in order to discuss the draft resolution and adopt it at the very next session of the congress.

In conclusion I would like to express the hope that the proposed variant for staffing our working organs is acceptable to the deputies to the congress, that it will be approved by them, and that it will produce doubtless benefit by excluding unrelated issues and complaints and thus conserving the precious time of USSR people's deputies. Thank you. (Applause).

A.V. Gorbunov: Comrades, anyone else who....

Ye.A. Gayer, scientific associate of the Institute of History, Archeology, and Ethnography of the Far Eastern Department of the USSR Academy of Sciences, Vladivostok (Far Eastern National-Territorial Election District, RSFSR): One minute, please.

M.S. Gorbachev: Oh, let her speak.

From the floor: Yes, let her speak, of course.

A.V. Gorbunov: One minute, please, you asked for one minute.

Ye.A. Gayer: Dear comrades, I want to know by what grounds I have been deprived of gaining the floor. The Soviet of Nationalities will meet after lunch, and the Soviet of the Union and the Soviet of Nationalities will meet jointly tomorrow. When am I going to be able to speak?

A.V. Gorbunov: You will speak at the next general meeting.

Ye.A. Gayer: There is something else I wish to say. Dear comrades, it was after last Friday that the terrible tragedy which threw our congress off schedule occurred in our country. It was Friday evening, as we recall, after our congress concluded its work. I would like to say something concerning the contempt that was voiced in the name of all the people publicly toward Academician Sakharov. On what basis can one person say that he

STENOGRAPHIC RECORD

Tenth Session

5–6 June 1989

speaks for all the people? I have telegrams, a pile of telegrams from the Far East, in which people ask me to extend support, respect, and admiration to Andrey Dmitriyevich Sakharov. (Tumultuous applause). Here is what I would like to say.... Please hold the applause!

A.V. Gorbunov: Excuse me, allow me to speak to you as well. You asked for one minute....

Ye.A. Gayer: It took me that much time just to get up to the podium. I will now speak.

A.V. Gorbunov: Respected colleague, I deny you the floor. You asked for one minute, and I have to keep the congress moving. I am showing you the red card. You are still among the speakers. Thank you. (Applause).

Comrades! I now have a very brief but very important announcement. It has been proposed that all of us now go and pay our respects to Lenin and lay wreaths on behalf of our congress at Vladimir Ilich Lenin's mausoleum and at the Tomb of the Unknown Soldier. (Applause).

It is proposed that we lay the wreaths now, right after the conclusion of our meeting. USSR people's deputies may convene at Red Square, by the mausoleum, at 1420. There is enough time. Exit through Spasskiy and Nikolskiy gates.

Now very briefly about our subsequent work:

First: Today at 1600 the first organizational meeting of the Soviet of Nationalities of the USSR Supreme Soviet will be held in the chamber meeting hall.

Second: Tomorrow at 1000 the first joint meeting of the chambers of the USSR Supreme Soviet is to be held there as well.

The editorial commission asks those deputies who will not participate in the meeting of the Soviet of Nationalities to convene at 1600 in the Hall of Mirrors.

Excuse me, but there is one more announcement: The commission on the events in Tbilisi will convene in the presidium room, here, at 1530.

Our next meeting, a general meeting of the congress, will be held here tomorrow at 1600. So, until that time, a recess of the general meeting is announced.

STENOGRAPHIC RECORD

FIRST CONGRESS OF PEOPLE'S DEPUTIES OF THE USSR
ELEVENTH SESSION
WEDNESDAY, 7 JUNE 1989
THE KREMLIN PALACE OF CONGRESSES

During the final days of the Congress, new ethnic violence erupted in the Fergana Valley of Uzbekistan. The immediate target of the pogroms was the region's Meskhetian Turks. By the end of the first week of June, Soviet authority was under attack throughout the area. Militia and reinforced internal troops were unable to control the riots and they themselves were frequently the object of rioters in search of weapons and ammunition. When Gorbachev opened the Eleventh Session with an appeal for calm and respect for law and order, the cities of Fergana, Tashlak, Kuvasay, and Margilan were in chaos and the violence was spreading to Kokand and Yaypan. Camps were being set up to protect the thousands of Turkish refugees who were eventually airlifted out of the region and resettled in Tadjikistan, southern Kazakhstan, and central Russia.

Due to the opening of the Supreme Soviet, the Congress's sole order of business was the presentation of the government's program by prime minister-designate N. I. Ryzhkov. Admitting that restructuring was not as simple or quick to achieve as originally thought, he asserted that the government was committed to a complete overhaul of the industrial sector and a general reorientation of investment policies to fund long-neglected social needs. Part of the financing of social programs would come from the reallocation of military expenditures, although Ryzhkov defended the generally unpopular space program as an economically sound investment. He declared that the government would triple its current allocation for environmental protection in each of the next three five-year plans. The general goal, he said, was to transfer economic control to the republics and local soviets and to remove the restrictions that inhibited individual opportunities. The road ahead would be difficult and painful, he warned, due to low productivity, a shortage of hard currency and the means to acquire it, and the perennial budget and trade deficits. Nevertheless the government's first objective was to raise the nation's standard of living and then to address the country's financial problems.

ELEVENTH SESSION
WEDNESDAY, 7 JUNE 1989
STENOGRAPHIC RECORD

M.S. Gorbachev, chairman of the USSR Supreme Soviet, is in the chair.

M.S. Gorbachev: Esteemed comrade deputies! Let the work of the congress continue. Before we tackle the questions on the agenda I would like, on behalf of the presidium, to inform the congress about the situation in Uzbekistan, how it is shaping up and developing, and what state it is in.

The situation at the moment is complex. The government commission set up in the republic under the leadership of Comrade Kadyrov, chairman of the Council of Ministers, involving all local and republic organs and with the help of the country's administrative organs, is at work. Much explanatory work is being done, measures are being taken within the sphere of the administrative organs to safeguard people's security and to maintain public order. Nevertheless, one way or another, this situation erupts in one place or another and is accompanied by clashes which lead to injuries or deaths. Instances of arson, though fewer, are continuing. In any event, even though the situation is under control, it has still not acquired a stable character and is not changing resolutely for the better. This worries us all very much, of course. This is yet another signal that we must be patient, restrained, and attentive and that we must show responsibility for our actions and for the situation in the country and in all the regions.... Especially with regard to interethnic relations. I would like to invite you all once

Eleventh Session
7 June 1989

more on behalf of the congress to issue to Uzbekistan's working people a fervent appeal to remain composed and calm, and most important of all to do everything necessary to ensure that these events do not get out of control, that the section of the population which, one way or another—and I must say this—is now being incited to extreme methods and using firearms in the process, that the situation is taken firmly in hand and these people are stopped. [sentence as published] We hope that the republic and working people have sufficient strength and that they heed our appeal. In turn, I think, we should issue an instruction that the law enforcement organs of the Soviet Union in cooperation with the republic commission and the republic's working people should do everything possible to protect people's lives so that they are not threatened by the extremist manifestations that are taking place there.

I believe that working people in all republics will hear us and will align themselves with the congress and this wording of the appeal of the first Congress of People's Deputies. If you share this concern, and I am sure that you do, I would ask you to support this appeal and the instruction which we are issuing here by raising your mandate cards.

Please lower them. That is agreed. We will keep the congress informed of events.

Comrades, the first sittings of the USSR Supreme Soviet and its chambers have been held and have resolved the main organizational questions: The chairmen of the chambers have been elected, the standing commissions have been formed, and opinions have been exchanged on the committees common to both chambers. This still has to be definitively resolved at the joint sittings. Nevertheless, the work in this direction goes on. At the joint sitting of the Soviet of the Union and the Soviet of Nationalities today, the chairman of the USSR Council of Ministers was appointed and the chairman of the People's Control Committee was elected.

The USSR Supreme Soviet has appointed Comrade Nikolay Ivanovich Ryzhkov chairman of the USSR Council of Ministers. (Applause).

Comrade Kolbin has been elected chairman of the USSR People's Control Committee. (Applause).

I give the floor to Deputy Nikolay Ivanovich Ryzhkov for the report on the forthcoming activity of the USSR Government.

From the floor: (Inaudible).

M.S. Gorbachev: He will speak, then ask your question. The discussion will continue.... And I intend to speak again.

N.I. Ryzhkov, chairman of the USSR Council of Ministers:
Esteemed comrade deputies! Everything that is happening in this chamber, to which the attention of Soviet people is riveted, really does signify the beginning of a qualitatively new stage in the development of our society, and a transition to genuine people's power in one of the most ethnically varied states in the world. It is precisely thus, understanding the peculiarities and the significance of the current moment, with a feeling of immense responsibility and profound gratitude, that I perceived my nomination for the post of head of government.

In light of the sharp debates that have developed at the congress, it goes without saying that I need, apart from setting forth the basic guidelines for the forthcoming work of the USSR Council of Ministers, to give an analysis of the country's socioeconomic development. This will enable the deputies to penetrate further into the work of the government, and to make an all-round analysis of the steps which were undertaken to resolve the difficult problems which faced our economy and to get an idea of the platform of the new composition of the USSR Council of Ministers. Taking this as a premise, it will be evidently be correct to begin with an analysis of the economic situation in the country. It is not unambiguous and it can be assessed in different ways. Such assessments have been audible during the principled conversation on the topic at the congress.

The consumer market is in a complicated situation. Financial and money circulation are in an extremely disordered state. Agriculture and capital construction are emerging from stagnation too slowly, and there is no substantial breakthrough in speeding up scientific and technological progress. That is one point of view, and it has a right to exist. There can be another; I would call it the traditional approach: The national income and the rates of growth of production are increasing, and to no small extent. The whole of the growth in industrial output has been achieved thanks to labor productivity, something that it has not been possible to achieve throughout the history of the development of our economy. Profit is increasing at an unprecedented rate. Wages and social consumption funds are growing, and we have turned a corner in speeding up housing construction, and in building of schools, hospitals and kindergartens. These are realities, and such an appraisal of them also has the right to exist. Finally, there is the third approach: The contrast between these processes, their contradictoriness and unusual properties, stem from the profound transformations upon which we have consciously embarked, from the immense complexities which are inevitable when society is in transition to a new qualitative level.

So the assessments vary. But it is only in combination that they can provide a real idea of the true state of affairs and that they will enable us to understand the sources of our difficulties and work out correct paths for further movement and, on this basis, determine both the

Eleventh Session
7 June 1989

urgent tasks for the coming year or 2 and those for the whole program for the new government.

People have a right to ask why the country is emerging from the economic crisis slowly. The reply to this and many other questions, whether we like it or not, is objectively contained both in our past and in the present.

During the debates on the report by Chairman of the USSR Supreme Soviet Mikhail Sergeyevich Gorbachev, we did not avoid the question of what we inherited up to April, 1985.

We must (?realize quite clearly) that the iceberg of colossal problems and difficulties which had amassed in the economy over many decades cannot be melted by 4 years of even the most active restructuring. Therefore, once again, I want to focus the attention of the people's deputies on the need to thoroughly weight the situation that existed when restructuring began. Facing the congress, we must admit with all frankness that the burden which was dragging the country to the depths of crisis turned out to be considerably heavier than the government had previously imagined. In the mid-eighties, the economy, because of its extensive development, was unable to guarantee the implementation to the equal extent of the three main tasks which faced the country at one and the same time: the raising of the people's welfare and the resolution of the social problems which had come to a head; the effective development of the national economy, allowing the tasks of the current period and also of the future to be resolved; and the guaranteeing of the high level of the state's defense capabilities. First, the development of the economy. It was held back by an insuperable barrier of the inertia of all economic systems, and the lack of receptivity to intensification, to scientific and technical progress. In all spheres of the national economy an expenditure-orientated mechanism prevailed. Mechanical engineering lagged behind. The economy's raw materials thrust and the underdevelopment of the consumer sector intolerably deformed the structure of public-sector production and set it aside for the solution of social problems. To this should be added the under-efficiency of the agro-industrial complex, and the country's growing dependence on imported foodstuffs.

The solution of defense tasks complicated the economic situation to no small extent. The need to guarantee the parity of the military potentials of the USSR and the United States demanded great efforts, the concentration here of the best specialists, and the most up-to-date technology and equipment: resources which were in short supply. Thus the expenditure-oriented economy and the defense complex swallowed up a considerable part of the national income. There was a constant shortage of resources for the main tasks connected with the satisfaction of people's demands. In the end result, by the middle of the last 5-year plan period the rise in the population's living standards had practically come to a halt, with complete stagnation of the social and cultural sphere. The financial deficit also rose continuously, although that circumstance was simply passed over in silence. Every year, the people were told that the budget income exceeded expenditures. In this very complex situation, the possibility had to be found primarily at least of halting or at the very least of slowing down the slide into the crisis. The country was, essentially, led into a dead end. There was no choice. Objectively, restructuring's time had come. Life pointed out to us the only true way: real economic reform. It rightly occupied the central place in the whole restructuring of Soviet society. We did not set about elaborating a program to implement it empty-handed. Ideas were gathered bit by bit, and we felt our way towards the theoretical foundations. Foreign experience was studied thoroughly, and experiments were carried out. I should say that at the beginning of that period, there was quite a bit of discord. But nevertheless, by 1987 we were able to complete that stage of work and to take up the creation of a new mechanism of economic management on a broad front.

The first steps did not come easily. Dogmatism and the residue from the periods of the cult, of voluntarism, and stagnation made it very difficult to move forward. There was no profound theoretical study of what we had to do. In many things we worked by trial and error, we learned and grew more mature for more radical decisions.

One of them was the working out of the law on state enterprises, a legal economic act of a fundamentally new kind. It has been the pivot for the modern system of management, and the foundation for its construction. Of course, not everything in the establishment of this system runs smoothly. Even the economic reforms are not going down a mirror-smooth road. There are examples of lack of coordination in specific elements of it. We are aware of them: Work in practice, and sometimes undesirable results, shed light on them. On the whole, the consistent application of the law on enterprises creates the essential conditions for changing the whole economic situation, and encourages the labor collectives to work efficiently.

It is clear that we have to seek an improvement in the economy persistently, overcoming one stage after another. The logic of the restructuring of production relations has led to it being essential to restore the cooperative movement in the country. In this sense one can, for example, speak boldly of the Law on Cooperatives of the USSR as another milestone on the road to renewal. It was a serious advance toward the further democratization of the economy. The cooperative movement is now suffering difficult growing pains: The future of the cooperative movement will depend to a large extent on how the healthy beginnings will develop in it, and what its prestige in society will be.

A year later, the Decree on Leasing. This shows that we are moving forward, consistently, step by step, to a new

Eleventh Session

7 June 1989

understanding of the role of various forms of ownership and management. We are making headway on questions about which, until not long ago, we still had such ossified ideas. What is particularly important is that the advance is happening not only on a theoretical level, but in concrete, practical deeds.

The consistent policy aiming at the democratization of management, the restructuring of the organizational structures in the national economy, and, the main thing, the social reorientating of the econmy, has brought us to the necessity of disseminating the principles of self-financing and self-recouping to the level of republican and local management.

Possible alternatives for implementing this idea have been worked out. The draft general provisions on the restructuring of the activity of the union republics has been published in the press, as is well known. In the process of debate, those provisions on the whole received support. But you know, comrades, the view of a number of republics on that question. It has been expressed more than once at the congress. I must say with all frankness, that a lot of how these republics see the problem in regional financial autonomy is attractive, and contains an element of healthy constructivism. At the same time, some of their proposals, which in many ways lead to economic self-isolation, and also a number of other fundamental provisions, are very debatable, and in our opinion will not be of help to the republics.

Throughout the world there are powerful integrational processes going on. This is an objective vital demand. So we have to search for the true path to success in the consolidation of forces, in deepening the distribution of labor while taking into account the specifics and potential of each one of the republics, the expansion of economic ties on a mutually advantageous basis, and the formation of an all-union market as quickly as possible.

Obviously there is no need to dwell on an analysis of the virtues and shortcomings of individual elements of the proposed mechanism of regional financial autonomy, the more so since much work lies ahead in drafting and debating the appropriate bill. The government's opinion on this question is that given the diversity of forms and methods of socioeconomic development of any region of the country, we should, on a political level, not violate the federative arrangement of the USSR, and, on an economic level, not permit splintering of the national economy complex in its new content. It would seem that these questions need to be examined only as a whole.

One must act in such a way that from 1991 all republics and regions may change to work under conditions of self-financing, and all law-making acts being drafted for the next 5-year plan period must be in keeping with these principles. But this does not exclude the possibility of working out in 1990 the most important elements of regional financial autonomy in individual republics.

I would like to speak in somewhat more detail about such a major section of the reform as perfection of the organizational structure of administration, to which the congress gave the closest attention. What has the government done here? Our efforts have been directed primarily toward the creation of various structures in the main link of the economy. For instance, about 800 new production and scientific-production and other associations of a similar kind have been created. There are already several state concerns, consortiums, and the first non-departmental corporations in operation. Here things have not proceeded without mistakes, either. Remember the sad experience of the state production associations: One thing was intended, but in fact what was created were offices. The provisions for them had to be cancelled. You live and learn.

Amendments in the primary link made it possible to start perfecting the upper echelons of administration. A number of ministries and departments have been abolished. Some of them have been transformed into all-union departments. The apparatus of state administration in the country as a whole has been reduced by 600,000 persons.

Undoubtedly, as the new forms of management are created at the level of the main link of production, the system of administration of the economy and the development of direct links in wholesale trade will be further improved. The number of industrial ministries will be reduced and their functions will undergo substantial changes.

In keeping with the USSR Constitution, the chairman of the Council of Ministers, endorsed by the congress, will submit to the Supreme Soviet specific proposals on this question.

To sum up what I have said, I would especially like to stress that while fully sharing the point of view of the comrades who have spoken here, radical restructuring of the economy is proceeding with difficulty. A number of adopted decisions, in connection with the real conditions of management, are half-baked. The reform is now at the most difficult and responsible stage. It is being tested for its durability under the complex conditions of the transition period, when methods of central direction and economic methods of leadership are coexisting. In many respects it is conditioned by the fact that while consistently advancing tne reform and refining its main principles, we must not at the same time allow violations of the country's economic stability. In this connection, I wish to stress quite categorically and with all certainty my commitment to truly economic methods of management. I have already had occasion to talk about the fact that in the course of implementing the radical reform we will be drawing ever nearer to forming a new model of the socialist system of economic management. Now,

Eleventh Session
7 June 1989

among the scientific public and in the press, a great discussion is taking place on the main principles of this economic model. The position of the government is based on recognizing the role of the socialist market and competition in our economy. I am firmly convinced, however, that this market will be able to develop successfully under the new system of economic management, and will be serving for the good of man only if we create an efficient economic mechanism for regulating it, which ensures reliable protection of the interests of citizens from market spontaneity.

A most important condition for the development of the market is the overcoming of monopolism. It is still very strong, and is at the basis in many respects of the troubles and shortcomings that exist in our country, especially in questions concerning price formation.

Now more than a thousand major and super-large industrial enterprises dictate their conditions to consumers. It is clear that the policy aimed at developing competition in all spheres is exceedingly necessary. For this, in our view, anti-trust legislation will have to be developed. At present the Institute of Economics and the Institute of the United States and Canada of the USSR Academy of Sciences are working on a draft for this law. The draft will, it appears, be submitted to the Supreme Soviet as early as this year.

Giving a summary of the tasks of the new government in such an important sphere as the deepening of the economic reform, I believe that key directions here should become: First, the restructuring of the work of the union republics and local soviets on the principles of regional financial autonomy. I am putting this problem in the forefront as it is not only of economic but also of great political importance. Second, the improvement of the financial autonomy model on the basis of using various forms of ownership and new structural formations. Legislative bodies and the executive authorities will have to elaborate the forms of economic and judicial regulation—and in a number of cases even to opt for reconsideration of operating laws—with the aim of creating equal conditions for the development of all forms of economic management on the basis of competitiveness and competition. Third is the creation of up-to-date, effective methods of controlling market relations. State regulation under conditions of a developed market should be carried out with the aim of solving tasks of raising the well-being of the people and its social security. Fourth, the working out of new principles of taxation policy to ensure a just financial relationship between the state, the republics, local soviets, enterprises and the populace. Undoubtedly inherent in the process of deepening and perfecting the economic reform are its own dialectic, logic, and stages of development. Our task is to have full clarity and accuracy in all this. At the same time, comrades, it is perfectly obvious that the radical economic reform must be carried out simultaneously with the implementation of major measures for profound structural restructuring of the national economy. The structure of the economy's management that has come about remains extremely conservative and overweight. This can be gauged by the fact that in national economic complexes producing raw material, i.e. intermediate produce, there is a concentration of over 60 percent of all fixed industrial production assets, while in industries providing for people's everyday needs there is a paltry amount: Light industry has only 4, and the food industry 6 percent. Without breaking the trends which have come into being historically for primarily developing the production of the means of production, the economy cannot turn its face to the people. This is the reason for implementing a cardinal structural shift in the national economy. Another aspect of this important problem: For decades, since the times of the industrialization, we have had the idea that the production of technical potential of our country is one of the most powerful and up-to-date in the world. As for the power, it is truly so. It was precisely this which allowed the country to become one of the strongest and most influential states. As for being progressive and up-to-date, an analysis of the true state of affairs has shown that of the R1.9 trillion worth of fixed production assets, 40 percent are worn out. Unquestionably, such a situation has an extremely negative influence on the efficiency of the economy. It affects everything, starting from the mastering of progressive forms of production, productivity and working conditions, and quality of output, and ending with the ecological position in many regions of the country.

The technical re-equipment of basic assets will, of course, be one of the main questions. However, it is necessary to realistically evaluate our resources, because we cannot advance on a wide front to resolve this task at present time. Objectively, the necessary conditions for this do not exist in the country. The task consists in selecting the main directions—first and foremost the direction which is linked with people's life. To create the conditions for modernization and re-equipment of the national economy, we need a powerful and modern machine-building industry. Proceeding from this fact, it must be this industry which should be given a priority development in the future, too.

Comrades! The principal and, I would say, also the most difficult task was to make a structural turn aimed at the implementation of the social re-orientation of the entire national economy. For decades we had understood the development of our society mainly in the light of the prism of quantitative indicators: how much coal and ore was extracted, how much steel and cast iron were smelted, how many hectares of plowed fields were had, etc. We missed the moment when in the whole developed world it was not the arithmetical growth, but the qualitative content of these volumes which became the genuine yardstick for the achievements of the nations. As a result, we have arrived at extremely unsatisfactory social indicators. These are first and foremost the conditions of people's life. Behind these words lie the pictures known to all: the shortage of housing, the overloading of transport, the chronic shortage of goods, the disrespectful

FIRST CONGRESS OF PEOPLE'S DEPUTIES OF THE USSR

Eleventh Session

7 June 1989

attitude toward people, and the growing social tension in society. The lack of good order in everyday life gives rise to the feeling of hopelessness in many people and puts an excessive burden on aged and disabled persons, children, and women. I should stress, in view of the huge scale of such a complex and inert system as is our economy, that the process of its improvement is not at all simple, but it was important to break the trends of stagnation. Certain positive shifts for the better were achieved only in 1988.

Let us take the distribution of the national income. In the past the steady growth of that part of it that was channelled toward the creation of production capacities prevailed, and the poportion of the resources directed to consumption was correspondingly reduced. This situation has begun to change. This can be graphically seen in the expenditures of the country's state budget. While they have on the whole grown by 26.4 percent in 1989 in comparison with 1985, the expenditures on social and cultural measures have grown by almost 33 percent—including those on education, which have grown by 34 percent, on health care, by 45 percent, and on housing construction—counting of all sources of financing—by 37 percent.

Today it can be said with conviction that in the current 5-year plan period it has proved possible to overcome the residual principle in the development of the material base of the socio-cultural sphere. Rates of growth of investment channelled into non-production construction are more than two times outstripping the increase in production capital investment. The addition to the funds for this kind of construction as against the last 5-year plan period will amount in the years 1986-90 to some R80 billion. If, say, in the tenth 5-year plan period, as compared with the previous one, the commissioning of housing even fell by 17.5 million square meters, and in the eleventh 5-year plan period practically failed to grow, in the current 5-year plan period the growth will amount, however, to nearly 100 million square meters. A similar picture is taking shape also for the general education schools. In the tenth 5-year plan period commissioning of them was reduced by nearly 1.3 million places, in the 11th by 1.5 million places, but in the current one a growth of 2.5 million will be secured. The commissioning of hospitals in the two previous 5-year plan periods fell by 28,000 beds. In this 5-year period it will increase by 65,000.

It should be especially stressed that the housing program will undoubtedly be among the constant cares of the new government. For to cope with the set task it is necessary to build some 30 million apartments or houses. From this it follows that already in the next 5-year plan period it is necessary to ensure the commissioning of 850 million square meters of housing, against 650 in the current one. But it would be better still to go for 900 million square meters. This will make it possible to improve housing conditions for 18 million families.

The strengthening of the social bias of the economy has been given a substantial boost in the current 5-year plan period. To solve even the most acute social problem of society, it is necessary to embark on a major economic restructuring of the nature of investment structure, never before carried out in our country on such a scale. This will be a difficult and even an extremely painful process, but it has to be embarked upon.

Undoubtedly, the newly-formed Council of Ministers of the USSR will subordinate all its work to the achievement of the aims most important for each person and society as a whole, and the satisfaction of the requirements of food, goods and services, housing, health, and education, ensuring the possibilities for the spiritual growth of the people and preservation of the natural environment. Already in the current 5-year plan period the government's attention has been centred on questions of the production of nonfood goods. In the first 3 years their output has increased by 32 billion rubles, or by 18 percent, which is practically equal to the growth in the whole previous 5-year plan period. Nevertheless, this turned out to be insufficient for the normalization of the situation. The state of the consumers market was also affected by reductions in the import of nonfood goods, as a result of which their market allocations of 1988 were at the 1985 level. This called for taking additional measures toward increasing the production of goods, and for building up and improving the material base for their production.

A program for technically re-equipping enterprises of the light industry was drawn up and adopted in 1988. For the purchase of up-to-date equipment and technology for this industry we took the step of arranging credits abroad worth over R1 billion, despite our difficulties with foreign currency.

To speed up the normalization of the situation on the consumer market the decision was taken to redesignate many enterprises in operation. The conversion of defense plants is also aimed at this.

As calculations show, we need to increase the production of nonfood goods in 1990, as compared with 1989, by no less than R45-50 billion, or by 20 percent, which exceeds the average annual increases over the past 3 years almost fivefold. In preparing the draft plan for 1990, USSR ministries and departments and the councils of ministers of the union republics took as a target precisely the achievement of such an aim.

Preliminary studies show that next year an increase can be achieved in production against the plan for 1989 of washing machines by one-third, of sewing machines by 20 percent, of radio equipment and tape recorders by 16 percent, and of furniture by 12 percent.

Measures have been taken by the government to expand paid services to the population. Over the 3 years of the 5-year plan period their volume has risen by almost 38 percent and exceeded R62 billion in 1988, as against

STENOGRAPHIC RECORD

Eleventh Session

7 June 1989

R58 billion under the 5-year plan. But we still virtually have to create a services industry.

The USSR Supreme Soviet chairman's report noted the efforts to develop public health and education. Sharp criticism on these matters was heard from people's deputies. Constructive proposals were voiced. The government, which is being formed anew, will undoubtedly take them as the basis in resolving urgent problems. I will only add that what we need to do is to bring the entire system of health protection up to qualitatively new limits. Calculations show that the concentration here of resources, including through the reduction of expenditures on defense, are opening up possibilities for building new hospitals for 500,000 beds, polyclinics for 1 million visits per shift, for re-equipping treatment and prevention establishments, and for increasing by 2.5 times the supply of up-to-date medical equipment.

Questions of satisfying the population's needs for medicines, an acute shortage of which is now being experienced, are to be studied thoroughly. It must be said that our pharmaceutical industry is providing only 45 percent of the country's needs for medicines. We must implement a complex of major measures to develop Soviet pharmaceutics. Here serious efforts are needed on the part of the union republics, since at the present time the exacerbation of the ecological situation has led to a number of enterprises being shut down, which has aggravated the situation with medicaments even more. Nor do we exclude at the same time the possibility, for the purpose of solving the problem swiftly, of building, on a turn-key basis, three or four pharmaceutical factories as well seeking out a possibility for increasing import purchases of made-up medicines.

Now I would like to specially single out questions that have caused extraordinary concern among the people's deputies. This concerns those to whom no one can and should be indifferent. This is a question of supplying the material needs of certain groups of the population. During the years of the 12th Five-Year Plan a number of urgent, centralized measures have been put into effect, aimed at solving this problem. The wages of some categories of the working people have been raised. I must say that here, in spite of the unfavorable financial situation, we have to a considerable extent paid old debts, which were formed right at the time of the 24th party congress. We consider it exceptionally important to at least render partial assistance to families that are poorly provided for, to mothers and children.

In 3 years the per capita payments of benefits from the social consumption funds have risen by R87 and attained R613 in 1988. When speaking of a social policy, I consider it necessary—although a great deal has already been said about this here—to especially stress the question of the responsibility of society and the state for the material situation of the groups of the population that are the least protected socially, such as pensioners, invalids, and young married couples, and families with many children. Many people's deputies have made requests to me regarding this issue. The government understands that almost 40 million people are today living below the poverty line. Therefore, of all the varied social problems which have taken shape in the country, this is the sorest, testifying to social injustice, especially with respect to those people who have given everything for society. Therefore we attribute special importance to the law on the provision of pensions, on which active work is now being conducted. Here we take a firm stand.

We must wait a little for the solution of other social issues, but the problem of pension provision must be solved in the course of the 13th 5-year plan. [applause]

At the same time it is quite evident that some issues are pressing ones. This has been repeatedly emphasized at the congress with particular poignancy and anguish. The Central Committee Politburo and the government have thoroughly weighed the possibility of bringing closer the term for resolving some of the most acute and pressing problems, which should be resolved within the framework of the future pension law. I think the people's deputies will uphold the position of the Central Committee Politburo and the USSR Council of Ministers regarding the fact that it is quite possible that already from January 1 of next year the minimum pension of blue and white collar workers and collective farmers could be raised to R70 per month, with abolition of the differences in pension provision—that is, to the level of the minimum wage of blue and white collar workers effective at the present time. [applause]

This will enable us to improve the material situation of 20 million people, including 8 million collective farmers. [applause] To increase the minimum amount of pensions to invalids of the first group to R80, and invalids of the second group to R60—this is more than 1 million people. [applause] To increase the amount of pensions to widows of perished servicemen to R60 a month for losing a breadwinner, and also to give them the same status for privileges as participants in the Great Patriotic War—this is 800,000 people. [applause] To pay to war invalids supplements to retirement pensions, set by the legislations, [word indistinct] in the sum of R15 a month, regardless of their maximum amount—this is 300,000 people. [applause] To give the right of free medicines to participants of the Great Patriotic War and to widows of perished servicemen—this is 7 million people. To give the right to free public transport in towns to participants of the war, and also to people awarded orders and medals for unselfish work in the war period—this is almost 6 million people. [applause] As a result of this, almost 22 million people will be able to feel already next year the social changes in their lives. Taking into acount numerous requests, it is planned to remove from 1990 all

STENOGRAPHIC RECORD

Eleventh Session

7 June 1989

earnings restrictions for workers and pensioners on payment for work, regardless of the amount of the pensions they are receiving. [applause]

For all this, comrades, almost R6 billion are needed. The Government will, in the near future, define sources, and will examine them jointly with commissions and committees of the USSR Supreme Soviet. At the same time it is quite obvious that the solution of the given problem is the concern of the entire society, of every enterprise and organization. Of course, all these and other acute social problems that have come to a head in the society will require great financial resources. They can be obtained only if there is a growth of efficiency of the economy; only then will their solution become a reality. One more question: In the course of the work of the congress, as proposed by Mikhail Sergeyevich Gorbachev, a commission is to be set up of people's deputies to examine the complex of questions relating to the benefits system that has been created in the state. Taking this into account, the country's leadership is submitting the proposal that the distinction which exists in the upkeep of patients in different medical establishments, and also in departmentally run sanatoria and holiday homes, including the USSR Ministry of Health's fourth main administration, be eliminated right away, proceeding from principles of social justice. [applause]

Comrade people's deputies! I am touching separately on the issues of the development of the agro-industrial complex and food supply for the population. It is extremely difficult to speak on this topic. So much has been said about it, so many decisions have been adopted, that it would seem that they only need all be implemented, and the problem would disappear. However, it remains, and is even becoming worse. That means that for decades the measures adopted have not attained their goals; they have not matched up to the interests of the main link, and, first and foremost, of the peasantry. It appeared that the country was undertaking immense efforts to extract this sector of the economy from failure. More investment, equipment, and material resources were put into it, and so-called sponsoring assistance from the town for the country was organized. It seemed that it was all being done on a global scale, but the person working directly on the land was lost behind all this. Moreover, many initiatives originating from the center, and regional initiatives, led to the peasant everywhere being turned into the subject of all kinds of experiments, such as the consolidation and fragmentation of farms, settlement of farmsteads and small villages, cutting in half of subsidiary plots, elimination of cattle in the private farmyard, and so on. The rate of growth of output in rural areas started falling without restraint. While at the end of the 1960's the average annual growth was R27,000 million, and the hope emerged for Soviet people that some extra provisions would appear on their tables, later on this hope kept dwindling, and came to nothing. In the 9th 5-year plan period, the annual average growth fell to R20 billion, in the 10th 5-year plan to R15 billion, and by the end of the 11th 5-year plan to R10 billion. However, despite all this, the sorrows of the rural areas did not then truly become the sorrow of the whole state. They were spoken of everywhere, but they were perceived in abstract fashion at all levels of management. There began the ever more obvious manifestations of the extreme vulnerability of our agro-industrial complex. Because of the absence of sufficient reserves and insurance stocks, the state was compelled to opt for large purchases of food. In 1964, imports of food amounted to R1.4 billion.

In the midseventies it grew to R6 billion, and in 1981 it amounted to R15 billion. In 1985, of R111 billion of food products marketed by state and cooperative treade, about R16 billion were imports of food products. The food situation in recent years has not in practice improved. Imports have to be preserved as before, and alongside this, the unsatisfied requirements of the population for foodstuffs have increased, and are now assessed at more than R20 billion. The further exacerbation in this issue of late is evident from the following figures: While in 1987 the country was producing food products worth R134.4 billion, or an increase of 5.8 percent over 1986, in 1988 there was virtually no increase. It is perfectly clear that a serious improvement can be attained only on the basis of a radical further improvement in production relations and of further radical restructuring of the economic mechanism in the rural areas. I must stress, with complete conviction, that the interests of the peasantry must be put at the foundations of this most important matter. It is only here that there are realistic opportunities to substantitally increase production of food and raw materials using the already created material-technical base. At the same time, we have to attain a qualitative renovation of the material base of the agro-industrial complex, the supply to rural areas of the equipment and resources they need, and an improvement in the utilization of the achievements of scientific-technological progress. In this regard, I totally support the statements of the people's deputies concerning changes to legislation on land tenure and use.

The issues are truly topical. The criticism of the decree on lease contracting that has been heard from this rostrum has, in the main, been justified. The decree is a temporary document, and hence it could not, was not capable of solving all the problems connected with lease contracting. We need more extensive legislative acts, and I would like to hope that due attention will be paid to this issue in the new Supreme Soviet. But in my view, neither now nor in the future should we set up the collective or state farm in opposition to the independent peasant farm or the cooperative of leaseholders. The most important thing is to give the peasants the opportunity to manage their affairs independently on the basis of different forms of holding and managing property. [applause] Decisions directed toward this were also adopted in March of this year, concerning further improvement of the management of the agro-industrial complex. They match up to the new regional policy, and are aimed at expanding the rights and enhancing the responsibilities of local bodies for providing the population of territories with food.

Eleventh Session
7 June 1989

Along with the changes in economic relations, overcoming the major shortcomings in the countryside's social development is the central, I would even say the fundamental issue for the countryside. Here, too, we also need fundamentally new approaches. The March plenum set the task of improving the provision of rural families with well-appointed housing in the near future. A number of specific measures regarding road construction have been determined. The volumes of capital investments for these purposes in the new 5-year plan must increase 2.4 times.

I also want to support the numerous statements by people's deputies which were heard from this rostrum to the effect that it is necessary to sharply raise the electrification and the level of gas supply to rural settlements and to radically change their entire social infrastructure.

For all this, in our view, over R120 billion of capital investments in the future 5-year plan must be used. This is 1.5 times more than envisioned for the current 5-year plan.

We must concentrate our efforts even more on the key problems of the country's agro-industrial complex, which are directly hindering our potential and the improvement of the provision of the population with food products, and are not allowing social tension in society to be removed. Above all this holds true for the transportation, processing, and storage of agricultural raw materials. Losses here are reaching astronomical figures. Up to one-quarter of what is grown by the countryside—this is according to modest calculations—does not reach the consumer. The extensive action program in this sphere is well known. It was the subject of a special examination in October 1987. The main aim which was set then is to ensure profound changes in the structure of the processing sectors of industry, to lay the main emphasis on strengthening its material and technical base. To implement this program in accordance with the government's decision it is planned to assimilate R77 billion. For all intents and purposes we must in many respects create anew the industry of processing, storage, and transportation of agricultural raw materials and food products.

I want to remind you that through the development of processing and the introduction of wastless technologies which rule out losses, output of up to R40 billion, or 60 percent of the entire increase in food goods in the country, should be obtaned additionally in 1995.

The question of land improvement in agriculture is now being completely revised. The system that existed for many years resulted in huge expenditures that did not yield the desired results, and was detrimental to nature in many respects. In this respect the criticism addressed to the former leadership of the Ministry of Land Reclamation and Water Resources is absolutely valid. The USSR Council of Ministers has drawn conclusions from this and believes that all questions of water resources should not be concentrated in the hands of a single organization. This ministry must become purely a construction organization.

As for construction projects, it is the collective and state farms and the union republics—those who know best what the land needs—who should be placing the orders. The center should be left to decide problems only of statewide and inter-republican significance. [applause]

Persistent work in all these areas will in the final analysis allow us already in the 13th 5-year plan to bring production of foodstuffs up to R200 billion a year, or increase it in comparison with last year by almost R70 billion. This is possible only with an annual increment of not less than 5 percent. Only in that case will there be a real change in the foodstuffs market.

I believe that the tasks of the new government to create conditions aimed at a radical improvement of the country's food supply should be directly taken from the appeal to the congress by the agrarian workers people's deputies. It is a code, the fulfillment of which should in effect transform the peasant, as he is all over the world, into a respected, prestigious figure. Everything must be done to ensure that he occupies a worthy position in our society. [applause] This concerns the social conditions of his life, including material supply, consumer services, medical facilities, education, and culture. It also concerns everything else covered in living conditions, production of the infrastructure, provision of machinery—in a word everything an urban resident has today.

For improvements in supplying the the populace with foodstuffs, a weighty contribution should also be made by other sectors of the economy. This applies first and foremost to such a powerful sector as fisheries, which is doing much to solve the tasks mentioned, but which also has quite a few problems. The main orientation in the government's activity in relation to the agrarian sector will be fulfilling the instruction from the people's deputies to turn the country's economy toward the need of the countryside. Only such concern for rural workers will provide the possibility to substantially change in a short period of time the state of affairs of foodstuffs on the consumer market.

Now to deal with the financial position of the state. Special attention was paid to this at the congress. The deputies should have exhaustive information at their disposal on this most important question. Over the three preceding 5-year plans, in connection with the drop in efficiency of social production, over R150 billion of income failed to be obtained, at a time when state expenditure was also above what was planned by R150 billion. Precisely here lies the source of our financial difficulties today. The shortage of financial resources at the time was made up from above-plan income from foreign trade to the extent of R103 billion. It was recovered due to the favorable situation of the world

STENOGRAPHIC RECORD

Eleventh Session
7 June 1989

market for fuel and energy resources. At the same time there was a direct raise in retail prices of R54 billion, and about R20 billion came from a hidden price rise for consumer goods by means of lowering their quality.

A further R106 billion was borrowed from the banking system. Over that period, the issues of money reached unprecedented levels, and the amount of money in circulation increased by almost three times. Such is the actual picture. Superficially, all was well. The expenditures were equal to the revenues, and consequently there were no problems here. At the same time, against this favorable background of financial balance, enterprises and industries were stripped bare. They were in effect deprived of any chance of using the resources which they had earned. The vast majority of accumulated resources, with the exception of sums regulated by the plan, were returned to the budget.

Such was the economic system, one which superficially balanced overall the national economy, and actually stifled the economic initiative of work collectives. I ask you to pay special attention to this, because the financial situation which has formed today in the country can largely be explained by precisely a fundamental break with the principles which used to exist. This is the financial legacy with which the country entered the 12th 5-year plan. Much time was required in order to come to terms deeply and comprehensively with the state of affairs in this zone which was once secret and inaccessible for all. It became clear that if we would not implement radical measures to develop new principles for financial relations between enterprises and the state—and now the question of regions is also on the agenda—then we would not be able to achieve the necessary socioeconomic transformations and we would undermine the economic reform.

Finding ourselves in such a financial position, we had to answer frankly the question: What strategy were we to select in order to get out of this most difficult situation? Various roads were proposed. The first was to cut social programs and to increase retail prices. The government had a firm position on this. It is the Politburo's position. That road is not acceptable from any point of view. The second was to take away from the enterprises the remainder of earned resources and to balance the state budget thereby, as was done previously. And this road was also rejected, because it directly undermines the foundations of the economic reform and violates the Law on Enterprises. The third was to increase the external debt. But that would have signified transformation of the domestic debt into a foreign economic debt. The latter had already reached a dangerous level, beyond which the country might end up in a most grave situation. Proceeding from all of this, a task was formulated: Relying on an increase in the efficiency of public-sector production and intensification of it, the growing expenditures of the state are to be covered only by increasing revenues, thereby stabilizing the financial situation in the country. And all this came against a background of a slump in world fuel prices which had already taken shape.

What are the results? Evidently, the 12th 5-year plan may turn out to be the first when the planned indicators for profit are achieved. An active process of recovery of the finances of enterprises has begun, and over half of profit now remains in their control. Currently, approximately R250 billion is concentrated in the hands of enterprises, taking into consideration the remainder of resources for economic incentive funds. This is the same amount as the Union Budget has this year.

However, it is necessary to note that, if we are seeing a strengthening of finances of the main production link, then the state of affairs with the state finances continues to grow worse. What is the reason for this? Overall, in the first 4 years of the 5-year plan, the state has not managed to receive the planned revenues and to stop the growth in expenditures. When working out the 5-year plan, the government expected a worsening in the state of the world market. However, the actual situation has turned out much worse than we had forecast. As a result, the revenues from foreign economic activity will be R30 billion less than was planned. The consequences of the antialcohol campaign which was forced along have also had an effect. As a result, state revenue, taking into consideration receipts from all sources, is expected to be R40 billion less. At the same time, over the years 1986-1989, expenditures will exceed those which were anticipated by R62 billion.

A significant portion of resources, in accordance with the decisions of the 27th party congress, has been allocated to implement measures for the country's social development. Could we have refrained from such expenditure? Judge for yourselves. I will name them for you.

The state has allocated over the 4 years R21 billion over and above what was estimated in the 5-Year Plan just in implementing the reforms in the health service and in general and higher education, in increasing to a minimum extent the pension provision of various population groups, in improving assistance to children in low-income families, and in improving the material provision of orphans, plus other expenditure. This, I stress, does not include capital investment in housing and other nonproduction construction.

Moreover, almost R10 billion has gone in additional assistance to agriculture. As you already know, more than R8 billion was required after the Chernobyl accident. The expenditure to eliminate the consequences of the earthquake in Armenia is also substantial. We spent approximately R5 billion annually in Afghanistan. The state of monetary circulation has deteriorated badly.

What is happening here? First, let us speak about the incomes of the population. In the first 3 years of the 5-Year plan they exceeded by R20 billion the plan figure, and almost the entire increment occurred in 1988. The growth in wages alone proved to be R14.5 billion more than was planned. The point is that, in availing themselves of the right granted them to manage the resources

Eleventh Session

7 June 1989

being earned, many enterprises lost an economically substantiated connection between work remuneration and labor productivity, thus violating a most important requirement of the law on state enterprises. The national economy was, of course, not ready to increase the production of goods and services which could compensate for such an explosion in incomes as happened in 1988. As a result, an extremely acute situation formed on the consumer market, particularly in 1988 and early in 1989. This has given impetus to inflation processes. Such, comrades, is the actual situation in finances and monetary circulation.

The government has examined a program for the financial recovery of the economy. It is to be implemented in two stages.

The first stage covers 1989-90. It is envisaged, as I have already said, to increase significantly over that period the production of goods, to reduce production, investment, and expenditure on defense, to reduce expenditure on the maintenance of the administrative apparatus, and to toughen the economic drive, along with a number of other measures. In particular, the problem of loss-making enterprises should be singled out. There were approximately 9,000 of them in 1988 in the spheres of material production. And that is not counting collective farms [kolkhozes]. More than R5 billion was required to cover the losses. But that is just one aspect of the matter, the purely financial aspect.

Another aspect, one which is probably no less important, is that the existing economic system, in which leveling tendencies are still preserved, enables such enterprises to live at the expense of work collectives which are working well, and about which Deputy Bunich has spoken here so graphically.

The government adheres to the firm position that 1990 must be the last year for such an economic phenomenon, which is inadmissible under our conditions. Comrades, all these measures will allow the budget deficit in the current year to be reduced by R29 billion and next year by R34 billion. In the second stage, in the 13th 5-year plan, the task is set not only to stabilize the financial position but also to overcome the budget deficit. In our opinion, it is necessary to draw up a program for making finances healthier in the 13th 5-year plan while preparing the concepts and main directions of the economic and social development of the country for the forthcoming period, to consider it in the USSR Supreme Soviet and discuss it at the second Congress of People's Deputies.

I cannot but speak about that situation that is taking shape in society around the cooperative movement. The processes developing here are being perceived by the people in different ways, since they are contradictory in many respects and have beneath them not only a healthy foundation, but also the completely negative strivings of individual categories of cooperative workers. This is doing irremediable harm to the very nature of cooperatives, to which elements such as self-seeking, unearned gain, personal enrichment, self-interest, and ignoring the interests of citizens are unacceptable. Unfortunately, all this exists in our cooperative movement and arouses the anger of working people. They are demanding that order be introduced. Things are getting to the state that demands are being put forward to close public catering and trade cooperatives and cooperatives carrying out intermediary activity, to leave them only in the sphere of production and domestic services. [applause]

I have to say, comrades, that nevertheless we need here a well-considered approach and painstaking consistent work to make cooperatives healthy [applause] and we need liberation from all the scum that has appeared during these 2 years of stormy development. And this work must be carried out locally in the most energetic manner, above all by the soviets of people's deputies, which give cooperatives the authorization to exist when their statutes are registered. The soviets have now been given the most extensive rights and possibilities to influence the establishment of new types of cooperatives that are necessary to society, of course in conformity with local conditions, and also to regulate their activity by means of an effective system of taxation. The basis in this matter is clear: the development of the cooperative movement on the principles of social justice.

Comrade deputies, the investment policy has been subjected to particularly sharp criticism. We should get right to the bottom of this matter and change the situation that has come about and bring the position into a healthy state. The principal peculiarity of the contemporary investment policy consists in the fact that enterprises, as a result of carrying out reforms, have received large financial resources. Thus, if in 1986 the proportion of investment from enterprises' own resources constituted approximately 3 percent of the overall volume of state capital investment, in 1989 it will reach 41 percent.

This fundamentally changes the whole organization of the investment process. The insistent need for substantial changes in the running of the construction complex has peaked throughout the country. Excessive centralization has fettered the initiative of republican and local bodies and has prevented fully accounting for their requirements and regional possibilities from being used.

No less important is the fact that the republics' responsibility has been sapped. Decisions were made on the decentralization of the management of construction production. Administrative functions have been transferred to the union republics. The only exception now is the Russian Federation, where the basic contract work is carried out by the union ministries. But facts have shown that here too a similar step must be taken.

STENOGRAPHIC RECORD

Eleventh Session

7 June 1989

The production of building materials has also basically been transferred to the union republics. This approach is in full accord with the principles of the new regional policy. Nevertheless, the situation remains difficult. The economic mechanism currently in operation in construction has not eliminated the former gross-output approaches and has only a feeble effect on the time-scale and quality of work.

At the start of the 5-year plan, in order to restrict the extent of construction, tough administrative measures were adopted as a forced step, but they produced only temporary results. Subsequently, during the changeover in economic methods, the situation of earlier years was repeated due to the imperfections of the economic mechanism. In 1988, as compared with 1985, the number of newly-started construction projects, the plans for which are now independently formulated and confirmed by ministries and enterprises, again rose by 31 percent.

Thus, the scattering of capital investment occurred once again. The time required to erect buildings today is more than double the accepted standard. Uncompleted construction is on the increase. Assignments relating to the commissioning of a great deal of capacity regularly fail to be made. As a result, the national economy is approaching the 13th 5-year plan with far less productive potential than was envisaged in the 5-year plan.

A future government will have to tackle highly complex tasks concerning investment policy. An assessment of the possibilities, bearing in mind the country's financial position, shows that realistically the overall volume of investment from all sources of finance during the next 5-year plan period can grow by no more than 10 percent.

At the same time, it is necessary to carry out major structural changes in the national economy, primarily in capital construction. First, we are to guarantee a fundamental turn-around in the economy toward the achievement of social tasks, which requires a major economic maneuver with the country's resources. This signifies, in effect, a need for outstripping growth in all kinds of capital investments which are directed at strengthening the material basis of the social and cultural sphere. Estimates show that their portion in the overall volume of investments in the national economy in real terms can grow in the 13th 5-year plan to 34 percent compared to 26 percent in the 12th 5-year plan, and the increment will be 1.5 times that in the current 5-Year plan.

Second, it is necessary to give priority to investments in the agrarian complex, and especially its social sphere.

Third, in the coming period, the main efforts should be concentrated on a radical reconstruction of branches in all spheres of the economy which are directly working for people. As for the reequipment of capital-intensive, basic branches of the national economy, the scale thereof will have to be substantially reduced; correspondingly, the efficiency of the existing production potential will have to be sharply increased, although here there are likewise problems which—and we must take this into consideration—could have an effect on the work of the entire national economy. Under such conditions, a tough approach will naturally be required in drawing up the investment program.

It will be necessary to stop or to postpone until a later date the accomplishment of a number of major projects and the fulfilment of a number of decisions on the development of certain branches and regions. It is difficult to do this, and this most difficult process will be most painful. Suffice it to say that preliminary estimates show that it would be possible to reduce the level of investment by R27 billion at individual major construction sites and installations alone. And it will be necessary, of course, together with the union republics, to carry out a package of vigorous measures to cut down the number of incomplete construction works. We need this very much, primarily because, given a slight growth in capital investments, it will be possible to increase in real terms the introduction of fixed assets.

Alongside the implementation of measures for structural reconstruction of investment activity, we are to pass over to using a fundamentally new economic mechanism which is directed at improvement in all qualitative features in the construction industry, because the currently operating mechanism has major inadequacies. Many troubles in capital construction are a consequence of the practice which has formed in financing whereby money for the erection of individual installations is not earned but allocated according to the desires of higher organizations. Of course, all this must resolutely be changed. To put it figuratively, money must have its master. Only then will it be used in a thrifty way.

The main provisions for the economic mechanism in construction have been elaborated. Of course, they must be clarified, taking into consideration the opinions of all the union republics. The new government will draw the right conclusions from the sharp but justified criticism which there has been at the congress. We must come to a civilized level in the sphere of capital construction. We are building installations which will live for decades and even centuries, and it is they which will reflect the intellectual and technical level of contemporary society.

Comrade deputies, let me speak briefly about the problems in the development of science and technology. An immense unevenness and degree of contrast are typical of the scientific and technical sphere of the national economy. On the one hand, there are great achievements in some spheres of science and technology, and on the other hand, there is a deep scientific and technical backwardness in many spheres, one which simply contradicts common sense in today's terms. The reasons here have an objective and subjective character, but the main reason is the economic management mechanism. It does not contain a motivational system that would stimulate any collective to seek new things and make it

Eleventh Session

7 June 1989

impossible to have material prosperity without mastering the achievements of science and technology. We must carry out in a precise way the policy for deepening financial autonomy and self-financing in the sphere of scientific and design activity.

Scientific establishments in 23 industries worked in 1988 under such conditions. This year all establishments are switching over, and this includes academies and higher educational establishments and the scientific organizations of the defense complex. Given this, it is exceptionally important to find a deep economic validity in the correlation between budget financing and business contract financing in the development of applied and fundamental research works. It is absolutely clear that, by switching scientific establishments over to working under the new economic management conditions, promising fundamental development work which has state-wide, national and long-term significance must not in any way suffer. As previsouly, it must be financed mostly from the budget.

A year of work by industrial scientific organizations under the new conditions has shown that the principles contained in the economic mechanism are generally correct and efficient. True, it still shows some negative traits. Notably, an unjustified growth in wages and the setting of excessive prices for scientific-technical output are causing a reduction in pilot works and works to lay down scientific groundwork.

These impediments can be overcome, however. The main thing is to get the country engaged as quickly as possible in those development processes which are taking place today throughout the world. This concerns, primarily, the technological revolution which is objectively developing abroad. And great efforts and the concentration of our immense intellectual potential will be required here.

Comrades, problems connected with the creation of a favorable environment for human habitation are causing grave strains in the country. The movement which has developed in favor of environmental security is adopting a more and more acute social and political thrust. The vigor of the mass information media and of the population are totally understandable here. The practice of allowing the public to judge ecological issues in specific regions did not exist in the past. One must note that a considerable number of existing industrial enterprises—especially those which went into operation in the 1930's, 40's, and 50's—in the majority of cases, did not meet ecological standards. And technological processes at many industrial installations which have been freshly introduced lag behind contemporary requirements.

As a result, the ecological situation in a number of major industrial centers has proved very unfavorable. Emissions of harmful substances into the air alone now comprise approximately 100 million tonnes. During 1985-1988 decisions were passed by the government on the protection and the rational use of the natural resources of Lake Baykal and Lake Ladoga, and on additional measures to prevent air and water pollution in the towns of Chelyabinsk, Magnitogorsk, Karabash, Fergana, Kemerovo, Salavat, Sterlitamak, Tolyatti, and others. Work connected with the diversion of a party of the Northern and Siberian rivers and the construction of Rzhevskiy Hydro-Center and of the Volga-Chogray Canal has ceased. An all-embracing decision has also been made on nature conservation measures in the Aral Sea basin. Proposals on the Volga and Caspian Sea basins are being prepared. In comparison with 1985 the areas of reserves have increased from 18 to 21 million hectares.

As we can see, things are already being done. However, the burden of the accumulated problems is so great that it would be extremely difficult in a short period of time improve the current unfavorable ecological situation. Significant monetary and material resources are required for this. Thus, according to the preliminary calculations, R135 billion need to be assimilated, allotted and used during the course of three 5-year plans for implementing the long-term state nature conservation draft program while ensuring the necessary development of the productive forces of the country. That is an average of R45 million in each 5-year plan period as against the R15 billion of the current plan.

But it is not just a question of finances. To assimilate such resources, the specialized capacities of construction organizations need to be developed as well, and perhaps the most important thing is to create ecologically clean technologies and appropriate equipment.

Of all the acute problems which are being debated by the public today, the issues of atomic and hydropower engineering come to the fore. Many deputies' questions and addresses were received on them. The sources of such concern are understandable—they are Chernobyl, lowland hydroelectric power stations, and so on. The questions are so profound and so fundamental, they affect so directly the future development of the country, and so directly influence the living conditions of Soviet people that in our view, they deserve special scrutiny.

In our view, it is necessary to make suitable modifications to the USSR's current long-term power-supply program, to discuss it in the Supreme Soviet and to submit it for discussion by the whole people. [applause] It is also necessary to give special consideration once again to the whole package of issues associated with the situation in Belorussia, the Ukraine, and Russia that has arisen since the Chernobyl accident. In other words, the ecological problems confronting the country should be tackled by the whole production-technical and intellectual potential, including the scientific resources of the academies, higher educational establishments, and sectors of industry. It is essential to proceed toward improving the ecological situation, step by step, throughout the country's regions.

STENOGRAPHIC RECORD

Eleventh Session
7 June 1989

Comrades, the basis for the government's activities will always be a profound respect for the freedom and constitutional rights, the honor, and dignity of every Soviet citizen, and firm adherence to the principle of the consolidation of society and of the various social and demographic groups. This is very important. Centrifugal tendencies have intensified in the country; strikes and rallies for dubious purposes have grown more frequent; nationalist sentiments are being aroused. Here I would like to state definitely that one cannot permit flouting of human rights by virtue of national or any other indicators, anarchy and irresponsibility, interruptions in the labor rhythm, and rising crime and corruption. Strictly maintaining all democratic liberties on a legal basis, the new government will display firmness in creating an atmosphere of legality in public order in the country, including on the basis of strengthening and further improving the activity of law-enforcement bodies.

The process of democratization is growing rapidly in the country. Moreover, it is constantly embracing new spheres of people's lives. Democratic principles are becoming a stable part of our everyday life. This applies both to production and to culture, and to citizens' dealings with each other. Our whole political system, economy, and regional relations are becoming more democratic.

In a word, the healthy processes of the emancipation of the individual are going on more and more actively in this country, which is experiencing with difficulty the transitional period to a new quality of growth. However, the dialectics of this state in society mean that pseudodemocratic processes are developing alongside democratic principles. They are having an extremely negative effect on the stability of the situation in the state, eroding discipline and leading, contrary to common sense, to violations of order in society. Many good undertakings in the country are not being seen through to the end, because of laxity, irresponsibility and gross violations of elementary requirements.

We are being haunted by tragic cases accompanied by large numbers of human victims. Irresponsibility, an immoral attitude to the tasks, and sometimes even a gross deviation from elementary human duty are not infrequently behind all this.

We will undoubtedly succeed in eliminating phenomena of this kind from our society's life if literally the whole people engage in this cause. Having put forward the democratization of society as a primary task, the party put into this concept, first of all, the lofty sense of and need for well-understood discipline and order when the citizens of our huge country, in building a democratic society and state based on the rule of law and the principles of consolidation of efforts, do everything necessary so the country will advance surely along the path of progress in a stable and uninterrupted manner. Comrade deputies, the issues of ensuring state security, and of the overall guidance of the construction of the USSR Armed Forces, constitute one of the most important areas of the government's work. When forming the plans for 1986-90, because of the international situation prevailing at the time and our military doctrine, we were compelled to envision a traditional growth of defense expenses at a pace exceeding the growth of the national income. The peaceful initiatives of the Soviet state, the signing of a number of treaties on reducing and limiting individual types of armaments, and the principles of the new military defense doctrine, however, have made it possible to implement a truly revolutionary maneuver. Including the proposed reduction of expenditure for the forthcoming 2 years, the overall saving of defense expenses in relation to the approved 5-year plan will amount to nearly R30 billion [Russian: 30 milliardov]. No doubt, the congress has to have full information about the real defense expenses. Only in this case people's deputies will be able to have a notion about them that will enable them to participate actively in examining the formulation of military expenses. Thus, in 1989, out of the overall expenses amounting to R77.3 billion, the following allocations have been envisioned:

R32.6 billion for purchasing armaments and hardware;
R15.3 billion for research and development;
R20.2 billion for the upkeep of the Army and Navy;
R4.6 billion for military construction;
R2.3 billion for pensions for servicemen; and
R2.3 billion for other expenses.

I think there is no need to comment on these data. We intend to continue persistently along the path of disarmament and to strive for reducing by one-third to one-half the relative share of defense expenses in the national income by 1995. One assumes that this issue will occupy a special place in the activity of the USSR Supreme Soviet.

Taking into account the consistent reduction in spending on defense needs, the government will aspire to provide the Soviet Armed Forces with everything necessary while at the same time implementing the principle of reasonable sufficiency. The Army is a creation of the Soviet people and it deserves support with all the means at one's disposal. [applause]

There is a pressing need for a speedy conversion of military production, and for released capacities and resources to be directed to tackle social and economic tasks. These measures are creating the possibility to substantially increase by 50 to 100 percent the output of equipment for the agro-industrial complex, light industry, trade, and public catering. These sorts of measures have led this year to a change in the production structure of the defense complex. The pace of the output growth of civilian products and consumer goods is here double the growth of military output. Under the influence of the conversion, the production structure of the military complex is radically changing. While at present the relative share of civilian products is 40 percent of the general output of industry, in the current 5-year plan

Eleventh Session

7 June 1989

period, by the end of the current 5-year plan period, it will be 46 percent, and in 1995 more than 60 percent.

Guided by the decision on the reorientation of the national economy to meet social demands, defense industries have been instructed to ensure the speedy creation of new high technology types of civilian products and complex everyday goods. Above all, this applies to medical equipment. In 1989 its production by enterprises of defense industries will reach almost R240 billion [as heard] and in the longer term, annual output will reach not less than R1 billion. Taking into account special acuteness in the sphere of providing invalids with various medical equipment and also difficulties with providing prosthetic appliances, something which was discussed quite justly and with great sadness at the congress, the Council of Ministers has recently adopted a decision to hand over production in this sphere to leading enterprises engaged in the sphere of space. [applause]

The defense complex must make a much greater contribution in meeting the demands of the population for cultural and consumer goods. Now, defense industries are manufacturing this type of goods to the value of about 30 billion rubles, or 22 percent of the general output in the country. In 1990 their growth is to be 33 percent. We hope that in the 13th 5-year plan period the amount of such goods manufactured by the complex will be to the value of R250-270 billion, and will double the task of the current 5-year plan period. I consider it necessary to dwell also on the question of creating and using space equipment in the interests of defense and the national economy.

Clearly, just as is expenditure for defense purposes, information should also be presented to the congress about expenditure connected with the implementation of our space programs. So, what sums are being directed toward this? I will quote figures in thousands of millions of rubles. They are broken down as follows: national-economic and scientific space: 1.7; military space: 3.9; the Buran space shuttle system: 1.3; total R6.9 billion. The question arises: Is this expenditure justified? It is possible to say in this respect that the implementation of space programs of a military purpose alone, according to the calculations of Ministry of Defense specialists, will enhance the combat efficiency of our Armed Forces by 1.5-2 times. At the same time, the main thing is to place the achievements of space technology at the service of the national economy and to make them increasingly directed toward social issues. The possibilities here are immense. Let us take just one issue: the development of telephone communications. We will not be able to solve this problem in the conditions of our country by conventional traditional means for many years. Space will provide us with the opportunity to proceed along another, more rapid path, as was decided, for example, with television, which now reaches 94 percent of the population of our country.

I must also talk about the following. In the spirit of restructuring and the development of glasnost the procedure for working out and adopting decisions on defense questions will alter substantially. They will undoubtedly be examined in the same way as the state plan and budget. Our main duty before the people is to ensure peaceful living conditions for the present and future generations of Soviet people on the basis of the implementation of a foreign policy which has been profoundly considered and thoroughly adjusted. Soviet peace initiatives will undoubtedly increase. The policy toward a radical improvement in international relations will continue to be actively developed. The government sees as one of its most important commitments to persistently put it into practice and to serve in every way the noble cause of asserting the spirit of trust, mutual understanding, and cooperation between all countries.

Comrades, a few words about foreign-economic activity and the country's foreign currency situation. The measures which have been taken here have been directed toward making our economy more open and providing all enterprises, associations and organizations, including cooperatives, with the opportunity of participating in the international division of labor. At the present time, when all have been granted the right to enter foreign markets, over 2,000 participants in foreign economic activity have already been registered in the country.

About 460 joint enterprises have been founded on the territory of the USSR. Two thousand contracts or direct ties with partners from the CEMA countries have been concluded. A strategy has been elaborated for the development of the USSR's foreign economic ties. The main thing in it is the transition from traditional forms of trading to the most broad cooperation in science, technology, and production. We envision a substantial change in the structure of exports, and a sharp rise in the proportion of manufactured goods among them. In imports, the priority is being given to purchases of equipment for modernization and reconstruction. However, the situation in foreign economic activity at present remains very complex. In 1988, as compared with 1985, exports had fallen by 7.6 percent, and imports by 6.3 percent. We have not managed to compensate with an increase in incomes for export of manufactured products the losses connected with the fall in world oil prices, from R160 per tonne in 1985 to R60 in 1988, and that for petroleum products and gas, amounting to about R25 billion in freely convertible currency alone over the past 3 years. The situation does not permit us to avoid the purchase abroad of many kinds of production. Thus, over the first 3 years of the 5-year plan, we imported food products and raw materials for their manufacture worth nearly R31 billion. This year about R22 billion will be spent on import of consumer goods and food, including over R5 billion in hard currency for grain and food alone. The continuing high demand for imports along with restricted ability to pay has led to the USSR's hard currency debts being more than double the annual

STENOGRAPHIC RECORD

Eleventh Session

7 June 1989

incomes from exports of goods and services. In connection with this, we have been compelled to take short-term credits, and to an ever greater extent of late. But even all the incomes from oil do not cover the interest payments. The government has calculated that the extraordinary hard currency debt is fraught with serious economic and political consequences. We have overstepped to such an extent, speaking figuratively, the red mark of the 25-percent correlation between payments for credit and currency incomes tolerated in international practice. It is clear that we must approach the questions of loans with the maximum circumspection. On the whole, I see the task in that the work of the new government must be directed toward decisively overcoming the alienation of our economy from the processes going on in the world economy, artificially created in the course of many years. As before, priority attention will be devoted to strengthening relations with socialist countries and to socialist economic integration.

In conclusion, I would like to say that we have to implement our work in a qualitatively changed political situation, and work with genuinely democratic soviets of people's deputies and their supreme organ of power.

The principal distinguishing feature of the government which will be appointed will be the fact that in new conditions it will really become a people's power organ enjoying the full rights. Only then it can be a reliable guarantee of the strict fulfillment of people's will. The party has made an irrevocable choice in favor of the Leninist concept of socialism as the living creativity of the masses, as a society developing on the basis of new genuinely humane goals. As of now, we can lean on all the experience and energy of people, the unbreakable unity between the policy and the everyday needs and interests of people. It was only yesterday when personal initiative, special regional features, cultural differences and nonstandard thinking were only obstacles for the bureaucratic management, but today they are the main sources for our hopes and optimism. I am convinced that by advancing firmly and consistently along the route of political and economic changes we shall at the end solve our urgent social problems. No matter how important is all that which will be done in the material sphere, we must not lose the most precious property—the cultural and spiritual heritage of the people—because people who lose their spiritual material have no historical prospects. On this level, I am supporting with all sincerity the position outlined at the Congress by the Deputy Dmitriy Sergeyvich Likhachev. He said that without culture in society there is no principled morality either, and without the elementary morality social and economic laws do not function. A low level of culture has a negative effect on public life, state work, on interethnic relations. The government will do everything possible to develop the material base of culture, press, and other mass information media and any useful initiatives and creative efforts to enrich the cultural heritage of the people; and the intellecutual potential of the society will receive our support. [applause]

Comrades! Many socioeconomic problems have accumulated in the country and this is also obvious from the discussion at the congress. All of them deserve the most serious attention. Their solution is only possible with intensive and very productive work of the entire national economy, every person. We have to consolidate ourselves for the solution of these problems. Only the cohesion and wisdom of the people can get the country out of the complex situation. We have ahead of us enormous work in the implementation of the party's course toward the renewal of the Soviet society. It is possible to fulfil it only under conditions of political stability in the state, and through the coordinated efforts of all peoples of our country. The new composition of the USSR Council of Ministers will make use of all the useful things accumulated in the past years and all that which is being worked out by the Congress of People's Deputies, and on this basis will strive for a steady and dynamic movement of the country on the path of restructuring and progress. In this lies the entire essence of our work. Thank you. [applause]

M.S. Gorbachev: Comrades, at the stage that we have reached in the work of our congress we need to consult with one another. We in the Presidium have exchanged opinions and want to convey our thoughts to you. We would like to end the sitting of the congress at this point now and resume the joint sitting of the Supreme Soviet chambers at 1800. There are impassioned and very meaningful discussions there, too. That is the first point, that is for today. As for subsequent days, I would ask you, dear comrades, to listen to how we in the presidium see the situation and how we propose proceeding subsequently.

Tomorrow, Thursday 8 June—debates on the question of the basic guidelines of the USSR's domestic and foreign policy and the program of the USSR Government's forthcoming activity. This is my answer to the question which arose before the report. We shall work from 1000 to 1400. At 1400 we shall have a recess, and we in the Presidium are going to discuss the list of questions for inclusion on the agenda under the heading "any other business." This can be done right now, because many questions which were proposed for discussion in this section at some point are already being resolved and are even being reflected in the main decision—the draft decision. It is our intention, and the commission we created together is working toward that, to issue before the sitting a draft resolution "On the Basic Guidelines of Domestic and Foreign Policy" so that deputies have the time to work on them thoroughly.

After that, the evening session will examine the question of the confirmation of the chairman of the Council of Ministers, the election of the Constitutional Oversight Committee, the confirmation of the chairman of the USSR People's Control Committee, the chairman of the USSR Supreme Court, the USSR Prosecutor General, and the Chief State Arbiter.

Eleventh Session

7 June 1989

Day 13. Friday 9 June. The morning sitting—the debates continue. But the debates will end, too, and the congress resolution will be adopted. That is all from 1000 to 1400. The adoption of the congress resolution "On the Basic Guidelines of the Domestic and Foreign Policy of the USSR" and the adoption of the congress resolution "On the formation of the Constitutional Commission." The evening sitting's agenda: items under "any other business." And the congress will finish work on Friday [9 June] evening.

For the Supreme Soviet: The second sitting of the Soviet of the Union is to be held starting at 1000, 10 June, at which the deputy chairman of the Soviet of the Union will be elected (both chairmen of the chambers are presently working with deputies to prepare proposals). The election of standing commissions of the Soviet of the Union. Examination of proposals on the composition of the committees of the USSR Supreme Soviet. At 1300 there will be the second sitting of the Soviet of Nationalities. The same agenda. And at 1600 the second joint sitting of the chambers. The agenda as follows: Election of committees of the USSR Supreme Soviet, examination of the proposals of the chairman of the USSR Council of Ministers on the composition of the USSR Government and also of proposals on the composition of the USSR People's Control Committee, the USSR Supreme Court, and the collegium of the Prosecutor's Office. These proposals are just being submitted now, but subsequently, as we have already said today, to examine these proposals in the Supreme Soviet deputies will clearly need a couple of weeks, because it is necessary to meet with everyone in all the commissions, to get to know one another, to elucidate everything, and to produce a conclusion in order to reach a decision. After the second joint sitting of the chambers, where these proposals will be heard, a recess is declared in the work of the Supreme Soviet until 20 June this year. That will be on 10 June, that is to say, for 10 days.

A.I. Lukyanov: But the commissions will be working.

M.S. Gorbachev: They will. These are the proposals. Can we take them as our basis?

Deputies: We can.

M.S. Gorbachev: Do you need to be given time to consider this, or can we adopt it right now? And if something arises in the meantime, will we introduce modifications at the congress? You need to think about it?

From the hall: Yes.

M.S. Gorbachev: Perhaps we'll resolve it this way, comrades, if it is acceptable? I propose that this be accepted as the basis. Comrades can think about it, and if they have any substantive proposals, they will send them to the Presidium.

From the hall: (Inaudible).

M.S. Gorbachev: No, discussion will continue, Andrey Dmitriyevich, discussion will go on. This is the framework of our work.

From the hall: (Inaudible).

M.S. Gorbachev: But, you know, as far as "any other business" is concerned, we will be working in the Presidium tomorrow and report to you. The point is that many questions have been submitted under "any other business," but we have already set up commissions on three of them, the most important ones. And a number of others questions remain: on standing orders, and several others which are being submitted. The Presidium will submit these proposals for your discussion. I have only set out the framework here, and as far as "any other business" is concerned, there will be another separate proposal on this question.

Who is in favor of adopting these proposals as the basis? Please vote.

Please lower your hands.

Against?

Lower your hands, please.

Abstentions?

Carried. Well, comrades, this basis will give us the opportunity to work and creatively approach and consider possible serious, cogent proposals. Okay?

From the hall: Yes.

M.S. Gorbachev: Fine. A recess in the congress work is declared until 1000 tomorrow. The Supreme Soviet session starts here, where we have been working, at 1800.

FIRST CONGRESS OF PEOPLE'S DEPUTIES OF THE USSR
TWELFTH SESSION
THURSDAY, 8 JUNE 1989
THE KREMLIN PALACE OF CONGRESSES

The morning of the Twelfth Session was spent on discussion of the government's program outlined by N. I. Ryzhkov on the previous day. Thirteen speakers offered a variety of perspectives, but their recurrent theme was a call for the devolution of power and responsibility from the center to local, regional, and republican soviets and enterprises.

The highlight of the session was the afternoon's debate over the creation of a new constitutional body, the Constitutional Oversight (or Compliance) Committee—a dispute that resulted in another Lithuanian boycott. Baltic opposition to the committee was expressed in a petition delivered and explained by Romas V. Gudaytis, a Lithuanian writer of Estonian extraction and member of the inner council of Sajudis. The basic objection of the Lithuanians and their allies stemmed from their concern that without constitutional reform the new committee might become a citadel for preserving the status quo in a highly centralized unitary state. Therefore they demanded a constitutional amendment giving veto power to each republican representative on the committee. Their basic demand, however, was to postpone the question to the fall or until the constitution had been perfected. Gorbachev, on the other hand, contended that other responsibilities of the Supreme Soviet Presidium would prevent it from effectively monitoring constitutional compliance. Only a committee of the country's leading jurists, he argued, could ensure that republics, collectives, central organs, and citizens were conforming to constitutional requirements and the policies of a socialist state committed to the rule of law. The proposal to form the committee was adopted over the opposition of 433 deputies and the abstention of 61, including 50 members of the Lithuanian delegation who then stalked out of the hall. That compelled the chair to postpone the actual appointment of the committee so that Gorbachev and the Congress Presidium could meet with the Lithuanians and allay their concerns.

The remainder of the session was devoted to the confirmation of the Supreme Soviet's nominees for constitutional office. N. I. Ryzhkov, Ye. A. Smolentsev, and Yu. G. Matveyev were easily confirmed in the posts of Chairman of the Council of Ministers, Chairman of the Supreme Soviet, and Chief State Arbiter of the USSR. There was significantly less enthusiasm for G. V. Kolbin's appointment to head the USSR People's Control Commission, and A. Ya. Sukharev, the nominee for USSR General Prosecutor, was vigorously challenged on numerous issues not least of which was his alleged role in squelching suspected Kremlin connections with persons convicted or implicated in the "Uzbek Case."

Texts of documents cited during the Twelfth Session are compiled in Appendices at the end of this volume: Constitution (Basic Law) of the USSR, Articles 114, 119, and 125 (Appendix A.1); Law on Criminal Liability for State Crimes, Article 11-1 (Appendix A.4).

TWELFTH SESSION
THURSDAY, 8 JUNE 1989
STENOGRAPHIC RECORD

USSR People's Deputy A.-M.K. Brazauskas is in the chair.

A.-M.K. Brazauskas: Comrades! We are continuing the work of the congress. Please take your seats. Today there are 2,082 people's deputies present at the morning session. We will continue the debates on questions regarding the basic directions of USSR domestic and foreign policy and the government's program of action.

Twelfth Session
8 June 1989

Some more information before we begin.... Later? We can do it later.

Comrade Gennadiy Vasilyevich Bykov has the floor. Comrade Shmelev should get ready.

G.V. Bykov, fitter-installer brigade leader, Leningrad I.I. Leps Scientific-Production Association "Znamya Truda" (Krasnogvardeyskiy Territorial Electoral District, Leningrad): Honorable comrade deputies! It is not easy for me, a worker, to step up to this podium for the first time, but I cannot keep silent, as I feel the need to bring to you all the urgent questions that concern the workers of the city of Leningrad. The electoral campaign and meetings with voters have shown that the people are clearly dissatisfied with the pace at which restructuring is proceeding. The growth of inflation, the shortage of food products and industrial goods, the waiting lines which insult human dignity, the increase in crime, and the general deterioration of the state of affairs in the country all evoke acute dissatisfaction. The reason for this is the lack of proper planning and haste in resolving a number of questions.

Let us recall at least the lack of consideration in the resolution on combatting drunkenness, the extremes in resolving questions regarding cooperatives or the agroprom [agro-industrial complex], and the frequently appearing incomplete legislative statutes. As you well understand, it is the people who must pay for all this. The working class supports restructuring. It supports the quickest possible realization of economic and political reforms. Yet we, the workers, seem to have been left aside from it.

For 4 years, few have been interested in our problems, in those processes which were developing within the working environment, or in our opinion about the course of restructuring. Many organizations in our country are united into various kinds of unions. There is a union of teachers, writers, artists, and even cooperatives. Yet the most massive representative organization of workers does not have its own union. The time has come to recognize the need for bringing together representatives of the working class on a country-wide level. Therefore, I propose that the USSR Supreme Soviet create a union of workers in the very near future.

Comrades! You and I can see how slowly economic reform is developing and how poorly cost accounting is being realized, about which so much is said and written. Having absolved themselves of the responsibility for plan fulfillment, the ministries nevertheless retain in their hands all the resources and the right to distribute the profits we have earned. Talk about the independence and self-management of enterprises will remain merely empty words if these concepts are not backed by an appropriate financial base and a real possibility of making independent decisions. For this purpose, I propose that we review the functions of the ministries, limiting their capacities to decide everything for the enterprises. We also must review the question of reducing their number, thereby reducing the huge expenditures for their maintenance.

As a worker, I would especially like to deal with the question of technical retooling, as I believe that restructuring is impossible without it, just as the improvement in labor conditions of the workers and in the living standard of our people is impossible without it. At the present time, we have a great scientific-technical potential in our country. However, manual labor is retained at many enterprises and old equipment and technology are still being used. Can it be that there are no more bright minds in Russia? Of course not. It is just that we must interest people in thinking constructively.

We must develop conditions that not only stimulate but also activate the work of the scientific-research institutes and design bureaus in this direction on a competitive basis and with independent, objective expert opinion. Only this will enable us in the next few years to acquire new engineering and new technological production, to improve the labor conditions of the workers, and consequently to increase the volume and improve the quality of the manufactured products.

The improvement in working conditions must be combined with accelerated resolution of social questions. After a hard day of work, the worker must rest in normal home surroundings. Yet in Leningrad the general housing problem is very acute, including for the working class.

For many years, Leningrad and other large cities have been replenished with work cadres from rural areas. As a result, as you know, many villages have died out. There is an exodus of the population from the small cities in Russia. Part of Leningrad's working class is comprised of newcomers, former limit workers, who have lived for many years in dormitories and communal apartments under crowded conditions. A significant portion of the new generation of Leningraders was born and grew up under difficult housing conditions. At the same time, Leningrad residents have not yet fulfilled their sacred duty to the people who survived the blockade, the participants in the Great Patriotic War.

Despite the limitations, the influx of work cadres from other cities to Leningrad continues. Therefore, I propose that we take measures to reduce the growth of the large cities which are already difficult to manage, and not to expand in them the network of industrial enterprises. Each city must make do with its own efforts.

At the same time, we must improve the life of the people in small cities, settlements, and villages, and do everything possible to see that the population does not flee from there. Only these measures, in my opinion, will allow us to gradually resolve many problems in our country, including the housing problem in Leningrad.

Twelfth Session

8 June 1989

Comrades! In meetings with voters during the election campaign, the question of the Law on Cooperatives and their activity was constantly raised. Cooperatives are a good thing, and I support them. I will not dwell on the negative aspects, about which much has been said. This was especially well treated in the speech by Deputy Sherbakov, the chairman of the Moscow City Soviet of Trade Unions. I believe this is the opinion of all the workers. It must alert our government and motivate it to think seriously about this question.

I believe the time has come to review the law on the activity of the cooperatives. We know that the enterprises deduct over half of our income to the state budget. All the people use these funds, including the members of the cooperatives. Yet the cooperatives themselves symbolically transfer to the state budget in some cases 3-5 percent of their profits. Is this fair? Of course not. I support the proposals of the deputies that we place cooperatives under equal conditions with the enterprises and build all mutual relations on a competitive basis.

We, the deputies, like all the Soviet people, fervently greeted and support the announcement by Nikolay Ivanovich Ryzhkov regarding the fact that beginning in 1990 the pension for low-income pensioners will be increased. I believe this is a good beginning. Having corrected the state of affairs in the country, we will be able to further resolve all our social questions.

Comrades! At the beginning of my deputy activity, I encountered a number of questions and with my own eyes became convinced of the inability of the rayon soviet executive committee [rayispolkoms] to resolve certain problems. For example, it turned out that in the headlong rush to provide housing for the population, there was lack of integration in building up our Krasnogvardeyskiy Rayon. I know for a fact that the leaders of our rayispolkom literally had to tear away from the city the social facilities which were specified in the detailed plan outline. People wait for years for the resolution of many social questions, and lose faith in promises. The reason for this, I believe, is that the rayons are still entirely dependent on the city authorities and cannot resolve questions independently.

I know that such a situation has arisen not only here, but also in other regions of our country. Therefore, I propose that we quickly adopt the law on the development of full local self-government and the formulation of the budget of local organs of authority at the expense of enterprises located on their territory. This will allow the rayispolkoms to resolve many questions for themselves.

Comrades! Whatever aspects of restructuring we touch upon, we cannot forget the most important thing—man. I have believed and still believe that the people's deputy must strive toward realizing the basic interests of every honest person. Look for yourselves. Who if not the worker creates material values in our country, and who if not the worker has the shortest, 15-day, vacation? I myself am a worker and understand all too well that in this time it is impossible to restore one's powers so that after the vacation one can continue to work with full return. I believe that the law on vacations of workers and employees must have a clearly defined duration of time—24 work days. (Applause). This is not only the desire, but also the demand of the workers of Leningrad, and I believe all the workers of our country.

In concluding my presentation, I would like to say that the voters have set great tasks before us, and this is as it should be. I have touched upon only the smallest portion of them. Now we must do everything possible to bring these mandates to life. We must do everything possible to bring our country out of that difficult position in which it has found itself. We must do everything to see that the slogan which was proclaimed in 1917, "All power to the soviets!", is brought to life not merely in word, but in deed.

Comrades! Today we have democracy, glasnost, and pluralism of opinion. Everyone can say whatever he wants. Yet I was insulted and hurt to the depths of my soul by the speech of Deputy Karyakin, who spoke about re-intering the body of Vladimir Ilyich Lenin at Volkov cemetery. He said that the people would understand this. No, Comrade Karyakin, the people will not understand. And I, a worker, do not support your proposal. The interment of Vladimir Ilyich Lenin in the mausoleum in Red Square is the will of the people. It is the memory of the people, and we must preserve it in perpetuity. Thank you for your attention. (Applause).

A.-M.K. Brazauskas: Comrade Shmelev has the floor. Comrade Prunskene should get ready.

N.P. Shmelev, doctor of economic sciences, section head at the USSR Academy of Sciences United States of America and Canada Institute, Moscow (from the USSR Academy of Sciences): Honorable Comrade Chairman! Honorable colleagues! I would like to begin by saying that I as an economist am not too concerned about the long-term prospects for our development. I believe that we as a nation and as a country do not intend to commit suicide and, having tried all thinkable and unthinkable methods of organizing our economic life, we cannot help but enter upon that path which Vladimir Ilyich Lenin defined in the 20's, in the last 2 years of his life, and in his fundamental ideas. Specifically, in the 70 years of our history we have had only 7-8 years of a really effective economy, and we simply cannot avoid returning to this road. We have no other alternative. Yet this requires time. In the West, an average of 8-10 years are needed to bring back a bankrupt, dying company to something viable. Of course, a considerably longer time is needed for such a gigantic economic organism as the Soviet economy.

Yet I am very much concerned with our short-term prospects. I am concerned about the next 2-3 years. I must express my fear that if we do not stop this snowballing

Twelfth Session

8 June 1989

inflation, if we do not stop the disintegration of the consumer market and the monstrous, world-record (in relation to the gross national product) budget deficit, within 2-3 years we may be faced with economic collapse.

What awaits us in this case? The scenario for development of events was written 200 years ago, during the time of the French revolution. It has been repeated several times since in history, and we are repeating it with the same sequence as before. We will be faced with a general rationing system, sharp devaluation of the ruble, unbridled expansion of the black market and a shadow economy, disintegration of the consumer market and a forced, I emphasize, forced return to administrative-command discipline in our national economy for some time.

After the speech presented by Nikolay Ivanovich Ryzhkov, I once again became convinced that the country's government and leadership understand that we are faced with such a danger. Yet I have grave doubts as to whether or not they understand the degree of acuteness of this danger. The Council of Ministers has outlined measures for levelling out the market and for reducing the budget deficit. Yet these measures, in my opinion, are insufficient and too long drawn out. While our budget deficit is somewhere on the level of over R100 billion, the measures for economy for this year will reduce it by less than R30 billion, and next year by slightly over R30 billion. The rest will again be the production of the printing presses, again forced loans from our investment holders in savings banks and from our enterprises. I am afraid that our economy will not be able to withstand such a gigantic mass of new monetary additions over what we already have.

Why has this situation arisen? The explanation commonly given is that the rapid growth of wages is responsible for everything. This is not fair. As we saw from yesterday's speech, the increase in wages over the last year was R14 billion, while the budget deficit is in excess of R100 billion. Moreover, comrades, whether we want it or not and regardless of the conditions, our specific conditions, a great historical process has begun. The degree of exploitation of the work force in our country is the highest of all the industrial countries. In our country, about 37-38 percent of the gross national product goes for wages. In the industrial world this indicator comprises 70 or more percent. Our working class has the moral right to increase its share in the gross national product, and it is approaching the resolution of this task by all possible means. Therefore, we must consider this for the future, because to stop this process is impossible. A second commonly given explanation which has resounded here and from the tribunal of the congress is that the co-operators are at fault for everything, that they turn noncash funds into cash. This is a totally incompetent explanation. The annual income of our population is on the order of R430 billion. All the income paid out for wages to co-operators comprises around R2 billion, and of these over a billion is simply a redistribution of money which they already have. Thus, co-operators share less than a fourth of a percent of the blame for the fact that the printing presses are running.

What has led to this situation? Yesterday, Nikolay Ivanovich Ryzhkov rightfully spoke of the heavy legacy which we have inherited. This is true. We have inherited the traditional factors of the budget deficit, and they are retained to the present day. Yet we cannot help but see the situation, which is that over those 3 5-year plans to which our premier referred, the budget deficit averaged R20 billion, while today it is more than R100 billion. This is already a new quality. These are already new reasons, reasons which have emerged in the last 3-4 years, and I would like to point out the most important of these. This, first of all, is the absolutely unqualified statute on the sale of alcoholic beverages which was often mentioned here. This was a noble statute, but as they say, stupidity is often worse than thievery. With good intentions, we dealt a great blow to the equilibrium of the market and to the balance of the budget deficit. The second mistake was the short-term but very painful campaign of 1986 in the struggle against so-called non-labor income, which dealt a painful blow to our agriculture. The third mistake, which we also could have avoided, was necessitated by the drop in oil prices, the sharp decline in prices, and our forced reduction of imports. Yet we preferred to reduce not grain imports, but the imports of machines and equipment. In doing so, we slashed at the most vital thing on which our state budget was based. We slashed at the import of consumer goods, where a ruble of currency spent on import yields from R8 to R10 of income in the budget, and with proper smart combination of the import structure this coefficient may be increased even more. And finally, there is the last mistake which I cannot explain by any rational arguments. While last year our budget deficit was somewhere at the level of R50-60 billion, this year it has skyrocketed past R100 billion. At the same time, our capital investments have also skyrocketed. Where did this money come from? This means that from the very beginning the government opted for covering all these expenses with the printing press. There have been no other sources for this growth in capital investments. This was a conscious step toward inflation.

Of course, I do not envy Nikolay Ivanovich Ryzhkov's position. He is being pressured by our not too knowledgeable ministers, who have gold stars in their eyes, and in this case they rush, as they say, as if to a buffet table. But do we have central authority or not? Could Nikolay Ivanovich and Boris Ivanovich Gostev have said: "No, there is no money. We are not going to print any more money"? I believe such a possibility existed.

In order to avoid a financial catastrophe, a financial crash, we need to cure our economy, and primarily to revitalize our financial system. This means levelling the market, balancing the supply of goods and monetary

STENOGRAPHIC RECORD

Twelfth Session
8 June 1989

means, and primarily eliminating the budget deficit. Why is this so necessary for us? Primarily to raise the living standard of the people—workers, peasants, the intelligentsia, and pensioners. If today we created such a commodity situation in the country where a person could spend each ruble for what he wants, this would mean approximately a 1.5-time increase in the living standard for all categories of the population. Second, every ruble must finally begin to work in the economy, so that people would want to earn this ruble. And thirdly, we must create a situation in which the supply of goods exceeds the demand so as to put into effect all the incentives of the new economic system, and primarily such a stimulus as the competition of producers.

How can we achieve the treatment and revitalization of our financial system? As far as I understand, the government is placing all its hopes on the sharp growth of consumer goods production this year and in 1990. Without going into detail, I can only say that this envisioned growth is not enough. It will barely be enough to cover the growth of the monetary mass. Yet that huge amount of money which is not backed by commodity goods and which the population has accumulated cannot touch this growth in any way.

There is another proposal: To perform radical reform of consumer prices. It is correct in itself. Yet in the current situation, when the social situation is so tense, I believe that we cannot risk taking such a step for some time, at least until the market is saturated even to a slight degree. It is no accident that according to surveys, only one-third of the population favors the reform of retail prices, and only under the condition that the stores begin to stock everything.

There is one other desperate proposal. It is the proposal to confiscate excess money from the population. From this tribunal I would like to address Deputy Viktor Afanasyev, the editor in chief of PRAVDA. I would like to ask him and his editorial staff what they were thinking when they published Chekalin's article, in which PRAVDA openly calls for taking personal money away from the population. Truly no CIA, no class enemy, can bring us so much harm as we can do to ourselves through our own, we might say, imprudence. Such appeals during such a heated situation, when everything disappears from the store shelves, when people, sensing impending inflation, grab whatever they can—these mean throwing another bucket of oil into the fire and increasing the alarm. As if all these incidents with soap, with salt, and matches were not enough for us. To add to this, PRAVDA—the central organ (we might add, in spite of the assurances of the government)—fans the emotions of the people: Spend money before it turns into simple pieces of paper. And the very confiscation of money (I do not even take a moral side), what can it give under current conditions? It will plug the budget hole for 6 months or so, and then we will again return to things as they were before. Not to mention how this would undermine the attitude and trust of the people toward restructuring.

Thus, whether we want to or not, in the matter of revitalizing our financial situation we must resort to normal economic measures. Not to confiscation in one form or another, but specifically to the application of those commodity-monetary relations which we have today.

I will try to present, comrades, that program which seems realistic to me. If I take one or two extra minutes, please forgive me. I warn you from the start that many may not like this program, and that it will probably not gain the support of the government.

What measures seem necessary now? First of all, to return to normal trade in alcoholic beverages. We must stifle the bootleggers not with the militia (the militia is powerless here), but with economic measures. These bootleggers, first of all, have taken away state income, and, second, they are destroying the entire social stability of our society. I would like to turn here to the writer Vasiliy Belov. If I called him an ideologue of the mafia, of the black economy, of rampant speculation, he would probably be very offended. But in fact that is how it is. Today, even if we refer to the official publications, half of the alcoholic beverages in the country (you have this reference at hand, comrade deputies) are already produced by bootleggers. This is only from sugar, not counting the tomato paste, "taburetovka" [the cheapest, most inferior ingredients], various bug exterminating fluids containing alcohol, and everything else. Drinking has not declined. That is an illusion. And people generally do not drink because of price. They drink because of depression, because of lies, and because of nothing to do. Here we must seek methods of solving the problem rather than destroying one of the sources of commodity and budget equilibrium in the country. (Applause).

The second factor is equalizing the market situation. Today in our country, according to the evaluations of specialists, there is somewhere around R150 billion in "hot" money. This is money which is waiting for goods to appear on the market. These are not savings for the future. Throw the goods on the store shelf, and this money will immediately jump out onto the market. To dislodge this R150 billion, we need approximately $15 billion worth of various imported consumer goods. Plus, for the next 2-3 years, while the economy is in such a state of imbalance, while there is a danger of collapse, we need artificial, I emphasize, artificial import on the order of $5-6 billion a year to maintain the commodity equilibrium. Where will we get this money? Yesterday we heard the very serious report by Nikolay Ivanovich Ryzhkov that there is no money like this in the country. I dare to affirm that if we want to, this money can be found.

First of all, will the government ever seriously present our collective farm [kolkhoz] chairmen with the notion that if they submit grain and meat in excess of a certain customary level, they will be paid in currency, with the

STENOGRAPHIC RECORD

Twelfth Session

8 June 1989

right to spend this currency wherever they like? (Applause). We might add that our people are humble. I am convinced that we do not have to pay them $200 per tonne. They will settle for 75, and will sell it at that price. This is the first source of a colossal savings in currency. Here is the second source: Year in and year out we have a carry-over reserve of uninstalled machinery and equipment which, if recalculated into dollars, is somewhere on the order of 10 billion. Perhaps we should stop the import of equipment for all of our gigantic projects for 5 or 10 years? (Applause).

The third source. Unfortunately, I am forced to use foreign statistics here, as we do not publish this information. We might ask: Has anyone ever thought how much our interests in Latin America cost us, for example? According to American professional estimates, it is $6-8 billion annually. A considerable part of this is in hard currency. And we do not know what a considerable part is for when we, for example, pay 400 percent for Cuban sugar (as compared with the world price), we pay this in hard currency. This source alone would be enough to keep the consumer market in equilibrium for those few years which we need to somehow get by and to truly embark upon the road to reform.

Finally, there are loans. Nikolay Ivanovich says that he does not want to leave any debts for his grandchildren. I can understand him, but nevertheless there is something provincial in this. Today the whole world borrows with one hand and repays with the other. Everyone lives, so to speak, on credit. And if we borrow a certain sum (less than that debt which today hangs over us, and again if we believe Western sources, the net debt hanging over us is somewhere on the order of $30 billion), nothing terrible will happen. How can we repay it? If we speak in business terms (any financier will understand me), the fact is that today no one repays debts. They do not have to repay them. They only have to maintain the interest payments, and in order to service the additionally borrowed money, any of the three sources which I have mentioned above would be sufficient. These, I repeat, are the reduction in imports of agricultural products, the reduction in the import of heavy equipment, and the reduction of our expenditures on international obligations.

Furthermore, if we are thinking about equalizing the market, we must make the decision to sell land or at least to give it on permanent lease to anyone who wants. This is a great source of extracting money. (Applause). We must make the decision not merely to talk about, but already to really sell apartments, to sell trucks, to sell tractors, to sell everything which is held in reserve. Let the government sell anything it can so as to somehow equalize the market. And finally, there is such a factor as stockholding, stocks and standard 30-year state loans at high interest. This would also paralyze a certain considerable portion of the unstable money held by the population.

Yet here is what else I would like to emphasize: Those funds which we can receive from increased import of consumer goods—this money should be destroyed, written off. Only in this case will we finally achieve a precedence of supply over demand on the market, which will allow us to change over to normal economic conditions and to normal competition. We can and must also extract excess money from the enterprises and also write it off and destroy it. By what means? By means of auctions. Go ahead, if you please, sell your automobile to your neighbor, if he wants, for 10 times the price. But you will then hand over half of this price to the budget, and the budget will destroy this money. And, of course, there are state loans: Empty money not secured by commodities which held by the enterprises may also be involved in the stable state structure, selling them obligations for long-term state loans at high interest.

We have already spoken here about the other sources of reducing our expenditures. Of course, we must reduce industrial capital investments. For example, yesterday I was glad to hear that, thank God, we will finally increase pensions. Yet does anyone even understand that if we stopped only one of the "projects of the century"—the Tyumen project—this money would be enough to increase pensions and to increase payments to all our underprivileged strata of the population already this year? And how many such "Tyumen projects" are we still realizing or just barely beginning to realize? We must understand that the state is bankrupt, that for the next 10 years there cannot be any "building of communism", that we can build only that which yields rapid comsumer effect. (Applause). No "building of communism"! (Applause). And I believe that the banks, through increased interest rates, must today also hold back the capital investments of enterprises.

Defense expenditures were also mentioned here. There is also one other factor—a very delicate one. I do not know if our farmers will support me or not. Of course, our agriculture needs additional injections of state funds. It needs support. Yet we have thought up the most ineffective, the most inept form of state aid to agriculture, where to one who works well we pay a ruble for a kilogram of produce, but to one who is all thumbs we pay 2 rubles (Applause). We need to eliminate this. (Applause). And this expenditure is no joke. It comprises almost one-third of the state budget deficit. We must rid ourselves of this expenditure as soon as possible. I do not want to say that for 3 years, until we treat and revitalize our financial position, we must apply the brakes to economic reform. No, revitalization and reform must proceed in parallel. Yet today the most acute thing is not the future, but the present day. In connection with this, I am presenting several proposals.

First of all, it seems to me that the budget is such an important, acute matter that already in October or November, when we meet, the adoption of the budget must fall under the competency of the Congress of People's Deputies. (Applause).

Twelfth Session
8 June 1989

The second thing. Nikolay Ivanovich Ryzhkov promises to eliminate the budget deficit sometime in the mid-90's. I believe we can and must shorten this time. Of course, it would be unrealistic this year. Yet if we take Draconian, radical measures for next year, we can reduce the deficit at least to that level which was customary for us for 15 years—at least to R10-20 billion as opposed to that colossal level at which it stands today. Therefore, I am presenting the following proposal: To provide in the congress recommendations for eliminating or principally reducing the budget deficit not at the end of the next five- year plan, but in 1991.

Furthermore, in order for us to understand where we stand, what is happening to us, and in what position the state finds itself, I believe that it is absolutely necessary to make public the real scope of the state debt. For many years we have borrowed secretly from the public as well as from enterprises. The state debt is huge, but we do not admit it. We must know this picture, how much the state has collected, how much it owes the population today, including the deductions from the savings banks and the deductions from the enterprise savings funds. It is just as necessary to publicize our foreign debt and our balance of payments. Otherwise, we are just guessing, feeling out our way as we go, but not really knowing the real state of affairs.

Finally, the last thought, and on this I will conclude with my final proposal. The country's Central Bank cannot find itself in the position in which it exists today—in the role of a department of the Ministry of Finance or a department of the Council of Ministers. In the situation which has emerged, the Central Bank must take the entire problem of the issuance of money and inflation into its own hands. In all normal states the Central Bank is just as independent as the supreme court or the constitutional supervision. The president of the Central Bank should not be subordinate to anyone, including Nikolay Ivanovich Ryzhkov. He must be subordinate only to the congress. (Applause). Thank you for your attention.

A.-M.K. Brazauskas: Kazimira Danute Prano Prunskene has the floor.

K.D.P. Prunskene, rector of the Institute for Advanced Training of Specialists in the National Economy under the Lithuanian SSR Council of Ministers (Shyaulyayskiy Territorial Electoral District, Lithuanian SSR): Honorable president! Honorable deputies! Many years of practical application of partial economic reforms have convincingly proven their inconsistency under conditions of super-centralized economic management of the great power which the Soviet Union has become. Revitalizing this gigantic economic organism, bringing it out of stagnation, or even overcoming its decline are becoming unthinkable under the old methods of long-distance management from a far-away great power center, regardless of how strong and even wise it may be.

The Baltic conception of economic reform is based on the principle of localizing the solution of problems, transferring [this problem solving] to that level where the economic and social processes are taking place, where there is real information and where these processes are implemented by interested people. We view the economic independence of the republics as the primary and necessary condition for reorganizing the economic management of individual republics as well as the Soviet Union as a whole. The need for this is determined by an entire series of circumstances.

First of all, decentralization and democratization of the economy can take place only in all of its cross-sections. This cannot be done selectively, such as by striving toward independence of enterprises while leaving the republics as a whole and their local Soviets without any rights. In that way the entire sense of the appeal—all power to the Soviets—is lost.

Second, the so-called unity of the national economic complex implemented at the will of the center and through it—and the results of this are well known to all—must be replaced by direct ties between the republics, and primarily their enterprises. Nothing unifies peoples and their economies more than the market.

Third, the economic development of any republic and region must consider the principle of regionalism—that is, the century of traditions in economic thought and motivation for actions of a specific people, the character of its interaction with a specific social and natural environment. Ignoring this fact and efforts to seek out and make unified decisions in the center inflicts a great and irreplaceable loss upon all the peoples of the union and tears out the natural roots of development and participation in international division of labor, with its own inimitable contribution. Is it not this that has led to the dying off of the Aral and to many other ecological catastrophes?

Fourth, restructuring may be implemented only by an interested person, and not simply by the work force or by an enterprise or department. In the production collectives this interest is one-sided. It does not encompass the ecological, socio-demographic, cultural, or national aspects of life which can and must be regulated within the framework of a socially visible territorial community. Such are the small republics which are capable of becomings masters of their own life and of responsibly directing their economic development for the good of man, the people of the republic and the Union as a whole.

Fifth. restructuring is proceeding an a non-uniform pace in the individual republics as well as in the regions. The readiness to change over to self government is also not uniform. This non-uniformity is natural, and it cannot be overlooked. We sense this also at the congress. Artificial inhibition of the processes of socio-political

STENOGRAPHIC RECORD

Twelfth Session

8 June 1989

activity and economic enterprise leads to underutilization of the domestic potential of the republics and regions and gives nothing but loss—for each individual as well as for the entire Union. By marching in unison we can go only in the direction of downfall, and it is possible to untangle ourselves from the routine of stagnation only by developing initiative.

Sixth. The right of the republics to independently manage their economy is natural, as is the right of a people or a person to existence and self-determination. The actual absence of rights in the sphere of economics, and not only in this sphere, as well as in the question of the return of these rights is, in our opinion, the most sore and burning question. Even if we do not touch upon those specific circumstances which are associated with the deals made by Stalin and Hitler in regard to the Baltic. If we circumvent these rights, then democratization itself and the idea of a legal state and union become speculative.

And finally, in order to attract people to investing their labor and means to the individual peasant farm, even to leasing which has little prospect in the Baltic, or to stock acquisition and other forms of demonopolization of the economy, it is necessary to protect the rights of people and enterprises, to provide guarantees and instill trust in the laws. To restore the lost trust in the laws and in authority at the republic level is much easier than to do so on a Union scale. Today the Lithuanian peasant is ready to believe his deputies, but will he trust the voting of the congress? That is the big question. For now, we, too, will not be able to convince him without being hypocritical, since that which is obvious for most people in the Baltic is still unclear or unacceptable for many congress deputies from other republics. Yet can all the Lithuanian, Estonian, or any other people be wrong or irrationally emotional? And who can take upon himself the mission of evaluating this?

Let us speak briefly about the very content of economic independence as presented in the draft of the law submitted to the congress, which has already been handed out to the deputies. I will note: The law was developed on the basis of an integral conception. If we apply or extract only individual parts, then the mechanism simply will not work. According to the outline, it is within the jurisdiction of the republics to adopt legislative statutes on regulating the republic's economy and on ownership, application and management of state property in the republic. This means decentralization of state ownership itself. The republics are becoming full-fledged masters of their land, their underground resources, their forests and other resources which were created not only during the years of Soviet rule. Thus, they are finally attaining an ownership interest. The republic organs of state authority implement state regulation of all spheres, including the monetary-credit and finance system, the formulation of the republic's state budget and the local budgets, foreign economic activity, the determination of principles for labor wages, pensions, and stipends, the order of price formation, and the principles of economic activity of the enterprises, equal for all sectors including the cooperative, whose flaws are caused specifically by the economy itself and by the absence of a normal market.

One of the arguments presented by the center and other opponents of the idea of an independent republic is the fear that regional differences might intensify. It seems to me that it is better to live differently but well than all the same but poorly. (Applause).

We have already experienced levelling. It holds back not only those who are more developed, but also facilitates a continuation of the weaknesses of those who are lagging behind. Many deputies from the Baltic, to put it mildly, are surprised at Comrade Ryzhkov's repeated statements which cause unfriendliness toward us on the part of other republics. Supposedly more profitable conditions have been created for us and we, using the cheap raw material, are pocketing the end product and realizing a great profit. (Noise in the audience). According to unreliable price estimates, Lithuania is "sentenced" to a negative balance in inter-republic trade. It would seem we are becoming dependents. I cannot believe that the prime minister does not know the real state of affairs about who is ultimately pocketing the considerable profits from industry. After all, around 95 percent of the deductions from the profits of enterprises of union subordination are accumulated by the center. The prices on agricultural produce are extremely unprofitable, and Lithuania is obligated to supply almost half of [this produce] to the union funds. Is it not a paradox that the increase in deliveries to the union fund leads to an increase in the republic's debts to the union treasury, which are already approaching the billion mark? If we produced less, we would not have any debts. After all, it is not we, but the center itself which by the departmental method sets the prices, the state orders, limits and other instruments of economic management. If, for example, Lithuania underpays Uzbekistan or Tadzhikistan for cotton due to unsubstantiated prices, under economic independence the agreements would be made according to mutually beneficial prices. And this would not lead to any isolation of the economy, as certain leaders fear. Rather, it would lead merely to correction of irrational, often distorted, structures and ties imposed by the center. Finally, integration will take on a natural basis.

We realize that under deficit conditions, a certain time will be needed to create an effective inter-republic market, under which there will no longer be a need for direct intrusion of the state into trade dealings between enterprises. Our conception provides for a transitional period of maintaining the inter-republic ties which have become established. They are to be implemented through mutually beneficial agreements and contracts between the individual republics, as well as between

STENOGRAPHIC RECORD

Twelfth Session

8 June 1989

them and the union apparatus. Here, a portion of the specific interests of producers and consumers will be represented in the form of a summary order and supply by the republics for equivalent commodity exchange. In the transition of all republics and regions to self-management, the process of formulating independent, self-financing enterprises interacting on the union market will also be accelerated.

Economic independence of the republic is in no way combined either with the currently effective principle of formulating the Union state budget, or with the one proposed by the USSR Council of Ministers. The mutual relations must be structured as follows: The republic budget—the union budget, since the union unites not economic enterprises, but sovereign republics. They have the right to know and to jointly determine what kind of budget is needed, how we formulate it, how much we spend and for what, including also for the free-wheeling of the departmental bureaucratic apparatus, the super-needs of the Armed Forces, the conquest of space, etc. The poverty of the people obligates us to become prudently thrifty and to resolve budgetary questions—union as well as republic—at the will of the people.

The people of my republic, as well as many other peoples, are capable of creative building. They are industrious and aim toward a better life. They do not want to appropriate someone else's labor or live off of handouts from the center. And where does the center get this? We insist on the general principle: By working better, one should also have the right to live better. This is not an exceptional, but a common right of every people. Lack of recognition of this in regard to the people of Lithuanian or of any other republic is a departure from the most sacred thing that a person and a people have—the right to free self determination.

We have dared to express an initiative for transforming the Union from a supra-republic, republic-managing strong center into an alliance of sovereign republics with an inter-republic apparatus which represents their interests and which they themselves formulate. This relates also to economic relations within the Union. The wisdom and the democratizing, restructuring force of the center may be evaluated by whether it will be able to rise above the egotistic interests of self-preservation and aid in the process of democratization, or whether it intends to continue along the tradition of determining the fate of large and small peoples, and even their minor economic affairs.

Associated with this is the essence of the so-called Baltic problem, which even in the course of the congress inevitably spills over into the general problem of building the Union and its prospects. As yet, we have not seen any shifts in the direction of constructive solutions to the question of recognizing economic independence either in Comrade Ryzhkov's speech or in the actions of the government. Rather, they speak of increasing only certain rights for the republics, whose people have expressed their firm will in this regard. We cannot put off the resolution of this problem even as long as fall. The people cannot long be in a state of political tension building up due to the foot-dragging and hindrances of the center, which is acting under the aegis of defending the conquests of socialism and internationalism. We declare that the economic models developed by the Baltic republics are very close to the statements of Moscow scientists, and they contain much more socialism than we have today. The Baltic republics are ready to assume responsibility—and this responsibility is needed primarily before one's own people, and not before some autocratic center. They are ready, if you will, to become experimental, turning the economy onto the natural and sensible path of development. There is simply no other way out for us and, it seems to me, there is also no other way out for the center. Thank you. (Extensive applause).

From the audience: I propose that we give the floor to economists from the Moscow group, to economic leaders... (the rest is inaudible).

A.-M.K. Brazauskas: Well, it seems to me, comrades, that is how it is working out. Up to now, as you see, the speakers have been economists. I think that we are not straying too far from the line. As I have already said, Comrade Nazarov has the floor, and Comrade Yegorova should get ready.

I.A. Nazarov, first secretary of the CPSU Russko-Polyanskiy Raykom, Omsk Oblast, village of Russkaya Polyana (from the CPSU): Honorable deputies! Honorable members of the presidium! There are many problems today in our state and much to discuss at the congress, but I would once again like to focus your attention on rural problems. I believe that I am not exaggerating when I say that food provision is the most sensitive point of economic reform and all of restructuring. The strength of authority of the government, as well as yours and mine, will depend on how completely and quickly this problem is resolved. Yet my voters and I are concerned by the fact that many of the decisions on agriculture in recent years bear a declarative character. This, I believe, can explain the fact that the country's agrarian sector has been marching in place, which gives reason for many publicists and agronomist-scientists to give a negative evaluation of the rural population. The reason for this, of course, may be the extended food crisis in the country. However, the main thing is that it characterizes the attitude of our society toward the peasantry.

Today it is quite the fashion to discuss and give advice on how to work the land. Even people who are not associated with agriculture do this, people who know the farm only from two or three trips which they have made there, or from folklore. Where does such disrespect

FIRST CONGRESS OF PEOPLE'S DEPUTIES OF THE USSR

Twelfth Session

8 June 1989

toward the people come from? I would like to ask such people to stop and think about the fact that this is simply not ethical, and that in general agriculture is not such a simple matter as some may think. You must understand, the peasant has never had and still does not have the decisive word. There is always someone to decide for him. Today he is asking for respect and consideration.

I am often asked by machinery operators, livestock raisers, and workers: Why is it that, in preparing their decisions and in speaking of agriculture, the central organs are not interested in the opinion of the rural residents? Why is it that the fate of the farm is often decided without considering the opinions of people living on the farm? Perhaps this can explain the frequent changes in the signboards by organs of farm management which have taken place in the country in recent years? This causes mistrust and skepticism among the peasants. We must put an end to this practice.

Comrades! I support the appeal of the farmers to the congress, the speech by Comrade Starodubtsev. This is not a desire to open another discussion on agriculture, but a soulful cry for help, a demand for us to take a sober approach to the problems of the farm and to undertake them in priority order. (Applause).

I support the proposal to create a USSR Supreme Soviet Committee on agrarian questions and food products, and propose that we charge it with the responsibility of protecting the interests of the agrarian sector. Specifically, this would entail protection of agrarian interests against departments, against the bureaucracy, against ill-planned voluntaristic decisions, and finally against incompetent management. This committee must have broad powers.

I also propose that at the Fall meeting of the USSR Congress of People's Deputies we consider the information presented by the government regarding the realization of our proposals and statements.

The farm workers also do not quite understand the opinion formed today among the country's leadership that an adequate amount of resources has been invested into agriculture. However, if the acuteness in technical provision of the farm with modern machinery has not been removed, if many villages and entire regions have become depopulated, and this has taken place due to distortions in the social infrastructure, how can we speak of adequacy? People do not run from good to bad. I might suggest that any one of us sitting in this auditorium go to visit a farm village, and not to a model one, as if sometimes done. There we will see a picture of the 18th-19th centuries. The statistical growth of capital investments in the agrarian sector is due to the increase in the cost of construction, the cost of fertilizers and technology.

But what about the problem of the quality of technology? Seventeen years ago I came to the farm and encountered this problem, yet even to this very day the machine builders manufacture outdated and poor quality "products".

The level of mechanization is not increasing. Its current state is somewhere in the 1960's. But where is automation? Where is electronics? Could it be that this is why farm labor is not held in esteem?

Here is the next point. As far as I know, the agrarian sector of Siberia is a sizeable part of the country's agricultural complex both in volume and in level of intensity of its development. For example, Omsk Oblast not only supplies itself with food, but also makes food deliveries to over 50 points throughout the country. Practically over half of the produce raised here is sent outside the oblast. And this is in spite of the very high industrial potential of the city of Omsk itself.

However, we Siberians see that the attitude of the center toward the development of the Siberian region is not entirely fair. There is no real state policy, which leads here to a serious imbalance in the economy. As before, Siberia is the raw material appendage of the country. Social outlays, the low level of the labor wage, the extremely inadequate capital investments in the Siberian village, the Siberian climate—all these factors lead to a constant migration of the population, and this creates difficulties in organization of production.

Today, Siberia's agrarian sector needs principle sizeable capital investments, and primarily for social development, road construction, water supply, gasification, and heat supply. Near Tyumen there are huge reserves of natural gas which is burned off in torches, while we are forced to heat our houses with firewood. The lack of resolution of these and other questions may lead to depopulation of the Siberian village. We see the tendencies toward this even now. What if Siberia turns into a Non-Chernozem Zone, and then billions would have to be invested to resurrect it?

A specific discussion centers around the virgin lands region. After all, here for many years much was built on the enthusiasm of the people. Yet today a new generation has come, and it has begun demanding not an advance, not slogans, but a real improvement in the living standard. Is the return offered by the virgin lands great? Yes, it is! Despite the fact that there are affirmations stating that it was supposedly a mistake to develop the virgin lands. Well, that is nothing new. Today we will hardly find a period in Soviet rule which has not been placed in doubt or some effort made to cross it out of history. The virgin Russko-Polyanskiy rayon alone supplies the state with 150,000-200,000 tonnes of grain a year, as well as 80 percent of the strong and hard wheat, 30,000 tonnes of milk, 5,000 tonnes of meat, and 200 tonnes of pure wool fiber.

There are many disagreements today about the forms of farm management. I believe that the March plenum of

STENOGRAPHIC RECORD

Twelfth Session

8 June 1989

the party Central Committee acted wisely in adopting the decision on different forms of organization of agricultural production. The peasant will himself decide how he should work. Therefore, we do not quite understand the categorical demands for general farm leasing and for organization of peasant farms. And what should we do with the current specialized enterprises and regions where full specialization and concentration of production have been implemented, and which, we might add, yield good results?

For example, in this same Omsk Oblast, where all the sheep raising is concentrated at only 30 state farms [sovkhozes] and vegetable farming—at 5 sovkhozes, a few poultry farms provide for the oblast's needs and export meat and fowl outside the oblast. The same is true for hog raising and dairy farming. What should we do if the area of arable land in each sovkhoz of this same Russko-Polyanskiy rayon where I work comprises 30,000 hectares, while the size of a field is 400 hectares and the annual production is R8-9 million of agricultural produce?

Each sovkhoz is a highly organized socialist enterprise with a high level of social development and a stable labor collective. In speaking of leasing and of peasant farms, we do not always stop to think that an appropriate material-technical base and technical equipment are needed for this. To count on manual labor is to discredit ahead of time this important cause, which is the new form of farming. And if today the labor of the peasant is one of the most difficult forms of labor, then what will it be tomorrow?

I raise these questions not for the purpose of somehow showing my attitude and opinion on farm leasing. My opinion is synonymous: This is one of the effective methods of revitalizing work on the farm, particularly when a collective is the leaseholder. However, we cannot allow working in fits and starts or categorical refusals, as was the case in times that were not the best. Perhaps we will need more than one year for this. Well, that is still better than concluding the matter with nothing more than catchy slogans. The practice of emotional decisions rather than rational ones is still prevalent today.

We are also concerned by the fact that the prerequisites have been created for economic stifling of the sovkhozes and kolkhozes. There have already been cases of reduced investments into this sector. The changeover by the sovkhozes and kolkhozes to self financing, which we might add was voluntary, without any improvement in price formation and without bringing about order in the ties between the city and the farm, has already brought this decision to discreditation, turning it, as they say, to false self-financing.

I would also like to address the people engaged in the governmental development of agrarian policy. Why is it that today we have so readily accepted independence for the leaseholder and the co-operator? This is good. We need this. But we still do not trust the socialist enterprise's labor collective, its council or its manager. (Applause).

Despite the numerous discussions and decisions, there is no local economic independence, and I can testify to this from my own practical experience. How long will this continue? How many more breakthroughs and revolutions do we need?

I had occasion to hear the speech of Comrade Murakhovskiy. At times he would say with indignation that, supposedly, the central departments do not interfere in local matters. Full independence has been granted. The criticism addressed at [these central departments] is not objective and, supposedly, the fault lies with the local sites. This prompted me to ask the question which has no answer: Either this is a matter of not knowing the state of affairs or a desire to lead us, mildly speaking, into confusion? Why do we not tear down the system of general mistrust and irresponsibility formulated within our society? How long will we build our case only on personalities, and not on systems? After all, just take a look. Leading agrarian practice is upheld by such pillars as Comrades Vagin, Starodubtsev, Veprev, and many others. And, luckily, it is good that there are many such people in the country and that they, as far as I know, are primarily distinguished by courage and firm will in standing up for their views. Yet where will we find enough such Starodubtsevs for the entire country? We need a system of economic management, and primarily economic independence in deed, which will undoubtedly be accompanied by the highest responsibility of the cadres.

I am in favor of regional cost accounting and local self government, and of the centralization of economic management, but only under the condition of centralized political management. This ultimately will allow people to manifest their abilities and to see who is capable of doing what. After all, everyone is tired of always being the eccentric!

Comrades! The voters have asked me also to convey their concern regarding the deterioration of labor and social discipline in the country and the removal of the anti-alcohol policy. For some people the words "discipline", "order", and "organization" are for some reason associated with the word "Stalinism". This is a misconception, and one which we do not understand. After all, any civilized society has inherent organization and conscious discipline. Otherwise, it is but a stone's throw away from anarchy. The process of democracy in the country is irreversible, but this process must be accompanied by organization and order. Those people for whom the word "discipline" causes an allergic reaction evidently never go to the labor collectives and do not see the laxness and irresponsibility which reign in many places. And for the present day the saying that we

Twelfth Session

8 June 1989

do not know how to work has become widespread. No, we do know how to work! It is just that we no longer want to work well.

I believe that the Soviet people will view with satisfaction that part of the speech which discussed pension provision. It is a very complex problem, but it must be resolved at any cost, sparing no money for this cause, and perhaps even to the detriment of certain other programs. This will significantly revitalize the moral atmosphere in the country. I say this because recently, more precisely in the past few days, we have received numerous telegrams and phone calls in which the people demand that we solve the problem of pension provision at this congress once and for all.

An entirely correct decision has been made in the country regarding social re-orientation of the economy. The people perceived this with satisfaction, but are beginning to be concerned by the absence of any real change in the state of affairs in this sphere, and this is inadmissible under the current tense situation in society.

It seems to me that today the question of fulfillment must be a very important one. We have learned so well to write decisions and orders (there are very many such documents), that we have forgotten entirely that these decisions must also be implemented. And it is especially bad when one cannot even find the creators of these documents.

It has become the rule in recent times to print memoirs in journals and newspapers some 20-30 years after the fact, to tell about how certain decisions were made at one time. Today we must all know who stands at the source of the decisions which are being made. This practice of management has become particularly widespread in the last decade.

The people are concerned with the possibility of realizing the program for housing construction to the year 2000, as well as the program for paved roads, since the resolution of the food program has dragged on since 1982. We need an all-people's referendum on developing the programs, and all-people's control of their implementation.

Comrades! The work of the congress has shifted into a constructive vein. The haste of the first few days is over. The Soviet people and the country's leaders have evidently become convinced that our USSR Congress of People's Deputies, the present membership of people's deputies, is capable of specific action, and is capable of imposing strict demands. We would like to believe that we all stand on one platform and have one goal, even though each one of us may have different tactical means of achieving this goal. This is the essence of each person's participation in restructuring.

The congress will be evaluated not only by political scientists, but primarily by all the people. The evaluation cannot be given according to specific decisions and specific results. Unfortunately, we have spent a long time formulating a society of general fault-finding, and at the same time general irresponsibility. For many years we have placed the blame on tsarism. Today we place it on the years of stagnation. Yet each one of us should simply answer for his own deeds. I believe that the decisions of the congress will give all of us new strength and decisiveness in overcoming those difficulties which arise in the path of restructuring.

Finally, the demands of most of my comrades from the Omsk delegation, as well as numerous telephone conversations and telegrams, obligate me to announce the following. In his speech from this podium, one of our honorable comrades spoke of the nondemocratic nature of nominating members of our Omsk delegation to the membership of the Supreme Soviet. I understand that this was one of the attempts to confuse the congress and to sidetrack it. Therefore, I must explain that the elections in our delegation were held by secret ballot, on an alternative basis. And if someone's wishes were not fulfilled, then that is an entirely different matter.

Thank you for your attention. (Applause).

A.-M.K. Brazauskas: Yegorova has the floor. Comrade Yemelyanov should get ready.

I.A. Yegorova, section head at the Altay Kray Clinical Hospital, city of Barnaul (from the women's councils united by the Committee of Soviet Women): Honorable chairman! Honorable comrades! We have come to the congress with our own concerns and with the concerns of our fellow citizens and colleagues. Perhaps I will be redundant on a number of problems, but I cannot help but express my point of view.

As you know, the solution of many social problems depends on the socio-economic capacities of the region. Altay Kray is one of the most important support bases for the national economic assimilation of the eastern rayons of the country. The kray's agriculture is also of all-union significance. Nevertheless, the methods of planning the development of the social sphere ("from what has been formed") do not correspond to the peculiarities of the region. The kray is huge in its territory, has a low population density and a weakly developed infrastructure. There is an acute problem with the farms, especially the small ones. It requires comprehensive solution. In many ways, credits would help in solving this problem, but unfortunately there are not enough of them.

I would like to express from this podium the desire of our Altay delegation and the Belorussian delegation that we need to raise society's respect toward bread. We probably all remember the words to the song which goes: "Son, remember the golden words—bread is the head of

STENOGRAPHIC RECORD

Twelfth Session

8 June 1989

everything". At the present time, unfortunately, we do not have the proper respect for bread. This, our dear, golden bread, is being frittered away too easily. We must finally raise the prestige and the price of bread.

Comrades! To this very day, Siberia, including the Altay, is viewed by some as a colony, the private domain of the departments. Who, for example, can tell us why Siberian gas goes to the European part of the country and to the West, but in practice is little used in Siberia? Yet its use would play a great economic and socio-ecological role in the lives of Siberians. For example, we in Altay are offered gas in exchange for supporting the construction of the nitrogen mineral fertilizer plant in the city of Zarinsk, which already lives in difficult ecological conditions due to the presence of a coke chemical plant there. We cannot help but ask the question: Should we build new plants for the production of mineral fertilizers if, as we know, the plants which already exist in the country are not working to their full capacity? With such an attitude of the departments, we will not be able to raise the social sphere not only in Altay Kray, but probably in the entire Siberian region. The time has come to hand over all the funds for disposition by the local Soviets. Today it is no secret to anyone that the local Soviets do not have sufficient economic capacities in their command to be the sole masters of their territory. The Soviets still act in the role of petitioners of the enterprises located on their territory.

Today there are enterprises of over 50 ministries operating on the territory of the kray, and there is friction with each of them during allocation of funds for the kray's integrated development, particularly for the development of the social sphere. The centralized management of resources has taken on such a scope that it is not accessible either to deputy control or to the community. We must provide a mechanism of independence of the local Soviet in the form of a law on local self-government. However, the existing legal draft on local self-government must be reworked in detail. A certain percentage of the monetary funds of the enterprises must be deducted for the local Soviets' fund. The expenditure of these funds must be conducted openly and publicly. First and foremost, the efforts and means must of course be directed toward satisfying the needs of man.

As a doctor, let me deal with several problems in public health. As we know, this sector does not receive significant development. For example, the people's deputies from Altay were given 35 mandates on public health—more than on any other direction. We must radically change the strategy and tactics of planning the development of public health, and we must also change our approach to planning methods. The basic principle must be the quality of life or health in the full sense of the word, referring to the state of total physical, spiritual and social well-being.

Today we cannot be satisfied with approaches to public health planning without consideration for the environment in which we live, the culture, the entire social infrastructure of the region, as well as the material-technical base of public health. The growth of expenditures for public health is within the limits of 1.5 percent—from 3.2 to 4.7 percent of the gross national product, as planned according to the basic principles. This is clearly insufficient. In the developed countries this indicator equals 8-12 percent. We were glad to hear in N.I. Ryzhkov's speech that there are plans to transfer the public health budget over to the level of the republic and the region. This will allow the local organs to themselves maneuver their own forces and funds. However, the per capita indicator remains different for different regions, and does not consider their peculiarities. For example, in Altay 88 percent of the rural hospitals have outdated facilities and are housed in make-shift buildings without water supply or sewer lines, not to mention hot water. We cannot make do with the financial norms for maintaining these buildings, and we are always having to take funds from the article entitled "capital repairs".

Despite the government resolution, we do not have a full wage fund in accordance with the staff roster. This fund comprises 82 percent of that which is required. This ties the hands of the doctors and inhibits the development of new services.

Restructuring in public health is taking very timid steps. No clear mechanism of economic management has been developed. The experiment being conducted in a number of oblasts is not entirely satisfactory. In essence, only medical workers are participating in it, while the health of the people depends not only on us, but on the conditions of work, every-day life, and the environment—that is, on the entire living environment and on the quality of life. It should become profitable for an enterprise to have a healthy worker. After all, today it is no secret to anyone that the sick leave rolls are paid out not from the profits of the enterprises, but from the social security funds, from the social funds. Therefore, a paradoxical situation arises: The more sick people there are, the greater the savings for the wage fund. Only when the labor collective will itself pay for a worker who has gotten sick will the capacities and funds be found for improving labor conditions and everyday production conditions. (Applause).

We must also interest every citizen in caring for his own health. We do not have a health cult. We must pay for maintaining health, then everyone will think: Should he run for a bottle of vodka, or should he run to the stadium?

Despite the fact that the prestige of medical workers has recently been on the upswing and allocations are increasing, there has been no significant improvement in health treatment or in the quality of mercy. The reason for this, in my opinion, is the absence of incentive motives. The wages of medical workers remain low, particularly those of the large army of therapists. The wages of nurses and medical assistants are extremely

STENOGRAPHIC RECORD

Twelfth Session

8 June 1989

low. These young girls receive a wage which borders on the poverty level. We have not worked out sufficiently clear criteria for evaluating the quality of a doctor's work. One can do nothing and receive his wages, or one can work well and still receive the same money. Therefore, comrades, we must finally approach the economic levers for evaluating the activity of the entire medical service.

Here is the next question. We should think about reducing the doctor's work load and providing him with technical support. First of all, the following question demands solution. Today many kolkhozes and sovkhozes are able to buy a car for their medical-obstetrics stations. However, the existing resolution prohibits them from doing so. Yet these cars are obtained primarily to give first aid to the village residents themselves. I think that this limitation must be removed.

I will express some very serious pretensions to the GiproNIIzdrav [State Planning and Scientific-Research Institute for Planning Public Health Institutions]. We have no current projects for hospitals at the kray or village levels. How long will we have to coordinate with the ministries how and what we can build? If a hospital costs 5 million, then we can build it at the expense of the local budget, and everything over this cost must be approved. So we build a hospital without a polyclinic, without domestic services, and then we must once again eek out money for all of this. We build a dormitory, and then we re-classify it as a hospital or polyclinic, pretending that nothing is happening. Comrades, whom are we fooling? Do we really have to coordinate with Moscow something, for example, that we must build in Barnaul?

I am a surgeon, comrades, and today I am afraid to stand at the operating table, not having sufficient support. I am afraid for the patient because we do not have the most necessary things. Why is this? Why, it is because the average annual growth rate for a number of medicines in the past 3 years have not increased but, unfortunately, have declined. We can feel all of this ourselves. Therefore, I propose that we specify a group of medicinal preparations, such that a person cannot live without today. This is insulin, derivatives, hormonal preparations, heart medications, and a number of others—15-20-30 titles. If a billion is needed for them, then let us vote today and grant it. We will agree to live today without prestigeous machines, without consumer goods, just so we can have these necessary medications.

Dear enterprise managers, people's deputies sitting in this auditorium, and those who, perhaps, are hearing us today on television, those who have currency funds! I appeal to you: Let us allocate part of these currency funds for buying much-needed medications. Because it is simply criminal not to have the most necessary medicines. In this case, all the preparations purchased abroad must be placed under public control. Their import must be publicized in the press, and their expenditure must be publicly known. At the same time, I would like to reprimand our medical industry. We export abroad very much raw material for medicine production. It is time we started to manufacture these medicines ourselves. I am speaking specifically about insulin, which could probably be produced here at home, as well as about trenthal, for whose manuifacture we also export raw material abroad.

The debates go on: Should we or should we not include medicines and instruments as consumer goods. I believe that everyone must include this in his conscience. We say that the dearest thing a person has is his life and his health. Therefore, the Council of Ministers must find the wherewithall to give the green light to whatever public health needs. Thus, we must avoid the situation whereby the Council of Ministers decides in December of 1988 to include medicines in the list of consumer goods, while the Gosplan [State Planning Committee] leaves in this section only the ready-made forms. It is unclear who manages whom.

And in general, how long will the sub-legal statutes of the departments negate the laws adopted by the Supreme Soviet? We will never achieve order in the country that way!

Comrades! Here is what disturbs us. Why is it that our group interests have in many cases been placed above our state interests? Some, covering themselves with the decision of the labor collective, refuse to manufacture cheap instruments. Others, in their race for currency, take raw materials abroad instead of developing production at home. Yet all of us together are supposedly fighting for restructuring. Maybe we have had enough of engaging in empty words? Let us do our deed, each in his own place and all together! We must demand from the government, the Minmedbioprom [Ministry of the Medical and Microbiological Industry], Minpribor [Ministry of Instrument Marking, Automation Equipment, and Control Systems] that they resolve the questions on the need for increasing the medicines and medical technology in our country, and also recommend to the Russian Federation Minzdrav [Ministry of Health] that it take control of the distribution of imported equipment which is in short supply.

Comrade deputies! We cannot speak of the success of our society if we do not have a respectful attitude toward women and motherhood. Why does society forget that the woman bears the burden of reproducing mankind, a burden which can and must be eased by preventative health and social measures? Equal rights certainly do not presuppose carrying equal physical burdens. We have thrown the woman into the crucible of the labor front. We are the only country in the world where there are more women than men working in the national economy. In our country the woman is not protected by

Twelfth Session

8 June 1989

law against the violation of her guaranteed rights. For example, can a woman plan her family? No, and no again. After all, these are not merely contraceptives that we are talking about. This is primarily the quality of life. It is an apartment which she will have to wait almost to retirement to receive. It is kindergartens and nursery schools. It is the patching of holes in the family budget. To create and preserve a family, and then also to give birth to three to four children—that requires extreme bravery on the part of a woman. (Applause).

We have spoken much about the benefits for our women. We have spoken, but not acted. Dear comrades, is this not why our socialist countries and other countries of the world live better than us, because they care more about their citizens? Let us think about this. It is clear that today we cannot exclude women from the sphere of material production. However, we can and must take them out of the night shifts and the hazardous shops. We cannot long put off the concern for the health and for the working and everyday living conditions of women. Today more than ever before, the state needs healthy women. It needs strong and stable families. (Applause).

I would also like to mention the following. Today all the ills of modern production affect primarily women. They, especially the ones with many children, are the first to be dismissed from work. They become unprofitable for the enterprises, since they cannot always work with full return. Therefore, it is necessary to increase the social protection of women. We need a social protection fund. I propose that we create such a fund. If a woman cannot devote herself entirely to work, then the enterprise should receive a certain sum from this fund. This will allow the woman to work in peace, without inflicting a loss upon the enterprise. It is very easy to put [a worker] out the door. If we are building a humanistic society, then let us show some humanity toward our women. Let us show some concern for the woman. This will speak of the culture of our society. As yet, unfortunately, we still have a shortage of such culture! I support the proposal to create government-level departments or sectors for protecting the rights and the social position of women. (Applause).

Comrade deputies! In the kray, as well as in the country, an unfavorable ecological situation is being formulated which is having an ever more negative effect on the health of our generations. We will never achieve success in preventing illnesses if we do not stop environmental pollution. We cannot continue to risk our health and our future for the sake of the immediate interests of production and localism. We must ensure full openness regarding environmental questions! People have the right to know what they are breathing and what they are eating. We have spoken for many years about the pollution of food products with pesticides. Today we are throwing out tens of thousands of tonnes of vegetables and fruits which have an increased nitrate content. Our country still has no conception of the study, prediction and control of the consequences of environmental pollution as related to the health status of the people. Yet today such a program is becoming a vital necessity.

Dear comrades, for a number of years the passions have flared around the Katun GES [hydroelectrical station]. Yet no one will make a final decision, either in Altay kray or in the government. The representatives from the Baltic have spoken from this podium about the Katun GES. The honorable Comrade Rasputin has spoken. Only our dear fellow countrymen, the Gorno-Altay residents themselves, have not yet had a chance to speak. Therefore, I have a request for the presidium: To give the floor today to the representatives of the Gorno-Altay Autonomous Oblast. Today it is absolutely necessary to solve the problem of providing power to Gorniy Altay. People cannot continue to live in indeterminacy, because this indeterminacy has inhibited the development of many social spheres in Gorniy Altay.

And finally, here is the last proposal which I would like to express. At the pre-electoral meetings, many voters raised the question of closing the nuclear test site in Semipalatinsk. We cannot ignore public opinion and the protests by the population of this huge region. We must respond to the voters when we return home and tell them what we decided here at the congress. They are awaiting our positive decision. We must stop all nuclear tests in Semipalatinsk! Thank you. (Applause).

A.-M.K. Brazauskas: Comrades, Deputy Yemelyanov has the floor. Comrade Gayer should get ready. We are receiving notes whose authors ask that we read a list of those comrades who will speak. Before 1400, I believe, six people will be able to speak, in addition to those previously announced. Yet, this is a preliminary list. In order, they are: Comrades Gumbaridze, Yablokov, Chebanov, Zalygin, Gvozdev, and Suleymenov. That is how many will speak before 1400.... Attention, comrades, we give the floor to Aleksey Mikhaylovich Yemelyanov.

A.M. Yemelyanov, head of the department of agricultural economics, M.V. Lomonosov MGU [Moscow State University] (Lenin Territorial Electoral District, Moscow, Russian Soviet Federated Socialist Republic [RSFSR]): Comrade deputies! Honorable voters, who tie your last vital hopes to our congress! Our congress will largely determine the fate of restructuring and the fate of the entire country. Restructuring has currently come to its critical point. Four years has not produced any improvement in the real living conditions of the population. In the recent period, a number of negative tendencies in the democratization of society have become apparent. The situation today generally stands as follows: Either we continue along the path of revolutionary democratic renovation of society, or a movement will begin along a new turn, which is well known to us from the past, and with its inevitable period of reactionary vengeance.

STENOGRAPHIC RECORD

Twelfth Session

8 June 1989

Of course, it would be incorrect to place the blame for the difficulties which have arisen on the current leadership alone. The legacy which we have inherited is too heavy. The abyss in which we have found ourselves is too great. Yet for the sake of objectivity we must say that the current difficulties are largely explained by inconsistencies in policy. We talk a lot about the new thinking. Yet it seems that we have really applied it only in foreign policy, where we have seen real results. As for the development of the economy and the social sphere, here the former approaches still prevail, the movement from what has been achieved, stop-gap measures, and therefore we have no real results. Nikolay Petrovich Shmelev has already presented specific examples of this. I would like to present one or two from the agrarian sphere. Really, why is that that every year we find huge resources, both currency and natural resources, for buying up large amounts of bread and meat, and why are there no such resources for reducing the losses of crops which we ourselves raise? Why do we have enough oil to buy grain, but when it comes time for harvest the combines and trucks stand idle because we have used up our limits of fuel? (Applause). What kind of a policy do we need here? These are questions which the rank-and-file worker, the rank-and-file peasant, would surely resolve if he were in charge. Yet they are beyond the comprehension of our high-ranking bureaucrats.

The main thing, perhaps, is that in recent years, in the 4 years of restructuring, we have made very little progress in resolving the basic question—the formulation of the political system, the political mechanism which would truly make the people the masters of the country. And it is clear that if the people were the masters, we would never have found ourselves in our current position. Today, unfortunately, the tendency is such that the farther up you go from the people, the more evident the extinguishing of democratic principles becomes. This, specifically, is understandable. Our restructuring (the initiators of restructuring and the Politburo have long ago stated this in their documents) is a revolution, and any revolution is a radical change in power—that is, a struggle for power. Yet history teaches us that the ruling class, the ruling elite, has never voluntarily or enthusiastically given up its power. Our 4 years of restructuring are a clear confirmation of this fact.

The administrative-bureaucratic apparatus at all levels, especially at the upper echelons of power, has set up its defense perimeters and is doing everything possible to preserve its monopolistic position, in which it holds only rights and no responsibilities, in which it determines everything, decides everything, and yet bears no responsibility for the consequences of its decisions (applause). Rather, it passes down these consequences onto the lower segments, and ultimately onto the people. I can imagine how difficult it is for the initiators of restructuring, for the secretary general and for other democratically minded leaders in the upper echelons of power, to more or less consistently implement the idea of restructuring and the idea of democratic renovation of our society.

Specifically, today we speak much about the independence of the lower levels and the enterprises. Yet it is elementally clear: It is impossible to accomplish this without limiting the functions of the upper levels. The wolves cannot be satisfied if the sheep are safe. Yet look at what is happening. There are plenty of models for cost accounting, but only a handful of enterprises get more or less real cost accounting independence. Just stop and think—which enterprises are these? They are those enterprises which can reliably prove that they are not only unprofitable, but that they are dying, that they have one foot in the grave. Only then do the bureaucrats meet, discuss the matter, and give some of these enterprises relatively complete cost accounting independence. Yet as long as they are still breathing, we let our ironclad state bureaucratic mechanism bring them to their deathbed. Yet why not take measures in time? What kind of science can compensate for these elementary absurdities? We must, and I believe that we can and should long ago have done this, extend to the state enterprises those elementary principles which have justified themselves in cooperative management: interest and independence. These are not purely cooperative principles. Rather, they are principles of elementary normal economic management, and they must exist at any state enterprise. (Applause).

We can understand why this is not done. If such independence were given to all state enterprises, then the superfluousness of our entire huge bureaucratic superstructure would immediately become apparent. And who wants to sign their own death sentence? I believe that we must radically change the principles of the management system's approach to restructuring. We must proceed not from the top down. We must engage not in the changing of signboards, not in stop-gap measures or in repainting of facades. Rather, we must proceed from the bottom up. At each management level there must be only those organs of management, with those functions and with that number of employees in the apparatus as are necessary to the lower levels. The existence of any management organ is justified only if the need for it is dictated from below by the interests of production development. (Applause).

Such a principle, in my opinion, is contained, although timidly, in the appeal of farmers, in the appeal which reflects the pain and soulful cries of our peasantry. I believe that this principle should perhaps be introduced not only into economic management, but also into the system of party leadership. Then we will be able to place the management pyramid in our country on a sound footing, when the entire management apparatus will be at the service of the people, and not the people at the service of the apparatus, as is in fact the case today. (Applause).

STENOGRAPHIC RECORD

Twelfth Session

8 June 1989

The tenacity of the administrative-bureaucratic system and apparatus is largely fed by the existence of social privileges in the distribution of material and spiritual benefits. This question is not new, and it has arisen also at our congress. I cannot deal in detail with this question. However, I would like to stress the following: When certain leaders tell us that these privileges supposedly do not exist, translated into simple everyday language this means only one thing. It means they think that all the people live as they do and are provided for as they are. How can we think of politics, and what can we expect? We spoke here about creating a commission on this matter. I do not oppose a commission, comrades, but commissions have one major characteristic—to drag out the solution of any question. I propose that our congress include in its resolution a categorical, unequivocal decision on eliminating these privileges in principle. And the commission could then determine the specific mechanism for realizing these principles adopted by the congress. (Applause).

Within the framework of this major problem, I would like to stress one specific question, which nevertheless is of general importance. I am a deputy from the Lenin electoral district of the capital city, including the Leninskiy and Kievskiy rayons. Not many Moscow residents, and moreover non-Moscow residents, know that 40-60 percent of the residents of the capital's historical center live in communal flats. They were born here and here they are living out their days. However, when it comes time for them to get an apartment, they are offered one in the outlying rayons of the capital. Meanwhile, comfortable houses for the Council of Ministers, the Central Committee, and other high-ranking departments are erected here. This is not only ignoring the interests of the pupulation, but, I believe, a direct challenge to the people. And I, as a deputy, am relaying a persistent demand, and not simply a request (our people are tired of acting in the role of beggars before the leaders). I am relaying the persistent demand of the voters that those houses which are today in various stages of progress toward completion do not go to those for whom they were intended, but rather to the residents of this microrayon. (Applause).

In principle we must strive to see that under the order of self- government, not one department has the right to do something on the territory of a given rayon or a given area without coordinating its actions with the residents of this rayon and without their agreement. Otherwise there can be no self-government.

I fully support the proposals expressed here regarding the provision for socially unprotected strata of the population. I would only like to emphasize that to this group we should also add the students, since their stipends, like the pensions of pensioners, have lost their value under conditions of runaway inflation, and do not provide for an elementary existence. (Applause).

There are many economic and social questions. However, their resolution has its roots in the formulation of a democratic political system. Things for us have not always been bad. There have been certain rays of light between the cults after the change of the country's head political leader—the secretary general. This period was approximately 1953-1957, as well as the 8th 5-Year Plan (1966-1970). But why later, after 4, 5, 6 years, did the economy and the social sphere go downhill?

Primarily because the political mechanism was changing. From a relative democracy and collective management we went to a regime of personal power, to authoritarian rule. We had no political defense mechanism for the democratic life of the country. And as long as we have no such mechanism, we still, even now, do not have any guarantees of the irreversibility of restructuring. Therefore, the formulation of such a mechanism is our number one task. (Applause).

Today we often stress the fact that the party itself is the guarantor of the irreversibility of restructuring. Allow me to doubt this principle. We have always had the party, but all the same we have reached our current state. Strictly speaking, it is not the people themselves who have come to the current crisis situation. They have come to it led by the party, often forced to realize its course. We must take this into consideration if we are to soberly evaluate the past and draw from it lessons for the present and for the future. The one-party system also presupposes one-party responsibility. We have already made considerable steps in formulating the new political mechanism. What more must we do? The first question is the delimitation of functions of state and party power and from this—dual office holding. Comrades, we must not adapt the system to a certain leader, but rather we must integrate the leader into a system based on democratic principles. The principles here are as follows: The one-party system—already there is monopolization of power, and if the leader of the single party is also the president—this is monopolization of power squared. And if for now we must temporarily have such dual office holding (and I understand why, because transferring power from the party to the people is a very difficult and long drawn out process), then we should not present this temporary combination of duties as a principle of socialism. We must specify this in the congress documents and each time return to the resolution of this question. Who then, you might say, will head up the party? What kind of a party do we have, if we reduce everything to one leader? And then, if there is no such leader in the Politburo, we must look farther. And in principle, what kind of a system is this, what kind of a mechanism is it when we do not know the members of the Politburo very well? After all, they have almost the same political face. They often express the same ideas, and sometimes even in the same words. Under Lenin it was not like that. We must put an end to this, too. (Applause).

As for the combination of party and state power at the lower segments, we must firmly secure the inadmissability of such combination in the resolutions of our

Twelfth Session

8 June 1989

congress. Otherwise there will be an even more unforeseen monopolization of power. (Applause).

Here is the next question. We must approach the upcoming elections to the republic and local Soviets with a more well-developed system.

First of all, the elections of all deputies must be equal.

Second, we must not permit an unopposed candidate to appear on the ballot, since this is a loophole for easily promoting a number of functionaries to the position of deputy.

Third, we must be ready to change over in the future to electing the president by direct vote, by all the people on a competitive alternative basis. I fully support the proposal which was presented here regarding the direct election of the editor-ion-chief of the newspaper IZVESTIYA and the chairman of Goskomteleradio [State Committee for Television and Radio Broadcasting]. I support the proposal to publish the book "Pamyat" [Memory], in which we can record the names of all those who died in Afghanistan. Yet in addition I would say that we must record there also the names of those who made the decisions on Afghanistan and specify who voted on this question and how. (Applause). It seems that this question has somehow been extinguished. The voters ask, as they asked me yesterday evening, why no commission on Afghanistan has been created, and the question has been hushed up.

Finally, the transition to true people's power largely changes the position of the party in our social and political system. Let me explain. Honorable party and political leaders, let us perceive all this correctly. Otherwise, any effort to formulate this question is already evaluated (as resounded also at the congress) almost as an attempt to drive a wedge between the party and the people, to reduce the authority of the party. No, this is not the case. Of course, the authority of the party has declined. That is a fact. But it has declined primarily as a result of the party's activity during the past period. And we must say directly that even now the democratization of the intra-party life lags behind the democratization of society. It is expressed in the party elections (I am referring to 100 for 100). It is the directives about which much has been said here. It is the decision of the March plenum regarding Comrade Yeltsin, a decision under whose aegis the last stage of the election campaign in Moscow was run, and evidently not only in Moscow. The people have given their evaluation of this decision, specifically, also through their meetings. It is just too bad that the members of the Politburo and the members of the Central Committee did not come to these people's meetings, bringing with them the leading, in their opinion, representative of the working class, Comrade Tikhomirov. So that, as was done in Lenin's time, they could themselves explain to the people the essence of their decisions, and not push this task off onto the raykoms and the lower-level party organizations. (Applause).

In conclusion I would once again like to stress the main idea. As long as we are moving toward people's power (and this is the basic content of restructuring), then we must redefine the place of the party in the social structures. The voters present the problem: What can you, the deputies, do? Almost all of you communists and the Central Committee will make a decision, and you will have to vote according to the party Charter, and all our will of the people will be extinguished. This question is repeated at almost all the meetings. I believe that this stems from former notions, when the party held undivided power, and the people were essentially deprived of it. Yet now the situation is drastically changing in connection with the transfer of power to the Soviets. The people stand above the party. Our congress stands above the party congress. The Supreme Soviet stands above the party Central Committee, and the constitution stands above the party charter. The party functions within the framework of the constitution developed by the people's representatives. And this determines our priorities. Each of us is first of all a deputy, and then a party member. And this must determine his behavior. Such a relation of party and people's organs must find its reflection in the USSR Constitution, the party charter, and in the documents of our congress. (Applause).

We must express the priorities which we have presented in everything, including also in the ranking of the organs in various documents. As it is, yesterday the voters presented me with the following question: "Why is it that in a recent information bulletin the Central Committee is listed first, and then the Supreme Soviet?" This also stems from the past. Here too we must change the stereotypes which have already been created.

In conclusion, I would like to say: Comrades, you and I are living in such a time of restructuring when objectively, and I stress, objectively all the roads lead to true people's power. We must do everything possible to remove any obstacles from this path, no matter who has placed them there.... Only then will we be able to use that last chance which history has given us for rehabilitation before our people and before the world community. We will not have another such possibility. Thank you for your attention. (Applause).

A.-M.K. Brazauskas: Attention, comrades! We are continuing the discussion. Comrade Gayer has the floor. Comrade Gumbaridze will speak after the recess.

Ye.A. Gayer, scientific associate of the USSR Academy of Sciences Far East Department Institute of History, Archaeology and Ethnography, Vladivostok (Far Eastern National-Territorial Electoral District, RSFSR): Honorable Chairman! Honorable deputies! Many of you are

Twelfth Session

8 June 1989

probably thinking: Why is this woman so eager to get up to the podium? The fact is not so much that I personally wanted to have the floor, but that thousands of my fellow countrymen from the Far East and the native peoples of the Far East tie their hopes for success of restructuring with my presentation at this congress. They are the Nanay, the Ulchi, the Nivkhi, the Vegidaltsy, Orochi, Oroki, Udegey, and others—even the names of these peoples some of you, perhaps, are hearing for the first time. I understand that it is very difficult to be the last speaker before the recess. But I hope that you will have patience and will listen to what I have to say.

Seeing me off to the congress, the people who for 70 years of Soviet rule have never had the chance to speak in full voice about their rights said: Be sure that you get to speak, and tell them about everything that has troubled us all these years, and that for us is most important! So tell me, please, how can I not justify their hopes?! Therefore, honorable chairman and honorable deputies, forgive me for such fervor, which perhaps has been manifested in the preceding days.

We have become accustomed to always speaking about our achievements and our victories. I believe today is not the time to talk about this. We know about our victories and achievements. Today I would like to tell about the problems which affect our peoples. It so happens that the epicenter of public interest toward the problems of national relations has been shifted in the direction of the Transcaucasus and our Baltic republics. On the background of general international conflicts in these regions, the problems of those Soviet peoples which we traditionally call the peoples of the Far East and the Far North remain almost unnoticed.

No, they cannot organize mass meetings and demonstrations today. I believe there is no need for this. But does this mean that their weak voice cannot be heard here? I would like to focus the attention of the country on their complex fate, particularly since the discussion in most cases centers not simply around their problems, but around the question of whether or not these peoples are to remain on earth. Names of disappearing species of animals and plants are being placed on the endangered species list. Yet we are speaking here about peoples!

Every people has its own ecological niche. The life and health of each people depend entirely on the condition of the natural environment. Yet the ecological problem in the Far East is no less acute than in the European part of our country. The intervention of the ministries and departments has turned out to be more terrible than anything else: The Minlesprom [Ministry of the Timber Industry], Mintsvetmet [Ministry of Ferrous Metallurgy], Minvostokstroy [Ministry of Construction in the Eastery Regions of the USSR] and other "bums" [papermaking industries] and "proms" [industrial administrations]. Through their efforts, such an export directionality has been created for the Far Eastern economy in which even Japan enjoys on our land that which it would have in the case of full annexation of the Far East, specifically—a raw material appendage. All Far Easterners suffer from this departmental invasion. As for the native peoples, for them the practice of economic management which has come about spells real tragedy. Let us take, for example, the recent struggle of the Udegey to protect the forest areas in the rayon where they live. Dallesprom [Far Eastern Timber Industry Administration] was planning to develop several large lespromkhozes [timber industry collective farms] there. This was in a region Khabarovsk Kray where the Udegey lived for centuries. This was a tragedy in the making, which could hardly have been averted were it not for the intervention of CPSU Central Committee Secretary Comrade Baklanov. Yet the situation could have arisen in which some Soviet writers had to urgently sit down to write a novel entitled "Really the Last of the Udegey".

Today once again the troubles of the Udegey have become aggravated in Primorskiy Kray. I have received a number of telegrams in which the people write: Please, Yevdokiya Aleksandrovna, you are our deputy. Help us! The invasion of the timber industry collective farms and the Ministry of the Timber Industry is now so severely reflected in the life of the Udegey of Primorskiy kray, that they are ready to defend their virgin forests and the place where they live with gun in hand. I do not think that it will come to this. (Applause).

Why do I present the example of the Udegey people? The Udegey in the Far East live in four settlements, and these settlements are located in four rayons and two krays. Their fates are determined by different ministries which are located in the Far East. Therefore, you can imagine how difficult it is for this people to solve its problems. Yet the fate of the Udegey people is analogous to the fates of all other native peoples and all Far Easterners. According to scientific terminology, we call those Far Easterners who came to these areas from the 17th century to the present day "non-natives". Yet they have been Far Easterners for a long time, and this problem is just as dear to them as to our native peoples.

The fact is that the lifestyle of the native peoples is tied with the taiga and the tundra. When the forest is cut down, when rivers are poisoned, when industry undermines the raw material base of the hunting and fishing trade—all this is not simply imprudent management. We are speaking here of the unregulated, uncontrolled destruction of the very basis of existence of these peoples. The economic development of the region in the last decades has completely ignored the legal rights of the native peoples. It has not taken into consideration the peculiarities of their labor resources, their ethnocultural characteristics, or their specific national interests. The consolidation of collective farms, their reorganization into sovkhozes and goskomkhozes, as well as many other ill-planned innovations, have contradicted the experience of labor activity and the peculiarities of life and

Twelfth Session

8 June 1989

everyday existence which have been formulated within the framework of national culture. Do you know how many small settlements, which were considered ineffective, were destroyed in the last 20 years! If we take only part of the region—from Khabarovsk to Nikolaevsk, it is so small, yet along the banks of the Amur River there were around 50 settlements destroyed, where native residents of the Far East had lived.

The reduction in the sphere of traditional labor, the uncontrolled, and sometimes even encouraged, influx of worshippers of the "long ruble" from other rayons of the country, gradually displaced the native population from the spheres of prestigeous labor. As a result, fishing—the primordeal occupation of many peoples of the Far East—has become the work of a select few. There is a catastrophic decline in the portion of participation of local residents in the hunting trade. With the exception of two or three villages, the marine animal hunting trade has ceased to exist.

At first glance it may seem that the peoples of the North have not received the concern and attention of the state. Actually, at the union and republic level in the last 30 years there have been tens of resolutions adopted which begin with the words "On the future development"...and so forth, and are directed at accelerating the socio-economic development of the northern peoples. However, most of them have merely remained on paper. Particular hopes were pinned on the resolution of 1980. Over 40 union ministries and departments were to have participated in its realization. But what do the ministries and departments care about the needs and concerns of the remote national villages?!

The next resolution turned out to be the next lie for them, and this, in essence, was recently admitted on the pages of SOVETSKAYA KULTURA by CPSU Central Committee worker Aleksandr Sergeyevich Filin. Having visited the Amur villages, he was forced to ask the question: If over R2 million have been invested since 1980 in Khabarovsk Kray for the development of the rayons where the northern peoples live, then why has not one single ruble found its way to those places where these peoples actually dwell? The lion's share of the capital expenditures settles in the rayon centers, in the large industrial settlements where there are singular representatives of the northern peoples. After all this, is it any wonder than 57 percent of the children in the national villages of this same Khabarovsk Kray go to school in unimproved buildings? Before coming to the congress, I toured the rayons of the region and visited the national villages and settlements of the Slavic peoples, our Far Easterners. The schools were in a sad state. The outward appearance of the wooden structures was pitiful. They were so decayed by wood rot and time that the holes had to be plugged with undershirts. I asked: Will something be done this summer, so that next winter the children can go to school in good buildings? I was told: No, this winter they will again study in such schools.

We have already spoken from this podium about the life expectancy of the native peoples. When one becomes acquainted with the illness rate of tuberculosis and infant mortality, there is something to think about. I am thankful to Klara Semenovna Khallik from Estonia, who understands very well the problems of the native peoples of our country. She spoke painfully. Yet the pain of these peoples to me, a representative of one of the native peoples, is even more painful. That is why I am speaking about it today.

Much in the culture of the northern people has been irretrievably lost, but much can still be saved. For this, first of all, we must secure specific territories for each of the aboriginal peoples and for individual groups of these peoples. We must also secure their exclusive right to economic assimilation, the right to engage in hunting and fishing, the right to pasturelands, inland water reservoirs, and coastal waters. Only in this way can we stop the assault of the union departments and ministries on the remnants of the traditional economy of these peoples and preserve them, at least in those boundaries which have been formed today. In the development of ideas expressed at the 19th all-union party conference on questions of reform of the political system, it would be expedient to return to such forms of national-administrative division as the national rayon and the national rural Soviet, which existed in the 1930's. Such national-territorial units must have elements of national sovereignty and be independent in resolving questions of local significance. The electoral organs of such microautonomies should have broader rights and powers than in ordinary administrative-territorial units, and they must have the real possibility of defining the character of the national life in the territories subordinate to them. Their decisions in the sphere of national-specific interests of the population—language, culture, labor, traditions, etc.—must not be rescinded by superior organs of authority. In the Amur basin, where almost half of the native population of the southern Far East lives, there has long been a need to have one of the forms of political autonomy of northern peoples. I personally believe that this should be not an okrug, as is customary for the northern peoples today, but an autonomous oblast. The population numbers, its national make-up, economic potential, degree of industrial assimilation, acuteness of the ecological situation, and character of social and national problems in this region are such that the autonomous okrug, even with consideration for the future expansion of its rights and competencies, would hardly be able to handle all of this.

Equality of peoples should not merely be a constitutional phrase. First of all this equality must be expressed in the status and the rights of the peoples. If 10,000 Jews in the Jewish Autonomous Oblast have their own national-political autonomy, then why can't the over 20,000 native residents of Khabarovsk kray have it too? In any case, I as a scientist-ethnographer cannot give any persuasive answer to this question posed by my countrymen.

Twelfth Session

8 June 1989

Recently among specialists in northern studies and among the northern peoples themselves there has been a growing conviction as to the need for creating an association of northern peoples in the country, a special social organization supported by the government. Such an organization would facilitate the political consolidation of all the northern peoples, the recognition of their rights, and the growth of their self-awareness, political, and social activity.

People's Deputy Kugultinov quite correctly spoke of the need for a legislative statute on the rights of the Soviet people. I fully support this proposal. An analysis of the conflict situations in various rayons of the country convinces us that the absence of constitutional principles on the rights of peoples and the absence of a mechanism guaranteeing their unequivocal adherence, is today the primary source of national problems.

In many Soviet republics today there are heated arguments over the question of which language should be the state language—Russian or the native language. For us this problem does not exist, since the languages of the northern peoples are disappearing. Many have practically disappeared. We hardly need to say that the disappearance of a language means the disappearance of a people. Wherever this is still possible, this process must be stopped today at any cost.

I would like to speak about the mandates of my Far Easterners. Dear deputies, allow me to speak for 3 minutes more. I will not get up to the podium again. (Excitement in the auditorium).

Honorable ministers! In the Far East there is a Far Eastern northern wage coefficient. This northern coefficient is given for the severe climatic conditions. But in no case it is given because some ministry or department decides. However, it turns out that some enterprises receive a coefficient of 1.2, while others receive 1.8, depending on their departmental affiliation. I believe that this injustice should be eliminated and that the northern coefficients should be granted equally. I also believe that difficult climatic conditions give me the right to say that these coefficients should be reflected in pensions, stipends and grants to Far Easterners.

I also want to say that I am a totally peaceful person. My opponent was Lieutenant-General Viktor Ivanovich Novozhilov. I believe that our 8th national-territorial district, on whose territory one can place many European states, deserves to be represented not by one, but by two deputies. There are more than enough problems there not only for one deputy, but probably even for two—both civilian problems, as well as a set of military problems.

No, we cannot depart from the law. Yet I believe it would be right to make a correction in the Law on Elections so that there would be a deputy from the Far Eastern military district as well as from the 8th national-territorial district. Then it would be easier to resolve both the military problems and the civilian ones.

As a candidate for people's deputy, I spoke in military units and on military vessels during the electoral meetings. My electors asked that I relate to the congress the fact that it must necessarily review the question of our sons who are serving in the army. In 2-3 years they will go on reserve. But how will they return—poor as church mice! I believe we should today raise the question of giving them a state aid grant for the initial period after their demobilization. How can we resolve this? I think the minister of defense will find a way. We cannot leave the situation as it is. (Applause).

And here is the last question. When the bulletin was read, deputies spoke up and said that their words had been distorted. They asked that they be corrected. I asked a question at the Soviet of Nationalities as to whether the material of the international Convention of 1957 was familiar. Much depended on this question and on the answer by the chairman of the Soviet of Nationalities. Yet in the bulletin I did not find either my questions or the answers to them. I ask that the Secretariat be very attentive to such problems. Thank you for your attention. (Applause).

A.-M.K. Brazauskas: Comrades, a few announcements.

First. Here is a request that all agrarian deputies, as it is written here, remain in the auditorium now. That is one thing.

Second. Today at 1440 the mandate commission will meet in the Granovit Hall.

Third. The commission to investigate the events in Tbilisi is meeting during the recess near the secretariat on the second floor.

That is all. We will have a 30-minute recess.

A.-M.K. Brazauskas: Comrades, we are continuing our work. Comrade Givi Grigoryevich Gumbaridze has the floor. Comrade Aleksey Vladimirovich Yablokov should get ready.

G.G. Gumbaridze, first secretary of the Georgian Communist Party Central Committee, Tbilisi (Zestafonskiy National-Territorial Electoral District, Georgian SSR): Honorable comrade deputies! Our dialogue with each other is primarily an open discussion with the people and the country. Perhaps never before has the price of the resounding word been so high. Thinking about this, I always see the faces of my fellow countrymen, for whom everything that is said from this rostrum is not simply direct speech, but a matter of their dignity and honor, their hope and faith in justice. The atmosphere of our

Twelfth Session
8 June 1989

congress largely reflects the complex and sometimes contradictory picture of the state of our society.

We have gathered here to discuss the short and long-term prospects for the country's foreign and domestic policy, the constructive program presented by the government. This means we have gathered to determine the most rational methods for moving ahead, so that the anomalies in economics, social and spiritual life, demography, ecology, and international relations, and the questions of political, legal and cultural sovereignty of nations do not arise as an insurmountable obstacle in the path of restructuring.

All of them make themselves known also in the life of Georgia. I have something to say about them, and I had intended to do so, but the content of the preceding discussion and the political situation in the republic force me to review and restructure my presentation. There is an entire series of important circumstances which motivate me to once again return to the April events in Tbilisi.

For us the Tbilisi tragedy holds deep personal pain. Nevertheless, we must rise above our emotions and examine everything that has happened in a broad political context, since we are speaking not only about the authority of power, but also about the prestige of our very restructuring. We bravely exposed the rotten springs of the authoritarian regime, but it is specifically for this reason that the basis for our new political model must from the beginning be high humanitarian and moral standards which determine the foundation of the theoretical searches of Vladimir Ilyich Lenin.

From these positions, the following conclusion is inevitable: Under conditions of democracy, the decision adopted in the republic which has led to such severe consequences, to a crisis of trust and to moral-political detriment, cannot in any case be acknowledged as being politically correct. And each of us feels the responsibility for this.

It is incorrect, or at least politically naive, to qualify the April meetings and demonstrations in Tbilisi as "public merry-making". This was a political action which the demonstrators primarily tried to tie in with the question of national self-determination. The affirmation that supposedly there were no slogans and appeals of a rather extreme direction is also incorrect.

However, all this cannot justify the bloody tragedy which took place on that night. It is easy to accuse a 70-year old woman and a 10-year old youth of extremism, but such an approach holds no prospects, and we have become convinced as to where it might lead. It is also irresponsible to ascribe anti-Russian sentiments to an entire people. There have not been and are not such sentiments of Russophobia in Georgia. We know that the Russian people, the Russian intelligentsia, like all the fraternal peoples, are suffering the pain of the Tbilisi tragedy. Indignation at the bureaucratic dictate really should not be confused with anti-Russian sentiments.

The congress adopted the decision to investigate the causes and circumstances surrounding the events of 9 April, and has created an authoritative commission. I am sure that it will scrupulously study all the materials and will determine the full truth, as Mikhail Sergeyevich Gorbachev demanded, and that the guilty parties, regardless of what position they occupy or where they work, will bear the punishment they deserve. This conviction is shared by all the deputies from Georgia with whom Mikhail Sergeyevich found time to meet during the course of the work of the congress. This meeting served as a characteristic example of a truly open, honest, and much needed dialogue. When the inability to conduct a dialogue leads to placing the wage on power—this is a blow to restructuring. And without saying this truth, we will find no other.

In creating a legal state, we are obligated to instill in the citizens, and especially in the youth, a respect for the law. And it is the party organs and state institutions which must primarily set the examples for the scrupulous adherence to this law. Decisions which are not made collectively, which are made hastily and contrary to the standards of party and official ethics, are always fraught with fateful errors and violations of the law.

Public order is the concern of society. In the extreme case there is the militia and the powers of protecting public order. The involvement of paratrooper units in such civil actions for the purpose of performing functions which are not characteristic of them is difficult even to explain, let alone justify, which certain people have tried to do in vain. Were it not for this, we would today not have any worries about the Army's role in the tragedy. The military prosecutor would not have to open a criminal case, especially since, as has now become clear, the Army units and their commanders had directive orders to implement only protective measures.

There were severe consequences even from the introduction of the curfew, which was announced to the people only 4 minutes before it went into effect.

The phrase also resounded here that we cannot turn the Army against the people. I would say the following: All of us are obligated to protect our Army, not to place on its shoulders the political problems which we have not solved. My fellow countrymen, whose grandfathers and fathers bravely fought at the battle of Borodino and in the battle of Stalingrad, have sacred respect for this tradition. The funerals from the Afghan war also did not bypass our mothers. That is why the republic perceived so acutely and painfully the series of inadmissable evaluations and expressions allowed from this rostrum by a former Afghan fighter. I speak about this with a peculiar personal feeling, as a person who grew up in the family of a Soviet officer and political worker.

STENOGRAPHIC RECORD

Twelfth Session

8 June 1989

Really, elementary ethics and humanity obligated Colonel-General Rodionov, who allowed himself to call the Tbilisi tragedy "Tbilisi provocation", "a Georgian variant of restructuring", to find in his lexicon words which expressed at least some sorrow and compassion for the victims and their relatives. (Applause).

His presentation may be perceived differently. However, how can we justify the harshness, the excess zeal which was not demanded by anyone? Was it not this excessive zeal which served as the reason for the subsequent insincerity and misinformation? How can we justify our actions by referring to a publication in the newspaper ZARYA VOSTOKA in the days of the curfew, if the real facts were distorted even before the official institutions? Only on the third day was the use of sapper shovels verified, only on the fifth—the use of gases, and only after almost a month did the chemical content of these gases become known, although this was extremely important for treatment of the victims. These facts were stubbornly denied in the daily meetings not only to us, but to the two representatives of the CPSU Central Committee Politburo- -Comrades Z. A. Sheverdnadze and G. P. Razumovskiy, as well as to the high leadership of the country. Perhaps not everyone knows, but it was only their persistence and only the principle of Mikhail Sergeyevich Gorbachev that allowed us to make headway in seeking the truth. We are grateful to him also for his help in sending to the republic highly trained medical specialists from Moscow, Leningrad and other cities, as well as from abroad, the representatives of the Soviet and International Red Cross.

Reorganization of society must be accompanied by the reorganization of institutions of power. Primarily it must be accompanied by the development, and sometimes even the radical change in style, forms and methods of the work of party organizations. It is unthinkable without renovation. It cannot be decreed by volitional decisions. Under conditions of glasnost, we must condemn efforts at forceful pressure on any unsanctioned manifestations of thought, word, or national sentiment. We must successively overcome the genes of authoritarianism which have long been lodged in us. We must learn to talk with people, to find convincing and precise arguments in any difficult dialogue.

When the principle positions of restructuring take on a declarative character, the public initiative which they awaken, not finding a natural outlet, begins to take on the form of open protest, as happened in our case. Therefore, consolidation, prudent compromise, and integration of all the potential possibilities of society—that is the only way to avoid unnecessary intellectual and physical victims in the process of revolutionary break-up.

Experience confirms that one of the most effective forms for this is constructive dialogue. We cannot divide society into formals and informals, and then even to instill a strictly political meaning into these concepts. We must at least from now on work in such a way as to convince of our sincerity even those who have become disinchanted in the prospect of such dialogue. We must convince them that we stand together with the people in deed, and not just in words, that we share their social and political ideals, that we give [the people] everything, not thinking of our own official success.

Restructuring has expanded the framework and the forms of manifesting national sentiments and interests, and it is time to remove many outdated stereotypes from our ideological baggage. Recently in the republic, for the first time since the Leninist period, the Day of Restoration of the Georgian State was celebrated, and this is as it should be. Historical dates are a tribute to events, and they do not disappear from the memory at someone's whim. By depriving the people of them, we take away their spiritual and moral foundations, and disrupt the continuity of their historically formulated political orientation.

Events such as those in Tbilisi are most easily explained as the flaring of national emotions. But did they not manifest in some measure the results of those well-known deformations of socialism and especially the constitutionally secured federal principles in Soviet statehood which had been allowed for many decades in the country? There was a bankrupting of the existing thousand-year old traditions and ideals of Georgian statehood, with which the sole desire of the people for cultural, linguistic and physical survival are equated, and to whose defense the political and military energy of tens of generations was devoted.

During the years of repression, the flower of the Georgian nation was destroyed. Tens of thousands of innocent people were thrown into jails and imprisoned in camps. Among the fabricated judicial processes there were the so-called "cases" of Georgian writers, theatre artists, scientific and technical intelligentsia, and many others. The gloom of the 30's, 40's and 50's cast its shadow even beyond the boundary of Stalinism, to the year 1956, when the deceived youth perished on these very same streets of Tbilisi. We cannot overlook all this in a political work during the epoch of glasnost.

Today, when the party is successively conducting a rehabilitation of slandered names and principally filling in the gaps in our history, we must everywhere objectively get to the bottom of our past, especially the recent past, without elevating scientific studies and arguments to the rank of big politics. In order to really give power to the Soviets, it is time we knew how this power was ratified in Georgia in 1918-1921, to have a fair historical evaluation of the violation of the agreement between Georgia and Soviet Russia which was approved by Vladimir Ilyich Lenin. We must objectively examine the basic principles of this agreement as applied to the present day and soberly restore the political portraits of well-known leaders of this contradictory epoch.

STENOGRAPHIC RECORD

Twelfth Session

8 June 1989

The rapid growth of national awareness testifies to the fact that the people have begun believing in restructuring, and that they strive to realize their sacred hopes by means of it. Today, in my opinion, we need not so much recipes, as a continuous scientific interpretation of all the processes, without any haste or prejudice.

Thus, the community is perceiving the questions of political sovereignty with particular acuteness. We must continue to develop work on creating its reliable economic and constitutional basis, as well as the sociopolitical mobilization of the people in a creative vein. We have begun, although with some delay, the development of the conception of republic cost accounting for the purpose of more rational ownership, management, and use of local natural resources. Work on the outline of the Georgian Constitution, in our opinion, must be directed at harmonizing the relations with the center, their correct combination with the real political and economic sovereignty of the republic.

In our opinion, the need has arisen to perform in-depth development in the multinational republics and regions on the question of ensuring the balance of inter-national interests with the interests of the native nation, primarily through language, culture, and other national values. This, undoubtedly, would facilitate increased trust.

I would like to stress that the republic has all the capacities, provided there is mutual agreement and respect, for solving all intranational problems, primarily those which concern the Abkhaz people, with whom the Georgian people have been closely tied by age-old fraternal relations. There are also problems which especially today disturb the youth and the republic as a whole, and which are in the stage of imminent solution. We must all learn how to resolve questions so as not to lead society into a dead end and not to inflict detriment upon the progress of our common cause.

In order to indeed promote restructuring, we must work out principally new conceptions of the national question. National energy is a huge reserve which we must learn to correctly manage. This is why today the consolidation on the basis of true pluralism of political, economic and national interests is as necessary as air, so that the collective intellect of our party and the Soviets may triumph everywhere over mediocrity and conservatism.

I would like to say one more thing from this rostrum. Our moral sense must not betray us, so as not to discredit that political force thanks to which both the 19th Party Conference and our congress embarked specifically upon a democratic path. I believe that the attitude toward party authority at the current turning-point stage is also a choice: Either in favor of restructuring, or not in favor of it. The party is the initiator of renovation of our society. It is the one who must stand at the avant-garde of restructuring. Thank you for your attention. (Applause).

A.-M.K. Brazauskas: Deputy Yablokov has the floor. Comrade Chabanov should get ready.

A.V. Yablokov, USSR Academy of Sciences corresponding member, head of laboratory at the USSR Academy of Sciences N.K. Koltsov Institute of Developmental Biology, Moscow (representing the scientific societies and associations under the USSR Academy of Sciences): Honorable congress! Honorable Comrade Chairman! I speak in the name of the entire group of delegates from the Far East, from Siberia, Leningrad, Podmoskovye, Moscow, Zaporozhye and other places associated with problems of the ecology. We support the basic principles presented in the speeches of Comrades Gorbachev and Ryzhkov. However, we believe that an analysis of the ecological problems does not in full measure reflect the alarming state of affairs in this sphere of our country. In the presentations of the overwhelming majority of deputies, ecological problems were rightly listed among the primary and most important ones. The situation is such: 20 percent of our country's population lives in zones of ecological distress, and another 35-40 percent lives in ecologically unfavorable conditions. As a result, there is a rapid increase in the illness rate associated with deterioration of the quality of the environment. One in every three men living in such rayons will contract cancer sometime during his life. Every year the number of cancer victims increases. Infant mortality is higher in some regions than in a number of African countries, while our average life expectancy is 4-8 years lower than in the developed countries of the world. In some regions, as for example in Zaporozhye, it is declining. In this day and age, comrades, it is declining!

The main reasons for the deterioration of the ecological situation in the country are both political and economic. As a result of many years of distortions in the political system, the Soviets have lost real power in the local areas. We have experienced, one might say, not only depeasantization, of which we have already spoken, but also "desovietization". As was determined even by the 27th party congress, the intervention of the party apparatus into economic management functions has been unjustifiably broad. Another part of the power of the soviets, possibly even the largest part, has been taken over by the ministries and departments. The soviets have been placed in the position of petitioners, and often agree to ecologically dangerous projects against their will, since it is only through them that they see a possibility for development of the territories. There are no effective economic incentives for resource conservation at the department level. An inevitable consequence of this is the extensive character of exploitation of natural resources and the extensive character of development of the departments themselves, about which less is said. Under conditions of departmental monopoly, the development of each sector proceeds without consideration for the pressure on the environment of neighboring sectors. With lack of power by the soviets, this leads to the elemental, ecologically dangerous development of entire regions.

STENOGRAPHIC RECORD

Twelfth Session

8 June 1989

A second group of reasons for deterioration of the ecological situation in the country may be considered ideological. We have erred in believing that the socialist system of economic management automatically ensures rational utilization of nature. Having been raised on this thesis, we at one time refused to participate in many world programs for saving the environment. According to the estimates of our diplomats, the USSR does not participate in several tens of over 100 ecologically oriented international agreements. While criticizing capitalist use of nature, we overlooked the fact that the leading capitalist countries have to a significant degree been able to manage those ecological problems with which we are currently faced. The process of socialization of nature is rapidly proceeding in all the developed countries of the world, while in our country a reverse tendency might sooner be noted—"desocialization". Natural resources are monopolistically used by departments or even groups of persons. A clear example of this is the fencing off of beaches in the resort zones of the Ukrainian SSR, and the directly opposite development of the right to beach access for any citizen as compared with, say, the United State of America or Italy.

The absence of precise information on the status of the environment also complicates the ecological situation. The absence of information is sometimes caused by departmental concealment of data. I support the proposal previously expressed here that we should consider such concealment a real ecological crime. We have already justifiably and repeatedly condemned here the secrecy of data on radiation pollution. Sometimes data are not secret, but are not accessible to the public. Not many people know, for example, that in 1987, one-fifth of all the sausage goods inspected in the Soviet Union (official Ministry of Health inspection) contained toxic chemicals in quantities which were harmful to the health. The same is true also for 42 percent of the products in children's milk kitchens (just think—children's milk kitchens!), and of 30 percent of all the food products in Leningrad.

These data are not secret, but they were published in a circulation of 18 copies. However, basically we simply do not have the necessary information in general. For example, even Goskomstat [State Committee for Statistics] does not know how many millions of hectares of arable land have been flooded over by water reservoirs. One does not need to be a prophet to say that the ecological crisis in the country will increase and intensify in the next few years. The social tension associated with the ecology will also increase. Ecology is already today placing strict limitations on the development of the national economy, and in some places it is even determining the domestic policy situation. Last year, over 2 million people stopped work, signed petitions, or participated in meetings for reasons of ecology.

There is only one solution. The party, which has voluntarily taken upon itself the heavy burden of political leadership, must quickly and decisively "turn green"— that is, it must face the problems of ecology. (Applause). Otherwise, ecological discontent will be politicized outside the framework of the party. At all levels we must recognize the fact that the time of ecologically incompetent managers is past. If, as Comrade Gorbachev stated in his speech, those not very great funds which were allocated by the state for ecology were spent ineffectively or not spent at all, the reason for this is not the absence of technology or funds, but rather it is the ecological-political short-sightedness of the leaders in local areas and in the center.

What must we do in the country to improve the ecological situation?

First of all, we must return local power to the soviets. The soviets must become the real masters of the natural resources in their territory. At the same time, we must engage such mechanisms of nature utilization which would ensure the protection of the environment against pilferage. Such mechanisms do exist. They are—introducing payments for natural resources which would ensure the financial independence of the soviets and would serve as one of the basics for regional cost accounting.

Another mechanism is the real implementation of the principle used throughout the world: "The polluter pays" for real compensation of the loss inflicted by the enterprises to nature as well as to the health of man. We often forget about the latter.

The central departments which have been liberated from economic management functions must become the scientific-technical headquarters of the sectors. And even the Council of Ministers itself must become the scientific-technical headquarters for restructuring. One of the main ecological requirements for such reorganization is not only the construction of purification structures, but also the transition to progressive and ecologically safe low-waste and waste-free technology.

I believe that the search for some special laws for our economy (individual deputies have spoken about this here) which differ from the laws of world economy has lead to an administrative-command style of development of the national economy and to an endless succession of party-government resolutions on the development of the sectors. Our national economy has become reminiscent of a jumping frog, if you will forgive me, as a biologist, such a comparison. Each jump is a resolution. Sometimes the jump is forward, sometimes to the right, and sometimes to the left, depending on what frightens it at the given moment.

The permanently operating Supreme Soviet and budget control will, I hope, allow us to forever reject such a style of national economic development. The Supreme Soviet must demand of the Council of Ministers that it sharply improve control over the quality of our environment. It is indicative that out of more than 300 toxic chemicals

Twelfth Session

8 June 1989

which have been approved for application, all the control services in the country can account for no more than 120 of them. But where are the other 180? We simply do not know. We need an all-encompassing state ecological expert investigation. The decision on it was made by the Supreme Soviet back in 1985, at the first session after the beginning of restructuring. Yet in fact this decision has not been implemented. I participated in a number of state ecological expert investigations: of the South Ukraine Atomic Power Station, the second phase of the Astrakhan Gas Condensate Complex, and the territorial integrated scheme for the Baykal region. And I must say that such a commission of experts is yet in fact powerless, and the investigation is conducted on semi-public principles.

Without an ecological expert investigation at the stage of pre-design development (before sizeable funds have been spent), we will always have immobilization of vast capital, as is the case today. After all, the people will ultimately, by the most primitive but also the most effective method, simply by the method of mass disobedience and demonstrations, conduct the final, people's, expert investigation without us.

How is it that the Council of Ministers allows the construction of major enterprises not only without an ecological expert investigation, but even without projects, sometimes even without technical-economic substantiation? That is what is happening today with the Tyumen petrochemical complex. This has already been mentioned several times. Yet the expenditures for it will be several times greater than the expenditures for the BAM [Baykal-Amur Main Line]. There is no project, there are no technical-economic substantiations, but the Council of Ministers adopts the decision to open financing. Even the term "privilege financing" has arisen, which means that construction is beginning without the necessary project documents required by law.

We speak of creating a legal state, yet the highest executive authority turns out to be the main violator of the laws. Both the law and reason state: We cannot build without allocation of land. Yet, for example, the Mingasprom [Ministry of the Gas Industry] willfully seizes plots of land in the Yamal, physically displacing the native residents from it. It conducts drilling operations and builds roads without allocation of land. And all this is done with the sanction of the Council of Ministers! I did not believe it, asked to see the documents, and they sent them to me by messenger from Salekhard. The documents state: The Council of Ministers has extended the privilege financing for the Mingazprom even this year. We must send the most serious instructions to the Supreme Soviet and the Council of Ministers to urgently put an end to this barbarism (the term which, by the way, was used by Nikolay Ivanovich Ryzhkov himself) in the application of our natural resources. (Applause).

The Supreme Soviet must take under its permanent control the matter of radically restructuring state management in the sphere of environmental protection, which was begun with the creation of the USSR Goskompriroda [State Committee for the Protection of Nature]. Increasing the status of this committee (which was repeatedly mentioned in the press prior to the congress, and then also discussed at the congress itself) is a vitally necessary task. Today this committee is almost powerless. This is not the kind of committee we expected!

World experience tells us that for stabilization of the ecological situation we must spend around 2 percent of the gross national product on environmental protection. And in order to improve the quality of the environment (that which is an extreme necessity for us today) we must spend no less than 5 percent. As yet, we are spending only around 1 percent. And those R135 billion for the next few five-year plans about which Nikolay Ivanovich spoke here are a ridiculously small amount. We must admit this. The basic financial reserves, perhaps, are found not only in conversion. I believe that the basic reserves may be found in the rejection of the extensive development of sectors. We can drill 15,000 wells each year, as we have been doing. Or we may obtain 5-10, and even 20 times more oil from each skillfully drilled well. Specialists believe that we can save several billion rubles a year on oil well drilling alone.

I am convinced that tens of billions of rubles are spent ineffectively in the national economy. Let us take the problem of buying pesticides. Three years ago we bought half a billion rubles worth of pesticides. This was in spite of the fact that one-third of the pesticides is lost along the road to the field, while the other two-thirds poison our health. This is where the deputies who will work on the budget in the Supreme Soviet commissions and committees can really get down to business.

Among other instructions to the Supreme Soviet for solving ecological problems are the following: We must put our environmental protection legislation in order. There are many gaps and oversights here. We still do not have an all-union law on the protection of nature. Although, perhaps, now it is more important to speak about a law to protect the environment in which we live. We must join numerous international conventions and agreements on environmental protection and honestly fulfill the responsibilities which we have assumed. Here is a small example. The World Charter on Nature which was adopted with the support of the USSR in 1982 has still not been publicized in our country.

We need a legislative mechanism for realizing the inalienable right of native residents to use their territory. The local soviet authorities must have the right of "veto" in questions concerning the life supporting systems of the small peoples and their national culture. (Applause). We must not be afraid that such a right of "veto" will

Twelfth Session

8 June 1989

hinder the development of the territory. The local sites will be interested in its development, and specifically its development, but not its pilferage. Everyone will benefit—both man and nature.

Finally, there is one more thing that we could do, right here at this congress. In developing the sections on environmental protection in the speeches under discussion, and taking into consideration the many presentations of the deputies, we must give ecological problems first priority importance. It would probably be expedient to adopt a special resolution, announcement or declaration of the congress on the ecological status of the environment. This is not a law on which jurists must work for a long time, verifying every comma. Such a resolution would become a testimony to the fact that the congress perceives the ecological danger as being very serious and tells the people that these problems will be solved. Perhaps it would be good to adopt similar documents on the economy, on the national question, and on the status of deputies. There is a basis for these documents. Without them it would be difficult for me, and for you too, comrade deputies, to report to the voters on the work of the congress. (Applause).

In conclusion, I would like to present two short questions. The ecological problem is so important for the USSR that it seems expedient to make the proposed Supreme Soviet Committee on Ecology a congress committee. This may relate also to the committees on the economy and the national question. The Constitution does not prohibit this. We have the right to create a congress committee, particularly since there are currently few ecology specialists in the Supreme Soviet. Most of them (30-40 people) who would like to work actively on this committee were not included in the Supreme Soviet. In order to involve them in solving these most important problems, perhaps we should create a congress committee, in the way of an exception. (Applause).

Here is the last thing about which I wanted to speak. Part of the deputies still believe that Moscow residents have certain specific interests. Comrades, 85 percent of the Moscow delegation is comprised of deputies elected from all-union organizations. I, for example, was nominated by the scientific societies from Kiev, Minsk, and Saratov. And so it was with most of them. There are, after all, problems, common problems for the entire country, and they must be solved. Our congress mail speaks of this. I have received tens of requests for ecological help from Kaliningrad, Leningrad, Sochi, Salekhard, Nikolayev, Vladimir and Ryazan Oblasts, Novosibirsk, Volgograd, and Odessa. All these materials, of course, will be forwarded to the Committee on Ecology, which will give them close examination.

Yet here the question arises: How will the committee be formulated? The congress is coming to a close. All the committees must begin their work, but we do not know how they are to be formulated. Judging by the agenda, this will take place on Saturday [10 June], when the congress finishes its work. Perhaps the presidium should think about at least appointing the committee chairmen, and then they can formulate [the committees]. Because we are at a loss, in any case, the ecologists.

The ecology, along with the economy and national relations, has become one of the country's main problems. We believe that the set of measures which was briefly outlined in this presentation would be an important step towards sharply improving the ecological situation.

If we cannot breathe the air, cannot drink the water, and cannot eat the food, then all social problems lose their meaning. If we do not solve the ecological problem, housing construction and the fulfillment of the food program are also cast into doubt. The solution of ecological problems is exceptionally important also from a political standpoint, since it leads to the consolidation of society. Both the "left" and "right-wingers" are in favor of the immediate solution of ecological problems. We must necessarily seek ways of consolidating our society. Thank you for your attention. (Applause).

A.-M.K. Brazauskas: Deputy Chabanov has the floor. Comrade Zalygin should get ready.

A.I. Chabanov, general director of the "Rotor" Science and Production Association (Cherkasskiy Territorial Electoral Okrug, Ukrainian Soviet Socialist Republic): Esteemed comrades, I had prepared a dry, critically constructive speech, but during the break my comrades asked me to take a couple of minutes to reply to Comrade Yemelyanov's speech. This is what I would like to say: Many "industrialists" know me, they know that I speak sincerely, honestly, and firmly. It may be that nobody else in this hall has more scars than I, caused by the party apparatus and individual party apparatus officials and taking the form of reprimands, severe reprimands, and attempts at expulsion from the party. I was chased out of one job—I moved on to another, and people again started expelling me. But I would like to say, comrades, that it is individual apparatus officials who are behind this. And none of this has anything to do with the party itself. While we were conducting the election campaign, the overwhelming majority of people asked me about my attitude to the party's position today. I explained this position and gained total approval. What I would like to say, dear comrades, is that the communist party and the communist ideology do not belong to our country alone; they are the result of the world civilization's development. The Communists' ideology took shape in ancient times, beginning with the revolt of Spartacus. Humane ideas have built up over the centuries—people thought of better ways to live and offered theoretical proof that this could be achieved under socialism. So we have no right, comrades, to adopt a frivolous attitude to the burden we are carrying on behalf of all mankind, to the responsibility for developing the worldwide gain that is communist ideology.

Twelfth Session

8 June 1989

I want to say a few words about constructiveness. What actually is the task facing a Communist, especially a Communist in leadership position? Primarily to take responsibility and to struggle, to take it on and to struggle. I have no desire to sound like the comrades who spoke on the subject of Popov's and Afanasyev's speeches: They should to get out, it was said, and get their hands dirty. This has happened many times before, people said these things and got applauded, but the outcome was bad. But in this specific instance, in my capacity as leader and scientist, for example, I would like to tell Comrade Yemelyanov how I would act in this instance as a Communist. I would take a rayon or at least a collective farm—being an academician you have the knowledge—and, as a Communist, get down to overcoming the resistance of individual apparatus officials, struggle against them, even incur their displeasure, but make that kolkhoz better than the farms in the Netherlands. That, I believe, is how a Communist ought to act. (Applause)

Of course we have problems with the apparatus, or rather with individual apparatus officials. They are, so to speak, products of the old "stagnation" period or even of the personality cult period. We must realize this. I would also say that such people are still to be found everywhere. I would cite the following example of obsolete thinking. Budennyy, for example, was a progressive commander during the civil war, but by the time of the Patriotic War he was unable to apply his concepts to produce anything substantial, to be of benefit to our people. I want to say that people with an obsolete mentality and obsolete methodology, like Budennyy, are still to be found in our country, at the bottom and at the top alike. It would be desirable for comrades among them who can see the similarity between themselves and those who have "grown old," as Budennyy did by the time of the Patriotic War, to make up their minds to depart. And as for those who are unwilling to depart—it is our task to help them depart through a verdict secured in struggle. (Applause)

And now, from the viewpoint of criticisms we will be making here on Nikolay Ivanovich Ryzhkov's report. I would like to say that this will not be simply a criticism of some positions taken in the report. This, the way I understand it, is the task of our congress, whose duty it is to continue work in order to correct shortcomings, and not in the sense of accepting that things are bad and there is nothing to be done about it. I would propose that we vote for Nikolay Ivanovich, and I recommend that we support his candidacy. But we must also help him in many respects, and we must take on a lot of things we used to leave alone. We are different people and, of course, there are many among us in this hall who could stand as alternative candidates for election. I know many general directors, like Comrade Volskiy, for example, who has been kept on in Nagorno-Karabakh Oblast—he is also a major specialist who could work here. I am in favor of alternative candidates for election and I believe that here it would of course be correct to consult in the first place, to consider proposals and recommendations for candidacies submitted to the congress, then to consult the Politburo, and to nominate someone as candidate. We would support this. The methodology does need to be amended somewhat—we sense this.

I think that the meaning of my remark at the Supreme Soviet sitting is clear. Much of what Comrade Shmelev said was also on my mind. And I wanted to say it clearly right there, at the Supreme Soviet. My remarks on the report. First, working on machine building with the Council of Ministers, with the Bureau for Machine Building, I want to say that there have been great changes there: New people, new ideas, new machines have emerged. I think that this is a guarantee of imminent change in the state of affairs in machine building. There have been major changes also along a number of other avenues of the Council of Ministers' work. On the other hand, I would say that Nikolay Ivanovich Ryzhkov's report today is, generally speaking, little different from previous speeches and previous reports. As if the specific figure of R6 billion allocated for social needs had only just been added. As a matter of fact, Nikolay Ivanovich, R6 billion is crumbs, it is very little. The data given about our expenditures on defense—R77 billion—is also just a figure; it has now been made public and we know about it. The report makes no promises that we will have built communism in 20 years' time. And all the rest is very similar to everything we have heard before. Like the winged phrase about gross output [val], for example. We have been criticizing all this ever since the sixties, and it was back in the sixties that the phrase "overwhelming gross output" [devyatyy val—meaning "the ninth wave," an untranslatable pun on 'val' in the sense of gross output and 'val' in the sense of wave] appeared in our country. "Industrialists" and "agriculturalists" alike remember it well. And now Nikolay Ivanovich says that he will be unable to cope with these gross volume indicators and abolish them in the current 5-Year Plan period. I think, Nikolay Ivanovich, that the indicator of volume accountability ought to be abolished as of 1 July. (Applause) And there are no problems in this regard.

Take another winged expression—the lack of a mechanism ensuring the introduction of scientific achievements. Here we are, saying this in the 4th year of restructuring, in the late eighties! Cast your minds back to the sixties, when Academician Kapitsa wrote his booklets, explaining and telling us the meaning of introduction and the pedagogical problems associated with it. Have we really been lacking such a mechanism all this time? First of all, we do have it and it must be utilized, even though not everything has been fully worked out from the viewpoint of the democratization of economic life. Even in the "Rotor" Science and Production Association we organized—with difficulty, of course, but we did it—science and production firms, we have no problems as regards the introduction of scientific results, and we seek innovations. Therefore, the mechanism is already in existence, and your definition is incorrect. Let

STENOGRAPHIC RECORD

Twelfth Session
8 June 1989

me emphasize this in particular: We cannot drag over from 1960 to 1989 the problem of lacking a mechanism for introduction.

Take another question for example—the dissipation of capital investments. It is something else we have known about since the sixties. What does this indicate? It indicates, of course, that a fresh influx of people is needed in the Council of Ministers. We have been saying this since the sixties. And now, in 1988 compared with 1985, there has been a 31-percent increase in new construction. But we cannot find capital investment funds for the breakthrough avenues in machine building. As a matter of fact, we did not fulfill the resolution on machine building, which was of crucial importance. This is because we divide the work among departments, and they are understandably unwilling to relinquish anything of theirs. Once again we spoke, just as we did in the sixties, about departmental barriers. There was just a slight variation, an amplification: You said that several ministries were eliminated and 600,000 persons were released from the state management apparatus. First, it is necessary to look and see to what use these 600,000 persons have been put. They must be properly transferred into the system of the national economy to ensure that they are put to good use, without moral or material loss. As a matter of fact, I know exactly where these 600,000 persons have ended up. They have not been put to sufficiently effective use.

Or, by way of another example, there was nothing in the report about the anticipated budget for 1989 or a forecast for 1990. And yet we are a parliament, not some sort of conference. We can spend 3-4 hours listening, with a break if need be, and should without fail look and see what sort of a budget we'll have this year and what are the prospects for next year; we should exchange opinions. Or another question that has been overlooked—the political question concerning restructuring. The problem made no mention of the following problem: Some 20-30 categories of mass consumer goods are in short supply, goods like soap, detergents, socks, and so on. During the transition period (is this so hard to understand?) the Council of Ministers must have an apparatus to monitor this work, to review state orders, to apply economic levers—an eye must be kept on all this. This enormous political work has been overlooked, and seems to be altogether missing from the report. This is trivial as far as we are concerned, but it must be resolved. It is easy to resolve, otherwise we would blow restructuring apart.

I would like to say, comrades, that we certainly have no right to play down the importance of our congress. I would say that our congress was meant to lay down the strategic tasks of our society's development in this century, in other words through the year 2000. This is the first Congress of People's Deputies. I think that we must bear in mind Lenin's idea that it is necessary to define the general before moving on to the specific. Anyone working on specifics, looking at the next 1-2 years, would always come up against specific problems. And I believe that our society's task through the year 2000 is, comrades, to create a new socialist civilization, to ensure people's happiness and the harmonious development of all nations in our multinational society. I would say that man's happiness—since time immemorial—has been the main issue and has stemmed from the community: food, gemstones for your woman, procreation of the species. This is why we must treat our ethnic groups, even the tiniest ones, in a way we have never treated them before. This is a question of fundamental importance.

I wish to say that there is one point in economic problems on which I disagree with Comrade Shmelev—that we have to spend 10 years doing nothing but "clearing the debris." Our strength, comrades, is immeasurable and we are totally different from the way critics depict us. We can and must boost the economy and solve the overall task of building a socialist civilization if we are to get society to respond.

We realize how this should be done. We can force our pace forward, and there are many examples of this being done. Nonetheless, I believe that the task of our deputies' corps, of our congress for its 5-year term, is to lay the foundations of a socialist civilization along the paths of restructuring and overcoming pseudosocialist distortions engendered by the personality cult and stagnation periods. We can under no circumstances wait 18 months until the start of the next 5-Year Plan Plan. We cannot allow the word "acceleration," which was correctly used, to disappear from our vocabulary. It is a certain section of the executive apparatus that has eroded this word. And it seems to me that, in all likelihood, people who prepared the material for Nikolay Ivanovich Ryzhkov are still sticking to the old "Budennyy style." This is how it seems to me, comrades. (Applause)

I wish to emphasize, comrades, that we here are not now questioning the fact that socialism enjoys great advantages over the capitalist method of economic management. We must develop this, we must prove it by utilizing society's response. But upholding the advantages of socialism is no joke for us—it is, after all, a gain for world civilization. We must develop it skillfully, and yet we distort it and then say that the time has come to move on to a different system and so on. This is not right.

Let me cite an example. We do a lot of work with partners abroad, with the capitalist world. There they are, in the course of conversations, saying that they are in favor of our restructuring, they are helping it, they sympathize with it. Why is this, one might ask? They say: Imagine a well cared-for small house and garden, and next to it a skyscraper which is about to collapse. If it collapses, its debris will fall all over the small home and its garden. It appears that the European countries are this well cared-for home, while the skyscraper which might collapse is our own country, so it must be helped, restructuring must be helped.

Twelfth Session
8 June 1989

It is said that bad things will happen if restructuring suffers defeat in our country. And if restructuring is defeated, it will make a tremendous contribution to the development of world civilization [sentence as published]. We know that.

I want to say, comrades, that we must certainly resolve the following task. And it should have figured in the text of the report. The first section concerns the restoration of the state's intellectual power. Many of us have spoken here about pensions, about the elderly, about pensioners, about mothers—figures, only the figures by which aid must be increased. And the same with education, medicine, ecology, and so on. The first point in all our reports must be the restoration of the state's intellectual potential, and everything must be put down in figures and time schedules, in figures and time schedules.

I would like to make special mention of the ecology, of the fact that ecology of course involves a major program, but there is no need to take so long working on it, with Nikolay Ivanovich saying that some time by years' end we shall have it prepared and submitted for approval. It took our own "Rotor" Association just a few months to prepare such a program from the Cherkassy region. It envisages the development of our city into a resort within a 10-year period. Enterprises themselves should take on such tasks.

We even have a supplementary decision concerning the Aral Sea. Thus it cannot be said that bringing the Aral Sea back to normal is an insoluble problem. Quite the contrary: We realize and we know that this problem can be solved and we can play a part in this work, and we can work out how it could be done.

Of course, the next question is the proper provision of financial resources. We can examine it objectively. Proposals were made here, but they are far from complete. We know how it should be done, we realize the tremendous funds that can be made available right now. But the most fundamental question here concerns changing the functions of ministries and departments. We do not advocate the mandatory elimination of ministries. It is a question of changing their functions. Ministries should not deal with gross volumes. They should be the think-tanks. They should adopt purely economic, exclusively economic approaches—from the viewpoint of developing specific categories of output, output quality, antimonopoly alternatives, transportation shipments, and so on. This is why the questions of changing ministries' functions must be resolved without fail in time for the next congress. One last point. What is more, enterprises under departmental jurisdiction, Mikhail Sergeyevich, must be given within 1 month the right to withdraw from departments and join other associations, other enterprises, while retaining the state orders allocated to them. An all-union arbitration commission must be set up to monitor enterprises' direct economic ties. This is of fundamental importance. Thank you for your attention. (Applause).

A.-M.K. Brazauskas: So, comrades, we have three more speakers remaining. As you can see, each one takes a little time away from the next. Nevertheless, I ask you to keep to the schedule and keep your speeches as short as possible. The floor is given to Sergey Pavlovich Zalygin, writer. Comrade Vladimir Matveyevich Gvozdev should get ready.

S.P. Zalygin, writer, editor-in-chief of the journal NOVYY MIR, secretary of the USSR Union of Writers governing board, Moscow (representing the USSR Union of Writers): Comrade deputies! It so happened that recently I was looking into an old encyclopedia and read the following text there: "In 1682-1690 the Kremlin witnessed violent disputes about "faith". The streltsy [Russian regular army soldiers] and people from the settlements gathered here with demands to expand their rights and to replace the rulers. (Excitement in auditorium). You understand the matter: From time to time, every 50 or 100 years, perhaps, is it a custom in Russia to meet like this. And this would be good were it not for one circumstance: Each time everything we must begin everything all over again. It is as if this huge country, with its most varied national shadings and customs, had no historical experience. Yes, each time we begin all over again.

I was listening now to the speeches of our economists. That is wonderful. That is, perhaps, the most serious thing that we have heard here. It made a great impression on me. Yet I would like to say: I am an elderly person. In 1929-30 I attended a technical school and studied agricultural economics from Chayanov's textbook, and you know, to this very day I have perhaps not read anything as interesting in this sense. (Applause).

Today we are creating an agrarian committee. Dear comrades, peasants, you know that we are now solving ecological and economic problems. It may very well be that we will now be faced with very serious trials and difficult years. But one thing we can say: If we preserve the land, if we preserve the peasant—we will survive. If not—there is no way out. (Applause).

And it seems to me that it would be very good for our new agrarian committee to borrow very very much—and I will not specify this question now—from the work experience of the Russian zemstvo. After all, this was an unusual democratic social organism. Perhaps today part of the funds which we are directing to public health, education and road construction may be handed over directly to these agrarian committees, if they should develop. They would manage these funds better than someone from the center manages them. Every now and then, a downright fantasmagorical situation is created. On one hand, we are launching a "Buran", and on the other—in these very same days some "Aunt Motya" forgets to shut off the valve and for 55 minutes pours fuel onto the fire from a broken pipeline, which is near Ufa.

Twelfth Session

8 June 1989

That is the combination. And very often we cannot find our way out of those problems, out of those crises, which no one creates for us. We create them ourselves, with our own hands. In connection with this, we cannot help but recall the very angry man that Churchill was. Yet he was probably correct. In any case, we must consider his words to the effect that the Bolsheviks successfully overcome those same difficulties which they create for themselves.

Well, let us say, we are talking about the problem of the Aral. This, comrades, is a world catastrophe. The words of Deputy Kailbergenov resounded here on this subject, but no one stopped to think, or perhaps did think but somehow never quite expressed himself about the fact that this is a catastrophe of which there has yet been no equal in the world. You think that this is simply some kind of accidental oversight—that they wanted to get one thing, but got something else instead? I do not know if that is correct. I do not know how to evaluate this fact. I can also think that, after all, this catastrophe was planned. When this project arose, all this work on the Aral, scientists warned us, as for example Academician Dorodnitsin, that we cannot build a dam on the Amur-Darya. But they built it anyway. The planners were told ahead of time: Let the Aral die off beautifully. So it has died. Only it has not been beautiful. They were told ahead of time: If necessary, we will take the Aral for irrigation to the last drop. And so they have taken it. So what is the value of our planning, if we foresee such consequences and nevertheless go forward, butt our heads against all obstacles to make something that is worthless? In this regard I have a direct inquiry to the Minvodkhoz [Ministry of Land Reclamation and Water Resources]. Since it is no longer there, then I will direct it to the Council of Ministers. Is someone at fault for this catastrophe, or are there no guilty parties? Let us, after all, get to the bottom of this. Who did this? Why? So that we do not repeat such grievous events. We do not need any repressions here. I am not advocating that. I merely believe that we should know all the "heroes of our time". (Applause.)

Now another commission on saving the Aral is being created. To whom is this commission subordinate? Why, to the Soyuzgiprovodkhoz [All-Union State Project-Research Institute on Waterway Management]. The very same organization that destroyed the Aral. Can we give it more billions as a reward for this destruction? Moreover, the saving of the Aral today depends not on hydrotechnical measures. It requires agricultural, forest, and chemical reclamation. Institutions such as Giprozem [State Institute for Planning Land Reclamation] should be working there, and not hydrotechnical builders. Here we need specifically that land reclamation which Soyuzgiprovodkhoz and Minvodkhoz (its name has been changed now) have disdained. They gave 2-3 percent of the funds for land reclamation as such, and all the rest they spent on hydrotechnical construction, on canals which are 10 times more profitable for the builders. And we are once again entrusting this matter to these same people? People such as Voropayev? That is a very dubious decision.

We have spent R130 billion over the last 20 years for land reclamation through the former Minvodkhoz. If we had given these 130 billion not to the department, but directly to those kolkhozes and sovkhozes, those farms which themselves would have managed this money, we would have seen more benefit from it. Yet for us, all measures have to go through departments. Why is this?

People always tell me that I am against land reclamation. I am not against it. I am in favor of that land reclamation which the farms themselves want. But I am against that land reclamation which is forced upon us. That is all. Even now we are imposing an entire series of such projects on our peasantry, on our agriculture. We must avoid this order, or else things will come to a bad end. I am against earmarked funds. For example, we allocate billions for some ministry, for this same land reclamation (two times more than for public health), and no one else can spend these funds for anything else. Yet this is not right—to distribute everything down to the last kopek from the center. Once again I repeat: Give the money to the consumer, directly to the managers, and they will know what to do with it. Whether to develop land reclamation or livestock raising—that is their business. In this sense I am in full agreement with Comrade Shmelev, who spoke about the role of the banks. Once again we may recall the pre-revolutionary land bank which subsidized farmers and subsidized them only in accordance with their requests, their true needs, but not with those which were imposed upon them.

It seems to me that our economy is sorely lacking—and we have not even heard about this at this congress—about the importance of the credit system. Yet without it, how can we plan and distribute funds?

We have no legislation on ecology. Comrade Yablokov just spoke about this. Comrades, 100 countries already have [this legislation], over 100, but we still do not. And we will not have it in the near future, probably because we still have not established forms of ownership. What kind of economic and ecology laws can there be if we have not established one form of ownership or another? Any law is primarily a regulation of ownership. I believe it would be very beneficial to think about the proposal which was presented here, the proposal to, perhaps, sell land to private individuals. So what if 5 or, say, 6 percent of our land fund belongs to someone? Let the private owner compete, let him work, let him invest money in his endeavor.

Public opinion plays, and must play, a very large role in our ecology movement. Yet we have not learned to listen to it, this widespread movement. We ignore the opinion of very many competent people. They say that public opinion is formed by dilettantes. Nothing of the kind. The concept of the "public" includes also all sorts of

STENOGRAPHIC RECORD

Twelfth Session

8 June 1989

specialists and scientists, and it is often more knowledgeable than the departments. Let me present the following idea. I have engaged in questions of economics for quite a long time, but had my first encounter with the departments in 1962, when the project for flooding the entire West-Siberian lowland during construction of the Lower Ob GES was being developed. If the project had been implemented, all our present oil and gas riches would have been flooded over, or at least a significant portion of them. We would have flooded an area of 135,000 square kilometers, or an area equal to the size of Czechoslovakia. And now I across these projects once again.

Do you know, comrades, when it was easier to resolve these problems, then or now? As strange as it may seem, it was easier for me then. Why? Because then the departments, the bureaucrats, were not as refined as they are now. First of all, they were afraid of their superiors. Secondly, they were afraid of the press. Today our bureaucratic workers are not afraid of anything in the world. And so, when I suggested to one high-ranking official that we meet on television and discuss our ecological problems, he answered: "I do not want to participate in this show." There is an evaluation of public opinion and our participation in public life for you. At the same time, we are destroying a whole series of wonderful public endeavors. In Volgograd, for example, a group of engineers headed by Comrade Tregubov, each with a seniority of 30-40 years and over half of them heroes of socialist labor, is sending out to all addresses, including also to the Council of Ministers, wonderful and precise conclusions. This is a public commission of experts which, if convened in official order, would cost a huge amount of money. And it is all done most conscientiously. And so what? So nothing. All this gets bogged down somewhere. Can it be that we will again ignore the experience of these most knowledgeable builders? I have visited many countries, many hydrotechnical construction sites, and I believe that I have never anywhere encountered such specialists as this Volgograd group. (Bell rings). I will only be one more minute, a minute and a half. I would like to say that the Gosplan [State Planning Committee] is not working normally. The Gosplan is the headquarters staff of our socialist economic management. But what has it turned into? It does not command the ministries today. Rather, it is the ministries which command it. It is specifically through the Gosplan that our departments become a state. When the Volkhov GES was being planned, the Gosplan was charged with working out the initial data, but on this basis it was already giving contracts to syndicates and builders. Today the Gosplan has been turned into a distribution department. It distributes the budget and that is all. Thank you for your attention. (Applause).

A.-M.K. Brazauskas: Deputy Gvozdev has the floor. Comrade Suleymenov should get ready.

V.M. Gvozdev, brigade leader of an integrated mechanized brigade at the "Raspadskaya" mine, "Yuzhkuzbassugol" Production Association, Kemerovo Oblast, city of Mezhdurechensk (representing the CPSU): Comrades, it is very difficult to speak after those who have spoken before me. Honestly, it is difficult. But today we, the deputies from the Kuzbass, get no peace from the calls, telegrams, and letters. Our constituents demand very little, especially for the Kuzbass and Siberia. They demand that we get down to specific deeds and decisions as quickly as possible. In the mine it is much easier when there is solid ground under your feet, and a mountain overhead. Yes, many of the thoughts and problems which I wanted to touch upon have already been brought up several times. I will try not to be redundant, but nevertheless I will repeat some things. This speaks of the fact that we all have the same concerns, we all have the same problems. In short, the diagnosis has been established. It is time to take scalpel in hand and begin the operations. We cannot procrastinate. After all, we must survive.

I never thought that I would be elected a USSR people's deputy. And now one thought worries me: How to justify that trust, what to do so that my deeds and actions do not disappoint the expectations of my comrades in labor?

Our country is on the road of restructuring and renovation, but unfortunately the great number of unresolved tasks and problems is not declining, but rather increasing. Economic difficulties are becoming more acute. The shortage of goods is increasing. Interethnic conflicts are arising, and the crime rate is going up. And, thinking about all these burning problems, I say to myself: "Don't worry, Gvozdev, don't panic, don't get distressed!" No matter what happens, all the current difficulties are difficulties of a temporary nature. Yet this temporary disorder has somehow dragged on. However, it cannot be that the wonderful ideas of restructuring will not conquer; that the feelings of the working man which are being reborn—to be the master of his land—would dare be trampled and destroyed by someone.

Let us look truth in the eye. In recent years, on the wave of democratization and glasnost, discipline has been shaken quite a bit. Many good decisions remain on paper, since there is no strict executive discipline. Some have understood democracy in their own way: As all-permissiveness of their rights and negation of any, even the most elementary, responsibilities. (Applause). I believe that this was facilitated to some degree by certain publications in the newspapers, in journals, and in television broadcasts.

Our congress must adopt a law, and a workable law at that, which states that parallel with the development of democracy there must be a steady growth in responsibility both by the manager and the managed for strict and unconditional fulfillment of the adopted decisions.

I am often asked: "How do you see your main task as people's deputy elected from the CPSU?" I answer briefly: [I see it] in the struggle for implementing the

Twelfth Session

8 June 1989

party platform, which was presented in the CPSU Central Committee's appeal to the people, and in its directives. In these documents I see everything that is needed for a better life of the simple Soviet people. And, if we speak honestly, I, a worker, have no heart for all those discussions about the fact that we supposedly need some other parties, factions, groups, or some other programs. In my opinion, disorder and vascillation, and especially lack of coordination in actions, never have and never will lead to anything good. Today as never before, we need unity and cohesion of all forces of restructuring. And what, deputies, should we focus our priority attention on?

I believe first of all on the adoption of laws, without which a legal state would be unthinkable. I am concerned that there are gross violations of the law under the guise of glasnost and democracy. The people who elected us expect much of us and of the congress decisions. We will not solve everything at once, but we have already approached the resolution of one important question—that of increasing the minimal amounts of pensions. That is wonderful.

We must continue to pursue specific decisions. People are tired of waiting. We must affirm through legislation the development of the social sphere, without which we cannot continue to live. And although numerous decisions have been adopted on this question, in practice the social sphere continues to be in a state of neglect, which evokes the just indignation of the workers.

Let me refer to several examples. My entire life has been associated with the Kuzbass. This is a mighty industrial complex with a well developed coal sector. It also has metallurgy, chemistry, and machine building. One-fifth of the country's coal is mined here. Millions of tonnes of cast iron, steel, rolled metal stock, and coke are produced here, as well as hundreds of thousands of tonnes of mineral fertilizers and cement. Iron ore is mined here.

However, the steady growth of the basic sectors of heavy industry in the Kuzbass has for many years been accompanied by a lagging behind in the development of the social sphere. Despite the fact that it is 13th in the republic in its volume of industrial production, the oblast is in 43rd place in housing provision, in 58th place in terms of children's preschool institutions, and in 70th place in terms of club facilities.

The problems of ecology and heat and water supply have reached a critical state in our basin, especially in the mining villages and settlements. In most of them even water is distributed by rationing. There is not enough of it to supply to the upper stories of houses. There is an acute shortage in many types of foodstuffs and goods. These are the unfortunate conditions in which the workers of the twice-medal winning Kuzbass live, including the residents of my native city of Mezhdurechensk.

Yet it is not only the Kuzbass that lives this way, but our entire rich region of Siberia and the Far East. Judging by everything, the ministries, pardon the expression, could spit on the social needs of the Siberians. As before, they continue to direct 70 percent of the capital investments toward production needs in top priority order. And as for the development of the social sphere, there is nothing good about it here. We might ask, what kind of a policy is this by the masters from the center, and primarily the Minugleprom [Ministry of the Coal Industry] managers, who do not notice all the acute social problems of the Kuzbass. We also believe that it is time we stopped going to Moscow for handouts, begging for all that is necessary for the normal life of the miners, metallurgists and chemists of the Kuzbass and Siberia. It is time we ourselves finally got the right to solve our own problems locally.

Here is what else I would like to say: These problems must be solved in such a way that those who occupy high positions do not flee to Moscow, and the miners themselves do not go away to warm regions. Rather, they must be solved in such a way that will make people have a great desire to come here to Siberia to work and live permanently.

Now, about the next question. Yes, we need cost accounting, but prudent and effective cost accounting. So that our prices would be brought in line with world prices. The way things are now, it will not do. We buy everything for millions, but sell our coal for kopeks.

Comrades, today the living standard, particularly that of the Kuzbass miners, is declining significantly. And here we cannot judge by wages alone, since they do not fully determine the living standard. For the money they earn, the miners cannot buy everyday items: valenki [felt boots], sheepskin coats, warm clothing and footwear which are so necessary in Siberia. There is a great shortage of refrigerators, washing machines and television sets.

Yet here we unexpectedly learn that for 1989 they have again reduced the funds for the Kuzbass on certain food and non-food items. People have felt this and express their bewilderment at such inequities in planning.

A difficult situation has arisen with food products, although we are taking measures for developing personal subsidiary farms and for overall improvement of the farm. Yet we cannot solve the food problem by ourselves in such an industrial region as our oblast, where less than 6 percent of the population works on the farm.

In short, there has long been an acute need for reviewing the prospects for our oblast's development, with all the problems that have accumulated there. The guidelines in doing so should not be the plans for continued growth of production. Rather, we must proceed from the situation which has arisen in terms of the living and working conditions of our people. (Applause).

STENOGRAPHIC RECORD

Twelfth Session
8 June 1989

A.-M.K. Brazauskas: Comrade Suleymenov has the floor. (Noise in the auditorium; voices).

O.O. Suleymenov, writer, first secretary of the Kazakhstan Union of Writers governing board, Alma-Ata (Ayaguzskiy Territorial Electoral District, Semipalatinsk Oblast): We, writers, speak not only about flowers, but more about the berries. Among the many aspects of restructuring for me the main one is the continuation of the process of decolonization, which was frozen in the 20's. It is taking place with all the manifestations characteristic for this process.

The originality of the historical situation is that the former parent state—Russia, on par with the other republics, has itself become a colony of the Center. We are seeing that which is customary in a new light. The interests of the state were always above the interests of the people and the individual. I was elected in Semipalatinsk Oblast, in the land of ancient historical tradition. That is where the great Kazakh writers were born, in these steppes and mountains—our Yasnaya Polyana, Mikhaylovskoye, Tarkhany. And it is in these very areas that the atomic test sites are now operating.

In the United States there is one test site, in China—one, while other countries test their bombs thousands of miles away from their territories, paying compensation to the atoll residents. In the USSR there are several test sites. The oldest of these is the one in Semipalatinsk. And it is also the most active—18 blasts a year. It is located practically in the center of the country. For 15 years, open tests were conducted on the ground and in the atmosphere. According to the most conservative estimates, charges with a total capacity of 2,500 Hiroshima bombs have been detonated in this region. Could all of this have taken place without some effect on the health of the population in these rayons and on the surrounding objects? Even if official specialists say so, we do not believe them. The experts of the public movement Nevada-Semipalatinsk have other, more frightening, data at their disposal. The Third Main Administration of the USSR Ministry of Health is keeping the materials from the studies a secret. Today, Hiroshima and Nagasaki have perhaps the highest indicator of average life expectancy in the world—thanks to the directed increase in the level of public health and the social sphere in these cities, and from them—throughout Japan. We must admit that our state has shown less compassion and respect for its own citizens. In the areas surrounding the test site, in the 40 years of testing, not a single health facility has been built at the expense of the center, not a single rural hospital has been equipped, not to mention anything else. The consequences of the open test blasts will long have an effect on the health of the entire country. In 1963, an agreement to cease testing in several spheres was finally signed. For the sake of fairness, we must pay due respect to the position of our scientists, and especially Academician Sakharov, who convinced the government to insist upon such an agreement. (Applause). This happened after the testing of the largest hydrogen bomb with a capacity of 60 megatons. Scientists realized what a nightmare for the world their invention holds. It combines both genius and evil, with increasing predominance of the latter. This combination is seen today even in the fact that Kurchatov and Lavrentiy Beriya were ordered to be the organizers of the Semipalatinsk test site.

Underground blasts are also unsafe, a fact which is evidenced by the emission of radioactive gases on 12 February of this year. The same thing also happened earlier, for example last summer. Thousands of children were afflicted in one day, with the hastily pronounced diagnosis of ORZ [ear-nose-throat disorders], nosebleeds, dizziness and other sympsoms which are rather characteristic of more than just a cold.

The world is changing. We have fewer enemies in the West and in the East. That means we have fewer defense expenditures. The Soviet world arsenals are overfilled. The nuclear defenses of the super powers have taken on colossal proportions and are capable of destroying those whom they are called upon to defend. Mikhail Sergeyevich Gorbachev's announcement at the London Guild Hall that our country is ceasing production of fission materials has added hopes for a nuclear-free 21st century, and is adding to the assurance that we are becoming a peaceful state. (Applause).

The fact that there is a new situation in the country, that the center already hears us, may be judged by the following. The birth of the Nevada-Semipalatinsk movement has led to a cessation of testing. For the fourth month the test sites are quiet. It is a fragile silence. We have great hopes that the government and the public anti-nuclear movement in the countries of the atomic club will hear us, will understand and support us, and will create conditions for signing a final agreement on banning testing in all spheres. (Applause).

After the 19th party congress it is now particularly evident that our development will ever more depend on the degree of openness of the dialogue between the people and the state, in the process of which at times different positions must be developed. We must remember that the country's troubles began at the beginning of the 20's specifically with the persecution of differences of opinion. In order for democratization and glasnost to continue, it is important to legislatively express the state attitude toward difference of opinion. We must acknowledge it to be a creative factor, rather than a hostile one. (Applause). Either in a resolution or in individual documents, we must condemn the crimes of the Stalinist clique against socialism, specifically such crimes as the physical extermination of the opposition. We must proclaim as being criminal the leftist theory and the practice of "rapid development", manifested in the rates and methods of sadly well-known reforms. How many times have the fresh winds of change turned to destructive hurricanes as a result of such "accelerations". The Kazakhs lost 350,000 lives in the war, yet in

Twelfth Session

8 June 1989

the time of the so-called period of "rapid acceleration" they lost over 4 million. Every people can recall similar occurrences in its biography. History is senselessly repeated if its lessons go for naught. Finally, we must publish a "white", or more precisely, a "black" book of Stalin's tyranny, with data on all the republics.

We do not want to indiscriminately reject all of our history. After all, aside from the dark aspects, there were also general spiritual values. Along with the sorrowful there is also positive experience, which must be preserved and continued. Yet it is specifically for this reason that we must separate the pure from the bloody. Yes, millions perished without a voice. Today our memory shouts about them. Today we are in a position to condemn the tyranny. This is a testimony to the speed of development of our morals and legal consciousness. The Alma-Ata students and workers were the first in the country to hold unsanctioned meetings. If the Alma-Ata events of December 1986 had been broadly and democratically discussed and understood, perhaps 9 April would never have happened in Tbilisi. I believe it would be correct to examine the circumstances of the tragic Alma-Ata incident in light of a new humanistic approach. I am forwarding all the telegrams and letters to the appropriate Supreme Soviet commission, where I am prepared to present a speech on this question. And I call upon my fellow countrymen—Kazakhs, Russians, Germans, Ukrainians, Uygurs, Koreans, and the people of Kazakhstan who have experienced all this to understand the gravity of the moment, to believe that justice is possible if only we maintain our self-control and understanding of the value of our common interests.

How much pain has accumulated in the country, and how strong the return. There is not a single people whose consciousness does not contain bleeding wounds. Many of us have on our hands the shouting demands of the Turks-Meskhetin, the Crimean Tatars, the Abkhaz, Ingush, Chechen, and Gagauz. The Supreme Soviet commission on interethnic relations has much work ahead of it, and at least some of these difficulties must be overcome before the next congress. The Karabakh knot is being ever more tightly drawn. Ever broader factors are becoming involved: ethnic, religions, and others. Academician Likhachev rightly spoke of the role of culture in interethnic disputes. This role is limited without a full, overall knowledge of the history of the question. The unidirectional knowledge with which the peoples have been raised is the reason for many national insults and ambitions. We must publish a special series of collections and documents on these heated topics. Culture presupposes taking steps toward each other. Such a collection should include, aside from objective historical information, also the harsh truth about Sumgait, and the information about the crash of the airplane from Baku which was carrying 50 Azerbaijani soldiers who had volunteered to help their neighbors in need and were on their way to help the earthquake disaster victims. These fellows wanted to make their contribution to the cause of restoring friendship, and they contributed what they could—their lives. There is no memorial to them. Their names did not resound in the press. Only their mothers know of their fate. There are probably many such unknown cases of nobility, and we must constantly work to publicize them. (Applause.) So that we will learn to sympathize with each other. What happened in Uzbekistan was no accident. What happened in Bashkiria was no accident. It is a sign, a painful, terrible metaphor which we have been given to read. One thing is clear: We cannot turn up the pressure when there are so many hole-ridden pipelines in the country. The concentrated fuel of national and social dissatisfaction flows toward the roads along which trains carrying children pass. Let us not leave a legacy of bitterness for our children and grandchildren. We have earned the right, and they simply must be happy. Thank you. (Applause.)

A.-M.K. Brazauskas: Comrades a few announcements before we end our meeting. I have some notes here. Deputies who did not have time to speak at our congress ask whether their proposals will be included in the stenographic record of the congress. Yes, they will be included. Therefore, since our congress is already coming to an end, I ask that you submit your presentations to the secretariat in written form. That is the first thing. Second, the organizational meeting of the commission investigating the case of Comrades Gdlyan and Ivanov will be held at 1515 today in the building of the editorial commission.

M.S. Gorbachev: Not the case.

A.-M.K. Brazauskas: That is how it is written. Of course: Not the case, but the question. Also, Aleksandr Nikolayevich Yakovlev asked me to say that the commission for evaluating the agreement of 1939 will meet after the evening session of the congress in the Granovit Palace.

We have also received a proposal from a large number of people's deputies—more than 200. They propose a procedural question: How to organize roll-call voting. The Presidium consulted on the matter. The procedure is new, and probably we will not have time to assimilate it in one day. Therefore, it is proposed that we analyze this system and use it at the next congress if possible.

And some more information, very briefly. Aside from the announced speaker, there were 89 people participating in the discussions. Of these, 32 were from union republics. From the autonomous republics—there are notes here that there were very few—there were seven, from the autonomous oblasts—2, from the oblasts of the Russian Federation—20 speakers, and from public organizations—27. Thus, deputies from more or less all groups and all territories were represented. Now we have proposals on speeches 2-3 minutes in length. The presidium proposes that the time for such presentations be given at the end of today's evening meeting, because now there is little time and many commissions will be

Twelfth Session

8 June 1989

working. So, the comrades who have signed up will have an opportunity to speak at the end of our evening session. Shall we begin the discussion now?

Voices: No.

A.-M.K. Brazauskas: Who is in favor of not beginning the discussion? I ask for a vote. Thank you. Who is opposed? It has been decided.

From the floor: I have an announcement.

A.-M.K. Brazauskas: We will yield the floor for an announcement.

Deputy (did not introduce himself): The group of people's deputies—241 people—who proposed the roll-call vote will conduct it without preliminary permission. The secretariat has the materials. Whoever did not get them may do so. Despite the opinion of others, we want the entire country to know our opinion. Many are dissatisfied, and therefore we propose to all who are not afraid to say their name and share the responsibility for any decisions which will be adopted—they will satisfy some, and not others—to join in our opinion. It will be published and circulated in the press. Thank you for your attention.

(Recess).

8 June 1989. Kremlin Palace of Congresses. 1600.

USSR Supreme Soviet Chairman M.S. Gorbachev presiding.

M.S. Gorbachev: Honorable comrade deputies! We continue the work of our congress. As we agreed yesterday, we will examine the following questions on the agenda: The first question is that of ratification of the USSR Council of Ministers chairman.

As you know, the USSR Supreme Soviet has appointed Nikolay Ivanovich Ryzhkov to serve as chairman of the USSR Council of Ministers. Yesterday we heard his speech and began our discussion. I introduce for your consideration the proposal to ratify Comrade Ryzhkov in the office of chairman of the USSR Council of Ministers. Do the deputies have any questions for Comrade Ryzhkov?

Yesterday, those who heard this discussion remember that the Supreme Soviet held a rather thorough discussion. I believe the participants in the debates, both today and probably tomorrow, will express many of their ideas, critical comments and evaluations addressed at the government, and not only the government. Nevertheless, within the framework and within the context of such an approach to this question, I would like to ask you: May I present my proposal for a vote, or will there be some questions here too... So, yes? That is the attitude? Good.

From the floor: There were some written questions for Nikolay Ivanovich....

M.S. Gorbachev: They were about the speech, yes?

From the floor: Yes.

M.S. Gorbachev: I believe we have decided that on the questions which were asked in connection with Nikolay Ivanovich's speech we will give him a chance to answer at the end of the discussion. Is that right, comrades?

From the auditorium: Yes.

M.S. Gorbachev: That is right. As that is the general attitude, comrades, I present the question for a vote. Who is in favor of ratifying Comrade Nikolay Ivanovich Ryzhkov as chairman of the USSR Council of Ministers? Please raise your cards. Please lower them.

Who is opposed? I request a count.

M.S. Gorbachev: While the comrades are counting up the results...I would like to announce that we in the Supreme Soviet have agreed that each presiding chairman will conduct the meeting while seated, which is generally accepted. There were some requests to consider this fact addressed here to me, and not just to me alone, so that the presiding chairman does not hang over the hall and, pardon me, does not move onto it. What do you think, comrades?

From the hall: (Indistinct).

M.S. Gorbachev: We have to agree here, so that there will be no misunderstanding. That is so, is it not?

From the hall: Yes.

M.S. Gorbachev: Good.

A.G. Kostenyuk: Honorable deputies, there were 59 votes against.

M.S. Gorbachev: Who abstained?

A.G. Kostenyuk: There were 87 deputies abstaining.

M.S. Gorbachev: Thus, the Congress of People's Deputies ratifies Comrade Ryzhkov in the position of chairman of the Council of Ministers. (Applause). Comrade Ryzhkov asks to speak.

N.I. Ryzhkov, chairman of the USSR Council of Ministers (representing the CPSU): Honorable people's deputies! Allow me to express my sincere thanks for ratifying me in this high state office of our country.

This is the second time I have been appointed to this office. However, I must say that the process of this appointment differs sharply from the old practice of

Twelfth Session

8 June 1989

making appointments to high posts in our country. I see this as the result of the great changes that have taken place in our country in recent years, in the years of restructuring, which have allowed us specifically to discuss on a democratic basis all the questions of our life and our society and to appoint the leaders of our state.

The discussion of questions at the congress, the numerous meetings, and the inquiries which we received during these days indicate that a great number of problems have come to a head in our country, problems we must solve. I believe it is specifically the congress which will determine the basic directions along which our society and our entire country must progress.

I understand what a difficult time it is in which I am assuming the leadership of the new government. I understand what great tasks face the country, and I understand how difficult it will be to resolve them.

Yet I am deeply convinced that if we can correctly select the line, select the correct policy both in a strategic and in a tactical plane, we will be able to solve the principle questions that have come to a head in our society and which were so heatedly discussed these days at our congress. I hope that we will work in close contact with the Supreme Soviet, which will be working continuously, as well as with its commissions, its committees, and with all the people's deputies. The executive authority will clearly implement this line, which will be ratified by our country's highest legislative organ. This I firmly promise you.

In conclusion I thank you once again. I thank all the Soviet people, who are showing me such great trust today. Thank you. (Applause).

M.S. Gorbachev: The next question. The election of the USSR Committee for Constitutional Control. In accordance with the Constitution, the USSR Committee for Constitutional Control is elected by the USSR Congress of People's Deputies for a 10-year term from among specialists in the field of politics and law. It includes a chairman, a deputy chairman, and 21 committee members, including representatives from each of the union republics.

Honorable comrade deputies, we are very careful in our approach to ensure that this very important organ, which is formulated by and directly subordinate to the congress, is composed of respected and competent people, as we associate the success of our endeavor on the road to formulating a legal socialist state with the work of this organ. Many of you, not only Communists but also non-party affiliated deputies, were present at the meeting of the party group, and at that time this topic was within the field of vision, specifically the question of membership and nominations of candidates for chairman. There were some rather convincing conclusions expressed as to the need for having an authoritative and competent person at the head of this new and very important organ. Therefore, I am now presenting the proposal to elect Comrade Vladimir Nikolayevich Kudryavtsev, who is currently vice-president of the USSR Academy of Sciences, to the position of chairman of the USSR Committee for Constitutional Control. I also propose that we elect Comrade Boris Mikhaylovich Lazarev, currently section chief of the USSR Academy of Sciences State and Law Institute, to serve as deputy chairman.

You have been given the materials on the candidates for Committee membership, as well as a draft of the resolution on election of the Committee for Constitutional Control. I hope you have had a chance to acquaint yourselves with them. As you can see, we propose including representatives from all the union republics and leading specialists from the field of politics and law in the membership of the committee. That is my brief speech. What thoughts, comments, or judgements do the deputies have? Please....

N.N. Vorontsov, doctor of biological sciences, chief scientific associate at the USSR Academy of Sciences N.K. Koltsov Institute of Developmental Biology, Moscow (representing the scientific societies and associations under the USSR Academy of Sciences): I would like to say that the list of members itself and the chairman of the proposed new organ—not a single person—evokes no objections from me. That is, we see here, as far as one can judge by these biographical data, specialists either in the field of jurisprudence or in history. That is all fine. Yet I have one principle comment regarding the membership of this important organ and regarding the subsequent organs.

Our society is made up of members of the Communist Party, as well as non-party members. I did not see here, among the proposed candidacies, a single non-party member. I have one question: Are there any doctors of juridical sciences in our country who are not party members? Are there any specialists in the field of state and law who are not party members? I am in no way trying to question this membership. Moreover, I will vote for this make-up, but I would like these comments to be taken into consideration in formulating other organs of the congress. It seems to me that we must reflect, at least to a certain degree, the make-up of society in formulating the leading organs. We in the USSR do not have a single minister who is not a party member. We have or practically have, as far as I know, no deputy ministers who are not party members. We practically do not have any directors of large enterprises who are not party members. This does not indicate any disrespect on my part to the majority of party members who are present here, but we must consider the fact that our society is heterogeneous. And we must reflect this heterogeneity, at least to a small degree, also in the make-up of the leading organs of the country. Thank you for your attention. (Applause).

M.S. Gorbachev: Please introduce yourself.

STENOGRAPHIC RECORD

FIRST CONGRESS OF PEOPLE'S DEPUTIES OF THE USSR

Twelfth Session

8 June 1989

V.I. Kolotov, editor of the newspaper VYBORGSKIY KOMMUNIST, city of Vyborg (Vyborg territorial electoral district, RSFSR): I am not personally acquainted with Vladimir Nikolayevich Kudryavtsev. However, our acquaintance by correspondence was made long ago, particularly in the period of the pre-electoral campaign, as well as in connection with the so-called case of Gdlyan and Ivanov. Comrade Kudryavtsev, I feel, is a a juridically trained person. His biographical report attests to this fact. But here is what puts me on guard. In his speeches on television and in his articles in the press, Vladimir Nikolayevich clearly exhibits a desire to always please the authorities, to always be in harmony with the official opinion. This cannot be concealed, it seems to me, by any outwardly strong and supposedly independent phrase. Therefore, I express my dissent against this candidacy and my mistrust of Comrade Kudryavtsev. We have long grown tired of yes-men. A person with such a character, it seems to me, cannot be the chairman of such a vitally important organ as the Committee for Constitutional Control, even if he is super-educated in law. That is my opinion. (Applause).

M.S. Gorbachev: Please.

R.V. Gudaytis, writer, literary consultant for the Lithuanian SSR Union of Writers, Vilnius (Kapsukskiy national-territorial electoral district, Lithuanian SSR): Comrade deputies, you will probably view my proposal not to create a Committee for Constitutional Control as an obstruction or an effort to hinder a pre-outlined scenario for the conclusion of the congress. Yet nevertheless, expressing the will of my constituents and the citizens of Lithuania, I must say: A hastily created committee will inevitably become an instrument of pressure on the national rebirth of the union republics, a pressure on their sovereignty.

We are not even reassured by the high juridical qualification of the Chairman and the committee members, including the authoritative and respected Lithuanian specialist Stachekas, with apologetics to the centralism of the unitarian state which retains the most important peculiarities of the Stalinist imperialist model. Reassure us and tell us that the USSR Committee for Constitutional Control will not become the "legal" guarantor for those forces who want to grip national problems with an iron hand. Reassure us and say that the Committee will not speak out against the creation of new democratic constitutions in the republics, will not challenge the rights of nations to their own land and, most importantly, to their own self determination. No outside force has the right to intervene in the constitutional position of a certain republic. No institution can put itself above the interests of the people of my Latvia, and moreover stop the effect of the laws of a sovereign republic, specifically the recently adopted amendments to the Lithuanian SSR Constitution.

As a test we might propose the amendment to Article 125 of the USSR Constitution: "The Committee for Constitutional Control is elected from among the number of specialists in law, comprised of 15 chairmen and 15 committee members from each union republic. The leadership is determined by the principle of strict sequence order. If the sovereignty of a union republic is infringed upon, it has the right of veto".

Let this serve as food for thought for the future, yet the present formulation is unacceptable to us. The overwhelming majority of the Lithuanian delegation, as well as a large group of deputies from Latvia and Estonia, address the congress with the following petition.

"Keeping in view the fact that:

first—the congress has defined a constitutional crisis in the form of internal contradictions between the Basic Law which dates back to the time of stagnation and the need for creating a new USSR Constitution, rather than implementing control over adherence to the outdated one;

secondly—as yet there is no law on constitutional control in the USSR;

thirdly—the powers of the USSR Committee for Constitutional Control as they are presented in the Constitution with the corresponding amendments allow this organ to infringe upon the sovereign rights of the union republics;

fourth—already last fall the population of Latvia, Lithuania and Estonia, through collective protests which gathered around 4 million signatures, expressed its disapproval of the latest undemocratic corrections and amendments to the USSR Constitution;

fifth—even now the voters have entrusted us with their concern for the sovereignty of our republics.

We consider the elections of the USSR Committee for Constitutional Control to be inexpedient, and we will not participate in them." Thank you. (Applause).

A.O. Dobrovolskiy, engineer-designer at a design bureau for precision electronic machine building, Minsk (Minsk-Lenin territorial electoral district, Minsk Oblast, Belorussian SSR): In order to make a responsible and important decision, we must know not only our own opinion, but also the opinion of others, of specialists. Therefore, I took upon myself the responsibility of calling to the city of Minsk and consulting on the question of the membership of the Committee for Constitutional Control. I would like to express my opinion and the opinion of the legal community. I gave the jurists half an hour for discussion. This candidacy was discussed also at the BSSR Academy of Sciences Philosophy and Law Institute, as well as at the juridical faculty of Belorussian State University. In general, all the jurists whom I was able to survey spoke out against the candidacy of Comrade Yemenov who was nominated from the Belorussian SSR. Several different sources proposed

Twelfth Session

8 June 1989

another name—that of Valeriy Guryevich Tikhin, a doctor of juridical sciences and pro-rector of Belorussian State University. This nomination was signed by 18 people's deputies from the Belorussian SSR, and I am handing it over to the Presidium with the belief that the opinion of the juridical community of the city of Minsk—the center of juridical science in Belorussia—must necessarily be taken into consideration. I insist that a separate vote be taken on the candidacy from Belorussia. Thank you.

Z.G. Balayan, LITERATURNAYA GAZETA special correspondent to the Armenian SSR, Yerevan (Askeranskiy national-territorial district, Nagorno-Karabakh Autonomous Oblast): The Constitution—the Basic Law—was written, as we know, in a lapidary fashion, and there we may include, as they say, only that which bears certain weight. Naturally, there are appropriate codes of laws and commentaries to the Constitution to allow to us understand all the details. The publishing house "Politicheskaya literatura" [political literature] in 1982 published a book entitled "The USSR Constitution, A Political-Legal Commentary". The following text appears on page 250 of this book: "An autonomous oblast is named after the name of the people who have selected the autonomous oblast as the form of realization of their right to self determination". Vladimir Nikolayevich Kudryavtsev, Vadim Konstantinovich Sobakin, and Anatoliy Ivanovich Lukyanov participated in the collective authorship of this code of laws, this political-legal commentary on the USSR Constitution. Seven years have passed since that time. As you know, the only oblast—the Nagorno-Karabakh Autonomous Oblast—in violation of the Constitution bears its name not by the national indicator, but by the geographical. As you know, there is no such nationality as the Nagorno-Karabakhs. There are Armenians, Azerbaijanis, Kurds, Talysh, Greeks, and Russians living there... I quote once again: "The autonomous oblast is named after the name of the people who have selected the autonomous oblast as the form of realization of their right to self determination". I would like to ask the candidate for chairman of the Committee for Constitutional Control, Vladimir Nikolayevich Kudryavtsev, a professor, a vice-president of the Academy of Sciences, and the director of the State and Law Institute for 15 years, to give an explanation of this question. Thank you.

M.S. Gorbachev: Comrades, perhaps we can agree to keep our comments to a maximum of 2-3 minutes, yes?

From the auditorium: Yes.

S.B. Kalagin, engineer-adjuster at the Perm Ya.M. Sverdlov production association "Motorostroitel," Perm (Sverdlov territorial district, Perm Oblast): Comrades! Now we are to elect the Committee for Constitutional Control now, but we are not to ratify it. This seems very significant to me, at least in terms of the candidacy of the committee chairman. At one of the meetings I heard several names of well-known jurists mentioned from the audience. I propose that the congress once again repeat these names, discuss them, and only after doing so conduct the election for committee chairman. Thank you.

M.S. Gorbachev: Very well. So, I repeat, recommended for election to the office of committee chairman are Comrade Vladimir Nikolayevich Kudoyavtsev, academician, vice-president of the USSR Academy of Sciences, doctor of juridical sciences, and professor. And to the office of deputy committee chairman—Comrade Boris Mikhaylovich Lazarev, section head at the USSR Academy of Sciences State and Law Institute, doctor of juridical sciences, and professor. Is this what you wanted? Or not this? That means I did not understand the question. Then excuse me, I will be more precise. But for now other comrades will speak.

D.A.A. Kerinov, department chairman at the Academy of Social Sciences under the CPSU Central Committee, Moscow (Shakhbuzskiy national-territorial district, Nakhichevan ASSR): Honorable comrade deputies! I did not intend to speak, but the comment by one of the comrades regarding the fact that Kudryavtsev supposedly "makes up" to his superiors, as was stated not very elegantly, simply amazed me and evoked a sense of strange bewilderment. I have known Vladimir Nikolayevich for many years. We are colleagues. We have worked together. We get along as colleagues and as friends. And never in my life have I noticed that he has ever "made up" to anyone. It is simply amazing to say such things. I must say that Vladimir Nikolayevich is one of the leading Soviet jurists. He is known throughout the world. He is a very decent and very interesting and original man. Therefore, I ask you to listen to the voice of a jurist who knows his colleagues quite well, and primarily Vladimir Nikolayevich. Thank you. (Applause).

A.M. Yakovlev, doctor of juridical sciences, section head at the USSR Academy of Sciences State and Law Institute, Moscow (representing the USSR Academy of Sciences): Actually, comrades, I understand all the concern which is being shown in this auditorium regarding the membership and functions of the Committee for Constitutional Control. Yet I would like to alleviate the suspicions that the Committee for Constitutional Control will somehow stand in the way of positive and constructive changes to our Constitution. We must not confuse two things, comrades—respect for that which is accepted as the Constitution, and the possibility of its goal-oriented, planned amendment by democratic means. These are two equally existing functions. Therefore, I wanted to alleviate any suspicions against this committee that supposedly it will take a stand against development of the Constitution. At the same time, we will be voting for a commission on developing a new Constitution. We cannot say that it will be an anti-constitutional commission. That is the first thing.

STENOGRAPHIC RECORD

Twelfth Session

8 June 1989

Secondly, I have known Vladimir Nikolayevich for a relatively short time—since about 1954. I myself, as you can see, am a rather elderly person and must say that I was hurt by the comments to the effect that he "makes up" to someone. I will tell you directly. Of course, all of us, as they say, are children of our time, why deny it? But for Kudryavtsev ever to have lied, or to have made up to someone or to have been dishonest in regard to his colleagues, as well as on principle questions?.. We do not always have the courage to say the truth in time. We have not always risen to the level of, say, Academician Sakharov, who was the only one to speak the truth when we remained silent. All this is true. And of this we are all, perhaps, guilty. But that he ever said anything against his conscience or against truth and honor—that never happened.

I will cite only two episodes. Even before our current president was the secretary general of the party, Vladimir Nikolayevich Kudreyavtsev, I, and a number of other colleagues raised the question of how shocking the state of affairs was in our fight against crime. At that time we sent a report to our current president, where we wrote about that which today, finally, we are beginning to overcome: The crime rate is not recorded, the militia is doing nothing, the courts are powerless, two people's assessors headed by a judge form that very same, so to speak, perfect troika with which we have galloped through the terrible years...

All these questions we raised even then, but excuse us, we raised them in a report, because, of course, no one would have published such, so to speak, jibberish. And at that time the current president placed the following resolution on this—I believe that this is already not an official secret: "I believe that the questions which are presented here are questions raised by honest communists on principle questions of our justice system". And this was forwarded to the minister of internal affairs, the general procurator, and the supreme court justice with the request to look into the matter and develop specific proposals for improving the work of our criminal justice system.

Well, as is always the case, of course, some things were done and some things were not. You might recall that the improvement began with registration. At least, the idea emerged of creating a single investigative committee, which we will today decide. That is the first episode. Here is the second episode. You know all of our infamous ukases and the shameful Article 11. And I will tell you one more secret here. Of course, it would have been correct to stand up and announce to the world about what an anti-constitutional article this was. But I must tell you that our future chairman of the Committee for Constitutional Control, if he is elected of course, stated on the second or third day at our country's highest party forum, at the Politburo, that this article was no good, and that it must be changed. To this he received verbal agreement and a blessing. I believe that the members of the highest party forum who are present here can confirm this episode.

M.S. Gorbachev: That is correct.

A.M. Yakovlev: There, you see, I have a witness to back me up, as they say. In short, I believe that in Kudryavtsev we are getting a man who, by the logic of his thinking, by his entire biography, and by his scientific authority was created specifically for occupying this office. That is my opinion. (Applause).

A.M. Obolenskiy, engineer-designer at the USSR Academy of Sciences Kolsk Scientific Center Polar Geophysical Institute, city of Apatity in Murmansk Oblast (Leningrad rural national-territorial district): Honorable comrades. I would like to direct your attention to the fact that this is our last chance to elect someone at the congress. The Constitution is compiled in such a way that we had the opportunity to elect the chairman of the Supreme Soviet, and the only place in which we can manifest our choice is the Committee for Constitutional Control. All other positions we merely ratify. I call on you to approach this with all responsibility. Once again we are being offered elections without competition.

First of all, I consider it disrespectful when we are given outlines of resolutions which are not signed by anyone. Anonymous, once again. We do not know their authorship. That about which much has been said is unclear.

Secondly, I would like to point out that the [time limit] Regulations are being systematically violated. We get these documents just before the vote is held. It is good that the comrade from Belorussia had enough time to call his constituents, evidently during the lunch break, and to consult with them somehow and learn their opinion. We elect these people for a term of 10 years. If we had a competition for the office of chairman, there would be two or three candidates here. Each one would get up to the podium and answer our questions. He would have to fight for our votes. I, for one, have questions to ask. I believe many of us do. What is Comrade Kudryavtsev's attitude toward those drafts of laws which were recently adopted by ukase? What is his attitude toward the revelry of departmental standard-setting in our country? And there are many other questions which might be asked. I point out that he is not a novice in legal work, and consequently, as one who has occupied key posts—he was an institute director—he bears certain responsibility for the quality of laws in our country which have now been adopted. We should talk about this.

I believe that now, under such conditions, we do not have the right to elect the Committee for Constitutional Control. The Constitution does not specify that it must be elected specifically at the first congress. Therefore, I submit the outline of the following resolution for your consideration. The USSR Congress of People's Deputies resolution "On the question of electing the Committee for Constitutional Control". Having reviewed the proposals of the congress Presidium on the personnel make-up of the committee, the congress notes a violation in the

Twelfth Session
8 June 1989

regulations of work of the congress: The draft of the resolution was handed out to the deputies on the day of voting, 8 June. The information presented to the deputies was brief, the biographies and references presented were insufficient for election to such an important organ, especially considering the long term of its tenure—10 years. Considering the above-mentioned facts, the congress resolves:

First. To put off examination of the question of electing the Committee for Constitutional Control to the Fall of 1989, to the second Congress of People's Deputies. (Applause).

Second. The elections of the committee and especially its leadership must necessarily be conducted on a competitive basis after thorough discussion of the candidacies.

Third. We must publicize the recommendations of the Presidium on the personnel make-up of the committee for the purpose of open public discussion of the proposed candidacies.

Fourth. We must entrust the Committee for Legislation and Law and Order to verify the comments of the workers on the proposed candidacies and to bring them to the attention of all the deputies.

Fifth. We must give groups of deputies in certain numbers (well, the number may be specified), I propose no less than 100 persons, the right to nominate additional candidates to the Committee for Constitutional Control.

That is all I have to say. Thank you. I would only like to add that this is introduced in the order of a legislative initiative on the basis of Article 114 of the Constitution. Each of us has the right to such legislative initiative. Therefore, I ask the chairman to put my proposal to a vote. (Applause).

K.V. Kogan, chief of the thermotechnical laboratory at the "Estrybprom" association, Tallinn (Tallin-Kalinin national-territorial district, Estonian SSR): Honorable deputies! I am sorry for the delay, but I would like to express my opinion on the question under discussion. One of the deputies from the Baltic who spoke signed his name here for all three republics, for all the voters there. There is a clearly apparent desire and attempt to shorten the reach of the yet uncreated Committee so that it will not be able to review matters in the union republics. It is assumed that this, perhaps, will infringe upon someone's rights. Yet it seems to me that the Committee is being created to guarantee against infringement on the rights of everyone living in our country. In connection with this I would like to say to you that already now the rights of many residents in these republics are being infringed upon. Such laws have been adopted, and I would like the Committee for Constitutional Control to begin its work with the Baltic, and specifically—with Estonia. (Applause).

I would like the Committee to review the correspondence of the USSR Constitution with all the amendments which were adopted in Estonia on 16 November 1988. I would like it to review the constitutionality of that conception which was adopted on the basis of all these amendments to the Constitution. I would like this Committee to determine the legality of our laws—the so-called laws on language, where education in one language is guaranteed, and in another—merely allowed. Moreover, the knowledge of a language is still the basis for concluding and extending labor agreements. That is the main thing. And finally, I would like to point out the following documents. This, it seems to me, is work specifically for the Committee. I will permit myself to quote them.

The newspaper SOVETSKAYA ESTONIA, 12 October 1988: "One other moment which, to put it mildly, causes puzzlement. On 5 October the newspaper NOORTE KHYAEL published an interview with the chief of the People's Front security service, A. Evele, who said that they have 80 persons who have mastered karate and judo, plus 400 guards".

Secondly, the newspaper SOVETSKAYA ESTONIA, 20 October 1988. I quote: "You, Comrade Zaytsev, are concerned about the creation of a security service within the Estonian People's Front. Well, you are not alone. This concern has resounded in several other newspaper publications, as for example in the newspaper VIRU SYNA on 7 October of this year, which cited the outrageous case where during the Estonian People's Front Congress the guards did not allow Estonian SSR Supreme Soviet Presidium Chairman A. Ryuytel into the press center".

The next item. The newspaper SOVETSKAYA LATVIA, 6 October 1988, V. Steshenko: "I will say honestly, it is difficult for me to imagine how to look for mutual understanding with people who at their meetings express and applaud racist misanthropic views, and who train the violence groups about which V. Turnis spoke. He himself is leaving, but what is he leaving behind for us? Storm troopers?"

The newspaper ATMODA dated 29 May 1989: "The question of creating people's detachments of the Latvian People's Front for protecting public order was discussed for the first time at the governing board level. The leadership of the group which will work on these questions was placed on Int Upmatsis". Next...

M.S. Gorbachev: Your time is up.

Ye.V. Kogan: One second, literally... The newspaper VETSPILSITAS ZINES, and I quote. "Today, when our Soviet society is concerned about the tyranny of the army, and specifically the free reign of tanks, the average Soviet man has the overwhelming desire to learn how to fight this peculiar defender of peace and restructuring. Already in the second issue of IZVESTIYA STAROGO

Twelfth Session
8 June 1989

GODA they began quoting the outstanding book "Military Basic Training". And today we have decided not to break the tradition which was started. Young comrades, read these quotes and use the knowledge which you obtain in the struggle for Soviet rule".

Finally, my request. I ask that a group of independent jurists be created which would get to the bottom of all these matters. I believe that this could be the very first and very worthwhile work for the new Committee for Constitutional Control. I would not like to argue now about the election procedures, but the need for such a commission or committee has grown very acute, dear comrades. Thank you for your attention.

A.A. Plotyaneks, professor at Latvian P. Stuchka State University Riga (Yelgavskiy national-territorial district, Latvian SSR): Honorable people's deputies! Honorable Chairman! The country's leading jurists and political scientists are being proposed for membership in the Committee for Constitutional Control. We announce that we have complete trust and respect toward these candidacies, including also toward Academician Vladimir Nikolayevich Kudryavtsev as the future chairman of this Committee. Yet at the same time, the conditions and circumstances under which this question is being resolved are rather unique. The proposals of the USSR people's deputies to introduce changes and amendments into the USSR Constitution are as yet not only unsubstantiated, but we do not even have a Constitutional Commission yet. The USSR Constitution of 1977 remains in effect, and the standards of the reorganizational law of 1 December of last year are embedded into it as individual fragments. Today the effective union Constitution contains an abundance of problems and contradictions.

The development of a new USSR Constitution still lies ahead. At the same time, in order to promote restructuring in the union republics, in the very near future we must introduce rather significant changes into the republic constitutions. This process is taking place, specifically, in all three of the Baltic republics and in other union republics as well. The new constitutional standards which are today being born in the union republics cannot coincide in meaning and in letter with the standards of the old union Constitution. The task of the USSR Committee for Constitutional Control is to implement control over the correspondence of the USSR Constitution with the constitutions of the union republics. Thus, the Committee will be called upon to "measure by a single level" the Constitutions of the union republics, achieving the elimination from them of all innovations for which we have created no normative analog at the federation level. But, of course, we will have to do so.

You might object: What is the hurry? We will adopt the new USSR Constitution, and then we will take up the constitutions of the union republics. Such an approach, unfortunately, is fraught with many dangers.

First of all, the all-union market, republic cost accounting, the transition to economic methods of management, the saturation of the market with goods, and many of our everyday needs which have been discussed from this rostrum, require their own solution. Economists are proposing various prescriptions for curing these economic ills, but without a change in the constitutions of the union republics these prescriptions will not work, and treatment is impossible.

Secondly, the logical process of renovating constitutional legislation in the socialist federative state must begin at the republic level, and the most successful innovations must then be generalized at the level of the union Constitution. What is the answer? We see the answer in the congress giving a limited interpretation to Article 125 of the USSR Constitution. We present for your consideration the draft of the following statute—it is very short:

"Resolution of the USSR Congress of Deputies on the order of application of Article 125 of the USSR Constitution."

"The USSR Congress of People's Deputies resolves: to specify that the right of the USSR Committee for Constitutional Control granted by Article 125 of the USSR Constitution to stop implementation of normative-legal statutes which contradict the USSR Constitution or the USSR Law, does not extend to the Constitutions of the union republics". (Applause).

What does this entail? This is not a disparagement of the role of the USSR Committee for Constitutional Control. It will be able to present its conclusions on the correspondence or lack of correspondence of the constitution of any union republic to the USSR Constitution.

The USSR Supreme Soviet Presidium will implement constitutional control. Our congress will retain the last word on these questions, but at the same time consideration will be given to the fact that the adoption of a union republic constitution, as well as the introduction of changes into it, remains the sovereign right of the union republic. And to give a certain, even the most competent federative organ, the right to stop its action, means to deprive the republic of its sovereignty with a single stroke of the pen.

Our concern is not unfounded, particularly after yesterday's speech by Nikolay Ivanovich Ryzhkov about the upcoming activity of the USSR government, which places the emphasis specifically on the unitarian, and not the federative, organization of our state. Giving the Committee for Constitutional Control the power to sanction or refute the Basic Laws of the union republics is a blow to the very idea of a legal state. A large part of the people's deputies from the Baltic republics (and not only them) who have promised their constituents that they would defend the reorganizational laws of their republics, want to and will keep this promise. Today we are creating a state organ which will be able to "burn"

Twelfth Session

8 June 1989

many new articles in the republic constitutions. What should we do? To vote against, to abstain, or to leave the auditorium... Yet we are in favor of this membership, we are in favor of this Committee. Thank you for your attention. (Applause).

Yu.V. Golik, deacon of the juridical faculty at Kemerovo State University, Kemerovo (Central Territorial-Electoral district, Kemerovo Oblast): First a few words about the Committee for Constitutional Control. Comrades! The Committee for Constitutional Control, or our variant of the constitutional court, is just as necessary to us as air. We have been striving for this for many years, and therefore I consider to be inadmissable the efforts (under supposedly democratic slogans) to torpedo the creation of this Committee. (Applause). In general, of course, the ideal variant is for this Committee to begin work tomorrow, or at least—on Monday. After all, we are suffocating from departmental standard-setting. And the faster we put an end to it, the easier it will be for all of us to breathe. I must say a few words also about that ultimatum, in essence, which our colleagues from the Baltic have issued, and not for the first time. Comrades, any effort to present an ultimatum to the Congress of People's Deputies is simply inadmissable. (Applause). We and we alone are capable of deciding all the questions which stand before us. We may be three times in disagreement with the general opinion. We may refute it, but we may not present an ultimatum.

And the final point: About the possible candidacy of Academician Kudryavtsev to the office of chairman of the Committee for Constitutional Control. I know Vladimir Nikolayevich Kudryavtsev, though not personally, from his works dating back to November of 1969. I specify this time so precisely for the simple reason that this was when I first read one of his books. I met him personally only here, at the congress. Therefore, I cannot be accused of any sympathies or antipathies built on personal experience. I consider him to be a principled man, and in essence, an ideal candidate for this position. (Applause).

M.S. Gorbachev: Deputy Tarazevich, Belorussia.

G.S. Tarazevich, chairman of the Belorussian SSR Supreme Soviet Presidium, Minsk (Molodechnenskiy national-territorial district, Belorussian SSR): First of all, I would like to express my opinion and support the opinion already expressed here about the fact that, of course, it is specifically at this congress that we must (and really must) elect the Committee for Constitutional Control. And now about the candidacy of Yevmenov from Belorussia. I know Comrade Yevmenov, and know him very well. He is a highly learned man, a very knowledgeable specialist, a social scientist, philosopher, and doctor of sciences with extensive experience in public work. He worked in Komsomol and party organs, spent much time in teaching work, worked in international organizations, specifically UNESCO, engaged specifically in problems of public relations, and has a good knowledge of international law. At the present time he is working in the Academy of Sciences, where he heads up the section on information on social sciences of our Belorussian Academy of Sciences. He is engaged in the study of public relations in the current, very complex, period of restructuring. He is principled, honest, and fair. We believe that he would be a worthy representative of Belorussia in the Committee for Constitutional Control, and I ask that you support his candidacy.

D.G. Smirnov, design engineer at the production association "KhEMZ", Kharkov (Kharkov-Moscow territorial electoral district, Kharkov Oblast): Comrades! I also have no pretensions against the make-up of the committee or its proposed chairman. However, I generally share the concern of the deputy who spoke before Comrade Tarazevich. Unfortunately, if we read the USSR Constitution closely, we will see that Article 125, which defines the activity of this committee, states: "The organization and order of activity of the USSR Committee for Constitutional Control is determined by the Law on Constitutional Control in the USSR". Yet there is no such law. How can we now create a committee which will not know how it should act and what it should do, other than be guided by general phrases from the Constitution? Let us put off this question for 6 months. Let us bring to Moscow these people who have been proposed for membership in the Committee for Constitutional Control. They will work for these 6 months as a constitutional committee under the USSR Supreme Soviet. First of all, all of us who are part of the Supreme Soviet will have a chance to meet them. We will know specifically what kind of people they are, and their work qualities. Moreover, we must use these 6 months to create a law which would regulate the activity of the committee. Thank you for your attention. (Applause).

A.T. Kruglov, assistant flight detachment commander at Syktyvkarskiy Aviation Enterprise, city of Syktyvkar (Syktyvkar territorial electoral district, Komi ASSR): Comrades! I have nothing against the candidacies which have been presented. They are all respectable and worthy people, and I approve of them. However, I would like to point out that the honorable comrades which are numbered in this committee have one, maybe only one, shortcoming. Yet it is a significant one. All of them are over 60, and some even far past 60. (Applause).

Furthermore, during my election campaign which I presented to the voters, my program contained the following point: The renovation of party, economic and state apparatus through the army of capable youth on a competitive basis. During the course of the entire congress, I see no alternative choice and no rejuvenation. Therefore, I support the proposals of the comrades who spoke before me not to hurry with this matter. Especially since we are electing them for a term of 10 years. We should hold the elections on a competitive basis and try to elect younger and more able-bodied people. Thank you for your attention. (Applause).

Twelfth Session

8 June 1989

N.V. Fedorov, senior instructor at Chuvash State University, city of Cheboksary (Moscow national-territorial electoral district, Chuvash ASSR): Honorable people's deputies! We must surely be very responsible to our constituents. It is remarkable that we resolve questions by acquainting ourselves with them on the same day as the question arises. And now once again we are hurrying. Yet the question being resolved is about how constitutional development and legislative development will proceed for at least the next 10 years. Perhaps many of us will not be around then, at least not in this auditorium. Yet the members of the Committee for Constitutional Control will be working and answering to our constituents. Under these conditions, the suggestion made by a number of the people's deputies seems very expedient: Not to hurry in deciding this question which bears such a principle and strategic character, and to be responsible before our constituents.

I am in no way casting doubt upon the candidacy of the well-known Academician Vladimir Nikolayevich Kudryavtsev. Moreover, perhaps not everyone has noticed that Deputy Kudryavtsev in essence has admitted at this congress the unconstitutionality of the USSR Supreme Soviet Presidium's ukase dated 8 April, referring to the understanding of just such an evaluation by Anatoliy Ivanovich Lukyanov.

The fact is that, actually, the USSR Supreme Soviet Presidium's ukase dated 8 April 1989 grossly contradicts Article 119 of the USSR Constitution. And in this respect the candidacy of Deputy Kudryavtsev is very fitting.

Yet perhaps I would not be fulfilling my responsibility to those who elected me if I did not say that after the television broadcast of 10 May ("Legal Channel", I believe) on which Professors Yakovlev and Guliyev spoke, a proposal was presented at the okrug electoral meetings to nominate Professor Vladimir Yevgenyevich Guliyev as an alternative candidate. He was the first to publicly give to the entire country a very well thought-out and qualified political and legal evaluation of the 8 April ukase. They spoke here of the fact that Academician Kudryavtsev also gave such an evaluation at a meeting of the CPSU Central Committee Politburo, but we must probably take into consideration the fact that evaluations must, ultimately, be given before all the people.

In support of the proposal made by a number of people's deputies to provide for the possibility of a real choice, I, expressing the interests of my constituents, propose as one of the candidacies (along with the other, very worthy ones)—the candidacy of Professor Vladimir Yevgenyevich Guliyev. I believe that many specialists know him. Thank you.

N.I. Timashova, pensioner, Tatar ASSR, city of Kazan (representing the All-Union Organization of Veterans of War and Labor): Honorable Comrade Chairman, honorable comrade deputies! We have been meeting for quite a long time now. And how many commissions we have already created! I join here the preceding comrades who said that the creation of a Committee for Constitutional Control is as necessary now, in our current situation, as is the air we breathe. That is the first thing.

Secondly, I join in the opinion that all the comrades proposed for membership in the committee are worthy, although many of them we do not know. Yet I have a request from the autonomous republics. One of the main thoughts expressed here was that there are many problems in the autonomous republics, okrugs and oblasts. Therefore, our request is that the membership of the committee include a candidacy from the autonomous republics. This is a large request. (Applause).

I cannot today name the candidacy. Therefore, I propose that we, perhaps, put off the ratification for a day, so that the comrades could once again take a look at their groups of deputies. Alright? But this committee should be ratified at this congress. Thank you.

People's deputy (Did not introduce himself): Comrade Chairman, honorable colleagues! The Estonian delegation of the Estonian deputy corps here comprises 48 people. Among them, unfortunately, there are 2-3 who, first of all, want to present themselves as representatives of all the Russian-speaking residents of the republic—that is one thing. And secondly—they contrapose themselves to the remaining portion of the delegation, the Estonian SSR government, the Estonian SSR Supreme Soviet, and the Estonian CP Central Committee. These people represent those forces which would like to, if they could, drive a deeper wedge between the population of the republics, supposedly proceeding from national contradictions. They want to introduce this line toward a schism here and to expand it in such a way as to set the representatives of one republic against another.

Comrades, let us think about what this means. This can lead to the situation whereby the centrifugal tendencies, which are also present, will receive such an additional impetus that later there will be no way that we will be able to "eat this porridge".

As for the Russian-speaking population of Estonia, pardon me, but I represent it in the same measure. If I speak personally for myself, my wife is from Leningrad, my children studied in a Russian school, and half of my constituents are Russians or Russian-speaking. For some reason, some people believe that they have a monopoly on representing the interests of the Russian-speaking population, and they want to make it appear as if others, who were also elected from the entire population (we do not discriminate, people are people), represent only the Estonians. This is not correct. It is a deeply erroneous and, unfortunately, conscious and goal-oriented position.

As for the Committee for Constitutional Control, I am not a jurist. I am a chemist. Therefore, I will express only my own subjective impression. Evidently, the matter

Twelfth Session

8 June 1989

stands as follows: We want to do it in the worst way. Comrades, perhaps we should put it off until the fall? Let us not do something in haste which will later be difficult to correct. Thank you for your attention. (Applause).

Yu.Yu. Voldyrev, senior engineer at the Central Scientific-Research Institute of Shipbuilding Electronics and Technology, Leningrad (Moscow territorial electoral district, Leningrad): We spoke here about the fact that certain comrades are trying to torpedo the elections. I believe that the ones who are torpedoing the election of the Committee for Constitutional Control are those who prepared these elections in this manner. (Applause).

I believe most of you went through an election campaign, and that it lasted more than one month. Today they are telling us to vote within the course of one day for people whom many of us do not know. Here I am in full and complete agreement with the position of the Lithuanian deputies which was expressed somewhat earlier, that this is principally amoral, and that we do not have the right, being responsible to our constituents, to vote for people whom we do not know. This is particularly important when we are electing an organ such as the Committee for Constitutional Control for a term of 10 years.

Why is this happening? Why has such a thing occurred? I believe to a significant degree the reason for this is the fact (and this was mentioned at the party group) that for us the committee is a political instrument. Thus, as long as the Committee for Constitutional Control is for us a political instrument, such things will continue. Moreover, you have probably noticed that today in discussing the question of electing the Committee for Constitutional Control, questions are being posed, essentially, on the mechanism of functioning of authority—those questions which we did not have time to discuss.

I believe that we can in no way elect the Committee for Constitutional Control in such a manner. We cannot elect it until we have seriously discussed the questions of the mechanism of functioning of our authority and the structure of this authority. These are the questions which we have not yet seriously discussed at this congress. Thank you. (Applause).

L.M. Sandulik, head of the biology faculty at Chernovtsy State University (Chernovtsy territorial electoral district, Ukrainian SSR): Most honorable Chairman! Most honorable USSR People's deputies! The USSR Committee for Constitutional Control is a vital state organ, and its election is perhaps the first step toward creating a legal state. I solemnly promised my constituents that if I should have to make crucial state decisions—exercise the authority granted to me by my constituents—I would necessarily study the question, consult with specialists, and ask the opinion of my constituents. It seems to me that today this is just such a case, when we can make a decision only after having studied the opinion of our constituents. I am not speaking of a referendum, but I propose that we put this question off until the next congress, since it is one for which we have not sufficiently prepared, as we received the documents an hour before voting.

In all probability, I will not have the opportunity to speak here again. If we will be ratifying the chairman of the Committee for People's Control, then I say now that I will speak out against the ratification of the candidacy of Comrade Kolbin as a man who took it upon himself to make the decision to "execute or to pardon"—he granted amnesty to people who had violated the law. In doing so, he exhibited lawlessness and still does not understand that he committed an illegal act. Thank you for your attention. (Applause).

Ye.A. Yevtushenko, poet, secretary of the USSR Writer's Union governing board (Kharkovskiy-Dzerzhinskiy territorial electoral district, Ukrainian SSR): Comrades, I was never brought to trial, and never asked for Comrade Kudryavtsev's protection. Moreover, I am not even personally acquainted with him, and our paths have never crossed. However, here is what I would like to say. It seems to me that to the Committee for Constitutional Control we must elect the most immaculate and honest people. This does not mean that I suspect Comrade Kudryavtsev of something dishonest. However, I believe that the proof of professional cleanliness for people of his profession is the behavior of these people at the time when human rights were being violated. I know many people—not professionals in this matter—among our writers and scientists who spoke out in defense of the so-called "dissidents". These, simply speaking, were merely free-thinking people. They defended [these dissidents], got them out of jails and out of mental institutions. I never heard the voice of Comrade Kudryavtsev in this struggle. Yet nevertheless, I would not have spoken up, except that I believe that if we are to vote him in, he must answer my question and tell us what he did to save people from jails, from camps, and from mental institutions.

I would also like to say the following. Recently LITERATURNAYA GAZETA published an article about how a former apprentice of Ryumin, if I am not mistaken his name is Grishayev, excuse me if I make a mistake here, is still teaching law, jurisprudence, etc. Why did I not hear the indignant voice of Comrade Kudryavtsev at this moment?

Yet the main thing that I want to say to you is this. I do not know what Comrade Kudryavtsev said in the lobby of the Politburo, and I do not think that this has any decisive significance for me and for the people in determining whether or not to elect him to this responsible position, just as it is of no importance what I whisper in my wife's ear or what I talk about in the kitchen with my mother-in-law. I heard about how Comrade Kudryavtsev commented on the ukase of 8 April which included the infamous Article 11, which enraged not

Twelfth Session

8 June 1989

only my Kharkov voters, but also all the working people—the working class, the peasantry, and the intelligentsia. Practically under the guise of mild criticism of this ukase there was a hidden advocacy of it and of Article 11, where criticism by a worker—a director or a rank-and-file party member—of a Central Committee Secretary and so forth may be declared a criminally punishable discreditation. Therefore, I would like you to focus attention on these qualities of Comrade Kudryavtsev and on his tendency to such advocacy of rather dubious ukases. I believe that this position should be filled by an impeccable person, and this cleanliness also includes the struggle for which one may lose his head.

And moreover, Mikhail Sergeyevich, I would like to say that we would nevertheless like to have leaders who are a bit younger... I am 56 years old. When I was 30, I fought to become the editor of a journal. Now I will not take this position. Mikhail Sergeyevich, we need people younger than you to lead this committee. This too we must take into consideration. Thank you. (Applause).

People's deputy (did not introduce himself): Honorable comrade Chairman, comrade deputies! Previously, we explained the serious shortcomings in state life by the fact that our system of the Soviet socialist state had no special organ which would implement control over its proper and continuous implementation. Now, when we are creating such a constitutional organ, we hear various voices which explain this way and that, and in general reduce the matter to the fact that we must take our time in creating this committee. We must, they say, wait and see how it will turn out, and so forth. I am in complete disagreement with such a point of view. I believe that specifically at the first congress we must create a Committee for Constitutional Control, and in the make-up which is proposed to us. And as for Comrade Vladimir Nikolayevich Kudryavtsev specifically, the vice-president of the USSR Academy of Sciences, although I am not a jurist and do not know him personally, as a current and, well, enlightened person, if you will not consider this immodest, and as one who keeps abreast of the events in our country, I have known him from afar for at least 15-20 years. And evidently recently, when the question of strengthening the leadership of the USSR Academy of Sciences was being resolved, there was probably good reason to elect him vice-president, who resolves questions associated with the development of the social sciences, including law, in our country. I believe this is one of the most worthy candidates for this important position. I propose that you vote for him, comrade deputies.

Now, as for the representative from our Kazakhstan, we have no doubt about him—about doctor of juridical sciences, Professor Gayrate Sapargaliyev. He is a well-trained and qualified man, who will successfully handle this assignment and will be worthy of representing the interests of our Kazakh Soviet Socialist Republic. Thank you. (Applause).

M.S. Gorbachev: We should probably bring this discussion to a close. We will have just a few more speakers.

V.I. Alksnis, lieutenant-colonel, senior engineer-inspector of a military unit, Baltic Military District (Yuglskiy national-territorial electoral district, Latvian SSR): Many representatives from the Baltic have already spoken from this rostrum. They spoke very loud words about returning to the Leninist principles of federalism. However, I would like to specify that, while their words speak for federalism, they are in fact proposing confederation.

I would like to address the Supreme Soviet Presidium with the request that the jurists give us, the deputies, a report on the basic indicators of confederation and federation so that the deputies could clearly distinguish when they are trying to push through the ideas of confederation veiled in pretty words. Moreover, I would like to bring to your attention the following information. On 31 May of this year, during the work of our congress, the Duma of the Latvian People's Front appealed to all the People's Front members. Up until now, the Latvian People's Front, in all of its activities, based on the principles adopted at the constituent congress and on its program, emphasized the first alternative—the principle of federation. However, the events of recent months testify to the fact that the efforts of all of the Baltic and Latvia in achieving this goal are encountering ever-increasing political, economic, and ideological counteraction from the center and the internal reactionary forces, up to the application of open violence, as was evidenced by the tragic events of 9 April in Tbilisi.

The course of the USSR Congress of People's Deputies testifies to the fact that the conservative majority which has been formed here speaks out against the union republic aspirations aimed at full state sovereignty. In connection with this, the Latvian People's Front duma governing board presents a question which is vitally important to our people for discussion in all the groups and sections of the Latvian People's Front. This is the question of beginning the struggle of the Latvian People's Front for full political and economic independence of Latvia. That is, for the first time the mask has been cast aside and the primary goal of the Latvian People's Front has been defined—this is the struggle for secession from the USSR. On 16 June we will hold a session of the Latvian SSR Supreme Soviet. Thus, the following task is presented in this appeal—to see that the 16 June session of the Lithuanian SSR Supreme Soviet adopts a declaration on the state sovereignty of Latvia, the amendments to the Constitution of the Latvian SSR regarding the right of ownership of the Latvian SSR, and ratification of USSR laws, so that the Latvian SSR Supreme Soviet immediately adopts the law on economic independence of Latvia. Latvia is today the only one of the Baltic republics which has no such amendments to its constitution. Yet the Latvian People's Front is now forcing the adoption of such a legal draft upon the Latvian SSR Supreme Soviet.

Twelfth Session

8 June 1989

In the name of my constituents, who specified one of my main tasks as fighting for strengthening our Soviet Federation, I spoke out against these aspirations, and I appeal to you: Comrades, it is true that in the Baltic republics, by means of adoption of discriminatory laws which belittle human dignity, a system of national oppression is indeed being formed. From this high tribunal I turn to the representatives, including also to international organizations on human rights, with a request to come to the Baltic republics and evaluate the correspondence of these laws to the standards of international law. (Applause).

I also speak out for the need to create a USSR Committee for Constitutional Control which could verify the implementation of the Constitution and other USSR laws on the territory of the Baltic. (Applause).

R.A. Bratun, writer (Lvov-Zaliznichnyy territorial electoral district, Ukrainian SSR): I, by the way, acquainted myself with the materials which our Baltic comrades presented to us, and I saw there no desire to secede from the Soviet Union. The struggle for their sovereignty and for republic cost accounting is not a struggle against Soviet authority. (Applause).

I am surprised by the speeches of Comrade Kogan and our countryman who spoke yesterday, I believe, and talked about the existence of storm trooper detachments. If this is so, then it is really shocking. But are these not simply worker's detachments, which are tagged with the label of storm detachments? (Noise in the auditorium.) I know that, for example, many workers collectives have delegated their representatives to worker detachments. I think our comrades from the Baltic should explain this to us. If this is so, this is really scandalous, and we must condemn this. But perhaps this is not so. I somehow doubt your interpretation. I personally believe that the question of constitutional control is a very important question. It is the first big step by our Union toward a legal state. Therefore, we should not make hasty decisions here today. We must consult with our constituents who have sent us here and who have instructed us to fight for a legal state and for such an organ of it as constitutional control. It is very important. I think that if we wait until the fall, nothing terrible will happen. (Applause).

I.N. Gryazin, section head at the Estonian SSR Academy of Sciences Institute of Philosophy, Sociology and Law, Tartu (Pyarnuskiy rural national-territorial electoral district, Estonian SSR): It is very difficult for me to keep from answering, but I would like to respond to certain of the colleague-deputies, including Kogan, for example. Yet I will not do so, because, whether we want to or not, this discussion must lead to some kind of compromise. If I were to respond, then I would continue to fan that argument which has already arisen. Yet we must come to some kind of result. Is that not so?

As far as I understand, two positions have become delineated. The first position is to reject the election of a Committee for Constitutional Control in general. The second position is not only to elect the committee, but to tell it how it must punish poor Estonia. These are two extremes. There is also a central position. For the sake of fairness I must say that I am inclined toward the first position. But that is not the question. I am not defending this position. Here we need a compromise.

I realistically envision such a compromise now. The status of the formed committee really does evoke some doubts in a juridical plane, particularly coordination of its status with certain other articles of the Constitution, including the principle of sovereignty of the union republic.

Therefore, I support the idea which was repeatedly expressed here, and specifically: Since the question is serious, dear deputies, it is oh-so serious!—let us not be hasty. The second congress is not far away. Let us examine this complex question with the constitutional status of the committee itself. Thank you. Let us live as friends!

I.V. Sorokin, senior officer in charge of criminal investigation operations, internal affairs section, Kuybyshev station, Kuybyshev (Lenin territorial electoral district, Kuybyshev Oblast, RSFSR): I am in favor of creating a Committee for Constitutional Control. Yet there is one thing—none of us know those candidates which are presented in this list. That is one thing. Secondly, we must think through, I believe, the mechanism of competitive selection.

And finally, we plan and implement these committee elections. I would like to propose the candidacy of Comrade Sobachak from Leningrad for membership in the committee. Thank you.

M.S. Gorbachev: Just a second. Let us allow the two comrades who are here to speak. With this we will conclude the discussion and will summarize. Alright?

A.Ya. Tsirulis, editor-in-chief of the newspaper PADOMYU YAUNATNE, Riga (Bauskiy national-territorial electoral district, Latvian SSR): I understand your indignation. When you listen to our "Interfront" representatives, what they say really does appear awful. I would truly be an unhappy man if this were really so. Yet even on the day of registration, speaking on Central Television, I suggested that it organize a direct broadcast from the Baltic republics on which questions could be answered. There are also other ways. Yet it is very difficult to judge about Latvcia, Lithuania and Estonia, as we have heard here at the congress, as well as about the life of the other republics; only from the pages of the central newspapers and from the broadcasts of Central radio and television. After all, a very broad spectrum of opinions must be presented here.

Twelfth Session

8 June 1989

I liked very much the proposal by Comrade Alksnis, who spoke of inviting international representatives for verification. They are very much needed in Latvia, Lithuania and Estonia, and this would bring much benefit. We are very much in need of glasnost. And we would be very grateful for this. (Applause).

R.A. Medvedev, historian, writer, Moscow (Voroshilovskiy territorial electoral district, Moscow, RSFSR): I would like, comrades, in the discussion of such a delicate question, to refer to the authority of Vladimir Ilyich Lenin and to read only three short excerpts in connection with that confrontation which has arisen here between the majority of the delegations and the delegations from the Baltic republics.

Lenin wrote: "...We must distinguish... the nationalism of a large nation from the nationalism of a small nation."

"In regard to the second form nationalism, almost always in historical practice we, the nationals of a large nation, are guilty of an endless number of coersions, and even more than that. We unwittingly perform an endless number of coersions and insults—we have only to recall them...". I will list the facts later.

"Therefore," wrote Lenin, "internationalism on the part of the oppressor or so-called 'great' nation (although it is great only in its coercion...) must consist not only of maintaining the formal equality of nations, but also of such inequality which would compensate on the part of the ... large nation... that inequality which in fact arises in life. Whoever has not understood this has not understood the truly proletarian attitude toward the national question. He has remained, in essence, at the viewpoint of the petty bourgeois and therefore cannot help but descend each minute to the bourgeois point of view."

This is why for Lenin in this case, in examining the relations between a large and a small nation, "...it is better to overdo in the direction of concessions and softness toward the national minorities than not to give enough attention to them. This is why in this case the basic interest of proletarian solidarity, and consequently also the proletarian class struggle, demands that we never have a formal attitude toward the national question, but always consider the necessary difference in the attitude of the proletariat of a small nation... and a large one... Lenin. Written 3 December." (Applause). Therefore, I propose: Since here the opinion of the majority of the Baltic delegation and the delegations of the Baltic republics to put this question off until the next session has become apparent, we will not be doing anything criminal if we examine this extremely important problem and select a constitutional commission for a term of 10 years at the fall session of the USSR Congress of People's Deputies. (Applause).

M.S. Gorbachev: I do not take upon myself the entire burden of responsibility for this decision. Let us seek it together. I believe.. Ah yes, excuse me, Comrade Kudryavtsev wanted to speak. Please.

V.N. Kudryavtsev, vice president of the USSR Academy of Sciences, Moscow (representing the CPSU): Dear comrades, I would like to answer those questions which you have presented to me and also to say a few words about how I understand this difficult work. You see, the work, if you speak about me and the Committee, is in general extremely difficult, as is already evident from the debates. But first I would like to speak on specific questions. First of all, Comrade Balayan, who read a quote here from a political-legal commentary on the name of the autonomous oblast. He is right. We must say that, of course, it was not written correctly there, unfortunately. I do not remember this text, but he probably quoted it correctly, that the autonomous oblast is supposedly named after the name of the people who live there. You see for yourselves that this is not quite so, and does not always correspond to reality. Therefore, we must admit that it is a mistake. (Applause).

I will not say who the author of this text was. There is no need to applaud, because I am not the author of this section. I simply do not know who the author there was. Yet I was a member of the editorial staff, and of course, I should have noticed this.

Secondly, regarding Yevgeniy Aleksandrovich Yevtushenko. Since he had such a serious reproach addressed to me, I would like to deal, Yevgeniy Aleksandrovich, with some of your comments.

Regarding saving [people] from prisons. Here is what I must say... Different people act differently in such cases, utilizing their different capacities. One person does this by means of speaking out at meetings and making appeals for freeing someone, while someone else does so in the form of letters to a newspaper or some other presentations. And if this concerns a jurist, especially the director of the State and Law Institute, naturally he has certain other channels for this purpose. I cannot recount them all now. Aleksandr Maksimovich Yakovlev, who spoke here, and I once counted during his election campaign how many people he had freed. We cannot say exactly, but in any case he aided in liberating many people from jails, because he is approached by about 5-6 people a month on this question. Overall, around 20 people a month turn to the institute, and for the most part we help them, because about 50 percent of these appeals, unfortunately, are rightful. Unfortunately in the sense that, it seems to us, many people are being imprisoned illegally and unfairly. In these cases we always take measures to restore justice by those means which are accessible to us. We do not write to newspapers or turn to the Procurator General, to the USSR Supreme Court or the USSR Supreme Soviet Presidium if it is a question of amnesty, or use other similar channels. That is one side of the question. The other side of the question also deals

Twelfth Session
8 June 1989

with the work of the institute. And of the director, obviously. This work is the preparation of legislation which proceeds along the line of humanization. Yevgeniy Aleksandrovich, I cannot see where you are sitting. There—at the end? It is better to talk to a person when you can see him.

I will tell you now about legislation, including that concerning political prisoners. After all, you are not a professional, Yevgeniy Aleksandrovich. One must know certain details here. You, perhaps, do not know that a year ago a resolution was adopted concerning the mental institutions. The document is a rather serious one. Although I think that it has not been 100 percent perfected. We fought to see that it be brought 100 percent to the end, up to world standards. In any case, that which was done there was, of course, a great step forward. After all, you do not know of the participation here of either myself or my associates. Why should I advertise myself here?

I can also tell you about one other document, where I headed up the commission. This was the draft of the Principles of Criminal Legislation for the USSR and the union republics, which was published in the press. This draft is currently being subjected to criticism for humanism, which you prehaps know, because this has been rather broadly illuminated in the press.

Now I must mention the ukase of 8 April. Here, I might add, is a note which I just received. It says: "At the request of my constituents, I ask that you tell us whether Deputy Kudryavtsev was one of the authors of the 8 April ukase on criminal responsibility for state crimes, Article 11." First of all, I will say directly that I am not the author, and secondly I would like to explain the situation a bit so that it is clear to all the deputies.

The ukase of 8 April is a fragment or, I would say, an element of another document—the draft of the Law on State Crimes. Such a draft had been prepared for about 6 months or 2 years. Many jurists participated in its preparation, including some from our institute. I can assure you (I just do not have the text with me now) that this draft was quite democratic, and its main purpose was to replace the former Law on State Crimes, which was based on former Stalinist legislation. That was its main purpose. And this group, I believe, achieved its goals. I speak of the draft which existed prior to the 8 April ukase. This can all be confirmed. There are no state secrets here.

When the ukase came out, it was just as unexpected for me as, I think, for all those present here. Anatoliy Ivanovich Lukyanov already spoke about this ukase when he was asked questions. I spoke out with the first commentary, about which Yevgeniy Aleksandrovich Yevtushenko spoke here. Only he is wrong when he affirms what I supposedly said there about Article 11. I did not say that. This too is not hard to verify. Seeing the shortcomings of Article 11, I did not mention it in my commentary. Perhaps this was wrong on my part, to keep quiet about it. But on that very same day I mentioned this to several leading officials. And then, as mentioned here by Aleksandr Maksimovich Yakovlev, at the meeting of the CPSU Central Committee Politburo I also openly spoke about this—about the shortcomings of this article. Judge for yourselves whether I did right or wrong... After all, the congress judges. I do not have to judge. I only want to say that discussions in the Politburo are not discussions "with my mother-in-law in the kitchen." (Applause).

One other comment of yours, Yevgeniy Aleksandrovich, I fully accept. That is about my age. It is a bad age. I am old already, born in 1923. There is nothing I can do about it. I personally believed that it is much better to be young within the membership of this committee. But if this trust is given to me, and as long as I am alive, then that means I must work. That is how I understand this matter. (Applause).

Now, Mikhail Sergeyevich, excuse me, perhaps I am dragging this out too long, but I would like to say a few words of a more general nature. I also believe that this is a necessary institution. This, strictly speaking, is an element of a legal state and a continuation of the line toward separation of powers and, if you will, toward the creation of those "checks and balances" which we as yet do not have in our political mechanism. Of course it will not simply work and will not simply counteract various forces, which even today are being manifested in this auditorium. Yet the committee has certain capacities, specifically independence. As you remember, according to the USSR Constitution the committee is subordinate only to the congress. It is not subordinate even to the USSR Supreme Soviet. The only organ to which the committee is responsible is the congress. And I believe that the committee must, of course, adopt the line toward legality, toward democratization, toward the preservation of rights of citizens and toward the struggle against departmental lawmaking.

There is one difficult question. It was raised by the deputies from the Baltic. And of course, it should not be circumvented. The difficulty lies in the fact that our Constitution is old, while the legislation will be renewed. Honorable comrade deputy from the Baltic, you could have presented another example. Well, let us say, for example, a law on leasing is issued, while the Constitution contains nothing on lease agreements. Does this mean that the Committee for Constitutional Control must, consequently, put an end to the law on leasing and find it anti-constitutional? This is not a simple question, perhaps because we must be prudent here in our practical application. As concerns, let us say, republic legislation, I believe that we must change over to the new federalism and restore the Leninist principles of federal relations between the Union and the republics. My point of view is that in this difficult situation, in connection with the republic and Union Constitutions, we may fully

STENOGRAPHIC RECORD

Twelfth Session
8 June 1989

find prudent juridical decisions which are not as unattainable as some believe. We may find a normal solution to this question which would satisfy, I believe, both the Union and the republics.

And finally. I must say here that after all, the committee is a collective organ. It is not the chairman who decides something there. He cannot decide anything by himself. It is 23 people. I might add that I believe the committee should work openly and rest on the will of the congress, on its resolutions and those laws which it will adopt. And, of course, we must create a law on constitutional control, which we do not have at the present time. Obviously, the congress should assign this matter to one or another membership of the committee and to the Supreme Soviet. I believe that the matter here is not one of position, but of that responsible work which muist be performed within one membership group or another, because this organ is a step forward on the road to a legal and democratic state. Thank you! (Applause).

M.S. Gorbachev: We agreed to stop the exchange of opinions with this. Is that right?

Voices from the audience: Yes, it is.

M.S. Gorbachev: Allow me to summarize the discussion of this question. In general, comrades, it seems to me that there is no reason for us to be suspicious of one another, both of the deputies and the republics. I would like to remove this [suspicion] right now. After all, in general we have never had a Committee for Constitutional Control, and we survived. The USSR Supreme Soviet Presidium previously implemented control over adherence to the USSR Constitution and ensured the correspondence of the constitutions and laws of the union republics to the Constitution and laws of the USSR, and it continues to do so now, after the amendment to the USSR Constitution. That is how it was prior to the amendment in November. That is how it is now, after the amendment in November. Thus, we may remove entirely the question of the Committee for Constitutional Control. Yet let us recall why this question arose. Because it was hoped that through this mechanism—this very serious, constitutional mechanism created by the congress itself and subordinate only to it—we might create such an instrument which would strengthen the Constitution and aid in strengthening the line toward implementation of laws and legal principles, and so that this committee, this instrument, might act in such a way that no one, under the guise of implementation and development of a certain law, could render it lifeless at the stage of its realization. Yet you and I already have this experience, and comments to this effect have resounded at the congress. There is a law on State Enterprise and there are decisions (the comrades even gave an example, I do not know how accurate it is, that even the government somewhere undermined a law, despite the fact that it authored the draft of this law which was introduced for discussion). The departments have created many instructions for interpreting the application of a law, by which they have even more greatly limited the essence of the law and "bridled" it.

Thus, the existence of such a juridical organ is a very important instrument enabling us to stand strictly in defense of laws. This is very necessary, because the USSR Supreme Soviet Presidium, despite all its capacities and all of its authority, simply does not always encompass the entire set of problems for the purpose of working out these questions in detail. Therefore, the debates were extensive. The question of the Committee for Constitutional Control was raised. There was a discussion about the constitutional court, what form to establish in order to strengthen specifically this part of our legal mechanism, which would stand firm in guarding the Constitution and the laws. Therefore, it seems to me that we are going toward the creation of a Committee for Constitutional Control. This merely strengthens the capacities of our entire federation—all our citizens and labor collectives, republics and autonomous formations, etc—to clarify through this mechanism our concerns, to use it as a competent organ. I might add that this would be an independent organ compiled in this way, democratically, whose purpose would be to achieve a correct sequence in the realization of constitutional principles.

I believe, comrades, that to argue over this question, and moreover to refute or cast doubt upon the need for creating a Committee for Constitutional Control, is to cut the branch on which we are all sitting. Therefore, dear friends from the Baltic, let us get down to the essence of the matter. Perhaps we will not create a committee at all. Let us decide together. I told about how we came to the necessity of its creation. Yet as long as we have the USSR Supreme Soviet Presidium, it will control everything. Nevertheless, the best forces of our jurisprudence are concentrated in the Committee for Constitutional Control. We are taking here the most mature jurists, authoritative people who will help the republics as well as the citizens, the collectives and the central organs to solve this very important problem. This corresponds to our line for the creation of a socialist legal state.

Now, as for your concerns, and including also the formulas which certain deputies have proposed here. How should we act on this? I have here the signatures of Comrades Gorbunov, Bisher, Bresis and others. And this has resounded here in proposals.

I believe, comrades, that naturally we are faced with the need of having a new USSR Constitution. The outline of the resolution which you have received, the main decision on the discussion of the questions of foreign and domestic policy, provides for the creation of a Constitutional Commission. It will begin work. Then we will be able to address it.

STENOGRAPHIC RECORD

Twelfth Session

8 June 1989

Secondly, even before the Constitutional Commission prepares a project and submits it for discussion by the congress, and later, evidently, the congress (if it sees fit) will submit it for referendum or public discussion (we will decide this), we must travel a certain path. Yet, evidently, the need for moving along the path of political and economic reform, along the path of restructuring, will present us with questions which we must resolve through the preparation and introduction of amendments to the Constitution. These are the proposals which are being born. Based on the fact that we are proceeding along the road of restructuring, we will have to catch all the needs for changes in the entire system of our institutions created today, so that outdated laws (I am speaking in this case not only about the Constitution) do not stand in our way.

The law always lags behind. This is an old rule. It is natural. Yet at the same time I believe that we cannot formulate the matter in such a way that we have some kind of bacchanalia in regard to our own Constitution. Whatever it may be. If proposals arise which are necessary for restructuring to be realized and to move ahead, that means that amendments and changes are needed in the Constitution. Having prepared certain proposals, we formulate them and introduce them in an established order. For this we now have mechanisms which will help us to quickly and competently develop and introduce the question of amendments to the Constitution.

In other words, I would reason with you as follows. First of all, it is no accident that we have come to the point where we need such a very important organ. Secondly, I believe that we, embarking upon the path of implementing restructuring and engaging for this purpose all the mechanisms—the Supreme Soviet, the Committee for Constitutional Control, and the Constitutional Commission—will find a way to catch the questions which are coming to a head and find for them the correct solutions.

I believe, comrades, if we adhere to the cause of revitalizing and strengthening our federation on Leninist principles and proceed on this path, then we will find all the answers and resolve all the questions. Therefore, on this part I would agree with the comrades: Let us not now pose one or another question to each other, so that this would appear as a dictate, as an ultimatum. Yet by the essence of the questions, we will have to one way or another compare any proposals, whoever they emanate from. That is as it should be. That is a normal legal process. Does this correspond do the current laws or not? If it does not correspond, then we must improve [these laws], since we consider correct and justified the proposals which are associated with our progress along the road of reform.

Therefore, I would think that the creation of a Committee for Constitutional Control would give us just this opportunity to better resolve the questions which are coming to a head. And this should not, I believe, in any sense foster any doubts in anyone's mind as to the possibility that something can stand in the way of reform.

Yet now two proposals remain. To create the committee now or in the fall? (Animation in the auditorium).

From the audience: (Inaudible).

M.S. Gorbachev: They ask, why are we electing the committee members for 10 years, while deputies are elected for only 5 years? This, comrades, is the generally accepted practice, in order to give stability to their work. As a rule, I might add—as was mentioned at the Supreme Soviet yesterday—in the whole world they try to select the wisest and most competent people for this institution and for the Supreme court.

I might add that everyone who becomes a member of the Committee for Constitutional Control must give up his deputy duties. They should not be deputies. This too is a clear question.

Thus, we have to decide all this. I considered it possible to introduce this proposal, comrades. I ask for your attention. I understand—the question is a heated one, and evokes discussion. Yet we can work in such an auditorium only when there is a certain order. Otherwise this would be the Novgorod vetche [popular assembly in ancient Russia].

I believe and am convinced that we acted correctly in introducing the proposal to decide this question today. Why? I will tell you. After all, nothing is done well if its pros and cons are not first considered and thought out. The question of the make-up of this organ was worked out already in preliminary order (this was assigned to the USSR Supreme Soviet Presidium) over the period of the last 3 months, and the proposals from the republics were formulated as a result of discussion. These were the proposals of the republics themselves, and if from 21 people we subtract the representatives of the republics, then a small part remains—6 people, about whom we are speaking. These are: the chairman, his deputy, and certain representatives of the center. In essence, this is a well thought out, well developed question, and absolutely no mistrust emerged toward the opinion of the republics. And, in my opinion, no one raised such a question. It arose in regard to Belorussia, but Comrade Tarazevich, speaking in the name of Belorussia, removed this question, as I understand. Therefore, you know, it seems to me that we can decide this question, considering all the comments and argumentation of all the comrades. Only here is what I want to say, comrades. Am I getting the mistaken impression that someone has a certain understanding that some of us are supposedly in a hurry to conclude this congress? I believe we worked normally and this was not the case. Yet I am beginning to

STENOGRAPHIC RECORD

Twelfth Session

8 June 1989

question whether there is a desire here to drag out the congress under any pretext. To impose, so to speak, these particular discussions. Especially since the circle of orators is the same.

M.S. Gorbachev: So, comrades, let us do this. Let no one suspect that we want to conclude the congress in haste. We can even call a recess in its work, if that is what the congress decides. And come back again in a few days... Yet it seems to me that yesterday on the basis of a collective exchange of opinions we were able to come to the conclusion that we have already solved the primary tasks which we presented for the first congress. Yet we cannot solve all the problems. It seems, we must be realists. This first congress has thrown out so many opinions, so many proposals, that we still have to digest all that was said. It is good that we have come to an agreement that in the fall—this means soon—there will be another congress, etc. Let us not be suspicious of one another and back each other into a corner. Let us nevertheless together—as the comrade from Estonia, I believe, just said—let us work together as friends, I am for that. I am in favor of that! So that no one will feel himself to be the victor or the vanquished at this congress. It is our democracy that wins. The process of political reform wins. Through this congress and through the struggle of opinions we are entering a difficult— perhaps we are not happy with everything—but already a new stage of development of democracy, glasnost, and the political process in the country in general. I apologize for discoursing before you, but you must know my opinion, and now you have the right to decide for yourselves.

So, there is the first proposal—to decide the question of the committee. And the second proposal—to put it off. A compromise.

Voices from the audience: Let us vote. Why worry needlessly?

M. S. Gorbachev: Yes.

People's deputy (Does not introduce himself): Well, here is what I want to say. I have a proposal to elect this committee now, but as a committee to prepare its status—after all, it does not yet exist. We will verify them in deed, and in the fall, perhaps, we will also ratify them in the form of this committee. (Noise, applause).

M.S. Gorbachev: Let us conclude, comrades.

V.N. Korneyenko, digital program machine tool adjuster, Gomel Radio Plant, Gomel (Gomel city national-territorial electoral district, Belorussian SSR): Deputy Tarazevich spoke here in the name of the Belorussian delegation. In connection with this, I would like to make the following announcement. The Belorussian delegation has not discussed the candidacy of Comrade Yemenov. Therefore, I believe, he does not have the right to pose the question this way. That is all I have to say.

M.S. Gorbachev: Let us first decide how we will build the bridge—in length or in breadth—and then the personal questions will come later. Thus, comrades, the first proposal—to formulate the Committee for Constitutional Control now. Who is in favor of proceeding with this, I ask you to raise your cards.

Now we must decide in principle: Will we formulate the committee or not? And then all the rest. I ask you to raise your cards. Please lower them. Opposed? Comrades, there is no need to count here: It is a clear minority.

Voices from the audience: (Inaudible).

M.S. Gorbachev: You do not understand what we are voting on? I thought I had formulated it clearly. I repeat. We must now decide the question of whether to begin work on formulating the committee or to put it off until the fall. The first proposal is to formulate it now. Who is in favor of doing this now...

Voices from the audience: (Inaudible).

M.S. Gorbachev: The comrade is in favor of the proposal, but with different powers.

Thus, the first proposal is to formulate now, to begin formulating the membership of the Committee for Constitutional Control.

Everyone in favor of this proposal, please raise your cards. Please lower them.

Everyone opposed? Comrades, do we need a count? No?

Voices from the audience: Yes, we do.

M. S. Gorbachev: We do. Count the votes.

A. G. Kostenyuk: Honorable deputies! 433 deputies have voted against the proposal.

M.S. Gorbachev: Who has abstained?

A.G. Kostenyuk: There were 61 deputies who abstained from the vote.

M.S. Gorbachev: Thus, the decision has been adopted.

A.G. Kostenyuk: The deputies from the Lithuanian republic did not participate in the voting. Fifty deputies.

M.S. Gorbachev: Out of?...

A.G. Kostenyuk: Comrades! Tell us how many are present altogether in the Lithuanian delegation. 58?

Voices from the audience: No....

A.G. Kostenyuk: Then, I am sorry. Please raise your hands so that we can count how many are present.

Twelfth Session
8 June 1989

Voices from the audience: (Inaudible).

M.S. Gorbachev: I simply say that we were deciding the processual question...

Comrades, I ask that you remain calm, because all of this is not so simple. We must not simplify it, and I would not simplify it in this case... It is all quite difficult. We must consult now on what to do further.

How will we act further, comrades?

People's deputy (did not introduce himself): Dear comrade deputies! Nevertheless, one of the important questions is the creation of a committee which does not have its own status. We cannot, we do not have the right to create a committee until a statute has been developed. A compromise decision has been expressed here, and now it is becoming particularly important to not create the Committee for Constitutional Control today... To create a commission (applause), to create a commission for working out the status of this committee. Perhaps in the same make-up, but a commission nevertheless. And based on how it will work, we will see whether it can be transformed into the Committee for Constitutional Control. That is my proposal. (Applause).

F. M. Burlatskiy, political observer for LITERATURNAYA GAZETA, Moscow (representing the Soviet Peace Fund in conjunction with eight Soviet committees speaking out for peace, solidarity, and international cooperation): Comrades! We must approach the moment we are living with all responsibility. Because we have convened this congress, our leaders have convened this congress in the name of democracy, in the name of developing restructuring, and in the name of unity. And we must seek means of achieving such unity. I propose that we put off the discussion of this question until tomorrow, and ask the congress Presidium and Mikhail Sergeyevich Gorbachev personally to enter into negotiations with the representatives of the Lithuanian delegations and to report on this question tomorrow here at the congress. Thank you. (Applause).

T.V. Moshnyaga, chief physician of the republic clinical hospital, Kishinev (Kishinev-Lenin national-territorial electoral district, Moldavian SSR): Honorable comrade deputies! From the standpoint of our delegation, the committee for Constitutional Control is a most important organ for the Congress of People's Deputies, since it will implement control over the adherence to the Constitution—the Basic Law of the country. And the Basic Law of the country provides for not infringing upon the interests of any other republic, not infringing upon the interests of any other Constitution. Consequently, this constitutional control will at the same time examine also questions of adherence to the constitutions of the union republics. Therefore, since there are differences of opinion on creating such a committee, on voting both on the principle and on the membership, I propose that we put off the examination of this question, at least until, as was proposed now, we can consult on it one more time. Thank you.

M.S. Gorbachev: Perhaps we should not develop the discussion now?

Voices from the audience: No.

M.S. Gorbachev: I would suggest Comrade Burlatskiy's proposal...

Voices from the audience: That is right.

M.S. Gorbachev: Nevertheless, comrades we, perhaps, have developed definite emotions and definite attitudes. There were probably many such emotions, and they will emerge many more times among us—that is not the worst thing. The worst thing is if our congress does not find such solutions which would correspond to the spirit of restructuring, the politics of restructuring, and the harmonization of interethnic relations, with consideration of the fact that we must also harmonize all points of view.

It seems to be the most simple question—to decide right away. Yet I think that the wisest decision would nevertheless be to accept Comrade Burlatskiy's proposal and to have the Presidium consult with the deputies from Lithuania and report on the results tomorrow. Alright? Yes, comrades?

Voices from the audience: Yes.

M.S. Gorbachev: Do we need a vote?

Voices from the audience: No.

M.S. Gorbachev: Good. And with those deputies who have left...

Voices from the audience: (Inaudible).

M.S. Gorbachev: Please.

Yu.Yu. Bredikis, chief of the 1st chair of surgery, Kaunas Medical Institute; head of the All-Union Center for Surgical Treatment of Serious Disruptions in Cardiac Rhythm, Lithuanian SSR, Kaunas (Representing the All-Union "Znaniye" Society): As we were coming to the congress, we of course understood that during voting there may always be a majority of votes, and our opinion, even though we may stubbornly defend it, may not always be heard. That is what has happened now.

Yet I agree that we should continue the discussion some more. Of course, the opinion that we should put off the question would be, in my mind, the most logical. But now I have a question. Are those results neutralized which were just voted on, until tomorrow?

FIRST CONGRESS OF PEOPLE'S DEPUTIES OF THE USSR

Twelfth Session

8 June 1989

M.S. Gorbachev: I think for now the question of the results of voting is not removed. We will hold the talks... And, naturally, with the deputies from Latvia.

From the audience: (Inaudible).

M.S. Gorbachev: Are you speaking on this question? Well, comrades, in general we have decided. Do we need to continue the discussion? Comrades, let us consider this question resolved. That is all. You and I must all adhere to the decision that has been adopted. Let us not suspect that some are Leninists, and others are not. Otherwise, we could, you know, go too far....

We still have many questions [to discuss]. Let us recess until 1900, and then work some more. We will recess until 1900.

(Recess).

Gorbachev: Esteemed comrades! Let us continue work. We have agreed as follows: After today's sitting we shall meet with comrades from the Lithuanian delegation and talk with them. A proposal is already taking shape here which we shall possibly submit tomorrow after more detailed discussion.

But now—back to the agenda. On the chairman of the USSR Supreme Soviet. The USSR Supreme Soviet has elected Comrade Yevgeniy Aleksandrovich Smolentsev. Comrade Smolentsev is an experienced man who has worked for several years on the USSR Supreme Court. Recently he has been working as chairman of the Russian Soviet Federated Socialist Republic [RSFSR] Supreme Court. Is Comrade Smolentsev here?

From the floor: Yes.

M.S Gorbachev: Comrade Smolentsev, come on up. What thoughts or questions are there for him? We listened for an hour in the Supreme Soviet yesterday to his answers to quite a lot of questions. But nevertheless, I want to present Comrade Smolentsev to you. I repeat: If there are no questions, may we proceed to the vote.... No?

From the floor: One question.

M.S. Gorbachev: Please, go ahead. Put your question, Comrade Aparin. Switch on microphone 2.

I.V. Aparin, first secretary of Kytmanovskiy CPSU Rayon Committee raykom, Kytmanovo settlement (Novoaltayskiy Territorial Electoral Okrug, Altay Kray): Yevgeniy Alekseyevich, for 10 years you were deputy chairman of the USSR Supreme Court. Many questions are arising now in connection with the so-called Gdlyan case and charges are being leveled at that group of investigators. But do we really not have here a court of ultimate jurisdiction which examines all such cases and draws the final conclusion: that either the charge is right or the accused is? Are you and the Supreme Court together not involved in what has happened and the stage that we have now reached in connection with the Gdlyan case? Should the investigators alone bear the responsibility for this? Thank you.

Ye.A. Smolentsev, chairman of the RSFSR Supreme Court: I do not quite understand the question. I believe that deputies have created a very authoritative commission here which is to investigate these questions in the broad sense. That is, not just the conduct of the investigators engaged in the investigation of well-known cases and those cases of bribery which are now being tried. I do not think that this is the right time for perhaps the future chairman of the USSR Supreme Court and the present chairman of the RSFSR Supreme Court to make any comment because it is not impossible that I shall have to examine some of these cases.

I.V. Aparin: Excuse me, you have probably not quite understood me: I would like the opinion not of the present chairman of the RSFSR Supreme Court but of the deputy chairman of the USSR Supreme Court in which capacity you worked for 10 years. Is that right?

Ye.A. Smolentsev: Yes.

I.V. Aparin: Well then: All these cases—the Khint case and others in connection with which the Gdlyan group is now being accused of a breach of procedure—have been examined at the Supreme Court. Were there no appeals about violations having occurred in the process? After all, ultimately Supreme Courts passed sentence. My question is: Do they not bear responsibility for the violations which occurred?

Ye.A. Smolentsev: The Supreme Court of the union has examined a whole series of cases involving responsible workers from Uzbekistan. Sentences have been passed in those cases which have been examined. In some cases partial decisions were made on the violations which occurred. As for the so-called Churbanov case, all the violations were committed, so to speak, in the sentence itself. And in connection with that one of the accused was acquitted while the case of a second was directed for further investigation. I was not directly involved in the examination of those cases, I was working at the RSFSR Supreme Court at that time, and it is simply difficult for me to comment on them now.

M.S. Gorbachev: Good. Can I put the question of confirmation to the vote? Those in favor of the confirmation of Comrade Smolentsev as chairman of the USSR Supreme Court, please raise your mandate cards. Lower them, please. Those against? (The votes are counted). Hands down please.

A.G. Kostenyuk: Esteemed deputies, 14 deputies voted against.

M.S. Gorbachev: Who abstained? (Votes are counted).

STENOGRAPHIC RECORD

FIRST CONGRESS OF PEOPLE'S DEPUTIES OF THE USSR

Twelfth Session
8 June 1989

A.G. Kostenyuk: There are 77 abstentions.

M.S. Gorbachev: The question is settled. Comrade Smolentsev has been confirmed as chairman of the USSR Supreme Court. (Applause).

On the USSR chief state arbiter. The USSR Supreme Soviet has appointed Comrade Yuriy Gennadiyevich Matveyev to this post. There was quite a broad exchange of opinions on the discussion of this question, too. Is Comrade Matveyev here? Come up here and introduce yourself to the congress, please.

I present Comrade Yuriy Gennadiyevich Matveyev to you. Deputies may ask him questions if they want. Do I have your support?

From the hall: Yes.

M.S. Gorbachev: Good. Thank you. Those in favor of the confirmation of Comrade Yuriy Gennadiyevich Matveyev as USSR chief state arbiter, please raise your cards. Lower them. Those against? (Votes are counted).

A.G. Kostenyuk: Esteemed deputies, there are 6 votes against.

M.S. Gorbachev: Abstentions? (Votes are counted).

A.G. Kostenyuk: There are 28 abstentions.

M.S. Gorbachev: In that case, Comrade Matveyev has been confirmed as USSR chief state arbiter. (Applause).

Comrades! The USSR Supreme Soviet has elected Gennadiy Vasilyevich Kolbin chairman of the USSR People's Control Committee. If any of the deputies are unfamiliar with the discussion held at the USSR Supreme Soviet sitting, I would say that the discussion was most extensive and principled. Nevertheless, this is the result.

Comrade Kolbin is sure to be somewhere in the hall. Gennadiy Vasilyevich, please.

I know that you are familiar with Comrade Kolbin but even so I am going to present him to you and invite you to ask him questions if there is anything that needs clarification.

G.V. Kolbin, first secretary of the Kazakh Communist Party Central Committee, Alma-Ata city (Prikaspiyskiy Territorial Electoral Okrug, Guryev Oblast): Mikhail Sergeyevich, I would like to answer a rejoinder expressed during the first half of the evening sitting. Namely, that I am high-handed. I have never been high-handed wherever I have worked and I have not interfered in court proceedings or investigations. As for recovering money in Kazakhstan related to the misrepresentation of statistics, all that was done according to strict legal procedure and by decision of the court. (Applause).

M.S. Gorbachev: I must confirm that yesterday generally speaking such clarity was lacking. And therefore comrades correctly said to you....

G.V. Kolbin: Mikhail Sergeyevich, I would like to explain further. I do not hide the fact that people are not calm when they stand on this platform, they become nervous. I was nervous, too. And I probably committed a few inaccuracies in my account of this case.

M.S. Gorbachev: Good. Comrades have some questions....

From the floor: Comrades! I am not acquainted with Kolbin but I have closely followed the course of restructuring and the way that Comrade Kolbin worked in Ulyanovsk Oblast. He is one of the few oblast party committee [obkom] secretaries who stood in line for milk along with everyone else. After he visited the stores order was always established there. (Noise in hall). I have closely followed his way of working in Kazakhstan, too. There, too, his work may be assessed positively. But today (if each of us were asked this question) who can prove that bribery took place, who can resolve those questions which have not been settled in our legislation? That is all I have to say. I must say, comrades, that restructuring (and this is my personal opinion) needs people like Comrade Kolbin. (Applause).

M.S. Gorbachev: I asked for questions....

From the floor: (Inaudible).

M.S. Gorbachev: If there are any then, of course, ask them. Go ahead.

Switch on microphone 2.

A.K. Izmodenov, secretary of Sukhoy Log CPSU City Committee [gorkom], Sukhoy Log City (Kamyshlovskiy Territorial Electoral Okrug, Sverdlovsk Oblast): Gennadiy Vasilyevich! People in the Urals have long known your professional qualities. But at the same time a number of voters ask: Do you think that restructuring and the development of democracy are helped by the fact, according to our press reports, that immediately before the elections on March 26 virtually all Kazakh Communist Party Obkom first secretaries were left unopposed by alternative candidates? What is your attitude to that?

G.V. Kolbin: It must be said that initially there were alternative candidates to all the contenders without exception. What you are talking about happened at the okrug voters' meetings. Of course it must have been better with competition. But that is what happened, and the people supported it.

From the floor: Did that happen by chance? Was it a coincidence?

STENOGRAPHIC RECORD

FIRST CONGRESS OF PEOPLE'S DEPUTIES OF THE USSR

Twelfth Session

8 June 1989

G.V. Kolbin: By chance. (Applause, noise in the hall).

M.S. Gorbachev: Gennadiy Vasilyevich, do you have something else to say on this matter?

G.V. Kolbin: No, Mikhail Sergeyevich, what I want to say is this, comrades. It is correct to raise the question that there must unfailingly be an alternative and that there must be 5 or 40 candidates from the viewpoint of democracy and the observance of the constitution. But there were no violations anywhere. That was people's will. And how many candidates should there be? Two, five, three? There were two, five, and then one each remained. And they were not only party workers....

M.S. Gorbachev: Fine. Further questions, please.

From the floor: Gennadiy Vasilyevich, I am not very satisfied with your answer. You were asked this question at the Supreme Soviet sitting, too. How do you view the People's Control Committee? As a system of control in the country? Then it is necessary. But if it is some kind of separate committee, as you said, and given that 90 commissions visit our enterprise a year such a committee is not necessary.

G.V. Kolbin: I would like to answer in the following way, comrades: This question requires thorough consideration because there are about 40 organizations which carry out interdepartmental control alone. There were thoughts of amalgamating them all into one but doubts appeared. I haven't been to the USSR People's Control Committee building yet, as you can guess.... All these questions must be considered in greater depth.

M.S. Gorbachev: Next please.

L.I. Sukhov, vehicle driver at the Kharkov Road Transport Enterprise No 16301, Kharkov city (Kharkovskiy-Leninskiy Territorial Electoral Okrug, Kharkov Oblast): Tell me, please, what will you do in your work to ensure that we don't have the lines of people which now greet us around hotels? How will you check the work of organs subordinate to you? How do you think that you will check that? How will work with letters be conducted?

G.V. Kolbin: I think we all have to work on this: those who are deputies, those who are not, and everyone else. (Applause).

L.I. Sukhov: That is quite clear. But how do you check whether the people's control organs lower down are working correctly? (Disturbance in the auditorium).

M.S. Gorbachev: Gennadiy Vasilyevich, is the question clear?

G.V. Kolbin: No, I did not understand the question.

L.I. Sukhov: How will you check the correctness of work by people's control organs lower down?

G.V. Kolbin: I think it is necessary first to do some work to study this.

M.S. Gorbachev: Next, please.

N.N. Koryugin, chief of the economic research laboratory at the Cherepovets 50th Anniversary of the USSR Metallurgical Combine, Cherepovets City (Cherepovetskiy Territorial Electoral Okrug, Vologda Oblast): Gennadiy Vasilyevich, at the Supreme Soviet session yesterday Comrade Ye.A. Smolentsev, who has now been elected chairman of the USSR Supreme Court, described your actions in connection with the handing back of money as unlawful. What is your view on that?

G.V. Kolbin: Comrades, I think I have answered that question. After all, Comrade Smolentsev was asked: Without a decision by the court, is this action lawful or unlawful? He said: Unlawful. But there were decisions by the courts. And therefore these actions were lawful....

M.S. Gorbachev: Fine. That is all clear. We can put it to a vote.

Sh.A. Amonashvili, general director of an experimental science and production association of the Georgian Soviet Socialist Republic [SSR] Ministry of Public Education (from the USSR trade unions): Esteemed deputies, yesterday, when Gennadiy Vasilyevich's candidacy for this post was under discussion, it was said that he worked in Georgia in the early eighties. It so happened that we did not have time to speak then, the debate was ended. So allow me to add this to what was said yesterday: Gennadiy Vasilyevich acquitted himself very well in Georgia. He is a very principled, sensitive comrade. And another thing that gratified us: He studied the Georgian language and knew how to approach people. I think he will justify all our hopes. I am speaking here on behalf of the Georgian group of deputies. Thank you. (Applause).

M.S. Gorbachev: Let us conclude on that note.

From the floor: I have a different view.

R.A. Medvedev, writer, Moscow City (Voroshilovskiy Territorial Electoral Okrug, Moscow City): Comrades, at the Supreme Soviet session yesterday I came out against Comrade Kolbin's candidacy, and since this is not the Supreme Soviet, but the Congress of People's Deputies, I would like to explain my view in more detail.

In our country there is no truly authoritative People's Control Committee. A real, authoritative People's Control Committee is an institution no less important for our country than the USSR Council of Ministers. When Vladimir Ilich Lenin wrote his testament, the last letter he wrote was the letter "How We Should Reorganize the Workers' and Peasants' Inspectorate." Lenin wrote about the party control organ and the people's control organ that existed at that time. Both of these organs were

STENOGRAPHIC RECORD

Twelfth Session
8 June 1989

operating disgracefully badly. Lenin thought the two organs should be combined, making the people's control organ (which was called the Workers' and Peasants' Inspectorate at the time) paramount and attaching to it 75-100 people from the party control organ (Central Control Commission). The Workers' and Peasants' Inspectorate, combined with the Central Control Commission, should be headed by someone who would not be restrained by any authority: neither the authority of the party Central Committee, nor the authority of the party general secretary. And this person, the leader of the combined control organ, should be able to demand absolutely any document, any documentation, any reply.

Yesterday, answering our questions, Comrade Kolbin failed to show that kind of firmness and principledness. I had no confidence that he would be the kind of person who will be absolutely independent in his judgments and will show, as chairman of the people's control organ of the Congress of People's Deputies, a degree of principle that will rise above even decisions of the Central Committee—I did not have that confidence, and therefore I voted against him yesterday. And I consider it necessary to do the same again.

M.S. Gorbachev: Fine. Comrades, shall we continue the debate?

Voices from the floor: No!

M.S. Gorbachev: Fine. Who is in favor of confining ourselves to the opinions already expressed and ending now the exchange of opinions on the candidacy for the post of chairman of the People's Control Committee? Please raise your credentials cards. Please lower them. Against? Please lower them. Abstentions? The vast majority is in favor of ending the discussion.

May we decide the question of confirmation?

Voices from the floor: Yes!

M.S. Gorbachev: Who is in favor of confirming Comrade Kolbin as chairman of the USSR People's Control Committee? Please raise your credentials cards. Please lower them. Against? Count, please.

A.G. Kostenyuk: Esteemed deputies, 252 deputies voted "against."

M.S. Gorbachev: Comrades, who abstained from voting?

A.G. Kostenyuk: There were 138 abstentions.

M.S. Gorbachev: So Comrade Kolbin is confirmed as chairman of the USSR People's Control Committee. (Applause).

Yesterday, comrades, the candidacy for the post of USSR general prosecutor was discussed heatedly at the Supreme Soviet. As a result of the discussion, the USSR Supreme Soviet appointed Comrade Aleksandr Yakovlevich Sukharev USSR general prosecutor, by an overwhelming majority of votes.

Is Comrade Sukharev here? What questions do we have for him? Comrades, please introduce yourselves and ask your questions.

V.V. Guliy, special correspondent of the newspaper SOVETSKIY SAKHALIN, Yuzhno-Sakhalinsk City (Yuzhno-Sakhalinskiy Territorial Electoral Okrug, Sakhalin Oblast): In my years of work on the newspaper I have collected a great many questions for the prosecutor's office, including some complaints. I will single out briefly a few of those that I regard as particularly fundamental.

Aleksandr Yakovlevich, it is important to me to know whether you think that amendments should be made to the existing law on the USSR Prosecutor's Office? If so, which articles of the law should, in your view, be changed first? Do you consider it possible for alternative candidacies for local prosecutors to be discussed before the general prosecutor appoints them? What, in your view, should be done drastically to reduce the influx of recurrent complaints to the USSR Prosecutor's Office and the law enforcement organs in general? What has been done to this end at the USSR Prosecutor's Office while you have been working there?

And one last thing. Since all my questions to you have hitherto remained unanswered (I would like to observe that I am not leaving here without answers from you), I ask you now to answer a question from a voter of mine, Military Prosecutor Butov. The point of the question is this. When will his letters about criminal abuses by Chief Military Prosecutor Lieutenant General of Justice Popov and his senior assistant Major General of Justice (if I am not mistaken about the name) Kaunin and other officials be examined? The examination of this question, my voter reports, has been "tied up in red tape" (I quote him) for 5 months by the USSR Prosecutor's Office.

M.S. Gorbachev: Aleksandr Yakovlevich, before you begin your reply.... Let us agree, comrades, to formulate the questions concisely and answer them concisely. And let us agree on how many minutes we will allow for questions and answers. Is half an hour too little? An hour? No limit?

Voices from the floor: No.

M.S. Gorbachev: Fine, then let us decide as we go along. Aleksandr Yakovlevich, go ahead, there are four questions for you.

A.Ya. Sukharev: I will answer the first question: My attitude to the law on the USSR Prosecutor's Office and whether it is necessary to amend this law. This is the 1979 law, with the amendments made on two occasions, most recently in 1987. I consider the basic principles of

FIRST CONGRESS OF PEOPLE'S DEPUTIES OF THE USSR

Twelfth Session

8 June 1989

this law to be correct. But I think it will be necessary to make amendments to this law because of the democratization of our life. This is a very large question, a question of principle, involving, in particular, a review, I would say, of the concept of prosecutor's supervision, so that this supervision ensures the monitoring of the rule of law over the entire field of social relations, rather than being merely narrow supervision relating mainly to criminal law. It is a question of supervision in the social sphere, supervision of legislation in the sphere of ecology, supervision of the rule of law in the economic sphere. Let me repeat: Supervision of the rule of law—and the laws should be improved in the sphere of human rights and the democratization of the process of our life. As I see it, there should be changes here. That is my answer to the first question.

Second. Do I admit the possibility of alternative candidates for the posts of prosecutors of republics, krays, and oblasts? Yes, I admit the possibility of alternatives.

The influx of complaints and letters. How do we intend to organize work with letters or complaints to the USSR Prosecutor's Office and what measures are we now adopting? Yesterday I expressed my fundamental position on this score. The essence of it is as follows. Our society is gradually turning into a society of petitioners and complainants. In the course of last year the USSR Prosecutor's Office alone satisfied 110,000 complaints, letters, and petitions from citizens. All of them, the bulk of them, should have been satisfied at the ministries, departments, and organizations in question, including social organizations. That is not right. So we are falling down somewhere here, there is a great deal of rust in our bureaucratic mechanism. Therefore we must do a great deal of very serious work to adjust this mechanism. We cannot go on like that, relying on complaints and good bosses higher up. Are we doing anything about it at the prosecutor's office? Yes, we are. We are stepping up monitoring and exactingness, becoming more demanding toward prosecutors lower down, but, to be frank, our increased toughness is not getting us very far. So it is not only a question of exactingness. We need a good legal mechanism. I advocate that a new law be adopted on work with complaints and on receiving citizens, especially in the conditions of democratization, when, to be frank, the influx of such complaints will increase. We must be prepared for that.

About military prosecutor Popov and his assistants. I will tell you frankly: I know these warnings, these complaints exist. I must look into this matter, and I am prepared, if I am given the floor, to report on it in more detail tomorrow.

M.S. Gorbachev: Any more questions?

A.L. Markevich, chief of the Obluchye freightcar depot, Obluchye City (Obluchenskiy City National-Territorial Electoral Okrug, Jewish Autonomous Oblast, RSFSR): Aleksandr Yakovlevich, as we know, the mafia and organized crime now have such means at their disposal that.... What do you think: First, is there not a real threat now that this mafia and organized crime will get their people onto the organs of power? Second. What do you think: What is the situation on this question now, do we not need a special state program to combat the mafia and corruption and the formation of a special committee, directly subordinate to the congress, on combating the mafia and corruption?

A.Ya. Sukharev: May I ask you to clarify: You are talking about the formation of a special committee?

A.L. Markevich: Yes.

A.Ya. Sukharev: Thank you. For all the significance of what we have in society now, especially when it comes to organized crime (and this kind of crime does exist, and unfortunately the trend toward an increasing proportion of organized crime in society is becoming more marked), all the same I would not wish to dramatize the situation in this respect. Still less would I say now that there is a real threat, that the mafia is, so to speak, already beginning to rule, or is close to appointing officials on the organs of power. I do not think that would reflect the actual state of affairs.

The fact that organized crime is growing, that for very many years we underestimated the significance of this kind of crime, that 57 percent of all crime in our country is mercenary crime, and that the various forms of parasitism, the various forms of this specific kind of crime have been underestimated both in the legal sphere and, I would say, in the moral, psychological, and political sphere—all this is true. We must formulate a whole program for combating the mafia, as you put it, for combating organized crime. But it should be a comprehensive program. I do not know whether we should create some kind of special committee, but at the CPSU Central Committee Legal Policy Commission recently, together with the minister of internal affairs, we reported on these proposals. We are now working on these proposals, because they are indeed very urgent.

M.S. Gorbachev: One moment, Comrade Ivanov is to ask a question. Will you read this? Well, fine. (Applause).

N.V. Ivanov, investigator for important cases under the USSR general prosecutor, Moscow City (Leningradskiy City National-Territorial Electoral Okrug, RSFSR): Since Aleksandr Yakovlevich and I are accomplices, I think one platform is enough for us both.

First question. You claim that party organs did not interfere in the course of the investigation? This was stated yesterday. Why are you misleading the people's deputies and the public, when you know that the matter

STENOGRAPHIC RECORD

FIRST CONGRESS OF PEOPLE'S DEPUTIES OF THE USSR

Twelfth Session

8 June 1989

came under discussion on three occasions at the Politburo and more than once at the CPSU Central Committee and the CPSU Central Committee Party Control Committee? Why did the Politburo adopt unlawful decisions on the case twice during your term as USSR general prosecutor alone?

Second question. When a case involving a group of people is being investigated, the law does not provide for the bringing of a separate criminal case with regard to each new accomplice. Cases were not and could not be brought against the three 19th party conference delegates who were arrested: Dzhabbarov, Radzhabov, and Smirnov. Nonetheless you are misleading the public to this day by claiming that at the time of the conference a case had not been brought against them, and that a case was brought later. Why are you lying?

Third question. At the USSR Supreme Soviet sitting yesterday you stated that when Gdlyan and I published the article "Opposition" in OGONEK, we already knew that criminal proceedings were to be brought against the conference delegates in the near future. Of the four delegates we had in mind, two were CPSU Central Committee workers. And you knew that for a long time we had been trying unsuccessfully to obtain the consent of the CPSU Central Committee and USSR Supreme Soviet Presidium for their arrest. Why did you mislead the public?

Another thing. Fourth question. Even after the party conference decision you stood in the way of a positive outcome to the question of the arrest of these delegates. The conference was in June, and the first two delegates were not arrested until October, and the third in January. How do you explain that?

Fifth question. Last summer you told me (I have 5 minutes under the standing orders, I am sorry, you voted for that yourselves) that Smirnov was working under the leadership of Comrade Ligachev, and that the latter has a good opinion of him. Does not this explain the fact that after receiving the consent of the USSR Supreme Soviet Presidium for criminal proceedings to be brought against Smirnov on 13 September 1988, for 4 months you refused to sanction his arrest?

Sixth question. CPSU Central Committee Secretary Comrade Ligachev is not addressing the congress. It must be assumed that he has no objections to make. How do you explain the fact that having a grievance against Ivanov, instead of going to the court with a complaint or suit, he went to you, the USSR general prosecutor, that is, his subordinate? Does this not show that Comrade Ligachev is sure that you will carry out all his instructions and wishes?

Next question. (Disturbance in the auditorium.) My 5 minutes are not up yet. On 18 May, over a 7-hour period, investigators of the prosecutor's office and Ministry of Internal Affairs [MVD] from our group totally exposed you and your deputy Vasilyev as having arranged, personally and through KGB Colonel Dukhanin, department prosecutor Titov, and other subordinates, for the evidence in the case to collapse. The defendants were taken to the USSR KGB prison of Lefortovo and asked to drop their truthful evidence on the payment of bribes to CPSU Central Committee workers. In response to dozens of reports from investigators and the exposure of your destruction of the case in the interests of your mafia patrons, you expelled from the investigation group 70 investigators, including all, without exception, who had criticized you. How do you explain that? And how does it tally with your assertion that you intend to take the case to its conclusion, if you have broken up the backbone of the group?

M.S. Gorbachev: Perhaps you could sit down for the time being. I feel the answers will be lengthy. Sit down for the time being.

N.V. Ivanov: And a last question. On 19 May, over a 6-hour period, representatives of the public from Zelenograd City, which elected Gdlyan as its deputy, took part in the work of the USSR Prosecutor's Office collegium. As general prosecutor you took everything into the realms of demagoguery, decided nothing, and even declared hypocritically that you are opposed to publications about the Gdlyan group. Yet the very next day all the central newspapers except PIONERSKAYA PRAVDA published defamatory items on the group. In response the Zelenograd labor collectives held a political strike. How objectively and with what principles were you acting in this situation? Since my time limit is up, thank you for your attention. (Applause).

M.S. Gorbachev: Go ahead.

A.Ya. Sukharev: Comrades, I have to pluck up my courage, so to speak, because, as you realize, it is easier to ask questions than to answer them. Especially since there are many of them. But I will try to answer you in the order in which the qeustions were put.

So, the first question. About the party conference delegates. At the USSR Supreme Soviet sitting yesterday, touching on this question, I said that Comrade Gdlyan knew already that the prosecutor's office leadership had raised the question of who the party delegates really were. I can confirm this now. It is true. Who are we talking about? Which delegates? Dzhabbarov and Radzhabov, party oblast committee [obkom] secretaries. Comrade Smirnov, second secretary of the Moldavian Communist Party Central Committee and former CPSU Central Committee apparatus worker. And, as I understand it, the comrades raised the question, and I feel they are raising it now, too, of Comrade Mogilnichenko. What are we actually talking about? I stated and I state now: During my term in office as USSR general prosecutor there were and are no obstacles raised by the Supreme Soviet Presidium and CPSU Central Committee to the investigation, the bringing of cases, and the

STENOGRAPHIC RECORD

FIRST CONGRESS OF PEOPLE'S DEPUTIES OF THE USSR

Twelfth Session

8 June 1989

arrest of individuals if there were grounds for it. You know what happened subsequently: Radzhabov and Dzhabbarov were arrested, as well as others who were not conference delegates—Usmankhodzhayev, former first secretary of the Uzbek Communist Party Central Committee, and Comrade Salimov, former chairman of that republic's Supreme Soviet Presidium. Four people were arrested, two of them delegates.

True, they were arrested rather later. This whole matter had to be studied very, very carefully. Although documents were indeed sent to the Supreme Soviet Presidium and Central Committee (since it was a question of Central Committee members and conference delegates) earlier. This whole matter had to be studied. And we are now convinced that we acted entirely correctly. Why did we act correctly? Because in my time (at that time I already held the post of USSR general prosecutor) four people were arrested, Comrade Smirnov among them. But now we have had to drop the case, because a skilled investigation was carried out with the participation of, you understand, very big lawyers, and not only good investigators, but skilled supervisory prosecutors and leaders in investigation work. And the prosecutor's office collegium discussed this matter. We came to the conclusion: What happened, comrades, was not merely a mistake, but, to call things by their names, a falsification of the case. And we apologized to Comrade Smirnov. We wrongfully arrested him (and I have to say it, so that the delegates know about this) because the whole investigation had an accusatory bias, if you like, the evidence was forced. That is the crux of the matter, that is where the differences of opinion are. I know the whole country and people beyond the bounds of our country are listening to us. Some people even said to me: Is there any need to raise these questions at the congress, could we perhaps go into it all calmly afterwards? Comrades, if I see that a man has been wrongfully arrested, if a tragic mistake has been made, then as a Communist and as a prosecutor I cannot allow an innocent man to remain in prison for a single hour. I hope that the commission that is to work on this matter will be convinced of that.

About Comrade Ligachev. You know, when two of our investigators for important cases under the USSR general prosecutor started saying openly in the mass media and before large audiences in Leningrad that certain persons from the country's highest political leadership figure in the case and then started naming names, you know, all of us who were involved, so to speak, in this case were simply perplexed. At first we did not understand what was going on. How could anyone who is not merely a lawyer, you understand, but a lawyer of such high qualifications ignore the presumption of innocence, when in fact certain things were indeed being hinted against people, and immediately unleash such things on public opinion?

I can state quite clearly that there were and are no legal grounds for such conclusions, and still less, you understand, for such public statements. And both Comrade Gdlyan and Comrade Ivanov know that very well. I think the comrades who are to be involved in the investigation, I mean the commission created by the congress, will also become convinced of this. I spoke about a case being brought against Smirnov. With regard to the commissions. Including, that is, the Central Committee commission, the Party Control Committee commission, the CPSU Central Committee Politburo commission, as was said here, and also the Supreme Soviet Presidium commission.

Comrades! What is this all about? I have only been general prosecutor for a year. Before that, I was first deputy for 3 months. You understand, I also had faith, with all my heart (I tell you this sincerely), and I still have faith. Because the so-called "Uzbek" case—I apologize to the Uzbek comrades—rather, the case of bribery in Uzbekistan involved a real interweaving of a great truth, the truth about the mafia, which exists, the truth about bribery, and a lie. You understand, a dangerous lie, as is now clear, unfortunately. Yes, a dangerous lie. Therefore when complaints began to reach the party Central Committee, and they began earlier—I said yesterday that back in 1986, in February, the prosecutor's office collegium discussed the impermissible methods used by Comrades Gdlyan and Ivanov. Yes, they were reprimanded then. This was not simply a complaint from an outsider or an injured party. No. It was the report of a supervising prosecutor, or rather, the prosecutor who was acting for the prosecution in court. But unfortunately, after these reprimands, legality was forgotten and the matter was not properly handled. Perhaps we could have saved the prosecutor's office, let me be frank, from the discomfort, to put it mildly, that it has suffered, and perhaps Comrades Gdlyan and Ivanov, too. Do you understand? That is why I am having to speak about it now. But this did not happen, although there were complaints. And they increased. There were more and more of them. So what should the party Central Committee and the Supreme Soviet Presidium have done? What should they have done with all these letters, complaints, and so forth?

Comrades, you know, yesterday I was informed that out of the nine charges in the Gaipov case, the Uzbekistan Supreme Court retained only one, and that one is dubious, and it has submitted a partial ruling to the general prosecutor. So now, comrades, the court has established and reported to the general prosecutor violations of the rule of law by Gdlyan and Ivanov. I have to respond—this is the reality.

I will tell you another thing. When we were preparing the Churbanov case, there was a hitch—the gray-haired lawyer who was prosecuting for the state (many of us saw him on television) came up to me and said: "Comrade General Prosecutor, I cannot go on with these charges, because there is much that is contrived, much that is not backed up by evidence." But all the same, he went along with it. And do you know what happened? One of the defendants was acquitted in the end. With regard to

STENOGRAPHIC RECORD

Twelfth Session

8 June 1989

another defendant, Yakhyayev, the case was singled out as a separate case. Why did they do this? Because, to be frank, our investigators acted unlawfully when they saved up, so to speak, in reserve, the Yakhyayev case, concerning his moral and ethical qualities and violations of the rule of law while he was Uzbek minister of internal affairs. And of course, the Supreme Court (as general prosecutor I have to acknowledge this) acted correctly. You cannot do things like that, that is the point, and we have to reckon with it. Legality is paramount, if we really want to create a rule-of-law state, however hard we may find it. I realize that this concerns the department, its prestige and authority. I understand all that, but we cannot postpone these questions "to a later date." We must resolve them immediately, once complaints come in. We are in favor of the fight against crime, but with clean hands and a clear conscience—that is the point. (Applause).

Comrades, I realize I am taking up too much of your time. Reproaches have been made here against the general prosecutor and the KGB. Absolutely unsubstantiated reproaches. What are we talking about, comrades? The name of investigator Dukhanin was mentioned. Who is Dukhanin? An investigator, a highly skilled investigator of the USSR KGB. Combined teams have long been the practice in the work of the USSR Prosecutor's Office, the USSR MVD, and the USSR KGB when it is a question of major crimes. And that is how we acted in this case. After all, you know that this case—it was reported in the press—began originally in 1983, when KGB workers and their investigators had already restored R10 million of stolen money to the state. Only later did the case come over to the prosecutor's office. Throughout the investigation team's work, the KGB helped us operationally. The question has now been raised, when did Dukhanin join the investigation team? He is not the only one, 12 of their investigators joined. They joined, comrades, because the case had been in progress for 6 years. World experience knows no other example of a crime investigation dragging on for 6 years. People were in prison, under guard, for 3 years (and in some cases more).

Therefore we could not go on allowing the case to drag on endlessly. We decided to work on it together. Comrade Dukhanin was one of those who worked on the case with regard to Usmankhodzhayev, Smirnov, Radzhabov, Dzhabbarov, and Salimov. As I said, we had 12 of these investigators from the KGB. There were approximately the same number of investigators from the Military Prosecutor's Office and the USSR Prosecutor's Office. Comrade Smirnov was in the KGB special prison, we had many people there under investigation. Very many, unfortunately, both there and in the USSR MVD fourth special prison. The question was one of interrogating the witnesses who are under guard and have given incriminating evidence against Smirnov, because from the very first Smirnov, while admitting various kinds of moral and ethical violations that he committed, has categorically denied bribe-taking or any involvement in it. They started interrogating the witnesses, because many things did not add up, there was much that was, you see, strange and erroneous, that much was obvious. Who came to that conclusion? It was not Cormade Dukhanin. It was the supervisory prosecutors who came to that conclusion, as they did, unfortunately, with regard to other defendants, too. They are a group of 12 people which I, as general prosecutor, set up back in December. And Comrades Gdlyan and Ivanov know very well what became of the charges when these independent prosecutors had a look to see what kind of evidence they had been given. Is there, as we say, a case to answer? That is the question. And when they began to look with, so to speak, the supervisory eye at all these matters, and when Comrade Dukhanin started to check the validity and strength of this evidence, it turned out that not only was there no evidence, but people even started to say: We were forced to incriminate ourselves, and forced to incriminate Comrade Smirnov, too. Forgive me, but this happened because of pressure, blackmail. Things must be called by their names. And I have already told you the outcome. Comrade Dukhanin honorably fulfilled his duty, and you will find that out for yourselves if you set up a commission to investigate.

You will excuse me, comrades, I may have forgotten something, I may have omitted to answer some of the questions, but I think I have said what is most important. That is the main thing. We must have the rule of law, the rule of law must triumph. (Applause).

You will excuse me, I have one more thing to say. Last year—in only 1 year (of course, it is not only a matter of Comrades Gdlyan and Ivanov, that is not the main point)—we were forced to release 2,182 people either from special prisons or from the courtroom, because these people had been wrongfully arrested, because they had been wrongfully repressed. That is a disgrace! In all, 6,500 of these people have suffered. I am only talking about the people who were, so to speak, under guard. This is a matter of principle. (Applause).

M.S. Gorbachev: Your question, please.

A.A. Yaroshinskaya, correspondent of the industry and capital construction department of the newspaper RADYANSKA ZHITOMIRSHCHINA (Zhitomirskiy Territorial Electoral Okrug, Ukrainian SSR): Esteemed Aleksandr Yakovlevich! This is my question. It is taken from letters from my voters, addressed to you personally and carrying thousands of signatures. You obviously know about the gross violations of the Law on Elections that occurred in Zhitomir City. Some 6 weeks ago I personally sent you a letter, as a deputy, to say that events in Zhitomir are gathering pace. Obviously you must know, if you read my letter, that in Zhitomir, after 26 March, 48 administrative cases were brought against my agents and the activists who helped me with the nomination and campaigning, others were expelled from the party, and 3 servicemen—2 lieutenant colonels and a colonel—ended up in hospital. Despite the fact that 6

Twelfth Session

8 June 1989

weeks have passed since I wrote to you, I have received no reply. From love of commissions, obviously, from our universal love of commissions, a commission came to our city of Zhitomir—four prosecutors. When I joyfully told my friends this, they retorted that four prosecutors could not come to Zhitomir and defend the truth just like that. I protested that they had come to defend the truth. You know, the four prosecutors were working in our city for nearly a week, if you multiply it out, that comes to nearly a month of work. I think a month was long enough to check and recheck several times the facts that were set forth in my voters' letter. But I repeat, more time passed, Zhitomir is in turmoil, people are indignant at the lawlessness, and we have received no clear reply from the USSR Prosecutor's Office. I would like to repeat our question today, and to receive a clear answer. Both I and my voters want to know when the lawlessness will end in Zhitomir, and if the prosecutor's office does not reply, who else should we turn to? Thank you. (Applause).

A.Ya. Sukharev: Tell me, please, if you can, when was your question submitted?

A.A. Yaroshinskaya: I sent my question via Comrade Nazemtsev, who came to Zhitomir. That was 6 weeks ago. There is a copy of the question in LITERATURNAYA GAZETA.

A.Ya. Sukharev: First, I wish to apologize on behalf of the prosecutor's office and my subordinates, and doubtless I myself am to blame here. But I want to tell you that we are currently receiving 2,000-2,500 letters a day (I am not complaining, as general prosecutor I am supposed to impose order). I understand what a deputy's question is, and once again I ask your forgiveness, I will look into it and give you a reply. But at the moment I am not able to answer this question.

A.A. Yaroshinskaya: Thank you, we will be waiting eagerly.

Yu.N. Afanasyev, rector of Moscow State Historical Archives Institute (Noginskiy Territorial Electoral Okrug, Moscow Oblast, RSFSR): Aleksandr Yakovlevich! More than a month ago a group of people's deputies, about 40 of them, submitted a question to you and a proposal on amending the preventive restrictions on the members of the "Karabakh" Committee. You met with this group just before your appointment to the post of general prosecutor. Until now, for more than a month, you have not favored us with any sign of attention. So we are addressing this question to you. We realize, of course, that some questions are difficult, even for the general prosecutor. But nonetheless, what do you have to say about these preventive restrictions on the members of the "Karabakh" Committee? That is the first thing. And, second, how would you react to the ethical problem: 40 deputies ask you a question, and you keep silent for more than a month? That is one question. A second question, on the case of Surgutskiy—former director of the "Tuchkovskiy" state farm [sovkhoz].

Proceedings were taken against him on unsubstantiated charges, and he was in the special prison for about 2 years, and then was entirely vindicated on the grounds of the absence of elements of a crime. He was also expelled from the party, but was subsequently reinstated in the party and reinstated in his job by a court decision. However, that court decision has not yet been implemented, after many months. He has sent letters and telegrams to you. And for many months you have not favored him with any reply. What do you have to say about the fact of the nonimplementation of the court decision, and also on the question of this ethical side of the matter? Why do you not answer Surgutskiy?

A.Ya. Sukharev: I understand your questions. I wish to answer you, Comrade Afanasyev, Deputy Afanasyev, as follows. When you sent a telegram to the USSR Prosecutor's Office on the subject of the "Karabakh" Committee, I did not learn of your message, unfortunately, until 8 days later. You were contacted and a discussion took place, as was reported to me. I believe you, of course, but I also place reliance on the reports of my comrades, my deputies and assistants, who handled this case. You said that you were about to leave for Leningrad and would entrust the matter to your agent, who works with you. His name was mentioned. The comrades telephoned twice more to say that your question was now being studied by the general prosecutor personally. Incidentally, I telephoned you, too. But at the time, I was told, you were on a foreign trip.

The question itself has been resolved. The preventive restrictions on the members of the "Karabakh" Committee against whom a criminal case was brought have been amended. The comrades are now in Armenia. You know that. I have nothing more to add here. I agree with you that it is better if the general prosecutor responds to such complaints, however busy, so to speak, he may be. But I will be frank with you, the volume of work is colossal. And all the same, I must think about how I should respond in such situations now, when we are discussing deputies' questions.

For instance, I have already received 500 questions from deputies here. Well, what of it? That is what the general prosecutor is for, people say, so that every day he has the opportunity to answer all questions in full. I am considering this matter and I ask your forgiveness, Comrade Afanasyev.

And as for the case concerning the director of the "Tuchkovskiy" sovkhoz, my position here is unequivocal: If there is a court decision, it should be implemented. That is the law. That is my position. I simply cannot tell you why it has not yet been fulfilled. I must investigate to see what the problem is here.

A.B. Demin, captain, troop unit deputy company commander for political affairs, Siberian Military District, Kochenevo Urban Settlement (Barabinskiy Territorial Electoral Okrug): Aleksandr Yakovlevich, I also want to

Twelfth Session

8 June 1989

ask you a question. A voter of mine who was the victim of an attack in 1985 has appealed to me. He is a militia worker. The attack was carried out by militia workers—his bosses. And from that day to this he has wanted the culprits to be punished. But wherever he turns—the MVD, the USSR Prosecutor's Office, the RSFSR Prosecutor's Office—no measures have been adopted. These people who committed the attack on him were dismissed from the militia organs. But recently they have been reinstated, and he has begun to receive various threatening notes.

The man is under protection. A militiaman, his cousin, is protecting him. Therefore I would like to ask: Why have you not replied to my deputy's question, which I submitted to the congress secretariat? And why have no measures been taken all this time on this case?

A.Ya. Sukharev: Comrades, I can....

A.B. Demin: I wanted to add something. An investigator came, he was there for 3 days, he said: No one is to blame. You are not Bukharin, he said, that you should be investigated, and he went away. That is it—that is all that was done.

A.Ya. Sukharev: I did not catch that, forgive me, could you say it again?

A.B. Demin: I want to know, why were no measures adopted all that time?

A.Ya. Sukharev: Fine. Comrades, in order to reply to the deputy, and these are often quite complicated cases—both criminal and civil cases— in substance and not merely formally, or at least to indicate the thrust, so to speak, of what has been done in connection with the complaint, I need time. You may resent this, you may demand more organization and discipline on my part. But I will tell you frankly: I cannot do this in 3 days. It would be frankly blasphemous, do you understand? I think, if I am not mistaken, you have already asked me about this, and I told you what I know, that an investigation into instances of red tape is now taking place on this question. And I said that we will certainly adopt measures if we find red tape, if we find a culprit we will certainly punish people. You will receive a reply.

A.B. Demin: Thank you, I hope he will be released from his fear.

(Disturbance in the auditorium).

M.S. Gorbachev: Comrades, one moment. I hear people wanting to stop the questions. But please take note of the fact that there are six comrades at one microphone, and four more over here. In all there are 11, no, 12. There are 12 people wanting to ask questions, so you must take a decision in the light of this.... Now there are 13. What shall we do, shall we continue the questions?... Fine. One moment, you are asked to allow Deputy Sakharov to ask a question. Voices from the floor: Let him.

M.S. Gorbachev: So shall we give Academician Sakharov the floor, and then stop?

Voices from the floor: Yes.

M.S. Gorbachev: Those in favor of this proposal, please vote. Please lower your cards. Against? A lot, comrades, a lot.... Comrades, I must bring this information to your notice. I see that approximately—something in the region of—nearly 40 percent are opposed to limiting the discussion. In this situation I would continue the questions.

Voices from the floor: Yes.

M.S. Gorbachev: I simply think that would be the right thing to do. (Applause). And let us not be in a hurry here, comrades. Please be patient. Go ahead.

A.D. Sakharov, academician, chief scientific staffer of the P.N. Lebedev Physics Institute of the USSR Academy of Sciences, Moscow City (from the USSR Academy of Sciences): My first question is this. For a long time the idea has been expressed in the press and in public circles that the prosecutor's office should not conduct investigations at all, that the sole task of the prosecutor's office is to monitor compliance with the law. And that in cases where investigations are carried out by the prosecutor's office, this task cannot be effectively carried out with regard to the way in which investigations are carried out. That is my first question.

Second question. What is your personal view of the idea that an attorney should without fail be involved in the investigation from the moment that charges are brought?

Third question. What is your view of the idea that an extension of the period spent in detention during investigations should be permitted only in absolutely exceptional cases, which require the very highest sanction and the most overriding arguments? That is one group of questions.

Second group of questions. For many years I have been receiving a great many letters from people who, in their view, were unjustly convicted. These people sent me documents concerning matters on which they have appealed to the prosecutor's office, attaching detailed arguments from attorneys' statements and their own explanations as to why they were wrongfully convicted. And the replies from the prosecutor's office were also attached. They always went like this: "There are no grounds for a review of the case." No arguments to support this were cited, and we know from the press that in a number of cases these replies were written purely automatically. My question to Comrade Sukharev: What is his view of this practice, and will order be achieved in the work of the prosecutor's office so that all replies to

Twelfth Session
8 June 1989

complaints are not merely formal, but really carefully argued? As for my personal experience, I wrote a supervisory complaint to the prosecutor's office on the conviction of my wife and I received precisely the same reply, in the same form.

Next question. What is Comrade Sukharev's view of his close colleagues, prosecutors Katusev and Galkin? The point is that I have important information that a public statement by Katusev was one of the triggers leading to the Sumgait tragedy, while Galkin virtually folded up the investigation and the entire conduct of this case. Is that so? Perhaps my information is incorrect, but I would like an answer to this question.

Finally, my last question: What is Comrade Sukharev's view on the article—it was an interview, apparently—that he gave in 1975, on the subject of the case of Sergey Kovalev?

A.Ya. Sukharev: Thank you, Comrade Sakharov. First question: What is my view on the status of the investigative apparatus within the framework of the prosecutor's office? My view is negative. I think the investigative apparatus should be autonomous, and the job of the prosecutor's office, as Lenin conceived of it, is to exercise prosecutor's supervision, and not only in legal proceedings on criminal and civil cases, but, as I have already said, on the entire range of social relations that are regulated by the law. That is a colossal task. (Applause).

My attitude to the attorneys' service and their involvement at the stage of investigation: This is not only necessary, it is absolutely essential. If this had been done consistently, perhaps today we would not be talking about the things that we are talking about with great regret.

The third question. On extending the period of detention only in exceptional cases. I entirely agree with Comrade Sakharov. This is the only way, the only way. I think it is possible for us, if we are really creating a rule-of-law state, to work in this way. So that this is indeed the exception, rather than the rule, as it has become in a number of components of the prosecutor's office investigative apparatus, and MVD workers, too.

About letters from those unjustly convicted, and replies lacking substantiation. I think you are right here, Comrade Sakharov. There are very many such letters. Even now there are very many. I myself, when these letters reach me, try to provide the arguments, and I demand the same of my subordinates. But it is a colossal task, and there is a great deal of formalism and, I would say, callousness, although, of course, the climate is changing for the better in this respect, and so is the work.

Next question. My view on Cornrade Katusev and Comrade Galkin, especially as regards Comrade Katusev's statement on the Sumgait events. I would simply like to ask you, Comrade Sakharov, to understand my position correctly. I think there is an element of misunderstanding here. Of course, the events were fairly complex, in many ways unexpected, and people were demanding interviews and immediate glasnost. I suppose Comrade Katusev may, so to speak, have made a bit of a blunder or been inaccurate in his expressions, but to say that this was what sparked off the turn of events in this tragic way is, of course, wrong.

Voices from the floor: (Inaudible).

A.Ya. Sukharev: Absolutely right. And as for Comrade Galkin, I simply urge you to understand. I believe that Comrade Galkin has done everything necessary, that in less than a year he and his group have investigated all the Sumgait cases and all these cases have been passed on to the court. And many of them have already been tried. This is the same Comrade Galkin who is now the leader of the group investigating the Uzbek cases and I must tell you, comrades, about the Galkin who is engaged in such complex work, because not a single line has yet been written about him. That is to add to the portrait of Comrade Galkin. Further, I accept and do not rule out that in 1975, in giving an interview, I may have given the relevant assessment. Comrade Sakharov, I want you to understand my credo, my attitude toward cases of so-called "anti-Soviet agitation and propaganda" under the well known article 190/1. This attitude has long been known. Many lawyers present here know it. It is a principled attitude, we must review a lot in these questions, and I was one of the authors of their solution on democratic lines. I think that is right.

A.N. Boyko, department chief at Donetsk State University, Donetsk City (Donetskiy-Voroshilovskiy territorial electoral okrug, Donetsk Oblast): Esteemed Aleksandr Yakovlevich, yesterday and today you spoke of how the prosecutor's office and investigation should act with clean hands. That is pleasant to hear. But many voters are coming with complaints that their appeals go through the USSR Prosecutor's office twice, three times, or more, to the people against whom they are complaining and your department is not interested in whether they were acted against with clean or dirty hands. The question is as follows. What do you intend to do to eliminate this violation of the well-known USSR Supreme Soviet Decree? That is the first question. Second question. It is well known that in the quite recent past many people found themselves in psychiatric institutions for political reasons. But it emerges from 31 May LITERATURNAYA GAZETA items that the practice of involving psychiatrists in investigations is continuing and there is a question here for you. I shall go on to quote how these people were acted against dishonestly and with dirty hands. I quote: "Society is to blame with regard to these people and must redeem all its guilty, I am sure of it. I think that without waiting for any requests or petitions from the victims we must review absolutely all political cases of those years and with them the psychiatric diagnoses of all 'socially dangerous individuals' as well."

STENOGRAPHIC RECORD

Twelfth Session
8 June 1989

The question is as follows. What is your opinion, will you review these cases, since many people are turning to me and are, naturally, seeking truth and justice in this matter.

A.Y. Sukharev: I understand. I shall answer the first question, about complaints. This practice is continuing, I have already mentioned it. There are cases when complaints eventually find their way to be resolved to the very people against whom the complaints are leveled. That practice does exist. What is the way out? Despite the organizational measures to enhance responsibility, and that is being done now, I can see that this is of little benefit. I have already spoken on this subject. We need a new, renewed law, with a consideration for democratization, so that everyone in our country can indeed work to satisfy complaints, to satisfy complaints at the initial stage, when they are merely appearing, and then I think we will have order. We should have a good normative base so that even if someone initially wanted to avoid resolving a complaint, it would be difficult to do so. Yet this is being done without ceremony right now. Here is the point: A new law is needed. I am sure of it.

With regard to the LITERATURNAYA GAZETA article and to this entire problem as a whole, although in my view Academician Kudryavtsev has already spoken about it. We have a new normative base which makes it possible to monitor more stringently the facts which actually took place. Now we have created a special team as a result of these new alerts to check everything in the press and what complaints there are on this score. Our position is that in these matters there should not only be no violations but not even any doubts on this score. Today the line in the state and in law enforcement practice is very firm and precise.

M.S. Gorbachev: Please go ahead.

From the floor: I have the following question. In 1962-1970 you worked in the CPSU Central Committee Administrative Organs Department and at that time many of us appealed to that department about the exile of the great poet and now Nobel Prize winner Iosif Brodskiy. I would like to know your attitude toward the matter. At that time, in 1968, when you were chief of the sector for the prosecutor's office, court, and justice organs in the CPSU Central Committee, there was a trial of five participants in a demonstration connected with the invasion of Czechoslovakia. I would like to know your attitude toward that and also toward the toughening of the regimes in the camps which took place in those years when the supply of food to concentration camp stores in fact became the same or even worse than in Stalin's time. I would like to know all this because at the time, obviously with the aid of the administrative organs, an attempt was made to turn back the thaw and the positive phenomena of the "Prague spring" and to end it. Do you assess this negatively now and what is your position on these questions now?

A.Ya. Sukharev: Yes, of course. With regard to my work in the CPSU Central Committee Administrative Organs Department in the seventies. Yes, I was indeed deputy chief of the administrative organs department and later, in the years of which you speak, I became chief of a sector of that department and was concerned with the justice organs. We had a sector for questions of the Internal Affairs Ministry, and I mean by that that I had access to the solution of questions which were assigned to me on the basis of my department. Now, as for the poet Brodskiy. I had nothing to do with those questions. I shall say frankly that I had no access to that case. I have already formulated my attitude now absolutely precisely. Much of what happened in our country was wrong and deformed, not only did we lack the proper legal base, but we had very serious misinterpretations and distortions. I have already spoken about this. About Czechoslovakia. I was not in Czechoslovakia, I was not sent there. I visited Czechoslovakia later, as a member of a delegation in connection with my legal work. That is all I can say about that.

People's deputy (no name given): I ask you to touch on the trial of the five people who protested on this score. They were tried in Moscow. In particular Larisa Bogoraz and....

A.Ya. Sukharev: You want to know my attitude? Now? But I have already stated my attitude. Today I would approach these questions in an absolutely different way from what what was the case on that occasion. But, I repeat, I had nothing to do with that trial.

M.S. Gorbachev: Please, your question.

People's deputy (no name given): Please tell us, you are president of the Association of Jurists of the Soviet Union. That post obliges you to spend a long time abroad. It follows from your answers to questions that very many questions have accumulated in the country which must be resolved today. Next, why, although you live in Moscow and are in this auditorium today as a USSR people's deputy, are you sitting among the delegation from the Checheno-Ingush Autonomous Soviet Socialist Republic [ASSR]? A question in this connection: Why did you run as a USSR people's deputy for the Checheno-Ingush ASSR?

A.Ya. Sukharev: You know, I am and remain for the time being president of the Association of Jurists of the USSR. Soon we will have a jurists' union and in the near future there will be an all-union constituent conference. I head the Association of Soviet Jurists. But I do not think that the president of the Association of Soviet Jurists should spend a long time abroad. I have been abroad and established contacts on various questions, especially with regard to the struggle for peace, the humanization of our domestic policy, and the consolidation of cooperation. I shall say frankly that we have done a lot through the channels of the Association of Soviet Jurists. But I do not think that its future president

Twelfth Session

8 June 1989

should mainly devote his activity to foreign ties. We have very many domestic problems. We must engage primarily in legal culture and many other matters.

With regard to my position as a deputy. I am not a deputy from the Checheno-Ingush ASSR. I have the seventh national-territorial okrug, which unites the Checheno-Ingush ASSR, the Dagestan ASSR, and Astrakhan Oblast, where an enormous population mass lives. I was elected there and I am standing here and sitting among among this group of deputies because the okrug itself and that okrug's headquarters were and are in Groznyy City. I am sitting with the entire delegation. Thank you.

M.S. Gorbachev: Questions, please. Shall we stop?

Voice from the floor: Yes.

Voices from the floor: No, no, it's still quite early.

M.S. Gorbachev: Good. I was in favor of stopping, comrades, but I can see that the deputies feel otherwise. Comrade Sukharev, please sit down. Good, I think that in this case we must give the floor to Comrade Gdlyan.

T.Kh. Gdlyan, senior investigator for particularly important cases at the USSR General Prosecutor's Office, Moscow City (Tushinskiy Territorial Electoral Okrug, Moscow City): Miracles are taking place, comrades. We are working closely here with the general prosecutor.

M.S. Gorbachev: Comrade Gdlyan, you have 5 minutes. Is that alright?

T.Kh. Gdlyan: Why 5 minutes?

M.S. Gorbachev: In accordance with the standing order.

T.Kh. Gdlyan: These are complex questions and they should be heard by the deputies and the eminent congress. It is to elect the country's general prosecutor. A complex question. A quite controversial figure, to put it mildly, and naturally the deputies want to know who to vote for, what [as published] to abstain from and who to vote against. How can all this be done in 5 minutes? And in general, we are in a very great haste, Mikhail Sergeyevich.

M.S. Gorbachev: Please begin, Comrade Gdlyan.

T.Kh. Gdlyan: Comrades, this is what is at issue. I would like to put a question to Aleksandr Yakovlevich Sukharev, the aspirant for the post of USSR general prosecutor. Aleksandr Yakovlevich, you still have not answered the question of whether or not party organs, including the CPSU Central Committee, and the USSR Supreme Soviet Presidium intervened.

A.Ya. Sukharev: I reply that during my work as USSR general prosecutor and when I was first deputy general prosecutor for 3 months there were no such cases (Comrade Rekunkov, the former USSR general prosecutor, told me this). I declare this with total responsibility, and this can be established from documents.

T.Kh. Gdlyan: I must responsibly expose the USSR general prosecutor in the presence of everyone.

M.S. Gorbachev: Wait, you are to ask questions.

T.Kh. Gdlyan: One moment, why questions?

M.S. Gorbachev: You will make a statement later.

T.Kh. Gdlyan: Today?

M.S. Gorbachev: Yes, today. Now ask your questions.

T.Kh. Gdlyan: Right. Because they are fundamental questions. Understand, comrades, we are in a hurry, we.... But....

M.S. Gorbachev: Ask questions.

T.Kh. Gdlyan: Tell me, Aleksandr Yakovlevich, why did you yourself participate together with your subordinates in causing the collapse of the case that you and other comrades quite unjustly call for some reason "Uzbek," although there is no "Uzbek case?" Remember, general prosecutor, it is, rather, a "Moscow, Kremlin case, not an Uzbek" one.

M.S. Gorbachev: Comrade Gdlyan, listen....

T.Kh. Gdlyan: Please.

A.Ya. Sukharev: Well, comrades, what I think, some things I already....

M.S. Gorbachev: Comrade Gdlyan, formulate your questions, and the general prosecutor will answer them.

T.Kh. Gdlyan: I have said that.

M.S. Gorbachev: Ask all your questions.

T.Kh. Gdlyan: Together with his subordinates and workers, certain workers of the USSR KGB, he participated, as USSR general prosecutor, in causing the case to collapse, committing unlawful actions in respect of what he called the "Uzbek" case, although I have said what kind of case it is. This is a specific question.

M.S. Gorbachev: Have you any other questions?

Voices from the floor: Yes, ask questions!...

STENOGRAPHIC RECORD

Twelfth Session

8 June 1989

T.Kh. Gdlyan: We will not get to the bottom of it like this, comrades. You understand how it is. One asks—another answers.

(Noise in the hall).

M.S. Gorbachev: Comrade Gdlyan, this is not a television debate. You ask as many questions as you have, and we will listen to the answers.

T.Kh. Gdlyan: Good. Tell me with what the dismissal of Gdlyan and Ivanov from the leadership of the USSR Prosecutor's Office investigative group was connected. Were there, to put it more accurately, legitimate grounds for this, or were you carrying out someone's instructions, someone's social imperative? I mean in this case the party organs in the form of the CPSU Central Committee. Precisely those circles, I emphasize, so that there is no demagoguery here, those circles that are not interested in further investigating this now generally tragicomic affair.

Fourth. If you beat your breast with regard to your principledness, stating that you declared war on mafioso groups and you will see all this through to the end—in particular, the case that we were investigating—then say why approximately 70 investigators, the very best investigators of this investigative group, people who spent years going through this school and who knew everything, were sent packing by your orders. Professional specialists will understand what it means to change horses half-way into a crossing, so to speak. Why did you do this, and will new people ever understand, particularly when, as you put it, people sit for many years in custody? We, too, are against people sitting in custody for many years. This is my question, please.

M.S. Gorbachev: Do you have any other questions, Comrade Gdlyan?

T.Kh. Gdlyan: Yes.

M.S. Gorbachev: Go ahead.

T.Kh. Gdlyan: He still has not answered the questions. (Noise in the hall). Wait, it is necessary to answer when questions are asked. When he gave an answer at the 19th party conference as general prosecutor, he misled the entire party forum. He said that criminal proceedings were not instituted, and so no investigation was conducted. This is a question of principle, comrades. Why? Because it just will not do when the general prosecutor lies. And we will prove this, because there are jurists here who will give a conclusion. One moment. They will give a conclusion on whether or not criminal proceedings must be instituted. And now, in order to confirm this, I will tell you....

M.S. Gorbachev: Ask questions, Comrade Gdlyan. Have you asked them all?

T.Kh. Gdlyan: No, not all.

M.S. Gorbachev: Well, ask them, ask all the questions.

T.Kh. Gdlyan: When will I make a statement? Today?

M.S. Gorbachev: Today, today.

T.Kh. Gdlyan: One moment, comrades. Tell me, Aleksandr Yakovlevich, why did you go out of work time, so to speak, behind the back of the investigative group, to Usmankhodzhayev, former first secretary of the Uzbek Communist Party Central Committee, in the investigation prison and together with Vasilyev, your deputy, persuade him to renounce his incriminating testimony against Moscow bribetakers, above all party bribetakers, that is, bribetakers in the CPSU Central Committee? Why did you need to do this? And after you reflected this in the minutes of the interrogation, your deputy spent another 4 days going to the investigation prison on your orders and extorting from the former first secretary of the Uzbek Central Committee a statement written in his own hand that he renounced that testimony. Why did you need to do this, and whose orders were you carrying out? Moreover....

M.S. Gorbachev: Please put questions.

T.Kh. Gdlyan: The sixth question. When you were convinced that it was awkward for the general prosecutor and his deputy to go and extort testimonies, that is, to demand that the accused people renounce the testimonies, then you and Vasilyev, your deputy, instructed Prosecutor Titov and KGB Investigator Dukhanin to move the accused from the No 4 investigation prison of the USSR Ministry of Internal Affairs to a USSR KGB investigation prison in order there, by using the most unlawful methods (noise in the hall)—one moment—by using the most unlawful methods, to try to secure a renunciation of incriminating testimonies once again and above all in respect of Moscow bribetakers. Why did you do that?

Further. When the case collapsed in such an unlawful manner in front of everyone's eyes, we were taken off the investigation. At that time, when agents were messing up the criminal case behind our backs, we repeatedly came to you and raised the question—not only we but also the entire investigative group, in which there were approximately 60 investigators from all ends of the country, as well as militia and prosecutor's office workers—asked and demanded that this lawlessness be ended. You took no measures. Why?

Voices from the floor: That's enough.

A.Ya. Sukharev: Good, thank you. I believe, comrades, that I have already answered in part, and I want to say it once again. We can argue endlessly over whether or not there was intervention. I urge you to turn to the documents. I say once again that there was no intervention by

FIRST CONGRESS OF PEOPLE'S DEPUTIES OF THE USSR

Twelfth Session

8 June 1989

the Central Committee or the Supreme Soviet Presidium. I even think that if the Supreme Soviet Presidium had intervened, it would have been intervention in a good sense, because we are, after all, an accountable organ. If there had been alerts, it would have been necessary to react sooner. I blame myself, too, because I am the general prosecutor. I must answer for legality. Perhaps there was no need to speak of many things today, I will say frankly. There was no intervention. The commission will report everything to you documentarily. This is the answer to the first question.

Now with regard to the collapse of the case. You see, when a charge is worded in such a general form, if I may put it this way, then it is, of course, very complex to reply. Do you understand? With what was the dismissal of Comrade Gdlyan and Ivanov from work precisely on the investigation into the case of bribes in Uzbekistan linked? I took that step with the greatest of difficulty.

I realized what the response might be. I realized all this perfectly, but my colleagues—members of the collegium, members of the party committee—said to me: Comrade Sukharev, you are the general prosecutor, why do you not take measures? Because these workers in the investigative section—this applies not just to Comrades Gdlyan and Ivanov, for there were other investigators there, who will be mentioned—are completely evading prosecutor's office supervision. That very group of supervising prosecutors, which was set up for the first time last December, established that it was not just a question of innocent people sitting there. It was established there that the charges had been preprogramed, to put it crudely, and a very great deal was adjusted to fit that.

And then comrades' eyes began to open. They said: Listen, how is it possible to work like this? But what happened then? When alarm signals came in and it was necessary to set these alarm signals in legal motion and check them, Comrades Gdlyan and Ivanov demonstratively said: No commissions, no checks. Fine, no commissions. But there is the general prosecutor, give him an opportunity to check. Complaints may be addressed to me, but under the constitution I am responsible for my subordinates. No, they closed the safe, closed the files, closed the complaints—the very ones that we must check. They closed the documentation connected with all kinds of valuables. That is all, there are none.

What is more, reports from my deputies, from leaders of other subdivisions began to reach me. What is being done in the prosecutor's office? Whoever you say this to, they will not believe this. Therefore we had difficulty and pain in our soul, because we knew how this might affect the Uzbek case.... I beg your forgiveness for such an expression; once again excuse me. But this really was so. And only after this did we invite Comrade Gdlyan to the collegium and say—let us conduct a professional conversation. Perhaps you are right in some way that you are, in fact, nervous and afraid. "No, we will go to the people." But, comrades, are such questions of justice really decided by the crowd? You will excuse me, I greatly respect the voters, I understand their feelings now, I very much understand these feelings. But, as general prosecutor, when it is a question of the great social truth, I cannot defer these questions from today until tomorrow. If that's the way you want it, let me go, I will never agree to such a thing. This is the question. It was for these reasons that they were dismissed. (Applause).

Now with regard to the 65 investigators. Comrades, this is not a discussion for the unenlightened. There are 209 people in this investigative group, a giant, huge group. Of course, I realize how all this was presented and, probably, to begin with maybe, all this was necessary and essential. But why, one wonders, keep such a number of people for many years? Not just anyone but precisely a supervising prosecutor who was in the investigative group—Comrade Popova, she is probably listening to me now—came herself some 6 weeks ago; yes, Comrade Popova, whom Comrade Gdlyan trusts fully, wrote a report: Many investigators do not work at all, there is no organization or control, and the group must be reduced by—I do not remember now—30 or 40 people. But when we began really investigating the organization of this work, we arrived at the conclusion that a maximum of 100 people are needed there, particularly at the concluding stage of the work. But they must work, really work, and not like this—work 1 day and rest for 2. We have already seen excesses there, when people sit idle for years.

For many years it was not a permanent staff, as Gdlyan and Ivanov say. No, people changed. I will say frankly that some of these comrades, too, worked for too long, and we dismissed them. I will say frankly that we had very serious complaints against some comrades.

Allow me, Comrade Gdlyan, to answer the next question with regard to the fact that the general prosecutor went to Usmankhodzhayev in prison behind your back, began dissuading him, and so forth. I wish to speak straightaway so as to avoid misunderstandings. If the general prosecutor is trusted, then under the constitution he not only can but is obliged to check everything and must take nothing on trust. It has been like this with us for too long. (Applause). Nothing else is permitted. (Applause).

After you, Comrade Gdlyan, very suspiciously—you will excuse my use of this expression—visited Usmankhodzhayev, I was sent a statement. We had established a special work procedure. Not because these are some special people, no. There was simply no order before. Three people worked with these last five, because they were arrested under me. This is what is at issue. And it turned out that Comrade Gdlyan was there precisely on his day off, on a Sunday. We do not practice such a thing at all. After that move I was sent a statement. What kind of statement, do you think? First. This at once put me on my guard. "I trust Gdlyan alone and I want him to investigate my case, and not the three investigators who were doing so hitherto." A very peculiar coincidence, let us state frankly. It very much put me on my guard. And

STENOGRAPHIC RECORD

Twelfth Session

8 June 1989

second—a whole string of all kinds of names appeared. When I and the deputy general prosecutor, at Usmankhodzhayev's own request, invited him, since he was asking to say something very serious, he said—You know, much of what I wrote did not happen. I said, but you yourself admit that you really engaged in bribes. Yes, he replied, I admit it, but what I wrote did not happen. I said: "All of it?" No, not all of it, but a great deal. As regards certain names. Once the names cropped up in some mysterious circumstances. Then there were none. I met with Usmankhodzhayev at his request only 6 months later. I regret that three statements from him were addressed to me but for some reason reached me only 3 weeks later. And when I met with him again, not only had his position been confirmed but much had been said, too. In the sense that he was not to blame for everything and not as guilty as people tried to portray, I will say frankly—even to compel this person. A very great deal is now coming to light.

Now with regard to Security Committee workers' messing up the case. Comrades! I would not like to repeat yet again what I have already said. They are, believe me, honest, decent, and, I would say, selfless people. We live in different times and will properly assess all organs—both justice and KGB organs. But, believe me, they are working people, they are honest people. And I am not ashamed to speak about these people, to say that they were doing and did do a great thing together with us, under the leadership of the prosecutor's office, under our supervision. (Applause). Need I answer?

From the floor: No.

M.S. Gorbachev: That's all. Good. Thank you.

A.Ya. Sukharev: Then, the comrades who asked me questions please approach, and I will gladly answer them. (Applause).

M.S. Gorbachev: So, comrades? Shall we go on? We can still listen to comments or statements. But, perhaps, this is what we will do. We appointed Comrade Sukharev at the Supreme Soviet. Perhaps we should examine this now?

Our commission has begun working and will check everything, including the actions both of the general prosecutor and of the investigators and the facts relating to how things stand with the involvement of high-ranking persons in bribetaking, that is, it will investigate everything. If the commission's conclusions are such that we must draw the necessary conclusions on the basis of this, including with regard to the general prosecutor, we will draw them. But does the question arise now of casting doubt on the Supreme Soviet decision to appoint the general prosecutor?

From the hall: No.

M.S. Gorbachev: One minute. I told Comrade Gdlyan that in addition to questions, he may take the floor later to make a statement. Well, comrades? Good. Thus, I understand correctly that we are ending the discussion.

The hall: Yes.

M.S. Gorbachev: Whoever is in favor of confining ourselves at this stage to this exchange of opinions that has taken place, please vote. Please lower your identity cards. Against? Please lower. Abstentions?

We are ending. Now the question of appointing Comrade Sukharev to the post of USSR general prosecutor. Will we decide now?

Deputies: Yes.

M.S. Gorbachev: One minute. The question has already been decided. Comrades, I heard everything when you spoke. That was why I asked whether or not we will continue the discussion and speeches. The congress advocated confining ourselves to this. Let us work like this.

Who is in favor of approving the USSR Supreme Soviet's appointment of Comrade Aleksandr Yakovlevich Sukharev as USSR general prosecutor? Please vote. Please lower your identity cards. Who is against? Please count.

(The votes are counted).

M.S. Gorbachev: We will have a short closed session. Therefore I ask the guests and the press, while we vote, to give us an opportunity to hold a brief session. We thank you for participating in the work today. I ask the deputies to remain in the hall.

A.G. Kostenyuk: Comrade deputies, 330 deputies voted against.

M.S. Gorbachev: Who abstained, comrades? Please count. The opinion has arisen in the Presidium.... I am told that in this case it is necessary to count who voted "for." Why? Because the Presidium has formed the opinion that some people are both voting "against" and abstaining. The same people are voting. Yes, yes. Well, this is the opinion of members of the Presidium. Therefore we will count who was in favor of approval.

A.I. Lukyanov: Then we will know.

A.G. Kostenyuk: Precisely 273 deputies abstained.

M.S. Gorbachev: Comrades, please understand me, I must return to the voting. Whoever favors approving Comrade Aleksandr Yakovlevich Sukharev, please vote. Please count.

(The votes are counted).

STENOGRAPHIC RECORD

FIRST CONGRESS OF PEOPLE'S DEPUTIES OF THE USSR
THIRTEENTH SESSION
FRIDAY, 9 JUNE 1989
THE KREMLIN PALACE OF CONGRESSES

Seven commentators concluded the Congress's discussion of the direction of domestic and foreign policy before N. I. Ryzhkov and M. S. Gorbachev reappeared—Ryzhkov to respond to questions about the government's program, Gorbachev to deliver a peroration on perestroika and the significance of the Congress of People's Deputies. Heresies previously propounded in the Kremlin Palace were trifles compared to economist Gavril Popov's declaration that Marxism itself was irrelevant to the solution of modern economic and financial problems and his advice that Soviet economists and leaders would profit more from Keynesian and neo-Keynesian analysis. From V. A. Ostroukhov the Congress heard a rare defense of the cooperative movement. Although Ryzhkov reaffirmed the government's commitment to union republic financial autonomy, the prime minister emphasized the need for continued heavy industrial development, evaded any direct assurance on controversial nuclear and hydroelectric power projects, and generally left environmentalists dissatisfied. To emphasize the country's serious plight, Ryzhkov revealed publicly for the first time that the foreign debt of the USSR then stood at 34 billion rubles.

The General Secretary's sometimes eloquent speech came from his heart as well as his head and revealed the core of the man and his policy. His businesslike review of the achievements and failures of perestroika was attended, perhaps in response to Popov, by his affirmation of the scientific validity of Marxism-Leninism and his confidence in the "boundless possibilities of socialism." To those fearful of his concentration of power, he protested "no other policy than that of restructuring, democratization, and glasnost" which constituted "the meaning of my life and work."

The final segment of the Congress found the deputies wrangling over how to prepare the final report on domestic and foreign policy. The formation of a constitutional drafting commission produced a nasty episode in which Gorbachev rather arbitrarily excluded the liberal A. M. Obolensky while cavalierly admitting others to a body of unspecified size. The General Secretary was able to report a compromise with the Lithuanian and Estonian delegations on the drafting of a law to govern the Constitutional Oversight Committee. "Other Business" produced a flood of disparate proposals until the chair finally called an end and ordered those waiting to speak to submit their proposals in writing to the editing commission. As its last major act the First Congress formally rescinded the controversial Article 11-1 of the Law on Criminal Liability for State Crimes, which made it a crime punishable by fine or imprisonment to insult or defame the Soviet government or its officials publicly. Andrei Sakharov then took the stage for a final ugly scene. Admitted over protests to speak for five minutes, Sakharov attempted to present a draft "decree on power" but exceeded his time limit and had to be driven from the rostrum. Thereupon the Congress heard and approved its "message to the peoples of the world" and concluded its business to the solemn chords of the national anthem.

Texts of documents cited during the Thirteenth Session are compiled in Appendices at the end of this volume: Constitution (Basic Law) of the USSR, Articles 6, 14, 18, 20, 21, 40, 114 (Appendix A.1); Law on Criminal Liability for State Crimes, Article 11-1 (Appendix A.4); Decree on the Duties and Rights of USSR MVD Internal Troops in the Protection of Public Order (Summary) (Appendix A.5); Law on Elections of USSR People's Deputies (Appendix A.2); Draft Law on Status of USSR People's Deputies (Summary) (Appendix A.6).

THIRTEENTH SESSION
FRIDAY, 9 JUNE 1989
STENOGRAPHIC RECORD

Comrade A. I. Lukyanov, first deputy chairman of the USSR Supreme Soviet, presiding.

A.I. Lukyanov: Comrade deputies, let us continue the congress's work. Let us continue discussing questions pertaining to the basic guidelines for the USSR's domestic and foreign policy and the program for the forthcoming activities of the USSR Government.

The floor is granted to Deputy Beyshekeyeva. Comrade Popov, Moscow, will be next.

Z. Beyshekeyeva, senior shepherd at the Dzhety-Oguz Special State Farm, Dzhety-Oguz, Issyk-Kul Oblast, Kirghiz Soviet Socialist Republic [SSR] (from the CPSU): Esteemed chairman, esteemed deputies! Restructuring is the only correct path for the revolutionary renewal of Soviet society. That is why it is supported by the people. Each of us is experiencing the first visible results. Step by step our state's foreign policy is reaching more and more new frontiers. We learned with satisfaction of the results of Comrade Gorbachev's visit to China, with which Kirghiziya has a more than 800-km border.

Noticeable changes that are taking place in the countryside are evident to me, a woman shepherd. Thanks to the introduction of the new economic mechanism, output has shown a tendency to increase. The most important thing is that we are becoming genuine proprietors of the land.

However, it would be wrong to close our eyes to the difficulties and problems that exist. The working and living conditions of livestock workers seriously worry us. This is especially noticeable in sheep raising, the leading branch of our republic's economy. You know how hard the work of a livestock worker, especially a shepherd, is. Almost year-around nomadic life at an altitude of more than 3,000 meters with a drastically continental climate, unsettled conditions, separation from family and cultural life, and work without vacations, days off, or holidays. There is no mechanization. Thanks to our forefathers for inventing pitchforks. They are our chief "mechanization." This negatively affects the prestige of our occupation, and young people are not going to work in sheep raising and animal husbandry.

It would seem that in such a situation we should receive especially sensitive attention, but that is not happening. Industry has not yet organized the production of all-weather mobile shepherd's homes, tents, and high-quality work clothes; the automatic supply of electric power has not been arranged; and the wage coefficients for livestock workers working in high mountain areas have not been revised. Shepherds are demanding that a year's work be counted as 18 months', as it is for border guards. We, who live alongside them, are in worse conditions, yet the benefits are not extended to us. I believe that the pension age should be set at 50 years for us shepherds, too.

These questions pertain equally to all regions of the country where sheep raising is developed. They were repeatedly raised before the former USSR Supreme Soviet and Council of Ministers. But the ministries and departments concerned continue to remain deaf to our justifiable requests and complaints. Therefore, if the country needs wool, these problems, esteemed deputies, esteemed Mikhail Sergeyevich, must be tackled.

I also appeal to you, Mikhail Sergeyevich, because you worked in Stavropol Kray and know what the shepherd's work is like.

Comrades! Kirghiziya is one of the main suppliers of fine wool and mutton in the country. At present more than 63 percent of our total volume of washed wool is shipped out of the republic, some for export. We earn only about R230,000 million from its sale. Calculations show that if it were processed locally the republic could receive a real income of four to five times as much.

A high-quality suit that takes about 1 kg of wool to make now costs around R200, yet we sell 1 kg of wool for R8-10. And if you consider how much prices have been raised for farm machinery, spare parts, feed, building materials, and other manufactured goods, it works out that our collective farms [kolkhozes] and state farms [sovkhozes] and we shepherds are working for practically nothing.

In the course of numerous preelection meetings, my constituents and colleagues gave me a directive—to put before the government the question of revising procurement prices for agricultural products, especially wool and meat. We ask you, Nikolay Ivanovich, to take this into account in the work of the newly formed government.

In recent years the ecological situation surrounding Lake Issyk-Kul, a unique gift of nature that is an all-union cultural resort, has been deteriorating. The uncontrolled withdrawal of water for irrigation from the rivers feeding it is resulting in a lowering of the lake's level. The unregulated construction of vacation establishments without treatment installations, and many other factors are creating a real danger that the sad fate of the Aral will be repeated. The republic itself will not solve this problem. Today it is necessary to establish an all-union coordinating agency and draw up recommendations on Issyk-Kul's problems. This is all the more important in that, in my view, Lake Issyk-Kul can become a major tourism and vacation center for Soviet people.

Thirteenth Session
9 June 1989

Comrades! We are all witnesses of how democratization and glasnost have provided a powerful stimulus for the growth of national consciousness. That, of course, is good. The representatives of 80 nations and nationalities live and work in our mountainous region, Issyk-Kul Oblast. We have had no internationality frictions in the form in which they are manifesting themselves in other regions of the country. But we are concerned over the fact that certain groups of people are creating tension in internationality relations in the country. This has been clear at this congress, among other places.

In any situation one must remember that our strength lies in cohesiveness and unity, in the consolidation of all nations and nationalities. The mass news media should be oriented toward this, too. People are tired of reading all sorts of negative reports and disinformation. They expect articles and television programs that objectively disclose ways to solve the problems that have accumulated in internationality relations, and elucidations of the key issues in internationality policy.

And we, the people's chosen representatives, should use all of our powers to promote the stabilization of the situation and the strengthening of Leninist internationality friendship among Soviet peoples. Thank you for the attention. (Applause).

A.I. Lukyanov: The floor is granted to Comrade Gavril Kharitonovich Popov. Comrade Yakubov, Uzbekistan, will be next.

G.Kh. Popov, chief editor of the journal VOPROSY EKONOMIKI, Moscow City (from the USSR Union of Scientific and Engineering Societies): Comrade deputies, I would like to dwell on the platform set forth in the government's report. My task has been made much easier by the fact that we have already elected Nikolay Ivanovich, and, correspondingly, my remarks on the platform will not be personal. I was very worried that yesterday might have seen the emergence of the effect which we saw at the elections. I would call it the "peripheral effect" [effekt kraynego]—this was when a considerable group of our local leaders to all intents and purposes had to answer to voters at the elections for issues which they were essentially unable to resolve: answers for empty shelves, for unresolved housing questions, for the slow progress of restructuring, and for much else besides. Though they were "peripheral," they had to answer for all this personally. I was very worried that this might happen here, too. Moreover, I would like to say that we must also take account of the fact that we have a special kind of government. I remember I attended a Council of Ministers session 15 years ago chaired by Aleksey Nikolayevich Kosygin. I was struck then by the fact that Aleksey Nikolayevich became heated and spoke vigorously for almost an hour, yet during this time two ministers coolly remained seated. Only later did I realize that Aleksey Nikolayevich was addressing ministers whom he had not appointed, whom he had not chosen, and, above all, whom he knew for certain he could not remove.

Now the head of government has already been elected and, it seems to me, we can calmly discuss government problems and the platform as a platform. There are two aspects to this platform. The aspect linked with urgent tasks for the next 1-2 years, and the whole program.

I will discuss the urgent tasks first. The question of the financial crisis and the improvement of it is at the forefront. How do I see this question? If I am R1,000 in debt, I must make a list and see whom I own money to. I think roughly the same about our deficit. If it is R100 billion, there should be a table stating under what specific headings this R100 billion debt came about. I must say that over the past year, when there have been discussions about this deficit, I have still not seen such a table. But if there is no analysis, it is very hard to think about a cure.

The report attempted to show how the deficit came about. It stated in particular that an additional R21 billion was spent on social programs over the past 4 years. Last year R14.5 billion went on wages, and R8 billion on Chernobyl. These, of course, are specific figures, but they relate to different timeframes. One figure covers 4 years, the second covers 1 year, and the third figure is a one-shot figure, but, nonetheless, they do provide some kind of guide and make it possible to assess the situation. What is the upshot? Look, spending on agriculture went R10 billion over, it cannot be reduced. The report said that we should increase it. Spending on social needs was exceeded, it cannot be reduced, the report said that it should be increased.

Spending on Afghanistan, too, will clearly not decrease, since, on the one hand, we have to pay the people of this country for not listening to Andrey Dmitriyevich Sakharov and listening too much to our generals. (Applause). And on the other hand, we should nonetheless really pay all war veterans so we do not feel ashamed to look them in the eye. Furthermore, it seems to me that it will not be possible to make savings on Chernobyl, because in its wake a great deal more money will have to be invested in the Ukraine and Belorussia. And, above all, we will have to develop a safety system for stations and pipelines to prevent any repetition of the Chernobyl effect. In general it turns out that new spending is needed everywhere. How then can we eliminate our difficulties?

Nikolay Petrovich Shmelev has already said here yesterday that the cooperative system has not created any particular problems with regard to the deficit and that it is essentially a patch covering 2 percent of the hole.

I want to dwell on another point—the so-called overpayments which have emerged at our enterprises. Although these overpayments amounted to just R14 billion, and this is small change compared with the R100 billion deficit, we should take a look at them nonetheless.

Many trade union representatives have spoken here. They have decried cooperatives and economists very vigorously. But when it came to defending labor collectives' interests before the government, they kept their

STENOGRAPHIC RECORD

Thirteenth Session
9 June 1989

heads down for some reason. Yet I have a pile of telegrams from labor collectives, letters in which they ask for the question of these controls over the correlation between labor productivity and wages to be raised. Here is what workers at Moscow's "Pluton" plant wrote—they sent me a collective letter. They wrote: "The imposition of the ban on wage growth exceeding productivity growth is preventing us from reducing prime cost." I will explain that for the noneconomists among us. For instance, I have an article costing R1,000, and now I can reduce its prime cost to R950 by saving materials. But in order to obtain this saving in materials I have to pay R25 to those who save the materials. From the boss' standpoint the situation is quite elementary. I gain 50, I spend 25. From the standpoint of the authors of this restriction, it seems that the price is the same—R1,000—but wages have gone up by R25. This means that this road must not be followed. They reject this saving.

Moreover, the workers' letter states that this correlation reduces the incentive to cut staff; they write that a desire emerges to employ more lower-paid workers so as to maintain average wage levels. Let me explain once again. For instance, 6 people work in a section and earn R200 each. Now they decide to work as a team of five, but they ask that the five who remain be paid not an extra R200 in place of the sixth worker, but R250, for instance. Again, from the economic standpoint this is an entirely beneficial operation because, although I pay the five R50 more, I gain a worker who can be used in another section. But in this case, from the standpoint of the authors of the correlation, this approach is completely unacceptable because average wages increase.

Therefore, the workers conclude in their letter—I'll read it since it's very interesting (the letter is interesting in general; it is hand-written, but there are many signatures on it): "In December the Council of Ministers introduced an anti-inflationary correlation which, from our standpoint as workers, demonstrated complete ignorance of the subject on the part of high-ranking officials." (Applause).

Now I would like to add some comments of my own. Say I manufacture 10 refrigerators in my section. Suppose wages account for 50 percent of the cost of each refrigerator. It transpires that an 11th refrigerator can be manufactured in the section. But wages will account for more than 50 percent of the cost of this 11th refrigerator.

Of course, in this case state profits will fall, but, on the other hand, there will be an additional refrigerator, demand will be met, shortages will be reduced, there will be something to spend money on, and a blow will be struck against inflation. But the idea of controls over the correlation between labor productivity and wages proceeds from a different premise. Its premise is that wages should account for the same proportion of each additional refrigerator. That is, in other words, they are not interested in additional output but in maintaining state income.

Personally, it seems to me that even if the state doesn't earn a ruble from extra meat, an extra refrigerator, or an extra pair of shoes they should be produced, regardless of any correlations. (Applause).

Measures to control the correlation between labor productivity and wages suit only the apparatus, they do not eliminate any shortages, they merely create the semblance of combating shortages. But to all intents and purposes this is an attempt to lumber labor collectives with the leadership's inability to resolve economic problems.

How else is it suggested that we eliminate our crisis? There is talk of additional production of goods. Production of this will increase, production of that will grow, and so forth. What I want to ask is: Has our country ever had a government which did not promise to increase production of something or other? No it hasn't. Has there been a government in the country which has not found itself faced with growing shortages after a few years? Again no. Just why, one wonders?

Because it is not a question of the government, or of leaders, or of good intentions. Our economic science has been decried here probably also because it has demonstrated that the reason lies in the objective economic management mechanism. As long as the existing social relations in production continue, as long as the existing economic base continues, as long as the existing economic mechanism continues, as long as the existing political superstructure continues, there will be no adequate effect, however many extra billions of the people's money we invest in production. That is a fact of past experience, and we should make it our starting point. (Applause).

That is why it seems to me that it would be entirely insufficient for deputies to take promises of additional production at face value.

If the report had shown that we have now created a new economic mechanism capable of creating rather than spending, then it could have been believed. If the report had proved that we now have a machine capable not only of burning fuel but of going somewhere, then its promises could have been believed, too. For the time being all the remedies for the next 2 years as a whole have been taken from the arsenal of bureaucratic administration. But how can the consequences of administrative measures be cured by administrative measures? It seems to me that we want to act like a drug addict who cures his shakes with another fix. These, as has been said here, are draconian measures. I am not about to particularly go into them any further. I am comforted by the fact that we do not actually have a Draco, and consequently the draconian measures will most likely remain on paper. In practice they are unlikely to do any great damage. To be serious, the financial crisis is a reflection of the economic crisis. That is why the extensive criticism of the Ministry of Finance or the State Committee on Prices is only relatively fair. We latch onto the outward manifestations of the disease. Finances are the thermometer. They show

Thirteenth Session

9 June 1989

the patient's temperature. If we are going to fight, why fight the thermometer and the temperature? We should cure the disease.

In general it is time to stop portraying ourselves as trailblazers. Inflation has been a feature of all 20th-century economies in all countries. Starting with Keynes, whole schools of economists have studied this process. The bourgeois states have many years of experience of efforts in this area. They have learned to live with inflation. Anyone who travels abroad can see when you go back the next time that prices have risen. But everyone can also see something else—people live better. Yet the very word "inflation" throws us into a panic. Why? Because we live by the ideas of "Das Kapital"—a brilliantly analytical book, but one which reflects the situation a century ago. Who among our economic managers has ever studied neo-Keynesianism?

On the whole the problem itself—improving the economy and getting out of the crisis—is incorrectly formulated. If we improved the economy and emerged from the crisis, we would not need any restructuring. Isn't the reason why certain figures cling so vigorously to the idea of emergency measures that they want to dodge the actual problem of restructuring?

It has to be said with the utmost clarity: Emergency measures will not provide either a genuine improvement or a genuine overcoming of the financial crisis. (Applause). And this will emerge quite quickly.

Realistic tasks must be set for these measures. Not the improvement of the economy—that is a task beyond the power of emergency measures. But the creation of the preconditions for accelerating restructuring is feasible. It is from that viewpoint that we should approach the whole problem of emergency measures—what among these emergency measures will help to accelerate restructuring.

In the next part of my speech I would like to dwell on the model of restructuring. In order to create some emergency programs, it is necessary to know exactly what our aim is. As the saying goes, if you don't know which way to head, no wind can be a fair wind.

I would like to elucidate a few points when discussing this problem of the model which we should espouse.

The first problem relates to the subject who is to implement the package of restructuring measures.

The government's view is that all parameters should be worked out here, at the center. It will be necessary to issue 50 laws—but I think 50 will not be enough, we will need 100. If our Supreme Soviet works from morning to night and discusses them article by article, these 100 laws on restructuring may be ready in about 5 years.

Representatives from the Baltic republics think that we should hand over the decisive, overwhelming proportion of the economy to the republics, and then each republic will determine which economic model will be introduced. One republic may hang on to kolkhozes [collective farms], another may favor individual farmsteads, and so forth.

I think we should follow a path whereby the center issues just a few fundamental acts defining the general principles of the economic mechanism and creating a common economic basis in all republics. But the bulk of the legislation must nonetheless be handed over to the republics. (Applause).

Comrades, I need another 10 minutes, but I could also cut it short. (Noise in the auditorium).

A.I. Lukyanov: What do you think, comrades?

Auditorium: The standing orders!

A.I. Lukyanov: The standing orders? Gavriil Kharitonovich, the standing orders. (Noise in the auditorium). Please pay attention. Shall we put it to a vote?

Voices from the floor: Yes.

A.I. Lukyanov: Then I'm ready to vote.

Who is in favor of giving Comrade Popov 10 minutes? The majority. Ten minutes, go ahead.

G.Kh. Popov: Thank you, 10 minutes will be enough.

Comrades, talking about the republics, I think in general that it is time we abandoned the Stalinist interpretation of dividing republics into autonomous republics and union republics. I think that the overwhelming majority of our autonomous republics should become normal union republics and function as such. (Applause).

The second problem of the model. This is the problem of changing ownership relations and their content. The report included the concept of changing production relations. But we should no longer talk in general terms, we have to be specific. And, specifically, the problem is the following. If we proceed on the basis of Marxism, it is necessary to bring production relations and ownership relations into line with productive forces.

In our administrative system there has been, first, a general statization [ogosudarstvleniye] and, second, a general centralization. Both have done violence to the objective economy.

One wonders, for instance, what state ownership relations or centralization are needed by the person who sells us our newspapers on the newsstand? Why should there be rayon, city, oblast, and republic Soyuzpechat [Main Administration for the Distribution of Printed Matter] departments on top of a single news vendor? To make sure that there are ultimately two bureaucrats for each newspaper-seller?

It seems to me that this system is, of course, not entirely Marxist. We need to take a realistic approach to the problem of ownership.

STENOGRAPHIC RECORD

Thirteenth Session

9 June 1989

The experience of the developed capitalist countries shows that the state sector accounts for approximately 30-40 percent in economically developed countries. I think that bearing in mind our traditions and the interests of social orientation, it is enough for the state to retain control of 50 percent of the economy. The remaining 50 percent should be handed over to cooperatives and the private, individual sector.

We should also pursue decentralization within the framework of state ownership itself. Clearly, two-fifths of this ownership should be concentrated in the hands of the local soviets, two-fifths in the hands of the republics, and one-fifth in the hands of the center, the entire union.

Incidentally, we will then really resolve the problem of centralism. Here I wholly agree with Nikolay Ivanovich, when he said that we should concentrate on shock areas where a breakthrough can be made. In particular, I resolutely support all those who say that space spending should not be cut back but increased. This is an area where we have surged forward and where we can and should make some money in the world market. (Applause).

I would think it could be quite normal for us to buy cars from those who have long since outpaced us and whom we will never catch.

But, in order for Nikolay Ivanovich to concentrate on space, he has to be relieved of washing powder and dozens of other matters which are currently the government's concern. That is why the restructuring of ownership relations is the foundation of all other changes.

The next problem in the future economic management model is the problem of family peasant farms.

For me this is one of the central questions of our restructuring. The idea expressed here that the choice between kolkhoz, sovkhoz [state farm], and family peasant farm should be made in the market and in the course of competition is correct.

But when I listened to this correct statement, I could not tell whether equal conditions for all will be created to ensure that this market and this competition exist.

What kind of equality is there if some have land and others do not? Where will local soviets get the land to lease out? We are told that they will get it from farms which go bankrupt. But I have learned from our agrarian specialists' letter that apparently all farms should have all their debts written off. Where will the bankrupts come from if everyone has their debts written off?

It seems to me that we need to think harder about our country's experience. In 1861, when the reform was carried out, there was an opportunity to free the peasants and settle them on the land. Then they would feed themselves and the state. A different decision was made—to suit the landowners. The peasants were emancipated, but the landowners retained the land, the peasants had to lease land from the landowners, feed themselves, and, in addition, feed the state and the landowners. It is not very hard to imagine which road it is proposed that we follow now. The only thing I want to say is that this road ultimately led to three Russian revolutions. (Applause).

I am scared by our stubborn reluctance to take account of world agricultural experience. The entire experience of all prosperous countries shows that family peasant farms and farmers are the basis of the economy.

We have followed a different path from the very beginning of our history. At the end of the last century it was discovered that the Marxist theory that in agriculture large-scale production will triumph over small-scale production was not vindicated. Then Marxists—Kautskiy and Lenin—instead of admitting the facts, started criticizing the theory of stable small-scale peasant farms.

The struggle against family peasant farms was on our banners in 1917 and doomed our country to civil war.

Distrust of family peasant farms wrecked the New Economic Policy.

The slander alleging that family farms constantly give rise to capitalism led to the dispossession of the kulaks and collectivization.

Once again distrust of family farms led Comrade Khrushchev to combat personal plots and ultimately doomed all Khrushchev's reforms to failure. How long are we going to fail to take account of reality?

The March plenum has now finally stated that socialism is incompatible with private farms. But this theoretical conclusion has not been embodied in a specific program of action.

I am scared by the latest readiness to spend more billions. These billions were previously spent on chemicalization, then they were spent on land reclamation, now they must allegedly be spent on the social sphere on the grounds that this will apparently produce some results.

Why send people to the countryside, if 5 percent of a population can feed an entire country anywhere in the world under normal production relations? (Applause).

This is a key issue, comrades. If we feed the country with the help of family peasant farms, we will avoid having to import food. By avoiding food imports, we will release hard currency for ruble convertibility. We will further release capital investment from the excessive development of the oil and gas industry, which is plundering our natural resources and polluting our environment. There is a whole string of consequences.

I oppose any bureaucratic system of administration. I am confident that very many kolkhozes, kolkhoz members, sovkhozes, and sovkhoz workers will be efficient economic managers if the fetters of bureaucratic administration are removed from them. I am in favor of one thing only—actually ensuring the equality of all masters in the countryside. This is what needs to be ensured in

Thirteenth Session

9 June 1989

practice. Competition and the market will show who is most efficient. I am absolutely sure that competition in this country will have the same effect as it has worldwide. Tens of thousands of farmers go bust in the United States every year, but their place is taken not by large farms but by other farmers.

One final problem on which I would like to dwell. This is the problem of distribution according to labor and social guarantees.

I am somewhat troubled by the abundance of various measures in the social sphere contained in the program. Why? Well, I can understand why candidates campaigning for votes put this forward.

But what do one-shot additional money payments mean? Today they are either compensation for price growth in the past or a certain advance for price growth in the future. If prices rise, if it is hard to get cheap goods, the additional money becomes worthless in a year or two. That is quite obvious.

If we are really concerned about the less well-off we need not just a one-shot payment (which is necessary in itself) but a constant coefficient for annually adjusting all firm payments in the national economy in line with a cost-of-living index. This would be real concern. (Applause).

Second, it is necessary to set up guaranteed systems for the less well-off to obtain access to cheap goods. This is also a very substantive and important issue.

But nonetheless the most important thing is that the people should not be given the impression that our state has some kind of granary, and that if they pressure the state, kick up a fuss, and take to the streets the state will draw something out of the granary and make everybody happy. (Applause). This is an entirely impermissible policy.

The people have to be told the truth. Even if you repair your apartment there are loads of problems. And if we are to engage in restructuring, we will have a very hard time. Any statements to the effect that we will carry out restructuring while increasing prosperity are essentially direct deceptions of the people, deliberate or not. (Applause).

We deputies and the congress must say: We have one way out—real, hard, difficult work. What must we do? We must give everyone who wants to work the opportunity to work efficiently. We must concentrate on that. The crux of the problem is not what should be divided up and how, but that those who want to work should be given the opportunity to do so.

An enormous section of our society needs social protection. There are people who cannot work. Invalids, large families, and so forth naturally need an entire aid program. But the vast majority of our population needs to be given the chance to work, not social security and aid.

Dozens of people continually grab us by the hand near the Kremlin and thrust letters upon all deputies. What do these letters contain? Mainly people ask for apartments. Just think: A healthy man leaves a city somewhere in the Ukraine, comes here, and stands outside for hours. Why? To change something with regard to his apartment problem instead of working for this apartment. We have created a system under which people cannot solve the problem through their own labor.... (Applause).

Nikolay Andreyevich Kasyan—someone whom I very much respect—has spoken here. He called for an end to rallies, saying that we must work.

When I hear such statements from leaders, what I understand is "You work, I'll go on leading you." But when this is said by such a great worker as Nikolay Andreyevich, I nonetheless have to say to him: Nikolay Andreyevich, my dear fellow, I visited you more than 10 years ago. Then we discussed the construction of your center, and some prosecutors or financial organs were taking you to court. Now more than 10 years have passed. In any other country of the world a doctor such as yourself would now have dozens of centers. What is the case here? As I understood it from your speech, the same old discussions about construction and the same old attempts to take you to court are still going on. Why have you accomplished considerably less than you could have during these last few years, despite working unremittingly? Because the same thing has been happening to you as has been happening to all of us. We all work in a system in which our work produces considerably smaller returns than similar work in other countries. People go to rallies not because they want to hold rallies. They see no guarantees for their future and no way out in work. Their wants are very small. They want a system in which they can earn clothes, housing, and food through their own work.

In order to make our work efficient, unlike the current situation, we need to restructure our society. We will be unable to achieve material benefits for our voters, but we must create a system in society under which working people can depend on themselves alone and on their labor. Thank you! (Applause).

A.I. Lukyanov: The floor is granted to Comrade Yakubov. Deputy Ostroukhov will be next.

A. Yakubov, writer, first secretary of the board of the Uzbekistan Writers' Union, and secretary of the board of the USSR Writers' Union, Tashkent (from the USSR Writers' Union): Dear comrades! Time is valuable, and therefore I am omitting the entire intellectual part of my speech on lofty, global problems. I am getting down to business. Among the many values that we have increasingly lost in the course of 70 long years because of the eternal disorganization of our everyday life, our inadequate nutrition, and our kilometer-long lines that demean human dignity, there is one that is difficult to replace. That is the loss of the most noble of human qualities—mercy and compassion. They are being

STENOGRAPHIC RECORD

Thirteenth Session
9 June 1989

crowded out by embitterment and an unwillingness to listen to one another and sympathize with another person's misfortune.

On Friday [9 June], while walking past two very attractive, pretty women in the lobby, I involuntarily heard the following conversation: "Why are the Uzbeks always complaining about their cotton?" one of them said. "You get sick of it; they have nothing spiritual," the other added. And I thought with bitterness: So who is to blame for the fact that our once courageous, proud Uzbek peasant and his beautiful black-browed women find themselves in such a tragic situation?

But how can they be spiritually developed when, because of the infamous slogan of the "father of all times and peoples," Stalin, concerning the country's independence in cotton, they have been deprived of everything? All of their land, hundreds of thousands of hectares of marvelous fruit orchards, eternally green alfalfa fields, and even shady nut and almond groves—all that was cruelly cut down, plowed up, and sown to unrewarding cotton, as Chingiz Aytmatov has called it.

From the vast flood of sensational materials in the press that have rained down like a hail storm on the republic, I suppose you have already figured out to the kopek how much money each of our embezzlers stole. Embezzlers must be punished. There can be no two opinions about that. But what person who does not live in Uzbekistan can cross his heart and say with a clear conscience what sort of position our cotton grower has found himself in because of that same unrewarding cotton, cotton which the State Planning Committee [Gosplan] claims is a strategic raw material, brings vast revenues to the state, constitutes the lion's share of our foreign-exchange income, and without which, that same Gosplan admits, the state cannot get by? What are the living conditions of that peasant and his unfortunate wife, who is crushed by relentless toil? How much do these people receive?

Our women are employed at work that is not intended for women, under the radiation of the sun. That sun, as well as the insane use of toxic chemicals, has resulted in a sharp increase in cancerous, gastrointestinal, and women's illnesses, and women's and child mortality.

And how is their everyday life arranged? It is arranged in such a way that our women cotton growers, returning from the fields at twilight, cook broth for their children by burning antediluvian, filthy dried dung in their fireplaces. And it is hard not to cry when you look at these swarthy women, who in some respects resemble fire-scorched birches, in whom nothing feminine remains—neither breasts, nor bottom—to look at their eyes, filled with hopeless grief and sadness.

I recognize that all the country's peasants have it hard, Russian peasants especially, and I am glad that our government is taking fundamental measures to rectify this situation. But for all that, comrades, cotton is a special case. Let us recall those white, cruel-hearted farmers from the American South who, not wanting to work in the cotton fields themselves, and protecting their women and children from this inhuman labor, brought hundreds of thousands of Negroes from Africa in shackles. But in all fairness, let us also recall that, while motivated by the goal of not working, protecting their children from hard labor in those cotton fields, and receiving the healthy working offspring of the slaves, these cruel farmers fed them amply. And up sprung strapping, two-meter tall blacks whose descendants today are the flower of American sports, and the arts as well.

And what about our village children? How can one talk of sports or of their spiritual development? Because of malnutrition (20 kg of meat per capita) and work that is unsuited for children, they are not even accepted into the Army, and if they are accepted, it is only into construction battalions. And so, after this account, which is not even complete, of the dramatic situation of our peasant, I want to ask you, esteemed Nikolay Ivanovich: Is Gosplan's claim that the country needs cotton so much, that it is a strategic raw material and provides the lion's share of foreign-exchange revenues, true? And if it is true, then why is our price for cotton the lowest in the world? (Applause).

After all, Nikolay Ivanovich, we know from the prerevolutionary TURKESTANSKIYE VEDOMOSTI that the Russian merchant (the same one who brought this unrewarding crop to our region) would give 18 poods of wheat for one pood of cotton. Yet our own socialist state pays an average of 50 kopeks per kilogram, which is exactly what a half-kilogram of cucumbers costs at the Alayskiy Market in Tashkent (let's not forget, comrades, that two shirts costing at least R50 each can be sewn from the fabric produced from a kilogram of cotton).

It is stated back in the historical annals that in terms of its climatic and natural conditions Central Asia has no equals in the world, that the sweetest fruits and vegetables on the planet are grown there, and that its melons and watermelons are priceless for their taste and aroma.

Over the 70 years of our state's existence, as the result of the thoughtless, antiscientific, cruel exploitation of its natural resources, our region has been brought to the brink of ecological disaster.

Comrades, yesterday you did not listen to me fully; more precisely, you did not fully listen to the idea that Academician Aganbegyan expressed. Last year at a conference in the CPSU Central Committee devoted to the problem of the Aral, Academician Aganbegyan said that no one knows the real cause of the anomalies that have occurred in Uzbekistan with respect to its nature, its land and, finally, its people. And, he said, in setting any given tasks for the republic, Gosplan and the country's State Agroindustrial Committee are sailing in the fog. Therefore, the academician proposed, it is necessary to set up a special, authoritative economic commission consisting of the most prominent economists, ecologists, and medical and agricultural specialists, a commission which, after a

Thirteenth Session

9 June 1989

thorough study of matters, would present the government with a full and clear picture of what is happening in Uzbekistan.

I am convinced that Uzbekistan can feed half the country, comrades, and not in the distant future but in the next few years. For this to happen the republic must resolutely be freed from the domination of monoculture, and its industrious people must be helped to distance themselves from the shock of the stagnation years and straighten their shoulders.

My time is out, and I shall end on this. But I ask you to adopt my proposal for the establishment of a special commission. Thank you. (Applause).

A.I. Lukyanov: The floor is granted to Deputy Ostroukhov. Deputy Bykov will be next.

V.A. Ostroukhov, secretary of the party committee of the Sibkabel Production Association, Tomsk (from the Communist Party of the Soviet Union). Comrade deputies! Our congress is approaching its end. On the whole, it has been a new and unprecedented event. We obviously have yet to appraise it and interpret it. However, it is already clear that this event will move us considerably forward along the path of restructuring.

Comrades, for 20 years I worked as a mill operator in one of the hardest shops in cable production. Now I have been elected secretary of the party committee, that is, to translate it into the language of some who have been speaking now—into an apparatchik. And we have a good many of such people in the party. Like many others, I cannot conceive of my work without people, their needs and concerns. Therefore, such statements on the part of some speakers affect me in a rather unpleasant way. After all, what is happening today? Many Communists, workers, are keeping quiet out of modesty, recognizing their responsibility both for the party's past and for the present, while others are putting themselves forward as the ideologists of restructuring. Yet we all know that the generators of the ideas of restructuring are the CPSU Central Committee and Mikhail Sergeyevich Gorbachev. And to speak in a general way, it is all of us together, our entire party. Some speakers have correctly noted here that the party continues to be society's guiding force under the new conditions. While restructuring itself, it invites all public organizations and movements to join in concerted actions to renew our country.

Restructuring, as we have all felt, is difficult but interesting work. The importance of the political reform that is being carried out in the country is especially great. But the fate of restructuring, and I am certain of this, will in many respects be decided, nonetheless, in the area of the economy. Let us improve the economic situation, and I am certain that all other areas of restructuring will start proceeding more dynamically. I became convinced of this once again in listening to Nikolay Ivanovich Ryzhkov's report.

It turns out that in more than 70 years of the Soviet regime we have still not sorted out what state ownership, public ownership, and ownership by the people are. In the final analysis, as many economists have rightfully noted here in their interesting speeches, we have created ownership by no one. And ownership by no one means no one's property. That is the reason for the indifferent attitude toward it.

What is the solution here? Our plant's collective is coming out, in its deeds, for the new forms of economic management, the broadest introduction of cost accounting at all levels of the state structure—from the shop to the ministry—and the introduction of leasing and cooperative relations. What are we afraid of? After all, this is our socialist path.

Today five shops in our association are working under leasing arrangements, and three shops have been turned into production cooperatives. Let me note from the outset that one of the chief points of their contracts with the association's management is the maintenance of existing prices for the output they produce. Our party organization, the labor collective's council, and all the workers are opposed in principle to those cooperatives that receive unearned income by sharply raising prices. I believe this is an issue of state importance. We favor cooperatives that, by combining personal interest and independence, increase their income by increasing production volumes, improving quality, and updating products. Let us carefully think once again about the meaning of the speech by Deputy Shcherbakov from Moscow, who spoke of the fact that some cooperatives are discrediting the generally noble ideas of the cooperative movement in our country.

Our collective's goal is to create a lease-based cooperative association. And we are getting support from the ministry in this regard. But in the development of the cooperative movement there are a good many problems, which have been mentioned more than once here.

First of all, there is the unequal position of state cooperative enterprises, especially in the distribution of income, which is having negative consequences. Extremely serious and prompt changes and filling in of omissions are required in this part of the Law on Cooperatives.

Secondly, I believe that normative rates for the distribution of profits have been set unfairly. This is preventing collectives from moving on from the first model of cost accounting to the second. Let's say a collective in our country is left only 30 percent of the profits. We favor a flexible approach but oppose the mentality according to which any additional thousand rubles that a collective keeps for itself is equated with an act of sabotage against socialism. In this connection the Law on the State Enterprise also needs clarification. And, of course, it needs to be carried out.

The USSR State Committee for Labor and Social Problems recently created serious obstacles to the development

Thirteenth Session
9 June 1989

of the cooperative movement by adopting a decision to eliminate all social benefits for cooperative movements, including pension benefits connected with hazardous working conditions. Here I am mainly speaking of cooperatives created on the basis of industrial enterprises, and I believe that this measure is premature; it is a matter of jumping the gun. Such an approach only impedes the development of the cooperative movement in industry. The new government and the All-Union Council of Trade Unions must resolutely remove the barriers to leasing arrangements and cooperatives that have been erected in the quiet of Moscow offices.

At our congress people have spoken of the role of scientific and technological progress somehow under their breath. Yet the West has made a leap forward by introducing scientific advances into production. We all know examples of this. I think that the present strained situation in our economy has come about primarily because the country has not yet created an effective economic mechanism that provides incentives for the introduction of advanced accomplishments into practice. We hoped that the shift to cost accounting would bring a revolution in technological progress along with it. But, as we see, today these hopes have not been borne out. I think that the economists should still speak their minds here. This is the area in which we should accomplish a breakthrough.

Comrades! We listened closely to Nikolay Ivanovich Ryzhkov's report. I think that no one disputes the fact that it is a logical continuation of Mikhail Sergeyevich Gorbachev's report. The Tomsk delegation fully supports the election of Nikolay Ivanovich Ryzhkov as chairman of the USSR Council of Ministers. But we also have very great complaints against the work of the government, especially in solving the problem of Siberia. I speak with confidence precisely of solving a problem, and not of resolving questions, because in the past few years that problem really has revealed itself distinctly. Deputies from the Far East, the Altay, and the Kuznetsk Basin have also spoken of this here.

The vast territory from the Urals to the Pacific Ocean really does continue to be a raw-materials appendage. Trains carrying coal, timber, and metal come from there day and night. Pipelines pump hundreds of millions of tonnes of oil and billions of cubic meters of gas. But against that background, under the most severe natural and climatic conditions, the living standard of Siberians has not been improving, and by many indicators it remains lower than in the country's center. One must not forget the extreme Siberian cold, the mosquitoes, and the other bloodsucking insects of our short summer. There are no roads or schools. Villagers cannot utilize the gas that runs by the village through a gas pipeline. Today it is no longer necessary to put quotation marks around the notion of hardy Siberian health. Yet the problem of the Siberian countryside is another whole big topic of discussion. And all of these problems come from a departmental approach to the development of natural resources.

It is this consumeristic approach that has given rise to a number of serious environmental problems. It is perfectly obvious that the country should have a comprehensive program for the development of Siberia's natural resources with emphasis on the thorough local processing of extracted raw materials. And the main thing is to create the social conditions that are needed to attract people and keep them there. I want to say one more time, loud and clear, at this congress: If a drastic improvement is not made in people's lives in Siberia in the near future, this mighty source of raw materials will prove to be lost to the country. There will be no one to cut timber, mine coal, extract gas, etc.

I especially want to mention various shortages. They create inconveniences and cause irritation among people in any part of the country and, believe me, especially in Siberia. I realize that interruptions in supply can occur, but when the most basic consumer items are lacking (and for a year, or 2 years, and under the conditions of restructuring), you get flustered and cannot find any explanation when you are asked about this in labor collectives. And so you think: Just where is Nikolay Ivanovich with his government, and where are Gosplan and the ministries, of which we have more than enough? It would be a good idea to create a service in the country for responding to such acute situations, which affect the interests of millions of people.

In conclusion I would like once more, comrades, to speak about the party. I believe that it is in the critical stages of the history of our party and society as a whole that the Communist's steadfastness, conviction, and faith in his ideals are tested. In this connection I am disturbed and concerned by attempts, and they have been heard here at the congress, to belittle the party's role in our life and in restructuring. Such attempts do not follow the channel of restructuring. They are pursuing some sort of other goals. Just yesterday that sort of "nod" was made in the direction of the Kremlin leadership. In general, comrades, we need more trust in one another. After all, we are working for the common cause.

For example, I have known Yegor Kuzmich Ligachev for many years. I know him as an energetic, businesslike person who is devoted to the party's cause. And when we speak here of Comrade Ligachev, whether we want to or not, we cast a shadow on Mikhail Sergeyevich Gorbachev, as well. That is how I understand it. Therefore, let us respect one another and trust and support the Politburo, which is at our party's head, more. Thank you for your attention. (Applause).

A.I. Lukyanov: The floor is granted to Deputy Bykov. Next will be Comrade Bresis.

R.A. Bykov, artistic director of the Yunost Association of Mosfilm [Moscow Film Studio], secretary of the Board of the USSR Cinematographers' Union, Moscow (from the V.I. Lenin Soviet Children's Foundation): Esteemed comrade chairman, and dear colleagues, people's deputies! I have taken the floor in order to propose that we

Thirteenth Session

9 June 1989

take a look at the problems under discussion with one adjustment—through the prism of culture, spirituality, childhood, and the human being. It seems to me that it is time to speak this word at the congress. It seems to me that in our great congress marathon, in this huge television show the likes of which the world has never seen and the significance of which, in my opinion, we have not yet comprehended, because it entails solving the problems of democracy in full public view, the results of our work will echo in people's hearts through a purely real-life analysis. And if we do not yet know right now how we have done, depending on what sort of situation comes about in the country, we will realize that it represents our contribution to all that is good and all that is bad.

When I say that we should think of the human being, I say it in order that we recognize that among other, extremely important shortages, there is a shortage of intelligence, a shortage of education, a shortage of responsibility, a shortage of discipline, kindness and mercy, a shortage of beautiful relations. And when we speak of the economy and speak of the means of production and resources, we realize that all this is set into motion only in a system of production relations. And production relations are human relations.

I played a role in "Pisma mertvovogo cheloveka" [Letters of a Dead Man] and sat for a year in a cellar thinking about the end of the world—that was necessary in the course of working on the part. For a whole year I thought about the fact that humanity was supposed to be on the point of perishing, and that gave me a new perspective, and I would ride around Leningrad every evening and look at people, who were so carefree, and think: Can it be that they do not realize where we are going? After all, the same unprecedented transmutations that are taking place in the soil and taking place in the air are taking place in our souls. After all, the instinct for self-preservation, which used to move civilization, is being supplanted before our very eyes by the instinct for self-destruction. This is the beginning of an apocalyptic consciousness. We speak of the fact that we are having difficulty with the economy, and we say: Here are additional difficulties—Chernobyl, the disaster in Bashkiria, the harsh circumstances that existed in Sumgait, the harsh circumstances that came about in Uzbekistan. Of course, this reflects a lack of discipline, laxness, the intensity of the nationality struggle, and omissions. But all of that also has its own reasons—a shortage of general culture and morality, and human relations that we wrote off, that we have failed to take into account economically. And how has it happened that in our country children, culture, and education have ended up in the so-called sphere of the residual principle?

We are now asking about nuclear energy and the chemicalization of the country, and we will soon be talking about biological technologies that are no less dangerous, but very effective. And I want to ask whether we have thought these matters through from the standpoint of the human being. After all, if equipment for the education of schoolchildren in Sweden is reckoned at a thousand dollars, and R58 is spent for the education of one of our schoolchildren, that represents a definite sort of preparation of the future specialist. Whereas we spend R12,000 a year to train a specialist in our best higher schools, and one-third to one-half that amount in our pedagogical institutes, the developed capitalist countries spend $80,000 to train a specialist. So what are they doing, wasting money? And how is it that we want to do for R12,000 what costs $80,000? I think that what one can turn out for that sort of money is not a specialist but a model of a specialist, and a nonworking model at that. With that sort of specialists, that sort of culture of relations, just where are we going in the age of atomic energy, the age of chemicalization and biological technologies? This is a degree of risk that is no longer warranted. In present-day technologies there is a concept known as the human degree of risk; without it an economy is not modern; without taking the present-day human being into account, an economy becomes backward.

Our ruble should be backed up in human terms, because when we invest a ruble in production, we should know that R10 or R20 must be invested in the intellectual and human support for production. That is where it gets its backing from, and the malicious words once spoken by Saltykov-Shchedrin come to mind: Right now intelligent people give a 50-kopek piece for our ruble, and soon they will give a sock in the face. (Applause).

It is extremely important to call attention to how we approach the problems of our children. First of all, politically. Here very great changes have taken place in the past 50 years, within my lifetime. I was brought up in the Moscow City Pioneers' House, for which a palace had been turned over; it had been the palace of a count, and it had marble and circular staircases. And I would come from the Zamoskvorechye district, from the communal apartment where I lived—43 rooms with one kitchen—and I knew that this had been given to children by our state and our revolution. The palaces had been turned over to children. I arrived in the city of Naberezhnyye Chelny and saw the sole palace in the middle of the city. It was built of white stone, and I was told with pride that the largest square in Europe would be built right there. It would be built on landfill; of course, it was necessary there in the city of Naberezhnyye Chelny. We would not have understood that, if we had not recalled that it had recently been named the city of Brezhnev. And so there stands that white stone palace, and it is occupied, of course, not by children but by the city party committee and soviet executive committee, while the Pioneers' House—that is, the Pioneers' Palace—is located in the entryway to a prefabricated five-story apartment building in a housing tract. It's not a Pioneers' Palace, it's a Pioneers' entryway. (Applause). A speaker just now said that one must not belittle the role of the party. Dear friends, party members, and nonmembers! The role of the party can be belittled only by the party itself through its actions. (Applause). And one does not need to cast a shadow on the party; that shadow is cast of its own accord by that palace in Naberezhnyye Chelny. I spoke with a secretary of the city party committee [gorkom], a

STENOGRAPHIC RECORD

Thirteenth Session
9 June 1989

young, worthy, intelligent man; I don't know, maybe he is listening to me. I want to say to him: We did not speak of it, but I guessed from his eyes that he was dreaming of coming forth with an initiative—to turn that palace over to the children. (Laughter, applause).

If we are speaking of the economics of our children, which are also reflected in our entire economy, then allow me to ask you: How has it happened, our dear friends, that, while we have the slogans "All the best for children!" and "Children are a privileged class!" everything has been taken away from children. Two percent of all the money the budget allocates for sports goes to children, and the rest has been taken by you adults.

How has it happened that the average cost of a public building in the country is R250 per square meter, while the average cost of a school is R37 per square meter, and the average cost of a fully equipped hog barn is R43 a square meter? How has it happened, and what do we expect from a generation, if club doors are closed to them, if access to books is practically closed to them, and if there are 42 of them in a classroom? This is a special accomplishment of our pedagogy. I remember how during the war we Leningraders and Muscovites came to the city of Yoshkar-Ola, and there were not enough schools. And they made a third shift, and classes were held in the boiler rooms, but it never occurred to anyone to put more than 25 children in a classroom. It has long occurred to me that the person who thought up that idea of putting 42 children in a single room and letting them work there for 10 years is figuring out how to arrange things so that perhaps there can be a second shift.

We are presently organizing committees of the Supreme Soviet. I would like to express disagreement with the preliminary decision; the committee on children should be separate, although I myself realize that that is very complicated. One committee for science, public education, culture and upbringing; and of course, it should include children. But there is another committee—on the family and motherhood, and it, too, of course, should include children. I think that the approach to committees from the standpoint of linear structures has long since become obsolete. Shouldn't we propose a matrix system to our Supreme Soviet, so that committees will be local, and so that a combination of committees can be put together and assigned to a specific, individual problem?

We say: There is an inseparable link between "mother" and "child," "mother" and "family." Of course, but today we have come to such a state of moral decline of society that this link has been broken in our country. We say that there are no children without a mother. There are, dear friends! There are children without a mother, and a good many of them. More than a million children have been turned over to children's homes and orphanages, which is more than after the war; this is a moral disaster on the level of the Great Patriotic War, the most terrible war in history and in the history of our people. Our mothers did not abandon us, although they had it harder. Why, then, can a mother abandon a child today? It is because that sort of moral climate exists in society. Because if a mother abandoned us, everyone would turn their backs on her, her parents would not let her across the threshold of their home, she would never marry, and all her friends would turn their backs on her. But now the mother and father will confer, and her friends will help, and an intelligent young man will take her for a wife, because she's no dumb girl.

I want to say that the main thing today is to understand that the problems of children and culture, economics, finances, and restructuring as a whole are the problems of our human relations. We can build yet more electric power plants, endeavor to solve problems, and endeavor to create democracy; but democracy is not an order, it is a level of culture, a level of education, a level of kindness. The state itself should become moral, and the law should become moral. If wages do not respect work, if no one respects work, then we will never, through any lessons of work, teach people to respect work. (Applause).

A.I. Lukyanov: The floor is granted to Deputy Bresis. Next will be Deputy Marinichev.

V.-E.G. Bresis, chairman of the Latvian SSR [Soviet Socialist Republic] Council of Ministers, Riga City (Yekabpilsskiy National-Territorial Electoral Okrug, Latvian SSR): Esteemed deputies, I am sure that one of the merits of our congress is that it has conducted a thorough analysis of the state of the country's social and economic life. It is as if we have chosen the construction site for a new building and intend to start drawing up the plans in the near future.

However, a sense of incompleteness and contradiction on some questions is a source of concern to us. It is true that we have mastered the constructive methods of new political thinking in foreign policy. We have looked confidently into the 21st century and reassured and convinced the whole world with our confidence. But here at home we have embarked on economic restructuring without the most important thing—a scientifically substantiated concept. Consequently, decisions made by the government lack clear strategic guidelines and are often contradictory or even wrong.

It seems to me that two approaches are emerging at our congress. The first approach is to patch up the old mechanism, the second is to create a qualitatively new one. We are unconditionally in favor of the latter, a part of which is the idea of decentralizing the economy and increasing initiative and responsibility at all levels, on the basis of local conditions. The report also talked of the need to transfer the republics to economic accountability. If this idea is not distorted in practice, along with other economic actions it will undoubtedly lead to a new state of our economy.

However, at times feelings run high over the question of economic accountability for the republics. Especially when some deputies, including from our republic, give their own distorted interpretation of this question. That is why I feel it necessary to dwell on this subject again.

Thirteenth Session

9 June 1989

Indeed, the exceptionally high degree of centralization of production management and the mobilization of most resources in the hands of the administrative system have essentially created an extremely powerful braking and apathy mechanism. For example, 82 percent of all output produced in the republic is still distributed on a centralized basis. One wonders who has any interest in showing local initiative in these conditions? The notorious formula "initiative is punishable" operates strictly and rigorously. Newly produced output will once again be distributed by the center and only an insignificant proportion of this output or, at best, some of the above-plan output will be left for the initiators. What is more, Latvia has reached a period of economic development when most of the factors for increasing production, such as labor, energy, raw material, and ecological resources, are virtually exhausted, leaving the intensification factor as the main one. Consequently, our economic well-being in the future lies not in production per se but in producing more output of better quality and value. However, we will be able to realize our efforts and improve the republic's standard of living only on the basis of equivalent commodity exchange in the conditions of a union market. And by equivalent exchange we mean not only the exchange of material wealth but also the provision of services and finance and credit relations with the union. The crux of the issue is very simple. Whoever gives more to society will be able to have more himself.

Together with its neighboring republics and on the basis of approximately similar principles, Latvia is switching to a new model of socioeconomic development in 1990. An accord was reached on this with the country's government. We assumed that the central planning organs would work out the new elements of the future economic mechanism on the basis of our example. However, so-called acceptance of the plan for 1990 is literally now in progress—once again following the rules of the period of stagnation and braking.

Unfortunately, other examples also show that the country's Gosplan [State Planning Committee] is in no hurry to work out the elements of the new mechanism but, on the contrary, is continuing to strengthen centralization in planning. We ask the country's Supreme Soviet to adopt the law on regional economic accountability as quickly as possible in order to put an end to this practice. We suggest that in the new conditions, economic relations with the country's central organs and with other republics and regions be built and regulated on a mutually advantageous contract basis. It should be an economic contract under which the two sides assume the appropriate commitments.

Under the present planning system it has not been possible and will not be possible to ensure balanced plans. The main concern of Riga's numerous apparatchiks and the even more numerous apparatchiks in Moscow is still to assay, seek out, and limit. Clearly, every method is used here except a scientific method. This year, for example, despite the 100-percent state order, the plan for the republic's State Committee for Industry alone failed to balance out to the tune of R85 million. One wonders who is going to compensate the collectives? There are a mass of such instances—in other words, it has now become a system. This suits the bureaucratic apparatus. More than that, it is the circulatory system of the bureaucratic machine. It uses this to elevate itself to the pinnacle of the pyramid of economic power, while simultaneously belittling the working man. I will be frank, our specialists are not very good at wheedling and prying things out of people but they are also unaccustomed to kowtowing. That is why we are in favor of contractual principles and economic accountability. But republic economic accountability is not a subsistence economy and not economic self-isolation, as some comrades here try to make out. It is even quite the reverse: It leads to the formation of an all-union market and to the search for effective forms of all-union division of labor. Republic economic accountability also implies the right to price formation, independent management of credit resources, and the creation of mechanisms to protect the population from the vagaries of the market.

Economic sovereignty also means independent international ties and foreign currency cost-recovery. The foreign currency payments system introduced 2 and ½ years ago does not guarantee foreign currency self-financing even at the level of most enterprises, because the state takes up to 70 percent of foreign currency revenue. Territorial bodies get only about 5 percent. A great deal of dissatisfaction has been caused by decisions recently adopted by the USSR Government which, on the one hand, permit the development of foreign economic activity but, on the other, introduce rigid centralization and licensing, which sharply restricts even border trade.

Very important government documents and normative acts on these matters are being adopted without the republics' consent. I believe that the part of the output which is the property of the republic must be at the disposal of the republic's Council of Ministers. It, after all, issues the licenses. The republics must also keep all foreign currency proceeds generated by the republic—proceeds from tourism, for example, trade activity, joint ventures, and so forth. We must also establish fair normatives, based on world practice, with regard to foreign currency payments for freight transit via the republic's ports and the processing of petrochemical and ordinary freight. The absence of such payments does not make it possible to maintain freight transit routes and ports at the appropriate technical standard, leads to their irresponsible technical and ecological operation, and holds back the social sphere.

We ask the new government to abolish and revise both obsolete and new normative acts and instructions on the basis of the republics' transition to economic accountability and self-financing, including foreign currency self-financing.

STENOGRAPHIC RECORD

Thirteenth Session

9 June 1989

The country's new economic mechanism represents various forms of ownership. I support the theory voiced in both reports that the main, decisive point today is the absence of exploitation.

Improving forms of ownership means improving production relations. The role and importance of production relations are demonstrated to some extent by comparing the indicators of agricultural development in Latvia and Finland. In prewar years, the level of agricultural production in Latvia was higher than in Finland. However, in the postwar years the rate of growth in agricultural output in Finland has been considerably higher, while other indicators have been approximately equal. Finland resolved the food problem long ago and the upper level of production is now restricted. I should just add that the average field in Finland is about 15 hectares, and there is no exploitation, nor any category of people such as production organizers of various ranks, of whom there are approximately 4 million in our own country's agro-industrial complex. Evidently we need to more actively adopt world experience and abandon outmoded dogmas in some areas. Yes, we are in favor of a diversity of forms of ownership, of efficiently operating kolkhozes, sovkhozes, agrarian combines, or agrarian firms, but we are also in favor of the peasant as independent producer. I fully go along with the agrarian workers' appeal to the congress. What is more, the country's government must immediately take real measures to stop the exodus of people from the countryside and the dying of villages. Neglected and vacant land should be returned to agricultural production. It is paradoxical that there are millions of hectares of such land in a country where the food problem is still unsolved.

I think it is impossible to solve this problem without allocating extra material, financial, and labor resources. Latvia has adopted a law on peasant farms. Land is allocated to peasants to use in perpetuity. All their property can be inherited. There is now a hope that the land will gain a master. This year alone, there have been approximately 1,000 such masters in our republic. But life is extremely difficult for the peasantry today. In order to set up a normal family farm it is necessary to amass funds—even as much as R100,000—yet at the moment it does not seem possible to provide the peasants with sufficient credit, equipment, and materials. The Union of Latvian Agricultural Workers we have set up has begun to concern itself with protecting the interests of all agricultural workers. This economic organization seriously intends to help the peasantry. However, we are very concerned by what is now happening with purchase prices for agricultural products. It seems that indifferent functionaries intend to stifle even the very latest party decisions on agriculture. For example, with the projected prices, kolkhozes and sovkhozes will have their profits halved next year in comparison with 1988. While all farms in our republic have been profitable since 1983, with the introduction of the new prices one-quarter of them will become unprofitable. Here I would like to refer to the proposal by Deputy Popov, who suggested that debts not be written off. I do not totally agree with this idea and think that the state should write off the debts of bankrupt kolkhozes and also sovkhozes, in other words, of state enterprises. Then the land could be handed over free of debts to a peasant or leaseholder. (Applause).

Comrades! It seems to me that the prices system must be revised and reworked again. The peasants must not be coolly deceived for the umpteenth time. A group of deputies is submitting a question to the government on this matter.

Comrade deputies! We are accumulating a substantial bank of ideas. Along with our activeness, the store of creative, constructive ideas on our country's future is also growing and it seems to me that this is our main capital, this is the future of our country. Thank you for your attention. (Applause).

A.I. Lukyanov: The floor is granted to Deputy Marinichev.

Yu.M. Marinichev, chairman of the board of the Moscow Oblast Union of Russian Soviet Federated Socialist Republic [RSFSR] Consumers' Cooperatives, Moscow Oblast (from the USSR Consumers' Cooperatives): Esteemed comrade deputies! The questions of the Food Program and the problems of the countryside are being raised in trenchant fashion at our congress. For employees of consumers' cooperatives, they are especially close, since we form part of a single whole with the country's agrarian complex. And therefore, we support the appeal of the agrarian deputies concerning the need to radically change our attitude toward the countryside in actual deeds, and not just in words. We apply this appeal to ourselves, as well: A great deal depends on the consumers' cooperatives. And above all, the peasants' everyday life.

The consumers' cooperatives have existed for more than 90 years now in order to meet the interests of rural workers. Of course, the winds of history did not bypass us, either, and tremendous damage was done by the deviation from the true principles of the cooperative movement and the many years of a dogmatic approach to evaluating the role of cooperative ownership. Under the powerful pressure of the administrative-command system, the state assumed control over consumers' cooperatives. Nonetheless, relying on their democratic roots and traditions, they survived and preserved their viability. Today they employ 3.5 million sales clerks, cooks, procurement agents, bakers, and workers in the other common occupations. They provide 27 percent of the total retail trade, serve 40 percent of the country's population, purchase half of the potatoes and a third of the vegetables that become included in state resources, and bake one in every third kilogram of bread. Moreover, they produce nearly R10 billion worth of consumer goods at their enterprises annually.

At the same time, we are very concerned that the great potential inherent in the nature of this form of cooperatives is far from being fully utilized. There are reasons

STENOGRAPHIC RECORD

Thirteenth Session
9 June 1989

for that. The cooperatives' vulnerability and many of their problems are attributable to their long-standing, absolute legal defenselessness. Therefore, naturally, we placed great hopes on the promulgation of the Law on Cooperatives. Unfortunately, I must say that it failed to address many vitally important interests of consumers' cooperatives. For example, our system can take practically no advantage of the economic freedoms that the law grants to cooperatives in the sphere of production and services. For all intents and purposes, in both the center and at the local level (and this is since the law was adopted), the attitude toward consumers' cooperatives has remained unchanged. Gosplan, the Ministry of Finance, the State Committee for Labor and Social Problems, the State Committee on Prices, and other departments continue to try to draw consumers' cooperatives into the system of state regulation and control and to restrict their independence even in the use of their own money. In many decisions and, most importantly, in practical actions, essentially no distinctions are made between state enterprises and consumers' cooperatives. On the other hand, consumers' cooperatives are often confused with the new cooperatives, and the fundamental differences that stem from the social functions that their organizations perform in the countryside are forgotten. For many years, just as today, consumers' cooperatives have painfully experienced a shortage of state attention in matters of material and technical supply. Sales equipment, refrigeration equipment, and production equipment are allocated at a level of 30-50 percent of their requirements. This is seriously holding back any enhancement of the role of consumers' cooperatives in regions' attainment of self-sufficiency with regard to food supply, and in the establishment of relatively small procurement and processing enterprises and shops in every rural rayon. Today the share of rural workers' own resources in their food supply comes to 50 percent, but it could be substantially higher. Complaints regularly come in from the public concerning difficulties in turning in berries, fruits, and vegetables for processing. The situation with regard to the supply of production equipment has become especially acute since the branch that specialized in its production was eliminated, and the process of enlisting defense-industry enterprises in its production has been excessively delayed. While they mainly use their own personnel to build their facilities in the countryside, consumers' cooperative organizations have practically no possibility of buying the necessary construction machinery. In the final analysis, all this negatively affects the provision of services to rural inhabitants.

In our view, one cannot speak of repaying debts to the countryside unless equal conditions are created for rural and urban inhabitants to obtain goods. Given the acute shortage of commodity resources, it is very important to distribute them correctly and fairly. But what do we have in reality? Per capita retail trade turnover in the countryside is lower than in the city by a factor of 2.2.

The procedures for the distribution of resources through organizations of the Ministry of Trade that have developed in unplanned fashion in the country in recent years clearly infringe on the countryside's interests and are resulting in widening the gap in consumption levels between city and countryside. We are trying to find a solution and are increasing the production of goods and foodstuffs at our own enterprises, but our initiative is proving to be punishable. In Russia, for example, in 2 years consumers' cooperatives were deprived of R1.5 billion worth of resources for sale in the countryside. This was exactly the amount by which they had increased the production of similar goods at their own enterprises.

One gets the impression that Gosplan and the other planning agencies are not really supporting the interests of the countryside, and are taking the course of balancing resources on paper without reflecting on the consequences of what they are doing. The USSR Ministry of Trade is stubbornly holding onto its monopoly position in the market. In violation of the Law on the State Enterprise, it dictates to suppliers and customers who should conclude contracts with whom, and who should coordinate their assortment and how, while in practice it interferes with the development of direct ties between consumers' cooperatives and industry. Such a monopoly has not led to any good and will not do so in the future.

I would like to direct some critical remarks toward Comrade Voronin, the chairman of the USSR State Committee for Material and Technical Supply. He repeatedly has personally assured the public that the consumers' market would be supplied with timber and building materials. Several government decisions have been adopted on these matters, but the situation not only is not improving, it is becoming even more strained. In Moscow Oblast, for example, the need for commercial wood for the current year has been met by only half. On paper, in the form of unrealistic allocations, the need for standardized houses has been met by 100 percent, but in reality it has been met by only 5 percent. Shortages persist of plumbing products, ceramic tiles, and many other materials. This is especially troubling since solution of the extremely acute social problem of housing depends directly on accomplishment of the task of saturating the market with building materials.

I permit myself to express great apprehension concerning the feasibility of providing every family with a separate apartment or house by the year 2000, if we do not create all the conditions for citizens' widespread participation in the construction of their own individual housing—in both the countryside and the city.

The supply of small-scale machinery for rural workers is extremely unsatisfactory. The process of putting mini-tractors into series production is being dragged out, which is holding back growth in the number of lessees and of individual farmsteads and farms. The state of affairs in the commercial market causes one to reflect on another phenomenon in our life: Many people have

STENOGRAPHIC RECORD

Thirteenth Session
9 June 1989

responded to the Law on the State Enterprise from a position of narrow group interests, which have frequently come to dominate over the interests of the country and interests of the people. That is the reason for the washing out of inexpensive goods and the unwillingness to undertake production of items that are needed. A tendency toward the further alienation of producer and consumer has manifested itself. We cannot continue to simply watch while the supply of goods melts away, while whole groups of goods that we had in sufficient supply not just yesterday, but practically always, disappear. I think that we should not begin to shift to a market mechanism for regulating the economy without taking the actual conditions that exist in the state into account. This process should be carefully weighed, gradual, and well thought-out, and it should be accomplished on a step-by-step basis. Before shifting to the new economic relations, it would be useful, in addition to stepping up supervision of the work of trade organizations (which is being done today for good reason), to focus the attention of the public, and also to increase accountability at the state level for the assortment and quality of output produced by enterprises in all branches of the economy.

Comrade deputies! We are exceptionally concerned today by the question of the fairness of taxation of consumers' cooperatives. We pay an income tax on profits. We pay taxes on turnover, taxes on buildings, a land tax, a road tax, taxes on above-plan profits—and we even pay taxes on the part of profits that we allocate for the construction of social facilities in the countryside. Is this sort of taxation policy, which has been in place from time immemorial, rational? Does it suit the state, and most importantly, does it suit rural inhabitants? I think not.

Only 1.7 billion rubles annually is allocated for development of the exceptionally weak physical facilities and equipment of rural trade, while its payments to the budget amount to 3 billion rubles. And that is in a situation in which consumers' cooperatives are the system whose own money, without state participation, largely funds the construction of rural stores, food-service enterprises, and many social and cultural facilities.

One could reconcile oneself to that situation if the money taken from us went for rural needs. Yet, to all intents and purposes, it is transferred, through taxes, from the countryside to the city or channeled into various "projects of the century." Yet everywhere throughout the countryside there is a shortage of trade enterprises, and a considerable number of those that do exist are located in dilapidated, unsuitable buildings. In the 72d year of the Soviet regime about 100,000 rural communities have no stores. After hard work in the fields and livestock sections, people are forced to waste substantial amounts of time searching for basic necessities in cities and rayon centers and at central farmsteads. We ask the government to resolve the question of regularizing and reducing consumers' cooperatives' payments to the state budget in order to thereby increase their contributions to the social development of the countryside.

The further development of consumers' cooperatives' foreign economic ties would help improve the supply of consumer goods to the rural population. They were practically the first in the country to engage in foreign trade, back in the early 1920s. Direct and barter operations have developed especially actively in recent years, when the government has adopted a number of unquestionably correct decrees aimed at decentralizing foreign economic ties.

This is making it possible not only to enrich the assortment of goods for rural localities but also to provide incentives for individuals who sell their agricultural products. However, a number of recent decrees by the USSR Council of Ministers are at odds with those that were previously adopted and once again tend toward the monopolization of foreign economic ties. As a result of this, consumers' cooperative organizations have been deprived of the right to conduct barter operations and have been forced to cancel previously concluded agreements, and even long-term contracts, that are advantageous to us. These restrictions on the part of the state are not in the spirit of the Law on Cooperatives.

Several words about the new cooperatives. Numerous complaints about their work and the lack of public acceptance of many of them are forcing us to draw the conclusion that it is necessary to return to the legal status of those cooperatives and not to let conditions continue that allow the interests of the cooperatives and those of the consumer to become separated. We support those cooperatives that are created for the production of additional goods by using resources other than those intended for sale to the public, and that do not place their personal enrichment above everything else. We favor cooperation with such cooperatives, and we have experience in doing so.

The ideas of the diversity of forms of ownership that have found reflection in the reports and speeches at the congress seem to us to be correct in principle and to be very important for the further development of the country's economy. We see the future of consumers' cooperatives as lying in their self-development and the strengthening of their democratic principles and their ties with shareholders—with sovkhozes, kolkhozes, lessees, and local soviet agencies. This will allow us to increase our real contribution to accomplishing our society's urgent tasks.

The issues that we have raised concerning help from the state are needed not by the consumer cooperatives but by the countryside and the people who plant, plow, and feed us. It is a matter of restoring social justice for them.

We have prepared a draft decree of the USSR Council of Ministers that provides for resolvng the questions of enhancing the role of consumers' cooperatives in the social development of the countryside. What is troubling is that, because of the numerous approvals required (in the spirit of the old times), the decree has not yet come out, and its content is being emasculated. Therefore, the deputies from the consumers' cooperatives have made a

Thirteenth Session

9 June 1989

request—we are asking the government to examine the draft that has been submitted and resolve the questions raised in it. In practical terms it is extremely important to create an economically substantiated system of taxation, remove restrictions on foreign economic activity, and finally solve the problems of the state's providing real in matters of material and technical supply. In this connection, we would ask Nikolay Ivanovich Ryzhkov, chairman of the Council of Ministers, to receive a group of deputies from the cnsumers' cooperatives to discuss these matters.

Comrade deputies! In comrade Nikolay Ivanovich Ryzhkov's report we heard an analysis of the processes taking place in the country, candid admissions of errors that have been made, and a program of actions in the economic and social sphere that takes the actual situation and potential into account. This permits us to hope that the new government, relying on the positive and negative experience that has been gained in the first years of restructuring, and generalizing a number of interesting and unconventional proposals by people's deputies, will work out the sort of program of actions that will have a real impact on improving the country's economy.

Evidently, the discussions at the congress are drawing to a close. In returning home or getting down to work in the USSR Supreme Soviet, we should concert our efforts on deepening the restructuring processes. And in this responsible mission, we should always remember the supreme trust that the people has placed in us. Allow me to wish everyone success in performing his duties as a deputy. Thank you for the attention. (Applause).

A. I. Lukyanov: Comrades, we have received fairly many notes from deputies requesting that we announce the whole list of speakers. Altogether, 781 people have submitted requests to speak in the debates, and notes from another 11 people have just been given to me. For your information, I want to report that 96 deputies have spoken in the debates on the reports "On the Basic Guidelines of the USSR's Domestic and Foreign Policy" and "On the Program of Anticipated Activities of the USSR Government," and during the congress as a whole more than 500 deputies, which is practically one in every four congress participants, has spoken. If we follow the procedures that we stipulated 2 days ago for concluding the congress, we must evidently heed those deputies who have sent notes expressing a wish to close debate (here are those notes), and give the floor only to those who have specific proposals regarding the congress's draft resolution, for 3-5 minutes. (Deputy Bobritskiiy and others have written this).

Therefore, I should evidently put the question of closing debate to a vote. I want to remind you that according to our provisional rules of order, the closure of debate is done by a decision of the USSR Congress of People's Deputies made by no less than a two-thirds majority of the people's deputies. Therefore, whoever is in favor of closing debate on the report on the Basic Guidelines for the country's domestic and foreign policy and on the government's program of anticipated activities, I ask you to raise your credentials. Please lower them. Opposed? I ask for a count. (A vote count is taken.)

A.G. Kostenyuk: Esteemed deputies, 290 deputies voted against the motion.

A.I. Lukyanov: Who obstained? I ask for a count. (A vote count is taken).

A.G. Kostenyuk: 36 deputies obstained.

A.I. Lukyanov: This morning 2,131 deputies registered at the congress. Thus, by a majority of more than two-thirds, the debate on the reports is closed. In accordance with the congress's provisional rules of order, the texts of speeches by dpeuties who have been unable to speak in connection with the closure of debate may be included, by decision of the congress, in the stenographic record of the sessions. I am grateful to Deputy Ananyev and other deputies who are turning over their speeches to be included in the stenographic record of the congress. Are there no objections, comrades?

From the hall: No.

A. I. Lukyanov: It is agreed. The floor is granted to Nikolay Ivanovich Ryzhkov, chairman of the USSR Council of Ministers, for concluding remarks and answers to questions.

N. I. Ryzhkov, chairman of the USSR Council of Ministers:

Comrade people's deputies, in the debate that unfolded at the congress an objective appraisal has been given of our country's domestic and foreign policy, including the government's forthcoming activities. In our view, these debates have been very fruitful. We have received a good foundation for the elaboration of further steps to rectify the state of affairs in the economy both at the present stage of national economic development and in the long term. Of course this dialogue of people's deputies with the government both from this rostrum and via direct contacts during the congress has been in many respects very instructive and has taught us a great deal. It has been at first glance an unusual opportunity to see problems not only from above but also, as they say, to get a feeling for them from below—that is, directly from the people. Unfortunately, I have not been able to meet many of the deputies I wanted to meet to discuss various problems. You have seen how compressed our time has been. However, I am certain that there will be such an opportunity in the future, and I consider, of course, that it is necessary to follow the practice of personal exchanges of opinions. It will only be of great benefit.

During the meetings that have occurred there have been—in addition to the questions that hae been raised from this rostrum—very many questions, letters, and notes from people's deputies. Many of them have of course been repetitive and deal with various problems.

Thirteenth Session

9 June 1989

For this reason we obviously do not have the opportunity today to give a specific answer to every question. I would like to formulate a few positions of principle and express my thoughts on these matters.

As regards specific individual questions, they are connected with the development of the economy of particular regions of the country and the solution of various social problems.

They concern the allocation of resources—equipment, capital and production investments, construction—or on the contrary the cessation of construction. All of them will be without exception thoroughly examined. Instructions on many of them have already been issued and the government was instructed to find the best possible positive solutions.

I want to say that a great number of questions came in on halting the construction of chemical plants and production, and on the construction of nuclear power stations, such as the Krymskaya, Yuzhno-Ukrainskaya, Gorkiy Rostov, Tatar, and nuclear heat supply plants, etc. On the whole I spoke about the situation in the country's power generation industry at the Supreme Soviet session. The situation developing in this respect is extremely serious and should, frankly speaking, be a cause of worry for us. The country may find itself in a very serious situation with regard to power generation. Therefore, competent groups of specialists are now working on the individual power stations that comrades mentioned here. And, as final conclusions become available, appropriate decisions will be adopted and will be brought to the attention of both people's deputies and the public.

I would also like to dwell on some questions that to a greater degree touch on people's interest. This is in the first place the issue of ecology. In my report I made certain generalizations on this issue; I outlined the government's views and stances in the sphere of ecology. But seemingly, the length of the report and the time allocated for the report did not make it possible to cover this problem in depth. I agree with Comrade Yablokov, deputy, who spoke about this issue, that on the whole all of us must become ecologically minded—all of us! Starting from the chairman of the council of ministers [applause] right up to each individual. [applause] I think that the proposals that were voiced here with regard to organizational forms, in my view should be—this is what I think—they should be as follows: Of course, there should be a very powerful committee in the government that should deal with these issues and there should, of course, be a committee or commission of no lesser power in the Supreme Soviet. It is precisely upon these principles that we should start looking into all contradictions in the ecological sphere. In deciding any particular issues.

As far as the money is concerned, the R135 billion for 3 5-year plans or beyond, I think right now there is no need to argue; we have to sit around the table and look into the matter.

Comrades, I would like to answer two specific questions related to ecology. The first question worries very many people. I received a lot of notes on this question, and the speakers touched on it, too. Of late, this problem is being very vigorously touched on by mass media. The conversation...[loud noise from the hall]

[Lukyanov] Comrades, I ask you, I ask for your attention. Hand all your speeches in to the Congress Secretariat. [noise from the hall]

[Lukyanov] I am sorry, Nikolay Ivanovich. [noise from the hall]

[Ryzhkov] What's the matter?

[Lukyanov] Go ahead, Nikolay Ivanovich.

[Lukyanov] Please go ahead, Nikolay Ivanovich. [calls from the audience asking for an interval] Nikolay Ivanovich, what will we do? Shall we announce an interval?

[Ryzhkov] Please do. [audience says "no"]

[Lukyanov] No. The text will be published and that's it. [bell sounds] Please go ahead.

[Ryzhkov] I do not understand. This means that I can go on? All right. Thank you. Now I understand what is required of me. So, I have said that the issue of the construction of the gas and chemical complex in West Tyumen, in the Tyumen Oblast of West Siberia, is giving rise to many questions. And I should evidently give an exhaustive reply now. Let us decide together how to resolve this problem. The first principle-based question is that of whether or not we can go on managing without the development of the chemical industry in our country. My opinion is firm: Without the development of the chemical industry, the country is not in a position to progress any further, not in agriculture, in consumer goods production, in construction, or in industry. Without the chemical industry we will not move ahead. We will fell the forests, we will spend a long time on construction, and so forth. Therefore, the question is a principle-based one. And I think that we should take on this.

Second, certain scientists, specialists—and that was mentioned first and foremost in the press—proposed an option under which capacities should not be created, should not be built in Tyumen Oblast, but should be carried out—the processing of chemical raw materials, of gas and other hydrocarbon elements—should be carried out in the European region. I ask you: Is it possible today—I am speaking to you; I am speaking to the towns,

STENOGRAPHIC RECORD

Thirteenth Session

9 June 1989

to the people of Volgograd, Dzerzhinsk, Gorkiy, Ufa, Sterlitamak; I can list very many towns and cities where there is more than enough of the chemical industry today—can one seriously ask whether we should build new plants there or expand the existing ones? I believe that is not a legitimate formulation of the question. [applause] If these towns agree to this, I will be the first to agree to do away with that problem.

Second [as heard]: Why is it that we think this should happen in Tyumen Oblast? Comrades, over a period of 25 years we have invested absolutely enormous amounts; we have created an infrastructure. We have set up towns there. And today West Siberia is a resource region, a raw materials province. There is no processing industry there today. Therefore, that gas that we extract is six, it contains six percent ethane. Today it is considered normal in the world to extract ethane if there is 1.5 percent in an area. We leave this ethane in the gas, as they say.

We burn it and disrupt the ecological environment in the Soviet Union. Foreigners are more clever: They receive our natural gas, collect the ethane, make plastics and other chemical products, and sell them to us ten times dearer. So we are obliged to do it.

Second [as heard]: 15 billion cubic meters of gas are being burned today in western Siberia. It's burned in flares. I will tell you that this generates 10 million tonnes of soot, and burns up 30 billion cubic meters of oxygen. Can one really permit such a squandering of our means, our natural resources? For that reason, the government really has been thinking for a long time. And it was, incidentally, an initiative from the localities that, step by step, production facilities should be built there that would enable chemical products to be made on the spot. The program is to cover 15 years. During the next 5-year plan period, the maximum that can be built is to extend the Tobolsk factory and make chemical products there, and in Surgut, too. That is the maximum that the country can do. There are no financial resources in the country today.

But the main thing is that we have no ecologically clean chemical technology today. So we are obliged to negotiate with foreigners. We have only the wish, and we have the natural resources. We have nothing else. That's why we hold such talks. But we have imposed very rigorous economic terms. We have imposed very rigorous ecological terms, and when, in the fourth quarter, or in the first quarter of next year, the two projects about which talks are being held today are submitted to us, well, if necessary, let's set up an international ecological situation, as they say, and see whether it is or is not in accordance with ecological cleanliness.

The second question concerns the construction of the Katun hydroelectric power station. On this, claims have been made to the government and to me personally in connection with the project, about what the media are supposed to have reported. I want to quote, comrades, what the newspaper PRAVDA said on 15 March, when I was in Altay Kray: Ryzhkov was informed, I quote, that, following repeated consultation with experts, the USSR Academy of Sciences rejected the fear that the ground water would carry into the reservoir dangerous concentrations from the mercury deposits found here. There was nothing to support the fear that the water balance of the Ob would be disrupted by the damming of the Katun. Nor does the dam threaten the local landscape. The canyon is virtually free of woodland. However, the head of the government, after listening attentively to these new arguments, refrained nevertheless from making a final decision. It can be made, he declared, only on the basis of in-depth study, bearing in mind the views of the population and proceeding from all the ecological consequences and the economic effect. End of quotation. I still maintain that point of view. [applause]

Comrades, there have been a great many notes and personal addresses and speeches here concerning the fact that, well, the government, they say, has broken the law on state enterprises and introduced very stringent regulatory measures on wages and labor productivity. I have to report to the congress that in this respect the government has not broken the law. If the law is evoked, those who have a copy of it look under Article No 14, point 4, where it is stated clearly. Therefore, we realize that the regulation of wages and of labor productivity and the production of consumer goods is not really effective; is not the ideal way. And in this respect I agree with Comrade Popov. And it is my opinion, too, that it is not the ideal way. But then, let's find the ideal system, the ideal system of taxation—I am not speaking of citizens' personal taxation, I am speaking of the taxation of expenditure on wages, reproduction [as heard], and so forth. We do not have such a system today. Well, let us create such an effective system of taxation. I think that it must be effective for state enterprises, for leasing, and for cooperatives. We must find a universal system of taxation, then we would not require the measures that we are taking today to regulate these processes to some extent.

Now the pricing question. A great many questions were also raised about this. Obviously, I am repeating myself. As far as retail prices are concerned, I support the position expressed recently by many scholars. And I say recently because it was completely different in the beginning. You know the Politburo's position, the government's position, on this question. We consider that for the next 2 or 3 years there is no need for us at present to embark on considering retail prices. The consumer market must be balanced to a certain extent, and then this issue may be approached, but it is necessary to think within the framework of the next 5-year plan period.

As far as wholesale prices are concerned, there are questions here. After the congress, we obviously will have to carefully evaluate and weigh everything again. There are many problems. Among these, the problems of

Thirteenth Session

9 June 1989

purchase prices on agricultural raw materials are acute. Among these, the question of the purchase price of cotton is very acute—and there was talk of that there today. Incidentally, I will give you some information. We sell for freely convertible currency 100,000 [unit not specified] of cotton, in order to buy from Egypt the same 100,000, but long-fibred ones, to make threads. We do not earn anything in hard currency on cotton. Delivery is made only to CEMA member countries. That is why we must thoroughly think things through as far as wholesale prices go, and decide once and for all. But, obviously, we still have to work a bit on that.

I am giving information. When I said in my report that restrictions should be abolished on wages for retired workers, I said workers but the next day very many notes appeared. I would like to confirm again that just as in Moscow, that refers to unskilled and skilled workers. Comrades, yet another question. With regard to teachers, yes, we have received a question. It is a new one for us. It needs to be studied thoroughly; we will return to it.

Comrades, I want to dwell on yet another question, excuse me, on two questions. I have evidently already gone over the time allotted me. I would like to request the time to deal with two more questions.

[Lukyanov] Shall we give him the time? [audience roars yes]

[Ryzhkov] Several people, comrades who have made speeches, have asked a principle-based question: Should we end the 5-year plan in 1989, even in the next few months? I am convinced that during the 1 and a ½ years that remain until 1991 we must concentrate every effort, both of science and of those doing practical work, of absolutely all the economists and sociologists, to work out an efficient economic mechanism for the next 5-year plan. The errors that we have been allowing, have allowed to happen, must be taken into account. We must take into account the fact that we have accumulated experience. The main thing is that we should transfer the republics over to complete financial autonomy. To carry out such absolutely enormous groundwork—which will radically change our situation even for those principles, economic principles that is, which are in effect today—we need time and we need to concentrate efforts.

If we now allow ourselves, in the middle of 1989, to be drawn into breaking up this perhaps imperfect economic management model, we will first of all be wasting time and, what is most important, today every working collective is engaged in and knows that it has its norms, good or bad, on which it has made all its plans until the end of the current 5-year plan.

If we disturb this today, we will disturb our economic stability, and I think that will do more harm than good.

And the last question: Very many notes—proposals—were submitted and there were speeches, too—Comrade Shmelev spoke—to the effect that when taking into account the difficult situation which has arisen on the consumer market, it is necessary to take foreign credits, not to be afraid to increase foreign economic debt in the name of balancing the consumer market. I would like the people's deputies to be fully informed and clear on our opportunities in this direction. I will cite some data:

So I do not use foreign sources of information on our foreign currency debt, I—perhaps for the first time today—report that the country's foreign debt is now R34 billion. [uproar in the hall] I am convinced even now that it is necessary to approach the problems of the growth of debt and in particular of taking credits in a very carefully weighed manner. For many years we have been living in debt. How is the hard currency situation developing in the country? I am talking about freely convertible currency. For example, it is expected that in the current year the foreign currency revenue will be approximately R16 billion.

That's all we have: R16 billion. And now I would like you to turn your attention to the following figures. Of that amount, more than R5 billion goes to purchase grain and foodstuffs—that's one-third. Can we make a reduction here? Can we? [noise in hall] Well, then it is necessary. If we make a decision like that, taking into account the situation that nowadays still persists in our agriculture, then I think we will sharply worsen the supply of foodstuffs in our country. We will sharply worsen it! Second, R2.5 billion goes to acquire equipment and new technologies; R2.6 billion goes to purchase chemical materials. We are forced to buy them abroad. R1.5 billion goes to purchase raw materials for light industry. R2 billion goes to purchase rolled metal, especially cold-rolled metal, and special pipes, etc. Thus, even a simple calculation will show that approximately R2.5 billion remain. And simply to service the debt that we already have, taking into account that we have to pay interest [kredity] on this debt, we need R12 billion. This means that we are again taking on debt. Is it possible to further aggravate things? Comrades, I think, that we need a very well-balanced position regarding this question.

And in conclusion, esteemed comrades, I would like to say that the government, in close cooperation with the USSR Supreme Soviet and the people's deputies, will do all to ensure that our country embarks upon the path of stable development. The support in this is the trust of the people—the enormous credit which it gave us today. Thank you. [applause]

A.I. Lukyanov: Comrades! During the break a meeting will be held of the congress's editorial committee. Members of the editorial committee are requested to gather during this break in the Hall of Facets.

A second announcement. The committee for investigating the circumstances connected with events in Tbilisi is meeting during this break in the room of the congress Secretariat on the second floor.

Thirteenth Session

9 June 1989

And finally, the committee for inspecting materials connected with the work of the USSR Procuracy's investigative group headed by T.Kh. Gdlyan is meeting now in the editorial committee's room.

A 30-minute break is announced.

(Break).

A.I. Lukyanov: Comrade deputies! The floor is granted to Mikhail Sergeyevich Gorbachev. (Applause).

M. S. Gorbachev, chairman of the USSR Supreme Soviet Presidium:

Esteemed comrade deputies! We are completing the examination of the main areas of domestic and foreign policy at the first Congress of People's Deputies. The work of the congress is drawing toward its conclusion. Using the right of rapporteur, I would like to share my most preliminary impressions of the work of the congress. I think that we are still going to have to do a lot of thorough work on its results and the discussions that have taken place here, and anyone who was to try now, during the congress or immediately after it, to take upon himself that kind of mission, then I think he would be displaying arrogance, all the more so in view of the fact that many comrades who have not spoken are giving their speeches to the Secretariat. Overall, as a result of the discussions we are receiving an enormous amount of material which requires an appropriate, profound, and serious attitude and study.

Nevertheless I think—I am convinced of this, moreover—that this present congress of ours takes us into a new stage of the development of democracy and glasnost in the country, into a new stage in the development of restructuring itself. No doubt each one of us has his own opinion about the congress, his own observations, and his own assessments of the various sessions, the various discussions, and the various decisions. I consider that to be perfectly normal and natural. But you will evidently agree that this congress, notwithstanding all our differences in its assessment, can, nevertheless, be regarded as a major event in the whole history of the Soviet state [applause]

I know that there are different opinions about the character and the content of the discussions that have been taking place at the congress, but you must agree that we are the living witnesses and participants in the free comparison taking place in the atmosphere of the congress of views and points of view on the processes taking place in our society, on its past, present, and future.

This gives us a unique opportunity, not only us deputies but all the working people who are observing the work of the congress, the whole of our society, to have a clear idea of the real state of affairs, of the achievements and shortcomings, the reasons for this or that phenomenon taking place in the country. And this is very important. It gives us the opportunity once again to confirm what I already mentioned before: That in the framework of broad democratization and glasnost, there are real possibilities opening up for taking account of and for implementing the most varied interests of all strata of society. It is in precisely such an atmosphere of democratization and glasnost that our principle of pluralism of views is being put into practice. And this shows the enormous potential of our political system and our social system.

I felt it necessary to emphasize this at the very beginning in sharing my impressions of the congress, since as the congress has proceeded, guided by the discussions at the congress and assessing them, some people are throwing up the idea of a constructive opposition, of political pluralism, not pluralism of views, but political pluralism. I think that the congress, the entire work of the congress, is a convincing argument in favor of this, that in the framework of our political system and social system, but along the paths of democratization and glasnost, it is possible to have broad discussion and opposition of views, dissent, the elaboration on the basis of the comparison of points of view and agreed decisions, finding compromises, on all questions dealing with the fate of the country and the fate of the people.

Our congress is showing enormous possibilities for collective searches for the necessary decisions both for accelerating restructuring and accelerating socioeconomic development. And if anything should be said again about anything, comrades, it is that we must go further along the path of democratization and glasnost, towards people's power, along the path of deepening the revolutionary transformations. I have formed the opinion—and I want to tell you—that the congress, as I see it, firmly takes this line. [applause] And another thing, comrades. To tell the truth, many of us were psychologically and perhaps intellectually unready for such a turn of the discussions at the congress.

This also concerns the problems of social life as they have been raised here, and economic and political reform, and legislative activity, the essence of and the prospects for our union state, and an assessment of certain events in our distant and recent history. But I would not overdramatize all of that, in so far as everything that is happening is a reflection of the powerful democratic flow which is gaining speed in our country. We must delve into everything calmly and in a well measured manner, evaluate everything and, on the basis of collective discussions, come to coordinate conclusions, and we must transform them into a policy and into practical action.

We must seriously evaluate the critical remarks and proposals that were made in the speeches by the delegates of which I have already spoken at the beginning of my speech. Everything that is wise, innovative, constructive, and useful must be made use of without any prejudices. There is only one criterion here: the interests of restructuring, the interests of the people.

Thirteenth Session
9 June 1989

Probably something else needs to be spoken of once again: Any time of change requires search; it requires a breakthrough in thinking, in science and practice, and nonstandard decisions. Restructuring precisely sets the task of finding new ways to ensure the renewal of society. We must seek out these ways together, not fearing novelty and boldness if it moves us forward along the path of restructuring and solving urgent probems in our society.

Over the past few days, we have heard sharp, harsh, and emotional speeches by deputies and, over and over again, one can sense the burden of problems, their vast weight, and the fact that for the most part, the main and essentially the most important work still lies ahead of us. The deputies have brought to the congress rostrum major and specific issues, a critical spirit, fresh thinking and, I would say that this is perhaps the most important thing, dissatisfaction with the state of affairs in the labor collectives, in the regions, in the industrial sectors, and in the country as a whole.

True, opinions have been expressed that too much has been said at the congress about unresolved problems, but a lack of concrete proposals can be felt. I have even seen that in some telegrams coming in to the congress, there is very much criticism leveled at the center and little self-criticism. What would be my attitude to such judgments? I rather think that the merit of our congress has precisely been that on the basis of a broad discussion we are, as it were, obtaining a full idea of the real processes taking place in all the spheres of our country's life and of the moods among the people. That is the first point. Second, the congress makes it possible for us to see how restructuring is faring in life itself, how the political directives and decisions adopted by central bodies are being implemented, how the people themselves are appraising this restructuring and what stands in the way of an implementation of the reforms, lowers their effectiveness, and slows down or else simply puts the brake on our transforming activities. All of this, comrades, provides us with the knowledge, which is essential to tackling problems fruitfully and successfully, moving ahead, and improving our work. This knowledge then—and the debate provides us with considerably more in this regard than other meetings and forums—gives us the opportunity to assess our past work, detect shortcomings, draw lessons, and take all this into account in the elaboration of policy and where decisions have already been taken, they need to be adjusted to make these adjustments.

People's deputies have been saying sharply and uncompromisingly that there can be no talk of restructuring unless radical changes occur in the sphere of production and consumption, unless foodstuffs and goods appear on the shop shelves in sufficient quantity, and unless there is an improvement in housing, the provision of pensions, and in the sphere of health care and services, and so on. I do not regard as a shortcoming the fact that the discussion of these matters was the main theme both in the reports and in the speeches of deputies, although I am aware that many deputies are dissatisfied with both reports, in that they were too down to earth. I feel that even taking into account the debate that has taken place here, that indeed the reports were obviously directed nonetheless at what is concerning society at the present time.

It would be incomprehensible if in the context of the acute problems existing in our country at the moment and in the context of what troubles the people and creates great social tension in society, we should now engage in discussing how we envisage the nature of the renewed society, how we see it, what its main features are, and how and what stages we must go through to reach this goal, leaving without due attention and consideration all that is the subject of primary concern of the people today.

I believe that discussion of all these vitally important and urgent issues increases our conviction that the solution of these urgent—or as we say "crying out"—tasks is possible in the near future. Why am I talking about this? You see I haven't found, overall, any great divergences of principle on these matters. The subjects raised here were in fact the ones we have grown accustomed to and which have long been at the center of attention in discussions at previous congresses. Although—and this is very important and should be noted, so that it should not be understood from this that the congress has somehow not produced anything—there is a difference in approach, particularly with regard to the level of radicalism of the measures proposed by the government and of those proposed by the deputies. And this difference is quite substantial and deserves very serious political and scientific analysis and assessment.

From this, I feel, comrades, there follows just one thing: Work must be continued on a program of urgent measures for resolving pressing, vitally important socioeconomic problems and improving the economy as a whole. This must be done, moreover, without delay both by the USSR Supreme Soviet and the government, involving scientists, economists, and practical workers. I do not want to repeat myself comrades, but the exchange of opinions on approaches to the solution of tasks of developing our economy which took place here at the congress makes it necessary, in my view, to speak my mind on one or two, or three issues.

At the congress the deputies said a lot about shortcomings in the development of our economy, the national economy. This concerned labor collectives, regions, branches of the national economy, and the principle of economic management itself. I personally take all of this seriously and evaluate it as an important contribution to the search for solutions. But I would like to say the following: We will not move resolutely forward and we will not be able to achieve the goals that have been set if we do not carry out a cardinal restructuring of socialist property relationships. We need restructuring of a kind under which the person, the labor collective, is put in

Thirteenth Session
9 June 1989

real terms into the position of the master of production with all the deep and serious consequences that flow from this. [applause] Without that, comrades, we will not solve anything, and our structural measures, the reorganization of management, and all our slogans will not produce anything either. But if we breathe a living spirit into the economic activity of people and collectives, then the situation will change radically. This is something of which I am deeply convinced and I share the opinions of those who hold this position. And overall I think that this is not just the fruit of scientific and intellectual exercises, it is also the result of certain experience that has been built up.

Here I have to say that so far we have been feeling our way with difficulty toward ways of solving this cardinal problem. The search for the most efficient forms of financial autonomy and progressive models of it is proceeding with difficulty. But it seems to me that a general approach toward the reforming of socialist property is nevertheless gradually appearing in outline. I would support the ideas expressed here by deputies about regenerating the social character of state property, uniting it with the person and the collective via relations of socialist leasing in the very widest meaning of the word. In other words, the issue is this: society remaining the proprietor of the property of the whole people places it at the disposal of labor collectives and individual people through various kinds of leasing relationships—and they assume utter and complete responsibility for its use, they bear definite economic obligations to the state, they run their enterprise independently, on their own account and with the help of credits, and they form the income of the collective according to the result of their economic activity.

In doing so they act on the socialist market as independent producers of goods. [applause] The substantial difference between public and cooperative enterprises are being overcome with this approach, although, of course, the forms of management can and will be different. On this basis, on the basis of the large-scale introduction of leasing relations and the development of cooperatives, incentives will be created for the effective, dynamic, interested running of the economy.

I would only say once again—we have nevertheless heard the topic, even though it was not covered as frankly as it was on the eve of the congress during the past few months: How are we to approach resolving the problem of the market? I firmly think and I speak for this, for the market. [sentence as heard] I have already said so. But I think that it is impossible to agree with the comrades who believe that everything needs to be left to the market. Almost dropping all questions of regulation—naturally, regulation not within the framemwork of the administrative system but within the framework of new approaches, using economic methods. It seems to me that such reliance on the market which, so to speak, automatically must decide everything, I think that this is not serious. Even the capitalist market does not accept this. Doing things in this way means demolishing this entire market tomorrow and creating even greater strain, and then tomorrow we will talk—then already all will be on the streets and at meetings—with the working class, with all working people of the country.

So, we must follow our road to the market, preserving plan regulation, preserving economic methods of influence on processes taking place on the market, while at the same time stimulating the economic independence of primary production collectives as much as possible.

Comrades, evidently we have come right up to a fundamental turning point in the development of the economic reform. We must recognize this. We have positive experience, we have negative experience, we have accumulated quantitative—so to speak—experience, and we must understand all this in order to take a decision of principle on how to act further.

In this sense, I highly appreciate the discussion and the exchange of views that has taken place on these matters here at the congress. Taking account of the broad exchange of opinions that has taken place here at the congress, the government needs to thoroughly work through these issues and present them for the consideration of the USSR Supreme Soviet. That is the first thing that I would like to emphasize.

Further, improving the finances of the national economy is of decisive importance for the fate of restructuring the implementation of economic reform. While supporting the government's proposals in this respect, at the same time I think it expedient for the thoughts expressed here by deputies on this issue to be attentively considered by the government and the Supreme Soviet. It seems to be that here, too, as a result of the more in-depth considerations, taking into account the proposals that have been expressed, we shall be able to reach optimal solutions which will answer the real situation and the tasks of stabilizing the monetary and financial situation in the country. Indeed, those deputies who have been saying that half measures will not do in this regard are correct, and for this they have justly been criticizing the government and our economic departments. Much of what has been said on this matter by the economists deserves the most attentive consideration.

Comrades, I would like to say something further about the agrarian issue. Serious things have been heard at the congress on this issue, and not just because all of us, the entire country and the people, are concerned over food supplies in the country but also because of the energetic stance that the agrarian deputies have presented to the congress. In principle, I would like to support them, but, as people say, words alone in this respect are not very much support. This issue is of such a scale, since it concerns the fate of the peasantry and, in general, if you like, the fate of the country, that it needs to be approached in that way in the formulation of policy and in the carrying out of practical work.

We have been saying, and have been saying for a long time now, that the revival of the agrarian sector and its

STENOGRAPHIC RECORD

Thirteenth Session
9 June 1989

transformation into a highly developed sector of the economy capable of providing the country with everything needed is a task involving the whole people, but nearly always we have the peasant, the agricultural worker, and the rural inhabitant to face many problems on their own, the lack of amenities in rural life and the lack of the necesary funding for the conduct of agricultural production. The March plenum of the Central Committee, I am convinced, chose the right path. We must, on the basis of a radical restructuring of economic relationships in the countryside, finally remove all the fetters from the collective and state farms, from agricultural workers. We must provide them with wide opportunities for independence, that is how we must act. At the plenum, we recognized that it was necessary first and foremost to also solve the question of providing the countryside with social amenities. Moreover, large resources are to be directed to those ends. Already in the near future, people should start feeling real changes in their living conditions, and they should be firmly assured of a reliable prospect for life in the countryside. The accelerated development of storage and processing bases in the countryside has been recognized as one of the important and urgent tasks; for any efforts to increase agricultural output, agricultural produce, and the production of agricultural goods simply lose their raison d'etre unless these questions are solved urgently. Here, too, much has been determined in advance and is already being done. But, as I have understood from the speeches of the agrarian deputies and from their appeal, the needs of the agrarian sector to strengthen the material and technical basis require additional attention and examination both by the government and the Supreme Soviet.

But in general they require the attention of the whole of society, and this is how we must approach it—at the rayon, town, oblast, and republic level. We must make sure a change. [applause] Comrades, using all the economic power of our economy, we must go for a speedy solution of all these vitally important problems of the development of the countryside. I understand that on this account we have a common opinion here at the congress. [applause] We are all agreed, comrades, that we must resolutely carry out, more resolutely carry out the process of economic and political transformations. But this requires great legislative work, and it has started. I agree, as deputies have said here, and primarily Deputy Alekseyev, that it would be useful to work out and be guided in it by a defined strategy. That is correct. It even seems to me—not just seems, I am convinced—that a lagging behind in this area of the activity of the legislative organs is already hindering the advance of the transformation processes in our federal state.

Hence we get artificial clashes between the center and the republics; some seem to get the feeling they are misunderstood and others, in the center, that they are being pressured, without being given the opportunity to understand. All this demonstrates that life is leaving us behind, so to speak, with regard to our legislative work, and embarking on new legislative acts to correspond with the current stage of restructuring. And this stage is a very important one—both economic reform is a crucial stage, and political reform has reached its second stage, touching now upon issues of our federation, sovereignty of republics, autonomous formations, the life of national okrugs, and so on. Also of local soviets. Local soviets as well.

Clearly comrades no issue has been discussed as broadly at our present congress as the issue of interethnic relations. We have all clearly felt this, and felt it strongly, experienced quite a few uneasy moments even during the congress. There is much that troubles us here. It is essential to resolve these issues in an integrated way, an all-embracing way, boldly and at the same time tactfully and respectfully. But this also presupposes at the same time, comrades, that we cannot allow any compromise with attempts to resolve these generally very important, vitally important issues—without which restructuring will not go forward—affecting, to put it plainly, all peoples and nations of our country. We cannot agree, even for a single moment, with attempts by certain groups to resolve these problems, to settle, so to speak, the interethnic issues by criminal methods, disregarding morals and laws, and sometimes embarking on the road to anarchy.

This is unacceptable not only in interethnic issues, but in restructuring, in our lives as a whole. We must steer a constructive path, through democracy and glasnost, through mutual understanding and cooperation. These are essential prerequisites. And especially, frankly speaking, through dialogue.

And therefore, I, as chairman of the USSR Supreme Soviet, appeal to you, dear comrade people's deputies, and to all the citizens of our country, let us show wisdom, responsibility, restraint, and farsightedness in tackling these very important questions. [applause] Let us not allow outbursts of spur-of-the-moment emotions to gain the upper hand over concern for the future of our peoples, our children, grandchildren, and great-grandchildren. And only on the soil of wisdom and the law—and I repeat once again—of a broad dialogue, is it possible to solve—and we certainly can solve—all the problems which have accumulated in this important—and now acute—sphere of human relations. We must firmly and resolutely apply the law with regard to those who do not heed the arguments of common sense and the norms of the law.

In the deputies' speeches, questions were asked on the correlation between the center and the republics which are fundamental for our federation. As a result of the discussions which took place one may state that there is accord on two positions, it seems to me. First, on the vital need to strengthen the USSR as a multinational socialist state within the framework of which the free development of all the peoples which make up its population is ensured. And second, we must fill the Soviet federation with real content and ensure the sovereignty

Thirteenth Session

9 June 1989

of the union republics, broad independence, and autonomy, and the rights of the individual whatever his national affiliation. [applause]

In the debates, in a general sense, we have been all the time in one way or another been discussing cardinal questions and new questions. At the same time, we have been returning to questions which are, as it were, ordinary ones. But their importance lies in their ordinariness. I have in mind questions of law and order and discipline. I would like to again say a few words on this question. Restructuring and democracy are unthinkable without discipline and self-discipline and without a high sense of responsibility. Everywhere and in everything, and at all times, one of the bulwarks of democracy has been a developed civic sense, inseparable from the ability and readiness to control one's own actions, and to answer for them to oneself and to society.

In recent years the public has witnessed more than one tragedy which has stunned the country. Many human lives have been lost, mainly because of basic slovenliness and criminal dereliction of one's direct duties on the part of someone. That was the case with Chernobyl, with the "Admiral Nakhimov," at Sverdlovsk and Arzamas, near Alma-Ata, and in other places—and the latest tragedy with the trains in the Urals. These, comrades, are only the most glaring examples—and how many are there of the kind that you and I have become accustomed to? And behind every catastrophe are human lives, not to mention economic losses.

What we need is firm production and technological discipline. We must get rid of slovenliness and irresponsibility. It is our duty to work toward developing a conscious sense of discipline in society. I believe that the attention of the congress and all its bodies should be constantly drawn toward this. That is what I feel, and in my recent visit with Comrade Ryzhkov to Bashkiria and Chelyabinsk Oblast, that was the mood of the people, comrades. The people are very worried by this.

Closely connected with the viability of democracy, discipline, and self-discipline, is the problem of crime. The growth in crime gives rise to just anger among Soviet people, and all of us, especially in the localities, must direct maximum efforts to fighting this plague, especially against such a challenge to the very foundations of our society as organized crime.

The government and the law-and-order bodies, and all of our public, are obliged to adopt exhaustive measures on this question. That was the opinion of the congress, and I would just like to support that opinion. [applause]

Comrades, the urgency of solving many problems must not, of course, push restructuring—the future of restructuring—into the background, unless we want to repeat a deadlocked verion of development. Immediate and urgent decisions today must serve as a bridge to tomorrow, a bridgehead for the advance of restructuring and the success of further transformations.

I listened with great interest to Comrade Shmelev's speech, but as for his phrase—he spoke too lightly—that I am not interested in what we do tomorrow, only today, I think he was wrong in treating this subject in such a light-hearted fashion!

A policy that concentrates only on short-range objectives and does not combine the present and the future is not going to be of full value. Party policy is, to use an expression from the Marxist classics, tactics that never lose sight of the great obectives. This is a serious matter, comrades. Ever since it became a science, socialism has demanded to be treated as a science. That was Lenin's view. Trenchant, publicist phrases and poetic metaphors will not help here, although it is always interesting. Serious scientific analysis is necessary, and the party carries it out as it tackles the new problems confronting the theory of socialism. We must conduct our scientific investigations and discussions even more intensively, as we interpret the society in which we live. What have we built? What are we restructuring? Finally, what are the social aims and intentions of restructuring? How do we see the new targets of the revolutionary renewal of society and of socialism?

We have been long accustomed to taking as our starting-point the view that we have created the best of all possible social systems. This conclusion emerged from the idea that there was only one model of socialism, an idea that was formulated by the fact of building socialism in one country. We now know that this is not so. We have both seen in practice and recognized in theory the diversity of the roads of socialist development. We have discovered the real dangers of deviations from the essence of the socialist idea and of its distortions through dogmatism and impracticable, speculative plans, to say nothing of arbitrary rule and lawlessness.

But we also see something else: the inexhaustible riches contained in the idea of socialism, riches that can only be revealed by a diversity of practical solutions, united by the humanist ideas of service to mankind. I believe in the boundless possibilities of socialism—and this is not just a belief, but a matter of my own knowledge—and I think we must seek answers to all the questions that modern life has posed for us and which the broad discussion of all problems will pose within the framework of our system, on the roads of democratization and glasnost, rather than seeking somewhere from which to borrow other values in order to resolve our own problems. I think that that is the wrong road. I wanted to state my own position on this categorically at the congress. [applause]

We do not yet know the full richness of the forms of the society toward which we are moving. But we do know that these forms will continually arise from practice, from past, present and future knowledge, and through assimilation of all the achievements of human civilization.

STENOGRAPHIC RECORD

Thirteenth Session

9 June 1989

When Marxism was formed as a theory it did not stay aside from all the processes taking place in the world, nor did it arise on the roadside of the development of human civilization but on its highway of it. And all the more so, today it cannot but draw upon all the achievements of human civilization. That is why we cannot embark upon the path of isolation from the world and of restricting ties and cooperation with the world. No, that would contradict Leninist ideas.

We know that this society in all its relations and manifestations will be oriented toward man. It will be shaped and developed by the initiative of the masses, will be created by their creativity, and will open up vast expanses to man. Colossal forces are latent in socialism and we must give them an outlet on the basis of democracy and glasnost, the humanization of social relations, the recognition of values common to all mankind and of simple standards of morality and justice, the social and legal protection of the individual, of course, on the basis of an efficient and dynamic economy relying on economic methods and a diversity of forms of social ownership, and on the basis of professionalism, competence, conscientiousness of work, discipline, and self-discipline. That means on the basis of culture, comrades, in its broadest interpretation.

In essence, it is the problem of the spirituality of society. This has been spoken of at the congress, although not a very great deal. Socialism by its nature must be a society of spiritually rich, genuinely intelligent people, no matter what they do, no matter what social group they belong to. We must be extremely sensitive and attentive to spiritual problems. Otherwise, comrades, the renewal of society will not succeed. For everything is through man, and the main deciding force, and the main acting figure of restructuring is man. [applause] Many characteristics of the future are being formed in the course of restructuring.

It has taken us 4 years to recognize in the atmosphere of democratic discussions the real state of society, to elaborate new approaches in the economy and in the political sphere, and to begin restructuring in practice. I think that this work should be deepened, supported by what the present stage of restructuring gives us, and especially by what the present Congress of People's Deputies has given. As I see it, this is a major direction of party work on the threshold of the 28th CPSU Congress. In this sense the first Congress of USSR People's Deputies has worked well for restructuring, and therein lies its great service in the revolutionary renewal of socialism. [applause]

Comrades, I accept the criticism addressed to me, addressed to the political leadership, first and foremost over the slowness that has occurred in carrying out reforms. We have been late in many respects. This has had a serious effect on all the transformation processes.

I think that there would have been fewer shortcomings and omissions if the Central Committee had displayed more exactingness in the execution of the instructions both of the party congress and of the 19th party conference. This also applies to no less extent to the USSR Government. One of the gravest omissions has been the slow dismantling of the obsolete management structure, the attempts to solve pressing questions—and many of them have acquired a chronic nature—with old methods which have already more than once doomed us to failure.

In approaching a number of problems there has not been enough due principledness and timeliness in reacting to this or that topical problem of internal life. Today we are all better aware that restructuring is a fairly long-term matter. It is a historic transitional period in the development of socialism. It is necessary to stress once more: We are against skipping stages, losing touch with reality, even for the most noble of motives connected with an understandable impatience in society. But we must fight, and fight resolutely, also against gradualism, against Oblomovite [passive] behavior, against voluntary or involuntary application of the brakes on restructuring. In the last analysis the two extremes, both conservatism and ultra-leftism meet. The result, if one places either of these extremes at the basis of political activity can be the same: an irreparable blow to restructuring. I favor a vigorous, but at the same time balanced, realistic policy. The CPSU proposes it, without claiming infallibility and the absolute truth. On the contrary, it is inviting all our society, all the intellectual forces of our society to enrich it. We must self-critically—we are becoming increasingly successful at this—analyze every step we make, subjecting to public discussion the party's activity.

Restructuring has not been, nor will it be beyond criticism, and that is why it is restructuring. However, analyzing its lessons in the most impartial way, one cannot forget a good saying: Don't throw the baby out with the bathwater. It is unlikely, comrades—let's be realists and honest to ourselves and to our working people—it is unlikely that this congress would have taken place but for the April plenum of the Central Committee, the 27th party congress, and the 19th conference. [applause] Notwithstanding all the diversity of opinions, judgements, and proposals which there have been at the congress, one cannot be blind to this or fail to realize it, provided, of course, one does not take a biased stand. That has happened here, too.

One of the obvious results of restructuring consists in the fact that we have attained a normal and open political life after long years of despotism of the administrative-command system. Or perhaps I will put it like this, mostly normal. This is an achievement gained through hard suffering. We would have ruined restructuring had we not preserved it, and would have cut off its air.

Comrades, I would like to speak about another matter, too. There have been heated disputes at our congress and

Thirteenth Session
9 June 1989

opposing opinions have been expressed. This is a natural phenomenon strengthening the constructive basis of restructuring. I, and probably many deputies, too, cannot agree unconditionally with all the critical pronouncements. But for all that, there is discussion. We cannot agree particularly when one or another individually-adopted reason, phenomenon, or aspect of life which really do exist are made absolute. I think that such an approach is capable of distorting our view, of negatively influencing our appraisals and conclusions, thereby giving rise to new errors.

In the first few days here, quite a few sharp and scathing words were said about the apparatus. I do not want to defend bureaucracy, inflated staffing levels, or negligent and incompetent workers. Moreover, I think that we are waging the battle against bureaucracy without the necessary resoluteness and are resolving slowly the cadres questions which are dictated by restructuring itself. [applause]

However, I am convinced, convinced that the breaking of the command-administrative system must not be identified with a struggle against the apparatus. The overcoming of bureaucracy will not bring us success if it is confined to a campaign directed against the apparatus in general. Without a qualified, competent, well-organized apparatus of government in the center and in the provinces, we will not achieve anything sensible, comrades. And, incidentally, those who criticize and who speak on these problems, are themselves preparing generally to enter a new apparatus [applause]

So, overall this is what is at issue. [applause] And I am adding nothing surprising here, either. Let's put it like this; we need a new apparatus. I agree with that. [applause]

Comrades, I shall touch on yet another question which is worrying all of us. It also worries me. Because of historical reasons and distressing experience, we are especially sensitive to the question of excessive concentration of power in the hands of one leader. And this has been heard here at the congress; this concern is present. Since the question exists, I think it is necessary clearly and unambiguously to express one's attitude to it. You would probably simply not understand if I did not react to this theme which was present both on the eve of the congress and at the congress.

As a Communist I categorically do not accept the hints expressed - if not very plainly—alleging that I am trying to concentrate all the power in my hands. This is alien to me, to my views, my outlook, and indeed my character—I hope that you are already somewhat familiar with my style and character. It was not for this that the sharp about-turn to the new policy was made at the April plenum. It was not for this that the party and people embarked on the hard work of democratization, glasnost, cleansing, and renewal of our society and public life. As general secretary and chairman of the Supreme Soviet I have no other policy than that of restructuring, democratization, and glasnost and I declare again to the congress, to the working people, to the entire people my unwavering loyalty to that policy, for it is only on the basis of that that we shall be able to consolidate our society and resolutely accelerate movement along the path of restructuring. [applause] I see the meaning of my life and work in this. [applause]

Comrades, Marx and Lenin considered a critical attitude to one's own activity to be essential for a revolutionary party. I think that we can say in our party and society this is becoming a norm of life. But in this connection, as a Communist, I categorically reject attacks on the party. [applause] I repeat, so that it will be clear: I consider that we have raised the question at the very beginning and thus it must stand, and that must be our approach. The party is at the service of the people. That is the main thing. It is responsible for its policy, and it cannot be beyond the criticism, judgement, and assessments of the people. [applause]

But it is quite a different thing when it is a matter of attacks on the party simply as a party, a political party. Of course, in its history, the party's history, there have been various pages, including also tragic ones.

Our party has honestly owned up to the mistakes made, and soon there will be something more to tell you when we conclude on these matters in the near future. The party has assumed responsibility for them, has acted as the initiator of restructuring, of the radical renewal of society. I am confident that the 20 million Communists and the Central Committee will be to prove, in restructuring, that they are equal to the difficult tasks of the time and are capable of fulfilling in the future also the role of Soviet society's political vanguard.

Yes, the party, just as society as a whole, must restructure itself. As general secretary of the Central Committee I wish to tell the deputies that the Politburo firmly intends to put into effect the line of the 27th congress and the 19th party conference toward restructuring in society. I think that we must carry out a vast amount of work in preparing for the 28th party congress, a vast amount of work.

But the comrades have, evidently, been right in saying that the party is lagging behind and if it wants to be the vanguard of society and fulfill this mission—and society needs such a vanguard force, a bearer of program goals—the party must also restructure itself more quickly than society. [applause]

Comrades, I want—alarming rumors of what is supposedly taking place in the Central Committee and in the Politburo have been heard here—I want to say: The Central Committee holds the same position which I stated when describing the position of the Politburo, and I assure you that dangers of coups or of something similar do not at all exist here. This I state firmly. [applause] Let us be finished with rumors of all kinds, for

Thirteenth Session

9 June 1989

in 4 years I have died 7 times and my family has already been slain 3 times. [laughter]

And all this is rife, going around you understand. And they bring me family trees [skhemy rodovyye] of some kind and I look at them.

Comrades, let us be finished with these rumors, and above all the deputies and people involved in state matters should not rely on all this chatter which they are frequently being fed with. [applause]

There is a task facing us, comrades, which is exceptionally important in scale and newness, and that is to unite in an organic way the efforts of renewed Soviet power and the political work of a renewed party, so that the gigantic potential to be found in the socialist social system can be fully revealed. Yes, we are in a complex situation, but we are not in gloom or darkness. I want to say this bluntly, not in gloom and not in darkness, as it might seem to some people, even among those sitting here in this hall. We have a clear policy. The party will succeed in fulfilling its historic mission—the renewal of socialism—by working out a policy and offering it to society and I am sure that the Soviet system which is being regenerated on new principles of democracy will make its decisive contribution to the implementation of the tasks which we have drawn up.

At the congress, and many comrades have probably drawn attention to this, little has been said about foreign policy. It has been said that at the present stage of restructuring we have truly achieved considerable results which are welcomed by our people and the public throughout the world, results which have changed in many ways not just the image of the Soviet Union but the situation in the world, too. This is indeed so. What has been accomplished in the field of foreign policy is not as a result of a change in notions, concepts, or even doctrines. From what we have inherited, much that is musty, harmful, and vicious has been discarded.

But nobody will bring us positive changes in world affairs as a gift, any more than to other peoples. No, comrades, each step on the path to a new and more civilized world must be conquered in a difficult struggle, even though outwardly it may not always be so noticeable.

Let us take note of one other thing: In order that the positive advancements in international affairs may become irreversible, we must always remember that we are speaking with partners who take account of facts and facts alone, and we must always present them with facts which will convince them, for a long time I hope, that it is better to get along well with us, just as we hope to get along well with all neighbors, near and far. [applause]

And so, comrades, a difficult yet clear path lies ahead, if we assess it in a composed and stately manner, as we—people's deputies—are expected to do. Power to the soviets, comrades, means creating a system of democratic institutions, a system for the sovereignty of the people—orderly, efficient, and functioning in all conditions and under all circumstances. Power to the soviets is unattainable without the return of the land to the peasants. Power to the soviets cannot be unless each one of us feels himself to be a part of society and nature, health care and the education service, prosperity and well-being. The sovereignty of the people will not become firmly established until it displays a higher degree of efficiency than any other form of power. It follows from this that in politics, we shall have to learn much, assimilate much, and get used to much. The congress that has taken place has taught us a lot. We shall, no doubt, derive the necessary lessons from it and will part all the wiser. There is also no doubt that we shall come better prepared to the next congress. In short, all of us together have to become familiar with the school of soviet sovereignty of the people. I am sure that we shall manage this.

Allow me to express the conviction that by combined effort and through the deeds of each deputy, we shall cope with the obligations that have been placed upon us by the people and by our common fatherland. [applause]

A.I. Lukyanov: Comrade deputies, the editorial committee has prepared the draft resolution of the Congress of People's Deputies "On the Basic Guidelines of the USSR's Domestic and Foreign Policy." The floor is granted to Deputy Vadim Andreyevich Medvedev, chairman of the editorial committee.

V.A. Medvedev, member of the CPSU Central Committee Politburo and secretary of the CPSU Central Committee, Moscow City, (from the CPSU): Comrade deputies! The editorial commission you elected, which comprises 68 people representing all social strata of our society and all republics, has worked intensively these past few days and submits for your examination a draft congress resolution on the basic guidelines for Soviet domestic and foreign policy.

Four plenary sittings of the commission were held during the work. The working group worked virtually constantly throughout this time. We made no preliminary drafts, it is all the fruit of the work of the editorial commission—from the first line to the last.

The question of the nature of the document arose from the outset. Various viewpoints were voiced on this score. It was proposed, in particular, to impart to the document the nature of a congress declaration. This was also mentioned in certain deputies' speeches at the congress itself. On the other hand, the viewpoint was also expressed that the resolution, our document, should be purely pragmatic and should only generalize the concrete proposals made in the course of the congress' work. As a result of the exchange of opinions and—and this is the main thing—as a result of practical work we in the editorial commission drew the conclusion that the document should constitute a synthesis, that is, it should

Thirteenth Session
9 June 1989

incorporate the sum total of the political conclusions, assessments of the situation within the country, and formulas defining the directives for our future domestic and foreign policy.

At the same time it must also be quite specific, contain a practical solution of a number of problems, and provide the Supreme Soviet Presidium, the USSR Council of Ministers, and other organs with instructions for the elaboration and adoption of decisions on numerous questions.

The structure of the resolution was also determined on the basis of this premise. It begins with a preamble proclaiming that the Congress of People's Deputies assumes full supreme state power within the country. Thus it responds to the proposals from a number of deputies that the congress should adopt a declaration on this score. The first section of the draft provides a harsh but realistic assessment of the persisting difficult situation within the country, an assessment based on the report and deputies' speeches. The roots of this situation lie in the accumulated deformations and distortions of past periods and the inconsistency and sometimes even halfheartedness of recent measures, which have not as yet enabled the country to emerge from the crisis in which it found itself in the early 1980's. The commission was unanimous that the account of our state's domestic policy should begin with a detailed social program that would provide an integral account of questions linked with the material prosperity, spiritual development, and moral health of society and each of its members. In turn the social program has been set out, as I believe you have seen for yourselves, in such a way that the most pressing and topical questions in need of immediate solution are brought to the fore. They include questions of normalizing the market and easing the position of the least well-off strata of our society. Subsequent sections are devoted to our state's policy in the economic sphere, in the sphere of state and legal building, and in the sphere of national relations, and lastly, to international policy. The document ends with a conclusion whose leitmotiv is the unification of all strata of our people around the party in order to implement restructuring and raise our country to modern levels of socioeconomic development. We were guided by the basic provisions of Comrade M.S.Gorbachev's report "On the Basic Guidelines for the USSR's Domestic and Foreign Policy" and Comrade N.I.Ryzhkov's report "On the Program for the Upcoming Activity of the USSR Government," and also by the theses voiced at the congress from this platform by people's deputies. The commission analyzed the vast number of proposals and comments voiced here. All in all, 702 proposals and questions relating to specific problems were registered, including 72 on changes and additions to the constitution, 309 on socioeconomic problems, 87 on improving current legislation, 83 on interethnic relations, 18 on enhancing the role and prestige of the soviets and stepping up their real sovereignty, 19 on organization and on strengthening discipline, legality, and law and order, and 18 on monitoring accountable organs. They were all carefully systematized and a considerable number of them have been taken into consideration in the draft. Of course, some proposals and comments have not been reflected in this document either because they are too specific or because they require further study and discussion. They will all be handed over for further examination by the Supreme Soviet, its commissions, the government, and other state and public organs. The draft, comrades, also systematizes appeals from individual groups of deputies on various topical problems, including the appeal from a group of deputies from the agrarian sector, appeals on various problems of interethnic relations, and others that are reflected in the draft and proposed for your attention.

I would like to stress—to conclude these brief explanations—that the commission's work took place in an atmosphere of lively and sometimes quite keen debate and comparison of opinions and viewpoints. In this respect it continued the congress' work and reflected its spirit. There were debates on both general questions and specific questions like investment policy, leasing, the role of republic and local organs in solving social problems, the restructuring of the financial and credit system, and so on. By and large the debates were conducted in a constructive spirit, and the document which has been submitted to you emerged as a result.

Comrades, since this document was distributed new questions have appeared in our work and some omissions from the document have emerged. So permit me first to report on proposals from the editorial commission itself regarding additions and changes to the text. May I? A.I. Lukyanov: Yes, please do.

V.A. Medvedev: It is proposed to make obvious changes on page 3. At the beginning it alludes to the report by Comrade Gorbachev, chairman of the USSR Supreme Soviet. It is proposed to also include a reference to the report made by Comrade N.I. Ryzhkov, chairman of the Council of Ministers. "Statement" is a more accurate word for the report delivered by the chairman of the Council of Ministers on the program for the USSR Government's upcoming activity.

At the end of the first section it is proposed to include a paragraph instructing the Supreme Soviet and the Council of Ministers to analyze and generalize all the specific proposals made by deputies on economic, social, and other questions, take them into consideration in legislative work and in the practical activity of ministries and departments, and present people's deputies with a report on this. I believe that this should not arouse irritation.

On this same page, in accordance with the clarification made in Comrade N.I. Ryzhkov's closing speech today, it is proposed to include the following clarification in the fifth paragraph from the bottom: "Lift restrictions for pensioned workers and skilled workers." (Noise in the auditorium).

M.S. Gorbachev: Could you repeat that?

V.A. Medvedev: Fifth paragraph from the bottom: "Lift restrictions on labor remuneration for pensioned

FIRST CONGRESS OF PEOPLE'S DEPUTIES OF THE USSR

Thirteenth Session

9 June 1989

workers and skilled workers irrespective of the size of the pension they receive." (Noise in the auditorium). The proposal from the Council of Ministers is formulated exactly as it now sounds. As for other questions, the next page mentions the need to elaborate a law on pensions in general. (Noise in the auditorium).

The following proposal is submitted with regard to the text on page 7, second paragraph from the bottom. This paragraph says: "The congress on the whole approves the proposals set out in the reports (minor amendment here) by Comrades M.S. Gorbachev and N.I. Ryzhkov to improve the national economy, drastically reduce the budget deficit, regulate money circulation, and saturate the consumer market with goods and services and demands...." Now there is an addition in view of the proposals voiced by people's deputies: "...that additional steps be taken to stabilize the country's economic situation." The speeches yesterday and today from this platform also contain proposals. They should also be taken into consideration when solving these problems.

I ask you to turn to page 8. The third paragraph from the top, which begins with the words: "Seek additional resources to develop the economy and resolve social tasks by reducing military spending to the level of reasonable sufficiency." It is proposed to delete the words which follow—"and expenditure on space programs." And to say instead: "...increasing the effectiveness of space research, making broad use...," thereafter following the text: "...in the national economy of the achievements of space technology."

The third paragraph from the bottom, which begins with the words: "The congress deems it necessary to devote particular attention to the development of agriculture and all sectors of the agro-industrial complex." The following is to be inserted after this: "The USSR Supreme Soviet is instructed to substantially renew legislation on the land and land use." It goes on: "It is necessary to embark more boldly on transferring land to the lease...." Thereafter it follows the text.

Page 10. Fourth section. The words from the second paragraph "form a commission to prepare a new USSR Constitution..." should be moved to the previous paragraph, which will thus begin as follows: "The congress advocates unanimously that work begin immediately on preparing a new constitution—the fundamental law of the USSR." It goes on: "The congress resolves to form a commission to prepare a new USSR Constitution." Then it says: "The congress proceeds on the premise that the new constitution should embody the principles..."—thereafter following the text. The penultimate paragraph should be worded as follows: "The USSR Supreme Soviet is instructed to prepare amendments to the current constitution by the next session of the congress of People's Deputies..."—thereafter following the text.

I ask you to turn to page 12. The second paragraph, which ends with the words "concerning a unified tax system," should be supplemented with the following sentence: "The USSR Supreme Soviet and Council of Ministers must examine proposals from the Estonian and Lithuanian SSR's on the economic independence of these union republics and their transfer to republic economic accountability as of 1 January 1990." This proposal was submitted to the congress and requires attention.

Fifth paragraph from the top. After the words "the congress instructs" the words "the Constitutional Oversight Committee" should be omitted. They should be replaced with the words: "the USSR Supreme Soviet to examine the question of the consonance with the USSR Constitution..."—thereafter following the text.

Page 13. Third paragraph from the bottom. Add the following words to the middle of the paragraph: "The congress instructs the USSR Supreme Soviet Soviet of Nationalities and the supreme soviets of the appropriate republics to examine the question of measures to normalize the situation in Nagorno-Karabakh Autonomous Oblast, the proposal to restore the rights of the Volga Germans, the Crimean Tatars, and the Meskhetian Turks, and the development problems of small ethnic groups raised at the congress." (Noise in the auditorium).

I ask you to turn to page 14. The penultimate paragraph. If you swap the last and penultimate sentences in this paragraph it will end with the words: "The withdrawal of the Soviet troops from Afghanistan was a most important foreign policy step in recent years." The following sentence should be added to this paragraph: "The congress calls on parliaments and the international public to do everything possible to promote the return of the Soviet soldiers and officers who failed to return from the Afghan war and who are languishing in foreign lands."

Page 15, first paragraph. Before the last sentence of the paragraph, after the sentence "In such conditions ensuring the reliable defense of the country is one of our state's most important functions," the following sentence is to be inserted: "The congress advocates the further qualitative development of the Soviet Army, which is raised in the spirit of patriotism, closely linked with the entire Soviet people, and devoted to their interests." Then would come the final sentence: "Concern must continue to be shown for the Soviet Army and for enhancing its prestige."

There is one more proposal with regard to the text of this page. Second paragraph. End of this paragraph, three lines from the bottom. After the words "in the Asia-Pacific region," the gerundive clause "devoting particular attention to friendly relations with India" should be added.

Those are the additions that the editorial commission is making to its own draft.

A.I. Lukyanov: Are there any questions for Comrade Medvedev? There are questions? Please. Comrades, let us agree on how to conduct our work further. Perhaps that is what we should do now. I think that that this draft resolution with the amendments that have been entered should be taken as a basis. What do you think? Can we

STENOGRAPHIC RECORD

Thirteenth Session

9 June 1989

take it as a basis? And secondly, if anyone has any arguments against taking it as a basis, I ask him to speak up. Is there anyone who wants to speak up against taking this draft as a basis?

Voices from the hall. No.

A.I. Lukyanov: Then I ask you to vote. Whoever is for taking the draft as a basis, I ask you to vote. Opposed? I request a count. This is a serious matter.

A.G. Kostenyuk: Esteemed deputies, nine deputies voted "no."

A.I. Lukyanov: Who abstained? I request a count.

A.G. Kostenyuk: Forty deputies obstained.

A.I. Lukyanov: Thus, comrades, by majority vote the draft resolution of the USSR Congress of People's Deputies "On the Basic Guidelines of the USSR's Domestic and Foreign Policy" is taken as a basis.

Before declaring a break, I want to say that 29 notes have been received with requests to speak on the draft resolution. They are very diverse. In some notes comrades propose absolutely specific wordings to enter into the draft, which makes it possible for the editorial committee to work on the basis of such notes. Others ask to speak. From my viewpoint, Deputy N.A. Shibik took the best approach: He entered all of his amendments on the printed draft. It is very easy to work with such a document. I think that if anyone proposes his amendments in that form he will make our common, concerted work much easier. (Applause).

I would like to announce that deputies interested in the work of the Ecology Committee are asked to remain here in the hall after the end of this session.

A break is announced until 1600.

M. S. Gorbachev, Chairman of the USSR Supreme Soviet, presiding.

M. S. Gorbachev: Esteemed comrades! As we have agreed, a group of deputies has handed in texts containing their criticisms. We have turned them over to the editorial committee for action on the ideas expressed in the drafts. Now we have to agree on another matter. There are already about 30 who have signed up to speak. According to our rules of order, three minutes is allotted for that. Thus, we already need more than an hour for this. But as I understand it, once comrades have signed up, their requests are not to be withdrawn. Let us grant the floor, according to the rules, for up to three minutes, comrades, whether a speaker has finished or not. Many comrades have conveyed their criticisms to the editorial committee, and it is acting on them.

Let us continue our work. The floor is granted to Deputy Grigoriy Nikolayevich Podberezskiy.

G. N. Podberezskiy, director of Large-Panel Housing Construction Plant No 2 of the 50th Anniversary of the USSR Minsk Industrial Housing Construction Production Association (Minsk-Frunze National Territorial Election District): Esteemed deputies! I want to dwell on the following matter. If there is one thing we have plenty of in our country, as they say, it is controllers. There is state control, people's control, and worker control. If you try to count, you probably won't have enough fingers. I shall cite just one example—state acceptance. To be honest, I do not know what learned person thought that up. I am a builder. In Minsk we spend 1 million rubles a year and 700,000 rubles in wages on state acceptance. One can figure out how many pensions we could pay, and how we could help families that are not well-off. And there are no results, because the materials that come in are no good. I believe that instead of these controllers, there should be one controller—the Soviet ruble. If it hits people in the pocket, that means that the control will also be obvious. Therefore, I propose that the USSR Supreme Soviet prepare the question of unified control in the Soviet Union for the next congress. (Applause).

And a second matter, comrades. People in Belorussia are actively preparing for the shift to regional cost accounting as of 1 January 1990. But for some reason today we heard in the draft that only the Baltic republics will make the shift. I ask for an explanation.

A third matter. I carefully read the draft decree. It is written there that we should create a new Constitution. Is it possible that we have created enough new Constitutions? Let us bring the old one up to par, make amendments in it, and accept it at the next congress. That is all I have. Thank you. (Applause).

M. S. Gorbachev: The floor is granted to Deputy Ternyuk. Deputy Zaslavskiy is next.

N. E. Ternyuk: deputy chief technologist at the Plant imini Malyshev Production Association (Kharkov-Ordzhonikidze Territorial Election District, Ukrainian SSR): Esteemed comrades! We have very many laws that are very easy for executives to carry out. And the higher the executive's rank, the easier it is. For a worker, ordinary engineer, or economist, it is sometimes difficult to exercise his rights and take advantage of his possibilities, and sometimes difficult even to defend his honor and dignity. Therefore, I propose that the following be included on page 10, in the next-to-last paragraph: "The new draft Constitution must include mechanisms for the exercise of basic rights and freedoms that will guarantee equal possibility for exercising them to all of the USSR's citizens." This pertains to Articles 14, 18, 20, 21, 40 and others where this issue must be noted and resolved.

Furthermore, an economic system of economic management is impossible without a statewide information system; therefore, I believe that an addition must be made on page 9, third paragraph from the bottom, stating the need to establish a statewide information system.

Comrades, plant workers will go away dissatisfied with this draft, because it contains practically no specific

Thirteenth Session

9 June 1989

decisions on granting enterprises broad rights and possibilities. Therefore, I propose that the following matter be considered—page 10, before the third paragraph from the top: "The congress deems it necessary that the USSR Council of Ministers revoke the planning system based on gross indices. The Supreme Soviet, together with the USSR Council of Ministers, is charged with drawing up, on a priority basis, a set of laws regulating the economic and economic-management relations of enterprises among themselves, as well as between ministries and enterprises, in order to eliminate diktat."

Furthermore, the following words should be added to page 6, third paragraph from the top: "The production of medical equipment is to be given the status of the production of priority consumer goods, with provision for the appropriate material and technical supply." Our enterprises have the possibility of helping, and it must be done.

I believe that we should express ourselves more specifically with regard to cooperatives that engage in speculation. Therefore, I propose the following addition on page 9, fourth paragraph from the bottom: "to order local soviets to promptly halt the operations of cooperatives in which direct or indirect speculation takes place."

On page six, before the fifth paragraph, an additional point must be included with regard to instructions to the Council of Ministers regarding the implementation of social programs: "To work out a program for granting a 24-day vacation to workers." This is a serious question of social justice. On the same page, fifth paragraph from the top: "...including by providing for the granting of a three-year leave to mothers for childcare." I realize that that means approximately 18 billion rubles, but this matter must be adopted. Right now such a point can already be adopted, and women's work in child rearing recognized as state business.

M. S. Gorbachev: Deputy Zaslavskiy, please. Comrade Vladimir Nikolayevich Stepanov will be next to speak.

I. I. Zaslavskiy: scientific associate at the Moscow A.N. Kosygin Textile Institute (Oktyabr Territorial Election district, Moscow): Esteemed chairman, esteemed deputies! I would like to add a proposal to the resolution connected with the life of disabled people and assistance to the disabled. In general, I had prepared a large, substantial report, but I did not have a chance to present it in the debates, and therefore I cannot provide detailed substantiation. I shall cite only the two basic principles according to which I prepared my proposals.

First, disabled persons must be included to the greatest extent possible in the country's working and social life, so that they can work and earn money to support themselves. That is very important from both a moral standpoint and even a purely economic standpoint.

The second point: We do not have it easy with finances. We can manage to do something to help disabled persons and pensioners, and it is very important that everything allocated is used in optimal fashion. Proceeding on this premise, I submit the following proposals. On page 5, where mention is made of removing the restrictions on pay for pensioned workers, regardless of the amount of the pensions they receive, I propose to add the words: "and all employed disabled persons," that is, to remove restrictions for pensioned workers and all employed disabled persons. (Applause). That, first of all, will be humane. Secondly, a pension in this case compensates a person for the loss of health, since it is harder for him to work than for anyone else. And the reasons for which a disabled person often finds it disadvantageous to work will be removed. That is useful not only for the people who have lost their health, but for our country's economy.

Furthermore, on page 5, following the words "enhancing the physical facilities and equipment of the agroindustrial complex," I propose adding the following entire paragraph: "To work out by 1990 a comprehensive program for the physical, labor, social and psychological rehabilitation of disabled persons, in order that these people can become actively involved in life, and restore, to the extent possible, their ability to work, and in purely psychological terms, receive support." There has long been talk of this, and proposals have been submitted by the society of disabled persons, but unfortunately, they have not been included in a single state program.

To the following paragraph, on page 6, "To create the necessary social, economic and other prerequisites for improving the starting conditions for the inclusion of young people in independent labor and sociopolitical life," I propose adding: "young people, including the disabled." This pertains to the training system, so that people may acquire a specialty in technicums and higher educational institutions. Special boarding schools must be established in ordinary higher schools. Having acquired a specialty, a disabled person will be able to remove himself from society's books and become an active, full-fledged member of society. At this same place, on the sixth page, following the words, "taking the cost-of-living index into account," I propose adding, as an instruction to the Supreme Soviet: "to draw up a program for improving the sphere of social services provided to pensioners and the disabled on the basis of utilizing progressive economic methods for organizing production, while preserving existing benefits for the pensioners and disabled persons themselves."

Let me explain through an example. The prosthesis industry pursues gross output, and its products are very inconvenient. A disabled person has nowhere to get a different prosthesis, because practically all of them come from one enterprise or another—there is no choice. If there is competition among enterprises, it will be possible to choose the products of one or of another. Social funds will pay for them, and the disabled person will be able to select what he needs. If prostheses are kept cost-free for the disabled, and these enterprises are shifted, say, to leasing arrangements, it will become possible to utilize the money that already exists more efficiently, because right now it is being allocated but not fully used. Thank you for your attention. (Applause).

STENOGRAPHIC RECORD

Thirteenth Session

9 June 1989

M. S. Gorbachev: The floor is granted to Deputy Stepanov. Deputy Shchelkanov will speak next.

V. N. Stepanov, director of the Vidlitskiy State Wild-Animal Farm, Olonetskiy Rayon (Petrozavodsk Territorial Election District, Karelian ASSR): I have the following specific proposals. On the 10th page, the words: "To strengthen the role and increase the independence of the USSR State Bank, to study the question of its place in the economic system. To promote the establishment of cooperative and commercial banks, including republic and regional banks...." I believe that at the present time it is premature and mistaken to promote the development of cooperative and commercial banks. As examples show, in a situation where there is an acute shortage of resources, they are already being allocated, unfortunately, to cooperative and commercial banks. And they, in turn, offer them to enterprises and organizations at a higher interest rate than special banks offer. This primarily hurts agricultural enterprises and light-industry enterprises, and throught them—the buyer of their products. Relationships between these banks and the budget have not yet been established. And finally, lacking their own bank personnel, since there is a shortage of them, the cooperative and commercial banks will bleed the USSR state banks and special banks and their divisions by offering them different wages. Therefore, I believe that it is premature to adopt the point regarding the establishment of new banks, and that it must be postponed until the time when we adopt the Law on USSR Banks and when the Council on Economic Development gives us proposals.

To continue, page 11, the following proposition: "In the sociopolitical and economic life of citizens, public organizations, cooperatives and enterprises, the following general legal principle should be consistently established: 'everything that is not prohibited by law is permitted.'" In my view, this expression somewhat distorts our idea—the moral idea of socialism and communism, especially since not everything is in order with regard to our laws, as we have already said here. I would propose a different expression: "The actions of all citizens, organizations, enterprises, and cooperatives should be directed toward improving the well-being of our people, excluding the slightest exploitation of man by man."

Furthermore, on that same page, at the bottom: All of us together here have talked a great deal about the role of the local soviets. But the last proposition cancels out any sort of minimal rights of our soviets and proposes participation, so to speak, in various movements only thorugh public organizations and citizens' initiative. I propose to include the following proposition: "No ministries or departments have the right to be introduced in a territory without taking the opinion of the territory's residents into account."

And finally, at the Supreme Soviet session Yevgeniy Aleksandrovich Smolentsev expressed the view, when he was asked about trial by jury, that in general it has not justified itself, and that it is being rejected even in the capitalist countries. That is a very serious statement. Should we introduce trial by jury through a decision of the congress? Thank you.

M. S. Gorbachev: The floor is granted to Deputy Shchelkanov. Deputy Burltskiy is next.

A. A. Shchelkanov, loader at Store No 20 of the Leningrad Berezka Trading Firm (Kirov Territorial Election District, Leningrad): Comrade Deputies! I did not get the chance to speak, and therefore my proposals will be somewhat on the order of theses. There is no time, so I will have to make them that way.

Fifth page, first paragraph: "The congress orders the USSR Supreme Soviet and the USSR Council of Ministers it forms to draw up on an alternative basis and present for consideration by the following congress a detailed program of restructuring with specification of the basic areas, priorities and stages, and with dates and the criteria used in drafting." Extensive work with the public has shown that people do not even know at what stage we are, and have no notion of what lies behind and what lies ahead, and therefore potential is falling off sharply. A second aspect. On that same fifth page, where we propose raising the amounts of pensions. The wording of the first two points on raising does not cover a whole range of the population, for example, those who receive pensions for the loss of a breadwinner who has not been in the military. We have a huge number of people who receive pensions of 28-34 rubles. In particular, the letter of Galina Yevgenyevna Masova is about that. Therefore, I propose the wording: "To seek out funds for raising the minimum pensions and allowances of all citizens who are unable to work because of health or old age to 75 rubles." In order that all people be covered here and that we do not once again have doubts as to the humane nature of socialism.

Another point. Sixth page, in the middle: "to give increased attention to the participants in and veterans of war, and participants in the war in Afghanistan." I propose including: "internationalist military personnel." This spectrum is broader; it does not yet include but should include, in particular, military personnel who took part in events in Czechoslovakia in 1968 and in Damanskiy in 1969.

To continue, I beg the pardon of economists, but at the beginning of the third section on page 7, in connection with the fact that it was stated several times during the speeches and discussions that we have no economic concept, I propose ending the second paragraph in the third section on the seventh page with the words: "economic state of the country." And to add before the third paragraph: "To convene an open congress of economists before 1 September for the purpose of working out alternative guidelines for the country's economic development. The alternative variants are to be proposed for consideration by the Supreme Soviet and approval by the congress."

Two more general points. In the fourth section on the 10th page, we speak of the transfer of power to the

STENOGRAPHIC RECORD

Thirteenth Session
9 June 1989

soviets. In connection with the fact that Mikhail Sergeyevich's speech today contained a sentence about whether society needed the party, I propose the following addition at the end of the second section of that paragraph: "Over the course of 1989 to hold a broad nationwide discussion (or debate) concerning the role and place of the CPSU in present-day socialist society, to be concluded with a referendum." On page 11, third paragraph from the top, second and third lines. I consider it necessary to clarify: "the human rights to life, freedoms (in the plural, not "freedom"), the inviolability and security of the person, and housing." Thank you.

M. S. Gorbachev: The floor is granted to Comrade Burlatskiy. Next is Comrade Minasbekyan.

F. M. Burlatskiy, political commentator for LITERATURNAYA GAZETA, Moscow (from the Soviet Peace Fund, jointly with eight Soviet committees advocating peace, solidarity and international cooperation): Comrade deputies! I would first of all like to express regrets that the problems of the development of the political reform have been inadequately discussed by us at the congress. I hope that this will be done more thoroughly at the next session.

Now for specific proposals. On page 3, where the purposes of our development are discussed, the formula "to give socialism present-day forms" is used. The party documents from the 19th Party Conference and Mikhail Sergeyevich Gorbachev's speech at the UN contain what in my view are better and fundamentally more important characteristics: to carry out the transition from state bureaucratic forms and methods to a democratic, humane, civil socialist society.

On page 11, where human rights are mentioned, a reference is made to the Vienna meeting, which is very important. I propose adding a reference to the 1948 Universal Declaration of Human Rights and the Helsinki Act on the basis of the principle of the priority of the norms of interantional law over national norms, which was also stated in a decree of the Politburo of the CPSU Central Committee.

And finally, on page 14, where Afghanistan is discussed. I propose adding the following characterization to this provision: "To order the USSR Supreme Soviet to draw up guarantees against the repetition of such actions in the future." Thank you for your attention.

M. S. Gorbachev: The floor is granted to Deputy Mikhail Sergeyevich Minasbekyan. Next will be Comrade Mikhail Nikiforovich Poltoranin.

From the hall: Is a point of order possible?

M. S. Gorbachev: We are following the rules of order; the comrades are even cutting their remarks, and they are acting correctly.

From the hall: No, I wanted to make a criticism.

M. S. Minasbekyan, first secretary of the Yerevan Gorkom [city party committee] of the Armenian Communist Party (Yerevan-Ordzhonikidze National Territorial Election District, Armenian SSR): Esteemed comrade chairman! Esteemed comrade people's deputies! I want to make a number of proposals. The first concerns Nagorno-Karabakh. This problem has already been mentioned more than once here. But what is the reason that it is still not being solved? In my view, until the very concept used in considering important problems pertaining to practically the entire population of the oblast is changed, those problems will not be fully solved. The point is that attempts are still being made to solve them without the active participation of the people of Karabakh, and it should be just the other way around. If our goal is democracy, and if that is not simply a declaration, we must boldly undertake implementation of the right to self-determination.

In his report, Mikhail Sergeyevich Gorbachev, speaking about the acuteness of the nationality question, stressed that restructuring is creating the conditions for correcting any mistakes and deformations committed in the past. So let us give the people of Karabakh the opportunity to correct them themselves, and to determine their destiny. That will make it possible to stabilize the situation in Nagorno-Karabakh and create confidence that the principles of justice are being restored in our country.

Second, the following will unquestionably contribute to stabilization of the situation. At present the correct course of eliminating the blank spots in history has been adopted in the country. It is important not just to state facts but also to give them a fitting evaluation. It is known that in Western Armenia in 1915 Ottoman Turkey destroyed and deported about 1.5 million Armenians. Therefore, I propose that the congress recognize and condemn that fact as genocide. I am certain that if this had been done earlier a great deal of what is negative that has already been discussed here might never have happened. However, even now it is not too late. There is no statute of limitations for crimes against humanity.

Third, as you know, the democratization of our society has evoked an unprecedented upsurge of social activeness among the people, which of course, requires the utmost support and direction into a constructive channel. Therefore, among many problems I would single out the need to promptly adopt a Law on Voluntary Societies and Associations, that is, on nonformal organizations, which have sprung up in our republic and, evidently, throughout the entire country. Because of the lack of legal regulation and, let us say frankly, the unusualness of their emergence, noticeable difficulties are arising in their relations with bodies of authority. Yet many nonformal organizations support the positions of restructuring, and a prejudiced attitude toward them can only drive them away. And here, obviously, there should be only one optimal path—that is the path of dialogue and the consolidation of all progressive forces.

Thirteenth Session
9 June 1989

And finally, in the fifth section, where it is stated that justice has not yet been restored with regard to a number of nationalities, "nations and nationalities" should be written, since it is true that justice has not been restored everywhere. Thank you.

M. S. Gorbachev: The floor is granted to Deputy Poltoranin.

From the hall: I still have something to say about the procedures being followed.

M. S. Gorbachev: Fine, Comrade Poltoranin will now speak, and you....

M. N. Poltoranin, political commentator for the NOVOSTI Press Agency, Moscow (from the USSR Journalists' Union): This resolution contains a series of what I would say are illogical propositions. Take, for example, the words on the fourth page: "the positive trends that developed in the economy are being reduced to naught by the disorganization of the financial system, the imbalance of the market, and the increase in shortages of many goods...," and so forth. Since there are shortages, and shortages are growing, and the market is out of balance, evidently there is hardly any reason for speaking of positive changes in this proposition. I would make certain amendments here; I will convey them to the secretariat.

A second point: Unfortunately, in the entire resolution we do not mention the word "glasnost." And here on page 7, the second paragraph, I would propose the following alteration: "...cannot be achieved without a decisive upswing in culture and without a deepening of glasnost," and so forth. In general, incidentally, since we have spoken here about the Law on the Press, and we know that such a law—or more accurately, draft law—has been prepared in the CPSU Central Committee for publication, we journalist deputies (there are more than 50 of us here at the congress), would ask that an alternative draft of the law, which we have given to the secretariat, be published. And a final point concerning this draft resolution. Attention has already been called here to page 5, the first paragraph, where the congress instructs the Supreme Soviet "to take exhaustive measures." There are a lot of generalities here. I propose to edit these words to read as follows: "The congress instructs the Supreme Soviet to draw up a program for the dismantling of the administrative-command system and creation of stable structures for the self-organization of society. The program is to be based on the radical ideas expressed in the report of the Chairman of the Supreme Soviet and in deputies' speeches. In the political part of the program, first and foremost, mechanisms are to be worked out for the democratization of power, that is, the transfer of power to the soviets and their governing agencies, and the stages of this process and to be specified. To this end, the legal codification of the leading role of the CPSU that is stipulated in Article 6 of the Constitution is to be carried out within the framework of the Law on Public Organizations. That law should separate the jurisdications of the political and state authorities. The Supreme Soviet will present the draft program for first reading at the autumn session of the congress. The document is to be adopted following nationwide public discussion." Thank you for your attention.

M. S. Gorbachev: Comrade Grigoryan, please—shall Comrade Dmitriyev go first?

N. G. Dmitriyev, acting chairman of the Presidium of the All-Union Academy of Agricultural Sciences' Division for the RSFSR Nechernozem Zone, director of the All-Union Research Institute for the Breeding and Genetics of Agricultural Animals, Leningrad (from the V.I. Lenin All Union Academy of Agricultural Sciences): Since not a single proposal that is being submitted orally or in writing today is being voted on, it makes no sense to continue submitting proposals. The Presidium will decide. And since that is the case, the proposals ought to be turned over to the Presidium and we should end the matter at that. (Applause).

M. S. Gorbachev: Esteemed deputies! This idea was also included in our announcement and invitation before the break. And some of the comrades took advantage of that and turned their proposals in to the Presidum. Nonetheless, we clarified the situation during the break, and the comrades nonetheless consider it necessary to set forth their ideas before the congress. But since a proposal has been made, let us return to the point of departure.

At first, I will tell you this. Evidently, our process of drawing up this document will proceed further as follows: In one form or another we will express ideas and additions—changes in either wording or substance. And the editorial committee is supposed to continue its work over the course of several days together with the Presidium. The editorial committee—absolutely, together with the Presidium. If such a decision is made, following that work of the editorial committee and Presidium, the draft can be distributed to the deputies in order for them all to look it over and voice their views one more time. Those are the sort of options we have.

I am then returning to an old proosal, comrades, which the deputy from Leningrad has repeated, in order to give this process a more organized and efficient character. So, we can hear out speeches before the congress, or we can ask all the comrades to put their ideas in writing and turn them in for work. I call for a vote on the proposal from the deputy from Leningrad. Let us decide right now, comrades. (Commotion in the hall). So some of the deputies are insisting. Therefore, I will nonetheless put the proposal that has been made to a vote. Who is in favor of having ideas, criticisms, editorial corrections, and additions turned over to the editorial committee and Presidium for further work on the draft in written form—I ask you to raise your credentials. Opposed? Put them down. Abstentions? The absolute, overwhelming majority favors the option of submitting additions, criticisms and ideas in written form. Therefore, I ask all the comrades who insisted on speaking to support us all the same and agree.

Thirteenth Session
9 June 1989

Good. Now we should decide: Do we assign the job of producing the final document to the editorial committee and the Presidium, or should the draft be distributed to the deputies after work on it is finished? (Commotion in the hall). Distribute it. Fine, we have agreed, comrades. I see that the deputies are disposed to look at the final version. We then will set a deadline, to keep this process from dragging out. Fine, we have finished with this issue.

Yes, Comrade Grigoryan, you speak, since I announced you.

A. G. Grigoryan, architect, chairman of the board of the Armenian Architects' Union (from the USSR Architects' Union): I asked the floor for a point of information. Esteemed comrade chairman, esteemed comrade deputies! Permit me first to provide a point of information concerning the speech of Deputy Suleymenov from Kazakhstan, who said, in part, that in the difficult days for Armenia following the tragic earthquake, a plane carrying military personnel flying from Baku suffered a crash in the disaster zone, and who added that the memory of those who perished remains only in the memory of their mothers.

During those days a plane flying to us from Yugoslavia also crashed. The republic press wrote about these tragedies repeatedly, and with a sense of deep distress. And from the very first days, mountains of eternally living flowers were put up at the site of the death of people who had rushed to Armenia's aid. During those days a collection of money for the construction of monuments to the dead was begun throughout all Armenia, and a competition was announced for designs for the monuments. A decree of the Armenian Communist Party Central Committee and republic Council of Ministers was adopted on these matters. And there is no need to rekindle passions without knowing the real state of affairs. Especially since gratitude is a characteristic trait of the Armenian people, who have experienced too much grief in their tragic history not to understand their neighbor's grief, especially in these days of planetwide sharing of our grief.

And if the deputy who spoke was not pursuing other goals, why didn't he come up to us before his speech and clarify the facts? And just how can one speak that way about a people that has been dragging corpses from under the ruins for more than a half a year now, a people that precisely with the help of the fraternal peoples is restoring its destroyed hearth today.

I would further like to submit two specific proposals. A great deal has been said here about ecology, and in this sense Armenia, like our entire union, is no exception. I believe that in this connection it is extremely important to introduce into the criminal code articles pertaining to ecological crimes and ecological criminals and providing criminal liability for officials who reduce society's vital resources and the life of people themselves, regardless of the cities in which they live. Otherwise we will accomplish nothing. Let a few people, so to speak, sit for a while and think things over. The ecological situation will only benefit from that, and nature will somewhat recover.

I also want to discuss the role of the intelligentsia in such a fundamentally important and delicate question as internationality relations. We do not mean to condemn the Azerbaijani people for what happened and is happening in the Azerbaijan SSR, particularly for the atrocities of Sumgait. The young people who took to the streets yesterday or today were brought up for decades, and continue to be brought up, unfortunately, on numerous studies, articles and speeches by an intelligentsia that is purposefully poisoning their minds. I think that a resolution of the just demand of the Nagorno-Karabakh Autonomous Oblast, a demand in which the entire Armenian people joins, could be helped by the establishment of a committee to examine the whole set of issues that have been raised, as specified in the congress's draft resolution. Only that must be carried out without delay.

V.L. Ginzburg, academician and adviser to the directors of the USSR Academy of Sciences' P.N. Lebedev Physics Institute (from the USSR Academy of Sciences): A correct decision was made, I think, as the proposals submitted are not being voted on, to submit them to the Presidium. But I believe that there is a big difference here: The whole country knows those who have spoken and what they have said, but it does not know those who have not spoken. I am not talking about myself, comrades. But I believe that all the proposals that have been submitted and turned over to the Presidium should be published and distributed to the deputies; after all, some things will be included, and some things will not be included.

M.S. Gorbachev: Fine. Comrade Abasov, please.

M.T. Abasov, director of the Azerbaijan SSR Academy of Sciences' Institute for the Problems of Deep Petroleum and Gas Deposits (Shamkhor Natiional Territorial Election District, Azerbaijan SSR): Esteemed deputies! The situation in Nagorno-Karabakh has been spoken of repeatedly here in the hall. Taking advantage of the fact that many of the people's deputies are inadequately informed about various aspects of the problem of the Nagorno-Karabakh Autonomous Oblast, certain deputies have been continually trying to create a distorted idea of the essence of the conflict. Attempts are being made to draw us into a fruitless debate over a so-called historical right, primordial ancient lands, and so forth. Where these people want to lead the congress is understandable. I will limit myself to the following consideration. It is typical that the deputies who have spoken here, when recalling the decision on Nagorno-Karabakh, have avoided citing that document in full. Yet it spoke not of removal and not of separation from Armenia, but of the fact that it had been decided to leave Nagorno-Karabakh within Azerbaijan.

Another matter. In his speech Deputy Rasputin spoke with heightened bitterness and offense of how unfair attempts are to heap the blame for the contradictions

Thirteenth Session
9 June 1989

that have grown aggravated in the country on the Russian people, and to make them to blame for all of our problems. We fully share the writer's feeling and understand his sense of offense. The same sort of situation exists in Azerbaijan. On the whole, the times of stagnation severely affected the social and spiritual state of all peoples. The callous administrative-bureaucratic machine made no distinction as to people's national affiliation, and granted no one advantages and privileges. (Applause).

Some deputies are insisting that the issue of the Nagorno-Karabakh Autonomous Oblast be taken up in the congress, and that a commission be set up to investigate the events in Sumgait. But there have also been proposals from deputies from Azerbaijan, who also request that the circumstances leading to the departure of all Azerbaijanis from the Armenian SSR and the death of many people in the process be examined. I believe that these issues are extremely controversial and complex, and that they demand the most serious, thorough and comprehensive study. You understand, of course, that we have something to say in this connection.

M. S. Gorbachev: Comrade Abasov, all....

M. T. Abasov: However, I believe that in the common interest and in the interest of a complete elucidation of the truth, the Presidium's proposal that all these issues be turned over to the appropriate commissions and committees of the Supreme Soviet is correct. And that must be taken up promptly. (Applause).

M. S. Gorbachev: Fine. That is all, comrades! Comrade Ginzburg's proposal. His proposal, too, must be regarded with understanding.

Dear comrades! Since, within the framework of our chief resolution, we have a proposal to establish a Constitutional Commission and proposals concerning its personnel, I should inform you what sort of observations have been made concerning the commission's composition. The delegations from the Ukrainian and Belorussian SSRs proposed making two amendments: from the Ukrainian SSR, it is proposed to introduce Comrade Talanchuk, rector of Kiev Polytechnical Institute, as an additional candidate; and from Belorussia it is proposed to include comrade Platonov, president of the republic's Academy of Sciences, in place of Comrade Tkacheva. Can that be supported, comrades? Let us honor the request of the republics themselves.

Hall: Yes!

M.S. Gorbachev: Fine. For the time being, that is for inclusion, and later on we will define matters as a whole. A letter has been received from Deputy Obolenskiy. He writes on the issue of the membership of the Constitutional Commission: "To the first Congress of People's Deputies. Esteemed colleague deputies! I entreat you to include me on the Constitutional Commission...."

Hall: (Commotion).

M.S. Gorbachev: (continuing to read) "...I have long been interested in the issue of improving the Constitution, and I have already sent a number of proposals to the previous Supreme Soviet. I would like to take part directly in preparing the draft of a new version of our country's Basic Law. I ask you not to refuse my request. With esteem, Obolenskiy."

What do you think, comrades?

From the hall: (Commotion).

M.S. Gorbachev: Fine, then let's.... From the noise, I can't tell.... Whoever favors including Comrade Obolenskiy on the list and honoring his request, I ask you to raise your credentials. I ask for a count.

From the floor: Comrade deputies! Nine hundred thirty-four deputies voted "yes."

M.S. Gorbachev: Who is opposed?

From the floor: Nine hundred three voted "no."

M.S. Gorbachev: What does that mean for us? Does it mean that the question of including him has been decided? No?

From the floor: We need to find out who has abstained.

M.S. Gorbachev: Who has abstained?

From the floor: Dear comrades, while the commission is counting, I would like to take advantage....

M.S. Gorbachev: Yes, please.

From the floor: One hundred fourteen deputies abstained. Can we have a clarification?

M.S. Gorbachev: I'll give you one right now. Point 4 of the congress's Provisional Rules of Order, which we approved, states: "USSR Laws and resolutions of the USSR Congress of People's Deputies are adopted at sessions of the congress by a majority of votes of the total number of people's deputies." Thus, the proposal does not pass. (Applause).

Comrades! The group of deputies from Kirghizia is proposing to include Comrade Akayev, vice-president of the Kirghiz SSR Academy of Sciences, in place of Comrade Orozova. That is the view of the group of deputies from Kirghizia. I think we shall meet their request?

Hall: Yes!

M.S. Gorbachev: And another matter. The deputies' group from the autonomous okrugs submits the following proposal for consideration by the congress: "We ask that one representative of the small nationalities of the North, Deputy Vladimir Vladimirovich Kosygin, Koryak Autonomous Okrug, be included on the commission for drafting the new constitution." Let's honor their request.

Hall: Yes!

STENOGRAPHIC RECORD

Thirteenth Session
9 June 1989

M.S. Gorbachev: Are there no objections to this?

Hall: No!

M.S. Gorbachev: No.

From the hall: (Inaudible).

A.I. Lukyanov: We'll have to take a vote.

M.S. Gorbachev: Here we have a request from republics and deputies, and we will make a final decision. Yes, the resolution on establishment of a Conslitutional Commission—Since I see no objections, I will not put it to a vote. Although we could vote, comrades.

Hall: No!

M.S. Gorbachev: So far, it is not necessary—Fine, you keep track: We have still not mastered everything, comrades. I take responsibility here. Now we have a request, and first I will give the floor to Comrade Sagdeyev, and then to Comrade Andreyev; he has submitted a note requesting to speak.

R. Z. Sagdeyev, academician, director of the Scientific Methods Center for Analytical Research of the USSR Academy of Sciences' Institute of Space Reserch (from the USSR Academy of Sciences): Comrades! I have a proposal to somewhat strengthen the nonparty stratum, if such a thing even exists on the commission, and I hope to significantly strengthen its prestige. I propose including Academician Andrey Dmitriyevvich Sakharov on it.

M.S. Gorbachev: Comrades! Are there no objections to including him?

From the floor: No!

M. S. Gorbachev: There is no need to vote? No. Later on we will vote on the commission as a whole. Comrade Andreyev.

Yu. E. Andreyev, chief engineer at Mosgiprotrans, the Moscow State Design and Surveying Institute for Transportation Construction, Moscow (Babushkin Territorial Election District, Moscow, RSFSR): Esteemed comrade deputies! Concerning the membership of the Constitutional Commission. I express a lack of confidence in the candidacy of Comrade Aleksandr Sergeyevich Samsonov, based on the position he set forth in his speech. He showed himself today to be a fervent supporter of the methods of the Cultural Revolution in China, which we have condemned. I have in mind his invitation to leading economists to come to his enterprise for reeducation. (Applause). In his place, if a decision has already been made that there should be a director on the Constitutional Commission, I propose a different director—Comrade Mikhail Aleksandrovich Bocharov. (Applause).

M.S. Gorbachev: Comrades from Moscow, can you express your attitude? We would like to hear you. I have in mind the proposal to remove the candidacy of comrade Samsonov. I see that no one else is asking for the floor, therefore—You are asking for it? Concerning Samsonov?

From the floor: No.

M.S. Gorbachev: No, we need to settle matters, since there is a disagreement here. Please.

From the floor: Deeply esteemed comrade deputies, Muscovites have sent me numerous telegrams and letters. I have received more than 3,000 of them. They include several letters. What do these letters talk about? "Esteemed people's deputies, we ask you to explain what procedures we can follow to recall Deputy Samsonov as a people's deputy." In the first place, because he proposed carrying out reeducation work, and in the second place, because he proposed establishing a court of deputy's honor. Therefore, although I am not a Muscovite, I also favor his removal. Thank you.

M.S. Gorbachev: No one else will take the floor concerning the candidacy of Comrade Samsonov? That is all. One minute, one minute—The removal is being voted on.

From the floor: Why? You speak, then.

M.S. Gorbachev: Why that?

A.I. Lukyanov: No need.

M.S. Gorbachev: No, comrades, this is the congress's business. I ask you one more time: who from Moscow wants to speak? Please. Take the floor. We will listen to you. Please.

From the floor: I was in Proletarskiy Rayon when Samsonov was elected. I can say that a simply indecent incident happened there. In addition to Samsonov, Nuykin, the writer Pristavkin and Father Yakunin were running from that district. I was Nuykin's representative. As soon as we came in, we were told: "Comrades, that elderly woman over there is about to speak and say that people who do not live in this rayon should be excluded from the voting," although these people were chosen by the rayon. Indeed, that woman rose and spoke. A vote was taken instantly, and Samsonov remained practically the only candidate. That is how the person who has asked here for a "court of honor" got elected. (Applause).

M.S. Gorbachev: Comrades! (Commotion in the hall).

From the floor: Esteemed comrade deputies! I would like to say that not a single one of these candidacies has been discussed by the Moscow delegation, the way that the comrades from Belorussia, for example, discussed them. As you know, the Moscow delegation is very large. It comprises a group of deputies from rayons that went through the first and, in some cases, second rounds of voting. And Moscow's huge population of millions stands behind these deputies. People take different attitudes toward the result. Some had different sympathies. And here, when we were coming out of the Palace of Congresses—and I was among those who did not remove

FIRST CONGRESS OF PEOPLE'S DEPUTIES OF THE USSR

Thirteenth Session
9 June 1989

their badges—I did not hear a protest against a single candidacy of a Moscow deputy, except concerning Samsonov. I think that this reflects some sort of real situation. Comrade Samsonov was approved by the Credentials Commission, and he is a member of our assembly. In this case there are no questions, but the point is that deputies who enjoy the maximum support of Muscovites should be represented on the Constitutional Commission. In particular, I strongly ask you to support the candidacy of Comrade Bocharov, director of a building materials plant, whom we have elected to the USSR Supreme Soviet. He has worked actively in our editorial commission. I think that Comrade Bocharov will be a useful representative. (Applause).

M.S. Gorbachev: Concerning Comrade Samsonov?

From the floor: Comrades! I am a deputy from Kazakhstan. I am not acquainted at all with either Comrade Samsonov or Comrade Bocharov, but I must express my viewpoint, in particular, about Comrade Samsonov.

In discussing various issues in such a democratic forum, we may from time to time find ourselves in the minority. And if his concept of a court of honor is adopted, in the course of five years everyone will be in that court of honor. And it will easily turn into another punitive agency, of which we have no shortage. (Applause).

M.S. Gorbachev: Comrade Samsonov.

A.S. Samsonov, director of the Moscow S.M. Kirov Clock and Watch Plant, Moscow (Proletarskiy Territorial Election District, RSFSR): Esteemed deputies! I do not know why this question has been brought up today. My candidacy on that commission was not being discussed. Frankly speaking, I never thought that I would serve on it, but it is absolutely clear to me whose this proposal was to raise my candidacy here, in order that I might once more tell about myself and how I became a deputy.

What is the question? The question is that comrades here are carrying on a discussion about the correctness of my election. An esteemed comrade deputy spoke here talking about how some sort of rule had been violated from the standpoint of the election principle. I can report here that during the district meeting and during the elections, I was not in Moscow at all; at the time I was on a business trip abroad. And how everything took place, and how the matter was organized is another question. There is a Credentials Commission, and there is an election commission, which have been given the right to decide this question.

A second proposition. I want to say once again here, and today I can confirm once again, that what I was advocating was not holding any sort of trial of anyone who is absolutely innocent. Today the voters, my voters, who elected me, told me that what ought to be set up is not a court of honor but a commission on ethics. We will work for a few years and will come to this question, because the question is not a simple one. It requires a certain order; it requires a certain discipline. Therefore, I repeat once again: no issues should be distorted, and I firmly support the idea that we should have a certain order. Both in the congress, and in the country. (Applause).

N.T. Knyaznyev, first secretary of the Kustanay Obkom of the Kazakh Communist Party (Kustanay Territorial Election District, Kazakh SSR): Esteemed comrade deputies! I am a member of the Credentials Commission. Twice, and very closely, the Credentials Commission examined the results of the voting for the district where Comrade Samsonov ran. We submitted a decision to recognize Comrade Samsonov's authority, but in the process of our examination, instances of the flagrant violation of the Statute on Elections were discovered. In the process of the elections, there were so many obstructions against Comrade Samsonov that a normal person simply cannot conceive of them. We are serious people who have gathered, and we are simply wasting our time. I believe that this is a hounding of deputy Samsonov. (Applause).

V.A. Logunov, deputy editor of the newspaper MOSKOVSKAYA PRAVDA, Moscow (Kuntsevskiy Territorial Election District, RSFSR): I am one of those, whom Deputy Adamovich did not name, who was nominated in the Proletarskiy Election District. I was nominated by the Kometa collective, which includes many thousands. I attended that antidemocratic district meeting. In my opinion, there were 17 people there, including the writer Pristavkin, Gleb Yakunin, a retired officer, and me, a deputy editor. Literally in the very first minutes (I do not attribute this to Deputy Samsonov; he really was not at that district meeting), literally in the very first minutes it was announced that all the candidates for deputy who did not work and live in the rayon could leave. And thus, we left. I say this because we should nonetheless return to that period of the preelection campaign and to the district meetings and examine their work, because there were very many violations.

M.S. Gorbachev: Comrades! Can it be that this is enough?

From the hall: Yes!

M.S. Gorbachev: The picture is clear. Please.

From the floor: Comrade deputies! Since the questiion of Comrade Samsonov's candidacy primarily concerns the Moscow group, since he is in our group, I submit a proposal that the Moscow group vote separately.

From the hall: (Commotion).

From the floor: That is my proposal.

M.S. Gorbachev: Well, can it be that's enough?

Zh.I. Alferov, academician, director of the USSR Academy of Sciences' A.F. Ioffe Physics and Engineering Institute, Leningrad (from the USSR Academy of Sciences): From Comrade Samsonov's speech I understood that he did not intend to serve on the Constitutional

STENOGRAPHIC RECORD

Thirteenth Session
9 June 1989

Commission. I understood that he was simply withdrawing his own name.

M.S. Gorbachev: Fine. That's all. I will put the question to a vote. The question of the withdrawal of the candidacy of Comrade Samsonov.

Comrades! I am putting to a vote the withdrawal made by Comrade Samsonov. Whoever is in favor of not including the candidacy of Comrade Samsonov on the membership list for the Constitutional Commission, I ask you to raise your credentials. I ask for a count.

From the floor: Comrade deputies! 555 deputies voted "yes."

M.S. Gorbachev: Who is opposed, opposed to this proposal, opposed to the withdrawal?

From the floor: 1,188 voted "no." (Applause).

M.S. Gorbachev: Who abstained?

From the floor: 101 deputies abstained.

From the floor: Mikhail Sergeyevich, this is a deputy from Kazan.

M.S. Gorbachev: The question is decided. Please. You will be next.

O.P. Borodoin, staff correspondent of the newspaper IZVESTIYA (Yakutsk City National Terriitorial Election District, Yakut ASSR): We made an analysis of the list of candidates for this commission, and it turned out as follows: 17 people are first secretaries of obkoms and of the CPSU Central Committee; another 31 are employees and members of the Central Committee—these are people who have a relation, so to speak, to the top party leadership. Altogether it turns out that we have on this commission 55 percent candidates from the top party leadership, comrades. I have a question. What are getting ready to create: new Party Statutes, or a new Constitution? (Applause). In the second place, no one consulted me in the Yakutsk delegation, either, as to whether Yuriy Nikolayevich Prokopyev, the secretary of the party obkom, ought to be included on this commission. I have nothing against it, but that is also a violation of our democracy. I think that the commission should include people who are endowed with living, vital experience. That is the first point. the second point is that I propose, in general, to create an alternative commission. (Commotion in the hall). And that we have two draft Constitutions, so that we can choose. For the second commission, I propose, first of all, Yevtushenko. He has formulated. (Commotion in the hall). He has already done a fine job of formulating one point for the draft of the new constitution. I have everything.

V.M. Minin, chief of a repair and maintenance shop at the Glebovskiy Poultry Production Association, Kholshcheviki Settlement, Istrinskiy Rayon, Moscow Oblast, RSFSR (from the All-Union Leninist Communist Youth League): The voice of the young people has been heard very little at this congress, and that is probably noticeable: we are constantly be included on all the commissions at our request. We request that our comrade Sergey Zvonov, a deputy from the All-Union Komsomol [Leninist Communist Youth League], be included on this commission. (Applause).

M.S. Gorbachev: Well, comrades, what about the request by the deputies from the Komsomol?

Voices: No!

Yu. V. Golik, dean of the Division of Law of Kemerovo State University (Central Territorial Election District, Kemerovo Oblast): Comrades, we are not bound by any sort of quantitative limits in forming this commission; therefore, I propose to include Candidate of Legal Sciences Yuriy Alekseyevich Yevtyukhin, a docent at Kemerovo University, on it. Why him? To all intents and purposes, as of today he is the only theoretician who specializes in congresses of soviets. We need to develop this form of work, and therefore it would be a good idea to know what we had up until those congresses existed. Thank you.

M.S. Gorbachev: Comrades, that can be accepted. What do the legal specialists say? Do they support that? I see Comrade Kudryavtsev there, and Comrade Yakovlev. Do they agree with that? No one objects?

L. I. Sukhov, driver at Motor Transport Enterprise No 16301 (Kharkov Territorial Election District, Kharkov Oblast): I actually woke up early today, although I went to bed late, and I was thinking about what we are creating and how. Here we are all the time saying this person is good, and that person is good, but the "good" people have already been running things, and today we are mired down. And I appeal not so much to this hall as to the television viewers: take a look and what awaits us tomorrow if we really do not include on the commissions the people who really are reflecting about what our motherland should be like. I know that commotion will start up in the hall now, and that is also something that brought me here. We do not know how to conduct ourselves. I am a simple driver, but I have not once stamped my feet or shouted in this hall. So how is it you do not want to hear your comrades out? Can you possibly understand what he is talking about? Can you possibly think that your opinion is the only correct one? I also wanted to speak but was afraid that in that way each of us would start pushing his own line. I promised my voters, so I did it. And we should become a single monolith, but through agreements that are not without principle. We should know how to hear out everyone's opinion. And we are not doing that. We shout—let's have it, faster! And what's really putting us in a spot? Here's what. Yesterday we discussed candidacies at 11:30 p.m., when people already wanted to sleep and they were ready to accept anyone, just to have a nomination. That sounded like this: Shcherbitskiy—he was recommended to us. Everything was like it was before—

Thirteenth Session

9 June 1989

once again, someone had been recommended. Yet it is time, most likely, to get away from that—time! I propose Vlasov and Yevtushenko for the commission. I think that they will at least stimulate its work a bit. Thank you for the attention. (Applause).

M.S. Gorbachev: Andrey Dmitriyevich, just a minute. Let's decide this at the outset, so that things won't build up. Comrades, regarding Comrade Sukhov's proposals. He has proposed putting Comrade Yevtushenko on the commission. How do you view that? (Commotion in the hall). We'll have to vote. Whoever is in favor of supporting Comrade Sukhov's proposal and including Deputy Yevtushenko on the Constitutional Commission, I ask you to raise your credentials. (Vote count is taken).

M.S. Gorbachev: Andrey Dmitriyevich, sit down; I will give you the floor. Please.

A.D. Sakharov, academician, chief scientific associate at the P.N. Lebedev USSR Academy of Sciences' Physics Institute (from the USSR Academy of Sciences): I suspect that on all the fundamental issues that will arise in drafting the text of the constitution, I will be in the minority. That will put me in a difficult position, if it is not agreed upon in advance that the commission is to propose two alternative drafts that will be considered on an equal basis. I think that is very important.

M.S. Gorbachev: Please.

A.G. Kostenyuk: Esteemed deputies! 449 deputies voted "yes."

M.S. Gorbachev: Opposed? A clear majority; there is no point in taking a count. Abstentions, comrades? The question of the candidacy of Comrade Yevtushenko is decided—he is not included. Now for Comrade Vlasov, concerning his inclusion on the commission. Whoever is in favor of accepting Deputy Sukhov's proposal and including Comrade Vlasov on the Constitutional Commission, I ask you to raise your credentials.

(Vote count is taken).

A.G. Kostenyuk: 830 deputies voted "yes."

M.S. Gorbachev: Opposed?

(Vote count is taken).

A.G. Kostenyuk: 934 deputies voted "no." (Applause).

M.S. Gorbachev: Abstentions? Well, okay. Comrade Vlasov's candidacy does not pass. (Applause).

M. A. Mikheyev, leader of an all-purpose brigade with the Uglestroy-1 [Coal Construction-1] Construction Administration, Neryungri (Neryungri National Territorial Election District, Yakut ASSR): Comrade deputies! I am speaking on the matter that Deputy Borodin brought up here. He seemingly expressed a lack of trust in the party—the secretaries of the oblast party committees and the Central Committee. I fundamentally disagree with him. He said that these people supposedly do not know life. I will say two words in defense of my obkom party secretary Prokopyev. I am a Communist, a worker and a builder, and I have known him for a long time, since before he served as obkom secretary. I know how much he has done for the republic, and therefore I support Prokopyev's candidacy. Thank you. (Applause).

M.S. Gorbachev: Comrades, may I announce? Please.

From the floor: Comrades, we have voted on the candidacies of Yevtushenko, Vlasov, and Obolenskiy. Let us also vote on each candidate on the list. That would be normal. (Applause).

M.S. Gorbachev: The congress will decide that. So, comrades, with that we can consider that we have concluded the discussion. I remind you that the Ukraine and Belorussia have submitted changes; you remember, I announced them. Additions: to add Comrades Yevtyukhin, Sergey Zvonov from the Komsomol, Academician Sakharov and Akhayev. So we are adding to the list. Now we have a list of the candidates who were submitted (you have that list in your hands) and the comrades who are being added. So we must actually make a decision concerning the formation of the commission in the membership that has been presented. Before putting the adoption of this decision to a vote, I must, as we have agreed, consider the proposals of the comrades who have spoken here. Should we vote on them individually?

Individually. As you know, in this case the congress determines by majority whether to vote on them individually or as a list. Since a proposal has been received from Deputy Kirillov to vote on them individually, I ask whoever is in favor of his proposal to raise your credentials. I ask you to lower them. Opposed? I think that it is not just a majority but an overwhelming majority. The question is decided. Therefore, I submit a proposal: Whoever is in favor of adopting the resolution on the formation of the Constitutional Commission in the membership on which we have agreed, I ask you to raise your credentials. I ask you to lower them. Opposed? Count, please.

(Vote count is taken).

A.G. Kostenyuk: 106 deputies voted "no."

M.S. Gorbachev: Abstentions?

A.G. Kostenyuk: 94 deputies abstained.

M.S. Gorbachev: Fine, the question is decided, comrades. The decision on the formation of the Constitutional Commission has been adopted.

Dear comrades! Yesterday evening we did not fully decide one issue—the issue of the Constitutional Oversight Committee. In order to get out of the situation that arose among us—and we are all witnesses to it—we had to conduct discussions yesterday evening. And this morning I met with the deputies from Lithuania on this

Thirteenth Session

9 June 1989

matter. We had the same sort of discussions, and proposals also came in from the deputies from Estonia.

The following proposal is made, and I ask you to support it. It is this: to form a commission on the preparation of a draft Law on the Constitutional Oversight Committee in the USSR. (Applause).

For this purpose it is proposed to include the following comrades on this commission: A. Akayev, vice-president of the Kirghiz SSR Academy of Sciences (the Urals, Sverdlovsk; you have heard his speeches); V.G. Badamyants, chairman of the Armenian SSR State Security Committee; T.P. Buachidze, chairman of the Georgian Culture Foundation; Yu.V. Golik, dean of the Division of Law at Kemerovo State University; I.N. Gryazin, a department head at the Estonian SSR Academy of Sciences' Institute of Philosophy, Sociology, and Law; G.I. Yeremey, chairman of the Moldavian Republic Council of Trade Unions; Yu.Kh. Kalmykov, head of a division at D.I. Kurskiy Saratov Institute of Law; D.A. Kerimov, head of a department at the CPSU Central Committee's Academy of Social Sciences; G.K. Kryuchkov, first secretary of the Odessa Obkom of the Ukrainian Communist Party; V.N. Kudryavtsev, vice-president of the USSR Academy of Sciences; S.Kh. Negmatulloyev, president of the Tajik SSR Academy; O. Ovezgeldyyev, president of the Turkmen SSR Academy of Sciences; A.S. Pavlov, chief of the CPSU Central Committee's Department of State and Law; Z.K. Rustamov, member of the Syr-Darya Oblast Court, Uzbek SSR; V.I. Semenko, chairman of the Ivanovo Oblast Court; V.Ya. Skudra, Latvian SSR Minister of Justice; A.Yu. Smaylis, head of a laboratory at the Z. Yanushkyavichus Research Institute for the Physiology and Pathology of the Cardiovascular System, Lithuania; A.A. Sobchak, a department head in the Division of Law at Leningrad State University; U.M. Sultangazin, president of the Kazakh SSR Academy of Sciences; A.Ya. Sukharev, USSR procurator general; G.S. Tarnavskiy, Belorussian SSR procurator; A.M. Yakovlev, sector head at the USSR Academy of Sciences' Institute of State and Law. Okay?

Deputies: Yes.

M.S. Gorbachev: Can we put it to a vote?

Deputies: Yes.

M.S. Gorbachev: Whoever is in favor of forming this commission with this membership, I ask you to raise your credentials. I ask you to lower them. Are there any opposed? Count, please.

A.G. Kostyenyuk: Comrade deputies! 10 deputies voted "no."

M.S. Gorbachev: Abstentions?

A.G. Kostenyuk: 25 deputies abstained.

M.S. Gorbachev: The question is decided. Now, comrades, we have to consult with you. We on the Presidium, foreseeing such a course of development and the limitations on our time, drew up a proposal: to take a 30-minute break right now (we still have 15 minutes until 1800), and then hold debates on questions of "other business" until 2000. You have probably picked up on the fact that the problems of "other business" that have been put forward by deputies have turned into the main question. And we have several important questions. Two hours will be enough for us, since these matters of "other business" incorporate many proposals by deputies. And on that we could then conclude the congress's work. What about it, comrades? A 30-minute break.

M.S. Gorbachev: Comrades! Before going on to the next question, there is something we must agree on. I think that it is perfectly natural and in the deputies' interest. In order that a situation does not develop in which we have left seemingly without having concluded our work by adopting the main document and without having voted on the entire document. In order to take that document as a basis, we have already voted for the main things in it, which were prepared and were taken into account in the process, and have adopted them. Nonetheless, we are feeling uncomfortable and sensing some sort of delicate situation. So, if we asked you about the following. Let's vote for the resolution as a whole with instructions to the Presidium and the commission to work out the final wording of that resolution. As it turns out, so let it be.

If you are of that opinion, deputies, you can decide that way. And you can, as I have said. To be precise: We already have adopted the main basis, and a lot of additions, a great many; in the course of a week we could carry out the whole process and work out the final wording of the document in the Presidium commission and, at the end of that week, distribute the new draft, finally worded in accordance with the deputies observations, to the deputies, and receive your consent. And that means that sometime in about a week, 10 days at the most, because it is a large resolution encompassing all the fundamental issues, it would be published.

Thus, there can be two options. Either we stand with the version on which we have agreed, so that no later than within 10 days that resolution will be completed and published, but with the requirement that deputies be informed, without fail, of its final version. Or we can adopt different instruction.

So we are in favor of voting for the resolution as a whole and instructing the Editorial Commission and the Presidium to take the proposals that have been made into account to the greatest extent possible and, upon the completion of that work, publish it?

Yu.Yu. Boldyrev, senior engineer at the Central Research Institute for Ship Electronics and Technology, Leningrad (Moscow Territorial Election District, Leningrad): Comrades! I call your attention to the fact that we cannot and should not turn the authority to decide something for us over to the Editorial Commission, according to its status.

Thirteenth Session
9 June 1989

The Editorial Commission is a purely staff body that is supposed to offer us only versions, and we should vote on the proposals that we submit. Therefore, I submit a third proposal, which in my view is the only normal one: The principal controversial proposals must be put to a vote. Otherwise, it will not be the resolution of the congress; it will be only the resolution of the Editorial Commission. (Applause).

M.S. Gorbachev: And so, from this third version it follows—extend the work of the congress. No, I am saying that about the first option. And Comrade Boldyrev's proposal, as I understand it, is that the work of the congress must be continued. Is that right, Comrade Boldyrev? He just did not carry the idea through, and I always carry things through so they will be clear. So, continue the work of the congress until a decision is made?

So, three proposals.

The first proposal, which we discussed in the previous session. Whoever is in favor of acting in the manner on which we agreed, with the clarification that the document should be published no later than in 10 days, I ask you to raise your credentials.

What, it's not understandable? The first proposal, on which we agreed: Instruct the commission and the Presidium to work out the final wording of the text and distribute it to the deputies, and do all this in such a way that the resolution is published within 10 days, and no later. That is the proposal on which I am asking you to vote. I ask you to lower your credentials. Who is opposed? Perhaps we should count? It's a fundamental question.

M.S. Gorbachev: Andrey Dmitriyevich asks me to say that when the comrades receive the final draft with observations, and all the additions are expressed in it, that each deputy could express his opinion individually on each change. Fine. We are agreed. Please.

From the floor: Esteemed deputies, 121 deputies voted "no."

M.S. Gorbachev: Are there any comrades who abstained? In my opinion, no. No, there are. Comrades, while a count is being taken I want to say that the deputies are still of the following mind: That which we have now already discussed and taken as a basis, there is a proposal to vote for that or consider that those provisions have been adopted.

From the floor: We have voted. The basis has already been adopted.

M.S. Gorbachev: Therefore, the option about which we agreed remains. We will be given the figures in just a minute, but the question, in principle, has been decided.

From the floor: Will all proposals be received?

M.S. Gorbachev: Absolutely. But you have in mind that there will be identical proposals. We have already brought them to light here, during yesterday's work, and last night. There are a great many duplications and overlappings.

From the floor: 32 deputies abstained.

M.S. Gorbachev: The question is decided.

Comrades, now for a brief word of introduction concerning the point on the agenda known as "Other Business," I give the floor to Comrade Lukyanov. He will speak on behalf of the Presidium, since we have discussed this matter two or three times.

A.I. Lukyanov: Comrade deputies! During the preparations for the congress and in the course of its work, delegations from republics and regions, and people's deputies submitted proposals to examine a whole series of issues at the congress that were not on the preliminary agenda. Therefore, as you recall, at the first session of the congress a decision was made to add the point "Other Business" to the agenda.

The congress Presidium examined all these proposals very closely, and more than 20 of them were received. These questions were looked at three times in the congress Presidium before any sort of conclusion was reached.

It must be said, first of all, that many of the proposals have already been decided in the congress in one form or another. Many questions that the deputies have raised have been acted on. Thus, in what we have adopted, by and large, as a basis for the resolution "On the Basic Guidelines of Foreign and Domestic Policy," appropriate instructins have been given to the Supreme Soviet, the government and other bodies on a whole series of questions pertaining to the implementation of economic reform and the development of the social sphere, and provisions have been made for a radical renewal of legislation on the soviets of peoples deputies and for strenghtening the foundations of the rule-of-law state.

The preamble incorporates proposals that it was proposed to draw up in the form of a decree of the congress. The resolution reflects, in particular, deputies' proposals concerning the need to check on the conformity of certain ukases of the Presidium of the USSR Supreme Soviet to the Constitution, and that has also been expressed in a specific point in our resolution.

Substantial attention has been given to matters that were connected with proposals from the republics. In particular, they are reflected in our basic resolution, and evidently it will be necessary to decide whether to set up a special commission on this matter. I am referring to regional cost accounting and to carrying out the reform in the republics.

In connection with deputies' request that changes and additions be made in the existing Constitution and a new

STENOGRAPHIC RECORD

Thirteenth Session

9 June 1989

Constitution drawn up, as you know, today a Constitutional Commission has been formed that has been instructed to carefully study all the issues that the deputies raised and make appropriate proposals. You also know that commissions to work out a political and legal evaluation of the 1939 Soviet-German nonaggression treaty, to investigate the circumstances connected with events in Tbilisi, to investigate materials connected with the work of the USSR Procuracy's investigative group headed by T.Kh. Gdlyan, and other commissions have been formed by the congress and are already functioning.

Taking what has been said into account, the congress Presidium, after long discussion, reached the conclusion that under "Other Business" the following matters could be examined, taking the proposals from deputies and delegations into account. First, the question of preparing a draft Law on the Status of USSR People's Deputies. You know that proposals on this were expressed in the speeches of many USSR People's Deputies. Some deputies submitted proposals in written form—for example, Deputies K.D. Lubenchenko, A.F. Nazarenko, Yu.A. Koltsov and A.Ye. Sebentsov presented their ideas in the form of whole drafts of a USSR Law on the Status of USSR People's Deputies. That has already been mentioned here. As you know, the principal rights and duties of USSR people's deputies are established by the existing Law on the Status of People's Deputies in the USSR. But many norms in that law can already be applied and implemented, since they are not contrary to the new provisions of the Constitution and apply to all deputies and all representative bodies of state authority. This pertains to such institutions as deputy's immunity, the ties between deputies and constituents, the deputy's request for information, the right of legislative initiative, and a number of other provisions of that law. At the same time, USSR People's Deputies rightfully raise the question of the need to draft a new Law on the Status, and the Presidium fully agrees with that. That law, and it must be drawn up, should strengthen the guarantees of the rights of people's deputies, clarify the legal bases of deputies' relations with bodies of state authority and administration, and deal in detail with all matters connected with the implementation and exercise of deputies' powers.

Taking that into account, a draft resolution of the congress has been submitted for your consideration and will be distributed to you in advance; it proposes that the USSR Supreme Soviet be instructed to prepare a draft USSR Law on the Status of People's Deputies with a view to its adoption at the USSR Congress of People's Deputies to be held at the end of this year.

The resolution also proposes that certain additional norms be established right now, for the transitional period, so to speak, until the new law is adopted. These norms are aimed at creating conditions in which people's deputies can effectively carry out their deputy's activities right away. The resolution refers, in particular, to the provision of appropriate materials to deputies, and to deputies' priority right to speak and write in the mass media, and it provides that a deputy may have a secretary paid out of funds from the estimated expenses of the USSR Supreme Soviet. Deputies, and this is also stated in the draft resolution, should be provided with the space necessary for performance of their deputy's duties. It is established that officials are subject to disciplinary penalties up to and including dismissal for failure to fulfill their duties with regard to USSR people's deputies.

Naturally, the norms that are concentrated in the draft that has been distributed to you are norms of a temporary nature, until the next USSR Congress of People's Deputies adopts a new law on the deputies' status, which will be drawn up by the Supreme Soviet and presented for your consideration at the next congress. Moreover, it is natural that these temporary norms will be appropriately further refined, evidently taking into account the experience that we gain.

I have spoken with many comrades, and they have already submitted certain of their ideas concerning this draft, and I think that their ideas are justifiable. The only thing that is needed is for our law to gradually grow with the practice of the 2,250 USSR People's Deputies elected to our congress.

You have the draft congress decree on the preparation of a draft law on the deputies' status, and I hope that you have had the opportunity to become acquainted with it.

Now a second question. A substantial number of deputies' proposals for items to be included under "Other Business" on the agenda were connected with the need to draw up laws that are required to support the active work of our congress, as well as of the Supreme Soviet, committees, commissons and, in general, each people's deputy. Thorough work is required here, as it is on the law on the status. In this connection, the Presidium proposes that, after discussion, a resolution be adopted concerning this issue on the preparation of several draft laws regulating the procedures for the activities of the USSR Congress of People's Deputies, the Supreme Soviet, and its bodies. The draft of this resolution has been distributed to you. It calls for giving instructions to the Supreme Soviet to draw up and submit for consideration by the second congress draft regulations of the USSR Congress of People's Deputies, a Law on the Compensation of USSR Congress of People's Deputies for Expenses Associated With Deputy's Activities, and a Law on Procedures for Recalling USSR People's Deputies. In this regard, we have only a Law on the Procedures for Recalling a Deputy of the Supreme Soviet, and there are as yet no such procedures for a deputy who is a USSR People's Deputy.

As for (and there was another law there, and you have seen it) as for the preparation of a draft Law on USSR Constitutional Oversight, we could give such an instruction to a commission that we created specially today. We

Thirteenth Session
9 June 1989

gave it today. Therefore, this draft law obviously should not be included in the general resolution on instructions to the Supreme Soviet and in the drafts that it is to prepare. Although today some comrades submitted a rather interesting proposal that a program of legislative work be drawn up. And that proposal has also been reported to the deputies. In my opinion, it is a useful undertaking. And in addition, in the course of our debates a number of deputies expressed the idea that the USSR Congress of People's Deputies address a Message to the World's Peoples in which we could set forth our attitude toward restructuring and the principles of our foreign policy. So there are three major questions that could be considered in the section of our work on the agenda that consists of "Other Business."

I would like to emphasize one more time that all the remaining questions that we have considered in the Presidium with great thoroughness have in one way or another found reflection in the congress's main resolution, including a number of decisions concerning the nationalities question, with mention of certain painful knots that exist in our country with regard to the resolution of nationality relations.

So there is a proposal that the congress Presidium has instructed me to bring to your attention.

M.S. Gorbachev: Comrades! There are all the proposals that the Presidium is submitting for discussion at this session of ours. A question? Please.

From the hall: We have received a draft Law on Taxation, but when will that be?

A.I. Lukyanov: Comrades! You received several draft laws today: on taxation, on inventions, etc. Some of them have been put in finished form with due regard to their discussion by the public, and some have not yet been put in finished form. We believed that the deputies should receive these draft laws in their hands, as we agreed, so that you would know what lay ahead and what the Supreme Soviet would be doing. They are the drafts that will go for consideration by the Supreme Soviet and its commissions. There is not yet any need to consider them at the congress.

M.S. Gorbachev: Please.

A.Ye. Antifeyev, general dierctor of the Tyazhmash [Heavy Machinery] Production Association (Ilyichevskiy Territorial Election District, Donetsk Oblast): During the debates certain deputies proposed that the editor in chief of the newspaper IZVESTIYA be elected at the congress. A mass of telegrams came in from my constituents; I got 28 of them. I do not know about others, whether they support that proposal, but I would like this question also to be taken up under "Other Business" on the agenda. (Applause).

M.S. Gorbachev: Comrades! Please. An addition to the agenda, right?

Yu.A. Levykhin, scientific associate at the USSR Academy of Sciences' Institute of Spectroscopy, Troitsk (Podpolskiy Territorial Election District, Moscow Oblast): I believe that we could also consider at the congress the question of rescinding Article 11 of the 8 April ukase. I think that it has already been adequately worded and, to all intents and purposes, has been expressed in the resolution itself. Therefore, I think that we can adopt such decisions now. That is not just my opinion but the opinion of the people who signed the appeal on this subject. I propose that this question be decided right now as a legislative initiative. (Applause).

B.N. Nikolskiy, editor in chief of the magazine NEVA, Leningrad (Smolniy Territorial Election Distrrict, Leningrad): Back before the congress, the Leningrad group of deputies proposed that the question be included on the agenda of establishing a commission to investigate all the circumstances leading to the involvement of the Soviet Armed Forces in the war in Afghanistan. The course of the congress has shown that this question continues to be timely. One of the most dramatic moments in the congress arose over precisely the discussion of this problem. Therefore we Leningrad people's deputies submit the following proposal. I think that it will be difficult for the congress to set up a commission right now, and therefore I propose a draft of the following resolution: "To instruct the USSR Supreme Soviet to establish a commission to investigate and evaluate the circumstances that led to the Soviet Armed Forces' participation in the war in Afghanistan. (Applause).

V.A. Martirosyan, colonel, commander of a military unit, Carpathian Military District, Rovno (Rovno Territorial Election District): Mikhail Sergeyevich, by status, many of us deputies have initiative groups and authorized representatives. These are people who gave us a great deal of help during the election campaign. We need these people very much in order to work effectively. That requires that you declare here whether we can use these people's services, and whether they can officially give us assistance. That is the first thing.

Secondly, it has been directed here that space be allocated. I think that the people's deputies, especially those who are unable to receive people at their work places, should be allocated permanent offices, so that representatives of their initiative groups can sit there along with the people's deputies, because the people have an exceptionally large number of requests and very many urgent questions that need to be resolved. In particular, I have four rayons, and in each one of them space should also be allocated, since I should be there with an initiative group in each. I think that it would be advisable and simultaneouly would enhance the authority of our people's deputies. Thank you.

M.S. Gorbachev: Fine. Comrades, let us first finish setting the agenda, since discussion and proposals have already begun. Are there any more additions to the agenda?

A.G. Zhuravlev, professor at the Republic Interbranch Institute for the Advanced Training of Executives and

Thirteenth Session
9 June 1989

Specialists, Minsk (Minsk-Soviet Territorial Election District, Minsk Oblast): I propose that the question of changes that need to be made in the Law on Elections be included under "Other Business" on the agenda. Many of us have personally experienced all the shortcomings of that law. We are presently approaching elections to local soviets. And there are at least some points of the existing law that we have no right to leave unchanged. In particular, I would propose changing at least one point (we have the right to do that) by vote. It is the point on district election commissions. (Applause).

In addition, I believe that we should express ourselves absolutely clearly as to the impermissibility of substituting open voting for elections. We should clearly go on record as saying that elections without a choice of candidates are impermissible.

And finally, third and last. We could, in this connection, discuss the question of what is preventing us, in general, from holding elections where a choice of candidates is offered. I think that one shortcoming and one reason for this is that we lack such experience at the bottom. It seems to me that we are presently prepared, at least in many regions of our country, to begin electing the principal leaders of regions on the basis of a choice of candidates through direct secret balloting among the entire population. That is all I have to say. Thank you for your attention. (Applause).

M.S. Gorbachev: Deputy Sobchak.

A.A. Sobchak, department head in the Division of Law at Leningrad State University, Leningrad (Vasileostrovskiy Territorial Election District, Leningrad): Comrade deputies! In the newspaper KOMSOMOLSKAYA PRAVDA for this 2 June a number of USSR People's Deputies- -Comrades Batynskaya, Yemelyanov and Sokolov—reminded us of events in Novocherkassk in 1962. In connection with these events, seven people received death sentences, and a substantial number of people were sentenced to various terms of deprivation of freedom. I propose that we include on the agenda under "Other Business" a resolution of the congress instructing the USSR Procurator General to protest that judicial decision and take steps to rehabilitate the persons involved (Applause).

A.L. Plotnikov, foreman at the Kirovo-Chepetsk Repair and Maintenance Shop, Kirov Oblast (from the All-Union Leninist Communist Youth League): Comrades! During the time the congress has been in session we deputies have frequently met with Moscow's young people. There are permanent telephone hookups connecting us with our people back home. By way of carrying out our constituents' directives, in light of the positive reaction our hall gave the proposal made in Yuriy Vlasov's speech, and also taking into account the immense importance of the offices of chairman of the State Committee for Television and Radio Broadcasting and the editor in chief of the newspaper IZVESTIYA, we support the proposal that has been made here and propose that that question be included on the agenda under "Other Business." I think that step would be a concrete contribution by the congress to the development and irreversibility of the processes of the democratization of our mass media. (Applause).

M.S. Gorbachev: Please, please.

I.A. Andreyeva, chief art specialist at the All-Union House of Garment Patterns, and secretary of the board of the USSR Designers' Union, Moscow (from the USSR Designers' Union): I have several questions and proposals. How will we find out about the plans, the questions discussed, and in general, the agenda of the Supreme Soviet?

M.S. Gorbachev: We will send out....

I.A. Andreyeva: So that the possibility exists, I am asking not so much about myself, because we are in Moscow. But what about people outside of Moscow?

M.S. Gorbachev: We will send out materials. And more than that: so that the deputies will know about the plans for the work of commissions and committees, and not just the congress.

I.A. Andreyeva: Yes, yes. So that we can exercise our right. Secondly, we have never finished discussing questions pertaining to the state of affairs with regard to the 8 April ukase, the Law on Internal Troops, and other recent legislative acts that raised doubts and apprehensions among many deputies concerning their application. Therefore, I have the following proposal. I would like to include it on the agenda, raising for discussion under "Other Business" the possibility of the application of these laws until their wording is changed. And at the same time, raising the question of the deadlines for changes to be made in their wording, and of applying these laws and the ukase only with the authorization of the USSR Supreme Soviet or the USSR Congress of People's Deputies.

Thirdly, I consider it necessary, in confirmation of what Anatoliy Ivanovich has just said, to give all the people's deputies a list of the priority draft laws, as Comrade Lukyanov called them, that will be literally knocking on the door, in order that the people's deputies can determine their order of priority, and that that order of priority serve as the foundation for the Supreme Soviet's work.

And finally, I believe that under "Other Business" we must, at the end of the agenda (deputies have just handed me this request), allocate time for announcements and statements by deputies' groups, if deputies' groups or individual deputies have any. Thank you.

M.S. Gorbachev: Please.

A.V. Levashev, lecturer in the Department of Political Economy at Leningrad Soviet Leningrad Technological

Thirteenth Session

9 June 1989

Institute Leningrad, Pushkin (Kolpinskiy Territorial Election District, Leningrad): On behalf of more than 130 people's deputies, by way of carrying out numerous directives from our constituents, and on the basis of Article 114 of our USSR Constitution, as a legislative initiative we submit for consideration of the congress a draft resolution aimed at improving the material situation of the low-income segments of the population. We request that this resolution be submitted and examined under "Other Business."

M.S. Gorbachev: I do not understand. About what?

A.V. Levashev: A resolution on improving the situation of low- income segments.

I.B. Shamshev, senior instructor at Yaroslavl State University, Yaroslavl (Leninskiy Territorial election District, Yaroslavly Oblast): Comrades, I support the Leningrad deputies' proposal to discuss the question of the Afghan war, but in a slightly different form. I think that what we should be talking about here is not a comission, since we are not, say, talking about Tbilisi, where about 19 people died and several hundred people were wounded. In this case, tens of thousands, or even millions, of people died (about a million Afghans died), and here what we need is not a commission but to hold an open hearing in the USSR Supreme Soviet on the development, course and results of that war. To identify the people who were to blame for launching it, and present a report of the Supreme Soviet to the second USSR Congress of People's Deputies. Moreover, I think that the congress should perhaps go ahead today and discuss that war, which was started on the basis of the decision of a narrow circle of the country's leaders and waged illegally, contrary to the Constitution of the USSR and without the sanction of the Supreme Soviet. In addition, I think that we should adopt a decision to the effect that the congress categorically forbids the sending of contingents of USSR Armed Forces beyond the borders of the USSR without the discussion of this matter in the USSR Supreme Soviet and the adoption of a decision by a two-thirds majority in a roll-call vote. (Applause).

V.I. Kirillov, senior scientific associate at Voronezh Polytechnical Institute, Voronezh (Leninskiy Territorial Election District, Voronezh Oblast): We are constantly talking about imminent ecological disaster. In international practice an effective means of preventing such a disaster is to hold regional referendums. My colleague Deputy Sokolov from Voronezh and I have directives from my voters demanding that we absolutely establish procedures whereby regional referendums are held on ecological problems. I submit a proposal that we adopt a resolution that the holding of regional referendums on ecological problems be put into practice—until the adoption of a Law on Referendums, in connection with the importance and urgency of this task. Thank you.

K.A. Antanavichyus, department head at the Lithuanian SSR Academy of Sciences' Institute of Economics, Vilnius (Vilnius-Oktyabr Territorial Election District, Lithuanian SSR): The deputies have proved indefatigable. I nonetheless think that we must continue to consider the problems of the economic reform. We have submitted for consideration, over the signature of 109 deputies, a draft law on the economic autonomy of republics. There has been no response on this issue. Instead, general principles of the restructuring of the management of the economy and the social sphere, etc. are being proposed to us for consideration. We have already been considering that since the beginning of January, and even earlier. Indeed, this is only the restructuring of the management, and that cannot suit anyone. There is no talk of autonomy here and, most importantly, there is no talk of economic reform, of the reform of economic relations. Relations remain the same—command relations. So I propose that discussion of the draft law on economic autonomy, including the reform of economic relations, be mandatorily included on the agenda. In the first day it was also proposed by Academician Sakharov that a decree titled "All Power to the Soviets" be considered and adopted. I believe that we cannot leave such a question without attention. This is also consonant with the proposal by Deputy Rasputin, who spoke earlier and raised the question of holding a referendum on nuclear power plants. I believe that this question should also be included. Thank you for your attention.

From the floor: (Inaudible).

M.S. Gorbachev: Please. One minute. On a point of order, we give the floor to Comrade Yanayev—out of turn, since he observes that we have coming up, that, in my opinion, there will be another 20-30 or so people.

G.I. Yanayev, secretary of the All-Union Central Council of Trade Unions, Moscow (from the USSR Trade Unions): Excuse me, comrades who are in line, for requesting the floor out of turn on a point of order. Mikhail Sergeyevich, the first question is to you. If my memory does not fail me (and I hope it does not fail me), you said that the time until 0800 would be assigned to the discussion of "Other Business."

M.S. Gorbachev: That's right.

G.I. Yanayev: In that connection, maybe my proposal will help the comrades orient themselves, because we have already put forward so many proposals under "Other Business" that the discussion of each of them will require holding debates for as much time as those that we have already held. Perhaps, my esteemed colleague deputies, we ought to be realists. We think that most of us, if not so long ago, then at least recently, left our youth behind. So let's not put forward proposals in accordance with youthful maximalism. Let's be realists. Perhaps we should limit the discussion to those questions that have already been raised. Thank you. (Applause).

M.S. Gorbachev: Just a minute. Let's consider Comrade Yanayev's proposal. His proposal comes down to the following: cut off the list of questions...

FIRST CONGRESS OF PEOPLE'S DEPUTIES OF THE USSR

Thirteenth Session

9 June 1989

From the floor: Mikhail Sergeyevich, but I have already come up to the rostrum.

M.S. Gorbachev: Just a minute. To cut off the list of questions and begin considering whether or not to include on the agenda the proposals that the comrades have made. Is the proposal clear, comrades?

From the hall: Yes.

M.S. Gorbachev: I put to a vote: Whoever is in favor of adopting that proposal and taking up the question of whether to include the questions that have already been put forward on the agenda, I ask you to vote. I ask you to lower them. Opposed? I ask you to lower them. Abstentions? The list is cut off; the question is decided. Thank you.

From the floor: Mikhail Sergeyevich....

M.S. Gorbachev: No, just a minute. If you are going to speak on a question that has already been included, you take the floor, but now we will go no further. That is all, comrades, that is all.

Now I want to discuss with you what we will leave. Our time is moving on. We have already been working for 55 minutes, and I want to discuss what we will leave on the agenda. The first question—on the status of the deputy. Leave it for discussion?

From the hall: Yes.

M.S. Gorbachev: Good. The second question, on drafting laws that are required for supporting the active work of the congress. They include regulations of the USSR Congress of People's Deputies, a law on the compensation of people's deputies for expenses connected with their work as deputies, and a law on the procedures for recalling a USSR People's Deputy. Leave them? Leave them.

The third question concerns appeals. Such a proposal was made back at the beginning of our congress. Now I want to enumerate from memory and notes; although I may not repeat the authors' wording correctly, the essence will be clear. Comrades submitted a proposal that we consider the question of confirming the editor in chief of IZVESTIYA and the director of radio and television. Then to resolve the question of Article 11. There was also discussion at the same time of the ukases. After that came the question of setting up a commission on Afghanistan. The question of services to deputies—offices, and so forth—is covered by the discussion of the status and all that is provided there. Changes in the Law on Elections also need to be discussed—as well as events in Novocherkassk. Time must be set aside for statements. Comrades are submitting a draft resolution on low-income families; they believe that what the government has submitted is inadequate. It has also been proposed that we decide the question of referendums on ecological problems before the law on referendums is adopted. And finally, the question of economic reform. As I understand it, it is an initiative by the Baltic republics and Belorussia. Is that right? Do I understand correctly? So there are these 11 questions. Let's look and see what we will leave for discussion. So there are proposals that the Presidium has made—three of them. And there are questions that the comrades have submitted. I would not hurry, comrades, but all the same give attention to this. There are a lot of substantive questions here.

I do not believe that we have to resolve the question of the newspaper editor and the chairman of the Committee for Television and Radio Broadcasting at the congress. One is a member of the government. The other, in essence, will be higher than the government in our country. The government and all the rest are confirmed by the Supreme Soviet, and the editor—by the congress. Here is something that we need to sort out, comrades. I do not think that these questions should be decided in an emotional state. As for establishing a commission on Afghanistan, we could, I would submit the following proposal: to instruct the Supreme Soviet to decide this question and submit proposals, and then we will decide what sort of hearings to hold.

On changes in the Law on Elections. I do not think that we need to open debates at the congress on this matter. We should instruct the Supreme Soviet to take this matter up and prepare a draft law that takes everything into account. This, after all, is very serious, comrades. I am confident that we should have a better Law on Elections than we had in this election campaign. And the republics, incidentally, are themselves adopting them.

Now time must be allocated for statements. I think that this is already beyond the capabilities of this congress. And as for events in Novocherkassk, I would also turn the question over for consideration by the Supreme Soviet. There remains Article 11.1; I am leaving it separate. Those are the sort of explanations with which I would turn over all these questions for consideration to the Supreme Soviet, listing them in a certain order, and instruct it to resolve these questions. That is how.

If you have been listening closely, and if you have read our basic resolution, it begins with the statement that the USSR Congress of People's Deputies takes power into its hands. That is our basic document.

And so, we are deciding the question of what we will leave on the agenda under "Other Business." So, concerning the first three questions, I would support the proposal that the Presidium submitted: create a commission for the resolution of questions connected with republic cost accounting and economic autonomy—what we have included here in the basic draft, and Belorussia has added to it. To establish a comission for this work. So include those four questions. Consider the question of Article 11.1 right now. And turn over all the

Thirteenth Session

9 June 1989

remaining questions to the Supreme Soviet with appropriate commentaries and instructions, which I have mentioned. Okay, comrades?

From the hall: Okay.

M.S. Gorbachev: Whoever favors that approach, I ask you to vote. I ask you to lower them. Opposed? Abstentions? Adopted. And so, according to the agenda. On the status of deputies. Please, Comrade Krayko. The rules, I think, allow one or two minutes for observations, comrades.

A.N. Krayko, department chief in a division of the P.I. Baranov Central Institute of Aviation Engine Design Moscow (Bauman Territorial Election District, RSFSR): I ask for three minutes. In the draft that we have here, I propose making the following changes: to replace Article 9, which speaks about the secretary, with the following article: "In order to fulfill his duties as a deputy, a USSR People's Deputy may be released from his principal work and rely on aides who act as his official representatives, as well as on consultants and technical specialists. Their work, as well as mailing expenses, expenses for duplicating documents, etc. are paid for out of the deputy's budget, the upper limit of which is set by the USSR Supreme Soviet. The part of the deputy's budget that is not spent in the current year is returned to the state budget and cannot be spent for deputies' personal needs. In carrying out his work as a deputy, a USSR People's Deputy is provided with transportation. The local soviets provide permanent space, with telelphones, for the work of a people's deputy and his aides."

Now another important point, which has repeatedly been raised here at the congress. It concerns the so-called party-state collision. I recall an incident from the experience of Lenin. At the eighth congress of soviets a preliminary Central Committee decision was adopted on one of the questions, and the deputies asked Vladimir Ilyich what would happen to them if they voted against it. Vladimir Ilyich replied by referring to the Party Statutes. Here is the quote from the Party Statutes: "In questions pertaining to its internal life and current work, the faction is autonomous." Here were Lenin's words: "So, all members of the faction have the right and are obliged to vote according to their consciences, and not according to the Central Committee's instructions."

In accordance with this, I propose to add an additional, 14th point to the draft; it reads as follows: "In the USSR Congress of People's Deputies and the Supreme Soviet, the people's deputy is guided solely by the law, the will of his constituents, and his own convictions, and is autonomous in relation to other state, political and public bodies."

Finally, the first point. In accordance with what I have said, I propose the following wording: "To instruct the USSR Supreme Soviet to prepare a draft of a new Law on the Status of the USSR People's Deputy and to consider it at the USSR Congress of People's Deputies in the fourth quarter of 1989. In addition to the following, that law should provide for the division of authority among the deputies of soviets of various levels, the right to collective and individual investigation of the actions of state and public organizations and their representatives, the provision of up-to-date information, including the right to use printing and duplicating equipment, and the criminal liability of officials for knowingly providing deputies with false information. The draft law is to be sent to USSR People's Deputies in September 1989."

What I have said is the result of the work of a large group of Moscow deputies. I ask all these points to be put to a vote. (Applause).

A.I. Lukyanov: Aleksandr Nikolayevich, how much will your proposal cost?

A.N. Krayko: The problem is, you have set the budget.

A.I. Lukyanov: No, but you say. We have set it, but you.... (Inaudible).

A.N. Krayko: How much our proposal costs depends on the sort of budget we are given. R200 is not enough for us. That's for sure.

M.S. Gorbachev: Just a minute. Perhaps since the proposal is of a carefully considered, fundamental nature, we should consider these questions? But I think that we have a case of jumping the gun here. If we take that path and make decisions that way, I guarantee that we will produce such decisions that afterwards no one will be able to give an accounting for them. If we have discovered that we have many serious shortcomings in the process of preparation and in the adoption of decisions and their implementation in the past, that approach no longer merits cheers, comrades. I think and am convinced that we should proceed on the basis of the following. We should prepare a good, well-substantiated Law on the Status of the Deputy and submit it to the congress. Moreover, I think, that law should be thoroughly prepared, so that the deputy is given the proper status, and protected, and provided for. I will say bluntly—all those points should be included. (Applause).

Right now, I think, the question is already resolved in the draft. In addition to what already exists in the status of the deputy (since we have some deputies who are members of the Supreme Soviet, and some who are not), in order to preserve the deputy's lofty status, a number of provisions are being added, and they are being codified. Incidentally, for the most part they have been taken from the proposals of Comrade Krayko and his fellow deputies. Only they want to act on the entire draft right now, and we cannot do that just like that. Although I should say that I do not want to reject everything. But to take everything and immediately adopt it right now—Our people will say: Well, look, that way they will squander the country, too. (Applause).

I am certain that the question of the deputy's material situation needs to be resolved without delay, and that he

Thirteenth Session
9 June 1989

should be provided with transportation, without fail, should have an office for receiving people, and should have a secreatry on a permanent basis. He should receive general information from any agency. So, until there is a law, that will be enough.

Incidentally, transportation does not mean a private car. Transportation costs should be covered.

On this question, comrades, we have two approaches. In my opinion, this is very serious, and we should not look ridiculous before our people. I would put the question this way: everything that requires immediate resolution in order to provide the conditions for deputies' work should be used from these proposals, and all the rest should be used in preparing the draft law. Okay, comrades?

But Comrade Krayko was ahead of me here, and he submitted a proposal. We should either accept his proposal or reject it.

Who is in favor of adopting those proposals right now in their complete form? I ask you to raise your credentials. I ask you to lower them.

Opposed? Essentially the whole congress is opposed, comrade Krayko. But all the same your proposals, I assure you, will be used. Because there is a great deal of value in them.

Please.

A.V. Minzhurenko, department head at Omsk State Pedagogical Institute, Omsk (Central Territorial Election District, Omsk Oblast): I have more modest proposals. And I think that they can be adopted immediately. The point is that in this case I am acting according to precedent. We have now been working for three weeks, comrades. And we have people back home who have addressed their complaints and petitions to us. We, for example, with our authorized representatives, tried to do as follows: I left one of my authorized representatives, a qualified legal specialist with a higher education, a notarized authorization to continue the business that I had not finished when I left for the congress. We acted on our own without yet knowing whether we could do that or not. But it turned out that in some organizations that authorization has been treated with confidence, and he has continued to work, while in others it has not. Therefore, I think that we can establish this right now, without a lot of fuss. Many of us go on business trips and are simply busy people. We could leave notarized authorizations with our authorized representatives, and they could continue our affairs. I think that is not a very complicated matter.

M.S. Gorbachev: Your proposal is clear.

Comrades, I do not know: Either a comrade voluntarily turns over his authority, or we want to have three, four, seven deputies in one district. Comrades, this is a special authority that we receive from the people through an election campaign. It must not be oversimplified; that will not do. That is simply unacceptable. And I do not think that we need to vote here. We should simply explain that.

V.A. Zubanov, secretary of the party committee at the Khartsyzsk Steel Wire and Cable Plant, Khartsyzsk (Makeyevka-Gornyatskoye Territorial Election District, Donetsk Oblast): I have two questions about the work of a people's deputy that, in my opinion, need to be resolved right away.

The first question: I would still like to receive additional explanation of how the work of deputies who are not on a committee, a commission, or the Supreme Soviet but want to have the right to express their views without actually voting will be carried out. The question is this: Who will issue the summons to do so? How will questions concerning that deputy's place of work be resolved? A business assignment, leave from work—how will all these procedural questions be decided? I want Mikhail Sergeyevich to provide some additional explanation of this matter.

The second question has already been raised here: the provision of transportation. We all know that deputies are provided with free travel on transport. But the problem is there are rural rayons where means of transportation run to villages once a day, and sometimes only official vehicles go to them. If you take up such matters, it turns out that a deputy will be busy a whole day just to visit one village. I have three rayons, for example. Each rayon has a party raykom, a rayispolkom, and a rayon Komsomol committee. They all have means of transportation. I believe that, at least for the initial period, until we adopt the Law on the Status of the People's Deputy, the executive committees should provide a vehicle to a people's deputy upon request for various specific needs.

M.S. Gorbachev: Fine. Comrades, I think that we have already clarified this matter, and I want to say something once again.

First, deputies who work on the Supreme Soviet—on commissions and committees—have rights equal to those of members of the Supreme Soviet who serve on those commissions and committees. Moreover, those who are enlisted in regular work on those commissions will be materially provided for on the same level as regular members of the Supreme Soviet. But all that must be resolved.

Deputies who consider it necessary to take part in the discussion of questions that are of special interest to them will have, as we have already said, information about the meetings of a commission, etc. They will send a telegram to the Presidium of the USSR Supreme Soviet. On the basis of agreement with the Presidium, they will go. Those who work, including those who work at a machine tool, will be compensated for their average earnings out of the budget. That is mentioned in the status. As for transportation, let us preserve the record as it is. I think that people at the local level will be attentive to the resolution of these

Thirteenth Session

9 June 1989

questions, since that has been noted by the congress. We will live for these 3 or 4 months, and everything will probably become clear, and then provisions that will resolve all the questions and difficulties that have arisen will be incorporated in the law.

V.A. Shapovalenko, head of a laboratory at the Orenburggazprom [Orenburg Gas Industry] Production Association's Volga-Urals Research and Design Institute for the Extraction and Processing of Hydrogen Sulfide Gases, Orenburg (Orenburg City Election District, Orenburg Oblast): I have a small correction. In point 6, where it lists what a people's deputy has a right to request information about, nothing is said—and it should be said—about the organization of the information that is required to be given to him.

Further, the second paragraph: At the instruction of the USSR Congress of People's Deputies or the Supreme Soviet, public organizations have the right to show documents. But why should I have to ask authorization from the Supreme Soviet or the congress, when I should exercise that right within my district without the Supreme Soviet? Otherwise I won't be allowed at a single trade outlet; people will say: Give us the authorization from the chairman of the Presidium of the USSR Supreme Soviet. I believe that that should absolutely be included.

And, I am hurrying, the ninth point: "The USSR People's Deputy has the right to have a secretary." I would propose "assistant-secretary"; one could call it that. In connection with the fact that I still have a whole minute, I will make one announcement.

The first USSR Congress of People's Deputies is concluding. The discussion that has been held at the congress has been unprecedented in candor and has had a strong impact on public attitudes and on the whole internal situation in the country. At the same time, in preparations for holding the congress there was a great deal that left a feeling of dissatisfaction and concern. It seems to us that at the congress we have still not managed to create a mechanism for identifying and comparing points of view and bringing them closer together. Many key problems in the country's life either have not been considered, or have been discussed hastily. A good many valuable proposals have not been noticed or have been rejected without adequate grounds for doing so.

We believe that the chief source of the difficulties the congress has encountered is, in the first place, the lack of adequate advance preparation and, in the second place, the lack of proper mutual understanding among deputies and their inability to discuss and understand alternate points of view. We should draw lessons for the future from this. Taking into account the experience gained by the Moscow club of deputies, who did serious preparatory work just before the congress, as well as the experience of the groups of agrarian deputies and deputies who are Komsomol members, public-education employees and ecologists, who have done a great deal during the congress out of a desire to establish close contacts and mutual understanding among deputies from various regions of the country, and in an effort to create favorable conditions for dialogue and compromise agreements, we announce the establishment of an interregional group of people's deputies. The group's chief purpose is to begin preparations for the next, autumn 1989 congress, and to draw up proposals and draft documents, especially in the following areas—Okay, I'm finishing.

More than 150 deputies have signed this paper.

M.S. Gorbachev: I ask Comrade Lukyanov to formulate our proposal on the question under discussion, which comes from all the deputies.

A.I. Lukyanov: Comrades! On the eve of the congress we in the Presidium of the USSR Supreme Soviet carefully studied the question of the 8 April ukase. The Presidium of the Supreme Soviet believes that in Article 7 of that ukase it could be indicated, to put it bluntly, that public appeals for the violent overthrow of the social and state system established by our constitution are punishable under criminal law. The Presidium of the USSR Supreme Soviet has carefully studied the question of Article 11.1 and believes it possible to presently propose to the congress that this article be rescinded and simultaneously, if the designation of such a crime is required in the future, that it be examined—and this will evidently be approved by the congress—in the context of ratifying the Basic Principles of Criminal Legislation and the Law on State Crimes. (Applause).

M.S. Gorbachev: But this is a legal point; we must vote, comrades.

S.M. Ryabchenko, head of a laboratory at the Ukrainian SSR Academy of Sciences Physics Institute, Kiev (Moscow Territorial Election District, Ukrainian SSR): I would still like to add to Anatoliy Ivanovich's remarks one small detail. It seems to me that he is correct in saying that the Presidium of the USSR Supreme Soviet deems it possible to rescind the article. But I would like for that to read: "at the insistence of the congress." (Applause).

M.S. Gorbachev: Correct. Only, I think precisely that has been stated, that there is complete understanding and a unanimous position here. Whoever is in favor of the proposal that has been submitted and in favor of the adoption of a resolution on this matter, I ask you to raise your credentials. I ask you to lower them. Opposed? I ask for a count. (A count is taken). Comrades, I ask you immediately to keep in mind that following the close of the congress there will be announcements. Life goes on.

A.G. Kostenyuk: Esteemed deputies, seven voted "no."

M.S. Gorbachev: Abstentions?

A.G. Kostenyuk: Six deputies abstained.

Thirteenth Session
9 June 1989

M.S. Gorbachev: The question is decided. A resolution rescinding that article has been adopted. (Applause).

Comrades, I must inform you, because the Presidium and I, we cannot undertake the resolution of such a matter. Andrey Dmitriyevich Sakharov urgently requests the floor. (Commotion in the hall).

Wait just a minute. We on the Presidium have conferred on this account; we did not have the opportunity to do so in the course of the debates; moreover, it was taken into account that Deputy Sakharov has spoken several times, seven times in all, and we had to take that into account; such was the Presidium's collective opinion, but I must inform you that we have had such a request from Deputy Sakharov; he asks for 15 minutes— (Commotion in the hall).

Comrades, let's determine our will. Will we give him the floor? (Commotion in the hall). Just a minute. It seems to me that we should ask Andrey Dmitriyevich to condense and express his views in 5 minutes. (Commotion in the hall). Just a minute, comrades. There's no need—Here is another request that, for example, the Society of Theater Workers considers it abnormal that, despite insistent requests, Comrade Lavrov has not been allowed to speak once. (Commotion in the hall). So there's our situation. Fine, let's decide the question this way. I submit a compromise proposal: Whoever is in favor of giving Deputy Sakharov 5 minutes for a speech, I ask you to raise your credentials. Must we count? Opposed? A minority, a clear minority. Please, Andrey Dmitriyevich, 5 minutes.

A.D. Sakharov: As it turns out, comrades. It's not always possible. I have not spoken in conceptual terms. I would say that my proposal is, in any event, a little unusual; I recognize that and feel my responsibility for it. Therefore I will speak as I prepared to speak.

Esteemed people's deputies! I am speaking to explain why I voted against the proposed final document, despite the fact that it contains extremely many very important ideas and is extremely useful. But nonetheless, I believe that this document reflects the congress's work, and that the congress did not accomplish its main task—the establishment of power, the establishment of the sort of system of power that would provide for the accomplishment of other tasks—the economic task, the social task, and the task of overcoming ecological madness. The congress elected a chairman of the USSR Supreme Soviet on the first day, without a broad political discussion or at least a symbolic alternative. In my opinion, the congress committed a serious mistake, substantially reducing its ability to influence the formation of the country's policy, and thereby rendering poor service to the elected chairman, as well. According to the existing constitution, the chairman of the Presidium of the USSR Supreme Soviet possesses absolute, practically unlimited personal power. The concentration of such power in the hands of a single person is extremely dangerous, even if that person is the initiator of restructuring. In saying this, I have the utmost respect for Mikhail Sergeyevich Gorbachev, but this is not a personal question; it is a political question. Sometime it will be someone else. The construction of the house of state has begun with the roof, which is clearly not the best way to proceed. The same thing was repeated in electing the Supreme Soviet. For the majority of delegations what took place was simply the appointment, followed by the pro forma confirmation by the congress, of people among whom many are unprepared for legislative activity. Members of the Supreme Soviet are supposed to leave their previous jobs "as a rule"; this is the deliberately vague wording whereby they turn out to be "ceremonial generals"—more than 50 percent of them—on the Supreme Soviet. Such a Supreme Soviet will be, one can fear, simply a screen for the real power of the chairman of the Supreme Soviet and the party and state apparatus.

In the country, under the conditions of an approaching economic disaster and the tragic deterioration of international relations, powerful, dangerous processes are taking place, one manifestation of which is a general crisis of confidence among the people in the country's leadership. If we float downstream consoling ourselves with the hope of gradual changes for the better in the remote future, the growing tension may tear our society apart, with the most tragic consequences.

Comrade deputies! A tremendous historical responsibility rests on you; political decisions are needed; without them it will be impossible to strengthen the power of local soviet agencies and solve economic, social, ecological, and nationality problems. If the USSR Congress of People's Deputies cannot take power into its hands here, there is not the slightest hope that the soviets in the republics, oblasts, rayons, and villages will be able to take it.

M.S. Gorbachev: One minute.

A.D. Sakharov: Without strong local soviets, it will be impossible to carry out land reform and, in general, any sort of effective agrarian policy that differs from the senseless infusions of money aimed at reviving unprofitable kolkhozes. Further, I will omit my arguments and read the text of a decree on power that I propose we adopt.

Decree on power.

Proceeding from the principles of democracy, the USSR Congress of People's Deputies declares:

1. Article 6 of the USSR Constitution is rescinded.

2. The adoption of USSR laws is the exclusive right of the USSR Congress of People's Deputies. On the territory of a union republic, USSR laws acquire legal force following their ratification by the republic's supreme legislative body. (Applause).

3. The USSR Supreme Soviet is the congress's working body. I'll omit a point in order to speed up.

Thirteenth Session

9 June 1989

5. The election and recall of the supreme officials of the USSR, to wit, the chairman of the USSR Supreme Soviet, the deputy chairman of the USSR Supreme Soviet, the chairman of the USSR Ministry of Foreign Affairs, the chairman and members of the Constitutional Oversight Committee, the chairman of the USSR Supreme Court, the USSR procurator general, the USSR supreme arbitrator, the chairman of the Central Bank, as well as the chairman of the USSR KGB, the chairman of the State Committee for Television and Radio Broadcasting, and the editor in chief of the newspaper IZVESTIYA, are the exclusive right of the congress. The aforementioned officials are accountable to the congress and independent of the decisions of the CPSU and its agencies.

6. Candidates for the post of deputy—

I am omitting another point. Lastly.

The seventh point. The functions of the KGB are limited to the tasks of protecting the USSR's international security.

I ask that an editorial commission be established and that this decree be taken up at a special session of the congress.

I appeal to the USSR's citizens with a request to support the decree on an individual and collective basis, as they did in the case of the attempt to compromise me and divert attention from responsibility for the Afghan war.

I omit arguments.

I continue. For a long time now there has been no danger of a military attack against the USSR. (Commotion in the hall, applause). We have the largest Army in the world, larger than those of the United States or China taken together. I propose the establishment of a commission for the preparation of a decision on reducing periods of service in the Army by approximately half for privates and sergeants, with corresponding reductions of all types of arms, but with a substantially smaller reduction in the officers' corps and with a view to shifting to a professional army. Such a decision would have tremendous international significance for confidence-building and disarmament, including the complete prohibition of nuclear weapons, as well as tremendous economic and social significance.

My speech is of general significance, and I am continuing. (Commotion in the hall, applause).

Nationality problems. We inherited from Stalinism a national constitutional structure that bears the imprint of imperial thinking and the imperial policy of "divide and conquer." The victims of this legacy are the small union republics and the small national formations that belong to the union republics according to the principle of administrative subordination. They have been subjected to national oppression over the course of decades. Now these problems have dramatically burst out onto the surface.

But the large people, including the Russian people, who have borne the principal burden of imperial ambitions and the consequences of adventurism and dogmatism in foreign and domestic policy, have also been a victim of this legacy. Urgent measures are needed. I propose discussion of a transition to a federal, horizontal system of national constitutional structure. This system provides for granting all the existing national territorial formations, regardless of their size and present status, equal political, legal, and economic rights, with the preservation of present borders. In time, it may be necessary to adjust the borders.

M.S. Gorbachev: Anyway, finish up, Andrey Dmitriyevich. You've used two time allotments already, two allotments.

A.D. Sakharov: I'm finishing. I am omitting arguments. I have left out a great deal.

M.S. Gorbachev: That's all. Your time, two time allotments, has run out. I beg your pardon. That is all.

A.D. Sakharov: (Inaudible).

M.S. Gorbachev: That's all, Comrade Sakharov. Do you respect the congress? Good. That's all.

A.D. Sakharov: (Inaudible).

M.S. Gorbachev: All!

A.D. Sakharov: (Inaudible).

M.S. Gorbachev: I ask you to finish. I ask you to conclude. That's all! Take away your speech, please! (Applause). I ask you to sit down. Turn on the third microphone.

Voice from the floor: (Inaudible)

M.S. Gorbachev: What do you want?

A.Ya. Troitskiy, head of an office at the Kalinin Oblast Institute for Advanced Teacher Training, RSFSR (from the All-Union Organization of War and Labor Veterans): I want to express some surprise over the fact that the Presidium is for some reason dividing us, people's deputies with equal rights. Some have been able to speak seven or eight times each. Why should we listen to Comrade Sakharov now? Why is he permitted to address the people of the Soviet Union from the rostrum of this congress? Isn't he assuming too much? (Applause).

M.S. Gorbachev: We are continuing the congress's work. Permit me to ask USSR People's Deputy Valentina Adamovna Kiseleva to read the draft message of the USSR Congress of People's Deputies to the Peoples of the World, on which we have agreed.

V.A. Kiseleva, operator at the 60th Anniversary of the USSR Grodno Khimvolokno [Chemical Fiber] Production Association Grodno (Grodno National Territorial Election District, Belorussian SSR):

STENOGRAPHIC RECORD

Thirteenth Session
9 June 1989

"Message of the USSR Congress of People's Deputies to the Peoples of the World.

"We USSR People's Deputies have gathered for our first congress in order, in a situation of glasnost and openness, to lay the legal foundation for the comprehensive democratic renewal of our socialist society. As authorized representatives of the millions-strong Soviet people, we fully recognize the historic responsibility that rests on us. We recognize that the problems that have arisen before our homeland today are immense, and we proceed on the premise that there is no alternative to the radical restructuring of all spheres of our life. We have chosen this path thoughtfully and firmly, and we will not depart from it.

"In the center of our attention is the human being with his joys, sadness, cares and hopes. We are convinced that a socialist society does not and cannot have any moral alternative to the interests of the people and the aspirations and rights of the free human being.

"Restructuring is the internal affair of the peoples of the Soviet Union; it has been born of our country's urgent needs. But we do not separate ourselves from the world community and from the processes that are determining the face of present-day civilization, and we take freedom of the individual, democracy, and social justice as fundamental values on which the life of our society should be built.

"We regard restructuring as part of the democratization of the entire world order that is gathering force, as the Soviet Union's contribution to solving the global problems that are hanging over humanity. They are all closely interconnected, interwoven into a dangerous and tight knot. It can and must be untangled, but that requires that the world community concert its efforts in the name of its survival.

"Restructuring is fundamentally changing our attitude toward the surrounding world. Today we are open to the world and prepared to cooperate with everyone for whom human life and dignity are the supreme values, and we count on mutual understanding

"In the presently rapidly changing world, it is impossible to live according to old rules and standards. One cannot count on strengthening one's own security and providing for one's own well-being while disregarding the interests of others. It is senseless to turn international relations into an arena of ideological wars. It is criminal to exhaust the world economy with an arms race and to shun concern for preserving the human environment. No matter what barriers separate us, we are all children of mother earth, and we have one common destiny. Therefore, we call for an end to hostility and discord among peoples. A new peaceful period in the history of humanity is possible, and this possibility must be turned into reality.

"The congress solemnly assures the planet's peoples that it assumes responsibility for the Soviet state's strict observance of the principles of peaceful coexistence with regard to all the earth's states and peoples.

"On the basis of the new political thinking, the USSR Congress of People's Deputies has affirmed the principles by which our state should be guided in international affairs. They come down to the following:

"—the security of our country must be ensured, first and foremost, by political means, as a constituent element of universal and equal security in the process of the demilitarization, democratization, and humanization of international relations, relying on the authority and capabilities of the United Nations;

"—nuclear weapons should be eliminated as the result of negotiations oriented toward disarmament and the reduction of a state's defense potential to the limits of reasonable sufficiency;

"—the use of force and threat of the use of force for the purposes of attaining any political, economic, or other goals are intolerable; in relations with other countries, respect for sovereignty, independence, and territorial integrity are mandatory;

"—not confrontation, but dialogue and negotiations with an orientation toward a balance of interests should become the sole means of solving international problems and settling conflicts;

"—the Soviet economy should be organically included in the world economy on the basis of mutual advantage and equality, and should actively participate in the development and observance of the rules of the present-day international division of labor, scientific, and technological exchange, and trade.

"Our congress, as the supreme body of state authority, declares: the Soviet Union intends to strictly adhere to these principles in its foreign policy. Such is our foreign-policy strategy henceforth and forever. Such is the open and honest line of the Soviet Union and restructuring in the world arena. Such is the choice of the Soviet people.

"We appeal to the world's peoples and to world public opinion to develop the exchange of ideas and people, cultural and spiritual values, contacts, and dialogue in every way possible, at all levels and in all spheres, and to work together to seek and find mutually acceptable compromises for the sake of preserving peace on earth, for the sake of the prosperity and progress of all humanity." (Applause).

M.S. Gorbachev: That can be discussed. What do you think, comrades? If anyone has any clarifications or improvements, a request to approach the Presidium, in order that you can present your proposals. In principle I can put the question of adopting the draft message that has been read to a vote. Whoever is in favor of adopting the draft, I ask you to raise your documents. I ask you to lower them. Opposed? Abstentions? Two people. It is adopted. (Applause).

Thirteenth Session

9 June 1989

Dear comrades, the congress is concluding; this is the 13th day of its work. I once again want to thank you, the USSR People's Deputies, for the tremendous contribution that you have made to its preparation and conduct. We have all agreed on this, and in this case I reject Deputy Sakharov's negative opinions aimed at disparaging the congress and disparaging its role and landmark significance in our country's destiny. (Applause). Nonetheless, I welcome the open, direct discussion that has taken place here, for perhaps the first time in our entire history, of all the problems that trouble our people and the peoples of the world. (Applause). Quite likely we, as the first congress, have, as it was foreseen, been unable to exhaust all the problems. Therefore, many of us have remained outside the boundaries of the congress. But after all, we are just beginning our work. After the congress, on the basis of its instructions and the decisions it has adopted, the USSR Supreme Soviet will begin its work as a standing body, a legislative body, and its committees and its immense number of deputies will begin their work. This is opening up a great opportunity for the ideas that have been heard here and the proposals that have been submitted here to receive the most thorough and attentive consideration and embodiment in legislative acts or in the activities of the executive authority, or to be discussed at subsequent stages of the activity of the congress, the Supreme Soviet, and the bodies that they create.

I am extremely satisfied with the fact that, thanks to openness and pluralism of opinions, we for the first time have come to sense all the problems that characterize our society's present state. And perhaps for the first time we are recognizing, at this congress, the immensity, importance, and scale of the tasks that will need to be accomplished by the new bodies of Soviet power that have been created now at the top echelon, and that will be created on the basis of the new approaches and under the conditions of openness, democracy, and glasnost at the next stage of the political reform. We are armed with better knowledge. This gives us the hope and confidence that we will make the right decisions and better act to resolutely advance restructuring in all areas, especially in those sectors whose activity is connected with the satisfaction of our peoples' urgent needs and requirements. We are certain that all the basic ideas expressed here, including those that are debatable, will find their resolution in the further activities of the bodies of Soviet power.

Allow me, comrade deputies, to wish you great successes. We have tremendous work ahead of us. And we are confident that this corps of deputies will be up to the business that we have begun with regard to the renewal of our society in the interests of the people, on the basis of the principles of democracy and glasnost, and in the interests of our people's life. I wish you great successes.

The agenda is finished. The first USSR Congress of People's Deputies is declared closed. (Applause).

The national anthem of the Soviet Union is played.

STENOGRAPHIC RECORD

NOTES TO THE EIGHTH SESSION

2 ...the second secretary of the Moldavian Party Central Committee...arrested: V.I. Smirnov served as second secretary from August 1984 to October 1988. His arrest apparently came later. He was forced to resign because of high-handed methods which "complicated restructuring," but at the time he was not charged with criminal activity. FBIS-SOV 89-054 (22 March 1989), 93-94.

3 ...General Rodionov...the Tbilisi problem: Referring to exchanges during the Sixth and Seventh Sessions, 1: 224-37 and 292-95.

3 ...Yekaterina Alekseyevna Furtseva: Minister of Culture, 1960-74.

4 ...Metropolitan Aleksey: (A.M. Ridiger), above 1: 269.

4 ...a delicate problem raised by Deputy Oleynik: Above, 1: 260.

6 ...facts given here by Academician Likhanov: Apparently referring to the speech of D.S. Likhachev, above, 1: 210-212.

7 ...when Comrade Drutse compares bilingualism: Above 2.

10 ...children and mothers from Elista infected with AIDS: See above the note to 1: 253.

12 ...Trishka's caftan: An allusion to an eighteenth-century play, *Nedorosl'* (The Minor) by D.I. Fonvizin. The tailor Trishka was given a kaftan to mend but had no material. Therefore he pulled yarn from one section of the coat to make the repairs in another, and in the end of course, nothing was accomplished.

12 ...Zaslavsky has not enrolled me in the "Black Hundred:" The Black Hundreds were proto-fascist gangs that emerged during the 1905 Revolution to defend Russia, Orthodoxy, and the tsar against Jews and liberals. The speaker apparently refers to Moscow deputy I.I. Zaslavsky.

13 ...two Leningrad deputies who offered to give up their candidacies: A.A. Sobchak and A.A. Denisov made the offer in order to resolve the issue of NKAO representation in the Soviet of Nationalities.

14 ...Murakhovsky: Probably Vsevolod S. Murakhovsky, First Deputy Chairman of the USSR Council of Ministers and Chairman of the State Agroindustrial Committee (Gosagroprom) since January 1985; also a member of the CPSU CC Commission on Questions of Agrarian Policy, created in December 1988.

17 ...Evens, Yukagirs, Niykhi, Nantsy: Paleo-Siberian peoples of northeastern Siberia.

19 ...Amur-Yakut Mainline...BAM: Funding for the AYaM was cut off at the end of 1986 (*Izvestiya*, 24 Jan 1987). BAM—the Baikal-Amur Mainline, a 2,250-mile spur of the Trans-Siberian, shortens the distance between Taishet, west of Lake Baikal, and Komsomolsk on the Amur River by eliminating the route along the great bend of the Amur. The route also lies generally 600 miles north of the Chinese border. Construction on "the engineering project of the century" began in 1974, the line opened in 1984, and it was scheduled to become fully operational in November 1989.

20 ...belittled Pasternak, slandered Tvardovsky: In 1958 Boris Pasternak (1890-1960) was compelled to renounce the Nobel Prize for Literature for his novel *Doctor Zhivago*. Alexander Tvardovsky (1910-71) made *Novy mir* the leading liberal journal of the 1960s by opening it to the works of Alexander Solzhenitsyn and others. (*Novy mir* published Solzhenitsyn's *One Day in the Life of Ivan Denisovich* in November 1962.) But he was constantly hounded for his non-conformity and in February 1970 was finally forced to resign as editor.

20 ...People's Commissar Kraski: The speaker probably means L.B. Krasin (1870-1926), an Old Bolshevik who served as People's Commissar for Foreign Trade from 1920 to 1923.

21 ...a man who understands nothing of this, and who has failed in ideology: Ligachev was elevated into the central leadership by Yuri Andropov and given several portfolios, including ideology. In September 1988, Gorbachev removed him from the Politburo and placed him at the head of a new agricultural commission.

22 ...the agrarian note read to you yesterday: By V.A. Gontar, above, 1: 250.

28 ...Law Governing the State Enterprise: Law on State Enterprise, see 1: 303 (n147).

28 ...Law Governing the Cooperative System: Law on Cooperatives in the USSR, see the note to 1: 301 (n100).

31 ...a special treaty with the emigre Polish government (in London): On 30 July 1941, following the Nazi invasion of the USSR, the Soviet government and the Polish government-in-exile established diplomatic relations. That troubled relationship ended, de facto, in 1943. In June 1944, Moscow backed the communist Lublin Committee which established itself in eastern Poland in the train of the Red Army. In January 1945, after the reconquest of Poland, the Lublin Poles moved to Warsaw, reconstituted themselves as the Provisional Government of the Polish Republic, and immediately gained recognition from the USSR.

34 ...Law Governing Public Organizations: Probably the "Law on Voluntary Societies, Public Grass-roots Agencies, and Voluntary Grass-roots Associations." CDSP (15 Jun 1988), 9.

34 ...a large "replenishment" of internationalist fighting men: Veterans of the war in Afghanistan.

37 ...October 1964: The ouster of Nikita Khrushchev as First Secretary of the CPSU and Chairman of the Council of Ministers.

38 ...the representative from Soviet Uzbekistan: R.N. Nishanov, above, 1: 253-54.

41 ...Chapter 9 of the USSR Constitution: Chapter 9, consisting of Articles 76-81, defines the powers, rights, and duties of a Union Republic.

41 ...Continuing Adamovich's idea: Above, 1: 101.

41 ...Supporting Starodubtsev: Above, 1: 247.

42 ...citizens ...have the right to work: Under the "anti-parasite" legislation of the USSR, citizens are required to work. See above, 1: 306 (n195).

42 ...Chapter 7 of the Constitution: Articles 39-69 concerning "The Basic Rights, Freedoms, and Duties of Citizens of the USSR."

43 ...Sergey Zalygin: Editor of *Novy Mir*.

45 ...the 26 Baku commissars: Meshadi Azizbekov was the Bolshevik commissar of Baku province and a member of the radical Baku Commune that held power from April to July 1918. Ousted from power, the commissars fled the city as Turkish troops closed in. They were captured by forces of the Social Revolutionary government of Transcaspia and held in Krasnovodsk until 20 September 1918. Then, while ostensibly being taken by train to Astrakhan, they were murdered and their corpses were buried in the desert. At the end of the civil war, the bodies were recovered and reinterred under an eternal flame in the center of Baku. Cf. Ronald Grigor Suny, *The Baku Commune, 1917-1918* (Princeton University Press, 1972).

45 ...M.N. Rakhmanova: Above, 1: 219.

47 ...comrades Ryzhkov and Maslyukov: N.I. Ryzhkov, Chairman of the USSR Council of Ministers; Yu.D. Maslyukov, Chairman of the State Planning Committee (Gosplan).

48 ...the appeal...adopted in Tallinn on 14 May: A declaration of economic independence which asserted that the principle of regional accountability and autonomy was more appropriate to relations between republics and the center than the government's current proposal. See 1: 308 (n277).

The Baltic assembly, combining representatives of the Estonian and Latvian People's Fronts and the Lithuanian Sajudis, met in Tallinn on 13-14 May 1989 to forge a common front on economic and political sovereignty. It was there that the Baltic people's deputies agreed on the proposals that they presented to the Congress of People's Deputies, including a condemnation of the Nazi-Soviet pact as contrary to international law and, therefore, as invalid from the outset. CDSP (14 June 1989), 15 and 17.

49 ...Deputy Rodionov was pining for 1937: Above, 1: 229.

52 ...Deputy Alksnis's request: Above, 1: 25.

55 ...Deputy Sukharev: Minister of Justice; see above, 1: 304 (n152).

NOTES TO THE NINTH SESSION

65 ...stanitsa: A cossack village.

69 ...the article to which General Rodionov referred: In *Zarya Vostok*, the voice of the Georgian CP CC, discussed above, 1: 227*ff*.

73 ...accusation levelled again yesterday by Comrade Ivanov: Above, 1: 55.

74 ...draft of the Law on Local Self-Administration and Local Economy: The object of the law was to "revive" the sovereignty of local soviets as the representatives of state power. *Pravda*, 14 April 1989, in CDSP (10 May 1989), 24.

77 ...draft of the USSR Law on Youth: See "Youth Policy: Beginning of the Road," *Izvestiya*, 15 June 1989, in CDSP (12 July 1989), 30.

79 ...PO-2 airplane: originally the Polikarpov U-2, a single engine biplane which entered full production in 1927; the Red Air Force's primary trainer before the war, it saw some service as a night bomber in World War II.

81 ...all-union subbotnik: Voluntary unpaid work or service rendered on one's day off, originally and usually on Saturday, the sabbath (*subbota*).

84 ...Declaration of the Rights of the Peoples of Russia: A statement of principles adopted by the Council of People's Commissars on 15 November 1917. Together with the decrees on land and peace, this document was one of the first acts of the new Soviet government. It declared that henceforth the following principles would govern relations among the peoples of Russia: "(1) the equality and sovereignty of the peoples of Russia; (2) the right of the people of Russia to free self-determination up to and including separation and the formation of an independent state; (3) the abolition of each and every national and national-religious privilege and restriction; (4) the free development of national minorities and ethnic groups inhabiting the territory of Russia." These principles were incorporated into the 1918 Constitution, which defined the Soviet state as a federation of republics united by treaties.

Unresolved political, constitutional, and jurisdictional conflicts between the RSFSR, Georgia, and the Ukraine, however, led to a new definition, the **Declaration on the Formation of the USSR**, which was adopted by the First Congress of Soviets of the USSR in December 1922 and incorporated into the 1924 Constitution of the USSR. That document expressed the Leninist theory of "self-determination"—an idea frequently hailed during the First Congress of People's Deputies. Leninist self-determination promised every nation the right to form its own independent state, as promised in the Declaration of the Rights of the Peoples of Russia, but by "nation" Lenin meant only the proletariat and, of course, its vanguard, the Communist Party. Lenin reasoned that the overthrow of capitalism in the Russian Empire meant an end to the oppression of nationalities and, therefore, that the old social foundations of nationalism and national separatism would dissolve. In fact, he appealed to the nationalism of the peoples of the borderlands by offering them equality with the Russian nation in a new unified state.

Centrists contended that Lenin's argument was theoretically and practically flawed. It ran counter, they asserted, to a basic Marxist doctrine which held that nationalism and boundaries were manifestations and consequences of bourgeois mentality—relics of a historical past. Furthermore, they contended, the Soviet state depended in fact upon the military and industrial might of the RSFSR. The centrist alternative was Stalin's plan of "autonomization"—the incorporation into the RSFSR of the independent union republics as well as the existing autonomous republics, with the result that all would be autonomous in theory but, in fact, subordinate constituents of the RSFSR.

Cf. Richard Pipes, *The Formation of the Soviet Union* (Harvard University Press, 1964); S.V. Kharmandarya et al., *Obrazovaniye Soyuza Sovyetskikh sotsialisticheskikh respublik: Sbornik dokumentov* (Moscow, 1972); *Istoriya sovyetskoy konstitutsii: Sbornik dokumentov 1917-1957* (Moscow, 1957); *Sovyetskaya istoricheskaya entsiklopediya*, s.v. "Deklaratsiya prav narodov Rossii" and "Deklaratsiya ob obrazovanii Soyuza SSR."

87 ...Azizbekova has sketched a picture of Azerbaijani-Armenian friendship: Above, 326-27.

87 ...Foreign Minister Molotov: Vyacheslav M. Molotov (1890-1986), USSR Minister of Foreign Affairs, 1941-49, 1953-57. The young Transcaucasian Republic, under the presidency of the Georgian Menshevik Akaki Chkenkeli, abandoned Kars to the Turks in April 1918, and the Armenians never forgave him or the Georgians for their "betrayal."

92 ...60-letiye SSSR: sixtieth anniversary of the USSR.

96 ...the viewpoint of Deputy Bunich: V.P. Bunich, above, 1: 282.

96 ...Academician Aganbegyan, Comrade Abalkin, and others: Reform economists who enjoyed Gorbachev's confidence in and after 1988 included Abel G. Aganbegyan, Leonid Abalkin, Viktor Belkin, Pavel Bunich, Gavril Popov, N.P. Shmelev, Vladimir Tikhonov, and others. Aganbegyan directed the Institute for Production Forces and National Resources, Abalkin the USSR Academy of Sciences Institute of Economics. See below, 108.

96 ...the network of Berezka stores has been prohibited: In December 1988 the Politburo closed approximately one thousand Beriozka stores, which sold foreign goods to Soviet citizens who presented special coupons. The foreign currency stores, closed to Russians, were untouched. Richard Sakwa, *Gorbachev and His Reforms, 1985-1990* (Prentice-Hall, 1990), 86.

98 ...state acceptance: A quality control program put into effect on 1 January 1987. All executives were to be

NOTES TO THE TENTH SESSION

held responsible for the quality of the goods produced by their enterprises, and a state product acceptance committee was created to oversee the program. See Gorbachev's speech, CDSP (17 December 1986), 11.

99 ... then Markov himself received the title of Hero of Socialist Labor: G.M. Markov (1911-) became First Secretary of the Union of Writers in 1971; altogether he received two Orders of Lenin and one Order of the Red Banner of Labor.

99 ... our current impeachment is something like 14 October 1964: The date on which a plenum of the CPSU CC removed Khrushchev from power.

99 ... the Iron Lady: Margaret P. Thatcher who headed the British government from May 1979 until November 1990.

99 ... we will not forgive ourselves the notion...voiced for the first time by Astafyev: Viktor Petrovich Astafyev (1924-), author of *The Snows are Melting* and other works dealing with the inner lives of working-class people.

100 ... on Lubyanka...we should inscribe the names of the 40 millions of dead: The seven-story Lubyanka is the Moscow headquarters of the secret police. The inner courtyard contains a prison were the most prominent Moscow victims of the Great Purge were "processed". Also in the Moscow area is the Lefortovo Prison, which was the main torture center, and the Butyrka, which at one time held up 30,000 prisoners packed three per square yard.

102 ... the Democratic Union: *Demokraticheskii soyuz*— DS was formed in February 1988 and, despite police harassment, held its founding congress in May and adopted an overtly anti-socialist and pro-western program calling for full freedom and civil rights for citizens, a multi-party parliamentary system, free trade unions, national self-determination, etc. Sakwa, *Gorbachev and his Reforms*, 207-8; and Hosking, *The Awakening of the Soviet Union*, 74-75.

103 ... the "Progress-95" program: A program of social and economic development, involving all enterprises in the Moscow region, initiated by the Moscow City Party Committee. *Pravda*, 29 April 1989, in CDSP (24 May 1989), 25.

104 ... Law on Pensions: Final text, CDSP (18 October 1989), 20.

104 ... Comrade Dadamyan...we will ask him to speak: See below, 116.

109 ... Article 13 of the Congress Procedural Rules: See Appendix B.1: Provisional Standing Orders.

109 ... Tikhonov, Abalkin, Shmelev, and Burlatsky: See above, 292 (n96).

112 ... yesterday's speech by Vlasov: Yu.P. Vlasov at 1: 277.

NOTES TO THE TENTH SESSION

117 ... Cypriot model: In the 1960 compromise which produced the independence of Cyprus, the Greek majority renounced union with Greece while the Turk minority dropped its demand for partition. However, civil war in 1964, 1967, and 1974 resulted in a precariously partitioned state with Greek Cypriots insisting on a unitary state while Turks demanded a federal arrangement.

119 ... Comrade Shcherbin's responses: Boris E. Shcherbin (Ukrainian by birth) headed the USSR Bureau for the Fuel and Energy Complex and may have had some responsibility for nuclear safety. Cf. *Soviet Nomenklatura*, compiled by Albert L. Weeks, second edition (Washington: Washington Institute Press, 1987), 73.

119 ... the speech by Gennady Maksimovich Khodyrev: Above, 1: 108-9.

120 ... this has already been discussed: By A.I. Trudolyubov, above, 75.

120 ... the speech by...Chervonopisky, and the statement by Comrade Mazurov: Above, 90 and 24.

121 ... Blasphemous words...with regard to the Lenin mausoleum: By Yury Karyakin at 99.

121 ... the other side of the so-called "Russian coin"...discussed by Deputies Oleynik and Belov: Above, 1: 260 and 2: 13.

122 ... the concept of a "common blanket" proposed by Deputy Sokolov: Above, 1: 207-8.

124 ... ORBITA: An eleven-satellite telecommunications system inaugurated in 1967.

126 ... Griboyedov...who wrote the famous "Woe from Wit": Aleksandr S. Griboyedov (1795-1829). *Woe* *from Wit*, his most famous work, is generally regarded as one of the best comedies in the Russian language.

127 ...Deputy Kazannik, who voluntarily gave up his seat [to Yeltsin]: Above, 1: 184-87.

128 ...the tragedy in Bashkiria: See Headnote to Session Ten.

131 ...the accusation flung from this podium toward...Ligachev: By N.V. Ivanov, above, 55.

131 ...a deputy from our oblast who...raised suspicions about me [and made] accusations ...against the Committee for State Security: Referring to N.A. Strukov's remarks at 1: 179.

132 ...Kursk Magnetic Anamoly: The USSR's largest deposit of iron ore (about 45 billion tons) situated in Kursk, Belgorod, and Orel oblasts; though discovered in the late eighteenth century, industrial exploitation began only in 1952.

134 ...pursuing your kibitka over the steppes: A *kibitka* is a large sled or sledge.

138...make the twenty-fifth of May the holiday of democracy and law?—The Congress of People's Deputies opened on May 25.

139 ...Olzhas Suleymenov's idea: Above, 1: 120-21.

140 ...Roy Medvedev's accusations [of an anti-Gorbachev conspiracy in the Kremlin]: Above, 1: 156.

140 ...our own Kerenskyites—Milyukov, Guchkov, Chkeidze: Hardly an accurate classification of some of 1917's leading politicians: attorney Aleksandr F. Kerensky (1881-1968), the sometime Socialist Revolutionary who headed the Provisional Government from July to October; professor Pavel N. Milyukov (1859-1953), a British-style liberal who led the Constitutional Democratic Party and served as foreign minister in the Provisional Government's first coalition from March to May 1917; industrialist Aleksandr I. Guchkov (1862-1936), who founded and led the conservative Octobrist Party and held the post of war minister in the first coalition; and revolutionary Nikolay S. Chkeidze (1864-1926), a Georgian Menshevik, who chaired the rival Petrograd Soviet from May to August 1917.

140...famous words...slightly edited: "You, sirs, need great upheavals—we need a great country": From a speech by Prime Minister Petr A. Stolypin to the radical Second Duma on 10 May 1907, although Stolypin concluded, "...we need a great *Russia*!" Those words frequently appeared on banners at conservative national and monarchist marches and rallies, which were also part of glasnost and democratization.

141 ...Boris Oleynik, Ion Drutse, and others...who said those kind words about the Russian language and Russia: Oleynik at 1: 260, Drutse at 2: 2.

142 ...on 16 November [1988]...the Estonian Supreme Soviet adopted the well-known amendments: Affirming Estonian sovereignty and the right of republics to veto any central decision affecting their territory; these acts, declared unconstitutional by the USSR Supreme Soviet, were subsequently reaffirmed by Estonia.

146 ...the noted international figure of Comrade Kolbin: the controversial Gennady V. Kolbin, who subsequently resigned as First Secretary of the Kazakhstan CP to become Chairman of the USSR People's Control Commission. His confirmation is reported below, 220-22.

147 ...the name of Yury Chemodanov so painfully familiar: Chemodanov's arbitrary exclusion from the list of candidates for the Soviet of Nationalities was a major issue in the Fourth Session, 1: 102-19 *passim*.

NOTES TO THE ELEVENTH SESSION

149 ...Comrade Kadyrov: Gairat K. Kadyrov—Chairman of the Uzbekistan SSR Council of Ministers and candidate member of the CPSU CC.

NOTES TO THE TWELFTH SESSION

168 ...the speech by Deputy Sherbakov: I.e., V.P. Shcherbakov, 102.

168 ...Karyakin who spoke about re-intering the body of Lenin: Above, 99-100.

169 ...the speech by...Ryzhkov: Eleventh Session.

169 ...Nikolay Ivanovich and Boris Ivanovich Gostev: N.I. Ryzhkov and USSR finance minister B.I. Gostev.

170 ...return to normal trade in alcoholic beverages: In April 1985 the government launched an anti-alcohol campaign as a means of increasing worker productivity; the program apparently was inspired and certainly spurred on by Ligachev. State production of spirits was curtailed, vineyards were destroyed, taverns were closed, the number of state liquor stores was reduced and the operating hours of those that remained were shortened. The campaign cost the government about R10 billion per year in lost revenue; it created another black market and led to severe shortages of sugar, grain, potatoes, and other commodities used by illegal private distillers and brewers. By 1988 the program was an admitted failure, and early in 1990 it was abandoned.

170 ...writer Vasily Belov: An author known, like V.G. Rasputin, for his strong nationalist sentiments. Although a supporter of *Pamyat*, Belóv was not a member of it. His most recent novel, *Everything Lies Ahead*, was attacked for being antisemitic. The Secretary of the RSFSR Writers Union, Belov addressed the Eighth Session, above, 13-16.

175 ...the speech by Comrade Starodubtsev: At 1: 247-50.

176 ...Comrade Murakhovskiy: See above, 290 (n14).

180 ...Comrade Rasputin has spoken: Above, 138*ff*.

181 ...the appeal of farmers: Resolutions of 417 agrarian deputies submitted by V.A. Gontar, above, 250.

181 ...CPSU Central Committee Secretary Comrade Baklanov: Oleg Dmitriyevich Baklanov, a Ukrainian, coopted into the Central Committee in February 1988; also USSR Minister of General Machine-Building (Minobshchemash).

185 ...Khallik from Estonia who...spoke painfully...of native peoples: Above, 121-23.

186 ...Kugultinov...need for a legislative statute on the rights of the Soviet people: Above, 134.

188 ...elementary ethics and humanity obligated Colonel-General Rodionov: Above, 1: 229.

188 ...1956, when the deceived youth perished on these very same streets of Tbilisi: Army gunfire killed several Georgian students who were protesting the removal of a monument to Stalin, a native of Georgia. Moscow subsequently, and without calling attention to them, made several concessions to "the cult of Stalin" in the Georgian SSR.

191 ...Nikolay Ivanovich: N.I. Ryzhkov.

193 ...Popov's and Afanasyev's speeches: Above, 1: 97-99.

193 ...general directors, like Comrade Volskiy: Arkady I. Volsky, sent by the CPSU CC and USSR Supreme Soviet Presidium to head the special commission to supervise administration of the NKAO; former head of the CPSU CC Machine-building Department.

193 ...Academician Kapitsa: Apparently the noted physicist, Peter Leonidovich Kapitsa, a Hero of Socialist Labor and member of the Presidium of the USSR Academy of Sciences.

195 ...In 1682-1690 the Kremlin witnessed violent disputes: The regency of Sophia and her favorite, Prince Vasily V. Golitsyn, during the minorities of the co-tsars Ivan V and Peter I, later known as "the Great." This period saw continual turmoil due to the dynastic ambitions of the Miloslavsky and Naryshkin families. In 1689 Sophia was ousted, and Peter eventually gathered full power.

195 ...the Russian zemstvo: Zemstvo, from *zemskoe uchrezhdenie* (rural institution), was the agency of rural government created in 1864 at the district (*uezd*) and provincial level as part of the Great Reforms of Alexander II. A zemstvo consisted of an elected assembly and executive board. Their independence was severely restricted after 1890, but the zemstvo movement was responsible for the development of public education and health in rural Russia.

198 ...Kuzbass: Kuznetsk River basin, the major industrial region of western Siberia lying generally southeast of Novosibirsk and Tomsk with its center at Novokuznetsk (formerly Stalinsk). The region boasts huge deposits of bituminous coal.

199 ...Nevada-Semipalatinsk movement: A pressure-group of Soviet and American nuclear scientists whose goal was to ban nuclear testing.

199-200 ...The Kazakhs...lost over 4 million in the time of the so-called "rapid acceleration": I.e., the era of the first three five-year plans (1929-41) which witnessed the drive for rapid industrialization and its corollary, the collectivization of agriculture which, altogether, claimed as many as 20 million lives.

200 ...the Alma-Ata events of December 1986: Three days of rioting in the capital of Kazakhstan precipitated by Moscow's removal of Dinmukhamed Kunayev as First Secretary of the Kazakh CP and his replacement by the Russian, G.V. Kolbin.

200 ...Likachev rightly spoke of the role of culture in interethnic disputes: Above, 1: 210.

206 ...amendments adopted in Estonia on 16 November 1988: Acts of the Estonian Supreme Soviet affirming Estonian sovereignty and the right of a union republic to veto any decision by Moscow that affected its territory.

207 ...the reorganizational law of 1 December of last year: The Law on Amendments and Additions to the USSR Constitution. The changes are reflected in the constitutional provisions in Appendix A.1.

210 ...If we will be ratifying the Chairman of the Committee for People's Control: The CPD's confirmation of G.V. Kolbin is reported below, 220-22.

212 ...our countryman who spoke yesterday: I.e., on 6 June, the "countryman" being N.A. Kasyan, recorded at 126.

225 ...Churbanov case: In December 1988, Leonid Brezhnev's son-in-law, Yury M. Churbanov, was sentenced to twelve years hard labor for accepting R650,000 in bribes from Uzbekistan officials while he was serving as Deputy Minister of Internal Affairs in 1980-84.

NOTES TO THE THIRTEENTH SESSION

236 ...Gorbachev's visit to China: 15-19 May 1989.

237 ...Shmelev has already said: Above, 168.

241 ...Kasyan has spoken: Above, 126.

243 ...the speech by Deputy Shcherbakov: Above, 102.

245 ...Saltykov-Shchedrin: Mikhail E. (1826-89), famed writer and satirist.

248 ...the proposal by Deputy Popov: Above, 237.

262 ...draft resolution on the basic guidelines for Soviet domestic and foreign policy: Appendix B.4.

270 ...the speech of Deputy Suleymenov: Above, 199.

270 ...Deputy Rasputin spoke: Above, 138.

276 ...preparation of a draft Law on the Constitutional Oversight Committee: In December 1989 the Congress of People's Deputies adopted a law on constitutional oversight and formed the Constitutional Oversight Committee under the chairmanship of S.S. Alekseyev. Baltic opposition dissolved when the majority agreed to exclude republic legislation from supervision until the relationship between union republics and the USSR had been constitutionally redefined.

278 ...Supreme Soviet be instructed to prepare a draft USSR Law on the Status of People's Deputies: In December 1989 the Congress of People's Deputies rejected the draft law prepared by the Supreme Soviet; see Appendix B.3.

WORKS CITED

Aspaturian, Vernon V., "The Soviet Constitutional Order," in Roy C. Macridis and Robert E. Ward, editors, *Modern Political Systems: Europe*. 3rd Edition. Englewood Cliffs, N.J., 1972.

Current Digest of the Soviet Press, 1987-88.

Foreign Broadcast Information Service, *Daily Reports. Soviet Union*. 1988-89.

Hosking, Geoffrey, *The Awakening of the Soviet Union*. Cambridge, Mass., 1990.

Istoriya sovyetskoy konstitutsii. Sbornik dokumentov 1917-1957. Moscow, 1957.

Izvestiya. 1987-88.

Kharmandarya, S.V., et al., *Obrazovaniye Soyuza Sovyetskikh sotsialisticheskikh respublik. Sbornik dokumentov*. Moscow, 1972.

Mann, Dawn, *Paradoxes of Soviet Reform. The Nineteenth Communist Party Conference*. Foreword by Michel Tatu. Washington, 1988.

Moscow News, 1987-88.

The Nationalities Factor in Soviet Politics and Society. Edited by Lubomyr Hajda and Mark Beissinger. Boulder, Colo., 1990.

Pipes, Richard, *The Formation of the Soviet Union*. Cambridge, Mass., 1964.

Pervyi syezd narodnykh deputatov SSSR, 25 maya– 9 iyunya 1989 g. Stenograficheskii otchet. 6 tt. Moskva: Izdanie Verkhovnogo sovyeta SSSR, 1989.

Radio Liberty/Radio Free Europe, *Report on the USSR*. 1989.

Sakwa, Richard, *Gorbachev and His Reforms, 1985-1990*. New York, 1990.

Soviet Nomenklatura. Compiled by Albert L. Weeks. Second edition. Washington, 1987.

Sovyetskaya istoricheskaya entsiklopediya. Moscow, 1960-78.

Suny, Ronald Grigor, *The Baku Commune, 1917-1918*. Princeton, N.J., 1972.

The Supreme Soviet. A Biographical Directory. Compiled by Dawn Mann, Robert Monyak, and Elizabeth Teague. Munich, 1989.

Urban, Michael E., *More Power to the Soviets. The Democratic Revolution in the USSR*. Hants, England, 1990.

USSR Calendar of Events Annual, 1987, 1988. Edited by Joseph P. Mastro. Gulf Breeze, Fla.: Academic International Press, 1988, 1989.

USSR Documents Annual, 1987. The Gorbachev Reforms; 1988: Perestroika—The Second Stage. Edited by J.L. Black. Gulf Breeze, Fla.: Academic International Press, 1988, 1989.

APPENDIX A.1
CONSTITUTION (BASIC LAW) OF THE USSR
ARTICLES CITED

Note: This section incorporates modifications introduced into the 1977 Constitution of the USSR by the Law on Changes and Amendments to the Constitution (Basic Law) of the USSR of 1 December 1988. The following Articles, cited in this work, were amended: 108, 110, 111, 112, 113, 114, 119, 120, 124, 125, 151, 174.

Preamble. The Great October Socialist Revolution, accomplished by the workers and peasants of Russia under the leadership of the Communist Party headed by Lenin, overthrew capitalist and landowner rule, broke the chains of oppression, established the dictatorship of the proletariat, and created the Soviet state, a new type of state, the basic instrument for defending the gains of the revolution and for building socialism and communism. Humanity thereby began the epoch-making turn from capitalism to socialism.... A developed socialist society has now been built in the USSR. At this stage, when socialism is developing on its own foundations, the creative forces of the new system and the advantages of the socialist way of life are becoming increasingly evident, and the working people are more and more widely enjoying the fruits of their great revolutionary gains....

Art. 6. The leading and guiding force in Soviet society and the nucleus of its political system, of all state organizations and public organizations, is the Communist Party of the Soviet Union. The CPSU exists for the people and serves the people.

Art. 9. State property, i.e., the common property of the Soviet people is the principal form of socialist property. The land, its minerals, waters and forests are the exclusive property of the state. The state owns the basic means of production in industry, construction, and agriculture; means of transport and communication; the banks; the property of state-run trade organizations and public utilities, and other state-run undertakings; most urban housing; and other property necessary for state purposes.

Art. 14. The source of growth of social wealth and of the well-being of the people, and of each individual, is the labor, free from exploitation, of the Soviet people. The state exercises control over the measure of labor and of consumption in accordance with the principle of socialism: "From each according to his ability, to each according to his work." It fixes the rate of taxation on taxable income.

Socially useful work and its results determine a person's status in society. By combining material and moral incentives and encouraging innovation and a creative attitude toward work, the state helps to transform labor into the prime vital need of every Soviet citizen.

Art. 18. In the interest of the present and future generations, the necessary steps are being taken in the USSR to protect, and make scientifically substantiated, rational use of the land and its mineral and water resources and the plant and animal kingdoms; to preserve the purity of air and water; ensure the reproduction of natural wealth; and improve the human environment.

Art. 19. The social basis of the USSR is the unbreakable alliance of the workers, peasants, and intelligentsia. The state helps enhance the social homogeneity of society, namely the elimination of class differences and of the essential distinctions between town and country and between mental and physical labor, and the all-round development and drawing together of all the nations and nationalities of the USSR.

Art. 20. In accordance with the communist ideal, "The free development of each is the condition of the free development of all," the state pursues the aim of giving citizens more and more extensive opportunities to apply their creative energies, abilities, and talents, and to develop their personalities in every way.

Art. 21. The state concerns itself with improving working conditions, safety, and labor protection and the scientific organization of work and with reducing and ultimately eliminating all arduous physical labor through comprehensive mechanization and automation of production processes in all branches of the economy.

Art. 22. A program is being consistently implemented in the USSR to convert agricultural work into a form of industrial work, to extend the network of educational, cultural, and medical institutions, as well as of trade, public catering, community service, and public utility facilities in rural localities, and to transform hamlets and villages into well-planned and well-appointed settlements.

Art. 31. Defense of the socialist motherland is one of the most important functions of the state and is the concern of the whole people.

In order to defend the gains of socialism, the peaceful labor of the Soviet people, and the sovereignty and territorial integrity of the state, the USSR maintains Armed Forces and has instituted universal military service. The duty of the Armed Forces of the USSR to the people is to provide reliable defense of the socialist motherland and to maintain constant combat readiness, thereby guaranteeing that any aggressor is instantly repulsed.

Art. 35. Women and men have equal rights in the USSR. Exercise of these rights is ensured by according women equal access with men to education and vocational and professional training; equal opportunities in employment, equal remuneration and promotion; equality in social, political, and cultural activity; and through special labor and health protection measures for women; by providing conditions enabling mothers to work; by legal protection, and by material and moral support for mothers and children, including paid leaves and other benefits for mothers and expectant mothers, and a gradual reduction of working time for mothers with small children.

Art. 40. Citizens of the USSR have the right to work (that is, the right to guaranteed employment and pay in accordance with the quantity and quality of their work, and not below the state-established minimum), including the right to choose their trade or profession, type of job or work, in accordance with their inclinations, abilities, training and education, with due account for the needs of society.

This right is ensured by the socialist economic system, the steady growth of productive forces, free vocational and professional training, improvement of skills, training in new trades or professions, and development of the systems of vocational guidance and job placement.

Art. 48. Citizens of the USSR have the right to take part in the management and administration of state and public affairs and in the discussion and adoption of laws and measures of All-Union and local significance.

This right is ensured by the opportunity to vote and to be elected to Soviets of People's Deputies and other elective state bodies, to take part in nationwide discussions and referendums, in people's control, in the work of state bodies, public organizations, and local community groups, and in meetings at one's place of work or residence.

Art. 70. The Union of Soviet Socialist Republics is an integral, federal multinational state formed on the principle of socialist federalism as a result of the free self-determination of nations and the voluntary association of equal Soviet Socialist Republics. The USSR embodies the state unity of the Soviet people and draws all its nations and nationalities together for the purpose of jointly building communism.

Art. 73. The jurisdiction of the Union of Soviet Socialist Republics, as represented by its highest bodies of state authority and administration, shall cover:

1. the admission of new republics to the USSR; endorsement of the formation of new autonomous republics and autonomous regions within Union Republics;

2. determination of the state boundaries of the USSR and approval of changes in the boundaries between Union Republics;

3. establishment of the general principles for the organization and functioning of Republic and local bodies of state authority and administration;

4. insurance of uniformity of legislative regulations throughout the USSR and establishment of the fundamentals of the legislation of the USSR and Union Republics;

5. pursuance of a uniform social and economic policy; administration of the country's economy; determination of the main lines of scientific and technological progress and of general measures for the rational exploitation and conservation of natural resources; the drafting and approval of state plans for the economic and social development of the USSR, and endorsement of reports on their fulfillment;

6. the drafting and approval of the consolidated State Budget of the USSR, and endorsement of the report on its execution; management of a single monetary and credit system; determination of the taxes and revenues forming the Budget of the USSR; and formulation of the price and wage policy;

7. administration of the sectors of the economy and of enterprises and amalgamations under Union jurisdiction, and general guidance of industries under Union Republic jurisdiction;

8. issues of war and peace, defense of the sovereignty of the USSR and the safeguarding of its frontiers and territory, and organization of defense; direction of the Armed Forces of the USSR;

9. state security;

10. representation of the USSR in international relations; the USSR's relations with other states and with international organizations; establishment of the general procedure for, and coordination of, the relations of Union

Republics with other states and with international organizations; foreign trade and other forms of external economic activity on the basis of state monopoly;

11. control over the observance of the Constitution of the USSR and insurance of conformity of the constitutions of Union Republics to the Constitution of the USSR;

12. settlement of other matters of All-Union importance.

Art. 74. The laws of the USSR shall have the same force in all Union Republics. In the event of a discrepancy between a Union Republic law and an All-Union law, the law of the USSR shall prevail.

Art. 75. The territory of the Union of Soviet Socialist Republics is a single entity and comprises the territories of the Union Republics. The sovereignty of the USSR extends throughout its territory.

Art. 76. A Union Republic is a sovereign Soviet socialist state that has united with other Soviet Republics in the Union of Soviet Socialist Republics. Outside the spheres listed in Article 73 of the Constitution of the USSR, a Union Republic shall have its own constitution conforming to the Constitution of the USSR, with specific features of the Republic taken into account.

Art. 78. The territory of a Union Republic may not be altered without its consent. The boundaries between Union Republics may be altered by mutual agreement of the Republics concerned, subject to ratification by the Union of Soviet Socialist Republics.

Art. 80. A Union Republic has the right to enter into relations with other states, conclude treaties with them, exchange diplomatic and consular representatives, and take part in the work of international organizations.

Art. 81. The sovereign rights of Union Republics shall be safeguarded by the USSR.

[Amended Articles]

Art. 108. The highest body of state authority of the USSR shall be the Congress of People's Deputies of the USSR. The Congress of People's Deputies of the USSR is empowered to consider and resolve any issue within the jurisdiction of the Union of Soviet Socialist Republics. The exclusive prerogative of the Congress of People's Deputies of the USSR shall be:

1. The adoption and amendment of the Constitution of the USSR;

2. Decision-making on question of the national and state structure of the USSR within the jurisdiction of the Union of Soviet Socialist Republics;

3. The determination of the state borders of the USSR; endorsement of border changes between the Union Republics;

4. The definition of guidelines for the domestic and foreign policies of the USSR;

5. The approval of long-term state plans and most important national programs for the economic and social development of the USSR;

6. The election of the Supreme Soviet of the USSR;

7. The election of the Chairman of the Supreme Soviet of the USSR;

8. The election of the First Vice-Chairman of the Supreme Soviet of the USSR;

9. The endorsement of the Chairman of the Council of Ministers of the USSR;

10. The endorsement of the Chairman of the People's Control Committee of the USSR, the Chairman of the Supreme Court of the USSR, the Procurator-General of the USSR, and the Chief State Arbiter of the USSR;

11. The election of the Constitutional Oversight Committee of the USSR;

12. The revocation of legislative acts passed by the Supreme Soviet of the USSR;

13. Decision-making on holding a nationwide vote (referendum).

The Congress of People's Deputies of the USSR shall adopt laws of the USSR and decrees by a majority vote of People's Deputies of the USSR.

Art. 109. The Congress of People's Deputies of the USSR shall consist of 2,250 deputies, to be elected in the following order:

750 deputies from territorial electoral districts with equal numbers of voters;

750 deputies from national-territorial electoral districts on the basis of the following representation: 32 deputies from each Union Republic, 11 deputies from each Autonomous Republic, 5 deputies from each Autonomous Region, and 1 deputy from each Autonomous Area;

750 deputes from All-Union public organizations on the basis of the representation established by the Law on the Election of People's Deputies of the USSR.

Art. 110. The Congress of People's Deputies of the USSR, upon recommendation of the Credentials Commission elected by it, shall decide on the eligibility of deputies, and, in cases where the election law has been violated, shall declare the election of the deputies null and void.

The Congress of People's Deputies of the USSR is called by the Supreme Soviet of the USSR.

Regular sessions of the Congress of People's Deputies of the USSR shall be held once a year. Special sessions shall be called upon the initiative of the Supreme Soviet of the USSR on the proposal of one of the Chambers of the Supreme Soviet of the USSR, the

Presidium of the Supreme Soviet of the USSR, the Chairman of the Supreme Soviet of the USSR, at least one-fifth of the People's Deputies of the USSR, or upon the initiative of a Union Republic as represented by its highest body of state authority.

The first post-election session of the Congress of People's Deputies of the USSR shall be chaired by the Chairman of the Central Electoral Commission for Election of People's Deputies of the USSR, and subsequent ones by the Chairman of the Supreme Soviet of the USSR or his deputy.

Art. 111. The Supreme Soviet of the USSR shall be the permanent legislative, administrative, and control body of state authority of the USSR.

The Supreme Soviet of the USSR shall consist of two Chambers: the Soviet of the Union and the Soviet of Nationalities, each having equal numbers of deputies. The Chambers of the Supreme Soviet of the USSR shall have equal rights.

The Chambers shall be elected by the Congress of People's Deputies of the USSR by general ballot. The Soviet of the Union shall be elected from among the People's Deputies of the USSR representing territorial electoral districts and public organizations, taking into account the size of the electorate in a Union Republic or region. The Soviet of Nationalities shall be elected from among the People's Deputies of the USSR representing national-territorial electoral districts and from among People's Deputies of the USSR representing public organizations on the basis of the following representation: 11 deputies from each Union Republic, 4 deputies from each Autonomous Republic, 2 deputies from each Autonomous Region, and 1 deputy from each Autonomous Area.

The Congress of People's Deputies shall annually re-elect one-fifth of the deputies to the Soviet of the Union and the Soviet of Nationalities.

Each Chamber of the Supreme Soviet of the USSR shall elect a Chairman and two Deputy Chairmen. The Chairmen of the Soviet of the Union and the Soviet of Nationalities shall preside over the sittings of their respective chambers and conduct their affairs.

Joint sittings of the Chambers shall be presided over by the Chairman of the Supreme Soviet of the USSR or his First Deputy, or alternately by the Chairman of the Soviet of the Union and the Chairman of the Soviet of Nationalities.

Art. 112. The Supreme Soviet of the USSR shall be convened annually by the Presidium of the Supreme Soviet of the USSR for its recurrent spring and autumn sessions, which are to last, as a rule, for three to four months each.

A session of the Supreme Soviet of the USSR shall consist of separate and joint sittings of the Chambers, and of meetings of the standing commissions of the Chambers and committees of the Supreme Soviet of the USSR held between the sittings of the Chambers. A session may be opened or closed at either separate or joint sittings of the Chambers.

Upon expiration of the mandate of the Congress of People's Deputies of the USSR, the Supreme Soviet of the USSR shall retain its mandate until the formation of a new Supreme Soviet of the USSR by a newly elected Congress of People's Deputies of the USSR.

Art. 113. The Supreme Soviet of the USSR shall:

1. Name the date of elections of People's Deputies of the USSR and approve the composition of the Central Electoral Commission for Election of People's Deputies of the USSR;

2. Appoint the Chairman of the Council of Ministers of the USSR and on his proposal it shall approve the composition of the Council of Ministers of the USSR and make changes in it, and form and abolish Ministries and State Committees of the USSR on the proposal of the Council of Ministers of the USSR;

3. Form the Council of Defense of the USSR and confirm its composition; appoint and dismiss the high command of the Armed Forces of the USSR;

4. Elect the People's Control Committee of the USSR and the Supreme Court of the USSR, appoint the Procurator-General of the USSR and the Chief State Arbitrator of the USSR, and approve the composition of the Board of the Procurator's Office of the USSR and the Board of State Arbitration of the USSR;

5. Regularly hear the reports of the bodies that it forms or elects and of the officials whom it appoints or elects;

6. Ensure uniformity of legislative regulation on the whole territory of the USSR and establish the fundamentals of legislation of the USSR and the Union Republics;

7. Carry out legislative regulation of relations of ownership, organization or management of the national economy and social and cultural development, the budget and financial system, work remuneration and price formation, taxation, protection of the environment and use of natural resources, and exercise of the constitutional rights, freedoms and duties of citizens, and other relations whose regulation is within the competence of the USSR;

8. Interpret the laws of the USSR;

9. Establish the general principles of the organization and the activity of republican and local bodies of state authority and administration, and determine the fundamentals of the legal status of public organizations;

10. Submit the drafts of long-term state plans and the most important All-Union programs of economic and social development of the USSR for endorsement by the Congress of People's Deputies of the USSR; approve state plans for economic and social development of the USSR and the State Budget of the USSR; exercise control over the course of the fulfillment of the plan and budget; approve the reports of the fulfillment; in case of necessity make changes in the plan and the budget;

11. Ratify and renounce international treaties of the USSR;

12. Exercise control over the granting loans that render economic and other assistance to foreign states and over the concluding of agreements on state loans and credits received from sources abroad;

13. Determine the main measures in the sphere of defense and assurance of state security; order general or partial mobilization; proclaim a state of war in the event of armed attack on the USSR or when necessary to meet international treaty obligations involving mutual defense against aggression;

14. Adopt decision on using contingents of the Armed Forces of the USSR when it is necessary to meet international treaty obligations relating to the maintenance of peace and security;

15. Institute military and diplomatic ranks and other special titles;

16. Institute orders and medals of the USSR and honorific titles of the USSR;

17. Issue All-Union acts of amnesty;

18. Have the right to revoke Decrees and decisions of the Presidium of the Supreme Soviet of the USSR, directives of the Chairman of the Supreme Soviet of the USSR, and decisions and directives of the Council of Ministers of the USSR;

19. Revoke decisions and directives of the Councils of Ministers of the Union Republics should they fail to conform to the Constitution and laws of the USSR;

20. Resolve other questions within the competence of the USSR except those which are within the exclusive competence of the Congress of People's Deputies of the USSR.

The Supreme Soviet of the USSR adopts laws of the USSR and decisions. The laws and decisions adopted by the Supreme Soviet of the USSR may not contradict the laws and other acts adopted by the Congress of People's Deputies of the USSR.

Art. 114. The right to initiate legislation at the Congress of People's Deputies of the USSR and in the Supreme Soviet of the USSR is vested in People's Deputies of the USSR, the Soviet of the Union, the Soviet of Nationalities, the Presidium of the Supreme Soviet of the USSR, the Chairman of the Supreme Soviet of the USSR, the Constitutional Oversight Committee of the USSR, the Council of Ministers of the USSR, the Union Republics through their highest bodies of state authority, the committees of the Supreme Soviet of the USSR and the standing commissions of its Chambers, the People's Control Committee of the USSR, the Supreme Court of the USSR, the Procurator-General of the USSR, and the Chief State Arbitrator of the USSR.

The right to initiate legislation is also vested in public organizations through their All-Union bodies and in the Academy of Sciences of the USSR.

Art. 119. The Presidium of the Supreme Soviet of the USSR shall:

1. Convene sessions of the Supreme Soviet of the USSR;

2. Organize preparations for sessions of the Congress of People's Deputies of the USSR and the Supreme Soviet of the USSR;

3. Coordinate the activity of the standing commissions of the Chambers and committees of the Supreme Soviet of the USSR;

4. Give assistance to the People's Deputies of the USSR in the exercise of their powers, and provide necessary information to them;

5. Exercise control over the observance of the Constitution of the USSR and ensure the constitutions and laws of the Union Republics correspond to the Constitution and laws of the USSR;

6. Organize the preparation and holding of nationwide votes (referendums) as well as nationwide discussions of draft laws of the USSR and other most important matters of state;

7. Confer the highest military and diplomatic ranks and other special titles;

8. Award orders and medals of the USSR and confer honorific titles of the USSR;

9. Grant citizenship of the USSR and rule on matters concerning the renunciation or deprivation of citizenship of the USSR and of granting asylum;

10. Exercise the right of pardon;

11. Appoint and recall diplomatic representatives of the USSR to other countries and to international organization;

12. Receive letters of credence and recall of the diplomatic representatives of foreign states accredited to it;

13. Between sessions of the Supreme Soviet of the USSR order general or partial mobilization, proclaim a state of war in the event of armed attack upon the USSR or when necessary to meet international treaty obligations relating to mutual defense against aggression;

14. In the interests of defense of the USSR and the security of its citizens, proclaim martial law or a state of

emergency throughout the country or in particular localities, provided that the issue is considered with the Presidium of the Supreme Soviet of the relevant Union Republic; in the above cases it may introduce special forms of government run by state bodies of the USSR and the Union Republics;

15. Publish laws of the USSR and other acts approved by the Congress of People's Deputies of the USSR, the Supreme Soviet of the USSR, its Chambers, the Presidium of the Supreme Soviet of the USSR, and the Chairman of the Supreme Soviet of the USSR in the languages of the Union Republics.

The Presidium of the Supreme Soviet of the USSR issues Decrees and adopts decisions.

Art. 120. The Chairman of the Supreme Soviet of the USSR shall be the highest-ranking official in the Soviet state and shall represent the Union of Soviet Socialist Republics inside the country and in international relations.

The Chairman of the Supreme Soviet of the USSR shall be elected by the Congress of People's Deputies of the USSR from among the People's Deputies of the USSR by secret ballot for a term of five years and for not more than two consecutive terms. He may be recalled at any time by secret ballot by the Congress of People's Deputies of the USSR.

The Chairman of the Supreme Soviet of the USSR shall be accountable to the Congress of People's Deputies of the USSR and to the Supreme Soviet of the USSR.

Art. 124. A People's Deputy of the USSR has the right, at meetings of the Congress of People's Deputies of the USSR and at sessions of the Supreme Soviet of the USSR, to make an inquiry to the Chairman of the Supreme Soviet of the USSR, to the Council of Ministers of the USSR, and to the heads of other organs formed or elected by the Congress of People's Deputies of the USSR and by the Supreme Soviet of the USSR. The organ or the official to whom the inquiry is addressed must give an oral or written answer at the very same meeting of the Congress or Session of the Supreme Soviet of the USSR within three days at the most.

The People's Deputies of the USSR shall be released from their employment or production duties for the appropriate term, to exercise their duties in the Congress of People's Deputies of the USSR, in the Supreme Soviet of the USSR, in its Chambers, commission, and committees, and also among the population. People's Deputies of the USSR elected to the Supreme Soviet of the USSR shall be released from their employment or production duties for the whole duration of their term of office in the Supreme Soviet of the USSR.

A People's Deputy of the USSR cannot be criminally prosecuted, arrested, or subjected to measures of administrative punishment imposed by court order without the consent of the Supreme Soviet of the USSR or, in the period between its sessions, without the consent of the Presidium of the Supreme Soviet of the USSR.

Art. 125. The Constitutional Oversight Committee of the USSR shall be elected by the Congress of People's Deputies of the USSR from among specialists in politics and law, and shall consist of a Chairman, Vice-Chairman, and 21 members, including representatives of every Union Republic; members are elected for terms of ten years.

Persons elected to the Constitutional Oversight Committee of the USSR cannot simultaneously be members of organs whose acts are subject to review by the committee.

In performing their duties, those elected to the Constitutional Oversight Committee of the USSR are independent and obey only the Constitution of the USSR.

The Constitutional Oversight Committee of the USSR shall:

1. On its own initiative or on instructions from the Congress of People's Deputies of the USSR submit to the Congress its conclusions on the conformity to the Constitution of the USSR of draft laws of the USSR before the Congress;

2. On its own initiative, on instructions from the Congress of People's Deputies, or at the suggestion of the Supreme Soviet of the USSR or the highest bodies of state authority of the Union Republics submit to the Supreme Soviet of the USSR its conclusions on the conformity to the Constitution of the USSR and to the laws adopted by the Congress of People's Deputies of the USSR of acts of the Supreme Soviet of the USSR and its Chambers and of draft legislation prepared by those bodies.

3. See to it that the constitutions and laws of the Union Republics and the decrees of the Council of Ministers of the USSR and of the Councils of Ministers of the Union Republics conform to the Constitution and laws of the USSR;

4. Offer conclusions—on its own initiative, on instructions of the Congress of People's Deputies of the USSR or, at the suggestion of the Supreme Soviet of the USSR or its Chambers, the Presidium of the Supreme Soviet of the USSR, the Chairman of the Supreme Soviet of the USSR, or the standing commission of the Chambers and committees of the Supreme Soviet of the USSR, the Council of Ministers of the USSR, or the highest bodies of state authority of the Union Republics—

on the conformity of the acts of other state bodies and public organizations with the Constitution and laws of the USSR.

Upon discovering contradictions between an act or its individual provisions and the Constitution or laws of the USSR, the Constitutional Oversight Committee of the USSR shall direct to the organ that has issued that act its conclusion of the need to correct the violation. The dispatch of such a directive by the Committee suspends the effect of the act or its individual provisions that contradict the Constitution or laws of the USSR.

The Constitutional Oversight Committee of the USSR has the right to table motions in the Congress of People's Deputies of the USSR, the Supreme Soviet or Council of Ministers of the USSR concerning the revocation of acts by organs or officials accountable to them and which contradict the Constitution or laws of the USSR.

Art. 174. The Constitution of the USSR may be amended by decision of the Congress of People's Deputies of the USSR, adopted by a majority of not less than two-thirds of the total number of Congress of People's Deputies of the USSR.

APPENDIX A.2
LAW ON THE ELECTION OF PEOPLE'S DEPUTIES OF THE USSR
1 DECEMBER 1988

I. GENERAL PROVISIONS
Art. 1. Fundamental Principles of Electing People's Deputies of the USSR

People's Deputies of the USSR shall be elected in one-candidate electoral districts on the basis of universal, equal and direct suffrage by secret ballot. In order to ensure the representation of public organizations in accordance with the quotas established by this law, one-third of the People's Deputies of the USSR shall be elected from public organizations — the Communist Party of the Soviet Union, trade unions, co-operative organizations, the All-Union Leninist Young Communist League [Komsomol], associations of women, war and labor veterans, and scientists, artistic unions and other organizations created in accordance with the Law and having all-Union bodies. People's Deputies from public organizations shall be elected at the congresses or conferences of these organizations, or at the plenums of their all-Union bodies.

Art. 2. Universal Suffrage

People's Deputies of the USSR from electoral districts shall be elected on the basis of universal suffrage: citizens of the USSR who have reached the age of 18 shall have the right to vote. Deputies from public organizations shall be elected by all delegates of their congresses or conferences or the participants in the plenums of their all-Union bodies.

To be eligible for election as People's Deputy of the USSR a citizen of the USSR must have reached the age of 21.

Any direct or indirect limitation of the citizens' right to vote on the grounds of origin, social and property status, race, nationality, sex, education, language, attitude to religion, duration of residence in a given locality or type and nature of occupation is prohibited.

The mentally ill, pronounced unfit by a court and those serving a term of imprisonment or sent by a court to a place of forcible treatment shall not participate in the elections.

Art. 3. Equal Suffrage

People's Deputies of the USSR from electoral districts shall be elected on the basis of equal suffrage: each voter in each electoral district shall have one vote; all voters shall participate in the elections on an equal footing.

In electing People's Deputies from a public organization, each delegate to its congress or conference or each participant in the plenum shall have one vote and all these voters participate in the election on an equal footing.

Women and men shall have equal electoral rights.

Servicemen shall exercize the right to vote on an equal footing with other citizens.

Art. 4. Direct Suffrage

People's Deputies of the USSR from electoral districts shall be elected by direct suffrage:

People's Deputies shall be elected by citizens by direct vote.

People's Deputies from public organizations shall be elected by the delegates of their congresses or conferences or the participants in the plenums of their all-Union bodies by direct vote.

Art.5. Secret Ballot

People's Deputies of the USSR shall be elected by secret ballot: any control over voters' exercize of the franchise is inadmissible.

Art.6. The Conduct of Elections by Electoral Commissions

Elections of People's Deputies of the USSR shall be conducted by electoral commissions consisting of representatives of work collectives, public organizations, neighborhood meetings and meetings of servicemen in military units.

Art.7. Openness in the Preparations and Holding of Elections of People's Deputies of the USSR

Electoral commissions, work collectives and public organizations shall prepare and hold the elections of People's Deputies of the USSR openly and publicly.

Electoral commissions shall inform the public about their work, about the creation of electoral districts, about the composition of electoral commissions, their location and working hours and about lists of voters. Electoral commissions shall inform the public about the results of the registration of candidates for election as deputies, the *curricula vitae* of the candidates registered for election as deputies, the results of the voting for each candidate and the election returns.

Representatives of work collectives, public organizations, voters' meetings, authorized representatives as well as representatives of the press, television and radio shall have the right to be present at meetings of electoral commissions, including during the registration of candidates, the counting of votes at a polling station, the determining of the results of the voting in a district and the summing up of the general results of the election.

The mass media shall cover the preparation and holding of the elections of People's Deputies of the USSR and shall be guaranteed free access to all meetings and sessions connected with the elections. Electoral commissions, state and public bodies and work collectives shall provide them with information on the preparation and holding of the elections.

Art.8. Participation of Citizens, Work Collectives and Public Organizations in the Preparation and Holding of Elections of People's Deputies of the USSR

Citizens of the USSR shall participate in the preparation and holding of the elections of People's Deputies of the USSR through work collectives, public organizations, neighborhood meetings and meetings of servicemen in military units, and election meetings at district level, or through direct participation.

Work collectives and public organizations shall take part in preparing and holding the election of People's Deputies of the USSR through their representatives in electoral commissions or through direct participation.

Art.9. The Right to Nominate Candidates for Election as People's Deputies of the USSR

The right to nominate candidates for election as People's Deputies of the USSR from electoral districts shall belong to work collectives, public organizations, neighborhood meetings and meetings of servicemen in military units, and the right to nominate candidates from public organizations—to their all-Union bodies, which shall take into account the proposals on candidates for deputies put forward by local bodies, grass-root collectives and members of these organizations.

Art.10. Mandates of Voters and Public Organizations to People's Deputies of the USSR

Voters and public organizations shall give mandates to their deputies.

The procedure of presenting, summarizing and examining mandates and organizing their fulfilment shall be established by the Law of the USSR.

Art.11. Incompatibility of the Status of People's Deputy of the USSR with Official Position

Members of the Council of Ministers of the USSR, with the exception of the Chairman of the Council of Ministers of the USSR, heads of government departments of the USSR, Chairman and members of the Supreme Court of the USSR, Chief State Arbitrator and state arbitrators of the USSR, Chairman and members of the USSR Committee for Constitutional Supervision cannot be simultaneously People's Deputies of the USSR.

Art.12. The Expenses Involved in the Election of People's Deputies of the USSR. Financing the Elections

The expenses involved in the preparation and holding of the elections of People's Deputies of the USSR shall be met by the state.

Enterprises, institutions and organizations, and state and public bodies shall provide electoral commissions with premises and equipment for the preparation and holding of the elections.

Candidates nominated for election as People's Deputies of the USSR and voters shall bear no expenses involved in the preparation and holding of the elections.

Art.13. Responsibility for Violations of Legislation on the Election of People's Deputies of the USSR

Those who, by means of force, deception, intimidation or any other means, hinder citizens of the USSR in freely exercizing their right to elect, be elected as People's Deputies of the USSR and to engage in election campaigning, or members of electoral commissions and officials of state and public bodies who have forged electoral documents, falsified election returns, violated the secrecy of balloting or committed any other offence against this Law, are answerable under the law. Those who have published or spread by any means false information about candidates nominated for election as deputies shall also be punished by law.

II. THE PROCEDURE OF CALLING THE ELECTIONS AND CREATING ELECTORAL DISTRICTS

Art.14. The Calling of Elections of People's Deputies of the USSR

Elections of People's Deputies of the USSR shall be called by the Supreme Soviet of the USSR not later than four months before the expiry of the term of People's Deputies of the USSR.

Elections of People's Deputies of the USSR from public organizations shall be held at their congresses or conferences or at the plenums of their all-Union bodies not earlier than 20 days before the election day and not later than the election in electoral districts.

The date of the elections in electoral districts and the date and venue of the congresses or conferences of public organizations or the plenums of their all-Union bodies shall be published in the press.

Art.15. The Formation of Electoral Districts

For the election of People's Deputies of the USSR from electoral districts 750 territorial and 750 national-territorial electoral districts shall be formed.

Electoral districts shall be formed by the Central Electoral Commission for Election of People's Deputies of the USSR upon submission by the highest bodies of state authority of the Union Republics.

One People's Deputy of the USSR shall be elected from each electoral district.

The lists of electoral districts, indicating their borders and the addresses of the district electoral commissions, shall be published by the Central Electoral Commission not later than nine days after the calling of the election.

Art.16. Territorial Electoral Districts

Territorial electoral districts for the election of People's Deputies of the USSR shall be formed with an equal number of voters throughout the territory of the USSR. The administrative division of the territories of the Union Republics shall be taken into account in determining the borders of the electoral districts. The number of voters for the electoral district shall be established by the Supreme Soviet of the USSR for each election.

Art.17. National-territorial Electoral Districts

National-territorial electoral districts for the election of People's Deputies of the USSR shall be formed in accordance with the following quotas: 32 districts in each Union Republic, 11 districts in each Autonomous Republic, five districts in each Autonomous Region and one electoral district in each Autonomous Area.

National-territorial electoral districts shall be formed with an equal number of voters throughout the territory of the corresponding Union Republic, Autonomous Republic and Autonomous Region. The territory of an Autonomous Area constitutes one national-territorial electoral district.

Art.18. Representation Quotas for Public Organizations in the Election of People's Deputies of the USSR

50 People's Deputies of the USSR shall be elected from all-Union public organizations, including:

— 100 deputies from the Communist Party of the Soviet Union;

— 100 deputies from the trade unions of the USSR;

— 100 deputies from co-operative organizations (collective farms, consumers' societies and other co-operative associations of citizens);

— 75 deputies from the All-Union Leninist Young Communist League;

— 75 deputies from women's councils united by the Soviet Women's Committee;

— 75 deputies from organizations of war and labor veterans united by their all-Union Council;

— 75 deputies from scientists' associations (all-Union academic institutions, and scientific societies and associations), the Union of Scientists' and Engineers' Societies of the USSR and the All-Union Society of Innovators and Rationalizers;

— 75 deputies from artistic unions of the USSR (the Architects' Union, Designers' Union, Journalists' Union, Film Makers' Union, Composers' Union, Writers' Union, Theatre Workers' Union and Artistic Union).

— 75 deputies from other public organizations that have been set up in accordance with the law and have all-Union bodies.

Representation of each public organization shall be established, within these quotas, at a joint meeting of the elective leading bodies of these organizations or of their authorised representatives convened by the Central Electoral Commission, or, in case of disagreement, by the Central Electoral Commission.

III. ELECTORAL WARDS

Art.19. The Setting up of Electoral Wards

To hold the voting and count votes during the elections of People's Deputies of the USSR in their electoral districts, the territories of districts, cities and city districts as part of electoral districts shall be divided into the same electoral wards as for the elections of People's Deputies in territorial and national-territorial electoral districts.

Electoral wards shall also be set up in military units and shall be part of electoral districts in which the units are stationed.

In sanatoria, rest homes, hospitals and other in-patient medical establishments, in remote and inaccessible areas, and on board ships at sea on election day, electoral wards may be established as part of the electoral district to which the sanatoria, etc. belong according to their place of location or, in the case of vessels, to the port of registration. Electoral wards may be set up at polar stations and at Soviet agencies abroad, provided the appropriate conditions exist.

Art.20. The Order and Quotas for the Setting up of Electoral Wards

Electoral wards shall be set up by district, city (except cities of district subordination), and city district Soviets of People's Deputies or their presidiums in coordination with district electoral commissions. Electoral wards on board ships at sea on election day shall be set up by the respective Soviets of People's Deputies or their presidiums in the ports of registration of vessels. Electoral wards in military units shall be set up by the local Soviets of People's Deputies or their presidiums upon submission by commanders of units and larger formations.

Electoral wards shall be set up not later than two months before the elections. Electoral wards in military units, as well as in remote and inaccessible areas, on board ships at sea on election day, and at polar stations, shall be set up within the same time limits, and, in extraordinary situations, not later than five days before the elections.

Electoral wards shall be set up for electorates of not less than 20 but not more than 3,000 voters.

The respective local Soviet of People's Deputies or its presidium shall inform the electorate about the boundaries of the ward and the whereabouts of the ward's electoral commission and the polling station.

IV. ELECTORAL COMMISSIONS

Art.21. The System of Electoral Commissions

Electoral commissions shall be set up for holding elections of People's Deputies of the USSR;

the Central Electoral Commission for Election of People's Deputies of the USSR;

district electoral commissions for election of People's Deputies of the USSR by territorial constituencies;

district electoral commissions for election of People's Deputies of the USSR by national-territorial constituencies;

ward electoral commissions;

electoral commissions for election of People's Deputies of the USSR by public organizations.

Art.22. The Setting up of the Central Electoral Commission for Election of People's Deputies of the USSR

The Central Electoral Commission for Election of People's Deputies of the USSR shall be set up by the Supreme Soviet of the USSR with due account of the proposals by the higher bodies of state authority of the Union Republics and by all-Union bodies of public organizations not later than four months before the elections, and shall consist of a Chairman, two Deputy Chairmen, a Secretary and 31 members.

The Central Electoral Commission shall be set up for a term of five years.

Art.23. The Powers of the Central Electoral Commission for Election of People's Deputies of the USSR

The Central Electoral Commission for Election of People's Deputies of the USSR shall:

1. Exercize control throughout the entire territory of the USSR over the observance of this Law and ensure its uniform application; submit, if necessary, proposals to the Supreme Soviet of the USSR on interpretations of this Law;

2. Steer the activity of electoral commissions; establish the procedure of introducing changes in the composition of electoral commissions;

3. Set up territorial and national-territorial electoral districts;

4. Deal with issues pertaining to the inclusion of electoral wards outside the USSR in electoral districts within the territory of the USSR;

5. Distribute funds between electoral commissions; supervise the provision of electoral commissions with premises, means of transportation and communications facilities, and review other questions of providing the elections with funds and equipment;

6. Establish the forms of ballots cast during the election of People's Deputies of the USSR, voters' lists, minutes of election meetings and sessions of electoral commissions, other election documents, samples of ballot boxes and stamps of electoral commissions, and the order of filing election documents;

7. Hear reports by ministers, state committees and government departments of the USSR, and by other state and public organs on questions pertaining to the preparations and holding of elections;

8. Register the elected deputies, sum up the results of elections on a nationwide scale and publish in the press information on the results of elections and lists of the elected People's Deputies of the USSR;

9. Hand the documents necessary for checking the powers of deputies over to the Credentials Commission of the Congress of People's Deputies of the USSR;

10. Deal with questions of holding repeat elections;

11. Deal with questions pertaining to the procedure of recalling People's Deputies of the USSR;
12. Call by-elections to seats of People's Deputies of the USSR and supervise their holding;
13. Consider petitions and complaints against decisions and actions of electoral commission and make final rulings on them;
14. Exercize other powers as stipulated by this and other laws of the USSR.

Art.24. The Setting up of District Electoral Commissions

A district electoral commission shall be set up in every territorial and national-territorial electoral district for the election of People's Deputies of the USSR not later than three and a half months before the elections, and shall consist of 11-17 members.

Members of a district electoral commission shall be nominated by work collectives and their councils and republic, territory, region, area (Autonomous Area), district, city and city district bodies of public organizations, by meetings of voters in neighborhoods and of servicemen in military units. To name work collectives and public organizations nominating their representatives as members of commissions, the relevant Soviet of People's Deputies or their representatives may, if necessary, convene meetings of authorized representatives or work collectives and public organizations in their respective electoral districts.

District electoral commissions for electing People's Deputies of the USSR from territorial electoral districts shall be formed:
— in the Union republics which have territorial and regional divisions, and in the cities of republic subordinates — by the respective territorial, regional and city soviets of People's deputies or their presidiums;
— in the Union republics which have no territorial and regional divisions and in the Autonomous republics — by the Supreme Soviet of the respective Union or Autonomous republic or its Presidium.

District electoral commissions for electing People's Deputies of the USSR from national-territorial electoral disrtricts shall be formed respectively by the Supreme Soviet of People's deputies of an Autonomous region or Autonomous area, or their presidiums.

Art.25. Powers of a District Electoral Commission

1. Exercize control over the execution of this Law on the territory of the district;
2. Direct the activity of the ward electoral commissions;
3. Hear reports by the executive and administrative bodies of the local Soviets of People's Deputies and by the heads of enterprises, institutions and organizations on matters relating to the preparation and holding of the elections;
4. Supervise the drawing up of the list of voters and submittance of them for general cognizance;
5. Organize nomination of candidates for election;
6. Call ands hold district election meetings;
7. Register the candidates nominated for election and give the appropriate certificates to them, and see to the issuance of posters carrying the biographies of the candidates for elections;
8. Organize, jointly with work collectives and public organizations, meetings of the candidates for election with the voters both in work collectives and in neighborhoods;
9. Endore the text of the ballots for the electoral district and see to the issuance of ballots and provision of the ward electoral commissions with them;
10. Establish the results of the elections in the electoral district and publish them in the press, and give certificates to the elected deputies;
11. Organize repeat voting or repeat elections, as well as by-elections to replace the deputies who have vacated their posts;
12. Resolve questions relating to recalling a deputy;
13. Consider statements on and complaints against decisions and actions of ward electoral commissions and adopt decisions on them;
14. Exercize other powers vested in it by this Law.

Art.26. Formation of Ward Electoral Commissions

A ward electoral commission — to be of the same type for electing People's deputies of the USSR from territorial and national-territorial electoral distroicts — shall be formed not later than 45 days before the elections and shall consist of 5-19 members. The number of its members may be increased or decreased in case of necessity.

Representatives for participation in a ward electoral commission shall be proposed by work collectives or their councils, district, city and city district bodies of public organizations, and their primary organizations, the population's public initiative bodies and by meetings of voters in neighborhoods and of servicemen in military units.

Ward electoral commissions shall be formed by the district, city (except cities of district subordination) and city district Soviets of People's Deputies and their presidiums.

Art.27. Powers of Ward Electoral Commissions

Ward electoral commissions shall:
1. Draw up the list of voters;
2. Familiarize the voters with the electoral roll, accept and consider applications on errors in the roll, and decide on making respective changes in it;
3. Give certificates of the right to vote to the voters;
4. Inform the population of the day and place of the voting;

5. Ensure the preparation of the premises for the voting and ballot boxes;
6. Organize the voting at the polling station on election day;
7. Count the ballots cast at the polling station;
8. Consider statements and complaints concerning matters of the preparation of the elections and organization of the poll, and adopt decisions on them;
9. Exercize other powers as stipulated by this Law.

Art. 28. Formation of Electoral Commissions for Electing People's Deputies of the USSR from Public Organizations

Electoral commissions for electing People's deputies of the USSR from public organizations shall consist of 7-13 members and be formed by the all-Union bodies of these organizations not later than three and a half months before the day of the elections in electoral districts.

If necessary, several public organizations may form one electoral commission.

Art. 29. Powers of an Electoral Commission for Electing People's Deputies of the USSR from a Public Organization

An electoral commission for electing People's deputies of the USSR from a public organization shall:
1. Register the candidates for election and issue appropriate credentials for them;
2. Publish the list of the candidates for the election;
3. Summarize the proposals and views concerning the candidates for election voiced by local bodies, grass-roots collectives and members of public organizations and by citizens, and report on them to the congress or conference of the public organization or to the plenum of its all-Union body;
4. Endorse the text of the ballots for electing People's deputies of the USSR;
5. Ensure the preparation of the premises for the voting and the ballot boxes, and organize the voting at the congress or conference of the public organization or at the plenum of its all-Union body;
6. Count the votes and determine the results of the election of the deputies, and issue certificates to the elected deputies;
7. Organize repeat voting and by-elections to replace deputies who have vacated their posts;
8. Resolve questions relating to recalling deputies;
9. Exercize other powers vested in it by the Law.

Art. 30. Organization of the Work of Electoral Commissions

The chairman, vice-chairman and secretary of an electoral commission shall be elected at a meeting of the respective commission.

A sitting of an electoral commission shall be considered to have a quorum if at least two-thirds of the commission members participate in it. Decisions of a commission shall be adopted by a show of hands, by a vote of a majority of the total membership of the commission. Members of the commission who disagree with its decisions are entitled to voice a separate opinion, which is appended in written form to the record of proceedings.

The decisions of electoral commissions, adopted within the limits of their powers, are binding on all state and public bodies, enterprises, institutions and organizations.

The decisions and actions of an electoral commission may be appealed to a higher electoral commission and, in cases stipulated by this Law, also in court.

By decision of an electoral commission, a member of it may be released from his regular employment or duties for the period of the preparation and holding of the elections, with retention of his average earnings paid from the funds allocated for the elections.

Art. 31. Assistance to Electoral Commissions in Exercizing their Powers

State and public bodies, enterprises, institutions, organizations and officials are obliged to help electoral commissions exercize their powers and to provide them with information and materials necessary for their work.

On matters relating to the preparation and holding of elections, the electoral commission has the right to approach state and public bodies, enterprises, institutions, organizations and officials, who are obliged to consider the issue raised and to reply to the electoral commission within three days.

V. VOTING LISTS

Art. 32. The Voting List and its Compilation

A voting list, of the same type for the election of People's deputies by territorial and national-territorial electoral districts, shall be compiled for every electoral ward and signed by the chairman and secretary of the ward commission. The ward commission may invite members of the public to participate in compiling voting lists.

The executive committees of Soviets in cities and city districts, towns and rural communities shall ensure the registration of voters and provide ward commissions with information about the constituents, necessary to compile voting lists.

The voting lists of constituents who are military personnel staying with their units, as well as members of their families and other voters residing on military posts, shall be prepared on the basis of information provided by the commanding officers of the units concerned. Military personnel residing outside their units shall be put on the voting list at the place of their residence.

Voting lists for wards formed in holiday and resort centers, clinics and other in-patient establishments, as well as on board ships at sea on election day, at polar stations and in Soviet agencies abroad, shall be compiled on the basis of information submitted by the heads of these organizations and ships' captains.

Voters' names shall be put on ther voting list in an order convenient for balloting.

Art.33. Registering Citizens for Voting

The voting list shall include all Soviet citizens who have reached the age of 18 by election day, residing, permanently or temporarily, in the ward area at the time of the list's compilation, and eligible for voting.

A voter may not be registered for voting except in his ward.

Art.34. Acquainting Citizens with Voting Lists and the Right to Complain Against Inaccuracies Therein

Voting lists shall be displayed for general information at wards fifteen days before election day, except at holiday and resort centers, clinics and other in-patient establishments where they shall be displayed two days before the voting.

Citizens must be enabled to acquaint themselves with voting lists and check on their correctness on the ward premises.

A citizen may complain against not being included, incorrectly included on, or excluded from the voting list, or against inaccuracies therein. A complaint against voting list inaccuracies shall go to the ward commission, which must: consider the complaint within two days after receiving it, or immediately — should it reach the commission the day before or on election day, correct the list or provide the applicant, in writing, with the reasons for rejecting the claim. The decision by the ward commission can be appealed against to the district (city) people's court not later than five days before election day; the court must examine the complaint within three days.

Its decision shall be final. The ward commission shall correct the voting list immediately upon receiving the court decision.

Art.35. The Voting Certificate. An Additional Voting List

Should a voter, between the day the voting list is displayed for public notice and election day, move to another place the ward commission shall, at his request and upon presentation of a passport or other identity papers, issue him a voting certificate, and make the corresponding note on the list.

On the strength of the voting certificate, on election day the bearer shall be put on the additional voting list of the ward to which he has been relocated.

Art.36. The Voting List for the Election of People's Deputies from a Public Organization and its Compilation

The voting list relative to the election of People's deputies from a public organization shall be compiled by the all-Union body of that public organization and passed to the electoral commission not later than three days before election day.

The voting list shall include the delegates to a congress or a conference of the organization or the participants in a plenum of its all-Union body. All questions involved in compiling the voting list shall be handled by the electoral commission. The names of voters shall be listed alphabetically.

VI. NOMINATION AND REGISTRATION OF CANDIDATES

Art.37. The Procedure of Nominating Candidates for People's Deputies of the USSR in Electoral Districts

Nomination of candidates for People's Deputies of the USSR in territorial and national-territorial electoral districts shall begin three months and end two months before elections.

Nomination of candidates for deputies shall be made at general meetings (conferences) of work collectives.

Nomination of candidates for deputies from public organizations in electoral districts shall be made by their republican, territorial, regional, area, district, city and city district bodies.

Neighborhood meetings to nominate candidates for deputies shall be called by the corresponding Soviets of People's Deputies or their presidiums in conjunction with district electoral commissions. A meeting shall have a quorum of at least 500 voters residing in the territory of the electoral district.

Nomination meetings of servicemen shall be called by the command of military units.

Conditions shall be provided at meetings for nominating an unlimited number of candidates. Every participant in a meeting has the right to propose candidates for deputies, take part in the discussion on them, and support or oppose nominations. A meeting participant may propose himself as a candidate. The decision on nominating a candidate for a deputy shall be taken by open or secret ballot at the meeting's discretion.

A nomination shall be valid if it receives the votes of more than one half of the participants in the meeting or of the majority of the members of the appropriate body of a public organization. The nomination decision shall be formalized in a certificate and communicated to the candidate within two days at the most.

Candidates for People's deputies of the USSR shall, as a rule, be nominated from among citizens working or residing in the territory of the corresponding electoral district in the case of elections from territorial electoral districts, and in the territory of the corresponding Union Republic, Autonomous Republic, Autonomous Region or Autonomous Area in the case of elections from national-territorial districts.

A citizen of the USSR may not be elected to more than two Soviets at a time.

Art.38. District Electoral Meeting

Under the USSR Constitution, a district election meeting may be held to discuss candidates and pass nominations for registration to the corresponding electoral commission. The meeting shall be called by the district electoral commission once candidates have been proposed. Should there be no more than two candidates, the meeting shall not take place.

The work collectives, public organizations bodies, neighborhood meetings and meetings of servicemen in their units that have advanced candidatures shall send equal numbers of representatives to the district election meeting in accordance with the representation quotas fixed by the district electoral commission. At least half of the participants in the meeting shall be voters from the constituency concerned. They shall be sent by work collectives, neighborhood meetings and meetings of servicemen in military units.

Participants in the district election meeting shall have the list of the candidates and their *curriculum vitae* in advance.

At the meeting a candidate may make a statement of intent. Any participant in the meeting may discuss candidates and put forward proposals about them.

Any number of nominations may be presented for registration. The decision shall be taken by a majority vote by open or secret ballot, the voting procedure to be established by the meeting. The decision shall be passed if it receives over 50 percent of the votes. The results of the discussion of candidatures shall be reflected in the protocol of the meeting.

The meeting's decision may be appealed against to the district electoral commission, or to the Central Electoral Committee within three days.

Art.39. The Procedure of Nominating Candidates for People's Deputies of the USSR from Public Organizations

Candidates for People's deputies of the USSR from public organizations shall be proposed by the plenums of their all-Union bodies as required by the present Law. Nomination plenums shall be held not later than two months before the election day in the corresponding public organization.

Conditions shall be created during nominations that ensure that there be no limitation on the number of candidatures. Participants in the plenum may be any member of the given public organization, including a religious figure.

The decision to advance candidates shall be by open or secret ballot, as chosen by the plenums. Nomination shall require over half of the votes of the body of the public organization concerned. Candidates shall be informed about nomination decisions.

The plenums shall decide on the convening of congresses, conferences or plenums of all-Union bodies to elect People's Deputies from the given public organization.

Art.40. Registration of Candidates for People's Deputies of the USSR

Nominees from electoral districts shall be registered by the electoral commission upon submission from work collectives, public organizations bodies, neighborhood meetings and meetings of servicemen in their units which have made the nominations, or from a district election meeting if it was held.

Nominees from public organizations shall be registered by the electoral commissions for elections from public organizations upon submission from the all-Union bodies of the organizations concerned.

The registration of nominees from electoral districts shall begin two months and end one month before election day. The registration of nominees from public organizations shall begin not later than on the fifth day following the nomination meeting.

The registration shall require the protocols of district nomination meetings in the given electoral district, the protocols of the district election meeting, it it was held, the decisions of the all-Union body of the public organization, and the written consent of the candidates to stand for election in a given election district or from a public organization. Persons listed in Article 11 of the present Law, when nominated for deputies, shall, in their written statements, indicate their intention to leave their jobs when they are elected as deputies, or announce withdrawal of their candidatures. The local electoral commission shall forward the registration protocol; along with the nominees' consent to stand for election, to the Central Electoral Commission.

The corresponding electoral commission shall register all candidates nominated in accordance with the present Law. A registration refusal may be appealed against to the Central Electoral Commission within three days.

The nominee may seek election only from one territorial or national-territorial electoral district or one public organization.

The nominee may not be a member of the Central Electoral Commission or the district or ward electoral commission or the electoral commission for elections from public organizations that have registered his nomination. A person serving on such commissions shall resign the day his nomination has been registered.

Not later than on the fourth day following the registration, the electoral commission shall publish in the press a registration report, containing the nominees' *curricula vitae*.

Art.41. Cancelling the Nomination Decision. The Nominee's Own Withdrawal of his Candidature

The nominator, whether a working collective, a public organization body, a meeting of neighborhood voters of or servicemen of a military unit, or the all-Union body of a public organization, may annul a nomination at any time before the election. The decision to annul the nomination shall comply with nomination regulations and go to the appropriate electoral commission.

The nominee may withdraw his own candidature at any time before the election by applying to the corresponding electoral commission.

Art.42. Procedure for Nominating Candidates to fill Vacated Posts of People's Deputies

Should a vacancy open after the nominations registration has ended and other nominations have not been made, the district electoral commission shall request the above-mentioned nominators to propose new candidates. Should a vacancy occur less than a month before the regular election, a by-election shall be held within two months after the regular election.

Should vacancies occur before the election of nominees from public organizations and the number of contenders be smaller than the number of seats, the local electoral commission shall request the all-Union body of the public organization concerned to name new candidates.

New nominations shall be made as required by the present Law.

Art.43. Ballot

The ballot shall alphabetically list the registered candidates, stating their full names, post (occupation), the place of employment and of residence. The ballot shall be in the language of the electorate.

VII. GUARANTEES FOR THE ACTIVITIES OF CANDIDATES NOMINATED FOR PEOPLE'S DEPUTIES OF THE USSR

Art.44. The Right of Candidates Nominated for People's Deputies of the USSR to Address Public Meetings, to Use the Mass Media and to Receive Information

Once registered by electoral commissions, candidates have equal rights to address election and other meetings and conferences, and to use the press, radio and television.

Government and public bodies, industrial managers and heads of other establishments, and public self-government bodies shall assist candidates in organizing meetings with the constituents and members of public organizations and in providing the necessary reference material and other information.

Art.45. Candidate's Election Platform

Candidates shall set out their election platform, which must conform to the USSR Constitution and Soviet Law.

Art.46. Candidate's Campaign Assistants

The candidate may have up to ten campaign assistants, who help the candidate in the election campaign, canvassing for the candidate and looking after his interests in dealing with government and public bodies, constituents, members of public organizations, and in election commissions.

The candidate selects his campaign assistants himself and registers them with the district electoral commission or with an electoral commission formed by a public organization. Thereupon, the electoral commission issues credentials to the campaign assistants.

Campaign assistants cannot be members of a relevant electoral commission.

Art.47. Canvassing

The work collectives, constituents and public organizations which have nominated candidates have the right to freely campaign for them.

Electoral commissions provide to the work collectives, constituents and public organizations free use of premises for meetings and of the mass media in the course of the election campaign.

Citizens of the USSR, work collectives and public organizations are guaranteed the opportunity to discuss freely and comprehensively the political, business and personal qualifications of candidates, as well as the right to canvass for or against a candidate at meetings, in the press, on radio and television.

Candidates meet with the constituents either at election rallies or in some other way convenient to the voters. Voters' meetings are organised by the electoral commission jointly with the relevant Soviet of People's Deputies or its presidium and with public organizations.

The time and place of meetings and rallies are made known in advance.

No campaigning is allowed on election day.

Art.48. Absence of Work During Election Activities

After registration, candidates may take time off to meet with voters, to address rallies and to speak on radio and television, with retention of their average pay, the money coming from the election fund.

Art.49. The Right to Free Travel

After registration, candidates shall enjoy the right to

travel free on all types of public transport, except by taxi, within their electoral district. A candidate living outside his electoral district enjoys this right to travel to the electoral district and back to the place of residence.

The order of travel to election campaign events and ways of covering the travelling expenses of candidates nominated by public organizations shall be specified by the all-Union bodies of these organizations.

Art.50. The Inviolability of the Candidate

No criminal proceedings may be instituted against candidates, nor may they be put into custody or subjected to administrative punishment by court injunction without the consent of the Central Electoral Commission.

VIII. THE VOTING PROCEDURE AND VOTE COUNTING

Art.51. The Time and Place of Voting

Elections of People's Deputies at electoral districts are held on election day from 7 a.m. to 8 p.m. local time. The ward electoral commissions announce the time and place of voting at least ten days before the election. At polling stations set up on ships at sea, in military units, at Arctic and Antarctic stations, in remote and inaccessible areas, and at Soviet establishments abroad, the electoral commission may announce the voting process completed at any time if all the registered voters have cast their votes.

During the election of deputies from public organizations, voting takes place at a congress or conference of the public organization or at a plenum of its all-Union body, with the possibility of plenums involving members of other elective bodies of these organizations. In this case, all participants in the plenum may have decisive vote. The election of People's Deputies may also take place at joint congresses, conferences or plenums of the all-Union bodies of several public organizations.

Art.52. Arrangements

Voting takes place in premises with polling booths or rooms for secret voting, ballot boxes and specially designated places for issuing ballots. Ballot boxes shall be set up so that the voters pass through booths or rooms for secret voting before reaching the ballot boxes.

Organization of the voting process, guarantees of its secrecy, provision of the necessary equipment and maintenance of the premises where the event takes place is the responsibility of the ward electoral commission or of the electoral commission of the public organization.

Before the voting starts on election day, the chairman of the electoral commission shall check and seal the ballot boxes in the presence of all members of the commission.

Each constituent or delegate to the congress, conference or plenum votes in person, voting by proxy being prohibited. Ballots are issued by the electoral commission in accordance with the lists of constituents, a certificate giving the right to vote or the list of people voting at the congress or conference of the public organization or the plenum of its all-Union body, with the passport or any other identification paper to be shown. A mark is made on the list of constituents or in the list of voters to indicate the issue of ballots. Certificates giving the right to vote are attached to the additional list of constituents.

If some constituents cannot travel to the polling station on account of ill health or for any other reason, at their request the ward electoral commission instructs some members of the commission to organize voting at the place where the constituents may be at the moment.

Art.53. Procedure

The ballot is filled in by the voter in a polling booth or room for secret voting. The presence of any other person beside the voter is not allowed during this process. Constituents unable to fill in the ballot themselves have the right to invite any other person to the booth or room, with the exception of members of the electoral commission.

In elections of People's Deputies at electoral districts, the voters shall cross out on the ballot the names of the candidates he is voting against.

During the election of People's Deputies from public organizations, the voter shall cross out on the ballot the names of the candidates he is voting against.

Thereupon, the voter drops the filled ballot into the ballot box.

Art.54. Vote Counting

In elections of People's Deputies at electoral districts, the counting of votes at the polling station shall be carried out separately for each electoral district and for each candidate.

Ballot boxes shall be opened by the ward electoral commission after the announcement by the commission chairman of the end of voting. The opening of the ballot boxes before the end of voting is prohibited. Before the opening of the ballot boxes all unused ballots shall be counted and voided by the ward electoral commission.

Using the main and the additional voting lists, the ward electoral commission shall establish the general number of voters in the ward and also the number of voters who have received ballots. On the basis of the ballots in the ballot boxes, the commission shall establish for each electoral district (within the given electoral ward) the total number of voters to have taken part in the voting; the number of votes cast for and against each candidate; and the number of ballots declared void. No counts of votes are made for the additional names written by voters in their ballots.

Ballots of unauthorized forms and also ballots where more than one candidate is left shall be declared void. In the case of doubts regarding the validity of a ballot, the matter shall be resolved by the ward electoral commission by voting.

The results of the count of votes shall be reviewed at a sitting of the ward electoral commission and entered in a certificate drawn up separately for each electoral district. The certificate shall be signed by the chairman, vice-chairman, secretary and members of the commission and sent to the corresponding district electoral commission as prescribed by the Central Electoral Commission.

Art.55. Establishment of Election Results in the Electoral District

On the basis of the certificates of the ward electoral commissions, the district electoral commission shall establish: the total number of voters in the district; the number of voters to have received ballots; the number of voters to have taken part in the voting; the number of votes cast for and against each candidate; the number of ballots declared void.

A candidate shall be regarded elected if he has received more than a half of the votes of the electors who have taken part in the voting.

The district electoral commission may declare the elections invalid because of breaches of this Law in the course of the elections or during the count of votes.

Elections shall be declared invalid if less than a half of the electors entered in the voters' list have taken part in them, or in connection with the death of a candidate if he is the only one nominated in his district.

The results of the elections in the electoral district shall be established at a sitting of the district electoral commission and entered in the certificate, which shall be signed by the chairman, vice-chairman, secretary and members of the commission and sent to the Central Electoral Commission as prescribed by it.

The announcement of the results of the elections in the district shall be published in the press by the corresponding district electoral commission within terms set by the Central Electoral Commission. The announcement shall specify the total number of citizens included in the voters' list; the number of voters to have taken part in the elections; the number of votes cast for and against each candidate; the number of voided ballots; the full name, the post (occupation) and the places of work and residence of the elected deputy.

Art.56. Counting of Votes and Establishment of the Results of the Elections of People's Deputies of the USSR from Public Organizations

The counting of votes in the elections of Peoples' Deputies of the USSR from public organizations shall be done by electoral commissions for elections of candidates from public organizations for each candidate as prescribed by this Law for ward electoral commissions.

Ballots of any unauthorised form shall be null and void.

Candidates shall be considered elected if they receive more votes than any other candidates standing for the seats contested and more than a half of the votes of the delegates to the congresses and conferences of public organizations or of the participants in the plenums of their all-Union bodies who have taken part in the voting.

Elections shall be declared invalid if less than a half of the delegates to congresses and conferences of public organizations or participants in the plenums of their all-Union bodies, entered in the voters' lists, have taken part in them.

The returns shall be established at a sitting of the electoral commission concerned and entered in a certificate, this to be signed by the chairman, vice-chairman, secretary and members of the electoral commission and transmitted to the Central Electoral Commission as prescribed by the latter.

Announcements on the results of the elections of People's Deputies of the USSR from public organizations shall be published in the press by the electoral commissions by the deadline set by the Central Electoral Commission. The announcement shall give the number of delegates to the congress or conference of the public organization or the number of participants in the plenum of its all-Union body who have taken part in the elections; the full name, post (occupation), Party membership, and places of work and residence of each elected deputy; and the number of votes for and against the deputy.

IX. PROCEDURE FOR THE ASSESSMENT AND PUBLICATION OF THE RESULTS OF ELECTION OF PEOPLE'S DEPUTIES OF THE USSR

Art.57. Registration of People's Deputies of the USSR

The Central Electoral Commission for Election of People's Deputies of the USSR shall register the elected People's Deputies of the USSR on the basis of the certificates sent in by the electoral commissions.

The Central Electoral Commission shall have the power to declare the elections invalid if there be breaches of this Law in the course of the elections, in the counting of votes or in the determination of the electoral results, and to refuse registration to a People's Deputy of the USSR.

Art.58. Publication of the Results of the Elections of People's Deputies of the USSR

The announcement of the results of the elections in the country as a whole and the list of the elected People's Deputies of the USSR shall be printed in the press by the

Central Electoral Commission within ten days of the elections in alphabetical order, giving the full name, post (occupation), Party membership, and places of work and residence of each deputy, as well as the electoral district or public organization from which the deputy has been elected.

Art.59. The Credentials and the Badge of People's Deputy of the USSR

After the publication in the press of the list of People's Deputies of the USSR registered by the Central Electoral Commission, the district electoral commission or the electoral commission for a public organization shall issue a certificate of election to each deputy-elect.

After the confirmation by the Congress of People's Deputies of the USSR of the powers of the deputies-elect, the certificates of election issued to them shall be replaced with credentials of People's Deputy of the USSR. The deputies shall also be issued a badge of People's Deputy of the USSR.

X. REPEAT VOTING, REPEAT ELECTIONS AND BY-ELECTIONS TO SEATS OF PEOPLE'S DEPUTIES OF THE USSR

Art.60. Repeat Voting

If more than two candidates run for election as People's Deputy of the USSR for an electoral district and none of them be elected, the district electoral commission shall call a repeat vote in the district for the two candidates who have received the most votes. The district commission shall notify that decision to the Central Electoral Commission and the district's electorate. The repeat vote in the electoral district shall be held within two weeks' time in compliance with the prescriptions of this Law.

Repeat voting in the elections of People's Deputies of the USSR from public organizations shall be held if there be an equal number of votes preventing the determination of who has been elected. The repeat voting for those candidates shall be held at congresses or conferences of the public organizations concerned or at plenums of their all-Union bodies on the same or next day in compliance with the prescription of this Law.

In the event of a repeat vote that candidate shall be elected who has the greatest number of votes from constituents or delegates to a congress or conference of a public organization or from participants in the plenum of its all-Union body who have taken part in the voting.

Art.61. Repeat Elections

If no more than two candidates for People's Deputy of the USSR run in an electoral district and none of them be elected, or if the elections in that district be ruled as not having taken place or invalid, or else the repeat voting fail to determine the deputy-elect, the Central Electoral Commission shall ask the district electoral commission to hold repeat elections in the district. In such a case it may decide on the need for those elections to be held by district and ward electoral commissions of a new composition. The voting shall take place at the same polling stations and based on the same voters' list as used initially.

Repeat elections shall be held within two months of the initial elections. The formation of the electoral commissions, registration of candidates and other procedures shall be handled as prescribed by this Law.

In cases when the number of elected deputies proves smaller than the number of seats, or when the elections from a public organization are ruled invalid, the Central Electoral Commission shall call repeat elections in that public organization, the purpose in the former case being to fill the remaining seats, and in the latter, to put up all seats for a new election. The Central Electoral Commission may either order the repeat elections to be held by the appropriate electoral commission in its previous composition or propose to the all-Union body of the public organization concerned that it form a new electoral commission.

Art.62. By-elections to Seats of People's Deputies of the USSR

If the powers of individual People's Deputies of the USSR be revoked by the Congress of People's Deputies of the USSR or if a deputy be recalled or his powers be terminated for other reasons, new elections shall be held in the corresponding electoral districts or public organizations within three months of the departure of the deputy. The elections shall be announced by the Central Electoral Commission at least two months before their holding and shall be organized as prescribed by this Law. The district electoral commission or the electoral commission for electing deputies from a public organization shall be formed 50 days before the elections, and the ward electoral commission, one month before the elections, with the registration of candidates to be completed one month before the elections.

In case a People's Deputy of the USSR leaves office less than a year before the termination of the tenure of the whole body of People's Deputies of the USSR, no election shall be held to fill the vacancy.

M.S. Gorbachev
Chairman of the Presidium
of the Supreme Soviet of the USSR
T. Menteshashvili
Secretary of the Presidium
of the Supreme Soviet of the USSR

Moscow, the Kremlin, 1 December 1988

"Zakon SSSR. O vyborakh narodnykh deputatov SSSR," *Pravda* and *Izvestiya*, 4 December 1988; in J. L. Black, editor, *USSR Documents Annual, 1988. Perestroika—The Second Stage* (Academic International Press, 1989), 163-77. *Izvestiya*, 7 December 1988, lists the 750 territorial and national-territorial electoral districts. See also Viktor Yasmann, "Quotas of Seats in Congress of People's Deputies for Public and Professional Organizations," RF/RFE *Report on the USSR* (27 January 1989), 9-10.

APPENDIX A.3
DECREE ON THE PROCEDURE FOR ORGANIZING AND HOLDING MEETINGS, RALLIES, STREET PROCESSIONS, AND DEMONSTRATIONS IN THE USSR BY THE PRESIDIUM OF THE USSR SUPREME SOVIET, 28 JULY 1988

In accord with the interests of the people and for the purpose of strengthening and developing the socialist system, the USSR Constitution guarantees USSR citizens the freedom to hold meetings, rallies, street processions, and demonstrations. The exercise of these political freedoms is ensured by giving working people and their organizations access to public buildings, streets, squares and other facilities.

With a view toward regulating the procedure for organizing and holding meetings, rallies, street processions, and demonstrations, the Presidium of the USSR Supreme Soviet resolves that:

1. An application to hold a meeting, rally, street procession, or demonstration must be submitted to the executive committee of the appropriate local soviet.

An application to hold a meeting, rally, street procession, or demonstration may be submitted by persons, at least 18 years of age, who are authorized representatives of labor collectives and enterprises, institutions and organizations, of agencies of cooperatives and other public organizations, of public grass-roots agencies, and of certain other groups of citizens.

2. An application to hold a meeting, rally, street procession, or demonstration must be submitted in writing no later than 10 days in advance of the planned date of the event. The application must indicate the purpose and form of the event, the place where it is to be held or its route, the time it is to begin and end, the estimated number of participants, the last names, first names and patronymics of the authorized representatives (organizers), their places of residence and work (or study), and the date on which the application is submitted.

3. The soviet executive committee will examine the application and inform the authorized representatives (organizers) of its decision no less than five days before the date of the event, as stated the application. The soviet executive committee has the right, if necessary, to suggest another time and place for the event to the sponsors of the application. The decision can be appealed to a higher-level executive or administrative agency, in accord with procedures set forth in current legislation.

The soviet executive committee will ensure that the necessary conditions exist for holding the meeting, rally, street procession, or demonstration.

4. Meetings, rallies, street processions, and demonstrations are to be held for the purpose and at the time and place stated in the application.

When meetings, rallies, street processions, and demonstrations are held, the authorized representatives (organizers), as well as other participants, must observe Soviet laws and maintain public order. Participants are prohibited from carrying weapons or any specially prepared or modified instruments that could endanger people's lives and health or cause material damage to state and public organizations or citizens.

5. State and public organizations and officials, as well as citizens, have no right to obstruct meetings, rallies, street processions and demonstrations that are conducted in accordance with established procedure.

6. The soviet executive committee will prohibit a meeting, rally, street procession, or demonstration if the purpose for staging it varies from the USSR Constitution or union and autonomous-republic constitutions or if the demonstration threatens public order and the safety of citizens.

7. Meetings, rallies, street processions and demonstrations will be halted at the request of representatives of organs of power if no application has been submitted, if the authorities have decided to prohibit the event, if the procedure for holding the event, as stipulated in Art. 4

above, is violated, if there is danger to the lives and health of citizens, or if public order is disrupted.

8. Persons who violate the established procedure for organizing and holding meetings, rallies, street processions and demonstrations bear liability as prescribed by USSR and union-republic legislation.

In the event of material damage to state, cooperative, or other public organizations or to citizens during meetings, rallies, street processions, and demonstrations, the participants in such events shall be required to make restitution in accord with procedures established by law.

9. The presidiums of the union and autonomous-republic supreme soviets and the territory, province, region, district and city soviets may adopt additional measures to regulate the holding meetings, rallies, street processions, and demonstrations in the light of local conditions, union and autonomous-republic constitutions, and the stipulations of this decree.

10. The procedure for organizing and holding meetings and rallies set forth in this decree does not extend to meetings and rallies of labor collectives and public organizations, provided they are held in conformity with legislation and with their charters and statutes.

A. GROMYKO, Chairman
Presidium of the USSR Supreme Soviet
T. MENTESHASHVILI, Secretary
Presidium of the USSR Supreme Soviet

The Kremlin, Moscow, 28 July 1988

Source: *Izvestiya*, 29 July 1988, p. 2; and CDSP, No. 30 (1988), 15.

APPENDIX A.4
LAW ON CRIMINAL LIABILITY FOR STATE CRIMES (25 DECEMBER 1958)
ARTICLES 7 AND 11 AS AMENDED AND SUPPLEMENTED BY DECREE OF THE USSR SUPREME SOVIET PRESIDIUM OF 8 APRIL 1989

The USSR Supreme Soviet Presidium resolves:

I. To introduce the following amendments and addenda to the USSR Law "On Criminal Liability for State Crimes" dated 25 December 1958 ....

1. Articles 7 and 11 are to read as follows:

Article 7. Appeals to Overthrow or Change the Soviet State and Social System

(1) Public appeals to overthrow the Soviet state and social system or to change them by methods contrary to the USSR Constitution, or to obstruct the execution of Soviet laws for the purpose of undermining the USSR political and economic system, and equally to prepare for purposes of dissemination or to actually disseminate material containing such appeals are punishable by deprivation of freedom for a period of up to 3 years or a fine of up to R2,000.

(2) The same actions, committed repeatedly by an organized group or by using technical means designed or adapted for large print runs are punishable by deprivation of freedom for a period of up to 7 years or a fine of up to R5,000.

(3) Actions falling within paragraphs (1) or (2) of this article committed on instructions from foreign organizations or their representatives or involving the use of material assets or technical means received from such organizations are punishable by deprivation of freedom for a period between 3 and 10 years.

Article 11. Infringement of National or Racial Equality

(1) Actions deliberately intended to incite national or racial enmity or dissension, to degrade national honor and dignity, and to directly or indirectly restrict the rights, or directly or indirectly create privileges for citizens on the basis of their race or nationality are punishable by deprivation of freedom for a period of up to 3 years or a fine of up to R2,000.

(2) Those same actions when combined with violence, fraud, or threats, or when committed by officials are punishable by deprivation of freedom for a period of up to 5 years or a fine of up to R5,000.

(3) Actions covered by paragraphs (1) and (2) of this article, when committed by a group of persons or when involving loss of human life or other grave consequences, are punishable by deprivation of freedom for a period of up to 10 years.

2. To supplement the Law with Articles 7-1 and 11-1, reading as follows:

Article 7-1. Calls for Commission of Crimes against the State

Public appeals to betray the motherland or to commit an act or terrorism or sabotage are punishable by deprivation of freedom for a period of up to 3 years or a fine of up to R2,000.

Article 11-1. Insulting or Defaming State Organs and Public Organizations

The public insulting or defamation of the USSR supreme organs of state power and government, other state organs constituted or elected by the USSR Congress of People's Deputies or the USSR Supreme Soviet, or by officials appointed, elected, or confirmed in office by the USSR Congress of People's Deputies or the USSR Supreme Soviet, or public organizations and their all-Union organs constituted according to law and acting in conformity with the USSR Constitution is punishable by deprivation of freedom for a period of up to 3 years or a fine of up to R2,000.

. . . .

III. The Supreme Soviet Presidiums of the Union Republics are ordered to bring union republic legislation into conformity with the present decree.

IV. The present decree comes into force on the day of its publication.

M. GORBACHEV, Chairman,
USSR Supreme Soviet Presidium
T. Menteshashvili, Secretary,
USSR Supreme Soviet Presidium

The Kremlin, Moscow, 8 April 1989

Source: *Izvestiya*, 11 April 1989, p. 3.

APPENDIX A.5
DECREE ON THE DUTIES AND RIGHTS OF INTERNAL TROOPS OF THE USSR MINISTRY OF INTERNAL AFFAIRS IN SAFEGUARDING PUBLIC ORDER, 28 JULY 1988 (SUMMARY)

Note: This appendix is a composite of statements by Colonel General Yu. V. Shatalin, Commander of Internal Troops of the USSR Ministry of Internal Affairs; Major General A. Griyenko, Chief of the Internal Troops Political Directorate; and T. N. Menteshashvili, Secretary of the USSR Supreme Soviet.

The decree codifies duties and rights that previously existed in the form of MVD regulations and directives, and it extends to Internal Troops powers formerly granted only to the police (*militsia*).

MVD Internal Troops are components of the USSR Armed Forces and as such are governed by the regulations that govern the garrison and guard services.

The responsibility for maintaining public order belongs primarily to local and republic soviets and to the police, but when disturbances assume a mass character, the Minister of Internal Affairs may order Internal Troops to assist in the restoration of order. The authority to deploy Internal Troops rests exclusively with the USSR Minister of Internal Affairs, although under certain circumstances he must obtain the consent of the USSR Council of Ministers. Under no circumstances is it permissible to place Internal Troops under the command of local or republic authorities.

The Internal Troops are responsible for guarding state facilities, special freight, and corrective-labor and rehabilitation colonies and centers. They may assist other agencies in enforcing medical quarantines and in maintaining public order and safety during fires and natural disasters.

They may also be required to assist other agencies in the preservation of public order. In that respect, their duty is to suppress "large-scale disturbances of public order that threaten the lives or health of citizens, that disrupt the operation of enterprises, organizations, and institutions, or that threaten the destruction of state, public, or personal property."

Internal troops are provided with [unspecified] "special equipment and weapons" which they are authorized to use in the following circumstances:

1. to protect citizens from attacks that threaten their lives or well-being;

2. to protect servicemen, militiamen, and members of people's voluntary detachments whose lives are threatened while they are acting in the line of duty;

3. to detain persons who have committed particularly dangerous crimes or who have been apprehended in the commission of such crimes, when no other means of detaining them are available. Handcuffs may be used when escorting dangerous criminals and, under exceptional circumstances, to control unruly detainees.

Weapons may not be used against women and minors or against citizens accompanied by minors, except when they are participating in an armed attack; they may not be used in crowded streets or squares or other public places where they would endanger the lives or safety of bystanders.

Internal Troops have the authority to examine the documents of persons suspected of committing crimes, to make free use of communications facilities, to use state-owned vehicles in pursuit of criminals, to arrest persons who have violated administrative regulations, to enter residential buildings and enterprises in hot pursuit of suspects or to stop a crime in progress, to enter a home if they have seen a person who has committed a crime in hiding there or if someone is calling for help, and to cordon off and secure areas, buildings, and facilities. If no military patrol is available, they have the authority to detain servicemen engaged in the "malicious breach of public order" and turn them over to military authorities.

Sources: *Pravda*, 18 October 1988, p. 6; and *Izvestiya*, 29 October 1988, pp. 5-6; in CDSP (1988), No. 42, pp. 8-9, and No. 46, pp. 13-14; *Krasnaya zvezda*, 3 November 1988, pp. 1-2, in FBIS-SOV, 9 November 1988, 86-88.

APPENDIX B.1

PROVISIONAL STANDING ORDERS FOR SESSIONS OF THE CONGRESS OF PEOPLE'S DEPUTIES OF THE USSR

1. In line with the USSR Constitution, sessions of the USSR Congress of People's Deputies will be held once a year. Extraordinary sessions will be convened on the initiative of the USSR Supreme Soviet, at the request of one of the chambers of the USSR Supreme Soviet, the USSR Supreme Soviet Presidium, the USSR Supreme Soviet chairman, at least one-fifth of the USSR people's deputies, or on the initiative of a union republic in the shape of its supreme organ of state power (Article 110, part 4 of the USSR Constitution).

2. USSR Congress of People's Deputies sessions will examine all matters placed by Article 108 of the USSR Constitution under the exclusive jurisdiction of the USSR Congress of People's Deputies. (Article 108, part 3 of the USSR Constitution).

The USSR Congress of People's Deputies is entitled to scrutinize and resolve any matter that is under the jurisdiction of the Union of Soviet Socialist Republics. (Article 108, part 2 of the USSR Constitution).

3. The right of legislative initiative at the USSR Congress of People's Deputies is possessed by USSR people's deputies, the USSR Supreme Soviet Soviet of the Union, Soviet of Nationalities, and Presidium, the chairman of the USSR Supreme Soviet, the USSR Constitutional Oversight Committee, the USSR Council of Ministers, union republics in the shape of their supreme organs of state power, the chambers' standing commissions and committees of the USSR Supreme Soviet, the USSR Committee of People's Control, the USSR Supreme Court, the USSR prosecutor general, and the USSR chief state arbiter. (Article 114, part 1 of the USSR Constitution).

The right of legislative initiative is also possessed by public organizations in the shape of their all-union organs and by the USSR Academy of Sciences. (Article 114, part 2 of the USSR Constitution).

4. USSR laws and resolutions of the USSR Congress of People's Deputies will be adopted at congress sessions by a majority of the total number of USSR people's deputies and USSR laws on amendments to the USSR Constitution by a majority of at least two-thirds of the total number of USSR people's deputies. (Article 108, part 4 and Article 174 of the USSR Constitution).

Laws and other decisions of the USSR Congress of People's Deputies will be adopted, as a rule, after a preliminary discussion of the drafts by the relevant chambers' standing commissions and committees of the USSR Supreme Soviet. (Article 123, part 1 of the USSR Constitution).

USSR laws and other acts adopted by the USSR Congress of People's Deputies will be signed by the chairman of the USSR Supreme Soviet. (Article 121, part 1 of the USSR Constitution).

5. The USSR Congress of People's Deputies will elect the USSR Supreme Soviet by secret ballot from the USSR people's deputies in accordance with the demands of Article 111 of the USSR Constitution. (Article 108, part 3, Article 111, parts 2 and 4 of the USSR Constitution).

Every year the USSR Congress of People's Deputies will replace one-fifth of the members of the Soviet of the Union and Soviet of Nationalities. (Article 111, part 5 of the USSR Constitution).

6. The USSR Congress of People's Deputies will elect a USSR Supreme Soviet chairman by secret ballot from the USSR people's deputies. (Article 108, part 3, Article 120, part 2 of the USSR Constitution).

7. The USSR Congress of People's Deputies will elect a first deputy chairman of the USSR Supreme Soviet and the USSR Constitutional Oversight Committee. Candidates for election to the post of first deputy chairman of the USSR Supreme Soviet and proposals on the composition of the USSR Constitutional Oversight Committee will be submitted to the USSR Congress of People's Deputies by the USSR Supreme Soviet chairman. (Article 108, part 3 and Article 121, part 1 of the USSR Constitution).

8. Approval by the USSR Congress of People's Deputies of the chairman of the USSR Council of Ministers, chairman of the USSR People's Control Committee, chairman of the USSR Supreme Court, USSR prosecutor general, and USSR chief state arbiter will take place at the behest of the chairman of the USSR Supreme Soviet and following their election and appointment by the USSR Supreme Soviet. (Article 108, part 3 and Article 121, part 1 of the USSR Constitution).

9. The work of the USSR Congress of People's Deputies will be organized by the USSR Supreme Soviet Presidium. The chairman of the USSR Supreme Soviet will be

in overall charge of the preparation of questions to be examined by the USSR Congress of People's Deputies. (Article 118, part 1, Article 121, part 1 of the USSR Constitution).

10. USSR Congress of People's Deputies sessions will take place in the Kremlin Palace of Congresses in Moscow.

The USSR people's deputies will be seated in the stalls of the hall of sessions in accordance with the territorial principle: deputies from territorial and national-territorial okrugs in accordance with the republics, krays, or oblasts they represent; deputies from public organizations in accordance with the republics, krays, or oblasts in which they live or work.

11. The first session of the USSR Congress of People's Deputies after the elections will be chaired by the chairman of the Central Electoral Commission on the Election of USSR People's Deputies and subsequently the chairman of the USSR Supreme Soviet or his deputy. (Article 110, part 5 of the USSR Constitution).

12. At the first session after the elections the USSR Congress of People's Deputies will elect a Credentials Commission from the USSR people's deputies.

At the behest of the Credentials Commission the USSR Congress of People's Deputies will adopt a decision recognizing deputies' powers and, in the event of a breach of legislation on elections, declaring the election of certain deputies void. (Article 110, part 2 of the USSR Constitution).

13. The morning sessions of the USSR Congress of People's Deputies will take place between 1000 and 1400 hours with a 30-minute break and the evening sessions between 1600 and 1800 hours. The congress can decide to fix different times for the sessions.

As a rule, a maximum of 1 hour 30 minutes will be allowed for reports and 30 minutes for co-reports. Speakers in debates on reports and co-reports will be allowed 15 minutes; 7 minutes for a further contribution in debates; 5 minutes for speeches about candidates, and 3 minutes for speeches concerned with procedure, reasons for voting, and information.

14. Applications to speak in the debate will be submitted in advance to the USSR Supreme Soviet Presidium or during the work of the USSR Congress of People's Deputies to the person chairing the session.

When important questions are being discussed USSR people's deputies speaking for union and autonomous republics, regions, and also public organizations will be given an opportunity to speak.

Each union republic has the right to demand that at least three USSR people's deputies be given the opportunity to speak on the main items on the agenda.

15. The USSR Congress of People's Deputies will decide, by a majority of at least two-thirds of the total number of USSR people's deputies, when a debate should be ended.

When deciding the question of ending a debate deputies elected from a union republic have the right to insist that deputies from that republic be allowed to speak if this request is backed by at least two-thirds of the deputies elected from that republic. In the aforesaid event it will require a repeat vote to end the debate, conducted in accordance with part one of the present article.

16. Proposals on amendments to draft laws and other acts will be submitted in written form.

17. At sessions of the USSR Congress of People's Deputies a deputy can make a request to the USSR Supreme Soviet chairman, the USSR Council of Ministers, and the leaders of other organs formed or elected by the USSR Congress of People's Deputies and USSR Supreme Soviet. USSR people's deputies' requests can be submitted in written form and verbally. An answer to a request must be given at the congress within no more than 3 days. (Article 124, part 1 of the USSR Constitution).

18. At sessions of the USSR Congress of People's Deputies decisions on the questions under discussion will be taken by an open vote. In cases envisaged by the USSR Constitution, or if the congress so decides, there will be a secret ballot.

When there is an open vote a group of people's deputies, whose size is determined by the congress, will be instructed to add up the votes. A Tellers' Commission will be elected from the people's deputies to organize and hold a secret ballot.

Individual voting [poimennoye golosovaniye] can be conducted if the USSR Congress of People's Deputies so decides.

19. A USSR people's deputy will be assured the opportunity to actively participate in sessions of the USSR Congress of People's Deputies.

A USSR people's deputy has the right to participate in debates, make proposals, comments, and amendments concerning the questions under discussion, express his or her views on the composition of organs being set up by the congress and on candidates for official posts to be elected or approved by the congress, and to make requests, ask questions, and provide information. They will also have other rights in accordance with the USSR Constitution and other USSR laws.

A USSR people's deputy has the right to have a deciding vote on all matters to be examined at USSR Congress of People's Deputies sessions. A USSR people's deputy who is not a member of the USSR Supreme Soviet can participate with the right of a consultative voice in sessions of the USSR Supreme Soviet and its chambers. A USSR people's deputy who is not a member of a chamber commission or committee of the USSR Supreme Soviet can participate in a session of a chamber commission or committee of the USSR Supreme Soviet with the right of consultative voice.

A USSR people's deputy will be presented with draft laws, resolutions, and other documents submitted for discussion by the USSR Congress of People's Deputies in advance, as a rule at least 2 weeks in advance.

In line with Article 118 of the USSR Constitution, the USSR Supreme Soviet Presidium, in organizing the work of the USSR Congress of People's Deputies, can, at the request of at least 20 USSR people's deputies, disseminate materials it has prepared as official documents of the USSR Congress of People's Deputies.

A USSR people's deputy will be provided with the requisite material on the activity of the USSR Congress of People's Deputies, the USSR Supreme Soviet, its Presidium, and chambers' standing commissions and committees of the USSR Supreme Soviet.

During the work of the USSR Congress of People's Deputies, deputies will be provided with stenographic accounts of the sessions. The congress can decide to include in the stenographic accounts the texts of speeches of people's deputies who were unable to speak before the debate ended.

20. Sessions of the USSR Congress of People's Deputies will be open.

Representatives of state organs, public organizations, labor collectives, the press, television, and radio, and some individuals as well will be invited to attend sessions.

A closed session can be held if the USSR Congress of People's Deputies so decides.

APPENDIX B.2

RESOLUTION ON PROPOSALS, STATEMENTS, AND COMPLAINTS FROM CITIZENS RECEIVED BY THE CONGRESS OF PEOPLE'S DEPUTIES

1. To instruct the Congress of USSR People's Deputies Presidium and Secretariat to expeditiously examine and take account of proposals from citizens addressed to the congress when drawing up corresponding materials and decisions.

2. To submit personal requests and complaints from citizens to the congress for examination by the relevant state and social organs under the procedure laid down by the law. Notice of the measures taken to resolve issues raised in citizens' appeals should be given to the citizens concerned and to the USSR Supreme Soviet Presidium.

APPENDIX B.3

RESOLUTION ON THE PREPARATION OF A USSR DRAFT LAW ON THE STATUS OF PEOPLE'S DEPUTIES IN THE USSR

The Congress of USSR People's Deputies **resolves**:

1. To instruct the USSR Supreme Soviet to elaborate a new USSR Draft Law on the Status of People's Deputies in the USSR with a view to examining it at the second Congress of USSR People's Deputies in the fourth quarter of 1989.

The Draft Law is to be sent to USSR People's Deputies in September 1989.

2. Pending the adoption of the new USSR Law on the Status of People's Deputies in the USSR, USSR people's deputies enjoy all the rights and guarantees of deputies' activity, bear all the obligations envisaged by the USSR Constitution and by the present resolution as well as by those statutes of the USSR law of 20 September 1972 "On the Status of People's Deputies in the USSR" in the version of the USSR Law of 19 April 1979 (USSR Supreme Soviet Gazette, 1979, No 17, page 277) which do not contradict the USSR Constitution and the present resolution.

3. A USSR People's Deputy is obliged at least once a year to report back on his work and the work of the Congress of USSR People's Deputies to the voters, collectives, and social organizations which nominated him as candidate deputy or to the social organization which elected him. A USSR People's Deputy elected to the USSR Supreme Soviet is also obliged to report back on the work of the USSR Supreme Soviet.

4. USSR People's Deputies possess the right of legislative initiative, the right to participate in debates at sessions of the Congress of USSR People's Deputies, the USSR Supreme Soviet, its committees, and chambers' commissions, to present proposals, remarks, and amendments on the substance of the questions under discussion, to express an opinion on the personnel composition of the organs created by the Congress and USSR Supreme Soviet and on the candidacies of officials elected, appointed, or approved by the Congress of USSR People's Deputies and the USSR Supreme Soviet, to submit requests, raise questions, and present information.

5. A USSR People's Deputy who is not a member of USSR Supreme Soviet may take part in sessions of the USSR Supreme Soviet and its chambers with the right of a consultative voice.

A USSR People's Deputy who is not a member of the USSR Supreme Soviet and is elected to a committee of the USSR Supreme Soviet or a commission of a chamber takes part in committee or commission sessions with the right to vote.

A USSR People's Deputy who is not a member of a USSR Supreme Soviet committee or a standing commission of a chamber may take part in committee or commission sessions with the right of a consultative voice.

6. A USSR People's Deputy has the right to ask for and receive from state and social organs, enterprises, institutions, and organizations information necessary for his activity as a deputy.

On the instructions of the Congress of USSR People's Deputies, the USSR Supreme Soviet, and their organs a USSR People's Deputy is entitled to first-hand familiarization with documentation in state and public organs, at enterprises, institutions, and organizations.

7. Draft laws, resolutions, and other documents presented for the examination of the Congress of USSR People's Deputies are to be submitted to the USSR People's Deputy in good time and as a rule at least 2 weeks in advance.

A USSR People's Deputy is to be provided with documents adopted by the Congress of USSR People's Deputies and the USSR Supreme Soviet and information on their organs' work and also has the right to legal and other consultations necessary for the exercise of his powers.

8. The USSR People's Deputy has a preferential right to publish articles on questions of his activity as a deputy on the radio and television and in newspapers and journals published in his electoral okrug or by the social organization which elected him.

9. A USSR People's Deputy is entitled to an assistant—a secretary who is on the staff of an enterprise, institution, organization, or local soviet executive committee [ispolkom]. The secretary's work is paid for by money from the USSR State Budget according to scales determined by the USSR Law on the reimbursement of expenses incurred by USSR People's Deputies during their activity as deputies.

10. A USSR People's Deputy is given the opportunity to use official premises for participation in the work of the Congress of USSR People's Deputies, the USSR Supreme Soviet, its committees, and chambers' commissions, as well as of library stocks, communications facilities, computers and office equipment which the USSR Supreme Soviet possesses.

11. Local soviet ispolkoms, enterprises, institutions, and social organizations provide USSR People's Deputies with premises for receiving voters and discharging other deputy's duties and provide them with hotels when they are carrying out their activity as deputies away from their permanent place of residence.

12. Officials of state and social organs, enterprises, and organizations who do not meet their obligations toward USSR People's Deputies shall bear disciplinary responsibility up to and including dismissal from their post.

13. A USSR People's Deputy who is elected a member of the USSR Supreme Soviet and is freed from his official or production duties for his term in the USSR Supreme Soviet is guaranteed that his former job (post) will be kept open or that that he will be offered an equivalent job (post) on completion of his permanent work in the USSR Supreme Soviet.

Note: On 20 December 1988 the Second Congress of People's Deputies rejected the draft law on the Status of USSR People's Deputies prepared by the Supreme Soviet and returned it for further work. The basic provisions of the proposed legislation were outlined by R. N. Nishanov, Chairman of the Soviet of Nationalities, in a report to the Second Congress on 18 December. Nishanov's statement appeared in *Pravda* on 19 December 1988 and in translation in FBIS-SOV (21 December 1988), 45-49.

APPENDIX B.4
RESOLUTION ON BASIC GUIDELINES
FOR THE DOMESTIC AND FOREIGN POLICY OF THE USSR

The USSR Congress of People's Deputies, expressing the people's will, takes upon itself the full plenitude of the highest state power in the country.

The people have entrusted their future to the deputies, and there is no higher duty than to fulfill their instructions.

I.
Having heard and discussed the reports of M.S. Gorbachev, chairman of the USSR Supreme Soviet, on the Basic Guidelines for the Domestic and Foreign Policy of the USSR, and of N.I. Ryzhkov, chairman of the USSR Council of Ministers, on the program for future government activity, the congress notes that the country is living through an exceptionally crucial time in its history, on which the fate of restructuring and the future of our multinational motherland depend.

The profound restructuring of all aspects of social life that has begun on the party's initiative is designed to lead the country out of the highly serious crisis in which it found itself in the early eighties, to do away resolutely with everything that retards its development, to give socialism a modern face, and to open up for Soviet society new horizons of social progress.

The wave of renewal has stimulated and roused the whole people. A process of assimilating new forms of social life in politics, the economy, and culture is under way, although it is no easy process. The economic reform is taking its first steps. A reconstruction of the political system has begun. The foundations of a rule-of-law state are being laid. Profound changes are taking place in the public consciousness. A turbulent process of politicization of all strata of the population is developing.

Expressing the people's will, the congress calls for steady progress along the path of restructuring. At the same time the congress stresses that the restructuring process is taking place with difficulty and with contradictions, and the situation in the country remains complex and tense. The country has not yet emerged from the crisis. The renewal of social life comes into conflict with the tenacity of the old structures and methods of work and stereotyped ways of thinking. On the one hand, the resistance of conservative forces has to be overcome, and on the other, radical sentiments are declaring themselves and demands are made, without taking objective conditions into account, for all the problems to be resolved at a stroke.

Restructuring has aroused great hopes, but has not yet yielded the desired results, especially in the economic and social spheres. Some problems have even been aggravated, stepping up the social tension in society. The positive changes that have taken shape in production are negated by the disordered state of the financial system, the lack of balance in the market, and the growth in shortages of many goods and services. Despite the efforts being made, the food and housing problems remain acute. The ecological situation is becoming more complex. All this has a negative effect on living conditions, especially for the low-paid strata of the population.

The national economy's turn toward satisfying people's needs is being carried out only slowly. There has been no substantial progress in improving the scientific and technical standard and the efficiency of production. The scattering of capital investments and the growth in the volume of uncompleted construction continue.

Serious defects are occurring in the implementation of the economic reform and the formation of the new economic mechanism because of the absence of a comprehensive approach, inconsistency, and irresolute actions. The administrative edict system, adapting to the conditions of restructuring, is continuing to fetter economic development. The cumbersome management apparatus blocks the introduction of economic accountability relations and other progressive forms of organization of economic life, and blocks the masses' initiative. Leveling in labor remuneration, dependence, parochialism and departmentalism, and group egotism have not been eradicated.

Serious problems are also arising along the path of political reform and the democratization of society. In the work of the soviets and their executive organs, new functions and methods of leadership are being assimilated only slowly, the growing level of social activeness among the masses is not taken into account, and the positive potential of unofficial movements of working people is underestimated. The practice of overadministration with regard to enterprises, collective farms [kolkhozes] and state farms [sovkhozes], and cooperatives and lease operators has not stopped.

The congress notes as extremely alarming the weakening of discipline and responsibility and the growth in infringements of the law and crime in the country. There are major shortcomings in the work of law enforcement organs in the struggle against organized crime and corruption.

In the atmosphere of democratization and glasnost, the problems of interethnic relations that had accumulated over the years have come to light in all their urgency. Dangerous seats of conflict have opened up, and are developing into major excesses. Many years of deformation and distortion of the Leninist nationalities policy and prolonged disregard for the legitimate interests of the country's nations and ethnic groups have had their effect. Major distortions have arisen in the socioeconomic development of a number of republics and regions, along with uncontrolled migration processes. Many unresolved problems have come to light in the development of national languages and cultures, especially those of small peoples.

The USSR Congress of People's Deputies notes that the Soviet people—the working class, peasantry, and intelligentsia, all social strata, and all nations and ethnic groups of our country—fully supported the policy of restructuring at the elections of people's deputies. At the same time the voters firmly demanded that the policy be pursued more resolutely and consistently.

The congress instructs the USSR Supreme Soviet and the USSR Council of Ministers formed by it to formulate and implement exhaustive measures to consolidate and develop the positive changes that have begun, halt the growth of negative trends, resolve urgent problems in the shortest possible space of time, and lay firm foundations for the country's subsequent advance along the path of progress.

The USSR Supreme Soviet and the USSR Council of Ministers are to analyze thoroughly and summarize the concrete proposals put forward by deputies at the congress, take account of them in legislative practice and in the activity of the government, ministries, and departments, and keep the people's deputies informed of this.

II.

The highest purpose of the Soviet state's activity is the material prosperity, spiritual development, and moral health of society and every one of its members. The congress demands from state organs a decisive turn toward focusing attention on man, the further democratization and humanization of all spheres of social life, its spiritual renewal, and the consistent implementation of the principle of social justice.

To achieve a radical improvement in the people's living standard requires time, a substantial increase in production efficiency, and daily creative efforts by labor collectives, economic organs, and the whole of the public. But there are questions that demand speedy resolution.

The congress instructs the USSR Supreme Soviet and USSR Council of Ministers to adopt urgent measures in the near future to stabilize the situation on the consumer market and eliminate the shortage of essential goods and services. The congress considers it necessary without delay, no later than 1 January 1990, without waiting for the adoption of a new pension law:

—to increase the minimum level of the old-age pension for all citizens to the level of the minimum wage, eliminating the differences in pension provision for kolkhoz members, workers, and employees;

—to increase the minimum level of pensions for Group One and Group Two invalids and the widows and bereaved parents of servicemen, bringing them into line with benefits for participants in the Great Patriotic War;

—to grant the right to free medical supplies to participants in the Great Patriotic War and widows and bereaved parents of servicemen, and also to grant the right to the free use of urban transportation (excluding cabs) to participants in the war and to persons awarded orders and medals for selfless labor in the war years;

—to eliminate the discrepancies that exist in the maintenance of patients in medical institutions, as well as in departmental sanatoriums and leisure homes;

—to lift restrictions on the payment of pensions to pensioners working as workers and foremen, and also to all invalidity pensioners employed in the national economy, irrespective of the level of their wages.

Concrete proposals on these questions, including sources of financial provision, should be submitted by the USSR Council of Ministers for examination by the USSR Supreme Soviet within a 3-month period.

With a view to improving the whole range of social conditions for Soviet people's life and work, the congress instructs the USSR Supreme Soviet and USSR Council of Ministers, according to their competence, to implement the following measures:

—to accelerate the resolution of the food problem on the basis of the implementation of a modern agrarian policy incorporating a profound restructuring of socialist production relations, a radical improvement in living conditions in the countryside, and the strengthening of the material base of agro-industrial production;

—to ensure a rapid increase in the production of consumer goods and services of high quality, creating the appropriate economic structures to this end. To involve defense industry and heavy and construction industry enterprises in this work;

—substantially to expand housing construction, primarily cooperative and individual. To release the necessary capacities of construction organizations and material and financial resources for this purpose, by means of reducing production construction. To adopt measures to strengthen the construction industry's base, increase the production of cosntruction materials, and radically improve the architectural face of cities and rural settlements, the provision of amenities in the existing housing stock, and municipal services;

—to achieve a substantial improvement in the quality of health care and the supply of drugs to the population. To seek additional sources of funds and to ensure the rational assimilation of resources already appropriated for the expansion of the network of hospitals and clinics fitted with modern equipment, as well as enterprises to produce modern drugs and medical equipment; to give the production of medical equipment the status of priority consumer goods, and to develop mass physical culture and sport in every way as an effective means of boosting health and reducing morbidity;

—to examine the question of the possibility of increasing the minimum annual leave to 24 working days and child-care leave to the age of 3;

—to improve the social, economic, and other conditions for involving young people in independent labor and sociopolitical life; to formulate and implement the necessary measures to provide financial, legal, and organizational backing for the state youth policy. To formulate and submit for discussion in the USSR Supreme Soviet a question on the state of youth;

—to accelerate the resolution of numerous urgent problems encountered by women. To draw up a state program for improving the position of women in the USSR, including questions of the family, maternity and childhood, the protection of women's work and health, and the alleviation of housework and daily life;

—to step up attention toward war and labor veterans and participants in the war in Afghanistan, and to resolve their pressing problems as a matter of priority;

—to promote to the maximum extent the physical, labor, and social rehabilitation of invalids, their education and professional training, and their involvement in working life, while preserving their existing benefits;

—to approve the initiative of republics and labor collectives providing additional benefits for women, war and labor veterans, and invalids out of their own sources and funds;

—to complete in 1990 the formulation of a statewide ecology program, incorporating both priority and long-term measures to clean up the natural environment. To devote particular attention to ecological disaster zones. To ensure the thorough examination of plans and monitoring of the construction of canals, chemical enterprises, and nuclear power stations from the viewpoint of ecological safety and taking into account economic requirements. To step up state monitoring of the utilization of natural resources and ensure glasnost in information on the quality of the environment.

The congress expresses serious concern in connection with the scale of drunkenness, which is not declining, the ineffectiveness of antialcohol measures, and the spread of home distilling and drug addiction, and demands a resolute struggle against these phenomena.

One of the most important avenues of the activity of all organs of state power and administration and social organizations must be the consistent implementation of the principle of social justice and the complete overcoming of wage leveling and padding. The congress considers wages growth justified only where wages are in line with the results and quality of labor, subject to progressive income tax.

The congress instructs the USSR Council of Ministers, by the end of 1989, to:

—work out questions relating to the introduction of a new system of pension provision incorporating both a mechanism for adjusting pensions at the end of each year, taking account of the cost of living index, and also proposals submitted by USSR people's deputies for improving pension provision for individual categories of the population;

—elaborate a system of compensation measures (supplementary payments, subsidies on the acquisition of medicines and the purchase of children's clothing, and so forth) for people whose income per family member is lower than the subsistence minimum and organize, as of 1990, annual computations of the subsistence minimum per family member;

—submit to the USSR Supreme Soviet an analysis of the present system of benefits and privileges in all forms, and ensure maximum openness in resolving any question linked with benefits and privileges.

The congress considers the comprehensive development of political, spiritual, and labor standards embodied in scientific knowledge, artistic values, folk traditions, and norms of daily conduct to be am important condition for the renewal, humanization, and moral elevation of Soviet society. Without a decisive upsurge in standards or the expansion of glasnost, stable successes cannot be achieved in the democratization of society and the mobilization of human talents, abilities, and gifts.

The USSR Congress of People's Deputies states its commitment to a cultural policy and practice ensuring freedom of artistic creativity and unlimited access by working people to cultural achievements which enrich people's spiritual world.

The congress considers it essential to consistently implement Leninist principles in attitudes to culture and the creative intelligentsia, principles which rule out any manifestations of bureaucratic administration and make the norm a solicitous attitude to the legacy of the past, its best traditions, and state symbols and things sacred to nationalities. With a view to developing culture and spiritually enriching society, the USSR Supreme Soviet and USSR Council of Ministers are instructed to formulate a long-term program in which provision will be made for preserving and augmenting society's spiritual potential, introducing increasingly broad strata of the population to cultural values, renewing and creating a modern system of education and instruction, strengthening the material base of culture, science, education, and publishing, and immediately raising the living standard of low-paid workers in this sphere. Funds for sociocultural purposes are to be allocated on a priority basis.

The qualitative renewal of the entire system of education and instruction—the main source for augmenting society's intellectual potential—is assuming priority significance under present-day conditions. The congress resolutely urges the creation of a modern education system; the strengthening of its material base, including the provision of computer equipment; and the enhancement of the social status of public education teachers and all workers in the education system. In addition to implementing statewide measures it is necessary to more actively involve republic and local bodies, labor collectives, social movements, and charitable foundations in resolving these tasks.

III.
The congress attaches priority significance to the implementation of radical transformations in the economic sphere, regarding them as the foundation of restructuring and a decisive factor for for achieving its objectives. Without fundamental changes in the economy, property relationships, and the economic mechanism it is impossible to fulfill the social program advanced by the congress.

The congress on the whole approves the proposals put forward in the reports by M.S. Gorbachev and N.I. Ryzhkov for restoring the national economy to health, sharply reducing the budget deficit, regularizing the money supply, and filling the market with consumer goods and services, and demands that additional measures to stabilize the country's economic situation be adopted, taking into account the proposals expressed by people's deputies. The corresponding proposals are to be examined and considered by the Soviet of the Union Planning, Budget, and Financial Commission and other commissions of the chambers and committees of the USSR Supreme Soviet when the progress of the fulfillment of the 1989 targets and the draft plan and budget for 1990 are being discussed. After detailed, comprehensive, and public discussion by the committees and commissions, all questions linked with the establishment of budget income and expenditure must be taken up by the USSR Supreme Soviet.

In resolving strategic economic development tasks particular attention should be paid to the radical retooling of production on the basis of the latest Soviet and world scientific achievements and the introduction of advanced technology, primarily electronics, information science, and biotechnology. The congress stresses the need to develop both basic and applied research on a broad scale in all fields of scientific knowledge in the quest for breakthroughs in the most promising areas of scientific exploration, ensuring the improvement of social relations and qualitative changes in equipment and technology.

There will have to be a radical renewal of the structure of public education, a radical change in investment policy, a sharp reduction in the number of projects under construction at any one time, and a reduction in the volume of incomplete construction to the normative level by the beginning of the 13th 5-Year Plan. There must be a substantial reduction in capital investments in production needs. The corresponding commissions and committees of the USSR Supreme Soviet should analyze the situation and determine the advisability of large-scale projects which are under construction or in the planning stage.

The government is instructed to make changes to the USSR Energy Program and carry out widespread discussion of it.

Additional resources are to be sought to develop the economy and resolve social tasks by reducing military expenditure to the level of reasonable sufficiency, increase the effectiveness of space research, and make wide use of the achievements of space technology in the national economy. The USSR Council of Ministers is to elaborate a defense industry conversion program by the end of 1989. The capacities and material resources thus released are to be used to produce consumer goods and equipment for light industry, the agro-industrial complex, trade, public catering, and health care. Some of the funds released in connection with the reduction of the Armed Forces are to be used to improve the material and everyday living conditions of servicemen and members of their families.

The congress expresses serious concern in connection with the enormous losses in the national economy and the numerous instances of violation of labor and production discipline and labor safety regulations, and blatant mismanagement and irresponsibility. It demands that the USSR Government and soviet and economic organs take resolute measures to put a stop to such phenomena, and urges the Congress of People's Deputies, social organizations and movements, and labor collectives to develop a nationwide struggle against losses and mismanagement and for the strengthening of labor and executive discipline.

The congress considers it necessary to devote particular attention to the development of agriculture and all sectors of the agro-industrial complex. The USSR Supreme Soviet is to substantially update legislation on land and land use. It is necessary to begin more boldly to hand over the land for lease, including indefinite lease, to those who cultivate it. The resolution of questions connected with land leasing is to be entrusted to local soviets, with their powers being expanded by legislation. Diverse forms of economic management are to be developed in conjunction with the kolkhozes and sovkhozes—agro-industrial firms, cooperatives, lease collectives, and peasant farms—and the conditions are to be created for equal competition among them. Equivalent relations are to be ensured between agriculture and industry, agriculture is to be supplied with material and technical resources on a priority basis, and the production of agricultural machines is to be restructured in the light of changes in the structure of agriculture. The social base of the agrarian sector is to be strengthened. Any attempts to exercise command over agricultural enterprises are to be resolutely nipped in the bud.

The appeal of the group of agriculturalist people's deputies to the congress is to be supported, and the USSR

Government is to embark without delay on resolving the radical problems of development of the countryside that it raises.

The USSR Council of Ministers is to conduct an experiment in stimulating additional deliveries of high quality output by farms by paying for this output in currency saved as a result of reducing imports of grain and food.

The USSR Supreme Soviet, its committees and the commissions of the chambers, and the USSR Council of Ministers are to embark on the formulation of the concept and basic guidelines for the 5-year plan for the economic and social development of the USSR for 1991-1995 and for the period through 2005. In the process of this work particular attention is to be devoted to the social reorientation of economic growth, the attainment of full balance in the 5-year plan, the expansion of the autonomy of republics and local soviets, questions of resource-saving, and the creation of the conditions for full and efficient employment of the population. The use of gross volume indicators in planning and in assessing the results of the economic activity of enterprises and territories is to be abandoned.

The congress considers it necessary steadily to put into practice the radical economic reform, and to implement interconnected steps to change planning methods, financial levers, prices, taxes, and labor remuneration conditions, and to introduce territorial economic accountability. In the light of accumulated experience and past mistakes, it is necessary radically to improve the management of the actual process of implementation of the reform, and to prevent deviations from its principles. It is deemed necessary to form a State Commission for Economic Reform in the government.

With a view to further deepening the economic reform, the congress instructs the USSR Supreme Soviet and USSR Council of Ministers:

—to ensure the development of diverse forms of social ownership that exclude exploitation or alienation of the worker from the means of production. To create equal conditions for the development and free competition of the following forms of ownership: statewide, local (communal), cooperative, that based on the lease and share principles (the joint-stock form), that based on individual labor activity, and also various mixed forms; to adopt measures to eliminate negative phenomena in the development of the cooperative movement;

—to implement in the next few years a phased transition to wholesale trade in the means of production and to create the conditions for the formation of a socialist market, including a market in securities and investment resources. To adopt the necessary measures for the wide development of economic competition and the struggle against monopoly phenomena;

—to define ways of resolving the problem of loss-making and low-profit enterprises, in particular by handing them over for leasing, transferring them to the cooperative ownership of labor collectives, or in a number of cases closing them down;

—to implement a radical restructuring of the financial system and go over to a system of payments for resources and progressive taxation of profit (income). To strengthen the role and increase the autonomy of the USSR State Bank. To promote the creation of cooperative and commercial banks, including republican and regional banks;

—to formulate and consistently implement a program for reducing exports of fuel, energy, and raw material resources, and changing the structure of imports on the basis of increasing the efficiency of foreign economic activity and carrying out a phased switch to convertibility of the ruble.

The congress supports the course of all-around development of the initiative and autonomy of production enterprises (associations) as the starting point for economic reform. It is necessary to ensure their consistent, steady transfer to full economic accountability and the opportunity to use various models of economic accountability, and to stimulate the development of the contract system, the lease system, and joint-stock fellowships.

The voluntary creation of socialist concerns, intersector associations, unions, and other societies should be promoted in every way. The development of these forms will make it possible to radically change the functions of ministries and steadily reduce their numbers.

In an economic system based not on administrative instructions and decrees, but on economic methods of management regulated by the law, the role of the center should consist in the creation of the economic and legal conditions for efficient economic activity at every level, the development of the unionwide infrastructure, the implementation of a statewide scientific, technical, financial, and taxation policy, and the social protection of citizens.

The authenticity and fullness of statistical information and its reliability is to be ensured, and the same applies to all other information coming from official sources. The publication of objective data on the level and rate of inflation is to be organized. The comparability of statistical indicators of the country's economic development with corresponding indicators that are accepted in international practice is to be ensured.

IV.

The congress reaffirms: In the USSR all state power belongs to the people and is exercised by them through the soviets of people's deputies.

The congress supports the line formulated by the 19th all-union party conference on the clear demarcation of functions between party and state organs at all levels, the formation of a socialist rule-of-law state, and the consistent implementation of the principle whereby all social organizations, including the CPSU, operate within the framework of the USSR Constitution and Soviet laws.

The congress comes out unanimously in favor of beginning without delay work on preparing a new Constitution—the Fundamental Law of the USSR—forming a Constitutional Commission for that purpose. The new Constitution should embody the principles of humane, democratic socialism and lay down the socioeconomic and political foundations of the formation of the Soviet state, its Leninist federal structure, the treaty-based and constitutional nature of relations between the USSR and the union republics, and the development of all forms of autonomy, the high status of the soviets, the inalienable rights of man, and the security and legal protection of the individual. The new Constitution should embody a socioeconomic and state structure that would make it impossible for a personality cult or authoritarianism to spring up, or for administrative edict methods of managing society to persist.

The USSR Supreme Soviet is instructed to prepare, for the next Congress of People's Deputies, the necessary amendments to the existing USSR Constitution in the light of the proposals put forward by deputeis at the congress.

The congress declares its determination to assert the supremacy of the law in all spheres of state and social life and the quality of all citizens, officials, and organizations before the law, without exception. All citizens are responsible before the law for their actions. But the state, in the person of its organs and officials, should also be responsible for its actions and decisions before every citizen and the whole Soviet people. This principle should be consistently asserted in the sociopolitical and economic activity of citizens, social organizations, cooperatives, and enterprises: "Everything is permitted, except what is prohibited by law."

The main aspects of the activity of state organs and officials should be strictly regulated by the law. Unlawful individual or collegial actions by any officials that infringe citizens' rights may be the subject of an appeal to the court. The law is the basis of a rule-of-law state, the defender of citizens' freedom and equality and of order and organization in society, and the guarantor of the principle of social justice.

The congress proceeds on the basis of recognizing as immutable and sacred the inalienable human rights to life, freedom, the inviolability and security of the person and the home, and the right of peoples to self-determination. Any infringement of human rights and the rights of peoples is impermissible. The Soviet legislative system, the court, and all law enforcement organs are called upon consistently and strictly to implement and defend these rights.

Acting on the basis of international norms and principles, including those contained in the Universal Declaration of Human Rights, the Helsinki agreements, and the accords at the Vienna meeting, and bringing its domestic legislation into line with them, the USSR will promote the creation of a world community of rule-of-law states.

The congress notes that in accordance with the existing USSR Constitution it is empowered to take under consideration and resolve any question that falls within the jurisdiction of the USSR. At the same time the congress believes that the main bulk of legislative acts should be drafted, discussed, and adopted by the permanently operating USSR Supreme Soviet with the active participation of its committees and the commissions of the chambers, in accordance with a carefully formulated democratic procedure making provision for glasnost and openness in discussion and the presentation of alternative versions of decisions and proposals.

The congress instructs the USSR Supreme Soviet to formulate by the next congress a proposal on the procedure for annual renewal of the composition of the USSR Supreme Soviet.

The congress instructs the USSR Supreme Soviet to prepare by the beginning of 1990 legislative acts in which the principle of full power of the soviets in the economic, social, and political spheres of life, as well as measures to overcome departmentalism and parochialism, are expressed in consistent and concrete form. The reconstruction of the soviets of people's deputies at all levels, the democratization of their methods of activity, the all-around widening of their rights and powers, and the unconditional subordination of the executive apparatus to them are necessary conditions for the return of the real levers of power to the soviets. The governments of the USSR and the union and autonomous republics must be entirely subordinate to the supreme organs of power—the congresses and supreme soviets—and responsible to them. Leadership of all local affairs should take place on the basis of the principles of self-management, with maximum development of citizens' initiative and the stepping up of the role of social organizations and democratic movements. The successful resolution of these tasks should be furthered by the forthcoming elections to republican and local organs of power, whose powers expire in February 1990.

It is necessary to strengthen the constitutional guarantees of the constructive development of the democratic process in the country, to consistently democratize the eklectoral system, and to take experience of past elections of USSR people's deputies more fully into account when elaborating republic electoral laws.

An equally urgent task in the legislative field is the provision of legal backup for economic reform. The congress instructs the USSR Supreme Soviet to elaborate a unified law on the socialist enterprise and also to expedite the preparation of laws on leasing and leasing relationships, a unified tax system, republic economic accountability, and self-management and the local economy. The USSR Supreme Soviet and Committee for Economic Reform Questions is to be instructed to examine with the appropriate chamber commissions republics' proposals on questions of expanding their economic independence and the Lithuanian and Estonian Soviet Socialist Republic [SSR] Supreme Soviets' proposals on these republics' transition to economic accountability in 1990, submitted under the legislative initiative procedure.

In the very near future there must be legislative regulation of the activity of the mass media and social organizations, amalgamations, and associations. A law on freedom of conscience and religious organizations must be formulated and adopted.

The congress considers it necessary to resolutely strengthen law and order in the country. Democratic development can be undermined both by administrative tyranny and restrictions on the people's freedom to express their will, and also by the substitution of violence and tyranny by extremists for such freedom of expression.

The congress revokes Article 11-1 and considers it necessary to hone the wording of Article 7 of the USSR Supreme Soviet Presidium Decree of 8 April 1989, and also to instruct the USSR Supreme Soviet to exzamine the question of the conformity with the USSR Constitution of the USSR Supreme Soviet Presidium decrees on the procedure for organizing and conducting rallies and demonstrations and the obligations and rights of USSR Ministry of Internal Affairs [MVD] internal troops.

The congress demands the consistent continuation and intensification of the struggle against corruption, organized crime, embezzlement, and graft, which involves the eradication of these shameful phenomena at every level and the elimination of their causes. The USSR Council of Ministers is to elaborate a unionwide program to combat crime and submit it to the USSR Supreme Soviet. The state has an obligation to safeguard citizens against encroachments on their life, health, honor, and property, and to take all necessary measures to increase and strengthen the material and technical facilities available to the courts and prosecution, investigation, and militia agenies and improve the conditions of their workers' lives.

A most important element of the proposed judicial and legal reform must be to resolutely strengthen the independence of the courts, increase the effectiveness of the investigation process, and remove it from the sphere of any departmental influence whatsover. No criminal must escape the punishment he deserves, but no innocent person must be condemned. Only full protection of citizens' legal rights at all stages of the criminal process, including access by a defense attorney from the very beginning of an investigation, can resolve this task. An objective investigation, a strong defense, and an independent court make up the triune formula of socialist justice. The congress instructs the USSR Supreme Soviet to ensure the implementation of the judicial reform by the middle of next year in order to create a really independent and authoritative judicial system, which will involve the possibility of utilizing such a democratic form of court procedure as juries. The union republics' judicial systems must be structured with consideration for their political, legal, and cultural traditions while complying with all the principles of democratic justice.

V.
The congress draws particular attention to the nationalities question, the present state of interethnic relations, the urgent need for a fundamental renewal of nationalities policy, and the creation of a political mechanism capable of ensuring a reasonable and just approach to questions of interethnic relations. The federal structure of our multinational state must have real political and economic substance. We have an obligation to restore interethnic relations to full health and free them from everything that contradicts our morality and ideology and the humane principles of socialism.

The competence of the USSR, the sovereign rights of the republics, and the rights of autonomous entities need a modern precise juridical definition. The principle of national self-determination advanced by Lenin as the cornerstone of the voluntary unification of the republics in the USSR must be restored to its authentic significance, and provided with the requisite democratic legal guarantees.

The congress states: In creating the legal mechanism for protecting republics' sovereign rights which is essential in a rule-of-law state it is necessary to proceed from present-day realities. The economy, demography, and social and ethnic structure of all the republics have changed, national self-awareness has grown, and new requiremnents have emerged in spiritual life. All this requires the strengthening of political guarantees designed to ensure a reasonable and just approach to questions of interethnic relations, the free and comprehensive development of all the Soviet nations and ethnic groups within the framework of the federal union state, a full life for national languages, and the blossoming of culture.

The congress demands of central and local organs of power that they find mutually acceptable solutions to the nationalities problems, which are yet another heavy legacy bequeathed to us from the times of tyranny and lawlessness. To this day justice has not been restored for a number of nations and ethnic groups. While acknowledging the complexity of the situation and the specific characteristics of the situation in individual republics and regions, the Congress of Peoples' Deputies cannot fail to express a firm standpoint here: In line with the new nationalities policy being formulated in accordance with this resolution, a solution must be found by democratic means as quickly as possible. The congress instructs the USSR Supreme Soviet Soviet of Nationalities to get together with the supreme soviets of the relevant republics and study and submit proposals on questions raised at the congress relating to the restoration of the rights of the Volga Germans, Crimean Tatars, and Meskhetian Turks, and the development of small ethnic groups. The Commission for Nationalities Policy and Interethnic Relations of the Soviet of the Union is to examine the situation in the Nagorno-Karabakh Autonomous Oblast and report the results to the USSR Supreme Soviet.

The congress regards as essential:

—in the political sphere: the unswerving observance and substantial expansion of the rights of union and autonomous republics and other national entities, and the intensification of republic and local organs' independence and responsibility. All this must be regarded as the first step. We must advance consistently toward the implementation of the principle that union republics independently exercise state power on their territory, handling all questions not under the jurisdiction of the USSR. The constitutional provision that the competence of the Union includes the establishment of fundamentals and general principles of legislation, whereas the adoption of laws with direct force is the republics' prerogative, must be observed as one of the axiomatic principles of the functioning of the federal state. The constitutional reform of the Union is intended to resolve the most acute nationalities questions in such a way as to create the legal basis of a self-managing democratic society where each nation is guaranteed the development most in line with its historical, cultural, and other characteristics;

—in the economic sphere: the improvement of relations between the Union and the republics on the basis of the organic combination of their economic autonomy and active participation in the unionwide division of labor. It is necessary in this way to restructure the regulation of the country's integrated national economic complex, organically incorporating the transfer of republics, regions, krays, and oblasts to self-management and self-financing in the general process of renewal of our economy. All nations and ethnic groups should have the opportunity fully to express and realize their sovereign economic, social, and other interests, and to coordinate them reciprocally, on an equal footing, with a view to the harmonious development of the national economy of the regions and the country as a whole;

—in the spiritual sphere: the recognition of the very great social and historical value of the full diversity of national cultures. These are not only our country's property, they are a unique and irreplaceable part of mankind's spiritual assets, and the congress emphasizes the need for an equally solicitous attitude toward the cultures of all the Soviet peoples, both big and small, and the development and enrichment of national languages.

The congress points to the need to create legal forms of resolving the clashes that may and do arise in interethnic relations. In view of the complexity of such clashes, which touch on people's most delicate feelings, the congress appeals to representatives of all nations and ethnic groups for mutual understanding and goodwill, restraint, and tolerance. We should all work together to protect and respect each other's rights and interests, so as to exclude forever the use of violence in resolving nationality problems and ensure the democratic development of the entire multinational Soviet people.

VI.
The Congress of People's Deputies approves and assesses highly the international activity of the Soviet state in the years of restructuring.

The renunciation of dogmatic ideas, realism in the approach to various phenomena and processes of international life, the restoration to common human values of their lost significance, the deideologization of interstate relations, the organic reunification of a policy aimed at protecting the country's interests with morality—all these are distinctive features of the new thinking, in accordance with which a radical change has taken place in the USSR's foreign policy course. Today this course is firmly based on the historic conclusions of the 27th CPSU Congress on the mortally dangerous nature of the nuclear arms race for mankind's survival, the integral nature and growing interdependence of the modern world, and the inalienable right of peoples to a free sociopolitical choice.

The congress notes that in the years of restructuring, as a result of the implementation of the principles of the new political thinking, international tension has decreased considerably, and a reduction has begun in nuclear arsenals and the numerical strength of Soviet forces in the allied countries. The withdrawal of Soviet troops from Afghanistan was a very important foreign policy step in recent years. The congress appeals to parliaments and the international public to promote in every way the return of the Soviet soldiers and officers who did not return from the Afghan war and are languishing in a foreign land.

At the same time the congress notes that guarantees of the irreversibility of the positive changes that have begun in the sphere of disarmament and the strengthening of confidence-building measures have not yet become established. Under these conditions, ensuring the reliable defense of the country is one of the most important functions of our state. The congress advocates the further qualitative development of the Soviet Army in accordance with the existing principles of its formation. It is necessary to continue to show concern for the Soviet Army, which is educated in the spirit of patriotism, has close links with all the Soviet people, and is devoted to their interests.

The congress welcomes the normalization of Soviet-Chinese relations as an event of worldwide significance. It advocates the further development of equal and mutually beneficial cooperation with all socialist countries. It instructs the USSR Government to seek to further improve Soviet-American relations, which are of key significance in the cause of ending the arms race and strengthening universal peace; to ensure still more active Soviet participation in the building of the "common European home" and in the continuation of the Vladivostok line in the Asian and Pacific region, devoting particular attention to friendly relations with India; to develop fruitful contacts with Latin America and Africa; and to strengthen good-neighborly relations with all contiguous states.

The congress considers that the Soviet Union's foreign policy course born out of restructuring must continue to develop on the basis of the following principles:

—the country's security should be ensured first and foremost by political means, as an integral part of general and equal security, in the process of demilitarization, democratization, and humanization of international relations, and with reliance on the authority and potential of the United Nations;

—nuclear weapons should be eliminated in the course of a negotiation process oriented toward disarmament and the reduction of the defense potential of the state within the limits of reasonable sufficiency;

—the use of force and the threat of force with a view to achieving any political, economic, or other objectives are impermissible; in relations with other countries respect for sovereignty, independence, and territorial integrity are essential;

—not confrontation, but dialogue and talks based on the balance of interests should be adopted as the sole means of resolving international problems and settling conflicts;

—the integration of the Soviet economy into the world economy presupposes our active participation in the modern international division of labor, scientific and technical exchange, world trade, and cooperation with all who so wish.

The congress draws particular attention to the need to create reliable guarantees capable of totally ruling out in future the undemocratic adoption, without glasnost, of foreign policy decisions that are of vital significance for the country and its peoples. In future all such decisions should be adopted only after their discussion in the USSR Supreme Soviet, its committees, and the commissions of the chambers, and the most important decisions, for instance those concerning allied relations or the conclusion of very important treaties, should be submitted for examination by the USSR Congress of People's Deputies. The congress instructs the USSR Supreme Soviet to formulate a political assessment of the decision taken in the past to send Soviet troops into Afghanistan, and to report on that assessment at the second USSR Congress of People's Deputies. The formulation and implementation of the Soviet state's foreign policy should be under the people's control.

The congress declares before the whole world: The USSR's foreign policy course, based on the new thinking, is of a fundamental and permanent nature. It is not a tactical step, not a zigzag, not a concession to anyone, but a profoundly substantiated strategic line expressing the interests of the Soviet people and in accordance with the interests of all mankind. The congress again reaffirms the nationwide support for this course and comes out resolutely in favor of its continued active implementation.

The congress addresses all citizens of the country:

Compatriots! Before your eyes and with your participation we, the people's deputies, have discussed the problems of Soviet society's development. We perceived how serious these problems are and what efforts they will require of us all. We also perceived how great our common determination is to overcome the difficulties and enable the motherland to scale the heights of contemporary socioeconomic development. No one will do this for us. It is our country, our land, our socialist fatherland.

Our interests may be different, our opinions may not always coincide. But we agree that only revolutionary restructuring can lead to a renewed, humane, democratic socialism oriented in all its manifestations toward man. Such a society will draw its strength from the autonomy and creativity of the masses, and will offer them full scope.

We are on the right path. We understand the full importance of the consolidating role of the CPSU as the ruling party and the political vanguard of society. It began restructuring, and is its guarantor. It alone, renewing and improving itself, can head the movement toward the implementation of the people's aspirations.

The first USSR Congress of People's Deputies calls on you: Let us strengthen our will, redouble our efforts, and advance restructuring more vigorously, so that we can live better and become better!

APPENDIX B.5

FINDINGS OF THE COMMISSION TO INVESTIGATE THE CIRCUMSTANCES CONNECTED WITH EVENTS IN TBILISI CITY ON 9 APRIL 1989

On 24 December 1989 the Second Congress of People's Deputies heard the report of the commission set up by the First Congress of USSR People's Deputies to investigate the events which took place in Tbilisi 9 April 1989.

In accordance with the resolution that was adopted we publish the text of the statement for the press on the results of the investigation of the Tbilisi events.

Deputy Anatoliy Aleksandrovich Sobchak, chairman of the commission, was given the floor to report on the results of the investigation.

The commission on the investigation of the events which occurred in the city of Tbilisi, the speaker said, was set up by the First Congress and had 24 members. It included major scientists, famous writers and public figures, military personnel, representatives of the clergy and the new social movements of people's fronts, and Communists and nonparty people. In its work the commission was guided by the Congress' instructions—to fully investigate everything and to get down to the very roots, no matter what or who might be affected. As Comrade M.S. Gorbachev said at the First Congress, this is a major, special, far-reaching, political question concerning what, so to speak, the very foundations of our country's existence.

The events of 9 April 1989 must be examined in the context of the general processes of national and democratic movements now under way in the country. These processes were also under way in Georgia. In these conditions, the republic's party and state leadership was faced with a most important task: to justify its role as political vanguard and to act in the spirit of perestroyka. But the leadership of the Georgian Communist Party Central Committee failed to establish contacts and enter into a dialogue with public and, on the contrary, embarked on the path of confrontation with informal movements. This was especially vividly manifested during the November 1988 events during the discussion of constitutional amendments. It must be said that, according to many direct participants in these events, the November 1988 demonstrations in Tbilisi were perhaps on an even larger scale and the situation was even tenser than in April 1989. Even at that time, in November, the republic's leadership was inclined to resort to military force to terminate rallies and demonstrations in the city. Even then the country's leadership was faced with the question of the need to introduce a curfew and a special situation in the republic.

But a tragedy was avoided at the time because the country's leadership insisted on the need to resolve the prevailing situation by political means. Specifically, a beneficial role was played by M.S. Gorbachev's address to the Georgian people and the active and positive role played by the Georgian intelligentsia. We note, however, that the republic's leadership did not draw the proper conclusions from November's lessons, and this ultimately was one of the causes of the 9 April tragedy.

On 4 April 1989 Georgia's informal associations launched several days of unauthorized rallies outside Government House in Tbilisi. It must be emphasized that the holding of unauthorized rallies had become a general rule in the republic largely because the authorities did not authorize the holding of any rallies. Having failed to obtain permission to hold official rallies, representatives of the public and the informal organizations opted for holding unauthorized rallies.

It is sufficient to cite the following fact. Following the adoption of the well known legislative acts on the procedure for holding rallies and demonstrations in August 1988, the republic's local organs of power received 33 applications for permission to hold sundry mass events, but local soviet executive committees gave permission for only 6 such events. Despite this, 28 unauthorized rallies were held, and the holding of such rallies became the general rule from then on.

Numerous most diverse slogans were displayed at the rally organized 4 April, mainly along the following lines:
"End Discrimination Against Georgians in Georgia!", "Occupation Troops, Get Out of Georgia!", "We Demand Full Independence for Georgia!", "Long Live Free Georgia!", "Down With the Russian Empire!", "No to the Russian Communist Empire!", "USSR Is the Jail of the Peoples!", "Russian Invaders, Go Home!", "Down With the Turkish Agents!", and so on and so forth.

By 7 April, the republic's party leadership had already concluded that it was necessary to terminate the rally since it disrupted normal life in the city, normal transportation traffic, and the normal work of state institutions and various organizations.

The republic's leadership raised with the union leadership the question of the need to terminate this rally by means of force and of the need to introduce a curfew. That was the topic of telephone conversations with the CPSU Central Committee and other union organs. A coded message containing a detailed list of proposed measures and a request for consent for their implementation was sent to the CPSU Central Committee and was later read out at the First Congress.

A conference of several Central Committee secretaries and Politburo members, attended by the minister of defense, the KGB chairman, a deputy minister of internal affairs, and a number of senior officials from the party Central Committee was held in the CPSU Central Committee 7 April under the leadership of Comrade Ligachev, member of the Politburo and secretary of the CPSU Central Committee, and adopted a decision on the need to give assistance to the republic and to send units of Internal Troops and the Soviet Army there to protect installations and prevent possible disorders. When this decision was made, the utmost emphasis was placed on the need to solve questions by political means, and it was suggested that Internal Troops and Soviet Army subdivisions be sent in (this was said in a General Staff directive issued on that same day in the name of the defense minister) only in the event of the situation being exacerbated, only in the event of mass disturbances developing, for the purpose of controlling movement in and out of the city and protecting the most important state and public buildings in the city of Tbilisi. Consequently, subunits of Internal Troops and the Soviet Army and special militia subunits (OMON) started arriving in the city of Tbilisi already on 7 April. The republic's leadership was informed that it was necessary to act according to prevailing circumstances. Identical instructions were issued by the Ministry of Defense to General Rodionov, commander of the Transcaucasus Military District. Furthermore, General Kochetov, first deputy defense minister, arrived in Tbilisi from Armenia 7 April and attended all republic-level conferences which discussed questions associated with the need to terminate the unauthorized rally and made the appropriate decisions. It follows from this that the decision to terminate the rally by force was adopted at a sitting of the Georgian Communist Party Central Committee Bureau and was afterwards discussed at a meeting of the republic's party aktiv and supported by this aktiv (we would like to note the following detail: Gen Kochetov's arrival at this aktiv meeting was greeted with tumultuous applause by those taking part). This was followed by a sitting of the republic's Defense Council, which also discussed this question. But the decision on the specific operation plan and the specific timing of the operation was made by a narrow circle of persons including Comrades Patiashvili and Nikolskiy, former first and second secretary of the Communist Party Central Committee respectively, and by Generals Rodionov and Kochetov. It was decided that the action in question should take place at 0400 hours 9 April.

Several questions arise in connection with the subsequent development of events, and we must answer these questions. Why was it decided to terminate the rally at that precise time—early in the morning? Why were there so many women and adolescents among the rally participants? And finally, why was there such a large concentration of people in the square outside Government House at 0400 hours? Rough estimates speak of 8,000-10,000 people.

Answering the first question, it has to be said that the decision to terminate the rally actually at 0400 hours was made because that was the time when the number of people in the square had been at its lowest every day—just the hunger strikers (the rally was accompanied by a mass hunger strike with more than 100 young people taking part) and those who assisted and guarded them. Usually the number of people was no more than 200-300. These were the calculations on which the entire operation was planned.

But how come the crowd numbered 8,000-10,000 instead of 200-300? That was actually preceded by events associated with the entry of military subunits in the city and a show of military strength at noon on 8 April: Armored personnel carriers and infantry fighting vehicles carrying assault troops drove three abreast along the streets past participants in the rally, while three squadrons of combat helicopters overflew the city at low altitude. The population was thus warned that troops had entered the city and were ready for action. But this actually provoked exactly the opposite reaction.

It was after the show of strength had taken place that the number of people in the square started swelling, kept on swelling, and reached its peak by 0400 hours. Operation leaders Generals Rodionov and Yefimov, having come up against an unfamiliar situation, did not in any way amend the original operation plan. It can be boldly asserted that had the operation been amended in good time, had its procedure and timing been redefined, such serious and tragic consequences would not have ensued. It must be said in all fairness that, immediately before the operation's start, individual members of the Georgian Communist Party Central Committee Bureau were already making attempts to postpone the operation but these approaches were not heeded by the republic's leadership.

Finally, why were there so many women and adolescents in the square? The point is that the whole city knew of the forthcoming use of force and that the troops were meant to use force against the participants in the rally and disperse them. Therefore, family members and friends of the hunger strikers made their way to the square, reasoning that the larger the number of people, the less likely it would be that force would be used. The following episode occurred. A rather large number of women assembled in a rally outside Patiashvili's home in the afternoon of 8 April, demonstrated for several hours, demanded that someone come out to talk with them, and called for military force not to be used against the city residents. But since nobody came out for a heart-to-heart talk with them, the women moved from Patiashvili's home to the square and joined the rally.

I would like to draw your attention to the following fact. The entire rally, which had lasted several days around the clock, was conducted with the help of ordinary bullhorns. The square was equipped with a powerful public-address system but, for some unknown reason, nobody in the party leadership or the republic's state leadership thought of the possibility of switching on this public-address system and speaking to the people for however long it took for their words to be heeded.

And finally, there was one more opportunity, right before the operation started, for the republic's leaders and party officials to come out in the square and call on the rally participants to disperse and terminate the rally. I will not speak in detail about the way the operation to clear the square was conducted. It can only be said that the rally participants were cleared from the square in record time. The place where all that happened can only loosely be described as the square outside Government House. To all intents and purposes, it is not really a square but a widening of Rustaveli Prospekt, a pocket-handerkchief area where such a multitude of people had assembled.

It must be borne in mind that, at the time the rally was being terminated, all side streets along Rustaveli Prospekt were blocked off by trucks, buses, and trolleybuses. That had been done by the leaders of informal organizations the previous day in order to prevent a further movement of military equipment, as they explained to us subsequently. This was also one of the causes of the tragedy because the large numbers of people crammed within a small area were simply unable to quickly leave the square when the columns of soldiers moved in on them, and this resulted in a confrontation which subsequently developed into a real battle.

The making of wrong decisions, the inability to properly conduct the operation, the use, in addition to Internal Troops appropriately equipped and trained to some extent, though obviously not enough for this type of action, the bringing into play of companies of assault troops—all this led to the grave and tragic consequences which occurred as a result of this operation. [sentence as published]

I will not cite specific figures for the victims of the action in question. Different documents cite different figures. If we take just the data placed at our disposal by the Main Military Prosecutor's Office at various times—in May, June, or October for example—we will see that these data are completely different. We received different data on the number of victims among the civilian population, servicemen, and militia staffers from the Ministry of

Internal Affairs [MVD] and the Ministry of Health. Ultimately, it is up to the investigative organs and the courts to determine the precise number of victims, the specific nature of the wounds, and the nature of the injuries suffered by these victims.

I would like to raise a different matter today. Namely, the use of entrenching tools and toxic substances, of which so much was said by the periodical press in connection with these events. At this point I would like to draw attention to the following. Immediately after the events in question, representatives of the command and the commanders of subunits which took part in terminating the rally concealed the fact that entrenching tools, special means, and chemical substances had been used. This fact resulted in the loss of public trust in them and in all subsequent statements by representatives of the Armed Forces and the Internal Troops about the 9 April events. It has to be said that the use of chemical substances and special means like "Cheremukha" and "CS" gases was admitted only stage by stage. For example, it was only in early May that the military admitted to the use of "CS" gas, and the use of different types of "Cheremukha" gas was also admitted stage by stage. As for the use of entrenching tools, representatives of the military command continued to deny that entrenching tools had been used even until our commission members arrived back from Tbilisi, which was already at the end of June. However, as a result of the hearings of explanations and meetings with officers and soldiers of the paratroop regiment which took part in these events, we reliably established that entrenching tools had been used. This was said by many officers and soldiers of the paratroop regiment. They objectively could not but have been used in the prevailing situation. That was because, in direct violation of the defense minister's orders, a paratroop company was thrown right in the thick of it all, in the vortex of events unfolding in the square. Moreover, whereas Internal Troops soldiers were equipped in a certain fashion with bulletproof vests, shields, protective helmets, and rubber truncheons, the paratroopers had nothing of the sort. Their normal weapons were taken away from them prior to the start of the operation. Entrenching tools were their only means of attack and of protection against attack. These tools were used by the soldiers in the conditions in which they found themselves. I think that it is up to the courts and the investigative organs to determine the number of people who actually suffered from the use of entrenching tools. Our task is different—to establish the actual fact of the use of these tools and to condemn it. The specific number of people injured by them does not matter. Their use against the civilian population, against one's own people, is impermissible. The use of chemical means like "CS" gas is equally impermissible. The commission established that this means is not part of the Internal Troops weaponry, it is not an authorized means. The use of these means is a gross violation of current rules and regulations. There was an equally gross violation of instructions, standing orders, and rules governing the use of rubber truncheons and prohibiting the use of such truncheons against women and children, their use to beat people about the head, and so on. There were many such violations in the prevailing situation. In exactly the same way, many of the injured rally participants, as well as militia staffers and servicemen, spoke of "Cheremukha" special means being squirted from aerosol containers directly in the face of or close to rally participants, which is also categorically prohibited by instructions. It can thus be asserted that a multitude of violations were committed in the process of terminating the unauthorized rally, ranging from a violation of the defense minister's order prohibiting the use of servicemen to disperse the rally and authorizing their use only for guard duties, in order to guard installations, to a multitude of violations of standing orders, rules, and instructions in the process of terminating this rally. It is also necessary to mention the gross violations committed in the introduction of the curfew. The announcement that curfew was being introduced was made literally a few minutes before it was due to start. This was fraught with much unpleasantness for citizens who did not even suspect the existence of a curfew.

In the commission's opinion, the serious consequences ensuing after the introduction of the curfew, including the death of one person and the wounding of a number of citizens, were largely preconditioned by violations in the introduction of the curfew. One of the most serious questions arising in connection with the 9 April events in Tbilisi is the question of what caused the people's deaths. There are different conclusions and different opinions, including expert opinions, on the question of the causes of death. For this reason, to clarify this question, the commission invited a group of specialists, scientists in pathological anatomy and forensic medicine, and scientists known throughout the union and the world. They concluded that asphyxia (suffocation) was the immediate cause of the death of all who lost their lives in the square, with the exception of one case of serious craniocerebral injury. But conclusions differ as regards the type of suffocation which caused people's deaths, whether it was due to the use of special means or to crushing by the crowd. Specifically, a conclusion was drawn about the simultaneous effect of various factors, like the body being crushed in a tightly packed crowd and the inhalation of chemical substances. The inhalation of chemical substances coupled with the body being crushed aggravated the negative effect on the organism and this, in the specialists' opinion, caused the death of the victims.

The commission believes that the final conclusion on the causes of the victims' death is up to the investigative organs and the courts, which alone are in a position to evaluate the conclusions of the different specialists and different expert opinions and arrive at a verdict. However, regardless of the immediate causes of the victims' death, it is clear that the common causes of the tragic deaths of innocent people—mainly women, 16 of the 19 persons in question were women—were the violations and errors, the serious mistakes committed both when it was decided to terminate the rally and directly in the process of carrying out the operation to terminate the rally.

In conclusion, I would like to read out the conclusions and proposals contained in our commission's findings, in order to once more draw attention to the results of our commission's work.

On the basis of the available material, the Congress of USSR People's Deputies Commission arrives at the following conclusions.

The causes of the tragic events in the city of Tbilisi on 9 April 1989 are rooted in the fact that, in the conditions of democratization of our society's entire sociopolitical life, the republic's leadership proved unable to head the sharply and dynamically developing perestroyka processes in Georgia, to properly appraise the situation in the republic, and to make the appropriate decisions.

Political responsibility for the tragic consequences of the 9 April 1989 events in the city of Tbilisi rests with the leadership of the Georgian Communist Party Central Committee, primarily with Comrades Patiashvili and Nikolskiy, former first and second secretary of the Georgian Communist Party Central Committee respectively.

Political, moral, and other responsibility, including legal responsibility for their actions, must rest with Tsereteli, Gonsakhurdiya, Chenturiya, and other informal organization leaders who were the organizers of the unauthorized rally outside Government House and committed sundry breaches of public order when organizing and holding the rally: They called for noncompliance with legitimate demands by the authorities and, when a real threat emerged that armed force might be used, they took no measures to terminate the rally and did not attempt thus to prevent the tragic outcome of events.

In the commission's opinion, the decisions to send subunits of Internal Troops and the Soviet Army and special militia subunits to Georgia, formulated on the basis of defense minister's orders and USSR MVD orders following the 7 April 1989 conference in the CPSU Central Committee—to the extent that these orders concerned not simply the movement of troops but in fact the performance of actions introducing individual aspects of a special situation regime in the city of Tbilisi involving controls on movement in and out of the city and the installation of guards at the most important public and state buildings and other facilities—all these decisions were made in gross violation of the law.

The Georgian Council of Ministers order dated 8 April 1989 about clearing the square outside Government House of rally participants and implementing other measures to protect public order—and this, incidentally, is the only document adopted by a state organ in the case—is unlawful as regards the use of Internal Troops and Soviet Army servicemen since the current legislation gives no such powers to the republic's government. It must be noted, however, that this order was actually not performed by the organ to which it was addressed, namely the Georgian MVD.

Serious violations were committed when preparing and conducting the operation to clear the square and, in our opinion, these found expression in the fact that the operation plan was not amended to conform with the real existing situation. It was insufficiently worked out by subunit commanders, no reconnaissance was conducted, and the men, equipment, and facilities of the Tbilisi City Soviet Executive Committee Internal Affairs Administration and the Georgian MVD were not involved in the operation to the due extent. Contrary to the USSR defense minister's order, paratroop subunits were used not to guard installations but to clear the rally participants. Personal responsibility for the aforementioned violations and errors, which led to tragic consequences, rests with Generals Kochetov, Rodionov, and Yefimov. An appropriate share of responsibility also rests with Gorgodze, Georgian minister of internal affairs, who ducked the performance of his direct duties and whose actions resulted in a certain lack of coordination in the actions of servicemen and militia forces, which also had certain tragic consequences on that day. The commission perceives the need to institute criminal proceedings against the specific persons guilty of people's deaths or of causing grievous bodily harm.

It is also necessary to resolve the question about the liability of persons who violated Article 59 of the Internal Troops Combat Service Regulations, which prohibits the use of "Cheremukha" special means against women, adolescents, children, and in other specifically defined cases. The commission raises the question of the liability of persons who committed violations of the citizens' constitutionally guaranteed rights and legitimate interests in introducing and operating a curfew in the city of Tbilisi. Political, moral, and whenever necessary also legal responsibility must rest with the party and state organ officials who allowed the coverup or distortion of information about the 9 April 1989 events, as well as with commanders of Internal Troops subunits who tried to conceal the fact that special means of the "Cheremukha" variety and K-52 products containing "CS" gas had been used. The commission notes that the periodical press carried a lot of material which was based on rumors, conjectures, and false reports and presented a distorted picture of the events which actually took place. Some of that material was also used in official documents. For example, the commission found no proof of the existence and action of groups of fighters specially formed from among persons with extremist leanings in the square, nor of the claim that the first deaths and injuries occurred before the troops clashed with rally participants. Nor was there any confirmation of widespread reports about a multitude of people who supposedly disappeared without trace after 9 April, about the murder of women with entrenching tools, and so on. The commission notes that there are no facts to confirm Gen Rodionov's claim at the First Congress of USSR People's Deputies that a real threat that some of the republic's vitally important installations might be captured had emerged by 9 April. We studied secret KGB reports and official reports by the republican MVD, and not a single one of these or any other documents brought to our knowledge contains specific facts to this effect.

The commission notes that organized actions by former internationalist servicemen in Afghanistan, which helped to normalize the situation in the city, proved a positive factor in the settlement of conflicts between citizens and servicemen while the curfew was in effect in Tbilisi. The commission also notes that many militia staffers, performing their service duties in complex and extraordinary circumstances, not only assisted medical personnel in the evacuation of casualties but also gave any necessary assistance to injured and hunger-striking citizens.

In conclusion, the commission submits the following proposals for consideration by competent state organs and the Congress:

First. The party organs either consenting to, or making at union or republic level, the decision to send in the troops and conduct the operation in question, acted contrary to the 19th party conference decisions "On the Need To Demarcate the Functions of Party and State Organs." In a rule-of-law state, decisions by party organs at any level can become binding on organs of state power and administration, including the army, only after they are incorporated in a legal act by the competent state organ, either a law or a government resolution.

Second. The 9 April events in the city of Tbilisi demonstrated clear gaps in current legislation and the practice of making some most important state decisions on the introduction of special or emergency situations and curfews, and on the use of Soviet Army subunits to protect and restore pubic order inside the country. There is a need for clear and exhaustive legislative regulations governing the maintenance and procedures for the introduction of military (in the event of armed conflicts), special (in the event of internal disturbances), and emergency (in the event of natural disasters) situations which would rule out the possibility of any recurrence of the situation prevailing in Tbilisi, when the introduction of the curfew faced Soviet Army servicemen with the task of maintaining public order, which ought to be performed only by MVD forces.

It appears expedient to examine the question of increasing the strength of the Internal Troops and staffing them primarily on professional principles. It is necessary to legislatively define the procedure and mechanism for using Internal Troops subunits under republic and union subordination.

Third. It is necessary to legislatively prohibit the use of the Soviet Army to put down mass disturbances, making provision for the possible use of army subunits for this purpose only by way of exception, in cases directly envisaged by the law, and in each individual case by decision of the chairman of the USSR Supreme Soviet with subsequent notification to the USSR Supreme Soviet.

Fourth. There is a need to legislatively enshrine the rights and duties of militia and Internal Troops personnel in the performance of their duties involving the termination of unlawful actions and mass disturbances.

Fifth. There is also a need to legislatively enshrine the powers of parliamentary commissions set up by the Congress of People's Deputies and the USSR Supreme Soviet. Specifically, it is necessary to provide for officials' liability in the event of supplying commissions with deliberately false information. Unfortunately, we came up against this in our work.

And last. The commission draws attention to the need to reinforce the investigative group on the case in question by recruiting officials from the Prosecutor's Office of the Georgian Soviet Socialist Republic and other republics and appointing a special prosecutor for this case, in other words making this a comprehensive investigation and taking other measures for the earliest possible conclusion of preliminary investigations into the case instituted in connection with the 9 April 1989 events in the city of Tbilisi.

Finally, on the commission's behalf, I would like to call on people's deputies not to perceive events in Tbilisi as an event discrediting the Soviet Army and pitting the army against the people. Unfortunately, in the recent past we have only too often come across situations when, as soon as some official or party or state functionary is assailed, this is identified with the party itself. In just the same way, I do not think that it is necessary to identify any wrong decisions made by some military commander, leader, or official with the army. And I do not think that events in Tbilisi ought to serve as an excuse for pitting the people against the army.

Source: *Izvestiya*, 30 December 1989, p. 2; in FBIS-SOV 90-006 (9 January 1990), 71-76.

APPENDIX B.6
RESOLUTION OF THE USSR CONGRESS OF PEOPLE'S DEPUTIES ON THE REPORT OF THE COMMISSION TO INVESTIGATE THE CIRCUMSTANCES CONNECTED WITH EVENTS IN TBILISI CITY ON 9 APRIL 1989

Having heard the conclusions of the commission for investigating the events that took place in the city of Tbilisi on 9 April, 1989, the USSR People's Deputies Congress notes that the tragedy connected with the death of innocent people reflected the inability of the republic's former leadership, under conditions of a serious aggravation of the sociopolitical situation in the Georgian Soviet Socialist Republic, to relieve the prevailing situation through political means, as well as serious miscalculations and errors committed at every level of all-union and republican leadership in making and implementing the decision about putting an end to the unauthorized rally in the square outside the government building. The congress draws attention to the absence of clear legislation regulating the procedure and practice for using the armed forces to resolve internal conflicts.

The USSR Congress of People's Deputies resolves:

1. To take cognizance of the conclusion of the USSR Congress of People's Deputies commission for investigating the events which took place in Tbilisi on 9 April 1989.

2. To condemn the use of force against the participants in the 9 April 1989 demonstration in Tbilisi.

3. To instruct the USSR Supreme Soviet Presidium to dispatch the proposals of the commission for investigating the events which took place in Tbilisi on 9 April 1989 for the consideration and decision of the appropriate bodies, and to ensure control [kontrol] over their execution.

To prepare the text of the report on the results of the investigation into the Tbilisi events for the press, taking account of the discussion which has taken place.

[Signed] M. Gorbachev, chairman of the USSR Supreme Soviet.
The Kremlin, Moscow.
24 December 1989.

Source: TASS International Service, 24 December 1989; in FBIS-SOV 89-246 (26 December 1989), 33-34.

APPENDIX B.7
REPORT OF A. N. YAKOVLEV, CHAIRMAN OF THE COMMISSION ON THE POLITICAL AND LEGAL ASSESSMENT OF THE 1939 SOVIET-GERMAN TREATY OF NON-AGGRESSION, TO THE SECOND CONGRESS OF USSR PEOPLE'S DEPUTIES
23 DECEMBER 1989

I will begin with some historical information: On 23 August 1939 the Soviet-German Nonaggression Treaty was signed and on 31 August it was ratified by the USSR Supreme Soviet. On 24 August it was published, and on 24 Setember the exchange of the ratified documents took place. The existence of the secret protocol was first mentioned in 1946 at the Nuremburg trials. On 23 May 1946 the protocol was published by the SAINT LOUIS POST DISPATCH newspaper and in 1948 it appeared in a book published in the United States "The National Socialist Party of Germany and the Soviet Union 1939-41." The public did not know the contents of the protocol before this; neither did the USSR Supreme Soviet or the party's Central Commitee Politburo. Since 1939 no information concerning this was published here. The reasons for this silence are understandable. The essence of the secret protocol boils down to the fact that Stalin and Hitler divided up spheres of influence, which included neighboring sovereign states.

All this cost us dearly, both politically and morally. Until now all kinds of hypotheses have been devised as to how events would have developed in Europe without the treaty and the protocol. One particular question is whether war would have begun on 1 September 1939. Public opinion even today is being fed with ideas to the effect that certain aspects of the contemporary situation in Europe—moreover concerning not only the Soviet Union—look as if they were formed on the basis of, or under the influence of, the treaty of 23 August 1939 and the secret protocols of August and September.

All this spurred the First Congress of People's Deputies to create on 2 June 1989 a commission of 26 People's Deputies. I want to stress that we touched only on 1939, but not the following years. I stress this because many statements of various sorts and notes concerning 1940 and the following years were received by the commission. So I would like to stress once more that the competence of the commission is confined to 1939, and it is not competent to answer other questions or make judgements on events.

Such is background history. The commission came to an agreement on the conclusions, but I will say straight away that it was not easy to reach a consensus. There were many arguments and clashes of opinions, but they did not undermine the general constructive atmosphere of discussions. Notwithstanding all the variety of approaches, viewpoints, and emotional nuances, the striving to bring to light episodes of the past which are beyond contention did prevail. At the same time, there was the striving to interpret the prewar reality comprehensively, bearing in mind its real interconnections and the circumstances which bound it.

Nor were matters made easier by the fact that for a long time our official stenographic record avoided shedding light on many pages of the USSR's foreign policy during the whole post-October period.

Of course, there are conventions and restrictions here linked with the interests of third countries, but there are also a lot of things that lie under a bushel by virtue of the inertia of the stereotypes that came into being. At any rate, some key documents from the Soviet archives relating to the subject under discussion became available only very recently.

In passing let me observe that the current opinion that Britain and the United States allegedly revealed their file of documents without reservation is no more than a myth. London, for example, has established that a part of the government archives, considerable in its size and extremely important for grasping what happened, will remain secret until the year 2017. And Washington has not named any time restrictions whatsoever for a number of documents.

Nevertheless, the stock of reliable data that has already been accumulated makes it possible to reproduce a picture of the way in which mankind and individual states slipped into World War II and to make sufficient conclusions upon the basis of an analysis of the totality of the facts.

Some more observations of a preliminary nature. First, in embarking upon an analysis and assessment of the past we are understandably not in a position even for a moment to tear from our hearts the events that followed 1939. Our conscience is still tormented by grief for the millions and millions of workers and peasants, scientists, and poets who died and who are not with us today.

Nor does the anger against fascism and contempt for those who demonstrated their inability to curb the murderers abate. Here it is not easy to keep strictly to the clear channel of the facts and not give in to the onslaught of natural feelings. But it is too easy to reject something or condemn it. One must also understand—understand how agreements, deals, and compacts came into being, what moved those who inspired and created them—to understand in order to protect oneself from a repetition of what has already been gone through.

As applied to the past, time has stopped. It is possible to grasp any event, regardless of the emotional train that it pulls behind it, if the analysis of it is carried out in the specific context of historic development. But we often find ourselves in the power of a priori views, not of facts; the prisoners of schemes that are to our liking; tempted to whitewash what is one's own and blacken what belongs to someone else; or, what is no better, of ideologizing history to the extent that it loses its true content. Only a sober, honest analysis, devoid of blinding emotions and prejudice that lowers true worth, is capable of pacifying a troubled sea of passions.

Battles for truth are the motive force of history. The historical conscience is called upon to protect progress from equivocation and from the diabolical temptation to play hide-and-seek with the past. We would be committing a double error if we attempted to sweep inconvenient themes under the carpet. Justifying your own degradation by the sins of others is not the way to honest self-knowledge and renewal but to a lack of historical awareness.

Second, during the process of the commission's work we once again became convinced of how far the world has come over the past half century, of how strong is the difference between the political, legal, and moral norms of the contemporary world and of that in which Europe lived 5 decades ago. All of this had to be taken into consideration when we were delving into the past in the hope of returning to the politics of the present day. The main thing was not to confuse outward appearances with the real essence.

Of course, this report does not aspire to full coverage of the prewar period. Its logic and contents are bound up to the maximum degree with the events of 1939, although it is obvious to any unbiased person that it was far from being a suprise at the time. Therefore, without making a digression into the past, it is difficult to reach an objective assessment of what ensued. Everything of which I shall proceed to speak is based on documentary sources. The problem itself and its numerous nuances require detailed and sometimes minute analysis of the circumstances. And the congress undoubtedly expects well-constructed arguments from the commission.

So, what was the international situation in which the Soviet-German Nonaggression Treaty came into being?

What occurred immediately prior to its being concluded? What were the aims of the treaty in the plans of its creators and initiators? It is impossible to find unambiguous answers to this. In evaluating the agreement we cannot fail to dwell upon at least three circumstances: the suddenness of the turn-around in relations with the fascist regime; the secret accords with it which affected the interests of third countries; and the concealment of the true content and meaning of the agreement from Soviet people, the party, and the constitutional bodies of authority.

How and why did all of this become possible? Germany's attack on Poland on 1 September 1939 was the start of the tragedy, but it was also the finale of a policy towards German imperialism, a course which, as a rule, was pursued without the Soviet Union and frequently against its interests. This was the root of the historical perfidy. British Prime Minister Baldwin declared in 1936: We are all aware of Germany's wish to move eastwards. If he—that is Hitler—were to move east, I wouldn't be heartbroken. If it were to come to a fight in Europe, I would like it to be a fight between the Bolsheviks and the Nazis. Paris subsequently came to echo what London was saying. This position combined into one the policy of appeasement of aggressors and indulgence of Nazism's plans for *lebensraum*.

This led to the annexation of Austria and the betrayal of Czechoslovakia in Munich in 1939. In sacrificing Czechoslovakia, London at that time considered that it had bought Berlin's promise to never again wage war against Britain and to remove possible sources of disagreement by means of consultations. That is parenthetical.

France, the other participant in the Munich tragedy, drew up a similar agreement with the Reich. For Paris the Soviet-French mutual assistance treaty virtually ceased to exist.

The Munich agreement radically altered the situation in Europe, substantially strengthened Germany's position, crushed the beginnings of the system of collective security, and opened the way to aggression on a European-wide scale. The Munich pact was no hasty improvisation: It continued the political line charted by the Treaty of Locarno of 1925 and the 1933 Quadripartite Pact. The small and medium-sized countries of Europe realized that the democracies had betrayed them, and in fear they began to lean towards Germany.

The USSR found itself isolated internationally. Taking account of the support for Munich from the United States, the direct participation of Poland and Hungary in the dismemberment of Czechoslovakia, and Japan's approval of the agreement, the Soviet leadership could not but think of the threat of a single anti-Soviet coalition being created. Hasty decisions and a mystifying irrationality in perception of reality were a widespread disease at that time. The fact that London and Paris hailed Germany as a peacemaker guaranteeing the democracies comfort and tranquility for years and decades to come, was taken by Hitler to be a frank signal for a battle by force for hegemony in Europe.

After Munich there was in effect no question of whether or not there would be war: it was a matter of something quite different, namely of who would become the next victim, and when. The most amazing thing, perhaps, which confuses many people even today, is that the Western powers knew in detail about Germany's preparations for an armed encounter. They knew, yet thought that the Nazis would not encroach upon the interests of the Western democracies until they had settled accounts with the Soviet Union. They clung to their delusions even in the spring of 1939 when the Hitlerites occupied the remnants of Czechoslovakia and seized Klaipeda, and Italy attacked Albania.

What, from the point of view of Soviet interests, was the signifiance of the annexation of Austria, the transfer of Czechoslovakia to the control of Germany, the Nazi penetration of Hungary, Romania, and Bulgaria, the activization of the Reich's military intelligence services in Estonia, Latvia, Lithuania, and Finland if one takes these as a whole rather than separately? Soviet foreign policy was presented with the following basic possibilities:

- a) to try and conclude an alliance between the USSR, Britain, and France that might impede the aggressor;
- b: establish mutual understanding with neighboring states which also found themselves threatened.
- and c: in the event that it was impossible to avoid war with Germany, to try to avoid a war on two fronts—in the West and in the Far East.

Work began officially on the first possibility in March-April 1939, when the USSR tried to involve the Western powers in cooperation aimed at averting aggression. Second, during the visits of Potemkin, then deputy minister of foreign affairs, to Turkey and Poland in April-May 1939 and the diplomatic actions in March 1939 aimed at showing the governments of Latvia and Estonia that the USSR had an interest in averting aggression in the Baltic, the question of normalizing relations with Germany remained open. In the diplomatic documentation of the USSR for 1937 and 1938, no evidence has been found to suggest a Soviet intention to come to an understanding with Berlin. On Germany's part, from the end of 1938 or the beginning of 1939, soundings began of the possibilities of improving relations with the USSR. Hitler called this setting the scene for a new Rapallo stage. Judging by the documentary data, the Soviet leadership had reliable information of military preparations by the Nazi regime, and also of the line of conduct of the Western powers. For example, information on the contents of Hitler's conversation with Chamberlain on 15 September 1938 reached Stalin on the following day. The available materials gave reason to believe that if Germany's aggression against the USSR became inevitable, it would be carried out either in alliance with Poland, with a Polish rear loyal to the Reich, or with the submission of Poland. In any event, it would be with the use of the territory of Lithuania, Latvia, and Estonia.

The Weiss operation, the plan for the attack upon Poland which was confirmed on 11 April 1939, presupposed the seizure of Lithuania, the inviolability of which had in no way been guaranteed by Britain and France.

The appetites of the Reich were not satisfied by Lithuania, however. As early as 16 March 1939 the Latvian envoy in Berlin was told that his country should follow Germany, and then the Germans—and I quote—would not compel it by force to come under the protection of the Fuehrer. Speaking to the Generalitaet in May 1939, Hitler set the task of solving the Baltic problem as well as the Polish one.

As in other similar cases, Berlin had a minimum and a maximum program. If the West surrendered Poland to it without a fight, as it had previously surrendered Czechoslovakia, Hitler could stretch out the implementation of the Weiss plan time-wise; that data is available.

However, the leadership of the Reich understood that the run of easy victories was coming to an end, particularly when Poland, which had assisted during the Anschluss of Austria and the seizure of Czechoslovakia, became more stubborn. Indeed, as long as other people's territories were the object of the bargaining, Poland's Minister of Foreign Affairs Beck and those who thought like him did not shun dialogue with Berlin. But when they were invited to give up Danzig to Germany and take out of Polish lands a transportation corridor to Eastern Prussia, the desire to share the Soviet Ukraine diminished. The Nazis' promise to reserve for Poland an exit to the Black Sea, with Odessa in the bargain, also stopped being so very attractive.

The British military proved to Chamberlain that the threat of Nazi aggression was no myth and that military cooperation with the Soviet Union was the most expedient means of countering it. The relevant documents for this exist. In reply Chamberlain said he would rather resign than enter into an alliance with the USSR. Describing this stance on the part of his government, (?Collier), a member of the staff of Britain's Foreign Office wrote: London has no desire to link itself with the Soviet Union, but it wants to give Germany an opportunity to carry out aggression in the East at Russia's expense.

In some contemporary publications, particularly in the most recent months, one encounters a lot of complaint about the inflexibility of Soviet diplomacy, about missed alternatives, and so on. That kind of thing possibly did occur. More likely, even, it evidently did occur. But something else, too, ensues from the documents. Whenever the USSR moved to meet the Western powers, instructions were given to the British and French delegates not to record a drawing together of the positions but to build up demands and aggravate the disproportionate nature of the conditions and thereby block an agreement. Finally, on 11 July Britain decided to reject the Soviet Government's invitation to sign political and military agreements simultaneously.

At the sittings of the Chamberlain cabinet, where the position of the British delegation at the military talks in Moscow was worked out in July 1939, it was determined that the main thing was to draw out the time: the agreement itself—and I am quoting the Foreign Secretary Halifax—is not as important as it appeared at first sight.

Extensive British and French documentation covering the period from May to August 1939 shows that the Chamberlain cabinet found partnership with the USSR undesirable and military cooperation impossible. Although the British leaders knew precisely from Canaris, the chief of the Nazi military espionage service, that the attack on Poland had been fixed for the last week in August, the British delegation at the Moscow military negotiations was instructed to engage in arguments about wording until October, if possible.

The Anglo-French views were supported by the American representatives in Europe. The U.S. Ambassador in London, Kennedy, was convinced that the Poles had to be cast to the mercy of fate and the Nazis given the possibility to implement their aim in the East. A conflict between the USSR and Germany, to quote his words, would bring great advantage to the whole Western world. The U.S. Ambassador in Berlin, Wilson, also considered an attack by Germany on Russia with the tacit agreement of the Western powers and even with their approval to be the best alternative. The Soviet Union is now being reproached because it did not manage to induce the Polish Government to cooperate, conceding that part of the work to London and Paris. But even in a situation where there remained only a few days before the German attack, Poland did not want to hear anything about any cooperation with the USSR. On 20 August 1939 Beck declared: We do not have a military agreement with the USSR and we do not need such an agreement.

On the eve of the 50th anniversary of the attack by Germany on Poland, many hypotheses were put forward as to how events would have developed if the Soviet Union had adopted the tactics of Britain and France calculated to create an appearance of activity by the three powers in connection with the agreement, although there was no such thing, to act in response should there be aggression by Germany. Diametrically opposed views are being expressed on this subject. One of them says that there would not have been a war at all. Others imagine that in such a case the USSR could have fallen into the whirlpool of war as early as 1939 in which Britain and France, in the most optimistic scenario, would only have figured as our allies.

Now, of course, it is difficult to surmise. History does not recognize the subjunctive mood. History has already happened. Even suppositions are not subject to normal logic, insofar as the behavior of all the subjects of the policy could not be predicted. One cannot get rid of the impression that it was players and not politicians who were play acting on the stage of history. One thing is clear: A sense of responsibility, not to mention wisdom, was lacking in all of them, for which mankind paid a cruel price. In the same context one could examine this question: Was there a real threat of an attack by fascist Germany on our country in 1939? Naturally, an answer to this goes beyond the framework of the possibiltiies and aims of our commission. It is for scholars to answer. No real analysis of this problem was given either then or later. Nevertheless, the documents say that Soviet policy was then built more often on tactical reports than on profound strategic computations.

The question of Hitler's readiness for aggression against the USSR in 1939 has at least three aspects to it. Was

Germany objectively ready for war? Did it consider its military machine ready? And was the threat of an invasion taken as probable by the Soviet leadership?

Only the latter can be answered with confidence. Undoubtely, yes. It can be assumed that this perception was remedied in Stalin's psychological make-up by the hope that Hitler might get bogged down in the European theater of combat, which probably had an influence on his capacity to see and assess the possible alternatives objectively. It is, of course, difficult to talk of these facts even slightly categorically, but we are within our rights in allowing for their occurrence. Allegations that the Reich would not have begun the Polish campaign if the nonaggression pact with the USSR had not existed cannot be proven.

To refute these assertions one can cite more than one statement by Hitler himself. Moreover, Germany had gone too far in its preparations for war, especially by the middle of August, for the Fuehrer to sound the retreat without serious political risk to himself. The argument of those who adhere to the view that Stalin had exaggerated the threat of war amounts to the fact that in August 1939 there was no plan of military action against our country prepared at the German General Staff. However, to start with, this was only discovered after 1945, and second, at that time there were no plans for operations against Britain and France either. The staffs received the task of preparing such plans on 10 October 1939, once the Western powers had rejected Hitler's proposal to make peace.

Third, the pause from preparations for combat action on the Western front is not without its peculiar subtext. In the euphoria of a quick victory over Poland, Hitler for some time nursed the idea of breaking off the recent nonaggression treaty with the Soviet Union and making a sudden attack on our country. Fourth, the members of the Reich's General Staff sometimes needed only weeks to transfer conceptual developments into operational directives.

In analyzing the alternatives of 1939, it should be borne in mind that the Soviet leadership did have information on the content of the directives determining the line of the British and French delegations in war negotiations with us. Nor was the fact of the backstage contacts maintained between London and Berlin top secret. A careful reading of the documents reveals a fairly simple game. Berlin tried to get around us or, on the contrary, withdraw its advances, in precise correspondence with each twist in the Anglo-French-Soviet talks. So, after the first sounding out of Soviet intentions and Molotov's cautious reaction to the German appeal on 20 May, Ribbentrop gave the order to retire. However, it took only the differences with regard to the guarantees for the Baltic states that emerged at the tripartite talks in Moscow for the Germans to get moving.

In order to fix talks on an Anglo-Franco-Soviet military convention, it was sufficient for Berlin to suggest the idea on 26 July of renewing the Treaty on Neutrality of 1926, and to state its readiness to respect the inviolabilty of the Baltic states and to come to an agreement on finding a balance of their mutual interests. But when a date was fixed for opening military talks in Moscow, Ribbentrop immediately invited Astakhov, the charge d'affaires ad interim of the USSR in Berlin, to see him and he came out directly in favor of delimiting Soviet and German interests from the Baltic to the Black Sea. These ideas were repeated the next day, 3 August, by Ambassador Schulenburg in a conversation in Moscow.

The period from 26 July to 3 August 1939 is a landmark of fundamental importance. It was at this time that contacts were being stepped up in all areas, in both number and content. It was at this time that pressure from preliminary positions and real circumstances was growing, which led to the necessity for the final choice: Was there to be an accord or not? If there was to be, then with whom? With the Western democracies or with fascist Germany? It was at this time that those hazardous elements of the political game, which were in accordance with the psychology of the main actors in the drama, and as a result predetermined the appearance and essence of the secret protocol, were introduced into the political game.

How did events develop at this point and up to the opening of Soviet-German talks? The first move was made by the German side. For the first time Berlin legalized the idea of a treaty for a new settlement of interstate relations with the USSR, abandoning its slighting of our national interests. Let me remind you that after the coming to power of the Nazis, Germany sought to get the Soviets ostracized wherever it could. So the Soviet Union did not have any realistic alternative to cooperation with Britain and France before the beginning of August 1939, and had nothing to set against that cooperation. It is indicative that even after Ribbentrop's revelations, the Soviet side did not change its tactics. For another whole week it limited itself to listening to the German proposals, and Schulenburg was constantly sending telegraphs to Berlin about the profound mistrust by the Soviet Government of Germany, and its—and I quote—resolve to come to an agreement with Britain and France.

Now we know that Stalin suspected everyone and everything. His mistrust of Hitler was no less than his mistrust of Chamberlain or Daladier. And not only as a result of his personal vigilance: His concept of imperialist war focused on the lack of difference between the two groups that were competing on the world arena, seeing in each of them first and foremost an aspiration to remake the world and destroy the Soviet Union.

During the fateful days of August this concept played no small role. It is unlikely that Stalin was deceived about the real intentions of London and Paris, but it looks as if he was afraid of missing a possible chance for reaching an agreement. According to the testimony of (Dmitrov) on 7 September 1939, that is, 7 days after war began, Stalin, having referred to the talks with the Western powers, noted: We preferred accords with the so-called democratic countries, and for this reason conducted talks, but the English and the French wanted to treat us as farm laborers and at the same time to pay nothing for this. We, of course, would not become farm laborers, even less for nothing in return.

Schnurre, an official from the German Foreign Ministry, declared to Astakhov on 26 July 1939: Let Moscow think about what England has to offer it. At best, participation in a European war and hostility with Germany is hardly a desirable goal for Russia. But what can we offer? Neutrality and nonparticipation in the possible European conflict, and if Moscow wants it, a German-Soviet accord on mutual interests. What specifically was meant? Berlin replied: Germany's renunciation of claims on the Ukraine, of claims for dominance in the Baltics and plans for expansion in those regions in Eastern and southeastern Europe where the USSR has appreciable interests.

Soviet intelligence reported the fact that Germany's attack on Poland might occur at the end of August or the beginning of September to the leadership during the first days of July 1939. News was received from Ribbentrop's immediate entourage that in Hitler's opinion the Polish issue really must be resolved. Hitler said, I quote: What will occur if there is a war with Poland will exceed and will eclipse the Huns. This lack of restraint in German military operations is essential for demonstrating to the states of the east and southeast by example of the annihilation of Poland what it means under present day conditions to contradict the wishes of the Germans and provoke Germany into bringing in military forces. [end quote]

On 7 August 1939 it was reported to Stalin that Germany would be in a position to begin armed operations any day after 25 August. On 11 August 1939 the situation was considered by the Politburo of the VKP(B) [All-Russian Communist Party (of Bolsheviks)] Central Committee. Not without taking into account the reports about Hitler's attempt to restore a direct link with Chamberlain and the pessimistic predictions concerning the Moscow military talks, it was recognized as expedient to join in the official discussion of the issues raised by the Germans and to inform Berlin about this.

As a result, the Soviet-German negotiations commenced with a meeting between Molotov and Schulenburg in Moscow on 15 August 1939. The Germans proposed either the confirmation of a neutrality treaty or the conclusion of a nonaggression treaty. Stalin settled for the latter option. The final stage of the Soviet-German negotiations does not lend itself easily to reconstruction, comrades. No shorthand records were made. All the preliminary drafts brought to Moscow by Ribbentrop were destroyed, on his instruction. It is known that Von Ribbentrop set off for the meeting on 23 August in complete doubt as to the outcome of his mission, although he had Hitler's authority to satisfy any conceivable demands from Moscow. Preparatory Soviet material on the treaties has not yet been revealed to exist: It has not been found in the archives. All that is known is that it was not intended at the start to make the document of intent secret. Evidently, there was no need to do so, for Molotov was talking about things which were fairly well-known: joint guarantees of the independence of the Baltic states, mediation by the Germans aimed at stopping Japanese military actions against the USSR, and the development of German-Soviet economic relations. No kind of territorial claims affecting Poland or anyone—and especially no sort of questions of the fate of any specific country—were raised at that stage. Hitler offered more than Stalin was expecting.

Is there an explanation for that? Some sort of light may be shed by the directive of the Comintern Executive Committee of 22 August 1939, the contents of which became known to Berlin. It noted that the USSR was entering into negotiations with Germany on the subject of concluding a nonaggression treaty, intending to impel Britain and France to get down to business at the negotiations on a military alliance with our country. By all appearances, Hitler decided to render worthless at a stroke any British and French maneuvers, seeking to prompt Stalin to burn his bridges. The stage favored the show performed by the Nazis. On 19 and 20 August 1939 Stalin received documentary confirmation that Britain, France, and Poland did not intend to change their positions. Evidently, Stalin hoped to use the nonaggression treaty to influence Britain and France, but he miscalculated. After the signing of the treaty, the Western powers lost all constructive interest in us.

Was it possible to limit the negotiations with Berlin to just the conclusion of the nonaggression treaty? The analysis shows that it certainly was. In the form in which the treaty was signed on 23 August 1939, it would have supplemented the extensive catalogue of settlements which were familiar in world politics. Germany had by that time exchanged similar mutual obligations, drawn up in different ways, with, in particular, Poland in 1934, Britain and France in 1938, and Lithuania, Latvia, and Estonia in 1939. The conclusion of this treaty, obviously, altered the configuration of forces and enabled Berlin to close up one of the unknown quantities in the complex political equation. That is how it was.

But it would not be fair to break off the thought here. Stalin, for all his imperial ways, could not fail to understand the amoral and explosive nature of the secret deal with Hitler. Even after the war Stalin and Molotov covered up the traces of the existence of the secret protocol. The original of the protocol has not been discovered in our archives.

According to Khrushchev's testimony, Stalin's reasoning was as follows: A game is being carried out here, a game of who is going to outwit whom, who is going to deceive whom. And he added: I deceived them. By all appearances Stalin was not embarrassed by the price he paid in betraying the lofty moral foreign policy principles laid down by Lenin. Along with the German wording of the protocol, he accepted postulates like spheres of interest, territorial and political reconstruction, and other things which until then had been the offspring of the politics of imperialist divisions and redivisions of the world.

Hitler intended an exclusively territorial role for the second Rapallo, that of excluding the USSR as a potential enemy of Germany for up to 2 years. It is not clear why Stalin failed to attach importance to information received through various channels that in 24 months at most the Nazis would trample their obligations and attack the Soviet Union. As recently as July 1939, Soviet intelligence warned that the pretence of goodneighborliness toward the USSR and, in particular, respect for its interests in the Baltic, were intended to last just for a 2-year period. This was the same time for which the Germans concluded all their economic agreements with us. Stalin did not want to investigate these facts thoroughly.

In giving his wording to the protocol, Hitler was preparing the ground for bringing the Soviet Union into a collision not only with Poland, but with Britain and France, too. Thank God things did not go that far! Although at times our country was within a hair's breadth of a turn of events of that kind, particularly after units of the Red Army entered western Belorussia and the western Ukraine. All of this could have happened had the Soviet units not stopped on the Curzon line which, under the Treaty of Versailles, was determined as the eastern frontier of Poland.

Let us return, however, to the subject of 23 August. Hitler was not inspired by the scheme for the protocol set out by Molotov because it remained unclear how the Soviet side would react if Germany was to be on the western frontier of the USSR instead of Poland. Judging by intelligence material, the uncertainty of the Soviet position moved Hitler not to overstrain the neutrality of the USSR by unfolding the Ukrainian problem. Moreover, in August the Nazis let it be understood that they sympathized with the desire of the Ukrainians and Belorussians to live in reunited families.

The fact that the restoration of justice with regard to the Ukraine and Belorussia took place alongside social and political reconstruction in other lands did not worry Stalin. Let me summarize what has been said: Unlike the assessment of the secret protocols on which the commission was fully united, various opinions were expressed regarding the treaty itself. First: that in the specific conditions of the day the treaty was legitimate in political terms. The policies of Germany and Japan and the position of the Western democracies did not leave the Soviet Union with any other option. The leadership of the USSR was obliged to take measures to guarantee the country's safety, even if only to delay the start of the war and make use of the time gained to strengthen the economy and defense. Another point of view is that Stalin undertook to conclude a nonaggression treaty for other reasons. His main motive was not the agreement itself but what became the subject of the secret protocols, i.e. the possibility of taking troops into the Baltic republics, Poland, and Bessarabia and even, in the long-term, into Finland. That is, imperialist ambitions were the central motive behind the treaty. By weighing up the components of the past and drawing lessons for the future, the Commission of the Congress of USSR People's Deputies for a Political and Legal Assessment of the Soviet-German Nonaggression Treaty of 23 August 1939 has reached the following conclusions:

In itself, the treaty did not, from the legal viewpoint, go beyond the framework of agreements adopted at that time and did not violate the domestic legislation or international obligations of the USSR. It lost legal force on 22 June 1941. All Soviet-German agreements in existence at that time were completely erased by the first volley of fire at dawn on 24 June. [corrects himself] I'm sorry, on 22 June 1941. This is not just our position, it is an accepted norm of international law. As for postwar Europe, it was built on international legal norms which have different sources, as is reflected primarily in the United Nations Charter and the Final Act of the all-European conference of 1975. It is another matter that Stalin and some people in his entourage could, even at that time, toy with imperialist designs alien to the principles of socialism. This, however, goes beyond the framework of the actual treaty as an international legal document. In the same way, the assessment has nothing to do with those people to whom Stalin entrusted himself, by all accounts, after the conclusion of the 1939 treaty, nor with those who did not allow the obtained breathing space of peace to be made use of properly, who, to a large extent, demobilized and disoriented the anti-fascist forces, which could not fail to damage the subsequent struggle against Hitlerism and its allies.

At the same time, it is clear that with the conclusion of the treaty some deep-seated elements in the democratic attitude as a whole were violated. Neither the communists nor the overwhelming majority of the other left-wing forces and movements of prewar days—without even knowing about and without suspecting the existence of the secret protocols—were willing to admit the very possibility of an accord with Hitler about anything at all. Failing to take into account the frame of mind and the ethical convictions of the public means taking up positions which, sooner or later, will turn into moral and ideological-social losses, which is what actually happened.

A political and legal assessment of the Soviet-German nonaggression treaty is given in the conclusion of the commission and in the draft decision put forward for the attention of the congress. This is the result of an analysis of the facts and a synthesis of opinions which the members of the commission believe adequately convey the particular features of the extremely contradictory situation of that time and our attitude toward it from the stance of the new political thinking.

The commission has also formulated assessments with regard to the protocol. These are as follows.

First: The secret additional protocol of 23 August 1939 did exist, although the original has been discovered neither in the Soviet nor in foreign archives. Copies in the possession of the Governments of the USSR and the FRG can, at the level of present-day knowledge, be considered reliable. Indeed, subsequent events unfolded precisely according to the protocol.

Second: The initial protocol was compiled in the German Ministry of Foreign Affairs and accepted by Stalin and Molotov with small amendments. The Soviet participants in the talks—and this is not to their credit—forgot their original desires for two-fold guarantees of the independence of the Baltic countries. They did not insist upon Germany's willingness to bring Japan to reason being reflected in the protocol, being satisfied with oral promises by Ribbentrop to that effect.

Third: The political and state bodies [instantsiya] of the Soviet Union were not informed of the fact that the protocol was being prepared. Molotov did not have properly formulated authority to sign it. The protocol was taken out of the ratification procedures and was not confirmed by the country's legislative or executive bodies.

Fourth: Having been adopted in circumvention of the internal laws of the USSR and in violation of its treaty liabilities to third countries, the protocol in the juridical sense was an illegal document from the very first and was a deal that expressed the intentions of the physical forces that signed it.

Fifth and finally, the method of elaborating the protocol and the categories and concepts, such as territorial and political reconstruction, etc., applied in it were a patent diversion from the Leninist principles of Soviet foreign policy. It is true that the peoples of the Ukraine and Belorussia have regained their territorial unity. But using the same criteria common to all mankind, can one not understand the feelings of those who turned out to be a powerless plaything at the hands of the more powerful, and who started to assess their entire subsequent history through the prism of the injustices committed by Stalin?

Having embarked upon the path of dividing the loot with the predators, Stalin began to speak with the neighboring, especially small countries, in the language of ultimatums and threats. He did not consider it shameful to resort to force. This happened in the argument with Finland. With great power arrogance he brought Bessarabia back within the borders of the union, and restored Soviet power in the Baltic republics. All this deformed Soviet policy and state morality. Perhaps this is the first time that the events of the hard prewar times are described in such tough and unconditional terms. But the whole truth, even the bitterest, must be told some time.

The secret protocol of 23 August 1939 reflected precisely the inner essence of Stalinism. This is not the only one, but one of the most dangerous delayed action mines from the minefield we have inherited, and which we are now trying to clear with such difficulty and complexities. It is necessary to do this. The public mines do not simply fade away on their own. We must do it in the name of perestroyka, and for the sake of affirming the new political thinking in order to restore the honor of socialism trampled upon by Stalinism.

The commission believes that, as a result of the work carried out, certainty is being introduced into a number of issues which beset people's minds. A verdict correct in legal and moral terms has been passed, above all on the secret protocol. The commission members have conveyed their conclusions, weighing every word and checking them against their convictions. If the congress considers it possible to agree with the commission's proposals, this will provide additional service to clearing the atmosphere of relics of the past that are incompatible with socialism and justice.

Comrade deputies, in conclusion I wish to say the following. History is its own procurator and its own judge. But immersing ourselves in it, we must not lose sight of the fact that the prewar times were developing in different dimensions. At that time the countries did not yet think of themselves as part of the single stream of humanity. Neither the pan-European ideals nor the world ideals of justice and humanism made their way into the public, and especially the state, consciousness. The voice of the thinkers who saw the limit of civilization was drowned in the clatter of soldiers' boots and ovations in honor of leaders. The fate of the world was governed by the closed groups of politicians and pseudo-politicians with their ambitions, selfishness, demagogy, and detachment from the masses. Many wished to make service to these groups, as well as participation in mutual extermination, the lot of the peoples for ever.

It was necessary to cause the world to fall into the abyss of madness before the idea that destinies and collective action are interconnected in the name of ridding the earth of tyranny and restoring peace began to be asserted as an objective truth. Sooner or later the truth will win out on God's earth and deception will be unlocked. Without such moral cleansing the development of civilization is inconceivable. Today it is more important than ever before to recognize this. The peoples can live calmly and with confidence in the future only if everyone is together and in no way in confrontation with each other. Thank you for your attention.

Moscow, Kremlin, 24 December 1989.

Source: Moscow Television Service, 23 December 1989; in FBIS-SOV 89-248 (28 December 1989), 52-59.

APPENDIX B.8

RESOLUTION OF THE USSR CONGRESS OF PEOPLE'S DEPUTIES ON THE POLITICAL AND LEGAL ASSESSMENT OF THE SOVIET-GERMAN TREATY OF NON-AGGRESSION OF 1939

1. The Congress of USSR People's Deputies takes note of the conclusions of the Commission on the Political and Legal Assessment of the Soviet-German Nonaggression Treaty of 23 August 1939.

2. The Congress of USSR People's Deputies agrees with the commission's opinion that the nonaggression treaty with Germany was concluded in a critical international situation, in the conditions of the growing danger from fascist aggression in Europe and Japanese militarism in Asia, and had as one of its objectives to deflect the threat of approaching war from the USSR. Ultimately this objective was not achieved, and the errors arising from the existence of Germany's commitments to the USSR exacerbated the consequences of the perfidious Nazi aggression. At that time the country faced a difficult choice.

The commitments under the treaty came into force immediately it was signed, although the treaty itself was subject to ratification by the USSR Supreme Soviet. A resolution on ratification was adopted in Moscow on 31 August, and the instruments of ratification were exchanged on 24 September 1939.

3. The Congress believes that the content of this treaty was not at variance with the international legal norms and the treaty practice of states that were customary for settlements of this kind. However, both in the conclusion of the treaty and in the course of its ratification, the fact that a "secret additional protocol" was signed at the same time as the treaty, dividing the "spheres of interests" of the contracting parties from the Baltic to the Black Sea and from Finland to Bessarabia, was concealed.

The originals of the protocol have not been discovered in Soviet or foreign archives. However, expert graphological, photographic, and lexical analyses of copies, maps, and other documents and the fact that subsequent events are in accordance with the content of the protocol confirm the fact of its signing and its existence.

4. The Congress of USSR People's Deputies hereby confirms that the 23 August 1939 nonaggression treaty, as well as the friendship and border treaty between the USSR and Germany that was concluded on 28 September of the same year, along with other Soviet-German accords, lapsed—in accordance with the norms of international law—at the moment of Germany's attack on the USSR, that is, 22 June 1941.

5. The Congress notes that the 23 August 1939 protocol and other secret protocols signed with Germany in 1939-1941 were a departure from the Leninist principles of Soviet foreign policy both in the method of their compilation and in their content. Their demarcations of the USSR's and Germany's "spheres of interests" and other actions were, from the legal viewpoint, in conflict with the sovereignty and independence of a number of third countries.

The Congress notes that in that period the USSR's relations with Latvia, Lithuania, and Estonia were governed by a system of treaties. Under the 1920 peace treaty and the nonaggression treaties concluded in 1926-1933, the parties pledged mutually to respect each other's sovereignty, territorial integrity, and inviolability in all circumstances. The Soviet Union had similar commitments to Poland and Finland.

6. The Congress notes that the talks with Germany on the secret protocols were conducted by Stalin and Molotov in secret from the Soviet people, the All-Union Communist Party (Bolsheviks) Central Committee and the entire party, and the USSR Supreme Soviet and Government, and that these protocols were left out of the ratification procedures. Thus the decision to sign them was, in form and in essence, an act of personal power, and in no way reflected the will of the Soviet people, which is not responsible for this act of collusion.

7. The Congress of USSR People's Deputies condemns the fact of the signing of the 23 August 1939 "secret additional protocol" and other secret accords with Germany. The Congress deems the secret protocols to be legally invalid and null from the moment of their signing.

The protocols did not create a new legal basis for the Soviet Union's relations with third countries, but were used by Stalin and his entourage to issue ultimatums and impose pressure on other states in violation of the legal commitments made to them.

8. The Congress of USSR People's Deputies proceeds on the basis that the recognition of a complex and contradictory past is a part of the process of perestroyka, which is designed to give every people of the Soviet Union the opportunity for free and equal development in the conditions of an integral, interdependent world and increasingly wide mutual understanding.

[Signed] M. Gorbachev, chairman of the USSR Supreme Soviet.

Source: *Pravda*, 28 December 1989, p. 3; in FBIS-SOV 89-248 (28 December 1989), 59-60.

APPENDIX B.9
REPORT OF A. S. DZASOKHOV, CHAIRMAN OF THE USSR SUPREME SOVIET
COMMITTEE ON INTERNATIONAL AFFAIRS,
TO THE SECOND CONGRESS OF USSR PEOPLE'S DEPUTIES
ON THE POLITICAL ASSESSMENT OF THE DECISION TO SEND
SOVIET TROOPS INTO AFGHANISTAN IN DECEMBER 1979

Esteemed people's deputies! In line with the instructions of the First Congress of People's Deputies to formulate a political assessment of the decision to send Soviet troops into Afghanistan, the USSR Supreme Soviet Committee on International Affairs deems it necessary to report the following:

The committee members have acquainted themselves with Soviet government and CPSU Central Committee documents, and with material belonging to the USSR Foreign Ministry, the Defense Ministry, and the Committee for State Security, which relate to the commitment of the troops. They have had discussions with many people who, at the end of the 1970s, occupied high posts in party and state bodies, with military commanders, diplomats, and the leaders of various departments connected with the development of Soviet-Afghan relations. On a number of occasions this issue has been discussed at sittings of the committee in what has, at times, been a very hard-hitting manner. USSR people's deputies, representatives of other Supreme Soviet committees, soldiers who lived through the years of Afghanistan, and a whole number of experts have all participated in them.

Following detailed analysis of the available information, the committee has come to the conclusion that the decision to send Soviet troops into Afghanistan merits moral and political condemnation.

The overall international situation was, at the time when the decision was made, undoubtedly difficult and was marked by acute political confrontation. Given that situation, there was some idea that certain quarters in the United States of America were intending to take revenge for the loss of their positions following the fall of the Shah's regime in Iran. The facts indicated that such a train of events was possible. In the official statements that followed the deployment of the troops, one of the reasons for the action that had been taken was given as a desire to strengthen the Soviet Union's security on the approaches to her southern borders, and in this way to protect her positions in the region because of the tension that had developed by then in Afghanistan. Elements of armed interference from outside were on the increase, and the Afghan Government had issued appeals for help to the Soviet leadership. Documentary evidence has established that since March 1979, the Afghan Government had, on more than ten occasions, asked for Soviet troop detachments to be sent into the country. The Soviet's response had been to reject that form of assistance, stating that the Afghan revolution must defend itself. However, in the long run this stance underwent what was, frankly, a dramatic change. The December 1979 decision was undoubtedly affected by the excessive ideologization of Soviet foreign policy activity which had occurred over a period of many years under the direct influence of the ideological tenets that held sway at the time. It was in light of this that, to a considerable extent, our attitude toward the April Revolution itself developed. It was a premise which accorded with this view that was placed at the heart of the address from the Soviet leadership to the heads of foreign states in connection with the announcement that a contingent of our troops had been sent into Afghanistan. This pointed out that it was a matter of a limited task, assistance in protecting communications and individual installations. However, all these circumstances cannot justify the decision to send in troops.

Everyone knows how events actually developed further. The clashes became more intense and widespread. The Soviet military contingent found itself drawn into an escalation of large-scale military actions. International tension and distrust and military-political rivalry between East and West were heightened. The use of methods of force damaged the authority of Soviet policy among a substantial part of the world public.

By this action we set ourselves against the majority of the world community and against the norms of conduct which should be accepted and observed in international relations. The numerous violations of these norms by other states—including recently, regrettably—which took place at that time, too, cannot justify such actions on the part of our state.

The committee concludes that the decision to send in troops was made in violation of the USSR Constitution, the provisions of Article 73, paragraph 8, according to which (I quote) questions of peace and war, defense of sovereignty, protection of state borders and territories of the USSR, organization of defense, and the leadership of the USSR Armed Forces come under the jurisdiction of the Union of Soviet Socialist Republics in the person of its supreme organs of state power and government. In this context, we report that the USSR Supreme Soviet and its Presidium did not examine the question of sending troops to Afghanistan. The decision was made by a narrow circle of people. The International Affairs Committee has ascertained that the Politburo did not even assemble in its full complement to discuss this matter and make a decision on it.

In giving a political and moral assessment of the dispatch of troops into Afghanistan, it is essential—it is our duty—to name those engaged in dealing with the major foreign policy issues starting from the mid-1970s, who did indeed make the decision to send Soviet troops into Afghanistan. They are Leonid Ilyich Brezhnev, who at that time occupied the posts of General Secretary of the CPSU Central Committee, Chairman of the Presidium of our country's Supreme Soviet, Chairman of the Council of Defense, and Supreme Commander-in-Chief of the USSR Armed Forces; [Marshal D.F.] Ustinov, former USSR defense minister; [Yu.V.] Andropov, chairman of the State Security Committee [KGB]; and [Andrei A.] Gromyko, USSR foreign minister.

However, at the same time it would not be enough to reduce the matter to the personal responsibility of individual politicians alone. It was possible to carry out such a significant and truly dramatic action, circumventing the supreme organs of state power, without the people's participation, as a result of serious defects in the system of determining practical policy and the mechanism of adopting decisions. However, it must be pointed out that in accordance with the established practice at the time, had the aforementioned decision been submitted for discussion at any of the forums, whether political or state, it would most likely have been approved. The party and the people, and our foreign friends, were essentially presented with a fait accompli.

The policy based upon the new thinking intends excluding the possibility of any repetition of anything like the 1979 action. The determining guarantee should be the establishment of real control by the supreme organs of power over the processes of formation and implementation of the Soviet state's foreign policy course. Foreign policy should always be under the people's control. It seems to us, of particular importance is reliable and absolute control over the drawing up and adoption of decisions connected with the use of the USSR Armed Forces. Clear and precise constitutional norms must exist in this regard.

The Soviet Union's foreign policy, which made possible the conclusion of the Geneva accords on Afghanistan and the withdrawal of Soviet troops from that country, corresponds to the spirit and tasks of perestroika, and is an organic part of it. The time that has elapsed since the return of Soviet troops from Afghanistan demonstrates that the government and the Afghan national forces are capable independently of determining the destiny of their own country, and are rebuffing—and many reports on this have been coming in recently—the attempts of the armed opposition to impose a military solution. It should be pointed out that President Najibullah of Afghanistan perceived with understanding, and, most importantly, gave active backing to the Soviet approach to the issue of a withdrawal of the Soviet military contingent.

Political and diplomatic activity is gathering strength in the Republic of Afghanistan. Taking account of all the circumstances, it is considered well-founded to continue political and moral support to the neighboring Afghan people and to continue rendering assistance to the Republic of Afghanistan and developing cooperation with that country, in accordance with the bilateral state agreements.

Esteemed people's deputies, in both politically and morally censuring the decision to send in Soviet troops, the committee deems it necessary to declare that this in no way casts any aspersion upon the men and officers who were sent to Afghanistan. True to their oaths, and convinced that they were defending the interests of the motherland and rendering friendly aid to a neighboring people, they were merely fulfilling their military duty. The Soviet people lost thousands of their sons in Afghanistan. It is our sacred duty to preserve the memory of them, true sons of the fatherland. I beg you to observe a minute's silence in honor of the memory of those of our comrades who perished. [Brief silence]

It is our duty to give due recognition to the courage of those who underwent grave ordeals, to show concern for them, to help them to realize their plans for their lives, and to render help and support in very possible way to the disabled and the families of the dead.

The International Affairs Committee considers it necessary to add a number of practical suggestions to the political assessment of the decision to send Soviet troops to Afghanistan. As yet, the USSR Constitution and legislative acts do not define the mechanism for adopting decisions on the use of the Armed Forces beyond the bounds of our country. The Constitution contains only general provisions, in accordance with which they Supreme Soviet makes decisions on employing contingents of the USSR Armed Forces in the event of the need to fulfill international treaty obligations to maintain peace and security. What is evidently needed is for the procedure for employing the Armed Forces to be specified by means of a special legislative act, and, furthermore, for the clauses on the USSR Defense Council to be brought solidly into conformity with constitutional norms. This urgent task could be realized in the context of the work on the future, new Constitution of our country.

The committee also deems it expedient to examine the possibility of setting up a commission, within the framework of the USSR Supreme Soviet, on the affairs of former servicemen of the contingent of Soviet troops in Afghanistan. Similar measures should also, it seems to us, be taken with regard to the USSR Council of Ministers.

We deem it necessary to inform the Second Congress of the suggestion from many people's deputies and representatives of the public of our country that the day the withdrawal of troops from Afghanistan was completed, namely, 15 February, should be a day of remembrance.

Thus, esteemed people's deputies, the committee, basing itself upon the mandate it was given by the First Congress of People's Deputies, has striven to illuminate only the political assessment of the actual fact of sending troops into Afghanistan. The existing documentation gives sufficient grounds, in our opinion, for the basic conclusions submitted to you by the committee.

Concluding my report, I will point out that in historical perspective, the war in Afghanistan is today's living history, of which many political and social forces are participants, in addition to the Soviet Union. A great deal of multifaceted work lies ahead on the part of politicians, diplomats, and scholars, to make all-around evaluations of this historical event so full of drama.

Thank you for your attention.

Source: Moscow Television Service, 24 December 1989; in FBIS-SOV 89-248 (28 December 1989), 72-74.

APPENDIX B.10
RESOLUTION OF THE USSR CONGRESS OF PEOPLE'S DEPUTIES ON THE POLITICAL ASSESSMENT OF THE DECISION TO SEND SOVIET TROOPS INTO AFGHANISTAN IN DECEMBER 1979

1. The Congress of USSR People's Deputies supports the political assessment given by the USSR Supreme Soviet International Affairs Committee of the decision to send Soviet troops into Afghanistan in 1979, and believes that this decision deserves moral and political condemnation.

2. The Congress instructs the Constitutional Commission, in preparing the draft new USSR Constitution, to take into account the proposal to clarify the basic principles of the adoption of decisions on the use of USSR Armed Forces contingents contained in points 13 and 14 of Article 113 and point 13 of Article 119 of the existing USSR Constitution, in conjunction with the formulation of the Provision on the USSR Defense Council.

3. The USSR Supreme Soviet is to examine the question of setting up a commission for the affairs of former servicemen of the contingent of Soviet troops in Afghanistan.

4. The USSR Council of Ministers is instructed to draw up a state program aimed at resolving questions connected with organizing the lives and living conditions of former servicemen and others who formed part of the contingent of Soviet troops in Afghanistan, as well as the families of servicemen who died. [Signed]M. Gorbachev, chairman of the USSR Supreme Soviet.
Moscow, Kremlin, 24 December 1989.

Source: *Pravda*, 28 December 1989, p. 3; in FBIS-SOV 89-248 (28 December 1989), 64.

APPENDIX C.1
PRESIDIUM OF THE USSR CONGRESS OF PEOPLE'S DEPUTIES

Ambartsumyan, Viktor Amazaspovich, President of the Armenian SSR Academy of Sciences

Aytmatov, Chingiz T., Chairman of the Board of the Kirghiz SSR Writers Union and editor-in-chief of the magazine *Inostrannaya literatura*

Azizbekova, Pyusta Azizagakyzy, Director of the Museum for the History of Azerbaijan of the Azerbaijan SSR Academy of Sciences

Brazauskas, Algirdas-Mikolas Kaze, First Secretary of the Lithuanian CP CC

Gorbachev, Mikhail Sergeyevich, Chairman of the USSR Supreme Soviet and General Secretary of the CPSU CC

Gorbunov, Anatoly Valeriyanovich, Chairman of the Latvian SSR Supreme Soviet Presidium

Ishanov, Khekim, Chief Engineer of the Turkmenneft Production Association, Turkmen SSR

Kiseleva, Valentina Adamovna, Machine operator, Grodno 60th Anniversary of the USSR Khimvolokno Production Association, Belorussian SSR

Kozhakhmetov, Ibraimzhan, Chairman of the Kirov Kolkhoz, Panfilovsky Rayon, Taldy-Kurgan Oblast, Kazakh SSR

Kurashvili, Zeynab Giviyevna, Sewing machine operator, Gldani Knitwear Production Association, Tbilisi, Georgian SSR

Lippmaa, Endel Teodorovich, Director of the Institute of Chemical and Biological Physics, Estonian SSR Academy of Sciences

Lukyanov, Anatoly Ivanovich, First Deputy Chairman of the USSR Supreme Soviet Presidium

Mukhabatova, Soniyabibi Kushvakhtova, Livestock team leader, Khayeti-Nav Sovkhoz, Garmsky Rayon, Tajik SSR

Nishanov, Rafik Nishanovich, First Secretary of the Uzbekistan CP CC

Orlov, Vladimir Pavlovich, Chairman of the USSR Central Electoral Commission

Paton, Boris Yevgenyevich, President of the Ukrainian SSR Academy of Sciences

Rotar, Svetlana Anatolyevna, Mechanized milking foreman, Moldova Kolkhoz, Dondyushany Rayon, Moldavian SSR

Vorotnikov, Vitaly Ivanovich, Member of the CPSU CC Politburo and Chairman of the Presidium of the RSFSR Supreme Soviet

APPENDIX C.2
SECRETARIAT OF THE USSR CONGRESS OF PEOPLE'S DEPUTIES

Apostol, Veniamin Gavrilovich, chief producer at the Kishinev Chekhov Russian Drama Theater, Moldavian Soviet Socialist Republic [SSR].

Bocharov, Mikhail Aleksandrovich, director of the Butovo construction materials combine, Moscow city.

Vare, Vello Iosifovich, leading scientific associate of the Estonian SSR Academy of Sciences History Institute.

Yeraliyev, Zholdasbay, director of the state farm named for the 30th anniversary of October, Chimkent Oblast, Kazakh SSR.

Igrunov, Nikolay Stefanovich, second secretary of the Belorussian Communist Party Central Committee.

Kapto, Aleksandr Semenovich, chief of the CPSU Central Committee Ideology Department, Moscow city.

Krylova, Zoya Petrovna, chief editor of the journal RABOTNITSA, Moscow City.

Kudarauskas, Sigitas Yozovich, chief of department at the Kaunas Polytechnical Institute, Lithuanian SSR.

Mamedov, Suleyman Farkhad ogly, first secretary of Kirovabad Azerbaijan Communist Party City Committee.

Medvedev, Sergey Aleksandrovich, director of the Kirghiz mining and metallurgy combine.

Nazarov, Talbak, Tajik SSR minister of public education.

Nazaryan, Spartyon Yegoyevich, chairman of the "Maralik" agrofirm-collective farm, Armenian SSR.

Orazmuradova, Orazgul Mukhiyevna, pediatrician at the Serakhskiy Rayon Central Hospital, Turkmen SSR.

Pirtskhalaishvili, Zurab Georgiyevich, turner at the Tbilisi electrical railroad car repairs plant, Georgian SSR.

Plotniyeks, Andris Adamovich, professor at Latvia's P. Stuchka State University.

Usmanov, Rustamzhon Kazakevich, Russian language and literature teacher at the No 20 school named for Furkat, Uzbek SSR.

Shcherbak, Yuriy Nikolayevich, writer, and secretary of the Ukrainian Writers Union Board.

APPENDIX C.3
CREDENTIALS COMMISSION

Chairman of the Commission

Gidaspov, Boris Veniaminovich, general director of the "GIPKH" Science and Production Association, chairman of the board of the "Tekhnokhim" intersectorial state association, Leningrad City.

Deputy Chairmen of the Commission

Ivashko, Vladimir Antonovich, second secretary of the Ukrainian Communist Party Central Committee.

Klikunene, Vanda Styaponovna, deputy chairman of the Lithuanian Soviet Socialist Republic [SSR] Supreme Soviet Presidium, Vilnius City.

Commission Secretary

Oripov, Abdulla, writer, secretary of the Uzbek Writers Union Board.

Commission Members

Agrba, Violetta Zosimovna, laboratory leader at the USSR Academy of Medical Sciences Research Institute of Experimental Pathology and Therapeutics, Georgian SSR.

Akramova, Tamara Musoyevna, department chief at Matchinskiy Rayon Hospital, Leninabad Oblast, Tajik SSR.

Amzarakov, Vladimir Grigoryevich, automobile driver at the Kalinin State Farm [sovkhoz], Askizskiy Rayon, Khakass Autonomous Oblast, Krasnoyarsk Kray.

Bosenko, Nikolay Vasilyevich, pensioner, Moscow City.

Vasilenko, Mikhail Fedorovich, chief of the Kirghiz Communist Party Central Committee Party Organization and Cadre Work Department, Frunze City.

Vladislavlev, Aleksandr Pavlovich, first secretary of the Board of the USSR Union of Scientific and Engineering Societies, Moscow City.

Vorobyeva, Anastasiya Nikolayevna, leader of a team of plasterers of the Mobile Mechanized Column No 1, Kashira City, Moscow Oblast.

Geyba, Yanis Aloizovich, first secretary of Daugavpilsskiy Latvian Communist Party Rayon Committee [raykom].

Grishchenkov, Grigoriy Zakharovich, chairman of the Belorussian Union of Consumer Trade Cooperatives Board, Minsk City.

Gromov, Boris Vsevolodovich, colonel general, commander of the Red Banner Kiev Military District.

Gubin, Viktor Aleksandrovich, technology engineer at the "Solombalskiy Tsellyulozno-Bumazhnyy Kombinat" Production Association, Arkhangelsk City.

Guskova, Lidiya Mikhaylovna, chairman of the Astrakhan Oblast Trade Union Council, Astrakhan City.

Dementey, Nikolay Ivanovich, secretary of the Belorussian Communist Party Central Committee.

Dovlatyan, Frunzik Vaginakovich, artistic leader of "Armenfilm" Movie Studio, Yerevan City.

Dumbravan, Mikhail Georgiyevich, chairman of Ryshkanskiy Rayon's Kirov Collective Farm [kolkhoz], Moldavian SSR.

Zhivotov, Aleksey Aleksandrovich, chairman of the "Rossiya" Kolkhoz, Oktyabrskiy Rayon, Rostov Oblast.

Zaslavskiy, Ilya Iosifovich, scientific staffer at the Moscow A.N. Kosygin Textiles Institute.

Klimuk, Petr Ilich, major general of aviation, chief of the Yu.A. Gagarin Cosmonaut Training Center Political Department, Zvezdnyy Gorodok, Shchelkovskiy Rayon, Moscow Oblast.

Knyazev, Nikolay Trifonovich, first secretary of Kustanay Kazakh Communist Party Oblast Committee [obkom].

Konovalov, Aleksandr Ivanovich, rector of Kazan State University.

Korshunov, Aleksandr Aleksandrovich, team leader at the Tashkent V.P. Chkalov Aircraft Production Association, Uzbek SSR.

Kublashvili, Vakhtang Vladimirovich, assembly fitter at the Tbilisi Aircraft Production Association named for Dimitrov.

Kukushkin, Nikolay Timofeyevich, director of the "Severnyy Klyuch" Sovkhoz, Pokhvistnevskiy Rayon, Pokhvistnevskiy Rayon, Kuybyshev Oblast.

Kukhar, Ivan Ivanovich, chairman of the Vladimir Ilich Kolkhoz, Leninskiy Rayon, Moscow Oblast.

Kucher, Valeriy Nikolayevich, editor of the newspaper MAGNITOGORSKIY RABOCHIY, Chelyabinsk Oblast.

Laurinkus, Mechis Mechko, scientific worker at the Lithuanian SSR Academy of Sciences Institute of Philosophy, Sociology, and Law.

Marchenko, Georgiy Aleksandrovich, chief physician at the Nizhnyaya Tura City Central Hospital, Sverdlovsk Oblast.

Medikov, Viktor Yakovlevich, prorector of the Siberian Metallurgical Institute, Novokuznetsk City, Kemerovo Oblast.

Pamfilova, Ella Aleksandrovna, chairman of the trade union committee at the "Mosenergo" production association's central mechanical repair plant, Moscow City.

Polozkov, Ivan Kuzmich, first secretary of the Krasnodar CPSU Kray Committee.

Rasputin, Valentin Grigoryevich, writer, secretary of the USSR Writers' Union Board, Irkutsk City.

Rzayev, Firudin Orudzh ogly, fitter at the Baku Tire Plant named for the 40th anniversary of the Azerbaijan Communist Party.

Ryzhov, Aleksey Andreyevich, chief designer at the Ufa machine building design office, Bashkir ASSR.

Savitskiy, Mikhail Andreyevich, artist, leader of the USSR Academy of Arts Painting Workshop, Belorussian SSR.

Salykov, Kakimbek, first secretary of Karakalpak Uzbek Communist Party Obkom, Nukus City.

Selimov, Nurnazar, first secretary of Kizyl-Arvatskiy Turkmen Communist Party Raykom.

Fedorov, Svyatoslav Nikolayevich, general director of the "Mikrokhirurgiya Glaza" Intersector Scientific and Technical Complex, chairman of the Soviet Charity and Health Foundation, Moscow City.

Khaug, Arvo Voldemarovich, senior physician at the Tallinn Republic Psychoneurology Hospital.

Khokhlov, Aleksandr Fedorovich, rector of Gorkiy State University named for N.I. Lobachevskiy.

Tsybukh, Valeriy Ivanovich, first secretary of the Ukrainian Komsomol Central Committee.

Shulyak, Vasiliy Korneyevich, chairman of the "Trud" Kolkhoz, Teofipolskiy Rayon, Khmelnitskiy Oblast.

Yakovlev, Aleksandr Maksimovich, doctor of juridical sciences, sector chief at the USSR Academy of Sciences Institute of State and Law, Moscow City.

Yakushin, Ivan Nikitovich, chairman of the Lenin Kolkhoz, Lyuberetskiy Rayon, Moscow Oblast.

APPENDIX C.4
TELLERS COMMISSION

Abdurakhimov, Abdurakhman, chief economist of Namanganskiy Rayon's Sverdlov Collective Farm [kolkhoz], Namangan Oblast, Uzbek Soviet Socialist Republic [SSR].

Abutalipov, Shamil Abdulazhanovich, director of the Pavlovskiy Children's Home, Ulyanovsk Oblast.

Azizova, Zenfila Aziz kyzy, milkmaid at the M.F. Akhundov Kolkhoz, Kutkashenskiy Rayon, Azerbaijan SSR.

Akramov, Ernst Khashimovich, head of department at the republic clinical hospital, Frunze City.

Anishchev, Vladimir Petrovich, second secretary of the Uzbek Communist Party Central Committee, Tashkent City.

Anufriyeva, Lidiya Alekseyevna, director of the Povenets Secondary School, Medvezhyegorskiy Rayon, Povenets Settlement, Karelia Autonomous Soviet Socialist Republic [ASSR].

Apostol, Veniamin Gavrilovich, chief producer of the Kishinev Russian Drama Theater named for Chekhov, chairman of the Moldavian Union of Theater Workers, Kishinev City.

Arbatov, Georgiy Arkadyevich, academician, director of the USSR Academy of Sciences United States and Canada Institute, Moscow City.

Bayramova, Narmina Aliman kyzy, cotton grower at the Fizuli Kolkhoz, Udzharskiy Rayon, Azerbaijan SSR.

Barannikova, Olga Vyacheslavovna, student at the Tula Polytechnical Institute, Tula City.

Batiashvili, Stanislav Andreyevich, worker at the Lagodekhi machine building plant, Lagodekhi City, Georgian SSR.

Begeldinov, Talgat Yakubekovich, pensioner, Alma-Ata City.

Bekhtereva, Natalya Petrovna, academician, director of the USSR Academy of Medical Sciences Scientific Research Institute of Experimental Medicine, Leningrad City.

Vorobyev, Nikolay Nikolayevich, first secretary of Pytalovskiy CPSU Rayon Party Committee [raykom], Pskov Oblast.

Gorelkina, Valentina Alekseyevna, chairman of the Krasnoyarsk Public Education and Science Workers' Trade Union Kray Committee [kraykom], Krasnoyarsk City.

Grigoryan, Artsvin Gaykovich, architect, chairman of the Armenian Union of Architects Board, Yerevan City.

Gummyyev, Otuz, team leader at the "Sovyet Turkmenistana" kolkhoz, Oktyabrskiy Rayon, Tashauz Oblast, Turkmen SSR.

Danilova, Lyubov Andreyevna, deputy director for educational work at a secondary school, Meleuz City, Bashkir ASSR.

Derevyanko, Boris Fedorovich, editor of the VECHERNYAYA ODESSA newspaper, Odessa City.

Yerokhovets, Irina Yakovlevna, fitter at the G.K. Ordzhonikidze Computer Plant at the Minsk Computer Equipment Production Association, Minsk City.

Yeseykin, Nikolay Viktorovich, mechanic at the lease subdivision of the "Dobrovolets" kolkhoz, Shilovskiy Rayon, Ryazan Oblast.

Zakis, Yuris Roderikhovich, rector of the Latvian State University P. Stuchka, Riga City.

Zolotareva, Lyudmila Aleksandrovna, actress at the Voronezh Academy Drama Theater Koltsov, Voronezh City.

Ibrayeva, Kulzhariya, team leader at the "Sarykumskiy" state farm [sovkhoz], Alakulskiy Rayon, Taldy-Kurgan Oblast, Kazakh SSR.

Ivanenko, Nikolay Ilich, team leader at the "Primorskiy" kolkhoz, Shcherbinskiy Rayon, Krasnodar Kray.

Karimov, Dzhamshed Khilolovich, first secretary of the Dushanbe Tajik Communist Party City Committee, Dushanbe City.

Kobaliya, Larisa Nodariyevna, mechanic at the "Sabchota chay" tea growing sovkhoz, Galskiy Rayon, Abkhaz ASSR.

Koberidze, Vardisheli Georgiyevich, chairman of the Rustavi Voluntary Society for the Promotion of the Army, Aviation, and Navy [DOSAAF] Gorkom, Rustavi City, Georgian SSR.

Kosarchuk, Valeriy Petrovich, chief technologist of the "Moldselmash" production association, Beltsy City, Moldavian SSR.

Lasuta, Yelena Petrovna, shop chief of the Pinsk Spinning and Knitting Production Association named for the 60th anniversary of Great October, Pinsk City, Brest Oblast, Belorussian SSR.

Leksin, Nikolay Sergeyevich, pensioner, Raychikhinsk City, Amur Oblast.

Lukyanenko, Olga Fedotovna, animal specialist at the "Svitanok" kolkhoz, Manevichskiy Rayon, Volyn Oblast, Ukrainian SSR.

Magomadov, Lecha Dobachevich, chairman of the Chechen-Ingush ASSR State Committee for Prices, Groznyy City.

Mansurov, Rafis Khamzeyevich, drilling expert at the Aznakayevskiy Drilling Work Administration, Aznakayevo City, Tatar ASSR.

Markevich, Anatoliy Lavrentyevich, chief of the Obluchye train car depot, Obluchye City, Jewish Autonomous Oblast, Khabarovsk Kray.

Melnikov, Aleksandr Ivanovich, team leader at the V.I. Lenin kolkhoz, Syzransky Rayon, Kuybyshev Oblast.

Melnikov, Aleksandr Ilich, metal hull assembler at the Leningrad Admiralty Association, Leningrad City.

Misrikhanov, Kerimkhan Zamrudinovich, fitters' team leader at Makhachkala Machine-Building Plant, Makhachkala City, Dagestan ASSR.

Mitalene, Ona Antanovna, chief nurse at Klaypeda City Hospital, Klaypeda City, Lithuanian SSR.

Nazarenko, Arnold Filippovich, leading engineer at the "Yuzhnoye" Design Bureau, Dnepropetrovsk City.

Neff, Erika Matveyevna, machine milking operative on the "Proletarskiy" Sovkhoz, Ulyanovskiy Rayon, Karaganda Oblast, Kazakh SSR.

Nurm, Khasso Erikovich, engineer at the republic "Estagrostroy" Association, Tallinn City.

Novozhilov, Genrikh Vasilyevich, general designer at the Moscow S.V. Ilyushin Plant, Moscow City.

Ninnas, Toyvo Adolfovich, chief of the Estonian Maritime Shipping Company, Tallinn City.

Ozolinsh, Leopold Alfredovich, senior scientific staffer at the Latvian Scientific Research Institute of Traumatology and Orthopedics, Riga City.

Osipov, Anatoliy Konstantinovich, secretary of the party committee of the Mordovian N.P. Ogarev State University, Saransk City.

Osipyan, Yuriy Andreyevich, academician, vice president of the USSR Academy of Sciences, director of the USSR Academy of Sciences Institute of Solid-State Physics, Moscow City.

Oskin, Anatoliy Dmitriyevich, director of the Sosnogorsk Timber Procurement Establishment of the "Ukhtales" Production Association, Sosnogorsk City, Komi ASSR.

Pavlenko, Viktor Pavlovich, director of the "Maslovskiy" State Livestock Breeding Center, Novousmanskiy Rayon, Voronezh Oblast.

Pavlov, Anatoliy Vasilyevich, turner at Kungur Machine-Building Plant, Kungur City, Perm Oblast.

Pashyan, Stepa Andranikovich, radio apparatus regulator at the Abovyan "Izmeritel" Plant, Abovyan City, Armenian SSR.

Petrov, Nikifor Nikolayevich, director of the 50-letiye SSSR Sovkhoz, Srednekolymskiy Rayon, Srednekolymsk City, Yakutsk ASSR.

Prikhodko, Yekaterina Stepanovna, chairman of the board of Velikochernetchanskoye Consumer Society, Sumskiy Rayon, Ukrainian SSR, Sumy Oblast, Sumy City.

Pylin, Boris Filippovich, lieutenant colonel, senior lecturer at the Kacha Myasnikov Higher Military Aviation School for Pilots, Volgograd City.

Pyndyk, Galina Vladimirovna, machine milking operative on the Chapayev Kolkhoz, Zolochevskiy Rayon, Lvov Oblast.

Rynka, Anatoliy Andreyevich, chairman of Novograd-Volynskiy City Soviet Executive Committee, Novograd-Volynskiy City, Zhitomir Oblast.

Savostina, Zinaida Semenovna, director of Chelyabinsk Oblast Universal Scientific Library, Chelyabinsk City.

Samayev, Petr Lidzhiyevich, deputy chief of Elista Housebuilding Combine of the "Kalmstroy" Planning Construction and Installation Association, Kalmyk ASSR.

Sarkisyan, Sos Artashesovich, artiste of the Sundukyan State Academy Theater, Yerevan City.

Skokov, Yuriy Vladimirovich, general director of the "Kvant" Science-and-Production Association, Moscow City.

Snegur, Mircha Ivanovich, secretary of the Moldavian Communist Party Central Committee.

Solovyev, Yuriy Borisovich, chairman of the board of the USSR Designers' Union, Moscow City.

Strukov, Nikolay Alekseyevich, senior investigator of Kursk Oblast Prosecutor's Office, Kursk City.

Sychev, Yuriy Petrovich, lieutenant colonel, lecturer in a department of the Leningrad Yu.V. Andropov Higher Military Political School of Air Defense.

Tarnavskiy, Georgiy Stepanovich, Belorussian SSR prosecutor, Minsk City.

Tkemaladze, Grigoriy Abelovich, deputy chairman of the trade union committee of the "Chiaturmarganets" Production Association, Chiatura City, Georgian SSR.

Umarkhodzhayev, Mukhtar Ishankhodzhayevich, rector of Andizhan State Pedagogic Institute of Languages, Andizhan City, Uzbek SSR.

Usichenko, Ivan Ignatyevich, chairman of the Ukrainian SSR Red Cross Society Central Committee, Kiev City.

Chernyshova, Lyubov Petrovna, machine operator on the Karl Marx Kolkhoz, Novoaleksandrovskiy Rayon, Stavropol Kray.

Sherali, Loik, poet, chief editor of the journal SADOI SHARK, Dushanbe City.

Shlichite, Zita Leonovna, attorney of Klaypeda Legal Advice Bureau, Klaypeda City, Lithuanian SSR.

Ezizov, Atabay, team leader on the Lenin Kolkhoz, Turkmen-Kalinskiy Rayon, Mary Oblast, Turkmen SSR.

Ergeshov, Abdimanap Ergeshovich, team leader on the Frunze Kolkhoz, Bazar-Korgonskiy Rayon, Osh Oblast, Kirghiz SSR.

Yusupov, Erkin Yusupovich, vice president of the Uzbek SSR Academy of Sciences, Tashkent City.

Yanenko, Arkadiy Petrovich, rector of Novosibirsk Engineering and Construction Institute, Novosibirsk City.

APPENDIX C.5

COMMISSION TO INVESTIGATE THE CIRCUMSTANCES CONNECTED WITH EVENTS IN TBILISI CITY ON 9 APRIL 1989

Aasmyae, Khardo Yulovich, sector chief at the "Maynor" Design Bureau of the "Estlegprom" Association, Tallinn City.

Andronati, Sergey Andreyevich, director of the A.V. Bogatskiy Physico-Chemical Institute of the Ukrainian SSR Academy of Sciences, Odessa City.

Bekhtereva, Natalya Petrovna, director of the USSR Academy of Medical Sciences Experimental Medicine Research Institute, Leningrad City.

Borovik, Genrikh Avizzerovich, chairman of the Soviet Committee for the Defense of Peace, Moscow City.

Gazenko, Oleg Georgiyevich, academician, adviser to the directorate of the USSR Ministry of Health Institute of Medico-Biological Problems, Moscow City.

Vasilyev, Boris Lvovich, screenplay writer, Moscow City.

Golyakov, Aleksandr Ivanovich, first deputy chairman of the All-Union Council of War and Labor Veterans, Moscow City.

Govorov, Vladimir Leonidovich, chief of civil defense and deputy USSR defense minister, Moscow City.

Likhachev, Dmitriy Sergeyevich, chief of a sector of the USSR Academy of Sciences Russian Literature Institute, Leningrad City.

Lukin, Vladimir Petrovich, gas cutter at the Kolomna V.V. Kuybyshev Diesel Locomotive Building Plant, Moscow Oblast.

Martirosyan, Vilen Arutyunovich, commander of a troop unit, Rovno Oblast.

Miroshnik, Viktor Mikhaylovich, chairman of the Kazakh SSR KGB.

Nazarbayev, Nursultan Abishevich, chairman of the Kazakh SSR Council of Ministers.

Nechayev, Konstantin Vladimirovich, metropolitan Pitirim of Volokolamsk and Yuryev, Moscow City.

Odzhiyev, Rizoali Kadamshoyevich, deputy chairman of the "Internatsionalist" Cooperative Association, Dushanbe City.

Sagdeyev, Roald Zinnurovich, leader of the analytical research scientific methodology center at the USSR Academy of Sciences Institute of Space Research, Moscow City.

Sobchak, Anatoliy Aleksandrovich, department chief in the Leningrad State University law faculty.

Stankevich, Sergey Borisovich, senior scientific staffer at the USSR Academy of Sciences Institute of General History, Moscow City.

Tolpezhnikov, Vilen Fedorovich, consulting room chief at the N. Burdenko First Riga City Emergencies Teaching Hospital.

Tomkus, Vitas Pyatrovich, journalist, Vilnius City.

Fedotova, Valentina Ivanovna, chief editor of the journal SOVETSKAYA ZHENSHCHINA, Moscow City.

Shengelaya, Eldar Nikolayevich, chairman of the Georgian Cinema Workers' Union, Tbilisi City.

Shetko, Pavel Vadimovich, lecturer at the Minsk Oblast Belorussian Komsomol [Communist Youth League] Committee Propaganda Department.

Yakovlev, Aleksandr Maksimovich, sector chief at the USSR Academy of Sciences Institute of State and Law, Moscow City.

APPENDIX C.6
COMMISSION TO VERIFY THE MATERIALS CONNECTED WITH THE ACTIVITIES OF THE USSR PROSECUTOR'S OFFICE INVESTIGATIVE GROUP HEADED BY T. Kh. GDLYAN

Adylov, Vladimir Tuychiyevich, team leader at the Tashkent V.P. Chkalov Aviation Production Association.

Aleksandrin, Valeriy Grigoryevich, chairman of Yoshkar-Ola City People's Court, Mari Autonomous Soviet Socialist Republic.

Baranov, Aleksandr Ivanovich, chairman of the trade union committee of Leningrad City's "Izhorskiy Zavod" Production Association, Kolpino City.

Bichkauskas, Egidiyus Vitautovich, investigator of particularly important cases under the Lithuanian Soviet Socialist Republic [SSR] prosecutor, Vilnius City.

Bisher, Ilmar Olgertovich, professor of the Latvian P. Stuchka State University, Riga City.

Golik, Yuriy Vladimirovich, dean of the law faculty of Kemerovo State University.

Ignatovich, Nikolay Ivanovich, investigator of particularly important cases under the Belorussian SSR prosecutor, Minsk City.

Lubenchenko, Konstantin Dmitriyevich, docent of the law faculty of the Moscow M.V. Lomonosov State University.

Medvedev, Roy Aleksandrovich, writer, historian, publicist, Moscow City.

Pokhla, Vello Paulovich, member of the editorial collegium of the "Estonskiy telefilm" Main Editorial Board of the Estonian SSR State Committee for Television and Radio Broadcasting, Tallinn City.

Semenov, Vitaliy Aleksandrovich, senior scientific staffer of the Technical Mechanics Institute of the Ukrainian SSR Academy of Sciences, Dnepropetrovsk City.

Sorokin, Igor Viktorovich, senior criminal investigation commissioner of Kubyshev Station's Line Internal Affairs Department, Kuybyshev City.

Strukov, Nikolay Alekseyevich, Kursk Oblast Prosecutor's Office senior investigator, Kursk City.

Suleymenov, Olzhas Omarovich, writer, first secretary of the Kazakhstan Writers Union Board, Alma-Ata City.

Fedorov, Svyatoslav Nikolayevich, general director of the "Mikrokhirurgiya glaza" Intersectoral Scientific and Technical Complex, chairman of the Soviet Charity and Health Fund, Moscow City.

Yarin, Veniamin Aleksandrovich, operator at the Nizhniy Tagil V.I. Lenin Metallurgical Combine, Nizhniy Tagil City.

APPENDIX C.7
COMMISSION TO PREPARE THE RESOLUTION ON BASIC GUIDELINES FOR THE DOMESTIC AND FOREIGN POLICY OF THE USSR

Chairman of the Commission

Medvedev, Vadim Andreyevich, member of the CPSU Central Committee Politburo and secretary of the CPSU Central Committee.

Members of the Commission

Abalkin, Leonid Ivanovich, director of the USSR Academy of Sciences Economics Institute, Moscow city.

Adamovich, Aleksandr Mikhaylovich, director of the All-Union Scientific Research Institute of Movie Art, Moscow city.

Aytmatov, Chingiz, writer and chairman of the Kirghiz Soviet Socialist Republic [SSR] Writers Union Board.

Aleskerova, Rukhi Mursal kyzy, chairman of the Lagich Settlement Soviet of People's Deputies Executive Committee [ispolkom], Ismaillinskiy Rayon, Azerbaijan SSR.

Ayubov, Nazhmiddin, director of the Frunze Interkolkhoz [intercollective farm] Complex, Gissarskiy Rayon, Tajik SSR.

Bazarova, Roza Atamuradovna, chairman of the Turkmen SSR Supreme Soviet Presidium.

Borovkov, Vyacheslav Aleksandrovich, fitter at the Kirovskiy Zavod production association, Leningrad city.

Bunich, Pavel Grigoryevich, corresponding member of the USSR Academy of Sciences and faculty chief at the Moscow S. Ordzhonikidze Institute of Management, Moscow city.

Vasilyev, Ivan Afanasyevich, writer, Pskov Oblast.

Venglovskaya, Vanda Sergeyevna, weaver at the Zhitomir 60th Anniversary of the Great October Socialist Revolution Flax Combine, Ukrainian SSR.

Volskiy, Arkadiy Ivanovich, chairman of the Nagorno-Karabakh Autonomous Oblast Special Administration Committee and chief of a CPSU Central Committee department.

Voskanyan, Grant Mushegovich, chairman of the Armenian SSR Supreme Soviet Presidium.

Gavrilov, Andrey Petrovich, editor of the newspaper VECHERNYAYA KAZAN, Tatar ASSR [Autonomous SSR].

Gorbunov, Anatoliy Valeryanovich, chairman of the Latvian SSR Supreme Soviet Presidium.

Grossu, Semen Kuzmich, first secretary of the Moldavian Communist Party Central Committee.

Dudko, Tamara Nikolayevna, chairman of Partizanskiy Rayon Soviet Ispolkom, Minsk city, Belorussian SSR.

Yeltsin, Boris Nikolayevich, member of the CPSU Central Committee, Moscow city.

Zaykov, Lev Nikolayevich, member of the CPSU Central Committee Politburo, secretary of the CPSU Central Committee, and first secretary of the Moscow City CPSU Committee.

Ibragimov, Mirzaolim Ibragimovich, chairman of the Uzbek SSR Supreme Soviet Presidium.

Ivans, Daynis Evaldovich, chairman of the Latvian People's Front.

Kaipbergenov, Tulepbergen, chairman of the Karakalpak ASSR Writers Union Board.

Kakadzhikov, Chary, team leader at the 40th Anniversary of the Turkmen SSR Kolkhoz, Ashkhabadskiy Rayon, Turkmen SSR.

Kolesnikov, Vladimir Ivanovich, faculty chief at the Rostov Railroad Transport Engineers Institute.

Kontselidze, Marina Rizayevna, citrus fruit grower at the Khala Village Kolkhoz, Kobuletskiy Rayon, Georgian SSR.

Kryuchenkova, Nadezhda Aleksandrovna, teacher at the Inzhavina No 2 Secondary School, Tambov Oblast.

Kubilyus, Ionas Pyatrovich, rector of Vilnius State University, Lithuanian SSR.

Kudryavtsev, Vladimir Nikolayevich, vice president of the USSR Academy of Sciences and director of the

USSR Academy of Sciences Institute of State and Law, Moscow city.

Kuzubov, Vladimir Fedorovich, shop chief at the Gorkiy S. Ordzhonikidze aircraft production association, Gorkiy city.

Lavrov, Kirill Yuryevich, artist of the Leningrad Gorkiy Bolshoy Academy Drama Theater and chairman of the USSR Theater Workers Union Board.

Laptev, Ivan Dmitriyevich, chief editor of IZVESTIYA, Moscow city.

Lauristin, Maryu Yokhannesovna, faculty chief at Tartu State University, Estonian SSR.

Likhachev, Dmitriy Sergeyevich, academician, sector chief at the USSR Academy of Sciences Russian Literature Institute, and chairman of the Soviet Culture Foundation Board, Leningrad city.

Lukyanov, Anatoliy Ivanovich, first deputy chairman of the USSR Supreme Soviet and candidate member of the CPSU Central Committee Politburo.

Mazurov, Kirill Trofimovich, chairman of the All-Union Council of War and Labor Veterans, Moscow city.

Marchuk, Guriy Ivanovich, president of the USSR Academy of Sciences, Moscow city.

Masol, Vitaliy Andreyevich, chairman of the Ukrainian SSR Council of Ministers.

Matyukha, Vyacheslav Nikolayevich, team leader of a comprehensive team of the No 36 Construction Administration of the Mamontovnefteproromstroy trust, Tyumen Oblast.

Medvedev, Roy Aleksandrovich, writer, Moscow city.

Melekhin, Sergey Tikhonovich, mill operator in the large-sections shop at the Nizhniy Tagil Metallurgical Combine, Sverdlovsk Oblast.

Minin, Viktor Mikhaylovich, machineshop chief at the Glebovskiy poultry production association, Kholshcheviki settlement, Istrinskiy Rayon, Moscow Oblast.

Moiseyev, Mikhail Alekseyevich, chief of the USSR Armed Forces General Staff and USSR first deputy defense minister, Moscow city.

Nazarbayev, Nursultan Abishevich, chairman of the Kazakh SSR Council of Ministers.

Nechayev, Konstantin Vladimirovich, Metropolitan Pitirim of Volokolamsk and Yuryev and chairman of the Moscow Patriarchate publishing department, Moscow city.

Nechetnaya, Nadezhda Petrovna, spinner at the Lenin Factory, Bryansk Oblast.

Pallayev, Gaibnazar, chairman of the Tajik SSR Supreme Soviet Presidium.

Pivovarov, Nikolay Dmitriyevich, chairman of the Rostov Oblast Soviet Ispolkom.

Platon, Semen Ivanovich, chairman of the Kaluga City Soviet Ispolkom, Moldavian SSR.

Popov, Gavriil Kharitonovich, chief editor of the journal VOPROSY EKONOMIKI, Moscow city.

Primakov, Yevgeniy Maksimovich, director of the USSR Academy of Sciences Institute of World Economy and International Relations, Moscow city.

Pupkevich, Tadeush Karlovich, mobile excavator operator at the Narvskiy open-cut mine of the Estoslanets production association, Sillamyae city, Estonian SSR.

Razumovskiy, Georgiy Petrovich, candidate member of the CPSU Central Committee Politburo and secretary of the CPSU Central Committee.

Rakhimov, Murtaza Gubaydullovich, director of the Ufa 22d CPSU Congress Petroleum Refinery, Bashkir ASSR.

Ryzhkov, Nikolay Ivanovich, chairman of the USSR Council of Ministers and member of the CPSU Central Committee Politburo.

Sabirova, Nazira, team leader at the Yangiabad Sovkhoz [state farm], Gurlenskiy Rayon, Khorezm Oblast, Uzbek SSR.

Sbitnev, Anatoliy Mitrofanovich, steel smelter at the Kommunarsk metallurgical combine, Voroshilovgrad Oblast.

Sokolov, Yefrem Yevseyevich, first secretary of the Belorussian Communist Party Central Committee.

Starodubtsev, Vasiliy Aleksandrovich, chairman of the Lenin stud kolkhoz, Novomoskovskiy Rayon, Tula Oblast.

Stoumova, Galina Ivanovna, shop chief at the "Gatchinskiy" Sovkhoz, Leningrad Oblast.

Stupina, Yekaterina Davydovna, pediatrician at the Tavricheskiy Rayon hospital, Omsk Oblast.

Suleymenov, Olzhas Omarovich, writer and first secretary of the Kazakhstan Writers Union Board.

Tereshkova, Valentina Vladimirovna, chairman of the Presidium of the Union of Soviet Societies for Friendship and Cultural Relations With Foreign Countries, Moscow city.

Trefilov, Viktor Ivanovich, vice president of the Ukrainian SSR Academy of Sciences and director of the Ukrainian SSR Academy of Sciences Institute of Problems of Material Science.

Khachatryan, Vilesha Khachaturovich, truck driver at the Zangezurskiy copper and molybdenum combine, Armenian SSR.

Engver, Nikolay Nikolayevich, leading scientific staffer at the USSR Academy of Sciences Urals Department Physico-Technical Institute, Izhevsk city.

Yusupov, Adamali Koshokovich, unit leader of breakage face miners at the Lenin Komsomol Pit of the Kyzyl-Kiyskoye Mining Administration, Kirghiz SSR.

Yavkovlev, Aleksandr Nikolayevich, member of the CPSU Central Committee Politburo and secretary of the CPSU Central Committee.

Yanenko, Arkadiy Petrovich, rector of the Novosibirsk Engineering Construction Institute.

APPENDIX C.8
CONSTITUTIONAL COMMISSION

Commission Chairman:

Gorbachev, Mikhail Sergeyevich—chairman of the USSR Supreme Soviet, general secretary of the CPSU Central Committee.

Commission Deputy Chairman:

Lukyanov, Anatoliy Ivanovich—first deputy chairman of the USSR Supreme Soviet, candidate member of the CPSU Central Committee Politburo.

Commission Members:

Akayev, Askar—USSR people's deputy, vice president of the Kirghiz Soviet Socialist Republic [SSR] Academy of Sciences, Frunze City.

Aleksandrin, Valeriy Grigoryevich—USSR people's deputy, chairman of Yoshkar-Ola City People's Court, Mari Autonomous Soviet Socialist Republic [ASSR].

Alekseyev, Sergey Sergeyevich—USSR people's deputy, corresponding member of the USSR Academy of Sciences, director of the USSR Academy of Sciences Urals Department, Sverdlovsk City.

Ambartsumyan, Sergey Aleksandrovich—USSR people's deputy, rector of Yerevan State University.

Arutyunyan, Suren Gurgenovich—USSR people's deputy, first secretary of the Armenian Communist Party Central Committee.

Barabashev, Georgiy Vasilyevich—USSR people's deputy, chief of department at the Moscow State University named for M.V. Lomonosov Law Faculty, doctor of juridical sciences.

Berger, Arnold Vladimirovich—USSR people's deputy, director of the Kustanay Agricultural Institute Training and Experimental Farm named for Gagarin, Kazakh SSR.

Bikkenin, Nail Bariyevich—USSR people's deputy, chief editor of the journal KOMMUNIST.

Bisher, Ilmar Olgertovich—USSR people's deputy, professor at the Latvian State University named for P. Stuchka, Riga City.

Bogdanov, Igor Mikhaylovich—USSR people's deputy, school director, Gorkiy City.

Bogomolov, Oleg Timofeyevich—USSR people's deputy, director of the USSR Academy of Sciences Economics of the World Socialist System Institute, Moscow City.

Brazauskas, Algirdas-Mikolas Kaze—USSR people's deputy, first secretary of the Lithuanian Communist Party Central Committee.

Bunich, Pavel Grigoryevich—USSR people's deputy, corresponding member of the USSR Academy of Sciences, chief of department at the Moscow S. Ordzhonikidze Management Institute.

Burlatskiy, Fedor Mikhaylovich—USSR people's deputy, political observer of LITERATURNAYA GAZETA, Moscow City.

Vagris, Yan Yanovich—USSR people's deputy, first secretary of the Latvian Communist Party Central Committee.

Vezirov, Abdul-Rakhman Khalil ogly—USSR people's deputy, first secretary of the Azerbaijan Communist Party Central Committee.

Velikhov, Yevgeniy Pavlovich—USSR people's deputy, vice president of the USSR Academy of Sciences, Moscow City.

Vilkas, Eduardas Yono—USSR people's deputy, director of the Lithuanian SSR Academy of Sciences Economics Institute.

Vlasov, Aleksandr Vladimirovich—USSR people's deputy, chairman of the Russian Soviet Federated Socialist Republic [RSFSR] Council of Ministers, candidate member of the CPSU Central Committee Politburo.

Volskiy, Arkadiy Ivanovich—USSR people's deputy, chairman of the Nagorno-Karabakh Autonomous Oblast Special Administration Committee.

Vorotnikov, Vitaliy Ivanovich—USSR people's deputy, chairman of the RSFSR Supreme Soviet Presidium, member of the CPSU Central Committee Politburo.

Vyalyas, Vayno Iosipovich—USSR people's deputy, first secretary of the Estonian Communist Party Central Committee.

Gamzatov, Rasul Gamzatovich—USSR people's deputy, writer, chairman of the Dagestan ASSR Writers Union Board.

Golik, Yuriy Vladimirovich—USSR people's deputy, dean of the Kemerovo State University Law Faculty.

Grossu, Semen Kuzmich—USSR people's deputy, first secretary of the Moldavian Communist Party Central Committee.

Gryazin, Igor Nikolayevich—USSR people's deputy, chief of department at the Estonian SSR Academy of Sciences Philosophy, Sociology, and Law Institute.

Gumbaridze, Givi Grigoryevich—USSR people's deputy, first secretary of the Georgian Communist Party Central Committee.

Yevtyukhin, Yuriy Alekseyevich, docent at the Kemerovo State University, candidate of juridical sciences.

Yeltsin, Boris Nikolayevich—USSR people's deputy, Moscow City.

Zalygin, Sergey Pavlovich—USSR people's deputy, chief editor of the journal NOVYY MIR, secretary of the USSR Writers Union Board.

Zaslavskaya, Tatyana Ivanovna—USSR people's deputy, academician, director of the All-Union Center for the Study of Public Opinion on Socioeconomic Questions under the All-Union Central Council of Trade Unions [AUCCTU] and the USSR State Committee for Labor and Social Problems.

Zvonov, Sergey Nikolayevich—USSR people's deputy, director of Ivanovo's No 2 Motor Vehicle Passenger Transportation Enterprise.

Iskhaki, Yusuf Bashirkhanovich—USSR people's deputy, rector of the Tajik State Medical Institute.

Kalmykov, Yuriy Khamzatovich—USSR people's deputy, chief of department at the Saratov D.I. Kurskiy Law Institute.

Kerimov, Dzhangir Ali Abbas ogly—USSR people's deputy, chief of department at the CPSU Central Committee Academy of Social Sciences, Moscow city.

Kiyamov, Nurgaziz Vagizovich—USSR people's deputy, chairman of the Tatar ASSR Vakhitov Collective Farm [kolkhoz].

Kolbin, Gennadiy Vasilyevich—USSR people's deputy, chairman of the USSR Committee for People's Control.

Kosygin, Vladimir Vladimirovich—USSR people's deputy, own correspondent of Kamchatka Oblast Committee for Television and Radio Broadcasting, Koryak Autonomous Okrug.

Kryuchkov, Vladimir Aleksandrovich—chairman of the USSR KGB.

Kryuchkov, Georgiy Korneyevich—USSR people's deputy, first secretary of the Odessa Oblast Ukrainian Communist Party Committee [obkom].

Kudryavtsev, Vladimir Nikolayevich—USSR people's deputy, vice president of the USSR Academy of Sciences, Moscow City.

Kutafin, Oleg Yemelyanovich—rector of the All-Union Extramural Legal Studies Institute, doctor of juridical sciences.

Kyabin, Tiyt Reynkholdovich—USSR people's deputy, scientific secretary of the Estonian SSR Academy of Sciences Presidium Social Sciences Department.

Laptev, Ivan Dmitriyevich—USSR people's deputy, chief editor of the newspaper IZVESTIYA.

Lizichev, Aleksey Dmitriyevich—USSR people's deputy, chief of the Soviet Army and Navy Main Political Directorate.

Likhanov, Albert Anatolyevich—USSR people's deputy, chairman of the V.I. Lenin Soviet Children's Foundation Board, writer.

Marchuk, Guriy Ivanovich—USSR people's deputy, president of the USSR Academy of Sciences.

Masaliyev, Absamat Masaliyevich—USSR people's deputy, first secretary of the Kirghiz Communist Party Central Committee.

Matveyev, Yuriy Gennadiyevich—USSR people's deputy, USSR chief state arbiter.

Makhkamov, Kakhar—USSR people's deputy, first secretary of the Tajik Communist Party Central Committee.

Medvedev, Vadim Andreyevich—USSR people's deputy, member of the CPSU Central Committee Politburo, secretary of the CPSU Central Committee.

Mironenko, Viktor Ivanovich—USSR people's deputy, first secretary of the All-Union Lenin Communist Youth League Central Committee.

Nechayev, Konstantin Vladimirovich—USSR people's deputy, Metropolitan Pitirim of Volokolamsk and Yuryev, chairman of the Moscow Patriarchate Publishing Department.

Nikonov, Aleksandr Aleksandrovich—USSR people's deputy, president of the V.I. Lenin All-Union Academy of Agricultural Sciences.

Nishanov, Rafik Nishanovich—chairman of the USSR Supreme Soviet Soviet of Nationalities.

Niyazov, Saparmurad Atayevich—USSR people's deputy, first secretary of the Turkmen Communist Party Central Committee.

Ovezgeldyyev, Orazgeldy—USSR people's deputy, president of the Turkmen SSR Academy of Sciences.

Pavlov, Aleksandr Sergeyevich—USSR people's deputy, chief of the CPSU Central Committee State-Law Department.

Platon, Semen Ivanovich—USSR people's deputy, chairman of Kagul City Soviet of People's Deputies Executive Committee, Moldavian SSR.

Platonov, Vladimir Petrovich, USSR people's deputy, academician, president of the Belorussian SSR Academy of Sciences.

Pokrovskiy, Valentin Ivanovich—USSR people's deputy, president of the USSR Academy of Medical Sciences.

Polozkov, Ivan Kuzmich—USSR people's deputy, first secretary of Krasnodar Kray CPSU Committee.

Popov, Gavriil Kharitonovich—USSR people's deputy, chief editor of the journal VOPROSY EKONOMIKI.

Primakov, Yevgeniy Maksimovich—chairman of the USSR Supreme Soviet Soviet of the Union.

Prokopyev, Yuriy Nikolayevich—USSR people's deputy, first secretary of Yakutsk CPSU Obkom.

Pukhova, Zoya Pavlovna—USSR people's deputy, chairman of the Soviet Women's Committee.

Razumovskiy, Georgiy Petrovich—USSR people's deputy, candidate member of the CPSU Central Committee Politburo, secretary of the CPSU Central Committee, chief of the CPSU Central Committee Party Building and Cadre Work Department.

Rustamova, Zukhra Karimovna—USSR people's deputy, member of Syrdarya Oblast Court, Uzbek SSR.

Ryzhkov, Nikolay Ivanovich—USSR people's deputy, chairman of the USSR Council of Ministers, member of the CPSU Central Committee Politburo.

Sagdiyev, Makhtay Ramazanovich—USSR people's deputy, chairman of the Kazakh SSR Supreme Soviet Presidium.

Salayev, Eldar Yunis ogly—USSR people's deputy, president of the Azerbaijan SSR Academy of Sciences.

Salykov, Kakimbek—USSR people's deputy, first secretary of the Karakalpak Uzbek Communist Party Obkom.

Samsonov, Aleksandr Sergeyevich—USSR people's deputy, director of Moscow's No 1 Timepiece Plant named for S.M. Kirov.

Sakharov, Andrey Dmitriyevich—USSR people's deputy, academician, chief scientific associate of the USSR Academy of Sciences P.N. Lebedev Physics Institute, Moscow City.

Sbitnev, Anatoliy Mitrofanovich—USSR people's deputy, steel worker at the Kommunarsk metallurgical combine, Voroshilovgrad Oblast.

Sergiyenko, Valeriy Ivanovich—USSR people's deputy, chairman of Krasnoyarsk Kray Soviet of People's Deputies Executive Committee.

Simonov, Sergey Borisovich—USSR people's deputy, fitter and assembly worker at the Ufa motor-building production association.

Skudra Viktor Yanovich—USSR people's deputy, Latvian SSR minister of justice.

Slyunkov, Nikolay Nikitovich—USSR people's deputy, member of the CPSU Central Committee Politburo, secretary of the CPSU Central Committee.

Smolentsev, Yevgeniy Alekseyevich—chairman of the USSR Supreme Court.

Sobchak, Anatoliy Aleksandrovich—USSR people's deputy, chief of department at the Leningrad State University Law faculty.

Sokolov, Yefrem Yevseyevich—USSR people's deputy, first secretary of the Belorussian Communist Party Central Committee.

Suleymenov, Olzhas Omarovich—USSR people's deputy, writer, first secretary of the Kazakh SSR Writers Union Board.

Sukharev, Aleksandr Yakovlevich—USSR people's deputy, USSR general prosecutor.

Sychev, Nikolay Yakovlevich—USSR people's deputy, chairman of the Moscow City War and Labor Veterans Council.

Talanchuk, Petr Mikhaylovich—USSR people's deputy, rector of the Kiev Polytechnical Institute.

Tarazevich, Georgiy Stanislavovich—USSR people's deputy, chairman of the Belorussian SSR Supreme Soviet Presidium.

Tarnavskiy, Georgiy Stepanovich—USSR people's deputy, Belorussian SSR prosecutor.

Tkachuk, Vasiliy Mikhaylovich—USSR people's deputy, chairman of the "Prapor Kommunizmu" Kolkhoz, chairman of the "Prut" Agrofirm, Ivano-Frankovsk Oblast, Ukrainian SSR.

Topornin, Boris Nikolayevich—director of the USSR Academy of Sciences State and Law Institute, corresponding member of the USSR Academy of Sciences, Moscow City.

Umarkhodzhayev, Mukhtar Ishankhodzhayevich—USSR people's deputy, rector of the Andizhan State Language Teacher Training Institute.

Fokin, Vitold Pavlovich—USSR people's deputy, deputy chairman of the Ukrainian SSR Council of Ministers, chairman of the Ukrainian SSR State Planning Committee, Kiev City.

Khallik, Klara Semenovna—USSR people's deputy, leading scientific associate of the Estonian SSR Academy of Sciences Philosophy, Sociology, and Law Institute, Tallinn City.

Chebrikov, Viktor Mikhaylovich—USSR people's deputy, member of the CPSU Central Committee Politburo, secretary of the CPSU Central Committee.

Shalayev, Stepan Alekseyevich—USSR people's deputy, chairman of the AUCCTU.

Shakhnazarov, Georgiy Khosroyevich—USSR people's deputy, corresponding member of the USSR Academy of Sciences, aide to the general secretary of the CPSU Central Committee, Moscow City.

Shevardnadze, Eduard Amvrosiyevich—USSR foreign minister, member of the CPSU Central Committee Politburo.

Shevchenko, Valentina Semenovna—USSR people's deputy, chairman of the Ukrainian SSR Supreme Soviet Presidium.

Shinkaruk, Vladimir Illarionovich—USSR people's deputy, director of the Ukrainian SSR Academy of Sciences Philosophy Institute, Kiev City.

Shinkuba, Bagrat Vasilyevich—USSR people's deputy, poet, Georgian SSR.

Shlichite, Zita Leonovna—USSR people's deputy, attorney with the Klaypeda Legal Advice Service, Lithuanian SSR.

Shcherbitskiy, Vladimir Vasilyevich—USSR people's deputy, first secretary of the Ukrainian Communist Party Central Committee, member of the CPSU Central Committee Politburo.

Yakovlev, Aleksandr Maksimovich—USSR people's deputy, chief of section at the USSR Academy of Sciences State and Law Institute, Moscow City.

Yakovlev, Aleksandr Nikolayevich—USSR people's deputy, member of the CPSU Central Committee Politburo, secretary of the CPSU Central Committee.

Yakovlev, Veniamin Fedorovich—director of the All-Union Scientific Research Institute for Soviet State Building and Legislation, doctor of juridical sciences.

APPENDIX C.9
COMMISSION TO DRAFT LEGISLATION ON THE CONSTITUTIONAL OVERSIGHT COMMITTEE OF THE USSR

Akayev, A., Vice President of the Kirghiz Academy of Sciences

Badamyants, V. G., Chairman of the Armenian State Security Committee

Buachidze, T. P., Chairman of the Georgian Cultural Foundation

Golik, Yu. V., Dean of the Division of Law, Kemerovo State University

Gryazin, I. N., Department head, Estonian SSR Academy of Sciences Institute of Philosophy, Sociology, and Law

Kalmykov, Yu. Kh., Division head, D. I. Kursky Saratov Institute of Law

Kerimov, D. A., Department head, CPSU CC Academy of Social Sciences

Kryuchkov, G. K., First Secretary, Odessa obkom, Ukrainian Communist Party

Kudryavtsev, V. N., Vice-President of the USSR Academy of Sciences

Negmutalloyev, S. Kh., President, Tajik SSR Academy of Sciences

Ovezgeldyyev, O., President, Turkmen SSR Academy of Sciences

Pavlov, A. S., Chief of the CPSU CC Department of State and Law

Rustamov, Z. K., Member of the Syr-Darya Oblast Court, Uzbek SSR

Semenko, S. I., Chairman of the Ivanovo Oblast Court, RSFSR

Skudra, V. Ya., Minister of Justice, Latvian SSR

Smaylis, A. Yu., Laboratory head, Z. Yanushkyavichus Research Institute for the Physiology and Pathology of the Cardiovascular System, Lithuanian SSR

Sobchak, A. A., Department head, Division of Law, Leningrad State University

Sukharev, A. Ya., USSR Procurator General

Sultangazin, U. M., President of the Kazakh SSR Academy of Sciences

Tarnavsky, G. S., Procurator, Belorussian SSR

Yakovlev, A. M., Sector head, USSR Academy of Sciences Institute of State and Law

Yeremey, G. I., Chairman of the Moldavian Republic Council of Trade Unions

APPENDIX C.10
COMMISSION TO RENDER A POLITICAL AND LEGAL APPRAISAL OF THE SOVIET-GERMAN NON-AGGRESSION TREATY OF 1939

Chairman of the commission: Aleksandr Nikolayevich Yakovlev, Politburo member and CPSU Central Committee secretary.

Members of the commission:

Chingiz Aytmatov, writer and chairman of the board of the writers union, Kirghiz Soviet Socialist Republic [SSR].

Arbatov, director of the United States and Canada Institute.

Lyudmila Okopovna Arutyunyan, a department head at Yerevan State University.

Yuriy Nikolayevich Afanasyev, rector of the Moscow State Historical Archives Institute.

Vasiliy Vladimirovich Bykov, writer and secretary of the board of the USSR Writers Union, Minsk.

Mavrik Germanovich Vulfson, senior teacher of the Latvian Academy of Arts, Riga.

Igor Nikolayevich Gryazin, head of a department of the Institute of Philosophy, Sociology and Law of the Estonian SSR Academy of Sciences, Tartu.

Ion Panteleyevich Drutse, writer, Moldavia SSR, Moscow.

Grigoriy Sidorovich (?Yeremey), chairman of the Moldavian Republic Trade Union Council.

Aleksey Ivanovich Kazannik, faculty lecturer at Omsk State University.

Ivar Yanovich Kezbers, secretary of the Latvian Communist Party Central Committee.

Vitaliy Alekseyevich Korotich, editor-in-chief of OGONEK magazine.

Vladimir Alekseyevich Kravets, foreign minister of the Ukrainian SSR.

Sergey Borisovich Lavrov, a department head of Leningrad State University.

Vitautas Vitautovich Landsbergis, professor at the Lithuanian SSR state conservatory.

Maryu Yokhannesovna Lauristin, a department head at Tartu State University.

Endel Teodorovich Lippmaa, director of the Institute of Chemical and Biological Physics of the Estonian SSR Academy of Sciences.

Yustinas Moteyevich Martsinkyavichyus, writer, Lithuanian SSR.

Kazimir Vladislavovich Moteka, lawyer at Vilnius No 1 legal consultation office.

Nikolay Vasilyevich Neyland, deputy foreign minister, Latvian SSR.

Aleksey Mikhaylovich Ridiger, Metropolitan Aleksey of Leningrad and Novgorod.

Edgar Elmarovich Savisar, deputy director of the Mainor special planning and design office, Tallinn.

Valentin Mikhaylovich Falin, head of the International Department of the CPSU Central Committee.

Vladimir Ilarionovich Shinkaruk, director of the Institute of Philosophy of the Ukrainian SSR Academy of Sciences.

Zina Leonovna Shlichite, lawyer with the Klaipeda legal advice office.

APPENDIX D
DIRECTORY OF USSR PEOPLE'S DEPUTIES

Aare, Yukhan Yokhannesovich, commentator of Estonian Television Chief Propaganda Editorial Office, CPSU member, Tallinn city. From Pyarnuskiy City National-Territorial Okrug No 472, Estonian Soviet Socialist Republic [SSR].

Aasmyae, Khardo Yulovich, sector chief at the "Maynor" Planning and Design Bureau of the "Estlegprom" Estonian Territorial Production and Trade Association, CPSU member, Tallinn city. From Paydeskiy National-Territorial Okrug No 470, Estonian SSR.

Abakirov, Emilbek, chairman of the Kirghiz Republican Trade Unions Council, CPSU member, Frunze city. From the USSR trade unions.

Abalkin, Leonid Ivanovich, director of the USSR Academy of Sciences Institute of Economics, CPSU member, Moscow city. From the CPSU.

Abasov, Kurban Abas Kuli ogly, general director of the "Kaspmorneftegaz" Production Association, CPSU member, Baku city. From Ilichevskiy National-Territorial Okrug No 619, Nakhichevan Autonomous Soviet Socialist Republic [ASSR].

Abasov, Mitat Teymur ogly, director of the Azerbaijan SSR Academy of Sciences Institute of Problems of Deep Oil and Gas Deposits, CPSU member, Baku city. From Shamkhorskiy National-Territorial Okrug No 222, Azerbaijan SSR.

Abbasov, Yashar Isag ogly, steel worker at the Azerbaijan V.I. Lenin Pipe Rolling Mill, CPSU member, Sumgait city, Azerbaijan SSR. From the USSR trade unions.

Abbasova, Khuraman Zeynal kyzy, chairman of the Lenin Collective Farm [Kolkhoz], Agdamskiy Rayon, CPSU member, Agdam city. From Agdamskiy National-Territorial Okrug No 202, Azerbaijan SSR.

Abdalova, Muyassar Vaisovna, kolkhoz member of the Kalinin Kolkhoz, Koshkupyrskiy Rayon, CPSU candidate member, Uzbekyan Kishlak, Koshkupyrskiy Rayon. From Khivinskiy Territorial Okrug No 610, Khorezm Oblast, Uzbek SSR.

Abdimuratova, Shukir, family contract worker on the "Pravda" State Farm [Sovkhoz], Shumanayskiy Rayon, Kirovskiy Aul, Shumanayskiy Rayon. From Leninabadskiy National-Territorial Okrug No 567, Karakalpak ASSR.

Abdulguseyev, Mukail, team leader on the "Tabasaranskiy" State Farm [sovkhoz], Tabasaranskiy Rayon, CPSU member, Syrtych Village, Tabasaranskiy Rayon. From Derbentskiy Territorial Okrug No 363, Dagestan Autonomous Soviet Socialist Republic [ASSR].

Abdullayev, Ilkham Aziz ogly, team leader at the Zhdanov Kolkhoz, Ilichevskiy Rayon, CPSU member, Alyshar village, Ilichevskiy Rayon. From Yengidzhinskiy National-Territorial Okrug No 618, Nakhichevan ASSR.

Abdulmazhidova, Patimat Razakovna, unit leader on the Sverdlov Kolkhoz, Botlikhskiy Rayon, Tlokh village, Botlikhskiy Rayon. From Botlikhskiy National-Territorial Okrug No 527, Dagestan ASSR.

Abdurakhimov, Abdurakhman, chief economist on the Sverdlov Kolkhoz, Namanganskiy Rayon, CPSU member, Grivan settlement, Namanganskiy Rayon, Namangan Oblast. From Namanganskiy National-Territorial Okrug No 104, Uzbek SSR.

Abdykarimov, Sadulla, lathe operator at the Turtkulskiy Cotton Ginning Plant, CPSU member, Turtkul city. From Turtkulskiy National-Territorial Okrug No 565, Karakalpak ASSR.

Abzianidze, Givi Sergeyevich, first secretary of Kutaisi Georgian Communist Party City Committee [Gorkom], CPSU member, Kutaisi city. From Kutaisskiy National-Territorial Okrug No 178, Georgian SSR.

Abiatari, Taliko Ivanovna, milkmaid at the Manglisskiy Livestock Sovkhoz, Tetritskaroyskiy Rayon, Manglisi settlement, Tetritskaroyskiy Rayon. From Tetritskaroyskiy National-Territorial Okrug No 188, Georgian SSR.

Ablameyko, Igor Vasilyevich, electric welder at the Minsk S.I. Vavilov Machine Plant, CPSU member, Minsk city. From the All-Union Leninist Communist Youth League [Komsomol].

Aboyev, Aleksandr Safarbekovich, department chief at the Alagirskiy Central Rayon Hospital, CPSU member, Ordzhonikidze city. From Alagirskiy National-Territorial Okrug No 629, North Osetian ASSR.

Abramovich, Mariya Tikhonovna, machine operator at the "Metcha" Sovkhoz, Borisovskiy Rayon, CPSU member, Yartsevki village, Borisovskiy Rayon. From Borisovskiy National-Territorial Okrug No 568, Minsk Oblast, Belorussian SSR. Abramyan, Khoren Babkenovich, artistic leader of the Sundukyan Drama Theater, chairman of the board of the Armenian Theater Workers' Union, Yerevan city. From the USSR Theater Workers' Union.

Abramyan, Derenik Nshanovich, head of the Pedagogical Psychology Problems Laboratory at the Armenian Pedagogical Institute, candidate CPSU member, Yerevan City. From the USSR Society of Friends of the Cinema.

Abrashkina, Lidiya Mikhaylovna, packer at the Baku No 2 Footwear Factory, CPSU member, Baku city. From Bakinskiy-Nizaminskiy National-Territorial Okrug No 201, Azerbaijan SSR.

Abuladze, Tengiz Yevgenyevich, producer-director at the "Gruziya-Film" movie studio, CPSU member, Tbilisi city. From the CPSU.

Abutalipov, Shamil Abdulazhanovich, director of the Pavlovka Children's Home, CPSU member, Pavlovka Urban settlement, Ulyanovsk Oblast, Russian Soviet Federated Socialist Republic [RSFSR]. From the All-Union Komsomol.

Achilov, Aliboy, director of the Chepturinskiy Poultry Farm named for the 60th Anniversary of the USSR, CPSU member, Oktyabrskiy settlement, Gissarskiy Rayon. From Gissarskiy National-Territorial Okrug No 362, Tajik SSR.

Adamovich, Aleksandr Mikhaylovich, director of the All-Union Research Institute of Cinematic Art, Moscow city. From the USSR Cinematographers' Union.

Advadze, Valerian Sergeyevich, director of the Georgian SSR State Planning Committee [Gosplan] Research Institute of Economics, Planning, and Management of the National Economy, CPSU member, Tbilisi city. From Tbilisskiy-Oktyabrskiy National-Territorial Okrug No 163, Georgian SSR.

Adleyba, Boris Viktorovich, first secretary of Abkhaz Georgian Communist Party Oblast Committee [obkom], CPSU member, Sukhumi city. From Sukhumskiy Territorial Okrug No 669, Georgian SSR.

Adomaytis, Regimantas Vaytekovich, artist of the Vilnius Academic Drama Theater, chairman of the board of the Lithuanian Theater Workers' Union, Vilnius city. From the USSR Theater Workers' Union.

Adylov, Vladimir Tuychiyevich, lathe operators' team leader at the Tashkent V.P. Chkalov Aircraft Production Association, CPSU member, Tashkent city. From the CPSU.

Afanasyev, Viktor Grigoryevich, chief editor of PRAVDA, chairman of the USSR Journalists' Union Board, CPSU member, Moscow city. From the CPSU.

Afanasyev, Georgiy Nikolayevich, chief physician at the "Seregovo" resort under the Arkhangelsk Territorial Council for the Administration of Trade Union Resorts,
CPSU member, Seregovo settlement, Knyazhpogostskiy Rayon. From Knyazhpogostskiy National-Territorial Okrug No 585, Komi ASSR.

Afanasyev, Yuriy Nikolayevich, rector of the Moscow State Historical Archives Institute, CPSU member, Moscow city. From Noginskiy Territorial Okrug No 36, Moscow Oblast, RSFSR.

Afonin, Veniamin Georgiyevich, first secretary of Kuybyshev CPSU Obkom, CPSU member, Kuybyshev city. From Promyshlennyy Territorial Okrug No 206, Kuybyshev Oblast, RSFSR.

Agapova, Nina Ivanova, yarn twister at the Namangan 50th anniversary of the Uzbek SSR Silk Production Association, Namangan city, Uzbek SSR. From the USSR trade unions.

Agrba, Violetta Zosimovna, laboratory leader at the USSR Academy of Medical Sciences Research Institute of Experimental Pathology and Therapeutics, CPSU member, Sukhumi city, Abkhaz ASSR. From Sukhumskiy City National-Territorial Okrug No 185, Georgian SSR.

Aguzarova, Stella Borisovna, fitter at the Ordzhonikidze 50th Anniversary of the Komsomol Electric Light Plant, CPSU member, Ordzhonikidze city. From Sovietskiy National-Territorial Okrug No 627, North Osetian ASSR.

Akayev, Askar, vice president of the Kirghiz SSR Academy of Sciences, CPSU member, Frunze city. From Naukatskiy National-Territorial Okrug No 339, Kirghiz SSR.

Akebayev, Zhangeldy, chairman of Sarkandskiy Rayon Committee [Raykom] of the Voluntary Society for the Promotion of the Army, Air Force, and Navy [DOSAAF], CPSU member, Sarkand city, Taldy-Kurgan Oblast, Kazakh SSR. From the All-Union Voluntary Society for the Promotion of the Army, Air Force, and Navy (USSR DOSAAF).

Akentyev, Anatoliy Vasilyevich, chief of the Central House of the Soviet Army winter sports branch, CPSU member, "Tysovets" Sports Center, Skolevskiy Rayon, Lvov Oblast, Ukrainian SSR. From the USSR public sports organizations.

Akhmedov, Oktay Ali ogly, regulator at Baku's "Radiostroyeniye" Production Association, CPSU member, Baku city. From Bakinskiy-Shaumyanovskiy National-Territorial Okrug No 200, Azerbaijan SSR.

Akhmedov, Rakhmatullo, director of a cotton products combine, CPSU member, Kuva city. From Ferganskiy Territorial Okrug No 608, Fergana Oblast, Uzbek SSR.

Akhmetova, Rushangul Sunurovna, teacher at Ch. Valikhanova Secondary School, Kaynazar village, Enbekshikazakhskiy Rayon, Alma-Ata Oblast. From Alma-Atinskiy-Talgarskiy National-Territorial Okrug No 131, Kazakh SSR.

Akhromeyev, Sergey Fedorovich, adviser to the chairman of the USSR Supreme Soviet Presidium, CPSU member, Moscow city. From Beltsskiy Territorial Okrug No 697, Moldavian SSR.

Akhunov, Pulatzhan Alimovich, deputy director for educational work at School No 4, Shakhrikhan city, Moskovskiy Rayon, Andizhan Oblast, Uzbek SSR. From the All-Union Komsomol.

Akimenko, Vasiliy Savelyevich, chairman of the board of the Bryansk Oblast Union of Consumer Trade Cooperatives [Potrebsoyuz], CPSU member, Bryansk city, RSFSR. From the USSR Consumer Cooperative System.

Akmamedov, Geldy Mamedmuradovich, master baker at the No 1 Bakery of the "Ashkhabadkhleb" Production Association, CPSU member, Ashkhabad city. From Ashkhabadskiy-Pervomayskiy National-Territorial Okrug No 418, Turkmen SSR.

Akmataliyeva, Urukan Kalilovna, silk reeler at the Osh All-Union Komsomol Silk Industrial and Trade Association, CPSU member, Osh city. From Oshskiy City National-Territorial Okrug No 340, Kirghiz SSR.

Akmatov, Tashtanbek, chairman of the Kirghiz SSR Supreme Soviet Presidium, CPSU member, Frunze city. From Issyk-Kulskiy National-Territorial Okrug No 329, Kirghiz SSR.

Akramov, Ernst Khashimovich, department chief at the republican clinical hospital, Frunze city. From Frunzenskiy-Sverdlovskiy National-Territorial Okrug No 324, Kirghiz SSR.

Akramova, Tamara Musoyevna, department chief at Matchinskiy Rayon Hospital, CPSU member, Buston city, Matchinskiy Rayon, Leninabad Oblast. From Matchinskiy National-Territorial Okrug No 374, Tajik SSR.

Aksenov, Ivan Mikhaylovich, chairman of the Krupskaya Kolkhoz, Topchikhinskiy Rayon, CPSU member, Chistyunka village, Topchikhinskiy Rayon, Altay Kray, RSFSR. From the kolkhozes united by the Union Kolkhoz Council.

Aksenov, Vyacheslav Ivanovich, team leader of the "Nizhneangarsktransstroy" Trust's No 608 construction and installation train, CPSU member, Kichera settlement, Severo-Baykalskiy Rayon. From Barguzinskiy National-Territorial Okrug No 518, Buryat ASSR.

Aleksandrin, Valeriy Grigoryevich, chairman of Yoshkar-Ola City People's Court, CPSU member, Yoshkar-Ola city. From Sverdlovskiy National-Territorial Okrug No 594, Mari ASSR.

Aleksankin, Aleksandr Vasilyevich, deputy chairman of the RSFSR Council of Ministers, chairman of the RSFSR Nonchernozem Zone State Agro-Industrial Committee [Gosagroprom], CPSU member, Moscow city. From Tulskiy National-Territorial Okrug No 29, RSFSR.

Alekseyev, Anatoliy Aleksandrovich, chief of the production dispatch section at the Kaspiyskiy Machine Building Plant, Kaspiyskiy city. From Kaspiyskiy National-Territorial Okrug No 551, Kalmyk ASSR.

Alekseyev, Boris Grigoryevich, chairman of Nizhne-Ilimskiy Rayispolkom, CPSU member, Zheleznogorsk-Ilimskiy City. From Ust-Kutskiy Territorial Electoral Okrug No 175, Russian Soviet Federated Socialist Republic [RSFSR].

Alekseyev, Sergey Sergeyevich, corresponding member of the USSR Academy of Sciences, director of the USSR Academy of Sciences Urals Department Institute of Philosophy and Law, CPSU member, Sverdlovsk city, RSFSR. From the USSR Academy of Sciences.

Alekseyeva, Lidiya Mikhaylovna, secretary of the party committee of the "Serp i Molot" Kolkhoz, Dmitriyevskiy Rayon, CPSU member, Pogodino village, Dmitriyevskiy Rayon, Kursk Oblast, RSFSR. From the CPSU.

Alekseyenko, Mikhail Grigoryevich, chief of the geological prospecting section of the "Tuvakobalt" Combine mining shop, CPSU member, Khovu-Aksy Urban settlement, Tandinskiy Rayon. From Tandinskiy National-Territorial Okrug No 654, Tuva ASSR.

Aleskerova, Rukhi Mursal kyzy, chairman of Lagich settlement Soviet of People's Deputies Executive Committee [ispolkom], CPSU member, Lagich settlement, Ismaillinskiy Rayon. From Geokchayskiy National-Territorial Okrug No 205, Azerbaijan SSR.

Aleshin, Yevgeniy Pavlovich, director of the All-Union Rice Research Institute, CPSU member, Krasnodar city, RSFSR. From the V.I. Lenin All-Union Academy of Agricultural Sciences.

Aliyeva, Gyullyu Bayram kyzy, milkmaid at the Dimitrov Kolkhoz, Kasum-Ismailovskiy Rayon, CPSU member, Samedabad settlement, Kasum-Ismailovskiy Rayon. From Kasum-Ismailovskiy National-Territorial Okrug No 209, Azerbaijan SSR.

Aliluyev, Nikolay Ivanovich, machine operator at the Kuybyshev Railroad Ruzayevka Station locomotive depot, CPSU member, Ruzayevka city. From Ruzayevskiy National-Territorial Okrug No 610, Mordovian ASSR.

Alimbetov, Iskendir Abdireymovich, senior shepherd at Takhtakupyrskiy Rayon's "Zhanadarya" Sovkhoz, CPSU member, Takhtakupyrskiy Rayon. From Takhtakupyrskiy National-Territorial Okrug No 564, Karakalpak ASSR.

Alimov, Saydullo, chairman of Kabodiyenskiy Rayon's Karl Marx Kolkhoz, CPSU member, Kabodiyenskiy

Rayon, Khatlon Oblast. From Shaartuzskiy National-Territorial Okrug No 383, Tajik SSR.

Alimova, Khalimakhan, chairman of the Uzbek Republic Trade Union Council, CPSU member, Tashkent city. From the USSR's trade unions.

Allamuradov, Buri Allamuradovich, first secretary of Namangan Uzbek Communist Party Obkom, CPSU member, Namangan city. From Namanganskiy Territorial Okrug No 583, Namangan Oblast, Uzbek SSR.

Allayarov, Redzhapbay Allayarovich, chairman of Tashauzskiy Rayon's Kalinin Kolkhoz, CPSU member, Voroshilov settlement, Tashauzskiy Rayon, Tashauz Oblast. From Tezebazarskiy National-Territorial Okrug No 443, Turkmen SSR.

Almazov, Vladimir Andreyevich, director of the RSFSR Ministry of Health Cardiology Research Institute, CPSU member, Leningrad city. From the USSR Academy of Medical Sciences and 40 scientific medical societies.

Alferov, Zhores Ivanovich, academician, director of the USSR Academy of Sciences A.F. Ioffe Physical and Technical Institute, CPSU member, Leningrad city. From the USSR Academy of Sciences.

Alybekov, Asanbek, senior shepherd at Toktogul Sovkhoz, Toktogulskiy Rayon, CPSU member, Kara-Kungey settlement, Toktogulskiy Rayon, Osh Oblast. From Toktogulskiy National-Territorial Okrug No 348, Kirghiz SSR.

Amaglobeli, Nodari Sardionovich, rector of Tbilisi State University, CPSU member, Tbilisi city. From Tbiliskiy-Ordzhonikidzevskiy Territorial Okrug No 657, Georgian SSR.

Amanbayev, Dzhumgalbek Beksultanovich, first secretary of Issyk-Kul Kirghiz Communist Party Obkom, CPSU member, Rybache city. From Narynskiy National-Territorial Okrug No 338, Kirghiz SSR.

Amangeldinova, Galina Aleksandrovna, teacher at No 22 secondary school, CPSU member, Pavlodar city, Kazakh SSR. From the USSR's trade unions.

Amanov, Akif Mami ogly, drilling foreman at the Ali-Bayramly Drilling Work Administration, CPSU member, Ali-Bayramly city. From Akhsuinskiy Territorial Okrug No 675, Azerbaijan SSR.

Amanov, Tulkin, chief of the "Shurtangaz" Gasfield Administration, CPSU member, Beshkent city, Kashka-Darya Oblast. From Karshinskiy National-Territorial Okrug No 102, Uzbek SSR.

Amanova, Maral Bazarovna, department head at the Turkmen A.M. Gorkiy University, CPSU member, Ashkhabad city. From the women's councils united in the Soviet Women's Committee.

Ambartsumyan, Viktor Amazaspovich, president of the Armenian SSR Academy of Sciences, CPSU member, Yerevan city. From Ashtarakskiy National-Territorial Okrug No 404, Armenian SSR.

Ambartsumyan, Sergey Aleksandrovich, rector of Yerevan State University, CPSU member, Yerevan city. From Yerevanskiy-Myasnikyanskiy National-Territorial Okrug No 392, Armenian SSR.

Amonashvili, Shalva Aleksandrovich, general director of the Georgian SSR Ministry of Public Education Experimental Science and Production Association, CPSU member, Tbilisi city. From the USSR's trade unions.

Amosov, Nikolay Mikhaylovich, honorary director of Cardio-Vascular Surgery Research Institute, Kiev city. From Leninskiy Territorial Okrug No 464, Kiev.

Amzarakov, Vladimir Grigoryevich, automobile driver at Askizskiy Rayon's Kalinin Sovkhoz, Askiz-1 Kishlak, Askizskiy Rayon. From Askizskiy National-Territorial Okrug No 372, Khakassy Autonomous Oblast.

Ananyev, Anatoliy Andreyevich, writer, editor in chief of OKTYABR journal, CPSU member, Moscow city. From the peace movement, the Soviet Committee for the Defense of Peace, and the USSR United Nations Association.

Andreyev, Anatoliy Yevgenyevich, chairman of the Belorussian SSR Supreme Soviet Presidium Commission for the Affairs of Former Partisans and Members of the Underground, CPSU member, Minsk city. From the All-Union Organization of War and Labor Veterans.

Andreyev, Khristofor Grigoryevich, chief state engineer and, inspector at Strashenskiy Rayon Agro-Industrial Association, member of the CPSU, Strasheny Urban settlement. From Strashenskiy National-Territorial Okrug No 282, Moldavian SSR.

Andreyeva, Irina Aleksandrovna, chief art critic at the Union House of Fashion, secretary of the USSR Designers' Union, Moscow city. From the USSR Designers' Union.

Andronati, Sergey Andreyevich, director of the Ukrainian SSR Academy of Sciences A.V. Bogatskiy Physics and Chemistry Institute, CPSU member, Odessa city. From Odesskiy-Kiyevskiy Territorial Okrug No 498, Odessa Oblast, Ukrainian SSR.

Angapov, Semen Vasilyevich, pensioner, member of the CPSU, Ulan-Ude, Buryat ASSR. From the All-Union Organization of War and Labor Veterans.

Angarkhayev, Ardan Lopsonovich, writer, artistic director of the theater workshop in the Khuzhir House of Culture, Tunkinskiy Rayon, Kyren village, Tunkinskiy Rayon. From Dzhidinskiy National-Territorial Okruk No 520, Buryat ASSR.

Anisimov, Aleksandr Ivanovich, chief of a workshop at Groznyy Chemical Plant named for the 50th anniversary of the USSR, CPSU member, Groznyy city. From the Zavodskiy National-Territorial Okrug No 669, Chechen Ingush ASSR.

Anisimova, Galina Anatolyevna, deputy chief of a Northern Maritime Steamship Company computer center department, CPSU member, Arkhangelsk city, RSFSR. From the women's councils united in the Committee of Soviet Women.

Anishchev, Vladimir Petrovich, second secretary of the Uzbek Communist Party Central Committee, CPSU member, Tashkent city. From Nukusskiy Territorial Okrug No 611, Karakalpak ASSR.

Annamukhamedov, Atakhodzhamengli, deputy commander of Turkmen Civil Aviation Administration head enterprise first flying division air squadron, CPSU member, Ashkhabad city. From Ashkhabadskiy-Leninskiy National-Territorial Okrug No 417, Turkmen SSR.

Annamukhamedov, Ovezmukhamed, chairman of the Turkmen Republic Trade Union Council, CPSU member, Ashkhabad city. From the USSR's trade unions.

Antanavichyus, Kazimeras Antano, chief of a department at the Lithuanian SSR Academy of Sciences Economics Institute, Vilnius city. From Vilnyusskiy-Oktyabrskiy National-Territorial Okrug No 228, Lithuanian SSR.

Antanaytis, Vaydotas Vito, head of a department of the Lithuanian Agricultural Academy, Noreykishkes Rural Soviet, Kaunasskiy Rayon. From Kaunasskiy Rural Territorial Okrug No 689, Lithuanian SSR.

Antifeyev, Anatoliy Yevgenyevich, general director of "Tyazhmash" Production Association, CPSU member, Mariupol city. From Ilichevskiy Territorial Okrug No 439, Donetsk Oblast, Ukrainian SSR.

Anufriyev, Vladislav Grigoryevich, secretary of the Kazakh Communist Party Central Committee, CPSU member, Alma-Ata city. From Dzhetysuskiy National-Territorial Okrug No 140, Kazakh SSR.

Anufriyev, Gennadiy Panteleyevich, deputy chief at Rovno Nuclear Power Station [AES] centralized repair shop, CPSU member, Kuznetsovsk city. From Sarnenskiy Territorial Okrug No 511, Rovno Oblast, Ukrainian SSR.

Anufriyeva, Lidiya Alekseyevna, director of Povenets Secondary School, CPSU member, Povenets settlement, Medvezhyegorskiy Rayon. From Medvezhyegorskiy National-Territorial Okrug No 575, Karelian ASSR.

Aparin, Ivan Vasilyevich, first secretary of Kytmanovskiy CPSU Raykom, CPSU member, Kytmanovo village, Altay Kray. From Novoaltayskiy Territorial Okrug No 70, Altay Kray RSFSR.

Apostol, Veniamin Gavrilovich, chief director of Kishinev's A.P. Chekhov Russian Drama Theater, chairman of the Moldavian Union of Theater Workers Board, CPSU member, Kishinev city. From the USSR Union of Theater Workers.

Arbatov, Georgiy Arkadyevich, director of the USSR Academy of Sciences United States and Canada Institute, CPSU member, Moscow City. From the USSR Academy of Sciences.

Ardzinba, Vladislav Grigoryevich, director of the Georgian SSR's Abkhaz Institute of Language, Literature, and History named for D.I. Gulia, CPSU member, Eshera village, Sukhumskiy Rayon. From Gudautskiy City National-Territorial Okrug No 486, Abkhaz ASSR.

Aripdzhanov, Makhmut Maripovich, first secretary of the Andizhan Uzbek Communist Party Oblast Committee [obkom], CPSU member, Andizhan City. From Leninskiy Territorial Okrug No 577, Andizhan Oblast, Uzbek Soviet Socialist Republic [SSR].

Arkhipov, Petr Mikhaylovich, chairman of the Turkmen SSR KGB, CPSU member, Ashkhabad city. From Nebit-Dagskiy Territorial Okrug No 744, Turkmen SSR.

Arkhipova, Irina Konstantinovna, soloist at the USSR State Academic Bolshoy Theater, chairman of the All-Union Music Society Central Board, CPSU member, Moscow city. From the All-Union Music Society.

Arshba, Ruslan Ardevanovich, shaft-sinker at "Tkvarchelskoye" Mining Administration Mine No 2, CPSU member, Tkvarcheli city. From Tkvarchelskiy National-Territorial Okrug No 491, Abkhaz ASSR.

Arslonov, Aliyer Kumriyevich, team leader at Papskiy Rayon's kolkhoz named for the 22d party congress, CPSU member, Pap city. From Chustskiy Territorial Okrug No 585, Namangan Oblast, Uzbek SSR.

Artemenko, Gennadiy Ivanovich, leader of a team of gas arc welders at the No 140 Mechanization and Specialized Work Administration of the No 9 Construction Trust, Vitebsk City. From Vitebskiy City Territorial Okrug No 551, Vitebsk Oblast, Belorussian SSR.

Aruvald, Andres Evald-Eduardovich, chairman of the Estonian Potrebsoyuz, CPSU member, Tallinn city. From the USSR's Consumer Cooperatives.

Arutyunyan, Avetik Beniaminovich, fitter at "Agrostroy" No 7 Trust's No 2 mobile mechanized column, CPSU member, V. Getashen village, Martuninskiy Rayon. From Martuninskiy National-Territorial Okrug No 410, Armenian SSR.

Arutyunyan, Lyudmila Akopovna, head of department at Yerevan State University, CPSU member, Yerevan city. From the women's councils united in the Soviet Women's Committee.

Arutyunyan, Martin Karapetovich, chairman of the Armenian Republic Trade Union Council, CPSU member, Yerevan city. From the USSR's trade unions.

Arutyunyan, Suren Gurgenovich, first secretary of the Armenian Communist Party Central Committee, CPSU member, Yerevan city. From Leninakanskiy Territorial Okrug No 737, Armenian SSR.

Arutyunyan, Elmir Tatulovich, leader of a team of tool makers at Yerevan's "Elektropribor" Production Association, CPSU member, Yerevan city. From Yerevanskiy-Shaumyanskiy National-Territorial Okrug No 391, Armenian SSR.

Arystanbayev, Sagin Tileshovich, driver at Yeril Motor Transport Dispatch Enterprise, CPSU member, Yesil city. From Yesilskiy Territorial Okrug No 648, Tselinograd Oblast, Kazakh SSR.

Asankulov, Dzhumabek, chairman of the Kirghiz SSR KGB, CPSU member, Frunze city. From Kyzyl-Kiyskiy National-Territorial Okrug No 335, Kirghiz SSR.

Askarov, Atakul, section leader at Uzgenskiy Rayon's "Shoro-Bashat" Sovkhoz, CPSU member, Shoro-Bashat village, Uzgenskiy Rayon, Osh Oblast. From Uzgenskiy National-Territorial Okrug No 351, Kirghiz SSR.

Askarov, Yuldashboy Akbarovich, director of "Madaniyat" Sovkhoz, Pakhtaabadskiy Rayon, CPSU member, Pakhtaabadskiy Rayon, Andizhan Oblast. From Izbaskanskiy Territorial Okrug No 576, Uzbek SSR.

Astafyev, Vasiliy Mikhaylovich, pensioner, CPSU member, Perm city, RSFSR. From the All-Union Organization of War and Labor Veterans.

Astafyev, Viktor Petrovich, writer, Krasnoyarsk city, RSFSR. From the USSR Union of Writers.

Astakhova, Maryana Maryanovna, senior technician at Krasnodar's chemical plant named for the 60th anniversary of the USSR, CPSU member, Belorechensk city, Krasnodar Kray, RSFSR. From the women's councils united in the Soviet Women's Committee.

Atadzhanov, Alikhan Rakhmatovich, first deputy chairman of the Uzbek SSR Council of Ministers, chairman of the Uzbek SSR Gosplan, CPSU member, Tashkent city. From Chartakskiy National-Territorial Okrug No 105, Uzbek SSR.

Atayev, Seyitiniyaz, deputy chairman of the Turkmen Committee for Solidarity with the Countries of Asia and Africa, CPSU member, Ashkhabad city. From the All-Union Organizationof War and Labor Veterans.

Atdayev, Khodzhamukhamed, blacksmith at Ashkhabad's Petroleum Machine Building Plant named for the 50th anniversary of the USSR, CPSU member, Ashkhabad city. From Ashkhabadskiy-Zheleznodorozhniy National-Territorial Okrug No 420, Turkmen SSR.

Auyelbekov, Yerkin Nurzhanovich, first secretary of Kzyl-Orda Kazakh Communist Party Obkom, CPSU member, Kzyl-Orda city. From Kzyl-Ordinskiy National-Territorial Okrug No 144, Kazakh SSR.

Aushev, Ruslan Sultanovich, lieutenant colonel, commander of a motorized rifle regiment, Far East Military District, CPSU member, Maritime Kray. From Ussuriyskiy National-Territorial Okrug No 102, Maritime Kray, RSFSR.

Avaliani, Teymuraz Georgiyevich, deputy director of the capital construction directorate at the "Kiselevskugol" Production Association, CPSU member, Kiselevsk city. From Belovskiy Territorial Okrug No 193, Kemerovo Oblast, RSFSR.

Averintsev, Sergey Sergeyevich, chief of a sector at the USSR Academy of Sciences Institute of World Literature, Moscow City. From the USSR Academy of Sciences.

Averkin, Vladimir Nikolayevich, director of the No 1 Boarding School, CPSU member, Novgorod city, RSFSR. From the CPSU.

Avotin, Viktor Matisovich, executive secretary of the journal DAUGAVA, CPSU member, Riga city. From Ogrskiy National-Territorial Okrug No 311, Latvian SSR.

Avtorkhanov, Supyan Evterbiyevich, chairman of Nozhay-Yurtovskiy Rayon Soviet Executive Committee [rayispolkom] Rayon Planning Commission, CPSU member, Nozhay-Yurt village. From Nozhay-Yurtovskiy National-Territorial Okrug No 676, Chechen-Ingush Autonomous Soviet Socialist Republic [ASSR].

Aydak, Arkadiy Pavlovich, chairman of the "Leninskaya Iskra" Kolkhoz, Yadrinskiy Rayon, CPSU member, Verkhniye Achaki village, Yadrinskiy Rayon. From Yadrinskiy National-Territorial Okrug No 689, Chuvash ASSR.

Aydamirov, Abuzar Abdulkhakimovich, writer, CPSU member, Meskety village, Nozhay-Yurtovskiy Rayon. From Gudermesskiy Territorial Okrug No 397, Chechen-Ingush ASSR.

Aypin, Yeremey Danilovich, senior editor at the okrug House of Creativity of the Northern Ethnic Groups, CPSU member, Khanty-Mansiysk city. From Khanty-Mansiyskiy National-Territorial Okrug No 747, Khanty-Mansiysk Autonomous Okrug.

Aytmatov, Chingiz, writer, chairman of the board of the Kirghiz SSR Writers' Union, chief editor of the journal INOSTRANNAYA LITERATURA, CPSU member, Frunze city. From the CPSU.

Aytkhozhina, Nagima Abenovna, acting director of the Kazakh SSR Academy of Sciences Institute of Molecular Biology, CPSU candidate member, Alma-Ata city. From the women's councils united by the Soviet Women's Committee.

Ayubov, Nazhmiddin, director of the Frunze Interkolkhoz Complex, Gissarskiy Rayon, CPSU member, Shakhrinau settlement, Gissarskiy Rayon. From Gissarskiy Territorial Okrug No 725, Tajik SSR.

Azarov, Viktor Yakovlevich, pensioner, CPSU member, Moscow city. From the All-Union Organization of War and Labor Veterans.

Azarov, Sergey Ignatyevich, assistant general director of the "Vinnitsaenergo" Energy Production Association, CPSU member, Vinnitsa city, Ukrainian SSR. From the All-Union Organization of War and Labor Veterans.

Azizbekova, Pyusta Azizaga kyzy, director of the Azerbaijan History Museum, CPSU member, Baku city. From Bakinskiy-Azizbekovskiy National-Territorial Okrug No 199, Azerbaijan SSR.

Azizova, Zenfila Aziz kyzy, milkmaid at the M.F. Akhundov Kolkhoz, Kutkashenskiy Rayon, Sultan Nukha village, Kutkashenskiy Rayon. From Agdashskiy National-Territorial Okrug No 203, Azerbaijan SSR.

Babanov, Toktogul Babanovich, chairman of Kirovskiy Rayon's "Rossiya" Kolkhoz, CPSU member, Amanbayevo village, Kirovskiy yn, Kirghiz SSR. From kolkhozes united in the Union Kolkhoz Council.

Babayev, Ismail Adil ogly, combine and machine operator at Shamkhorskiy Rayon's 26th Party Congress Sovkhoz, Ugerli village, Shamkhorskiy Rayon. From Tauzskiy Territorial Okrug No 683, Azerbaijan SSR.

Babeshko, Vladimir Andreyevich, rector of Kubanskiy State University, CPSU member, Krasnodar city, RSFSR. From the "Znaniye" All-Union Society.

Babich, Valentina Mitrofanovna, chairman of Kiev Agro-Industrial Complex Workers Trade Union Gorkom, CPSU member, Kiev city. From the USSR's trade unions.

Babchenko, Nikolay Ivanovich, chairman of Dnepropetrovskiy Local Industry and Municipal and Consumer Service Enterprise Workers Trade Union Obkom, CPSU member, Dnepropetrovsk city, Ukrainian SSR. From the USSR's trade unions.

Babynin, Genrikh Vladimirovich, sector chief at the "Strela" Scientific Research Institute, Tula city. From Proletarskiy Territorial Okrug No 315, Tula Oblast, RSFSR.

Bachinskiy, Dmitriy Grigoryevich, senior engineer at the Lvov Polytechnical Institute, CPSU member, Lvov city, Ukrainian SSR. From the All-Union Organization of War and Labor Veterans.

Badalbayeva, Patima, chief physician at Shakhrisabz Central Rayon Hospital, CPSU member, Shakhrisabz city, Kashka-Darya Oblast, Uzbek SSR. From the women's councils united in the Soviet Women's Committee.

Badamyants, Valeriy Georgiyevich, chairman of the Armenian SSR KGB, CPSU member, Yerevan city. From Kafanskiy National-Territorial Okrug No 406, Armenian SSR.

Badzhelidze, Nino Usupovna, tea grower at Khutsubani village Kolkhoz, Khutsubani village, Kobuletskiy Rayon. From Chakvskiy National-Territorial Okrug No 501, Adzhar ASSR.

Bagirov, Tofik Guseyn ogly, locomotive engineer at the Baladzhary Locomotive Depot named for A.A. Dzhafarov, Azerbaijan Railroad, CPSU member, Baku city. From Bakinskiy-8ovskiy National-Territorial Okrug No 195, Azerbaijan SSR.

Bagirova, Seyran Kyamil kyzy, vine-dresser at Babekskiy Rayon's kolkhoz named for Dzh. Mamedkuli-zade, Nizhniy Uzunoba village, Babekskiy Rayon. From Dzhagrinskiy National-Territorial Okrug No 616, Nakhichevan ASSR.

Baklanov, Viktor Vasilyevich, machine operator at Magdalinovskiy Rayon's "Gigant" Kolkhoz, CPSU member, Zhdanovka village, Magdalinovskiy Rayon, Dnepropetrovsk Oblast, Ukrainian SSR. From kolkhozes united in the Union Kolkhoz Council.

Baklanov, Oleg Dmitriyevich, secretary of the CPSU Central Committee, CPSU member, Moscow city. From the CPSU.

Bakradze, Akakiy Viktorovich, artistic leader of the K. Mardzhanishvili State Academic Theater in Tbilisi, CPSU member, Tbilisi city. From Tbilisskiy-Saburtalinskiy National-Territorial Okrug No 167, Georgian SSR.

Bakulin, Valentin Ivanovich, team leader of fitters at the "Krasnaya Talka" Spinning and Finishing Factory in Ivanovo, CPSU member, Ivanovo city, RSFSR. From the USSR's trade unions.

Balayan, Zoriy Gaykovich, LITERATURNAYA GAZETA own correspondent in the Armenian SSR, CPSU member, Yerevan city. From Askeranskiy National-Territorial Okrug No 729, Nagorno-Karabakh Autonomous Oblast [NKAO].

Balenko, Aleksandra Georgiyevna, engineer and economist at the "Kamchatavtotrans" Territorial Production Association, Petropavlovsk-Kamchatskiy city, Kamchatka Oblast, RSFSR. From the All-Union Komsomol.

Baleshev, Nikolay Fedorovich, first secretary of Ashkhabad Turkmen Communist Party Gorkom, CPSU member, Ashkhabad city. From Ashkhabadskiy-Sovietskiy National-Territorial Okrug No 419, Turkmen SSR.

Baltayeva, Roza, deputy chief physician at the Beruni Central Rayon Hospital, CPSU member, Beruni city. From Beruniyskiy National-Territorial Okrug No 559, Kara-Kalpak ASSR.

Baluyev, Veniamin Georgiyevich, chairman of the Belorussian SSR KGB, CPSU member, Minsk city. From Mozyrskiy National-Territorial Okrug No 87, Belorussian SSR.

Barabanov, Vyacheslav Ivanovich, livestock unit chief at Dzheti-Oguzskiy Rayon's "Kommunizm" Kolkhoz, CPSU member, Pokrovka village, Dzheti-Oguzskiy Rayon, Issyk Kul Oblast. From Przhevalskiy National-Territorial Okrug No 341, Kirghiz SSR.

Barannikova, Olga Vyacheslavovna, 4th-year student at the Tula Polytechnical Institute, candidate CPSU member, Tula city, RSFSR. From the All-Union Komsomol.

Baranov, Aleksandr Yefimovich, pensioner, CPSU member, Kirov city, RSFSR. From the All-Union Organization of War and Labor Veterans.

Baranov, Aleksandr Ivanovich, trade union committee chairman at Leningrad's "Izhorskiy Zavod" Production Association, CPSU member, Kolpino city, Leningrad city, RSFSR. From the USSR's trade unions.

Baranova, Galina Timofeyevna, deputy chief physician for treatment at Berdsk Central City Hospital, CPSU member, Berdsk city, Novosibirsk Oblast, RSFSR. From the women's councils united in the Soviet Women's Committee.

Baranovskiy, Vasiliy Vasilyevich, pensioner, CPSU member, Simferopol city, Ukrainian SSR. From the All-Union Organization of War and Labor Veterans.

Baravikas, Gediminas Vatslavovich, Vilnius city chief architect, chief of the Main Administration for Architecture and Urban Development, CPSU member, Vilnius city. From the USSR Architects' Union.

Barbolova, Kalamkas Zhakudayevna, machine operator at Dzhetysayskiy Rayon's "Dzhetysayskiy" Sovkhoz, CPSU member, Dzhetysayskiy Rayon, Chimkent Oblast, Kazakh SSR. From the All-Union Komsomol.

Barsov, Aleksey Ivanovich, milking machine operator at Kastorenskiy Rayon's Aleksandrovskiy State Stud Farm No 12, Nikolskoye village, Kastorenskiy Rayon. From Shchigrovskiy Territorial Okrug No 219, Kursk Oblast, RSFSR.

Barusheva, Lyubov Vasilyevna, seamstress at the Volodarskiy Sewn Goods Factory, Baku city. From Bakinskiy-Nasiminskiy National-Territorial Okrug No 198, Azerbaijan SSR.

Baryshnikov, Ivan Antonovich, marker at the Volga Motor Vehicle Plant named for the 50th anniversary of the USSR, CPSU member, Tolyatti city, Kuybyshev Oblast, RSFSR. From the CPSU.

Bashev, Nikolay Alekseyevich, director of Yashkinskiy Rayon's "Kolmogorovskiy" Poultry Breeding Sovkhoz, CPSU member, Kolmogorovo village, Yashkinskiy Rayon. From Mariinskiy Territorial Okrug No 189, Kemerovo Oblast, RSFSR.

Bashirova, Lala Mir Gasan kyzy, laboratory worker at the Novo-Bakinskiy Oil Refinery named for Vladimir Ilich, Baku city. From Bakinskiy-Narimanovskiy Territorial Okrug No 672, Azerbaijan SSR.

Bashmakov, Yevgeniy Fedorovich, first deputy chairman of the Kazakh SSR Council of Ministers, CPSU member, Alma-Ata city. From Uralskiy National-Territorial Okrug No 154, Kazakh SSR.

Baskova, Valentina Aleksandrovna, milkmaid at the "Molochnoye" State Livestock Breeding Center, CPSU member, Vologda city, RSFSR. From the women's councils united in the Soviet Women's Committee.

Batiashvili, Stanislav Andreyevich, worker at the Lagodekhi Machine Building Plant, CPSU member, Lagodekhi city. From Gurdzhaanskiy Territorial Okrug No 662, Georgian SSR.

Batorov, Oleg Borisovich, second secretary of the Osinskiy CPSU Rayon Committee [raykom], CPSU member, Osa Village, Osinskiy Rayon, Irkutsk Oblast, Russian Soviet Federated Socialist Republic [RSFSR]. From Ust-Ordynskiy Buryatskiy National-Territorial Okrug No 746, Ust-Ordynskiy Buryatskiy Autonomous Okrug.

Batrachenko, Svetlana Vasilyevna, pioneer leader at the "Artek" All-Union Pioneer Camp named for V.I. Lenin, Gurzuf Urban settlement, Yalta city, Crimean Oblast, Ukrainian SSR. From the All-Union Komsomol.

Batynskaya, Lyudmila Ivanovna, editor of the KRASNOYARSKIY KOMSOMOLETS newspaper, CPSU member, Krasnoyarsk city, RSFSR. From the USSR Journalists' Union.

Batyshev, Sergey Yakovlevich, academician of the USSR Academy of Pedagogical Sciences, adviser to the USSR Academy of Pedagogical Sciences Presidium, CPSU member, Moscow City. From the USSR Academy of Pedagogical Sciences jointly with the Soviet Association of Pegagogical Researchers.

Bavula, Valentina Stepanovna, inspector at the 60th Anniversary of October Plant, CPSU member, Vinnitsa city. From Vinnitskiy Territorial Okrug No 404, Vinnitsa Oblast, Ukrainian SSR.

Bazarova, Roza Atamuradovna, chairman of the Turkmen SSR Supreme Soviet Presidium, CPSU member, Ashkhabad city. From Kunya-Urgenchskiy National-Territorial Okrug No 436, Turkmen SSR.

Bazhanov, Nikolay Nikolayevich, faculty chief at the I.M. Sechenov First Moscow Medical Institute, CPSU member, Moscow city. From the USSR Academy of Medical Sciences together with 40 scientific medical societies.

Bayramova, Nadezhda Nikiforovna, link leader at the "Pravda" Sovkhoz, Izhevsk city. From Leninskiy National-Territorial Okrug No 657, Udmurt ASSR.

Bayramova, Narmina Aliman-kyzy, cotton grower at Udzharskiy Rayon's Fizuli Kolkhoz, Bolt village, Udzharskiy Rayon. From Yevlakhskiy Territorial Okrug No 676, Azerbaijan SSR.

Bayzhanov, Sabit Mukanovich, first secretary of Dzhambul Kazakh Communist Party Obkom, CPSU member, Dzhambul city. From Chuyskiy National-Territorial Okrug No 158, Kazakh SSR.

Bedulya, Vladimir Leontyevich, chairman of Kamenetskiy Rayon's "Sovetskaya Belorussiya" Kolkhoz, CPSU member, Ryasna village, Kamenetskiy Rayon, Brest Oblast, Belorussian SSR. From the Soviet Peace Fund together with eight Soviet committees advocating peace, solidarity, and international cooperation.

Begeldinov, Talgat Yakubekovich, pensioner, CPSU member, Alma-Ata city. From the All-Union Organization of War and Labor Veterans.

Bekbosinov, Nurlikhan Uteuovich, general director of the "Mangyshlakneft" Production Association, CPSU member, Shevchenko city. From Mangyshlakskiy Territorial Okrug No 623, Guryev Oblast, Kazakh SSR.

Bekbulatova, Gulchekhra, sewing machine operator at the Gulistan sewing association named for the 50th anniversary of the Uzbek Komsomol, CPSU member, Gulistan city. From Gulistanskiy Territorial Okrug No 593, Syrdarya Oblast, Uzbek SSR.

Bekh, Nikolay Ivanovich, general director of the Kama Heavy Truck Production Association, CPSU member, Naberezhnyye Chelny City. From Tukayevskiy National-Territorial Okrug No 642, Tatar ASSR.

Bekhtereva, Natalya Petrovna, academician, director of the USSR Academy of Medical Sciences Experimental Medicine Scientific Research Institute, CPSU member, Leningrad city. From scientific societies and associations under the USSR Academy of Sciences.

Bekishiyev, Akhmad Dzhumangaziyevich, team leader on Tarumovskiy Rayon's kolkhoz named for the 17th party congress, CPSU member, Novodmitriyevka village, Tarumovskiy Rayon. From Kizilyurtovskiy Territorial Okrug No 364, Dagestan ASSR.

Beknazarov, Soibnazar, first secretary of the Gorno-Badakhshan Tajik Communist Party Obkom, CPSU member, Khorog city. From Badakhshanskiy National-Territorial Okrug No 357, Tajik SSR.

Belenkov, Yuriy Nikitich, director of the USSR Academy of Medical Sciences All-Union Cardiological Scientific Center, CPSU Member, Moscow city. From the USSR Academy of Medical Sciences jointly with 40 scientific medical societies.

Belikov, Mikhail Aleksandrovich, producer-director at the movie studio named for A.P. Dovzhenko, Kiev city. From the USSR Cinematography Workers' Union.

Belina, Anna Vasilyevna, teacher at the Ytyk-Kyuyel secondary school, Ytyk-Kyuyel village, Alekseyevskiy Rayon. From Megino-Kangalasskiy National-Territorial Okrug No 697, Yakut ASSR.

Belogolov, Aleksandr Konstantinovich, director of Shelopuginskiy Rayon's "Mironovskiy" State Farm [sovkhoz], CPSU member, Mironovo village, Shelopuginskiy Rayon, Chita Oblast. From Shilkinskiy Territorial Okrug No 344, RSFSR.

Belozertsev, Sergey Vladimirovich, senior lecturer at Karelia State University, CPSU member, Petrozavodsk City. From Kalininskiy National-Territorial Okrug No 570, Karelian ASSR.

Belous, Nikolay Petrovich, gas-arc welder with the "Strezhevoyneft" Administration named for the 50th anniversary of the USSR, CPSU member, Strezhevoy City. From Kolpashevskiy Territorial Okrug No 314, RSFSR.

Belov, Vasiliy Ivanovich, writer, secretary of the RSFSR Writers' Union Board, CPSU member, Vologda city, RSFSR. From the CPSU.

Belyakov, Anatoliy Mikhaylovich, first secretary of Buryat CPSU Obkom, CPSU member, Ulan-Ude city. From Ulan-Udenskiy Rural Territorial Okrug No 360, Buryat ASSR.

Belyakov, Oleg Sergeyevich, chief of a CPSU Central Committee department, CPSU member, Moscow city. From Volzhskiy National-Territorial Okrug No 595, Mari ASSR.

Belyakova, Galina Fedorovna, engineer at the "Bratskgesstroy" Administration "Bratskzhelezobeton" Combine, CPSU member, Bratsk city, Irkutsk Oblast, RSFSR. From the All-Union Komsomol.

Belyayev, Vitaliy Sergeyevich, tractor driver on "Gomontovo" Sovkhoz, Volosovskiy Rayon, CPSU member, Begunitsy settlement, Volosovskiy Rayon. From Kingiseppskiy Territorial Okrug No 63, Leningrad Oblast, RSFSR.

Belyayev, Vladimir Nikitich, dean of the Moscow Physical Engineering Institute, CPSU member, Moscow city. From Kantemirovskiy Territorial Okrug No 8, Moscow city.

Belyayev, Sergey Vladimirovich, lieutenant, assistant chief for Komsomol work of a border detachment political department in the Far Eastern Military District, CPSU member, Amur Oblast, RSFSR. From the All-Union Komsomol.

Berdzenishvili, Merab Isidorovich, sculptor, professor at the Tbilisi Academy of Art, Tbilisi city. From Leninogorskiy National-Territorial Okrug No 740, South-Ossetian Autonomous Oblast.

Berezin, Anatoliy Ivanovich, first secretary of the Mordovian CPSU Obkom, CPSU member, Saransk city. From Chamzinskiy Territorial Okrug No 378, Mordovian ASSR.

Berezov, Vladimir Antonovich, second secretary of the Lithuanian Communist Party Central Committee, CPSU member, Vilnius city. From Tauragskiy National-Territorial Okrug No 249, Lithuanian SSR.

Berger, Arnold Vladimirovich, director of the Kustanay Agricultural Institute experimental teaching farm named for Gagarin, CPSU member, Sadchikovka village, Kustanayskiy Rayon, Kustanay Oblast. From Rudnenskiy National-Territorial Okrug No 149, Kazakh SSR.

Berikashvili, Vissarion Georgiyevich, tractor driver on Chandari village kolkhoz, Gurdzhaanskiy Rayon, CPSU member, Chandari village, Gurdzhaanskiy Rayon. From Gurdzhaanskiy National-Territorial Okrug No 174, Georgian SSR.

Berko, Mikhail Dmitriyevich, chairman of Drogobychskiy Rayon's "Pershe Travnya" Collective Farm [kolkhoz], CPSU member, Rykhtychi village, Drogobychskiy Rayon. From Drogobychskiy Territorial Okrug No 488, Ukrainian SSR.

Beyshekeyeva, Zayna, senior shepherd at the Dzhety-Oguz State Special Farm, CPSU member, Dzhety-Oguz village, Dzhety-Oguz Rayon, Issyk-Kul Oblast, Kirghiz SSR. From the CPSU.

Bezbakh, Yakov Yakovlevich, team leader at the Nizhnedneprovskiy K. Liebknecht Pipe-Rolling Plant open-hearth shop basic production section, CPSU member, Dnepropetrovsk City. From Industrialnyy Territorial Okrug No 423, Ukrainian Soviet Socialist Republic [SSR].

Bichenov, Roland Romanovich, stock unit chief on "Kavkaz" Kolkhoz, CPSU member, Elkhotovo village, Kirovskiy Rayon. From Kirovskiy National-Territorial Okrug No 631, North Osetian ASSR.

Bichkauskas, Egidiyus Vitautovich, investigator for especially important cases under the Lithuanian SSR Prosecutor's Office, CPSU member, Vilnius city. From Shilutskiy National-Territorial Okrug No 254, Lithuanian SSR.

Bigunets, Nikolay Vasilyevich, chief physician at the Dubovskaya City Precinct Hospital, CPSU member, Dubovoye village, Tyachevskiy Rayon, Transcarpathian Oblast. From Zakarpatskiy National-Territorial Okrug No 45, Ukrainian SSR.

Bikkenin, Nail Bariyevich, chief editor of the journal KOMMUNIST, CPSU member, Moscow city. From the CPSU.

Bilyukovich, Yevgeniya Georgiyevna, teacher at No 3 secondary school, Pruzhany city, Brest Oblast. From Kobrinskiy National-Territorial Okrug No 76, Belorussian SSR.

Bimbayev, Vyacheslav Matsakovich, chief of the "Kamselkhozvodoprovod" Design Planning and Construction Production Association, CPSU member, Elista city. From Tselinnyy National-Territorial Okrug No 555, Kalmyk ASSR.

Biryukov, Vitaliy Aleksandrovich, fitter at the metallurgical plant named for A.K. Serov, CPSU member, Serov city. From Serovskiy Territorial Okrug No 304, Sverdlovsk Oblast, RSFSR.

Bisher, Ilmar Olgertovich, professor at the Latvian State University named for P. Stuchka, CPSU member, Riga city. From Stuchkinskiy National-Territorial Okrug No 317, Latvian SSR.

Biyushkin, Sergey Nikolayevich, excavator operator at the Mikhaylovskiy mining and enriching combine mining administration, CPSU member, Zheleznogorsk city, Kursk Oblast, RSFSR. From the All-Union Komsomol.

Blayev, Boris Khagutsirovich, director of the Tyrnyauz tungsten-molybdenum combine, CPSU member, Tyrnyauz city. From Kommunisticheskiy Territorial Okrug No 367, Kabardino-Balkar ASSR.

Blazhiyevskiy, Viktor Borisovich, chief of the Transcaucasus Railroad, CPSU member, Tbilisi city. From Sukhumskiy Rural National-Territorial Okrug No 186, Georgian SSR.

Blinova, Alevtina Aleksandrovna, chairman of the Shkalanskiy Rural Soviet of People's Deputies Ispolkom, CPSU member, Skalanka village, Yaranskiy Rayon, Kirov Oblast, RSFSR. From the USSR Consumer Cooperatives.

Bliznov, Leonid Yevgenyevich, fitter-repairman at Moscow's kerchief production association, CPSU member, Pavlovskiy Posad city. From Orekhovo-Zuvevskiy Territorial Okrug No 38, Moscow Oblast, RSFSR.

Blokhin, Yuriy Vitalyevich, deputy director of the Moldavian SSR State Planning Committee Scientific Resrach Institute for Planning, CPSU member, Kishinev City. From Kishinevskiy-Oktyabrskiy National-Territorial Okrug No 259, Moldavian SSR.

Blums, Guntis Valdovich, director of the "Stari" Sovkhoz, Gulbenskiy Rayon, CPSU member, Zemdegas village, Gulbenskiy Rayon, Latvian SSR. From the USSR DOSAAF.

Bobadzhanov, Mirzo, pensioner, CPSU member, Dushanbe city. From the All-Union Organization of War and Labor Veterans.

Bobrik, Boris Fedorovich, manager of the "Vostoknefteprovodstroy" Trust, CPSU member, Ufa City. From Belebeyevskiy Territorial Okrug No 353, Bashkir ASSR.

Bobritskiy, Nikolay Grigoryevich, deputy general director of the "Bobruyskshina" Production Association, CPSU member, Bobruysk city. From Bobruyskiy Territorial Okrug No 573, Mogilev Oblast, Belorussian SSR.

Bobyleva, Yevdokiya Fedorovna, director of the Odoyev Secondary School, CPSU member, Odoyev village, Tula Oblast, RSFSR. From the All-Union Organization of War and Labor Veterans.

Bocharov, Mikhail Aleksandrovich, director of the Butovskiy Construction Materials Combine, CPSU member, Razvilka settlement, Moscow Oblast, RSFSR. From Sovetskiy Territorial Okrug No 23, Moscow city.

Bochkov, Oleg Aleksandrovich, Major, chief of staff of a troop unit, CPSU member, Kaluga Oblast. From Maloyaroslavetskiy Territorial Okrug No 186, Kaluga Oblast, RSFSR.

Bogdanov, Igor Mikhaylovich, director of School No 94, CPSU member, Gorkiy city. From Leninskiy Territorial Okrug No 156, Gorkiy Oblast, RSFSR.

Bogdanov, Radik Garifullovich, chief physician at Ufa City No 21 Clinical Hospital, CPSU member, Ufa City. From Sovetskiy Territorial Okrug No 352, Bashkir ASSR.

Bogomolov, Oleg Timofeyevich, director of the USSR Academy of Sciences Economics of the World Socialist System Institute, CPSU member, Moscow city. From Sevastopolskiy Territorial Okrug No 22, Moscow city.

Bogomolov, Yuriy Aleksandrovich, director of the "Yevlashevskiy" Sovkhoz, Kuznetskiy Rayon, CPSU member, Yevlashevo village, Kuznetskiy Rayon. From Kuznetskiy Territorial Okrug No 254, Penza Oblast, RSFSR.

Bokuchava, Natella Terentyevna, director of the No 4 Secondary School, CPSU member, Sukhumi city, Abkhaz ASSR. From the USSR Academy of Pedagogical Sciences jointly with the Soviet Association of Pedagogical Research Workers.

Bolbasov, Vladimir Sergeyevich, chief scientific associate, deputy chief of laboratory at the Belorussian SSR Academy of Sciences Electronics Institute, CPSU member, Minsk city. From the All-Union Society of Inventors and Rationalizers.

Boldin, Valeriy Ivanovich, chief of a CPSU Central Committee department, CPSU member, Moscow city. From Pravoberezhnyy National-Territorial Okrug No 633, North Osetian ASSR.

Boldyrev, Ivan Sergeyevich, first secretary of the Stavropol CPSU Kray Party Committee [Kraykom], CPSU member, Stavropol city. From Budennovskiy Territorial Okrug No 104, Stavropol Kray, RSFSR.

Boldyrev, Yuriy Yuryevich, senior engineer at the Central Scientific Research Institute for Shipbuilding Electrical Equipment and Technology, CPSU member, Leningrad city. From Moskovskiy Territorial Okrug No 54, Leningrad city.

Bondarenko, Boris Viktorovich, senior navigator from the Borispol amalgamated aviation detachment, CPSU member, Borispol city. From Pereyaslav-Khmelnitskiy Territorial Okrug No 474, Kiev Oblast, Ukrainian SSR.

Borisov, Andrey Savvich, producer at the Yakutsk Oyunskiy Drama Theater, CPSU member, Yakutsk City. From Vilyuyskiy National-Territorial Okrug No 695, Yakutsk ASSR.

Borisovskiy, Vladimir Zakharovich, deputy chairman of the Ukrainian SSR Council of Ministers, CPSU member, Kiev city. From Dnepropetrovskiy National-Territorial Okrug No 39, Ukrainian SSR.

Borisyuk, Nadezhda Petrovna, machine operator at the "Sibir" Central Enriching Factory, CPSU member, Myski city, Kemerovo Oblast, RSFSR. From the women's councils united in the Soviet Women's Committee.

Borkovets, Vladimir Ivanovich, team leader at the "Sayanmramor" Production Association, Sayanogorsk city. From Khakasskiy Territorial Okrug No 96, Krasnoyarsk Kray, RSFSR.

Borovik, Genrikh Aviezerovich, writer, political observer of the USSR State Committee for Television and Radio Broadcasting, chairman of the Soviet Committee for the defense of Peace, CPSU member, Moscow city. From the Peace Movement united by the Soviet Committee for the Defense of Peace, jointly with the USSR United Nations Association.

Borovikov, Georgiy Georgiyevich, clerk of works at the "Sochispetsstroy" Territorial-Construction Association No 10 Mechanized Works Administration, CPSU member, Sochi city. From Sochinskiy Territorial Okrug No 83, Krasnodar Kray, RSFSR.

Borovkov, Vyacheslav Aleksandrovich, machine assembly works fitter at the "Kirovskiy Zavod" Production Association, CPSU member, Leningrad city. From the USSR Trade Unions.

Borodin, Nikolay Vasilyevich, chairman of "Pervoye Maya" Kolkhoz, Shilkinskiy Rayon, CPSU member, Bogomyakov village, Shilkinskiy Rayon, Chita Oblast, RSFSR. From the CPSU.

Borodin, Oleg Petrovich, IZVESTIYA own correspondent, CPSU member, Yakutsk city. From Yakutskiy City National-Territorial Okrug No 690, Yakutsk ASSR.

Borodin, Yuriy Ivanovich, chairman of the USSR Academy of Medical Sciences Siberian Department Presidium, CPSU member, Novosibirsk city, RSFSR. From the USSR Academy of Medical Sciences jointly with 40 scientific medical societies.

Borodulin, Anatoliy Vladimirovich, leader of a team of fitters and assembly workers at the Balashikha mechanical casting plant, CPSU member, Balashikha city. From Balashikhinskiy Territorial Okrug No 28, Moscow Oblast, RSFSR.

Bosenko, Nikolay Vasilyevich, pensioner, CPSU member, Moscow city. From the All-Union Organization of War and Labor Veterans.

Botandayev, Iosif Nikiforovich, automobile driver at the "Tuimskiy" Sovkhoz, Shirinskiy Rayon, CPSU member, Shira settlement, Shirinskiy Rayon. From Shirinskiy National-Territorial Okrug No 735, Khakass Autonomous Oblast.

Boyars, Yuriy Rudolfovich, lecturer at the Latvian P. Stuchki State University, CPSU member, Riga city. From Dobelskiy National-Territorial Okrug No 303, Latvian SSR.

Boyko, Aleksey Nikolayevich, head of department at Donetsk State University, CPSU member, Donetsk city. From Donetskiy-Voroshilovskiy Territorial Okrug No 432, Donetsk Oblast, Ukrainian SSR.

Boykov, Sergey Vladimirovich, leader of a fitters' team from the No 154 mechanized column of the "Bamstroymekhanizatsiya" Trust, Aldan city. From Aldanskiy National-Territorial Okrug No 693, Yakut ASSR.

Boztayev, Keshrim Boztayevich, first secretary of the Semipalatinsk Kazakh Communist Party Obkom, CPSU member, Semipalatinsk city. From Semipalatinskiy Territorial Okrug No 641, Semipalatinsk Oblast, Kazakh SSR.

Bragin, Anatoliy Stepanovich, chairman of the DOSAAF primary organization of the Leninskiy Komsomol Ship-Building Plant, CPSU member, Komsomolsk-na-Amure city, Khabarovsk Kray, RSFSR. From the All-Union Voluntary Society for the Promotion of the Army, Aviation, and Navy (USSR DOSAAF).

Bragish, Dmitriy Petrovich, first secretary of the Moldavian Komsomol Central Committee, CPSU member, Kishinev city. From Faleshtskiy National-Territorial Okrug No 285, Moldavian SSR.

Bratun, Rostislav Andreyevich, writer, CPSU member, Lvov City. From Lvovskiy-Zaliznichnyy Territorial Okrug No 487, Lvov Oblast, Ukrainian SSR.

Braun, Andrey Georgiyevich, first secretary of the Tselinograd Kazakh Communist Party Obkom, CPSU member, Tselinograd city. From Tselinogradskiy-Atbasarskiy National-Territorial Okrug No 155, Kazakh SSR.

Brazauskas, Algirdas-Mikolas Kaze, first secretary of the Lithuanian Communist Party Central Committee, CPSU member, Vilnius city. From Vilniusskiy-Leninskiy Territorial Okrug No 685, Lithuanian SSR.

Bredikis, Yurgis Yuozovich, head of the First Surgical Department at the Kaunas Medical Institute, head of the All-Union Center for the Surgical Treatment of Complex Heart Disorders, CPSU member, Kaunas city, Lithuanian SSR. From the All-Union "Znaniye" Society.

Bresis, Vilnis-Edvins Gedertovich, chairman of the Latvian SSR Council of Ministers, CPSU member, Riga City. From Yekabpilsskiy National-Territorial Okrug No 305, Latvian SSR.

Breurosh, Boris Sergeyevich, combine operator at the "Druzhba" Kolkhoz, Maloviskovskiy Rayon, CPSU member, Paliyevka settlement, Maloviskovskiy Rayon. From Znamenskiy Territorial Okrug No 479, Kirovograd Oblast, RSFSR.

Britvin, Nikolay Vasilyevich, Lieutenant General, chief of the USSR KGB Political Directorate of Border Forces, CPSU member, Moscow city. From Moskovskiy National-Territorial Okrug No 375, Tajik SSR.

Brodavskiy, Anitset Petrovich, director of the Vilnius Sovkhoz-Technical College of the Lithuanian SSR, CPSU member, Pagiryay Village, Vilnyusskiy Rayon. From Vilnyusskiy Rural National-Territorial Okrug No 230, Lithuanian SSR.

Bronshteyn, Mikhail Lazarevich, head of department at Tartu State University, CPSU member, Tartu city. From Tartuskiy-Sovetskiy National-Territorial Okrug No 477, Estonian SSR.

Brovkin, Valentin Mikhaylovich, chief of the No 2 paper production unit at "Syktyvkarskiy Lesopromyshlennyy Kompleks" Production Association named for the Lenin Komsomol, CPSU member, Syktyvkar City. From Ezhvinskiy National-Territorial Okrug No 581, Komi ASSR.

Bruss, Ayvar Pavlovich, chief agronomist at the "Tervete" Kolkhoz, Dobelskiy Rayon, Apiri village, Dobelskiy Rayon, Latvian SSR. From kolkhozes united in the Union Kolkhoz Council.

Bryukhanova, Natalya Viktorovna, teacher at the Sheragulskiy Secondary School, CPSU member, Sheragul village, Tulonskiy Rayon, Irkutsk Oblast, RSFSR. From the USSR Consumer Cooperatives.

Buachidze, Tengiz Pavlovich, chairman of the Georgian Culture Fund, CPSU member, Tbilisi city. From

Batumskiy-Shaumyanskiy National-Territorial Okrug No 493, Adzhar ASSR.

Buburuz, Petr Dmitriyevich, senior priest at the Trinity Cathedral in Kishinev City, Kishinev City. From Kishinevskiy-Leninskiy Territorial Okrug No 695, Moldavian SSR.

Bulatov, Vladimir Kondratyevich, elementary military training teacher at Secondary School No 4, Igra settlement, Igrinskiy Rayon, Udmurt ASSR. From the All-Union Komsomol.

Bunich, Pavel Grigoryevich, head of department at the S. Ordzhonikidze Management Institute in Moscow, CPSU member, Moscow City. From the USSR Academy of Sciences.

Burachas, Antanas Yono, chairman of the Scientific and Technical Information Council attached to the Lithuanian SSR Academy of Sciences Presidium, CPSU member, Vilnius city. From Alitusskiy Territorial Okrug No 687, Lithuanian SSR.

Buravov, Gennadiy Vladimirovich, diesel engine driver at the Bugulma Locomotive Depot of the Kuybyshev Railroad, Bugulma city. From Bugulminskiy National-Territorial Okrug No 638, Tatar ASSR.

Burayev, Ivan Zambayevich, head of the "40 Let Oktyabrya" Kolkhoz machine workshops, Sarpinskiy Rayon, Umantsevo village, Sarpinskiy Rayon. From Sarpinskiy National-Territorial Okrug No 554, Kalmyk ASSR.

Burbulis, Gennadiy Eduardovich, deputy director of the All-Union Institute for Improving the Qualifications of Specialists of the USSR Ministry of Nonferrous Metallurgy, CPSU member, Sverdlovsk city. From Leninskiy Territorial Okrug No 292, Sverdlovsk Oblast, RSFSR.

Burduzhan, Valeriyan Vasilyevich, chairman of the "Pogranichnik" Kolkhoz, Brichanskiy Rayon, CPSU member, Larga village, Brichanskiy Rayon, Moldavian SSR. From kolkhozes united in the Union Kolkhoz Council.

Burlatskiy, Fedor Mikhaylovich, political observer for LITERATURNAYA GAZETA, CPSU member, Moscow city. From the Soviet Peace Fund together with eight Soviet committees in favor of peace, solidarity, and international cooperation.

Burskiy, Viktor Ivanovich, chairman of the Brest Oblast Soviet Executive Committee [oblispolkom], CPSU member, Brest City. From Pinskiy Territorial Okrug No 550, Brest Oblast, Belorussian SSR.

Burtsev, Mikhail Petrovich, director of the Kashkinskiy Lumber Unit, CPSU member, Kolpakovka settlement, Shalinskiy Rayon. From Krasnoufimskiy Territorial Okrug No 300, Sverdlovsk Oblast, RSFSR.

Burykh, Yuriy Yevgenyevich, chief of the technical department of the Gorlovskiy Chemical Plant, CPSU member, Gorlovka city. From Gorlovskiy Territorial Okrug No 436, Donetsk Oblast, Ukrainian SSR.

Bushuyev, Vitaliy Vasilyevich, director of the Siberian Energy Research Institute, CPSU member, Novosibirsk city, RSFSR. From the USSR Union of Scientific and Engineering Societies.

Byakova, Lyudmila Stepanovna, seamstress at the Kurganskiy Trade and Industry Sewn Goods Association, CPSU member, Kurgan city, RSFSR. From women's councils iunited in the Soviet Women's Committee.

Byazyrova, Valentina Timofeyevna, teacher at Secondary School No 5, CPSU member, Ordzhonikidze city. From Leninskiy National-Territorial Okrug No 624, North Osetian ASSR.

Bykanov, Prokopiy Innokentyevich, team leader of bulldozer operators at the Deputatskiy Mining and Enriching Combine of the "Yakutzoloto" Production Association, CPSU member, Deputatskiy settlement, Ust-Yanskiy Rayon, Yakutsk ASSR. From USSR professional unions.

Bykov, Vasiliy Vladimirovich, writer, secretary of the USSR Union of Writers Board, Minsk city. From the USSR Union of Writers.

Bykov, Gennadiy Vasilyevich, leader of fitters team at the Leningrad I.I. Lepse "Znamya Truda" Hardware Science-and-Production Association, CPSU member, Leningrad city. From Krasnogvardeyskiy Territorial Okrug No 53, Leningrad city.

Bykov, Roland Anatolyevich, artistic leader of the Mosfilm "Yunost" Association, secretary of the USSR Union of Cinematographers Board, Moscow city. From the V.I. Lenin Soviet Children's Fund.

Bykovskikh, Nina Grigoryevna, senior foreman of a machine plant, CPSU member, Staryy Oskol city, Belgorod Oblast, RSFSR. From women's councils united in the Soviet Women's Committee.

Chabanov, Alim Ivanovich, general director of the "Rotor" science and production association, CPSU member, Cherkassy city. From Cherkasskiy Territorial Okrug No 535, Cherkassy Oblast, Ukrainian SSR.

Chausova, Yelena Vladimirovna, foreman confectioner at the Proletarskiy rayon bread combine production association, CPSU member, Proletarsk city, Rostov Oblast, RSFSR. From the USSR Consumer Cooperatives.

Chayenkov, Vladimir Afanasyevich, pensioner, CPSU member, Yaroslavl city, RSFSR. From the All-Union Organization of War and Labor Veterans.

Chayka, Kalistrat Fedorovich, deputy chairman of the Cherkassy Oblast Department of the Organization for the Protection of Historical and Cultural Monuments, CPSU member, Cherkassy city, Ukrainian SSR. From the All-Union Organization of War and Labor Veterans.

Chebanu, David Parfenovich, crane-truck driver at the Yedinetskiy "Rayagrostroy" mechanization and transport cooperative, CPSU member, Yedintsy city. From Yedinetskiy National-Territorial Okrug No 267, Moldavian SSR.

Chebotar, Valeriy Pavlovich, chairman of the Kotovskiy Rayon "Agrostroy" association, CPSU member, Kotovsk city. From Kotovskiy National-Territorial Okrug No 272, Moldavian SSR.

Chebrikov, Viktor Mikhaylovich, member of the Politburo and secretary of the CPSU Central Committee, CPSU member, Moscow city. From the CPSU.

Chekhoyev, Anatoliy Georgiyevich, first secretary of the South Osetian Georgian Communist Party Obkom, CPSU member, Tskhinvali city. From Tskhinvalskiy City National-Territorial Okrug No 736, South Osetian Autonomous Oblast.

Chekov, Nikolay Vasilyevich, colonel general, USSR deputy defense minister for construction and billeting of troops, CPSU member, Moscow city. From the USSR DOSAAF.

Chekuolis, Algimantas Yurgis Yurgio, chief editor of the weekly GIMTASIS KRASHTAS, CPSU member, Vilnius city. From Utenskiy Territorial Okrug No 692, Lithuanian SSR.

Chelyshev, Vitaliy Alekseyevich, senior correspondent for the newspaper INDUSTRIALNOYE ZAPOROZHYYE, CPSU member, Zaporozhyye City. From Zaporozhskiy-Zhovtnevoy Territorial Okrug No 455, Ukrainian SSR.

Chemodanov, Yuriy Martynovich, teacher at Kuanpamashskiy Incomplete-Grade Secondary School, CPSU candidate member, Kuanpamash village, Novotoryalskiy Rayon, Mari ASSR. From the All-Union Komsomol.

Chentsov, Nikolay Ivanovich, arc welder at the "Oktyabrugol" production association's "Komsomolskoye" mine administration, Kirovskoye city. From Torezskiy Territorial Okrug No 445, Donetsk Oblast, Ukrainian SSR.

Chepanis, Alfred Kazimirovich, deputy chairman of the Latvian SSR Council of Ministers, CPSU member, Riga City. From Daugavpilsskiy Territorial Okrug No 709, Latvian SSR.

Chepurnaya, Margarita Aleksandrovna, organizer of extracurricular and extramural educational work at Popovskiy Secondary School, CPSU member, Popovka village, Konotopskiy Rayon. From Konotopskiy Territorial Okrug No 514, Sumy Oblast, Ukrainian SSR.

Cherednichenko, Fedor Grgiroyevich, director of the "Rostovskiy" sovkhoz, Rodionovo-Nesvetayskiy Rayon, CPSU member, Veselyy village, Rodionovo-Nesvetayskiy Rayon. From Novoshakhtinskiy Territorial Okrug No 275, Rostov Oblast, RSFSR.

Cherepovich, Vladimir Anatolyevich, secretary of the party committee of the Dneprovskiy "Era" enterprise, CPSU member, Kherson city. From Khersonskiy Territorial Okrug No 528, Kherson Oblast, Ukrainian SSR.

Cherkasova, Antonina Fedorovna, electric fitter at the Volga truck plant, CPSU member, Tolyatti city, Kuybyshev Oblast, RSFSR. From the women's councils united in the Committee of Soviet Women.

Cherkeziya, Otar Yevtikhiyevich, chairman of the Georgian SSR Supreme Soviet Presidium, CPSU member, Tbilisi city. From Ochamchirskiy City National-Territorial Okrug No 489, Abkhaz ASSR.

Chernavin, Vladimir Nikolayevich, fleet admiral, commander in chief of the Navy and USSR deputy defense minister, CPSU member, Moscow city. From Lenkoranskiy Territorial Okrug No 678, Azerbaijan SSR.

Chernenko, Vladimir Timofeyevich, mechanic at the "Pobeda" Kolkhoz, Gulkevichskiy Rayon, CPSU member, Verbovyy Village, Gulkevichskiy Rayon, Krasnodar Kray. From Kropotkinskiy Territorial Okrug No 77, Krasnodar Kray, RSFSR.

Chernyak, Vladimir Kirillovich, department chief at the Ukrainian SSR Academy of Sciences' Economics Institute, Kiev City. From Kiev City National-Territorial Okrug No 33.

Chernykh, Aleksandr Grgiroyevich, chief agronomist at the Unginskiy sovkhoz, Krapivinskiy Rayon, CPSU member, Zelenovskiy settlement, Krapivinskiy Rayon. From Rudnichnyy Territorial Okrug No 191, Kemerovo Oblast, RSFSR.

Chernykh, Galina Aleksandrovna, director of the Obyachevo Secondary School, CPSU member, Obyachevo village, Priluzskiy Rayon. From Sysolskiy National-Territorial Okrug No 588, Komi ASSR.

Chernyshev, Oleg Viktorovich, department chief of the Belorussian State Theatrical Art Institute, CPSU member, Minsk city. From the USSR Designers Union.

Chernyshova, Lyubov Petrovna, machine operator at the Karla Marksa Kolkhoz, Novoaleksandrovskiy Rayon, CPSU member, Rasshevatskaya village, Novoaleksandrovskiy Rayon, Stavropol Kray, RSFSR. From the kolkhozes united in the Union Council of Kolkhozes.

Chernyayev, Anatoliy Sergeyevich, aide to the CPSU Central Committee general secretary, CPSU member, Moscow city. From the CPSU.

Chernyayev, Nikolay Fedorovich, machine operator at the "Krasnoye Znamya" kolkhoz, Karsunskiy Rayon, CPSU member, Karsun Urban settlement, Karsunskiy

Rayon. From Ulyanovskiy Territorial Okrug No 329, Ulyanovsk Oblast, RSFSR.

Chervonopiskiy, Sergey Vasilyevich, first secretary of the Cherkassy Ukrainian Komsomol Gorkom, CPSU member, Cherkassy city, Ukrainian SSR. From the All-Union Komsomol.

Chetberova, Marziyat Gasankyzy, milkmaid at the Ordzhonikidze Kolkhoz, Belokanskiy Rayon, Katekh village, Belokanskiy Rayon. From Zakatalskiy National-Territorial Okrug No 207, Azerbaijan SSR.

Chigogidze, Guram Yegorovich, chairman of the Adzhar ASSR Council of Ministers, CPSU member, Batumi city. From Kobuletskiy National-Territorial Okrug No 498, Adzhar ASSR.

Chizhov, Anatoliy Alekseyevich, director of the "Progress" plant, CPSU member, Kuybyshev city. From Kirovskiy Territorial Okrug No 205, Kuybyshev Oblast, RSFSR.

Chiladze, Otar Ivanovich, writer, Tbilisi city. From the USSR Writers' Union.

Chilaya, Yelena Georgiyevna, teacher at the Tskhakaya Fourth Russian Secondary School, Tskhakaya city. From Tskhakayevskiy National-Territorial Okrug No 189, Georgian SSR.

Chilebayev, Toktogul Bekbolotovich, chairman of the board of the Kirghiz potrebsoyuz, CPSU member, Frunze city. From USSR consumer cooperatives.

Chimpoy, Mikhail Ilich, writer, secretary of the board of the Moldavian SSR Writers Union, Kishinev city. From Kishinevskiy-Dnestrovskiy National-Territorial Okrug No 258, Moldavian SSR.

Chitin, Anzor Antonovich, electric locomotive driver at the Semtredia locomotive depot, Transcaucasus railroad, CPSU member, Samtredia city. From Samtredskiy National-Territorial Okrug No 183, Georgian SSR.

Chichik, Yuriy Mikhaylovich, director of the "Krasnorechenskiy" Sovkhoz, Khabarovskiy Rayon, CPSU member, Krasnorechenskoye village, Khabarovskiy Rayon. From Khabarovskiy Rural Territorial Okrug No 111, Khabarovsk Kray, RSFSR.

Chobanu (Cheban) Ivan Konstantinovich, writer, first secretary of the board of the Moldavian Writers Union, secretary of the board of the USSR Writers Union, CPSU member, Kishinev city. From the USSR Writers' Union.

Cholokyan, Karzui Sarkisovna, kolkhoz member at the Rustavli Kolkhoz, Vtoraya Bagazhyashta village, Gulripshskiy Rayon, CPSU member, Vtoraya Bagazhyashta village, Gulripshskiy Rayon. From Gulripshskiy National-Territorial Okrug No 488, Abkhaz ASSR.

Chursina, Pavlina Mikhaylovna, weaver at the Kargalinskiy cloth combine, Fabrichnyy settlement, Dzhambulskiy Rayon, Alma-Ata Oblast, Kazakh SSR. From the women's councils united in the Soviet Women's Committee.

Chukhrayev, Aleksandr Mikhaylovich, chief doctor at the Kursk Oblast No 1 clinical hospital, CPSU member, Kursk city. From Zheleznogorskiy Territorial Orkug No 217, Kursk Oblast, RSFSR.

Chkheidze, Zurab Amvrosiyevich, chairman of the Georgian SSR Council of Ministers, CPSU member, Tbilisi city. From Batumskiy-Leninskiy National-Territorial Okrug No 492, Adzhar ASSR.

Chkheidze, Temur Nodarovich, television theater artistic leader, CPSU member, Tbilisi city. From the USSR Union of Theatrical Workers.

Chyapas, Vitautas Yonovich, senior teacher at the Klaypeda faculty of preschool education of the Shyaulyayskiy K. Preykshas pedagogical institute, Klaypeda city. From Klaypedskiy-Tsentralnyy National-Territorial Okrug No 240, Lithuanian SSR.

Dabizha (Chobanu), Nikolay Trofimovich, writer, chief editor of the LITERATURA SHI ARTA weekly, CPSU member, Kishinev city. From Orgeyevskiy National-Territorial Okrug No 276, Moldavian SSR.

Davlyatov, Sergey Ikromovich, driver at the No 11 Khatlon Production Automotive Transport Association automotive transport enterprise, CPSU member, Dusti settlement, Kumsangirskiy Rayon, Khatlon Oblast. From Kumsangirskiy National-Territorial Okrug No 370, Tajik SSR.

Davronov, Akhtam, team leader on the XXII Partsezd Kolkhoz, Kyzyltepinskiy Rayon, CPSU member, Kyzyltepinskiy Rayon, Samarkand Oblast. From Navoiyskiy National-Territorial Okrug No 108, Uzbek SSR.

Davranov, Narzi, physician at the Sverdlovsk Central Rayon Hospital, CPSU member, Zhondor settlement, Sverdlovskiy Rayon, Bukhara Oblast. From Gizhduvanskiy National-Territorial Okrug No 101, Uzbek SSR.

Dadamyan, Boris Vartanovich, general director of Stepanakert Motor Transport Production Association, CPSU member, Stepanakert city. From Stepanakertskiy National-Territorial Okrug No 218 Azerbaijan SSR.

Dadov, Khamita Aubekirovich, machine operator at Terskiy Rayon's "Zarya Kommunizma" Kolkhoz, CPSU member, Terskoye village, Terskiy Rayon. From Terskiy National-Territorial Okrug No 543, Kabardino-Balkar ASSR.

Dambayev, Dambi Bazarovich, chairman of Yeravninskiy Rayon's "Pobeda" Kolkhoz, CPSU member, Ust-Yegita settlement, Yeravninskiy Rayon. From Khorinskiy National-Territorial Okrug No 524, Buryat ASSR.

Dambis, Ayvar Albertovich, leader of a team of pipe stackers at "Latinzhstroymekhanizatsiya" Trust Administration No 10, CPSU member, Riga city. From the USSR's trade unions.

Dandzberg, Andrey Karlovich, chairman of the "Padomyu Zveyniyeks" Fishing Kolkhoz, Tukumskiy Rayon, CPSU member, Kapas village, Tukumskiy Rayon. From Tukumskiy National-Territorial Okrug No 318, Latvian SSR.

Danilenko, Anatoliy Stepanovich, chairman of Mironovskiy Rayon's Buznitskiy Kolkhoz, CPSU member, Mironovka city, Kiev Oblast, Ukrainian SSR. From the kolkhozes united in the Union Council of Kolkhozes.

Danilov, Valeriy Nikolayevich, foreman at Pridneprovsk Railroad Sinelnikovo Refrigerated Freightcar Depot, CPSU member, Sinelnikovo city. From Sinelnikovskiy Territorial Okrug No 430, Dnepropetrovsk Oblast, Ukrainian SSR.

Danilov, Vener Mikhaylovich, assistant foreman at Krasnodar's Cotton Fabric Combine, CPSU member, Krasnodar city. From Leninskiy Territorial Okrug No 73, Krasnodar Kray, RSFSR.

Danilov, Leonid Ivanovich, chief of Cherepovets Metallurgical Combine Administration for the Development, Creation, and Introduction of Prototype Models of Equipment and Promising Equipment and Technology, CPSU member, Cherepovets city, Vologod Oblast, RSFSR. From the All-Union Society of Inventors and Rationalizers.

Danilov, Sergey Nikolayevich, livestock farmer and leaseholder at Yukamenskiy Rayon's "Shafeyevskiy" Sovkhoz, CPSU member, Verkh-Uni village, Yukamenskiy Rayon. From Glazovskiy National-Territorial Okrug No 663, Udmurt ASSR.

Danilova, Lyubov Andreyevna, deputy director of educational and instructional work at Secondary School No 3, CPSU member, Meleuz city, Bashkir ASSR. From Ufimskiy National-Territorial Okrug No 31, RSFSR.

Danilyuk, Igor Vasilyevich, chairman of Podvolovhisskiy Rayon's "Radyanska Ukraina" kolkhoz, CPSU member, Kamenki village, Podvolochisskiy Rayon, Ternopol Oblast. From Ternopolskiy National-Territorial Okrug No 57, Ukrainian SSR.

Danilyuk, Nikolay Nikolayevich, chairman of Khabarovsk Kray Soviet Executive Committee [Krayispolkom], CPSU member, Khabarovsk city, RSFSR. From Smidovichskiy National-Territorial Okrug No 720, Yevreyskaya Autonomous Oblast.

Darsigov, Musa Yusupovich, team leader at Malgobekskiy Rayon's "Alkhanchurtskiy" Sovkhoz, CPSU member, Novy Redant village, Malgobekskiy Rayon. From Nazranovskiy National-Territorial Okrug No 674, Chechen Ingush ASSR.

Dedeneva, Nina Nikolayevna, weaver at "Vostok" Cotton Fabric Production Association, CPSU member, Omsk city, RSFSR. From the women's councils united in the Committee of Soviet Women.

Dedyukhin, Leonid Stepanovich, leader of a team of workers adjusting computerized program-controlled tools at the "Sverdlovskiy M.I. Kalinin Machine Building Plant" Science-and-Production Association, CPSU member, Sverdlovsk city, RSFSR. From the All-Union Society of Inventors and Rationalizers.

Degeyev, Aminat Magomedovna, milkmaid at Levashinskiy Rayon's A. Bogatyrev Sovkhoz, Mekegi village, Levashinskiy Rayon. From Lakskiy National-Territorial Okrug No 532, Dagestan ASSR.

Degtyarev, Mikhail Pavlovich, leader of a team of stonemasons at Construction Trust No 4 interfarm mobile mechanized column No 223, CPSU member, Slutsk city. From Slutskiy National-Territorial Okrug No 72, Belorussian SSR.

Demakov, Nikolay Andreyevich, deputy commander of Novosibirsk Combined Air Detachment, CPSU member, Novosibirsk city. From Novosibirskiy National-Territorial Okrug No 21, RSFSR.

Demchenko, Fedor Mikhaylovich, leader of a team at Poltava Housing Construction Combine, Poltava city. From Poltavskiy Territorial Okrug No 504, Poltava Oblast, Ukrainian SSR.

Demchuk, Anna Demyanovna, deputy director of educational and instructional work at Lukov Secondary School, CPSU member, Lukov settlement, Turiyskiy Rayon, Volyn Oblast, Ukrainian SSR. From the USSR Consumer Cooperatives.

Demchuk, Mikhail Ivanovich, Belorussian SSR minister of public education, CPSU member, Minsk city. From the All-Union "Znaniye" Society.

Dementey, Nikolay Ivanovich, secretary of the Belorussian Communist Party Central Committee, CPSU member, Minsk city. From Polotskiy Territorial Okrug No 554, Vitebsk Oblast, Belorussian SSR.

Demidov, Gennadiy Ilich, chief surgeon at Penza Oblispolkom health department, CPSU member, Penza city. From Leninskiy Territorial Okrug No 252, Penza Oblast, RSFSR.

Demidov, Mikhail Vasilyevich, first secretary of Kalevalskiy Rayon CPSU Committee [raykom], CPSU member, Kalevala Settlement. From Kemskiy National-Territorial Okrug No 573, Karelian ASSR.

Demin, Aleksandr Borisovich, captain, company deputy commander for political affairs, Siberian Military District, CPSU member, Novosibirsk Oblast. From Barabinskiy Territorial Okrug No 234, Novosibirsk Oblast, RSFSR.

Demurchiyeva, Flora Musa kyzy, worker at Marneulskiy Rayon's Algetskiy Viticultural Sovkhoz, CPSU member, Algetskiy Viticultural Sovkhoz settlement, Marneulskiy Rayon. From Bolnisskiy National-Territorial Okrug No 171, Georgian SSR.

Denisenko, Anatoliy Grigoryevich, chairman of Akimovskiy Rayon's Kalinin Kolkhoz, CPSU member, Chervonoarmeyskoye village, Akimovskiy Rayon, Zaporozhye Oblast, Ukrainian SSR. From the kolkhozes united in the Union Kolkhoz Council.

Denisov, Vladimir Ilich, general director of "Povolzhskoye" Experimental Production Association, CPSU member, Tolyatti city. From Tolyattinskiy Territorial Okrug No 212, Kuybyshev Oblast, RSFSR.

Denisov, Nikolay Petrovich, machine operator at Arzamasskiy Rayon's "Borba" Kolkhoz, candidate member of the CPSU, Abramovo village, Arzamasskiy Rayon, Gorkiy Oblast, RSFSR. From the All-Union Komsomol.

Derevyanko, Boris Fedorovich, editor of VECHERNYAYA ODESSA, CPSU member, Odessa city. From Odesskiy-Primorskiy Territorial Okrug No 499, Odessa Oblast, Ukrainian SSR.

Desyatov, Vladimir Mikhaylovich, engineer and designer at Komsomolsk-na-Amurye's Lenin Komsomol Plant, CPSU member, Komsomolsk-na-Amurye city. From Komsomolskiy Territorial Okrug No 113, Khabarovsk Kray, RSFSR.

Dikhtyar, Anatoliy Dmitriyevich, leader of a multipurpose team at "Tbilgorstroy" Association's No 5 Housing Construction Combine, CPSU member, Tbilisi city. From Tbilisskiy-Zavodskiy National-Territorial Okrug No 165, Georgian SSR.

Dikul, Valentin Ivanovich, director of the Center for the Rehabilitation of Patients Suffering From Spinal and Brain Injuries and the Consequences of Infantile Cerebral Palsy, Moscow city. From Krasnogvardeyskiy Territorial Okrug No 10, Moscow city.

Dikusarov, Vladimir Grigoryevich, first secretary of Khmelnitskiy Ukrainian Communist Party Obkom, CPSU member, Khmelnitskiy city. From Volochisskiy Territorial Okrug No 532, Khmelnitskiy Oblast, Ukrainian SSR.

Dilekov, Khudayberdy, petroleum extractor at "Kamyshldzhaneft" Oil and Gas Extracting Administration, candidate CPSU member, Kamyshldzha settlement, Kizyl-Atrekskiy Rayon. From Kizyl-Atrekskiy National-Territorial Okrug No 434, Turkmen SSR.

Dmitriyev, Aleksey Aleksandrovich, machine operator at Yalchikskiy Rayon's "Slava" Kolkhoz, CPSU member, Lash-Tayaba village, Yalchikskiy Rayon. From Batyrevskiy National-Territorial Okrug No 683, Chuvzsh ASSR.

Dmitriyev, Vladimir Vasilyevich, worker at Maykopskiy Rayon's Pervomayskiy Timber Procurement Establishment, CPSU member, Pervomayskiy settlement, Maykopskiy Rayon. From Maykopskiy Rural National-Territorial Okrug No 702, Adyge Autonomous OBlast.

Dmitriyev, Nikolay Grigoryevich, acting chairman of the V.I. Lenin All-Union Academy of Agricultural Sciences RSFSR Non-Chernozem Zone Department, director of the All-Union Agricultural Livestock Breeding and Genetics Research Institute, CPSU member, Leningrad city, Pushkin city [as published]. From the V.I. Lenin All-Union Academy of Agricultural Sciences.

Dmitriyeva, Valentina Dmitryevna, milkmaid at Kanashkiy Rayon's "Motor" Kolkhoz, CPSU member, Askhva village, Kanashskiy Rayon, Chuvash ASSR. From the All-Union Organization of War and Labor Veterans.

Dobrotolyubov, Veniamin Mikhaylovich, troubleshooter for machine tools with digital program control at "Stankostroitelnyy Zavod" V.I. Lenin Production Association, Frunze City. From Frunzenskiy Territorial Okrug No 714, Kirghiz SSR.

Dobrovolskaya, Taisiya Nikolayevna, chairman of Pregornyy Rayon's V.I. Lenin Kolkhoz trade union committee, CPSU member, Goryachevodskiy settlement, Predgornyy Rayon, Stavropol Kray, RSFSR. From the USSR's trade unions.

Doga, Yevgeniy Dmitriyevich, composer, first deputy chairman of the Moldavian SSR Union of Composers Board, CPSU member, Kishinev city. From Chimishliyskiy National-Territorial Okrug No 288, Moldavian SSR.

Dolganov, Aleksandr Vasilyevich, director of Lyambirskiy Rayon's "Rossiya" State Livestock Breeding Center, CPSU member, Aleksandrovka village, Lyambirskiy Rayon. From Romodanovskiy National-Territorial Okrug No 609, Mordovian ASSR.

Donchak, Yaroslav Antonovich, leader of a drift-winning team at the mine named for the 60th anniversary of the October Revolution, CPSU member, Karaganda city. From Karagandinskiy-Kirovskiy Territorial Okrug No 628, Karaganda Oblast, Kazakh SSR.

Donchenko, Yuriy Anatolyevich, leader of a comprehensive team at the "Konstantinovpromstroy" Trust's No 1 Construction Administration, CPSU member, Konstantinovka city. From Konstantinovskiy Territorial Okrug No 440, Donetsk Oblast, Ukrainian SSR.

Dondup, Mariy-ool Vasilyevich, director of the Sagly Secondary School named for the 50th anniversary of

October, CPSU member, Sagly village, Ovyurskiy Rayon. From Ovyurskiy National-Territorial Okrug No 652, Tuva ASSR.

Dorokhov, Ivan Vasilyevich, first secretary of Bobrovskiy CPSU Raykom, CPSU member, Bobrov city. From Liskinskiy Territorial Okrug No 153, Voronezh Oblast, RSFSR.

Doronina, Zinaida Nikolayevna, department chief at the central rayon hospital, Turan city, Piy-Khemskiy Rayon. From Piy-Khemskiy National-Territorial Okrug No 653, Tuva ASSR.

Dovlatyan, Frunzik Vaginakovich, artistic leader of "Armenfilm" Movie Studio, CPSU member, Yerevan city. From Yerevanskiy-Mashtotsskiy National-Territorial Okrug No 390, Armenian SSR.

Drunina, Yuliya Vladimirovna, poetess, secretary of the USSR Writers' Union Board, secretary of the RSFSR Writers' Union Board, Moscow city. From the women's councils united in the Soviet Women's Committee.

Drutse, Ion Panteleyevich, writer, CPSU member, Moscow city. From Drokiyevskiy National-Territorial Okrug No 265, Moldavian SSR.

Druz, Petr Antonovich, pensioner, CPSU member, Belovo city, Kemerovo Oblast, RSFSR. From the All-Union Organization of War and Labor Veterans.

Druzhinina, Lyubov Nikolayevna, sewing machine operator at the 1 May Sewn Goods Production Association, Frunze city. From the USSR trade unions.

Dubko, Aleksandr Iosifovich, chairman of the "Progress" Agro-Industrial Kolkhoz-Combine, CPSU member, Vertelishki village, Grodnenskiy Rayon, Grodno Oblast, Belorussian SSR. From kolkhozes united in the All-Union Kolkhoz Council.

Dubnikov, Valeriy Danilovich, director of the Paranga peat enterprise in Paranginskiy Rayon, Mary ASSR, CPSU member, Paranga Settlement, Paranginskiy Rayon. From Sernurskiy National-Territorial Okrug No 601, Mari ASSR.

Dubovitskiy, Gennadiy Anisimovich, gas-arc welder at the "Nizhnevolzhskneft" Production Association's Korobkovskiy Oil and Gas Extraction Administration, CPSU member, Kotovo city. From Kamyshinskiy Territorial Okrug No 143, Volgograd Oblast, RSFSR.

Dudko, Tamara Nikolayevna, chairman of Minsk city's Partizanskiy Rayon Soviet Executive Committee [Rayispolkom], CPSU member, Minsk city. From the women's councils united in the Soviet Women's Committee.

Dumbravan, Mikhail Georgiyevich, chairman of Ryshkanskiy Rayon's Kirov Kolkhoz, CPSU member, Lyadoveny village, Ryshkanskiy Rayon. From Ryshkanskiy National-Territorial Okrug No 279, Moldavian SSR.

Dumitrash, Ivan Pavlovich, chairman of the Moldavian SSR Red Cross Society Central Committee, CPSU member, Kishinev city. From the Union of USSR Red Cross and Red Crescent Societies.

Dusmyatov, Abdubako, trade union committee chairman at the Isfara Chemical Plant, CPSU member, Kulkunt village, Isfarinskiy Rayon, Leninabad Oblast, Tajik SSR. From the USSR trade unions.

Dyachenko, Aleksandr Nikolayevich, chief of a housing construction combine, CPSU member, Tiraspol city. From Tiraspolskiy National-Territorial Okrug No 283, Moldavian SSR.

Dyadenko, Nikolay Sergeyevich, chairman of Stavropol RSFSR Red Cross Society Kraykom, CPSU member, Stavropol city, RSFSR. From the Union of USSR Red Cross and Red Crescent Societies.

Dyakov, Ivan Nikolayevich, first secretary of Astrakhan CPSU Obkom, CPSU member, Astrakhan city. From Astrakhanskiy Territorial Okrug No 122, Astrakhan Oblast, RSFSR.

Dygay, Gleb Grigoryevich, pensioner, CPSU member, Kishinev city. From the All-Union Organization of War and Labor Veterans.

Dylevich, Galina Petrovna, chairman of Zalesskiy Rural Soviet Ispolkom, CPSU member, Luchayka village, Glubokskiy Rayon, Vitebsk Oblast, Belorussian SSR. From USSR consumer cooperatives.

Dyusembayev, Vakhit, mining foreman at the blasthole drilling section of the Leninogorsk polymetallic combine's Tishinskiy Mine, CPSU member, Leninogorsk City. From Zaysanskiy National-territorial Okrug No 141, Kazakh SSR.

Dyusov, Leonid Leonovich, lathe operator and borer at the "Minskiy Motornyy Zavod" Production Association, CPSU member, Minsk city. From Minskiy-Partizanskiy Territorial Okrug No 565, Minsk Oblast, Belorussian SSR.

Dzasokhov, Aleksandr Sergeyevich, first secretary of North Osetian CPSU Obkom, CPSU member, Ordzhonikidze city. From Ordzhonikidzevskiy Territorial Okrug No 379 North Osetian ASSR.

Dzidzariya Vakhtang Valikoyevich, machine operator at Tsalendzhikhskiy Rayon's Tsalendzhikhskiy Tea Agro-Industrial Combine, Tsalendzhikhskiy Rayon's Tsalendzhikhskiy Agro-Industrial Combine settlement. From Zugdidskiy Territorial Okrug No 664 Georgian SSR.

Dzhafarov, Vagif Dzhafar ogly, first secretary of Shushinskiy Party Raykom, CPSU member, Shusha city. From Shushinskiy National-Territorial Okrug No 730, NKAO.

Dzhanasbayev, Azhibzhan Tokenovich, leader of a team of drillers at "Kazvolfram" Production Association's

Akzhal Mine, CPSU member, Akzhal settlement, Agadyrskiy Rayon. From Dzhezkazganskiy Territorial Okrug No 627, Dzhezkazgan Oblast, Kazakh SSR.

Dzharimov, Aslan Aliyevich, first secretary of Agyde CPSU Obkom, CPSU member, Maykop city. From Koshekhablskiy National-Territorial Okrug No 703, Adyge Autonomous Oblast.

Dzhimov, Magamet Shumafovich, machine operator at Krasnogvardeyskiy Rayon's V.I. Lenin Kolkhoz, Dzhambichi Aul, Krasnogvaredeyskiy Rayon, Adyge Autonomous Oblast. From the All-Union Komsomol.

Dzhorayev, Kurbanbay, team leader at Deynauskiy Rayon's Frunze Kolkhoz, CPSU member, Zergeleyen settlement, Deynauskiy Rayon, Chardzhou Oblast. From Deynauskiy National-Territorial Okrug No 426, Turkmen SSR.

Dzhumagulov, Apas, chairman of the Kirghiz SSR Council of Ministers, CPSU member, Frunze city. From Sulyuktinskiy National-Territorial Okrug No 344, Kirghiz SSR.

Dzhumatova, Menslu Duisenbayevna, head doctor at Chapayevskiy Rayon's Dzhambul Rural District Hospital, Dzhambul settlement, Chapyevskiy Rayon, Uralsk Oblast, Kazakh SSR. From the USSR's trade unions.

Dzhumayeva, Saparsoltan Mukhamedovna, milkmaid at Maryyskiy Rayon's Chkalov Kolkhoz, CPSU member, Kersagyr settlement, Maryyskiy Rayon, Mari Oblast. From Maryyskiy Rural National-Territorial Okrug No 438, Turkmen SSR.

Dzhunaydov, Ismat, chief agronomist at Kommunisticheskiy Rayon's Karl Marx Kolkhoz, CPSU member, "Leskhoz" village, Kommunisticheskiy Rayon, Khatlon Oblast. From Kommunisticheskiy National-Territorial Okrug No 368, Tajik SSR.

Dzhusoyty, Nafi Grigoryevich, chief of the History, Osetian Literature, and Folklore Department at Georgian SSR Academy of Sciences South Osetian Research Institute, CPSU member, Tskhinvali city. From Tsinkhvalskiy National-Territorial Okrug No 191, Georgian SSR.

Egnatashvili, Ketevan Giviyevna, canning association canning plant worker, Gori city. From Goriyskiy National-Territorial Okrug No 173, Georgian SSR.

Emiridze, Guram Khuseynovich, first secretary of Adzhar Georgian Communist Party Obkom, CPSU member, Batumi city. From Khelvachaurskiy National-Territorial Okrug No 499, Adzhar ASSR.

Engver, Nikolay Nikolayevich, leading scientific staffer at the USSR Academy of Sciences Urals Department, CPSU member, Izhevsk city. From Industrialnyy National-Territorial Okrug No 658, Udmurt ASSR.

Ergashev, Bakhromzhon Makhmudovich, chairman of the Engels Kolkhoz, Leningradskiy Rayon, CPSU member, Kaltatoy village, Leningradskiy Rayon, Fergana Oblast, Uzbek SSR. From the kolkhozes united by the Union Kolkhoz Council.

Ergeshov, Abdimanap Ergeshovich, team leader at the Frunze Kolkhoz, Bazar-Korgonskiy Rayon, CPSU member, Zhash-Lenina village, Bazar-Korgonskiy Rayon, Osh Oblast. From Dzhalal-Abadskiy Territorial Okrug No 715, Kirghiz SSR.

Esambayev, Makhmud Alisultanovich, ballet soloist of the Chechen-Ingush State Philharmonic Society, Groznyy city. From Shalinskiy National-Territorial Okrug No 678, Chechen-Ingush ASSR.

Eshpay, Andrey Yakovlevich, composer, secretary of the USSR Composers' Union Board, Moscow city. From the USSR Composers' Union.

Esirgapov, Abdugappar Dzhurobekovich, leader of a cotton growing team on the "Krasnaya Zarya" Kolkhoz, Gulistanskiy Rayon, CPSU member, Gulistanskiy Rayon, Syr-Darya Oblast. From Gulistanskiy National-Territorial Okrug No 114, Uzbek SSR.

Eyzan, Andrey Vilisovich, deputy chief physician at the Ventspilsskiy Central Rayon Hospital, CPSU member, Ventspils city. From Ventspilsskiy National-Territorial Okrug No 300, Latvian SSR.

Ezizov Atabay, team leader at the Lenin Kolkhoz, Turkmen-Kalinskiy Rayon, CPSU member, Kemine settlement, Turkmen-Kalinskiy Rayon, Mary Oblast. From Bayram-Aliyskiy National-Territorial Okrug No 422, Turkmen SSR.

Falin, Valentin Mikhaylovich, chief of a CPSU Central Committee department, CPSU member, Moscow city. From the Union of Soviet Societies for Friendship and Cultural Relations With Foreign Countries and the Soviet Society for Cultural Ties with Compatriots Abroad (the "Rodina" Society).

Falin, Mikhail Ivanovich, pensioner, CPSU member, Leningrad city. From the All-Union Organization of War and Labor Veterans.

Falk, Petr Petrovich, lieutenant colonel, senior navigation officer with a military unit, [puncutation as published] Air Force, CPSU member, Orenburg Oblast. From Buzulukskiy Territorial Okrug No 246, Orenburg Oblast, RSFSR.

Fargiyev, Khamzat Akhmedovich, teacher at No 18 Secondary School, Malgobek City. From Sunzhenskiy Territorial Okrug No 398, Chechen-Ingush ASSR.

Fatullayev, Mirbako, deputy chief physician at the Ura-Tyube Central Rayon Hospital, CPSU member, Ura-Tyube city. From Ura-Tyubinskiy National-Territorial Okrug No 381, Tajik SSR.

Fazletdinov, Mukmin Galyaitdinovich, chairman of Abzelilovskiy Rayon's "Put Lenina" kolkhoz, CPSU member, Mikhaylovka village, Abzelilovskiy Rayon, Bashkir ASSR. From the kolkhozes united in the All-Union Kolkhoz Council.

Fedirko, Pavel Stefanovich, chairman of the USSR Tsentrosoyuz Board, CPSU member, Moscow city. From the USSR consumer cooperatives.

Fedorin, Roman Nikolayevich, writer, chief editor of the journal ZHOVTEN, CPSU member, Lvov city. From Drogobychskiy National-Territorial Okrug No 51, Ukrainian SSR.

Fedorov, Aleksandr Pavlovich, general director of the "Akhangarantsement" production association, CPSU member, Akhangaran city. From Akhangaranskiy Territorial Okrug No 601, Tashkent Oblast, Uzbek SSR.

Fedorov, Nikolay Vasilyevich, senior teacher at the Chuvash State University, CPSU member, Cheboksary. From Moskovskiy National-Territorial Okrug No 681, Chuvash ASSR.

Fedorov, Svyatoslav Nikolayevich, general director of the "Mikrokhirurgiya Glaza" intersector scientific and technical complex, chairman of the Soviet Charity and Health Foundation, CPSU member, Moscow city. From the CPSU.

Fedotova, Valentina Ivanovna, chief editor of SOVETSKAYA ZHENSHCHINA magazine, CPSU member, Moscow city. From the women's councils united in the Soviet Women's Committee.

Fedyashin, Viktor Ivanovich, chairman of the council of the "Mordovagropromstroy" Republic Cooperative and State Association, CPSU member, Saransk city. From Kovylkinskiy National-Territorial Okrug No 608, Mordovian ASSR.

Feskov, Nikolay Stepanovich, director of Yelskiy Rayon's Kochishche Secondary School, CPSU member, Kochishche village, Yelskiy Rayon. From Mozyrskiy Territorial Okrug No 558, Gomel Oblast, Belorussian SSR.

Filippov, Viktor Pavlovich, director of the "Pechornipineft" Institute, CPSU member, Ukhta city. From Timanskiy National-Territorial Okrug No 589, Komi ASSR.

Filippova, Valentina Gavrilovna, deputy chairman of the "Aley" kolkhoz, CPSU member, Staroaleyskoye village, Tretyakovskiy Rayon, Altay Kray, RSFSR. From the CPSU.

Filonov, Georgiy Nikolayevich, academician-secretary at the USSR Academy of Pedagogical Sciences Theory and History of Pedagogy Department, chief editor of the journal SOVETSKAYA PEDAGOGIKA, CPSU member, Moscow city. From the USSR Academy of Pedagogical Sciences along with the Soviet Association of Pedagogical Research Workers.

Filshin, Gennadiy Innokentyevich, department chief at the USSR Academy of Sciences Siberian Department's Economics and Organization of Industrial Production Institute, CPSU member, Irkutsk city. From Irkutskiy Territorial Okrug No 171, Irkutsk Oblast, RSFSR.

Finogenov, Vladimir Vyacheslavovich, tool shop foreman at the "Elektroavtomat" plant, CPSU member, Alatyr city, Chuvash ASSR. From the All-Union Komsomol.

Firsov, Anatoliy Vasilyevich, senior trainer at the "Kirovets" Experimental Youth Association, CPSU member, Moscow city. From Medvedkovskiy Territorial Okrug No 16, Moscow city.

Fisinin, Vladimir Ivanovich, general director of the "Soyuzptitseprom" science and production association, director of the All-Union Poultry Farming Scientific Research and Technological Institute, CPSU member, Zagorsk city, Moscow Oblast. From the VaskhniL.

Fokin, Vitold Pavlovich, deputy chairman of the Ukrainian SSR Council of Ministers, chairman of the Ukrainian SSR Gosplan, CPSU member, Kiev city. From Lisichanskiy National-Territorial Okrug No 38, Ukrainian SSR.

Fomenko, Vladimir Leonidovich, deputy shop chief at the Mogilev V.I. Lenin "Khimvolokno" Production Association's V.V. Kuybyshev artificial fiber plant, Mogilev city. From Mogilevskiy city Territorial Okrug No 571, Mogilev Oblast, Belorussian SSR.

Fomenko, Galina Ivanovna, deputy editor of the KOMMUNIST rayon newspaper, CPSU member, Chernyakhovsk city, Kaliningrad Oblast, RSFSR. From the women's councils united in the Soviet Women's Committee.

Fomin, Vladimir Ivanovich, team leader at Urmarskiy Rayon's "Musirminskiy" Sovkhoz, CPSU member, Musirmy village, Urmarskiy Rayon. From Urmarskiy National-Territorial Okrug No 687, Chuvash ASSR.

Fominykh, Viktor Nikolayevich, arc welder at the "Aktyubinskselmash" plant, Aktyubinsk city. From Aktyubinsk city Territorial Okrug No 618, Aktyubinsk Oblast, Kazakh SSR.

Foteyev, Vladimir Konstantinovich, first secretary of the Chechen-Ingush CPSU Obkom, CPSU member, Groznyy city. From Nauskiy National-Territorial Okrug No 675, Chechen-Ingush ASSR.

Frolov, Ivan Timofeyevich, aide to the general secretary of the CPSU Central Committee, CPSU member, Moscow city. From Tulchinskiy Territorial Okrug No 409, Vinnitsa Oblast, Ukrainian SSR.

Frolov, Konstantin Vasilyevich, director of the USSR Academy of Sciences Machine Science Institute named for A. Blagonravov, vice president of the USSR Academy of Sciences, CPSU member, Moscow city. From the

Union of Soviet Societies for Friendship and Cultural relations with Foreign Countries and the Soviet Society for Cultural Ties with Compatriots Abroad (the "Rodina" Society).

Fuzhenko, Ivan Vasliyevich, lieutenant general, commander of the Red Banner Turkestan Military District, CPSU member, Tashkent city. From Termezskiy Territorial Okrug No 592, Surkhandarya Oblast, Uzbek SSR.

Fyuk, Ignar Vladislavovich, architect, chief of the Estonian SSR Main Administration for Architecture, Tallinn city. From Pylvaskiy National-Territorial Okrug No 471, Estonian SSR.

Gabitova, Mavziga Gaffanovna, chairman of Burangulovo village Soviet Ispolkom, CPSU member, Burangulovo village, Abzelilovskiy Rayon, Bashkir ASSR. From the women's councils united by the Soviet Women's Committee.

Gabriyelyan, Vagan Mikhaylovich, first secretary of Mardakertskiy party raykom, CPSU member, Mardakert city. From Mardakertskiy National-Territorial Okrug No 728, NKAO.

Gabrusev, Sergey Artemovich, chief of synthetic fiber production at the Mogilev V.I. Lenin "Khimvolokno" Production Association, CPSU member, Mogilev city. From Mogilevskiy City National-Territorial Okrug No 93, Belorussian SSR.

Gadzhiyev, Mazakhir Nushiravan ogly, adjusters team leader at the Baku S.M. Kirov Machine-Building Plant, CPSU member, Baku city. From the USSR trade unions.

Gagloyev, Alan Sardionovich, marker for a North Osetian ASSR mechanized forestry establishment, CPSU member, Kambilevskoye village, Prigorodnyy Rayon, North Osetian ASSR. From the All-Union Komsomol.

Galoyan, Galust Anushavanovich, secretary of the Armenian Communist Party Central Committee, CPSU member, Yerevan city. From Akhuryanskiy National-Territorial Okrug No 403, Armenian SSR.

Galstyan, Samvel Surenovich, chairman of the S. Shaumyan Kolkhoz, Artashatskiy Rayon, CPSU member, Kakhtsrashen village, Artashatskiy Rayon. From Artashatskiy National-Territorial Okrug No 401, Armenian SSR.

Gamkrelidze, Tamaz Valerianovich, director of the Georgian SSR Academy of Sciences Oriental Studies Institute, CPSU member, Tbilisi city. From Akhalshenskiy National-Territorial Okrug No 496, Adzhar ASSR.

Gams, Eduard Sergeyevich, captain, junior scientific associate of a scientific research institute, CPSU member, Shikhany Urban Settlement, Srataov Oblast. From Balakovskiy Territorial Okrug No 286, RSFSR.

Gamzatov, Rasul Gamzatovich, writer, chairman of the Dagestan ASSR Writers Union Board, secretary of the RSFSR Writers Union Board, secretary of the USSR Writers Union Board, CPSU member, Makhachkala city. From Oktyabrskiy Territorial Okrug No 365, Dagestan ASSR.

Gaponov-Grekhov, Andrey Viktorovich, academician, director of the USSR Academy of Sciences Applied Physics Institute, Gorkiy city. From the USSR Academy of Sciences.

Gasanova, Shamama Makhmudaly kyzy, chairman of the "1 May" Kolkhoz, Fizulinskiy Rayon, CPSU member, Arayatyly village, Fizulinskiy Rayon. From Agdzhabedinskiy Territorial Okrug No 674, Azerbaijan SSR.

Gashper, Mikhail Alekseyevich, mechanized team leader of the "Dnestr" scientific-production association "Ivancha" Sovkhoz, CPSU member, Furcheny village, Orgeyevskiy Rayon, Moldavian SSR. From the USSR trade unions.

Gausknekht, Yuriy Gennadyevich, drilling expert at the Izhevsk drilling work administration at the "Udmurtneft" production association, CPSU member, Izhevsk city. From Ustinovskiy National-Territorial Okrug No 661 Udmurtskiy ASSR.

Gavrilov, Andrey Petrovich, editor of the newspaper VECHERNYAYA KAZAN, CPSU member, Kazan city. From Baumanskiy Territorial Okrug No 382, Tatar ASSR.

Gayda, Mikhail Mikhaylovich, captain, aircraft technician at the Chernigov Military Pilots School Aviation Training regiment, CPSU member, Uman City. From Umanskiy Territorial Okrug No 539, Ukrainian SSR.

Gayduchenya, Sergey Nikolayevich, procurement worker for Maloviskovskiy Rayon Potrebsoyuz Procurement Office, CPSU member, Malaya Viska city, Kirovograd Oblast, Ukrainian SSR. From the USSR Consumer Cooperatives.

Gayer, Yevdokiya Aleksandrovna, scientific staffer of the Institute of History, Archeology, and Ethnography of the USSR Academy of Sciences Far Eastern Branch, CPSU member, Vladivostok city. From Dalnevostochnyy National-Territorial Okrug No 8, RSFSR.

Gazenko, Oleg Georgiyevich, academician, adviser to the directors of the USSR Health Ministry Institute of Medicobiological Problems, CPSU member, Moscow city. From scientific societies and associations under the USSR Academy of Sciences.

Gdlyan, Telman Khorenovich, senior investigator for especially important cases at the USSR General Prosecutor's Office, CPSU member, Moscow. From Tushinskiy Territorial-Electoral Okrug No 25, Moscow city.

Geda, Sigitas Zigmas Zigmovich, poet, secretary of the Lithuanian SSR Writers Union Board, Vilnius. From

Alitusskiy National-Territorial Okrug No 231, Lithuanian SSR.

Gelman, Aleksandr Isaakovich, movie dramatist, CPSU member, Moscow. From the USSR Cinematographers' Union.

Genzyalis, Bronislavas Konstantinovich, professor at the Vilnius State University named for V. Kapsukas, CPSU member, Vilnius city. From Kretingskiy National-Territorial Okrug No 243, Lithuanian SSR.

German (Granin), Daniil Aleksandrovich, writer, secretary of the USSR Writers' Union Board, CPSU member, Leningrad city. From the CPSU.

German, Natalya Fedorovna, team leader of the "Shabo" sovkhoz-plant, Belgorod-Dnestrovskiy Rayon, candidate CPSU member, Shabo village, Belgorod-Dnestrovskiy Rayon. From Belgorod-Dnestrovskiy Territorial Okrug No 500, Odessa Oblast, Ukrainian SSR.

Germel, Stanislav Vladimirovich, link leader at the Kolkhoz named for Thaelmann, CPSU member, Gorodishche village, Gomel Oblast, Belorussian SSR. From kolkhozes united in the USSR Kolkhoz Council.

Gerzanich, Mariya Vasilyevna, chief of the Vinogradov Central Rayon Hospital, Vinograd city. From Mukachevskiy Territorial Okrug No 452, Transcarpathian Oblast, Ukrainian SSR.

Geyba, Yanis Aloizovich, first secretary of the Daugavpilsskiy Latvian Communist Party Raykom, CPSU member, Daugavpils City. From Daugavpilsskiy Rural National-Territorial Okrug No 302, Latvian SSR.

Gezhin, Konstantin Georgiyevich, electrician at the No 5 "Stavropolkhimstroy" construction and installation administration, CPSU member, Nevinnomyssk city, Stavropol Kray, RSFSR. From the All-Union Komsomol.

Gibadullin, Marat Rashatovich, operator in the "Tatneft" production association's "Primkamneft" oil and gas extraction administration, CPSU member, Yelabug city, Tatar ASSR. From the All-Union Komsomol.

Gidaspov, Boris Veniaminovich, general director of the "GIPKH" Science and Production Association, chairman of the board of the "Tekhnokhim" intersectorial state association, CPSU member, Leningrad city. From Petrogradskiy Territorial Okrug No 56, Leningrad city.

Gidirim, Georgiy Petrovich, department head of the Kishinev Medical Institute, CPSU member, Kishinev city. From Kaushanskiy National-Territorial Okrug No 270, Moldavian SSR.

Gil, Yaroslav Yakovlevich, chief physician at the Kremenetskiy Central Rayon Hospital, CPSU member, Kremenets city. From Zbarazhskiy Territorial Okrug No 517, Ukrainian SSR.

Gilalzade, Dzhangir Gadi ogly, team leader in No 32 Construction Administration in No 3 Construction and Installation Trust, CPSU member, Kirovabad city. From Kirovabadskiy Territorial Okrug No 677, Azerbaijan SSR.

Ginzburg, Vitaliy Lazarevich, adviser to the directors of the P.M. Lebedev Physics Institute of the USSR Academy of Sciences, CPSU member, Moscow City. From the USSR Academy of Sciences.

Girenko, Andrey Nikolayevich, first secretary of the Crimean Ukrainian Communist Party Obkom, CPSU member, Simferopol city. From Krymskiy National-Territorial Okrug No 49, Ukrainian SSR.

Giyasova, Perzad Gamid kyzy, worker at the Khachmas Canned Goods Combine, Khachmas city. From Khachmasskiy National-Territorial Okrug No 221, Azerbaijan SSR.

Glavatskikh, Mikhail Vladimirovich, combine operator on the "Kommunar" Sovkhoz in Glazovskiy Rayon, Udmurtskiye Klyuchi village, Glazovskiy Rayon. From the Severnyy Territorial Okrug No 395, Udmurt ASSR.

Glazkov, Nikolay Semenovich, foreman and team leader at the Moscow Decorative Timepiece Plant, CPSU member, Moscow city. From Pervomayskiy Territorial Okrug No 18, Moscow city.

Glazunov, Aleksandr Nikolayevich, technician at the "Lipetskiy Traktornyy Zavod" Production Association's Lipetsk Tracklaying Tractor Plant, CPSU member, Lipetsk city. From Lipetskiy Territorial Okrug No 220, Lipetsk Oblast, RSFSR.

Glazunov, Vladimir Ivanovich, director of the "Prigorodnoye" Experimental Production Farm in Saratovskiy Rayon, CPSU member, Kleshchevka village, Saratovskiy Rayon, Saratov Oblast, RSFSR. From the All-Union Komsomol.

Glazunov, Ivan Fedorovich, director of the Anzobskiy Mining and Enriching Combine, CPSU member, Zarafshan-I settlement, Ayninskiy Rayon, Leninabad Oblast. From Pendzhikentskiy National-Territorial Okrug No 379, Tajik SSR.

Gnatyuk, Viktoriya Vyacheslavovna, physician at the Kalinovka Central Rayon Hospital, CPSU member, Kalinovka city, Vinnitsa Oblast. From Vinnitskiy National-Territorial Okrug No 35, Ukrainian SSR.

Gninenko, Yuriy Ivanovich, laboratory chief at the Kazakh Scientific Research Institute for Forestry, CPSU member, Shchuchinsk City. From Shchuchinskiy National-Territorial Okrug No 159, Kazakh SSR.

Godzhayeva, Safiya Abdurakhman kyzy, tobacco grower on the S. Vurgun Kolkhoz in Zakatalskiy Rayon, Ashagi

Tala village, Zakatalskiy Rayon. From Shchekinskiy Territorial Okrug No 680, Azerbaijan SSR.

Gogeshvili, Aleko Rafayelovich, transformer assembly worker at the Batumi Transformer Plant, CPSU member, Batumi city. From Batumskiy-Primorskiy National-Territorial Okrug No 495, Adzhar ASSR.

Gogua, Aleksey Nochevich, writer, chief editor of the children's magazine AMTSABZ, CPSU member, Sukhumi city. From Ochamchirskiy Rural National-Territorial Okrug No 490, Abkhaz ASSR.

Goldanskiy, Vitaliy Iosifovich, director of the N.N. Semenov Institute of Chemical Physics of the USSR Academy of Sciences, chairman of the Soviet Pugwash Committee, CPSU member, Moscow City. From the Soviet Peace Foundation plus eight Soviet committees advocating peace, solidarity, and international cooperation.

Golev, Anatoliy Vasilyevich, engineer at Prigorodnyy Rayon's Lenin Kolkhoz, CPSU member, Kambileyevskoye village, Prigorodnyy Rayon. From Prigorodnyy National-Territorial Okrug No 634, North Osetian ASSR.

Golik, Yuriy Vladimirovich, dean of the Law Faculty at Kemerovo State University, CPSU member, Kemerovo city. From Tsentralnyy Territorial Okrug No 190, Kemerovo Oblast, RSFSR.

Golov, Ivan Alekseyevich, chairman of Talovskiy Rayon's "Gigant" Kolkhoz, CPSU member, Tishanka village, Talovskiy Rayon, Voronezh Oblast, RSFSR. From kolkhozes united in the All-Union Kolkhoz Council.

Golovin, Stanislav Pavlovich, radio apparatus tuner at the Mari Machine-Building Plant, CPSU member, Yoshkar-Ola City. From Yoshkar-Olinskiy Territorial Okrug No 374, Mari ASSR.

Golovlev, Yevgeniy Leonidovich, laboratory chief at the Institute of Biochemistry and the Physiology of Microorganisms, Pushchino city, CPSU member, Pushchino city, Moscow Oblast. From Serpukhovskiy Territorial Okrug No 41, Moscow Oblast, RSFSR.

Golovnev, Vasiliy Yefimovich, military unit technical, CPSU member, Mogilev Oblast. From Krichevskiy National-Territorial Okrug No 96, Belorussian SSR.

Golovnitskiy, Lev Nikolayevich, artist, academician-secretary of the USSR Academy of Arts' Siberian and Far East Department, CPSU member, Krasnoyarsk city, RSFSR. From the USSR Academy of Arts.

Golubeva, Valentina Nikolayevna, general director of the Ivanovo cotton production combine, CPSU member, Ivanovo city, RSFSR. From the CPSU.

Golushko, Nikolay Mikhaylovich, chairman of the Ukrainian SSR KGB, CPSU member, Kiev city. From Korostyshevskiy Territorial Okrug No 449, Zhitomir Oblast, Ukrainian SSR.

Golyakov, Aleksandr Ivanovich, first deputy chairman of the All-Union Council of War and Labor Veterans, CPSU member, Moscow city. From the All-Union Organization of War and Labor Veterans.

Gonchar, Aleksandr Nikolayevich, major, party committee secretary in a motorized rifle regiment in the Leningrad Military District, CPSU member, Pechenga city, Murmansk Oblast, RSFSR. From the CPSU.

Gonchar, Aleksandr Terentyevich, writer, secretary of the USSR Writers Union Board, CPSU member, Kiev city. From the USSR Writers Union.

Goncharik, Vladimir Ivanovich, chairman of the Belorussian Republican Trade Unions Council, CPSU member, Minsk city. From the USSR Trade Unions.

Goncharov, Viktor Vasilyevich, first secretary of Yenakiyevo Leninist Communist Youth League [Komsomol] city committee [gorkom], CPSU member, Yenakiyevo City. From Yenakiyevskiy Territorial Okrug No 437, Ukrainian SSR.

Gorbachev, Aleksandr Grigoryevich, director of the "Rossiya" Sovkhoz, Kizlyarskiy Rayon, CPSU member, Bolshaya Areshevka village, Kizlyarskiy Rayon. From Kizlyarskiy National-Territorial Okrug No 531, Dagestan ASSR.

Gorbachev, Mikhail Sergeyevich, general secretary of the CPSU Central Committee and chairman of the USSR Supreme Soviet Presidium, CPSU member, Moscow city. From the CPSU.

Gontar, Valentina Alekseyevna, chairman of the "Shlyakh do Komunizmu" Kolkhoz, Chernobayevskiy Rayon, CPSU member, Novoukrainka village, Chernobayevskiy Rayon, Cherkassy Oblast, Ukrainian SSR. From kolkhozes united in the Union Kolkhoz Council.

Gorbatko, Viktor Vasilyevich, major general, chief of faculty in the Air Force Engineering Academy named for N.Ye. Zhukovskiy, chairman of the All-Union Society of Philatelists, CPSU member, Moscow city. From the All-Union Society of Philatelists.

Gorbenko, Anatoliy Pavlovich, link leader on the kolkhoz named for Lenin, Ustinovskiy Rayon, CPSU member, Berezovatka village, Ustinovskiy Rayon, Kirovograd Oblast. From Kirovogradskiy National-Territorial Okrug No 48, Ukrainian SSR.

Gorbunov, Anatoliy Valeryanovich, chairman of the Latvian SSR Supreme Soviet Presidium, CPSU member, Riga city. From Tsesisskiy Territorial Okrug No 713, Latvian SSR.

Gorbunov, Gennadiy Nikolayevich, director of the Irkutsk aviation plant named for the 60th anniversary of the USSR, CPSU member, Irkutsk city. From Leninskiy Territorial Okrug No 170, Irkutsk Oblast, RSFSR.

Gorbunov, Yuriy Gerasimovich, chief of the "OshKPDproyektstroy" Association, CPSU member, Osh city. From Oshskiy Territorial Okrug No 721, Kirghiz SSR.

Gordeyev, Ivan Dementyevich, chairman of the "Leninskiy put" Kolkhoz, Sosnovskiy Rayon, CPSU member, Olkhi village, Sosnovskiy Rayon. From Michurinskiy Territorial Okrug No 310, Tambov Oblast, RSFSR.

Gordeyev, Vladimir Sergeyevich, chairman of the Aginskiy Okrug Economically Accountable Young People's Association, CPSU member, Aginskoye Urban settlement, Aga Buryat Autonomous Okrug, Chita Oblast, RSFSR. From the All-Union Komsomol.

Gordeyeva, Valentina Ivanovna, leader of a stock unit contract collective on "Peredovik" Kolkhoz, Pskovskiy Rayon, CPSU member, Kholstovo village, Pskovskiy Rayon, Pskov Oblast, RSFSR. From kolkhozes united in the Union Kolkhoz Council.

Gorelkina, Valentina Aleksandrovna, chairman of the Krasnoyarsk Kray Committee of the Public Education and Scientific Workers Trade Union, CPSU member, Krasnoyarsk city, RSFSR. From the USSR Trade Unions.

Gorelovskiy, Ivan Ivanovich, chairman of the Azerbaijan SSR KGB, CPSU member, Baku city. From Masallinskiy National-Territorial Okrug No 214, Azerbaijan SSR.

Gorinchey, Vitaliy Vasilyevich, chairman of the kolkhoz named for Lenin, Ungenskiy Rayon, CPSU member, Pyrlitsa village, Ungenskiy Rayon. From Ungenskiy National-Territorial Okrug No 284, Moldavian SSR.

Gorinov, Trofim Iosifovich, pensioner, CPSU member, Yoshkar-Ola city, Mari ASSR. From the All-Union Organization of War and Labor Veterans.

Gorlov, Grigoriy Kirillovich, deputy director of the "Stavropolvodmelioratsiya" Association Training Combine, CPSU member, Stavropol city, RSFSR. From the All-Union Organization of War and Labor Veterans.

Gorokhov, Vladislav Andreyevich, director of "Losinyy Ostrov" State National Nature Park, CPSU member, Moscow City. From Mytishchinskiy Territorial Okrug No 35, RSFSR.

Gorozhaninov, Yuriy Ivanovich, general director of the "UralAZ" Production Association, CPSU member, Miass city. From Zlatoustovskiy Territorial Okrug No 335, Chelyabinsk Oblast, RSFSR.

Gorshkov, Leonid Aleksandrovich, deputy chairman of the RSFSR Council of Ministers, CPSU member, Moscow city. From Severnyy National-Territorial Okrug No 26, RSFSR.

Gorynin, Igor Vasilyevich, director of the "Prometey" Central Scientific Research Institute for Construction Materials, CPSU member, Leningrad city. From the USSR Union of Scientific and Engineering Societies.

Govorov, Vladimir Leonidovich, Army General, chief of Civil Defense and deputy defense minister of the USSR, CPSU member, Moscow city. From Groznenskiy Rural National-Territorial Okrug No 672, Chechen-Ingush ASSR.

Grachev, Nikolay Petrovich, troubleshooter at the "Tretiy Gosudarstvennyy Podshipnikovyy Zavod" Production Association, CPSU member, Saratov city. From Zavodskoy Territorial Okrug No 284, Saratov Oblast, RSFSR.

Gracheva, Galina Petrovna, director of the "Sverdlovskiy" State Poultry Breeding Center, Sysertskiy Rayon, CPSU member, Kashino village, Sysertskiy Rayon, Sverdlovsk Oblast, RSFSR. From women's councils united in the Soviet Women's Committee.

Grakhovskiy, Aleksandr Adamovich, chairman of the Gomel Oblast Soviet Executive Committee [Oblispolkom], CPSU member. From Rechitskiy National-Territorial Okrug No 88, Belorussian SSR.

Grebneva, Tatyana Fedorovna, chief of the No 15 children's combine, CPSU member, Kamenka city, Penza Oblast, RSFSR. From women's councils united in the Soviet Women's Committee.

Gretsov, Sergey Nikolayevich, leasing link leader on "Sudbishchenskiy" Sovkhoz, Novoderevenkovskiy Rayon, Sudbishchi village, Novoderevenkovskiy Rayon, Orel Oblast, RSFSR. From the All-Union Komsomol.

Grib, Aleksandr Vasilyevich, blast furnace attendant at the "Zaporozhstal" Metallurgical Combine, CPSU member, Zaporozhye city. From Zaporozhskiy-Leninskiy Territorial Okrug No 454, Zaporozhye Oblast, Ukrainian SSR.

Grigoryan, Artsvin Gaykovich, architect, chairman of the Armenian Architects Union Board, CPSU member, Yerevan city. From the USSR Architects Union.

Grigoryan, Nyutyun Arushanovich, first secretary of the Kirovakan Armenian Communist Party Gorkom, CPSU member, Kirovakan city. From Kirovakanskiy National-Territorial Okrug No 397, Armenian SSR.

Grigoryan, Vachagan Santurovich, first secretary of the Martuninskiy party raykom, CPSU member, Martuni city. From Martuninskiy National-Territorial Okrug No 727, NKAO.

Grigoryev, Vladimir Viktorovich, director of Shumerlinskiy Rayon's "Kombinat" Sovkhoz, CPSU member, Shumerlya City. From Tsivilskiy Territorial Okrug No 401, Chuvash ASSR.

Grigoryev, Firs Grigoryevich, chief physician at Kanashskiy Rayon Central Hospital, CPSU member, Shikhazany village, Kanashskiy Rayon, Chuvash ASSR.

From Kazanskiy National-Territorial okrug No 11, RSFSR.

Grigoryev, Vladimir Viktorovich, first secretary of the Vitebsk Belorussian Communist Party Obkom, CPSU member, Vitebsk city. From Glubokskiy National-Territorial Okrug No 80, Belorussian SSR.

Grinovskis, Ervid Yanovich, professor at the Latvian Agricultural Academy, CPSU member, Yelgava city. From Yelgavskiy Territorial Okrug No 710, Latvian SSR.

Grintsov, Ivan Grigoryevich, secretary of the Ukrainian Communist Party Central Committee, CPSU member, Kiev city. From Akhtyrskiy Territorial Okrug No 513, Sumy Oblast, Ukrainian SSR.

Gritsenko, Nikolay Nikolayevich, rector of the All-Union Central Council of Trade Unions [AUCCTU] Higher School of the Trade Union Movement named for N.M. Shvernik, CPSU member, Moscow city. From the USSR Trade Unions.

Grishchenko, Petr Semenovich, first secretary of the Udmurt CPSU Obkom, CPSU member, Izhevsk city. From Igrinskiy National-Territorial Okrug No 664, Udmurt ASSR.

Grishchenkov, Grigoriy Zakharovich, chairman of the Belorussian Potrebsoyuz Board, CPSU member, Minsk city. From the USSR Consumer Cooperatives.

Grishchuk, Valeriy Pavlovich, senior lecturer at Kiev State University named for T.G. Shevchenko, CPSU member, Kiev City. From Dneprovskiy Territorial Okrug No 465, Ukrainian SSR.

Grezhdiyeru, Anton Gavrilovich, chief editor of the newspaper YNVETSEMYNTUL PUBLIK, CPSU member, Kishinev city. From Floreshtskiy National-Territorial Okrug No 286, Moldavian SSR.

Gromov, Boris Fedorovich, engineer at the First Northern Railroad Vologda Station Locomotive Depot, CPSU member, Vologda city, RSFSR. From the All-Union Organization of War and Labor veterans.

Gromov, Boris Vsevolodovich, lieutenant general, commander of the Red-Banner Kiev Military District, CPSU member, Kiev city. From Prilukskiy Territorial Okrug No 542, Chernigov Oblast, Ukrainian SSR.

Gromov, Viktor Ivanovich, rotary lathe operator at the Verkhnesaldinskiy metallurgical production association named for V.I. Lenin, CPSU member, Verkhnyaya Salda city, Sverdlovsk Oblast, RSFSR. From the CPSU.

Gromyan, Roman Teodorovich, chief of department at the Ternopol state teacher training institute named for Ya. Galan, CPSU member, Ternopol city. From Ternopolskiy Territorial Okrug No 516, Ternopol Oblast, Ukrainian SSR.

Gross, Viktor Ivanovich, general director of the "Bryanskiy Avtomobilnyy Zavod" Production Association, CPSU member, Bryansk city. From Bryanskiy Territorial Okrug No 129, Bryansk Oblast, RSFSR.

Grossu, Semen Kuzmich, first secretary of the Moldavian Communist Party Central Committee, CPSU member, Kishinev city. From Yedinetskiy Territorial Okrug No 699, Moldavian SSR.

Grozdev, Stepan Vasilyevich, first secretary of the Komratskiy Moldavian Communist Party Raykom, CPSU member, Komrat city. From Komratskiy National-Territorial Okrug No 271, Moldavian SSR.

Grudinina, Anna Kornilovna, chief of section in the Borisoglebskaya Central Rayon Hospital, Borisoglebsk city. From Borisoglebskiy Territorial Okrug No 151, Voronezh Oblast, RSFSR.

Grudinina, Svetlana Vladimirovna, team leader at the Kazakh machine testing station experimental farm, Kaskelenskiy Rayon, CPSU member, Oktyabr village, Kaskelenskiy Rayon, Alma-Ata Oblast. From Alma-Atinskiy-Iliyskiy National-Territorial Okrug No 129, Kazakh SSR.

Gruzdov, Ivan Pavlovich, chairman of the "Zarya Kommunizma" Kolkhoz, Korenevskiy Rayon, CPSU member, Korenevo village, Korenevskiy Rayon, Kursk Oblast, RSFSR. From kolkhozes united in the Union Kolkhoz Council.

Gryazin, Igor Nikolevich, chief of department at the Estonian SSR Academy of Sciences Philosophy, Sociology, and Law Institute, CPSU member, Tartu city. From Pyarnuskiy Rural National-Territorial Okrug No 473, Estonian SSR.

Gubarev, Viktor Andreyevich, deputy director of the "Neftetermmash" Prototype-Experimental Machine Building Plant, CPSU member, Chernomorskiy village, Severskiy Rayon, from Krymskiy Territorial Okrug No 78, Krasnodar Kray, RSFSR.

Gubin, Viktor Aleksandrovich, technonology engineer at the "Solombalskiy Tsellyulozno-Bumazhnyy Kombinat" Production Association, CPSU member, Arkhangelsk city, RSFSR. From the All-Union Komsomol.

Gudaytis, Romas Vitautovich, writer, literary consultant to the Lithuanian SSR Writers Union, CPSU member, Vilnius city. From Kapsukskiy National-Territorial Okrug No 235, Lithuanian SSR.

Gudzhabidze, Avtandil Valeryanovich, chairman of the kolkhoz named for PRAVDA in Tkhinvali village, Makharadzevskiy Rayon, CPSU member, Tkhinvali village, Makharadzevskiy Rayon. From Makharadzevskiy National-Territorial Okrug No 179, Georgian SSR.

Guguchiya, Dzhoto Iosifovich, chairman of the kolkhoz named for K. Marx, Zugdidskiy Rayon, CPSU member,

Kakhati village, Zugdidskiy Rayon, Georgian SSR. From kolkhozes united in the Union Kolkhoz Council.

Gudilina, Valentina Grigoryevna, chief of department in the Solnechnogorskaya Central Rayon Hospital, Solnechnogorsk city. From Solnechnogorskiy Territorial Okrug No 42, Moscow Oblast, RSFSR.

Gudushauri, Otar Naskidovich, general director of the Georgian SSR Ministry of Health Scientific Traumatology and Orthopedics Center, CPSU member, Tbilisi city. From Samtredskiy Territorial Okrug No 668, Georgian SSR.

Gukasov, Erik Khristoforovich, first deputy chairman of the Kazakh SSR Council of Ministers, chairman of the Kazakh SSR Gosagroprom, CPSU member, Alma-Ata city. From Saryagachskiy National-Territorial Okrug No 150, Kazakh SSR.

Gulamov, Rasul, pensioner, CPSU member, Tashkent city. From the All-Union Organization of Veterans of War and Labor.

Guliy, Vitaliy Valentinovich, special correspondent for the SOVETSKIY SAKHALIN newspaper, CPSU member, Yuzhno-Sakhalinsk city. From the Yuzhno-Sakhalinskiy Territorial Okrug No 290, Sakhalin Oblast, RSFSR.

Gulchenko, Ivan Mikhaylovich, department head of the Karaganda Polytechnical Institute Petropavlovsk branch, Petropavlovsk city. From Petropavlovsk city Territorial Okrug No 639, North Kazakhstan Oblast, Kazakh SSR.

Gulova, Zulaykho Sokhibnazarovna, field crop cultivation team leader of the "XXII Party Congress" Kolkhoz in Ordzhonikidzeabadskiy Rayon, CPSU member, Ordzhonikidzeabadskiy Rayon, Tajik SSR. From the CPSU.

Gulyayev, Yuriy Vasilyevich, director of the USSR Academy of Sciences Radio Engineering and Electronics Institute, CPSU member, Moscow city. From the USSR Union of Scientific and Engineering Societies.

Gumbaridze, Givi Grigoryevich, chairman of the Georgian SSR KGB, CPSU member, Tbilisi city. From Zestafonskiy National-Territorial Okrug No 175, Georgian SSR.

Gumennaya, Zinaida Leonidovna, senior salesperson at the Vladimiro-Aleksandrovskiy Rayon Consumer Society store, CPSU member, Zolotaya Dolina village, Partizanskiy Rayon, Maritime Kray, RSFSR. From the USSR consumer cooperatives.

Gummyyev, Otuz, team leader at the Oktyabrskiy Rayon "Sovet Turkmenistany" kolkhoz, CPSU member, Gazakdegish settlement, Oktyabrskiy Rayon, Tashauz Oblast. From Tashauzskiy Territorial Okrug No 745, Turkmen SSR.

Gundogdyyev, Yazgeldi Potayevich, first secretary of the Turkmen Komsomol Central Committee, CPSU member, Ashkhabad city. From Vekil-Bazarskiy National-Territorial Okrug No 424, Turkmen SSR.

Gurenko, Stanislav Ivanovich, secretary of the Ukrainian Communist Party Central Committee, CPSU member, Kiev city. From Zaporozhskiy-Shevchenkovskiy Territorial Okrug No 456, Zaporozhye Oblast, Ukrainian SSR.

Guruleva, Nina Grigorevna, procurement worker in the Nerchinskiy Rayon Consumer Society rayon procurement office, Olensk village, Nerchinskiy Rayon, Chita Oblast, RSFSR. From the USSR consumer cooperatives.

Gusev, Vladimir Vasilyevich, first secretary of the Gorno-Altay CPSU Obkom, CPSU member, Gorno-Altaysk city. From Katunskiy National-Territorial Okrug No 706, Gorno-Altay Autonomous Oblast.

Guskova, Lidiya Mikhaylovna, chairman of the Astrakhan Oblast Trade Union Council, CPSU member, Astrakhan city, RSFSR. From women's councils united in the Soviet Women's Committee.

Gustov, Vitaliy Vladimirovich, oil and gas extraction foreman at the "Yuganskneftegaz" production association's "Mamontovneft" oil and gas extraction administration, CPSU member, Nefteyugansk city, Tyumen Oblast, RSFSR. From the USSR trade unions.

Gutskalov, Nikolay Ivanovich, captain-director of the Murmansk Trawler Fleet Administration's large autonomous trawler "Marshal Yeremenko," CPSU member, Murmansk city, RSFSR. From the USSR trade unions.

Gvenetadze, Avtandil Davidovich, chief physician of the Tkibuli children's hospital-polyclinic association, CPSU member, Tkibuli city. From Tskhaltubskiy National-Territorial Okrug No 190, Georgian SSR.

Gvozdev, Vladimir Matveyevich, comprehensive mechanized team leader of the "Yuzhkuzbassugol" production association "Raspadskaya" mine, CPSU member, Mezhdurechensk city, RSFSR Kemerovo Oblast. From the CPSU.

Ibragimbekov, Rustan Mamed Ibragim ogly, writer, secretary of the Azerbaijan SSR Cinematographers Union Board, secretary of the USSR Cinematographers Union Board, CPSU member, Moscow city. From Nakhichevansky Second City National-Territorial Okrug No. 614, Nakhichevan ASSR.

Ibragimov, Guseyn Rustam ogly, driller at the "Neftyanyye Kamni" maritime drilling operations administration of the 22d CPSU Congress Oil and Gas Recovery Administration of the "Kaspmorneftegaz" Production Association, CPSU member, Baku city. From the CPSU.

Ibragimov, Mirza Azhdar ogly, department chief at the Nizami Institute of Literature of the Azerbaijan SSR

Academy of Sciences, CPSU member, Baku city. From Nakhichevanskiy Territorial Okrug No 679, Azerbaijan SSR.

Ibragimov, Mirzaolim Ibragimovich, permanent representative of the Uzbek SSR Council of Ministers to the USSR Council of Ministers, CPSU member, Moscow city. From Muynakskiy National-Territorial Okrug No 562, Karakalpak ASSR.

Ibrayeva, Kulzhariya, link leader on "Sarykumskiy" Sovkhoz, Alakulskiy Rayon, CPSU member, Kazakhstan village, Alakulskiy Rayon. From Taldy-Kurganskiy Rural Territorial Okrug No 644, Taldy-Kurgan Oblast, Kazakh SSR.

Ibraimova, Raisa Belekovna, chairman of the Kirghiz SSR Red Cross Society Central Committee, CPSU member, Frunze city. From the USSR Union of Red Cross and Red Crescent Societies.

Igityan, Genrikh Surenovich, general director of the Republican Aesthetic Education Center, director of the Armenian Museum of Modern Art, CPSU member, Yerevan city. From the USSR Artists Union.

Ignatov, Stepan Vladimirovich, chief economist on "Pomozdinskiy" Sovkhoz, CPSU member, Pomozdino village, Ust-Kulomskiy Rayon. From Ust-Kulomskiy National-Territorial Okrug No 590, Komi ASSR.

Ignatovich, Nikolay Ivanovich, investigator for important cases under the Belorussian SSR prosecutor, CPSU member, Minsk City. From Minskiy-Zavodskoy National-Territorial Electoral Okrug No 65, Belorussian SSR.

Ignatyev, Innokentiy Gavrilovich, permanent representative of the Yakutsk ASSR Council of Ministers on the RSFSR Council of Ministers, CPSU member, Moscow City. From Bulunskiy National-Territorial Orkug No 694, Yakutsk ASSR.

Igrunov, Nikolay Stefanovich, second secretary of the Belorussian Communist Party Central Committee, CPSU member, Minsk city. From Volkovysskiy National-Territorial Okrug No 90, Belorussian SSR.

Igumnov, Oleg Aleksandrovich, teacher at the No 6 secondary school, Frunze city. From Frunzenskiy-Pervomayskiy National-Territorial Okrug No 323, Kirghiz SSR.

Ikayev, Georgiy Dzambulatovich, first secretary of Digorskiy CPSU Raykom, CPSU member, Digora city. From Digorskiy National-Territorial Okrug No 630, North-Osetian ASSR.

Ikramov, Anvar Salikhovich, first secretary of the Samarkand Uzbek Communist Party Obkom, Samarkand city. From Bulungurskiy National-Territorial Okrug No 106, Uzbek SSR.

Ikramova, Mukhabbat, milkmaid at the "Uzbekistan" Kolkhoz, Khatyrchinskiy Rayon, CPSU member, Changir Village, Khatyrchinskiy Rayon, Samarkand Oblast. From Kattakurganskiy Territorial Okrug No 587, Samarkand Oblast, Uzbek SSR.

Ilakov, Aleksandr Vasilyevich, first secretary of Ongudayskiy CPSU Raykom, CPSU member, Onguday village, Altay Kray. From Ongudayskiy National-Territorial Okrug No 708, Gorno-Altay Autonomous Oblast.

Ilin, Aleksey Nikolayevich, first secretary of Pskov CPSU Obkom, CPSU member, Pskov City. From Ostrovskiy Territorial Okrug No 266, Pskov Oblast, RSFSR.

Ilizarov, Gavriil Abramovich, general director of the Kurgan "Vosstanovitelnaya travmatologiya i ortopediya" All-Union Scientific Center, CPSU member, Kurgan city, RSFSR. From the CPSU.

Inkens, Edvins Edmundovich, senior editor at the Latvian SSR State Committee for Television and Radio Broadcasting Main Television News Broadcasts Editorial Office, CPSU member, Riga city. From Tsesisskiy National-Territorial Okrug No 319, Latvian SSR.

Inochkin, Anatoliy Mikhaylovich, lathe and drill operator at the Saratov aviation plant, CPSU member, Saratov city, RSFSR. From the All-Union Organization of War and Labor Veterans.

Iovlev, Dmitriy Mikhaylovich, fitter at the "Moskvich" Production Association automobile plant named for the Lenin Komsomol, CPSU member, Moscow city. From the CPSU.

Irgashev, Akram Kurbanovich, manager of "Uzbekgidroenergostroy" Trust, CPSU member, Tashkent City. From Tashkentskiy-Oktyabrskiy National-Territorial Okrug No 117, Uzbek SSR.

Isakadze, Liana Aleksandrovna, artistic director and chief producer with the Georgian State Chamber Orchestra, soloist with the Moscow State Philharmonic Orchestra, Moscow city. From women's councils united in the Soviet Women's Committee.

Isakov, Bektur Sydykovich, teacher at the Aral secondary school, Talasskiy Rayon, CPSU member, Aral village, Talasskiy Rayon. From Talasskiy National-territorial Okrug No 345, Kirghiz SSR.

Isakov, Ismanali Ismailovich, face worker at the Khaydarkan mercury combine, CPSU member, Khaydarkan settlement, Frunzenskiy Rayon, Osh Oblast. From Frunzenskiy National-Territorial Okrug No 352, Kirghiz SSR.

Isayev, Geydar Isa ogly, first secretary of the Nakhichevan Azerbaijan Communist Party Obkom, CPSU member, Nakhichevan city. From Vanandskiy National-Territorial Okrug No 615, Nakhichevan ASSR.

Isayev, Yuriy Alekseyevich, general director of the "AvtoUAZ" Production Association, CPSU member, Ulyanovsk city. From Ulyanovskiy National-Territorial Okrug No 30, RSFSR.

Isayeva, Antonina Ivanovna, milking machine operator on the kolkhoz named for S.M. Kirov, Zolochevskiy Rayon, CPSU member, Berezovka village, Zolochevskiy Rayon, Kharkov Oblast, Ukrainian SSR. From kolkhozes united in the Union Kolkhoz Council.

Ishanov, Khekim, chief engineer at the "Turkmenneft" Production Association, CPSU member, Nebit-Dag city. From Nebit-Dagskiy National-Territorial Okrug No 439, Turkmen SSR.

Ishin, Aleksandr Yakovlevich, first secretary of Shakhty CPSU Gorkom, CPSU member, Shakhty city, Rostov Oblast, RSFSR. From the CPSU.

Iskakov, Kubanychbek Duyshenbekovich, team leader on "Arashan' Sovkhoz, Ak-Suyskiy Rayon, Issyk-Kul Oblast, CPSU member, Dzhol-Kolot village, Ak-Suyskiy Rayon, Issyk-Kul Oblast. From Tyupskiy National-Territorial Okrug No 349, Kirghiz SSR.

Iskakova, Bayan Seilkhanovna, chief of department at the Kzyltu Rayon Hospital, CPSU member, Kzyltu Workers settlement, Kzyltuskiy Rayon. From Shchuchinskiy Territorial Okrug No 633, Kokchetav Oblast, Kazakh SSR.

Iskaliyev, Nazhameden, first secretary of the Uralsk Kazakh Communist Party Obkom, CPSU member, Uralsk city. From Chapayevskiy Territorial Okrug No 646, Uralsk Oblast, Kazakh SSR.

Iskandarov, Inom Nazarovich, general director of the Uzbek "Uzbekrezinotekhnika" Production Association, CPSU member, Angren city, Tashkent Oblast. From Akhangaranskiy National-Territorial Okrug No 118, Uzbek SSR.

Iskander, Fazil Abdulovich, writer, Moscow city. From Sukhumi City National-Territorial Okrug No 482, Abkhaz ASSR.

Iskhaki, Yusuf Bashirkhanovich, rector of the Tajik State Medical Institute named for Abuali ibn Sino, CPSU member, Dushanbe city. From Dushanbinskiy-Oktyabrskiy National-Territorial Okrug No 354, Tajik SSR.

Ismailov, Tofik Kyazim ogly, general director of the Azerbaijan SSR Academy of Sciences space research science and production association, CPSU member, Baku city. From Nakhichevanskiy National-Territorial Okrug No 215, Azerbaijan SSR.

Ivanov, Kliment Yegorovich, general director of the "Sever" Agro-Combine, CPSU member, Yakutsk city. From Yakutskiy Severnyy Territorial Okrug No 402, Yakutsk ASSR.

Ivanov, Nikolay Veniaminovich, investigator for important cases under the USSR general prosecutor, CPSU member, Moscow City. From Leningradskiy City National-Territorial Okrug No 19, RSFSR.

Ivanov, Valentin Borisovich, first deputy director of the Nuclear Reactors Scientific Research Institute named for V.I. Lenin, CPSU member, Dimitrovgrad city. From Dimitrovgradskiy Territorial Okrug No 330, Ulyanovsk Oblast, RSFSR.

Ivanov, Viktor Vasilyevich, fitter at the Crimea "Titan" Production Association named for the 50th anniversary of the USSR, Krasnoperekopsk city. From Yevpatoriyskiy Territorial Okrug No 482, Crimean Oblast, Ukrainian SSR.

Ivanov, Viktor Vasilyevich, procurement worker at the Luzhskiy Rayon Consumer Cooperative cooperative procurement enterprise, Luga city, Leningrad Oblast, RSFSR. From the USSR consumer cooperatives.

Ivanov, Vitaliy Pavlovich, admiral, commander of the Twice Red-Banner Baltic Fleet, CPSU member, Kaliningrad city. From Kaliningradskiy Rural Territorial Okrug No 178, Kaliningrad Oblast, RSFSR.

Ivanov, Vyacheslav Vasilyevich, chairman of the Krasnoyarsk Kray Potrebsoyuz, CPSU member, Krasnoyarsk city, RSFSR. From the USSR consumer cooperatives.

Ivanov, Vyacheslav Vsevolodovich, sector chief at the USSR Academy of Sciences Slavic and Balkan Studies Institute, Moscow City. From the USSR Academy of Sciences.

Ivans, Daynis Evaldovich, chairman of the Latvian People's Front, CPSU member, Riga city. From Madonskiy National-Territorial Okrug No 310, Latvian SSR.

Ivashko, Vladimir Antonovich, second secretary of the Ukrainian Communist Party Central Committeem CPSU member, Kiev city. From the CPSU.

Ivchenko, Ivan Mikhaylovich, link leader on the "Oktyabr" Kolkhoz, Chertkovskiy Rayon, CPSU member, Setraki village, Chertkovskiy Rayon. From Millerovskiy Territorial Okrug No 273, Rostov Oblast, RSFSR.

Izvekov, Sergey Mikhaylovich, Patriarch Pimen of Moscow and All Russia, Moscow city. From the Peace Movement united in the Soviet Committee for the Defense of Peace, jointly with the USSR UN Association.

Izmodenov, Andrey Konstantinovich, secretary of Sukhoy Log CPSU Gorkom, CPSU member, Sukhoy Log city. From Kamyshlovskiy Territorial Okrug No 299, Sverdlovsk Oblast, RSFSR.

Kabakov, Viktor Stepanovich, rector of the Leningrad Engineering-Economic Institute named for P. Togliatti, CPSU member, Leningrad city. From Frunzenskiy Territorial Okrug No 59, Leningrad city.

Kabanov, Yevgeniy Nikolayevich, captain-director of the "Kamchatrybprom" Production Association's freezer-trawler "Sokolovo," CPSU member, Petropavlovsk-Kamchatskiy city, Kamchatka Oblast, RSFSR. From the CPSU.

Kabasin, Gennadiy Sergeyevich, first secretary of the Voronezh CPSU Obkom, CPSU member, Voronezh city. From Kalacheyevskiy Territorial Okrug No 152, Voronezh Oblast, RSFSR.

Kachalovskiy, Yevgeniy Viktorovich, first deputy chairman of the Ukrainian SSR Council of Ministers, CPSU member, Kiev city. From Kharkovskiy Rural National-Territorial Okrug No 59, Ukrainian SSR.

Kadannikov, Vladimir Vasilyevich, general director of the "AvtoVAZ" Production Association, CPSU member, Tolyatti city. From Avtozavodskiy Territorial Okrug No 211, Kuybyshev Oblast, RSFSR.

Kadyrov, Gayrat Khamidullayevich, chairman of the Uzbek SSR Council of Ministers, CPSU member, Tashkent city. From Yangiyerskiy Territorial Okrug No 595, Syrdarya Oblast, Uzbek SSR.

Kafarova, Elmira Mikail kyzy, deputy chairman of the Azerbaijan SSR Council of Ministers, CPSU member, Baku city. From Shemakhinskiy National-Territorial Okrug No 224, Azerbaijan SSR.

Kaipbergenov, Tulepbergen, writer, chairman of the Karakalpak ASSR Writers Union Board, CPSU member, Nukus city. From Khodzheyliyskiy National-Territorial Okrug No 566, Karakalpak ASSR.

Kaira, Nikolay Ivanovich, chairman of the kolkhoz named for Shchors, Volodarskiy Rayon, CPSU member, Boyevoye village, Volodarskiy Rayon. From Zhovtnevoy Territorial Okrug No 438, Donetsk Oblast, Ukrainian SSR.

Kakadzhikov, Chary, team leader on the "40 let TSSR" Kolkhoz, Ashkhabadskiy Rayon, CPSU member, Bezmein city, Ashkhabadskiy Rayon. From Ashkhabadskiy Rural National-Territorial Okrug No 421, Turkmen SSR.

Kakhirov, Kurbanmagomed Zulfikarovich, teamleader at Magaramkentskiy Rayon's "Leninskiy" Sovkhoz, CPSU member, Gilyar village, Magaramkentskiy Rayon. From Suleyman-Stalskiy National-Territorial Okrug No 533, Dagestan ASSR.

Kakhn, Yuriy Kharriyevich, senior scientific staffer at the Estonian SSR Academy of Sciences Economics Institute, CPSU member, Tallinn city. From the All-Union Komsomol.

Kalandarov, Abdukhakim Ochilovich, chairman of the Kolkhoz named for Karl Marx, Pakhtachiyskiy Rayon, Samarkand Oblast, Uzbek SSR. From kolkhozes united in the Union Kolkhoz Council.

Kalandarov, Bagibek, leader of a cotton growing team on the "Pravda" Kolkhoz, Khankinskiy Rayon, CPSU member, Khankinskiy Rayon, Khorezm Oblast. From Urgenchskiy National-Territorial Okrug No 126, Uzbek SSR.

Kalachev, Leoinid Mikhaylovich, captain of an IL-62 aircraft from the Far East Civil Aviation Administration of Khabarovsk combined aviation detachment, CPSU member, Khabarovsk city, RSFSR. From the USSR Trade Unions.

Kalachik, Vladimir Mikhaylovich, general director of the "Molodechnenskiy" Agrocombine, CPSU member, Molodechno city. From Molodechnenskiy Territorial Okrug No 569, Minsk Oblast, Belorussian SSR.

Kalashnikov, Sergey Fedorovich, deputy director in charge of youth work at the Bobruyskiy Sewn Goods Factory Named for F.E. Dzerzhinskiy, CPSU member, Bobruysk city, Mogilev Oblast, Belorussian SSR. From the All-Union Komsomol.

Kalashnikov, Vladimir Ilich, first secretary of the Volgograd CPSU Obkom, CPSU member, Volgograd city. From Krasnoarmeyskiy Territorial Okrug No 138, Volgograd Oblast, RSFSR.

Kalashnikov, Vladimir Yakovlevich, director of "Erdem" Sovkhoz, Mukhorshibirskiy Rayon, CPSU member, Tugnuy settlement, Mukhorshibirskiy Rayon. From Gusino-Ozerskiy National-Territorial Okrug No 519, Buryat ASSR.

Kalimullina, Raisa Masobekhovna, milkmaid at Bakalinskiy Rayon's Karl Marx Kolkhoz, Novyy Tumutuk village, Bakalinskiy Rayon. From Dyurtyulinskiy National-Territorial Okrug No 508, Bashkir ASSR.

Kalin, Ivan Petrovich, chairman of the Moldavian SSR Council of Ministers, CPSU member, Kishinev city. From the Novoanenskiy National-Territorial Okrug No 275, Moldavian SSR.

Kalinichenko, Aleksandr Ivanovich, link leader at the "Salnenskiy" Sovkhoz, Nezhinskiy Rayon, CPSU member, Salnoye village. From Nezhinskiy Territorial Okrug No 541, Chernigov Oblast, Ukrainian SSR.

Kalinichenko, Vladimir Mikhaylovich, head of department at the Novocherkasskiy Polytechnic Institute, CPSU member, Novocherkassk city. From Novocherkasskiy Territorial Okrug No 274, Rostov Oblast, RSFSR.

Kalinin, Nikolay Vasilyevich, colonel general, commander of the Moscow Order of Lenin Military District, CPSU member, Moscow city. From the CPSU.

Kalish, Vitaliy Nikolayevich, steel worker at the "Dneprospetsstal" Electrometallurgical Plant Named for A.N. Kuzmin, CPSU member, Zaporozhye city, Ukrainian SSR. From the CPSU.

Kallas, Siym Udovich, deputy editor of the newspaper RAKHVA KHYAYAL, CPSU member, Tallinn city. From Rakvereskiy Severniy National-Territorial Okrug No 474, Estonian SSR.

Kalmykov, Aleksey Nikolayevich, leader of a construction team at the "Terbunskaya" Cooperative-State Construction Organization of the "Lipetskagropromstroy" Association, CPSU member, Terbuny settlement, Lipetsk Oblast, RSFSR. From the USSR trade unions.

Kalmykov, Yuriy Khamzatovich, chief of department at the Saratov Law Institute Named for D.I. Kurskiy, CPSU member, Saratov city. From Leninskiy Territorial Okrug No 283, Saratov Oblast, RSFSR.

Kalnynsh, Arnys Antonovich, director of the Latvian Scientific Research Institute of the Economics of the Agroindustrial Complex, CPSU member, Riga city. From Kekavskiy National-Territorial Okrug No 315, Latvian SSR.

Kalyagin, Sergey Borisovich, engineer and machine-setter at the Permskiy "Motostroitel" Production Association Named for Ya.M. Sverdlov, CPSU member, Perm city. From Sverdlovskiy Territorial Okrug No 258, Perm Oblast, RSFSR.

Kamenshchikova, Galina Nikolayevna, chief physician at the children's association of the Zelenodolskiy Tsentralniy Rayon Hospital, CPSU member, Zelenodolsk city. From Zelenodolskiy National-Territorial Okrug No 640, Tatar ASSR.

Kanarovskaya, Anna Matveyevna, deputy director and chief economist at the Sovkhoz-Plant Named for Dzerzhinskiy, Dubossarskiy Rayon, CPSU member, Dubossary city. From Dubossarskiy National-Territorial Okrug No 266, Moldavian SSR.

Kangliyev, Andrey Yakhyayevich, truck driver at the "Erken-Shakharskiy" Fruit Sovkhoz, Adyge-Khablskiy Rayon, CPSU member, Erken-Shakhar settlement, Adyge-Khablskiy Rayon. From Adyge-Khablskiy National-Territorial Okrug No 722, Karachayevo-Cherkess Autonomous Oblast.

Kandaurov, Sergey Nikolayevich, welder at the Kurskiy "Elektroagregat" Science and Production Association, CPSU member, Kursk city. From Kurskiy National-Territorial Okrug No 18, RSFSR.

Kanibalotskiy, Viktor Ivanovich, general director of the "Ulan-Udenskiy" Meat Combine, CPSU member, Ulan-Ude city. From Zagorskiy National-Territorial Okrug No 515, Buryat ASSR.

Kalin, Vasiliy Ivanovich, leader of a team of drivers at the Voronezhskiy Auto Combine, CPSU member, Voronezh city, RSFSR. From the USSR trade unions.

Kanoatov, Muminsho, writer, first secretary of the Tajik SSR Writers' Union Board, CPSU member, Dushanbe city. From Garmskiy Territorial Okrug No 724, Tajik SSR.

Kanchaveli, Shorena Shalvovna, seamstress at Combine No 1 of the Kutaisskiy Local Industry Interrayon Production Association, Kutaisi city. From Kutaisskiy Territorial Okrug No 665, Georgian SSR.

Kanchukoyeva, Rimma Khamidovna, teacher at Nartkalinskiy Secondary School No 1, CPSU member, Nartkala city, Urvanskiy Rayon. From Urvanskiy National-Territorial Okrug No 544, Kabardino-Balkar ASSR.

Kapitsa, Mikhail Stepanovich, director of the USSR Academy of Sciences Oriental Studies Institute and chairman of the Soviet Committee for Solidarity with Asian and African Countries, CPSU member, Moscow City. From the Soviet Peace Fund in conjuction with eight Soviet committees working for peace, solidarity, and international cooperation.

Kapto, Aleksandr Semenovich, chief of a CPSU Central Committee department, CPSU member, Moscow city. From the All-Union Znaniye Society.

Kapustin, Anatoliy Vladimirovich, chairman of the Sakhalinskiy Territorial Committee of the Coal Industry Workers Union, CPSU member, Yuzhno-Sakhalinsk city, Sakhalin Oblast, RSFSR. From the USSR trade unions.

Karaganov, Sergey Vasilyevich, director of Secondary Vocational and Technical College No 6, CPSU member, Okha city, Sakhalin Oblast, RSFSR. From the All-Union Komsomol.

Kara-Sal, Damdyn Bazyyyevich, director of the "Tuvinskiy" Sovkhoz, Dzun-Khemchikskiy Rayon, CPSU member, Teve-Khaya village, Dzun-Khemchikskiy Rayon. From Dzun-Khemchikskiy National-Territorial Okrug No 650, Tuva ASSR.

Karasev, Valentin Ivanovich, faculty chief at the Kramatorsk Industrial Institute, CPSU member, Kramatorsk City. From Kramatorskiy Territorial Okrug No 441, Donestk Oblast, Ukrainian SSR.

Karaulov, Aleksandr Olegovich, physician at the "Predgorye Kavkaza" Sanatorium, Goryachiy Klyuch city. From Tuapsinskiy Territorial Okrug No 86, Krasnodar Kray, RSFSR.

Karepin, Vladimir Yevgenyevich, fitter at the East Siberian Railroad Ulan-Ude Locomotive Depot Named for Kalinin, Ulan-Ude city. From Ulan-Ude city Territorial Okrug No 359, Buryat ASSR.

Karimberdiyeva, Nasiba Salimovna, worker at the Cotton-Growing Sovkhoz Named for A.S. Pushkin, Bayautskiy Rayon, Syr-Darya Oblast, Uzbek SSR, CPSU member. From the All-Union Komsomol.

Karimov, Dzhamshed Khilolovich, first secretary of Dushanbe Tajik Communist Party City Committee [gorkom], CPSU member, Dushanbe City. From Dushanbinskiy-Tsentralnyy National-Territorial Okrug No 356, Tajik SSR.

Karimov, Islam Abduganiyevich, first secretary of the Kashka-Darya Uzbek Communist Party Obkom, CPSU member, Karshi city. From Shakhrisabzskiy Territorial Okrug No 582, Kashka-Darya Oblast, Uzbek SSR.

Karimov, Khurshed Khilolovich, director of the Tajik SSR Academy of Sciences Institute of Plant Physiology and Biophysics, CPSU member, Dushanbe city. From the All-Union Znaniye Society.

Kariyeva, Bernara Rakhimovna, soloist at the Uzbek SSR Bolshoy State Academy Theater of Opera and Ballet, chairman of the Board of the Uzbek Theater Workers Union, CPSU member, Tashkent city. From the USSR Theater Workers' Union.

Karyakin, Yuriy Fedorovich, senior scientific staffer at the USSR Academy of Sciences Institute of the International Workers' Movement, CPSU member, Moscow City. From the USSR Academy of Sciences.

Karlov, Nikolay Vasilyevich, corresponding member of the USSR Academy of Sciences and rector of the Moscow Physical Technical Institute, CPSU member, Moscow city. From the USSR Academy of Sciences.

Karmanovskiy, Viktor Yevgenyevich, chief of the "Komitermneft" Oil and Gas Extracting Administration, CPSU member, Usinsk city. From Intinskiy National-Territorial Okrug No 584, Komi ASSR.

Karpenko, Valentin Filippovich, leader of a team of fitters at the Nalchik Remote-Control Equipment Plant, CPSU member, Nalchik city. From the Promyshlenniy National-Territorial Okrug No 538, Kabardino-Balkar ASSR.

Karpenko, Mariya Yosifovna, chief editor of the republic magazine RABOTNITSA I SELYANKA, CPSU member, Minsk city. From the peace movement united in the Soviet Committee for the Defense of Peace together with the USSR UN Association.

Karpenko, Nikolay Ivanovich, deputy chief physician of the Minsk Oblast Teaching Hospital, CPSU member, Lesnoy settlement, Minskiy Rayon. From Minskiy Rural Territorial Okrug No 567, Minsk Oblast, Belorussian SSR.

Karpenko, Svetlana Yuryevna, teacher, organizer of extracurricular work at Konotopskiy Rayon's Shevchenkovskaya Secondary School, CPSU candidate member, Konotop city, Sumy Oblast, Ukrainian SSR. From the All-Union Komsomol.

Karpov, Anatoliy Yevgenyevich, senior scientific staffer at Moscow's M.V. Lomonosov State University, editor in chief of the journal 64. SHAKHMATNOYE OBOZRENIYE, chairman of the Soviet Peace Foundation Board, CPSU member, Moscow city. From the Soviet Peace Foundation and eight Soviet committees in favor of peace, solidarity, and international cooperation.

Karpov, Vladimir Vasilyevich, writer, first secretary of the USSR Writers Union Board, CPSU member, Moscow city. From the CPSU.

Karpochev, Vladimir Andreyevich, chairman of Volzhskiy Rayon's "Put Lenina" Kolkhoz, CPSU member, Polevaya village, Volzhskiy Rayon. From Zvenigovskiy National-Territorial Okrug No 597, Mari ASSR.

Kartashov, Lev Petrovich, head of a department at Orenburg Agricultural Institute, CPSU member, Orenburg city. From Kuybyshevskiy National-Territorial Okrug No 17, RSFSR.

Karyagin, Vladimir Yakovlevich, director of Kolkhozabadskiy Rayon's No 1 Secondary School, CPSU member, Kolkhozabad settlement, Khatlon Oblast. From Kolkhozabadskiy National-Territorial Okrug No 367, Tajik SSR.

Kashnikov, Nikolay Ilich, senior departmental lecturer at the Ufa Sergo Ordzhonikidze Aviation Institute's Kumertau Evening Studies Faculty, CPSU member, Kumertau City. From Kumertauskiy Territorial Okrug No 356, Bashkir ASSR.

Kasymova, Dilbar Mirzayevna, weaver at Tashkent Textile Combine No 1 Weaving and Textile Plant, CPSU member, Tashkent city. From Tashkentskiy-Frunzenskiy National-Territorial Okrug No 116, Uzbek SSR.

Kashauskas, Stasis Feliksovich, writer, CPSU member, Vilnius city. From Telshyayskiy National-Territorial Okrug No 250, Lithuanian SSR.

Kashperko, Vladimir Konstantinovich, machine operator at Khoynikskiy Rayon's "Strelichevo" Sovkhoz, CPSU member, Strelichevo village, Khoynikskiy Rayon. From Rechitskiy Territorial Okrug No 559, Gomel Oblast, Belorussian SSR.

Kasyan, Vladimir Vasilyevich, section chief at Anapskiy Rayon's "Pervomayskiy" Sovkhoz, CPSU member, Chernyy village, Anapskiy Rayon. From Novorossiyskiy Territorial Okrug No 81, Krasnodar Kray, RSFSR.

Kasyan, Nikolay Andreyevich, chief of a department at Leshchinovskiy Boarding School, Kobelyaki, Poltava Oblast, Ukrainian SSR. From the Soviet Charity and Health Foundation.

Kasyanov, Anatoliy Vasilyevich, chairman of Voroshilovgrad Oblispolkom, CPSU member, Voroshilovgrad city. From Stakhanovskiy Territorial Okrug No 420, Voroshilovgrad Oblast, Ukrainian SSR.

Kasyanov, Anatoliy Fedorovich, chairman of Novoazovskiy Rayon's Karl Marx Kolkhoz, CPSU member, Mariupol city, Donetsk Oblast, Ukrainian SSR. From the kolkhozes united in the Union Kolkhoz Council.

Katayev, Abduzhabor, workshop chief at Isfarinskiy Hydrometallurgical Plant, CPSU member, Navgilem Kishlak Soviet, Isfarinskiy Rayon. From Isfarinskiy National-Territorial Okrug No 364, Tajik SSR.

Katilevskiy, Sergey Mikhaylovich, blacksmith at "Voroshilovgradteplovoz" Production Association, CPSU member, Voroshilovgrad city. From Voroshilovgradskiy National-Territorial Okrug No 37, Ukrainian SSR.

Katolikov, Aleksandr Aleksandrovich, director of Syktyvkar No 1 Residential School for Orphans, CPSU member, Syktyvkar city, Komi ASSR. From the V.I. Lenin Soviet Children's Foundation.

Katorgin, Boris Ivanovich, deputy chief designer at a power-engineering machine building design bureau, CPSU member, Khimki city. From Khimkinskiy Territorial Okrug No 44, Moscow Oblast, RSFSR.

Katrinich, Vasiliy Antonovich, team leader at Sholdaneshtskiy Rayon's kolkhoz named for the 50th anniversary of October, CPSU member, Kushmirka village, Sholdaneshtskiy Rayon. From Rybnitskiy Territorial Okrug No 702, Moldavian SSR.

Kauls, Albert Ernestovich, chairman of Rizhskiy Rayon's "Adazhi" agrofirm, CPSU member, Rizhskiy Rayon poste restante Adazhi. From Siguldskiy National-Territorial Okrug No 314, Latvian SSR.

Kavun, Vasiliy Mikhaylovich, first secretary of the Zhitomir Ukrainian Communist Party Obkom, CPSU member, Zhitomir city. From Berdichevskiy Territorial Okrug No 447, Zhitomir Oblast, Ukrainian SSR.

Kayumova, Tozhinor Isakhanovna, teacher at Ishtykhanskiy Rayon's No 33 School, Frunze Kolkhoz, Ishtykhanskiy Rayon. From Bulungurskiy Territorial Okrug No 586, Samarkand Oblast, Uzbek SSR.

Kazachenko, Petr Petrovich, chairman of "Voskhod" Kolkhoz, Uzlovskiy Rayon, CPSU member, Donskoy city. From Bogoroditskiy Territorial Okrug No 317, Tula Oblast, RSFSR.

Kazakov, Vasiliy Ivanovich, deputy chairman of the RSFSR Council of Ministers, CPSU member, Moscow city. From Stavropolskiy National-Territorial Okrug No 28, RSFSR.

Kazakova, Tursun Dzhumoboyevna, teacher at the No 22 secondary school named for G. Gulyam, Gazalkent city, Bostanlykskiy Rayon. From Chirchikskiy Territorial Okrug No 603, Tashkent Oblast, Uzbek SSR.

Kazamarov, Aleksandr Aleksandrovich, chief project designer, deputy general director of the "Geofizika" Science and Production Association, CPSU member, Moscow city. From Kuybyshevskiy Territorial Okrug No 12, Moscow city.

Kazannik Aleksey Ivanovich, faculty lecturer at Omsk State University, Omsk city. From Omskiy National-Territorial Okrug No 22, RSFSR.

Kazarezov, Vladimir Vasilyevich, first secretary of the Novosibirsk CPSU Obkom, CPSU member, Novosibirsk city. From Tatarskiy Territorial Okrug No 236, Novosibirsk Oblast, RSFSR.

Kazarin, Aleksey Aleksandrovich, carpenter and concrete worker at the "Sharyadrev" Timber Processing Production Association, CPSU member, Sharya city, Kostroma Oblast, RSFSR. From the All-Union Komsomol.

Kazmin, Gennadiy Petrovich, first secretary of the Khakass CPSU Obkom, CPSU member, Abakan city. From Abakanskiy National-Territorial Okrug No 731, Khakass Autonomous Oblast.

Kaznin, Yuriy Fedorovich, lecturer at the Kemerovo State Medical Institute, Kemerovo city. From Topkinskiy Territorial Okrug No 192, Kemerovo Oblast, RSFSR.

Kebich, Vyacheslav Frantsevich, deputy chairman of the Belorussian SSR Council of Ministers, chairman of the Belorussian SSR Gosplan, CPSU member, Minsk city. From Mogilevskiy Rural National-Territorial Okrug No 94, Belorussian SSR.

Kemova, Tamara Nikolayevna, assembly worker at the Cherkessk Industrial Rubber Goods Plant, CPSU member, Cherkessk City. From Cherkesskiy National-Territorial Okrug No 721, Karachayevo-Cherkess Autonomous Oblast.

Kenesbayeva, Kaziza Kuzhanovna, machine operator at Krasnoarmeyskiy Rayon Specialized Association, "Tednik" Sovkhoz, Krasnoarmeyskiy Rayon, Kokchetav Oblast, Kazakh SSR. From the women's councils united in the Soviet Women's Committee.

Kerimbekov, Teldibek Abdiyevich, driver at Talas Passenger Motor Transport Enterprise, CPSU member, Talas city. From Talasskiy Territorial Okrug No 722, Kirghiz SSR.

Kerimov, Dzhangir Ali Abbas ogly, head of a department at the CPSU Central Committee Academy of Social Sciences, CPSU member, Moscow city. From Shakhbuzskiy National-Territorial Okrug No 623, Nakhichevan ASSR.

Kezbers, Ivar Yanovich, secretary of the Latvian Communist Party Central Committee, CPSU member, Riga City. From Kuldigskiy Territorial Okrug No 711, Latvian SSR.

Khabibullin, Ravmer Khasanovich, first secretary of the Bashkir CPSU Obkom, CPSU member, Ufa city. From Tuymazinskiy Territorial Okrug No 358, Bashkir ASSR.

Khachatryan, Vilesha Khachaturovich, driver at the Zangezurskiy copper-molybdenum combine. CPSU member, Kadzharan city. From Masisskiy Territorial Okrug No 735, Armenian SSR.

Khachirov, Ismail Azretovich, chairman of the "Rodina" kolkhoz, Prikubanskiy Rayon. CPSU member, Chapayevskoye village, Prikubanskiy Rayon. From Karachayevo-Cherkesskiy Territorial Okrug No 106, Stavropol Kray, RSFSR.

Khadipash, Yusuf Ramazanovich, truck driver on "Adygeyskiy" Sovkhoz, Oktyabrskiy Rayon. Enem settlement, Oktyabrskiy Rayon. From Teuchezhskiy National-Territorial Okrug No 704, Adyge Autonomous Oblast.

Khadyrke, Ion Dimitriyevich, secretary of the Moldavian SSR Writers Union party organization bureau. CPSU member, Kishinev city. From Kalarashskiy National-Territorial Okrug No 269, Moldavian SSR.

Khadzhiyev, Salambek Naibovich, general director of the "Grozneftekhim" science and production association. CPSU member, Groznyy city. From Groznenskiy Territorial Okrug No 396, Chechen-Ingush ASSR.

Khaknazarov, Salmonzhon, team leader on the "Ganiabad" Sovkhoz, Uzbekistanskiy Rayon, Okmachit Village, Uzbekistanskiy Rayon, Fergana Oblast. From Kokandskiy National-Territorial Okrug No 122, Uzbek SSR.

Khalilov, Salikh Khalilovich, senior lecturer at the Dagestan Agricultural Institute. CPSU member, Makhachkala city, Dagestan ASSR. From the All-Union Organization of War and Labor Veterans.

Khalilova, Solma Musa kyzy, fitter-electrical assembly worker at the "Bakelektroavtomat" plant. CPSU member, Baku city. From women's councils united in the Soviet Women's Committee.

Khalimov, Izatullo, first secretary of the Khatlon Tajik Communist Party Obkom. CPSU member, Kurgan-Tyube city. From Kolkhozabadskiy Territorial Okrug No 727, Tajik SSR.

Khallik, Klara Semenovna, leading scientific staffer at the Estonian SSR Academy of Sciences Institute of Philosophy, Sociology, and Law. CPSU member, Tallinn City. From Tallinnskiy-Mustamyaeskiy National-Territorial Okrug No 454, Estonian SSR.

Khandzhyan, Grigor Sepukhovich, painter, Yerevan city. From Yerevanskiy 26 Komissarov National Territorial Okrug No 389, Armenian SSR.

Khanzadyan, Sero Nikolayevich, writer, CPSU member, Yerevan City. From Echmiadzinskiy National-Territorial Okrug No 416, Armenian SSR.

Kharchenko, Grigoriy Petrovich, first secretary of the Zaporozhye Ukrainian Communist Party Obkom, CPSU member, Zaporozhye city. From Melitopolskiy Territorial Okrug No 459, Zaporozhye Oblast, Ukrainian SSR.

Kharchenko, Konstantin Aleksandrovich, major, deputy subunit commander for political affairs, Moscow Military District. CPSU member, Kalinin city. From Kalinin city Territorial Okrug No 180, Kalinin Oblast, RSFSR.

Kharchuk, Boris Ignatyevich, major general, chairman of the Ukrainian SSR DOSAAF Central Committee, CPSU member, Kiev city. From the USSR DOSAAF.

Kharif, Semen Lvovich, general director of the "Gornozavodskisement" Production Association, CPSU member, Gornozavodsk City, Perm Oblast. From Chusovskiy Territorial Okrug No 263, Perm Oblast.

Kharitonov, Viktor Fedorovich, director of the Murom Dzerzhinskiy Plant, CPSU member, Murom City, Vladimir Oblast. From Muromskiy Territorial Okrug No 137, Vladimir Oblast, RSFSR.

Khashimov, Abdullodzhon, director of the Leninabad woolen headscarf experimental factory, CPSU member, Leninabad city. From Leninabadskiy National-Territorial Okrug No 372, Tajik SSR.

Khaug Arvo Voldemarovich, chief physician of the Tallinn republican psychoneurology hospital, CPSU member, Tallinn city. From Tallinnskiy-Yysmyazskiy National Territorial Okrug No 457, Estonian SSR.

Khayeyev, Izatullo, chairman of the Tajik SSR Council of Ministers, CPSU member, Dushanbe city. From Voseyskiy National-Territorial Okrug No 359, Tajik SSR.

Khitron, Pavel Sbramovich, director of "Amurskiy" sovkhoz, Oktyabrskiy Rayon, CPSU member, Amurzet village, Oktyabrskiy Rayon. From Leninskiy National-Territorial Okrug No 717, Jewish Autonomous Oblast.

Khitrun, Leonid Ivanovich, first secretary of the Ryazan CPSU Obkom, CPSU member, Ryazan city. From Ryazhskiy Territorial Okrug No 281, Ryazan Oblast, RSFSR.

Khlebtsov, Konstantin Aleksandrovich, milking machine operator at the "Nosovichi" breeding center, Dobrushskiy Rayon, CPSU member, Nosovichi village, Dobrushskiy Rayon. From Novobelitskiy National-Territorial Okrug No 85, Belorussian SSR.

Khloponina, Irina Valentinovna, experimental shop tailor at the Artemovsk sewn-goods factory named for 8 March, Artemovsk city. From Artemovskiy Territorial Okrug No 434, Donetsk Oblast, Ukrainian SSR.

Khmel, Valentina Petrovna, leader of an integrated team of finishers at the Angarsk Construction Administration No 5 construction and installation administration,

CPSU member, Angarsk city, Irkutsk Oblast, RSFSR. From the CPSU.

Khmura, Valeriy Vasilyevich, chairman of the Olginskiy Rural Soviet Ispolkom, CPSU member, Olginskaya village, Primorsko-Akhtarskiy Rayon. From Timashevskiy Territorial Okrug No 84, Krasnodar Kray, RSFSR.

Khodzhakov, Ovlyakuli, first secretary of the Tashauz Turkmen Communist Party Obkom, CPSU member, Tashauz city. From Ilyalinskiy National-Territorial Okrug No 427, Turkmen SSR.

Khodzhamuradov, Annamurad, chairman of the Turkmen SSR Council of Ministers, CPSU member, Ashkhabad city. From Krasnovodskiy National-Territorial Okrug No 435, Turkmen SSR.

Khodyrev, Gennadiy Maksimovich, first secretary of the Gorkiy CPSU Obkom, CPSU member, Gorkiy city. From Pavlovskiy Territorial Okrug No 163, Gorkiy Oblast, RSFSR.

Khokhlov, Aleksandr Fedorovich, rector of Gorkiy State University named for N.I. Lobachevskiy, CPSU member, Gorkiy city. From Nizhegorodskoy Territorial Okrug No 158, Gorkiy Oblast, RSFSR.

Kholamkhanova, Nazifa Khakimovna, cutter at the "Nalchikgorshveytrikotazhbyt" Association's "Dom Mody" studio, CPSU member, Nalchik city. From Leninskiy Territorial Okrug No 366, Kabardino-Balkar ASSR.

Kholboyeva, Zukhro Akramovna, salesperson at the Ura-Tyubinskiy Rayon Potrebsoyuz "Guli-Surkh" Department Store, Ura-Tyube city, Leninabad Oblast, Tajik SSR. From the USSR Consumer Cooperatives.

Khomenyuk, Aleksey Pavlovich, leader of an intensive labor collective on the "50 let KPSS" Sovkhoz, Uyarskiy Rayon, CPSU member, Novonikolayevka village, Uyarskiy Rayon. From Zaozernovskiy Territorial Okrug No 91, Krasnoyarsk Kray, RSFSR.

Khomyakov, Aleksandr Aleksandrovich, first secretary of the Saratov CPSU Obkom, CPSU member, Saratov city. From Yershovskiy Territorial Okrug No 288, Saratov Oblast, RSFSR.

Khomyakov, Aleksandr Ivanovich, chairman of the "Rodina" Kolkhoz, Kochevskiy Rayon, CPSU member, B. Kocha village, Kochevskiy Rayon. From Komi-Permyatskiy National-Territorial Okrug No 742, Komi-Permyak Autonomous Okrug.

Khorolskaya, Nina Ivanovna, milking machine operator at Mashevskiy Rayon's "Ukraina" Kolkhoz, CPSU member, Mashevka Urban Settlement, Poltava Oblast. From Novosanzharskiy Territorial Okrug No 508, Poltava Oblast, Ukrainian SSR.

Khrennikov, Tikhon Nikolayevich, composer, first secretary of the USSR Composers' Union Board, CPSU member, Moscow city. From the USSR Composers' Union.

Khripunov, Nikolay Fedorovich, general director of the Voskresensk "Minudobreniya" production association, CPSU member, Voskresensk city. From Yegoryevskiy Territorial Okrug No 30, Moscow Oblast, RSFSR.

Khubayev, Vasiliy Aleksandrovich, machine operator at the seed cultivation sovkhoz named for Kost Khetagurov, Tskhinvalskiy Rayon, CPSU member, Khetagurovo village, Tskhinvalskiy Rayon. From Tskhinvalskiy Rural National-Territorial Okrug No 737, South Osetian Autonomous Oblast.

Khubiyev, Khadzhibek Nanakovich, chairman of Moskovskiy Rayon's "Rossiya" Kolkhoz, CPSU member, Sretenka village, Moskovskiy Rayon, Kirghiz SSR. From Kalininskiy Territorial Okrug No 717, Kirghiz SSR.

Khudaybergenova, Rimadzhon Matnazarovna, first secretay of Khorezmskiy Uzbek Communist Party Obkom, CPSU member, Urgench city. From Khivinskiy National-Territorial Okrug No 127, Uzbek SSR.

Khudayerov, Parda, director of the "Iskra" Sovkhoz, Gagarinskiy Rayon, Surkhan-Darya Oblast, Uzbek SSR. From Termezskiy National-Territorial Okrug No 112, Uzbek SSR.

Khudonazarov, Davlatnazar, first secretary of the Tajik SSR Cinematographers' Union Board, CPSU member, Dushanbe city. From Khorogskiy National-Territorial Okrug No 711, Gorno-Badakhshan Autonomous Oblast.

Khudyakova, Retoriya Mikhaylovna, department manager at the "Rekonstruktor" sovkhoz, CPSU member, Muskatnyy settlement, Aksayskiy Rayon, Rostov Oblast, RSFSR. From the women's councils united in the Soviet Women's Committee.

Khugayeva, Diana Varlamovna, leader of a lease collective at the Kirovskiy Sovkhoz Chasavalskiy stock unit, Dzhavskiy Rayon, Chasavaya village, Dzhavskiy Rayon. From Dzhavskiy National-Territorial Okrug No 738, South Osetian Autonomous Oblast.

Khurtsiya, Marina Vakhtangovna, store assistant at the Tskhaltubskiy Rayon Potrebsoyuz, CPSU member, Gvishtibi village, Tskhaltubskiy Rayon, Georgian SSR. From the USSR Consumer Societies.

Khusanbayev, Mutallim Abdumuminovich, caster and molder at the Nauskiy "Leninabadselmash" plant, Kushtegirman Kishlak, Nauskiy Rayon. From Nauskiy National-Territorial Okrug No 376, Tajik SSR.

Khusanov, Abduzhabbar Ulmasovich, senior secretary at the editorial office of the oblast newspaper KOMMUNA, CPSU member, Fergana City. From Ferganskiy National-Territorial Okrug No 125, Uzbek SSR.

Khuzhamuratova, Sanobar Ismailovna, teacher at the Secondary School named for Papanin, CPSU candidate member, kolkhoz named for Lenin, Amudarinskiy Rayon. From Amudarinskiy National-Territorial Okrug No 558, Karakalpak ASSR.

Khvorov, Aleksey Ivanovich, chief physician at the oblast children's clinical hospital named for V.I. Lenin, CPSU member, Chita city. From Chitinskiy city territorial Okrug No 342, Chita Oblast, RSFSR.

Kiknadze, Shalva Davidovich, senior staffer at the Georgian SSR Council of Ministers, CPSU member, Tbilisi city. From the All-Union Organization of War and Labor Veterans.

Kim Yen Un, senior scientific staffer at Omsk State University, CPSU member, Omsk city. From Sovetskiy Territorial Okrug No 238, Omsk Oblast, RSFSR.

Kimketov, Psabida Davletovich, team leader at the "Yuzhnyy" Sovkhoz Combine, Ust-Dzhegutinskiy Rayon, CPSU member, Ust-Dzheguta City, Stavropol Kray. From Ust-Dzhegutinskiy National-Territorial Okrug No 725, Karachayevo-Cherkess Autonomous Oblast.

Kirakosyan, Armenak Balasanovich, lathe operator at "Luys" Production Association's Kirovakan Lighting Engineering Plant, candidate CPSU member, Kirovakan city, Armenian SSR. From the All-Union Komsomol.

Kirgizbayev, Tukhtakhon Bazarovna, teamleader at Syrdarinskiy Rayon's "Malik" Sovkhoz, CPSU member, Syrdarinskiy Rayon, Syr-Darya Oblast, Uzbek SSR. From the CPSU.

Kirilenko, Nikolay Aleksandrovich, workshop chief at "Kondopogabumprom" Production Association, CPSU member, Kondopoga city. From Kondopozhskiy National-Territorial Okrug No 574, Karelian ASSR.

Kirilov, Vladimir Ivanovich, senior scientific staffer at Voronezh Polytechnical Institute, Voronezh city. From Leninskiy Territorial Okrug No 149, Voronezh Oblast, RSFSR.

Kiriyak, Nellya Pavlovna, secretary of the Moldavian SSR Supreme Soviet Presidium, CPSU member, Kishinev city. From the women's councils united in the Soviet Women's Committee.

Kiselev, Aleksandr Aleksandrovich, second secretary of Volgograd Komsomol Obkom, CPSU member, Volzhskiy city, Volgograd Oblast. From Volgogradskiy National-Territorial Okrug No 4, RSFSR.

Kiselev, Gennadiy Nikolayevich, second secretary of the Kirghiz Communist Party Central Committee, CPSU member, Frunze city. From Dzhalal-Abadskiy National-Territorial Okrug No 327, Kirghiz SSR.

Kiseleva, Valentina Adamovna, employee at Grodno "Khimvolokno" Production Association named for the 60th anniversary of the USSR, Grodno city. From Grodnenskiy National-Territorial Okrug No 89, Belorussian SSR.

Kisin, Viktor Ivanovich, chief of Moscow's I.A. Likhachev, Automobile Plant New Technology Administration, CPSU member, Moscow city. From the All-Union "Znaniye" Society.

Kislitsyn, Vyacheslav Aleksandrovich, chairman of Medvedevskiy Rayon's "Pobeditel" Kolkhoz, CPSU member, Medvedevo settlement, Medvedevskiy Rayon. From Medvedevskiy National-Territorial Okrug No 598, Mari ASSR.

Kistanov, Aleksey Timofeyevich, workshop chief at Taranovskiy Rayon's Taranovskiy Poultry Sovkhoz, CPSU member, Mayskoye village, Taranovskiy Rayon, Kustanay Oblast, Kazakh SSR. From the USSR Consumer Cooperatives.

Kiyamov, Nurgaziz Vagizovich, chairman of Alekseyevskiy Rayon's Vakhitov Kolkhoz, CPSU member, Stepnaya Shentala village, Alekseyevskiy Rayon. From Alekseyevskiy Territorial Okrug No 385, Tatar ASSR.

Kiysk, Kalye Karlovich, director and producer at "Tallinnfilm" Movie Studio, CPSU member, Tallinn city. From the USSR Union of Cinema Workers.

Klepikov, Aleksandr Fedorovich, first secretary of Syr-Darya Uzbek Communist Party Obkom, CPSU member, Dzhizak city, Syr-Darya Oblast. From Dzhizakskiy National-Territorial Okrug No 113, Uzbek SSR.

Klepikov, Mikhail Ivanovich, leader of a multi-purpose team at Ust-Labinskiy Rayon's "Kuban" Kolkhoz, CPSU member, Ust-Labinsk city, Krasnodar Kray, RSFSR. From the CPSU.

Klepikov, Yuriy Nikolayevich, movie scriptwriter, Leningrad city. From the USSR Union of Cinema Workers.

Kletskov, Leonid Gerasimovich, first secretary of Grodno Belorussian Communist Party Obkom, CPSU member, Grodno city. From Oshmyanskiy National-Territorial Okrug No 92, Belorussian SSR.

Klibik, Valentina Sergeyevna, secretary of the Latvian SSR Supreme Soviet Presidium, CPSU member, Riga city. From the women's councils united in the Soviet Women's Committee.

Klikunene, Vanda Styaponovna, deputy chairman of the Lithuanian SSR Supreme Soviet Presidium, CPSU member, Vilnius city. From the women's councils united in the Soviet Women's Committee.

Klimentova, Lidiya Alekseyevna, chairman of the Kuybyshev UMedical Workers Trade Union Obkom, CPSU member, Kuybyshev city, RSFSR. From the USSR trade unions.

Klimov, Mikhail Valeryevich, assistant chief physician at Vyshnevolotskiy Central Rayon Hospital, Vyshniy Volochek city. From Vyshnevolotskiy Territorial Okrug No 183, Kalinin Oblast, RSFSR.

Klimova, Galina Nikolayevna, leader of a team of plasterers at No 3 "Engelskhimstroy" Trust No 38 Construction and Installation Administration, CPSU member, Engels city. From Engelsskiy Territorial Okrug No 289, Saratov Oblast, RSFSR.

Klimuk, Petr Ilich, major general of aviation, chief of the Yu.A. Gagarin Cosmonaut Training Center Political Department, CPSU member, Zvezdnyy Gorodok, Shchelkovskiy Rayon, Moscow Oblast, RSFSR. From the USSR DOSAAF.

Klishchuk, Petr Martynovich, teamleader at Chistopolskiy Rayon's "Salkynkolskiy" Sovkhoz, CPSU member, Salkynkol village, Chistopolskiy Rayon, Kokchetav Oblast. From Kokchetavskiy National-Territorial Okrug No 145, Kazakh SSR.

Klochkov, Ivan Frolovich, chief of Leningrad State History Museum military-patriotic work sector, CPSU member, Leningrad city. From the All-Union Organization of War and Labor Veterans.

Klokov, Vsevolod Ivanovich, chief scientific staffer at the Ukrainian SSR Academy of Sciences History Institute, CPSU member, Kiev city. From the All-Union Organization of War and Labor Veterans.

Klumbis, Egidiyus Lyaonovich, chief of Kaunas Medical Institute Central Research Laboratory Neurosurgery Laboratory, Kaunas city. From Kaunas city Territorial Okrug No 688, Lithuanian SSR.

Klushin, Oleg Gennadyevich, general director of the V.I. Lenin "Krengolmskaya Manufaktura" Cotton Fabric Combine, CPSU member, Narva city. From Krengolmskiy National-Territorial Okrug No 468, Estonian SSR.

Klyukin, Viktor Valentinovich, deputy chief controller at the Kirov 20th Party Congress Machine Building Production Association, CPSU member, Kirov city. From Kirovskiy Territorial Okrug No 197, Kirov Oblast, RSFSR.

Knyazev, Nikolay Trifonovich, first secretary of Kustanay Kazakhstan Communist Party Obkom, CPSU member, Kustanay city. From Kustanayskiy Territorial Okrug No 634, Kustanay Oblast, Kazakh SSR.

Knyazev, Yuriy Ivanovich, chairman of the "Yantar" Production Association trade union committee, CPSU member, Orel city, RSFSR. From the USSR trade unions.

Kobaliya, Larisa Nodariyevna, machine operator at the "Sabchota Chay" Tea Sovkhoz, Galskiy Rayon, CPSU candidate member, Kvemo-Bargebi village, Galskiy Rayon. From Galskiy National-Territorial Okrug No 485, Abkhaz ASSR.

Koberidze, Vardisheli Georgiyevich, chairman of Rustavi DOSAAF Gorkom, CPSU member, Rustavi city, Georgian SSR. From the USSR DOSAAF.

Kobzon, Iosif Davydovich, artist of the Moscow Concert Association, CPSU member, Moscow city. From the USSR trade unions.

Kochetov, Konstantin Alekseyevich, army general, USSR first deputy defense minister, CPSU member, Moscow city. From Odintsovskiy Territorial Okrug No 37, Moscow Oblast, RSFSR.

Kochmuradov, Garyagdy Yagmurovich, fitter at the "40 Let Turmenskoy SSR" repair plant, CPSU member, Tashauz city. From Tashauzskiy City National-Territorial Okrug No 442, Turkmen SSR.

Kodyrov, Barakatulo Kamarovich, senior herdsman at the Khasan Sovkhoz, Leninskiy Rayon, CPSU member, Varmonik Kishlak, Leninskiy Rayon. From Leninskiy National-Territorial Okrug No 373, Tajik SSR.

Kokarev, Mikhail Andreyevich, electric welders' team leader at the "Neftemash" Plant, CPSU member, Izhevsk city. From Pervomayskiy National-Territorial Okrug No 660, Udmurt ASSR.

Kolbeshkin, Aleksey Yefimovich, tool makers' team leader at the Voronezh "Elektronika" Science and Production Association, CPSU member, Voronezh city, RSFSR. From the CPSU.

Kolbin, Gennadiy Vasilyevich, first secretary of the Kazakh Communist Party Central Committee, CPSU member, Alma-Ata city. From Prikaspiyskiy Territorial Okrug No 624, Guryev Oblast, Kazakh SSR.

Kolchukova, Nina Mikhaylovna, chairman of the board of the Oktyabrskiy village Consumer Society, Engelsskiy Rayon Potrebsoyuz, CPSU member, Karl Marx Sovkhoz, Engelsskiy Rayon, Saratov Oblast, RSFSR. From the USSR Consumer Cooperative System.

Kolesnik, Anatoliy Ivanovich, machine operator at the "Bratslavskiy" Sovkhoz, Adamovskiy Rayon, CPSU member, Bratslavka village, Adamovskiy Rayon. From Tselinnyy Territorial Okrug No 248, Orenburg Oblast, RSFSR.

Kolesnik, Nikolay Dmitriyevich, chairman of the "Krasnaya Zvezda" Kolkhoz, Dinskiy Rayon, CPSU member, Plastunovskaya Village, Dinskiy Rayon, Krasnodar Kray. From Pervomayskiy Territorial Okrug No 74, Krasnodar Kray, RSFSR.

Kolesnikov, Sergey Ivanovich, chairman of the presidium of the East Siberian Branch of the USSR Academy of Medical Sciences Siberian Department, CPSU member, Irkutsk City. From Irkutskiy National-Territorial Okrug No 10, RSFSR.

Kolesnikov, Vladimir Ivanovich, faculty chief at the Rostov Railroad Transport Engineers Institute, CPSU member, Rostov-na-Donu city. From Oktyabrskiy Territorial Okrug No 268, Rostov Oblast, RSFSR.

Kolinichenko, Aleksey Nikolayevich, lieutenant general, CPSU member, Ulan-Ude city. From Zheleznodorozhnyy National-Territorial Okrug No 514, Buryat ASSR.

Kolodeznikov, Aleksandr Semenovich, captain, assistant chief of department at the Yakutsk city Military Commissariat, Yakutsk city. From the All-Union Komsomol.

Kolomiyets, Yuriy Afanasyevich, chairman of the Ukrainian SSR Gosagroprom, CPSU member, Kiev city. From Kotovskiy Territorial Okrug No 502, Odessa Oblast, Ukrainian SSR.

Kolotov, Vasiliy Ilich, editor of VYBORGSKIY KOMMUNIST, CPSU member, Vyborg City. From Vyborgskiy Territorial Okrug No 61, RSFSR.

Kolpakova, Nyura Zakharovna, milkmaid at the "Krasnoselskiy" Sovkhoz, Krasnoselskiy Rayon, Krasnoselsk Urban settlement, Krasnoselskiy Rayon. From Vardenisskiy National-Territorial Okrug No 405, Armenian SSR.

Koltsov, Yuriy Arsenyevich, colonel, deputy commander of a troop unit, Odessa Military District, CPSU member, Crimean Oblast. From Kerchenskiy Territorial Okrug No 483, Crimean Oblast, Ukrainian SSR.

Komarov, Georgiy Alekseyevich, director of the Kirghiz Research Institute of Ecology and Prevention of Infections Diseases, CPSU member, Frunze city. From Frunzenskiy-Oktyabrskiy National-Territorial Okrug No 322, Kirghiz SSR.

Komarov, Yuriy Trofimovich, general director of the V.I. Lenin "Tuvaasbest" Combine, CPSU member, Ak-Dovurak city. From Barun-Khemchikskiy National-Territorial Okrug No 649, Tuva ASSR.

Kondratyev, Aleksey Ivanovich, Mordovian ASSR minister of health, CPSU member, Saransk city. From Torbeyevskiy National-Territorial Okrug No 612, Mordovian ASSR.

Kondratenko, Nikolay Ignatovich, chairman of Krasnodar Kray Soviet of People's Deputies Executive Committee, CPSU member, Krasnodar City. From Tikhoretskiy Territorial Okrug No 85, Krasnodar Kray, RSFSR.

Konev, Sergey Ivanovich, clinical house surgeon with the Dnepropetrovsk Medical Institute's Infectious Diseases Department, Dneprodzerzhinsk City. From Dneprodzerzhinskiy Territorial Okrug No 427, Ukrainian SSR.

Konkov, Pavel Ivanovich, pensioner, CPSU member, Krasnoyarsk city, RSFSR. From the All-Union Organization of War and Labor Veterans.

Konovalov, Vladimir Petrovich, electric locomotive engineer at Dema Station Depot of the Bashkir branch of the Kuybyshev Railroad, CPSU member, Ufa city. From Leninskiy Territorial Okrug No 349, Bashkir ASSR.

Kononenko, Leonid Alekseyevich, fitter at the Kiev Artem Production Association, CPSU member, Kiev city. From the All-Union Komsomol.

Kontselidze, Marina Rizayevna, citrus fruit grower on the Khala village Kolkhoz, Kobuletskiy Rayon, CPSU member, Gorgadzeyebi village, Kobuletskiy Rayon. From Batumskiy Territorial Okrug No 659, Georgian SSR.

Kopylova, Aleksandra Vasilyevna, chief of the Mtsensk city Soviet of People's Deputies Ispolkom Public Education Department, CPSU member, Mtsensk city. From Mtsenskiy Territorial Okrug No 250, Orel Oblast, RSFSR.

Kopysov, Nikolay Mikhaylovich, controller at the Izhevsk Radio Plant, CPSU member, Izhevsk city. From Avtozavodskiy Territorial Okrug No 392, Udmurt ASSR.

Korbutov, Ivan Ivanovich, colonel general, CPSU member, Moscow city. From Bobruyskiy National-Territorial Okrug No 95, Belorussian SSR.

Kordiyak, Yevgeniy Konstantinovich, hull workers' team leader at the ship repair plant, CPSU member, Chardzhou City. From Chardzhouskiy-Amudarinskiy National-Territorial Okrug No 447, Turkmen SSR.

Korenev, Aleksandr Anatolyevich, truck drivers' team leader at the Kurgan No 1 Motor Transport Production Association, CPSU member, Kurgan city, RSFSR. From the USSR trade unions.

Korneva, Svetlana Ivanovna, director of the Kiev "Kiyevlyanka" Knitwear Factory, CPSU member, Kiev city. From the women's councils united by the Soviet Women's Committee.

Korniyenko, Anatoliy Ivanovich, chief of the Ukrainian Communist Party Central Committee Organizational Party and Cadre Work Department, CPSU member, Kiev city. From Rovenskiy National-Territorial Okrug No 55, Ukrainian SSR.

Korneyenko, Viktor Nikolayevich, troubleshooter for machine tools with digital program control at the Gomel Radio Plant, Gomel City. From Gomelskiy City National-Territorial Okrug No 84, Belorussian SSR.

Korobkin, Vladimir Vladimirovich, chief of the normalization and standardization department at the "Izhevskiy Motozavod" Production Association, CPSU member, Izhevsk city. From Oktyabrskiy National-Territorial Okrug No 659, Udmurt ASSR.

Korobtsev, Viktor Pavlovich, pensioner, CPSU member, Tambov city, RSFSR. From the All-Union Organization of War and Labor Veterans.

Koromyslov, Georgiy Fedorovich, general director of a sector scientific complex and director of the All-Union Research Institute of Experimental Veterinary Science, CPSU member, Moscow city. From the V.I. Lenin All-Union Academy of Agricultural Sciences.

Korostelev, Aleksandr Fedorovich, automatic machine operator at the "Kurganarmkhimmash" Production Association, CPSU member, Kurgan city. From Kurganskiy Territorial Okrug No 213, Kurgan Oblast, RSFSR.

Korotich, Vitaliy Alekseyevich, chief editor of the magazine OGONEK, CPSU member, Moscow City. From Kharkovskiy City National-Territorial Okrug No 58, Ukrainian SSR.

Korotkin, Vladimir Ivanovich, machine operator at the "Chyrvony Kastrychnik" Kolkhoz, Shklovskiy Rayon, Litovsk village, Shklovskiy Rayon. From Mogilevskiy Rural Territorial Okrug No 572, Mogilev Oblast, Belorussian SSR.

Korovyatskiy, Vladimir Vasilyevich, milking machine operator at the "Krasnyy Poselok" Kolkhoz, CPSU member, Zheleznyak village, Monastyrshchinskiy Rayon, Smolensk Oblast, RSFSR. From the kolkhozes united by the Union Kolkhoz Council.

Korshunov, Aleksandr Aleksandrovich, team leader at the Tashkent V.P. Chkalov Aircraft Production Association, CPSU member, Tashkent city. From the USSR trade unions.

Korshunov, Anatoliy Ivanovich, cutter at the Popasnaya Railcar Repair Plant, CPSU member, Popasnaya city. From Lisichanskiy Territorial Okrug No 417, Voroshilovgrad Oblast, Ukrainian SSR.

Koryugin, Nikolay Nikolayevich, chief of the economic research laboratory at the Cherepovets 50th Anniversary of the USSR Metallurgical Combine, CPSU member, Cherepovets city. From Cherepovetskiy Territorial Okrug No 148, Vologda Oblast, RSFSR.

Kosarchuk, Valeriy Petrovich, chief technologist at the "Moldselmash" Production Association, CPSU member, Beltsy city. From Beltskiy National-Territorial Okrug No 262, Moldavian SSR.

Koshlakov, Georgiy Vadimovich, first deputy chairman of the Tajik SSR Council of Ministers, CPSU member, Dushanbe city. From Rushanskiy National-Territorial Okrug No 715, Gorno-Badakhshan Autonomous Oblast.

Kostenetskaya, Marina Grigoryevna, writer, Riga city. From Preylskiy National-Territorial Okrug No 312, Latvian SSR.

Kostenko, Anatoliy Ivanovich, lieutenant general, commander of the Red Banner Belorussian Military District, CPSU member, Minsk city. From Borisovskiy National-Territorial Okrug No 70, Belorussian SSR.

Kostenko, Viktor Ivanovich, instrument control man at the Shebekino Chemicals Plant of the "SintezPAV" Science and Production Association, CPSU member, Shebekino city. From Belgorodskiy city Territorial Okrug No 125, Belgorod Oblast, RSFSR.

Kostenyuk, Aleksandr Grigoryevich, chairman of Orenburg Oblast Soviet of People's Deputies Ispolkom, CPSU member, Orenburg city. From Buguruslanskiy Territorial Okrug No 245, Orenburg Oblast, RSFSR.

Kostishin, Nikolay Anatolyevich, fitter at the "Pribor" Plant, Bendery city. From Benderskiy National-Territorial Okrug No 263, Moldavian SSR.

Kotik, Vasiliy Dmitriyevich, leader of an amalgamated comprehensive logging team at the De-Kastri Logging Combine, CPSU member, De-Kastri village, Ulchskiy rayon. From Severnyy Territorial Okrug No 114, RSFSR.

Kotlovtsev, Nikolay Nikiforovich, colonel general, chairman of the USSR DOSAAF Central Committee, CPSU member, Moscow city. From the USSR DOSAAF.

Kotlyakov, Vladimir Mikhaylovich, corresponding member of the USSR Academy of Sciences, director of the USSR Academy of Sciences Geography Institute, CPSU member, Moscow city. From the scientific societies and associations attached to the USSR Academy of Sciences.

Kotov, Yuriy Stepanovich, chief of department at Kazan State University, CPSU member, Kazan City. From Sovetskiy Territorial Okrug No 383, Tatar ASSR.

Kovalev, Mikhail Vasilyevich, chairman of the Belorussian SSR Council of Ministers, CPSU member, Minsk city. From Polotskiy National-Territorial Okrug No 83, Belorussian SSR.

Kovalev, Vladimir Grigoryevich, milling machine operator at the Safonovo Plastics Plant, CPSU member, Safonovo city. From Vyazemskiy Territorial Okrug No 306, Smolensk Oblast, RSFSR.

Kovalev, Vladimir Nikolayevich, pilot instructor at the Mineralnyye Vody Combined Aviation Detachment, CPSU member, Mineralnyye Vody city. From Mineralovodskiy Territorial Okrug No 107, Stavropol Kray, RSFSR.

Kovalevskiy, Yevgeniy Mikhaylovich, chief architect of Minsk city, chairman of the Belorussian Architects' Union Board, CPSU member, Minsk city. From the USSR Architects' Union.

Kozachko, Anatoliy Vasilyevich, first secretary of Yashaltinskiy CPSU Raykom, CPSU member, Yashalta Worker settlement, Yashaltinskiy Rayon. From Yashaltinskiy National-Territorial Okrug No 556, Kalmyk ASSR.

Kozhakhmetov, Ibraimzhan, chairman of the Kirov Kolkhoz, Panfilovskiy Rayon, CPSU member, Altyuy village, Panfilovskiy Rayon, Taldy-Kurgan Oblast, Kazakh SSR. From the kolkhozes united by the Union Kolkhoz Council.

Kozhauov, Zhanbyrbay, team leader at the Dzhambul Sovkhoz, Syrdarinskiy Rayon, CPSU member, Oktyabr village, Syrdarinskiy Rayon, Kzyl-Orda Oblast, Kazakh SSR. From the USSR trade unions.

Kozhedub, Ivan Nikitovich, marshal of aviation, military inspector and adviser of the USSR Defense Ministry Group of General Inspectors, CPSU member, Moscow city. From the USSR DOSAAF.

Kozik, Aleksandr Mikhaylovich, chief of the Brest DOSAAF Combined Technical School, CPSU member, Brest city, Belorussian SSR. From the USSR DOSAAF.

Kozin, Eduard Gennadiyevich, senior lecturer of the Kharkov V.I. Lenin Polytechnical Institute's Sumy Branch, CPSU member, Sumy City. From Sumskiy Territorial Okrug No 512, Ukrainian SSR.

Kozlov, Valter Viktorovich, director of the Maritime State Regional Electric Power Station, CPSU member, Luchegorsk settlement, Pozharskiy Rayon. From Spasskiy Territorial Okrug No 101, Maritime Kray, RSFSR.

Kozyrev, Nikolay Kuzmich, teacher at the Krasnyy Luch Mining Technical School, Krasnyy Luch city. From Krasnoluchskiy Territorial Okrug No 416, Voroshilovgrad Oblast, Ukrainian SSR.

Kraft, Yuriy Andreasovich, general director of the "Estlegprom" Association, first deputy chairman of the Estonian SSR State Committee for Industry, minister of the Estonian SSR, CPSU member, Tallinn city. From Tallinskiyn Rural Territorial Okrug No 748, Estonian SSR.

Krasilnikov, Yuriy Georgiyevich, deputy chief engineer at the Kazan Motor Building Production Association, CPSU member, Kazan City. From Leninskiy Territorial Okrug No 381, Tatar ASSR.

Kravchenko, Galina Ivanovna, team leader at the "Pioner" Sovkhoz, Sudogoskiy Rayon, CPSU member, Muromtsevo settlement, Sudogodskiy Rayon. From Gus-Khrustalnyy Territorial Okrug No 134, Vladimir Oblast, RSFSR.

Kravchenko, Konstantin Fedorovich, pensioner, CPSU member, Vladivostok city, RSFSR. From the All-Union Organization of War and Labor Veterans.

Kravchenko, Leonid Petrovich, general director of TASS, CPSU member, Moscow city. From the USSR Journalists' Union.

Kravchenko, Nalina Vasilyevna, party committee secretary of the "Gryazinskiy" Sovkhoz, CPSU member, Sinyavka village, Gryazinskiy Rayon, Lipetsk Oblast, RSFSR. From the CPSU.

Kravets, Vladimir Alekseyevich, Ukrainian SSR foreign minister, CPSU member, Kiev city. From Kharkovskiy National-Territorial Okrug No 523, Kharkov Oblast, Ukrainian SSR.

Kravtsov, Nikolay Ivanovich, director of the "Karbid" Production Association, CPSU member, Temirtau city, Karaganda Oblast. From Temirtauskiy National-Territorial Okrug No 153, Kazakh SSR.

Krasnova, Lyudmila Mikhaylovna, chief doctor of the Tula Oblast hospital, CPSU member, Tula city, RSFSR. From the women's councils united in the Soviet Women's Committee.

Krayko, Aleksandr Nikolayevich, department chief of a branch of the Central Institute of Aeroengine Building named for P.I. Baranov, Moscow city. From Baumanskiy Territorial Okrug No 3, Moscow city.

Kreshtak, Valeriy Ivanovich, gas-arc welder of the "Fosfor" Production Association in Chimkent, CPSU member, Chimkent city. From the Chimkentskiy Territorial Okrug No 650, Chimkent Oblast, Kazakh SSR.

Krivenko, Viktor Mikhaylovich, chairman of the trade union committee of the Grebenka locomotive depot of the Poltava branch of the Southern Railroad, CPSU member, Grebenka city, Poltava Oblast, Ukrainian SSR. From the USSR trade unions.

Krivorotov, Vladimir Ivanovich, chairman of the "Rossiya" Kolkhoz, Krasnogvardeyskiy Rayon, CPSU member, Voskhod village, Krasnogvardeyskiy Rayon, Crimea Oblast, Ukrainian SSR. From the kolkhozes united in the Union Kolkhoz Council.

Krivoruchko, Yekaterina Vasilyevna, machine operator of the Chimkent cement plant, CPSU member, Chimkent city, Kazakh SSR. From the women's councils united in the Soviet Women's Committee.

Krivov, Gennadiy Ivanovich, general director of the "Kboper" agro-industrial combine, Balashovskiy Rayon, CPSU member, Balashov city. From Balashovskiy Territorial Okrug No 287, Saratov Oblast, RSFSR.

Krishevich, Valeriy Pavlovich, engine driver of the Korosten locomotive depot of the Southwestern Railroad, CPSU member, Korosten city. From Korostenskiy Territorial Okrug No 448, Zhitomirskiy Oblast, Ukrainian SSR.

Krotkov, Ivan Maksimovich, leader of a crop cultivation team on Vurnarskiy Rayon's "Gvardeyets" Kolkhoz, Pileshkasy village, Vurnarskiy Rayon. From the Shumerlinskiy National-Territorial Okrug No 688, Chuvash ASSR.

Kruchina, Nikolay Yefimovich, administrator of affairs of the CPSU Central Committee, CPSU member, Moscow city. From Gorno-Altayskiy Territorial Okrug No 68, Altay Kray, RSFSR.

Kruglov, Albert Timofeyevich, deputy commander of a flying detachment at the Syktyvkar aviation enterprise, CPSU member, Syktyvkar City. From Syktyvkarskiy Territorial Okrug No 371, Komi ASSR.

Krumin, Viktor Mikhaylovich, adviser of the Latvian SSR Council of Ministers, CPSU member, Riga city. From the All-Union Organization of War and Labor Veterans.

Krutov, Aleksandr Nikolayevich, commentator with Central Television in Moscow city, CPSU member, Moscow city. From Zagorskiy Territorial okrug No 31, RSFSR.

Krylova, Zoya Petrovna, chief editor of the journal RABOTNITSA, CPSU member, Moscow city. From the women's councils united in the Soviet Women's Committee.

Kryshkin, Anatoliy Makarovich, lathe operator of the "Dormekhanizatsiya" Administration of the "Blagoustroystvo" Production Construction Association, CPSU member, Alma-Ata city. From Alma-Atinskiy-Leninskiy National-Territorial Okrug No 130, Kazakh SSR.

Kryuchenkova, Nadezhda Aleksandrovna, teacher at the Inzhavinskiy Secondary School No 2, CPSU member, Inzhavino Worker settlement. From Zherdevskiy Territorial Okrug No 309, Tambov Oblast, RSFSR.

Kryuchkov, Vitaliy Ivanovich, chief of the "Volgogradavtodor" No 5 road construction administration, CPSU member, Novoanninskiy city. From the Mikhaylovskiy Territorial Okrug No 144, Volgograd Oblast, RSFSR.

Kryuchkov, Georgiy Korneyevich, first secretary of Odessa Ukrainian Communist Party Obkom, CPSU member, Odessa city. From the Razdelnyanskiy Territorial Okrug No 503, Odessa Oblast, Ukrainian SSR.

Kryzhanovskiy, Dmitriy Pavlovich, team leader at the "Veselopodolskiy" Sovkhoz, Uritskiy Rayon, CPSU member, Veselyy Podol village, Uritskiy Rayon, Kustanay Oblast. From the Kustanayskiy National-Territorial Okrug No 146, Kazakh SSR.

Kryzhkov, Boris Vasilyevich, deputy chief of production of the "Kaprolaktam" Dzerzhinskiy Production Association, CPSU member, Dzerzhinsk city. From the Dzerzhinskiy Territorial Okrug No 162, Gorkiy Oblast, RSFSR.

Kubdasheva, Kulyash, chief of a branch of the health and hygiene unit at the "Karatau" Production Association, CPSU member, Zhanatas city. From Dzhambulskiy Territorial Okrug No 625, Dzhambul Oblast, Kazakh SSR.

Kubilyus, Ionas Pyatrovich, rector of the Vilnius State University named for V. Kapsukas, CPSU member, Vilnius city. From the Radvilishkskiy National-Territorial Okrug No 247, Lithuanian SSR.

Kublashvili, Vakhtang Vladimirovich, assembly fitter at the Tbilisi Aircraft Production Association named for Dimitrov, CPSU member, Tbilisi city. From Tbilisskiy 26 Kommissarov Territorial Okrug No 656, Georgian SSR.

Kucharova, Mukaddas, milkmaid at the "Ok-Oltyn" Kolkhoz, Altynsayskiy Rayon, CPSU member, Altynsayskiy Rayon. From Denauskiy Territorial Okrug No 591, Surkhandarya Oblast, Uzbek SSR.

Kucher, Valeriy Nikolayevich, editor of the newspaper MAGNITOGORSKIY RABOCHIY, CPSU member, Magnitogorsk city, Chelyabinsk Oblast, RSFSR. From the USSR Journalists' Union.

Kucherenko, Viktor Grigoryevich, chairman of Donetsk Oblispolkom, CPSU member, Donetsk city. From Donetskiy-Kirovskiy Territorial Okrug No 433, Donetsk Oblast, Ukrainian SRR.

Kucherskiy, Nikolay Ivanovich, director of the Navoi mining and metallurgical combine named for the 50th anniversary of the USSR, CPSU member, Navoi city. From Navoiyskiy Territorial Okrug No 588, Samarkand Oblast, Uzbek SSR.

Kucheyko, Aleksandr Petrovich, multiskilled team leader at construction trust No 19 construction administration No 104, CPSU member, Lida city, Grodno Oblast. From Lidskiy National-Territorial Okrug No 91, Belorussian SSR.

Kuchinskas, Lyaonas-Antanas Antanovich, Vilnius State University department lecturer, Vilnius city. From the USSR Designers' Union.

Kudarauskas, Sigitas Yozovich, chief of the electrical engineering department of the Kaunas Polytechnical Institute's Klaypeda faculties, CPSU member, Klaypeda city. From Klaypedskiy-Baltiyskiy National-Territorial Okrug No 241, Lithuanian SSR.

Kudryavtsev, Aleksandr Petrovich, rector of the Moscow Architectural Institute, CPSU member, Moscow city. From the USSR Architects' Union.

Kudryavtsev, Vladimir Nikolayevich, vice president of the USSR Academy of Sciences, director of the USSR Academy of Sciences Institute of State and Law, CPSU member, Moscow city. From the CPSU.

Kugultinov, David Nikitich, writer, chairman of the Kalmyk ASSR Writers' Union Board, CPSU member, Elista city. From the Iki-Burulskiy National-Territorial Okrug No 550, Kalmyk ASSR.

Kukayn, Rita Aleksandrovna, director of the Latvian SSR Academy of Sciences A. Kirkhenshteyn Institute of Microbiology, CPSU member, Riga city. From Yurmalskiy National-Territorial Okrug No 320, Latvian SSR.

Kukhar, Ivan Ivanovich, chairman of the Vladimir Ilich kolkhoz, Leninskiy Rayon, Moscow Oblast, CPSU member, Moscow city. From kolkhozes united in the Union Kolkhoz Council.

Kukushkin, Nikolay Timofeyevich, director of the "Severnyy Klyuch" sovkhoz, Pokhvistnevskiy Rayon, CPSU member, Savrukha village, Pokhvistnevskiy Rayon. From Sergiyevskiy Territorial Okrug No 209, Kuybyshev Oblast, RSFSR.

Kulagin, Vladimir Konstantinovich, general director of the "Teplokontrol" production association, CPSU member, Kazan city. From Privolzhskiy National-Territorial Okrug No 637, Tatar ASSR.

Kulakova, Rauza Gafurovna, chairman of the Ulyanovsk communications workers trade union obkom, CPSU member, Ulyanovsk city, RSFSR. From the USSR trade unions.

Kuldyshev, Mamidali Sagimbekovich, "Tash-Kumyrstroy" trust mobile mechanized column No 370 Komsomol-youth team leader, Tash-Kumyr city. From Tash-Kumyrskiy National-Territorial Okrug No 346, Kirghiz SSR.

Kuleshov, Aleksey Antonovich, chairman of Altay Krayispolkom, CPSU member, Barnaul city. From Shebalinskiy National-Territorial Okrug No 710, Gorno-Altay Autonomous Oblast.

Kulibayev, Askar Altynbekovich, first secretary of Guryev Kazakhstan Communist Party Obkom, CPSU member, Guryev city. From Guryevskiy National-Territorial Okrug, No 138, Kazakh SSR.

Kuliyev, Adil Guseynovich, Azerbaijan Potrebsoyuz department deputy chief, CPSU member, Baku city. From the All-Union War and Labor Veterans' Organization.

Kulikov, Fedor Mikhaylovich, first secretary of Penza CPSU Obkom, CPSU member, Penza city. From Kamenskiy Territorial Okrug No 255, Penza Oblast, RSFSR.

Kuliyev, Sultan Oyusovich, livestock unit chief at the Lenin Kolkhoz, Chegemskiy Rayon, CPSU member, Chegem Pervyy settlement, Chegemskiy Rayon. From Chegemskiy National-Territorial Okrug No 545, Kabardino-Balkarsk ASSR.

Kulikov, Viktor Georgiyevich, Marshal of the Soviet Union, general inspector of the USSR Defense Ministry General Inspectors' Group, CPSU member, Moscow city. From the All-Union War and Labor Veterans' Organization.

Kulikov, Yakov Pavlovich, scientific consultant at a branch of the Central Scientific Research Institute of Ferrous Metallurgy Economics, CPSU member, Dnepropetrovsk city, Ukrainian SSR. From the All-Union War and Labor Veterans' Organization.

Kulikov, Yevgeniy Andreyevich, chairman of the Lenin Kolkhoz, Dubenskiy Rayon, CPSU member, Povodimovo village, Dubenskiy Rayon. From Bolshebereznikovskiy National-Territorial Okrug No 606, Mordovian ASSR.

Kulmatov, Renat Satarovich, first secretary of Osh Kirghiz Communist Party Obkom, CPSU member, Osh city. From Alayskiy National-Territorial Okrug No 325, Kirghiz SSR.

Kupin, Aleksey Danilovich, machine operator at the "Rossiya" kolkhoz, Giaginskiy Rayon, CPSU member, Giaginskaya village, Giaginskiy Rayon. From Maykopskiy Territorial Okrug No 80, Krasnodar Kray, RSFSR.

Kuptsov, Valentin Aleksandrovich, first secretary of Vologda CPSU Obkom, CPSU member, Vologda city. From Velikoustyugskiy Territorial Okrug No 146, Vologda Oblast, RSFSR.

Kurashvili, Zeynab Giviyevna, sewing machine operator at the "Gldani" knitwear production association in Tbilisi, CPSU member, Tbilisi city. From Tbilisi-Gldanskiy National-Territorial Okrug No 162, Georgian SSR.

Kurbanov, Khayrullo, team leader at the "Urgut" sovkhoz, Urgutskiy Rayon, CPSU member, Muminabad Kishlak, Khamzinskiy Kishlak Soviet. From Pastdargomskiy Territorial Okrug No 589, Samarkand Oblast, Uzbek SSR.

Kurbanov, Sukhrob Usmanovich, artist, chairman of the board of the Tajik SSR Artists' Union, CPSU member, Dushanbe City. From the USSR Artists' Union.

Kurbanova, Amangozel, carpet maker at the "Turkmenkover" production association in Ashkhabad. From women's councils united in the Soviet Women's Committee.

Kurilenko, Viktor Trifonovich, machine operator at the "Ukraina" kolkhoz, Pologovskiy Rayon, CPSU member, Pologi city, Zaporozhye Oblast. From Zaporozhskiy National-Territorial Okrug No 46, Ukrainian SSR.

Kurochka, Grigoriy Mikhaylovich, chairman of the Komi ASSR Supreme Court permanent session, CPSU member, Vorkuta City. From Vorkutinskiy National-Territorial Okrug No 582, Komi ASSR.

Kurtashin, Vladimir Yegorovich, general director of the "Kriogenmash" science and production association, CPSU member, Balashikha city, Moscow Oblast, RSFSR. From the USSR trade unions.

Kushnerenko, Mikhail Mikhaylovich, first secretary of Kherson Ukrainian Communist Party Obkom, CPSU member, Kherson city. From Novotroitskiy Territorial Okrug No 530, Kherson Oblast, Ukrainian SSR.

Kushchenko, Yevdokiya Petrovna, member of the "Bilshovik" Kolkhoz, Kamenskiy Rayon. From Smelyanskiy

Territorial Okrug No 538, Cherkassy Oblast, Ukrainian SSR.

Kutashov, Nikolay Anatolyevich, laboratory chief at the Scientific Research Institute for Shale, CPSU member, Kokhtla-Yarve city. From Kokhtla-Yarveskiy National-Territorial Okrug No 467, Estonian SSR.

Kutepov, Yevgeniy Aleksandrovich, chief design engineer at the Taganrog machinebuilding plant, CPSU member, Taganrog city. From Taganrogskiy Territorial Okrug No 277, Rostov Oblast, RSFSR.

Kutsenko, Nikolay Antonovich, legal adviser with the Kremenchug No 3 housing construction combine, Kremenchug City. From Poltavskiy National-Territorial Okrug No 54, Ukrainian SSR.

Kutuzov, Petr Petrovich, chairman of the "Krasnaya Zvezda" Kolkhoz, Svobodnenskiy Rayon, CPSU member, Chernigovka village, Svobodnenskiy Rayon. From Svobodnenskiy Territorial Okrug No 117, Amur Oblast, RSFSR.

Kuznetsov, Valeriy Pavlovich, leader of a team of face workers at the "Ognevka" mine of the Belogorskiy Mining Enrichment Combine, Ognevka settlement, Ulanskiy Rayon, East Kazakhstan Oblast, Kazakh SSR. From the USSR trade unions.

Kuznetsov Lev Aleksandrovich, senior teacher of the Leningrad State Pedagogical Institute named for A.I. Herzen, CPSU member, Leningrad city. From scientific societies and associations under the USSR Academy of Sciences.

Kuzovlev, Anatoliy Tikhonovich, chairman of the Kolkhoz named for Kalinin, Kanevskiy Rayon, CPSU member, Kanevskaya village, Kanevskiy Rayon, Krasnodar Kray, RSFSR. From the kolkhozes united in the Union Kolkhoz Council.

Kuzmin, Aleksandr Nikolayevich, sector chief at the Central Scientific Research Institute of Automation and Hydraulics, Moscow city. From Kirovskiy Territorial Okrug No.9, Moscow city.

Kuzmin, Petr Ignatyevich, general director of the "Lovzhanskoye" science and production association, Shumilinskiy Rayon, CPSU member, Nikitikha village, Shumilinskiy Rayon. From Vitebskiy Rural National-Territorial Okrug No 81, Belorussian SSR.

Kuzmin, Fedor Mikhaylovich, lieutenant general, commander of the Red-Banner Baltic Military District, CPSU member, Riga city. From Leninskiy Territorial Okrug No 706, Latvian SSR.

Kuzubov, Vladimir Fedorovich, chief of a shop of the Gorkiy Aviation Production Association named for S. Ordzhonikidze, CPSU member, Gorkiy city. From Sormovskiy Territorial Okrug No 159, Gorkiy Oblast, RSFSR.

Kvaratskhelia, Gucha Shalvovna, senior scientific staffer at the Georgian SSR Academy of Sciences Linguistics Institute, professor of Tbilisi State Pedagogical Institute, CPSU member, Tbilisi city. From the women's councils united in the Soviet Women's Committee.

Kyabin, Tiyt Reynkholdovich, academic secretary of the Estonian SSR Academy of Sciences presidium social sciences department, CPSU member, Tallinn city. From the Tallinnskiy-Matrosovskiy National-Territorial Okrug No 452, Estonian SSR.

Kyazimova, Zuriyya Guseyn kyzy, team leader of the Ordubad silk spinning factory, CPSU member, Ordubad city. From Ordubadskiy National-Territorial Okrug No 622, Nakhichevan ASSR.

Laak, Tynu Khugovich, first secretary of the Tartu Estonian Communist Party Gorkom, CPSU member, Tartu city. From the Tartuskiy-Universitetskiy National-Territorial Okrug No 478, Estonian SSR.

Labunov, Vladimir Arkhipovich, academician-secretary of the Belorussian SSR Academy of Sciences Physics, Mathematics and Information Technology Department, CPSU member, Minsk city. From the Minskiy-Pervomayskiy National-Territorial Okrug No 66, Belorussian SSR.

Lakman, Teodor Yakovlevich, chairman of the "Pobeda" Kolkhoz, Kalininskiy Rayon, CPSU member, Poltavka village, Kalininskiy Rayon. From the Kalininskiy National-Territorial Okrug No 330, Kirghiz SSR.

Landsbergis, Vitautas Vitautovich, professor at the Lithuanian SSR State Conservatoire, Vilnius city. From Panevezhis City National-Territorial Okrug No 245, Lithuanian SSR.

Lapkin, Viktor Alekseyevich, chairman of the "Borodino" kolkhoz, Mozhayskiy Rayon, CPSU member, Mozhayskiy Rayon. From the Istrinskiy Territorial Okrug No 32, Moscow Oblast, RSFSR.

Laptev, Ivan Dmitriyevich, chief editor of the IZVESTIYA newspaper, CPSU member, Moscow city. From the CPSU.

Lapygin, Vladimir Lavrentyevich, general designer and director of an automation and instrument-making science-production association, CPSU member, Moscow city. From the Ulug-Khemskiy National-Territorial Okrug No 656, Tuva ASSR.

Larionov, Vladimir Petrovich, deputy chairman of the USSR Academy of Sciences Siberian Department Yakutsk Scientific Center Presidium, director of the Institute of Arctic Physical and Technical Problems, CPSU member, Yakutsk city. From the CPSU.

Lashchenov, Semen Yakovlevich, manager of the "Tadzhikgidroenergostroy" trust, CPSU member, Dushanbe city. From the Yavanskiy National-Territorial Okrug No 384, Tajik SSR.

Lashchin, Petr Konstantinovich, tractor driver on the Lenin Kolkhoz, Kurganinskiy Rayon, Mikhaylovskaya village, Kurganinskiy Rayon. From Labinskiy Territorial Okrug No 79, Krasnodar Kray, RSFSR.

Lasuta, Yelena Petrovna, shop chief of the Pinsk production spinning and knitting association named for the 60th anniversary of Great October, Pinsk city, Brest Oblast. From the Pinskiy National-Territorial Okrug No 78, Belorussian SSR.

Laurinkus, Mechis Mechko, scientific worker at the Lithuanian SSR Academy of Sciences Institute of Philosophy, Sociology and Law, Pagiryay settlement, Vilniusskiy Rayon. From Tauragskiy Territorial Okrug No 693, Lithuanian SSR.

Lauristin, Maryyu Yokhannesovna, Tartu State University department head, CPSU member, Tartu city. From the Tartuskiy Territorial Okrug No 750, Estonian SSR.

Laurushas, Vitautas Antanovich, composer, chairman of the Lithuanian SSR Composers Union Board, CPSU member, Vilnius city. From the USSR Composers Union.

Lautsis, Uldis Volfgangovich, chairman of the Latvian SSR Red Cross Society Central Committee, CPSU member, Valmiera city. From the USSR Union of Red Cross and Red Crescent Societies.

Laverov, Nikolay Pavlovich, president of the Kirghiz SSR Academy of Sciences, CPSU member, Moscow city. From the Sokulukskiy National-Territorial Okrug No 342, Kirghiz SSR.

Lavrenishina, Valentina Aleksandrovna, chief of the Kostomuksha mining and enrichment combine first aid unit department, Kostomuksha city. From the Segezhskiy Territorial Okrug No 370, Karelian ASSR.

Lavrentyev, Aleksandr Petrovich, general director of the Kazan helicopter production association named for the USSR's 60th anniversary, CPSU member, Kazan city. From the Kirovskiy National-Territorial Okrug No 635, Tatar ASSR.

Lavrov, Kirill Yuryevich, artiste of the Leningrad Great Academy Theater named for M. Gorkiy, chairman of the USSR Union of Theater Workers Board, CPSU member, Leningrad city. From the USSR Union of Theater Workers.

Lavrov, Sergey Borisovich, Leningrad State University department head, CPSU member, Leningrad city. From scientific societies and associations under the USSR Academy of Sciences.

Layus, Alvidas-Yuozas Pyatrovich, chairman of the Lithuanian "Sigma" production association trade union committee, CPSU member, Vilnius city. From the USSR Trade Unions.

Lazarev, Valentin Nikolayevich, cutter at the Alatyr Mechanics Plant, CPSU member, Alatyr city. From the Alatyrskiy National-Territorial Okrug No 682, Chuvash ASSR.

Lebedev, Aleksandr Timofeyevich, pensioner, CPSU member, Ivanovo city, RSFSR. From the All-Union Organization of War and Labor Veterans.

Leksin, Nikolay Sergeyevich, pensioner, CPSU member, Raychikhinsk city, Amur Oblast, RSFSR. From the All-Union Organization of War and Labor Veterans.

Lemesheva, Natalya Vasilyevna, chairman of the Vitebskiy Rayon kolkhoz named for Kirov, CPSU member, Kirovskiy settlement, Vitebskiy Rayon, Vitebsk Oblast, Belorussian SSR. From women's councils united in the Soviet Women's Committee.

Leonchev, Vladimir Aleksandrovich, fitter team leader at the Novokuybyshevsk "50-letiye SSR" petrochemical combine, CPSU member, Novokuybyshevsk city. From Novokuybyshevskiy Territorial Okrug No 208, Kuybyshev Oblast, RSFSR.

Lesnichenko, Valentin Yegorovich, first secretary of the Karachayevo-Cherkessk CPSU Obkom, CPSU member, Cherkessk city. From Karacheyevskiy National-Territorial Okrug No 724, Karachayevo-Cherkessk Autonomous Oblast.

Lesyuk, Yaroslav Stepanovich, chairman of the Gnezdychevskiy settlement soviet ispolkom, CPSU member, Gnezdychev settlement, Zhidachovskiy Rayon, Lvov Oblast, Ukrainian SSR. From USSR Consumer Cooperatives.

Levakin, Vyacheslav Alekseyevich, director general of the Saransk "Svetotekhnika" production association, CPSU member, Saransk city. From Proletarskiy National-Territorial Okrug No 604, Mordovian ASSR.

Levashev, Aleksey Vladimirovich, assistant lecturer at the Leningrad Technological Institute named for Leningrad City Soviet Political Economy Department, Leningrad City, Pushkin City [as published]. From Kolpinskiy Territorial Okrug No 52, RSFSR.

Levitskas, Vitautas Yuozovich, director general of the Kaunas fur production association named for K. Gedris, CPSU member, Kaunas city. From the CPSU.

Levykin, Yuriy Alekseyevich, scientific staffer at the USSR Academy of Sciences Spectroscopy Institute, Troitsk city. From Podolskiy Territorial Okrug No 39, Moscow Oblast, RSFSR.

Lezhenko, Grigoriy Filippovich, tunneler at the V.I. Lenin Mine of the V.I. Lenin Mining Administration of the "Krivbassrud" Production Association, CPSU member, Krivoy Rog City, Dnepropetrovsk Oblast. From Krivorozhskiy National-Territorial Okrug No 40, Ukrainian SSR.

Lezhnev, Mikhail Aleksandrovich, director of the "Sosnovskaya" poultry unit at the Sosnovskiy Rayon "Chelyabinskoye" poultry breeding association, CPSU member, Roshchino settlement, Sosnovskiy Rayon. From Traktorozavodskiy Territorial Okrug No 334, Chelyabinsk Oblast, RSFSR.

Ligachev, Yegor Kuzmich, member of the CPSU Central Committee Politburo, secretary of the CPSU Central Committee, CPSU member, Moscow city. From the CPSU.

Likhanov, Albert Anatolyevich, writer, chairman of the V.I. Lenin Soviet Children's Fund Board, CPSU member, Moscow city. From the V.I. Lenin Soviet Children's Fund.

Likhachev, Dmitriy Sergeyevich, academician, chief of a sector of the Institute of Russian Literature (Pushkin House) of the USSR Academy of Sciences, chairman of the board of the Soviet Culture Foundation, Leningrad city. From the Soviet Culture Foundation.

Lippmaa, Endel Teodorovich, director of the Estonian SSR Academy of Sciences Institute of Chemical and Biological Physics, Tallinn city. From Tallinnskiy-Tsentralnyy National-Territorial Okrug No 456, Estonian SSR.

Lisichkin, Gennadiy Stepanovich, sector chief at the USSR Academy of Sciences Institute of Economics of the World Socialist System, CPSU member, Moscow City. From the USSR Academy of Sciences.

Lisitskiy, Viktor Ivanovich, deputy director for economic affairs of the "Chernomorskiy Sudostroitelnyy Zavod" Production Association, CPSU member, Nikolayev City. From Zavodskoy Territorial Okrug No 494, Ukrainian SSR.

Lisnichiy, Dmitriy Vasilyevich, leader of an equipment overhaul team at the Nikolayev alumina plant, CPSU member, Nikolayev city. From Leninskiy Territorial Okrug No 493, Nikolayev Oblast, Ukrainian SSR.

Lisov, Nikolay Ivanovich, chairman of the Shatkovskiy Rayon "Krasnaya Zvezda" kolkhoz, CPSU member, Panovo village, Shatkovskiy Rayon, Gorkiy Oblast, RSFSR. From kolkhozes united in the Union Council of Kolkhozes.

Litskevich, Mariya Nikolayevna, painter team leader of the "Tomskzhilstroy" trust's "Otdelstroy" construction administration, Tomsk city, RSFSR. From women's councils united in the Soviet Women's Committee.

Litvinov, Ivan Aleksandrovich, pensioner, CPSU member, Volgograd city, RSFSR. From the All-Union Organization of War and Labor Veterans.

Litvinov, Valeriy Vyacheslavovich, director of the Khabarovsk heating equipment plant, CPSU member, Khabarovsk City. From Khabarovskiy City Territorial Okrug No 110, RSFSR.

Litvintsev, Yuriy Ivanovich, first secretary of the Tula CPSU Obkom, CPSU member, Tula city. From Shchekinskiy Territorial Okrug No 319, Tula Oblast, RSFSR.

Litvintseva, Galina Nikolayevna, interior decorator team leader of the "Zhilgrazhdanstroy" trust's No 7 construction and installation administration, CPSU member, Ulan-Ude city. From Oktyabrskiy National-Territorial Okrug No 516, Buryat ASSR.

Lizichev, Aleksey Dmitriyevich, army general, chief of the Soviet Army and Navy Main Political Directorate, CPSU member, Moscow city. From the CPSU.

Lobov, Vladimir Nikolayevich, army general, first deputy chief of the USSR Armed Forces General Staff, CPSU member, Moscow city. From Ayaguzskiy National-Territorial Okrug No 135, Kazakh SSR.

Lobov, Oleg Ivanovich, second secretary of the Armenian Communist Party Central Committee, CPSU member, Yerevan city. From National-Territorial Okrug No 409 named for Kamo, Armenian SSR.

Lochmelis, Adolf Adamovich, chairman of Kraslavskiy Rayon's "Briviba" kolkhoz, CPSU member, Dagda settlement, Kraslavskiy Rayon. From Ludzenskiy National-Territorial Okrug No 309, Latvian SSR.

Logeyko, Andrey Vladimirovich, leader of basic military training at Poltavskaya Secondary School, Kartalinskiy Rayon, Kartaly city. From Kartalinskiy Territorial Okrug No 336, Chelyabinsk Oblast, RSFSR.

Logunov, Valentin Andreyevich, deputy editor of MOSKOVSKAYA PRAVDA, CPSU member, Moscow City. From Kuntsevskiy Territorial Okrug No 13, RSFSR.

Lokotunin, Valeriy Ivanovich, first secretary of the Kazakh Communist Party Karaganda Obkom, CPSU member, Karaganda city. From Karagandinskiy-Leninskiy Territorial Okrug No 629, Karaganda Oblast, Kazakh SSR.

Lopatin, Vladimir Nikolayevich, captain, troop unit propagandist, CPSU member, Vologda city. From Vologodskiy Territorial Okrug No 145, Vologda Oblast, RSFSR.

Lubenchenko, Konstantin Dmitriyevich, reader at Moscow M.V. Lomonosov State University, CPSU member, Zhukovskiy city. From Ramenskiy Territorial Okrug No 40, Moscow Oblast, RSFSR.

Luchenok, Igor Mikhaylovich, composer, chairman of the Belorussian SSR Composers Union Board, CPSU member, Minsk city. From USSR Trade Unions.

Luchinskiy, Petr Kirillovich, second secretary of the Tajik Communist Party Central Committee, CPSU member, Dushanbe city. From Kanibadamskiy Territorial Okrug No 726, Tajik SSR.

Lukin, Vladimir Petrovich, oxyacetylene cutter at the Kolomna diesel engine building plant named for V.V. Kuybyshev, CPSU member, Kolomna city. From Moskovskiy rural National-Territorial Okrug No 2, RSFSR.

Lukkoyev, Yuriy Prokhorovich, machine operator at the Volomskiy timber unit of the Padanskiy comprehensive timber procurement enterprise of the "Karellesprom" territorial production association, CPSU member, Shalgovaary settlement, Medvezhyegorskiy Rayon, Karelian ASSR. From the CPSU.

Lukyanenko, Olga Fedotovna, animal specialist on Manevichskiy Rayon's "Svitanok" kolkhoz, CPSU member, Borovichi village, Manevichskiy Rayon, Volyn Oblast. From Volynskiy National-Territorial Okrug No 36, Ukrainian SSR.

Lukyanov, Anatoliy Ivanovich, candidate member of the CPSU Central Committee Politburo, first deputy chairman of the USSR Supreme Soviet Presidium, CPSU member, Moscow city. From the CPSU.

Lukyanov, Anatoliy Sergeyevich, chief physician at Asino central rayon hospital, Asino city. From Leninskiy Territorial Okrug No 312, Tomsk Oblast, RSFSR.

Lunev, Viktor Andreyevich, lathe operator at the Moscow "Kompressor" production association's "Kompressor" refrigeration machine building plant, CPSU member, Moscow city. From the CPSU.

Lunkov, Dmitriy Alekseyevich, producer at the Saratov Oblast committee for television and radio broadcasting, CPSU member, Saratov city. From the USSR Cinematographers Union.

Lutsans, Yanis Petrovich, chairman of the Limbazhskiy Rayon "Komunars" kolkhoz-agrocombine, CPSU member, Klintsleyas village, Rizhskiy Rayon. From Limbazhskiy National Territorial Okrug No 308, Latvian SSR.

Lutsik, Ivan Aleksandrovich, chairman of the Minusinskiy Rayon "Iskra Lenina" kolkhoz, CPSU member, Tes village, Minusinskiy Rayon, Krasnoyarsk Kray, RSFSR. From kolkhozes united in the Union Council of Kolkhozes.

Lushev, Petr Georgiyevich, army general, USSR first deputy minister of defense, commander in chief of the Warsaw Pact Joint Armed Forces, CPSU member, Moscow city. From the USSR DOSAAF.

Lushnikov, Vladimir Petrovich, drifter at the "Intaugol" production association's "Vostochnaya" mine, CPSU member, Inta city. From Pechorskiy Territorial Okrug No 372, Komi ASSR.

Lyzo, Ivan Stepanovich, chairman of the trade union committee at the "Gosudarstvennyy Soyuznyy Zavod 'Dvigatel' im. V.I. Lenina" production association, CPSU member, Tallinn city. From the USSR Trade Unions.

Machavariani, Mukhran Ivanovich, writer, chairman of the Georgian Writers' Union Board, CPSU member, Tbilisi city. From Kobuletskiy National-Territorial Okrug No 177, Georgian SSR.

Made, Tiyt Raymondovich, lecturer at the Republic Institute for further teacher training, CPSU member, Tallinn city. From Rakvereskiy Yuzhnyy National-Territorial Okrug No 475, Estonian SSR.

Madivarova, Kalzhan, leasing team member on Kungradskiy Rayon's Sovkhoz XXIV S'yezda KPSS, CPSU member, Kungradskiy Rayon, Karakalpak ASSR. From the USSR Consumer Cooperatives.

Magomedov, Sapiyula Aliyevich, carpenter and concrete layer at the "Promgrazhdanstroy" construction administration of the Chirkeygesstroy construction administration, CPSU member, Dubki settlement, Kizilyurtovskiy Rayon, Dagestan ASSR. From USSR Trade Unions.

Magomedov, Gadzhimurad Mamedovich, first secretary of the Sergokalinskiy CPSU Raykom, CPSU member, Sergokala village, Sergokalinskiy Rayon. From Izberbashskiy National-Territorial Okrug No 529, Dagestan ASSR.

Makashov, Albert Mikhaylovich, lieutenant general, commander of the Red-Banner Urals Military District, CPSU member, Sverdlovsk city. From Irbitskiy Territorial Okrug No 297, Sverdlovsk Oblast, RSFSR.

Makhanov, Turganbay, chief physician at Kzyl-Orda Oblast Hospital, CPSU member, Kzyl-Orda City. From Kzyl-Ordinskiy Territorial Okrug No 631, Kzyl-Orda Oblast, Kazakh SSR.

Maksimov, Valeriy Nikolayevich, team leader at "Vorkutaugol" production association's "Severnaya" mine, Vorkuta city. From Vorgashorskiy National-Territrorial Okrug No 583, Komi ASSR.

Maksimov, Yuriy Pavlovich, army general, commander in chief of the missile forces, USSR deputy defense minister, CPSU member, Moscow city. From Krasnoyarskiy National-Territorial Okrug No 16, RSFSR.

Malikova, Liliya Avkhadiyevna, director of a public catering association of the Yanaulskiy Rayon Consumer Society, CPSU member, Yanaul settlement, Yanaulskiy Rayon, Bashkir ASSR. From the USSR consumer cooperatives.

Malmygin, Aleksandr Aleksandrovich, chief doctor at the Kizner Central Rayon Hospital, CPSU member, Kizner settlement. From Mozhginskiy National-Territorial Okrug No 665, Udmurt ASSR.

Makharashvili, Beglar Dmitriyevich, first secretary of Tbilisi Georgian Communist Party Gorkom. CPSU member, Tbilisi city. From Tbilisskiy 26 Komissarov National-Territorial Okrug No 164, Georgian SSR.

Makhkamov, Kakhar, first secretary of the Tajik Communist Party Central Committee, CPSU member, Dushanbe city. From Dushanbinskiy Territorial Okrug No 723, Tajik SSR.

Makhmudov, Ubaydillo Nurmakhmadovich, cotton-growing team leader on the "Moskva" Kolkhoz. CPSU member, Khorkash village, Romintanskiy Rayon, Bukhara Oblast, Uzbek SSR. From the kolkhozes united by the Union Kolkhoz Council.

Malkova, Yevgeniya Kirillovna, foreman of workshop No 5 at Clothing Production and Repair Factory No 1 of the Moscow city "Siluet" Production Association. CPSU member, Moscow city. From the USSR trade unions.

Malkovskaya, Vera Mikhaylovna, leader of a team of plasterers at Construction and Assembly Line No 3 of Construction and Assembly Trust No 4 of the "Tatneftegazstroy" Association. CPSU member, Leninogorsk city. From Oktyabrskiy National-Territorial Okrug No 644, Tatar ASSR.

Malofeyev, Anatoliy Aleksandrovich, first secretary of the Minsk Belorussian Communist Party Obkom, CPSU member, Minsk city. From Stolbtsovskiy National-Territorial Okrug No 73, Belorussian SSR.

Maltsev, Yevgeniy Demyanovich, painter, deputy chairman of the board of the Leningrad organization of the RSFSR Union of Artists, Leningrad city. From the USSR Union of Artists.

Maltsev, Innokentiy Ivanovich, planer at the Moscow Yefremov "Krasnyy Proletariy" Machine Tool Manufacturing Plant, CPSU member, Moscow city. From the All-Union Organization of War and Labor Veterans.

Malyuta, Oleg Lavrentyevich, head of department at the Kirovograd Oblast Children's Hospital, CPSU member, Kirovograd city. From Kirovogradskiy Territorial Okrug No 476, Kirovograd Oblast, Ukrainian SSR.

Mamarasulov, Salidzhan, first secretary of the Surkhan-Darya Uzbek Communist Party Obkom, CPSU member, Termez city. From Denauskiy National-Territorial Okrug No 111, Uzbek SSR.

Mambetov, Azerbayzhan Madiyevich, artistic leader of the M. Auezov Drama Theater, chairman of the board of the Kazakh Union of Theater Workers, CPSU member, Alma-Ata city. From the USSR Union of Theater Workers.

Mamedov, Anver Musa ogly, chairman of the board of the Akhsuinskiy Rayon Consumer Society, CPSU member, Akhsu city, Azerbaijan SSR. From the USSR consumer cooperatives.

Mamedov, Veli Guseyn ogly, first secretary of the 26 Baku Commissars Azerbaijan Communist Party Raykom, Baku city, CPSU member, Baku city. From Bakinskiy 26 Bakinskikh Kommissarov National-Territorial Okrug No 194, Azerbaijan SSR.

Mamedov, Muslum Radzhab ogly, first secretary of the Baku Azerbaijan Communist Party Gorkom, CPSU member, Baku city. From Bakinskiy-Oktyabrskiy National-Teritorial Okrug No 196, Azerbaijan SSR.

Mamedov, Rafik Dzhabbar ogly, welder at Mobile Mechanized Column No 101 of Trust No 5, CPSU member, Nakhichevan city. From Nakhichevanskiy First City National-Territorial Okrug No 613, Nakhichevan ASSR.

Mamedov, Suleyman Farkhad ogly, first secretary of the Kirovabad Azerbaijan Communist Party Gorkom, CPSU member, Kirovabad city. From Kirovabadskiy National-Territorial Okrug No 210, Azerbaijan SSR.

Mamedov, Firidun Arykh ogly, member of the apparatus of the "Orgsintez" Production Association, CPSU member, Sumgait city. From Sumgaitskiy National-Territorial Okrug No 219, Azerbaijan SSR.

Mamedov, Etibar Pasha ogly, assistant drill operator at the Maritime Administration of Exploratory Drilling and Specialized Technical Facilities of the "Kaspmorneftegaz" Production Association, Baku city. From the All-Union Komsomol.

Mamonov, Anatoliy Grigoryevich, tractor driver at the 1 May Kolkhoz, Dobropolskiy Rayon, Zavidovo-Borzenka village, Dobropolskiy Rayon, Donetsk Oblast, Ukrainian SSR. From the USSR consumer cooperatives.

Manko, Nikolay Mikhaylovich, assembly worker at Construction and Assembly Administration No 3 of the "Dushanbezhilstroy" Planning and Construction Administration, CPSU member, Dushanbe city. From Dushanbinskiy-Frunzenskiy National-Territorial Okrug No 355, Tajik SSR.

Manayenkov, Yuriy Alekseyevich, first secretary of the Lipetsk CPSU Obkom, CPSU member, Lipetsk city. From Lebedyanskiy Territorial Okrug No 222, Lipetsk Oblast, RSFSR.

Manonov, Khasan, director of the Tursunzade Ginning Association, CPSU member, Tursunzade city. From Tursunzadevskiy National-Territorial Okrug No 380, Tajik SSR.

Mansurov, Rafis Khamzeyevich, drilling foreman at the Aznakayevo Drilling Works Administration, Aznakayevo city. From Zainskiy National-Territorial Okrug No 639, Tatar ASSR.

Manyakin, Sergey Iosifovich, chairman of the USSR People's Control Committee, CPSU member, Moscow city. From the CPSU.

Marchenko, Georgiy Aleksandrovich, chief doctor at the Nizhnyaya Tura city Central Hospital, CPSU member, Nizhnyaya Tura city. From Kushvinskiy Territorial Okrug No 301, Sverdlovsk Oblast, RSFSR.

Marchuk, Guriy Ivanovich, president of the USSR Academy of Sciences, CPSU member, Moscow city. From the CPSU.

Margaryan, Sanam Mushegovna, secondary school teacher in Gladzor village, Yekhegnadzorskiy Rayon, CPSU member, Yekhegnadzor Urban settlement. From Yekhegnadzorskiy National-Territorial Okrug No 407, Armenian SSR.

Margvelashvili, Parmen Ioramovich, senior department lecturer at Tbilisi State University, CPSU member, Tbilisi city. From Tbilisskiy-Ordzhonikidzevskiy National-Territorial Okrug No 166, Georgian SSR.

Maresyev, Aleksey Petrovich, first deputy chairman of the Soviet War Veterans Committee, CPSU member, Moscow city. From the All-Union Organization of War and Labor Veterans.

Marinichev, Yuriy Mikhaylovich, chairman of the Board of the Moscow Oblast Potrebsoyuz, CPSU member, Balashikha city, Moscow Oblast, RSFSR. From the USSR consumer cooperatives.

Markaryants, Vladimir Surenovich, chairman of the Armenian SSR Council of Ministers, CPSU member, Yerevan city. From Yerevanskiy-Leninskiy Territorial Okrug No 732, Armenian SSR.

Markevich, Anatoliy Lavrentyevich, chief of the Obluchye Railroad Car Depot, CPSU member, Obluchye city, Khabarovsk Kray. From Obluchenskiy City National-Territorial Okrug No 718, Jewish Autonomous Oblast.

Markin, Nikolay Alekseyevich, design engineer at the Urals "Omega" Instrument-Making Plant, Uralsk city. From Uralskiy Territorial Okrug No 645, Uralsk Oblast, Kazakh SSR.

Markov, Oleg Ivanovich, arc welder at the "Sibenergomash" Production Association, CPSU member, Barnaul city. From Leninskiy Territorial Okrug No 65, Altay Kray, RSFSR.

Martinaytis, Martseliyus-Teodoras Izidorovich, senior lecturer at the Vilnius V. Kapsukas State University, Vilnius city. From Rokishkskiy National-Territorial Okrug No 248, Lithuanian SSR.

Martirosyan, Vilen Arutyunovich, colonel, commander of a troop unit, Carpathian Military District, CPSU member, Rovno Oblast. From Rovenskiy Territorial Okrug No 509, Rovno Oblast, Ukrainian SSR.

Martynov, Fedor Nikolayevich, director of the Novovyatsk Wallboard Combine, CPSU member, Novovyatsk city. From Pervomayskiy Territorial Okrug No 198, Kirov Oblast, RSFSR.

Martsinkyavichyus, Yustinas Moteyevich, writer, CPSU member, Vilnius city. From the USSR Writers' Union.

Masaliyev, Absamat Masaliyevich, first secretary of the Kirghiz Communist Party Central Committee, CPSU member, Frunze city. From Issyk-Kulskiy Territorial Okrug No 716, Kirghiz SSR.

Maselskiy, Aleksandr Stepanovich, chairman of Kharkov Oblispolkom, CPSU member, Kharkov city. From Lozovskiy Territorial Okrug No 527, Kharkov Oblast, Ukrainian SSR.

Mashbashev, Iskhak Shumafovich, writer, responsible secretary of the Adyge Writers Organization, CPSU member, Maykop city. From Shovgenovskiy National-Territorial Okrug No 705, Adyge Autonomous Oblast.

Masko, Galina Ignatyevna, deputy director of the No 3 Secondary School, CPSU member, Slonim city, Grodno Oblast, Belorussian SSR. From the CPSU.

Maslakova, Anna Polikarpovna, team leader at Saransk "Rezinotekhnika" Plant, CPSU member, Saransk city. From Oktyabrskiy National-Territorial Okrug No 603, Mordovian ASSR.

Masliy, Mariya Dmitriyevna, instrument controller at Kalush "Khlorvinil" Production Association, Kalush city, Ivano-Frankovsk Oblast, Ukrainian SSR. From the USSR trade unions.

Maslin, Vladimir Petrovich, first deputy chairman of the Soviet Peace Fund Board, CPSU member, Moscow city. From the Soviet Peace Fund jointly with eight Soviet committees advocating peace, solidarity, and international cooperation.

Masol, Vitaliy Andreyevich, chairman of the Ukrainian SSR Council of Ministers, CPSU member, Kiev city. From Donetskiy-Leninskiy Territorial Okrug No 431, Donetsk Oblast, Ukrainian SSR.

Matveyev, Yevgeniy Ivanovich, leader of a carpenters' team with the "Gidromontazh" Trust No 63 Construction and Installation Administration, CPSU member, Selyatino Settlement, Naro-Fominskiy Rayon. From Leninskiy Territorial Okrug No 27, RSFSR.

Matveyev, Yuriy Gennadiyevich, chief state arbiter of the Ukrainian SSR, CPSU member, Kiev city. From Kalushskiy Territorial Okrug No 461, Ivano-Frankovsk Oblast, Ukrainian SSR.

Matveychuk, Sergey Ivanovich, fitter-repairman at Vladimir-Volynskiy Cannery, CPSU member, Vladimir-Volynskiy city. From Vladimir-Volynskiy Territorial Okrug No 411, Volyn Oblast, Ukrainian SSR.

Matviyenko, Valentina Ivanovna, deputy chairman of Leningrad Gorispolkom, CPSU member, Leningrad city. From the women's councils united by the Soviet Women's Committee.

Mateushuk, Zinaida Kondratyevna, shop chief at Brest Electromechanical Plant named for the 25th CPSU Congress, CPSU member, Brest city. From Brestskiy National-Territorial Okrug No 74, Belorussian SSR.

Matiyko, Lidiya Timofeyevna, team leader at Fastov No 37 Construction and Installation Administration, CPSU member, Fastov city. From Fastovskiy Territorial Okrug No 475, Kiev Oblast, Ukrainian SSR.

Matkovski, Dumitru Leontyevich, writer, chief editor of the journal NISTRU, CPSU member, Kishinev city. From Rezinskiy National-Territorial Okrug No 277, Moldavian SSR.

Matyukha, Vyacheslav Nikolayevich, comprehensive team leader at the "Mamontovneftepromstroy" Trust's No 36 Construction Administration, CPSU member, Nefteyugansk city. From Tobolskiy Territorial Okrug No 326, Tyumen Oblast, RSFSR.

Matyukhin, Leonid Ivanovich, chief of the Gorkiy Railroad, CPSU member, Gorkiy city. From Gorkovskiy National-Territorial Okrug No 6, RSFSR.

Mayboroda, Viktor Alekseyevich, cutter-polisher at the Ust-Katavskiy freightcar building plant, Ust-Katav city. From Satkinskiy Territorial Okrug No 340, Chelyabinsk Oblast, RSFSR.

Mazurov, Kirill Trofimovich, pensioner, chairman of the All-Union Council of War and Labor Veterans, CPSU member, Moscow city. From the All-Union Organization of War and Labor Veterans.

Medeubekov, Kiylybay Usenovich, chairman of the V.I. Lenin All-Union Academy of Agricultural Sciences [VaskhniL] Eastern Branch Presidium, CPSU member, Alma-Ata city. From the Vaskhnil.

Medikov, Viktor Yakovlevich, prorector of the Siberian Metallurgical Institute, CPSU member, Novokuznetsk city. From Novokuznetskiy Territorial Okrug No 195, Kemerovo Oblast, RSFSR.

Medvedev, Vadim Andreyevich, member of the CPSU Central Committee Politburo, secretary of the CPSU Central Committee, CPSU member, Moscow city. From the CPSU.

Medvedev, Nikolay Nikolayevich, sector chief of Kaunas Scientific Research Institute of Radio Measuring Eguipment, CPSU member, Kaunas city. From Kaunasskiy-Panyamunskiy National-Territorial Okrug No 237, Lithuanian SSR.

Medvedev, Svyatoslav Aleksandrovich, first secretary of North Kazakhstan Kazakh Communist Party Obkom, CPSU member, Petropavlovsk city. From Severo-Kazakhstanskiy National-Territorial Okrug No 151, Kazakh SSR.

Medvedev, Sergey Aleksandrovich, director of the Kirghiz Mining and Metallurgical Combine, CPSU member, Orlovka settlement, Keminskiy Rayon. From Kantskiy Territorial Okrug No 718, Kirghiz SSR.

Mekheda, Mikhail Ilich, pensioner, CPSU member, Khmelnitskiy city, Ukrainian SSR. From the All-Union Organization of War and Labor Veterans.

Meleyev, Kaka, chief agronomist of the "Leningrad" Kolkhoz, Takhtinskiy Rayon, Khankala settlement, Takhtinskiy Rayon, Tashauz Oblast. From Takhtinskiy National-Territorial Okrug No 441, Turkmen SSR.

Melekhin, Sergey Tikhonovich, operative at Nizhniy Tagil V.I. Lenin Metallurgical Combine, CPSU member, Nizhniy Tagil city, Sverdlovsk Oblast, RSFSR. From the USSR trade unions.

Meliyev, Abdurashid, galvanizer at Samarkand Elevator-Building Plant, CPSU member, Samarkand city, Uzbek SSR. From the All-Union Komsomol.

Melikov, Arif Dzhangirovich, composer, department chief at the Azerbaijan U. Gadzhibekov State Conservatoire, CPSU member, Baku city. From Salyanskiy Territorial Okrug No 681, Azerbaijan SSR.

Melnik, Konstantin Alekseyevich, chairman of the Moldavian Potrebsoyuz Board, CPSU member, Kishinev city. From the USSR consumer cooperatives.

Melnikov, Aleksandr Ivanovich, team leader on the V.I. Lenin Kolkhoz, Syzranskiy Rayon, CPSU member, Novaya Racheyka village, Syzranskiy Rayon. From Syzranskiy Territorial Okrug No 210, Kuybyshev Oblast, RSFSR.

Melnikov, Aleksandr Ilich, assembler at Leningrad Admiralty Association, CPSU member, Leningrad city. From Leninskiy Territorial Okrug No 46, Leningrad city.

Melnikov, Vasiliy Pavlovich, director of Rostov Oblast Volgodonskiy Rayon's "Pobeda" Sovkhoz, CPSU member, Pobeda settlement. From Volgodonskiy Territorial Okrug No 270, RSFSR.

Melnikov, Vladimir Ivanovich, first secretary of the Komi CPSU Obkom, CPSU member, Syktyvkar city. From Ukhtinskiy Territorial Okrug No 373, Komi ASSR.

Memanishvili, Omar Aleksandrovich, senior smelter at Zestafoni Ferroalloy Plant, CPSU member, Rupoti village, Terzholskiy Rayon. From Zestafonskiy Territorial Okrug No 663, Georgian SSR.

Mendybayev, Marat Samiyevich, second secretary of the Kazakh Communist Party Central Committee, CPSU member, Alma-Ata city. From the CPSU.

Menshatov, Aleksey Dmitriyevich, director of the "Azinskiy" State Pedigree Stud Farm, Chernushinskiy Rayon, CPSU member, Azinskiy settlement, Chernushinskiy Rayon. From Chaykovskiy Territorial Okrug No 262, Perm Oblast, RSFSR.

Menshikov, Vadim Vladimirovich, first deputy chairman of the Soviet Charity and Health Fund Board, CPSU member, Moscow city. From the Soviet Charity and Health Fund.

Menteshashvili, Tengiz Nikolayevich, secretary of the USSR Supreme Soviet Presidium, CPSU member, Moscow city. From Mtskhetskiy National-Territorial Okrug No 180, Georgian SSR.

Mergenov, Yerkin Tlekovich, sculptor, chairman of the Kazakh SSR Artists' Union Board, CPSU member, Alma-Ata city. From the USSR Artists' Union.

Merkulov, Ivan Andreyevich, chairman of the Shumakov Kolkhoz, Zmeinogorskiy Rayon, CPSU member, Baranovka village, Zmeinogorskiy Rayon. From Rubtsovskiy Territorial Okrug No 71, Altay Kray, RSFSR.

Meshalkin, Yevgeniy Nikolayevich, director of the RSFSR Health Ministry Scientific Research Institute of Pathology and Blood Circulation, CPSU member, Novosibirsk city. From the peace movement united by the Soviet Committee for the Defense of Peace jointly with the UN Association in the USSR.

Meshcheryakov, Yuriy Alekseyevich, first secretary of Pavlodar Kazakh Communist Party Obkom, CPSU member, Pavlodar city. From Pavlodarskiy Territorial Okrug No 637, Pavlodar Oblast, Kazakh SSR.

Mesyats, Valentin Karpovich, first secretary of Moscow CPSU Obkom, CPSU member, Moscow city. From Stupinskiy Territorial Okrug No 43, Moscow Oblast, RSFSR.

Metonidze, Guram Archilovich, integrated electricians team leader at the "Elektrovozostroitel" Production Association, CPSU member, Tbilisi city. From Tbilisskiy-Leninskiy Territorial Okrug No 654, Georgian SSR.

Mezentsev, Aleksandr Moiseyevich, vehicle driver at Alma-Ata No 1 Bus Pool, CPSU member, Alma-Ata city. From Alma-Atinskiy - Oktyabrskiy Territorial Okrug No 614, Alma-Ata city.

Mezhelaytis, Eduardas Benyaminovich, poet, CPSU member, Vilnius city. From the All-Union Organization of War and Labor Veterans.

Mgaloblishvili, Nodar Mikhaylovich, architect, chairman of the Georgian Architects' Union Board, CPSU member, Tbilisi city. From the USSR Architects' Union.

Mgeladze, Guram Davidovich, first deputy chairman of the Georgian SSR Council of Ministers, chairman of the Georgian SSR Gosagroprom, CPSU member, Tbilisi city. From Gegechkorskiy National-Territorial Okrug No 172, Georgian SSR.

Mikiver, Mikk Arnoldovich, chairman of the Estonian SSR Theater Figures' Union Board, CPSU member, Tallinn city. From Tallinnskiy city Territorial Okrug No 747, Estonian SSR.

Militenko, Svetlana Aleksandrovna, department chief at the "Lesnaya polyana" Sanatorium, CPSU member, Pyatigorsk city. From Pyatigorskiy Territorial Okrug No 109, Stavropol Kray, RSFSR.

Mikhaylov, Vladlen Mikhaylovich, Colonel General, deputy chief of the USSR Armed Forces General Staff, CPSU member, Moscow city. From Buynakskiy National-Territorial Okrug No 528, Dagestan ASSR.

Mikhaylova, Lidiya Ivanovna, teacher at the Shorshely Secondary School, CPSU member, Shorshely village, Mariinsko-Posadskiy Rayon. From Kugeskiy National-Territorial Okrug No 685, Chuvash ASSR.

Mikheyev, Mikhail Alekseyevich, leader of a comprehensive team at the "Yakutuglestroy" Combine's "Uglestroy-1" Trust, CPSU member, Neryungri city. From Neryungrinskiy National-Territorial Okrug No 699, Yakut ASSR.

Milkin, Anatoliy Vasilyevich, first secretary of East Kazakhstan Kazakh Communist Party Obkom, CPSU member, Ust-Kamenogorsk city. From Zyryanovskiy Territorial Okrug No 621, East Kazakhstan Oblast, Kazakh SSR.

Miloserdnyy, Anatoliy Kirillovich, director of Orsha "Krasnyy borets" Machine Tool Building Plant, CPSU member, Orsha city. From Orshanskiy Territorial Okrug No 553, Vitebsk Oblast, Belorussian SSR.

Milyutin, Aleksandr Stepanovich, chief engineer at the Teploozersk Cement Plant, CPSU member, Teploozersk settlement, Obluchenskiy Rayon. From Obluchenskiy Rural National-Territorial Okrug No 719, Jewish Autonomous Oblast.

Minasbekyan, Mikhail Sergeyevich, first secretary of Yerevan Armenian Communist Party Gorkom, CPSU member, Yerevan city. From Yerevanskiy-Ordzhonikidzevskiy National-Territorial Okrug No 388, Armenian SSR.

Minayev, Valentin Fedorovich, laboratory chief at the Krasnoarmeysk Mechanization Research Institute, CPSU member, Krasnoarmeysk City, Pushkinskiy Rayon. From Dmitrovskiy Territorial Okrug No 29, RSFSR.

Minzhurenko, Aleksandr Vasilyevich, chief of department at the Omsk State Teacher Training Institute, CPSU member, Omsk city. From Tsentralnyy Territorial Okrug No 239, Omsk Oblast, RSFSR.

Minin, Viktor Mikhaylovich, chief of mechanical shop at the Glebovskoye Poultry Production Association, CPSU member, Kholshcheviki settlement, Istrinskiy Rayon, Moscow Oblast, RSFSR. From the All-Union Komsomol.

Minnullin, Tufan Abdullovich, writer, chairman of the Tatar ASSR Writers Union Board, CPSU member, Kazan city. From Kukmorskiy National-Territorial Okrug No 643, Tatar ASSR.

Miraliyeva, Elmira Mirzoyevna, radio apparatus assembly worker at the "Elektrosignal" Plant, Derbent city. From Kalininskiy National-Territorial Okrug No 530, Dagestan ASSR.

Mirgazyamov, Marat Parisovich, chairman of the Bashkir ASSR Council of Ministers, CPSU member, Ufa City. From Birskiy National-Territorial Okrug No 503, Bashkir ASSR.

Mirkadirov, Mirsali, team leader on the "Azatlyk" Kolkhoz in Tyulkubasskiy Rayon, CPSU member, Azatlyk settlement, Tyulkubasskiy Rayon. From Chimkentskiy National-Territorial Okrug No 157, Kazakh SSR.

Mirkasymov, Mirakhmat Mirkhadzhiyevich, first secretary of Tashkent Uzbek Communist Party Obkom, CPSU member, Tashkent city. From Yangiyulskiy Territorial Okrug No 604, Tashkent Oblast, Uzbek SSR.

Mirkhalikov, Temurbay, first secretary of Leninabad Tajik Communist Party Obkom, CPSU member, Leninabad city. From Leninabadskiy Territorial Okrug No 730, Tajik SSR.

Mironenko, Viktor Ivanovich, first secretary of the All-Union Komsomol Central Committee, CPSU member, Moscow city. From the All-Union Komsomol.

Mironov, Nikolay Sergeyevich, general director of the "Mashinostroitelnyy Zavod 'Molniya'" Production Association, CPSU member, Moscow city. From Volgogradskiy Territorial Okrug No 5, Moscow city.

Mironova, Dagmara Sergeyevna, weaver at the Barnaul Cotton Textile Combine, CPSU member, Barnaul city, RSFSR. From the USSR trade unions.

Mironova, Svetlana Leonidovna, director of No 38 Secondary School, CPSU member, Makhachkala city. From Makhachkalinskiy Territorial Okrug No 362, Dagestan ASSR.

Miroshin, Boris Vladimirovich, chairman of Sovetskiy Rayispolkom, Orsk City, CPSU member, Orsk City. From Orskiy Territorial Okrug No 247, RSFSR.

Miroshnik, Viktor Mikhaylovich, chairman of the Kazakh SSR KGB, CPSU member, Alma-Ata city. From Dzhambulskiy National-Territorial Okrug No 139, Kazakh SSR.

Mirrakhimov, Mirsaid Mirkhamidovich, director of the Kirghiz Cardiology Research Institute, CPSU member, Frunze city. From Kara-Suyskiy National-Territorial Okrug No 332, Kirghiz SSR.

Mirzabekov, Abdurazak Mardanovich, chairman of the Dagestan ASSR Council of Ministers, CPSU member, Makhachkala city. From Khasavyurtovskiy National-Territorial Okrug No 534, Dagestan ASSR.

Mirzoyev, Ramazon Zarifovich, first secretary of Dangarinskiy Tajik Communist Party Raykom, CPSU member, Dangara settlement, Dangarinskiy Rayon. From Dangarinskiy National-Territorial Okrug No 363, Tajik SSR.

Mirzoyan, Melanya Andranikovna, secretary of Kirovakan Armenian Communist Party Gorkom, CPSU member, Kirovakan city, Armenian SSR. From women's councils united by the Soviet Women's Committee.

Mirzoyan, Edvard Mikhaylovich, composer, chairman of the Armenian SSR Composers Union Board, CPSU member, Yerevan. From the USSR Composers Union.

Misrikhanov, Kerimkhan Zamrudinovich, leader of a team of fitters and assembly workers at the Makhachkala Machine-Building Plant, CPSU member, Makhachkala city. From Leninskiy National-Territorial Okrug No 525, Dagestan ASSR.

Misuna, Ivan Ivnaovich, production foreman at the Krasnoyarsk Aluminum Plant, Krasnoyarsk City. From Tsentralnyy Territorial Okrug No 89 RSFSR.

Mitalene, Ona Antanovna, chief nurse at the Klaypeda city Hospital, CPSU member, Klaypeda city, Lithuanian SSR. From the Soviet Charity and Health Fund.

Mitin, Boris Sergeyevich, rector of the Moscow K.E. Tsiolkovskiy Aviation Technology Institute, CPSU member, Moscow city. From the USSR trade unions.

Mitin, Viktor Stepanovich, chief of surgery at the Neryungri Central City Hospital. From Yakutskiy Yuzhnyy Territorial Okrug No 403, Yakutsk ASSR.

Mitskis, Algis Matovich, chief of department at the Kaunas Medical Institute, CPSU member, Kaunas city. From Kaunasskiy-Leninskiy National-Territorial Okrug No 236, Lithuanian SSR.

Mishuk, Stanislav Mikhaylovich, leader of a team of fitters at the Khust Industrial Equipment Plant, CPSU member, Khust city. From Khustskiy Territorial Okrug No 453, Transcarpathian Oblast, Ukrainian SSR.

Mkhitaryan, Rafik Yervandovich, general director of the Kirovakan Sewn Goods Production Association, CPSU member, Kirovakan city. From Kirovakanskiy Territorial Okrug No 736, Armenian SSR.

Mkrtumyan, Gragat Tigranovich, chairman of the Norashen village Kolkhoz in Shamshadinskiy Rayon, CPSU member, Norashen village, Shamshadinskiy Rayon. From Idzhevanskiy National-Territorial Okrug No 408, Armenian SSR.

Mkrtchyan, Misak Levonovich, first secretary of Leninakan Armenian Communist Party Gorkom, CPSU member, Leninakan city. From the CPSU.

Mkatsakanyan, Bavakan Gagikovna, chairman of the Arshaluys Rural Soviet of People's Deputies, CPSU member, Arshaluys village, Echmiadzinskiy Rayon, Armenian SSR. From USSR consumer cooperatives.

Mogilevets, Yuriy Klimentyevich, first deputy chairman of the Turkmen SSR Council of Ministers, chairman of the Turkmen SSR Gosagroprom, CPSU member, Ashkhabad city. From Bakhardenskiy National-Territorial Okrug No 423, Turkmen SSR.

Moiseyev, Mikhail Alekseyevich, Colonel General, chief of the USSR Armed Forces General Staff and USSR first deputy defense minister, CPSU member, Moscow city. From the CPSU.

Moiseyev, Nikolay Andreyevich, Colonel General, member of the Military Council and chief of the Political Directorate of the Group of Soviet Forces in Germany, CPSU member. From Tsentralnyy Territorial Okrug No 316, Tula Oblast, RSFSR.

Mokanu, Aleksandr Aleksandrovich, chairman of the Moldavian SSR Supreme Soviet Presidium, CPSU member, Kishinev city. From Kotovskiy Territorial Okrug No 701, Moldavian SSR.

Moldobayev, Alimbek Tologonovich, senior shepherd on the Kolkhoz named for Karl Marx in Leninskiy Rayon, candidate CPSU member, Byurgendyu village, Leninskiy Rayon, Osh Oblast. From Lenin-Dzholskiy National-Territorial Okrug No 336, Kirghiz SSR.

Moldobasanov, Kalyy Moldobasanovich, composer, chairman of the Kirghiz SSR Composers Union Board, CPSU member, Frunze city. From the USSR Composers Union.

Mollaniyazov, Kurbanmamed, foreman at the "Turkmenneft" Production Association's "Nebitdagneft" Oil and Gas Extraction Administration, CPSU member, Nebit-Dag city, Turkmen SSR. From the USSR trade unions.

Molotkov, Nikolay Vasilyevich, adjustor at the Ryazan Mechanical Plant, Ryazan City. From Ryazanskiy Territorial Okrug No 279, RSFSR.

Momotova, Tamara Vasilyevna, deputy chief engineer at the Zhlobin Artificial Fur Production Association, CPSU member, Zhlobin city, Gomel Oblast. From Zhlobinskiy National-Territorial Okrug No 86, Belorussian SSR.

Moroz, Dmitriy Vasilyevich, chairman of the Lenin Kolkhoz, Nesterovskiy Rayon, CPSU member, Podlesnoye village, Nesterovskiy Rayon, Lvov Oblast. From Chervonogradskiy Territorial Okrug No 492, Ukrainian SSR.

Morozov, Ivan Sergeyevich, colonel general, commander of the Red-Banner Odessa Military District, CPSU member, Odessa city. From Tiraspolskiy Territorial Okrug No 704, Moldavian SSR.

Moshnyaga, Timofey Vasilyevich, chief physician at the republic clinical hospital, CPSU member, Kishinev city. From Kishinevskiy-Leninskiy National-Territorial Okrug No 257, Moldavian SSR.

Moskalenko, Galina Semenovna, link leader at Pogrebishchenskiy Rayon's Lenin Kolkhoz, Monchin village, Pogrebishchenskiy Rayon. From Kazatinskiy Territorial Okrug No 407, Vinnitsa Oblast, Ukrainian SSR.

Moskalik, Mariya Nikolayevna, cook at the Gorodenkovskiy Rayon Potrebsoyuz Canteen, CPSU member, Gorodenka city, Ivano-Frankovsk Oblast, Ukrainian SSR. From USSR consumer cooperatives.

Mostovoy, Pavel Ivanovich, chairman of the Ukrainian SSR State Committee for Material and Technical Supply, CPSU member, Kiev City. From Leninskiy Territorial Okrug No 413, Voroshilovgrad Oblast, Ukrainian SSR.

Moteka, Kazimir Vladislavovich, lawyer at the First Vilnius Legal Consultation Office, Vilnius city. From Varenskiy National-Territorial Okrug No 232, Lithuanian SSR.

Motornyy, Dmitriy Konstantinovich, chairman of the S.M. Kirov Kolkhoz, CPSU member, Chernobayevka village, Belozerskiy Rayon, Kherson Oblast, Ukrainian SSR. From kolkhozes united in the All-Union Kolkhoz Council.

Mukhabatova, Soniyabibi Khushvakhtovna, livestock unit team leader at Garmskiy Rayon's "Khayeti-Nav" Sovkhoz, CPSU member, Zarafshan Kishlak, Garmskiy Rayon. From Garmskiy National-Territorial Okrug No 361, Tajik SSR.

Mukhamedzhanov Bektas Gafurovich, scientific worker at the Kazakh SSR Academy of Sciences M.A. Aytkhozhin Institute of Molecular Biology and Biochemistry, CPSU member, Alma-Ata city. From the All-Union Komsomol.

Mukhametzyanov, Aklim Kasimovich, general director of the "Tatneft" Production Association named for V.D. Shashin, CPSU member, Almetyevsk city. From Almetyevskiy Territorial Okrug No 386, Tatar ASSR.

Mukhametzyanov, Mukharam Timergaliyevich, chairman of Buinskiy Rayon's "Iskra" Kolkhoz, CPSU member, Novyye Tinchali village, Buinskiy Rayon, Tatar ASSR. From kolkhozes united in the All-Union Kolkhoz Council.

Mukhammad-Yusuf, Mukhammad-Sodik, chairman of the Spiritual Administration of Muslims of Central Asia and Kazakhstan, Tashkent City. From Tashkentskiy-Kirovskiy Territorial Okrug No 598, Tashkent Oblast, Uzbek SSR.

Mukhidinov, Khayrullo Irgashevich, chief of the "Leninabadvodstroy" Trust's Mobile Mechanized Column No 34, CPSU member, Vodnik settlement, Khodzhentskiy Rayon, Leninabad Oblast. From Khodzhentskiy National-Territorial Okrug No 382, Tajik SSR.

Mukhtarov, Akhmedzhan Gulyamovich, editor of the republic newspaper KISHLOK KHAKIKATI ("Rural Truth"), CPSU member, Tashkent city. From the USSR Journalists Union.

Mukhtarov, Lyatif Ismail ogly, team leader at Tauzskiy Rayon's M.B. Kasumov Sovkhoz-Technical College, CPSU member, Kovlyar settlement, Tauzskiy Rayon. From Tauzskiy National-Territorial Okrug No 220, Azerbaijan SSR.

Mukishev, Vladimir Zhalelovich, excavator operator at the "Bogatyr" Opencut Mine of the "Ekibastuzugol" Production Association, CPSU member, Ekibastuz City. From Ekibastuzskiy Territorial Okrug No 638, Pavlodar Oblast, Kazakh SSR.

Muntyan, Mikhail Ivanovich, soloist with the A.S. Pushkin Moldavian State Academy Opera and Ballet Theater, CPSU member, Kishinev city. From the CPSU.

Muradyan, Vardanush Aramovna, worker at the Masis "Gofrotara" Factory, CPSU member, Masis settlement, Masisskiy Rayon. From Nairiyskiy National-Territorial Okrug No 411, Armenian SSR.

Muradyan, Norik Grigoryevich, first secretary of Spitak Armenian Communist Party Raykom, CPSU member, Spitak city. From Gugarkskiy National-Territorial Okrug No 398, Armenian SSR.

Murashev, Arkadiy Nikolayevich, scientific worker at the USSR Academy of Sciences High Temperature Institute, candidate CPSU member, Moscow city. From Timiryazevskiy Territorial Okrug No 24, Moscow city.

Murashov, Vladimir Konstantinovich, team leader at Seltinskiy Rayon's Lenin Kolkhoz, CPSU member, Selty village, Seltinskiy Rayon. From Uvinskiy National-Territorial Okrug No 667, Udmurt ASSR.

Muravko, Mikhail Mikhaylovich, director of the "Sozh" Sovkhoz-Combine, Gomelskiy Rayon, CPSU member, Novaya Guta Population Center. From Novobelitskiy Territorial Okrug No 556, Belorussian SSR.

Musayeva, Gyulkhanum Eyyub kyzy, milkmaid at Lerikskiy Rayon's 20th Party Congress Sovkhoz, CPSU member, Gosmolyan village, Lerikskiy Rayon. From Lenkoranskiy National-Territorial Okrug No 213, Azerbaijan SSR.

Mutalibov, Ayae Niyazi ogly, chairman of the Azerbaijan SSR Council of Ministers, CPSU member, Baku city. From Kubatlinskiy National-Territorial Okrug No 211, Azerbaijan SSR.

Muzafarov, Sabir Bakir ogly, drilling worker at the "Leninneft" Oil and Gas Extraction Administration, CPSU member, Baku city. From Bakinskiy-Leninskiy National-Territorial Okrug No 193, Azerbaijan SSR.

Mylnikov, Andrey Andreyevich, artist, faculty chief at the I.Ye. Repin Institute of Art, Sculpture, and Architecture in Leningrad. From the USSR Academy of Arts.

Mylnikov, Vladimir Vasilyevich, pensioner, CPSU member, Ternopol city, Ukrainian SSR. From the All-Union War and Labor veterans Organization.

Mysnichenko, Vladislav Petrovich, first secretary of Kharkov Ukrainian Communist Party Obkom, CPSU member, Kharkov city. From Bogodukhovskiy Territorial Okrug No 524, Kharkov Oblast, Ukrainian SSR.

Myakota, Aleksey Sergeyevich, first secretary of Poltava Ukrainian Communist Party Obkom, CPSU member, Poltava city. From Mirgorodskiy Territorial Okrug No 507, Poltava Oblast, Ukrainian SSR.

Nabiyeva, Yulduz, senior commodity expert at the Fergana Oblast Potrebsoyuz, Fergana city, Uzbek SSR. From USSR consumer cooperatives.

Nadelyuyev, Vladimir Ivanovich, chairman of the Nizhneudinskiy Rayon's Lenin Kolkhoz, CPSU member, Solontsy village, Nizhneudinskiy Rayon. From Nizhneudinskiy Territorial Okrug No 174, RSFSR.

Nagiyev, Ramazan Shamy ogly, engineer at the Azerbaijan Railroad's Dzhulfa Locomotive Depot, CPSU member, Dzhulfa city. From Dzhulfinskiy National-Territorial Okrug No 617, Nakhichevan ASSR.

Namazova, Adilya Avaz kyzy, faculty chief at the Azerbaijan Medical Institute, CPSU member, Baku city. From the women's councils united in the Soviet Women's Committee.

Napalkov, Nikolay Pavlovich, director of the Oncological Scientific Research Institute named for Professor Petrov, CPSU member, Leningrad city. From the All-Union "Znaniye" Society.

Narmatov, Begaly Yzayevich, senior shepherd at Chatkalskiy Rayon's "Kanysh-Kiya" Sovkhoz, CPSU member, Aygyr-Dzhal settlement, Chatkalskiy Rayon, Osh Oblast. From Dzhany-Dzholskiy National-Territorial Okrug No 328, Kirghiz SSR.

Naumov, Sergey Yakovlevich, chairman of Argayashskiy Rayon's "Marksist" Kolkhoz, CPSU member, Baygazina village, Argayashskiy Rayon. From Kyshtymskiy Territorial Okrug No 338, Chelyabinsk Oblast, RSFSR.

Navruzov, Sherkhonbek, team leader at Ishkashimskiy Rayon's "Vakhon" Sovkhoz, CPSU member, Darshay Kishlak, Ishkashimskiy Rayon. From Ishkashimskiy National-Territorial Okrug No 713, Gorno-Badakhshan Autonomous Oblast.

Naydenov, Nikolay Andreyevich, drift-winning team leader at the "Vorkutaugol" Production Association's "Tsentralnaya" Mine, CPSU member, Vorkuta city, Komi ASSR. From the CPSU.

Nazarbayev, Nursultan Abishevich, chairman of the Kazakh SSR Council of Ministers, CPSU member, ALma-Ata city. From Alma-Atinskiy-Iliyskiy Territorial Okrug No 617, Alma-Ata Oblast, Kazakh SSR.

Nazarenko, Arnold Filippovich, chief engineer at the "Yuzhnoye" Design Bureau, Dnepropetrovsk. From Leninskiy Territorial Okrug No 421, Dnepropetrovsk Oblast, Ukrainian SSR.

Nazarov, Ivan Aleksandrovich, first secretary of Russko-Polyanskiy CPSU Raykom, CPSU member, Russkaya Polyana settlement, Omsk Oblast, RSFSR. From the CPSU.

Nazarov, Talbak, Tajik SSR minister of public education, CPSU member, Dushanbe city. From Ordzhonikidzeabadskiy National-Territorial Okrug No 378, Tajik SSR.

Nazaryan, Spartion Yegoyevich, chairman of the "Maralik" Agricultural Firm and Kolkhoz, CPSU member, Maralik settlement, Aniyskiy Rayon, Armenian SSR. From kolkhozes united in the All-Union Kolkhoz Council.

Nechayev, Konstantin Vladimirovich, Metropolitan Pitirim of Volokolamsk and Yuryevskiy, chairman of the Moscow Patriarchate's Publications Department, Moscow city. From the Soviet Cultural Foundation.

Nechetnaya, Nadezhda Petrovna, spinning machine operator at the Lenin Factory, CPSU member, Klintsy city. From Klintsovskiy Territorial Okrug No 131, Bryansk Oblast, RSFSR.

Neduzhko, Mikhail Ivanovich, sector chief at the "Rostovoblgrazhdanstroy" Association's No 6 Construction and Installation Administration, candidate CPSU member, Taganrog city, Rostov Oblast, RSFSR. From the All-Union Komsomol.

Nefedov, Oleg Matveyevich, academician, vice president of the USSR Academy of Sciences, CPSU member, Moscow city. From the USSR Academy of Sciences.

Neff, Erika Matveyevna, milking machine operator at Ulyanovskiy Rayon's "Proletarskiy" Sovkhoz, Proletarskoye settlement, Ulyanovskiy Rayon. From Karagandinskiy-Telmanskiy National-Territorial Okrug No 143, Kazakh SSR.

Negmatulloyev, Sabit Khabibuloyevich, president of the Tajik SSR Academy of Sciences, CPSU member, Dushanbe city. From Kurgan-Tyubinskiy Territorial Okrug No 729, Tajik SSR.

Nekhayevskiy, Arkadiy Petrovich, first secretary of Vinnitsa Ukrainian Communist Party Obkom, CPSU member, Vinnitsa city. From Gaysinskiy Territorial Okrug No 405, Vinnitsa Oblast, Ukrainian SSR.

Nemkova, Lyubov Georgiyevna, flying instructor at the V.P. Chkalov USSR DOSAAF Central Flying Club, CPSU member, Moscow city. From the USSR DOSAAF.

Nemtsev, Yevgeniy Ivanovich, leader of a repair team at the "Orgtekhnika" Production Association's "Elektropribor" Plant, CPSU member, Groznyy. From Staropromyslovskiy National-Territorial Okrug No 671, Chechen-Ingush ASSR.

Nesterenko, Yevgeniy Yevgenyevich, soloist with the USSR State Academic Bolshoy Theater, professor at the P.I. Tchaikovsky Moscow State Conservatory, CPSU member, Moscow city. From the CPSU.

Nesterenko, Sergey Mikhaylovich, second secretary of the Turkmen Communist Party Central committee, CPSU member, Ashkhabad city. From Chardzhouskiy Territorial Okrug No 746, Turkmen SSR.

Neumyvakin, Aleksandr Yakovlevich, chairman of All-Russian Society for the Blind Central Board, CPSU member, Moscow city. From the Soviet Charity and Health Foundation.

Nevolin, Sergey Innokentyevich, chief physician at Novokuznetsk city Hospital No 11, CPSU member, Novokuznetsk city. From Kemerovskiy National-Territorial Okrug No 13, RSFSR.

Neyelov, Yuriy Vasilyevich, chairman of Surgutskiy Rayispolkom, CPSU member, Surgut city. From Surgutskiy Territorial Okrug No 325, Tyumen Oblast, RSFSR.

Neyland, Nikolay Vasilyevich, Latvian SSR deputy foreign minister, CPSU member, Riga city. From Darztsiyemskiy National-Territorial Okrug No 292, Riga city.

Nivalov, Nikolay Nikolayevich, first secretary of Chernovtsy Ukrainian Communist Party Obkom, CPSU member, Chernovtsy city. From Storozhinetskiy Territorial Okrug No 546, Chernovtsy Oblast, Ukrainian SSR.

Nikanorov, Igor Alekseyevich, lathe operator at Ryazan Machine Tool Plant, CPSU member, Ryazan city, RSFSR. From the All-Union Komsomol.

Nikitin, Vladilen Valentinovich, first deputy chairman of the RSFSR Gosagroprom, RSFSR minister, CPSU member, Moscow city. From Priozerniy National-Territorial Okrug No 553, Kalmyk ASSR.

Nikitin, Rudolf Ivanovich, general director of "Izotop" Production Association, CPSU member, Yoshkar-Ola city. From Zavodskiy National-Territorial Okrug No 593, Mari ASSR.

Nikishin, Nikolay Petrovich, machine operator at the kolkhoz named for the 50th anniversary of the Ukrainian Communist Party, CPSU member, Chuginka village, Stanichno-Luganskiy Rayon, Voroshilovgrad Oblast, Ukrainian SSR. From the kolkhozes united in the Union Kolkhoz Council.

Nikolayev, Aleksandr Aleksandrovich, chairman of the Yukhnovskiy Rayon's "45 Let Oktyabrya" Kolkhoz, Kaluga Oblast, CPSU member, Shchelkanovo village, Yukhnovskiy Rayon. From Smolenskiy National-Territorial Okrug No 27, RSFSR.

Nikolayev, Vasiliy Vasilyevich, employee at Sterlitamak "Kaustik" Production Association, CPSU member, Sterlitamak city,. From Meleuzovskiy National-Territorial Okrug No 509, Bashkir ASSR.

Nikolayenko, Anatoliy Fedorovich, chief of a mechanized brigade at Chaplinskiy Rayon's "Rossiya" Kolkhoz, CPSU member, Novonatalovka village, Chaplinskiy Rayon, Kherson Oblast. From Khersonskiy National-Territorial Okrug No 60, Ukrainian SSR.

Nikolaychuk, Vadim Fedorovich, director of Norilsk A.P. Zavenyagin Mining and Metallurgical Combine "Zapolyarnyy" Mine, CPSU member, Norilsk city. From Norilskiy Territorial Okrug No 95, Krasnoyarsk Kray, RSFSR.

Nikolskiy, Boris Vasilyevich, second secretary of the Georgian Communist Party Central Committee, CPSU member, Tbilisi city. From Rustavskiy Territorial Okrug No 667, Georgian SSR.

Nikonov, Aleksandr Aleksandrovich, president of VASKHNIL, deputy chairman of the USSR Gosagroprom, CPSU member, Moscow city. From VASKHNIL.

Nikonov, Viktor Petrovich, member of the CPSU Central Committee Politburo, secretary of the CPSU Central Committee, CPSU member, Moscow city. From the CPSU.

Nimbuyev, Tsyren, general chairman of the "Mogoytuyskoye" Agro-Industrial Association, CPSU member, Mogoytuy settlement. From Aginskiy Buryatskiy National-Territorial Okrug No 741, Aginskiy Buryatskiy Autonomous Okrug.

Nishanov, Rafik Nishanovich, first secretary of the Uzbek Communist Party Central Committee, CPSU member, Tashkent city. From Leningradskiy National-Territorial Okrug No 123 Uzbek SSR.

Niyazov, Dzhumamrat Yagmurovich, driver at Chardzhou Oblast Potrebsoyuz Service Station, CPSU member, Chardzhou city, Turkmen SSR. From the USSR Consumer Cooperatives.

Niyazov, Saparmurad Atayevich, first secretary of the Turkmen Communist Party Central Committee, CPSU member, Ashkhabad city. From Ashkhabadskiy Rural Territorial Okrug No 741, Turkmen SSR.

Norikhin, Vladimir Aleksandrovich, radio equipment controller at "Elektropribor" Plant, CPSU member, Vladimir city, RSFSR. From the All-Union Komsomol.

Noroyan, Ashot Gaykovich, machine operator and teamleader at "Artiktuf" Production Association facing slab workshop, CPSU member, Artik city. From Artikskiy National-Territorial Okrug No 402, Armenian SSR.

Nosov, Konstantin Grigoryevich, general director of the V.I. Lenin "Krivorozhstal" Metallurgical Combine, CPSU member, Krivoy Rog city. From Dzerzhinskiy Territorial Okrug No 426, Dnepropetrovsk Oblast, Ukrainian SSR.

Nosov, Vavil Petrovich, chief of the machine repair workshop at Ust-Tsilemskiy Rayon's "Tsilemskiy" Sovkhoz, CPSU member, Trusovo village. From Nizhnepechorskiy National-Territorial Okrug No 586, Komi ASSR.

Novikov, Grigoriy Fedorovich, sector chief at an electronic equipment production association, CPSU member, Votkinsk City. From Votkinskiy National-Territorial Okrug No 662, Udmurt ASSR.

Novikov, Vladimir Mikhaylovich, chairman of Tuzha Interfarm Construction Organization, CPSU member, Tuzha settlement. From Sovetskiy Territorial Okrug No 201, Kirov Oblast, RSFSR.

Novikov, Yevgeniy Fedorovich, chairman of Dubovskiy Rayon's kolkhoz named for the 50th anniversary of the USSR, CPSU member, Olenye village, Dubovskiy Rayon, Volgograd Oblast, RSFSR. From the kolkozes united by the Union Kolkhoz Council.

Novikov, Igor Georgiyevich, miner at "Donetskugol" Production Association Ye.T. Abakumov Mine clearing pit face, Donetsk city, Ukrainian SSR. From the All-Union Komsomol.

Novozhilov, Genrikh Vasilyevich, general designer at Moscow's S.V. Ilyushin Machine Building Plant, CPSU member, Moscow city. From the CPSU.

Nozdrya, Viktor Alekseyevich, leader of a team of fitters and installattion workers at the "S. Ordzhonikidze Sevastopolskiy Morskoy Zavod" Production Association, CPSU member, Sevastopol city. From Sevastopolskiy Territorial Okrug No 484, Crimean Oblast, Ukrainian SSR.

Nugis, Yulo Iokhannesovich, general director of "Estoplast" Production Association, CPSU member, Tallinn city. From Tallinnskiy-Leninskiy National-Territorial Okrug No 449, Estonian SSR.

Nuzhnyy, Vladimir Pavlovich, lease collective leader at Apanasenkovskiy Rayon's "Rossiya" Kolkhoz and Breeding Plant, CPSU member, Manychskoye village, Apanasenkovskiy Rayon. From Ipatovskiy Territorial Okrug No 105, Stavropol Kray, RSFSR.

Nurm, Khasso Erikovich, engineer at "Estagrostroy" Republic Association, CPSU member, Tallinn city. From Tallinnskiy-Oktyabrskiy National-Territorial Okrug No 455, Estonian SSR.

Nyrkov, Anatoliy Ivanovich, machine setter at Ordzhonikidze Glass Works, Ordzhonikidze city. From Kosta-Khetagurovskiy National-Territorial Okrug No 625, North Osetian AsSR.

Nyuksha, Konstantin Ivanovich, fitter and tool maker at "Rizhskiy Elektromashinostroitelnyy Zavod" Production Association, CPSU member, Riga city. From the CPSU.

Obolenskiy, Aleksandr Mitrofanovich, design engineer at the USSR Academy of Sciences Kola Scientific Center's Polar Geophysic Institute, Apatity City, Murmansk Oblast. From Leningradskiy Rural National-Territorial Okrug No 20, RSFSR.

Oborin, Anatoliy Vasilyevich, chairman of Kozmodemyansk city People's Court, CPSU member, Kozmodemyansk city. From Gornomariyskiy National-Territorial Okrug No 596, Mari ASSR.

Oborok, Konstantin Mikhaylovich, chairman of the Nisporenskiy Settlement Ispolkom, CPSU member, Varzareshty village, Nisporenskiy Rayon. From Ungenskiy Territorial Okrug No 705, Moldavian SSR.

Obraz, Vasiliy Sidorovich, pensioner, CPSU member, Poltava city, Ukrainian SSR. From the All-Union Organization of Veterans of War and Labor.

Obraztsov, Ivan Filippovich, RSFSR minister of higher and secondary special education, CPSU member, Moscow city. From the All-Union "Znaniye" Society.

Ochirov, Valeriy Nikolayevich, colonel, air force regiment commander, CPSU member. From Universitetskiy National-Territorial Okrug No 548, Kalmyk ASSR.

Ochirov, Vasiliy Mandzhiyevich, senior shepherd at the "Gashunskiy" sovkhoz, CPSU member, Gashun settlement, Yashkulskiy Rayon. From Yashkulskiy National-Territorial Okrug No 557, Kalmyk ASSR.

Odzhiyev, Rizoali Kadamshoyevich, deputy chairman of the "Internatsionalist" Cooperative Association, Dushanbe city. From the All-Union Komsomol.

Oganesyan, Myasnik Vaganovich, teamleader at Akhalkalakskiy Rayon's Chamdzvrala Livestock Farming Sovkhoz, CPSU member, Chamdzvrala village, Akhalkalakskiy Rayon. From Akhalkalakskiy National-Territorial Okrug No 168, Georgian SSR.

Oganesyan, Rafik Gevorkovich, stone mason at "Lenstroy" Trust No 46 Construction Administration, Leninakan city. From Leninakanskiy-Moskovskiy National-Territorial Okrug No 395, Armenian SSR.

Oganesyan, Samvel Vidokovich, coordinator at "Razdanmash" Production Association instrument shop, CPSU member, Kakhsi village, Razdanskiy Rayon. From Razdanskiy National-Territorial Okrug No 413, Armenian SSR.

Oganesyan, Edgar Sergeyevich, composer, rector of Yerevan's Komitas State Conservatoire, CPSU member, Yerevan city. From Yerevanskiy-Spandaryanskiy Territorial Okrug No 733, Armenian SSR.

Ogarok, Valentin Ivanovich, first deputy chairman of the Uzbek SSR Council of Ministers, CPSU member, Tashkent city. From Karshinskiy Territorial Okrug No 581, Kashka-Darya Oblast, Uzbek SSR.

Okeyev, Tolomush Okeyevich, director and producer at "Kirghizfilm" Movie Studio, CPSU member, Frunze city. From the USSR Union of Cinema Workers.

Oleynik, Boris Ilich, poet, secretary of the Ukrainian SSR Writers Union Board, CPSu member, Kiev city. From the CPSU.

Olekas, Yuozas Yuozovich, senior scientific staffer at Vilnius State University Microsurgery Problems Institute, Vilnius city. From Vilkavishkskiy National-Territorial Okrug No 233, Lithuanian SSR.

Omelichev, Bronislav Aleksandrovich, colonel general, first deputy chief of the USSR Armed Forces General Staff, CPSU member, Moscow city. From Iolotanskiy National-Territorial Okrug No 428, Turkmen SSR.

Omelyanenko, Konstantin Sergeyevich, chairman of Volnovakhskiy Rayon's "Rossiya" Kolkhoz, Zlatoustovka village. From Volnovakhskiy Territorial Okrug No 435, Ukrainian SSR.

Oplanchuk, Vladimir Yakovlevich, director of Leninabadskiy Mining and Chemical Combine, CPSU member, Chkalovsk city. From Kayrakkumskiy National-Territorial Okrug No 365, Tajik SSR.

Opolinskiy, Vladimir Aleksandrovich, teamleader at Chernomorskiy Ship Building Plant, CPSU member, Nikolayev city, Ukrainian SSR. From the USSR trade unions.

Oragvelidze, Roman Titevich, fitter and assmbler at Tbilisi Tool Making Production Association, CPSU member, Tbilisi city. From the USSR trade unions.

Orazbayev, Amangeldi, teamleader at Kungradskiy Rayon's Chapayev Sovkhoz, CPSU member, Kungradskiy Rayon, Karakalpak ASSR. From Nukusskiy National-Territorial Okrug No 128, Uzbek SSR.

Orazberdiyev, Abdyrakhman, first secretary of Turkmen Communist Party Karakumskiy Raykom, CPSU member, Yagty-Yel settlement, Karakumskiy Rayon, Mari Oblast. From Karakumskiy National-Territorial Okrug No 431, Turkmen SSR.

Orazliyev, Meretgeldy, painters team leader at specialized small-scale mechanization administration of the "Turkmentsentrostroy" Construction Administration's Construction Department, CPSU member, Ashkhabad City. From Ashkhabadskiy Territorial Okrug No 740, Turkmen SSR.

Orazov, Kurban Muradovich, first secretary of the Turkmen Communist Party Mari Obkom, CPSU member, Mari city. From Sakar-Chaginskiy National-Territorial Okrug No 440, Turkmen SSR.

Orekhov, Anatoliy Pavlovich, chairman of Karymskiy Rayispolkom, CPSU member, Karymskoye settlement, Karymskiy Rayon. From Chitinskiy Rural Territorial Okrug No 343, Chita Oblast, RSFSR.

Oripov, Abdulla, writer, secretary of the Uzbek Writers Union Board, CPSU member, Tashkent city. From Tashkentskiy-Khamzinskiy National-Territorial Okrug No 115, Uzbek SSR.

Orlik, Mariya Andreyevna, deputy chairman of the Ukrainian SSR Council of Ministers, CPSU member, Kiev city. From the women's councils united in the Soviet Women's Committee.

Orlov, Aleksandr Kondratyevich, director of the Chelyabinsk branch of the N.M. Shvernik Trade Union Movement Higher School, CPSU member, Chelyabinsk City. From Leninskiy Territorial Okrug No 332, RSFSR.

Orlov, Vladimir Mikhaylovich, director of the "Lipovaya Gora" Academic Experimental Farm, CPSU member, Perm city. From Motovilikhinskiy Territorial Okrug No 257, Perm Oblast, RSFSR.

Orozova, Umtul Sheysheyevna, chairman of the Kirghiz SSR State Committee for Television and Radio Broadcasting, CPSU member, Frunze city. From the women's councils united in the Soviet Women's Committee.

Orunbekova, Begaim Madanbekovna, milkmaid at Suzakskiy Rayon's Oktyabrskiy Viticultural Sovkhoz Combine, CPSU member, Frunze village, Suzakskiy Rayon, Osh Oblast. From Suzakskiy National-Territorial Okrug No 343, Kirghiz SSR.

Osipov, Anatoliy Konstantinovich, secretary of the party committee of the N.P. Ogarev Mordovian State University, CPSU member, Saransk city. From Leninskiy National-Territorial Okrug No 602, Mordovian ASSR.

Osipov, Vladimir Vasilyevich, colonel general, CPSU member, Moscow city. From Benderskiy Territorial Okrug No 698, Moldavian SSR.

Osipov, Prokopiy Dmitriyevich, secretary of the party committee of the Vilyusk Hydroelectric Power Station, CPSU member, Chernyshevskiy settlement, Mirninskiy Rayon. From Mirninskiy National-Territorial Okrug No 696, Yakutsk ASSR.

Osipyan, Yuriy Andreyevich, academician, vice president of the USSR Academy of Sciences, director of the USSR Academy of Sciences Solid-State Physics Institute, member of the CPSU, Moscow city. From the USSR Academy of Sciences.

Oskin, Anatoliy Dmitryevich, director of the "Ukhtales" Production Association's Sosnogorsk Logging Combine, CPSU member, Sosnogorsk City. From Sosnogorskiy National-Territorial Okrug No 587, Komi ASSR.

Ostrozhinskiy, Valentin Yevgenyevich, first secretary of the Ternopol Ukrainian Communist Party Obkom, CPSU member, Ternopol city. From Chortkovskiy Territorial Okrug No 518, Ternopol Oblast, Ukrainian SSR.

Ostroukhov, Viktor Alekseyevich, secretary of the "Sibkabel" production association party committee, CPSU member, Tomsk city, RSFSR. From the CPSU.

Otarashvili, Guram Zakharyevich, leader of a leaseholder team of viticulturalists, Kurdgelaurskiy Kolkhoz, Telavskiy Rayon, CPSU member, Kurdgelauri village, Telavskiy Rayon. From Telavskiy National-Territorial Okrug No 187, Georgian SSR.

Otsason, Reyn Augustovich, deputy chairman of the Estonian SSR Council of Ministers, chairman of the Estonian SSR Gosplan, CPSU member, Tallinn city. From Valgaskiy National-Territorial Okrug No 458, Estonian SSR.

Ovezgeldyyev, Orazgeldy, president of the Turkmen SSR Academy of Sciences, CPSU member, Ashkhabad city. From Kalininskiy National-Territorial Okrug No 430, Turkmen SSR.

Ovchinnikov, Aleksandr Ivanovich, lieutenant general, Military Council member, chief of the Turkestan Military District Political Directorate, CPSU member, Tashkent city. From Chirchikskiy National-Territorial Okrug No 120, Uzbek SSR.

Ovchinnikov, Aleksandr Nikolayevich, director of Kineshma "Elektrokontakt" Plant, CPSU member, Kineshma city. From Kineshemskiy Territorial Okrug No 168, Ivanovo Oblast, RSFSR.

Ovchinnikov, Vladimir Petrovich, repairman at the Altay Units Plant, CPSU member, Barnaul City. From Barnaulskiy Territorial Okrug No 66, RSFSR.

Oyun, Vadim Orambalovich, director of the "Pobeda" sovkhoz, Kyzylskiy Rayon, CPSU member, Tselinnoye village, Kyzylskiy Rayon. From Kyzylskiy Rural National-Territorial Okrug No 651, Tuva ASSR.

Ozolas, Romualdas Alfredovich, deputy editor in chief of "Mintis" Publishing House, CPSU member, Vilnius city. From Shyaulyayskiy Rural National-Territorial Okrug No 256, Lithuanian SSR.

Ozolinsh, Leonid Alfredovich, senior scientific staffer at the Latvian Traumatology and Orthopedics Research Institute, Yurmala city. From Leninskiy National-Territorial Okrug No 289, Latvian SSR.

Pal, Oskar Maksimovich, director of the "Sovetskaya" agricultural firm, Vozvyshenskiy Rayon, CPSU member, Sovetskoye village, Vozvyshenskiy Rayon. From Petropavlovskiy Rural Territorial Okrug No 640, North Kazakhstan Oblast, Kazakh SSR.

Palagnyuk, Boris Timofeyevich, director of the pedigree poultry breeding sovkhoz named for the 60th anniversary of the USSR, Rybnitskiy Rayon, CPSU member, Rybnitsa city. From Rybnitskiy National-Territorial Okrug No 278, Moldavian SSR.

Palchin, Semen Yakovlevich, director of the "Tukhard" sovkhoz, Ust-Yeniseyskiy Rayon, CPSU member, Tukhard settlement, Ust-Yeniseyeskiy Rayon. From Taymyrskiy National-Territorial Okrug No 745, Taymyrsk (Dolgako-Nenetsk) Autonomous Okrug.

Paldzhyan, Vazgen Abramovich, Supreme Patriarch, Catholicos of All Armenia Vazgen I, Echmiadzin city. From Echmiadzinskiy Territorial Okrug No 739, Armenian SSR.

Pallayev, Gaibnazar, chairman of the Tajik SSR Supreme Soviet Presidium, CPSU member, Dushanbe city. From Vakhskiy National-Territorial Okrug No 358, Tajik SSR.

Palm, Viktor Alekseyevich, department chief at Tartu State University, CPSU member, Tartu city. From Keylaskiy National-Territorial Okrug No 464, Estonian SSR.

Paltyshev, Nikolay Nikolayevich, chairman of the No 1 secondary vocational and technical college, CPSU member, Odessa city, Ukrainian SSR. From USSR Academy of Pedagogical Sciences jointly with the Soviet Association of Pedagogical Research Workers.

Pamfilova, Ella Aleksandrovna, chairman of the trade union committee at the "Mosenergo" production association's central mechanical repair plant, CPSU member, Moscow city. From the USSR trade unions.

Panasenko, Taras Ivanovich, first secretary of the Rovno Ukrainian Communist Party Obkom, CPSU member, Rovno city. From Dubnovskiy Territorial Okrug No 510, Rovno Oblast, Ukrainian SSR.

Panov, Ivan Mitrofanovich, chief editor of KRASNAYA ZVEZDA, CPSU member, Moscow city. From the USSR Journalists' Union.

Panov, Nikolay Nikolayevich, commander of an An-26 at the Pskov Combined Air Detachment, Pskov City. From Pskovskiy Territorial Okrug No 264, RSFSR.

Panteleyev, Nikolay Vasilyevich, lathe operator at the Kirov Lepse electrical machine building plant, CPSU member, Kirov city, RSFSR. From the USSR trade unions.

Pantykin, Viktor Pavlovich, chairman of the kolkhoz XXII Sezda KPSS, Suzdalskiy Rayon, CPSU member, Novoye village, Suzdalskiy Rayon. From Kolchuginskiy Territorial Okrug No 136, Vladimir Oblast, RSFSR.

Panchenko, Emiliya Andreyevna, section chief of the "Ukrainian state museum of the history of the 1941-1945 Great Patriotic War" memorial complex, CPSU member, Kiev city. From the All-Union Organization of War and Labor Veterans.

Paplevchenkov, Ivan Mikhaylovich, chairman of the "Krasnyy Putilovets" kolkhoz, Kashinskiy Rayon, CPSU member, Kashin city, Kalinin Oblast, RSFSR. From the kolkhozes united in the Union Kolkhoz Council.

Parachev, Valentin Petrovich, chairman of the Ulyanova Kolkhoz, Trubchevskiy Rayon, CPSU member, Yurovo village, Trubchevskiy Rayon. From Pochepskiy Territorial Okrug No 132, Bryansk Oblast, RSFSR.

Parubok, Yemelyan Nikonovich, link leader at the Suvorova Kolkhoz, CPSU member, Bashtechki village, Zhashkovskiy Rayon, Cherkassy Oblast, Ukrainian SSR. From the CPSU.

Parusnikov, Vladimir Alekseyevich, leader of a team of tool makers at the Omsk television plant, CPSU member, Omsk city, RSFSR. From the USSR trade unions.

Pasha-zade, Allakhshukyur Gummat ogly, Sheykh-ul-islam, chairman of the Spiritual Administration of Muslims of the Transcaucasus, Baku city. From Negramskiy National-Territorial Okrug No 621, Nakhichevan ASSR.

Pashaly, Mikhail Konstantinovich, chairman of the Chadyr-Lungskiy Rayon agro-industrial association, CPSU member, Chadyr-Lunga city. From Chadyr-Lungskiy National-Territorial Okrug No 287, Moldavian SSR.

Pashyan, Stepa Andranikovich, radio apparatus regulator at the Abovyan "Izmeritel" plant, CPSU member, Abovyan city. From Abovyanskiy National-Territorial Okrug No 399, Armenian SSR.

Pastorov, Ivan Ivanovich, director of the "Uralets" sovkhoz-technical college, Vereshchaginskiy Rayon, CPSU member, Zyukayka settlement, Vereshchaginskiy Rayon. From Kudymkarskiy Territorial Okrug No 260, Perm Oblast, RSFSR.

Patiashvili, Dzhumber Ilich, first secretary of the Georgian Communist Party Central Committee, CPSU member, Tbilisi city. From Tbilisskiy-Pervomayskiy Territorial Okrug No 655, Georgian SSR.

Patrakhin, Aleksandr Aleksandrovich, department chief of the Moskovskiy central rayon hospital, CPSU member, Belovodskoye village. From Moskovskiy National-Territorial Okrug No 337, Kirghiz SSR.

Paton, Boris Yevgenyevich, president of the Ukrainian SSR Academy of Sciences, director of the Ye.O. Paton Institute of Electric Welding, general director of the Ukrainian SSR Academy of Sciences "Ye.O. Paton Institute of Electric Welding" intersectorial scientific and technical complex, CPSU member, Kiev city. From the CPSU.

Patsalyuk, Mikhail Prokofyevich, chairman of the "Druzhba" kolkhoz, Kitsmanskiy Rayon, CPSU member, Brusnitsa village, Kitsmanskiy Rayon, Chernovitsy Oblast, Ukrainian SSR. From the kolkhozes united in the Union Kolkhoz Council.

Patsatsiya, Otari Ambakovich, general director of the "Gruzbumprom" production association, Zugdidi city, CPSU member, Inguri village, Zugdidskiy Rayon. From Zugdidskiy National-Territorial Okrug No 176, Georgian SSR.

Pauls, Raymond Voldemarovich, composer, chairman of the Latvian SSR State Committee for Culture, Riga City. From Liyepayskiy City National-Territorial Okrug No 306, Latvian SSR.

Pavlenko, Leonid Ivanovich, first secretary of the Volyn Ukrainian Communist Party Obkom, CPSU member, Lutsk city. From Lutskiy Territorial Okrug No 410, Volyn Oblast, Ukrainian SSR.

Pavlenko, Viktor Pavlovich, director of the "Maslovskiy" State Stud Farm, Novousmanskiy Rayon, CPSU member, Novousmanskiy Rayon, Voronezh Oblast. From Semilukskiy Territorial Okrug No 155, Voronezh Oblast, RSFSR.

Pavlevich, Ivan Borisovich, leader of the Kamenetsk-Podolskiy housing operation association trade union committee's "Desantnik" military sports and patriotic club, CPSU member, Kamenetsk-Podolskiy city. From Kamenetsk-Podolskiy Territorial Okrug No 533, Khmelnitskiy Oblast, Ukrainian SSR.

Pavliashvili, Zoya Alekseyevna, kolkhoz member at Kheltubani village kolkhoz, Goriyskiy Rayon. CPSU member, Tartiza village, Goriyskiy Rayon. From Goriyskiy Territorial Okrug No 661, Georgian SSR.

Pavliy, Aleksandr Andreyevich, senior consultant of the Donetsk Oblispolkom, CPSU member, Donetsk city, Ukrainian SSR. From All-Union Organization of War and Labor Veterans.

Pavlov, Aleksandr Sergeyevich, CPSU Central Committee department chief, CPSU member, Moscow city. From Bukinskiy Territorial Okrug No 602, Tashkent Oblast, Uzbek SSR.

Pavlov, Anatoliy Vasilyevich, lathe operator at the Kungur Machine-Building Plant, CPSU member, Kungur City, Perm Oblast. From Kungurskiy Territorial Okrug No 261, Perm Oblast, RSFSR.

Pavlov, Vladimir Aleksandrovich, smith and stamp operator at the "Novocherkasskiy elektrovozostroitelnyy zavod" production association, Novocherkassk city, Rostov Oblast, RSFSR. From the USSR trade unions.

Payziyev, Duysenbay, leader of a team of tunnelers at the "Achpolimetall" combine "Ansay" mine, CPSU member, Kentau city. From Turkestanskiy Territorial Okrug No 652, Chimkent Oblast, Kazakh SSR.

Payshchikov, Vyacheslav Vasilyevich, chairman of the Gorkiy Obkom of the trade union of ship building industry workers, CPSU member, Gorkiy city, RSFSR. From the USSR trade unions.

Pchelka, Nikolay Fedorovich, cylinder-packaging machine operator at the "Tomlesprom" production association's Komsomolsk timber facility, CPSU member, Komsomolsk settlement, Pervomayskiy Rayon, Tomsk Oblast, RSFSR. From the USSR trade unions.

Pegarkov, Nikolay Grigoryevich, chairman of the "Velikiy Oktyabr" kolkhoz, CPSU member, Khokholskiy Urban settlement, Voronezh Oblast, RSFSR. From the All-Union Organization of War and Labor Veterans.

Penyagin, Aleksandr Nikolayevich, refractory maker at the Chelyabinsk electrometallurgy combine, CPSU candidate member, Chelyabinsk city. From Metallurgicheskiy Territorial Okrug No 333, Chelyabinsk Oblast, RSFSR.

Perelygina, Lyudmila Fedorovna, chairman of the Ukrainian Republican Committee of the trade union of cultural workers, CPSU member, Kiev city. From the USSR trade unions.

Pershilin, Konstantin Georgiyevich, director of the Novosibirsk agricultural institute's "Tulinskoye" training and experimental farm, CPSU member, Tulinskiy settlement, Novosibirskiy Rayon, Novosibirsk Oblast, RSFSR. From the USSR trade unions.

Pershin, Andrey Leonidovich, excavator operator at the Kungradskiy Rayon production repair and operation association, Kungrad city. From Kungradskiy National-Territorial Okrug No 561, Karakalpak ASSR.

Peters, Yanis Yanovich, writer, chairman of the board of the Latvian SSR Writers Union, CPSU member, Riga city. From Valmiyerskiy National-Territorial Okrug No 299, Latvian SSR.

Petkel, Vladimir Viktorovich, chairman of the Tajik SSR KGB, CPSU member, Dushanbe city. From Murgabskiy National-Territorial Okrug No 714, Gorno-Badakhshan Autonomous Oblast.

Petrakov, Nikolay Yakovlevich, deputy director of the USSR Academy of Sciences Central Economics and Mathematics Institute, CPSU member, Moscow City. From the USSR Academy of Sciences.

Petrenko, Anatoliy Filippovich, general director of the "Vladimirmebel" veneer furniture production association, CPSU member, Vladimir city. From Vladimirskiy Territorial Okrug No 133, Vladimir Oblast, RSFSR.

Petrov, Aleksandr Petrovich, first secretary of the Chuvash CPSU Obkom, CPSU member, Cheboksary city. From Kanashskiy Territorial Okrug No 400, Chuvash ASSR.

Petrov, Andrey Pavlovich, composer, chairman of the board of the Leningrad composers' organization of the RSFSR Composers Union, CPSU member, Leningrad city. From the USSR Composers' Union.

Petrov, Nikifor Nikolayevich, director of the sovkhoz named for the 50th anniversary of the USSR, Srednekolymskiy Rayon, CPSU member, Srednekolymsk city. From Kolymskiy National-Territorial Okrug No 696, Yakutsk ASSR.

Petrova, Lyudmila Nikolayevna, general director of the "Niva Stavropolya" Science-and-Production Association, CPSU member, Stavropol city, RSFSR. From Vaskhnil.

Petrova, Raisiya Arkadyevna, party organization secretary on the "Bolshevik" Kolkhoz, Sovetskiy Rayon, CPSU member, Lyupersola village, Sovetskiy Rayon, Mari ASSR. From the women's councils united in the Soviet Women's Committee.

Petrukovich, Aleksey Stepanovich, instrument building plant fitter and pattern maker, CPSU member, Izyum city, Kharkov Oblast, Ukrainian SSR. From the All-Union Organization of War and Labor Veterans.

Petrushenko, Nikolay Semenovich, lieutenant colonel, propaganda and agitation instructor in a military unit political department, Central Asian Military District, CPSU member, East Kazakhstan Oblast. From Leninogorskiy Territorial Okrug No 622, East Kazakhstan Oblast, Kazakh SSR.

Pfeyfer, Aleksandr Genrikhovich, lease team leader at the "Iskra" sovkhoz, CPSU member, Sovet settlement, Akbulakskiy Rayon, Orenburg Oblast, RSFSR. From the USSR consumers cooperatives.

Pichuzhkin, Mikhail Sergeyevich, permanent representative of the Ukrainian SSR Council of Ministers to the USSR Council of Ministers, CPSU member, Moscow city. From Pervomayskiy Territorial Okrug No 496, Nikolayev Oblast, Ukrainian SSR.

Pilipets, Ivan Nikolayevich, chairman of the "Pravda" Kolkhoz, Koropskiy Rayon, CPSU member, Atyusha village, Koropskiy Rayon, Chernigov Oblast, Ukrainian SSR. From the kolkhozes united in the Union Kolkhoz Council.

Pilnikov, Stanislav Vasilyevich, teacher at the No 1 secondary school, CPSU member, Pitkyaranta city. From Olonetskiy National-Territorial Okrug No 576, Karelian ASSR.

Pirnazarov, Rozygeldy, chief of a department at the Chardzhou Oblast Ophthalmological Hospital, Chardzhou City. From Chardzhouskiy City National-Territorial Okrug No 446, Turkmen SSR.

Pirov, Makhmaruzi, Kurgan-Tyube Oblast Hospital chief of department, "Navruz" Sovkhoz, Vakhshskiy Rayon. From Kurgan-Tyubinskiy National-Territorial Okrug No 371, Tajik SSR.

Pirtskhalaishvili, Zurab Georgiyevich, lathe operator at the Tbilisi electrical railroad car repair plant, CPSU member, Tbilisi city. From Tbilisskiy-Leninskiy National-Territorial Okrug No 161, Georgian SSR.

Piryazeva, Nina Mikhaylovna, electrical assembly worker at Novosibirsk's "Sibselmash" Production Association, Novosibirsk city. From Leninskiy Territorial Okrug No 229, Novosibirsk Oblast, RSFSR.

Pisanets, Viktor Alekseyevich, machine operator on the "Zarya" Kolkhoz, Veselovskiy Rayon, CPSU member, Zaporozhye village, Veselovskiy Rayon. From Vasilyevskiy Territorial Okrug No 458, Zaporozhye Oblast, Ukrainian SSR.

Pisarenko, Viktor Andreyevich, colonel, first deputy chief of the Siberian Military District Air Force Political Department, CPSU member, Novosibirsk city. From Kamenskiy Territorial Okrug No 69, Altay Kray, RSFSR.

Piskunovich, Georgiy Petrovich, machine operator on the "Geroy Truda" Kolkhoz, Glubokskiy Rayon, Derkovshchina village, Glubokskiy Rayon. From Glubokskiy Territorial Okrug No 552, Vitebsk Oblast, Belorussian SSR.

Pivovarov, Nikolay Dmitriyevich, chairman of the Rostov Oblispolkom, CPSU member, Rostov-na-Donu city. From Kamenskiy Territorial Okrug No 272, Rostov Oblast, RSFSR.

Plamadyala, Anna Andreyevna, chief of the Novoanenskiy Rayon Potrebsoyuz Speyskiy rural consumer cooperative store, Pugacheny village, Novoanenskiy Rayon, Moldavian SSR. From the USSR trade unions.

Platon, Semen Ivanovich, chairman of the Kagul Gorispolkom, CPSU member, Kagul city. From Kagulskiy National-Territorial Okrug No 268, Moldavian SSR.

Platonov, Vladimir Petrovich, academician, president of the Belorussian SSR Academy of Sciences, CPSU member, Minsk city. From the USSR Academy of Sciences.

Platonov, Yuriy Pavlovich, architect, first secretary of the USSR Architects' Union Board, CPSU member, Moscow city. From the USSR Architects' Union.

Pletenetskiy, Dmitriy Yefimovich, director of the "Paspaulskiy" Sovkhoz, Choyskiy Rayon, CPSU member, Paspaul village, Choyskiy Rayon. From Mayminskiy National-Territorial Okrug No 707, Gorno-Altay Autonomous Oblast.

Plekhanov, Aleksandr Nikolayevich, first secretary of the Kurgan CPSU Obkom, CPSU member, Kurgan city. From Lebyazhyevskiy Territorial Okrug No 214, Kurgan Oblast, RSFSR.

Plotnieks, Andris Adamovich, professor at the Latvian State University named for P. Stuchka, CPSU member, Riga city. From Yelgavskiy National-Territorial Okrug No 304, Latvian SSR.

Plotnikov, Andrey Leonidovich, foreman at the Kirovocherepetsk mechanical repairs plant, Kirov Oblast, Kirovocherepetsk city, RSFSR. From the All-Union Komsomol.

Plyutinskiy, Vladimir Antonovich, chairman of the "Zarya" Agrifirm's "Zarya kommunizma" Kolkhoz, Rovenskiy Rayon, CPSU member, Zorya village, Rovenskiy Rayon, Rovno Oblast, Ukrainian SSR. From the kolkhozes united in the Union Kolkhoz Council.

Podberezskiy, Grigoriy Nikolayevich, director of the No 2 large-panel housing construction plant of the Minsk industrial housing construction production association named for the 50th anniversary of the USSR, CPSU member, Minsk city. From Minskiy-Frunzenskiy National-Territorial Okrug No 67, Belorussian SSR.

Podobayev, Sergey Aleksandrovich, general director of the "Tikhinich" Agrifirm, Rogachevskiy Rayon, CPSU member, Tikhinichi village, Rogachesvskiy Rayon. From Zhlobinskiy Territorial Okrug No 557, Gomel Oblast, Belorussian SSR.

Podolskiy, Yevgeniy Mikhaylovich, first secretary of the Tambov CPSU Obkom, CPSU member, Tambov city. From Rasskazovskiy Territorial Okrug No 311, Tambov Oblast, RSFSR.

Podolyanina, Yelena Ivanovna, chairman of the kolkhoz named for Zhdanov, CPSU member, Zhdanovo village, Shargorodskiy Rayon, Vinnitsa Oblast, Ukrainian SSR. From the kolkhozes united in the Union Kolkhoz Council.

Podziruk, Viktor Semenovich, lieutenant colonel, senior instructor, navigator-researcher in a military unit, CPSU member, Ivanovo Oblast. From Ivanovskiy National-Territorial Okrug No 9, RSFSR.

Pogorelov, Vladimir Grigoryevich, director of the sovkhoz named for the 26th CPSU Congress, Nikolayevskiy Rayon, CPSU member, Stepovoye village, Nikolayevskiy Rayon, Nikolayev Oblast. From Nikolayevskiy National-Territorial Okrug No 52, Ukrainian SSR.

Pogosyan, Genrikh Andreyevich, pensioner, CPSU member, Stepanakert city. From Stepanakertskiy National-Territorial Okrug No 726, NKAO.

Pokhitaylo, Yevgeniy Dmitriyevich, first secretary of the Omsk CPSU Obkom, CPSU member, Omsk city. From Tarskiy Territorial Okrug No 242, Omsk Oblast, RSFSR.

Pokhodnya, Grigoriy Semenovich, shop chief of the Frunze kolkhoz, Belgorodskiy Rayon, CPSU member, Bessonovka village, Belgorodskiy Rayon, Belgorod Oblast, RSFSR. From the CPSU.

Pokrovskiy, Boris Aleksandrovich, Chamber Music Theater artistic director, Moscow city. From the USSR Theatrical Workers' Union.

Pokrovskiy, Valentin Ivanovich, president of the USSR Academy of Medical Sciences, director of the USSR Ministry of Health Central Epidemiology Scientific Research Institute, CPSU member, Moscow city. From the USSR Academy of Medical Sciences jointly with 40 scientific medical societies.

Polikarpov, Nikolay Aleksandrovich, director of Mokshanskiy Rayon's "Yelizevetinskiy" Sovkhoz, CPSU member, Yelizavetino village. From Oktyabrskiy Territorial Okrug No 253, RSFSR.

Polikarpov, Nikolay Platonovich, chief of the Zelenogorsk timber combine's Zelenogorsk timber station, Morkinskiy Rayon, CPSU candidate member, Zelenogorsk village, Morkinskiy Rayon. From Morkinskiy National-Territorial Okrug No 599, Mari ASSR.

Polozkov, Ivan Kuzmich, first secretary of the Krasnodar CPSU Kraykom, CPSU member, Krasnodar city. From Krasnodarskiy National-Territorial Okrug No 15, RSFSR.

Poltoranin, Mikhail Nikiforovich, APN political observer, CPSU member, Moscow city. From the USSR Journalists' Union.

Poluektov, Aleksandr Sergeyevich, bureau chief at the Kozelskiy Branch of the Automation and Instrument Building Research Institute Plant, CPSU member, Sosenskiy settlement, Kozelskiy Rayon. From Sukhinichskiy Territorial Okrug No 187, Kaluga Oblast, RSFSR.

Polyachenko, Mikhail Naumovich, chief physician at the Khabarovsk Kray Dermo-Venereology Dispensary, CPSU member, Khabarovsk City. From Amurskiy Territorial Okrug No 112, RSFSR.

Polyanichko, Viktor Petrovich, second secretary of the Azerbaijan Communist Party Central Committee, CPSU member, Baku city. From Khachmasskiy Territorial Okrug No 684, Azerbaijan SSR.

Polyanskaya, Polina Alekseyevna, painter-decorator of the "Tsentrobamstroy" Trust No 585 installation train, CPSU member, Tynda city, Amur Oblast, RSFSR. From the USSR trade unions.

Pometun, Grigoriy Konstantinovich, foreman-instructor at Zaporozhye city No 35 vocational and technical school, CPSU member, Zaporozhye city, Ukrainian SSR. From the All-Union Organization of War and Labor Veterans.

Ponomarev, Aleksey Filippovich, first secretary of the Belgorod CPSU Obkom, CPSU member, Belgorod city. From Valuyskiy Territorial Okrug No 127, Belgorod Oblast, RSFSR.

Ponomarev, Vladimir Matveyevich, fitter in the "Salavatnefteorgsintez" Production Association Control and Measuring Instruments and Automation Shop, CPSU member, Salavat city, Bashkir ASSR. From the USSR trade unions.

Ponomarenko, Lyudmila Vladimirovna, section chief at the "Azovtyazhmash" Production Association Design department, CPSU member, Mariupol city, Donetsk Oblast, Ukrainian SSR. From the women's councils united in the Soviet Women's Committee.

Popadyuk, Stepan Alekseyevich, machine operator on the kolkhoz named for 17 Veresnya, Stryyskiy Rayon, CPSU member, Yosipovichi village, Stryyskiy Rayon. From Stryyskiy Territorial Okrug No 491, Lvov Oblast, Ukranian SSR.

Popov, Viktor Andreyevich, deputy shop chief at the Yelets "Elta" Plant, Yelets city. From Yeletskiy Territorial Okrug No 221, Lipetsk Oblast, RSFSR.

Popov, Gavriil Kharitonovich, chief editor of the journal VOPROSY EKONOMIKI, CPSU member, Moscow city. From the USSR Union of Scientific and Engineering Societies.

Popov, Nikolay Ivanovich, army general, CPSU member, Moscow city. From Kyvraksiy National-Territorial Okrug No 620, Nakhichevan ASSR.

Popov, Filipp Vasilyevich, first secretary of the Altay CPSU Kraykom, CPSU member, Barnaul city. From Slavgorodskiy Territorial Okrug No 72, Altay Kray, RSFSR.

Popov, Yuriy Vasilyevich, deputy science director of Leningrad's V.M. Bekhterev Psychoneurology Scientific Research Institute, CPSU member, Leningrad City. From Nevskiy Territorial Okrug No 55, RSFSR.

Popova, Nadezhda Vasilyevna, pensioner, CPSU member, Moscow city. From the All-Union Organization of War and Labor Veterans.

Portnov, Gennadiy Aleksandrovich, fitter-assembly worker at the "Zavod Transportnogo Mashonostroyeniya" Production Association, CPSU member, Omsk city. From Leninskiy Territorial Okrug No 237, Omsk Oblast, RSFSR.

Poshkus, Bolyus Ignovich, director of the Lithuanian Agricultural Economics Scientific Research Institute, CPSU member, Vilnius city. From VASKHNIL.

Posibeyev, Grigoriy Andreyevich, first secretary of the Mariy CPSU Obkom, CPSU member, Yoshkar-Ola city. From Sovetskiy Territorial Okrug No 375, Mari ASSR.

Postnikov, Viktor Ivanovich, general director of "Stavropolskoye" Broiler Production Association, CPSU member, Stavropol city, RSFSR. From the CPSU.

Postnikov, Stanislav Ivanovich, army general, CPSU member, Moscow city. From Brestskiy Territorial Okrug No 547, Brest Oblast, Belorussian SSR.

Postoronko, Ivan Grigoryevich, first secretary of the Ivano-Frankovsk Ukrainian Communist Party Obkom, CPSU member, Ivano-Frankovsk city. From Snyatynskiy Territorial Okrug No 463, Ivano-Frankovsk Oblast, Ukrainian SSR.

Potapov, Aleksandr Serafimovich, chief of editor of TRUD, CPSU member, Moscow city. From the USSR trade unions.

Potapov, Vladimir Ivanovich, first secretary of Irkutsk CPSU Obkom, CPSU member, Irkutsk city. From Cheremkhovskiy Territorial Okrug No 176, Irkutsk Oblast, RSFSR.

Pozharskiy, Boris Ivanovich, chairman of the Perm Oblast Trade Union Council, CPSU member, Perm city, RSFSR. From the USSR trade unions.

Pribylova, Nadezhda Nikolayevna, department head and professor at the Kursk Medical Institute, CPSU member, Kursk city, RSFSR. From women's councils united by the Soviet Women's Committee.

Prikhodko, Yekaterina Stepanovna, chairman of the Sumskiy Rayon Velikochernetchanskiy Consumer Society Board, CPSU member, Sumy city, Ukrainian SSR. From the USSR consumer cooperatives.

Prikhodko, Zinaida Semenovna, first secretary of the Perechinskiy Ukrainian Communist Party Raykom, CPSU member, Perechin Urban settlement, Transcarpathian Oblast, Ukrainian SSR. From the women's councils united by the Soviet Women's Council.

Priymachenko, Nikolay Ivanovich, first secretary of the Polesskiy Ukrainian Communist Party Raykom, CPSU member, Polesskoye Urban settlement, Polesskiy Rayon. From Ivankovskiy Territorial Okrug No 471, Kiev Oblast, Ukrainian SSR.

Primakov, Yevgeniy Maksimovich, director of the USSR Academy of Sciences Institute of World Economics and International Relations, CPSU member, Moscow city. From the CPSU.

Prokopchuk, Boris Vasilyevich, oblispolkom first deputy chairman, chairman of the oblast agricultural committee, CPSU member, Tyumen City. From Ishimskiy Territorial Okrug No 322, RSFSR.

Prokopyev, Yuriy Nikolayevich, first secretary of the Yakutsk CPSU Obkom, CPSU member, Yakutsk city. From Ordzhonikidzevskiy National-Territorial Okrug No 700, Yakutsk ASSR.

Prokushev, Vladimir Ivanovich, PRAVDA correspondent for the Bashkir ASSR, CPSU member, Ufa City. From Sovetskiy National-Territorial Okrug No 505, Bashkir ASSR.

Pronin, Gennadiy Viktorovich, fitters team leader at the "Pobedit" plant named for the USSR's 50th anniversary, CPSU member, Ordzhonikidze city. From Promyshlennyy National-Territorial Okrug No 626, North Osetian ASSR.

Prudnikov, Igor Vasilyevich, mechanical equipment repairs engineer at the Nevyansk Mechanics Plant, Nevyansk city. From Alapayevskiy Territorial Okrug No 296, Sverdlovsk Oblast, RSFSR.

Prunskene, Kazimera Danute Prano, rector at the Lithuanian SSR Council of Ministers Institute for

Improving the Qualifications of National Economic Specialists, CPSU member, Vilnius city. From Shyaulyayskiy Territorial Okrug No 694, Lithuanian SSR.

Prusak, Mikhail Mikhaylovich, director of Kholmskiy Rayon's "Trudovik" sovkhoz, CPSU member, Kholm city, Novgorod Oblast, RSFSR. From the All-Union Komsomol.

Pshenichnikov, Vyacheslav Konstantinovich, second secretary of the Moldavian Communist Party Central Committee, CPSU member, Kishinev city. From Kagulskiy Territorial Okrug No 700, Moldavian SSR.

Pugo, Boris Karlovich, chairman of the CPSU Central Committee Party Control Committee, CPSU member, Moscow city. From the CPSU.

Pukhova, Zoya Pavlovna, chairman of the Soviet Women's Committee, CPSU member, Moscow city. From the women's councils united by the Soviet Women's Committee.

Pupkevich, Tadeush Karlovich, mobile excavator operator at the "Estonslanets" production association's "Narvskiy" open pit, CPSU member, Sillamyae city. From Yykhviskiy National-Territorial Okrug No 463, Estonian SSR.

Pyankov, Boris Yevgenyevich, colonel general, commander of the Red Banner Siberian Military District, CPSU member, Novosibirsk City. From Dzerzhinskiy Territorial Okrug No 230k RSFSR.

Pyankov, Pavel Pavlovich, senior rolling-press operator at the Pervouralsk New Pipe Plant, CPSU member, Pervouralsk city. From Pervouralskiy Territorial Okrug No 303, Sverdlovsk Oblast, RSFSR.

Pylin, Boris Filippovich, lieutenant colonel, senior teacher at the Kachinskiy Higher Military Aviation Pilots' School named for Myasnikov, CPSU member, Volgograd city. From Sovetskiy Territorial Okrug No 139, Volgograd Oblast, RSFSR.

Pyndyk, Galina Vladimirovna, milking machine operator at Zolochevskiy Rayon' kolkhoz named for Chapayev, Gorodilov village, Zolochevskiy Rayon. From Zolochevskiy Territorial Okrug No 489, Lvov Oblast, Ukrainian SSR.

Radzhabaliyev, Tadzhimurot, director at the Ganchinskiy Rayon "Leningrad" sovkhoz, CPSU member, Dam Kishlak, Ganchinskiy Rayon. From Ganchinskiy National-Territorial Okrug No 360, Leninabad Oblast, Tadzhik SSR.

Radzhabov, Rakhmon Radzhabovich, chief doctor at the Vanch Central Rayon Hospital, CPSU member, Vanch settlement, Vanchskiy Rayon. From Vanchskiy National-Territorial Okrug No 712, Gorno-Badakhshan Autonomous Oblast.

Rakhimov, Azim, deputy manager of the "Bukharaoblagropromstroy" No 2 oblast state cooperative association, CPSU member, Bukhara city, Uzbek SSR. From the All-Union Organization of War and Labor Veterans.

Rakhimov, Murtaza Gubaydullovich, director of the Ufa oil refinery named for the 22d CPSU Congress, CPSU member, Ufa city. From Ordzhonikidzevskiy Territorial Okrug No 351, Bashkir ASSR.

Rakhimova, Bikhodzhal Fatkhitdinovna, secretary of the Leninabad Tadzhikistan Communist Party Obkom, CPSU member, Leninabad city, Tadzhik SSR. From the women's councils united by the Soviet Women's Committee.

Rakhimova, Damilya Sagyndykovna, chairman of the Karaganda Obkom of the Kazakh SSR Red Cross Society, CPSU member, Karaganda city, Kazakh SSR. From the USSR Union of Red Cross and Red Crescent Societies.

Rakhimova, Sanobar Khalimovna, worker on the S. Rakhimov sovkhoz, Karshinskiy Rayon, Kashkadarya Oblast, Uzbek SSR. From the All-Union Komsomol.

Rakhmadiyev, Yerkegali, composer, first secretary of the Kazakhstan Composers' Union board, CPSU member, Alma-Ata city. From Arkalykskiy National-Territorial Okrug No 134, Kazakh SSR.

Rakhmankulova, Tupa, team leader on the Navoi Kolkhoz, Dzhizakskiy Rayon, CPSU member, Dzhizak city. From Dzhizakskiy Territorial Okrug No 594, Syr-Darya Oblast, Uzbek SSR.

Rakhmanov, Bazor, team leader on the "40 Let Oktyabrya" Kolkhoz, Termezskiy Rayon, CPSU member, Termezskiy Rayon, Surkhandarya Oblast, Uzbek SSR. From the USSR trade unions.

Rakhmanova, Marina Nikolayevna, department head at the Orenburg Medical Institute, CPSU member, Orenburg city, RSFSR. From the V.I. Lenin Soviet Children's Foundation.

Rakhmatullin, Makhmut Zubairovich, driver at the Sibayskiy Sovkhoz, Baymakskiy Rayon, CPSU member, Staryy Sibay village, Baymakskiy Rayon. From Sibayskiy National-Territorial Okrug No 513, Bashkir ASSR.

Ramanauskas, Vitautas Anuprovich, chairman of the Lithuanian Potrebsoyuz Board, CPSU member, Vilnius city. From the USSR consumer cooperatives.

Rasputin, Valentin Grigoryevich, writer, secretary of the USSR Writers' Union Board, Irkutsk city, RSFSR. From the USSR Writers' Union.

Rastrogina, Nina Alekseyevna, weaver at the 8 March Cotton Spinning and Weaving Factory, Mary city. From Maryyskiy City National-Territorial Okrug No 437, Turkmen SSR.

Raud, Irina Paulovna, chief design architect at the "Estonproyekt" State Design Institute, deputy chairman of the Estonian SSR Architects' Union Board, Tallinn city. From the USSR Architects' Union.

Rayg, Ivar Khelmutovich, senior scientific worker at the Estonian SSR Academy of Sciences Economics Institute, CPSU member, Saku settlement, Kharyuskiy Rayon. From Vilyandiskiy Yuzhniy National-Territorial Okrug No 460, Estonian SSR.

Razbivnaya, Galina Anatolyevna, director of the city Palace of Young Pioneers and Schoolchildren named for Yu.V. Andropov, CPSU member, Petrozavodsk city, Karelian ASSR. From the women's councils united by the Soviet Women's Committee.

Razuvayeva, Galina Petrovna, polisher at the "Kvant" production association, CPSU member, Nevinnomyssk city. From Nevinnomyssk Territorial Okrug No 108, Stavropol Kray, RSFSR.

Razumovskiy, Vasiliy Grigoryevich, academician-secretary of a department of the USSR Academy of Pedagogical Sciences, CPSU member, Moscow city. From the USSR Academy of Pedagogical Sciences in conjunction with the Soviet Pedagogical Research Workers Association.

Razumovskiy, Georgiy Petrovich, candidate member of the CPSU Central Committee Politburo, secretary of the CPSU Central Committee, CPSU member, Moscow city. From the CPSU.

Rebane, Karl Karlovich, academician, president of the Estonian SSR Academy of Sciences, CPSU member, Tallinn city. From the USSR Academy of Sciences.

Rekus, Viktor Maksimovich, chairman of the "Pamyat Kirova" kolkhoz, Kagalnitskiy Rayon, CPSU member, Kirovskaya village, Kagalnitskiy Rayon, Rostov Oblast, RSFSR. From kolkhozes united in the Union Kolkhoz Council.

Reshetnikov, Anatoliy Vasilyevich, deputy shop chief at the Kaluga engine building production association, Kaluga city. From Kaluzhskiy Territorial Okrug No 185, Kaluga Oblast, RSFSR.

Reshetnikova, Anna Safronovna, chief agronomist at the "Druzhba" Kolkhoz, Kiliyskiy Rayon, CPSU member, Mirnoye village, Kiliyskiy Rayon, Odessa Oblast. From Odesskiy National-Territorial Okrug No 53, Ukrainian SSR.

Reshetova, Nataliya Yuryevna, Obninsk city deputy prosecutor, CPSU member, Obninsk city, Kaluga Oblast, RSFSR. From women's councils united in the Soviet Women's Committee.

Revenko, Grigoriy Ivanovich, first secretary of Kiev Ukrainian Communist Party Obkom, Kiev city. From Belotserkovskiy Territorial Okrug No 470, Kiev Oblast, Ukrainian SSR.

Revnivtsev, Vladimir Ivanovich, general director of the "Mekhanbor" intersectoral scientific-technical complex, CPSU member, Leningrad city. From the All-Union Society of Inventors and Rationalizers.

Reysh, Bruno Erikhovich, oblast health department chief surgeon, department chief at the oblast hospital, Ust-Kamenogorsk. From Vostochno-Kazakhstanskiy National-Territorial Okrug No 137, Kazakh SSR.

Reznik, Aleksandr Ivanovich, chairman of the "Mir" Kolkhoz, Gayvoronskiy Rayon, CPSU member, Chervonoye village, Gayvoronskiy Rayon, Kirovograd Oblast, Ukrainian SSR. From kolkhozes united in the Union Kolkhoz Council.

Ridiger, Aleksey Mikhaylovich, member of the Holy Synod of the Russian Orthodox Church, Metropolitan Aleksiy of Leningrad and Novgorod, Leningrad city. From the Soviet Charity and Health Foundation.

Rodionov, Igor Nikolayevich, colonel general, commander of the Red-Banner Transcaucasus Military District, CPSU member, Tbilisi city. From Borzhomskiy Territorial Okrug No 660, Georgian SSR.

Rogatin, Boris Nikolayevich, chairman of the the All-Union Council of the All-Union Trade Unions' Voluntary Physical Education and Sports Society, CPSU member, Moscow city. From USSR public sports organizations.

Rogozhina, Vera Aleksandrovna, senior scientific assistant at the USSR Academy of Sciences Siberian Department Institute of the Earth's Core, CPSU member, Irkutsk city, RSFSR. From women's councils united in the Soviet Women's Committee.

Romazan, Ivan Kharitonovich, director of the Magnitogorsk V.I. Lenin Metallurgical Combine, CPSU member, Magnitogorsk city, Chelyabinsk Oblast, RSFSR. From the CPSU.

Romazanov, Kabdulla Zakiryanovich, steelworker at the Karaganda Metallurgical Combine, CPSU member, Temirtau city, Karaganda Oblast, Kazakh SSR. From the CPSU.

Romanenko, Viktor Dmitriyevich, director of the Ukrainian SSR Academy of Sciences Institute of Hydrobiology, CPSU member, Kiev city. From the USSR trade unions.

Romanov, Vasiliy Ivanovich, chairman of the Kemerovo Oblast Trade Unions Council, CPSU member, Kemerovo city, RSFSR. From the USSR trade unions.

Romanov, Grigoriy Nikolayevich, fitter at the "Khimzavod im. L.Ya. Karpova" production association, CPSU member, Mendeleyevsk city, Mendeleyevskiy Rayon. From Komsomolskiy National-Territorial Okrug No 641, Tatar ASSR.

Romanov, Yuriy Vasilyevich, second secretary of Gubkin Komsomol Gorkom, CPSU member, Gubkin city,

Belgorod Oblast, RSFSR. From the All-Union Komsomol.

Rotar, Svetlana Anatolyevna, mechanized milking foreman at the "Moldova" kolkhoz, CPSU member, Skayany village, Dondyushanskiy Rayon, Moldavian SSR. From the All-Union Komsomol.

Rozanov, Yevgeniy Grigoryevich, chairman of the State Committee for Civil Construction and Architecture under the USSR Gosstroy, academic secretary at the USSR Academy of Arts Architecture Department, CPSU member, Moscow city. From the USSR Academy of Arts.

Rubiks, Alfreds Petrovich, Riga Gorispolkom chairman, CPSU member, Riga city. From Leningradskiy National-Territorial Okrug No 290, Latvian SSR.

Ruchkin, Aleksey Stepanovich, chairman of the "Avangard" Kolkhoz, Ustyuzhenskiy Rayon, CPSU member, Sobolevo village, Ustyuzhenskiy Rayon. From Sokolskiy Territorial Okrug No 147, Vologda Oblast, RSFSR.

Rugin, Roman Prokopyevich, writer, senior methodologist at the okrug Institute of Culture of the Northern Peoples, CPSU member, Salekhard City. From Yamalo-Nenetskiy National-Territorial Okrug No 750, Yamalo-Nenetsk Autonomous Okrug.

Rusanov, Anatoliy Ivanovich, department head at Leningrad State University, Leningrad city. From the USSR Union of Scientific and Engineering Societies.

Russkikh, Vladimir Georgiyevich, skidding machine operator at the Komsomolskiy timber procurement establishment, Sovietskiy Rayon, CPSU member, Komsomolskiy settlement, Sovetskiy Rayon. From Urayskiy Territorial Okrug No 327, Tyumen Oblast, RSFSR.

Rustamova, Zukhra Karimovna, member of Syr-Darya Oblast People's Court, CPSU member, Gulistan city, Syr-Darya Oblast, Uzbek SSR. From the USSR trade unions.

Russu, Georgiy Sergeyevich, chief clinic physician at the Scientific Research Institute for Protecting the Health of Mothers and Children, CPSU Member, Kishinev city. From Kishinevskiy-Sovetskiy National-Territorial Okrug No 260, Moldavian SSR.

Russu, Ion Nikolayevich, first secretary of Slobodzeyskiy Moldavian Communist Party Raykom, CPSU member, Slobodzeya urban settlement, Slobodzeyskiy Rayon. From Slobodzeyskiy National-Territorial Okrug No 280, Moldavian SSR.

Ruzhitskiy, Aleksandr Antonovich, first secretary of Cherkassy Ukrainian Communist Party Obkom, CPSU member, Cherkassy city. From Zvenigorodskoy Territorial Okrug No 536, Cherkassy Oblast, Ukrainian SSR.

Ryabchenko, Sergey Mikhaylovich, laboratory chief at the Ukrainian SSR Academy of Sciences Institute of Physics, Kiev city. From Moskovskiy Territorial Okrug No 468, Kiev city.

Ryabkov, Vitaliy Makarovich, rector of the G.I. Nosov Mining and Metallurgy Institute in Magnitogorsk, CPSU member, Magnitogorsk City. From Chelyabinskiy National-Territorial Okrug No 32, RSFSR.

Ryabtsov, Boris Ivanovich, senior foreman at the Chkalovskiy section of the "Agroprommekhmontazh" Trust's Ilinogorskiy Interfarm Mobile Mechnaized Column, CPSU member, Chkalovsk City. From Gorodetskiy Territorial Okrug No 161, Gorkiy Oblast, RSFSR.

Ryazanova, Galina Ivanovna, production engineer at the Perm V.I. Lenin machine building plant, CPSU member, Perm city, RSFSR. From women's councils united in the Soviet Women's Committee.

Rybakov, Vladimir Ivanovich, automatic machine operator at the Maykop "Stankonromal" plant, CPSU member, Maykop city. From Maykop City National-Territorial Okrug No 701, Adygey Autonomous Oblast.

Rybyanchenko, Lidiya Ivanovna, general director of the Kamyshin A.N. Kosygin cotton combine, CPSU member, Kamyshin city, Volgograd Oblast, RSFSR. From women's councils united in the Soviet Women's Committee.

Rychin, Yevgeniy Sergeyevich, general director of the "Moskva" agroindustrial combine, Lyuberetskiy Rayon, Moscow Oblast, CPSU member, Moscow city. From the CPSU.

Rynka, Anatoliy Andreyevich, Novograd-Volynskiy Gorispolkom chairman, CPSU member, Novograd-Volynskiy city. From Novograd-Volynskiy Territorial Okrug No 450, Zhitomir Oblast, Ukrainian SSR.

Ryuytel, Arnold Feodorovich, chairman of the Estonian SSR Supreme Soviet Presidium, CPSU member, Tartu city. From Tartuskiy Rural National-Territorial Okrug No 479, Estonian SSR.

Ryumin, Valeriy Viktorovich, deputy chief designer at the "Energiya" science and production organization, CPSU member, Moscow city. From the CPSU.

Ryzhikov, Mikhail Borisovich, AUCCTU secretary, chairman of the agroindustrial complex workers' trade union Central Committee, CPSU member, Moscow city. From the USSR trade unions.

Ryzhkov, Nikolay Ivanovich, member of the CPSU Central Committee Politburo, chairman of the USSR Council of Ministers, CPSU member, Moscow city. From the CPSU.

Ryzhov, Aleksey Andreyevich, chief designer at the Ufa machine building design office, CPSU member, Ufa city,

From Duvanskiy National-Territorial Okrug No 504, Bashkir ASSR.

Rzayev, Anar Rasul ogly, writer, first secretary of the Azerbaijan Writers' Union Board, CPSU member, Baku city. From Bakinskiy 26 Bakinskikh Komissarov Territorial Okrug No 671, Azerbaijan SSR.

Rzayev, Firudin Orudzh ogly, fitter at the Baku tire plant named for the 40th anniversary of the Azerbaijan Communist Party, CPSU member, Baku city. From Bakinskiy-Narimanovskiy National-Territorial Okrug No 197, Azerbaijan SSR.

Saar, Vyayno Aleksandrovich, multiskilled team leader at "Tallinnstroy" trust construction administration No 4, CPSU member, Tallinn city. From the CPSU.

Sabirov, Abdurakhman Ganiyevich, department chief at the Bekabad central rayon hospital, CPSU member, Zafar settlement, Bekabadskiy Rayon, Tashkent Oblast. From Bukinskiy National Territorial Okrug No 119, Uzbek SSR.

Sabirova, Nazira, team leader at the "Yangiabad" sovkhoz, Gurlenskiy Rayon, CPSU member, Sholikor Kishlak Soviet, Gurlenskiy Rayon. From Urgenchskiy Territorial Okrug No 609, Khorezm Oblast, Uzbek SSR.

Sbitnev, Anatoliy Mitrofanovich, steel worker at the Kommunarskiy Metallurgical Combine, CPSU member, Perevalsk city. From Kommunarskiy Territorial Okrug No 414, Voroshilovgrad Oblast, Ukrainian SSR.

Sadygova, Nazaket Shamil kyzy, chief of the children's consultant unit at the Sabirabad Combined Children's Hospital, CPSU member, Sabirabad city. From Sabirabadskiy National-Territorial Okrug No 216, Azerbaijan SSR.

Safarov, Bozorali Solikhovich, shift engineer at the Kulyab Airport Aviation Technology Base, CPSU candidate member, Kulyab city. From Kulyabskiy National-Territorial Okrug No 369, Tajik SSR.

Safarov, Ilkhom, chairman of the Lenin Kolkhoz, Kumsangirskiy Rayon, Council of Ministers, Kumsangirskiy Rayon, Khatlon Oblast, Tajik SSR. From the kolkhozes united by the Union Kolkhoz Council.

Safarov, Yusup Odinayevich, tractor operator at the Usmal Yusupov Kolkhoz, Bukharskiy Rayon, CPSU member, Losha Kishlak, Bukharskiy Rayon. From Bukharskiy Territorial Okrug No 578, Bukhara Oblast, Uzbek SSR.

Safarova, Ramiya Nizameddin kyzy, worker on the Michurin Sovkhoz, Kusarskiy Rayon, CPSU member, Nizhniy Leger village, Kusarskiy Rayon. From Kubinskiy National-Territorial Okrug No 212, Azerbaijan SSR.

Safiyeva, Gulrukhsor, poet, chairman of the Tajik Republican Branch of the Soviet Culture Foundation, CPSU member, Dushanbe city. From the Soviet Culture Foundation.

Safin, Minikhalaf Mustafaivich, chairman of the Lenin Kolkhoz, Krasnokamskiy Rayon, CPSU member, Neftekamsk city. From Neftekamskiy National-Territorial Okrug No 510, Bashkir ASSR.

Safiullin, Mars Giniyatovich, metal caster at the Kazan Motor Building Production Association, CPSU member, Kazan city. From the USSR trade unions.

Safiullin, Rafgat Fayzullovich, chairman of the Tatar Potrebsoyuz Board, CPSU member, Kazan city. From the USSR Consumer Cooperative System.

Safonov, Anatoliy Kirillovich, chief of the Alma-Ata House Building Combine Design and Construction Association, CPSU member, Alma-Ata city. From Alma-Atinskiy-Alatauskiy Territorial Okrug No 613, Alma-Ata city.

Sagaanday, Galina Sandakovna, kindergarten chief, CPSU member, Chaa-Khol settlement, Ulug-Khemskiy Rayon, Tuva ASSR. From the women's councils united by the Soviet Women's Committee.

Sagdeyev, Roald Zinkurovich, leader of the scientific methodological center of analytical research at the USSR Academy of Sciences Space Research Institute, CPSU member, Moscow City. From the USSR Academy of Sciences.

Sagdiyev, Makhtay Ramazanovich, first secretary of Kokchetav Kazakh Communist Party Obkom, CPSU member, Kokchetav city. From Kokchetavskiy Territorial Okrug No 632, Kokchetav Oblast, Kazakh SSR.

Saidov, Kakhraman Mukhamadiyevich, chief of the city health department of Aktash city Soviet of People's Deputies Ispolkom, CPSU member, Aktash city, Samarkand Oblast. From Kattakurganskiy National-Territorial Okrug No 107, Uzbek SSR.

Saydaliyev, Saidkul, plasterers' team leader at No 14 Special Construction Administration of the "Dushanbestroy" Trust, CPSU member, Dushanbe city. From the USSR trade unions.

Sayfitdinova, Masturakhon, director of the "Anor" Sovkhoz, Kuvinskiy Rayon, CPSU member, Talmazor village, Kuvinskiy Rayon, Fergana Oblast, Uzbek SSR. From the women's councils united by the Soviet Women's Committee.

Sakandelidze, Iamze Binalovna, tobacco grower on the Merisi village Kolkhoz, Kedskiy Rayon, Merisi village, Kedskiy Rayon. From Kedskiy National-Territorial Okrug No 497, Adzhar ASSR.

Sakharov, Andrey Dmitriyevich, member of the USSR Academy of Sciences Presidium and chief scientific staffer of the USSR Academy of Sciences P.N. Lebedev Physics Institute, Moscow City. From the USSR Academy of Sciences.

Salayev, Eldar Yunis ogly, president of the Azerbaijan SSR Academy of Sciences, CPSU member, Baku city. From Shekinskiy National-Territorial Okrug No 223, Azerbaijan SSR.

Salakhyan, German Sarkisovich, tool maker at the Yerevan V.I. Lenin "Armelektromash" Production Association, CPSU member, Yerevan city. From Yerevanskiy-Leninskiy National-Territorial Okrug No 385, Armenian SSR.

Salikhov, Murodali, chairman of the Tajik Republican Trade Unions Council, CPSU member, Dushanbe city. From Kulyabskiy Territorial Okrug No 728, Tajik SSR.

Salimov, Alibala Khanakhmed ogly, chairman of the N. Narimanov Kolkhoz, Neftechalinskiy Rayon, CPSU member, Mursagullu village, Neftechalinskiy Rayon, Azerbaijan SSR. From the kolkhozes united by the Union Kolkhoz Council.

Saltykov, Nikolay Pavlovich, team leader at the "Prokatstroy-1" Construction Administration of the "Cherepovetsmetallurgstroy" Trust, Cherepovets city, Vologda Oblast, RSFSR. From the USSR trade unions.

Salukvadze, Revaz Georgiyevich, director of the Sukhumi I.N. Vekua Physico-Technical Institute, CPSU member, Sukhumi city. From Sukhumskiy-Leninskiy National-Territorial Okrug No 481, Abkhaz SSR.

Salykov, Kakimbek, first secretary of Karakalpak Uzbek Communist Party Obkom, CPSU member, Nukus city. From Turtkulskiy Territorial Okrug No 612, Karakalpak ASSR.

Samarin, Vladimir Ivanovich, own correspondent for the newspaper ORLOVSKAYA PRAVDA, CPSU member, Orel City. From Orlovskiy Territorial Okrug No 249, Orel Oblast, RSFSR.

Samayev, Petr Lidzhiyevich, deputy chief of the Elista House Building Combine of the "Kalmstroy" Design, Construction, and Installation Association, CPSU member, Elista city. From Elistinskiy National-Territorial Okrug No 547, Kalmyk ASSR.

Samedova, Guncha Sabirkyzy, team leader at the K. Samedov Kolkhoz, Salyanskiy Rayon, Sarvan village, Salyanskiy Rayon. From Salyanskiy National-Territorial Okrug No 217, Azerbaijan SSR.

Samilyk, Nikolay Ignatyevich, first secretary of Kirovograd Ukrainian Communist Party Obkom, CPSU member, Kirovograd city. From Dobrovelichkovskiy Territorial Okrug No 478, Kirovograd Oblast, Ukrainian SSR.

Samodichenko, Ivan Ivanovich, machine operator, lease collective leader on the "Orlovskiy" Sovkhoz, Tatarskiy Rayon, CPSU member, Orlovka village, Tatarskiy Rayon, Novosibirsk Oblast, RSFSR. From the CPSU.

Samoplavskiy, Valeriy Ivanovich, Ukrainian SSR minister of forestry, CPSU member, Kiev city. From Starosamborskiy Territorial Okrug No 490, Lvov Oblast, Ukrainian SSR.

Samoylov, Aleksandr Ivanovich, milking machine operator at the "Chervonyy Veleten" State Stock Breeding Farm, Gotvaldovskiy Rayon, CPSU candidate member, Pershotravnevoye city, Gotvaldovskiy Rayon. From Izyumskiy Territorial Okrug No 525, Kharkov Oblast, Ukrainian SSR.

Samoylov, Ivan Danilovich, director of the Nizhnyaya Sinyachikha Museum of Wooden Architecture and Folk Art, CPSU member, Alapayevsk city, Sverdlovsk Oblast, RSFSR. From the Soviet Culture Foundation.

Samsonov, Nikolay Alekseyevich, lathe operator at the Mari 50th Anniversary of the USSR "Kontakt" Plant, Yoshkar-Ola city. From Zarechnyy National-Territorial Okrug No 592, Mari ASSR.

Samsonov, Aleksandr Sergeyevich, director of the S.M. Kirov First Moscow Timepiece Plant, CPSU member, Moscow City. From Proletarskiy Territorial Okrug No 20, RSFSR.

Samsonov, Yuriy Grigoryevich, first secretary of Ulyanovsk CPSU Obkom, CPSU member, Ulyanovsk city. From Novospasskiy Territorial Okrug No 331, Ulyanovsk Oblast, RSFSR.

Sandulyak, Leontiy Ivanovich, faculty chief at Chernovitsy State University, CPSU member, Chernovtsy city. From Chernovitskiy Territorial Okrug No 544, Chernovitsy Oblast, Ukrainian SSR.

Sandurskiy, Boguslav Florionovich, general director of the "Bashneft" Production Association, CPSU member, Ufa city. From Burayevskiy Territorial Okrug No 355, Bashkir ASSR.

Sanchat, Aleksandr Sandanovich, first secretary of Tes-Khemskiy Komsomol Raykom, CPSU member, Samagaltay village, Tes-Khemskiy Rayon. From Tes-Khemskiy National-Territorial Okrug No 655, Tuva ASSR.

Saparov, Khydyr, machine operator at the K. Marx Kolkhoz, Geok-Tepinskiy Rayon, CPSU member, Kurmantgekdzhe settlement, Geok-Tepinskiy Rayon. From Geok-Tepinskiy National-Territorial Okrug No 425, Turkmen SSR.

Sapegin, Aleksey Andreyevich, electric locomotive engineer at the Smolensk Locomotive Depot of the Belorussian Railroad, CPSU member, Smolensk city. From Smolenskiy Territorial Okrug No 305, Smolensk Oblast, RSFSR.

Saprykin, Aleksey Viktorovich, steel caster at the Novolipetsk Yu.V. Andropov Metallurgical Combine, CPSU member, Lipetsk city, RSFSR. From the All-Union Komsomol.

Sarakayev, Archil Totrazovich, chairman of the Kalinin Kolkhoz, Irafskiy Rayon, CPSU member, Chikola village, Irafskiy Rayon. From Terskiy Territorial Okrug No 380, North Osetian ASSR.

Sarayev, Sergey Borisovich, high-voltage power line repair and operation service chief on the Tuva Grid, Kyzyl City. From Kyzylskiy Vostochnyy National-Territorial Okrug No 646, Tuva ASSR.

Sarkisyan, Sos Artashesovich, artist at the Sundukyan State Academic Theater, Yerevan City. From Yerevanskiy-Sovetskiy Territorial Okrug No 734, Armenian SSR.

Sarsenov, Malik Abilbekovich, chief of the "Aralvodstroy" Specialized Construction Association, CPSU member, Nukus city. From Chimbayskiy National-Territorial Okrug No 568, Karakalpak ASSR.

Sarsenov, Umirzak, chairman of the Kazakh Potrebsoyuz Board, CPSU member, Alma-Ata city. From the USSR Consumer Cooperative System.

Sarychev, Anatoliy Ivanovich, chairman of the "Proletarskaya Pobeda" Kolkhoz, Gorodovikovskiy Rayon, CPSU member, Vinogradnoye city, Gorodovikovskiy Rayon. From Gorodovikovskiy National-Territorial Okrug No 549, Kalmyk ASSR.

Satin, Boris Fedorovich, first secretary of Tashkent Uzbek Communist Party Gorkom, CPSU member, Tashkent city. From Tashkentskiy-Chilanzarskiy Territorial Okrug No 600, Tashkent Oblast, Uzbek SSR.

Satybaldiyev, Rayymkul Altybayevich, chief physician at the Kirovskiy Central Rayon Hospital, CPSU member, Kirovskoye village, Kirovskiy Rayon. From Kirovskiy National-Territorial Okrug No 333, Kirghiz SSR.

Saunin, Anatoliy Nikolayevich, faculty lecturer at Makeyevka Engineering Construction Institute, CPSU member, Donetsk city. From Makeyevskiy Territorial Okrug No 443, Donetsk Oblast, Ukrainian SSR.

Savchenko, Natalya Vladimirovna, chairman of the "Chernomorets" Fishing Kolkhoz, CPSU member, Novorossiysk city, Krasnodar Kray, RSFSR. From the All-Union Association of Fishing Kolkhozes.

Savinova, Yevgeniya Isidorovna, physician at the water-transport workers' hospital, Chistopol city. From Chistopolskiy National-Territorial Okrug No 645, Tatar ASSR.

Savinykh, Viktor Petrovich, rector of the Moscow Institute of Geodesy, Aerial Photography, and Cartography Engineers, CPSU member, Moscow city. From Kirovskiy National-Territorial Okrug No 14, RSFSR.

Savisaar, Edgar Elmarovich, deputy director of the Estonian SSR Light Industry Ministry "Maynor" special planning and design office, CPSU member, Tallinn city. From Vilyandiskiy Severnyy National-Territorial Okrug No 459, Estonian SSR.

Savitskaya, Svetlana Yevgenyevna, test pilot-cosmonaut, deputy chief of the "Energiya" science and production association chief designer's department, CPSU member, Moscow city. From the Soviet Peace Foundation in conjunction with eight Soviet committees supporting peace, solidarity, and international cooperation.

Savitskiy, Mikhail Andreyevich, artist, leader of the USSR Academy of Arts painting workshop, Minsk city. From the Soviet Cultural Foundation.

Savkov, Vladimir Aleksandrovich, chief agronomist at the "Ukraina" kolkhoz, CPSU member, Makov village, Dunayevetskiy Rayon, Khmelnitskiy Oblast, Ukrainian SSR. From kolkhozes united in the Union Kolkhoz Council.

Savostina, Zinaida Semenovna, director of the Chelyabinsk Oblast General Science Library, CPSU member, Chelyabinsk city, RSFSR. From the women's councils united by the Soviet Women's Committee.

Savostyuk, Oleg Mikhaylovich, graphic artist, secretary of the USSR Artists' Union Board, chairman of the board of the Moscow Organization of the RSFSR Artists' Union, CPSU member, Moscow city. From the USSR Artists' Union.

Saydakhmedov, Isakzhan Mamadzhanovich, commander of the Samarkand Combined Air Detachment, CPSU member, Samarkand City. From Samarkandskiy National-Territorial Okrug No 110, Uzbek SSR.

Sazonova, Zoya Vladimirovna, packer at the Groznyy Sewn Goods Production Association, CPSU member, Groznyy city. From Leninskiy National-Territorial Okrug No 668, Chechen-Ingush ASSR.

Sebentsov, A. Ye., department head, Moscow Searchlight Plant. From the Perovsky Territorial Election District, RSFSR.

Sefershayev, Fikret, leader of a cotton-growing team on the "30 Let Uzbekskoy SSR" Kolkhoz in Chinazskiy Rayon, CPSU member, Yallama kishlak, Chinazskiy Rayon. From Yangiyulskiy National-Territorial Okrug No 121, Uzbek SSR.

Seyitkuliyeva, Ogulbike Arnamukhammedovna, machine operator at the "Lenin Yely" Kolkhoz, Iolotanskiy Rayon, CPSU member, Khudayberdyyev settlement, Iolotanskiy Rayon, Mary Oblast. From Bayram-Aliyskiy Territorial Okrug No 742, Turkmen SSR.

Sekacheva, Raisa Ivanovna, machine milking foreman on the Lenin Kolkhoz, Spasskiy Rayon, CPSU member, Gavrilovo village, Spasskiy Rayon, Ryazan Oblast, RSFSR. From the women's councils united by the Soviet Women's Committee.

Seleznev, Aleksandr Ivanovich, first secretary of Kursk CPSU Obkom, CPSU member, Kursk city. From Lgovskiy Territorial Okrug No 218, Kursk Oblast, RSFSR.

Seleznev, Igor Sergeyevich, chief designer at the "Raduga" Machine Building Design Bureau, CPSU member, Dubna city, Moscow Oblast, RSFSR. From the CPSU.

Seleznev, Stanislav Vitalyevich, lecturer at the "Nizhnevartovskkhimstroy" Construction and Installation Trust's Study Course Combine, CPSU member, Nizhnevartovsk city. From Nizhnevartovskiy Territorial Okrug No 323, Tyumen Oblast, RSFSR.

Selimov, Nurnazar, first secretary of Kizyl-Arvatskiy Turkmen Communist Party Raykom, CPSU member, Kizyl-Arvat city. From Kizyl-Arvatskiy National-Territorial Okrug No 433, Turkmen SSR.

Semenikhin, Aleksandr Vasilyevich, electric locomotive driver at Tselinograd Station's locomotive depot on the Virgin Lands Railroad, CPSU member, Tselinograd city. From Tselinogradskiy Territorial Okrug No 647, Tselinograd Oblast, Kazakh SSR.

Semenko, Valentina Ivanovna, chairman of Ivanovo Oblast Court, CPSU member, Ivanovo city, RSFSR. From the V.I. Lenin Soviet Children's Fund.

Semenov, Vitaliy Aleksandrovich, senior scientific staffer at the Ukrainian SSR Academy of Sciences' Technical Mechanics Institute, Dnepropetrovsk. From Zhovtnevoy Territorial Okrug No 422, Ukrainian SSR.

Semenov, Vladimir Magomedovich, Colonel General, commander of the Order of Lenin Transbaykal Military District, CPSU member, Chita city. From Kyakhtinskiy National-Territorial Okrug No 523, Buryat ASSR.

Semenov, Vladimir Mikhaylovich, secretary of Grodno Belorussian Communist Party Obkom, CPSU member, Grodno City. From Grodnenskiy Territorial Okrug No 560, Belorussian SSR.

Semenova, Galina Vladimirovna, chief editor of the magazine KRESTYANKA, CPSU member, Moscow city. From women's councils united by the Soviet Women's Committee.

Semenova, Galina Illarionovna, deputy director of the Belomorsk State Fishery Base, CPSU member, Belomorsk city. From Belomorskiy National-Territorial Okrug No 572, Karelian ASSR.

Semenova, Nina Mikhaylovna, grader at the Novgorod Lenin Komsomol Plant, CPSU member, Novgorod city, RSFSR. From women's councils united by the Soviet Women's Committee.

Semukha, Vladimir Iosifovich, chairman of the Belorussian SSR Red Cross Society Central Committee, CPSU member, Minsk city. From the USSR Union of Red Cross and Red Crescent Societies.

Serdyukovskaya, Galina Nikolayevna, director of the USSR Ministry of Health All-Union Scientific Center for Preventive Medicine Child and Adolescent Health and Disease Prevention Research Institute, CPSU member, Moscow city. From the USSR Academy of Medical Sciences together with 40 scientific medical societies.

Seredkin, Vladimir Stepanovich, director of the Klyuyevka Lumber Transshipment Base, CPSU member, Klyuyevka Settlement, Kabanskiy Rayon. From Kabanskiy National-Territorial Okrug No 522, Buryat ASSR.

Sergiyenko, Valeriy Ivanovich, chairman of the Krasnoyarsk Krayispolkom, CPSU member, Krasnoyarsk city. From Minusinskiy Territorial Okrug No 94, Krasnoyarsk Kray, RSFSR.

Setkin, Yuriy Borisovich, commander of a parachute training unit at the Voluntary Society for the Promotion of the Army, Aviation, and Navy's Cheboksary Air Sports Club, CPSU member, Cheboksary City. From Leninskiy National-Territorial Okrug No 679, Chuvash ASSR.

Sevryukov, Vladimir Vasilyevich, deputy chief for youth work and secretary of the Komsomol committee of the Black Sea Shipping Line, CPSU member, Odessa city, Ukrainian SSR. From the All-Union Komsomol.

Shabalin, Gennadiy Georgiyevich, chairman of the "Chudinovskiy" Kolkhoz, Khalturinskiy Rayon, CPSU member, Chudinovo village, Khalturinskiy Rayon. From Kotelnichskiy Territorial Okrug No 200, Kirov Oblast, RSFSR.

Shabanov, Talgat Khatipyanovich, drivers team leader at the Uchaly Mining and Enrichment Combine, Uchaly City. From Beloretskiy Territorial Okrug No 354, Baskirian ASSR.

Shabanov, Vitaliy Mikhaylovich, army general, USSR deputy defense minister, CPSU member, Moscow. From Khmelnitskiy Territorial Okrug No 531, Khmelnitskiy Oblast, Ukrainian SSR.

Shagiyev, Khaydar Khzyrovich, chairman of the Frunze Kolkhoz, Sterlitamakskiy Rayon, CPSU member, Tyuryushlya village, Sterlitamakskiy Territorial Okrug No 357, Bashkir ASSR.

Shakhanov, Mukhtar, writer, secretary of the Kazakh SSR Writers Union Board, chief editor of the journal ZHALYN, CPSU member, Alma-Ata city. From Alma-Atinskiy-Talgarskiy Territorial Okrug No 616, Alma-Ata Oblast, Kazakh SSR.

Shakhnazarov, Georgiy Khosroyevich, corresponding member of the USSR Academy of Sciences, aide to the CPSU Central Committee general secretary, CPSU member, Moscow city. From the scientific societies and associations under the USSR Academy of Sciences.

Shalayev, Stepan Alekseyevich, chairman of the AUCCTU, CPSU member, Moscow city. From the USSR trade unions.

Shalyyev, Atabally Bapbayevich, drilling foreman at the South Turkmen exploratory drilling administration of the "Turkmengazprom" production association's

"Turkmenburgaz" trust, CPSU member, Kirov Kolkhoz, Murgabskiy Rayon, Mary Oblast, Turkmen SSR. From the CPSU.

Shamanadze, Shadiman Nodariyevich, senior editor of the Georgian Writers Union Main Editorial Collegium, Tbilisi city. From the All-Union Komsomol.

Shamba, Taras Mironovich, secretary of the party committee of the CPSU Central Committee Academy of Social Sciences, CPSU member, Moscow city. From Gudautskiy Rural National-Territorial Okrug No 487, Abkhaz ASSR.

Shamiladze, Vakhtang Mamiyevich, faculty chief at Tbilisi State University, CPSU member, Tbilisi City. From Batumskiy-Leonidze National-Territorial Okrug No 494, Adzhar ASSR.

Shamin, Nikolay Vasilyevich, leader of the "Respublika bodrykh" Teenagers' Military-Patriotic Club under Tomsk city DOSAAF Aviation Sports Club, Tomsk city, RSFSR. From the USSR DOSAAF.

Shamikhin, Albert Mikhaylovich, responsible organizer of the Automotive and Agricultural Machine-Building Workers Trade Union Central Committee, CPSU member, Riga city. From the USSR trade unions.

Shamshev, Igor Borisovich, senior teacher at Yaroslavl State University, CPSU member, Yaroslavl City. From Leninskiy Territorial Okrug No 345, Yaroslavl Oblast, RSFSR.

Shamyrbekov, Kuttubek Imankozhoyevich, herdsmen's team leader on the Tort-Kul Kolkhoz, Temir-Kanat village, Tonskiy Rayon, Issyk-Kul Oblast, Kirghiz SSR. From the All-Union Komsomol.

Shapkhayev, Sergey Gerasimovich, senior lecturer at the East Siberia Technological Institute, Ulan-Ude City From Sovetskiy National-Territorial Okrug No 517, Buryat ASSR.

Shapovalenko, Vladislav Aleksandrovich, laboratory chief at the Volga-Urals Scientific Research and Planning Institute for the Extraction and Processing of Hydrogen Sulfide Gases at the "Orenburggazprom" Production Association, Orenburg city. From Orenburg city Territorial Okrug No 243, Orenburg Oblast, RSFSR.

Shapulin, Nikolay Petrovich, electric welders' team leader at the Stavropol Truck Trailer Plant of the Kama Large-Capacity Trucks Association, Stavropol City. From Stavropolskiy Territorial Okrug No 103, Stavropol Kray, RSFSR.

Sharayev, Leonid Gavrilovich, first secretary of Nikolayev Ukrainian Communist Party Obkom, CPSU member, Nikolayev city. From Voznesenskiy Territorial Okrug No 495, Nikolayev Oblast, Ukrainian SSR.

Sharin, Leonid Vasilyevich, first secretary of Amur CPSU Obkom, CPSU member, Blagoveshchensk city. From Belogorskiy Territorial Okrug No 116, Amur Oblast, RSFSR.

Sharipov, Yuriy Kamalovich, general director of Ufa S.M. Kirov Production Association, CPSU member, Ufa city. From Ufimskiy National-Territorial Okrug No 506, Bashkir ASSR.

Sharipova, Fazolat, family contract leader on the "Shafirkan" Kolkhoz dairy goods farm, Shafirkanskiy Rayon, CPSU member, Talidzha settlement, Shafirkanskiy Rayon, Bukhara Oblast. From Gizhduvanskiy Territorial Okrug No 579, Bukhara Oblast, Uzbek SSR.

Sharonov, Andrey Vladimirovich, secretary of the Ufa Ordzhonikidze Aviation Institute Komsomol Committee, CPSU member, Ufa city, Bashkir ASSR. From the All-Union Komsomol.

Sharyy, Grigoriy Ivanovich, chairman of the "Zapovit Lenina" Kolkhoz, CPSU member, Pervozvanovka village, Chutovskiy Rayon, Poltava Oblast, Ukrainian SSR. From the All-Union Komsomol.

Shashkov, Nikolay Vladimirovich, manager of the Nikitinskoye department of the "Vasilyevskiy" Sovkhoz, Shuyskiy Rayon, Vasilyevskoye village, Shuyskiy Rayon. From Shuyskiy Territorial Okrug No 169, Ivanovo Oblast, RSFSR.

Shaydulin, Midkhat Idiyatovich, pensioner, CPDU member, Ufa city, Bashkir ASSR. From All-Union Organization of War and Labor Veterans.

Shatornyy, Stanislav Ivanovich, deputy chief engineer of the "Askold" Machine-Building Plant, CPSU member, Arsenyev city. From Artemovskiy Territorial Okrug No 99, Maritime Kray, RSFSR.

Shatrovenko, Yuriy Nikolayevich, cadet at Voroshilovgrad Higher Military Aviation School for Navigators Named for the Donbass Proletariat, Voroshilovgrad city, Ukrainian SSR. From the All-Union Komsomol.

Shchapov, Yuriy Stepanovich, director of the "Chernogorskiy" opencut mine, CPSU member, Chernogorsk city. From Chernogorskiy National-Territorial Okrug No 734, Khakass Autonomous Oblast.

Shchedrin, Rodion Konstantinovich, composer, chairman of the RSFSR Composers' Union Board, Moscow city. From the USSR Composers' Union.

Shchelkanov, Aleksandr Aleksandrovich, loader at the Leningrad "Berezka" Trading Firm's No 20 Store, Leningrad City. From Kirovskiy Territorial Okrug No 51, RSFSR.

Shchelkonogov, Anatoliy Afanasyevich, director of the Solikamsk magnesium plant, CPSU member, Solikamsk city. From Bereznikovskiy Territorial Okrug No 259, Perm Oblast, RSFSR.

Shchepanovskiy, Adam Mikhaylovich, chairman of the "Prapor Lenina" Agro-Industrial Firm and Kolkhoz, Borshchevskiy Rayon, CPSU member, Volkovtsy village, Borshchevskiy Rayon, Ternopol Oblast, Ukrainian SSR. From the kolkhozes united by the Union Kolkhoz Council.

Shcherbak, Yuriy Nikolayevich, writer, secretary of the Ukrainian Writers' Union Board, Kiev city. From Shevchenkovskiy Territorial Okrug No 469, Kiev city.

Shcherbakov, Vladimir Pavlovich, chairman of Moscow city Trade Unions Council, CPSU member, Moscow city. From the USSR trade unions.

Shcherbina, Mariya Yemelyanovna, milkmaid at the "Berezki" Stud Farm, Gomelskiy Rayon, Zalyadye settlement, Gomelskiy Rayon, Gomel Oblast, Belorussian SSR. From the USSR trade unions.

Shcherbitskiy, Vladimir Vasilyevich, member of the CPSU Central Committee Politburo, first secretary of the Ukrainian Communist Party Central Committee, CPSU member, Kiev city. From Verkhnedneprovskiy Territorial Okrug No 424, Dnepropetrovsk Oblast, Ukrainian SSR.

Shekhovtsov, Viktor Afanasyevich, deputy deacon of the Far Eastern State University, Vladivostok city. From Vladivostokskiy Territorial Okrug No 97, Maritime Kray, RSFSR.

Sheklycheva, Dzhumagozel, leader of a team of plasterers and painters in the Maryoblagropromstroy No 22 interfarm mobile mechanized column, CPSU member, Dogryyel settlement, Sakar-Chaginskiy Rayon. From Maryyskiy Territorial Okrug No 743, Turkmen SSR.

Shelistov, Nikolay Mikhaylovich, chief of surgery at the Ostrogozhsk Central Rayon Hospital, CPSU member, Ostrogozhsk City. From Rossoshanskiy Territorial Okrug No 154, RSFSR.

Shelukhin, Yuriy Sergeyevich, deputy chief metallurgist of Ulyanovsk Machine Tool Building Production Association of Heavy and Unique Machine Tools, CPSU member, Ulyanovsk city. From Zasviyazhskiy Territorial Okrug No 328, Ulyanovsk Oblast, RSFSR.

Shengelaya, Eldar Nikolayevich, producer-director at the "Gruziya-Film" Movie Studio, CPSU member, Tbilisi city. From the USSR Cinematographers Union.

Shenin, Oleg Semenovich, first secretary of Krasnoyarsk CPSU Kraykom, CPSU member, Krasnoyarsk city. From Kanskiy Territorial Okrug No 92, Krasnoyarsk Kray, RSFSR.

Sherali, Loik, poet, chief editor of the journal SADOI SHARK, CPSU member, Dushanbe city. From Ura-Tyubinskiy Territorial Okrug No 731, Tajik SSR.

Sheraliyev, Abdurazak, teacher at the No 41 Secondary School, Sirmok settlement, Uchkurganskiy Rayon. From Chartakskiy Territorial Okrug No 584, Namangan Oblast, Uzbek SSR.

Shergoziyev, Mamatgazi, chairman of the "Leningrad" Kolkhoz, Bagdadskiy Rayon, CPSU member, Karakchital village, Bagdadskiy Rayon. From Leningradskiy Territorial Okrug No 606, Fergana Oblast, Uzbek SSR.

Shetko, Pavel Vadimovich, lecturer for the Minsk Belorussian Komsomol Obkom Propaganda Department, Minsk city. From the All-Union Komsomol.

Shevchenko, Aleksandra Fedorovna, director of the "Donskoy" Sovkhoz, Trunovskiy Rayon, CPSU member, Donskoye village, Trunovskiy Rayon, Stavropol Kray, RSFSR. From the women's councils united by the Soviet Women's Committee.

Shevchenko, Vladimir Antonovich, first secretary of Sumy Ukrainian Communist Party Obkom, CPSU member, Sumy city. From Shostkinskiy Territorial Okrug No 515, Sumy Oblast, Ukrainian SSR.

Shevchenko, Vladimir Ivanovich, milk production foreman on the "Shlyakh Illicha" Kolkhoz, Repkinskiy Rayon, CPSU member, Grabov village, Repkinskiy Rayon, Chernigov Oblast. From Chernigovskiy National-Territorial Okrug No 63, Ukrainian SSR.

Shevchenko, Valentina Semenovna, chairman of the Ukrainian SSR Supreme Soviet Presidium, CPSU member, Kiev city. From Kiyevskiy Rural National-Territorial Okrug No 34, Ukrainian SSR.

Shevlyuga, Vladimir Yakovlevich, molder at the "Rostselmash" Production Association, CPSU member, Rostov-na-Donu City. From Proletarskiy Territorial Okrug No 269, RSFSR.

Sheyko, Anatoliy Vasilyevich, chief agronomist at Starobelskiy Rayon's "Pervoye Maya" Kolkhoz, CPSU member, Bondarevo village. From Starobelskiy Territorial Okrug No 419, Ukrainian SSR.

Sheyn, Yelizaveta Vasilyevna, senior engineer of Krasnoyarsk "Krastyazhmash" Production Association, Krasnoyarsk city, RSFSR. From the women's councils united by the Soviet Women's Committee.

Shibik, Nikolay Aleksandrovich, editor of the republican RABOCHAYA GAZETA, CPSU member, Kiev city. From the USSR Journalists Union.

Shinelev, Vladimir Viktorovich, work superintendent for the No 4 Construction and Installation Trust's No 32 Construction Administration, CPSU member, Novocheboksarsk city. From Novocheboksarskiy National-Territorial Okrug No 686, Chuvash ASSR.

Shinkaruk, Vladimir Ilarionovich, director of the Ukrainian SSR Academy of Sciences Institute of Philosophy, CPSU member, Kiev city. From the All-Union "Znaniye" Society.

Shinkevich, Ivan Artemovich, chairman of the Railroad Transport and Transport Construction Workers Trade Union Central Committee, CPSU member, Moscow city. From the USSR trade unions.

Shinkuba, Bagrat Vasilyevich, poet, chairman of the Abkhaz ASSR Council of Ministers Commission for Conferring Abkhaz ASSR D.I. Gulia State Prizes in the

Spheres of Literature, Art, and Abkhaz Studies. CPSU member, Sukhumi city. From Ochamchirskiy National-Territorial Okrug No 181, Georgian SSR.

Shipitko, Gennadiy Ivanovich, IZVESTIYA correspondent in the Kirghiz SSR, CPSU member, Frunze city. From Frunzenskiy-Leninskiy National-Territorial Okrug No 321, Kirghiz SSR.

Shirokopoyas, Anatoliy Danilovich, chairman of the Krasnodar Kray Trade Union Council, CPSU member, Krasnodar city, RSFSR. From USSR trade unions.

Shirshin, Grigoriy Chooduyevich, first secretary of the Tuva CPSU Obkom, CPSU member, Kyzyl city. From Tuvinskiy Territorial Okrug No 391, Tuva ASSR.

Shishov, Aleksey Alekseyevich, pensioner, CPSU member, Krasnodar city, RSFSR. From the All-Union Organization of War and Labor Veterans.

Shishov, Viktor Aleksandrovich, director of the Velskiy Rayon "Vazhskiy" Sovkhoz, CPSU member, Blagoveshchenskoye village, Velskiy Rayon. From Kotlasskiy Territorial Okrug No 119, Arkhangelsk Oblast, RSFSR.

Shishov, Yevgeniy Illarionovich, director of the Tselinogradskiy Rayon "Zarechnyy" Sovkhoz, CPSU member, Prigorodnoye village, Tselinogradskiy Rayon, Tselinograd Oblast. From Tselinogradskiy-Shortandinskiy National-Territorial Okrug No 156, Kazakh SSR.

Shkanakin, Vladimir Gennadyevich, lieutenant general, commander of a military unit, Turkestan Military District, CPSU member, Tashkent city. From Tashkentskiy-Leninskiy Territorial Okrug No 597, Tashkent Oblast, Uzbek SSR.

Shkolnik, Leonid Borisovich, chief of the press sector of the Jewish Autonomous Oblast CPSU Obkom Ideological Department, CPSU member, Birobidzhan city. From Birobidzhanskiy National-Territorial Okrug No 716, Jewish Autonomous Oblast.

Shlifer, Leonid Iosifovich, chairman of the "Zarya Kommunizma" Kolkhoz, CPSU member, Nadlak village, Novoarkhangelskiy Rayon, Kirovograd Oblast, Ukrainian SSR. From the All-Union Organization of War and Labor Veterans.

Shlichite, Zina Leonovna, lawyer with the Klaypeda legal advice service, Klaypeda city. From Klaypedskiy Territorial Okrug No 690, Lithuanian SSR.

Shlyakota, Voldemar Viktorovich, director of the Balvskiy Rayon "Vetsumi" Sovkhoz, CPSU member, Vilyaka city. From Aluksnenskiy National-Territorial Okrug No 297, Latvian SSR.

Shmal, Yuriy Yakovlevich, director of the Maslyaninskiy Rayon "Maslyaninskiy" Sovkhoz, CPSU member, Maslyanino Urban settlement. From Iskitimskiy Territorial Okrug No 235, Novosibirsk Oblast, RSFSR.

Shmelev, Nikolay Petrovich, section chief at the USSR Academy of Sciences Institute of the United States of America and Canada, CPSU member, Moscow City. From the USSR Academy of Sciences.

Shmonina, Tatyana Nikolayevna, director of No 17 Secondary School, CPSU member, Magadan city, RSFSR. From women's councils united in the Soviet Women's Committee.

Shmotyev, Valeriy Ivanovich, heat specialist at the Verkh-Isetskiy metallurgical plant, CPSU member, Sverdlovsk city. From Chkalovskiy Territorial Okrug No 295, Sverdlovsk Oblast, RSFSR.

Shnyukas, Domiyonas Yurgevich, PRAVDA correspondent in the Lithuanian SSR and Kaliningrad Oblast, CPSU member, Vilnius city. From the USSR Journalists Union.

Shorokhov, Viktor Nikolayevich, tuner at the Tula "V.M. Ryabikov" machine-building plant, CPSU member, Tula city, RSFSR. From the CPSU.

Shoyubov, Zakhid Gamil ogly, director of the Khaldanskaya rural comprehensive secondary school, CPSU member, 1-Salamabad village, Yevlakhskiy Rayon. From Bardinskiy National-Territorial Okrug No 204, Azerbaijan SSR.

Shtepo, Viktor Ivanovich, director general of the Volgograd "Volgo-Don" specialized production association, CPSU member, Bereslavka settlement, Kalachevskiy Rayon, Volgograd Oblast, RSFSR. From the CPSU.

Shtoyk, Garri Gvidovich, director of the East Kazakhstan copper and chemical combine of the "Kazpolimetall" production association, CPSU member, Ust-Talovka settlement, Shemonaikhinskiy Rayon, East Kazakhstan Oblast, Kazakh SSR. From the CPSU.

Shubin, Veniamin Ilich, pensioner, CPSU member, Arkhangelsk city, RSFSR. From the All-Union Organization of War and Labor Veterans.

Shubin, Vladimir Aleksandrovich, team leader and tutor at the Chita machine-building plant, CPSU member, Chita city, RSFSR. From the All-Union Organization of War and Labor Veterans.

Shuvalov, Sergey Gavrilovich, first deputy chairman of the Central Board of the All-Union Voluntary Society of Bibliophiles, CPSU member, Moscow city. From the All-Union Voluntary Society of Bibliophiles.

Shukshin, Anatoliy Stepanovich, grinder at the Far East Power machine-building plant, CPSU member, Khabarovsk city, RSFSR. From the CPSU.

Shulgin, Ivan Ivanovich, senior lieutenant, assistant chief of a troop unit political department for Komsomol work, Pacific Fleet, CPSU member, Maritime Kray, RSFSR. From the All-Union Komsomol.

Shuldeshova, Valentina Alekseyevna, painters' team leader at No 29 Specialized Administration of the "Tyumengazstroy" Trust, CPSU member, Tyumen city, RSFSR. From the women's councils united by the Soviet Women's Committee.

Shulyak, Vasiliy Korneyevich, chairman of the "Trud" Kolkhoz, Teofipolskiy Rayon, CPSU member, Teofipol urban settlement, Khmelnitskiy Oblast. From Khmelnitskiy National-Territorial Okrug No 61, Ukrainian SSR.

Shundeyev, Ivan Nikandrovich, director of the "Koyelginskiy" Sovkhoz, Yetkulskiy Rayon, CPSU member, Koyelga village, Yetkulskiy Rayon. From Kopeyskiy Territorial Okrug No 337, Chelyabinsk Oblast, RSFSR.

Shushkevich, Stanislav Stanislavovich, proctor of the V.I. Lenin Belorussian State University, CPSU member, Minsk City. From Minskiy-Moskovskiy Territorial Okrug No 564, Belorussian SSR.

Shust, Anna Andreyevna, livestock unit chief at the "Mayak" Kolkhoz, Sumskiy Rayon, CPSU member, V. Sirovatka village, Sumskiy Rayon, Sumy Oblast, Ukrainian SSR. From the women's councils united by the Soviet Women's Committee.

Shustko, Lev Sergeyevich, colonel general, commander of the Red Banner North Caucasus Military District, CPSU member, Rostov-na-Donu city. From Zaterechnyy National-Territorial Okrug No 628, North Osetian ASSR.

Shvets, Aleksandr Mikhaylovich, chairman of the trade union committee of Novokrivorozhskiy Lenin Komsomol Mining and Enriching Combine, CPSU member, Krivoy Rog city, Dnepropetrovsk Oblast, Ukrainian SSR. From the USSR trade unions.

Sidor, Ivan Nikolayevich, chief doctor at Volyn Oblast Hospital, CPSU member, Lutsk city, Volyn Oblast, Ukrainian SSR. From the USSR trade unions.

Sidorchuk, Tatyana Vasilyevna, upholsterer at the Carpathian furniture combine, Ivano-Frankovsk city. From Ivano-Frankovskiy Territorial Okrug No 460, Ivano-Frankovsk Oblast, Ukrainian SSR.

Sidoreyko, Vasiliy Larionovich, drilling foreman at the "Surgutneftegaz" Production Association's No 2 Surgut Drilling Operation Administration, CPSU member, Surgut city, Khanty-Mansiyskiy Autonomous Okrug. From the CPSU.

Sidorenko, Viktor Dmitriyevich, painter, chairman of the board of the Ukrainian SSR Artists Union Kharkov organization, CPSU member, Kharkov city. From the USSR Artists Union.

Sidorov, Aleksey Anatolyevich, pensioner, CPSU member, Sverdlovsk city, RSFSR. From the All-Union Organization of War and Labor Veterans.

Sidorov, Vasiliy Pavlovich, tractor driver on the Ilich Kolkhoz in Pestrechinskiy Rayon, CPSU member, Yantsevary village, Pestrechinskiy Rayon. From Arskiy Territorial Okrug No 387, Tatar ASSR.

Silantyev, Aleksandr Petrovich, Marshal of Aviation, military inspector and adviser in the USSR Defense Minister Inspectors General Group, CPSU member, Moscow city. From the All-Union Organization of War and Labor Veterans.

Simvolokov, Vyacheslav Vladimirovich, coach and lecturer at the Krasnogvardeyskoye Children's and Young People's Sports School, Krasnogvardeyskoye settlement. From Dzhankoyskiy Territorial Okrug No 481, Crimean Oblast, Ukrainian SSR.

Simonov, Mikhail Petrovich, general designer at the P.O. Sukhoy Machine Building Plant, CPSU member, Moscow city. From the USSR DOSAAF.

Simonov, Sergey Borisovich, fitter and assembly worker at the Ufa Motor Building Production Association, CPSU member, Ufa city. From Kalininskiy Territorial Okrug No 350, Bashkir ASSR.

Simonyan, Karen Aramovich, deputy chief editor of the journal VOZROZHDENNAYA ARMENIYA, CPSU member, Yerevan City. From Yerevanskiy-Zeytunskiy National-Territorial Okrug No 394, Armenian SSR.

Simonyan, Valeriy Vaganovich, machine operator on Kokhpinskiy Sovkhoz in Noyemberyanskiy Rayon, CPSU member, Kokhp village, Noyemberyanskiy Rayon. From Tumanyanskiy National-Territorial Okrug No 415, Armenian SSR.

Sinelnikov, Viktor Makarovich, machine operator on the "Novoannovskiy" Sovkhoz in Krasnodonskiy Rayon, CPSU member, Khryashchevatoye settlement, Krasnodonskiy Rayon. From Krasnodonskiy Territorial Okrug No 415, Voroshilovgrad Oblast, Ukrainian SSR.

Siradze, Viktoriya Moiseyevna, chairman of the Georgian Republic Trade Union Council, CPSU member, Tbilisi city. From Signakhskiy National-Territorial Okrug No 184, Georgian SSR.

Sirman, Vasiliy Vladimirovich, tractor driver on the Shevchenko Kolkhoz in Severinovka village, Zhmerinskiy Rayon, CPSU member, Severinovka village, Zhmerinskiy Rayon. From Zhmerinskiy Territorial Okrug No 406, Vinnitsa Oblast, Ukrainian SSR.

Sitnikov, Aleksandr Prokofyevich, pensioner, CPSU member, Rostov-na-Donu city, RSFSR. From the All-Union Organization of War and Labor Veterans.

Skakun, Galina Fedorovna, milking machine operator on the Zhdanov Kolkhoz in Brestskiy Rayon, Borisy village, Brestskiy Rayon, Brest Oblast, Belorussian SSR. From kolkhozes united by the Union Kolkhoz Council.

Skarulis, Regimantas Ionovich, deputy director of the Lithuanian SSR Ministry of Health Experimental and Clinical Medicine Research Institute, CPSU member, Vilnius city. From the USSR Academy of Medical Sciences together with 40 scientific medical societies.

Skiba, Ivan Ivanovich, chief of a CPSU Central Committee department, CPSU member, Moscow city. From kolkhozes united by the Union Kolkhoz Council.

Skokov, Viktor Vasilyevich, Colonel General, commander of the Red Banner Carpathian Military District, CPSU member, Lvov city. From Kovelskiy Territorial Okrug No 412, Volyn Oblast, Ukrainian SSR.

Skrobuk, Ivan Ivanovich, Lieutenant Colonel, CPSU member, Grodno Oblast. From Slonimskiy Territorial Okrug No 562, Grodno Oblast, Belorussian SSR.

Skudra, Viktor Yanovich, Latvian SSR minister of justice, CPSU member, Riga city. From Saldusskiy National-Territorial Okrug No 316, Latvian SSR.

Skulme, Dzhemma Otovna, painter, chairman of the Latvian SSR Union of Artists Board, secretary of the USSR Union of Artists Board, CPSU member, Riga city. From the USSR Union of Artists.

Skvortsov, Vladimir Vitalyevich, chief of a shop at the Vyazniki Motor Vehicle Lighting Equipment Plant, CPSU member, Vyazniki city. From Kovrovskiy Territorial Okrug No 135, Vladimir Oblast, RSFSR.

Sleptsov, Sergey Yefimovich, machine operator at "Churovichskiy" Sovkhoz, Churovichi village, Klimovskiy Rayon, Bryansk Oblast, RSFSR. From the All-Union Komsomol.

Slyunkov, Nikolay, Nikitovich, member of the CPSU Central Committee Politburo, secretary of the CPSU Central Committee, CPSU member, Moscow city. From the CPSU.

Smailova, Kaken, head of Issyk-Kul Oblast Hospital No 1, Naryn city, Issyk-Kul Oblast. From Narynskiy Territorial Okrug No 720, Kirghiz SSR.

Smaylis, Alfredas Yuozovich, head of a laboratory at the Z. Yanushkyavichyus Cardio-Vascular System Physiology and Pathology Research Institute, Kachergine urban settlement, Kaunasskiy Rayon. From Kaunasskiy Rural National-Territorial Okrug No 239, Lithuanian SSR.

Smirnov, Dmitriy Genrikhovich, engineer and designer at "KhEMZ" Production Association, CPSU member, Kharkov city. From Kharkovskiy-Moskovskiy Territorial Okrug No 521, Kharkov Oblast, Ukrainian SSR.

Smolina, Zoya Pavlovna, chairman of the Ivanovo CPSU Obkom Party Control Commission, CPSU member, Ivanovo city, RSFSR. From the women's councils united in the Soviet Women's Committee.

Smorodin, Ivan Mikhaylovich, controller at Novgorod "Volna" Production Association, Novgorod city. From Novgordskiy Territorial Okrug No 227, Novgorod Oblast, RSFSR.

Smyk, Nikolay Mikhaylovich, leader of a multi-purpose team at Krasnoyarsk's V.I. Lenin Metallurgical Plant, CPSU member, Krasnoyarsk city, RSFSR. From the CPSU.

Snegur, Mircha Ivanovich, secretary of the Moldavian Communist Party Central Committee, CPSU member, Kishinev city. From Sorokskiy Territorial Okrug No 703, Moldavian SSR.

Sobolev, Valerian Markovich, chief designer, chief of the "Barrikada" Production Association Design Bureau, CPSU member, Volgograd city. From Tsentralnyy Territorial Okrug No 141, Volgograd Oblast, RSFSR.

Sobolev, Vitaliy Pavlovich, second secretary of the Latvian Communist Party Central Committee, CPSU member, Riga city. From Daugavpilsskiy City National-Territorial Okrug No 301, Latvian SSR.

Sobolev, Vladimir Vasilyevich, fitter and driver at Krasnoyarsk's "Yenisey" Chemical Combine, CPSU member, Krasnoyarsk city. From Leninskiy Territorial Okrug No 87, Krasnoyarsk Kray, RSFSR.

Sokolov, Aleksandr Aleksandrovich, chairman of Gorkiy Oblispolkom, CPSU member, Gorkiy city. From Sergachskiy Territorial Okrug No 164, Gorkiy Oblast, RSFSR.

Sokolov, Viktor Ivanovich, deputy chief mechanic at "Kirovskiy Zavod" Production Association "Transmash" Plant, CPSU member, Tikhvin city. From Tikhvinskiy Territorial Okrug No 64, Leningrad Oblast, RSFSR.

Sokolov, Yefrem Yevseyevich, first secretary of the Belorussian Communist Party Central Committee, CPSU member, Minsk city. From Korbinskiy Territorial Okrug No 549, Brest Oblast, Belorussian SSR.

Sokolov, Yuriy Ivanovich, senior scientific staffer at "Elektronika" Production Association, CPSU member, Voronezh city. From Levoberezhnyy Territorial Okrug No 150, Voronezh Oblast, RSFSR.

Sokolova, Yuliya Yuryevna, senior instructor at the Soviet Army and Navy Main Political Directorate, CPSU member, Moscow city. From the women's councils united in the Soviet Women's Committee.

Solntsev, Roman Kharisovich, writer, CPSU member, Krasnoyarsk city. From Kirovskiy Territorial Okrug No 88, Krasnoyarsk Kray, RSFSR.

Solovyev, Yuriy Borisovich, chairman of the USSR Designers Union Board, CPSU member, Moscow city. From the USSR Designers Union.

Solodilov, Yuriy Ivanovich, commander of the Murmansk combined air detachment, CPSU member, Murmansk city. From Severomorskiy Territorial Okrug No 226, Murmansk Oblast, RSFSR.

Soltanov, Bereket, petroleum and gas extraction worker in the Sakar-Chaginskiy Rayon Gasfield Administration, CPSU member, Sakar-Chaginskiy Rayon, Mary Oblast, Turkmen SSR. From the All-Union Komsomol.

Sopyyev, Muratberdy, chairman of Ashkhabadskiy Rayon's "Sovet Turkmenistany" Kolkhoz, CPSU member, Gyami village, Ashkhabadskiy Rayon, Turkmen SSR. From the kolkhozes united in the Union Kolkhoz Council.

Sorochik, Yuriy Yuryevich, department chief at Lvov Ukrainian Komsomol Gorkom, CPSU member, Lvov City. From Lvovskiy National-Territorial Okrug No 50, Ukrainian SSR.

Sorokin, Aleksey Andreyevich, teamleader at "Lisakovskrudstroy" Trust" "Promstroy-1" Construction Administration, Lisakovsk city. From Rudnenskiy Territorial Okrug No 636, Kustanay Oblast, Kazakh SSR.

Sorokin, Aleksey Ivanovich, fleet admiral, first deputy chief of the Soviet Army and Navy Main Political Directorate, CPSU member, Moscow city. From the All-Union War and Labor Veterans' Organization.

Sorokin, Mikhail Ivanovich, army general, USSR deputy defense minister, chief inspector of the USSR Defense Ministry, CPSU member, Moscow city. From Altayskiy National-Territorial Okrug No 3, RSFSR.

Soskovets, Oleg Nikolayevich, general director of Karaganda Metallurgical Combine, CPSU member, Temirtau city. From Temirtauskiy Territorial Okrug No 630, Karaganda Oblast, Kazakh SSR.

Sotnikov, Nikolay Ivanovich, director of Leningrad Ceramics Plant, CPSU member, Leningrad city. From Volkhovskiy Territorial Okrug No 60, Leningrad Oblast, RSFSR.

Sozinov, Aleksey Alekseyevich, chairman of the VASKHNIL Southern Branch Presidium, CPSU member, Kiev city. From VASKHNIL.

Spanderashvili, Tamaz Mikhaylovich, steel worker at Rustavi Metallurgical Plant, CPSU member, Rustavi city. From Rustavskiy National-Territorial Okrug No 182, Georgian SSR.

Spasskiy, Igor Dmitriyevich, general designer and chief of Leningrad's "Rubin" Design and Installation Bureau, CPSU member, Leningrad city. From the CPSU.

Spiridonov, Mikhail Vasilyevich, chairman of the kolkhoz named for the 22d party congress, Orlovskiy Rayon, Orel Oblast, CPSU member, Orel city, RSFSR. From the kolkhozes united in the Union Kolkhoz Council.

Stadnik, Vladimir Yakovlevich, workshop chief at Lukhovitsy Machine Building Plant, CPSU member, Lukhovitsy city. From Kolomenskiy Territorial Okrug No 33, Moscow Oblast, RSFSR.

Stakvilyavichyus, Mindaugas Yozo, associate professor at Shyaulyay Pedagogical Institute, CPSU member, Shyaulyay city. From Shyaulyay City National-Territorial Okrug No 225, Lithuanian SSR.

Stankovich, Yevgeniy Fedorovich, secretary of the Ukrainian SSR Union of Composers Board, CPSU member, Kiev city. From the USSR Union of Composers.

Starovoytov, Vasiliy Konstantinovich, chairman of Kirovskiy Rayon's "Rassvet" Kolkhoz named for Orlovskiy, CPSU member, Kirovskiy Rayon, Mogilev Oblast, Belorussian SSR. From the All-Union War and Labor Veterans' Organization.

Starovoytova, Galina Vasilyevna, senior scientific staffer at the USSR Academy of Sciences Presidium Center for the Study of Interethnic Relations, Moscow City. From Yerevanskiy-Sovetskiy National-Territorial Okrug No 393, Armenian SSR.

Starodubtsev, Vasiliy Aleksandrovich, chairman of Novomoskovskiy Rayon's Lenin Kolkhoz and Breeding Farm, CPSU member, Sokolniki city, Novomoskovskiy Rayon, Tula Oblast, RSFSR. From the kolkhozes united in the Union Kolkhoz Council.

Starodubtsev, Dmitriy Aleksandrovich, director of Yaroslavskiy Rayon's Dzerzhinskiy Sovkhoz, Makeyevskoye settlement, Yaroslavskiy Rayon. From Yaroslavskiy Territorial Okrug No 346, Yaroslavl Oblast RSFSR.

Starostina, Tatyana Andreyevna, professor of the First Moscow Medical Institute named for I.M. Sechenov, Moscow city. From the USSR Academy of Medical Science and 40 scientific medical societies.

Statulyavichyus, Vitautas Antano, vice president of the Lithuanian SSR Academy of Sciences, director of the Lithuanian Academy of Sciences Mathematics and Cybernetics Institute, CPSU member, Vilnius city. From Utenskiy National-Territorial Okrug No 253, Lithuanian SSR.

Stefanenko, Ivan Denisovich, pensioner, CPSU member, Gorkiy city, RSFSR. From the All-Union Organization of Veterans of War and Labor.

Stelmashonok, Vladimir Ivanovich, artist, chairman of the board of the Belorussian SSR Artists' Union, CPSU member, Minsk City. From the USSR Artists' Union.

Stepanenko, Aleksandr Vasilyevich, vice president of the Belorussian SSR Academy of Sciences, CPSU member, Minsk city. From the USSR Union of Scientific and Engineering Societies.

Stepanov, Vladimir Nikolayevich, director of Olonetskiy Rayon's "Vidlitskiy" Animal Sovkhoz, CPSU member, Vidlitsy village. From Petrozavodskiy Territorial Okrug No 369, Karelian ASSR.

Stepanova, Galina Sambuyevna, organizer of extracurricular and extramural educative work at Onokhoy Secondary School, CPSU member, Onokhoy settlement, Zaigrayevskiy Rayon. From Zaigrayevskiy National-Territorial Okrug No 521, Buryat ASSR.

Stepanova, Galina Sergeyevna, chief of the N.G. Bezrukov Kolkhoz Dairy Product Complex, CPSU member, Oktyabrskoye village, Poretskiy Rayon, Chuvash ASSR. From the women's councils united in the Soviet Women's Committee.

Stepnadze, Telman Sergeyevich, team leader at Khashurskiy Rayon's Alskiy Viticultural Sovkhoz, CPSU member, Brili village, Khashurskiy Rayon. From Akhaltsikhskiy National-Territorial Okrug No 169, Georgian SSR.

Stipakov, Yevgeniy Grigoryevich, chief medic at No 2 Municipal Clinical Hospital, CPSU member, Ivanovo city. From Ivanovskiy city Territorial Okrug No 166, Ivanovo Oblast, RSFSR.

Stolbunov, Valeriyan Konstantinovich, director of Ordzhonikidzevskiy Rayon's "Pokrovskiy" Breeding Farm, CPSU member, Pokrovka village, Ordzhonikidzevskiy Rayon. From Arkalykskiy Territorial Okrug No 635, Kustanay Oblast, Kazakh SSR.

Stoumova, Galina Ivanovna, workshop chief at Gatchinskiy Rayon's "Gatchinskiy" Sovkhoz, CPSU member, Bolshiye Kolpany village, Gatchinskiy Rayon. From Gatchinskiy Territorial Okrug No 62, Leningrad Oblast, RSFSR.

Strautin, Ivar Fritsevich, chairman of the Latvian Potrebsoyuz Board, CPSU member, Riga city. From the USSR Consumer Cooperatives.

Strelkov, Aleksandr Iosifovich, teamleader at "Avtokran" Production Association Power-Driven Crane Plant, CPSU member, Ivanovo city. From Ivanovskiy Rural Territorial Okrug No 167, Ivanovo Oblast, RSFSR.

Stroyev, Yegor Semenovich, first secretary of Orel CPSU Obkom, CPSU member, Orel city. From Livenskiy Territorial Okrug No 251, Orel Oblast, RSFSR.

Strukov, Nikolay Alekseyevich, senior investigator at the Kursk Oblast Prosecutor's Office, CPSU member, Kursk City. From Kurskiy Territorial Okrug No 216, Kursk Oblast, RSFSR.

Studenikin, Mitrofan Yakovlevich, director of the USSR Academy of Medical Science Pediatric Research Institute, CPSU member, Moscow city. From the USSR Academy of Medical Science and 40 scientific medical societies.

Stupin, Yuriy Vasilyevich, chairman of the Trade Union Central Council For the Administration of Health Resorts, CPSU member, Moscow city. From the USSR's trade unions.

Stupina, Yekaterina Davydovna, pediatrician at Tavricheskiy Rayon Hospital, Tavricheskoye urban settlement, Tavricheskiy Rayon. From Tavricheskiy Territorial Okrug No 241, Omsk Oblast, RSFSR.

Subbi, Olev Iokhannesovich, painter, acting professor of the Estonian SSR's State Art Institute Fine Art Department, Tallinn city. From the USSR Union of Artists.

Subbotina, Olga Grigoryevna, deputy director in charge of educational and training work at Ardatov's Eighth-Grade School, CPSU candidate member, Ardatov city. From Ardatovskiy National-Territorial Okrug No 605, Mordovian ASSR.

Sulakshin, Stepan Stepanovich, laboratory chief at the Nuclear Physics Scientific Research Institute, CPSU member, Tomsk City. From Tomskiy Territorial Okrug No 313, RSFSR.

Suleymenov, Olzhas Omarovich, writer, first secretary of the Kazakhstan Writers' Union Board, CPSU member, Alma-Ata City. From Ayaguzskiy Territorial Okrug No 642, Semipalatinsk Oblast, Kazakh SSR.

Sultangazin, Umirzak Makhmutovich, president of the Kazakh SSR Academy of Sciences, CPSU member, Alma-Ata city. From Karagandinskiy-Oktyabrskiy National-Territorial Okrug No 142, Kazakh SSR.

Sumarokov, Ilya Alekseyevich, general director of the "Usolye" Agro-Industrial Combine, director of the 60th Anniversary of the USSR Sovkhoz, Usolskiy Rayon, CPSU member, Belorechenskiy settlement, Usolskiy Rayon. From Angarskiy Territorial Okrug No 172, Irkutsk Oblast, RSFSR.

Suntsov, Sergey Dmitriyevich, deputy chief engineer of an automobile plant under the "Izhmash" Production Association, CPSU member, Izhevsk city. From Izhevskiy Territorial Okrug No 393, Udmurt ASSR.

Suprunov, Leonid Yakovlevich, chairman of the Maritime Kray Motor Transport and Highway Workers Trade Union Commitee, CPSU member, Vladivostok city, Maritime Kray, RSFSR. From the USSR trade unions.

Surkov, Mikhail Semenovich, major general, chief of the political department of a troop unit, CPSU member, Yerevan city. From Leninakanskiy-Shirakskiy National-Territorial Okrug No 396, Armenian SSR.

Sukharev, Aleksandr Yakovlevich, USSR Prosecutor General, CPSU member, Moscow city. From Groznenskiy National-Territorial Okrug No 7, RSFSR.

Sukhinin, Vladimir Yuryevich, electric locomotive driver at the North Kazakhstan Railroad's Groznyy

Locomotive Depot, CPSU member, Groznyy city. From Oktyabrskiy National-Territorial Okrug No 670, Chechen-Ingush ASSR.

Sukhov, Leonid Ivanovich, vehicle driver at the Kharkov 16301 Motor Transport Enterprise, Solonitsevka settlement, Dergachevskiy Rayon. From Kharkovskiy-Leninskiy Territorial Okrug No 519, Kharkov Oblast, Ukrainian SSR.

Sukhorukov, Dmitriy Semenovich, army general, USSR deputy defense minister for personnel and chief of the USSR Defense Ministry Main Personnel Directorate, CPSU member, Moscow city. From Lubenskiy Territorial Okrug No 506, Poltava Oblast, Ukrainian SSR.

Surmanidze, Tsiala Otarovna, kolkhoz member at the Skhalta Village Kolkhoz, Khuloyskiy Rayon, Skhalta Village, Khuloyskiy Rayon, Adzhar ASSR. From Khuloyskiy National-Territorial Okrug No 500, Adzhar ASSR.

Sushko, Boris Ivanovich, smelter at the 50th Anniversary of the USSR Pure Metals Plant, CPSU member, Svetlovodsk city, Kirovograd Oblast, Ukrainian SSR. From the All-Union Society of Inventors and Rationalizers.

Svatkovskiy, Vladimir Vasilyevich, chairman of the V.I. Lenin Fishing Kolkhoz, CPSU member, Petropavlovsk-Kamchatskiy city, Kamchatka Oblast, RSFSR. From the All-Union Association of Fishing Kolkhozes.

Svid, Georgiy Semenovich, chairman of the "Avangard" Kolkhoz, Ryazanskiy Rayon, CPSU member, Ryazan city, RSFSR. From the kolkhozes united by the Union Kolkhoz Council.

Sydykov, Usen, first deputy chairman of the Kirghiz SSR Council of Ministers and chairman of the Kirghiz SSR State Agro-Industrial Committee, CPSU member, Frunze City. From Kochkorskiy National-Territorial Okrug No 334, Kirghiz SSR.

Syrgiy, Afanasiy Alekseyevich, director of the "Dumbraveny" Sovkhoz, Sorokskiy Rayon, CPSU member, Dumbraveny village, Sorokskiy Rayon. From Sorokskiy National-Territorial Okrug No 281, Moldavian SSR.

Sysoyev, Valeriy Sergeyevich, chairman of the Central Council of the All-Union "Dinamo" Physical Culture and Sports Society, CPSU member, Moscow city. From USSR public sports organizations.

Sysoyev, Viktor Andreyevich, director of the Tambov Oblast Palace of Pioneers and Schoolchildren, CPSU member, Tambov city, RSFSR. From the All-Union Komsomol.

Sychev, Nikolay Yakovlevich, pensioner, CPSU member, Moscow city. From the All-Union Organization of War and Labor Veterans.

Taabaldiyev, Esenkadyr, senior shepherd at the "Uchnura" Kolkhoz, Tyan-Shanskiy Rayon, CPSU member, Tyan-Shanskiy Rayon, Issyk-Kul Oblast. From Tyan-Shanskiy National-Territorial Okrug No 350, Kirghiz SSR.

Tabeyev, Fikryat Akhmedzhanovich, first deputy chairman of the RSFSR Council of Ministers, CPSU member, Moscow city. From Rzhevskiy Territorial Okrug No 184, Kalinin Oblast, RSFSR.

Tabukashvili, Revaz Shalvovich, leader of the "Gruziyafilm" Movie Studio Screenplay Association, CPSU member, Tbilisi city. From Batumskiy National-Territorial Okrug No 170, Georgian SSR.

Tagandurdyyev, Bayramgeldy, first secretary of the Chardzhou Turkmen Communist Party Obkom, CPSU member, Chardzhou city. From Kerkinskiy National-Territorial Okrug No 432, Turkmen SSR.

Talanchuk, Petr Mikhaylovich, rector of the Kiev Polytechnical Institute, CPSU member, Kiev city. From Zhovtnevyy Territorial Okrug No 466, Kiev city.

Talashin, Igor Stepanovich, troubleshooter at an assembly workshop in the Savelovskiy "Progress" Production Association, CPSU member, Kimry city, Kalinin Oblast. From Bezhetskiy Territorial Okrug No 182, Kalinin Oblast, RSFSR.

Tamberg, Eyno Martinovich, composer, professor of the Tallinn State Conservatory, Estonian SSR Composers' Union Board secretary, Tallinn city. From the USSR Composers' Union.

Tapanyan, Srbui Mkrtichevna, team leader of a sewn goods unit at Yerevan's A. Myasnikyan No 1 Knitwear Production Association, Yerevan city. From the USSR trade unions.

Taranov, Ivan Tikhonovich, chairman of the Stavropol Krayispolkom, CPSU member, Stavropol city. From Zelenchukskiy National-Territorial Okrug No 723, Karachayevo-Cherkess Autonomous Oblast.

Tarasov, Aleksey Pavlovich, director of Yermolayevo Secondary School No 1, CPSU member, Yermolayevo Urban settlement, Kumertauskiy Rayon. From Salavatskiy National-Territorial Okrug No 512, Bashkir ASSR.

Tarasov, Igor Stepanovich, chairman of the Dnepropetrovsk Oblast Committee of the Ukrainian SSR Red Cross Society, CPSU member, Dnepropetrovsk city. From the USSR Union of Red Cross and Red Crescent Societies.

Tarazevich, Georgiy Stanislavovich, chairman of the Belorussian SSR Supreme Soviet Presidium, CPSU member, Minsk city. From Molodechnenskiy National-Territorial Okrug No 71, Belorussian SSR.

Tarnavskiy, Georgiy Stepanovich, Belorussian SSR prosecutor, CPSU member, Minsk city. From Slutskiy Territorial Okrug No 570, Minsk Oblast, Belorussian SSR.

Tashev, Saburbay Mavlyanovich, chief of the "Turkmengeologiya" Association's Kushtang Geological Prospecting Expedition, CPSU member, Gaurdak Settlement, Charshanginskiy Rayon, Chardzhou Oblast. From Khodzhambasskiy National-Territorial Okrug No 445, Turkmen SSR.

Tatarchuk, Valentin Ivanovich, director of the Solikamsk 60th Anniversary of the USSR Pulp and Paper Combine, CPSU member, Solikamsk city, Perm Oblast, RSFSR. From the CPSU.

Tatarchuk, Nikolay Fedorovich, first secretary of the Kalinin CPSU Obkom, CPSU member, Kalinin city. From Kalininskiy Rural Territorial Okrug No 181, Kalinin Oblast, RSFSR.

Tavkhelidze, Albert Nikiforovich, president of the Georgian SSR Academy of Sciences, CPSU member, Tbilisi city. From Sukhumskiy Rural National-Territorial Okrug No 483, Abkhaz ASSR.

Tazhimuratova, Aisulyu, teacher at S.M. Kirov Secondary School No 4, Nukus city. From Nukusskiy National-Territorial Okrug No 563, Kara-Kalpak ASSR.

Tedeyev, Lev Razhdenovich, machine operator at the Znaurskiy Rayon Machine and Tractor Pool Repair and Operation Enterprise, Dzagina Village, Znaurskiy Rayon, South Osetian Autonomous Oblast. From Znaurskiy National-Territorial Okrug No 739, South Osetian Autonomous Oblast.

Telegin, Viktor Leonidovich, chairman of the "Votkinskiy Zavod" Production Association Trade Union Committee, CPSU member, Votkinsk city, Udmurt ASSR. From the USSR trade unions.

Telezin, Anna Fedorovna, link leader at Tlumachskiy Rayon's Moskalev Kolkhoz, Podverbtsy village, Tlumachskiy Rayon. From Kolomyyskiy Territorial Okrug No 462, Ivano-Frankovsk Oblast, Ukrainian SSR.

Temirbayev, Valeriy Batayevich, first secretary of the Chimkent Kazakh Communist Party Obkom, CPSU member, Chimkent city. From Lengerskiy Territorial Okrug No 651, Chimkent Oblast, Kazakh SSR.

Temnogrudova, Zinaida Sergeyevna, doctor at Penza Oblast Hospital No 4, Penza city, RSFSR. From the All-Union Organization of War and Labor Veterans.

Ten, Radiy Lavrentyevich, director of the Tokmak Worsted Spinning Factory, CPSU member, Tomsk City. From Tokmakskiy National-Territorial Okrug No 347, Kirghiz SSR.

Terekhova, Elvira Ivanovna, head of a dairy farm at the V.I. Lenin Kolkhoz, Tambovskiy Rayon, CPSU member, Tolstovka village, Tambovskiy Rayon. From Amurskiy Territorial Okrug No 115, Amur Oblast, RSFSR.

Tereshkova, Valentina Vladimirovna, chairman of the presidium of the Union of Soviet Societies for Friendship and Cultural Relations with Foreign Countries, CPSU member, Moscow city. From the Union of Soviet Societies for Friendship and Cultural Relations With Foreign Countries and the Soviet Society for Cultural Relations With Compatriots Abroad (the "Rodina" Society).

Ternyuk, Nikolay Emmanuilovich, deputy chief technologist at the "Zavod im. Malysheva" Production Association, CPSU member, Kharkov City. From Kharkovskiy-Ordzhonikidzevskiy Territorial Okrug No 522, Kharkov Oblast, Ukrainian SSR.

Tertyshnyy, Yevgeniy Alekseyevich, chief of the "Chuvashstroy" Territorial Construction Association, CPSU member, Cheboksary city. From the Cheboksarskiy Territorial Okrug No 399, Chuvash ASSR.

Tetenov, Valentin Afanasyevich, first deputy chief of the Perm branch of the Sverdlovsk Railroad, CPSU member, Perm city. From Dzerzhinskiy Territorial Okrug No 256, Perm Oblast, RSFSR.

Tileubayeva, Kulzada Tleubayevna, senior shepherdess of the "Aydarminskiy" Sovkhoz, Moyynkumskiy Rayon, CPSU member, Kenes village, Moyynkumskiy Rayon. From Chuyskiy Territorial Okrug No 626, Dzhambul Oblast, Kazakh SSR.

Timashova, Nadezhda Ivanovna, pensioner, CPSU member, Kazan city, Tatar ASSR. From the All-Union Organization of War and Labor Veterans.

Timchenko, Vladimir Mikhaylovich, milling machine operator of the "Azovskiy Optiko-Mekhanicheskiy Zavod" Production Association, Azov city. From the Zernogradskiy Territorial Okrug No 271, Rostov Oblast, RSFSR.

Timchenko, Mikhail Andreyevich, director of the "Marushinky" Sovkhoz, Tselinny Rayon, CPSU member, Druzhba settlement, Tselinnyy Rayon. From the Biyskiy Territorial Okrug No 67, Altay Kray, RSFSR.

Tikhonenkov, Ernst Petrovich, deputy director of the Institute of Mineral Resources, CPSU member, Simferopol city. From the Simferopolskiy Territorial Okrug No 480, Crimea Oblast, Ukrainian SSR.

Tikhonov, Vladimir Aleksandrovich, professor at the USSR Council of Ministers Academy of the National Economy, CPSU member, Moscow city. From VASKHNIL.

Tikhonov, Georgiy Ivanovich, chief of the Department of Capital Construction and Modernization of the USSR Council of Ministers Bureau for the fuel and energy complex, CPSU member, Moscow city. From the Rogunskiy National-Territorial Okrug No 377, Tajik SSR.

Tkachenko, Stanislav Nikolayevich, deputy chief physician at Pavlodar Oblast Hospital, Pavlodar City. From Pavlodarskiy National-Territorial Okrug No 148, Kazakh SSR.

Tkacheva, Zoya Nikolayevna, chief of a department of the Slavgorod Central Rayon Hospital, Slavgorod city. From Krichevskiy Territorial Okrug No 574, Mogilev Oblast, Belorussian SSR.

Tkachuk, Vasiliy Mikhaylovich, chairman of the "Prapor Komunizmu" Kolkhoz, chairman of the "Prut" Agricultural Firm, Kolomyyskiy Rayon, CPSU member, Podgaychiki village, Kolomyyskiy Rayon, Ivano-Frankovsk Oblast. From the Ivano-Frankovskiy National-Territorial Okrug No 47, Ukrainian SSR.

Tkemaladze, Grigoriy Abelovich, deputy chairman of the trade union committee of the "Chkaturmarganets" Production Association, CPSU member, Chkatura city. From the Chkaturskiy National-Territorial Okrug No 192, Georgian SSR.

Tkhor, Aleksey Ivanovich, leader of a team of face workers of the M.V. Frunze mining administration of the "Rovenkiantratsit" Production Association, CPSU member, Antratsit city, Voroshilovgrad Oblast, Ukrainian SSR. From the USSR trade unions.

Tlostanov, Vladimir Kalimetovich, rector of Kabardino-Balkar State University, CPSU member, Nalchik City. From Oktyabrskiy National-Territorial Okrug No 537, Kabardino-Balkar ASSR.

Tolpezhnikov, V. F., manager, Consultation Office No.1 of the N. Burdenko Riga City Emergency Medical Assistance Clinical Hospital. From the Proletarian National Territorial Election District, Latvian SSR.

Tolstoukhov, Igor Arkadyevich, first secretary of Yaroslavl CPSU Obkom, CPSU member, Yaroslavl city. From Rostovskiy Territorial Okrug No 347, Yarosavl Oblast, RSFSR.

Tomkus, Vitas Pyatrovich, journalist, Vilnius city. From the Panevezhskiy Territorial Okrug No 691, Lithuanian SSR.

Toome, Indrek Kherbertovich, chairman of the Estonian SSR Council of Ministers, CPSU member, Tallinn city. From the Vyruskiy National-Territorial Okrug No 461, Estonian SSR.

Tozik, Leonid Afanasyevich, leader of a comprehensive team at the "Minskpromstroy" Construction and Installation Association, CPSU member, Minsk city. From the USSR trade unions.

Travkin, Nikolay Ilich, student at the Moscow Higher Party School, CPSU member, Moscow City. From Shchelkovskiy Territorial Okrug No 45, Moscow Oblast, RSFSR.

Tretyak, Ivan Moiseyevich, Army General, commander in chief of the country's air defense forces, USSR deputy defense minister, CPSU member, Moscow city. From the All-Union Organization of War and Labor Veterans.

Trefilov, Viktor Ivanovich, vice president of the Ukrainian SSR Academy of Sciences, director of the Institute of the Problems of Materials Science of the Ukrainian SSR Academy of Sciences, CPSU member, Kiev city. From the USSR Union of Scientific and Engineering Societies.

Troitskiy, Andrey Yakovlevich, chief of an office of the Kalinin Oblast teachers' in-service training institute, CPSU member, Kalinin city, RSFSR. From the All-Union Organization of War and Labor Veterans.

Trofimov, Aleksey Vasilyevich, director of the "Rugozerskiy" Animal Sovkhoz, CPSU member, Rugozero village, Muyezerskiy Rayon, Karelian ASSR. From Suoyarvskiy National-Territorial Okrug No 579, Karelian ASSR.

Trofimov, Valeriy Ivanovich, chief of a shop of the Malovisherskiy glass works, CPSU member, Malaya Vishera city. From Borovichskiy Territorial Okrug No 228, Novgorod Oblast, RSFSR.

Trokhimets, Mikhail Anatolyevich, machine operator at the 1 May Kolkhoz in Rakitinyanskiy Rayon, CPSU member, Nastashka village, Rakitinyanskiy Rayon, Kiev Oblast, Ukrainian SSR. From the All-Union Komsomol.

Trubilin, Nikolay Timofeyevich, deputy chairman of the RSFSR Council of Ministers, CPSU member, Moscow city. From the All-Union Voluntary Society for the Struggle for Sobriety.

Trubin, Andrey Dmitriyevich, steel founder at the Nizhnyy Tagil metallurgical combine named for V.I. Lenin, CPSU member, Nizhniy Tagil city, Sverdlovsk Oblast, RSFSR. From the All-Union Komsomol.

Trudolyubov, Aleksandr Ivanovich, chairman of the "Dnepr" Kolkhoz in Kholm-Zhirkovskiy Rayon, CPSU member, Steshino village, Kholm-Zhirkovskiy Rayon, Smolensk Oblast, RSFSR. From the All-Union Komsomol.

Tsalko, Aleksandr Valeryanovich, colonel, military unit commander, Moscow Military District, CPSU member, Kalinin Oblast. From Kalininskiy National-Territorial Okrug No 12, RSFSR.

Tsarenko, Aleksandr Mikhaylovich, chairman of the "Mir" kolkhoz, Putivlskiy Rayon, CPSU member, Mazevka village, Putivlskiy Rayon, Sumy Oblast. From Sumskiy National-Territorial Okrug No 56, Ukrainian SSR.

Tsarevskiy, Aleksandr Leonidovich, faceworker at the "Stakhanovugol" production association's mine named for the 22d CPSU Congress, CPSU member, Stakhanov city, Voroshilovgrad Oblast, Ukrainian SSR. From the All-Union Komsomol.

Tsavro, Yuriy Stanislavovich, head of department at Yaltinskiy City Hospital, CPSU member, Yalta city. From Yaltinskiy Territorial Okrug No 485, Crimea Oblast, Ukrainian SSR.

Tsereteli, Zurab Konstantinovich, painter and sculptor, chairman of the Georgian SSR Designers' Union Board, CPSU member, Tbilisi city. From the USSR Designers Union.

Tsigelnikov, Aleksandr Sergeyevich, deputy director of capital construction management at the "Leninskugol" production association, CPSU member, Leninsk-Kuznetskiy city, Kemerovo Oblast, RSFSR. From the All-Union Komsomol.

Tsintsadze, Sulkhan Fedorovich, composer, chairman of the Georgian SSR Composers Union Board, CPSU member, Tbilisi city. From the USSR Composers Union.

Tsirulis, Andrey Yanovich, chief editor of the newspaper PADOMYU YAUNATNE, CPSU member, Riga city. From Bauskiy National-Territorial Okrug No 298, Latvian SSR.

Tso, Vasiliy Ivanovich, general director of the Akhunbabayevskiy cotton-wool production association, CPSU member, Andizhan city. From Leninskiy National-Territorial Okrug No 98, Uzbek SSR.

Tsoy, Konstantin Nikolayevich, chief physician at the republic antituberculosis clinic, CPSU member, Kyzyl city. From Kyzylskiy Tsentralnyy National-Territorial Okrug No 648, Tuva ASSR.

Tsybukh, Valeriy Ivanovich, first secretary of the Ukrainian Komsomol Central Committee, CPSU member, Kiev city. From Mogilev-Podolskiy Territorial Okrug No 408, Vinnitsa Oblast, Ukrainian SSR.

Tsyganov, Viktor Ivanovich, chairman of the Kalinin Oblast Trade Union Council, CPSU member, Kalinin city, RSFSR. From the USSR trade unions.

Tsykalo, Rostislav Ivanovich, deputy party committee secretary at the "Krasnoyarskgesstroy Construction Administration, CPSU member, Sayanogorsk City. From Sayanogorskiy National-Territorial Okrug No 733, Khakass Autonomous Oblast.

Tsyplayev, Sergey Alekseyevich, scientific secretary to the State Optical Institute named for S.I. Vavilov, CPSU member, Leningrad city. From the All-Union Komsomol.

Tsyrenov, Zhargal Tsydenzhapovich, machine operator at Bichurskiy Rayon's "Bichurskiy" Sovkhoz, CPSU member, Dabatuy village. From Selenginskiy Territorial Okrug No 361, Buryat ASSR.

Tsyu, Nikolay Antonovich, first secretary of Kishinev party gorkom, CPSU member, Kishinev City. From Kishinevskiy-Oktyabrskiy Territorial Okrug No 696, Moldavian SSR.

Tsyurupa, Viktor Aleksandrovich, head of department at city hospital No 15, Moscow city. From Veshnyakovskiy Territorial Okrug No 4, Moscow city.

Tyminskiy, Grigoriy Aleksandrovich, chairman of Kelmenetskiy Rayon's "Druzhba Narodov" Kolkhoz, CPSU member, Vartikovtsy village, Kelmenetskiy Rayon. From Novoselitskiy Territorial Okrug No 545, Chernovitsy Oblast, Ukrainian SSR.

Tynspoyeg, Gustav Augustovich, first deputy chairman of the Estonian SSR Council of Ministers, chairman of the Estonian SSR Gosagroprom, CPSU member, Tallinn city. From Yygevaskiy National-Territorial Okrug No 462, Estonian SSR.

Tyugu, Enn Kharaldovich, academician-secretary at the Estonian SSR Academy of Sciences Computer Science and Technical Physics Department, CPSU member, Tallinn city. From the USSR Union of Scientific and Engineering Societies.

Tyulebekov, Kasym Khazhibayevich, first secretary of Alma-Ata Kazakh Communist Party Obkom, CPSU member, Alma-Ata city. From Alma-Altinskiy-Frunzenskiy National-Territorial Okrug No 132, Kazakh SSR.

Tyulyandin, Aleksey Dmitriyevich, first deputy chairman of the Union of USSR Red Cross and Red Crescent Societies Ispolkom, CPSU member, Moscow city. From the Union of USSR Red Cross and Red Crescent Societies.

Tyupa, Sergey Viktorovich, director of the Rzhishchev "Radiator" Plant, CPSU member, Rzhishchev Urban settlement, Kagarlykskiy Rayon. From Mironovskiy Territorial Okrug No 473, Kiev Oblast, Ukrainian SSR.

Tyurina, Tamara Vasilyevna, chief of the technology bureau of the "Elektrovypryamitel" Production Association, Saransk City. From Saranskiy Territorial Okrug No 376, Mordovian ASSR.

Tyutryumov, Aleksandr Mikhaylovich, trade union committee chairman at the "Kondopogabumprom" Production Association, CPSU member, Kondopoga city, Karelian ASSR. From the USSR trade unions.

Tubolets, Irina Ivanovna, stamp operator at the Minsk Tractor Plant named for V.I. Lenin, CPSU member, Minsk city. From the USSR trade unions.

Tukhtabayev, Abdumutalib Tursinovich, joiner at the Altynkulskaya consumer goods factory, CPSU member, Pakhtaabad village, Andizhanskiy Rayon. From the Andizhanskiy Territorial Okrug No 575, Andizhan Oblast, Uzbek SSR.

Tumetova, Maysha Moldakarayevna, shepherdess of the "Tushchikudukskiy" Sovkhoz, Mangistauskiy Rayon, CPSU member, Tushchikuduk village, Mangistauskiy Rayon, Guryev Oblast. From the Mangyshlakskiy National-Territorial Okrug No 147, Kazakh SSR.

Tupolev, Aleksey Andreyevich, general designer, responsible leader of the "Opyt" Machine Building Plant in

Moscow, CPSU member, Moscow city. From the Union of Soviet Societies for Friendship and Cultural Relations With Foreign Countries and the Soviet Society for Cultural Ties with Fellow Countrymen Abroad (the "Rodina" Society).

Turabov, Gasan Sattar ogly, director and artistic director of the Azerbaijan State Academy Drama Theater named for M. Azizbekov, CPSU member, Baku city. From the Bakinskiy-Nasiminskiy Territorial Okrug No 673, Azerbaijan SSR.

Turayeva, Mukar, team leader at the "Kommunist" Sovkhoz in Yakkabagskiy Rayon, CPSU member, Samak kishlak, Yakkabagskiy Rayon, Kaskha-Darya Oblast. From the Shakhrisabzskiy National-Territorial Okrug No 103, Uzbek SSR.

Turenko, Vyacheslav Stepanovich, chief of the pediatric surgery department at the Central Medical and Hygiene Unit No 104, Stepnogorsk City, Tselinograd Oblast. From Yermentauskiy Territorial Okrug No 649, Tselinograd Oblast, Kazakh SSR.

Turganbayev, Danebay Tazhenovich, machine operator at the Kuybyshev Sovkhoz in Kegeyliyskiy Rayon, CPSU member, Kegeyliyskiy Rayon. From the Kegeyliyskiy National-Territorial Okrug No 560, Karakalpak ASSR.

Turysov, Karatay, secretary of the AUCCTU, CPSU member, Moscow city. From the USSR trade unions.

Tutov, Nikolay Dmitriyevich, senior lieutenant, secretary of the Komsomol committee of a military unit in the Air Force, CPSU member, Orenburg city. From the Orenburgskiy Rural Territorial Okrug No 244, Orenburg Oblast, RSFSR.

Tuzov, Vladimir Nikolayevich, chairman of the Radio and Electronics Industry Workers Union Central Committee, CPSU member, Moscow city. From the USSR trade unions.

Ubaydullayeva, Rano Akhatovna, deputy director of the Uzbek SSR Academy of Sciences Economics Institute, CPSU member, Tashkent city. From the women's councils united in the Soviet Women's Committee.

Udalov, Aleksandr Vladimirovich, deputy chief of the Northern Railroad's Buy Locomotive Depot, CPSU member, Buy city. From Sharinskiy Territorial Okrug No 203, Kostroma Oblast, RSFSR.

Ugarov, Boris Sergeyevich, artist, president of the USSR Academy of Arts, CPSU member, Moscow city. From the USSR Academy of Arts.

Ulasevich, Yelena Genrikhovna, milking machine operator at Ivyevskiy Rayon's V.I. Lenin Kolkhoz, CPSU member, Geraneny village, Ivyevskiy Rayon. From Oshmyanskiy Territorial Okrug No 561, Grodno Oblast, Belorussian SSR.

Ulyanov, Mikhail Aleksandrovich, artistic director of the Yevg. Vakhtangov State Academic Theater, chairman of the RSFSR Theater Workers' Union Board, CPSU member, Moscow city. From the CPSU.

Umalatova, Sazhi Zayndinovna, leader of an integrated team at the Groznyy "Krasnyy Molot" Machine Building Plant, CPSU member, Groznyy city. From the CPSU.

Umarkhodzhayev, Mukhtar Ishankhodzhayevich, rector of the Andizhan State Language Teacher Training Institute, CPSU member, F. Engels Sovkhoz, Andizhanskiy Rayon, Andizhan Oblast. From Andizhanskiy National-Territorial Okrug No 97, Uzbek SSR.

Umerenkov, Aleksey Mikhaylovich, chairman of Prokhladnenskiy Rayon's Zhuk Kolkhoz, CPSU member, Priblizhnaya village, Prokhladnenskiy Rayon. From Prokhladnenskiy Rural National-Territorial Okrug No 542, Kabardino-Balkar ASSR.

Uoka, Kazimeras Kosto, bulldozer driver at the "Kauno Statiba" Construction and Installation Trust's No 14 Mechanized Earth Work Administration, CPSU member, Kaunas city. From Kaunasskiy-Pozhelskiy National-Territorial Okrug No 238, Lithuanian SSR.

Urvant, Vadim Nikolayevich, major, full-time secretary of a military unit party bureau, Carpathian Military District, CPSU member, Khmelnitskiy Oblast. From Shepetovskiy Territorial Okrug No 534, Khmelnitskiy Oblast, Ukrainian SSR.

Usenbekov, Kaliynur Usenbekovich, pensioner, CPSU member, Frunze city. From the All-Union Organization of War and Labor Veterans.

Ushakov, Valeriy Sidorovich, tractor driver at Starooskolskiy Rayon's "Krasnaya Zvezda" sovkhoz, CPSU member, Lapygino village, Starooskolskiy Rayon. From Starooskolskiy Territorial Okrug No 128, Belgorod Oblast, RSFSR.

Usilina, Nina Andreyevna, chief veterinarian at Shakhunskiy Rayon's "Komsomolets" Sovkhoz, Luzhayki settlement, Shakhunskiy Rayon. From Urenskiy Territorial Okrug No 165, Gorkiy Oblast, RSFSR.

Usichenko, Ivan Ignatyevich, chairman of the Ukrainian SSR Red Cross Society Central Committee, CPSU member, Kiev city. From the Union of USSR Red Cross and Red Crescent Societies.

Usmanov, Gumer Ismagilovich, first secretary of Tatar CPSU Obkom, CPSU member, Kazan city. From Buinskiy Territorial Okrug No 388, Tatar ASSR.

Usmanov, Rustamzhon Kazakevich, teacher at the No 20 School named for Furkat, Lugumbek village, Izbaskanskiy Rayon, Andizhan Oblast. From Izbaskanskiy National-Territorial Okrug No 99, Uzbek SSR.

Usyan, Samvel Vazgenovich, instrument controller at the "Nairit" Science-and-Production Association, CPSU member, Yerevan city. From Yerevanskiy-Promyshlennyy National-Territorial Okrug No 386, Armenian SSR.

Utkin, Vladimir Fedorovich, general designer and general director of the "Yuzhnoye" Science-and-Production Association, CPSU member, Dnepropetrovsk city, Ukrainian SSR. From the CPSU.

Uvarov, Aleksandr Ivanovich, senior lieutenant, secretary of a military unit Komsomol committee, Moscow Military District, CPSU member, Kalinin Oblast, RSFSR. From the All-Union Komsomol.

Vagin, Mikhail Grigoryevich, chairman of the V.I. Lenin Kolkhoz, CPSU member, Sukhonoska village, Koverninskiy Rayon, Gorkiy Oblast, RSFSR. From the CPSU.

Vagris, Yan Yanovich, first secretary of the Latvian Communist Party Central Committee, CPSU member, Riga city. From Proletarskiy Territorial Okrug No 708, Latvian SSR.

Vakarchuk, Ivan Aleksandrovich, head of department at the Lvov I. Franko State University, CPSU member, Lvov city. From Lvovskiy-Leninskiy Territorial Okrug No 486, Lvov Oblast, Ukrainian SSR.

Vakhidov, Vakhob, first deputy chairman of the Tajik SSR Council of Ministers, chairman of the Tajik SSR Gosagroprom, CPSU member, Dushanbe city. From Kanibadamskiy National-Territorial Okrug No 366, Tajik SSR.

Vakhitov, Farit Mansafovich, chairman of Sterlibashevskiy Rayon "Pravda" kolkhoz, CPSU member, Bakeyevo village, Sterlibashevskiy Rayon. From Alsheyevskiy National-Territorial Okrug No 507, Bashkir ASSR.

Valeyeva, Zukhra Sibgatovna, team leader of painters of Construction Administration No 3 of the Ufimskiy Planning and Construction Association of Large-Panel House-Building, CPSU member, Ufa city. From the CPSU.

Valentinov, Leonid Fedorovich, road grader operator with the "Spetsstroymekhanizatsiya" Trust, CPSU member, Cheboksary city. From Kalininskiy National-Territorial Okrug No 680, Chuvash ASSR.

Valov, Vladimir Arkadyevich, general director of the "Vostok" Production Association, CPSU member, Vostochnyy Settlement, Omutninskiy Rayon, Kirov Oblast, RSFSR. From Zuyevskiy Territorial Okrug No 199, Kirov Oblast.

Vanag, Yanis Yanovich, first secretary of Madonskiy Latvian Communist Party Raykom, CPSU member, Madona city. From Rezeknenskiy Territorial Okrug No 712, Latvian SSR.

Vardanyan, Rafik Petrosovich, chairman of Araratskiy Rayon Ararat village Kolkhoz named for St. Shaumyan, CPSU member, Ararat village. From Araratskiy National-Territorial Okrug No 400, Armenian SSR.

Vare, Vello Iosifovich, leading scientific staffer at Estonian SSR Academy of Sciences Institute of History, CPSU member, Tallinn city. From the All-Union Organization of War and Labor Veterans.

Varek, Toomas Karlovich, chairman of Rakvereskiy Rayon "Viru" Kolkhoz, CPSU member, Khalyala settlement, Rakvereskiy Rayon, Estonian SSR. From kolkhozes united in the Union Kolkhoz Council.

Varennikov, Valentin Ivanovich, army general, commander in chief of the Ground Forces, USSR deputy defense minister, CPSU member, Moscow city. From Maloderbetovskiy National-Territorial Okrug No 552, Kalmyk ASSR.

Varzhin, Yevgeniy Dmitriyevich, chief agronomist on Yelnikovskiy Rayon "Rassvet" Kolkhoz, CPSU member, Yelniki village, Yelnikovskiy Rayon. From Staroshaygovskiy National-Territorial Okrug No 611, Mordovian ASSR.

Vasilchuk, Nikolay Parfenovich, chairman of the Board of the Khmelnitskiy Oblast Consumer Cooperative Union, CPSU member, Kmelnitskiy city, Ukrainian SSR. From the USSR consumer cooperatives.

Vasilenko, Mikhail Fedorovich, chief of the Kirghiz Communist Party Central Committee Party-Organizational and Cadre Work Department, CPSU member, Frunze city. From Kantskiy National-Territorial Okrug No 331, Kirghiz SSR.

Vasilets, Aleksandr Nikolayevich, electric engine driver at the Southern Railroad Kupyansk locomotive depot named for 25th CPSU Congress, CPSU member, Kupyansk city. From Kupyanskiy Territorial Okrug No 526, Kharkov Oblast, Ukrainian SSR.

Vasilyev, Boris Gennadyevich, general director of "Kostromaenergo" Association, CPSU member, Kostroma City. From Kostromskiy Territorial Okrug No 202, RSFSR.

Vasilyev, Boris Lvovich, movie dramatist, CPSU member, Moscow city. From the USSR Union of Cinematographers.

Vasilyev, Ivan Afanasyevich, writer, CPSU member, Borki village, Velikolukskiy Rayon, Pskov Oblast, RSFSR. From the CPSU.

Vasilyev, Ivan Vasilyevich, Pskov Oblast Civil Defense assistant chief of staff, CPSU member, Pskov city, RSFSR. From the All-Union Organization of War and Labor Veterans.

Vasilyev, Konstantin Sergeyevich, head of department at the Kamyzyak Central District Hospital, candidate CPSU member, Kamyzyak City, Astrakhan Oblast, RSFSR. From Primorskiy Territorial Okrug No 123, Astrakhan Oblast.

Vasilyev, Sergey Viktorovich, Tyumen State University lecturer, CPSU member, Tyumen city. From Leninskiy Territorial Okrug No 320, Tyumen Oblast, RSFSR.

Vasko, Nikolay Petrovich, director of Beskaragayskiy Rayon's "Semenovskiy" Sovkhoz, CPSU member, Semenovka village, Beskaragayskiy Rayon, Semipalatinsk Oblast. From Semipalatinskiy National-Territorial Okrug No 152, Kazakh SSR.

Vasnetsov, Andrey Vladimirovich, monumental artist, chairman of the USSR Union of Artists Board, CPSU member, Moscow city. From the USSR Union of Artists.

Vavakin, Leonid Vasilyevich, chief architect of Moscow city, chief of the Moscow Main Architecture Administration, CPSU member, Moscow city. From the USSR Union of Architects.

Vayshvila, Zigmas Zigmovich, senior teacher at the Institute for Improving the Qualifications of Leading Workers and Specialists in the National Economy attached to the Lithuanian SSR Council of Ministers, Vilnius city. From Mazheykskiy National-Territorial Okrug No 244, Lithuanian SSR.

Vdovkin, Nikolay Ivanovich, chief veterinary physician on the Udmurt ASSR Kiyasovskiy Rayon's Lenin Sovkhoz, CPSU member, Podgornoye village, Kiyasovskiy rayon. From Sarapulskiy National-Territorial Okrug No 666, Udmurt ASSR.

Vedenkina, Zinaida Alekseyevna, trolley bus transport administration trolley bus driver, Yoshkar-Ola city, Mari ASSR. From the USSR trade unions.

Vedmid, Alina Petrovna, chairman of Vasilkovskiy Rayon "Zarya Kommunizma" kolkhoz, CPSU member, Salivonki village, Vasilkovskiy Rayon, Kiev Oblast, Ukrainian SSR. From women's councils united in the Soviet Women's Committee.

Velikhov, Yevgeniy Pavlovich, vice president of the USSR Academy of Sciences, CPSU member, Moscow city. From the CPSU.

Velikonis, Virmantas Pyatrovich, chairman of the "Ramigala" Kolkhoz, Panevezhskiy Rayon, CPSU member, Garutskay village, Panevezhskiy Rayon. From Panevezhskiy Rural National-Territorial Okrug No 246, Lithuanian SSR.

Venglovskaya, Vanda Sergeyevna, weaver at the Zhitomirskiy Flax Combine named for the 60th anniversary of the Great October Socialist Revolution, CPSU member, Zhitomir city. From Zhitomirskiy National-Territorial Okrug No 44, Ukrainian SSR.

Venediktov, Dmitriy Dmitriyevich, chairman of the Executive Committee of the USSR Union of Societies of the Red Cross and Red Crescent, CPSU member, Moscow city. From the USSR Union of Societies of the Red Cross and Red Crescent.

Veprev, Arkadiy Filimonovich, director of the "Nazarovskiy" Sovkhoz, Nazarovskiy Rayon, CPSU member, Stepnoy settlement, Nazarovskiy Rayon. From Achinskiy Territorial Okrug No 90, Krasnoyarsk Kray, RSFSR.

Vertebniy, Ivan Andreyevich, chairman of the Kolkhoz Named for Gorkiy, Globinskiy Rayon, CPSU member, Velikiye Krinki village, Globinskiy Rayon, Poltava Oblast, Ukrainian SSR. From the kolkhozes united in the Union Kolkhoz Council.

Vershedenko, Anna Mikhaylovna, milkmaid at the "Ogni Kommunizma" Kolkhoz, Bashtanskiy Rayon, CPSU member, Khristoforovka village, Bashtanskiy Rayon, Nikolayev Oblast, Ukrainian SSR. From the kolkhozes united in the Union Kolkhoz Council.

Vezirov, Abdul-Rakhman Khalil ogly, first secretary of the Azerbaijan Communist Party Central Committee, CPSU member, Baku city. From Imishlinskiy National-Territorial Okrug No 206, Azerbaijan SSR.

Vezirova, Sara Mustafa kyzy, operator at the oil and gas extraction administration named for Serebrovskiy, CPSU member, Baku city. From Bakinskiy-Leninskiy Territorial Okrug No 670, Azerbaijan SSR.

Veyser, Ledzher Marovich, secretary of the Komsomol Committee of the Secondary School Named for Masanchi, Kurdayskiy Rayon, CPSU member, Masanchi village, Kurdayskiy Rayon, Dzhambul Oblast, Kazakh SSR. From the All-Union Komsomol.

Vidiker, Vladimir Ivanovich, director of the "Suvorovskiy" Sovkhoz, Irtyshskiy Rayon, CPSU member, Suvorovo village, Irtyshskiy Rayon, Pavlodar Oblast. From Ekibastuzskiy National-Territorial Okrug No 160, Kazakh SSR.

Viktorovich, Anton Alekseyevich, assistant foreman at the Baranovichi cotton production association, Baranovichi City. From Baranovichskiy Territorial Okrug No 548, Belorussian SSR.

Vilkas, Eduardas Yono, director of the Lithuanian SSR Academy of Sciences Institute of Economics, CPSU member, Vilnius city. From Vilnyusskiy-Leninskiy National-Territorial Okrug No 225, Lithuanian SSR.

Vilkova, Mariya Sergeyevna, foreman at Gorkiy's "Rekord" Footwear Factory, CPSU member, Gorkiy city, RSFSR. From the women's councils united in the Soviet Women's Committee.

Viltsans, Andris Petrovich, junior scientific staffer at the Latvian SSR Academy of Sciences Institute of Microbiology Named for A. Kirkhenshteyn, CPSU member, Riga city. From the All-Union Komsomol.

Vindizhev, Arsen Khasanbiyevich, machine operator at the "Krasnaya Kabarda" Kolkhoz, Baksanskiy Rayon. CPSU member, Kyzburuk-2 village, Baksanskiy Rayon. From Baksanskiy National-Territorial Okrug No 539, Kabardino-Balkar ASSR.

Vinnik, Anatoliy Yakovlevich, first secretary of the Donetsk Ukrainian Communist Party Obkom, CPSU member, Donetsk Oblast. From Gorlovskiy National-Territorial Okrug No 43, Ukrainian SSR.

Vladislavlev, Aleksandr Pavlovich, first secretary of the Board of the USSR Union of Scientific and Engineering Societies, CPSU member, Moscow city. From the USSR Union of Scientific and Engineering Societies.

Vlasenko, Anatoliy Aleksandrovich, first secretary of the Smolensk CPSU Obkom, CPSU member, Smolensk city. From Roslavlskiy Territorial Okrug No 307, Smolensk Oblast, RSFSR.

Vlasov, Aleksandr Vladimirovich, candidate member of the CPSU Central Committee Politburo, chairman of the RSFSR Council of Ministers, CPSU member, Moscow city. From Rostovskiy National-Territorial Okrug No 24, RSFSR.

Viyeru, Grigoriy Pavlovich, poet, CPSU member, Kishinev city. From Kishinevskiy-Frunzenskiy National-Territorial Okrug No 261, Moldavian SSR.

Viznyuk, Vasiliy Petrovich, excavator operator with the "Chernovitsstroy" Trust Mechanization Administration, CPSU member, Chernovtsy City. From Chernovitskiy National-Territorial Okrug No 64, Ukrainian SSR.

Vlasov, Yuriy Petrovich, writer, CPSU member, Moscow City. From Lyublinskiy Territorial Okrug No 15, RSFSR.

Vlazneva, Mariya Ivanovna, milkmaid at the "Rossiya" Kolkhoz, Torbeyevskiy Rayon, Slaim village, Torbeyevskiy Rayon. From Krasnoslobodskiy Territorial Okrug No 377, Mordovian ASSR.

Vnebrachniy, Ivan Semenovich, diesel engine driver at the Oktyabrskiy Railroad Velikolukskiy Locomotive Depot, CPSU member, Velikiye Luki city. From Velikolukskiy Territorial Okrug No 265, Pskov Oblast, RSFSR.

Voblikov, Vladimir Aleksandrovich, chief of the Baltiyskiy CPSU Gorkom Organizational Department, CPSU member, Leningrad city. From Chernyakhovskiy Territorial Okrug No 179, Kaliningrad Oblast, RSFSR.

Voystrochenko, Anatoliy Fomich, first secretary of the Bryansk CPSU Obkom, member of the CPSU, city of Bryansk. From Volodarskiy Territorial Okrug No 130, Bryansk Oblast, RSFSR.

Volkov, Vladimir Anatolyevich, secretary of the party committee at the Sverdlovsk Machine Building Plant Named for M.I. Kalinin, CPSU member, Sverdlovsk city. From Ordzhonikidzevskiy Territorial Okrug No 294, Sverdlovsk Oblast, RSFSR.

Volodin, Boris Mikhaylovich, first secretary of the Rostov CPSU Obkom, CPSU member, Rostov-na-Donu city. From Salskiy Territorial Okrug No 276, Rostov Oblast, RSFSR.

Volodichev, Viktor Vasilyevich, leader of a team of construction workers on the "Angarstroy" Construction Administration's Construction-Work Train No 274, CPSU member, Vikhorevka city, Bratskiy Rayon. From Bratskiy Territorial Okrug No 173, Irkutsk Oblast, RSFSR.

Volodko, Adolf Adolfovich, chairman of the Kolkhoz named for Suvorov, Postavskiy Rayon, CPSU member, Novoselki village, Postavskiy Rayon, Vitebsk Oblast, Belorussian SSR. From the kolkhozes united in the Union Kolkhoz Council.

Vologzhin, Valentin Mikhaylovich, general director of the "Konveyer" Production Association Named for the 60th Anniversary of the Great October Socialist Revolution, CPSU member, Lvov city, Ukrainian SSR. From the USSR Union of Scientific and Engineering Societies.

Voloshin, Anatoliy Vladimirovich, link leader at "Leninskiy Put" Kolkhoz, Mozdokskiy Rayon, CPSU member, Troitskoye village, Mozdokskiy Rayon. From Mozdokskiy National-Territorial Okrug No 632, North Osetian ASSR.

Voloshkina, Lyudmila Fedotovna, teacher at Secondary School No 14, Armavir city. From Armavirskiy Territorial Okrug No 75, Krasnodar Kray, RSFSR.

Volskiy, Arkadiy Ivanovich, chairman of the NKAO Special Administration Committee, chief of a CPSU Central Committee department, CPSU member, Moscow city. From Stepanakertskiy Territorial Okrug No 682, Azerbaijan SSR.

Vooglayd, Yulo Vakhurovich, scientific leader at the Raplaskiy Rayon Agro-Industrial Complex Data Processing and Computer Training Center, Tallinn city. From Raplaskiy National-Territorial Okrug No 476, Estonian SSR.

Vorobyev, Andrey Ivanovich, director of the USSR Ministry of Health All-Union Hematology Scientific Center, Moscow city. From the USSR Academy of Medical Sciences along with 40 scientific medical societies.

Vorobyev, Nikolay Nikolayevich, first secretary of the Pytalovskiy CPSU Raykom, CPSU member, Pytalovo city, Pskov Oblast, RSFSR. From the CPSU.

Vorobyev, Eduard Arkadyevich, colonel general, commander of the Central Group of Forces, CPSU member, Moscow city. From Uzhgorodskiy Territorial Okrug No 451, Transcarpathian Oblast, Ukrainian SSR.

Vorobyeva, Anastasiya Nikolayevna, leader of a team of plasterers of the Mobile Mechanized Column No 1,

CPSU member, Kashira city, Moscow Oblast, RSFSR. From the women's councils united in the Soviet Women's Committee.

Voronezhtsev, Yuriy Ivanovich, senior scientific associate of the Belorussian SSR Academy of Sciences Institute of the Mechanics of Metal Polymer Systems, CPSU member, Gomel City. From Gomelskiy City Territorial Okrug No 555, Belorussian SSR.

Voronina, Lyubov Mikhaylovna, team leader at the Kolkhoz named for the 50th Anniversary of October, Primorskiy Rayon, CPSU member, Zelenovka village, Primorskiy Rayon. From Berdyanskiy Territorial Okrug No 457, Zaporozhye Oblast, Ukrainian SSR.

Voronina, Raisa Grigoryevna, glassblower at the Ryazan Electronic Instruments Association, CPSU member, Ryazan city, RSFSR. From the USSR trade unions.

Voronov, Sergey Ivanovich, machine operator at the "40 Let Oktyabrya" Kolkhoz, Kashirskiy Rayon, CPSU member, poste restante Dankovo, Kashirskiy Rayon, Voronezh Oblast, RSFSR. From the All-Union Komsomol.

Voronov, Yuriy Petrovich, writer, chief editor of LITERATURNAYA GAZETA; CPSU member, Moscow city. From the USSR Union of Writers.

Vorontsov, Anatoliy Yevgenyevich, chairman of the "Leninets" Kolkhoz, Bryanskiy Rayon, CPSU member, Glinishchevo village, Bryanskiy Rayon, Bryansk Oblast, RSFSR. From the kolkhozes united in the Union Kolkhoz Council.

Vorontsov, Nikolay Nikolayevich, doctor of biological sciences, chief scientific staffer at the USSR Academy of Sciences Institute of the Biology of Development Named for N.K. Koltsov, Moscow city. From the USSR Academy of Sciences scientific societies and associations.

Vorontsov, Sergey Aleksandrovich, chairman of the "Zavety Lenina" Kolkhoz, Spasskiy Rayon, CPSU member, Vyzheles village, Spasskiy Rayon. From Oktyabrskiy Territorial Okrug No 280, Ryazan Oblast, RSFSR.

Vorotnikov, Vitaliy Ivanovich, member of the CPSU Central Committee Politburo, chairman of the RSFSR Supreme Soviet Presidium, CPSU member, Moscow city. From Voronezhskiy National-Territorial Okrug No 5, RSFSR.

Voskanyan, Grant Mushegovich, chairman of the Armenian SSR Supreme Soviet Presidium, CPSU member, Yerevan city. From Sevanskiy Territorial Okrug No 738, Armenian SSR.

Voskoboynikov, Valeriy Ivanovich, Mi-8 helicopter flight engineer of the 25th Flight Detachment of Novyy Urengoy Combined Air Detachment, Novyy Urengoy city. From Novourengoyskiy Territorial Okrug No 324, Tyumen Oblast, RSFSR.

Vostrukhov, Oleg Vasilyevich, director of the No 49 Secondary School, Pechora Station on the Northern Railroad, CPSU member, Pechora city, Komi ASSR. From the All-Union Komsomol.

Vulfson, Mavrik Germanovich, senior teacher at the Latvian Academy of Arts, CPSU member, Riga City. From Kirovskiy National-Territorial Okrug No 296, Latvian SSR.

Vyucheyskiy, Aleksandr Ivanovich, chief of the rolling and repair shop of the Khoreyver Oil and Gas Prospecting Expedition, CPSU member, Naryan-Mar city. From Nenetskiy National-Territorial Okrug No 744, Nenetsk Autonomous Okrug.

Vyali, Arder Ivanovich, first secretary of Khaapsaluskiy Estonian Communist Party Raykom, CPSU member, Khaapsalu city. From Khaapsaluskiy National-Territorial Okrug No 480, Estonian SSR.

Vyalyas, Vayno Iosipovich, first secretary of the Estonian Communist Party Central Committee, CPSU member, Tallinn city. From Pyarnuskiy Territorial Okrug No 749, Estonian SSR.

Vyatkina, Galina Ivanovna, director of Orsha Pilot-Experimental Sewn Goods Factory, CPSU member, Orsha city. From Orshanskiy National-Territorial Okrug No 82, Belorussian SSR.

Yablokov, Aleksey Vladimirovich, corresponding member of the USSR Academy of Sciences, laboratory chief at the USSR Academy of Sciences N.K. Koltsov Institute of Developmental Biology, CPSU member, Moscow city. From the scientific societies and associations attached to the USSR Academy of Sciences.

Yablonko, Nikolay Vasilyevich, director of Temryukskiy Rayon's "Chernomorskiy" Vineyard Sovkhoz, CPSU member, Taman village. From Slavyanskiy Territorial Okrug No 82, RSFSR.

Yadgarov, Damir Salikhovich, first secretary of Bukhara Uzbek Communist Party Obkom, CPSU member, Bukhara city. From Bukharskiy National-Territorial Okrug No 100, Uzbek SSR.

Yagmyrov, Govshut, team leader at the Engels Kolkhoz, Sayatskiy Rayon, CPSU member, Erdzhel settlement, Sayatskiy Rayon, Chardzhou Oblast. From Chardzhouskiy Rural National-Territorial Okrug No 448, Turkmen SSR.

Yakimenko, Anatoliy Nikolayevich, chairman of the "Zhovten" Kolkhoz, Novgorod-Severskiy Rayon, CPSU member, Degtyarevka village, Novgorod-Severskiy Rayon. From Sosnitskiy Territorial Okrug No 543, Chernigov Oblast, Ukrainian SSR.

Yakovlev, Aleksandr Maksimovich, sector chief at the USSR Academy of Sciences Institute of State and Law, CPSU member, Moscow City. From the USSR Academy of Sciences.

Yakovlev, Aleksandr Nikolayevich, member of the CPSU Central Committee Politburo, secretary of the CPSU Central Committee, CPSU member, Moscow city. From the CPSU.

Yakovlev, Albert Mikhaylovich, chairman of the Construction and Construction Materials Industry Workers Trade Union Central Committee, CPSU member, Moscow city. From the USSR Trade Unions.

Yakovlev, Makar Makarovich, chief of an investigation unit at the Yakut ASSR Proseuctor's Office, CPSU member, Yakutsk City. From Yakutskiy Rural National-Territorial Okrug No 691, Yakut ASSR.

Yakovlev, Yegor Vladimirovich, chief editor of the newspaper MOSKOVSKIYE NOVOSTI, CPSU member, Moscow city. From the USSR Cinematographers' Union.

Yakubov, Adyl, writer, first secretary of the Uzbek Writers' Union Board, secretary of the USSR Writers' Union Board, CPSU member, Tashkent city. From the USSR Writers' Union.

Yakubov, Yusupdzhan Raimdzhanovich, director of a butterfat combine, CPSU member, Kokand city. From Kokandskiy Territorial Okrug No 605, Fergana Oblast, Uzbek SSR.

Yakutis, Vladislav Stanislavovich, comprehensive team leader at the Pinchuga "Boguchanles" Timber Association, CPSU member, Pinchuga settlement, Boguchanskiy Rayon. From Lesosibirskiy Territorial Okrug No 93, Krasnoyarsk Kray, RSFSR.

Yakushin, Ivan Nikitovich, chairman of the Lenin Kolkhoz, Lyuberetskiy Rayon, CPSU member, Lytkarino city. From Lyuberetskiy Territorial Okrug No 34, Moscow Oblast, RSFSR.

Yakushkin, Viktor Vladimirovich, teacher at No 147 Secondary Vocational and Technical School, CPSU member, Vitebsk city. From Vitebskiy City National-Territorial Okrug No 79, Belorussian SSR.

Yanayev, Gennadiy Ivanovich, AUCCTU secretary, CPSU member, Moscow city. From the USSR trade unions.

Yaneks, Yuris Aleksandrovich, first deputy chairman of Liyepayskiy Rayon Soviet of People's Deputies Ispolkom, chairman of the "Liyepaya" Agro-Industrial Association, CPSU member, Liyepaya city. From Liyepayskiy Rural National-Territorial Okrug No 307, Latvian SSR.

Yanenko, Arkadiy Petrovich, rector of Novosibirsk Engineering Construction Institute, CPSU member, Novosibirsk city. From Oktyabrskiy Territorial Okrug No 233, Novosibirsk Oblast, RSFSR.

Yangyshev, Vladimir Mikhaylovich, first secretary of Lenskiy CPSU Raykom, CPSU member, Lensk City. From Leninskiy National-Territorial Okrug No 692, Yakut ASSR.

Yanshin, Aleksandr Leonidovich, academician, adviser to the USSR Academy of Sciences Presidium, chairman of the USSR Academy of Sciences Scientific Council on Problems of the Biosphere and the Academy of Sciences Commission for the Study of the Quaternary Period, Moscow city. From the scientific societies and associations attached to the USSR Academy of Sciences.

Yarin, Veniamin Aleksandrovich, operator at the Nizhniy Tagil V.I. Lenin Metallurgical Combine, CPSU member, Nizhniy Tagil city. From Nizhnetagilskiy Territorial Okrug No 302, Sverdlovsk Oblast, RSFSR.

Yarovaya, Olga Pavlovna, milkmaid at the "Krasnaya Zvezda" training farm, Atkarskiy Rayon, CPSU member, Turgenevo village, Atkarskiy Rayon. From Atkarskiy Territorial Okrug No 285, Saratov Oblast, RSFSR.

Yarovoy, Vladimir Ivanovich, director of the "Gosudarstvennyy Soyuznyy Zavod 'Dvigatel' Im. V.I. Lenina" production association, CPSU member, Tallinn city. From Tallinnskiy-Lasnamyaeskiy National-Territorial Okrug No 451, Estonian SSR.

Yashin, Sergey Aleksandrovich, electric welders' team leader at the mechanized operations administration of the "Shkapovneftestroy" Trust, CPSU member, Belebey city. From Oktyabrskiy National-Territorial Okrug No 511, Bashkir ASSR.

Yastrebov, Aleksey Zakharovich, deputy chief technologist at the Sarapul Ordzhonikidze Radio Plant, CPSU member, Sarapul city. From Kamskiy Territorial Okrug No 394, Udmurt ASSR.

Yastrebtsov, Sergey Vyacheslavovich, captain, commanding officer of a troop unit company, Odessa Military District, CPSU member, Odessa Oblast. From Izmailskiy Territorial Okrug No 501, Odessa Oblast, Ukrainian SSR.

Yavorivskiy, Vladimir Aleksandrovich, writer, secretary of the Ukrainian Writers' Union Board, CPSU member, Kiev City. From Minskiy Territorial Okrug No 467, Kiev City, Ukrainian SSR.

Yazdurdiyeva, Rozbibi, leader of a cotton growing team on the Zhdanov Kolkhoz, Termezskiy Rayon, CPSU member, Termezskiy Rayon, Surkan-Darya Oblast, Uzbek SSR. From the kolkhozes united by the Union Kolkhoz Council.

Yefimov, Aleksandr Nikolayevich, marshal of aviation, commander in chief of the Air Force, USSR deputy defense minister, CPSU member, Moscow city. From the All-Union Organization of War and Labor Veterans.

Yefimov, Anatoliy Stepanovich, chairman of the Uzbek SSR People's Control Committee, CPSU member, Tashkent city. From Pastdargomskiy National-Territorial Okrug No 109, Uzbek SSR.

Yefimov, Vladimir Gordeyevich, chief engineer at Yantikovskiy Rayon's "Krasnaya Chuvashiya" Kolkhoz, Yantikovo-Norvati village, Yantikovskiy Rayon, Chuvash ASSR. From Zheleznodorozhnyy National-Territorial Okrug No 684, Chuvash ASSR.

Yefimov, Nikolay Vasilyevich, leader of an installation workers' team at the "Stalkonstruktsiya" Specialized Trust's Vyksa Construction and Installation Administration, CPSU member, Vyksa city. From Arzamasskiy Territorial Okrug No 160, Gorkiy Oblast, RSFSR.

Yefremov, Aleksandr Grigoryevich, director of Shadrinskiy Rayon's "Krasnaya Zvezda" Sovkhoz, CPSU member, Krasnaya Zvezda village, Shadrinskiy Rayon. From Shadrinskiy Territorial Okrug No 215, Kurgan Oblast, RSFSR.

Yefremov, Oleg Nikolayevich, artistic director of the Moscow Arts Academic Theater of the USSR, first secretary of the USSR Theater Workers' Union Board, CPSU member, Moscow city. From the USSR Theater Workers Union.

Yegizekova, Aysaule Naurzbayevna, machine operator in a Komsomol-youth team on Khobdinskiy Rayon's "Akrabskiy" Sovkhoz, CPSU member, Akrab village, Khobdinskiy Rayon, Aktyubinsk Oblast. From Aktyubinskiy National-territorial Okrug No 133, Kazakh SSR.

Yegorov, Oleg Mikhaylovich, second officer aboard the Kaliningrad Refrigerator and Transport Fleet Administration's "Primorskiy Bereg" refrigerator ship, CPSU member, Kaliningrad city, RSFSR. From the All-Union Komsomol.

Yegorova, Iya Andreyevna, department chief at the Altay Kray Clinical Hospital, CPSU member, Barnaul city, RSFSR. From the women's councils united in the Soviet Women's Committee.

Yegorshin, Viktor Vladimirovich, log truck driver with the Northern Logging Company, CPSU member, Letneozerskiy settlement, Plesetskiy Rayon. From Plesetskiy Territorial Okrug No 120, Arkhangelsk Oblast, RSFSR.

Yelagin, Valeriy Fedorovich, metal heater at the Volzhskiy Pipe Plant, CPSU member, Volzhskiy city. From Volzhskiy Territorial Okrug No 142, Volgograd Oblast, RSFSR.

Yelchenko, Yuriy Nikiforovich, secretary of the Ukrainian Communist Party Central Committee, CPSU member, Kiev city. From Kanevskiy Territorial Okrug No 537, Cherkassy Oblast, Ukrainian SSR.

Yeliseyev, Aleksey Stanislavovich, rector of the N.E. Bauman Moscow Higher Technical College, chairman of the "Rodina" Society Presidium, CPSU member, Moscow city. From the Union of Soviet Societies for Friendship and Cultural Relations With Foreign Countries and the Soviet Society for Cultural Ties with Compatriots Abroad (the "Rodina" Society).

Yeliseyev, Yevgeniy Aleksandrovich, first secretary of Kabardino-Balkar CPSU Obkom, CPSU member, Nalchik city. From Zolskiy National-Territorial Okrug No 540, Kabardino-Balkar ASSR.

Yelistratov, Yevgeniy Nikolayevich, machine operator at the Maslov Kolkhoz, Sorochinskiy Rayon, CPSU member, Ivanovka Vtoraya village, Sorochinskiy Rayon, Orenburg Oblast, RSFSR. From the All-Union Komsomol.

Yeltsin, Boris Nikolayevich, first deputy chairman of the USSR State Committee for Construction [Gosstroy], USSR minister, CPSU member, Moscow city. From Moscow City National-Territorial Okrug No 1, RSFSR.

Yemelyanov, Aleksey Mikhaylovich, faculty chief at the M.V. Lomonosov Moscow State University, CPSU member, Moscow city. From Leninskiy Territorial Okrug No 1, Moscow city.

Yemelyanov, Petr Yemelyanovich, lecturer at the Orshanka Teacher Training College, CPSU member, Orshanka settlement. From Orshanskiy National-Territorial Okrug No 600, Mari ASSR.

Yenokyan, Goarik Agabekovna, general director of Yerevan's "Garun" Sewn Goods Production Association, CPSU member, Yerevan city. From Yerevanskiy-Spandaryanskiy National-Territorial Okrug No 387, Armenian SSR.

Yenshakov, Engels Vasilyevich, chairman of Magadan Oblast Trade Union Council, CPSU member, Magadan city, RSFSR. From the USSR trade unions.

Yeraliyev, Zholdasbay, director of Kirovskiy Rayon's 30th Anniversary of October Sovkhoz, CPSU member, Kirovskiy Rayon. From Chardarinskiy Territorial Okrug No 653, Chimkent Oblast, Kazakh SSR.

Yeraliyev, Tokhtar Yeraliyevich, architect, chairman of the Kazakh Architects' Union Board, Alma-Ata city. From the USSR Architects' Union.

Yerelina, Valentina Kuzukovna, director of Sugash Secondary School, Sugash village, Ust-Koksinskiy Rayon. From Ust-Kanskiy National-Territorial Okrug No 709, Gorno-Altay Autonomous Oblast.

Yeremenko, Stepan Fedorovich, deputy chief of the "Yelabuzhskiy Avtomobilnyy Zavod" Production Association's Planning Administration, CPSU member, Yelabuga city. From Nizhnekamskiy Territorial Okrug No 390, Tatar ASSR.

Yeremey, Grigoriy Isidorovich, chairman of the Moldavian Republic Trade Unions Council, CPSU member, Kishinev City. From Brichanskiy National-Territorial Okrug No 264, Moldavian SSR.

Yermakov, Valentin Filippovich, chairman of the Russian Potrebsoyuz Board, CPSU member, Moscow city. From the USSR consumer cooperatives.

Yermakov, Nikolay Vasilyevich, chief of a mechanized detachment at Tengushevskiy Rayon's "Obnovleniye" Kolkhoz, CPSU member, Kurayevo village, Tengushevskiy Rayon. From Zubovo-Polyanskiy National-Territorial Okrug No 607, Mordovian ASSR.

Yermilov, Nikolay Kuzmich, director of Osinnikovskiy Rayon's "Kuzedeyevskiy" Sovkhoz, CPSU member, Kuzedeyeva settlement, Osinnikovskiy Rayon. From Zavodskiy Territorial Okrug No 196, Kemerovo Oblast, RSFSR.

Yermolayev, Gennadiy Mikhaylovich, director of Kormilovskiy Rayon's "Mikhaylovskiy" Livestock Breeding Sovkhoz, CPSU member, Mikhaylovka village, Kormilovskiy Rayon. From Omskiy Territorial Okrug No 240, Omsk Oblast, RSFSR.

Yerokhin, Vasiliy Aleksandrovich, major, deputy subunit commander, Kiev Military District, CPSU member, Kirovograd Oblast. From Aleksandriyskiy Territorial Okrug No 477, Kirovograd Oblast, Ukrainian SSR.

Yerokhin, Vladimir Lavrentyevich, shift engineer at the Gorkiy Combined Air Detachment's Aircraft Equipment Base, Gorkiy city. From Avtozavodskiy Territorial Okrug No 157, Gorkiy Oblast, RSFSR.

Yerokhovets, Irina Yakovlevna, installation worker at the Minsk Computer Equipment Production Association's G.K. Ordzhonikidze Computer Plant, CPSU member, Minsk city. From the CPSU.

Yeseykin, Nikolay Viktorovich, machine operator at a lease subunit of Shilovskiy Rayon's "Dobrovolets" Kolkhoz, CPSU member, Inyakino village, Shilovskiy Rayon. From Sasovskiy Territorial Okrug No 282, Ryazan Oblast, RSFSR.

Yetylen, Vladimir Mikhaylovich, postgraduate student at the CPSU Central Committee Social Sciences Academy, CPSU member, Anadyr city. From Chukotskiy National-Territorial Okrug No 748, Chukotka Autonomous Okrug.

Yevtukh, Vladimir Gavrilovich, first deputy chairman of the Belorussian SSR Council of Ministers, CPSU member, Minsk city. From Minskiy Rural National-Territorial Okrug No 69, Belorussian SSR.

Yevtushenko, Yevgeniy Aleksandrovich, poet, secretary of the USSR Writers' Union Board, Moscow City. From Kharkovskiy-Dzerzhinskiy Territorial Okrug No 520, Kharkov Oblast, Ukrainian SSR.

Yevtushkov, Mikhail Grigoryevich, chief agronomist at Yalutorovskiy Rayon's "Yalutorovskiy" Sovkhoz, CPSU member, Berkut village, Yalutorovskiy Rayon. From Kalininskiy Territorial Okrug No 321, Tyumen Oblast, RSFSR.

Yezhelev, Anatoliy Stepanovich, chief of IZVESTIYA's Leningrad Correspondent Center, CPSU member, Leningrad city. From the USSR Journalists' Union.

Yezhikov-Babakhanov, Yevgeniy Georgiyevich, first secretary of Dzhezkazgan Kazakh Communist Party Obkom, CPSU member, Dzhezkazgan city. From Balkhashskiy National-Territorial Okrug No 136, Kazakh SSR.

Yorga, Lyubov Ivanovna (Lari, Leonida), consultant at the current affairs department of the Moldavian SSR Writers' Union, Kishinev City. From Kutuzovskiy National-Territorial Okrug No 273, Moldavian SSR.

Yotsas, Aloizas Povilovich, chairman of "Pirmin" Kolkhoz, Shyaulyayskiy Rayon, CPSU member, Sutkunay village, Shyaulyayskiy Rayon, Lithuanian SSR. From kolkhozes united in the Union Kolkhoz Council.

Yudin, Vladimir Dmitriyevich, chief of the Northeastern Geological Production Association Central Geophysical Expedition Central Geochemical Group, CPSU member, Khasyn settlement, Khasynskiy Rayon. From Magadanskiy Territorial Okrug No 223, Magadan Oblast, RSFSR.

Yudov, Aleksandr Yevgenyevich, agronomist at the "Bolshevik" Sovkhoz, CPSU member, Sortavala city, Khaapalampi settlement. From Sortavalskiy National-Territorial Okrug No 578, Karelian ASSR.

Yuldashev, Shavkat Mukhitdinovich, first secretary of Fergana Uzbek Communist Party Obkom, CPSU member, Fergana city. From Margilanskiy National-Territorial Okrug No 124, Uzbek SSR.

Yulin, Boris Yegorovich, chairman of the Kalyagin Kolkhoz, Kinelskiy Rayon, CPSU member, N. Sarbay village, Kinelskiy Rayon, Kuybyshev Oblast, RSFSR. From the kolkhozes united by the Union Kolkhoz Council.

Yunyayev, Petr Alekseyevich, director of Gorodishchenskiy Rayon's "Kamenskiy" Sovkhoz, CPSU member, Kamennyy Settlement. From Traktorozavodskiy Territorial Okrug No 140, RSFSR.

Yusupov, Adamali Koshokovich, breakage face miners' unit leader at the Lenin Komsomol mine of the "Kyzyl-Kiyskoye" mining administration, Uch-Kurgon village, Frunzenskiy Rayon, Osh Oblast. From Kyzyl-Kiyskiy Territorial Okrug No 719, Kirghiz SSR.

Yusupov, Magomed Yusopovich, first secretary of Dagestan CPSU Obkom, CPSU member, Makhachkala city. From Khunzakhskiy National-Territorial Okrug No 535, Dagestan ASSR.

Yusupov, Erkin Yusupovich, vice president of the Uzbek SSR Academy of Sciences, CPSU member, Tashkent city. From the All-Union "Znaniye" Society.

Zagaynov, Yevgeniy Arkadyevich, department chief at the Republican Hospital, CPSU member, Yoshkar-Ola city. From Leninskiy National-Territorial Okrug No 591, Mari ASSR.

Zabrodin, Ivan Aleksandrovich, Ukrainian SSR minister of finance, CPSU member, Kiev city. From Artemovskiy National-Territorial Okrug No 42, Ukrainian SSR.

Zadoya, Nikolay Kuzmich, first secretary of Dnepropetrovsk Ukrainian Communist Party Obkom, CPSU member, Dnepropetrovsk city. From Gornyatskiy Territorial Okrug No 425, Dnepropetrovsk Oblast, Ukrainian SSR.

Zadyrko, Viktor Ivanovich, deputy general director of the "Gibrid-1" Industrial Production System, CPSU member, Niva Trudovaya village, Apostolovskiy Rayon. From Nikopolskiy Territorial Okrug No 428, Dnepropetrovsk Oblast, Ukrainian SSR.

Zakaryan, Valya Zavenovna, kolkhoz member at the Aykavan village Kolkhoz, Oktemberyanskiy Rayon, CPSU member, Aykavan village. From Oktemberyanskiy National-Territorial Okrug No 412, Armenian SSR.

Zakharenko, Aleksandr Antonovich, director of Sakhnovka Secondary School, Korsun-Shevchenkovskiy Rayon, CPSU member, Sakhnovka village, Korsun-Shevchenkovskiy Rayon, Cherkassy Oblast. From Cherkasskiy National-Territorial Okrug No 62, Ukrainian SSR.

Zakharov, Mark Anatolyevich, artistic leader and director of the Moscow Lenin Komsomol Theater, secretary of the board of the USSR Theater Workers' Union, CPSU member, Moscow city. From the USSR Theater Workers' Union.

Zakharov, Vladimir Andreyevich, first secretary of Kalmyk CPSU Obkom, CPSU member, Elista city. From Kalmytskiy Territorial Okrug No 368, Kalmyk ASSR.

Zakharov, Viktor Viktorovich, test driver at the Kremenchug Motor Vehicle Plant of the "Avtokraz" Production Association, CPSU member, Kremenchug City. From Kremenchugskiy Territorial Okrug No 505, Poltava Oblast, Ukrainian SSR.

Zakharova, Galina Ivanovna, tester at the Prokhladnyy Semiconductor Instruments Plant, CPSU member, Prokhladnyy city. From Prokhladnenskiy City National-Territorial Okrug No 541, Kabardino-Balkar ASSR.

Zakharchenko, Vera Fedorovna, milkmaid at the Krupskaya Kolkhoz, Kakhovskiy Rayon, Lyubimovka village, Kakhovskiy Rayon. From Kakhovskiy Territorial Okrug No 529, Kherson Oblast, Ukrainian SSR.

Zakhayev, Lechi, chief of a mechanized detachment at the "Lermontovskiy" Sovkhoz, Achkhoy-Martanovskiy Rayon, CPSU member, Achkhoy-Martan village. From Achkhoy-Martanovskiy National-Territorial Okrug No 673, Chechen-Ingush ASSR.

Zakis, Yuris Roderikhovich, rector of the Latvian P. Stuchka State University, CPSU member, Riga city. From Moskovskiy Territorial Okrug No 707, Latvian SSR.

Zalikhanov, Mikhail Chokkayevich, director of the Alpine Geophysics Institute, CPSU member, Nalchik city. From Elbrusskiy National-Territorial Okrug No 546, Kabardino-Balkar ASSR.

Zalygin, Sergey Pavlovich, writer, chief editor of the journal NOVYY MIR, secretary of the board of the USSR Writers' Union, Moscow city. From the USSR Writers' Union.

Zalomay, Vladimir Aleksandrovich, secretary of Brest Belorussian Communist Party Obkom, CPSU member, Brest City. From Baranovichskiy National-Territorial Okrug No 75, Belorussian SSR.

Zamanyagra, Mikhail Fedorovich, truck drivers' team leader at the "Beltsytrans" Production Association, Beltsy city, Moldavian SSR. From the USSR trade unions.

Zanokha, Aleksandr Ivanovich, chairman of the Lenin Kolkhoz, Alamedinskiy Rayon, CPSU member, Leninskoye village, Alamedinskiy Rayon. From Alamedinskiy National-Territorial Okrug No 326, Kirghiz SSR.

Zarin, Indulis Avgustovich, artist, rector of the Latvian SSR State Academy of Arts, CPSU member, Riga city. From the USSR Academy of Arts.

Zaslavskiy, Ilya Iosifovich, scientific staffer at the Moscow A.N. Kosygin Textiles Institute, Moscow city. From Oktyabrskiy Territorial Okrug No 17, Moscow city.

Zaslavskaya, Tatyana Ivanovna, academician, director of the AUCCTU and USSR State Committee for Labor and Social Questions All-Union Center for the Study of Public Opinion on Socioeconomic Questions, CPSU member, Moscow city. From the scientific societies and associations attached to the USSR Academy of Sciences.

Zavizion, Olga Vasilyevna, chairman of the board of the Staroderevyankovskaya village consumer society of the Kanevskiy Rayon Potrebsoyuz, CPSU member, Staroderevyankovskaya village, Kanevskiy Rayon, Krasnodar Kray, RSFSR. From the USSR Consumer Cooperative System.

Zaykov, Lev Nikolayevich, member of the CPSU Central Committee Politburo, secretary of the CPSU Central Committee, first secretary of Moscow CPSU Gorkom, CPSU member, Moscow city. From the CPSU.

Zaynalkhanov, Dalgat Gadzhiyevich, docker-machine operator at Makhachkala Maritime Commercial Port, Makhachkala city. From Kirovskiy National-Territorial Okrug No 526, Dagestan ASSR.

Zbykovskiy, Ivan Ignatyevich, director of the Donetsk S.M. Kirov Coke and Chemicals Plant, CPSU member, Donetsk city. From Donetskiy National-Territorial Okrug No 41, Ukrainian SSR.

Zelenovskiy, Anatoliy Antonovich, first secretary of Brest Belorussian Communist Party Obkom, CPSU member, Brest city. From Luninetskiy National-Territorial Okrug No 77, Belorussian SSR.

Zelinskiy, Igor Petrovich, rector of Odessa I.I. Mechnikov State University, CPSU member, Odessa city. From Odesskiy-Leninskiy Territorial Okrug No 497, Odessa Oblast, Ukrainian SSR.

Zemskova, Aleksandra Vladimirovna, senior investigator at Moskovskiy Rayon Soviet of People's Deputies Ispolkom Internal Affairs Department, Kaluga city, CPSU member, Kaluga city, RSFSR. From the All-Union Komsomol.

Zenko, Mikhail Fedorovich, excavator operator on the Petrozavodsk Mobile Mechanized Column, Meliorativnyy settlement, Prionezhskiy Rayon. From Prionezhskiy National-Territorial Okrug No 577, Karelian ASSR.

Zgerskaya (Yaroshinskaya), Alla Aleksandrovna, correspondent for the newspaper RADYANSKA ZHITOMIRSHCHINA, Zhitomir city. From Zhitomirskiy Territorial Okrug No 446, Zhitomir Oblast, Ukrainian SSR.

Zhakselekov, Ermek, chairman of the Kazakh Republic Trade Union Council, CPSU member, Alma-Ata city. From the USSR trade unions.

Zhanybekov, Shangerey Zhanybekovich, first deputy chairman of the Kazakh Republican Society for Cultural Relations With Compatriots Abroad, CPSU member, Alma-Ata city. From the All-Union Organization of War and Labor Veterans.

Zhdakayev, Ivan Andreyevich, bulldozer operator at the Pervomaysk Timber Industry Enterprise, CPSU member, Pervomaysk village, Smirnykhovskiy Rayon. From Tymovskiy Territorial Okrug No 291, Sakhalin Oblast, RSFSR.

Zhdanov, Aleksandr Georgiyevich, first secretary of Lazovskiy Moldavian Communist Party Raykom, CPSU member, Lazovsk settlement, Lazovskiy Rayon. From Lazovskiy National-Territorial Okrug No 274, Moldavian SSR.

Zhgeriya, Irma Akakiyevna, tea grower on the Goraberezhouli village Kolkhoz, Chokhataurskiy Rayon, CPSU member, Goraberezhouli village, Chokhataurskiy Rayon. From Potiyskiy Territorial Okrug No 666, Georgian SSR.

Zhigulin, Anatoliy Sergeyevich, first secretary of Taldy-Kurgan Kazakh Communist Party Obkom, CPSU member, Taldy-Kurgan city. From Taldy-Kurganskiy city Territorial Okrug No 643, Taldy-Kurgan Oblast, Kazakh SSR.

Zhigunova, Lyudmila Tazretovna, chief of the children's department of the city first-aid teaching hospital, Nalchik city. From Dolinskiy National-Territorial Okrug No 536, Kabardino-Balkar ASSR.

Zhitkov, Oleg Alekseyevich, tunneler of the "Tsentroshakhtorudstroy" Trust Yakovlevskoye Specialized Mine Construction Administration, CPSU member, Yakovlevo Settlement, Yakovlevskiy Rayon. From Belgorodskiy Rural Territorial Okrug No 126, RSFSR.

Zhivotov, Aleksey Aleksandrovich, chairman of the "Rossiya" Kolkhoz, Oktyabrskiy Rayon, CPSU member, Krasnyy Kut village, Oktyabrskiy Rayon. From Shakhtinskiy Territorial Okrug No 278, Rostov Oblast, RSFSR.

Zhonkuvvatova, Rano Normuradovna, team leader at the Kuybyshev Sovkhoz, Guzarskiy Rayon, CPSU member, Zarbdor Kishlak, Guzarskiy Rayon. From Guzarskiy Territorial Okrug No 580, Kashka-Darya Oblast, Uzbek SSR.

Zhuk, Aleksandr Vladimirovich, professor of a faculty at the Leningrad I.Ye. Repin Institute of Painting, Sculpture, and Architecture, Leningrad city. From the USSR Architects' Union.

Zhukov, Aleksandr Aleksandrovich, drilling foreman on the Buzuluk oil and gas prospecting expedition of the "Orenburggeologiya" Geological Production Association, CPSU member, Buzuluk city, Orenburg Oblast, RSFSR. From the USSR trade unions.

Zhukova, Tatyana Petrovna, teacher at the Moscow Oblast House of the Child, Vidnoye city, Leninskiy Rayon, Moscow Oblast, RSFSR. From the All-Union Komsomol.

Zhukovskaya, Lyudmila Leonovna, director of the Mozyr Sewn Goods Factory, CPSU member, Mozyr city, Gomel Oblast, Belorussian SSR. From the women's councils united by the Soviet Women's Committee.

Zhurabayeva, Tozhikhon, chief of the rural medical outpatients' clinic of the "Nayman" Kishlak Soviet, Tashlakskiy Rayon, Nayman Kishlak, Tashlakskiy Rayon. From Margilanskiy Territorial Okrug No 607, Fergana Oblast, Uzbek SSR.

Ziatdinov, Nazip Ziatdinovich, director of the "Gigant" Sovkhoz, Tukayevskiy Rayon, CPSU member, Novyy settlement, Tukayevskiy Rayon, Tatar ASSR. From the CPSU.

Zoidze, Nanuli Tariyelovna, tobacco grower on Brili Village Kolkhoz, Shuakhevskiy Rayon, Brili Village, Shuakhevskiy Rayon, Adzhar ASSR. From Shuakhevskiy National-Territorial Okrug No 502, Adzhar ASSR.

Zokirov, Munavarkhon Zakriyayevich, chief of the Kasansayskiy Rayon DOSAAF Sports and Technical Club, Kasansay city, Namangan Oblast, Uzbek SSR. From the USSR DOSAAF.

Zolnikov, Fedor Fedorovich, engineer at the electrification and mechanization enterprise of the Kalininskiy Rayon Agro-Industrial Association, CPSU member, Kalinino city. From Stepanavanskiy National-Territorial Okrug No 414, Armenian SSR.

Zolotareva, Lyudmila Aleksandrovna, actress at the Voronezh A.V. Koltsov Academic Drama Theater, CPSU member, Voronezh city, RSFSR. From the women's councils united by the Soviet Women's Committee.

Zolotukhin, Vladimir Petrovich, permanent correspondent of the Turkestan Military District newspaper FRUNZEVETS, CPSU member, Tashkent city. From Tashkentskiy-Kuybyshevskiy Territorial Okrug No 599, Tashkent Oblast, Uzbek SSR.

Zorina, Violetta Semenovna, needlewomen's teamleader at the Tbilisi "Komsomolka" Textile and Haberdashery Factory, CPSU member, Tbilisi city. From Tbilisskiy-Kirovskiy Territorial Okrug No 658, Georgian SSR.

Zubanov, Vladimir Aleksandrovich, secretary of the Khartsyzsk Steel Wire and Cable Plant party committee, CPSU member, Khartsyzsk city. From Makeyevskiy-Gornyatskiy Territorial Okrug No 444, Donetsk Oblast, Ukrainian SSR.

Zubkov, Vladimir Nikolayevich, chief physician at the No 5 Maternity Association, CPSU member, Rostov-na-Donu city. From Leninskiy Territorial Okrug No 267, Rostov Oblast, RSFSR.

Zubov, Ilya Ivanovich, deputy chief of the finance administration of Omsk Oblast Soviet of People's Deputies Ispolkom, CPSU member, Omsk city, RSFSR. From the All-Union Organization of War and Labor Veterans.

Zukhbaya, Otar Georgiyevich, chairman of the Abkhaz ASSR Council of Ministers, CPSU member, Sukhumi city. From Gagrsky National-Territorial Okrug No. 484, Abkhaz ASSR

Zumakulova, Tanzilya Mustafayevna, poet, CPSU member, Nalchik city, Kabardino-Balkar ASSR. From the women's councils united by the Soviet Women's Committee.

Zuykov, Vladimir Parmenovich, editor of the in-house newspaper STROITEL, CPSU member, Tyumen city, RSFSR. From the USSR Journalists' Union.

Zykova, Lyubov Vasilyevna, cook at the Gribanovsky Rayon consumer society canteen, Verkhny Karazhan village, Gribanovsky Rayon, Voronezh Oblast, RSFSR. From the USSR Consumer Cooperative System.

Zverev, Vladimir Viktorovich, breakage face mine worker at the "Dobropolskaya" Mine of the "Dobropolyeugol" Production Association, Dobropolye city. From Krasnoarmeyskiy Territorial Okrug No 442, Donetsk Oblast, Ukrainian SSR.

Zvonov, Sergey Nikolayevich, director of the Ivanovo Passenger Motor Transport Enterprise No 2, Ivanovo city, RSFSR. From the All-Union Komsomol.

INDEX OF SPEAKERS
VOLUMES 1-2

M.T. Abasov **2:** 227
A.M. Adamovich **1:** 17, 101, 231
Yu.N. Afanaseyev **1:** 97; **2:** 227
S.B. Aguzarova **1:** 149
Yu.T. Akbarov **1:** 54
S.F. Akhromeyev **2:** 94
P.A. Akhunov **2:** 111
S.S. Alekseyev **2:** 137
Zh.I. Alferov **2:** 29, 273
V.I. Alksnis **1:** 25; **2:** 211
R.A. Allayarov **1:** 34
G.A. Amangeldinova **1:** 164
S.A. Ambartsumyan **1:** 86
V.A. Ambartsumyan **1:** 220
Sh.A. Amonashvili **2:** 68, 221
Yu.E. Andreyev **1:** 82; **2:** 272
I.A. Andreyeva **1:** 56; **2:** 280
K.A. Antanavichyus **1:** 11; **2:** 281
A.Ye. Antifeyev **2:** 279
I.V. Aparin **2:** 219
V.G. Ardzinba **2:** 81
E.T. Arutyunyan **1:** 117
L.A. Arutyunyan **1:** 35, 114
S.G. Arutyunyan **1:** 118, 266
Kh.N. Atdayev **2:** 97
A.P. Aydak **1:** 20; **2:** 146
Ch.T. Aytmatov **1:** 27ff, 128; **2:** 69
P.A. Azizbekova **1:** 290; **2:** 44

V.V. Bakatin **1:** 53
V.I. Bakulin **1:** 270
Z.G. Balayan **2:** 204
Yu.A. Barashkov **1:** 181
A.I. Baranov—see V.A. Vrovkov
L.V. Barusheva **1:** 219
R. A. Bazarova **1:** 164
V.L. Bedulya **1:** 29
N.P. Bekhtereva **1:** 34
A.V. Belina **1:** 232
V.I. Belov **2:** 13
S.V. Belozertsev **1:** 44, 180; **2:** 57
V.N. Belyayev **1:** 10
V.A. Berezov **1:** 47; **2:** 30
Z. Beyshekeyeva **2:** 236
Ya.Ya. Bezbakh **1:** 61
E.B. Bichkauskas **1:** 162
V.A. Biryukov **1:** 30

I.O. Bisher **1:** 66
O.T. Bogomolov **1:** 62
Yu.Yu. Boldyrev **1:** 11; **2:** 31, 276
V.I. Borkovets **1:** 58
O.P. Borodin **2:** 274
G.A. Borovik **1:** 238
G.G. Borovikov **1:** 291
Yu.R. Boyars **1:** 15, 232
A.N. Boyko **1:** 60; **2:** 229
R.A. Bratun **1:** 227, **2:** 212
A.-M.K. Brazauskas **2:** 166, 180, 186, 200
Yu.Yu. Bredikis **2:** 218
V.-E.G. Bresis **2:** 246
P.G. Bunich **1:** 282
A.Y. Burachas **1:** 77
G.E. Burbulis **1:** 45
F.M. Burlatsky **1:** 66, 186; **2:** 218, 268
Yu.Ye. Burykh **1:** 173
V.V. Bushuyev **1:** 291
G.V. Bykov **2:** 167
R.A. Bykov **2:** 244

A.I. Chabanov **2:** 192
V.A. Chelyshev **1:** 46
Yu.M. Chemodanov **1:** 118
Yu.D. Chernichenko **2:** 19
O.V. Chernyshev **1:** 175
S.V. Chervonopisky **2:** 91
M.I. Chimpoy **1:** 176

B.V. Dadamyan **2:** 116
A.I. Demidov **1:** 147
A.B. Demin **2:** 227
V.F. Derevyanko **2:** 109
N.G. Dmitriyev **1:** 134; **2:** 269
A.O. Dobrovolsky **1:** 243; **2:** 203
F.V. Dovlatyan **1:** 52
I.P. Drutse **2:** 2
A.I. Dubko **1:** 81
V.V. Dyusembayev **2:** 66
A.S. Dzasokhov **2:** 100
V.D. Dzhafarov **1:** 218

A.Ya. Eshpay **1:** 244
A.V. Eyzan **2:** 93

P.P. Falk **1:** 38
Kh.A. Fargiyev **1:** 149
S.N. Fedorov **1:** 60
N.V. Fedorov **1:** 36; **2:** 209
V.P. Filippov **1:** 54
G.I. Filshin **1:** 134
V.L. Fomenko **1:** 45, 82

S.A. Gabrusev **1:** 219
T.V. Gankrelidze **1:** 162, 224
Ye.A. Gayer **2:** 115, 147, 183
T.Kh. Gdlyan **1:** 137, 150, 240, 294
B.V. Gidaspov **1:** 19, 23, 26, 80, 222; **2:** 52, 53
V.L. Ginzburg **1:** 57; **2:** 270
V.A. Giro **1:** 71
V.I. Goldansky **2:** 145
Yu.V. Golik **2:** 208, 274
S.P. Golovin **1:** 102, 110
Ye.L. Golovlev **1:** 33
V.V. Goncharov **1:** 34
V.A. Gontar **1:** 250
M.S. Gorbachev—see ANNOTATED LIST OF SPEECHES
A.V. Gorbunov **1:** 168, 238, 255; **2:** 132, 148
G.N. Gorbunov **2:** 94
A.A. Grakhovsky **2:** 26
A.G. Grigoryan **2:** 270
V.S. Grigoryan **1:** 82
V.P. Grishchuk **1:** 68
I.N. Gryazin **2:** 30, 212
R.V. Gudaytis **2:** 203
V.V. Guly **1:** 65; **2:** 203
G.G. Gumbaridze **2:** 186
V.V. Gustov **2:** 46
V.M. Gvozdez **2:** 197

M.A. Ibragimov **1:** 114
G.S. Igityan **1:** 24
E.E. Inkens **2:** 31
G.I. Isayev **1:** 163
N.V. Ivanov **1:** 154; **2:** 54, 55, 223
V.V. Ivanov **2:** 30
D.E. Ivans **1:** 32
A.K. Izmodenov **2:** 220

INDEX OF SPEAKERS

T. Kaipbergenov **1:** 223
G.A. Kakaras **1:** 56
S.B. Kalagin **2:** 204
S.F. Kalashnikov **1:** 159
V.N. Kalish **2:** 22
S.B. Kalyagin **1:** 82
Ya.S. Kanovich **1:** 79
S.V. Karaganov **1:** 68
N.V. Karlov **1:** 240
V.Ye. Karmanovsky **1:** 81
A.Ye. Karpov **2:** 39
V.V. Karpov **1:** 238
Yu.F. Karyakin **1:** 232; **2:** 99
V.I. Kasarev **1:** 104
N.I. Kashnikov **1:** 175
N.A. Kasyan **2:** 112, 126
T.I. Kayumova **1:** 34
T.K. Kazakova **2:** 94
A.I. Kazannik **1:** 185, 187, 243
V.V. Kazarezov **1:** 271
D.A. Kerinov **2:** 204
I.Ya. Kezbers **2:** 30
S.N. Khadzhiyev **1:** 171
K.S. Khallik **2:** 121
V.P. Khmel **1:** 30
V.V. Khmura **2:** 64
G.M. Khodryrev **2:** 108
D. Khudonazarov **2:** 88
A.U. Khusanov **2:** 58
Ye.U. Kim **1:** 221
V.I. Kirillov **1:** 58, 125; **2:** 281
N.P. Kiriyak **1:** 164
V.N. Kiselev **1:** 172
V.A. Kiseleva **2:** 207
N.T. Knyaznyev **2:** 273
I.D. Kobzon **1:** 221
Ye.V. Kogan **1:** 34; **2:** 206
G.V. Kolbin **2:** 220, 221
S.I. Kolesnikov **1:** 80
V.I. Kolesnikov **1:** 251
V.I. Kolotov **1:** 80; **2:** 203
Yu.A. Koltsov **1:** 148
S.I. Konev **1:** 37, 126
A.I. Konovalov **1:** 59, 144
V.N. Korneyenko **2:** 217
A.A. Korshunov **1:** 44, 293; **2:** 36
N.N. Koryugin **2:** 221
G.V. Koshlakov **1:** 242
G.I. Kravchenko **1:** 124
L.P. Kravchenko **2:** 94
A.N. Krayko **1:** 45, 127, 186, 220; **2:** 283
A.T. Kruglov **2:** 208
V.V. Krychkov **1:** 240
B.V. Kryzhkov **1:** 29, 240, 291
V.N. Kudryavtsev **1:** 69, 156; **2:** 213

D.N. Kugultinov **1:** 64; **2:** 133
I.I. Kukhar **1:** 38
A.G. Kuliyev **1:** 78
G.M. Kurochka **1:** 17, 81, 243; **2:** 58
N.A. Kutsenko **1:** 23; **2:** 58
L.A. Kuznetsov **1:** 187

V.V. Landsbergis **1:** 12, 76, 79; **2:** 47
V.P. Larionov **2:** 17
M.Y. Lauristan **1:** 30
V.A. Leonchev **1:** 110
A.V. Levashov **1:** 13; **2:** 280
Yu.A. Levykin **1:** 64; **2:** 58, 279
M.A. Lezhnev **1:** 80
D.S. Likhachev **1:** 210
A.A. Likhanov **2:** 9, 60
E.T. Lippmaa **2:** 28, 29
A.D. Lizichev **2:** 134
V.A. Logunov **1:** 29; **2:** 274
K.D. Lubenchenko **1:** 18, 38
V.P. Lukin **1:** 7

A.A. Makanu **2:** 62
K.N. Makhkamov **1:** 285
V.P. Malyshev **2:** 111
A.M. Mambetov **1:** 295
M.R. Mamedov **1:** 26, 103 (V.G. Mamedov)
Ya.A. Manayenkov **1:** 234
Yu.M. Marinichev **2:** 248
A.L. Markevich **2:** 223
V.A. Martirosyan **1:** 38, 114; **2:** 279
A.M. Masaliyev **1:** 280
V.A. Masol **1:** 209
K.T. Mazurov **2:** 24
N.N. Medvedev **2:** 109
R.A. Medvedev **1:** 76, 156; **2:** 31, 213, 221
V.A. Medvedev **2:** 262
S.T. Melekhin **1:** 205
Ye.N. Meshalkin **1:** 9, 102
M.A. Mikheyev **2:** 275
M.S. Minasbekyan **2:** 268
V.M. Minin **2:** 274
T.A. Minnullin **2:** 128
A.V. Minzhurenko **1:** 63; **2:** 284
V.I. Mironenko **1:** 37
B.V. Miroshin **1:** 186
B.S. Mitin **2:** 5
T.V. Momotova **1:** 105
M.I. Mongo **2:** 123
T.V. Moshnyaga **1:** 131, 241; **2:** 218
Mukhammad–Yusuf **1:** 30
A.G. Mukhtarov **1:** 241; **2:** 57
A.N. Murashev **1:** 62
A.N. Mutalibov **1:** 257

N.A. Nazarbayev **1:** 7, 215, 294
I.A. Nazarov **2:** 174
S.Kh. Negmatulloyev **1:** 163
A.Ya. Neumyvakin **2:** 33
B.N. Nikolsky **2:** 279
R.N. Nishanov **2:** 54, 59
S.A. Niyazov **2:** 6
V.P. Nosov **1:** 147
S.I. Novotny **1:** 80

A.M. Obolensky **1:** 10, 38, 44, 47, 182; **2:** 205
A.V. Oborin **1:** 113, 136 (V.A. Shapovalenko)
V.S. Obraz **1:** 122
V.N. Ochirov **2:** 93
R.K. Odzhiyev **1:** 242
Yu.Yu. Olekaf **1:** 242
B.I. Oleynik **1:** 260
V.P. Orlov **1:** 4
V.A. Ostroukhov **2:** 243

K.D. P. Prunskene **2:** 172
V.A. Palm **1:** 130
D.I. Patiashvili **1:** 234
Ya.Ya. Peters **2:** 84
N.S. Petruchenko **1:** 123, 233
V.A. Pisarenko **1:** 67
Pitirim **1:** 294 (Metropolitan)
Yu.P. Platonov **2:** 77
A.L. Plotnik **2:** 147, 280
A.L. Plotnikov **1:** 80, 291
A.A. Plotniyeks **1:** 13; **2:** 207
G.N. Podberezsky **2:** 265
G.A. Pogosyan **1:** 110, 218
N.A. Polikarpov **2:** 94
M.N. Poltoranin **1:** 241, 293; **2:** 269
V.P. Polyanichko **1:** 82
G.Kh. Popov **1:** 98, 132, 184; **2:** 237
F.V. Popov **1:** 8
G.A. Posibeyev **1:** 111
Ye.M. Primakov **1:** 242
Z.P. Pukhova **1:** 262
B.F. Pylin **1:** 59

M.N. Rakhmanova **1:** 219
V.G. Rasputin **2:** 138
V.I. Revnitsev **1:** 19
A.M. Ridiger **1:** 269
I.N. Rodionov **1:** 227
V.D. Romanenko **1:** 78
Z.K. Rustamova **2:** 57
S.M. Ryabchenko **1:** 243; **2:** 286
N.I. Ryzhkov **2:** 150, 201, 252

INDEX OF PERSONS

A.K. Safonov **1:** 293
R.Z. Sagdeyev **1:** 69; **2:** 272
A.D. Sakharov **1:** 7, 19, 31, 54, 133, 241; **2:** 59, 93, 228, 275, 286a
V.I. Samarin **1:** 58, 181
A.S. Samsonov **2:** 273
A.S. Samsonov **1:** 55, 130; **2:** 210
L.I. Sandulyak **1:** 44
A.N. Saunin **1:** 18
N.V. Savchenko **1:** 83
O.M. Savostyuk **1:** 110
N.S. Sazonov **1:** 119, 295; **2:** 108
A.Ye. Sebentsov **1:** 17, 150
A.I. Seleznev **2:** 131
V.M. Semenov **2:** 30
V.I. Sergiyenko **2:** 72
V.V. Sevryukov **1:** 82
M. Shakhanov **2:** 145
T.M. Shamba **1:** 293
I.B. Shamshev **2:** 281
V.A. Shapovalenko **1:** 243; **2:** 285
Yu.K. Sharipov **2:** 11
A.V. Sharonov **1:** 112
R.K. Shchedrin **1:** 82
A.A. Shchelkanov **1:** 32, 143; **2:** 267
V.P. Shcherbakov **2:** 102
E.N. Shengelaya **1:** 23, 232
P.V. Shetko **2:** 92
V.S. Shevchenko **2:** 55
V.Ya. Shevlyuga **1:** 65
N.P. Shmelev **2:** 168
I.N. Shundeyev **1:** 155
S.S. Shushkevich **1:** 81
A.A. Sidorov **1:** 242
A.Yu. Smaylis **1:** 71
D.G. Smirnov **2:** 208
Ye.A. Smolentsev **2:** 219
A.A. Sobchak **1:** 44, 112, 116, 185; **2:** 58, 118, 279
Ye.Ye. Sokolov **1:** 84, 207
R.Kh. Solntsev **1:** 157
Yu.B. Solovyev **1:** 31; **2:** 110

I.V. Sorokin **2:** 212
M.V. Spiridonov **1:** 37
S.B. Stankevich **1:** 14, 19, 54
V.A. Starodubtsev **1:** 247
V.K. Starovoytov **1:** 162
G.V. Starovoytova **1:** 111, 135
V.A. Statulyavichyus **1:** 57
V.N. Stepanov **1:** 100; **2:** 267
G.I. Stoumova **2:** 16
Ye.S. Stroyev **1:** 52
N.A. Strukov **1:** 179; **2:** 56
L.I. Sukhov **1:** 33; **2:** 221, 274
S.S. Sulakshin **1:** 45; **2:** 59
O.O. Suleymenov **1:** 120; **2:** 199

R.Sh. Tabukashvili **1:** 294
G.S. Tarazevich **2:** 208
A.N. Tavkhelidze **1:** 293
N.E. Ternyuk **2:** 265
N.I. Timashova **2:** 209
Z.N. Tkacheva **2:** 80
A.I. Tkhor **1:** 63
V.F. Tolpezhnikov **1:** 5, 100, 294
V.P. Tomkus **1:** 231
I.Kh. Toome **1:** 288
A.Ya. Troitsky **2:** 288
A.I. Trudolyubov **2:** 75
A.Ya. Tsirulis **2:** 212
S.A. Tsyplyayev **1:** 73

R.A. Ubaydullayeva **2:** 109

B.L. Vasilyev **1:** 239
Z.Z. Vayshvila **1:** 53
Ye.P. Velikhov **1:** 38
L.M. Veyser **1:** 220
A.Kh. Vezirov **1:** 117
Yu.P. Vlasov **1:** 277
V.A. Voblikov **1:** 31, 234
Yu.Yu. Voldyrev **2:** 210
A.I. Volsky **1:** 221
R.G. Voronina **1:** 46

N.N. Vorontsov **1:** 115; **2:** 202
V.I. Voskoboynikov **1:** 33
V.A. Vrovkov **1:** 138 (aka A.I. Baranov)

A.V. Yablokov **2:** 189
Ye.V. Yakovlev **1:** 121
A.M. Yakovlev **2:** 204
A. Yakubov **1:** 158; **2:** 241
V.V. Yakushkin **2:** 94
G.I. Yanayev **1:** 138; **2:** 282
A.P. Yanenko **1:** 186, 212
V.A. Yarin **1:** 137
V.I. Yarovoy **2:** 29, 139
A.A. Yarshinskaya **2:** 226 (see also Zgerskaya)
A.Z. Yastrebov **1:** 178
V.A. Yavorivsky **1:** 30
I.A. Yegorova **2:** 177
B.N. Yeltsin **1:** 46, 263
A.F. Yemelyanenkov **1:** 36
A.M. Yemelyanov **2:** 180
G.A. Yenokyan **1:** 117
N.V. Yeseykin **1:** 37
Ye.A. Yevtushenko **2:** 41, 210
V.D. Yudin **1:** 184
E.Yu. Yusupov **2:** 56

A.A. Zakharov **1:** 241
M.Ch. Zalikhanov **1:** 44
S.P. Zalygin **1:** 78; **2:** 195
T.I. Zaslavskaya **1:** 53
I.I. Zaslavsky **1:** 26, 137, 177; **2:** 266
A.A. Zgerskaya **2:** 110 (see also Yarshinskaya)
T.P. Zhukova **1:** 83
A.G. Zhuravlev **1:** 147; **2:** 279
V.P. Zolotukhin **1:** 61
V.A. Zubanov **1:** 113; **2:** 284
V.N. Zubkov **1:** 83
S.N. Zvonov **1:** 35

INDEX OF PERSONS

VOLUMES 1–2

Aare, Yu.Y. **1:** 93, 95
Aasmyae, K.Y. **1:** 10, 231, 292
Abalkin, L.I. **1:** 132, 271, 290; **2:** 20, 38, 97, 109, 292(n96)
Abasov, K.A. **1:** 93, 96

Abbasov, Ya.I. **1:** 92, 95
Abdimuratova, Sh. **1:** 93, 96
Abovyan, K. **1:** 115
Abramov, F. **1:** 102, 301(n102)
Abramyan, Kh.B. **1:** 93, 95

Adamovich, A.M. **1:** 53, 91, 119, 125, 127, 128-29, 146, 175, 215, 232, 234, 290, 297(n1b), 300(n45); **2:** 41
Adomaytis, R.V. **1:** 71

INDEX OF PERSONS

Advadze, V.S.   **1:** 92, 95
Adylov, V.T.   **1:** 92, 94;   **2:** 54, 57
Afanasyev, V.G.   **2:** 144, 170
Afanasyev, Yu.N.   **1:** 91, 100-105, 119-26, 129, 130, 131, 132, 146, 154, 174, 181-84, 278, 297(n1b), 300(n45);   **2:** 20, 29, 105, 193
Afanasyeva, L.V.   **1:** 93, 96
Aganbegyan, A.G.   **2:** 38, 154, 242, 292(n96)
Aguzarova, S.B.   **1:** 93, 96
Akayev, A.   **1:** 93, 95;   **2:** 272, 276
Akhmatova, A.   **1:** 304(n158)
Akhometova, R.S.   **1:** 92, 94
Akmamedov, G.M.   **1:** 93, 95
Akmataliyeva, U.K.   **1:** 93, 95
Akmatov, T.   **1:** 93, 95
Aleksandr II   **2:** 295(n195)
Aleksandrin, V.G.   **1:** 239
Aleksandrin, V.G.   **2:** 54
Aleksandrovna, Y.   **2:** 184
Aleksey, Metropolitan—see Ridiger
Alekseyev, S.S.   **1:** 244;   **2:** 258, 296 (n276)
Aleskerova, R.M.   **1:** 92, 95, 290
Aliluyev, N.I.   **1:** 93, 96
Aliyev   **1:** 267, 303(n137)
Alksnis, V.I.   **1:** 33, 148, 184, 299 (n25), 304(n148), 305(n183);   **2:** 2, 52, 53, 213
Allayarov, R.A.   **1:** 93, 95
Amangeldinova, G.A.   **1:** 10
Ambartsumyan, S.A.   **1:** 93, 95
Ambartsumyan, V.A.   **1:** 5, 93, 95
Amonashvili, Sh.A.   **1:** 92, 95;   **2:** 89
Anagapov, S.V.   **1:** 93, 95
Anamukhamedov, A.   **1:** 93, 95
Ananyev, A.A.   **2:** 251
Andreyev, Yu.E.   **1:** 10
Andreyevna, N.   **1:** 46, 156, 157, 217; 300(n46), 304(n156)
Andronati, S.A.   **1:** 231, 243, 245, 292
Andropov, Yu.A.   **1:** 302(n117);   **2:** 290(n21)
Anishchev, V.P.   **1:** 47
Antanavichyus, K.A.   **1:** 3, 77-78
Anufriyev, S.   **2:** 11
Anufriyev, V.G.   **2:** 107
Apostol, V.G.   **1:** 89
Arbatov, G.A.   **2:** 28, 105
Ardzinba, V.G.   **1:** 93, 95
Arshba, R.A.   **1:** 93, 95
Arutyunyan, E.T.   **1:** 93, 95, 118
Arutyunyan, L.A.   **1:** 93, 95;   **2:** 28, 105
Arutyunyan, S.G.   **1:** 246
Astafyev, V.P.   **2:** 99, 293(n99)

Atadzhanov, A.R.   **1:** 92, 94
Atdayev, Kh.   **1:** 93, 95
Auyelbekov, Ye.N.   **1:** 92, 94
Ayazyrova, V.Y.   **1:** 93, 96
Aypin, Ye.D.   **1:** 97
Aytmatov, Ch.T.   **1:** 5, 36, 37, 93, 95, 133, 216, 290, 291, 295;   **2:** 29, 31, 86, 105, 143, 242
Ayubov, N.   **1:** 290
Azizbekov, M.   **1:** 291;   **2:** 45, 291 (n45)
Azizbekova, P.A.   **1:** 5, 92, 95;   **2:** 33, 87

Babchenko, N.I.   **2:** 441
Babich, V.M.   **1:** 10
Badalbayeva, P.   **1:** 92, 94
Badamyants, V.G.   **2:** 276
Badrutdinov, G.   **2:** 129
Badzhelidze, N.U.   **1:** 93, 95
Bakatin, V.V.   **1:** 50;   **2:** 108
Baklanov, G.   **1:** 300(n45)
Baklanov, O.D.   **2:** 184, 295(n184)
Bakrdze, A.V.   **1:** 92, 95
Bakulin, V.I.   **1:** 246
Balayan, Z.G.   **1:** 82, 91, 111, 189, 218, 219, 221, 222, 244, 274, 302(n111);   **2:** 213
Baleshev, N.F.   **1:** 93, 95
Baranov, A.I.   **1:** 10;   **2:** 54, 59
Baranovsky, V.V.   **2:** 106
Barbanov, V.I.   **1:** 93, 95
Barusheva, L.V.   **1:** 92, 95
Batalin, Yu.P.   **2:** 106
Batorov, A.B.   **1:** 94, 97
Batynskaya, L.I.   **1:** 94, 96;   **2:** 280
Batyuk   **2:** 92
Bazarova, R.A.   **1:** 93, 95, 290
Bedulya, V.   **1:** 36
Bekhtereva, N.P.   **1:** 231, 292
Belenkov, Yu.N.   **1:** 10
Belinsky, V.G.   **1:** 254
Belkin, V.   **2:** 292(n96)
Belousov   **1:** 194
Belov, V.I.   **1:** 92, 94, 97, 184;   **2:** 27, 41, 43, 45, 67, 121, 170, 295(n170)
Belyayev, V.N.   **1:** 10, 297(n11a);   **2:** 107
Berezov, V.A.   **2:** 109
Beria, L.   **2:** 199
Bespalov   **1:** 259
Beyshekeyeva, Z.   **1:** 93, 95
Bezbakh, Ya.Ya.   **1:** 51
Bezuglyy, D.K.   **1:** 149
Bichkhauskas, E.V.   **1:** 10, 92, 95, 242;   **2:** 54
Biryukov, V.A.   **1:** 45

Bisher, A.I.   **2:** 54, 215
Bisher, I.O.   **1:** 93, 95, 239;   **2:** 29
Bobritsky, N.G.   **2:** 251
Bocharov, M.A.   **1:** 89, 140;   **2:** 92, 272, 273
Bodrenkov, A.   **2:** 75
Bogatsky, A.V.   **1:** 231, 292
Bogdanov, I.M.   **2:** 107
Bogmolov, O.T.   **2:** 20
Bogoraz. L.   **2:** 230
Boka   **1:** 146
Bokov, Kh.Kh.   **1:** 149
Bolbasov, V.S.   **1:** 92, 94
Boldyrev, Yu.Yu.   **1:** 15, 297(n11a);   **2:** 277
Borodin, O.P.   **1:** 241
Borodin, O.T.   **2:** 275
Borodin, Yu.I   **1:** 81
Borontsov   **1:** 245
Borovik, G.A.   **1:** 85, 219, 231, 232, 238, 292
Borovikov, G.G.   **1:** 86
Borovkov, V.A.   **1:** 245, 290
Bosenko, N.V.   **1:** 92, 94, 97
Botandayev, I.N.   **1:** 94, 96
Boyars, Yu.R.   **1:** 1, 3, 76, 300(n76)
Boykov, S.V.   **1:** 94, 96
Bratun   **1:** 294
Brazauskas, A.-M.K.   **1:** 5, 246;   **2:** 6, 109
Bresis, V.-E.G.   **2:** 215
Brezhnev, L.I.   **1:** 38, 278, 279, 302 (n137);   **2:** 2, 37, 99, 101, 126, 139
Britvin, N.V.   **1:** 93, 95
Brodsky, I.   **2:** 230
Bronshteyn, M.L.   **1:** 93, 95, 125
Brutsa   **1:** 294
Buachidze, T.P.   **1:** 93, 95;   **2:** 276
Budenny, S.   **2:** 193, 194
Bukharin   **1:** 156
Bunich, P.G.   **1:** 291;   **2:** 109, 138, 292(n96)
Buravov, G.V.   **1:** 93, 96
Burayev, I.Z.   **1:** 93, 96
Burlatsky, F.M.   **1:** 57, 69, 71, 101;   **2:** 109, 218
Burlitsky   **1:** 167
Bursky, V.I.   **1:** 10
Burtin, Yu.   **1:** 297(n1b)
Burykh, Yu.Ye.   **1:** 104, 171
Bush, G.H.   **2:** 99
Butov   **2:** 222
Bykov, V.V.   **1:** 300(n45);   **2:** 29, 105, 106

Catherine the Great   **1:** 299(n38)
Chaadayev, Peter   **1:** 280

INDEX OF PERSONS

Charles XII **2:** 133
Chazov, E.I. **2:** 106, 114
Chebrikov, V.M. **1:** 235, 301(n102a), 304(n154)
Chekalin **2:** 10, 170
Chekov, Anton **2:** 4
Chemodanov, Yu. **1:** 91, 102, 109-11, 112-14, 116, 120
Chepik **2:** 92
Chernenko, K.A. **1:** 302(n117); **2:** 2, 99
Chernichenko, F.G. **2:** 67, 73
Chernichenko, Yu.D. **1:** 101, 131, 296, 297(n1b), 301(n101); **2:** 1
Chernikov, I. **2:** 10
Chernomyrdin **2:** 106
Chernov, V. **1:** 1
Chernykh, G.A. **1:** 91, 93, 96, 227
Chernyshev **1:** 171
Chervonopisky, S.V. **2:** 120
Chimpoy, M.I. **1:** 93, 95, 171
Chkeidze **2:** 51
Chkeidze, N.S. **2:** 140, 294(n140)
Chkenkeli, A. **2:** 292(n87)
Cholokyan, K.S. **1:** 93, 95
Churbanov, Yu.M. **1:** 302(n137); **2:** 219, 225, 296(n225)
Churchill, W. **2:** 196
Churchill, W. (wife) **2:** 91
Clausewitz, Carl von **2:** 95
Clines, F.X. **2:** 61

Dadamyan, B.V. **1:** 218; **2:** 105
Danilov, S.N. **1:** 93, 96
Danilyuk, N.I. **1:** 94, 96
Darsigov, M.Yu. **1:** 93, 96
Davranov, N. **1:** 92, 94
Dekanozov, V.G. **2:** 85
Demakov, N.A. **1:** 79, 80, 85
Demchuk, M.I. **2:** 106
Demidov, M.V. **1:** 93, 96
Denisov, A.A. **1:** 112, 184, 218, 221; **2:** 290(13)
Dickens, Charles **1:** 121
Dikhtyar, A.D. **1:** 92, 94
Dmitriyev, A.A. **1:** 94, 96
Dmitriyev, V.V. **1:** 93, 96
Dobrovolsky, A.O. **1:** 81, 82
Doga, Ye.D. **1:** 93, 95
Dorodnitsin **2:** 196
Dostoyevsky, F.M. **2:** 99
Drutse, I.P. **1:** 93, 95, 177; **2:** 7, 23, 29, 43, 105
Druzhinin **2:** 106
Dubko, A.I. **1:** 92, 94
Dudko, T.N. **1:** 290
Dukhanin **2:** 226, 232
Dzhabbarov **2:** 224, 225, 226

Dzhafarov, V.D. **1:** 82, 91, 94, 96, 117, 120, 189, 218, 219, 212, 244, 274
Dzhumatova, M.D. **1:** 92, 94

Engver, N.I. **1:** 93, 96, 291
Eshpay **1:** 109
Evele, A. **2:** 206

Falin, V.M. **1:** 92, 94, 97; **2:** 29, 105
Fargiyev, Kh.A. **2:** 107
Fateyev, V.K. **1:** 93, 96
Fatullayev, M. **1:** 93, 95
Fedorov, N.V. **1:** 71, 93, 96, 172, 305(n171)
Fedorov, S.N. **2:** 54
Fedotova, V.I. **1:** 231, 292
Fetisov **2:** 92
Filin, A.S. **2:** 185
Filshin, G.N. **2:** 106
Flotnikov **1:** 146
Fomenko **1:** 81
Fonvizin, D.I. **2:** 290(n12)
Furtseva, Y.A. **2:** 3, 290(n3)

Gabrielan, V.M. **1:** 222
Gabrusev, S.A. **1:** 62, 81, 82
Gadzhiyev, MM. **1:** 92, 95-96
Gaipov **2:** 225
Galkin **2:** 58, 229
Gamzatov, I.G. **1:** 244
Gamzatov, R.G. **1:** 244
Gankrelidze, T.V. **1:** 189, 227, 232
Gavrilov, A.P. **1:** 290, 145
Gayer, Ye.A. **1:** 92, 94, 97
Gazenko, O.G. **1:** 245, 292
Gdlyan, T.Kh. **1:** 30, 82, 85, 136-38, 150, 152, 153-54, 155, 158, 159, 164, 179, 183, 239, 240, 241, 242-44, 302-3(n137), 304 (nn150, 156); **2:** 54-59, 106, 200, 225-26, 232
Gelman, A.A. **2:** 106
Genchev, A.A. **1:** 93, 96
Genzyalis, B.K. **1:** 92, 95
Gidaspov, B.V. **1:** 19, 80; **2:** 2
Gidirin, G.P. **1:** 241
Ginzburg, V.L. **1:** 63
Giro, A.V. **1:** 10, 51
Gladky **2:** 106
Glazkov, N.S. **2:** 33
Gnatyuk, V.V. **1:** 92, 94
Goborov, V.L. **1:** 292
Gogeshvili, A.R. **1:** 93, 96
Golik, Yu.V. **1:** 239; **2:** 54, 276
Golovnev, V.Ye. **1:** 92, 94
Golyakov, A.I. **1:** 231, 292
Gonchar, O. **1:** 260

Goncharik, V.I. **2:** 106
Gontar, V.A. **1:** 246; **2:** 295(n181)
Gorbachev, A.G. **1:** 93, 96
Gorbachev, M.S. **1:** 1, 2, 3, 5, 8, 9, 14, 18, 19, 24, 26-28, 29, 30, 31, 33-38, 43, 44, 45, 46, 47, 48-49, 51, 52, 58, 62, 67, 77, 78, 91, 99, 101, 103, 113, 114, 118, 121, 124, 125, 130, 135, 139, 140, 146, 147, 148, 149, 150, 154-59 passim, 161-64 passim, 170, 171, 173, 175, 176, 179, 180, 181, 182, 184, 207, 208, 210, 212, 214, 219, 222, 223, 232, 237, 246, 253, 254, 255, 257, 258, 259, 262, 263, 264, 266, 269, 272, 278, 280, 282, 285-87, 297(n11b), 299(n45), 300(n59), 302(n117), 303(nn142, 147), 304(n150b), 305(n154); **2:** 2, 4, 5, 6, 7, 9, 15, 20, 22, 23, 26, 37, 43, 44, 45, 46, 48, 49, 53, 61, 69, 72, 75, 78, 86, 87, 97, 99, 100, 110, 113, 116, 117, 123, 126, 131, 132, 134, 136, 143, 149, 156, 166, 187, 190, 199, 218, 235, 236, 243, 244, 263, 268, 290(n21)
Gorbacheva, R.M. **1:** 35, 46
Gorbunov, A.V. **1:** 5, 140, 166, 170, 171, 222, 246, 265, 290; **2:** 113, 215
Gorbunov, G.N. **2:** 96
Gorinov, T.I. **1:** 15, 58
Gostev, B.I. **1:** 284; **2:** 169, 295 (n169)
Govorov, V.L. **1:** 233
Grakhovsky, A. **2:** 1
Granin, D.A. **1:** 183, 231
Griboyedov, A.S. **2:** 294(n126)
Griboyedov, I.I. **2:** 126
Grigoryan **1:** 110, 218, 221
Grishayev **2:** 210
Grishin **1:** 303(n137)
Gromov, B.F. **2:** 107
Grossu, S.K. **1:** 290
Gryazin, I.N. **1:** 93, 95; **2:** 1, 29, 105, 276
Gubarev, V.A. **1:** 83
Gubin, V.A. **2:** 147
Guchkov, A.I. **2:** 140, 294(n140)
Gudaytis, R.V. **1:** 92, 95; **2:** 166
Guguchiya, D.I. **1:** 92, 95
Guliyev, V.Y. **2:** 209
Gulova, Z.S. **1:** 93, 95
Guly, V.V. **1:** 65, 68, 241
Gumbaridze, G.G. **1:** 92, 95, 292, 294

INDEX OF PERSONS

Gumilev, N.S. **1:** 158, 304(158)
Gundogdyyev, Ya.P. **1:** 93, 95
Gusev, V.K. **1:** 259

Hitler, A. **2:** 173

Ibragimov, G.R. **1:** 10, 92, 95
Ibragimov, M.I. **1:** 93, 96, 290
Igantovich, N.I. **2:** 54
Igityan, G.S. **1:** 26, 93, 95, 163, 305(n163); **2:** 106
Ignatov, S.V. **1:** 93, 96
Ignatovich, N.I. **1:** 92, 94, 232, 244
Ikayev, G.D. **1:** 93, 96
Iliya II (Georgia) **1:** 227
Isakov, I.I. **1:** 93, 95
Isayev, G.I. **1:** 93, 96
Ishanov, Kh. **1:** 5, 93, 95, 287
Ismailov, T.K. **1:** 92, 95
Ivan V **2:** 295(n195)
Ivanov, N.V. **1:** 30, 80, 85, 155, 158, 159, 164, 182, 240, 241, 302-3(137); **2:** 54, 56-58, 73, 106, 200, 225
Ivans, D.E. **1:** 290; **2:** 107
Ivashko, V.A. **1:** 92, 94

Kadyrov, G.K. **2:** 149, 294(n149)
Kafarova, E.M. **1:** 92, 95
Kaipbergenov, T. **1:** 93, 96, 189, 290; **2:** 196
Kakadzhivov, C. **1:** 290
Kakhirov, K.Z. **1:** 93, 96
Kakhn, Yu.Kh. **1:** 93, 95
Kalashnikov, V.Ya. **1:** 93, 95, 160
Kallas, S.U. **1:** 93, 95
Kalmykov, Yu.Kh. **2:** 276
Kalyagin, S.B. **1:** 300(n82)
Kamenshchikova, G.N. **1:** 93, 96
Kanarovskaya, A.M. **1:** 93, 95
Kangliyev, A.Ya. **1:** 94, 96
Kapitsa, P.L. **2:** 193, 295(n193)
Kaplan **1:** 206
Kapto, A.S. **1:** 89, 92, 94
Kapustin, A.V. **1:** 65
Kara-Sal, D.B. **1:** 93, 96
Karaganov, S.V. **1:** 65
Karpenko, V.F. **1:** 93, 96
Karpochev, V.A. **1:** 58, 93, 96
Karpov, A.Ye. **1:** 121, 244, 302(n121); **2:** 33
Karpov, V.V. **1:** 121, 231, 232, 234, 237, 238, 240, 241, 302(n121)
Kartashov, L.P. **2:** 107
Karyakin, Yu.F. **1:** 102, 302(n102); **2:** 168
Kashnikov, N.I. **1:** 170
Kashperk **2:** 106

Kasyan, N.A. **2:** 33, 113, 127, 241
Kasyan, V.V. **1:** 83
Katilevsky, S.M. **1:** 92, 94
Katusev **2:** 229
Kaunin **2:** 222
Kazakova, T.K. **2:** 61
Kazannik, A.I. **1:** 92, 94, 97, 139, 160, 185-85, 188, 189, 190, 241, 274; **2:** 13, 29, 105, 127
Kazarezov, V.V. **1:** 246
Kerensky, A.F. **2:** 294(n140)
Kergilov, S. **2:** 84
Kerimov, D.A. **1:** 93, 96; **2:** 276
Kerimov, A.O. **1:** 239
Kezbers, I.Y. **2:** 105
Khachatryan, V.K. **1:** 291
Khadzhiyev, S.N. **1:** 171
Khallik, K.S. **1:** 93, 95; **2:** 113, 185
Khanzadyan, S.N. **1:** 93, 95
Khazanov, G. **2:** 25
Khint **1:** 154
Khitrov, P.A. **1:** 94, 96
Khlebstov, K.A. **2:** 81
Khmura, V.V. **1:** 83, 294; **2:** 33
Khodyrev, G.M. **2:** 119
Khomyakov, A.I. **1:** 71, 94, 96
Khrushchev, N.S. **1:** 155; **2:** 126, 240, 291(n37)
Khudayberenova, R.M. **1:** 92, 94
Khudonazarov, D. **1:** 94, 96
Khugayeva, D.V. **1:** 94, 96
Khusanbayev, M.A. **1:** 93, 95
Kim **1:** 160, 244
Kirillov, V.I. **2:** 275
Kiriyak, N.P. **1:** 93, 95, 177
Kirov, S.M. **2:** 68
Kiselev, A.A. **1:** 79, 80, 83, 85
Kiselev, G.I. **1:** 93, 95
Kiselev, V.N. **1:** 241
Kiseleva, V.A. **1:** 5, 92, 94
Kislitsyn, V.A. **1:** 58
Klibik, V.S. **1:** 93, 95
Klishchuk, P.M. **1:** 92, 94
Kochetov, K.A. **1:** 234, 235
Kodyrov, B.K. **1:** 93, 95
Kogan, Ye.V. **2:** 145, 212
Kohl, H. **2:** 31
Kolbin, G.V. **2:** 146, 166, 210, 220, 221, 222, 294(n146), 296(n200)
Kolesnikov, V.I. **1:** 80, 290
Kolotov, V.I. **1:** 183
Koltsov, Yu.A. **1:** 152; **2:** 106, 278
Komarov, G.A. **2:** 106
Komarov, Yu.T. **1:** 93, 96
Konovalov, A.I. **1:** 145; **2:** 109
Kontselidze, M.R. **1:** 290
Korniyenko, V.N. **1:** 81, 82
Korobkin, V.V. **1:** 93, 96

Korotich, V.A. **1:** 300(n45); **2:** 29, 105, 106
Korpochev **1:** 15
Korshunov, A.A. **1:** 92, 94; **2:** 33, 40
Koryavin **2:** 92
Kostenetskaya, M.G. **1:** 93, 95
Kostenyuk, A.G. **1:** 10
Kostishin, N.A. **1:** 93, 95
Kosygin, A.N. **2:** 237
Kosygin, V.V. **1:** 94, 96; **2:** 271
Kotov **1:** 145
Kozhakhmatov, I. **1:** 5, 92, 94
Krasilnikov **1:** 145
Krasin, L.B. **2:** 290(n20)
Kravets, V.A. **2:** 105
Krayko, A.N. **2:** 283
Krupskaya, N.K. **2:** 100
Krylova, Z.P. **1:** 89, 140
Kryuchenkova, N.A. **1:** 290
Kryuchkov, G.K. **2:** 276
Kubilyus, I.P. **1:** 290
Kucheyko, A.P. **1:** 92, 94
Kudarauskas, S.Y. **1:** 89, 92, 95
Kudrin, L.S. **1:** 241, 242
Kudryavtsev, V.N. **1:** 50, 73, 160, 239, 240, 290; **2:** 202-3, 204, 207, 208, 209, 214, 230, 276
Kugultinov, D.N. **1:** 93, 96; **2:** 186
Kukayn, R.A. **1:** 93, 95
Kukhar, I.I. **1:** 127
Kuldyshev, M.S. **1:** 93, 95
Kulikov, Ye.A. **1:** 93, 96
Kuliyev, S.O. **1:** 93, 96
Kunayev, D. **2:** 296(n200)
Kuntsevich **2:** 110
Kuplyauskene, Yu.Y. **1:** 92, 95
Kurashvili, Z.G. **1:** 5, 92-93, 95
Kurbanov, K. **2:** 106
Kurbanova, A. **1:** 93, 95
Kurchatov **2:** 199
Kurilenko, V.T. **1:** 92, 94
Kurochka, G.M. **1:** 245
Kurochkin **1:** 244
Kuzovlev, A.T. **1:** 83
Kuzubov, V.F. **1:** 291
Kyabin, T.R. **1:** 93, 95
Kydyyev, V. **2:** 84

Labunov, V.A. **1:** 92, 94
Landsbergis, V.V. **1:** 1, 52, 100, 297(n12a); **2:** 29, 33, 105
Laptev, I.D. **1:** 290
Lapygin, V.L. **1:** 93, 96
Lari **1:** 177
Larionov, V.P. **1:** 94, 96
Lauristin, M.Y. **1:** 232, 290; **2:** 29, 105

INDEX OF PERSONS

Lavrov **2:** 286
Lavrov, K.Y. **1:** 290
Lavrov, S.B. **2:** 105
Lazarev, B.M. **2:** 194, 202
Lenin **1:** 1, 33, 37, 51, 150, 153, 162, 174, 175, 181, 200, 201, 204, 208, 215, 233, 234, 249, 252, 254, 271, 277, 281, 282, 300(n45), 305(n162); **2:** 7, 20, 42, 45, 49, 83, 95, 99, 100, 101, 102, 117, 121, 122, 129, 133, 134, 143, 148, 261, 292(n84)
Leonenkov **1:** 146
Leonov, I.M. **1:** 263
Leskov, N.S. **1:** 99, 301(n99)
Levakin, V.A. **1:** 93, 96
Levashev **1:** 183
Levsha **1:** 99
Levykin, Y.A. **2:** 107
Lezhenko, G.F. **1:** 92, 94
Lezhnev, M.A. **1:** 80
Ligachev, Ye.K. **1:** 20, 154, 300 (n46), 302-3(n137); **2:** 1, 21, 55, 73, 121, 131, 224, 225, 290(n21), 295(n170)
Likhachev, D.S. **1:** 219, 220, 231, 234, 269, 292, 295; **2:** 43, 200
Likhanov, A.A. **1:** 92, 94, 97, 294; **2:** 1, 40, 81
Likhanov, D. **2:** 6
Lippmaa, E.T. **1:** 5; **2:** 1, 29, 105
Lisichkin, G.S. **1:** 82, 85
Lisisky, D.V. **2:** 106
Lisnichy, D.V. **2:** 106
Litvintseva, G.N. **1:** 93, 95
Lomonosov, M. **1:** 274
Lubenchenko, K.D. **1:** 3, 239, 303 (n137); **2:** 54, 278
Luchenok, I.M. **2:** 108
Lukin, V.P. **1:** 92, 94, 231, 292
Lukyanenko, O.F. **2:** 106
Lukyanov, A.I. **1:** 1, 5, 71, 76, 77, 78, 81, 91, 105, 111, 117, 118, 133-35, 136, 139, 140, 144, 145, 147-48, 150-51, 154, 155, 157-59, 163-65, 167, 179, 182, 222, 290; **2:** 1, 19, 62, 139, 204
Lushchikov, S.G. **1:** 93, 96
Lutsans, Ya.P. **1:** 93, 95
Lyubimov, Yu.P. **1:** 102, 301(n102)

Magomedov, G.M. **1:** 93, 96
Mainullin, T.A. **1:** 93, 96
Makhamadaliyev **2:** 10
Maksimov, V.N. **1:** 93, 96
Mamedov, M.R. **1:** 302(n104)
Mamedov, V.G. **1:** 89, 91, 92, 95
Manko, N.M. **1:** 93, 95

Mao Zedong **2:** 20
Marchuk, G.I. **1:** 290; **2:** 106
Margvelashvili, P.I. **1:** 10, 89, 232
Markov, G.M. **2:** 293(n99)
Markov, O.I. **2:** 99
Martirosyan, V.A. **1:** 233, 292
Martsinkivichyus, Y.M. **2:** 105
Martynov **2:** 92
Marx, Karl **1:** 176, 215, 248; **2:** 261
Mashbashev, I.Sh. **1:** 94, 96
Maslakova, A.P. **1:** 93, 96
Maslyukov **2:** 47, 106, 291(n47)
Masol, V.A. **1:** 290
Masova, G.Y. **2:** 267
Mateushuk, Z.K. **1:** 92, 94
Matkovsky, D. **1:** 176
Matveychuk, Z.K. **2:** 106
Matveyev, Yu.G. **2:** 166, 220
Matyukha, V.N. **1:** 290
Matyukhin, L.I. **1:** 92, 94, 97
Mazepa **2:** 133
Mazurov, K.T. **1:** 290; **2:** 120
Medeubekov, K.U. **1:** 92, 94
Medikov, V.Ya. **1:** 86
Medvedev, N.N. **1:** 92, 95
Medvedev, R.A. **1:** 77, 78, 97, 121, 232, 233, 234, 239, 290, 300(n45); **2:** 56, 57, 140
Medvedev, S.A. **1:** 89
Medvedev, V.A. **1:** 290; **2:** 33
Melekhin, S.T. **1:** 290
Melzev, K. **1:** 93, 95
Menteshashvili, T.N. **1:** 93, 95
Meshalkin, Ye.N. **1:** 121, 127, 158, 174, 305(n179a); **2:** 22
Mikhaylova, L.I. **1:** 93, 96
Mikheyev, M.A. **1:** 94, 96
Milyukov, P.N. **2:** 140, 294(n140)
Minasbekyan, M.S. **1:** 64
Minin, V.M. **1:** 291; **2:** 147
Minzhurenko, A.V. **1:** 51
Mironenko, V.I. **2:** 92
Mironova, D.S. **1:** 94, 96
Miroshin, B.V. **1:** 241, 243; **2:** 59, 60
Miroshnik, V.M. **1:** 292
Mitin, B.S. **1:** 294; **2:** 1
Mnatsakanyan, B.G. **1:** 93, 95
Mogilnichenko **2:** 224
Moiseyev, M.A. **1:** 290
Mokan, A.A. **2:** 33
Molotov, V.M. **2:** 30, 31, 87, 143, 292(n87)
Momotova, T.V. **1:** 92, 94
Mongo, M.I. **1:** 94, 97
Morgun **2:** 67
Moshnyaga, T.V. **1:** 93, 95

Moteka, K.V. **1:** 92, 95; **2:** 29, 105
Mukhabatova, S.K. **1:** 5
Mukhametzyanov, M.T. **1:** 93, 96
Murakhovsky, V.S. **2:** 14, 15, 21, 176, 290(n14)
Murashov, V.K. **1:** 93, 96
Mutalibov, A.N. **1:** 246

Naan, G. **2:** 144
Nagiev, R.Sh. **1:** 93, 96
Nagornyuk, A.N. **1:** 153
Namazova, A.A. **1:** 92, 95
Napalkov, N.P. **1:** 80, 85
Napoleon **1:** 3, 33
Nasonov, A.F. **1:** 82, 85
Navruzov. Sh. **1:** 94, 96
Nazarbayev, N.A. **1:** 11, 290, 292, 293, 295
Nazarenko, A.F. **2:** 278
Nazarov, T. **1:** 10, 89
Nazaryan, S.Ye. **1:** 89
Nechayev, K.V. **1:** 290, 292
Nechetnaya, N.P. **1:** 290
Nefedov, O.L. **1:** 231
Negmatulloyev, S.Kh. **2:** 276
Nemtsev, Ye.I. **1:** 93, 96
Neumyvakin, A.Ya. **1:** 33
Nevolin, S.I. **1:** 92, 94, 97
Neyland, N.V. **1:** 93, 95; **2:** 29, 105
Nikitin, R.I. **1:** 93, 96
Nikitin, V.V. **1:** 93, 96
Nikolayev, V.V. **1:** 93, 95
Nikorsky, B. **1:** 226
Nikulin, Y. **2:** 25
Nimbuyev, Ts. **1:** 94, 96
Nishanov, R.N. **1:** 5, 92, 94, 116, 189, 246; **2:** 125
Niyazov, S.A. **1:** 294; **2:** 1
Norikhin, V.A. **1:** 241
Nosov **1:** 275
Novozhilov, V.I. **2:** 186
Nugis, Yu.I. **1:** 93, 95
Nyrkov, A.I. **1:** 93, 96
Nyuksha, K.I. **1:** 93, 95

Obolensky, A.M. **1:** 3, 44-45, 47, 80, 85, 134, 150, 166, 183, 184, 297(n11a), 304(n150); **2:** 235, 271
Oborin, A.V. **1:** 302(n136)
Ochirov, V.N. **1:** 93, 96
Odzhiyev, R.K. **1:** 93, 95, 292
Oganesyan, R.G. **1:** 93, 95
Olahansky **1:** 259
Olekas, Yu.Yu. **1:** 92, 95
Oleynik, B.I. **1:** 92, 94, 246; **2:** 4, 6, 26, 109, 121
Opolinsky **2:** 106

Orazmuradova, O.M. **1:** 89
Ordzhonikidze, G.K. **1:** 305(n162)
Orlov, V.P. **1:** 1, 2, 5, 222; **2:** 52, 55
Orozova, U.Sh. **1:** 93, 95; **2:** 271
Osetrov **2:** 55
Osipov, P.D. **1:** 94, 96
Osipyan, Y.A. **1:** 86, 91; **2:** 21
Ostroukhov, V.A. **2:** 235
Otsason, R.A. **1:** 78
Ovezgeldyyev, O. **2:** 276

Palagnyuk, B.T. **1:** 93, 95
Palchin, S.Ya. **1:** 94, 97
Pallayev, G. **1:** 93, 95, 290
Palm **1:** 165, 188
Pamfilova, E.A. **2:** 108
Panichev **2:** 106
Pashaly, M.K. **1:** 93, 95
Pasternak, B. **2:** 20, 290(n20)
Patiashvili, D. **2:** 1, 50, 51
Paton, B.Ye. **1:** 5, 116; **2:** 2
Pauls, R.V. **1:** 71; **2:** 43
Pavlov **1:** 284
Pavlov, A.S. **2:** 38, 276
Peregudov **2:** 5
Pershin, A.L. **1:** 93, 96
Peter I **1:** 123; **2:** 133, 295(n195)
Peters, Ya.Ya. **1:** 93, 95; **2:** 84
Petrakov, N.A. **1:** 82, 85
Petrakov, N.Y. **2:** 20, 107
Petrov **1:** 175, 183; **2:** 92
Petrova, L.N. **1:** 94, 96
Pilnikov, S.V. **1:** 93, 96
Pilyulkin **2:** 3
Piryazeva, N.M. **1:** 81
Pitirim (Nechayev) **1:** 72, 98, 148, 290, 292
Pitirim, N.N. **2:** 43, 45
Pivovarov, N.D. **1:** 290
Plato **2:** 139
Platon, S.I. **1:** 93, 95, 290
Platonov, V.P. **1:** 10
Plotniyeks, A.A. **1:** 16, 89
Plyanichko **1:** 99b
Podziruk, V.S. **1:** 92, 94, 97
Pogorelov, V.G. **2:** 106
Pogosyan, G.A. **1:** 82, 91, 94, 96, 111, 118, 120, 189, 218, 219, 222, 244, 274, 302(n110)
Pokhla, V.P. **1:** 240; **2:** 54
Pokhol **1:** 244
Popov, G.Kh. **1:** 1, 2, 9, 91, 100, 101, 119, 120-25 passim, 126, 129, 130, 146, 173, 181, 182, 186, 215, 271, 278, 290, 297(n1b); **2:** 20, 193, 235, 292 (n96)
Popov **2:** 92; **2:** 222

Poroshin **1:** 87
Posibeyev, G.A. **1:** 109
Presnyakov, A. **1:** 134
Primakov, Ye.M. **1:** 242, 290
Pristavkin **2:** 272, 274
Prokopyev, Yu.N. **2:** 274, 275
Prokushev, V.I. **1:** 93, 95
Promyslov **1:** 303(n137)
Pugacheva, A. **2:** 25
Pugo, B. **1:** 155
Pukhova, Z.P. **1:** 246
Pupkevich, T.K. **1:** 93, 95, 290
Pushkin **1:** 280; **2:** 99, 133, 134

Radzhabov, R.R. **2:** 224-26
Rakhimov, M.G. **1:** 290
Rakhimova, B.F. **1:** 93, 95, 244
Rakhmadiyev, Ye. **1:** 92, 94
Rakhmanova, M.N. **2:** 45
Rasputin, V.G. **2:** 15, 84, 113, 180, 270, 281, 295(n170)
Razumovsky, G.P. **1:** 40, 229, 236, 245, 290; **2:** 51, 188
Reagan, R. **2:** 99
Rekunkov, A.M. **1:** 151, 304(nn151, 152); **2:** 231
Reshetnikov, A.V. **1:** 10
Ribbentrop, Joachim von **2:** 30, 143
Ridiger, A.M. (Metropolitan Aleksey) **2:** 4, 29, 105
Rodionov, I.N. **1:** 24, 189, 225-26, 227, 232, 233, 234, 235, 236, 247, 293, 294; **2:** 3, 49, 69, 188, 290(n3)
Romanenko, V.D. **1:** 92, 94; **2:** 111
Romanov, G.V. **1:** 302-3(n137)
Romanov, V.F. **1:** 145; **2:** 32
Romazanov, K.Z. **1:** 92, 94
Rotar, S.A. **1:** 5
Rubiks, A.P. **1:** 93, 95
Rugin, R.P. **1:** 94, 97
Rustamov, Z.K. **2:** 276
Rybakov, A. **1:** 300(n45)
Rybakov, V.M. **1:** 79-80, 85, 239
Rykov, A.I. **2:** 21
Ryumin, V.V. **2:** 112, 210
Ryuytel, A.F. **1:** 93, 95; **2:** 206
Ryzhkov, N.I. **1:** 20, 173, 175, 213, 261, 284, 290, 301(n100); **2:** 34, 47, 107, 128, 141, 149, 150, 166, 168-71, 172, 173, 174, 178, 191, 193, 194, 195, 201, 235, 240, 242-44, 259, 263
Ryzhov **1:** 121

Sabirova, N. **1:** 290
Safarov, B.S. **1:** 93, 95
Safilulin, M.G. **2:** 108

Safin, M.M. **1:** 93, 95
Safiyeva, G. **1:** 93, 95
Sagdeyev, R.Z. **1:** 70, 231, 234, 292
Sakandelidze, I.B. **1:** 93, 95
Sakhadze, I. **2:** 25
Sakharov, A.D. **1:** 1, 2, 8, 9, 12, 13, 15, 53, 61, 122-23, 157, 160, 176, 179, 182, 227, 231, 234, 241, 243, 292, 294, 300(n45); **2:** 20, 61, 86, 92-94, 100, 101, 147, 197, 272, 276, 286, 289
Sakisyan **1:** 166
Salamanov **2:** 46
Salimov, A.K. **2:** 226
Saltykov-Shchedrin, M.E. **2:** 245, 296(n245)
Salukvadze, R.G. **1:** 93, 95
Samarin, V.I. **1:** 52
Samsonov, A.S. **1:** 55, 133, 173; **2:** 272, 273
Samsonov, N.A. **1:** 93, 96
Sanchat, A.S. **1:** 93, 96
Sapargaliyev, G. **2:** 211
Saunin, A.N. **1:** 105
Savinykh, V.P. **1:** 80, 85
Savisaar, E.E. **2:** 29, 105
Sebentsov, A.Ye. **2:** 278
Sefershayev, F. **1:** 92, 94
Seleznez, A.I. **1:** 178
Selyunin **1:** 271
Semenko, V.I. **2:** 276
Semenov, V.A. **1:** 239, 243; **2:** 54, 56
Semyashkin **1:** 146
Shalyyev, A.B. **1:** 93, 95
Shamikhin, A.M. **1:** 93, 95
Shapovalenko, V.A. **1:** 302(n136)
Sharipov, Yu.K. **1:** 93, 95; **2:** 46
Shatov **1:** 46
Shchedrin, R **1:** 97
Shchelkanov **1:** 183
Shchelokov **2:** 2
Shcherbak, Yu.N. **1:** 89; **2:** 106
Shcherbakov, V.P. **2:** 243
Shcherbin, B.E. **2:** 119, 293(n119)
Shcherbina, M.Y. **2:** 108
Shekhovstov **1:** 173
Shelev **2:** 20
Shengelaya, E.N. **1:** 231, 292
Sherbakov **2:** 168
Shetko, P.V. **1:** 231, 292
Shevardnadze, E.A. **1:** 40, 229, 235, 236; **2:** 1, 31, 32, 52, 85, 188
Shevchenko, T.G. **1:** 261
Shevchenko, V.S. **1:** 92, 94
Shevlyuga, V.Ya. **1:** 65, 83, 253

INDEX OF PERSONS

Shibik, N.A. **2:** 265
Shichite, Z.L. **2:** 29, 105
Shinkarak, V.I. **2:** 29, 105
Shipitko, G.I. **2:** 106
Shkabardnya **2:** 107
Shlyakota, V.V. **1:** 10
Shmal, Yu.Ya. **1:** 81
Shmelev, N.P. **1:** 132, 271; **2:** 109, 181, 193, 194, 237, 259, 292(n96)
Shorokhov, V.N. **1:** 239; **2:** 54, 59
Shostakovich, D.S. **1:** 301(n99)
Shtoyk, G.G. **1:** 92, 94
Shushkevich, S.S. **1:** 300(n81)
Sidor, I.N. **2:** 106
Skudra, V.Ya. **2:** 276
Smaylis, A.Yu. **2:** 276
Smirnov, D.G. **2:** 2, 55, 224-25, 226
Smirnov, V.I. **2:** 290(n2)
Smolentsev, Ye.A. **2:** 166, 219, 221, 267
Sobakin, V.K. **2:** 204
Sobchak, A.A. **1:** 116, 185, 218, 221, 232, 240, 292; **2:** 59, 89, 276, 290(n13)
Sokolov, Ye.Ye. **1:** 51; **2:** 122, 280, 281
Sokolov, Yu.I. **1:** 10
Solntsev, R.K. **1:** 160, 161
Solomenstev, M.S. **1:** 301(n102a), 302-3(n137)
Soloyvev **2:** 92
Solzhenitsyn, A. **2:** 99, 290(n20)
Sorokin, I.V. **1:** 239, 241; **2:** 54
Sorokin, M.I. **1:** 79
Spanderashvili, T.M. **1:** 93, 95
Spartacus **2:** 192
Stachekas **2:** 203
Stadnik, V.Y. **2:** 107
Stalin **1:** 33, 38, 91, 101, 125, 149, 155, 160, 299(n45), 300(n46), 304(n149); **2:** 2, 85, 116, 117, 121, 126, 133, 134, 143, 173, 230, 242, 295(n188)
Stankevich, S.B. **1:** 1, 3, 15, 50, 53, 54, 177, 292, 295
Starodubstev, D.A. **2:** 67, 75, 110
Starodubstev, V.A. **1:** 246, 290; **2:** 16, 41, 175, 176
Starovoytova, G.V. **1:** 163, 166, 305(n163)
Statulyavichyus, V.A. **1:** 51, 275
Stepanenko, A.V. **1:** 81
Stepanova, G.S. **1:** 93, 95
Stepnadze, T.S. **1:** 93, 95
Steshenko, V. **2:** 206
Stolypin, P.A. **1:** 274; **2:** 294(n140)
Stoumova, G. **2:** 1

Stoumova, G.I. **1:** 291
Stroyev, Ye.S. **1:** 50, 58
Strukov, N.A. **1:** 139; **2:** 54
Studenkin, M.Y. **2:** 106
Stupina, Y.D. **1:** 291
Sukharev, A.Ya. **2:** 55, 166, 222, 229, 231, 233, 276, 291(n55), 304(n152)
Sukhov, L.I. **1:** 3; **2:** 275
Suleymenov, O.O. **1:** 123, 177, 241, 291; **2:** 139, 270
Sultangazin, U.M. **2:** 276
Sviridov **2:** 10
Sychev, N.Ya. **1:** 47, 183

Tabukashvili, R.Sh. **1:** 93, 95
Tadinov, A. **2:** 84
Tarazevich, G.S. **1:** 92, 94, 237, 293, 294; **2:** 208, 216
Tarnavsky, G.S. **2:** 276
Tedeyev, L.R. **1:** 94, 96
Temnogrudova, Z.S. **2:** 107
Terebilov **1:** 154
Tereshkova, V.V. **1:** 291
Thatcher, M. **2:** 99, 293(n99)
Tikhin, V.G. **2:** 204
Tikhomirov **2:** 183
Tikhonov, V.A. **2:** 20, 109, 292(n96)
Titov **2:** 224, 232
Tkacheva, Z.N. **2:** 271
Tkhor, AI. **1:** 69
Tolbina, M. **2:** 84
Tolkachekov, A. **2:** 84
Tolkachenov, V.F. **2:** 106
Tolpezhnikov, V.F. **1:** 2, 232, 247, 292; **2:** 106
Tolstoy, L. **2:** 4, 99, 131
Tomkus, V.P. **1:** 292
Toome, I.K. **1:** 246
Trapeznikov **2:** 2
Travkin, N.I. **1:** 9, 82, 85, 97
Trefilov, V.I. **1:** 291
Trushin **1:** 230
Tsigelnikov, A.S. **1:** 110; **2:** 147
Tso, V.I. **1:** 92, 94; **2:** 107
Turchak, Cpt. **2:** 92
Turnis, V. **2:** 206
Tvardovsky, A. **2:** 20, 290(n20)
Tytkheu **2:** 133
Tyukhteneva, A. **2:** 84

Ulyanov, M. **1:** 300(n45)
Ulyanova, M.I. **2:** 100
Umalatova, S.Z. **1:** 93, 96
Umarkhodzhayev, M.I. **1:** 275
Umerenkov, A.M. **1:** 93, 96
Uoka, K.K. **1:** 92, 95
Upmatsis, I. **2:** 206

Usmankhodzhayev **2:** 226, 234
Usmanov, R.K. **1:** 89
Uvarov, A.I. **1:** 110; **2:** 147

Vagin, M.G. **2:** 176
Valentinov, L.F. **1:** 93, 96
Vardanyan, R.P. **1:** 93, 95
Vare, V.I. **1:** 89
Vasiliyev, L.B. **1:** 232, 239, 294, 295
Vasilyev **2:** 33, 224
Vasilyev, N.F. **2:** 15
Vasilyeva **2:** 106
Vasnetsov, A.V. **2:** 106
Vazgen I. **2:** 465a
Vedenkina, Z.A. **1:** 93, 96
Venglovskaya, V.S. **1:** 92, 94, 290
Veprev, A.F. **1:** 59, 102, 110, 112-13, 116; **2:** 107, 176
Veyser, L.M. **1:** 92, 94
Vezirov, A.Kh. **1:** 92, 95, 118
Vichkauskas **1:** 244
Vidiker, V.I. **1:** 10, 92, 94
Vilkas, E.Y. **1:** 92, 95
Viyeru, G.P. **1:** 176
Vlasov, A.V. **2:** 6
Vlasov, Yu.P. **2:** 88, 99, 112, 275, 280
Volsky, A.I. **1:** 221, 290, 302(117); **2:** 193, 295(n193)
Vooglayd, Yu.V. **1:** 93, 95
Voronezhtsev **1:** 81
Voronin, L.A. **2:** 249
Vorotnikov, V.I. **1:** 2, 3, 92, 94, 97, 101, 110, 112, 127, 186, 302(nn112, 127); **2:** 6
Voskanyan, G.M. **1:** 290
Vosnesensky, A. **1:** 300(n45)
Vshtuni, Azat **1:** 103b
Vulfson, M.G. **1:** 93, 95; **2:** 29, 105
Vydrin, A.V. **1:** 148
Vyshinsky, A.A. **2:** 85
Vyucheysky, A.I. **1:** 94, 97

Weizsacker, Carl von **1:** 269

Yablokov, A.V. **2:** 196, 252
Yakhyayev **2:** 226
Yakovlev, A.M. **1:** 220, 232, 239, 244, 292; **2:** 209, 213, 214, 276
Yakovlev, A.N. **1:** 102, 157, 222, 232, 237, 238, 291, 293, 301(n102a), 305(n165); **2:** 32, 54, 105, 140, 200
Yakovlev, M.M. **1:** 241, 242
Yakovlev, YeV. **1:** 2, 232
Yakubov, A. **1:** 160
Yakunin, G. **1:** 133; **2:** 273, 274

Yakushkin, V.V. **1:** 92, 94
Yamenko, A.P. **1:** 291
Yanenko, A.P. **2:** 109
Yarin, V.A. **1:** 154, 239; **2:** 54, 107
Yarkov **2:** 92
Yaroshenko **1:** 10
Yarovoy, V.I. **2:** 113, 145
Yavorsky, V.A. **1:** 227
Yazov, D.T. **1:** 230, 235; **2:** 106
Yefimov, A.S. **1:** 92, 94, 229
Yelemova, G. **2:** 84
Yeltsin, B.N. **1:** 3, 29, 45-46, 51, 60, 71, 92, 94, 113, 125, 127-28, 139, 150, 172, 185-86, 187, 188, 190, 246, 274, 281, 290, 297(n1b), 299(n29), 302(n128); **2:** 86, 109, 127, 183
Yemelyanov, A.M. **2:** 193, 280
Yemenov **2:** 203, 208, 217
Yenkyan, G.A. **1:** 93, 95
Yeraliyev, T.Y. **2:** 78

Yeraliyev, Z. **1:** 89
Yerelina, V.K. **1:** 94, 96
Yeremey, G.I. **2:** 105, 275
Yerokhin, V.A. **1:** 10
Yetylen, V.M. **1:** 94, 97
Yevtushenko, Ye.A. **1:** 300(n45); **2:** 1, 33, 44, 139, 214, 274, 275, 276
Yevtyukhin, Yu.A. **2:** 274, 275
Yudin, V.D. **1:** 241
Yurasov **2:** 92
Yusupov, A.K. **1:** 291
Yusupov, E.Yu. **1:** 158, 239

Zabrodin, I.A. **1:** 92, 94
Zadorzhnyy **2:** 92
Zakis, Y.R. **2:** 107
Zaletskas, K.V. **1:** 92, 95
Zalkhanov, M.Ch. **1:** 72
Zalygin, S.P. **1:** 97, 111; **2:** 43, 106, 291(n43)
Zamanyagra, M.F. **1:** 93, 95

Zanokha, A.I. **1:** 93, 95
Zaslavskaya, T.I. **1:** 50, 52, 53, 54-55, 67, 82, 297(n1b); **2:** 20, 38
Zaslavsky, I.I. **1:** 171, 181, 241; **2:** 12, 290(n12)
Zaykov, L.N. **1:** 98, 290, 297(n1b); **2:** 19
Zaynalkhanov, D.G. **1:** 93, 96
Zaytsev **2:** 206
Zbykovsky, I.I. **2:** 107
Zemskova, A.V. **1:** 239
Zhdakayev, I.A. **1:** 65, 68
Zhdanov, A.A. **2:** 85
Zhigunova, L.T. **1:** 93, 96
Zhuk, A.V. **1:** 183
Zhuravlev, A.G. **1:** 81, 82, 304(n150)
Zokirov, M.Z. **1:** 92, 94
Zolotukhin, V.P. **1:** 51, 76
Zubkov, V.N. **1:** 65, 83
Zvonov, S.N. **1:** 239; **2:** 274, 276
Zykina, L. **2:** 25

INDEX OF PLACE NAMES

VOLUMES 1–2

Abkhazian ASSR **1:** 235, 298(n16); **2:** 50, 82-84
Adzharian ASSR **1:** 298(n16)
Afghanistan **1:** 189, 202; **2:** 9, 15, 48, 87, 91, 92-93, 94, 100, 102, 136, 139, 140, 159, 237, 264, 267, 278-79, 291(n34)
Africa **1:** 202
Alma-Ata **2:** 40, 72, 146, 200, 296 (n200)
Altay **2:** 141
Altay Kray **2:** 177, 178
America **1:** 218
Amudarya River **1:** 224; **2:** 196
Amur basin **2:** 185
Amur River **2:** 290(n19)
Amur-Yakut Mainline (AYaM) **2:** 19, 290(n19)
Angara River **2:** 124, 141
Angarsk **2:** 95
Apatita **1:** 42, 183
Apsheron Peninsula **1:** 299(n24)
Aral region **1:** 189, 216, 223, 224, 255
Aral Sea **2:** 67, 88, 98, 161, 172, 195, 196

Arkhangelsk **1:** 181
Armenian SSR **1:** 22, 113, 117, 120, 163, 219, 220, 222, 230, 246, 258, 266, 268, 276, 307 (n268); **2:** 10, 44, 79, 81, 86, 87, 92, 116, 117, 128, 140, 159, 268, 270, 271, 292(n87)
Asha **2:** 114
Astrakhan **2:** 291(n45)
Austria **1:** 286
Austria **2:** 70
Azerbaijan SSR **1:** 22, 26, 38, 110, 114, 116, 117, 120, 218, 219, 220, 222, 230, 257, 268, 298(n16), 305(n162); **2:** 44, 81, 116, 136, 270, 271—see also Baku, Nagorno-Karabakh AO, Sumgait
Azov Sea **1:** 261, 306(n216); **2:** 66

Baikal, Lake **1:** 306(n214); **2:** 88, 161
Baikal region **2:** 67, 85, 191
Baikal-Amur Mainline (BAM) **2:** 19, 290(n19)
Baikalsk **2:** 95
Baikonur **1:** 216, 306(n216)

Baku **1:** 24, 26, 104, 258, 299(n24); **2:** 117, 200, 170, 291(n45)
Balakhna **2:** 119
Baltic Military District **2:** 4
Baltic republics **1:** 15, 35, 38, 41, 78, 100, 126, 130, 162, 184, 265, 276, 297(n1); **2:** 1, 4, 14, 29, 32, 86, 173, 184, 207, 212, 282
Basel, Switzerland **1:** 269, 297(n1)
Bashkiria **2:** 12-13, 113, 200, 245, 259
Beijing **2:** 133
Belgium **1:** 306(n196)
Belgorod Oblast **2:** 294(n132)
Belorussian SSR **1:** 22, 88, 101, 207, 244, 246, 260, 261, 274; **2:** 4, 14, 30, 75, 77, 136, 204, 216, 237, 282
Berkakit-Neryungra **2:** 19
Bessarabia **2:** 30
Black Sea **2:** 109
Bratsk **2:** 95
Brezhnev (city) **2:** 245
Bryansk **1:** 60, 261; **2:** 53
Bryukhovetsky Rayon **2:** 65

INDEX OF PLACE NAMES

Bulgaria **1:** 211
Buryat ASSR **1:** 109, 110
Butyrka Prison **2:** 293(n100)

Canada **1:** 306(n196); **2:** 70
Carpathian Military District **2:** 4
Caspian Sea **1:** 246, 259; **2:** 161
Caucasus region **1:** 297(n1); **2:** 31
Central Asia **1:** 163, 224, 287; **2:** 7, 10, 71, 31
Chapayevka River **2:** 110
Chapayevsk **2:** 110
Chechen-Ingush ASSR **1:** 111, 149, 304(n149)
Chelyabinsk **1:** 80, 85; **2:** 114, 161
Chelyabinsk Oblast **2:** 259
Cherkassy region **2:** 90-91, 195
Chernobyl **1:** 123, 191, 207, 208, 246, 261; **2:** 15, 81, 88, 92, 96, 108, 119, 237, 245, 259
Chigirin **1:** 261, 307(n261)
China **1:** 27, 35, 189, 202, 214, 255, 285; **2:** 102, 113, 132, 133, 140, 161, 236, 272, 290(n19), 296 (n236)
Chita **1:** 306(n214)
Chukchi Peninsula **2:** 124
Crimea **1:** 32, 41; **2:** 60, 88
Cuba **1:** 157; **2:** 15
Cyprus **2:** 117, 293(n117)
Czechoslovakia **1:** 166, 232, 238, 305(n166); **2:** 230, 267

Daghestan **1:** 259
Dalnevostok Okrug **1:** 80
Damansky **2:** 267
Denmark **1:** 306(n196)
Dnepr River **2:** 75
Dneprodzerzhinsk **1:** 37, 126
Dnepropetrovsk **2:** 3
Dnieper River **1:** 307(n261)
Donetsk Oblast **1:** 61
Dushanbe **2:** 89
Dzerzhinsk **2:** 119
Dzerzhinsky Square (Moscow) **1:** 280

East Kazakhstan Oblast **2:** 67-68
Eastern Europe **2:** 1
Ekibastuz **1:** 216; **2:** 106
Elitsa, Kalmyk ASSR **1:** 253, 307 (n253); **2:** 10
England **1:** 157, 301(n102), 305 (n162)
Estonian SSR **1:** 22, 40, 130, 277, 288; **2:** 13, 14, 30, 31, 48, 85, 121, 140, 142-43, 144, 209, 212, 213, 264, 294(n142), 296(n206) see also Baltic republics

Ethiopia **2:** 15
Europe **1:** 189
Europe, Eastern **1:** 300(n76)
European territories **2:** 72

Far East **1:** 273
Far Eastern Economic District **2:** 18
Fergana **2:** 143, 149, 161
Finland **1:** 211; **2:** 30, 70, 85, 248
France **1:** 225, 305(n162), 306 (n196); **2:** 4, 16, 31

Gachinsky Oblast **2:** 17
Gediminas Square (Vilnius) **1:** 231
Geneva **1:** 27
Georgian SSR **1:** 22, 38, 100, 143, 152, 157, 162, 228, 230, 234, 235, 237, 244, 276, 293, 298 (nn16, 23), 304-5(n162); **2:** 49-50, 68-69, 82, 92, 134, 140, 187, 188, 291(n69), 292(n84)—see also Tbilisi
Germany (FRG) **1:** 225, 255, 277, 306(n196); **2:** 1, 31
Germany (Nazi) **2:** 28
Gomel **1:** 81
Gomel Oblast **2:** 26
Gorky **2:** 93, 100, 108-9, 119, 136
Gorno-Badakhshan AO **1:** 298(n16)
Gorny Altay **2:** 180
Gorny Badakhshan **2:** 89
Great Britain **2:** 31
Greece **1:** 306(n196); **2:** 79
Groznyy **2:** 231
Gulsary **2:** 78

Hiroshima **2:** 199
Holland **2:** 70
House of Political Enlightenment (Moscow) **1:** 297(n1)
Hungary **1:** 166, 305(n166)

India **2:** 264
Ingush ASSR **2:** 107
Iran **2:** 9
Irkutsk **1:** 80, 214, 306(n214)
Irkutsk Oblast **2:** 95
Israel **1:** 301(n102)
Issyk-Kul, Lake **2:** 236
Issyk-Kul Oblast **2:** 237
Italy **1:** 255, 306(n196)
Ivanov **1:** 80

Japan **1:** 255, 306(n196); **2:** 199
Jewish AO **2:** 185

Kabardino-Balkar AR **1:** 72
Kali-Khumb **2:** 89

Kalinin **1:** 80
Kaliningrad **2:** 35
Kaliningrad Oblast **2:** 192
Kalmyk ASSR **1:** 109, 110, 307(n253); **2:** 134
Kaluga **2:** 52
Kama **2:** 129
Kamchatka **1:** 170, 174; **2:** 124
Kanev **1:** 261
Kara-Kalpak ASSR **1:** 223, 298 (n16)
Karaganda **1:** 306(n214)
Karelia **2:** 57
Kars region **2:** 87, 292(n87)
Katun River **2:** 141, 253
Kazakh SSR **1:** 22, 67, 124, 216, 217, 224, 259, 299(n38); **2:** 10, 72, 149, 220, 294(n146), 296 (nn199, 200)—see also East Kazakhstan Oblast
Kazan **2:** 21, 130
Kemerovo **2:** 161
Kerazhnyansky Rayon **1:** 262
Khabarovsk Kray **2:** 184, 185, 186
Khatyn **1:** 101
Khmelnitsky **1:** 261, 262
Kholm-Zhirkovsky Rayon **2:** 76
Khoreziya Oblast (Turkmenia) **1:** 223
Khorog **2:** 89
Kiev **1:** 261, 273; **2:** 3, 4, 77, 79, 192
Kiev Rayon **2:** 182
Kirghiz SSR **1:** 22, 281, 282; **2:** 111, 236
Kirov **1:** 80, 85
Kirovabad **1:** 229, 258; **2:** 91
Kirovakan **2:** 86
Kishinev **1:** 305(n176); **2:** 2, 4, 64
Kobelyaki **2:** 127
Kola Peninsula **1:** 42
Komi ASSR **1:** 81, 91
Komsomolsk **1:** 194; **2:** 290(n19)
Koryak AO **2:** 123a
Kostroma **1:** 80
Krasnodar **1:** 83
Krasnogvardeysky Rayon **2:** 168
Krasnovodsk **2:** 291(n45)
Krasnoyarsk **1:** 116, 133, 214, 306 (n214)
Krasnoyarsk Kray **1:** 59; **2:** 73, 74
Kremlin **1:** 128; **2:** 79
Kremlin, Georgyevsky Hall **1:** 111
Kremlin, Palace of Congresses **1:** 123, 124, 147, 174
Krylatskoye **2:** 80
Kstovo **2:** 119
Kuban **1:** 37, 83; **2:** 21, 65, 66
Kulunda **2:** 21

INDEX OF PLACE NAMES

Kulyab 2: 89
Kuropaty 1: 133, 306(n231)
Kursk Magnetic Anamoly 2: 132, 294(n132)
Kursk Oblast 2: 131, 132, 294(n132)
Kuvasay 2: 149
Kuybyshev Oblast 2: 35
Kuzbass 2: 197, 198, 295(n198)

Ladoga, Lake 2: 161
Latin America 1: 202; 2: 171
Latvian SSR 1: 22, 25, 232, 255-57, 277, 299(n24); 2: 14, 30, 31, 52, 84, 85, 143, 211, 212, 213, 238, 247—*see also* Baltic republics
Lefortovo Prison 2: 293(n100)
Lenin Mausoleum 1: 206; 2: 9, 100, 121, 128, 143, 148, 168
Leninakan 1: 220; 2: 86
Leningrad 1: 19, 30, 80, 85, 130, 131, 273, 282, 300(n46); 2: 16-17, 25, 40, 52, 53, 113, 160, 167, 209, 227, 245
Leningrad Oblast 2: 16, 75, 192
Lenino 1: 133
Leninogorsk 2: 68
Leninsk 1: 216
Leninsky Rayon 2: 182
Lithuanian SSR 1: 22, 52, 77, 78, 162, 231, 246, 277, 297(n12); 2: 1, 10, 14, 30, 31, 48, 77, 85, 140, 143, 173—*see also* Baltic republics
London Guild Hall 2: 199
Lubyanka 2: 100, 293(n100)
Luxembourg 1: 306(n196)
Luzhniki (Olympic) Stadium 1: 55, 300(n55)
Luzhniki district (Moscow) 1: 103, 104, 122, 123
Lvov 1: 261, 305(n175); 2: 4
Lykhny 2: 50, 83
Lyublinsky Rayon (Moscow) 1: 277

Mansiysk AO 2: 125
Margilan 2: 149
Mary ASSR 1: 109, 110, 112, 115, 116, 118-19, 177; 2: 24
Mezhdurechensk 2: 198
Mikhaylovskoye 2: 199
Minsk 1: 81, 84, 133, 306(n231); 2: 77, 192, 203, 265
Mogilev 1: 81
Moldavian SSR 1: 22, 305(n176); 2: 2, 3, 6, 62, 64, 107, 290(n2)
Mongolia 1: 157

Moscow 1: 1, 14, 16, 27, 30, 39, 50, 51, 52, 53, 54, 55, 61, 63, 66, 67, 76, 77, 78, 85, 87, 88, 89, 100, 109, 111, 120, 130, 132, 149, 157, 173, 211, 214, 215, 217, 219, 232, 252, 273, 277, 280, 282, 297(n1), 301(n102); 2: 2, 15, 21, 23, 37, 38, 52, 55, 80, 103, 107, 117, 120, 122, 136, 182, 183, 198, 208, 230, 247, 272, 273
Moscow Oblast 1: 9, 55, 64; 2: 75, 80, 249
Murgab Rayon 2: 89
Murmansk 2: 57

Naberezhnyye Chelny 2: 52, 53, 245
Nagasaki 2: 199
Nagorno-Karabakh AO 1: 82, 88-89, 91, 100, 111, 112, 113, 114, 116, 117, 120, 127, 163, 177, 185, 188, 189, 218, 219, 220, 221, 222, 230, 238, 246, 259, 260, 267, 268, 276, 298(n16), 302(n117), 307(n267); 2: 44, 45, 52, 87, 116-18, 133, 143, 193, 264, 267-71, 295(n193)
Nakhichevan ASSR 1: 229, 258, 298(n16); 2: 87, 116
Narew (Narev) River 2: 30
Narodichsky Rayon 2: 111
Nefteyugansk 2: 47
Netherlands 1: 306(n196); 2: 16
Nicaragua 2: 15
Nikolaevsk 2: 185
Nikolayev Oblast 2: 192
Nizhegorodsky Rayon 2: 120
Nizhnyaya Tunguska 2: 124
NKAO 2: *see* Nagorno-Karabakh AO
Nonchernozem zone 1: 37, 214, 217, 249, 271, 306(n214); 2: 75, 135
Northern Ossetia 1: 149, 304 (n149) *see also* Progorodny district
Norway 1: 306(n196); 2: 70, 85
Novgorod 2: 25
Novocherkassk 1: 166, 305(n166); 2: 280, 282
Novokuznetsk 1: 86; 2: 296(n198)
Novosibirsk 1: 79, 80, 81, 84, 214, 215, 306(n214); 2: 295(n198)
Novosibirsk Oblast 1: 272, 273

Ob River 2: 124, 253
Odessa 2: 109

Odessa Military District 2: 4
Oka River 2: 119
Omsk 1: 64, 80, 214, 306(n214)
Omsk Oblast 2: 175-76
Orel 1: 42, 58
Orenburg Oblast 1: 219

Pacific region 2: 264
Pamir Glacier 1: 224
Pamir region 2: 89
Pavlodar Oblast 1: 306(n214)
Petrozavodsk 2: 57
Pokrovskoye-Streshnevo 1: 280
Poland 1: 126, 166, 211, 305(n166), 307(n261); 2: 1, 86, 291(n31)
Poltava 1: 23
Portugal 1: 306(n196)
Primorsko-Akhtarsky Rayon 2: 65
Primorsky Kray 2: 184
Progorodny district (N.-Ossetia) 1: 304(n149)
Prut River 2: 63
Pushkin Square (Moscow) 1: 53, 55

Red Square 1: 53; 2: 100, 148
Reykjavik 1: 27
Riga 1: 232; 2: 4, 86, 247
Riga Market (Moscow) 2: 15
Rostov 1: 65, 83; 2: 10
Rovno 1: 261
Russian SFSR 1: 16, 22, 41, 58, 63, 66, 88, 91, 100, 109, 110, 112, 116, 118, 120, 169, 170, 211, 217, 228, 246, 247, 260, 270, 298(n16); 2: 6, 10, 15, 18, 30 34, 85, 91, 113, 120, 122, 131, 132, 140, 141, 149, 159, 161, 188, 199, 249, 252, 292(n84)
Russko-Polansky Rayon 2: 175
Rustaveli Prospekt (Tbilisi) 1: 227, 228, 235
Rustavi 2: 51
Ryazan 1: 37
Ryazan Oblast 2: 10, 192

Sakhalin 1: 52, 65, 68; 2: 124
Salavat 2: 161
Salekhard Oblast 2: 192
San Francisco 2: 79
San Marino 1: 113
San River 2: 30
Saratov 2: 10, 192
Semipalatinsk 2: 180
Semipalatinsk Nuclear Test Range 1: 216
Semipalatinsk Oblast 2: 199

Shelekhov **2:** 95
Siberia **1:** 103, 157, 158, 215, 272, 274, 299(n38), 305(n166), 307(n274); **2:** 14, 19, 46-47, 65, 74, 124, 161, 175, 178, 197, 198, 244, 253, 295(n198)
Smolensk **1:** 27, 60; **2:** 34, 52, 53, 75, 76
Sochi **1:** 86
Sochi Oblast **2:** 192
Sokolina Hill **2:** 134
South-Ossetian AO **1:** 298(n16)
Spain **2:** 70
Spitak **2:** 87
Stalin Mausoleum **2:** 100
Stalingrad **2:** 187
Stalinsk **2:** 296(n198)
Stavropol **1:** 37
Stavropol Kray **2:** 236
Sterlitamak **2:** 161
Sukhumi **2:** 83
Sumgait **1:** 24, 26, 40, 103, 135, 229, 246, 299(n24); **2:** 87, 52, 88, 118, 143, 229, 245, 270, 271
Surgut **2:** 46, 253
Sverdlovsk **1:** 31, 273, 306(n241); **2:** 58, 136, 259
Sweden **1:** 286, 301(n102); **2:** 70, 85
Switzerland **1:** 225; **2:** 70
Sykarya River **1:** 224

Taganka Theater (Moscow) **1:** 301 (n102)
Tagil **1:** 137
Taishet **2:** 290(n19)
Tajik SSR **1:** 22, 52, 163, 287; **2:** 89, 92, 111, 149, 173
Tallinn **1:** 261; **2:** 48, 86, 145, 291(n48)
Tambov **1:** 60
Tarkhany **2:** 199
Tashauz Oblast **1:** 223; **2:** 98
Tashkent **1:** 223; **2:** 242
Tashkent Oblast **2:** 57
Tashlak **2:** 149
Tataria **2:** 13, 17
Tbilisi **1:** 1, 5, 23-24, 31, 40, 103, 133, 135, 154, 157, 177, 179, 184, 224, 225, 226, 227, 229, 230, 231, 232, 233, 234, 235, 237, 238, 239, 241, 242, 243, 264, 280, 288, 292, 293, 294, 297(n5), 298(n23); **2:** 1, 3, 4, 49-55 passim, 59, 68-69, 83, 88, 91, 106, 136, 143, 148, 187, 188, 211, 278, 295(n188)
Tiananmen Square **2:** 113
Timashevsky Rayon **2:** 65
Tolyatti **2:** 161
Tomb of the Unknown Soldier **1:** 207; **2:** 148
Tommot **2:** 19
Tomsk **2:** 124, 295(n198)
Trans-Siberian Railway **2:** 290(n19)
Transcaspia **2:** 291(n45)
Transcaucasia **1:** 41, 116
Transcaucasian Military District **1:** 235; **2:** 4
Transcaucasian Republic **2:** 292 (n84)
Transcaucasus region **2:** 45, 184
Trubnaya Square (Moscow) **1:** 297 (n1)
Tula **1:** 247; **2:** 34
Turkey **1:** 152, 306(n196), 307 (n268); **2:** 88, 268
Turkmen SSR **1:** 22, 259; **2:** 6, 7, 9, 111
Tuva ASSR **1:** 109, 110, 111
Tyanshan (glacier) **1:** 224
Tynda **2:** 19
Tyumen **2:** 27, 46-47, 65, 124, 175
Tyumen Oblast **2:** 141, 253

Ufa **2:** 13
Ukraine, Western **1:** 307(n261)
Ukrainian SSR **1:** 22, 62, 88, 104, 209, 210, 246, 260, 261, 274, 305(n175), 306(n214); **2:** 7, 14, 30, 91, 109, 136, 161, 190, 237, 241, 292(n84)
Ulyanov Oblast **2:** 36
Union of Soviet Socialist Republics **1:** 152, 161, 162, 217, 255, 256, 266, 276, 277; **2:** 15, 30, 32, 38, 86, 99, 288
United Kingdom **1:** 306(n196) *see also* England
United States of America **1:** 27, 113, 202, 225, 238, 255, 301 (n102), 306(n196); **2:** 20, 39, 134

Urals **1:** 273
Urengoy **2:** 65
Ust-Kamenogorsk **2:** 52
Uzbek SSR **1:** 22, 61, 88, 224, 246, 287, 298(n16); **2:** 55, 57, 111, 150, 173, 200, 225, 245, 294 (n149), 296(n225)

Vakhsh River **1:** 286
Vietnam **1:** 225
Vilnius (Vilno) **1:** 231; **2:** 4, 30, 86
virgin lands **2:** 72
Vistula—see Wisla
Vladimir **2:** 54
Vladimir Oblast **2:** 192
Vladivostok **2:** 35
Vladivostok Line (Asian-Pacific Region) **1:** 202
Vnnitsa Oblast **1:** 262
Volga German ASSR **1:** 299(n38)
Volga Republic **2:** 134
Volga River **1:** 259; **2:** 110, 119, 129, 161
Volgodonsk **2:** 111
Volgograd **1:** 80, 85; **2:** 197
Volkov Cemetery **2:** 168
Vorkuta **1:** 81; **2:** 58
Voronezh **1:** 273
Vyksa **2:** 119
Vysotskoye **1:** 305(n175)

Washington, D.C. **1:** 157
West Siberia **1:** 273
West Siberian Lowland **2:** 197
West, The **1:** 101, 203
Wisla (Vistula) River **2:** 30

Yakutiya **1:** 242; **2:** 18
Yasnaya Polyana **2:** 199
Yaypan **2:** 149
Yenisey River **2:** 124
Yerevan **1:** 218, 219
Yoshkar-Ola **2:** 24, 246
Yugoslavia **1:** 157; **2:** 270

Zachepilovka **1:** 260
Zamoskvorechye Rayon **2:** 245
Zaporozhye **1:** 261; **2:** 22-23, 189
Zarinsk **2:** 178
Zhitomir **2:** 226, 227
Zhitomir Oblast **2:** 111
Zvartnots **1:** 229

SUBJECT INDEX

Abkhazia, Abkhazians, **2:** 189, 200; delegation, **2:** 107; relations with USSR, **2:** 82-84; "secession" of, **1:** 235, **2:** 50, 83-84; Likhny Appeal, **2:** 83; Abkhazian Bolshevik Commune (1918), **2:** 83;
Aboriginal people—*see* Far East, Peoples of; North, Peoples of
Academy of Medical Sciences, **1:** 273
Academy of Sciences, **1:** 273, **2:** 19, 95, 211; and Chernobyl disaster, **2:** 80; and CPD elections, **1:** 284, 297-98(n13), **2:** 138
Academy of Social Sciences (CPSU CC), **1:** 139
Accounting—*see* Cost accounting
Administrative-command system, **1:** 101, 126-27, 212, 214, 246, 249, 250, 258, 264, 276, 288, 289; **2:** 18, 62, 74, 78, 96, 141, 169, 175, 181, 239, 248, 260-61, 269, 271—*see also* Bureaucracy, Ministries
Admiral Nakhimov disaster, **2:** 259
Aeroflot, **1:** 284
Afanasyev-Popov attack on Congress majority, **1:** 91, 97-99, 100-104, 119, 120, 124, 125, 128, 129, 130, 131, 132-33, 146, 154, 180, 181, 278
Afghan War, **1:** 189, 195; **2:** 9, 15, 48, 102, 136, 139, 158, 188, 237, 264, 281; veterans, **2:** 91-94, 136, 237; *Commemorative Book,* **2:** 92, 183; responsibility, **2:** 92, 93, 94, 100, 183, 268, 281; commission on, **2:** 183, 279, Appendices B.9 and B.10
Africa, **1:** 202; **2:** 15
"Aggressive and obedient majority", **1:** 91, 98, 105—*see* Afanasyev-Popov attack
Agricultural policy, **1:** 20, 38, 42, 147, 189, 192-93, 210, 224, 247-50, 250-51, 303(n147), **2:** 146, 176; Resolution on, **1:** 250-51; **2:** 22; CPSU Commission on, **2:** 290(n14)
Agricultural Sciences, All-Union Academy of, **1:** 273
Agriculture, condition of, **1:** 101, 102, 146, 193, 210, 214, **2:** 16, 20, 71, 132, 181, 194, 257-58, 267; collectivization, **1:** 302(n102), **2:** 41, 88, 128; capital investment, **2:** 150, 156-57, 175, 237; equipment, **2:** 62, 156, 175, 266; imports, **2:** 169, 171—*see also* Rural conditions
Agroindustrial State Committee (Gosagroprom), **2:** 14, 27, 98, 242, 290(n14)
AIDS epidemic, **1:** 253, 307(n253); **2:** 10, 134
Air pollution, **2:** 22-23, 161—*see also* Pollution generally
Alcohol, alcoholism, **1:** 304(n152); **2:** 15, 68, 91, 135, 176; sale of spirits, **2:** 169, 170—*see also* Drunkenness
Aleuts, **2:** 125
Alliances, **1:** 202
Alma Ata riots (1986), **2:** 146, 200
Altai nation, **2:** 84; delegation, **2:** 177, 244
American Architects Union, **2:** 79
Amguemskaya Hydroelectric Power Station, **2:** 124
Amnesty International, **1:** 134
Andreyeva affair, **1:** 156-57
Animal husbandry, **2:** 236
Anthem, **1:** 143, **2:** 43, 235, 289
Anti-communism, **1:** 227, 234, 270, 282, **2:** 97, 99, 121, 126, 131, 261
Anti-Russianism, **1:** 227, **2:** 142, 187
Apparat, apparatchiks, **1:** 2, 30, 33, 34, 37, 43, 45, 58, 61, 63, 65, 73, 91, 98-99, 100, 101, 105, 113, 130, 135, 139, 141-42, 178, 179, 185, 198, 213, 240, 254, 264, 265, 279, 282, 287, **2:** 3, 4-5, 7, 20-21, 23, 36, 97, 192, 198, 202, 243, 247, 256, 261, 275—*see also* Afanasyev-Popov attack, Communist Party of Soviet Union
Appropriations, **1:** 142
April eighth decree—*see* State Crimes, Law on
Arable land, flooding of, **2:** 190, 197
Arbitration, **2:** 195; State Committee (Gosarbitrazh), **2:** 12
see also Chief State Arbiter
Architects Union, **2:** 78
Architecture (urban), **2:** 77-79
Archives, condition of, **1:** 211
Arctic region, peoples—*see* North, peoples of
Arkhstroy, **2:** 78
Armed Forces, **1:** 162, **2:** 25, 162, 264; General Staff, **2:** 92, 94; discipline, **2:** 135; agitation against, **2:** 136; Main Political Directorate, **2:** 135; "bullying," **2:** 135; force reductions, **2:** 135*ff.*, 144—*see also* Army
Armenia, Armenians, **1:** 24, 26, 114, 114-15, 120, 136, **2:** 204; delegation, **1:** 36, 79, 82, 115-16, 117, 188; **2:** 52; genocide of (1915), **1:** 268, 307(n268); **2:** 87-88, 268; foreign interest in, **2:** 266-67; diaspora, **2:** 267; refugees, **2:** 268; alleged poisoning of, **2:** 268; in Sumgait, **2:** 299 (n24)
Armenian earthquake, **2:** 86-87, 136, 158, 270; International Circle for Aiding the Young Victims of, **2:** 10
Armenian-Azeri conflict, **1:** 24, 26, 35, 38, 91, 189, 267; **2:** 52, 87-88, 116-18—*see also* Nagorno-Karabakh, Sumgait
Arms production, **1:** 189, 196

INDEX OF SUBJECTS

Army, and civil disorder, **1:** 31, 40, **2:** 3, 43, 48-49, 68, 85, 127, 146; in Vilnius, **1:** 231; in Tbilisi, **1:** 54, 225-26, 227-30, 234-36, 247, 298(n23); **2:** 49, 50-51, 92, 136, 187-88, and Appendix B.5—*see also* Internal Troops

Army, alleged slander by Sakharov, **2:** 92-95,100; professionalization of, **2:** 287

Article 11-1—*see* State Crimes, Law on

Asia, **1:** 202; **2:** 49

Astrakhan Gas Condensate Complex, **2:** 191

Athletes, black, **2:** 242

Atmoda (Latvia), **2:** 206

Atomic Power, Ministry of, **1:** 261, 262

AUCCTU—*see* Trade Unions, All-Union Central Council of

Autarky, **1:** 217

Automobiles, **2:** 240

"Autonomization", **2:** 44, 292(n84)

Autonomous national formations, **1:** 66, 298(n16), **2:** 17, 74-75, 82, 108, 123-24, 125-26, 143, 146, 185, 204, 213, 239, 264, 271

Azerbaijan, Azeris, **1:** 24, 26, 114-15, 120, 299(n24); **2:** 200, 204, 271; delegation, **1:** 79, 82, 91, 110-11, 114, 115-17, 120, 161, 188, 189; Communist Party of, **1:** 24, 115; Baku Commissars (1918), **2:** 45, 291(n45); refugees, **1:** 268—*see also* Nagorno-Karabakh, Soviet of Nationalities

Baikal Movement, **2:** 141
Balance of payments, **2:** 172
Balkar nation, **1:** 149
Baltic Assembly, **2:** 49, 143, 291 (n48)
Baltic republics, **1:** 38, 126, 130, 260; **2:** 1, 7, 37, 47-48, 113, 172 (reforms), 206, 207, 211-12, 239, 282—*see also* Estonia, Latvia, Lithuania, Nazi-Soviet Pact
Banks, banking, **2:** 73, 171, 172, 267, 287; Law on, **2:** 267
Bashkir nation, **2:** 129, 130, 133; delegation, **2:** 11

Bashkiria rail disaster, **2:** 113, 114-15, 136, 146, 259

Basic Guidelines for the Domestic and Foreign Policy of the USSR, Resolution on, **2:** 262-65; proposed amendments, **2:** 265-70; text, Appendix B.4—*see also* Gorbachev report

Belorussia, Belorussians: delegation, **1:** 79, 81, 82, 162, **2:** 177, 217, 271, 275, 282; Communist Party, **1:** 51; Belorussian Martyrology, **1:** 306(n231); Academy of Sciences, **2:** 203; State University, **2:** 203

Berezka, beriozka, **2:** 96, 292(n96)

Bilingualism—*see under* Language

Biophysics Institute, **2:** 81

Birth defects, **1:** 223

Birth rate, **2:** 14, 111

Black Hundreds, **2:** 12, 290(n12)

Black market, **1:** 258; **2:** 169, 170

Books, **2:** 6

Boundaries, **1:** 259, 287 (Central Asia)

Braille, **2:** 36—*and see subjects under* Disabled persons

Brezhnev, Brezhnevism, **1:** 146, 155, 278, 279, **2:** 37, 99, 100, 127, 139—*see also* Stagnation

Bribery, **1:** 151-52, 153, 200, 303(n137), 306(n195), **2:** 55, 103; in Uzbek affair, **2:** 231-33

Budget, **2:** 154, 158, 168, 171-72, 197; control of, **1:** 101, 213, **2:** 14, 17; deficit, **1:** 189, 191, **2:** 15, 95, 149, 151, 159, 169, 170, 172, 237

Building materials, **1:** 195; **2:** 160, 249

Buran (space shuttle), **2:** 195

Bureaucracy, state, **1:** 60, 180, 189, 193, 196, 246, 252, 264, 286, 289, 303(n142); **2:** 3-4, 21, 25, 91, 92, 101, 118, 121, 137, 140, 142, 159, 238, 240-41, 247—*see also* Administrative-command system

Burn-treatment centers, **2:** 114

Canada, **2:** 122
Canals, canal building, **1:** 261; **2:** 196

Cancer, in children, **2:** 9
Capital investment, **1:** 189, 191, 196, 265, 287, 303(n147), **2:** 73, 76, 107, 119, 150, 159-60, 169-70, 171, 175, 185, 194, 198, 240
Capitalism, **2:** 103, 168, 194
Caspian Institute, **1:** 259
Catholics, **2:** 122
Caucasian Bureau (1921), **2:** 116, 117, 118
CEMA—*see* Europe, East
Censorship, **1:** 151
Census (1979), **1:** 299(n38)
Central Asia: deputies, **1:** 254, 282; boundaries, **1:** 287; ecology, **2:** 122, 242
Central Electoral Commission, **1:** 2, 13, 18-19, 20-21, 25, 26, 165, 300(n59), **2:** 52-53
Centralism—*see* Power
Chapayev Plant, **2:** 35
Charity, **2:** 10-11
Charity and Health Foundation, **2:** 33, 36, 126
Chechen nation, **1:** 149, 152, **2:** 200; repression of, **1:** 304(n149)
Chechen-Ingush delegation, **1:** 170, **2:** 230-31
Chemical and Petroleum Machine Building, Ministry of, **2:** 47
Chemical industry, **1:** 298, 255, 261, **2:** 119-202, 252; weapons, **2:** 110; fertilizers, **1:** 193, 210, **2:** 132, 178, 190-91, 240; pesticides, **2:** 191; toxins, **2:** 242; imports, **2:** 254
Chernobyl disaster, **1:** 246, 261, **2:** 1, 15, 26-27, 30, 80-81, 136, 158, 237, 259—*see also* Children of Chernobyl
Chernobyl Nuclear Power Station, **1:** 261, **2:** 26, 27, 81
Chernozem soil zone, **2:** 132
Chief State Arbiter, **1:** 7, 181; **2:** 164, 287; confirmation of, **2:** 166, 220
Chigirin Nuclear Power Station, **1:** 261, 307(n261), **2:** 106
Children, **1:** 126, 212, 261, 284, **2:** 9-11, 16, 40, 42, 74, 77, 80, 91, 120, 131, 154, 158, 199, 242, 245-46; abuse of, **2:** 11, 107
Protective organizations: Association of the Soviet Intelligentsia

Children (cont.)
in the Defense of Childhood, **2:** 10; Children and AIDS Program, **2:** 10; Children of Chernobyl Program, **2:** 10; V.I. Lenin Children's Fund, **2:** 9, 10, 11, 40, 60, 81, 139; Children's Oncological Center, **2:** 9; Children's Protection Day, **2:** 2, 10

China: relations with, **1:** 27, 35, 189, 202, 255, **2:** 113, 132-33, 199, 236; "Chinese method" of social control, **2:** 75; Cultural Revolution, **2:** 272

Christianity, **1:** 27; **2:** 49, 122

Chuvash nation, **2:** 129

Circassian nation, **2:** 133

"Citizen" (term), **1:** 180, 181

Citizenship, **2:** 143

City planning, **2:** 77*ff.*

Civil disobedience, **2:** 102

Civil rights, **1:** 143, **2:** 162

Class solidarity, **2:** 45

Class struggle, **2:** 122

Coal miners, mining, **2:** 198

COCOM, **1:** 196, 306(n196)

Collective farms (kolkhozes), **1:** 249, 251, 301(n100), **2:** 14, 16, 65, 76, 159, 170, 193, 248, 258; Union Council of Kolkhozes, **1:** 38

Collective Labor Disputes, Law on Resolving, **1:** 304(n153)

Commissions, **2:** 182

Committee on State Security—*see* KGB

Communications, **2:** 163

Communism, **2:** 92, 117, 127, 192, 267

Communist Party of the Soviet Union—CPSU: **1:** 1, 22, 35, 37, 51, 59, 101, 161, 189, 198, 213, 246, 263, 264, 270, **2:** 6, 28, 36-37, 66, 67, 130, 140, 181, 183, 202, 244, 245, 260, 268, 274; Bolsheviks, **1:** 1, 91, 173; power monopoly of, **1:** 265, **2:** 20, 43, 182, 183—*see also* anti-communism, apparat, Article 6 *under* Constitution

General Secretary, **1:** 29-30*ff.*, 155, 178; report of, 190-205*ff.*—*see also* Gorbachev candidacy *under* Supreme Soviet, Chairman

Nineteenth Party Conference, **1:** 17, 30, 32, 41, 142, 163, 172, 190, 209, 247-48, 263, 270, 276, 288, 303(n142), **2:** 23, 37, 83, 97, 99, 101, 189, 199, 224, 232, 260, 261, 268

Party Congresses: Eighth Congress, **2:** 283; Tenth Congress, **1:** 91; Twelfth Congress, **2:** 121; Twenty-sixth Congress, **2:** 97; 27th Congress, **1:** 194, 207, 215, 270, 286, **2:** 83, 158, 260, 261; 28th Congress, **2:** 260, 261

CPSU Central Committee, **1:** 31, 33, 36, 46, 69, 100, 142, 146, 147, 151, 155, 166, 238, 259, 265, 270, 276, 279, 297(n1), 297(n2), 302(n117), 304 (n151), **2:** 9, 21, 22, 24, 32, 51, 92, 101, 107, 130, 132, 143, 146, 225, 242; and Uzbek affair, **2:** 231-33

Administrative Organs Department, **2:** 230

Commissions—*see* Agricultural Policy, International Policy, Legal Policy Questions, Nationalities

Control Committee, **1:** 155, 160, **2:** 55, 224

Plenums: April 1985, **1:** 198, **2:** 37; June 1986, **1:** 215; March 1988, **1:** 271; March 1989, **1:** 192-93, 248-49, 263, 267, 303(n147), **2:** 20, 22, 83, 90, 156-57, 175-76, 183, 240; April 1989, **1:** 307(n267), **2:** 99, 260

Politburo, **1:** 31, 37, 100, 121, 127, 147, 154, 155, 159, 161, 178, 182, 237, 261, 270, 293, **2:** 1, 27, 131, 140, 155, 158, 209, 214, 244, 268, 290(n21)

CPSU Central Control Commission, **2:** 222

CPSU Central Inspection Commission, **1:** 307(n267)

Communist Youth League—*see* Komsomol

Computers, computerization **1:** 124, 132, 142, **2:** 5-6

Congress of People's Deputies:
Agenda, **1:** 7-8, 9, 11, 12, 15, 16, 44, 100, 129, **2:** 2, 33, 49, 62, 105, 115, 164-65, 180, 203, 277

Composition of, **1:** 22, Appendix D

Commissions of investigation—*see* Gdlyan-Ivanov affair, Nazi-Soviet Pact, Tbilisi incident

Credentials Commission, **1:** 19-20, 25-26, 26, 60, 137, 179, 222, **2:** 2, 186, 273, Appendix C.3; reports, **1:** 20-23, **2:** 52-53

Decorum in, **1:** 2, 15, 17, 45, 54, 56, 58, 61, 67, 86, 98, 100, 127, 128, 130, 131, 146, 156, 168, 171-72, 174, 220, 221, 236, 279, 295, **2:** 13, 39, 109, 127, 128, 131, 143-44, 145, 256

Deputy status, **1:** 13, 16, 17, 59, 62, 64, 67, 68, 72, 104, 147, 148, 152, 175, 177, 187, 204, 252-53, 304(n148), 305(n165), **2:** 3, 13, 63, 137, 147, 183, 216, 278, 282, 283-85, Appendix B.3; services, compensation and support, **2:** 278, 279, 282, 283-85
see also Supreme Soviet, Deputy status

Editing Commission, **1:** 290-92, **2:** 33, 235, 251, 262-64, 269, 273, 276-77, Appendix C.7

Election of, **1:** 20-21, 99, 148, 165, 177, 280, 297(n1a), 297(n1b), 299(n29), **2:** 88, 183, 220-21—*see also* Electoral Law, Central Electoral Commission

Elections disputed, **1:** 21, 183; Latvia, **1:** 25, 299(n25), **2:** 2; Ukraine, **1:** 23; Moscow **1:** 26, **2:** 273; Smolensk, **1:** 26;

Microphones, **1:** 56, 148, 156, 165, 298(n17), **2:** 147

Participation, statistics, **1:** 4, 20-22; **2:** 108, 200, 250, 263, 286

Powers of, **1:** 1-2, 7-8, 12, 16, 18, 59, 61, 64-65, 67, 71, 75, 134, 155, 178, 181, 203, 252, 263-64, 280-81, 297(n13), **2:** 37, 138, 172, 214, 280, 282, 286-87

INDEX OF SUBJECTS

Preparation of, **1**: 100, 105, 123, 128, 130, 131, 134, 136, 139, 141-42, 147, 148, 155, 159, **2**: 285

Presidium, **1**: 2, 5-7, 16, 24, 33, 56, 72, 74, 78, 89, 91, 111, 117, 127, 136, 139, 260, 150, 155, 156, 177, 178, 189, 194, 240, 244, 292, 295, **2**: 29, 31, 32, 166, 269, 270, 271, 276, 278, 286, Appendix C.1

Procedures, **1**: 59-60, 64, 67, 68, 71-72, 99, 100, 101, 102, 104, 105, 110, 111, 114, 119, 124, 128, 129, 131, 131-32, 135, 136, 139, 275, 140, 144-45, 147, 148, 167*ff.*, 217-18, 227, 231-32, 243, 244, 270, 295-96, 297(n11), 298(n15), 298 (n17), **2**: 30, 32-33, 61, 104, 106, 107, 108, 109, 145, 164-65, 200, 205-6, 216, 265, 269-70, 276-77, 281-82

Representation in, **1**: 15-16, 21, 34, 58; women, 263

Resolution on Citizens' Proposals, **1**: 89, Appendix B.2

Second Congress, **1**: 298(n18), 304(n148), **2**: 143, 159, 175, 212, 213, 264, 278, 281, 283, 285

Secretariat, **1**: 56, 89, 119, 135, 139, 140, 146, 166, 167-68, 169, 243, 275, **2**: 255, Appendix C.2

Standing Orders, **1**: 2-3, 7, 11-12, 13-14, 15, 18, 19, 78, 144, 162, 168, 296, 304(n148), **2**: 109, 251, 271, Appendix B.1

Stenographic record, *Preface*, **2**: 200, 251

Television coverage, **1**: 18, 140, 150, 172, 179, 260, 282, 298(n18), **2**: 108, 245

Tellers Commission, **1**: 10-11, 47-48, 89, 91, 92, 97, 106, 179, 188, 244, Appendix C.4

Voting procedure in, **1**: 11, 14-15, 17, 45, 47-48, 51, 56, 64, 87-88, 113, 121, 134, 147, 148, 167, 173, 177, 179, 183, 214, 244, 297(n11), **2**: 2

Congress of Soviets (1917), **1**: 282

Conservation, **1**: 147, **2**: 189—*see also* Environmental issues

Constituent Assembly (1917), **1**: 1

Constitution (Basic Law) of the USSR

1977 Constitution amended, **1**: 1, 2, 8, 13, 19, 42, 66, 69, 71, 74, 76, 102, 113, 114, 134, 135, 139, 141, 148, 168, 172, 183, 246, 253, 255-56, 264, 268, 276, 278, 282, **2**: 9, 14, 42, 48, 52, 56, 137, 139, 142, 143, 203, 204, 207, 215, 264, 265, 271

Articles cited: Article 6, **1**: 182, **2**: 36, 43, 269, 286; Article 7, **2**: 42, 43; Article 9, **2**: 41; Article 14, **2**: 265; Article 18, **2**: 265; Article 19, **2**: 40-41; Article 20, **2**: 265; Article 21, **2**: 265; Article 22, **2**: 42; Article 31, **2**: 43; Article 35, **2**: 16; Article 36, **2**: 129; Article 40, **2**: 42, 265; Article 70, **1**: 256; Article 73, **1**: 256; Article 74, **1**: 256, **2**: 48; Article 76, **1**: 256, **2**: 85; Article 78, **1**: 259; Article 80, **2**: 85; Article 81, **2**: 85; Article 82, 2: 13; Article 96, **1**: 23; Article 108, **1**: 7, 181, 297(n13); Article 109, **2**: 129; Article 110, **1**: 13, 20, 59, 74, 300(n59); Article 111, **1**: 7, 51, 57, 61, 70, 129, 297(n13), 300(nn57 and 70); Article 113, **1**: 61, 297(n13), 300 (n61); **2**: 13; Article 114, **1**: 297(n13), **2**: 206; Article 118, **2**: 129; Article 119, **1**: 300(n71), **2**: 209; Article 121, **1**: 181; Article 124, **1**: 51, 73-74, 165, 300(n73), 304(n148), 305(n165); Article 125, **2**: 203, 207, 208; Article 174, **1**: 256; Article 199, **1**: 71; texts, Appendix A.1

1918 Constitution, **2**: 137, 292 (n84)

1924 Constitution, **1**: 66, 254, 299(n38), **2**: 137

1936 Constitution, **1**: 254, 305(n162), **2**: 137

Constitutional Commission, **2**: 165, 216, 271-76, 278, Appendix C.8; Samsonov candidacy, **2**: 272-74

Constitutional Oversight Committee, **1**: 7, 42, 143, 172, 181, 203, **2**: 59, 88, 164, 166, 264, 274, 287; election of **2**: 202-29, 235; commission to draft law on, **2**: 276, 278-79, Appendix C.9

Construction industry, **1**: 271, 303(n147), **2**: 62, 160; *Construction Norms and Regulations* (SNiP), **2**: 79; State Committee (Gosstroy), **1**: 192, 284, **2**: 47, 106

Consumer cooperatives, **2**: 248-51

Consumer goods and services, **1**: 189, 191, 192, 210, 214, 250, 270-71, 274, 281, **2**: 7, 12, 22, 73, 74, 95, 103, 104, 110, 150, 154-55, 158, 159, 169, 170, 171, 179, 249, 253, 263, 266

Cooperatives, **1**: 58, 100, 121, 153, 193, 207, 251, 271, 283, 285, 301(n100), **2**: 12, 15, 20, 23, 67, 103-4, 127, 159, 235, 237, 240, 243-44, 249, 266; Law on, **1**: 197, 249, 285, 301(n100), **2**: 28, 63, 138, 152, 168, 243, 249, 250—*see also* Consumer cooperatives

Correctional Affairs, Chief Administration for, **1**: 304(n153)

Corrective labor colonies, **1**: 153, 160, 304(n153)

Corruption, **1**: 151-52, 153, 200, 254, 258, 278, 302-3(n137), **2**: 101, 242—*see also* Gdlyan-Ivanov

Cossacks, **2**: 133

Cost accounting (*khozraschet*), **1**: 201, 210, 212, 215-16, 265, 266, 273, 281, 286, 288-89, **2**: 6, 12-13, 19, 38, 47, 62, 67, 73, 74, 92, 96, 98, 102, 138, 167, 176, 181, 198, 207, 212, 243, 246, 264, 265, 277, 282

Cost of living index, **2**: 104, 241

Cotton, production of, **1**: 224, 255, 286, 302(n137), **2**: 7, 98, 109, 241, 254

Cotton-growing region, **2**: 242-43; unemployment in, **2**: 109; standard of living in, **2**: 111; birthrate, **2**: 111

INDEX OF SUBJECTS

Council of Chief Architects, **2:** 77
Council of Ministers, **1:** 2, 7, 32, 213, 249, 252, 259, 272, 276, 287, 288, **2:** 12, 14, 125, 129, 154, 155, 179, 190, 194, 237, 238, 250, 263, 264, 267, 290(n14); Chairman, **1:** 7, 46, 104, 176, 181, 198, 249, **2:** 128, 164, 291(n47); confirmation of chairman, **2:** 166, 193, 201—*see also* Ryzhkov statement
Council on the National Economy, **1:** 133
Counting Commission—*see* Congress of People's Deputies, Tellers Commission
Coup, danger of, **2:** 261-62
Courts, **1:** 143, 178
Credit, **2:** 62, 171, 196, 247
Crime, **1:** 143, 151, 152, 153-54, 156, 159, 200, 207, 258, 264, 271, **2:** 77, 91, 108, 135, 139, 259; statistics, **1:** 304(n152), **2:** 205; organized, **1:** 303 (n137), 304(n151), **2:** 103, 223—*see also* "Mafia"
Crimean delegation, **1:** 148
Crimean Nuclear Power Station, **1:** 148, 261, **2:** 252
Crimean Tatars, **2:** 123, 130, 134, 146, 200, 264; repression of, **1:** 254, **2:** 66, 72, 107
Criminal Code (1958), **1:** 299(n35), 302(nn134-35), 306(n195); **2:** 270
Criminal Legislation, Principles of, **1:** 152, 207, 304(n152), **2:** 214
Cuba, **2:** 15, 171
Cult of personality, **1:** 29, 30, **2:** 41, 42, 82
Culture, state of, **1:** 210-12, 250, **2:** 15, 46; centers, **1:** 261
Currency, **1:** 215, 278, 285, **2:** 103, 158, 159, 163-64, 170-71, 179; devaluation, **2:** 169; convertible (hard), **2:** 240, 254, 254; foreign, **2:** 247; exchange rate, **2:** 265
Cyprus, partition, **2:** 117, 293(n117)
Czechoslovakia, intervention (1968), **1:** 166, **2:** 230, 267

Dacha, Gorbachev's, **1:** 32, 41
Damansky intervention (1969), **2:** 267

Debt, agrarian, **1:** 251; national, **1:** 143, **2:** 172, 254; foreign, **2:** 172, 235, 254
Decentralization, **2:** 172
Declaration of the Rights of the Peoples of Russia, **2:** 84, 292 (n84)
Declaration on the Formation of the USSR, **2:** 292(n84)
Defense and Security Questions, USSR Committee for, **2:** 135
Defense Council, **2:** 134
Defense industry, **2:** 12; conversion to civilian market, **1:** 210, 216, 251, 273, 303(n147), **2:** 39-40, 96, 154-55, 159, 162-63
Defense, Law on, **2:** 135
Defense, Ministry of, **1:** 238, **2:** 92, 94, 163—*see also* Space program
Defense policy, **1:** 202, **2:** 135-37, 151, 162; "reasonable sufficiency,", **1:** 202; **2:** 135, 264 *see also* Disarmament
Defense spending, **1:** 189, 196, 206, **2:** 162-63, 171, 199, 264; redirection of, **1:** 210, 212, 262, 273, **2:** 149
Democracy, democratization, **1:** 40, 44, 53, 63, 66, 71, 91, 98, 123, 124-25, 127, 130, 131, 133-34, 139, 143, 146, 156, 161, 164, 171, 175, 176, 180, 182, 198, 200, 204, 207, 209, 237, 246, 254, 255, 257, 260, 265, 270, 277, 303(n142), **2:** 7, 8-9, 28, 37, 48, 73, 90, 99, 123, 126, 162, 172, 180-81, 182, 197-98, 235, 237, 255ff.
Democratic Union, **2:** 37, 102, 293(n102)
Demonstrations—*see* rallies and demonstrations
Disabled persons, **1:** 126, **2:** 34-36, 38, 40, 120, 124, 154, 241, 266-67; veterans, **2:** 136; Society of, **2:** 34, 36; All-Russian Society of the Blind, **2:** 34, 35
Disarmament, **1:** 27, 202, **2:** 96, 135, 199
Disaster relief, **2:** 158
Discipline, need for, **1:** 91, 123, 125, 153, 200, 271, **2:** 19, 26, 28, 96, 119, 135, 176, 197, 259

Dissidents, **1:** 43 306(n195)
Distribution system, **1:** 189, **2:** 19
Donetsk delegation, **1:** 172
DOSAAF—*see* Voluntary Society for the Promotion of the Army, Aviation, and Navy
Drugs, drug addiction, **1:** 304(n152), **2:** 15, 68, 91, 135
Drunkenness, **1:** 153, 304(n152), **2:** 9, 167, 170—*see also* Alcohol, alcoholism
Dzerzhinsky Division, **1:** 54

Earthquakes, **1:** 163, 266, **2:** 79
Eastern Regions, Ministry of Construction in (Minvostokstroy), **2:** 184
Ecology—*see* Environmental issues
Economic development, **2:** 123, 125; incentives and disincentives, **1:** 284, 287; Council, **2:** 267
Economic Independence of Union Republics, Draft Law on, **1:** 277, **2:** 173
Economic management, **1:** 272-73, 283-84, 286, 288, 289, **2:** 38, 74, 152, 161, 172, 173, 176, 181, 190, 194, 243, 246, 260, 266, 281
Economic reform, general, **1:** 40, 125-26, 180, 197, 246, 276, **2:** 70, 73, 137, 171, 237-41, 256-58, 263, 282—*see also* Regionalism
Economics, Institute of, **2:** 153
Economists, economic advisors, **1:** 271, 272, 282, **2:** 15, 20, 23, 38, 103-4, 195, 267—*see also* Keynesian economics
Economy, general, **1:** 142, 189, 215-16ff., 246, 272, 288, 303 (n147), **2:** 7, 20-21, 89, 150ff., 168, 238, 257; inequities, **2:** 8; world, **1:** 203, 258, 270, 272
Education, **1:** 190, 122-23, 211-12, 250, 281, **2:** 5-6, 9, 15, 26, 41, 68-69, 107, 154, 155, 158, 245-46; Ministry of, **2:** 10
Efficiency, **1:** 197, **2:** 153, 241
Ekran Factory, **2:** 35
Elderly, **2:** 9, 40, 42, 107, 131, 153, 194, 267—*see also* Pensions, Veterans
Elders, Soviet of, **2:** 112, 146

Elections, Law on, **1:** 23, 25, 66, 75, 139, 253, **2:** 14, 17-18, 43, 52-53, 63, 88-89, 138-39, 186, 193, 226, 280, 282 — *see also* Central Electoral Commission; *see* Elections *under* Congress of People's Deputies, Supreme Soviet, Soviet of Nationalities and Soviet of the Union
Electric Industry, Ministry of, **2:** 12
Electrical Equipment Industry, Ministry of, **1:** 286, **2:** 12
Electrification, rural, **2:** 157
Electronics, **1:** 191, **2:** 21
Energy, **2:** 18, 74
Engineers, **1:** 291
Entsy nation, **2:** 125
Environmental issues, **1:** 189, 191, 194, 207, 208, 209, 216, 223, 246, 255, 259, 261, 265, 284, **2:** 7, 13, 18, 22, 38, 46, 48, 61, 63, 65, 73, 74, 95, 106, 109, 119, 124-25, 141, 149, 155, 161, 180, 184, 189, 192, 196-97, 235, 242, 244, 252-53, 270, 281; State Committee for the Protection of Nature, **2:** 13, 67, 95, 141, 191— *see also* Nuclear pollution, Pollution, Water quality, and INDEX OF PLACE NAMES
Equality, **1:** 215, 246, 264, **2:** 185; of republics, **2:** 185
Erosion—*see* Soil erosion
Estonia, Estonians, **1:** 130, 141, **2:** 122, 142-43, 206, 212; delegation, **1:** 57, 162, 288, **2:** 12, 29, 209; declaration of sovereignty, **2:** 121, 142; law on cost accounting, **1:** 288, 289, **2:** 13, 142; Academy of Sciences, **1:** 130; Supreme Soviet, **1:** 288, 308(n288), **2:** 142; Communist Party, **2:** 142; Labor Collectives Council, **2:** 142, 144; People's Front, **2:** 143, 291(n48)
Ethane, **2:** 8
Ethiopia, **2:** 15
Ethnic—*see* Interethnic
Europe, Eastern, **2:** 163-64, 254
Europe, Western, **1:** 189, 203, **2:** 194; Economic Community, **1:** 210; Christian Ecumenical Assembly, **1:** 269;

"homeland," **2:** 49; Parliament, **2:** 88;
Evenks, **2:** 17, 124, 290(n17)
Extortion, **1:** 200, 306(n195)

Factionalism, **1:** 91, 100, 103-4, 121, 124, 128-29, 131, 132, 133, 252, 270, 282, **2:** 283—*see also* Afanaseyev-Popov attack
Families, **1:** 262, **2:** 1, 155, 241, 246; farms, **1:** 303(n147), **2:** 240
Far East, peoples of, **2:** 184-86, 198
Far Eastern Department, USSR Academy of Sciences, **2:** 19
Far Eastern Timber Industry Administration (Dallesprom), **2:** 184
February (1917) Revolution, comparison, **2:** 140
Federalism, **1:** 66, 198, 201, 246, 256-57, 258, 285, **2:** 152, 174, 207, 211, 287—*see also* Union of Soviet Socialist Republics
Fergana riots, **2:** 115, 149-50
Ferrous Metallurgy, Ministry of (Mintsvetmet), **2:** 184
Fertilizers, **1:** 193, 210, **2:** 178
Finance, Ministry of, **1:** 192, 284 (ministers), 285, **2:** 103, 104, 127, 172, 238, 249
Financial system, conditions, **1:** 191, **2:** 118, 157-59, 257, 269
Financing, regional, **1:** 288, **2:** 153, 235
Finland, **2:** 122, 248
Finno-Ugric languages, nations, **2:** 122, 123
Fishing industry, **2:** 18, 65, 66, 124, 185
Five-Year Plans: Ninth, **2:** 156; Twelfth, **1:** 191, 215, 265, 306(n215), **2:** 98, 155, 158, 160, 162-63, 254; Thirteenth, **1:** 195, 197, 208, 209, 306(n195), **2:** 155, 157, 159, 160, 194; Fourteenth, **1:** 195, 306(n195)
Flag, **1:** 143
Food contamination, **2:** 180
Food processing, **1:** 192, 303(n147), **2:** 66, 132, 153, 157
Food supply, **1:** 191, 223, 265, 271, 281, 286, **2:** 22, 95, 118, 131, 132, 151, 156, 157, 174, 177, 240, 248, 254; in Siberia, **1:** 274; around Chernobyl, **2:** 27—*see also* Rationing

Foreign Affairs, Ministry of, **2:** 29, 287
Foreign economic activity, **2:** 163; aid, **1:** 212, **2:** 171; concessions, **2:** 15
Foreign investment, Armenia, **1:** 267
Foreign policy, **1:** 202, 255, 277, 283, **2:** 9, 102, 129, 145, 163, 262, 264, 278; and New Thinking, **1:** 201-2—*see also* Trade
Foreign relations, **2:** 8; with China, **2:** 102; with the capitalist world, **2:** 194
Fuel and Energy Complex, Bureau of, **2:** 293(n119)
Fuel, prices, **2:** 157-58; supply, **2:** 65, 98;
Furniture, **1:** 194

Gagauz nation, **2:** 123, 200
Gas industry, **2:** 252; Ministry of, **2:** 191; Ministry for Construction of Petroleum and Gas Industry Enterprises, **2:** 47
Gas pipeline disaster (Bashkiria), **2:** 113, 114-15, 200
Gasification, rural, **2:** 132, 157, 175; Siberia, **2:** 178, 252
Gdlyan-Ivanov affair, **1:** 30, 137-38, 150-55, 158-59, 159-60, 164, 304(n156), **2:** 72-73, 223-26, 231-34; and public opinion, **1:** 302(n137); Commission, **1:** 137-38, 178, 182, 189, **2:** 2, 200, 251, 278; nominations, **1:** 238-45; election of, **2:** 53-60, Appendix C.6—*see also* "Uzbek affair"
Geological Sciences, Ukrainian Institute of, **1:** 261
Georgia, Georgians, **1:** 38, 152, 294, 297(n5), **2:** 188-89; delegation, **1:** 115, 161, 162, **2:** 139, 221; annexation of (1921), **1:** 162, 228, 304-5(n162), **2:** 188; Supreme Soviet, **1:** 23, 226, 232; Communist Party, **1:** 226, 234-35, **2:** 50-51; Patriarch of, **1:** 227—*see also* Tbilisi incident
Germans—*see* Volga Germans
Glasnost, **1:** 17, 27, 34, 39, 91, 143, 146, 165, 171, 200, 209, 257, 265, 270, 279, 283, 298(n13),

Glasnost (cont.)
   300(n55), 303(n142), **2:** 28, 37, 163, 197-98, 213, 235, 237, 255-56, 269
Gold mining, **1:** 287
"Golden boys," case of, **1:** 153— *see also* Gdlyan-Ivanov, Uzbek affair
Gorbachev report, **1:** 190-205 (text); 246, 257, 259, 262, 264, 269, 270, 280, 307(n247), **2:** 2, 22, 44, 131, 151, 155, 164, 165, 235, 263; follow-up, **2:** 255-62—*see also Basic Guidelines for the Domestic and Foreign Policy of the USSR* and Congress of People's Deputies, Editing Commission
Gorky Nuclear Power Station, **2:** 252
Gosagroprom—*see* Agroindustrial, State Committee
Gosarbitrazh—*see* Arbitration, State Committee
Goskompriroda—*see under* Environment: State Committee for the Protection of Nature
Goskomstat—*see* Statistics, State Committee on
Goskomtsen—*see* Prices, State Committee on
Gosplan—*see* Planning, State Committee
Gossnab—*see* Supply, State Committee for Material and Technical
Gosstroy—*see* Construction, State Committee
Gostelradio—*see* Television and Radio Broadcasting, State Committee for
Gradualism, **2:** 260
Grass-roots agencies—*see* Public Organizations, Law on
Great Patriotic War, **1:** 195, 261, 287, **2:** 5, 24 (veterans), 25 (museum), 43, 76, 88, 129, 133, 155, 167, 193, 246—*see also* World War II
Greeks, **2:** 204
Groznensky rabochy, **1:** 149

Health, health care, **1:** 189, 191, 193-94, 266, **2:** 38, 106, 154, 158 *see also* Medical services, Public health
Heat, **1:** 272, **2:** 198
Helsinki Act, **1:** 202, **2:** 268
Herbicides, **2:** 65
Highways, Ministry of (Minavtodor), **2:** 14
History curriculum, **2:** 68-69, 116
Homelessness, **2:** 1, 10
"Hooliganism", **1:** 200, **2:** 15
Housing, **1:** 250, 271, 281, **2:** 9, 12, 35-36, 66, 73, 98, 106, 120, 124, 125, 150, 154, 158, 177, 182; Armenia, **1:** 268; Siberia, **1:** 274; Moscow, **1:** 277; rural, **2:** 17; Tyumen, **2:** 27, 46; military, **2:** 136; Leningrad, **2:** 167; Housing-2000 Program, **2:** 78, 79, 177, 249
Human rights, **1:** 143, 199, **2:** 90, 162, 268; and Criminal Code, 299(n35); UN General Declaration, **1:** 134, **2:** 268 *see also* Helsinki process
Hungary, intervention, **1:** 166
Hunting, **2:** 185
Hydroelectric power, **1:** 286, **2:** 124, 132, 141, 161, 197, 235
Hydrotechnical construction—*see* Canals, Irrigation, Land Reclamation

Impeachment, **1:** 102, 103, 278, **2:** 99
India, **1:** 202, **2:** 264
Industrial "aggression", **1:** 261, 271, **2:** 18, 184, 240
Industrialization, **1:** 248, **2:** 120, 141; and agriculture, **1:** 249, 258, 303(n147); excessive, **1:** 206, 209, 246, 255, 286, **2:** 27, 46, 65, 95, 118-19, 120, 132
Industry, heavy, **1:** 189, **2:** 235, 171; output, **1:** 272; investment in, **1:** 196, **2:** 149; obsolescence of, **2:** 46, 167
Industry, light, **1:** 192, **2:** 104, 153, 154, 254, 267; Ministry of, **1:** 271
Infant mortality, **1:** 266, **2:** 7, 10, 189; infanticide, **2:** 1, 11
Inflation, **1:** 193, 205, 215, 264, **2:** 95, 102, 158, 159, 169-70, 238, 239
Ingush nation, **1:** 149, 152, **2:** 200 *see also* Chechen-Ingush
Instrumentation, Automation Equipment, and Control Systems, Ministry of (Minpribor) **2:** 106, 179
Intelligentsia, **1:** 63, 65, 156, 217, 265, 308(n280), **2:** 5, 86, 89, 122, 187—*see also* Association of, *and* Moscow Group
Interethnic relations, **1:** 141, 142, 152, 162, 163, 176, 200, 217, 254, 259, 261, 267, 280, 281, 287, 303(n142), **2:** 4, 7, 13, 17-18, 23, 44-45, 62, 63, 71, 101, 124, 130, 164, 218, 258, 268, 287; Latvia, **1:** 299 (n25); Abkhazia, **2:** 83-84; and Criminal Code, **2:** 299 (n35)
Interethnic tension, **1:** 40-41, 160, 210, 252, 264, 268, 276, 280, 293, **2:** 3, 23, 136 (armed forces), 146, 200, 237; causes, **1:** 126, 277, **2:** 14, 48, 89, 141
Internal Affairs, Ministry of, **1:** 178, 179, 233, 238, 280, 306 (n231), **2:** 50, 224, 226, 228, 293(n100)
Internal Troops, **1:** 53, 141, **2:** 3, 146, 149; Decree on, **1:** 133, 139, 179, 264, 302(n133), 305(n179), **2:** 280, Appendix A.5; in Tbilisi, **1:** 229, 235, 297(n5), **2:** 50, 51; in Vilnius, **1:** 231
International Policy, Commission on, **1:** 305(n65)
International Red Cross, **1:** 225
Interregional Group of Deputies, **1:** 91, 297(n1), 301(n101), **2:** 285
Intolerance, **1:** 279
Intourist, **1:** 212
Iran, **2:** 9
Irresponsibility, **1:** 278-79, 283
Irrigation, **2:** 14, 15, 65, 132, 196, 236
Islam, **2:** 49
Ivanovo-Voznesensk Soviet (1905), **1:** 270
Iveriya Hospital, **1:** 235
Izvestiya, cited, **1:** 63, 160, 177, 179, 189, 244, 305(n171), **2:** 64, 144; editor, **1:** 278, **2:** 183, 279, 282, 287

INDEX OF SUBJECTS

Izvestiya Starogo Goda, **2:** 206-7
Izvestiya TsK KPSS, **2:** 60

Japan, Japanese, **1:** 123, **2:** 141, 184
Jews, **1:** 66, **2:** 185
Joint (foreign) enterprises, **2:** 96
Journalists, **1:** 241; *see also* Press
Judges, Law on, **1:** 152, 158, 304 (n152)
Judicial oversight, **1:** 204
Judicial reform, **1:** 199-200, 304 (n153), **2:** 153; trial by jury, **2:** 267
Jurists, **2:** 166, 211; Association of, **2:** 230
Justice, Ministry of, **1:** 304(n152)
Juvenile delinquency, **2:** 11

Kalinin delegation, **1:** 110
Kalmyk nation, **1:** 149, **2:** 133-34
Kama River Nuclear Power Station, **2:** 129
Kansk-Achinsk Fuel-Power Project—KATEK, **2:** 107
Das Kapital, **2:** 239
Karabakh Committee, **1:** 166, **2:** 227
Karacharovo Mechanical Plant, **2:** 104
Karachay nation, **1:** 149
Katun Hydroelectric Power Station, **2:** 84, 141, 180, 253
Kazakhstan, Kazakhs, **2:** 146 (nationalism), 200; delegation, **1:** 67, 123, 163, 293, **2:** 146
Kazannik resignation, **1:** 184-88, 274-75, **2:** 13
Ket nation, **2:** 125
Keynesian economics, **2:** 235, 239
KGB—Committee on State Security, **1:** 152, 178, 238, 279-80, **2:** 23, 127, 131, 224, 226, 232, 287
Khint case, **1:** 154
Khmelnitsky Nuclear Power Station, **2:** 106
Khrushchev, **1:** 155, **2:** 240
Kirghiz delegation, **1:** 79, 281, **2:** 271
Kirishi Biochemical Plant, **2:** 106
Kirov delegation, **1:** 79
Kolkhoz—*see* Collective farms
Komi delegation, **1:** 81-82
Komsomol, **1:** 157, 159, 166, 195, 212, **2:** 25, 54, 60, 208, 274; women in, **1:** 263; Komsomol Youth Affairs Committee, **2:** 147

Komsomolskaya Pravda, **2:** 72, 93, 144, 280
Koreans, **2:** 200
Krasnaya Talka Factory, **1:** 271
Krays, **1:** 298(n16); Kraykom secretaries, **1:** 58
Kulaks, **1:** 102
Kurds, **2:** 204

Labor, **1:** 143; discipline, **1:** 192; veterans, **1:** 195; surplus, **1:** 258; women, **1:** 262; collectives, **1:** 207, 252, 259, 289, **2:** 80, 102, 142, 143, 176, 179, 237-38; colonies, **1:** 304(n153)—*see also* Collective Labor Disputes, Productivity, Wages, Workers
Labor and Social Questions, State Committee for, **1:** 284, **2:** 243-44, 249
Land reclamation, **1:** 259, **2:** 196, 240
Land Reclamation and Water Resources, Ministry of (Minvodkhoz), **2:** 14, 157, 176; expenditures, **2:** 196
Land Reclamation, Institute for Planning (Giprozem), **2:** 196
Land reform, **1:** 251, **2:** 22; "Land to the peasant", **1:** 265, **2:** 41
Landownership, **1:** 42, 143, 248, 251, 285; **2:** 13, 14, 67, 131, 156, 196—*see also* Property
Language, language policy, **1:** 35, 41, 281, **2:** 4, 63, 68, 130, 186; bilingualism, **1:** 260, 261, 265, **2:** 4, 7, 15, 71, 122, 141, 146; Moldavia, 305 (n176)
Latin America, **1:** 202, **2:** 171
Latvia, Latvians, **2:** 122, 248; delegation, **1:** 57, 66, 76, 79, 168, 175, **2:** 107; People's Front, **1:** 25, 33, 141, 299(n25), **2:** 211, 291(n48); economic reform, **2:** 247; Communist Party, **1:** 25, 257; Supreme Soviet, **1:** 25, 299(n25), **2:** 211
Law and order, **1:** 40, 91, 124, 125, 130, 200, 139, 200, 207, 217, 281, **2:** 198, 259; law enforcement, **1:** 151, 152-53, 178, 189; telephone law, **1:** 303 (n137)—*see also* Crime
Laws—*see* Banks, Collective Labor Disputes, Cooperatives, Defense, Economic Independence of Union Republics, Elections, Estonian Law on Cost Accounting, Judges, Legal Profession, Local Self-Government, Pensions, Press, Psychiatric Assistance, Public Organizations, Repression—Draft Law on Extrajudicial Mass Repression of the Period of Stalinism, State Crimes, State Enterprise, Union Republics—Law on Economic Independence of
Leasing, **1:** 42, 100, 121, 193, 248, 251, 284-85, 301(n100), **2:** 12, 20, 138, 152, 156, 173, 176, 264
Leasing and Leasing Relations, Legislative Principles of, **1:** 301(n100)
Legal Policy Questions, Commission on, **1:** 154, 304(n154), **2:** 223
Legal profession, **1:** 298(n19); Law on, **1:** 153, 158; lawyers, **2:** 20, 57, 228
Legal system, **1:** 255, **2:** 137; reform, **1:** 199, 303(n142)
Lenin, Leninism, **1:** 1, 51, 91, 150, 153, 165, 173, 174, 216, 249, 254, 281, **2:** 22, 37, 42, 84, 86, 121, 126, 133-34, 136, 143, 146, 164, 183, 187, 188, 194, 199, 213, 221-22, 235, 237, 240, 259-60, 261, 283; national policy of, **1:** 200, 201, 208, 217, 254, 257, 267, **2:** 41, 82-83, 84, 87, 101, 117, 129, 144, 211, 214 292(n84); Mausoleum, **1:** 206, **2:** 99-100, 121, 128, 143, 148, 168 293(n121); Prize for Literature, **2:** 99
Leningrad delegation, **1:** 80, 112, 154, 174, 182, 218, 282
Leningrad Pumped Storage Power Plant, **2:** 106
Leningrad State University Library, **1:** 211
Leninogorsk Polymetals Combine, **2:** 67
Libraries, condition of, **1:** 211
Library of Congress, **1:** 211
Life expectancy, **2:** 185, 189

Literaturnaya Gazeta, **2:** 210, 227, 229, 230

Lithuania, delegation, **1:** 51, 55, 57, 132, 161, **2:** 48, 142; *Sajudis*, **1:** 141, 297(n12), **2:** 49, 166, 291(n48); ultimatum on Supreme Soviet election, **1:** 76-79, 97; autonomy proposal, **1:** 276-77; constitution, **2:** 48; boycott of Constitutional Oversight Committee election, **2:** 166, 203, 208, 217-19, 235, 275-76; Communist Party, **1:** 277; Supreme Council, **1:** 297(n12); Supreme Soviet, **2:** 211; annexation of, **2:** 1—*see also* Nazi-Soviet Pact

Loans, state, **1:** 142, 205; foreign, **2:** 71

Local Self-Government, Law on, **2:** 13, 19, 48, 74, 77, 178, 291(n74)

Lower Ob Hydroelectric Station, **2:** 197

Lumbering, **2:** 18

Machine tool industry, **1:** 191, 273; Ministry of Machine Tool and Tool Building Industry (Minstankoprom), **2:** 106; Bureau of Machine Building, **2:** 193

Machine tractor stations (MTS), **2:** 128

"Mafia", **1:** 151, 156, 200, 304 (n151), **2:** 67, 170, 223, 232

Malnutrition, **2:** 242

Mandate Commission—*see* Congress of People's Deputies, Credentials Commission

Mankurtism, **2:** 86

Manual Therapy Center, **2:** 126

Market, market system, **1:** 189, 191, 192, 197, 249, 264, 285, 288, 306(n195), 307(n271), **2:** 8, 12, 19, 26, 73, 103, 119, 137, 152-53, 169-71, 247, 257, 269; world, **2:** 157-58, 240

Marxism, **1:** 60, 216, 248, **2:** 7, 235, 239, 240, 260, 261, 292(n84)

Mary nation, **2:** 129; delegation, **1:** 109-10, 111-13, 115, 116, 118-19, 177—*see also* Chemodanov candidacy *under* Soviet of the Union election

Maternity leave, **2:** 266

Meat production, **2:** 12, 22

Media—*see* Press, Television

Medical and Microbiological Industry, Ministry of the (Minmedbioprom), **2:** 106, 179

Medical services and facilities, **1:** 206, 250, 277, 307(n253), **2:** 9-11, 27, 46, 80, 98, 106, 125, 132, 150, 154, 155, 163, 266; military, **2:** 136; medicine, **1:** 277, **2:** 155, 179; medical workers, wages, **2:** 178-79—*see also* Prostheses

Memorial (*Pamyat*), **2:** 37

Memorial, All-Union Historical-Educational Society, **1:** 45, 299(n45);

Mental institutions—*see* Psychiatric hospitals

Mental retardation, **2:** 10

Meskhetian Turks, **1:** 152, 162, **2:** 149, 200, 264; repression of, **1:** 254

Message to the Peoples of the World, **1:** 171, **2:** 235, 279, 288 (text)

Metallurgical industry, **1:** 209, 255, **2:** 22-23, 67

Migration, **1:** 256; Siberia, **1:** 175, 274, 307(n274); Latvia, **1:** 299 (n25), **2:** 85-86; Yakutia, **2:** 18; Non-chernozem zone, **2:** 75-76; rural, **2:** 131, 167

Military—*see also* Armed forces, Defense, Disarmament

Military sports clubs, **2:** 91

Militia, **1:** 40, 50, 53, 54, 67, 141, 235, 300(n55), **2:** 149, 228

Mining, **2:** 18; conditions, **2:** 67

Ministries, as monopolies, **1:** 125-26, 208, 212, 216, 246, 265, 286, **2:** 18, 74, 89, 98, 119, 122, 138, 153, 173, 176, 178, 181, 189, 197, 202, 256, 267; and environment, **1:** 257, 261, **2:** 8, 18, 185, 190, 244; decrees of, **1:** 147, **2:** 179; reduction of, **2:** 152, 194

Ministry—*see* Atomic Power, Chemical, Construction, Education, Electric Industry, Electrical Equipment, Ferrous Metallurgy, Finance, Gas Industry, Highways, Instrumentation, Internal Affairs, Internal Affairs, Justice, Land Reclamation, Machine Tool, Medical, Pensions, Personal Services, Power, Public Health, Railroads, Timber Industry, Trade

Moldavian delegation, **1:** 79, 131, 176, **2:** 218; Communist Party, **2:** 224; corruption in, **2:** 2, 290(n2)

Molodezh Gruzii, **1:** 230

Molotov-Ribbentrop—*see* Nazi-Soviet pact

Mongol Yoke, **2:** 141

Monopolies, **1:** 125

Morality, **1:** 269, **2:** 19, 38, 90, 123, 139, 164, 267

Mortality, **2:** 124

Moscow, **1:** 132, 151, **2:** 103; Muscovites, **1:** 172-73, **2:** 19, 130 (Tatars), 273; delegation, **1:** 59, 63, 64, 66, 67, 69, 79, 82, 84-85, 98, 100, 105, 123-24, 124, 127, 130-31, 142, 174, 175, 282, **2:** 192, 272; Moscow Group, **1:** 1, 3, 9, 34, 45, 51, 58, 59, 60, 67, 82, 83, 98, 103, 129-30, 278, 297(n1), 301(n101), **2:** 12, 19-20, 22, 23-24, 37, 103, 283, 285; People's Front, **1:** 299 (n45); city soviet, **1:** 53, 54, 55, 98, **2:** 130; city party committee, **1:** 297(n1), 299 (n29), **2:** 293(n103); State University, **1:** 1: 156, 157 *see also* Muscovites

Moscow Tribune, **1:** 297(n1)

Moskovskaya Pravda, **2:** 46

Moskovskiye Novosti, **2:** 14; *Moscow News*, **1:** 2, 297(n1)

Moskovsky universitet (yearbook), **1:** 157

Mothers, **1:** 126, 266

Murder, **1:** 153

Museums, condition of, **1:** 211

Muslims, **1:** 30

MVD—*see* Internal Affairs, Ministry of; *see also* Internal Troops

Mytishchi Plant, **2:** 47

Nagorno-Karabakh: conflict, **1:** 36, 104, 114, 116, 117, 120, 163, 259, 267, **2:** 40, 44-45, 52, 87, 115, 200, 264, 268, 270-71; delegation, **1:** 76, 82, 88-

INDEX OF SUBJECTS

Nagorno-Karabakh (Cont.) 89, 91, 110-11, 112, 114-15, 116-18, 120, 127, 176, 184, 187, 188, 189, 218, 274; history, **2:** 116-18; economy, **2:** 117; resolution on, **2:** 118; special administration of, **1:** 267, 268, 302(n110), **2:** 117—*see also* Karabakh Committee

Nanay nation, **2:** 184

National Resources, Institute, **2:** 292 (n96)

National self-determination, **1:** 139, 141, **2:** 123, 173, 187, 204
  see also Lenin, national policy

Nationalism—*see* Interethnic relations *and also* specific nations and issues

Nationalities, Commission on Problems of, **1:** 267

Nationalities—*see* Soviet of; *see also* Declaration of the Rights of the Peoples of Russia

Nationality-State Formations, Principles of, **2:** 18, 125

Natives, **2:** 191, 264—*see also* Far East, Peoples of; North, Peoples of; and specific nations

NATO, Georgian appeal to, **1:** 228

Natural gas, **1:** 193, 214, **2:** 8

Natural resources, **2:** 124 (Siberia), 190

Nature, Conservancy Commission, **1:** 72; State Committee for the Protection of (Goskompriroda), **2:** 13, 67, 95, 141, 191—*see also* Environmental issues

Nazi-Soviet pact, **1:** 162, 165, 246, 277, 288, 305(n165), 307 (n261), **2:** 1, 31, 49, 85-86, 173 291(n49); CPD commission, **1:** 165, **2:** 28-32, 49, 105 (approved), 200, 278, Appendix C.10; report of, Appendix B.7; resolution on, Appendix B.8

Nedorosl' (The Minor), **2:** 290(n12)

Negidal nation, **2:** 125

Negroes, **2:** 242

Nekrasov Library, **1:** 211

NEP—New Economic Policy (1921-1929), **1:** 283, 285, **2:** 20, 240

Nevada-Semipalatinsk movement, **2:** 199

New York Times, **2:** 61

Nganasan nation, **2:** 125

Nihilism, **2:** 72, 140

Nivkh nation, **2:** 133, 184

No-confidence vote, **1:** 61, 101, 246, 294

Nomenklatura, **1:** 189, 266, 304 (n151), **2:** 43, 156
  see also Privileges

Nonchernozem, Agricultural Committee for, **1:** 249

Noorte Khyael, **2:** 206

North, people of the, **2:** 17-19, 122, 123-26, 185-86, 271; children **2:** 11; Council on, **2:** 17; decree on, **2:** 125; Resolution of, **2:** 125-26

Novocherkassk riot (1962), **1:** 166, **2:** 280, 282

Novosibirsk delegation, **1:** 81

Novosti, **1:** 238

Novoye delo, **1:** 45

Nuclear contamination, **1:** 261, **2:** 15, 80, 111, 199—*see also* Chernobyl disaster

Nuclear power, **1:** 148, 209, 252, 262, **2:** 15-16, 106, 107, 108, 119, 129, 161, 235, 252, 281

Nuclear weapons, **1:** 189, 202; testing, **1:** 216, **2:** 106, 180, 199—*see also* Disarmament

Obedience, **1:** 102

Obkom secretaries, **1:** 58, 61, 63, 69

Oblasts, **1:** 298(n16)

October Revolution, **1:** 252, 287, **2:** 129, 130

Ogonek, **2:** 224

Oil and gas industry, **1:** 283, **2:** 46-47, 98, 240, 244; oil prices, **2:** 169

Okrugs, **1:** 298(n16)

Old Bolsheviks, **2:** 290(n20)

Omsk delegation, **1:** 63-64, **2:** 177

Omsk State University, **1:** 185

One Day in the Life of Ivan Denisovich, **2:** 290(n20)

ORBITA, **2:** 124, 293(n124)

Orenburg delegation, **2:** 59

Oroki nation, **2:** 184

Orphans, **2:** 10

Ottawa Citizen, **2:** 61, 92

Ownership—*see* Landownership, Property

Paint, **1:** 248

Pamirian nation, **2:** 89

Pamyat, **1:** 299(n45)

"Parasitism," **1:** 195, 306(n195), **2:** 291(n42)

"Parliament" (term), **2:** 131, 138

Parochialism, **1:** 60, 252

Pastureland, **2:** 185

Peace Foundation, **2:** 39, 40

Peasant farms, **1:** 285, **2:** 173, 240, 248

Peasants, **1:** 247-48, 250, 262, 265, **2:** 98, 122, 129, 131, 132, 147, 155, 156-57, 176, 242; Appeal of, **1:** 246, 250-51, 275, **2:** 146, 157, 175, 181, 248

Pechora cartel, **1:** 153

Pensions, pensioners, **1:** 43, 143, 193, 205, 250, 262, 265, 277, **2:** 16, 24, 27, 37-38, 41, 103, 104, 106, 124, 155-56, 158, 168, 177, 194, 244, 266, 267; Law on, **2:** 38-39, 74, 104, 131, 293(n104)

People's Control Committee, **1:** 7, 8, 172, 181; confirmation of chairman, **2:** 150, 164, 210, 220-22

Perestroika—*see* Restructuring

Personal Services, RSFSR Ministry of, **2:** 130

Personality cult, **1:** 142

Pervyi syezd nardonykh deputatov SSSR: Stenograficheskii otchet, **1:** x, 297(nn11), 300 (n82), 302(n104), 303(n138), 305(n171)

Petrochemical industry, **1:** 209, 255, **2:** 141

Pharmaceutical industry, **2:** 155

Physicians for Human Rights, **1:** 225

Physicians without Borders, **1:** 225

Pioneers' House (Moscow), **2:** 245

Pionerskaya Pravda, **1:** 225, **2:** 224

Planning, State Committee on (Gosplan), **1:** 192, 214, 249, 255, 276, 284, 288, 306 (n214), **2:** 12, 20, 21, 27, 85, 104, 127, 179, 197, 242, 244, 249, 291(n47); RSFSR State Committee on, **2:** 141—*see also* State deliveries

Pluralism, **1:** 98, 103, 127, 183, 215, **2:** 14, 139, 189, 255

PO-2 aircraft, **2:** 79, 292(n79)

INDEX OF SUBJECTS

Poison gas, use of: Tbilisi, **1**: 225, 229, 235-36, 297(n5), 298 (n23); Armenia, **1**: 268

Poland, **1**: 166, **2**: 291(n31); Lublin Poles, **2**: 291(n31)

Political prisoners, **2**: 214—*see also* Dissidents

Politicheskaya literatura publishing house, **2**: 204

Pollution: Aral region, **1**: 223-24, 255, **2**: 161, 172, 194, 196, 242; Baikal region, **2**: 161, 191; Black Sea, **2**: 109; Caspian region, **1**: 246, 259, **2**: 161; industrial, **1**: 216, **2**: 95-96, 110, 240; Lake Issyk-Kul, **2**: 236; Lake Ladoga, **2**: 161; Moscow region, **1**: 277; Siberia, **2**: 161; Tyumen region, **2**: 191; Volga River, **2**: 161; polluters, **2**: 190, 270—*see also* nuclear contamination

Popov, Gavril—*see* Afanasyev-Popov

Popular front movements, **1**: 297 (n1), 299(n45)

Pornography, **2**: 15, 38

Poverty, **1**: 189, 205, 265, **2**: 39, 124, 132, 241, 281, 282

Power, centralization of, **1**: 126, 130, 132, 201, 208, 246, 256, 258, 260, 263-64, 272-73, 276, 283, 288, 303(n147), **2**: 13, 15, 42-43, 48, 88, 122, 159, 199, 203, 261; separation of powers, **1**: 42, 71, 101, 198, 203, **2**: 72, 88, 99, 101, 182, 214; Sakharov's draft decree on, **2**: 235, 286-87, 289

see also Soviets

Power industry, electrical, **1**: 272, **2**: 252

Power and Electrification, Ministry of, **1**: 272, **2**: 47, 124

Pravda, **1**: 130, 156, 160, 261, 299(24), 300(n46), **2**: 80, 86, 103, 144, 170, 253

Preservation, historical, **1**: 211-12

Presidency, **1**: 3, 101—*see* Supreme Soviet, Chairman

Press, **1**: 151, 153, 162, 199, **2**: 15, 23, 63-64, 72, 91-92, 129, 130, 228; freedom of, **1**: 143, 265, 282; Law on, **2**: 269

Prices, pricing, **1**: 142, 205, 215-16, 249, 250, 284, 303(n147), **2**: 18, 38, 62, 95, 98, 170, 173, 236, 243, 248, 253; State Committee on (Goskomtsen), **2**: 38, 238, 249

Printed Matter, Main Administration for Distribution of, **2**: 239

Privileges, **1**: 43, 142, 178, 189, 195-96, 266, **2**: 6, 23, 42, 120-21, 156, 182

Procuracy, **1**: 153, 158, 166, 178, **2**: 222, 224, 228

Production Forces, Institute of, **2**: 292(n96)

Production, means of, **1**: 303 (n147), **2**: 62, 153

Productive relations, **1**: 265, **2**: 239

Productivity, **1**: 189, 192, 209, 215-16, 252, 270, 283, 284, 298(n18), **2**: 19, 96, 98, 102, 149, 151, 238, 241, 253

Progress-95, **2**: 103, 293(n103)

Property, **2**: 63, 73, 138, 156, 239, 243, 247, 257

Property: private, **1**: 199, 265, 289, **2**: 14, 67, 103, 240; socialist, **1**: 301(n100), **2**: 138, 173, 240; mixed, **2**: 12; peasant, **1**: 193; industrial, **1**: 252; cooperative, **2**: 301(n100)

Property—*see also* Cooperatives, Landownership, and Leasing

Prosecutor General, **1**: 7, 151-52, 172, 181, 182, 302-3(n137), 304(nn151, 152), 306(n231), **2**: 287

Prosecutor General, confirmation of, **2**: 166, 222-34

Prosecutor—*see also* Procuracy (Prosecutor's office)

Prostheses, prosthetics industry, **2**: 91, 93, 163, 266

Prostitution, **1**: 304(n152)

Psychiatric abuse, **2**: 43; hospitals, **1**: 153, **2**: 214

Psychiatric Assistance, Law on, **1**: 153

Public health, **2**: 155; Altai Kray, **2**: 178-79; Aral region, **1**: 223-24, 255

Public Health Institutions, Institute for Planning, **2**: 179

Public Health, Ministry of (Minzdrav), **1**: 261, 266, **2**: 10, 80, 81, 95, 127, 156, 190; and nuclear testing, **2**: 199; Georgian, **1**: 225; Ukrainian, **2**: 112; RSFSR, **2**: 179—*see also* Health care, Medical services

Public Opinion, Center for Study of, **1**: 50—*see also* Gdlyan-Ivanov

Public organizations, **1**: 58, 66, 168, 180, 199, 246, 282, **2**: 22; women and, **1**: 263; in elections, **1**: 284; Law on, **2**: 34, 268, 269, 291(n34)

Public transportation, **2**: 155

Quality control, **2**: 292-93(n98)

Railroads, **1**: 253, **2**: 135

Railroads, Ministry of, **2**: 106

Rallies and demonstrations: Decree on, **1**: 17-18, 35, 36, 50, 53, 54, 55, 133, 139, 141, 175, 264, 282, 298(n17), 299 (n35), **2**: 146; in Moscow, **1**: 50, 53-55, 130-31; **2**: 127

Rape, **1**: 153

Rationing, **1**: 247, 250, 278, **2**: 91, 197

Raykom secretaries, **1**: 58

Rayons, **1**: 298(n16)

Red Army—*see* Armed Forces, Army

Red Cross, **2**: 188

Referendum, **1**: 101, 102, 265, **2**: 141, 210, 281, 282

Refugees, **1**: 268, **2**: 44, 149

Regionalism, **2**: 172-74, 246-48, 265-66—*see also* Cost accounting, Union republics

Rehabilitation, political, **1**: 149, 152, 156, 160, **2**: 90, 188, 264; Commission on, **1**: 301 (n102); of Chechen-Ingush, **2**: 304(n149)

Religion, **1**: 122; and Tbilisi comission, **1**: 238; freedom of, **1**: 199, 269

Representation, **1**: 8-9, 58—*and see under* Congress of People's Deputies, Soviet of Nationalities, Soviet of the Union, and Supreme Soviet

Repression, **1**: 102, 149, 160, 279, 288, **2**: 82, 90, 100, 188, 199-200; Draft Law on

Repression (Cont.)
  Extrajudicial Mass Repression of the Period of Stalinism **1:** 308(n288)—*see also* Stalinism
Republics—*see* Union republics
Resolutions—*see under* Congress of Peoples Deputies
Restructuring, **1:** 7-8, 13, 27, 30, 31, 34, 35-36, 38, 39*ff.*, 46, 49, 125-26, 129, 130, 132, 175, 180, 190*ff.*, 215, 217, 246, 250, 254, 255, 257, 259, 261, 264, 272, 275-76, 278, 283, 285, 299(n29), 303(n142), **2:** 5, 15, 21, 24, 25, 39, 41, 43, 66, 70, 84, 97, 103-4, 121, 126, 134, 139, 142, 145, 150*ff.*, 163, 167, 177, 194-95, 207, 216, 235, 236, 239, 241, 243, 255-56*ff.*, 267, 279, 281; opponents of, **1:** 156-57, 226, 264, 270, 284, 300(n46), **2:** 1, 37, 45, 48, 139, 140, 180
Revolution (1905), **2:** 290(n12); (1917)—*see* October Revolution
Ribbentrop-Molotov—*see* Nazi-Soviet pact
Rigun Hydroelectric Power Plant, **1:** 286
Roads, **1:** 214, **2:** 14, 66, 76, 131, 135, 175, 177
Robbery, **1:** 153
Rock music, **2:** 15, 25
Rostov Nuclear Power Station, **1:** 252, **2:** 111, 252
Rovno Nuclear Power Station, **1:** 262
Ruble—*see* currency
"Rule-of-law state", **1:** 2, 35, 36, 42, 59, 66, 81, 143, 147, 149, 162, 171, 199, 254, 276, **2:** 37, 63
Rural conditions, **1:** 193, 214, 246, 247, 250, **2:** 1, 7, 15, 16-17, 64-65, 75, 76, 128, 129, 131-32, 156-57, 174-76, 236, 250, 258—*see also* Standard of living, urban-rural *and* "Unpromising villages"
Rural soviets, **2:** 64-65
Rus, **1:** 177, 305(n177)
Russia, Russians, **2:** 6, 122-23, 125, 131-32, 200, 204, 271, 287;

delegation, **1:** 16, 51, 59, 65, 66, 79-80*ff.*, 85-86, 116, 118, 164, 168, 183-84, 222; domination of USSR, **2:** 14; Supreme Soviet, **1:** 302(n127), **2:** 126; chauvinism of, **2:** 140 *see* Language; *see also* anti-Russianism
Russian Museum, Leningrad, **1:** 211
Russian Orthodox Church, **2:** 122
Russian Social Democratic Workers Party, **1:** 42
Russophobia, **2:** 14, 140, 142, 187
Ryazan delegation, **1:** 37
Ryzhkov statement, **2:** 149, 169, 201, 263; follow-up, **2:** 252-55, 263

Sajudis—*see* Lithuania
Sakharov and alleged slander of army, **2:** 92-95, 100, 147-48
Savings Bank (*Sberbank*), **2:** 98
School construction, **2:** 98, 125, 131, 136, 150, 185, 246
Science and technology, **1:** 132, 191, 272; **2:** 19, 23, 161-62, 190, 193; weaknesses of, **1:** 273, **2:** 19; Novosibirsk center, **1:** 273
Secrecy, **1:** 279
Semya, **1:** 279, **2:** 139
Senior citizens—*see* Elderly
Sergo Ordzhonikidze Plant, **2:** 104
Sheep-raising, **2:** 176, 236
Shevchenko—*see* Ukrainian Language Society
Shortages, **1:** 153, **2:** 23, 24, 27, 36, 38, 103, 120, 153-54, 170, 181, 194, 244, 245, 269
Siberian delegation, **1:** 30, 102-3, 157-58
Siberian Department, USSR Academy of Sciences, **2:** 19, 141
Slavs, **2:** 133
Smoking ban, **1:** 275
Soap, **1:** 247, 272, **2:** 23, 24, 38, 133, 194
Social consumption funds, **2:** 104, 155
Social development, **2:** 149, 151, 155, 168, 175, 193, 198, 237, 244
Social justice, injustice, **1:** 264, 271, 281, **2:** 97, 156 —*see also* Privileges

Social organizations—*see* public organizations
Social stratification, **1:** 33, 264, 271
Socialism, **1:** 123, 189, 198, 201, 249, 276, **2:** 19, 24, 26, 42, 64, 70-71, 84, 86, 102, 121, 122, 137, 164, 174, 188, 194, 235, 238-41, 259-62, 267
Socialist countries, **1:** 202—*see also* Europe, Eastern
Socialist legality, **1:** 152, 156, 182
Soil erosion, **2:** 132
South Ukrainian Nuclear Power Station, **1:** 262, **2:** 191, 252
Southern Urals Power Project, **2:** 106
Sovereignty, popular, **2:** 262—*see* Federalism, Power, Union of Soviet Socialist Republics, Union republics
Sovetskaya Estoniya, **2:** 122, 206
Sovetskaya Kultura, **2:** 25, 64, 185
Sovetskaya Latvia, **2:** 206
Sovetskaya Litva, **2:** 48
Sovetskaya Rossiya, **1:** 156, 300 (n46)
Soviet-German Friendship Treaty (1939), **2:** 1
Soviets, powers of, **1:** 37, 38, 63, 142-43, 156, 180, 181, 198-99, 208, 217, 263, 289, **2:** 14, 17, 63, 64, 73, 74, 76, 100-101, 118-19, 149, 153, 178, 181, 189, 191, 265, 267-68, 286-87, 291-92(n74); "All power to the Soviets", **1:** 180, 181, 198, 199, 216, 252, 275, 280, **2:** 22, 41, 126, 129, 168, 183, 262, 281; First Congress of, **2:** 282, 292(n84)
Soviet State Construction and Legislation, Scientific Research Institute of, **1:** 142;
Soviet of Nationalities, **2:** 112, 148 Commission, on interethnic relations, **2:** 17; on small nations, **2:** 125
Election of, **1:** 91; candidates, **1:** 92-94; deputies elected, **1:** 94-97; Yeltsin candidacy, **1:** 125, 127-28, 139, 150, 172-73, 179, 184-88, 274-75; **2:** 19-20—*see also* Kazannik resignation
Electoral process, **1:** 51, 52, 57-58, 60, 64, 70, 73, 79*ff.*, 85, 155, 274-75

INDEX OF SUBJECTS

Soviet of Nationalities (Cont.)
  Powers of, **1:** 259, **2:** 8, 48, 62-63
  Representation in, **2:** 129, 186; Kabardino-Balkar AO, **1:** 72; Nagorno-Karabakh, **1:** 76, 82, 88-89, 114-18, 218-22, 260, 274—*see also* Nagorno-Karabakh as main heading
Soviet of the Union
  Election of, **1:** 91; deputies elected, **1:** 106-8; Chemodanov candidacy, **1:** 91, 102, 108-10, 111-13, 115, 116, 118-19, 120, 177-78, **2:** 147
  Electoral process, **1:** 51, 52, 56, 57-58, 60, 64, 68, 69, 70, 79*ff.*
  Representation in, Latvia, **1:** 66; Moscow, **1:** 52-53, 60, 63, 75, 82, 85-86, 127; Rostov, **1:** 65, 83-84; Sakhalin, **1:** 52, 65, 68-69
Soyuz, **1:** 299(n25)
Space program, **1:** 196, 216, 306(n216), **2:** 149, 264; cost of, **2:** 163, 240; shuttle, **2:** 163, 195
Speculation, speculators, **2:** 103, 265
"Stagnation", **1:** 105, 125-26, 128-29, 142, 200, 209, 226, 253, 254, 264, 288, **2:** 2-3, 38, 44, 48, 100, 143, 144, 146, 193, 203, 243, 247, 271—*see also* Brezhnev
Stalin, Stalinism, **1:** 91, 98, 102, 125, 128, 146, 149, 152, 158, 160, 267, 277, 299-300(nn45, 46), 301-2(n102), 304(n149), 306(n231), **2:** 20, 37, 71, 82-83, 94, 99, 116, 117, 121, 126, 133-34, 139, 143, 144, 176, 199-200, 203, 214, 241, 287, 292(n84), 293(n100); "Stalinist-Brezhnevian" Supreme Soviet, **1:** 91, 98, 120, 124-25—*see* Afanaseyev-Popov attack
Standard of living, **1:** 43, 139, 191, 193, 264, 271, 271-72, 277, **2:** 38, 149, 151, 153-54, 170, 175; Azerbaijan, **1:** 257; Siberia, **1:** 274, **2:** 198; military families, **2:** 136-37; urban-rural comparisons, **1:** 246, 247, 249, 250, 262

State acceptance, **2:** 98, 292-93 (n98)
State and Law, Institute, **2:** 213
State Committees, *see* Agroindustrial, Arbitration, Construction, Nature, KGB, Labor and Social Questions, Planning, Prices, Statistics, Supply, Television and Radio
State Building and Legislation, All-Union Scientific Research Institute of Soviet **1:** 139
State Crimes, Law on, **1:** 134, 135, 139, 141, 154-55, 160, 179, 253, 264, 282, 302(nn134-35), 305(n179), 307(n253), **2:** 43, 49, 205, 209, 210, 214, 235, 279, 280, 282, 285-86; text: Appendix A.4; Article 11.1 rescinded, **2:** 285-86
State deliveries, **2:** 8, 73, 77, 119
State Enterprise, Law on, **1:** 147, 197, 249, 303(n147), **2:** 13, 28, 35, 46, 63, 98, 107, 118, 120, 138, 142, 152, 158, 159, 215, 243, 249, 250
State farms (sovkhoz), **1:** 249, 251, **2:** 14—*see also* Collective farms
State income, **2:** 238
State orders, **1:** 283, **2:** 47, 104, 173
State production associations, **2:** 152
Statistics, challenged, **1:** 214, 215-16, 272, 280, 304(n152), **2:** 38; State Committee on (Goskomstat), **1:** 214, 215, 280, 304 (n152), **2:** 5, 21, 38, 190
Streltsy, **2:** 195
Stroitelnaya Gazeta, **2:** 76
Students, **2:** 182
Subbotnik, **2:** 81, 292(n81)
Suicide, **1:** 304(n152), **2:** 1, 11
Sumgait riots, **1:** 24, 26, 103, 136, 268, 299(24), **2:** 40, 52, 87, 117-18, 229, 270, 271
Sumy Association, **2:** 47
Supply, State Committee for Material and Technical (Gossnab), **1:** 248, 287, **2:** 12, 249
Supreme Court, **1:** 7, 176, 181, **2:** 164, 213, 287; confirmation of chairman, **2:** 166, 219-20; of RSFSR, **2:** 219
Supreme Soviet of the USSR, **1:** 26, 27, 104, 113-14, 123, 127, 198, 246, 287, **2:** 28, 85, 107, 112, 132, 137, 148, 167, 190, 220, 231, 263, 264, 267, 269, 271, 280; and foreign policy, **1:** 203
  Chairman, **1:** 7, 9, 10, 48-49, 155, 157, 171, 174, 181, 264, 265, 266; report of, **1:** 130, 131 (*see also* Gorbachev report); nominations for position of: Gorbachev, **1:** 27-41; Obolensky, **1:** 42-45; Yeltsin, **1:** 45-47, **2:** 99, 134, 183, 205, 261, 286, 287; election, **1:** 48-49
  First Deputy Chairman, **1:** 7, 91; Lukyanov's candidacy, **1:** 133-36, 139, 140-67
  Commissions, **1:** 12, 14, 16, 51, 59, 62, 73, 75, 124, 132, 143, 195, 204, 249, 251, 259, 262, 275, 280, 289, 295, **2:** 90, 141, 146, 150, 156, 175, 192, 246, 252
  Deputy status, **1:** 56-57, 59, 60, 61, 62, 64, 66, 67, 68, 69, 69-70, 72, 73-74, 75, 121, 165*see also* CPD, Deputy status
  Electoral process, **1:** 7, 8, 9, 10, 13, 17, 50-51, 52, 57, 58, 59, 61, 63, 63-64, 65, 67, 68, 71, 72, 73, 76-89, 91, 97-98, 99, 159, 180, 181, 188, **2:** 89, 91, 142
  Powers of, **1:** 7-8, 11, 12, 13, 18, 36, 50-51, 57, 59, 61, 62, 67, 69, 69-70, 71, 72, 73, 75, 161, 203, 213, 252-53, 280-81, 297(n13), **2:** 183, 281
  Presidium, **1:** 1, 2, 11, 12, 36, 69-71, 78, 89, 139, 140, 158, 159, 171, 264, **2:** 49, 55, 143, 166, 207, 213, 215, 216, 224, 225, 232-33, 285; decrees of, **1:** 157, 282, **2:** 117, 278
  Representation in, **1:** 1-2, 12, 59, 60, 63, 66-67, 155, 174, 175, 253, **2:** 123-24; Belorussia, **1:** 81, 84; Lithuania, **1:** 76-79; Russia, **1:** 79-86, 91, 109-10; Tajikistan, **1:** 63, 71; Ukraine, **1:** 61-62, 104; Uzbekistan, **1:** 61—*see also* Soviet of Nationalities, Soviet of the Union

Taiga, **2:** 184-85
Tajikistan, Tajiks, **2:** 89, 136; delegation, **1:** 71, 79, 163; Communist Party, **1:** 51, 63, 71
Talysh nation, **2:** 204
Tatars, **2:** 128, 129, 130—*see also* Crimean Tatars
Taxes, taxation, **1:** 143, 249, 284-85, 289, **2:** 73, 96, 153, 250, 279; turnover tax, **2:** 8; income tax, **2:** 35
Tbilisi incident, **1:** 1, 2, 5, 23-24, 31, 40, 54, 103, 133, 136, 139, 154, 157, 162, 176, 178, 183, 189, 224-37, 264, 278, 280, 288, 297(n5), **2:** 1, 4, 40, 83, 88, 91, 187-88, 200; initial investigations, **1:** 51, 292-93, 298(n23); documents, **2:** 49-51; CPD Commission, proposed, **1:** 24, 136, 165, 230, 264, 295 (approved), 298(n24), **2:** 1, 4, 51, 55, 68, 106, 136, 148, 186, 251, 278; constituted, **1:** 230-44, 246-47, 292-95, Appendix C.5; report of, Appendix B.5; resolution on, Appendix B.6
Teachers, status and wages, **2:** 6
Technical standards, **1:** 270
Tekhnika cooperative, **2:** 103
Telephones, **2:** 11-12, 163
Television, **2:** 89, 92, 124, 129, 130, 212; power of, **2:** 15, 72 *see also under* Congress of People's Deputies
Television and Radio Broadcasting, State Committee for (Gostelradio), **1:** 278, **2:** 183; CPD control of chairmanship, **2:** 280, 282, 287
Textile industry, **1:** 270
Tiananmen Square, statement on, **2:** 113, 132-33
Timber Industry, Ministry of (Minlesprom), **2:** 184
Tobolsk factory, **2:** 253
Tofalars, **2:** 125
Tomsk delegation, **2:** 244
Trade deficit, **2:** 149
Trade, foreign, **2:** 8, 21, 46, 67, 95, 141; Ministry of, **2:** 35, 249; domestic—*see* Market
Trade unions, **1:** 58, 142, 143, **2:** 36, 71 (foreign), 237
Trade Unions, All-Union Central Council of, **2:** 95, 243

Trans-Siberian Railway, **1:** 307 (n274)
Transcaucasian Republic, **2:** 82, 292(n87)
Trishka, **2:** 12, 290(n12)
Trud, **2:** 144
Tseleteli Society (Georgia), **1:** 228
Tsentrosoyuz, **1:** 249
Tuberculosis, **2:** 11
Tundra, **2:** 184-85
Tungus, **2:** 133
Turkey, **1:** 152; 1921 treaty with, **2:** 116; and Armenian genocide (1915), **2:** 268
Turkmen delegation, **1:** 79, 163, 164
Turks, **2:** 133, 146 *see also* Meskhet Turks
Turukhanskaya Hydroelectric Power Station, **2:** 124
Tyura Tam Spaceport, **1:** 216

Udegey nation, **2:** 184
Ukraine, Ukrainians, **2:** 200; delegation, **1:** 30, 61-62, 78, 79, **2:** 56, 59, 271, 275; Language Society, **1:** 261, 307 (n261); Academy of Sciences, **1:** 307(n261)
Ulba Hydroelectric Power Station, **2:** 67
Ulchi nation, **2:** 184
Ulyanovsk Automotive Plant, **2:** 71
Unemployment, **2:** 109; 137; discharged officers, **2:** 144
Union of Soviet Socialist Republics, **1:** 122, 141, 161, 187, 201, 204, **2:** 49, 69, 71, 82, 142, 143, 152, 203, 207, 258-59, 287—*see also* Declaration on the Formation of
Union republics, financial powers, **2:** 8, 149, 153, 235, 254, 264; sovereignty of, **1:** 30, 33, 34, 40-41, 52, 76, 77, 126, 139, 141, 201, 259, 260, 266, 276, 288, 289, 300(n76), **2:** 13, 62-63, 71, 72, 86, 120, 173-74, 189, 203, 211-12, 246-47, 259, 264, 281, 282; status of, **2:** 17-18, 82; Law on Economic Independence of, **1:** 308(n277)
United Nations, **1:** 202, 261; Georgian appeal to, **1:** 228; convention on children's rights, **2:** 11; Khrushchev in, **2:** 126;

UNESCO, **2:** 208; Gorbachev's speech to, **2:** 268
United States, **2:** 13, 90, 122, 126-27, 199, 242; relations with, **1:** 27, 202, 203, **2:** 5; Congress, **1:** 124, 228, **2:** 39-40, 102; construction standards, **2:** 78, 79; medical assistance **2:** 110
United States and Canada, Institute of, **2:** 153
Unknown Soldier, Tomb of, **1:** 207
"Unpromising villages", **2:** 75, 120, 185
Urals Department, USSR Academy of Sciences, **2:** 19
USSR Constitution: A Political-Legal Commentary, **2:** 204
Uygur nation, **2:** 200
"Uzbek affair", **1:** 151-56, 158, **2:** 72, 166, 219, 223-26, 229, 231-34, 242—*see also* Gdlyan-Ivanov affair
Uzbekistan, Uzbeks, **2:** 242; delegation, **1:** 79, 158-59, **2:** 111; Communist Party, **1:** 61, 254, **2:** 225; Supreme Court, **2:** 225; Supreme Soviet, **1:** 61

Vacations, **2:** 168, 266
Vagrancy, **1:** 304(n152)
Veche (Novgorod), **2:** 216
Vechernyi Tallinn, **2:** 142-43
Vegidaltsy nation, **2:** 184
Veterans, **1:** 142, 189, 195, 205, **2:** 34, 40, 120, 124, 144-45, 267; pensions, **2:** 24-25, 39, 129; All-Union Council of, **2:** 24
Vetspilsitas Zines, **2:** 206
View (*Vzglyad*—tv program), **2:** 92
Virgin lands, **2:** 175
Virusyna, **2:** 206
Vladimir Ilyich Plant, **2:** 104
Volga Germans, **1:** 38, 123, 149, 152, 299(n38), **2:** 72, 107, 134, 200, 264
Volga River, Committee for Salvation of, **1:** 20
Volkhov Hydroelectric Station, **2:** 197
Voluntary societies—*see* Public organizations
Voluntary Society for the Promotion of the Army, Aviation, and Navy (DOSAAF) **2:** 91

Vremya (tv program), **1**: 24, 225, 278
Vysotsky, **1**: 175, 305(n175)

Wage coefficients, **2**: 185, 236
Wages, **1**: 189, 192, 205, 211, 215, 277, 283, 284, **2**: 16, 24, 40, 70-71, 74, 102, 150, 155, 158, 161, 178, 237, 238, 253; minimum wage, **2**: 104; comparison, **2**: 169; in Siberia, **2**: 175
Water quality, **1**: 209, 277, **2**: 65, 98, 161, 184, 253
Water supply, **1**: 163, 255, **2**: 3, 14, 119, 175, 198
Waterway Management, All-Union Institute on (Soyuzgiprovodkhoz), **2**: 196—*see also* Canals
White Sun of the Desert (film), **2**: 91
Widows, **1**: 262, **2**: 155

Women, **1**: 126, 164, 165, 189, 195, 205, 246, 262-63, **2**: 7, 10, 11, 16-17, 60, 98, 109, 154, 179, 242; deputies, **2**: 44; Soviet Committee of, **1**: 165, 246, 262, 263
Wool, **2**: 236
Workers, **1**: 63, 65, 189, **2**: 23, 89, 97, 167, 254; protection of, **1**: 197; shortage of, **2**: 16; exploitation of, **2**: 169
Workers and Peasants Inspectorate, **2**: 222
World Charter on Nature, **2**: 191
World Health Organization, **1**: 275
World market—*see* Market
World War II, relocation of Volga Germans, **1**: 299(n38); repressions during, 301(n102); relocation of Chechen-Ingush, 304(n149); veterans of, **2**: 24-25; graves, **2**: 25, 76; Poland in, 31, 291(n31) *see also* Great Patriotic War, Nazi-Soviet Pact, Veterans
Writers Union, **2**: 138, 293(n99)

Xerox machines, and power, **2**: 16, 43

Yakut Scientific Center, **2**: 19
Yakutsk delegation, **2**: 274
Youth, **1**: 141, 142, 159, 160, 189, 199, **2**: 15, 25, 77, 91; delinquency, **2**: 1; spiritual degeneration of, **2**: 140
Yukaghir nation, **2**: 125, 133

Zabota program, **2**: 36
Zaporozhye-Moscow telelink, **2**: 22
Zarya Vostok, **1**: 27-28, 298(n23), **2**: 188, 291(n69)
Zavolzhsky Chemical Plant, **2**: 106
Zemstvo, **2**: 195
Zhizn Natsionalnostei, **2**: 102

ABBREVIATIONS AND ACRONYMS

AES—Atomic Energy Station
AN—Academy of Sciences
AO—Autonomous Oblast
ASSR—Autonomous Soviet Socialist Republic
Atommash—Nuclear Machine building
AUCCTU—All-Union Central Council of Trade Unions
AYaM—Amur-Yakut Mainline
BAM—Baikal-Amur Mainline
bum—paper industry
CDSP—*Current Digest of the Soviet Press*
CMEA—Council for Mutual Economic Assistance (Comecon)
CPD—Congress of People's Deputies
CPSU CC—Communist Party of the Soviet Union Central Committee
Dallesprom—Far Eastern Timber Administration
FBIS-SOV—Foreign Broadcast Information Service, *Daily Report: Soviet Union*

GAES—pumped storage electric station
GES—hydroelectric power station
Giprozem—Institute for Land Reclamation Planning
GKNT—State Committee for Science and Technology
GOELRO—State Plan for the Electrification of Russia
gorispolkom—municipal soviet executive committee
gorkom—municipal party central committee
Gosagroprom—State Agroindustrial Committee
Gosarbitrazh—State Arbitration Committee
Gosbank—State Bank
Goskino—State Committee for Cinematography
Goskomizdat—State Committee for Publishing
Goskomnarobraz—State Committee for Public Education

Goskompriroda—State Committee for Environmental Protection
Goskomstat—State Committee on Statistics
Goskomteleradio—State Committee for Television and Radio Broadcasting
Goskomtrud—State Committee for Labor and Social Questions
Goskomtsen—State Committee on Prices
Gosleskhoz—State Committee for the Forest Industry
Gosobrazovanie—State Committee for Public Education
Gosplan—State Planning Committee
Gossnab—State Committee for Material and Supply
Gosstroy—State Committee on Construction
goszakaz—state orders
KGB—Committee for State Security
kolhkoz—collective farm

ABBREVIATIONS AND ACRONYMS

Komsomol—see VLKSM or YCL
krayispolkom—kray soviet executive committee
kraykom—kray party central committee
Minavtodor—Ministry of Highways
Minelektrotekhprom—Ministry of the Electrical Equipment Industry
Minenergo—Ministry of Power and Electrification
Mingasprom—Ministry of the Gas Industry
Minlesbumprom—Ministry of Timber, Pulp, Paper and Wood Processing Industry
Minmash—Ministry of Machine Production
Minmedbioprom—Ministry of the Medical and Microbiological Industry
Minpribor—Ministry of Instrumentation, Automation, and Control Systems
Minstantkoprom—Ministry of Machine Tool and Tool-building Industry
Mintiazmash—Ministry of Heavy Transport Machinery
Mintorg—Ministry of Trade
Mintsvetmet—Ministry of Nonferrous Metallurgy
Minvodkhoz—Ministry of Land Reclamation and Water Resources
Minvostokstroy—Ministry of Construction in Far Eastern Regions
Minvuz—Ministry of Higher and Specialized Secondary Education
MTS—machine tractor station
MVD—Ministry of Internal Affairs
NEP—New Economic Policy (1921-28)
NKAO—Nagorno-Karabakh Autonomous Oblast
nomenklatura—the privileged class; its members
NTT—scientific-technical center
obkom—oblast party central committee
oblispolkom—oblast soviet executive committee
perestroika—restructuring
proms—industries, industrial administrations
PTU—polytechnic institute
rayispolkom—district soviet executive committee
raykom—district party central committee
RL/RFE—Radio Liberty/Radio Free Europe
RSFSR—Russian Soviet Federated Socialist Republic
sovkhoz—state farm
Soyuzgiprovodkhoz—All-Union Research Institute on Waterway Management
Tsentrosoyuz—Central Union of Consumers Cooperatives
TsK—Central Committee (party)
VLKSM—All-Union Leninist Communist Youth League (Komsomol)
VUZ—institution of higher education
YCL—Young Communist League (Komsomol)
ZakVO—Trancaucasian Military District